Tuttle

Compact
Chinese
Dictionary

LI Dong 李冬

TUTTLE Publishing

Tokyo | Rutland, Vermont | Singapore

Published by Tuttle Publishing, an imprint of Periplus Editions (HK) Ltd.

www.tuttlepublishing.com

ISBN 978-0-8048-3993-8

North America, Latin America and Europe
Tuttle Publishing
364 Innovation Drive, North Clarendon,
VT 05759-9436 USA.
Tel: 1(802) 773-8930
Fax: 1(802) 773-6993
info@tuttlepublishing.com
www.tuttlepublishing.com

Asia Pacific
Berkeley Books Pte. Ltd.
61 Tai Seng Avenue #02-12, Singapore 534167
Tel: (65) 6280-1330
Fax: (65) 6280-6290
inquiries@periplus.com.sg
www.periplus.com

13 12 11 10
6 5 4 3 2 1

Printed in Singapore

Contents

Introducing Chinese

1 PRONUNCIATION

1.1 Vowels

SINGLE VOWELS

There are seven basic single vowels:

a similar to *a* in *ah*

e similar to *a* in *ago*

ě similar to *e* in *ebb* (this sound never occurs alone and is transcribed as **e**, as in **ei**, **ie**, **ue**)

i similar to *ee* in *cheese* (spelled **y** when not preceded by a consonant)

o similar to *oe* in *toe*

u similar to *oo* in *boot* (spelled **w** when not preceded by a consonant)

ü similar to German **ü** in *über* or French **u** in *tu*; or you can get **ü** by saying **i** and rounding your lips at the same time (spelled **u** after **j**, **q**, **x**; spelled **yu** when not preceded by a consonant)

VOWEL COMBINATIONS

These single vowels combine with each other or with the consonants of **n** or **ng** to form what are technically known as *diphthongs*. These combinations are pronounced as a single sound, with a little more emphasis on the first part of the sound.

You can learn these combinations in four groups:

Group 1:	diphthongs starting with **a/e/ê**
ai	similar to *y* in *my*
ao	similar to *ow* in *how*
an	
ang	
en	
eng	
ei	similar to *ay* in *may*
Group 2:	diphthongs starting with **i**
ia	
ie	similar to *ye* in *yes*
iao	
iou	similar to *you* (spelled **iu** when preceded by a consonant)
ian	
ien	similar to *in* (spelled **in** when preceded by a consonant)
ieng	similar to *En* in *English* (spelled **ing** when preceded by a consonant)
iang	similar to *young*
iong	
Group 3:	diphthongs starting with **u/o**
ua	

uo	
uai	similar to *why* in British English
uei	similar to *way* (spelled **ui** when preceded by a consonant)
uan	
uen	(spelled **un** when preceded by a consonant)
ueng	
uang	
ong	

Group 4:	diphthongs starting with **ü**	
üe	used only after **j, q, x**; spelled **ue**	
üen	used only after **j, q, x**; spelled **un**	
üan	used only after **j, q, x**; spelled **uan**	

1.2 Consonants

Consonants may be grouped in the following ways.

Group 1: These consonants are almost the same in Chinese and English.

CHINESE	ENGLISH
m	*m*
n	*n*
f	*f*
l	*l*
s	*s*
r	*r*
b	pronounced as hard *p* (as in *speak*)
p	*p* (as in *peak*)
g	pronounced as hard *k* (as in *ski*)
k	*k* (as in *key*)
d	pronounced as hard *t* (as in *star*)
t	*t* (as in *tar*)

Group 2: Some modification is needed to get these Chinese sounds from English.

CHINESE	ENGLISH
j	as *j* in *jeep* (but unvoiced, not round-lipped)
q	as *ch* in *cheese* (but not round-lipped)
x	as *sh* in *sheep* (but not round-lipped)
c	as *ts* as in *cats* (make it long)
z	as *ds* as in *beds* (but unvoiced, and make it long)

Group 3: No English counterparts

Chinese **zh**, **ch**, and **sh** have no English counterparts. You can learn to say **zh**, **ch** and **sh** starting from **z**, **c** and **s**. For example, say **s** (which is almost the same as the English *s* in *sesame*) and then roll up your tongue to touch the roof of your mouth. You get **sh**.

TONES

Chinese is a tonal language, i.e. a sound pronounced in different tones is understood as different words. So the tone is an indispensable component of the pronunciation of a word.

1.3 Basic tones

There are four basic tones. The following five-level pitch graph shows the values of the four tones:

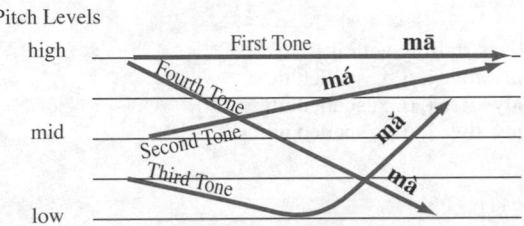

- The First Tone is a high, level tone and is represented as ¯, e.g. 妈 **mā** (meaning *mother*, *mom*).

- The Second Tone is a high, rising tone and is represented by the tone mark ´, e.g. 麻 **má** (*hemp* or *sesame*).

- The Third Tone is a falling, then rising tone. As you can see from the pitch graph it falls from below the middle of the voice range to nearly the bottom and then rises to a point near the top. It is represented by the tone mark ˇ, e.g. 马 **mǎ** (*horse*).

- The Fourth Tone is a falling tone. It falls from high to low and is represented by the tone mark ` , e.g. 骂 **mà** (*curse*).

In Chinese speech, as in English speech, some sounds are unstressed, i.e. pronounced short and soft. They do not have any of the four tones. Such sounds are said to have Neutral Tone. Sounds with the neutral tone are not marked. For example in 爸爸 **bàba** (*daddy*) the first syllable is pronounced in the fourth tone and the second syllable in the neutral tone, i.e. unstressed.

TONE CHANGES

Tones may undergo changes in actual speech ("tone sandhi"). The third tone, when followed by a first, second, fourth or neutral tone sound, loses its final rise and stops at the low pitch. Followed by another third tone sound, it becomes the second tone. This is a general rule and the notation of third tone sounds remains unchanged. For example, in 所以 **suǒyǐ** (*therefore*, *so*), notation remains the third tone for both syllables, but the word is actually pronounced like **suóyǐ**.

Two important words 不 **bù** (*no*) and 一 **yī** (*one*) also undergo tone changes. You will find the details of their tone changes under these entries.

1.4 Syllables: Distinct units

Normally a consonant and a vowel, said in a particular tone, merge to form a syllable in Chinese. Every syllable is a distinct unit in speech. Learners should say each syllable clearly and give full value to most syllables in speech. The general impression of Chinese speech, described in musical terms, is staccato rather than legato (which could be used to describe English).

1.5 *Pinyin:* the romanization scheme to show pronunciation

As Chinese writing normally does not indicate pronunciation, a romanization scheme, known as *pinyin*, is used to represent the sounds and tones of Chinese, as in this dictionary. *Pinyin* is useful for learning the phonetics of Mandarin.

2 WRITING CHINESE: 汉字 Hànzi

Chinese is not phonetic like most European languages (in varying degrees). Chinese is written in logograms, known as 汉字 (**Hànzi**) and generally referred to as "Chinese characters", or "Sinograms."

2.1 Chinese characters as syllables

Each Chinese character is pronounced as a syllable. It is of course important to be able to read a character with the correct pronunciation.

2.2 The composition of Chinese characters: Meaningful components

Chinese characters can be analyzed into components. It is acknowledged that there are three kinds of components. Of the three, the most interesting to learners of Chinese is a group of components that convey certain meanings. The presence of such a component in a character gives you some clue to its meaning of the character. Hence, learning the meaning of these component parts will deepen your understanding of characters you know, and help you guess the meaning of unfamiliar characters. See List 1 on page xviii.

2.3 The writing of Chinese characters

STROKES
Each Chinese character is composed of strokes. The table below shows the basic strokes. Recognizing the strokes in a character is helpful for finding a character or radical in the Stroke Index, List of Radicals and Radical Index. Each of the strokes shown in the table is counted as one stroke.

Stroke	Writing the stroke	Examples
Héng	left to right 一	千 主 女

Stroke	Writing the stroke	Examples
Shù	top to bottom 		千 山 北
Piě	top (right) to bottom (left) ノ	千 人 么
Nà	top (left) to bottom (right) ヽ	人 木 又
Diǎn	top to bottom 丶	主 心 习
Tí	bottom (left) to top (right) ノ	习 打 北
Stroke with hook	left to right, top to bottom ⼀ ノ ⼁ ⺄	买 打 以 心
Stroke with turn(s)	⼃ ⼄ ⼅ ⼆	山 马 女 么 又
Stroke with turn(s) and hook	⼇ ⼈ ⼉ ⼊ 乙	北 习 认 马

STROKE ORDER

For the character to look correct, its strokes should be written in the correct order. Knowing the order will also help you remember characters. The general rules of stroke order are as shown below.

Rule	Example	Stroke order
Top before bottom	三	一 二 三
Left before right	什	ノ イ 仁 什
Horizontal before vertical/downward	天	一 二 干 天
"Enter the room, then close the door"	日	丨 冂 冃 日
Vertical stroke before sides/bottom	小	亅 刂 小

SIMPLIFIED AND TRADITIONAL CHARACTERS

The Chinese government simplified hundreds of Chinese characters in mid-1950 by reducing the numbers of their strokes. Such simplified characters are called 简体字 **jiǎntǐzì**. This dictionary uses **jiantizi**. Traditional versions (also known as complicated characters) are still used in Taiwan and Hong Kong, and they are shown after "Trad" where applicable, e.g.:

学 xué Trad 學

3 VOCABULARY: Word-formation

Chinese words are either of one syllable or more than one syllable (mostly two syllables). When they are made up of two or more syllables, their meanings are usually transparent; that is, the way a word is formed tells you a lot about its meaning. Therefore it is very helpful to know the meanings of the components in a word and the way the word is formed, and it also makes understanding the word easier and more interesting.
There are six basic word-formation methods:

- **Compounding**: the components of a word are complementary to each other in meaning and are of the same status. For example:

    重 *once again* + 复 *repeat* → 重复 *repeat*

- **Modification**: one component modifies the other. For example:

    外 *outside* + 国 *country* → 外国 *foreign country*

- **Verb+object**: the word has a verb-and-object relationship. For example:

    发 *develop* + 烧 *burning, fever* → 发烧 *to run a fever*

- **Verb+complementation**: the word has a verb-and-complement relationship, that is, the first component is a verb or an adjective and the second one modifies it. For example:

    提 *raise* + 高 *high* → 提高 *raise*

- **Suffixation**: the word contains a suffix. For example:

    本 *a book* + 子 *nominal suffix* → 本子 *notebook*

- **Idioms**: the word is an idiomatic expression. For example:

    马上 → *at once, immediately*

4 GRAMMAR

4.1 Main features of Chinese grammar

TOPIC+COMMENT STRUCTURE

The basic principle in making Chinese sentences is to follow the "topic+comment" structure. "Topic" means the subject matter you want to talk about, and "comment" is the information you give about the subject matter. To make a Chinese sentence, you simply first mention the subject matter you want to talk about, and then say what you have to say about it. For example, you can say 那本书 **nà běn shū** (that book) first as the "topic" and then add "comment":

那本书 **Nà běn shū** (that book) + 很有意思 **hěn yǒu yìsi** (very interesting) → *That book is very interesting.*

那本书 **Nà běn shū** (that book) + 卖完了 **mài wán le** (sold out) → *That book has been sold.*

那本书 **Nà běn shū** (that book) + 你有吗 **nǐ yǒu ma** (do you have) → *Do you have that book?*

那本书 **Nà běn shū** (that book) + 语言很优美 **yǔyán hěn yōuměi** (language is beautiful) → *The language of that book is beautiful.*

ELLIPSIS OF SENTENCE ELEMENTS

Chinese speakers may leave out words that are supposed to be understood, and therefore need not be spoken. Subjects and conjunctions are often omitted. For example, you may translate the English sentence *If you like it, you may buy it, but if you don't like it, you don't have to*, into the Chinese sentence 喜欢就买, 不喜欢就别买。 **Xǐhuan jiùmǎi, bù xǐhuan jiù bié mǎi.** Literally, it means "Like it, and buy, don't like then don't buy." Compare the two sentences, and you will find that some English words, such as *if*, *you*, *it*, and *but* are not translated.

WORD CLASSES: FLEXIBILITY, NO INFLECTION

Chinese words do not have inflections, i.e. they do not change to indicate grammatical categories. For example, the verb 去 **qù** (*to go*) is invariably 去 **qù**; there is no past form or any other inflected form of this verb. Neither do Chinese words normally have formal markers of word class. Consequently it is rather easy for a word to be used in more than one word class. This relative flexibility in word classes, however, does not mean that Chinese does not have word classes (see Section 4.2).

MEASURE WORDS AND PARTICLES

Measure words (量词 **liàngcí**) and particles (助词 **zhùcí**) are two word classes found in Chinese but not in English and most other languages.

Measure words are usually required when a noun is modified by a numeral. For example, 两书 **liǎng shū** is unacceptable; you must use the measure word 本 **běn** between the numeral and the noun: 两本书 **liǎng běn shū** (*two books*). Furthermore, Chinese nouns require specific measure words to go with them. For example, the noun 书 **shū** (*book*) must be used with the measure word 本 **běn**. See List 2 on pages xiv–xv for the common measure words.

In Chinese grammar, particles are words attached to other words or at the end of a sentence to indicate grammatical concepts or to express emotions. For example, the particles 了 **le**, 着 **zhe**, 过 **guo** are attached to verbs to indicate, respectively, whether the actions denoted are completed, in progress or past experiences.

4.2 Word classes

Following are brief explanations of the basic terms in Chinese grammar used in this dictionary. (A word of warning: it is a rather complicated matter to define grammatical terms accurately. Here we will be content with some general but useful ideas.)

ADJECTIVE	a describing word, a word that describes people, things or actions, typically used before a noun
ADVERB	a word that modifies a verb, an adjective or another adverb
CONJUNCTION	a word used to link two words, phrases or sentences, indicating certain relationships between them
IDIOM	a set phrase, the meaning of which cannot be readily derived from its components
INTERJECTION	a word that expresses strong emotions
MEASURE WORD	a word that connects a numeral to a noun. Measure words are a special feature of Chinese; a list of measure words is given in List 2
MODAL VERB	a word used before a verb to indicate necessity, possibility, willingness, etc.
NOUN	a naming word, a word that names people, animals, plants, things, ideas, etc.
NUMERAL	a word that represents a number, typically used with a noun
ONOMATOPOEIA	a word that imitates the sounds of a thing or an action
PARTICLE	a word used with another word, phrase, or sentence to indicate certain grammatical meanings or to express strong emotions
PREPOSITION	a word used before a noun or pronoun to indicate time, place, direction, manner, reason of an action, etc.

PRONOUN	a word that is used in the place of a noun, a verb, an adjective, etc.
VERB	an action word, a word that indicates what somebody does or feels

4.3 Other grammar terms

ATTRIBUTE	the element that modifies the subject or object of a sentence; or, in word-formation analysis, a word that modifies a noun
ADVERBIAL	the element that is used before the predicate of a sentence and modifies it; or, in word-formation analysis, a word that precedes a verb or an adjective to modify it
COMPLEMENT	the element that is used after the predicate of a sentence and modifies it; or, in word-formation analysis, a word that follows a verb or an adjective to modify it
IMPERATIVE SENTENCE	a command or a request
OBJECT	the element that follows a predicative verb, typically to indicate the target of an action
PREDICATE	the comment or information about the subject, typically a verb or an adjective
PREFIX	an additional element that immediately precedes the word it is attached to
SUBJECT	the topic of a sentence, what the speaker wants to talk about, typically a noun or pronoun
SUFFIX	an additional element that closely follows the word it is attached to

List 1

Meaningful Character Components

冫 = freezing, ice (e.g. 冰 **bīng**, 冷 **lěng**, 寒 **hán**)

讠, 言 = word (e.g. 语 **yǔ**, 词 **cí**)

八 = dividing (e.g. 分 **fēn**, 半 **bàn**)

亻, 人 = man, person (e.g. 他 **tā**, 信 **xìn**)

刂, 刀 = knife (e.g. 利 **lì**, 剩 **shèng**)

力 = muscle, strength (e.g. 男 **nán**, 办 **bàn**)

阝 (on the left) = mound, steps (e.g. 院 **yuàn**, 附 **fù**)

阝 (on the right) = city, region (e.g. 部 **bù**, 邮 **yóu**)

氵, 水 = water (e.g. 河 **hé**, 海 **hǎi**)

忄, 心 = the heart, emotions (e.g. 情 **qíng**, 怕 **pà**, 感 **gǎn**)

宀 = roof, house (e.g. 家 **jiā**, 室 **shì**)

广 = roof, hut (e.g. 庭 **tíng**, 店 **diàn**)

门 = door, gate (e.g. 闻 **wén**, 间 **jiān**)

土 = earth (e.g. 场 **chǎng**, 城 **chéng**)

女 = woman (e.g. 妇 **fù**, 妈 **mā**)

饣, 食 = food (e.g. 饭 **fàn**, 饱 **bǎo**)

口 = the mouth, speech, eating (e.g. 问 **wèn**, 吃 **chī**)

囗 = boundary (e.g. 围 **wéi**, 园 **yuán**)

子, 孑 = child (e.g. 孩 **hái**, 学 **xué**)

艹 = plant, vegetation (e.g. 草 **cǎo**, 菜 **cài**)

纟 = silk, texture (e.g. 组 **zǔ**, 纸 **zhǐ**)

辶 = walking (e.g. 道 **dào**, 过 **guò**)

彳 = path, walking (e.g. 行 **xíng**, 往 **wǎng**)

巾 = cloth (e.g. 布 **bù**, 带 **dài**)

马 = horse (e.g. 骑 **qí**)

扌, 手, 攵 = the hand, action (e.g. 拿 **ná**, 擦 **cā**)

灬, 火 = fire, heat (e.g. 烧 **shāo**, 热 **rè**)

礻, 示 = spirit (e.g. 神 **shén**, 祖 **zǔ**)

户 = door, window (e.g. 房 **fáng**)

父 = father (e.g. 爸 **bà**)

日 = the sun (e.g. 晴 **qíng**, 暖 **nuǎn**)

月 = the moon (e.g. 阴 **yīn**, 明 **míng**)

月, 肉 = flesh, human organ (e.g. 脸 **liǎn**, 脚 **jiǎo**)

贝 = shell, treasure (e.g. 贵 **guì**)

止 = toe (e.g. 步 **bù**)

木 = tree, timber (e.g. 树 **shù**, 板 **bǎn**)

王, 玉 = jade (e.g. 理 **lǐ**, 球 **qiú**)

见 = seeing (e.g. 视 **shì**, 现 **xiàn**)

气 = vapor (e.g. 汽 **qì**)

车 = vehicle (e.g. 辆 **liàng**)

疒 = disease, ailment (e.g. 病 **bìng**, 疼 **téng**)

立 = standing (e.g. 站 **zhàn**, 位 **wèi**)

穴 = cave, hole (e.g. 空 **kōng**, 窗 **chuāng**)

衤, 衣 = clothing (e.g. 裤 **kù**, 袜 **wà**)

钅, 金 = metal (e.g. 银 **yín**, 钱 **qián**)

石 = stone, rock (e.g. 碗 **wǎn**, 磁 **cí**)

目 = the eye (e.g. 眼 **yǎn**, 睡 **shuì**)

田 = farm, field (e.g. 界 **jiè**, 里 **lǐ**)

瓜 = melon, gourd (e.g. 瓢 **piáo**, 瓣 **bàn**)

禾 = seedling, crop (e.g. 种 **zhǒng**, 秋 **qiū**)

鸟 = bird (e.g. 鸡 **jī**)

米 = rice (e.g. 糖 **táng**, 精 **jīng**)

竹 = bamboo (e.g. 筷 **kuài**, 笔 **bǐ**)

舌 = the tongue (e.g. 话 **huà**, 活 **huó**)

舟 = boat (e.g. 船 **chuán**)

酉 = fermentation (e.g. 酒 **jiǔ**)

走 = walking (e.g. 起 **qǐ**)

足 = the foot (e.g. 跳 **tiào**, 踢 **tì**)

List 2

Measure Words

Measure words are a special feature of Chinese. A particular measure word, or set of measure words, occurs with each noun whenever one is speaking of numbers. The measure word may function like a collective noun (like a *pride* [of lions] or a *school* [of fish]) or may be related to the shape of the object. Noun phrases using measure words often have the structure "number + measure word + noun," e.g.

□ 一把刀 **yì bǎ dāo** *a knife*
□ 两道难题 **liǎng dào nántí** *two difficult questions*

Some measure words occur with verbs, and may be related to the frequency or duration of the action. For verbs, the expression may have the structure "verb + number + measure word," e.g.

□ 看了三遍 **kànle sān biàn** *read three times*
□ 去过两次 **qùguo liǎng cì** *have been ... twice*

bǎ 把 for objects with handles; a handful

bān 班 class (in school)

bèi 倍 fold, time

běn 本 for books

bǐ 笔 for a sum of money

biàn 遍 times, indicating the frequency of an action done in its complete duration from the beginning to the end

cè 册 volume (books)

céng 层 story, floor

chǎng 场 for movies, sport events

chǐ 尺 a traditional Chinese unit of length (equal to ⅓ meter)

cì 次 time, expressing frequency of an act

cùn 寸 a traditional Chinese unit of length (equal to ¹⁄₃₀ meter)

dào 道 for questions in a school exercise, examination, etc.; for things in the shape of a line

dī 滴 drop (of liquid)

diǎn 点 o'clock

dù 度 degree (of temperature, longitude, latitude, etc.)

duàn 段 section of something long

dùn 顿 for meals

duǒ 朵 for flowers

fēn 分 Chinese currency (1 分 **fēn** = 0.1 角 **jiǎo** = 0.01 元 **yuán**), cent

fèn 份 for a set of things or newspapers, documents, etc.

fēng 封 for letters

fú 幅 for pictures, poster, maps, etc.

gè 个 the most commonly used measure word for nouns that do not take special measure words, or in default of any other measure word

gēn 根 for long, thin things

gōngchǐ 公尺 meter (formal)

gōngjīn 公斤 kilogram

gōnglǐ 公里 kilometer

háng 行 used with nouns that are formed in lines; line, row, queue

hù 户 used with nouns denoting households and families

huí 回 number of times

jiā 家 for families or businesses

jiān 间 for rooms

jiàn 件 for things, affairs, clothes or furniture

jiǎo 角 Chinese currency (0.1 **yuán** or 10 **fēn**), ten cents, a dime

jiē 节 a period of time

jīn 斤 a Chinese unit of weight equivalent to half a kilogram

jù 句 for sentences

kē 棵 for trees

kè 克 gram

kè 刻 quarter of an hour

kǒu 口 for members of a family

kuài 块 for things that can be broken into lumps or chunks; for money; yuan, dollar

lǐ 里 a Chinese unit of length, equivalent to 0.5 kilometers

lì 粒 for rice, pearls

liǎng 两 a traditional Chinese unit of weight, equivalent to 50 grams; ounce

liàng 辆 for vehicles

liè 列 for trains

máo 毛 a Chinese money unit, colloquialism for 角 **jiǎo** (= 0.1 元 **yuán** or 10 分 **fēn**)

mēn 门 for school subjects, languages, etc.

mǐ 米 meter (colloquial)

miàn 面 for flat objects

miǎo 秒 second (of time)

míng 名 for people, especially for those with a specific position or occupation

mǔ 亩 a traditional Chinese unit of area, especially in farming (equal to ⅟₁₅ hectare or 667 square meters)

pái 排 for things arranged in a row

pī 批 for a batch of goods, and for things/people arriving at the same time

pǐ 匹 for horses

piān 篇 for a piece of writing

piàn 片 for a thin and flat piece, slice

píng 瓶 a bottle of

qún 群 a crowd/group of

shēn 身 for clothes

shǒu 首 for songs and poems

shuāng 双 a pair of (shoes, chopsticks, etc.)

suì 岁 year (of age)

suǒ 所 for houses, or institutions housed in a building

tái 台 for machines, big instruments, etc.

tàng 趟 for trips

tào 套 a set of

tiáo 条 for things with a long, narrow shape

tóu 头 for cattle or sheep

wèi 位 a polite measure word for people

xià 下 used with certain verbs to indicate the number of times the action is done

xiàng 项 item, component

yè 页 for pages (of a book)

yīngchǐ 英尺 foot (as a measurement of length)

yīngcùn 英寸 inch

yuán 元 the basic unit of Chinese currency (1 元 **yuán** = 10 角 **jiǎo**/毛 **máo** = 100 分 **fēn**), dollar

zhāng 张 for paper, beds, tables, desks

zhèn 阵 for an action or event that lasts for some time

zhī 支 for stick-like things

zhī 只 for animals, utensils, or objects

zhǒng 种 kind, sort

zuò 座 for large and solid objects, such as a large building

Using the Dictionary

Note: You are recommended to read *Introducing Chinese* (pp. iv–xii) before using the dictionary.

1 Pronunciation

The pronunciation of Chinese words as transcribed in this dictionary uses the *pinyin* scheme, which is the official, internationally recognized Chinese romanization system. Every Chinese character in this dictionary is accompanied by its *pinyin* spelling so that you will know how to pronounce every word and say every sentence.

2 Word class

The word class of each headword is indicated immediately after the headword, e.g.

> 爱护 àihù v
> 阿姨 āyí N mother's sister

When a headword may be used in different word classes, they are shown by I, II, and so on, e.g.

> 爱好 àihào I v like, be interested in, have as a hobby II N hobby, interest

3 Traditional characters

If a character has a traditional version (传统字 **chuántǒng zì**, also known as 繁体字 **fántǐzì** "complicated character"), it is shown as part of the headword, preceded by Trad, e.g.:

> 爱 ài TRAD 愛

4 Definitions

For Chinese headwords English equivalents or near equivalents are given, in most cases, as definitions, e.g.

> 高兴 gāoxìng ADJ joyful, delighted, willing

For grammatical words that have no English equivalents, concise explanations are given in brackets, e.g.

> 的 de PARTICLE (attached to a word, phrase or clause to indicate that it is an attribute.
> 的 de is normally followed by a noun.)

When a headword has more than one meaning under the same word class, the different meanings are indicated by 1, 2, etc. For example:

> 月 yuè N 1 month 2 the moon

Homonyms (words pronounced and written the same but with different, unrelated meanings) are treated as separate words, e.g.

代 ¹ **dài** N **1** generation

代 ² **dài** v take the place of, perform on behalf of

5 Measure Words

After the definition of a Chinese noun, the specific measure word used with the noun is shown, if it is one of the headwords in the dictionary, e.g.

书 **shū** book (本 běn)

When the specific measure word is not within the scope of this dictionary and therefore is not shown, you can often use the default measure word 个 **ge**.

6 Common Collocations

Collocations are words habitually juxtaposed with each other. This dictionary shows common collocations related to the headwords, with clear definitions and necessary sample sentences. For example:

包 **bāo** N parcel, bag
　钱包 **qiánbāo** wallet, purse
　书包 **shūbāo** schoolbag
　邮包 **yóubāo** mailbag, parcel for posting

7 Example Sentences

Words become really meaningful only when used in sentences. That is why a host of example sentences are supplied for almost each and every headword in the dictionary. All the sentences are carefully constructed to be idiomatic and communicatively useful. For example, the headword **dàibiǎo** 代表 has two example sentences:

代表 **dàibiǎo I** N representative, delegate ■ 谁是你们的代表? Shuí shì nǐmen de dàibiǎo? *Who is your representative?* **II** v represent, indicate ■ 这只是他个人的意见，不代表公司的立场。Zhè zhǐ shì tā gèrén de yìjiàn, bú dàibiǎo gōngsī de lìchǎng. *This is only his personal opinion, which does not represent the view of the company.*

In the first example sentence the headword 代表 **dàibiǎo** functions as a noun, meaning "representative." In the second example sentence 代表 **dàibiǎo** functions as a verb, and has the meaning "to represent."

Studying the sentences carefully will help you learn how to use Chinese words in everyday communication.

The example sentences in the Chinese-English sentences are all composed of the Chinese words that are treated as headwords in the dictionary. This means that this dictionary is self-contained.

8 English Translation of Chinese Sentences

All Chinese example sentences are accompanied by an English translation. In some cases a second translation is provided in brackets to aid comprehension and idiomatic expression. → indicates a freer, more idiomatic translation and ←, a more literal translation. For example:

> 让 **ràng** ■ 你应该让那辆车先行。Nǐ yīnggāi ràng nà liàng chē xiānxíng. *You should let that vehicle go first. (→ You should give way to that vehicle.)*

9 Note

The Note presented in a color box gives essential information on cultural context, pronunciation, grammar and usage. These help you use the language in a socially acceptable and idiomatic way. For example:

> 肥 **féi**...
>
> NOTE: 肥 féi is normally used to describe animals. It is insulting to use it to describe humans.

10 How to find Chinese words

BY PINYIN SPELLING

Headwords are arranged alphabetically according to their *pinyin* spelling. So if you know how a word is pronounced, you can find it easily, just like the way you will look up an English word in an English dictionary.

If you do not know the pronunciation of a word you can find it either by its radical or the number of its strokes.

BY RADICALS

Radicals (部首 **bùshǒu**) are certain component parts of characters that have been used in Chinese dictionary-making for nearly 2,000 years. Characters sharing a radical are grouped together under the heading of that radical. To find a character in a dictionary, follow these steps:

(i)   In the List of Radicals, look up the character's radical according to the number of strokes in the radical. This gives a Radical Index number.

(ii) Turn to the number in the Radical Index.

(iii) Locate the character according to the number of remaining strokes needed to write the character (i.e. number of total strokes minus radical strokes = remaining strokes). You will find the *pinyin* by the character.

For example, to find 活 by Radical Index:

(i)   The radical group of 活 is 氵, which has three strokes. In the List of Radicals, look up 氵 in the section marked "3 strokes":

3 strokes

氵   34

(ii)   Turn to number 34 in the Radical Index.

(iii) As there are nine strokes in 活, and the radical has three strokes, six strokes remain
       to complete the character 活 (9 − 3 = 6). Look in the section "6 strokes" and locate
       活:
       6 strokes
       活   **huó**

(iv)   Turn to **huó** in the dictionary.
       huó 活 ...

BY STROKE NUMBERS
Unfortunately, looking for a character by its radical is not an entirely satisfactory method
as learners may not always know which part of the character is the radical. Therefore, this
section includes a Stroke Index to aid the learner further. Simply look for the character
according to the number of its strokes, and then locate the character by its first stroke.

For example, to find 活 by Stroke Index:
(i)   There are nine strokes in 活. Go to the section of nine strokes.
       9 strokes

(ii)   As the first stroke of 活 is " 、", locate 活 under " 、".

       `
       活   **huó**

(iii) Turn to **huó** in the dictionary.
       huó 活 ...

List of Radicals

1 stroke

、	1
一	2
丨	3
乙	4
亅	5
丿	6

2 strokes

亠	7
丷	8
冫	9
冖	10
二	11
十	12
厂	13
匚	14
卜	15
刂	16
勹	17
冂	18
勹	19
刀	20
力	21
八	22
亻	23
人	24
儿	25
几	26
又	27
凵	28
厶	29
辶	30
卩	31
阝(on left)	32
阝(on right)	33

3 strokes

氵	34

忄	35
小	36
宀	37
丬	38
广	39
门	40
辶	41
工	42
干	43
土	44
士	45
上	46
卄	47
艹	48
大	49
寸	50
扌	51
口	52
口	53
巾	54
山	55
彳	56
彡	57
夕	58
夂	59
犭	60
饣	61
彐	62
尸	63
已	64
己	65
巳	66
弓	67
女	68
子	69
纟	70
马	71

4 strokes

灬	72

文	73
方	74
心	75
户	76
斗	77
王,玉	78
木	79
犬	80
歹	81
瓦	82
车	83
比	84
日	85
曰	86
贝	87
见	88
父	89
攵	90
牛	91
手	92
毛	93
气	94
片	95
斤	96
爪	97
月	98
欠	99
天	100
风	101
殳	102
火	103
礻	104
戈	105
水	106
聿	107
止	108

5 strokes

龙	109
石	110

业	111
目	112
田	113
四	114
皿	115
钅	116
矢	117
禾	118
白	119
用	120
鸟	121
疒	122
立	123
穴	124
衤	125
示	126
母	127
去	128
疋	129
皮	130

6 strokes

老	131
耳	132
西	133
页	134
虍	135
虫	136
缶	137
舌	138
竹	139
自	140
舟	141
衣	142
羊	143
米	144
艮	145
羽	146
糸	147

7 strokes

麦	148
走	149
里	150
足	151
采	152
豸	153
身	154
角	155
言	156
辛	157
系	158
束	159
非	160
西	161
豆	162

8 strokes

隹	163
青	164
鱼	165
雨	166
齿	167

9 strokes

革	168
是	169
食	170
鬼	171
音	172

11 strokes

麻	173

12 strokes

黑	174

13 strokes

鼠	175

Radical Index

All characters are listed here under their radical plus the number of additional strokes needed to write them.

1　丶

举	jǔ
叛	pàn
为	wéi, wèi
永	yǒng
之	zhī
州	zhōu
主	zhǔ

2　一

一	yī, yí, yì

1–2 strokes

才	cái
丁	dīng
七	qī
三	sān
万	wàn
下	xià
于	yú
与	yǔ
丈	zhàng

3 strokes

不	bú, bù
丰	fēng
互	hù
世	shì
屯	tún
无	wú
五	wǔ
牙	yá
尤	yóu
专	zhuān

4 strokes

丙	bǐng
册	cè
东	dōng
甘	gān
可	kě
平	píng
正	zhēng, zhèng

5 strokes

而	ér
亚	yà
再	zài

6 strokes

辰	chén
更	gēng, gèng
来	lái
丽	lì
两	liǎng
求	qiú
巫	wū
严	yán

7–21 strokes

甬	béng
奉	fèng
哥	gē
耕	gēng
恭	gōng
柬	jiǎn
赖	lài
面	miàn
囊	náng
融	róng
甚	shèn
事	shì
爽	shuǎng
泰	tài
夏	xià
艳	yàn
枣	zǎo
奏	zòu

3　一

承	chéng
习	diāo
了	le, liǎo
买	mǎi
司	sī
习	xí
也	yě

4　乙

乙	yǐ

2–8 strokes

巴	bā
丑	chǒu
飞	fēi
幻	huàn
君	jūn
矛	máo
民	mín
乡	xiāng
予	yú
昼	zhòu

5　丨

串	chuàn
临	lín
且	qiě
申	shēn
师	shī
书	shū
央	yāng
由	yóu
中	zhōng

6　丿

1–2 strokes

川	chuān
瓜	guā
及	jí
九	jiǔ
久	jiǔ
么	me
乞	qǐ
千	qiān
丸	wán
义	yì

3–4 strokes

长	cháng, zhǎng
丹	dān
乏	fá

瓜	guā
乎	hū
乐	lè, yuè
丘	qiū
升	shēng
生	shēng
失	shī
氏	shì
甩	shuǎi
乌	wū

5 strokes

丢	diū
年	nián
乔	qiáo
向	xiàng
兆	zhào

6–14 strokes

重	chóng, zhòng
垂	chuí
囱	cōng
够	gòu
乖	guāi
甥	shēng
舞	wǔ
周	zhōu

7　亠

2–3 strokes

亢	kàng
六	liù
市	shì
亡	wáng

4–5 strokes

充	chōng
交	jiāo
亩	mǔ
齐	qí
弃	qì

6–7 strokes

哀	āi
帝	dì

京	jīng
亮	liàng
氓	máng
亭	tíng
弯	wān
享	xiǎng

8–9 strokes

高	gāo
竟	jìng
离	lí
率	lǜ, shuài
商	shāng

10–15 strokes

膏	gāo
豪	háo
就	jiù
敲	qiāo
衰	shuāi
童	tóng
赢	yíng
衷	zhōng

8　冫

2–4 strokes

冰	bīng
冲	chōng, chòng
次	cì
决	jué

5–6 strokes

冻	dòng
净	jìng
况	kuàng
冷	lěng
冶	yě

8–14 strokes

凑	còu
减	jiǎn
凉	liáng
凌	líng
凝	níng

5 strokes

劫 jié
劲 jìn
劳 láo
励 lì
努 nǔ

6–11 strokes

勃 bó
舅 jiù
勘 kān
勉 miǎn
勤 qín
势 shì
勇 yǒng
助 zhù

22 八

八 bā

2–4 strokes

半 bàn
并 bìng
分 fēn, fèn
公 gōng
共 gòng
关 guan
兰 lán
兴 xīng, xìng

5–6 strokes

兵 bīng
单 dān
弟 dì
典 diǎn
兑 duì
谷 gǔ
具 jù
其 qí

7–9 strokes

兼 jiān
前 qián
首 shǒu
兽 shòu
养 yǎng
益 yì

23 亻

1–2 strokes

仇 chóu
化 huà

仅 jǐn
仆 pú
仁 rén
仍 réng
什 shén
亿 yì

3 strokes

代 dài
付 fù
们 men
他 tā
仙 xiān
仪 yí
仔 zǐ

4 strokes

传 chuán, zhuàn
伐 fá
仿 fǎng
份 fèn
伏 fú
伙 huǒ
价 jià
件 jiàn
任 rèn
伤 shang
似 sì
伟 wěi
伪 wěi
伍 wǔ
休 xīu
仰 yǎng
伊 yī
优 yōu

5 strokes

伴 bàn
伯 bó
伺 cì, sì
但 dàn
低 dī
佛 fó, fú
估 gū
何 hé
你 nǐ
伸 shēn
体 tǐ
位 wèi
佣 yōng

住 zhù
作 zuò

6 strokes

侧 cè
侈 chǐ
供 gōng, gòng
佳 jiā
例 lì
侣 lǚ
佩 pèi
侨 qiáo
使 shǐ
侍 shì
修 xiū
依 yī
侦 zhēn
侄 zhí

7 strokes

保 bǎo
便 biàn, pián
促 cù
俄 é
俘 fú
俭 jiǎn
俊 jùn
俩 liǎ
俏 qiào
侵 qīn
俗 sú
侮 wǔ
信 xìn

8 strokes

倍 bèi
倡 chàng
倒 dǎo, dào
俯 fǔ
候 hòu
健 jiàn
借 jiè
俱 jù
倦 juàn
倾 qīng
倘 tǎng
倚 yǐ
债 zhài
值 zhí

9–10 strokes

傲 ào
傍 bàng
偿 cháng
储 chǔ
傅 fù
假 jiǎ, jià
偶 ǒu
偏 piān
停 tíng
偷 tōu
做 zuò

11–13 strokes

催 cuī
僵 jiāng
僚 liáo
僻 pì
傻 shǎ
像 xiàng

24 人

人 rén
入 rù

1–2 strokes

仓 cāng
从 cóng
个 gè
介 jiè
今 jīn
以 yǐ

3–4 strokes

丛 cóng
合 hé
会 huì, kuài
令 lìng
企 qǐ
全 quán
伞 sǎn
众 zhòng

5–10 strokes

含 hán
盒 hé
金 jīn
命 mìng
拿 ná
禽 qín
舍 shě, shè
舒 shū

余 yú

25 儿

儿 ér

4–9 strokes

兜 dōu
先 xiān

26 几

几 jī, jǐ

1–12 strokes

凳 dèng
凡 fán
凤 fèng
凰 huáng
凭 píng

27 又

又 yòu

1–2 strokes

叉 chā
反 fǎn
双 shuāng
友 yǒu

3–11 strokes

变 biàn
叠 dié
对 duì
发 fā
欢 huān
艰 jiān
难 nán, nàn
叔 shū
叙 xù

28 凵

凹 āo
出 chū
函 hán
画 huà
击 jī
凸 tū
凶 xiōng

29 厶

参 cān
能 néng
去 qù

叁	sān	随	suí	沸	fèi	浪	làng	滴	dī
台	tái	隧	suì	河	hé	涝	lào	滚	gǔn
县	xiàn	隙	xì	泪	lèi	流	liú	滥	làn
允	yǔn	隐	yǐn	泌	mì	润	rùn	溜	liū
		障	zhàng	沫	mò	涉	shè	漏	lòu
30 廴				泥	ní	涛	tāo	滤	lǜ
建	jiàn	**33 阝 (on right)**		泞	níng	涕	tì	满	mǎn
延	yán	邦	bāng	泡	pào	涂	tú	漫	màn
		鄙	bǐ	沛	pèi	消	xiāo	漠	mò
31 卩		部	bù	泼	pō	浴	yù	漂	piāo
即	jí	都	dōu, dū	泣	qì	涨	zhǎng	漆	qī
卷	juǎn	郊	jiāo	浅	qiǎn	**8 strokes**		溶	róng
卵	luǎn	郎	láng	泄	xiè	淡	dàn	滩	tān
却	què	邻	lín	泻	xiè	淀	diàn	滔	tāo
卫	wèi	那	nà, nèi	沿	yán	混	hùn	演	yǎn
卸	xiè	邪	xié	泳	yǒng	渐	jiàn	源	yuán
印	yìn	邮	yóu	油	yóu	淋	lín	**12–17 strokes**	
		郁	yù	泽	zé	清	qīng	澳	ào
32 阝 (on left)		郑	zhèng	沾	zhān	渠	qú	潮	cháo
2–5 strokes				沼	zhǎo	深	shēn	澄	chéng
阿	ā	**34 氵**		治	zhì	渗	shèn	灌	guàn
陈	Chén	**2–4 strokes**		注	zhù	淘	táo	激	jī
队	duì	沉	chén	**6 strokes**		添	tiān	潦	liáo
防	fáng	池	chí	测	cè	淆	xiáo	瀑	pù
附	fù	泛	fàn	洞	dòng	淹	yān	潜	qián
际	jì	沟	gōu	洪	hóng	液	yè	潭	tán
阶	jiē	汗	hàn	浑	hún	淫	yín	溪	xī
陆	lù	汉	hàn	活	huó	涌	yǒng	澡	zǎo
阳	yáng	沪	hù	济	jì	渔	yú	**35 忄**	
阴	yīn	汇	huì	浇	jiāo	**9 strokes**		**1–5 strokes**	
阵	zhèn	江	jiāng	洁	jié	渡	dù	怖	bù
阻	zǔ	沥	lì	津	jīn	溉	gài	怪	guài
6–8 strokes		没	méi	浓	nóng	港	gǎng	怀	huái
除	chú	泖	qī	派	pài	湖	hú	快	kuài
陡	dǒu	汽	qì	洽	qià	滑	huá	怜	lián
降	jiàng	沙	shā	洒	sǎ	溅	jiàn	忙	máng
隆	lóng	汰	tài	洗	xǐ	渴	kě	怕	pà
陋	lòu	汤	tāng	洋	yáng	浏	liú	怯	qiè
陌	mò	汪	wāng	洲	zhōu	湿	shī	性	xìng
陪	péi	沃	wò	浊	zhuó	湾	wān	忆	yì
陶	táo	污	wū	**7 strokes**		温	wēn	忧	yōu
险	xiǎn	汹	xiōng	涤	dí	游	yóu	**6–8 strokes**	
陷	xiàn	汁	zhī	浮	fú	渣	zhā	惭	cán
限	xiàn	**5 strokes**		海	hǎi	滞	zhì	惨	cǎn
院	yuàn	波	bō	浩	hào	滋	zī	悼	dào
9–12 strokes		泊	bó	浸	jìn	**10–11 strokes**		惦	diàn
隘	ài	法	fǎ	酒	jiǔ	滨	bīn		
隔	gé								

惯	guàn
恨	hèn
恒	héng
恢	huī
悔	huǐ
惊	jīng
惧	jù
恼	nǎo
恰	qià
悄	qiāo
情	qíng
惋	wǎn
悟	wù
惜	xī
悦	yuè

9–13 strokes

懂	dǒng
惰	duò
愤	fèn
憾	hàn
慌	huāng
慨	kǎi
慷	kāng
愧	kuì
懒	lǎn
愣	lèng
慢	màn
慎	shèn
惕	tì
愉	yú

36 小

小	xiǎo

1–3 strokes

尘	chén
当	dāng, dàng
光	guāng
尖	jiān
少	shǎo, shào

4–9 strokes

尝	cháng
党	dǎng
辉	huī
尚	shàng
省	shěng
肖	xiào

37 宀

2–4 strokes

安	ān
宏	hóng
牢	láo
宁	níng, nìng
守	shǒu
它	tā
完	wán
宇	yǔ
灾	zāi
宅	zhái
字	zì

5–6 strokes

宝	bǎo
宠	chǒng
定	dìng
宫	gōng
官	guān
客	kè
审	shěn
实	shí
室	shì
宪	xiàn
宣	xuān
宜	yí
宙	zhòu
宗	zōng

7–8 strokes

案	àn
宾	bīn
害	hài
寂	jì
寄	jì
家	jiā
寇	kòu
宽	kuān
容	róng
宿	sù
宵	xiāo
宴	yàn
宰	zǎi

9–11 strokes

察	chá
富	fù
寡	guǎ
寒	hán

蜜	mì
寞	mò
塞	sāi
寓	yù
寨	zhài

38 丬

鉴	jiàn
将	jiāng
妆	zhuāng
壮	zhuàng
状	zhuàng

39 广

广	guǎng

3–4 strokes

床	chuáng
库	kù
庆	qìng
序	xù
应	yīng, yìng
庄	zhuāng

5–6 strokes

底	dǐ
店	diàn
度	dù
废	fèi
府	fǔ
庙	miào
庞	páng
庭	tíng

7-16 strokes

腐	fǔ
康	kāng
廊	láng
廉	lián
鹿	lù
磨	mó
唐	táng
席	xí
鹰	yīng
庸	yōng
座	zuò

40 门

门	mén

2–4 strokes

闭	bì
闯	chuǎng
间	jiān, jiàn
闷	mēn, mèn
闪	shǎn
问	wèn
闲	xián

5–9 strokes

阐	chǎn
阀	fá
闺	guī
阂	hé
阔	kuò
闹	nào
闻	wén
阅	yuè
闸	zhá

41 辶

2–3 strokes

边	biān
达	dá
过	guò, guo
辽	liáo
迈	mài
迁	qiān
巡	xún
迅	xùn

4 strokes

迟	chí
返	fǎn
还	hái, huán
进	jìn
近	jìn
连	lián
迫	pò
违	wéi
迎	yíng
远	yuǎn
运	yùn
这	zhè, zhèi

5–6 strokes

迪	dí
迹	jì
迷	mí
逆	nì
适	shì

述	shù
送	sòng
逃	táo
退	tuì
选	xuǎn
逊	xùn
追	zhuī

7–8 strokes

逮	dài
递	dì
逗	dòu
逢	féng
逛	guàng
逻	luó
逝	shì
速	sù
通	tōng
透	tòu
途	tú
造	zào
逐	zhú

9–12 strokes

逼	bī
避	bì
遍	biàn
道	dào
遣	qiǎn
邀	yāo
遥	yáo
遗	yí
遇	yù
遭	zāo
遮	zhē
遵	zūn

42 工

工	gōng

2–6 strokes

功	gōng
攻	gōng
汞	gǒng
巩	gǒng
贡	gòng
巧	qiǎo
式	shì
项	xiàng
左	zuǒ

43 干		**9–17 strokes**		**5–6 strokes**		落	là, luò	套	tào
干	gān, gàn	堡	bǎo	草	cǎo	蓝	lán		
刊	kān	壁	bì	茶	chá	蔓	màn	**50 寸**	
		堤	dī	荡	dàng	蒙	méng	寸	cùn
44 土		堕	duò	范	fàn	蔑	miè	**4–9 strokes**	
土	tǔ	赫	hè	荒	huāng	幕	mù	封	fēng
2–3 strokes		境	jìng	茧	jiǎn	墓	mù	耐	nài
场	chǎng	堪	kān	荐	jiàn	慕	mù	辱	rǔ
地	de, dì	墙	qiáng	茎	jīng	葡	pú	寿	shòu
坑	kēng	壤	rǎng	苦	kǔ	蔬	shū	尊	zūn
圣	shèng	塑	sù	荔	lì	蒜	suàn		
寺	sì	塌	tā	茫	máng	蓄	xù	**51 扌**	
在	zài	塔	tǎ	茅	máo	蕴	yùn	**2–3 strokes**	
至	zhì	塘	táng	茂	mào	葬	zàng	扒	bá
4–6 strokes		填	tián	苗	miáo	蔗	zhè	打	dǎ
坝	bà	墟	xū	苹	píng	蒸	zhēng	扣	kòu
城	chéng	增	zēng	茄	qié	**13–16 strokes**		扩	kuò
赤	chì			荣	róng	薄	báo, bó	扑	pū
垫	diàn	**45 士**		若	ruò	藏	cáng	扔	rēng
坊	fāng	士	shì	药	yào	蕾	lěi	扫	sǎo, sào
坟	fén	**3–11 strokes**		英	yīng	蘑	mó	托	tuō
坏	huài	鼓	gǔ	**7–8 strokes**		薯	shǔ	扬	yáng
圾	jī	壶	hú	菠	bō	藤	téng	扎	zhā
坚	jiān	吉	jí	菜	cài	薪	xīn	**4 strokes**	
均	jūn	嘉	jiā	菇	gū			把	bǎ
垦	kěn	壳	ké	荷	hé	**48 廾**		扳	bān
垮	kuǎ	声	shēng	黄	huáng	弊	bì	扮	bàn
块	kuài	喜	xǐ	获	huò	开	kāi	报	bào
垃	lā	壹	yī	菊	jú	弄	nòng	抄	chāo
垒	lěi	志	zhì	菌	jūn	异	yì	扯	chě
垄	lǒng			莲	lián			抖	dǒu
坡	pō	**46 上**		萝	luó	**49 大**		扶	fú
坛	tán	上	shàng	萌	méng	大	dà, dài	抚	fǔ
坦	tǎn			莫	mò	**1–3 strokes**		护	hù
型	xíng	**47 艹**		萍	píng	夺	duó	技	jì
幸	xìng	**1–4 strokes**		萨	sà	夫	fū	拒	jù
址	zhǐ	艾	ài	萄	táo	夹	jiā	抗	kàng
坐	zuò	芭	bā	营	yíng	夸	kuā	抠	kōu
7–8 strokes		苍	cāng	著	zhù	太	tài	抡	lūn
埠	bù	芳	fāng	**9–12 strokes**		头	tóu	拟	nǐ
堵	dǔ	芬	fēn	蔼	ǎi	**5–9 strokes**		拧	níng, nǐng
堆	duī	花	huā	蔽	bì	奥	ào	扭	niǔ
基	jī	节	jié	葱	cōng	奔	bēn	抛	pāo
埋	mái, mán	芹	qín	董	dǒng	奋	fèn	批	pī
培	péi	苏	sū	葫	hú	奖	jiǎng	抢	qiǎng
堂	táng	芽	yá	蕉	jiāo	奇	qí	扰	rǎo
域	yù	艺	yì	葵	kuí	牵	qiān	投	tóu
		芝	zhī			奢	shē		

抑	yì	挑	tiāo, tiǎo	掩	yǎn	**52 口**		咙	lóng
折	zhē, zhé	挺	tǐng	掷	zhì	口	kǒu	呢	ne
找	zhǎo	挖	wā	**9 strokes**		**2 strokes**		味	wèi
执	zhí	挟	xié	插	chā	叭	bā	咏	yǒng
抓	zhuā	挣	zhēng, zhèng	搀	chān	叼	diāo	咋	zǎ
5 strokes		指	zhǐ	搓	cuō	叮	dīng	**6 strokes**	
拔	bá	拽	zhuài	搭	dā	号	hào	哆	duō
拌	bàn	**7 strokes**		搁	gē	叫	jiào	哈	hā
抱	bào	挨	ái	搅	jiǎo	另	lìng	哄	hǒng, hòng
拨	bō	捌	bā	揭	jiē	史	shǐ	哗	huá
拆	chāi	捕	bǔ	揪	jiū	叹	tàn	咳	ké
抽	chōu	挫	cuò	揽	lǎn	兄	xiōng	鸣	míng
担	dàn	捣	dǎo	搂	lǒu	叶	yè	哪	nǎ
抵	dǐ	捍	hàn	揉	róu	右	yòu	品	pǐn
拐	guǎi	换	huàn	搜	sōu	只	zhī, zhǐ	呻	shēn
拣	jiǎn	捐	juān	提	tí	**3 strokes**		虽	suī
拘	jū	捆	kǔn	握	wò	吃	chī	哇	wā
拉	lā	捞	lāo	援	yuán	吊	diào	响	xiǎng
拦	lán	捏	niē	揍	zòu	吗	ma	哑	yǎ
拢	lǒng	捎	shāo	**10 strokes**		吐	tǔ, tù	咽	yàn
抹	mā, mǒ	损	sǔn	摆	bǎi	吸	xī	咬	yǎo
拇	mǔ	捅	tǒng	搬	bān	吓	xià	咱	zán
拍	pāi	挽	wǎn	搏	bó	吁	yù	咨	zī
披	pī	振	zhèn	搞	gǎo	**4 strokes**		**7–9 strokes**	
抬	tái	捉	zhuō	摸	mō	吧	ba	啊	ā
拖	tuō	**8 strokes**		摄	shè	吵	chǎo	唉	āi
拓	tuò	捶	chuí	摊	tān	呈	chéng	唱	chàng
押	yā	措	cuò	携	xié	吹	chuī	喘	chuǎn
拥	yōng	掂	diàn	摇	yáo	呆	dāi	唇	chún
择	zé	掉	diào	**11–16 strokes**		吨	dūn	啡	fēi
招	zhāo	接	jiē	播	bō	吩	fēn	喊	hǎn
拙	zhuō	捷	jié	擦	cā	否	fǒu	喝	hē
6 strokes		据	jù	操	cāo	告	gào	哼	hēng
按	àn	掘	jué	撤	chè	吼	hǒu	喉	hóu
持	chí	控	kòng	撑	chēng	呕	ǒu	唤	huàn
挡	dǎng	掠	lüè	摧	cuī	听	tīng	啃	kěn
拱	gǒng	描	miáo	撵	niǎn	吞	tūn	喇	lǎ
挂	guà	捻	niǎn	撇	piē	吻	wěn	啦	la
挥	huī	排	pái	撒	sā	呜	wū	唠	láo
挤	jǐ	捧	pěng	擅	shàn	呀	yā, ya	啰	luō
挎	kuà	掐	qiā	摔	shuāi	员	yuán	哦	ǒ
括	kuò	授	shòu	撕	sī	**5 strokes**		喷	pēn
挠	náo	探	tàn	攒	zǎn	哎	āi	啤	pí
挪	nuó	掏	tāo	摘	zhāi	咐	fù	啥	shà
拼	pīn	推	tuī	撞	zhuàng	呵	hē	哨	shào
拾	shí	掀	xiān			呼	hū	唆	suō
拴	shuān					咖	kā	唾	tuò

唯	wéi	帆	fān
喂	wèi	帅	shuài
啸	xiào	帖	tiě
喧	xuān	希	xī
喻	yù	帐	zhàng
哲	zhé	帜	zhì
啄	zhuó	**7–12 strokes**	
10–17 strokes		常	cháng
嘲	cháo	幅	fú
嘿	hēi	帽	mào
嚼	jiáo	幢	zhuàng
嘛	ma		
嗯	ng	**55 山**	
噢	ō	山	shān
器	qì	**3–9 strokes**	
嚷	rǎng	岸	àn
嗓	sǎng	崩	bēng
嗽	sòu	岔	chà
嗦	suo	崇	chóng
嗡	wēng	岛	dǎo
嗅	xiù	峰	fēng
噪	zào	岗	gāng
嘱	zhǔ	峻	jùn
嘴	zuǐ	凯	kǎi
		岭	lǐng
53 囗		岂	qǐ
2–3 strokes		嵌	qiàn
回	huí	岁	suì
团	tuán	炭	tàn
因	yīn	峡	xiá
4–5 strokes		崖	yá
固	gù	岩	yán
国	guó	幽	yōu
困	kùn	屿	yǔ
图	tú	崭	zhǎn
围	wéi		
园	yuán	**56 彳**	
7–8 strokes		**3–5 strokes**	
圈	quān	彼	bǐ
圆	yuán	彻	chè
		行	háng, xíng
54 巾		径	jìng
巾	jīn	往	wǎng
2–6 strokes		役	yì
帮	bāng	征	zhēng
币	bì	**6–14 strokes**	
布	bù	待	dāi, dài
带	dài	得	dé, de, děi

德	dé	狮	shī
很	hěn	狭	xiá
衡	héng	犹	yóu
徊	huái	狱	yù
徽	huī	**7–10 strokes**	
街	jiē	猜	cāi
律	lù	猖	chāng
徘	pái	猴	hóu
徒	tú	猾	huá
微	wēi	狼	láng
衔	xián	狸	lí
循	xún	猎	liè
衍	yǎn	猫	māo
		猛	měng
57 彡		猿	yuán
彩	cǎi	猪	zhū
形	xíng		
须	xū	**61 饣**	
影	yǐng	**2–4 strokes**	
彰	zhāng	饭	fàn
		饥	jī
58 夕		饪	rèn
夕	xī	饮	yǐn
2–8 strokes		**5–10 strokes**	
多	duō	饱	bǎo
梦	mèng	饼	bǐng
名	míng	馋	chán
外	wài	饿	è
夜	yè	馆	guǎn
		饺	jiǎo
59 夂		馒	mán
备	bèi	饶	ráo
处	chǔ, chù	蚀	shí
冬	dōng	饰	shì
复	fù	饲	sì
各	gè	馅	xiàn
务	wù		
		62 彐	
60 犭		归	guī
3–6 strokes		录	lù
狈	bèi	寻	xún
独	dú		
犯	fàn	**63 尸**	
狗	gǒu	尸	shī
狠	hěn	**1–5 strokes**	
狐	hú	层	céng
狡	jiǎo	尺	chǐ
狂	kuáng	届	jiè

尽	jǐn, jìn		
居	jū		
局	jú		
尼	ní		
尿	niào		
屁	pì		
屈	qū		
屉	tì		
尾	wěi		
6–11 strokes			
屡	lǚ		
履	lǚ		
屏	píng		
屎	shǐ		
属	shǔ		
屠	tú		
屋	wū		
屑	xiè		
展	zhǎn		
64 已			
已	yǐ		
65 己			
己	jǐ		
66 巳			
导	dǎo		
卷	juǎn		
巷	xiàng		
67 弓			
弓	gōng		
1–13 strokes			
弹	dàn		
疆	jiāng		
弥	mí		
强	qiáng		
弱	ruò		
弦	xián		
引	yǐn		
张	zhāng		
68 女			
女	nǚ		
2–4 strokes			
妒	dù		
妨	fáng		

妇	fù	孤	gū	绒	róng	驻	zhù	**5–6 strokes**
好	hǎo, hào	孩	hái	统	tǒng			怠	dài
奸	jiān	孔	kǒng	**7–13 strokes**		**72 灬**		恶	ě, è, wù
妈	mā	孙	sūn	绷	bēng	**4–6 strokes**		恩	ēn
妙	miào	孝	xiào	编	biān	点	diǎn	急	jí
奶	nǎi	学	xué	缠	chán	杰	jié	悬	kěn
奴	nú	孕	yùn	绸	chóu	烈	liè	恐	kǒng
如	rú			锻	duàn	烹	pēng	恋	liàn
她	tā	**70 纟**		缝	féng, fèng	热	rè	虑	lù
妥	tuǒ	**2–4 strokes**		缚	fù	**8–10 strokes**		怒	nù
妄	wàng	纯	chún	缓	huǎn	熬	áo	思	sī
妖	yāo	纺	fǎng	继	jì	煎	jiān	息	xī
5 strokes		纷	fēn	绩	jì	焦	jiāo	怨	yuàn
姑	gū	纲	gāng	缴	jiǎo	然	rán	怎	zěn
姐	jiě	红	hóng	绢	juàn	熟	shú	总	zǒng
妹	mèi	级	jí	绿	lù	熊	xióng	**7–8 strokes**	
姆	mǔ	纪	jì	绵	mián	熏	xūn	悲	bēi
妻	qī	纠	jiū	渺	miǎo	燕	yàn	惫	bèi
始	shǐ	纳	nà	绳	shéng	照	zhào	惩	chéng
姓	xìng	纽	niǔ	缩	suō	煮	zhǔ	患	huàn
6–12 strokes		纱	shā	维	wéi			惠	huì
婚	hūn	丝	sī	绣	xiù	**73 文**		惑	huò
嫉	jí	纹	wén	续	xù	文	wén	您	nín
嫁	jià	纤	xiān	绪	xù			惹	rě
姜	jiāng	约	yuē	缘	yuán	**74 方**		悉	xī
娇	jiāo	纸	zhǐ	缀	zhuì	方	fāng	悬	xuán
姥	lǎo	纵	zòng	综	zōng	**4–10 strokes**		悠	yōu
媒	méi	**5 strokes**				放	fàng	**9–11 strokes**	
嫩	nèn	练	liàn	**71 马**		旅	lǚ	憋	biē
娘	niáng	络	luò	马	mǎ	旁	páng	愁	chóu
娶	qǔ	绍	shào	**3–14 strokes**		旗	qí	慈	cí
嫂	sǎo	绅	shēn	驳	bó	施	shī	感	gǎn
婶	shěn	细	xì	驰	chí	旋	xuán	慧	huì
耍	shuǎ	线	xiàn	驾	jià	族	zú	慰	wèi
娃	wá	织	zhī	骄	jiāo			想	xiǎng
媳	xí	终	zhōng	驴	lú	**75 心**		意	yì
嫌	xián	组	zǔ	骡	luó	心	xīn	愚	yú
姨	yí	**6 strokes**		骆	luò	**1–4 strokes**		愈	yù
姻	yīn	绑	bǎng	骂	mà	必	bì	愿	yuàn
婴	yīng	给	gěi, jǐ	骗	piàn	忽	hū		
娱	yú	绘	huì	骑	qí	忌	jì	**76 户**	
姿	zī	绞	jiǎo	驱	qū	念	niàn	户	hù
		结	jiē, jié	骚	sāo	忍	rěn	**3–8 strokes**	
69 子		经	jīng	驶	shǐ	态	tài	扁	biǎn
子	zǐ, zi	绝	jué	驼	tuó	忘	wàng	房	fáng
1–6 strokes		络	luò	验	yàn	忠	zhōng	雇	gù
存	cún	绕	rào	骤	zhòu			启	qǐ

扇　shàn

77 斗

斗　dòu
斜　xié

78 王，玉

王　Wáng
玉　yù

1–5 strokes

玻　bō
环　huán
玖　jiǔ
玲　líng
珑　lóng
玫　méi
珊　shān
玩　wán
现　xiàn
珍　zhēn

6–10 strokes

班　bān
斑　bān
瑰　guī
瑚　hú
璃　lí
理　lǐ
琴　qín
球　qiú
瑞　ruì
珠　zhū
琢　zuó

79 木

木　mù

1–2 strokes

本　běn
朵　duǒ
机　jī
末　mò
朴　pǔ
权　quán
杀　shā
术　shù
未　wèi
朽　xiǔ
杂　zá

3 strokes

材　cái
村　cūn
杆　gān, gǎn
杠　gàng
极　jí
李　Lǐ
枚　méi
条　tiáo
杏　xìng
杨　yáng
朱　zhū

4 strokes

板　bǎn
杯　bēi
构　gòu
柜　guì
果　guǒ
林　lín
枪　qiāng
松　sōng
枉　wǎng
枕　zhěn
枝　zhī

5 strokes

柏　bǎi
标　biāo
柄　bǐng
查　chá
栋　dòng
架　jià
栏　lán
柳　liǔ
某　mǒu
柠　níng
柒　qī
染　rǎn
柔　róu
柿　shì
树　shù
相　xiāng
柱　zhù

6 strokes

柴　chái
档　dàng
格　gé
根　gēn

梗　gěng
桂　guì
核　hé
栗　lì
桥　qiáo
桑　sāng
桃　táo
桅　wéi
校　xiào
样　yàng
株　zhū
桌　zhuō

7 strokes

检　jiǎn
梨　lí
梁　liáng
梅　méi
梢　shāo
梳　shū
梯　tī
桶　tǒng
械　xiè

8 strokes

棒　bàng
棺　guān
棍　gùn
椒　jiāo
棵　kē
棱　léng
棉　mián
棚　péng
棋　qí
森　sēn
椭　tuǒ
椅　yǐ
植　zhí
棕　zōng

9–12 strokes

榜　bǎng
槽　cáo
概　gài
横　héng
槐　huái
桨　jiǎng
橘　jú
枯　kū
榴　liú

楼　lóu
檬　méng
模　mó, mú
榷　què
橡　xiàng
樱　yīng
榨　zhà

80 犬

犬　quǎn

6–9 strokes

哭　kū
献　xiàn

81 歹

歹　dǎi

2–6 strokes

毙　bì
残　cán
歼　jiān
殊　shū
死　sǐ
殃　yāng
殖　zhí

82 瓦

瓦　wǎ

6 strokes

瓷　cí
瓶　píng

83 车

车　chē

1–6 strokes

轨　guǐ
轰　hōng
较　jiào
轮　lún
轻　qīng
轧　yà
载　zài
斩　zhǎn
转　zhuǎn

7–12 strokes

辈　bèi
辐　fú
辅　fú
辑　jí

辆　liàng
输　shū
辖　xiá
舆　yú

84 比

比　bǐ

2 strokes

毕　bì

85 旦

晋　jìn
量　liáng, liàng
曲　qū, qǔ
替　tì
显　xiǎn
暂　zàn
最　zuì

86 日

日　rì

1–4 strokes

昂　áng
昌　chāng
旦　dàn
旱　hàn
昏　hūn
旧　jiù
旷　kuàng
昆　kūn
明　míng
时　shí
旺　wàng
易　yì
早　zǎo
者　zhě
旨　zhǐ

5–6 strokes

春　chūn
晃　huǎng
昧　mèi
晒　shài
晓　xiǎo
星　xīng
映　yìng
晕　yùn
昨　zuó

7–11 strokes

培	àn
暴	bào
曾	céng
晨	chén
晶	jīng
景	jǐng
琼	liàng
暮	mù
暖	nuǎn
普	pǔ
晴	qíng
暑	shǔ
晚	wǎn
晤	wù
晰	xī
智	zhì

87 贝

贝	bèi

2–3 strokes

财	cái
贞	zhēn

4 strokes

败	bài
贬	biǎn
贩	fàn
贯	guàn
购	gòu
货	huò
贫	pín
贪	tān
贤	xián
责	zé
质	zhì

5 strokes

贷	dài
费	fèi
贵	guì
贺	hè
贱	jiàn
贸	mào
贴	tiē

6–12 strokes

赌	dǔ
贿	huì
赖	lài

赂	lù
赔	péi
赛	sài
赏	shǎng
赞	zàn
贼	zéi
赠	zèng
赚	zhuàn
资	zī

88 见

见	jiàn

2–5 strokes

观	guān
规	guī
觉	jiào, jué
览	lǎn

89 父

父	fù

2–6 strokes

爸	bà
爹	diē
斧	fǔ
爷	yé

90 攵

2–5 strokes

改	gǎi
故	gù
收	shōu
政	zhèng

6–7 strokes

敌	dí
敢	gǎn
教	jiāo, jiào
救	jiù
敏	mǐn
效	xiào
致	zhì

8–11 strokes

敞	chǎng
敷	fū
敬	jìng
散	sǎn, sàn
数	shǔ, shù

91 牛

牛	niú

4–7 strokes

犁	lí
牧	mù
牲	shēng
特	tè
物	wù
牺	xī

92 手

手	shǒu

5–15 strokes

掰	bāi
拜	bài
攀	pān
拳	quán
掌	zhǎng
挚	zhì

93 毛

毛	máo

6–10 strokes

毫	háo
耗	hào
髦	máo
毯	tǎn

94 气

气	qì

4–8 strokes

氮	dàn
氛	fēn
氢	qīng
氧	yǎng

95 片

片	piàn

4–8 strokes

版	bǎn
牌	pái

96 斤

斤	jīn

1–9 strokes

斥	chì
断	duàn

斯	sī
所	suǒ
欣	xīn
新	xīn

97 爪

爪	zhuǎ

4–6 strokes

爱	ài
采	cǎi
爬	pá
乳	rǔ
受	shòu

98 月

月	yuè

2–3 strokes

肠	cháng
肚	dù
肝	gān
肌	jī
有	yǒu

4 strokes

肪	fáng
肥	féi
肤	fū
服	fú
股	gǔ
肩	jiān
朋	péng
肾	shèn
胁	xié
育	yù
胀	zhàng
肢	zhī
肿	zhǒng

5 strokes

胞	bāo
背	bēi, bèi
胆	dǎn
肺	fèi
骨	gǔ
胡	hú
脉	mài
胖	pàng
胜	shèng
胃	wèi

6 strokes

脆	cuì
胳	gē
脊	jǐ
胶	jiāo
朗	lǎng
脑	nǎo
胸	xiōng
脏	zāng, zàng
脂	zhī

7–8 strokes

脖	bó
朝	cháo
脚	jiǎo
腊	là
脸	liǎn
脾	pí
期	qī
腔	qiāng
脱	tuō
望	wàng
朝	zhāo

9–16 strokes

膀	bǎng
臂	bì
膊	bó
腹	fù
膜	mó
膨	péng
腮	sāi
膛	táng
腾	téng
腿	tuǐ
膝	xī
腥	xīng
腰	yāo

99 欠

欠	qiàn

4–10 strokes

歌	gē
款	kuǎn
欧	ōu
欺	qī
歉	qiàn
软	ruǎn
歇	xiē

欲	yù

100 天

天	tiān

101 风

风	fēng

11 strokes

飘	piāo

102 殳

殿	diàn
段	duàn
毁	huǐ
殴	ōu
毅	yì

103 火

火	huǒ

2–5 strokes

灿	càn
炒	chǎo
炊	chuī
灯	dēng
灰	huī
灸	jiǔ
炕	kàng
烂	làn
炼	liàn
灵	líng
炉	lú
灭	miè
炮	pào
烁	shuò
炎	yán
灶	zào
炸	zhá

6–14 strokes

爆	bào
烦	fán
焊	hàn
烘	hōng
煌	huáng
烤	kǎo
煤	méi
燃	rán
熔	róng
烧	shāo

烫	tàng
熄	xī
烟	yān
焰	yàn
烛	zhú

104 衤

福	fú
祸	huò
礼	lǐ
社	shè
神	shén
视	shì
祥	xiáng
祝	zhù
祖	zǔ

105 戈

裁	cái
成	chéng
戴	dài
或	huò
截	jié
戒	jiè
威	wēi
我	wǒ
武	wǔ
戏	xì
栽	zāi
战	zhàn

106 水

水	shuǐ

5–6 strokes

浆	jiāng
泉	quán

107 聿

隶	lì
肆	sì
肃	sù

108 止

止	zhǐ

2–4 strokes

步	bù
此	cǐ
肯	kěn

歧	qí
歪	wāi

109 龙

龙	lóng

6 strokes

聋	lóng
袭	xí

110 石

石	shí

3–5 strokes

础	chǔ
砍	kǎn
矿	kuàng
码	mǎ
破	pò
砌	qì
砂	shā
研	yán
砸	zá
砖	zhuān

6–12 strokes

碍	ài
磅	bàng
碑	bēi
碧	bì
磁	cí
磋	cuō
碟	dié
硅	guī
碱	jiǎn
磕	kē
磷	lín
硫	liú
碌	lù
碰	pèng
确	què
硕	shuò
碎	suì
碳	tàn
碗	wǎn
硬	yìng

111 业

业	yè

7 strokes

凿	záo

112 目

目	mù

2–4 strokes

盯	dīng
盾	dùn
看	kān, kàn
盲	máng
冒	mào
眉	méi
盼	pàn
眨	zhǎ

5–13 strokes

睬	cǎi
瞪	dèng
督	dū
睛	jīng
瞒	mán
眯	mí
眠	mián
睦	mù
瞥	piē
瞧	qiáo
睡	shuì
瞎	xiā
眼	yǎn
瞻	zhān
睁	zhēng

113 田

田	tián

2–7 strokes

畅	chàng
电	diàn
番	fān
甲	jiǎ
界	jiè
累	lèi
留	liú
略	lüè
男	nán
畔	pàn
畏	wèi
畜	xù
野	yě

114 四

四	sì

4–8 strokes

罢	bà
罚	fá
暑	shǔ
罩	zhào
置	zhì
罪	zuì

115 皿

盗	dào
监	jiān
盟	méng
盘	pán
盆	pén
盛	shèng
血	xiě, xuè
衅	xìn
盐	yán
盈	yíng
盏	zhǎn

116 钅

2–4 strokes

钞	chāo
钓	diào
钉	dīng, dìng
钙	gài
钢	gāng
钩	gōu
钦	qīn
钥	yào
针	zhēn
钟	zhōng

5–6 strokes

铲	chǎn
铃	líng
铝	lǚ
铅	qiān
钱	qián
钳	qián
铁	tiě
铜	tóng
银	yín
铀	yóu
钻	zuān, zuàn

7 strokes

锄	chú
锋	fēng
锅	guō
链	liàn
铺	pū
锐	ruì
锁	suǒ
销	xiāo
锌	xīn
锈	xiù
铸	zhù

8–17 strokes

锤	chuí
错	cuò
镀	dù
锻	duàn
键	jiàn
锦	jǐn
镜	jìng
锯	jù
镰	lián
锣	luó
镁	měi
锹	qiāo
锡	xī
镶	xiāng
镇	zhèn
镯	zhuó

117 矢

矮	ǎi
短	duǎn
矩	jǔ
知	zhī

118 禾

禾	hé

2–4 strokes

秉	bǐng
和	hé
季	jì
科	kē
秒	miǎo
秋	qiū
私	sī
秃	tū

委	wěi
香	xiāng
秀	xiù
种	zhǒng, zhòng

5–6 strokes

称	chèn, chēng
乘	chéng
秤	chèng
积	jī
秘	mì
税	shuì
秧	yāng
移	yí
秩	zhì
租	zū

7–12 strokes

程	chéng
稠	chóu
稻	dào
稿	gǎo
稼	jià
穆	mù
稍	shāo
穗	suì
稳	wěn
稀	xī
稚	zhì

119 白

白	bái

1–9 strokes

百	bǎi
的	de, dí
皇	huáng
皆	jiē
魄	pò
皂	zào

120 用

用	yòng

121 鸟

鸟	niǎo

2–7 strokes

鹅	é
鸽	gē

鸡	jī
鹊	què
鸦	yā
鸭	yā

122 疒

2–5 strokes

疤	bā
病	bìng
疮	chuāng
疯	fēng
疾	jí
疗	liáo
疲	pí
疼	téng
疫	yì
症	zhèng

6–12 strokes

癌	ái
痹	bì
痴	chī
痕	hén
痪	huàn
瘤	liú
瘸	qué
瘦	shòu
瘫	tān
痰	tán
痛	tòng
瘟	wēn
痒	yǎng

123 立

立	lì

1–9 strokes

产	chǎn
端	duān
竭	jié
竟	jìng
亲	qīn
竖	shù
站	zhàn
章	zhāng

124 穴

穴	xué

2–11 strokes

穿	chuān
窗	chuāng
窜	cuàn
窖	jiào
究	jiū
空	kōng, kòng
窟	kū
帘	lián
窿	lóng
窃	qiè
穷	qióng
突	tū
窝	wō
窑	yáo
窄	zhǎi

125 衤

2–3 strokes

补	bǔ
衬	chèn
初	chū
衫	shān

4–7 strokes

袄	ǎo
被	bèi
袱	fú
裤	kù
袍	páo
裙	qún
袜	wà
袖	xiù
裕	yù

126 示

示	shì

8 strokes

禁	jìn

127 母

母	mǔ

2–4 strokes

毒	dú
每	měi

128 去

去	qù

129 疋

楚	chǔ
疏	shū

130 皮

皮	pí

5 strokes

皱	zhòu

131 老

考	kǎo
老	lǎo

132 耳

耳	ěr

2–8 strokes

耻	chǐ
聪	cōng
耽	dān
聚	jù
联	lián
聊	liáo
聘	pìn
取	qǔ
耸	sǒng
职	zhí

133 西

西	xī

3–12 strokes

覆	fù
票	piào
要	yāo, yào

134 页

页	yè

2–4 strokes

颁	bān
顶	dǐng
顿	dùn
顾	gù
顷	qǐng
顺	shùn
颂	sòng
顽	wán
项	xiàng
预	yù

5–13 strokes

颤	chàn
颠	diān
额	é
颊	jiá
颈	jǐng
颗	kē
领	lǐng
频	pín
颇	pō
颜	yán
颖	yǐng

135 虍

虎	hǔ
虏	lǔ
虚	xū

136 虫

虫	chóng

3–6 strokes

蚕	cán
蛋	dàn
虹	hóng
蚂	mǎ
蛮	mán
蛇	shé
蛙	wā
蚊	wén
虾	xiā
蚁	yǐ
蛀	zhù

7–15 strokes

蝉	chán
蠢	chǔn
蝶	dié
蛾	é
蜂	fēng
蝴	hú
蝗	huáng
蜡	là
螺	luó
蜜	mì
蜻	qīng
蝇	yíng
蜘	zhī

137 缶

缸	gāng
罐	guàn
缺	quē

138 舌

舌	shé

2–7 strokes

辞	cí
乱	luàn

139 竹

竹	zhú

3–5 strokes

笆	bā
笨	bèn
笔	bǐ
笛	dí
第	dì
符	fú
竿	gān
笼	lóng
笋	sǔn
笑	xiào

6–7 strokes

策	cè
筹	chóu
答	dā, dá
等	děng
简	jiǎn
筋	jīn
筷	kuài
签	qiān
筛	shāi
筒	tǒng
筝	zhēng
筑	zhù

8–13 strokes

簸	bǒ
管	guǎn
籍	jí
箭	jiàn
篮	lán
篱	lí
箩	luó
篇	piān

算	suàn
箱	xiāng

140 自

自	zì

4–8 strokes

鼻	bí
臭	chòu

141 舟

舟	zhōu

4–9 strokes

般	bān
舶	bó
舱	cāng
船	chuán
舵	duò
航	háng
舰	jiàn
艘	sōu
艇	tǐng

142 衣

衣	yī

2–8 strokes

表	biǎo
袋	dài
裂	liè
裳	shàng
装	zhuāng

143 羊

羊	yáng

3–8 strokes

差	chā, chà
盖	gài
美	měi
群	qún
善	shàn
羡	xiàn
翔	xiáng
羞	xiū
着	zháo, zhe, zhuó

144 米

米	mǐ

3–6 strokes

粗	cū
粉	fěn
粪	fèn
类	lèi
粒	lì
料	liào
籽	zǐ

7–11 strokes

粹	cuì
糕	gāo
糊	hú
精	jīng
糠	kāng
粮	liáng
糖	táng
粤	yuè
糟	zāo
粥	zhōu

145 艮

既	jì
良	liáng

146 羽

羽	yǔ

4–12 strokes

翅	chì
翠	cuì
翻	fān
翘	qiào
翁	wēng
翼	yì

147 糸

繁	fán
紧	jǐn
素	sù
索	suǒ
絮	xù
紫	zǐ

148 麦

麦	mài

149 走

走	zǒu

3–8 strokes

超	chāo
趁	chèn
赴	fù
赶	gǎn
起	qǐ
趋	qū
趣	qù
趟	tàng
越	yuè

150 里

里	lǐ

4 strokes

野	yě

151 足

足	zú

3–6 strokes

跌	diē
跺	duò
跟	gēn
跪	guì
践	jiàn
距	jù
跨	kuà
路	lù
趴	pā
跑	pǎo
跳	tiào
跃	yuè

7–13 strokes

蹦	bèng
踩	cǎi
蹈	dǎo
蹲	dūn
踏	tā, tà
踢	tì
蹄	tí
躁	zào
踪	zōng

152 釆

释	shì

153 豸			
貌	mào		

辟 pì

158 系

系 xì

154 身	
身	shēn

3–8 strokes

躲 duǒ
射 shè
躺 tǎng

159 束

束 shù

9 strokes

整 zhěng

155 角	
角	jiǎo

6 strokes

触 chù
解 jiě

160 非

非 fēi

7 strokes

靠 kào

156 言	
言	yán

6–13 strokes

警 jǐng
譬 pì
誓 shì
誉 yù

161 酉

酬 chóu
醋 cù
酱 jiàng
酷 kù
酶 méi
酿 niàng
配 pèi
酸 suān
醒 xǐng
酗 xù
酝 yùn
酌 zhuó
醉 zuì

157 辛	
辛	xīn

6–12 strokes

瓣 bàn
辨 biàn
辩 biàn
辫 biàn
辣 là

162 豆

豆 dòu

5–8 strokes

登 dēng
豌 wān

163 隹	
雌	cí
雕	diāo
集	jí
雀	què
售	shòu
雄	xióng
雅	yǎ
耀	yào

164 青	
青	qīng

6 strokes

静 jìng

165 鱼	
鱼	yú

4–8 strokes

鲸 jīng
鲁 lǔ
鲜 xiān

166 雨	
雨	yǔ

3–13 strokes

霸 bà
雹 báo
霍 huò

雷 léi
零 líng
露 lù
霉 méi
霜 shuāng
雾 wù
霞 xiá
需 xū
雪 xuě
震 zhèn

167 齿	
齿	chǐ

5 strokes

龄 líng

168 革	
革	gé

2–9 strokes

鞭 biān
鞠 jū
勒 lè
鞋 xié
靴 xuē

169 是	
是	shì

2–6 strokes

匙 chí, shi
题 tí

170 食	
食	shí

7 strokes

餐 cān

171 鬼	
鬼	guǐ

4 strokes

魂 hún

172 音	
音	yīn

4 strokes

韵 yùn

173 麻	
麻	má

4–9 strokes

摩 mó
魔 mó

174 黑	
黑	hēi

3–4 strokes

墨 mò
默 mò

175 鼠	
鼠	shǔ

Stroke Index

This index lists all characters in this dictionary according to the number of strokes used to write them. Characters with the same number of strokes are grouped together according to the first stroke used. These groups are listed in the following order:

1. 一 (including ⼅ ⼂)
2. 丨 (including 亅 丿)
3. 丿 (including 丿 乛 亅)

4. 丶 (including 丶 乀)
5. 乛 (including 乛 乛 ⻖ 乛 乁 乙 乚)
6. ⼃ (including 乚 乚 乚 乚 乚)

Within each group, characters are arranged alphabetically according to *pinyin*.

1–2 strokes					
一	工 gōng	亡 wáng	区 qū	仓 cāng	勿 wù
厂 chǎng	亏 kuī	之 zhī	犬 quǎn	长 cháng,	凶 xiōng
丁 dīng	三 sān	**亅**	市 shì	zhǎng	月 yuè
二 èr	尸 shī	叉 chā	世 shì	仇 chóu	勾 yún
弓 gōng	士 shì	飞 fēi	太 tài	从 cóng	爪 zhǎo
七 qī	土 tǔ	已 jǐ	天 tiān	丹 dān	**丶**
十 shí	万 wàn	马 mǎ	厅 tīng	乏 fá	订 dìng
一 yī, yí, yì	下 xià	刃 rèn	屯 tún	反 fǎn	斗 dòu
卜 bó, bǔ	于 yú	卫 wèi	瓦 wǎ	分 fēn, fèn	方 fāng
丿	丈 zhàng	习 xí	王 wáng	风 fēng	户 hù
八 bā	**丨**	也 yě	无 wú	凤 fèng	火 huǒ
儿 ér	巾 jīn	已 yǐ	五 wǔ	父 fù	讥 jī
几 jī, jǐ	口 kǒu	子 zǐ, zi	牙 yá	公 gōng	计 jì
九 jiǔ	山 shān		艺 yì	勾 gōu	亢 kàng
人 rén	上 shàng	女 nǚ	尤 yóu	化 huà	六 liù
入 rù	小 xiǎo	乡 xiāng	友 yǒu	介 jiè	认 rèn
乛	**丿**	与 yǔ	元 yuán	斤 jīn	为 wéi,
刀 dāo	川 chuān		云 yún	今 jīn	wèi
刁 diāo	凡 fán	**4 strokes**	扎 zhā	仅 jǐn	文 wén
了 le, liǎo	个 gè	**一**	支 zhī	毛 máo	心 xīn
力 lì	及 jí	不 bú, bù	专 zhuān	牛 niú	忆 yì
乙 yǐ	久 jiǔ	车 chē	**丨**	片 piàn	**乛**
又 yòu	么 me	歹 dǎi	贝 bèi	仆 pú	巴 bā
3 strokes	乞 qǐ	丰 fēng	见 jiàn	气 qì	办 bàn
一	千 qiān	夫 fū	内 nèi	欠 qiàn	尺 chǐ
才 cái	勺 sháo	戈 gē	日 rì	仁 rén	丑 chǒu
寸 cùn	丸 wán	互 hù	少 shǎo,	仍 réng	队 duì
大 dà, dài	夕 xī	井 jǐng	shào	什 shén	孔 kǒng
干 gān,	义 yì	巨 jù	水 shuǐ	升 shēng	劝 quàn
gàn	亿 yì	开 kāi	止 zhǐ	氏 shì	书 shū
	丶	历 lì	中 zhōng	手 shǒu	双 shuāng
	广 guǎng	木 mù	**丿**	乌 wū	引 yǐn
	门 mén	匹 pǐ	币 bì	午 wǔ	予 yú

乚
比 bǐ
幻 huàn
以 yǐ
允 yǔn

5 strokes

一

艾 ài
扒 bá
本 běn
丙 bǐng
布 bù
打 dǎ
东 dōng
甘 gān
功 gōng
古 gǔ
击 jī
节 jié
刊 kān
可 kě
厉 lì
龙 lóng
灭 miè
末 mò
平 píng
扑 pū
巧 qiǎo
切 qiè
去 qù
扔 rēng
石 shí
示 shì
术 shù
未 wèi
轧 yà
右 yòu
玉 yù
札 zhā
正 zhēng, zhèng
左 zuǒ

丨

凹 āo
叭 bā
北 běi

出 chū
旦 dàn
电 diàn
叼 diāo
叮 dīng
归 guī
号 hào
甲 jiǎ
叫 jiào
旧 jiù
卡 kǎ
另 lìng
目 mù
且 qiě
申 shēn
史 shǐ
帅 shuài
四 sì
叹 tàn
田 tián
凸 tū
兄 xiōng
央 yāng
叶 yè
业 yè
由 yóu
占 zhàn
只 zhǐ, zhǐ

丿

白 bái
包 bāo
册 cè
斥 chì
处 chǔ, chù
匆 cōng
丛 cóng
代 dài
冬 dōng
犯 fàn
付 fù
瓜 guā
禾 hé
乎 hū
饥 jī
句 jù
乐 lè, yuè
令 lìng

们 men
鸟 niǎo
丘 qiū
生 shēng
失 shī
甩 shuǎi
他 tā
外 wài
务 wù
仪 yí
印 yìn
用 yòng
孕 yùn
仔 zǐ

丶

半 bàn
必 bì
汉 hàn
汇 huì
记 jì
兰 lán
礼 lǐ
立 lì
宁 níng, nìng
让 ràng
闪 shǎn
市 shì
它 tā
讨 tǎo
头 tóu
写 xiě
穴 xué
讯 xùn
议 yì
永 yǒng
汁 zhī
主 zhǔ

乛

边 biān
对 duì
加 jiā
辽 liáo
矛 máo
民 mín
尼 ní
皮 pí

圣 shèng
司 sī
召 zhào

乚

发 fā
纠 jiū
母 mǔ
奶 nǎi
奴 nú
丝 sī
台 tái
幼 yòu

6 strokes

一

百 bǎi
邦 bāng
场 chǎng
臣 chén
成 chéng
存 cún
达 dá
地 de, dì
动 dòng
夺 duó
而 ér
耳 ěr
巩 gǒng
共 gòng
轨 guǐ
过 guò, guo
划 huá, huà
灰 huī
机 jī
圾 jī
吉 jí
夹 jiā
匠 jiàng
考 kǎo
扣 kòu
夸 kuā
扩 kuò
老 lǎo
列 liè
迈 mài
朴 pǔ

权 quán
扫 sǎo, sào
式 shì
死 sǐ
寺 sì
托 tuō
西 xī
协 xié
邪 xié
刑 xíng
朽 xiǔ
压 yā
亚 yà
厌 yàn
扬 yáng
页 yè
有 yōu
再 zài
在 zài
芝 zhī
执 zhí
至 zhì

丨

尘 chén
吃 chī
虫 chóng
此 cǐ
当 dāng, dàng
吊 diào
帆 fān
刚 gāng
光 guāng
回 huí
尖 jiān
劣 liè
虏 lǔ
吗 ma
岂 qǐ
曲 qū, qǔ
肉 ròu
师 shī
岁 suì
同 tóng
吐 tǔ, tù
团 tuán
网 wǎng

吸 xī
吓 xià
迅 xùn
因 yīn
屿 yǔ
吁 yù
早 zǎo
则 zé
贞 zhēn
妆 zhuāng
壮 zhuàng

丿

传 chuán, zhuàn
创 chuàng
丢 diū
多 duǒ
朵 duǒ
伐 fá
仿 fǎng
份 fèn
伏 fú
负 fù
各 gè
行 háng
合 hé
后 hòu
华 huá
会 huì, kuài
伙 huǒ
肌 jī
价 jià
件 jiàn
名 míng
年 nián
企 qǐ
迁 qiān
乔 qiáo
全 quán
任 rèn
伞 sǎn
色 sè
杀 shā
伤 shāng
舌 shé
似 sì

身 shēn	沥 lì	迟 chí	抽 chōu	妻 qī	贬 biǎn
私 sī	疗 liáo	附 fù	刺 cì	其 qí	昌 chāng
体 tǐ	没 méi	改 gǎi	担 dān	奇 qí	畅 chàng
条 tiáo	闷 mēn,	鸡 jī	到 dào	枪 qiāng	齿 chǐ
秃 tū	mèn	即 jí	抵 dǐ	茄 qié	迪 dí
妥 tuǒ	亩 mǔ	忌 jì	顶 dǐng	青 qīng	典 diǎn
位 wèi	判 pàn	际 jì	范 fàn	取 qǔ	贩 fàn
我 wǒ	沛 pèi	劲 jìn	奋 fèn	软 ruǎn	非 fēi
希 xī	评 píng	局 jú	奉 fèng	若 ruò	咐 fù
系 xì	沏 qī	君 jūn	构 gòu	丧 sāng,	购 gòu
仙 xiān	柒 qī	灵 líng	拐 guǎi	sàng	固 gù
秀 xiù	启 qǐ	陆 lù	规 guī	事 shì	国 guó
役 yì	弃 qì	驴 lú	柜 guì	势 shì	果 guǒ
饮 yǐn	汽 qì	屁 pì	轰 hōng	述 shù	呵 hē
迎 yíng	穷 qióng	驱 qū	画 huà	松 sōng	呼 hū
佣 yōng	饪 rèn	忍 rěn	环 huán	抬 tái	虎 hǔ
犹 yóu	沙 shā	删 shān	或 huò	态 tài	具 jù
余 yú	社 shè	屉 tì	拣 jiǎn	坦 tǎn	咖 kā
皂 zào	识 shí	尾 wěi	杰 jié	拖 tuō	凯 kǎi
针 zhēn	诉 sù	张 zhāng	茎 jīng	拓 tuò	肯 kěn
住 zhù	汰 tài	阻 zǔ	拘 jū	玩 wán	昆 kūn
作 zuò	完 wán		苦 kǔ	枉 wǎng	岭 lǐng
坐 zuò	汪 wāng	纯 chún	矿 kuàng	卧 wò	咙 lóng
`	忘 wàng	妒 dù	垃 lā	武 wǔ	虏 lǔ
补 bǔ	沃 wò	妨 fáng	拉 lā	现 xiàn	罗 luó
灿 càn	闲 xián	纺 fǎng	拦 lán	幸 xìng	明 míng
沉 chén	辛 xīn	纷 fēn	林 lín	押 yā	鸣 míng
初 chū	汹 xiōng	纲 gāng	垄 lǒng	英 yīng	呢 ne
床 chuáng	序 xù	妙 miào	拢 lǒng	拥 yōng	岐 qí
词 cí	言 yán	纳 nà	轮 lún	雨 yǔ	尚 shàng
弟 dì	冶 yě	纽 niǔ	抹 mǎ, mǒ	郁 yù	呻 shēn
冻 dòng	译 yì	努 nǔ	码 mǎ	枣 zǎo	肾 shèn
兑 duì	应 yīng,	纱 shā	卖 mài	责 zé	叔 shū
泛 fàn	yìng	纹 wén	茅 máo	择 zé	图 tú
沟 gōu	忧 yōu	妖 yāo	茂 mào	斩 zhǎn	旺 wàng
罕 hǎn	灾 zāi	纸 zhǐ	玫 méi	招 zhāo	味 wèi
宏 hóng	灶 zào		枚 méi	者 zhě	贤 xián
沪 hù	诈 zhà	**8 strokes**	苗 miáo	枕 zhěn	些 xiē
怀 huái	这 zhè,	一	拇 mǔ	枝 zhī	岩 yán
间 jiān,	zhèi	拔 bá	拧 níng,	直 zhí	易 yì
jiàn	诊 zhěn	板 bǎn	nǐng	转 zhuǎn	咏 yǒng
究 jiū	证 zhèng	抱 bào	欧 ōu	拙 zhuō	咋 zǎ
库 kù	ᄀ	杯 bēi	殴 ōu		帜 zhì
快 kuài	阿 ā	奔 bēn	拍 pāi	哎 āi	忠 zhōng
况 kuàng	驳 bó	表 biǎo	披 pī	岸 àn	卓 zhuó
牢 láo	层 céng	厕 cè	苹 píng	昂 áng	ノ
冷 lěng	陈 chén	拆 chāi	坡 pō	败 bài	爸 bà

版	bǎn	侵	qīn	房	fáng	视	shì	姑	gū	厚	hòu
饱	bǎo	乳	rǔ	放	fàng	祥	xiáng	贯	guàn	胡	hú
卑	bēi	刹	shā	废	fèi	享	xiǎng	姐	jiě	荒	huāng
备	bèi	舍	shě, shè	沸	fèi	泄	xiè	练	liàn	挥	huī
彼	bǐ	使	shǐ	府	fǔ	泻	xiè	妹	mèi	挤	jǐ
秉	bǐng	侍	shì	该	gāi	性	xìng	姆	mǔ	茧	jiǎn
采	cǎi	饰	shì	怪	guài	学	xué	叁	sān	柬	jiǎn
侧	cè	受	shòu	官	guān	询	xún	绍	shào	荐	jiàn
侈	chǐ	饲	sì	河	hé	沿	yán	绅	shēn	砍	kǎn
垂	chuí	所	suǒ	话	huà	炎	yán	始	shǐ	枯	kū
的	de, dí	贪	tān	剂	jì	夜	yè	细	xì	垮	kuǎ
钓	diào	兔	tù	肩	jiān	宜	yí	线	xiàn	挎	kuà
肪	fáng	往	wǎng	郊	jiāo	泳	yǒng	姓	xìng	括	kuò
肥	féi	委	wěi	京	jīng	油	yóu	织	zhī	栏	lán
肺	fèi	物	wù	净	jìng	育	yù	终	zhōng	厘	lí
氛	fēn	胁	xié	卷	juǎn	泽	zé	纵	zòng	荔	lì
肤	fū	欣	xīn	炕	kàng	闸	zhá	组	zǔ	玲	líng
服	fú	依	yī	刻	kè	沾	zhān			珑	lóng
斧	fǔ	鱼	yú	空	kōng,	沼	zhǎo	**9 strokes**		茫	máng
供	gōng,	胀	zhàng		kòng	郑	zhèng	一		面	miàn
	gòng	侦	zhēn			治	zhì	按	àn	某	mǒu
狗	gǒu	征	zhēng	郎	láng	宙	zhòu	柏	bǎi	耐	nài
谷	gǔ	知	zhī	帘	lián	注	zhù	帮	bāng	南	nán
股	gǔ	肢	zhī	怜	lián	宗	zōng	甭	béng	挠	náo
刮	guā	侄	zhí	泪	lèi			标	biāo	柠	níng
乖	guāi	制	zhì	炉	lú	丁		柄	bǐng	挪	nuó
和	hé	质	zhì	庙	miào	承	chéng	玻	bō	拼	pīn
忽	hū	肿	zhǒng	盲	máng	孤	gū	勃	bó	砌	qì
狐	hú	周	zhōu	氓	máng	函	hán	残	cán	牵	qiān
昏	hūn			泌	mì	驾	jià	草	cǎo	轻	qīng
货	huò	丶		沫	mò	艰	jiān	茶	chá	荣	róng
季	jì	宝	bǎo	闹	nào	建	jiàn	查	chá	砂	shā
佳	jiā	变	biàn	泥	ní	降	jiàng	城	chéng	珊	shān
金	jīn	波	bō	泞	níng	届	jiè	持	chí	甚	shèn
径	jìng	泊	bó	顷	qǐng	居	jū	春	chūn	拾	shí
例	lì	怖	bù	怕	pà	隶	lì	带	dài	柿	shì
侣	lǚ	诧	chà	庞	páng	陋	lòu	挡	dǎng	树	shù
命	mìng	炒	chǎo	泡	pào	录	lù	荡	dàng	耍	shuǎ
牧	mù	衬	chèn	泼	pō	弥	mí	垫	diàn	拴	shuān
念	niàn	诚	chéng	泣	qì	陌	mò	栋	dòng	挑	tiāo,
爬	pá	宠	chǒng	浅	qiǎn	屈	qū	毒	dú		tiǎo
佩	pèi	炊	chuī	怯	qiè	刷	shuā	封	fēng	挺	tǐng
朋	péng	单	dān	券	quàn	肃	sù	赴	fù	挖	wā
贫	pín	诞	dàn	衫	shān	弦	xián	革	gé	歪	wāi
凭	píng	底	dǐ	审	shěn	限	xiàn	拱	gǒng	威	wēi
迫	pò	店	diàn	诗	shī	驻	zhù	故	gù	咸	xián
侨	qiáo	定	dìng	实	shí	乚		挂	guà	相	xiāng
		法	fǎ	试	shì	参	cān				

效 xiào	**11 strokes**	萍 píng	逻 luó	脚 jiǎo	毫 háo
羞 xiū	一	戚 qī	眯 mí	梨 lí	痕 hén
袖 xiù	菠 bō	掐 qiā	啤 pí	犁 lí	谎 huǎng
畜 xù	埠 bù	球 qiú	圈 quān	脸 liǎn	祸 huò
烟 yān	菜 cài	娶 qǔ	雀 què	领 lǐng	混 hùn
宴 yàn	捶 chuí	啥 shà	蛇 shé	笼 lóng	寄 jì
谊 yì	措 cuò	梢 shāo	梳 shū	铝 lǚ	寂 jì
益 yì	掂 diān	奢 shē	堂 táng	猫 māo	剪 jiǎn
涌 yǒng	掉 diào	盛 shèng	唾 tuò	猛 měng	减 jiǎn
浴 yù	堵 dǔ	授 shòu	晚 wǎn	敏 mǐn	渐 jiàn
冤 yuān	堆 duī	爽 shuǎng	唯 wéi	您 nín	惊 jīng
悦 yuè	辅 fú	硕 shuò	晤 wù	偶 ǒu	竟 jìng
阅 yuè	副 fù	探 tàn	虚 xū	徘 pái	惧 jù
宰 zǎi	梗 gěng	掏 tāo	悬 xuán	盘 pán	康 kāng
窄 zhǎi	菇 gū	萄 tao	鸭 yā	偏 piān	寇 kòu
站 zhàn	硅 guī	梯 tī	崖 yá	售 shòu	廊 láng
涨 zhǎng	黄 huáng	桶 tǒng	眼 yǎn	停 tíng	粒 lì
症 zhèng	基 jī	推 tuī	野 yě	铜 tóng	梁 liáng
衷 zhōng	检 jiǎn	袭 xí	婴 yīng	偷 tōu	淋 lín
诸 zhū	教 jiāo, jiào	掀 xiān	跃 yuè	脱 tuō	鹿 lù
烛 zhú	接 jiē	厢 xiāng	崭 zhǎn	悉 xī	率 lǜ, shuài
准 zhǔn	捷 jié	械 xiè	睁 zhēng	衔 xián	麻 má
资 zī	救 jiù	酗 xù	蛀 zhù	馅 xiàn	谜 mí
座 zuò	菊 jú	雪 xuě		象 xiàng	密 mì
丁	据 jú	掩 yǎn	丿	斜 xié	谋 móu
剥 bāo, bō	掘 jué	营 yíng	笨 bèn	衅 xìn	烹 pēng
剧 jù	菌 jūn	域 yù	舶 bó	移 yí	清 qīng
恳 kěn	勘 kān	酝 yùn	脖 bó	银 yín	情 qíng
陪 péi	控 kòng	职 zhí	猜 cāi	悠 yōu	渠 qú
弱 ruò	勒 lè	掷 zhì	彩 cǎi	猪 zhū	商 shāng
桑 sāng	理 lǐ	著 zhù	铲 chǎn	做 zuò	深 shēn
陶 táo	辆 liàng		猖 chāng		渗 shèn
通 tōng	聊 liáo	丨	偿 cháng	丶	兽 shòu
陷 xiàn	聋 lóng	崩 bēng	船 chuán	惭 cán	宿 sù
屑 xiè	掠 lüè	蝉 chán	袋 dài	惨 cǎn	淘 táo
验 yàn	啰 luō	常 cháng	得 dé, de, děi	阐 chǎn	添 tiān
预 yù	萝 luó	唱 chàng	笛 dí	凑 còu	惋 wǎn
展 zhǎn	梅 méi	晨 chén	第 dì	粗 cū	望 wàng
乚	萌 méng	匙 chí, shi	舵 duò	淡 dàn	谓 wèi
继 jì	梦 mèng	崇 chóng	符 fú	盗 dào	惜 xī
绢 juàn	描 miáo	啡 fēi	竿 gān	悼 dào	淆 xiáo
能 néng	捻 niǎn	患 huàn	鸽 gē	惦 diàn	谐 xié
娘 niáng	排 pái	距 jù	够 gòu	淀 diàn	旋 xuán
射 shè	培 péi	啃 kěn	馆 guǎn	断 duàn	淹 yān
绣 xiù	捧 pěng	啦 la	盒 hé	袱 fú	痒 yǎng
娱 yú	票 piào	累 lèi	凰 huáng	盖 gài	窑 yáo
		略 lüè	假 jiǎ, jià	惯 guàn	液 yè
		啰 luō		焊 hàn	

淫 yín
庸 yōng
渔 yú
欲 yù
章 zhāng
着 zháo, zhe, zhuó
琢 zhuó
族 zú

乛
逮 dài
蛋 dàn
弹 dàn
兜 dōu
堕 duò
敢 gǎn
颈 jǐng
隆 lóng
颇 pō
骑 qí
随 suí
屠 tú
隐 yǐn

乚
绷 bēng
毙 bì
绸 chóu
婚 hūn
绩 jì
绿 lǜ
绵 mián
婶 shěn
绳 shéng
维 wéi
续 xù
绪 xù
缀 zhuì
综 zōng

12 strokes
一
斑 bān
棒 bàng
逼 bī
博 bó
裁 cái

插 chā
搀 chān
超 chāo
朝 cháo
趁 chèn
厨 chú
葱 cōng
搓 cuō
搭 dā
堤 dī
董 dǒng
搁 gē
辜 gū
棺 guān
棍 gùn
葫 hú
惠 huì
惑 huò
颊 jiá
椒 jiāo
搅 jiǎo
揭 jiē
敬 jìng
揪 jiū
堪 kān
棵 kē
款 kuǎn
葵 kuí
落 là, luò
揽 lǎn
棱 léng
联 lián
裂 liè
硫 liú
搂 lǒu
棉 mián
棚 péng
葡 pú
期 qī
欺 qī
棋 qí
翘 qiáo
琴 qín
趋 qū
确 què
惹 rě
揉 róu

萨 sà
散 sǎn, sàn
森 sēn
斯 sī
搜 sōu
塔 tǎ
提 tí
替 tì
椭 tuǒ
握 wò
喜 xǐ
雄 xióng
雅 yǎ
雁 yàn
壹 yī
椅 yǐ
硬 yìng
援 yuán
越 yuè
暂 zàn
葬 zàng
朝 zhāo
植 zhí
殖 zhí
煮 zhǔ
棕 zōng
揍 zòu
琢 zuó

丨
悲 bēi
辈 bèi
敞 chǎng
喘 chuǎn
跌 diē
赌 dǔ
幅 fú
喊 hǎn
喝 hē
黑 hēi
喉 hóu
辉 huī
践 jiàn
晶 jīng
景 jǐng
喇 lǎ
量 liáng, liàng

晾 liàng
帽 mào
跑 pǎo
赔 péi
喷 pēn
嵌 qiàn
晴 qíng
啥 shá
赏 shǎng
暑 shǔ
蛙 wā
喂 wèi
晰 xī
啸 xiào
喧 xuān
遗 yí
喻 yù
遇 yù
凿 záo
装 zhuāng
紫 zǐ
最 zuì

丿
傲 ào
奥 ào
掰 bāi
傍 bàng
惫 bèi
策 cè
馋 chán
程 chéng
惩 chěng
锄 chú
储 chǔ
答 dā, dá
氮 dàn
等 děng
短 duǎn
鹅 é
番 fān
锋 fēng
傅 fù
猴 hóu
猾 huá
集 jí
焦 jiāo
街 jiē

筋 jīn
腊 là
链 liàn
猎 liè
鲁 lǔ
牌 pái
脾 pí
铺 pū
腔 qiāng
禽 qín
然 rán
锐 ruì
筛 shāi
稍 shāo
甥 shēng
剩 shèng
释 shì
舒 shū
税 shuì
锁 suǒ
毯 tǎn
艇 tǐng
筒 tǒng
稀 xī
销 xiāo
锌 xīn
锈 xiù
循 xún
粤 yuè
智 zhì
筑 zhù
铸 zhù

丶
谤 bàng
遍 biàn
曾 céng
窗 chuāng
窜 cuàn
道 dào
渡 dù
惰 duò
愤 fèn
粪 fèn
富 fù
溉 gài
港 gǎng
割 gē

雇 gù
寒 hán
湖 hú
滑 huá
痪 huàn
慌 huāng
溅 jiàn
就 jiù
慨 kǎi
渴 kě
裤 kù
愧 kuì
阔 kuò
愣 lèng
蛮 mán
渺 miǎo
普 pǔ
谦 qiān
裙 qún
善 shàn
湿 shī
惕 tì
童 tóng
痛 tòng
湾 wān
温 wēn
窝 wō
羡 xiàn
翔 xiáng
谢 xiè
焰 yàn
谣 yáo
游 yóu
愉 yú
寓 yù
裕 yù
渣 zhā
掌 zhǎng
筝 zhēng
滞 zhì
滋 zī
尊 zūn

乛
隘 ài
登 dēng
隔 gé
屡 lǚ

膏 gāo
寡 guǎ
豪 háo
竭 jié
精 jīng
慷 kāng
辣 là
漏 lòu
慢 màn
漫 màn
蜜 mì
漂 piào
谱 pǔ
漆 qī
旗 qí
歉 qiàn
敲 qiāo
熔 róng
赛 sài
裳 shàng
瘦 shòu
瘟 wēn
熄 xī
演 yǎn
寨 zhài
彰 zhāng
遮 zhē

翠 cuì
凳 dèng
骡 luó
隧 suì

嫩 nèn
缩 suō
熊 xióng
疑 yí

15 strokes

磅 bàng
播 bǒ

槽 cáo
撤 chè
撑 chēng
聪 cōng
醋 cù
敷 fū
横 héng
慧 huì
蕉 jiāo
磕 kē
霉 méi
撵 niǎn
飘 piāo
趣 qù
撒 sā
蔬 shū
撕 sī
趟 tàng
踠 wān
橡 xiàng
鞋 xié
薪 xīn
樱 yīng
蕴 yùn
增 zēng
震 zhèn
撞 zhuàng
醉 zuì

暴 bào
憋 biē
踩 cǎi
嘲 cháo
蝶 dié
嘿 hēi
蝴 hú
蝗 huáng
瞒 mán
墨 mò
噢 ō
器 qì
遣 qiǎn
踏 tā, tà

踢 tī
题 tí
瞎 xiā
影 yǐng
嘱 zhǔ
幢 zhuàng
踪 zōng

稻 dào
德 dé
稿 gǎo
稼 jià
箭 jiàn
靠 kào
黎 lí
僻 pì
篇 piān
艘 sōu
膛 táng
躺 tǎng
膝 xī
箱 xiāng
镇 zhèn

澳 ào
潮 cháo
澄 chéng
懂 dǒng
额 é
糊 hú
潦 liáo
瘤 liú
摩 mó
潜 qián
熟 shú
瘫 tān
潭 tán
颜 yán
毅 yì
遵 zūn
履 lǚ
劈 pī

慰 wèi
豫 yù

16 strokes

薄 báo,
　　bó
操 cāo
颠 diān
霍 huò
橘 jú
蕾 lěi
融 róng
擅 shàn
薯 shǔ
醒 xǐng
燕 yàn
整 zhěng

餐 cān
默 mò
瞥 piē
蹄 tí
噪 zào
赠 zèng
嘴 zuǐ

雕 diāo
衡 héng
僵 jiāng
鲸 jīng
镜 jìng
篮 lán
篱 lí
穆 mù
膨 péng
邀 yāo
赞 zàn

辨 biàn
辩 biàn
糕 gāo
憾 hàn

激 jí
懒 lǎn
窿 lóng
磨 mó
凝 níng
瘸 qué
糖 táng
澡 zǎo

壁 bì
避 bì

缴 jiǎo

**17-23
strokes**

霸 bà
鞭 biān
擦 cā
蠢 chǔn
戴 dài
覆 fù
警 jǐng
鞠 jū
磷 lín
露 lù
檬 méng
蘑 mó
攀 pān
壤 rǎng
霜 shuāng
藤 téng
霞 xiá
攒 zǎn

蹦 bèng
蹈 dǎo
瞪 dèng
蹲 dūn
嚼 jiáo
螺 luó
瞧 qiáo

嚷 rǎng
蹋 tà
耀 yào
躁 zào
瞻 zhān

簸 bǒ
翻 fān
繁 fán
罐 guàn
徽 huī
籍 jī
镰 lián
穗 suì
镶 xiāng
镯 zhuó

癌 ái
瓣 bàn
爆 bào
辫 biàn
颤 chàn
灌 guàn
糠 kāng
魔 mó
囊 náng
瀑 pù
燃 rán
鹰 yīng
赢 yíng
糟 zāo
燥 zào

臂 bì
疆 jiāng
譬 pì
翼 yì
骤 zhòu

A

阿 **ā** PREFIX (used to address certain relatives or friends to convey sentiment of intimacy)
阿爸 **ā bà** daddy
阿婆 **ā pó** (maternal) granny
阿拉伯文 **Ālābówén** N the Arabic language (especially the writing)
阿拉伯语 **Ālābóyǔ** N the Arabic language
阿姨 **āyí** N mother's sister ■ 我妈妈有一个姐姐，一个妹妹，所以我有两个阿姨。Wǒ māma yǒu yí ge jiějie, yí ge mèimei, suǒyǐ wǒ yǒu liǎng ge āyí. *My mother has an elder sister and a younger sister, so I have two aunts.*

NOTES: (1) 阿姨 āyí is a form of address used by a child for a woman about his/her mother's age. (2) 阿姨 āyí is also used by adults and children for domestic helpers and female nursery staff.

啊 **ā** I INTERJ (used to express strong emotions such as surprise, admiration, regret etc.) oh, ah ■ 啊，海风多么凉爽！Ā, hǎifēng duōme liángshuǎng! *How refreshing the sea breeze is!* II PARTICLE (attached to a sentence to express strong emotions such as surprise, admiration, regret etc.) ■ 北京的冬天真冷啊！Běijīng de dōngtiān zhēn lěng a! *How cold the winter in Beijing is!*

哎 **āi** INTERJ (used to attract attention or express surprise) ■ 哎，你还在玩电子游戏？Āi, nǐ hái zài wán diànzǐ yóuxì? *Oh, you're still playing computer games?*
哎呀 **āiya** INTERJ (used to express surprise or annoyance) ■ 哎呀，我说了半天，你怎么还不明白？Āiya, wǒ shuōle bàntiān, nǐ zěnme hái bù míngbai? *Goodness, I've been explaining for ages, how come you still don't see the point?*
哎哟 **āiyō** INTERJ (used to express surprise or pain)

唉 **āi** INTERJ 1 (as a sigh) alas ■ 唉，孩子又病了。Āi, háizi yòu bìng le. *Alas, the child is sick again.* 2 (as a response) yes, right

哀 **āi** I V mourn II ADJ grieved
哀悼 **āidào** V mourn
哀求 **āiqiú** V entreat, implore

挨 **āi** V undergo (some painful or unpleasant experience) ■ 那个小偷挨了一顿打。Nàge xiǎotōu āi le yí dùn dǎ. *That thief was beaten up.*

癌 **ái** N cancer
肺癌 **fèi'ái** lung cancer

胃癌 **wèi'ái** stomach cancer

蔼 **ǎi** TRAD 藹 ADJ amiable, friendly (See 和蔼 hé'ǎi)

矮 **ǎi** ADJ (of a person or plant) of short stature, short ■ 他虽然长得矮，但是篮球打得挺好。Tā suīrán zhǎng de ǎi, dànshì lánqiú dǎ de tǐng hǎo. *Although he's short, he's a good basketball player.*

爱 **ài** TRAD 愛 V 1 love 2 like, be fond of ■ 她爱表现自己。Tā ài biǎoxiàn zìjǐ. *She likes to show off.*
爱戴 **àidài** V love and esteem
爱好 **àihào** I V like, be interested in, have as a hobby II N hobby, interest ■ 我的爱好比较广泛，不过我最大的爱好是玩电子游戏。Wǒde àihào bǐjiào guǎngfàn, búguò wǒ zuìdà de àihào shì wán diànzǐ yóuxì. *I have many hobbies, but my favorite is playing computer games.*
爱护 **àihù** V care for and protect, cherish ■ 父母都爱护自己的孩子。Fùmǔ dōu àihù zìjǐ de háizi. *All parents care for and protect their children.*
爱面子 **ài miànzi** V be overly concerned about one's image
爱情 **àiqíng** N romantic love ■ 年轻人都希望获得爱情。Niánqīngrén dōu xīwàng huòdé àiqíng. *Young people all yearn for love.*
爱情小说 **àiqíng xiǎoshuō** love story, romance fiction
爱人 **àirén** N husband or wife

NOTE: 爱人 àirén as husband or wife is only used in Mainland China as a colloquialism. On formal occasions 丈夫 zhàngfu (husband) and 妻子 qīzi (wife) are used instead. Now there is a decreasing tendency to use 爱人 àirén in China. In its place 先生 xiānsheng and 太太 tàitai are used to refer to husband and wife, a long established practice in Taiwan, Hong Kong and overseas Chinese communities.

爱惜 **àixī** V cherish, value highly
爱惜自己的名誉 **àixī zìjǐ de míngyù** treasure one's reputation

碍 **ài** TRAD 礙 V hinder
碍事 **àishì** V be in one's way

艾 **ài** N mugwort
艾滋病 **àizībìng** N AIDS

NOTE: 艾滋病 is a transliteration, i.e. reproducing the sounds of the English word AIDS.

隘 **ài** ADJ narrow (See 狭隘 xiá'ài)

安 ān

安 ān ADJ peaceful, safe

安定 āndìng ADJ peaceful and stable ■ 这个社会表面上安定, 其实矛盾很多。Zhège shèhuì biǎomiànshàng āndìng, qíshí máodùn hěn duō. *This society seems to be stable on the surface; actually there are many contradictions within.*

安静 ānjìng ADJ quiet, peaceful, serene ■ 这里很少有车开过, 环境很安静。Zhèlǐ hěn shǎo yǒu chē kāiguò, huánjìng hěn ānjìng. *There is very little traffic here. The environment is very peaceful.*

安乐死 ānlèsǐ N euthanasia

安宁 ānníng ADJ calm, composed

安排 ānpái V arrange, make arrangements, plan

安全 ānquán I N security, safety ■ 开车安全第一。Kāichē ānquán dì yī. *When you are driving, safety is the most important thing.*
安全带 ānquándài safety belt
安全帽 ānquánmào safety helmet
II ADJ safe, secure ■ 在这里夜里一个人在街上走, 安全吗? Zài zhèlǐ yèlǐ yí ge rén zài jiē shang zǒu, ānquán ma? *Is it safe to walk alone in the streets here at night?*

安慰 ānwèi V comfort, console ■ 他们失去了心爱的女儿, 心情悲痛, 朋友们都来安慰他们。Tāmen shīqùle xīn'ài de nǚ'ér, xīnqíng bēitòng, péngyoumen dōu lái ānwèi tāmen. *They are in deep sorrow as they have lost their beloved daughter. Their friends have all come to comfort them.*

安稳 ānwěn ADJ safe and secure

安详 ānxiáng ADJ (of facial expression) serene, composed

安心 ānxīn ADJ be relaxed and content ■ 她不安心在小学教书, 她想当电影演员。Tā bù ānxīn zài xiǎoxué jiāoshū, tā xiǎng dāng diànyǐng yǎnyuán. *She is not content to be a primary school teacher; she wants to be a movie star.*

安置 ānzhì V find an appropriate place (for people)

安装 ānzhuāng V install, fix
安装空调设备 ānzhuāng kōngtiáo shèbèi install an air-conditioner

岸 àn

岸 àn N bank or shore (of a river, lake, or sea) ■ 河的两岸是一个个小村子。Hé de liǎng àn shì yí gège xiǎo cūnzi. *The river is flanked by small villages.*
海岸 hǎi àn coast
河岸 hé'àn river bank
上岸 shàng àn go ashore

按 àn

按 àn PREP according to, in accordance with ■ 我一定按你说的做。Wǒ yídìng àn nǐ shuō de zuò. *I will definitely do as you say.*

按揭 ànjiē N mortgage

按期 ànqī ADV on schedule

按时 ànshí ADV according to a fixed time, on time ■ 你得按时吃药, 病才会好。Nǐ děi ànshí chī yào, bìng cái huì hǎo. *You've got to take the medicine at the specified times, or you won't get well.*

按照 ànzhào PREP according to, in accordance with (same as 按 àn)

案 àn

案 àn N case, plan

案件 ànjiàn N case, legal case
民事案件 mínshì ànjiàn civil case
刑事案件 xíngshì ànjiàn criminal case
调查案件 diàochá ànjiàn investigate a (police) case

暗 àn

暗 àn ADJ dark, dim ■ 房间里太暗了, 你要看书得开灯。Fángjiān li tài àn le, nǐ yào kàn shū děi kāi dēng. *The room is dim. Turn on the light if you want to read.*

暗暗 àn'àn ADV secretly
暗暗得意 àn'àn déyì secretly very pleased with oneself

暗淡 àndàn ADJ dim, gloomy
光线暗淡的房间 guāngxiàn àndàn de fángjiān a dimly-lit room

暗杀 ànshā V assassinate

暗示 ànshì I V drop a hint **II** N hint

暗室 ànshì N darkroom (for developing films)

暗中 ànzhōng ADV in the dark, in secret
暗中帮忙 ànzhōng bāngmáng secretly help

昂 áng

昂 áng V hold (the head) high

昂起头 ángqǐ tóu hold the head high
昂贵 ángguì ADJ very expensive, costly
昂扬 ángyáng ADJ in high spirits

凹 āo

凹 āo ADJ concave, sunken, dented

凹凸不平 āotū bùpíng rugged, full of bumps and holes

熬 áo

熬 áo V stew, boil

熬汤 áo tāng prepare soup by simmering

袄 ǎo

袄 ǎo Trad 襖 N a Chinese-style coat/jacket

棉袄 mián'ǎo padded coat

傲 ào

傲 ào ADJ arrogant (See 骄傲 jiāo'ào)

奥 ào

奥 ào ADJ deep, profound

奥秘 àomì N deep secret, profound mystery
探索奥秘 tànsuǒ àomì explore a mystery

澳 ào

澳 ào N deep waters

澳大利亚 Àodàlìyà N Australia

B

八 **bā** NUM eight ■ 八八六十四。Bā bā liùshísì. *Eight times eight is sixty-four.*

捌 **bā** NUM Same as 八 bā

扒 **bā** v **1** strip off, take off (clothes, etc.) **2** hold on to, cling to

叭 **bā** ONOMATOPEIA crack

巴 **bā** N cheek

巴结 **bājie** v flatter, fawn on

芭 **bā** N flower

芭蕾舞 **bāléiwǔ** N ballet

笆 **bā** N bamboo fence (See 篱笆 líbā)

疤 **bā** N scar (See 伤疤 shāngbā)

吧 **bā** N bar

酒吧 **jiǔbā** wine bar, bar, pub
网吧 **wǎngbā** Internet café

拔 **bá** v pull out, pull up

拔苗助长 **bá miáo zhù zhǎng** pull up a young plant to help it grow (→ spoil things by excessive enthusiasm)

把 1 **bǎ** PREP (used before a noun or pronoun to indicate it is the object of the sentence) ■ 哥哥把自行车修好了。Gēge bǎ zìxíngchē xiūhǎo le. *My elder brother has fixed the bike.*

把 2 **bǎ** I N handle II M. WD **1** (for objects with handles) **2** a handful of
一把刀 **yì bǎ dāo** a knife
一把米 **yì bǎ mǐ** a handful of rice
把柄 **bǎbǐng** N **1** handle **2** something that may be used against someone
抓住了他的把柄 **zhuāzhùle tāde bǎbǐng** have got evidence that may be used against him
把关 **bǎguān** v check on
把手 **bǎshǒu** N handle, handrail
把握 **bǎwò** I N being certain and assured, confidence ■ 你有成功的把握吗? Nǐ yǒu chénggōng de bǎwò ma? *Are you sure of success?* II v seize (an opportunity)
把握时机 **bǎwò shíjī** seize an opportunity
把戏 **bǎxì** N trick
玩把戏 **wán bǎxì** play a trick

爸 **bà** N dad, daddy, papa

爸爸 **bàba** N daddy, papa

坝 **bà** TRAD 壩 N dam, embankment

大坝 **dàbà** big dam

霸 **bà** I N tyrant II v dominate, rule by might

恶霸 **èbà** local tyrant
霸道 **bàdào** ADJ overbearing, high-handed
霸权 **bàquán** N hegemony
霸权主义 **bàquán zhǔyì** hegemonism
霸占 **bàzhàn** v occupy or possess by force
霸占民房 **bàzhàn mínfáng** seize possession of private property by force

罢 **bà** TRAD 罷 v stop

罢工 **bàgōng** v stage a strike, down tools

吧 **ba** PARTICLE **1** (used to make a suggestion) ■ 今天太冷了, 别去游泳吧! Jīntiān tài lěng le, bié qù yóuyǒng ba! *It's too cold today. Don't go swimming, OK?* **2** (used to indicate supposition) ■ 你是新加坡来的张先生吧? Nǐ shì Xīnjiāpō lái de Zhāng xiānsheng ba? *Aren't you Mr Zhang from Singapore?*

掰 **bāi** v break off with hands

白 **bái** I ADJ white ■ 下雪以后, 路上一片白。Xiàxuě yǐhòu, lù shang yí piàn bái. *The road was all white after the snowfall.* II ADV in vain, without any result ■ 我忘了在电脑里保存文件, 一个晚上的工作白做了。Wǒ wàngle zài diànnǎo li bǎocún wénjiàn, yí ge wǎnshang de gōngzuò dōu bái zuò le. *I forgot to save my document in the computer. An evening's work all came to nothing.* III ADV for free ■ 世界上没有白吃的午餐。Shìjiè shang méiyǒu bái chī de wǔcān. *There is no free lunch in the world.* (→There's no such thing as a free lunch.)

NOTE: In Chinese tradition, white symbolizes death and is the color for funerals.

白白 **báibái** ADV in vain, for nothing
白菜 **báicài** N cabbage (棵 kē)
白酒 **báijiǔ** N spirits usually distilled from sorghum or rice, white spirits
白开水 **báikāishuǐ** N plain boiled water ■ 感冒了要喝白开水。Gǎnmào le yào hē báikāishuǐ. *You should drink a lot of boiled water when you've got a cold.*
白领 **báilǐng** N white-collar worker
白人 **báirén** N Caucasian person, Caucasian people

白天 báitiān

白天 **báitiān** N daytime ■ 春天来了，白天越来越长了。Chūntiān lái le, báitiān yuèlaiyuè cháng le. *Spring has come. Days become longer and longer.*

百 **bǎi** NUM hundred

三百元 **sānbǎi yuán** three hundred yuan/dollars

NOTE: 百 bǎi may have the abstract sense of *a great deal of* and *a multitude of*. This sense can be found in many expressions, e.g. 百闻不如一见 Bǎi wén bùrú yí jiàn, which literally means *A hundred sounds are not as good as one sight* and may be translated as *Seeing is believing.*

百货 **bǎihuò** N general merchandise
百货商店 **bǎihuò shāngdiàn** department store
百日咳 **bǎirìké** N whooping cough
百姓 **bǎixìng** N common people

NOTE: 老百姓 lǎobǎixìng is also used to mean "common people".

柏 **bǎi** N cypress

柏树 **bǎishù** cypress tree, cypress

摆 **bǎi** TRAD 擺 V put, place, arrange ■ 吃饭了，你把碗筷摆好吧! Chīfàn le, nǐ bǎ wǎnkuài bǎihǎo ba! *It's mealtime, will you please set the table?*
摆动 **bǎidòng** V sway, swing
摆脱 **bǎituō** V break away from, shake off

败 **bài** TRAD 敗 V be defeated ■ 我们球队又败了，得研究一下原因。Wǒmen qiúduì yòu bài le, děi yánjiū yíxià yuányīn. *Our (ball) team was defeated again. We've got to look into the reason.*
败坏 **bàihuài** V ruin, corrupt
道德败坏 **dàodé bàihuài** rotten morals

拜 **bài** V do obeisance, pay respect to

拜访 **bàifǎng** V pay a visit (to a senior person), make a courtesy call
拜会 **bàihuì** V make an official call
拜年 **bài nián** V pay a New Year's call, wish someone a Happy New Year

班 **bān** N 1 class (in school) ■ 我们班有十二个男生，十四个女生。Wǒmen bān yǒu shí'èr ge nánshēng, shísì ge nǔshēng. *Our class has twelve male students and fourteen female students.* 2 shift (in a workplace)
加班 **jiābān** work overtime
上班 **shàngbān** go to work
下班 **xiàbān** finish work
班机 **bānjī** N airliner, flight ■ 我乘560班机去新加坡。Wǒ chéng wǔ-liù-líng bānjī qù Xīnjiāpō. *I'll go to Singapore by flight 560.*
班长 **bānzhǎng** N leader (of a class in school, a squad in the army, etc.)

斑 **bān** N spot, speck

斑点 **bāndiǎn** spot, stain
斑马 **bānmǎ** N zebra

般 **bān** N kind, sort (See 一般 yìbān)

搬 **bān** V move (heavy objects) ■ 我们把这张桌子搬到房间外面去吧。Wǒmen bǎ zhè zhāng zhuōzi bān dào fángjiān wàimiàn qù ba. *Let's move this table out of the room.*
搬不动 **bān bu dòng** cannot move/cannot be moved
搬得动 **bān de dòng** can move/can be moved
搬家 **bānjiā** V move (house) ■ 我们这个周末搬家。Wǒmen zhège zhōumò bānjiā. *We're moving house this weekend.*
搬运 **bānyùn** V transport, move
搬运工人 **bānyùn gōngrén** mover

颁 **bān** V issue, confer on

颁布 **bānbù** V promulgate, proclaim
颁发 **bānfā** V issue, distribute
颁发奖状 **bānfā jiǎngzhuàng** issue a certificate of merit

扳 **bān** V pull, turn

扳手 **bānshǒu** N spanner, wrench

板 **bǎn** N board

木板 **mùbǎn** wooden plank

版 **bǎn** N printing plate

第一版 **dìyī bǎn** the first edition

办 **bàn** TRAD 辦 V handle, manage ■ 你办事我很放心。Nǐ bànshì wǒ hěn fàngxīn. *I feel reassured when you're handling a matter. (→ I have confidence in you when you're in charge.)*
办法 **bànfǎ** N 1 way of doing things ■ 这些老办法都不行。Zhèxiē lǎo bànfǎ dōu bùxíng. *All these old methods won't work.* 2 method
想办法 **xiǎng bànfǎ** think up a plan, find a way of doing things
有办法 **yǒu bànfǎ** have a way with ..., be resourceful
没有办法 **méiyǒu bànfǎ** there's nothing we can do ■ 飞机票全卖完了，我们明天不能走，没有办法。Fēijī piào quán màiwán le, wǒmen

míngtiān bù néng zǒu, méiyǒu bànfǎ. *All the air tickets are sold out. We won't be able to leave tomorrow. There's nothing we can do.*

办公 **bàngōng** v work (as a white-collar worker, usually in an office) ■ 王经理在办公, 你有事可以给他留个话。 Wáng jīnglǐ zài bàngōng, nǐ yǒushì kěyǐ gěi tā liú ge huà. *Mr Wang, the manager, is working in his office. You can leave him a message, if you've any business.*

办公大楼 **bàngōng dàlóu** office building

办公时间 **bàngōng shíjiān** office hours, working hours

办公室 **bàngōngshì** N office (间 jiān) ■ 请你到我办公室来一下。 Qǐng nǐ dào wǒ bàngōngshì lái yíxià. *Please come to my office.*

办理 **bànlǐ** v deal with, go through ■ 我正在办理到中国去的签证。 Wǒ zhèngzài bànlǐ dào Zhōngguó qù de qiānzhèng. *I'm in the process of obtaining a visa for China.*

办事 **bànshì** v conduct affairs, manage affairs ■ 他很会办事。 Tā hěn huì bànshì. *He is very good at getting things done.*

办学 **bànxué** v run a school

半 **bàn** M. WD half ■ 我等她等了一个半小时。 Wǒ děng tā děngle yí ge bàn xiǎoshí. *I waited one and a half hours for her.*

半岛 **bàndǎo** N peninsula

九龙半岛 **Jiǔlóng bàndǎo** Kowloon Peninsula (in Hong Kong)

半径 **bànjìng** N radius

半路 **bànlù** N halfway, midway

半数 **bànshù** N half the number, half

半天 **bàntiān** N **1** half a day **2** a period of time felt to be very long; a very long time ■ 那本书我找了半天, 还没找到。 Nà běn shū wǒ zhǎole bàntiān, hái méi zhǎodào. *I've been looking for the book for a long time but I still haven't found it.*

半途而废 **bàntú ér fèi** IDIOM give up halfway

半夜 **bànyè** N midnight, at midnight

拌 **bàn** v mix

伴 **bàn** N companion

同伴 **tóngbàn** companion

伴侣 **bànlǚ** N companion (especially husband or wife)

终身伴侣 **zhōngshēn bànlǚ** life-long companion, husband and wife

伴随 **bànsuí** v go along with, keep company

伴奏 **bànzòu** v accompany with musical instrument

扮 **bàn** v disguise as

扮演 **bànyǎn** v play the role (of a character in a play, movie, etc.)

瓣 **bàn** N petal, segment

花瓣 **huābàn** petal, flower petal

帮 **bāng** TRAD 幫 v help, assist ■ 你能帮我找一下这本书吗? Nǐ néng bāng wǒ zhǎo yíxià zhè běn shū ma? *Can you help me find this book?*

NOTE: 帮 bāng, 帮忙 bāngmáng and 帮助 bāngzhù are synonyms. Their differences are: (1) 帮忙 bāngmáng is a verb that takes no object, while 帮 bāng and 帮助 bāngzhù are usually followed by an object. (2) As verbs, 帮 bāng and 帮助 bāngzhù are interchangeable, but 帮 bāng is more colloquial than 帮助 bāngzhù. (3) 帮助 bāngzhù can also be used as a noun.

帮忙 **bāngmáng** v help, help out ■ 上个周末, 他搬家, 很多朋友来帮忙。 Shàng ge zhōumò tā bānjiā, hěn duō péngyou lái bāngmáng. *Last weekend, he moved house. Many friends came to help out.*

NOTE: See note on 帮 bāng.

帮助 **bāngzhù** I v help, assist ■ 李先生帮助我们解决了很多困难。 Lǐ xiānsheng bāngzhù wǒmen jiějuéle hěn duō kùnnan. *Mr Li helped us overcome many difficulties.* II N help, assistance

NOTE: See note on 帮 bāng.

邦 **bāng** N country

绑 **bǎng** TRAD 綁 v tie, bind (with a rope)

绑架 **bǎngjià** v kidnap

榜 **bǎng** N list of names, honor roll

榜样 **bǎngyàng** N (positive) example, role model ■ 我们的老师是美国人, 说一口标准中文, 真是我们的好榜样! Wǒmen de lǎoshī shì Měiguórén, shuō yì kǒu biāozhǔn Zhōngwén, zhēn shì wǒmen de hǎo bǎngyàng! *Our teacher is an American and speaks standard Chinese. He really is a good role model for us.*

膀 **bǎng** N upper arm

翅膀 **chìbǎng** wing

傍 **bàng** v be close to

傍晚 **bàngwǎn** N dusk, at dusk

磅 **bàng** N (measurement for weight) pound

谤 bàng

两磅牛肉 liǎng bàng niúròu two pounds of beef

谤 bàng TRAD 謗 V slander

诽谤 fěibàng slander

棒 bàng I N stick, club (根 gēn)

铁棒 tiěbàng iron bar
II ADJ strong, very good ■ 他篮球打得真棒。Tā lánqiú dǎ de zhēn bàng. *He really plays basketball very well.* (→ *He is a wonderful basketball player.*)
棒球 bàngqiú N baseball
棒球场 bàngqiúchǎng baseball court
棒球运动员 bàngqiú yùndòngyuán baseball player

包 bāo I N parcel, bag ■ 他在路边拣到一个包，马上交给警察。Tā zài lùbiān jiǎn dào yíge bāo, mǎshàng jiāo gei jǐngchá. *He picked up a parcel by the roadside and immediately handed it over to the police.*

钱包 qiánbāo wallet, purse
书包 shūbāo schoolbag
邮包 yóubāo mailbag, parcel for posting
II V wrap up ■ 顾客: "请你把这只花瓶好好包起来。" Gùkè: "Qǐng nǐ bǎ zhè zhī huāpíng hǎohǎo bāo qǐlai." *Customer: "Could you please wrap up this vase carefully?"*
包办 bāobàn V assume full responsibility for, do entirely by oneself
包办宴席 bāobàn yànxí (of a restaurant) take care of everything for banquets
包袱 bāofu N a bundle wrapped in a cloth-wrapper
包裹 bāoguǒ N parcel, package
包含 bāohán V contain, have as ingredients
包括 bāokuò V include, embrace ■ 旅行团包括一名翻译，一共十五人。Lǚxíngtuán bāokuò yì míng fānyì, yígòng shíwǔ rén. *There are fifteen people in the tour group, including an interpreter.*
包围 bāowéi V surround, encircle, lay siege
包装 bāozhuāng N package, packaging
包装材料 bāozhuāng cáiliào packaging material
包子 bāozi N steamed bun with filling

胞 bāo N the placenta

细胞 xìbāo cell

剥 bāo V peel, peel off

薄 báo ADJ thin, flimsy ■ 天冷了，这条被子太薄，要换一条厚一点儿的。Tiān lěng le, zhè tiáo bèizi tài báo, yào huàn yì tiáo hòu yìdiǎnr

de. *It's getting cold. This blanket is too thin. You need a thicker one.*

NOTE: See note on 薄 bó.

雹 báo N hail

雹子 báozi hail

宝 bǎo TRAD 寶 N treasure

宝岛 bǎodǎo treasure island
宝库 bǎokù treasure house
宝贝 bǎobèi N treasured object, treasure
小宝贝 xiǎo bǎobèi (endearment for children) darling, dear
宝贵 bǎoguì ADJ valuable, precious ■ 世界上什么最宝贵? Shìjiè shang shénme zuì bǎoguì? *What is the most valuable thing in the world?*
宝剑 bǎojiàn N double-edged sword (把 bǎ)
宝石 bǎoshí N precious stone

保 bǎo V conserve, protect ■ 这房子用了新材料，特别保暖。Zhè fángzi yòngle xīn cáiliào, tèbié bǎo nuǎn. *This house uses a new type of material that is particularly good at keeping the house warm.*

保安 bǎo'ān N security guard
保持 bǎochí V keep, maintain ■ 他去年在学校运动会上得了长跑冠军，今年能保持吗? Tā qùnián zài xuéxiào yùndònghuì shang déle chángpǎo guànjūn, jīnnián néng bǎochí ma? *He was the champion in long-distance running at the school sports meet last year. Can he maintain it this year?* (→ *Can he defend his position this year?*)
保存 bǎocún V keep, save ■ 这个文件很重要，你好好以后，千万别忘了保存。Zhège wénjiàn hěn zhòngyào, nǐ dǎhǎo yǐhòu, qiānwàn bié wàngle bǎocún. *This is an important document. After you've done (← typed) it, do remember to save it.*
保管 bǎoguǎn V take charge of
保管员 bǎoguǎnyuán storekeeper
保护 bǎohù V protect, safeguard, conserve
保健 bǎojiàn N health care, health protection
保健食品 bǎojiàn shípǐn health food
妇幼保健 fùyòu bǎojiàn maternity and child care
保龄球 bǎolíngqiú N bowling
保留 bǎoliú V retain, reserve ■ 这张飞机票我们给你保留三天。Zhè zhāng fēijīpiào wǒmen gěi nǐ bǎoliú sān tiān. *We'll reserve this air ticket for you for three days.*
保密 bǎomì V keep ... secret ■ 这件事一定要保密。Zhè jiàn shì yídìng yào bǎomì. *This matter must be kept secret.*

保密文件 bǎomì wénjiàn classified document

保姆 bǎomǔ N (children's) nurse, nanny
当保姆 dāng bǎomǔ work as a nanny

保守 bǎoshǒu I v guard, keep ■ 你能保守一个秘密吗？Nǐ néng bǎoshǒu yí ge mìmì ma? *Can you keep a secret?* II ADJ conservative ■ 一个人年纪大了，往往会保守。Yí ge rén niánjì dà le, wǎngwǎng huì bǎoshǒu. *As one gets old, one tends to be conservative.*

保卫 bǎowèi v defend ■ 当外敌入侵时，每个人都应该保卫自己的国家。Dāng wài dí rùqīn shí, měi ge rén dōu yīnggāi bǎowèi zìjǐ de guójiā. *When an enemy invades our country, everybody should defend it.*

保温 bǎowēn v preserve heat

保险 bǎoxiǎn I ADJ safe, risk-free II v insure III N insurance
保险单 bǎoxiǎndān insurance policy
保险费 bǎoxiǎnfèi insurance premium
保险公司 bǎoxiǎn gōngsī insurance company

保养 bǎoyǎng v 1 take good care of one's health
(人)保养得很好 (rén) bǎoyǎng de hěn hǎo (of people) well preserved
2 maintain (automobiles, machines, etc.), keep in good state
车辆保养 chēliàng bǎoyǎng vehicle maintenance

保障 bǎozhàng v secure, insure, guarantee
社会保障 shèhuì bǎozhàng social security

保证 bǎozhèng I v guarantee, pledge II N guarantee ■ 你们能为产品提供保证吗？Nǐmen néng wèi chǎnpǐn tígòng bǎozhèng ma? *Can you provide a guarantee for your products?* 产品保证书 chǎnpǐn bǎozhèngshū (product) quality guarantee

保重 bǎozhòng v take good care of oneself ■ 您退休以后，多多保重身体。Nín tuìxiū yǐhòu, duōduō bǎozhòng shēntǐ. *(I hope) you will take good care of your health after retirement.*

堡 bǎo N fortress, castle

堡垒 bǎolěi N fort, fortress

饱 bǎo TRAD 飽 ADJ having eaten one's fill, full

饱吃一顿 bǎo chī yídùn have a square meal, eat to one's fill
吃得饱 chī de bǎo have enough to eat
吃不饱 chī bu bǎo not have enough to eat (→ not have enough food) ■ 您吃饱了吗？Nín chī bǎo le ma? *Have you had (← eaten) enough?*

NOTE: It is customary for a Chinese host to ask a guest who seems to have finished the meal: 您吃饱了吗？Nín chī bǎo le ma? *Have you had (eaten)*

enough? The guest is expected to reply: 吃饱了。多谢。您慢慢吃。Chī bǎo le. Duō xiè. Nín mànman chī. *Yes, I have. Thank you. Please take your time to eat.*

饱和 bǎohé ADJ saturated

饱满 bǎomǎn ADJ full, plump

报 bào TRAD 報 I N newspaper (same as 报纸 bàozhǐ)

看报 kànbào read a newspaper
II v respond, reciprocate

报仇 bàochóu v avenge, revenge

报酬 bàochou N renumeration, reward
报酬很高 bàochou hěn gāo well-paid

报到 bàodào v report for duty, register ■ 学校九月一日开学，学生从八月二十五日起报到。Xuéxiào Jiǔyuè yírì kāixué, xuésheng cóng Bāyuè èrshíwǔ rì qǐ bàodào. *The academic year begins on September 1, and students start registration on August 25.*

报道 bàodào (or 报导 bàodǎo) I v report (news), cover ■ 今天城里各家报纸都报道了昨天的交通事故。Jīntiān chéng li gè jiā bàozhǐ dōu bàodàole zuótiān de jiāotōng shìgù. *Today all the newspapers in the city covered yesterday's road accident.* II N news story
独家报道 dújiā bàodào exclusive report
深入报道 shēnrù bàodào in-depth report
现场报道 xiànchǎng bàodào on the spot ("alive") report

报恩 bào'ēn v pay a debt of gratitude

报复 bàofù v retaliate, revenge ■ 谁得罪了她，她一定要报复。Shéi dézuìle tā, tā yídìng yào bàofù. *She will retaliate against whoever has offended her.*

报告 bàogào I v report, make known ■ 播音员：“现在报告新闻。”Bōyīnyuán: "Xiànzài bàogào xīnwén." *Newscaster: "Now the news."* II N report, talk (at a large-scale meeting) (份 fèn)
财务报告 cáiwù bàogào financial report
秘密报告 mìmì bàogào confidential report

报刊 bàokān N newspapers and periodicals, the press

报考 bàokǎo v enter oneself for an examination

报名 bàomíng v enter one's name, sign up, apply for (a place in school) ■ 有六百多人报名参加星期天的长跑。Yǒu liùbǎi duō rén bàomíng cānjiā Xīngqītiān de chángpǎo. *Over 600 people have signed up for Sunday's long-distance run.*

报社 bàoshè N newspaper office

报销 bàoxiāo v submit an expense account, get reimbursement

报纸 bàozhǐ N newspaper (张 zhāng, 份 fèn) ■ 今天报纸上有什么重要消息？Jīntiān bàozhǐ shang yǒu shénme zhòngyào xiāoxi? *What important news is there in today's paper?*

抱 bào

NOTE: In colloquial Chinese, 报 bào is often used instead of 报纸 bàozhǐ, e.g.■ 你看得懂中文报吗? Nǐ kàndedǒng Zhōngwén bào ma? *Can you understand Chinese newspapers?*

抱 bào v hold ... in arms, embrace, hug ■ 妈妈抱着孩子。Māma bàozhe háizi. *The mother is holding her baby in her arms.*

抱负 **bàofù** N aspiration, ambition
抱歉 **bàoqiàn** ADJ apologetic, be sorry, regretful ■ 我忘了昨天的会议, 实在抱歉! Wǒ wàngle zuótiān de huìyì, shízài bàoqiàn! *I'm awfully sorry that I forgot the meeting yesterday.*
抱怨 **bàoyuàn** v complain, grumble

暴 bào ADJ fierce and brutal

暴动 **bàodòng** N rebellion, insurrection
暴力 **bàolì** N violence, brutal force
　暴力电影 **bàolì diànyǐng** violent movie
　有暴力倾向 **yǒu bàolì qīngxiàng** have a tendency to violence
暴露 **bàolù** v expose, lay bare
暴雨 **bàoyǔ** N rainstorm, torrential rain

爆 bào v explode

爆发 **bàofā** v break out, burst out ■ 火山爆发。Huǒshān bàofā. *A volcano erupted.*
爆破 **bàopò** v demolish with dynamite
爆炸 **bàozhà** I v explode II N explosion
　自杀炸弹爆炸 **zìshā zhàdàn bàozhà** the explosion of a suicide bomb

杯 bēi N cup, mug, glass (只 zhī)

杯子 **bēizi** cup, mug, glass
茶杯 **chábēi** teacup
酒杯 **jiǔbēi** wine glass
一杯茶/酒 **yì bēi chá/jiǔ** a cup of tea, a glass of wine

NOTE: 杯 bēi may denote either *cup*, *mug*, or *glass*. 杯 bēi is seldom used alone. It is usually suffixed with 子 zi: 杯子 bēizi, or combined with 茶 chá or 酒 jiǔ: 茶杯 chábēi, 酒杯 jiǔbēi.

背 bēi v carry ... on the back ■ 孩子每天高高兴兴背着书包上学校。Háizi měi tiān gāo-gāo-xìng-xìng bēizhe shūbāo shàng xuéxiào. *Every day the child goes to school happily, his schoolbag on his back.*

背包 **bēibāo** N backpack, knapsack

卑 bēi ADJ 1 low and humble 2 mean, contemptible

卑鄙 **bēibǐ** ADJ contemptible, despicable
　卑鄙小人 **bēibǐ xiǎorén** despicable person/people

碑 bēi N stone tablet

纪念碑 **jìniànbēi** monument

悲 bēi N grieved

悲哀 **bēi'āi** ADJ deeply grieved
悲惨 **bēicǎn** ADJ miserable, tragic
悲愤 **bēifèn** ADJ very sad and angry, filled with grief and indignation
悲观 **bēiguān** ADJ pessimistic ■ 你太悲观了, 情况不会这么坏吧。Nǐ tài bēiguān le, qíngkuàng bú huì zhème huài ba. *You're too pessimistic. Things can't be that bad.*
　悲观主义 **bēiguānzhǔyì** pessimism
　悲观者 **bēiguānzhě** pessimist
悲剧 **bēijù** N tragedy
悲伤 **bēishāng** ADJ deeply sorrowful
悲痛 **bēitòng** ADJ deeply grieved, agonized, with deep sorrow ■ 他在交通事故中失去了妻子、女儿, 悲痛极了。Tā zài jiāotōng shìgù zhōng shīqùle qīzi, nǚ'ér, bēitòng jíle. *He lost his wife and daughter in a road accident and is deeply grieved.*

北 bēi N north, northern

北极 **běijí** the North Pole (← the north extreme) ■ 在北半球, 刮北风, 天就冷。Zài běi bànqiú, guā běifēng, tiān jiù lěng. *In the northern hemisphere, the weather becomes cold when a north wind blows.*
北极星 **běijíxīng** the North Star, Polaris
北边 **běibian** N north side, to the north, in the north
北方 **běifāng** N northern region
北京 **Běijīng** N Beijing (Peking) (the capital of the People's Republic of China)
北面 **běimiàn** N Same as 北边 běibian

辈 bèi TRAD 輩 N generation, lifetime

贝 bèi TRAD 貝 N shellfish

贝壳 **bèiké** N shell

狈 bèi TRAD 狽 N a legendary beast, similar to the wolf

备 bèi TRAD 備 v prepare

备忘录 **bèiwànglù** N memorandum, memo
备用 **bèiyòng** v reserve, spare
　备用轮胎 **bèiyòng lúntāi** spare tire

惫 bèi TRAD 憊 ADJ fatigued

背 bèi I v 1 turn away, leave, go away 2 learn by heart II N back

背面 **bèimiàn** N reverse side, the back of an object

背叛 **bèipàn** V betray

背叛⋯的信任 **bèipàn...de xìnrèn** betray the trust of ...

背诵 **bèisòng** V repeat from memory ■ 他们六岁的孩子能背诵好几首唐诗。Tāmen liù suì de háizi néng bèisòng hǎojǐ shǒu Táng shī. *Their six-year-old child can recite quite a few Tang poems.*

背心 **bèixīn** N vest, waistcoat

被 **bèi** PREP by (introducing the doer of an action) ■ 花瓶被小明打破了。Huāpíng bèi Xiǎo Míng dǎpò le. *The vase was broken by Xiao Ming.*

被动 **bèidòng** ADJ passive

被动式 **bèidòngshì** (in grammar) the passive voice

被动吸烟 **bèidòng xīyān** passive smoking

被告(人) **bèigào(rén)** N defendant

被迫 **bèipò** V be forced to, be compelled to

被子 **bèizi** N quilt, blanket (条 tiáo)

倍 **bèi** M. WORD (-fold, times) ■ 这个学校的学生人数比我们学校多一倍。(这个学校的学生人数是我们学校的两倍。) Zhège xuéxiào de xuéshēng rénshù bǐ wǒmen xuéxiào duō yí bèi. (Zhège xuéxiào de xuéshēng rénshù shì wǒmen xuéxiào de liǎng bèi.) *The number of students in this school is twice as many as that of our school.* (→ *The student population of this school is twice of ours.*)

倍数 **bèishù** N (in math) multiple

奔 **bēn** V run fast

奔驰 **bēnchí** V (of animals and vehicles) run fast, speed

奔跑 **bēnpǎo** V run fast, whizz

奔腾 **bēnténg** V gallop

本 **běn** I N principal, capital

赔本 **péi běn** lose one's capital in investments or other business dealings

II M. WD (for books, magazines, etc.)

一本书 **yì běn shū** a book

III ADJ this one, one's own ■ 本店春节照常营业。Běn diàn chūnjié zhàocháng yíngyè. *This store will do business as usual during the Spring Festival.* (→ *We'll be open during the Chinese New Year.*)

NOTE: 本 **běn** in the sense of *this one* is only used on formal occasions.

本地 **běndì** N this locality

本来 **běnlái** ADV originally, at first ■ 这个旅馆本来是一个富商的家。Zhège lǚguǎn běnlái shì

yí ge fù shāng de jiā. *This hotel was originally a rich merchant's residence.*

本领 **běnlǐng** N skill, ability, capability ■ 他已经二十多岁了, 还没有本领独立生活。Tā yǐjīng èrshí duō suì le, hái méiyǒu běnlǐng dúlì shēnghuó. *He is over twenty, but still lacks the skills to live independently.*

本能 **běnnéng** N instinct, intuition

求生的本能 **qiúshēng de běnnéng** the instinct to survive

本钱 **běnqián** N the money with which one makes investments or conducts other business dealings, capital

本事 **běnshì** N ability, capability ■ 他自以为本事很大, 其实什么都做不好。Tā zì yǐwéi běnshì hěn dà, qíshí shénme dōu zuò bu hǎo. *He thinks himself very capable; actually he can't get anything done properly.*

NOTE: 本领 **běnlǐng** and 本事 **běnshì** are synonyms, but 本领 **běnlǐng** emphasizes skills while 本事 **běnshì** has a more general sense of "the ability to get things done" and may be used with negative connotations.

本性 **běnxìng** N natural character, inherent quality ■ 本性难改。Běnxìng nán gǎi. *It's difficult to change one's nature.* (→ *A leopard will not change its spots.*)

本质 **běnzhì** N innate character, true nature ■ 研究问题我们要透过表面现象看到本质。Yánjiū wèntí, wǒmen yào tòuguo biǎomiàn xiànxiàng kàndào běnzhì. *When studying a problem we should see beyond appearances and get to its essence.*

本子 **běnzi** N notebook (本 běn)

笨 **bèn** ADJ dumb, stupid ■ 千万不能对孩子说"你真笨!"这样的话。Qiānwàn bù néng duì háizi shuō "Nǐ zhēn bèn!" zhèyàng de huà. *Never, ever say to a child such things as "How stupid you are!"*

笨蛋 **bèndàn** N fool, idiot

笨重 **bènzhòng** ADJ heavy and cumbersome

笨拙 **bènzhuō** ADJ clumsy

崩 **bēng** V collapse

崩溃 **bēngkuì** V collapse, crumble

绷 **bēng** TRAD 繃 V stretch tight

绷带 **bēngdài** N bandage

甭 **béng** ADV (contraction of 不用 búyòng) don't ■ 甭客气! Béng kèqi! *Don't stand on ceremony! It's OK.*

蹦 **bèng** V jump

逼 bī

蹦床 **bèngchuáng** trampoline

蹦极跳 **bèngjítiào** bungee jump

逼 bī v 1 force, compel 2 get close to, press on towards

逼近 **bījìn** v close in on, gain on

逼迫 **bīpò** v force, coerce

鼻 bí N nose

鼻子 **bízi** the nose ■ 有些中国人叫西方人"大鼻子", 这是不礼貌的。Yǒuxiē Zhōngguórén jiào Xīfāngrén "dà bízi", zhè shì bù lǐmào de. *Some Chinese call Westerners "Big Noses"; this is impolite.*

鼻涕 **bítì** N nasal mucus

比 bǐ I PREP (introducing the object that is compared with the subject of a sentence), than ■ 你写汉字没有我写得快, 但是写得比我好看。Nǐ xiě Hànzì méiyǒu wǒ xiě de kuài, dànshì xiě de bǐ wǒ hǎokàn. *You write Chinese characters more slowly, but more beautifully than I do.*

II v compete, compare, contrast ■ 你们俩谁跑得快? 比一比! Nǐmen liǎ shuí pǎo de kuài? Bǐ yì bǐ! *Of you two, who runs faster? Let's see!*

比方 **bǐfang** N example, analogy

打比方 **dǎ bǐfang** make an analogy

比分 **bǐfēn** N score (of a game or sporting competition)

比价 **bǐjià** N 1 price ratio 2 exchange rate ■ 人民币和美元的比价是多少? Rénmínbì hé Měiyuán de bǐjià shì duōshǎo? *What is the exchange rate between Renminbi and U.S. dollar?*

比较 **bǐjiào** I v compare ■ 这两种方法哪个好, 我们要比较一下。Zhè liǎng zhǒng fāngfǎ nǎge hǎo, wǒmen yào bǐjiào yíxià. *Which of the two approaches is the better one? We need to compare them.*

和…比较 **hé…bǐjiào** compare … with

II ADV relatively, quite, to some degree ■ 这两天天气比较好。Zhè liǎng tiān tiānqì bǐjiào hǎo. *The weather these days is not bad.*

比例 **bǐlì** N percentage ■ 这个学校海外留学生在学生人数中占多少比例? Zhège xuéxiào hǎiwài liúxuéshēng zài xuéshēng rénshù zhōng zhàn duōshǎo bǐlì? *What percentage of this school's enrolment is from overseas students?*

比如 **bǐrú** CONJ for example ■ 今年我们都取得了很大进步, 比如约翰, 现在已经会用中文写电子邮件了。Jīnnián wǒmen dōu qǔdéle hěn dà jìnbù, bǐrú Yuēhàn, xiànzài yǐjīng huì yòng Zhōngwén xiě diànzǐ yóujiàn le. *We have all made good progress this year. Take John for example, now he can write e-mails in Chinese.*

NOTE: In spoken Chinese you can also use 比如说 bǐrúshuō.

比赛 **bǐsài** I v compete, have a match ■ 我们比赛一下, 看谁打字打得又快又好。Wǒmen bǐsài yíxià, kàn shéi dǎ zì dǎ de yòu kuài yòu hǎo. *Let's have a contest to see who types quickly and accurately. (→ Let's compete and see who types better.)* II N competition, match, game ■ 昨天晚上的篮球比赛精彩极了! Zuótiān wǎnshang de lánqiú bǐsài jīngcǎi jíle. *The basketball match yesterday evening was wonderful!*

比赛项目 **bǐsài xiàngmù** event (of a sports meet)

参加比赛 **cānjiā bǐsài** participate in a game (or sports event)

和/跟…比赛 **hé/gēn…bǐsài** have a match/race with

看比赛 **kàn bǐsài** watch a game/sports event

比喻 **bǐyù** N metaphor

比重 **bǐzhòng** N 1 specific gravity 2 proportion

鄙 bǐ ADJ low, base (See 卑鄙 bēibǐ)

笔 bǐ TRAD 筆 N writing instrument, pen, pencil (支 zhī)

钢笔 **gāngbǐ** fountain pen

画笔 **huàbǐ** paintbrush (for art)

毛笔 **máobǐ** Chinese writing brush

圆珠笔 **yuánzhūbǐ** ballpen

笔记 **bǐjì** N notes (taken in class or while reading) ■ 我昨天没来上课, 你的笔记能借我看一下吗? Wǒ zuótiān méi lái shàngkè, nǐ de bǐjì néng jiè wǒ kàn yíxià ma? *I was absent from class yesterday. Could you let me have a look at your notes?*

记笔记 **jì bǐjì** take notes (in class, at a lecture, etc.)

做笔记 **zuò bǐjì** make notes (while reading).

笔记本 **bǐjìběn** N notebook

笔记本电脑 **bǐjìběn diànnǎo** notebook computer

笔迹 **bǐjì** N handwriting

辨认笔迹 **biànrèn bǐjì** decipher someone's handwriting

笔试 **bǐshì** N written test, written examination

笔直 **bǐzhí** ADJ perfectly straight

彼 bǐ PRON that, the other

彼此 **bǐcǐ** PRON each other

碧 bì ADJ green

碧绿 **bìlǜ** ADJ green, dark green

蔽 bì v cover, conceal (See 隐蔽 yǐnbì)

毙 bì TRAD 斃 v die (See 枪毙 qiāngbì)

币 **bì** TRAD 幣 N currency (See 人民币 Rén-mínbì)

痹 **bì** N paralysis (See 麻痹 mábì)

必 **bì** I ADV certainly, inevitably II MODAL v must
必定 **bìdìng** ADV certainly, definitely
必将 **bìjiāng** ADV will surely
必然 **bìrán** ADJ inevitable, be bound to ■ 他因为骄傲而失败，这是必然的。Tā yīnwèi jiāo'ào ér shībài, zhè shì bìrán de. *He failed because he was conceited. This was inevitable.*
必胜客 **Bìshèngkè** N Pizza Hut (Restaurant)
必修 **bìxiū** ADJ compulsory (courses, subjects of study)
必修课 **bìxiūkè** compulsory subject, required course
必须 **bìxū** MODAL v must ■ 你要在那个大学学习，必须在半年前报名。Nǐ yào zài nàge dàxué xuéxí, bìxū zài bànnián qián bàomíng. *You must apply for enrolment half a year earlier if you want to study in that university.*
必需 **bìxū** v must have
必需品 **bìxūpǐn** daily necessities
必要 **bìyào** ADJ necessary ■ 你外出旅行两天，带这么多衣服，必要吗? Nǐ wàichū lǚxíng liǎngtiān, dài zhème duō yīfu, bìyào ma? *Is it necessary to take so many clothes with you for a trip of two days?*
必要条件 **bìyào tiáojiàn** necessary condition

毕 **bì** TRAD 畢 v finish

毕竟 **bìjìng** ADV after all, anyway
毕业 **bìyè** v graduate from school ■ 你哪一年毕业? Nǐ nǎ yì nián bìyè? *When will you graduate?*

闭 **bì** TRAD 閉 v close, shut up ■ 老人看报看累了，闭上眼睛休息一会。Lǎorén kàn bào kàn lèi le, bìshang yǎnjing xiūxi yíhuìr. *The old man was tired from reading the newspapers. He closed his eyes to rest for a while.* ■ 她愤怒地喊: "闭嘴!" Tā fènnù de hǎn: "Bì zuǐ!" *She shouted angrily, "Shut up!"*

NOTE: 闭嘴! Bìzuǐ! *Shut your mouth!* is a very impolite expression to tell people to stop talking. You can also say 闭上你的嘴! Bì shang nǐ de zuǐ! *Shut your mouth!*

闭幕 **bìmù** v the curtain falls (of a theatrical performance, an event, etc.), close
闭幕式 **bìmùshì** N closing ceremony
闭塞 **bìsè** ADJ cut off from the outside world, secluded

弊 **bì** N fraud, corrupt practice

作弊 **zuòbì** cheat (especially in examinations)
舞弊 **wǔbì** be engaged in fraud, misconduct or malpractice
弊病 **bìbìng** N malpractice, disadvantage

避 **bì** v evade, avoid ■ 很多人在商场里避雨。Hěn duō rén zài shāngchǎng li bì yǔ. *Many people are in the shopping mall to shelter from the rain.*
避免 **bìmiǎn** v avoid, avert
避孕 **bìyùn** N contraception, birth control
避孕套 **bìyùntào** condom
避孕药 **bìyùnyào** contraceptive pill

壁 **bì** N wall (See 隔壁 gébì)

臂 **bì** N arm

一臂之力 **yí bì zhì lì** a helping hand

鞭 **biān** N whip

鞭子 **biānzi** whip (条 tiáo)
鞭策 **biāncè** v spur on, urge on
鞭炮 **biānpào** N firecracker
放鞭炮 **fàng biānpào** set off firecrackers

边 **biān** TRAD 邊 N side, border ■ 山的这一边有很多树，那一边没有树。Shān de zhè yì biān yǒu hěn duō shù, nà yì biān méiyǒu shù. *On this side of the hill there are lots of trees, and on the other side there are no trees.*

NOTE: The most frequent use of 边 biān is to form "compound location nouns": 东边 dōngbian *east side*, 南边 nánbian *south side*, 西边 xībian *west side*, 北边 běibian *north side*, 里边 lǐbian *inside*, 外边 wàibian *outside*. 边 biān in such cases is often pronounced in the neutral tone.

边…边 **biān…biān** CONJ (used with verbs to indicate simultaneous actions) ■ 他们边走边谈，不一会儿就到市中心了。Tāmen biān zǒu biān tán, bùyíhuìr jiù dào shì zhōngxīn le. *They chatted while walking, and soon reached the city center.*
边防 **biānfáng** N frontier defense
边防部队 **biānfáng bùduì** frontier guards
边防检查站 **biānfáng jiǎncházhàn** frontier checkpoint
边疆 **biānjiāng** N border area
边疆地区 **biānjiāng dìqū** border area
边界 **biānjiè** N border (between two countries)
边界线 **biānjiè xiàn** boundary (between two countries)
边境 **biānjìng** N frontier, border
边缘 **biānyuán** N edge, periphery
边缘状态 **biānyuán zhuàngtài** borderline case

编 biān

编 biān TRAD 編 v compile, compose ■ 那本词典是一位有丰富教学经验的老教授编的。Nà běn cídiǎn shì yí wèi yǒu fēngfù jiàoxué jīngyàn de lǎo jiàoshòu biān de. *That dictionary was compiled by an old professor with rich teaching experience.*

编号 biānhào N serial number
护照编号 hùzhào biānhào passport's serial number

编辑 biānjí I v edit, compile II N editor
财经编辑 cáijīng biānjí finance editor
特约编辑 tèyuē biānjí contributing editor
总编辑 zǒngbiānjí chief editor

编制 biānzhì v 1 weave, braid 2 draw up (a plan, a computer programme, etc.)

贬 biǎn v reduce, derogate

贬低 biǎndī v belittle, play down
贬低别人的成绩 biǎndī biéren de chéngjì belittle someone's achievements

贬值 biǎnzhí v devalue, depreciate
货币贬值 huòbì biǎnzhí currency devaluation

扁 biǎn ADJ flat ■ 面包放在这么多菜的下面,都压扁了。Miànbāo fàng zài zhème duō cài de xiàmiàn, dōu yā biǎn le. *Placed under so many groceries, the bread was crushed flat.*

变 biàn TRAD 變 v transform, change ■ 世界上任何事情都在变。Shìjiè shang rènhé shìqing dōu zài biàn. *Everything in the world is changing.*

变成 biànchéng v change into ■ 几年不见, 小女孩变成了大姑娘。Jǐnián bújiàn, xiǎo nǚhái biànchéngle yí ge dà gūniang. *I hadn't seen her for several years and the little girl had changed into a young lady.*

变动 biàndòng v 1 alter, change 2 (of organizations) reshuffle, reorganize
人事变动 rénshì biàndòng reshuffle of personnel

变革 biàngé v transform, change

变更 biàngēng v alter, modify
变更旅行路线 biàngēng lǚxíng lùxiàn change one's itinerary

变化 biànhuà I v transform, change ■ 情况变化了,不能仍然用老办法。Qíngkuàng biànhuà le, bù néng réngrán yòng lǎo bànfǎ. *Things have changed. We cannot use old ways of doing things as before.* (→ *We cannot continue doing things the old way.*)
千变万化 qiānbiàn wànhuà always in a state of flux, everchanging
II N transfomation, change
巨大变化 jùdà biànhuà tremendous changes

NOTE: As a verb 变化 biànhuà is interchangeable with 变 biàn, 变化 biànhuà being a little more formal than 变 biàn.

变换 biànhuàn v vary, alternate

变迁 biànqiān v change, evolve

变形 biànxíng v deform, transfigure
变形金刚 biànxíng jīn'gāng transformer (a toy)

变质 biànzhì v change the nature of, deteriorate ■ 这些过期食品变质了。Zhèxiē guòqī shípǐn biànzhì le. *These foodstuffs are past their sell-by dates and have gone bad.*

便 biàn ADV Same as 就 jiù 3 ADV. Used only in written Chinese.

便道 biàndào N shortcut

便利 biànlì ADJ convenient, easy

便条 biàntiáo N informal written message
留便条 liú biàntiáo leave a note

便于 biànyú v be easy to, be convenient for

辩 biàn TRAD 辯 v argue, debate

辩个明白 biàn ge míngbai debate until the truth is out

辩护 biànhù v speak in defense of
辩护律师 biànhù lǜshī defense lawyer, defense counselor

辩解 biànjiě v try to defend oneself
无力的辩解 wúlì de biànjiě feeble excuses

辩论 biànlùn I v debate ■ 我不想和任何人辩论有关宗教的问题。Wǒ bùxiǎng he rènhé rén biànlùn yǒuguān zōngjiào de wèntí. *I don't want to debate with anyone on matters of religion.*
II N debate (场 chǎng)
举行一场辩论 jǔxíng yì chǎng biànlùn hold a debate

辨 biàn v distinguish, discriminate

辨别 biànbié v distinguish, tell ... from ...
辨别是非 biànbié shìfei distinguish what is right from what is wrong

辨认 biànrèn v identify, recognize
辨认罪犯 biànrèn zuìfàn identify a criminal

辫 biàn TRAD 辮 N pigtail, braid

辫子 biànzi pigtail, braid (条 tiáo)

遍 biàn M. WD (for frequency of an action done in its complete duration from start to end) ■ 这本书我看了三遍。Zhè běn shū wǒ kànle sān biàn. *I've read this book three times.*

遍地 biàndì N everywhere

标 biāo TRAD 標 v mark

标本 **biāoběn** N sample, specimen
采集标本 **cǎijí biāoběn** collect samples or specimen

标点 **biāodiǎn** N punctuation mark
标点符号 **biāodiǎn fúhào** punctuation marks ■ 你这个标点用得不对。Nǐ zhège biāodiǎn yòng de bú duì. *The punctuation mark you used is not correct. (→ You used a wrong punctuation mark.)*

标题 **biāotí** N title, heading
大标题 **dà biāotí** banner headline

标语 **biāoyǔ** N slogan

标志 **biāozhì** N sign, mark
社会地位的标志 **shèhuì dìwèi de biāozhì** status symbol

标准 **biāozhǔn** I N standard, criterion
符合标准 **fúhé biāozhǔn** conform to the standard ■ 这些产品不符合标准，不能出厂。Zhèxiē chǎnpǐn bù fúhé biāozhǔn, bù néng chū chǎng. *These products do not conform to the standard and cannot leave the factory. (→ These products do not meet the standard and cannot be shipped.)*
达到标准 **dádào biāozhǔn** reach the standard ■ 你们的汉语水平达到什么标准？Nǐmen de Hànyǔ shuǐpíng dádào shénme biāozhǔn? *What proficiency level has your Chinese reached?*
II ADJ standard, perfect ■ 外国人说汉语发音不太标准，问题不大。Wàiguórén shuō Hànyǔ fāyīn bú tài biāozhǔn, wèntí bú dà. *It doesn't matter if a foreigner doesn't speak Chinese with perfect pronunciation.*

表 1 **biǎo** TRAD 錶 N watch (块 kuài, 只 zhī)
■ 他戴了一块新表。Tā dàile yí kuài xīn biǎo. *He wears a new watch.*
男表 **nán biǎo** men's watch
女表 **nǚ biǎo** ladies' watch

表 2 **biǎo** N form (张 zhāng, 份 fèn) ■ 这张表我不会填，你能帮帮我吗？Zhè zhāng biǎo wǒ bú huì tián, nǐ néng bāngbang wǒ ma? *I don't know how to fill in this form. Could you help me?*

表 3 **biǎo** V express, show
表表心意 **biǎobiǎo xīnyì** show one's goodwill (or gratitude)
表达 **biǎodá** V express (thoughts or emotions) ■ 你能不能用简单的中文把意思表达清楚？Nǐ néng bu néng yòng jiǎndān de Zhōngwén bǎ yìsi biǎodá qīngchu? *Can you express the meaning clearly in simple Chinese?*
表面 **biǎomiàn** N surface
表面文章 **biǎomiàn wénzhāng** something done just for the show, pay lip service
表明 **biǎomíng** V make clear, demonstrate ■ 她一直不说话，表明她其实不赞成。Tā yìzhí

bù shuōhuà, biǎomíng tā qíshí bú zànchéng. *She was silent all the way, showing that actually she disapproved.*
表情 **biǎoqíng** N facial expression ■ 从她的表情可以看出她的内心的感情吗？Cóng tāde biǎoqíng kěyǐ kànchū tāde nèixīn de gǎnqíng ma? *Can you tell the feelings in her heart from her facial expression?*
一付严肃的表情 **yīfù yánsù de biǎoqíng** with a serious expression
表示 **biǎoshì** V express, show ■ 一般点头表示同意，摇头表示不同意。Yìbān diǎntóu biǎoshì tóngyì, yáotóu biǎoshì bù tóngyì. *Generally, nodding indicates agreement and shaking one's head indicates disagreement.*
表现 **biǎoxiàn** V 1 display, show 2 perform ■ 新工人表现很好，老板决定增加他的工资。Xīn gōngrén biǎoxiàn hěn hǎo, lǎobǎn juédìng zēngjiā tā de gōngzī. *The new worker performed well, and the boss decided to raise his wages.*
表演 **biǎoyǎn** I V put on (a show), perform, demonstrate ■ 他们星期六在这里表演歌舞。Tāmen Xīngqīliù zài zhèlǐ biǎoyǎn gēwǔ. *They perform singing and dancing here on Saturday.*
II N performance, show (场 cháng)
参加表演 **cānjiā biǎoyǎn** participate in a performance/demonstration
看表演 **kàn biǎoyǎn** watch a performance
表扬 **biǎoyáng** V praise, commend ■ 他学习进步很大，老师在班上表扬了他。Tā xuéxí jìnbù hěn dà, lǎoshī zài bān shang biǎoyángle tā. *He made great progress in his studies and the teacher praised him in class.*
表彰 **biǎozhāng** V commend, honor

憋 **biē** V suppress resentment with effort, contain oneself
憋不住 **biē bu zhù** cannot contain oneself, unable to hold oneself back

别 1 **bié** ADV don't ■ 别说话了，电影开始了。Bié shuōhuà le, diànyǐng kāishǐ le. *Don't talk. (→ Stop talking.) The movie has started.*

NOTE: 别 bié is a contraction of 不要 búyào in an imperative sentence. It is only used colloquially.

别 2 **bié** PRON other, the other
别处 **biéchù** N other place(s), elsewhere
别的 **biéde** PRON other ■ 他大学毕业以后一直在教书，没有做过别的工作。Tā dàxué bìyè yǐhòu yìzhí zài jiāoshū, méiyǒu zuòguo biéde gōngzuò. *He has been teaching since graduating from university and has not held any other job (← done any other work).*
别人 **biérén** PRON other people, others

别字 **biézì** N a character which is not written or pronounced correctly

别 3 **bié** N farewell

告别 **gàobié** bid farewell

别 **biè** See 别扭 **bièniu**

别扭 **bièniu** ADJ awkward, uncomfortable ■ 我感到挺别扭。Wǒ gǎndao tǐng bièniu. *I feel awkward.* (→ *I find the situation uncomfortable.*)
闹别扭 **nào bièniu** to be at odds with someone, to be difficult with someone; make difficulties for someone

宾 **bīn** TRAD 賓 N guest

嘉宾 **jiābīn** distinguished guest, guest speaker
宾馆 **bīnguǎn** N guesthouse ■ 这是政府宾馆，不对外开放。Zhè shì zhèngfǔ bīnguǎn, bú duì wài kāifàng. *This is a government guesthouse. It is not open to the public.*

滨 **bīn** TRAD 濱 N shore, bank

海滨 **hǎibīn** seashore

冰 **bīng** N ice ■ 水到零度就结成冰。Shuǐ dào líng dù jiù jiéchéng bīng. *Water freezes to ice at 0°C.*
冰棍儿 **bīnggùnr** N flavored popsicle
冰淇淋 **bīngqílín** N ice cream
冰箱 **bīngxiāng** N refrigerator
电冰箱 **diàn bīngxiāng** refrigerator

兵 **bīng** N soldier

当兵 **dāng bīng** be a soldier, serve in the armed forces ■ 她哥哥在部队当兵。Tā gēge zài bùduì dāng bīng. *Her brother is serving in the armed forces.*

饼 **bǐng** TRAD 餅 N cake (只 **zhī**)

大饼 **dàbǐng** sesame cake (a breakfast food)
烙饼 **làobǐng** pancake
月饼 **yuèbǐng** mooncake (for the Mid-Autumn Festival)
饼干 **bǐnggān** N cookie(s), biscuit(s) (片 **piàn**, 包 **bāo**)
一包饼干 **yì bāo bǐnggān** a package of cookies
一片饼干 **yí piàn bǐnggān** a cookie

丙 **bǐng** N the third of the "Celestial Stems," the third

柄 **bǐng** N handle, stem

秉 **bǐng** V hold in hand

并 **bìng** TRAD 並 I ADV (used before a negative word for emphasis) ■ 事情并不像你想像的那么简单。Shìqing bìng bú xiàng nǐ xiǎngxiàng de nàme jiǎndān. *Things are not at all as simple as you imagine.* II CONJ Same as 并且 **bìngqiě**. Used only in written Chinese. III V combine, incorporate

NOTE: 并 **bìng** is used to emphasize negation. It is not grammatically essential; without 并 **bìng** the sentences still stand. The following is perfectly acceptable: ■ 事情不象你想象的那么简单。Shìqing bú xiàng nǐ xiǎngxiàng de nàme jiǎndān. *Things are not as simple as you imagine.*

并存 **bìngcún** V co-exist
并非 **bìngfēi** ADV not, not at all
并非如此 **bìngfēi rúcǐ** not like that
并排 **bìngpái** V be side by side, be abreast with
并且 **bìngqiě** CONJ moreover, what's more, and ■ 技术员发现并且解决了问题。Jìshùyuán fāxiàn bìngqiě jiějuéle wèntí. *The technician discovered the problem and solved it.* (← *The technician discovered the problem; what's more, he solved it.*)

病 **bìng** I V fall ill, be ill ■ 我爸爸病了，在家休息。Wǒ bàba bìng le, zài jiā xiūxi. *My father's ill and is taking a rest at home.* II N illness, disease

肺病 **fèibìng** lung disease, tuberculosis
急性病 **jíxìngbìng** acute disease
慢性病 **mànxìngbìng** chronic disease
生病 **shēng bìng** to fall ill ■ 这一点儿小病，没关系。Zhè yìdiǎnr xiǎo bìng, méi guānxi. *This is a mild case (of illness); it doesn't matter.*
病床 **bìngchuáng** N hospital bed
病虫害 **bìngchónghài** N plant diseases and insect pests
病毒 **bìngdù** N virus
电脑病毒 **diànnǎo bìngdù** computer virus
病房 **bìngfáng** N (hospital) ward
小儿科病房 **xiǎo'érkē bìngfáng** pediatrics ward
重病房 **zhòngbìngfáng** intensive care ward
病假 **bìng jià** N sick leave
请病假 **qǐng bìngjià** ask for/apply for sick leave ■ 她请了三天病假。Tā qǐngle sāntiān bìngjià. *She asked for three days' sick leave.*
病菌 **bìngjūn** N pathogenic bacteria
病情 **bìngqíng** N patient's conditions
病人 **bìngrén** N patient ■ 病人要听医生的嘱咐。Bìngrén yào tīng yīshēng de zhǔfu. *Patients should take their doctors' advice.*

门诊病人 **ménzhěn bìngrén** outpatient
住院病人 **zhùyuàn bìngrén** inpatient (warded patient)
病史 **bìngshǐ** N medical record

剥 **bō** V peel, strip

波 **bō** N ripple, wave

波动 **bōdòng** V fluctuate (like a wave)
情绪波动 **qíngxù bōdòng** constantly changing moods
波浪 **bōlàng** N wave
波涛 **bōtāo** N high wave
汹涌波涛 **xiōngyǒng bōtāo** roaring waves

玻 **bō** N glass

玻璃 **bōli** N glass ■ 大楼的正面全部是玻璃。**Dàlóu de zhèngmiàn quánbù shì bōli.** *The front of the big building is all covered by glass.*
玻璃杯 **bōlibēi** glass
玻璃窗 **bōlichuāng** glass window, glass pane

菠 **bō** N spinach

菠菜 **bōcài** spinach

播 **bō** V 1 sow 2 broadcast

播放 **bōfàng** V broadcast (radio or TV programs)
播送 **bōsòng** V broadcast (radio programs)
播音 **bōyīn** V broadcast (radio programs)
播音员 **bōyīnyuán** newsreader
播种 **bōzhòng** V sow seeds

拨 **bō** Trad 撥 V 1 stir with a finger or stick 2 allocate

拨款 **bōkuǎn** V allocate funds, appropriate (money)

伯 **bó** N Same as 伯父 **bófù**

伯父 **bófù** N father's elder brother ■ 伯父只比爸爸大两岁，但是看来比爸爸老得多。**Bófù zhǐ bǐ bàba dà liǎng suì, dànshì kànlái bǐ bàba lǎo de duō.** *My father's elder brother is only two years older than he, but looks much older.*

NOTE: 伯父 **bófù** is also a form of address for men older than your father but not old enough to be your grandfather. The colloquialism for 伯父 **bófù** is 伯伯 **bóbo**.

伯母 **bómǔ** N father's elder brother's wife ■ 我的伯父伯母住在香港。**Wǒ de bófù bómǔ zhù zài Xiānggǎng.** *My uncle (← father's elder brother) and aunt (his wife) live in Hong Kong.*

NOTE: 伯母 **bómǔ** is also a form of address for women older than your mother but not old enough to be your grandmother. It is generally used by well-educated urban Chinese.

勃 **bó** ADJ vigorous

舶 **bó** N ship

泊 **bó** V (of ships) anchor, moor

驳 **bó** TRAD 駁 V refute

驳斥 **bóchì** V refute, rebut

脖 **bó** N neck

脖子 **bózi** neck

博 **bó** ADJ 1 plentiful, abundant 2 wide, extensive

博客 **bókè** N blogger
博客论坛 **bókè lùntán** blog

NOTE: 博客 **bókè** is a transliteration of *blogger*. To blog, i.e. write as a blogger, is 写博 **xiě bó**.

博览会 **bólǎnhuì** N exposition, exhibition, fair
世界博览会 **shìjiè bólǎnhuì** World Exposition, World Expo
博士 **bóshì** N doctor, Ph.D. ■ 张博士是一位中国著名的生物化学家。**Zhāng bóshì shì yíwèi Zhōngguó zhùmíng de shēngwùhuàxuéjiā.** *Dr Zhang is a well-known biochemist in China.*
博士生 **bóshìshēng** Ph.D. candidate
博士生导师 **bóshìshēng dǎoshī** Ph.D. supervisor
博士后 **bóshìhòu** post-doctorate
博士学位 **bóshì xuéwèi** Ph.D. degree
博物馆 **bówùguǎn** N museum
历史博物馆 **lìshǐ bówùguǎn** museum of history

膊 **bó** N arm (See 胳膊 **gēbo**)

搏 **bó** V be engaged in a hand-to-hand combat, fight
搏斗 **bódòu** V battle, wrestle

薄 **bó** ADJ meager, small
一份薄礼 **yí fèn bó lǐ** an insignificant gift

NOTE: The character 薄 has two pronunciations: báo and bó. While 薄 báo is used to describe material "thin-ness," (eg. 一条薄被子 **yì tiáo báo bèizi** *a thin blanket*), 薄 bó is used in a figurative sense. See 薄 báo for examples.

薄膜 **bómó** N membrane, film

薄弱 **bóruò** ADJ frail, weak

簸 **bǒ** V jerk (See 颠簸 diānbǒ)

卜 **bo** TRAD 蔔 (See 萝卜 luóbo)

捕 **bǔ** V catch, arrest

捕捞 **bǔlāo** V catch (fish)

卜 **bǔ** V divine, predict

未卜先知 **wèi bǔ xiān zhī** have foresight, foresee

补 **bǔ** TRAD 補 V mend, patch ■ 衣服破了，补一下还能穿。Yīfu pò le, bǔ yíxià hái néng chuān. *The coat is torn, but mend it and it can still be worn.*

补偿 **bǔcháng** V compensate, make up

补充 **bǔchōng** V make up, supplement ■ 刚才小李谈了这个问题，我想补充几句。Gāngcái Xiǎo Lǐ tánle zhège wèntí, wǒ xiǎng bǔchōng jǐ jù. *Just now Xiao Li spoke of this problem. I'd like to add a few points.*

补救 **bǔjiù** V remedy

补救办法 **bǔjiù bànfǎ** corrective measure, remedial measure

补课 **bǔkè** V make up for missed lessons

补贴 **bǔtiē** I N subsidy II V subsidize

补习 **bǔxí** V take or give supplementary lessons ■ 他英文不行，妈妈给他请家庭教师补习。Tā Yīngwén bù xíng, māma gěi tā qǐng jiātíng jiàoshī bǔxí. *He is poor at English, and his mother hired a home tutor to give him extra lessons.*

补习班 **bǔxíbān** (after school) class

补助 **bǔzhù** N subsidy, grant-in-aid

不 **bù** ADV no, not ■ 今天不冷。Jīntiān bù lěng. *It's not cold today.* ■ 你说得不对。Nǐ shuō de bú duì. *You're not correct.*

NOTE: When followed by a syllable in the fourth (falling) tone, 不 undergoes tone change (tone sandhi) from the normal fourth tone to the second (rising) tone, e.g. 不对 búduì, 不是 búshì.

不必 **búbì** ADV need not, not have to, unnecessarily ■ 你不必送这么贵重的礼物。Nǐ búbì sòng zhème guìzhòng de lǐwù. *You don't have to give such an expensive gift.*

不比 **bùbǐ** V unlike

不辞而别 **bù cí ér bié** IDIOM leave without saying good-bye, take French leave

不错 **búcuò** ADJ 1 not wrong ■ 你告诉我的电话号码不错。Nǐ gàosu wǒ de diànhuà hàomǎ bú cuò. *The telephone number you gave (← told) me is correct.* 2 quite right, not bad, quite

good ■ 这孩子画得真不错。Zhè háizi huà de zhēn búcuò. *This child really doesn't draw badly.* (→ *This child draws quite well.*)

NOTE: ...得不错 ...de búcuò is ambiguous. It may mean either ... *correctly* or ... *rather well.* For example, the sentence 你说得不错。Nǐ shuō de búcuò. may mean either *You spoke correctly.* (→ *You're right.*) or *You spoke quite well.* (→ *Well said.*)

不大 **búdà** ADV not very, not much

不但 **búdàn** CONJ not only ... (but also)

...不但..., 而且 **...búdàn..., érqiě** CONJ not only ..., but also ... ■ 这个电脑游戏不但小孩爱玩, 而且大人也爱玩。Zhège diànnǎo yóuxì búdàn xiǎohái ài wán, érqiě dàren yě ài wán. *Not only children but also grownups like to play this electronic game.*

不当 **búdàng** ADJ improper, unsuitable

不得不 **bùdébù** ADV have to, have no choice but ■ 这个星期去上海的飞机票全部卖完了, 我们不得不改到下星期去。Zhège xīngqī qù Shànghǎi de fēijīpiào quánbù màiwán le, wǒmen bùdébù gǎi dào xià xīngqī qù. *This week's air tickets to Shanghai are sold out, so we have no choice but to change our departure date to next week.*

不得了 **bùdéliǎo** I ADJ horrible, extremely serious ■ 不得了了, 对面房子着火了! Bùdéliǎo le, duìmiàn fángzi zháohuǒ le! *How terrible, the house opposite is on fire!* II ADV extremely (used after an adjective and introduced by 得 de) ■ 昨天热得不得了。Zuótiān rè de bùdéliǎo. *It was extremely hot yesterday.*

不得已 **bùdéyǐ** ADJ having no alternative but to ..., acting against one's will ■ 非到不得已的时候, 不能用这笔钱。Fēidào bùdéyǐ de shíhou, bù néng yòng zhè bǐ qián. *You're not allowed to use this money, unless you really have to.*

不等 **bùděng** V vary, differ

不定 **búdìng** ADJ indefinite, not sure

不断 **búduàn** ADV without interruption, continuously, incessantly ■ 只有不断努力, 才能永远进步。Zhǐyǒu búduàn nǔlì, cái néng yǒngyuǎn jìnbù. *Only by continuous efforts can one make progress forever.*

不法 **bùfǎ** ADJ illegal, lawless

不法分子 **bùfǎ fènzi** criminal

不法行为 **bùfǎ xíngwei** illegal act, illegal practice

不妨 **bùfáng** ADV might as well ■ 你不妨试试针灸, 看看有没有效果。Nǐ bùfáng shìshi zhēnjiǔ, kànkan yóuméiyǒu xiàoguǒ. *You might as well try your acupuncture to see if it is efficacious.*

不敢当 **bùgǎndāng** IDIOM Thank you, I don't dare to accept (a polite/modest reply to a compliment) ■ "您中文说得很标准。" "不敢当，还要不断练习。" "Nín Zhōngwén shuō de hěn biāozhǔn." "Bùgǎndāng, háiyào búduàn liànxí." *"You speak standard Chinese. (→ Your Chinese is perfect.)" "Thank you very much. I still need constant practice."*

不公 **bùgōng** ADJ unfair, unjust

不够 **búgòu** ADJ not enough, insufficient

不顾 **búgù** I V disregard II PREP in spite of

不管 **bùguǎn** CONJ no matter (what, who, how, etc.) ■ 不管你明天来不来，都给我一个电话。Bùguǎn nǐ míngtiān lái bu lái, dōu gěi wǒ yí ge diànhuà. *Whether you come or not tomorrow, give me a call.*

NOTE: 不管 bùguǎn may be replaced by 不论 búlùn or 无论 wúlùn, but 不管 bùguǎn is more colloquial.

不过 **búguò** CONJ Same as 但是 dànshì. Used colloquially.

不好意思 **bù hǎoyìsi** IDIOM I'm embarrassed (a polite phrase used when you are offering an apology, giving a gift, or receiving a gift or other acts of kindness) ■ 不好意思，我又迟到了。Bù hǎoyìsi, wǒ yòu chídào le. *I'm sorry I'm late again.* ■ 又让你送我礼物，真不好意思。Yòu ràng nǐ sòng wǒ lǐwù, zhēn bù hǎoyìsi. *Oh, you gave me a gift again, it's embarrassing.*

NOTE: 不好意思 bù hǎoyìsi literally means *I'm embarrassed*. It is easy to understand why you say it when you are apologizing or receiving a gift. When you are giving a gift, however, you also say it to imply that the gift is so insignificant that you feel embarrassed about it.

不见 **bújiàn** V disappear, be lost

不见得 **bú jiàndé** ADV not necessarily, unlikely ■ 这位医生的诊断不见得对，你最好再看另一位医生。Zhè wèi yīshēng de zhěnduàn bújiàndé duì, nǐ zuìhǎo zài kàn língyí wèi yīshēng. *This doctor's diagnosis is not necessarily correct, you've better see another one.*

不禁 **bùjīn** ADV cannot help oneself from, cannot refrain from

不仅 **bùjǐn** CONJ Same as 不但 búdàn. Tends to be used in writing.

不久 **bùjiǔ** ADV not long afterwards, in the near future, soon

不堪 **bùkān** I V cannot bear, cannot stand
　不堪设想 **bùkān shèxiǎng** (of consequences) too serious to face, very bad
　II ADV (used after an adjective) utterly
　混乱不堪 **hùnluàn bùkān** in utter chaos

不愧 **búkuì** V be worthy of, deserve to be called

不利 **búlì** ADJ unfavorable, disadvantageous

不料 **búliào** ADV unexpectedly

不论 **búlùn** CONJ Same as 不管 bùguǎn. Used more in writing.

不满 **bùmǎn** ADJ Same as 不满意 bùmǎnyì dissatisfied

不免 **bùmiǎn** ADV unavoidable, inevitable, would only be natural

不平 **bùpíng** N injustice, resentment ■ 不平则鸣。Bù píng zé míng. *Where there is injustice, there will be an outcry.*

不然 **bùrán** CONJ otherwise, or ■ 你别说了，不然我真要生气了。Nǐ bié shuō le, bùrán wǒ zhēn yào shēngqì le. *Don't say any more, or I'll really be angry.*

NOTE: To be more emphatic, you can use 不然的话 bùrán de huà instead of 不然 bùrán.

不容 **bùróng** V not tolerate, not allow

不如 **bùrú** V be not as good as, not as ... as ■ 走路不如骑车快。Zǒulù bùrú qíchē kuài. *Walking is not as fast as riding a bicycle.*

不少 **bùshǎo** ADJ quite a few ■ 我做了不少解释，她还是不原谅我。Wǒ zuòle bùshǎo jiěshì, tā háishì bù yuánliàng wǒ. *I have given many explanations, but she still won't forgive me.*

不是 **búshi** N fault, blame ■ 那是我的不是，不能怪你。Nàshi wǒde bú shì, bùnéng guài nǐ. *It's my fault, you're not to blame.*

不是…而是… **bú shì...ér shì...** CONJ not ... but ... ■ 他不是美国人，而是加拿大人。Tā bú shì Měiguórén, ér shì Jiānádàrén. *He is not an American, but a Canadian.*

不是…就是… **bú shì...jiùshì...** CONJ either ... or ... ■ 他不是美国人，就是加拿大人。Tā bú shì Měiguórén, jiùshì Jiānádàrén. *He is either an American or a Canadian.*

不时 **bùshí** ADV now and then, from time to time

不停 **bùtíng** ADV without letup, incessantly

不同 **bùtóng** ADJ not the same, different ■ 这两个字发音相同，写法不同，意思也不同。Zhè liǎng ge zì fāyīn xiāngtóng, xiěfǎ bùtóng, yìsi yě bùtóng. *These two characters have the same pronunciation but they are different in writing and meaning.* …和/跟…不同 **...hé/gēn...bùtóng ...** is/are different from ... ■ 我的意见跟他的意见不同。Wǒ de yìjiàn gēn tā de yìjiàn bùtóng. *My opinion is different from his.*

不惜 **bù xī** V not hesitate, not spare
　不惜工本 **bù xī gōngběn** spare neither labor or money, spare no expense

不像话 **búxiànghuà** ADJ totally unreasonable, outrageous

不相上下 **bù xiāng shàng xià** IDIOM equally matched, be as good as

不幸 **búxìng** ADJ unfortunate ■ 这次交通事故

死了一人，伤了三人，真是一件不幸的事。Zhè cì jiāotōng shìgù sǐle yì rén, shāngle sān rén, zhēn shì yí jiàn búxìng de shì. *One person died and three others were injured in this road accident, which is indeed an unfortunate event.*

NOTE: 不幸 búxìng is used to describe serious events or matters, often involving death. Do not use 不幸 búxìng for trivial matters. For example, even though in English it is acceptable to say, "Unfortunately, I haven't seen the film," in Chinese it would be wrong to say 我不幸没有看过那个电影。Wǒ búxìng méiyǒu kànguo nàge diànyǐng.

不行 bùxíng ADJ 1 will not do, not allowed ■ "妈妈，这个周末我带十几个同学来家里玩，行不行？" "不行。" "Māma, zhège zhōumò wǒ dài shí jǐ ge tóngxué lái jiālǐ wán, xíng bu xíng?" "Bù xíng." *"Mom, may I bring a dozen classmates home for a party this weekend?" "No, you may not."* 2 not (be) good (at ...) ■ 我的中文不行，请你多多帮助。Wǒ de Zhōngwén bù xíng, qǐng nǐ duōduō bāngzhù. *My Chinese is not good. Please help me.*

不朽 bùxiǔ ADJ immortal

不许 bùxǔ v not permitted, not allowed ■ 不许逃学。Bùxǔ táo xué. *Truancy is not allowed.*

不言而喻 bú yán ér yù IDIOM it goes without saying, it is self-evident

不要 búyào ADV (used in an imperative sentence or as advice) do not ■ 你不要着急，你孩子的病很快会好的。Nǐ búyào zháojí, nǐ háizi de bìng hěnkuài huì hǎo de. *Don't you worry, your child will recover soon.*

NOTE: See note on 别 bié.

不宜 bùyí ADV unsuitable ■ 这部电影儿童不宜。Zhè bù diànyǐng értóng bùyí. *This film is not suitable for chidren.* (→ *This is an adult movie.*)

不用 búyòng ADV no need, there's no need, don't have to ■ 不用麻烦了，我们一会儿就走。Búyòng máfan le, wǒmen yíhuìr jiù zǒu. *Don't bother. We'll be leaving soon.*

不由得 bù yóude ADV cannot but, cannot help

不在乎 búzàihu v not mind, not care 满不在乎 mǎn búzàihu not care at all, couldn't care less ■ 他这个学期考试门门不及格，但是他还是满不在乎。Tā zhège xuéqī kǎoshì ménmén bù jígé, dànshì tā háishi mǎnbúzàihu. *He failed in every subject this semester, but he couldn't care less.*

不怎么样 bù zěnmeyàng ADV not up to too much, not very

不止 bùzhǐ ADV more than, not limited to

不只 bùzhǐ ADV not only

不至于 búzhìyú ADV not as far as, not so bad as

不足 bùzú ADJ inadequate, insufficient

资金不足 zījīn bùzú insufficient funds

布 1 bù N cotton or linen cloth (块 kuài, 片 piàn) ■ 这块布很好看，做裙子正合适。Zhè kuài bù hěn hǎokàn, zuò qúnzi zhèng héshì. *This piece of cotton cloth looks good, it is just right for a skirt.*
棉布 miánbù cotton cloth, cotton material

布 2 bù TRAD 佈 v arrange, deploy

布告 bùgào I v announce publicly II N public announcement, bulletin

布局 bùjú layout, overall arrangement

布置 bùzhì v decorate, furnish ■ 他们马上要结婚了，这几天正在布置新房。Tāmen mǎshàng yào jiéhūn le, zhè jǐ tiān zhèngzài bùzhì xīnfáng. *They're getting married soon and are decorating their new home these days.*

埠 bù N dock, port

步 bù N step, pace ■ 走几步就到了，不用开车。Zǒu jǐ bù jiù dào le, bú yòng kāi chē. *It's just a few steps away. There's no need to drive.*

步子 bùzi step, pace

下一步 xià yí bù the next step, the next stage

步兵 bùbīng N infantry, infantryman

步伐 bùfá N step, pace

步骤 bùzhòu N procedure, steps ■ 她没有按照步骤关电脑，结果死机了。Tā méiyǒu ànzhào bùzhòu guān diànnǎo, jiéguǒ sǐjī le. *She didn't follow the procedures to shut down the computer and, as a result, it crashed.*

怖 bù v fear (See 恐怖 kǒngbù)

部 bù N part, unit

部队 bùduì N troops, the army

部分 bùfen N portion, part ■ 中国的中学分初中和高中两部分。Zhōngguó de zhōngxué fēn chūzhōng hé gāozhōng liǎng bùfen. *Chinese high schools consist of junior high and senior high schools.*

大部分 dà bùfen most of ..., the majority of ...

部件 bùjiàn N component, part

部门 bùmén N department

部署 bùshǔ I v map out, deploy II N plan

部位 bùwèi N in position, location

部长 bùzhǎng N (government) minister

教育部长 jiàoyù bùzhǎng minister of education

外交部长 wàijiāo bùzhǎng minister of foreign affairs, foreign minister

C

擦 cā v clean or erase by wiping or rubbing ■ 窗户脏了, 要擦一下。Chuānghu zāng le, yào cā yíxià. *The window is dirty and needs cleaning.*

猜 cāi v guess ■ "谁来了? 你猜猜看。" "我猜不着。告诉我吧。" "Shéi lái le? Nǐ cāicai kàn." "Wǒ cāi bu zháo. Gàosu wǒ ba." *"Guess who's come?" "I can't. Just tell me."*

猜测 **cāicè** v guess, conjecture
猜想 **cāixiǎng** v suppose, conjecture

才 1 cái TRAD 纔 ADV **1** (before a verb) a short time ago, just ■ 我才认识他, 对他还不了解。Wǒ cái rènshi tā, duì tā hái bù liǎojiě. *I came to know him not long ago, and I don't know him very well.* **2** (used before a word of time or quantity to indicate that the speaker feels the time is too early, too short or the quantity is too little), only, as early as, as few/little as ■ 我学中文才一年, 说得不好。Wǒ xué Zhōngwén cái yì nián, shuō de bù hǎo. *I've learned Chinese for only one year, and can't speak it very well.* **3** (used after a word of time to indicate that the speaker feels that the time is too late or there is too much delay) as late as ■ 妈妈等到孩子都回来了才睡觉。Māma děngdào háizi dōu huílai le, cái shuìjiào. *Mother did not go to bed until all her children came home.*

才 2 cái N talent, remarkable ability

才干 **cáigàn** N talent, competence
有才干 **yǒu cáigàn** capable and talented
才能 **cáinéng** N talent, ability
才智 **cáizhì** N talent and high intelligence, ability and wisdom

财 cái TRAD 財 N wealth, property

财产 **cáichǎn** N property, belongings
个人财产 **gèrén cáichǎn** private property, personal belongings
财富 **cáifù** N wealth, fortune
财经 **cáijīng** N finance and economy
财会 **cáikuài** N finance and accounting
财会专业 **cáikuài zhuānyè** the profession (or department) of finance and accounting

NOTE: 会 is pronounced kuài here, not huì.

财力 **cáilì** N financial capacity
财务 **cáiwù** N financial affairs, finance
财务部门 **cáiwù bùmén** department(s) of finance (in a company or an institution)

财务主任 **cáiwù zhǔrèn** director of finance (in a company or an institution)
财政 **cáizhèng** N public finance
财政部 **cáizhèngbù** the Ministry of Finance
财政年度 **cáizhèng niándù** fiscal year

材 cái N material

材料 **cáiliào** N **1** materials, e.g. steel, timber, plastic ■ 建筑材料越来越贵, 房子的造价也就越来越贵。Jiànzhù cáiliào yuèláiyuè guì, fángzi de zàojià yě jiù yuèláiyuè guì. *As building materials become more and more expensive, building houses also becomes more and more expensive.* **2** data (for a thesis, a report, etc.) ■ 报上提供的材料对我写文章很有帮助。Bào shang tígōng de cáiliào duì wǒ xiě wénzhāng hěn yǒu bāngzhù. *The data provided in the newspapers are very helpful to my writing.*

裁 cái v **1** cut into parts, cut down **2** judge, decide

裁缝 **cáifeng** N tailor, dressmaker
裁减 **cáijiǎn** v cut down, reduce
裁决 **cáijué** v judge, rule
裁判 **cáipàn** I v **1** (in law) judge **2** (in sports) act as referee or umpire II N referee, umpire (位 wèi, 名 míng) ■ 裁判不公平, 引起观众不满。Cáipàn bùgōngpíng, yǐnqǐ guānzhòng bùmǎn. *The referee was unfair and it made the spectators unhappy.*
当裁判 **dāng cáipàn** act as a referee
裁判员 **cáipànyuán** N Same as 裁判 cáipàn II
裁员 **cáiyuán** v reduce staff

采 cǎi TRAD 採 v pick, gather ■ 公园里的花, 是给大家看的, 任何人不能采。Gōngyuán li de huā shì gěi dàjiā kàn de, rènhé rén bù néng cǎi. *The flowers in the park are for everyone to admire. Nobody is allowed to pick them.*

采访 **cǎifǎng** v (of mass media) interview
采购 **cǎigòu** v (corporate) purchase
采购员 **cǎigòuyuán** purchasing agent
采集 **cǎijí** v gather, collect
采集标本 **cǎijí biāoběn** collect (plant, insect, etc.) specimen
采纳 **cǎinà** v accept, adopt
采纳建议 **cǎinà jiànyì** accept a proposal
采取 **cǎiqǔ** v adopt (a policy, a measure, an attitude, etc.) ■ 对这个重大的经济问题, 政府准备采取什么措施? Duì zhège zhòngdà de jīngjì wèntí, zhèngfǔ zhǔnbèi cǎiqǔ shénme cuòshī? *What measures is the government prepared to adopt to deal with this major economic problem?*
采用 **cǎiyòng** v use, employ
采用新技术 **cǎiyòng xīn jìshù** adopt a new technique

彩 **cǎi** ADJ colorful, multi-colored

彩票 **cǎipiào** N lottery, lottery ticket ■ 我赢彩票啦! Wǒ yíng cǎipiào la! *I've won the lottery!*

彩色 **cǎisè** ADJ multi-colored

踩 **cǎi** V step on, tread on ■ 你们在花园里玩球, 可别踩了花。Nǐmen zài huāyuán li wán qiú, kě bié cǎile huā. *When you play ball in the garden, don't step on the flowers.*

睬 **cǎi** V pay attention to

菜 **cài** N 1 vegetables ■ 一个人既要吃肉, 又要吃菜, 才能健康。Yí ge rén jì yào chī ròu, yòu yào chī cài, cái néng jiànkāng. *One should eat both meat and vegetables in order to be healthy.*
种菜 **zhòng cài** grow vegetables
2 any non-staple food such as vegetables, meat, fish, eggs etc
买菜 **mǎi cài** buy non-staple food, do grocery shopping ■ 妈妈每个星期五都要买很多菜, 有鱼、有肉、还有蔬菜。Māma měi ge Xīngqīwǔ dōu yào mǎi hěn dōu cài, yǒu yú, yǒu ròu, háiyǒu shūcài. *Every Friday, mother buys lots of food: fish, meat and vegetables.*
3 cooked dish ■ 这个菜又好看又好吃, 是谁做的? Zhège cài yòu hǎokàn yòu hǎochī, shì shuí zuò de? *This dish is both beautiful and delicious. Who cooked it?*
点菜 **diǎn cài** order a dish (in a restaurant)
中国菜 **Zhōngguócài** Chinese dishes, Chinese food
菜单 **càidān** N menu

参 **cān** TRAD 參 V call, enter

参观 **cānguān** V visit (a place) ■ 这个古迹十分有名, 每天有很多人来参观。Zhège gǔjì shífēn yǒumíng, měitiān yǒu hěn duō rén lái cānguān. *This historical site is well-known. Many people come to visit it every day.*

参加 **cānjiā** V 1 join ■ 我可以参加中文班吗? Wǒ kěyǐ cānjiā Zhōngwén bān ma? *May I join the Chinese class?* **2** participate, attend ■ 欢迎您来参加我们的晚会。Huānyíng nín lái cānjiā wǒmen de wǎnhuì. *You're welcome to our evening party.*

参考 **cānkǎo** V consult, refer to
参考书 **cānkǎo shū** reference book(s)
仅供参考 **jǐn gōng cānkǎo** for reference only

参谋 **cānmóu** I V offer advice II N 1 staff officer
参谋长 **cānmóuzhǎng** chief of staff
2 advice
给我当参谋 **gěi wǒ dāng cānmóu** give me advice

参议员 **cānyìyuán** N senator

参议院 **cānyìyuàn** N senate, the Senate

参与 **cānyù** V participate, involve

参阅 **cānyuè** V consult (a book, a periodical, etc.) ■ 请参阅下文。Qǐng cānyuè xiàwén. *Please also read the next article.*

参照 **cānzhào** V use as reference, refer to

餐 **cān** N meal

一日三餐 **yìrì sāncān** three meals a day

餐车 **cānchē** N dining car (on a train)

餐厅 **cāntīng** N restaurant ■ 旅馆的餐厅在十二楼。Lǚguǎn de cāntīng zài shí'èr lóu. *The restaurant in the hotel is on the twelfth floor.*

残 **cán** TRAD 殘 ADJ damaged, savage

残暴 **cánbào** ADJ ferocious, brutal
残暴的独裁统治 **cánbào de dúcái tǒngzhì** tyrannical dictatorship

残疾 **cánjí** ADJ disabled
残疾人 **cánjírén** disabled person(s) ■ 这个车位是残疾人专用的, 你的车不能停在这里。Zhège chēwèi shì cánjírén zhuānyòng de, nǐ de chē bùnéng tíng zài zhèlǐ. *This parking lot is only for the disabled; you can't park your car here.*

残酷 **cánkù** ADJ cruel, brutal

残忍 **cánrěn** ADJ cruel, merciless
使用残忍的手段 **shǐyòng cánrěnde shǒuduàn** with most cruel means

残余 **cányú** ADJ remnants, survivors

残障 **cánzhàng** Same as 残疾 **cánjí**

惭 **cán** TRAD 慚 N shame

惭愧 **cánkuì** ADJ be ashamed ■ 由于我的错误, 给你带来了不便, 我深感惭愧。Yóuyú wǒ de cuòwù, gěi nǐ dàiláile búbiàn, wǒ shēn gǎn cánkuì. *My error has caused you inconvenience. I feel deeply ashamed.*

蚕 **cán** TRAD 蠶 N silkworm (条 tiáo)

惨 **cǎn** TRAD 慘 ADJ miserable, tragic

灿 **càn** TRAD 燦 ADJ brilliant

灿烂 **cànlàn** ADJ magnificent, splendid

仓 **cāng** TRAD 倉 N storage

仓促 **cāngcù** ADJ hasty, hurried
仓促离去 **cāngcù líqù** leave in a hurry

仓库 **cāngkù** N warehouse

苍 **cāng** TRAD 蒼 N dark green

苍白 **cāngbái** ADJ pallid, pale
苍蝇 **cāngying** N housefly
　苍蝇拍 **cāngying pāi** flyswatter

舱 **cāng** TRAD 艙 N cabin (in a ship or an airplane)
　经济舱 **jīngjìcāng** economy class (on a plane)
　商务舱 **shāngwùcāng** business class (on a plane)
　头等舱 **tóuděngcāng** first class (on a plane)

藏 **cáng** v hide, conceal ■ 他把玩具藏在床下，不让妈妈看见。 Tā bǎ wánjù cáng zài chuáng xia, bú ràng māma kànjiàn. *He hid the toy under the bed so his mother wouldn't see.*
　捉迷藏 **zhuō mícáng** hide-and-seek

操 **cāo** N drill, exercise

操场 **cāochǎng** N sports ground, playground
　(在) 操场上 **(zài) cāochǎng shang** on the sports ground ■ 很多学生在操场上玩。 Hěn duō xuéshēng zài cāochǎng shang wán. *Many students are playing on the sports ground.*
操劳 **cāoláo** v toil, work very hard
操练 **cāoliàn** v drill, practice, train
操心 **cāoxīn** v deeply concern, be at pains
操纵 **cāozòng** v control, operate
操作 **cāozuò**] v operate ■ 你会操作这台机器吗？ Nǐ huì cāozuò zhè tái jīqì ma? *Do you know how to operate this machine?*
　操作手册 **cāozuò shǒucè** operating manual
　操作系统 **cāozuò xìtǒng** operating system

槽 **cáo** N trough

跳槽 **tiàocáo** abandon one's job in favor of another, get a new job

草 **cǎo** N grass, weed (棵 kē) ■ 你们每天给马喂几次草？ Nǐmen měi tiān gěi mǎ wèi jǐ cì cǎo? *How many times a day do you feed the horses?* (← *How many times a day do you feed the horses grass?*)
　野草 **yěcǎo** weed
草案 **cǎo'àn** N draft (of a plan, proposal, a document, etc.)
草地 **cǎodì** N 1 lawn ■ 我家房前有一片草地。 Wǒ jiā fáng qián yǒu yí piàn cǎodì. *There is a lawn in front of our house.* 2 meadow
草率 **cǎoshuài** ADJ careless, sloppy
草原 **cǎoyuán** N grassland, steppe, pasture

册 **cè** M. WD (used for books) volume

两千册图书 **liǎngqiān cè túshū** two thousand [volumes of] books

厕 **cè** TRAD 廁 N toilet

厕所 **cèsuǒ** N toilet ■ 请问，厕所在哪里？ Qǐngwèn, cèsuǒ zài nǎli? *Excuse me, where is the toilet?*
公共厕所 **gōnggòng cèsuǒ** public toilet
男厕所 **náncèsuǒ** men's toilet
女厕所 **nǔcèsuǒ** women's toilet

NOTE: See note on 洗手间 xǐshǒujiān (in 洗 xǐ).

测 **cè** TRAD 測 v measure, gauge

测定 **cèdìng** v determine (the position, speed, etc.) by measuring
测量 **cèliáng** v survey, measure
测试 **cèshì** v test
测算 **cèsuàn** v measure and calculate
　测算有害气体排放量 **cèsuàn yǒuhài qìtǐ páifàngliáng** calculate the emission of harmful gases
测验 **cèyàn** I v test (in a school) ■ 明天数学测验，请同学们好好准备。 Míngtiān shùxué cèyàn, qǐng tóngxuémen hǎohǎo zhǔnbèi. *There will be a mathematics examination tomorrow. Be well prepared, everyone.* II N test, examination ■ 这个学期一共有四次测验。 Zhège xuéqī yígòng yǒu sì cì cèyàn. *There will be four tests this semester.*
　测验题目 **cèyàn tímù** test questions.

侧 **cè** I N side

大楼的右侧 **dàlóu de yòucè** the right side of the building
II v incline, lean
侧面 **cèmiàn** N side, flank

策 **cè** N plan (See 政策 zhèngcè)

策划 **cèhuà** v plan (an event, a theatrical performance, etc.)
　策划人 **cèhuàrén** planner
策略 **cèlüè** N tactics
　有策略的 **yǒu cèlüè de** tactful

层 **céng** TRAD 層 M. WD story (storey), level, floor ■ "你住在第几层？" "我住在第三层。" "Nǐ zhù zài dì jǐ céng?" "Wǒ zhù zài dì sān céng." *"Which floor do you live on?" "I live on the third floor."*

NOTE: See note on 楼 lóu.

层次 **céngcì** N 1 administrative or educational level 2 arrangement of ideas in writing or colors in painting

曾 **céng** ADV Same as 曾经 céngjīng. Used more in writing.
曾经 **céngjīng** ADV once, formerly ■ 这位老人曾经是一位著名的科学家。 Zhè wèi lǎorén céngjīng shì yí wèi zhùmíng de kēxuéjiā. *That old gentleman was once a famous scientist.*

NOTE: 曾经 céngjīng is used to emphasize that an action or situation took place in the past.

叉 **chā** N fork (把 bǎ)

叉子 **chāzi** fork (把 bǎ)

差 **chā** N **1** difference, discrepancy

时差 **shíchā** time difference (between time zones)
2 mistake, error

差别 **chābié** N disparity, gap
城乡差别 **chéngxiāng chābié** the urban-rural gap

差错 **chācuò** N error, fault
没有差错 **méiyǒu chācuò** error-free

差距 **chājù** N gap, disparity
贫富差距 **pín-fù chājù** the gap between rich and poor

差异 **chāyì** N diversity, difference

插 **chā** V insert, stick in ■ 花瓶里要插一些花才好。Huāpíng li yào chā yìxiē huā cái hǎo. *It would be good to have some flowers in the vase.*

插花艺术 **chāhuā yìshù** the art of flower arrangement

插秧 **chāyāng** V transplant rice seedlings

插嘴 **chāzuǐ** V interrupt by saying something

茶 **chá** N tea ■ 您喝红茶还是绿茶？Nín hē hóngchá háishì lǜchá? *Do you drink black tea or green tea?*

茶杯 **chá bēi** teacup
茶袋 **chá dài** teabag
茶壶 **chá hú** teapot
茶叶 **cháyè** tea leaf
红茶 **hóngchá** black tea
绿茶 **lǜchá** green tea
喝茶 **hē chá** drink tea
茶馆 **cháguǎn** N teahouse
茶话会 **cháhuà huì** N tea party

查 **chá** V check, investigate, look up ■ 我可以用一下你的词典吗？我要查一个字。Wǒ kěyǐ yòng yíxià nǐ de cídiǎn ma? Wǒ yào chá yí ge zì. *May I use your dictionary? I want to look up a word.*

查词典 **chá cídiǎn** look up words in a dictionary

查办 **chábàn** V investigate and punish

查获 **cháhuò** V hunt down and seize (stolen goods, criminals, etc.)

查明 **chámíng** V investigate and clarify, prove after an investigation

查询 **cháxún** V inquire about
电话号码查询服务 **diànhuà hàomǎ cháxún fúwù** telephone directory service

查阅 **cháyuè** V search (reference books, documents, etc.)
查阅五年前的统计数字 **cháyuè wǔ nián qián de tǒngjì shùzì** search the statistics from five years ago

察 **chá** V examine, look over closely (See 观察 guānchá, 警察 jǐngchá)

岔 **chà** I N branching off

岔路 **chàlù** fork (in a road)
II V change the subject
打岔 **dǎchà** interrupt and change the subject (of a talk)

差 **chà** I V be short of, lack in ■ 我还差二十块钱，你可以借给我吗？Wǒ hái chà èrshí kuài qián, nǐ kěyǐ jiè gěi wǒ ma? *I'm still short of twenty dollars. Can you give me a loan?* II ADJ poor, not up to standard ■ 他身体很差，经常生病。Tā shēntǐ hěn chà, jīngcháng shēngbìng. *He is in poor health and often falls ill.*

差不多 **chàbuduō** ADV **1** more or less the same ■ 他们俩年龄差不多，经历也差不多，很快成了好朋友。Tāmen liǎ niánlíng chàbuduō, jīnglì yě chàbuduō, hěn kuài chéngle hǎo péngyou. *They were more or less of the same age and had more or less the same experiences, and soon became good friends.* **2** almost ■ 我们晚饭吃得差不多了，弟弟才回来。Wǒmen wǎnfàn chī de chàbuduō le, dìdi cái huílai. *We had almost finished dinner when my younger brother came home.*

差点儿 **chàdiǎnr** ADV almost, nearly ■ 今天是妻子的生日，陈先生差点儿忘了。Jīntiān shì qīzi de shēngrì, Chén xiānsheng chàdiǎnr wàngle. *Today is his wife's birthday. Mr Chen almost forgot it.* (→ *Mr Chen nearly forgot it is his wife's birthday today.*)

诧 **chà** TRAD 詫 V be surprised

诧异 **chàyì** V be surprised, be amazed

拆 **chāi** V take apart, demolish ■ 小孩把玩具拆开了，可是不知道怎样再装起来。Xiǎohái bǎ wánjù chāikāi le, kěshì bù zhīdào zěnyàng zài zhuāng qǐlai. *The child took the toy apart, but did not know how to reassemble it.*

拆除 **chāichú** V demolish and remove

拆穿 **chāichuān** V expose (a lie, a plot, etc.)

拆迁 **chāiqiān** V demolish (a dwelling) and relocate (inhabitants)

柴 **chái** N firewood (See 火柴 huǒchái)

柴油 **cháiyóu** N diesel oil

搀 **chān** TRAD 攙 V **1** help by the arm **2** mix, mingle

单 chán TRAD 蟬 N cicada

兔 chán TRAD 饞 ADJ too fond of eating, gluttonous
嘴馋 zuǐchán too fond of eating

缠 chán TRAD 纏 V 1 wind, twine 2 pester

产 chǎn TRAD 產 V produce

产地 chǎndì N origin of manufacturing
产量 chǎnliàng N (production) output, yield ■ 你们工厂去年的产量是多少? Nǐmen gōngchǎng qùnián de chǎnliàng shì duōshǎo? *What was the output of your factory last year?*
产品 chǎnpǐn N product ■ 我们必须不断研究和开发新产品。Wǒmen bìxū búduàn yánjiū hé kāifā xīn chǎnpǐn. *We must continually research and develop new products.*
产生 chǎnshēng V produce, give rise to, lead to ■ 新科技的应用产生了一些新的社会现象。Xīn kējì de yìngyòng chǎnshēngle yìxiē xīn de shèhuì xiànxiàng. *The use of new technology has given rise to some new social phenomena.*
产物 chǎnwù N outcome, result
产业 chǎnyè N property, estate
产值 chǎnzhí N output value

滻 chǎn TRAD 鏟 N spade

铲子 chǎnzi spade

阐 chǎn TRAD 闡 V explain

阐明 chǎnmíng V explain clearly, clarify
阐述 chǎnshù V elaborate, explain

颤 chàn TRAD 顫 V quiver, vibrate

颤动 chàndòng V quiver, shake
颤抖 chàndǒu V (of people) tremble, shake

昌 chāng V prosper

昌盛 chāngshèng ADJ prosperous, flourishing

倡 chāng ADJ ferocious

倡狂 chāngkuáng ADJ ferocious, savage

长 cháng TRAD 長 ADJ long ■ 你还年轻, 生活道路还长着呢。Nǐ hái niánqīng, shēnghuó dàolù hái chángzhe ne. *You're still young, and have a long way to go in life.*
长城 Chángchéng N the Great Wall (a historic landmark in Northern China)
长处 chángchu N strong point, merit, strength
长度 chángdù N length
长短 chángduǎn N 1 length 2 right and wrong

3 mishap, accident

NOTE: See note on 大小 dàxiǎo.

长江 Chángjiāng N the Yangtze River (China's longest river)
长跑 chángpǎo N long-distance running
长跑运动员 chángpǎo yùndòngyuán long-distance runner
长期 chángqī N a long period of time ■ 他长期研究汉语语法, 发表过很多文章。Tā chángqī yánjiū Hànyǔ yǔfǎ, fābiǎoguo hěn duō wénzhāng. *He has studied Chinese grammar for a long time, and has published many essays.*
长寿 chángshòu ADJ enjoying longevity ■ 祝您健康长寿! Zhù nín jiànkāng chángshòu! *Wishing you good health and longevity!* (said to an old person)
长途 chángtú N long distance ■ 我要打一个国际长途电话到纽约。Wǒ yào dǎ yí ge guójì chángtú diànhuà dào Niǔyuē. *I want to make an international call to New York.*
长途电话 chángtú diànhuà long-distance telephone call
国际长途电话 guójì chángtú diànhuà international telephone call
长途汽车 chángtú qìchē long-distance bus, coach
长远 chángyuǎn ADJ long-term, long-range
长远打算 chángyuǎn dǎsuàn long-term plan

尝 cháng TRAD 嘗 V taste ■ 这种水果我没有吃过, 想尝尝。Zhè zhǒng shuǐguǒ wǒ méiyǒu chīguo, xiǎng chángchang. *I've never eaten this fruit. I'd like to taste it.*
尝试 chángshì V try

偿 cháng TRAD 償 V make up, compensate

偿还 chánghuán V pay back (a debt)

常 cháng I ADV often

常常 chángcháng ADV often ■ 我常(常)去市图书馆借书。Wǒ cháng (cháng) qù shì túshūguǎn jiè shū. *I often go to the city library to borrow books.*

NOTE: Colloquially, 常常 chángcháng is often used instead of 常 cháng.

不常 bù cháng not often, seldom
II ADJ 1 common, regular 2 normal
常规 chángguī ADJ regular, conventional
常规武器 chángguī wǔqì conventional weapon
常年 chángnián ADV all year round
常识 chángshí N 1 common sense ■ 孩子从生活中学会很多常识。Háizi cóng shēnghuó zhōng

常务 **chángwù**

xuéhuì hěn duō chángshí. *Children learn a lot of common sense from life.* **2** basic knowledge ■ 我不是计算机专家，我只知道计算机的常识。Wǒ bú shì jìsuànjī zhuānjiā, wǒ zhǐ zhīdào jìsuànjī de chángshí. *I'm not a computer expert; I've only got some basic knowledge.*

常务 **chángwù** ADJ day-to-day
常务委员 **chángwù wěiyuán** member of a standing committee
常务委员会 **chángwù wěiyuánhuì** standing committee

肠 **cháng** TRAD 腸 N intestine

大肠 **dàcháng** large intestine
小肠 **xiǎocháng** small intestine
肠胃病 **chángwèibìng** N gastrointestinal disease
肠炎 **chángyán** N enteritis

厂 **chǎng** TRAD 廠 N factory, works, mill

钢铁厂 **gāngtiěchǎng** iron and steelworks
造纸厂 **zàozhǐchǎng** paper mill
厂房 **chǎngfáng** N factory building
厂商 **chǎngshāng** N **1** factory, firm **2** factory owner
厂长 **chǎngzhǎng** N factory manager

敞 **chǎng** V open

敞开 **chǎngkāi** V open wide

场 **chǎng** TRAD 場 **I** N ground, field

体育场 **tǐyùchǎng** stadium
飞机场 **fēijīchǎng** airport
市场 **shìchǎng** market
II M. WD (for movies, sport events, etc.)
一场电影 **yì chǎng diànyǐng** a show of film ■ 这个电影院一天放六场电影。Zhège diànyǐngyuàn yìtiān fàng liù chǎng diànyǐng. *This cinema has six film shows a day.*
一场球赛 **yì chǎng qiúsài** a ball game, a ball match
场地 **chǎngdì** N venue (especially for sports)
场合 **chǎnghé** N occasion, situation
场面 **chǎngmiàn** N scene (in a play, movie, etc.)
场所 **chǎngsuǒ** N place (for public activity)
公共场所 **gōnggòng chǎngsuǒ** public place(s)

倡 **chàng** V initiate

倡议 **chàngyì** **I** V propose **II** N proposal, suggestion (项 xiàng)

唱 **chàng** V sing

唱歌 **chànggē** sing songs, sing

畅 **chàng** TRAD 暢 ADJ uninhibited, unimpeded

畅快 **chàngkuài** ADJ carefree
畅谈 **chàngtán** V talk freely and openly
畅通 **chàngtōng** ADJ unimpeded, flowing freely and smoothly
畅销 **chàngxiāo** V sell well
畅销书 **chàngxiāoshū** bestseller

抄 **chāo** V copy by hand
抄写 **chāoxiě** V Same as 抄 chāo

超 **chāo** V go beyond, exceed

超产 **chāochǎn** V exceed production quota
超出 **chāochū** V go beyond, exceed
超额 **chāo'é** V exceed quotas
超过 **chāoguò** V **1** overtake ■ 我前面的车开得太慢，我要超过它。Wǒ qiánmiàn de chē kāi de tài màn, wǒ yào chāoguò tā. *The car in front of me is moving too slowly. I want to overtake it.* **2** exceed ■ 去年这个国家的旅游者超过了三百万。Qùnián dào zhège guójiā de lǚyóuzhě chāoguòle sānbǎiwàn. *The number of tourists visiting this country last year exceeded three million.*
超级 **chāojí** ADJ super
超级大国 **chāojí dàguó** superpower
超级公路 **chāojí gōnglù** super-highway, motorway
超级市场 **chāojí shìchǎng** supermarket
超声波 **chāoshēngbō** N ultrasonic wave, supersonic wave
超越 **chāoyuè** V transcend, surpass

钞 **chāo** TRAD 鈔 N paper money

现钞 **xiànchāo** cash, ready money
钞票 **chāopiào** N paper money, banknotes (张 zhāng)

朝 **cháo** **I** V face ■ 中国人的房子大多朝南。Zhōngguórén de fángzi dàduō cháo nán. *Chinese people's houses mostly face the south.* (→ *Most Chinese houses face south.*) **II** PREP towards, to ■ 你一直朝前走十分钟左右，就到公园了。Nǐ yìzhí cháo qián zǒu shí fēnzhōng zuǒyòu, jiù dào gōngyuán le. *Walk straight ahead for about ten minutes and you'll reach the park.* **III** N dynasty
朝代 **cháodài** N dynasty

潮 **cháo** ADJ wet

潮湿 **cháoshī** ADJ damp, humid
潮水 **cháoshuǐ** N tidewater

嘲 **cháo** V jeer, mock

嘲笑 **cháoxiào** V ridicule, sneer at

尘 chén

吵 **chǎo I** v (Same as 吵架 chǎojià) quarrel ■ 他们夫妻俩又吵了。Tāmen fūqī liǎ yòu chǎo le. *The couple quarreled again.* **II ADJ** (Same as 吵闹 chǎonào **II**) noisy

吵架 **chǎojià** v quarrel

NOTE: For "quarrel," 吵架 chǎojià is more commonly used than 吵 chǎo, for example ■ 他们夫妻俩又吵架了。Tāmen fūqī liǎ yòu chǎojià le. *The couple quarreled again.*

吵闹 **chǎonào I** v wrangle, raise hell **II ADJ** noisy, hustle and bustle

吵嘴 **chǎozuǐ** v bicker, quarrel

炒 **chǎo** v 1 stir-fry, roast 2 sensationalize, create a commotion

炒股票 **chǎo gǔpiào** speculate on the stock exchange

炒鱿鱼 **chǎo yóuyú** fire (an employee), send ... packing

车 **chē** TRAD 車 N vehicle, traffic (辆 liàng) ■ 我的车坏了。Wǒ de chē huài le. *My car (or bicycle) has broken down.* ■ 路上车很多。Lùshang chē hěn duō. *There is lots of traffic on the road.*

车牌 **chē pái** (vehicle) license plate

车牌号 **chē pái hào** (vehicle) license plate number

开车 **kāi chē** drive an automobile

骑车 **qí chē** ride a bicycle

停车场 **tíngchēchǎng** parking lot, carpark

修车 **xiū chē** repair a car/bicycle

修车行 **xiūchēháng** motor vehicle repair and servicing shop

学车 **xué chē** learn to drive (or to ride a bicycle)

车床 **chēchuáng** N machine tool

车间 **chējiān** N workshop (in a factory) ■ 这个车间有多少工人? Zhège chējiān yǒu duōshǎo gōngrén? *How many workers work in this workshop?*

车辆 **chēliàng** N vehicles, traffic ■ 街上车辆很多，jiēshang chēliàng hěn duō. *There is heavy traffic in the street.*

车辆管理 **chēliàng guǎnlǐ** vehicle administration

车厢 **chēxiāng** N carriage (in a train)

车站 **chēzhàn** N bus stop, coach station, railway station

长途汽车站 **chángtú qìchēzhàn** coach station

出租汽车站 **chūzū qìchēzhàn** taxi stand

火车站 **huǒchēzhàn** railway station

扯 **chě** v 1 pull 2 tear 3 chat

撤 **chè** v 1 remove 2 withdraw, retreat

撤退 **chètuì** v retreat

撤销 **chèxiāo** v cancel, revoke

彻 **chè** TRAD 徹 ADJ thorough

彻底 **chèdǐ** ADJ thorough, complete ■ 经过彻底调查，确定这个地区没有这种病。Jīngguò chèdǐ diàochá, quèdìng zhège dìqū méiyǒu zhè zhǒng bìng. *After a thorough investigation it is confirmed that this region is free from this disease.*

臣 **chén** N (in ancient times) minister, official

辰 **chén** N 1 celestial body 2 time

沉 **chén I** v sink ■ 一公斤铁在水里会沉，一公斤棉花沉吗? Yì gōngjīn tiě zài shuǐ li huì chén, yì gōng jīn miánhuā huì chén ma? *While a kilogram of iron will sink in water, will a kilogram of cotton?* **II ADJ** 1 deep, profound 2 heavy

沉淀 **chédiàn I** v (of a substance) precipitate, settle **II N** sediment

沉静 **chénjìng** ADJ serene, placid

沉闷 **chénmèn** ADJ 1 (of weather) depressing, oppressive 2 (of moods) in low spirit 3 (of ambiance, atmosphere) dull, boring

沉默 **chénmò** ADJ silent, reticent ■ 他总是很沉默，没人知道他到底在想什么。Tā zǒngshì hěn chénmò, méi rén zhīdào tā dàodǐ zài xiǎng shénme. *He is always reticent, and nobody knows what he is thinking.*

沉思 **chénsī** v ponder, be lost in thought

沉痛 **chéntòng** ADJ deeply grieved, in deep sorrow

沉重 **chénzhòng** ADJ heavy, serious

沉着 **chénzhuó** ADJ cool-headed, composed

陈 **chén** TRAD 陳 **I ADJ** old, stale **II** v display

陈酒 **chénjiǔ** N vintage wine

陈旧 **chénjiù** ADJ old-fashioned, outdated

陈列 **chénliè** v display, exhibit ■ 商店里陈列着最新的电子产品。Shāngdiàn li chénliè zhe zuìxīn de diànzǐ chǎnpǐn. *Latest electronic products are displayed in the store.*

陈列橱窗 **chénliè chúchuāng** showcase

陈列厅 **chénlièting** exhibition hall, showroom

陈述 **chénshù** v state (one's views, reasons, etc.)

晨 **chén** N early morning (See 早晨 zǎochén)

尘 **chén** TRAD 塵 N dust (See 灰尘 huīchén)

尘土 **chéntǔ** dust, dirt

衬 **chèn**

衬 **chèn** TRAD 襯 N (clothes) lining, underwear

衬衫 **chènshān** N shirt (件 jiàn) ■ 你去公司上班, 当然要每天换衬衫。Nǐ qù gōngsī shàngbān, dāngrán yào měitiān huàn chènshān. *If you work in a company, of course you should change shirts every day.*

衬衣 **chènyī** N shirt or similar underwear (件 jiàn)

趁 **chèn** PREP taking advantage of, while, when ■ 我想趁这个机会, 向大家说几句话。Wǒ xiǎng chèn zhège jīhuì, xiàng dàjiā shuō jǐ jù huà. *I'd like to take this opportunity to say a few words to you.*

称 **chèn** TRAD 稱 V suit, fit well

称心 **chènxīn** ADJ very much to one's liking, find ... satisfactory

称 **chēng** TRAD 稱 V **1** call, be known as, address ... as ■ 电脑又称计算机。Diànnǎo yòu chēng jìsuànjī. *"Diannao" is also known as "jisuanji."* **2** weigh ■ 他去飞机场之前, 称了一下行李, 看看有没有超重。Tā qù fēijīchǎng zhī qián, chēngle yíxià xíngli, kànkan yǒu méi yǒu chāozhòng. *He weighed his luggage before leaving for the airport to make sure it was not overweight.*

称号 **chēnghào** N honorific title

称呼 **chēnghu** I V call, address ■ 我见了你的父母, 该怎么称呼他们? Wǒ jiàn le nǐ de fùmǔ, gāi zěnme chēnghu tāmen? *How should I address your parents when I meet them?* II N form of address ■ 使用正确的称呼是很重要的。Shǐyòng zhèngquè de chēnghu shì hěn zhòngyào de. *It is very important to use correct forms of address.*

称赞 **chēngzàn** V compliment, praise

撑 **chēng** V prop up, support

成 **chéng** V become, turn into ■ 他是我小学时的同学, 没想到成了一位大人物。Tā shì wǒ xiǎoxué shí de tóngxué, méi xiǎngdào chéngle yí wèi dàrénwù. *He was my primary school classmate and, unexpectedly, has become a big shot.*

成本 **chéngběn** N (in business) cost ■ 生产厂家必须降低成本才能生存。Shēngchǎn chǎngjiā bìxū jiàngdī chéngběn cái néng shēngcún. *Manufacturers must reduce cost if they are to survive.*
生产成本 **shēngchǎn chéngběn** production cost

成分 **chéngfèn** N component part, ingredient (种 zhǒng) ■ 这种中药有哪些成分? Zhè zhǒng Zhōngyào yǒu nǎxiē chéngfèn? *What are the ingredients in this Chinese medicine?*

成功 **chénggōng** I V succeed ■ 祝你成功! Zhù nǐ chénggōng! *I wish you success!* II ADJ successful ■ 在一个成功的男人背后, 总有一位好妻子。Zài yí ge chénggōng de nánrén bèihou, zǒng yǒu yí wèi hǎo qīzi. *Behind a successful man, there stands a good wife.*

成果 **chéngguǒ** N positive result, achievement (项 xiàng) ■ 我们中文学习进步这么大, 都是老师辛苦工作的成果。Wǒmen Zhōngwén xuéxí jìnbù zhème dà, dōu shì lǎoshī xīnkǔ gōngzuò de chéngguǒ. *The rapid progress we have made in our Chinese studies is the result of our teachers' hard work.*

成绩 **chéngjì** N achievement, examination result ■ 他去年的考试成绩非常好。Tā qùnián de kǎoshì chéngjì fēicháng hǎo. *His examination results last year were very good.*
考试成绩 **kǎoshì chéngjì** examination result
取得成绩 **qǔdé chéngjì** make an achievement, get (positive, good) results

成见 **chéngjiàn** N prejudice

成交 **chéng jiāo** V complete a business deal

成就 **chéngjiù** N great achievement (项 xiàng) ■ 我们在经济发展方面取得了很大成就。Wǒmen zài jīngjì fāzhǎn fāngmiàn qǔdéle hěn dà chéngjiù. *We have won great achievements in economic development.*

成立 **chénglì** V establish, set up

成名 **chéng míng** V become famous ■ 她写了那本小说, 几乎一夜成名。Tā xiěle nà běn xiǎoshuō, jīhū yí yè chéng míng. *She wrote that novel and became famous almost overnight.*

成品 **chéngpǐn** N end product, finished product

成千上万 **chéng qiān shàng wàn** IDIOM thousands of, a large number of

成人 **chéngrén** N adult
成人教育 **chéngrén jiàoyù** adult education
成人电影 **chéngrén diànyǐng** adult movie

成熟 **chéngshú** I V mature ■ 秋天是很多水果成熟的季节。Qiūtiān shì hěn duō shuǐguǒ chéngshú de jìjié. *Autumn is the season when many fruits ripen.* II ADJ ripe, mature ■ 他虽然二十多岁了, 但是还不够成熟。Tā suīrán èrshí duō suì le, dànshì hái bú gòu chéngshú. *Although he is over twenty, he is not mature enough.*

成套 **chéngtào** ADJ in a complete set
成套设备 **chéngtào shèbèi** complete set of equipment (or machinery)

成天 **chéngtiān** ADV all day long, all the time

成为 **chéngwéi** V become ■ 这个小城已经成为著名的大学城。Zhège xiǎo chéng yǐjīng chéngwéi zhùmíng de dàxué chéng. *This town has become a well-known university town.*

成效 **chéngxiào** N desired effect, beneficial effect

成心 chéngxīn ADV intentionally, purposely

成语 chéngyǔ N idiom, set phrase

成员 chéngyuán N member

成长 chéngzhǎng V grow up ■ 他已经成长为一名优秀青年。Tā yǐjīng chéngzhǎng wéi yìmíng yōuxiù qīngnián. *He has grown into a fine young man.*

城 chéng N city, town (座 zuò)

城里 chénglǐ in town, downtown

城外 chéngwài out of town, suburban area

进城 jìn chéng go to town, go to the city center ■ 我今天下午进城，有什么事要我办吗？Wǒ jīntiān xiàwǔ jìn chéng, yǒu shénme shì yào wǒ bàn ma? *I'm going to town this afternoon. Is there anything you want me to do for you?*

城市 chéngshì N city, urban area (as opposed to rural area) (座 zuò) ■ 我喜欢住在大城市里。Wǒ xǐhuan zhù zài dà chéngshì li. *I like to live in big cities.*

城市生活 chéngshì shēnghuó city life

城市规划 chéngshì guīhuà city planning

大城市 dà chéngshì big city, metropolis

国际城市 guójì chéngshì cosmopolis

城镇 chéngzhèn N cities and towns, urban area

城镇人口 chéngzhèn rénkǒu urban population

诚 chéng TRAD 誠 ADJ sincere

以诚待人 yǐ chéng dài rén treat people with sincerity

诚恳 chéngkěn ADJ sincere ■ 我们诚恳地希望你提出批评建议。Wǒmen chéngkěn de xīwàng nǐ tíchū pīpíng jiànyì. *We sincerely hope you will give us your criticism and suggestions.*

诚实 chéngshí ADJ honest, simple ■ 爸爸从小教育我做人要诚实。Bàba cóng xiǎo jiàoyù wǒ zuòrén yào chéngshí. *Since my childhood, father has taught me to be an honest person.*

诚心诚意 chéngxīn chéngyì ADJ very sincerely

诚信 chéngxìn N sincerity and trust, trust

诚意 chéngyì N good faith, sincerity

诚挚 chéngzhì ADJ sincere, cordial

承 chéng V bear, undertake

承办 chéngbàn V undertake

承包 chéngbāo V contract ■ 我们公司承包了这项工程。Wǒmen gōngsī chéngbāo le zhè xiàng gōngchéng. *This project is contracted to our company.*

承包商 chéngbāoshāng contractor

承认 chéngrèn V 1 acknowledge, recognize ■ 大家都承认他是一位有成就的科学家。Dàjiā dōu chéngrèn tā shì yí wèi yǒu chéngjiù de kēxuéjiā. *Everyone acknowledges that he is a scientist who has made great achievements.* 2 admit (mistake, error, etc.) ■ 我承认自己不了解情况，批评错了。Wǒ chéngrèn zìjǐ bù liǎojiě qíngkuàng, pīpíng cuò le. *I admit that I did not know the situation well and made a wrong criticism.*

承受 chéngshòu V endure, bear

承受力 chéngshòulì endurance

乘 1 chéng V 1 use (a means of transport), travel (by car, train, plane, etc.) ■ 你打算乘火车，还是乘飞机到北京去？Nǐ dǎsuàn chéng huǒchē, háishì chéng fēijī qù Běijīng? *Do you plan to go to Beijing by train or by plane?* 2 take advantage of

乘人之危 chéng rén zhì wēi take advantage of the misfortune (or weakness) of others

乘 2 chéng V multiply ■ 二乘三等于六。(2 x 3 = 6) Èr chéng sān děngyú liù. *Two multiplied by three is six.*

乘客 chéngkè N passenger

乘机 chéngjī V seize an opportunity

乘务员 chéngwùyuán N attendant (on a train, coach, etc.)

呈 chéng V 1 appear, assume 2 present

呈现 chéngxiàn V appear, show

程 chéng N regulation, procedure

程度 chéngdù N level, degree ■ 汽车坏到这种程度，已经修不好了。Qìchē huài dao zhè zhǒng chéngdù, yǐjīng xiū bù hǎo le. *The car is damaged to such a degree that it cannot be repaired.*

程序 chéngxù N procedure

计算机程序 jìsuànjī chéngxù computer program

惩 chéng TRAD 懲 V punish

惩办 chéngbàn V (of the authorities) punish

惩罚 chéngfá V punish, penalize

澄 chéng ADJ (of water) clear, clean

澄清 chéngqīng V clarify

澄清事实 chéngqīng shìshí clarify a matter

秤 chèng N scale(s)

吃 chī V eat ■ "你吃过早饭没有？" "吃过了。" "Nǐ chī guo zǎofàn méiyǒu?" "Chī guo le." *"Have you had breakfast?" "Yes, I have."*

吃惊 chījīng V be shocked, be startled, be alarmed

大吃一惊 dà chī yì jīng greatly shocked, have the fright of one's life ■ 他回家时，发现家门大开，大吃一惊。Tā huíjiā shí, fāxiàn jiā

吃苦 chīkǔ

mén dà kāi, dà chī yì jīng. *When he got home, he had the fright of his life when he saw the door wide open.*

吃苦 **chīkǔ** v endure hardships, suffer
吃了很多苦 **chī le hěn duō kǔ** have suffered a lot
吃亏 **chīkuī** v suffer losses, be at a disadvantage ■ 不了解市场情况，就要吃亏。Bù liǎojiě shìchǎng qíngkuàng, jiùyào chīkuī. *If you don't know the market, you'll suffer losses.*
吃力 **chīlì** ADJ making or requiring great efforts

痴 **chī** ADJ foolish, stupid

白痴 **báichī** idiot

池 **chí** N pool, pond

游泳池 **yóuyǒngchí** swimming pool
池塘 **chítáng** N pond

迟 **chí** TRAD 遲 ADJ late

迟到 **chídào** v come late, be late (for work, school, etc.) ■ 对不起，我迟到了。Duìbuqǐ, wǒ chídào le. *I'm sorry I'm late.*
迟缓 **chíhuǎn** ADJ (of movement) slow, sluggish
迟疑 **chíyí** v hesitate, waver

持 **chí** v persevere

持久 **chíjiǔ** ADJ enduring, lasting
持续 **chíxù** v continue, sustain, persist
可持续发展 **kě chíxù fāzhǎn** sustainable development

匙 **chí** N spoon

汤匙 **tāngchí** soup spoon

驰 **chí** TRAD 馳 v move quickly, gallop

尺 **chǐ** I N ruler (把 bǎ)

尺子 **chǐzi** ruler
II M. WD a traditional Chinese unit of length (equal to ⅓ meter)
公尺 **gōngchǐ** meter
英尺 **yīngchǐ** foot (as a measurement of length)
尺寸 **chǐcun** N size, measurements ■ 你做衣服以前，要量一下尺寸。Nǐ zuò yīfu yǐqián, yào liáng yíxià chǐcun. *Before a garment is made for you, measurements should be taken.*
尺码 **chǐmǎ** N size (of shoes, shirts, ready-made clothing, etc.) ■ 我们有各种尺码的裙子，保证您满意。Wǒmen yǒu gè zhǒng chǐmǎ de qúnzi, bǎozhèng nín mǎnyì. *We have skirts of various sizes. Your satisfaction is guaranteed.*

侈 **chǐ** ADJ wasteful (See 奢侈 shēchǐ)

齿 **chǐ** TRAD 齒 N tooth, teeth

齿轮 **chǐlún** N gear wheel, gear

耻 **chǐ** TRAD 恥 N shame

可耻 **kěchǐ** shameful, disgraceful
耻辱 **chǐrǔ** N deep shame, humiliation

赤 **chì** ADJ red

赤道 **chìdào** N the equator
赤字 **chìzì** N the number in red, deficit

翅 **chì** N wing

翅膀 **chìbǎng** N wing (of a bird) ■ 这只鸟翅膀受伤了，不能飞了。Zhè zhī niǎo chìbǎng shòu shāng le, bù néng fēi le. *This bird's wing is injured, it can't fly.*

斥 **chì** v scold, shout at

冲 **chōng** TRAD 衝 v 1 clash 2 charge, rush, dash

冲锋 **chōngfēng** v (of troops) charge, assault
冲浪 **chōnglàng** v surf
冲破 **chōngpò** v break through, breach
冲突 **chōngtū** I v clash II N conflict, clash ■ 警察和抗议者在市政府大楼前发生了冲突。Jǐngchá hé kàngyìzhě zài shìzhèngfǔ dàlóu qián fāshēngle chōngtū. *The police and protesters clashed in front of the municipal government building.*
利益冲突 **lìyì chōngtū** conflict of interest

充 **chōng** ADJ sufficient, full

充分 **chōngfèn** ADJ abundant, ample, adequate ■ 对明天的会谈双方都做了充分的准备。Duì míngtiān de huìtán shuāngfāng dōu zuòle chōngfèn de zhǔnbèi. *Both parties made ample preparations for the talk tomorrow.*
充满 **chōngmǎn** ADJ full of, be filled with ■ 他充满了信心，一定能完成公司的任务。Tā chōngmǎnle xìnxīn, yídìng néng wánchéng gōngsī de rènwù. *He is full of confidence that he will complete the task set by the company.*
充沛 **chōngpèi** ADJ abundant, plentiful
精力充沛 **jīnglì chōngpèi** full of vigor and vitality, very energetic
充实 **chōngshí** I ADJ substantial II v strengthen, enrich
充足 **chōngzú** ADJ sufficient, adequate, enough ■ 他们有充足的资金研究和开发这项新技术。

Tāmen yǒu chōngzú de zījīn yánjiū hé kāifā zhè xiàng xīn jìshù. *They have sufficient funds to research and develop this new technology.*

虫 chóng TRAD 蟲 N insect, worm

虫子 **chóngzi** N insect, worm (只 zhī)

重 chóng ADV again, once again ■ 我在电脑上做的文件没有保存，只好重做。Wǒ zài diànnǎo shang zuò de wénjiàn méiyǒu bǎocún, zhǐ hǎo chóng zuò. *I failed to save the file in the computer, and had to redo [the work].*

重叠 **chóngdié** V overlap
重复 **chóngfù** V repeat ■ 我离家前，妈妈又把话重复了一遍。Wǒ lí jiā qián, māma yòu bǎ huà chóngfùle yí biàn. *Before I left home, mother repeated what she had said.*
重新 **chóngxīn** ADV Same as 重 chóng

崇 chóng ADJ high, lofty

崇拜 **chóngbài** V worship, adore
崇高 **chónggāo** ADJ lofty, sublime ■ 不少人不相信世界上有什么崇高的东西。Bùshǎo rén bù xiāngxìn shìjiè shang yǒu shénme chónggāo de dōngxi. *Quite a few people do not believe there is anything lofty in the world.*
崇敬 **chóngjìng** V hold in high esteem, revere

宠 chǒng TRAD 寵 V pamper, indulge

宠物 **chǒngwù** N pet

冲 chòng ADJ strong, forceful

抽 chōu V take out (from in-between)

抽空 **chōukòng** V manage to find time
抽水机 **chōushuǐjī** N water pump
抽屉 **chōuti** N drawer
抽象 **chōuxiàng** ADJ abstract ■ 这么抽象的道理，有多少人听得懂？Zhème chōuxiàng de dàoli, yǒu duōshǎo rén tīng de dǒng? *How many people understand such abstract concepts?*
抽烟 **chōuyān** V smoke a cigarette (cigar), smoke

绸 chóu TRAD 綢 N silk (See 丝绸 sīchóu)

愁 chóu V worry ■ 你别愁，大伙儿会帮助你的。Nǐ bié chóu, dàhuǒr huì bāngzhù nǐ de. *Don't worry. We'll all help you.*

酬 chóu V reward

稠 chóu ADJ thick, dense

稠密 **chóumì** ADJ dense
人口稠密 **rénkǒu chóumì** densely populated

筹 chóu TRAD 籌 V prepare

筹备 **chóubèi** V prepare (a conference, an event, etc.)
筹建 **chóujiàn** V prepare to construct (a factory, a school, etc.)

仇 chóu N deep hatred

仇恨 **chóuhèn** intense hatred

丑 chǒu TRAD 醜 ADJ ugly ■ 他很丑，但是他很温柔。Tā hěn chǒu, dànshì tā hěn wēnróu. *He's ugly, but he's gentle and sweet.*

丑恶 **chǒu'è** ADJ ugly, hideous
丑闻 **chǒuwén** N scandal ■ 丑闻暴露后，市长只能辞职。Chǒuwén bàolù hòu, shìzhǎng zhǐ néng cízhí. *When the scandal was exposed, the mayor had to resign.*

臭 chòu ADJ smelly, stinking ■ 臭豆腐，闻闻臭，吃起来香。Chòu dòufu, wénwen chòu, chī qǐlai xiāng. *The preserved beancurd smells bad but tastes delicious.*

出 chū V emerge from, go out, exit

出版 **chūbǎn** V publish ■ 这本词典由一家国际出版公司出版。Zhè běn cídiǎn yóu yì jiā guójì chūbǎn gōngsī chūbǎn. *This dictionary is published by an international publishing house.*
出差 **chūchāi** V be on a business trip, leave town on business
出产 **chūchǎn** V produce, manufacture
出动 **chūdòng** V set out, go into action
出发 **chūfā** V set off (on a journey), start (a journey) ■ "我们明天什么时候出发？""早上八点。" "Wǒmen míngtiān shénme shíhou chūfā?" "Zǎoshang bā diǎn." *"When do we set off tomorrow?" "Eight o'clock in the morning."*
出发点 **chūfādiǎn** starting point, point of departure
出国 **chūguó** V go abroad, go overseas
出境 **chūjìng** V leave the country, exit
办理出境手续 **bànlǐ chūjìng shǒuxù** go through exit formalities
出口 **chūkǒu** I V 1 export ■ 这个国家出口大量工业品到世界各地。Zhège guójiā chūkǒu dàliàng gōngyèpǐn dào shìjiè gè dì. *This country exports large amounts of industrial products to various places in the world.*
出口公司 **chūkǒu gōngsī** export company
出口贸易 **chūkǒu màoyì** export business in foreign trade
2 speak, utter **II** N exit ■ 这是停车场的出

口，不能从这里进。Zhè shì tíngchēchǎng de chūkǒu, bù néng cóng zhèlǐ jìn. *This is the car-park exit. You can't enter from here.*

出来 chūlai v come out ■ 请你出来一下。Qǐng nǐ chūlai yíxià. *Would you please step out for a while?*

出路 chūlù N outlet, way out

出卖 chūmài v 1 sell, be for sale ■ 工厂倒闭以后，出卖机器还债。Gōngchǎng dǎobì yǐhòu, chūmài jīqì huán zhài. *After the factory went bankrupt, the machines were sold to pay back debts.* 2 betray, sell out ■ 犹大为了三十块金币出卖耶稣。Yóudà wèile sānshí kuài jīnbì chūmài Yēsū. *Judas sold out Jesus for 30 pieces of gold.*

出门 chūmén v leave home, go out

出面 chūmiàn v act in the name of

出名 chūmíng ADJ famous, well-known ■ 他出名了。Tā chūmíng le. *He's become famous.*

出纳 chūnà N Same as 出纳员 chūnà yuán

出纳员 chūnàyuán N cashier

出品 chūpǐn N product

出去 chūqu v go out ■ 请你出去一下。Qǐng nǐ chūqu yíxià. *Please go out for a while. (→ Please leave us for a while.)*

出入 chūrù I v go in and come out II N inconsistency, discrepancy

出色 chūsè ADJ outstanding, remarkable

出身 chūshēn N family background, (a person's) social origin

出神 chūshén v be lost in thought, be spellbound

出生 chūshēng v be born ■ 他于1980年出生在中国。Tā yú yāo-jiǔ-bā-líng nián chūshēng zài Zhōngguó. *He was born in China in the year 1980.*

出生地 chūshēng dì place of birth

出生日期 chūshēng rìqī date of birth

出生证 chūshēng zhèng birth certificate

出事 chūshì v (an accident) take place

出事地点 chūshìdìdiǎn the scene of an accident

出席 chūxí v attend (a meeting, a court trial, etc.) ■ 你出席明天的会议吗？Nǐ chūxí míngtiān de huìyì ma? *Are you going to attend the meeting tomorrow?*

出息 chūxi N (a person's) future

有出息 yǒu chūxi (especially of a young person) have a bright future, promising

出现 chūxiàn v come into view, appear, emerge ■ 开车两小时，一座漂亮的小山城出现在我们面前。Kāichē liǎng xiǎoshí, yí zuò piàoliang de xiǎo shānchéng chūxiàn zài wǒmen miànqián. *After two hours' drive, a beautiful small mountain town appeared before us.*

出洋相 chūyángxiàng v make a fool of oneself, cut a ridiculous figure

出院 chūyuàn v be discharged from hospital

出租 chūzū v have ... for hire, rent ■ 这家商店出租电视机。Zhè jiā shāngdiàn chūzū diànshìjī. *This store has TV sets for hire.*

房屋出租 fángwū chūzū house for rent, house to let

出租汽车 chūzū qìchē N taxi ■ 我要一辆出租汽车去飞机场。Wǒ yào yí liàng chūzū qìchē qù fēijīchǎng. *I need a taxi to go to the airport.*

NOTE: The slang expression 打的 dǎdī, which means *to call a taxi* or *to travel by taxi*, is very popular in everyday Chinese.

初 chū I N beginning

月初 yuèchū at the beginning of a month

年初 niánchū at the beginning of a year

II ADJ at the beginning, for the first time ■ 我初来贵国，情况还不熟悉。Wǒ chū lái guì guó, qíngkuàng hái bù shúxī. *I have just arrived in your country, and do not know much about it.* III PREFIX (used for the first ten days of a lunar month), the first

初一 chū yī the first day (of a lunar month)

五月初八 Wǔyuè chū bā the eighth day of the fifth lunar month

年初一／大年初一 nián chū yī/dà nián chū yī the first day of the first lunar month (Chinese New Year's Day)

初步 chūbù ADJ initial, tentative ■ 这仅仅是我们的初步打算。Zhè jǐnjǐn shì wǒmen de chūbù dǎsuàn. *This is but our tentative plan.*

初级 chūjí ADJ elementary, initial

初级小学／初小 chūjí xiǎoxué/chūxiǎo elementary school (from Grade 1 to Grade 4 of a primary school)

初级中学／初中 chūjí zhōngxué/chūzhōng junior high school

初期 chūqī N initial stage

除 chú I v get rid of II PREP except, apart from

除草 chú cǎo v to weed

除草剂 chúcǎojì weed killer, herbicide

除虫 chú chóng I v to kill insects II N insecticide

除此以外 chúcǐ yǐwài PREP apart from this, besides

除非 chúfēi CONJ unless, only if ■ 除非他们正式邀请我，否则我是不会去参加他们的婚礼的。Chúfēi tāmen zhèngshì yāoqǐng wǒ, fǒuzé wǒ shì bú huì qù cānjiā tāmen de hūnlǐ de. *I'm not going to attend their wedding, unless they send me a formal invitation.*

除了⋯(以外) chúle ... (yǐwài) PREP except, besides ■ 这个动物园除了圣诞节每天开

放。Zhège dòngwùyuán chúle Shèngdànjié měitiān kāifàng. *This zoo is open to the public all year round except on Christmas Day.*

NOTE: (1) While *except* and *besides* are two distinct words in English, 除了…以外, chúle…yǐwài may mean either *except* or *besides*, as is shown in the examples. (2) 以外 yǐwài may be omitted, i.e. 除了…以外 chúle…(yǐwài) and 除了… chúle are the same.

除夕 chúxī N New Year's eve

NOTE: In colloquial Chinese, the Chinese New Year's eve is called 大年夜 dàniányè. The dinner on the Chinese New Year's eve is 年夜 饭 niányèfàn, or 团圆饭 tuányuánfàn, a family reunion dinner.

厨 chú TRAD 廚 N kitchen

厨房 chúfáng N kitchen
厨房设备 chúfáng shèbèi kitchen equipment
厨房用具 chúfáng yòngjù kitchen utensils
厨师 chúshī N chef
大厨师 dàchúshī master chef

锄 chú TRAD 鋤 I N hoe

锄头 chútou hoe (把 bǎ)
II v do hoeing

处 chǔ TRAD 處 v handle, deal with

处罚 chǔfá v penalize, discipline
处方 chǔfāng N (doctor's) prescription
处方药 chǔfāng yào prescribed medicine
非处方药 fēi chǔfāng yào over-the-counter medicine
开处方 kāi chǔfāng write out a prescription
处分 chǔfèn I N disciplinary action ■ 十名官员 因接受贵重礼物受到处分。Shí míng guānyuán yīn jiēshòu guìzhòng lǐwù shòudào chǔfèn. *Disciplinary action was taken against the ten officials who had accepted expensive gifts.*
警告处分 jǐnggào chǔfèn disciplinary warning
II v take disciplinary action ■ 处分这名学生 是为了教育全校所有的学生。Chǔfèn zhè míng xuésheng shì wèile jiàoyù quán xiào suǒyǒu de xuésheng. *The purpose of taking disciplinary action against this student is to educate all the students of the school.*
处分服用兴奋剂的运动员 chǔfèn fúyòng xīngfènjì de yùndòngyuán take disciplinary action against athletes who have taken stimulants
处境 chǔjìng N (usually) bad situation, plight
处境危险 chǔjìng wēixiǎn in a dangerous situation

处决 chǔjué v put to death, execute
处理 chǔlǐ v 1 handle, deal with ■ 对于顾客提 出的意见，我们都会认真处理。Duìyú gùkè tíchū de yìjiàn, wǒmen dōu huì rènzhēn chǔlǐ. *We deal with customers' suggestions seriously.* 2 sell at reduced prices
处理品 chǔlǐpǐn goods sold at reduced prices
3 take disciplinary action
处理违反校纪的学生 chǔlǐ wéifǎn xiào jì de xuésheng take disciplinary action against students who have violated school regulations
处于 chǔyú v be in state of, be situated at
处置 chǔzhì v dispose of, handle, deal with

础 chǔ TRAD 礎 N plinth (See 基础 jīchǔ)

楚 chǔ ADJ clear, neat (See 清楚 qīngchu)

储 chǔ TRAD 儲 v store

储备 chǔbèi v store away
储存 chǔcún v 1 store away, keep in reserve
2 (in computing) save a file
储蓄 chǔxù v save (money), deposit (money)
定期储蓄 dìngqī chǔxù fixed deposits, term deposit
活期储蓄 huóqī chǔxù checking account

处 chù TRAD 處 N place, location ■ 你知道他 现在的住处吗？Nǐ zhīdào tā xiànzài de zhùchù ma? *Do you know where he lives now?*
处处 chùchù ADV everywhere

触 chù TRAD 觸 v touch, contact

触电 chùdiàn v get an electric shock
触犯 chùfàn v violate (law), offend (a person)

穿 chuān v 1 wear (clothes, shoes), be dressed in ■ 你穿黑衣服去参加中国人的婚礼，不合 适。Nǐ chuān hēi yīfu qù cānjiā Zhōngguórén de hūnlǐ, bù héshì. *It is not appropriate for you to go to a Chinese wedding in black.*
穿着 chuānzhe be dressed in
2 put on (clothes, shoes) ■ 这个小孩会穿衣服 了，可是还不会穿鞋子。Zhège xiǎohái huì chuān yīfu le, kěshì hái bú huì chuān xiézi. *This child can put on his clothes, but still can't put on his shoes.*

川 chuān N river

船 chuán N boat, ship ■ 从香港坐船到上海 去，只要两天。Cóng Xiānggǎng zuòchuán dào Shànghǎi qù, zhǐ yào liǎng tiān. *It takes only two days to travel from Hong Kong to Shanghai by sea.*

船舶 chuánbó

划船 **huá chuán** row a boat

坐船 **zuò chuán** travel by boat/ship

船舶 **chuánbó** N boats and ships

船舶公司 **chuánbó gōngsī** shipping company

传 **chuán** TRAD 傳 V **1** pass (something) on, transmit **2** spread (news, rumor) ■ 好事不出门，坏事传千里。Hǎo shì bù chūmén, huài shì chuán qiān lǐ. *Good news stays at home, but bad news travels far and wide.*

传播 **chuánbō** V propagate, disseminate ■ 学校不仅仅是传播知识的地方。Xuéxiào bù jǐnjǐn shì chuánbó zhīshi de dìfang. *A school is more than a place to disseminate knowledge.*

传达 **chuándá** V pass on, relay, transmit

传达室 **chuándá shì** reception office

传达总公司的指令 **chuándá zǒnggōngsī de zhǐlìng** pass on instructions from the company's HQ

传递 **chuándì** V transmit, deliver

传媒 **chuánméi** N media, mass media

大众传媒 **dàzhòng chuánméi** mass media

传染 **chuánrǎn** V infect ■ 验血表明，他被传染上艾滋病毒了。Yànxuè biǎomíng, tā bèi chuánrǎn shàng àizībìngdú le. *Blood tests indicate that he is infected with the AIDS virus.*

传染病 **chuánrǎnbìng** infectious (contagious) disease

传授 **chuánshòu** V teach, pass on (knowledge, skill, etc.)

传说 **chuánshuō** I N legend, folklore

民间传说 **mínjiān chuánshuō** folktale

II V it is said, they say

传送 **chuánsòng** V convey, deliver

传送带 **chuánsòngdài** conveyor belt

传统 **chuántǒng** N tradition, heritage ■ 每个民族都有自己的传统。Měi ge mínzú dōu yǒu zìjǐ de chuántǒng. *Every ethnic group has its own traditions.*

传统服装 **chuántǒng fúzhuāng** traditional costume

传销 **chuánxiāo** N pyramid selling

传真 **chuánzhēn** N fax ■ 我发了一份传真给他。Wǒ fāle yí fèn chuánzhēn gei tā. *I sent him a fax.*

喘 **chuǎn** V breathe with difficulty, pant

串 **chuàn** V string together

疮 **chuāng** N sore, open sore

冻疮 **dòngchuāng** chilblain

疮疤 **chuāngbā** N scar

窗 **chuāng** N window (扇 shàn)

玻璃窗 **bōlichuāng** glass window

窗户 **chuānghu** N window (扇 shàn)

打开窗户 **dǎkāi chuānghu** open a window

关上窗户 **guānshang chuānghu** close a window

窗口 **chuāngkǒu** N window

窗帘 **chuānglián** N (window) curtain (块 kuài) ■ 天黑了，把窗帘拉上吧。Tiān hēi le, bǎ chuānglián lā shàng ba. *It's getting dark. Let's close the curtains.*

窗台 **chuangtái** N window sill

床 **chuáng** N bed (张 zhāng) ■ 这张床很舒服。Zhè zhāng chuáng hěn shūfu. *This bed is very comfortable.*

单人床 **dānrénchuáng** single bed

双人床 **shuāngrénchuáng** double bed

床单 **chuángdān** N bedsheet (条 tiáo)

床铺 **chuángpù** N bed (in school dormitories, army barracks, etc.) (张 zhāng)

床位 **chuángwèi** N bed (in a hospital, ship, train, etc.) (张 zhāng)

闯 **chuǎng** TRAD 闖 V charge, rush

闯祸 **chuǎnghuò** V cause disasters, get into trouble

创 **chuàng** TRAD 創 V create

创建 **chuàngjiàn** V found (a company, an institution, etc.)

创立 **chuànglì** V set up, found

创业 **chuàngyè** V start an undertaking

创业精神 **chuàngyè jīngshen** pioneering spirit

创造 **chuàngzào** V create ■ 有人说神创造了天地。Yǒurén shuō shén chuàngzàole tiān-dì. *Some people say God created the universe.*

创造性 **chuàngzàoxìng** N creativity ■ 创造性是艺术作品的生命。Chuàngzàoxìng shì yìshù zuòpǐn de shēngmìng. *Creativity is the life of a work of art.*

创作 **chuàngzuò** I V create (works of art and literature) ■ 这位作家创作了反映农民生活的小说。Zhè wèi zuòjiā chuàngzuòle fǎnyìng nóngmín shēnghuó de xiǎoshuō. *This author wrote novels about peasant lives.* II N work of art or literature

吹 **chuī** V blow, puff ■ 风吹草动。Fēng chuī cǎo dòng. *Winds blow and the grass stirs.* (→ *There are signs of disturbance/trouble.*)

吹牛 **chuīniú** V brag, boast

吹牛大王 **chuīniú dàwáng** braggart

吹捧 **chuīpěng** V lavish praise on, flatter

相互吹捧 **xiānghù chuīpěng** flatter each other

炊 **chuī** v cook

炊事员 **chuīshìyuán** N cook, kitchen staff (in a school, a factory, etc.)

垂 **chuí** v hang down

垂直 **chuízhí** ADJ vertical
垂直线 **chuízhíxiàn** vertical line

锤 **chuí** v hammer

锤子 **chuízi** hammer (把 bǎ)

捶 **chuí** v beat with a fist or stick

春 **chūn** N spring

春季 **chūnjì** spring (season)
春节 **Chūnjié** N Spring Festival (the Chinese New Year) ■ 春节是中国人最重要的节日。 Chūnjié shì Zhōngguórén zuì zhòngyào de jiérì. *The Spring Festival is the most important festival for the Chinese.*
春天 **chūntiān** N spring ■ 春天来了，花园里的花都开了。 Chūntiān lái le, huā-yuán lǐ de huā dōu kāi le. *Spring is here. The flowers in the garden are in full bloom.*

纯 **chún** TRAD 純 ADJ pure

纯粹 **chúncuì** ADJ unadulterated, pure and simple ■ 这纯粹是谎言! Zhè chúncuì shì huǎngyán! *This is a lie, pure and simple!*
纯洁 **chúnjié** ADJ pure, ingenuous

唇 **chún** TRAD 脣 N lip

嘴唇 **zuǐchún** (mouth) lip
嘴唇皮儿 **zuǐchúnpír** (mouth) lip

蠢 **chǔn** ADJ stupid, foolish

蠢事 **chǔnshì** an act of folly
干蠢事 **gān chǔnshì** do a stupid thing, commit a folly

雌 **cí** ADJ (of animals) female ■ 我不知道家里的狗是雌的还是雄的。 Wǒ bù zhīdào jiālǐ de gǒu shì cí de háishì xióng de. *I don't know whether our family dog is female or male.*

词 **cí** TRAD 詞 N word ■ 现代汉语的词一般是由两个字组成。 Xiàndài Hànyǔ de cí yìbān shì yóu liǎng ge zì zǔchéng. *Modern Chinese words generally consist of two characters.*
词典 **cídiǎn** N dictionary (本 běn) ■ 这本词典对我们很有帮助。 Zhè běn cídiǎn duì wǒmen hěn yǒu bāngzhù. *This dictionary is very helpful to us.*
查词典 **chá cídiǎn** consult a dictionary

瓷 **cí** N porcelain

瓷器 **cíqì** N porcelain

磁 **cí** N magnetism

磁带 **cídài** N magnetic tape, audio tape (盘 pán) ■ 这一盘磁带是我爷爷最喜欢的，几乎每天都听。 Zhè yì pán cídài shì wǒ yéye zuì xǐhuan de, jīhu měi tiān dōu tīng. *This is my granddad's favorite tape. I listen to it almost every day.*
磁卡 **cíkǎ** N magnetic card (for making telephone calls, etc.)
磁盘 **cípán** N magnetic disc

慈 **cí** ADJ kind and loving

慈爱 **cí'ài** N love and affection (from an elderly person, e.g. a grandmother)
慈祥 **cíxiáng** ADJ (of an elderly person's countenance) kindly

辞 **cí** TRAD 辭 v take leave

辞职 **cízhí** v resign (from job, position)

此 **cǐ** PRON 1 this ■ 此路不通。 Cǐ lù bù tōng. *This road is blocked. (→ No through road.)* 此时此地 **cǐshícǐdì** here and now
2 here ■ 会议到此结束。 Huìyì dào cǐ jiéshù. *The meeting ends here/at this point. (→ This is the end of the meeting.)*
此后 **cǐhòu** CONJ after this, ever after
此刻 **cǐkè** N this moment
此时 **cǐshí** ADV right now
此外 **cǐwài** CONJ besides, apart from (that), as well ■ 他买了一台新电脑，此外，还买了一些软件。 Tā mǎile yì tái xīn diànnǎo, cǐwài, hái mǎile yìxiē ruǎnjiàn. *He bought a new computer and some software as well.*

次 **cì** 1 M. WD time (expressing frequency of an act) ■ 这是我第一次出国旅行。 Zhè shì wǒ dì-yī cì chūguó lǚxíng. *This is my first trip abroad.*
下次 **xiàcì** next time
次数 **cìshù** N number of times

次 **cì** 2 ADJ inferior

次品 **cìpǐn** N substandard product, seconds (used goods)
次要 **cìyào** ADJ next in importance, of secondary importance

次 **cì** 3 N order, sequence

次序 **cìxù** N order, sequence

伺 **cì** v wait on

伺候 **cìhou**

伺候 **cìhou** v wait on, serve

刺 **cì** I v prick ■ 花儿很美, 但是会刺人。Huār hěn měi, dànshì huì cì rén. *The flower is beautiful, but it may prick you.* II n thorn

刺激 **cìjī** v 1 irritate ■ 强烈的阳光刺激我的眼睛, 很不舒服。Qiángliè de yángguāng cìjī wǒ de yǎnjing, hěn bù shūfu. *The strong sunlight irritates my eyes; it's very uncomfortable.* 2 stimulate, give incentive to ■ 公司决定增加加班费, 来刺激工人的积极性。Gōngsī juédìng zēngjiā jiābānfèi, lái cìjī gōngrén de jījíxìng. *The company decided to increase overtime pay in order to arouse workers' enthusiasm.*

囱 **cōng** n chimney (See 烟囱 yāncōng)

聪 **cōng** TRAD 聰 n acute hearing

聪明 **cōngmíng** ADJ clever, bright, intelligent ■ 他不但聪明, 而且用功, 所以考试总是第一名。Tā búdàn cōngmíng, érqiě yònggōng, suǒyǐ kǎoshì zǒngshi dì-yī míng. *He is not only clever, but also hardworking, so he always comes out first in the exams.*

匆 **cōng** TRAD 怱 ADJ hurriedly

匆匆 **cōngcōng** ADJ hurriedly, in a rush
匆忙 **cōngmáng** ADJ in a hurry, in haste

葱 **cōng** n onion, scallion

大葱 **dàcōng** green Chinese onion
洋葱 **yángcōng** onion
小葱 **xiǎocōng** spring onion

从 **cóng** TRAD 從 PREP following, from ■ "你从哪里来?" "我从很远的地方来。" "Nǐ cóng nǎlǐ lái?" "Wǒ cóng hěn yuǎn de dìfang lái." *"Where did you come from?" "I came from a faraway place."*

从···出发 **cóng...chūfā** set out from ...
从不 **cóngbù** ADV never
从此 **cóngcǐ** CONJ since then, from then on ■ 我上次跟他开玩笑, 他竟生气了, 从此我不跟他开玩笑了。Wǒ shàng cì gēn tā kāi wánxiào, tā jìng shēngqì le, cóngcǐ wǒ bù gēn tā kāi wánxiào le. *He got angry when I joked with him the last time. Since then I have never joked with him.*
从···到··· **cóng...dào...** PREP from ... to ..., from ... till ... ■ 我从上午九点到下午三点都要上课。Wǒ cóng shàngwǔ jiǔ diǎn dào xiàwǔ sān diǎn dōu yào shàngkè. *I've classes from nine o'clock in the morning till three o'clock in the afternoon.*
从早到晚 **cóng-zǎo-dào-wǎn** from morning till night, many hours in a day ■ 夏天他从早到晚都在农场工作。Xiàtiān tā cóng-zǎo-dào-

wǎn dōu zài nóngchǎng gōngzuò. *In summer he works on the farm from morning till night.*
从古到今 **cóng-gǔ-dào-jīn** from the remote past till now
从而 **cóng'ér** CONJ thus, thereby ■ 我要认真学好中文, 从而了解中华文化。Wǒ yào rènzhēn xué hǎo Zhōngwén, cóng'ér liǎojiě Zhōnghuá wénhuà. *I will study the Chinese language earnestly, thereby gaining an understanding of Chinese culture.*
从来 **cónglái** ADV always, ever
从来不 **cónglái bù** never ■ 我从来不喝酒。Wǒ cónglái bù hē jiǔ. *I never drink wine.*
从···起 **cóng...qǐ** PREP starting from ... ■ 我决定从明年一月一日起每天早上跑步。Wǒ juédìng cóng míngnián Yīyuè yírì qǐ měi tiān zǎoshang pǎobù. *I've decided to jog every morning starting from January 1 next year.*
从前 **cóngqián** n 1 past, in the past ■ 我从前不知道学中文多么有意思。Wǒ cóngqián bù zhīdào xué Zhōngwén duōme yǒu yìsi. *I did not know how interesting it is to learn Chinese.* 2 once upon a time (used in story-telling)
从容 **cóngróng** ADJ unhurried, leisurely
从事 **cóngshì** v be engaged in (business, education, law, etc.)
从未 **cóngwèi** ADV never in the past

丛 **cóng** TRAD 叢 n shrub, thicket

丛书 **cóngshū** n a series of books on a specific topic

凑 **còu** v put together, pool

凑钱 **còu qián** pool money
凑合 **còuhe** v make do, make do with
凑巧 **còuqiǎo** ADV luckily, as luck would have it

粗 **cū** ADJ thick, crude ■ 这根绳子太细了, 要粗点儿的。Zhè gēn shéngzi tài xì le, yào cū diǎnr de. *This rope is too thin. We need a thicker one.*

粗暴 **cūbào** ADJ rough, brutal
粗鲁 **cūlǔ** ADJ rude, boorish
粗细 **cūxì** n degree of thickness

NOTE: See note on 大小 dàxiǎo.

粗心 **cūxīn** ADJ careless ■ 她太粗心了, 考试的时候竟然漏了一道题目。Tā tài cūxīn le, kǎoshì de shíhou jìngrán lòule yí dào tímù. *She was so careless she missed a question in the exam.*

促 **cù** v urge

促进 **cùjìn** v promote, advance ■ 让我们为促进友谊努力。Ràng wǒmen wèi cùjìn yǒuyì nǔlì. *Let's work hard to promote our friendship.*
促使 **cùshǐ** v impel, urge

醋 **cù** N vinegar ■ 他喜欢吃酸的, 什么东西都放醋。Tā xǐhuan chī suān de, shénme dōngxi dōu fàng cù. *He is fond of sour flavors, and adds vinegar to whatever he eats.*

窜 **cuàn** TRAD 竄 V 1 rush about 2 falsify, fabricate

催 **cuī** V urge, hurry ■ 别催她, 时间还早。Bié cuī tā, shíjiān hái zǎo. *Don't hurry her. There's enough time.*

摧 **cuī** V break, destroy

摧残 **cuīcán** V devastate, wreck
摧毁 **cuīhuǐ** V destroy completely

脆 **cuì** ADJ crisp

脆弱 **cuìruò** ADJ fragile, frail

粹 **cuì** ADJ pure

翠 **cuì** N green, bluish green

村 **cūn** N village

村庄 **cúnzhuāng** N village
村子 **cūnzi** N village (座 zuò)

存 **cún** V store, keep ■ 她一有钱就存在银行里。Tā yì yǒu qián jiù cún zài yínháng lǐ. *As soon as she gets some money, she deposits it in the bank.*
存储 **cúnchǔ** V 1 save a file (in computing) 2 store
存放 **cúnfàng** V leave in someone's care
存款 **cúnkuǎn** N savings ■ 她从银行取出一些存款, 给女儿办婚礼。Tā cóng yínháng qǔchū yìxiē cúnkuǎn, gěi nǚ'ér bàn hūnlǐ. *She withdrew some money from her savings in the bank for her daughter's wedding.*
存盘 **cún pán** V save (a computer file)
存在 **cúnzài** V exist ■ 这家公司存在严重问题。Zhè jiā gōngsī cúnzài yánzhòng wèntí. *There are serious problems with this company.*

寸 **cùn** M. WD a traditional Chinese unit of length (equal to 1/30 meter)
英寸 **yīngcùn** inch

磋 **cuō** V consult

磋商 **cuōshāng** V consult, discuss

搓 **cuō** V rub with the hands

错 **cuò** TRAD 錯 ADJ wrong ■ 我错了, 我不应该那么做。Wǒ cuò le, wǒ bù yīnggāi nàme zuò. *I was wrong. I shouldn't have done that.*

错字 **cuòzì** wrong character
错误 **cuòwù** I N mistake, error ■ 你这次作业有很多错误。Nǐ zhè cì zuòyè yǒu hěn duō cuòwù. *You've made many mistakes in this assignment.*
犯错误 **fàn cuòwù** make a mistake
纠正错误 **jiūzhèng cuòwù** correct a mistake
II ADJ wrong, erroneous ■ 这是一个错误的决定。Zhè shì yí ge cuòwù de juédìng. *This is a wrong decision.*

措 **cuò** V arrange, handle

措施 **cuòshī** N measure, step ■ 由于措施不当, 问题更加严重了。Yóuyú cuòshī bú dàng, wèntí gèngjiā yánzhòng le. *Owing to inappropriate measures, the problem became even more serious.*

挫 **cuò** V frustrate, defeat

受挫 **shòucuò** be frustrated, be defeated
挫折 **cuòzhé** N setback, frustration

D

答 **dā** V answer

答应 **dāying** V 1 answer, reply ■ 我按了半天门铃, 也没人答应。Wǒ ànle bàntiān ménlíng, yě méi rén dāying. *I pressed the doorbell for a long time, but nobody answered.* 2 promise ■ 爸爸答应给他买一台笔记本电脑。Bàba dāying gěi tā mǎi yì tái bǐjìběn diànnǎo. *Father has promised to buy him a notebook computer.*

搭 **dā** V put up, build

搭配 **dāpèi** I V arrange in pairs or groups II N (word) collocation

达 **dá** TRAD 達 V reach, attain

达成 **dáchéng** V reach (an agreement, an understanding, a business deal, etc.)
达到 **dádào** V reach, achieve ■ 不能为了达到目的, 而不择手段。Bù néng wèile dádào mùdì, ér bù zé shǒuduàn. *One shouldn't stop at nothing in order to achieve one's aim. (→ The end doesn't always justify the means.)*

答 **dá** V answer, reply ■ 这个问题我不会答。Zhège wèntí wǒ bú huì dá. *I can't answer this question.*
答案 **dá'àn** N answer (to a list of questions) ■ 关于这个问题, 还是没有答案。Guānyú zhège wèntí, háishì méiyǒu dá'àn. *There is still no answer to this question.*

答辩 **dábiàn** v speak in self-defense
论文答辩 **lùnwén dábiàn** (postgraduate students') oral examination in defense of a thesis
答复 **dáfù I** v (formally) reply **II** N (formal) reply
答卷 **dájuàn** N answer sheet

打 **dǎ** v 1 strike, hit ■ 不能打人。Bù néng dǎ rén. *You can't hit people.* 2 play (certain games)
打高尔夫球 **dǎ gāo'ěrfūqiú** play golf
打篮球 **dǎ lánqiú** play basketball
打台球 **dǎ táiqiú** play pool
打败 **dǎbài** v defeat, beat
打扮 **dǎbàn** v dress up, make up ■ 新娘打扮得很漂亮。Xīnniáng dǎbàn de hěn piàoliang. *The bride was beautifully dressed.*
打车 **dǎ chē** v call a taxi ■ 时间很紧了, 我们得打车。Shíjiān hěn jǐn le, wǒmen děi dǎ chē. *We don't have much time now; we've got to call a taxi.*
打倒 **dǎdǎo** v strike down, overthrow, down with ...
打的 **dǎ dī** v Same as 打车 dǎ chē
打电话 **dǎ diànhuà** v make a telephone call
打发 **dǎfa** v dispatch, send away
打工 **dǎgōng** v work (especially as a manual laborer)
打击 **dǎjí** v strike a blow against (a crime, a bad tendency, etc.), deal with and punish severely
打击盗版 **dǎjí dàobǎn** attack the crime of piracy (of intellectual products)
打架 **dǎjià** v fight (between people), come to blows
打交道 **dǎ jiāodao** v to have dealings with, negotiate with
和各式各样的人打交道 **hé gèshìgèyàng de rén dǎ jiāodao** deal with all kinds of people
打卡 **dǎkǎ** v punch a card, record attendance at work by punching a time machine
打瞌睡 **dǎ kēshuì** v doze, doze off
打一会儿瞌睡 **dǎ yíhuìr kēshuì** have a doze-off
打量 **dǎliang** v measure with the eye, size up
打猎 **dǎliè** v hunt
打破 **dǎpò** v break
打破花瓶 **dǎpò huāpíng** break a vase
打破世界纪录 **dǎpò shìjiè jìlù** break a world record
打球 **dǎ qiú** v play baseball/basketball/volley-ball, etc.
打扰 **dǎrǎo** v disturb, interrupt ■ 爸爸在写一份重要的报告, 你别去打扰他。Bàba zài xiě yí fèn zhòngyào de bàogào, nǐ bié qù dǎrǎo tā. *Daddy is working on an important report. Don't disturb him.*

NOTE: You can use 打搅 dǎjiǎo instead of 打扰 dǎrǎo, with the same meaning. When you call on someone, especially at their home, you can say 打扰你们了 Dǎrǎo nǐmen le as a polite expression.

打扫 **dǎsǎo** v clean up ■ 中国人在过春节前, 要打扫屋子。Zhōngguórén zài guò chūnjié qián, yào dǎsǎo wūzi. *Before the Spring Festival, Chinese people clean up their houses.*
打算 **dǎsuàn** v plan, contemplate ■ 我不打算买什么。Wǒ bù dǎsuàn mǎi shénme. *I don't intend to buy anything.*
打听 **dǎtīng** v inquire, ask ■ 您从北京大学来, 我想跟您打听一位教授。Nín cóng Běijīng Dàxué lái. Wǒ xiǎng gēn nín dǎtīng yí wèi jiàoshòu. *As you're from Beijing University, I'd like to ask you about a professor.*
打压 **dǎyā** v press hard, oppress
打仗 **dǎzhàng** v go to war, fight in a war
打招呼 **dǎ zhāohu** v 1 greet, say hello to 2 let know, notify
打针 **dǎzhēn** v give (or get) an injection
打字 **dǎzì** v type

大 **dà** ADJ big, large ■ 中国实在大。Zhōngguó shízài hěn dà. *China is indeed big.*
大半 **dàbàn** ADV more than half
大便 **dàbiàn I** N solid waste from the body, stool **II** v move the bowels
大臣 **dàchén** N official (in a royal court), minister
大大 **dàdà** ADV greatly, enormously
大胆 **dàdǎn** ADJ bold, courageous ■ 你可以大胆地试验, 失败了不要紧。Nǐ kěyǐ dàdǎn de shìyàn, shībàile búyàojǐn. *You can experiment boldly. It doesn't matter if you fail.*

NOTE: See note on 胆 dǎn.

大道 **dàdào** N main road, thoroughfare
大地 **dàdì** N land, the earth
大都 **dàdōu** Same as 大多 dàduō
大多 **dàduō** ADV mostly ■ 商场里卖的衣服大多是中国制造的。Shāngchǎng li mài de yīfu dàduō shì Zhōngguó zhìzào de. *Most of the garments sold in shopping malls are made in China.*
大多数 **dàduōshù** N great majority, overwhelming majority ■ 大多数人支持新政府。Dàduōshù rén zhīchí xīn zhèngfǔ. *Most of the people support the new government.*
大方 **dàfang** ADJ 1 generous, liberal
出手大方 **chūshǒu dàfang** spend money freely, very generous
2 elegant and natural
式样大方 **shìyàng dàfang** elegant style
大概 **dàgài I** ADJ general, more or less ■ 他的话我没听清楚, 但是大概的意思还是懂的。Tā de huà wǒ méi tīng qīngchu, dànshì dàgài de

yìsi háishì dǒng de. *I did not catch his words clearly, but I understood the general idea.* **II** ADV probably

大锅饭 **dàguōfàn** N food prepared in a big pot
吃大锅饭 **chī dàguōfàn** IDIOM everyone getting the same reward regardless of different functions and contributions

大后天 **dàhòutiān** N three days from now

大会 **dàhuì** N assembly, congress, rally
■ 全国人民代表大会每年三月在北京举行会议。Quánguó Rénmín Dàibiǎo Dàhuì měi nián Sānyuè zài Běijīng jǔxíng huìyì. *The National People's Congress [of China] holds meetings in Beijing in March every year.*

大伙儿 **dàhuǒr** PRON everybody, all the people

NOTE: 大伙儿 dàhuǒr is a very colloquial word. For general use, 大家 dàjiā is preferred.

大家 **dàjiā** PRON all, everybody ■ 请大家安静一下，我有一件重要的事跟大家说。Qǐng dàjiā ānjìng yíxià, wǒ yǒu yí jiàn zhòngyào de shì gēn dàjiā shuō. *Please be quiet, everybody. I've something important to say to you all.*
我们大家 **wǒmen dàjiā** all of us ■ 我们大家都想去参观那个展览会。Wǒmen dàjiā dōu xiǎng qù cānguān nàge zhǎnlǎnhuì. *We all want to visit that exhibition.*
你们大家 **nǐmen dàjiā** all of you
他们大家 **tāmen dàjiā** all of them

大街 **dàjiē** N main street
逛大街 **guàng dàjiē** take a stroll in the streets, do window-shopping

大局 **dàjú** N overall public interest

大理石 **dàlǐshí** N marble

大力 **dàlì** ADJ vigorous, energetic

大量 **dàliàng** ADJ a large amount of, a large number of ■ 人们可以从英特网获取大量信息。Rénmen kěyǐ cóng yīngtèwǎng huòqǔ dàliàng xìnxī. *People can obtain a great deal of information from the Internet.*

大陆 **dàlù** N continent, mainland ■ 亚洲大陆是世界上人口最多的地方。Yàzhōu dàlù shì shìjiè shang rénkǒu zuì duō de dìfang. *The Asian continent is the most populated place in the world.*
中国大陆 **Zhōngguó dàlù** mainland China

大米 **dàmǐ** N rice

大拇指 **dàmǔzhǐ** N the thumb

NOTE: 拇指 mǔzhǐ can also be used to denote *the thumb*. In Chinese the thumb is considered one of the fingers—手指 shǒuzhǐ.

大脑 **dànǎo** N cerebrum, brain

大牌 **dàpái** N celebrity, hotshot
大牌明星 **dàpái míngxīng** celebrity movie star

大炮 **dàpào** N cannon

大批 **dàpī** ADJ a large quantity of, lots of ■ 大

批农民离开农村，到城市找工作。Dàpī nóngmín líkāi nóngcūn, dào chéngshì zhǎo gōngzuò. *Large numbers of peasants leave their villages to seek jobs in cities.*

大片 **dàpiān** N blockbuster
好莱坞大片 **Hǎoláiwù dàpiān** Hollywood blockbuster

大气 **dàqì** N atmosphere

大人 **dàren** N adult, grown-up ■ 小孩儿都希望很快变成大人。Xiǎoháir dōu xīwàng hěn kuài biànchéng dàren. *Children all hope to become adults very soon.* (→ *All children hope to grow up quickly.*)

NOTE: 大人 dàren is a colloquialism. The general word for *adult* is 成年人 chéngnián rén.

大人物 **dà rénwù** great personage, big shot, very important person (VIP)

大厦 **dàshà** N super-big, imposing building (座 zuò)

大声 **dàshēng** ADJ in a loud voice ■ 请你大声点，我听不清。Qǐng nǐ dàshēng diǎn, wǒ tīng bu qīng. *Speak up, please. I can hardly hear you.*

大师 **dàshī** N master (of art or scholarship)
国画大师 **guóhuà dàshī** master of traditional Chinese art

大使 **dàshǐ** N ambassador
中国驻美国大使 **Zhōngguó zhù Měiguó dàshǐ** Chinese ambassador in the U.S.

大使馆 **dàshǐguǎn** N embassy

大事 **dàshì** N matter of importance

大肆 **dàsì** ADV wantonly, without restraint

大体 **dàtǐ** N on the whole, in the main
大体来说 **dàtǐ láishuō** on the whole

大小 **dàxiǎo** N size ■ 你知道那间房间的大小吗？Nǐ zhīdào nà jiān fángjiān de dàxiǎo ma? *Do you know the size of that room?*

NOTE: 大 dà and 小 xiǎo are opposites. Put together, 大小 dàxiǎo means *size*. There are other Chinese nouns made up of antonyms e.g. 长短 chángduǎn *length*, 粗细 cūxì *thickness*, 好坏 hǎohuài *quality*, 高低 gāodī *height*.

大型 **dàxíng** ADJ large-scale, large-sized ■ 今年十月这个城市要举行一个大型汽车展览会。Jīnnián Shíyuè zhège chéngshì yào jǔxíng yí ge dàxíng qìchē zhǎnlǎnhuì. *In October this year a large-scale auto show will be held in this city.*

大学 **dàxué** N university (座 zuò, 所 suǒ) ■ 这座大学很有名。Zhè zuò dàxué hěn yǒumíng. *This university is well-known.*
考大学 **kǎo dàxué** sit for the university entrance examination
考上大学 **kǎo shàng dàxué** pass the university entrance examination ■ 我今年一定要考上大学。Wǒ jīnnián yídìng yào kǎo shàng

dàxué. *I'm determined to pass the university entrance examination this year.*
上大学 **shàng dàxué** go to university, study in a university
大洋洲 **Dàyángzhōu** N Oceania ■ 新西兰在大洋洲。Xīnxīlán zài Dàyángzhōu. *New Zealand is in Oceania.*
大衣 **dàyī** N overcoat
大意 **dàyì** N rough idea
大约 **dàyuē** ADJ, ADV approximate, approximately, about, nearly ■ 昨天下午大约四点钟有人给你打电话。Zuótiān xiàwǔ dàyuē sì diǎnzhōng yǒu rén gěi nǐ dǎ diànhuà. *Someone telephoned you at about four o'clock yesterday afternoon.*
大致 **dàzhì** ADJ rough, general
大众 **dàzhòng** N the masses
大众媒体 **dàzhòng méitǐ** mass media
大自然 **dàzìrán** N Nature, Mother Nature

呆 **dāi** I ADJ foolish, stupid ■ 她很呆，竟会相信这个广告。Tā hěn dāi, jìng huì xiāngxìn zhège guǎnggào. *It is foolish of her to believe the commercial.*
呆子 **dāizi** idiot
II V Same as 待 dāi

待 **dāi** V stay ■ 我这次来只待两三天。Wǒ zhè cì lái zhǐ dāi liǎng-sān tiān. *For this visit I'll stay only a couple of days.*

NOTE: 待 dāi in the sense of *stay* may be replaced by 呆 dāi.

歹 **dǎi** ADJ bad, evil

歹徒 **dǎitú** N bad guy, criminal

大 **dài** as in 丈夫 dàifu.

大夫 **dàifu** N doctor (位 wèi). Same as 医生 yīshēng, used more as a colloquialism.

代 1 **dài** N 1 generation ■ 李家在这个村子里住了好几代了。Lǐ jiā zài zhège cūnzi li zhùle hǎo jǐ dài le. *The Lis have been living in this village for generations.* 2 dynasty ■ 唐代中国是当时世界上最强大的国家。Táng dài Zhōngguó shì dāngshí shìjiè shang zuì qiángdà de guójiā. *China during the Tang Dynasty was the most powerful country in the world at that time.*

NOTE: The major Chinese dynasties are 秦 Qín, 汉 Hàn, 唐 Táng, 宋 Sòng, 元 Yuán, 明 Míng, 清 Qīng.

代 2 **dài** V take the place of, perform on behalf of ■ 这件事你得亲自做，别人不能代你做。Zhè jiàn shì nǐ děi qīnzì zuò, biérén bù néng dài nǐ zuò. *You must do it by yourself; nobody can do it on your behalf.*

代课老师 **dàikè lǎoshī** relief teacher
代校长 **dài xiàozhǎng** acting principal
代部长 **dài bùzhǎng** acting minister
代办 **dàibàn** I V do or act for another II N charge d'affaires
代表 **dàibiǎo** I N representative, delegate ■ 谁是你们的代表? Shuí shì nǐmen de dàibiǎo? *Who is your representative?* II V represent, indicate ■ 这只是他个人的意见，不代表公司的立场。Zhè zhǐ shì tā gèrén de yìjiàn, bú dàibiǎo gōngsī de lìchǎng. *This is only his personal opinion, which does not represent the view of the company.*
代表团 **dàibiǎotuán** N delegation, mission
美国商业代表团 **Měiguó shāngyè dàibiǎotuán** U.S. trade mission
代词 **dàicí** N pronoun
人称代词 **rénchēng dàicí** personal pronoun
代号 **dàihào** N code name
代价 **dàijià** N price (for achieving something), cost
代理 **dàilǐ** V act on behalf of, act as agent
代理人 **dàilǐrén** agent
代数 **dàishù** N algebra
代数方程式 **dàishù fāngchéngshì** algebraic formula
代替 **dàitì** V substitute for, replace ■ 这次家长会你爸爸妈妈一定要出席，不能请人代替。Zhè cì jiāzhǎnghuì nǐ bàba māma yídìng yào chūxí, bù néng qǐng rén dàitì. *Your parents must attend this parents' meeting and nobody can go on their behalf.*

贷 **dài** TRAD 貸 V loan

贷款 **dàikuǎn** I N loan
无息贷款 **wúxī dàikuǎn** interest-free loan
II V loan money to, borrow money from
款给一家小企业 **dàikuǎn gěi yì jiā xiǎo qǐyè** loan money to a small business
向银行贷款 **xiàng yínháng dàikuǎn** ask the bank for a loan

带 1 **dài** TRAD 帶 V bring, take

带动 **dàidòng** V spur on
带劲 **dàijìn** ADJ 1 interesting, exciting 2 energetic, forceful
带来/带…来 **dàilái/dài...lái** V bring ... ■ 明天上课的时候，把词典带来。Míngtiān shàngkè de shíhou, bǎ cídiǎn dàilái. *Please bring your dictionary with you when you come to class tomorrow.*
带领 **dàilǐng** V lead, guide ■ 教授要带领学生去非洲作野外调查。Jiàoshòu yào dàilǐng xuésheng qù Fēizhōu zuò yěwài diàochá. *The professor will take his students to Africa to do a field study.*

带去/带…去 **dàiqu/dài…qù** v take ■ 你不知道图书馆在哪儿？我带你去。Nǐ bù zhīdào túshūguǎn zài nǎr? Wǒ dài nǐ qù. *You don't know where the library is? I'll take you there.*

带头 **dàitóu** v take the lead, be the first
带头发言 **dàitóu fāyán** be the first to speak (at a meeting), set the ball rolling

带 2 **dài** TRAD 帶 N belt, ribbon, band

安全带 **ānquándài** safety belt
皮带 **pídài** leather belt
丝带 **sīdài** silk ribbon

带 3 **dài** TRAD 帶 N zone, area

寒带 **hándài** frigid zone
热带 **rèdài** tropical zone, tropics
温带 **wēndài** temperate zone

待 **dài** v 1 treat, deal with ■ 他待朋友很热心。Tā dài péngyou hěn rèxīn. *He is warmhearted in dealing with friends.* 2 wait for
待业 **dài yè** wait for a job opportunity
待遇 **dàiyù** N 1 treatment 2 remuneration ■ 这个职务责任非常重，但是待遇很好。Zhège zhíwù zérèn fēicháng zhòng, dànshì dàiyù hěn hǎo. *This position carries heavy responsibilities, but pays well.*

逮 **dài** v catch

逮捕 v arrest, take into custody

袋 **dài** N sack, bag (只 zhī)

口袋 **kǒudài** pocket

> NOTE: 袋 dài is seldom used alone. It is either used with the nominal suffix 子 zi to form 袋子 dài zi, or with another noun to form a compound word, e.g. 口袋 kǒudài (pocket).

戴 **dài** v wear, put on ■ 外面很冷，戴上帽子吧! Wàimiàn hěn lěng, dàishang màozi ba! *It's cold outside. Put on your cap.*
戴手套儿 **dài shǒutàor** wear gloves
戴眼镜 **dài yǎnjìng** wear spectacles

怠 **dài** ADJ idle, slack

怠工 **dàigōng** N slowdown (as workers' protest)
怠慢 **dàimàn** v slight, give the cold shoulder to

单 **dān** TRAD 單 ADJ single, separate ■ 他不习惯和别人合住，一定要单住一个房间。Tā bù xíguàn hé biérén hézhù, yídìng yào dān zhù yí ge fángjiān. *He is not used to sharing a room with another person and insists on having a room to himself.*
单人床 **dānrénchuáng** single bed

单人房间 **dānrén fángjiān** (hotel) room for a single person
单数 **dānshù** odd number
单纯 **dānchún** ADJ simple-minded, ingenuous
单词 **dāncí** N word ■ 光学单词用处不大，一定要把单词放在句子中学。Guāng xué dāncí yòngchu bú dà, yídìng yào bǎ dāncí fàng zài jùzi zhōng xué. *Learning words in insolation is not very useful. You must learn words in sentences.*
单调 **dāndiào** ADJ monotonous
单独 **dāndú** ADJ alone, on one's own ■ 经过半年培训，她能单独工作了。Jīngguò bànnián péixùn, tā néng dāndú gōngzuò le. *After six months' training, she can now work all by herself.*
单亲家庭 **dānqīn jiātíng** N single-parent family
单身贵族 **dānshēn guìzú** N a single person with lots of money to spend, yuppy
单位 **dānwèi** N work unit, e.g. a factory, a school, a government department
单元 **dānyuán** N unit (in an apartment house), apartment, flat

丹 **dān** N red color

担 **dān** TRAD 擔 v carry on the shoulder, take on (responsibility, burden etc)
担保 **dānbǎo** v guarantee, vouch for
担保人 **dānbǎorén** guarantor
担负 **dānfù** v take on (responsibility), meet (expenditure), hold (a position)
担负使命 **dānfù shǐmìng** undertake a mission
担负子女的教育费 **dānfù zǐnǚ de jiàoyùfèi** meet children's educational costs
担任 **dānrèn** v assume the office of, act in the capacity of
担心 **dānxīn** v worry, fret ■ 他担心考试不及格。Tā dānxīn kǎoshì bù jígé. *He is worried that he may fail the exam.* ■ 我为爸爸的身体担心。Wǒ wèi bàba de shēntǐ dānxīn. *I'm worried about daddy's health.*
担忧 **dānyōu** v worry

耽 **dān** v delay

耽误 **dānwù** v delay ■ 你们没有按时交货，耽误了我们的生产。Nǐmen méiyǒu ànshí jiāohuò, dānwùle wǒmen de shēngchǎn. *Your failure to deliver the goods on time has delayed our production.*
耽误时间 **dānwù shíjiān** waste time

胆 **dǎn** TRAD 膽 N 1 gallbladder 2 courage

胆子 **dǎnzi** courage
胆子大 **dǎnzi dà** be brave, be bold

胆量 dǎnliàng

胆子小 **dǎnzi xiǎo** be timid, be cowardly

NOTE: The ancient Chinese believed that the gall-bladder was the organ of courage—if one had a big gallbladder it meant that the person was endowed with courage and daring, and if one was timid it was because he had a small gallbladder. Therefore, 他胆子很大 Tā dǎnzi hěn dà and 他很大胆 Tā hěn dàdǎn means *He is bold*; 他胆子很小 Tā dǎnzi hěn xiǎo and 他很胆小 Tā hěn dǎnxiǎo means *He is timid*.

胆量 dǎnliàng N courage, guts
试试他的胆量 **shìshi tāde dǎnliàng** test his courage, see how brave he is
胆怯 dǎnqiè ADJ timid, cowardly

旦 dàn N dawn (See 元旦 yuándàn)

但 dàn CONJ Same as 但是 dànshì. Used in writing.
但是 dànshì CONJ but, yet ■ 这个女孩子长得很漂亮，但是大家都不喜欢她。Zhège nǚháizi zhǎng de hěn piàoliang, dànshì dàjiā dōu bù xǐhuan tā. *This girl is quite pretty, but nobody likes her.*

担 dàn TRAD 擔 N load, burden
担子 dànzi load, burden
担子重 dànzi zhòng great burden, heavy responsibility

淡 dàn ADJ 1 not salty, tasteless, bland ■ 汤太淡了，得放些盐。Tāng tài dàn le, děi fàng xiē yán. *The soup is tasteless. Put some salt in it.*
2 (of tea, coffee) weak

氮 dàn nitrogen
氮肥 dànféi nitrogenous fertilizer

蛋 dàn N egg (especially chicken egg) ■ 鸡蛋营养丰富。Jīdàn yíngyǎng fēngfù. *Eggs are very nutritious.*
蛋白质 dànbáizhì N protein
蛋糕 dàngāo N (western-style) cake

诞 dàn TRAD 誕 V be born
诞辰 dànchén N birthday ■ 十二月二十五日是耶稣基督的诞辰。Shí'èryuè èrshí wǔ rì shì Yēsū Jīdū de dànchén. *December 25th is the birthday of Jesus Christ.*
诞生 dànshēng V be born

弹 dàn TRAD 彈 N bullet
弹药 dànyào N ammunition
弹药库 dànyàokù arms depot

当 1 dāng TRAD 當 PREP at the time of, when ■ 当他赶到火车站，火车已经开走了。Dāng tā gǎndào huǒchēzhàn, huǒchē yǐjīng kāizǒu le. *When he hurried to the railway station, the train had already left.*
当…的时候 dāng...de shíhou CONJ when ... ■ 当我在工作的时候，不希望别人来打扰我。Dāng wǒ zài gōngzuò de shíhou, bù xīwàng biérén lái dǎrǎo wǒ. *When I am working, I don't want to be disturbed.*

NOTE: 当 dāng may be omitted, especially colloquially, e.g. 我在工作的时候，不希望别人来打扰我。Wǒ zài gōngzuò de shíhou, bù xīwàng biérén lái dǎrǎo wǒ.

当 2 dāng TRAD 當 V work as, serve as ■ "你长大了想当什么？" "我想当医生。" "Nǐ zhǎngdàle xiǎng dāng shénme?" "Wǒ xiǎng dāng yīshēng." *"What do you want to be when you grow up?" "I'd like to be a doctor."*
当场 dāngchǎng N on the spot
当场抓获 **dāngchǎng zhuāhuò** catch red-handed
当初 dāngchū N originally, at the outset
当代 dāngdài ADJ contemporary, present-day
当地 dāngdì N at the place in question, local
当地人 **dāngdì rén** a local ■ 他来自一个小城市，当地没有大学。Tā láizi yí ge xiǎo chéngshì, dāngdì méiyǒu dàxué. *He came from a small city, where there was no university.*
当地时间 dāngdì shíjiān local time
当局 dāngjú N the authorities
当面 dāngmiàn ADV to someone's face, in the very presence of
当面撒谎 **dāngmiàn sāhuǎng** tell a bare-faced lie
当年 dāngnián N in those years, then ■ 想当年，亲戚朋友之间主要靠写信联系。哪有什么电子邮件？Xiǎng dāngnián, qīnqi péngyou zhī jiān zhǔyào kào xiě xìn liánxì. Nǎyǒu shénme diànzǐ yóujiàn? *In those years, relatives and friends mainly relied on letter-writing to keep in touch with each other. How could there be e-mails?* (→ There was no such thing as e-mails.)
当前 dāngqián N at present, now
当然 dāngrán ADV of course ■ "你到了北京别忘了给我发一份电子邮件。" "那当然，忘不了。" "Nǐ dàole Běijīng bié wàngle gěi wǒ fā yí fèn diànzǐ yóujiàn." "Nà dāngrán, wàng bu liǎo." *"Don't forget to send me an e-mail when you arrive in Beijing." "Of course, I won't forget."*
当时 dāngshí N at that time, then
当事人 dāngshìrén N person/people concerned, party (to a lawsuit)
当心 dāngxīn V be cautious, take care

当选 **dāngxuǎn** v be elected
当选为代表 **dāngxuǎn wéi dàibiǎo** be elected a delegate
当中 **dāngzhōng** n right in the middle, in the center

挡 dǎng TRAD 擋 v block, keep off ■ 记者被挡在门外。Jìzhě bèi dǎng zài ménwài. *The reporters were barred from the house.*

党 dǎng TRAD 黨 n political party

NOTE: As China is under a one-party rule, when people mention 党 dǎng in China, they usually refer to 中国共产党 Zhōngguó Gòngchǎn Dǎng *the Chinese Communist Party.*

党派 **dǎngpài** n political party, political group
党委 **dǎngwěi** n (Chinese Communist) Party committee
党委书记 **dǎngwěi shūjì** (Chinese Communist) Party committee secretary, (Chinese Communist) Party chief

NOTE: The Chinese Communist Party Committee in a province is called 省委 shěngwěi, and that in a city 市委 shìwěi. These are the most powerful organs in a Chinese province or city (not the local governments—政府 zhèngfǔ).

党员 **dǎngyuán** n party member

荡 dàng TRAD 蕩 v swing, sway

荡秋千 **dàng qiūqiān** play on the swings

当 dàng TRAD 當 v 1 treat as, regard as ■ 他非常节省，一块钱当两块钱用。Tā fēicháng jiéshěng, yí kuài qián dàng liǎng kuài qián yòng. *He is very thrifty and wishes he could make one dollar go twice as far.* 2 think ■ 你中文说得这么好，我还当你是中国人呢! Nǐ Zhōngwén shuōde zhème hǎo, wǒ hái dàng nǐ shì Zhōngguórén ne! *You speak Chinese so well that I thought you were a Chinese!*
当天 **dàngtiān** n the same day
当做 **dàngzuò** v treat as, regard as

档 dàng TRAD 檔 n 1 shelf, cabinet 2 grade, class
档案 **dàng'àn** n (份 fèn) file, archive
档次 **dàngcì** n standard or level of quality, grade, class

刀 dāo n knife (把 bǎ)

刀子 **dāozi** a small knife
铅笔刀 **qiānbǐ dāo** pencil sharpener
水果刀 **shuǐguǒ dāo** penknife
刀刃 **dāorèn** n edge of a knife

岛 dǎo TRAD 島 n island ■ 新西兰有两个大岛：南岛和北岛。Xīnxīlán yǒu liǎng ge dà dǎo: nán dǎo hé běi dǎo. *New Zealand has two big islands: South Island and North Island.*
岛屿 **dǎoyǔ** n island, islet

捣 dǎo TRAD 搗 v beat, smash

捣蛋 **dǎodàn** v make trouble (in a mischievous way)
故意捣蛋 **gùyì dǎodàn** be deliberately mischievous
捣乱 **dǎoluàn** v make trouble, sabotage
捣乱公共秩序 **dǎoluàn gōnggòng zhìxù** disrupt public order

蹈 dǎo v dance (See 舞蹈 wúdǎo)

导 dǎo TRAD 導 v lead, guide (See 辅导 fǔdǎo, 领导 lǐngdǎo, 指导 zhǐdǎo)
导弹 **dǎodàn** n guided missile (枚 méi)
导航 **dǎoháng** n navigation (by electronic devices)
导师 **dǎoshī** n supervisor (for postgraduate students)
导演 **dǎoyǎn** I n director (for films or play) ■ 名导演 míng dǎoyǎn famous director II v direct (a film or play) ■ 这部电影是谁导演的? Zhè bù diànyǐng shì shéi dǎoyǎn de? *Who directed this movie?*
导游 **dǎoyóu** n tourist guide
导致 **dǎozhì** v lead to, cause

倒 dǎo v fall, topple ■ 风大极了，把很多树都刮倒了。Fēng dà jíle, bǎ hěn duō shù dōu guā dǎole. *The winds were so strong that many trees were blown down.*
倒闭 **dǎobì** go bust, cease operations
倒卖 **dǎomài** v resell at a profit
倒霉 **dǎoméi** v have bad luck, be out of luck

到 dào v arrive, come to, up to ■ 我们已经学到第十八课了。Wǒmen yǐjīng xué dào dìshíbā kè le. *We've studied up to Lesson 18.*
到处 **dàochù** adv everywhere ■ 王老师家里到处都是书。Wáng lǎoshī jiā lǐ dàochù dōu shì shū. *There are books everywhere in Teacher Wang's home.* ■ 他到处游览名胜古迹 Tā dàochù yóulǎn míngshèng gǔjì. *He visits well-known scenic spots and historical sites everywhere.*

NOTE: 到处 dàochù is always placed before a verbal phrase, and is often followed by 都 dōu.

到达 **dàodá** v arrive, reach
到底 **dàodǐ** adv 1 in the end, finally ■ 她到底还是找到了理想的丈夫。Tā dàodǐ háishì zhǎodàole lǐxiǎng de zhàngfu. *Finally she found her ideal husband.* 2 after all (used in a ques-

tion) ■ 他到底想要什么? Tā dàodǐ xiǎng yào shénme? *What does he want after all?*

到来 **dàolái** v arrive

到期 **dàoqī** v become due, expire

到…为止 **dào...wéizhǐ** PREP until, by, up to ■ 到上个月底为止, 公司今年的收入已经超过八百万。 Dào shànggè yuè dǐ wéizhǐ, gōngsī jīnnián de shōurù yǐjīng chāoguò bābǎiwàn. *By the end of last month, the company revenue this year has exceeded eight million yuan.*

倒 **dào** I v 1 put upside down ■ 他把画挂倒了。 Tā bǎ huà guà dào le. *He hung the picture upside down.* 2 pour (water), make (tea) ■ 她给客人倒了一杯水。 Tā gěi kèrén dàole yì bēi shuǐ. *She gave the visitor a glass of water.* II ADV contrary to what may be expected (used before a verb or an adjective to indicate an unexpected action or state) ■ 弟弟倒比哥哥高。 Dìdi dào bǐ gēge gāo. *The younger brother is unexpectedly taller than his elder brother.*

倒计时 **dàojìshí** N countdown

倒退 **dàotuì** v go backward, regress

悼 **dào** v mourn

悼念 **dàoniàn** v mourn, grieve over

盗 **dào** N robber, bandit (See 强盗 qiángdào, 盗版 dàobǎn)

盗版 **dàobǎn** I N pirated edition, pirated copy 盗版书 dàobǎn shū pirated edition of a book 盗版电影 dàobǎn diànyǐng pirated movie II v make pirated copies

盗窃 **dàoqiè** v steal, embezzle, commit larceny 盗窃犯 dàoqièfàn thief, one who commits larceny

道 1 **dào** N way, path

道德 **dàodé** N morals, ethics ■ 赚钱也要讲道德。 Zhuànqián yě yào jiǎng dàodé. *When making money you should also pay attention to ethics.* 不道德 bú dàodé immoral

道理 **dàoli** N principle, reason, hows and whys ■ 这个道理人人都懂。 Zhège dàoli rénrén dōu dǒng. *Everybody understands this principle.* (→ *Everybody understands why this is true/correct.*) 讲道理 jiǎng dàoli (of a person) be reasonable ■ 他这个人很不讲道理。 Tā zhège rén hěn bù jiǎng dàoli. *This man is very unreasonable.* 有道理 yǒu dàoli reasonable, true ■ 你说的话很有道理。 Nǐ shuō de huà hěn yǒu dàoli. *What you said is reasonable/true.*

NOTE: 道 dào and 理 lǐ are two important concepts in Chinese thought. The original meaning of 道 dào is

path, way. By extension it denotes "the fundamental principle of the universe." 理 lǐ originally meant *the grain of a piece of jade* and came to mean "the underlying logic of things."

道路 **dàolù** N road, path ■ 车辆把前面的道路堵住了。 Chēliàng bǎ qiánmiàn de dàolù dǔzhù le. *Traffic has blocked the road ahead.*

道 2 **dào** M. WD 1 (for things in the shape of a line) 一道光线 yí dào guāngxiàn a ray of sunshine 2 (for questions in a school exercise, examinations, etc.) 两道难题 liǎng dào nántí two difficult questions

道 3 **dào** v Same as 说 shuō, used only in old-fashioned writing 能说会道 néng shuō huì dào eloquent, glib

道歉 **dàoqiàn** v apologize, say sorry ■ 你应该向他们道歉。 Nǐ yīnggāi xiàng tāmen dàoqiàn. *You should apologize to them.*

稻 **dào** N rice, paddy

稻子 **dàozi** rice, paddy rice

得 **dé** v get, obtain ■ 她去年英文考试得了A。 Tā qùnián Yīngwén kǎoshì déle A. *She got an A for the English examination last year.*

得到 **dédào** v succeed in getting/obtaining ■ 他得到一个去中国学汉语的机会。 Tā dédào yí ge qù Zhōngguó xué Hànyǔ de jīhuì. *He got a chance to go to China to study Chinese.*

NOTE: The verb 得 dé is seldom used alone. It is often followed by 到 dào, grammatically a complement, to mean *get* or *obtain*.

得病 **débìng** v fall ill, contract a disease

得力 **délì** ADJ competent and efficient, very capable 得力助手 délìzhùshǒu very capable assistant, indispensable right-hand assistant

得失 **déshī** N gain and loss, success and failure

得以 **déyǐ** MODAL v so that, can

得意 **déyì** ADJ complacent, deeply pleased with oneself

得意忘形 **déyì wàng xíng** be dizzy with success

得意洋洋 **déyì yángyáng** show extreme self-complacency, be elated

得罪 **dézuì** v offend, incur displeasure of ... 得罪不起 dézuì bùqǐ can't afford to offend

德 **dé** N virtue

德国 **Déguó** N Germany

德文 **Déwén** N the German language (especially the writing)

德语 **Déyǔ** N the German language

地 **de** PARTICLE (attached to a word or phrase to indicate that it is an adverb. 地 de is normally followed by a verb or an adjective.)

慢慢地说 **mànman de shuō** speak slowly

愉快地旅行 **yúkuài de lǚxíng** travel pleasantly

NOTE: See note on 的 de.

得 **de** PARTICLE (introducing a word, phrase or clause to indicate that it is a complement. 得 de is normally preceded by a verb or an adjective.)

说得大家都笑了起来 **shuō de dàjiā dōu xiàole qǐlái** talk in such a way that everybody starts laughing

贵得很 **guì de hěn** very expensive

来得很早 **lái de hěn zǎo** come early

NOTE: See note on 的 de.

的 **de** PARTICLE (attached to a word or phrase to indicate that it is an attribute. 的 de is normally followed by a noun.)

我的电脑 **wǒ de diànnǎo** my computer

最新型的电脑 **zuì xīnxíng de diànnǎo** the latest computer model

学校刚买来的电脑 **xuéxiào gāng mǎilai de diànnǎo** the computer that the school just bought

NOTE: 的, 得, 地 have different functions and are three distinct words. However, as they are pronounced the same (de) in everyday speech, some Chinese speakers do not distinguish them.

…的话 **…de huà** CONJ if ■ 明天下雨的话，就改期举行。**Míngtiān xià yǔ de huà, jiù gǎigī jǔxíng.** If it rains tomorrow, we'll change the date for the meeting.

NOTE: See note on 要是 yàoshì.

得 **děi** MODAL V have to ■ 时间不早了，我们得走了。**Shíjiān bù zǎo le, wǒmen děi zǒu le.** It's quite late. We've got to go.

灯 **dēng** TRAD 燈 N lamp, lighting

电灯 **diàndēng** light, electric light

关灯 **guān dēng** turn off the light

开灯 **kāi dēng** turn on the light

日光灯 **rìguāngdēng** fluorescent lamp

台灯 **táidēng** desk lamp

灯火 **dēnghuǒ** N lights

灯火通明 **dēnghuǒ tōngmíng** (of a building) brightly lit

灯笼 **dēnglóng** N lantern

灯泡 **dēngpào** N light bulb (只 zhī)

登 **dēng** V 1 publish (in a newspaper, a journal, etc.) ■ 今天各大报纸都登了这条新闻。**Jīntiān gè dà bàozhǐ dōu dēngle zhè tiáo xīnwén.** This news is published in all the major newspapers today.

登广告 **dēng guǎnggào** place an advertisement, advertise

2 go up, ascend

登机 **dēngjī** V board a plane

登机卡 **dēngjīkǎ** boarding card

登记 **dēngjì** V register, check in ■ 在旅馆里住，都要登记。**Zài lǚguǎn li zhù, dōu yào dēngjì.** To stay in a hotel, one has to register.

登陆 **dēnglù** V land (from waters, especially by troops)

登山 **dēngshān** V climb a mountain or hill

登山运动 **dēngshān yùndòng** mountaineering

登山运动员 **dēngshān yùndòngyuán** mountaineer

等 1 **děng** V wait, wait for ■ 我昨天等你等了半小时。**Wǒ zuótiān děng nǐ děngle bàn xiǎoshí.** I waited for you for half an hour yesterday.

等一下 **děng yíxià** wait a minute

等待 **děngdài** V wait (usually used in writing) ■ 你不能总是等待机会，要主动寻找机会。**Nǐ bù néng zǒngshì děngdài jīhuì, yào zhǔdòng xúnzhǎo jīhuì.** You mustn't always wait for an opportunity; you should proactively search for it.

等到 **děngdào** CONJ by the time, as late as ■ 等到发现问题，已经太晚了。**Děngdào fāxiàn yǒu wèntí, yǐjīng tài wǎn le.** It was too late by the time the problem was identified.

等候 **děnghòu** V Same as 等待 děngdài

等 2 **děng** N grade, rank, class ■ 我们商店只卖一等品。**Wǒmen shāngdiàn zhǐ mài yì-děng pǐn.** Our store sells first-class goods only. (→ We sell only the best here.)

等级 **děngjí** N grade, rank

确定（商品的）等级 **quèdìng (shāngpǐn de) děngjí** determine the grades (of a commodity)

等于 **děngyú** V be equal to, equal, amount to ■ 一加二等于三。**Yī jiā èr děngyú sān.** One plus two equals three.

等 3 **děng** PARTICLE **1** and so on and so forth, et cetera ■ 我们在中国参观了北京、上海、西安等地。**Wǒmen zài Zhōngguó cānguānle Běijīng, Shànghǎi, Xī'ān děng dì.** In China we visited Beijing, Shanghai, Xi'an and other places.

瞪 **dèng**

2 (used at the end of a list) ■ 我们在中国游览了北京、上海、西安等三个大城市。Wǒmen zài Zhōngguó yóulǎn le Běijīng, Shànghǎi, Xī'ān děng sān ge dà chéngshì. *We toured the three major cities of Beijing, Shanghai and Xi'an.*

瞪 **dèng** v open one's eyes wide, stare, glare

凳 **dèng** N stool (low chair)

凳子 **dèngzi** stool (个 gè)

低 **dī I** ADJ low ■ 她说话声音很低，你得仔细听才行。Tā shuōhuà shēngyīn hěn dī, nǐ děi zǐxì tīng cái xíng. *She speaks in a low voice. You've got to listen attentively.* **II** v lower ■ 他低着头，离开校长办公室。Tā dīzhe tóu, líkāi xiàozhǎng bàngōngshì. *He left the principal's office with his head hung low.*

低调 **dīdiào** ADJ low key
低估 **dīgū** v underestimate
低级 **dījí** ADJ **1** elementary **2** vulgar
低级趣味 **dījí qùwèi** vulgar interests, base taste
低劣 **dīliè** ADJ inferior

堤 **dī** N dike, embankment

滴 **dī** M. WORD drop (used for liquids) ■ 节约每一滴水。Jiéyuē měi yì dī shuǐ. *Save every drop of water.*

敌 **dí** TRAD 敵 N enemy

敌对 **díduì** ADJ hostile, antagonistic
敌对的态度 **díduì de tàidu** hostile attitude
敌人 **dírén** N enemy
敌视 **díshì** v be hostile to

笛 **dí** N flute

笛子 **dízi** flute
吹笛子 **chuī dízi** play the flute

涤 **dí** TRAD 滌 v wash, wash away

的 **dí** as in 的确 díquè

的确 **díquè** ADV really, truly ■ 这个名胜的确美丽。Zhège míngshèng díquè měilì. *This well-known scenic spot is truly beautiful.*
的士 **díshì** N taxi

迪 **dí** v enlighten

迪斯科 **dísīkē** N disco

底 **dǐ** N base, bottom

底片 **dǐpiàn** N (film) negative

底下 **dǐxia** N underneath, under ■ 孩子躲在桌子底下。Háizi duǒ zài zhuōzi dǐxia. *The child hid under the table.*
底线 **dǐxiàn** N bottom line

抵 **dǐ** v **1** arrive **2** resist

抵偿 **dǐcháng** v compensate for
抵达 **dǐdá** v arrive at
抵抗 **dǐkàng** v resist
抵押 **dǐyā** v pledge ... as security for a loan, mortgage
抵押品 **dǐyāpǐn** security (for a loan)
抵制 **dǐzhì** v boycott, reject

地 **dì** N earth, ground

地板 **dìbǎn** N floor, timber floor
地步 **dìbù** N **1** extent **2** (poor) condition
地带 **dìdài** N region, zone
地道 **dìdào** N tunnel, underpass (条 tiáo) ■ 请走地道。Qǐng zǒu dìdao. *Please use the underpass.*
地道 **dìdao** ADJ genuine, authentic
地道的中国菜 **dìdao de Zhōngguócài** authentic Chinese cuisine
地点 **dìdiǎn** N the place for an event or activity, venue ■ 展览会的时间和地点决定以后，我会立即通知你。Zhǎnlǎnhuì de shíjiān hé dìdiǎn juédìng yǐhòu, wǒ huì lìjí tōngzhī nǐ. *After the time and venue of the exhibition are decided on, I will inform you immediately.*
地方 **dìfang** N **1** place, location, area (个 gè) ■ 他们正在找开会的地方。Tāmen zhèngzài zhǎo kāihuì de dìfang. *They're looking for a venue for their conference.* **2** part of, aspect ■ 这本书我有些地方不大明白。Zhè běn shū wǒ yǒuxie dìfang búdà míngbai. *I'm not quite clear about parts of this book.*

NOTE: 地方 dìfang is a word of wide application. It has both concrete, specific senses and abstract, general senses, as in the following examples: ■ 医生: 你什么地方不舒服? Yīshēng: Nǐ shénme dìfang bù shūfu? *Doctor: What spot ails you?* (→ *What's wrong with you?*) ■ 照顾不到的地方，请多多原谅。Zhàogù búdào de dìfang, qǐng duōduō yuánliàng. *If there's anything not well attended to, please accept my sincere apology.*

地理 **dìlǐ** N geography
地理学家 **dìlǐxuéjiā** geographer
国家地理学会 **Guójiā Dìlǐ Xuéhuì** National Geographic Society
地面 **dìmiàn** N the earth's surface, ground ■ 这里的地面比海平面高出二百公尺。Zhèlǐ de dìmiàn bǐ hǎipíngmiàn gāochū èrbǎi gōngchǐ. *The ground here is 200 meters above sea level.*

地球 **dìqiú** N the earth

地球科学 **dìqiú kēxué** earth science

地区 **dìqū** N region, area ■ 这个国家东部地区比西部地区发达。Zhège guójiā dōngbù dìqū bǐ xībù dìqū fādá. *In this country, the eastern regions are more developed than the western regions.*

地势 **dìshì** N physical features of a place, terrain

地毯 **dìtǎn** N carpet (张 zhāng)

地铁 **dìtiě** N underground railway, subway

地图 **dìtú** N map (张 zhāng)

地图册 **dìtúcè** atlas

地位 **dìwèi** N status, position ■ 他在公司里有很高的地位。Tā zài gōngsī li yǒu hěn gāo de dìwèi. *He holds a high position in the company.*

地下 **dìxià** N underground

地下商场 **dìxià shāngchǎng** underground shopping center

地下铁路 (地铁) **dìxià tiělù (dìtiě)** underground railway, subway

地下停车场 **dìxià tíngchēchǎng** parking garage, underground carpark

地形 **dìxíng** N topography, terrain

地震 **dìzhèn** N earthquake, seism (场 cháng) ■ 在南太平洋发生了里氏六级地震。Zài nán Tàipíngyáng fāshēng le Lǐ shì liù jí dìzhèn. *An earthquake, measuring 6 on the Richter scale, occurred in the South Pacific Ocean.*

地址 **dìzhǐ** N address ■ 这是我的地址和电话号码。Zhè shi wǒ de dìzhǐ he diànhuà hàomǎ. *Here are my address and telephone number.*

地质 **dìzhì** N geology

地质调查 **dìzhì diàochá** geological survey

地质学家 **dìzhìxuéjiā** geologist

帝 **dì** N the Supreme Being

帝国 **dìguó** N empire

帝国主义 **dìguózhǔyì** imperialism

弟 **dì** N younger brother

弟弟 **dìdi** younger brother ■ 我弟弟比我小两岁。Wǒ dìdi bǐ wǒ xiǎo liǎng suì. *My younger brother is two years younger than me.*

弟妹 **dìmèi** N 1 younger brother and younger sister 2 younger brother's wife

弟兄 **dìxiōng** N brothers

递 **dì** TRAD 遞 V hand over, pass on ■ 请你把那本词典递给我。Qǐng nǐ bǎ nà běn cídiǎn dì gěi wǒ. *Please pass me that dictionary.*

快递 **kuàidì** fast delivery (of mail)

快递服务 **kuài dì fúwù** fast delivery service

递交 **dìjiāo** V hand over, present

递增 **dìzēng** V increase progressively

第 **dì** PREFIX (used before a number to form an ordinal number)

第一 **dì-yī** the first

第一天 **dì-yī tiān** the first day

第十 **dì-shí** the tenth

第十课 **dì-shí kè** the tenth lesson, Lesson 10

第三者 **dì-sānzhě** N third party, one who has an affair with a married person

颠 **diān** TRAD 顛 V bump, jolt

颠簸 **diānbǒ** V bump, bump along

颠倒 **diāndǎo** V turn upside down, reverse

颠倒黑白 **diāndǎo hēibái** confound black and white, confuse right and wrong

颠覆 **diānfù** V subvert or overturn in an illegal way

掂 **diān** TRAD 㨄 V weigh in the hand

点 **diǎn** TRAD 點 I N 1 drop, point, dot ■ 雨点打在窗户上。Yǔdiǎn dǎ zài chuānghu shang. *Raindrops beat on the window pane.*

墨点 **mò diǎn** ink stain

水点 **shuǐ diǎn** water stain

2 (indicating decimal)

三点四 **sān diǎn sì** 3.4 (three point four)

十二点三五 **shí'èr diǎn sān wǔ** 12.35 (twelve point three five)

II M. WD 1 a little, a bit

有(一)点儿… **yǒu (yì) diǎnr...** a bit ..., a little ... (used before nouns and adjectives) ■ 我有一点儿累，想休息一会儿。Wǒ yǒu yìdiǎnr lèi, xiǎng xiūxi yíhuìr. *I'm a bit tired. I want to take a little break.*

2 o'clock ■ "现在几点?" "三点正。" "Xiànzài jǐdiǎn?" "Sān diǎn zhèng." *"What time is it?" "Three o'clock sharp."* III V drip, put a dot, touch ■ 你给我点眼药水，行吗? Nǐ gěi wǒ diǎn yǎnyàoshuǐ, xíng ma? *Could you please put my eye drops in for me?*

点火 **diǎnhuǒ** V light a fire

点名 **diǎnmíng** V call the roll, do roll-call

点燃 **diǎnrán** V kindle, ignite

点心 **diǎnxīn** N snack, light refreshments

NOTE: The Cantonese pronunciation of 点心 is "dim sum." Many Chinese restaurants overseas sell Cantonese-style refreshments or snack known as "dim sum." To have such refreshments for a meal is "yum cha," the Cantonese pronunciation of 饮茶 yǐnchá, which literally means *drink tea*.

点钟 **diǎnzhōng** N o'clock ■ "现在几点钟?" "三点钟。" "Xiànzài jǐ diǎnzhōng?" "Sān diǎnzhōng." *"What time is it?" "Three o'clock."*

NOTE: In colloquial Chinese 点钟 diǎnzhōng can

be shortened to 点 diǎn, e.g. "现在几点?" "三点。"
"Xiànzài jǐ diǎn?" "Sān diǎn." "What time is it?"
"Three o'clock."

点缀 **diǎnzhuì** v embellish, decorate
点子 **diǎnzi** N idea
　鬼点子 **guǐdiǎnzi** wicked idea, trick
　出点子 **chū diǎnzi** come up with ideas

典 diǎn N standard, law

典礼 **diǎnlǐ** N ceremony ■ 王先生、王太太要
到美国来参加他们女儿的大学毕业典礼。Wáng
xiānsheng, Wáng tàitai yào dào Měiguó lái cānjiā
tāmen nǚ'ér de dàxué bìyè diǎnlǐ. *Mr and Mrs
Wang are coming to the States to attend their
daughter's commencement.*
　结婚典礼 **jiéhūn diǎnlǐ** wedding ceremony
典型 **diǎnxíng** ADJ typical, representative
　典型事例 **diǎnxíng shìlì** typical case

电 diàn TRAD 電 N electricity, power, electronics ■ 我们这里电比较便宜。Wǒmen zhèlǐ
diàn bǐjiào piányi. *Power is rather cheap here.*
电报 **diànbào** N telegram, cable (份 fèn)
电车 **diànchē** N trolley bus, streetcar (辆
liàng) ■ 他每天坐电车上班。Tā měitiān zuò
diànchē shàngbān. *He goes to work by trolley
bus every day.*
电池 **diànchí** N battery, electrical cell (节 jié)
　可充电电池 **kě chōngdiàn diànchí** rechargeable battery
电灯 **diàndēng** N electric light (个 gè) ■ 你会
装电灯吗? Nǐ huì zhuāng diàndēng ma? *Do you
know how to install an electric light?*
　关电灯 **guān diàndēng** turn off the light
　开电灯 **kāi diàndēng** turn on the light
电动机 **diàndòngjī** N (electric) motor (台 tái)
电风扇 **diànfēngshàn** N Same as 电扇 diàn
shàn
电话 **diànhuà** N telephone, telephone call (个
gè) ■ "我可以用一下你的电话吗?" "Wǒ kěyǐ
yòng yíxià nǐ de diànhuà ma?" *"May I use your
telephone?"*
　无绳电话 **wú shéng diànhuà** cordless
telephone
　移动电话 **yídòng diànhuà** mobile phone
　打电话 **dǎ diànhuà** use the telephone, be
on the phone. ■ 王先生在打电话。Wáng
xiānsheng zài dǎ diànhuà. *Mr Wang is on the
phone.*
　给…打电话 **gěi...dǎ diànhuà** call ... on the
telephone, ring ...
　听电话 **tīng diànhuà** answer a telephone call
■ 李小姐, 请你听电话。Lǐ xiǎojiě, qǐng nǐ tīng
diànhuà. *Miss Li, you're wanted on the phone.*
电缆 **diànlǎn** N (electric) cable (条 tiáo)

电力 **diànlì** N electric power, power
电铃 **diànlíng** N electric bell
电炉 **diànlú** N electric stove, hot plate
电路 **diànlù** N electric circuit
电脑 **diànnǎo** N computer (台 tái) ■ 我会用电
脑写汉字。Wǒ huì yòng diànnǎo xiě Hànzì. *I
can input Chinese characters on a computer.*
　笔记本电脑 **bǐjìběn diànnǎo** notebook computer
电钮 **diànniǔ** N switch (on an electrical appliance)
电器 **diànqì** N electrical appliance
　电器商店 **diànqì shāngdiàn** electrical appli-
ances store
电扇 **diànshàn** N electric fan (台 tái) ■ 夜里
热极了, 我得开着电扇睡觉。Yèlǐ rè jíle, wǒ děi
kāizhe diànshàn shuìjiào. *It's so hot at night that I
have to sleep with the electric fan on.*
电视 **diànshì** N television
　电视机 **diànshìjī** TV set (台 tái)
　电视台 **diànshìtái** TV station
　有线电视 **yǒuxiàn diànshì** cable TV
　看电视 **kàn diànshì** watch TV ■ 我很少看电
视。Wǒ hěn shǎo kàn diànshì. *I seldom watch TV.*
电台 **diàntái** N radio station
电梯 **diàntī** N elevator, lift (部 bù) ■ 大楼着火
的时候, 千万不能用电梯。Dàlóu zháohuǒ de
shíhou, qiānwàn bù néng yòng diàntī. *Do not use
the elevator when there is a fire in the building.*
　乘电梯 **chéng diàntī** go up/down by elevator
电影 **diànyǐng** N movie, film (场 chǎng, 部 bù,
个 gè)
　电影票 **diànyǐngpiào** film ticket
　电影院 **diànyǐngyuàn** cinema, cinema complex, movie theater (座 zuò)
　看电影 **kàn diànyǐng** watch a film, go to the
movies. ■ 他常常和女朋友一起看电影。Tā
chángcháng hé nǚpéngyou yìqǐ kàn diànyǐng. *He
often goes to the movies with his girlfriend.*
电源 **diànyuán** N power supply, mains
电子 **diànzǐ** N electron
　电子工业 **diànzǐ gōngyè** electronics industry
　电子贺卡 **diànzǐ hèkǎ** e-card
　电子邮件 **diànzǐ yóujiàn** e-mail ■ 我今天
收到两个电子邮件, 发了三个电子邮件。Wǒ
jīntiān shōudào liǎng ge diànzǐ yóujiàn, fāle sān
ge diànzǐ yóujiàn. *I received two e-mail messages and sent three today.*
　电子游戏 **diànzǐ yóuxì** electronic game

垫 diàn TRAD 墊 I v put something under
something else to raise it or make it level
II N mat, pad, cushion
　垫子 **diànzi** mat, pad, cushion

店 diàn N Same as 商店 shāngdiàn

店员 **diànyuán** N sales clerk, shop assistant

惦 **diàn** v keep thinking about, remember with concern

惦记 **diànjì** v keep thinking about, remember with concern

淀 **diàn** as in 淀粉 diànfěn

淀粉 **diànfěn** N starch, amylum

殿 **diàn** N hall (in a palace, temple, etc.)

雕 **diāo** v carve

浮雕 **fúdiāo** relief (sculpture)
石雕 **shídiāo** stone carving
雕刻 **diāokè** v carve, engrave (a work of art)
雕塑 **diāosù** N sculpture
雕像 **diāoxiàng** N statue

刁 **diāo** ADJ sly, tricky

刁难 **diāonàn** make things unnecessarily difficult in order to harrass

叼 **diāo** v hold in the mouth

掉 **diào** v fall, drop ■ 杯子从桌子上掉到地上。Bēizi cóng zhuōzi shang diàodao dì shang. *The cup fell from the table to the floor.*

NOTE: 掉 diào is often used after a verb, as a complement to mean *finish (doing ...)*, e.g.
吃掉 **chīdiào** eat up ■ 水果都吃掉了。Shuǐguǒ dōu chīdiào le. *The fruit is all eaten up.*
卖掉 **màidiào** sell out ■ 那些书还没有卖掉。Nà xiē shū hái méiyǒu màidiào. *Those books aren't sold out yet.*
扔掉 **rēngdiào** throw away, discard ■ 这件衣服太小了,不能穿了,你扔掉吧! Zhè jiàn yīfu tài xiǎo le, bù néng chuān le, nǐ rēngdiào ba! *This dress is too small for you. You'd better throw it away.*
忘掉 **wàngdiào** forget ■ 这件事我怎么也忘不掉。Zhè jiàn shì wǒ zenme yě wàng bu diào. *I can't forget this incident, no matter how hard I try.*

钓 **diào** TRAD 釣 v to fish with hook and line, angle ■ 你钓到几条鱼? Nǐ diàodao jǐ tiáo yú? *How many fish have you caught [with hook and line]?*

调 **diào** TRAD 調 v 1 exchange, swap ■ 你想和我调一下座位吗? Nǐ xiǎng hé wǒ diào yíxià zuòwèi ma? *Would you like to swap seats with me?* 2 transfer

调查 **diàochá** I v investigate ■ 政府有关部门正在调查这家公司的商业活动。Zhèngfǔ yǒu-guān bùmén zhèngzài diàochá zhè jiā gōngsī de shāngyè huódòng. *The relevant government departments are investigating this company's commercial activities.* II N investigation ■ 关于这个事件,警察正在进行调查。Guānyú zhège shìjiàn, jǐngchá zhèngzài jìnxíng diàochá. *The police are conducting an investigation of this incident.*

调查团 **diàochátuán** investigation team
调查人员 **diàochá rényuán** investigator
调动 **diàodòng** v transfer to another post
申请调动工作 **shēnqǐng diàodòng gōngzuò** apply for a job transfer
调度 **diàodù** v dispatch (vehicles or workers)
调换 **diàohuàn** v exchange (a purchase, a seat, etc.)

吊 **diào** TRAD 弔 v hang, suspend

上吊 **shàngdiào** hang oneself (to commit suicide)
吊车 **diàochē** N crane (a heavy machine)
吊环 **diàohuán** N rings (in gymnastics)
吊销 **diàoxiāo** v revoke (a license, a permit, a certificate, etc.)
吊销营业执照 **diàoxiāo yíngyè zhízhào** revoke a business permit

跌 **diē** v 1 fall, tumble ■ 老人跌了一交,摔断了左腿。Lǎorén diēle yì jiāo, shuāiduànle zuǒ luǐ. *The old man fell down and broke his left leg.* 2 (prices) fall, drop ■ 昨天股票跌了,还是升了? Zuótián gǔpiào diē le, háishì shēng le? *Did the shares fall or rise yesterday?*

爹 **diē** N dad, daddy

爹爹 **diēdie** dad, daddy

碟 **dié** N small dish, small plate

碟子 **diézi** small dish
茶碟 **chádié** saucer

蝶 **dié** N butterfly

叠 **dié** TRAD 疊 v pile up

丁 **dīng** N small cube

肉丁 **ròudīng** diced meat

钉 **dīng** TRAD 釘 N (metal) nail

叮 **dīng** v 1 (of mosquitos) bite 2 remind repeatedly

叮嘱 **dīngzhǔ** v urge repeatedly, exhort

盯 **dīng** v gaze, stare ■ 你别老盯着人家看, 多不礼貌! Nǐ bié lǎo dīngzhe rénjiā kàn, duō bù lǐmào! *You shouldn't stare at people. How rude!*

顶 **dǐng** TRAD 頂 I N top (of the head), peak, summit
山顶 **shāndǐng** peak
头顶 **tóudǐng** crown of the head
屋顶 **wūdǐng** roof
II v carry on the head, hit with the head ■ 九号队员顶球入门。Jiǔhào duìyuán dǐng qiú rù mén. *No. 9 headed the ball into the goal.*
顶点 **dǐngdiǎn** N zenith, apex
顶端 **dǐngduān** N top, peak

订 **dìng** TRAD 訂 v book
订房间 **dìng fángjiān** reserve a hotel/motel room ■ 我想订一个双人房间。Wǒ xiǎng dìng yí ge shuāngrén fángjiān. *I'd like to book a double room.*
订票 **dìng piào** book tickets
订座 **dìng zuò** book a table (at a restaurant), book a seat (in a theater)

NOTE: 定 dìng can also be used in this sense, e.g. 定房间 = 订房间.

订购 **dìnggòu** v place an order
订户 **dìnghù** N subscriber (to a newspaper or magazine)
订婚 **dìnghūn** v be engaged (for marriage)
订婚戒指 **dìnghūn jièzhǐ** engagement ring (枚 méi, 只 zhī)
和···订婚 **hé...dìnghūn** be engaged to ...
订货 **dìnghuò** v order goods (in bulk), order
订货单 **dìnghuòdān** (written) order (份 fèn)
订阅 **dìngyuè** v subscribe (a newspaper or magazine)

钉 **dìng** TRAD 釘 v drive a nail into

定 **dìng** I v fix, set, determine ■ 你去北京的日期定了吗? Nǐ qù Běijīng de rìqī dìngle ma? *Have you decided on the date to leave for Beijing?* II ADJ fixed, set, decided
定额 **dìng'é** N quota (for sales, production, etc.)
完成销售定额 **wánchéng xiāoshòu dìng'é** fill a sales quota
定价 **dìngjià** N fixed price, price
定居 **dìngjū** v start living in a place, settle down
定理 **dìnglǐ** N theorem (条 tiáo)
定量 **dìngliàng** v determine the quantity of
定量分析 **dìngliàng fēnxī** quantitative analysis
定律 **dìnglǜ** N (scientific) law
定期 **dìngqī** ADV at regular intervals
定期维修车辆 **dìngqī wéixiū chēliàng** regular maintenance of vehicles

定位 **dìngwèi** v determine the position of
定位仪 **dìngwèiyí** GPS navigation system, GPS
定性 **dìngxìng** v determine the quality of
定性分析 **dìngxìng fēnxī** qualitative analysis
定义 **dìngyì** N definition
下定义 **xià dìngyì** give a definition

丢 **diū** v lose, throw away ■ 我的表丢了。Wǒ de biǎo diū le. *I've lost my watch.*
丢脸 **diūliǎn** lose face, be disgraced
丢三落四 **diū-sān-là-sì** v be forgetful, be scatter-brained ■ 年纪大了, 容易丢三落四的。Niánjì dà le, róngyì diū-sān-là-sì de. *When one gets old, one tends to be more forgetful.*

NOTE: 落 here is pronounced as là, not its usual luò.

丢失 **diūshī** v lose

东 **dōng** TRAD 東 N east, eastern ■ 一直往东走, 就是我们的学校。Yìzhí wàng dōng zǒu, jiùshì wǒmen de xuéxiào. *Walk straight towards the east and you'll come to our school.*
东北 **dōngběi** N northeast, the Northeast ■ 中国东北天气非常冷。Zhōngguó Dōngběi tiānqì fēicháng lěng. *It's very cold in Northeast China.*

NOTE: 东北 dōngběi as a specific geographical term refers to the northeastern part of China, which used to be known in the West as Manchuria.

东边 **dōngbian** N the east side, to the east, in the east
东道 **dōngdào** N host
东道国 **dōngdàoguó** N host country
东道主 **dōngdàozhǔ** N host (usually for an official function)
东方 **dōngfāng** N the East, the Orient ■ 东方文化和西方文化有很大的不同。Dōngfāng wénhuà hé xīfāng wénhuà yǒu hěn dà de bùtóng. *There are major differences between the cultures of East and West.*
东面 **dōngmiàn** N Same as 东边 dōngbian
东南 **dōngnán** N southeast ■ 中国东南地区经济发达, 人口很多。Zhōngguó dōngnán dìqū jīngjì fādá, rénkǒu hěn duō. *The southeastern regions in China are economically well-developed and densely populated.*
东西 **dōngxi** N 1 thing, things (个 gè, 件 jiàn, 种 zhǒng) ■ 我没有看到过这种东西。Wǒ méiyǒu kàndàoguo zhè zhǒng dōngxi. *I've never seen such a thing.* 2 a person or animal (used affectionately or disapprovingly in colloquial Chinese) ■ 你这个坏东西又在骗人了。Nǐ zhè ge huài dōngxi yòu zài piànrén le. *You rascal! You're trying to deceive me again.*

NOTE: 东西 dōngxi, which literally means *east and*

west, is an extremely common "all-purpose" noun that can denote any object or objects in Chinese. More examples: ■ 妈妈出去买东西了。Māma chūqu mǎi dōngxi le. *Mother's gone shopping.* ■ 图书馆里不能吃东西。Túshūguǎn lǐ bù néng chī dōngxi. *No food in the library.*

冬 dōng N winter

冬季 **dōngjì** winter season
冬天 **dōngtiān** N winter ■ 今年的冬天比去年冷。Jīnnián de dōngtiān bǐ qùnián lěng. *This year's winter is colder than last year's.*

董 dǒng as in 董事 dǒngshì

董事 **dǒngshì** N director (of a company), trustee
董事长 **dǒngshìzhǎng** chairman of the board of directors ■ 大华公司王董事长在记者招待会上宣布了重大消息。Dàhuá Gōngsī Wáng dǒngshìzhǎng zài jìzhě zhāodàihuì shang xuānbù le zhòngdà xiāoxi. *Mr Wang, chairman of the board of Da Hua Company, announced important news at the press conference.*

懂 dǒng V comprehend, understand ■ 我不懂你的意思。Wǒ bù dǒng nǐ de yìsi. *I don't understand what you mean.*

NOTE: 懂 is often used after another verb as a complement, e.g.

读懂 **dúdǒng** read and understand ■ 这本书我读了两遍才读懂。Zhè běn shū wǒ dúle liǎng biàn cái dúdǒng. *I understood this book only after reading it twice.*
看懂 **kàndǒng** see (or read) and understand ■ 这个电影我没有看懂。Zhège diànyǐng wǒ méiyǒu kàndǒng. *I didn't understand that movie.*
听懂 **tīngdǒng** listen and understand ■ 我听得懂一些简单的中文。Wǒ tīng de dǒng yìxiē jiǎndān de Zhōngwén. *I can understand a little simple spoken Chinese.*

懂事 **dǒngshì** ADJ be sensible

动 dòng I HAD 動 V move, act ■ 别动，我给你照张像。Bié dòng, wǒ gěi nǐ zhào zhāng xiàng. *Stay put, I'll take your picture.*

动工 **dònggōng** V begin construction ■ 计算机房什么时候动工? Jìsuànjī fáng shénme shíhòu dònggōng? *When will the building of the computer lab start?*
动机 **dòngjī** N motive, intention ■ 他的动机是好的，可惜效果不那么好。Tā de dòngjī shì hǎo de, kěxī xiàoguǒ bù nàme hǎo. *His intention was good; it's a shame the effect was not so good.*
动机不纯 **dòngjī bùchún** with hidden motives
动静 **dòngjing** N signs of activity

动力 **dònglì** N **1** source of power, power **2** driving force (to do something), motivation
动乱 **dòngluàn** N (social) turmoil, upheaval
动脉 **dòngmài** N artery
主动脉 **zhǔ dòngmài** main artery
动人 **dòngrén** ADJ moving, touching ■ 这个电影的故事十分动人。Zhège diànyǐng de gùshi shífēn dòngrén. *This film has a moving storyline.*
动身 **dòngshēn** V start (a journey), set off (on a journey) ■ 你如果要在天黑前到达，就得早上动身。Nǐ rúguǒ yào zài tiān hēi qián dàodá, jiù děi zǎoshang dòngshēn. *If you want to arrive before dark, you've got to set off early in the morning.*
动手 **dòngshǒu** V start work ■ 我们现在动手，一定能在七点前完成任务。Wǒmen xiànzài dòngshǒu, yídìng néng zài qī diǎn qián wánchéng rènwù. *If we start work now we're sure to be able to finish the job before seven o'clock.*
动态 **dòngtài** N general tendency of affairs, developments
科技动态 **kējì dòngtài** developments in science and technology, what's new in science and technology
动物 **dòngwù** N animal (只 zhī)
动物学 **dòngwùxué** zoology
动物园 **dòngwùyuán** zoo ■ 下星期五我们班参观动物园。Xià Xīngqīwǔ wǒmen bān cānguān dòngwùyuán. *Our class will visit the zoo next Friday afternoon.*
动摇 **dòngyáo** V waver, vacillate
决不动摇 **jué bù dòngyáo** will not waver, be very firm and determined
动用 **dòngyòng** V put to use, draw on
动用预备金 **dòngyòng yùbèi jīn** draw on reserve fund
动员 **dòngyuán** V mobilize
动作 **dòngzuò** N movement (of the body) ■ 你跳舞的动作真优美! Nǐ tiàowǔ de dòngzuò zhēn yōuměi! *The movements of your dance are really beautiful! (→ You're a graceful dancer!)*

冻 dòng TRAD 凍 V freeze ■ 天这么冷，我真冻坏了。Tiān zhème lěng, wǒ zhēn dòng huài le. *It's so cold. I'm frozen to death.*

冻肉 **dòngròu** frozen meat
肉冻 **ròudòng** jellied meat
水果冻 **shuǐguǒdòng** fruit jelly
冻结 **dòngjié** V freeze
工资冻结 **gōngzī dòngjié** wage freeze

栋 dòng TRAD 棟 M. WD (for buildings)

一栋古典风格的小楼 **yí dòng gǔdiǎn fēnggé de xiǎo lóu** a nice house in classical style

49

洞 **dòng** N hole, cave, cavity ■ 你敢进这个山洞吗? Nǐ gǎn jìn zhège shāndòng ma? *Do you dare to enter this mountain cave?*

都 **dōu** ADV all, both, without exception ■ 我每天都跑步。Wǒ měitiān dōu pǎobù. *I jog every day.*

NOTE: When words like 每天 měitiān (every day), 每个 měi ge (every one), 大家 dàjiā (everybody) or 所有的 suǒyǒu de (all) are used, they usually occur with the adverb 都 dōu.

兜 **dōu** I N pocket, bag II V 1 wrap up 2 move around 3 canvass, solicit

抖 **dǒu** V shake, tremble

陡 **dǒu** ADJ steep, precipitous

斗 **dòu** TRAD 鬥 V fight

斗争 **dòuzhēng** I V struggle, fight ■ 为世界和平而斗争! Wèi shìjiè hépíng ér dòuzhēng! *Struggle for world peace!* II V struggle, fight
斗志 **dòuzhì** N will to fight, militancy

豆 **dòu** N bean, pea

豆子 **dòuzi** bean, pea
豆腐 **dòufu** N bean curd, tofu
豆浆 **dòujiāng** N soybean milk

逗 **dòu** V play with, tease ■ 他下班以后, 最爱逗孩子玩。Tā xiàbān yǐhòu, zuì ài dòu háizi wán. *After work, the thing he likes to do best is play with the baby.*
逗留 **dòuliú** V stay briefly

都 **dū** N big city, metropolis

首都 **shǒudū** capital city, capital
都市 **dūshì** N big city, metropolis

督 **dū** V supervise

督促 **dūcù** V supervise and urge

毒 **dú** N 1 poison, toxin

毒蛇 **dúshé** poisonous snake
蛇毒 **shédú** snake's venom
有毒 **yǒudú** poisonous, venomous
2 narcotic drug (e.g. heroin, cocaine, etc.)
贩毒 **fàndú** drug trafficking
吸毒 **xīdú** drug taking
毒害 **dúhài** V poison
毒害青少年 **dúhài qīng shàonián** poison the minds of young people
毒品 **dúpǐn** Same as 毒 dú 2

毒药 **dúyào** N poison, toxicant

独 **dú** TRAD 獨 ADJ solitary, alone

独裁 **dúcái** V establish a dictatorship, rule arbitrarily
独裁者 **dúcáizhě** dictator
独裁政权 **dúcái zhèngquán** dictatorial regime
独唱 **dúchàng** N (singing) solo
男高音独唱 **nángāoyīn dúchàng** tenor solo
独立 **dúlì** V be independent ■ 孩子大了都想独立, 父母不用太担心。Háizi dàle dōu xiǎng dúlì, fùmǔ búyòng tài dānxīn. *When children grow up, they all want to be independent. Parents should not be too worried.*
独特 **dútè** ADJ unique, distinctive
独特的风格 **dútè de fēnggé** unique style
独自 **dùzì** ADV all by oneself, alone
独自旅游 **dúzì lǚyóu** have a holiday all by oneself
独奏 **dùzòu** N solo performance on an musical instrument
萨克斯管独奏 **sà kè sī guǎn dúzòu** saxophone solo

读 **dú** TRAD 讀 V 1 read, read aloud ■ 他正在读一份重要文件。Tā zhèng zài dú yí fèn zhòngyào wénjiàn. *He is reading an important document* 2 attend (a school), study (in a school)
读小学/中学/大学 **dú xiǎoxué/ zhōngxué/ dàxué** attend a primary school/high school/ university

NOTE: (1) In colloquial Chinese, 读 dú may be replaced by 看 kàn when used in the sense of *read*, e.g. 看书 kàn shū, 看报 kàn bào. (2) When used in the sense of *attend (school)* or *study (in a school)* 读 dú may be replaced by 念 niàn to become 念小学/中学/大学 niàn xiǎoxué/zhōngxué/ dàxué, which is more colloquial.

读书 **dúshū** V 1 read ■ 这孩子喜欢读书。Zhè háizi xǐhuan dúshū. *The child likes reading.* 2 be a student, study (in a school) ■ 我姐姐工作了, 可是我妹妹还在读书。Wǒ jiějie gōngzuò le, kěshì wǒ mèimei háizài dúshū. *My elder sister is working but my younger sister is still a student.*
读物 **dùwù** N reading material
儿童读物 **értóng dúwù** children's books
读者 **dúzhě** N reader ■ 今天报上登了很多读者来信, 对这个问题发表意见。Jīntiān bào shang dēng le hěn duō dúzhě láixìn, duì zhège wèntí fābiǎo yìjian. *Today's newspaper publishes many readers' letters airing views on this issue.*

堵 **dǔ** V block ■ 什么东西堵住了下水道? Shénme dōngxi dǔzhùle xiàshuǐdào? *What is blocking the sewer?*

堵塞 **dǔsè** v block ■ 水管堵塞了。Shuǐguǎn dǔsè le. *There is a blockage in the waterpipe.*
交通堵塞 **jiāotōng dǔsè** traffic jam

赌 **dǔ** v gamble

赌博 **dǔbó** v gamble
赌场 **dǔchǎng** N gambling house, casino

肚 **dù** N stomach

肚子 **dùzi** abdomen, stomach, belly

度 **dù** I N limit, extent

难度 **nándù** degree of difficulty ■ 这篇课文难度太高。Zhè piān kèwén nándù tài gāo. *This text is too difficult.*
II M. WD degree (of temperature, longitude, latitude, etc.) ■ 今天最高气温是二十五度。Jīntiān zuì gāo qìwēn shì èrshíwǔ dù. *The highest temperature today is 25 degrees.*
度过 **dùguò** v spend (a period of time) ■ 孩子们在爷爷奶奶家度过了愉快的暑假。Háizimen zài yéye nǎinai jiā dùguòle yí ge yúkuài de shǔjià. *The children spent a pleasant summer vacation with their grandpa and grandma.*

渡 **dù** v cross (a body of water, e.g. a river, a strait, etc.)

渡船 **dùchuán** N ferry boat, ferry (条 tiáo)
渡口 **dùkǒu** N a place where people or things are carried across, ferry landing
渡轮 **dùlún** N ferry boat, ferry (艘 sōu)

镀 **dù** TRAD 鍍 v plate

镀金 **dùjīn** v get gilded

妒 **dù** v be jealous

妒忌 **dùjì** v be jealous of
妒忌别人的财富/成就 **dùjì biéren de cáifù/chéngjiù** be jealous of someone's wealth/achievements
妒忌心 **dùjìxīn** N jealousy ■ 他的妒忌心很重。Tā de dùjì xīn hěn zhòng. *He is prone to jealousy.*

端 **duān** v carry ... level with one or both hands ■ 她端了一大盘水果走了进来。Tā duānle yí dà pán shuǐguǒ zǒule jìnlai. *She came in, carrying a big plate of fruit.*
端正 **duānzhèng** ADJ upright, proper

短 **duǎn** ADJ (of length, time) short ■ 这条街很短，只有十几座房子。Zhè tiáo jiē hěn duǎn, zhǐ yǒu shíjǐ zuò fángzi. *This is a short street, with only a dozen houses.*
短处 **duǎnchù** N shortcoming, defect
短促 **duǎncù** ADJ very brief

短期 **duǎnqī** N short-term ■ 这个目标不可能在短期内达到。Zhège mùbiāo bù kěnéng zài duǎnqī nèi dádào. *This goal cannot be reached in a short time.*
短信 **duǎnxìn** N text message (by cell phone), text
短信息服务 **duǎnxìnxī fúwù** short message service (SMS) ■ 我昨天收到他发来的两份短信。Wǒ zuótiān shōudao tā fālai de liǎng fèn duǎnxìn. *I received two text messages from him yesterday.*
短暂 **duǎnzàn** ADJ short and temporary, momentary

段 **duàn** M. WD section (for something long)

一段经历 **yí duàn jīnglì** an experience in life
一段路 **yí duàn lù** a section of a road/street, part of a journey

断 **duàn** TRAD 斷 v 1 break, snap ■ 我和她的联系断了，我不知道她在哪里。Wǒ hé tā de liánxì duàn le, wǒ bù zhīdào tā zài nǎli. *I have lost contact with her. I do not know where she is.*
2 break off, cut off
断电 **duàn diàn** cut off electricity ■ 一场大雪使这个地区断电三天。Yì chǎng dà xuě shǐ zhège dìqū duàn diàn sān tiān. *A heavy snow cut off electricity supply to this region for three days.*
断奶 **duàn nǎi** wean (a child)
断水 **duàn shuǐ** cut off water supply
断定 **duàndìng** v conclude
断断续续 **duàn-duàn-xù-xù** ADV off and on, intermittently
断绝 **duànjué** v break off, sever
断绝贸易关系 **duànjué màoyì guānxì** break off trade relations

锻 **duàn** TRAD 鍛 v forge, shape metal

锻炼 **duànliàn** v undergo physical training, do physical exercises

缎 **duàn** TRAD 緞 See 绸缎 chóuduàn satin, 缎子 duànzi satin

堆 **duī** v heap up, pile up ■ 你要扔的东西都堆在墙角，明天打扫出去。Nǐ yào rēng de dōngxi dōu duī zài qiángjiǎo, míngtiān dǎsǎo chūqu. *Pile up whatever you want to dump in the corner. Tomorrow we'll get rid of it.*
堆积 **duījī** v pile up

对 1 **duì** TRAD 對 v treat, deal with ■ 我的批评是对事不对人。Wǒ de pīpíng shì duì shì bú duì rén. *My criticism concerns the issue, not the person.*

对 2 **duì** TRAD 對 PREP 1 opposite 2 Same as 对于 duìyú

对岸 duì'àn

对岸 duì'àn N the other side of the river, lake or sea

对比 duìbǐ v compare and contrast ■ 你对比一下中文和英文，就会发现很多有趣的问题。Nǐ duìbǐ yíxià Zhōngwén hé Yīngwén, jiù huì fāxiàn hěn duō yǒuqù de wèntí. *If you compare and contrast Chinese and English, you will find many interesting issues.*

对不起 duìbuqǐ IDIOM I'm sorry, I beg your pardon ■ 对不起，打错电话了。Duìbuqǐ, dǎ cuò diànhuà le. *Sorry, I've dialed a wrong number.*

NOTE: 对不起 duìbuqǐ is a very useful idiomatic expression in colloquial Chinese. It is used when you've done something wrong or caused some inconvenience to others. For more formal occasions, use 请原谅 qǐng yuánliàng *please forgive me.*

对策 duìcè N countermeasure

对称 duìchèn ADJ symmetrical
不对称 búduìchèn asymmetrical

对待 duìdài v treat (people), approach (matters)

对得起 duìdeqǐ v be worthy of, not let down
对得起良心 duìdeqǐ liángxīn be at peace with one's conscience

对方 duìfāng N the other side, the other party ■ 你必须清楚地了解对方的企图。Nǐ bìxū qīngchu de liǎojiě duìfāng de qìtú. *You must have a clear idea of the other party's intention.*

对付 duìfu v cope with, deal with ■ 这种不讲道理的人，实在难对付。Zhè zhǒng bù jiǎng dàoli de rén, shízài nán duìfu. *It is indeed difficult to deal with such unreasonable people.*

对话 duìhuà I v have a dialogue ■ 他能够流利地用中文对话。Tā nénggòu liúlì de yòng Zhōngwén duìhuà. *He is able to have a dialogue in fluent Chinese.* II N dialogue ■ 工人已经和老板进行了两次对话。Gōngrén yǐjīng he lǎobǎn jìnxíng le liǎng cì duìhuà. *Workers have conducted two rounds of talks with the boss.*

对抗 duìkàng v antagonize, oppose vigorously

对立 duìlì v oppose, be hostile

对联 duìlián N antithetical couplet written on scrolls

对面 duìmiàn N opposite, the opposite side

对手 duìshǒu N opponent
竞争对手 jìngzhēng duìshǒu opponent in a competition, rival

对象 duìxiàng N 1 person or thing to which action or feeling is directed, object ■ 她研究的对象是学前儿童。Tā yánjiū de duìxiàng shì xuéqián értóng. *Preschool children are the object of her study.* 2 marriage partner, fiancé(e) ■ 找对象 zhǎo duìxiàng look for a marriage partner

对应 duìyìng ADJ corresponding

对应词 duìyìng cí corresponding word ■ 这个英文词在中文里几乎没有对应词。Zhège Yīngwén cí zài Zhōngwén lǐ jīhū méiyǒu duìyìng cí. *You can hardly find a word in Chinese that corresponds to this English word.*

对照 duìzhào v contrast and compare, refer to

对于 duìyú PREP 1 (introducing the object of an action) regarding ■ 我对于这个理论还没有完全理解。Wǒ duìyú zhège lǐlùn hái méiyǒu wánquán lǐjiě. *I still haven't fully understood this theory.* 2 (indicating a certain relationship) to, towards ■ 学习中文对于了解中国人和中国文化很有帮助。Xuéxí Zhōngwén duìyú liǎojiě Zhōngguórén he Zhōngguó wénhuà hěn yǒu bāngzhù. *Learning Chinese is very helpful towards understanding the Chinese people and Chinese culture.*

对 3 **duì** TRAD 對 ADJ correct, true ■ 你的话很对。Nǐ de huà hěn duì. *Your words are correct.* (→ *You're right.*) ■ 你说得很对。Nǐ shuō de hěn duì. *You spoke correctly.* (→ *You're right.*)

NOTE: 对不对 duì bu duì is used at the end of a sentence to form a question, e.g. ■ 他回答得对不对? Tā huídá de duì bu duì? *Did he answer correctly?* ■ 中华文明是世界上最古老的文明，对不对? Zhōnghuá wénmíng shì shìjiè shang zuì gǔlǎo de wénmíng, duì bu duì? *Chinese civilization is the oldest in the world, isn't it?*

对头 duìtóu ADJ correct, on the right track
不对头 búduìtóu wrong, not right ■ 你的想法不对头。Nǐde xiǎngfǎ búduìtóu. *Your ideas are not quite right.*

对 4 **duì** TRAD 對 M. WD pair, two (matching people or things)
一对花瓶 yí duì huāpíng two matching vases
一对夫妻 yí duì fūqī a couple (husband and wife)

队 duì TRAD 隊 N team
篮球队 lánqiúduì basketball team
足球队 zúqiúduì soccer team

队伍 duìwu N troops ■ 队伍天黑后进了村。Duìwu tiānhēi hòu jìnle cūn. *The troops entered the village after dark.*

队员 duìyuán N member of a team

队长 duìzhǎng N team leader

兑 duì v exchange, convert

兑换 duìhuàn v (of currency) exchange, convert
兑换率 duìhuànlǜ exchange rate

兑现 duìxiàn v cash (a check)

吨 dūn TRAD 噸 M. WD ton ■ 一吨等于一千公斤。Yí dūn děngyú yìqiān gōngjīn. *One ton equals 1,000 kilograms.*

蹲 **dūn** v squat

盾 **dùn** N shield (See 矛盾 máodùn)

顿 **dùn** TRAD 頓 M. WD (for meals) ■ 我们一天吃三顿饭：早饭、午饭、晚饭。Wǒmen yì tiān chī sān dùn fàn: zǎofàn, wǔfàn, wǎnfàn. *We have three meals a day: breakfast, lunch and supper (or dinner).*

顿时 **dùnshí** ADV immediately, at once

多 **duō** I ADJ many, much ■ 今天的作业不多。Jīntiān de zuòyè bù duō. *There isn't much homework today.*

比…得多 **bǐ...de duō** much more ... than ■ 今天比昨天热得多。Jīntiān bǐ zuótiān rè de duō. *Today is much hotter than yesterday.*

II NUM more, over ■ 他在台湾住了八个多月。Tā zài Táiwān zhùle bā ge duō yuè. *He lived in Taiwan for over eight months.* III ADV how ...! ■ 要是我能去北京学中文，多好啊! Yàoshì wǒ néng qù Běijīng xué Zhōngwén, duō hǎo a! *How nice it would be if I could go to Beijing to study Chinese!*

多半 **duōbàn** ADV probably, most likely

多亏 **duōkuī** ADV luckily, fortunately

多么 **duōme** ADV Same as 多 III ADV. Used in colloquial Chinese.

多媒体 **duōméitǐ** N multimedia

多少 **duōshǎo** PRON how many, how much ■ 你们班多少人学中文? Nǐmen bān duōshǎo rén xué Zhōngwén? *How many in your class are studying Chinese?*

…多少钱 **...duōshǎo qián** How much is ...? ■ 这本书多少钱? Zhè běn shū duōshǎo qián? *How much is this book?*

没有多少 **méiyǒu duōshǎo** not many, not much ■ 他没有多少钱，可是要装出很有钱的样子。Tā méiyǒu duōshǎo qián, kěshì yào zhuāngchū hěn yǒuqián de yàngzi. *He hasn't got much money, but he pretends to be rich.*

NOTE: See note on 几, 讠.

多数 **duōshù** N majority ■ 世界上多数国家都实行民主制度。Shìjiè shang duōshù guójiā dōu shíxíng mínzhǔ zhìdù. *The majority of countries in the world practice democracy.*

多余 **duōyú** ADJ surplus

哆 **duō** as in 哆嗦 duōsuo

哆嗦 **duōsuo** v tremble, shiver

夺 **duó** TRAD 奪 v take by force, win ■ 我们队夺得了冠军。Wǒmen duì duódéle guànjūn. *Our team has won the championship.*

夺取 **duóqǔ** v capture, seize

朵 **duǒ** M. WD (for flowers) ■ 送给你一朵花。Sòng gei nǐ yì duǒ huā. *I'll give you a flower.*

躲 **duǒ** v hide (oneself) ■ 他躲在门背后。Tā duǒ zài mén bèihòu. *He hid behind the door.*

躲避 **duǒbì** v hide, avoid, keep away from
躲避债主 **duǒbì zhàizhǔ** hide from the creditor

躲藏 **duǒcáng** v go into hiding

跺 **duò** v stamp (one's foot)

舵 **duò** N rudder, helm

惰 **duò** ADJ be lazy ■ 教不严，师之惰。Jiào bù yán, shī zhī duò. *If the teaching is not rigorous, it's because the teacher is lazy.*

堕 **duò** TRAD 墮 v fall

堕落 **duòluò** v (of one's morals or behavior) become worse, degenerate

E

俄 **é** N (a shortened form of 俄国 Russia or 俄语 Russian)

俄国 **éguó** N Russia

俄文 **éwén** N the Russian language (especially the writing)

俄语 **éyǔ** N the Russian language ■ 俄语的语法很复杂。Éyǔ de yǔfǎ hěn fùzá. *Russian grammar is complicated.*

鹅 **é** TRAD 鵝 N goose (只 zhī)

天鹅 **tiān'é** swan

蛾 **é** N moth

蛾子 **ézi** moth (个 gè)

额 **é** TRAD 額 N forehead

额外 **éwài** ADJ additional, extra
额外的开支 **éwài de kāizhī** extra expenditure

讹 **é** TRAD 訛 v extort, blackmail

讹诈 **ézhà** v extort, blackmail

恶 **ě** TRAD 惡 v vomit

恶心 **èxīn** v 1 feel sick, be sickened ■ 我看到那种食物，就感到恶心。Wǒ kàndào nà zhǒng

53

shíwù, jiù gǎndào ěxīn. *I feel sick at the sight of the food.* **2** feel disgusted, be nauseated ■ 她拍老板马屁的样子, 真叫人恶心! Tā pāi lǎobǎn mǎpì de yàngzi, zhēn jiào rén ěxīn! *The way she fawns over the boss is really nauseating!*

恶 è TRAD 惡 ADJ bad, wicked ■ 人性是善, 还是恶? Rénxìng shì shàn, háishi è? *Is human nature good or bad?*

恶毒 **èdú** ADJ vicious, malicious
恶化 **èhuà** V get worse, aggravate
恶劣 **èliè** ADJ very bad, abominable
恶性 **èxìng** ADJ malicious
   恶性肿瘤 **èxìng zhǒngliú** malignant tumor, cancer
   恶性事件 **èxìng shìjiàn** vicious crime

饿 è TRAD 餓 ADJ hungry ■ 我饿了, 我们去吃饭吧! Wǒ è le, wǒmen qù chī fàn ba! *I'm hungry. Let's go and eat.*

恩 ēn N kindness, grace

恩爱 **ēn'ài** ADJ (between husband and wife) deep, caring love
恩惠 **ēnhuì** N kindness that brings about great benefits
恩情 **ēnqíng** N lovingkindness
恩人 **ēnrén** N benefactor

儿 ér TRAD 兒 N child, son

儿女 **érnǚ** N son(s) and daughter(s), children
儿童 **értóng** N child(ren) ■ 这种电影不适合儿童看。 Zhè zhǒng diànyǐng bù shìhé értóng kàn. *This kind of film is not suitable for children.*
   儿童时代 **értóng shídài** childhood
儿子 **érzi** N son (个 gè) ■ 他希望妻子生一个儿子。 Tā xīwàng qīzi shēng yí ge érzi. *He hopes that his wife will give birth to a son.*

而 ér CONJ (indicating a contrast) but, yet, on the other hand ■ 学而不用, 等于没学。 Xué ér bú yòng, děngyú méi xué. *If you learn skills but do not use them, it is tantamount to not having learned them at all.*

而且 **érqiě** CONJ moreover, what's more ■ 这件衣服大了一点儿, 而且比较贵, 还是不买吧。 Zhè jiàn yīfu dàle yìdiǎnr, érqiě bǐjiào guì, háishi bù mǎi ba. *This dress is a bit too big and also expensive. You shouldn't buy it.*

耳 ěr N ear

耳朵 **ěrduo** N the ear (只 zhī) ■ 人有两只耳朵, 就说明应该听不同的声音。 Rén yǒu liǎng zhī ěrduo, jiù shuōmíng yīnggāi tīng bùtóng de shēngyīn. *A man has two ears, which means he should listen to different voices.* (→ *A man has*

two ears, which means he should hear out different opinions.)

二 èr NUM second, two ■ 我二哥去年结婚了。 Wǒ èrgē qùnián jiéhūn le. *My second elder brother got married last year.*
二千二百二十二 **èrqiān èrbǎi èrshí'èr** two thousand, two hundred and twenty-two (2,222)

NOTE: See note on 两 liǎng.

二奶 **èr-nǎi** N mistress, concubine, kept woman
   包二奶 **bāo èr-nǎi** keep a woman as mistress
二手 **èrshǒu** ADJ second-hand, used
   二手车 **èrshǒu chē** used car
   二手房 **èrshǒu fáng** second-hand housing
二氧化碳 **èryǎnghuàtàn** N carbon dioxide

F

发 fā TRAD 發 V **1** send out, release ■ 我上个星期给他发了一封信, 今天上午又发了一个传真。 Wǒ shàng ge xīngqī gěi tā fāle yì fēng xìn, jīntiān shàngwǔ yòu fāle yí ge chuánzhēn. *I sent him a letter last week and a fax this morning.*
发传真 **fā chuánzhēn** send a fax
发电子邮件 **fā diànzǐ yóujiàn** send an e-mail message
发 (手机) 短信 **fā (shǒujī) duǎnxìn** send a text message (by cell phone)
2 develop (into a state)
发表 **fābiǎo** V publicize, make known, publish ■ 请您发表对目前经济形势的看法。 Qǐng nín fābiǎo duì mùqián jīngjì xíngshì de kànfǎ. *Please express your views on the current economic situation.*
发布 **fābù** V release, issue
   发布通告 **fābù tōnggào** release an announcement
   发布新闻 **fābù xīnwén** release news
发财 **fācái** V make a fortune, become prosperous
发出 **fāchū** V **1** produce, emit, give off **2** send out ■ 学校已经向新生发出通知。 Xuéxiào yǐjīng xiàng xīnshēng fāchū tōngzhī. *The school has sent out notifications to the new students.*
发达 **fādá** ADJ developed, well-developed ■ 这个国家制造业很发达。 Zhège guójiā zhìzàoyè hěn fādá. *This country has a well-developed manufacturing industry.*
发电 **fādiàn** V generate electricity
   发电厂 **fādiànchǎng** power plant
   发电机 **fādiànjī** generator
   火力发电 **huǒlì fādiàn** thermal power
   水力发电 **shuǐlì fādiàn** hydro power

发动 **fādòng** v launch (a massive campaign)

发抖 **fādǒu** v tremble ■ 她冷得发抖。Tā lěng de fādǒu. *She trembled with cold.*

发挥 **fāhuī** v allow display, give free rein to ■ 这项工作能够充分发挥他在这方面的能力。Zhè xiàng gōngzuò nénggòu chōngfèn fāhuī tā zài zhè fāngmiàn de nénglì. *This job allows him to display his ability in this area fully.*

发火 **fāhuǒ** lose temper, get angry

发觉 **fājué** v find, find out, become aware of

发明 **fāmíng** I v invent ■ 飞机是谁发明的? Fēijī shì shuí fāmíng de? *Who invented the airplane?* II N invention (项 xiàng) ■ 这项新发明会给公司带来巨大的利益。Zhè xiàng xīn fāmíng huì gěi gōngsī dàilái jùdà de lìyì. *This new invention will bring tremendous benefits to the company.*

发脾气 **fā píqi** lose one's temper, flare up

发票 **fāpiào** N receipt (张 zhāng)

发起 **fāqǐ** v launch, initiate

发热 **fārè** v Same as 发烧 fāshāo

发烧 **fāshāo** v run a fever

发高烧 **fā gāoshāo** run a high fever

发射 **fāshè** v shoot, launch

发射嫦娥一号探月卫星 **fāshè Cháng'é yíhào tànyuè wèixīng** launch Chang'e No. 1 Lunar Orbiting Spacecraft

发生 **fāshēng** v take place, happen ■ 前面发生了交通事故, 车辆必须绕道。Qiánmiàn fāshēngle jiāotōng shìgù, chēliàng bìxū ràodào. *A road accident happened up ahead. Traffic must detour.*

发誓 **fāshì** v pledge, vow

发誓不再抽烟 **fāshì búzài chōuyān** vow not to smoke again

发现 **fāxiàn** v discover, find, find out ■ 我发现他爱打扮了, 是不是有女朋友了? Wǒ fāxiàn tā ài dǎbàn le, shì bu shì yǒu nǚpéngyou le? *I notice that he is paying more attention to his grooming. Has he gotten a girlfriend?*

发行 **fāxíng** v issue (books, stamps, etc.), publish

发言 **fāyán** I v speak (at a meeting), make a speech ■ 代表们在会上纷纷发言。Dàibiǎomén zài huìshang fēnfēn fāyán. *The delegates spoke at the meeting, one after another.* II N speech

发言人 **fāyánrén** spokesperson

发炎 **fāyán** v become inflamed

发扬 **fāyáng** v develop, carry forward ■ 希望你发扬优点, 克服缺点。Xīwàng nǐ fāyáng yōudiǎn, kèfú quēdiǎn. *I hope you will develop your strong points and overcome your shortcomings.*

发音 **fāyīn** N pronunciation ■ 他中文说得很流利, 虽然发音不太好。Tā Zhōngwén shuō de hěn liúlì, suīrán fāyīn bú tài hǎo. *He speaks Chinese fluently, though his pronunciation is not too good.*

发育 **fāyù** v (of humans) develop physically

发展 **fāzhǎn** v develop ■ 公司决定发展在这个地区的业务。Gōngsī juédìng fāzhǎn zài zhè ge dìqū de yèwù. *The company has decided to develop its business in this region.*

发展中国家 **fāzhǎnzhōng guójiā** developing country

乏 **fá** v lack (See 缺乏 quēfá.)

罚 **fá** TRAD 罰 v punish, penalize ■ 他因为超速驾车, 被罚了两百块。Tā yīnwéi chāosù jiàchē, bèi fále liǎngbǎi kuài. *He was fined 200 yuan for speeding.*

罚款 **fákuǎn** I v fine ■ 超速要罚款。Chāosù yào fákuǎn. *Speeding will be fined.* II N fine

罚款单 **fákuǎndān** fine notice

缴罚款 **jiǎo fákuǎn** pay a fine

伐 **fá** v fell, cut down

伐木 **fámù** fell trees, do logging

伐木工人 **fámù gōngrén** lumberjack

阀 **fá** TRAD 閥 N valve

阀门 **fámén** valve

法 **fǎ** N method, law

法定 **fǎdìng** ADJ required by law, legal

法定年龄 **fǎdìng niánlíng** legal age (for certain rights)

法定人数 **fǎdìng rénshù** quorum

法官 **fǎguān** N judge

法规 **fǎguī** N laws and regulations

法律 **fǎlǜ** N law ■ 每一个公民都必须遵守法律。Měi yí ge gōngmín dōu bìxū zūnshǒu fǎlǜ. *Every citizen must obey the law.*

违反法律 **wéifǎn fǎlǜ** violate the law

修改法律 **xiūgǎi fǎlǜ** amend a law

法人 **fǎrén** N legal person

法庭 **fǎtíng** N law court, court

法文 **Fǎwén** N the French language (especially the writing)

法西斯 **Fǎxīsī** N Fascism

法语 **Fǎyǔ** N the French language

法院 **fǎyuàn** N law court, court

高级人民法院 **gāojí rénmín fǎyuàn** supreme people's court

中级人民法院 **zhōngjí rénmín fǎyuàn** intermediate people's court

法则 **fǎzé** N rule, law

自然法则 **zìrán fǎzé** law of nature

法治 **fǎzhì** N rule of law

法制 **fǎzhì** N legal system, rule by law

法子 **fǎzi** N way of doing things, method
没法子 **méifǎzi** no way, there's nothing I can do

翻 **fān** V 1 turn, turn over 2 translate, interpret

翻译 **fānyì** I V translate, interpret ■ 这本小说已经被翻译成八种语言。Zhè běn xiǎoshuō yǐjīng bèi fānyì chéng bā zhǒng yǔyán. *This novel has been translated into eight languages.* 把…翻译成…bǎ…fānyì chéng… translate … into … ■ 你能不能把这封信翻译成中文? Nǐ néng bu néng bǎ zhè fēng xìn fānyì chéng Zhōngwén? *Can you translate this letter into Chinese?* II N translator, interpreter ■ 这位翻译中文英文都好极了。Zhè wèi fānyì Zhōngwén Yīngwén dōu hǎo jíle. *This translator (or interpreter) has very good command of both Chinese and English.* 当翻译 **dāng fānyì** to work as a translator (or interpreter)

帆 **fān** N sail

帆船 **fānchuán** N sailboat (艘 sōu)

番 **fān** ADJ foreign, outlandish

番茄 **fānqié** N tomato (只 zhī)

凡 **fán** ADV every

凡是 **fánshì** ADV every, all ■ 凡是我姐姐的朋友，我都认识。Fánshì wǒ jiějie de péngyou, wǒ dōu rènshi. *I know every one of my sister's friends.*

NOTE: 凡是 fánshì is used before a noun phrase to emphasize that what is referred to is all-embracing, without a single exception. The phrase introduced by 凡是 fánshì usually occurs at the beginning of a sentence, and 都 dōu is used in the second half of the sentence.

烦 **fán** TRAD 煩 ADJ annoyed

烦闷 **fánmèn** ADJ worried and unhappy
烦恼 **fánnǎo** ADJ annoyed and angry, vexed
烦躁 **fánzào** ADJ annoyed and impatient, fidgety

繁 **fán** ADJ numerous, abundant, complicated

繁多 **fánduō** ADJ numerous, various
品种繁多 **pǐnzhǒng fánduō** a great variety of
繁华 **fánhuá** ADJ flourishing, booming, bustling
繁忙 **fánmáng** ADJ busy, fully occupied
繁荣 **fánróng** ADJ prosperous, thriving
繁体字 **fántǐzì** N old-styled, unsimplified Chinese character, e.g. 門 for 门.

NOTE: As 繁体字 literally means *complicated style*

character, some people don't like the negative impli-cation, and prefer to use the term 传统字 *traditional character*. 繁体字 or 传统字 are used in Taiwan, Hong Kong and overseas Chinese communities.

繁殖 **fánzhí** V reproduce, breed
繁重 **fánzhòng** ADJ strenuous, onerous

反 **fǎn** I ADJ reverse, opposite ■ 请看反面。Qǐng kàn fǎnmiàn. *Please read the reverse side.* II V oppose

反驳 **fǎnbó** V argue against, refute, retort
反常 **fǎncháng** ADJ abnormal, unusual ■ 情况反常。Qíngkuàng fǎncháng. *We have an unusual situation here.*
反倒 **fǎndào** ADV Same as 反而 fǎn'ér
反动 **fǎndòng** ADJ reactionary
反动派 **fǎndòngpài** reactionaries
反对 **fǎnduì** V oppose, object to ■ 我不反对你的计划，但是我觉得很难做到。Wǒ bù fǎnduì nǐ de jìhuà, dànshì wǒ juéde hěn nán zuòdào. *I don't object to your plan, but I think it'll be dif-ficult to implement.*
反对意见 **fǎnduì yìjiàn** opposing opinion
反对党 **fǎnduìdǎng** the Opposition [party]
反而 **fǎn'ér** ADV on the contrary (to expecta-tions), instead ■ 他吃了药，病情反而恶化了。Tā chīle yào, bìngqíng fǎn'ér èhuà le. *Contrary to expectations his conditions worsene after he took the medicine.*
反复 **fǎnfù** ADV repeatedly, over and over again
反感 **fǎngǎn** ADJ feel disgusted, be averse to 对他的行为很反感 **duì tāde xíngwéi hěn fǎngǎn** feel disgusted with his behavior
反攻 **fǎngōng** N counterattack, counteroffen-sive II V launch a counterattack
反抗 **fǎnkàng** V resist, fight back, rebel ■ 当父母的如果管得太多，孩子会反抗。Dāng fùmǔ de rúguǒ guǎn de tài duō, háizi huì fǎnkàng. *If a parent is too bossy, the child will rebel.*
反馈 **fǎnkuì** N feedback
反射 **fǎnshè** V reflect
条件反射 **tiáojiàn fǎnshè** conditional reflec-tion
反思 **fǎnsī** V think from a new angle, reflect on
反问 **fǎnwèn** V ask a question as a reply ■ 她反问我："你说呢?" Tā fǎnwèn wǒ: "Nǐ shuō ne?" *She replied,"What do you think?"*
反问句 **fǎnwènjù** N rhetorical question (e.g. 难道不知道吗? Nǐ nándào bùzhīdào ma? *Don't you know?*)
反应 **fǎnyìng** N response, reaction ■ 病人还在昏迷中，医生问他话，没有反应。Bìngrén háizài hūnmí zhōng, yīshēng wèn tā huà, méiyǒu fǎnyìng. *The patient is still in a coma and gives n response to the doctor's questions.*

反映 **fǎnyìng** v **1** reflect, mirror ■ 这本小说反映了当代大学生的生活。Zhè běn xiǎoshuō fǎnyìngle dāngdài dàxuésheng de shēnghuó. *This novel reflects the life of contemporary university students.* **2** report, make known, convey

反正 **fǎnzhèng** ADV anyway, at any rate

返 **fǎn** v return

返回 **fǎnhuí** return to, come back to
返回主页 **fǎnhuí zhǔyè** return to the homepage

犯 **fàn** v violate, offend

犯错误 **fàn cuòwù** make a mistake, commit an offense ■ 他犯了一个严重错误，心里很难过。Tā fànle yí ge yánzhòng cuòwù, xīnli hěn nánguò. *He is very troubled that he made a serious mistake.*
犯法 **fàn fǎ** v break the law
犯规 **fàn guī** v foul (in sports), break a rule
犯人 **fànrén** N convict
犯罪 **fànzuì** v commit a crime, be engaged in criminal activities
犯罪分子 **fànzuì fènzi** criminal
犯罪现场 **fànzuì xiànchǎng** crime scene

范 1 **fàn** TRAD 範 N model (See 模范 mófàn)

范 2 **fàn** TRAD 範 N border, mould

范围 **fànwéi** N scope, range, limits ■ 这不属于我的工作范围。Zhè bù shǔyú wǒ de gōngzuò fànwéi. *This is outside my job description.*

饭 **fàn** TRAD 飯 N **1** cooked rice ■ 小王每顿吃两碗饭。Xiǎo Wáng měi dùn chī liǎng wǎn fàn. *Xiao Wang eats two bowls of rice every meal.* **2** meal (顿 dùn) ■ 我请你吃饭。Wǒ qǐng nǐ chīfàn. *I'll treat you to a meal.*

饭店 **fàndiàn** N **1** restaurant (家 jiā) ■ 这家饭店饭菜好吃，价钱也便宜。Zhè jiā fàndiàn fàncài hǎochī, jiàqián yě piányi. *The dishes in this restaurant are delicious and affordable.* **2** hotel (家 jiā)

NOTE: The original meaning of 饭店 **fàndiàn** is *restaurant*, but 饭店 is also used to denote *a hotel*. For example, 北京饭店 Běijīng fàndiàn may mean *Beijing Restaurant* or *Beijing Hotel*.

饭碗 **fànwǎn** N rice bowl, way of making a living, job

贩 **fàn** v buy to resell

贩卖 **fànmài** v buy and sell for a profit (usually in an illegal way)
贩卖毒品 **fànmài dúpǐn** drug trafficking
贩卖人口 **fànmài rénkǒu** human trafficking

泛 **fàn** I v **1** float **2** flood II ADJ general, extensive

泛滥 **fànlàn** v overflow, flood, go rampant ■ 假货泛滥市场。Jiǎhuò fànlàn shìchǎng. *The market is flooded with counterfeit goods.*

方 **fāng** ADJ square ■ 中国人传统在方桌或者圆桌上吃饭，不用长桌吃饭。Zhōngguórén chuántǒng zài fāngzhuō huòzhě yuánzhuō shang chīfàn, bú yòng chángzhuō chīfàn. *Traditionally, the Chinese use a square or round table, not at an oblong one, for their meals.*
长方 **chángfāng** oblong, rectangular
正方 **zhèngfāng** square

方案 **fāng'àn** N plan, program (for a major project) ■ 经过反复讨论，委员会通过了这个方案。Jīngguò fǎnfù tǎolùn, wěiyuánhuì tōngguòle zhège fāng'àn. *After repeated discussions the committee approved the program.*

方便 **fāngbiàn** ADJ convenient, handy ■ 你方便的话，请帮我找一下这本书。Nǐ fāngbiàn de huà, qǐng bāng wǒ zhǎo yíxià zhè běn shū. *If it's not too much trouble, please help me locate this book.*
方便面 **fāngbiàn miàn** instant noodles

NOTE: A euphemism for "going to the toilet" is 方便一下 fāngbiàn yíxià, e.g. ■ 我要方便一下。Wǒ yào fāngbiàn yíxià. *I'm going to use the restroom.*

方程 **fāngchéng** N equation
方程式 **fāngchéngshì** N Same as 方程 fāngchéng
方程式赛车 **fāngchéngshì sàichē** formula racing car
方法 **fāngfǎ** N method
方面 **fāngmiàn** N side, aspect ■ 政府应该考虑社会各方面的意见。Zhèngfǔ yīnggāi kǎolǜ shèhuì gè fāngmiàn de yìjiàn. *The government should consider viewpoints from various aspects of society.*
方式 **fāngshì** N manner, way ■ 说话的内容很重要，说话的方式同样重要。Shuōhuà de nèiróng hěn zhòngyào, shuōhuà de fāngshì tóngyàng zhòngyào. *What you say is important, and how you say it is equally important.*
生活方式 **shēnghuó fāngshì** way of life, lifestyle
方向 **fāngxiàng** N direction, orientation ■ 你的方向错了。Nǐ de fāngxiàng cuò le. *You're in the wrong direction.*
方针 **fāngzhēn** N guiding principle, policy ■ 你们国家的教育方针是什么? Nǐmen guójiā de jiàoyù fāngzhēn shì shénme? *What are the guiding principles of education in your country?*

坊 fāng N side street, lane

芳 fāng ADJ fragrant

芳香 **fāngxiāng** sweet-smelling, fragrant
芳香的玫瑰 **fāngxiāng de méigui** fragrant roses

肪 fáng N fat (See 脂肪 zhīfáng)

防 fáng V prevent, guard against

防火 **fánghuǒ** fire prevention
防火墙 **fánghuǒqiáng** firewall
防病 **fángbìng** disease prevention ■ 防火比救火重要，防病比治病重要。Fánghuǒ bǐ jiùhuǒ zhòngyào, fángbìng bǐ zhìbìng zhòngyào. *Preventing fires is more important than fire fighting; preventing diseases is more important than curing diseases.*
防盗 **fángdào** anti-burglary measures
防护 **fánghù** V protect, shelter
防护林 **fánghùlín** shelter forest
防守 **fángshǒu** V defend, guard
防线 **fángxiàn** N defense line
防汛 **fángxùn** N flood prevention
防疫 **fángyì** N epidemic prevention
防疫针 **fángyìzhēn** inoculation
打防疫针 **dǎ fángyìzhēn** be inoculated (against)
防御 **fángyù** V defend (usually in wars)
防止 **fángzhǐ** V prevent, guard against ■ 政府将采取措施防止人才外流。Zhèngfǔ jiāng cǎiqǔ cuòshī fángzhǐ réncái wàiliú. *The government will adopt measures to prevent brain drain.*
防治 **fángzhì** V prevent and treat (diseases)
防治病虫害 **fángzhì bìngchónghài** prevention and treatment of plant diseases and elimination of pests

妨 fáng V hinder, impede

妨碍 **fáng'ài** V hinder, hamper, disturb ■ 你们把车停在这里，会妨碍交通。Nǐmen bǎ chē tíng zài zhèlǐ, huì fáng'ài jiāotōng. *If you park your car here, it will block traffic.*

房 fáng N 1 house (幢 chuáng) ■ 他们打算明年买房。Tāmen dǎsuàn míngnián mǎi fáng. *They plan to buy a house next year.*
草房 **cǎofáng** thatched cottage
楼房 **lóufáng** house of two or more levels
平房 **píngfáng** single-story house, bungalow **2** room (间 jiān)
病房 **bìngfáng** sickroom, hospital ward
客房 **kèfáng** guestroom, spare room

房产 **fángchǎn** N real estate, property
房产商 **fángchǎnshāng** real estate agent, housing developer
房贷 **fángdài** N home loan, mortgage
房东 **fángdōng** N landlord, landlady
房间 **fángjiān** N room (间 jiān) ■ 这间房间不大，但是挺舒服。Zhè jiān fángjiān bú dà, dànshì tǐng shūfu. *This room is not big, but it's very comfortable.*
房屋 **fángwū** N houses, buildings
房子 **fángzi** N house, housing
房租 **fángzū** N rent (for housing)

仿 fǎng V imitate

仿佛 **fǎngfú** V be like, be alike ■ 他们俩年龄相仿佛，经历也差不多。Tāmen liǎ niánlíng xiāng fǎngfú, jīnglì yě chàbuduō. *The two of them are of similar age and share similar life experiences.*

纺 fǎng TRAD 紡 V spin (into thread/yarn)

纺织 **fǎngzhī** V spin and weave ■ 在这个山村里，还有老人会纺织土布。Zài zhège shāncūn lǐ, háiyǒu lǎorén huì fǎngzhī tǔbù. *In this mountain village there are old people who still make homespun cloth.*
纺织工业 **fǎngzhī gōngyè** textile industry
纺织品 **fǎngzhīpǐn** textile goods

访 fǎng TRAD 訪 V visit

访问 **fǎngwèn** V visit, interview ■ 已经有一百多万人访问过这个网站。Yǐjīng yǒu yìbǎi duō wàn rén fǎngwènguo zhège wǎngzhàn. *Over a million people have visited this website.*

放 fàng V put, put in ■ 请你不要把你的书放在我的桌子上。Qǐng nǐ bú yào bǎ nǐ de shū fàng zài wǒ de zhuōzi shang. *Please don't put your books on my desk.*
放大 **fàngdà** V enlarge, magnify ■ 这张照片请放大。Zhè zhāng zhàopiàn qǐng fàngdà. *Please enlarge this photo.*
放大镜 **fàngdàjìng** magnifying glass
放假 **fàngjià** V on holiday, have the day off
放弃 **fàngqì** V abandon, give up ■ 这个机会十分难得，你不要放弃。Zhège jīhuì shífēn nándé, nǐ bú yào fàngqì. *This is a very rare opportunity. Don't pass it up.*
放射 **fàngshè** V radiate
放射科 **fàngshèkē** department of radiology (in a hospital)
放射科治疗 **fàngshèkē zhìliáo** radiotherapy (= 放射疗法 fàngshè liáofǎ)
放松 **fàngsōng** V relax, rest and relax ■ 这星期工作太紧张了，周末我要好好放松放松。Zhè

xīngqī gōngzuò tài jǐnzhāng le, zhōumò wǒ yào hǎohǎo fàngsōng fàngsōng. *This week I've been really stressed out with work; I'll rest and relax over the weekend.*

放心 fàngxīn v set one's mind at ease, be at ease

放学 fàngxué v 1 (of schools) be over ■ 今天学校四点半放学。Jīntiān xuéxiào sì diǎn bàn fàngxué. *Today school will be over at half past four.* 2 (of pupils) return home after school ■ 你每天放学以后做什么? Nǐ měitiān fàngxué yǐhòu zuò shénme? *What do you do after school every day?*

放映 fàngyìng v show (a movie) ■ 这个周末电影院放映什么影片? Zhège zhōumò diànyǐngyuàn fàngyìng shénme yǐngpiàn? *What movies will the cinema show this weekend? (→ What's on at the cinema this weekend?)*

飞 fēi TRAD 飛 v fly ■ 小鸟飞走了。Xiǎo niǎo fēi zǒule. *The little bird flew away.*

飞机 fēijī N airplane (架 jià)
飞机票 fēijīpiào air ticket
飞机场 fēijīchǎng airport
开飞机 kāi fēijī pilot a plane
坐/乘飞机 zuò/chéng fēijī travel by plane
飞快 fēikuài ADJ with the speed of a flying object, very fast
飞翔 fēixiáng v circle in the air (like an eagle), hover
飞行 fēixíng v (of aircraft) fly
飞行员 fēixíngyuán N aircraft pilot
飞跃 fēiyuè I v go forward in leaps and bounds II N sudden and rapid development

非 fēi ADV not, do not

非…不可 fēi...bùkě ADV have no choice but to ..., simply must ... ■ 我今天非写完这个报告不可。Wǒ jīntiān fēi xiěwán zhège bàogào bùkě. *I simply must finish writing this report today.*

NOTE: 非…不可… fēi...bùkě is used to emphasize the verb after 非 fēi. 不可 bùkě may be omitted, e.g. 我今天非写完这个报告。Wǒ jīntiān fēi xiěwán zhège bàogào. *I simply must finish writing this report today.* Instead of 非, we can also use 非得 fēiděi 非得…不可…, e.g. 我今天非得写完这个报告(不可)。Wǒ jīntiān fēiděi xiěwán zhège bàogào (bùkě).

非常 fēicháng I ADV unusually, very ■ 我非常想去新加坡旅行。Wǒ fēicháng xiǎng qù Xīnjiāpō lǚxíng. *I very much want to take a trip to Singapore.* II ADJ unusual, out of the ordinary
非常事件 fēicháng shìjiàn unusual incident
非常措施 fēicháng cuòshī emergency measures

非但 fēidàn Same as 不但 búdàn
非法 fēifǎ ADJ illegal, unlawful
非法同居 fēifǎ tóngjū illegal cohabitation
非洲 Fēizhōu N Africa

啡 fēi as in 咖啡 kāfēi

肥 féi ADJ fat, fattened

NOTE: 肥 féi is normally used to describe animals. It is insulting to use it to describe humans.

肥料 féiliào N fertilizer
有机肥料 yǒujī féiliào organic fertilizer
肥沃 féiwò ADJ (of soil) fertile
肥皂 féizào N soap (块 kuài)
肥皂粉 féizàofěn detergent powder

匪 fěi N bandit

匪帮 fěibāng gang of bandits, criminal gang
匪徒 fěitú bandit, criminal gangster

诽 fěi TRAD 誹 v slander

诽谤 fěibàng v slander, libel

肺 fèi N the lungs ■ 吸烟伤害肺。Xīyān shānghài fèi. *Smoking harms the lungs.*
肺气肿 fèiqìzhǒng pulmonary emphysema
肺炎 fèiyán pneumonia

费 fèi TRAD 費 I N fee, charge ■ 我一个月要花很多钱交各种各样的费。Wǒ yí gè yuè yào huā hěnduō qián jiāo gè-zhǒng-gè-yàng de fèi. *I spend a lot of money on various fees every month.*
管理费 guǎnlǐfèi administration charge
机场费 jīchǎngfèi airport tax
水电费 shuǐdiànfèi water and electricity bill
学费 xuéfèi tuition fee
交费 jiāofèi pay fees, a charge, etc
II v cost, spend ■ 他费了很多钱才把车修好。Tā fèile hěn duō qián cái bǎ chē xiūhǎo. *Only after spending a small fortune did he get his car repaired.*
费了九牛二虎之力 fèile jiǔ-niú-èr-hǔ zhī lì IDIOM spend the strength of nine bulls and two tigers, make tremendous efforts ■ 我费了九牛二虎之力才完成这个任务。Wǒ fèile jiǔ-niú-èr-hǔ zhī lì cái wánchéng zhège rènwù. *It was with tremendous effort that I accomplished the task.*
费力 fèilì ADJ requiring great effort, painstaking
费力不讨好 fèilì bù tǎohǎo do a thankless job
费用 fèiyòng N expense, costs
生活费用 shēnghuó fèiyòng living expenses, cost of living
办公费用 bàngōng fèiyòng administration cost, overheads

废 fèi

废 **fèi** TRAD 廢 ADJ useless

废除 **fèichú** v abolish, abrogate
废话 **fèihuà** N nonsense, rubbish
废品 **fèipǐn** N 1 reject, useless product 2 junk
 废品回收 **fèipǐnhuíshōu** collecting junk, recycling
废气 **fèiqì** N waste gas
 减少废气排放 **jiǎnshǎo fèiqì páifàng** reduce waste gas emission
废物 **fèiwù** N 1 waste material ■ 这些录音带、录像带都是废物了。Zhè xiē lùyīndài, lùxiàngdài dōu shì fèiwù le. *All these audiotapes and videotapes are waste materials now.* 2 good-for-nothing ■ 她连这么简单的事都做不好，真是个废物! Tā lián zhème jiǎndān de shì dōu zuò buhǎo, zhēnshi gè fèiwù! *She can't even do well such simple jobs. What a good-for-nothing!*
废墟 **fèixū** N ruins, debris

沸 **fèi** v boil

沸腾 **fèiténg** v 1 boil 2 seethe with excitement

分 **fēn** I v 1 divide ■ 今天是你的生日，你来分生日蛋糕。Jīntiān shì nǐ de shēngrì, nǐ lái fēn shēngrì dàngāo. *Today's your birthday, come and cut your birthday cake.* 2 distribute 3 distinguish II N 1 point, mark (obtained in an exam) 2 minute ■ 现在是十点二十分。Xiànzài shì shí diǎn èrshí fēn. *It's 10:20 now.* III M. WD (Chinese currency: 1 分 fēn = 0.1 角 jiǎo = 0.01 元 yuán), cent
···分之··· **...fēnzhī...** NUM (indicating fraction)
 三分之二 **sān fēnzhī èr** two thirds
 八分之一 **bā fēnzhī yī** one eighth
···百分之··· **...bǎi fēnzhī** ... percent
 百分之七十 **bǎi fēnzhī qīshí** seventy percent
 百分之四十五 **bǎi fēnzhī sìshíwǔ** forty-five percent
分辨 **fēnbiàn** v distinguish, differentiate
 分辨不同的声调 **fēnbiàn bùtóng de shēngdiào** differentiate different tones (of Chinese syllables)
分辩 **fēnbiàn** v defend oneself (against a charge), make excuses
分别 **fēnbié** v 1 part with, be separated from 2 distinguish ■ 对于犯错误的人，我们要分别情况，不同对待。Duìyú fàn cuòwù de rén, wǒmen yào fēnbié qíngkuàng, bùtóng duìdài. *Regarding those who have made mistakes, we should distinguish between circumstances and deal with them accordingly.*
分布 **fēnbù** v be distributed (over an area)
分寸 **fēncùn** N proper limits for speech or action, sense of propriety

分割 **fēngē** v carve up, cut into pieces
分工 **fēngōng** v have a division of labor
分红 **fēnhóng** v pay or receive dividends
分化 **fēnhuà** v split up, break up
分解 **fēnjiě** v resolve, decompose
分类 **fēnlèi** v classify
 分类账 **fēnlèizhàng** ledger
 把文件分类存档 **bǎ wénjiàn fēnlèi cúndàng** classify and file documents
分离 **fēnlí** v separate, sever
分裂 **fēnliè** v split, break up
分泌 **fēnmì** v secrete
 分泌胃液 **fēnmì wèiyè** secrete gastric juice
分明 **fēnmíng** ADJ 1 sharply contoured 2 distinct ■ 我的家乡四季分明。Wǒ de jiāxiāng sìjì fēnmíng. *My hometown has four distinct seasons.*
分母 **fēnmǔ** N denominator (in a fraction, e.g. "3" in $^2/_3$)
分配 **fēnpèi** v distribute, allocate
分批 **fēnpī** ADV in batches, in groups
 分批送货 **fēnpī sònghuò** deliver goods in batches
分期 **fēnqī** ADV by stages, in instalments
 分期付款 **fēnqī fùkuǎn** pay (a bill) in instalments
分歧 **fēnqí** N difference (in opinions), divergence
 消除分歧 **xiāochú fēnqí** settle differences
分清 **fēnqīng** v distinguish
 分清主次 **fēnqīng zhǔcì** distinguish what is important from what is less so, prioritize
分散 **fēnsàn** I v disperse, scatter
 分散投资 **fēnsàn tóuzī** diversify one's investments
 II ADJ scattered
分数 **fēnshù** N 1 grade, point 2 fraction
分析 **fēnxī** I v analyze II N analysis ■ 经过分析他们知道了这个药的化学成分。Jīngguò fēnxī tāmen zhīdàole zhège yào de huàxué chéngfèn. *After an analysis, they learned the drug's chemical components.*
分享 **fēnxiǎng** v share (joy, benefits, etc.)
分钟 **fēnzhōng** N minute (of an hour) ■ 打长途电话，以每分钟计费。Dǎ chángtú diànhuà, yǐ měi fēnzhōng jìfèi. *The cost of long-distance telephone calls is calculated by the minute.*
分子 **fēnzǐ** N numerator (in a fraction, e.g. "2" in $^2/_3$)

芬 **fēn** N fragrance, sweet smell

芬芳 **fēnfāng** ADJ fragrant, sweet-smelling

吩 **fēn** v instruct

吩咐 **fēnfù** v instruct, tell (what to do) ■ 她

60

吩咐旅馆服务员把晚饭送到房间来。Tā fēnfù lǚguǎn fúwùyuán bǎ wǎnfàn sòngdào fángjiān lái. *She instructed the hotel attendant to deliver the dinner to her room.*

纷 fēn TRAD 紛 ADJ **1** numerous, varied **2** disorderly, confused
纷纷 fēnfēn ADJ numerous and disorderly ■ 对于这个处分，大家议论纷纷，有人说太重，有人说太轻。Duìyú zhège chǔfèn, dàjiā yìlùn fēnfēn, yǒurén shuō tài zhòng, yǒurén shuō tài qīng. *There is great controversy over this disciplinary action; some say it is too severe, others say it is too light.*

氛 fēn N fog, atmosphere

坟 fén N tomb
坟墓 fénmù N grave, tomb (座 zuò)

粉 fěn N powder
面粉 miànfěn wheat flour
奶粉 nǎifěn milk powder
药粉 yàofěn (medicinal) powder
粉笔 fěnbǐ N chalk (支 zhī)
粉末 fěnmò N powder, dust
粉碎 fěnsuì V smash, crush

分 fèn N **1** component **2** limit
糖分 tángfèn sugar content
分量 fènliàng N weight ■ 他在公司里工作了二十多年了，说话很有分量。Tā zài gōngsī li gōngzuòle èrshí duō nián le, shuōhuà hěn yǒu fènliàng. *He has been working in the company for over twenty years and what he says carries a lot of weight.*
分外 fènwài ADV especially, unusually
分子 fènzi N member or element (of a social group)
犯罪分子 fànzuìfènzi criminal element, criminal

份 fèn M. WD (for a set of things or newspapers, documents, etc.)
一份礼物 yí fèn lǐwù a present
一份晚报 yí fèn wǎnbào a copy of the evening paper
一份报告 yí fèn bàogào a report

奋 fèn TRAD 奮 V exert oneself
奋斗 fèndòu V fight, struggle, strive
奋勇 fènyǒng ADJ courageous, brave, fearless

粪 fèn TRAD 糞 N excrement, feces

愤 fèn TRAD 憤 N anger
愤恨 fènhèn V be angry and bitter, be very resentful
愤怒 fènnù ADJ enraged, angry ■ 她发现又受了欺骗，十分愤怒。Tā fāxiàn yòu shòule qīpiàn, shífēn fènnù. *She was enraged to discover that she had been cheated again.*

丰 fēng TRAD 豐 ADJ abundant, plentiful
丰富 fēngfù ADJ abundant, rich, plenty ■ 这本书的内容非常丰富，值得反复阅读。Zhè běn shū de nèiróng fēicháng fēngfù, zhídé fǎnfù yuèdú. *This book has very rich content and is worth repeated reading.*
丰满 fēngmǎn ADJ **1** plump **2** plentiful
身材丰满 shēncái fēngmǎn with a full (and attractive) figure
羽毛丰满 yǔmáo fēngmǎn full-fledged, developed well enough to be independent
丰收 fēngshōu N bumper harvest

封 fēng I M. WD (for letters) ■ 王先生，有你一封信。Wáng xiānsheng, yǒu nǐ yì fēng xìn. *Mr Wang, here's a letter for you.* II V seal, block ■ 大雪封山。Dà xuě fēng shān. *The heavy snow has blocked up all roads to the mountains.*
封闭 fēngbì V close, seal
封建 fēngjiàn ADJ **1** feudal **2** traditional (in a bad sense)
封锁 fēngsuǒ V block, seal off
封锁消息 fēngsuǒ xiāoxī news blackout

风 fēng TRAD 風 N wind ■ 冬天中国常常刮西北风。Dōngtiān Zhōngguó chángcháng guā xīběi fēng. *In winter a northwestern wind prevails in China.*
风向 fēngxiàng wind direction
风暴 fēngbào N windstorm (场 chǎng)
风度 fēngdù N bearing, (elegant) demeanor
很有风度 hěn yǒu fēngdù with elegant demeanor
风格 fēnggé N style (of doing things)
管理风格 guǎnlǐ fēnggé managerial style
建筑风格 jiànzhù fēnggé architectural style
风光 fēngguāng N scenery, sight
风景 fēngjǐng N landscape, scenery ■ 山顶上的风景特别优美。Shāndǐng shang de fēngjǐng tèbié yōuměi. *The scenery at the top of the mountain is particularly beautiful.*
风浪 fēnglàng I N high winds and big waves II ADJ stormy
风力 fēnglì N wind force, wind power ■ 今天风力很大，不能划船。Jīntiān fēnglì hěn dà, bù néng huáchuán. *Today the wind is too strong for us to go boating.*

风气 fēngqì

风气 fēngqì N general mood and common practice (of a society, a locality or an organization)
风趣 fēngqù N humor, wit
　有风趣 yǒu fēngqù witty, humorous
风沙 fēngshā N sand blown up by winds
风尚 fēngshàng N prevailing norm or practice (in a positive sense)
风俗 fēngsú N custom, social customs ■ 有些旧风俗正在渐渐消失。Yǒuxiē jiù fēngsú zhèngzài jiànjiàn xiāoshī. *Some old customs are gradually disappearing.*
风味 fēngwèi N special flavor, local color
风险 fēngxiǎn N risk
　冒风险 mào fēngxiǎn run a risk
风筝 fēngzheng N kite (只 zhī)
　放风筝 fàngfēngzheng fly a kite

疯 fēng TRAD 瘋 ADJ insane, crazy ■ 你疯啦？Nǐ fēng la? *Are you crazy?*
疯狂 fēngkuáng ADJ insane, frenzied
疯子 fēngzi N lunatic, a crazy guy

蜂 fēng N wasp, bee

蜂蜜 fēngmì N honey

峰 fēng N mountain peak, peak (See 山峰 shānfēng)

锋 fēng TRAD 鋒 N sharp point of a knife

锋利 fēnglì ADJ sharp

逢 féng V come upon, meet ■ 每逢结婚纪念日，他们夫妻总要庆祝一下。Měi féng jiéhūn jìniànrì, tāmen fūqī zǒngyào qìngzhù yíxià. *Every time their wedding anniversary comes around, that couple will celebrate it.*
逢年过节 féng-nián-guò-jié ADV on festival days and the New Year's Day, on festive occasions

缝 féng TRAD 縫 N sew ■ 现在很少人自己缝衣服了。Xiànzài hěn shǎo rén zìjǐ féng yīfu le. *Very few people make their own clothes nowadays.*

讽 fěng TRAD 諷 V satirize

讽刺 fěngcì I N satire II V use satire, satirize

奉 fèng V offer, obey, believe in

奉献 fèngxiàn V offer as a tribute, present with respect
奉行 fèngxíng V believe in and act upon, pursue (a policy, principle, etc.)

凤 fèng TRAD 鳳 N as in 凤凰 fènghuáng

凤凰 fènghuáng N a mythical bird symbolic of peace and prosperity, phoenix

缝 fèng TRAD 縫 N seam

见缝插针 jiànfèng chāzhēn IDIOM stick a needle in a seam (→ make full use of every minute available)

佛 Fó N Buddha

佛教 Fójiào N Buddhism

否 fǒu V negate

否定 fǒudìng V negate, deny ■ 我不想否定你们的成绩。Wǒ bù xiǎng fǒudìng nǐmen de chéngjì I don't want to deny your achievements.
否决 fǒujué V vote down, veto, overrule
否认 fǒurèn V deny, repudiate
否则 fǒuzé CONJ otherwise, or

夫 fū N man, husband

夫妇 fūfù N Same as 夫妻 fūqī
夫妻 fūqī N husband and wife
　夫妻关系 fūqī guānxi marital relationship
夫人 fūrén N (formal term for another person's) wife ■ 王董事长和夫人将出席宴会。Wáng dǒngshìzhǎng hé fūrén jiāng chūxí yànhuì. *Chairman Wang and his wife will attend the dinner party.*

肤 fū TRAD 膚 N skin (See 皮肤 pífū)

敷 fū V apply

敷药 fū yào apply medicine (to a wound)
敷衍 fūyǎn V go through the motions, be perfunctory

扶 fú V support with the hand

扶着老人过马路 fúzhe lǎorén guò mǎlù help an old person walk across the street

佛 fú (only used in 仿佛 fǎngfú)

服 fú I V obey II N clothing

服从 fúcóng V obey, submit to ■ 少数服从多数。Shǎoshù fúcóng duōshù. *The minority submits to the majority.*
服气 fúqì V be convinced
服务 fúwù V serve, work for
　为…服务 wèi...fúwù serve ..., work for .... ■ 我能为大家服务，感到很高兴。Wǒ néng wèi dàjiā fúwù, gǎndào hěn gāoxìng. *I'm happy to be able to serve you all.*
服务器 fúwùqì N (of computer) server
服务业 fúwùyè N service industry

服务员 **fúwùyuán** N attendant, waiter/wait-ress ■ 这位服务员态度不大好。Zhè wèi fúwùyuán tàidu bú dà hǎo. *This attendant's work attitude is not very good.*

NOTE: Though 服务员 fúwùyuán is used to refer to or address an attendant, a waiter or waitress, in everyday usage 小姐 xiǎojiě is more common (if the attendant is a woman).

服装 **fúzhuāng** N garments, apparel
服装工业 **fúzhuāng gōngyè** garment indus-try
服装商店 **fúzhuāng shāngdiàn** clothes store

浮 **fú** v float ■ 你说说铁做的大轮船为什么会浮在水上? Nǐ shuōshuo tiě zuò de dà lúnchuán wèishénme huì fú zài shuǐ shang? *Can you tell me why a big ship made of iron can float on water?*
浮雕 **fúdiāo** N relief sculpture
浮动 **fúdòng** v float, fluctuate
浮动汇率 **fúdòng huìlǜ** floating exchange rate

俘 **fú** v capture
战俘 **zhànfú** prisoner of war
俘虏 **fúlǔ** N captive, prisoner of war

幅 **fú** M. WD (for pictures, posters, maps, etc.)
一幅中国画 **yì fú Zhōngguó huà** a Chinese painting
幅度 **fúdù** N range, extent

福 **fú** N blessing, happiness
福利 **fúlì** N welfare, well-being
为职工谋福利 **wéi zhígōng móu fúlì** work for the welfare of the staff
福气 **fúqì** N good fortune
有福气 **yǒu fúqì** have good fortune, be very lucky

辐 **fú** TRAD 輻 N (of a wheel) spoke
辐射 **fúshè** v radiate, spread out

符 **fú** v be in accord
符号 **fúhào** N symbol, mark
符合 **fúhé** v conform to, accord with ■ 这种产品的质量不符合要求。Zhè zhǒng chǎnpǐn de zhìliàng bù fúhé yāoqiú. *The quality of this product does not meet the requirements.*

伏 **fú** v bend over

袱 **fú** TRAD 襆 N cloth-wrapper

抚 **fǔ** TRAD 撫 v 1 touch softly 2 foster (a child)

抚养 **fǔyǎng** v bring up (a child), provide for (a child)
抚育 **fǔyù** v bring up (a child), educate (a child)

府 **fǔ** N government office (See 政府 zhèngfǔ)

俯 **fǔ** v bow one's head, bend down

斧 **fǔ** N hatchet, ax
斧子 **fǔzi** hatchet, ax

辅 **fǔ** TRAD 輔 v assist, supplement
辅导 **fǔdǎo** v coach, tutor ■ 王老师, 您的辅导对我们很有帮助。Wáng lǎoshī, nín de fǔdǎo duì wǒmen hěn yǒu bāngzhù. *Teacher Wang, your tutorial is helpful to us.*
辅导课 **fǔdǎokè** tutorial class, tutorial
辅导老师 **fǔdǎo lǎoshī** tutor, teaching assist-ant
辅助 **fǔzhù** v assist, play an auxiliary role

腐 **fǔ** ADJ rotten, decayed
腐败 **fǔbài** I ADJ 1 badly decayed
腐败食品 **fǔbài shípǐn** food that has gone bad
2 corrupt ■ 腐败的官员人人恨。Fǔbài de guānyuán rénrén hèn. *Everyone hates corrupt officials.* II N corruption
腐化 **fǔhuà** ADJ degenerate, corrupt
腐烂 **fǔlàn** ADJ decomposed, putrid
腐蚀 **fǔshí** v 1 corrode, etch 2 make (people) corrupt
腐朽 **fúxiǔ** ADJ decayed, rotten

父 **fù** N father
父亲 **fùqin** N father ■ 您父亲作什么工作? Nín fùqin zuò shénme gōngzuò? *What does your father do?*

NOTE: 爸爸 bàba and 父亲 fùqin denote the same person. While 爸爸 bàba is colloquial, like *daddy*, 父亲 fùqin is formal, equivalent to *father*. When referring to another person's father, 父亲 fùqin is preferred. As a form of address to your own father, only 爸爸 bàba is normally used.

赴 **fù** v go to, attend

负 **fù** TRAD 負 v 1 carry on the back 2 shoulder, bear
负担 **fùdān** I v bear (costs)
负担旅费 **fùdān lǚfèi** bear travel expenses
II N burden, load
负伤 **fùshāng** v get wounded, get injured
负责 **fùzé** I v be responsible, be in charge ■ 你

妇 fù

现在负责哪一方面的工作? Nǐ xiànzài fùzé nǎ yì fāngmiàn de gōngzuò? *Which part of the job are you responsible for?*
负责人 **fùzérén** the person-in-charge
II ADJ responsible ■ 他做事非常负责。Tā zuòshì fēicháng fùzé. *He has a strong sense of responsibility.*

妇 fù TRAD 婦 N woman

妇女 **fùnǚ** N woman, womankind

付 fù V pay ■ 提供服务后请立即付费。Tígōng fúwù hòu qǐng lìjí fù fèi. *You are expected to pay as soon as a service is rendered. (→ Pay promptly for services rendered.)*
付出 **fùchù** V pay out, contribute
付款 **fùkuǎn** N pay a sum of money ■ 收到货后请马上付款。Shōudào huò hòu qǐng mǎshàng fùkuǎn. *Please pay promptly after receiving the goods.*

附 fù V 1 be close to 2 attach, add

附带 **fùdài** ADJ additional
附带条件 **fùdài tiáojiàn** additional condition
附和 **fùhé** V chime in with, echo
附加 **fujiā** ADJ extra
增值附加税 **zēngzhí fùjiāshuì** value-added tax
附近 **fùjìn** N the area nearby ■ 附近的学校都很好。Fùjìn de xuéxiào dōu hěn hǎo. *The schools nearby (or in this area) are all very good.*
附属 **fùshǔ** V attach, affiliate
北京师范大学附属中学 **Běijīng Shīfàn Dàxué Fùshǔ Zhōngxué** a middle school affiliated to Beijing Normal University

咐 fù V instruct (See 吩咐 fēnfù, 嘱咐 zhǔfu)

复 fù TRAD 復 ADJ repeat, complex, compound

复合 **fùhé** V compound
复活节 **Fùhuójié** N Easter
复述 **fùshù** V retell, repeat ■ 请你把她的话一个一个字地复述一下。Qǐng nǐ bǎ tā de huà yí ge yí ge zì de fùshù yíxia. *Please repeat what she says verbatim.*
复习 **fùxí** V review (one's lesson) ■ 下星期要考试, 这几天我在复习。Xià xīngqī yào kǎoshì, zhè jǐ tiān wǒ zài fùxí. *I'll be having an examination next week. I'm reviewing my lesson these days.*
复兴 **fùxīng** V revive, rejuvenate
复印 **fùyìn** V photocopy
复印机 **fùyìnjī** photocopier
复杂 **fùzá** ADJ complicated, complex ■ 这件事很复杂, 我说不清楚。Zhè jiàn shì hěn fùzá, wǒ

shuō bu qīngchu. *This is a complicated matter. I can't explain it clearly.*
复制 **fùzhì** N copy, clone

覆 fù V cover

覆盖 **fùgài** V cover, cover up

腹 fù N abdomen, belly

副 1 fù M. WD (for objects in pairs or sets) pair, set
一副手套儿 **yí fù shǒutàor** a pair of gloves
一副眼镜 **yí fù yǎnjìng** a pair of spectacles

副 2 fù ADJ 1 deputy, vice-... ■ 这几天校长生病, 有事可以找副校长。Zhè jǐtiān xiàozhǎng shēngbìng, yǒu shì kěyǐ zhǎo fù xiàozhǎng. *The principal is ill these days. You can go and talk to the deputy principal if there are any problems.* 2 secondary
副食 **fùshí** N non-staple foodstuffs
副业 **fùyè** N side occupation, sideline
副作用 **fùzuòyòng** N side effect

富 fù ADJ rich, wealthy ■ 这个地区很富, 房子都很漂亮。Zhège dìqū hěn fù, fángzi dōu hěn piàoliang. *This is a wealthy area with beautiful houses.*
富人 **fùrén** rich person, rich people

NOTE: In everyday Chinese, 富 fù is not used as much as 有钱 yǒuqián to mean *rich*.

富强 **fùqiáng** ADJ (of a country) rich and powerful
富有 **fùyǒu** ADJ rich, affluent
富裕 **fùyù** ADJ rich, well-to-do
富余 **fùyu** V have more and to spare

傅 fù N teacher, advisor (See 师傅 shīfu)

缚 fù TRAD 縛 V bind, tie up

G

该 1 gāi TRAD 該 MODAL V should, ought to ■ 他不该答应了你, 又不去办。Tā bù gāi dāyìngle nǐ, yòu bú qù bàn. *He shouldn't have made you a promise and then done nothing.*

该 2 gāi TRAD 該 V 1 be somebody's turn to do something ■ 今天该你洗碗。Jīntiān gāi nǐ xǐ wǎn. *It's your turn to wash the dishes today.* 2 deserve ■ 活该! Huógāi! *Serve you (or him/her/them) right!*

该 3 **gāi** Trad 該 PRON that, the said, the above-mentioned ■ 该校学生人数在五年内增加一倍。 Gāi xiào xuésheng rénshù zài wǔ nián nèi zēngjiā yí bèi. *The student population of that school has doubled in five years.*

NOTE: 该 gāi in this sense is used only in formal writing.

改 **gǎi** v alter, change, correct ■ 你这个坏习惯一定要改。 Nǐ zhège huài xíguàn yídìng yào gǎi. *You must break this bad habit.*

改行 **gǎiháng** change one's profession/ trade

改期 **gǎiqī** change a scheduled time, change the date (of an event)

改变 **gǎibiàn** I v transform, change ■ 我想改变一下我们的旅行路线。 Wǒ xiǎng gǎibiàn yíxià wǒmende lǚxíng lùxiàn. *I'd like to change our itinerary.* II N change, transformation

改革 **gǎigé** I v reform ■ 只有不断改革, 才能跟上时代。 Zhǐyǒu búduàn gǎigé, cáinéng gēnshàng shídài. *Only by constant reform can we keep abreast with the times.* II N reform ■ 改革开放是中国八十年代以来的两项重大政策。 Gǎigé, kāifàng shì Zhōngguó bāshí niándài yǐlái de liǎng xiàng zhòngdà zhèngcè. *Reform and opening-up have been two major policies in China since the 80s.*

改建 **gǎijiàn** v rebuild

改进 **gǎijìn** I v improve, make ... more advanced/sophisticated ■ 怎么样改进我们的服务? 请您多提意见。 Zěnmeyàng gǎijìn wǒmen de fúwù? Qǐng nín duō tí yìjiàn. *What should we do to improve our service? Please feel free to make suggestions.* II N improvement (项 xiàng) ■ 这项技术改进使产量大大增加。 Zhè xiàng jìshù gǎijìn shǐ chǎnliàng dàdà zēngjiā. *This technological improvement greatly increased production.*

改良 **gǎiliáng** v improve, reform

改善 **gǎishàn** I v ameliorate, make ... better/more favorable ■ 人人都想改善生活条件。 Rénrén dōu xiǎng gǎishàn shēnghuó tiáojiàn. *Everybody wants to improve their living conditions.* II N improvement, amelioration

改邪归正 **gǎi-xié-guī-zhèng** IDIOM give up evil and return to good, turn over a new leaf

改造 **gǎizào** I v remold, rebuild, reform ■ 这个城区要全面改造。 Zhège chéngqū yào quánmiàn gǎizào. *This urban district will undergo comprehensive rebuilding.* II N remolding, rebuilding

改正 **gǎizhèng** v put ... right, rectify ■ 改正下面句子中的错误。 Gǎizhèng xiàmiàn jùzi zhōng de cuòwù. *Correct the errors in the following sentences.*

改组 **gǎizǔ** v re-organize

盖 1 **gài** TRAD 蓋 v build ■ 我们学校明年要盖一座电脑中心。 Wǒmen xuéxiào míngnián yào gài yí zuo diànnǎo zhōngxīn. *Our school is going to build a computer center next year.*

盖 2 **gài** TRAD 蓋 N cover, lid

盖子 **gàizi** cover, lid

概 **gài** ADJ broadly, general

概况 **gàikuàng** N general situation, basic facts 中国概况 **Zhōngguó gàikuàng** basic facts about China, a profile of China

概括 **gàikuò** v summarize ■ 你能不能把这份报告概括成五百个字左右的短文? Nǐ néng bu néng bǎ zhè fèn bàogào gàikuò chéng wǔbǎi ge zì zuǒyòu de duǎn wén? *Can you summarize this report in about 500 Chinese characters?*

概念 **gàiniàn** N concept, notion ■ 你用老概念解释不了新现象。 Nǐ yòng lǎo gàiniàn jiěshì bù liǎo xīn xiànxiàng. *You cannot explain fresh phenomena with outdated concepts.*

概念车 **gàiniànchē** concept car

溉 **gài** v irrigate (See 灌溉 guàngài)

钙 **gài** N calcium

钙片 **gàipiàn** calcium tablet

甘 **gān** I v be willing, be convinced

甘拜下风 **gānbài xiàfēng** IDIOM accept willingly defeat or inferiority 不甘失败 **bùgān shībài** not be reconciled to defeat, not accept defeat II ADJ sweet, pleasant

甘心 **gānxīn** v be willing to, be ready to

甘蔗 **gānzhe** N sugar cane

干 **gān** TRAD 乾 ADJ dry

干杯 **gānbēi** v drink a toast, "Bottoms up!"

干脆 **gāncuì** I ADJ decisive, not hesitant, straight to the point II ADV just, simply ■ 你既然这么讨厌男朋友, 干脆不要他了! Nǐ jìrán zhème tǎoyàn nánpéngyou, gāncuì bú yào tā le! *Since you dislike your boyfriend so much, just dump him!*

干旱 **gānhàn** N drought, dry spell

干红 **gānhóng** N dry red wine 干红葡萄酒 **gān hóng pútaojiǔ** dry red wine

干净 **gānjìng** ADJ clean ■ 这些衣服很干净, 不用洗。 Zhèxiē yīfu hěn gānjìng, bú yòng xǐ. *These clothes are clean. They don't need washing.*

干涉 **gānshè** v intervene, interfere 干涉内政 **gānshè nèizhèng** interfere with the internal affairs (of a country)

干预 **gānyù** v intervene, meddle with
干预子女的婚姻 **gānyù zǐnǚ de hūnyīn** meddle in the marriage of (one's adult child)

干燥 **gānzào** ADJ dry, arid ■ 沙漠上天气干燥。*Shāmò shang tiānqì gānzào. In the desert, the weather is dry.*

杆 **gān** N pole

电线杆 **diànxiàn gān** electric pole, telephone/utility pole

肝 **gān** N the liver

竿 **gǎn** N pole, rod

钓鱼竿 **diàoyúgǎn** fishing rod

杆 **gǎn** N stick

枪杆 **qiānggǎn** the barrel of a rifle

赶 **gǎn** TRAD 趕 v 1 catch up with 2 hurry up, rush for, try to catch ■ 我得马上走，去赶最后一班公共汽车。*Wǒ děi mǎshàng zǒu, qù gǎn zuì hòu yìbān gōnggòng qìchē. I've got to go right now to catch the last bus.*
赶上 **gǎnshàng** catch up, catch up with
赶得上 **gǎn de shàng** can catch up
赶不上 **gǎn bu shàng** cannot catch up
没赶上 **méi gǎn shàng** fail to catch up

赶紧 **gǎnjǐn** ADV hasten (to do something) ■ 他母亲生重病住院了，他得赶紧回家。*Tā mǔqin shēng zhòngbìng zhùyuàn le, tā děi gǎnjǐn huíjiā. His mother is hospitalized owing to a severe illness and he has to rush back home.*

赶快 **gǎnkuài** ADV Same as 赶紧 **gǎnjǐn**
赶忙 **gǎnmáng** ADV hurriedly, hastily

敢 **gǎn** MODAL v dare ■ 这么多人，我不敢讲话。*Zhème duō rén, wǒ bù gǎn jiǎnghuà. There're so many people here, I don't dare to speak.*

敢于 **gǎnyú** v dare to, have the courage to

感 **gǎn** v feel

感到 **gǎndào** v feel ■ 我有机会访问你们的国家，感到很高兴。*Wǒ yǒu jīhuì fǎngwèn nǐmen de guójiā, gǎndào hěn gāoxìng. I feel very happy to have the opportunity to visit your country.*

感动 **gǎndòng** v move, touch emotionally

感化 **gǎnhuà** v reform ... through gentle persuasion and/or by setting a good example

感激 **gǎnjī** v feel deeply grateful ■ 你在我最困难的时候帮助我，我十分感激。*Nǐ zài wǒ zuì kùnnán de shíhou bāngzhù wǒ, wǒ shífēn gǎnjī. I'm grateful to you as you helped me in my most difficult times.*

感觉 **gǎnjué** I v feel ■ 我感觉他对我们不大友好。*Wǒ gǎnjué tā duì wǒmen bú dà yǒuhǎo. I feel that he is not very friendly to us.* II N feeling, impression

感慨 **gǎnkǎi** v sigh with deep inner feelings (over a revelation, an experience, etc.)

感冒 **gǎnmào** v catch a cold ■ 突然变冷，很多人感冒了。*Tūrán biàn lěng, hěn duō rén gǎnmào le. It suddenly became cold, so quite a few people caught colds.*

感情 **gǎnqíng** N 1 feelings, emotion 2 affection, love ■ 他们在一起工作多年，渐渐产生了感情。*Tāmen zài yìqǐ gōngzuò duō nián, jiànjiàn chǎnshēng le gǎnqíng. Having worked together for quite a few years, they have gradually become fond of each other.*

感染 **gǎnrǎn** v 1 (of a wound) become infected 2 (of a movie, a story, music, etc.) affect

感受 **gǎnshòu** N impression or lesson learned from personal experiences

感想 **gǎnxiǎng** N impressions, reflections ■ 请问，您参观了这个学校，有什么感想? *Qǐngwèn, nín cānguānle zhège xuéxiào, yǒu shénme gǎnxiǎng? Could you please tell us your impressions of the school you've just visited?*

感谢 **gǎnxiè** v be grateful, thank

感兴趣 **gǎn xìngqù** v be interested (in) ■ 我对小说不感兴趣。*Wǒ duì xiǎoshuō bù gǎn xìngqù. I'm not interested in fiction.*

干 **gàn** TRAD 幹 v do, work ■ 你干了一下午了，该休息休息了。*Nǐ gànle yíxiàwǔ le, gāi xiūxi xiūxi le. You've been working for the entire afternoon. You should take a break.*

干部 **gànbù** N cadre, official (位 **wèi**)

NOTE: 干部 **gànbù** is a communist party term, denoting party (or government) officials. It is not commonly used today. In its stead, 官员 **guānyuán** is the word for government officials.

干劲 **gànjìn** N drive and enthusiasm (for a job)
干劲不足 **gànjìn bùzú** lack of enthusiasm
干劲十足 **gànjìn shízú** with enormous enthusiasm

干吗 **gànmá** ADV 1 why ■ 他干吗生气? *Tā gànmá shēngqì? Why is he angry?* 2 Same as 做什么 **zuò shénme** ■ 咱们明天干吗? *Zánmen míngtiān gànmá? What are we going to do tomorrow?*

NOTE: 干吗 **gànmá** is a highly colloquial expression, used in casual conversational style.

缸 **gāng** N vat, jar (只 **zhī**)

刚 **gāng** TRAD 剛 ADV just, barely ■ 他去年考试刚及格。*Tā qùnián kǎoshì gāng jígé. He barely passed the exam last year.*

刚才 **gāngcái** N a short while ago, just

刚刚 **gānggāng** ADV Same as 刚 gāng, but more emphatic

钢 **gāng** TRAD 鋼 N steel

钢笔 **gāngbǐ** N fountain pen (支 zhī)

钢材 **gāngcái** N steel products, rolled steel

钢琴 **gāngqín** N piano (架 jià)

弹钢琴 **tán gāngqín** play the piano

钢铁 **gāngtiě** N iron and steel, steel ■ 钢铁制造是基础工业。Gāngtiě zhìzào shì jīchǔ gōngyè. *Steel and iron manufacturing is a basic (or primary) industry.*

纲 **gāng** TRAD 綱 N guiding principle, outline

纲领 **gānglǐng** N fundamental principle, guideline

纲要 **gāngyào** N outline, essentials

岗 **gǎng** TRAD 崗 N sentry post

岗位 **gǎngwèi** N post (as a job)

脱离工作岗位 **tuōlí gōngzuò gǎngwèi** leave one's job

港 **gǎng** N port, harbor

海港 **hǎigǎng** seaport ■ 上海港是中国最重要的海港之一。Shànghǎi gǎng shì Zhōngguó zuì zhòngyào de hǎigǎng zhī yī. *The Port of Shanghai is one of the most important seaports in China.*

港口 **gǎngkǒu** port, harbor

杠 **gàng** N big, thick stick, bar

杠杆 **gànggǎn** N lever

高 **gāo** ADJ 1 tall, high ■ 那座高高的楼房是一座新医院。Nà zuò gāogāo de lóufáng shì yí zuò xīn yīyuàn. *That tall building is a new hospital.* 2 above average, superior

高超 **gāochāo** ADJ (of skills) superior, consummate

高潮 **gāocháo** N high tide, high water

高大 **gāodà** ADJ tall and big ■ 他们有三个儿子，都长得很高大。Tāmen yǒu sān ge érzi, dōu zhǎng de hěn gāodà. *They have three sons who are all tall and big.*

高档 **gāodàng** ADJ top grade, high quality

高档家具 **gāodàng jiājù** fine furniture

高等 **gāoděng** ADJ advanced, higher

高等教育 **gāoděng jiàoyù** higher education

高等学校 **gāoděng xuéxiào** institution of higher education, colleges and universities

高低 **gāodī** N 1 height 2 difference in quality, skills, etc. ■ 比一比高低。Bǐyibǐ gāodī. *Compete to see which one is better.*

NOTE: See note on 大小 dàxiǎo.

高度 **gāodù** I N altitude, height II ADJ a high degree ■ 日本的汽车制造工业高度发达。Rìběn de qìchē zhìzào gōngyè gāodù fādá. *Japan has a highly developed car manufacturing industry.*

高峰 **gāofēng** N peak, summit

高峰会议 **gāofēng huìyì** summit meeting

高贵 **gāoguì** ADJ 1 (of moral) noble, admirable 2 (of people) aristocratic, elitist

出身高贵 **chūshēn gāoguì** of an aristocratic or elitist family background

高级 **gāojí** ADJ advanced, high-level

高级小学 (高小) **gāojí xiǎoxué (gāoxiǎo)** higher primary school (Grades 5 and 6)

高级中学 (高中) **gāojí zhōngxué (gāozhōng)** senior high school

高级旅馆 **gāojí lǚguǎn** exclusive hotel

高考 **gāokǎo** N university entrance examinations

NOTE: 高考 gāokǎo is the shortened form of 高等学校入学考试 gāoděng xuéxiào rùxué kǎoshì. In everyday use of the language the Chinese have a tendency to shorten a long-winding term into a two-character word, e.g. 股市 gǔshì from 股票市场 gǔpiào shìchǎng *share market*; 人大 Réndà from 人民代表大会 Rénmín Dàibiǎo Dàhuì *the People's Congress*.

高空 **gāokōng** N high altitude

高粱 **gāoliang** N sorghum

高明 **gāomíng** ADJ (of ideas or skills) brilliant, consummate

高尚 **gāoshàng** ADJ (of moral, behavior, etc.) noble, lofty

高烧 **gāoshāo** N high fever

发高烧 **fā gāoshāo** run a high fever

高深 **gāoshēn** ADJ (of learning) profound, recondite, obscure

高速 **gāosù** ADJ high-speed

高速公路 **gāosù gōnglù** superhighway, motorway

高兴 **gāoxìng** ADJ joyful, delighted, willing ■ 见到你，我很高兴。Jiàndào nǐ, wǒ hěn gāoxìng. *I'm delighted to see you.*

高血压 **gāoxuèyā** N high blood pressure

高压 **gāoyā** N high pressure

高压手段 **gāoyā shǒuduàn** high-handed measure

高雅 **gāoyǎ** ADJ elegant, refined

高原 **gāoyuán** N highland, plateau

高涨 **gāozhàng** V upsurge, rise

高中 **gāozhōng** N See 高级 gāojí.

膏 **gāo** N paste, ointment (See 牙膏 yágāo.)

糕 gāo

糕 gāo N cake (See 蛋糕 dàngāo, 糕糕 zāogāo.)

搞 gǎo V do, be engaged in (a trade, profession, etc.) ■ 搞了半天，你原来不是我要找的人。Gǎole bàntiān, nǐ yuánlái bú shì wǒ yào zhǎo de rén. *After so much ado, you turn out not to be the person I'm looking for.*

搞鬼 **gǎoguǐ** V play dirty tricks on the sly
搞活 **gǎohuó** V vitalize, invigorate

稿 gǎo N draft (of an essay, a painting, etc.)

稿子 **gǎozi** draft
打稿子 **dǎgǎozi** draw up a draft
初稿 **chūgǎo** initial draft
稿件 **gǎojiàn** N manuscript, contribution (to a magazine, a publisher, etc.)

告 gào V **1** tell, inform ■ 我告你一件事，你别对别人说。Wǒ gào nǐ yí jiàn shì, nǐ bié duì biérén shuō. *I'll tell you something. Don't tell others.* **2** sue, bring a legal action against ■ 有人告他偷东西。Yǒurén gào tā tōu dōngxi. *He was charged with theft.*

告别 **gàobié** V bid farewell to, part with ■ 我告别父母到中国来学汉语，已经八个月了。Wǒ gàobié fùmǔ dào Zhōngguó lái xué Hànyǔ, yǐjīng bā ge yuè le. *It is eight months since I bade my parents farewell and came to China to study Chinese.*
告辞 **gàocí** V bid farewell formally
告诫 **gàojiè** V warn sternly, exhort, admonish
告诉 **gàosu** V tell, inform ■ 这件事千万别告诉他。Zhè jiàn shì qiānwàn bié gàosu tā. *You mustn't tell him about this matter.*
告状 **gàozhuàng** V **1** file a lawsuit **2** bring a complaint (with someone's superior), report someone's wrongdoing

哥 gē N elder brother

哥哥 **gēge** N elder brother

歌 gē N song (首 shǒu) ■ 这首歌很好听，我想再听一遍。Zhè shǒu gē hěn hǎotīng, wǒ xiǎng zài tīng yí biàn. *This song is beautiful. I want to hear it once more.*
唱歌 **chànggē** sing a song ■ 你会唱中文歌吗？Nǐ huì chàng Zhōngwén gē ma? *Can you sing Chinese songs?*
歌词 **gēcí** N words of a song
歌剧 **gējù** N opera
歌剧院 **gējù yuàn** opera house
歌曲 **gēqǔ** N song
流行歌曲 **liúxíng gēqǔ** pop song
歌手 **gēshǒu** N singer
歌颂 **gēsòng** V sing the praise of, eulogize
歌星 **gēxīng** N pop star

歌咏 **gēyǒng** N singing
歌咏队 **gēyǒngduì** N singing group, chorus

胳 gē N arm

胳膊 **gēbo** N arm (只 zhī) ■ 这位举重运动员胳膊特别粗。Zhè wèi jǔzhòng yùndòngyuán gēbo tèbié cū. *This weightlifter has unusually thick arms.*

搁 gē V put, place ■ 你先把脏衣服搁在洗衣机里。Nǐ xiān bǎ zāng yīfu gē zài xǐyījī li. *You put the dirty clothes in the washing machine first.*

割 gē V cut ■ 夏天割草，冬天可以喂牛羊。Xiàtiān gē cǎo, dōngtiān kěyǐ wèi niúyáng. *Grass is cut in summer to feed cattle and sheep in winter.*

鸽 gē N dove (只 zhī)

鸽子 **gēzi** dove

革 gé V **1** expel, remove **2** transform, change

革命 **gémìng** N revolution (场 chǎng)
革新 **géxīn** V innovate, reform
技术革新 **jìshù géxīn** technological innovation

格 gé N pattern, standard

格格不入 **gé-gé-bú-rù** IDIOM like a square peg in a round hole, incompatible
格局 **géjú** N arrangement pattern, layout
格式 **géshì** N format, form
格外 **géwài** ADV exceptionally, unusually

隔 gé V separate, partition ■ 隔一条江就是另一个国家。Gé yì tiáo jiāng jiù shì lìng yí ge guójiā. *Beyond the river is another country.*
隔壁 **gébì** N next door ■ 我们家隔壁住着一对老夫妻。Wǒmen jiā gébì zhùzhe yí duì lǎo fūqī. *Next door to our home lives an old couple.*
隔阂 **géhé** N feelings of alienation or estrangement, often caused by misunderstanding
消除隔阂 **xiāochú géhé** banish feelings of estrangement by clearing up a misunderstanding
隔绝 **géjué** V be completely cut off, be isolated
与世隔绝 **yǔ shì géjué** be isolated from the outside world
隔离 **gélí** V isolate (a patient, a criminal), quarantine
隔离病房 **gélí bìngfáng** isolation ward

个 gè TRAD 個 M. WD (the most common measure word)
一个人 **yí ge rén** a person
两个苹果 **liǎng ge píngguǒ** two apples
三个工厂 **sān ge gōngchǎng** three factories

NOTE: 个 gè can be used as a "default" measure word, i.e. if you do not know the correct measure word to go with a noun, you can use this one. It is normally pronounced in the neutral tone.

个别 gèbié ADJ 1 very few, exceptional ■ 这是个别现象。Zhè shì gèbié xiànxiàng. *This is an isolated case.* 2 individual, one-to-one ■ 对学习特别困难的学生，老师个别辅导。Duì xuéxí tèbié kùnnán de xuésheng, lǎoshī gèbié fǔdǎo. *The teacher gives individual tutoring to students with special difficulties.*

个儿 gèr N size (of a person)
高个儿 gāogèr tall guy

NOTE: 个儿 gèr is only used in an informal situation.

个人 gèrén N 1 individual ■ 个人利益和集体利益产生矛盾时，怎么处理? Gèrén lìyì hé jítǐ lìyì chǎnshēng máodùn shí, zénme chùlǐ? *How should we handle cases where there is a conflict between an individual's interest and the collective interest?* 2 personal ■ 这是我个人的意见，不代表公司。Zhè shì wǒ gèrén de yìjiàn, bú dàibiǎo gōngsī. *This is my personal opinion and it does not represent that of the company.*

个人所得税 gèrénsuǒdé shuì personal income tax
个人隐私 gèrén yǐnsī personal and confidential matter, privacy
个体 gètǐ N individual
个性 gèxìng N personality
个性开朗 gèxìng kāilǎng an outgoing personality
个子 gèzi N height and size (of a person), build ■ 他因为营养不良，个子很小。Tā yīnwèi yíngyǎng bùliáng, gèzi hěn xiǎo. *Due to malnutrition, he is of small build.*

各 gè PRON each, every ■ 爸爸妈妈各有主张，他不知道该听谁的。Bàba māma gè yǒu zhǔzhāng, tā bù zhīdào gāi tīng shuí de. *Dad and mom each have their own views. He doesn't know whom to listen to.*

各别 gèbié ADV individually
各别会见 gèbié huìjiàn meet individually
各别情况 gèbié qíngkuàng isolated case
各行各业 gè-háng-gè-yè N every trade and profession
各式各样 gè-shì-gè-yàng ADJ all kinds of, of every description
各式各样的电子产品 gèshì gèyàng de diànzǐ chǎnpǐn all kinds of electronic products
各种 gè zhǒng ADJ all kinds of
各自 gèzì PRON each
各自为政 gè zì wéi zhèng each doing things

in his/her/their own way, administer autonomously

给 gěi TRAD 給 I V give, provide ■ 在我写论文的过程中，王老师给了我很多指导。Zài wǒ xiě lùnwén de guòchéng zhōng, Wáng lǎoshī gěile wǒ hěn duō zhǐdǎo. *In the course of writing this thesis, Teacher Wang gave me a great deal of guidance.* II PREP for, to ■ 她给我们做了一顿很好吃的中国饭。Tā gěi wǒmen zuòle yí dùn hěn hǎochī de Zhōngguó fàn. *She cooked us a delicious Chinese meal.*

给以 gěiyǐ V be given
给以支持 gěiyǐ zhīchí be given support

根 gēn I N root ■ 这棵树非常大，根一定很深。Zhè kē shù fēicháng dà, gēn yídìng hěn shēn. *This tree is very big. Its roots must be deep.* II M. WD (for long, thin things)
一根筷子 yì gēn kuàizi a chopstick
根本 gēnběn I N essence, what is fundamental II ADJ essential, fundamental, basic ■ 我们不能头痛医头，脚痛医脚，而必须找到一个根本的解决方法。Wǒmen bù néng tóutòng yī tóu, jiǎotòng yī jiǎo, ér bìxū zhǎodào yí ge gēnběn de jiějué fāngfǎ. *We cannot just take temporary and cosmetic measures, but must find a fundamental solution.*
根据 gēnjù I V do according to, on the basis of ■ 我们根据最新情况，对计划作了修改。Wǒmen gēnjù zuìxīn qíngkuàng, duì jìhuà zuòle xiūgǎi. *We have amended our plan according to the latest situation.* II N grounds, basis ■ 你对我的批评没有根据。Nǐ duì wǒ de pīpíng méiyǒu gēnjù. *Your criticism of me is groundless.*
根深蒂固 gēnshēn dìgù IDIOM deep-rooted, ingrained
根深蒂固的种族偏见 gēnshēn dìgùde zhǒngzú piānjiàn deep-rooted racial prejudice
根源 gēnyuán N root cause, origin
宗教的根源 zōngjiào de gēnyuán the root cause of religion

跟 gēn I V follow II PREP with ■ 老师: "请大家跟我念。" Lǎoshī: "Qǐng dàjiā gēn wǒ niàn." *Teacher: "Read after me, please."*
跟上 gēnshàng V catch up with, keep abreast with
跟前 gēnqián N near, nearby
跟随 gēnsuí V Same as 跟 gēn (= follow)
跟头 gēntou N 1 fall
跌跟头 diēgēntou have a fall, fall down 2 somersault
翻跟头 fāngēntou do a somersault
跟…一起 gēn...yìqǐ PREP together with ...
跟踪 gēnzōng V follow the tracks of, trail, shadow, stalk

耕 gēng

发现被人跟踪 fāxiàn bèi rén gēnzōng find oneself be followed

耕 gēng v plough

耕地 gēngdì I v plough the field II N farmland
可耕地 kěgēngdì arable land
耕种 gēngzhòng v farm, raise crops

更 gēng v change

更改 gēnggǎi v change, alter
更换 gēnghuàn v replace
更换旧电脑 gēnghuàn jiù diànnǎo replace old computer(s)
更新 gēngxīn v renew, replace
设备更新 shèbèi gēngxīn renewal of equipment
更正 gēngzhèng v make corrections
更正错误的数据 gēngzhèng cuòwù de shùjù correct wrong data

梗 gěng N stem, stalk

更 gèng ADV still more, even more ■ 美国很大，加拿大更大。Měiguó hěn dà, Jiānádà gèng dà. America is big and Canada is even bigger.
更加 gèngjiā ADV Same as 更 gèng

工 gōng N 1 work 2 worker

汽车修理工 qìchē xiūlǐ gōng automobile repairman (→ mechanic)
工厂 gōngchǎng N factory, works (座 zuò, 家 jiā) ■ 这座工厂生产什么? Zhè zuò gōngchǎng shēngchǎn shénme? What does this factory make?
办工厂 bàn gōngchǎng run a factory
建工厂 jiàn gōngchǎng build a factory
开工厂 kāi gōngchǎng set up a factory
工程 gōngchéng N 1 project, construction work (项 xiàng) ■ 这项工程从设计、施工到完成一共花了三年半时间。Zhè xiàng gōngchéng cóng shèjì, shīgōng dào wánchéng yígòng huāle sānnián bàn shíjiān. From design, construction till completion, this project took three and a half years. 2 engineering
土木工程 tǔmù gōngchéng civil engineering
水利工程 shuǐlì gōngchéng water conservancy project
工程师 gōngchéngshī N engineer (位 wèi)
总工程师 zǒnggōngchéngshī chief engineer
工地 gōngdì N worksite, construction site
工夫 gōngfu N 1 time ■ 他用了一个晚上的工夫把报告修改了一遍。Tā yòngle yí ge wǎnshang de gōngfu bǎ bàogào xiūgǎile yí biàn. He spent an entire evening revising this report. 2 efforts

工会 gōnghuì N labor union, trade union
工具 gōngjù N tool (件 jiàn) ■ 没有合适的工具, 这活儿没法干。Méiyǒu héshì de gōngjù, zhè huór méifǎ gàn. This job can't be done without the proper tools.
工具箱 gōngjùxiāng tool box
工龄 gōnglíng N length of service
工钱 gōngqián N Same as 工资 gōngzī
工人 gōngrén N workman, worker ■ 这道门坏了, 要请工人来修一下。Zhè dào mén huài le, yào qǐng gōngrén lái xiū yíxià. Something is wrong with this door. We should ask a worker to fix it.
当工人 dāng gōngrén be a worker
工伤 gōngshāng N industrial injury
工伤事故 gōngshāng shìgù industrial injury industrial accident
工事 gōngshì N defense works
工薪阶层 gōngxīn jiēcéng N wage or salary earners
工序 gōngxù N industrial procedure
工业 gōngyè N (manufacturing) industry ■ 这个国家没有汽车工业。Zhège guójiā méiyǒu qìchē gōngyè. This country does not have an automobile industry.
轻工业 qīnggōngyè light industry
新兴工业 xīnxīng gōngyè sunrise industry
重工业 zhònggōngyè heavy industry
工艺品 gōngyìpǐn N handicraft (件 jiàn)
工资 gōngzī N wages, salary ■ 你们是每月发工资, 还是每两个星期发工资? Nǐmen shì měi yuè fā gōngzī, háishì měi liǎng ge xīngqī fā gōngzī? Do you pay wages every month or every fortnight?
工作 gōngzuò I v work ■ 我们一星期工作五天。Wǒmen yì xīngqī gōngzuò wǔ tiān. We work five days in a week. II N work, job (件 jiàn) ■ 这件工作不太难。Zhè jiàn gōngzuò bú tài nán. This job is not too difficult.
工作餐 gōngzuò cān N staff meal

功 gōng N 1 skill 2 achievement, merit

功夫 gōngfu N 1 Same as 工夫 gōngfu (= efforts) 2 martial arts
功夫片 gōngfu piàn martial arts film
练功夫 liàn gōngfu practice martial arts ■ 每天一大早他就起来练功夫。Měitiān yí dà zǎo tā jiù qǐlái liàn gōngfu. Every day he gets up in the early morning and practices martial arts.
功绩 gōngjì N merits and achievements
功课 gōngkè N 1 schoolwork ■ 他功课不错, 考试成绩总是很好。Tā gōngkè búcuò, kǎoshì chéngjì zǒngshì hěn hǎo. His schoolwork is quite good, and his examination results are always very good. 2 homework
做功课 zuò gōngkè do homework.
功劳 gōngláo N contribution, credit ■ 没有功

劳，也有苦劳。Méiyǒu gōnglao, yě yǒu kǔláo. *I've worked hard, even if my contributions are not great.*

功能 **gōngnéng** N function
功能键 **gōngnéngjiàn** function key(s)

功效 **gōngxiào** N effect, efficacy

攻 **gōng** V attack

攻读 **gōngdú** V study hard, specialize
攻读博士学位 **gōngdúbóshì xuéwèi** work hard to gain a Ph.D. degree

攻克 **gōngkè** V attack and capture (a city, a fortress, etc.)

攻心 **gōngxīn** V win the hearts and minds of ■ 攻心为上。Gōngxīn wéi shàng. *To win the hearts and minds is of primary importance.*
攻心战 **gōngxīnzhàn** psychological warfare

公 1 **gōng** ADJ male (of certain animals)

公 2 **gōng** ADJ 1 public ■ 天下为公。Tiānxià wéi gōng. *The world is for public interests.* (→ *The world is for the people.*) 2 open, public 3 fair

公安 **gōng'ān** N public security
公安局 **gōng'ān jú** public security bureau (police bureau)
公安人员 **gōng'ān rényuán** public security personnel, policeman

NOTE: See note on 警察 jǐngchá.

公报 **gōngbào** N communiqué, bulletin
公布 **gōngbù** V make a public announcement, publish
公尺 **gōngchǐ** M. WD (unit of measurement) meter
公道 **gōngdào** ADJ fair, just, impartial
公费 **gōngfèi** N (at) public expense
公费医疗 **gōngfèi yīliáo** medical care paid by the government (→ *free medical care for government officials and others*)
公分 **gōngfēn** M. WD centimeter
公告 **gōnggào** N announcement (by a government agency)
公共 **gōnggòng** ADJ public, communal ■ 这是一座公共图书馆，任何人都可以进去看书。Zhè shì yí zuò gōnggòng túshūguǎn, rènhé rén dōu kěyǐ jìnqù kàn shū. *This is a public library. Anybody can go on and read.*
公共关系 **gōnggòng guānxì** N public relations
公共汽车 **gōnggòng qìchē** bus

NOTE: The word for *bus* in Taiwan is 公车 gōngchē. In Hong Kong, *bus* is 巴士 bāshì, obviously a transliteration of the English word *bus*.

公斤 **gōngjīn** M. WD kilogram
公关 **gōngguān** N (shortening of 公共关系 gōnggòng guānxì) public relations
公开 **gōngkāi** I ADJ open, public ■ 他发表公开谈话，反对政府的计划。Tā fābiǎo gōngkāi tánhuà, fǎnduì zhèngfǔ de jìhuà. *He gave a public talk opposing the government plan.* II V make public, reveal ■ 希望你能公开自己的观点。Xīwàng nǐ néng gōngkāi zìjǐ de guāndiǎn. *I hope you will make your views known.*
公里 **gōnglǐ** N kilometer
公路 **gōnglù** N public road, highway (条 tiáo)
高速公路 **gāosù gōnglù** motorway, expressway
公民 **gōngmín** N citizen ■ 你拿哪个国家的护照，你就是那个国家的公民。Nǐ ná nǎge guójiā de hùzhào, nǐ jiù shì nàge guójiā de gōngmín. *You are a citizen of the country whose passport you hold.*
公平 **gōngpíng** ADJ fair, impartial
买卖公平 **mǎimai gōngpíng** fair trade
公顷 **gōngqǐng** N hectare (= 10,000 square meters)
公然 **gōngrán** ADV brazenly, openly
公然撒谎 **gōngrán sāhuǎng** tell a bare-faced lie
公认 **gōngrèn** V generally acknowledge, universally accept
公社 **gōngshè** N commune
公式 **gōngshì** N formula
数学公式 **shùxué gōngshì** mathematics formula
公司 **gōngsī** N commercial firm, company, corporation (家 jiā) ■ 贵公司是哪一年成立的? Guì gōngsī shì nǎ yì nián chénglì de? *In which year was your company founded?*
分公司 **fēn gōngsī** branch of a company
总公司 **zǒng gōngsī** company headquarters
公务 **gōngwù** N public affairs, official duty
公务员 **gōngwùyuán** N civil servant, government office holders
公用 **gōngyòng** ADJ for public use
公用电话 **gōngyòng diànhuà** N public telephone, payphone ■ 现在很多人都有手机，公用电话不象从前那样重要了。Xiànzài hěn duō rén dōu yǒu shǒujī, gōngyòng diànhuà búxiàng yǐqián nàyàng zhòngyào le. *Nowadays many people have cell phones, so public telephones are not as important as before.*
公元 **gōngyuán** N of the Christian/common era, AD (Anno Domini)
公元前 **gōngyuán qián** BC (before Christ), BCE (before the Christian/common era) ■ 他生于公元前二十五年，死于公元三十一年。Tā shēng yú gōngyuán qián èrshíwǔ nián, sǐ yú

公园 gōngyuán

gōngyuán sānshíyī nián. *He was born in 25 BC and died in AD 31.*

公园 **gōngyuán** N public garden, park (座 zuò)

公约 **gōngyuē** N 1 agreement, convention, pact
2 pledge
　服务公约 **fúwù gōngyuē** service pledge

公债 **gōng zhài** N government bonds
　公债券 **gōngzhài quàn** bond

公证 **gōngzhèng** V notarize
　公证处 **gōngzhèngchù** notary office
　公证人 **gōngzhèngrén** notary public, notary

恭 gōng ADJ deferential, reverent

恭敬 **gōngjìng** ADJ very respectful, deferential

供 gōng V supply ■ 供大于求。Gōng dà yú qiú. *Supply exceeds demand.* ■ 供不应求。Gōng bú yìng qiú. *Supply falls short of demand.*

供给 **gōngjǐ** V supply, provide ■ 对于经济特别困难的学生，政府供给生活费。Duìyú jīngjì tèbié kùnnan de xuésheng, zhèngfǔ gōngjǐ shēnghuófèi. *The government provided a living stipend to students with special financial difficulties.*

NOTE: 给 in 供给 is pronounced as jǐ, not its usual gěi.

宫 gōng N palace

宫殿 **gōngdiàn** palace
王宫 **wánggōng** royal palace

弓 gōng I N bow II V bend, arch

弓箭 **gōngjiàn** bow and arrows

汞 gǒng N mercury

巩 gǒng TRAD 鞏 V consolidate

巩固 **gǒnggù** I V consolidate, strengthen ■ 我们这次会谈是为了巩固和发展我们之间的合作关系。Wǒmen zhè cì huìtán shì wèile gǒnggù hé fāzhǎn wǒmen zhī jiān de hézuò guānxi. *The purpose of our talks is to strengthen and develop cooperation.* II ADJ solid, firm· ■ 他们夫妻之间关系很巩固。Tāmen fūqī zhī jiān guānxi hěn gǒnggù. *Their marital relationship has a solid foundation.*

拱 gǒng N arch

拱门 **gǒngmén** arched gate, arched door

共 gòng ADV 1 altogether, in total ■ 那座大学共有学生一万三千五百四十名。Nà zuò dàxué gòng yǒu xuésheng yíwàn sānqiān wǔbǎi

sìshí míng. *That university has a total student population of 13,540.* 2 jointly, together (used only in writing)

共产党 **gòngchǎndǎng** N communist party

共和国 **gònghéguó** N republic ■ 什么样的国家才是真正的共和国？Shénmeyàng de guójiā cái shì zhēnzhèng de gònghéguó? *What kind of country is a genuine republic?*

共计 **gòngjì** V total, add up to

共鸣 **gòngmíng** N 1 resonance 2 sympathetic response
　引起共鸣 **yǐnqǐ gòngmíng** find a ready echo

共青团 **Gòngqīngtuán** N (shortening from 中国共产主义青年团 Zhōngguó gòngchǎnzhǔyì qīngniántuán) the Chinese Communist Youth League

共识 **gòngshí** N common understanding
　达成共识 **dáchéng gòngshí** achieve common understanding

共同 **gòngtóng** I ADJ common, shared II ADV together, jointly ■ 我们之间缺乏共同语言，就不必多谈了。Wǒmen zhī jiān quēfá gòngtóng yǔyán, jiù bú bì duō tán le. *As we do not have a common language, there is no need for further conversation.*

共性 **gòngxìng** N generality, common characteristics

供 gòng V 1 confess, own up

口供 **kǒugòng** (criminal) confession
2 lay (offerings)

贡 gòng TRAD 貢 N tribute

贡献 **gòngxiàn** I V contribute, dedicate II N contribution, devotion, dedication
　为…作出贡献 **wèi…zuòchu gòngxiàn** make a contribution to .... ■ 这位科学家为环境保护贡献了自己的一生。Zhè wèi kēxuéjiā wèi huánjìng bǎohù gòngxiàn le zìjǐ de yìshēng. *This scientist dedicated his life to environmental protection.*

勾 gōu V 1 strike out with a pen 2 delineate (the outline of a drawing) 3 induce, evoke

勾结 **gōujié** V collaborate secretly with (on criminal matters)

沟 gōu TRAD 溝 N ditch, trench (条 tiáo)

沟通 **gōutōng** V link up, connect
　沟通意见 **gōutōng yìjiàn** exchange ideas

钩 gōu TRAD 鉤 N hook (只 zhī)

钩子 **gōuzi** hook

狗 gǒu N dog (只 zhī, 条 tiáo)

母狗 **mǔ gǒu** bitch
小狗 **xiǎo gǒu** puppy

构 **gòu** TRAD 構 v construct, form

构成 **gòuchéng** v make up, form ■ 远山近
水构成了美丽的风景。Yuǎn-shān-jìn-shuǐ
gòngchéngle měilì de fēngjǐng. *Hills in the background and a lake in the foreground make up a
beautiful landscape.*
构件 **gòujiàn** N component, part
构思 **gòusī** v (of writers or artists) work out the
plot of a story or composition of a picture
构造 **gòuzào** N structure ■ 小小的手机构造
极其复杂。Xiǎoxiǎo de shǒujī gòuzào jíqí fùzá.
*The cell phone, small as it is, has an extremely
complex structure.*

购 **gòu** v purchase

购买 **gòumǎi** v purchase
购买采矿设备 **gòumǎi cǎi kuàng shèbèi**
purchase mining equipment
购买力 **gòumǎilì** purchasing power

够 **gòu** ADJ enough, sufficient ■ 够了, 够了, 谢
谢你! Gòu le, gòu le, xièxie nǐ! *That's enough.
Thank you!*

孤 **gū** ADJ lonely

孤儿 **gū'ér** N orphan
孤儿院 **gū'éryuàn** orphanage
孤立 **gūlì** ADJ isolated, without support or
sympathy

辜 **gū** v (as in 辜负 **gūfù**)

辜负 **gūfù** v fail to live up to, let down
辜负父母的期望 **gūfù fùmǔ de qīwàng** fail
to live up to parents' expectations

估 **gū** v estimate

估计 **gūjì** I v estimate, reckon, size up ■ 我估计
整个工程要花三百万元。Wǒ gūjì zhěngge gōng-
chéng yào huā sānbǎiwàn yuán. *I estimate the
entire project will cost three million yuan* II N estimate, approximate calculation, appraisal ■ 根
据专家估计, 今年经济增长可达百分之五。Gēnjù
zhuānjiā gūjì, jīnnián jīngjì zēngzhǎng kě dá
bǎifēn zhī wǔ. *According to expert estimates, economic growth will reach five percent this year.*

姑 **gū** N aunt, woman

姑姑 **gūgu** N Same as 姑妈 **gūmā**, especially as
a colloquialism
姑妈 **gūmā** N father's sister, aunt

姑母 **gūmǔ** N Same as 姑妈 **gūmā**, especially
used in writing.
姑娘 **gūniang** N unmarried young woman, girl,
lass ■ 那个姑娘是谁家的孩子? Nàge gūniang
shì shuí jiā de háizi? *Whose child is that girl?*
大姑娘 **dàgūniang** young woman (usually
unmarried), lass
小姑娘 **xiǎo gūniang** little girl

NOTE: 姑娘 **gūniang** is a colloquial word. When
used to mean *unmarried young lady*, 姑娘
gūniang is used together with the word 小伙子
xiǎohuǒzi (young man), e.g. ■ 姑娘小伙子都爱
热闹。Gūniang xiǎohuǒzi dōu ài rènao. *Young
people all like having fun.*

姑且 **gūqiě** ADV tentatively, for the time being

菇 **gū** N mushroom

香菇 **xiānggū** dried mushroom

古 **gǔ** ADJ ancient ■ 中国是一个文明古国, 有
很多古建筑。Zhōngguó shì yí ge wénmíng
gǔguó, yǒu hěnduō gǔ jiànzhù. *China is a
country of ancient civilization and boasts a large
number of ancient buildings.*
古代 **gǔdài** N ancient times
古典 **gǔdiǎn** ADJ classical
古典音乐 **gǔdiǎn yīnyuè** classical music
古董 **gǔdǒng** N antique, old curio (件 jiàn)
老古董 **lǎogǔdǒng** old fogey (个 gè)
古怪 **gǔguài** ADJ weird, queer
行为古怪 **xíngwéi gǔguài** behave strangely
古迹 **gǔjì** N historic site, place of historic interest ■ 这个古迹每年吸引几万人参观。Zhège
gǔjì měi nián xīyǐn jǐ wàn rén cānguān. *This
historic site attracts tens of thousands of visitors
every year.*
古老 **gǔlǎo** ADJ ancient, time-honored ■ 中国
的苏州有两千五百多年的历史, 真是一座古老
的城市。Zhōngguó de Sūzhōu yǒu liǎngqiān
wǔbǎi duō nián de lìshǐ, zhēn shì yí zuò gǔlǎo
de chéngshì. *The city of Suzhou in China has a
history of over 2,500 years. It is indeed an ancient
city.*

鼓 **gǔ** N drum

鼓吹 **gǔchuī** v advocate, preach (usually wrong
and harmful ideas)
鼓励 **gǔlì** v encourage ■ 新加坡政府鼓励华人说
华语。Xīnjiāpō zhèngfǔ gǔlì Huárén shuō Huáyǔ.
*The Singapore government encourages ethnic
Chinese to speak Mandarin.*
物质鼓励 **wùzhì gǔlì** material incentive
精神鼓励 **jīngshén gǔlì** moral incentive,
moral encouragement

鼓舞 gǔwǔ

鼓舞 **gǔwǔ** v inspire, fire up … with enthusiasm, hearten ■ 这个消息真是鼓舞人心! Zhège xiāoxi zhēn shì gǔwǔ rénxīn. *This news is really inspiring!*

鼓掌 **gǔzhǎng** v applaud

骨 gǔ N bone

骨头 **gǔtou** N bone (根 gēn)
骨干 **gǔgàn** N backbone (denoting people)
公司的骨干 gōngsī de gǔgàn the backbone (most important staff) of a company
骨肉 **gǔròu** N one's flesh and blood
骨折 **gǔzhé** v fracture a bone

股 gǔ N share, stock (in a company)

股东 **gǔdōng** N shareholder, stockholder
股份 **gǔfèn** N share, stock
股票 **gǔpiào** N share, stock (份 fèn) ■ 他上个月买了这家公司十万股票。Tā shàngge yuè mǎile zhè jiā gōngsī shíwàn gǔpiào. *He bought 10,000 shares of the company last month.*
股市 **gǔshì** N share market

谷 gǔ TRAD 穀 N grain, cereal

谷子 **gǔzi** grain (粒 lì)
谷物 **gǔwù** N grain, cereal (collectively)
谷物价格 gǔwù jiàgé grain prices

雇 gù TRAD 僱 v employ, hire

雇佣 **gùyōng** v hire, employ

NOTE: 雇佣 gùyōng is used when hiring low-rank employees, e.g. unskilled workers. To employ a professional, the verb to use is 聘用 pìnyòng.

雇员 **gùyuán** N employee, staff member

故 gù I ADJ old, former II ADV on purpose, deliberately

故事 **gùshi** N story, tale
讲故事 jiǎng gùshi tell a story ■ 他每天晚上都给孩子讲一个故事。Tā měitiān wǎnshang dōu gěi háizi jiǎng yí ge gùshi. *He tells his child a story every evening.*
听故事 tīng gùshi listen to a story
故乡 **gùxiāng** N native place, hometown
故意 **gùyì** ADV deliberately, intentionally, on purpose ■ 他犯的错误是无意的, 不是故意的。Tā fàn de cuòwù shì wúyì de, búshì gùyì de. *He did not commit this mistake deliberately, but by accident.*
故障 **gùzhàng** N breakdown (of a machine)
排除故障 páichú gùzhàng troubleshooting

顾 gù TRAD 顧 v attend to, care for ■ 他忙得顾不上吃饭。Tā máng de gù bu shàng chīfàn.

He was so busy that he did not have time for meals.

顾此失彼 **gùcǐ shībǐ** IDIOM pay too much attention to one thing at the expense of another
顾客 **gùkè** N customer, client (位 wèi)
顾虑 **gùlù** v have misgivings, worry
顾虑重重 gùlù chóngchóng be filled with misgivings
顾问 **gùwèn** N advisor, consultant (位 wèi)

固 gù I ADJ secure, solid II v secure, consolidate, strengthen

固定 **gùdìng** v fix, make immovable
固定资产 gùdìng zīchǎn fixed assets
固然 **gùrán** CONJ granted (that), although
固体 **gùtǐ** N solid matter, solid
固有 **gùyǒu** ADJ inherent, innate
固执 **gùzhí** ADJ obstinate, stubborn
固执己见 gùzhí jǐjiàn stubbornly stick to one's opinions, pigheaded

瓜 guā N melon, gourd (只 zhī)

瓜子 **guāzǐ** N melon seeds (颗 kē)

刮 guā v (of a wind) blow ■ 这儿冬天经常刮西北风。Zhèr dōngtiān jīngcháng guā xīběi fēng. *A northwestern wind often blows here in winter.*

寡 guǎ ADJ 1 few, insufficient 2 widowed

孤儿寡母 gū'ér guǎmǔ orphan and widow
寡妇 **guǎfu** N widow

挂 guà TRAD 掛 v hang ■ 墙上挂着一幅世界地图。Qiáng shang guàzhe yì fú shìjiè dìtú. *A map of the world hung on the wall.*

挂钩 **guàgōu** v hook up, couple together
挂号 **guàhào** v register (at a hospital) ■ 在中国看病的第一件事就是挂号。Zài Zhōngguó kànbìng de dì-yí jiàn shì jiù shì guàhào. *In China, when you go to see a doctor the first thing to do is to register.*
挂号费 **guàhào fèi** registration fee, doctor's consultation fee
挂号处 **guàhào chù** registration office

NOTE: In China if you are sick you go to a hospital where doctors work in their specialist departments, e.g. internal medicine, gynecology and dermatology. 挂号 guàhào means *to tell a receptionist which department you want to go to and pay the consultation fee*. Dentistry is usually one of the departments and a dentist is generally considered just another doctor.

挂念 **guàniàn** v miss and worry about (a person)

乖 guāi ADJ (of children) be good, be well-behaved
乖孩子 guāi háizi a well-behaved child

拐 guǎi v turn, make a turn ■ 往前走，再向左拐，就是火车站。Wàng qián zǒu, zài xiàng zuǒ guǎi, jiù shì huǒchēzhàn. Walk straight on, then turn left, and you will find the railway station.
拐弯 guǎiwān v turn a corner
拐弯抹角 guǎiwān mòjiǎo IDIOM talk in a roundabout way, beat around the bush

怪 guài I ADJ strange, odd, queer ■ 昨天我碰到了怪事。Zuótiān wǒ pèngdàole guài shì. Something strange happened to me yesterday. II v blame ■ 你们别怪来怪去的，看看该怎么办吧。Nǐmen bié guài-lái-guài-qù de, kànkan gāi zénme bàn ba. Don't blame each other. Try to find out what should be done.
怪不得 guàibudé ADV no wonder, so that's why

关 guān TRAD 關 v 1 close ■ 你离开的时候，请把灯关掉，把门关上。Nǐ líkāi de shíhou, qǐng bǎ dēng guāndiào, bǎ mén guānshàng. When you leave, please turn off the lights and close the door. 2 turn off, switch off
把电灯/电视机/录音机/机器关掉 bǎ diàndēng/diànshì jī/ lùyīnjī/jīqì guāndiào turn off the lights/TV/recorder/machine 3 v concern, involve
关闭 guānbì v close down, shut down
关闭机场 guānbì jīchǎng shut down the airport
关怀 guānhuái v be kindly concerned about, show loving care to
关键 guānjiàn N what is crucial or critical ■ 一家公司的成功，关键在于人力资源。Yì jiā gōngsī de chénggōng, guānjiàn zàiyú rénlì zīyuán. The success of a company lies in its human resources.
关键词 guānjiàncí keyword
关节炎 guānjiéyán N arthritis
风湿性关节炎 fēngshīxìng guānjiéyán rheumatic arthritis
关切 guānqiè v be deeply concerned
关头 guāntóu N juncture, moment
在紧要关头 zài jǐnyào guāntóu at a critical juncture, at a crucial moment
关系 guānxi I N connection, relation ■ 我和他只是一般朋友关系。我希望保持这种关系。Wǒ hé tā zhǐ shì yìbān péngyou guānxi. Wǒ xīwàng bǎochí zhè zhǒng guānxi. He and I are merely ordinary friends, and I intend to keep it that way.
和…有关系 hé...yǒu guānxi have something to do with
没(有)关系 méi(yǒu)guānxi it doesn't matter, it's OK ■ 这两件事有没有关系? Zhè liǎng jiàn shì yǒu méiyǒu guānxi? Is there any connec-

tion between these two matters? (→ Are these two matters related?)
II v affect, have bearing on ■ 能不能考上大学，关系到青年人的前途。Néng bù néng kǎoshàng dàxué, guānxi dào qīngniánrén de qiántú. Whether a young person passes the university entrance examination or not has bearing on his/her future.
关心 guānxīn v be concerned about, care for ■ 妈妈总是关心孩子的健康。Māma zǒngshì guānxīn háizi de jiànkāng. Mothers are always concerned about their children's health.
关于 guānyú PREP about, on
关照 guānzhào v 1 look after, take care of ■ 这里的工作请你关照一下。Zhèlǐ de gōngzuò qǐng nǐ guānzhào yíxià. Please keep an eye on the work here. 2 notify, inform ■ 我已经关照服务员叫出租汽车了。Wǒ yǐjīng guānzhào fúwùyuán jiào chūzū qìchē le. I've already asked the attendant to call a taxi.

NOTE: "请你多关照。" "Qǐng nǐ duō guānzhào." is often said by someone who has just arrived or started working in a place, to someone who has been working there longer. It is a polite expression meaning something to the effect of "I'd appreciate your guidance."

观 guān TRAD 觀 I v look at, observe II N view, outlook
观测 guāncè v observe
观测市场动向 guāncè shìchǎng dòngxiàng pay close attention to the market trend
观察 guānchá v observe, watch ■ 对于市场情况，他观察得很仔细。Duìyú shìchǎng qíngkuàng, tā guānchá de hěn zǐxì. He watches the market very carefully.
观察员 guāncháyuán observer (at a conference, especially an international conference)
观点 guāndiǎn N viewpoint, view ■ 对问题有不同的观点，是很正常的。Duì wèntí yǒu bù tóng de guāndiǎn, shì hěn zhèngcháng de. It is normal to have different views on an issue.
观光 guānguāng v go sightseeing, visit and observe
观看 guānkàn v watch (a theatrical performance, sports event)
观念 guānniàn N concept, sense
是非观念 shìfēi guānniàn the sense of what is right and what is wrong
观赏 guānshǎng v view and admire (beautiful flowers, rare animals, etc.)
观赏野生动物 guānshǎng yěshēng dòngwù observe wild animals
观众 guānzhòng N audience (in a theater, on TV, etc.), spectator

官 guān

官 guān N (government) official ■ 很多中国人想当官。Hěn duō Zhōngguórén xiǎng dāng guān. *Many Chinese want to be officials.*

NOTE: 官 guān is a colloquial word. For more formal occasions, use 官员 guānyuán.

官方 guānfāng ADJ official
官方消息 guānfāng xiāoxi official news, news released by the authorities
官僚 guānliáo N bureaucrat
官僚主义 guānliáozhǔyì bureaucracy
官员 guānyuán N official (位 wèi) ■ 这位官员很负责任。Zhè wèi guānyuán hěn fùzérèn. *This official has a strong sense of responsibility.*

NOTE: See note on 干部 gànbù.

棺 guān N coffin

棺材 guāncái coffin (口 kǒu)

管 1 guǎn V be in charge of, take care (of) ■ 王老师管一年级的教学。Wáng lǎoshī guǎn yī-niánjí de jiàoxué. *Teacher Wang is in charge of the first-year courses.*
管理 guǎnlǐ V manage, administer ■ 他管理工厂很有办法。Tā guǎnlǐ gōngchǎng hěn yǒu bànfǎ. *He is resourceful and efficient in managing the factory.*
商业管理 shāngyè guǎnlǐ business administration
管辖 guǎnxiá V have jurisdiction over

管 2 guǎn N tube, pipe

管子 guǎnzi tube, pipe (根 gēn)
管道 guǎndào N pipeline, conduit

馆 guǎn TRAD 館 N building (for a specific purpose)

饭馆 fànguǎn restaurant
体育馆 tǐyùguǎn gymnasium
图书馆 túshūguǎn library
馆子 guǎnzi N restaurant (colloquial) (家 jiā)

冠 guàn N the best

冠军 guànjūn N champion, championship ■ 我们学校获得了全市中学生篮球邀请赛冠军。Wǒmen xuéxiào huòdéle quán shì zhōngxuéshēng lánqiú yāoqǐngsài guànjūn. *Our school has won the city high school basketball invitational tournament championship.*

贯 guàn V pass through

贯彻 guànchè V implement, carry out ■ 贯彻这项新政策，大约要半年时间。Guànchè zhè xiàng xīn zhèngcè, dàyuē yào bànnián shíjiān. *Implementing the new policy will take about half a year.*

惯 guàn I ADJ accustomed to II N custom, convention

惯例 guànlì N usual practice, convention
打破惯例 dǎpò guànlì break with convention
惯用语 guànyòngyǔ N idiomatic expression
惯于 guànyú V be used to, habitually
惯于撒谎 guànyú sāhuǎng be a habitual liar

灌 guàn V fill (water, air), pour

灌溉 guàngài V irrigate
灌木 guànmù N bush

罐 guàn N tin, jar

罐头 guàntou N can, tin
罐头食品 guàntou shípǐn canned food

光 1 guāng I N light ■ 发光的不一定是金子。Fā guāng de bù yídìng shì jīnzi. *All that glitters is not gold.*
灯光 dēngguāng lamplight
阳光 yángguāng sunlight
月光 yuèguāng moonlight
II ADJ smooth, shiny
光彩 guāngcǎi I N luster, splendor II ADJ honorable
觉得光彩 juéde guāngcǎi feel proud
光碟 guāngdié N compact disk (CD) (盘 pán)
光滑 guānghuá smooth, glossy
光辉 guānghuī I N brilliance, radiance ■ 云挡不住太阳的光辉。Yún dǎng bu zhù tàiyang de guānghuī. *The clouds cannot shut out the brilliance of the sunlight.* II ADJ brilliant, splendid ■ 他在医学研究上取得了光辉的成绩。Tā zài yīxué yánjiū shang qǔdéle guānghuī de chéngjì. *He achieved brilliant results in medical research.*
光亮 guāngliàng ADJ bright, shiny
光临 guānglín V (a polite expression) be present, come
欢迎光临! Huānyíng guānglín! You're cordially welcome! We welcome you.
光明 guāngmíng ADJ bright, promising ■ 只要努力就会有光明的前途。Zhǐyào nǔlì jiùhuì yǒu guāngmíng de qiántú. *If only you work hard, you will have a bright future.*
光荣 guāngróng ADJ glorious, honorable ■ 他代表全校参加这次比赛，是很光荣的。Tā dàibiǎo quánxiào cānjiā zhè cì bǐsài, shì hěn guāngróng de. *He represented the school in the competition, which was a great honor.*
光线 guāngxiàn N light, ray (道 dào)

光 2 guāng ADV only, sole ■ 光有钱就能幸福吗? Guāng yǒu qián jiù néng xìngfú ma? *Can money alone make you happy?*

光棍儿 **guānggùnr** N unmarried man, bachelor
打光棍儿 **dǎ guānggùnr** remain unmarried, be a bachelor

广 **guǎng** TRAD 廣 ADJ extensive, wide

广播 **guǎngbō** I V broadcast ■ 今天早上广播了一条重要新闻。**Jīntiān zǎoshang guǎngbōle yì tiáo zhòngyào xīnwén.** *A piece of important news was broadcast early this morning.* II N broadcasting ■ 这位老人每天都听新闻广播。**Zhè wèi lǎorén měitiān dōu tīng xīnwén guǎngbō.** *This old man listens to the news broadcast every day.*
广播电台 **guǎngbō diàntái** radio station
广播公司 **guǎngbō gōngsī** broadcasting company
英国广播公司 **Yīngguó Guǎngbō Gōngsī** the British Broadcasting Company (BBC)
广播员 **guǎngbōyuán** newsreader
广场 **guǎngchǎng** N square
广大 **guǎngdà** ADJ vast, extensive ■ 中国西北广大地区还没有充分开发。**Zhōngguó xīběi guǎngdà dìqū hái méiyǒu chōngfèn kāifā.** *The vast area of China's northwest is yet to be fully developed.*
广泛 **guǎngfàn** ADJ widespread, wide-ranging, extensive ■ 他们对市场进行了广泛的调查。**Tāmen duì shìchǎng jìnxíng le guǎngfàn de diàochá.** *They conducted an extensive market investigation.*
广告 **guǎnggào** N advertisement
广阔 **guǎngkuò** ADJ vast, wide ■ 中国东北有一片广阔的平原。**Zhōngguó dōngběi yǒu yí piàn guǎngkuò de píngyuán.** *China's northeast boasts a vast plain.*

逛 **guàng** V stroll, take a random walk

逛公园 **guàng gōngyuán** stroll in the park
逛街 **guàng jiē** stroll around the streets, do window shopping

瑰 **guī** as in 玫瑰 méigui

规 **guī** TRAD 規 N compass, regulation, rule

规定 **guīdìng** I V stipulate, prescribe ■ 政府规定，珍贵文物不能带出国。**Zhèngfǔ guīdìng, zhēnguì wénwù bù néng dàichū guó.** *The government stipulates that precious cultural relics may not be taken out of the country.* II N regulation
规范 **guīfàn** N standard, norm
符合规范 **fúhé guīfàn** meet the standard
规格 **guīgé** N specifications (of a product), norm
规划 **guīhuà** V 1 long-term program
五年发展规划 **wǔ nián fāzhǎn guīhuà** five-year development plan

2 draw up a long-term program
规矩 **guīju** I N rule, established practice
老规矩 **lǎoguīju** well-established practice
II ADJ well behaved, behave within the norm
规律 **guīlǜ** N law, regular pattern ■ 经济活动十分复杂，但是还是有规律的。**Jīngjì huódòng shífēn fùzá, dànshì háishì yǒu guīlǜ de.** *Economic activities are very complicated, but they also follow regular patterns.*
规模 **guīmó** N scale ■ 这次航空展览会规模很大。**Zhè cì hángkōng zhǎnlǎnhuì guīmó hěn dà.** *This is a large-scale air show.*
规则 **guīzé** N rule, regulation
交通规则 **jiāotōng guīzé** traffic regulations
游戏规则 **yóuxì guīzé** game rules
规章 **guīzhāng** N rules, regulations
规章制度 **guīzhāng zhìdù** rules and regulations (of an organization, an institution, etc.)

归 **guī** TRAD 歸 V return, go back to

归根结底 **guī-gēn-jié-dǐ** in the final analysis
归还 **guīhuán** V return, revert
归还原主 **guīhuán yuánzhǔ** be returned to the original owner
归结 **guījié** V sum up, put in a nutshell
归纳 **guīnà** V sum up, induce
归纳法 **guīnàfǎ** inductive method

硅 **guī** N silicon

硅谷 **guīgǔ** silicon valley

龟 **guī** N turtle

海龟 **hǎiguī** sea turtle

闺 **guī** N boudoir, a lady's chamber

闺女 **guīnǚ** N 1 girl, maiden 2 daughter

鬼 **guǐ** N ghost ■ 我根本不相信有鬼。**Wǒ gēnběn bù xiāngxìn yǒu guǐ.** *I don't believe in ghosts at all.*

鬼故事 **guǐ gùshi** ghost story
鬼屋 **guǐ wū** haunted house
鬼话 **guǐhuà** N wild and ridiculous talk, nonsense (aimed to deceive)
鬼话连篇 **guǐhuà liánpiān** a pack of lies

轨 **guǐ** N rail

出轨 **chūguǐ** (of a train) derail
轨道 **guǐdào** N track, orbit
上了轨道 **shàng le guǐdào** settle into normal routine

桂 **guì** N cassia, bay tree, sweet-scented asmanthus

桂冠 **guìguān** N laurel (emblem of victory or success)

柜 guì TRAD 櫃 N cupboard, cabinet

柜台 **guìtái** N counter, bar

贵 guì TRAD 貴 ADJ **1** expensive, of great value ■ 这家商店的东西很贵。Zhè jiā shāngdiàn de dōngxi hěn guì. *The goods in this shop are all very expensive.* **2** extremely valuable, precious
贵金属 **guìjīnshǔ** rare metal, precious metal **3** of noble birth, high-ranking

贵宾 **guìbīn** N distinguished guest (位 wèi)

贵姓 **guìxìng** IDIOM your family name ■ "请问，您贵姓？" "我姓王。" "您大名是…？" "我叫宝华。" "Qǐng wèn, nín guìxìng?" "Wǒ xìng Wáng." "Nín dàmíng shì…?" "Wǒ jiào Bǎohuá." *"What's your family name?" "Wang." "And your given name is…?" "It's Baohua."*

NOTE: (1) While 贵姓 guìxìng is the polite form when asking about somebody's family name, the polite way to ask somebody's given name is "请问, 您大名是…？" "Qǐngwèn, nín dàmíng shì…?" 大名 literally means *big name*. The answer to this question is "我叫XX。" "Wǒ jiào XX." (2) The word 贵 guì in the sense of *valuable* is added to certain nouns to mean *your …*, e.g. 贵姓 guìxìng *your family name*, 贵国 guìguó *your country*, 贵校 guìxiào *your school*. They are only used in formal and polite contexts.

贵重 **guìzhòng** ADJ valuable, precious
贵族 **guìzú** N aristocrat, aristocracy

跪 guì V kneel

跪下去 **guìxià qù** kneel down

滚 gǔn V roll ■ 球滚到沙发下面去了。Qiú gǔn dào shāfā xiàmiàn qù le. *The ball rolled under the armchair.*

NOTE: 滚 gǔn is used to tell somebody "get out of here" or "beat it," e.g. ■ 滚! 滚出去! Gǔn! Gǔn chūqu! *Get lost! Get out of here!* ■ 滚开! Gǔn kāi! *Beat it!* These are highly offensive.

滚动 **gǔndòng** V roll

棍 gùn N stick, rod

棍子 **gùnzi** stick, rod (根 gēn)

锅 guō TRAD 鍋 N pot, pan, wok

锅炉 **guōlú** N boiler

国 guó TRAD 國 N country, nation ■ 国与国之间应该是平等的。Guó yú guó zhī jiān yīnggāi shì píngděng de. *There should be equality among nations.*

德国 **Déguó** Germany
俄国 **Éguó** Russia
法国 **Fǎguó** France
美国 **Měiguó** the United States of America
英国 **Yīngguó** England, the United Kingdom
中国 **Zhōngguó** China
国法 **guófǎ** N the law of a country
国防 **guófáng** N national defense
国防部 **guófángbù** Ministry of National Defense
国会 **guóhuì** N (the U.S.) Congress, Parliament
国会议员 **guóhuì yìyuán** Congressman, member of Parliament (MP)
国籍 **guójí** N nationality
加入美国国籍 **jiārù Měiguó guójí** be naturalized as a U.S. citizen
国际 **guójì** ADJ international ■ 反对恐怖活动已经成为一个国际问题。Fǎnduì kǒngbù huódòng yǐjīng chéngwéi yí ge guójì wèntí. *Anti-terrorism has become an international issue.*
国家 **guójiā** N country, state ■ 他代表国家参加运动会。Tā dàibiǎo guójiā cānjiā yùndònghuì. *He represented his country in the sports meet.*

NOTE: It is significant that the Chinese word meaning *country*—国家 guójiā—is composed of the word 国 guó (country) and the word 家 jiā (family). In traditional Chinese thought, China was one big family and the country was ruled as such, with the emperor as the patriarch.

国库 **guókù** N national treasury
国民 **guómín** N national (of a country)
国民党 **Guómíndǎng** N the Kuomintang (KMT, the political party which ruled China before 1949 and is now a major party in Taiwan.)
国旗 **guóqí** N national flag (面 miàn)
国情 **guóqíng** N the conditions of a country
国庆节 **guóqìngjié** N National Day (October 1st in the People's Republic of China)
国王 **guówáng** N king, monarch
国务卿 **guówùqīng** N (the U.S.) Secretary of State
国务院 **guówùyuàn** N (Chinese) State Council, (the U.S.) State Department
国务院总理 **Guówùyuàn Zǒnglǐ** N (Chinese) Premier
国营 **guóyíng** ADJ state-operated
国有 **guóyǒu** ADJ state-owned

果 guǒ N fruit

果断 **guǒduàn** ADJ resolute
采取果断措施 **cǎiqǔ guǒduàn cuòshī** take decisive measures

果然 guǒrǎn ADV sure enough, as expected

果实 guǒshí N fruit

果树 guǒshù N fruit tree (棵 kē)

果园 guǒyuán N orchard (座 zuò)

过 guò TRAD 過 V 1 pass, cross ■ 过马路，一定要小心。Guò mǎlù, yídìng yào xiǎoxīn. *You must be very careful when crossing the street.*

过来 guòlai come over, come across (towards the speaker) ■ 公共汽车开过来了。Gōnggòng qìchē kāi guòlai le. *A bus is coming over.*

过去 guòqu go over, go across (away from the speaker) ■ 河水很急，我游不过去。Héshuǐ hěn jí, wǒ yóu bù guòqu. *The river runs swiftly. I can't swim across it.*

2 spend (time), live (a life), observe (a festival) ■ 他在国外过了这么多年，生活习惯有些改变了。Tā zài guówài guòle zhème duō nián, shēnghuó xíguàn yǒu xiē gǎibiàn le. *He has spent so many years overseas that some of his habits have changed.* ■ 从此以后，他们俩过得很幸福。Cóngcǐ yǐhòu, tāmen liǎ guò de hěn xìngfú. *They lived happily ever after.*

过日子 guò rìzi live a life

过年 guò nián observe New Year's Day

过节 guò jié observe a festival

过程 guòchéng N process, course

过度 guòdù ADJ excessive, over-

饮酒过度 yǐnjiǔ guò dù drink excessively

过渡 guòdù N transition

过分 guòfèn ADJ excessive, going overboard

过分的要求 guòfèn de yāoqiú excessive demands

过后 guòhòu ADV afterwards, later

过劳死 guòláosǐ N death from overwork

过滤 guòlù V filter

过去 guòqù N (something) in the past ■ 过去的事，不要多想了。Guòqù de shì, bú yào duō xiǎng le. *Don't keep thinking about what's past. (→ Let bygones be bygones.)* ■ 他过去常常生病，现在身体好多了。Tā guòqù chángcháng shēngbìng, xiànzài shēntǐ hǎo duō le. *He was often sick in the past. Now he is in much better health.*

过失 guòshī N fault, error

过问 guòwèn V take an interest in, concern oneself with

过于 guòyú ADV too, excessively

过 guo TRAD 過 PARTICLE (used after a verb or an adjective to emphasize a past experience) ■ "你去过中国没有？" "去过，我去过中国很多地方。" "Nǐ qùguo Zhōngguó méiyǒu?" "Qùguo, wǒ qùguo Zhōngguó hěn duō dìfang." *"Have you been to China?" "Yes, I've been to many parts of China."*

H

哈 hā ONOMATOPOEIA (sound of loud laughter)

哈哈 hāha ONOMATOPOEIA (representing loud laughter) ■ 听了孩子天真的话，老人哈哈大笑起来。Tīngle háizi tiānzhēn de huà, lǎorén hāhā dàxiào qǐlai. *Hearing the child's naïve words, the old man burst into laughter.*

哈欠 hāqian V yawn

打哈欠 dǎhāqian give a yawn

还 hái TRAD 還 ADV still, as before ■ 时间还早，我还想看一会儿书再睡。Shíjiān hái zǎo, wǒ xiǎng kàn yíhuìr shū zài shuì. *It's still early. I want to do a little reading before going to bed.*

还是 háishi I ADV still, as before ■ 老师说了两遍，我还是不大懂。Lǎoshī shuōle liǎng biàn, wǒ háishi bú dà dǒng. *The teacher has explained twice, but I still don't quite understand.* II CONJ or ■ 你喝茶还是喝咖啡？Nǐ hē chá háishi hē kāfēi? *Would you like tea or coffee?*

孩 hái N child, children

孩子 háizi child, children

海 hǎi N sea ■ 这个国家任何地方都离海很近。Zhège guójiā rènhé dìfang dōu lí hǎi hěn jìn. *Anywhere in this country is close to the sea.*

海岸 hǎi'àn N seashore, sea coast

海岸线 hǎi'ànxiàn coastline

海拔 hǎibá N height above sea level, elevation

海拔一百米 hǎibá yìbǎi mǐ 100 meters from sea level

海报 hǎibào N playbill, poster

贴海报 tiē hǎibào put up a poster

海滨 hǎibīn N seaside

海带 hǎidài N seaweed, kelp

海港 hǎigǎng N seaport (座 zuò)

海关 hǎiguān N customs, customs house ■ 通过海关的时候，要检查护照。Tōngguò hǎiguān de shíhou, yào jiǎnchá hùzhào. *Your passport will be examined when you pass through customs.*

海关检查 hǎiguān jiǎnchá customs inspection, customs examination

海关手续 hǎiguān shǒuxù customs formalities

海关人员 hǎiguān rényuán customs officer

海军 hǎijūn N navy

海面 hǎimiàn N sea/ocean surface

海鸥 hǎi'ōu N seagull (只 zhī)

海外 hǎiwài ADJ overseas

海外华侨 hǎiwài Huáqiáo overseas Chinese

海峡 hǎixiá N straits, channel

台湾海峡 **Táiwān hǎixiá** Taiwan Straits
海鲜 **hǎixiān** N seafood
海鲜馆 **hǎixiān guǎn** seafood restaurant
海啸 **hǎixiào** N tsunami
海洋 **hǎiyáng** N seas, ocean ■ 地球表面十分
之七是海洋。Dìqiú biǎomiàn shí fēnzhī qī shì
hǎiyáng. *Seven-tenths of the Earth's surface is
covered by seas and oceans.*
海洋生物 **hǎiyáng shēngwù** marine creatures
海员 **hǎiyuán** N seaman, sailor
海运 **hǎiyùn** N sea transportation, ocean shipping
海蜇 **hǎizhé** N jellyfish

害 **hài** I v harm, cause harm to ■ 吸烟不但害
自己, 而且害别人。Xīyān búdàn hài zìjǐ, érqiě
hài biérén. *Smoking not only harms the smoker, it
harms others too.* II N harm
有害 **yǒuhài** harmful ■ 吸烟有害健康。Xīyān
yǒuhài jiànkāng. *Smoking is harmful to health.*
害虫 **hàichóng** N pest (insect)
害处 **hàichu** N harm ■ 对孩子严格一点, 只有
好处, 没有害处。Duì háizi yángé yìdiǎn, zhǐyǒu
hǎochu, méiyǒu hàichu. *To be strict with children
has only benefits, and will cause no harm.*
害怕 **hàipà** v fear, be fearful
害羞 **hàixiū** ADJ be bashful, be shy

含 **hán** v 1 hold in the mouth ■ 孩子嘴里含着
一块糖, 说不清话。Háizi zuǐ li hánzhe yí kuài
táng, shuō bu qīng huà. *The child had a piece
of candy in his (or her) mouth and couldn't speak
clearly.* 2 contain, have ... as ingredient
含糊 **hánhu** ADJ vague, ambiguous
含量 **hánliàng** N amount of ingredient, content
含义 **hányì** N implied meaning, meaning

寒 **hán** ADJ cold

寒带 **hándài** N frigid zone
寒假 **hánjià** N winter vacation
寒冷 **hánlěng** ADJ freezing cold, frigid ■ 世
界上最寒冷的地方在南极。Shìjiè shang zuì
hánlěng de dìfang zài Nánjí. *The coldest place on
earth is in the Antarctic.*
寒流 **hánliú** N cold current
寒暄 **hánxuān** v exchange greetings (at the
beginning of a meeting)

函 **hán** N letter

公函 **gōnghán** official letter
函授 **hánshòu** v teach by correspondence
函授学校 **hánshòu xuéxiào** correspondence
school

喊 **hǎn** v shout ■ 有人在外面喊你。Yǒu rén
zài wàimiàn hǎn nǐ. *Someone is calling for you
outside.*

喊叫 **hǎnjiào** v cry out, shout

罕 **hǎn** ADV rarely, seldom

罕见 **hǎnjiàn** ADJ rare

汗 **hàn** N sweat, perspiration

出汗 **chūhàn** to sweat, to perspire ■ 这个房间
热得我出汗。Zhège fángjiān rè de wǒ chūhàn.
The room was so hot that I perspired.

汉 **Hàn** TRAD 漢 N the Han people (the main
ethnic group among the Chinese)
汉奸 **hànjiān** N traitor (to China), Chinese collaborator (with a foreign country)
汉人 **Hànrén** N a Han Chinese, Han Chinese
people
汉学 **Hànxué** N Sinology
汉学家 **Hànxuéjiā** sinologist
汉语 **Hànyǔ** N the language of the Han people,
the Chinese language ■ 你学了几年汉语了? Nǐ
xuéle jǐ nián Hànyǔ le? *How many years have you
been learning Chinese?*

NOTE: In Chinese there are a number of words denoting "the Chinese language." 汉语 Hànyǔ literally
means *the language of the Han Chinese people*, in
contrast with the languages of the non-Han peoples
in China. 汉语 Hànyǔ is therefore the accurate,
scientific term for the language. However, the
most popular term for the Chinese language is 中
文 Zhōngwén. In Singapore and other Southeast
Asian countries, the standard Chinese language is
often referred to as 华语 Huáyǔ in contrast to the
various Chinese dialects spoken there. Also see
note on 普通话 Pǔtōnghuà.

汉字 **Hànzì** N Chinese character, sinogram
常用汉字 **chángyòng Hànzì** frequently used
Chinese characters, common Chinese characters
汉族 **Hànzú** N the Han nationality, Han Chinese
people

旱 **hàn** ADJ (of climate) dry

旱冰场 **hànbīngchǎng** N roller-skating rink
旱灾 **hànzāi** N drought

焊 **hàn** v weld

电焊工 **diànhàngōng** welder

捍 **hàn** v defend, guard

捍卫 **hànwèi** v defend, protect
捍卫公司的利益 **hànwèi gōngsī de lìyì**
defend the interests of a company

感 hàn N regret (See 遗憾 yíhàn)

行 háng I M. WD line, row, queue (used with nouns that are formed in lines)
第四页第二行 dì-sì yè dì-èr háng line two on page 4
十四行诗 shísì háng shī sonnet
II N profession, trade
行情 hángqíng N price quotations ■ 黄金的行情看涨。Huángjīn de hángqíng kànzhǎng. *The price for gold is expected to rise.*
行业 hángyè N trade and profession, industry
各行各业 gè-háng-gè-yè every trade and profession

航 háng V navigate

航班 hángbān N flight, flight number
105航班 yāo-líng-wǔ hángbān Flight No 105
飞往广州的航班 fēiwǎng Guǎngzhōu de hángbān the flight to Guangzhou
航道 hángdào N waterway, channel
航海 hánghǎi N (ocean) navigation
航海家 hánghǎijiā (great) navigator
航空 hángkōng N aviation
航空公司 hángkōng gōngsī aviation company, airline
航空信 hángkōngxìn airmail letter
航空学校 hángkōng xuéxiào aviation school
航天 hángtiān N spaceflight
航天飞机 hángtiān fēijī space shuttle, spaceship
航线 hángxiàn N ocean or air route
航行 hángxíng V (of a ship) sail, (of an aircraft) fly
航运 hángyùn N shipping
航运公司 hángyùn gōngsī shipping company

豪 háo ADJ bold and unrestrained

豪华 háohuá ADJ luxurious, sumptuous

毫 háo N fine long hair

毫不 háo bù ADV not in the least, not at all ■ 他读书不用功，考试成绩不好毫不奇怪。Tā dúshū bú yònggōng, kǎoshì chéngjì bù hǎo háo bù qíguài. *He didn't study hard, so it's no wonder he got very poor grades at the exams.*

NOTE: 毫不 háo bù is an adverb used before an adjective of two or more syllables. For example, you can say 毫不奇怪 háo bù qíguài *not at all strange*, but you cannot say 毫不怪 háo bú guài.

毫米 háomǐ N millimeter

毫无 háo wú V have no … at all, be in total absence of ■ 他心很硬，对不幸的人毫无同情心。Tā xīn hěn yìng, duì búxìng de rén háo wú tóngqíngxīn. *He is hardhearted, and has no sympathy at all for less fortunate people.*

NOTE: The object of 毫无 háo wú usually takes a word of two or more syllables, and usually refers to something abstract, like 同情心 tóngqíngxīn *sympathy.*

好 1 hǎo ADJ good, all right ■ 我爸爸身体很好。Wǒ bàba shēntǐ hěn hǎo. *My father is in good health.*
好比 hǎobǐ V may be compared as, be like, same as
好吃 hǎochī ADJ delicious ■ 王太太做的这个菜，好吃极了! Wáng tàitai zuò de zhège cài, hǎochī jíle! *This dish cooked by Mrs Wang is really delicious!*
好处 hǎochu N benefit, advantage ■ 经常锻炼对身体有很多好处。Jīngcháng duànliàn duì shēntǐ yǒu hěnduō hǎochu. *Regular physical exercise is very beneficial to health.*
对…有好处 duì...yǒu hǎochu be beneficial to
好感 hǎogǎn N favorable impression, fondness (for somebody)
对他有好感 duì tā yǒu hǎogǎn be fond of him, have a soft spot for him
好汉 hǎohàn N brave man, hero ■ 不到长城非好汉。Búdào Chángchéng fēi hǎohàn. *You're not a hero until you've been to the Great Wall.*
好好儿 hǎohāor ADJ normal, nothing wrong ■ 她昨天还好好儿的，今天怎么病了呢? Tā zuótiān hái hǎohāor de, jīntiān zěnme bìng le ne? *She was quite well yesterday. How come she should fall ill today?*
好坏 hǎohuài N what is good and what is bad (for somebody)
不知好坏 bùzhī hǎohuài don't know what is good and what is bad for oneself, be insensible
好久 hǎojiǔ ADV a long time ■ 我好久没玩得这么痛快了。Wǒ hǎojiǔ méi wán de zhème tòngkuai le. *I haven't had such fun for a long time.*
好看 hǎokàn ADJ 1 pleasant to the eye, good-looking, pretty ■ 她妈妈年轻的时候很好看。Tā māma niánqīng de shíhou hěn hǎokàn. *Her mother was beautiful when young.* 2 interesting, absorbing ■ 这本小说好看不好看? Zhè běn xiǎoshuō hǎokàn bu hǎokàn? *Is this novel interesting?*
好容易 hǎo róngyì ADV with great difficulty ■ 我好容易找到他家，他偏不在。Wǒ hǎo róngyì zhǎodào tā jiā, tā piān bú zài. *I found his home with great difficulty, and he had to be out.*

NOTE: 好容易 hǎo róngyì is an idiomatic expression. You can also say 好不容易 hǎo bù róngyì, with exactly the same meaning, e.g. ■ 我好不容易找到他家，他偏不在。Wǒ hǎo bù róngyì zhǎodào tā jiā, tā piān bú zài. *I found his home with great difficulty, and he had to be out.*

好听 **hǎotīng** ADJ pleasant to the ear, melodious

好玩儿 **hǎowánr** ADJ great fun ■ 这个游戏很好玩儿。Zhège yóuxì hěn hǎowánr. *This game is great fun.*

好像 **hǎoxiàng** v be like, similar to ■ 天边的白云好像一座雪山。Tiānbiān de bái yún hǎoxiàng yí zuò xuěshān. *The white cloud on the horizon looks like a snow mountain.*

好心 **hǎoxīn** ADJ kindhearted ■ 她是个好心人。Tā shì ge hǎoxīn rén. *She is a kindhearted person.*

好在 **hǎozài** ADV fortunately, luckily

好转 **hǎozhuǎn** v take a turn for the better, improve

好 **2 hǎo** ADV 1 very, very much 2 How…! ■ 你这件新衣服好漂亮! Nǐ zhè jiàn xīn yīfu hǎo piàoliang! *How pretty your new dress is!*

好多 **hǎo duō** ADJ a good many, many, much ■ 我生日那天，好多朋友都送给我贺卡和礼物。Wǒ shēngrì nà tiān, hǎo duō péngyou dōu sòng gei wǒ hèkǎ hé lǐwù. *Many friends gave me greeting cards and gifts on my birthday.*

好些 **hǎoxiē** ADJ a good many, a large number of, lots of

NOTE: 好些 hǎoxiē is a colloquial word, only used in casual, familiar styles.

好 **hào** v be fond of

好吃 **hào chī** ADJ fond of eating, gluttonous

好动 **hào dòng** ADJ hyperactive

好客 **hàokè** ADJ hospitable
热情好客 **rèqíng hàokè** warm and hospitable

好奇 **hào qí** ADJ be curious, inquisitive ■ 这个孩子对什么都好奇。Zhège háizi duì shénme dōu hàoqí. *This child is curious about everything.*

好色 **hào sè** ADJ oversexed, lewd

好学 **hào xué** ADJ fond of learning, thirsty for knowledge ■ 这个学生虚心好学，进步很快。Zhège xuésheng xūxīn hào xué, jìnbù hěn kuài. *This student is modest and fond of learning. He is making rapid progress.*

耗 **hào** v consume

耗费 **hàofèi** v consume (especially in a wasteful way), cost (a large amount of money, time, etc.)

号 **hào** TRAD 號 N 1 order of sequence ■ 小王住在三号楼五号房间。Xiǎo Wáng zhù zài sān hào lóu, wǔ hào fángjiān. *Xiao Wang lives ir Building 3, Room 5.* 2 date of month ■ 今天二十号，九月二十号。Jīntiān èrshí hào, Jiǔyuè èrsh hào. *Today's the 20th, September 20th.*

NOTE: See note on 日 rì.

号称 **hàochēng** v be known as (something great), claim to be

号码 **hàomǎ** N serial number, size ■ "你穿多大号码的衬衫?" "我穿四十码。" "Nǐ chuān duō dà hàomǎ de chènshān?" "Wǒ chuān sìshí mǎ." *"What size shirt do you wear?" "Size 40."*

号召 **hàozhào** v call upon, appeal ■ 中国政府号召一对夫妻只生一个孩子。Zhōngguó zhèngf hàozhào yí duì fūqī zhǐ shēng yí ge háizi. *The Chinese government appeals to each couple to have only one child.*

浩 **hào** ADJ vast, numerous

浩大 **hàodà** ADJ huge, gigantic
浩大的工程 **hàodà de gōngchéng** a huge engineering project

呵 **hē** v blow a puff of breath, exhale through the mouth

喝 **hē** v drink ■ 中国人一般先吃饭后喝汤，或者边吃饭边喝汤。Zhōngguórén yìbān xiān chī fàn hòu hē tāng, huòzhě biān chī fàn biān hē tāng. *The Chinese usually have the main course before soup, or have the main course and soup a the same time.*

NOTE: 喝 hē (drink) 和 渴 kě (thirsty) look similar. Be careful not to confuse the two characters.

合 **hé** v 1 close ■ 他太累了，一合上眼就睡着了。Tā tài lèi le, yì hé shang yǎn jiù shuìzháo le. *He was so tired that he fell asleep the moment he closed his eyes.* 2 co-operate, do in partnership
合办企业 **hébàn qǐyè** run an enterprise in partnership
3 conform with
不合我的口味 **bùhé wǒde kǒuwèi** not to my taste
4 be equal to

合法 **héfǎ** ADJ legal, legitimate ■ 他是个有妇之夫，和另一个女人同居是不合法的。Tā shì gè yǒu fù zhī fū, hé lìng yī ge nǚrén tóngjū shì bùhé fǎ de. *He is a married man, and it is not legal for him to live with another woman.*

合格 **hégé** ADJ qualified, up to standard

合乎 **héhū** v conform with, correspond to
合乎惯例 **héhū guànlì** conform with normal practice

合伙 **héhuǒ** v form a partnership, work in a partnership
和老同学合伙开公司 **hé lǎo tóngxué**

héhuǒ kāi gōngsī set up a company in partnership with an old classmate

合金 héjīn N alloy

合理 hélǐ ADJ conforming to reason, reasonable, logical ■ 对于你们的合理要求，我们会尽力满足。Duìyú nǐmen de hélǐ yāoqiú, wǒmen huì jìnlì mǎnzú. *We will do our best to meet your reasonable demands.*

合适 héshì ADJ suitable, appropriate ■ 他做这个工作非常合适。Tā zuò zhège gōngzuò fēicháng héshì. *He is very suitable for this job.*

合算 hésuàn ADJ worthwhile paying ■ 这笔生意做得不合算。Zhè bǐ shēngyi zuò de bù hésuàn. *This business deal didn't pay.*

合同 hétóng N contract, agreement (份 fèn)

合资 hézī V pool capital to run a business
合资企业 hézī qǐyè joint venture

合作 hézuò I V cooperate, work together ■ 我们非常高兴和你们合作。Wǒmen fēicháng gāoxìng hé nǐmen hézuò. *We're very happy to cooperate with you.* II N cooperation ■ 我们应该加强合作。Wǒmen yīnggāi jiāqiáng hézuò. *We should enhance our cooperation.*

盒 hé N box ■ 她的铅笔盒子里有四支铅笔。Tāde qiānbǐ hézi li yǒu sì zhī qiānbǐ. *There are four pencils in her pencil box.*
盒子 hézi box (只 zhī)

何 hé PRON which, what

何等 héděng I ADJ what kind II ADV how, what
何况 hékuàng CONJ 1 what's more, moreover 2 let alone

荷 hé N lotus

荷花 héhuā lotus flower

河 hé N river (条 tiáo) ■ 这条河太宽，我游不过去。Zhè tiáo hé tài kuān, wǒ yóu bu guòqu. *This river is too broad. I can't swim across it.*

NOTE: In modern Chinese, 江 jiāng and 河 hé both mean *river*. Usually (not always) rivers in the south are known as 江 jiāng and rivers in the north are 河 hé.

河道 hédào N river course
河流 héliú N rivers

阂 hé V hinder, obstruct

禾 hé N seedling, (especially) rice seedling

禾苗 hémiáo N seedling (of cereal crops)

和 hé I CONJ and ■ 我和你都在学中文。Wǒ hé nǐ dōu zài xué Zhōngwén. *You and I are both learning Chinese.* II PREP with

和…一起 hé...yìqǐ together with … ■ 昨天我和朋友一起吃中饭。Zuótiān wǒ hé péngyou yìqǐ chī zhōngfàn. *Yesterday I had lunch with a friend of mine.*

核 hé N kernel, core, pit

核电站 hédiànzhàn N nuclear power plant
核桃 hétao N walnut (颗 kē)
核武器 héwǔqì N nuclear weapon
核心 héxīn N core, kernel

贺 hè TRAD 賀 V congratulate

贺词 hècí N speech of congratulations
贺卡 hèkǎ N greeting card (张 zhāng)

赫 hè ADJ conspicuous, grand

显赫 xiǎnhè distinguished and influential, illustrious
赫赫 hèhè ADJ illustrious, impressive
赫赫有名 hèhè yǒumíng very famous, illustrious

黑 hēi ADJ black, dark ■ 天快黑了, 他们还在踢球。Tiān kuài hēi le, tāmen hái zài tīqiú. *It's almost dark, but they're still playing soccer.*
黑暗 hēi'àn ADJ dark ■ 他很天真, 不知道社会的黑暗面。Tā hěn tiānzhēn, bù zhīdào shèhuì de hēi'àn miàn. *He is naïve, and is unaware of the seamy side of society.*
黑板 hēibǎn N blackboard
黑夜 hēiyè N night
白天黑夜 báitiān hēiyè day and night

嘿 hēi INTERJ 1 (used to attract someone's attention in a casual or impolite manner) ■ 嘿, 这里不准吸烟。Hēi, zhèli bùzhǔn xīyān. *Hey! You can't smoke here.* 2 (used to indicate admiration) ■ 嘿, 昨天的球赛咱们队打得真棒! Hēi, zuótiān de qiúsài zánmen duì dǎ de zhēn bàng! *Hey, our team played marvelously in yesterday's match!*

痕 hén N trace

伤痕 shānghén scar
痕迹 hénjì N trace, mark, stain

狠 hěn ADJ 1 cruel, relentless

心毒手狠 xīndú shǒuhěn with a vicious mind and cruel means
2 severe, stern
狠狠地批评 hěnhěnde pīpíng criticize severely
狠毒 hěndú ADJ cruel and vicious
狠心 hěnxīn I ADJ ruthless II V make a painful decision

83

下狠心 xià hěnxīn make a tough decision resolutely

很 hěn ADV very, quite ■ 我很讨厌下雨天。Wǒ hěn tǎoyàn xià yǔ tiān. *I hate rainy days.*

NOTE: When used as predicates, Chinese adjectives normally require an adverb. For example, 我高兴 Wǒ gāoxìng sounds unnatural, while 我很高兴 Wǒ hěn gāoxìng (I'm [very] happy), 我不高兴 Wǒ bù gāoxìng (I'm not happy) or 我非常高兴 Wǒ fēicháng gāoxìng (I'm very happy) are normal sentences. The adverb 很 hěn is often used as a default adverb before an adjective. In such cases the meaning of 很 hěn is very weak.

恨 hèn v 1 hate, be angry with ■ 她恨男朋友欺骗了她。Tā hèn nánpéngyou qīpiàn le tā. *She hates her boyfriend for cheating on her.* 2 regret deeply ■ 他恨自己念书不用功, 但是太晚了。Tā hèn zìjǐ niànshū bú yònggōng, dànshì tài wǎn le. *He deeply regrets not having studied hard, but it's too late.*

恨不得 hènbude ADV how … wish to ■ 他恨不得马上回家过年。Hā hènbude mǎshàng huíjiā guònián. *How he wishes he could go home right now for the spring festival.*

NOTE: We use 恨不得 to express a wish that is very strong but cannot be fulfilled. If we say 他恨不得马上回家过年。 Hā hènbude mǎshàng huíjiā guònián, it means *it is quite impossible for him to go back home right now*.

哼 hēng v 1 snort 2 hum

衡 héng I N weighing instrument II v weigh, measure
衡量 héngliáng v judge, consider
衡量利弊 héngliáng lìbì consider the pros and cons

恒 héng I ADJ permanent, forever II N perseverance
恒心 héngxīn N perseverance
恒星 héngxīng N star (颗 kē) ■ 太阳是一颗恒星, 地球是一颗行星。Tàiyáng shì yìkē héngxīng, dìqiú shì yìkē xíngxīng. *While the sun is a star, the earth is a planet.*

横 héng ADJ 1 horizontal 2 violent, fierce
横行 héngxíng v play the tyrant, run amok

轰 hōng TRAD 轟 v rumble, explode
轰动 hōngdòng v cause a sensation
轰炸 hōngzhà v bomb
轰炸机 hōngzhàjī bomber

烘 hōng v dry or warm by the fire, roast
烘干机 hōnggānjī (clothes) dryer

红 hóng TRAD 紅 ADJ 1 red ■ 中国人传统上喜欢红颜色。Zhōngguórén chuántǒng shang xǐhuan hóng yánsè. *Traditionally the Chinese love the color red.* 2 popular, favored
红包 hóngbāo N a red envelope (containing money), bribe
收红包 shōu hóngbāo take bribes
红茶 hóngchá N black tea
红绿灯 hónglǜdēng N traffic lights, stoplights
红人 hóngrén N a trusted and favored employee or member of an organization
红外线 hóngwàixiàn N infrared ray
红血球 hóngxuèqiú N red blood cell, erythrocyte
红眼病 hóngyǎnbìng N 1 conjunctivitis (eye disease) 2 envy, jealousy

虹 hóng N rainbow
彩虹 cǎihóng rainbow (道 dào)

宏 hóng ADJ grand, magnificent
宏大 hóngdà ADJ great, grand
宏观 hóngguān ADJ macroscopic
宏观经济学 hóngguān jīngjìxué macroeconomics
宏伟 hóngwěi ADJ magnificent, grand

洪 hóng N big
洪水 hóngshuǐ flood

哄 hǒng v 1 coax 2 cheat, hoodwink
哄骗 hǒngpiàn v lie in order to cheat

哄 hòng N horseplay
起哄 qǐhòng start a horseplay

喉 hóu N throat
喉咙 hóulóng N throat, larynx
喉咙疼 hóulóng téng have a sore throat

猴 hóu N monkey
猴子 hóuzi N monkey (只 zhī)

吼 hǒu v roar, howl

后 hòu TRAD 後 N back, rear) ■ 请用后门。Qǐng yòng hòumén. *Please use the back door.*
后边 hòubian N back, rear ■ 听课的时候我喜欢坐在前边, 不喜欢坐在后边。Tīng kè de shíhou,

wǒ xǐhuan zuò zài qiánbian, bù xǐhuan zuò zài hòubian. *When attending lectures, I like to sit in the front row, not the back row.*

后代 **hòudài** N succeeding generations, posterity

后方 **hòufāng** N rear, behind

后果 **hòuguǒ** N consequences ■ 你愿意承受这一行动的后果吗? Nǐ yuànyì chéngshòu zhè yī xíngdòng de hòuguǒ ma? *Are you willing to bear the consequences of this action?*

后悔 **hòuhuǐ** V regret, feel sorry (for having done something) ■ 我真后悔，没听爸爸的话。Wǒ zhēn hòuhuǐ, méi tīng bàba de huà. *I really regret not taking father's advice.*

后来 **hòulái** N afterwards, later on ■ 他刚到北京的时候，不爱吃中国菜，后来就慢慢习惯了。Tā gāng dào Běijīng de shíhou, bú ài chī Zhōngguó cài, hòulái mànman xíguàn le. *When he first came to Beijing he did not like Chinese food, but later on he gradually got used to it.*

后面 **hòumian** N Same as 后边 hòubian

后年 **hòunián** N the year after next

后期 **hòuqī** N later stage, later periods

后勤 **hòuqín** N logistics, support services

后台 **hòutái** N 1 backstage 2 behind-the-scenes supporter

后天 **hòutiān** N the day after tomorrow

后头 **hòutou** N Same as 后面 hòumian or 后边 hòubian, used colloquially.

后退 **hòutuì** V retreat, draw back

厚 **hòu** ADJ thick ■ 这么厚的小说，她两天就看完了。Zhème hòu de xiǎoshuō, tā liǎng tiān jiù kànwán le. *It took her only two days to finish reading such a thick novel.*

厚度 **hòudù** N thickness

候 **hòu** V wait

候补 **hòubǔ** V be a candidate (for a position) 候补委员 **hòubǔ wěiyuán** alternative member of a committee

候选人 **hòuxuǎnrén** N candidate (for an election or selection)

乎 **hū** PARTICLE (added to another word to express strong emotions) (See 几乎 jīhū, 似乎 sìhū.)

呼 **hū** V 1 exhale 2 shout, cry out

呼声 **hūshēng** N 1 call, crying 2 public voice, expression of public opinion

呼吸 **hūxī** V breathe ■ 我刚才不大舒服，在花园里呼吸了新鲜空气，感到好多了。Wǒ gāngcái búdà shūfu, zài huāyuán li hūxīle xīnxiān kōngqì, gǎndào hǎo duō le. *I didn't feel well just now. I'm feeling much better now that I've had some fresh air in the garden.*

呼吁 **hūyù** V appeal, call on

忽 **hū** ADV suddenly

忽略 **hūlüè** V neglect, overlook

忽然 **hūrán** ADV suddenly ■ 刚才天气还好好儿的，忽然下起大雨来了。Gāngcái tiānqì hái hǎohǎor de, hūrán xià qǐ dà yǔ lái le. *Just now the weather was still fine. Suddenly it's raining hard.*

忽视 **hūshì** V overlook, neglect ■ 他们忽视了一个细节，使计划失败。Tāmen hūshì le yí ge xìjié, shǐ jìhuà shībài. *They overlooked a detail, which doomed the plan.*

胡 1 **hú** TRAD 鬍 N beard, mustache

胡子 **húzi** beard, whiskers
刮胡子 **guā húzi** shave (beard, whiskers)

胡 2 **hú** ADJ foreign, outlandish

NOTE: In ancient China, 胡 hú was used to refer to foreigners, especially the nomadic tribesmen from Central Asia. A number of words with 胡 hú were created to denote objects introduced to China by or through these people. Words with 胡 hú may also have derogatory meanings.

胡来 **húlái** V fool with, mess up

胡乱 **húluàn** ADV rashly, carelessly

胡萝卜 **húluóbo** N carrot

胡闹 **húnào** V act noisily and willfully, create a scene

胡琴 **húqin** N a traditional musical instrument with two strings, also called 二胡 èrhú (把 bǎ) 拉胡琴 (二胡) **lā húqin (èrhú)** play the *erhu*

胡说 **húshuō** I V talk nonsense ■ 你别胡说，我和她只是朋友关系。Nǐ bié húshuō, wǒ hé tā zhǐ shì péngyou guānxi. *Don't talk nonsense, she and I are only friends.* II N nonsense
胡说八道 **húshuo bādào** pure nonsense

胡同 **hútòng** N narrow lane in Beijing

瑚 **hú** as in 珊瑚 shānhú

葫 **hú** as in 葫芦 húlu

葫芦 **húlu** N bottle gourd, calabash

糊 **hú** I V paste II N mush, gruel

糊涂 **hútu** ADJ muddle-headed, muddled, confused
糊涂虫 **hútu chóng** N muddle-headed person, bungler

湖 **hú** N lake ■ 中国最大的湖是青海省的青海湖。Zhōngguó zuì dà de hú shì Qīnghǎi Shěng de Qīnghǎi Hú. *China's biggest lake is Qinghai Lake in Qinghai Province.*

湖泊 húpō

湖泊 **húpō** N lakes

蝴 hú as in 蝴蝶 húdié

蝴蝶 **húdié** N butterfly

壶 hú TRAD 壺 N kettle (把 bǎ)

水壶 **shuǐhú** kettle ■ 壶里还有水吗? Hú li hái yǒu shuǐ ma? *Is there any water left in the kettle?*

狐 hú N fox

狐狸 **húli** fox

虎 hǔ N tiger (See 老虎 lǎohǔ, 马虎 mǎhu)

互 hù I ADJ reciprocal II ADV mutually, each other

互利 **hùlì** ADJ of mutual benefit

互联网 **hùliánwǎng** N the Internet, the World Wide Web ■ 有了互联网, 信息交流方便多了。 Yǒule hùliánwǎng, xìnxi jiāoliú fāngbiàn duōle. *With the Internet, information exchange is so much more convenient.*

互相 **hùxiāng** ADV each other, one another

互助 **hùzhù** V help each other

户 hù M. WD (used with nouns denoting households and families) ■ 这条街上有三十几户人家。 Zhè tiáo jiē shang yǒu sānshí jǐ hù rénjiā. *There are over 30 households [living] along this street.*

户口 **hùkǒu** N registered permanent residence
城镇户口 **chéngzhèn hùkǒu** urban residence
农村户口 **nóngcūn hùkǒu** rural residence

护 hù TRAD 護 V protect

护士 **hùshi** N nurse ■ 护士按照医生的嘱咐给病人吃药。 Hùshi ànzhào yīshēng de zhǔfu gěi bìngrén chī yào. *Nurses administer medicine to patients according to doctors' instructions.*

NOTE: In China nurses are almost exclusively women. To address a nurse politely, use 护士小姐 hùshì xiǎojiě, e.g. ■ 护士小姐, 我还需要吃这个药吗? Hùshì xiǎojiě, wǒ hái xūyào chī zhè ge yào ma? *Nurse, do I still need to take this medicine?* or you can put her family name before 护士 hùshì, e.g. 张护士 Zhāng hùshì, 李护士 Lǐ hùshì.

护照 **hùzhào** N passport (份 fèn)
申请护照 **shēnqǐng hùzhào** apply for a passport

沪 hù TRAD 滬 N a shortened form for the metropolis of Shanghai

沪东 **Hù-Dōng** East Shanghai

花1 huā N flower (朵 duǒ)

种花 **zhòng huā** plant flowers, do gardening

NOTE: In colloquial Chinese 花儿 huār may be used instead of 花 huā, e.g. ■ 去医院看病人, 可以带一些花儿。 Qù yīyuàn kàn bìngrén, kěyǐ dài yìxiē huār. *You can take some flowers with you when you visit a patient in the hospital.*

花朵 **huāduǒ** N flowers

花瓶 **huāpíng** N vase (只 zhī) ■ 花瓶里插了几朵美丽的花。 Huāpíng li chāle jǐ duǒ měilì de huā. *Some beautiful flowers were placed in the vase.*
瓷器花瓶 **cíqì huāpíng** porcelain vase

花儿 **huār** I N Same as 花 huā II ADJ full of colors, mottled, loud ■ 这条裙子太花儿了, 你穿不合适。 Zhè tiáo qúnzi tài huār le, nǐ chuān bù héshì. *This skirt is too flashy. It's unsuitable for you to wear.*

花色 **huāsè** N 1 (of fabric) design and color 2 (of a commodity) variety of designs, colors, sizes, etc.

花生 **huāshēng** N peanut
花生酱 **huāshēngjiàng** peanut butter

花纹 **huāwén** N decorative pattern, pattern

花样 **huāyàng** N 1 pattern, variety
花样溜冰 **huāyàngliūbīng** figure skate 2 trick
和我玩花样 **hé wǒ wán huāyang** play tricks on me

花园 **huāyuán** N garden (座 zuò) ■ 这里几乎每座房子都有一个小花园。 Zhèli jīhū měi zuò fángzi dōu yǒu yí ge xiǎo huāyuán. *Almost every house here has a small garden.*

花2 huā V 1 spend ■ 你每天花多少时间做作业? Nǐ měitiān huā duōshǎo shíjiān zuò zuòyè? *How much time do you spend on assignments every day?* 2 cost (money) ■ 在英国留学一年要花多少钱? Zài Yīngguó liúxué yì nián yào huā duōshǎo qián? *How much would it cost to study in the UK for a year?* 3 take (time) ■ 写这篇文章花了我整整两天。 Xiě zhè piān wénzhāng huāle wǒ zhěngzhěng liǎng tiān. *It took me two full days to write this essay.*

NOTE: In writing, the character 化 huā can be used instead of 花 huā as a verb meaning *spend, cost,* etc.

花费 **huāfèi** I V consume, spend
花费大量心血 **huāfèi dàliàng xīnxuè** put in a great deal of effort
II N money spent, expenses

划 huá TRAD 劃 V 1 row, paddle

划船 **huáchuán** row a boat

2 scratch or scrape with a sharp object ■ 我的手划破了，不能在花园里干活了。Wǒ de shǒu huá pò le, bù néng zài huāyuán li gànhuó le. *I've scratched my hand. I can't work in the garden any more.* **3** be worth the money spent

划算 huásuàn ADJ worth it, getting money's worth

滑 huá ADJ slippery ■ 下雪以后，路上很滑。Xià xuě yǐhòu, lù shang hěn huá. *After a snowfall, roads are slippery.*

滑冰 huábīng V skate (on ice), ice-skating

滑头 huátóu I ADJ crafty, shifty II N a crafty, shifty person

滑雪 huáxuě I V ski II N skiing

猾 huá as in 狡猾 jiǎohuá

华 huá TRAD 華 I N China II ADJ magnificent, gorgeous

华丽 huálì ADJ gorgeous, magnificent

华侨 huáqiáo N overseas Chinese

华人 huárén N ethnic Chinese

华氏 huáshì N Fahrenheit scale

华氏温度计 huáshì wēndùjì Fahrenheit thermometer

哗 huá TRAD 嘩 N noise

化 huà I V 1 melt ■ 太阳出来，雪很快化了。Tàiyang chūlai, xuě hěn kuài huà le. *When the sun came out, the snow melted very quickly.* **2** transform II N chemistry

化肥 huàféi N chemical fertilizer

化工 huàgōng N chemical industry

化工厂 huàgōngchǎng chemical plant

化合 huàhé N chemical combination

化石 huàshí N fossil

化纤 huàxiān N chemical fiber

化学 huàxué N chemistry ■ 他对化学感兴趣，以后想当化学工程师。Tā duì huàxué gǎn xìngqu, yǐhòu xiǎng dāng huàxué gōngchéngshī. *He is interested in chemistry, and hopes to become a chemical engineer.*

化学家 huàxuéjiā chemist

化学工业(化工) huàxué gōngyè (huàgōng) chemical industry

化验 huàyàn N chemical test, laboratory test ■ 你必须化验一下血。Nǐ bìxū huàyàn yíxià xuè. *You must have your blood tested.*

化验报告 huàyàn bàogào laboratory test report

化验单 huàyàn dān laboratory test application (a form signed by a doctor for the patient to have a test done in a laboratory)

化验室 huàyàn shì laboratory

化验员 huàyàn yuán laboratory assistant, laboratory technician

化妆 huàzhuāng V put on make-up

化妆品 huàzhuāngpǐn cosmetics

划 huà TRAD 劃 V 1 plan 2 delimit

划分 huàfēn V divide, differentiate

画 huà TRAD 畫 V draw, paint ■ 这个小孩喜欢画各种动物，而且画得挺好。Zhège xiǎohái xǐhuan huà gè zhǒng dòngwù, érqiě huà de tǐng hǎo. *This child likes to draw animals, and is very good at it.*

国画 guóhuà traditional Chinese painting

铅笔画 qiānbǐ huà pencil drawing

水彩画 shuǐcǎi huà watercolor (painting)

油画 yóuhuà oil painting

中国画 Zhōngguóhuà Same as 国画 guóhuà

画儿 huàr N picture, drawing (张 zhāng, 幅 fú) ■ 这张画儿画得真好! Zhè zhāng huàr huà de zhēn hǎo! *This picture is so well done!*

NOTE: You can use 画 huà instead of 画儿 huàr, e.g. ■ 这张画画得真好! Zhè zhāng huà huà de zhēn hǎo! *This picture is so well done!*

画报 huàbào N illustrated magazine, pictorial (份 fèn, 本 běn) ■ 星期天的报纸大多有一份画报。Xīngqītiān de bàozhǐ dàduō yǒu yí fèn huàbào. *Most Sunday newspapers carry a pictorial (or color) supplement.*

画家 huàjiā N painter, artist (位 wèi)

画面 huàmiàn N image on the screen or the canvas

画蛇添足 huà shé tiān zú IDIOM add legs to a snake (→ do superfluous things, thus causing damage or attracting ridicule)

话 huà TRAD 話 N speech, what is said, words (句 jù) ■ 你这句话很有道理。Nǐ zhè jù huà hěn yǒu dàoli. *Your words are very reasonable.* (→ You're quite right there.) ■ 别忘了我的话。Bié wàngle wǒ de huà. *Don't forget what I said.*

话剧 huàjù N stage play (as opposed to opera)

话题 huàtí N topic of conversation, subject of a talk, theme

槐 huái N Chinese scholar tree

槐树 huáishù Chinese scholar tree (棵 kē)

徊 huái V walk to and fro (See 徘徊 páihuái)

怀 huái TRAD 懷 I N bosom II V 1 keep in mind 2 miss, think of

怀念 huáiniàn V think of tenderly

怀疑 huáiyí V 1 disbelieve, doubt ■ 我怀疑他说的话是不是真的。Wǒ huáiyí tā shuōde huà shì-

bushì zhēn de. *I doubt if he was telling the truth.*
2 think something is unlikely, suspect ■ 我怀疑他在撒谎。Wǒ huáiyí tā zài sāhuǎng. *I suspect that he was lying.*

NOTE: 怀疑 huáiyí has two seemingly contradictory meanings – *disbelieve* and *think something is unlikely*, but the context will make the meaning clear.

怀孕 **huáiyùn** v be pregnant

坏 **huài** TRAD 壞 **I** ADJ bad ■ 小孩子看电影，总爱问谁是好人，谁是坏人。Xiǎoháizi kàn diànyǐng, zǒng ài wèn shéi shì hǎorén, shéi shì huàirén. *When children watch movies, they like to ask who the good guy is and who the bad guy is.* **II** v break down, be out of order ■ 电视机坏了，今天没法看电视新闻了。Diànshìjī huài le, jīntiān méi fǎ kàn diànshì xīnwén le. *The TV set has broken down. There's no way we can watch the TV news today.*

坏处 **huàichu** N negative effect, disadvantage ■ 这样做好处很多，但是也有不少坏处。Zhèyàng zuò hǎochu hěn duō, dànshì yě yǒu bù shǎo huàichu. *This way of doing things has many advantages, but it also has quite a few disadvantages.*

NOTE: 坏处 huàichu and 害处 hàichu both refer to the undesirable effects of an action or actions. 坏处 huàichu connotes general negativity while 害处 hàichu emphasizes the harm that results.

坏蛋 **huàidàn** N bad person, villain, rascal

欢 **huān** TRAD 歡 ADJ joyful

欢呼 **huānhū** v cheer, hail
欢乐 **huānlè** ADJ joyful, happy
欢送 **huānsòng** v send off (a guest) ■ 我们明天到机场去欢送中国公司的代表。Wǒmen míngtiān dào jīchǎng qù huānsòng Zhōngguó gōngsī de dàibiǎo. *We're going to the airport tomorrow to send off the representative from the Chinese company.*
欢送会 **huānsònghuì** a send-off party (e.g. a farewell tea party)
欢喜 **huānxǐ** ADJ joyful, happy, delighted
欢笑 **huānxiào** v laugh heartily
欢迎 **huānyíng** v welcome ■ 热烈欢迎您! Rèliè huānyíng nín! *A warm welcome to you!*

还 **huán** TRAD 還 v return, pay back ■ 他向银行借了十万元，要在五年内还清。Tā xiàng yínháng jièle shíwàn yuán, yào zài wǔ nián nèi huán qīng. *He borrowed 100,000 yuan from a bank and must repay the loan within five years.* ■ 有借有还，再借不难。Yǒu jiè yǒu huán, zài jiè bù nán. *Return what you borrowed, and it won't be difficult to borrow again.*
还原 **huányuán** v return to the original, restore

环 **huán** TRAD 環 N circle, ring

环节 **huánjié** N link
重要环节 **zhòngyào huánjié** important link
环境 **huánjìng** N environment ■ 这家造纸厂污染环境，引起当地居民的强烈不满。Zhè jiā zàozhǐ chǎng wūrǎn huánjìng, yǐnqǐ dāngdì jūmín de qiángliè bùmǎn. *This paper mill pollutes the environment, arousing the local people's great displeasure.*
环境保护 **huánjìng bǎohù** environmental protection

缓 **huǎn** TRAD 緩 ADV leisurely

缓和 **huǎnhé** **I** v ease up, alleviate ■ 她说了一个笑话，让会场上的紧张气氛缓和下来。Tā shuōle yí ge xiàohua, ràng huìchǎng shàng de jǐnzhāng qìfen huǎnhé xiàlai. *She told a joke, which defused tension at the meeting.* **II** ADJ relaxed, gentle
口气缓和 **kǒuqì huǎnhé** with a gentle, mild tone
缓慢 **huǎnmàn** ADJ slow, unhurried

换 **huàn** TRAD 換 v change, replace ■ 她的地址换了，我不知道她的新地址。Tā de dìzhǐ huàn le, wǒ bù zhīdào tā de xīn dìzhǐ. *She has changed her address. I don't have her new one.*
换取 **huànqǔ** v exchange for, get in return

唤 **huàn** v call out

瘫 **huàn** N paralysis (See 瘫痪 tānhuàn)

幻 **huàn** ADJ illusory

幻灯 **huàndēng** N slide show
幻灯机 **huàndēngjī** slide projector
幻灯片 **huàndēngpiàn** slide, lantern slide (张 zhāng)
幻想 **huànxiǎng** v fantasize, have illusions

患 **huàn** v suffer (from a disease)

患者 **huànzhě** N patient
精神病患者 **jīngshénbìng huànzhě** one who suffers from a mental disorder

荒 **huāng** **I** ADJ barren, desolate **II** N crop falure, famine
荒地 **huāngdì** N uncultivated land, wasteland,
荒凉 **huāngliáng** ADJ bleak, desolate
荒谬 **huāngmiù** ADJ absurd, preposterous
荒谬至极 **huāngmiù zhìjí** absolutely absurd
荒唐 **huāngtáng** ADJ preposterous, way off the mark

荒唐透顶 **huāngtáng tòudǐng** incredibly silly, totally unreasonable

慌 **huāng** ADJ flustered, panic-stricken ■ 他考试要迟到了, 慌得坐错了车。Tā kǎoshì yào chídào le, huāng de zuòcuòle chē. *As he was about to be late for the examination, he was so flustered that he took the wrong bus.*

慌了手脚 **huāngle shǒu jiǎo** be so flustered as to not know what to do, be at a loss as to what to do

慌乱 **huāngluàn** ADJ panic-stricken, flustered

慌张 **huāngzhāng** ADJ in frantic haste, flustered

皇 **huáng** N emperor

皇帝 **huángdì** N emperor ■ 中国历史上第一个皇帝是秦始皇帝。Zhōngguó lìshǐ shang dì yī ge huángdì shì Qín Shǐ Huángdì. *The first emperor in Chinese history was Qin Shi Huangdi.*

皇后 **huánghòu** N wife of an emperor, empress

蝗 **huáng** N locust

蝗虫 **huángchóng** locust
蝗灾 **huángzāi** locust disaster

凰 **huáng** N female phoenix

煌 **huáng** ADJ intensely bright

黄 **huáng** ADJ yellow

黄瓜 **huángguā** N cucumber (根 gēn) ■ 我夏天爱吃新鲜黄瓜。Wǒ xiàtiān ài chī xīnxiān huángguā. *I love to eat fresh cucumber in summer.*

黄色 **huángsè** I N the yellow color II ADJ pornographic

黄色电影 **huángsè diànyǐng** pornographic movie
黄色网站 **huángsè wǎngzhàn** pornographic website

黄油 **huángyóu** N butter ■ 在新鲜面包上涂一层黄油, 可好吃了! Zài xīnxiān miànbāo shang tú yì céng huángyóu, kě hǎo chī le! *If you spread a thin layer of butter on freshly baked bread, how delicious it is!*

晃 **huǎng** V sway, shake

谎 **huǎng** N lie

谎话 **huǎnghuà** lie (especially used in speech)
谎言 **huǎngyán** lie (especially used in writing)

徽 **huī** N emblem, sign

国徽 **guóhuī** national emblem
校徽 **xiàohuī** school badge

灰 **huī** I ADJ gray ■ 这个城市污染很严重, 天空总是灰灰的。Zhège chéngshì wūrǎn hěn yánzhòng, tiānkōng zǒng shì huīhuī de. *This city has a serious pollution problem. Its sky is always gray.* II N ash, dust

灰尘 **huīchén** N dust

灰心 **huīxīn** ADJ disheartened, discouraged ■ 他虽然遭到失败, 但是没有灰心。Tā suīrán zāodào shībài, dànshì méiyǒu huīxīn. *Although he failed, he was not disheartened.*

恢 **huī** ADJ extensive, vast

恢复 **huīfù** V recover, restore ■ 祝你早日恢复健康! Zhù nǐ zǎorì huīfù jiànkāng! *I wish you a speedy recovery of health!*

挥 **huī** TRAD 揮 V 1 wave (See 发挥 fāhuī.) 2 scatter, disperse

挥霍 **huīhuò** V spend money carelessly, be a spendthrift, squander

辉 **huī** TRAD 輝 N splendor

辉煌 **huīhuáng** ADJ brilliant, splendid

回 I **huí** 1 V return (to a place), go back ■ 小陈在英国大学毕业以后, 就回中国找工作。Xiǎo Chén zài Yīngguó dàxué bìyè yǐhòu, jiù huí Zhōngguó zhǎo gōngzuò. *After graduating from university in the UK, Xiao Chen returned to China to look for a job.* 2 reply, answer

回电话 **huí diànhuà** call back

回避 **huíbì** V evade, dodge

回避问题 **huíbì wèntí** evade a question

回答 **huídá** V reply, answer ■ 警察说: "我问你几个问题, 你要老实回答。" Jǐngchá shuō: "Wǒ wèn nǐ jǐ ge wèntí, nǐ yào lǎoshí huídá." *The policeman said, "I'm going to ask you some questions. You must answer truthfully."*

回顾 **huígù** V look back, review

回国 **huíguó** V return to one's home country

回击 **huíjī** V counterattack

回来 **huílai** V return to a place (coming towards the speaker) ■ 哥哥要从国外回来过圣诞节。Gēge yào cóng guówài huílai guò shèngdànjié. *My elder brother is coming home from abroad for Christmas.*

回去 **huíqu** V return to a place (away from the speaker) ■ 你回去以后, 要常常给我们发电子邮件, 保持联系。Nǐ huíqu yǐhòu, yào chángcháng gěi wǒmen fā diànzǐ yóujiàn, bǎochí liánxì. *After you've returned home, you should send us e-mail often to keep in touch.*

回收 **huíshōu** V reclaim, recover

废品回收 **fèipǐn huíshōu** collect junk for recycling

回头 **huítóu** ADV later ■ 回头再说。**Huítóu zài shuō.** *I'll talk to you later.*

NOTE: 回头 **huítóu** is a colloquialism, used only in very informal styles.

回想 **huíxiǎng** V recall, recollect

回信 **huíxìn** N reply (either spoken or written) ■ 我们上个月送去了报价, 还没有收到他们回信。**Wǒmen shàng ge yuè sòngqule bàojià, hái méiyǒu shōudào tāmen huíxìn.** *We sent them quotes last month, and still haven't gotten a reply from them.*

回忆 **huíyì** I V recall, recollect ■ 你回忆一下, 最后一次是在哪里用那把钥匙的。**Nǐ huíyì yíxià, zuìhòu yí cì shì zài nǎli yòng nà bǎ yàoshi de.** *Try to remember where you used that key for the last time.* II N recollection, memory

回 2 **huí** M. WD number of times (of doing something) ■ 我去看了他们两回了, 他们一次都没有来过。**Wǒ qù kànle tāmen liǎng huí le, tāmen yí cì dōu méiyǒu láiguo.** *I've visited them twice, but they haven't come to see me even once.*

毁 **huǐ** V destroy

毁坏 **huǐhuài** V do irreparable damage
毁坏名誉 **huǐhuài míngyù** destroy one's reputation

毁灭 **huǐmiè** V exterminate
毁灭罪证 **huǐmiè zuìzhèng** destroy incriminating evidence

悔 **huǐ** V repent, regret

悔改 **huǐgǎi** V repent and mend one's way
悔恨 **huǐhèn** V repent bitterly

惠 **huì** N benefits, kindness (See 恩惠 **ēnhuì**)

慧 **huì** ADJ wise, intelligent (See 智慧 **zhìhuì**)

贿 **huì** TRAD 賄 V bribe

贿赂 **huìlù** I V bribe ■ 在这个国家, 贿赂官员是常见的事吗? **Zài zhège guójiā, huìlù guānyuán shì chángjiàn de shì ma?** *Is it commonplace to bribe officials in this country?* II N bribery

汇 **huì** TRAD 匯 V 1 converge, gather 2 remit

汇报 **huìbào** V report (to one's superior)

汇集 **huìjí** V compile, collect, gather
汇集有关的文件 **huìjí yǒuguān de wénjiàn** compile relevant documents

汇款 **huìkuǎn** V remit money, send remittance

汇率 **huìlù** N (currency) exchange rate

会 1 **huì** TRAD 會 I MODAL V 1 know how to, can ■ 我会游泳, 但是今天不能去游泳, 因为我感冒了。**Wǒ huì yóuyǒng, dànshì jīntiān bù néng qù yóuyǒng, yīnwèi wǒ gǎnmào le.** *I can swim, but I'm not able to today because I've got a cold.* 2 probably, will ■ 我看夜里会下雨。**Wǒ kàn yèlǐ huì xiàyǔ.** *I think it will rain tonight.* II V have the ability or knowledge ■ 你会日文吗? **Nǐ huì Rìwén ma?** *Do you speak (or write) Japanese?*

NOTE: 会 **huì** as a full verb meaning *have the ability* or *knowledge* is used with a limited range of nouns, such as nouns denoting languages. Using 会 **huì** in this way is colloquial.

会 2 **huì** TRAD 會 N 1 meeting, conference

大会 **dàhuì** an assembly, a rally
开会 **kāi huì** have a meeting ■ 明天的会非常重要, 请您一定参加。**Míngtiān de huì fēicháng zhòngyào, qǐng nín yídìng cānjiā.** *The meeting tomorrow is very important. Please be sure to attend it.*

2 association
读书会 **dúshū huì** book club
工会 **gōnghuì** labor union
学生会 **xuéshenghuì** students union

会场 **huìchǎng** N venue for a meeting, conference, assembly or rally

会话 **huìhuà** I V talk, hold a conversation ■ 我和她一天用中文会话, 一天用英文会话。**Wǒ hé tā yìtiān yòng Zhōngwén huìhuà, yìtiān yòng Yīngwén huìhuà.** *She and I talk in Chinese one day, and in English the next day.* II N conversation ■ 中文会话不太难, 难的是写汉字。**Zhōngwén huìhuà bú tài nán, nán de shì xiě hànzì.** *Chinese conversation is not too difficult. What is difficult is writing Chinese characters.*

会见 **huìjiàn** V (formal) meet

会客 **huìkè** V receive visitors ■ 今天市长有重要会议, 不能会客。**Jīntiān shìzhǎng yǒu zhòngyào huìyì, bù néng huì kè.** *Today the mayor is at an important conference and is not able to receive visitors.*

会谈 **huìtán** V hold (formal) talks ■ 两个大学的校长将举行会谈, 讨论怎样加强合作。**Liǎng ge dàxué de xiàozhǎng jiāng jǔxíng huìtán, tǎolùn zěnyàng jiāqiáng hézuò.** *The presidents of the two universities will hold a talk to discuss how to strengthen cooperation.*

会晤 **huìwù** V meet (formally)

会议 **huìyì** N meeting, conference ■ 这次会议讨论什么问题? **Zhè cì huìyì tǎolùn shénme wèntí?** *What questions will be discussed at the* conference? (→ What is on the conference agenda?)

参加会议 cānjiā huìyì participate in a meeting or conference

出席会议 chūxí huìyì attend a meeting or conference ■ 教育部长和几位重要人物出席了会议。Jiàoyù bùzhǎng hé jǐ wèi zhòngyào rénwù chūxíle huìyì. *The Minister of Education and several other VIPs attended this conference.*

举行会议 jǔxíng huìyì hold a meeting or conference

取消会议 qǔxiāo huìyì cancel a meeting or conference ■ 你知道为什么取消这次会议吗？Nǐ zhīdào wèishénme qǔxiāo zhè cì huìyì ma? *Do you know why this meeting was canceled?*

召开会议 zhàokāi huìyì convene a meeting or conference ■ 校长召开全体教师会议，讨论学生纪律问题。Xiàozhǎng zhàokāi quántǐ jiàoshī huìyì, tǎolùn xuéshēng jìlǜ wèntí. *The principal convened a teachers' meeting to discuss the issue of student discipline.*

会员 huìyuán N member of an asspciation

会员证 huìyuánzhèng membership card

工会会员 gōnghuì huìyuán labor union member

俱乐部会员 jùlèbù huìyuán club member

绘 huì v paint, draw

绘画 huìhuà N painting, drawing

昏 hūn v faint

昏迷 hūnmí v fall into a coma ■ 他在交通事故中受伤，昏迷了一天一夜才醒来。Tā zài jiāotōng shìgù zhōng shòule shāng, hūnmíle yìtiān-yí-yè cái xǐnglai. *He was injured in a traffic accident and was unconscious for twenty-four hours.*

婚 hūn N marriage

婚姻 hūnyīn N marriage ■ 婚姻是人生大事。Hūnyīn chì rénshēng dà shì. *Marriage is an important event in one's life.*

魂 hún N soul (See 灵魂 línghún)

浑 hún ADJ 1 muddy 2 whole, all over

浑身 húnshēn ADJ from head to foot, all over the body

浑身疼痛 húnshēn téngtòng ache all over

混 hùn v 1 mix up ■ 这两个词发音相同，意思不同，你别把它们混起来。Zhè liǎng ge cí fāyīn xiāngtóng, yìsi bù tóng, nǐ bié bǎ tāmen hùn qǐlai. *These two words have the same*

pronunciation, but different meanings. Do not mix them up.

混为一谈 hùn wéi yì tán lump different things together, fail to make a distinction between different things

2 pass for, pass off as **3** get along, get along with

混合 hùnhé v mix, blend, mingle

混乱 hùnluàn ADJ chaotic, confused

混凝土 hùnníngtǔ N cement, concrete

混淆 hùnxiáo v eliminate differences in order to confuse, mix up

混淆是非 hùnxiáo shìfēi confuse right and wrong

混浊 hùnzhuó ADJ murky, turbid

活 huó I v 1 be alive 2 work II ADJ alive, living ■ 很多中国人只吃活鱼，不吃死鱼。Hěn duō Zhōngguórén zhǐ chī huó yú, bù chī sǐ yú. *Many Chinese only eat live (→ freshly caught) fish, not dead ones.*

活动 huódòng I v do physical exercise II N activity

参加活动 cānjiā huódòng participate in an activity

活该 huógāi v serve one right, deserve ■ 他活该! Tā huógāi! *Serves him right!*

活力 huólì N vitality, vigor

活泼 huópo ADJ lively, vivacious ■ 她性格活泼，爱交朋友，到处受欢迎。Tā xìnggé huópo, ài jiāo péngyou, dàochù shòu huānyíng. *She is vivacious by nature and likes to make friends, so she is popular wherever she goes.*

活儿 huór N work, job

干活儿 gàn huór work, do a job ■ 没有适当的工具，这活儿没法干。Méiyǒu shìdàng de gōngjù, zhè huór méi fǎ gàn. *This job can't be done without the proper tools.*

NOTE: 活儿 huór and 干活儿 gàn huór are very colloquial, and usually refer to manual work.

活跃 huóyuè ADJ active, brisk ■ 这两天股票市场十分活跃。Zhè liǎng tiān gǔpiào shìchǎng shífēn huóyuè. *The share market is very brisk these days.*

火 huǒ N fire ■ 生了火，房间里就暖和了。Shēngle huǒ, fángjiān li jiù nuǎnhuo le. *After a fire was lit, the room became warm.*

着火 zháo huǒ catch fire, be caught on fire ■ 着火了! 着火了! Zháo huǒ le! Zháo huǒ le! *Fire! Fire!*

火柴 huǒchái N match (根 gēn, 盒 hé)

火柴盒 huǒchái hé a matchbox

划火柴 huá huǒchái strike a match

火车 huǒchē N train (辆 liàng, 列 liè) ■ 我们坐

火箭 huǒjiàn

火车到北京去。Wǒmen zuò huǒchē dào Běijīng qù. *We'll go to Beijing by train.*

火车站 **huǒchē zhàn** railway station
火车票 **huǒchē piào** train ticket
火车时刻表 **huǒchē shíkè biǎo** railway timetable
火箭 **huǒjiàn** N rocket (枚 méi)
发射火箭 **fāshè huǒjiàn** launch a rocket
火力 **huǒlì** N 1 fire power 2 thermal energy
火力发电 **huǒlì fādiàn** thermal power
火山 **huǒshān** N volcano (座 zuò)
火山爆发 **huǒshān bàofā** the eruption of a volcano
活火山 **huó huǒshān** active volcano
死火山 **sǐ huǒshān** dormant volcano
火焰 **huǒyàn** N flame
熊熊火焰 **xióngxióng huǒyàn** raging flames
火药 **huǒyào** N gunpowder
火灾 **huǒzāi** N fire disaster, fire (场 cháng)

伙 huǒ TRAD 夥 N partner

伙伴 **huǒbàn** N partner, mate
伙食 **huǒshí** N meals (provided by a school, a factory, etc.)

霍 huò as in 霍乱 huòluàn

霍乱 **huòluàn** N cholera

祸 huò TRAD 禍 N disaster, calamity

祸害 **huòhài** I N disaster, scourge II V bring disaster to, ruin

或 huò CONJ Same as 或者 huòzhě. Used more in writing.

或多或少 **huòduō huòshǎo** ADV more or less, somehow
或许 **huòxǔ** ADV perhaps, maybe
或者 **huòzhě** CONJ or, either ... or ■ 你明天一定要给我回信,可以打电话,或者发电子邮件。Nǐ míngtiān yídìng yào gěi wǒ huíxìn, kěyǐ dǎ diànhuà, huòzhě fā diànzǐ yóujiàn. *You must give me a reply tomorrow, either by phone or by email.*

惑 huò V confuse (See 迷惑 míhuo)

货 huò TRAD 貨 N goods ■ 暂时没有货,过两天再来问吧。Zànshí méiyǒu huò, guò liǎng tiān zài lái wèn ba. *We're out of stock for the time being. Do come and inquire after a couple of days.*

货币 **huòbì** N currency
货币贬值 **huòbì biǎnzhí** currency devaluation
货币升值 **huòbìshēngzhí** currency appreciation
货物 **huòwù** N goods, commodities, merchandise

CHINESE-ENGLISH

获 huò TRAD 獲 V gain, win

获得 **huòdé** V win, obtain, get ■ 他工作努力,获得了优秀成绩。Tā gōngzuò nǔlì, huòdéle yōuxiù chéngjì. *He works hard and has won excellent achievements.*
获取 **huòqǔ** V gain, obtain

J

击 jī TRAD 擊 V strike (See 打击 dǎjī)

几 jī TRAD 幾 ADV nearly

几乎 **jīhū** ADV almost, nearly ■ 这个国家的人几乎都会说一点英语。Zhège guójiā de rén jīhū dōu huì shuō yìdiǎn Yīngyǔ. *Almost everyone in this country speaks some English.*

饥 jī TRAD 飢 ADJ starved

饥饿 **jī'è** ADJ starved, hungry

机 jī TRAD 機 N 1 machine 2 opportunity

机场 **jīchǎng** N airport ■ "机场离这里还不远?" "不远,大概十公里。" "Jīchǎng lí zhèli yuǎn bu yuǎn?" "Bù yuǎn, dàgài shí gōnglǐ." *"Is the airport far from here?" "Not very far. About ten kilometers."*
机车 **jīchē** N locomotive (辆 liàng)
机床 **jīchuáng** N machine tool (台 tái)
机动 **jīdòng** ADJ 1 flexible
机动资金 **jīdòng zījīn** emergency fund, reserve fund
2 motorized, machine-powdered
机动车 **jīdòngchē** motorized vehicle (e.g. automobiles, motorcycles)
机构 **jīgòu** N government agency, organization
机关 **jīguān** N government office, state organ ■ 这一地区有很多重要的政府机关。Zhè yí dìqū yǒu hěn duō zhòngyào de zhèngfǔ jīguān. *There are many important government offices in this district.*
机会 **jīhuì** N opportunity, chance ■ 你有没有机会去北京学中文? Nǐ yǒu méiyǒu jīhuì qù Běijīng xué Zhōngwén? *Do you have any chance of going to Beijing to learn Chinese?*
放弃机会 **fàngqì jīhuì** give up an opportunity
抓住机会 **zhuāzhù jīhuì** grasp an opportunity
错过机会 **cuòguò jīhuì** miss an opportunity
机灵 **jīlíng** ADJ quick-witted
机密 **jīmì** ADJ secret, classified, confidential

92

机密文件 **jīmìwénjiàn** classified document
机器 **jīqì** N machine (台 **tái**)
使用机器 **shǐyòng jīqì** operate a machine
修理机器 **xiūlǐ jīqì** repair a machine
机器人 **jīqì rén** N robot
机体 **jītǐ** N organism
机械 **jīxiè** N machine, machinery ■ 建筑机械已经进入工地，马上要开工了。Jiànzhù jīxiè yǐjīng jìnrù gōngdì, mǎshàng yào kāigōng le. *Construction machinery has entered the construction site. (→ Construction machinery is on the site now.) Work will begin soon.*
机遇 **jīyù** N rare opportunity, favorable situation
机智 **jīzhì** I N wit II ADJ sharp-witted

肌 **jī** N muscle, flesh

肌肉 **jīròu** N muscle

讥 **jī** TRAD 譏 V sneer, mock

讥笑 **jīxiào** V sneer at, laugh at, ridicule

鸡 **jī** TRAD 雞 N chicken (只 **zhī**) ■ 我最爱喝鸡汤。Wǒ zuì ài hē jītāng. *Chicken soup is my favorite food.*
公鸡 **gōngjī** rooster
母鸡 **mǔjī** hen
小鸡 **xiǎojī** chick
肯德基烤鸡 **Kěn dé jī kǎojī** Kentucky Fried Chicken (KFC)

NOTE: 鸡 jī, as a general term, may denote either a hen, a rooster or chick, though they may be specified by 公鸡 gōngjī cock, 母鸡 mǔjī hen and 小鸡 xiǎojī chicken. As food, it is always 鸡 jī.

鸡蛋 **jīdàn** N hen's egg (只 **zhī**, 个 **gè**)

积 **jī** TRAD 積 V accumulate, amass

积极 **jījí** ADJ 1 enthusiastic, active ■ 王老师积极推广普通话。Wáng lǎoshī jījí tuīguǎng Pǔtōnghuà. *Teacher Wang is very enthusiastic about popularizing Putonghua.* 2 positive ■ 对于困难，我们应该采取积极的态度。Duìyú kùnnán, wǒmen yīnggāi cǎiqǔ jījí de tàidu. *We should adopt a positive attitude towards difficulties.*
积极性 **jījíxìng** N initiative, enthusiasm, zeal ■ 要使我们的公司成功，每一名职工必须发挥积极性。Yào shǐ wǒmen de gōngsī chénggōng, měi yì míng zhígōng bìxū fāhuī jījíxìng. *To make our company a success, every staff member must exercise initiative.*
积累 **jīlěi** V accumulate, build up
积压 **jīyā** V keep too long in store, overstock
积压物资 **jīyā wùzī** overstocked supplies

基 **jī** N (earthen) foundation

基本 **jīběn** ADJ fundamental, basic ■ 这件事的基本情况我已经知道了。Zhè jiàn shì de jīběn qíngkuàng wǒ yǐjīng zhīdào le. *I've learned the basic facts of this matter (or event).*
基本上 **jīběn shang** basically, on the whole
基层 **jīcéng** N primary level, grass-roots
基础 **jīchǔ** N foundation, basis ■ 学中文，第一年是打基础。Xué Zhōngwén, dì-yī nián shì dǎ jīchǔ. *The first year of your Chinese studies lays the foundation.*
基地 **jīdì** N base
基金 **jījīn** N fund
教育基金 **jiàoyù jījīn** educational fund
基金会 **jījīnhuì** N foundation
儿童福利基金会 **értóng fúlì jījīnhuì** Foundation for Children's Welfare
基因 **jīyīn** N gene

激 **jī** I V arouse, excite II ADJ violent, fervent

激动 **jīdòng** I V arouse, excite ■ 比赛结束前两分钟，他踢进一球，真是激动人心! Bǐsài jiéshù qián liǎng fēnzhōng, tā tī jìn yì qiú, zhēnshi jīdòng rénxīn! *Two minutes before the end of the match he scored a goal. How exciting!* II ADJ excited, very emotional ■ 我妹妹听了这个消息激动得一夜没睡。Wǒ mèimei tīngle zhège xiāoxi jīdòng de yíyè méi shuì. *After hearing the news my sister was so excited that she didn't sleep the entire night.*
激发 **jīfā** V arouse, stir up
激发爱国主义 **jīfā àiguózhǔyì** arouse patriotism
激光 **jīguāng** N laser
激光打印机 **jīguāng dǎyìnjī** laser printer
激励 **jīlì** V excite and urge, strongly encourage
激烈 **jīliè** ADJ fierce, intense ■ 运动会上运动员之间的竞赛十分激烈。Yùndònghuì shang yùndòngyuán zhī jiān de jìngsài shífēn jīliè. *At the sports meet competition between athletes was very fierce.*
激情 **jīqíng** N intense emotion, passion
激素 **jīsù** N hormone

圾 **jī** N garbage (See 垃圾 lājī.)

及 **jí** I CONJ and, with ■ 他父亲、伯父、及祖父都是商人。Tā fùqin, bófù, jí zǔfù dōu shì shāngrén. *His father, uncle and grandfather were all businessmen.* II V reach, come up to III ADV in time for

及格 **jígé** V pass (a test, an examination etc.) ■ "王老师，我这次测验及格吗?" "Wáng lǎoshī, wǒ zhè cì cèyàn jígé ma?" *"Teacher Wang, did I pass the test?"*
及时 **jíshí** I ADJ timely, at the proper time ■ 这

场雨下得真及时，农民高兴极了。Zhè cháng yǔ xià de zhēn jíshí, nóngmín gāoxìng jíle. *This rain came at the right time. Farmers are delighted.*
II ADV immediately, promptly, without delay
及早 **jízǎo** ADV as soon as possible, promptly

籍 jí N 1 registration 2 membership

会籍 **huìjí** membership of an association
籍贯 **jíguàn** N place of one's birth or origin

级 jí TRAD 級 N grade, rank ■ 他是一级教师。Tā shì yì-jí jiàoshī. *He is a first-class teacher.*
级别 **jíbié** N grade, scale
工资级别 **gōngzījíbié** wage/salary scale

极 jí TRAD 極 ADV extremely, highly ■ 今天天气极好。Jīntiān tiānqì jí hǎo. *The weather is extremely good today.*
极端 **jíduān** ADV extremely
走极端 **zǒu jíduān** go to extremes
极了 **jíle** ADV extremely, very ■ 这两天我忙极了。Zhè liǎng tiān wǒ máng jíle. *I'm extremely busy these days.*

NOTE: 极了 jíle is used after adjectives or some verbs to mean *extremely ... or very ...* For example: ■ 忙极了 máng jíle *extremely busy* ■ 高兴极了 gāoxìng jíle *very happy, delighted*

极力 **jílì** ADV to one's utmost
极力劝他戒烟 **jílì quàn tā jiè yān** try all one can to persuade him to give up smoking
极其 **jíqí** ADV extremely, highly ■ 我们极其重视产品质量。Wǒmen jíqí zhòngshì chǎnpǐn zhìliàng. *We attach great importance to the quality of our products.*
极限 **jíxiàn** N the ultimate, the limit

吉 jí ADJ lucky, fortunate, auspicious

吉普车 **jípǔchē** N jeep (辆 liàng)
吉祥 **jíxiáng** ADJ lucky, auspicious
吉祥物 **jíxiángwù** N mascot

辑 jí V compile, edit (See 编辑 biānjí)

疾 jí N disease

疾病 **jíbìng** N disease, illness

嫉 jí V be jealous

嫉妒 **jídù** V be jealous
嫉妒她妹妹的美貌 **jídù tā mèimei de měimào** be jealous of her younger sister's beauty

即 jí V be, mean

非此即彼 **fēicǐ jíbǐ** if it is not this one, it must be that one
即便 **jíbiàn** CONJ even if, even though
即将 **jíjiāng** ADV soon
即使 **jíshǐ** CONJ even if, even though ■ 他即使非常忙，也要抽工夫学中文。Tā jíshǐ fēicháng máng, yě yào chōu gōngfu xué Zhōngwén. *Even though he is very busy, he will try and find time to learn Chinese.*

急 jí ADJ 1 anxious ■ 他心里很急。Tā xīnlǐ hěn jí. *He's very anxious.* 2 urgent ■ 他家里有急事，今天没来上班。Tā jiāli yǒu jíshì, jīntiān méi lái shàngbān. *He has an urgent family matter [to attend to] and did not come to work today.*
急剧 **jíjù** ADJ sudden and intense, abrupt
急忙 **jímáng** ADJ hurried, hasty ■ 听说孩子病了，她急忙赶回家。Tīngshuō háizi bìng le, tā jímáng gǎn huíjiā. *Hearing that her child was sick, she rushed back home.*
急切 **jíqiè** ADJ eager and impatient, urgent
急性子 **jíxìngzi** N an impatient or impetuous person ■ 我妈妈是个急性子，爸爸是个慢性子，但是他们俩好像很合得来。Wǒ māma shì ge jíxìngzi, bàba shì ge mànxìngzi, dànshì tāmen liǎ hǎoxiàng hěn hé de lái. *My mother is an impatient person while my father moves slowly. However, they seem to get along quite well.*
急于 **jíyú** V be eager to, be anxious to
急于求成 **jí yú qiú chéng** eager to have immediate success
急躁 **jízào** ADJ impetuous, impatient ■ 他有一个缺点，就是性情急躁。Tā yǒu yí ge quēdiǎn, jiùshì xìngqíng jízào. *He has a shortcoming; that is, he is rather impatient.*

集 jí V gather

集合 **jíhé** V gather together, assemble
集会 **jíhuì** N meeting, assembly
集市 **jíshì** N country fair, market
集体 **jítǐ** ADJ collective
集团 **jítuán** N group, grouping
集邮 **jíyóu** N stamp collecting, philately
集中 **jízhōng** I V concentrate, focus ■ 这个国家的重工业集中在一个很小的地区。Zhège guójiā de zhònggōngyè jízhōng zài yí ge hěn xiǎo de dìqū. *The heavy industry of this country is concentrated in a small region.* II ADJ concentrated, focused ■ 这个学生上课时注意力不集中。Zhège xuésheng shàngkè shí zhùyìlì bù jízhōng. *This student's attention is not focused in class. (→ This student doesn't pay attention in class.)*
集资 **jízī** V raise funds

几 **jǐ** TRAD 幾 PRON **1** several, some ■ 我上星期买了几本书。Wǒ shàng xīngqī mǎile jǐ běn shū. *I bought several books last week.* **2** how many ■ 你上星期买了几本书? Nǐ shàng xīngqī mǎile jǐ běn shū? *How many books did you buy last week?*

NOTE: When 几 jǐ is used in a question to mean *how many*, it is presumed that the answer will be a number less than ten. Otherwise 多少 duōshǎo should be used instead. Compare: ■ 你有几个哥哥? Nǐ yǒu jǐ ge gēge? *How many elder brothers do you have?* ■ 你们学校有多少学生? Nǐmen xuéxiào yǒu duōshǎo xuésheng? *How many students are there in your school?*

几何 **jǐhé** N geometry

脊 **jǐ** N spine, backbone

脊梁 **jǐliang** N spine, backbone
脊椎 **jǐzhuī** N vertebra

己 **jǐ** PRON self (See 自己 zìjǐ.)

挤 **jǐ** TRAD 擠 **I** V squeeze, crowd ■ 他再忙也要挤出时间和孩子玩玩。Tā zài máng yě yào jǐchu shíjiān hé háizi wánwan. *No matter how busy he is, he always finds time to play with his children.* **II** ADJ crowded

给 **jǐ** TRAD 給 V provide (See 供给 gōngjǐ)

计 **jì** TRAD 計 V **1** plan **2** calculate

计划 **jìhuà** N, V plan ■ 这个计划不可行。Zhè ge jìhuà bù kěxíng. *This plan is not feasible.* ■ 我计划明年去美国旅游。Wǒ jìhuà míngnián qù Měiguó lǚyóu. *I plan to tour the States next year.*
制定计划 zhìdìng jìhuà draw up a plan
执行计划 zhíxíng jìhuà implement a plan
计较 **jìjiào** V **1** be fussy, haggle over **2** argue, dispute
斤斤计较 jīnjīn jìjiào haggle over insignificant things, quibble over trivia
计算 **jìsuàn** V calculate ■ 请你计算一下这个班去年考试的平均成绩。Qǐng nǐ jìsuàn yíxià zhège bān qùnián kǎoshì de píngjūn chéngjì. *Please calculate the average marks of this class for last year's examination.*
计算机 **jìsuànjī** Same as 电脑 diànnǎo. Used as a more formal term.

记 **jì** TRAD 記 V **1** remember, recall ■ 那条街叫什么,我记不清了。Nà tiáo jiē jiào shénme, wǒ jì bu qīng le. *I don't remember clearly the name of that street. (→ I can't quite recall the name of that street.)* **2** record (usually by writing down), bear in mind ■ 我把她要我买的东西都记下来了。Wǒ bǎ tā yào wǒ mǎi de dōngxi dōu jì xiàlai le. *I've written down the things she wants me to buy.*

记得 **jìde** V can remember, can recall ■ 我们第一次是在什么地方见面的,你还记得吗? Wǒmen dì-yī cì shì zài shénme dìfang jiànmiàn de, nǐ hái jìde ma? *Do you still remember where we first met?*
记不得 **jìbude** cannot remember, cannot recall ■ 我记不得了。Wǒ jìbude le. *I can't remember.*
记笔记 **jì bǐjì** V take notes
记号 **jìhao** N mark, sign
做记号 zuò jìhao put a mark
留下记号 liúxia jìhao leave a mark
记录 **jìlù** V, N record ■ 护士把病人的体温记录下来。Hùshi bǎ bìngrén de tǐwēn jìlù xiàlai. *The nurse recorded the patient's temperature.*
会议记录 huìyì jìlù minutes (of a meeting)
记性 **jìxing** N ability to memorize things, memory
记忆 **jìyì** **I** V remember, memorize ■ 童年的经历老人还记忆犹新。Tóngnián de jīnglì lǎorén hái jìyì yóuxīn. *The old man still vividly remembers his childhood experiences.* **II** N memory ■ 他们俩在海边共度的夏天,成了他难忘的记忆。Tāmen liǎ zài hǎibiān gòngdù de xiàtiān, chéngle tā nánwàng de jìyì. *The summer they spent together by the seaside has become an indelible memory for him.*
记载 **jìzǎi** V written record
记者 **jìzhě** N correspondent, reporter
记者招待会 **jìzhě zhāodàihuì** press conference, news conference
新闻记者 **xīnwén jìzhě** news reporter, journalist
记住 **jìzhù** V learn by heart, bear in mind ■ 你要记住我的话,别忘了! Nǐ yào jìzhù wǒ de huà, bié wàng le! *You should bear in mind what I said. Don't forget it.*

纪 **jì** TRAD 紀 N **1** discipline **2** record

纪律 **jìlǜ** N discipline (条 tiáo) ■ 他违反学校纪律,受到了批评。Tā wéifǎn xuéxiào jìlǜ, shòudàole pīpíng. *He violated school discipline and was reprimanded.*
纪念 **jìniàn** V commemorate ■ 中国的端午节纪念一位伟大的爱国诗人。Zhōngguó de Duānwǔ jié jìniàn yí wèi wěidà de àiguó shīrén. *The Chinese boat festival commemorates a great patriotic poet.*
纪要 **jìyào** N major points, summary, digest

技 **jì** N skill, ability

技能 jìnéng

技能 **jìnéng** N skill, technical skill

技巧 **jìqiǎo** N skill, craftsmanship
写作技巧 **xiězuòjìqiǎo** writing skills

技术 **jìshù** N technique, technology, skill
技术工人 **jìshù gōngrén** skilled worker

技术员 **jìshùyuán** N technician (位 wèi) ■ 车
床出问题了，要请技术员来看一下。Chēchuáng
chū wèntí le, yào qǐng jìshùyuán lái kàn yíxià.
*Something has gone wrong with the machine
tool. Please send for the technician.*

际 jì TRAD 際 N boundary, border (See 国际
guójì, 实际 shíjì.)

季 jì N season

季度 **jìdù** N quarter (of a year)

季节 **jìjié** N season ■ 春夏秋冬, 你最喜欢哪
个季节? Chūn-xià-qiū-dōng, nǐ zuì xǐhuan nǎge
jìjié? *Spring, summer, autumn and winter—which
season do you like best?*

济 jì TRAD 濟 V aid (See 经济 jīngjì.)

剂 jì TRAD 劑 N medicine

剂量 **jìliàng** N dose, dosage

迹 jì N remains, trace (See 古迹 gǔjì.)

迹象 **jìxiàng** N sign, indication
地震的迹象 **dìzhèn de jìxiàng** signs of a
(forthcoming) earthquake

既 jì CONJ 1 same as 既然 jìrán. Used more in
writing. 2 both ... and ...

既…又… **jì...yòu...** both ... and .... ■ 她既要
上班, 又要管孩子。Tā jì yào shàngbān, yòu yào
guǎn háizi. *She has to both work and care for the
children.*

既…也… **jì...yě...** both ... and .... ■ 你既要看
到一个人的优点, 也要看到一个人的缺点。Nǐ jì
yào kàndao yí ge rén de yōudiǎn, yěyào kàndao
yí ge rén de quēdiǎn. *You should see both the
merits and shortcomings of a person.*

既然 **jìrán** CONJ now that, since, as

忌 jì V 1 avoid, shun 2 be jealous

忌酒 **jìjiǔ** avoid wine, refrain from drinking
wines

忌妒 **jìdu** Same as 嫉妒 jídù

绩 jì TRAD 績 N accomplishment (See 成绩
chéngjì.)

继 jì TRAD 繼 V continue

继承 **jìchéng** V inherit, carry on
继承人 **jìchéngrén** N heir, successor

继续 **jìxù** V continue ■ 这种情况不能再继续
下去了。Zhè zhǒng qíngkuàng bùnéng zài jìxù
xiàqu le. *This situation must not be allowed to
go on.*

寂 jì ADJ lonely

寂静 **jìjìng** ADJ peaceful and quiet, still
寂寞 **jìmò** ADJ lonely

寄 jì V 1 send by mail, post ■ 请你马上把这些
书寄给王先生。Qǐng nǐ mǎshàng bǎ zhèxiē
shū jǐgei Wáng xiānsheng. *Please post these
books to Mr Wang immediately.*
寄快件 **jì kuàijiàn** send by express mail
2 entrust
寄托 **jìtuō** V entrust
寄托希望 **jìtuō xīwàng** place one's hope on

加 jiā V 1 add, plus ■ 一加二等于三。Yì jiā èr
dēngyú sān. *One plus two equals three.*
2 increase

加班 **jiābān** V work overtime
加班费 **jiābān fèi** overtime pay

加工 **jiāgōng** V process (unfinished products) ■ 这个工厂主要做来料加工。Zhège
gōngchǎng zhǔyào zuò láiliào jiāgōng. *This factory mainly processes supplied materials.*
来料加工 **láiliào jiāgōng** processing of supplied materials
食品加工 **shípǐn jiāgōng** food processing

加紧 **jiājǐn** V intensify, speed up
加紧准备 **jiājǐn zhǔnbèi** speed up preparations

加剧 **jiājù** V aggravate, exacerbate

加拿大 **Jiānádà** N Canada

加强 **jiāqiáng** V strengthen, reinforce ■ 我们要
加强研究开发工作。Wǒmen yào jiāqiáng yánjiū
kāifā gōngzuò. *We should strengthen research
and development work.*

加热 **jiārè** V heat, heat up

加入 **jiārù** V 1 become a member of 2 add in
加入网球俱乐部 **jiārù wǎngqiú jùlèbù** join
a tennis club

加深 **jiāshēn** V deepen
加深两国之间的相互理解 **jiāshēn liǎngguó
zhījiān de xiānghù lǐjiě** deepen mutual
understanding between the two countries

加速 **jiāsù** V accelerate, quicken
加速器 **jiāsù qì** accelerator

加以 **jiāyǐ** I V (used before a verb to indicate
what should be done) ■ 这个问题应及时加以
解决。Zhège wèntí yīng jíshí jiāyǐ jiějué. *This
problem should be solved promptly.* II CONJ in
addition, moreover ■ 他身体很差, 加以工作
太辛苦, 终于病倒在床上。Tā shēntǐ hěn chà,
jiāyǐ gōngzuò tài xīnkǔ, zhōngyú bìngdǎo zài

chuáng shang. *He was in poor health; moreover, he worked too hard and was finally bedridden with illness.*

NOTE: 加以 jiāyǐ as a verb smacks of officialese and is chiefly used in writing. The sentence still stands when 加以 jiāyǐ is omitted, e.g. ■ 这个问题应及时解决。Zhège wèntí yīng jíshí jiějué. *This problem should be solved promptly.*

加油 **jiāyóu** v **1** add fuel, fuel up
　加油站 **jiāyóuzhàn** gas station, service station
2 make extra efforts
　加油干 **jiāyóugàn** double one's efforts, put more effort into one's work

NOTE: 加油 jiāyóu is the colloquial expression used to cheer on a sportsperson or a sporting team in a competition, equivalent to *Come on!*, or *Go! Go!*

加重 **jiāzhòng** v increase the amount, aggravate
　加重负担 **jiāzhòng fùdān** increase the burden

嘉 **jiā** ADJ good, fine
　嘉宾 **jiābīn** honored guest
　嘉奖 **jiājiǎng** v commend, cite

佳 **jiā** ADJ good, fine, beautiful
　佳节 **jiājié** joyous festival

夹 **jiā** v pinch, squeeze, wedge between, sandwich
　夹杂 **jiāzá** v be mixed up with
　夹子 **jiāzi** N tong, clip
　衣服夹子 **yīfu jiāzi** clothes pin

家 **jiā** I N **1** family, household ■ 我家有四口人: 父亲, 母亲, 姐姐和我。Wǒ jiā yǒu sì kǒu rén: fùqin, mǔqin, jiějie hé wǒ. *There're four people in my family: my father, my mother, my sister and I.* **2** home ■ 下课以后我就回家。Xià kè yǐhòu wǒ jiù huíjiā. *I go home as soon as school is over.* II M. WD (for families or businesses)
　四家人家 **sì jiā rénjiā** four families
　一家商店 **yì jiā shāngdiàn** a store
　两家工厂 **liǎng jiā gōngchǎng** two factories III SUFFIX (denoting an accomplished expert)
　画家 **huàjiā** painter, artist
　教育家 **jiàoyùjiā** educator
　科学家 **kēxuéjiā** scientist
家常 **jiācháng** ADJ everyday life, commonplace
　谈家常 **tán jiācháng** have a chitchat
　家常便饭 **jiācháng biànfàn** simple meal, usually home-cooked
家畜 **jiāchù** N domesticated animal (头 tóu)
家教 **jiājiào** N **1** private tutor ■ 他们的女儿数学不行, 他们要给她找一位家教。Tāmen de nǚ'ér shùxué bùxíng, tāmen yào gěi tā zhǎo yí wèi jiājiào. *Their daughter is not good at math, so they're going to find a private tutor for her.* **2** family upbringing
家具 **jiājù** N furniture (套 tào, 件 jiàn)
家属 **jiāshǔ** N family member, one's dependent (名 míng)
家庭 **jiātíng** N family (个 gè) ■ 中国人比较重视家庭。Zhōngguórén bǐjiào zhòngshì jiātíng. *The Chinese attach much importance to the family.*

NOTE: 家 jiā has more meanings than 家庭 jiātíng. While 家庭 jiātíng means only *family*, 家 jiā may mean *family*, *household* or *home*.

家务 **jiāwù** N household chores, housework (件 jiàn)
家乡 **jiāxiāng** N hometown, home village ■ 这几年家乡发生了巨大变化。Zhè jǐ nián, jiāxiāng fāshēngle jùdà biànhuà. *In the past few years great changes have taken place in my hometown.*
家喻户晓 **jiā yù hù xiǎo** IDIOM be a household name, widely known
家长 **jiāzhǎng** N **1** head of a family **2** parent

颊 **jiá** N cheek

甲 1 **jiǎ** N first

甲 2 **jiǎ** N shell, nail
　指甲 **zhǐjia** fingernail
　甲板 **jiǎbǎn** N deck (of a ship)

假 **jiǎ** ADJ **1** false, untrue ■ 他说的这些话都是假的。Tā shuō de zhèxiē huà dōu shì jiǎ de. *All he said was untrue.* **2** artificial
假定 **jiǎdìng** v Same as 假设 jiǎshè
假话 **jiǎhuà** N falsehood, lie
假货 **jiǎhuò** N fake (goods), forgery, counterfeit
假冒 **jiǎmào** v pass off as genuine
假如 **jiǎrú** CONJ supposing, if
假若 **jiǎruò** CONJ Same as 假如 jiǎrú
假设 **jiǎshè** v suppose, assume
假腿 **jiǎtuǐ** N artificial leg
假牙 **jiǎyá** N dentures
假装 **jiǎzhuāng** v pretend, feign

稼 **jià** N crops (See 庄稼 zhuāngjià.)

价 **jià** TRAD 價 N price, value
价格 **jiàgé** N price ■ 新汽车价格合理, 卖得很快。Xīn qìchē jiàgé hélǐ, màide hěn kuài. *The new car is reasonably priced and sells quickly.*
价钱 **jiàqian** N price ■ 他只是问一下价钱, 没打算买。Tā zhǐshì wèn yíxià jiàqian, méi dǎsuàn

mǎi. *He only asked the price and didn't intend to buy it.*

价值 **jiàzhí** N value

价值观 **jiàzhíguān** N values ■ 对不起，我的价值观和你不一样。Duìbuqǐ, wǒ de jiàzhíguān hé nǐ bù yíyàng. *Sorry, my values are different from yours.*

驾 **jià** TRAD 駕 V drive, pilot

驾驶 **jiàshǐ** V drive, pilot
　驾驶轮船 **jiàshǐ lúnchuan** pilot a ship
　驾驶飞机 **jiàshǐ fēijī** pilot a plane
　驾驶汽车 **jiàshǐ qìchē** drive an automobile
驾驶员 **jiàshǐyuán** N driver, pilot

架 1 **jià** M. WD (used for machines, aircraft etc.)
　一架客机 **yí jià kèjī** a passenger plane

架 2 **jià** N shelf, stand
　书架 **shūjià** bookshelf

嫁 **jià** V (of a woman) marry ■ 他们的女儿嫁给了一个美国人。Tāmen de nǚér jiàgeile yí ge Měiguórén. *Their daughter married an American.*

NOTE: 嫁 jià means specifically (for a woman) *to marry*, while (for a man) *to marry* is 娶 qǔ. However more and more people simply use the verb 和…结婚 hé…jiéhūn to mean *marry*, e.g. 他们的女儿和一个美国人结婚。Tāmen de nǚér he yí ge Měiguórén jiéhūn. *Their daughter married an American.*

假 **jià** N holiday, leave

假期 **jiàqī** N holiday period, leave
假条 **jiàtiáo** N an application for leave, a leave form ■ 明天家里有重要的事不能来上课，这是假条。Míngtiān jiāli yǒu zhòngyào de shì, bù néng lái shàngkè, zhè shì jiàtiáo. *I can't come to class tomorrow as there's important family business to attend to. Here's my leave application.*
病假条 **bìngjiàtiáo** an application for sick leave, a doctor's certificate of illness, a medical certificate

尖 **jiān** ADJ sharp, pointed ■ 这孩子耳朵尖, 我们这么小声说话她都听见了。Zhè háizi ěrduo jiān, wǒmen zhème xiǎoshēng shuōhuà tā dōu tīngjiànle. *This child has sharp ears. We talked in such low voices but she heard us.*

尖端 **jiānduān** I N pointed end II ADJ sophisticated
　尖端产品 **jiānduān chǎnpǐn** technologically advanced product
　尖端科学 **jiāoduānkēxué** sophisticated science

尖端技术 **jiānduān jìshù** most advanced technology
尖锐 **jiānruì** ADJ 1 very sharp, penetrating ■ 多家报纸对政府提出尖锐批评。Duō jiā bàozhǐ duì zhèngfǔ tíchū jiānruì pīpíng. *Several newspapers made biting criticism of the government.* 2 fierce, uncompromising ■ 他们之间的矛盾很尖锐。Tāmen zhī jiān de máodùn hěn jiānruì. *There is bitter conflict between them.*
尖子 **jiānzi** N the pick (of a group), top student

坚 **jiān** TRAD 堅 ADJ hard, firm

坚持 **jiānchí** V uphold, persist (in) ■ 不管刮风下雨, 他坚持每天跑步。Bùguǎn guāfēng xià yǔ, tā jiānchí měi tiān pǎobù. *He persists in jogging every day no matter how wet or windy it is.*
坚定 **jiāndìng** ADJ firm ■ 我坚定地相信公司的决定是正确的。Wǒ jiāndìng de xiāngxìn gōngsī de juédìng shì zhèngquè de. *I'm firmly convinced that the company's decision is correct.*
坚固 **jiāngù** ADJ solid, sturdy
坚决 **jiānjué** ADJ resolute, determined ■ 我坚决执行公司的决定。Wǒ jiānjué zhíxíng gōngsī de juédìng. *I will resolutely carry out the company's decision.*
坚强 **jiānqiáng** ADJ strong, staunch
　性格坚强 **xìnggé jiānqiáng** strong character
坚实 **jiānshí** ADJ solid, substantial
　打下坚实的基础 **dǎxià jiānshí de jīchǔ** lay a solid foundation
坚硬 **jiānyìng** ADJ solid and hard

间 **jiān** TRAD 間 I N room (for a special purpose)
　洗澡间 **xǐzǎo jiān** bathroom
　手术间 **shǒushù jiān** operating theater, surgical room
II M. WD (for rooms)
　一间教室 **yì jiān jiàoshì** a classroom
　两间办公室 **liǎng jiān bàngōngshì** two offices

肩 **jiān** N the shoulder ■ 我左肩疼。Wǒ zuǒ jiān téng. *My left shoulder hurts.*

艰 **jiān** TRAD 艱 ADJ difficult

艰巨 **jiānjù** ADJ (of a big and important task) very difficult, strenuous
艰苦 **jiānkǔ** ADJ difficult, hard, tough ■ 城里人往往不了解很多农民的艰苦生活。Chénglírén wǎngwǎng bù liáojiě hěnduō nóngmín de jiānkǔ shēnghuó. *People in the city usually do not know the hard life many peasants live.*
艰难 **jiānnán** ADJ arduous, hard
　艰难的任务 **jiānnán de rènwu** arduous task
艰险 **jiānxiǎn** ADJ hard and difficult, perilous

兼 **jiān** ADV concurrently ■ 他是这家公司的董事长兼总经理。Tā shì zhè jiā gōngsī de dǒngshìzhǎng jiān zǒngjīnglǐ. *He is chairman of the board and concurrently CEO of the company.*

监 **jiān** TRAD 監 **I** v supervise, inspect **II** N prison, jail
监察 **jiānchá** v supervise, monitor
监督 **jiāndū** v **1** supervise, superintend **2** have under surveillance, watch over
监视 **jiānshì** v keep under surveillance, monitor ■ 在入口处安装了摄像机，来监视进出人员。Zài rùkǒuchù ānzhuāngle shèxiàngjī, lái jiānshì jìnchū rényuán. *A camera has been installed at the entrance to keep a watch on the people coming and going.*
监狱 **jiānyù** N jail, prison (座 zuò)

歼 **jiān** v wipe out
歼击机 **jiānjījī** N fighter plane
歼灭 **jiānmiè** v annihilate, wipe out

奸 **jiān** **I** ADJ wicked and treacherous **II** N traitor
汉奸 **hànjiān** traitor to the Han people, traitor to the Chinese people

煎 **jiān** v fry, shallow-fry

剪 **jiǎn** v cut (with scissors), shear
剪彩 **jiǎncǎi** v cut the ribbon at an opening ceremony
剪刀 **jiǎndāo** N scissors, shears (把 bǎ)

茧 **jiǎn** TRAD 繭 N **1** callus **2** cocoon
老茧 **lǎojiǎn** callus

柬 **jiǎn** N letter
请柬 **qǐngjiǎn** letter of invitation, invitation

检 **jiǎn** TRAD 檢 v examine
检测 **jiǎncè** v check and measure, verify
检查 **jiǎnchá** v examine, inspect, check ■ 先生，我要检查一下你的行李。Xiānsheng, wǒ yào jiǎnchá yíxià nǐ de xínglǐ. *I need to inspect your luggage, sir.*
检察 **jiǎnchá** N procuratorial work
检察员 **jiǎncháyuán** procurator
检察院 **jiǎncháyuàn** procuratorate
最高人民检察院 **Zuìgāo Rénmín Jiǎncháyuàn** the Supreme People's Procuratorate
检讨 **jiǎntǎo** **I** v **1** examine **2** review **II** N self-criticism

书面检讨 **shūmiàn jiǎntǎo** written self-criticism
做检讨 **zuò jiǎntǎo** make a self-criticism
检修 **jiǎnxiū** v examine and repair (a machine), maintain
大检修 **dàjiǎnxiū** overhaul
汽车检修工 **qìchē jiǎnxiū gōng** car mechanic
检验 **jiǎnyàn** **I** v examine, test **II** N examination, testing ■ 我们的产品都是经过严格的质量检验的。Wǒmen de chǎnpǐn dōu jīngguò yángé de zhìliàng jiǎnyàn de. *All our products undergo strict quality control.*

捡 **jiǎn** TRAD 撿 v pick up ■ 把垃圾捡起来。Bǎ lājī jiǎn qǐlái. *Pick up the litter.*

俭 **jiǎn** TRAD 儉 ADJ thrifty (See 勤俭 qínjiǎn)

拣 **jiǎn** TRAD 揀 v **1** choose, select ■ 这么多漂亮衣服，她不知道拣哪一件好。Zhème duō piàoliang yīfu, tā bù zhīdào jiǎn nǎ yí jiàn hǎo. *There were so many pretty dresses, she did not know which to choose.* **2** Same as 捡 jiǎn

减 **jiǎn** v **1** subtract, deduct ■ 三百六十七减二百八十六是多少? Sānbǎi liùshíqī jiǎn èrbǎi bāshíliù shì duōshǎo? *How much is 367 minus 268?*
减数 **jiǎnshù** subtrahend (e.g. 268 in the example)
被减数 **bèi jiǎnshù** minuend (e.g. 367 in the example)
2 reduce, lighten
减轻 **jiǎnqīng** v lighten, alleviate ■ 使用电脑以后，人们的工作量并没有减轻。Shǐyòng diànnǎo yǐhòu, rénmen de gōngzuò liàng bìng méiyǒu jiǎnqīng. *With the use of the computer, people's workload has not in fact been lightened.*
减弱 **jiǎnruò** v weaken, reduce in force
减少 **jiǎnshǎo** v make fewer, make less, reduce

简 **jiǎn** TRAD 簡 ADJ simple
简便 **jiǎnbiàn** ADJ simple and convenient, handy
简称 **jiǎnchēng** **I** v be called ... for short, be abbreviated as **II** N shortened form, shortening
简单 **jiǎndān** ADJ simple, uncomplicated
简短 **jiǎnduǎn** ADJ simple and short, brief
简短的发言 **jiǎnduǎn de fāyán** a brief speech, a short talk
简化 **jiǎnhuà** v simplify
简化手续 **jiǎnhuà shǒuxù** simplify formalities
简陋 **jiǎnlòu** ADJ simple and crude
简明 **jiǎnmíng** ADJ simple and clear, concise
简体字 **jiǎntǐzì** N simplified Chinese character

简讯 jiǎnxùn N news in brief, bulletin
简要 jiǎnyào ADJ brief and to the point
简要提纲 jiǎnyào tígāng brief outline
简易 jiǎnyì ADJ simple and easy ■ 这台机器操作简易。Zhètái jīqí cāozuò jiǎnyì. *The operartion of the machine is easy.*
简直 jiǎnzhí ADV simply, virtually
简直叫人不敢相信 jiǎnzhí jiào rén bùgǎn xiāngxìn simply unbelievable

碱 jiǎn N alkali, soda

件 jiàn M. WD (for things, clothes or furniture)
一件东西 yí jiàn dōngxi a thing, something ■ 我有一件东西忘在机场了。Wǒ yǒu yí jiàn dōngxi wàng zài jīchǎng le. *I've [inadvertently] left something in the airport.*
一件事情 yí jiàn shìqing a matter
一件衣服 yí jiàn yīfu a piece of clothing (e.g. a jacket, dress)

见 jiàn TRAD 見 V see, perceive ■ 经理, 有一位小姐要见你。Jīnglǐ, yǒu yí wèi xiǎojiě yào jiàn nǐ. *There's a young lady here who wants to see you, sir (← manager).*
见解 jiànjiě N opinion, view
提出见解 tíchū jiànjiě voice one's opinion
见面 jiànmiàn V meet, see (a person) ■ 这个周末她要带男朋友回家和父母见面。Zhège zhōumò tā yào dài nánpéngyou huíjiā hé fùmǔ jiànmiàn. *This weekend she will bring her boy-friend home to meet her parents.*
见识 jiànshi N knowledge, experience
见效 jiànxiào V produce the desired result, be effective

舰 jiàn TRAD 艦 N warship (艘 sōu)
航空母舰 hángkōng mǔjiàn aircraft carrier
驱逐舰 qūzhújiàn destroyer
巡洋舰 xúnyángjiàn cruiser
舰队 jiànduì N fleet of warships

剑 jiàn TRAD 劍 N sword (把 bǎ)

建 jiàn V 1 build, construct ■ 在新区里要建两座学校。Zài xīnqū li yào jiàn liǎng zuò xuéxiào. *Two schools will be built in the new district.* 2 found, set up ■ 这座大学建于1950年。Zhè zuò dàxué jiàn yu yījiǔwǔlíng nián. *This university was founded in 1950.*
建交 jiànjiāo V establish diplomatic relations
建立 jiànlì V 1 establish, set up ■ 我们希望和你们建立友好合作关系。Wǒmen xīwàng hé nǐmen jiànlì yǒuhǎo hézuò guānxi. *We hope to establish a relationship of friendly cooperation with you.* 2 Same as 建 jiàn (= build, construct)
建设 jiànshè V build, construct ■ 真难想象, 在一片沙漠上建设起这样一座城市。Zhēn nán xiǎngxiàng, zài yí piàn shāmò shang jiànshèqi zhèyàng yí zuò chéngshì. *It's hard to imagine that such a city could have been built in the desert.*
建议 jiànyì V suggest, propose ■ 他的建议没有被采用, 甚至没有被考虑。Tā de jiànyì méiyǒu bèi cǎiyòng, shènzhì méiyǒu bèi kǎolǜ. *His suggestion was not adopted; it was not even considered.*
建造 jiànzào V construct, build
建造一座大水库 jiànzào yízuò dà shuǐkù build a big reservoir
建筑 jiànzhù N 1 building, edifice (座 zuò) ■ 这座古代建筑具有很高的艺术价值。Zhè zuò gǔdài jiànzhù jùyǒu hěn gāo de yìshù jiàzhí. *This ancient building has high artistic value.* 2 architecture
建筑师 jiànzhùshī N architect
建筑物 jiànzhùwù N architectural structure, building
建筑学 jiànzhùxué N (the discipline of) architecture

健 jiàn ADJ strong
健儿 jiàn'ér N athlete (as a term of approbation) (位 wèi)
健康 jiànkāng I N health ■ 生了病才知道健康多么宝贵。Shēngle bìng cái zhīdào jiànkāng duōme bǎoguì. *You don't know how precious good health is until you are ill.* II ADJ healthy, in good health ■ 祝您健康! /祝您身体健康! Zhù nín jiànkāng! / Zhù nín shēntǐ jiànkāng! *I wish you good health.*
健美 jiànměi ADJ vigorous and graceful, of athletic beauty
健美操 jiànměicāo N calisthenics
健全 jiànquán I ADJ sound, perfect
身心健全 shēn-xīn jiànquán a healthy body and a sound mind
健全的税收制度 jiànquán de shuìshōu zhìdù a sound tax system
II V make perfect, improve
健身 jiànshēn V do physical exercises, have a work-out
健身房 jiànshēnfáng N gymnasium, health club
健壮 jiànzhuàng ADJ healthy and strong, robust

键 jiàn N key (See 关键 guānjiàn.)
键盘 jiànpán N keyboard

荐 **jiàn** TRAD 薦 v recommend (See 推荐 tuījiàn.)

鉴 **jiàn** TRAD 鑒 **I** N mirror

以史为鉴 **yǐ shǐ wéi jiàn** take history as a mirror (→ learn from history)
II v inspect, examine
鉴别 **jiànbié** v distinguish, discern
鉴别古画 **jiànbié gǔhuà** appraise an ancient painting, study an ancient painting to determine its authenticity and/or value
鉴于 **jiànyú** PREP in view of, considering

贱 **jiàn** TRAD 賤 ADJ cheap

溅 **jiàn** TRAD 濺 v splash, spatter

践 **jiàn** TRAD 踐 v trample

践踏 **jiàntà** v trample underfoot
践踏公民权利 **jiàntà gōngmín quánlì** trample on civil rights

渐 **jiàn** TRAD 漸 ADV Same as 渐渐 jiànjiàn

渐渐 **jiànjiàn** ADV gradually, by and by

箭 **jiàn** N arrow ■ 你会射箭吗? Nǐ huì shè jiàn ma? *Do you know how to shoot an arrow?*
箭头 **jiàntóu** N **1** arrow head **2** sign of an arrow to show direction

间 **jiàn** TRAD 間 v separate

间隔 **jiàngé** **I** N interval, space between **II** v have intervals
间接 **jiànjiē** ADJ indirect

江 **jiāng** N river (条 tiáo) ■ 这条江从西向东流。Zhè tiáo jiāng cóng xī xiàng dōng liú. *This river flows from west to east.*

NOTE: The most famous 江 jiāng in China is 长江 Cháng jiāng, the longest river in China. 长江 Cháng jiāng, which literally means *long river*, is also known as the Yangtze River. See note on 河 hé.

疆 **jiāng** N border, boundary

僵 **jiāng** ADJ stiff and numb, deadlocked

冻僵 **dòngjiāng** frozen stiff

姜 **jiāng** TRAD 薑 N ginger

将 1 **jiāng** TRAD 將 PREP Same as 把 bǎ, but only used in writing.

将 2 **jiāng** TRAD 將 ADV will, shall, be going to, be about to ■ 张部长将在下周二出席会议, 并发表重要讲话。Zhāng bùzhǎng jiāng zài xià zhōuèr chūxí huìyì, bìng fābiǎo zhòngyào jiǎnghuà. *Minister Zhang will attend the conference next Tuesday and deliver an important speech.*
将近 **jiāngjìn** ADV be close to, near
将军 **jiāngjūn** N (armed forces) general
将来 **jiānglái** N future ■ 将来的世界会怎么样? 谁也不知道。Jiānglái de shìjiè huì zěnmeyàng? Shéi yě bù zhīdào. *What will the world be like in the future? Nobody knows.*
将要 **jiāngyào** ADV Same as 将 jiāng 2 ADV

浆 **jiāng** TRAD 漿 N thick liquid

豆浆 **dòujiāng** soybean milk, soy milk

讲 **jiǎng** TRAD 講 v **1** talk **2** tell

讲故事 **jiǎng gùshi** tell a story
3 pay attention to, attach importance to
讲卫生 **jiǎng wèishēng** pay attention to personal hygiene
讲话 **jiǎnghuà** N speech, talk ■ 我的讲话只是代表我个人的意见, 不代表公司立场。Wǒ de jiǎnghuà zhǐshì dàibiǎo wǒ gèrén de yìjiàn, bú dàibiǎo gōngsī lìchǎng. *My talk expresses only my personal opinion, and does not reflect the stand of the company.*
讲解 **jiǎngjiě** v explain orally
讲究 **jiǎngjiu** **I** v be particular about, pay much attention to ■ 她十分讲究穿着。Tā shífēn jiǎngjiu chuānzhuó. *She pays much attention to clothes.* **II** ADJ exquisite, of very high standard
讲课 **jiǎngkè** v lecture, teach
讲理 **jiǎnglǐ** v Same as 讲道理 jiǎng dàoli
讲述 **jiǎngshù** v give an account of, narrate, tell about
讲演 **jiǎngyǎn** v deliver a speech
讲义 **jiǎngyì** N lecture notes, teaching materials
讲座 **jiǎngzuò** N lecture, course of lectures ■ 李教授在下学期要做当代中国经济讲座, 共分十二讲。Lǐ jiàoshòu zài xià xuéqī yào zuò dāngdài Zhōngguó jīngjì jiǎngzuò, gòng fēn shí'èr jiǎng. *Next semester, Professor Li will offer a course in Contemporary Chinese Economy, which will be given in twelve lectures.*

奖 **jiǎng** TRAD 獎 **I** N prize, award ■ 这个电影得过奖, 不过一点也不好看。Zhège diànyǐng déguo jiǎng, búguò yìdiǎn yě bù hǎokàn. *This film has won an award, but isn't at all interesting.* **II** v award
奖杯 **jiǎngbēi** N trophy, cup (given as a prize)
奖金 **jiǎngjīn** N **1** prize money (笔 bǐ) **2** bonus (笔 bǐ) ■ 到年底, 公司里的职工每人多发一个月的

奖励 jiǎnglì

工资作为奖金。Dào niándǐ, gōngsī lǐ de zhígōng měirén duō fā yí gè yuè de gōngzī zuòwéi jiǎngjīn. *At the end of the year, every staff member in the company is paid one extra month wages as bonus.*

奖励 jiǎnglì v reward in order to encourage
奖励助人为乐者 **jiǎnglì zhù-rén-wéi-lè zhě** reward and encourage a good Samaritan

奖品 jiǎngpǐn N prize, award (份 fèn, 件 jiàn)
颁发奖品 **bānfā jiǎngpǐn** present a prize/an award
领取奖品 **lǐngqǔ jiǎngpǐn** receive a prize/an award

奖学金 jiǎngxuéjīn N scholarship

奖状 jiǎngzhuàng N certificate of award, certificate of merit (张 zhāng)

桨 jiǎng TRAD 槳 N oar

降 jiàng v fall, lower ■ 一天中气温降了十度。Yì tiān zhōng qìwēn jiàngle shí dù. *The temperature fell by ten degrees within a day.*

降低 jiàngdī v lower, cut down, reduce ■ 顾客很少，他们只能降低价格。Gùkè hěn shǎo, tāmen zhǐnéng jiàngdī jiàgé. *As there were few customers, they had to reduce prices.*

降价 jiàngjià v reduce prices
降临 jiànglín v befall, arrive

酱 jiàng TRAD 醬 N soy paste

酱油 jiàngyóu N soy sauce

匠 jiàng N craftsman

交 jiāo v 1 hand over, pay (bills, fees) ■ 这个月的电费你交了吗？Zhè ge yuè de diànfèi nǐ jiāole ma? *Have you paid this month's electricity bill?* 2 cross, intersect

交叉 jiāochā v intersect, cross
交叉点 **jiāochādiǎn** Same as 交点 jiāodiǎn

交错 jiāocuò v crisscross, interlock

交代 jiāodài v 1 leave word, hand over
交代任务 **jiāodài rènwu** give information about a job, brief on a task
2 confess (a wrongdoing)

交待 jiāodài Same as 交代 jiāodài
交点 jiāodiǎn N point of intersection
交付 jiāofù v pay, hand over
交换 jiāohuàn v exchange ■ 主客交换了礼物。Zhǔ-kè jiāohuànle lǐwù. *The host and the guest exchanged gifts.*

交际 jiāojì I N social contact, social intercourse, communication ■ 她和外人没有什么交际。Tā hé wàirén méiyǒu shénme jiāojì. *She doesn't have many social contacts.* II v make social contacts ■ 和不同的人交际要用不同的方法。Hé

bùtóng de rén jiāojì yào yòng bùtóng de fāngfǎ. *You should use different ways to maintain social contact with different people.*

交际费 jiāojìfèi N entertainment expense
交际花 jiāojìhuā N social butterfly
交际舞 jiāojìwǔ N ballroom dancing
交流 jiāoliú v exchange, communicate
交涉 jiāoshè v negotiate
交手 jiāoshǒu v fight hand to hand, cross swords with

交谈 jiāotán v have a conversation, talk with
用中文交谈 **yòng Zhōngwén jiāotán** have a conversation in Chinese

交替 jiāotì v 1 replace 2 alternate

交通 jiāotōng N transport, transportation, traffic ■ 火车仍然是中国最主要的交通工具。Huǒchē réngrán shì Zhōngguó zuì zhǔyào de jiāotōng gōngjù. *The railway remains China's chief means of transport.*
交通事故 **jiāotōng shìgù** traffic accident, road accident
交通警察 **jiāotōng jǐngchá** traffic policeman, traffic police

交往 jiāowǎng v associate with, be in contact with

交易 jiāoyì N business transaction, business deal (笔 bǐ)
做一笔交易 **zuò yìbǐ jiāoyì** do a business deal

胶 jiāo TRAD 膠 N rubber

胶卷 jiāojuǎn N roll of film
胶片 jiāopiàn N film (for a camera)

郊 jiāo N outskirts, suburbs

郊区 jiāoqū N suburbs, outskirts (of a city) ■ 在西方人们一般都喜欢居住在郊区。Zài Xīfāng rénmen yìbān dōu xǐhuan jūzhù zài jiāoqū. *In the West, people generally prefer to live in the suburbs.*

浇 jiāo TRAD 澆 v water

浇花 jiāohuā water flowers
浇水 jiāoshuǐ supply water to plants or crops
浇灌 jiāoguàn v irrigate, water

教 jiāo v teach ■ 请你教教我怎么使用这台新电脑。Qǐng nǐ jiāojiao wǒ zěnme shǐyòng zhè tái xīn diànnǎo. *Please teach me how to use this new computer.*

骄 jiāo TRAD 驕 ADJ conceited

骄傲 jiāo'ào ADJ proud, conceited, arrogant ■ 他为自己的孩子感到骄傲。Tā wèi zìjǐ de háizi gǎndào jiāo'ào. *He is proud of his children.*

娇 **jiāo** ADJ **1** tender and beautiful **2** Same as 娇气 jiāoqi

娇惯 **jiāoguàn** V pamper, spoil

娇气 **jiāoqì** ADJ **1** finicky, squeamish **2** fragile, delicate

焦 **jiāo** ADJ **1** scorched, burnt **2** anxious, worried

焦点 **jiāodiǎn** N focus

焦急 **jiāojí** ADJ anxious, very worried
　焦急地等待 jiāojí de děngdài wait anxiously

蕉 **jiāo** N banana (See 香蕉 xiāngjiāo)

椒 **jiāo** N hot spice plant (See 辣椒 làjiāo)

嚼 **jiáo** V chew, munch

角 **1 jiǎo** N corner ■ 不少人常常在公园的一角练习英语口语, 那地点就成了 "英语角"。Bùshǎo rén chángcháng zài gōngyuán de yì jiǎo liànxí Yīngyǔ kǒuyǔ, nà dìdiǎn jiù chéngle "Yīngyǔ Jiǎo". Many people often practice oral English in a corner of the park, and that spot becomes the "English Corner."

角度 **jiǎodù** N angle, point of view

角落 **jiǎoluò** N corner, nook

角 **2 jiǎo** M. WD (Chinese currency: 1 角 jiǎo = 0.1 元 yuán = 10 分 fēn) ten cents, a dime
　两角钱 liǎng jiǎo qián two jiao, twenty cents
　八块九角五分 bā kuài jiǔ jiǎo wǔ fēn eight yuan nine jiao and five fen = eight dollars and ninety-five cents

NOTE: In colloquial Chinese 毛 máo is often used instead of 角 jiǎo, e.g. 两毛钱 liǎng máo qián is equivalent to two jiao twenty cents

饺 **jiǎo** TRAD 餃 N Same as 饺子 jiǎozi

饺子 **jiǎozi** N stuffed dumpling, jiaozi
　包饺子 bāo jiǎozi make jiaozi

狡 **jiǎo** ADJ sly, cunning

狡猾 **jiǎohuá** ADJ cunning, crafty

脚 **jiǎo** N foot (只 zhī) ■ 我的脚很大, 穿不下这双鞋。Wǒ de jiǎo hěn dà, chuān bú xià zhè shuāng xié. My feet are big. This pair of shoes doesn't fit.

脚步 **jiǎobù** N footstep, step

搅 **jiǎo** TRAD 攪 V **1** mix **2** confuse, disturb

搅拌 **jiǎobàn** V stir, mix

缴 **jiǎo** V **1** pay, hand in **2** capture

缴纳 **jiǎonà** V pay, hand in
　缴纳罚款 jiǎonà fákuǎn pay a fine

绞 **jiǎo** V wring, twist
　把毛巾绞干 bǎ máojīn jiǎo gān wring a towel dry

轿 **jiào** TRAD 轎 N sedan chair

轿车 **jiàochē** N sedan car, car

叫 **1 jiào** V call, address, shout, cry out ■ 大家都叫他小王。Dàjiā dōu jiào tā Xiǎo Wáng. Everybody calls him Xiao Wang.

叫喊 **jiàohǎn** V shout, call out

叫唤 **jiàohuan** V cry out, call out

叫嚷 **jiàorǎng** V yell, howl

叫做 **jiàozuò** V be called, be known as, be referred to as ■ 这种病叫做百日咳。Zhè zhǒng bìng jiàozuò bǎirìké. This illness is called the "hundred-day cough" (or whooping cough).

叫 **2 jiào** PREP Same as 被 bèi. Used more in colloquialisms.

教 **jiào** N teaching

教材 **jiàocái** N teaching material, textbook, coursebook (份 fèn, 本 běn)

教导 **jiàodǎo** V instruct, give moral guidance

教会 **jiàohuì** N organized religious group, church
　天主教会 Tiānzhǔ Jiàohuì the Catholic Church

教练 **jiàoliàn** N (sports) coach

教师 **jiàoshī** N teacher (位 wèi, 名 míng) ■ 在中国人的传统中, 严格的教师才是好教师。Zài Zhōngguórén de chuántǒng zhōng, yángé de jiàoshī cái shì hǎo jiàoshī. In the Chinese tradition, only a strict teacher was a good teacher.

教室 **jiàoshì** N classroom (间 jiān) ■ 我们在那间教室上数学课。Wǒmen zài nà jiān jiàoshì shàng shùxué kè. We have our mathematics class in that classroom.

教室大楼 **jiàoshì dàlóu** classroom block

教授 **jiàoshòu** N university professor

副教授 **fùjiàoshòu** associate professor

教唆 **jiàosuō** V instigate and abet

教堂 **jiàotáng** N church building, church
　大教堂 dàjiàotáng cathedral
　上教堂 shàng jiàotáng go to church (for worship)

教条 **jiàotiáo** N dogma

教学 **jiàoxué** N teaching, education ■ 老师们每月开会, 讨论教学中出现的问题。Lǎoshīmen měi yuè kāihuì, tǎolùn jiàoxué zhong chūxiàn de wèntí. The teachers have a monthly meeting to discuss problems encountered in teaching.

教训 jiàoxun I v lecture, talk down to ■ 你可以不同意别人的意见，可别老是教训别人。Nǐ kěyǐ bù tóngyì biérén de yìjiàn, kě bié lǎoshì jiàoxun biérén. *You may hold different opinions from others, but you shouldn't always talk down to them.* **II** N lesson (learnt from mistakes or experience), moral

教养 jiàoyǎng N upbringing, education 有教养 yǒu jiàoyǎng well brought up, well-bred

教育 jiàoyù I v educate, teach ■ 父母应该教育自己的孩子。Fùmǔ yīnggāi jiàoyù zìjǐ de háizi. *Parents should educate their children.* **II** N education ■ 教育关系到国家的将来。Jiàoyù guānxì dào guójiā de jiānglái. *Education has an important bearing on the future of a country.*

教员 jiàoyuán N teacher (in a particular school)

觉 jiào TRAD 覺 See 睡觉 shuìjiào

较 jiào TRAD 較 **I** PREP Same as 比 bǐ **1** PREP. Used only in writing. **II** ADV **1** Same as 比较 bǐjiào **2** Used only in writing.

较量 jiàoliàng v test the strength of, compete

窖 jiào N cellar

地窖 dìjiào cellar, pit

阶 jiē TRAD 階 N steps, grade

阶段 jiēduàn N period, stage ■ 这项工程正处在开始阶段。Zhè xiàng gōngchéng zhèng chù zài kāishǐ jiēduàn. *This project is just at an initial stage.*

阶级 jiējí N social class ■ 今天的中国社会有哪些阶级? Jīntiān de Zhōngguó shèhuì yǒu nǎxiē jiējí? *What classes does today's Chinese society have?*

揭 jiē v take off, reveal

揭发 jiēfā v expose, uncover 揭发一起逃税案 jiēfā yìqǐ táoshuì àn expose a case of tax evasion

揭露 jiēlù v uncover, reveal 揭露阴谋 jiēlù yīnmóu uncover a conspiracy

揭示 jiēshì v bring to light, reveal 揭示真相 jiēshì zhēnxiàng reveal the truth

皆 jiē PRON all, both ■ 人人皆知。Rénrén jiē zhī. *Everyone knows.*

结 jiē TRAD 結 v bear (fruit)

结实 jiēshi ADJ sturdy, strong, robust ■ 他们做的家具都很结实。Tāmen zuò de jiājù dōu hěn jiēshi. *The furniture they make is very sturdy.* ■ 他身体很结实。Tā shēntǐ hěn jiēshi. *He has a robust body.*

接 jiē v **1** receive (a letter, a telephone call) ■ 我要休息一会儿，谁的电话都不接。Wǒ yào xiūxi yíhuìr, shuí de diànhuà dōu bù jiē. *I'll have a rest and take no calls.* **2** meet and greet (a visitor) ■ 王先生是第一次到这里来，你应该去机场接他。Wáng xiānsheng shì dì-yī cì dào zhèlǐ lái, nǐ yīnggāi qù jīchǎng jiē tā. *This is the first time that Mr Wang's coming here. You should go and meet him at the airport.*

接班 jiēbān v take over from, carry on

接触 jiēchù v get in touch (with) ■ 我先和他们初步接触一下，了解他们的想法。Wǒ xiān hé tāmen chūbù jiēchù yíxià, liǎojiě tāmen de xiǎngfǎ. *I'll first get in touch with them tentatively to find out their thoughts.*

接待 jiēdài v receive (a visitor)

接到 jiēdao v have received ■ 我还没有接到会议邀请信。Wǒ hái méiyǒu jiēdao huìyì yāoqǐngxìn. *I have not yet received a letter of invitation to the conference.*

接见 jiējiàn v receive (somebody), meet (somebody), give an audience ■ 教育部长昨天接见了中学教师代表。Jiàoyù bùzhǎng zuótiān jiējiànle zhōngxué jiàoshī dàibiǎo. *The Minister of Education received representatives of secondary school teachers yesterday.*

NOTE: 接见 jiējiàn meaning *receive* or *meet* is only used for formal or official occasions. It implies that the receiving party is superior in status to the one being received.

接近 jiējìn v be close to, be near

接连 jiēlián ADV successively, one after another ■ 我接连收到公司三个电子邮件，催我马上付款。Wǒ jiēlián shōu dào gōngsī sān gè diànzǐ yóujiàn, cuī wǒ mǎshàng fùkuǎn. *I received three e-mail messages from the company in a row, urging me to pay the bill immediately.*

接洽 jiēqià v arrange with

接受 jiēshòu v accept ■ 我们不接受礼物。Wǒmen bù jiēshòu lǐwù. *We do not accept gifts.*

接受批评 jiēshòu pīpíng accept criticism, take criticism

接着 jiēzhe CONJ and immediately, then, at the heels of (a previous action or event) ■ 我先听到有人叫我，接着小王跑了进来。Wǒ xiān tīngdao yǒu rén jiào wǒ, jiēzhe Xiǎo Wáng pǎole jìnlai. *I first heard someone calling me, and then Xiao Wang ran into the room.*

街 jiē N street (条 tiáo) ■ 我家前边的那条街总是很安静。Wǒ jiā qiánbian de nà tiáo jiē zǒngshì hěn ānjìng. *The street in front of my home is always quiet.*

街上 **jiē shang** on the street

步行街 **bùxíng jiē** pedestrian street

逛大街 **guàng dàjiē** stroll the streets, do window shopping

街道 **jiēdào** N street (条 tiáo)

街道委员会 **jiēdào wěiyuánhuì** neighborhood committee

街坊 **jiēfang** N neighbor

街头 **jiētóu** N street

街头流浪汉 **jiētóu liúlànghàn** a homeless being in the street

节 jié TRAD 節 **I** N **1** festival ■ 这个地方一年有好几个节。**Zhège dìfang yì nián yǒu hǎo jǐ ge jié.** *There're quite a number of festivals in this area.*

过节 **guò jié** observe a festival, celebrate a festival

中秋节 **zhōngqiūjié** Mid-Autumn Festival (on the fifteenth day of the eighth lunar month) **2** section, division **II** M. WD a period of time

一节课 **yì jié kè** a period of class

III V save, economize

节目 **jiémù** N program ■ 这个节目是谁编的? 谁演的? **Zhège jiémù shì shuí biān de? Shuí yǎn de?** *Who wrote this program? Who acted it?*

儿童节目 **értóng jiémù** children's program

体育节目 **tǐyù jiémù** sports program

文艺节目 **wényì jiémù** theatrical program

新闻节目 **xīnwén jiémù** news program (on TV or radio)

节日 **jiérì** N festival day ■ 中国人最重要的节日是春节, 也就是中国人的新年。**Zhōngguórén zuì zhòngyào de jiérì shì chūnjié, yě jiùshì Zhōngguórén de xīnnián.** *The most important festival for the Chinese is the Spring Festival, which is the Chinese New Year.*

节省 **jiéshěng** V save, be frugal with ■ 你平时节省一点钱, 几年下来就可能有一大笔钱。**Nǐ píngshí jiéshěng yìdiǎn qián, jǐ nián xiàlai jiù kěnéng yǒu yídà bǐ qián.** *If you save a little money routinely, after several years you may have a substantial sum of money.*

节约 **jiéyue** V economize, save, practice thrift ■ 我们应当节约用电, 节约用水。**Wǒmen yīngdāng jiéyuē yòngdiàn, jiéyuē yòngshuǐ.** *We should cut down electricity and water consumption.*

节约能源 (节能) **jiéyuē néngyuán (jiénéng)** conserve energy

节制 **jiézhì** V control, be moderate in

节制生育 (节育) **jiézhì shēngyù (jiéyù)** birth control, family planning

节奏 **jiézòu** N rhythm, tempo

结 jié TRAD 結 V **1** tie, end **2** form, congeal

结构 **jiégòu** N structure, construction

结果 **jiéguǒ I** N result, consequence ■ 这次试验的结果很鼓舞人心。**Zhè cì shìyàn de jiéguǒ hěn gǔwǔ rénxīn.** *The result of this test is heartening.* **II** ADV as a result, consequently, finally ■ 技术员连续工作二十小时, 结果解决了问题。**Jìshùyuán liánxù gōngzuò èrshí xiǎoshí, jiéguǒ jiějuéle wèntí.** *Technicians worked for twenty hours continuously, and finally solved the problem.*

结合 **jiéhé** V combine, integrate ■ 热情的态度要和冷静的头脑相结合。**Rèqíng de tàidu yào hé lěngjìng de tóunǎo xiāng jiéhé.** *Enthusiasm should be combined with a cool head.* ■ 他们俩终于结合为一对幸福的夫妻。**Tāmen liǎ zhōngyú jiéhéwéi yí duì xìngfú de fūqī.** *They were finally joined as a happy couple.*

结婚 **jiéhūn** V marry ■ 他和中学时的女朋友结婚。**Tā hé zhōngxué shí de nǚpéngyou jiéhūn.** *He married his high school sweetheart.*

结晶 **jiéjīng** N **1** crystallization **2** fruit, result

多年努力的结晶 **duōnián nǔlì de jiéjīng** the fruit of many years' painstaking efforts

结局 **jiéjú** N outcome, final result

结论 **jiélùn** N verdict, conclusion ■ 经过调查, 我们的结论如下。**Jīngguò diàochá, wǒmen de jiélùn rú xià.** *As a result of the investigation, our conclusions are as follows.*

结束 **jiéshù** V end, terminate ■ 第二次世界大战是哪一年结束的? **Dì-èr cì shìjiè dàzhàn shì nǎ yì nián jiéshù de?** *In which year did World War II end?*

结算 **jiésuàn** V settle an account, close an account

结业 **jiéyè** V complete a course of study, graduate

洁 jié TRAD 潔 ADJ clean

洁白 **jiébái** ADJ pure white, spotless

截 jié V intercept, stop

截止 **jiézhǐ** V end, up to ■ 招标日期本星期五截止。**Zhāobiāo rìqī běn Xīngqīwǔ jiézhǐ.** *Invitation to public bidding will end by this Friday.*

劫 jié V rob, raid

劫持 **jiéchí** V kidnap, hijack

杰 jié TRAD 傑 ADJ outstanding, excellent

杰出 **jiéchū** ADJ outstanding, distinguished

杰作 **jiézuò** N outstanding work (of art, music or literature)

捷 jié ADJ quick (See 敏捷 mǐnjié)

竭 jié V exhaust

竭力 jiélì

竭力 jiélì v do one's utmost, do everything within one's power
竭力满足顾客 jiélì mǎnzú gùkè do all one can to satisfy customers

姐 jiě N Same as 姐姐 jiějie

姐姐 jiějie N elder sister

解 jiě v untie, undo ■ 医生: 请你把上衣解开, 我要听听你的心肺。*Yīshēng: Qǐng nǐ bǎ shàngyī jiě kāi, wǒ yào tīngting nǐ de xīnfèi. Doctor: Please undo your jacket. I want to listen to your heart and lungs.*
解答 jiědá v provide an answer, give an explanation ■ 这个问题谁会解答? *Zhè ge wèntí shuí huì jiědá? Who can answer this question?*
解放 jiěfàng I v set free, liberate, emancipate ■ 美国南北战争解放了南方的黑人。*Měiguó nánběi zhànzhēng jiěfàngle nánfāng de hēirén. The American South-North War (→ the American Civil War) emancipated Black people in the South.* **II** N liberation, emancipation
解雇 jiěgù v dismiss (an employee), discharge
解决 jiějué v solve (a problem), settle (an issue) ■ 要解决目前的困难, 必须和各方面合作。*Yào jiějué mùqián de kùnnán, bìxū hé gè fāngmiàn hézuò. We must cooperate with all parties if the present difficulties are to be overcome.*
解剖 jiěpōu v **1** dissect **2** analyse, probe
解散 jiěsàn v dismiss, disband
解释 jiěshì I v explain, account for ■ 请你解释一下这个句子。*Qǐng nǐ jiěshì yíxià zhè ge jùzi. Please explain this sentence to me.* **II** N explanation, interpretation

介 jiè v lie between, interpose

介绍 jièshào v **1** introduce ■ 我来介绍一下, 这位是李先生, 这位是王小姐。*Wǒ lái jièshào yíxià, zhè wèi shì Lǐ xiānsheng, zhè wèi shì Wáng xiǎojiě. Let me introduce [the people here]. This is Mr. Li. This is Miss Wang.* **2** provide information, brief ■ 你刚从中国回来, 请你介绍一下中国的情况。*Nǐ gāng cóng Zhōngguó huílai, qǐng nǐ jièshào yíxià Zhōngguó de qíngkuàng. As you've just come back from China, please tell us something about the current situation in China.*
介绍人 jièshào rén matchmaker, sponsor (for membership in a club, a political party, an association etc.)
介绍信 jièshàoxìn letter of recommendation

届 jiè M. WD (used for a conference or congress held at regular intervals, for graduating classes) ■ 我是那个中学九九届的毕业生。*Wǒ*

shì nà ge zhōngxué jiǔjiǔ jiè de bìyèshēng. *I was a graduate of the class of '99 of that high school.*

界 jiè N **1** border, boundary **2** realm, circle

商业界 shāngyè jiè business circle
体育界 tǐyù jiè sporting circle
界限 jièxiàn N dividing line, limits
界线 jièxiàn N boundary line, demarcation line
把球打出界线 bǎ qiú dǎchū jièxiàn send the ball outside (the court)

借 jiè v borrow, lend ■ 他借给我一百元。*Tā jiègei wǒ yìbǎi yuán. He lent me one hundred dollars.*

NOTE: This verb may mean either *borrow* or *lend*, depending on the patterns in which it occurs: A 借给B… A jiègei B… *A lends B ...* A向B借… A xiàng B jiè… *A borrows ... from B*

借鉴 jièjiàn v use for reference, learn (lessons) from
借口 jièkǒu I v use as an excuse
借口身体不好不上班 jièkǒu shēntǐ bùhǎo bù shàngbān use poor health as an excuse for not going to work
II excuse, pretext
找借口 zhǎo jièkǒu make up an excuse, invent an excuse
借助 jièzhù v have the aid of, make use of

戒 jiè v guard against

戒严 jièyán I N curfew, martial law **II** v enforce martial law, impose a curfew

诫 jiè TRAD 誡 v admonish, warn (See 告诫 gàojiè)

巾 jīn N towel (See 毛巾 máojīn.)

今 jīn N now, the present

今后 jīnhòu N from today, from now on
今年 jīnnián N this year
今天 jīntiān N today ■ 今天天气很好。*Jīntiān tiānqì hěn hǎo. The weather's fine today.* ■ 我今天要上五节课。*Wǒ jīntiān yào shàng wǔ jié kè. I have five classes today.*

筋 jīn N tendon, vein

津 jīn v ferry

津贴 jīntiē N subsidy, stipend

斤 jīn N jin (a traditional Chinese unit of weight equal to half a kilogram) ■ 这条鱼重八斤。*Zhè tiáo yú zhòng bā jīn. This fish weighs eight jin.*

金 jīn N 1 gold (两 liǎng ounce) ■ 这块金表价值极高，你要好好保存。Zhè kuài jīn biǎo jiàzhí jí gāo, nǐ yào hǎohǎo bǎocún. *This gold watch is very valuable. You must keep it well.*
金子 jīnzi gold
2 money ■ 他每两周拿五百块退休金。Tā měi liǎng zhōu ná wǔbǎi kuài tuìxiū jīn. *He gets five hundred dollars as pension money every fortnight.*
金额 jīn'é N sum of money (笔 bǐ)
一大笔金额 yí dàbǐ jīn'é a large sum of money
金黄 jīnhuáng ADJ golden (color)
金牌 jīnpái N gold medal
金牌获得者/金牌得主 jīnpái huòdézhě/jīnpái dezhǔ gold medalist
金钱 jīnqián N money
金融 jīnróng N finance, banking
金属 jīnshǔ N metal ■ 金、银、铜、铁都是金属。Jīn, yín, tóng, tiě dōu shì jīnshǔ. *Gold, silver, copper and iron are all metals.*
金鱼 jīnyú N goldfish (条 tiáo)
金鱼缸 jīnyúgāng goldfish bowl
养金鱼 yǎng jīnyú keep goldfish
金字塔 jīnzìtǎ N the pyramid

仅 jīn TRAD 僅 ADV only, merely ■ 她一个月的工资仅够付房租和吃饭。Tā yí ge yuè de gōngzī jǐn gòu fù fángzū hé chīfàn. *Her monthly wages are only enough for rent and food.*
仅仅 jǐnjǐn ADV Same as 仅 jǐn, but more emphatic.

尽 jǐn TRAD 盡 V to the greatest extent ■ 这事要尽快办。Zhè shì yào jǐnkuài bàn. *This matter must be handled as soon as possible.*
尽管 jǐnguǎn I ADV feel free to, not hesitate ■ 有什么问题，尽管和我联系。Yǒu shénme wèntí, jǐnguǎn hé wǒ liánxì. *If you have any questions, do not hesitate to contact me.* II CONJ even though ■ 尽管她很聪明，但是念书不用功，结果成绩不好。Jǐnguǎn tā hěn cōngmíng, dànshì niànshū bú yònggōng, jiéguǒ chéngqì bùhǎo. *Even though she is quite intelligent, she does not study hard and consequently fails to get good results in exams.*
尽量 jǐnliàng ADV to the best of one's capacity, to the greatest extent
尽量⋯⋯一点 jǐnliàng...yìdiǎn as ... as possible, as soon as possible ■ 对孩子你要尽量耐心一点。Duì háizi nǐ yào jìnliàng nàixīn yìdiǎn. *In dealing with children you should try your best to be patient.*

锦 jǐn N brocade
锦绣 jǐnxiù ADJ splendid, beautiful

谨 jǐn ADJ cautious
谨慎 jǐnshèn ADJ cautious, careful
谨慎驾驶 jǐnshèn jiàshǐ drive carefully

紧 jǐn TRAD 緊 ADJ 1 tight, taut ■ 今天的活动安排得比较紧。Jīntiān de huódòng ānpái de bǐjiào jǐn. *Today's activities are scheduled rather tightly.* 2 urgent, tense
握紧方向盘 wòjǐn fāngxiàngpán grip the steering wheel firmly
3 be close to
紧靠着地铁站 jǐn kàozhe dìtiězhàn very close to a subway station
4 in short supply ■ 时间很紧。Shíjiān hěn jǐn. *Time is in short supply.* (→ *We're pressed for time.*) 5 pressing, urgent
紧急 jǐnjí ADJ urgent, pressing
紧急任务 jǐnjírènwu urgent task
紧急状况 jǐnjí zhuàngkuàng emergency situation, contingency
紧密 jǐnmì ADJ very close, intimate
紧密配合 jǐnmì pèihé in close coordination
紧缩 jǐnsuō V tighten, reduce
紧缩开支 jǐnsuō kāizhī cut back expenditure
紧张 jǐnzhāng ADJ tense, nervous ■ 明天要考试了，我没有很好准备，心里很紧张。Míngtiān yào kǎoshì le, wǒ méiyǒu hěn hǎo zhǔnbèi, xīnli hěn jǐnzhāng. *We're having an examination tomorrow. I'm not well prepared, and feel really nervous.*

晋 jìn V go forward, advance
晋升 jìnshēng V promote (to a higher position)
晋升为教授 jìnshēng wéi jiàoshòu be promoted to professorship level

尽 jìn TRAD 盡 V exhaust, use up ■ 我已经尽了最大努力。Wǒ yǐjīng jìnle zuì dà nǔlì. *I've already exhausted my energies [on this]. (→ I've done my very best.)*
尽力 jìnlì V do all one can

进 jìn TRAD 進 V move forward, enter ■ 请进！Qǐng jìn! *Please come in! (or Please go in!)*
进步 jìnbù I ADJ progressive ■ 社会上的进步力量一定会取胜。Shèhuì shang de jìnbù lìliàng yídìng huì qǔshèng. *The progressive forces in society will surely prevail.* II N progress ■ 你们的中文学习有了很大进步。Nǐmen de Zhōngwén xuéxí yǒule hěn dà jìnbù. *You have made very good progress in your Chinese studies.*
进程 jìnchéng N course (of progress), process
进而 jìn' ér ADV and then, subsequently
进攻 jìngōng V advance and attack, attack
进化 jìnhuà V evolve, develop ■ 人是从猴子进

进化论 jìnhuàlùn

化来的, 你信不信? Rén shì cóng hóuzi jìnhuà lái de, nǐ xìn bú xìn? *Man evolved from the monkey. Do you believe this?*

进化论 **jìnhuàlùn** N (Charles Darwin's) theory of evolution

进军 **jìnjūn** V march, advance

进口 **jìnkǒu** I V import ■ 这个国家每年进口大量农产品。Zhège guójiā měi nián jìnkǒu dàliàng nóngchǎnpǐn. *This country imports large quantities of farm produce every year.* II N entry, entrance

进来 **jìnlai** V come in, come into ■ 进来吧, 我们在等你呢! Jìnlai ba, wǒmen zài děng nǐ ne! *Please come in. We've been waiting for you.*

进取 **jìnqǔ** V be enterprising, be aggressive and ambitious

进取心 **jìnqǔxīn** enterprising spirit

进去 **jìnqu** V go in, go into ■ 他们在开会, 请不要进去。Tāmen zài kāihuì, qǐng bú yào jìnqu. *They're having a meeting. Please don't go in.*

进入 **jìnrù** V enter, enter into

进行 **jìnxíng** V conduct, carry out ■ 孩子做错了事, 应该进行教育。Háizi zuò cuòle shì, yīnggāi jìnxíng jiàoyù. *When a child makes a mistake, he should be educated.*

NOTE: The object that 进行 jìnxíng takes must be a noun of two or more syllables. 进行 jìnxíng is used only in formal Chinese.

进修 **jìnxiū** V do advanced studies, undergo in-service advanced training ■ 我们的中文老师要去北京进修半年。Wǒmen de Zhōngwén lǎoshī yào qù Běijīng jìnxiū bànnián. *Our Chinese teacher will go to Beijing for half a year's advanced studies.*

进一步 **jìnyíbù** ADV advancing a step further, further, more deeply ■ 对于这个问题, 我们还要进一步研究。Duìyú zhège wèntí, wǒmen hái yào jìnyíbù yánjiū. *We need to study this problem further.*

近 jìn ADJ close to, close by

离⋯近 **lí...jìn** be close to ■ 爸爸的办公室离家很近。Bàba de bàngōngshì lí jiā hěn jìn. *Father's office is close to home.*

近代 **jìndài** N modern times (usually from the year 1840)

近来 **jìnlái** ADV recently, nowadays, these days

近年 **jìnnián** N recent years

近期 **jìnqī** N in the near future

近视 **jìnshì** N nearsightedness, shortsightedness

近视眼镜 **jìnshì yǎnjìng** spectacles for nearsightedness

近似 **jìnsì** ADJ similar, approximate

近似值 **jìnsì zhí** approximate value, approximation

劲 jìn TRAD 勁 N physical strength ■ 这位举重运动员真有劲! Zhè wèi jǔzhòng yùndòngyuán zhēn yǒu jìn! *This weight lifter is really powerful!*

没劲 **méijìn** dull, boring, bored ■ 这日子过得真没劲! Zhè rìzi guòde zhēn méijìn! *Life is so boring!*

劲头 **jìntóu** N 1 strength, energy 2 zeal, vigor

劲头十足 **jìntóu shízú** full of vigor, in high spirits

浸 jìn V soak, steep

禁 jìn V forbid

禁区 **jìnqū** N forbidden zone

军事禁区 **jūnshì jìnqū** military zone

禁止 **jìnzhǐ** V forbid, prohibit ■ 禁止吸烟。Jìnzhǐ xīyān. *No smoking.*

京 jīng N 1 capital city 2 (shortened for) Beijing

京剧 **jīngjù** N Beijing (Peking) opera

鲸 jīng N whale

鲸鱼 **jīngyú** whale (条 tiáo)

晶 jīng N crystal (See 结晶 jiéjīng)

茎 jīng N stem or stalk (of a plant)

经 jīng TRAD 經 V pass through, experience

经常 **jīngcháng** ADV often ■ 你经常迟到, 这样不好。Nǐ jīngcháng chídào, zhèyàng bù hǎo. *You're often late, which is not good.*

经典 **jīngdiǎn** N classic

经费 **jīngfèi** N outlay, fund (for a specific purpose or the regular running of an organization)

经过 **jīngguò** I V go through, pass ■ 没有亲自经过, 就不知道多难。Méiyǒu qīnzì jīngguò, jiù bù zhīdào duō nán. *Without experiencing it personally, you wouldn't know how difficult it is.* II PREP through, after ■ 经过这件事, 他变得聪明了。Jīngguò zhè jiàn shì, tā biàn de cōngmíng le. *He was more sensible after this incident.*

经济 **jīngjì** N economy ■ 这个国家的经济不太好。Zhège guójiā de jīngjì bú tài hǎo. *This country's economy is not in very good shape.*

经济学 **jīngjìxué** economics

经济学家 **jīngjìxuéjiā** economist

市场经济 **shìchǎng jīngjì** market economy

经纪人 **jīngjìrén** N agent, manager

经理 **jīnglǐ** N manager (位 wèi) ■ 他是管人力资源的经理。Tā shì guǎn rénlì zīyuán de jīnglǐ. *He is the manager in charge of human resources.*

副经理 **fùjīnglǐ** deputy manager

市场经理 **shìchǎng jīnglǐ** marketing manager

总经理 **zǒngjīnglǐ** general manager, chief executive officer (CEO)

经历 **jīnglì** I v experience, undergo ■ 这位老人经历了很多困难，才获得幸福的晚年。Zhè wèi lǎorén jīnglìle hěn duō kùnnan, cái huòdé xìngfú de wǎnnián. *This old man has experienced many troubles before enjoying a blissful old age.* II N personal experience

经商 **jīngshāng** v engage in business, be a businessman

经受 **jīngshòu** v undergo, withstand

经受考验 **jīngshòu kǎoyàn** face a test, undergo a test

经销 **jīngxiāo** v sell, deal with

经销豪华汽车 **jīngxiāo háohuá qìchē** deal with luxury cars

经验 **jīngyàn** N experience, lesson (learnt from experiences) ■ 这个经验对我很有价值。Zhège jīngyàn duì wǒ hěn yǒu jiàzhí. *This experience is very valuable to me.*

取得经验 **qǔdé jīngyàn** acquire experience

有经验 **yǒu jīngyàn** experienced

经营 **jīngyíng** v operate (a business)

惊 **jīng** TRAD 驚 v startle, surprise

惊动 **jīngdòng** v disturb, alarm

惊慌 **jīnghuāng** ADJ panic-stricken, alarmed

惊慌失措 **jīnghuāng shīcuò** be panic-stricken

惊奇 **jīngqí** v be surprised and incredulous, be amazed

惊讶 **jīngyà** v be astonished, be surprised

惊异 **jīngyì** v be astounded and puzzled

睛 **jīng** N the pupil of the eye (See 眼睛 yǎnjing.)

精 **jīng** ADJ choice, refined

精彩 **jīngcǎi** ADJ (of a theatrical performance or sports event) brilliant, thrilling, wonderful ■ 昨天的足球比赛真精彩啊! Zuótiān de zúqiú bǐsài zhēn jīngcǎi a! *The football match yesterday was really wonderful!*

精打细算 **jīngdǎ xìsuàn** IDIOM be very careful in budgeting to save every cent

精华 **jīnghuá** N the cream of the crop, the very best

精简 **jīngjiǎn** v trim and prune (an organization), reduce staffing

精力 **jīnglì** N energy, vigor ■ 我父亲年纪大了，精力不如以前了。Wǒ fùqin niánjì dà le, jīnglì bùrú yǐqián le. *My father is getting old and is not so energetic as before.*

精美 **jīngměi** ADJ exquisite and beautiful

精密 **jīngmì** ADJ precise

精密仪器 **jīngmì yíqì** precision instrument

精确 **jīngquè** ADJ accurate, precise

精神 **jīngshén** N 1 vigor, vitality ■ 这位老人八十多岁了，但是精神很好。Zhè wèi lǎorén bāshí duō suì le, dànshì jīngshén hěn hǎo. *This old man (or woman) is over eighty, but is energetic and alert.* 2 spirit, the mind

精神病 **jīngshénbìng** N mental illness

精神病院 **jīngshénbìngyuàn** mental institution

精神病医生 **jīngshénbìng yīshēng** psychiatrist

精通 **jīngtōng** ADJ having great proficiency in, be master of

精细 **jīngxì** ADJ paying attention to details, meticulous

精益求精 **jīng yì qiú jīng** v seek perfection

精致 **jīngzhì** ADJ exquisite, fine

景 **jǐng** N view, scenery

景色 **jǐngsè** N view, scenery

景象 **jǐngxiàng** N sight, scene

警 **jǐng** I v alert II N 1 police 2 alarm

警车 **jǐngchē** police car

火警 **huǒjǐng** fire alarm

警察 **jǐngchá** N policeman, police ■ 这里发生了交通事故，快叫警察! Zhèli fāshēngle jiāotōng shìgù, kuài jiào jǐngchá! *A traffic accident has happened here. Call the police quickly!*

NOTE: In China the police bureau is called 公安局 gōng'ānjú *Public Security Bureau*, which should be distinguished from 国安局 guó'ānjú *Bureau of National Security*.

警告 **jǐnggào** I v warn, caution ■ 路旁有牌子警告，前面是弯曲山路，必须减速。Lùpáng yǒu páizi jǐnggào, qiánmian shì wānqū shānlù, bìxū jiǎnsù. *A poster by the roadside warns motorists to reduce speed as the road ahead is zigzagging and hilly.* II N warning

警戒 **jǐngjiè** v guard against, be on alert

警惕 **jǐngtì** v be vigilant

警卫 **jǐngwèi** v guard and defend (a military installation, a VIP, etc.)

井 **jǐng** N well, (water) well

水井 **shuǐjǐng** water well

油井 **yóujǐng** oil well

颈 **jǐng** TRAD 頸 N neck

头颈 **tóujǐng** the neck

长颈鹿 **chángjǐnglù** (long-neck-deer) giraffe

竞 jìng

竞 jìng TRAD 競 v compete

竞赛 jìngsài v contest, compete
竞选 jìngxuǎn v run for office
竞争 jìngzhēng I v compete II N competition

竟 jìng ADV unexpectedly

竟然 jìngrán ADV unexpectedly, contrary to expectation ■ 这个小孩下棋竟然胜了他爸爸。Zhège xiǎohái xiàqí jìngrán shèngle tā bàba. *Quite unexpectedly the child should beat his father in chess.*

境 jìng N boundary, place

国境 guójìng territory (of a country), border
国境线 guójìngxiàn national boundary line
境地 jìngdì N situation, plight
危险的境地 wēixiǎn de jìngdì dangerous position

镜 jìng TRAD 鏡 N mirror

镜子 jìngzi mirror (面 miàn)
照镜子 zhào jìngzi look at oneself in a mirror
镜头 jìngtóu N 1 camera lens 2 shot, scene

径 jìng TRAD 徑 N track (See 田径 tiánjìng)

敬 jìng v respect

敬爱 jìng'ài v respect and love ■ 有多少孩子敬爱自己的父母？Yǒu duōshǎo háizi jìng'ài zìjǐ de fùmǔ? *How many children respect and love their parents?*
敬而远之 jìng-ér-yuǎn-zhī IDIOM keep a respectful distance from, give a wide berth to
敬酒 jìngjiǔ v propose a toast
敬礼 jìnglǐ v salute

静 jìng ADJ quiet, peaceful, silent ■ 请大家静一静，我要宣布一件事。Qǐng dàjiā jìng yi jìng, wǒ yào xuānbù yí jiàn shì. *Be quiet, everybody. I have an announcement to make.*

静悄悄 jìngqiāoqiāo ADJ perfectly quiet and hushed
静坐 jìngzuò v 1 meditate
静坐养生 jìngzuò yǎngshēng meditate to keep in good health
2 stage a sit-in

净 jìng ADJ clean (See 干净 gānjing.)

净化 jìnghuà v purify
净化废水 jìnghuà fèishuǐ purify waste water

究 jiū v investigate, probe

究竟 jiūjìng ADV Same as 到底 dàodǐ

纠 jiū TRAD 糾 v rectify

纠纷 jiūfēn N dispute
纠正 jiūzhèng v rectify, correct

揪 jiū TRAD 揫 v hold tight, seize

九 jiǔ NUM nine ■ 九九八十一。Jiǔjiǔ bāshíyī. *Nine times nine is eighty-one.*
九一一 jiǔ-yāo-yāo 9/11 September 11
九千九百九十九 jiǔqiān jiǔbǎi jiǔshíjiǔ 9,999

NOTE: See note on 一 yī regarding pronunciation of 一 as yāo.

玖 jiǔ NUM nine

久 jiǔ ADV for a long time ■ 时间太久了，我记不清了。Shíjiān tài jiǔle, wǒ jìbuqīng le. *It was too long ago. I can't remember it clearly.* ■ 日久见人心。Rì jiǔ jiàn rénxīn. *As time goes on, you will know a person's nature.*

灸 jiǔ N moxibustion (See 针灸 zhēnjiǔ.)

酒 jiǔ N alcoholic beverage (种 zhǒng, 瓶 píng) ■ 我不喝酒，我还要开车。Wǒ bù hē jiǔ, wǒ háiyào kāichē. *No alcoholic drinks for me. I'll be driving.*
白酒 bái jiǔ colorless spirit distilled from grains
葡萄酒 pútaojiǔ (grape) wine
黄酒 huáng jiǔ yellow rice wine
酒吧 jiǔ bā N (wine) bar, pub
酒店 jiǔ diàn N 1 wine shop 2 restaurant 3 hotel

NOTE: Although 酒店 jiǔ diàn literally means *wine shop*, it is sometimes used to mean *a hotel*, usually a luxury one. This usage is especially common in Hong Kong, e.g. 香港半岛酒店 Xiānggǎng bàndǎo jiǔdiàn *The Peninsula Hong Kong Hotel*. Also see note on 饭店 fàndiàn.

酒会 jiǔhuì N cocktail party, reception
酒精 jiǔjīng N alcohol

旧 jiù TRAD 舊 ADJ (of things) old, second-hand ■ 他把旧车卖了一千块钱。Tā bá jiù chē màile yìqiān kuài qián. *He sold his old car for one thousand dollars.*

舅 jiù N mother's brother, uncle

舅父 jiùfù mother's brother, uncle
舅舅 jiùjiù Same as 舅父 jiùfù, used as a form of address
舅妈 jiùmā Same as 舅母 jiùmǔ, used as a form of address

舅母 jiùmǔ mother's brother's wife, aunt

救 **jiù** V save, rescue ■ 他在河中大叫，"救命! 救命!" Tā zài hé zhong dà jiào, "Jiù mìng! Jiù mìng!" *He cried out in the river, "Help! Help!"*

救火 jiùhuǒ put out a fire, fire fighting
救火车 jiùhuǒchē fire engine
救护车 jiùhùchē ambulance
救济 jiùji V provide relief

就 1 **jiù** PREP **1** with regard to, concerning ■ 商业部长就物价问题发表谈话。Shāngyè bùzhǎng jiù wùjià wèntí fābiǎo tánhuà. *The Minister of Commerce delivered a talk on prices.* **2** as far as ... is concerned, in terms of ■ 就人口来说，中国是世界上第一大国。Jiù rénkǒu láishuō, Zhōngguó shì shìjiè shang dì-yī dà guó. *In terms of population, China is the biggest country in the world.*

就 2 **jiù** ADV as early as ..., as soon as ... (used before a verb to emphasize that the action takes place very early, very quickly or only for a very short period of time) ■ 他今天早上六点钟就起床了。Tā jīntiān zǎoshang liù diǎnzhōng jiù qǐchuáng le. *He got up as early as six o'clock this morning.*

一···就··· yī...jiù... as soon as ... ■ 妈妈一下班就做晚饭。Māma yí xiàbān jiù zuò wǎnfàn. *Mom prepared supper as soon as she got off work.*

就餐 jiùcān V take a meal
就地 jiùdì ADV on the spot
就近 jiùjìn ADV nearby
就是 jiùshì CONJ even if ■ 我就是不睡觉，也要做完这个作业。Wǒ jiùshì bú shuìjiào, yě yào zuòwán zhège zuòyè. *Even if I don't sleep, I must finish this assignment.*
就算 jiùsuàn CONJ even if, even though
就业 jiùyè V obtain employment
就职 jiuzhí V take office

居 **jū** V **1** occupy (See 邻居 línjū, 居民 jūmín, 居住 jūzhù.) **2** inhabit, dwell

居留 jūliú V reside, live
居留权 jūliúquán right of residency, residency
居留证 jūliúzhèng residency permit
居民 jūmín N resident, inhabitant
居民委员会 jūmín wěiyuánhuì neighborhood committee

NOTE: 居民委员会 jūmín wěiyuánhuì is the grassroot organization in Chinese cities, under government supervision. In colloquial Chinese it is shortened to 居委会 jūwěihuì.

居然 jūrán ADV unexpectedly
居室 jūshì N bedroom

一套三居室的公寓 yítào sān jūshì de gōngyù a three-bedroom apartment
居住 jūzhù V reside, inhabit, live

拘 **jū** V **1** detain, arrest **2** limit

拘留 jūliú V detain by the police
拘留所 jūliúsuǒ detention center, detention camp
拘束 jūshù ADJ restrained, ill at ease

鞠 **jū** V as in 鞠躬 jūgōng

鞠躬 jūgōng V bow, take a bow

菊 **jú** N chrysanthemum

菊花 júhuā chrysanthemum
菊花展览 júhuā zhǎnlǎn chrysanthemum show
秋菊 qiū jú chrysanthemum

局 **jú** N office

局部 júbù ADJ part (not whole), local ■ 今天本市局部停电。Jīntiān běnshì júbù tíngdiàn. *Today parts of this city will not have power supply.*
局面 júmiàn N situation, phase
打开局面 dǎkāi júmiàn usher in a new phase, make a breakthrough
局势 júshì N situation
局限 júxiàn V limit, confine
局长 júzhǎng N director/chief of a bureau ■ 一个部下面有几个局，所以一位部长下面有几位局长。Yí ge bù xiàmiàn yǒu jǐ ge jú, suǒyǐ yí wèi bùzhǎng xiàmian yǒu jǐ wèi júzhǎng. *As there are several bureaus under a ministry, there are several bureau chiefs under a minister.*

橘 **jú** N tangerine

橘树 jú shù tangerine tree
橘子 júzi tangerine

NOTE: 橘子 júzi can also be written as 桔子 júzi.

矩 **jǔ** N carpenter's square (See 规矩 guīju)

举 **jǔ** TRAD 舉 V hold high, raise, lift ■ 举头望明月，低头思故乡 (李白) Jǔ tóu wàng míng yuè, dī tóu sī gùxiāng (Lí Bái) *I raise my head to gaze at the bright moon and hang my head yearning for my hometown (lines from a poem by Li Bai)*
举办 jǔbàn V conduct (a meeting, an event)
举动 jǔdòng N (body) movement, act
一举一动 yìjǔ yídòng every movement (of a person)
举世闻名 jǔshì wénmíng IDIOM world-renowned

举行 jǔxíng

举行 jǔxíng v hold (a meeting, a ceremony) ■ 下个月将举行国际会议，讨论这个问题。Xiàge yuè jiāng jǔxíng guójì huìyì, tǎolùn zhège wèntí. *An international conference will be held next month to discuss this issue.*

聚 jù v assemble, get together

聚会 jùhuì n social gathering, (social) party
举行生日聚会 jǔxíng shēngri jùhuì throw a birthday party

NOTE: See note on 派对 pàiduì.

聚集 jùjí v gather, collect
聚集资金（集资）jùjí zījīn (jízī) collect funds, raise funds
聚精会神 jùjīng huìshén IDIOM give undivided attention to

句 jù M. WD (for sentences)

一句话 yí jù huà one sentence
这句话 zhè jù huà this sentence
句子 jùzi n sentence (句 jù, 个 gè) ■ 这句句子语法不对。Zhè jù jùzi yǔfǎ bú duì. *The grammar of this sentence is wrong.*

拒 jù v resist, refuse

拒不认错 jù bù rèncuò refuse to admit to a mistake

具 jù v own, possess

具备 jùbèi v possess, be provided with ■ 这个小城市不具备建立大学的条件。Zhège xiǎo chéngshì bú jùbèi jiànlì dàxué de tiáojiàn. *This small city does not possess the conditions necessary for establishing a university.*
具体 jùtǐ ADJ specific, concrete ■ 你说他这个人不好，能不能说得具体些? Nǐ shuō tā zhège rén bù hǎo, néng bù néng shuōde jùtǐ xiē? *You say he is not a good man. Can you be more specific?*
具有 jùyǒu v have, possess, be provided with ■ 中国文化具有哪些特点? Zhōngguó wénhuà jùyǒu nǎxiē tèdiǎn? *What characteristic features does Chinese culture have?*

俱 jù ADV together

俱乐部 jùlèbù n club ■ 这个俱乐部每年要交多少会费? Zhège jùlèbù měi nián yào jiāo duōshǎo huìfèi? *What are the annual dues of this club?*

惧 jù TRAD 懼 v fear

惧内 jùnèi fear one's wife, be henpecked

剧 jù TRAD 劇 I n drama, play II ADJ severe, intense

剧本 jùběn n script of a play
电影剧本 diànyǐng jùběn script of a film, scenario
剧场 jùchǎng n theater (座 zuò) ■ 今晚在剧场里有精彩演出。Jīnwǎn zài jùchǎng li yǒu jīngcǎi yǎnchū. *There will be a wonderful performance in the theater this evening.*
剧烈 jùliè ADJ fierce, severe
剧烈的疼痛 jùliè de téngtòng acute pain
剧团 jùtuán n theatrical company
剧院 jùyuàn n playhouse, theater (座 zuò)

据 jù TRAD 據 PREP according to

据说 jùshuō IDIOM it is said, they say, rumor has it ■ 据说王小姐现在在美国工作。Jùshuō Wáng xiǎojiě xiànzài zài Měiguó gōngzuò. *It is said that Miss Wang is working in America.*

锯 jù n saw

锯子 jùzi hand saw (把 bǎ)
电锯 diànjù chainsaw

巨 jù ADJ gigantic

巨大 jùdà ADJ huge, gigantic, tremendous ■ 我们国家的经济发展取得了巨大的成绩。Wǒmen guójiā de jīngjì fāzhǎn qǔdéle jùdà de chéngjì. *Our country has made tremendous achievements in economic development.*

拒 jù v repel, resist

拒绝 jùjué v refuse, reject ■ 她拒绝了他的邀请。Tā jùjuéle tā de yāoqǐng. *She turned down his invitation.* ■ 他拒绝承认错误。Tā jùjué chéngrèn cuòwù. *He refused to admit to any wrong.*

距 jù n a stretch of distance

距离 jùlí n distance ■ 她和谁都保持一定距离。Tā hé shuí dōu bǎochí yídìng jùlí. *She keeps a distance from everybody. (→ She gives everyone a wide berth.)*

捐 juān v donate, contribute

捐款 juānkuǎn I v contribute money, make a cash donation II n cash donation, financial donation
捐献 juānxiàn v donate (something of considerable value)
捐赠 juānzèng v contribute as a gift, donate

卷 juǎn v roll up ■ 他把地图卷起来，放在书架上。Tā bǎ dìtú juǎn qǐlai, fàng zài shūjià shang. *He rolled the map up and placed it on the bookshelf.*

绢 juàn TRAD 絹 N silk (See 手绢 shǒujuàn.)

卷 juàn ADJ tired (See 疲倦 píjuàn)

掘 jué v dig

掘土机 juétǔjī excavation machine, earth mover

决 1 jué ADV definitely, under any circumstance used before a negative word, e.g. 不 bù) ■ 我决不做任何对社会有害的事。Wǒ jué bú zuò rènhé duì shèhuì yǒuhài de shì. *I would never, ever, do anything that is harmful to society.*

决 2 jué v decide, determine

决策 juécè I v decide on a policy, formulate strategy II N policy decision, strategic decision (项 xiàng)

决定 juédìng I v decide, determine, make up one's mind ■ 你有没有决定买哪一辆汽车？Nǐ yǒu méiyǒu juédìng mǎi nǎ yí liàng qìchē? *Have you decided which car to buy?* II N decision 做决定 zuò juédìng make a decision ■ 买哪一座房子，他们还没有做决定。Mǎi nǎ yí zuò fángzi, tāmen hái méiyǒu zuò juédìng. *They haven't decided which house to buy.*

决赛 juésài N final game, final round, finals

决心 juéxīn N determination ■ 我们有决心，有信心，一定按时完成计划。Wǒmen yǒu juéxīn, yǒu xìnxīn, yídìng ànshí wánchéng jìhuà. *We are determined, and we are confident, that we will fulfill the plan according to schedule.*
下决心 xià juéxīn make up one's mind, be determined
II v be determined, make up one's mind

决议 juéyì N resolution
提出决议 tíchū juéyì put forward a resolution
作出决议 zuòchū juéyì adopt a resolution

决战 juézhàn I v wage a decisive battle II N decisive battle

觉 jué TRAD 覺 v feel, sense

觉察 juéchá v detect, perceive

觉得 juéde v feel, find, think ■ 我觉得你说的话很有道理。Wǒ juéde nǐ shuō de huà hěn yǒu dàolǐ. *I think what you said is quite true (or reasonable).* ■ 你觉得他的想法行不行？Nǐ juéde tā de xiǎngfǎ xíng bu xíng? *Do you think his idea will work?*

觉悟 juéwù v gain understanding, become aware of

觉醒 juéxǐng v be awakened (to truth, reality, etc.)

绝 jué TRAD 絕 I ADJ absolute II v cut off, sever
绝对 juéduì ADV absolutely ■ 我告诉你的消息绝对准确。Wǒ gàosù nǐ de xiāoxi juéduì zhǔnquè. *The news I told you is absolutely correct.*
绝对多数 juéduì duōshù absolute majority

绝望 juéwàng v despair, give up all hope

绝缘 juéyuán v (of electricity) insulate

绝症 juézhèng N terminal illness

军 jūn TRAD 軍 N army, armed forces
海军 hǎijūn navy
空军 kōngjūn air force
陆军 lùjūn army

军备 jūnbèi N weapons and equipment, armaments

军队 jūnduì N armed forces, troops (支 zhī)

军官 jūnguān N military officer, officer (名 míng, 位 wèi)

军火 jūnhuǒ N arms and ammunition

军舰 jūnjiàn N warship (艘 sōu)

军人 jūnrén N serviceman, soldier (名 míng)

军事 jūnshì N military affairs ■ 军事上的事，我不大懂。Jūnshì shang de shì, wǒ bú dà dǒng. *I don't know much about military affairs.*

军需 jūnxū N military supplies

军用 jūnyòng ADJ for military use

军装 jūnzhuāng N army uniform

君 jūn N 1 monarch 2 gentleman

君主 jūnzhǔ N monarch
君主立宪 jūnzhǔ lìxiàn constitutional monarchy

君子 jūnzǐ N cultured and honorable man, gentleman

NOTE: In Confucianism 君子 jūnzǐ refers to *a cultured gentleman and a man of virtue.* 君子 jūnzǐ is in contrast with 小人 xiǎorén, *a mean person or an inferior being.*

均 jūn ADJ equal

均匀 jūnyún ADJ well distributed, evenly applied

菌 jūn N fungus, bacterium (See 细菌 xìjūn.)

峻 jùn ADJ harsh, stern (See 严峻 yánjùn.)

俊 jùn ADJ handsome (See 英俊 yīngjùn.)
美女俊男 měinǚ jùnnán beautiful women and handsome men

K

咖 **kā** used in 咖啡 kāfēi only

咖啡 **kāfēi** N coffee (杯 bēi) ■ 这种咖啡很好喝。 Zhè zhǒng kāfēi hěn hǎohē. *This kind of coffee tastes good.*
浓咖啡 **nóng kāfēi** espresso
速溶咖啡 **sùróng kāfēi** instant coffee
冲咖啡 **chōng kāfēi** make (instant) coffee
煮咖啡 **zhǔ kāfēi** brew coffee

NOTE: 咖啡 kāfēi is one of the few transliterations (音译词 yīnyìcí) in Chinese vocabulary, as it represents more or less the sound of "coffee."

卡 **kǎ** N card (张 zhāng) ■ 这张卡很重要，你要放好了。 Zhè zhāng kǎ hěn zhòngyào, nǐ yào fànghǎo le. *This is a very important card. Keep it safely.*
贺卡 **hèkǎ** greeting card
借书卡 **jièshū kǎ** library card
信用卡 **xìnyòng kǎ** credit card
银行卡 **yínháng kǎ** banking card
卡车 **kǎchē** N lorry, truck (辆 liàng)

NOTE: The composition of 卡车 kǎchē is a semi-transliteration (半音译词 bàn yīnyìcí): 卡 kǎ represents the sound of the English word "car" and 车 chē means *vehicle*. See 咖啡 kāfēi for an example of transliteration.

卡片 **kǎpiàn** N card (张 zhāng)

开 **kāi** TRAD 開 V 1 open, open up ■ 开开门! Kāikai mén! *Open the door, please!* 2 turn on, switch on 3 drive (a vehicle), pilot (a plane) ■ 我会开汽车，不会开飞机。 Wǒ huì kāi qìchē, bú huì kāi fēijī. *I can drive a car, but I can't pilot a plane.* 4 start
开采 **kāicǎi** V mine, excavate
开除 **kāichú** V expel
被学校开除 **bèi xuéxiào kāichú** be expelled from the school
开刀 **kāidāo** V perform a medical operation
开发 **kāifā** V develop (land, resources, products, etc.)
开发商 **kāifāshāng** (real estate, land) developer
开放 **kāifàng** V open, open up ■ 这个展览会从下周起对外开放。 Zhège zhǎnlǎnhuì cóng xià zhōu qǐ duìwài kāifàng. *This exhibition will open to the public next week.*
开工 **kāigōng** V (of a factory) start production, (of a construction project) start building
开关 **kāiguān** N switch

开会 **kāihuì** V attend a meeting, hold a meeting ■ 我们最好开个会，讨论一下这个问题。 Wǒmen zuìhǎo kāi ge huì, tǎolùn yíxià zhège wèntí. *We'd best have a meeting to discuss this issue.*
开课 **kāikè** V introduce a course, teach a subject
开垦 **kāikěn** V reclaim (wasteland)
开口 **kāikǒu** V start to talk
难以开口 **nányǐ kāikǒu** find it difficult to bring up a matter
开阔 **kāikuò** ADJ open and wide, expansive, spacious
开朗 **kāilǎng** ADJ broad-minded and outspoken always cheerful
性格开朗 **xìnggé kāilǎng** of a cheerful disposition
开门 **kāimén** V open for business ■ "这里的商店什么时候开门?" "九点钟开门。" "Zhèli de shāngdiàn shénme shíhou kāimén?" "Jiǔ diǎnzhōng kāimén." *"When do stores here open for business?" "Nine o'clock."*
开明 **kāimíng** ADJ civilized, enlightened
开幕 **kāimù** V (of a play, a ceremony, conference, etc.) open, start
开幕式 **kāimùshì** opening ceremony
开辟 **kāipì** V open up, start ■ 这里要开辟成特别经济区。 Zhèli yào kāipì chéng tèbié jīngjìqū. *A special economic zone will be started here.*
开设 **kāishè** V 1 offer (a course in a college) 2 open (an office, a factory, etc.)
开始 **kāishǐ** I V begin, commence II N beginning start ■ 我开始觉得中文非常难，现在觉得不太难了。 Wǒ kāishǐ juéde Zhōngwén fēicháng nán, xiànzài juéde bú tài nán le. *At the beginning I found Chinese very difficult, but now I think it's not too difficult.*
开头 **kāitóu** N Same as 开始 kāishǐ, used colloquially.
开拓 **kāituò** V open up
开玩笑 **kāi wánxiào** V joke ■ 这是很严肃的事，你不要开玩笑。 Zhè shì hěn yánsù de shì, nǐ bú yào kāi wánxiào. *This is a very serious matter. Don't joke about it. (→ This is no laughing matter.)*
跟/和···开玩笑 **gēn/hé...kāi wánxiào** joke with ..., make fun of ....
开心 **kāixīn** ADJ feeling happy, delighted
开学 **kāixué** V start (school) ■ 中国的学校一般九月一日开学。你们国家的学校哪一天开学? Zhōngguó de xuéxiào yìbān Jiǔyuè yírì kāixué. Nǐmen guójiā de xuéxiào nǎ yì tiān kāixué? *Schools in China usually start on September 1. On which day does school begin in your country?*
开演 **kāiyǎn** V start (a performance, a film, etc.) ■ 电影什么时候开演? Diànyǐng shénme shíhou kāiyǎn? *When does the film start?*

开夜车 **kāi yèchē** v burn the midnight oil ■ 明天要交作业，今天晚上我得开夜车。*Míngtiān yào jiāo zuòyè, jīntiān wǎnshang wǒ děi kāi yèchē. I must hand in my assignment tomorrow. I'll have to burn the midnight oil tonight.*

开展 **kāizhǎn** v launch, develop, expand

开支 **kāizhī** I v pay (expenses) II N expenditure, expenses
日常家用开支 **rìcháng jiāyòng kāizhī** daily household expenses

凯 **kǎi** ADJ triumphant
凯旋 **kǎixuán** v return in triumph

慨 **kǎi** ADJ deeply touched (See 感慨 gǎnkǎi)

刊 **kān** v publish
刊登 **kāndēng** v publish (in a newspaper, magazine, etc.)
刊物 **kānwù** N periodical, journal, magazine

勘 **kān** v survey, investigate
勘探 **kāntàn** N prospecting, exploration
石油勘探队 **shíyóukāntàn duì** oil prospecting team

堪 **kān** MODAL V may, can

看 **kān** v look after, take care of
看孩子 **kān háizi** look after children, baby-sit

NOTE: This verb 看 is pronounced in the first tone when used in this sense.

砍 **kǎn** v chop, hack

看 **kàn** v 1 look, watch ■ 我看看你的新衣服。*Wǒ kànkan nǐ de xīn yīfu. Let me have a look at your new dress.* 2 read ■ "你每天看报吗？" "我不每天看报。" "*Nǐ měi tiān kàn bào ma?" "Wǒ bù měi tiān kàn bào." "Do you read newspapers every day?" "No."*
看电视 **kàn diànshì** watch TV
看电影 **kàn diànyǐng** watch a film
看体育比赛 **kàn tǐyù bǐsài** watch a sport event

NOTE: See note on 看见 kànjiàn.

看病 **kànbìng** v see a doctor ■ 我下午要请半天假，去看病。*Wǒ xiàwǔ yào qǐng bàn tiān jià, qù kànbìng. I'll ask for half a day leave to see a doctor this afternoon.*
看不起 **kànbuqǐ** v look down upon, despise
看得起 **kàndeqǐ** respect, hold in esteem

NOTE: In colloquial Chinese, 瞧不起 qiáobuqǐ can

be used instead of 看不起 kànbuqǐ. Likewise 看得起 kàndeqǐ may be replaced by 瞧得起 qiáodeqǐ.

看待 **kàndài** v look upon, regard, treat ■ 所有的职工都一律看待。*Suǒyǒu de zhígōng dōu yílù kàndài. All staff members are treated alike.*
看法 **kànfǎ** N 1 way of looking at things, view ■ 你的看法不一定对。*Nǐ de kànfǎ bù yídìng duì. Your view is not necessarily correct.* 2 negative opinion ■ 他对我有看法。*Tā duì wǒ yǒu kànfǎ. He has a negative opinion of me.*
看见 **kànjiàn** v see, get sight of ■ 我朝山上看了很久，才看见一个人在爬山。*Wǒ cháo shān shang kànle hěn jiǔ, cái kànjiàn yí ge rén zài pá shān. I looked at the hills for a long time before I saw a man climbing.*
看不见 **kàn bu jiàn** cannot see
看得见 **kàn de jiàn** can see
没(有)看见 **méi (yǒu) kànjiàn** fail to see ■ 我没看见他在图书馆里。*Wǒ méi kànjiàn tā zài túshūguǎn li. I did not see him in the library.*

NOTE: While 看 kàn is *to look* or *to look at*, 看见 kànjiàn is *to see* or *to catch sight of*. For example ■ 我朝窗外看，没有看见什么。*Wǒ cháo chuāng wài kàn, méiyǒu kànjiàn shénme. I looked out of the window and did not see anything.*

看来 **kànlái** ADV it looks as if, it seems as if ■ 看来要下大雨了。*Kànlái yào xià dà yǔ le. It seems that a downpour is coming our way.*
看望 **kànwàng** v call on, pay a visit to ■ 我每年过年都要看望中学时的老师。*Wǒ měi nián guònián dōu yào kànwàng zhōngxué shí de lǎoshī. I pay a visit to my high school teacher every New Year's Day.*
看样子 **kànyàngzi** ADV Same as 看来 kànlái
看做 **kànzuò** v regard as, look upon as
把你看做我的好朋友 **bǎ nǐ kàn zuò wǒde hǎo péngyou** (I) regard you as my good friend, take you for my good friend

康 **kāng** N good health (See 健康 jiànkāng.)

慷 **kāng** as in 慷慨 kāngkài
慷慨 **kāngkài** ADJ generous, liberal

糠 **kāng** N husk, bran, chaff

抗 **kàng** v resist (See 反抗 fǎnkàng, 抗议 kàngyì.)
抗击 **kàngjī** v beat back, resist by fighting
抗议 **kàngyì** v, N protest ■ 许多居民抗议建造新机场。*Xǔduō jūmín kàngyì jiànzào xīn jīchǎng. Many residents protested against the building of a new airport.*

亢 **kàng** ADJ high, haughty

炕 **kàng** N a heatable brick bed, *kang*

考 **kǎo** V examine, test ■ 下星期二考中文。 Xià Xīngqī'èr kǎo Zhōngwén. *There will be an examination on Chinese next Tuesday.*
考察 **kǎochá** V 1 inspect, make an on-the-spot investigation 2 test and judge (a person)
考古 **kǎogǔ** V do archaeological studies
考古学 **kǎogǔxué** archaeology
考核 **kǎohé** V examine and check
年终考核 **niánzhōng kǎohé** annual (staff) performance review
考虑 **kǎolǜ** V think over carefully, consider, contemplate ■ 他正在考虑转到另一个学校去。Tā zhèngzài kǎolǜ zhuǎndào lìng yí ge xuéxiào qu. *He is contemplating transferring to another school.*
考取 **kǎoqǔ** V pass an examination for admission to employment or study
考取名牌大学 **kǎoqǔ míngpái dàxué** gain admission to a famous university by passing an examination
考试 **kǎoshì** I V examine, test ■ 我们明天考试。Wǒmen míngtiān kiaoshì. *We're having an examination tomorrow.*
考得好 **kǎo de hǎo** do well in an examination
考得不好 **kǎo de bù hǎo** do poorly in an examination
II N examination, test (次 cì, 场 cháng) ■ 这次考试太难了! Zhè cì kǎoshì tài nán le! *This test was really difficult!*
高等学校入学考试 (高考) **gāoděng xuéxiào rùxué kǎoshì (gāokǎo)** university entrance examination
汉语水平考试 **Hànyǔ Shuǐpíng Kǎoshì (HSK)** Chinese Proficiency Test
考验 **kǎoyàn** I V test, put through rigorous testing II N rigorous test, trial

烤 **kǎo** V bake, roast ■ 中国人很少吃烤牛肉。Zhōngguórén hěn shǎo chī kǎo niúròu. *The Chinese rarely eat roast beef.*

靠 **kào** V rely on, depend on ■ 做事不能靠运气。Zuòshì bù néng kào yùnqi. *You cannot rely on luck to get things done.*
靠得住 **kàodezhù** trustworthy, reliable
靠不住 **kàobuzhù** untrustworthy, unreliable
靠近 **kàojìn** V close to, near

科 **kē** N 1 section (of an administration office)
财务科 **cáiwùkē** finance section

2 branch (of academic study)
工科 **gōngkē** faculty of engineering
理科 **lǐkē** faculty of (natural) sciences
文科 **wénkē** faculty of arts
3 shortening for 科学 **kēxué**
科技 **kējì** science and technology
科目 **kēmù** N (school) subject, course
科学 **kēxué** N science ■ 科学能解决世界上所有的问题吗? Kēxué néng jiějué shìjiè shang suǒyǒu de wèntí ma? *Can science solve all the problems in the world?*
科学研究 (科研) **kēxué yánjiū (kēyán)** scientific research
科学家 **kēxuéjiā** N scientist (位 wèi)
科学院 **kēxuéyuàn** N academy of science
科长 **kēzhǎng** N section head

棵 **kē** M. WD (for plants)
三棵树 **sān kē shù** three trees
一棵草 **yì kē cǎo** a blade of grass

颗 **kē** M. WD (for beans, pearl, etc.)
一颗黄豆 **yìkē huángdòu** a soybean

磕 **kē** V knock
磕头 **kētóu** V kowtow

咳 **ké** V cough
咳嗽 **késou** V cough ■ 你咳嗽很厉害, 得去看病。Nǐ késou hěn lìhai, děi qù kànbìng. *You've got a bad cough. You need to see a doctor.*
咳嗽药水 **késou yàoshuǐ** cough syrup
咳嗽糖 **késou táng** cough lozenge/drop

壳 **ké** N shell
鸡蛋壳 **jīdànké** egg shell

可 **kě** I ADV 1 indeed (used before an adjective for emphasis) ■ 当父母可不容易呢! Dāng fùmǔ kě bù róngyì ne! *Being a parent is indeed no easy job!* 2 after all (used before a verb for emphasis) ■ 我可找到你了! Wǒ kě zhǎodào nǐ le! *I've found you after all.* 3 be sure to (used in an imperative sentence for emphasis) ■ 可别忘了给他发一份电子邮件。Kě bié wàngle gěi tā fā yí fèn diànzǐ yóujiàn! *Be sure not to forget to send him an e-mail.* (→ *Be sure to send him an e-mail.*) II MODAL V can be, may be III CONJ Same as 可是 **kěshì**

NOTE: 可 **kě** is only used colloquially. When using 可 **kě** to emphasize an adjective or a verb, 啦 la, 呢 ne or 了 le is often used at the end of the sentence.

可爱 **kě'ài** ADJ lovable, lovely ■ 这小女孩真

可爱! Zhè xiǎo nǚhái zhēn kě'ài! *What a lovely little girl!*

NOTE: 可 in the sense of *can be, may be* plus a verb forms an adjective, similar to English adjectives of *v+-able/ible*. For example, 可爱 kě'ài is similar to *lovable*. Quite a number of Chinese adjectives are formed in the same way as 可爱 kě'ài.

可耻 kěchǐ ADJ shameful, disgraceful
可观 kěguān ADJ considerable, sizeable
一笔可观的现金 yìbǐ kěguān de xiànjīn a considerable sum of cash
可贵 kěguì ADJ valuable, recommendable
可见 kějiàn CONJ it can be seen, it is thus clear
可靠 kěkào ADJ reliable, trustworthy
可口 kěkǒu ADJ palatable, tasty
可口可乐 kěkǒukělè N Coca-Cola (瓶 píng)
百事可乐 bǎishìkělè Pepsi[-Cola]

NOTE: 可口可乐 kěkǒukělè is a transliteration of "Coca-Cola." It can be shortened into 可乐 kělè.

可怜 kělián ADJ pitiful, pitiable ■ 这小孩的父母在交通事故中死了，真可怜! Zhè xiǎohái de fùmǔ zài jiāotōng shìgù zhong sǐ le, zhēn kělián! *Both his parents died in a road accident, the poor child!*
可能 kěnéng I MODAL V may, possible, possibly ■ 他两天没来上课，可能病了。Tā liǎng tiān méi lái shàngkè, kěnéng bìng le. *He's been absent from class for two days. He may be ill.* II N possibility ■ 这种可能是有的。Zhè zhǒng kěnéng shì yǒu de. *This is possible.*
(没)有可能 (méi) yǒu kěnéng (im)possible, (im)possibly ■ "这件事有解决的可能吗?" "Zhè jiàn shì yǒu jiějué de kěnéng ma?" *"Is it possible to solve this matter?"*
可怕 kěpà ADJ fearsome, frightening
可是 kěshì CONJ Same as 但是 dànshì, used colloquially.
可恶 kěwù ADJ detestable, hateful
可惜 kěxī ADJ be a pity, be a shame ■ 真可惜! Zhēn kěxī! *What a shame!*
可喜 kěxǐ ADJ gratifying, heartening
可笑 kěxiào ADJ laughable, ridiculous
可行 kěxíng ADJ can be done, feasible
可行性 kěxíngxìng feasibility
可行性报告 kěxíngxìng bàogào feasibility report
可疑 kěyí ADJ suspicious
可疑分子 kěyífènzǐ a suspect
行为可疑 xíngwéi kěyí suspicious behavior
可以 kěyǐ MODAL V giving permission, may, can, be allowed ■ 你不可以把阅览室的书带回家。Nǐ bù kěyǐ bǎ yuèlǎnshì de shū dàihuí jiā. *You are not allowed to take books home from the reading room.*

渴 kě ADJ thirsty ■ 我渴了，请给我一杯水。Wǒ kě le, qǐng gěi wǒ yì bēi shuǐ. *I'm thirsty. Please give me a glass of water.*
口渴 kǒukě thirsty

NOTE: See note on 喝 hē.

渴望 kěwàng V thirst for, long for

克 kè M. WD gram
五百克 wǔbǎi kè 500 grams
克服 kèfú V overcome, conquer ■ 我相信一定能克服这些暂时的困难。Wǒ xiāngxìn yídìng néng kèfú zhèxiē zànshí de kùnnan. *I am convinced that we are surely able to overcome these temporary difficulties.*

刻 1 kè V carve ■ 他在石头上刻上自己的名字。Tā zài shítou shang kè shang zìjǐ de míngzi. *He carved his name on the rock.*

刻 2 kè M. WD quarter of an hour
一刻钟 yí kè zhōng a quarter of an hour, 15 minutes
三点一刻 sān diǎn yí kè a quarter past three
刻苦 kèkǔ ADJ hardworking, assiduous, painstaking ■ 这位科学家刻苦研究十几年，终于找到了答案。Zhè wèi kēxuéjiā kèkǔ yánjiū shí jǐ nián, zhōngyú zhǎodào le dá'àn. *The scientist researched arduously for a dozen years and finally found the answer.*

客 kè N guest
客车 kèchē N 1 passenger train 2 coach
客观 kèguān ADJ objective
客观的报道 kèguān de bàodào objective report
客户 kèhù N client, buyer
客气 kèqi ADJ 1 polite, standing on ceremony ■ 您跟我们一起吃午饭吧，别客气。Nín gēn wǒmen yìqǐ chī wǔfàn ba, bié kèqi. *Have lunch with us. Don't stand on ceremony.* 2 modest ■ 你唱歌唱得这么好，还说不好，太客气了。Nǐ chànggē chàng de zhème hǎo, hái shuō bù hǎo, tài kèqi le. *You sing so well but you still say you don't sing well. You're too modest.*
客人 kèrén N guest, visitor
客厅 kètīng N living room, sitting room

课 kè TRAD 課 N lesson, class, lecture ■ 今天的课你听懂没有? Jīntiān de kè nǐ tīngdǒng méiyǒu? *Do you understand today's lesson?*
上课 shàng kè go to class
下课 xià kè finish class
课本 kèběn N textbook, course book (本 běn)
课程 kèchéng N course, a program of study

■ 医学课程花的时间比其他课程长。Yīxué kèchéng huā de shíjiān bǐ qítā kèchéng cháng. *A course in medicine takes more time than other courses.*

课时 **kèshí** N class hour
课堂 **kètáng** N classroom
课题 **kètí** N research topic
课文 **kèwén** N text (篇 piān) ■ 这篇课文写得真好。Zhè piān kèwén xiě de zhēn hǎo. *This text is really well written.*

肯 kěn MODAL V be willing to ■ 中国的父母一般肯为孩子作出牺牲。Zhōngguó de fù-mǔ yìbān kěn wèi háizi zuòchu xīshēng. *Generally speaking, Chinese parents are willing to make sacrifices for their children.*

肯定 **kěndìng** I v confirm, acknowledge ■ 总公司充分肯定你们的成绩。Zǒnggōngsī chōngfèn kěndìng nǐmen de chéngjì. *The company's head office fully acknowledges your achievements.* II ADJ affirmative, positive, definite ■ 很抱歉，我不能给你一个肯定的回答。Hěn bàoqiàn, wǒ bù néng gěi nǐ yí ge kěndìng de huídá. *I'm sorry, but I'm not in a position to give you a definite reply.*

啃 kěn v gnaw, nibble

恳 kěn TRAD 懇 ADJ sincere

恳切 **kěnqiè** ADJ earnest, sincere
恳求 **kěnqiú** v implore, entreat

垦 kěn TRAD 墾 v cultivate (land)

垦荒 **kěnhuāng** v reclaim wasteland

坑 kēng N pit, hollow

空 kōng I ADJ empty ■ 箱子是空的，里面什么也没有。Xiāngzi shì kōng de, lǐmiàn shénme yě méiyǒu. *The suitcase is empty, there's nothing in it.* II N sky

空洞 **kōngdòng** ADJ hollow, devoid of content
空洞的承诺 **kōngdòng de chéngnuò** hollow promise
空话 **kōnghuà** N empty talk, hollow words
空间 **kōngjiān** N space, room ■ 要给孩子留一些空间，让他做自己喜欢做的事。Yào gěi háizi liú yìxiē kōngjiān, ràng tā zuò zìjǐ xǐhuan zuò de shì. *Leave a child room (or time) to let him do what he enjoys doing.*
空军 **kōngjūn** N air force
空气 **kōngqì** N air ■ 这里的空气真好！Zhèlǐ de kōngqì zhēn hǎo! *The air here is really fresh.*
空前 **kōngqián** ADJ unprecedented ■ 这种经济增长的速度是空前的。Zhè zhǒng jīngjì

zēngzhǎng de sùdù shì kōngqián de. *This kind of economic growth rate is unprecedented.*
空调 **kōngtiáo** N air conditioning
空调机 **kōngtiáojī** air conditioner
有空调的房间 **yǒu kòngtiáo de fángjiān** air-conditioned room
空想 **kōngxiǎng** N pipe-dream, fantasy
空心 **kōngxīn** ADJ hollow
空虚 **kōngxū** ADJ void, empty
生活空虚 **shēnghuó kōngxū** live a life devoid of any meaning, a meaningless existence
空中 **kōngzhōng** N in the sky, in the air

恐 kǒng v fear

恐怖 **kǒngbù** ADJ horrible, terrifying ■ 这个电影太恐怖了，小孩子不能看。Zhège diànyǐng tài kǒngbù le, xiǎo háizi bù néng kàn. *This film is too frightening for children to see.*
恐怖电影 **kǒngbù diànyǐng** horror movie
恐怖分子 **kǒngbù fènzi** terrorist
恐怖活动 **kǒngbù huódòng** terrorist activity
恐怖主义 **kǒngbù zhǔyì** terrorism
恐惧 **kǒngjù** v be in great fear of, dread
恐怕 **kǒngpà** ADV I'm afraid, perhaps ■ 他的病恐怕两三天好不了。Tā de bìng kǒngpà liǎng-sān tiān hǎobuliǎo. *I'm afraid he won't recover in a couple of days.*

NOTE: 恐怕 kǒngpà and 也许 yěxǔ may both mean *perhaps*, but 恐怕 kǒngpà implies that what might perhaps happen is undesirable.

孔 kǒng N aperture, hole

孔夫子 **Kǒngfūzǐ** N Confucius

NOTE: (1) 孔夫子 Kǒngfūzǐ—also called 孔子 Kǒngzǐ in Chinese—is the most influential Chinese philosopher. His Europeanized name is *Confucius*. The great ancient philosopher 孟子 Mèngzǐ also has a Europeanized name, viz. *Mencius*. His teachings are referred to as 孔子学说 Kǒngzǐ xuéshuō or 儒家学说 Rújiā xuéshuō.

孔雀 **kǒngquè** N peacock (只 zhī)

空 kòng I ADJ unoccupied, vacant

空房 **kòngfáng** vacant room
II N free time ■ 你今天晚上有空吗? Nǐ jīntiān wǎnshang yǒukòng ma? *Are you free this evening?*
空白 **kòngbái** ADJ blank space
空白支票 **kòngbái zhīpiào** blank check
空缺 **kòngquē** N vacant position
空隙 **kòngxì** N narrow gap, brief interval
空闲 **kòngxián** I ADJ be free II N free time, leisure

空子 **kòngzi** N loophole
钻空子 **zuān kòngzi** take advantage of a loophole

控 **kòng** V **1** control **2** accuse

控告 **kònggào** V accuse, sue
控股公司 **kònggǔ gōngsī** N holding company
控制 **kòngzhì** V control, dominate ■ 她控制不住自己的感情，大哭起来。Tā kòngzhì bú zhù zìjǐ de gǎnqíng, dàkū qǐlai. *She couldn't control her emotions and began to cry loudly.*

抠 **kōu** V dig with a finger

口 **kǒu** I N mouth ■ 病从口入。Bìng cóng kǒu rù. *Disease enters your body by the mouth.* (→ *Bad food causes disease.*) ■ 我家有四口人。Wǒ jiā yǒu sì kǒu rén. *There're four people in my family.*
口岸 **kǒu' àn** N port
口才 **kǒucái** I N the ability to speak well, gift of gab II ADJ eloquent
有口才 **yǒu kǒucái** be eloquent
口吃 **kǒuchī** V stammer, stutter
口齿 **kǒuchǐ** N the ability to pronounce sounds and words clearly
口齿清楚 **kǒuchǐ qīngchǔ** with clear enunciation
口袋 **kǒudài** N pocket (只 zhī)
口号 **kǒuhào** N slogan (条 tiáo) ■ 这种政治口号已经没有人喊了。Zhè zhǒng zhèngzhì kǒuhào yǐjīng méiyǒu rén hǎn le. *Nobody shouts such political slogans any more.*
口气 **kǒuqì** N **1** tone (of speech)
温和的口气 **wēnhé de kǒuqì** gentle tone
2 manner of speaking
听他的口气 **tīng tāde kǒuqì** judging by the way he spoke
口腔 **kǒuqiāng** N oral cavity
口试 **kǒushì** N oral examination
口头 **kǒutóu** ADJ oral, spoken
口头协议 **kǒutóu xiéyì** oral agreement
口语 **kǒuyǔ** N spoken language, speech ■ 要学好口语，就要多听，多说。Yào xué hǎo kǒuyǔ, jiù yào duō tīng, duō shuō. *To learn the spoken language well, one should listen a lot and speak a lot.*

扣 **kòu** I N **1** button
扣子 **kòuzi** button
2 knot
系个扣儿 **xì gè kòur** make a knot
II V **1** button up
扣扣子 **kòu kòuzi** do up the buttons
2 detain, arrest **3** deduct
扣除 **kòuchú** V deduct

扣留 **kòuliú** V detain, hold in custody
扣留驾驶执照 **kòuliú jiàshǐ zhízhào** suspend a driving license
扣押 **kòuyā** V distrain, detain
扣压 **kòuyā** V withhold, pigeonhole

寇 **kòu** N bandit

哭 **kū** V cry, weep, sob ■ 别哭了，有话好好说。Bié kū le, yǒu huà hǎohǎo shuō. *Don't cry. Speak up if you have something to say.*

枯 **kū** ADJ withered

枯燥 **kūzào** ADJ dull and dry
枯燥乏味 **kūzào fáwèi** dull and insipid

窟 **kū** N cave, hole

窟窿 **kūlong** N hole, cavity

苦 **kǔ** ADJ **1** bitter ■ 这杯咖啡太苦了，要放点儿糖。Zhè bēi kāfēi tài kǔ le, yào fàng diǎnr táng. *This coffee is too bitter. Put a bit of sugar in it.* **2** (of life) hard, miserable ■ 经济不好，不少人生活很苦。Jīngjì bù hǎo, bù shǎo rén shēnghuó hěn kǔ. *As the economy is not in good shape, many people's lives are very hard.*
吃苦 **chīkǔ** suffer hardships, endure hardships
苦闷 **kǔmèn** ADJ depressed, dejected
苦难 **kǔnàn** N great suffering, misery
苦恼 **kǔnǎo** ADJ vexed, troubled

库 **kù** TRAD 庫 N warehouse (See 仓库 cāngkù)

库存 **kùcún** N stock, reserve

裤 **kù** TRAD 褲 N trousers

裤子 **kùzi** N trousers (条 tiáo) ■ 这条裤子短了一点儿。Zhè tiáo kùzi duǎnle yìdiǎnr. *This pair of trousers is a bit too short.*

酷 **kù** ADJ **1** cruel
酷刑 **kùxíng** cruel torture, torture
2 cool ■ 太酷了！Tài kù le! *It's really cool!*

夸 **kuā** V **1** exaggerate, boast **2** praise

夸大 **kuādà** V exaggerate
夸奖 **kuājiǎng** V praise, commend

垮 **kuǎ** V collapse, break down

打垮 **dǎkuǎ** defeat, rout, smash

跨 **kuà** V take big strides ■ 他再向前跨一步，就要滚下楼梯了。Tā zài xiàngqián kuà yí bù, jiùyào gǔnxia lóutī le. *If he took another step forward he would tumble down the staircase.*

挎 kuà

跨国公司 kuàguó gōngsī multinational company

挎 kuà v carry on the arm

快 kuài ADJ quick, fast ■ 他跑得很快。Tā pǎo de hěn kuài. *He runs very fast.*
快餐 kuàicān N fast food
快车 kuài chē N express train
快递 kuàidì N express delivery
快乐 kuàilè ADJ joyful, happy ■ 在这个快乐的节日里, 人们暂时忘了生活中种种不愉快的事。Zài zhège kuàilè de jiérì li, rénmen zànshí wàngle shēnghuó zhōng zhǒng-zhǒng bù yúkuài de shì. *At this happy festival, people forget for the time being the unpleasant things in life.*
快速 kuàisù ADJ highspeed

会 kuài as in 会计 kuàijì

会计 kuàijì N **1** accounting
会计年度 kuàijì niándù fiscal year
2 accountant
会计主任 kuàijì zhǔrèn chief accountant

块 kuài TRAD 塊 M. WD **1** (for things that can be broken into lumps or chunks)
一块蛋糕 yí kuài dàngāo a piece/slice of cake
两块面包 liǎng kuài miànbāo two pieces of bread
2 (for money) yuan, dollar (only in spoken Chinese)
三块钱 sǎn kuài qián three yuan (or dollars)

NOTE: See note on 元 yuán.

筷 kuài N chopstick

筷子 kuàizi chopstick, chopsticks
一双筷子 yì shuāng kuàizi a pair of chopsticks

宽 kuān TRAD 寬 ADJ **1** wide, broad ■ 江面很宽, 我游不过去。Jiāngmiàn hěn kuān, wǒ yóu bu guòqu. *The river is too wide for me to swim across.* **2** lenient, generous **3** well-off
宽敞 kuānchang ADJ spacious
宽大 kuāndà ADJ **1** roomy, spacious **2** lenient
宽带 kuāndài N broadband
宽广 kuānguǎng ADJ extensive, expansive
宽阔 kuānkuò ADJ broad, wide

款 kuǎn N sum of money (笔 bǐ) ■ 你可以用这张卡取款, 或者存款。Nǐ kěyǐ yòng zhè zhāng kǎ qǔ kuǎn, huòzhē cún kuǎn. *You can withdraw or deposit money with this card.*
款待 kuǎndài v entertain hospitably

狂 kuáng ADJ mad, wild

狂风 kuángfēng N terrible wind, strong fast wind
狂人 kuángrén N madman, maniac
狂妄 kuángwàng ADJ outrageously conceited

况 kuàng N situation (See 情况 qíngkuàng, 状况 zhuàngkuàng.)
况且 kuàngqiě CONJ moreover, besides

矿 kuàng TRAD 礦 N (coal, gold, etc.) mine (座 zuò), mineral
金矿 jīnkuàng gold mine
煤矿 méikuàng coal mine
油矿 yóukuàng oilfield
矿藏 kuàngcáng N mineral resources
矿产 kuàngchǎn N mineral products
矿工 kuànggōng N miner
矿区 kuàngqū N mining area
矿山 kuàngshān N mine
矿石 kuàngshí N mineral ore
矿物 kuàngwù N mineral

旷 kuàng ADJ free from worries

旷工 kuànggōng v absent from work without leave
旷课 kuàngkè v absent from school without leave

亏 kuī I N loss
转亏为盈 zhuǎn kuī wéi yíng turn loss into gain
II v **1** lose, be deficient **2** thank to
亏待 kuīdài v treat shabbily
亏损 kuīsǔn N loss, deficiency

葵 kuí as in 葵花 kuíhuā

葵花 kuíhuā N sunflower

愧 kuì ADJ ashamed (See 惭愧 cánkuì.)

昆 kūn as in 昆虫 kūnchóng

昆虫 kūnchóng N insect (只 zhī)

捆 kǔn I v bundle up, tie II M. WD bundle

困 kùn I v be stranded, be in a tough spot ■ 由于突然发大水, 人们被困在那个小山村。Yóuyú tūrán fā dàshuǐ, rénmen bèi kùn zài nàge xiǎo shāncūn. *Because of a sudden flood, people were stranded in the small mountain village.* II ADJ sleepy
困苦 kùnkǔ ADJ poverty-stricken, destitute
困难 kùnnan I N difficulty ■ 困难是有的, 但是

没有关系。Kùnnan shì yǒu de, dànshì méiyǒu guānxi. *There are difficulties, but it doesn't matter.*
克服困难 kèfú kùnnan overcome difficulty
II ADJ difficult ■ 我们现在的情况比较困难。Wǒmen xiànzài de qíngkuàng bǐjiào kùnnan. *Our situation is rather difficult.*

扩 kuò TRAD 擴 V spread out

扩充 kuòchōng V strengthen, reinforce
扩大 kuòdà V expand, enlarge
扩散 kuòsàn V spread, proliferate
扩张 kuòzhāng V expand, extend

括 kuò V include, embrace (See 概括 gàikuò.)

阔 kuò ADJ wide (See 广阔 guǎngkuò.)

L

拉 lā V pull ■ 请你拉这个门，别推这个门。Qǐng nǐ lā zhège mén, bié tuī zhège mén. *Please pull this door, not push it.*

垃 lā as in 垃圾 lājī

垃圾 lājī N rubbish, garbage ■ 请不要乱扔垃圾。Qǐng bú yào luàn rēng lājī. *Please do not litter.*
垃圾处理 lājī chǔlǐ rubbish disposal
垃圾袋 lājī dài rubbish bag
垃圾箱 lājī xiāng rubbish bin
垃圾邮件 lājī yóujiàn N junk mail
阻止垃圾邮件 zǔzhǐ lājī yóujiàn prevent junk mail

喇 lǎ as in 喇叭 lǎba

喇叭 lǎba N 1 horn, trumpet 2 loudspeaker
吹喇叭 chuī lǎba blow the horn, play the trumpet

蜡 là TRAD 蠟 N wax

蜡烛 làzhú N candle (支 zhī)
点蜡烛 diǎn làzhú light a candle

腊 là TRAD 臘 ADJ 1 of the twelfth month of the lunar year 2 (of meat) salted and dried, cured

腊肉 làròu N cured meat, ham
腊月 làyuè N the twelfth (and last) month of the lunar year

落 là V 1 leave out 2 lag behind

NOTE: When used in these senses, 落 is pronounced as là, not as luò, which it usually is.

辣 là ADJ spicy hot, peppery

辣椒 làjiāo N red pepper, chilli

啦 la PARTICLE (an exclamation indicating completion of an action and/or emergence of a new situation; 了 le + 啊 a) ■ 我们赢啦! Wǒmen yíng la! *We've won!*

NOTE: 啦 la is the combination of 了 le and 啊 a. It is only used at the end of a sentence. You can replace 啦 la with 了 le but then the strong emotive coloring of 啊 a is lost. Compare: 我赢啦! Wǒ yíng la! *I won!* and 我赢了。Wǒ yíng le. *I won.*

来 1 lái TRAD 來 V come, come to, move towards to the speaker ■ 他是三年前来新西兰的。Tā shì sān nián qián lái Xīnxīlán de. *He came to New Zealand three years ago.*
来宾 láibīn N guest, visitor
来不及 láibují V not have enough time (to do something), there isn't enough time (to do something) ■ 到那时候，哭都来不及。Dào nà shíhou, kū dōu láibují. *Should such a moment come, there would be no time even to cry (→ it would be too late to regret).*

NOTE: The opposite to 来不及 láibují is 来得及 láidejí, e.g. ■ 还来得及吃早饭。Hái láidejí chī zǎofàn. *There is still enough time to have breakfast.*

来访 láifǎng V come to visit, come to call
来回 láihuí V make a around trip, make a return journey
来客 láikè N guest, customer (to a restaurant, hotel, etc.)
来历 láilì N origin, background
来历不明 láilì bùmíng of uncertain origin, of dubious background
来临 láilín V arrive, approach
来年 láinián N the coming year
来往 láiwang N dealings, connection
和他们没有来往 hé tāmen méiyǒu láiwang have had no dealings with them
来信 láixìn N letter received, incoming letter ■ 来信早已收到。Láixìn zǎo yǐ shōudào. *I received your letter long ago.*
来源 láiyuán N source, origin
消息来源 xiāoxi láiyuán source of the news
来自 láizì V come from ■ 这个中文班的学生来自世界各国。Zhège Zhōngwén bān de xuésheng láizì shìjiè gè guó. *The students of this Chinese class came from all over the world.*

来 2 **lái** TRAD 來 NUM approximately, more or less, close to (used after the number 10 or a multiple of 10 to indicate approximation)
十来辆车 **shí lái liàng chē** about ten cars
五十来个学生 **wǔshí lái ge xuésheng** approximately fifty students
三百四十来块钱 **sānbǎi sìshí lái kuài qián** about 340 yuan

赖 **lài** TRAD 賴 V rely (See 依赖 yīlài)

兰 **lán** TRAD 蘭 N orchid
兰花 **lánhuā** orchid

栏 **lán** TRAD 欄 N railing, fence
栏杆 **lángān** N railing, banister, balustrade

拦 **lán** TRAD 攔 V stop, block, hold back ■ 你要去就去, 没人拦你。 **Nǐ yào qù jiù qù, méi rén lán nǐ.** If you want to go, go ahead. Nobody is trying to stop you.

蓝 **lán** TRAD 藍 ADJ blue ■ 天很蓝, 因为空气很干净。 **Tiān hěn lán, yīnwèi kōngqì hěn gānjing.** The sky is blue because the air is clean.

篮 **lán** TRAD 籃 N basket
篮球 **lánqiú** N basketball
篮球比赛 **lánqiú bǐsài** basketball match
篮球队 **lánqiú duì** basketball team
打篮球 **dǎ lánqiú** play basketball
篮子 **lánzi** N basket

览 **lǎn** TRAD 覽 V view (See 游览 yóulǎn, 阅览室 yuèlǎnshì, 展览 zhǎnlǎn.)

揽 **lǎn** TRAD 攬 V 1 pull into one's arms, take into one's arms 2 take on
揽生意 **lǎn shēngyì** canvass for business

懒 **lǎn** TRAD 懶 ADJ lazy, indolent ■ 你真太懒了, 收到他来信两个星期了, 还不回信。 **Nǐ zhēn tài lǎn le, shōudào tā láixìn liǎng ge xīngqī le hái bù huíxìn.** You're really lazy. It's two weeks since you received his letter and you still haven't replied.
懒惰 **lǎnduò** ADJ lazy
懒骨头 **lǎn gútou** N lazybones

烂 **làn** TRAD 爛 I V rot, go bad II ADJ rotten ■ 这个苹果烂了, 扔了吧。 **Zhège píngguǒ làn le, rēng le ba.** This apple is rotten. Throw it away.

滥 **làn** TRAD 濫 I V overflow, flood (See 泛滥 fànlàn.) II ADJ excessive, indiscriminate
滥用 **lànyòng** V abuse, misuse
滥用职权 **lànyòng zhíquán** abuse one's power

狼 **láng** N wolf (只 zhī)
披着羊皮的狼 **pīzhe yángpí de láng** a wolf in sheep's clothing
一群狼 **yì qún láng** a pack of wolves
狼狈 **lángbèi** ADJ in an awkward position
狼狈为奸 **lángbèi wéijiān** V act in collusion with each other

廊 **láng** N corridor

郎 **láng** SUFFIX (for certain nouns of people)
放羊郎 **fàng yángláng** shepherd

朗 **lǎng** ADJ loud and clear
朗读 **lǎngdú** V read in a loud and clear voice ■ 学外语, 一定要朗读课文。 **Xué wàiyǔ, yídìng yào lǎngdú kèwén.** To learn a foreign language, one should read texts aloud.
朗诵 **lǎngsòng** V recite (a poem) theatrically

浪 **làng** I N wave ■ 风急浪高, 不能出海。 **Fēng jí làng gāo, bù néng chūhǎi.** The winds are strong and the waves high. We can't go out to sea. II ADJ uncontrolled, dissolute
浪潮 **làngcháo** N tide, tidal wave
浪费 **làngfèi** V waste ■ 浪费时间就是浪费生命。 **Làngfèi shíjiān jiùshì làngfèi shēngmìng.** To waste time is to waste life.
浪漫 **làngmàn** ADJ romantic

捞 **lāo** TRAD 撈 V pull or drag out of water ■ 孩子们在小河里捞什么呢? **Háizimen zài xiǎo hé li lāo shénme ne?** What are the children trying to scoop out of the stream?
打捞 **dǎlāo** salvage (a sunken ship, etc.)

劳 **láo** TRAD 勞 V toil
劳动 **láodòng** V do manual labor ■ 他夏天在父亲的农场劳动。 **Tā xiàtiān zài fùqin de nóngchǎng láodòng.** In summer he works on his father's farm.
脑力劳动 **nǎolì láodòng** mental work
体力劳动 **tǐlì láodòng** physical (manual) labor
劳动节 **láodòng jié** N Labor Day (on May 1)
劳动力 **láodònglì** N work force, manpower
劳动力不足 **láodònglì bùzú** short of manpower
劳驾 **láojià** IDIOM Excuse me, Would you mind (doing ... for me) ■ 劳驾, 请您让一下。 **Láojià, qǐng nín ràng yíxià.** Excuse me, would you please make way?

NOTE: 劳驾 **láojià** is a northern dialect expression. To say *Excuse me*, 对不起 **duìbuqǐ** is more widely used.

唠 láo as in 唠叨 láodao

唠叨 láodao ADJ be garrulous
唠唠叨叨说个没完 láoláo dāodāo shuō gè méiwán chatter on and on

牢 láo I ADJ firm, fast II N shortening for 牢房 láofáng
坐牢 zuòláo serve jail term
牢房 láofáng N Same as 监狱 jiānyù, used only informally.
牢固 láogù ADJ firm, solid
牢骚 láosāo N discontent, grumbling
发牢骚 fāláosāo grumble

老 lǎo I ADJ 1 old, elderly ■ 他在帮一位老太太过马路。Tā zài bāng yí wèi lǎo tàitai guò mǎlù. *He's helping an old lady cross the street.*
老太太 lǎo tàitai old lady, old woman
老先生 lǎo xiānsheng old gentleman, old man
2 long-standing ■ 这个老问题一直没有办法解决。Zhè ge lǎo wèntí yìzhí méiyǒu bànfǎ jiějué. *This perennial problem has remained unsolved for a long time.*
老朋友 lǎopéngyou long-standing friend ■ 我们在小学的时候就认识了，是老朋友。Wǒmen zài xiǎoxué de shíhou jiù rènshi le, shì lǎo péngyou. *We've known each other since primary school. We're old friends.*
II PREFIX (added to numbers to indicate seniority among siblings)
老大 lǎo dà the eldest child
老二 lǎo èr the second child

NOTE: Chinese tradition values and respects old age. Today, people still attach 老 lǎo to a family name as a form of address to show respect and friendliness to an older person, e.g. 老李 Lǎo Lǐ, 老王 Lǎo Wáng. See note on 小 xiǎo.

老百姓 lǎobǎixìng N common people, ordinary folk
老板 lǎobǎn N 1 boss ■ 他是我的老板，他要我做什么我就做什么。Tā shì wǒ de lǎobǎn, tā yào wǒ zuò shénme wǒ jiù zuò shénme. *He is my boss; I do what he tells me to do.* **2** owner of a store, a business, etc.
老成 lǎochéng ADJ (of a youngster) mature and experienced
老大娘 lǎodàniáng N (a respectful form of address or reference to an old woman) (位 wèi)

NOTE: 老大娘 lǎodàniáng has a rustic flavor. It is normally not used in cities or among better-educated people. 老太太 lǎotàitai is a more appropriate word.

老大爷 lǎodàye N (a respectful form of address or reference to an old man) (位 wèi)

NOTE: 老大爷 lǎodàye has a rustic flavor. It is normally not used in cities or among better-educated people. 老先生 lǎoxiānsheng is a more appropriate word.

老汉 lǎohàn N old man, old fellow
老虎 lǎohǔ N tiger (头 tóu, 只 zhī)
小老虎 xiǎo lǎohǔ tiger cub
老化 lǎohuà V 1 becoming old
人口老化 rénkǒulǎohuà ageing of the population
2 becoming outdated
知识老化 zhīshi lǎohuà outdated knowledge
老家 lǎojiā N native place
老龄 lǎolíng N old age, people of old age
老年 lǎonián N old age
老年人 lǎoniánrén N old person
老婆 lǎopó N (vulgarism) wife, old girl
老人 lǎorén N old person, elderly person (位 wèi) ■ 这位老人人老心不老，还在学中文和武术。Zhè wèi lǎorén rén lǎo xīn bù lǎo, háizài xué Zhōngwén hé wǔshù. *This old person is young at heart. He/She is still learning Chinese and martial arts.*
老人家 lǎorenjia N (respectful form of address for an old person) ■ 您老人家身体好吗？Nín lǎorenjia shēntǐ hǎoma? *Are you in good health, sir (or ma'am)?*
老师 lǎoshī N teacher (位 wèi) ■ 我的中文老师是北京人。Wǒ de Zhōngwén lǎoshī shì Běijīngrén. *My Chinese teacher is from Beijing.*

NOTE: 老师 lǎoshī, usually prefixed by a family name, is the standard form of address to a teacher, e.g. 王老师 Wáng Lǎoshī. There is no equivalent of 王老师 Wáng Lǎoshī in English. This dictionary uses the literal translation *Teacher Wang*.

老是 lǎoshi ADV always, constantly ■ 他老是写错这个字。Tā lǎoshi xiěcuò zhège zì. *He always writes this character wrongly.*
老实 lǎoshi ADJ honest ■ 说老实话，做老实人。Shuō lǎoshi huà, zuò lǎoshi rén. *Speak the truth and be an honest person.*
老实话 lǎoshi huà plain truth
老实人 lǎoshi rén honest person
老实说 lǎoshi shuō frankly, to tell the truth
老鼠 lǎoshǔ N mouse, mice, rat, rats (只 zhī)
老太婆 lǎotàipó N old woman

NOTE: See note on 老头儿 lǎotóur.

老太太 lǎotàitai N (a respectful form of address or reference to an old woman) (位 wèi) ■ 老太太，您找谁？Lǎotàitai, nín zhǎo shuí? *Who are you looking for, ma'am?*
老天爷 lǎotiānyé N the Old Lord of Heaven, Heaven, God ■ 我的老天爷! Wǒde lǎotiānyé! *My God! Goodness gracious!*

老头儿 lǎotóur

老头儿 lǎotóur N old man (个 gè) ■ 几个老头儿在树下打牌。Jǐ ge lǎotóur zài shù xia dǎpái. *Some old men were playing cards under the tree.*

NOTE: (1) 老头儿 lǎotóur is an impolite way of referring to *an old man*. As a form of address, 老头儿 lǎotóur is very rude. Instead, use the neutral term 老人 lǎorén or the polite terms 老先生 lǎoxiānsheng or 老大爷 lǎodàyé. (2) The corresponding impolite word for *an old woman* is 老太婆 lǎotàipó. Use 老太太 lǎotàitai or 老大娘 lǎodàniáng instead.

老外 lǎowài N foreigner

NOTE: 老外 lǎowài is a familiar term for *foreigner* in China. It is quite informal, but not really impolite. The formal term is 外国人 wàiguórén.

老先生 lǎoxiānsheng N (a respectful form of address or reference to an old man) (位 wèi) ■ 老先生，请您让我看看您的票子。Lǎoxiānsheng, qǐng nín ràng wǒ kànkan nín de piàozi. *Please show me your ticket, sir.*

老爷 lǎoye N (old fashioned) lord, sir

姥 lǎo as in 姥姥 lǎolao

姥姥 lǎolao N (maternal) granny

涝 lào N waterlogging, flooding

旱涝保收 hànlào bǎoshōu (of crops) sure to reap a good harvest even if there is drought or flooding

乐 lè TRAD 樂 ADJ happy, delighted, joyful

乐观 lèguān ADJ optimistic ■ 根据乐观的估计，今年经济增长可以达到百分之五。Gēnjù lèguān de gūjì, jīnnián jīngjì zēngzhǎng kěyǐ dádào bǎifēn zhī wǔ. *According to an optimistic estimate, the economy will grow by five percent this year.*

乐观主义 lèguān zhǔyì optimism
乐观主义者 lèguānzhǔyìzhě optimist
乐趣 lèqù N pleasure, joy
乐意 lèyì ADJ be happy to, be willing to

勒 lè V rein in

勒索 lèsuǒ V extort, blackmail

了 le PARTICLE 1 (used after a verb to indicate the completion of an action) ■ 他吃了晚饭就上网玩游戏。Tā chīle wǎnfàn jiù shàngwǎng wán yóuxì. *As soon as he had eaten supper, he went online to play games.* 2 (used at the end of a sentence to indicate the emergence of a new situation) ■ 秋天来了，树叶黄了。Qiūtiān lái le, shùyè huáng le. *Autumn has come and leaves have turned yellow.*

雷 léi N thunder ■ 昨天又打雷，又闪电，挺吓人的。Zuótiān yòu dǎ léi, yòu shǎndiàn, tǐng xiàrén de. *There was thunder and lightning yesterday. It was rather frightening.*

打雷 dǎléi thunder
雷达 léidá N radar
雷雨 léiyǔ N thunderstorm

蕾 lěi N (flower) bud

垒 lěi TRAD 壘 N as in 垒球 lěiqiú

垒球 lěiqiú N softball
垒球棒 lěiqiúbàng softball bat (根 gēn)

泪 lèi TRAD 淚 N teardrop, tear (See 眼泪 yǎnlèi.)

类 lèi TRAD 類 N kind, category, class ■ 这两类不同的情况，不要混为一谈。Zhè liǎng lèi bùtóng de qíngkuàng, bú yào hùnwéi yìtán. *These are two different situations. Don't lump them together.*

类似 lèisì ADJ similar
类型 lèixíng N type (种 zhǒng)

累 lèi ADJ exhausted, tired ■ "你劳动了半天，累不累？" "不累，一点都不累。" "Nǐ láodòngle bàntiān, lèi bu lèi?" "Bú lèi, yìdiǎn dōu bú lèi." *"Are you tired after doing manual labor for such a long time?" "No, I'm not the least tired."*

棱 léng N edge

冷 lěng ADJ cold ■ 他每天都洗冷水澡。Tā měi tiān dōu xǐ lěngshuǐ zǎo. *He takes a cold bath every day.*

冷淡 lěngdàn ADJ cold, indifferent, apathetic ■ 商业界对政府的新政策很冷淡。Shāngyè jiè duì zhèngfǔ de Xīnzhèngcè hěn lěngdàn. *The business circle is indifferent to the new policies of the government.*

冷静 lěngjìng ADJ calm, sober ■ 你冷静一些，别这么激动。Nǐ lěngjìng yìxiē, bié zhème jīdòng. *Calm down; don't be so agitated.*

冷却 lěngquè I V to make cool II N cooling
冷却剂 lěngquèjì coolant, cooler
冷饮 lěngyǐn N cold drink, ice-cream

愣 lèng ADJ stupefied, blank

发愣 fālèng look stupefied, stare blankly

厘 lí M. WD one thousandth of a foot

厘米 límǐ M. WD centimeter

离 lí TRAD 離 I V depart, leave ■ 他每天很早就离家，很晚才回家。Tā měitiān hěn zǎo jiù

lí jiā, hěn wǎn cái huí jiā. *He leaves home early and returns late every day.* **II PREP** (indicating distance in space or time) away from, from ■ 现在离寒假只有两个星期了。Xiànzài lí hánjià zhǐyǒu liǎngge xīngqī le. *There are only two weeks before the winter holiday.*
离…近 **lí…jìn** close to
离…远 **lí…yuǎn** far away from
离别 **líbié** v leave, bid farewell
离婚 **líhūn** v divorce
　离婚协议 **líhūn xiéyì** divorce settlement
　申请离婚 **shēnqǐng líhūn** file a divorce, sue for a divorce
离开 **líkāi** v **1** depart, leave ■ 我离开一会儿，马上就回来。Wǒ líkāi yíhuìr, mǎshàng jiù huílai. *Excuse me for a minute. I'll be back soon.* **2** do without
离不开 **líbukāi** cannot do without ■ 孩子还小，离不开妈。Háizi hái xiǎo, líbukāi mā. *The child is too young to be without his mother.*
离休 **líxiū** v (of officials) retire

篱 **lí** TRAD 籬 N hedge, fence
篱笆 **líba** N bamboo fence, twig fence

黎 **lí** as in 黎明 **límíng**
黎明 **límíng** N dawn, daybreak

狸 **lí** N racoon dog

梨 **lí** N pear (只 zhī)

犁 **lí** N plough

璃 **lí** N glass (See 玻璃 bōli.)

李 **Lǐ** N (a family name)

礼 **lǐ** TRAD 禮 N **1** rite, ceremony **2** gift
礼拜天 **Lǐbàitiān** N Same as 星期天 Xīngqītiān. A rather old-fashioned word.
礼节 **lǐjié** N etiquette, protocol
礼貌 **lǐmào** ADJ polite, courteous ■ 礼貌待客。Lǐmào dài kè. *Treat customers with courtesy.*
礼品 **lǐpǐn** N gift (件 jiàn)
礼堂 **lǐtáng** N auditorium, assembly hall (座 zuò)
礼物 **lǐwù** N gift, present (件 jiàn) ■ 今天是你的生日，我送你一件小礼物。Jīntiān shì nǐ de shēngrì, wǒ sòng nǐ yí jiàn xiǎo lǐwù. *Today's your birthday. I'll give you a little gift.*

结婚礼物 **jiéhūn lǐwù** wedding present
生日礼物 **shēngrì lǐwù** birthday present
新年礼物 **xīnnián lǐwù** New Year present

里 1 **lǐ** TRAD 裏 N inside ■ 生活里总会出现种种麻烦。Shēnghuó li zǒng huì chūxiàn zhǒng-zhǒng máfan. *You are bound to encounter various troublesome situations in life.*
里边 **lǐbian** N inside
里面 **lǐmiàn** N Same as 里边 lǐbian

里 2 **lǐ** M.WD (a traditional Chinese unit of distance, equivalent to half a kilometer) ■ 从市中心到飞机场有二十里，也就是十公里。Cóng shìzhōngxīn dào fēijīchǎng yǒu èrshí li, yě jiù shì shí gōnglǐ. *From the city center to the airport it's twenty li, or ten kilometers.*

理 **lǐ** I N pattern, reason II v manage, handle
理睬 **lǐcǎi** v (usu. negative sense) show interest in, pay attention to
理发 **lǐfà** v have a haircut and shampoo, have one's hair done
　理发店 **lǐfàdiàn** barbershop, hair salon
　理发师 **lǐfàshī** barber, hairdresser, hairstylist

理会 **lǐhuì** v **1** comprehend, understand **2** take notice of
不理会 **bùlǐhuì** take no notice of, ignore
理解 **lǐjiě** v understand, comprehend ■ 我理解你的心情。Wǒ lǐjiě nǐ de xīnqíng. *I understand how you feel.*
理亏 **lǐkuī** ADJ be in the wrong
　自知理亏 **zìzhī lǐkuī** know oneself to be in the wrong, realize that justice is not on one's side
理论 **lǐlùn** N theory
理念 **lǐniàn** N notion, ideal
理事 **lǐshì** N member of a council
理所当然 **lǐsuǒdāngrán** ADJ naturally, as should be expected
理想 **lǐxiǎng** N ideal, aspiration ■ 我小时候的理想是当个旅行家。Wǒ xiǎoshíhou de lǐxiǎng shì

dāng ge lǚxíngjiā. *When I was a child, I dreamed of being a traveler.*

理想主义 lǐxiǎng zhǔyì idealism

实现理想 shíxiàn lǐxiǎng realize an ideal

理由 lǐyóu N reason, justification, ground, argument ■ 我们有充分的理由处分他。Wǒmen yǒu chōngfèn de lǐyóu chǔfèn tā. *We have sufficient reason to discipline him.*

理直气壮 lǐzhíqìzhuàng ADJ bold and assured that justice is on one's side

力 lì N strength, force, might ■ 我全身无力，恐怕生病了。Wǒ quánshēn wú lì, kǒngpà shēngbìng le. *I feel weak all over; I'm afraid I'm ill.*

力量 lìliang N 1 strength ■ 人多力量大。Rén duō lìliang dà. *Strength lies in numbers.* 2 efforts, ability ■ 我们尽最大的力量克服当前的困难。Wǒmen jìn zuì dà de lìliang kèfú dāngqián de kùnnan. *We are making maximum efforts to overcome the present difficulties.*

力气 lìqi N physical strength

力求 lìqiú V strive for, do one's best for

力求完美 lìqiú wánměi strive for perfection

力图 lìtú V try hard, try one's best to

力图改善处境 lìtú gǎishàn chǔjìng try hard to improve one's situation

力争 lìzhēng V work hard for, do all one can to

历 lì TRAD 歷 N past experience

历代 lìdài N successive dynasties

历来 lìlái ADV all through the ages, always, ever since

历史 lìshǐ N history ■ 中国的历史非常长，有三千多年。Zhōngguó de lìshǐ fēicháng cháng, yǒu sānqiān duō nián. *China has a very long history of over three thousand years.*

历史学家 lìshǐxuéjiā historian

沥 lì TRAD 瀝 V drip, trickle

沥青 lìqīng N asphalt

荔 lì as in 荔枝 lìzhī

荔枝 lìzhī N litchi, lichee

隶 lì N slave (See 奴隶 núlì)

栗 lì chestnut

栗子 lìzi chestnut (颗 kē)

立 lì I V stand ■ 你立在门口干什么? Nǐ lì zài ménkǒu gàn shénme? *Why are you standing by the door?*

坐立不安 zuò-lì-bù-ān on pins and needles, on tenterhooks, anxious

II ADV immediately, at once

立场 lìchǎng N position, standpoint

立方 lìfāng M. WD (mathematics) cube

三立方米/公尺 sān lìfāng mǐ/gōngchǐ 3 cubic meters

立即 lìjí ADV immediately, without delay ■ 王董事长要我立即飞往上海处理一件事。Wáng dǒngshìzhǎng yào wǒ lìjí fēiwǎng Shànghǎi chǔlǐ yí jiàn shì. *Chairman Wang wants me to fly to Shanghai immediately to handle an emergency.*

立交桥 lìjiāoqiáo N flypast, flyover (座 zuò)

立刻 lìkè ADV at once, immediately ■ 我接到你的电话, 立刻就来了。Wǒ jiēdào nǐ de diànhuà, lìkè jiù lái le. *I came immediately after getting your call.*

立体 lìtǐ ADJ three-dimensional

厉 lì TRAD 厲 ADJ severe, strict

厉害 lìhai ADJ severe, fierce, formidable ■ 这个人说话很厉害。Zhège rén shuōhuà hěn lìhai. *This person has a sharp tongue.*

NOTE: (1) 厉害 lìhai is often used with 得 de to indicate a very high degree, e.g. ■ 这两天热得厉害。Zhèliǎngtiān rède lìhai. *These days are terribly hot.* ■ 情人节花儿贵得厉害。Qíngrénjié huār guìde lìhai. *Flowers are terribly expensive on Valentine's Day.* (2) 厉害 lìhai may be written as 利害 lìhai.

丽 lì TRAD 麗 ADJ beautiful (See 美丽 měilì.)

励 lì TRAD 勵 V encourage (See 鼓励 gǔlì.)

利 lì N 1 benefit, advantage 2 profit, interest

利弊 lìbì N pros and cons

利害 lìhai Same as 厉害 lìhai

利率 lìlǜ N interest rate

利润 lìrùn N profit ■ 这家公司今年第一季度的利润下降了百分之十二。Zhè jiā gōngsī jīnnián dìyī jìdù de lìrùn xiàjiàngle bǎifēnzhī shí'èr. *The company profits decreased by 12 percent in the first quarter this year.*

利息 lìxī N interest (on a loan)

利益 lìyì N benefit, interest ■ 每个人都为了个人利益而工作, 但也要考虑社会的利益。Měi gè rén dōu wèile gèrén de lìyì ér gōngzuò, dàn yě yào kǎolǜ shèhuì de lìyì. *Everybody works for their personal interest, but should also take into consideration the interests of society.*

利用 lìyòng V make use of, benefit from ■ 我们要合理地利用自然资源。Wǒmen yào hélǐ de lìyòng zìrán zīyuán. *We should make use of natural resources in a rational way.*

例 **lì** N example

例子 **lìzi** N example (个 gè) ■ 王老师举了很多例子, 说明这个词的用法。 Wáng lǎoshī jǔle hěn duō lìzi, shuōmíng zhège cí de yòngfǎ. *Teacher Wang gave many examples to illustrate the way this word is used.*
举例子 **jǔ lìzi** give an example
例如 **lìrú** CONJ for example, such as
例外 **lìwài** N exception

粒 **lì** M. WD (for rice, pearls, etc)

一粒米 **yí lì mǐ** a grain of rice

俩 **liǎ** TRAD 倆 NUM two people ■ 这件事你们夫妻俩好好商量一下。 Zhè jiàn shì nǐmen fūqī liǎ hǎohǎo shāngliang yíxià. *(To a couple) I hope you two will discuss this matter properly.*

连 **lián** TRAD 連 I v connect, join ■ 海洋把世界连成一片。 Hǎiyáng bǎ shìjiè lián chéng yípiàn. *Oceans and seas connect the entire world.* II ADV in succession, repeatedly ■ 我连发了三份电子邮件给他, 他都没有回。 Wǒ lián fāle sān fèn diànzǐ yóujiàn gěi tā, tā dōu méiyǒu huí. *I sent him three e-mail messages in succession but there has been no reply.* III PREP even ■ 你连中文报纸都会看了! Nǐ lián Zhōngwén bàozhǐ dōu huì kàn le! *You can even read Chinese language newspapers!*
连…都… **lián...dōu...** IDIOM even ■ 连三岁小孩都知道。 Lián sān suì xiǎohái dōu zhīdào. *Even a toddler (← a three-year-old) knows this.*

NOTE: (1) 连…都… lián...dōu... is an emphatic expression, stressing the word after 连 lián. (2) 都 dōu may be replaced by 也 yě, i.e. 连…也… lián...yě... is the same as 连…都… lián...dōu..., e.g. ■ 连三岁小孩也知道。 Lián sān suì xiǎohái yě zhīdào. *Even a toddler knows this.*

连队 **liánduì** N company (in the army)
连连 **liánlián** ADV repeatedly, again and again
连忙 **liánmáng** V make haste, hasten without the slightest delay ■ 她听说老父亲跌倒了, 连忙回家。 Tā tīngshuō lǎo fùqin diēdǎo le, liánmáng huíjiā. *Hearing that her old father had had a fall, she hastened back home.*
连绵 **liánmián** V continue, be continuous, be uninterrrupted
连同 **liántóng** CONJ together with
连续 **liánxù** V be continuous, in succession, in a row
连续剧 **liánxùjù** N TV series
连夜 **liányè** ADV that very night

莲 **lián** N lotus

莲子 **liánzǐ** lotus seed

廉 **lián** ADJ 1 inexpensive, cheap 2 morally clean
廉价 **liánjià** ADJ low-priced, inexpensive
廉价出售 **liánjià chūshòu** sell at low prices
廉洁 **liánjié** ADJ (of officials) honest and clean, not corrupt

镰 **lián** N sickle

镰刀 **liándāo** sickle (把 bǎ)

帘 **lián** N curtain (See 窗帘 chuānglián)

怜 **lián** TRAD 憐 V pity (See 可怜 kělián.)

联 **lián** TRAD 聯 V connect

联邦 **liánbāng** N federation, union
联合 **liánhé** V unite, get together (to do something) ■ 两国要联合开发海洋资源。 Liǎng guó yào liánhé kāifā hǎiyáng zīyuán. *The two countries will jointly develop their ocean resources.*
联合国 **Liánhé Guó** the United Nations
联合国部队 **Liánhé Guó bùduì** United Nations troops
联欢 **liánhuān** V have a get-together, have a gala/party ■ 明天中外学生联欢, 你表演什么节目? Míngtiān zhōngwài xuésheng liánhuān, nǐ biǎoyǎn shénme jiémù? *At the gala for Chinese and overseas students tomorrow, what item will you be performing?*
联络 **liánluò** V liaise, get in touch with
联络员 **liánluòyuán** liaison officer
联盟 **liánméng** N alliance, coalition
联系 **liánxì** I v get in touch, contact ■ 你有什么事, 可以用电子邮件和张小姐联系。 Nǐ yǒu shénme shì, kěyǐ yòng diànzǐ yóujiàn hé Zhāng xiǎojiě liánxì. *You can contact Miss Zhang by e-mail if you've an issue.* II N connection, relationship
联想 **liánxiǎng** V make a connection in the mind, associate with

脸 **liǎn** TRAD 臉 N face (张 zhāng) ■ 顾客来了, 她总是笑脸相迎。 Gùkè lái le, tā zǒngshì xiào liǎn xiāngyíng. *When a customer comes, she always smiles a welcome.* ■ 出了这样的事, 他觉得没脸见人。 Chūle zhèyang de shì, tā juéde méi liǎn jiàn rén. *After this event, he felt too ashamed to face anyone.*
丢脸 **diūliǎn** be disgraced, lose face
脸盆 **liǎnpén** N wash basin (只 zhī)
脸色 **liǎnsè** N 1 complexion
脸色苍白 **liǎnsè cāngbái** pale complexion
2 facial expression

链 liàn N chain

练 liàn TRAD 練 V practice, drill ■ 他早晨五点起床，先练武术，再练中文口语。Tā zǎochén wǔ diǎn qǐchuáng, xiān liàn wǔshù, zài liàn Zhōngwén kǒuyǔ. *He gets up at five o'clock in the morning, practices martial arts first and then oral Chinese.*

练习 liànxí I V exercise, train, drill ■ 你常常练习汉语口语吗? Nǐ chángcháng liànxí Hànyǔ kǒuyǔ ma? *Do you often practice oral Chinese?* II N exercise, drill ■ 我数学练习做好了，还有三道英文练习没有做。Wǒ shùxué liànxí zuò hǎo le, hái yǒu sān dào Yīngwén liànxí méiyǒu zuò. *I've finished my mathematics exercises. I haven't done the three English exercises.*

炼 liàn TRAD 煉 V smelt (See 锻炼 duànliàn, 训练 xùnliàn.)

恋 liàn TRAD 戀 N infatuation, love

恋爱 liàn'ài I V be in romantic love, be courting ■ 他们俩恋爱了两年，在上个月结婚了。Tāmen liǎ liàn'ài le liǎngnián, zài shàng ge yuè jiéhūn le. *They courted for two years and got married last month.* II N romantic love
谈恋爱 tán liàn'ài be in courtship, in love

良 liáng ADJ good

良好 liánghǎo ADJ good, fine, commendable ■ 这种药经过试验，证明效果良好。Zhè zhǒng yào jīngguò shìyàn, zhèngmíng xiàoguǒ liánghǎo. *After testing, this medicine proved to have good effects.*
良种 liángzhǒng N fine breed, improved variety

凉 liáng ADJ cool, chilly ■ 尽管中午很热，早上和夜里还是挺凉的。Jǐnguǎn zhōngwǔ hěn rè, zǎoshang hé yèlǐ háishì tǐng liáng de. *Even though it is hot at noon, it is still cool in the early morning and at night.*
凉菜 liángcài N cold dish, salad
凉快 liángkuai ADJ pleasantly cool

量 liáng V measure, take measurements ■ 你量一量，这个房间有多大。Nǐ liáng yi liáng, zhège fángjiān yǒu duō dà. *Measure the room, find out how big it is.*

粮 liáng TRAD 糧 N grain

粮食 liángshi N grain, cereal, staple food

梁 liáng TRAD 樑 N beam (in structure) (See 桥梁 qiáoliáng.)

两 1 liǎng TRAD 兩 M. WD (a traditional Chinese unit of weight equivalent to 50 grams), ounce ■ 我买二两茶叶。Wǒ mǎi èr liǎng cháyè. *I want two liang of tea.*

两 2 liǎng TRAD 兩 NUM 1 two

两个人 liǎng ge rén two people
两本书 liǎng běn shū two books
2 (as an approximation) a couple of, a few ■ 我来说两句话。Wǒ lái shuō liǎng jù huà. *Let me say a few words.*

NOTE: Both 两 liǎng and 二 èr may mean *two*, but are used differently. 二 èr must be used in mathematics or when saying the number 2 in isolation, e.g. ■ 一、二、三、四…yī, èr, sān, sì… *1, 2, 3, 4 …* ■ 二加三是五。Èr jiā sān shì wǔ. *2 plus 3 is 5.* Use 两 liǎng when referring to "two something," e.g. ■ 两张桌子 liǎng zhāng zhuōzi *two tables*

亮 liàng ADJ bright ■ 天亮了! Tiān liàng le! *Day is breaking!*
亮丽 liànglì ADJ spectacularly beautiful

谅 liàng TRAD 諒 V forgive (See 原谅 yuánliàng.)

晾 liàng V dry in the sun, dry in the air

辆 liàng M. WD (for vehicles)

一辆汽车 yí liàng qìchē a car
两辆自行车 liǎng liàng zìxíngchē two bicycles

量 liàng N quantity, capacity

酒量 jiǔliàng capacity for liquor, how much wine one can hold
保质保量 bǎozhì bǎoliàng ensure both the quality and quantity (of products)

聊 liáo V chat

聊天 liáotiān V chat ■ 奶奶常去邻居家聊天。Nǎinai cháng qù línjū jiā liáotiān. *My granny often goes to her neighbor's home for a chat.*
聊天室 liáotiānshì N (Internet) chatroom

僚 liáo N official (See 官僚 guānliáo)

潦 liáo ADJ slovenly

潦草 liáocǎo ADJ (of handwriting) illegible, done hastily and carelessly

辽 liáo TRAD 遼 ADJ vast

辽阔 liáokuò ADJ vast, extensive

疗 **liáo** TRAD 療 v treat, cure

疗养 **liáoyǎng** v recuperate, convalesce
疗养院 **liáoyǎngyuàn** sanitorium

了 **liǎo** v finish, be done with ■ 这么多工作，一星期也做不了。Zhème duō gōngzuò, yì xīngqī yě zuò bu liǎo. *So much work can't be finished even in a week.*

NOTE: 了 liǎo, together with 得 de or 不 bu, is often used after a verb as a complement to mean *can ... or cannot ...* e.g. ■ 这件事我干得了，那件事我干不了。Zhè jiàn shì wǒ gàn de liǎo, nà jiàn shì wǒ gàn bu liǎo. *I can do this job, but I can't do that job.*

了不起 **liǎobuqǐ** ADJ wonderful, terrific ■ 这个孩子门门功课第一名，真了不起! Zhège háizi ménmén gōngkè dì-yī míng, zhēn liǎobuqǐ! *This child came out first in all the subjects. How wonderful!*

了解 **liǎojiě** v know, understand, find out ■ 我来是要了解这一地区的市场情况。Wǒ lái shì yào liǎojiě zhè yí dìqū de shìchǎng qíngkuàng. *I've come to find out the marketing situation in this region.*

料 1 **liào** N material (See 材料 cáiliào, 燃料 ránliào, 染料 rǎnliào, 塑料 sùliào, 饮料 yǐnliào, 原料 yuánliào, 资料 zīliào.)

料 2 **liào** v anticipate, expect

料事如神 **liàoshìrúshén** predict accurately as if one were a god

列 **liè** M. WD (for trains)

一列火车 yí liè huǒchē a train

烈 **liè** ADJ intense

烈火 **lièhuǒ** N raging flame
烈士 **lièshì** N martyr (位 wèi)

裂 **liè** v crack, splint

猎 **liè** TRAD 獵 v hunt

猎人 **lièrén** hunter
打猎 **dǎliè** go hunting, hunt

劣 **liè** ADJ inferior, bad (quality) (See 恶劣 èliè)

磷 **lín** N phosphorus (P)

邻 **lín** TRAD 鄰 N neighbor

邻居 **línjū** N neighbor ■ 和邻居保持良好的关系、很重要。Hé línjū bǎochí liánghǎo de guānxi, hěn zhòngyào. *It is important to maintain good relations with the neighbors.*

林 **lín** N forest, woods

林场 **línchǎng** N forestry center
林区 **línqū** N forest, forest land
林业 **línyè** N forestry industry, timber industry

淋 **lín** v drench, pour

淋浴 **línyù** N shower (bath)
洗淋浴 xǐ línyù take a shower

临 **lín** TRAD 臨 v arrive

临时 **línshí** ADJ tentative, provisional ■ 这是临时措施，正式办法还要研究制定。Zhè shì línshí cuòshī, zhèngshì bànfǎ hái yào yánjiū zhìdìng. *This is only a tentative measure. We need to study and devise formal measures.*

灵 **líng** TRAD 靈 I N fairy II ADJ agile, quick

灵魂 **línghún** N soul, spirit
灵活 **línghuó** ADJ flexible, agile ■ 他头脑灵活，能迅速对付各种不同的情况。Tā tóunǎo línghuó, néng xùnsù duìfù gè zhǒng bùtóng de qíngkuàng. *He is quick-witted and can cope with various situations promptly.*

零 **líng** I NUM zero

一百零二 yìbǎi líng èr 102
四千零五 sìqiān líng wǔ 4,005
II ADJ fractional, fragmentary

NOTE: (1) No matter how many zeros there are between digits, only one 零 líng is used. For example, 4005 is 四千零五 sìqiān líng wǔ, not 四千零零五 sìqiān líng líng wǔ. (2) 零 líng can also be written as O, e.g 四千O五 sìqiān líng wǔ *4005*.

零件 **língjiàn** N part, spare part
零钱 **língqián** N allowance, pocket money, small change

铃 **líng** TRAD 鈴 N bell ■ 门铃响了，看看是谁来了。Mén líng xiǎng le, kànkan shì shéi lái le. *The doorbell is ringing. Go and see who's there.*

玲 **líng** as in 玲珑 línglóng

玲珑 **línglóng** ADJ 1 (of things) exquisite 2 (of people) clever and nimble

龄 **líng** TRAD 齡 N age (See 年龄 niánlíng.)

凌 **líng** v approach

凌晨 **língchén** N the time before dawn

岭 **lǐng** N mountain range, ridge

领 **lǐng** TRAD 領 V lead, take ■ 服务员领客人到他们预订的桌子。Fúwùyuán lǐng kèrén dào tāmen yùdìng de zhuōzi. *The waiter led the customers to the table they had reserved.*

领导 **lǐngdǎo** I V 1 lead, provide leadership ■ 政府领导人民发展经济。Zhèngfǔ lǐngdǎo rénmín fāzhǎn jīngjì. *The government provides leadership for the people to develop the economy.* 2 have jurisdiction over II N leader, the person in charge ■ 我要找你们的领导。Wǒ yào zhǎo nǐmen de lǐngdǎo. *I want to see the person in charge here.*

NOTE: (1) 领导 **lǐngdǎo** as a verb is somewhat pompous, appropriate only for grand occasions. (2) As a noun 领导 **lǐngdǎo** is no longer very popular in China and has never been very popular in other Chinese-speaking communities. To refer to "the person in charge," many Chinese use 老板 **lǎobǎn** (boss) or specific terms such as 厂长 **chǎngzhǎng** (factory manager) or 校长 **xiàozhǎng** (headmaster, school principal, university president).

领土 **lǐngtǔ** N territory
领袖 **lǐngxiù** N leader (位 wèi) ■ 他是这个国家的一位重要政治领袖。Tā shì zhège guójiā de yí wèi zhòngyào zhèngzhì lǐngxiù. *He is an important political leader of this country.*

令 **lìng** V command, cause to (See 命令 mìnglìng.)

另 **lìng** ADJ Same as 另外 lìngwài. Used before a monosyllabic verb.
另外 **lìngwài** ADJ other, another ■ 这个方法不行，得另外想办法。Zhège fāngfǎ bù xíng, děi lìngwài xiǎng bànfǎ. *This method doesn't work. We've got to find another way.*

溜 **liū** V 1 slide, glide 2 sneak off, slip away

留 **liú** V remain (in the same place), stay behind ■ 你们先回家吧，我再留一会儿做完这件事。Nǐmen xiān huíjiā ba, wǒ zài liú yíhuìr zuòwán zhè jiàn shì. *You go home first. I'll stay behind for a while to finish this job.*
留学 **liúxué** V study abroad ■ 很多亚洲学生在美国留学。Hěn duō Yàzhōu xuéshēng zài Měiguó liúxué. *Many Asian students are studying in America.*
留学生 **liúxuéshēng** international students (especially in a university)

瘤 **liú** N tumor

榴 **liú** N pomegranate
石榴 **shíliu** pomegranate

硫 **liú** N sulfur
硫酸 **liúsuān** sulfuric acid

流 **liú** V flow ■ 河水慢慢地向东流去。Hé shuǐ mànmàn de xiàng dōng liúqù. *The river flows slowly to the east.*
流动 **liúdòng** V flow, move from place to place
流动人口 **liúdòng rénkǒu** floating population, migrant population
流利 **liúlì** ADJ fluent ■ 我什么时候才能流利地说中文呢? Wǒ shénme shíhou cái néng liúlì de shuō Zhōngwén ne? *When will I be able to speak Chinese fluently?*
流氓 **liúmáng** N hooligan, gangster
流行 **liúxíng** V be fashionable, be popular
流行歌手 **liúxíng gēshǒu** pop singer
流行音乐 **liúxíng yīnyuè** pop music
流行病 **liúxíngbìng** N epidemic
流行性感冒(流感) **liúxíngxìng gǎnmào (liúgǎn)** N influenza, flu

浏 **liú** as in 浏览 liúlǎn
浏览 **liúlǎn** V browse
浏览器 **liúlǎnqì** N (computer) browser

柳 **liǔ** N willow
杨柳 **yángliǔ** willow
柳树 **liǔshù** willow, willow tree (棵 kē)

六 **liù** NUM six
六十六 **liùshí liù** sixty-six
六十五岁 **liùshí wǔ suì** sixty-five years of age

龙 **lóng** TRAD 龍 N dragon (条 tiáo) ■ 中国人把自己称作"龙的传人"。Zhōngguórén bǎ zìjǐ chēngzuò "lóng de chuánrén". *The Chinese call themselves "descendants of the dragon."*

聋 **lóng** TRAD 聾 ADJ deaf, hard of hearing
聋子 **lóngzi** deaf person
聋哑人 **lóngyǎrén** N deaf and dumb person, deaf mute

笼 **lóng** TRAD 籠 N cage
笼子 **lóngzi** cage
鸟笼 **niǎolóng** bird cage

窿 **lóng** N pit, hole (See 窟窿 kūlong)

隆 **lóng** ADJ grand

隆重 **lóngzhòng** ADJ grand, ceremonious

咙 **lóng** TRAD 嚨 N as in 喉咙 hóulóng

珑 **lóng** TRAD 瓏 ADJ as in 玲珑 línglóng

垄 **lǒng** TRAD 壟 N ridge

垄断 **lǒngduàn** V monopolize

拢 **lǒng** TRAD 攏 V hold together

楼 **lóu** TRAD 樓 N **1** building with two or more stories (座 zuò) ■ 这座楼是去年建的。Zhè zuò lóu shì qùnián jiàn de. *This building was built last year.* **2** floor (层 céng)
楼上 **lóushàng** upstairs
楼下 **lóuxià** downstairs
大楼 **dàlóu** a big building (especially a high-rise building)
高楼 **gāolóu** high-rise

NOTE: In naming floors, the Chinese system is the same as the American system but different from the British one, i.e. 一楼 yī-lóu is the American first floor, and the British ground floor.

楼房 **lóufáng** N multi-storied building (cf. 平房 píngfáng one-story building, bungalow)

楼梯 **lóutī** N stairs, stairway, staircase ■ 别站在楼梯上讲话，会妨碍别人上下。Bié zhàn zài lóutī shang jiǎnghuà, huì fáng'ài biérén shàng-xià. *Do not stand talking on the stairs. It'll obstruct people going up and down.*

搂 **lǒu** TRAD 摟 V embrace, hold in arms

漏 **lòu** V **1** leak ■ 屋顶漏了，要找人修理。Wūdǐng lòu le, yào zhǎo rén xiūlǐ. *The roof leaks. We'll have to find someone to fix it.* **2** leave out by mistake

漏洞 **lòudòng** N loophole, inconsistency (in argument)

漏税 **lòushuì** I V evade tax II N tax evasion

陋 **lòu** ADJ ugly (See 简陋 jiǎnlòu)

炉 **lú** TRAD 爐 N stove, furnace

炉子 **lúzi** stove, furnace

虏 **lǔ** TRAD 虜 N captive (See 俘虏 fúlǔ)

鲁 **lǔ** ADJ rash (See 粗鲁 cūlǔ)

陆 **lù** TRAD 陸 N land

陆军 **lùjūn** N army

陆续 **lùxù** ADV one after another, in succession ■ 开会的代表陆续到达。Kāihuì de dàibiǎo lùxù dàodá. *Congress delegates arrived one after another.*

录 **lù** TRAD 錄 V record

录取 **lùqǔ** V enroll (students), appoint (job applicants)

录像 **lùxiàng** V record with a video camera or video recorder ■ 他们的婚礼全录像了。Tāmen de hūnlǐ quán lùxiàng le. *Their wedding ceremony was videotaped.*
录像机 **lùxiàngjī** video recorder

录音 **lùyīn** V make a recording of sounds (e.g. music, reading) ■ 这里在录音，请安静! Zhèlǐ zài lùyīn, qǐng ānjìng! *Recording is in progress. Please be quiet.*
录音机 **lùyīnjī** audio recorder, sound recorder

录用 **lùyòng** V employ (staff)

碌 **lù** ADJ busy (See 忙碌 mánglù)

路 **lù** N road (条 tiáo) ■ 这条路很长，一直通到山里。Zhè tiáo lù hěn cháng, yìzhí tōngdào shān li. *This road is very long and leads all the way into the hills.*
马路 **mǎlù** road (in a city)
路程 **lùchéng** N distance traveled, journey
路过 **lùguò** V pass, pass by, pass through
路口 **lùkǒu** N intersection, crossing
路面 **lùmiàn** N road surface
路上 **lùshang** N **1** on one's way (to) ■ 她去学校的路上，要经过一座公园。Tā qù xuéxiào de lùshàng, yào jīngguò yí zuò gōngyuán. *On her way to school, she passes by a park.* **2** on the road
路线 **lùxiàn** N route, itinerary ■ 这是不是去那里最近的路线? Zhè shì bu shì qù nàli zuì jìn de lùxiàn? *Is this the shortest route to that place?*
路子 **lùzi** N way and means of doing things
很有路子 **hěn yǒu lùzi** very resourceful

露 **lù** V show, reveal ■ 她笑的时候，露出雪白的牙齿。Tā xiào de shíhou, lùchū xuěbái de yáchǐ. *When she smiles, white teeth show.*

赂 **lù** TRAD 賂 V bribe (See 贿赂 huìlù)

鹿 **lù** N deer

驴 **lǘ** N donkey

驴子 **lǘzi** donkey

铝 **lǚ** N aluminum (Al)

侣 **lǚ** N companion (See 伴侣 bànlǚ)

旅 **lǚ** V travel

旅馆 **lǚguǎn** N hotel (座 zuò, 家 jiā)
汽车旅馆 **qìchē lǚguǎn** motel
五星旅馆 **wǔxīng lǚguǎn** five-star hotel
旅客 **lǚkè** N hotel guest, passenger (of coach, train, plane, etc.)
旅途 **lǚtú** N journey, travels ■ 他把旅途看到，听到的都写下来。 Tā bǎ lǚtú kàndào, tīngdào de dōu xiě xiàlái. *He wrote down all he saw and heard on his travels.*
旅行 **lǚxíng** V travel ■ 我在中国旅行的时候，学到不少知识。 Wǒ zài Zhōngguó lǚxíng de shíhou, xuédào bùshǎo zhīshi. *I gained a lot of knowledge when I traveled in China.*
旅行社 **lǚxíngshè** travel agency
旅游 **lǚyóu** V travel for pleasure ■ 我有了钱，就到国外去旅游。 Wǒ yǒule qián, jiù dào guówài qù lǚyóu. *I'll go overseas for a holiday when I've got the money.*
旅游车 **lǚyóuchē** tour bus
旅游公司 **lǚyóu gōngsī** travel company
旅游路线 **lǚyóu lùxiàn** tour itinerary
旅游团 **lǚyóutuán** tour group
旅游业 **lǚyóuyè** the tourism industry, tourism
旅游者 **lǚyóuzhě** tourist, holiday-maker

履 **lǚ** I N shoe II V carry out, fulfill

履历 **lǚlì** N résumé
履行 **lǚxíng** V fulfill (one's promise), perform (one's obligation)

屡 **lǚ** TRAD 屢 ADV repeatedly

屡次 **lǚcì** ADV repeatedly

率 **lǜ** N rate (See 效率 xiàolǜ.)

绿 **lǜ** TRAD 綠 ADJ green ■ 春天到了，树木都绿了。 Chūntiān dào le, shùmù dōu lǜ le. *Spring has come; the trees are all green.*
绿党 **lǜdǎng** the Green Party
绿化 **lǜhuà** V make green by planting trees, afforest
绿卡 **lǜkǎ** N green card (permanent residency permit in the U.S.A. and some other countries)

律 **lǜ** N law

律师 **lǜshī** N lawyer

律师事务所 **lǜshī shìwùsuǒ** law firm

虑 **lǜ** TRAD 慮 V ponder (See 考虑 kǎolǜ.)

滤 **lǜ** TRAD 濾 V filter

卵 **luǎn** N egg (a cell)

卵子 **luǎnzǐ** egg

乱 **luàn** TRAD 亂 ADJ 1 disorderly, chaotic 2 at will, random ■ 你别乱说。 Nǐ bié luànshuō. *Do not talk irresponsibly.*
乱码 **luànmǎ** N crazy code, confusion code
乱七八糟 **luànqībāzāo** IDIOM in an awful mess, very messy

略 **lüè** V capture (See 侵略 qīnlüè.)

略微 **lüèwēi** ADJ slight

掠 **lüè** V plunder

掠夺 **lüèduó** V plunder, rob

抡 **lūn** TRAD 掄 V brandish, swing

轮 **lún** TRAD 輪 I N wheel II V take turns

轮船 **lúnchuán** N steamship, ship ■ 现在很少人坐轮船旅行。 Xiànzài hěn shǎo rén zuò lúnchuán lǚxíng. *Few people travel by ship now.*
轮廓 **lúnkuò** N outline, contour
轮流 **lúnliú** V take turns
轮流值班 **lúnliú zhíbān** be on duty by turns
轮子 **lúnzi** N wheel

论 **lùn** TRAD 論 V discuss

论点 **lùndiǎn** N argument, point of contest . (个 gè)
提出两个论点 **tíchū liǎng gè lùndiǎn** put forward two arguments
论述 **lùnshù** V explain (an argument), discuss
论文 **lùnwén** N dissertation, thesis, essay (篇 piān) ■ 张教授发表了多篇关于中国历史的论文。 Zhāng jiàoshòu fābiǎole duō piān guānyú Zhōngguó lìshǐ de lùnwén. *Professor Zhang has published several theses on Chinese history.*
论证 **lùnzhèng** V prove (an argument), demonstrate, discuss

啰 **luō** as in 啰唆 luō suō

啰唆 **luōsuō** ADJ long-winded, wordy, verbose

螺 **luó** N snail

螺丝 **luósī** screw

螺丝刀 luósīdāo N screwdriver (把 bǎ)
螺丝钉 luósīdīng N screw (颗 kē)

骡 luó N mule

骡子 luózi mule (头 tóu)

锣 luó N gong (面 miàn)

箩 luó N bamboo basket

箩筐 luókuāng N large bamboo or wicker basket (只 zhī)

萝 luó TRAD 蘿 N trailing plant

萝卜 luóbo N turnip, radish, carrot (根 gēn, 个 gè)
白萝卜 bái luóbo turnip
红萝卜 hóng luóbo radish
胡萝卜 hú luóbo carrot

逻 luó V petrol

逻辑 luóji N logic

骆 luò as in 骆驼 luòtuo

骆驼 luòtuo N camel (头 tóu)

络 luò TRAD 絡 N net

络绎不绝 luòyì bùjué ADV, ADJ in an endless stream, endless

落 luò V fall, drop ■ 秋天, 树叶落了。Qiūtiān, shùyè luò le. In autumn, leaves fall.
落成 luòchéng V (of a building or engineering project) be completed
落后 luòhòu ADJ backward, outdated ■ 你这种观点太落后了。Nǐ zhè zhǒng guāndiǎn tài luòhòu le. Your views are outdated.
落实 luòshí V (of a policy or idea) be implemented, be fulfilled
落选 luòxuǎn V lose an election, fail to be chosen

M

妈 mā TRAD 媽 N ma, mom

妈妈 māma N mom, mommy

抹 mā V wipe, wipe off

抹桌子 mā zhuōzi wipe the table
抹布 mābù N rag (块 kuài)

麻 má I N hemp

麻袋 mádài sack (只 zhī)
II ADJ numb
麻痹 mábì I V benumb, lull II N paralysis
小儿麻痹症 xiǎoér mábìzhèng infantile paralysis
麻烦 máfan I V bother ■ 这封信我能翻译, 不用麻烦陈先生了。Zhè fēng xìn wǒ néng fānyì, búyòng máfan Chén xiānsheng le. I can translate this letter. We don't have to bother Mr Chen.
II ADJ troublesome, complicated ■ 这件事很麻烦, 我不一定能做好。Zhè jiàn shì hěn máfan, wǒ bù yídìng néng zuò hǎo. This matter is complicated. I'm not sure I can get it done well.

NOTE: 麻烦您 máfan nín is a polite expression to request somebody's service or to ask a favor. Another example: ■ 麻烦您把盐递给我。Máfan nín bǎ yán dì gei wǒ. Please pass the salt [to me].

麻将 májiàng N (the game) mahjong
打麻将 dǎmájiàng play mahjong
麻木 mámù ADJ unable to feel anything, numb
麻雀 máquè N sparrow (只 zhī)
麻醉 mázuì I V anesthetize II N anesthesia
麻醉师 mázuìshī anesthetist, anesthesiologist
局部麻醉 júbù mázuì localized anesthesia
全身麻醉 quánshēnmázuì general anesthesia

马 mǎ TRAD 馬 N horse (匹 pǐ) ■ 你会骑马吗? Nǐ huì qí mǎ ma? Can you ride a horse?
马达 mǎdá N motor
马虎 mǎhu ADJ sloppy, careless ■ 你这个作业作得太马虎了。Nǐ zhège zuòyè zuò de tài mǎhu le. You did this assignment carelessly.

NOTE: 马马虎虎 mǎ-mǎ-hū-hū is a common idiomatic expression meaning so-so, not too bad or just managing. For example ■ "去年你考试成绩怎么样?" "马马虎虎。" "Qùnián nǐ kǎoshì chéngjì zénmeyàng?" "Mǎ-mǎ-hū-hū." "How did you do in the exams last year?" "So-so."

马力 mǎlì N horse power
马铃薯 mǎlíngshǔ N potato
马路 mǎlù N street, avenue (条 tiáo) ■ 这条马路从早到晚车很多。Zhè tiáo mǎlù cóng-zǎo-dào-wǎn chē hěn duō. This street has lots of traffic from morning till night.
马路上 mǎlù shang in the street, on the road
过马路 guò mǎlù walk across a street ■ 过马路要特别小心。Guò mǎlù yào tèbié xiǎoxīn. One should be especially careful when crossing the street.
马上 mǎshàng IDIOM ADV at once, immediately ■ 他要我们马上回信。Tā yào wǒmen mǎshàng huíxìn. He demands a prompt reply.

马戏 mǎxì

马戏 mǎxì N circus performance (场 cháng)
马戏团 mǎxìtuán circus

码 mǎ TRAD 碼 V stack up

码头 mǎtóu N dock, wharf ■ 船马上要靠码头了。Chuán mǎshàng yào kào mǎtóu le. *The ship will soon anchor at the dock.*
码头工人 mǎtóu gōngrén docker, long-shoreman

蚂 mǎ TRAD 螞 as in 蚂蚁 mǎyǐ

蚂蚁 mǎyǐ ant (只 zhī)

骂 mà TRAD 罵 V curse, swear ■ 你怎么骂人? Nǐ zěnme mà rén? *How can you swear at people?*

嘛 ma PARTICLE surely, that goes without saying (used at the end of a sentence to indicate that the truth of the statement is obvious) ■ 农村的空气就是比城市干净嘛! Nóngcūn de kōngqì jiùshì bǐ chéngshì gānjìng ma! *The air in rural areas is surely cleaner than that in cities.*

吗 ma TRAD 嗎 PARTICLE (used at the end of a sentence to turn it into a yes-or-no question) ■ 你会说中文吗? Nǐ huì shuō Zhōngwén ma? *Do you speak Chinese?*

埋 mái V bury ■ 他把死狗埋在树下。Tā bǎ sǐ gǒu mái zài shù xia. *He buried his dead dog under the tree.*
埋没 máimò V stifle (talent)
埋头 máitóu V devote wholeheartedly to, be engrossed in
埋头苦干 máitóukǔgàn devote oneself to hard work without complaint and for a long time

买 mǎi TRAD 買 V buy ■ 你这本书在哪儿买的? Nǐ zhè běn shū zài nǎr mǎi de? *Where did you buy this book?*
买卖 mǎimai N trade, business ■ 最近店里的买卖怎么样? Zuìjìn diànlǐ de mǎimai zěnmeyàng? *How is business at your shop recently?*
做买卖 zuò mǎimai do business, be engaged in business ■ 几乎每一家大公司都想跟中国做买卖。Jīhū měi yì jiā dà gōngsī dōu xiǎng gēn Zhōngguó zuò mǎimai. *Almost every corporation wants to do business with China.*

迈 mài TRAD 邁 V step forward ■ 完成了这项任务,我们就朝工厂自动化迈了一大步。Wánchéngle zhè xiàng rènwù, wǒmen jiù cháo gōngchǎng zìdònghuà màile yí dà bù. *After completing this project, we will have made a big stride towards automation of the factory.*

麦 mài TRAD 麥 N wheat (See 小麦 xiǎomài.)

卖 mài TRAD 賣 V sell ■ 他把汽车卖了。Tā bǎ qìchē mài le. *He sold his car.* ■ 你们这里卖水果吗? Nǐmen zhèlǐ mài shuǐguǒ ma? *Do you sell fruit here?*

脉 mài TRAD 脈 N blood vessel

脉搏 màibó N pulse

埋 mán as in 埋怨 mányuàn

埋怨 mányuàn V blame, complain

瞒 mán TRAD 瞞 V conceal truth from ■ 这件事你不该瞒我。Zhè jiàn shì nǐ bù gāi mán wǒ. *You shouldn't have hidden this matter from me.*

馒 mán as in 馒头 mántou

馒头 mántou N steamed bun (只 zhī)

蛮 mán TRAD 蠻 ADJ unrestrained and wild

蛮不讲理 mán bù jiǎnglǐ totally unreasonable and behaving atrociously

满 mǎn TRAD 滿 I ADJ 1 full, full to the brim ■ 碗里的水满了。Wǎn lǐ de shuǐ mǎn le. *The bowl is full of water.* ■ 房间里挤得满满的。Fángjiān li jǐ de mǎnmǎn de. *The room is packed.* 2 satisfied II V reach the limit
满额 mǎn'é ADJ reaching full quota
满意 mǎnyì ADJ satisfied, pleased ■ 我们要让顾客高兴地来,满意地走。Wǒmen yào ràng gùkè gāoxìng de lái, mǎnyì de zǒu. *We should ensure customers arrive happy and leave satisfied.*
对…满意 duì...mǎnyì be satisfied with
满月 mǎnyuè I V (of a newborn baby) be one month old
满月酒 mǎnyuè jiǔ dinner party in celebration of a baby's first month
II N full moon
满足 mǎnzú V meet the needs of, satisfy ■ 我们要增加产量,满足市场的需要。Wǒmen yào zēngjiā chǎnliàng, mǎnzú shìchǎng de xūyào. *We should increase output to satisfy the needs of the market.*

慢 màn ADJ slow ■ 你说得慢,我就听得懂。Nǐ shuō de màn, wǒ jiù tīng de dǒng. *If you speak slowly, I can understand you.*
慢性 mànxìng ADJ 1 (of diseases) chronic
慢性肝炎 mànxìng gānyán chronic hepatitis
2 Same as 慢性子 mànxìngzi
慢性子 mànxìngzi ADJ (of a person) slow or indolent

漫 màn V overflow

漫长 **màncháng** ADJ long, endless

蔓 **màn** as in 蔓延 mànyán

蔓延 **mànyán** V spread, extend

忙 **máng** ADJ busy ■ 你在忙什么? Nǐ zài máng
shénme? *What are you busy with?*

NOTE: When friends meet in China, a common conversation opener is 你最近忙吗? Nǐ zuìjìn máng ma? *Have you been busy lately?*

忙碌 **mánglù** ADJ busy

忙忙碌碌 **mángmáng lùlù** very busy, always engaged in doing something

茫 **máng** ADJ boundless and indistinct

茫茫 **mángmáng** boundless and blurred, vast
茫然 **mángrán** ADJ knowing nothing about, ignorant, in the dark

盲 **máng** ADJ blind

盲从 **mángcóng** V follow blindly
盲人 **mángrén** N blind person
盲人学校 **mángrén xuéxiào** school for the blind
盲文 **mángwén** N braille

氓 **máng** N man (See 流氓 liúmáng)

猫 **māo** TRAD 貓 N cat (只 zhī) ■ 我家有一只
小白猫。 Wǒ jiā yǒu yì zhī xiǎo bái māo. *We keep a white kitten at home.*

猫头鹰 **māotóuyīng** N owl (只 zhī)

毛 1 **máo** N hair

羊毛 **yángmáo** wool
毛笔 **máobǐ** N traditional Chinese writing brush
(支 zhī, 管 guǎn)
毛病 **máobìng** N 1 illness ■ 我什么毛病也没
有, 身体健康得很。 Wǒ shénme máobìng yě
méiyǒu, shēntǐ jiànkāng de hěn. *I have no complaints at all; I am in excellent health.* 2 trouble, breakdown
毛巾 **máojīn** N towel (条 tiáo) ■ 他拿着一条大
毛巾进浴室洗澡。 Tā názhe yì tiáo dà máojīn jìn
yùshì xǐzǎo. *He went into the bathroom with a big towel to take a bath.*
毛衣 **máoyī** N woolen sweater, woolen pullover
(件 jiàn)

毛 2 **máo** 1 M. WD Same as 角 jiǎo 2 M WD.
Used colloquially.

髦 **máo** long hair (See 时髦 shímáo)

矛 **máo** N spear, lance

矛盾 **máodùn** I N contradiction, conflict ■ 他们
之间有很大的矛盾。 Tāmen zhījiān yǒu hěn dà
de máodùn. *There is a big rift between them.*
II ADJ contradictory, inconsistent
自相矛盾 **zìxiāng máodùn** self-contradictory,
inconsistent ■ 这篇文章前后自相矛盾。 Zhè
piān wénzhāng qiánhòu zìxiāng máodùn. *This
article is inconsistent in its argument.*

NOTE: 矛盾 máodùn is a colorful word derived
from an ancient Chinese fable. A man who sold
spears (矛 máo) and shields (盾 dùn) boasted that
his spears were so sharp that they could penetrate
any shield, and that his shields were so strong
that no spear could ever penetrate them. As there
seemed to be a contradiction there, 矛盾 máodùn
came to mean *inconsistency* or *contradiction*.

茅 **máo** N cogongrass

茅屋 **máowū** N thatched cottage (间 jiān)

茂 **mào** ADJ luxuriant

茂密 **màomì** ADJ (of vegetation) luxuriant,
thick, dense
茂盛 **màoshèng** ADJ (of vegetation) luxuriant,
lush

冒 **mào** V 1 emit, send forth, give off ■ 开水
冒着热气。 Kāishuǐ màozhe rè qì. *Boiling water gives off steam.* 2 risk 3 make false claims
冒牌 **màopái** V counterfeit, forge
冒牌货 **màopáihuò** (goods) counterfeit, fake,
forgery
冒险 **màoxiǎn** V risk, take a risk

帽 **mào** N hat, cap

帽子 **màozi** hat, cap (顶 dǐng)
戴帽子 **dài màozi** put on/wear a hat (or a cap)
■ 今天外面很冷, 你要戴帽子。 Jīntiān wàimiàn
hěn lěng. Nǐ yào dài màozi. *It's very cold outside.
You'd better wear a hat.*
脱帽子 **tuō màozi** take off a hat (or a cap)

贸 **mào** TRAD 貿 N trade

贸易 **màoyì** N trade, exchange ■ 搞制造和搞贸
易, 那个更赚钱? Gǎo zhìzào hé gǎo màoyì, nǎge
gèng zhuànqián? *Manufacturing or trade, which
is more profitable?*
贸易公司 **màoyì gōngsī** trading company
对外贸易 **duìwài màoyì** foreign trade
国际贸易 **guójì màoyì** international trade

貌 mào

貌 mào N appearance (See 礼貌 lǐmào, 面貌 miànmào.)

么 me TRAD 麼 PARTICLE (used to form certain words) (See 多么 duōme, 那么 nàme, 什么 shénme, 为什么 wèishénme, 怎么 zěnme, 怎么样 zěnmeyàng, 这么 zhème.)

眉 méi N eyebrow

眉毛 méimao eyebrow

没 méi ADJ Same as 没有 méiyǒu, used colloquially.

没错 méicuò ADJ quite right
没关系 méi guānxi See 关系 guānxi.
没什么 méishénme IDIOM nothing serious, it doesn't matter ■ "你不舒服吗?" "没什么, 就是有点儿头疼。" "Nǐ bù shūfu ma?" "Méishénme, jiùshì yǒudiǎnr tóuténg." "Aren't you feeling well?" "Nothing serious, just a bit of headache."
没说的 méishuōde ADJ above reproach, perfect
没意思 méi yìsi See 意思 yìsi.
没用 méiyòng ADJ useless ■ 他这个人太没用了, 连一个小孩都对付不了。 Tā zhège rén tài méiyòng le, lián yí ge xiǎohái dōu duìfu bù liǎo. That man is really useless. He can't even deal with a child.
没有 méiyǒu I v 1 do not have ■ 他没有兄弟, 只有一个姐姐。 Tā méiyǒu xiōngdì, zhǐyǒu yí ge jiějie. He has no brothers, only an elder sister. 2 there is/are no ■ 房间里没有人。 Fángjiān li méiyǒu rén. There is nobody in the room. II ADV did not, have not (indicating negation of past experiences, usually used before a verb or at the end of a question) ■ 我没有学过这个字。 Wǒ méiyǒu xuéguo zhège zì. I haven't learned this Chinese character.
还没有 hái méiyǒu not yet ■ "你去过中国没有?" "还没有。" "Nǐ qùguo Zhōngguó méiyǒu?" "Hái méiyǒu." "Have you ever been to China?" "Not yet."

NOTE: In spoken Chinese, 没有 méiyǒu is often shortened to 没 méi, but it cannot be replaced by 没 méi if it is used at the end of a sentence. For example, you can say: 你去过中国没有? Nǐ qùguo Zhōngguó méiyǒu? but not 你去过中国没? Nǐ qùguo Zhōngguó méi?

枚 méi M. WD (for small objects, such a coin)

一枚硬币 yìméi yìngbì a coin

玫 méi as in 玫瑰 méigui

玫瑰 méigui N rose (朵 duǒ)

两朵玫瑰花 liǎng duǒ méiguihuā two roses
一束玫瑰花 yí shù méiguihuā a bouquet of roses

煤 méi N coal

煤矿 méikuàng coal mine
煤矿工 méikuànggōng coal miner, collier
煤气 méiqì coal gas
煤田 méitián coalfield

媒 méi N 1 matchmaking

媒人 méirén matchmaker
2 go-between, intermediary
媒介 méijiè N medium
媒体 méitǐ N medium
大众媒体 dàzhòng méitǐ mass media

梅 méi N plum tree

梅花 méihuā plum blossom

NOTE: 梅花 méihuā is unique to China, as you cannot find this flower in other parts of the world. Therefore, though conventionally translated as plum, it is actually not the same thing.

酶 méi N enzyme

霉 méi N mold, mildew

发霉 fā méi go moldy

每 měi I ADV every, each ■ 卡车司机每工作两天, 休息一天。 Kǎchē sījī měi gōngzuò liǎng tiān, xiūxi yì tiān. The truck drivers have a day off after working for two days. II PRON every, each ■ 你每天都看电视新闻吗? Nǐ měitiān dōu kàn diànshì xīnwén ma? Do you watch TV news everyday?

NOTE: Usage in Chinese requires that 每 měi is followed by 都 dōu all, without exception.

美 měi ADJ beautiful ■ 她从小就是个美人儿。 Tā cóngxiǎo jiù shì ge měirénr. She has been a beauty since childhood.
美德 měidé N virtue, moral excellence
美观 měiguān ADJ pleasing to the eye
美国 Měiguó N the U.S.A., America ■ 中国和美国离得很远。 Zhōngguó hé Měiguó lí de hěn yuǎn. China and the U.S. are far apart.
美好 měihǎo ADJ (of abstract things) fine, beautiful ■ 世界上的事物并不都象人们希望的那样美好。 Shìjiè shang de shìwù bìng bù dōu xiàng rénmen xīwàng de nàyàng měihǎo. Things in the world are not all as fine as people wish them to be.
美丽 měilì ADJ beautiful

CHINESE-ENGLISH

美满 měimǎn ADJ (of marriage, family, etc.) totally satisfactory, happy ■ 她有美满的家庭、成功的事业，真是太幸福了。Tā yǒu měimǎn de jiātíng, chénggōng de shìyè, zhēnshì tài xìngfú le. *She has a happy family and a successful career. What a fortunate woman!*

美妙 měimiào ADJ wonderful, splendid

美容 měiróng I V make one's skin and face more beautiful II N comestics
美容师 měiróngshī beautician
美容院 měiróngyuàn beauty salon, beauty parlor

美术 měishù N fine arts ■ 她对美术非常感兴趣。Tā duì měishù fēicháng gǎn xìngqù. *She has a great interest in the fine arts.*
美术馆 měishùguǎn gallery, art museum
美术家 měishùjiā artist

美元 Měiyuán N U.S. dollar, greenback

美中不足 měizhōngbùzú IDIOM a blemish in something otherwise perfect

美洲 Měizhōu N continent of America, America

镁 měi TRAD 鎂 N magnesium (Mg)

妹 mèi N younger sister
妹妹 mèimei younger sister

昧 mèi ADJ ignorant (See 愚昧 yúmèi)

闷 mēn TRAD 悶 ADJ stuffy, close

门 1 mén TRAD 門 N door, gate (道 dào) ■ 我们学校的大门正对汽车站。Wǒmen xuéxiào de dàmén zhèng duì qìchē zhàn. *There is a bus stop directly opposite the gate of our school.*
大门 dàmén gate
门口 ménkǒu N doorway, by the door, by the gate
门市部 ménshìbù N sales department
门诊 ménzhěn N outpatient service
门诊部 ménzhěnbù outpatient department (of a hospital)

门 2 mén TRAD 門 M. WD (for school subjects, languages, etc.) ■ 要学会一门语言，非下功夫不可。Yào xuéhuì yì mén yǔyán, fēi xià gōngfu bùkě. *To learn a language, you simply must make great efforts.*

闷 mèn TRAD 悶 ADJ in low spirits, lonely, depressed

们 men TRAD 們 SUFFIX (indicating plural number) ■ 学生们都很喜欢这位新老师。Xuéshengmen dōu hěn xǐhuan zhè wèi xīn lǎoshī. *All the students like this new teacher.*

NOTE: As a plural number marker, 们 men is only used with nouns denoting people. It is not used when there are words indicating plurality, such as numbers or words like 一些 yìxiē, 很多 hěn duō. In many cases, the plural number of a personal noun is implicit without the use of 们 men. In the example sentence, 们 men is not obligatory, i.e. 学生都很喜欢这位新老师。Xuésheng dōu hěn xǐhuan zhè wèi xīn lǎoshī. *All the students like this new teacher.* is correct and idiomatic.

蒙 méng V cover

檬 méng as in 柠檬 níngméng

萌 méng V sprout
萌芽 méngyá V sprout, bud, shoot forth

盟 méng N alliance
结盟 jiéméng forge an alliance, form an alliance
盟国 méngguó N ally (country)

猛 měng ADJ fierce, violent
猛烈 měngliè ADJ fierce, furious

梦 mèng TRAD 夢 I N dream ■ 我昨天夜里做了一个奇怪的梦。Wǒ zuótiān yèlǐ zuòle yí ge qíguài de mèng. *I had a strange dream last night.*
做梦 zuòmèng have a dream
II V dream, have a dream
梦想 mèngxiǎng V dream of, have a pipe dream

眯 mī V narrow one's eyes

迷 mí V be lost, be deluded
迷糊 míhu ADJ 1 (of vision) blurred 2 muddle-headed
迷惑 míhuò V 1 puzzle, be puzzled 2 delude, be deluded
迷失 míshī V lose one's bearings
迷失方向 míshī fāngxiàng lose one's bearings
迷信 míxìn N superstition

谜 mí TRAD 謎 N riddle
谜语 míyǔ N riddle
猜谜语 (猜谜) cāi míyǔ (cāi mí) guess a riddle ■ 我给你猜一个谜语。Wǒ gěi nǐ cāi yí ge míyǔ. *Can you guess my riddle?*

弥 mí TRAD 彌 ADJ full, overflowing
弥补 míbǔ V make up, remedy

弥漫 **mímàn**

弥漫 **mímàn** ADJ fill (the air)

米 I **mǐ** M. WD meter (colloquial)

一米 **yì mǐ** one meter
三米半 **sān mǐ bàn** three and half meters.

NOTE: The formal word for meter is 公尺 **gōngchǐ**.

米 2 **mǐ** N rice, paddy rice (粒 lì) ■ 在中国南方，很多农民种米。**Zài Zhōngguó nánfāng, hěn duō nóngmín zhòng mǐ.** In South China many farmers grow rice.
米饭 **mǐfàn** N cooked rice (碗 wǎn) ■ 米饭煮好了，菜还没有做好。**Mǐfàn zhǔ hǎo le, cài hái méiyǒu zuò hǎo.** The rice is cooked, but the dishes are not ready yet.

NOTE: The staple food for southern Chinese (Chinese living south of the Yangtze River) is 米饭 **mǐfàn**, while northern Chinese mainly eat 面食 **miànshí** (food made of wheat flour), such as 面条儿 **miàntiáor** (noodles) and 馒头 **mántou** (steamed buns).

米酒 **mǐjiǔ** N rice wine

秘 **mì** ADJ secret

秘密 **mìmì** I N secret II ADJ secret, confidential ■ 她有一个秘密信箱。**Tā yǒu yí ge mìmì xìnxiāng.** She has a secret post office box.
秘密警察 **mìmì jǐngchá** secret police
秘密文件 **mìmì wénjiàn** classified document
秘书 **mìshū** N secretary ■ 要当秘书，一定要打字打得好。**Yào dāng mìshū, yídìng yào dǎzì dǎ de hǎo.** To be a secretary, one must have good typing skills.
私人秘书 **sīrén mìshū** private secretary

泌 **mì** V secrete (See 分泌 **fēnmì**)

密 **mì** ADJ close, dense

密度 **mìdù** N density, thickness
密封 **mìfēng** V seal, seal up
密切 **mìqiè** ADJ close, intimate ■ 这家人家的兄弟姐妹关系很密切。**Zhè jiā rénjiā de xiōngdì-jiě-mèi guānxi hěn mìqiè.** The siblings in this family are very close to each other.

蜜 **mì** N honey

蜜蜂 **mìfēng** N bee (只 zhī)

棉 **mián** N cotton

棉花 **miánhua** N cotton ■ 中国是棉花进口国，还是棉花出口国？**Zhōng-guó shì miánhua jìnkǒuguó, háishi miánhua chūkǒuguó?** Is China a cotton importer or cotton exporter?

棉衣 **miányī** N cotton-padded jacket (件 jiàn)
棉大衣 **miándàyī** cotton-padded overcoat

绵 **mián** TRAD 綿 N silk floss

绵羊 **miányáng** sheep (只 zhī)

眠 **mián** V sleep (See 睡眠 **shuìmián**)

免 **miǎn** V avoid, do without

免除 **miǎnchú** V be free from, be exempt from
免得 **miǎnde** CONJ so as not to, lest ■ 你要早作准备，免得临时匆忙。**Nǐ yào zǎo zuò zhǔnbèi, miǎnde línshí cōngmáng.** You should start preparing early, so as not to be in a hurry when the time comes.
免费 **miǎnfèi** ADJ free of charge, free ■ 世界上没有免费的午餐。**Shìjièshang méiyǒu miǎnfèi de wǔcān.** There is no free lunch in the world.

勉 **miǎn** V 1 strive 2 encourage, exhort 3 force

勉励 **miǎnlì** V encourage, urge
勉强 **miǎnqiǎng** I ADV grudgingly, barely ■ 他勉强答应了我的要求。**Tā miǎnqiǎng dāyìngle wǒ de yāoqiú.** He yielded to my demand grudgingly. II V force to do ■ 他不愿去，你就别勉强他。**Tā bú yuàn qù, nǐ jiù bié miǎnqiǎng tā.** If he's unwilling to go, don't force him to.

面 I **miàn** N 1 face 2 (maths) surface ■ 你们俩有矛盾，还是面对面地谈一下吧。**Nǐmen liǎ yǒu máodùn, háishì miàn-duì-miàn de tán yíxià ba.** If there is conflict between the two of you, you'd better discuss it face to face.
面对 **miànduì** V be faced with
面对一个复杂的问题 **miànduì yí ge fùzá de wèntí** be faced with a complicated problem
面积 **miànjī** N (mathematics) area ■ 这个房间的面积是二十平方公尺。**Zhège fángjiān de miànjī shì èrshí píngfāng gōngchǐ.** This room has an area of 20 square meters.
面孔 **miànkǒng** N (human) face, facial features
面临 **miànlín** V be faced with, be up against
面临新的挑战 **miànlín xīn de tiǎozhàn** be up against a new challenge
面貌 **miànmào** N appearance, state (of things)
面面俱到 **miànmiànjùdào** IDIOM cover every aspect (of a matter)
面目 **miànmù** N appearance, look
面前 **miànqián** N in the face of, in front of, before ■ 在我们面前摆着两种选择。**Zài wǒmen miànqián bǎizhe liǎng zhǒng xuǎnzé.** We are faced with two choices.
面容 **miànróng** N facial features
面子 **miànzi** N face, honor

爱面子 **ài miànzi** be keen on face-saving
丢面子 **diū miànzi** lose face
给…留面子 **gěi...liú miànzi** save face (for somebody)

面 2 **miàn** TRAD 麵 N 1 (面条儿 miàntiáor) noodle
方便面 **fāngbiàn miàn** instant noodles ■ 他中饭常常只吃一碗方便面。**Tā zhōngfàn chángcháng zhǐ chī yì wǎn fāngbiànmiàn.** *He often only has a bowl of instant noodles for lunch.*
2 wheat flour
和面 **huómiàn** knead dough
面包 **miànbāo** N bread (片 piàn, 只 zhī, 条 tiáo)
一片面包 **yípiàn miànbāo** a slice of bread
面包车 **miànbāochē** N minibus, van (辆 liàng)
面包房 **miànbāo fáng** bakery
面粉 **miànfěn** N flour
面条儿 **miàntiáor** N noodles (碗 wǎn) ■ 面条儿要趁热的才好吃。**Miàntiáor yào rè de cái hǎochī.** *Noodles must be eaten hot.* ■ 她是北方人，面条儿做得好，米饭做得不好。**Tā shì běifāngrén, miàntiáor zuò de hǎo, mǐfàn zuò de bù hǎo.** *She's a northerner. She makes good noodle meals, but doesn't cook rice well.*

面 3 **miàn** M. WD (for flat objects)
一面镜子 **yí miàn jìngzi** a mirror
两面旗子 **liǎng miàn qízi** two flags

苗 **miáo** N seedling

描 **miáo** V trace, copy
描绘 **miáohuì** V depict, describe
描述 **miáoshù** V describe, give an account of
描写 **miáoxiě** V describe (in writing) ■ 她在信中描写了那里的美丽风景。**Tā zài xìn zhōng miáoxiěle nàli de měilì fēngjǐng.** *In her letter she gives a description of the beautiful landscape there.*

秒 **miǎo** M. WD (of time) second ■ 我跑一百公尺要十四秒，你呢? **Wǒ pǎo yìbǎi gōngchǐ yào shísì miǎo, nǐ ne?** *It takes me 14 seconds to run 100 meters. How about you?*

渺 **miǎo** ADJ distant and indistinct
渺小 **miǎoxiǎo** ADJ tiny, insignificant

妙 **miào** ADJ wonderful, ingenious ■ 你的主意真妙! **Nǐ de zhǔyì zhēn miào!** *What a wonderful idea!*
不妙 **búmiào** not good, unpromising ■ 这两天情况不妙。**Zhè liǎngtiān qíngkuàng búmiào.** *Things are not good these days.*

妙不可言 **miào bùkěyán** IDIOM so wonderful as to beg description

庙 **miào** TRAD 廟 N temple (座 zuò)

灭 **miè** TRAD 滅 V extinguish, put out, go out ■ 火灭了。**Huǒ miè le.** *The fire was extinguished.*
灭火器 **mièhuǒqì** N fire extinguisher
灭亡 **mièwáng** V exterminate, be exterminated, become extinct

蔑 **miè** V disdain, smear
蔑视 **mièshì** V look upon with contempt

民 **mín** N 1 people 2 civilian
民兵 **mínbīng** N militia
民航 **mínháng** N civil aviation
民间 **mínjiān** ADJ 1 among common folks
民间故事 **mínjiān gùshi** folk tale
2 people-to-people
民间往来 **mínjiān wǎnglái** people-to-people exchange
民生 **mínshēng** N the people's (economic) life, economy
民事 **mínshì** ADJ (of law) civil
民事案件 **mínshì ànjiàn** civil case
民意 **mínyì** N the will of the masses
民意调查 **mínyì diàochá** opinion poll
民用 **mínyòng** ADJ for civilian use
民众 **mínzhòng** N the masses of the people
民主 **mínzhǔ** I N democracy ■ 世界上发达国家都实行真正的政治民主。**Shìjiè shang fādá guójiā dōu shíxíng zhēnzhèng de zhèngzhì mínzhǔ.** *All the developed countries in the world practice genuine political democracy.* II ADJ democratic ■ 没有民主的制度，不可能长期稳定。**Méiyǒu mínzhǔ de zhìdù, bù kěnéng chángqī wěndìng.** *There can be no long-term stability without a democratic system.*
民族 **mínzú** N ethnic group, nationality (个 gè) ■ 汉民族是中国最大的民族。**Hàn mínzú shì Zhōngguó zuì dà de mínzú.** *The Hans are the biggest ethnic group in China.*
少数民族 **shǎoshù mínzú** minority ethnic group
多民族文化 **duō mínzú wénhuà** multiculturalism

敏 **mǐn** ADJ quick, agile
敏感 **mǐngǎn** ADJ sensitive
敏捷 **mǐnjié** ADJ agile, nimble
敏锐 **mǐnruì** ADJ alert, sharp-witted

名 míng

名 1 **míng** N 1 name ■ 你记得他家的那条街名吗? Nǐ jìdé tā jiā de nà tiáo jiē míng ma? *Do you remember the name of the street where his home is?* 2 (personal) given name 3 reputation

出名 chūmíng become famous

国名 guómíng name of a country

名 2 **míng** M. WD (used for people, esp. those with a specific position or occupation)

一名军人 yì míng jūnrén a soldier

两名学生 liǎng míng xuésheng two students

名称 míngchēng N (non-personal) name

公司的名称 gōngsī de míngchēng company name

名单 míngdān N name list, roll (张 zhāng, 份 fèn)

学生名单 xuésheng míngdān class roll

名额 míng'é N the number of people assigned or allowed for a particular purpose, quota of people

大学招生名额 dàxué zhāoshēng míng'é university enrolment quota

名副其实 míngfùqíshí IDIOM be worthy of the name

名副其实的好老师 míngfùqíshí de hǎo lǎoshī a good teacher in every sense of the word

名贵 míngguì ADJ precious, of great value

名牌 míngpái N famous brand, branded name

名人 míngrén N famous person, well-known personality

名声 míngshēng N reputation

破坏我们的名声 pòhuài wǒmende míngshēng smear our reputation

名胜 míngshèng N famous scenic spot ■ 这个地区有很多名胜，每年吸引大批旅游者。 Zhège dìqū yǒu hěn duō míngshèng, měi nián xīyǐn dàpī lǚyóuzhe. *The area boasts many famous scenic spots and attracts large numbers of tourists every year.*

名义 míngyì N name, capacity

以我个人的名义 yǐ wǒ gèrén de míngyì in my own name

以总经理代表的名义 yǐ zǒngjīnglǐ dàibiǎo de míngyì in the capacity of the representative of the CEO

名誉 míngyù N reputation, honor

名誉博士 míngyù bóshì honorary doctorate

恢复名誉 huīfù míngyù restore one's honor

名字 míngzi N name, given name ■ 我的名字叫王小明。 Wǒ de míngzi jiào Wáng Xiǎo Míng. *My name is Wang Xiaoming.*

NOTE: To be exact, 名字 míngzi only means *given name*, but informally 名字 míngzi may also mean *full name* (family name + given name). The formal word for *full name* is 姓名 xìngmíng. See 姓 xìng.

明 míng ADJ bright

明白 míngbai I ADJ clear, obvious ■ 对不起，我没有说明白。 Duìbuqǐ, wǒ méiyǒu shuō míngbai. *Sorry, I didn't make it very clear.* II V understand, see the point ■ 老师又解释了一遍，我才明白了。 Lǎoshī yòu jiěshì yí biàn, wǒ cái míngbai le. *I only understood after the teacher explained it again.*

明亮 míngliàng ADJ bright, well-lit ■ 这间房间很明亮，我很喜欢。 Zhè jiān fángjiān hěn míngliàng, wǒ hěn xǐhuan. *This room is very bright. I like it.*

明明 míngmíng ADV clearly, obviously, as clear as day ■ 你明明知道，为什么要说不知道? Nǐ míngmíng zhīdào, wèishénme yàoshuō bùzhīdào? *You obviously knew it, why did you say you didn't?*

明年 míngnián N next year

NOTE: 明年 míngnián is next year relative only to this year 今年 jīnnián. For the year after another year, we use 第二年 dì-èr nián or 下一年 xià yì nián. For example ■ 他们在2002年结婚，第二年生了一个儿子。 Tāmen zài èr-líng-líng-èr nián jiéhūn, dì-èr nián shēngle yí ge érzi. *They married in 2002 and had a son the following year.* It would be wrong to use 明年 míngnián in this example.

明确 míngquè I ADJ definite and explicit ■ 他说得很明确，本月十五日下午三点二十五分到达北京机场。 Tā shuō de hěn míngquè, běnyuè shíwǔ rì xiàwǔ sān diǎn èrshíwǔ fēn dàodá Běijīng jīchǎng. *He made it very clear—he will be arriving at Beijing Airport at 3:25 p.m. on the fifteenth of this month.* II V make definite and explicit ■ 请你明确一下品种、数量和交货日期。 Qǐng nǐ míngquè yíxià pǐnzhǒng, shùliàng hé jiāohuò rìqī. *Please be definite about the product specifications, quantity and date of shipment.*

明天 míngtiān N tomorrow

明显 míngxiǎn ADJ obvious, apparent, evident ■ 你明显瘦了。 Nǐ míngxiǎn shòu le. *You've obviously lost weight.*

明信片 míngxìnpiàn N postcard (张 zhāng)

明星 míngxīng N movie star, star

体育明星 tǐyù míngxīng sports star

鸣 míng TRAD 鳴 V (of bird) chirp, crow

耳鸣 ěrmíng ringing in the ears

命 mìng N 1 life 2 fate, destiny

命令 mìnglìng N, V order ■ 军人必须服从命令

令。Jūnrén bìxū fúcóng mìnglìng. *A soldier must obey orders.*

命名 **mìngmíng** v give a name to, name

命题 **mìngtí** v set a question for an examination, assign a subject or topic for writing

命运 **mìngyùn** N fate, destiny ■ 有些传统的中国人相信出生的年、月、日、时决定一个人的命运。Yǒuxiē chuántǒng de Zhōngguórén xiāngxìn chūshēng de nián, yuè, rì, shí juédìng yí ge rén de mìngyùn. *Some traditional Chinese believe that the year, month, date and hour of one's birth determines a person's fate.*

谬 **miù** ADJ mistaken, absurd

谬论 **miùlùn** N fallacy, spurious argument

谬误 **miùwù** N mistake, error

摸 **mō** v 1 touch ■ 请不要摸展览品。Qǐng bú yào mō zhǎnlǎnpǐn. *Please do not touch the exhibits.* 2 grope

摸索 **mōsuǒ** v grope, search for, explore

模 **mó** I N model, copy II v imitate

模特儿(模特) **mótèr (mótè)** N (fashion) model

模范 **mófàn** N good example, model

模仿 **mófǎng** v imitate, ape, be a copycat ■ 小明喜欢模仿爸爸讲话,而且模仿得很像。Xiǎo Míng xǐhuan mófǎng bàba jiǎnghuà, érqiě mófǎng de hěn xiàng. *Xiao Ming likes to mimic his daddy, and he does it well.*

模型 **móxíng** N copy, model ■ 我父亲在中学的时候喜欢装飞机模型。Wǒ fùqin zài zhōngxué de shíhou xǐhuan zhuāng fēijī móxíng. *My father liked to assemble airplane models when he was a high school student.*

膜 **mó** N membrane

塑料薄膜 **sùliào bómó** plastic film

磨 **mó** v 1 grind

磨刀 **módāo** sharpen a knife

2 rub, wear 3 waste time

磨时间 **móshíjiān** stall, kill time

磨洋工 **móyánggōng** IDIOM loaf during working hours, stage a slow-down

蘑 **mó** N mushroom

蘑菇 **mógu** mushroom

摩 **mó** v rub, scrape

摩擦 **mócā** I v rub II N friction, clash

和同事发生摩擦 **hé tóngshì fāshēng mócā** generate friction among colleagues

摩托车 **mótuōchē** N motorcycle (辆 liàng)

魔 **mó** I N demon, monster II ADJ magic

魔鬼 **móguǐ** N monster, demon (个 gè)

魔术 **móshù** N magic

魔术师 **móshùshī** magician

变魔术 **biàn móshù** do magic (as entertainment)

抹 **mǒ** v 1 apply by smearing 2 strike out, erase

抹杀 **mǒshā** v totally ignore (one's merit, achievement, etc.)

莫 **mò** v don't ■ 莫谈国事。Mòtán guóshì. *Do not talk about state affairs.* (→ *Do not talk about politics.*)

莫名其妙 **mòmíng qímiào** IDIOM be utterly baffled

漠 **mò** N desert (See 沙漠 shāmò.)

寞 **mò** ADJ silent, desolate (See 寂寞 jìmò)

末 **mò** N end (See 周末 zhōumò)

沫 **mò** N foam, froth

啤酒沫 **píjiǔmò** beer froth

肥皂沫 **féizàomò** soapsuds, lather

墨 **mò** N ink

墨水 **mòshuǐ** N ink

默 **mò** ADJ silent

默默 **mòmò** ADV quietly, silently

陌 **mò** ADJ path

陌生 **mòshēng** ADJ unfamiliar

陌生人 **mòshēngrén** stranger ■ 很多小孩都知道不跟陌生人说话。Hěn duō xiǎohái dōu zhīdào bù gēn mòshēngrén shuōhuà. *Many children know not to talk to a stranger.*

谋 **móu** TRAD 謀 v plot, plan

谋害 **móuhài** v plot to murder

谋求 **móuqiú** v seek, be in quest of

谋求最大利润 **móuqiú zuìdà lìrùn** seek the maximum profits

某 **mǒu** PRON certain (used to denote an indefinite person or thing, usually in writing) ■ 在该国某地发生森林大火。Zài gāiguó mǒu dì fāshēng sēnlín dàhuǒ. *At a certain place in that country a forest fire broke out.*

某人 **mǒurén** N certain person, certain people, somebody

某事 **mǒushì** N certain thing or event, something

某些 **mǒuxiē** PRON some, certain ones

模 mú N mould, matrix

模样 **múyàng** I N appearance, look II ADV approximately, about

母 mǔ I ADJ 1 maternal, of a mother ■ 孩子需要母爱。Háizi xūyào mǔ'ài. *Children need maternal love.* 2 female (of certain animals) II N mother

母亲 **mǔqin** N mother ■ 母亲在家照顾孩子。Mǔqin zài jiā zhàogù háizi. *Mother takes care of her children at home.*

母亲节 **Mǔqinjié** Mother's Day

母性 **mǔxìng** N maternal instinct

母语 **mǔyǔ** N mother tongue ■ 她英语说得这么好，真让人不相信英语不是她的母语。Tā Yīngyǔ shuō de zhème hǎo, zhēn ràng rén bù xiāngxìn Yīngyǔ bú shì tā de mǔyǔ. *She speaks English so well that it's hard to believe that it isn't her mother tongue.*

姆 mǔ N woman tutor (See 保姆 bǎomǔ)

拇 mǔ N thumb

拇指 **mǔzhǐ** thumb

亩 mǔ TRAD 畝 M. WD (a traditional Chinese unit of area, especially in farming: 1 *mu* is equivalent to ¹⁄₁₅ hectare, about 667 square meters)

亩地（田）shí mǔ dì (tián) 10 *mu* of ground (paddy fields/farmland)

木 mù N 1 Same as 木头 mùtou 2 tree ■ 独木不成林。Dú mù bù chéng lín. *A single tree does not make a forest.* (→ *One swallow doesn't make a summer.*)

木材 **mùcái** N timber, wood

木匠 **mùjiang** N carpenter

木头 **mùtou** N wood, timber

目 mù N eye

双目失明 **shuāngmù shīmíng** having lost sight in both eyes, be blind

目标 **mùbiāo** N target, objective, goal ■ 她的目标是五年内存十万元。Tā de mùbiāo shì wǔ nián nèi cún shíwàn yuán. *Her goal is to save a hundred thousand dollars in five years.*

目的 **mùdì** N aim, purpose

目睹 **mùdǔ** V see with one's own eyes, witness

目光 **mùguāng** N sight, vision

目光远大 **mùguāng yuǎndà** farseeing, farsighted and ambitious

目录 **mùlù** N catalog

产品目录 **chǎnpǐn mùlù** product catalog

图书目录 **túshū mùlù** library catalog

目前 **mùqián** N at present ■ 目前的困难是暂时的。Mùqián de kùnnan shì zànshí de. *The present difficulties are only temporary.*

目中无人 **mùzhōng wúrén** IDIOM believe no one is better than oneself; overweening, conceited and arrogant

暮 mù I N dusk, evening twilight II ADJ late

暮年 **mùnián** old age

慕 mù V admire

慕名 **mùmíng** V be attracted by somebody's reputation

慕名而来 **mùmíng érlái** come out of admiration

墓 mù N tomb

公墓 **gōngmù** cemetery

墓地 **mùdì** N graveyard

幕 mù N curtain, screen

谢幕 **xièmù** answer a curtain call

穆 mù ADJ solemn

穆斯林 **Mùsīlín** N Muslim

牧 mù I V herd (cattle, horses, etc.)

牧羊 **mùyáng** herd sheep

II N animal husbandry

牧场 **mùchǎng** N grazing land, pastureland

牧民 **mùmín** N herdsmen

牧区 **mùqū** N pastoral area

牧业 **mùyè** N animal husbandry

睦 mù ADJ peaceful, harmonious

睦邻 **mùlín** N good neighborhood

N

拿 ná V hold, carry in hand ■ 我手里拿着很多书，不能开门，请你帮帮我。Wǒ shǒu li názhe hěn duō shū, bù néng kāi mén, qǐng nǐ bāngbang wǒ. *I'm holding lots of books and can't open the door. Please help me.* II PREP regarding, as to

拿…来说 ná...láishuō v take ... for example

拿手 náshǒu ADJ very good at, adept at

拿手好戏 náshǒu hǎoxì something that one is adept at, one's favorite game

拿主意 ná zhǔyi v make a decision ■ 这件事你得自己拿主意。Zhè jiàn shì nǐ děi zìjǐ ná zhǔyi. *You've got to make a decision about this matter by yourself.*

拿走 ná zǒu v take away, remove

哪 **nǎ** PRON 1 which ■ 这么多新车，你说哪辆最漂亮? Zhème duō xīn chē, nǐ shuō nǎ liàng zuì piàoliang? *Of so many new cars, which do you think is the most attractive?* 2 whatever, whichever ■ 下星期我都在家，你哪天来都可以。Xià xīngqī wǒ dōu zài jiā, nǐ nǎ tiān lái dōu kěyǐ. *I'll be home all next week. You may come any day.*

哪里 nǎli ADV where ■ 你住在哪里? Nǐ zhù zài nǎli? *Where do you live?*

NOTE: 哪里哪里 nǎli nǎli is an idiomatic expression used as a modest reply to a compliment, e.g. "你汉字写得真漂亮。" "哪里哪里。" "Nǐ Hànzì xiě de zhēn piàoliang." "Nǎli, nǎli." *"You write beautiful Chinese characters." "Thank you."*

哪怕 nǎpà CONJ even if, even though ■ 哪怕卖掉房子，王先生和王太太也要让孩子念大学。Nǎpà màidiào fángzi, Wáng xiānsheng hé Wáng tàitai yěyào ràng háizi niàn dàxué. *Even if they have to sell the house, Mr and Mrs Wang will put their child through university.*

NOTE: 哪怕 nǎpà introduces an exaggerated, rather unlikely situation to emphasize the statement of the sentence.

哪儿 nǎr ADV Same as 哪里 nǎli. Used colloquially.

哪些 nǎxiē PRON the plural form of 哪 nǎ ■ 你想看哪些书? Nǐ xiǎng kàn nǎxiē shū? *Which books do you want to read?*

那 **nà** I PRON that ■ 这辆自行车是我的，那辆自行车是我弟弟的。Zhè liàng zìxíngchē shì wǒ de, nà liàng zìxíngchē shì wǒ dìdi de. *This bike is mine. That one is my younger brother's.* II Same as 那么 nàme

那个 nàge PRON that one

那里 nàli ADV there, over there ■ 他在那里工作。Tā zài nàli gōngzuò. *He works there.* ■ 那里就是图书馆。Nàli jiù shì túshūguǎn. *Over there is the library.*

NOTES: (1) 那里 nàli is used after a personal noun or pronoun to make it a place word, as a personal noun or pronoun cannot be used immediately after a preposition, e.g. 我从张小姐听到这个消息。Wǒ cóng Zhāng xiǎojiě tīngdao zhège xiāoxi. is incorrect. 那里 nàli must be added after 张小姐 Zhāng

xiǎojiě (*Miss Zhang*): 我从张小姐那里听到这个消息。Wǒ cóng Zhāng xiǎojiě nàli tīngdao zhège xiāoxi. *I learned the news from Miss Zhang.* In this case 张小姐那里 Zhāng xiǎojiě nàli becomes a place word which can occur after the preposition 从 cóng. (2) Colloquially, 那儿 nàr may replace 那里 nàli.

那么 nàme I ADV like that ■ 你那么做，她会不高兴。Nǐ nàme zuò, tā huì bù gāoxìng. *If you behave like that, she'll be unhappy.* II CONJ in that case, then ■ 你不喜欢吃米饭，那么吃面包吧。Nǐ bù xǐhuan chī mǐfàn, nàme chī miànbāo ba. *You don't like rice; in that case eat bread.* (→ *Since you don't like rice, have bread instead.*)

NOTE: Although 那么 nàme as a conjunction is glossed as *in that case, then*, Chinese speakers tend to use it much more than English speakers use "in that case" or "then." In colloquial Chinese 那么 nàme is often shortened to 那 nà, e.g. 你不喜欢吃米饭，那吃面包吧。Nǐ bù xǐhuan chī mǐfàn, nà chī miànbāo ba. *You don't like rice; in that case eat bread.*

那儿 nàr PRON Same as 那里 nàli, used colloquially.

那些 nàxiē PRON those ■ 这些是中文书，那些是英文书。Zhèxiē shì Zhōngwén shū, nàxiē shì Yīngwén shū. *These are Chinese books. Those are English books.*

那样 nàyàng ADV Same as 那么 nàme 1 ADV

纳 **nà** v pay, offer

纳闷儿 nàmènr v be wondering (why, what, who, how, etc.), be perplexed

纳税 nàshuì v pay taxes

纳税人 nàshuìrén tax-payer

奶 **nǎi** N milk

奶粉 nǎifěn N milk powder

奶奶 nǎinai N paternal grandmother, granny

NOTE: The formal word for *paternal grandmother* is 祖母 zǔmǔ and that for *maternal grandmother* is 外祖母 wàizǔmǔ. While 奶奶 nǎinai is the colloquialism for 祖母 zǔmǔ, that for 外祖母 wàizǔmǔ is 姥姥 lǎolao, or 外婆 wàipó.

奶油 nǎiyóu N cream

耐 **nài** v able to endure

耐烦 nàifán ADJ patient ■ 尽管顾客东挑西拣，营业员也不能露出不耐烦的样子。Jìnguǎn gùkè dōng-tiāo-xī-jiǎn, yíngyè-yuán yě bù néng lùchu bú nàifán de yàngzi. *Even if the customer*

耐力 nàilì

is very choosy, the shop assistant mustn't appear impatient.

NOTE: 耐烦 nàifán is only used in its negative form, 不耐烦 bú nàifán.

耐力 **nàilì** N endurance, staying power
耐心 **nàixīn** I ADJ patient ■ 除了耐心地等待，没有别的办法。Chúle nàixīn de děngdài, méiyǒu biéde bànfǎ. *There is nothing you can do except wait patiently.* II N patience
耐用 **nàiyòng** ADJ durable ■ 我们的产品很耐用。Wǒmen de chǎnpǐn hěn nàiyòng. *Our products are durable.*

男 nán ADJ (of humans) male

男孩子 **nán háizi** boy ■ 那个男孩子是王先生的小儿子。Nàge nán háizi shì Wáng xiānsheng de xiǎo érzi. *That boy is Mr Wang's youngest son.*
男青年 **nán qīngnián** young man
男人 **nánrén** N man, men ■ 男人能做的事，女人也能做。Nánrén néng zuò de shì, nǚrén yě néng zuò. *What men can do, women also can.*
男生 **nánshēng** N male student/pupil
男性 **nánxìng** N the male gender, male
男子 **nánzǐ** N male adult
大男子主义 **dànánzǐzhǔyì** male chauvinisim
男子汉 **nánzǐhàn** N 1 man, men 2 hero

南 nán N south, southern ■ 很多老年人喜欢住在南方。Hěn duō lǎoniánrén xǐhuan zhù zài nánfāng. *Many old people like to live in the south.*

南边 **nánbian** N south side, to the south, in the south ■ "新西兰的南边还有什么国家吗？" "没有了。" "Xīnxīlán de nánbian hái yǒu shénme guójiā ma?" "Méiyǒu le." *"Is there any country to the south of New Zealand?" "No, there isn't."*
南部 **nánbù** N southern region (of a country)
南方 **nánfāng** N the southern part, the south of a country
南方人 **nánfāngrén** southerner
南面 **nánmiàn** N Same as 南边 nánbian

难 nán TRAD 難 ADJ difficult ■ 这道练习太难了，我不会做。Zhè dào liànxí tài nán le, wǒ bú huì zuò. *This exercise is too difficult. I can't do it.*

难产 **nánchǎn** N difficult childbirth, difficult labor
难道 **nándào** ADV (used at the beginning of a sentence or before a verb to make it a rhetorical question) ■ 难道你不知道吗？Nándào nǐ bù zhīdào ma? *Didn't you know?*
难得 **nándé** ADJ hard to come by, rare ■ 这个机会很难得，你别错过。Zhège jīhuì hěn nándé, nǐ bié cuòguo. *This is a rare opportunity; don't you miss it.*

难度 **nándù** N degree of difficulty
难怪 **nánguài** ADV no wonder
难关 **nánguān** N critical moment, crisis
度过难关 **dùguò nán guān** go through a crisis
难过 **nánguò** ADJ sad, grieved ■ 听到这个不幸的消息，我们非常难过。Tīngdào zhège búxìng de xiāoxi, wǒmen fēicháng nánguò. *On hearing this unfortunate news, we were all very sad.*

NOTE: 难过 nánguò is usually used as a predicate, and seldom as an attribute.

难堪 **nánkān** ADJ embarrassed, embarrassing
难堪的局面 **nánkān de júmiàn** embarrassing situation, awkward plight
难看 **nánkàn** ADJ ugly ■ 他穿这件衣服真难看。Tā chuān zhè jiàn yīfu zhēn nánkàn. *He really looks ugly in that suit.*
难免 **nánmiǎn** ADJ hardly avoidable
难受 **nánshòu** ADJ 1 feeling ill, uncomfortable ■ 他昨天晚上酒喝得太多，今天早上头疼难受。Tā zuótiān wǎnshang jiǔ hē de tài duō, jīntiān zǎoshang tóuténg nánshòu. *He drank too much last night. This morning he had a headache and felt terrible (→ had a hangover). 2 feeling sorry, feeling bad/sad ■ 我的错误给公司带来损失，我心里很难受。Wǒ de cuòwù gěi gōngsī dàilai sǔnshī, wǒ xīnli hěn nánshòu. *I feel bad that my mistake has caused loss to the company.*
难题 **nántí** N difficult issue, insoluble problem
难以 **nányǐ** ADV difficult to
难以理解 **nányǐ lǐjiě** difficult to understand, incomprehensible

难 nàn TRAD 難 N disaster, adversity

逃难 **táonàn** flee from war or natural disaster
难民 **nànmín** N refugee
难民营 **nànmínyíng** refugee camp

囊 náng N bag, pocket

挠 náo V scratch

挠痒痒 **náoyǎngyang** scratch at an itch

脑 nǎo TRAD 腦 N brain

脑外科 **nǎo wàikē** brain surgery
脑袋 **nǎodai** N Same as 头 tóu. Used only colloquially and in a derogatory sense.
脑筋 **nǎojīn** N brains, mental capacity
动脑筋 **dòng nǎojīn** rack one's brains
脑力 **nǎolì** N brain power
脑力劳动 **nǎolì láodòng** mental work
脑子 **nǎozi** N brain, mind ■ 他怎么会有这种想法？脑子出问题了吧？Tā zěnme yǒu zhè zhǒng

脑子出问题了吧？Tā zěnme yǒu zhè zhǒng

ING
144

xiǎngfǎ? Nǎozi chū wèntí le ba? *How come he has such ideas? Something wrong with his mind? (or He must be out of his mind./He must be crazy.)*

动脑子 **dòng nǎozi** use brains

囟 **nǎo** ADJ irritated, vexed

囟火 **nǎohuǒ** ADJ annoyed, angry

闹 **nào** TRAD 鬧 V make trouble, cause a disturbance ■ 别闹了，邻居该来提意见了。Bié nào le, línjū gāilái tí yìjiàn le. *Stop making such a noise. The neighbors will come to complain.*

闹脾气 **nào píqi** V throw a tantrum
闹事 **nào shì** V make trouble, provoke a disturbance
闹笑话 **nào xiàohua** V make a fool of oneself, cut a ridiculous figure

呢 **ne** PARTICLE 1 (used at the end of a question to soften the tone of an enquiry) ■ 你打算明年做什么呢? Nǐ dǎsuàn míngnián zuò shénme ne? *What do you intend to do next year?* 2 How about ...? Where is (are) ...? ■ 你们明天出去旅游，孩子呢? Nǐmen míngtiān chūqu lǚyóu, háizi ne? *You're going on holiday tomorrow. How about the kids?*

那 **nèi** Same as 那 nà. Used colloquially.

内 **nèi** N inside, within ■ 我一定在十天内还清借款。Wǒ yídìng zài shí tiān nèi huánqīng jièkuǎn. *I will pay off the debt within ten days.*
内部 **nèibù** N interior, inside
内部资料 **nèibù zīliào** document for internal circulation (e.g. within a government department)
内地 **nèidì** N the interior part (of a country), inland
内阁 **nèigé** N (government) cabinet
内行 **nèiháng** N expert, professional
内科 **nèikē** N department of internal medicine (in a hospital)
内幕 **nèimù** N inside story
内容 **nèiróng** N content, substance ■ 王董事长讲话的主要内容是什么? Wáng dǒngshìzhǎng jiǎnghuà de zhǔyào nèiróng shì shénme? *What is the main idea behind Chairman Wang's talk?*
内心 **nèixīn** N one's heart of hearts, one's inner world ■ 她内心很矛盾。Tā nèixīn hěn máodùn. *She suffers from conflicting thoughts.* (→ *She is torn by conflicting thoughts.*)
内在 **nèizài** ADJ inherent, intrinsic
内脏 **nèizàng** N internal organs
内战 **nèizhàn** N civil war
内政 **nèizhèng** N internal affairs, domestic affairs

干涉内政 **gānshè nèizhèng** interfere in the internal affairs (of another country)

嫩 **nèn** ADJ young and tender, tender ■ 请你把牛肉做得嫩一点。Qǐng nǐ bǎ niúròu zuò de nèn yìdiǎn. *Please make the beef tender.* (→ *Don't overcook the beef.*)

能 **néng** I MODAL V can, be able to ■ 这辆车加满汽油，能跑多少公里? Zhè liàng chē jiā mǎn qìyóu, néng pǎo duōshǎo gōnglǐ? *How many kilometers can this car run on a full tank?* II N energy

NOTE: See note on 会 huì *modal verb*.

能干 **nénggàn** ADJ (of people) able, capable, efficient ■ 他非常能干，别人一星期做的工作，他三天就完成了。Tā fēicháng nénggàn, biérén yì xīngqī zuò de gōngzuò, tā sān tiān jiù wánchéng le. *He is very efficient. He can finish in three days what takes others a week to do.*
能歌善舞 **nénggēshànwǔ** IDIOM be good at singing and dancing
能够 **nénggòu** MODAL V Same as 能 néng MODAL V
能力 **nénglì** N ability ■ 我们要求职工有使用电脑的能力。Wǒmen yāoqiú zhígōng yǒu shǐyòng diànnǎo de nénglì. *We require that our staff have computer competence.* (← *We require that our staff have the ability to use computers.*)
能量 **néngliàng** N energy, capabilities
能手 **néngshǒu** N expert, dab hand
能源 **néngyuán** N energy resources

嗯 **ng** INTERJ (used after a question to reinforce questioning) ■ 你把自行车借给谁了，嗯? Nǐ bǎ zìxíngchē jiègěi shuí le, ng? *Who did you lend your bicycle to, eh?*

尼 **ní** N Buddhist nun
尼庵 **ní'ān** Buddhist nunnery
尼姑 **nígū** Buddhist nun
尼龙 **nílóng** N nylon

泥 **ní** N mud ■ 他们在下雨天踢球，搞得身上都是泥。Tāmen zài xiàyǔtiān tīqiú, gǎode shēnshang dōushì ní. *They played soccer in the rain and got themselves all covered with mud.*
泥泞 **nínìng** ADJ muddy, miry
泥土 **nítǔ** N soil, earth, clay

拟 **nǐ** TRAD 擬 V draw up, draft
拟订 **nǐdìng** V draw up, work out
拟订计划 **nǐdìng jìhuà** draw up a plan

你 **nǐ** PRON you (singular) ■ 你好! Nǐ hǎo! *How do you do? Hello!* ■ 你好吗? Nǐ hǎoma? *How're you?*
你们 **nǐmen** PRON you (plural) ■ 我告诉你们一

个好消息。Wǒ gàosu nǐmen yí ge hǎo xiāoxi. *I'll tell you a piece of good news.*

逆 nì ADJ contrary, counter

逆流 nìliú N adverse current (of water)

年 nián N year (no measure word required) ■ 一年有十二个月。Yì nián yǒu shí'èr ge yuè. *There're twelve months in a year.*
今年 jīnnián this year
明年 míngnián next year
去年 qùnián last year

NOTE: No measure word is used with 年 nián, e.g. 一年 yì nián (one year), 两年 liǎng nián (two years), 三年 sān nián (three years).

年代 niándài N a decade of a century ■ 我爸爸妈妈喜欢听(二十世纪)七十年代的歌。Wǒ bàba māma xǐhuan tīng (èrshí shìjì) qīshí niándài de gē. *My dad and mom enjoy listening to songs of the seventies (of the twentieth century).*
年度 niándù I N year
财务年度 cáiwù niándù fiscal year
II ADJ annual
年度报表 niándù bàobiǎo annual report
年级 niánjí N grade (in school) ■ 这个年级有多少学生？Zhège niánjí yǒu duōshǎo xuésheng? *How many students are there in this grade?*
年纪 niánjì N age ■ "老先生，您多大年纪了？" "七十了。" "Lǎo xiānsheng, nín duōdà niánjì le?" "Qīshí le." *"How old are you, sir?" "Seventy."*

NOTE: 您多大年纪了？Nín duōdà niánjì le? is an appropriate way to ask the age of an elderly person. To ask a young child his/her age, the question should be: 你几岁了？Nǐ jǐ suì le? For people who are neither children nor elderly, the question to use is: 你多大岁数？Nǐ duō dà suìshù?

年龄 niánlíng N age (of a person or other living things)
年轻 niánqīng ADJ young ■ 你还年轻，有些事你还不大懂。Nǐ hái niánqīng, yǒuxiē shì nǐ hái bú dà dǒng. *You're still too young to understand some matters.*
年轻人 niánqīngrén young person, youth

撵 niǎn TRAD 攆 V drive away, oust

捻 niǎn V twist with the fingers

念 niàn I V 1 read, read aloud ■ 你每天念中文课文吗？Nǐ měi tiān niàn Zhōngwén kèwén ma? *Do you read your Chinese lessons everyday?* 2 study (in a school) ■ 他们的大儿子在英国念大学，他念数学。Tāmen de dà érzi zài Yīngguó niàn dàxué, tā niàn shùxué. *Their eldest son is studying in a university in the UK; he studies mathematics.* II N idea, thought

NOTE: See note on 读 dú.

念头 niàntou N idea, thought

娘 niáng N 1 mom, ma (used in the northern dialect) 2 girl (See 姑娘 gūniang.)

酿 niàng TRAD 釀 V brew, make (wine)

酿酒 niàngjiǔ make wine

鸟 niǎo TRAD 鳥 N bird (只 zhī)

尿 niào N urine

撒尿 sāniào piss, pee, go pee

NOTE: 撒尿 sāniào is a vulgar or childish word for *urinate*. The formal word for *urinate* is 小便 xiaopian.

捏 niē V 1 mold, knead 2 make up, fabricate

捏造 niēzào V fabricate, make up

您 nín PRON you (honorific)

NOTE: 您 nín is the honorific form of 你 nǐ. Use 您 nín when respect or deference is called for. Normally, 您 nín does not have a plural form. 您们 nínmen is absolutely unacceptable in spoken Chinese, and only marginally so in written Chinese. To address more than one person politely, you can say 您两位 nín liǎng wèi (two people), 您三位 nín sān wèi (three people), or 您几位 nín jǐ wèi (several people).

凝 níng V curdle, coagulate

凝结 níngjié V (of gas or hot air) condense
凝视 níngshì V look at steadily and for a long time, gaze fixedly, stare

宁 níng TRAD 寧 ADJ peaceful, tranquil

宁静 níngjìng ADJ tranquil and peaceful, serene

柠 níng TRAD 檸 as in 柠檬 níngméng

柠檬 níngméng N lemon (只 zhī)

泞 níng TRAD 濘 as in 泥泞 nínìng

拧 níng TRAD 擰 V wring, twist

拧毛巾 níng máojīn wring a towel

拧 nǐng TRAD 擰 V screw, wrench

女子 **nǚzǐ**

拧螺丝 **nǐng luósī** turn a screw (to tighten or loosen it)

宁 **nìng** TRAD 寧 MODAL V would rather

宁死不屈 **nìng sǐ bù qū** would rather die than succumb

宁可 **nìngkě** MODAL V Same as 宁肯 nìngkěn

宁肯 **nìngkěn** MODAL V would rather ■ 她宁肯走去, 也不搭他的车。Tā nìngkěn zǒuqù, yě bù dā tāde chē. *She would rather walk there than go in his car.*

NOTE: As is shown in the example sentence, 宁肯 nìngkěn is often used alongside with 也 yě: 宁肯…也… nìngkěn… yě…

宁愿 **nìngyuàn** MODAL V Same as 宁肯 nìngkěn

牛 **niú** N ox, cow (头 tóu)

牛奶 **niúnǎi** cow's milk, milk
牛肉 **niúròu** beef
公牛 **gōng niú** bull
黄牛 **huángniú** ox
奶牛 **nǎiniú** cow
水牛 **shuǐniú** water buffalo
小牛 **xiǎo niú** calf

NOTE: In the Chinese context, the ox (黄牛 huángniú) and the water buffalo (水牛 shuǐniú) are more important than the milk cow (奶牛 nǎiniú).

扭 **niǔ** V turn (one's head, back, etc.)

扭转 **niǔzhuǎn** V turn around, reverse

纽 **niǔ** TRAD 紐 N knob, button

纽扣 **niǔkòu** N button (颗 kē, 个 gè)

农 **nóng** TRAD 農 N farming

农产品 **nóngchǎnpǐn** N farm produce
农场 **nóngchǎng** N farm ■ 这个农场真大! Zhège nóngchǎng zhēn dà! *How big this farm is!*
农场主 **nóngchǎngzhǔ** farmer
农村 **nóngcūn** N farming area, rural area, countryside ■ 农村人口比较少, 生活不太方便。Nóngcūn rénkǒu bǐjiào shǎo, shēnghuó bú tài fāngbiàn. *In rural areas, the population is small and life is not very convenient.*
农户 **nónghù** N rural household
农具 **nóngjù** N farm implements
农贸市场 **nóngmào shìchǎng** N farm produce market
农民 **nóngmín** N peasant, farmer ■ 这个村子的农民生活相当困难。Zhège cūnzi de nóngmín shēnghuó xiāngdāng kùnnan. *The peasants in this village live a tough life.*

农田 **nóngtián** N farm land
农药 **nóngyào** N agricultural chemical, pesticide
农业 **nóngyè** N agriculture ■ 我们必须努力发展农业。Wǒmen bìxū nǔlì fāzhǎn nóngyè. *We must work hard to develop agriculture.*
农作物 **nóngzuòwù** N agricultural crop

浓 **nóng** TRAD 濃 ADJ (of gas/liquid) thick, dense, concentrated ■ 今天早上有浓雾。Jīntiān zǎoshang yǒu nóng wù. *There was dense fog this morning.*
浓厚 **nónghòu** ADJ 1 (of smoke, cloud, etc.) thick 2 (of atmosphere, interest, etc.) strong, heavy

弄 **nòng** V 1 do, manage, get … done ■ 我弄饭, 你去买点儿酒。Wǒ nòng fàn, nǐ qù mǎi diǎnr jiǔ. *I'll do the cooking, you go and buy some wine.* 2 fool with
弄虚作假 **nòngxū zuòjiǎ** IDIOM use deception, practice fraud

奴 **nú** N slave

奴隶 **núlì** N slave
奴役 **núyì** V enslave

努 **nǔ** V work hard

努力 **nǔlì** ADJ making great efforts ■ 我们大家努力工作, 为了更好的明天。Wǒmen dàjiā nǔlì gōngzuò, wèile gèng hǎo de míngtiān. *We all work hard for a better tomorrow.*

怒 **nù** ADJ angry, outraged

怒吼 **nùhǒu** N angry roar
怒火 **nùhuǒ** N fury

女 **nǚ** ADJ (of humans) female ■ 请问, 女洗手间在哪里? Qǐng wèn, nǚ xǐshǒujiān zài nǎlǐ? *Excuse me, where is the women's toilet?*
女孩子 **nǚ háizi** girl
女青年 **nǚ qīngnián** young woman
女生 **nǚshēng** female student
女儿 **nǚ'ér** N daughter (个 gè)
女人 **nǚrén** N woman, adult woman ■ 这条街都是卖女人穿的衣服, 所以叫 "女人街"。Zhè tiáo jiē dōu shì mài nǚrén chuān de yīfu, suǒyǐ jiào "nǚrén jiē". *The shops along this street all sell women's clothes, so it is known as "Women's Street."*
女士 **nǚshì** N (respectful form of address or reference to a woman) Madam, Ms, lady ■ 女士们, 先生们, 请允许我代表市政府热烈欢迎大家。Nǚshìmen, xiānshengmen, qǐng yúnxǔ wǒ dàibiǎo shì zhèngfǔ rèliè huānyíng dàjiā. *Ladies and gentlemen, allow me to extend to you a warm welcome on behalf of the city government.*
女子 **nǚzǐ** N female adult

暖 nuǎn ADJ warm ■ 在中国, 一到四月天就暖了。Zài Zhōngguó, yídào Sìyuè tiān jiù nuǎn le. *In China the weather becomes warm when April comes.*

暖和 nuǎnhuo ADJ pleasantly warm ■ 她的话说得我心里很暖和。Tā de huà shuō de wǒ xīnli hěn nuǎnhuo. *What she said warmed my heart.*

暖瓶 nuǎnpíng N thermos bottle (只 zhī)

暖气 nuǎnqì N central heating

暖水瓶 nuǎnshuǐpíng N Same as 暖瓶 nuǎnpíng

挪 nuó V move, shift

挪用 nuóyòng V divert (funds)
挪用公款 nuóyòng gōngkuǎn misappropriate public funds

O

噢 Ō INTERJ (used to indicate understanding or a promise) ■ 噢, 我明白了。Ō, wǒ míngbai le. *Oh, I see.* ■ 噢, 我忘不了。Ō, wǒ wàng bu liǎo. *Yes, I won't forget it.*

哦 Ǒ INTERJ (used to indicate doubt) ■ 哦, 他还会说日本话? Ǒ, tā hái huì shuō Rìběn huà? *Well, he also speaks Japanese?*

欧 ōu TRAD 歐 N Europe

欧元 Ōuyuán N Euro ■ 一百欧元可以换多少美元? Yìbǎi Ōuyuán kěyǐ huàn duōshǎo Měiyuán? *How many U.S. dollars can a hundred Euros be exchanged for?*

欧洲 Ōuzhōu N Europe ■ 我有了钱, 就去欧洲旅游。Wǒ yǒule qián, jiù qù Ōuzhōu lǚyóu. *When I have the money, I'll go to Europe for a holiday.*

殴 ōu TRAD 毆 V beat up (people)

殴打 ōudǎ V beat up (people)

呕 ǒu TRAD 嘔 V vomit

呕吐 ǒutù V vomit, be sick ■ 我想呕吐。Wǒ xiǎng ǒutù. *I feel sick.*

偶 ǒu 1 ADV 1 occasionally
偶尔 ǒu'ěr occasionally, once in a while
2 accidentally
偶然 ǒurán accidentally, by chance

偶 ǒu 2 N even number
偶数 ǒushù even number

P

趴 pā V lie on one's stomach

爬 pá V crawl, climb ■ 他们的儿子才一岁, 还不会走路, 只会在地上爬。Tāmen de érzi cái yí suì, hái bú huì zǒulù, zhǐ huì zài dì shang pá. *Their son is only a year old, he still can't walk and can only crawl on the floor.*

爬行 páxíng V crawl, creep
爬行动物 páxíng dòngwù N reptile

扒 pá V rake up

扒手 páshǒu N pickpocket ■ 火车站扒手很多; 要保管好自己的钱包。Huǒchēzhàn páshǒu hěn duō; yào bǎoguǎn hǎo zìjǐ de qiánbāo. *There're many pickpockets at the railway station; take very good care of your wallets.*

怕 pà I V fear, be afraid II ADV Same as 恐怕 kǒngpà, but with less force.

拍 pāi V pat, clap

拍马屁 pāi mǎpì V flatter sickeningly, lick the boots of

拍卖 pāimài V auction, sell at a reduced price ■ 这幢豪宅将在下星期拍卖。Zhè chuáng háo zhái jiāng zài xià xīngqī pāimài. *This luxury mansion will be auctioned next week.*

拍摄 pāishè V take a photo, shoot (a movie)

拍手 pāishǒu V clap, applaud ■ 孩子们拍手欢迎新老师。Háizimen pāishǒu huānyíng xīn lǎoshī. *The children gave the new teacher a big hand.*

拍照 pāizhào V take photos, have one's photo taken ■ 你的手机能拍照吗? Nǐde shǒujī néng pāi zhào ma? *Can your cell phone take photos?*

拍子 pāizi N 1 bat, racket
乒乓球拍子 pīngpāngqiú pāizi table tennis racket
羽毛球拍子 yǔmáoqiúpāi zi tennis racket
2 measurement of musical time, beat, time
打拍子 dǎpāizi beat time

排 pái I V 1 arrange in a definite order ■ 旅客排成一行, 等待登机前检查。Lǚkè pái chéng yì háng, děngdài dēngjī qián jiǎnchá. *The travelers stood in a line for the preflight inspection.* **2** reject, expel II N 1 row, rank ■ "你的票是几排几座?" "七排四座。" "Nǐ de piào shì jǐ pái jǐ zuò?" "Qī pái sì zuò." *"What is the seat and row in your ticket?" "Row 7, Seat 4."* **2** (army) platoon
排长 páizhǎng platoon leader
III M. WD (for things arranged in a row)
一排椅子 yì pái yǐzi a row of chairs

排斥 **páichì** v expel, reject

排除 **páichú** v rule out, eliminate
  排除这种可能性 **páichú zhè zhǒng kěnéngxìng** rule out this possibility
  排除障碍 **páichú zhàng'ài** surmount an obstacle

排队 **páiduì** v form a line, line up, queue up

排挤 **páijǐ** v elbow out, push aside, squeeze out

排列 **páiliè** v arrange, put in order
  按字母顺序排列 **àn zìmǔ shùnxù páiliè** arrange in alphabetical order

排球 **páiqiú** N volleyball (只 zhī)

徘 **pái** v as in 徘徊 páihuái

徘徊 **páihuái** v pace up and down, move hesitantly

牌 1 **pái** N playing cards (张 zhāng, 副 fù) ■ 他在火车上和别的旅客一起打牌。Tā zài huǒchē shang hé biéde lǚkè yìqǐ dǎpái. *He played cards with fellow passengers on the train.*
  打牌 **dǎpái** play cards
  发牌 **fāpái** deal cards
  洗牌 **xǐpái** shuffle cards

牌 2 **pái** N brand name, brand ■ 你买的汽车是什么牌的? Nǐ mǎi de qìchē shì shénme pái de? *What brand of car did you buy?*
  名牌 **míngpái** famous brand, branded name

牌子 **páizi** N 1 signboard (块 kuài) ■ 他在门口放了一块牌子, "减价出售"。Tā zài ménkǒu fàngle yí kuài páizi, "jiǎnjià chūshòu". *He put up a "Discount sale" signboard at the gate.* 2 brand, brand name

派 1 **pài** I v 1 dispatch ■ 公司派我到上海开发市场。Gōngsī pài wǒ dào Shànghǎi kāifā shìchǎng. *The company sent me to Shanghai to develop the market.* 2 assign (a job)

派 2 **pài** N faction, school (of thought) ■ 在这个问题上有很多派。Zài zhège wèntí shang yǒu hěn duō pài. *There are many schools of thought on this issue.*
  保守派 **bǎoshǒupài** the conservative faction, conservatives

派别 **pàibié** N faction, group, school (of thought)

派出所 **pàichūsuǒ** N police station

派对 **pàiduì** N (social) party ■ 我们搬进新房子以后要开一个派对。Wǒmen bānjìn xīnfángzi yǐhòu yào kāi yí ge pàiduì. *We'll give a party after moving into the new house.*

NOTE: 派对 pàiduì is a transliteration of (*social*) *party*, used among urban fashionable people. 聚会 jùhuì is a more formal word.

派遣 **pàiqiǎn** v send, dispatch (troops, formal delegate, etc.)

攀 **pān** v climb

攀登 **pāndēng** v climb, scale

盘 **pán** TRAD 盤 N dish, plate

盘子 **pánzi** plate, dish, tray (只 zhī)
盘旋 **pánxuán** v (of a bird or airplane) spiral, circle

判 **pàn** v judge, distinguish

判处 **pànchǔ** v (in a law court) sentence
  判处无期徒刑 **pànchǔ wúqī túxíng** sentenced to life imprisonment
判定 **pàndìng** v decide, come to a conclusion
判断 **pànduàn** I v judge, decide ■ 他判断是非的能力很强。Tā pànduàn shì-fēi de nénglì hěn qiáng. *He is very good at telling right from wrong.* II N judgment, verdict
判决 **pànjué** N court decision, judgment

盼 **pàn** v expect, hope for

盼望 **pànwàng** v look forward to, long for ■ 母亲盼望孩子们都回家过春节。Mǔqin pànwàng háizimen dōu huíjiā guò chūnjié. *The mother longed for the homecoming of all her children for Chinese New Year.*

畔 **pàn** N (river, lake, etc.) side, bank

叛 **pàn** v betray, revolt

叛变 **pànbiàn** v turn traitor, become a turncoat
叛徒 **pàntú** N traitor, turncoat

旁 **páng** N side ■ 路旁都摆着各种各样的小摊子。Lùpáng dōu bǎizhe gè-zhǒng-gè-yàng de xiǎo tānzi. *By the roadside are all kinds of stalls.*
旁边 **pángbiān** N side
旁观 **pángguān** v look on, observe ■ 旁观者清。Pángguānzhě qīng. *The onlooker sees most of the game.*

庞 **páng** TRAD 龐 ADJ huge

庞大 **pángdà** ADJ huge, enormous

胖 **pàng** ADJ fat, plump ■ 现在胖的人越来越多了。Xiànzài pàng de rén yuèláiyuè duō le. *There are more and more fat people now.*
胖子 **pàngzi** N fat person, "fatty"

抛 **pāo** v throw, hurl

抛弃 **pāoqì** v abandon, forsake

刨 **páo** v dig, unearth, excavate

袍 **páo** N gown, robe

袍子 **páozi** gown, robe

跑 **pǎo** v run ■ 我们比一比，看谁跑得快。Wǒmen bǐ yi bǐ, kàn shéi pǎo de kuài. *Let's compete and see who runs faster.*

跑步 **pǎobù** v jog

跑道 **pǎodào** N runway, track (in a sports ground)

炮 **pào** N cannon, gun (门 mén, 座 zuò)

炮兵 **pàobīng** N artillery man

炮弹 **pàodàn** N artillery shell (发 fā, 颗 kē)

炮火 **pàohuǒ** N artillery fire

泡 **pào** I N 1 bubble

肥皂泡 **féizàopào** soap bubble
2 blister II v soak, steep

泡沫 **pàomò** N foam, froth

泡沫塑料 **pàomò sùliào** N styrofoam

陪 **péi** v accompany ■ 我今天没有空陪你去看电影。Wǒ jīntiān méiyǒu kòng péi nǐ qù kàn diànyǐng. *I don't have time to go to the movies with you.*

陪同 **péitóng** v accompany

培 **péi** v cultivate

培训 **péixùn** I N training ■ 秘书们都要参加新电脑软件使用的培训。Mìshūmen dōu yào cānjiā xīn diànnǎo ruǎnjiàn shǐyòng de péixùn. *Secretaries will all have training in the use of a new computer software.*

培训班 **péixùnbān** training class, training course

培训生 **péixùn shēng** trainee
II v train

培训新职工 **péixùn xīn zhígōng** train new staff

培养 **péiyǎng** v 1 train, develop 2 cultivate, breed

培育 **péiyù** v bring up, nurture and educate

培育下一代 **péiyù xià yídài** bring up the next generation, bring up one's children

赔 **péi** TRAD 赔 v compensate, pay for (damage, loss, etc.) ■ 你借给我的书，我丢了。我赔你吧。Nǐ jiè gei wǒ de shū, wǒ diū le. Wǒ péi nǐ ba. *I've lost the book you lent me. Let me pay for it.*

赔偿 **péicháng** v compensate

赔款 **péikuǎn** N reparation, indemnity

佩 **pèi** v 1 wear 2 admire

佩服 **pèifu** v admire ■ 我佩服自学成才的人。Wǒ pèifu zì-xué-chéng-cái de rén. *I admire those who become a success from being self-taught.*

NOTE: You can utter 佩服 Pèifu or 佩服! 佩服! Pèifu! Pèifu! to express great admiration for a feat or a remarkable achievement, e.g. ■ "你五门功课都是一百分? 佩服! 佩服!" "Nǐ wǔ mén gōngkè dōu shì yìbǎi fēn? Pèifu! Pèifu!" *"You got full marks for all the five subjects? Wow!"*

配 **pèi** v 1 match, blend 2 be worthy of, deserve

配得上 **pèi de shàng** be worthy of, good enough to be

配不上 **pèi bushàng** not good enough to be, unworthy of

配备 **pèibèi** v allocate, provide with, be equipped with ■ 每个教室配备一台电脑。Měige jiàoshì pèibèi yìtái diànnǎo. *Equip each classroom with a computer.*

配方 **pèifāng** N medical prescription, formula

配合 **pèihé** v cooperate, coordinate ■ 病人要和医生密切配合，才能早日恢复健康。Bìngrén yào hé yīshēng mìqiè pèihé, cáinéng zǎorì huīfù jiànkāng. *A patient should cooperate closely with his doctor so as to achieve a speedy recovery.*

配偶 **pèi'ǒu** N spouse

配套 **pèitào** v make up a complete set

沛 **pèi** ADJ abundant (See 充沛 chōngpèi)

喷 **pēn** TRAD 噴 v sprinkle, spray ■ 这棵树上有虫子，要喷点儿药。Zhè kē shù shang yǒu chóngzi, yào pēn diǎnr yào. *This tree has insects on it and needs spraying.*

喷射 **pēnshè** v spurt, spray

喷水池 **pēnshuǐchí** N fountain

盆 **pén** N basin, pot (个 gè)

花盆 **huāpén** flower pot

洗脸盆 **xǐliǎnpén** washbasin

盆地 **péndì** N (in geography) basin

烹 **pēng** v boil, cook

烹饪 **pēngrèn** N cuisine, cooking

烹调 **pēngtiáo** v cook

烹调技术 **pēngtiáo jìshù** cooking skill

中华烹调 **Zhōnghuá pēngtiáo** Chinese cuisine

朋 **péng** N companion, friend

朋友 **péngyou** N friend ■ 朋友之间应该互相帮

助。Péngyou zhī jiān yīnggāi hùxiāng bāngzhù. *Friends should help one another.*

跟/和…交朋友 **gēn/hé…jiāo péngyou** make friends with …

男朋友 **nánpéngyou** boyfriend
女朋友 **nǚpéngyou** girlfriend

朋 **péng** N shed

棚子 **péngzi** shed

彭 **péng** v expand, inflate

彭胀 **péngzhàng** v expand, dilate

捧 **pěng** v 1 hold in both hands (with care, pride, etc.) ■ 他捧着一盆花回家。Tā pěngzhe yì pén huā huíjiā. *He came home with a pot of flowers in his hands.* 2 sing somebody's praise (especially insincerely), flatter ■ 你别捧我，我知道自己有几斤几两。Nǐ bié pěng wǒ, wǒ zhīdào zìjǐ yǒu jǐ jīn jǐ liǎng. *Don't flatter me. I know my worth.*

碰 **pèng** v bump into, touch

碰到 **pèngdao** meet unexpectedly, run into
碰钉子 **pèng dīngzi** IDIOM meet with a sharp rebuff, be given the cold shoulder ■ 她向老板要求加薪，可是碰了钉子。Tā xiàng lǎobǎn yāoqiú jiāxīn, kěshì pèngle dīngzi. *She asked the boss for a raise, but met with a sharp rebuff.*

批 **pī** I M. WD (for a batch of goods, and for things/people arriving at the same time)
一批新书 **yì pī xīn shū** a batch of new books (published at about the same time)
两批旅游者 **liǎng pī lǚyóuzhě** two groups of tourists
II v criticize, comment on, give instructions
批发 **pīfā** v sell wholesale
批改 **pīgǎi** v correct and grade (students' exercises, essays, etc.)
批判 **pīpàn** v criticize
批评 **pīpíng** I v criticize, scold ■ 老师批评他常常迟到。Lǎoshī pīpíng tā chángcháng chídào. *The teacher criticized him for being often late for class.* II N criticism ■ 我接受你对我的批评。Wǒ jiēshòu nǐ duì wǒ de pīpíng. *I accept your criticism.*
批示 **pīshì** I v write comments on a document (e.g. report, request) submitted by subordinates II N comments on a document (e.g. report, request) submitted by subordinates
批准 **pīzhǔn** v approve, ratify ■ 你的申请已经批准了。Nǐ de shēnqǐng yǐjīng pīzhǔn le. *Your application has been approved.*

劈 **pī** v chop to split

披 **pī** v drape over the shoulder ■ 他披着大衣，看孩子在雪地里玩。Tā pīzhe dàyī, kàn háizi zài xuědì li wán. *With an overcoat draped over his shoulders, he watched the children play in the snow.*

皮 **pí** N 1 skin 2 leather, hide

牛皮 **niúpí** ox hide
皮带 **pídài** N leather belt
系上皮带 **xìshang pídài** buckle up one's belt
皮肤 **pífū** skin (human) ■ 在海边住了一个夏天，他的皮肤晒黑了。Zài hǎibiān zhùle yí ge xiàtiān, tā de pífū shài hēi le. *After a summer day by the sea, he was tanned.*
皮革 **pígé** N leather, hide
皮革制品 **pígé zhìpǐn** leather product, leatherware
皮鞋 **píxié** N leather shoes
皮衣 **píyī** N fur coat, leather jacket

疲 **pí** ADJ fatigued

疲惫 **píbèi** ADJ physically and mentally exhausted
疲乏 **pífá** ADJ tired, weary
疲倦 **píjuàn** ADJ weary, tired
疲劳 **píláo** ADJ fatigued, tired ■ 我连续工作了六小时，实在疲劳。Wǒ liánxù gōngzuòle liù xiǎoshí, shízài píláo. *I have been working nonstop for six hours. I am indeed tired.*

啤 **pí** N beer

啤酒 **píjiǔ** N beer (瓶 píng, 杯 bēi) ■ 这种啤酒很好喝。Zhè zhǒng píjiǔ hěn hǎohē. *This beer tastes good.*

NOTE: 啤酒 píjiǔ is an example of a semi-transliteration: 啤 pí represents the sound of English word *beer* and 酒 jiǔ means *alcoholic drink*.

脾 **pí** N spleen

脾气 **píqi** N disposition, temper ■ 王医生脾气好，很少生气。Wáng yīshēng píqi hǎo, hěn shǎo shēngqì. *Dr Wang is good-tempered; he rarely gets angry.*
脾气坏 **píqi huài** have an irritable temper
发脾气 **fā píqi** throw a tantrum, lose one's temper

匹 **pǐ** M. WD (for horses)

一匹快马 **yì pǐ kuài mǎ** a fast horse

屁 **pì** N flatulence, fart

屁股 **pìgu** N bottom, buttocks

辟 pì

辟 pì TRAD 闢 V open up (See 开辟 kāipì.)

僻 pì ADJ unusual, out-of-the-way (See 偏僻 piānpì)

譬 pì N example

譬如 pìrú CONJ Same as 比如 bǐrú

偏 1 piān I ADJ not straight, slanting II V be prejudiced, show favoritism
偏爱 piān'ài v be partial, favor
偏爱他的小女儿 piān'ài tāde xiǎonǚ'ér favor one's youngest daughter
偏差 piānchā N deviation, error
偏见 piānjiàn N prejudice, bias
对同性恋者有偏见 duì tóngxìngliànzhě yǒu piānjiàn hold prejudice against homosexuals
偏僻 piānpì ADJ remote, out-of-the-way
偏向 piānxiàng I v show favoritism II N erroneous tendency

偏 2 piān ADV must (used to indicate that the action in question is contrary to one's expectation or wishes) ■ 明天有一个重要的考试，她偏今天病倒了。Míngtiān yǒu yí ge zhòngyào de kǎoshì, tā piān jīntiān bìngdào le. Just as there'll be an important exam tomorrow, what must she do but fall ill today?

NOTE: You can use 偏偏 piānpian instead of 偏 piān.

篇 piān M. WD (for a piece of writing)
一篇文章 yì piān wénzhāng an article/essay

便 pián as in 便宜 piányi
便宜 piányi ADJ inexpensive, cheap
便宜货 piányi huò cheap goods, bargain

片 piàn I N thin and flat piece ■ 王太太做的肉片特别好吃。Wáng tàitai zuò de ròupiàn tèbié hǎochī. The meat slices cooked by Mrs Wang are particularly delicious. II M. WD (for thin, flat pieces)
一片面包 yí piàn miànbāo a slice of bread
片面 piànmiàn ADJ one-sided, unilateral ■ 我们应该全面考虑问题，不要有片面的观点。Wǒmen yīnggāi quánmiàn de kǎolǜ wèntí, bú yào yǒu piànmiàn de guāndiǎn. We should approach an issue from all sides and not have a one-sided view.

骗 piàn V deceive, fool ■ 你受骗了! Nǐ shòu piàn le! You've been duped!
骗局 piànjú N hoax, fraud
揭穿一个骗局 jiēchuān yí ge piànjú expose a fraud

骗子 piànzi N swindler, con-man

漂 piāo V float, drift

飘 piāo TRAD 飄 V flutter ■ 彩旗飘飘。Cǎiqí piāopiāo. Colorful banners fluttered in the breeze.
飘扬 piāoyáng V (of banners, flags, etc.) flutter, wave

票 piào N ticket (张 zhāng) ■ 我买两张去香港的飞机票。Wǒ mǎi liǎng zhāng qù Xiānggǎng de fēijī piào. I want to buy two air tickets to Hong Kong.
电影票 diànyǐng piào movie ticket
飞机票 fēijī piào air ticket
火车票 huǒchē piào train ticket
门票 ménpiào admission ticket (to a show, sporting event, etc.)
汽车票 qìchē piào bus/coach ticket

漂 piào as in 漂亮 piàoliang

漂亮 piàoliang IDIOM ADJ pretty, good-looking ■ 你的汉字写得真漂亮。Nǐ de Hànzì xiě de zhēn piàoliang. Your Chinese characters are beautifully written.

撇 piē V 1 discard, abandon 2 skim off from the surface of a liquid

瞥 piē I v take a glance at, shoot a glance at II N glimpse

拼 pīn V 1 fight bitterly, risk one's life 2 put together
拼搏 pīnbó V fight hard against a formidable adversary (often figuratively)
拼搏精神 pīnbó jīngshen fierce fighting spirit
拼命 pīnmìng V do all one can, risk one's life ■ 他拼命赚钱，都是为了什么呢? Tā pīnmìng zhuànqián, dōushì wèile shénme ne? He does everything possible to earn money, but for what purpose?
拼音 pīnyīn I v spell, phonetize II N Romanized Chinese writing, pinyin
拼音文字 pīnyīn wénzì phonetic writing
汉语拼音方案 Hànyǔ pīnyīn fāng'àn Scheme for the Chinese Phonetic Alphabet

频 pín TRAD 頻 ADV frequently
频道 píndào N frequency channel, (TV) channe
频繁 pínfán ADJ frequent
频率 pínlǜ N frequency

贫 pín TRAD 貧 ADJ poor, lacking
贫乏 pínfá ADJ lacking in, deficient

152

资源贫乏 **zīyuán pínfá** poor in natural resources

贫苦 **pínkǔ** ADJ poor and miserable, poverty-stricken

贫困 **pínkùn** ADJ poor, destitute

贫民 **pínmín** N poor people, people living below the poverty line

贫穷 **pínqióng** ADJ poor, poverty-stricken

品 **pǐn** I N 1 article, product 2 quality, grade

上品 **shàngpǐn** superior quality, product of superior quality

II V savor

品尝 **pǐncháng** V savor, taste

品德 **pǐndé** N moral character

品德高尚 **pǐndé gāoshàng** of lofty (excellent) moral character

品行 **pǐnxíng** N moral character and conduct, behavior

品行不良 **pǐnxíng bùliáng** of poor moral standard and behave badly

品质 **pǐnzhì** N 1 (of people) moral character, intrinsic quality ■ 这个人很讨人喜欢, 但是品质不好。 Zhège rén hěn tǎorén xǐhuan, dànshì pǐnzhì bù hǎo. *This guy is quite pleasant, but has bad moral character.* 2 (of products) quality

品种 **pǐnzhǒng** N variety, breed ■ 超级市场里的水果品种多得不得了, 简直让人眼睛都看花了。 Chāojíshìchǎng li de chuǐguǒ pǐnzhǒng duō de bùdeliǎo, jiǎnzhí ràng rén yǎnjing dōu kànhuā le. *There is a huge variety of fruits in the supermarket. It is simply dazzling.*

聘 **pìn** V invite for service/employment

聘请 **pìnqǐng** V invite for service, employ

聘任 **pǐnrèn** V appoint (for a professional or managerial position)

聘书 **pìnshū** N letter of appointment (份 fèn)

乒 **pīng** N bang (sound)

乒乓球 **pīnqpānqqiú** N table tennis, table tennis ball (只 zhī)

平 **píng** ADJ 1 flat, level, smooth ■ 这张桌面不平。 Zhè zhāng zhuōmiàn bù píng. *This table surface is not level.* 2 be on the same level, equal 3 average, common

平安 **píng'ān** ADJ safe and sound ■ 高高兴兴上班, 平平安安回家。 Gāo-gāo-xìng-xìng shàngbān, píng-píng-ān-ān huíjiā. *Come to work in high spirits and return home safe and sound.* (A Chinese slogan urging workers to observe occupational safety.)

平常 **píngcháng** I ADJ ordinary, common ■ 那是我一生中最不平常的一天。 Nà shì wǒ yìshēng zhong zuì bù píngcháng de yì tiān. *That was the most unusual day of my life.* II ADV ordinarily, usually, normally ■ 我平常不喝酒, 只有节日的时候喝一点儿。 Wǒ píngcháng bù hē jiǔ, zhǐyǒu jiérì de shíhou hē yìdiǎnr. *I normally don't drink. I only drink a little on festive occasions.*

平等 **píngděng** I ADJ equal (in status) ■ 法律面前人人平等。 Fǎlù miànqián rénren píngděng. *Everyone is equal in the eyes of the law.* II N equality ■ 夫妻之间的平等是现代婚姻的基础。 Fūqī zhījiān de píngděng shì xiàndài hūnyīn de jīchǔ. *Equality between husband and wife is the foundation of modern marriages.*

平凡 **píngfán** ADJ ordinary, common

平方 **píngfāng** N (in maths) square

三平方公尺 **sān píngfāng gōngchǐ** 3 square meters

平衡 **pínghéng** I N balance, equilibrium II V to keep in balance

平静 **píngjìng** ADJ calm, quiet, uneventful ■ 老人平静的生活被这个消息打乱了。 Lǎorén píngjìng de shēnghuó bèi zhège xiāoxi dǎluàn le. *The old man's peaceful life was shattered by this news.*

平均 **píngjūn** ADJ average ■ 这个城市的人平均收入是一年一万元。 Zhège chéngshì de rén píngjūn shōurù shì yì nián yíwàn yuán. *The average per capita income of this city is 10,000 yuan a year.*

平面 **píngmiàn** N (in mathematics) plane

平面几何 **píngmiàn jǐhé** plane geometry

平民 **píngmín** N the common people, civilian (个 gè, 名 míng)

平日 **píngrì** ADV on an ordinary day (not a holiday or festival)

平时 **píngshí** ADV usually, under normal circumstances

平坦 **píngtǎn** ADJ level and broad

平稳 **píngwěn** ADJ smooth and stable

平行 **píngxíng** ADJ parallel

平行线 **píngxíngxiàn** parallel lines

平庸 **píngyōng** ADJ mediocre, ordinary

平原 **píngyuán** N flatland, plain ■ 中国东北地区是一个大平原。 Zhōngguó dōngběi dìqū shì yí ge dà píngyuán. *The northeast region of China is a huge plain.*

评 **píng** TRAD 評 V 1 comment 2 appraise

评比 **píngbǐ** V appraise through comparison

年终评比 **niánzhōng píngbǐ** end-of-the-year appraisal (of performance of a number of people or groups)

评定 **píngdìng** V evaluate, assess

评估 **pínggū** V assess, appraise

资产评估 zīchǎn pínggū assets appraisal
评价 píngjià **I** v appraise, evaluate **II** N evaluation
高度评价 gāodù píngjià place a high value on, speak highly of
评论 pínglùn **I** v comment ■ 我不想评论他们之间的矛盾。Wǒ bù xiǎng pínglùn tāmen zhījiān de máodùn. *I have no comment on the conflict between them.* **II** N comment, commentary
评选 píngxuǎn v appraise and select, select by public appraisal

苹 píng TRAD 蘋 N apple

苹果 píngguǒ N apple (个 gè)
苹果园 píngguǒ yuán apple orchard

萍 píng N duckweed

萍水相逢 píngshuǐ xiāngféng IDIOM (of strangers) meet by chance like drifting duckweed

凭 píng TRAD 憑 **I** N evidence, proof

真凭实据 zhēnpíng shíjù hard evidence
II v go by, base on
凭票入场 píngpiào rùchǎng admission by tickets

屏 píng N screen

屏风 píngfēng N partition
屏幕 píngmù N (movie, TV, computer) screen

瓶 píng **I** N bottle (个 gè)

瓶子 píngzi bottle ■ 给我一个空瓶子。Gěi wǒ yí ge kōng píngzi. *Give me an empty bottle.*
II M. WD a bottle of
一瓶啤酒 yì píng píjiǔ a bottle of beer
两瓶可口可乐 liǎng píng kěkǒukělè two bottles of Coca-Cola

坡 pō N slope ■ 骑自行车上坡很累。Qí zìxíngchē shàng pō hěn lèi. *Cycling up a slope is very tiring.*

泼 pō TRAD 潑 **I** v sprinkle **II** ADJ vigorous, bold (See 活泼 huópo.)

颇 pō ADV quite, rather

迫 pò v compel, oppress

迫害 pòhài v persecute
迫切 pòqiè ADJ urgent, pressing ■ 我们的迫切任务是了解市场情况。Wǒmen de pòqiè rènwù shì liǎojiě shìchǎng qíngkuàng. *Our urgent task is to understand the market situation.*
迫使 pòshǐ v compel, force

破 pò **I** v 1 break, damage 2 break, split ■ 你的衣服破了。Nǐ de yīfu pò le. *Your clothes are torn.* **II** ADJ torn, damaged ■ 花瓶打破了。Huāpíng dǎpò le. *The vase is broken.*
破产 pòchǎn **I** v go bankrupt **II** N bankruptcy ■ 没有想到，这家大公司会宣布破产。Méiyǒu xiǎngdào, zhè jiā dà gōngsī huì xuānbù pòchǎn. *It is quite unexpected that this big company should declare bankruptcy.*
破除 pòchú v do away with, eradicate
破坏 pòhuài v sabotage, damage
破获 pòhuò v solve (a criminal case), catch (criminals)
破旧 pòjiù ADJ old and worn-out, shabby ■ 不准破坏公共财物。Bù zhǔn pòhuài gōnggòng cáiwù *Vandalism of public property is not allowed.*
破旧的厂房 pòjiù de chǎngfáng run-down factory building
破烂 pòlàn ADJ worn-out, tattered
捡破烂 jiǎn pòlàn pick up what is valuable from among garbage, make a living by doing this
破裂 pòliè v split, break down
破碎 pòsuì **I** v break into pieces, smash **II** ADJ broken into pieces, smashed, crushed ■ 他的梦想破碎了。Tā de mèngxiǎng pòsuì le. *His dream was shattered.*

魄 pò N 1 soul, spirit 2 vigor

魄力 pòlì N daring, resolution

剖 pōu v cut open

剖析 pōuxī v dissect
剖析一个典型事例 pōuxī yí ge diǎnxíng shìlì study a typical case in great detail

扑 pū v 1 pounce on 2 flap

扑克 pūkè N playing cards
扑克牌 pūkèpái (张 zhāng, 副 fù)

NOTE: 扑克 pūkè is a transliteration of *poker*, to mean *playing cards*, not the card game. 扑克牌 pūkèpái, however, is more commonly used in everyday Chinese. We say 打扑克牌 dǎ pūkè pái, or 打牌 dǎ pái for the verb *to play cards*.

扑灭 pūmiè v extinguish, put out

铺 pū v spread, unfold ■ 桌子上铺着一块漂亮的桌布。Zhuōzi shang pūzhe yí kuài piàoliang de zhuōbù. *A beautiful tablecloth was spread over the table.*

葡 pú N as in 葡萄 pútao

葡萄 pútao N grape (颗 kē) ■ 这里的葡萄又

大又甜。Zhèli de pútao yòu dà yòu tián. *The grapes here are big and sweet.*
葡萄酒 pútaojiǔ grape wine
葡萄园 pútaoyuán vineyard

仆 **pú** TRAD 僕 N servant

仆人 púrén (domestic) servant (个 gè, 名 míng)

NOTE: 仆人 púrén is an old-fashioned word for *servant.* Use 用人 yòngrén or 保姆 bǎomǔ.

菩 **pú** as in 菩萨 Púsà

菩萨 Púsà N Buddha, Bodhisattva

朴 **pǔ** TRAD 樸 ADJ plain, simple

朴实 pǔshí ADJ **1** (of style) simple and plain, down-to-earth **2** (of people) sincere and honest
朴素 pǔsù ADJ simple and plain ■ 她喜欢穿朴素的衣服。Tá xǐhuan chuān pǔsù de yīfu. *She likes to dress simply.*

普 **pǔ** ADJ common, universal

普遍 pǔbiàn ADJ widespread, commonplace ■ 人们普遍认为这种做法是不对的。Rénmen pǔbiàn rènwéi zhè zhǒng zuòfǎ shì bú duì de. *People generally think this kind of behavior is wrong.*
普查 pǔchá N survey
人口普查 rénkǒu pǔchá census
普及 pǔjí v popularize, make commonplace
普通 pǔtōng ADJ common, commonplace, or-dinary ■ 在这个城市里一座普通的房子要多少钱? Zài zhège chéngshìli yí zuò pǔtōng de fángzi yào duóshǎo qián? *How much is an ordinary house in this city?*
普通话 Pǔtōnghuà N Standard Modern Chi-nese, Mandarin, Putonghua ■ 大多数中国人都听得懂普通话。Dàduōshù Zhōngguórén dōu tīng de dǒng Pǔtōnghuà. *Most Chinese people understand Putonghua.*

NOTE: Modern Standard Chinese is known as 普通话 Pǔtōnghuà in China, 国语 Guóyǔ in Taiwan and 华语 Huáyǔ in Singapore and other Southeast Asian countries. They refer to the same language, though slight differences do exist among them.

谱 **pǔ** I v set to music II N musical score

乐谱 yuèpǔ musical score
钢琴谱 gāngqín pǔ piano score
谱曲 pǔqǔ v set music to words

瀑 **pù** N waterfall

瀑布 pùbù N waterfall

Q

七 **qī** NUM seven

七个小矮人 qī ge xiǎo ǎirén the seven dwarves
七百七十七 qībǎi qīshíqī seven hundred and seventy-seven

柒 **qī** NUM seven

沏 **qī** v infuse

沏茶 qīchá make tea

妻 **qī** N wife

妻子 qīzi wife ■ 丈夫和妻子应当互相爱护,互相尊重。Zhàngfu hé qīzi yīngdāng hùxiāng àihu, hùxiāng zūnzhòng. *A couple should care for and respect each other.*

凄 **qī** ADJ chilly, cold

凄惨 qīcǎn ADJ miserable, wretched
凄凉 qīliáng ADJ desolate, dreary, miserable

漆 **qī** N lacquer, paint

漆黑 qīhēi ADJ pitch dark, pitch black
漆黑一团 qīhēiyìtuán pitch dark

期 **qī** I N fixed time

按期 àn qī according to the schedule, on time ■ 贵公司订购的货物我们一定按期送到。Guì-gōngsī dìnggòu de huòwù wǒmen yídìng àn qī sòngdào. *We will certainly deliver on time the goods your company ordered.*
到期 dàoqī expire, due
过期 guòqī overdue, expired
II v expect
期待 qīdài v expect, look forward to
期间 qījiān N period, time ■ 春节期间饭店的生意特别好。Chūnjié qījiān fàndiàn de shēngyi tèbié hǎo. *During the Chinese New Year holidays, restaurants have particularly good business.*
期刊 qīkān N periodical, journal (本 běn)
期望 qīwàng I v expect, hope II N expecations, hope
期望过高 qīwàng guògāo expect too much
期限 qīxiàn N deadline, time limit
超过期限 chāoguò qīxiàn exceed the time limit, become overdue
定一个期限 dìng yí ge qīxiàn set a deadline

戚 qī N relative (See 亲戚 qīnqi)

欺 qī V cheat, bully

欺负 **qīfu** V bully, take advantage of (someone) ■ 他有了一点儿权，就要欺负别人。Tā yǒu le yìdiǎnr quán, jiùyào qīfu biéren. *He tried to bully others once he'd got some power.*
欺骗 **qīpiàn** V deceive

歧 qí ADJ different, divergent

歧视 **qíshì** I V discriminate against
歧视残疾人士 **qíshì cánjírénshì** discriminate against the disabled
II N discrimination
种族歧视 **zhǒngzú qíshì** racial discrimination

齐 qí TRAD 齊 I ADJ neat, in a straight line ■ 书架上的书放得很齐。Shūjià shang de shū fàng de hěn qí. *The books in the bookshelf are neatly arranged.* II V reaching to the same height ■ 树长得齐屋顶了。Shù zhǎng de qí wūdǐng le. *The trees have grown as tall as the roof.* III ADV together, all ready
齐全 **qíquán** ADJ complete, all in readiness
品种齐全 **pǐnzhǒng qíquán** have a complete range of products (goods)

其 qí PRON this, that

其次 **qícì** ADV next, secondary, secondly ■ 他们离婚的原因首先是性格不合，其次是经济上有矛盾。Tāmen líhūn de yuányīn shǒuxiān shì xìnggé bù hé, qícì shì jīngjì shang yǒu máodùn. *The first reason they gave for divorcing was incompatibility of disposition and the second reason was financial conflict.*
其实 **qíshí** ADV actually, as a matter of fact
其他 **qítā** PRON other, else
其余 **qíyú** PRON the rest, the remainder ■ 我付了学费以后把其余的钱存进了银行。Wǒ fùle xuéfèi yǐhòu bǎ qíyú de qián cúnjìnle yínháng. *After paying the tuition fee, I deposited the remainder of the money in the bank.*
其中 **qízhōng** N among them, in it ■ 北京有很多名胜古迹，故宫是其中之一。Běijīng yǒu hěn duō míngshèng gǔjì, gùgōng shì qízhōng zhī yī. *There are many scenic spots and historical sites in Beijing. The Palace Museum is one of them.*

棋 qí N chess

下棋 **xiàqí** play chess
下一盘棋 **xià yìpánqí** play a game of chess
棋盘 **qípán** N chess board

棋子 **qízǐ** N chess piece

旗 qí N flag, banner (面 miàn)

旗杆 **qígān** flagstaff, flag pole
国旗 **guóqí** national flag
升旗 **shēngqí** hoist a flag
旗袍 **qípáo** N a woman's dress with high neck and slit skirt, cheongsam
旗帜 **qízhì** N banner (面 miàn)
旗子 **qízi** N flag, banner (面 miàn)

奇 qí ADJ strange

奇怪 **qíguài** ADJ strange, unusual, odd ■ 他一年到头戴着一顶黄帽子，真奇怪。Tā yì-nián-dào-tóu dàizhe yì dǐng huáng màozi, zhēn qíguài. *It is really odd that he wears a yellow cap all year long.*
奇花异草 **qíhuāyìcǎo** N rare, exotic flora
奇迹 **qíjì** N miracle, wonder
创造奇迹 **chuàngzào qíjì** perform a miracle, work wonders
奇妙 **qímiào** ADJ marvelous, intriguing
奇特 **qítè** ADJ peculiar, unique

骑 qí TRAD 騎 V ride (a horse, bicycle etc.)

骑马 **qí mǎ** ride a horse
骑自行车 **qí zìxíngchē** ride a bicycle

岂 qǐ TRAD 豈 ADV (forming a rhetorical question)

岂不 **qǐbù** ADV wouldn't it, doesn't it ■ 岂不浪费钱财? Qǐbù làngfèi qiáncái? *Wouldn't it be a waste of money?*
岂有此理 **qǐyǒucǐlǐ** IDIOM preposterous, outrageous ■ 真是岂有此理! Zhēnshi qǐyǒucǐlǐ! *How absurd! That's really outrageous!*

企 qǐ V hope, eagerly look forward to

企图 **qǐtú** I V attempt, try ■ 恐怖分子企图破坏铁路和公路，制造大规模交通事故。Kǒngbùfènzǐ qǐtú pòhuài tiělù hé gōnglù, zhìzào dà guīmó jiāotōng shìgù. *Terrorists attempted to sabotage railways and highways to cause large-scale traffic accidents.* II N attempt ■ 他们的企图失败了。Tāmen de qǐtú shībài le. *Their attempt failed*

NOTE: 企图 **qǐtú** is usually used for negative situations. For example, we usually do not say 他企图帮助我。Tā qǐtú bāngzhù wǒ. *He tried to help me.* but 他企图欺骗我。Tā qǐtú qīpiàn wǒ. *He tried to deceive me.*

企业 **qǐyè** N enterprise (家 jiā)
企业家 **qǐyèjiā** entrepreneur
国有企业 **guóyǒu qǐyè** state-owned enterprise

私有企业 **sīyǒu qǐyè** private enterprise

启 **qǐ** TRAD 啟 v **1** open **2** start, initiate

启程 **qǐchéng** v start a journey, set out

启发 **qǐfā** I v enlighten, arouse ■ 我们应该启发孩子的学习兴趣。**Wǒmen yīnggāi qǐfā háizi de xuéxí xìngqù.** *We should arouse an interest to learn in children.* II N enlightenment, inspiration

启示 **qǐshì** N revelation, inspiration, enlightenment

启事 **qǐshì** N public announcement

乞 **qǐ** v beg

乞丐 **qǐgài** N beggar

乞求 **qǐqiú** v implore, beg for
乞求宽恕 **qǐqiú kuānshù** beg for mercy

起 **qǐ** v rise, get up ■ 快十点钟了, 他还没起呢! **Kuài shí diǎnzhōng le, tā hái méi qǐ ne!** *It's almost ten o'clock and he still isn't up!*

从…起 **cóng...qǐ** starting from ... ■ 从晚上七点起, 网吧就特别忙。**Cóng wǎnshang qī diǎn qǐ, wǎngbā jiù tèbié máng.** *Starting from seven o'clock in the evening, the Internet cafe is particularly busy.*

NOTE: 起 **qǐ** is seldom used alone. To express *to get up (out of bed)*, 起床 **qǐchuáng** is more common than 起 **qǐ**. One can very well say: 快十点钟了, 他还没起床呢! **Kuài shí diǎnzhōng le, tā hái méi qǐchuáng ne!** *It's almost ten o'clock and he still isn't up!*

起草 **qǐcǎo** v make a draft of (a plan, a document, etc.)

起初 **qǐchū** ADV at first, at the onset

起床 **qǐchuáng** v get up (out of bed)

起点 **qǐdiǎn** N starting point

起飞 **qǐfēi** v (of a plane) take off

起伏 **qǐfú** I v undulate, fluctuate II N fluctuation, setback

起哄 **qǐhòng** v set up a commotion in a light-hearted or mocking manner

起劲 **qǐjìn** ADV enthusiastically, in high spirits

起来 **qǐlai** v get up (out of bed), stand up ■ 校长走进教室, 大家都站起来。**Xiàozhǎng zǒujìn jiàoshì, dàjiā dōu zhàn qǐlai.** *When the principal entered the classroom, everybody stood up.*

NOTE: 起来 **qǐlai** is often used after a verb as a complement to express various meanings. Among other meanings, 起来 **qǐlai** may be used after a verb to mean *begin to ...*, e.g. ■ 我们不等爸爸了, 吃起来吧。**Wǒmen bù děng bàba le, chī qǐlai ba.** *We're not going to wait for daddy any longer. Let's start eating.*

起码 **qǐmǎ** ADJ the very least, minimum

起身 **qǐshēn** v **1** get up **2** set out, set off

起诉 **qǐsù** v sue, file a lawsuit against

起诉书 **qǐsùshū** indictment

起义 **qǐyì** I v stage an uprising, revolt II N uprising
农民起义 **nóngmín qǐyì** peasants' uprising

起源 **qǐyuán** I N origin ■ 你知道人类的起源吗? **Nǐ zhīdào rénlèi de qǐyuán ma?** *Do you know the origin of humankind?* II v originate

砌 **qì** v lay (bricks), build by laying bricks

砌一堵墙 **qì yì dǔ qiáng** build a brick wall

泣 **qì** v sob, cry

哭泣 **kūqì** cry, weep and sob

气 I **qì** TRAD 氣 N **1** air, gas ■ 车轮没有气了。**Chēlún méiyǒu qì le.** *The tire is flat.* **2** breath **3** spirit, morale

NOTE: Apart from its concrete meaning of *air, gas*, 气 **qì** is an important concept in traditional Chinese thought, meaning something like *vital force of life*.

气喘 **qìchuǎn** I v gasp for air II N asthma
气喘病 **qìchuǎn bìng** asthma

气氛 **qìfēn** N atmosphere, ambiance ■ 我喜欢这家酒吧友好的气氛。**Wǒ xǐhuan zhè jiā jiǔbā yǒuhǎo de qìfēn.** *I like the friendly ambiance of this bar.*

气概 **qìgài** N lofty spirit, (heroic) mettle

气功 **qìgōng** N a form of exercises involving deep breath, *qigong*
练气功 **liàn qìgōng** practice exercises of deep breath, practice *qigong*

气候 **qìhòu** N climate ■ 地球上的气候在渐渐变暖。**Dìqiú shang de qìhòu zài jiànjiàn biàn nuǎn.** *The climate on earth is gradually becoming warmer.*

气力 **qìlì** N strength, energy
花很大气力 **huā hěn dà qìlì** make great efforts

气流 **qìliú** N air current

气魄 **qìpò** N daring, boldness

气球 **qìqiú** N balloon
热气球 **rèqìqiú** hot-air balloon

气势 **qìshì** N momentum

气体 **qìtǐ** N gas

气味 **qìwèi** N smell, odor

气温 **qìwēn** N atmospheric temperature ■ 受寒流影响, 今天夜里气温要下降十度左右。**Shòu hánliú yǐngxiǎng, jīntiān yèlǐ qìwēn yào xiàjiàng shí dù zuǒyòu.** *Owing to a cold current, the temperature will fall by about 10 degrees tonight.*

NOTE: See note on 温度 **wēndù**.

气息 **qìxī** N **1** breath, breathing **2** flavor

气象 **qìxiàng** N meteorological phenomena, weather

气压 **qìyā**

气象台 **qìxiàngtái** meteorological observatory
气象学 **qìxiàngxué** meteorology
气象预报 **qìxiàng yùbào** weather forecast
气压 **qìyā** N atmospheric pressure, air pressure

气 2 **qì** TRAD 氣 v be angry, make angry ■ 你干吗说这种话气她? **Nǐ gànmá shuō zhè zhǒng huà qì tā?** Why on earth did you say that and make her angry?
气愤 **qìfèn** ADJ very angry, fumingly mad

汽 **qì** N vapor, steam

汽车 **qìchē** N automobile, car (辆 liàng) ■ 我的汽车坏了。 **Wǒde qìchē huài le.** My car has broken down.
开汽车 **kāi qìchē** drive a car

NOTE: In everyday Chinese, 车 chē is often used instead of 汽车 qìchē to refer to a car, e.g. ■ 我可以把车停在这里吗? **Wǒ kěyǐ bǎ chē tíng zài zhèlǐ ma?** May I park my car here?

汽船 **qìchuán** N steamboat (艘 sōu)
汽水 **qìshuǐ** N soda water, soft drink, soda, pop (瓶 píng, 杯 bēi) ■ 我不喝汽水, 我喝矿泉水。 **Wǒ bù hē qìshuǐ, wǒ hē kuàngquánshuǐ.** I don't drink soft drinks. I drink mineral water.
汽油 **qìyóu** N gasoline, petroleum ■ 我们的汽油快用完了, 到前面的加油站要停下加油。 **Wǒmen de qìyóu kuài yòngwán le, dào qiánmiàn de jiāyóuzhàn yào tíngxia jiāyóu.** We've almost run out of gas. We'll have to stop for gas at the next gas station.

弃 **qì** TRAD 棄 v abandon (See 放弃 fàngqì.)

器 **qì** N utensil

器材 **qìcái** N equipment, material
器官 **qìguān** N (human and animal) organ
器械 **qìxiè** N apparatus, instrument
医疗器械 **yīliáo qìxiè** medical equipment

掐 **qiā** v pinch, nip

恰 **qià** ADV just, exactly

恰当 **qiàdàng** ADJ appropriate, suitable, proper
恰到好处 **qiàdào hǎochù** IDIOM just right, hitting the spot ■ 你说的话, 恰到好处。 **Nǐ shuōde huà, qià dào hǎochu.** What you said hit the nail on the head.
恰好 **qiàhǎo** ADV just right, in the nick of time
恰恰 **qiàqià** ADV exactly, precisely
恰巧 **qiàqiǎo** ADV as luck would have it, fortunately ■ 恰巧大家都在。 **Qiàqiǎo dàjiā dōu zài.** Fortunately everyone happened to be there.

恰如其分 **qiàrúqífèn** IDIOM no more no less, ap

洽 **qià** v consult, discuss

洽谈 **qiàtán** v hold a talk
和他们公司洽谈合作项目 **hé tāmen gōngs qiàtán hézuò xiàngmù** hold talks with their company over co-operation

牵 **qiān** v lead along by hand

牵扯 **qiānchě** v involve, implicate
牵引 **qiānyǐn** v tow, draw
牵制 **qiānzhì** v restrain, be bogged down

千 **qiān** NUM thousand

一千零一夜 **yìqiān líng yí yè** a thousand and one nights
四千五百八十 **sìqiān wǔbǎi bāshí** four thousand, five hundred and eighty, 4,580
千方百计 **qiānfāng bǎijì** IDIOM in a thousand and one ways, by every possible means
千克 **qiānkè** N kilogram (kg)
千瓦 **qiānwǎ** N kilowatt (kW)
千万 **qiānwàn** ADV be sure to, must never (used in an imperative sentence for emphasis) ■ 明天的会你千万别迟到。 **Míngtiān de huì nǐ qiānwàn bié chídào.** Be sure not to be late for tomorrow's meeting.

迁 **qiān** TRAD 遷 v move

迁就 **qiānjiù** v accommodate oneself to, yield to

签 **qiān** TRAD 簽 v sign, autograph

签订 **qiāndìng** v sign (a treaty, an agreement, etc.) ■ 那家建筑公司和市政府签订了两份合同。 **Nà jiā jiànzhù gōngsī hé shì zhèngfǔ qiāndìngle liǎng fèn hétóng.** The construction compan has signed two contracts with the city government
签发 **qiānfā** v (of an official) sign and issue (an document, certificate, etc.)
签名 **qiānmíng** I v autograph, sign one's name II N autograph, signature
请歌星签名 **qǐng gēxīng qiānmíng** ask a singer for his/her autograph
签署 **qiānshǔ** v sign (a treaty, a contract, etc.)
签证 **qiānzhèng** N visa
签证处 **qiānzhèngchù** visa section (of a consulate or embassy)
入境签证 **rùjìng qiānzhèng** entry visa
申请签证 **shēnqǐng qiānzhèng** apply for a visa
签字 **qiānzì** I v sign (a document)
在支票上签字 **zài zhīpiào shang qiānzì** sign a check
II N signature

铅 **qiān** TRAD 鉛 N lead (Pb)

铅笔 **qiānbǐ** N pencil (支 zhī)
铅笔盒 **qiānbǐ hé** pencil box
铅笔刀 **qiānbǐ dāo** pencil sharpener

谦 **qiān** TRAD 謙 ADJ modest

谦虚 **qiānxū** ADJ modest, self-effacing ■ 他对自己的成绩非常谦虚。Tā duì zìjǐ de chéngjì fēicháng qiānxū. *He is very modest about his achievements.*
谦逊 **qiānxùn** ADJ modest, unassuming

前 **qián** I N 1 front, in front of ■ 中国人的姓名，姓在前，名在后。Zhōngguórén de xìngmíng, xìng zài qián, míng zài hòu. *In a Chinese person's name, the family name comes before the given name.* 2 Same as 以前 yǐqián II ADV forward

NOTE: In everyday Chinese, 前 qián is seldom used alone to mean *front* or *in front of*. Often it is better to use 前边 qiánbiān.

前辈 **qiánbèi** N the older generation, elders, trailblazer
前边 **qiánbian** N front ■ 房子前边有一块草地。Fángzi qiánbian yǒu yí kuài cǎodì. *In front of the house is a lawn.*
前程 **qiánchéng** N future, prospects
远大前程 **yuǎndà qiánchéng** bright future
前方 **qiánfāng** N (in war) front, frontline
前后 **qiánhòu** ADV (of time) around, about
在2000年前后 **zài èr-líng-líng-líng nián qiánhòu** around the year 2000
前进 **qiánjìn** V go forward, advance ■ 我们的经济在过去一年又前进了一大步。Wǒmen de jīngjì zài guòqu yì nián yòu qiánjìn le yí dà bù. *Last year our economy took a big stride forward.*
前景 **qiánjǐng** N prospect, vista
前列 **qiánliè** N front rank, forefront
前面 **qiánmian** N Same as 前边 qiánbian
前年 **qiánnián** N the year before last ■ 前年我刚开始学中文。Qiánnián wǒ gāng kāishǐ xué Zhōngwén. *I just began to learn Chinese the year before last.*
前期 **qiánqī** N early stage, early days
工程的前期 **gōngchéng de qiánqī** the early stage of an engineering project
前人 **qiánrén** N predecessor, forefather ■ 前人栽树，后人乘凉。Qiánrén zāishù, hòurén chéngliáng. *The forefathers planted the trees, and their descendants enjoy the fruit of labor of our predecessors. (→ We all enjoy the fruit of labor of our predecessors.)*
前所未有 **qiánsuǒwèiyǒu** IDIOM unprecedented, hitherto unheard of

前提 **qiántí** N 1 prerequisite, the prime consideration 2 (in logic) premise
前天 **qiántiān** N the day before yesterday ■ 他前天去中国，今天我收到了他从中国发来的电子邮件。Tā qiántiān qù Zhōngguó, jīntiān wǒ shōudàole tā cóng Zhōngguó fālai de diànzǐ yóujiàn. *He left for China the day before yesterday, and today I got an e-mail he sent from China.*
前头 **qiántou** Same as 前面 qiánmian, used colloquially.
前途 **qiántú** N future, prospects, future prospects ■ 一个青年连中学都没有毕业，不可能有什么前途。Yí ge qīngnián lián zhōngxué dōu méiyǒu bìyè, bù kěnéng yǒu shénme qiántú. *A young man does not have much of future prospects if he does not even finish high school.*
前往 **qiánwǎng** V go to, proceed
前线 **qiánxiàn** N (in war) front, frontline
上前线 **shàng qiánxiàn** go to the front, go to war

钳 **qián** TRAD 鉗 N pincer, plier, forceps

钳子 **qiánzi** pincer, plier, forceps (把 bǎ)
老虎钳 **lǎohǔqián** plier, pincer

潜 **qián** TRAD 潛 ADJ hidden, latent

潜伏 **qiánfú** V hide, lie low
潜伏期 **qiánfúqī** (in medicine) incubation period
潜力 **qiánlì** N latent capacity, potential, potentiality
潜水 **qiánshuǐ** V go under water, dive
潜水员 **qiánshuǐyuán** diver
潜水艇 **qiánshuǐtǐng** N submarine (艘 sōu)

钱 **qián** TRAD 錢 N money (笔 bǐ) ■ 钱很重要，但不是万能的。Qián hěn zhòngyào, dàn bú shì wànnéng de. *Money is important, but it is not all-powerful.*
钱包 **qiánbāo** wallet, purse

浅 **qiǎn** TRAD 淺 ADJ 1 shallow ■ 这条河很浅，可以走过去。Zhè tiáo hé hěn qiǎn, kěyǐ zǒu guòqu. *This river is shallow. You can wade across it.* 2 easy, of low standard ■ 这本书太浅，你不用看。Zhè běn shū tài qiǎn, nǐ bú yòng kàn. *This book is too easy for you; you don't have to read it.*

遣 **qiǎn** V send, dispatch (See 派遣 pàiqiǎn)

谴 **qiǎn** TRAD 譴 V as in 谴责 qiǎnzé

谴责 **qiǎnzé** V condemn, denounce

嵌 **qiàn** V inlay, imbed

欠 qiàn

欠 qiàn v owe, be in debt to ■ 他欠我一百元。Tā qiàn wǒ yìbǎi yuán. *He owes me a hundred yuan.*

欠人情 qiàn rénqíng v owe a debt of gratitude

歉 qiàn N 1 apology 2 crop failure

歉意 qiànyì N apology, regret
深表歉意 shēn biǎo qiànyì offer one's profound apology

腔 qiāng N cavity

口腔 kǒuqiāng oral cavity

枪 qiāng TRAD 槍 N small arms, gun, pistol (支 zhī, 把 bǎ)
手枪 shǒuqiāng handgun (revolver, pistol)
枪毙 qiāngbì v execute by shooting

强 qiáng I ADJ strong ■ 她中文口语很强，但是写汉字的能力比较弱。Tā Zhōngwén kǒuyǔ hěn qiáng, dànshì xiě Hànzì de nénglì bǐjiào ruò. *She is strong in oral Chinese, but weak in writing characters.* **II** ADV by force

强大 qiángdà ADJ powerful ■ 谁都希望自己的祖国强大。Shéi dōu xīwàng zìjǐ de zǔguó qiángdà. *Everybody wants their motherland to be a powerful country.*

强盗 qiángdào N bandit, robber

强调 qiángdiào v emphasize, lay stress on ■ 王老师强调语音准确的重要性。Wáng lǎoshī qiángdiào yǔyīn zhǔnquè de zhòngyàoxìng. *Teacher Wang emphasized the importance of correct pronunciation.*

强度 qiángdù N intensity, strength ■ 这种材料的强度还不够。Zhè zhǒng cáiliào de qiángdù hái bú gòu. *This material does not have enough strength.*

强化 qiánghuà v strengthen, intensify

强奸 qiángjiān v rape
强奸幼女 qiángjiān yòunǚ rape an underage girl

强烈 qiángliè ADJ strong, intense, violent ■ 顾客们强烈要求退货。Gùkèmen qiángliè yāoqiú tuìhuò. *The customers firmly demanded a refund.*

强盛 qiángshèng ADJ (of a country) strong and prosperous, powerful and wealthy

强制 qiángzhì v coerce, force

墙 qiáng TRAD 牆 N wall (道 dào) ■ 墙上有一张世界地图。Qiáng shang yǒu yì zhāng shìjiè dìtú. *There's a map of the world on the wall.*

墙壁 qiángbì N wall

强 qiǎng v make an effort

强迫 qiǎngpò v force, coerce ■ 你能把马领到水边，但是不能强迫马喝水。Nǐ néng bǎ mǎ lǐng dào shuǐbian, dànshì bùnéng qiǎngpò mǎ hēshuǐ. *You can lead a horse to the water, but you can't force it to drink.*

抢 qiǎng TRAD 搶 v 1 seize, grab 2 rob, loot

抢劫 qiǎngjié v rob
抢劫银行 qiǎngjié yínháng rob a bank
抢救 qiǎngjiù v rescue, salvage
抢救病人 qiǎngjiù bìngrén rescue a patient, give emergency treatment to a patient

悄 qiāo ADJ quiet

悄悄 qiāoqiāo ADV quietly, on the quiet ■ 他悄悄对我说："别在这里买，太贵了。" Tā qiāoqiāo de duì wǒ shuō: "Bié zài zhèli mǎi, tài guì le." *He whispered to me, "Don't buy it here, it's too expensive."*

敲 qiāo v knock, rap ■ 有人敲门。Yǒu rén qiāo mén. *Someone is knocking at the door.*

锹 qiāo TRAD 鍬 N spade

铁锹 tiěqiāo spade (把 bǎ)

桥 qiáo TRAD 橋 N bridge (座 zuò) ■ 长江上有很多大桥。Chángjiāng shang yǒu hěn duō dà qiáo. *There are many big bridges across the Yangtze River.*
过桥 guò qiáo cross a bridge
桥梁 qiáoliáng N big bridge (座 zuò)

乔 qiáo TRAD 喬 disguise

乔装 qiáozhuāng v disguise
乔装成一个海盗 qiáozhuāng chéng yí ge hǎidào disguise oneself as a pirate

侨 qiáo TRAD 僑 v sojourn, live abroad

侨胞 qiáobāo N countrymen residing overseas

瞧 qiáo v Same as 看 kàn v 1. Used only as a colloquialism.

巧 qiǎo I ADV coincidentally ■ 真巧，我正要找他，他来了。Zhēn qiǎo, wǒ zhèngyào zhǎo tā, tā láile. *What a happy coincidence; he came just when I wanted to see him.* **II** ADJ skilled, clever ■ 他们的儿子手巧，女儿嘴巧。Tāmen de érzi shǒu qiǎo, nǚ'ér zuǐ qiǎo. *Their son is clever with his hands and their daughter has the gift of the gab.*

巧妙 qiǎomiào ADJ ingenious, very clever

翘 qiào TRAD 翹 v stick up, bend upward

俏 qiào ADJ pretty and cute

切 **qiē** v cut, slice ■ 爸爸把西瓜切成四块。 Bàba bǎ xīguā qiē chéng sì kuài. *Dad cut the watermelon into four pieces.*

茄 **qié** N eggplant

茄子 **qiézi** eggplant (只 zhī)

且 **qiě** CONJ moreover (See 而且 érqiě.)

怯 **qiè** ADJ timid (See 胆怯 dǎnqiè.)

切 **qiè** v be close to, tally with

切实 **qièshí** ADJ 1 feasible, practical 2 earnest 切实可行的办法 **qièshí kěxíng de bànfǎ** practical measure

窃 **qiè** TRAD 竊 v steal, pilfer

窃取 **qièqǔ** v steal, grab
窃听 **qiètīng** v eavesdrop, bug
窃听器 **qiètīngqì** listening-in device, bug

钦 **qīn** v admire

钦佩 **qīnpèi** v admire, esteem
令人钦佩 **lìngrén qīnpèi** admirable

亲 **qīn** TRAD 親 I N blood relation II ADJ close, intimate

亲爱 **qīn'ài** ADJ dear, beloved, darling ■ 我亲爱的祖母去年去世了，我难受了好久。Wǒ qīn'ài de zǔmǔ qùnián qùshì le, wǒ nánshòule hǎojiǔ. *My dear grandmother died last year; I was sad for a long time.*

NOTE: Although 亲爱 qīn'ài is glossed as *dear*, the Chinese reserve 亲爱(的) qīn'ài (de) for the very few people who are really dear and close to their hearts.

亲笔 **qīnbǐ** ADV (written) in one's own handwriting
亲密 **qīnmì** ADJ intimate, close
亲戚 **qīnqi** N relative, relation
亲戚朋友 **qīnqi péngyou** relatives and friends
走亲戚 **zǒu qīnqi** visit a relative
亲切 **qīnqiè** ADJ cordial
亲热 **qīnrè** ADJ affectionate, warm-hearted
亲人 **qīnrén** N family member ■ 我在故乡已经没有亲人了。Wǒ zài gùxiāng yǐjīng méiyǒu qīnrén le. *I haven't got any family member in my hometown.*
亲身 **qīnshēn** ADJ personal, firsthand
亲身经历 **qīnshēn jīnglì** personal experience
亲生 **qīnshēng** ADJ one's biological (parents or children)
她的亲生父亲 **tāde qīnshēng fùqin** her biological father

亲手 **qīnshǒu** ADV with one's own hands, by oneself, personally
亲眼 **qīnyǎn** ADV with one's own eyes
亲友 **qīnyǒu** N relatives and friends
走亲访友 **zǒu qīn fǎng yǒu** visit relatives and friends
亲自 **qīnzì** ADV by oneself, personally ■ 李校长亲自来征求对教学的意见。Lǐ xiàozhǎng qīnzì lái zhēngqiú duì jiàoxué de yìjiàn. *Mr Li, the principal, came himself to ask for our comments on teaching.*

侵 **qīn** v invade, intrude, encroach

侵略 **qīnlüè** v invade (by force) ■ 侵略别国在国际上是不允许的。Qīnlüè bié guó zài guójì shang shì bù yǔnxǔ de. *Invading another country is not permitted internationally.*
侵入 **qīnrù** v intrude into, make incursions into
侵蚀 **qīnshí** v corrode, erode
侵占 **qīnzhàn** v invade and occupy

琴 **qín** N (stringed) musical instrument

钢琴 **gāngqín** piano (架 jià)
提琴 **tíqín** violin (把 bǎ)

勤 **qín** ADJ diligent, hard-working

勤奋 **qínfèn** ADJ diligent, applying oneself to
勤俭 **qínjiǎn** ADJ diligent and frugal ■ 勤俭致富。Qínjiǎn zhìfù. *Industry and frugality leads to wealth.*
勤恳 **qínkěn** ADJ diligent and conscientious
勤劳 **qínláo** ADJ hard-working, industrious

芹 **qín** celery

芹菜 **qíncài** celery

禽 **qín** N bird, fowl

青 **qīng** ADJ green ■ 在新西兰草地一年到头都是青青的。Zài Xīnxīlán cǎodì yì-nián-dào-tóu dōu shì qīngqīng de. *In New Zealand the grass is green all year round.*

青菜 **qīngcài** N Chinese cabbage (棵 kē)
青春 **qīngchūn** N the quality of being young, youth
青春期 **qīngchūnqī** puberty
永葆青春 **yǒngbǎo qīngchūn** have eternal youth
青年 **qīngnián** N young person, young people, youth (especially male) (位 wèi, 个 gè)
青蛙 **qīngwā** N frog (只 zhī)

清 **qīng** I ADJ 1 clear (water), clean ■ 过去这条河的水很清，能看到河底的小石头。Guòqù zhè tiáo hé de shuǐ hěn qīng, néng kàndào hédǐ de xiǎo shítou. *In the past this river had very clear water and you could see the little stones on the riverbed.* **2** (of matters) clear, easy to understand ■ 这件事没有人能说得清。Zhè jiàn shì méiyǒu rén néng shuō de qīng. *Nobody can give a clear account of this matter.* **II** v make clear

清查 qīngchá v check thoroughly

清晨 qīngchén n early morning

清除 qīngchú v remove, clear away
清除垃圾邮件 qīngchú lājī yóujiàn delete junk mail

清楚 qīngchu ADJ clear (of speech or image)
■ 我说得清清楚楚，你怎么会误会呢? Wǒ shuōde qīng-qīng-chǔ-chǔ, nǐ zěnme huì wùhuì ne? *I said it very clearly. How could you misunderstand it?*

清洁 qīngjié v clean, clear up
清洁工 qīngjiégōng cleaner

清理 qīnglǐ v sort out, clear out
清理办公桌 qīnglǐ bàngōngzhuō clear out a desk

清晰 qīngxī ADJ very clear, distinct

清新 qīngxīn ADJ pure and fresh, refreshing
清新的空气 qīngxīn de kōngqì fresh air

清醒 qīngxǐng ADJ clear-headed, sober

轻 qīng TRAD 輕 ADJ **1** light (of weight) ■ 油比水轻。Yóu bǐ shuǐ qīng. *Oil is lighter than water.* **2** low, soft (of voice) **3** of a low degree ■ 对他的处分太轻了。Duì tā de chǔfèn tài qīng le. *The disciplinary action against him was not severe enough.*

轻便 qīngbiàn ADJ lightweight and handy, portable

轻工业 qīnggōngyè n light industry

轻快 qīngkuài ADJ **1** light-hearted, lively **2** light-footed, brisk

轻视 qīngshì v think ... unimportant, underestimate, belittle

轻松 qīngsōng ADJ (of a job) easy, not requiring much effort, relaxed ■ 这个工作很轻松，当然工资不高。Zhège gōngzuò hěn qīngsōng, dāngrán gōngzī bù gāo. *This job is easy and requires no real effort; of course it is poorly paid.*

轻微 qīngwēi ADJ slight, trifling
只有轻微的损失 zhǐyǒu qīngwēi de sǔnshī only slightly damaged

轻易 qīngyì ADV **1** easily, demanding little effort **2** without much consideration, rashly
轻易下结论 qīngyì xià jiélùn reach a hasty conclusion

轻音乐 qīng yīnyuè n light music

氢 qīng n hydrogen (H)

氢气 qīngqì hydrogen

倾 qīng v incline, lean

倾听 qīngtīng v listen attentively

倾向 qīngxiàng n tendency, inclination

倾销 qīngxiāo v dump (goods)
反倾销法 fǎn qīngxiāo fǎ anti-dumping regulation

倾斜 qīngxié v tilt, incline

蜻 qīng as in 蜻蜓 qīngtíng

蜻蜓 qīngtíng n dragonfly (只 zhī)

情 qíng n **1** circumstance **2** feeling, sentiment

情报 qíngbào n intelligence, information

情感 qínggǎn n emotion, feeling

情节 qíngjié n plot (of a story, movie, etc.)

情景 qíngjǐng n scene, occasion ■ 旅馆大楼在半夜着火了，人们从楼上跳下，真是可怕的情景。Lǚguǎn dàlóu zài bànyè zháohuǒ le, rénmen cóng lóushang tiàoxia, zhēn shì kěpà de qíngjǐng. *When the hotel caught fire at midnight, people jumped from the upper floors. It was indeed a frightening scene.*

情况 qíngkuàng n situation, circumstance ■ 他生病住院了，情况很严重。Tā shēng bìng zhùyuàn le, qíngkuàng hěn yánzhòng. *He's been hospitalized. His condition is very serious.*

情理 qínglǐ n accepted code of conduct, reason
不近情理 bù jìn qínglǐ violate the accepted code of conduct, unreasonable

情形 qíngxíng n circumstances, situation ■ 两列火车马上要相撞，情形十分紧张。Liǎng liè huǒchē mǎshàng yào xiāngzhuàng, qíngxíng shífēn jǐnzhāng. *The two trains were about to collide. It was an extremely nerve-racking situation.*

情绪 qíngxù n mood, feelings

情愿 qíngyuàn v would rather, prefer ■ 我情愿多花些钱，也要买到称心的东西。Wǒ qíngyuàn duō huā xiē qián, yě yào mǎidào chènxīn de dōngxi. *I'd rather spend more money in order to get things that satisfy me.*

NOTE: 情愿 qíngyuàn is usually used together with 也 yě, as shown in the example sentence. 也 yě may be replaced by 都 dōu, e.g. ■ 我情愿多花些钱，都要买到称心的东西。Wǒ qíngyuàn duō huā xiē qián, dōu yāomǎi dào chènxīn de dōngxi. *I'd rather spend more money in order to get things that satisfy me.*

晴 qíng ADJ (of weather) fine, clear ■ 今天上午晴，中午以后开始下雨了。Jīntiān shàngwǔ qíng, zhōngwǔ yǐhòu kāishǐ xià yǔ le. *It was fine this morning. It began raining in the afternoon.*

晴朗 **qínglǎng** ADJ fine, sunny
晴天 **qíngtiān** N fine day

请 **qǐng** TRAD 請 V **1** invite ■ 今天晚上我请你吃饭。 *Jīntiān wǎnshang wǒ qǐng nǐ chīfàn. I'll invite you to dinner tonight.* **2** ask, request

NOTE: 请 qǐng is used to start a polite request, equivalent to *Please ...*, e.g. ■ 请您别在这里吸烟。 Qǐng nín bié zài zhèli xīyān. *Please don't smoke here.* ■ 请坐! Qǐng zuò! *Sit down, please!*

请假 **qǐngjià** V ask for leave
请病假 **qǐng bìngjià** ask for sick leave
请事假 **qǐng shìjià** ask for leave of absence
请柬 **qǐngjiǎn** N letter of invitation, invitation card (份 fèn)
请教 **qǐngjiào** V ask for advice, consult

NOTE: 请教 qǐngjiào is a polite word, used when you want to ask for advice or information, e.g. ■ 请教，这个汉字是什么意思? Qǐngjiào, zhège Hànzì shì shénme yìsi? *Would you please tell me the meaning of this Chinese character?*

请客 **qǐngkè** V **1** invite to dinner ■ 张先生这个星期六在家里请客。 *Zhāng xiānsheng zhège Xīngqīliù zài jiāli qǐngkè. This Saturday Mr Zhang will give a dinner party at home.* **2** treat (someone to something) ■ 这次出去玩、车票、门票都是我请客。 *Zhè cì chūqu wán, chēpiào, ménpiào duō shì wǒ qǐngkè. On this date, I'll pay for bus fares and admission tickets.*
请客送礼 **qǐngkè sònglǐ** invite to dinner and give gift to, bribe by gifts and dinner parties
请求 **qǐngqiú** I V request, ask for ■ 我请求你原谅我的错误。 *Wǒ qǐngqiú nǐ yuánliàng wǒ de cuòwù. I ask for your forgiveness of my mistake.* II N request ■ 你们的请求已交委员会考虑。 *Nǐmen de qǐngqiú yǐ jiāo wěiyuánhuì kǎolù. Your request has been submitted to the committee for consideration.*
请示 **qǐngshì** V ask (a person of superior position) for instruction
请帖 **qǐngtiě** N letter of invitation, invitation card (份 fèn)
请问… **qǐng wèn...** Excuse me, ...

NOTE: When you want some information from someone, start your query with 请问… qǐng wèn..., e.g. ■ 请问, 去火车站怎么走? Qǐng wèn, qù huǒchēzhàn zěnme zǒu? *Excuse me, could you show me the way to the railway station?*

顷 **qǐng** TRAD 頃 N a unit of area (= 6.6667 hectares)

庆 **qìng** TRAD 慶 V celebrate

庆贺 **qìnghè** V congratulate, celebrate

庆祝 **qìngzhù** V celebrate ■ 下个月他们的女儿大学毕业。他们打算好好庆祝一下。 *Xià ge yuè tāmen de nǚ'ér dàxué bìyè, tāmen dǎsuàn hǎohǎo qìngzhù yíxià. Their daughter will graduate from university next month. They plan to celebrate lavishly.*

穷 **qióng** TRAD 窮 ADJ poor, poverty-stricken ■ 国家再穷也应该花足够的钱办教育。 *Guójiā zài qióng yě yīnggāi huā zúgòu de qián bàn jiàoyù. No matter how poor a country is, sufficient funds should be spent on education.*
穷苦 **qióngkǔ** ADJ poor, poverty-stricken
穷人 **qióngrén** poor person, the poor

秋 **qiū** N fall, autumn ■ 北京香山的秋景很美。 *Běijīng Xiāngshān de qiū jǐng hěn měi. The autumn scenery on Fragrance Hill in Beijing is very beautiful.*
秋收 **qiūshōu** N autumn harvest
秋天 **qiūtiān** N fall, autumn

丘 **qiū** N mound, low and small hill

丘陵 **qiūlíng** N hills, hilly land

求 **qiú** V beseech, beg, humbly ask for ■ 我求你再考虑考虑。 *Wǒ qiú nǐ zài kǎolù kǎolù. I beg you to give it further consideration.*
求婚 **qiúhūn** V propose marriage, make a marriage offer

球 **qiú** N **1** ball (只 zhī) **2** ball game (场 chǎng)
比球 **bǐ qiú** have a (ball game) match
棒球 **bàngqiú** baseball
打球 **dǎ qiú** play basketball or volleyball
看球 **kàn qiú** watch a ball game
篮球 **lánqiú** basketball
排球 **páiqiú** volleyball
踢球 **tī qiú** play soccer
足球 **zúqiú** soccer
球场 **qiúchǎng** N sports ground (especially where ball games are played)
球队 **qiúduì** N (ball game) team
球迷 **qiúmí** N (ball game) fan
足球迷 **zúqiúmí** soccer fan
球员 **qiúyuán** (ball game) player

曲 **qū** ADJ crooked, bent
曲线 **qūxiàn** N curve
曲线图 **qūxiàntú** line graph, graph
曲折 **qūzhé** ADJ tortuous, winding

区 **qū** TRAD 區 N district ■ 中国的城市一般分成几个区。 *Zhōngguó de chéngshì yìbān fēnchéng jǐ ge qū. A city in China is usually divided into several districts.*

区别 qūbié

商业区 **shāngyèqū** commercial area, business district

工业区 **gōngyèqū** industrial zone, industrial district

区别 **qūbié** I v set apart, differentiate ■ 你能区别美国英语和英国英语吗? Nǐ néng qūbié Měiguó Yīngyǔ hé Yīngguó Yīngyǔ ma? *Can you tell American English from British English?* II N difference

区分 **qūfēn** I v put in different categories, differentiate II N differentiation

区域 **qūyù** N region, area

驱 **qū** TRAD 驅 v drive

驱车前往 **qūchē qiánwǎng** drive (in a car) to

驱逐 **qūzhú** v drive out, banish

驱逐出境 **qūzhú chūjìng** deport, deportation

驱逐舰 **qūzhújiàn** N destroyer

趋 **qū** TRAD 趨 v tend (to become)

趋势 **qūshì** N tendency
令人担忧的趋势 **lìngrén dānyōu de qūshì** a worrying tendency

趋向 **qūxiàng** v tend to, incline to

屈 **qū** v bend, bow

屈服 **qūfú** v yield (to), knuckle under

渠 **qú** N 1 ditch, canal 2 medium, channel

灌溉渠 **guàngàiqú** irrigation channel

渠道 **qúdào** N 1 irrigation ditch 2 medium of communication, channel

曲 **qǔ** N melody, tune

曲调 **qǔdiào** N tune, melody

曲子 **qǔzi** N song, melody
熟悉的曲子 **shúxī de qǔzi** familiar tune

取 **qǔ** v fetch, collect ■ 我要找一个自动取款机取点钱。 Wǒ yào zhǎo yí ge zìdòng qǔkuǎnjī qǔ diǎn qián. *I'm looking for an ATM to withdraw some money.*

取款 **qǔkuǎn** withdraw money

取代 **qǔdài** v replace, substitute for

取得 **qǔdé** v obtain, achieve ■ 我们去年取得很大成绩。 Wǒmen qùnián qǔdé hěn dà chéngjì. *We made great achievements last year.*

取消 **qǔxiāo** v cancel, call off ■ 明天的会议已经取消了。 Míngtiān de huìyì yǐjīng qǔxiāo le. *The meeting for tomorrow has been called off.*

娶 **qǔ** v (of a man) marry

娶媳妇 **qǔ xífù** (of a man) marry, take a wife

NOTE: See note on 嫁 jià.

去 **qù** v leave for, go to ■ 你什么时候去中国? Nǐ shénme shíhou qù Zhōngguó? *When are you going to China?*

NOTE: 到 dào and 到…去 dào...qù have the same meaning and are normally interchangeable.

去年 **qùnián** N last year

去世 **qùshì** v die, pass away

NOTE: 去世 qùshì must be used when you want to show respect and/or love to the deceased. For instance, the normal word for *die*, 死 sǐ, would be totally inappropriate in the example sentence.

趣 **qù** N interest

趣味 **qùwèi** N 1 interest, delight 2 taste, preference

低级趣味 **dījí qùwèi** vulgar taste

圈 **quān** N circle, ring ■ 运动会的旗子上有五个圈。 Yùndònghuì de qízi shang yǒu wǔ ge quān. *There are five circles on the flag of the Games.*

圈套 **quāntào** N snare, trap

设下圈套 **shèxià quāntào** set a trap, lay a snare

落入圈套 **luòrù quāntào** be caught in a trap, be snared

圈子 **quānzi** N circle, ring

权 **quán** TRAD 權 N 1 authority, power 2 right, privilege

权利 **quánlì** N right ■ 你要享受权利, 就要尽一定的义务。 Nǐ yào xiǎngshòu quánlì, jiùyào jìn yídìng de yìwù. *If you want to enjoy rights, you will have to fulfil certain obligations.*

权力 **quánlì** N authority, power ■ 校长有权力解雇教师吗? Xiàozhǎng yǒu quánlì jiěgù jiàoshī ma? *Does a principal have the authority to dismiss a teacher?*

权威 **quánwēi** N authority, authoritativeness
国际法权威 **guójìfǎ quánwēi** an authority in international law

权限 **quánxiàn** N limits of one's authority, extent of one's authority
超出他的权限 **chāochū tā de quánxiàn** exceed the limit of his authority

权益 **quányì** N rights, rights and interests

全 **quán** ADJ whole, complete ■ 他说的不全是真话。 Tā shuō de bù quán shì zhēnhuà. *He did not tell the whole truth.*

全国 **quánguó** the whole country

全世界 **quánshìjiè** the entire world

全部 **quánbù** N all, without exception ■ 我爸爸全部的时间都放在工作上。 Wǒ bàba quánbù de shíjiān dōu fàng zài gōngzuò shang. *My father devotes all his time to work.*

全都 **quándōu** ADV all, without exception

全会 **quánhuì** N plenary session, plenary meeting ■ 中共中央十六届二中全会 Zhōnggòng Zhōngyāng shíliù jiè èr-zhōng quánhuì the second plenary meeting of the 16th Central Committee of the Chinese Communist Party

全集 **quánjí** N completed works (of an author)

全局 **quánjú** N overall situation

全力 **quánlì** ADV with all of one's strength, making every effort
全力以赴 **quánlì yǐfù** spare no efforts, go all out

全面 **quánmiàn** ADJ all-round, comprehesive ■ 对这个问题，我们要做全面的考虑。Duì zhège wèntí, wǒmen yào zuò quánmiàn de kǎolǜ. *We will give thorough consideration to this issue.*

全民 **quánmín** N the entire people (of a country)

全体 **quántǐ** N all, each and every one (of a group of people) ■ 她代表全体学生向老师表示感谢。Tā dàibiǎo quántǐ xuésheng xiàng lǎoshī biǎoshì gǎnxiè. *On behalf of all the students she expressed gratitude to the teacher.*

全心全意 **quánxīn quányì** IDIOM wholeheartedly

拳 **quán** N fist

拳头 **quántou** N fist

泉 **quán** N spring (a small brook)

矿泉 **kuàngquán** mineral water
温泉 **wēnquán** hot spring

犬 **quǎn** N dog

警犬 **jǐngquǎn** police dog

劝 **quàn** TRAD 勸 v 1 try to talk … into (or out of) doing something, advise 2 encourage ■ 他劝我不要把钱都存在那家银行。Tā quàn wǒ bú yào bǎ qián dōu cún zài nà jiā yínháng. *He adviced me not to put all my money in that bank.*

劝告 **quàngào** I v exhort, advise ■ 医生劝告他不要吸烟了。Yīshēng quàngào tā búyào xīyān le. *His doctor advised him to give up smoking.* II N advice

劝说 **quànshuō** v persuade, advise

劝阻 **quànzǔ** v dissuade from, advise … not to 劝阻无效 **quànzǔ wúxiào** try in vain to dissuade someone from doing something

券 **quàn** N ticket, certificate

入场券 **rùchǎngquàn** admission ticket

缺 **quē** v 1 lack, be short of ■ 要买笔记本电脑，我还缺三百块钱。Yào mǎi bǐjìběn diànnǎo, wǒ hái quē sānbǎi kuài qián. *I'm short of 300 yuan for the purchase of a notebook computer.*
缺人手 **quē rénshǒu** shorthanded
2 be incomplete, be absent

缺点 **quēdiǎn** N shortcoming, defect

缺乏 **quēfá** v be deficient in, lack ■ 人们往往缺乏道德勇气。Rénmen wǎngwǎng quēfá dàodé yǒngqì. *People often lack moral courage.*

缺口 **quēkǒu** N breach, indenture

缺少 **quēshǎo** v be short of, lack ■ 我们缺少一名球员，你愿意参加比赛吗? Wǒmen quēshǎo yì míng qiúyuán, nǐ yuànyì cānjiā bǐsài ma? *We're still short of one player. Are you willing to participate in the game?*

NOTE: 缺乏 quēfá and 缺少 quēshǎo are synonyms, but 缺乏 quēfá has abstract nouns as objects, while 缺少 quēshǎo takes as objects nouns denoting concrete persons or things.

缺席 **quēxí** v be absent from (a meeting, a class, etc.)

缺陷 **quēxiàn** N defect, shortcoming

瘸 **qué** v be lame

瘸子 **quézi** lame person, cripple

却 **què** TRAD 卻 ADV unexpectedly, contrary to what may be normally expected, but, yet ■ 他很有钱，却并不幸福。Tā hěn yǒuqián, què bìng bú xìngfú. *He is rich, but he is not happy.*

鹊 **què** TRAD 鵲 N magpie

喜鹊 **xǐquè** magpie (只 zhī)

榷 **què** v discuss

商榷 **shāngquè** discuss

雀 **què** N finch

麻雀 **máquè** sparrow (只 zhī)

确 **què** TRAD 確 I ADJ true, authentic II ADV firmly

确保 **quèbǎo** v ensure, guarantee

确定 **quèdìng** v confirm, fix, determine ■ 他出国的日期已经确定。Tā chūguó de rìqí yǐjīng quèdìng. *His date of departure overseas has been fixed.*

确立 **quèlì** v establish

确切 **quèqiè** ADJ precise, specific

确认 **quèrèn** v affirm, confirm

确实 **quèshí** ADJ verified to be true, indeed ■ 这个消息不确实。Zhège xiāoxi bú quèshí. *This news is not true.*

确信 quèxìn v firmly believe, be convinced

确凿 quèzáo ADJ conclusive, irrefutable

裙 qún N skirt

裙子 qúnzi N skirt (条 tiáo)

群 qún M. WD a crowd of, a group of (for people or animals)
一群狗 yì qún gǒu a pack of dogs
一群鸟 yì qún niǎo a flock of birds
一群牛 yì qún niú a herd of cattle
一群小学生 yì qún xiǎoxuésheng a group of primary schoolchildren

群岛 qúndǎo N archipelago

群体 qúntǐ N (social) group
弱势群体 ruòshì qúntǐ weak social group

群众 qúnzhòng N the masses (people), the general public ■ 在群众的帮助下，警察很快抓到了强盗。Zài qúnzhòng de bāngzhù xià, jǐngchá hěn kuài zhuādàole qiángdào. *With the help of the general public, the police soon caught the robber.*

R

然 rán CONJ however

然而 rán'ér CONJ Same as 但是 dànshì. Usually used in written Chinese.

然后 ránhòu IDIOM CONJ afterwards, ... and then
先…然后… xiān...ránhòu... first ... and then... ■ 他每天早上先跑步，然后吃早饭。Tā měitiān zǎoshang xiān pǎobù, ránhòu chī zǎofàn. *Every morning he first jogs and then has breakfast.*

燃 rán v burn

燃料 ránliào N fuel

燃烧 ránshāo v burn ■ 森林大火燃烧了三天三夜。Sēnlín dàhuǒ ránshāole sān tiān sān yè. *The forest fire raged three days and nights.*

染 rǎn v dye ■ 有些年轻人喜欢染头发。Yǒuxiē niánqīngrén xǐhuan rǎn tóufa. *Some young people like to dye their hair.*

染料 rǎnliào N dyestuff

壤 rǎng N soil (See 土壤 tǔrǎng)

嚷 rǎng v yell, shout ■ 别嚷了，有话好好说。Bié rǎng le, yǒu huà hǎohǎo shuō. *Stop yelling. Speak nicely if you have something to say.*

让 ràng TRAD 讓 v 1 let, give way ■ 你应该让那辆车先行。Nǐ yīnggāi ràng nà liàng chē xiānxíng. *You should let that vehicle go first.* (→ *You should give way to that vehicle*) 2 allow, make ■ 他的话让我明白了许多道理。Tā de huà ràng wǒ míngbaile xǔduō dàolǐ. *What he said made me understand many things.* (→ *What he said enlightened me.*)

饶 ráo TRAD 饒 v have mercy on, forgive

扰 rǎo TRAD 擾 v harass (See 打扰 dǎrǎo.)

绕 rào TRAD 繞 v make a detour, bypass ■ 前面施工，车辆绕道。Qiánmiàn shīgōng, chēliàng rào dào. *Road works ahead. Vehicles must detour.*

惹 rě v cause (something undesirable), invite (trouble etc.) ■ 别惹麻烦了。Bié rě máfan le. *Don't ask for trouble.*

热 rè TRAD 熱 ADJ 1 hot ■ 香港的夏天很热。Xiānggǎng de xiàtiān hěn rè. *Summer in Hong Kong is very hot.* 2 ardent, passionate

热爱 rè'ài v ardently love, be in deep love with ■ 我热爱我的祖国。Wǒ rè'ài wǒ de zǔguó. *I love my motherland.*

热潮 rècháo N upsurge, craze

热带 rèdài N the tropics, the tropical zone

热量 rèliàng N quantity of heat

热烈 rèliè ADJ warm, ardent ■ 热烈欢迎新同学。Rèliè huānyíng xīn tóngxué! *A warm welcome to the new students!*

热闹 rènao ADJ noisy and exciting in a pleasant way, boisterous, bustling, lively (of a scene or occasion) ■ 中国人过年非常热闹。Zhōngguórén guònián fēicháng rènao. *When the Chinese celebrate their New Year's Day, it is a noisy and exciting occasion.*

热情 rèqíng ADJ enthusiastic, warmhearted ■ 她对人很热情。Tā duì rén hěn rèqíng. *She's warmhearted towards others.* ■ 他常常热情地帮助朋友。Tā chángcháng rèqíng de bāngzhù péngyou. *He often helps his friends enthusiastically.*

热水瓶 rèshuǐpíng N thermos, thermos flask

热心 rèxīn ADJ warmhearted, enthusiastic
对… 热心 duì...rèxīn be warmhearted towards, be enthusiastic about ■ 他对朋友很热心。Tā duì péngyou hěn rèxīn. *He is warmhearted towards friends.*

人 rén N human being, person ■ 人和动物有什么区别？Rén hé dòngwù yǒu shénme qūbié? *What are the differences between humans and animals?*

人才 réncái N talented person, person of ability ■ 我们公司需要电脑人才。Wǒmen gōngsī xūyào diànnǎo réncái. *Our company needs people with computer skills.*

人才市场 **réncái shìchǎng** personnel market, job fair

人才外流 **réncái wàiliú** brain drain

人道主义 **réndàozhǔyì** N humanitarianism

人道主义援助 **réndàozhǔyì yuánzhù** humanitarian aid

人格 **réngé** N personality, moral quality

以我的人格担保 **yǐ wǒ de réngé dānbǎo** give (you) my personal guarantee

人工 **réngōng** I ADJ artificial, man-made

人工智能 **réngōng zhìnéng** artificial intelligence

II N manpower, man-day

人家 **rénjia** PRON 1 other people ■ 人家能做到的, 我也能做到。 Rénjia néng zuòdao de, wǒ yě néng zuòdao. *What others can achieve, I can too.* 2 he, she, they (used to refer to another person or other people) 3 I, me (used to refer to oneself, used only among intimate friends or family members)

人间 **rénjiān** N the earth, the human world

人间天堂 **rénjiān tiāntáng** paradise on earth

人均 **rénjūn** N average, per capita

人口 **rénkǒu** N population (human) ■ 很多发展中国家都在控制人口增长。 Hěn duō fāzhǎnzhōng guójiā dōu zài kòngzhì rénkǒu zēngzhǎng. *Many developing countries are controlling population increase.*

NOTE: It is interesting that the Chinese word for *population* is made up of 人 rén (human) and 口 kǒu (the mouth). It suggests that feeding people (mouths) has been the primary concern in China.

人类 **rénlèi** N humankind, mankind ■ 人类应该保护自然环境。 Rénlèi yīnggāi bǎohù zìrán huánjìng. *Mankind should protect the natural environment.*

人类学 **rénlèixué** N anthropology

人力 **rénlì** N manpower

人力资源 **rénlì zīyuán** human resource

人们 **rénmen** N people, the public ■ 春节那儿天, 人们都比较客气, 避免争吵。 Chūnjié nà jǐ tiān, rénmen dōu bǐjiào kèqi, bìmiǎn zhēngchǎo. *During the Chinese New Year, people are polite to each other so as to avoid quarrels.*

人民 **rénmín** N the people (of a state) ■ 政府应该为人民服务。 Zhèngfǔ yīnggāi wèi rénmín fúwù. *The government should serve the people.*

人民币 **Rénmínbì** N the Chinese currency, Renminbi (RMB)

人情 **rénqíng** N 1 common sense, reason 不近人情 **bú jìn rénqíng** unreasonable (in dealing with interpersonal matters)

2 human feelings

讲人情 **jiǎng rénqíng** resort to feeings (instead of regulations, law, etc.)

3 gift, favor

送人情 **sòng rénqíng** give a gift (in order to gain favors)

人权 **rénquán** N human rights

人蛇 **rénshé** N illegal (especially smuggled) immigrant

人参 **rénshēn** N ginseng

人生 **rénshēng** N (one's entire) life ■ 人生苦短。 Rénshēng kǔ duǎn. *It's sad that life is so short.*

人事 **rénshì** N human resources matters

人事部门 **rénshì bùmén** human resources department, personnel department

人寿 **rénshòu** N human lifespan

人寿保险 **rénshòu bǎoxiǎn** life insurance

人体 **réntǐ** N human body

人体解剖学 **réntǐ jiěpōuxué** human anatomy, anatomy

人为 **rénwéi** ADJ man-made, artificial

人物 **rénwù** N well-known and important person, figure, personage (位 wèi) ■ 这位大学校长是世界著名人物。 Zhè wèi dàxué xiàozhǎng shì shìjiè zhùmíng rénwù. *This university president is a famous figure in the world.*

人心 **rénxīn** N popular feelings, the will of the people

人性 **rénxìng** N human nature

人员 **rényuán** N personnel, staff ■ 我校有教学人员五十六名, 其他人员十八名。 Wǒ xiào yǒu jiàoxué rényuán wǔshí liù míng, qítā rényuán shíbā míng. *This school has a teaching staff of 56 people and 18 other staff members.*

人造 **rénzào** ADJ man-made, artificial ■ 第一颗人造卫星是哪一年上天的? Dì-yī kē rénzào wèixīng shì nǎ yì nián shàngtiān de? *In which year was the first man-made satellite launched?*

人质 **rénzhì** N hostage

扣留人质 **kòuliú rénzhì** hold a hostage

仁 **rén** I N benevolence, humanity II ADJ benevolent, humane

仁慈 **réncí** ADJ benevolent, merciful

忍 **rěn** V endure, tolerate, put up with ■ 你刚来, 有的地方不习惯, 还得忍一点。 Nǐ gāng lái, yǒude dìfang bù xíguàn, hái děi rěn yìdiǎn. *You're new here, so there may be things you're not used to and will have to put up with for a while.*

忍耐 **rěnnài** V bear, put up with, exercise patience ■ 没有办法, 只能忍耐。 Méiyǒu bànfǎ, zhǐ néng rěnnài. *There's nothing we can do, we can only put up with it.*

忍受 **rěnshòu** v tolerate, stand

忍心 **rěnxīn** v have the heart to (do), be hard-hearted

NOTE: 忍心 rěnxīn is usually used in its negative form of 不忍心 bùrěn xīn, which means *not have the heart to (do)*, e.g. ■ 我不忍心把这个可怕的消息告诉她。*Wǒ bù rěnxīn bǎ zhè ge kěpà de xiāoxi gàosu tā. I don't have the heart to tell her this terrible news.*

忍住 **rěnzhù** v endure, bear

忍不住 **rěnbuzhù** unable to bear, cannot help ■ 她在电话里听到妈妈的声音，忍不住哭起来。*Tā zài diànhuà li tīngdao māma de shēngyīn, rěnbuzhù kū qǐlai. Hearing mom's voice on the phone, she couldn't help crying.*

忍得住 **rěndezhù** can endure, can bear

韧 **rèn** TRAD 韌 ADJ strong and pliable, tenacious

认 **rèn** TRAD 認 v 1 recognize ■ 两年不见，我几乎认不出你了！*Liǎng nián bú jiàn, wǒ jīhū rèn bu chū nǐ le! I haven't seen you for two years, and I can hardly recognize you.* 2 identify ■ 你认一下，这里这么多自行车，哪辆是你的？*Nǐ rèn yíxià, zhèli zhème duō zìxíngchē, nǎ liàng shì nǐ de? Among so many bicycles here, can you identify which one is yours?*

认得 **rènde** v Same as 认识 rènshi

认定 **rèndìng** v be firmly convinced, maintain, decide on

认可 **rènkě** v approve
质量认可书 zhìliàng rènkě shū certificate of quality approval

认识 **rènshi** v know, understand ■ 你认识这个汉字吗？*Nǐ rènshi zhège Hànzì ma? Do you know this Chinese character?*

认为 **rènwéi** v think, consider (normally followed by a clause) ■ 我不这么认为。*Wǒ bú zhème rènwéi. I don't think so.*

认真 **rènzhēn** ADJ earnest, conscientious, serious ■ 他是在开玩笑，你不要太认真。*Tā shì zài kāiwánxiào, nǐ bú yào tài rènzhēn. He's joking. Don't take it too seriously.*

任 **rèn** I CONJ no matter II v 1 appoint, take up 2 give free rein to

任何 **rènhé** PRON any, whatever ■ 在任何情况下，都要遵守法律。*Zài rènhé qíngkuàng xia, dōu yào zūnshǒu fǎlù. One should abide by the law under any circumstances.*

任何人 **rènhé rén** anyone

任何事 **rènhé shì** any matter, anything, everything ■ 他做任何事都挺认真。*Tā zuò rènhé shì dōu tǐng rènzhēn. He does everything conscientiously.*

任命 **rènmìng** v appoint (to a position of importance)
任命他为副总裁 rènmìng tā wéi fùzǒngcái appoint him Vice-CEO

任务 **rènwù** N assignment, mission ■ 这个任务很难，不可能在一个月内完成。*Zhège rènwù hěn nán, bù kěnéng zài yí ge yuè nèi wánchéng. This is a difficult mission which cannot be accomplished in a month.*

任性 **rènxìng** ADJ willful, headstrong

任意 **rènyì** ADV randomly, at random

饪 **rèn** TRAD 飪 v cook (See 烹饪 pēngrèn)

刃 **rèn** N the edge of a knife, blade

扔 **rēng** v throw, toss ■ 不要乱扔垃圾。*Bú yào luàn rēng lājī. Do not discard rubbish. (→ Don't litter.)*

仍 **réng** ADV Same as 仍然 réngrán

仍旧 **réngjiù** ADV Same as 仍然 réngrán

仍然 **réngrán** ADV still, as before ■ 他有这么多钱，仍然不满足。*Tā yǒu zhème duō qián, réngrán bù mǎnzú. He has so much money but he is still not satisfied.*

日 **rì** N date, day

三月二十四日 Sānyuè èrshí sì rì the twenty-fourth of March

九月一日 Jiǔyuè yí rì the first of September

NOTE: In writing, 日 rì is used for dates as shown above. However, in speech it is more common to say 号 hào. For example, to say *the twenty-fourth of March* 三月二十四号 Sānyuè èrshí sì hào is more natural than 三月二十四日 Sānyuè èrshí sì rì.

日报 **rìbào** N daily newspaper, daily

日本 **Rìběn** N Japan ■ 你去过日本吗？*Nǐ qùguo Rìběn ma? Have you ever been to Japan?*

日常 **rìcháng** ADJ daily, routine ■ 他不希望有规律的日常生活被打乱。*Tā bù xīwàng yǒu guīlǜ de rìcháng shēnghuó bèi dǎluàn. He does not want his regular everyday life to be upset.*

日程 **rìchéng** N daily schedule, schedule ■ 今天的日程排得很满。*Jīntiān de rìchéng pái de hěn mǎn. We have a full schedule today.*

议事日程 yìshì rìchéng agenda

日程表 **rìchéngbiǎo** N timetable (for a schedule)

日光 **rìguāng** N sunlight

日记 **rìjì** N diary (本 běn, 篇 piān)

日记本 **rìjìběn** diary

记日记 jì rìjì keep a diary

日期 **rìqī** N date (especially of an event) ■ 请你

查一下这批饼干的过期日期。Qǐng nǐ chá yíxià zhè pī bǐnggān de guòqī rìqī. *Please check the "use by" date of this batch of biscuits.*

日文 **Rìwén** N the Japanese language (especially the writing)

日夜 **rìyè** ADV day and night, round the clock
日夜服务 **rìyè fúwù** round-the-clock service

日益 **rìyì** ADV day by day, increasingly

日用品 **rìyòngpǐn** N daily necessities

日语 **Rìyǔ** N the Japanese language

日元 **Rìyuán** N Japanese currency, yen ■ 十万美元是一大笔钱，十万日元不算一大笔钱。Shíwàn Měiyuán shì yí dà bǐ qián, shí wàn Rìyuán bú suàn yí dà bǐ qián. *While a hundred thousand American dollars is a big sum of money, a hundred thousand Japanese yen is not.*

日子 **rìzi** N **1** day, date ■ 今天是什么日子? 为什么街上那么多人? Jīntiān shì shénme rìzi? Wèishénme jiē shang nàme duō rén? *What day is today? Why are there so many people in the street?* **2** life ■ 我们家的日子比过去好多了。Wǒmen jiā de rìzi bǐ guòqù hǎo duō le. *The life of my family is much better than before. (→ My family is better off now.)* ■ 我只想安安静静地过日子。Wǒ zhǐ xiǎng ān-ān-jìng-jìng de guò rìzi. *I only want to live a quiet and peaceful life.*

融 **róng** V **1** melt, thaw **2** be in harmony, blend, fuse

融化 **rónghuà** V melt, thaw

融洽 **róngqià** ADJ harmonious, very friendly

荣 **róng** TRAD 榮 I ADJ glorious, flourishing II N glory, honor

荣誉 **róngyù** N honor, great credit
荣誉称号 **róngyù chēnghào** title of honor

容 **róng** V **1** tolerate **2** hold, accommodate

容积 **róngjī** N amount of space, volume

容量 **róngliàng** N the amount that something can hold, capacity

容纳 **róngnà** V have a capacity of, hold, contain

容器 **róngqì** N container, vessel

容忍 **róngrěn** V tolerate

容许 **róngxǔ** V permit, allow

容易 **róngyì** ADJ **1** easy, not difficult ■ 这么容易的问题, 你都不会回答? Zhème róngyì de wèntí, nǐ dōu bú huì huídá? *You even can't answer such an easy question?* **2** having a tendency to, likely ■ 刚到一个新地方, 容易生病。Gāngdào yí ge xīn dìfang, róngyì shēngbìng. *You're likely to fall ill when you first arrive in a new land.*

溶 **róng** V dissolve, melt

溶化 **rónghuà** V dissolve

溶解 **róngjiě** V dissolve, melt
溶液 **róngyè** N solution

熔 **róng** V melt, smelt

绒 **róng** TRAD 絨 N fine hair, down

鸭绒被 **yāróngbèi** duckdown quilt

柔 **róu** ADJ soft, gentle

柔和 **róuhé** ADJ soft and mild, gentle
柔和的口气 **róuhé de kǒuqì** a gentle and soothing voice

柔软 **róuruǎn** ADJ soft, lithe

揉 **róu** V rub, knead

揉面 **róumiàn** knead dough

肉 **ròu** N flesh, meat ■ 在我们这儿肉比鱼便宜。Zài wǒmen zhèr ròu bǐ yú piányi. *Pork is cheaper than fish.*

鸡肉 **jīròu** chicken meat
牛肉 **niúròu** beef
羊肉 **yángròu** mutton
鱼肉 **yúròu** fish meat
猪肉 **zhūròu** pork

NOTE: The most popular meat in China is pork. Unspecified, 肉 ròu often refers to *pork*.

如 **rú** I V **1** be like, be similar to **2** according to **3** for example, such as II CONJ Same as 如果 rúguǒ. Used only in writing.

如此 **rúcǐ** PRON so, such as
如此说来 **rúcǐ shuōlái** in that case, then, so

NOTE: See note on 如何 rúhé.

如果 **rúguǒ** CONJ if, in the event that ■ 如果明天下雨, 我们就不去海边游泳。Rúguǒ míngtiān xià yǔ, wǒmen jiù bú qù hǎibian yóuyǒng. *If it rains tomorrow, we won't go to the seaside to swim.*

NOTE: 如果 rúguǒ is usually used with 就 jiù.

如何 **rúhé** PRON how, what ■ 你以为如何? Nǐ yǐwéi rúhé? *What do you think?*

NOTE: 如何 rúhé is one of the few remnants of Classical Chinese still used in Modern Chinese, but it is usually used in writing only. The same is true with 如此 rúcǐ, 如今 rújīn and 如同 rútóng.

如今 **rújīn** PRON today, now

NOTE: See note on 如何 rúhé.

如同 **rútóng** V be like, as

NOTE: See note on 如何 rúhé.

如意 **rúyì** ADJ as one wishes

辱 rǔ

称心如意 chènxīn rúyì to one's heart's content

万事如意 wànshì rúyì best of luck for everything ■ 祝你万事如意! Zhù nǐ wànshì rúyì! *I wish you the best of luck!*

辱 rǔ v insult (See 侮辱 wǔrǔ)

乳 rǔ N 1 breast 2 milk

乳房 rǔfáng N female breast, udder
乳牛 rǔniú N dairy cattle, cow (头 tóu)
乳制品 rǔzhìpǐn N dairy product

入 rù v 1 enter, go in ■ 病从口入。Bìng cóng kǒu rù. *Disease enters the body by the mouth.* (→ *Bad food causes disease.*) 2 join, become a member of

入境 rùjìng v enter a country
入口 rùkǒu N entry, entrance
入侵 rùqīn v invade, make inroads
入手 rùshǒu v start with, proceed
入学 rùxué v start school

软 ruǎn TRAD 軟 ADJ 1 soft, supple 2 weak, feeble

软件 ruǎnjiàn N computer software, software ■ 他除了买这台新电脑以外，还买了一些软件。Tā chúle mǎi zhè tái xīn diànnǎo yǐwài, hái mǎile yìxiē ruǎnjiàn. *In addition to the new computer he also bought some software.*
软盘 ruǎnpán N floppy disk
软驱 ruǎnqū N floppy drive
软弱 ruǎn ruò ADJ weak, feeble ■ 她性格软弱，常常受人欺负。Tā xìnggé ruǎnruò, chángcháng shòu rén qīfu. *She has a weak character, and is often subject to bullying.*

锐 ruì TRAD 銳 ADJ sharp

锐利 ruìlì ADJ sharp, pointed

瑞 ruì ADJ auspicious

瑞雪 ruìxuě N timely snow

润 rùn TRAD 潤 v moisten, enrich (See 利润 lìrùn)

弱 ruò ADJ weak, feeble ■ 他年老体弱，不能在田里干活了。Tā nián-lǎo-tǐ-ruò, bù néng zài tián li gànhuó le. *He is old and feeble, and is unable to work in the fields.*

弱势群体 ruòshì qúntǐ N weak social group, the disadvantaged

若 ruò CONJ if

若干 ruògān NUM a certain number

S

撒 sā v cast, spread out

撒渔网 sā yúwǎng spread out a fishing net
撒谎 sā v Same as 说谎 shuōhuǎng

洒 sǎ TRAD 灑 v sprinkle, spray ■ 这片稻田有害虫，要洒一点儿药。Zhè piàn dàotián yǒu hàichóng, yào sǎ yìdiǎnr yào. *This paddy field is infested. You need to spray some pesticide on it.*

萨 sà TRAD 薩 as in 菩萨 Púsà

腮 sāi N cheek

塞 sāi v plug, stuff

把很多衣服塞进旅行袋 bǎ hěn duō yīfu sāijìn lǚxíngdài stuff lots of clothes in the duffel bag

赛 sài TRAD 賽 v compete (See 比赛 bǐsài, 竞赛 jìngsài.)

三 sān NUM three, 3

十三 shísān thirteen
三十 sānshí thirty

叁 sān NUM three

伞 sǎn TRAD 傘 N umbrella (把 bǎ) ■ 我的伞又丢了。Wǒ de sǎn yòu diū le. *I've lost my umbrella again.*

散 sǎn ADJ loose

散文 sǎnwén N prose, essay (篇 piān)

散 sàn v 1 disperse, scatter 2 disseminate, distribute

散步 sànbù v take a short leisurely walk, stroll ■ 他俩沿着小河散步，直到天快黑了。Tā liǎ yánzhe xiǎo hé sànbù, zhídào tiān kuài hēi le. *The two of them took a walk along the stream till it was almost dark.*
散布 sànbù v disseminate, spread
散布谣言 sànbù yáoyán spread rumors
散发 sànfā v distribute, give out
散发广告纸 sànfā guǎnggào zhǐ pass out fliers

丧 sāng TRAD 喪 N funeral

奔丧 bēnsāng travel to attend a funeral
丧事 sāngshì N funeral arrangements

170

办丧事 bàn sāngshì make funeral arrangements

桑 sāng N mulberry

桑树 sāngshù mulberry tree (棵 kē)
桑叶 sāngyè mulberry leaf (张 zhāng)
桑拿浴 sāngnàyù N sauna

NOTE: This is a case of a semi-transliteration. 桑拿 represents the sound of *sauna* and 浴 means *bath*.

嗓 sǎng N throat

嗓子 sǎngzi N **1** throat ■ 我嗓子疼。Wǒ sǎngzi téng. *I have a sore throat.* **2** voice

丧 sàng TRAD 喪 v lose

丧失 sàngshī v lose, forfeit

骚 sāo TRAD 騷 v disturb, upset

骚动 sāodòng **I** v disturb, cause a commotion **II** N social disturbance, commotion
骚乱 sāoluàn **I** v riot **II** N riot, disturbance
平息骚乱 píngxī sāoluàn put down a riot

嫂 sǎo N elder brother's wife

嫂子 sǎozi N elder brother's wife, sister-in-law ■ 他父母去世以后，嫂子对他非常关心。Tā fùmǔ qùshì yǐhòu, sǎozi duì tā fēicháng guānxīn. *After his parents' death, his sister-in-law was very concerned for him.*

NOTE: One's younger brother's wife is 弟妹 dìmèi.

扫 sǎo TRAD 掃 v sweep ■ 秋天我得常常扫院子里的落叶。Qiūtiān wǒ děi chángcháng sǎo yuànzi li de luòyè. *In autumn, I have to often sweep away the fallen leaves in my courtyard.*
扫地 sǎo dì sweep the floor
扫除 sǎochú v clean (a room, a courtyard, etc.)

扫 sào as in 扫帚 sàozhou

扫帚 sàozhou N broom (把 bǎ)

色 sè N **1** color ■ 那座白色的大楼就是医院。Nà zuò báisè de dàlóu jiù shì yīyuàn. *That white building is the hospital.* **2** sex
色彩 sècǎi N color, hue
色彩丰富 sècǎi fēngfù a riot of colors
色狼 sèláng N a lascivious man, sexual molester
色盲 sèmáng N color blindness, achromatopsia
色情 sèqíng N pornography
色欲 sèyù N lust, sexual lust

森 sēn N forest

森林 sēnlín N forest

杀 shā TRAD 殺 v kill ■ 你敢杀鸡吗? Nǐ gǎn shā jī ma? *Do you dare to kill chickens?*
杀害 shāhài v kill, murder

刹 shā as in 刹车 shāchē

刹车 shāchē **I** N brake **II** v apply brakes, brake
急刹车 jíshāchē brake suddenly

沙 shā N sand, grit

沙发 shāfā N upholstered chair, sofa, couch
沙漠 shāmò N desert ■ 沙漠里最需要的是水。Shāmò li zuì xūyào de shì shuǐ. *In a desert, what is most needed is water.*
沙滩 shātān N sandy beach
沙土 shātǔ N sandy soil
沙眼 shāyǎn N trachoma
沙子 shāzi N sand, grit (粒 lì) ■ 我右眼里恐怕有一粒沙子，难受极了。Wǒ yòuyǎn li kǒngpà yǒu yí lì shāzi, nánshòu jíle. *I'm afraid there is a grain of sand in my right eye. It's so irritating!*

砂 shā N grit, sand

纱 shā TRAD 紗 N yarn

棉纱 miánshā cotton yarn

傻 shǎ ADJ foolish, stupid ■ 你别看他模样傻，其实一点儿也不傻。Nǐ bié kàn tā móyàng shǎ, qíshí yìdiǎnr yě bù shǎ. *He may look stupid, but he is actually not at all stupid.*
傻子 shǎzi N fool, idiot

厦 shà N a tall building, mansion

高楼大厦 gāolóu dàshà tall buildings and great mansions

啥 shà PRON what

有啥吃啥 yǒu shà chī shà eat whatever you've got

NOTE: 啥 shà is a dialectal word, used on very casual occasions.

筛 shāi v sieve, sift

筛子 shāizi sieve

晒 shài TRAD 曬 v dry in the sun, bask

晒太阳 shài tàiyang sunbathe ■ 有的人喜欢在夏天晒太阳，这对皮肤有害。Yǒude rén xǐhuan zài xiàtiān shài tàiyang, zhè duì pífu yǒuhài. *In summer some people like to sunbathe, which is harmful to the skin.*

山 shān

山 shān N mountain, hill (座 zuò) ■ 这个美丽的小城，前面是大河，背后是青山。Zhège měilì de xiǎochéng, qiánmian shì dà hé, bèihòu shì qīng shān. *In front of this beautiful town is a big river and behind it are green hills.*

爬山 páshān mountain climbing, mountaineering ■ 星期六我们去爬山吧! Xīngqīliù wǒmen qù páshān ba! *Let's go mountain climbing this Saturday.*

山地 shāndì N hilly area, mountainous region

山地车 shāndìchē mountain bike (辆 liàng)

山峰 shānfēng N mountain peak (座 zuò)

山冈 shāngāng N low hill (座 zuò)

山沟 shāngōu N gully, ravine (条 tiáo)

山谷 shāngǔ N valley (条 tiáo)

山河 shānhé N mountains and rivers, land (of a country)

大好山河 dàhǎo shānhé the beautiful land (of a country)

山脚 shānjiǎo N the foot of a hill (mountain)

在山脚下 zài shānjiǎo xià at the foot of the hill (mountain)

山岭 shānlǐng N mountain ridge

山脉 shānmài N mountain range (条 tiáo) ■ 世界上最大的山脉—喜马拉雅山脉—是在中国。Shìjiè shang zuì dà de shānmài—Xǐmǎlāyǎ shānmài—shì zài Zhōngguó. *The biggest mountain range in the world—the Himalayas—is in China.*

山水 shānshuǐ landscape

游山玩水 yóu-shān-wán-shuǐ enjoy the landscape, go sightseeing

山头 shāntóu N hilltop (座 zuò)

山腰 shānyāo N halfway up the mountain, mountainside

衫 shān N shirt (See 衬衫 chènshān.)

珊 shān N as in 珊瑚 shānhú

珊瑚 shānhú N coral

删 shān v delete (words)

闪 shǎn TRAD 閃 v 1 flash, sparkle 2 glitter, twinkle

闪电 shǎndiàn N lightning ■ 昨天夜里又打雷，又闪电，真吓人。Zuótiān yèlǐ yòu dǎléi, yòu shǎndiàn, zhēn xiàrén. *Last night thunder boomed and lightning flashed. It was really frightening.*

闪盘 shǎnpán N (computing) flash memory disk

闪烁 shǎnshuò v twinkle, glitter

闪耀 shǎnyào v shine

扇 shàn N fan (See 电扇 diànshàn.)

善 shàn ADJ good, kind, friendly

善良 shànliáng ADJ kind-hearted, good-hearted

善于 shànyú v be good at ■ 他善于理解，不善于表达。Tā shànyú lǐjiě, bú shànyú biǎodá. *He is good at understanding, but not good at expressing himself.*

擅 shàn I v be good at II ADV (doing things) without authorization

擅长 shàncháng ADJ expert in, having a special skill

擅长谈判 shàncháng tánpàn be especially good at negotiation, be an expert negotiator

擅自 shànzì ADV without permission, without authorization

伤 shāng TRAD 傷 I v wound, injure, hurt ■ 他踢球的时候伤了脚。Tā tīqiú de shíhou shāngle jiǎo. *He injured his foot playing football.* II N wound, injury ■ 你的伤不重，很快就会好的。Nǐ de shāng bú zhòng, hěn kuài jiù huì hǎo de. *Your injury is not serious and will heal soon.*

受伤 shòushāng be wounded, be injured

伤疤 shāngbā N scar

伤风 shāngfēng v catch a cold

伤害 shānghài v harm, hurt ■ 她无意说的那句话，大大伤害了他的感情。Tā wúyì shuōde nà jù huà, dàdà shānghàile tā de gǎnqíng. *That casual remark of hers hurt him badly.*

伤痕 shānghén N bruise, scar

伤口 shāngkǒu N wound, cut

伤脑筋 shāng nǎojīn I v be vexed, be frustrated II ADJ troublesome, vexing

伤脑筋的问题 shāng nǎojīn de wèntí a very difficult problem, a thorny problem

伤心 shāngxīn ADJ heartbreaking, heartbroken ■ 当她三岁的儿子死了，她伤心得不想活。Dāng tā sān suì de érzi sǐ le, tā shāngxīn de bù xiǎng huó. *When her three-year-old son died, she was so heartbroken that she did not want to live.*

伤员 shāngyuán N wounded soldier (名 míng)

商 shāng I v discuss, consult II N commerce, business

商标 shāngbiāo N trademark

商场 shāngchǎng N 1 shopping center, mall (家 jiā, 座 zuò) 2 department store

商店 shāngdiàn N shop, store (家 jiā) ■ 我常去那家商店买东西。Wǒ cháng qù nàjiā shāngdiàn mǎi dōngxi. *I often shop at that store.*

开商店 kāi shāngdiàn open or keep a shop

商量 shāngliang v discuss, consult ■ 有重要的事，先和好朋友商量再决定。Yǒu zhòngyào de shì, xiān hé hǎo péngyou shāngliang zài juédìng. *When an important matter arises, discuss it with good friends before making a decision.*

商品 **shāngpǐn** N commodity (件 jiàn, 种 zhǒng) ■ 商品的价格是由什么决定的? Shāngpǐn de jiàgé shì yóu shénme juédìng de? *What determines the price of commodities?*

商榷 **shāngquè** V discuss politely, deliberate

商人 **shāngrén** N merchant, business person

商讨 **shāngtǎo** V exchange views in order to reach a consensus

商业 **shāngyè** N commerce, business ■ 这个城市商业十分发达。Zhège chéngshì shāngyè shífēn fādá. *Commerce is very well developed in this city.*

商业管理 **shāngyè guǎnlǐ** business administration

商业管理硕士 **shāngyè guǎnlǐ shuòshì** Master of Business Administration (MBA)

商业区 **shāngyèqū** N business district

商业中心区 **shāngyè zhōngxīnqū** central business district (CBD)

商议 **shāngyì** V discuss, confer

赏 **shǎng** TRAD 賞 V **1** admire, enjoy **2** reward, grant

赏罚分明 **shǎngfá fēnmíng** IDIOM rewarding merit and punishing mistake fairly, exercise discipline judiciously

赏识 **shǎngshí** V recognize and admire the talent of (people), appreciate the worth of (people)

上 1 **shàng** I N on top of, on, above II ADJ previous, last

上星期 **shàng xīngqī** last week

上一课 **shàng yí kè** the previous class (lesson)

NOTE: 上 shàng is often used after a noun to form words of location. While its basic meaning is *on top*, 上 shàng may have various, often semi-idiomatic meanings, e.g.

报纸上 **bàozhǐ shang** in the newspaper

地上 **dì shang** on the ground

工作上 **gōngzuò shang** in work

会上 **huì shang** at the meeting

世界上 **shìjiè shang** in the world

手上 **shǒu shang** in hand, in the hands of

上边 **shàngbian** N above, high up ■ 从那座大楼的上边可以看见飞机场。Cóng nà zuò dàlóu de shàngbian kěyǐ kànjiàn fēijīchǎng. *From the top of that high building, one can see the airport.*

上层 **shàngcéng** N upper stratum (of a society)

上层社会 **shàngcéng shèhuì** upper social class

上等 **shàngděng** ADJ (of products) superior, first-rate

上帝 **Shàngdì** N God

上级 **shàngjí** N higher authorities, superior ■ 你是我的上级, 我当然要完成你分配的任务。Nǐ shì wǒ de shàngjí, wǒ dāngrán yào wánchéng nǐ fēnpèi de rènwù. *You're my superior, so of course I will complete the task you assigned.*

上空 **shàngkōng** N overhead, in the sky

上面 **shàngmian** N Same as 上边 shàngbian

上升 **shàngshēng** V rise ■ 到了晚上, 病人的体温上升了。Dào le wǎnshang, bìngrén de tǐwēn shàngshēng le. *When evening came, the patient's temperature rose.*

上述 **shàngshù** N above-mentioned

上诉 **shàngsù** V appeal (to a higher court)

上午 **shàngwǔ** N morning (usually from 8 a.m. to noon)

NOTE: 上午 shàngwǔ does not mean the whole morning. It denotes the part of morning from about eight or nine o'clock to noon. The period before eight or nine o'clock is 早晨 zǎochén or 早上 zǎoshang.

上下 **shàngxià** N from top to bottom, up and down

上旬 **shàngxún** N the first 10 days of a month

上衣 **shàngyī** N upper garment, jacket (件 jiàn) ■ 你这件上衣很好看。Nǐ zhè jiàn shàngyī hěn hǎokàn. *Your jacket looks good.*

上游 **shàngyóu** N upper reaches (of a river)

上载 **shàng zài** V upload

上涨 **shàngzhǎng** V (of rivers, prices) rise, go up

上 2 **shàng** V **1** go upwards, ascend

上楼 **shàng lóu** go upstairs ■ 我坐电梯上楼。Wǒ zuò diàntī shàng lóu. *I take the lift upstairs.*

上来 **shànglai** come up ■ 楼上有空房间, 快上来吧! Lóu shang yǒu kòng fángjiān, kuài shànglai ba! *There's a vacant room upstairs, please come up!*

上去 **shàngqu** go up ■ 他们在楼上等你, 快上去吧! Tāmen zài lóu shang děng nǐ, kuài shàngqu ba! *They're waiting for you upstairs. Please go upstairs.*

2 get on (a vehicle), go aboard (a plane, ship)

上车 **shàng chē** get into a vehicle

上船 **shàng chuán** board a ship

上飞机 **shàng fēijī** get on the plane

3 attend (school), go to (work)

上大学 **shàng dàxué** go to university

上班 **shàngbān** V go to work ■ 我母亲每天九点上班, 五点下班。Wǒ mǔqin měi tiān jiǔ diǎn

上报 shàngbào

CHINESE-ENGLISH

shàngbān, wǔ diǎn xiàbān. *Every day my mother goes to work at nine and finishes at five.*

上报 **shàngbào** v 1 report to a higher body 2 appear in the newspapers

上当 **shàngdàng** v be fooled, be duped ■ 他太老实了，容易上当受骗。Tā tài lǎoshi le, róngyì shàngdàng shòupiàn. *He is too straightforward and easily duped.*

上课 **shàngkè** v go to class, have classes ■ 明天放假，不上课。Míngtiān fàngjià, bú shàngkè. *Tomorrow's a holiday. There will be no classes.*

上任 **shàngrèn** v assume office, take up a post

上市 **shàngshì** v be available on the market
上市公司 **shàngshì gōngsī** listed company

上台 **shàngtái** v 1 go on stage 2 come to power

上网 **shàngwǎng** v get on the Internet, surf the Internet ■ 他一般吃了晚饭，就上网半小时看看新闻。Tā yìbān chīle wǎnfàn jiù shàngwǎng bàn xiǎoshí kànkan xīnwén. *After supper he usually gets on the Internet for half an hour to read the news.*

上学 **shàngxué** v go to school

尚 **shàng** v worship, revere

裳 **shàng** N clothing (See 衣裳 yīshang)

烧 **shāo** TRAD 燒 v 1 burn ■ 市政府禁止烧垃圾。Shìzhèngfǔ jìnzhǐ shāo lājī. *The city government bans the burning of rubbish.* 2 cook ■ 今天我给你们烧个鱼。Jīntiān wǒ gěi nǐmen shāo ge yú. *Today I'll cook you a fish.* 3 have a fever

烧饼 **shāobǐng** N sesame seed cake (块 kuài)
烧毁 **shāohuǐ** v burn up

捎 **shāo** v take (something) along for (someone)
捎个话儿 **shāo gè huàr** take an (oral) message, relay a message

梢 **shāo** N the thin tip of a long-shaped object
树梢儿 **shùshāor** treetops

稍 **shāo** ADV Same as 稍微 shāowéi. Often used in written Chinese.

稍微 **shāowéi** ADV slightly, just a little bit ■ 你能不能把电视机的声音开得稍微大一点？Nǐ néng bu néng bǎ diànshìjī de shēngyin kāi de shāowéi dà yìdiǎn? *Could you turn the TV up a bit?*

勺 **sháo** N spoon

勺子 **sháozi** N ladle, spoon (把 bǎ) ■ 她用勺子把汤分给大家。Tā yòng sháozi bǎ tāng fēn gei dàjiā. *She gave soup to everyone with a ladle.*

少 **shǎo** I ADJ small in amount, few, little ■ 新西兰人少地多。Xīnxīlán rén shǎo dì duō. *New Zealand has a small population and much land.* II ADV not often, seldom ■ 我们虽然在同一个学校，但是很少见面。Wǒmen suīrán zài tóng yí ge xuéxiào, dànshì hěn shǎo jiànmiàn. *Although we're in the same school, we seldom see each other.* III v be short, be missing ■ 原来我有一百元，现在怎么少了二十元? Yuánlái wǒ yǒu yìbǎi yuán, xiànzài zěnme shǎole èrshí yuán? *I originally had one hundred dollars. How is it that I have twenty dollars less now?*

少量 **shǎoliàng** N small amount, little, few
少数 **shǎoshù** N minority
少数民族 **shǎoshù mínzú** minority nationality (non-Han ethnic group in China)

少 **shào** ADJ young

少年 **shàonián** N young man (from around 10 to 16 years old), adolescent ■ 自古少年出英雄。Zìgǔ shàonián chū yīngxióng. *Ever since ancient times, heroes have emerged from the young.*

NOTE: (1) A young woman of around 10 to 16 years old is called 少女 shàonǚ. (2) The word 青少年 qīngshàonián is often used to mean *young people collectively.*

少女 **shàonǚ** N teenage girl
少先队 **Shàoxiānduì** N the Young Pioneers

NOTE: 少先队 Shàoxiānduì is the shortened form of 少年先锋队 Shàonián Xiānfēngduì.

绍 **shào** TRAD 紹 v connect (See 介绍 jièshào.)

哨 **shào** N 1 sentry 2 whistle

哨兵 **shàobīng** N sentry, armed guard (名 míng)
哨子 **shàozi** N whistle
吹哨子 **chuī shàozi** blow a whistle

奢 **shē** ADJ excessive, luxurious

奢侈 **shēchǐ** ADJ luxurious ■ 他们有钱以后生活非常奢侈。Tāmen yǒuqián yǐhòu shēnghuó fēicháng shēchǐ. *They lived in luxury after becoming rich.*
奢侈品 **shēchǐpǐn** luxury item

舌 **shé** N tongue

舌头 **shétou** N the tongue ■ 医生: 你舌头伸出来, 我看看。Yīshēng: Nǐ shétou shēn chūlai, wǒ kànkan. *Doctor: Stick out your tongue and I'll have a look.* (→ *Show me your tongue.*)

174

蛇 shé N snake (条 tiáo) ■ 她最怕蛇。Tā zuì pà shé. *She finds snakes the most frightening [of all animals].*

舍 shě V give up

舍不得 **shěbude** V unwilling to give up, hate to part with

舍得 **shěde** V be willing to part with, not grudge ■ 她为了孩子, 舍得花钱花时间。Tā wèile háizi, shěde huā qián huā shíjiān. *She is willing to spend time and money on her children.*

设 shè TRAD 設 V equip, set up

设备 **shèbèi** N equipment, installation (件 jiàn, 套 tào) ■ 这套实验室设备是从国外进口的。Zhè tào shíyànshì shèbèi shì cóng guówài jìnkǒu de. *This set of laboratory equipment was imported from overseas.*

设法 **shèfǎ** V try to find a way, attempt to

设计 **shèjì** I V design ■ 工程师正在设计一种不用汽油的汽车。Gōngchéngshī zhèngzài shèjì yì zhǒng bú yòng qìyóu de qìchē. *Engineers are designing a car that does not use petrol.* II N design, plan

设立 **shèlì** V establish, set up

设施 **shèshī** N facilities, equipment

设想 **shèxiǎng** V conceive, envision
不堪设想的后果 **bùkān shèxiǎng de hòuguǒ** inconceivable consequences

设置 **shèzhì** V set up, establish

社 shè N association

社会 **shèhuì** N society ■ 我们每个人都应该关心社会。Wǒmen měi ge rén dōu yīnggāi guānxīn shèhuì. *Each of us should be concerned for society.*
社会上 **shèhuì shang** in society, the general public
社会学 **shèhuìxué** N sociology
社会主义 **shèhuì zhǔyì** N socialism
社交 **shèjiāo** N social life, social intercourse
社论 **shèlùn** N editorial (篇 piān)

舍 shè N hut, shed (See 宿舍 sùshè.)

摄 shè TRAD 攝 V photograph, shoot (movies, etc)

摄像 **shèxiàng** V make a video recording
摄像机 **shèxiàngjī** camcorder
摄氏 **shèshì** N Celsius, centigrade
摄氏温度计 **shèshì wēndùjì** centigrade thermometer

NOTE: China uses Celsius (摄氏 shèshì), not Fah-renheit (华氏 huáshì). In everyday speech, people usually do not mention 摄氏 shèshì. So if a Chinese person says 今天最高气温二十八度。Jīntiān zuìgāo qìwēn èrshíbā dù, it automatically means *The highest temperature today will be 28 degrees Celsius.*

摄影 **shèyǐng** N photography ■ 这个电影的摄影十分成功。Zhège diànyǐng de shèyǐng shífēn chénggōng. *The cinematography of this film is a spectacular success.*
摄影家 **shèyǐngjiā** accomplished photographer
摄影师 **shèyǐngshī** photographer
摄影作品 **shèyǐng zuòpǐn** a work of photography

射 shè V shoot (a gun, an arrow etc.)

射击 **shèjī** V shoot, fire

涉 shè V involve

涉及 **shèjí** V involve, touch on, have something to do with

谁 shéi TRAD 誰 PRON Same as 谁 shuí. Used colloquially.

身 shēn I N human body ■ 他身高175公分。Tā shēn gāo yìbǎi qīshíwǔ gōngfēn. *He is 175 centimeters tall.* II M. WD (for clothes)
一身新衣服 **yì shēn xīn yīfu** a suit of new clothes
身边 **shēnbiān** N close by one's side, on one's person ■ 我身边没有她的地址, 我发电子邮件告诉你。Wǒ shēnbiān méiyǒu tā de dìzhǐ, wǒ fā diànzǐ yóujiàn gàosu nǐ. *I don't have her address with me. I'll send it to you by email.*
身材 **shēncái** N stature, figure
身材苗条 **shēncái miáotiáo** with a slender figure
身分(份) **shēnfen** N social status, identity
身分不明 **shēnfen bùmíng** unknown identity
身分证 **shēnfenzhèng** N I.D. card
身体 **shēntǐ** N 1 human body ■ 少年儿童正处在长身体的时期。Shàonián értóng zhèng chǔ zài zhǎng shēntǐ de shíqī. *Children and adolescents are at a stage of physical development.* 2 health ■ 我爸爸年纪大了, 但是身体还很好。Wǒ bàba niánjì dà le, dànshì shēntǐ hái hěn hǎo. *My father is getting old, but is still in good health.*

NOTE: Although its original meaning is the *body*, 身体 shēntǐ is often used in colloquial Chinese to mean *health*. Friends often ask about each other's health in greeting: ■ 你身体好吗? Nǐ shēntǐ hǎo ma? *How's your health?* ■ 你最近身体怎么样? Nǐ zuìjìn shēntǐ zěnmeyàng? *How's your health been recently?*

深 shēn

深 **shēn** ADJ **1** deep **2** difficult to understand, profound ■ 这本书太深了，我看不懂。Zhè běn shū tài shēn le, wǒ kàn bu dǒng. *This book is too difficult. I can't understand it.*

深奥 **shēn'ào** ADJ profound, abstruse

深沉 **shēnchén** ADJ deep, heavy
深沉的爱 shēnchén de ài deep love

深处 **shēnchù** N depths, recesses
内心深处 nèixīn shēnchù one's innermost heart, one's most private feelings and thoughts

深度 **shēndù** N depth, how deep something is

深厚 **shēnhòu** ADJ deep, profound ■ 他对故乡有深厚的感情。Tā duì gùxiāng yǒu shēnhòu de gǎnqíng. *He has deep feelings for his hometown.*

深化 **shēnhuà** V deepen

深刻 **shēnkè** ADJ incisive, insightful, profound ■ 这位老人经历十分丰富，对人性有深刻的认识。Zhè wèi lǎorén jīnglì shífēn fēngfù, duì rénxìng yǒu shēnkè de rènshi. *This old man has had very rich experiences and has an incisive understanding of human nature.*

深浅 **shēnqiǎn** N **1** Same as 深度 shēndù **2** proper limit for speech or action, propriety

深切 **shēnqiè** ADJ heartfelt, earnest

深情 **shēnqíng** N deep feelings

深入 **shēnrù** V enter deeply into ■ 这一政策深入人心。Zhè yí zhèngcè shēnrù rénxīn. *This policy enters deeply into people's hearts.* (→ *This policy is extremely popular.*)

深入浅出 **shēn-rù-qiǎn-chū** IDIOM explain complicated theories or phenomena in simple, easy-to-understand language.

深信 **shēnxìn** V firmly believe, be deeply convinced

深远 **shēnyuǎn** ADJ profound and lasting, far-reaching

深重 **shēnzhòng** ADJ extremely serious, extremely grave

申 shēn V explain, state

申报 **shēnbào** V **1** declare (at customs) **2** submit an official report

申请 **shēnqǐng** V apply for (a visa, job, permit, etc.)
申请表 shēnqǐngbiǎo application form
申请人 shēnqǐngrén applicant
申请书 shēnqǐngshū letter of application

申述 **shēnshù** V give an official explanation

伸 shēn V stretch out, extend ■ 火车开的时候，你千万不要把头伸出车窗。Huǒchē kāi de shíhou, nǐ qiānwàn bú yào bǎ tóu shēnchū chēchuāng. *Never stick your head out of the window when the train is moving.*

伸展 **shēnzhǎn** V extend, stretch

绅 shēn TRAD 紳 as in 绅士 shēnshì

绅士 **shēnshì** N gentleman, gentry

呻 shēn as in 呻吟 shēnyín

呻吟 **shēnyín** V groan, moan

神 shén I N god, supernatural being

财神爷 **cáishényé** the god of money, Mammon

II ADJ magical, wondrous

神话 **shénhuà** N mythology, myth

神经 **shénjīng** N **1** nerve ■ 我牙神经疼。Wǒ yá shénjīng téng. *My tooth nerve hurts.* **2** The mind mental state ■ 他神经有毛病。Tā shénjīng yǒu máobìng. *There is something wrong with his mind.*

神经病 **shénjīngbìng** neuropathy, mental disorder, crazy

NOTE: The formal word for *mental disorder* is 精神病 jīngshénbìng but 神经病 shénjīngbìng may be used in everyday Chinese.

神秘 **shénmì** ADJ mysterious ■ 有些西方人觉得汉字很神秘。Yǒuxiē xīfāngrén juéde Hànzì hěn shénmì. *Some Westerners find Chinese characters quite mysterious.*

神奇 **shénqí** ADJ miraculous, mystical

神气 **shénqì** ADJ **1** arrogant and cocky **2** spirited and vigorous

神情 **shénqíng** N (facial) expression, look

神色 **shénsè** N appearance, expression ■ 那个人神色可疑。Nàge rén shénsè kěyí. *That man looks suspicious.*

神圣 **shénshèng** ADJ sacred, holy

神态 **shéntài** N bearing, appearance

神仙 **shénxiān** N immortal, celestial being (位 wèi)

什 shén PRON what

什么 **shénme** PRON what ■ 你要什么? Nǐ yào shénme? *What do you want?*

什么的 **shénmede** PRON and so on, and so forth ■ 他们要了很多菜，有鱼、肉、蔬菜、什么的。Tāmen yàole hěn duō cài, yǒu yú, ròu, shūcài, shénmede. *They ordered lots of dishes, fish, meat, vegetables and so on.*

审 shěn V **1** examine **2** interrogate

审查 **shěnchá** V examine, investigate

审定 **shěndìng** V examine and approve (a proposal, a plan, etc.)

审计 **shěnjì** V audit
审计员 shěnjìyuán auditor

审理 **shěnlǐ** v try (a legal case), handle (a legal case)

审美 **shěnměi** N appreciation of what is beautiful

审判 **shěnpàn** v bring to trial, try

审批 **shěnpī** v examine and approve

审问 **shěnwèn** v Same as 审讯 shěnxùn

审讯 **shěnxùn** v interrogate (by the police)

审议 **shěnyì** v deliberate, consider

婶 **shěn** N wife of one's father's younger brother

婶母 **shěnmǔ** wife of one's father's younger brother

婶婶 **shěnshen** Same as 婶母 shěnmǔ. Used as a form of address

肾 **shèn** N kidney

肾炎 **shènyán** N nephritis

甚 **shèn** ADV much, very much

甚至 **shènzhì** ADV even, so much so ■ 她到过中国很多地方，甚至西藏也去过。Tā dàoguo Zhōngguó hěn duō dìfang, shènzhì Xīzàng yě qù guo. *She has been to many places in China, even to Tibet.*

慎 **shèn** ADJ cautious

慎重 **shènzhòng** ADJ very cautious, discreet

渗 **shèn** v seep, ooze

渗透 **shèntòu** v seep into, permeate

升 **shēng** v rise, go up ■ 昨天股票升了百分之零点五。Zuótiān gǔpiào shēngle bǎifēn zhī líng diǎn wǔ. *Shares rose by half a percent yesterday.*

生 **shēng** I v 1 give birth to, grow ■ 他妻子上星期生了一个女儿。Tā qīzi shàng xīngqī shēng le yí ge nǚ'ér. *His wife gave birth to a girl baby last week.* 2 be born ■ 生在福中不知福。Shēng zài fú zhōng bùzhī fú. *Though born in luck, one doesn't appreciate how lucky he is.* 3 live, grow II ADJ alive, living

生病 **shēngbìng** v fall ill

生产 **shēngchǎn** v produce, manufacture

生产力 **shēngchǎnlì** N productive force

生产率 **shēngchǎnlǜ** N productivity

生存 **shēngcún** I v survive, be alive ■ 由于过分开发，野生动物在这里无法生存。Yóuyú guòfèn kāifā, yěshēng dòngwù zài zhèlǐ wúfǎ shēngcún. *Owing to excessive development, wildlife cannot survive here.* II N survival

生动 **shēngdòng** ADJ vivid, lively ■ 她在信里生动有趣地描写了旅行经历。Tā zài xìn li shēngdòng yǒuqù de miáoxiěle lǚxíng jīnglì. *In her letter she gives vivid and interesting accounts of her travel experiences.*

生活 **shēnghuó** I N life 日常生活 rìcháng shēnghuó daily life II v live, lead (a life) ■ 我小时候生活得很愉快。Wǒ xiǎoshíhou shēnghuó de hěn yúkuài. *I lived a happy life in childhood.* (→ *I had a happy childhood.*)

生活费 **shēnghuófèi** N living allowance, stipend

生活费用 **shēnghuó fèiyòng** N cost of living

生活水平 **shēnghuó shuǐpíng** N living standards 提高生活水平 tígāo shēnghuó shuǐpíng raise living standards

生机 **shēngjī** N 1 chance of survival, lease of life 一线生机 yíxiàn shēngjī a slim chance of survival 2 vitality 生机勃勃 shēngjī bóbó full of vigor and vitality

生理 **shēnglǐ** N the physical aspect of human life 生理上 shēnglǐ shàng physical, physically 生理学 shēnglǐxué physiology

生命 **shēngmìng** N life (条 tiáo) ■ 这只小猫也是一条小生命，不能眼看它死去。Zhè zhī xiǎo māo yě shì yì tiáo xiǎo shēngmìng, bù néng yǎnkàn tā sǐqu. *This kitten is also a life. We can't let it die without doing anything.*

生命科学 **shēngmìng kēxué** life science

生命力 **shēngmìnglì** N life force

生怕 **shēngpà** CONJ for fear of, so as not to

生气 **shēngqì** v get angry, be offended ■ 别对他生气，他不是故意的。Bié duì tā shēngqì, tā bú shì gùyì de. *Don't get angry with him. He did not mean it.*

生前 **shēngqián** N (of a dead person) during his/her lifetime

生日 **shēngrì** N birthday ■ 我忘了今天是我妻子的生日! Wǒ wàngle jīntiān shì wǒ qīzi de shēngrì! *I forgot it's my wife's birthday today.* 过生日 guò shēngrì celebrate a birthday ■ 你今年打算怎么过生日? Nǐ jīnnián dǎsuàn zěnme guò shēngrì? *How are you going to celebrate your birthday this year?*

生日贺卡 **shēngrì hékǎ** birthday card

生日礼物 **shēngrì lǐwù** birthday present

生态 **shēngtài** N ecology

生态学家 **shēngtàixuéjiā** ecologist

生态旅游 **shēngtài lǚyóu** ecotourism

生物 **shēngwù** N living things ■ 生物一般分为动物和植物两大类。Shēngwù yìbān fēnwéi dòngwù hé zhíwù liǎng dà lèi. *Living things are generally categorized into animals and plants.*

生物学 **shēngwùxué** biology

生物化学 **shēngwù huàxué** chemical biology, biochemistry

生效 **shēngxiào** V come into effect, become effective

生意 **shēngyi** N business, trade ■ 他每天上网做生意。Tā měi tiān shàngwǎng zuò shēngyi. *He does trading over the Internet every day.*

生育 **shēngyù** V give birth to, bear

生长 **shēngzhǎng** V grow, grow up ■ 这种植物在河边生长得很好。Zhè zhǒng zhíwù zài hébiān shēngzhǎng de hěn hǎo. *This kind of plant grows well by the river.*

生殖 **shēngzhí** V reproduce

生殖系统 **shēngzhí xìtǒng** reproductive system

生 2 **shēng** ADJ 1 raw, not cooked ■ 我不敢吃生鱼。Wǒ bù gǎn chī shēng yú. *I don't dare to eat raw fish.* 2 unripe ■ 苹果还太生，要等一段时间才能吃。Píngguǒ hái tài shēng, yào děng yí duàn shíjiān cái néng chī. *The apples are not ripe yet. It will be some time before they are edible.* 3 unfamiliar

生词 **shēngcí** N new words and phrases (in a language lesson) ■ 这个句子里有一个生词，我不认识，也不会念。Zhège jùzi li yǒu yí ge shēngcí, wǒ bú rènshi, yě bú huì niàn. *There's a new word in this sentence. I don't know it, nor do I know how to say it.*

记生词 **jì shēngcí** memorize new words

生人 **shēngrén** N stranger

生疏 **shēngshū** ADJ unfamiliar

人地生疏 **réndìshēngshū** unfamiliar with the place and the people, be a stranger in a place

甥 **shēng** N one's sister's child (See 外甥 wàishēng)

牲 **shēng** N domesticated animal

牲畜 **shēngchù** N livestock, domestic animal (头 tóu)

牲口 **shēngkou** N pack animal, draught animal (e.g. horse, buffalo, donkey) (头 tóu)

声 **shēng** TRAD 聲 N sound, noise, voice ■ 机器声太大，我听不清你说什么。Jīqì shēng tài dà, wǒ tīng bu qīng nǐ shuō shénme. *The noise from the machine is too loud; I can't hear what you're saying.*

声调 **shēngdiào** N tone of a Chinese character ■ "这个字是哪个声调？" "这个字读第二声。" "Zhège zì shì nǎge shēngdiào?" "Zhège

zì dú dì-èr shēng." *"Which tone should this character be read with?"* (or *"Which tone does this character have?"*) *"This character is read with the second tone."*

声明 **shēngmíng** I N formal statement II V make a statement, publicly declare ■ 我声明，他做的任何事情都与我无关。Wǒ shēngmíng, tā zuò de rènhé shìqing dōu yǔ wǒ wú guān. *I declare that whatever he does has nothing to do with me.*

声势 **shēngshì** N power and influence, momentum

声音 **shēngyīn** N voice, sound ■ 请你们说话声音轻一点。Qǐng nǐmen shuōhuà shēngyīn qīng yìdiǎn. *Please talk softly.* (or *Please don't talk so loudly.*)

声誉 **shēngyù** N reputation, prestige

绳 **shéng** TRAD 繩 N string, rope

绳子 **shéngzi** rope, cord (根 gēn, 条 tiáo) ■ 你拉一下这根绳子，窗子就会开。Nǐ lā yíxià zhè gēn shéngzi, chuāngzi jiù huì kāi. *Pull this cord and the window will open.*

省 1 **shěng** N province ■ 中国一共有多少个省？Zhōngguó yígòng yǒu duōshǎo ge shěng? *How many provinces are there in China?*

省会 **shěnghuì** provincial capital

省长 **shěngzhǎng** governor of a province

省 2 **shěng** V 1 save, economize ■ 他用钱很省。Tā yòng qián hěn shěng. *He is very frugal with money.* 2 leave out, omit

省得 **shěngde** CONJ in case, so as not to

省略 **shěnglüè** V omit, leave out

省略号 **shěnglüèhào** N (punctuation mark to indicate ellipsis ...), ellipsis

胜 **shèng** TRAD 勝 V triumph (over), be victorious, defeat ■ 上海队胜了北京队。Shànghǎi duì shèngle Běijīng duì. *The Shanghai team defeated the Beijing team.*

胜利 **shènglì** I V win a victory ■ 我们胜利了! Wǒmen shènglì le! *We've won!* II N victory ■ 我们的胜利来得不容易。Wǒmen de shènglì lái de bù róngyì. *Our victory was hard-won.*

剩 **shèng** V be left over, have as surplus ■ 我原来有五百块钱，用了四百块，还剩一百块。Wǒ yuánlái yǒu wǔbǎi kuài qián, yòngle sìbǎi kuài, hái shèng yìbǎi kuài. *I originally had five hundred dollars; I've used four hundred dollars and now have one hundred dollars left.*

剩菜 **shèng cài** N leftovers

剩余 **shèngyú** I N surplus, remainder II V Same as 剩 shèng

盛 **shèng** ADJ 1 flourishing, prosperous 2 magnificent, grand 3 popular, common

盛产 **shèngchǎn** v produce an abundance of, abound in

盛大 **shèngdà** ADJ grand, magnificent
盛大的典礼 **shèngdà de diǎnlǐ** a grand and elaborate ceremony

盛开 **shèngkāi** v bloom luxuriantly

盛情 **shèngqíng** N great kindness, lavish hospitality

盛行 **shèngxíng** v be in vogue, be very popular

圣 **shèng** TRAD 聖 ADJ sacred, holy

圣诞节 **shèngdànjié** N Christmas
圣诞夜 **shèngdànyè** Christmas eve

失 **shī** I v 1 lose 2 err, make mistakes II N slip, mishap, mistake

失败 **shībài** I v be defeated, lose, fail II N defeat, loss, failure ■ 失败是成功之母。Shībài shì chénggōng zhī mǔ. *Failure is the mother of success.*

失眠 **shīmián** I N insomnia II v suffer from insomnia

失去 **shīqù** v lose (something valuable) ■ 她渐渐对孩子失去耐心。Tā jiànjiàn duì háizi shīqù nàixīn. *She is running out of patience with the kids.*

失事 **shīshì** v have an accident

失望 **shīwàng** ADJ disappointed ■ 你们没有完成上个月的生产计划, 我非常失望。Nǐmen méiyǒu wánchéng shàng ge yuè de shēngchǎn jìhuà, wǒ fēicháng shīwàng. *I am bitterly disappointed that you failed to complete last month's production plan.*
对…失望 **duì…shīwàng** be disappointed with…

失误 **shīwù** I v make a mistake, muff II N fault, error, miscalculation

失效 **shīxiào** v (of documents) become invalid, expire, (of medicines) cease to be effective ■ 你的护照已经失效了。Nǐde hùzhào yǐjīng shīxiào le. *Your passport has expired.*

失学 **shīxué** v be unable to go to school, be deprived of education

失业 **shīyè** v lose one's job, become unemployed ■ 经济情况不好, 失业的人越来越多。Jīngjì qíngkuàng bù hǎo, shīyè de rén yuèláiyuè duō. *As the economy is weak, more and more people lose their jobs.*

失约 **shīyuē** v fail to keep an appointment

失踪 **shīzōng** v be missing, disappear
失踪人员 **shīzōng rényuán** missing person

师 **shī** TRAD 師 N master, teacher

师范 **shīfàn** teachers' education
师范学院 **shīfàn xuéyuàn** N teachers' college, college of education

师傅 **shīfu** N master worker (位 wèi) ■ 这位师傅技术很高。Zhè wèi shīfu jìshù hěn gāo. *This master worker is highly skilled.*

NOTE: 师傅 **shīfu** is also a polite form of address for *a worker*. For example, an electrician or mechanic can be addressed as 师傅 **shīfu** or, if his family name is 李 **Lǐ**, 李师傅 **Lǐ shīfu**.

师长 **shīzhǎng** N 1 teacher 2 division commander (in the army)

诗 **shī** N poem, poetry (首 shǒu) ■ 现在写诗、读诗的人越来越少了。Xiànzài xiě shī, dú shī de rén yuèláiyuè shǎo le. *Nowadays fewer and fewer people write or read poems.*

诗歌 **shīgē** N poem, poetry (首 shǒu)
诗人 **shīrén** N poet (名 míng)

施 **shī** v carry out, execute

施肥 **shīféi** v apply fertilizer

施工 **shīgōng** v (construction work) be underway, be in progress ■ 前面施工, 绕道通行。Qiánmiàn shīgōng, rào dào tōngxíng. *Road works ahead. Detour.*

施加 **shījiā** v exert, bring to bear on
对…施加压力 **duì…shījiā yālì** put pressure on …

施行 **shīxíng** v (of regulations, laws, etc.) put into force, implement, enforce

施展 **shīzhǎn** v put out to good use, give free play to

狮 **shī** TRAD 獅 N lion

狮子 **shīzi** lion (头 tóu)

湿 **shī** TRAD 濕 ADJ damp, wet ■ 昨夜下过雨, 早上路面还湿着。Zuóyè xiàguo yǔ, zǎoshang lùmiàn hái shīzhe. *It rained last night, so the roads were wet this morning.*

湿度 **shīdù** N humidity, moisture
湿润 **shīrùn** ADJ moist

尸 **shī** TRAD 屍 N dead body, corpse

尸体 **shītǐ** dead body, corpse (具 jù)

十 **shí** NUM ten

十五 **shíwǔ** fifteen
五十 **wǔshí** fifty
十分 **shífēn** ADV one hundred percent, totally, fully ■ 我十分理解你们的心情。Wǒ shífēn lǐjiě nǐmen de xīnqíng. *I understand your feelings completely.*
十全十美 **shíquán shíměi** IDIOM perfect in every way
十足 **shízú** ADV 100 percent, out-and-out

179

拾 1 **shí** NUM ten

拾 2 **shí** V pick up (from the ground)

石 **shí** N stone, rock

石灰 **shíhuī** N lime
石灰石 **shíhuīshí** limestone

石头 **shítou** N stone, rock (块 kuài) ■ 摸着石头过河。Mōzhe shítou guò hé. Cross a river by feeling for stones. (→ Make decisions as you go along, act without a premeditated plan.)

石油 **shíyóu** N petroleum, oil

蚀 **shí** V lose

蚀本 **shíběn** V lose one's capital (in business ventures)

识 **shí** TRAD 識 V know (See 认识 rènshi, 知识 zhīshi.)

识别 **shíbié** V distinguish, identify, recognize
识别敌友 **shíbié dí yǒu** tell enemies from friends

识字 **shízì** V learn to to read, become literate

时 **shí** TRAD 時 N Same as 点钟 diǎnzhōng. Used only in writing.

时常 **shícháng** ADV often, frequently

时代 **shídài** N a historical period, epoch, age ■ 人类从石器时代到电脑时代，花了几千年的时间。Rénlèi cóng shíqì shídài dào diànnǎo shídài, huāle jǐ qiān nián de shíjiān. It took mankind thousands of years to move from the Stone Age to the Computer Age.

时而 **shí'ér** ADV occasionally, sometimes

时光 **shíguāng** N time

时候 **shíhou** N a certain point in time, (the time) when ■ 飞机什么时候开? Fēijī shénme shíhou kāi? When will the plane depart?

时机 **shíjī** N opportunity, opportune moment

时间 **shíjiān** N a period of time ■ 时间不够，我没做完那道练习。Shíjiān bú gòu, wǒ méi zuòwán nà dào liànxí. As there wasn't enough time, I did not finish that exercise.

时节 **shíjié** N occasion, season
荷花盛开的时节 héhuā shèngkāi de shíjié the season when lotus flowers are in full bloom

时刻 **shíkè** N at a particular point in time ■ 在关键时刻，可以看出一个人的本性。Zài guānjiàn shíkè, kěyǐ kànchū yí ge rén de běnxìng. At critical moments, a person shows his true colors.

时刻表 **shíkèbiǎo** (railway, coach, etc.) time-table

时髦 **shímáo** ADJ fashionable, in vogue

时期 **shíqī** N period of time, stage ■ 他在少年时期受到良好的教育。Tā zài shàonián shíqī shòudao liánghǎo de jiàoyù. He received a very good education during his adolescence.

时时 **shíshí** ADV constantly, at all times

时事 **shíshì** N current affairs, current events

时装 **shízhuāng** N the latest fashion
时装表演 **shízhuāng biǎoyǎn** fashion show
时装设计 **shízhuāng shèjì** fashion design

实 **shí** TRAD 實 I ADJ real, true II N reality, fact

实话 **shíhuà** N true fact, truth
实话实说 **shíhuà shíshuō** tell the truth

实惠 **shíhuì** I N real benefit II ADJ substantial

实际 **shíjì** I N reality, actual situation ■ 我们的停车场停不了这么多的车，这是一个实际问题。Wǒmen de tíngchēchǎng tíng bu liǎo zhème duō de chē, zhè shì yíge shíjì wèntí. It is a real problem that our car park is too small to accommodate so many cars. II ADJ practical, realistic ■ 我们订计划要实际一点。Wǒmen dìng jìhuà yào shíjì yìdiǎn. We should be practical when drawing up a plan.

实践 **shíjiàn** I V put into practice, apply ■ 懂了这个道理，就要实践。Dǒngle zhège dàolǐ, jiù yào shíjiàn. After you've understood this principle, you should put it into practice. II N practice ■ 实践出真知。Shíjiàn chū zhēnzhī. Practice leads to genuine knowledge.

实况 **shíkuàng** N what is really happening
实况转播 **shíkuàng zhuǎnbō** live broadcast

实力 **shílì** N actual strength, strength
军事实力 **jūnshì shílì** military strength

实施 **shíshī** V put into effect, carry out

实事求是 **shíshìqiúshì** IDIOM find out truth from the facts, be realistic

实体 **shítǐ** N 1 entity 2 substance

实物 **shíwù** N real object
实物交易 **shíwù jiāoyì** barter

实习 **shíxí** N practice, fieldwork

实现 **shíxiàn** V materialize, realize

实行 **shíxíng** V put into practice, take effect, implement, carry out, institute ■ 他的新年决心实行了多久? Tā de xīnnián juéxīn shíxíngle duōjiǔ? How long did he put his New Year's resolutions into practice?

实验 **shíyàn** N experiment, test (项 xiàng, 次 cì) ■ 有人反对用动物做实验。Yǒurén fǎnduì yòng dòngwù zuò shíyàn. Some people oppose experiments on animals.

实验室 **shíyànshì** N laboratory

实验员 **shíyànyuán** N laboratory technician

实业 **shíyè** N industry and commerce, industry
实业家 **shíyèjiā** entrepreneur, industrialist

实用 **shíyòng** ADJ practical (for use), useful, handy ■ 这套工作服穿着不好看，但是十分实

用。Zhè tào gōngzuòfú chuānzhe bù hǎokàn, dànshì shífēn shíyòng. *This set of work clothes does not look beautiful, but it is very practical.* ■ 这本词典非常实用。Zhè běn cídiǎn fēicháng shíyòng. *This dictionary is very useful.*

实在 shízài I ADJ honest, truthful ■ 他说的话你听了可能不高兴, 但却很实在。Tā shuō de huà nǐ tīngle kěnéng bù gāoxìng, dàn què hěn shízài. *What he said may have made you unhappy, but it was truthful.* II ADV indeed, really ■ 我记不起你的名字了, 实在抱歉。Wǒ jì bu qǐ nǐ de míngzi le, shízài hěn bàoqiàn. *I'm really sorry I can't remember your name.*

实质 shízhì N substance, essence
实质上 shízhìshang in essence, practically, virtually

食 shí N food, meal ■ 食, 色, 性也。(孔子) Shí, sè, xìng yě. (Kǒngzǐ) *The need for food and sex is human nature. (Confucius)*
食品 shípǐn N foodstuff (as commodities) (件 jiàn) ■ 新西兰生产的食品质量很高。Xīnxīlán shēngchǎn de shípǐn zhìliàng hěn gāo. *The foodstuffs produced in New Zealand are of very high quality.*
食品工业 shípǐn gōngyè food industry
食品加工 shípǐn jiāgōng food processing
食品商店 shípǐn shāngdiàn provision shop, grocery
食堂 shítáng N dining hall
食物 shíwù N food ■ 空气、水和食物都是绝对必要的。Kōngqì, shuǐ hé shíwù dōu shì juéduì bìyào de. *Air, water and food are absolutely indispensable.*
食用 shíyòng ADJ used as food, edible
食欲 shíyù N appetite
没有食欲 méiyǒu shíyù have no appetite

史 shǐ N history
史料 shǐliào N historical data, historical materials

屎 shǐ N excrement

使 shǐ V 1 make, enable ■ 岁月使人老。Suìyuè shǐ rén lǎo. *Time makes one old.* 2 make use of, apply
使得 shǐdé V Same as 使 shǐ 1
使劲 shǐjìn V exert all one's strength
使命 shǐmìng N mission
不辱使命 bùrǔ shǐmìng mission accomplished
使用 shǐyòng V use, apply ■ 你会使用这台电脑吗? Nǐ huì shǐyòng zhè tái diànnǎo ma? *Do you know how to use this computer?*

驶 shǐ V sail, drive

始 shǐ V begin, start
始终 shǐzhōng ADV from beginning to end, throughout, ever ■ 我始终不明白她为什么这么恨那个地方。Wǒ shǐzhōng bù míngbai tā wèishénme zhème hèn nàge dìfang. *I have never ever understood why she should hate that place so much.*

示 shì V show, indicate
示范 shìfàn V set an example, demonstrate
教学示范 jiàoxué shìfàn teaching demonstration
示弱 shìruò V show signs of weakness
示威 shìwēi V put on a show of force, demonstrate
抗议示威 kàngyì shìwēi protest demonstration
示意图 shìyìtú N sketch map

士 shì N 1 scholar, gentleman (See 博士 bóshì, 护士 hùshì, 女士 nǚshì, 硕士 shuòshì, 学士 xuéshì, 战士 zhànshì.) 2 non-commisioned officer
士兵 shìbīng N rank-and-file soldier, private

誓 shì V vow, pledge
发誓 fāshì vow, swear, take an oath
誓言 shìyán N oath, pledge

氏 shì N family name

侍 shì V wait on, serve
侍女 shìnǚ N maid
侍候 shìhòu V wait on, look after

释 shì TRAD 釋 V 1 explain (See 解释 jiěshì) 2 let go, be relieved of
释放 shìfàng V release, set free

世 shì N 1 the world 2 lifetime 3 generation, era
世代 shìdài N generations
世代经商 shìdài jīngshāng have been businessmen for generations
世纪 shìjì N century ■ 公元两千年, 世界迎来了一个新世纪—二十一世纪。Gōngyuán liǎngqiān nián, shìjiè yínglái le yí ge xīn shìjì—èrshíyī shìjì. *In the year AD 2000, the world greeted a new century—the twenty-first century.*
世界 shìjiè N the world ■ 世界每天都在变。Shìjiè měitiān dōu zài biàn. *The world is changing every day.*

世界观 shìjièguān

世界上 shìjiè shang in the world ■ 世界上的事情都很复杂。Shìjiè shang de shìqing dōu hěn fùzá. *Everything in the world is complicated.*

世界博览会 Shìjiè Bólǎnhuì the World Exposition

世界贸易组织 Shìjiè Màoyì Zǔzhī the World Trade Organization (WTO)

世界卫生组织 Shìjiè Wèishēng Zǔzhī the World Health Organization (WHO)

世界观 shìjièguān N the way one looks at the world, world outlook, ideology

市 shì N 1 municipality, city ■ 下午我要到市里去。Xiàwǔ wǒ yào dào shìli qù. *I'm going to the city this afternoon.* 2 market

市场 shìchǎng N marketplace, market

市场经济 shìchǎng jīngjì market economy

菜市场 cài shìchǎng vegetable market, food market

市价 shìjià N market price

市民 shìmín N resident of a city, townsfolk

市长 shìzhǎng N mayor

式 shì N form, pattern

式样 shìyàng N style, type

事 shì N 1 affair, matter (件 jiàn) ■ 这件事很重要，一定要办好。Zhè jiàn shì hěn zhòngyào, yídìng yào bànhǎo. *This is an important matter and must be done well.* 2 job, work

找个事做 zhǎo ge shì zuò try to find something to do, try to find a job

3 accident, something bad

事变 shìbiàn N military or political incident of historical significance

事故 shìgù N accident, mishap (件 jiàn) ■ 有关部门正在调查事故的原因。Yǒuguān bùmén zhèngzài diàochá shìgù de yuányīn. *The departments concerned are investigating the cause of the accident.*

事故现场 shìgù xiànchǎng scene of an accident

工伤事故 gōngshāng shìgù industrial accident

交通事故 jiāotōng shìgù traffic accident, road accident

事迹 shìjì N deed, achievement

英雄事迹 yīngxióng shìjì heroic deeds

事件 shìjiàn N (historic) event, incident ■ 九一一是个可怕的事件。Jiǔ-yāo-yāo shì ge kěpà de shìjiàn. *9/11 was a terrible event.*

NOTE: 一 is pronounced as yāo here. See note on 一 yī for more information.

事例 shìlì N example, case

事情 shìqing N Same as 事 shì

NOTE: (1) In many cases, 事 shì may be replaced by 事情 shìqing, e.g. ■ 这件事情很重要，一定要办好。Zhè jiàn shìqing hěn zhòngyào, yídìng yào bànhǎo. *This is an important matter and must be done well.*
找个事情做 zhǎo ge shìqing zuò try to find something to do, try to find a job.
(2) 事 shì or 事情 shìqing is a noun that can be applied widely, denoting *any affair, matter or business to be done or considered*. Here are more examples ■ 我今天晚上没有事情做。Wǒ jīntiān wǎnshang méiyǒu shìqing zuò. *I've nothing to do this evening.* ■ 他们在路上出事了。Tāmen zài lùshang chūshì le. *They had an accident on the way.*

事实 shìshí N fact (件 jiàn) ■ 你应该先调查事实，再作结论。Nǐ yīnggāi xiān diàochá shìshí, zài zuò jiélùn. *You should check the facts before drawing a conclusion.*

事实上 shìshí shang in fact, as a matter of fact

事态 shìtài N state of affairs, situation

事先 shìxiān ADV beforehand, in advance ■ 他上星期去中国工作了，事先没有告诉任何人。Tā shàng xīngqī qù Zhōngguó gōngzuò le, shìxiān méiyǒu gàosu rènhé rén. *He went to work in China last week. He had not told anybody beforehand.*

事务 shìwù N matters to attend to, work

事务工作 shìwù gōngzuò routine work

事项 shìxiàng N item, matter

注意事项 zhùyì shìxiàng points for attention

事业 shìyè N 1 career ■ 要事业，还是要家庭？她决定不了。Yào shìyè, háishì yào jiātíng? Tā juédìng bù liǎo. *She can't make up her mind whether to pursue a career or have a family.* 2 cause, undertaking ■ 他为世界和平事业作出了巨大贡献。Tā wèi shìjiè hépíng shìyè zuòchūle jùdà gòngxiàn. *He made tremendous contributions to the cause of world peace.*

视 shì TRAD 視 V watch

视察 shìchá V (of a high-ranking official) inspect, observe

视觉 shìjué N the sense of sight

视力 shìlì N eyesight, sight

视力测验 shìlì cèyàn eyesight test

视频光盘 shìpín guāngpán video compact disc, VCD

视线 shìxiàn N line of sight

挡住了视线 dǎngzhù le shìxiàn block one's view

视野 shìyě N field of vision

是 **shì** v 1 be, yes ■ "你们的中文老师是不是北京人？" "是的。" "Nǐmen de Zhōngwén lǎoshī shì bu shì Běijīngrén?" "Shìde." *Is your Chinese teacher from Beijing?" "Yes."* 2 (indicating existence of), (there) be ■ 小学旁边是一座公园。 Xiǎoxué pángbian shì yí zuò gōngyuán. *There is a park by the primary school.* 3 (used to emphasize the words following it) ■ 那家饭店的菜是不错。 Nà jiā fàndiàn de cài shì búcuò. *That restaurant's food is indeed quite good.*

是非 **shìfēi** N 1 right and wrong, truth and falsehood

明辨是非 **míngbiàn shìfēi** distinguish clearly between right and wrong

2 trouble, quarrel

搬弄是非 **bānnòng shìfēi** sow discord, tell tales

布 **shì** TRAD 飾 v decorate (See 装饰 zhuāngshì)

室 **shì** N room (See 办公室 bàngōngshì, 教室 jiàoshì, 浴室 yùshì.)

市 **shì** N persimmon (See 西红柿 xīhóngshì.)

舌 **shì** TRAD 適 v suit, fit

舌当 **shìdàng** ADJ appropriate, suitable ■ 在中国送钟给老年人当礼物，是不适当的，因为"送钟"和"送终"同音。 Zài Zhōngguó sòng zhōng gěi lǎoniánrén dāng lǐwù, shì bú shìdàng de, yīnwèi "sòngzhōng" hé "sòngzhōng" tóngyīn. *In China it is not appropriate to give an old person a clock as a gift because "give a clock" (sòng zhōng) is pronounced the same as "pay last tribute" (sòng zhōng).*

舌合 **shìhé** v suit, fit ■ 他善于交际，适合做生意。 Tā shànyú jiāojì, shìhé zuò shēngyi. *He is good at social dealings, and is suited to be a businessman.*

舌宜 **shìyí** ADJ suitable, appropriate

舌应 **shìyìng** v adapt to ■ 她以前是教书的，现在当翻译，一时还不适应。 Tā yǐqián shì jiāoshū de, xiànzài dāng fānyì, yìshí hái bú shìyìng. *She used to teach. Now she works as an interpreter and has not quite adapted to it.*

舌用 **shìyòng** ADJ applicable, suitable ■ 你的方法很先进，但是在这里不适用。 Nǐ de fāngfǎ hěn xiānjìn, dànshì zài zhèli bú shìyòng. *Your method is very advanced, but it cannot be applied here.*

折 **shì** v pass, leave

逝世 **shìshì** v pass away, die

NOTE: See note on 去世 qùshì.

试 **shì** TRAD 試 v test, try ■ 这种新药，病人试过没有？ Zhè zhǒng xīnyào, bìngrén shìguo méiyǒu? *Has the patient tried this new drug?*

试试/试一下 **shìshì/shì yíxià** have a try

试卷 **shìjuàn** N examination paper, test paper (份 fèn)

试行 **shìxíng** v try out

试验 **shìyàn** v test, experiment (项 xiàng, 次 cì) ■ 研究人员正在动物身上试验这种新药。 Yánjiū rényuán zhèngzài dòngwù shēnshang shìyàn zhè zhǒng xīn yào. *Researchers are testing this new medicine on animals.*

试用 **shìyòng** v try out, be on probation

试用人员 **shìyòng rényuán** staff on probation

试用期 **shìyòngqī** probation period

势 **shì** TRAD 勢 N 1 power, force 2 situation, circumstances

势必 **shìbì** ADV be bound to, be sure to

势力 **shìlì** N (social) force

匙 **shi** N spoon (See 钥匙 yàoshi.)

收 **shōu** v 1 receive, accept

收到 **shōudao** receive ■ 我昨天收到一封信。 Wǒ zuótiān shōudao yì fēng xìn. *I received a letter yesterday.*

收下 **shōuxia** accept ■ 请你收下这件小礼物。 Qǐng nǐ shōuxia zhè jiàn xiǎo lǐwù. *Please accept this small gift.*

2 collect (fee), charge ■ 这种服务是要收费的。 Zhè zhǒng fúwù shì yào shōufèi de. *This service will incur a fee.*

收藏 **shōucáng** v collect (antiques, collectibles, etc.)

收藏中国明代花瓶 **shōucáng Zhōngguó Míngdài huāpíng** collect Chinese Ming vases

收成 **shōucheng** N harvest (of crops)

收复 **shōufù** v recover (lost territory)

收购 **shōugòu** v purchase, buy

收购价格 **shōugòu jiàgé** purchasing price

收回 **shōuhuí** v take back, recall

收回贷款 **shōuhuí dàikuǎn** recall a loan, call in a loan

收获 **shōuhuò** I v gather in crops, harvest ■ 今年这位农民收获了五千公斤小麦。 Jīnnián zhè wèi nóngmín shōuhuòle wǔqiān gōngjīn xiǎomài. *This year the farmer harvested five thousand kilograms of wheat.* II N gain (of work), achievement, reward ■ 这次试验取得了大量数据，收获很大。 Zhè cì shìyàn qǔdéle dàliàng shùjù, shōuhuò hěn dà. *A large amount of data has been obtained from the test, which is a big achievement.*

收集 shōují

收集 shōují v collect, gather ■ 他想把世界各国的邮票都收集到。Tā xiǎng bǎ shìjiè ge guó de yóupiào dōu shōují dào. *He wants to collect stamps from all the countries in the world.*

收买 shōumǎi v buy over, buy in

收入 shōurù I v earn, receive ■ 我不想告诉他我去年收入多少钱。Wǒ bù xiǎng gàosu tā wǒ qùnián shōurù duōshǎo qián. *I didn't want to tell him how much I earned last year.* II N income

收拾 shōushi v put in order, tidy up ■ 她做完饭，总要收拾一下厨房。Tā zuòwán fàn, zǒngyào shōushi yíxià chúfáng. *She will always tidy up the kitchen after cooking.*

收缩 shōusuō v contract, shrink

收益 shōuyì N profit, earnings

收音机 shōuyīnjī N radio (台 tái, 架 jià)

手 shǒu N hand (只 zhī, 双 shuāng) ■ 我的手不干净，要洗一下才能吃饭。Wǒ de shǒu bù gānjìng, yào xǐ yíxià cái néng chīfàn. *My hands are not clean. I have to wash them before I eat.*

手上 shǒu shang in the hand ■ 他手上拿着一本书。Tā shǒu shang názhe yì běn shū. *He's holding a book in his hand.*

右手 yòushǒu the right hand

左手 zuǒshǒu the left hand

手表 shǒubiǎo N wristwatch (块 kuài)

NOTE: In everyday usage, 手表 shǒubiǎo is often shortened to 表 biǎo: ■ 我的表慢了，你的表几点? Wǒ de biǎo màn le, nǐ de biǎo jǐ diǎn? *My watch is slow. What time is it by your watch?*

手电筒 shǒudiàntǒng N flashlight, torch (只 zhī)

手段 shǒuduàn N means, measure ■ 我不赞成使用不合理的手段来达到目的。Wǒ bú zànchéng shǐyòng bù hélǐ de shǒuduàn lái dádào mùdì. *I don't endorse the use of unjustifiable means to achieve one's ends.*

手法 shǒufǎ N trick, gimmick

手工 shǒugōng ADJ done by hand, made by hand, manual

手工业 shǒugōngyè handicraft industry

手工艺品 shǒugōngyìpǐn handicraft item

手机 shǒujī N cell phone, mobile telephone (只 zhī) ■ 上飞机以前，要关上手机。Shàng fēijī yǐqián, yào guānshang shǒujī. *Switch off your cell phone before boarding a plane.*

手巾 shǒujin N face towel, towel (条 tiáo)

手绢 shǒujuàn N handkerchief (块 kuài)

手枪 shǒuqiāng N pistol (把 bǎ)

手势 shǒushì N gesture, signal, sign

打手势 dǎ shǒushì make a gesture

手术 shǒushù N operation ■ 外科主任亲自做这个手术。Wàikē zhǔrèn qīnzì zuò zhè ge shǒushù. *The chief surgeon will perform the operation himself.*

手术间 shǒushùjiān operating room, surger room

做手术 zuò shǒushù perform an operation, operate

手套 shǒutào N glove (只 zhī, 副 fù) ■ 今天真冷，我戴了手套、帽子、还觉得冷! Jīntiān zhēn lěng, wǒ dàile shǒutào, màozi, hái juéde lěng! *It's really cold today. I'm wearing gloves and a hat, but still feel cold!*

手续 shǒuxù N formalities, procedures ■ 买卖房子，要办法律手续。Mǎimài fángzi, yào bàn fǎlǜ shǒuxù. *You will have to complete the legal formalities when you buy or sell a house.*

办手续 bàn shǒuxù go through the formaliti

手艺 shǒuyì N craftsmanship, workmanship

手指 shǒuzhǐ N finger, thumb

NOTE: In Chinese the thumb 拇指 mǔzhǐ, or 大拇指 dàmǔzhǐ is considered just one of the fingers. So it is correct to say: 我有十个手指。Wǒ yǒu shí ge shǒuzhǐ. *I have ten fingers.*

手镯 shǒuzhuó N bracelet

守 shǒu v 1 observe, abide by 2 guard, defend

守财奴 shǒucáinú N miser

守法 shǒufǎ v observe the law

守卫 shǒuwèi v guard, defend

首 I shǒu I N the head II ADJ first

首创 shǒuchuàng v initiate, pioneer

首创精神 shǒuchuàng jīngshén pioneering spirit

首都 shǒudū N capital city ■ 中国的首都是北京。Zhōngguó de shǒudū shì Běijīng. *China's capital city is Beijing.*

首领 shǒulǐng N leader, chieftain, chief

首脑 shǒunǎo N head

首脑会议 shǒunǎo huìyì summit meeting, summit

首席 shǒuxí ADJ chief, principal

首席小提琴手 shǒuxí xiǎotíqínshǒu the first violinist (of an orchestra)

首席执行官 shǒuxí zhíxíngguān chief executive officer (CEO)

首先 shǒuxiān ADV first, first of all ■ 首先，请允许我自我介绍一下。Shǒuxiān, qǐng yǔnxǔ wǒ zìwǒ jièshào yíxià. *First of all, allow me to introduce myself.*

首相 shǒuxiàng N prime minister

英国首相 Yīngguó shǒuxiàng the British Prime Minister

首要 shǒuyào ADJ of primary importance

首长 shǒuzhǎng N senior official, ranking officer

首 2 **shǒu** M. WD (for songs and poems)

一首歌 **yì shǒu gē** a song

寿 **shòu** TRAD 壽 N life, lifespan

长寿 **chángshòu** longevity ■ 祝您老人家健康
长寿! Zhù nín lǎorénjia jiànkāng chángshòu! (to
an elderly person) *Wish you good health and
longevity!*
寿命 **shòumìng** N lifespan
寿星 **shòuxing** birthday boy, birthday girl

受 **shòu** V 1 receive, accept ■ 每个人都有受
教育的权利。Měi ge rén dōu yǒu shòu jiàoyù
de quánlì. *Everyone has the right to receive an
education.* 2 suffer, be subject to
受苦 **shòukǔ** suffer from hardship
受罚 **shòufá** V be punished, be penalized ■ 拖
延付款要受罚。Tuōyán fùkuǎn yào shòufá. *Late
payment will be penalized.*
受理 **shòulǐ** V (of law courts or lawyers) accept
and handle a case
受聘 **shòupìn** V be appointed for a position
受聘担任首席法律顾问 **shòupìn dānrèn
shǒuxí fǎlǜ gùwèn** be appointed as chief
legal advisor
受伤 **shòushāng** V be wounded, be injured

受 **shòu** V give, award

授予 **shòuyǔ** V confer, award
授予学位 **shòuyǔ xuéwèi** confer an academic
degree

瘦 **shòu** ADJ thin, lean ■ 她比以前瘦多了。Tā
bǐ yǐqián shòu duō le. *She is thinner than
before.*
瘦肉 **shòuròu** N lean meat
瘦子 **shòuzi** N lean or thin person

售 **shòu** V sell

售货员 **shòuhuòyuán** N shop assistant, sales
clerk

兽 **shòu** TRAD 獸 N beast, animal

人面兽心 **rénmiàn shòuxīn** a human face
with a beast's heart—a beast in human shape
兽医 **shòuyī** N 1 veterinary science 2 veterinary
surgeon, veterinarian

殊 **shū** ADJ different (See 特殊 tèshū)

书 **shū** TRAD 書 I N 1 book (本 běn) ■ 这本书
很有意思,你看过没有? Zhè běn shū hěn yǒu
yìsi, nǐ kànguo méiyǒu? *This book is very interesting. Have you read it?* 2 style of calligraphy

3 letter II V write
看书 **kàn shū** read, do reading ■ 我喜欢看
书。Wǒ xǐhuan kàn shū. *I like reading.*
书包 **shūbāo** N schoolbag (只 zhī) ■ 小学生的
书包为什么这么重? Xiǎoxuéshēng de shūbāo
wèishénme zhème zhòng? *Why are children's
schoolbags so heavy?*
书本 **shūběn** N book
书呆子 **shūdāizi** N bookworm, nerd
书店 **shūdiàn** N bookstore, bookshop (家 jiā)
书法 **shūfǎ** N calligraphy
书法家 **shūfǎjiā** calligrapher
书籍 **shūjí** N books (collectively)
书记 **shūjì** N secretary of the Chinese Communist Party organizations
书架 **shūjià** N bookshelf ■ 王老师的办公室有
一个大书架。Wáng lǎoshī de bàngōngshì yǒu yí
ge dà shūjià. *There is a big bookshelf in Teacher
Wang's office.*
书刊 **shūkān** N books and periodicals
书面 **shūmiàn** ADJ in written form, written
书面邀请 **shūmiàn yāoqǐng** written invitation
书目 **shūmù** N booklist, (book) catalogue
参考书目 **cānkǎo shūmù** list of reference
books, bibliography
书评 **shūpíng** N book review
书市 **shūshì** N book fair, book market
书写 **shūxiě** V write
书信 **shūxìn** N letter
书展 **shūzhǎn** N book fair

NOTE: 书展 shūzhǎn is the shortening of 图书展销
túshū zhǎnxiāo.

叔 **shū** N father's younger brother

叔叔 **shūshu** N father's younger brother,
uncle ■ 我叔叔是设计电脑软件的。Wǒ
shūshu shì shèjì diànnǎo ruǎnjiàn de. *My father's
younger brother designs computer software.*

NOTE: 叔叔 shūshu is a form of address used by
a child for a man around his/her father's age. It is
common to put a family name before 叔叔 shūshu
e.g. 张叔叔 Zhāng shūshu. Also see note on 阿
姨 āyí.

梳 **shū** N comb

梳子 **shūzi** comb (把 bǎ)

舒 **shū** I ADJ relaxing, leisurely II V stretch,
unfold
舒畅 **shúchàng** ADJ free from worry
心情舒畅 **xīnqíng shūchàng** feel carefree
舒服 **shūfu** ADJ comfortable ■ 这把椅子很舒服,
你坐下去就不想起来了。Zhè bǎ yǐzi hěn shūfu,
nǐ zuò xiàqu jiù bù xiǎng qǐlái le. *This chair is*

very comfortable. Sit on it and you don't want to get up.

不舒服 **bù shūfu** (of a person) not very well, be under the weather ■ 我今天不舒服，想早点回家。Wǒ jīntiān bù shūfu, xiǎng zǎo diǎn huíjiā. *I'm unwell today. I want to go home early.*

舒适 **shūshì** ADJ comfortable, cosy

疏 **shū** I ADJ 1 sparse, scattered 2 (of relationships) not intimate, distant II v neglect, overlook

疏忽 **shūhu** I v neglect, overlook II N oversight, omission

疏漏 **shūlòu** N careless omission, slip

疏远 **shūyuǎn** ADJ (of relationships) not close, estranged

蔬 **shū** N vegetable

蔬菜 **shūcài** vegetable, greens ■ 多吃蔬菜，少吃肉，对健康有利。Duō chī shūcài, shǎo chī ròu, duì jiànkāng yǒulì. *Eating lots of vegetables and little meat is good for your health.*

输 1 **shū** TRAD 輸 v lose (a game, a bet) ■ 上回我们队输了，这回一定要赢! Shàng huí wǒmen duì shū le, zhè huí yídìng yào yíng! *Our team lost the game the last time; this time we must win!*

输 2 **shū** TRAD 輸 v transport

输出 **shūchū** v export

输送 **shūsòng** v transport, convey

输血 **shūxuè** N blood transfusion

熟 **shú** ADJ 1 ripe, cooked ■ 苹果还没有熟，很酸。Píngguǒ hái méiyǒu shú, hěn suān. *The apples are not yet ripe. They're sour.* 2 familiar with, well acquainted

熟练 **shúliàn** ADJ skilful, skilled ■ 我们工厂缺乏熟练工人。Wǒmen gōngchǎng quēfá shúliàn gōngrén. *Our factory is short of skilled workers.*

熟悉 **shúxi** ADJ familiar with, well acquainted with ■ 他和熟悉的人在一起的时候话很多。Tā hé shúxi de rén zài yìqǐ de shíhou huà hěn duō. *He is talkative in the company of the people he knows well.*

数 **shǔ** TRAD 數 v count ■ 我来数一下，这里有多少人，一、二、三、… Wǒ lái shǔ yíxià, zhèlǐ yǒu duōshǎo rén, yī, èr, sān… *Let me count to see how many people are here. One, two, three …*

暑 **shǔ** N heat, hot season

暑假 **shǔjià** N summer holiday, summer vacation

薯 **shǔ** N potato, yam

署 **shǔ** N government office

属 **shǔ** TRAD 屬 v 1 belong to 2 be born in the year of …

属相 **shǔxiang** N (lunar calendar) the tradition twelve animals that mark the cycle of years ■ "你知道中国的十二属相吗?" "知道，是鼠、牛、虎、兔、龙、蛇、马、羊、猴、鸡、狗和猪。" "Nǐ zhīdào Zhōngguó de shí'èr shǔxiang ma?" "Zhīdào, shì shǔ, niú, hǔ, tù, lóng, shé, mǎ, yáng, hóu, jī, gǒu he zhū." *"Do you know the twelve animals of the Chinese Zodiac?" "Yes. They are rat, ox, tiger, rabbit (or hare), dragon, snake, horse, sheep (or goat), monkey, rooster (o phoenix), dog and pig (or boar)."*

属于 **shǔyú** v belong to

鼠 **shǔ** N rat, mouse

老鼠 **lǎoshǔ** rat, mouse (只 zhī)

术 **shù** TRAD 術 N craft, skill

术语 **shùyǔ** N technical term, terminology

束 **shù** N knot

束缚 **shùfù** v bind up, fetter

述 **shù** v narrate

述评 **shùpíng** N commentary, review

树 **shù** TRAD 樹 I N tree (棵 kē) ■ 我爸爸在花园里种了两棵树。Wǒ bàba zài huāyuán li zhòngle liǎng kē shù. *My father planted two tree in the garden.* II v set up

树干 **shùgǎn** N tree trunk

树立 **shùlì** v set up, establish

树林 **shùlín** N woods

树木 **shùmù** N trees (collectively)

树皮 **shùpí** N bark

数 **shù** TRAD 數 I N number, figure ■ 说这种语言的人数在不断减少。Shuō zhè zhǒng yǔyán de rénshù zài búduàn jiǎnshǎo. *The number of speakers of this language is on the decline.* II AD a few, several

数额 **shù'é** N amount, quota

数据 **shùjù** N data ■ "你能肯定这些数据是准确的吗?" "能肯定。" "Nǐ néng kěndìng zhèxiē shùjù shì zhǔnquè de ma?" "Néng kěndìng." *"Are you sure these data are accurate?" "Positive."*

数据库 **shùjùkù** data base

数目 **shùmù** N number, figure

确切的数目 **quèqiè de shùmù** precise numbe

数量 **shùliàng** N quantity, amount ■ 电视节目的数量在增加, 但质量怎么样呢? Diànshì jiémù de shùliàng zài zēngjiā, dàn zhìliàng zěnmeyàng ne? *The quantity of TV programs is increasing, but how about their quality?*

数学 **shùxué** N mathematics

数学家 **shùxuéjiā** mathematician

数字 **shùzì** N 1 numeral, digit (in writing) ■ 我认为写中文的时候, 一般应该写中文数字, 如 "一"、"二"、"三". Wǒ rènwéi xiě Zhōngwén de shíhou, yìbān yīnggāi xiě Zhōngwén shùzì, rú "yī", "èr", "sān". *I think when we're writing Chinese, we should generally use Chinese numerals, such as 一, 二 and 三.* 2 figure, number ■ 每个月都节省一点钱, 几年以后就是一笔不小的数字. Měi ge yuè dōu jiéshěng yìdiǎn qián, jǐ nián yǐhòu jiùshì yìbǐ bù xiǎo de shùzì. *If you save some money every month, years later you will have quite a large sum.*

数字相机 **shùzì xiàngjī** digital camera

数字摄像机 **shùzì shèxiàngjī** digital camcorder

竖 **shù** ADJ vertical

竖立 **shùlì** V erect, set upright

刷 **shuā** V brush ■ 我每天睡觉前刷牙. Wǒ měitiān shuìjiào qián shuā yá. *I brush my teeth before going to bed every night.*

耍 **shuǎ** V play

摔 **shuāi** V 1 fall, fumble ■ 她从自行车上摔下来, 擦破了手. Tā cóng zìxíngchē shang shuāi xiàlai, cāpòle shǒu. *She fell off the bicycle and scraped her hand.* 2 fall and break, cause to fall and break

衰 **shuāi** V decline, decay

衰老 **shuāilǎo** ADJ old and in declining health

衰弱 **shuāiruò** ADJ feeble, very weak

衰退 **shuāituì** V become weaker, decline

经济衰退 **jīngjì shuāituì** economic recession

甩 **shuǎi** V swing, throw

帅 **shuài** TRAD 帥 I N commander in chief

元帅 **yuánshuài** marshal

II ADJ beautiful, handsome

率 **shuài** V lead, command

率领 **shuàilǐng** V lead, command (troops)

拴 **shuān** V tie, fasten

双 **shuāng** TRAD 雙 M. WD 1 two, double 2 a pair of (shoes, chopsticks, etc.)

一双鞋 **yì shuāng xié** a pair of shoes

两双筷子 **liǎng shuāng kuàizi** two pairs of chopsticks

双胞胎 **shuāngbāotāi** N twins

双方 **shuāngfāng** N both sides, both parties ■ 双方同意加强合作. Shuāngfāng tóngyì jiāqiáng hézuò. *Both parties agree to strengthen their cooperation.*

双人床 **shuāngrénchuáng** N double bed

霜 **shuāng** N frost, frostlike powder

爽 **shuǎng** ADJ 1 crisp, freshing 2 straightforward, open-hearted

爽快 **shuǎngkuài** ADJ 1 refreshed 2 straightforward, frank 3 readily, without hesitation

谁 **shuí** TRAD 誰 PRON 1 who, whom ■ 谁是你们的中文老师? Shuí shì nǐmen de Zhōngwén lǎoshī? *Who's your Chinese teacher?* 2 everyone, anybody, whoever, no matter who ■ 谁也不能保证永远不犯错误. Shuí yě bù néng bǎozhèng yǒngyuǎn bú fàn cuòwù. *Nobody can guarantee that he will never make a mistake.*

水 **shuǐ** N water ■ 我口渴, 要喝水. Wǒ kǒu kě, yào hē shuǐ. *I'm thirsty. I want to drink some water.*

自来水 **zìláishuǐ** running water, tap water

开水 **kāishuǐ** boiled water

水产 **shuǐchǎn** N aquatic product

水产品 **shuǐchǎnpǐn** aquatic product

水稻 **shuǐdào** N paddy rice, rice ■ 这些年, 水稻产量有了相当大的提高. Zhèxiē nián shuǐdào chǎnliàng yǒule xiāngdāng dà de tígāo. *The yield of paddy rice has increased considerably in recent years.*

水电 **shuǐdiàn** N Same as 水力发电 shuǐlì fādiàn

水电供应 **shuǐdiàn gōngyìng** water and electricity supply

水电站 **shuǐdiànzhàn** N Same as 水力发电站 shuǐlì fādiànzhàn

水分 **shuǐfèn** N moisture content

水果 **shuǐguǒ** N fruit ■ 水果人人都爱吃. Shuǐguǒ rénrén dōu ài chī. *Everybody loves to eat fruit.*

水果刀 **shuǐguǒ dāo** penknife

水果店 **shuǐguǒ diàn** fruit shop, fruiterer

水库 **shuǐkù** N reservoir

水利 **shuǐlì** N water conservancy, irrigation works

水利工程 **shuǐlì gōngchéng** water conservancy project

水力 **shuǐlì** N waterpower, hydraulic power

水力发电 shuǐlì fādiàn N hydraulic electricity
水力发电站 shuǐlì fādiànzhàn hydroelectric station, hydropower station

水泥 shuǐní N cement ■ 我要买两袋优质水泥，多少钱? Wǒ yào mǎi liǎng dài yōuzhì shuǐní, duōshǎo qián? *I want two sacks of quality cement. How much is it?*

水平 shuǐpíng N 1 level, standard ■ 政府努力提高人民的生活水平。Zhèngfǔ nǔlì tígāo rénmín de shēnghuó shuǐpíng. *The government is working hard to raise the people's standard of living.*
2 proficiency (in language) ■ 我的中文水平不高，请您多多帮助。Wǒ de Zhōngwén shuǐpíng bù gāo, qǐng nín duōduō bāngzhù. *My proficiency in Chinese is not very high. Please help me.*
生活水平 shēnghuó shuǐpíng living standard
提高生活水平 tígāo shēnghuó shuǐpíng raise the standard of living
文化水平 wénhuà shuǐpíng cultural level, educational experience ■ 这位老人的文化水平不高，但是说的话总是有道理。Zhè wèi lǎorén de wénhuà shuǐpíng bù gāo, dànshì shuō de huà zǒngshì hěn yǒu dàolǐ. *This old person is not very well educated, but what he says always has a lot of truth in it.*

水土 shuǐtǔ N water and soil
水土流失 shuǐtǔ liúshī soil erosion
水银 shuǐyín N mercury
水源 shuǐyuán N source of a river, headwater
水灾 shuǐzāi N disastrous flooding, inundation
水蒸气 shuǐzhēngqì N water vapor, steam
水准 shuǐzhǔn N Same as 水平 shuǐpíng

税 shuì N tax, duty ■ 每个公民都有交税的义务。Měi ge gōngmín dōu yǒu jiāo shuì de yìwù. *Every citizen has an obligation to pay taxes.*
税务局 shuìwùjú tax bureau, Inland Revenue Service
关税 guānshuì tariff, customs duty
税率 shuìlǜ N tax rate
税收 shuìshōu N tax revenue

睡 shuì V sleep ■ 我昨天没睡好，因为心里有事。Wǒ zuótiān méi shuì hǎo, yīnwèi xīnli yǒushì. *I did not sleep well last night as I had something on my mind.*
睡觉 shuìjiào V sleep, go to bed ■ 这么晚了，你还不睡觉? Zhème wǎn le, nǐ hái bú shuìjiào? *It's so late. You're not going to bed?*

NOTE: (1) 睡 shuì and 睡觉 shuìjiào are often interchangeable. (2) 觉 is pronounced jiào in 睡觉 shuìjiào, but jué in 觉得 juéde.

睡眠 shuìmián N sleep
睡眠不足 shuìmián bùzú sleep deficiency

睡衣 shuìyī N pajamas, dressing gown
睡着 shuìzháo V fall asleep ■ 昨天我十点上床，到十二点左右才睡着。Zuótiān wǒ shí diǎnzhōng shàngchuáng, dào shí'èr diǎn zuǒyòu cái shuì zháo. *I went to bed at ten yesterday and didn't fall asleep until about twelve o'clock.*

顺 shùn TRAD 順 I ADJ smooth II V 1 arrange, plan 2 do at one's convenience
顺便 shùnbiàn ADV in passing, incidentally ■ 你回家的路上，顺便给我买一份晚报，好吗? Nǐ huíjiā de lùshang, shùnbiàn gěi wǒ mǎi yífèn wǎnbào, hǎo ma? *Could you buy me an evening paper on your way home?*
顺利 shùnlì ADJ smooth, without a hitch, successful ■ 他一生都很顺利。Tā yìshēng dōu hěn shùnlì. *All his life has been plain sailing.* (→ *He has had an easy life.*)
顺手 shùnshǒu ADJ 1 smooth, without hitches 2 convenient, without much trouble
顺序 shùnxù N sequence, order

说 shuō TRAD 說 V 1 say, speak ■ 他说今天晚上没有时间。Tā shuō jīntiān wǎnshang méiyǒu shíjiān. *He said he did not have time this evening.* 2 explain, tell ■ 你说说，这个菜怎么做? Nǐ shuōshuo, zhège cài zěnme zuò? *Will you tell me how to cook this dish?*
说笑话 shuō xiàohua tell a joke
说法 shuōfǎ N 1 wording 2 statement, version
说服 shuōfú V 1 persuade ■ 妈妈说服了爸爸提前退休。Māma shuōfú le bàba tí qián tuìxiū. *Mom has persuaded Dad to have an early retirement.* 2 convince ■ 他说的话没有道理，我没有被说服。Tā shuōde huà méiyǒu dàoli, wǒ méiyǒu bèi shuōfú. *What he said was not reasonable; I was not convinced.*
说谎 shuōhuǎng V tell lies, lie
说理 shuōlǐ V reason things out, argue
说明 shuōmíng I V 1 explain ■ 我来说明一下，为什么我最近有时候迟到。Wǒ lái shuōmíng yíxià, wèishénme wǒ zuìjìn yǒu shíhou chídào. *Let me explain why I've been sometimes late recently.* 2 prove, show ■ 你考试取得了好成绩，这说明你学习很努力。Nǐ kǎoshì qǔdéle hǎo chéngjì, zhè shuōmíng nǐ xuéxí hěn nǔlì. *You got a good grade at the examination. This shows you studied very hard.* II N explanation, manual
说情 shuōqíng V plead for mercy (for someone)

烁 shuò TRAD 爍 V glitter (See 闪烁 shǎnshuò)

硕 shuò TRAD 碩 ADJ large, big

硕士 shuòshì N holder of a master's degree
硕士学位 shuòshì xuéwèi master's degree, masterate

司 **Sī** v take charge of

司法 sīfǎ N administration of justice, judicature
司法机关 sīfǎ jīguān judicial office, judicial system
司机 sījī N (professional) automobile driver, train driver
司令 sīlìng N commander, commanding officer
司令部 sīlìngbù N (military) headquarters

斯 **Sī** PRON this

NOTE: This character was used in Classical Chinese to mean *this*. In Modern Chinese it is normally used just to transliterate foreign names, e.g. 查尔斯 Chá'ěrsī for the English name *Charles*.

撕 **Sī** v tear (a piece of paper)

撕得粉碎 sī dé fěnsuì tear into tiny pieces, tear up

私 **Sī** ADJ private

私人 sīrén I ADJ private, personal ■ 私人财产受到法律保护。Sīrén cáichǎn shòudào fǎlǜ bǎohù. *Private property is protected by the law.* II N personal relationship
私营 sīyíng ADJ privately operated, private owned
私有 sīyǒu ADJ privately owned, private
私自 sīzì ADV without permission, secretly
私自决定 sīzì juédìng make a decision all by oneself and without permission from the authorities

思 **Sī** v think

思潮 sīcháo N trend of thought, ideological trend
思考 sīkǎo v ponder over, think seriously
思念 sīniàn v miss, think of longingly
思前想后 sīqián xiǎnghòu IDIOM ponder over, weigh pros and cons
思索 sīsuǒ v think hard, beat one's brains
思维 sīwéi N thought, thinking, the process of thinking
思想 sīxiǎng N thought, thinking ■ 这个孩子怎么会有这种思想呢? Zhège háizi zěnme huì yǒu zhè zhǒng sīxiǎng ne? *How did the child have this kind of thinking?*
思想家 sīxiǎngjiā thinker
思绪 sīxù N train of thought, thinking

丝 **Sī** TRAD 絲 N **1** silk **2** threadlike things

丝绸 sīchóu N silk, silk cloth ■ 我要买一些丝绸产品, 带回去送朋友。Wǒ yào mǎi yìxiē sīchóu chǎnpǐn, dài huíqu sòng péngyou. *I want to buy some silk products to take home as gifts for friends.*
丝毫 sīháo N the slightest, in the least
没有丝毫变化 méiyǒu sīháo biànhuà without the slightest change, haven't changed in the least

NOTE: 丝毫 sīháo is usually used alongside with a negative word, as is shown in the example.

死 **Sǐ** v die ■ 我家的狗昨天死了。Wǒ jiā de gǒu zuótiān sǐ le. *Our family dog died yesterday.*

NOTE: See note on 去世 qùshì.

死亡 sǐwáng N death
死亡证 sǐwáng zhèng death certificate
死刑 sǐxíng N death sentence

四 **Sì** NUM four ■ 四海为家。Sì hǎi wéi jiā. *Make the four seas one's home.* (→ *Make one's home wherever one is.*)
四十四 sìshí sì forty-four
四处 sìchù ADV here and there, in all directions, everywhere
四方 sìfāng N the four directions of east, west, north and south, all sides
四季 sìjì N the four seasons, all the year round
四季如春 sìjì rú chūn (warm and pleasant) like spring all the year round
四面八方 sìmiàn bāfāng IDIOM in all directions, from all over
四肢 sìzhī N the four limbs, arms and legs
四肢发达 sìzhī fādá physically strong
四周 sìzhōu ADV all around, on all sides

肆 **Sì** NUM four

饲 **Sì** v TRAD 飼 raise (animals)

饲料 sìliào N (animal) feed, fodder
饲养 sìyǎng v raise (animals) ■ 这位农民饲养了一百多头猪。Zhè wèi nóngmín sìyǎng le yìbǎi duō tóu zhū. *This farmer raises over 100 pigs.*

伺 **Sì** v watch, await

伺机 sìjī v wait for one's chances

似 **Sì** v seem

似乎 sìhū ADV it seems, as if ■ 他听了我的话, 似乎不大高兴。Tā tīngle wǒ de huà, sìhū bú dà gāoxìng. *He seemed unhappy after hearing what I had to say.*

似是而非 **sìshì'érfēi** IDIOM sound right but is actually wrong
似是而非的理论 **sìshì'érfēi de lǐlùn** a plausibly deceptive theory, a specious theory

寺 **sì** N monastery, temple

清真寺 **qīngzhēnsì** mosque

松 1 **sōng** TRAD 鬆 I ADJ lax, weak ■ 这个学校对学生的要求太松。 **Zhège xuéxiào duì xuésheng de yāoqiú tài sōng.** *This school demands too little of the students.* (→ *This school does not set a high standard for students.*) II v loosen, slacken ■ 带子太紧了，要松一下。 **Dàizi tài jǐn le, yào sōng yíxià.** *The belt is too tight. It needs to be loosened.*

松 2 **sōng** N pine

松树 **sōngshù** pine tree (棵 **kē**)

耸 **sǒng** TRAD 聳 v 1 alarm, alert 2 rise up

耸耸肩膀 **sǒngsǒng jiānbǎng** shrug one's shoulders
耸人听闻 **sǒngrén tīngwén** IDIOM exaggerate (news) in order to sensationalize

颂 **sòng** TRAD 頌 v praise, extol

颂扬 **sòngyáng** v sing praises of, eulogize

讼 **sòng** TRAD 訟 v file a lawsuit (See 诉讼 **sùsòng**)

送 **sòng** v 1 give as a gift ■ 去年圣诞节，爸爸送给他一辆自行车。 **Qùnián shèngdànjié, bàba sòng gei tā yí liàng zìxíngchē.** *Last Christmas his father gave him a bike.* 2 deliver ■ 我们可以把你买的电脑送到你家。 **Wǒmen kěyǐ bǎ nǐ mǎi de diànnǎo sòngdào nǐ jiā.** *We can deliver the computer you've bought to your home.*

3 accompany, take, escort
送礼 **sònglǐ** v present a gift to
送大礼 **sòng dà lǐ** give an expensive gift
送行 **sòngxíng** v see off
到机场送行 **dào jīchǎng sòngxíng** see ... off at the airport

诵 **sòng** TRAD 誦 v chant, recite (See 背诵 **bèisòng.**)

艘 **sōu** M. WD (used with nouns denoting boats and ships)

一艘渔轮 **yì sōu yúlún** a fishing boat

搜 **sōu** v search

搜查 **sōuchá** v search, ransack
搜查证 **sōucházhèng** search warrant
搜集 **sōují** v collect, gather

搜集资料 **sōují zīliào** collect data, data-gathering
搜索 **sōusuǒ** v search
搜索队 **sōusuǒduì** search party
搜索引擎 **sōusuǒ yǐnqíng** search engine

嗽 **sòu** N cough (See 咳嗽 **késou.**)

苏 **sū** TRAD 蘇 v revive

苏打 **sūdǎ** N soda
苏醒 **sūxǐng** v regain consciousness, come to

俗 **sú** N custom, convention

俗话 **súhuà** N traditional saying, saying

诉 **sù** TRAD 訴 v tell (See 告诉 **gàosu.**)

诉讼 **sùsòng** v lawsuit, litigation
对…提出诉讼 **duì...tíchū sùsòng** file a lawsuit against

肃 **sù** TRAD 肅 I ADJ solemn (See 严肃 **yánsù.**)
II v clean up, eliminate
肃清 **sùqīng** v eliminate, clean up

速 **sù** N speed

速度 **sùdù** N speed, velocity ■ 你开车超过了限定的速度。 **Nǐ kāichē chāoguòle xiàndìng de sùdù.** *You have exceeded the speed limit.*

素 **sù** ADJ 1 plain, simple 2 vegetarian

吃素 **chīsù** eat vegetarian food only, be a vegetarian
素菜 **sùcài** N vegetarian dish, vegetarian food
素食 **sùshí** N vegetarian food
素食主义 **sùshí zhǔyì** vegetarianism
素食主义者 **sùshí zhǔyìzhě** vegetarian (a person)
素质 **sùzhì** N (of a person) true quality, basic nature

宿 **sù** v stay overnight

宿舍 **sùshè** N hostel, dormitory
学生宿舍 **xuésheng sùshè** students' hostel (dormitory)

塑 **sù** v mold

塑料 **sùliào** N plastic
塑造 **sùzào** v sculpture, portray

酸 **suān** ADJ sour ■ 我不喜欢吃酸的东西。 **Wǒ bù xǐhuan chī suān de dōngxi.** *I don't like to eat sour food.* ■ 这种酒太酸了一点儿。 **Zhè zhǒng jiǔ tài suānle yìdiǎnr.** *This wine is a bit too sour.*

算 **suàn** v 1 calculate ■ 完成这项工程需要多少人工, 你算过没有? Wánchéng zhè xiàng gōngchéng xūyào duōshǎo réngōng, nǐ suànguo méiyǒu? *Have you calculated how many man-hours will be needed to finish this project?* 2 regard, consider ■ 今天不算冷, 昨天才冷呢! Jīntiān bú suàn lěng, zuótiān cái lěng ne! *Today can't be considered cold. Yesterday was really cold.*

算了 **suànle** v forget about it, let it pass
算盘 **suànpán** N abacus (把 bǎ)
算是 **suànshì** ADV at last
算术 **suànshù** N arithmetic
算数 **suànshù** v count ■ 我说话是算数的。Wǒ shuōhuà shì suàn shù de. *Whatever I say counts.* (→ *I mean what I say.*)

蒜 **suàn** N garlic

大蒜 **dàsuàn** garlic

虽 **suī** TRAD 雖 CONJ although

虽然 **suīrán** CONJ although, though ■ 虽然已经是秋天了, 这两天天气还是很热。Suīrán yǐjīng shì qiūtiān le, zhè liǎng tiān tiānqì háishì hěn rè. *Although it's already autumn, it's still hot these days.*
虽说 **suīshuō** Same as 虽然 suīrán, used colloquially

随 **suí** TRAD 隨 v let (somebody do as he pleases), as you wish ■ 这件事和我没有关系, 随你处理。Zhè jiàn shì hé wǒ méiyǒu guānxi, suí nǐ chǔlǐ. *This matter is none of my business. You can deal with it any way you like.*

随便 **suíbiàn** ADJ casual, informal ■ 中饭我们随便一点, 晚上我请你到饭店去好好吃一顿。Zhōngfàn wǒmen suíbiàn chī yìdiǎn, wǎnshang wǒ qǐng nǐ dào fàndiàn qu hǎohǎo chī yí dùn. *For lunch we'll have a casual meal. In the evening I'll take you to a restaurant for a square meal.*

NOTE: 随便 suíbiàn is often used in casual conversation to mean *like as you wish*, *anything you like*, or *I have no objection whatsoever.* e.g. ■ "你喝红茶还是绿茶?" "随便。" "Nǐ hē hóngchá háishì lùchá?" "Suíbiàn." *"Do you want to drink black tea or green tea?" "Anything's fine with me."*

随后 **suíhòu** ADV immediately afterwards
随即 **suíjí** ADV immediately, soon after
随时 **suíshí** ADV whenever, at any moment
随时随地 **suíshí suídì** IDIOM anytime and anywhere, ever
随手 **suíshǒu** ADV 1 immediately ■ 请随手关门。Qǐng suíshǒu guānmén. *Please close the door after you.* 2 casually, without much thought

随手乱放 **suíshǒu luàn fàng** put ... somewhere casually and without much thought
随意 **suíyì** I ADV as one pleases, casually II ADJ random
随意抽样 **suíyì chōuyàng** random sampling
随着 **suízhe** PREP along with, in the wake of

岁 **suì** TRAD 歲 M. WD year (of age) ■ 我小弟弟今年八岁。Wǒ xiǎo dìdi jīnnián bā suì. *My younger brother is eight years old.*

NOTE: See 年纪 niánjì.

岁数 **suìshu** N years of age ■ 你今年多大岁数? Nǐ jīnnián duōdà suìshu? *How old are you?*
上了岁数的人 **shàngle suìshu de rén** elderly person
岁月 **suìyuè** N years

碎 **suì** ADJ broken, fragmentary ■ 车窗的玻璃被一块石头打碎了。Chēchuāng de bōli bèi yí kuài shítou dǎ suì le. *The car window was shattered by a stone.*

穗 **suì** N the ear of grain

麦穗 **màisuì** ear of wheat, wheat head

隧 **suì** N tunnel

隧道 **suìdào** N tunnel

孙 **sūn** TRAD 孫 N grandchild

孙女 **sūnnǚ** N granddaughter
孙子 **sūnzi** N grandson

笋 **sǔn** N bamboo shoot

竹笋 **zhúsǔn** bamboo shoot

损 **sǔn** TRAD 損 v damage

损害 **sǔnhài** v harm, damage, injure
损耗 **sǔnhào** I v undergo wear and tear, deplete II N loss
损坏 **sǔnhuài** v damage as to render unusable, damage
损坏公物 **sǔnhuài gōngwù** damage public property
损人利己 **sǔnrénlìjǐ** IDIOM harm others to benefit oneself
损伤 **sǔnshāng** v damage, harm, hurt
损失 **sǔnshī** I v lose, suffer from damage and/or loss II N loss, damage ■ 这次水灾造成巨大损失。Zhè cì shuǐzāi zàochéng jùdà sǔnshī. *This flooding caused huge losses.*

唆 **suō** v instigate, abet

唆使 **suōshǐ** v abet, instigate

缩 suō TRAD 縮 V shrink ■ 棉布下水以后会缩。Miánbù xiàshuǐ yǐhòu huì suō. *Cotton cloth will shrink in the wash.*

缩短 suōduǎn V shorten, cut down

缩小 suōxiǎo V reduce in size, shrink

所 1 suǒ M. WD (for houses or institutions housed in a building)
一所医院 **yì suǒ yīyuàn** a hospital
两所大学 **liǎng suǒ dàxué** two universities

所 2 suǒ I N place II PARTICLE indicating passive voice

所得 suǒdé N income, earnings
所得税 **suǒdéshuì** income tax

所谓 suǒwèi ADJ what is called, so-called ■ 他所谓的 "理由" 完全站不住脚。Tā suǒwèi de "lǐyóu" wánquán zhàn bu zhù jiǎo. *His so-called "reason" does not have a leg to stand on.*

所以 suǒyǐ CONJ therefore, so ■ 我上星期病了，所以没有来上班。Wǒ shàng xīngqī bìng le, suǒyǐ méiyǒu lái shàngbān. *I was sick last week, so I did not come to work.*

所有 suǒyǒu IDIOM ADJ all ■ 所有的朋友都反对他的计划。Suǒyǒu de péngyou dōu fǎnduì tā de jìhuà. *All his friends opposed his plan.*

NOTE: 所有 suǒyǒu is (1) used only as an attribute, (2) always followed by 的 de and (3) often used together with 都 dōu.

所有制 suǒyǒuzhì N ownership

所在 suǒzài N place, location

索 suǒ V search, search for

索赔 suǒpéi V claim indemnity

索取 suǒqǔ V ask for, exact
索取报名单 **suǒqǔ bàomíngdān** ask for an application form

索性 suǒxìng ADV might as well, simply

锁 suǒ TRAD 鎖 I N lock II V lock ■ 离开以前一定要把办公室的门锁上。Líkāi yǐqián yídìng yào bǎ bàngōngshì de mén suǒ shàng. *Before you leave, make sure you lock the office door.*

嗦 suo as in 罗嗦 luósuo

T

他 tā PRON he, him ■ 我不喜欢他。Wǒ bù xǐhuan tā. *I don't like him.*

他们 tāmen PRON they, them ■ 他们有困难，我们要帮助他们。Tāmen yǒu kùnnan, wǒmen yào bāngzhù tāmen. *As they're in difficulty, we should help them.*

他人 tārén PRON another person, other people

它 tā PRON it ■ 它是我的小狗。Tā shì wǒ de xiǎo gǒu. *It's my puppy.*

它们 tāmen PRON (non-human) they, them (plural form of 它 tā)

她 tā PRON she, her ■ 她是我班上的女同学。Tā shì wǒ bānshang de nǚ tóngxué. *She's a girl student from my class.*

她们 tāmen PRON (female) they, them

塌 tā V collapse, cave in

踏 tā as in 踏实 tāshi

踏实 tāshi ADJ 1 reliable 2 free from anxiety, reassured

塔 tǎ N pagoda, tower (座 zuò) ■ 在中国几乎每一个城市都有一座古塔。Zài Zhōngguó jīhū měi yí ge chéngshì dōu yǒu yí zuò gǔ tǎ. *In China almost every town has an ancient tower.*

踏 tà V step on, tread ■ 脚踏实地。Jiǎo tà shídì. *The feet step on firm ground. (→ be earnest and down-to-earth)*

蹋 tà V as in 糟蹋 zāota

台 tái TRAD 檯 I N table, desk (张 zhāng) ■ 董事长坐在一张大写字台后面。Dǒngshìzhǎng zuò zai yì zhāng dà xiězìtái hòumiàn. *The chairman of the board sat behind a large desk.* II M. WD (for machines, big instruments, etc.)
一台机器 **yì tái jīqì** a machine

台风 táifēng N typhoon (场 cháng)

台阶 táijiē N flight of steps, steps

台湾 Táiwān N Taiwan

抬 tái TRAD 擡 V lift, raise ■ 这几个小姑娘怎么抬得动这台电脑呢？Zhè jǐ ge xiǎogūniang zěnme tái de dòng zhè tái diànnǎo ne? *How could these little girls carry this computer?*
抬高 (物价) **táigāo (wùjià)** raise (prices)

泰 tài ADJ peaceful ■ 国泰民安。Guó tài mín ān. *The country is prosperous and the people live in peace.*

泰然 tàirán ADJ calm, composed
泰然自若 **tàirán zìruò** behave with great composure

太 tài ADV 1 excessively, too ■ 这个房间太小，坐不下二十个人。Zhège fángjiān tài xiǎo, zuò bu xià èrshí ge rén. *This room is too small. It can't seat twenty people.* 2 extremely, really ■ 你们现在抬高物价，太不讲道理了。Nǐmen *xiànzài táigāo wùjià, tài bù jiǎng dàolǐ le. It is extremely unreasonable of you to raise prices now.*

太空 tàikōng N outer space

太平 tàipíng ADJ peaceful and orderly

太平间 tàipíngjiān N mortuary

太平洋 Tàipíngyáng N the Pacific Ocean

太太 tàitai N 1 Mrs, Madam ■ 王先生和王太太常常在家里请客吃饭。Wáng xiānsheng hé Wáng tàitai chángcháng zài jiā li qǐngkè chīfàn. *Mr and Mrs Wang often give dinner parties in their home.* 2 wife ■ 今天是我太太生日，我要早一点回家。Jīntiān shì wǒ tàitai shēngrì, wǒ yào zǎo yìdiǎn huíjiā. *Today's my wife's birthday. I need to go home earlier.*

NOTE: (1) While *Mrs* is used in English-speaking countries regardless of class or social status, its counterpart 太太 tàitai is only used in middle-class or upper-class circles. Similarly, 太太 tàitai meaning *wife* is also only used in such circles. (2) Although Chinese women often retain their family names after marriage, 太太 tàitai as a form of address must be prefixed by the husband's family name: 王太太 Wáng tàitai *Mrs Wang (the wife of Mr Wang).*

太阳 tàiyang N the sun, sunshine

NOTE: (1) Put together, 太 tài (meaning *big, great* in Classical Chinese) and 阳 yáng (meaning the Yang of ancient Chinese thought) mean the ultimate Yang, as the sun is the ultimate symbol of Yang. The ultimate symbol of Yin is the moon 月 yuè. (2) In 太阳 tàiyang, 阳 yang is pronounced in the neutral tone.

太阳能 tàiyángnéng N solar energy

态 tài TRAD 態 N stance

态度 tàidu N attitude, approach ■ 这位服务员的服务态度不好。Zhè wèi fúwùyuán de fúwù tàidu bù hǎo. *This attendant's work attitude is not good.*

NOTE: Though 态度 tàidu is glossed as *attitude* or *approach*, it is more commonly used in Chinese than its equivalents in English.

汰 tài V eliminate (See 淘汰 táotài)

摊 tān TRAD 攤 N trader's stand, stall ■ 路两边摆了很多摊子，有卖吃的，也有卖工艺品的。Lù liǎngbian bǎile hěn duō tānzi, yǒu mài chī de, yě yǒu mài gōngyìpǐn de. *There are many stands on the two sides of the street; some sell food and others sell small handicraft articles.*

滩 tān TRAD 灘 N beach, shoal (See 沙滩 shātān)

瘫 tān TRAD 癱 V be paralyzed

瘫痪 tānhuàn I V be paralyzed II N paralysis 全身瘫痪 quánshēn tānhuàn complete paralysis

贪 tān V 1 be greedy 2 be corrupt, practice graft

贪官 tānguān corrupt official

3 covet, hanker after

贪婪 tānlán ADJ greedy, avaricious

贪图 tāntú V hanker after, covet

贪污 tānwū I V embezzle, be involved in corruption

贪污公款 tānwū gōngkuǎn embezzle public funds

II N graft, corruption

贪污犯 tānwūfàn embezzler, grafter

贪心 tānxīn N greed, avarice

贪嘴 tānzuǐ ADJ greedy for food

坛 tán TRAD 壇 N altar

天坛 Tiāntán the Temple of Heaven (in Beijing)

潭 tán N deep pool

痰 tán N phlegm, sputum

吐痰 tǔtán spit

谈 tán TRAD 談 V talk, discuss ■ 我想跟你谈一件事。Wǒ xiǎng gēn nǐ tán yí jiàn shì. *I'd like to discuss something with you.*

谈一下 tán yíxià talk briefly about, give a brief talk about

谈话 tánhuà V have a (serious, formal) talk ■ 校长找我谈话。Xiàozhǎng zhǎo wǒ tánhuà. *The principal summoned me for a talk.*

谈论 tánlùn V talk about

谈判 tánpàn I V negotiate, hold talks ■ 双方正在为签订一项合同谈判。Shuāngfāng zhèngzài wèi qiāndìng yí xiàng hétong tánpàn. *The two sides are negotiating the signing of a contract.*

II N negotiation (项 xiàng) ■ 这项谈判在进行了三个星期以后终于取得双方满意的结果。Zhè xiàng tánpàn zài jìnxíng sān ge xīngqī yǐhòu zhōngyú qǔdé shuāngfāng mǎnyì de jiéguǒ. *After three weeks the negotiations finally reached a conclusion that satisfied both parties.*

谈天 tántiān V talk about everything under the sun, shoot the breeze, chitchat ■ 上班的时候，不能谈天。Shàngbān de shíhou, bù néng tántiān. *You are not supposed to chat during working hours.*

毯 tǎn N carpet, rug, blanket

地毯 dìtǎn carpet, rug
挂毯 guàtǎn tapestry
毯子 tǎnzi N blanket (条 tiáo)

坦 tǎn ADJ **1** candid, frank **2** level, smooth

平坦 píngtǎn (of land) level, flat
坦白 tǎnbái V **1** confess to (crimes or wrongdoing) **2** be frank, be candid
坦白地说 tǎnbáide shuō to be frank with you, to tell the truth
坦克 tǎnkè N tank (military vehicle)

炭 tàn N charcoal

碳 tàn N carbon (C)

二氧化碳 èryǎnghuàtàn carbon dioxide

叹 tàn TRAD 嘆 V sigh

叹气 tànqì V heave a sigh

探 tàn V **1** explore **2** spy **3** visit

探测 tàncè V survey, probe
探亲 tànqīn V visit one's parents, visit relatives
探索 tànsuǒ V explore, seek, search for ■ 医生们正在探索医治这种疾病的方法。Yīshēngmen zhèngzài tànsuǒ yīzhì zhè zhǒng jíbìng de fāngfǎ. *Doctors are searching for a way to cure this disease.*
探讨 tàntǎo V explore and discuss, inquire into
探讨...的可行性 tàntǎo...de kěxíngxìng explore the feasibility of ...
探望 tànwàng V go to see, visit
探望病人 tànwàng bìngrén visit someone who is sick, visit a patient
探险 tànxiǎn V venture into, explore
探险队 tànxiǎnduì exploration team
探险家 tànxiǎnjiā explorer

汤 tāng TRAD 湯 N soup (碗 wǎn) ■ 妈妈做的汤真好喝。Māma zuò de tāng zhēn hǎohē. *The soup mom prepared is really delicious.*
喝汤 hē tāng eat soup
汤匙 tāngchí N tablespoon (把 bǎ)
汤圆 tāngyuán N stuffed dumpling made of glutinous rice

堂 táng I N **1** main room, hall (See 食堂 shítáng.) **2** relationship between cousins of the same paternal grandfather
堂兄弟 tángxiōngdì male children of one's father's brothers
II M. WD (for a period of lessons)

上午有三堂课 shàngwǔ yǒu sān táng kè three classes in the morning

膛 táng N chest

唐 táng N the Tang Dynasty (AD 618–907)

唐人街 tángrénjiē N Chinatown

塘 táng N dyke, embankment

糖 táng N sugar, candy (块 kuài) ■ "你的咖啡里要放糖吗？" "Nǐ de kāfēi li yào fàng táng ma?" *"Do you want sugar in your coffee?"*
糖果 tángguǒ N candy, sweets

倘 tǎng CONJ if, in case

倘若 tǎngruò CONJ if, in case

躺 tǎng V lie ■ 她喜欢躺在床上看书。Tā xǐhuan tǎng zài chuángshang kànshū. *She likes to lie on the bed and read.*

趟 tàng M. WD (for trips) ■ 我去了两趟，都没找到他。Wǒ qùle liǎng tàng, dōu méi zhǎodao tā. *I made two trips but did not find him.*

烫 tàng TRAD 燙 ADJ boiling hot, scalding hot, burning hot ■ 这碗汤太烫了，没法喝。Zhè wǎn tāng tài tàng le, méifǎ hē. *This bowl of soup is too hot to eat.*

涛 tāo N big waves

滔 tāo V inundate, flood

滔滔不绝 tāotāo bùjué ADJ talking on and on in a flow of eloquence

掏 tāo V pull out, draw out

掏耳朵 tāo ěrduo pick one's ears

陶 táo N pottery

陶瓷 táocí N pottery and porcelain, ceramics

萄 táo N as in 葡萄 pútao

淘 táo V wash in a pan or basket

淘金 táojīn pan for gold
淘气 táoqì ADJ naughty, mischievous
淘气鬼 táoqìguǐ a naughty child, an imp
淘汰 táotài V eliminate through competition
淘汰赛 táotàisài (in sports) elimination series

桃 táo N peach

桃花 táohuā peach blossom

桃树 táoshù peach tree
桃子 táozi peach (只 zhī)

逃 táo v 1 flee, run away (from danger, punishment, etc.) ■ 警察来的时候, 强盗已经逃走了。 Jǐngchá lái de shíhou, qiángdào yǐjīng táozǒu le. *By the time the policemen arrived, the robbers had fled.* 2 evade, escape
逃避 táobì v evade, shirk
逃避责任 táobì zérèn evade responsibility
逃跑 táopǎo v run way, take flight
逃税 táoshuì I v evade paying taxes ■ 有不少公司冒险逃税。 Yǒu bùshǎo gōngsī màoxiǎn táoshuì. *Some companies risk evading tax payments.* II N tax evasion ■ 逃税是要进监狱的。 Táoshuì shì yào jìn jiānyù de. *Tax evasion is punishable by imprisonment.*
逃学 táoxué v play truant
逃走 táozǒu Same as 逃跑 táopǎo

讨 tǎo TRAD 討 v ask for, demand
讨好 tǎohǎo v 1 fawn on, toady to 2 be rewarded with good results
吃力不讨好 chīlì bù tǎohǎo work hard only to get negative results, do a thankless job
讨价还价 tǎojià huánjià v haggle over prices, bargain
讨论 tǎolùn I v discuss, talk over ■ 老师们在讨论明年的工作。 Lǎoshīmen zài tǎolùn míngnián de gōngzuò. *The teachers are discussing next year's work.* II N discussion (次 cì)
讨厌 tǎoyàn I ADJ vexing, disgusting ■ 这种电视广告讨厌得很。 Zhè zhǒng diànshì guǎnggào tǎoyàn de hěn. *This kind of TV commercial is disgusting.* II v find vexing, find disgusting ■ 我讨厌连续下雨的天气。 Wǒ tǎoyàn liánxù xiàyǔ de tiānqì. *I hate incessant rain.*
讨债 tǎozhài v press for repayment of a debt

套 tào M. WD set, suit, suite (for a collection of things)
一套衣服 yí tào yīfu a suit of clothes
两套家具 liǎng tào jiājù two sets of furniture

特 tè ADV particularly, especially

特别 tèbié I ADJ special ■ 他病得很重, 住在特别病房。 Tā bìng de hěn zhòng, zhù zài tèbié bìngfáng. *He's seriously ill and stays in the special ward.* II ADV especially ■ 我特别喜欢吃新西兰的苹果。 Wǒ tèbié xǐhuan chī Xīnxīlán de píngguǒ. *I especially like New Zealand apples.*
特别行政区 tèbié xíngzhèngqū special administrative region
特产 tèchǎn N special local product or produce
特此 tècǐ ADV hereby

特点 tèdiǎn N special features, characteristics
特定 tèdìng ADJ specific, specified, special
特定的条件 tèdìngde tiáojiàn special condition
特快 tèkuài ADJ express
特快火车 tèkuài huǒchē express train
特快专递 tèkuài zhuān dì express delivery
特区 tèqū N special zone
特权 tèquán N privilege
特色 tèsè N distinguishing feature
特殊 tèshū ADJ special, unusual, exceptional ■ 你只有在特殊情况下才能采取这一措施。 Nǐ zhǐyǒu zài tèshū qíngkuàng xia cái néng cǎiqǔ zhè yí cuòshī. *Only under special circumstances can you take this step.*
特殊教育 tèshū jiàoyù special education
特务 tèwù N special agent, spy
特意 tèyì ADV for a special purpose, specially
特征 tèzhēng N salient feature

藤 téng N vine, rattan

藤椅 téngyǐ rattan chair
葡萄藤 pútaoténg grape vine

腾 téng v gallop, jump

疼 téng v 1 ache, hurt
头疼 tóu téng headache, have a headache 2 love dearly, dote on ■ 我小时候, 我奶奶可疼我了。 Wǒ xiǎoshíhou, wǒ nǎinai kě téng wǒ le. *When I was a child, my granny really doted on me dearly.*

NOTE: 疼 téng in the sense of *ache, hurt* is a colloquial word. You can use 痛 tòng instead of 疼 téng to mean *ache, hurt*.

疼痛 téngtòng ADJ pain, ache, soreness
全身疼痛 quánshēn téngtòng aches and pains all over

梯 tī N ladder, steps (See 电梯 diàntī, 楼梯 lóutī.)

踢 tī v kick

踢球 tī qiú play soccer
踢足球 tī zúqiú play soccer

提 tí v 1 carry in the hand (with the arm down) ■ 我可以提这个小皮箱上飞机吗? Wǒ kěyǐ tí zhège xiǎo píxiāng shàng fēijī ma? *Can I carry this small bag on board the plane?* 2 mention, raise ■ 你见到他的时候, 别提这件事。 Nǐ jiàndao tā de shíhou, bié tí zhè jiàn shì. *Don't mention this matter when you see him.*
提建议 tí jiànyì put forward a proposal, make a suggestion

提问题 **tí wèntí** raise a question

提案 **tí'àn** n proposal (份 **fèn**)

提拔 **tíbá** v promote (to a higher position)
提拔为部门经理 **tíbá wéi bùmén jīnglǐ** be promoted to branch manager

提包 **tíbāo** n handbag, shopping bag (只 **zhī**)

提倡 **tíchàng** v advocate, recommend

提纲 **tígāng** n outline

提高 **tígāo** v raise, advance, improve ■ 我们不断提高产品的质量。**Wǒmen búduàn tígāo chǎnpǐn de zhìliàng.** *We work constantly to improve the quality of our products.*

提供 **tígōng** v provide, supply ■ 我们提供售后服务。**Wǒmen tígōng shòuhòu fúwù.** *We provide after-sales service.*

提交 **tíjiāo** v submit to, refer to

提炼 **tíliàn** v extract and purify, refine

提名 **tímíng** v nominate (for a/an position/election)

提前 **tíqián** v put ahead of schedule, advance, bring forward ■ 长途汽车提前半小时到达。**Chángtú qìchē tíqián bàn xiǎoshí dàodá.** *The coach arrived half an hour ahead of the schedule.*

提取 **tíqǔ** v withdraw, collect
提取存款 **tíqǔ cúnkuǎn** withdraw money from a bank account
提取行李 **tíqǔ xíngli** collect luggage

提升 **tíshēng** v promote (to a higher position)

提示 **tíshì** v hint, tip ■ 给我一个提示, 好吗? 给我一个提示, hǎoma? *Can you give me a hint?*

提问 **tíwèn** v put questions to

提醒 **tíxǐng** v remind, call attention to

提要 **tíyào** n abstract, synopsis

提议 **tíyì** I v propose II n proposal

提早 **tízǎo** v Same as 提前 **tíqián**

题 **tí** trad 題 n 1 topic, title 2 question, problem

题材 **tícái** n subject matter, theme

题目 **tímù** n 1 question for an examination, school exercises, etc. (道 **dào**) ■ 这次测验一共有十道题目。**Zhè cì cèyàn yígòng yǒu shí dào tímù.** *There will be ten questions in this test.* 2 title, subject ■ 他要给文章取一个好题目。**Tā yào gěi wénzhāng qǔ yí ge hǎo tímù.** *He will give his essay a good title.*

蹄 **tí** n hoof

体 **tǐ** trad 體 I n 1 body 2 substance II v personally do or experience

体操 **tǐcāo** n gymnastics

体会 **tǐhuì** I v learn, realize, gain intimate knowledge through personal experience ■ 他当了一年爸爸, 体会到当父母是多么不容易。**Tā dāngle yì nián bàba, tǐhuì dào dāng fùmǔ shì duōme**

bù róngyì. *After being a father for a year, he realized how difficult parenting was.* II n personal understanding ■ 请你谈谈你在中国工作的体会。**Qǐng nǐ tántan nǐ zài Zhōngguó gōngzuò de tǐhuì.** *Please tell us what you have learned from working in China.*

体积 **tǐjī** n volume (mathematics) ■ 这个箱子体积不大, 为什么这么重? **Zhège xiāngzi tǐjī bú dà, wèishénme zhème zhòng?** *This box is not big. Why is it so heavy?*

体力 **tǐlì** n physical strength

体谅 **tǐliàng** v show understanding towards, be sympathetic to, make allowance for
体谅他人的难处 **tǐliang tārén de nánchu** understand and sympathize with other people's difficulties, empathize

体面 **tǐmiàn** I adj respectable, decent II n dignity, face

体贴 **tǐtiē** v give every consideration to, give loving care to

体温 **tǐwēn** n body temperature, temperature

体现 **tǐxiàn** v give expression to, embody

体验 **tǐyàn** I n personal experience II v learn through one's personal experience

体育 **tǐyù** n physical education, sports

体育场 **tǐyùchǎng** n stadium, sports field

体育馆 **tǐyùguǎn** n gymnasium ■ 这个体育馆有多少座位? **Zhège tǐyùguǎn yǒu duōshǎo zuòwèi?** *How many seats are there in this gymnasium?*

体育课 **tǐyù kè** n physical education (PE) lesson ■ 今天下午上体育课, 我不能穿皮鞋。**Jīntiān xiàwǔ shàng tǐyù kè, wǒ bù néng chuān píxié.** *I'm having a PE class this afternoon, so I can't wear leather shoes today.*

体制 **tǐzhì** n (organizational) system, structure

体质 **tǐzhì** n physique, constitution

体重 **tǐzhòng** n (body) weight

惕 **tì** adj be on the alert (See 警惕 **jǐngtì**)

剃 **tì** v shave
剃胡子 **tì húzi** shave one's beard

涕 **tì** n 1 tears 2 snivel (See 鼻涕 **bítì**)

屉 **tì** n drawer (See 抽屉 **chōutì**)

替 **tì** v 1 replace, substitute ■ 万一他生病了, 谁来替他呢? **Wànyī tā shēngbìng le, shuí lái tì tā ne?** *If he falls ill, who will replace him?* 2 Same as 给 **gěi** prep

替代 **tìdài** v substitute for, replace

替换 **tìhuàn** v replace, displace

天 **tiān** N 1 sky, heaven 2 day ■ 我在朋友家住
了三天。Wǒ zài péngyou jiā zhùle sān tiān. *I
stayed with my friend for three days.* 3 weather
■ 农民还是靠天吃饭。Nóngmín háishì kào tiān
chīfàn. *Farmers still depend on the weather to
make a living.*

老天爷 **Lǎotiānyé** Heavens (a colloquial term
that denotes "God" or "Nature")

天才 **tiāncái** N genius ■ 他们的儿子非常聪
明，但是并不是天才。Tāmen de érzi fēicháng
cōngming, dànshì bìng bù shì tiāncái. *Their son is
very smart, but he isn't a genius.*

天地 **tiāndì** N field of activity, scope of operation

天空 **tiānkōng** N sky

天气 **tiānqì** N weather ■ 明天的天气怎么样？
Míngtiān de tiānqì zěnmeyàng? *How will the
weather be tomorrow?*

天然 **tiānrán** ADJ natural
　天然气 **tiānránqì** natural gas

天色 **tiānsè** N time of the day ■ 天色还早。
Tiānsè hái zǎo. *It's still early.*

天上 **tiānshang** N in the sky

天生 **tiānshēng** ADJ inherent, natural

天堂 **tiāntáng** N paradise

天天 **tiāntiān** N every day
　天天向上 **tiāntiān xiàngshàng** make
progress every day

天文 **tiānwén** N astronomy
　天文台 **tiānwéntái** astronomical observatory
　天文学家 **tiānwénxuéjiā** astronomer

天下 **tiān xià** N under heaven, in the world, on
earth

天线 **tiānxiàn** N antenna

天知道！ **Tiān zhīdao!** IDIOM Only God knows!

天真 **tiānzhēn** ADJ 1 simple and unaffected,
ingenuous ■ 和天真的孩子说话，是一种享
受。Hé tiānzhēn de háizi shuōhuà, shì yì zhǒng
xiǎngshòu. *Talking with innocent children is an
enjoyment.* 2 naïve, gullible ■ 你怎么会相信
这种广告？太天真了！Nǐ zěnme huì xiāngxìn zhè
zhǒng guǎnggào? Tài tiānzhēn le! *How could you
believe such advertisements? You're too naïve!*

天主教 **tiānzhǔjiào** N the Catholic Church,
Catholicism
　天主教徒 **Tiānzhǔjiàotú** member of the
Catholic Church, Catholic

添 **tiān** V add ■ 你这么忙，我不想给你添麻烦。
Nǐ zhème máng, wǒ bù xiǎng gěi nǐ tiān máfan. *You're so busy. I don't want to trouble you.*

田 **tián** N farmland (esp. paddy fields), fields
　种田 **zhòngtián** grow crops, farm

田地 **tiándì** N farmland, field

田野 **tiányě** N farmland and open country ■ 城
里人有时候喜欢到田野走走。Chénglǐrén yǒu-
shíhou xǐhuan dào tiányě zǒuzǒu. *City people like
to take an occasional stroll in the open country.*

填 **tián** V fill in (a form, blanks as in an exercise) ■ 进入一个国家要填表，离开一个国家
也要填表。Jìnrù yí ge guójiā yào tián biǎo, líkāi
yí ge guójiā yě yào tián biǎo. *To enter a country
you need to fill in a form, and to leave a country
you need to fill in a form as well.*

填补 **tiánbǔ** V fill, fill up

填写 **tiánxiě** V fill out (a document)

挑 **tiāo** V take one's pick, choose, select ■ 商
店里这么多鞋子，你还挑不到一双喜欢的？
Shàngdiàn li zhème duō xiézi, nǐ hái tiāo bu dào
yì shuāng xǐhuan de? *There are so many shoes in
the store, and you still can't choose a pair you like?*
　东挑西拣 **dōng-tiāo-xī-jiǎn** choose this and
pick that, spend a long time choosing, be very
choosy

挑选 **tiāoxuǎn** V select ■ 董事会要从经理中
挑选出一名总经理。Dǒngshìhuì yào cóng jīnglǐ
zhong tiāoxuǎnchu yì míng zǒngjīnglǐ. *The board
of directors will select a chief executive officer
from the executives.*

条 **tiáo** TRAD 條 I M. WD (for things with a
long, narrow shape)
　一条河 **yì tiáo hé** a river
　两条鱼 **liǎng tiáo yú** two fish
II N 1 strip 2 item, article

条件 **tiáojiàn** N 1 condition ■ 这个地区的自然
条件不好。Zhège dìqū de zìrán tiáojiàn bù hǎo.
*The natural conditions of this region are rather
poor.*
　生活条件 **shēnghuó tiáojiàn** living conditions ■ 他们那里的生活条件比较差。Tāmen
nàlǐ de shēnghuó tiáojiàn bǐjiào chà. *Their living
conditions are rather poor.*
　工作条件 **gōngzuò tiáojiàn** working conditions ■ 工人们要求改善工作条件。Gōngrén-
men yāoqiú gǎishàn gōngzuò tiáojiàn. *Workers
demand that their working conditions be
improved.* 2 requirement, prerequisite ■ 对方
的条件太高，我们无法合作。Duìfāng de tiáojiàn
tài gāo, wǒmen wúfǎ hézuò. *The other party's
requirements are too high for us to work with
them.*

条款 **tiáokuǎn** N clause (in a contract, an agreement, etc.) (项 xiàng)

条理 **tiáolǐ** N orderliness
　有条理 **yǒu tiáolǐ** well-organized

条例 **tiáolì** N regulation, rule

条文 **tiáowén** N clause, article, item

条约 **tiáoyuē** N treaty, pact (份 fèn) ■ 两国
将签订条约，以加强合作。Liǎng guó jiāng

qiāndìng tiáoyuē, yǐ jiāqiáng hézuò. *The two countries will sign a treaty in order to strengthen cooperation.*

条子 **tiáozi** N informal note (张 zhāng)
给他留一张条子 **gěi tā liú yì zhāng tiáozi** leave a brief note for him

调 **tiáo** TRAD 調 V **1** adjust **2** mediate **3** provoke, tease

调和 **tiáohé** V **1** mediate, reconcile **2** compromise
调剂 **tiáojì** V adjust, regulate
调节 **tiáojié** V regulate, moderate
调节器 **tiáojiéqì** regulator, conditioner
调解 **tiáojiě** V mediate, make peace
调解纠纷 **tiáojiě jiūfēn** mediate disputes
调皮 **tiáopí** ADJ naughty, mischievous
调整 **tiáozhěng** V adjust, rectify ■ 教育部打算调整中小学的师生比例。Jiàoyùbù dǎsuàn tiáozhěng zhōng-xiǎoxué de shīshēng bǐlì. *The Ministry of Education plans to adjust the teacher-student ratio in schools.*

挑 **tiǎo** V **1** poke, pick up **2** stir up, instigate

挑拨 **tiǎobō** V instigate, sow discord
挑拨同事之间的关系 **tiǎobō tóngshì zhījiān de guānxi** sow discord among colleagues
挑衅 **tiǎoxìn** I V provoke II N provocation
故意挑衅 **gùyì tiǎoxìn** deliberate provocation
挑战 **tiǎozhàn** V challenge to battle, challenge to a contest, throw down the gauntlet

跳 **tiào** V jump, leap, hop

跳动 **tiàodòng** V move up and down, beat
跳高 **tiào gāo** N high jump
撑杆跳高 **chēnggǎn tiàogāo** pole vault, pole jump
跳绳 **tiào shéng** N rope-skipping, rope-jumping
跳水 **tiào shuǐ** N diving
跳板跳水 **tiàobǎn tiàoshuǐ** springboard diving
跳台跳水 **tiàotái tiàoshuǐ** platform diving
跳远 **tiào yuǎn** N long jump
三级跳远 **sānjí tiàoyuǎn** hop, step and jump, triple jump
跳舞 **tiàowǔ** V dance ■ 她跳舞跳得很美。Tā tiàowǔ tiào de hěn měi. *She dances beautifully.*
跳跃 **tiàoyuè** V jump, leap
跳蚤 **tiàozǎo** N flea (只 zhī)

贴 **tiē** TRAD 貼 V paste, stick ■ 他回到办公室，发现门上贴了一张便条。Tā huídào bàngōng-shì, fāxiàn mén shang tiēle yì zhāng biàntiáo. *When he came back to the office he found a note stuck on the door.*

帖 **tiě** N invitation card

请帖 **qǐngtiě** invitation card

铁 **tiě** TRAD 鐵 N iron ■ 花园里的那条长椅是铁做的。Huāyuán li de nà tiáo chángyǐ shì tiě zuò de. *The bench in the garden is made of iron.*

铁道 **tiědào** N Same as 铁路 tiělù
铁路 **tiělù** N railway (条 tiáo)

厅 **tīng** TRAD 廳 N hall (See 餐厅 cāntīng.)

听 **tīng** TRAD 聽 V **1** listen ■ 他每天早上都听广播。Tā měi tiān zǎoshang dōu tīng guǎngbō. *He listens to the radio early every morning.*
听见 **tīngjiàn** hear ■ 我听见有人在花园里叫我。Wǒ tīngjiàn yǒu rén zài huāyuán li jiào wǒ. *I heard somebody calling me in the garden.*
2 heed, obey ■ 你不听他的话，会后悔的。Nǐ bù tīng tā de huà, huì hòuhuǐ de. *You will be sorry if you don't heed his advice (or warning).*
听话 **tīnghuà** V heed, be obedient
听讲 **tīngjiǎng** V listen to a talk (or lecture)
听取 **tīngqǔ** V hear (one's subordinate's report, complaint, etc.)
听说 **tīngshuō** V hear of, it is said ■ 听说张先生一家搬走了。Tīngshuō Zhāng xiānsheng yìjiā bānzǒu le. *I've heard that Mr Zhang's family has moved.*
听写 **tīngxiě** N dictation, do dictation
听众 **tīngzhòng** N audience (of a radio, a concert, etc.)

NOTE: See note on 观众 guānzhòng.

亭 **tíng** N pavilion, kiosk

亭子 **tíngzi** pavilion, kiosk

停 **tíng** V **1** stop, park (a vehicle) ■ 路上车辆太多了，我们停停开开，花了一个小时才回到家。Lùshang chēliàng tài duō le, wǒmen tíng tíng kāi kāi, huāle yí ge xiǎoshí cái huídao jiā. *Traffic was heavy. We were continually stopping and it took us one hour to arrive home.*
停下来 **tíng xiàlai** come to a stop
2 stay over
停泊 **tíngbó** V (of ships) lie at anchor, anchor
停车 **tíngchē** V stop a car, park a car
停车场 **tíngchēchǎng** parking lot, car park
停顿 **tíngdùn** V pause
停留 **tíngliú** V stop and stay for a short while, stop over
停职 **tíngzhí** V suspend from one's duties (as a disciplinary action)
停止 **tíngzhǐ** V stop, cease ■ 请你们立即停止这种影响他人的行为。Qǐng nǐmen lìjí tíngzhǐ zhè zhǒng yǐngxiǎng tārén de xíngwéi. *Stop such disruptive behavior immediately, please.*
停滞 **tíngzhì** V stagnate, be at a standstill

庭 **tíng** N front courtyard

庭院 **tíngyuàn** N courtyard and garden

艇 **tǐng** N light boat (艘 sōu)

救生艇 **jiùshēngtǐng** lifeboat

挺 **tǐng** I ADV very ■ 她学习挺认真。Tā xuéxí tǐng rènzhēn. *She studies conscientiously.* II ADJ tall, upright, erect

NOTE: 挺 tǐng and 很 hěn share the same meaning, but 挺 tǐng is a colloquial word.

挺拔 **tǐngbá** ADJ tall and straight
挺立 **tǐnglì** V stand upright

通 **tōng** I V 1 (of roads, railways) lead to, go to ■ 条条大路通罗马。Tiáotiáo dàlù tōng Luómǎ. *All roads lead to Rome.* 2 go through without blockage ■ 下水道不通了。Xiàshuǐdào bùtōng le. *The sewer is blocked up.* 3 understand, comprehend 4 notify, give notice II ADJ 1 (of language) grammatical, logical ■ 这句话不通，但是我说不出错在哪里。Zhè jù huà bù tōng, dànshì wǒ shuō bu chū cuò zài nǎlǐ. *This sentence is not quite right, but I can't identify where the mistake is.* 2 in general use

通报 **tōngbào** I V (of government offices) circulate a notice II N circular, bulletin
通常 **tōngcháng** ADJ general, usual
通道 **tōngdào** N thoroughfare, passageway
通风 **tōngfēng** N ventilation
通风口 **tōngfēngkǒu** ventilation opening
通风系统 **tōngfēng xìtǒng** ventilation system
通告 **tōnggào** I V give public notice, announce II N public notice, announcement
通过 **tōngguò** I V pass through ■ 从我家到机场，要通过城里。Cóng wǒ jiā dào jīchǎng, yào tōngguò chénglǐ. *Going from my home to the airport, one has to pass through the city center.* II PREP through, as a result of ■ 通过这次访问，我更了解中国了。Tōngguò zhè cì fǎngwèn, wǒ gèng liǎojiě Zhōngguó le. *As a result of this visit, I understand China better.*
通航 **tōngháng** V be open to navigation or air traffic
通红 **tōnghóng** ADJ very red
通货膨胀 **tōnghuò péngzhàng** N inflation
抑制通货膨胀 **yìzhì tōnghuò péngzhàng** check inflation
通奸 **tōngjiān** V commit adultery
通商 **tōngshāng** V (of countries) have trade relations
通顺 **tōngshùn** ADJ (of writing) coherent and smooth

通俗 **tōngsú** ADJ easily understood and accepted by common folks, popular
通俗读物 **tōngsúdúwù** light reading, popular literature
通信 **tōngxìn** V exchange letters with, correspond
通行 **tōngxíng** V pass through
通行证 **tōngxíngzhèng** pass, permit
通讯 **tōngxùn** N communication ■ 这几年通讯技术迅速发展，传真、电子邮件、手机等越来越普及。Zhè jǐ nián tōngxùn jìshù xùnsù fāzhǎn, chuánzhēn, diànzǐ yóujiàn, shǒujī děng yuèláiyuè pǔjí. *In recent years communication technology has seen rapid development. Fax, e-mail, cell phones and so on are becoming more and more widely used.*
通讯社 **tōngxùn shè** N news service
通用 **tōngyòng** V be in general use
通知 **tōngzhī** I V notify, inform ■ 代表团什么时候来，请及时通知。Dàibiǎotuán shénme shíhou lái, qǐng jíshí tōngzhī. *Please let us know promptly when the delegation will come.* II N notice ■ 市政府在报上发了一个通知。Shì zhèngfǔ zài bào shang fāle yí ge tōngzhī. *The city government has published a notice in the paper.*

童 **tóng** N child

童年 **tóngnián** N childhood

同 **tóng** I ADV together, in common II PREP with, along with ■ 我们正在同那家公司商量合办食品加工厂的计划。Wǒmen zhèngzài tóng nà jiā gōngsī shāngliang hébàn shípǐn jiāgōngchǎng de jìhuà. *We are discussing a plan with that company to open a food-processing plant.* III ADJ same, alike IV CONJ and ■ 这件事已经分别通知了教育局长同卫生局长。Zhè jiàn shì yǐjīng fēnbié tōngzhī le jiàoyù júzhǎng tóng wèishēng júzhǎng. *The director of the education bureau and the director of the public health bureau respectively have been informed of this matter.*
同伴 **tóngbàn** N companion
同胞 **tóngbāo** N fellow countryman, compatriot
同步 **tóngbù** ADJ at the same time, synchronic, simultaneous
同步卫星 **tóngbùwèixīng** synchronous satellite
同等 **tóngděng** ADJ of the same rank (status, grade, etc.)
同行 **tóngháng** ADJ of the same trade or occupation ■ 同行是冤家。Tóngháng shì yuānjia. *People of the same trade hate each other.*
同类 **tónglèi** ADJ of the same category (kind)
同盟 **tóngméng** N alliance, league

同情 tóngqíng

同情 **tóngqíng** I v sympathize with ■ 我很同情这位在交通事故中失去儿子的母亲。Wǒ hěn tóngqíng zhè wèi zài jiāotōng shìgù zhong shīqù érzi de mǔqin. *I sympathize with the mother who lost her son in the traffic accident.* II n sympathy

同时 **tóngshí** ADV at the same time, simultaneously ■ 我和她同时开始学中文。Wǒ hé tā tóngshí kāishǐ xué Zhōngwén. *She and I began to learn Chinese at the same time.*

同事 **tóngshì** N colleague, co-worker

同屋 **tóngwū** N roommate, flatmate ■ 他是我的同学，也是我的同屋。Tā shì wǒ de tóngxué, yě shì wǒ de tóngwū. *He is my classmate, and my roommate as well.*

同性恋 **tóngxìngliàn** N 1 homosexuality, homosexual love 2 (a person) homosexual, gay, lesbian

同学 **tóngxué** N classmate, schoolmate ■ 我的朋友大多是我的同学。Wǒ de péngyou dàduō shì wǒ de tóngxué. *Most of my friends are my schoolmates.*

老同学 **lǎotóngxué** former schoolmate

NOTE: In Chinese schools, teachers address students as 同学们 tóngxuémen, e.g. ■ 同学们，我们现在上课了。Tóngxuémen, wǒmen xiànzài shàngkè le. *Class, we're starting class now.*

同样 **tóngyàng** ADJ same, similar ■ 他和妻子有同样的爱好，同样的理想。Tā hé qīzi yǒu tóngyàng de àihào, tóngyàng de lǐxiǎng. *He and his wife share the same hobby and the same dream.*

同一 **tóngyī** ADJ identical, same

同意 **tóngyì** v agree, approve ■ 我不同意你说的话。Wǒ bù tóngyì nǐ shuō de huà. *I don't agree with what you said.*

同志 **tóngzhì** N comrade

NOTE: 同志 tóngzhì used to be the most common form of address in China before 1980. Now it is seldom used. 同志 tóngzhì is almost never used between a Chinese and a foreigner. The common forms of address in China today are 先生 xiānsheng (to men) and 小姐 xiǎojiě (to women, especially young women). In some places 同志 tóngzhì has acquired the meaning for *a fellow homosexual.*

铜 **tóng** TRAD 銅 N copper, bronze ■ 铜是一种重要金属。Tóng shì yì zhǒng zhòngyào jīnshǔ. *Copper is an important metal.*

筒 **tǒng** N section of thick bamboo

竹筒 **zhútǒng** a thick bamboo tube

捅 **tǒng** v poke, stab

桶 **tǒng** N bucket, pail (只 zhī) ■ 他提了一桶水去洗汽车。Tā tíle yì tǒng shuǐ qù xǐ qìchē. *He carried a bucket of water over to wash his car.*

统 **tǒng** TRAD 統 ADV together

统称 **tǒngchēng** v generally be known as

统筹 **tǒngchóu** v plan as a whole

统计 **tǒngjì** I v add up II n statistics

统一 **tǒngyī** I v unify, integrate ■ 关于这个问题，我们需要统一认识。Guānyú zhège wèntí, wǒmen xūyào tǒngyī rènshi. *We need to reach a common understanding on this issue.* II ADJ unified ■ 这些国家已经形成一个统一的市场。Zhèxiē guójiā yǐjīng xíngchéng yí ge tǒngyī de shìchǎng. *These countries have already formed a common market.*

统治 **tǒngzhì** v rule

统治阶级 **tǒngzhì jiējí** ruling class

痛 **tòng** v Same as 疼 téng v 1

痛苦 **tòngkǔ** ADJ painful, tortuous

痛快 **tòngkuai** ADJ overjoyed, very delighted ■ 我在会上说了一直想说的话，心里很痛快。Wǒ zài huìshang shuōle yìzhí xiǎng shuō de huà, xīnli hěn tòngkuai. *At the meeting I said what I'd been wanting to say, and felt extremely pleased.*

偷 **tōu** v steal, pilfer ■ 我的钱包让人偷了！Wǒ de qiánbāo ràng rén tōu le! *My wallet's been stolen!*

偷窃 **tōuqiè** v steal, pilfer

偷税 **tōushuì** v evade taxes

偷偷 **tōutōu** ADV stealthily, on the quiet ■ 我看见一个人偷偷走进校长办公室。Wǒ kànjiàn yí ge rén tōutōu zǒujìn xiàozhǎng bàngōngshì. *I saw a figure walking stealthily into the principal's office.* (→ *I saw someone sneak into the principal's office.*)

头 **tóu** TRAD 頭 I N 1 the head 2 head, chief, leader ■ 你们的头儿呢？我要找他说话。Nǐmen de tóur ne? Wǒ yào zhǎo tā shuōhuà. *Who's your head? (or Who's in charge here?) I want to talk to him.* II ADJ first, first few ■ 我刚来的头几个星期，几乎天天下雨。Wǒ gāng lái de tóu jǐge xīngqī, jīhū tiāntiān xiàyǔ. *The first few weeks after I arrived, it rained almost every day.* III M. wD (for cattle or sheep) 一头牛 **yì tóu niú** a head of cattle (or buffalo/cow) 两头羊 **liǎng tóu yáng** two sheep

头发 **tóufa** N hair (on the human head) (根 gēn)

头脑 **tóunǎo** N brains ■ 她很有头脑。Tā hěn yǒu tóunǎo. *She's got plenty of brains.*

头脑简单 **tóunǎo jiǎndān** simple-minded

投 **tóu** v **1** throw, toss **2** join

投标 **tóubiāo** v make a bid, lodge a tender
投产 **tóuchǎn** v go into production
投放 **tóufàng** v **1** throw in, put in **2** put (goods, funds) on the market
投机[1] **tóujī** I v **1** engage in speculation
货币投机 **huòbì tóujī** currency speculation
2 be opportunistic **II** ADJ opportunistic
投机分子 **tóujīfènzǐ** opportunist
投机[2] **tóujī** ADJ agreeable, of the same mind
谈得很投机 **tán de hěn tóujī** have a most agreeable conversation
投票 **tóupiào** v cast a vote, vote
投入 **tóurù** v put into, invest ■ 他们在孩子的教育上投入很多钱。Tāmen zài háizi de jiàoyù shang tóurù hěn duō qián. *They put lots of money into their children's education.*
投诉 **tóusù** I v complain formally **II** N formal complaint ■ 公共汽车公司收到很多投诉，说汽车不准时。Gōnggòng qìchē gōngsī shōu dào hěn duō tóusù, shuō qìchē bù zhǔnshí. *The bus company has received lots of complaints about the buses not being punctual.*
投降 **tóuxiáng** v surrender, capitulate
投掷 **tóuzhì** v throw, hurl
投资 **tóuzī** I v invest
投资在一家合资企业 **tóu zī zài yì jiā hézī qǐyè** invest in a joint venture
II N investment
投资的回报 **tóuzī de huíbào** return on an investment

透 **tòu** I v penetrate, pass through ■ 月光透进房间。Yuèguāng tòujìn fángjiān. *Moonlight came into the room.* **II** ADJ thorough ■ 王老师把这个语法问题讲得很透。Wáng lǎoshī bǎ zhège yǔfǎ wèntí jiǎng de hěn tòu. *Teacher Wang explained this grammar point thoroughly.*
透明 **tòumíng** ADJ transparent
透明度 **tòumíngdù** transparency

凸 **tū** ADJ protruding

秃 **tū** ADJ bald, bare

突[1] **tū** ADJ protruding

突出 **tūchū** I v give prominence, highlight, emphasize ■ 他在这篇文章中突出了市场调查的重要性。Tā zài zhè piān wénzhāng zhong tūchūle shìchǎng diàochá de zhòngyàoxìng. *In this article he emphasizes the importance of market research.* **II** ADJ prominent, conspicuous

■ 火车上只有他一个外国人，显得很突出。Huǒchē shang zhǐyǒu tā yí ge wàiguórén, xiǎnde hěn tūchū. *He is the only foreigner on the train and is very conspicuous.*

突[2] **tū** ADV suddenly, unexpectedly

突击 **tūjī** N sudden attack **II** v make a sudden attack
突破 **tūpò** I N breakthrough **II** v achieve a breakthrough
突然 **tūrán** ADJ sudden, abrupt, unexpected

图 **tú** TRAD 圖 N **1** picture **2** chart, diagram (张 zhāng) ■ 他画了一张图，说明这种药不同成分的比例。Tā huàle yì zhāng tú, shuōmíng zhè zhǒng yào bùtóng chéngfèn de bǐlì. *He drew a chart to show the proportion of the various ingredients in this medicine.*
图案 **tú'àn** N pattern, design
图表 **túbiǎo** N chart, diagram, graph (张 zhāng)
图画 **túhuà** N picture, painting, drawing (张 zhāng)
图片 **túpiàn** N picture, photograph
图书 **túshū** N books
图书馆 **túshūguǎn** N library (座 zuò) ■ 图书馆里不准吃东西。Túshūguǎn lǐ bù zhǔn chī dōngxi. *Eating in the library is not allowed.* (→ No food in the library.)
图像 **túxiàng** N picture, image
图形 **túxíng** N graph
图纸 **túzhǐ** N blueprint

徒 **tú** N apprentice

徒弟 **túdì** N apprentice, pupil

屠 **tú** v slaughter

屠夫 **túfū** N butcher
屠杀 **túshā** N massacre

涂 **tú** TRAD 塗 v smear, spread on ■ 她在面包上涂了一层黄油。Tā zài miànbāo shang túle yì céng huángyóu. *She spread butter on the bread.*

途 **tú** N way, route

途径 **tújìng** N way, channel

土 **tǔ** N soil, earth ■ 你鞋上怎么全是土？Nǐ xié shang zěnme quán shì tǔ? *How come your shoes are covered with dirt?*
土地 **tǔdì** N land ■ 对农民来说，最重要的资源是土地。Duì nóngmín lái shuō, zuì zhòngyào de zīyuán shì tǔdì. *To farmers, the most important resource is land.*
土豆 **tǔdòu** N potato (只 zhī, 块 kuài)
土壤 **tǔrǎng** N soil

吐 tǔ

肥沃的土壤 féiwò de tǔrǎng fertile soil

吐 tǔ v spit, exhale ■ 她吓得半天才吐出一口气。Tā xià de bàntiān cái tǔ chū yì kǒu qì. *She was so terrified that she held her breath.*

吐 tù v vomit, throw up ■ 他酒喝得太多，吐了。Tā jiǔ hē de tài duō, tù le. *He vomited because he drank too much.*

兔 tù N rabbit, hare

兔子 tùzi rabbit, hare (只 zhī)

团 tuán TRAD 團 I N (military) regiment, group, team ■ 你打算参加旅行团，还是自己一个人去中国？Nǐ dǎsuàn cānjiā lǚxíngtuán, háishi zìjǐ yígerén qù Zhōngguó? *Do you plan to tour China in a tour group or all by yourself?*
代表团 dàibiǎotuán delegation
歌舞团 gēwǔtuán song and dance troupe
旅行团 lǚxíngtuán tour group
II v unite, get together
团结 tuánjié v unite, be in solidarity with ■ 团结就是力量。Tuánjié jiù shì lìliàng. *Unity is strength.*
团聚 tuánjù v reunite
和老同学团聚 hé lǎo tóngxué tuánjù reunite with old classmates
团体 tuántǐ N organization, group
团员 tuányuán N 1 member of a delegation, group, etc. 2 member of the Chinese Communist Youth League
团圆 tuányuán v reunite with family members
团长 tuánzhǎng N 1 head of a delegation 2 (in the army) regiment commander

推 tuī v 1 push, shove ■ 你要推这个门，不要拉。Nǐ yào tuī zhège mén, bú yào lā. *You should push this door, not pull it.* 2 shirk, shift 3 infer, reason 4 put off, defer
推测 tuīcè v infer, suppose
推迟 tuīchí v postpone ■ 旅行团出发的日期要推迟三天。Lǚxíngtuán chūfā de rìqī yào tuīchí sān tiān. *The date of the tourist group departure will be postponed for three days.*
推动 tuīdòng v push forward, promote ■ 中国迅速的经济发展推动了中文教学。Zhōngguó xùnsù de jīngjì fāzhǎn tuīdòngle Zhōngwén jiàoxué. *China's rapid economic development has promoted teaching and learning of the Chinese language.*
推翻 tuīfān v overturn, overthrow
推广 tuīguǎng v popularize, spread ■ 中国大力推广普通话，已经取得了成功。Zhōngguó dàilì tuīguǎng Pǔtōnghuà, yǐjīng qǔdéle chénggōng. *China's tremendous efforts to popularize Putonghua have been successful.*

推荐 tuījiàn v recommend ■ 你能不能给我推荐一位会说英语的牙医？Nǐ néng bu néng gěi wǒ tuījiàn yí wèi huì shuō Yīngyǔ de yáyī? *Could you recommend me a dentist who speaks English?*
推进 tuījìn v promote, advance
推理 tuīlǐ I v infer, reason II N reasoning by way of inference, inference
推论 tuīlùn I v infer, deduce II N conclusion based on inference
推算 tuīsuàn I v work out (with figures), calculate II N calculation
推销 tuīxiāo v promote (sale), market
推销新产品 tuīxiāo xīnchǎnpǐn promote a new product
推行 tuīxíng v carry out, pursue, implement
推选 tuīxuǎn v elect, choose

腿 tuǐ N leg (条 tiáo) ■ 他腿长，跑得快。Tā tuǐ cháng, pǎo de kuài. *He's got long legs and runs fast.*

退 tuì v move back, retreat ■ 请你退到黄线后面。Qǐng nǐ tuìdao huángxiàn hòumiàn. *Please step back behind the yellow line.*
退步 tuìbù v retrogress, fall behind
退还 tuìhuán v return
退还礼物 tuìhuán lǐwù return a gift
退款 tuìkuǎn v refund, ask for refund ■ 你对商品不满意，可以退款。Nǐ duì shāngpǐn bù mǎnyì, kěyǐ tuìkuǎn. *If you are not satisfied with your purchase, you can ask for a refund.*
退休 tuìxiū I v retire ■ 张校长决定在年底退休。Zhāng xiàozhǎng juédìng zài niándǐ tuìxiū. *Mr Zhang, the Principal, has decided to retire at the end of the year.* II N retirement
退休金 tuìxiūjīn N pension

吞 tūn v swallow

屯 tún N village

托 tuō v entrust, ask ■ 你进城吗？我托你办一件事，行吗？Nǐ jìnchéng ma? Wǒ tuō nǐ bàn yí jiàn shì, xíng ma? *Are you going to town? May I ask you to do something?*
托儿所 tuō'érsuǒ N nursery, child-care center (所 suǒ)

拖 tuō v drag on, defer, procrastinate ■ 这件事不能再拖了，得马上决定。Zhè jiàn shì bù néng zài tuō le, děi mǎshàng juédìng. *We cannot defer any longer but have to make an immediate decision on this matter.*
拖延 tuōyán v delay, put off

脱 tuō v 1 take off (clothes, shoes, etc.)

脱衣服 tuō yīfu take off clothes ■ 这个小孩儿会自己脱衣服吗? Zhège xiǎoháir huì zìjǐ tuō yīfu ma? Can the child take off his clothes by himself? (→ Can this child undress himself?)
脱帽子 tuō màozi take off one's hat
脱鞋 tuō xié take off one's shoes
2 get out of
脱离 tuōlí v break away from, sever
脱落 tuōluò v drop, come off

驼 **tuó** N camel

椭 **tuǒ** as in 椭圆 tuǒyuán

椭圆 tuǒyuán N oval
椭圆形 tuǒyuánxíng oval shape

妥 **tuǒ** ADJ appropriate, proper

妥当 tuǒdàng ADJ appropriate, proper
妥善 tuǒshàn ADJ appropriate and satisfactory
妥协 tuǒxié v, N compromise ■ 双方达成妥协。Shuāngfāng dáchéng tuǒxié. The two sides have reached a compromise.

拓 **tuò** v open up (See 开拓 kāituò)

唾 **tuò** N saliva

唾沫 tuòmo saliva, spittle

W

挖 **wā** v dig, scoop, excavate

挖掘 wājué v dig, excavate, unearth

哇 **wā** PARTICLE Same as 啊 a II

蛙 **wā** N frog (See 青蛙 qīngwā.)

娃 **wá** N baby, child

娃娃 wáwa baby, child (个 gè)

瓦 **wǎ** N tile (片 piàn)

瓦解 wǎjiě v disintegrate, collapse

袜 **wà** TRAD 襪 N sock, stocking

袜子 wàzi stocking, sock (只 zhī, 双 shuāng) ■ 我的袜子破了。Wǒ de wàzi pò le. My socks have holes.
穿袜子 chuān wàzi put on socks, wear socks

脱袜子 tuō wàzi take off socks

歪 **wāi** ADJ not straight, askew, crooked ■ 这幅画挂歪了。Zhè fú huà guà wāi le. The picture hangs askew.
歪曲 wāiqū v distort, misinterpret ■ 我不是那个意思, 你歪曲了我的话。Wǒ bú shì nàge yìsi, nǐ wāiqūle wǒde huà. That's not what I meant; you've distorted my remarks.

外 **wài** N outside ■ 墙外是一条安静的小街。Qiáng wài shì yì tiáo ānjìng de xiǎo jiē. Beyond the wall is a quiet by-street.
外边 wàibian N outside ■ 外边凉快, 我们到外边去吧。Wàibian liángkuai, wǒmen dào wàibian qù ba. It's cool outside. Let's go outside.
外表 wàibiǎo N outward appearance, exterior
外宾 wàibīn N foreign guest, foreign visitor (位 wèi)
外部 wàibù N exterior, what is external
外出 wàichū v go outside, leave town
外地 wàidì N parts of the country other than where one is ■ 他经常到外地去开会。Tā jīngcháng dào wàidì qù kāihuì. He often travels to other parts of the country to attend conferences.
外地人 wàidìrén one who is from other parts of the country, not a native
外观 wàiguān N exterior, surface, outward appearance
外国 wàiguó N foreign country ■ 你去过外国吗? Nǐ qùguo wàiguó ma? Have you ever been abroad?
外国货 wàiguóhuò foreign products, foreign goods
外国人 wàiguórén foreigner
外行 wàiháng I ADJ lay, not trained II N layman
外汇 wàihuì N foreign exchange
外汇储备 wàihuì chǔbèi foreign currency reserve
外汇兑换率 wàihuì duìhuànlǜ exchange rate
外交 wàijiāo N foreign affairs, diplomacy
外交部 Wàijiāo bù Ministry of Foreign Affairs
外交官 wàijiāo guān diplomat
外界 wàijiè N the external world
外科 wàikē N department of external medicine, surgery
外科医生 wàikē yīshēng surgeon
外力 wàilì N external force
外流 wàiliú v outflow
人才外流 réncái wàiliú brain drain
外面 wàimiàn N Same as 外边 wàibian
外婆 wàipó N (maternal) granndma
外甥 wàishēng N one's sister's son
外甥女 wàishēngnǚ N one's sister's daughter
外事 wàishì N foreign affairs

外事处 **wàishìchù** foreign affairs office

外头 **wàitou** N outside, outdoors

外文 **wàiwén** N foreign language (especially its writing) (门 mén) ■ 这本书已经翻译成多种外文。Zhè běn shū yǐjīng fānyì chéng duō zhǒng wàiwén. *This book has been translated into many foreign languages.*

外向型 **wàixiàngxíng** ADJ export-oriented

外向型经济 **wàixiàngxíng jīngjì** export-oriented economy

外形 **wàixíng** N appearance, external form

外衣 **wàiyī** N coat, outer clothing

外语 **wàiyǔ** N foreign language (门 mén) ■ 懂一门外语很有用。Dǒng yì mén wàiyǔ hěn yǒuyòng. *Knowing a foreign language is useful.*

外资 **wàizī** N foreign capital, foreign investment

外祖父 **wàizǔfù** N (maternal) grandfather

外祖母 **wàizǔmǔ** N (maternal) grandmother

豌 wān as in 豌豆 wāndòu

豌豆 **wāndòu** N pea

弯 wān TRAD 彎 ADJ curved, tortuous ■ 你这条线划得不直，划弯了。Nǐ zhè tiáo xiàn huà de bù zhí, huà wān le. *You did not draw this line straight; it's curved.*

弯曲 **wānqū** ADJ curved, zigzagging

湾 wān TRAD 灣 N bay, gulf (See 台湾 Táiwān.)

顽 wán ADJ naughty, stubborn

顽固 **wángù** ADJ 1 stubborn, pig-headed 2 difficult to cure ■ 这种皮肤病很顽固。Zhè zhǒng pífūbìng hěn wángù. *This skin disease is difficult to cure.*

顽皮 **wánpí** ADJ naughty, impish

顽强 **wánqiáng** ADJ indomitable, tenacious

丸 wán N bolus, pill (粒 lì, 颗 kē)

完 wán V finish, end ■ 电影什么时候完？Diànyǐng shénme shíhou wán? *When will the movie end?*

吃完 **chīwán** finish eating, eat up ■ 我吃完饭就去开会。Wǒ chīwán fàn jiù qù kāihuì. *I'm going to a meeting as soon as I finish my meal.*

看完 **kànwán** finish reading/watching ■ 我昨天看完电视已经十二点了。Wǒ zuótiān kànwán diànshì yǐjīng shí'èr diǎn le. *It was already twelve o'clock when I finished watching TV last night.*

用完 **yòngwán** use up ■ 我的钱用完了，我要到银行去取钱。Wǒ de qián yòngwán le, wǒ yào dào yínháng qu qǔ qián. *I've used up my money. I'll go to the bank to get some cash.*

做完 **zuòwán** finish doing ■ 你什么时候可以做完作业? Nǐ shénme shíhou kěyǐ zuòwán zuòyè? *When can you finish your homework?*

完备 **wánbèi** ADJ perfect, complete

完毕 **wánbì** V complete, finish

完成 **wánchéng** V accomplish, fulfill ■ 我们完成这个任务后要好好庆祝一下。Wǒmen wánchéng zhège rènwù hòu yào hǎohǎo qìngzhù yíxià. *We will have a good celebration after we have accomplished this task.*

完蛋 **wándàn** V be done for, be finished

完全 **wánquán** ADJ complete ■ 你完全不懂我的意思。Nǐ wánquán bù dǒng wǒ de yìsi. *You completely fail to see my point.*

完善 **wánshàn** V make perfect, perfect

完整 **wánzhěng** ADJ complete, integrated ■ 请你用一个完整的句子来回答。Qǐng nǐ yòng yí ge wánzhěng de jùzi lái huídá. *Please answer in a complete sentence.*

玩 wán V have fun, play

玩具 **wánjù** N toy (个 gè)

玩弄 **wánnòng** V play with

玩儿 **wánr** V play, have fun ■ 我们一块儿到公园去玩儿吧。Wǒmen yíkuàir dào gōngyuán qù wánr ba. *Let's go to the park to have fun!*

NOTE: Though 玩儿 wánr is often glossed as *to play*, its basic meaning is *to relax* or *to have a good time*. It can refer to many kinds of activities and therefore has a very wide application. More examples: ■ 上星期天我们在海边玩儿得真高兴! Shàng Xīngqītiān wǒmen zài hǎibiān wánr de zhēn gāoxìng. *We had a wonderful time by the seaside last Sunday.* ■ 我想去香港玩儿。Wǒ xiǎng qù Xiānggǎng wánr. *I want to have a holiday in Hong Kong.*

玩笑 **wánxiào** N joke, jest

开玩笑 **kāi wánxiào** play a prank, crack a joke, pull someone's leg ■ 他喜欢跟别人开玩笑，有时候太过分了。Tā xǐhuan gēn bié rén kāi wánxiào, yǒushi tài guò fènle. *He likes to play jokes on people, sometimes he would go too far.*

玩意儿 **wányìr** N 1 plaything 2 stuff, thing

NOTE: 玩意儿 wányìr is normally used with some contempt to suggest "insignificance" or "unworthiness", similar to 东西 dōngxi. The expletives 什么玩意儿? Shénme wányìr? and 他是个什么玩意儿? Tā shì ge shénme wányìr? may be roughly translated respectively into *What trash!* and *Who does he think himself is?*

挽 wǎn V salvage, draw, pull

挽救 **wǎnjiù** V rescue, save

晚 **wǎn** I ADJ late, not on time ■ 时间太晚了，我得走了。Shíjiān tài wǎn le, wǒ děi zǒu le. *It's very late; I've got to go.* II N evening, night

晚报 **wǎnbào** N evening paper (份 fèn)

晚餐 **wǎncān** N Same as 晚饭 wǎnfàn, used formally.

晚饭 **wǎnfàn** N evening meal, dinner, supper (顿 dùn) ■ 你们家一般什么时候吃晚饭? Nǐmen jiā yìbān shénme shíhou chī wǎnfàn? *When do you usually have supper at home?*
做晚饭 zuò wǎnfàn prepare supper

晚会 **wǎnhuì** N evening party, an evening of entertainment

晚年 **wǎnnián** N old age ■ 他的晚年生活很幸福。Tāde wǎnnián shēnghuó hěn xìngfú. *He had a happy old age.*

晚上 **wǎnshang** N evening ■ 你今天晚上打算做什么? Nǐ jīntiān wǎnshang dǎsuàn zuò shénme? *What do you plan to do this evening?*
今天晚上 (今晚) jīntiān wǎnshang (jīnwǎn) this evening
昨天晚上 (昨晚) zuótiān wǎnshang (zuówǎn) yesterday evening

惋 **wǎn** V be sorry for, sigh

惋惜 **wǎnxī** V feel sorry (for someone or about something)
为浪费人才而惋惜 wéi làngfèi réncái ér wǎnxī feel sorry about the waste of talents

碗 **wǎn** N bowl (只 zhī) ■ 中国人吃饭一般用碗，大碗放菜，小碗放米饭。Zhōngguórén chīfàn yìbān yòng wǎn, dà wǎn fàng cài, xiǎo wǎn fàng mǐfàn. *Chinese people usually use bowls for meals: big bowls for dishes and small ones for cooked rice.*
…碗饭 …wǎnfàn … bowl(s) of rice
菜碗 càiwǎn a dish bowl, big bowl
饭碗 fànwǎn rice bowl, livelihood, job

万 **wàn** TRAD 萬 I NUM ten thousand
一万两千三百 (12,300) yíwàn liǎngqiān sānbǎi twelve thousand and three hundred
二十万 (200,000) èr shí wàn two hundred thousand
II N a very large number III ADV (negative sense) absolutely

NOTE: 万 wàn (ten thousand) is an important number in Chinese. While English has four basic digits (one, ten, hundred and thousand) Chinese has five (个 gè one, 十 shí ten, 百 bǎi hundred, 千 qiān thousand, 万 wàn ten thousand). The Chinese use 万 wàn to mean ten thousand. Therefore a hundred thousand is 十万 shí wàn. In Chinese-speaking communities in Southeast Asia, some people use 十千 shíqiān for ten thousand, e.g. 三十千 sānshíqiān 30,000. This is, however, not acceptable in standard Chinese.

万分 **wànfēn** ADV extremely

万岁 **wànsuì** INTERJ Long Live ■ 祖国万岁! Zǔguó wànsuì! *Long live the motherland!*

万万 **wànwàn** ADV under no circumstances, never ever ■ 万万不可掉以轻心。Wànwàn bù kě diàoyǐqīngxīn. *Under no circumstances should you relax your vigilance.*

万一 **wànyī** I CONJ in the unlikely event of, in case ■ 万一飞机失事，不要惊慌。Wànyī fēijī shīshì, búyào jīnghuāng. *In case of an air accident, do not panic.* II N a possible but unlikely event, contingency
对付万一的情况 duìfu wànyī de qíngkuàng cope with a contingency

万维网 **wànwéiwǎng** N World Wide Web (WWW)

汪 **wāng** ADJ (of water) vast

汪洋 **wāngyáng** N vast expanse of water

王 1 **wáng** N king

王国 **wángguó** N kingdom
丹麦王国 Dānmài wángguó the Kingdom of Denmark

王 2 **Wáng** N (a family name)

亡 **wáng** V perish, die

枉 **wǎng** V treat unfairly, wrong (See 冤枉 yuānwang)

网 **wǎng** TRAD 網 N net, network

网吧 **wǎngbā** N Internet café (座 zuò, 家 jiā) ■ 这家网吧吸引很多年轻人。Zhè jiā wǎngbā xīyǐn hěn dūo niánqīngrén. *This Internet café attracts many young people.*

网络 **wǎngluò** N Internet
网络电话 wǎngluò diànhuà Internet phone
网络警察 (网警) wǎngluò jǐngchá (wǎngjǐng) Internet police

网球 **wǎngqiú** N tennis
网球场 wǎngqiúchǎng tennis court

网页 **wǎngyè** N web page

网站 **wǎngzhàn** N website ■ 欢迎您访问我的个人网站。Huānyíng nín fǎngwèn wǒ de gèrén wǎngzhàn. *You are welcome to visit my personal website.*

往 **wǎng** I PREP towards, in the direction of ■ 你往前走，到红绿灯的地方，往左拐，就可以

往常 wǎngcháng

到火车站。Nǐ wǎng qián zǒu, dào hónglǜdēng
de dìfang, wǎng zuǒ guǎi, jiù kěyǐ dào huǒchēzhàn. *Walk straight on, and turn left at the traffic
lights. Then you'll reach the railway station.*
II v go **III** ADJ previous, past

往常 wǎngcháng ADV habitually in the past,
used to

往返 wǎngfǎn v journey to and from, make a
round trip

往后 wǎnghòu ADV from now on
往后的日子 wǎnghòu de rìzi the days to
come

往来 wǎnglái **I** v come and go **II** N contact,
dealings
业务往来 yèwù wǎnglái business dealings

往年 wǎngnián N (in) former years

往日 wǎngrì N in former times, in the past

往事 wǎngshì N past events, the past
回忆往事 huíyì wǎngshì recollect past
events, reflect upon the past

往往 wǎngwǎng ADV very often, usually

旺 wàng ADJ flourishing

妄 wàng ADJ preposterous

妄图 wàngtú v try in vain

妄想 wàngxiǎng **I** v attempt in vain **II** N vain
hope

忘 wàng v forget, overlook ■ 别忘了寄这封
信。Bié wàng le jì zhè fēng xìn. *Don't forget
to post this letter.*

忘记 wàngjì v forget, overlook

忘却 wàngquè v forget

望 wàng v look at, gaze into the distance
■ 举头望明月。Jǔ tóu wàng míngyuè. *I look
up to gaze at the bright moon.* (a line from a
poem by Tang dynasty poet Li Bai)

望远镜 wàngyuǎnjìng N telescope, binoculars

危 wēi **I** ADJ perilous **II** ADV by force

危害 wēihài **I** v harm severely, jeopardize
■ 降低农产品价格会危害农民的利益。Jiàngdī
nóngchǎnpǐn jiàgé huì wēihài nóngmín de lìyì.
*Lowering the prices of agricultural produce will
severely harm the farmer's interest.* **II** N severe
harm, damage ■ 森林面积的减少给环境造
成很大危害。Sēnlín miànji de jiǎnshǎo gěi
huánjìng zàochéng hěn dà wēihài. *The reduction of forest areas causes great damage to the
environment.*

危机 wēijī N crisis ■ 要解决危机, 先要了解
危机是怎么发生的。Yào jiějué wēijī, xiān yào
liáojiě wēijī shì zěnme fāshēng de. *In order to*

*resolve a crisis, one should first of all learn how it
came into being.*

危急 wēijí ADJ in acute danger, critical, perilous

危险 wēixiǎn **I** ADJ dangerous, risky **II** N danger,
risk ■ 病人已经脱离危险。Bìngrén yǐjīng tuōlí
wēixiǎn. *The patient is out of danger.*

威 wēi N awesome force

威风 wēifēng N power and prestige, manner or
style showing power and prestige
耍威风 shuǎ wēifēng throw one's weight
around

威力 wēilì N formidable force, power

威望 wēiwàng N enormous prestige

威胁 wēixié **I** v threaten ■ 森林面积越来越小,
威胁到野生动物的生存。Sēnlín miànji yuèlaiyuè
xiǎo, wēixié dào yěshēng dòngwù de shēngcún.
*Forests are getting smaller and smaller, which
threatens the survival of wild animals.* **II** N threat
构成威胁 gòuchéng wēixié pose a threat

威信 wēixìn N popular trust, prestige
在同事中享有很高威信 zài tóngshì zhōng
xiǎngyǒu hěn gāo wēixìn enjoy high prestige among colleagues

微 wēi ADJ tiny, of extremely small amounts,
minute

微不足道 wēi bùzú dào IDIOM negligibly small,
extremely tiny

微观 wēiguān ADJ microcosmic, micro-

微小 wēixiǎo ADJ tiny, of very small amounts

微笑 wēixiào v smile ■ 她微笑着说, "谢谢你
了。" Tā wēixiàozhe shuō, "Xièxie nǐ le." *She
said, smiling, "Thank you."*

桅 wéi as in 桅杆 wéigān

桅杆 wéigān N mast

围 wéi TRAD 圍 v enclose, surround ■ 他建
了一道墙, 把自己的房子围起来。Tā jiànle yí
dào qiáng, bǎ zìjǐ de fángzi wéi qǐlai. *He built a
wall to enclose his home.*

围攻 wéigōng v besiege, lay siege to

围巾 wéijīn N scarf (条 tiáo)

围棋 wéiqí N weiqi (a Chinese chess game, also
known as go)
下围棋 xiàwéiqí play weiqi

围绕 wéirào v **1** move around, encircle ■ 地球
围绕太阳转。Dìqiú wéirào tàiyang zhuàn. *The
earth moves around the sun.* **2** center on, focus
on ■ 请大家围绕这个问题谈, 不要离题。Qǐng
dàjiā wéirào zhè ge wèntí tán, bú yào lítí. *Please
focus on this question. Do not digress.*

唯 wéi ADV only

NOTE: In some cases, 唯 is also written as 惟 wéi.

唯独 wéidú ADV only, alone

唯物论 wéiwùlùn N materialism

唯心论 wéixīnlùn N idealism

唯一 wéiyī ADJ the only one, sole ■ 他唯一的爱好是打麻将, 一有空就打。Tā wéiyī de àihào shì dǎ májiàng, yì yǒukòng jiù dǎ. *His only hobby is playing mahjong. He plays mahjong whenever he has time.*

维 **wéi** TRAD 維 V preserve, safeguard

维护 wéihù V safeguard, defend ■ 为了维护国家安全, 必须要有一支强大的军队。Wèile wéihù guójiā ānquán, bìxū yào yǒu yì zhī qiángdà de jūnduì. *To ensure national security, we must maintain strong armed forces.*

维生素 wéishēngsù N vitamin

维修 wéixiū V keep in good repair, maintain (a machine, a house, etc.)

违 **wéi** TRAD 違 V disobey, violate

违背 wéibèi V go against, violate ■ 你们这样做, 违背了总公司的意愿。Nǐmen zhèyàng zuò, wéibèile zǒnggōngsī de yìyuàn. *What you've done goes against the will of the headquarters.*

违法 wéifǎ V violate the law, break the law

违反 wéifǎn V run counter to, violate

违犯 wéifàn V break (the law, regulations, etc.)
违犯财务规定 wéifàn cáiwù guīdìng breach financial regulations

为 **wéi** TRAD 為 V 1 be, become 2 do, act

为难 wéinán V 1 make things difficult for ■ 我不想为难你。Wǒ bùxiǎng wéinán nǐ. *I don't want to make things difficult for you.* 2 feel awkward
为难的事情 wéinán de shìqíng something one finds difficult to cope with, some perplexing matter

为期 wéiqī ADV (to be completed) by a definite date
为期不远 wéi qī bù yuǎn will take place soon
为期一星期 wéiqī yì xīngqī will last a week

为首 wéishǒu V be headed by
以董事长为首的代表团 yǐ dǒngshìzhǎng wéishǒu de dàibiǎotuán a delegation headed by the chairman of the Board of Trustees

为止 wéizhǐ V up to, till
到…为止 dào...wéizhǐ up to, until

尾 **wéi** N tail, end

尾巴 wěiba N tail (条 tiáo)

委 **wěi** V entrust

委托 wěituō V entrust ■ 公司委托律师正式回答用户的投诉。Gōngsī wěituō lǜshī zhèngshì huídá yònghù de tóusù. *The company has entrusted its lawyer to give a formal reply to the consumers' complaint.*

委员会 wěiyuánhuì N committee (个 gè)

伟 **wěi** TRAD 偉 ADJ big

伟大 wěidà ADJ great ■ 孙中山是中国历史上的一位伟大人物。Sūn Zhōngshān shì Zhōngguó lìshǐ shang de yí wèi wěidà rénwù. *Dr Sun Yat-sen is a great man in Chinese history.*

伪 **wěi** ADJ false

伪造 wěizào V forge, counterfeit
一份伪造的文件 yí fèn wěizào de wénjiàn a forged document

卫 **wèi** TRAD 衛 V defend, protect

卫生 wèishēng N hygiene, sanitation ■ 保持个人卫生和公共卫生, 有利于人民的身体健康。Bǎochí gèrén wèishēng hé gōnggòng wèishēng, yǒulì yú rénmín de shēntǐ jiànkāng. *Maintaining good personal hygiene and public sanitation is beneficial to the health of the citizens.*
个人卫生 gèrén wèishēng hygiene, personal hygiene
公共卫生 gōnggòng wèishēng sanitation, public sanitation
环境卫生 huánjìng wèishēng environmental sanitation

卫生间 wèishēngjiān N bathroom, (private) toilet

卫生局 wèishēngjú N (government) health department

卫星 wèixīng N satellite
卫星电视 wèixīng diànshì satellite TV
人造卫星 rénzào wèixīng man-made satellite

为 **wèi** TRAD 為 PREP (do, work) for the benefit of, in the interest of ■ 我为人人, 人人为我。Wǒ wèi rénrén, rénrén wèi wǒ. *I work for everybody as everybody works for me. (→ One for all and all for one.)*

为何 wèihé ADV what for, why

为了 wèile PREP for the purpose of ■ 为了健康, 他不吸烟不喝酒, 每天锻炼身体。Wèile jiànkāng, tā bù xīyān bù hē jiǔ, měi tiān duànliàn shēntǐ. *In order to keep fit he does not smoke or drink, and exercises every day.*

NOTE: Both 为 wèi and 为了 wèile can be used as prepositions and have similar meanings, but 为了 wèile is more commonly used in everyday Chinese.

为什么 wèishénme

为什么 wèishénme ADV why, what for

未 wèi ADV have not, did not ■ 该生未经批准不来上课，将受处分。Gāishēng wèi jīng pīzhǔn bù lái shàngkè, jiāng shòu chǔfèn. *This student was absent from class without permission and will be disciplined.*

NOTE: 未 wèi is only used in rather formal, written styles. In everyday Chinese, 没有 méiyǒu is used instead.

未必 wèibì ADV not necessarily, may not
未来 wèilái N future ■ 少年儿童是国家的未来。Shàonián értóng shì guójiā de wèilái. *The youth and children are the future of a nation.*
未免 wèimiǎn ADV rather, a bit too

位 wèi I M. WD (polite term used for people)
一位老师 yí wèi lǎoshī a teacher ■ 那位先生是谁？Nà wèi xiānsheng shì shuí? *Who is that gentleman?*
II N position, location
位于 wèiyú v be situated in, be located in
位置 wèizhi N 1 place, location ■ 没有人能确定沉船的位置。Méiyǒu rén néng quèdìng chénchuán de wèizhì. *Nobody can determine the location of the sunken ship.* 2 (abstract) position ■ 人力资源经理是公司里一个极其重要的位置。Rénlì zīyuán jīnglǐ shì gōngsī li yí ge jíqí zhòngyào de wèizhi. *The human resources manager holds an extremely important position in a company.*

味 wèi N taste, flavor

味道 wèidao N taste ■ 我觉得这个菜味道太淡，我喜欢味道浓一点的菜。Wǒ juéde zhège cài wèidao tài dàn, wǒ xǐhuan wèidao nóng yìdiǎn de cài. *I find this dish too bland. I like strongly-flavored dishes.*
味精 wèijīng N monosodium glutamate (MSG), gourmet powder

胃 wèi N stomach

谓 wèi v be called (See 所谓 suǒwèi.)

慰 wèi v console

慰问 wèiwèn v express sympathy and solicitude for

畏 wèi v fear

畏惧 wèijù v fear, dread

喂 1 wèi INTERJ 1 hey ■ 喂，你的票呢？Wèi, nǐ de piào ne? *Hey, where's your ticket?* 2 hello, hi ■ 喂，这里是大华公司，您找谁？Wèi, zhèlǐ shì Dàhuá Gōngsī, nín zhǎo shuí? *Hello, this is Dahua Company. Who would you like to speak to?*

NOTE: In telephone conversations 喂 wèi is equivalent to *hello*. In other contexts, 喂 wèi is a rude way of getting people's attention. It is more polite to say 对不起 duìbuqǐ, e.g. ■ 对不起，先生，您的票呢？Duìbuqǐ, xiānsheng, nín de piào ne? *Excuse me, sir, where's your ticket?*

喂 2 wèi v feed ■ 她夜里起来给孩子喂奶。Tā yèli qǐlai gěi háizi wèi nǎi. *Every night she gets up to feed her baby.*

温 wēn I ADJ warm II v 1 warm up 2 review (one's lessons)
温带 wēndài N temperate zone ■ 中国和美国部分领土都在北温带。Zhōngguó hé Měiguó bùfen lǐngtǔ dōu zài běi wēndài. *Most of the territories of China and the U.S. are in the North Temperate Zone.*
温度 wēndù N temperature (atmospheric) ■ 今天温度比较低，但是没有风，所以不觉得怎么冷。Jīntiān wēndù bǐjiào dī, dànshì méiyǒu fēng suǒyǐ bù juéde zěnme lěng. *The temperature is rather low today, but it is not windy, so you don't feel very cold.*

NOTE: 温度 wēndù generally refers to *atmospheric temperature* only. For *body temperature* the expression is 体温 tǐwēn, e.g. ■ 人的正常体温是多少？Rénde zhèngcháng tǐwēn shì duōshǎo? *What is the normal temperature of a human being?* When a person has a fever, however, 热度 rèdù is used to refer to his/her temperature, e.g. ■ 他今天热度还很高。Tā jīntiān rèdù hái hěn gāo. *He is still running a fever.*

温度计 wēndùjì N thermometer
温和 wēnhé ADJ 1 (of climate) temperate, without extreme temperatures
温和的气候 wēnhé de qìhòu mild, intemperate climate
2 (of people) gentle, mild
语气温和 yǔqì wēnhé mild tone
温暖 wēnnuǎn ADJ warm
温柔 wēnróu ADJ (of people) gentle and soft, soothing

瘟 wēn N plague

瘟疫 wēnyì N epidemic, pandemic (场 cháng)

文 wén N 1 writing, script 2 culture

文化 wénhuà N culture ■ 语言中有很多文化知

208

识。Yǔyán zhong yǒu hěn duō wénhuà zhīshi. *A language contains a great deal of cultural knowledge.*

文化部 **Wénhuàbù** the Ministry of Culture

文件 **wénjiàn** N 1 document (份 fèn) 2 (computer) file ■ 这个文件你保留在电脑里了吗? Zhège wénjiàn nǐ bǎoliú zài diànnǎo li le ma? *Have you saved this file in the computer?*

文盲 **wénmáng** N illiterate person

文明 **wénmíng** I N civilization, culture II ADJ civilized ■ 在文明社会不应该存在这种现象。 Zài wénmíng shèhuì bù yīnggāi cúnzài zhè zhǒng xiànxiàng. *Such a phenomenon should not exist in a civilized society.*

文凭 **wénpíng** N diploma, certificate of academic achievements (张 zhāng)

文人 **wénrén** N man of letters, literati

文物 **wénwù** N cultural relic, historical relic

文物商店 **wénwù shāngdiàn** antique shop

文献 **wénxiàn** N document, literature

文学 **wénxué** N literature ■ 我姐姐在大学念英国文学。 Wǒ jiějie zài dàxué niàn Yīngguó wénxué. *My elder sister studies English literature in university.*

文学家 **wénxué jiā** (great) writer

文雅 **wényǎ** ADJ refined and elegant

文言 **wényán** N Classical Chinese

文言文 **wényánwén** Classical Chinese writing

NOTE: Before the 20th century mainstream Chinese writing was done in 文言 wényán Classical Chinese, which was based on ancient Chinese and divorced from everyday speech of the time. A literate revolution took place in early 20th century, which succeeded in replacing 文言 wényán with 白话 báihua, plain speech, vernacular.

文艺 **wényì** N literature and art, performing arts

文艺晚会 **wényì wǎnhuì** an evening of entertainment, soirée

文章 **wénzhāng** N essay, article (篇 piān) ■ 他文章写得又快又好。 Tā wénzhāng xiě de yòu kuài yòu hǎo. *He writes good essays, and he writes them quickly.*

文字 **wénzì** N written language, script, character ■ 这本小说已经翻译成六种文字了。 Zhè běn xiǎoshuō yǐjīng fānyì chéng liù zhǒng wénzì le. *This novel has been translated into six languages.*

文字处理 **wénzì chǔlǐ** word processing

纹 **wén** TRAD 紋 N ripple (See 皱纹 zhòuwén)

蚊 **wén** N mosquito

蚊子 **wénzi** mosquito (只 zhī)

闻 **wén** TRAD 聞 N what is heard

闻名 **wénmíng** ADJ well-known

吻 **wěn** V, N kiss ■ 每天晚上儿子睡觉前, 她都要吻吻他。 Měitiān wǎnshang érzi shuìjiào qián, tā dōu yào wěn wěn tā. *Before her son went to sleep every evening, she would kiss him.*

稳 **wěn** TRAD 穩 ADJ steady, stable ■ 等车停稳了再下车。 Děng chē tíng wěnle zài xià chē. *Do not get off the car (or bus) before it comes to a complete stop.*

稳当 **wěndang** ADJ reliable, safe 一个稳当的办法 yí ge wěndang de bànfǎ a reliable method

稳定 **wěndìng** ADJ stable ■ 现在的形势十分稳定。 Xiànzài de xíngshì shífēn wěndìng. *The present situation is very stable.*

稳妥 **wěntuǒ** ADJ safe and appropriate

问 **wèn** TRAD 問 V 1 ask (a question), inquire 2 ask after, send regards

问答 **wèndá** N questions and answers

问答题 **wèndátí** (in tests, exercises, etc.) question requiring an answer in writing (not a multiple-choice question)

问好 **wèn hǎo** V ask after, give greetings to ■ 请代问您父母亲好。 Qǐng dài wèn nín fùmǔqin hǎo. *Please give my regards to your parents.*

问候 **wènhòu** V give regards to, send regards to, ask after

问路 **wèn lù** V ask the way ■ 你会用中文问路吗? Nǐ huì yòng Zhōngwén wènlù ma? *Can you ask the way in Chinese?*

问世 **wènshì** V be published, come into being

问题 **wèntí** N 1 question (道 dào, for school examinations only) 2 problem ■ 出问题了! Chū wèntí le! *Something's gone wrong!* 没有问题 méiyǒu wèntí no problem

翁 **wēng** N old man

嗡 **wēng** ONOMATOPOEIA buzz

窝 **wō** N nest, lair

鸟窝 **niǎowō** bird's nest

窝囊 **wōnang** I V feel vexed and annoyed 受窝囊气 shòu wōnangqì be subject to petty annoyances

II ADJ (of people) useless, good-for-nothing

我 **wǒ** PRON I, me ■ 我叫张明, 我是中国人。 Wǒ jiào Zhāng Míng, wǒ shì Zhōngguórén. *My name is Zhang Ming. I'm Chinese.*

我们 **wǒmen** PRON we, us

卧 wò v lie

卧床休息 wòchuáng xiūxi lie in bed and rest
卧室 wòshì N bedroom (间 jiān)

沃 wò ADJ (of land) fertile

握 wò v hold, grasp

握手 wòshǒu v shake hands ■ 他和新认识的朋
友握手。Tā hé xīn rènshi de péngyou wòshǒu.
He shook hands with his new friends.

乌 wū ADJ black, dark

乌鸦 wūyā N crow (只 zhī)
乌云 wūyún N dark clouds

呜 wū v toot, hoot

呜咽 wūyè v sob

污 wū I N filth II v smear, defile

污蔑 wūmiè v slander
污染 wūrǎn I v pollute ■ 这家化工厂严重
污染环境，必须关闭。Zhè jiā huàgōngchǎng
yánzhòng wūrǎn huánjìng, bìxū guānbì. *This
chemical plant is seriously polluting the environment and must be closed down.* II N pollution

巫 wū N witch

巫术 wūshù witchcraft
巫婆 wūpó N witch

诬 wū TRAD 誣 v accuse falsely

诬告 wūgào v file a false charge against
诬蔑 wūmiè I v slander, vilify II N slander
诬陷 wūxiàn v frame
诬陷好人 wūxiàn hǎorén frame an innocent
person

屋 wū N house, room

屋子 wūzi N room (间 jiān) ■ 这个房子有几间
屋子? Zhège fángzi yǒu jǐ jiān wūzi? *How many
rooms are there in the house?*

NOTE: 屋子 wūzi in the sense of *room* is only used
in north China. To southern Chinese 屋子 wūzi
may mean *house*. To avoid ambiguity, it is better to
use the word 房间 fángjiān for *room*.

无 wú TRAD 無 I N nothing, nil

从无到有 cóng wú dào yǒu grow out of
nothing
II v have no ■ 我们无法解决这个问题。Wǒmen
wú fǎ jiějué zhège wèntí. *We have no way to
solve this problem.*

无比 wúbǐ ADJ matchless, unparalleled
无偿 wúcháng ADJ free, gratis
无偿服务 wúcháng fúwù voluntary service
无耻 wúchǐ ADJ shameless, brazen
无从 wúcóng ADV having no way (of doing
something), being in no position to
无从说起 wúcóng shuōqǐ don't know where
to begin
无法 wúfǎ MODAL v unable to
无非 wúfēi ADV nothing but, no more than
■ 他无非是为了钱。Tā wúfēi shì wèile qián. *He
wants nothing but money.*
无话可说 wú huà kě shuō IDIOM have nothing
to say
无可奉告 wú kě fènggào IDIOM No comment
无可奈何 wú kě nàihé IDIOM have no alternative (but)
无理 wúlǐ ADJ unreasonable, unjustifiable
无理取闹 wúlǐ qǔnào make trouble without
any justification, provoke deliberately
无聊 wúliáo ADJ 1 bored 2 silly, meaningless
无论 wúlùn CONJ Same as 不管 bùguǎn. Tends
to be used in writing.
无论如何 wúlùn rúhé IDIOM no matter what, at
any rate
无能为力 wú néng wéi lì IDIOM be totally
powerless
无情 wúqíng ADJ ruthless, heartless
无情无义 wú qíng wú yì IDIOM cold-hearted
and merciless
无穷 wúqióng ADJ infinite, boundless
无绳电话 wú shéng diànhuà N cordless
telephone
无数 wúshù ADJ innumerable, countless ■ 无
数事实证明，那种社会制度是行不通的。Wúshù
shìshí zhèngmíng, nà zhǒng shèhuì zhìdù shì
xíngbutōng de. *Innumerable facts have proven
that kind of social system does not work.*
无所谓 wúsuǒwèi v doesn't matter ■ 他同意
不同意，无所谓；反正我已经决定。Tā tóngyì bù
tóngyì, wúsuǒwèi; fǎnzheng wǒ yǐjing juédìng. *It
doesn't matter whether he approves or not—I've
made up my mind anyway.*
无所作为 wú suǒ zuòwéi IDIOM make no effort,
be in a state of inertia
无微不至 wú wēi bù zhì IDIOM meticulous, spar-
ing no effort, paying attention to every detail
无微不至的照顾 wú wēi bù zhì de zhàogù
meticulous care and attention
无限 wúxiàn ADJ infinite, limitless
无线电 wúxiàndiàn N (wireless) radio
无线因特网 wúxiàn yīntèwǎng wireless
Internet

无效 **wúxiào** ADJ invalid ■ 你的签证已经无效
了。Nǐde qiānzhèng yǐjing wúxiào le. *Your visa is
now invalid.*

无疑 **wúyí** ADV undoubtedly, beyond any doubt

无意 **wúyì** ADJ unintentional
无意之中发现 **wúyì zhīzhōng fāxiàn** discover by chance

五 **wǔ** NUM five ■ 五五二十五。Wǔ wǔ
èrshíwǔ. *Five times five is twenty-five.*
五星红旗 **wǔ xīng hóng qí** the five-star red
flag (the Chinese national flag)

伍 **wǔ** NUM five

午 **wǔ** N noon
午饭 **wǔfàn** N lunch (顿 dùn)
午间 **wǔjiān** N lunchtime
午间休息 **wǔjiān xiūxi** lunchtime break

武 **wǔ** N military
武力 **wǔlì** N military force
武力解决 **wǔlì jiějué** deal with (a situation)
by force
武器 **wǔqì** N weapon (件 jiàn) ■ 不准带任何武
器上飞机。Bù zhǔn dài rènhé wǔqì shàng fēijī.
*It is forbidden to bring a weapon of any kind on
board the plane.*
大规模杀伤武器 **dàguīmó shāshāng wǔqì**
weapon of mass destruction (WMD)
武术 **wǔshù** N martial arts ■ 他在中国学了三年
武术。Tā zài Zhōngguó xuéle sān nián wǔshù.
He studied martial arts in China for three years.
武术大师 **wǔshù dàshī** martial arts master
武术馆 **wǔshù guǎn** martial arts school
武装 **wǔzhuāng** I v arm, equip
武装到牙齿 **wǔzhuāng dào yáchǐ** be armed
to the teeth
II N arms
解除武装 **jiěchú wǔzhuāng** lay down arms,
be disarmed

侮 **wǔ** v insult
侮辱 **wǔrǔ** I v insult, humiliate ■ 我不能容忍
别人侮辱我的父母。Wǒ bùnéng róngrěn biéren
wǔrǔ wǒde fùmǔ. *I can't tolerate someone insulting my parents.* II N insult ■ 你这么说，是对
我的侮辱。Nǐ zhème shuō, shì duì wǒde wǔrǔ.
What you said was an insult to me.

舞 **wǔ** N dance
舞弊 **wǔbì** I N fraud, fraudulent practice
舞弊案 **wǔbì àn** a case of fraud
II v commit a fraud ■ 一名年轻人因利用计算

机舞弊而被逮捕。Yì míng niánqīngrén yīn lìyòng
jìsuànjī wǔbì ér bèi dàibǔ. *A young man was arrested for computer fraud.*
舞蹈 **wǔdǎo** N dance
舞会 **wǔhuì** N ball
化装舞会 **huàzhuāng wǔhuì** fancydress party
舞台 **wǔtái** N stage, theater
舞厅 **wǔtīng** N dance hall
迪斯科舞厅 **dísīkē wǔtīng** discothèque, disco

晤 **wù** v meet (people)

勿 **wù** ADV do not, don't ■ 请勿吸烟。Qǐngwù
xīyān. *Please do not smoke.* (→ *No smoking.
Smoke-free.*)

物 **wù** N 1 things, objects 2 material
物价 **wùjià** N price, commodity price ■ 最近的
物价比较稳定。Zuìjìn de wùjià bǐjiào wěndìng.
Prices have been quite stable recently.
物理 **wùlǐ** N physics ■ 我弟弟物理、数学都挺
好。Wǒ dìdi wùlǐ, shùxué dōu tǐng hǎo. *My younger brother is good at physics and mathematics.*
物力 **wùlì** N material resources
物品 **wùpǐn** N article, goods
物体 **wùtǐ** N object, substance
物业 **wùyè** N real estate, property
物业管理 **wùyè guǎnlǐ** property management
物资 **wùzī** N goods and materials, supplies

务 **wù** TRAD 務 I v work, to spend one's efforts
on II ADV must, be sure to
务必 **wùbì** ADV must, be sure to

雾 **wù** TRAD 霧 N fog, mist ■ 今天早上有大雾，
很多人迟到。Jīntiān zǎoshang yǒu dà wù, hěn
duō rén chídào. *Many people were late for work
this morning because of the heavy fog.*

悟 **wù** v realize
悟出了道理 **wùchūle dàoli** come to see the
light, begin to understand
顿悟 **dùnwù** epiphany

误 **wù** TRAD 誤 ADJ erroneous
误差 **wùchā** N (in physics) error
误会 **wùhuì** I v misunderstand, misconstrue
II N misunderstanding ■ 我没有说清楚，造
成了误会，很抱歉。Wǒ méiyǒu shuō qīngchu,
zàochéngle wùhuì, hěn bàoqiàn. *I did not make
it clear, which has caused a misunderstanding. I
apologize.*
误解 **wùjiě** v misunderstand

恶 **wù** v loathe (See 厌恶 yànwù)

X

西 **Xī** N west, western ■ 河东是一座小城, 河西是一大片农场。Hé dōng shì yí zuò xiǎo chéng, hé xī shì yí dà piàn nóngchǎng. *East of the river is a small town, and on the west is a big farm.*

西北 **xīběi** N northwest, the Northwest

西边 **xībian** N west side, to the west, in the west

西餐 **xīcān** N Western-style meal ■ 走, 我请你吃西餐。Zǒu, wǒ qǐng nǐ chī xīcān. *Let's go. I'll treat you to a Western-style meal.*

西餐馆 **xīcānguǎn** N Western-style restaurant

西方 **xīfāng** N the West, Occident ■ 西方文明有什么重要特点? Xīfāng wénmíng yǒu shénme zhòngyào tèdiǎn? *What are the major characteristics of Western civilization?*

西服 **xīfú** N Western-style clothes, men's suit

西瓜 **xīguā** N watermelon (只 zhī)

西红柿 **xīhóngshì** N tomato (只 zhī)

西南 **xīnán** N southwest, the Southwest ■ 中国西南地方有很多少数民族。Zhōngguó xīnán dìfang yǒu hěn duō shǎoshù mínzú. *There are many national minorities in China's southwestern region.*

西面 **xīmiàn** Same as 西边 xībian

西医 **xīyī** N 1 Western medicine 2 doctor trained in Western medicine (位 wèi)
中西医结合治疗 **Zhōngxīyī jiéhé zhìliáo** treat (patients) with a combination of Chinese and Western medicine

晰 **Xī** ADJ clear, distinct (See 清晰 qīngxī)

锡 **Xī** N (metal) tin (Sn)

吸 **Xī** V 1 inhale, suck 2 absorb, suck up

吸毒 **xīdú** I V take drugs II N drug-taking, substance abuse

吸取 **xīqǔ** V absorb, draw in
吸取教训 **xīqǔ jiàoxun** learn a lesson (from past experience)

吸收 **xīshōu** V suck up, absorb ■ 我们要吸收别人的好经验。Wǒmen yào xīshōu biérén de hǎo jīngyàn. *We should draw from other people's positive experiences.*

吸烟 **xīyān** I V smoke II N smoking ■ 这里不准吸烟。Zhèlǐ bù zhǔn xīyān. *Smoking is not allowed here.*

吸引 **xīyǐn** V attract ■ 我们想吸引更多的旅游者来我国游览。Wǒmen xiǎng xīyǐn gèng duō de lǚyóuzhě lái wǒguó yóulǎn. *We want to attract more tourists to our country.*

吸引力 **xīyǐnlì** N attraction

有吸引力 **yǒu xīyǐnlì** attractive

希 **Xī** V wish, hope

希望 **xīwàng** I V hope, wish ■ 我希望你常给我打电话。Wǒ xīwàng nǐ cháng gěi wǒ dǎ diànhuà. *I hope you'll ring me often.* II N hope ■ 孩子是父母的希望。Háizi shì fùmǔ de xīwàng. *Children are their parents' hope.*

稀 **Xī** ADJ 1 rare, scarce 2 watery

稀饭 **xīfàn** N rice porridge

稀少 **xīshǎo** ADJ scarce, few and far between
人烟稀少 **rényān xīshǎo** sparsely populated

稀有 **xīyǒu** ADJ rare
稀有金属 **xīyǒujīnshǔ** a rare metal

夕 **Xī** N dusk, twilight

夕阳 **xīyáng** the setting sun

惜 **Xī** V 1 cherish, treasure (See 珍惜 zhēnxī) 2 have pity on (See 可惜 kěxī)

牺 **Xī** TRAD 犧 N sacrifice

牺牲 **xīshēng** I V sacrifice, give up ■ 他们为子女牺牲了大量时间和金钱。Tāmen wèi zǐnǚ xīshēngle dàliàng shíjiān hé jīnqián. *They gave up a great deal of time and money for their children.* II N sacrifice

悉 **Xī** V know (See 熟悉 shúxī.)

溪 **Xī** N small stream

小溪 **xiǎoxī** a small stream

膝 **Xī** N knee

膝盖 **xīgài** knee

息 **Xī** V cease (See 消息 xiāoxi, 休息 xiūxi.)

熄 **Xī** V extinguish (fire)

熄灭 **xīmiè** V (of fire) die out, be extinguished

媳 **Xí** daughter-in-law

媳妇 **xífù** N daughter-in-law
儿媳妇 **érxífù** daughter-in-law

NOTE: In some dialects, 媳妇 xífù may also refer to *a wife*, e.g. 娶媳妇 qǔ xifu *to get a wife*, *(for men) to get married.*

袭 **Xí** TRAD 襲 V attack, raid

袭击 **xíjī** V (of troops) attack, raid

突然袭击 tūrán xíjī sudden attack, launch a sudden attack

习 **xí** TRAD 習 I v practice, exercise II N custom, habit

习惯 **xíguàn** I N habit II v be accustomed to, be used to ■ 很多中国人不习惯吃西餐。Hěn duō Zhōngguórén bù xíguàn chī xīcān. *Many Chinese are not used to eating Western-style meals.*
习惯上 **xíguàn shang** habitually
习俗 **xísú** N accepted custom, custom
习题 **xítí** N exercises (in school work)

席 **xí** N seat

来宾席 **láibīnxí** visitors' seats
席位 **xíwèi** N seat

洗 **xǐ** v wash, bathe ■ 吃饭前要洗手。Chīfàn qián yào xǐ shǒu. *You should wash your hands before having a meal.*
洗尘 **xǐchén** v give a welcome dinner
洗涤 **xǐdí** v wash, cleanse
洗涤剂 **xǐdíjì** detergent
洗手间 **xǐshǒujiān** N toilet, restroom, washroom

NOTE: 洗手间 xǐshǒujiān is a common euphemism for *toilet*. The formal word for *toilet* is 厕所 cèsuǒ, e.g. 男厕所 nán cèsuǒ (Men's room, Gents'), 女厕所 nǚ cèsuǒ (Ladies' room, Ladies').

洗衣机 **xǐyījī** N washing machine (台 tái)
洗澡 **xǐzǎo** v take a bath, take a shower ■ 他习惯临睡前洗一个热水澡。Tā xíguàn línshuì qián xǐ yí ge rèshuǐ zǎo. *He is used to taking a hot bath just before going to bed.*
洗澡间 **xǐzǎojiān** bathroom, shower room (Same as 浴室 yùshì.)

喜 **xǐ** I v be fond of II ADJ happy, glad

喜爱 **xǐ'ài** v be fond of, love
喜欢 **xǐhuan** v like, be fond of ■ 他喜欢一边喝啤酒，一边看体育节目。Tā xǐhuan yìbiān hē píjiǔ, yìbiān kàn tǐyù jiémù. *He likes to drink beer while watching sports programs.*
喜鹊 **xǐque** N magpie (只 zhī)

NOTE: In Chinese folklore, 喜鹊 xǐque *the magpie* is an auspicious bird, the harbinger of good tidings, hence 喜鹊 xǐque.

喜事 **xǐshì** N happy event (especially a wedding)
办喜事 **bànxǐshì** arrange a wedding
喜讯 **xǐxùn** N good news, good tidings
喜悦 **xǐyuè** ADJ happy, joyful

隙 **xì** N narrow gap (See 空隙 kòngxì)

戏 **xì** TRAD 戲 N drama, play (出 chū) ■ 今天晚上我们去看戏。Jīntiān wǎnshang wǒmen qù kàn xì. *We're going to watch a play this evening.*
戏剧 **xìjù** N drama

系 **xì** N department (of a university) ■ 这座大学有十二个系，最大的是电脑系。Zhè zuò dàxué yǒu shí'èr ge xì, zuì dà de shì diànnǎo xì. *This university has twelve departments; the biggest is the Computing Science Department.*
系主任 **xì zhǔrèn** chair of a (university) department
系列 **xìliè** N series
一系列 **yíxìliè** a series of
系统 **xìtǒng** N a group of items serving a common purpose, system (套 tào)

细 **xì** TRAD 細 ADJ 1 thin, slender (of objects shaped like a strip) ■ 中国的面条又细又长，是我最喜欢吃的东西。Zhōngguó de miàntiáo yòu xì yòu cháng, shì wǒ zuì xǐhuan chī de dōngxi. *Chinese noodles are thin and long; they are my favorite food.* 2 small, tiny
细沙 **xìshā** fine sand
3 meticulous ■ 他把计划的各个方面都考虑得很细。Tā bǎ jìhuà de gè ge fāngmiàn dōu kǎolǜ de hěn xì. *He considered every single aspect of the plan very carefully.*
细胞 **xìbāo** N (in biology) cell
细节 **xìjié** N details ■ 这件事的细节我不清楚。Zhè jiàn shì de xìjié wǒ bù qīngchu. *I'm not clear about the details of this matter.*
细菌 **xìjūn** N bacterium, germ
细小 **xìxiǎo** ADJ tiny
细心 **xìxīn** ADJ very careful, meticulous ■ 她做完数学练习后总要细心地检查一遍。Tā zuòwán shùxué liànxí hòu zǒngyào xìxīn de jiǎnchá yíbiàn. *After finishing her mathematics exercises she checks every question very carefully.*
细致 **xìzhì** ADJ careful, meticulous

瞎 **xiā** ADJ blind

虾 **xiā** TRAD 蝦 N prawn, shrimp (只 zhī)

峡 **xiá** N gorge

峡谷 **xiágǔ** N gorge, canyon

狭 **xiá** ADJ narrow

狭隘 **xiá'ài** ADJ narrow
狭窄 **xiázhǎi** ADJ narrow, narrow and limited
心胸狭窄 **xīnxiōng xiázhǎi** narrow-minded, intolerant

霞 **xiá** N rosy clouds, morning or evening glow

辖 **xiá** TRAD 轄 v govern (See 管辖 guǎnxiá)

213

下 xià

下 1 **xià** I PREP below, under, underneath ■ 树下很凉快。 Shù xià hěn liángkuài. *It's cool under the tree.*

山下 **shānxia** at the foot of a hill or hills II V 1 go/come down 2 leave off, finish 3 issue, deliver III ADJ low, inferior

下班 **xiàbān** V get off work

下边 **xiàbian** N below, under ■ 椅子下边有几本书，是谁的? Yǐzi xiàbian yǒu jǐ běn shū, shì shéi de? *There are some books under the chair. Whose are they?*

下车 **xiàchē** V get off a vehicle

下达 **xiàdá** V make known to lower levels

下岗 **xiàgǎng** V be laid off, be unemployed ■ 张师傅下岗好几年了，生活很困难。 Zhāng shīfu xiàgǎng hǎo jǐ nián le, shēnghuó hěn kùn-nan. *Master worker Zhang was laid off several years ago and has been living a hard life.*

下岗工人 **xiàgǎng gōngrén** a worker who has been laid off, an unemployed worker

下级 **xiàjí** N lower level, subordinate

下降 **xiàjiàng** V fall, descend

下课 **xiàkè** V finish class ■ 你们每天几点钟下课? Nǐmen měi tiān jǐ diǎnzhōng xiàkè? *When do you finish school everyday?*

下来 **xiàlái** V come down ■ 晚饭做好了，快下来吃吧! Wǎnfàn zuòhǎo le, kuài xiàlai chī ba! *Supper is ready. Come down and eat!*

下列 **xiàliè** ADJ listed below

下令 **xiàlìng** V issue an order

下落 **xiàluò** N what has happened (to someone), whereabouts

打听…的下落 **dǎting...de xiàluò** inquire about (someone's) whereabouts, try to find what has happened to (someone)

下面 **xiàmiàn** Same as 下边 xiàbian

下去 **xiàqù** V go down ■ 时间不早了，我们(从山上)下去吧。 Shíjiān bù zǎo le, wǒmen (cóng shānshang) xiàqu ba. *It's quite late. Let's go down [the hill].*

下台 **xiàtái** V 1 step down from the stage 2 lose a position, fall from power

下午 **xiàwǔ** N afternoon

下乡 **xiàxiāng** V go to the countryside

下旬 **xiàxún** N the last ten days of a month

下游 **xiàyóu** N lower reaches (of a river)

下载 **xià zài** V download

下 2 **xià** M. WD (used with certain verbs to indicate the number of times the action is done) ■ 我试了几下，都不行。 Wǒ shìle jǐ xià, dōu bù xíng. *I tried several times, but it didn't work.*

吓 xià TRAD 嚇 V 1 frighten, scare ■ 我不是吓你，你父亲的病极其严重。 Wǒ bú shì xià nǐ,

nǐ fùqin de bìng jíqí yánzhòng. *I don't want to frighten you, but your father's illness is extremely severe.* 2 be frightened, be scared ■ 她看到强盗手里拿着刀，吓得尖叫起来。 Tā kàndao qiángdào shǒuli názhe dāo, xià de jiānjiào qǐlai. *When she saw the robber holding a knife in hand, she was so frightened that she screamed.*

吓人 **xiàrén** ADJ frightening, terrible

夏 xià N summer

夏天 **xiàtiān** N summer ■ 北京的夏天热吗? Běijīng de xiàtiān rè ma? *Is summer in Beijing hot?*

掀 xiān V lift, lift up

掀起 **xiānqǐ** V set off, start

先 xiān ADV first (in time sequence) ■ 您先请。 Nín xiān qǐng. *After you.*

先…再… **xiān...zài...** first ... and then ... ■ 他早上先跑步，再吃早饭。 Tā zǎoshang xiān pǎo-bù, zài chī zǎofàn. *Early in the morning he first jogs and then has breakfast.*

先锋 **xiānfēng** N pioneer

先后 **xiānhòu** ADV one after another, successively ■ 他们四个孩子大学毕业后先后离家。 Tāmen sì ge háizi dàxué bìyè hòu xiānhòu lí jiā. *After graduation from university their four children left home one after another.*

先进 **xiānjìn** ADJ advanced ■ 这种照相机使用最先进的技术。 Zhè zhǒng zhàoxiàngjī shǐyòng zuì xiānjìn de jìshù. *This camera uses the most advanced technology.*

先前 **xiānqián** ADV previously

先生 **xiānsheng** N 1 teacher 2 Mister (Mr) 3 sir, gentleman ■ 先生，有事吗? Xiānsheng, yǒu shì ma? *Is there anything I can do for you, sir?* 4 husband ■ 您先生在哪儿工作? Nín xiānsheng zài nǎr gōngzuò? *Where does your husband work?*

先行 **xiānxíng** V go ahead, precede

鲜 xiān TRAD 鮮 ADJ 1 fresh ■ 她买了几根鲜黄瓜回家做凉菜。 Tā mǎile jǐ gēn xiān huáng-gua huíjiā zuò liángcài. *She bought several fresh cucumbers and brought them home to prepare a cold dish.* 2 bright, brightly-colored 3 delicious ■ 这鱼汤真鲜! Zhè yútāng zhēn xiān! *The fish soup is really delicious!*

鲜红 **xiānhóng** N bright red, scarlet

鲜花 **xiānhuā** N fresh flower, flower (朵 duǒ) ■ 他采了路边的一朵鲜花，送给女朋友。 Tā cǎile lùbiān de yì duǒ xiānhuā, sòng gei nǚpéngyou. *He picked a fresh flower by the roadside and gave it to his girlfriend.*

鲜明 **xiānmíng** ADJ bright, clear, distinct

鲜血 **xiānxuè** N blood

鲜艳 **xiānyàn** ADJ gaily-colored

纤 **xiān** TRAD 纖 N fiber

纤维 **xiānwéi** N fiber

仙 **xiān** N fairy, immortal

仙女 **xiānnǚ** N fairy maiden

仙人 **xiānrén** N immortal, celestial

贤 **xián** TRAD 賢 ADJ virtuous

贤惠 **xiánhuì** ADJ (of women) kind and wise, virtuous

衔 **xián** TRAD 啣 I v 1 hold in the mouth 2 join, link up II N rank, title

军衔 **jūnxián** military rank

衔接 **xiánjiē** v link up, join

弦 **xián** N string (of a musical instrument), bowstring

咸 **xián** TRAD 鹹 ADJ salty

闲 **xián** TRAD 閒 ADJ idle, unoccupied ■ 有的人挺忙, 有的人闲着: 分工不合理。 Yǒude rén tǐng máng, yǒude rén xiánzhe: fēngōng bù hélǐ. *While some are very busy, others are idle. The division of labor is irrational.*

清闲 **qīngxián** leisurely, carefree

闲话 **xiánhuà** N chat, gossip

闲人 **xiánrén** N idler, uninvolved person ■ 闲人免入。 Xiánrén miǎn rù. *No Admittance.*

闲事 **xiánshì** N matter that does not concern you ■ 你别管闲事。 Nǐ bié guǎn xiánshì. *It's none of your business.*

嫌 **xián** I v dislike, complain II N suspicion

避嫌 **bìxián** avoid suspicion

嫌疑 **xiányí** N suspicion

显 **xiǎn** TRAD 顯 v appear, look

显得 **xiǎnde** v appear to be, seem to be ■ 他穿了黑衣服显得更瘦。 Tā chuānle hēi yīfu xiǎnde gèng shòu. *Dressed in a black suit, he appeared all the thinner.*

显然 **xiǎnrán** ADV clearly, obviously

显示 **xiǎnshì** v show, manifest

显著 **xiǎnzhù** ADJ remarkable, outstanding, notable ■ 今年我们公司在开发新产品方面取得了显著成就。 Jīnnián wǒmen gōngsī zài kāifā xīn chǎnpǐn fāngmiàn qǔdéle xiǎnzhù chéngjiù. *This year our company has made notable achievements in developing new products.*

险 **xiǎn** TRAD 險 ADJ dangerous (See 危险 wēixiǎn.)

县 **xiàn** TRAD 縣 N (rural) county ■ 中国有两千左右个县。 Zhōngguó yǒu liǎngqiān zuǒyòu ge xiàn. *China has around 2,000 counties.*

县城 **xiànchéng** N county town, county seat

县长 **xiànzhǎng** N mayor of a county

现 **xiàn** TRAD 現 N now, at present

现场 **xiànchǎng** N 1 (crime, accident, disaster, etc.) scene 2 on the site, on the spot

事故现场 **shìgù xiànchǎng** accident scene

现成 **xiànchéng** ADJ ready-made

现代 **xiàndài** N modern times, the contemporary age ■ 在这座古庙前, 盖了这么一个现代建筑, 很不合适。 Zài zhè zuò gǔ miào qián, gàile zhème yí ge xiàndài jiànzhù, hěn bù héshì. *It is inappropriate to put up such a modern building in front of this ancient temple.*

现代化 **xiàndàihuà** I v modernize ■ 我们的教学手段应该现代化。 Wǒmen de jiàoxué shǒuduàn yīnggāi xiàndàihuà. *Our means of teaching and learning should be modernized.* II N modernization ■ 办公设备的现代化提高了工作效率。 Bàngōng shèbèi de xiàndàihuà tígāole gōngzuò xiàolǜ. *The modernization of office equipment has increased work efficiency.*

现金 **xiànjīn** N cash

现钱 **xiànqián** Same as 现金 xiànjīn

现实 **xiànshí** I N what is real, reality, actuality ■ 现实往往不那么美好。 Xiànshí wǎngwǎng bú nàme měihǎo. *The reality is often not so perfect.* II ADJ realistic ■ 这个计划不太现实。 Zhège jìhuà bú tài xiànshí. *This plan is not very realistic.*

现象 **xiànxiàng** N phenomenon

现行 **xiànxíng** ADJ currently in effect, in effect

现行法令 **xiànxíngfǎlìng** decrees in effect, current laws

现在 **xiànzài** N the present time, now ■ 现在几点钟? Xiànzài jǐ diǎn zhōng? *What time is it?*

现状 **xiànzhuàng** N current situation

陷 **xiàn** v 1 get bogged down 2 get trapped, be framed

陷害 **xiànhài** v make a trumped-up charge against, frame

陷入 **xiànrù** v get trapped, be caught in

馅 **xiàn** N filling, stuffing

馅儿 **xiànr** filling, stuffing

线 **xiàn** TRAD 線 N string, thread, wire (根 gēn) ■ 这根线太短, 有没有长一点的? Zhè gēn xiàn tài duǎn, yǒu méi yǒu cháng yìdiǎn de? *This string is too short. Do you have a longer one?*

215

线路 **xiànlù** N circuit, route

线索 **xiànsuǒ** N clue, lead (in a police case)
发现线索 **fāxiàn xiànsuǒ** discover a clue, find a lead

限 **xiàn** v limit

限度 **xiàndù** N limitation, limit
超过限度 **chāoguò xiàndù** exceed the limit
限期 **xiànqī** I N time limit, deadline II v set a time limit, impose a deadline
限期完成 **xiànqī wánchéng** must be done (finished, completed, etc.) by the deadline
限于 **xiànyú** v be confined to, be limited to
限于时间关系 **xiànyú shíjiān guānxì** owing to the time limitation
限制 **xiànzhì** v limit, restrict, confine ■ 为了减肥，她限制自己一天吃两顿饭。Wèile jiǎnféi, tā xiànzhì zìjǐ yì tiān chī liǎng dùn fàn. *To reduce weight she restricted herself to two meals a day.*

宪 **xiàn** TRAD 憲 N statute

宪兵 **xiànbīng** N military police
宪法 **xiànfǎ** N constitution ■ 根据宪法，公民享有言论自由。Gēnjù xiànfǎ, gōngmín xiǎngyǒu yánlùn zìyóu. *According to the Constitution, citizens enjoy freedom of speech.*

羡 **xiàn** v admire, envy

羡慕 **xiànmù** v envy ■ 她的家庭这么美满，真让人羡慕。Tā de jiātíng zhème měimǎn, zhēn ràng rén xiànmù! *Her perfectly happy family really makes one envious.*

献 **xiàn** TRAD 獻 v offer, dedicate

献身 **xiànshēn** v give one's life for, devote oneself to

乡 **xiāng** TRAD 鄉 N rural town ■ 乡比县小，比村大。Xiāng bǐ xiàn xiǎo, bǐ cūn dà. *A rural town is smaller than a county, but bigger than a village.*

乡村 **xiāngcūn** N rural area, countryside
乡下 **xiāngxia** N countryside, rural area
乡镇 **xiāngzhèn** N townships and villages
乡镇企业 **xiāngzhèn qǐyè** township and village enterprise, rural industry

相 **xiāng** ADV each other, mutually

相比 **xiāngbǐ** v compare
相差 **xiāngchà** v differ, differ from
相当 **xiāngdāng** I ADJ suitable, appropriate ■ 我在翻译的时候，常常想不出一个相当的词。Wǒ zài fānyì de shíhou, chángcháng xiǎng bu chū yí ge xiāngdāng de cí. *When I do transla-tion I often cannot find a suitable word.* II ADV fairly, rather, quite ■ 他中文说得相当不错。Tā Zhōngwén shuō de xiāngdāng búcuò. *He speaks Chinese rather well.*
相等 **xiāngděng** v be equal
相对 **xiāngduì** ADV relatively, comparatively
相对来说 **xiāngduì láishuō** relatively speaking
相对论 **xiāngduìlùn** the theory of relativity
相反 **xiāngfǎn** ADJ opposite, contrary ■ 不同的意见，甚至相反的意见都要听。Bùtóng de yìjiàn, shènzhì xiāngfǎn de yìjiàn dōu yào tīng. *We should hear out different, even opposing, opinions.*
相符 **xiāngfú** v conform to, agree with, tally with
与事实相符 **yǔ shìshí xiāngfú** conform with the facts
相关 **xiāngguān** v be related to, be interrelated
相互 **xiānghù** ADJ mutual, each other ■ 一对年轻人必须相互了解才能考虑婚姻。Yíduì niánqīngrén bìxū xiānghù liǎojiě cái néng kǎolǜ hūnyīn. *A young man and a young woman must know each other well before contemplating marriage.*
相继 **xiāngjì** ADV in succession, one after another
相交 **xiāngjiāo** v intersect
相识 **xiāngshí** v be acquainted with, come to know
老相识 **lǎoxiāngshí** someone you have known for a long time, an old acquaintance
相似 **xiāngsì** ADJ similar to, be alike ■ 他们姐妹俩长得很相似，但是脾气性格不一样。Tāmen jiě-mèi liǎ zhǎng de hěn xiāngsì, dànshì píqì xìnggé bù yíyàng. *The two sisters resemble each other, but have different temperaments.*
相通 **xiāngtōng** I v be linked with each other II ADJ mutually comprehensible, compatible with
相同 **xiāngtóng** ADJ identical, same ■ 相同的年龄，相同的经历使他们有很多共同语言。Xiāngtóng de niánlíng, xiāngtóng de jīnglì shǐ tāmen yǒu hěn duō gòngtóng yǔyán. *The same age and the same experiences give them lots of common language.*
相信 **xiāngxìn** v believe, believe in
相应 **xiāngyìng** ADJ corresponding, relevant
相应措施 **xiāngyìng cuòshī** appropriate measures

镶 **xiāng** TRAD 鑲 v 1 set into, set 2 mount

香 **xiāng** ADJ 1 fragrant, sweet-smelling, aromatic ■ 我闻到烤肉的香味。Wǒ wéndào

kǎoròu de xiāngwèi. *I smell the delicious aroma of roast beef.* **2** savoury, appetizing

香肠 **xiāngcháng** N sausage (根 gēn)

香港 **Xiānggǎng** N Hong Kong ■ 香港是买东西的好地方。Xiānggǎng shì mǎi dōngxi de hǎo dìfang. *Hong Kong is a good place for shopping.*

香蕉 **xiāngjiāo** N banana (根 gēn)

香味 **xiāngwèi** N sweet smell, fragrance

香烟 **xiāngyān** N cigarette (支 zhī)

香皂 **xiāngzào** N toilet soap, bath soap (块 kuài) ■ 这块香皂很好闻。Zhè kuài xiāngzào hěn hǎowén. *This soap smells nice.*

箱 **xiāng** N box, chest, trunk

箱子 **xiāngzi** N trunk, chest, box, suitcase (只 zhī) ■ 这个箱子是她奶奶传给她的。Zhège xiāngzi shì tā nǎinai chuán gěi tā de. *This trunk was passed down to her from her grandmother.*

厢 **xiāng** N wing (of a house), wing room

车厢 **chēxiāng** (train) carriage

详 **xiáng** TRAD 詳 ADJ detailed

详细 **xiángxì** ADJ in detail, detailed ■ 他详细说明了全部经过。Tā xiángxì shuōmíngle quánbù jīngguò. *He told the whole story in detail.*

祥 **xiáng** ADJ auspicious (See 吉祥 jíxiáng)

翔 **xiáng** V circle in the air, fly (See 飞翔 fēixiáng)

享 **xiǎng** V enjoy

享福 **xiǎngfú** V enjoy a happy life, live a blessed life

享乐 **xiǎnglè** V indulge in material comfort 享乐主义 **xiǎnglè zhǔyì** hedonism

享受 **xiǎngshòu** I V enjoy ■ 在有些方面现代人享受的比古代皇帝还多。Zài yǒuxiē fāngmiàn xiàndàirén xiǎngshòu de bǐ gǔdài huángdì hái duō. *In some respects modern man enjoys more things than an emperor did in ancient times.*
II N enjoyment, pleasure
精神享受 **jīngshén xiǎngshòu** spiritual pleasure

享有 **xiǎngyǒu** V enjoy (rights, prestige, etc.)

响 **xiǎng** TRAD 響 I ADJ loud, noisy ■ 教室里在考试，你们说话声音别这么响。Jiàoshì li zài kǎoshì, nǐmen shuōhuà shēngyīn bié zhènme xiǎng. *There's an examination in progress in the classroom. Don't talk so loudly.* II N sound, noise

响亮 **xiǎngliàng** ADJ loud and clear, resounding

响声 **xiǎngshēng** N sound (especially loud sounds)

响应 **xiǎngyìng** V respond, answer

想 **xiǎng** V **1** think ■ 我想这个手续不会太麻烦。Wǒ xiǎng zhè shǒuxù bú huì tài máfan. *I don't think this procedure will be very complicated.*
想一下 **xiǎng yíxià** think for a while, give ... some thought ■ 明天晚上跟不跟他一块儿去看电影？让我想一下。Míngtiān wǎnshang gēn bu gēn tā yíkuàir qù kàn diànyǐng? Ràng wǒ xiǎng yíxià. *Shall I go to the movie with him tomorrow evening? Let me think it over.*
2 think back, recall **3** miss, remember with longing

想办法 **xiǎng bànfǎ** V think of a way (to do something) ■ 没关系，我来想办法。Méiguānxi, wǒ lái xiǎng bànfǎ. *It's OK. I'll think of a way.*

想法 **xiǎngfa** N what one thinks, idea, opinion ■ 老师想了解一下学生对开口语课的想法。Lǎoshī xiǎng liǎojiě yíxià xuésheng duì kāi kǒuyǔ kè de xiǎngfa. *The teacher wants to find out what the students think of introducing an oral Chinese class.*

想方设法 **xiǎng fāng shè fǎ** IDIOM try every means, do all one can

想念 **xiǎngniàn** V miss, remember with longing ■ 祖母去世两年了，我还非常想念她。Zǔmǔ qùshì liǎng nián le, wǒ hái fēicháng xiǎngniàn tā. *It's over two years since Granny died, but I still miss her very much.*

想像 **xiǎngxiàng** V imagine
想像力 **xiǎngxiànglì** imaginative power

相 **xiàng** as in 相声 xiàngsheng

相声 **xiàngsheng** N comic dialogue, comic cross-talk

巷 **xiàng** N narrow street, alley (条 tiáo)

一条深巷 **yìtiáo shēn xiàng** a long alley

项 1 **xiàng** TRAD 項 N the neck

项链 **xiàngliàn** N necklace (条 tiáo)
戴一条珍珠项链 **dài yì tiáo zhēnzhū xiàngliàn** wear a pearl necklace

项 2 **xiàng** TRAD 項 M. WD item of something (for things that are composed of items or things considered to be components)
一项任务 **yí xiàng rènwù** a mission

项目 **xiàngmù** N item ■ 他负责一个重要的研究项目。Tā fùzé yíge zhòngyào de yánjiū xiàngmù. *He is in charge of an important research project.*

象 1 **xiàng** N elephant (头 tóu, 只 zhī)

象棋 xiàngqí

> **NOTE:** Chinese often fondly refer to elephants as 大象 dàxiàng.

象棋 **xiàngqí** N chess (副 fù, 盘 pán)
国际象棋 **guójì xiàngqí** Western chess
中国象棋 **Zhōngguó xiàngqí** Chinese chess
下一盘象棋 **xià yì pán xiàngqí** play a game of chess

象 2 **xiàng** Same as 像 xiàng **I** v

象征 **xiàngzhēng I** N symbol **II** v symbolize

像 **xiàng I** v resemble, take after, be like **II** N likeness of (a human being), portrait (幅 fú) ■ 墙上挂着祖父的像。Qiáng shang guàzhe zǔfù de xiàng. *On the wall hangs a portrait of their grandfather.*

像样 **xiàngyàng** ADJ presentable, up to the standard

橡 **xiàng** N rubber, rubber tree, oak, oak tree

橡胶 **xiàngjiāo** N rubber
橡胶树 **xiàngjiāoshù** rubber tree
橡皮 **xiàngpí** N eraser (a piece of rubber) (块 kuài)

向 **xiàng I** v face ■ 这个房间有两个窗子, 一个向南, 一个向东。Zhège fángjiān yǒu liǎng ge chuāngzi, yí ge xiàng nán, yí ge xiàng dōng. *There are two windows in the room. One faces south and the other faces east.* **II** PREP in the direction of, towards ■ 中国的长江, 黄河都向东流。Zhōngguó de Chángjiāng, Huánghé dōu xiàng dōng liú. *China's Yangtze River and Yellow River flow to the east.* **III** ADV all along, always

向导 **xiàngdǎo** N guide
旅游向导 **lǚyóu xiàngdǎo** tourist guide
向来 **xiànglái** ADV always, all along
向往 **xiàngwǎng** v yearn for, look forward to

消 **xiāo** v 1 vanish, disappear 2 dispel, remove

消除 **xiāochú** v clear up, dispel ■ 我跟他好好谈了一次, 消除了我们之间的误会。Wǒ gēn tā hǎohǎo tánle yícì, xiāochúle wǒmen zhījiān de wùhuì. *I had a good talk with him and cleared up the misunderstanding between us.*
消毒 **xiāodú** v disinfect, sterilize
消费 **xiāofèi** v consume ■ 生活水平提高了, 人们消费的商品就越来越多。Shēnghuó shuǐpíng tígāole, rénmen xiāofèi de shāngpǐn jiù yuèláiyuè duō. *As people's living standard rises, they consume more and more goods.*
消费品 **xiāofèipǐn** consumer commodities, consumer goods
消费者 **xiāofèizhě** consumer

消化 **xiāohuà** v digest ■ 我中饭还没有消化呢, 不想吃晚饭。Wǒ zhōngfàn hái méiyǒu xiāohuà ne, bù xiǎng chī wǎnfàn. *I still haven't digested my lunch. I don't want to eat supper.*
消化不良 **xiāohuà bùliáng** indigestion
消化系统 **xiāohuà xìtǒng** digestive system
消极 **xiāojí** ADJ lacking enthusiasm, passive
消灭 **xiāomiè** v eliminate, wipe out ■ 这种害虫在本地区基本消灭。Zhè zhǒng hàichóng zài běn dìqū jīběn xiāomiè. *This pest has been mainly exterminated in this region.*
消失 **xiāoshī** v disappear, vanish ■ 太阳出来以后, 雾渐渐消失了。Tàiyang chūlai yǐhòu, wù jiànjiàn xiāoshī le. *As the sun came out, the fog dissipated.*
消息 **xiāoxi** N news (条 tiáo) ■ 我告诉你一个好消息。Wǒ gàosu nǐ yí ge hǎo xiāoxi. *I'll tell you a piece of good news.*

宵 **xiāo** N night (See 元宵 yuánxiāo)

销 **xiāo** TRAD 銷 v 1 sell, market

畅销书 **chàngxiāoshū** bestseller (book)
2 cancel, annual
销毁 **xiāohuǐ** v destroy (especially by burning)
销毁罪证 **xiāohuǐ zuìzhèng** destroy incriminating evidence
销路 **xiāolù** N market, sale
销路很好 **xiāolù hěn hǎo** (of a commodity) have a good market
销售 **xiāoshòu** N sale, market ■ 你们销售这家汽车制造厂的零件吗? Nǐmen xiāoshòu zhè jiā qìchē zhìzàochǎng de língjiàn ma? *Do you sell parts from this auto manufacturer?*
销售部 **xiāoshòubù** sales department
销售额 **xiāoshòu'é** revenue from sales, sales takings
销售量 **xiāoshòuliàng** sales volume

削 **xiāo** v peel with a knife

削苹果 **xiāo píngguǒ** peel an apple

淆 **xiáo** v confuse (See 混淆 hùnxiáo)

小 **xiǎo** ADJ 1 small, little ■ 这双鞋太小了, 有没有大一点儿的? Zhè shuāng xié tài xiǎo le, yǒu méiyǒu dà yìdiǎnr de? *This pair of shoes is too small. Do you have a bigger size?* **2** being a child, young ■ 我小时候, 放暑假的时候, 常常住在奶奶家。Wǒ xiǎo shíhou, fàng shǔjià de shíhou, chángcháng zhù zai nǎinai jiā. *When I was a child, I often stayed with granny during the summer holidays.* ■ 我姓李, 您就叫我小李吧。Wǒ xìng Lǐ, nín jiù jiào wǒ Xiǎo Lǐ ba. *My*

family name is Li. You can call me Xiao Li.
小孩儿 **xiǎoháir** young child, child

NOTE: "小 xiǎo + family name," like 小李 Xiǎo Lǐ, is a casual, friendly form of address to a person younger than oneself. See note on 老 lǎo for forms of address like 老李 Lǎo Lǐ.

小便 **xiǎobiàn I** N urine
小便池 **xiǎobiànchí** urinal
II V urinate
小费 **xiǎofèi** N tip, gratuity
小伙子 **xiǎohuǒzi** N young man, lad

NOTE: See note on 姑娘 gūniang.

小姐 **xiǎojiě** N **1** young lady **2** Miss ■ 王先生，王太太和他们的女儿王小姐都在美国旅行。Wáng xiānsheng, Wáng tàitai hé tāmen de nǚ'ér Wáng xiǎojiě dōu zài Měiguó lǚxíng. *Mr and Mrs Wang, with their daughter Miss Wang, are all traveling in the United States.*

NOTE: 小姐 xiǎojiě is a common form of address to a young (or not so young) woman. If her family name is not known, just use 小姐 xiǎojiě. 小姐 xiǎojiě is also the form of address for *a waitress* or *female attendant*, e.g. ■ 小姐，请给我一杯水。Xiǎojiě, qǐng gěi wǒ yì bēi shuǐ. *Miss, please give me a glass of water.*

小康 **xiǎokāng** ADJ fairly prosperous, well-off, well-to-do
小康社会 **xiǎokāng shèhuì** a well-off society
小麦 **xiǎomài** N wheat ■ 在中国北方粮食以小麦为主。Zài Zhōngguó běifāng liángshí yǐ xiǎomài wéi zhǔ. *In northern China, wheat is the main cereal crop.*
小米 **xiǎomǐ** N millet
小朋友 **xiǎopéngyou** N (a friendly form of address or reference) child ■ 小朋友，你们校长办公室在哪里? Xiǎopéngyou, nǐmen xiàozhǎng bàngōngshì zài nǎlǐ? *Where's your headmaster's office, children?*
小气 **xiǎoqì** ADJ stingy, miserly
小区 **xiǎoqū** N residential community, neighborhood
小时 **xiǎoshí** N hour
半小时 **bàn xiǎoshí** half an hour
小时工 **xiǎoshígōng** N (domestic) worker paid on an hourly basis
小数 **xiǎoshù** N decimal
小说 **xiǎoshuō** N novel (本 běn, 篇 piān) ■ 这篇小说语言优美，但是没有多大意思。Zhè piān xiǎoshuō yǔyán yōuměi, dànshì méiyǒu duō dà yìsi. *The language of this story is beautiful but it is not very meaningful.*
小说家 **xiǎoshuōjiā** (accomplished) novelist

爱情小说 **àiqíng xiǎoshuō** romance novel
长篇小说 **chángpiān xiǎoshuō** novel
短篇小说 **duǎnpiān xiǎoshuō** short story, story
历史小说 **lìshǐ xiǎoshuō** historical novel
小提琴 **xiǎotíqín** N violin
小提琴手 **xiǎotíqínshǒu** violinist
拉小提琴 **lā xiǎotíqín** play the violin
小偷 **xiǎotōu** N thief, pickpocket ■ 抓小偷! 抓小偷! Zhuō xiǎotōu! Zhuō xiǎotōu! *Stop thief! Stop thief!*
小心 **xiǎoxīn** ADJ careful, cautious ■ 他说话，做事都很小心。Tā shuōhuà, zuòshì dōu hěn xiǎoxīn. *He is cautious in speech and action.*
小型 **xiǎoxíng** ADJ small-sized
小学 **xiǎoxué** N primary school (座 zuò, 所 suǒ)
小学生 **xiǎoxuésheng** primary school student, pupil
小子 **xiǎozi** N son, boy
小组 **xiǎozǔ** N small group

晓 **xiǎo** TRAD 曉 V know

晓得 **xiǎode** V Same as 知道 zhīdào. Only used in colloquial Chinese.

孝 **xiào** N filial piety

孝顺 **xiàoshùn** V perform one's filial duties faithfully, be obedient and considerate of one's parents

效 **xiào** N effect

效果 **xiàoguǒ** N effect, result ■ 对孩子太严格，往往效果不好。Duì háizi tài yángé, wǎngwǎng xiàoguǒ bù hǎo. *Being too strict with children often gives poor results.*
效力 **xiàolì** N desired effects, intended results
效率 **xiàolǜ** N efficiency ■ 我们必须不断提高工作效率。Wǒmen bìxū búduàn tígāo gōngzuò xiàolǜ. *We must constantly improve work efficiency.*
效益 **xiàoyì** N beneficial (economic) results, economic benefits

校 **xiào** N school

校徽 **xiàohuī** N school badge
校园 **xiàoyuán** N school ground, campus
校长 **xiàozhǎng** N headmaster, principal, university president, university vice chancellor ■ 在中文里，小学、中学、大学的负责人都叫"校长"。Zài Zhōngwén li, xiǎoxué, zhōngxué, dàxué de fùzérén dōu jiào "xiàozhǎng". *In Chinese, people in charge of primary schools, high schools or universities are all called "xiaozhang."*

NOTES: (1) While in Chinese *the chief of any school* is called 校长 xiàozhǎng, different terms are required in English. (2) In an English-system university, the vice-chancellor is its chief executive officer. *Vice-chancellor* should therefore be translated as 校长 xiàozhǎng while *chancellor*, being largely an honorary position, should be 名誉校长 míngyù xiàozhǎng.

笑 **xiào** v **1** laugh, smile ■ 笑一笑，十年少。 Xiào yi xiào, shí nián shào. *Laugh and you'll be ten years younger.* (→ *Laughter is the best medicine.*)
大笑 **dàxiào** laugh
2 laugh at, make fun of
笑话 **xiàohua** I N joke ■ 我来讲个笑话。Wǒ lái jiǎng ge xiàohua. *I'll tell you a joke.* II v laugh at ■ 我中文讲得不好，你们别笑话我。Wǒ Zhōngwén jiǎng de bù hǎo, nǐmen bié xiàohua wǒ. *I don't speak Chinese very well. Please don't laugh at me.*
笑容 **xiàoróng** N smiling expression, smile
笑容满面 **xiàoróng mǎnmiàn** be all smiles

肖 **xiào** v resemble, be like

肖像 **xiàoxiàng** N portrait (幅 fú)

啸 **xiào** v howl, roar

些 **xiē** M. WD some, a few, a little ■ 午饭我吃了一些面包。Wǔfàn wǒ chīle yìxiē miànbāo. *I had some bread for lunch.*
好些 **hǎoxiē** quite a few, lots of ■ 昨天晚上他和老朋友谈了很久，喝了好些酒。Zuótiān wǎnshang tā hé lǎo péngyou tánle hěn jiǔ, hēle hǎoxiē jiǔ. *Yesterday evening he chatted with his old friends for a long time and drank lots of wine.*

歇 **xiē** v take a rest ■ 我走不动了，歇会儿吧。Wǒ zǒu bu dòng le, xiē huìr ba. *I can't walk any further. Let's take a break.*

协 **xié** TRAD 協 v **1** join **2** assist

协定 **xiédìng** N agreement, treaty ■ 两家公司签订了技术合作的协定。Liǎng jiā gōngsī qiāndìng-le jìshù hézuò de xiédìng. *The two companies signed an agreement on technological cooperation.*
协会 **xiéhuì** N association (an organization)
环境保护者协会 **huánjìng bǎohùzhě xiéhuì** Environmentalists Association
协力 **xiélì** v join in a common effort, work together
协商 **xiéshāng** v discuss and seek advice, consult
协调 **xiétiáo** v coordinate, harmonize
协议 **xiéyì** N agreement (a document)

协议书 **xiéyìshū** agreement (a document) (份 fèn)
达成协议 **dáchéng xiéyì** reach an agreement
协助 **xiézhù** N assistance ■ 由于当地居民的协助，警方很快逮捕了罪犯。Yóuyú dāngdì jūmín de xiézhù, jǐngfāng hěn kuài dàibǔle zuìfàn. *Thanks to the asssitance by local residents, the police arrested the criminal in no time.*
协作 **xiézuò** v cooperate

胁 **xié** TRAD 脅 v threaten (See 威胁 wēixié)

斜 **xié** ADJ oblique, slanting ■ 他斜穿过马路。Tā xié chuānguo mǎlù. *He crossed the street diagonally.*

挟 **xié** v hold under the arm

挟持 **xiéchí** v **1** seize by force **2** detain under duress

携 **xié** v **1** carry, take along with **2** take by the hand
携带 **xiédài** v carry, take along ■ 以下物品不准携带上机:… Yǐxià wùpǐn bùzhǔn xiédài shàngjī: … *It is forbidden to carry the following objects on the plane: …*
携手 **xiéshǒu** ADV hand in hand
携手并进 **xiéshǒu bìngjìn** go forward hand in hand, advance side by side

邪 **xié** ADJ evil, heretical

邪教 **xiéjiào** N religious cult, cult

鞋 **xié** N shoe (只 zhī, 双 shuāng)

凉鞋 **liáng xié** sandals
皮鞋 **pí xié** leather shoes
拖鞋 **tuō xié** slippers
雨鞋 **yǔ xié** rubber boots
运动鞋 **yùndòng xié** sports shoes
鞋带 **xiédài** N shoelace, shoestring (根 gēn, 副 fù)
系鞋带 **jì xiédài** tie shoelace

谐 **xié** TRAD 諧 ADJ harmonious (See 和谐 héxié)

血 **xiě** N Same as 血 xuè. Used only in colloquial Chinese.

写 **xiě** TRAD 寫 v write, write with a pen ■ 这个汉字怎么写？Zhège Hànzì zěnme xiě? *How do you write this Chinese character?*
写作 **xiězuò** v write as a professional writer, compose essays

泻 **xiè** v flow swiftly

腹泻 **fùxiè** have diarrhea

卸 **xiè** V 1 unload 2 remove, strip (See 装卸 zhuāngxiè)

泄 **xiè** V allow air or liquid to escape, let out, leak

泄露 **xièlòu** V leak (information)

泄气 **xièqì** V lose heart, be discouraged

谢 **xiè** TRAD 謝 V 1 thank 2 decline

谢谢 **xièxie** V thank ■ "谢谢你。" "不客气。" "Xièxie nǐ." "Bú kèqi." *"Thank you." "You're welcome."*

NOTE: There are many ways of replying to 谢谢你 xièxie nǐ, e.g. ■ 不客气。Bú kèqi. *You don't have to be so polite.* ■ 不用谢。Bú yòng xiè. *You don't have to thank me.* ■ 没关系。Méi guānxi. *It doesn't matter.*

谢绝 **xièjué** V decline (an invitation, an offer, etc.), refuse politely

械 **xiè** N tool (See 机械 jīxiè.)

屑 **xiè** N butts, scraps

面包屑 **miànbāo xiè** crumbs (of bread)

心 **xīn** N 1 the heart ■ 这个人心真好! Zhège rén xīn zhēn hǎo! *This person is really kindhearted.* 用心 **yòngxīn** apply oneself to ■ 你学习不太用心。Nǐ xuéxí bú tài yòngxīn. *You don't really apply yourself to studying.*
放心 **fàngxīn** feel relieved, be assured, at ease ■ 你一个人去爬山, 我不放心。Nǐ yí ge rén qù páshān, wǒ bú fàngxīn. *I'd be worried if you go mountain-climbing all by yourself.*
开心 **kāixīn** be joyous
痛心 **tòngxīn** pained, agonized
伤心 **shāngxīn** heartbroken
2 mind, feeling 3 core, center

心爱 **xīn'ài** ADJ beloved, treasured

心得 **xīndé** N what one has learned from work, study, etc, gain in understanding

心理 **xīnlǐ** N mentality, psychology ■ 夫妻常常吵架, 会对孩子的心理造成不良影响。Fūqī chángcháng chǎojià, huì duì háizi de xīnlǐ zàochéng bùliáng yǐngxiǎng. *Frequent quarrels between husband and wife will have undesirable effects on their child's mental well-being.*
心理分析 **xīnlǐ fēnxi** psychoanalysis
心理学 **xīnlǐxué** (the science of) psychology
心理咨询 **xīnlǐ zīxún** psychological consultation

心里 **xīnli** ADV in the heart, in the mind
心里有事 **xīnliyǒushì** have something on one's mind

心灵 **xīnlíng** I N soul, spirit
心灵深处 **xīnlíng shēnchù** deep down in one's heart
II ADJ quick-witted, agile-minded, bright
心灵手巧 **xīnlíng shǒuqiǎo** intelligent and capable, clever and deft

心目 **xīnmù** N mental view, mind
在他的心目中 **zài tāde xīnmùzhōng** in his eyes, in his opinion and judgment

心情 **xīnqíng** N state of mind, mood

心事 **xīnshì** N worry, something on one's mind ■ 你好像有什么心事, 怎么啦? Nǐ hǎoxiàng yǒu shénme xīnshì, zěnme la? *You seem to be worrying about something, what is it?*

心思 **xīnsi** N 1 idea, thought 2 state of mind, mood
没有心思出去玩儿 **méiyǒu xīnsi chūqu wánr** not in a mood to go out

心疼 **xīnténg** V 1 love dearly 2 feel sorry

心头 **xīntóu** N mind, heart
牢记心头 **láojì xīntóu** bear firmly in mind

心血 **xīnxuè** N painstaking effort
付出很大心血 **fùchū hěn dà xīnxuè** put a great deal of painstaking efforts

心血来潮 **xīnxuè láicháo** IDIOM be seized by an impulse, have a brainstorm

心眼儿 **xīnyǎnr** N heart, mind, intention
没安什么好心眼儿 **méi ān shénme hǎo xīnyǎnr** do not mean well, have some bad intention

心意 **xīnyì** N regard, warm feelings, good intention ■ 您的心意我领了, 但是礼物不能收。Nín de xīnyì wǒ lǐng le, dànshì lǐwù bùnéng shōu. *I appreciate your kindness, but I can't take your gift.*

心愿 **xīnyuàn** N wish, aspiration

心脏 **xīnzàng** N the heart (as a medical term)
心直口快 **xīnzhí kǒukuài** ADJ frank and outspoken

欣 **xīn** ADJ joyful

欣赏 **xīnshǎng** V admire, appreciate ■ 秋天, 人们到北京附近的香山欣赏美丽的红叶。Qiūtian, rénmen dào Běijīng fùjìn de xiāng shān xīnshǎng měilì de hóng yè. *In fall, people go to the Fragrance Hill near Beijing to admire the beautiful red leaves.*

欣欣向荣 **xīnxīn xiàng róng** IDIOM flourishing, prosperous

辛 **xīn** ADJ 1 spicy hot 2 laborious, hard

辛苦 **xīnkǔ** I ADJ 1 hard and toilsome (job) ■ 你们辛苦了。Nǐmen xīnkǔ le. *You've been working hard.* 2 harsh, difficult (life) II V (used

to request somebody's service) ■ 辛苦你把
这几只箱子搬到楼上去。Xīnkǔ nǐ bǎ zhè jǐ zhī
xiāngzi bān dào lóu shang qù. *Would you please
carry these suitcases upstairs?*

NOTE: "你们辛苦了!" "Nǐmen xīnkǔ le!" is used
by a superior to express appreciation of hard work
done by subordinate(s). When somebody has done
you a service, you can say: "辛苦你了!" "Xīnkǔ
nǐ le!"

辛勤 xīnqín ADJ industrious

锌 xīn N zinc (Zn)

新 xīn I ADJ new ■ 旧的不去, 新的不来。Jiù
de bú qù, xīn de bù lái. *If old stuff doesn't
go away, new stuff won't come. (→ If you don't
discard old things, you won't be able to use new
things.)* II ADV newly, recently
新陈代谢 xīnchéndàixiè IDIOM metabolism
新房 xīnfáng N bridal bedroom
新近 xīnjìn ADV recently, lately
新加坡 Xīnjiāpō N Singapore
新郎 xīnláng N bridegroom
新年 xīnnián N New Year ■ 祝您新年快乐! Zhù
nín xīnnián kuàile! *I wish you a happy New Year!*
新年贺卡 xīnnián hèkǎ New Year card
新娘 xīnniáng N bride
新生 xīnshēng N 1 newborn
新生儿 xīnshēng'ér newborn baby
2 new student
新生报到 xīnshēng bàodào new students
registration
3 new life, a new leaf (in one's life)
开始新生 kāishǐ xīnshēng turn over a new
leaf
新式 xīnshì N new type, new style
新闻 xīnwén N news (of current affairs) (条 tiáo)
■ 你是怎么样得到新闻的—读报纸, 听广播,
还是看电视? Nǐ shì zěnmeyàng dédào xīnwén
de—dú bàozhǐ, tīng guǎngbō, háishì kàn diànshì?
*How do you get the news—by reading newspa-
pers, listening to radio or watching television?*
新西兰 Xīnxīlán N New Zealand ■ 每年很
多外国人到新西兰去旅游。Měi nián hěn duō
wàiguórén dào Xīnxīlán qù lǚyóu. *Every year
many foreigners go to New Zealand on holiday.*
新鲜 xīnxiān ADJ fresh ■ 我们每天都要吃新
鲜蔬菜。Wǒmen měi tiān dōu yào chī xīnxiān
shūcài. *We should eat fresh vegetables every day.*
新兴 xīnxīng ADJ new and fast developing,
burgeoning
新兴产业 xīnxīng chǎnyè fast growing
industry, sunrise industry
新型 xīnxíng N new type, new pattern

新颖 xīnyǐng ADJ new and original

薪 xīn N 1 firewood 2 salary

高薪养廉 gāoxīn yǎnglián the policy of high
salary for civil servants in order to cultivate a
clean government
薪金 xīnjīn Same as 薪水 xīnshui
薪水 xīnshui N salary, wages

信 1 xìn I V believe, trust ■ 我不信他一天能
干这么多活。Wǒ bú xìn tā yì tiān néng gàn
zhème duō huó. *I don't believe he could have
done so much work in a day.* II N trust
信贷 xìndài N (in banking) credit
信赖 xìnlài V trust, have faith in
可以信赖的 kěyǐ xìnlài de trustworthy, reliable
信念 xìnniàn N faith, conviction
信任 xìnrèn I V trust, have confidence in ■ 你
既然请他做这么重要的工作, 一定很信任他。Nǐ
jìrán qǐng tā zuò zhème zhòngyào de gōngzuò,
yídìng hěn xìnrèn tā. *Since you've asked him to
do such an important job, you must really trust
him.* II N trust, confidence
信心 xìnxīn N confidence, faith ■ 我对公司
的前途充满信心。Wǒ duì gōngsī de qiántú
chōngmǎn xìnxīn. *I have full confidence in the
company's future.*
信用 xìnyòng N 1 trustworthiness
讲信用 jiǎngxìnyòng keep one's word, be
trustworthy
2 credit
信用卡 xìnyòngkǎ credit card
信誉 xìnyù N reputation, prestige

信 2 xìn N 1 letter, mail ■ 现在人们很少写
信。Xiànzài rénmen hěn shǎo xiě xìn. *People
don't often write letters now.*
寄信 jì xìn post a letter
介绍信 jièshàoxìn letter of recommendation,
reference
收到信 shōudào xìn receive a letter
祝贺信 zhùhèxìn letter of congratulation
2 sign, evidence
信封 xìnfēng N envelope
信号 xìnhào N signal
信件 xìnjiàn N letters, mail
信息 xìnxī N information ■ 你有关于他的信息
吗? Nǐ yǒu guānyú tā de xìnxī ma? *Do you have
any information about him?*
信息产业 xìnxī chǎnyè N information industry

衅 xìn N quarrel, dispute

挑衅 tiǎoxìn provoke

兴 **xīng** TRAD 興 **I** v **1** promote **2** start, begin **II** ADJ flourishing

兴办 **xīngbàn** v set up, initiate

兴奋 **xīngfèn** ADJ excited, overjoyed ■ 她们得了冠军，兴奋得跳了起来。Tāmen déle guànjūn, xīngfèn de tiàole qǐlai. *When they won the championship, they were so overjoyed that they jumped.*

兴奋剂 **xīngfènjì** N stimulant

兴建 **xīngjiàn** v build, construct

兴起 **xīngqǐ** v start and become popular, rise

兴旺 **xīngwàng** ADJ prosperous, thriving

星 **xīng** N star (颗 kē)

行星 **xíngxīng** planet

NOTE: In everyday Chinese 星星 xīngxīng is normally used instead of 星 xīng, e.g. ■ 今天晚上的星星真亮。Jīntiān wǎnshang de xīngxing zhēn liàng. *Tonight the stars are really bright.*

星期 **xīngqī** N week (个 gè) ■ 一年有五十二个星期。Yì nián yǒu wǔshí èr ge xīngqī. *There're fifty-two weeks in a year.*

星期一 **Xīngqīyī** Monday
星期二 **Xīngqī'èr** Tuesday
星期三 **Xīngqīsān** Wednesday
星期四 **Xīngqīsì** Thursday
星期五 **Xīngqīwǔ** Friday
星期六 **Xīngqīliù** Saturday
星期日/星期天 **Xīngqīrì/ Xīngqītiān** Sunday
上星期 **shàng xīngqī** last week
下星期 **xià xīngqī** next week

腥 **xīng** N fishy smell

行 1 **xíng** **I** v **1** travel, go ■ 三人行，必有我师。(孔子) Sān rén xíng, bì yǒu wǒ shī. (Kǒngzǐ) *When three people are walking together, at least one of them can be my teacher. (→ One can always find someone good enough to be one's teacher.)* **2** practice, carry out **II** N **1** trip, travel **2** act, behavior

行程 **xíngchéng** N route, distance traveled

行动 **xíngdòng** **I** v move around ■ 老人行动不便，不愿多外出。Lǎorén xíngdòng búbiàn, bú yuàn duō wàichū. *The old man has difficulty moving about and is reluctant to go out very often.* **II** N action, behavior ■ 不但要听他说什么，而且要看他的行动。Búdàn yào tīng tā shuō shénme, érqiě yào kàn tā de xíngdòng. *We should not only listen to what he says but also look at what he does.*

行贿 **xínghuì** v offer a bribe, bribe

行径 **xíngjìng** N disgraceful conduct, deviant behavior

行军 **xíng jūn** v (of troops) march

行李 **xíngli** N luggage, baggage (件 jiàn)

行人 **xíngrén** N pedestrian

行人道 **xíngréndào** sidewalk

行人横道线 **xíngrén héngdàoxiàn** pedestrian crossing

行使 **xíngshǐ** v exercise (rights, power, etc.)

行使公民权利 **xíngshǐ gōngmín quánlì** exercise one's civil rights

行驶 **xíngshǐ** v (of a vehicle or ship) travel

行为 **xíngwéi** N behavior, conduct, act ■ 他的行为不符合教师的身分。Tāde xíngwéi bù fúhé jiàoshī de shēnfēn. *His behavior does not befit his status as a teacher.*

行星 **xíngxīng** N planet

行政 **xíngzhèng** N administration

行政部门 **xíngzhèng bùmén** administrative department

行政命令 **xíngzhèng mìnglìng** executive order

行 2 **xíng** **I** v all right, OK, (that) will do ■ "我可以用一下你的词典吗？" "行。" "Wǒ kěyǐ yòng yíxià nǐ de cídiǎn ma?" "Xíng." *"May I use your dictionary?" "OK."* **II** ADJ competent, capable ■ 我踢足球不行，打篮球还可以。Wǒ tī zúqiú bù xíng, dǎ lánqiú hái kěyǐ. *I'm not good at soccer but I'm not too bad at basketball.*

刑 **xíng** ADJ penal, criminal

刑场 **xíngchǎng** N execution ground

刑罚 **xíngfá** N torture

上刑罚 **shàngxíng fá** torture

刑法 **xíngfǎ** N penal code, criminal law

刑事 **xíngshì** ADJ criminal, penal

刑事犯 **xíngshìfàn** criminal offender, convict

刑事案件 **xíngshì ànjiàn** criminal case

形 **xíng** N form, shape

形成 **xíngchéng** v take shape, form ■ 习惯形成以后，就很难改变。Xíguàn xíngchéng yǐhòu, jiù hěn nán gǎibiàn. *After a habit is formed, it is difficult to break it.*

形容 **xíngróng** v describe

形式 **xíngshì** N form, shape ■ 道歉是必要的，用什么形式还要考虑。Dàoqiàn shì bìyào de, yòng shénme xíngshì háiyào kǎolǜ. *While an apology is necessary, we need to think over the form it should take.*

形势 **xíngshì** N situation

形态 **xíngtài** N form, pattern

形象 **xíngxiàng** N image ■ 公司要注意公共关系，改善社会形象。Gōngsī yào zhùyì gōnggòng guānxi, gǎishàn shèhuì xíngxiàng. *The company should pay attention to public relations and improve its public image.*

形状 xíngzhuàng

形状 **xíngzhuàng** N appearance, shape, form

型 **xíng** N model, type

型号 **xínghào** N model (of a car, airplane, etc.)

醒 **xǐng** V wake, wake up ■ 我今天很早就醒了。Wǒ jīntiān hěn zǎo jiù xǐng le. *I woke up very early this morning.*

睡醒 **shuìxǐng** have enough sleep ■ 睡醒了没有? Shuì xǐngle méiyǒu? *Have you had enough sleep?*

叫醒 **jiàoxǐng** wake somebody up ■ 你明天早上五点钟叫醒我, 好吗? Nǐ míngtiān zǎoshang wǔ diǎnzhōng jiàoxǐng wǒ, hǎo ma? *Could you wake me up tomorrow morning at five?*

兴 **xìng** TRAD 興 ADJ joyful

兴趣 **xìngqù** N interest ■ 我对别人的私事没有兴趣。Wǒ duì biéren de sīshì méiyǒu xìngqù. *I'm not interested in other people's private matters.*

对···（不）感兴趣 **duì...(bù) gǎn xìngqù** be (un)interested in ...

对···（没）有兴趣 **duì...(méi) yǒu xìngqù** be (un)interested in ...

杏 **xìng** N apricot

杏花 **xìnghuā** apricot blossom (朵 duǒ)

杏树 **xìngshù** apricot tree

杏子 **xìngzi** apricot (个 gè)

性 **xìng** N 1 nature, character

本性 **běnxìng** (of a human being) innate quality, character

2 sex, gender

男性 **nánxìng** male

性别 **xìngbié** N gender, sex

性病 **xìngbìng** N sexually transmitted disease (STD)

性格 **xìnggé** N person's character, disposition ■ 她性格很坚强。Tā xìnggé hěn jiānqiáng. *She has a strong character.*

性工作者 **xìng gōngzuòzhě** N sex worker

性交 **xìngjiāo** N sexual intercourse

性命 **xìngmìng** N (human) life ■ 这是性命交关的是啊! Zhè shì xìngmìngjiāoguān de shì a! *This is a matter of life and death.*

性能 **xìngnéng** N function, performance

性能良好 **xìngnéng liánghǎo** (of a machine) perform well, with satisfactory performance

性情 **xìngqíng** N temperament

性情温和 **xìngqíng wēnhé** with a gentle, mild temperament

性骚扰 **xìng sāorǎo** N sexual harassment

性质 **xìngzhì** N nature (of a matter, an event,

etc.), basic quality ■ 这一事件的性质是新旧力量之间的一场政治斗争。Zhè yí shìjiàn de xìngzhì shì xīn jiù lìliang zhījiān de yì chǎng zhèngzhì dòuzhēng. *This incident is in nature a political struggle between the new and old forces.*

幸 **xìng** N good fortune

幸福 **xìngfú** ADJ happy, fortunate ■ 她实现了自己的理想, 感到很幸福。Tā shíxiàn le zìjǐ de lǐxiǎng, gǎndao hěn xìngfú. *She feels happy as she has realized her aspiration.*

NOTE: 幸福 **xìngfú** is used in a sublime sense, denoting a profound and almost perfect happiness. So it has a much more limited use than its English equivalents *happy* or *fortunate*. The usual Chinese word for *happy*, as in "I'm happy to hear the news," is 高兴 gāoxìng, e.g. ■ 听到这个消息, 我很高兴。Tīngdào zhège xiāoxi, wǒ hěn gāoxìng. *I'm happy to hear this news.*

幸好 **xìnghǎo** ADV fortunately, luckily

幸亏 **xìngkuī** ADV fortunately, luckily

幸运 **xìngyùn** ADJ fortunate, lucky

姓 **xìng** N family name ■ 中国人最常用的三个姓是李、王、张。Zhōngguórén zuì chángyòng de sān ge xìng shì Lǐ, Wáng, Zhāng. *The three most common family names of the Chinese are Li, Wang and Zhang.*

贵姓 **guìxìng** your family name (polite usage, normally in a question) ■ "您贵姓?" "我姓王。" "Nín guìxìng?" "Wǒ xìng Wáng." *"What's your family name?" "Wang."*

NOTE: The character 姓 xìng has 女 nǚ, meaning *female*, in it—an indication that the Chinese once had a matriarchal society.

姓名 **xìngmíng** N full name

兄 **xiōng** N elder brother

兄弟 **xiōngdì** N brother(s)

胸 **xiōng** N chest, thorax ■ 医生, 我胸口疼。Yīshēng, wǒ xiōngkǒu téng. *Doctor, I have a pain in the chest.*

胸怀 **xiōnghuái** I N mind, heart

胸怀宽广 **xiōnghuái kuānguǎng** be broad-minded

II V cherish, harbor

胸怀大志 **xiōnghuái dàzhì** cherish great ambition

胸膛 **xiōngtáng** N chest (of the human body)

凶 **xiōng** TRAD 兇 ADJ ferocious, fierce ■ 有话好好说, 别这么凶。Yǒu huà hǎohǎo shuō, bié zhème xiōng. *If you've got something to say, say it nicely; don't be so ferocious.*

凶恶 xiōng'è ADJ ferocious, fierce

凶狠 xiōnghěn ADJ fierce and malicious

凶猛 xiōngměng ADJ ferocious, violent

汹 xiōng TRAD 洶 as in 汹涌 xiōngyǒng

汹涌 xiōngyǒng ADJ turbulent

雄 xióng ADJ 1 male (of animals) ■ 雄狮子比雌狮子大得多。Xióng shīzi bǐ cí shīzi dà de duō. *Male lions are much bigger than female ones.* 2 grand, imposing

雄厚 xiónghòu ADJ abundant, rich
资金雄厚 zījīnxiónghòu with abundant funds, very well-financed

雄伟 xióngwěi ADJ grand, magnificent ■ 这个城市有很多雄伟的建筑。Zhège chéngshì yǒu hěn duō xióngwěi de jiànzhù. *This city boasts many grand buildings.*

雄壮 xióngzhuàng ADJ full of power and grandeur, magnificent

熊 xióng N bear (只 zhī)

熊猫 xióngmāo N panda, giant panda (只 zhī)

修 xiū v 1 Same as 修理 xiūlǐ 2 build, construct (a building, bridge, road, etc.) ■ 这条江上还要修一座大桥。Zhè tiáo jiāng shang háiyào xiū yí zuò dà qiáo. *A big bridge will be built across this river.* 3 study, cultivate

修订 xiūdìng v revise
修订版 xiūdìngbǎn revised edition

修复 xiūfù v restore (a work of art)

修改 xiūgǎi v amend, revise ■ 这份报告要修改一下, 再送董事会。Zhè fèn bàogào yào xiūgǎi yíxià, zài sòng dǒngshìhuì. *This report needs some revision before it is submitted to the board of directors.*

修建 xiūjiàn v build, construct

修理 xiūlǐ v repair, fix ■ 这台机器很旧了, 不值得再修理了。Zhè tái jīqì hěn jiù le, bù zhídé zài xiūlǐ le. *This machine is very old and is not worth repairing any more.*

修养 xiūyǎng N 1 accomplishment, training
文化修养 wénhuà xiūyǎng cultural accomplishment
2 self-cultivation, good behavior and manners

修正 xiūzhèng v amend, revise

修筑 xiūzhù v build, construct

羞 xiū v be shy, be bashful

羞耻 xiūchǐ N sense of shame
羞耻心 xiūchǐ xīn sense of shame
不知羞耻 bùzhī xiūchǐ have no sense of shame, shameless

休 xiū I N leisure II v stop, cease, rest

休息 xiūxi v rest, take a rest, have a day off

休闲 xiūxián N leisure
休闲服 xiūxiánfú casual clothes

休养 xiūyǎng v recuperate, convalesce

朽 xiǔ v decay

不朽 bùxiǔ immortal

嗅 xiù v smell, sniff

秀 xiù ADJ elegant

秀丽 xiùlì ADJ elegantly beautiful

锈 xiù TRAD 鏽 N rust

绣 xiù TRAD 繡 v embroider

袖 xiù N sleeve

袖子 xiùzi sleeve

须 xiū TRAD 須 MODAL v must

须知 xūzhī N (important) notice, essential information
考生须知 kǎoshēng xūzhī important notice to examinees

虚 xū ADJ 1 void 2 of frail health 3 false 4 modest

虚假 xūjiǎ ADJ false, sham

虚拟 xūnǐ ADJ invented, fictitious
虚拟现实 xūnǐ xiànshí virtual reality

虚弱 xūruò ADJ debilitated, weak

虚伪 xūwěi I ADJ hypocritical II N hypocrisy
虚伪的人 xūwěi de rén hypocrite

虚心 xūxīn ADJ open-minded and modest ■ 他很不虚心, 总是认为自己了不起。Tā hěn bù xūxīn, zǒngshì rènwéi zìjǐ liǎobuqǐ. *He is very arrogant, always thinking himself terrific.*

墟 xū N ruins (See 废墟 fèixū)

需 xū v need

需求 xūqiú N demand, requirement

需要 xūyào v need, be in need of ■ 我需要一本中文词典。Wǒ xūyào yì běn Zhōngwén cídiǎn. *I need a Chinese dictionary.*

许 xǔ TRAD 許 I v 1 promise 2 allow II ADJ approximate, rough

许多 xǔduō ADJ many, much ■ 妈妈买回来许多好吃的东西。Māma mǎi huílai xǔduō hǎochī de dōngxi. *Mom bought lots of delicious food.*

许可 xǔkě v permit, allow

序 xù

序 xù N 1 sequence, order 2 preface

序言 **xùyán** N preface

续 xù TRAD 續 v continue (See 继续 jìxù, 连续 liánxù, 陆续 lùxù, 手续 shǒuxù.)

绪 xù TRAD 緒 N mood (See 情绪 qíngxù.)

絮 xù as in 絮叨 xùdao

絮叨 **xùdao** I ADJ garrulous, long-winded II v talk too much, be a chatterbox

畜 xù v keep domesticated animals

畜产品 **xùchǎnpǐn** N animal products
畜牧 **xùmù** v raise livestock
畜牧业 **xùmùyè** animal husbandry

蓄 xù v save up

蓄电池 **xùdiànchí** N battery

酗 xù as in 酗酒 xùjiǔ

酗酒 **xùjiǔ** v drink excessively, get drunk

叙 xù v 1 chat 2 narrate

叙述 **xùshù** v narrate, recount
叙谈 **xùtán** v chat ■ 让我们好好叙谈叙谈。Ràng wǒmen hǎohǎo xùtán xùtán. *Let's have a nice chat.*

宣 xuān v declare, announce

宣布 **xuānbù** v declare, announce ■ 校长在大会上宣布了对他的处分。Xiàozhǎng zài dàhuì shang xuānbùle duì tā de chǔfèn. *At the assembly the principal announced the disciplinary action to be taken against him.*
宣称 **xuānchēng** v assert, profess
宣传 **xuānchuán** I v 1 disseminate, publicize ■ 卫生部正在大力宣传吸烟的害处。Wèishēngbù zhèngzài dàlì xuānchuán xīyān de hàichu. *The Ministry of Health is making efforts to disseminate information on the harm that smoking does.* 2 propagandize II N 1 dissemination 2 propaganda ■ 这完全是宣传，不能相信。Zhè wánquán shì xuānchuán, bù néng xiāngxìn. *This is propaganda, pure and simple. You mustn't believe it.*
宣读 **xuāndú** v read out in public
宣告 **xuāngào** v declare, proclaim
宣誓 **xuānshì** v swear an oath
宣誓仪式 **xuānshì yíshì** swearing-in ceremony
宣言 **xuānyán** N declaration, manifesto

宣言书 **xuānyánshū** declaration (份 fèn)
宣扬 **xuānyáng** v publicize, promote

喧 xuān ADJ noisy

喧闹 **xuānnào** ADJ noisy and full of activities, very noisy

悬 xuán TRAD 懸 v hang, suspend

悬案 **xuán'àn** N unsettled case, cold case
悬挂 **xuánguà** v hang
悬念 **xuánniàn** N suspense
悬崖 **xuányá** N overhanging cliff, precipice
悬崖勒马 **xuányá lèmǎ** rein in at the brink of the precipice (→ avoid an imminent danger at the last moment)

旋 xuán v circle, spin

旋律 **xuánlǜ** N melody
旋转 **xuánzhuǎn** v revolve, spin

选 xuǎn TRAD 選 v 1 Same as 选举 xuǎnjǔ 2 select, choose ■ 不同牌子的电视机都差不多，很难选。Bùtóng páizi de diànshìjī dōu chàbuduō, hěn nán xuǎn. *TV sets of different brands are more or less the same; it is difficult to select one.*
选拔 **xuǎnbá** v select, choose
选定 **xuǎndìng** v select, decide on
选购 **xuǎngòu** v choose and buy
选购年货 **xuǎngòu niánhuò** shop for the Chinese New Year
选举 **xuǎnjǔ** I v elect, vote ■ 我们下午选举班长。Wǒmen xiàwǔ xuǎnjǔ bānzhǎng. *We're going to elect a class monitor this afternoon.* II N election, voting
选民 **xuǎnmín** N voter, electorate
选手 **xuǎnshǒu** N (of sports) selected contestant, player, athlete, competing athlete
选用 **xuǎnyòng** v select for use
选择 **xuǎnzé** I v select, choose II N choice ■ 我们除此以外，别无选择。Wǒmen chú cǐ yǐwài, bié wú xuǎnzé. *We have no choice but to do this.*

削 xuē v cut, pare

削减 **xuējiǎn** v cut down, reduce
削弱 **xuēruò** v weaken

靴 xuē N boots

靴子 **xuēzi** boots (只 zhī, 双 shuāng)

穴 xué N cave

学 xué TRAD 學 I v learn, study ■ "你在大学学什么？" "学电脑。" "Nǐ zài dàxué xué shénme?" "Xué diànnǎo." *"What do you study at university?" "Computer science."* II N 1 learning, knowledge 2 school, course of study

学费 xué fèi N tuition, tuition fee

学会 xuéhuì V learn (to do something), master

学科 xuékē N subject for study, discipline

学年 xuénián N academic year

学派 xuépài N school of thought

学期 xuéqī N semester, term ■ 中国的学校一般分上学期和下学期两个学期。Zhōngguó de xuéxiào yìbān fēn shàng xuéqī he xià xuéqī liǎng ge xuéqī. *Chinese schools generally have two terms: the first term and the second term.*

学生 xuésheng N student, pupil (个 gè, 名 míng)

学时 xuéshí N class hour, period

学术 xuéshù N learning, scholarship

学术会议 xuéshù huìyì (scholarly or scientific) conference, symposium

学说 xuéshuō N theory, doctrine

学位 xuéwèi N academic degree

学士学位 xuéshì xuéwèi bachelor degree

硕士学位 shuòshì xuéwèi master's degree, masterate

博士学位 bóshì xuéwèi PhD degree, doctorate

学问 xuéwen N learning, knowledge ■ 这位老教授很有学问。Zhè wèi lǎo jiàoshòu hěn yǒu xuéwen. *This old professor has a great deal of learning.*

学习 xuéxí I V study, learn ■ 学生不但从书本中学习，而且在社会上学习。Xuésheng búdàn cóng shūběn zhong xuéxí, érqiě zài shèhuì shang xuéxí. *A student learns not only from books but also from society.*

向…学习 xiàng...xuéxí learn from ..., emulate ... ■ 你工作很认真，我要向你学习。Nǐ gōngzuò hěn rènzhēn, wǒ yào xiàng nǐ xuéxí. *You work conscientiously. I must emulate you.* II N study ■ 学生应该把学习放在第一位。Xuésheng yīnggāi bǎ xuéxí fàng zai dì-yī wèi. *Students should give priority to their studies.*

学校 xuéxiào N school (座 zuò)

学院 xuéyuàn N college, institute ■ 在中国有些高等学校叫"学院"，例如"教育学院"。Zài Zhōngguó yǒuxiē gāoděng xuéxiào jiào "xuéyuàn", lìrú "jiàoyù xuéyuàn". *In China some institutions of higher learning are called "college," for example "college of education."*

学者 xuézhě N scholar

学制 xuézhì N 1 educational system 2 term of study

雪 xuě N snow

下雪 xià xuě to snow ■ "香港冬天下雪吗?" "不下。" "Xiānggǎng dōngtiān xià xuě ma?" "Bú

xià." *In Hong Kong, does it snow in winter?" "No."*

雪白 xuě bái ADJ snow-white

雪花 xuěhuā N snowflake (片 piàn)

血 xuè N blood ■ 流了一点血，不要紧。Liúle yìdiǎn xuè, bú yàojǐn. *It's just a little bleeding, nothing serious.*

输血 shūxuè blood transfusion

血管 xuèguǎn N blood vessel

动脉血管 dòngmài xuèguǎn artery

静脉血管 jìngmài xuèguǎn vein

血汗 xuèhàn N blood and sweat, sweat and toil

血汗工厂 xuèhàn gōngchǎng sweatshop

血库 xuèkù N blood bank

血型 xuèxíng N blood type ■ "你是什么血型？" "我是O型。" "Nǐ shì shénme xuèxíng?" "Wǒ shì O xíng." *"What's your blood type?" "Type O."*

血压 xuèyā N blood pressure

高血压 gāoxuèyā high blood pressure, hypertension

低血压 dīxuèyā low blood pressure, hypotension

血液 xuèyè N blood (as a technical term) ■ 你要化验血液。Nǐ yào huàyàn xuèyè. *You should have your blood tested.*

熏 xūn V treat with smoke, smoke

熏鱼 xūnyú smoked fish

循 xún V abide by, follow

循环 xúnhuán V circulate

血液循环 xuèyè xúnhuán blood circulation

循序渐进 xúnxù jiànjìn IDIOM proceed step by step in an orderly way

寻 xún TRAD 尋 V seek, search

寻求 xúnqiú V seek, go in quest of

寻找 xúnzhǎo V look for, seek ■ 他家的猫不见了，他们正在到处寻找。Tā jiā de māo bú jiàn le, tāmen zhèngzài dàochù xúnzhǎo. *Their cat has disappeared, and they are looking for it everywhere.*

旬 xún N a period of ten days in a month

上旬 shàngxún the first ten days in a month

中旬 zhōngxún the second ten days in a month

下旬 xiàxún the last ten days in a month

询 xún TRAD 詢 V inquire (See 咨询 zīxún)

询问 xúnwèn V inquire, ask about

巡 xún V patrol

巡逻 **xúnluó** v patrol, go on patrol
巡逻艇 **xúnluótǐng** patrol boat

讯 xùn N message (See 通讯 tōngxùn.)

迅 xùn ADJ rapid

迅速 **xùnsù** ADJ rapid, speedy, swift ■ 这件
事很急，要迅速处理。Zhè jiàn shì hěn jí, yào
xùnsù chǔlǐ. *This is an urgent matter, and should
be dealt with without delay.*

训 xùn v train

军训 **jūnxùn** military training
训练 **xùnliàn** v train ■ 全国运动会快开了，运动
员正在紧张训练。Quánguó yùndònghuì kuài kāi
le, yùndàngyuán zhèngzài jǐnzhāng xùnliàn. *The
national games will be held soon. Athletes are
engaged in intense training.*

逊 xùn TRAD 遜 ADJ modest (See 谦逊
qiānxùn)

Y

压 yā TRAD 壓 v press, push down ■ 这纸盒不
能压。Zhè zhǐhé bù néng yā. *This paper box
mustn't be crushed.*
压价 **yājià** v undersell with reduced prices
压力 **yālì** N pressure ■ 他的父母一定要他上名牌
大学，他觉得压力很大。Tā de fùmǔ yídìng yào
tā shàng míngpái dàxué, tā juéde yālì hěn dà.
*He is under tremendous pressure as his parents
insist on him going to a famous university.*
压迫 **yāpò** I v oppress ■ 在有些国家，妇女仍
然受到压迫。Zài yǒuxiē guójiā, fùnǚ réngrán
shòudao yāpò. *In some countries, women still
suffer from oppression.* II N oppression
压缩 **yāsuō** v compress, condense
空气压缩机 **kōngqì yāsuōjī** air compressor
压抑 **yāyì** v suppress, bottle up
压抑自己的愤怒 **yāyì zìjǐ de fènnù** bottle up
one's anger
压制 **yāzhì** v repress, stifle

呀 yā INTERJ oh, ah (expressing surprise) ■ 呀，
你还会说上海话! Yā, nǐ hái huì shuō Shànghǎi
huà! *Oh, you also speak the Shanghai dialect!*

鸦 yā N crow (See 乌鸦 wūyā)

鸦片 **yāpiàn** N opium
抽鸦片 **chōu yāpiàn** smoke opium

鸭 yā TRAD 鴨 N duck

鸭子 **yāzi** duck (只 zhī)

押 yā v 1 escort (goods, criminal) 2 pawn,
pledge as security

牙 yá N tooth, teeth (颗 kē) ■ 我牙疼。Wǒ yá
téng. *I have a toothache.*
牙齿 **yáchǐ** N tooth, teeth (颗 kē)
牙膏 **yágāo** N toothpaste (管 guǎn)
牙科 **yákē** N dentistry
牙科医生 **yákē yīshēng** dentist (位 wèi)
牙刷 **yáshuā** N toothbrush (把 bǎ)
牙医 **yáyī** N Same as 牙科医生 yákē yīshēng

芽 yá N sprout, bud

发芽 **fāyá** germinate, to bud, to sprout

崖 yá N cliff (See 悬崖 xuányá)

雅 yǎ ADJ elegant, cultured (See 文雅 wényǎ)

雅思 **Yǎsī** N International English Language
Testing System (IELTS)

哑 yǎ TRAD 啞 ADJ dumb, mute

哑巴 **yǎba** N mute person, mute
哑语 **yǎyǔ** N sign language

亚 yà ADJ second

亚军 **yàjūn** N (in sports) second place, runner-up
亚洲 **Yàzhōu** N Asia ■ 亚洲是世界上最大的一
个洲。Yàzhōu shì shìjiè shang zuì dà de yí ge
zhōu. *Asia is the largest continent in the world.*

讶 yà v be surprised (See 惊讶 jīngyà)

轧 yà TRAD 軋 v run over, roll

呀 ya PARTICLE Same as 啊 ā 2 PARTICLE (Used
after a, e, i, o, u) ■ 这个苹果真大呀! Zhège
píngguǒ zhēn dà ya! *How big this apple is!*

淹 yān v submerge, inundate

淹没 **yānmò** v submerge, flood

烟 yān N 1 smoke 2 Same as 香烟 xiāngyān
■ 请勿吸烟。Qǐng wù xīyān. *No smoking.*
禁烟区 **jìnyānqū** smoke-free area, "No
Smoking" area
烟草 **yāncǎo** N tabacco
烟囱 **yāncōng** N chimney
烟雾 **yānwù** N mist, smoke, smog

严 yán TRAD 嚴 ADJ strict, severe

严格 **yángé** I ADJ strict, stringent, rigorous
II v make ... strict, make ... stringent ■ 工厂决

定严格产品质量检查制度。Gōngchǎng juédìng yángé chǎnpǐn zhìliàng jiǎnchá zhìdù. *The factory has decided to make the product quality control system more stringent.*

严寒 yánhán N severe cold

严禁 yánjìn V strictly forbid ■ 此处严禁停车。 Cǐchù yánjìn tíngchē. *Parking is strictly forbidden here.*

严厉 yánlì ADJ stern, severe
严厉的警告 yánlì de jǐnggào a stern warning

严密 yánmì ADJ tight, watertight

严肃 yánsù ADJ serious, solemn ■ 李校长为 什么总是这么严肃? Lǐ xiàozhǎng wèishénme zǒngshì zhème yánsù? *Why does Mr Li, the principal, always look so serious?*

严重 yánzhòng ADJ serious, critical ■ 她的病 情很严重。 Tā de bìngqíng hěn yánzhòng. *She is critically ill.*

岩 yán N rock

岩石 yánshí rock (块 kuài)

炎 yán ADJ scorching

炎热 yánrè ADJ scorching hot

延 yán V extend, delay, postpone

延长 yáncháng V prolong, extend ■ 会议延长 两天。 Huìyì yáncháng liǎng tiān. *The conference was extended two more days.*

延缓 yánhuǎn V put off, delay

延期 yánqī V postpone, defer

延伸 yánshēn V stretch, extend

延续 yánxù V 1 continue, go on 2 last

言 yán I N speech II V talk, say

言论 yánlùn N remark, expression of opinion
言论自由 yánlùn zìyóu freedom of speech

言语 yányǔ V speak, reply

沿 yán PREP along ■ 你沿着公园一直走, 就到 市中心了。 Nǐ yánzhe gōngyuán yì zhí zǒu, jiù dào shìzhōngxīn le. *Walk along the park and you will get to the city center.*

沿儿 yánr N edge, border

沿岸 yán'àn N bank, coast

沿海 yánhǎi N coast
沿海城市 yánhǎi chéngshì coastal city

沿途 yántú N (places) on the way
沿途的见闻 yántú de jiànwén what one sees and learns on the way

研 yán V study, research

研究 yánjiū I V research, study, consider carefully ■ 公司已经研究了你的计划, 认为是可行

的。 Gōngsī yǐjīng yánjiūle nǐ de jìhuà, rènwéi shì kěxíng de. *The company has considered your plan carefully and believes it is feasible.*
II N research, study (项 xiàng)
做气候变化的研究 zuò qìhou biànhuà de yánjiū do research on climate change

研究生 yánjiūshēng N graduate student, post-graduate student

研究生院 yánjiūshēng yuàn graduate school (of a university)

研究所 yánjiūsuǒ N research institute, research unit

NOTE: The difference between 研究所 yánjiūsuǒ and 研究院 yánjiūyuàn is that the former is usually smaller in scale.

研究院 yánjiūyuàn N research institute

NOTE: See note on 研究所 yánjiūsuǒ.

研制 yánzhì N research and development, R&D

盐 yán TRAD 鹽 N salt ■ 我吃得比较淡, 你菜 里少放点盐。 Wǒ chī de bǐjiào dàn, nǐ cài li shǎo fàng diǎn yán. *I prefer my food to be bland. Please don't put too much salt in the dish.*

颜 yán TRAD 顏 N complexion, color

颜色 yánsè N color ■ 我们有各种颜色的墙纸。 Wǒmen yǒu gè zhǒng yánsè de qiángzhǐ. *We have wallpaper in various colors.*

掩 yǎn V cover, cover up

掩盖 yǎngài V cover, cover up ■ 漂亮的统计数 字掩盖不了事实真相。 Piàoliang de tǒngjì shùzì yǎngài bùliǎo shìshí zhēnxiàng. *Attractive statistics cannot cover up the truth of the matter.*

掩护 yǎnhù V cover, shield

掩饰 yǎnshì V cover up, gloss over, conceal
掩饰错误 yǎnshì cuòwù gloss over a mistake

眼 yǎn N eye

左眼 zuǒyǎn the left eye

右眼 yòuyǎn the right eye

眼光 yǎnguāng N eye, way of looking at things, point of view
很有审美眼光 hěn yǒu shěnměi yǎnguāng have an eye for what is beautiful
用老眼光看新问题 yòng lǎo yǎnguāng kàn xīn wèntí look at a new problem from an old point of view

眼镜 yǎnjìng N glasses, spectacles (副 fù)
太阳眼镜 tàiyang yǎnjìng sunglasses

眼镜店 yǎnjìngdiàn N optician's shop

眼镜盒 yǎnjìnghé N glasses case

眼睛 yǎnjing N eye ■ 打电脑的时间太长, 我

眼看 yǎnkàn

的眼睛累了。Dǎ diànnǎo de shíjiān tài cháng, wǒ de yǎnjing lèi le. *I've been working on the computer for too long; my eyes are tired.*

眼看 **yǎnkàn** ADV soon, in a moment

眼科 **yǎnkē** N department of ophthalmology
眼科医生 **yǎnkē yīshēng** ophthalmologist

眼泪 **yǎnlèi** N tear (滴 dī)
流下一滴眼泪 liúxia yì dī yǎnlèi shed a drop of tear ■ 她用手绢擦眼泪。Tā yòng shǒujuàn cā yǎnlèi. *She wiped the tears away with her handkerchief.*

眼力 **yǎnlì** N 1 eyesight
眼力好 yǎnlì hǎo good eyesight
2 discerning power, judgment
有眼力 yǒu yǎnlì be discerning

眼前 **yǎnqián** ADV 1 before one's eyes ■ 那件交通事故就发生在他眼前。Nà jiàn jiāotōng shìgù jiù fāshēng zài tā yǎnqián. *The road accident happened right in front of him.* **2** at present, at this moment

眼色 **yǎnsè** N meaningful glance
交换眼色 jiāohuàn yǎnsè exchange meaningful glances

眼神 **yǎnshén** N expression in one's eyes

眼下 **yǎnxià** ADV at the moment, now

演 yǎn I V act, perform, show ■ 他很会演戏。Tā hěn huì yǎn xì. *He is good at acting.* II N show (a film) ■ 今天电影院演什么电影? Jīntiān diànyǐngyuàn yǎn shénme diànyǐng? *What movies are being shown at the cinema today?*

演变 **yǎnbiàn** V evolve, unfold

演出 **yǎnchū** I V put on a theatrical performance, perform ■ 这次音乐会有两位有名的歌唱家演出。Zhè cì yīnyuèhuì yǒu liǎng wèi yǒumíng de gēchàngjiā yǎnchū. *Two well-known singers will perform at the concert.* II N theatrical performance ■ 他们的演出精彩极了! Tāmen de yǎnchū jīngcǎi jíle! *How wonderful their performance was!* ■ 昨天晚上的演出让人失望。Zuótiān wǎnshang de yǎnchū ràng rén shīwàng. *The performance last night was disappointing.*

演说 **yǎnshuō** V deliver a formal speech

演算 **yǎnsuàn** V perform mathematical calculations

演习 **yǎnxí** N exercise, drill
军事演习 jūnshì yǎnxí military exercise

演员 **yǎnyuán** N actor, actress, performer

演奏 **yǎnzòu** V give an instrument performance

衍 yǎn V spread out (See 敷衍 fūyan)

厌 yàn TRAD 厭 V detest, loathe

厌恶 **yànwù** V detest, be disgusted with

艳 yàn ADJ fresh and attractive (See 鲜艳 xiānyàn)

燕 yàn N (bird) swallow
燕子 **yànzi** swallow (只 zhī)

雁 yàn N wild goose
大雁 **dàyàn** wild goose

焰 yàn N flame (See 火焰 huǒyàn)

咽 yàn V swallow ■ 我要喝一点水, 才能把药片咽下去。Wǒ yào hē yìdiǎn shuǐ, cái néng bǎ yàopiàn yàn xiàqu. *I must drink a bit of water to be able to swallow the pill.*

宴 yàn I N feast II V entertain
宴会 **yànhuì** N banquet, feast ■ 明天晚上我要去参加朋友的结婚宴会。Míngtiān wǎnshang wǒ yào qù cānjiā péngyou de jiéhūn yànhuì. *Tomorrow night I'll be attending a friend's wedding banquet.*
参加宴会 cānjiā yànhuì attend a banquet
告别宴会 gàobié yànhuì farewell banquet
欢迎宴会 huānyíng yànhuì welcome banquet
结婚宴会 jiéhūn yànhuì wedding banquet
宴请 **yànqǐng** V entertain with a feast
宴席 **yànxí** N banquet, feast

验 yàn TRAD 驗 V examine
验光 **yànguāng** N optometry
验光师 **yànguāngshī** optometrist
验收 **yànshōu** V check and accept, check upon delivery
验证 **yànzhèng** V test to verify

央 yāng N center (See 中央 zhōngyāng)

秧 yāng N seedling
插秧 **chāyāng** transplant rice seedlings
秧苗 **yāngmiáo** N rice seedling

殃 yāng N calamity (See 遭殃 zāoyāng)

羊 yáng N sheep, goat, lamb (头 tóu)
山羊 **shānyáng** goat
小羊 **xiǎoyáng** lamb
羊毛 **yángmáo** N wool
羊皮 **yángpí** N sheepskin
羊肉 **yángròu** N mutton

阳 yáng TRAD 陽 N what is open, overt, masculine, the sun

阳光 **yángguāng** N sunshine, sunlight

阳性 **yángxìng** ADJ (of medical test) positive

扬 **yáng** TRAD 揚 v raise, make known (See 表扬 biǎoyáng, 发扬 fāyáng.)

杨 **yáng** N poplar

杨树 **yángshù** poplar tree (棵 kē)

洋 **yáng** N ocean (See 大洋洲 Dàyángzhōu, 海洋 hǎiyáng.)

养 **yǎng** TRAD 養 v **1** provide for, support ■ 爸爸妈妈辛辛苦苦地工作，把我养大。Bàba māma xīn-xīn-kǔ-kǔ de gōngzuò, bǎ wǒ yǎng dà. *Dad and mom worked hard to provide for me.* **2** raise, keep as pet ■ 我一直想养一只狗。Wǒ yìzhí xiǎng yǎng yì zhī gǒu. *I have always wanted to have a dog.* **3** form, cultivate **4** recuperate one's health

养成 **yǎngchéng** v form (a habit)
养成每天锻炼的好习惯 **yǎngchéng měitiān duànliàn de hǎo xíguàn** form the good habit of doing exercises every day

养分 **yǎngfèn** N nutrient

养活 **yǎnghuo** v provide for, support, sustain

养料 **yǎngliào** N nourishment, nutriment

养育 **yǎngyù** v bring up (a child), rear

养殖 **yǎngzhí** N breed or cultivate (aquatic products, plants, etc.)
水产养殖场 **shuǐchǎn yǎngzhíchǎng** aquatic farm

氧 **yǎng** N oxygen (O$_2$)

氧气 **yǎngqì** oxygen

氧化 **yǎnghuà** v oxidize, oxidate

痒 **yǎng** v itch, tickle

发痒 **fāyǎng** itch ■ 我背上发痒。Wǒ bēishang fāyǎng. *My back itches.*

仰 **yǎng** v face upward

仰望 **yǎngwàng** v **1** look up to **2** revere

样 **yàng** TRAD 樣 I M. WD kind, category, type ■ 他做了几样菜，招待朋友。Tā zuòle jǐ yàng cài, zhāodài péngyou. *He prepared several dishes to entertain his friends.* II N appearance, looks

样子 **yàngzi** N appearance, manner ■ 几年不见，你还是以前的样子。Jǐ nián bú jiàn, nǐ hái shì yǐqián de yàngzi. *It's been years since I last saw you and you still look the same as before.*

要 **yāo** as in 要求 yāoqiú

要求 **yāoqiú** I v ask, demand, require ■ 老师要求我们每天都读课文。Lǎoshī yāoqiú wǒmen měi tiān dōu dú kèwén. *The teacher requires us to read the texts every day.* II N demand, requirement ■ 我想提两个要求，可以吗？Wǒ xiǎng tí liǎng ge yāoqiú, kěyǐ ma? *May I ask for two requirements?*

腰 **yāo** N waist, small of the back

妖 **yāo** N evil spirit

妖怪 **yāoguài** N monster, bogey man

邀 **yāo** v invite

邀请 **yāoqǐng** I v invite ■ 他邀请很多朋友来参加他的二十一岁生日宴会。Tā yāoqǐng hěn duō péngyou lái cānjiā tā de èrshíyī suì shēngrì yànhuì. *He invited many friends to his twenty-first birthday dinner party.* II N invitation ■ 我昨天发出了邀请，他们大约明天会收到。Wǒ zuótiān fāchūle yāoqǐng, tāmen dàyuē míngtiān huì shōudao. *I sent the invitation yesterday, and they'll probably receive it tomorrow.*
邀请信 **yāoqǐngxìn** letter of invitation

摇 **yáo** v shake, wave ■ 点头表示同意，摇头表示不同意。Diǎn tóu biǎoshì tóngyì, yáo tóu biǎoshì bù tóngyì. *Nodding the head indicates agreement and shaking the head signals disagreement.*

摇头丸 **yáotóuwán** N Ecstasy pill (an addictive drug)

谣 **yáo** TRAD 謠 N **1** rumor **2** ballad, rhyme

民谣 **mínyáo** folk ballad, ballad
谣言 **yáoyán** N malicious rumor, rumor

遥 **yáo** ADJ faraway

遥远 **yáoyuǎn** ADJ faraway, remote

窑 **yáo** N kiln

砖窑 **zhuānyáo** brick kiln (座 zuò)

咬 **yáo** v bite ■ 我给蚊子咬了一口。Wǒ gěi wénzi yǎole yì kǒu. *I was bitten by a mosquito.*

药 **yào** TRAD 藥 N medicine, drug ■ 这种药你一天吃两次，每次吃一片。Zhè zhǒng yào nǐ yì tiān chī liǎng cì, měi cì chī yí piàn. *You should take this medicine twice a day, one pill each time.*
草药 **cǎoyào** herbal medicine
吃药 **chī yào** take medicine
西药 **xīyào** Western medicine
中药 **Zhōngyào** traditional Chinese medicine
药方 **yàofāng** N prescription
药房 **yàofáng** N pharmacist's, pharmacy
药片 **yàopiàn** N pill

231

药水 yàoshuǐ

药水 yàoshuǐ N liquid medicine

耀 yào V shine, dazzle (See 照耀 zhàoyào)

要 yào I V **1** want, would like ■ 我要一间安静的房间。Wǒ yào yì jiān ānjìng de fángjiān. *I want a quiet room.* **2** ask (somebody to do something) ■ 我哥哥要我问你好。Wǒ gēge yào wǒ wèn nǐ hǎo. *My brother asked me to give you his regards.* **II** ADJ important

要人 yàorén important person, VIP

III MODAL V should, must ■ 你想学好中文，就要多听，多讲。Nǐ xiǎng xuéhǎo Zhōngwén, jiù yào duō tīng, duō jiǎng. *If you want to learn Chinese well, you should listen more and speak more.*

IV CONJ suppose, if

要点 yàodiǎn N key point, major point

要好 yàohǎo ADJ on very good terms, very close

要紧 yàojǐn ADJ important, urgent, serious ■ 考试的时候，最要紧的是看清考题。Kǎoshì de shíhou, zuì yàojǐn de shì kànqīng kǎotí. *The most important thing at examinations is to understand the question clearly.*

不要紧 búyàojǐn it doesn't matter

要领 yàolǐng N main points, gist

要么 yàome CONJ either ... (or) ■ 你要么现在就去，要么别别去了。Nǐ yàome xiànzài jiù qù, yàome jiù bié qù le. *You either go right now, or don't go.*

要命 yàomìng ADV extremely ■ 我这两天忙得要命。Wǒ zhè liǎng tiān máng de yàomìng. *I'm extremely busy these days.*

要是 yàoshì CONJ if ■ 要是你明天不能来，请给我打个电话。Yàoshì nǐ míngtiān bù néng lái, qǐng gěi wǒ dǎ ge diànhuà. *If you're not able to come tomorrow, please give me a call.*

NOTE: Both 如果 rúguǒ and 要是 yàoshì mean *if*. While 如果 rúguǒ is for general use, 要是 yàoshì is a colloquialism.

要素 yàosù N essential element

钥 yào TRAD 鑰 N as in 钥匙 yàoshi

钥匙 yàoshi N key (把 bǎ)

爷 yé TRAD 爺 N paternal grandfather

爷爷 yéye N Same as 祖父 zǔfù. Used in colloquial Chinese.

也 yě ADV **1** also, too ■ 你想去北京学习，我也想去北京学习。Nǐ xiǎng qù Běijīng xuéxí, wǒ yě xiǎng qù Běijīng xuéxí. *You want to study in Beijing, so do I.* **2** neither, nor ■ 你没有看过这个电影，我也没看过这个电影。Nǐ méiyǒu kàn-guo zhège diànyǐng, wǒ yě méi kànguo zhège diànyǐng. *You haven't seen this movie, nor have I.*

也许 yěxǔ ADV perhaps, maybe

NOTE: See note on 恐怕 kǒngpà.

野 yě I N open country **II** ADJ wild

野蛮 yěmán ADJ savage, barbaric

野生 yěshēng ADJ wild (animal or plant)

野生动物 yěshēng dòngwù wildlife

野兽 yěshòu N wild beast

野外 yěwài N open country, field

野外作业 yěwài zuòyè field work

野心 yěxīn N wild ambition

冶 yě V smelt

冶炼 yěliàn smelt

冶金 yějīn N metallurgy

业 yè TRAD 業 N industry

业务 yèwù N **1** professional work, vocational work ■ 她业务水平很强。Tā yèwù shuǐpíng hěn qiáng. *She is very efficient professionally.* **2** business ■ 公司的业务开展很顺利。Gōngsī de yèwù kāizhǎn hěn shùnlì. *The business of the company has developed smoothly.*

业余 yèyú I N spare time **II** ADJ amateur ■ 他是一位中学老师，也是业余音乐家。Tā shì yí wèi zhōngxué lǎoshī, yě shì yèyú yīnyuèjiā. *He is a high school teacher and also an amateur musician.*

叶 yè TRAD 葉 N leaf

叶子 yèzi leaf (片 piàn)

页 yè TRAD 頁 N page ■ 请把书翻到二十页。Qǐng bǎ shū fān dào èrshí yè. *Please turn to page twenty of your book.*

夜 yè N night, evening ■ 他昨夜十一点钟才回家。Tā zuó yè shíyī diǎnzhōng cái huíjiā. *Last night he did not return home until eleven o'clock.* (→ *Last night he returned home as late as eleven o'clock.*)

半夜 bànyè midnight

夜班 yèbān N night shift

上夜班 shàng yèbān be on a night shift

夜车 yèchē N night train

夜里 yèli N at night ■ 这条大街夜里也车辆不断。Zhè tiáo dàjiē yèli yě chēliàng bú duàn. *There is constant traffic on this main street even at night.*

夜晚 yèwǎn N Same as 夜里 yèli

液 yè N liquid, fluid

液体 yètǐ N liquid

一 yī NUM one ■ 一万一千一百一十一 yíwàn yìqiān yìbǎi shíyī eleven thousand, one hundred and eleven 11,111

NOTE: (1) 一 undergoes tone changes (tone sandhi). When standing alone, 一 is pronounced with the first tone, i.e. yī. When followed by a sound in the fourth tone, 一 changes to the second tone, e.g. 一定 yídìng. 一 is pronounced in the fourth tone in all other circumstances, e.g. 一般 yìbān, 一同 yìtóng, 一起 yìqǐ. Pay attention to the various tones of 一 here and in the following words. (2) When saying a number (e.g. a telephone number) pronounce 一 as yāo for clarity, e.g. 我的电话号码是五八一三九。Wǒ de diànhuà hàomǎ shì wǔ-bā-yāo-sān-jiǔ. My telephone number is 58139.

一般 yìbān ADJ 1 generally speaking, normal 2 average, commonplace ■ 他的学习成绩一般。Tā de xuéxí chéngjì yìbān. His school record is average. 3 same as, as ... as ■ 哥哥长得和爸爸一般高了。Gēge zhǎng de hé bàba yìbān gāo le. My elder brother is now as tall as Daddy.

一半 yíbàn N half, one half ■ 他一半时间念书，一半时间做工。Tā yíbàn shíjiān niànshū, yíbàn shíjiān zuògōng. He spends half his time studying and the other half working.

一辈子 yíbèizi N one's entire life

一边 yìbiān N one side ■ 在这场争论中，我站在你们一边。Zài zhè chǎng zhēnglùn zhōng, wǒ zhàn zài nǐmen yìbiān. In this debate I am on your side.

一边…一边… yìbiān…yìbiān… CONJ while ..., at the same time ■ 不少大学生一边学习一边工作。Bùshǎo dàxuéshēng yìbiān xuéxí yìbiān gōngzuò. Quite a few university students study and work at the same time.

NOTE: 一边…一边… yìbiān…yìbiān… links two verbs to indicate that the two actions denoted by the verbs take place simultaneously. Another example: ■ 他常常一边做作业一边听音乐。Tā chángcháng yìbiān zuò zuòyè yìbiān tīng yīnyuè. He often does his homework while listening to music. When the verbs are monosyllabic, 边…边… biān…biān… may be used instead of 一边…一边… yìbiān…yìbiān…, e.g. ■ 孩子们边走边唱。Háizimen biān zǒu biān chàng. The children sang while walking. ■ 我们边吃边谈吧。Wǒmen biān chī biān tán ba. Let's carry on the conversation while eating.

一旦 yídàn CONJ once, in case ■ 一旦有她的消息，马上告诉我。Yídàn yǒu tāde xiāoxi, mǎshàng gàosu wǒ. Once you've got news about her, let me know immediately.

一道 yídào ADV Same as 一起 yìqǐ

一点儿 yìdiǎnr N a tiny amount, a bit ■ 那个菜不好吃，我只吃了一点儿。Nàge cài bù hǎo chī, wǒ zhǐ chīle yìdiǎnr. That dish is not tasty. I ate only a tiny bit of it.

一定 yídìng I ADJ 1 fixed, specified ■ 他吃饭没有一定的时间。Tā chīfàn méiyǒu yídìng de shíjiān. He has no fixed mealtimes. 2 to a certain degree, fair, limited ■ 你的中文已经达到了一定水平。Nǐ de Zhōngwén yǐjīng dádàole yídìng shuǐpíng. You've already reached a certain level of proficiency in Chinese. II ADV certainly, definitely

一度 yídù ADV for a time, on one occasion

一帆风顺 yìfān fēng shun IDIOM plain sailing

一方面…一方面… yìfāngmiàn…yìfāngmiàn… CONJ on the one hand ... on the other hand ... ■ 我们一方面要发展经济，一方面要保护环境。Wǒmen yìfāngmiàn yào fāzhǎn jīngjì, yìfāngmiàn yào bǎohù huánjìng. We should on the one hand develop the economy and on the other hand protect the environment

一概 yígài ADV all, without exception

一概而论 yígài ér lùn IDIOM lump everything together, make sweeping generalization

一共 yígòng ADV in all, total, altogether ■ 我们去年一共学了五百二十个汉字。Wǒmen qùnián yígòng xuéle wǔbǎi èrshí ge Hànzì. Last year we learned 520 Chinese characters in total.

一贯 yíguàn ADV all along, always

一会儿 yíhuìr ADV in a very short time ■ 不用麻烦倒茶，我一会儿就走。Bú yòng máfan dào chá, wǒ yíhuìr jiù zǒu. Please don't bother making tea. I'll be leaving in a moment.

一会儿…一会儿… yíhuìr…yíhuìr… CONJ one moment ... the next (moment) ■ 她一会儿哭，一会儿笑，到底怎么啦? Tā yíhuìr kū, yíhuìr xiào, dàodǐ zěnme la? One moment she was crying, and the next she was laughing—what's happened to her?

一…就… yī…jiù… CONJ as soon as, no sooner ... than ...

一口气 yìkǒuqì ADV (do something) in one breath, without a break ■ 他一口气开了三百英里。Tā yìkǒuqì kāile sānbǎi yīnglǐ. He drove 300 miles without a break.

一块儿 yíkuàir ADV Same as 一起 yìqǐ. Tends to be used in colloquial Chinese.

一连 yìlián ADV in a row, successively ■ 他一连输了三盘棋。Tā yìlián shū le sān pán qí. He lost three games of chess in a row.

一路平安 yílù píng'ān IDIOM have a good journey

一路顺风 yílù shùnfēng IDIOM Have a good trip!

一律 yílǜ ADV all, without exception

一毛不拔 yìmáo bù bá

一毛不拔 **yìmáo bù bá** IDIOM unwilling to give even a hair, very stingy

一旁 **yìpáng** N one side

一面···一面 **yímiàn...yímiàn** CONJ at the same time, while

一齐 **yìqí** ADV Same as 一起 yìqǐ

一起 **yìqǐ** ADV together ■ 我们一起去吃饭吧。Wǒmen yìqǐ qù chīfàn ba. *Let's have a meal together.*

一切 **yíqiè** I ADJ all, every and each without exception ■ 出国的一切手续都办完，要多长时间？Chūguó de yíqiè shǒuxù dōu bànwán yào duō cháng shíjiān? *How long will it take to go through all the formalities for going abroad?* II PRON all, everything ■ 他做的一切都是为了赚更多的钱。Tā zuò de yíqiè dōushì wèile zhuàn gèng duō de qián. *Everything he does, he does it to make more money.*

一生 **yìshēng** N all one's life, lifetime ■ 这位老人一生都住在这个山区。Zhè wèi lǎorén yìshēng dōu zhù zài zhège shānqū. *This old man has lived in this mountainous area all his life.*

一时 **yìshí** ADV for the time being, momentarily

一手 **yìshǒu** ADV single-handedly, all by oneself

一同 **yìtóng** ADV Same as 一起 yìqǐ

一系列 **yíxìliè** N a series of

一下 **yíxià** ADV (used after a verb to indicate the action is done briefly or casually) for a short while ■ 请您等一下，王先生马上就来。Qǐng nín děng yíxià, Wáng xiānsheng mǎshàng jiù lái. *Please wait for a while. Mr Wang will be here in a moment.*

NOTE: It is very common in spoken Chinese to use 一下 yíxià after a verb, especially as an informal request. Some Northern Chinese speakers use 一下儿 yíxiàr instead of 一下 yíxià. Another example: ■ 我们在这儿停一下儿吧。Wǒmen zài zhèr tíng yíxiàr ba. *Let's stop here for a while.*

一下子 **yíxiàzi** ADV all at once, all of a sudden ■ 这么多事一下子做不完，明天再做吧。Zhème duō shì yíxiàzi zuò bu wán, míngtiān zài zuò ba. *We can't finish so many things at once. Let's continue tomorrow.*

一向 **yíxiàng** ADV all along, always

一些 **yìxiē** M WD a small amount of, a bit of ■ 我这里有一些书，你看看还有没有用。Wǒ zhèlǐ yǒu yìxiē shū, nǐ kànkan hái yǒu méiyǒu yòng. *I have a few books here. Have a look to see if they are still useful.*

一心 **yìxīn** ADV single-mindedly, wholeheartedly ■ 她一心想当电影明星。Tā yìxīnxiǎng dāng diànyǐng míngxīng. *She has a single-minded determination to be a movie star.*

一样 **yíyàng** ADJ same, identical ■ "一下"和

"一下儿"是一样的。"Yíxià" hé "yíxiàr" shì yíyàng de. *"Yixia" and "Yixiar" are the same (i.e. have the same meaning).*

一再 **yízài** ADV time and again, repeatedly

一直 **yìzhí** ADV always, all the time ■ 他一直很关心你，常打听你的消息。Tā yìzhí hěn guānxīn nǐ, cháng dǎtīng nǐ de xiāoxi. *He is always concerned for you and frequently asks after you.*

一致 **yízhì** ADJ unanimous, identical ■ 会上没有取得一致的意见。Huìshang méiyǒu qǔdé yízhì de yìjiàn. *No consensus of opinion was reached at the meeting.*

壹 **yī** N one

衣 **yī** N clothing

衣服 **yīfu** N clothes, pieces of clothing (件 jiàn) ■ 她很会穿衣服。Tā hěn huì chuān yīfu. *She has good dress sense.*

NOTE: 衣服 yīfu may denote *clothes* or *pieces of clothing*. 一件衣服 yí jiàn yīfu may be a *jacket*, a *coat*, a *dress* or a *sweater*, but not a *pair of trousers*, which is 一条裤子 yì tiáo kùzi.

衣裳 **yīshang** N Same as 衣服 yīfu

伊 **yī** PRON she, her, he, his

伊斯兰教 **Yīsīlánjiào** N Islam

医 **yī** TRAD 醫 I V heal, cure ■ 他的病还能医吗？Tāde bìng hái néng yī ma? *Can his illness be treated?* II N medicine

医疗 **yīliáo** N medical care

公费医疗 **gōngfèi yīliáo** public health service

医生 **yīshēng** N medical doctor (位 wèi)

医务室 **yīwùshì** N clinic (in a school, factory, etc.) ■ 我们学校的医务室只有一位护士。Wǒmen xuéxiào de yīwùshì zhǐyǒu yí wèi hùshi. *There is only a nurse in our school clinic.*

医学 **yīxué** N medical science, medicine ■ 医学正在经历一场革命。Yīxué zhèngzài jīnglì yì chǎng gémìng. *Medical science is experiencing a revolution.*

医学院 **yīxuéyuàn** N medical school

医药 **yīyào** N medicine

医药费 **yīyàofèi** medical expenses

医院 **yīyuàn** N hospital (座 zuò) ■ 马上送医院！Mǎshàng sòng yīyuàn! *Take him to the hospital right now!*

送···去医院 **sòng...qù yīyuàn** take ... to the hospital

住(医)院 **zhù (yī) yuàn** be hospitalized ■ 他病得很重，得住医院。Tā bìng de hěn zhòng, děi zhù yīyuàn. *He's seriously ill and has to be hospitalized.*

医治 yīzhì v treat (a patient)

依 **yī** v **1** rely on **2** according to

依次 yīcì ADV in order, successively

依旧 yījiù ADV as before, still

依据 yījù I v be based on
依据最新资料 yījù zuìxīn zīliào based on the latest data
II N basis, foundation
没有依据的指控 méiyǒu yījù de zhǐkòng unfounded allegation

依靠 yīkào v rely on, depend on ■ 公司的成功依靠全体职工的努力。Gōngsī de chénggōng yào yīkào quántǐ zhígōng de nǔlì. *The success of the company depends on the efforts of all staff.*

依赖 yīlài v rely on, be dependent on

依然 yīrán ADV still, as before

依照 yīzhào PREP according to, based on

姨 **yí** N one's mother's sister (See 阿姨 āyí)

仪 **yí** TRAD 儀 N instrument, appearance

仪表 yíbiǎo N **1** appearance, bearing
仪表堂堂 yíbiǎo tángtáng look dignified, with imposing presence
2 gauge, meter

仪器 yíqì N instrument (件 jiàn)

仪式 yíshì N ceremony
举行仪式 jǔxíng yíshì hold a ceremony

宜 **yí** ADJ suitable (See 便宜 piányi.)

移 **yí** v move, shift ■ 窗前的阳光太强, 我要把桌子往边上移。Chuāngqián de yángguāng tài qiáng, wǒ yào bǎ zhuōzi wǎng biānshang yí. *The sunshine is too strong by the window. I want to move my desk to the side.*

移动 yídòng v move, shift ■ 强冷空气正在向东移动。Qiáng lěng kōngqì zhèngzài xiàng dōng yídòng. *Strong cold air is moving eastward.*
移动电话 yídòng diànhuà mobile telephone

移民 yímín I v immigrate, emigrate II N immigrant, emigrant, immigration
移民局 Yímínjú Immigration Services
新移民 xīn yímín new immigrant

疑 **yí** v doubt, disbelief

疑惑 yíhuò v feel uncertain, wonder

疑问 yíwèn N doubt ■ 这个计划一定要实现, 这是毫无疑问的。Zhège jìhuà yídìng yào shíxiàn, zhè shì háowú yíwèn de. *It is beyond any doubt that this plan will materialize.*

疑心 yíxīn N Same as 怀疑 huáiyí

遗 **yí** TRAD 遺 v **1** leave behind as legacy, inheritance **2** bequeath, hand down **3** lose, omit

遗产 yíchǎn N inheritance, legacy

遗传 yíchuán v pass to the next generation, be hereditary
遗传病 yíchuánbìng hereditary disease

遗憾 yíhàn I v regret II ADJ regretful ■ 我错过了那场音乐会, 真是很遗憾。Wǒ cuòguole nà chǎng yīnyuèhuì, zhēn shì hěn yíhàn. *It is a pity that I missed the concert.*

遗留 yíliú v leave behind, hand down

遗失 yíshī v lose, be lost ■ 那份遗失的文件找到了。Nà fèn yíshī de wénjiàn zhǎodào le. *The lost document was recovered.*

遗体 yítǐ N body of a dead person, remains
向遗体告别 xiàng yítǐ gàobié pay last tribute to a dead person

遗址 yízhǐ N remains (of a building), ruins

已 **yǐ** ADJ Same as 已经 yǐjīng. Used in written Chinese.

已经 yǐjīng ADV already ■ 她已经三十五岁了, 还没有结婚。Tā yǐjīng sānshíwǔ suì le, hái méiyǒu jiéhūn. *She is already thirty-five years old and is not married yet.*

乙 **yǐ** I N the second of the ten Heavenly Stems II ADJ second

以 **yǐ** I PREP **1** with, in the manner of ■ 我们要以高标准严格要求自己。Wǒmen yào yǐ gāo biāozhǔn yángé yāoqiú zìjǐ. *We should set high standards for ourselves.* **2** for, because of ■ 这个地方以风景优美著名。Zhège dìfang yǐ fēngjǐng yōuměi zhùmíng. *This place is famous for its beautiful scenery.*

以 **yǐ** 2 CONJ in order to, so as to ■ 应该推广新技术以提高工作效率。Yīnggāi tuīguǎng xīn jìshù yǐ tígāo gōngzuò xiàolǜ. *We should promote new technology so as to increase efficiency.*

以便 yǐbiàn CONJ so that, in order that ■ 请你尽早通知我们, 以便及时做好准备。Qǐng nǐ jǐn zǎo tōngzhī wǒmen, yǐbiàn jíshí zuò hǎo zhǔnbèi. *Please let us know as soon as possible so that we can get ready in time.*

以后 yǐhòu N after, later

以及 yǐjí CONJ Same as 和 hé 2 CONJ, used in formal Chinese.

以来 yǐlái N since, in the past ... ■ 三个月以来, 你的中文口语有了很大进步。Sān ge yuè yǐlái, nǐ de Zhōngwén kǒuyǔ yǒule hěn dà jìnbù. *In the past three months you have made good progress in spoken Chinese.*

以免 yǐmiǎn CONJ in order to avoid, so as not to

以内 yǐnèi N within, during ■ 三天以内我一

以前 yǐqián

定把报告交给你。Sān tiān yǐnèi wǒ yídìng bǎ bàogào jiāo gei nǐ. *I will definitely submit my report to you in three days.*

以前 yǐqián N before, some time ago ■ 不久以前 **bùjiǔ yǐqián** not long ago

以上 yǐshàng N over, more than ■ 中国人口百分之六十以上住在农村。Zhōngguó rénkǒu bǎifēn zhī liùshí yǐshàng zhù zài nóngcūn. *Over sixty percent of China's population lives in rural areas.*

以身作则 yǐshēn zuòzé IDIOM set a good example (for others to follow)

以外 yǐwài N beyond, outside, other than ■ 八小时以外你可以做自己喜欢做的事。Bā xiǎoshí yǐwài nǐ kěyǐ zuò zìjǐ xǐhuan zuò de shì. *You can do what you enjoy doing outside the eight working hours.*

以往 yǐwǎng N formerly, in the past

以为 yǐwéi V think (usually incorrectly) ■ 呀,你还在工作? 我以为你已经回家了。Yǎ, nǐ háizài gōngzuò? Wǒ yǐwéi nǐ yǐjīng huíjiā le. *Oh, you're still working. I thought you'd gone home.*

以下 yǐxià N below, less than ■ 他们的年收入在一万元以下。Tāmen de nián shōurù zài yíwàn yuán yǐxià. *Their annual income is less than 10,000 yuan.*

以至 yǐzhì CONJ 1 up to 2 so as to, so ... that

以至于 yǐzhìyú CONJ Same as 以至 yǐzhì

椅 yǐ N chair

椅子 **yǐzi** chair (把 bǎ) ■ 房间里有一张桌子和四把椅子。Fángjiān li yǒu yì zhāng zhuōzi hé sì bǎ yǐzi. *There is a table and four chairs in the room.*

倚 yǐ V lean on or against, rest on or against

蚁 yǐ N ant (See 蚂蚁 mǎyǐ)

亿 yì TRAD 億 NUM one hundred million ■ 中国有十三亿人口。Zhōngguó yǒu shísān yì rénkǒu. *China has a population of 1.3 billion.* 十亿 **shíyì** billion

亿万 yìwàn NUM millions upon millions, an astronomical number of 亿万富翁 **yìwàn fùwēng** billionaire, super-rich

艺 yì TRAD 藝 N art

艺术 yìshù N art ■ 他是搞艺术的。Tā shì gǎo yìshù de. *He is engaged in art.* (→ *He is an artist.*) 艺术家 **yìshùjiā** N (accomplished, recognized) artist

艺术作品 yìshù zuòpǐn N a work of art

忆 yì TRAD 憶 V recall (See 回忆 huíyì, 记忆 jìyì.)

异 yì TRAD 異 ADJ different, unusual

异常 yìcháng ADJ abnormal, unusual ■ 环境遭到破坏, 造成天气异常。Huánjìng zāodào pòhuài, zàochéng tiānqì yìcháng. *As the environment is damaged, abnormal weather results.*

毅 yì ADJ firm, resolute

毅力 yìlì N indomitable will, strong willpower 毅然 **yìrán** ADV resolutely

抑 yì V repress (See 压抑 yāyì)

役 yì N military campaign (See 战役 zhànyì)

疫 yì N epidemic (See 瘟疫 wēnyì)

亦 yì ADV also

译 yì TRAD 譯 V translate, interpret

译员 yìyuán N interpreter, translator (位 wèi, 名 míng)

易 yì I ADJ easy (See 容易 róngyì) II V exchange (See 贸易 màoyì)

益 yì N benefit (See 利益 lìyì.)

谊 yì TRAD 誼 N friendship (See 友谊 yǒuyì.)

意 yì N 1 idea, meaning 2 expectation, wish

意见 yìjiàn N 1 opinion, view (条 tiáo) ■ 在这个问题上我们已经取得了一致的意见。Zài zhège wèntí shang wǒmen yǐjīng qǔdéle yízhì de yìjiàn. *We have reached consensus on this issue.* 2 complaint, objection ■ 我对他处理这件事的方法很有意见。Wǒ duì tā chǔlǐ zhè jiàn shì de fāngfǎ hěn yǒu yìjiàn. *I have objections to the way he dealt with this matter.* 提意见 **tí yìjiàn** make a comment (on an issue, a proposal etc.), make a complaint

意料 yìliào V expect, anticipate 意料之中 **yìliào zhīzhōng** in line with expectations 出乎意料 **chūhū yìliào** out of expectations, not anticipated

意识 yìshi I N consciousness II V be conscious of, be aware of

意思 yìsi N meaning ■ 他的意思是你最好别

去。Tā de yìsi shì nǐ zuìhǎo bié qù. *What he meant is that you'd better not go.*

意图 yìtú N intention
了解他们的意图 liǎojiě tāmende yìtú find out their intentions

意外 yìwài I ADJ unexpected, unforeseen ■ 她平时常常迟到，今天这么早就来了，让人感到意外。Tā píngshí chángcháng chídào, jīntiān zhème zǎo jiù lái le, ràng rén gǎndao yìwài. *She is usually late for work, but she came so early today. It's quite unexpected.* II N mishap, accident ■ 我们要采取安全措施，以防止意外。Wǒmen yào cǎiqǔ ānquán cuòshī, yǐ fángzhǐ yìwài. *We should take safety measures to prevent accidents.*

意味着 yìwèizhe V mean, imply

意向 yìxiàng N intent, purpose
意向书 yìxiàngshū letter of intent, agreement of intent

意义 yìyì N significance ■ 这件事有很大的历史意义。Zhè jiàn shì yǒu hěn dà de lìshǐ yìyì. *This event has great historical significance.*

意愿 yìyuàn N will, wish

意志 yìzhì N will, willpower ■ 这位运动员意志坚强，受了伤还每天锻炼。Zhè wèi yùndòngyuán yìzhì jiānqiáng, shòule shāng hái měi tiān duànliàn. *This athlete is strong-willed. He trains every day despite his injury.*

义 yì TRAD 義 I ADJ righteous II N righteousness, justice

义务 yìwù N duty, obligation ■ 先生，我们没有义务为您提供这种服务。Xiānsheng, wǒmen méiyǒu yìwù wèi nín tígōng zhè zhǒng fúwù. *We are not obligated to provide you with this service, sir.*
义务工作(义工) yìwù gōngzuò (yìgōng) N voluntary work, voluntary worker
义务教育 yìwù jiàoyù N compulsory education

议 yì TRAD 議 V discuss, exchange views

议案 yì'àn N proposal, motion (份 fèn)
议程 yìchéng N agenda
议定书 yìdìngshū N protocol (a diplomatic document) (份 fèn)
议会 yìhuì N parliament
议论 yìlùn V comment, discuss, talk
议员 yìyuán N member of parliament (MP)

翼 yì N wing

因 yīn CONJ because

因此 yīncǐ CONJ therefore, so ■ 这种产品质量极好，因此价格比较高。Zhè zhǒng chǎnpǐn zhìliàng jí hǎo, yīncǐ jiàgé bǐjiào gāo. *This product is of excellent quality and is therefore rather expensive.*

因而 yīn'ér CONJ Same as 因此 yīncǐ

因素 yīnsù N factor, element ■ 坚强的意志是事业成功的因素。Jiānqiáng de yìzhì shì shìyè chénggōng de yīnsù. *A strong will is an important factor for a successful career.*

因特网 yīntèwǎng N Internet

因为 yīnwèi CONJ because ■ 因为大多数人都反对，所以这个计划放弃了。Yīnwèi dàduōshù rén dōu fǎnduì, suǒyǐ zhège jìhuà fàngqì le. *Because the majority opposed the plan, it was abandoned.*

NOTE: 因为 yīnwèi is usually followed by 所以 suǒyǐ: 因为…所以… yīnwèi…suǒyǐ… *because … therefore*

阴 yīn TRAD 陰 ADJ 1 cloudy, overcast ■ 昨天上午天晴，下午阴天，晚上下雨。Zuótián shàngwǔ tiānqíng, xiàwǔ yīntiān, wǎnshang xiàyǔ. *Yesterday it was fine in the morning, cloudy in the afternoon and it rained in the evening.* 2 hidden

阴暗 yīn'àn ADJ gloomy
生活中的阴暗面 shēnghuó zhōngde yīn'ànmiàn the seamy side of life

阴谋 yīnmóu N conspiracy
揭露一项国际阴谋 jiēlù yí xiàng guójì yīnmóu uncover an international conspiracy

阴天 yīntiān cloudy day

阴性 yīnxìng ADJ (of medical test) negative

姻 yīn N marriage (See 婚姻 hūnyīn.)

音 yīn N sound

音响 yīnxiǎng N sound, acoustics
音响设备 yīnxiǎng shèbèi sound system
音响效果 yīnxiǎng xiàoguǒ acoustic effects

音像 yīnxiàng N audio-video

音乐 yīnyuè N music ■ 星期天我常常跟朋友一块儿听音乐。Xīngqītiān wǒ chángcháng gēn péngyou yíkuàir tīng yīnyuè. *I often listen to music with my friends on Sundays.*
古典音乐 gǔdiǎn yīnyuè classical music
流行音乐 liúxíng yīnyuè pop music
轻音乐 qīng yīnyuè light music, easy listening
音乐会 yīnyuè huì concert (场 cháng)
音乐会门票 yīnyuèhuì ménpiào concert ticket
露天音乐会 lùtiān yīnyuèhuì open-air concert
音乐家 yīnyuè jiā musician
音乐学院 yīnyuè xuéyuàn (music) conservatory

银 yín TRAD 銀 I N silver ■ 银是一种贵金属。 Yín shì yì zhǒng guì jīnshǔ. *Silver is a precious metal.* II ADJ relating to money or currency
银行 yínháng N bank (家 jiā) ■ 这里的银行几点钟开始营业? Zhèlǐ de yínháng jǐ diǎnzhōng kāishǐ yíngyè? *What time do the banks here open for business?*
银行家 yínhángjiā banker
储备银行 chǔbèi yínháng reserve bank
商业银行 shāngyè yínháng commercial bank
投资银行 tóuzī yínháng investment bank
银幕 yínmù N projection screen, screen

淫 yín ADJ 1 pornographic 2 excessive
淫秽 yínhuì ADJ pornographic, obscene

引 yǐn V lead, provoke
引导 yǐndǎo V guide, lead
引进 yǐnjìn V introduce, import ■ 从国外引进技术和资金, 很有必要。 Cóng guówài yǐnjìn jìshù hé zījīn, hěn yǒu bìyào. *It is very necessary to introduce technology and capital from abroad.*
引起 yǐnqǐ V give rise to, lead to, cause, arouse ■ 连续三天大雨, 引起了水灾。 Liánxù sān tiān dà yǔ, yǐnqǐle shuǐzāi. *Three days of incessant heavy rain caused flooding.*
引人注目 yǐnrén zhùmù IDIOM eye-catching, conspicuous
引入 yǐnrù V lead into, introduce
引用 yǐnyòng V quote, cite
引诱 yǐnyòu V lure, seduce

隐 yǐn TRAD 隱 V hide, conceal
隐蔽 yǐnbì V take cover, conceal
隐藏 yǐncáng V hide
隐藏的地方 yǐncáng de dìfāng hideaway
隐瞒 yǐnmán V conceal (facts)
隐瞒真相 yǐnmán zhēnxiàng cover up the truth
隐约 yǐnyuē ADJ 1 indistinct, faint 2 vague

饮 yǐn TRAD 飲 V drink
饮料 yǐnliào N drink, beverage
饮食 yǐnshí N food and drink
饮食业 yǐnshíyè catering industry, catering
饮用水 yǐnyòngshuǐ N drinking water
非饮用水 fēi yǐnyòngshuǐ non-drinking water

印 yìn V print ■ 这张照片, 我想印三份。 Zhè zhāng zhàopiàn, wǒ xiǎng yìn sān fèn. *I want three prints of this photo.*
影印 yǐngyìn photocopy

影印机 yǐngyìnjī photocopier
印染 yìnrǎn V print and dye (textiles)
印刷 yìnshuā V print (books, pamphlets, etc.) ■ 本店印刷各类文件。 Běn diàn yìnshuā gè lèi wénjiàn. *This shop prints all kinds of documents.*
印刷厂 yìnshuāchǎng N print shop, printing press
印刷机 yìnshuājī N printing machine, press
印刷品 yìnshuāpǐn N printed matter
印象 yìnxiàng N impression
给…留下印象 gěi…liúxià yìnxiàng leave an impression on ... ■ 这个展览会给我留下深刻印象。 Zhège zhǎnlǎnhuì gěi wǒ liúxià shēnkè yìnxiàng. *This exhibition has left a deep impression on me.*

应 yīng TRAD 應 MODAL V Same as 应该 yīnggāi
应当 yīngdāng MODAL V Same as 应该 yīnggāi
应该 yīnggāi MODAL V should, ought to ■ 你应该早一点告诉我。 Nǐ yīnggāi zǎo yìdiǎn gàosu wǒ. *You should have told me earlier.*

英 yīng ADJ outstanding
英国 Yīngguó N England, Britain, the UK
英俊 yīngjùn ADJ (of men) handsome, attractive
英俊青年 yīngjùn qīngnián handsome young man
英明 yīngmíng ADJ wise, brilliant
英文 Yīngwén N the English language (especially the writing)
英雄 yīngxióng N hero ■ 是英雄创造历史, 还是历史产生英雄? Shì yīngxióng chuàngzào lìshǐ, háishì lìshǐ chǎnshēng yīngxióng? *Do heroes create history or does history produce heroes?*
英勇 yīngyǒng ADJ heroic
英语 Yīngyǔ N the English language ■ 你用英语说吧, 大家都听得懂。 Nǐ yòng Yīngyǔ shuō ba, dàjiā dōu tīng de dǒng. *You can say it in English. Everybody here understands it.*

婴 yīng TRAD 嬰 N baby
婴儿 yīng'ér baby (个 gè)

樱 yīng N oriental cherry
樱花 yīnghuā cherry blossom

鹰 yīng N eagle
老鹰 lǎoyīng eagle (只 zhī)
秃鹰 tūyīng bald eagle

迎 yíng V meet, receive, welcome
迎接 yíngjiē V meet, greet ■ 今天下午我们要

去机场迎接外国客人。Jīntiān xiàwǔ wǒmen yào qù jīchǎng yíngjiē wàiguó kèren. *This afternoon we are going to the airport to meet visitors from overseas.*

营 **yíng** TRAD 營 I v operate II N (military) battalion
营长 **yíngzhǎng** battalion commander
营养 **yíngyǎng** N nutrition, nourishment ■ 这种水果营养特别丰富。Zhè zhǒng shuǐguǒ yíngyǎng tèbié fēngfù. *This fruit is particularly rich in nutrition.*
营业 **yíngyè** v (of a commercial or service establishment) do business
营业员 **yíngyèyuán** N shop assistant, salesperson
营业时间 **yíngyè shíjiān** N business hours

盈 **yíng** N surplus
盈利 **yínglì** I v make profit, reap profit II N profit

蝇 **yíng** TRAD 蠅 N fly (See 苍蝇 cāngying.)

赢 **yíng** TRAD 贏 v win (a game), beat (a rival) ■ 昨天的球赛谁赢了？Zuótiān de qiúsài shéi yíng le? *Who won the ball game yesterday?*

影 **yǐng** N 1 shadow
影子 **yǐngzi** shadow
2 image, reflection
影片 **yǐngpiàn** N movie, film (部 bù)
影响 **yǐngxiǎng** I v influence, affect ■ 经济发展慢，影响了生活水平的提高。Jīngjì fāzhǎn màn, yǐngxiǎngle shēnghuó shuǐpíng de tígāo. *Slow economic development affects the improvement of living standards.* II N influence ■ 中学生受谁的影响大—父母，还是朋友？Zhōngxuéshēng shòu shuí de yǐngxiǎng dà—fùmǔ, háishì péngyou? *Who has more influence on high school students—parents or friends?*

颖 **yǐng** ADJ clever (See 新颖 xīnyǐng)

应 **yìng** TRAD 應 v respond
应酬 **yìngchou** v engage in social activities, entertain
应付 **yìngfu** v 1 cope with ■ 顾客多的时候，一个售货员应付不了。Gùkè duō de shíhou, yí ge shòuhuòyuán yìngfu bùliǎo. *When there're many cusomers, one sales clerk can't cope.* 2 do perfunctorily
应邀 **yìngyāo** ADJ at the invitation of, on invitation

应用 **yìngyòng** v apply ■ 这项新技术还不能应用在工业上。Zhè xiàng xīn jìshù hái bù néng yìngyòng zài gōngyè shang. *This new technology cannot be applied in industry yet.*
应用科学 **yìngyòng kēxué** N applied science

映 **yìng** v reflect (See 反映 fǎnyìng.)

硬 **yìng** ADJ (of substance) hard, tough ■ 这种材料非常硬。Zhè zhǒng cáiliào fēicháng yìng. *This material is very hard.*
硬件 **yìngjiàn** N (in computing) hardware

拥 **yōng** TRAD 擁 v 1 embrace 2 crowd, swarm 3 own, possess
拥抱 **yōngbào** v embrace, hug ■ 中国人一般不习惯和人拥抱。Zhōngguórén yìbān bù xíguàn hé rén yōngbào. *The Chinese are generally unaccustomed to hugging.*
拥挤 **yōngjǐ** I v push, push and shove ■ 不要拥挤，前面有小孩子! Búyào yōngjǐ, qiánmiàn yǒu xiǎoháizi! *Don't push, there're kids before me!* II ADJ crowded ■ 现在这个时候公共汽车很拥挤，我们还是叫出租汽车吧。Xiànzài zhège shíhou gōnggòng qìchē hěn yōngjǐ, wǒmen háishi jiào chūzū qìchē ba. *The buses are crowded at this moment, let's call a taxi.*
拥有 **yōngyǒu** v possess, own

佣 **yōng** N servant
女佣 **nǚyōng** woman servant
佣人 **yōngrén** N servant

庸 **yōng** ADJ 1 mediocre 2 second-rate, inferior
平庸 **píngyōng** mediocre, commonplace
庸俗 **yōngsú** ADJ vulgar

永 **yǒng** ADV forever
永久 **yǒngjiǔ** ADJ perpetual, everlasting
永远 **yǒngyuǎn** ADV forever ■ 他永远不会做对家庭有害的事。Tā yǒngyuǎn bú huì zuò duì jiātíng yǒuhài de shì. *He would never do anything that may harm his family.*

咏 **yǒng** v sing (See 歌咏 gēyǒng)

泳 **yǒng** v swim (See 游泳 yóuyǒng)

勇 **yǒng** ADJ courageous, bold, brave
勇敢 **yǒnggǎn** ADJ brave, bold, fearless ■ 他勇敢地从大火中救出两个孩子。Tā yǒnggǎn de cóng dà huǒ zhōng jiùchū liǎng ge háizi. *He bravely saved two children from the fire.*
勇气 **yǒngqì** N courage ■ 你要有勇气承认错

误。Nǐ yào yǒu yǒngqì chéngrèn cuòwù. *You should have the courage to admit your mistake.*

勇士 **yǒngshì** n heroic warrior, hero

勇于 **yǒngyú** v have the courage to
勇于认错 **yǒngyú rèncuò** have the courage to admit one's mistake

涌 **yǒng** v gush, surge

涌现 **yǒngxiàn** v emerge in large numbers

用 **yòng** I v 1 use, (do something) with 2 need II n use, usefulness

用不着 **yòngbuzháo** IDIOM 1 there is no need to ■ 这点小事，用不着请别人帮忙。Zhè diǎn xiǎo shì, yòngbuzháo qǐng biéren bāngmáng. *This is a trivial matter and there is no need to ask for help.* 2 useless ■ 用不着的书别放在书架上。Yòngbuzháo de shū bié fàng zài shūjià shang. *Don't put useless books on the bookshelf.*

用处 **yòngchu** n use

用法 **yòngfǎ** n the way to use, use, usage

用功 **yònggōng** ADJ hardworking, diligent (student) ■ 这学期我没有好好学习，下学期要用功点。Zhè xuéqí wǒ méiyǒu hǎohǎo xuéxí, xià xuéqí yào yònggōng diǎn. *I did not work hard in my studies this semester. I will work harder in the next semester.*

用户 **yònghù** n user (of a product), consumer

用具 **yòngjù** n utensil, appliance

用力 **yònglì** v exert oneself (physically)

用人 **yòngrén** n Same as 佣人 yōngrén

用途 **yòngtú** n use, function ■ 这种新型汽车用途很广。Zhè zhǒng xīnxíng qìchē yòngtú hěn guǎng. *This new model of automobile has a wide range of uses.*

用意 **yòngyì** n intention, purpose

幽 **yōu** ADJ 1 quiet, serene 2 dim, secluded

幽暗 **yōu'àn** ADJ dim, gloomy

幽静 **yōujìng** ADJ quiet and secluded, serene

幽默 **yōumò** n humor ■ 他很有幽默感。Tā hěn yǒu yōumògǎn. *He's got a good sense of humor.*

悠 **yōu** ADJ remote

悠久 **yōujiǔ** ADJ very long, long-standing, time-honored ■ 中国历史悠久，人口众多。Zhōngguó lìshǐ yōujiǔ, rénkǒu zhòngduō. *China has a long history and a large population.*

优 **yōu** TRAD 優 ADJ excellent, superior

优点 **yōudiǎn** n strong point, merit ■ 每个人都有优点和缺点。Měi ge rén dōu yǒu yōudiǎn hé quēdiǎn. *Everybody has their strong points and weak points.*

优惠 **yōuhuì** ADJ preferential, favorable
优惠价 **yōuhuìjià** preferential price

优良 **yōuliáng** ADJ fine, good ■ 她的儿子年年考试成绩优良。Tā de érzi niánnián kǎoshì chéngjì yōuliáng. *Her son gets good examination results every year.*

优美 **yōuměi** ADJ beautiful, graceful ■ 这里优美的风景吸引大批游览者。Zhèli yōuměi de fēngjǐng xīyǐn dàpī yóulǎnzhě. *The beautiful landscape here attracts large numbers of tourists.*

优胜 **yōushèng** ADJ winning
优胜者 **yōushèngzhě** winner

优势 **yōushì** n superiority, advantage ■ 这个国家人力资源丰富，是发展经济的优势。Zhège guójiā rénlì zīyuán fēngfù, shì fāzhǎn jīngjì de yōushì. *Rich human resources are an advantage the country has in economic development.*

优先 **yōuxiān** ADJ taking precedence, having priority

优秀 **yōuxiù** ADJ outstanding, excellent ■ 这位青年是我们公司的优秀人才。Zhè wèi qīngnián shì wǒmen gōngsī de yōuxiù réncái. *This young man is an outstanding talent of our company.*

优异 **yōuyì** ADJ outstanding, exceptional

优越 **yōuyuè** ADJ superior ■ 别以为自己比别人优越。Bié yǐwéi zìjǐ bǐ biéren yōuyuè. *Don't think you're superior to others (→ None of your "Holier-than-thou" attitude.)*
优越感 **yōuyuègǎn** superiority complex

优质 **yōuzhì** n superior quality, excellent quality

忧 **yōu** TRAD 憂 I v worry II n sorrow, anxiety

忧虑 **yōulǜ** v feel anxious, worry

忧郁 **yōuyù** ADJ melancholy, heavy-hearted

尤 **yóu** ADV especially

尤其 **yóuqí** ADV especially ■ 新西兰的天气很舒服，尤其是夏天。Xīnxīlán de tiānqì hěn shūfu, yóuqí shì xiàtiān. *The weather in New Zealand is very pleasant, especially in summer.*

由 **yóu** PREP 1 (introducing the agent of an action) by ■ 技术问题由你们解决。Jìshù wèntí yóu nǐmen jiějué. *Technical problems will be solved by you. (→ You are responsible for solving technical problems.)* 2 (introducing manner or cause of an action) with ■ 很多交通事故都是由车速太快造成的。Hěn duō jiāotōng shìgù dōu shì yóu chēsù tài kuài zàochéng de. *Many road accidents are caused by speeding.*

由此可见 **yóu cǐ kě jiàn** IDIOM it can be seen that, this shows

由于 **yóuyú** I PREP because of, owing to, due to ■ 由于家庭她不得不放弃事业。Yóuyú jiātíng tā bùdébù fàngqì shìyè. *She had no* choice but to give up her career because of her family. **II CONJ** because ■ 由于丈夫身体不好, 她不能出国工作。Yóuyú zhàngfu shēntǐ bù hǎo, tā bù néng chūguó gōngzuò. *She was not able to go abroad to work because her husband was in poor health.*

油 **yóu I N** oil ■ 油比水轻。Yóu bǐ shuǐ qīng. *Oil is lighter than water.* **II ADJ** greasy (food) ■ 这个菜太油了, 我不能吃。Zhège cài tài yóu le, wǒ bù néng chī. *This dish is too greasy. I can't eat it.*

食油 shíyóu edible oil, cooking oil
石油 shíyóu petroleum, oil
油画 yóuhuà **N** oil painting (幅 fú)
油料 yóuliào **N** oil material
油料作物 yóuliàozuòwù oil-bearing crops
油田 yóutián **N** oilfield

铀 **yóu N** uranium (U)

邮 **yóu TRAD** 郵 **N** mail, post

邮包 yóubāo **N** mailbag
邮购 yóugòu **N** mail order
邮寄 yóujì **V** mail, post ■ 邮寄支票给您。Yóujì zhīpiào gěi nín. *Mail you a check.*
邮局 yóujú **N** post office ■ 由于电脑的广泛使用, 邮局已经没有以前那么重要了。Yóuyú diànnǎo de guǎngfàn shǐyòng, yóujú yǐjīng méiyǒu yǐqián nàme zhòngyào le. *Thanks to the extensive use of the computer, the post office is no longer as important as before.*
邮票 yóupiào **N** postal stamp (张 zhāng)
邮政 yóuzhèng **N** mail service, postal service

犹 **yóu TRAD** 猶 **PREP** like, as

犹如 yóurú **PREP** just like, just as
犹豫 yóuyù **ADJ** hesitant, wavering, procrastinating ■ 去不去国外找工作, 我还有点犹豫。Qù bu qù guówài zhǎo gōngzuò, wǒ hái yǒudiǎn yóuyù. *I'm still wavering over going abroad to look for a job.*

游 **yóu V 1** play **2** tour

游击 yóujī **V** be engaged in guerrilla warfare
游击战 yóujīzhàn guerrilla warfare
游客 yóukè **N** tourist, visitor (to a tourist attraction) ■ 游客止步。Yóukè zhǐbù. *(in a tourist attraction) No admittance to visitors. No visitors*
游览 yóulǎn **V** go sightseeing, tour for pleasure ■ 每年很多人去香港游览。Měi nián hěn duō rén qù Xiānggǎng yóulǎn. *Every year many people go to Hong Kong on holiday.*
游览者 yóulǎnzhě tourist

游人 yóurén **N** tourist, visitor (to a tourist attraction)
游戏 yóuxì **N** game ■ 我们来做游戏! Wǒmen lái zuò yóuxì! *Let's play a game!*
(电脑) 游戏机 (diànnǎo) yóuxìjī (computer) play station, (electronic game) console
(儿童) 游戏室 (értóng) yóuxìshì (kids') playing room
电子游戏 diànzǐ yóuxì video game, electronic game
游行 yóuxíng **N 1** (celebratory) parade **2** (protest) demonstration
举行游行 jǔxíng yóuxíng hold a parade, hold demonstrations
游泳 yóuyǒng **V** swim ■ 他游泳游得很好。Tā yóuyǒng yóu de hěn hǎo. *He swims very well.* ■ 我一星期游两次泳。Wǒ yì xīngqī yóu liǎng cì yǒng. *I swim twice a week.*
蛙式游泳 (蛙泳) wāshì yóuyǒng (wāyǒng) breaststroke
自由式游泳 (自由泳) zìyóushì yóuyǒng (zìyóuyǒng) freestyle
游泳池 yóuyǒngchí **N** swimming pool
室内游泳池 shìnèi yóuyǒngchí indoor swimming pool (座 zuò)
游泳裤 yóuyǒngkù **N** swimming trunks (条 tiáo)
游泳衣 yóuyǒngyī **N** swimsuit (件 jiàn)

友 **yǒu N** friend

友爱 yǒu'ài **N** friendly affection
友好 yǒuhǎo **ADJ** friendly ■ 她对所有的人都很友好。Tā duì suǒyǒu de rén dōu hěn yǒuhǎo. *She is friendly to everyone.*
友情 yǒuqíng **N** friendly sentiments
友人 yǒurén **N** friend
友谊 yǒuyì **N** friendship ■ 友谊天长地久。Yǒuyì tiān-cháng-dì-jiǔ. *Our friendship will last forever.*

有 **yǒu V 1** possess, have ■ 他们有一座房子, 一辆汽车, 在银行里还有一些钱。Tāmen yǒu yí zuò fángzi, yí liàng qìchē, zài yínháng li háiyǒu yìxiē qián. *They have a house, a car and some money in the bank.* **2** exist, there is (are) ■ 世界上有多少国家? Shìjiè shang yǒu duōshǎo guójiā? *How many countries are there in the world?* 没有 méiyǒu do not possess, have no, do not exist, there is no ■ 教室里没有人。Jiàoshì li méiyǒu rén. *There is nobody in the classroom.*
有待 yǒudài **V** remain, await ■ 很多问题有待解决。Hěn duō wèntí yǒudài jiějué. *Many problems remain to be solved.*
有的 yǒude **PRON** some ■ 有的人喜欢体育, 有的人喜欢艺术, 也有的人什么也不喜欢。Yǒude rén xǐhuan tǐyù, yǒude rén xǐhuan yìshù, yě yǒude rén shénme yě bù xǐhuan. *Some people*

are fond of sports, others are fond of the arts and still others are not fond of anything.

有的是 **yǒudeshì** v be plenty of, be abundant, not in short supply ■ 大学毕业生有的是。Dàxué bìyèshēng yǒudeshì. *There are plenty of university graduates.*

有(一)点儿 **yǒu(yì)diǎnr** ADV slightly, a little, somewhat ■ 他这么回答，她有一点失望。Tā zhème huídá, tā yǒuyìdiǎn shīwàng. *She is somewhat disappointed at his reply.*

NOTE: 有点 yǒudiǎn, 有点儿 yǒudiǎnr, 有一点 yǒuyìdiǎn, 有一点儿 yǒuyìdiǎnr mean the same thing. 有点儿 yǒudiǎnr and 有一点儿 yǒuyìdiǎnr are only used in colloquial Chinese.

有关 **yǒuguān** v have bearing on, have something to do with, be related to ■ 这件事与你有关。Zhè jiàn shì yú nǐ yǒuguān. *This matter has something to do with you.* (→ *This matter concerns you.*)

有害 **yǒuhài** ADJ harmful

有机 **yǒujī** ADJ organic

有力 **yǒulì** ADJ forceful, powerful, strong ■ 我们要采取有力措施节水节电。Wǒmen yào cǎiqǔ yǒulì cuòshī jié shuǐ jié diàn. *We should take strong measures to save water and electricity.*

有利 **yǒulì** ADJ favorable, advantageous ■ 我们要在那里发展业务有有利条件，也有不利条件。Wǒmen yào zài nàli fāzhǎn yèwù yǒu yǒulì tiáojiàn, yě yǒu búlì tiáojiàn. *There are both favorable and unfavorable conditions for developing our business there.*

有名 **yǒumíng** ADJ famous, well-known ■ 这是一本很有名的小说。Zhè shì yì běn hěn yǒumíng de xiǎoshuō. *This is a well-known novel.*

有钱 **yǒuqián** ADJ rich, wealthy ■ 他爸爸很有钱，但是他从来不乱花钱。Tā bàba hěn yǒuqián, dànshì tā cónglai bú luàn huā qián. *His father is very wealthy, but he is quite frugal.*

NOTE: See note on 富 fù.

有趣 **yǒuqù** ADJ interesting, amusing ■ 他在旅行的时候，遇到很多有趣的事。Tā zài lǚxíng de shíhou, yùdao hěn duō yǒuqù de shì. *He had many interesting experiences during his tour.*

有时 **yǒushí** ADV Same as 有时候 yǒushíhou

有时候 **yǒushíhou** ADV sometimes ■ 他工作一般都很认真，但有时候也会马虎。Tā gōngzuò yìbān dōu hěn rènzhēn, dàn yǒushíhou yě huì mǎhu. *He is generally a conscientious worker, but he can be careless sometimes.*

有效 **yǒuxiào** ADJ 1 effective, efficacious 2 valid ■ 我的护照还有效。Wǒ de hùzhào hái yǒuxiào. *My passport is still valid.*

有效期 **yǒuxiàoqī** term of validity, expiration date

有些 **yǒuxiē** PRON Same as 有的 yǒude

有氧运动 **yǒuyǎng yùndòng** N aerobic exercise

有意 **yǒuyì** v 1 have a mind to, be inclined 2 Same as 故意 gùyì

有意思 **yǒu yìsi** ADJ meaningful, interesting ■ 这本书很有意思，每个人都应该看。Zhè běn shū hěn yǒu yìsi, měi ge rén dōu yīnggāi kàn. *This book is very meaningful. Everybody should read it.*

没有意思 **méiyǒu yìsi** uninteresting, meaningless ■ 那个电影没有意思。Nàge diànyǐng méiyǒu yìsi. *That movie isn't interesting.*

有益 **yǒuyì** ADJ beneficial

有用 **yǒuyòng** ADJ useful ■ 我相信中文会越来越有用。Wǒ xiāngxìn Zhōngwén huì yuèlaiyuè yǒuyòng. *I believe the Chinese language will be more and more useful.*

没有用 **méiyǒu yòng** useless ■ 这本书太旧了，没有什么用了。Zhè běn shū tài jiù le, méiyǒu shénme yòng le. *This book is too outdated, and is not of much use.*

诱 **yòu** v induce, seduce

诱惑 **yòuhuò** v entice, seduce

右 **yòu** N the right side

右边 **yòubian** N the right side, the right-hand side ■ 超级市场的右边是一个停车场。Chāojí shìchǎng de yòubian shì yí ge tíngchēchǎng. *On the right side of the supermarket is a parking lot.*

幼 **yòu** ADJ very young

幼儿 **yòu'ér** N young child between 2 and 6 years old

幼儿园 **yòu'éryuán** N kindergarten

幼稚 **yòuzhì** ADJ naïve, childish

又 **yòu** ADV 1 again ■ 电脑昨天刚修好，今天又坏了。Diànnǎo zuótiān gāng xiūhǎo, jīntiān yòu huài le. *The computer was fixed yesterday, but it broke down again today.* 2 moreover, additionally ■ 这个菜味道好，营养又丰富。Zhège cài wèidao hǎo, yíngyǎng yòu fēngfù. *This dish is tasty and also very nutritious.*

又…又… **yòu...yòu...** CONJ ... and also ..., both ... and ... ■ 他们的小女儿又聪明又可爱。Tāmen de xiǎo nǚ'ér yòu cōngmíng yòu kě'ài. *Their young daughter is both bright and lovely.*

NOTE: See note on 再 zài.

愚 **yú** ADJ foolish

愚蠢 **yúchǔn** ADJ foolish, stupid

愚昧 **yúmèi** ADJ ignorant and foolish

輿 **yú** N chariot

輿论 **yúlùn** N public opinion

余 **yú** TRAD 餘 V spare (See 其余 qíyú, 业余 yèyú.)

鱼 **yú** TRAD 魚 N fish (条 tiáo) ■ 河里有鱼吗? Hé li yǒu yú ma? *Is there any fish in the river?*

渔 **yú** N fishing ■ 授人以鱼，不如授之以渔。(老子) Shòu rén yǐ yú, bùrú shuò zhī yǐ yú. (Lǎozǐ) *Giving someone a fish is not so good as teaching him how to fish. (Laozi)*

渔船 **yúchuán** N fishing boat (艘 sōu)
渔民 **yúmín** N fisherman
渔网 **yúwǎng** N fishing net (张 zhāng)
渔业 **yúyè** N fishery

娱 **yú** V amuse, give pleasure to

娱乐 **yúlè** I V entertain, amuse II N entertainment, amusement
娱乐活动 **yúlè huódòng** recreation, recreational activities

愉 **yú** N pleasure

愉快 **yúkuài** ADJ 1 pleasant, joyful ■ 我永远不会忘记那段愉快的经历。Wǒ yǒngyuǎn bú huì wàngji nà duàn yúkuài de jīnglì. *I will never forget that pleasant experience.* 2 pleased, happy ■ 听到这句话，我很不愉快。Tīngdào zhè jù huà, wǒ hěn bù yúkuài. *I feel displeased to hear this.*

于 **yú** TRAD 於 PREP in, at (only used in written Chinese) ■ 他生于一九七零年。Tā shēng yú yì-jiǔ-qī-líng nián. *He was born in 1970.*

于是 **yúshì** CONJ as a result, hence ■ 他爸爸在上海找到了工作，于是全家搬到上海去了。Tā bàba zài Shànghǎi zhǎodao le gōngzuò, yúshì quán jiā bāndao Shànghǎi qù le. *His father found a job in Shanghai; as a result the family moved to Shanghai.*

予 **yǔ** V give

予以 **yǔyǐ** give

宇 **yǔ** N 1 space 2 building

宇宙 **yǔzhòu** N the universe

与 **yǔ** TRAD 與 Same as 和 hé and 跟 gēn. Only used in written Chinese.

与此同时 **yǔ cǐ tóngshí** IDIOM at the same time
与其…不如 **yǔqí…bùrú** CONJ would rather ... than
与其坐着谈，不如起而行 **yǔqí zuòzhe tán, bùrú qǐ ér xíng** would rather get up and do something than sit here talking

NOTE: Pay attention to the different word orders of 与其…不如 **yǔqí…bùrú** and *would rather ... than*; while it is 与其A不如B in Chinese, in English it is *would rather B than A.*

屿 **yǔ** TRAD 嶼 N islet (See 岛屿 dǎoyǔ)

雨 **yǔ** N rain ■ 这里夏天多雨。Zhèli xiàtiān duō yǔ. *It often rains here in summer.*
下雨 **xià yǔ** to rain ■ 我看马上要下雨了。Wǒ kàn mǎshàng yào xià yǔ le. *It seems to me that it's going to rain soon.*
雨天 **yǔtiān** rainy day
雨水 **yǔshuǐ** N rainwater, rainfall
雨衣 **yǔyī** N raincoat

羽 **yǔ** N feather

羽毛 **yǔmáo** N feather (根 gēn)
羽毛球 **yǔmáoqiú** N badminton, shuttlecock (只 zhī)
羽绒 **yǔróng** N eiderdown
羽绒衣 **yǔróngyī** eiderdown clothes, eiderdown coat

语 **yǔ** TRAD 語 I N language, words II V speak, say

语调 **yǔdiào** N intonation ■ 中文的声调不容易掌握，语调也很难。Zhōngwén de shēngdiào bù róngyì zhǎngwò, yǔdiào yě hěn nán. *While it is not easy to have a good command of Chinese tones, Chinese intonation is also difficult.*
语法 **yǔfǎ** N grammar ■ 我不大懂汉语语法，我想学一点儿。Wǒ bú dà dǒng Hànyǔ yǔfǎ, wǒ xiǎng xué yìdiǎnr. *I don't quite understand Chinese grammar; I want to learn a bit.*
语气 **yǔqì** N tone, manner of speaking ■ 同样一句话，语气不同，听了感觉就不同。Tóngyàng yí jù huà, yǔqì bùtóng, tīngle gǎnjué jiù bùtóng. *Saying the same sentence in different tones of the voice produces different feelings in the hearer.*
语文 **yǔwén** N speech and writing, language
语言 **yǔyán** N language (门 mén, 种 zhǒng) ■ 要了解一个民族，就要学它的语言。Yào liǎojiě yí ge mínzú, jiù yào xué tā de yǔyán. *If you want to understand an ethnic group, you should study its language.*

与 **yù** TRAD 與 V take part, participate

与会 **yùhuì** V be present at a meeting (conference)

域 **yù** N territory (See 领域 lǐngyù)

郁 **yù** TRAD 鬱 ADJ gloomy (See 忧郁 yōuyù)

吁 yù

吁 **yù** TRAD 籲 v appeal (See 呼吁 hūyù)

玉 **yù** N jade

玉手镯 **yùshǒuzhuó** jade bracelet
玉米 **yùmǐ** N corn, maize (根 gēn)

育 **yù** v educate, nurture (See 教育 jiàoyù, 体育 tǐyù, 体育场 tǐyùchǎng, 体育馆 tǐyùguǎn.)

浴 **yù** v bathe

浴室 **yùshì** N bathroom (间 jiān)

遇 **yù** v encounter

遇到 **yùdào** v encounter, come across ■ 我在国外旅行的时候，遇到不少好心人。Wǒ zài guówài lǚxíng de shíhou, yùdào bùshǎo hǎoxīnrén. *When I traveled overseas, I came across many kindhearted people.*

遇见 **yùjiàn** v meet (someone) unexpectedly, come across, run into ■ 我昨天在超级市场遇见一个老同学。Wǒ zuótiān zài chāojí shìchǎng yùjiàn yí ge lǎo tóngxué. *I ran into an old classmate of mine in the supermarket yesterday.*

喻 **yù** v explain (See 比喻 bǐyù)

愈 **yù** I v recover from illness

大病处愈 **dàbìng chù yù** have just recovered from a serious illness
II ADV more

欲 **yù** N desire

食欲 **shíyù** desire for food, appetite
性欲 **xìngyù** sex desire
欲望 **yùwàng** N desire
求知的欲望 **qiúzhī de yùwàng** desire to have more knowledge, hunger for knowledge

预 **yù** TRAD 預 ADV in advance

预报 **yùbào** N forecast, prediction ■ 你听过今天的天气预报吗？Nǐ tīngguo jīntiān de tiānqì yùbào ma? *Have you listened to the weather forecast for today?*

预备 **yùbèi** v prepare, get ready ■ 他们在春节前一个星期，就开始预备春节时的饭菜了。Tāmen zài chūnjié qián yí ge xīngqī, jiù kāishǐ yùbèi chūnjié shí de fàncài le. *They began preparing the food for the Spring Festival a week before.*

预备会议 **yùbèi huìyì** preparatory meeting
预备学校 **yùbèi xuéxiào** preparatory school
预测 **yùcè** v forecast, predict

预定 **yùdìng** v schedule, fix in advance ■ 代表团预定下周一到达。Dàibiǎotuán yùdìng xià zhōuyī dàodá. *The delegation is scheduled to arrive next Monday.*

预订 **yùdìng** v book, place an order

预防 **yùfáng** v take precautionary measures to prevent, prevent ■ 预防重于治疗。Yùfáng zhòngyú zhìliáo. *Prevention (of disease) is more important than treatment.*

预告 **yùgào** v announce in advance

预计 **yùjì** v project ■ 今年的销售额预计将达到一亿元。Jīnnián de xiāoshòu'é yùjì jiāng dádào yī yì yuán. *Sales for this year is projected to reach 100 million dollars.*

预见 **yùjiàn** v foresee ■ 我早就预见了这个结果。Wǒ zǎojiù yùjiàn le zhège jiéguǒ. *I foresaw this result long ago.*

预期 **yùqī** v expect, anticipate

预赛 **yùsài** v trial match, preliminary contest

预算 **yùsuàn** N budget

预习 **yùxí** v prepare lessons before class, preview

预先 **yùxiān** ADV in advance, beforehand

预言 **yùyán** I v predict II N prediction, prophecy
古代圣人的预言 **gǔdài shèngrén de yùyán** prophecy made by ancient sages
预约 **yùyuē** v make an appointment

狱 **yù** TRAD 獄 N prison (See 监狱 jiānyù)

誉 **yù** TRAD 譽 N honor (See 荣誉 róngyù)

裕 **yù** ADJ abundant (See 宽裕 kuānyù)

寓 **yù** I v imply II reside

公寓 **gōngyù** apartment, apartment building
寓言 **yùyán** N fable

豫 **yù** N comfort (See 犹豫 yóuyù.)

冤 **yuān** N injustice, wrong

冤枉 **yuānwang** v treat unfairly, wrong ■ 别冤枉好人。Bié yuānwang hǎorén. *Don't wrong innocent people.*

猿 **yuán** N ape

猿人 **yuánrén** N apeman
北京猿人 **Běijīng Yuánrén** Peking man

缘 **yuán** N reason

缘故 **yuángù** N reason, cause

元 I **yuán** ADJ first, primary

元旦 **yuándàn** N the New Year's Day

元件 **yuánjiàn** N component part, component

元首 **yuánshǒu** N head of state ■ 中华人民共和国主席是中国元首。Zhōnghuá Rénmín Gònghéguó zhǔxí shì Zhōngguó yuánshǒu. *The President of the People's Republic of China is China's head of state.*

元素 **yuánsù** N (chemical) element

元宵 **yuánxiāo** N 1 元宵节 Yuánxiāojié, the Lantern Festival (the 15th of the first month in the Chinese lunar calendar, when the full moon appears for the first time in a year.) 2 the traditional sweet dumpling for the Lantern Festival

元 2 **yuán** M. WD (the basic unit of Chinese currency 1 元 yuán = 10 角 jiǎo/毛 máo = 100 分 fēn), yuan, dollar

美元 **Měiyuán** U.S. dollar

日元 **Rìyuán** Japanese yen

NOTE: 元 yuán is the formal word for the basic unit of Chinese currency. In spoken Chinese 块 kuài is more common. For instance, the sum of 50 yuan is usually written as 五十元 wǔshí yuán, but spoken of as 五十块 wǔshí kuài or 五十块钱 wǔshí kuài qián.

员 **yuán** TRAD 員 N member (See 党员 dǎngyuán, 服务员 fúwùyuán, 官员 guānyuán, 技术员 jìshùyuán, 教员 jiàoyuán, 人员 rényuán, 售货员 shòuhuòyuán, 委员会 wěiyuánhuì, 演员 yǎnyuán, 运动员 yùndòngyuán.)

园 **yuán** TRAD 園 N garden (See 动物园 dòngwùyuán, 公园 gōngyuán, 花园 huāyuán.)

原 **yuán** ADJ original, former

原材料 **yuáncáiliào** N raw material

原告 **yuángào** N plaintiff, prosecutor

原来 **yuánlái** ADJ original, former ■ 她原来的计划是去英国工作一段时间。Tā yuánlái de jihuà shì qù Yīngguó gōngzuò yí duàn shíjiān. *Her original plan was to go to England and work there for a period of time.*

原理 **yuánlǐ** N principle, tenet

生物学原理 **shēngwùxué yuánlǐ** principles of biology

原谅 **yuánliàng** V pardon, excuse, forgive ■ 我今天上午没有能到飞机场去接你，请多原谅。Wǒ jīntiān shàngwǔ méiyǒu néng dào fēijīchǎng qù jiē nǐ, qǐng duō yuánliàng. *Please forgive me for not having been able to meet you at the airport this morning.*

原料 **yuánliào** N raw material

原始 **yuánshǐ** ADJ primitive

原因 **yuányīn** N cause, reason ■ 出了问题，一定要找出原因。Chūle wèntí, yídìng yào zhǎochū yuányīn. *When something has gone wrong we must identify the cause.*

原油 **yuányóu** N crude oil

原则 **yuánzé** N principle ■ 不管发生什么，我都不会放弃原则。Bùguǎn fāshēng shénme, wǒ dōu bú huì fàngqì yuánzé. *I will not abandon my principles, no matter what.*

原子 **yuánzǐ** N atom

原子弹 **yuánzǐdàn** atomic bomb

原子能 **yuánzǐnéng** atomic energy

源 **yuán** N source, fountainhead

源泉 **yuánquán** N source, fountainhead

圆 **yuán** TRAD 圓 ADJ round, circular ■ 在古代，人们不知道地球是圆的。Zài gǔdài rénmen bù zhīdào dìqiú shì yuán de. *In ancient times people did not know that the earth was round.*

圆满 **yuánmǎn** ADJ totally satisfactory, perfect

援 **yuán** V help

援助 **yuánzhù** V aid, support

远 **yuǎn** TRAD 遠 ADJ far, distant, remote

离…远… **lí...yuǎn...** ... is far from ... ■ 我家离学校不远。Wǒ jiā lí xuéxiào bù yuǎn. *My home is not far from school.*

远方 **yuǎnfāng** N distant place

远景 **yuǎnjǐng** N distant view, prospect

院 **yuàn** N courtyard

院子 **yuànzi** N courtyard, compound

愿 **yuàn** TRAD 願 V wish, hope

愿望 **yuànwàng** N wish, aspiration, desire ■ 我的愿望终于实现了。Wǒ de yuànwàng zhōngyú shíxiàn le. *My wish has come true at last!*

愿意 **yuànyì** I MODAL V be willing, will ■ 你愿意去就去，你不愿意去就别去。Nǐ yuànyì qù jiù qù, nǐ bú yuànyì qù jiù bié qù. *If you're willing to go, you can go; if you're not willing to go, you don't have to go.* II V wish, want ■ 父母都愿意自己的孩子幸福。Fùmǔ dōu yuànyì zìjǐ de háizi xìngfú. *All parents want their children to be happy.*

怨 **yuàn** V resent, complain (See 埋怨 mányuàn.)

约 **yuē** TRAD 約 ADV Same as 大约 dàyuē. Used in written Chinese.

约会 **yuēhuì** N (social) appointment, engagement, date ■ 她今天打扮得这么漂亮，看来有约会。Tā jīntiān dǎbàn de zhème piàoliang, kàn-

约束 yuēshù

lai yǒu yuēhuì. *She dressed up beautifully today, she probably has a date.*

约束 **yuēshù** v restrain, bind

月 **yuè** N 1 month ■ 我在那里住了八个月。Wǒ zài nàli zhùle bā ge yuè. *I stayed there for eight months.* 2 the moon
一月 **yīyuè** January
十二月 **shí'èryuè** December
月份 **yuèfèn** N month
四月份 **sìyuèfèn** April
月光 **yuèguāng** N moonlight
月亮 **yuèliang** N the moon ■ 今天晚上的月亮真好！Jīntiān wǎnshang de yuèliang zhēn hǎo! *What a fine moon it is tonight!*
月球 **yuèqiú** N the Moon (as a scientific term)

乐 **yuè** TRAD 樂 N music
乐队 **yuèduì** N band, orchestra
乐器 **yuèqì** N musical instrument
乐曲 **yuèqǔ** N melody

越 **yuè** I ADV even more II V get over, jump
越过 **yuèguò** v cross, surmount
越来越… **yuèláiyuè…** ADV more and more ■ 学中文的人越来越多。Xué Zhōngwén de rén yuèláiyuè duō. *More and more people are learning Chinese.*
越…越…yuè…yuè… ADV the more ... the more ... ■ 我越学越对中文感兴趣。Wǒ yuè xué yuè duì Zhōngwén gǎn xìngqù. *The more I study the more interested I am in Chinese.*

悦 **yuè** ADJ pleased (See 喜悦 xǐyuè)

阅 **yuè** TRAD 閱 V read
阅读 **yuèdú** v read seriously ■ 总经理每天花很多时间阅读各部门的报告。Zǒngjīnglǐ měi tiān huā hěn duō shíjiān yuèdú gè bùmén de bàogào. *The general manager spends a lot of time every day reading reports submitted by various departments.*
阅览室 **yuèlǎnshì** N reading room (间 jiān) ■ 阅览室里的图书杂志不能带出室外。Yuèlǎnshì li de túshū zázhì bù néng dàichū shìwài. *You are not allowed to take books and periodicals out of the reading room.*

跃 **yuè** TRAD 躍 V leap
跃进 **yuèjìn** v leap forward

粤 **yuè** N a shortened form for 广东 Guǎngdōng
粤语 **Yuèyǔ** Guangdong dialect, Cantonese

匀 **yún** v divide evenly, even up

云 **yún** TRAD 雲 N cloud ■ 蓝天白云，好看极了！Lán tiān bái yún, hǎokàn jíle! *White clouds in the blue sky, how beautiful!*
多云 **duōyún** cloudy ■ 今天多云。Jīntiān duōyún. *It's cloudy today.*
云彩 **yúncai** N clouds

允 **yǔn** v allow
允许 **yǔnxǔ** v allow, permit ■ 这里不允许停车。Zhèli bù yǔnxǔ tíng chē. *Parking is not allowed here.*

运 1 **yùn** TRAD 運 v transport, carry ■ 中国主要靠火车运货。Zhōngguó zhǔyào kào huǒchē yùn huò. *China mainly uses trains to transport goods.*
运动 **yùndòng** I v do physical exercises ■ 你经常运动吗？Nǐ jīngcháng yùndòng ma? *Do you exercise often?* II N physical exercises
运动会 **yùndònghuì** N sports meet, games 奥林匹克运动会 **Àolínpǐkè yùndònghuì** the Olympic Games
运动鞋 **yùndòngxié** N sport shoes
运动员 **yùndòngyuán** N athlete, sportsman, sportswoman ■ 我叔叔年轻的时候是一名长跑运动员。Wǒ shūshu niánqīng de shíhou shì yì míng chángpǎo yùndòngyuán. *In his younger days, my uncle was a long-distance runner.*
运输 **yùnshū** I v transport, carry ■ 你们用什么把煤运输到港口？Nǐmen yòng shénme bǎ méi yùnshū dào gǎngkǒu? *How do you transport coal to the port?* II N transportation
运送 **yùnsòng** v transport, ship
运算 **yùnsuàn** v operate (a mathematical problem)
运行 **yùnxíng** v move, be in motion
运用 **yùnyòng** v use, apply, put into use ■ 我们现在运用电脑控制生产过程。Wǒmen xiànzài yùnyòng diànnǎo kòngzhì shēngchǎn guòchéng. *Now we use computers to control the production process.*
运转 **yùnzhuǎn** v revolve, turn around

运 2 **yùn** TRAD 運 N fortune, luck
运气 **yùnqi** N good luck ■ 他运气真好，又中彩票了！Tā yùnqì zhēn hǎo, yòu zhòng cǎipiàole! *He is really luck—he has won the lottery again!*

蕴 **yùn** TRAD 蘊 v hold in store
蕴藏 **yùncáng** v hold in store, contain
石油蕴藏量 **shíyóu yùncángliàng** oil reserve

酝 yùn TRAD 醞 V brew, make wine

酝酿 yùnniàng V **1** brew, ferment **2** deliberate, prepare mentally

晕 yùn TRAD 暈 ADJ dizzy, giddy ■ 坐了十小时飞机, 我有点头晕。Zuòle shí xiǎoshí fēijī, wǒ yǒu diǎn tóuyùn. *After ten hours of flight, I feel dizzy.*

韵 yùn N rhyme

韵母 yùnmǔ N vowel

孕 yùn N pregnancy (See 怀孕 huáiyùn)

Z

砸 zá V smash, break

杂 zá TRAD 雜 ADJ **1** miscellaneous, sundry **2** mixed, mingled, disorderly

杂费 záfèi sundry charges

杂技 zájì N acrobatics ■ 听说中国的杂技很有名。Tīngshuō Zhōngguó de zájì hěn yǒumíng. *I've heard people say that Chinese acrobatics are very famous.*

杂技团 zájìtuán acrobatic troupe

杂技演员 zájì yǎnyuán acrobat

杂交 zájiāo V hybridize, cross

杂乱 záluàn ADJ disorderly, in a jumble

杂事 záshì N miscellaneous matters, odd jobs

杂文 záwén N essay of social commentary

杂志 zázhì N magazine (本 běn, 种 zhǒng) ■ 他订了两种杂志。Tā dìngle liǎng zhǒng zázhì. *He subscribes to two magazines.*

杂质 zázhì N (in chemistry) foreign substance

咋 zǎ ADV how, why (a Northern dialectal word)

栽 zāi V plant

栽培 zāipéi V cultivate and grow

灾 zāi TRAD 災 N disaster, calamity ■ 中国每年都有地方受灾。Zhōngguó měi nián dōu yǒu dìfang shòu zāi. *Every year there are places in China that are hit by calamities.*

旱灾 hànzāi drought

火灾 huǒzāi fire

水灾 shuǐzāi flooding, floods

灾害 zāihài N disaster, calamity ■ 由于各种灾害, 全国每年损失几十亿元。Yóuyú gè zhǒng zāihài, quánguó měi nián sǔnshī jǐ shí yì yuán. *Owing to disasters of all kinds the country loses billions of dollars every year.*

自然灾害 zìrán zāihài natural disaster

灾荒 zāihuāng N famine caused by a natural disaster

灾难 zāinàn N great suffering caused by a natural disaster, calamity (场 cháng)

灾难性后果 zāinànxìng hòuguǒ disastrous consequences

宰 zǎi V slaughter

载 zài V carry, be loaded with

载重 zàizhòng N load, carrying capacity

再 zài ADV again, once more ■ 你的电脑修好了, 要是再坏, 我就没有办法了。Nǐ de diànnǎo xiūhǎo le, yàoshì zài huài, wǒ jiù méiyǒu bànfǎ le. *Your computer has been repaired. If it breaks down again, there'll be nothing I can do.*

NOTE: 再 zài and 又 yòu are both glossed as *again*, but they have different usage. 又 yòu is used in the context of a past situation while 再 zài is used for a future situation. Here is a pair of examples: ■ 她昨天又迟到了。Tā zuótian yòu chídào le. *She was late (for work, school, etc.) again yesterday.* ■ 明天你不要再迟到了。Míngtiān nǐ bú yào zài chídào le. *Please do not be late again tomorrow.*

再见 zàijiàn V see you again, goodbye ■ "我回家了, 再见!" "再见, 明天见。" "Wǒ huíjiā le, zàijiàn!" "Zàijiàn, míngtiān jiàn." *"I'm going home, goodbye!" "Bye! See you tomorrow."*

再三 zàisān ADV over and over again ■ 她再三要求, 才让她参加了考试。Tā zàisān yāoqiú, cái ràng tā cānjiā le kǎoshì. *It was only after her repeated requests that she was allowed to sit for the examination.*

再说 zàishuō ADV **1** what's more, besides **2** later, some other time

在 I zài I PREP in, on, at ■ 在新加坡很多人会说中文。Zài Xīnjiāpō hěn duō rén huì shuō Zhōngwén. *In Singapore many people speak Chinese.*

在…里 zài...li in ■ 他在房间里休息。Tā zài fángjiān li xiūxi. *He's taking a rest in the room.*

在…上 zài...shang on ■ 在桌子上有两本书。Zài zhuōzi shang yǒu liǎng běn shū. *There are two books on the desk.*

在…下 zài...xia under ... ■ 在床下有一双鞋。Zài chuáng xia yǒu yì shuāng xié. *There's a pair of shoes under the bed.*

在…之间 zài...zhī jiān between ■ 我要在这两棵树之间种一些花。Wǒ yào zài zhè liǎng kē shù zhī jiān zhòng yìxiē huā. *I'm going to plant*

在乎 zàihu

some flowers between the two trees.
II v be in ■ "小明在哪里？" "他在操场上。"
"Xiǎo Míng zài nǎlǐ?" "Tā zài cāochàng shang."
"Where's Xiao Ming?" "He's on the sports ground."

在乎 zàihu v care, care about ■ 她不在乎别人的闲话。Tā bùzàihu biéren de xiánhuà. She doesn't care about people's gossip.

NOTE: 在乎 zàihu is normally used in a negative sentence, or a question. The same is true with 在意 zàiyì.

在意 zàiyì v take notice of, mind, care

NOTE: See note on 在乎 zàihu.

在于 zàiyú v lie in, rest with
在座 zàizuò v be present (at a meeting)

在 2 zài ADV (used to indicate an action in progress) ■ "你在做什么？" "我在找东西。"
"Nǐ zài zuò shénme?" "Wǒ zài zhǎo dōngxi."
"What are you doing?" "I'm looking for something."

咱 zán PRON Same as 咱们 zánmen

咱们 zánmen PRON we, us (including the person or persons spoken to) ■ 你在学中文，我也在学中文，咱们都在学中文。Nǐ zài xué Zhōngwén, wǒ yě zài xué Zhōngwén, zánmen dōu zài xué Zhōngwén. You're learning Chinese, I'm learning Chinese. We're both learning Chinese.

NOTE: 咱们 zánmen is only used in colloquial Chinese, and has a Northern dialect flavor. You can always just use 我们 wǒmen, even to include the person(s) spoken to. The following example is perfectly acceptable: ■ 你在学中文，我也在学中文，我们都在学中文。Nǐ zài xué Zhōngwén, wǒ yě zài xué Zhōngwén, wǒmen dōu zài xué Zhōngwén. You're learning Chinese. I'm learning Chinese. We're both learning Chinese.

攒 zǎn TRAD 攢 v save (money)

攒钱 zǎnqián save money

暂 zàn TRAD 暫 ADJ temporary

暂且 zànqiě ADV for the time being, for the moment
暂时 zànshí ADV temporarily, for the time being ■ 你暂时在这里住一下，大房间一空出来就可以搬进去。Nǐ zànshí zài zhèli zhù yíxià, dà fángjiān yí kòng chūlai jiù kěyǐ bān jìnqu. Please stay here for the time being. You can move to the bigger room as soon as it is vacated.

赞 zàn TRAD 讚 v **1** support, favor **2** praise, commend
赞成 zànchéng v approve of, support, be in favor of ■ 赞成的，请举手！Zànchéng de, qǐng jǔshǒu! Those in favor, please raise your hands.
赞美 zànměi v eulogize, praise highly
赞赏 zànshǎng v appreciate, admire
赞叹 zàntàn v gasp in admiration
赞同 zàntóng v endorse, approve of
赞扬 zànyáng v praise publicly
赞助 zànzhù v support, sponsor

脏 zāng TRAD 髒 ADJ dirty ■ 这些衣服脏了，要洗一下。Zhèxiē yīfu zāng le, yào xǐ yíxià. These clothes are dirty and need washing.

脏 zàng TRAD 臟 N internal organs (See 心脏 xīnzàng.)

葬 zàng v bury (a human body)

葬礼 zànglǐ N funeral

遭 zāo v meet with (misfortune)

遭到 zāodào v suffer, encounter, meet with
遭受 zāoshòu v suffer, be subjected to ■ 去年这个地区连续遭受自然灾害。Qùnián zhège dìqū liánxù zāoshòu zìrán zāihài. Last year this area suffered repeated natural disasters.
遭殃 zāoyāng v suffer disasters, be subject to terrible suffering
遭遇 zāoyù v encounter, meet with

糟 zāo ADJ messy, wretched

糟糕 zāogāo I ADJ in a mess, terrible, very bad ■ 我这次考试很糟糕。Wǒ zhè cì kǎoshì hěn zāogāo. I did very poorly in the exam.
II INTERJ How terrible! What bad luck! ■ 真糟，我的钥匙丢了。Zhēn zāogāo, wǒ de yàoshi diū le. How terrible! I've lost my keys!
糟蹋 zāota v **1** ruin, waste, spoil **2** abuse, violate

凿 záo v chisel

枣 zǎo N date (a fruit)

枣树 zǎoshù date tree
枣子 zǎozi date (颗 kē)
蜜枣 mìzǎo candied date

早 zǎo I ADJ early ■ 李先生每天很早上班，很晚下班。Lǐ xiānsheng měi tiān hěn zǎo shàngbān, hěn wǎn xiàbān. Every day Mr Li goes to work early and comes off work late. **II** good morning (See note below)

NOTE: A common greeting among the Chinese when they meet in the morning is 早 zǎo or 你早 Nǐ zǎo.

早晨 **zǎochén** N early morning (approximately 6–9 a.m.) ■ 很多人喜欢在早晨锻炼身体。Hěn duō rén xǐhuan zài zǎochén duànliàn shēntǐ. *Many people like to exercise in the early morning.*

早点 **zǎodiǎn** Same as 早饭 zǎofàn

早饭 **zǎofàn** N breakfast (顿 dùn) ■ 我今天起得太晚了，没有时间吃早饭。Wǒ jīntiān qǐ de tài wǎn le, méiyǒu shíjiān chī zǎofàn. *I got up too late today and didn't have time for breakfast.*

早期 **zǎoqī** N early stage, early phase

早日 **zǎorì** N at an early date, soon ■ 祝你早日康复! Zhù nǐ zǎorì kāngfù! *I wish you'll recover soon.* (→ *I wish you a speedy recovery.*)

早上 **zǎoshang** N Same as 早晨 zǎochén

早晚 **zǎowǎn** I N morning and evening II ADV sooner or later

早已 **zǎoyǐ** ADV long ago, for a long time

澡 **zǎo** N bath (See 洗澡 xǐzǎo.)

躁 **zào** ADJ rash, impetuous (See 急躁 jízào)

噪 **zào** ADJ noisy

噪音 **zàoyīn** N noise
噪音污染 **zàoyīnwūrǎn** noise pollution, white pollution

燥 **zào** ADJ dry (See 干燥 gānzào.)

皂 **zào** N soap (See 香皂 xiāngzào.)

造 **zào** V I make, build ■ 中国人在公元一世纪就会造纸。Zhōngguórén zài gōngyuán yí shìjì jiù huì zào zhǐ. *The Chinese knew how to make paper as early as in the first century.* 2 invent, fabricate

造反 **zàofǎn** V rise in rebellion, rebel

造价 **zàojià** N cost (of building or manufacturing)

造句 **zàojù** I V make sentences
用所给的词语造句 **yòng suǒ gěi de cíyǔ zàojù** make sentences with the given words II N sentence-making

造型 **zàoxíng** N modelling

灶 **zào** N stove

则 **zé** TRAD 則 CONJ in that case, then ■ 如果一切顺利，则工厂可在明年开工。Rúguǒ yíqiè shùnlì, zé gōngchǎng kě zài míngnián kāigōng. *If everything goes well, then the factory can start production next year.*

NOTE: 则 zé is only used in formal Chinese. In everyday Chinese, use 那 nà or 那么 nàme instead. See note on 那么 nàme.

责 **zé** TRAD 責 I N duty II V scold

责备 **zébèi** V reproach, blame
责备的口气 **zébèi de kǒuqì** a reproachful tone

责怪 **zéguài** V blame ■ 出了差错，他总是责怪别人。Chūle chācuò, tā zǒngshì zéguài biérén. *When something goes wrong, he would blame others.*

责任 **zérèn** N 1 responsibility, duty ■ 教育孩子是父母的责任。Jiàoyù háizi shì fùmǔ de zérèn. *It is the parents' responsibility to educate their children.* 2 responsibility for a fault or mistake ■ 这次交通事故责任主要在开快车的那一方。Zhè cì jiāotōng shìgù zérèn zhǔyào zài kāi kuàichē de nà yì fāng. *The person who was speeding is mainly to blame for this traffic accident.*

责任感 **zérèngǎn** N sense of responsibility

择 **zé** TRAD 擇 V choose (See 选择 xuǎnzé.)

泽 **zé** TRAD 澤 N pool, pond (See 沼泽 zhǎozé)

贼 **zéi** TRAD 賊 N thief

怎 **zěn** ADV how, why

怎么 **zěnme** ADV 1 how, in what manner ■ 对不起，请问去北京大学怎么走? Duìbuqǐ, qǐng wèn qù Běijīng Dàxué zěnme zǒu? *Excuse me, could you please tell me how to get to Beijing University?* 2 no matter how (used with 都 dōu or 也 yě) ■ 是这把钥匙吗? 我怎么都开不开这个门。Shì zhè bǎ yàoshi ma? Wǒ zěnme dōu kāi bu kāi zhège mén. *Is this the right key? No matter how I tried, I couldn't open the door.* 3 why, how come ■ 你怎么又迟到了? Nǐ zěnme yòu chídào le? *Why are you late again?* 4 how can ... ■ 这么多作业，我今天怎么做得完? Zhème duō zuòyè, wǒ jīntiān zěnme zuò de wán? *How can I finish so many assignments today?*

怎么办 **zěnmebàn** ADV what's to be done? ■ 要是飞机票卖完了，怎么办? Yàoshì fēijīpiào màiwán le, zěnmebàn? *What should we do if the air tickets are sold out?*

怎么了 **zěnmele** ADV what happened? ■ 怎么

怎么样 zěnmeyàng

了，她怎么哭了? Zěnmele, tā zěnme kū le?
What happened? Why is she crying?

怎么样 zěnmeyàng ADV 1 Same as 怎么 zěnme
1 (= how) 2 how ■ 你今天觉得怎么样? Nǐ
jīntiān juéde zěnmeyàng? *How are you feeling
today?* 3 how's that? is it OK? ■ 我们每个人
讲一个故事，怎么样? Wǒmen měi ge rén jiǎng
yí ge gùshi, zěnmeyàng? *We each tell a story,
how about that?*

怎样 zěnyàng ADV Same as 怎么样 zěnmeyàng.
Used in writing.

增 zēng v add, increase

增产 zēngchǎn v increase production
增加 zēngjiā v increase ■ 去年他家的收入增
加了两千元。 Qùnián tā jiā de shōurù zēngjiāle
liǎngqiān yuán. *Last year his family income
increased by 2,000 yuan.*
增进 zēngjìn v promote, enhance
增强 zēngqiáng v strengthen
增设 zēngshè v add (a new office, a new
department, etc.), introduce (a new course of
study)
增添 zēngtiān v provide (additional equipment,
evidence, etc.)
增添人员和设备 zēngtiān rényuán hé
shèbèi provide more personnel and equipment
增援 zēngyuán I N (military) reinforcements
II v send reinforcements
增长 zēngzhǎng v increase, grow ■ 大学生人
数在五年中增长百分之三十以上。 Dàxuéshēng
rénshù zài wǔ nián zhong zēngzhǎng bǎifēn zhi
sānshí yǐ shàng. *In the past five years the number
of university students has grown by more than
thirty percent.*

赠 zèng v present a gift

赠送 zèngsòng v present as a gift
向主人赠送礼物 xiàng zhǔrén zèngsòng
lǐwù present a gift to the host
赠阅 zèngyuè v give (a book, a publication) as
a complimentary copy

扎 zhā v prick, stab

扎实 zhāshi ADJ solid, sturdy

渣 zhā N dregs, residue

煤渣 méizhā coal cinders
渣滓 zhāzǐ N sediment, dregs, residue

闸 zhá N floodgate

闸门 zhámén N 1 sluice gate 2 throttle valve

眨 zhǎ v blink, wink

向我眨了眨眼 xiàng wǒ zhǎ le zhǎ yǎn
winked at me

炸 zhà v explode, burst

炸弹 zhàdàn N bomb (枚 méi)
扔炸弹 rēng zhàdàn drop a bomb
炸药 zhàyào N dynamite, explosives
引爆炸药 yǐnbào zhàyào set off an explosive

诈 zhà v cheat, swindle

诈骗 zhàpiàn v defraud, swindle
诈骗犯 zhàpiànfàn swindler

榨 zhà v press, extract

榨菜 zhàcài N hot pickled mustard tuber

摘 zhāi v pick, pluck ■ 星期天跟我们一起去

果园摘苹果吧。 Xīngqītiān gēn wǒmen yìqǐ qù
guǒyuán zhāi píngguǒ ba. *Do go to the orchard
with us on Sunday to pick apples.*
摘要 zhāiyào I N abstract, summary
论文摘要 lùnwén zhāiyào abstract of an
academic or scholarly paper
II v make a summary

宅 zhái N residence, house. (See 住宅 zhùzhá)

窄 zhǎi ADJ narrow ■ 这条街太窄，汽车开不

进去。 Zhè tiáo jiē tài zhǎi, qìchē kāi bu jìnqu
This street is too narrow for a car to enter.

债 zhài N debt ■ 借了债，就要还。 Jièle zhài,

jiùyào huán. *If you owe a debt, you'll have to
repay it.*
还债 huánzhài to pay off/settle a debt
借债 jièzhài to borrow money, to get a loan
欠债 qiànzhài to owe a debt ■ 她为了读完
大学，欠了一大笔债。 Tā wèile dú wán dàxué,
qiànle yí dà bǐzhài. *To finish her college education, she incurs a huge debt.*
要债 yào zhài to demand repayment of a deb
债务 zhàiwù N debt, liabilities
债务人 zhàiwùrén debtor
债主 zhàizhǔ N creditor

寨 zhài N stockade, stockaded village

瞻 zhān v look up or forward

瞻仰 zhānyǎng v look at with reverence

沾 zhān v be stained with

250

沾光 zhānguāng v benefit from association, sponge off

展 zhǎn v display

展出 zhǎnchū v be on show, put on display ■ 这两天商场展出最新夏装。Zhè liǎngtiān shāngchǎng zhǎnchū zuì xīn xiàzhuāng. *These days the latest summer wear is on display in the shopping center.*

展开 zhǎnkāi v carry out, launch ■ 政府将要展开交通安全的活动。Zhèngfǔ jiāngyào zhǎnkāi jiāotōng ānquán de huódòng. *The government will carry out activities to promote traffic safety.*

展览 zhǎnlǎn I v put on display, exhibit ■ 这个画儿画得真好，可以去展览。Zhège huàr huà de zhēn hǎo, kěyǐ qù zhǎnlǎn. *This picture is done so well that it can be put on display.* II N exhibition, show

展览会 zhǎnlǎnhuì Same as 展览 II N

展示 zhǎnshì v display, show

展望 zhǎnwàng I v look into the distance, look into the future

展望未来 zhǎnwàngwèilái foresee the future, predict the future II N general view regarding future developments

展现 zhǎnxiàn v present before one's eyes

展销 zhǎnxiāo v show and advertise (products) 汽车展销会 qìchē zhǎnxiāohuì automobile fair, auto fair

盏 zhǎn TRAD 盞 M. WD (for lamps)

斩 zhǎn TRAD 斬 v chop, cut

斩草除根 zhǎn cǎo chú gēn IDIOM cut the weeds and dig up the roots (→ destroy root and branch, remove the root of trouble completely)

崭 zhǎn TRAD 嶄 as in 崭新 zhǎnxīn

崭新 zhǎnxīn ADJ brand-new

占 zhàn v occupy ■ 你一个人不能占两个座位。Nǐ yí ge rén bù néng zhàn liǎng ge zuòwèi. *You're only one person and can't take two seats.*

占领 zhànlǐng v occupy, seize
占领军 zhànlǐngjūn occupation troops

占便宜 zhàn piányi v gain additional advantage at others' expenses

占有 zhànyǒu v possess, own
占有有利地位 zhànyǒu yǒulì dìwèi occupy an advantageous position

战 zhàn TRAD 戰 N 1 war, warfare 2 fight, battle

战场 zhànchǎng N battleground, battlefield

战斗 zhàndòu v combat, fight

战略 zhànlüè N military strategy, strategy

战胜 zhànshèng v triumph over, defeat ■ 人不可能战胜自然。Rén bù kěnéng zhànshèng zìrán. *It is impossible for man to triumph over nature.*

战士 zhànshì N soldier, fighter

战术 zhànshù N military tactics

战线 zhànxiàn N battle line

战役 zhànyì N military campaign

战友 zhànyǒu N army buddy

战争 zhànzhēng N war ■ 在二十一世纪，人类能避免大规模战争吗？Zài èrshíyī shìjì, rénlèi néng bìmiǎn dà guīmó zhànzhēng ma? *Can mankind avoid large-scale wars in the twenty-first century?*

站 1 zhàn v stand ■ 房间里有些人站着，有些人坐着。Fángjiān li yǒuxiē rén zhànzhe, yǒuxiē rén zuòzhe. *In the room some people are standing, and others are seated.*
站起来 zhàn qǐlai stand up
站岗 zhàngǎng v stand guard, be on sentry duty

站 2 zhàn N station, stop ■ 我要一辆出租汽车去火车站。Wǒ yào yí liàng chūzū qìchē qù huǒchē zhàn. *I need a taxi to go to the railway station.*
出租汽车站 chūzū qìchē zhàn taxi stand
火车站 huǒchē zhàn railway station
汽车站 qìchē zhàn coach/bus station, bus stop
站长 zhànzhǎng N railway/coach stationmaster

张 1 zhāng TRAD 張 v open, spread

张望 zhāngwàng v look around

张 2 zhāng TRAD 張 M. WD (for paper, bed, table etc.)
一张纸 yì zhāng zhǐ a piece of paper
两张床 liǎng zhāng chuáng two beds
三张桌子 sān zhāng zhuōzi three tables/desks

张 3 Zhāng TRAD 張 N a common family name
张先生/太太/小姐 Zhāng xiānsheng/tàitai/xiǎojiě Mr/Mrs/Miss Zhang

章 zhāng N chapter

章程 zhāngchéng N regulations (for an organization)

彰 zhāng v clear, evident (See 表彰 biǎozhāng)

掌 **zhǎng** N hand, palm

了如指掌 **liǎo rú zhǐzhǎng** know ... like the back of one's hand
掌管 **zhǎngguǎn** v be in charge of
掌上电脑 **zhǎngshàng diànnǎo** N palm-top, hand-held computer
掌声 **zhǎngshēng** N clapping, applause
掌握 **zhǎngwò** v have a good command of, know well ■ 要掌握一门外语是不容易的。Yào zhǎngwò yì mén wàiyǔ shì bù róngyì de. *It is not easy to gain a good command of a foreign language.*

长 1 **zhǎng** TRAD 長 v 1 grow ■ 孩子长大成人，父母也老了。Háizi zhǎngdà chéngrén, fùmǔ yě lǎo le. *The parents will be old when their children are grown up.* 2 grow to be, look ■ 今年的庄稼长得真好。Jīnnián de zhuāngjia zhǎng de zhēn hǎo. *The crops this year are really good.*

长 2 **zhǎng** TRAD 長 N chief (See 校长 xiàozhǎng)

涨 **zhǎng** TRAD 漲 v rise, go up ■ 水涨船高。Shuǐ zhǎng chuán gāo. *When the river rises the boat goes up. (→ When the general situation improves, particular things improve.)*

涨价 **zhǎngjià** v (of prices) rise

帐 1 **zhàng** TRAD 帳 N curtain, canopy

帐篷 **zhàngpeng** N tent
搭帐篷 **dā zhàngpeng** pitch a tent

帐 2 **zhàng** TRAD 賬 N account

查帐 **chá zhàng** examine an account, audit
算帐 **suàn zhàng** compute income and expense, settle accounts

NOTE: 帐 zhàng *account* is also written as 账, e.g. 查账, 算账.

帐单(账单) **zhàngdān** N bill
付电话帐单 **fù diànhuà zhàngdān** pay the phone bill
帐目(账目) **zhàngmù** N items of an account
帐目不清 **zhàngmù bùqīng** accounts not in order

胀 **zhàng** TRAD 脹 v swell

障 **zhàng** v hinder, obstruct

障碍 **zhàng'ài** N obstacle, barrier
排除障碍 **páichú zhàng'ài** clear an obstacle

丈 **zhàng** N 1 senior 2 husband

丈夫 **zhàngfu** N husband

招 **zhāo** v beckon, attract

招待 **zhāodài** v receive or entertain (a guest) ■ 他们用好酒好菜招待客人。Tāmen yòng hǎo jiǔ hǎo cài zhāodài kèren. *They entertained their guests with good wine and good food.*
招待会 **zhāodàihuì** N reception (a social function)
记者招待会 **jìzhě zhāodàihuì** press conference
招呼 **zhāohu** v call, shout at ■ 马路对面有人在招呼我。Mǎlù duìmiàn yǒurén zài zhāohu wǒ. *There's someone calling me on the other side of the road.*
打招呼 **dǎ zhāohu** 1 greet ■ 他进屋就跟大家打招呼。Tā jìn wū jiù gēn dàjiā dǎ zhāohu. *He greeted everybody when he came into the room.* 2 inform casually, tell ■ 他没跟我打招呼就把我的自行车骑走了。Tā méi gēn wǒ dǎ zhāohu jiù bǎ wǒ de zìxíngchē qízǒu le. *He rode off on my bicycle without telling me.*
招聘 **zhāopìn** v advertise for a position, recruit (employees)
招聘广告 **zhāopìn guǎnggào** advertisement for employment
招生 **zhāoshēng** v enrol new students, recruit students
招生办公室 **zhāoshēng bàngōngshì** (college and university) enrolment office
招收 **zhāoshōu** v recruit
招收工人 **zhāoshōu gōngrén** recruit workers
招收学生 **zhāoshōu xuésheng** enroll new students
招手 **zhāoshǒu** v wave (one's hand), beckon

朝 **zhāo** N early morning

朝气 **zhāoqì** N youthful spirit
朝气蓬勃 **zhāoqì péngbó** full of youthful spirit, full of vigor and vitality
朝夕 **zhāoxī** N morning and evening, daily
朝夕相处 **zhāoxī xiāngchǔ** be together from morning till night

着 **zháo** v catch ■ 着火了! 着火了! Zháohuǒ le! Zháohuǒ le! *Fire! Fire!*

着急 **zháojí** v be anxious, be worried ■ 已经十二点了，女儿还没有回家，妈妈很着急。Yǐjīng shí'èr diǎn le, nǚ'ér hái méiyǒu huíjiā, māma hěn zháojí. *It was almost twelve o'clock and her daughter was still not home. The mother felt very worried.*
着凉 **zháoliáng** v catch a cold

找 **zhǎo** v look for, search for ■ 你真的关心她，就帮她找个对象吧。Nǐ zhēn de guānxīn tā, jiù bāng tā zhǎo ge duìxiàng ba. *If you are really concerned for her, help her to find a fiancé.*

找到 zhǎodào v find ■ 我姐姐在香港找到了一个好工作。Wǒ jiějie zài Xiānggǎng zhǎodàole yí ge hǎo gōngzuò. *My elder sister has found a good job in Hong Kong.*

沼 zhǎo N pond

沼泽 zhǎozé N swamp, marsh
沼泽地 **zhǎozédì** swamp, marshland

召 zhào v summon

召集 zhàojí v call, convene
召集紧急会议 **zhàojí jǐnjí huìyì** convene an emergency meeting

召开 zhàokāi v convene (a conference) ■ 下星期校长要召开全体教师会议，讨论明年工作安排。Xià xīngqī xiàozhǎng yào zhàokāi quántǐ jiàoshī huìyì, tǎolùn míngnián gōngzuò ānpái. *Next week the [high school] principal will convene a meeting of all teaching staff to discuss next year's work.*

照 1 zhào v **1** take a photo ■ 这儿风景不错，我想照一张相。Zhèr fēngjǐng bú cuò, wǒ xiǎng zhào yì zhāng xiàng. *The scenery is good here. I'd like to have a picture taken.* **2** look in a mirror ■ 他们的小男孩从来不照镜子，小女孩老是照镜子。Tāmen de xiǎo nánhái cónglái bú zhào jìngzi, xiǎo nǚhái lǎoshì zhào jìngzi. *Their little boy never looks in the mirror but their little girl always looks in the mirror.* **3** shine, light up ■ 冬天的太阳照在脸上，暖暖的，很舒服。Dōngtiān de tàiyang zhào zài liǎnshang, nuǎnnuǎn de, hěn shūfu. *In winter when the sun shines on your face you feel warm and comfortable.*

照顾 zhàogu v look after, care for ■ 她每个星期六到老人院去照顾老人。Tā měi ge Xīngqīliù dào lǎorényuàn qù zhàogu lǎorén. *Every Saturday afternoon she goes to a senior citizens' home to look after the senior citizens there.*

照会 zhàohuì N (diplomatic) note

照料 zhàoliào v take care of, attend to
照料日常事务 **zhàoliào rìcháng shìwù** take care of day-to-day affairs

照明 zhàomíng N lighting, illumination
照明设备 **zhàomíng shèbèi** lighting equipment

照片 zhàopiàn N photograph, picture, snapshot (张 zhāng) ■ 老人常常看着老照片，回忆过去的生活。Lǎorén chángcháng kànzhe lǎo zhàopiàn, huíyì guòqù de shēnghuó. *The old man (or woman) often looks at old photos, recalling life in the past.*

照射 zhàoshè v shine on, light up

照相 zhàoxiàng v take a picture ■ 人们喜欢站在那幅画前照相。Rénmen xǐhuan zhàn zài nà fú huà qián zhàoxiàng. *People like to take photos standing in front of that painting.*

照相馆 zhàoxiàngguǎn N photographic studio

照相机 zhàoxiàngjī N camera (架 jià, 台 tái) ■ 明天出去玩，别忘了带照相机! Míngtiān chūqu wán, bié wàngle dài zhàoxiàngjī! *Don't forget to bring a camera with you on your outing tomorrow!*
数码照相机 **shùmǎ zhàoxiàngjī** digital camera

照耀 zhàoyào v shine, illuminate

照应 zhàoying v look after, take care of

照 2 zhào PREP according to, in the manner of ■ 我们还是照以前的方法付款。Wǒmen háishì zhào yǐqián de fāngfǎ fùkuǎn. *We will pay in the same way as before.*

照常 zhàocháng ADV as usual ■ 本店春节照常营业。Běn diàn chūnjié zhàocháng yíngyè. *Business as usual during the Spring Festival.*

照例 zhàolì ADV as usual, as a rule

照样 zhàoyàng ADV in the same old way

罩 zhào v cover, overspread

兆 zhào N sign, omen

预兆 yùzhào omen, presage

遮 zhē v hide from view

折 zhē as in 折腾 zhēteng

折腾 zhēteng v **1** do over and over again **2** cause suffering

折 zhé I v convert to, amount to ■ 一美元折多少日元? Yì Měiyuán zhé duōshǎo Rìyuán? *How many Japanese yen does an American dollar amount to?* II N discount, reduction (in price) ■ 这些书现在打八折。Zhèxiē shū xiànzài dǎ bā zhé. *These books are under a twenty percent discount now.*

折合 zhéhé v convert to, amount to

折磨 zhémo I v cause much mental or physical suffering II N suffering
受病痛的折磨 **shòu bìngtòng de zhémo** suffer terribly from the disease

哲 zhé ADJ wise

哲学 zhéxué N philosophy ■ 我对东方哲学感兴趣。Wǒ duì dōngfāng zhéxué gǎn xìngqù. *I am interested in Eastern philosophy.*

哲学家 zhéxuéjiā philosopher

者 **zhě** SUFFIX (a nominal suffix denoting a person or people) (See 读者 dúzhě, 记者 jìzhě, 作者 zuòzhě.)

这 **zhè** TRAD 這 PRON this ■ 这也不行, 那也不行, 你到底要我怎么办? Zhè yě bù xíng, nà yě bù xíng, nǐ dàodǐ yào wǒ zěnmebàn? *This won't do and that won't do either. What do you expect me to do?*

这个 **zhège** PRON this one, this ■ 这个太大, 给我小一点儿的。 Zhège tài dà, gěi wǒ xiǎo yìdiǎnr de. *This one is too big. Give me a smaller one.*

这会儿 **zhèhuìr** N now, this time

这里 **zhèli** N this place, here ■ 我刚来的时候, 不习惯这里的天气。 Wǒ gāng lái de shíhou, bù xíguàn zhèli de tiānqì. *When I first came, I wasn't used to the weather here.*

NOTE: In spoken Chinese 这里 zhèli can be replaced by 这儿 zhèr.

这么 **zhème** ADV like this, in this manner, so ■ 这件衣服这么贵, 我没想到。 Zhè jiàn yīfu zhème guì, wǒ méi xiǎngdào. *I did not expect this dress to be so expensive.*

这么着 **zhèmezhe** ADV like this, so

这些 **zhèxiē** PRON these ■ 这些书你都看过吗? Zhèxiē shū nǐ dōu kànguo ma? *Have you read all these books?*

这样 **zhèyàng** ADJ 1 such ■ 他就是这样的一个人, 根本靠不住。 Tā jiùshì zhèyàng de yí ge rén, gēnběn kào bu zhù. *He is just such a person (→ That's just typical of him). He is not reliable at all.* 2 Same as 这么 zhème. Used only in writing.

这样一来 **zhèyàng yìlái** ADV consequently

蔗 **zhè** N sugarcane (See 甘蔗 gānzhe)

着 **zhe** PARTICLE (used after a verb to indicate the action or state is going on) ■ 门开着, 灯亮着, 可是房间里没有人。 Mén kāizhe, dēng liàngzhe, kěshì fángjiān li méiyǒu rén. *The door was open and the light was on but there was no one in the room.*

这 **zhèi** TRAD 這 PRON. Same as 这 zhè. Used colloquially.

珍 **zhēn** ADJ valuable

珍贵 **zhēnguì** ADJ precious, valuable ■ 这些文物有两千年的历史, 多么珍贵啊! Zhè xiē wénwù yǒu liǎngqiān nián de lìshǐ, duōme zhēnguì a! *These cultural relics are 2,000 years old; how precious they are!*

珍惜 **zhēnxī** V cherish dearly, value highly

珍珠 **zhēnzhū** N pearl (颗 kē)

珍珠项链 **zhēnzhū xiàngliàn** pearl necklace

真 **zhēn** ADJ true, real ■ 这个电影是根据真人真事编写的。 Zhège diànyǐng shì gēnjù zhēn rén zhēn shì biānxiě de. *This movie is based on a real-life story.* ■ 中国真大呀! Zhōngguó zhēn dà ya! *China is really big!*

真诚 **zhēnchéng** ADJ sincere, genuine

真话 **zhēnhuà** N truth ■ 这家报纸很少说真话。 Zhè jiā bàozhǐ hěn shǎo shuō zhēnhuà. *This newspaper rarely tells the truth.*

真空 **zhēnkōng** vacuum

真理 **zhēnlǐ** N truth ■ 真理往往掌握在少数人手里。 Zhēnlǐ wǎngwǎng zhǎngwò zài shǎoshù rén shǒuli. *Truth is very often in the hands of the minority.*

真实 **zhēnshí** ADJ true, real, authentic ■ 到底发生了什么? 没有人知道真实的情况。 Dàodǐ fāshēngle shénme? Méiyǒu rén zhīdào zhēnshí de qíngkuàng. *What on earth happened? Nobody knows the true situation.*

真相 **zhēnxiàng** N the real situation, actual fact

真心 **zhēnxīn** N sincerity

真正 **zhēnzhèng** ADJ true, real, genuine ■ 真正的友谊是天长地久的。 Zhēnzhèng de yǒuyì shì tiān-cháng-dì-jiǔ de. *Genuine friendship is everlasting.*

针 **zhēn** N 1 needle (根 gēn) ■ 我要一根缝衣针。 Wǒ yào yì gēn féngyī zhēn. *I want a sewing needle.* 2 injection ■ 护士给他打了一针。 Hùshì gěi tā dǎ le yì zhēn. *The nurse gave him an injection.*

打针 **dǎzhēn** give an injection, get an injection

针对 **zhēnduì** V aim at, be aimed at ■ 这次反吸烟运动主要针对青少年。 Zhè cì fǎn xīyān yùndòng zhǔyào zhēnduì qīngshàonián. *This anti-smoking campaign is mainly aimed at teenagers.*

针灸 **zhēnjiǔ** I N acupuncture and moxibustion ■ 他学中文的目的是为了研究针灸。 Tā xué Zhōngwén de mùdì shì wèile yánjiū zhēnjiǔ. *His purpose in learning Chinese is to study acupuncture and moxibustion.* II V give or receive acupuncture and moxibustion treatment ■ 他针灸了几次, 肩就不疼了。 Tā zhēnjiǔle jǐ cì, jiān jiù bù téng le. *After a few sessions of acupuncture and moxibustion, his shoulder no longer hurts.*

贞 **zhēn** TRAD 貞 ADJ loyal, faithful

侦 **zhēn** TRAD 偵 V detect

侦察 **zhēnchá** V reconnoiter, scout

侦察卫星 zhēnchá wèixīng reconnaissance (spy) satellite
侦探 zhēntàn N detective
私人侦探 sīrén zhēntàn private detective, private eye

诊 zhěn TRAD 診 V examine (a patient)
诊断 zhěnduàn I V diagnose
诊断为良性肿瘤 zhěnduàn wéi liángxìng zhǒngliú diagnosed as a benign tumor
II N diagnosis
做出诊断 zuòchū zhěnduàn make a diagnosis

枕 zhěn N pillow
枕头 zhěntou pillow (只 zhī)

阵 I zhèn TRAD 陣 N column or row of troops
阵地 zhèndì N (military) position
阵容 zhènróng N layout of troops
阵线 zhènxiàn N (military) front
阵营 zhènyíng N military camp

阵 2 zhèn TRAD 陣 M. WD (for an action or event that lasts for some time) ■ 刮了一阵大风，院子里满是落叶。Guāle yí zhèn dà fēng, yuànzi li mǎnshì luòyè. A strong wind blew for a while and the courtyard was full of fallen leaves.
阵雨 zhènyǔ shower

振 zhèn V arouse to action
振动 zhèndòng V vibrate
振奋 zhènfèn V stimulate, excite
令人振奋的消息 lìngrén zhènfèn de xiāoxi exciting news
振兴 zhènxīng V promote, develop

镇 zhèn I N rural town II V suppress
镇定 zhèndìng ADJ composed, calm
镇定剂 zhèndìng jì sedative (a medicine)
镇静 zhènjìng ADJ calm, composed ■ 遇到危险，千万要保持镇静。Yùdào wēixiǎn, qiānwàn yào bǎochí zhènjìng. Be sure to keep calm when in danger.
镇痛 zhèntòng I V ease pain II N analgesia
镇痛药 zhèntòngyào analgesic medicine, pain-killer
镇压 zhènyā V suppress, put down

震 zhèn V shake
地震 dìzhèn earthquake
震荡 zhèndàng V vibrate
震动 zhèndòng V shake, quake

震惊 zhènjīng V be greatly surprised, be shocked

正 zhēng as in 正月 zhēngyuè
正月 zhēngyuè N the first month of the lunar year

蒸 zhēng V steam ■ 馒头刚蒸好，快来吃吧！Mántou gāng zhēng hǎo, kuài lái chībā! The steamed buns are just ready, come and eat them!
蒸发 zhēngfā V evaporate
蒸汽 zhēngqì N steam
蒸汽机 zhēngqì jī N steam engine
蒸气浴 zhēngqì yù N sauna

挣 zhēng as in 挣扎 zhēngzhá
挣扎 zhēngzhá V struggle desperately

征 zhēng TRAD 徵 V solicit
征求 zhēngqiú V solicit, ask for ■ 老师征求学生对教学的意见。Lǎoshī zhēngqiú xuéshengduì jiaoxué de yìjian. The teachers solicit students' comments on their teaching.

争 zhēng V 1 strive 2 argue ■ 别争了，争到明天也争不出结果来。Bié zhēng le, zhēng dào míngtiān yě zhēng bu chū jiéguǒ lai. Stop arguing. Even if you argue till tomorrow there will be no conclusion.
争论 zhēnglùn V dispute, debate
争气 zhēngqì V work hard to win honor
为父母争气 wéi fùmǔ zhēngqì work hard to win honor for one's parents
争取 zhēngqǔ V strive for, fight for ■ 我们争取提前完成计划。Wǒmen zhēngqǔ tíqián wánchéng jihuà. We strive to fulfill the plan ahead of schedule.
争议 zhēngyì N dispute
有争议的问题 yǒu zhēngyì de wèntí issue in dispute, a controversial matter

筝 zhēng N 1 a musical instrument, zheng 2 kite
风筝 fēngzheng kite

睁 zhēng V open (the eyes) ■ 奇怪，这个人怎么睁着眼睛睡觉？Qíguài, zhège rén zěnme zhēngzhe yǎnjing shuìjiào? Strange, how is it that this person sleeps with his eyes open?

整 I zhěng ADJ whole, full, entire ■ 雨下了整整两天两夜。Yǔ xiàle zhěngzhěng liǎng tiān liǎng yè. It rained incessantly for two days and two nights.
整个 zhěngge ADJ whole, entire ■ 整个工程都是他负责。Zhěngge gōngchéng dōu shì tā fùzé. He is in charge of the entire project.

整数 zhěngshù

整数 **zhěngshù** N (in maths) whole number, integer

整体 **zhěngtǐ** N whole, entirety, (something) as a whole

从整体上说 **cóng zhěngtǐ shàng shuō** on the whole

整天 **zhěngtiān** N the whole day, all the time

整天抱怨 **zhěngtiān bàoyuàn** grumble all the time

整整 **zhěngzhěng** ADJ whole, full

整整一个星期 **zhěngzhěng yí ge xīngqī** a full week, the entire week

整 2 **zhěng** I ADJ in good order, neat, tidy II V put in order

整顿 **zhěngdùn** V put in order, improve, re-organize

整顿纪律 **zhěngdùn jìlǜ** enforce discipline

整洁 **zhěngjié** ADJ clean and tidy

整理 **zhěnglǐ** V put in order, tidy up ■ 客人来前, 整理一下房间。**Kèren lái qián, zhěnglǐ yíxià fángjiān.** *Tidy up the rooms before guests arrive.*

整齐 **zhěngqí** ADJ in good order, neat and tidy

整整齐齐 **zhěng-zhěng-qí-qí** (an emphatic form of 整齐 **zhěngqí**) ■ 十几双鞋排得整整齐齐。**Shí jǐ shuāng xié páide zhěng-zhěng-qí-qí.** *Over a dozen pairs of shoes were arranged in a very orderly way.*

正 **zhèng** I ADJ 1 straight, upright ■ 帮我看看, 这幅画挂得正不正? **Bāng wǒ kànkan, zhè fú huà guà de zhèng bu zhèng?** *Have a look to see if this picture is hung straight.* 2 standard, normal, regular II ADV Same as 正在 **zhèngzài**

正常 **zhèngcháng** ADJ normal, regular ■ 在正常的情况下, 他一般给父母发一份电子邮件。**Zài zhèngcháng de qíngkuàng xià, tā yì zhōu gěi fùmǔ fā yí fèn diànzǐ yóujiàn.** *Under normal circumstances he sends his parents an e-mail once a week.*

正当 **zhèngdāng** CONJ just when, just as

正当 **zhèngdàng** ADJ proper, legitimate

正当权益 **zhèngdàng quányì** legitimate rights and interests

正规 **zhèngguī** ADJ regular, standard

正好 **zhènghǎo** I ADJ just right ■ 你来得正好, 我正要找你呢。**Nǐ lái de zhènghǎo, wǒ zhèngyào zhǎo nǐ ne.** *You've come at the right moment; I was just looking for you.* II ADV chance to, by co-incidence ■ 我正好那天下午没课, 可以陪她进城。**Wǒ zhènghǎo nà tiān xiàwǔ méi kè, kěyǐ péi tā jìnchéng.** *It happened that I did not have class that afternoon, so I could go to town with her.*

正经 **zhèngjing** ADJ 1 decent, proper 2 serious, not frivolous

一本正经 **yì běn zhèngjing** in all seriousness, sanctimonious

正面 **zhèngmiàn** I N facade, the obverse side II ADJ positive

正派 **zhèngpài** ADJ upright, decent

正派人 **zhèngpàirén** a decent person

正巧 **zhèngqiǎo** ADV as it happens, just at the right moment

正确 **zhèngquè** ADJ correct, accurate ■ 你要听各方面的意见, 才能形成正确的观点。**Nǐ yào tīng gè fāngmiàn de yìjiàn, cáinéng xíngchéng zhèngquè de guāndiǎn.** *You can form the correct viewpoint only after hearing out opinions from all sides.*

正式 **zhèngshì** ADJ formal, official ■ 公司正式通知职工, 明年一月起工资提高百分之十。**Gōngsī zhèngshì tōngzhī zhígōng, míngnián Yíyuè qǐ gōngzī tígāo bǎifēn zhī shí.** *The company has formally informed the staff that they will get a ten-percent raise starting next January.*

正在 **zhèngzài** ADV (used before a verb to indicate the action is in progress) ■ 他正在看电视。**Tā zhèngzài kàn diànshì.** *He's watching TV.*

正在…呢 **zhèngzài…ne** Same as 正在 **zhèngzài** but with a casual, friendly tone

证 **zhèng** TRAD 證 N proof, certificate

身分证 **shēnfen zhèng** ID card

学生证 **xuéshengzhèng** student ID card

证件 **zhèngjiàn** N paper or document proving one's identity, e.g a passport, an ID card

证据 **zhèngjù** N evidence, proof ■ 说话要有证据。**Shuōhuà yào yǒu zhèngjù.** *When you make a claim, you must have evidence.*

证明 **zhèngmíng** I V prove, testify ■ 事实证明, 他的想法行不通。**Shìshí zhèngmíng, tā de xiǎngfǎ xíng bu tōng.** *Facts have proven that his ideas do not work.* II N certificate ■ 你要请医生开一张病假证明。**Nǐ yào qǐng yīshēng kāi yì zhāng bìngjià zhèngmíng.** *You should ask your doctor to issue a certificate for medical leave.*

出证明 **chū zhèngmíng** issue a certificate

出生证明 **chūshēng zhèngmíng** birth certificate

证书 **zhèngshū** N certificate (份 **fèn**, 张 **zhāng**)

毕业证书 **bìyè zhèngshū** diploma

结婚证书 **jiéhūn zhèngshū** marriage license, marriage certificate

政 **zhèng** N governance, government

政变 **zhèngbiàn** N coup d'etat

政策 **zhèngcè** N government policy ■ 政府的移民政策可能会变化。**Zhèngfǔ de yímín zhèngcè kěnéng huì biànhuà.** *The government immigration policy may change.*

政党 **zhèngdǎng** N political party

政府 zhèngfǔ N government

政权 zhèngquán N 1 political power 2 government, regime ■ 军人发动政变，建立了新政权。Jūnrén fādòng zhèngbiàn, jiànlì le xīn zhèngquán. *Soldiers launched a coup d'etat, and established a new government.*

政治 zhèngzhì N politics, governance ■ 我对这个国家的政治情况了解不多。Wǒ duì zhège guójiā de zhèngzhì qíngkuàng liǎojiě bù duō. *I don't know much about the political situation in this country.*

症 zhèng N disease

急症 jízhèng acute disease, (medical) emergency
急症室 jízhèng shì emergency room (ER)
症状 zhèngzhuàng N symptom

挣 zhèng V work to earn (money)

挣钱养活全家 zhèngqián yǎnghuo quánjiā work to earn money so as to provide for the family

郑 zhèng TRAD 鄭 as in 郑重 zhèngzhòng

郑重 zhèngzhòng ADJ solemn, serious

之 zhī PARTICLE Same as 的 de. Used in written Chinese or certain set expressions.

之后 zhī hòu N after, behind ■ 他退休之后，要搬到故乡去住。Tā tuìxiū zhī hòu, yào bāndào gùxiāng qù zhù. *After his retirement he will move to his hometown.*

之间 zhī jiān N between ■ 我们之间存在着一些误会。Wǒmen zhī jiān cúnzàizhe yìxiē wùhuì. *There is some misunderstanding between us.*

之前 zhī qián N before ■ 你要在六月之前给我回信。Nǐ yào zài Liùyuè zhī qián gěi wǒ huíxìn. *You should give me a reply before June.*

之外 zhī wài N outside, apart from ■ 地球之外，还有其他地方有生命吗？Dìqiú zhī wài, háiyǒu qítā dìfang yǒu shēngmìng ma? *Apart from Earth, is there life anywhere else?*

之下 zhī xià N below, under ■ 三层楼之下是一个大餐厅。Sān-céng-lóu zhī xià shì yí gè dà cāntīng. *Below the third floor is a large restaurant.*

之一 zhī yī N one of

之中 zhī zhōng N between, among ■ 她的朋友之中，没有人会说中文。Tā de péngyou zhī zhōng, méiyou rén huì shuō Zhōngwén. *There is none among her friends who speaks Chinese.*

芝 zhī as in 芝麻 zhīma

芝麻 zhīma N sesame (粒 lì)

支 1 zhī I v 1 prop up, sustain 2 send away II N branch

支部 zhībù N branch (of a political party)

支撑 zhīchēng v prop up, shore up

支持 zhīchí v support ■ 同事之间要相互合作，相互支持。Tóngshì zhī jiān yào xiānghù hézuò, xiānghù zhīchí. *Colleagues should cooperate and support each other.*

支出 zhīchū I v pay, expend II N expenditure, expenses

支付 zhīfù v pay ■ 我可以用信用卡支付吗？Wǒ kěyǐ yòng xìnyòngkǎ zhīfù ma? *Can I pay by credit card?*

支流 zhīliú N tributary

支配 zhīpèi v 1 allocate, arrange 合理支配有限的资金 hélǐ zhīpèi yǒuxiàn de zījīn rationally allocate limited funds 2 control, determine

支票 zhīpiào N (in banking) check, cheque (张 zhāng)

兑现支票 duìxiàn zhīpiào cash a check

支援 zhīyuán v, N support, aid ■ 全国支援受灾地区。Quánguó zhīyuán shòuzāi dìqū. *The whole country aided the disaster-stricken region.* ■ 感谢你们给我们的宝贵支援。Gǎnxiè nimen gěi wǒmen de bǎoguì zhīyuán. *Our thanks for your precious aid.*

支柱 zhīzhù N mainstay, pillar

支 2 zhī M. WD (for stick-like things)

一支笔 yì zhī bǐ a pen

枝 zhī N twig, branch (根 gēn)

肢 zhī N limb

上肢 shàngzhī upper limbs
下肢 xiàzhī lower limbs

只 zhī TRAD 隻 M. WD (for animals, utensils, objects normally occurring in pairs, etc.)

一只手 yì zhī shǒu a hand
两只狗 liǎng zhī gǒu two dogs

知 zhī v know, be aware of

知道 zhīdào v know ■ 我不知道这件事。Wǒ bù zhīdào zhè jiàn shì. *I don't know about this matter.*

知觉 zhījué N consciousness, senses

知识 zhīshi N knowledge ■ 他这一方面的知识很丰富。Tā zhè yì fāngmiàn de zhīshi hěn fēngfù. *He has rich knowledge in this aspect.*

知识经济 zhīshi jīngjì knowledge economy

蜘 zhī as in 蜘蛛 zhīzhū

蜘蛛 zhīzhū N spider (只 zhī)
蜘蛛网 zhīzhūwǎng spider web

脂 zhī N fat, grease

脂肪 **zhīfáng** N fat

汁 zhī N juice

果汁 **guǒzhī** fruit juice

织 zhī TRAD 織 V weave (See 纺织 fǎngzhī, 组织 zǔzhī.)

执 zhí TRAD 執 V **1** grasp, persist **2** take charge, manage

执法 **zhífǎ** V enforce the law

执行 **zhíxíng** V carry out, implement, execute ■ 坚决执行上级交给我们的任务。Jiānjué zhíxíng shàngjí jiāo gei wǒmen de rènwù. *We will resolutely carry out the mission entrusted to us by the higher authorities.*

执行总公司的指示 **zhíxíng zǒnggōngsī de zhǐshì** carry out instructions from the company HQ

执照 **zhízhào** N license, permit

驾驶执照 **jiàshǐ zhízhào** driver's license

营业执照 **yíngyè zhízhào** business permit

执政 **zhízhèng** V (of a political party) govern, be in power

执政党 **zhízhèngdǎng** ruling party

直 zhí ADJ straight, direct ■ 这班航机直飞香港, 中间不停。Zhè bān hángjī zhí fēi Xiānggǎng, zhōngjiān bù tíng. *This airliner flies direct to Hong Kong without any stopover.*

直达 **zhídá** ADV nonstop, through ■ 这次航班直达纽约。Zhècì hángbān zhídá Niǔyuē. *This flight goes nonstop to New York.*

直到 **zhídào** PREP until, till ■ 孩子们在花园里玩, 直到天黑。Háizimen zài huāyuán li wán, zhídào tiānhēi. *The children played in the garden till it was dark.*

直接 **zhíjiē** ADJ direct ■ 你可以直接找房东, 不用通过中间人。Nǐ kěyǐ zhíjiē zhǎo fángdōng, bú yòng tōngguò zhōngjiānrén. *You can make direct contact with the landlord without going through the middleman.*

直径 **zhíjìng** N diameter

直辖市 **zhíxiáshì** N metropolis under the direct jurisdiction of the central government (the metropolises of Beijing, Shanghai, Tianjin and Chongqing)

直线 **zhíxiàn** N straight line (条 tiáo)

直至 **zhízhì** CONJ until

值 zhí I N value II V **1** be worth ■ 这辆旧车大约还值两千元。Zhè liàng jiùchē dàyuē hái zhí liǎngqiān yuán. *This old car probably is still worth 2,000 yuan.* **2** be on duty

值班 **zhíbān** V be on duty

值得 **zhíde** V be worth ■ 这本词典虽然不便宜, 还是值得买。Zhè běn cídiǎn suīrán bù piányi, háishì zhíde mǎi. *Although this dictionary is not cheap, it is worth buying.*

植 zhí V plant, grow

植物 **zhíwù** N plant, flora

植物学 **zhíwùxué** N botany

植物学家 **zhíwùxuéjiā** botanist

植物园 **zhíwùyuán** N botanical garden

殖 zhí V breed

殖民 **zhímín** V colonize

殖民地 **zhímíndì** N colony

殖民主义 **zhímín zhǔyì** colonialism

侄 zhí N one's brother's child

侄女 **zhínǚ** N one's brother's daughter

侄子 **zhízi** N one's brother's son

职 zhí TRAD 職 N job, profession, office

职称 **zhíchēng** N professional title

职工 **zhígōng** N staff (of a factory, a company, an enterprise, etc.), employee(s) ■ 我们公司总共有一千八百五十名职工。Wǒmen gōngsī zǒnggòng yǒu yìqiān bābǎi wǔshí míng zhígōng. *Our company has 1,850 employees in total.*

职能 **zhínéng** N function

职权 **zhíquán** N authority of office

职务 **zhíwù** N official duties and obligations, post

职业 **zhíyè** N occupation, profession, vocation ■ 他的职业是医生, 也是一位业余作家。Tā de zhíyè shì yīshēng, yě shì yí wèi yèyú zuòjiā. *He is a doctor by profession but he is also a writer in his spare time.*

职业病 **zhíyèbìng** N occupational disease

职业介绍所 **zhíyè jièshàosuǒ** N employment agency

职员 **zhíyuán** N office worker, clerk (名 míng)

止 zhǐ V stop (pain, cough, thirst, etc.) ■ 这个止痛药有没有副作用? Zhège zhǐtòngyào yǒu méiyǒu fùzuòyòng? *Does this painkiller have any side effects?*

只 zhǐ TRAD 祇 ADV only ■ 我只有一个弟弟, 没有哥哥, 也没有姐妹。Wǒ zhǐ yǒu yí ge dìdi, méiyǒu gēge, yě méiyǒu jiě-mei. *I've only got a younger brother. I don't have an elder brother or any sister.*

只得 **zhǐděi** V have got to, have to

只得照他说的做 **zhǐděi zhào tā shuōde zuò** have got no choice but do as he told

只顾 **zhǐgù** V care only about, be absorbed in

只顾赚钱 zhǐgù zhuànqián only care about making money

只管 zhǐguǎn v do as you wish, do not hesitate to ■ 有事只管来找我。Yǒushì zhǐguǎn lái zhǎo wǒ. *Do not hesitate to come to me if you've any problems.*

只好 zhǐhǎo ADV have no choice but ■ 他自行车坏了，只好走路去上学。Tā zìxíngchē huài le, zhǐhǎo zǒu lù qù shàngxué. *His bicycle has broken down, so he has to walk to school.*

只是 zhǐshì ADV only, just ■ 她只是想学几句旅游中文。Tā zhǐshì xiǎng xué jǐ jù lǚyóu Zhōngwén. *She only wants to learn some tourist Chinese.* ■ 我很想认真了解中国的历史，只是没有时间。Wǒ hěn xiǎng rènzhēn liǎojiě Zhōngguó de lìshǐ, zhǐshì méiyǒu shíjiān. *I'd like to learn Chinese history earnestly, it's just that I don't have the time.*

只要 zhǐyào CONJ so long as, provided that, if only ■ 只要打一个电话，饭店就会马上把菜送来。Zhǐyào dǎ yí ge diànhuà, fàndiàn jiù huì mǎshàng bǎ cài sònglai. *You only need to give the restaurant a call and they will deliver your order immediately.*

只有 zhǐyǒu I ADV can only, have no choice but ■ 既然答应帮助他，只有尽力而为了。Jìrán dāyìng bāngzhù tā, zhǐyǒu jìn lì ér wéi le. *Now that I've promised to help him, I can only do my best.* II CONJ only, only if ■ 只有认真地学，才能学好中文。Zhǐyǒu rènzhēn de xué, cáinéng xuéhǎo Zhōngwén. *Only if you study in earnest, can you gain a good command of Chinese.*

指 1 zhǐ I N finger

手指 shǒuzhǐ finger (根 gēn, 个 gè)
II v 1 point at, point to ■ 你不知道那东西叫什么，就用手指。Nǐ bù zhīdào nà dōngxi jiào shénme, jiù yòng shǒu zhǐ. *If you don't know what it's called, just point at it with your finger.* 2 refer to, allude to, mean ■ 他说有些工作不负责，不知道是指谁。Tā shuō yǒuxiē rén gōngzuò bú fùzé, bù zhīdào shì zhǐ shuí. *I don't know to whom he was referring when he said some people were not responsible in their work.*

指头(手指头) zhǐtou (shǒuzhítou) N Same as 手指 shǒuzhǐ

指标 zhǐbiāo N target, quota

指出 zhǐchū v point out ■ 老师指出了我发音中的问题。Lǎoshī zhǐchūle wǒ fāyīn zhōng de wèntí. *The teacher pointed out the problems in my pronunciation.*

指甲 zhǐjia N fingernail
修指甲 xiū zhǐjia do fingernails, manicure fingernails

指 2 zhǐ v 1 guide, refer to 2 reply on, count on

指导 zhǐdǎo v guide, direct, supervise ■ 工程师指导技术员修理机器。Gōngchéngshī zhǐdǎo jìshùyuán xiūlǐ jīqì. *The engineer supervised technicians in repairing the machine.*

指导员 zhǐdǎoyuán N political instructor (in the Chinese People's Liberation Army)

指导思想 zhǐdǎo sīxiǎng N guiding principle

指定 zhǐdìng v appoint, designate
指定法律代表 zhǐdìng fǎlǜ dàibiǎo appoint a legal representative

指挥 zhǐhuī v command, direct, conduct
指挥部 zhǐhuībù N headquarters

指令 zhǐlìng N instruction, order

指明 zhǐmíng v point out, show clearly

指南针 zhǐnánzhēn N compass

指示 zhǐshì I v 1 instruct 2 indicate II N 1 instruction 2 indication

指数 zhǐshù N index
琼斯指数 Dào Qióngsī zhǐshù Dow Jones Index

指望 zhǐwàng v count on, expect ■ 别指望他会来帮助你。Bié zhǐwàng tā huì lái bāngzhù nǐ. *Don't count on his help.*

指针 zhǐzhēn N (needle) indicator, pointer

纸 zhǐ TRAD 紙 N paper (张 zhāng) ■ 纸是古代中国人发明的。Zhǐ shì gǔdài Zhōngguórén fāmíng de. *Paper was invented by the ancient Chinese.*

纸张 zhǐzhāng N paper

址 zhǐ N location (See 地址 dìzhǐ)

旨 zhǐ N purpose (See 宗旨 zōngzhǐ)

挚 zhì ADJ sincere (See 诚挚 chéngzhì)

至 zhì PREP to, until (only used in written Chinese) ■ 银行营业时间是上午九时到下午五时。Yínháng yíngyè shíjiān shì shàngwǔ jiǔ shí zhì xiàwǔ wǔ shí. *The business hours of the bank are from nine in the morning till five in the afternoon.*

至多 zhìduō ADV at most, maximum

至今 zhìjīn ADV till now, to this day, so far ■ 至今已有七十多人报名学习中文。Zhìjīn yǐ yǒu qīshí duō rén bàomíng xuéxí Zhōngwén. *So far over seventy people have applied to study Chinese.*

至少 zhìshǎo ADV at least, minimum ■ 孩子至少懂得了为什么不应该说假话。Háizi zhìshǎo dǒngdele wèishénme bù yīnggāi shuō jiǎhuà. *At least the child has understood why one should not tell lies.*

至于 zhìyú

至于 **zhìyú** CONJ as to, as for

志 1 **zhì** TRAD 誌 N record (See 杂志 zázhì.)

志 2 **zhì** N will, aspiration

志气 **zhìqì** N aspiration, ambition
有志气 **yǒu zhìqì** have lofty aspirations
志愿 **zhìyuàn** I v volunteer
志愿者 **zhìyuànzhě** volunteer (a person)
II N wish, ideal

致 **zhì** V 1 send, extend 2 devote (time, efforts, etc)

致词 **zhìcí** v make a (short formal) speech
致富 **zhìfù** v become rich
勤劳致富 **qínláo zhìfù** become rich by working hard
致敬 **zhìjìng** v salute

治 **zhì** V 1 treat (disease) ■ 医生的责任是治病救人。Yīshēng de zérèn shì zhì bìng jiù rén. *It is the responsibility of a doctor to treat diseases and save lives.* 2 rule, govern

治安 **zhì'ān** N public order, public security
治理 **zhìlǐ** v govern, administrate
治疗 **zhìliáo** I v treat (a patient, a disease) II N medical treatment ■ 治疗无效。Zhìliáo wúxiào. *Medical treatment failed*

制 **zhì** TRAD 製 V 1 make, work out 2 control, restrict

制裁 **zhìcái** N sanction
制裁那个国家 **zhìcái nàge guójiā** establish sanction against that country
制定 **zhìdìng** v lay down, draw up ■ 他们在每年年底制定第二年的计划。Tāmen zài měi nián niándǐ zhìdìng dì-èr nián de jìhuà. *They draw up the plan for the next year at the end of a year.*
制度 **zhìdù** N system ■ 目前的教育制度存在很多问题。Mùqián de jiàoyù zhìdù cúnzài hěn duō wèntí. *There are many problems in the current educational system.*
制服 **zhìfú** N uniform (件 jiàn, 套 tào)
制品 **zhìpǐn** N products
乳制品 **rǔzhìpǐn** dairy product
制约 **zhìyuē** v constrain, restrain
受条件的制约 **shòu tiáojiàn de zhìyuē** constrained by one's circumstances
制造 **zhìzào** v make, manufacture ■ "中国制造" 的商品越来越多。"Zhōngguó zhìzào" de shāngpǐn yuèláiyuè duō. *There are more and more goods labeled "Made in China."*
制造业 **zhìzàoyè** manufacturing industry
制止 **zhìzhǐ** v stop, curb

帜 **zhì** TRAD 幟 N banner (See 旗帜 qízhì)

质 **zhì** TRAD 質 N nature, character

质变 **zhìbiàn** N qualitative change
质量 **zhìliàng** N quality ■ 这个牌子的汽车质量好，价格又便宜。Zhège páizi de qìchē zhìliàng hǎo, jiàgé yòu piányi. *Cars of this make are of good quality and inexpensive.*
质朴 **zhìpǔ** ADJ unaffected, ingenuous

秩 **zhì** N order, rank

秩序 **zhìxù** N order, proper sequence

置 **zhì** v place, put (See 布置 bùzhì)

掷 **zhì** TRAD 擲 v throw, hurl

智 **zhì** ADJ wise, intelligent

智者 **zhìzhě** wise man
智慧 **zhìhuì** N wisdom, intelligence
智力 **zhìlì** N intelligence, intellect
智力发达 **zhìlì fādá** highly intelligent
智谋 **zhìmóu** N tactic, clever scheme
智能 **zhìnéng** N intelligence and capability
人工智能 **réngōng zhìnéng** artificial intelligence
智商 **zhìshāng** N intelligence quotient (IQ)

稚 **zhì** ADJ childish (See 幼稚 yòuzhì)

滞 **zhì** v stagnate (See 停滞 tíngzhì)

终 **zhōng** TRAD 終 N end, finish

终点 **zhōngdiǎn** N end point, destination
终端 **zhōngduān** N terminal
终究 **zhōngjiū** ADV after all, in the end
终年 **zhōngnián** ADV all the year round, throughout the year
终身 **zhōngshēn** ADJ all one's life, lifelong ■ 王医生把终身献给了医疗事业。Wáng yīshēng bǎ zhōngshēn xiàngěile yīliáo shìyè. *Dr Wang gave all his life to medicine.*
终生大事 **zhōngshēng dàshì** marriage
终于 **zhōngyú** ADV finally, at last ■ 他终于实现了自己的愿望。Tā zhōngyú shíxiànle zìjǐ de yuànwàng. *He finally realized his aspirations.*
终止 **zhōngzhǐ** v terminate, end

中 **zhōng** I N center, middle

东南西北中 **dōng, nán, xī, běi, zhōng** the east, the south, the west, the north and the center

II ADJ **1** middle, medium **2** Chinese

中餐 **zhōngcān** N Chinese cuisine, Chinese food ■ 我们用中餐招待客人。 Wǒmen yòng zhōngcān zhāodài kèren. *We entertain guests with Chinese food.*

中餐馆 **zhōngcānguǎn** Chinese restaurant
中餐厅 **zhōngcāntīng** Chinese restaurant (in a hotel, etc.)

中国 **Zhōngguó** N China ■ 中国历史长，人口多。 Zhōngguó lìshǐ cháng, rénkǒu duō. *China has a long history and a large population.*

中华 **Zhōnghuá** N China, Chinese ■ 中华文明对东亚各国有很大影响。 Zhōnghuá wénmíng duì Dōng-Yà gè guó yǒu hěn dà yǐngxiǎng. *Chinese civilization has had great influence on countries in East Asia.*

NOTE: Both 中国 Zhōngguó and 中华 Zhōnghuá may refer to *China*, but 中华 Zhōnghuá has historical and cultural connotations

中间 **zhōngjiān** **I** N center, middle ■ 花园的中间有一棵大树。 Huāyuán de zhōngjiān yǒu yì kē dà shù. *In the center of the garden there is a very big tree.* **II** PREP among

中立 **zhōnglì** ADJ neutral
中立国 **zhōnglìguó** a neutral state
中年 **zhōngnián** N middle age
中年人 **zhōngniánrén** middle-aged person
中秋节 **Zhōngqiūjié** N Mid-Autumn Festival (the fifteenth day of the eighth lunar month)
中途 **zhōngtú** N halfway, mid-way
中文 **Zhōngwén** N the Chinese language (especially the writing) ■ 世界上有十几亿人用中文。 Shìjiè shang yǒu shí jǐ yì rén yòng Zhōngwén. *Over a billion people in the world use Chinese.*

NOTE: See note on 汉语 Hànyǔ.

中午 **zhōngwǔ** N noon ■ 我们中午休息一个小时。 Wǒmen zhōngwǔ xiūxi yí ge xiǎoshí. *We have a one-hour break at noon.*

中心 **zhōngxīn** N central part, center ■ 城市的中心是一座大公园。 Chéngshì de zhōngxīn shì yí zuò dà gōngyuán. *There is a big park in the center of the city.*

市中心 **shìzhōngxīn** city center
研究中心 **yánjiū zhōngxīn** research center
中型 **zhōngxíng** ADJ medium-sized
中学 **zhōngxué** N secondary school, high school, middle school (座 zuò, 所 suǒ)
中药 **zhōngyào** N traditional Chinese medicine (e.g. herbs) ■ 很多常见的植物都是有用的中药。 Hěn duō chángjiàn de zhíwù dōu shì yǒuyòng de zhōngyào. *Many common plants are useful traditional Chinese medicine.*

中医 **zhōngyī** N **1** traditional Chinese medicine (TCM) ■ 中医和古代哲学思想有关。 Zhōngyī hé gǔdài zhéxué sīxiǎng yǒuguān. *Traditional Chinese medicine is related to ancient Chinese philosophical thought.* **2** traditional Chinese medical doctor ■ 你这个病可以请一位中医看看。 Nǐ zhège bìng kěyǐ qǐng yí wèi zhōngyī kànkan. *You can consult a traditional Chinese doctor on your illness.*

中游 **zhōngyóu** N middle-reaches (of a river)

忠 **zhōng** ADJ loyal

忠诚 **zhōngchéng** ADJ loyal, faithful
忠实 **zhōngshí** ADJ loyal and faithful
忠于 **zhōngyú** V be loyal to
忠于祖国 **zhōngyú zǔguó** be loyal to one's motherland
忠贞 **zhōngzhēn** ADJ loyal (to one's country, spouse, etc.)

衷 **zhōng** N innermost feelings

言不由衷 **yánbùyóuzhōng** speak insincerely
衷心 **zhōngxīn** ADJ sincere, whole-hearted

钟 **zhōng** TRAD 鐘 N clock (座 zuò) ■ 这座钟慢了三分钟。 Zhè zuò zhōng mànle sān fēnzhōng. *This clock is three minutes slow.*

钟表 **zhōngbiǎo** N clocks and watches, time-piece
钟表店 **zhōngbiǎodiàn** watchmaker's shop
钟点 **zhōngdiǎn** N time, hour
钟点工 **zhōngdiǎngōng** Same as 小时工 xiǎoshígōng
钟楼 **zhōnglóu** N clock tower
钟头 **zhōngtóu** N Same as 小时 xiǎoshí. Used in spoken Chinese.

肿 **zhǒng** TRAD 腫 N swell

肿瘤 **zhǒngliú** N tumor
恶性肿瘤 **èxìng zhǒngliú** malignant tumor, cancer
良性肿瘤 **liángxìng zhǒngliú** benign tumor

种 **zhǒng** TRAD 種 **I** M. WD kind, sort, type ■ 这里有三种酒，你想喝哪一种? Zhèlǐ yǒu sān zhǒng jiǔ, nǐ xiǎng hē nǎ yì zhǒng? *Here are three kinds of wine. Which one would you like to drink?*

各种各样 **gè zhǒng gè yàng** all sorts of, all kinds of

II N **1** seed, breed **2** racial group
种类 **zhǒnglèi** N kind, category
种种 **zhǒngzhǒng** ADJ all sorts of
种子 **zhǒngzi** N seed
种族 **zhǒngzú** N race
种族主义 **zhǒngzúzhǔyì** racism

种 zhòng

种 zhòng TRAD 種 V plant ■ 爸爸在我家小花园里种了一些花。Bàba zài wǒ jiā xiǎo huāyuán li zhòngle yìxiē huā. *Dad planted some flowers in our little garden.*

种地 zhòngdì V grow crops, farm

种植 zhòngzhí V grow (crops)

重 zhòng ADJ 1 heavy ■ 这个机器太重了，我们两个人搬不动。Zhège jīqì tài zhòng le, wǒmen liǎng ge rén bān bu dòng. *This machine is too heavy for the two of us to move.* 2 considerable in value or quantity

重大 zhòngdà ADJ major, great ■ 去年国际上有哪些重大事件? Qùnián guójì shang yǒu nǎxiē zhòngdà shìjiàn? *What were the major international events last year?*

重点 zhòngdiǎn N main point, focal point, emphasis ■ 我今年要把重点放在学习语法上。Wǒ jīnnián yào bǎ zhòngdiǎn fàng zai xuéxí yǔfǎ shang. *This year I will focus on the study of Chinese grammar.*

重工业 zhònggōngyè N heavy industry

重量 zhòngliàng N weight ■ 称一下这件行李的重量。Chēng yíxià zhè jiàn xíngli de zhòngliàng. *Weigh this piece of luggage to see how heavy it is.*

重视 zhòngshì V attach importance to, value ■ 老年人一般比较重视身体健康。Lǎoniánrén yìbān bǐjiào zhòngshì shēntǐ jiànkāng. *Old people generally value good health.*

重心 zhòngxīn N 1 center of gravity 2 focus, point of emphasis

重型 zhòngxíng ADJ heavy-duty

重要 zhòngyào ADJ important ■ 我有一个重要的消息告诉你。Wǒ yǒu yí ge zhòngyào de xiāoxi gàosu nǐ. *I have important news to tell you.*

众 zhòng TRAD 衆 I N crowd II ADJ numerous

众多 zhòngduō ADJ numerous

众人 zhòngrén N all the people, everybody

众议院 Zhòngyìyuàn N (U.S.) House of Representatives

舟 zhōu N boat

周 1 zhōu I N 1 week ■ "你们学校寒假放几周?" "三周。" "Nǐmen xuéxiào hánjià fàng jǐ zhōu?" "Sān zhōu." *"How many weeks of winter holiday does your school have?" "Three weeks."* 2 circumference, cycle II ADV all around, all over

NOTES: (1) 周 zhōu and 星期 xīngqī both mean *week*, but 周 zhōu is usually used in writing only. Normally 星期 xīngqī is the word to use. (2) 周 zhōu is not used with any measure words.

周到 zhōudào ADJ thorough, thoughtful ■ 你们都准备好了，想得真周到。Nǐmen dōu zhǔnbèi hǎole, xiǎngde zhēn zhōudào. *It is really thoughtful of you to get everything ready.*

周密 zhōumì ADJ careful and thorough, attentive to every detail

周末 zhōumò N weekend ■ 这个周末我要进城买衣服和鞋子。Zhège zhōumò wǒ yào jìnchéng mǎi yīfu hé xiézi. *This weekend I'll go to town to buy clothes and shoes.*

周年 zhōunián N anniversary 结婚十周年 jiéhūn shí zhōunián the tenth anniversary of one's wedding

周期 zhōuqī N cycle, period

周围 zhōuwéi N surrounding area, all around ■ 新西兰周围都是大海。Xīnxīlán zhōuwéi dōu shì dàhǎi. *All around New Zealand is the sea.*

周折 zhōuzhé N twists and turns, setbacks

周转 zhōuzhuǎn N (of funds) flow, cash flow 周转不灵 zhōuzhuǎnbùlíng not have enough cash for business operation, have cashflow problems

周 2 Zhōu N a common family name

周先生/太太/小姐 Zhōu xiānsheng/tàitai/xiǎojiě Mr/Mrs/Miss Zhou

州 zhōu N 1 administrative district in ancient China 2 state (in the U.S.) 纽约州 Niǔyuēzhōu the State of New York

洲 zhōu N 1 island in a river 2 continent (See 大洋洲 Dàyángzhōu, 欧洲 Ōuzhōu, 亚洲 Yàzhōu.)

粥 zhōu N porridge, gruel

小米粥 xiǎomǐzhōu millet gruel 喝了半碗粥 hēle bàn wǎn zhōu ate half a bowl of gruel

皱 zhòu TRAD 皺 V wrinkle, crease

皱纹 zhòuwén N wrinkle (on skin), lines

昼 zhòu N daytime

昼夜 zhòuyè N day and night, round the clock 昼夜服务 zhòuyè fúwù round-the-clock (7/24) service

宙 zhòu N time (See 宇宙 yǔzhòu)

骤 zhòu N trot (See 步骤 bùzhòu)

猪 zhū N pig (头 tóu) ■ 中国人一般吃猪肉，不大吃牛肉、羊肉。Zhōngguórén yìbān chī zhūròu, bú dà chī niúròu, yángròu. *The Chinese*

normally eat pork and don't eat much beef or mutton.

诸 zhū ADJ all, various

诸位 zhūwèi PRON everybody, all of you

朱 zhū N 1 red 2 a common family name

珠 zhū N pearl (See 珍珠 zhēnzhū)

株 zhū M. WD (for plants and small trees)

竹 zhú N bamboo

竹子 zhúzi bamboo (棵 kē) ■ 院子里的一角种了几棵竹子。Yuànzi li de yì jiǎo zhòngle jǐ kē zhúzi. *There is some bamboo planted in a corner of the courtyard.*

逐 zhú ADV one after another, one by one

逐步 zhúbù ADV step by step, progressively, gradually ■ 我们的中文水平在逐步提高。Wǒmen de Zhōngwén shuǐpíng zài zhúbù tígāo. *Our Chinese proficiency is progressively improving.*

逐渐 zhújiàn ADV gradually, step by step ■ 地球正在逐渐变暖。Dìqiú zhèngzài zhújiàn biàn nuǎn. *The Earth is gradually warming up.*

逐年 zhúnián ADV one year after another, year by year

烛 zhú TRAD 燭 N candle (See 蜡烛 làzhú)

主 zhǔ I N 1 master, owner 2 host II ADJ dominant, principal

主办 zhǔbàn V host (a conference, an event, etc.) ■ 这个展览会由城市博物馆主办。Zhège zhǎnlǎnhuì yóu chéngshì bówùguǎn zhǔbàn. *This exhibition is hosted by the city museum.*

主编 zhǔbiān N editor-in-chief, editor

主持 zhǔchí V be in charge of, host (a TV program), chair (a meeting)
节目主持人 jiémù zhǔchírén host/hostess of a TV/radio show

主导 zhǔdǎo ADJ guiding, dominant

主动 zhǔdòng ADJ of one's own accord, taking the initiative ■ 他主动提出帮助我们。Tā zhǔdòng tíchū bāngzhù wǒmen. *He offered to help us without being asked.*

主观 zhǔguān ADJ subjective ■ 你这种说法只是建立在你个人的经历上，所以比较主观。Nǐ zhè zhǒng shuōfǎ zhǐshì jiànlì zài nǐ gérén de jīnglì shang, suǒyǐ bǐjiào zhǔguān. *Your arguments are rather subjective because they are based only on your personal experiences.*

主管 zhǔguǎn I V be in charge, be responsible for ■ 这位副校长主管财务工作。Zhè wei fùxiàozhǎng zhǔguǎn cáiwù gōngzuò. *This deputy principal is responsible for the finance of the school.* II N person in charge

主力 zhǔlì N main force

主流 zhǔliú N mainstream

主权 zhǔquán N sovereign rights, sovereignty

主人 zhǔrén N 1 host ■ 客人都来了，主人呢? Kèrén dōu lái le, zhǔrén ne? *The guests have all arrived, but where is the host?* 2 owner, proprietor

主人翁 zhǔrénwēng N master (of one's country, a society, etc.)

主任 zhǔrèn N chairman (of a committee), director (of a department) ■ 这个委员会的主任由一位教授担任。Zhège wěiyuánhuì de zhǔrèn yóu yí wèi jiàoshòu dānrèn. *The chair of this committee was held by a professor.*
办公室主任 bàngōngshì zhǔrèn office manager
车间主任 chējiān zhǔrèn head of a workshop (in a factory)

主任医生 zhǔrèn yīshēng N chief physician, chief surgeon

主食 zhǔshí N staple food

主题 zhǔtí N theme
(电影的) 主题歌 (diànyǐng de) zhǔtígē theme song (of a movie)

主体 zhǔtǐ N main body

主席 zhǔxí N chairman, chairperson
大会主席 dàhuì zhǔxí chairperson of an assembly

主要 zhǔyào ADJ major, chief, main ■ 纠正错误是主要的，谁该负责以后再说。Jiūzhèng cuòwù shì zhǔyào de, shuí gāi fùzé yǐhòu zài shuō. *Rectifying the mistake is the main thing. The question of who is to blame can wait till later.*

主义 zhǔyì N doctrine, -ism

主意 zhǔyi N definite view, idea ■ 这件事我没有什么主意，你看呢? Zhè jiàn shì wǒ méiyǒu shénme zhǔyi, nǐ kàn ne? *I don't have any definite views on this matter. What do you think?*

主张 zhǔzhāng I V advocate, stand for ■ 我主张立即恢复谈判。Wǒ zhǔzhāng lìjí huīfù tánpàn. *I advocate resuming negotiations immediately.*
II N proposition, idea, what one stands for

煮 zhǔ V boil, cook ■ 这块牛肉至少要煮一小时才能吃。Zhè kuài niúròu zhìshǎo yào zhǔ yì xiǎoshí cáinéng chī. *This piece of beef should be boiled for at least one hour before it is edible.*

嘱 zhǔ TRAD 囑 V advise

嘱咐 zhǔfu V exhort, tell (somebody to do

something) earnestly, advise ■ 老人去世前，嘱咐子女要互相爱护，互相照顾。Lǎorén qùshì qián, zhǔfu zǐnǚ yào hùxiāng àihu, hùxiāng zhàogu. *Before his death the old man exhorted his children to love and care for each other.*

嘱托 zhǔtuō v entrust

住 zhù v reside, stay ■ "你住在哪里？" "我住在学校附近。" "Nǐ zhù zài nǎlǐ?" "Wǒ zhù zài xuéxiào fùjìn." *"Where do you live?" "I live near the school."*

住房 zhùfáng N housing, accommodation

住所 zhùsuǒ N where one lives, lodge, residence

住院 zhùyuàn v be hospitalized

住宅 zhùzhái N residence, home

住宅区 **zhùzháiqū** residential quarters

助 zhù v assist, help

助理 zhùlǐ N assistant

助理局长 **zhùlǐ júzhǎng** assistant director of the bureau

局长助理 **júzhǎng zhùlǐ** assistant to the director of the bureau

助手 zhùshǒu N assistant

助长 zhùzhǎng v encourage, promote

注 zhù v 1 add, pour 2 fix, focus on 3 register, record 4 annotate, explain

注册 zhùcè v register

注册商标 **zhùcè shāngbiāo** registered trademark

注解 zhùjiě I v annotate, explain with notes II N explanatory note, note

注目 zhùmù v fix one's eyes on

引人注目 **yǐnrén zhùmù** eye-catching

注射 zhùshè v inject

注释 zhùshì N Same as 注解 zhùjiě

注视 zhùshì v look attentively, gaze at

注意 zhùyì v pay attention to, take notice of ■ 说话的时候，要注意语法。Shuōhuà de shíhou, yào zhùyì yǔfǎ. *One should pay attention to grammar when speaking.*

注重 zhùzhòng v 1 emphasize, stress 2 pay great attention to, attach importance to 注重售后服务 **zhùzhòng shòuhòufúwù** pay much attention to after-sale service

驻 zhù TRAD 駐 v stay

驻扎 zhùzhá v (of troops) be stationed

蛀 zhù v (of insects) eat into, bore through

蛀虫 zhùchóng N bookworm, termite

祝 zhù v express good wishes, wish ■ 祝你生日快乐！Zhù nǐ shēngrì kuàilè! *I wish you a happy birthday!*

祝福 zhùfú v give one's blessing to, wish somebody happiness

祝贺 zhùhè v congratulate ■ 祝贺你大学毕业！Zhùhè nǐ dàxué bìyè! *Congratulations on your graduation!*

祝愿 zhùyuàn I v wish ■ 祝愿你们生活美满幸福。Zhùyuàn nǐmen shēnghuó měimǎn xìngfú. *(to newly-weds) Wish you perfect happiness.* II N good wishes

著 zhù v write

著名 zhùmíng ADJ famous, well-known ■ 我们的中文老师是一位著名的小说家。Wǒmen de Zhōngwén lǎoshī shì yí wèi zhùmíng de xiǎoshuōjiā. *Our Chinese teacher is a famous novelist.*

著作 zhùzuò N writings, (literary) work ■ 他的著作被翻译为十多种语言。Tā de zhùzuò bèi fānyìwéi shí duō zhǒng yǔyán. *His works have been translated into a dozen foreign languages.*

筑 zhù TRAD 築 v build, construct (See 建筑 jiànzhù.)

柱 zhù N pillar, column

柱子 zhùzi pillar, column (根 gēn)

铸 zhù v cast

铸造 zhùzào cast, foundry

抓 zhuā v grab, seize ■ 他抓住小偷的胳膊。Tā zhuāzhù xiǎotōu de gēbo. *He grabbed the thief by the arm.*

抓紧 zhuājǐn v grasp firmly ■ 你要抓紧时间，在下星期一前写完报告。Nǐ yào zhuājǐn shíjiān, zài xià Xīngqīyī qián xiě wán bàogào. *You should make the best use of your time and write up the report before next Monday.*

爪 zhuǎ N paw, claw

爪子 zhuǎzi paw, claw (只 zhī)

拽 zhuài v fling, throw

专 zhuān TRAD 專 ADJ special, specific

专长 zhuāncháng N special skill, specialist field, expertise

专程 zhuānchéng ADV (make a trip) specially for

专家 zhuānjiā N expert, specialist ■ 他是计算机专家，关于计算机的事他没有不知道的。Tā shì jìsuànjī zhuānjiā, guānyú jìsuànjī de shì tā méiyǒu bù zhīdào de. *He is a computer expert and knows everything there is to know about computers.*

专科 **zhuānkē** N school (or college) for vocational training

专科学校 **zhuānkē xuéxiào** school (or college) for vocational training

专利 **zhuānlì** N patent

申请专利 **shēnqǐng zhuānlì** apply for a patent

专门 **zhuānmén** ADJ specialized, specialist ■ 他发表过很多语言学专门著作。Tā fābiǎoguo hěn duō yǔyánxué zhuānmén zhùzuò. *He has published many specialized works on linguistics.*

专心 **zhuānxīn** ADJ concentrate on, be absorbed in ■ 他做事不专心, 所以一事无成。Tā zuòshì bù zhuānxīn, suǒyǐ yí shì wú chéng. *He does everything half-heartedly and, as a result, has accomplished nothing.*

专业 **zhuānyè** N specialist field of study, specialty

专用 **zhuānyòng** v use for a special purpose

专款专用 **zhuānkuǎn zhuānyòng** earmark a fund for a specific purpose

专政 **zhuānzhèng** N dictatorship

专制 **zhuānzhì** N autocracy

砖 **zhuān** TRAD 磚 N brick

砖头 **zhuāntóu** brick (块 kuài)

转 **zhuǎn** TRAD 轉 v 1 turn, change ■ 今天下午雨转晴。Jīntiān xiàwǔ yǔ zhuǎn qíng. *This afternoon it'll change from a rainy day to a fine day.* 2 pass on, forward ■ 我已经把他的电子邮件转给他姐姐了。Wǒ yǐjīng bǎ tā de diànzǐ yóujiàn zhuǎn gei tā jiějie le. *I have forwarded his e-mail message to his sister.*

转变 **zhuǎnbiàn** v change, transform (usually for the better) ■ 他从一个小偷转变成一个对社会有用的公民。Tā cóng yí ge xiǎotōu zhuǎnbiàn chéng yí ge duì shèhuì yǒuyòng de gōngmín. *He has transformed from a thief to a useful member of society.*

转播 **zhuǎnbō** v relay a radio or TV broadcast

转车 **zhuǎnchē** v transfer to another train (or bus)

转达 **zhuǎndá** v pass on (a piece of information)

转动 **zhuǎndòng** v turn around, turn

转告 **zhuǎngào** v pass along (word)

转化 **zhuǎnhuà** v transform

转换 **zhuǎnhuàn** v transform, change

转基因 **zhuǎn jīyīn** N genetic modification, GM 转基因食品 **zhuǎnjīyīn shípǐn** transgenic food

转交 **zhuǎnjiāo** v pass on (something) ■ 小王要我把这本书转交给你。Xiǎo wáng yào wǒ bǎ zhè běn shū zhuǎnjiāo gěi nǐ. *Xiao Wang asked me to pass this book on to you.*

转让 **zhuǎnràng** v transfer (a property, rights, etc.)

转入 **zhuǎnrù** v switch over, turn to

转弯 **zhuǎnwān** v turn a corner, turn 向左转弯 **xiàngzuǒ zhuǎnwān** turn left

转向 **zhuǎnxiàng** v change direction

转学 **zhuǎnxué** v transfer to another school

转折 **zhuǎnzhé** N a turn in the course of events

转移 **zhuǎnyí** v shift, transfer

传 **zhuàn** TRAD 傳 N biography

自传 **zìzhuàn** autobiography

传记 **zhuànjì** N biography

赚 **zhuàn** TRAD 賺 v make money, make a profit ■ 这家小小的西餐馆去年赚了五万多。Zhè jiā xiǎoxiǎo de xīcānguǎn qùnián zhuànle wǔwàn duō. *This small Western-style restaurant made a profit of over 50,000 yuan last year.*

庄 **zhuāng** TRAD 莊 I N village II ADJ serious, grave

庄稼 **zhuāngjia** N crop ■ 光种庄稼, 很难富起来。Guāng zhòng zhuāngjia, hěn nán fù qǐlai. *It is difficult to get rich raising crops only*

庄稼地 **zhuāngjiadì** N farmland

庄稼人 **zhuāngjiarén** N farmer (especially one that grows crops)

庄严 **zhuāngyán** ADJ solemn, imposing

庄重 **zhuāngzhòng** ADJ serious, solemn

妆 **zhuāng** TRAD 妝 v apply make-up (See 化妆 huàzhuāng, 化妆品 huàzhuāngpǐn)

装 **zhuāng** TRAD 裝 I v 1 pretend ■ 她不想跟他说话, 所以装着没看见。Tā bù xiǎng gēn tā shuōhuà, suǒyǐ zhuāngzhe méi kànjian. *She did not want to talk to him, so she pretended not to see him.* 2 load and unload 3 fit, install II N clothing

装备 **zhuāngbèi** 1 v equip 2 N equipment 军事装备 **jūnshì zhuāngbèi** armament

装配 **zhuāngpèi** v assemble (parts) 装配线 **zhuāngpèixiàn** assembly line

装饰 **zhuāngshì** I v decorate ■ 他们用中国工艺品装饰客厅。Tāmen yòng Zhōngguó gōngyìpǐn zhuāngshì kètīng. *They decorated their living room with Chinese handicrafts.* II N decoration

装饰品 **zhuāngshìpǐn** article for decoration, ornament

装卸 **zhuāngxiè** v load and unload

装置 **zhuāngzhì** I v install II N installation, device

节能装置 **jiénéng zhuāngzhì** energy-saving device

壮 **zhuàng** TRAD 壯 ADJ 1 robust, sturdy 2 magnificent

壮大 **zhuàngdà** v grow in strength

壮观 **zhuàngguān** N magnificent sight

壮丽 zhuànglì

壮丽 **zhuànglì** ADJ beautiful and magnificent

壮烈 **zhuàngliè** ADJ heroic

壮志 **zhuàngzhì** N high aspirations

状 zhuàng TRAD 狀 N form, shape

状况 **zhuàngkuàng** N shape (of things), situation, condition ■ 你爷爷的身体状况怎么样？Nǐ yéye de shēntǐ zhuàngkuàng zěnmeyàng? *How is your grandpa's health?*

状态 **zhuàngtài** N state (of affairs), appearance ■ 运动员的精神状态非常重要。Yùndòngyuán de jīngshén zhuàngtài fēicháng zhòngyào. *It is important for an athlete to be in a good mental state.*

撞 zhuàng V bump against, collide ■ 两辆汽车相撞，造成重大交通事故。Liǎng liàng qìchē xiāng zhuàng, zàochéng zhòngdà jiāotōng shìgù. *The two cars collided and caused a major road accident.*

幢 zhuàng M. WD (for houses)

一幢大楼 **yí zhuàng dàlóu** a big (multi-storied) building

追 zhuī V **1** chase, run after ■ 孩子们在操场上你追我，我追你。Háizimen zài cāochǎng shang nǐ zhuī wǒ, wǒ zhuī nǐ. *Children chased one another on the playing ground.* **2** look into, get to the roots of

追查 **zhuīchá** V trace, investigate

追查谣言 **zhuīchá yáoyán** try to find out the source of a rumor

追悼 **zhuīdào** V mourn over (the death of somebody)

追悼会 **zhuīdàohuì** memorial service, memorial meeting

追赶 **zhuīgǎn** V run after, pursue

追究 **zhuījiū** V get to the roots, investigate the origin

追究责任 **zhuījiū zérèn** investigate to find out who is responsible for an accident

追求 **zhuīqiú** V pursue, seek ■ 人人追求幸福。Rénren zhuīqiú xìngfú. *Everyone pursues happiness.*

追上 **zhuīshang** V catch up with, catch ■ 我追不上他。Wǒ zhuī bu shang tā. *I can't catch up with him.*

追问 **zhuīwèn** V inquire in great details

缀 zhuì V sew, stitch (See 点缀 diǎnzhui)

准 zhǔn TRAD 準 I ADJ accurate, exact ■ 电子手表一般都很准。Diànzǐ shǒubiǎo yìbān dōu hěn zhǔn. *Electronic watches are usually quite accurate.* II V permit, allow III N norm, standard

准备 **zhǔnbèi** I V prepare ■ 明天考试，你们准

备好了吗？Míngtiān kǎoshì, nǐmen zhǔnbèi hǎo le ma? *There'll be an examination tomorrow. Are you well prepared?*

准备好 **zhǔnbèi hǎo** be well prepared II N preparation ■ 老师上课前要做很多准备。Lǎoshī shàngkè qián yào zuò hěn duō zhǔnbèi. *The teacher needs to do a lot of preparation before class.*

准确 **zhǔnquè** ADJ accurate, exact ■ 发音不准确，有时候会闹笑话。Fāyīn bù zhǔnquè, yǒushíhou huì nào xiàohua. *Inaccurate pronunciation can sometimes have comical effects.*

准时 **zhǔnshí** ADJ punctual, on time ■ 他每天准时九点钟到达办公室。Tā měitiān zhǔnshí jiǔ diǎnzhōng dàodá bàngōngshì. *Every day he arrives at his office punctually at nine o'clock.*

准许 **zhǔnxǔ** V permit, allow

准则 **zhǔnzé** N norm, standard

行为准则 **xíngwéi zhǔnzé** code of conduct

捉 zhuō V catch, capture ■ 你怎么捉得住猫？Nǐ zěnme zhuō de zhu māo? *How can you catch a cat?*

拙 zhuō ADJ clumsy (See 笨拙 bènzhuō)

桌 zhuō N table

桌子 **zhuōzi** table, desk (张 zhāng)

卓 zhuó ADJ outstanding

卓越 **zhuóyuè** ADJ brilliant, exceptional

啄 zhuó V peck

啄木鸟 **zhuómùniǎo** woodpecker

酌 zhuó V **1** weigh and consider **2** drink (wine)

酌情 **zhuóqíng** V take the circumstances into consideration

酌情处理 **zhuóqíng chǔlǐ** settle a matter as one sees fit

着 zhuó V apply, use

着手 **zhuóshǒu** V begin, set out

着想 **zhuóxiǎng** V consider (somebody's interest) ■ 我是为你着想。Wǒ shì wéi nǐ zhuóxiǎng. *I'm considering your interest.* (→ I'm doing this for your good.)

浊 zhuó TRAD 濁 ADJ turbid, muddy (See 浑浊 húnzhuó)

镯 zhuó N bracelet (See 手镯 shǒuzhuó)

姿 zī N looks, appearance

姿势 zīshì N posture

姿态 zītài N **1** posture **2** attitude, pose
保持低姿态 bǎochí dīzītài keep a low profile

资 zī consult

咨询 zīxún v seek advice, consult

资 zī TRAD 資 N money, capital

资本 zīběn N capital ■ 他开工厂的资本是从银行借来的。Tā kāi gōngchǎng de zīběn shì cóng yínháng jièlai de. *The capital with which he opened his factory was borrowed from the bank.*

资本家 zīběnjiā N capitalist

资本主义 zīběn zhǔyì N capitalism

资产 zīchǎn N asset, property

资产阶级 zīchǎnjiējí N bourgeoisie

资格 zīgé N qualification ■ 她通过考试，终于取得了教师资格。Tā tōngguò kǎoshì, zhōngyú qǔdé le jiàoshī zīgé. *She passed the exams and got her teaching qualification.*

资金 zījīn v fund

资料 zīliào N **1** material, data ■ 王老师从北京带回来很多中文教学的参考资料。Wáng lǎoshī cóng Běijīng dài huílai hěn duō Zhōngwén jiàoxué de cānkǎo zīliào. *Teacher Wang brought back from Beijing a great deal of reference materials for teaching and learning Chinese.* **2** means (of production) ■ 生产资料公有，是社会主义的特点。Shēngchǎn zīliào gōngyǒu, shì shèhuì zhǔyì de tèdiǎn. *Public ownership of the means of production is a special feature of socialism.*

资源 zīyuán N natural resources

资助 zīzhù v provide financial support, fund

滋 zī v grow

滋味 zīwèi N taste, flavor

滋长 zīzhǎng v grow, develop

子 zǐ N **1** son, child

长子 zhǎngzǐ the first son
2 something small and hard

子弹 zǐdàn N bullets

子弟 zǐdì N sons and younger brothers, children
高干子弟 gāogàn zǐdì children of high-ranking officials, "princelings"

子女 zǐnǚ N sons and daughters, children

子孙 zǐsūn N children and grandchildren, descendants
子孙后代 zǐsūn hòudài descendants, posterity

籽 zǐ N seed

仔 zǐ ADJ as in 仔细 zǐxì

仔细 zǐxì ADJ very careful, paying attention to details ■ 考试的时候一定要仔细看清题目。Kǎoshì de shíhou yídìng yào zǐxì kànqīng tímù. *At an examination be sure to read the questions very, very carefully.*

紫 zǐ ADJ purple ■ 他冻得脸都发紫了。Tā dòng de liǎn dōu fā zǐ le. *He was so cold that his face turned purple.*

自 I zì PRON self, one's own

自卑 zìbēi v feel oneself inferior
自卑感 zìbēigǎn inferiority complex, sense of inferiority

自动 zìdòng ADJ automatic
自动扶梯 zìdòng fútī escalator
自动化 zìdònghuà automatic, automation

自动柜员机 zìdòng guìyuánjī N automated teller machine (ATM)

自发 zìfā ADJ spontaneous

自费 zìfèi ADJ self-supporting, paid by myself ■ 我不明白，他们怎么有钱送孩子去国外自费留学？Wǒ bù míngbái, tāmen zěnme yǒu qián sòng háizi qù guówài zìfèi liúxué? *I don't understand how they could afford to send their child overseas as a self-supporting student.*
自费留学生 zìfèi liúxuéshēng self-supporting foreign student, fee-paying foreign student

自豪 zìháo v be very proud of oneself

自己 zìjǐ PRON self, one's own ■ 你不能只想到自己。Nǐ bù néng zhǐ xiǎngdao zìjǐ. *You mustn't think of yourself only.*
你自己 nǐ zìjǐ yourself
你们自己 nǐmen zìjǐ yourselves
他自己 tā zìjǐ himself
他们自己 tāmen zìjǐ themselves
我自己 wǒ zìjǐ myself
我们自己 wǒmen zìjǐ ourselves

自觉 zìjué ADJ being aware of, being conscious of, voluntary, conscientious ■ 他犯这个错误不是自觉的。Tā fàn zhège cuòwù bú shì zìjué de. *He made the mistake without being aware of it. (→ He unconsciously made the mistake.)*

自来水 zìláishuǐ N running water

自满 zìmǎn ADJ complacent

自然 zìrán I N nature ■ 哲学问题之一就是人和自然的关系。Zhéxué wèntí zhī yī jiù shì rén hé zìrán de guānxi. *One philosophical issue is the relationship between humankind and nature.*
自然保护区 zìrán bǎohùqū nature reserve
II ADJ natural ■ 父母爱子女是自然的。Fùmǔ ài zǐnǚ shì zìrán de. *It is only natural that parents love their children.*

自杀 zìshā

自杀 zìshā **I** v commit suicide **II** n suicide ■ 这件案子是自杀，还是他杀? Zhè jiàn ànzi shì zìshā, háishi tāshā? *Is this a case of suicide or homicide?*

自身 zìshēn n self, oneself

自私 zìsī adj selfish, egoistic ■ 独生子女往往比较自私，对不对? Dúshēngzǐ nǚ wǎngwǎng bǐjiào zìsī, duì búduì? *Is it true that an only child tends to be selfish?*

自私自利 zìsī zìlì idiom selfish, self-seeking

自卫 zìwèi n self-defense

自我 zìwǒ n oneself

自相矛盾 zìxiāng máodùn idiom self-contra-dictory

自信 zìxìn adj self-confident

缺乏自信 quēfá zìxìn lacking in self-confidence

自行 zìxíng adv by oneself

自行车 zìxíngchē n bicycle (辆 liàng)

自学 zìxué v study independently, teach oneself ■ 他自学日语三年，已经能看懂日文书了。Tā zìxué Rìyǔ sān nián, yǐjīng néng kàndǒng Rìwén shū le. *He taught himself Japanese for three years and is now able to read Japanese books.*

自由 zìyóu **I** n freedom, liberty ■ 那个国家缺乏新闻自由，受到人们的普遍批评。Nàge guójiā quēfá xīnwén zìyóu, shòudao rénmen de pǔbiàn pīpíng. *That country lacks freedom of the press and is widely criticized.* **II** adj free, unrestrained ■ 他觉得和父母住在一起不自由。Tā juéde hé fùmǔ zhù zài yìqǐ bú zìyóu. *Living with his parents, he does not feel free.*

自愿 zìyuàn v volunteer, of one's own accord

自治 zìzhì n autonomy

自治区 zìzhìqū n autonomous region

广西壮族自治区 Guǎngxī Zhuàngzú Zìzhìqū Guangxi Zhuang Autonomous Region

自主 zìzhǔ v act on one's own, keep the initiative in one's own hands

自助餐 zìzhùcān n buffet dinner

自 2 zì prep Same as 从 cóng. Only used in written Chinese.

自从 zìcóng prep from, since ■ 自从2001年9月11日，世界各地的飞机场都加强了行李检查。Zìcóng èr-líng-líng-yī nián Jiǔyuè shíyī rì, shìjiè gèdì de fēijīchǎng dōu jiāqiángle xínglǐ jiǎnchá. *Since September 11, 2001, airports all over the world have strengthened their luggage check system.*

自古 zìgǔ adv since ancient times

自始至终 zì shǐ zhì zhōng idiom from start to finish

字 zì n Chinese character, sinogram ■ 中国字很有意思。Zhōngguó zì hěn yǒu yìsi. *Chinese characters are very interesting.*

汉字 Hànzì Chinese character

字典 zìdiǎn n dictionary (本 běn)

字母 zìmǔ n letter (of an alphabet)

字母表 zìmǔbiǎo alphabet

子 zi particle (a nominal suffix) (See 杯子 bēizi, 被子 bèizi, 本子 běnzi, 鼻子 bízi, 脖子 bózi, 叉子 chāzi, 虫子 chóngzi, 村子 cūnzi, 刀子 dāozi, 电子 diànzi, 儿子 érzi, 房子 fángzi, 个子 gèzi, 孩子 háizi, 盒子 hézi, 猴子 hóuzi, 胡子 húzi, 饺子 jiǎozi, 橘子 júzi, 句子 jùzi, 裤子 kùzi, 筷子 kuàizi, 例子 lìzi, 帽子 màozi, 脑子 nǎozi, 牌子 páizi, 盘子 pánzi, 妻子 qīzi, 旗子 qízi, 裙子 qúnzi, 日子 rìzi, 嗓子 sǎngzi, 嫂子 sǎozi, 沙子 shāzi, 勺子 sháozi, 绳子 shéngzi, 狮子 shīzi, 毯子 tǎnzi, 兔子 tùzi, 袜子 wàzi, 蚊子 wénzi, 屋子 wūzi, 箱子 xiāngzi, 小伙子 xiǎohuǒzi, 样子 yàngzi, 叶子 yèzi, 一下子 yíxiàzi, 椅子 yǐzi, 院子 yuànzi, 种子 zhǒngzi, 竹子 zhúzi, 桌子 zhuōzi.)

宗 zōng n ancestor

宗教 zōngjiào n religion

宗教信仰 zōngjiào xìnyǎng religious belief

宗派 zōngpài n faction, sect

宗旨 zōngzhǐ n primary purpose, aim

棕 zōng n palm, palm fiber

棕色 zōngsè n brown

综 zōng adj comprehensive

综合 zōnghé adj comprehensive, synthetical

踪 zōng n footprint

跟踪 gēnzōng follow the tracks of, shadow (somebody)

踪迹 zōngjì n trace, track

总 zǒng trad 總 **I** adj 1 overall, total

总开关 zǒngkāiguān switch

2 chief, head

总书记 Zǒngshūjì Secretary-General

II adv 1 always, invariably ■ 他总觉得自己正确。Tā zǒng juéde zìjǐ zhèngquè. *He always thinks himself correct.* **2** anyway, after all

总得 zǒngděi modal v have got to, have to, must ■ 我们总得想个办法。Wǒmen zǒngděi xiǎng gè bànfǎ. *We've got to find a way put.*

总的来说 zǒngdeláishuō idiom generally speaking, on the whole

总督 zǒngdū n governor-general, governor

总额 zǒng'é n total (a sum of fund)

总而言之 zǒng'éryánzhī idiom Same as 总之 zǒngzhī

总共 zǒnggòng adv in all, altogether

总和 zǒnghé N sum total
总计 zǒngjì N grand total
总结 zǒngjié I v sum up, do a review of one's past work or life experiences ■ 每年年底, 公司都要总结一年的工作。Měi nián niándǐ, gōngsī dōuyào zǒngjié yì nián de gōngzuò. *At the end of every year the company does a general review of the work done.* II N summary, a general view of one's past work or life experiences ■ 这个计划已经完成, 我们应该做一个总结了。Zhège jìhuà yǐjīng wánchéng, wǒmen yīnggāi zuò yí ge zǒngjié le. *Now that this plan is fulfilled, we should do a general review.*
总理 zǒnglǐ N premier, prime minister ■ 中国的国务院总理是政府首脑。Zhōngguó de guówùyuàn zǒnglǐ shì zhèngfǔ shǒunǎo. *The premier of the Chinese State Council is China's head of government.*
总是 zǒngshì ADV Same as 总 II ADV 1
总数 zǒngshù N sum total
总司令 zǒngsīlìng N commander-in-chief
总算 zǒngsuàn ADV at long last, finally
总统 zǒngtǒng N president (of a country) ■ 美国每四年举行总统选举。Měiguó měi sì nián jǔxíng zǒngtǒng xuǎnjǔ. *The U.S.A. holds its presidential election every four years.*
总务 zǒngwù N general affairs
总务科 zǒngwùkē general affairs section
总之 zǒngzhī ADV in a word, in short ■ 总之, 你的计划是不可行的。Zǒngzhī, nǐde jìhuà shì bùkě xíng de. *Your plan, in short, is not feasible.*

纵 zòng ADV 1 from north to south 2 vertical, lengthwise
纵横 zònghéng ADJ in length and breadth

走 zǒu v 1 walk ■ 我家离学校很近, 我每天走到学校。Wǒ jiā lí xuéxiào hěn jìn, wǒ měi tiān zǒudao xuéxiào. *My home is close to the school. I walk to school every day.* 2 leave ■ 时间不早了, 我们得走了。Shíjiān bù zǎo le, wǒmen děi zǒu le. *It's quite late. We've got to go.* 3 visit
走亲戚 zǒu qīnqi visit a relative
4 escape, leak out
走道 zǒudào N sidewalk, footpath
走访 zǒufǎng v visit and interview, interview
走狗 zǒugǒu N running dog, flunkey
走廊 zǒuláng N corridor, hallway
走漏 zǒulòu v leak (information)
走私 zǒusī v smuggle
走私犯 zǒusīfàn smuggler
走弯路 zǒuwānlù v take a roundabout course
走向 zǒuxiàng N 1 alignment 2 trend
明年市场的走向 míngnián shìchǎng de zǒuxiàng the market trend next year

奏 zòu v play music (See 演奏 yǎnzòu)
揍 zòu v beat, hit
挨揍 áizòu get a thrashing

租 zū I v rent, hire ■ 在这座大楼租一个办公室, 要多少钱? Zài zhè zuò dàlóu zū yí ge bàngōngshì, yào duōshǎoqián? *How much is it to rent an office in this building?* II N rent (money)
房租 fángzū (housing) rent
租金 zūjīn N rent

足 zú I N foot II ADJ sufficient, enough
足球 zúqiú N soccer ■ 我爸爸年轻的时候, 常常踢足球, 现在还爱看足球比赛。Wǒ bàba niánqīng de shíhou, chángcháng tī zúqiú, xiànzài hái ài kàn zúqiú bǐsài. *My father often played soccer when he was young, and now he still enjoys watching soccer games.*
踢足球 tī zúqiú play soccer
足以 zúyǐ ADJ enough, sufficient

族 zú N clan, nationality (See 民族 mínzú.)

阻 zǔ v 1 resist, prevent 2 hinder, block
阻碍 zǔ'ài v hinder, obstruct
阻挡 zǔdǎng v block, stop
阻拦 zǔlán v bar the way, stop
阻力 zǔlì N resistance, obstacle
阻扰 zǔrǎo v obstruct, stand in the way

NOTE: 阻扰 zǔrǎo may also be 阻挠 zǔnáo. They are interchangeable.

阻止 zǔzhǐ v stop, hold back

祖 zǔ N ancestor
祖父 zǔfù N grandfather
祖国 zǔguó N motherland, fatherland ■ 他虽然住在国外, 但深深地关心祖国。Tā suīrán zhù zai guówài, dàn shēnshēn de guānxīn zǔguó. *Although living in a foreign country, he is still deeply concerned for his motherland.*
祖母 zǔmǔ N grandmother
祖先 zǔxiān N ancestor, ancestry

组 zǔ TRAD 組 I N group ■ 老师把全班分为三个组, 练习口语。Lǎoshī bǎ quán bān fēn wéi sān ge zǔ, liànxí kǒuyǔ. *The teacher divided the class into three groups for oral Chinese practice.* II v form, organize
组成 zǔchéng v make up, compose ■ 这个专家组由五名世界级科学家组成。Zhège zhuānjiāzǔ yóu wǔ míng shìjiè jí kēxuéjiā zǔchéng. *This expert panel is made up of five world-class scientists.*

组合 zǔhé v compose, combine

组织 zǔzhī I v organize ■ 学校正在组织去北京旅游。Xuéxiào zhèngzài zǔzhī qù Běijīng lǚyóu. *The school is organizing a trip to Beijing.* II N organization

钻 zuān TRAD 鑽 N drill

钻研 zuānyán v study in great depth, study intensively ■ 这位科学家有时候钻研一个问题而忘了吃饭。Zhè wèi kēxuéjiā yǒushíhou zuānyán yí ge wèntí ér wàngle chīfàn. *Sometimes this scientist studies a problem so intensively that he forgets his meals.*

钻 zuàn TRAD 鑽 N diamond

钻石 zuànshí diamond (粒 lì, 颗 kē)
一枚三克拉的钻石戒指 yìméi sān kèlā de zuànshí jièzhǐ a 3-carat diamond ring

嘴 zuǐ N mouth ■ 不要用嘴呼吸，要用鼻子呼吸。Bú yào yòng zuǐ hūxī, yào yòng bízi hūxī. *Breathe through the nose, not through the mouth.*

嘴巴 zuǐba N mouth
张开嘴巴 zhāngkāi zuǐba open one's mouth
嘴唇 zuǐchún N lip

最 zuì ADV most (used before an adjective or a verb to indicate the superlative degree) ■ 中国是世界上人口最多的国家。Zhōngguó shì shìjiè shang rénkǒu zuì duō de guójiā. *China is the most populous country in the world.*

最初 zuìchū ADV in the initial stage, initially ■ 最初我不习惯那里的生活。Zuìchū wǒ bù xíguàn nàli de shēnghuó. *Initially I was not used to the life there.*

最好 zuìhǎo I ADJ best, top-rate II ADV had better ■ 你最好常去看望奶奶。Nǐ zuìhǎo cháng qù kànwàng nǎinai. *You'd better visit your grandma often.*

最后 zuìhòu ADV in the final stage, finally ■ 笑得最后，才笑得最好。Xiào de zuìhòu, cái xiào de zuìhǎo. *He who laughs last laughs best.*

最近 zuìjìn ADV recently, in recent times ■ 我最近特别忙。Wǒ zuìjìn tèbié máng. *I'm particularly busy these days.*

罪 zuì N crime, offense ■ 被告不承认自己有罪。Bèigào bù chéngrèn zìjǐ yǒuzuì. *The defendant did not admit to any offense. (→ The defendant pleaded not guilty.)*

罪恶 zuì'è N crime, evil
罪犯 zuìfàn N criminal, convict ■ 警察在案发第二天就抓到了罪犯。Jǐngchá zài àn fā dì-èr tiān jiù zhuā dào le zuìfàn. *The police caught the criminal the day after the crime.*

罪名 zuìmíng N charge, accusation
逃税的罪名 táoshuì de zuìmíng tax evasion charge
罪行 zuìxíng N crime, offense
罪状 zuìzhuàng N facts about a crime, indictment

醉 zuì v get drunk, be intoxicated ■ 他昨天晚上喝醉了，今天头疼。Tā zuótiān wǎnshang hē zuì le, jīntiān tóuténg. *He was drunk last night and this morning he has a headache.*

尊 zūn v respect, esteem

尊敬 zūnjìng v respect, honor ■ 中国的传统是尊敬老人。Zhōngguó de chuántǒng shì zūnjìng lǎorén. *A tradition of the Chinese is to respect the aged.*
尊严 zūnyán N dignity, honor
尊重 zūnzhòng v respect, esteem ■ 我们非常尊重这位经验丰富的老教师。Wǒmen fēicháng zūnzhòng zhè wèi jīngyàn fēngfù de lǎo jiàoshī. *We hold this very experienced old teacher in high esteem.*

遵 zūn v obey

遵守 zūnshǒu v observe, abide by ■ 你既然在这个学校学习，就要遵守学校的各项规定。Nǐ jìrán zài zhège xuéxiào xuéxí, jiù yào zūnshǒu xuéxiào de gè xiàng guīdìng. *Since you are studying in this school, you should observe its regulations.*
遵循 zūnxún v follow faithfully, adhere to
遵照 zūnzhào v act in accordance with

昨 zuó N yesterday

昨天 zuótiān N yesterday ■ 你昨天晚上去哪里了? Nǐ zuótiān wǎnshang qù nǎli le? *Where were you yesterday evening?*

琢 zuó as in 琢磨 zuómo

琢磨 zuómo v turn over in one's mind, ponder

左 zuǒ N the left side ■ 我弟弟用左手吃饭，写字。Wǒ dìdi yòng zuǒshǒu chīfàn, xiězì. *My younger brother eats and writes with the left hand.*
左边 zuǒbian N the left side, the left-hand side
左右 zuǒyòu ADV approximately, nearly, about ■ 今天最高温度二十度左右。Jīntiān zuìgāo wēndù èrshí dù zuǒyòu. *Today's maximum temperature is about twenty degrees.*

做 zuò v 1 do ■ 这件事我不会做。Zhè jiàn shì wǒ bú huì zuò. *I don't know how to do this.*
2 make ■ 这张桌子是我爸爸做的。Zhè zhāng zhuōzi shì wǒ bàba zuò de. *This table was made by my father.*

做工 zuògōng do manual work, work ■ 今年夏天你要去哪里做工? Jīnnián xiàtiān nǐ yào qù nǎlǐ zuògōng? *Where are you going to work this summer?*

做法 zuòfǎ N way of doing things, method, practice ■ 他这种做法不讲原则，我不赞成。Tā zhè zhǒng zuòfǎ bù jiǎng yuánzé, wǒ bú zànchéng. *This kind of practice of his is unprincipled and I don't approve of it.*

做饭 zuòfàn cook, prepare a meal

做客 zuòkè v be a guest, visit ■ 在春节的时候，我们到亲戚家做客。Zài chūnjié de shíhou, wǒmen dào qīnqi jiā zuòkè. *In Spring Festival we visit our relatives.*

做梦 zuòmèng v dream ■ 我昨天夜里做了一个奇怪的梦。Wǒ zuótiān yèli zuò le yí ge qíguài de mèng. *I had a strange dream last night.*

做主 zuòzhǔ v be one's own master

作 zuò v Same as 做 zuò

NOTE: 做 zuò and 作 zuò have the same pronunciation and often the same meaning, but 做 zuò is much more commonly used while 作 zuò occurs only in certain set expressions.

作案 zuò'àn v commit a crime

作废 zuòfèi v become invalid

作风 zuòfēng N way of behavior, way of working, style
独断独行的领导作风 dúduàndúxíng de lǐngdǎo zuòfēng autocratic style of leadership

作家 zuòjiā N writer (especially of literary works, e.g. novels, stories) ■ 在过去，作家是很受人尊敬的。Zài guòqu, zuòjiā shì hěn shòu rén zūnjìng de. *In the past writers were very much respected.*
作家协会 Zuòjiā Xiéhuì Writers' Association

作品 zuòpǐn N literary or artistic work ■ 这位作家又有新作品了。Zhè wèi zuòjiā yòu yǒu xīn zuòpǐn le. *This writer has written another work.*

作为 zuòwéi PREP as, in the capacity of

作文 zuòwén N (student's) composition ■ 她的作文经常得到老师的表扬。Tā de zuòwén jīngcháng dédào lǎoshī de biǎoyáng. *Her compositions are often commended by the teacher.*

作物 zuòwù N crop

作业 zuòyè N school assignment, homework ■ 中国的中小学生每天要做很多作业。Zhōngguó de zhōngxiǎo xuésheng měi tiān yào zuò hěn duō zuòyè. *School children in China have lots of homework to do every day.*

作用 zuòyòng N function, role ■ 他在这次谈判中起了很大作用。Tā zài zhè cì tánpàn zhōng qǐle hěn dà zuòyòng. *He played a major role in the negotiations.*
在···中起作用 zài...zhōng qǐ zuòyòng play a role in ..., perform a function in ...

作者 zuòzhě N author ■ 这本书的作者是一位女作家。Zhè běn shū de zuòzhě shì yí wèi nǚzuòjiā. *The author of this book is a woman writer.*

坐 zuò v sit ■ 她正坐在窗边看书。Tā zhèng zuò zài chuāngbiān kànshū. *She's sitting by the window, reading.*

座 zuò I M. WD (for large and solid objects, such as a large building)
一座大楼 yí zuò dàlóu a big building
一座山 yí zuò shān a mountain, a hill
一座工厂 yí zuò gōngchǎng a factory
一座大学 yí zuò dàxué a university
一座桥 yí zuò qiáo a bridge
一座城市 yí zuò chéngshì a city

II N seat

座儿 zuòr N seat

座谈 zuòtán v have an informal discussion, have an informal meeting ■ 校长今天下午和一年级学生座谈。Xiàozhǎng jīntiān xiàwǔ hé yì niánjí xuésheng zuòtán. *The principal will have an informal discussion with first-year students this afternoon.*
座谈会 zuòtánhuì an informal discussion, forum

座位 zuòwèi N seat ■ 这个座位有人吗? Zhège zuòwèi yǒu rén ma? *Is this seat taken?*

座右铭 zuòyòumíng N motto ■ "为社会做贡献" 是我的座右铭。"Wéi shèhuì zuò gòngxiàn" shǐ wǒ de zuòyòumíng. *"Contribute to the society" is my motto.*

A

A N 优, 优等 yōuděng ■ *She got an "A" on her English test.* 她英文测验得了 "优"。 Tā Yīngwén cèyàn déle "yōu".

a, an ART 一 yī, 一个 yí ge
a boy 一个男孩 yí ge nánhái
an hour 一个小时 yí ge xiǎoshí

AA (= Associate of Arts) ABBREV 准文学士 zhǔn wénxuéshì

AAA (= American Automobile Association) ABBREV 美国汽车协会 Měiguó qìchē xiéhuì

abacus N 算盘 suànpán [M. WD 只 zhī]

abandon V 遗弃 yíqì, 抛弃 fàngqì, 中止 zhōngzhǐ

abashed ADJ 惭愧的 cánkuì de, 难为情的 nán-wéiqíng de

abate V 减轻 jiǎnqīng, 减少 jiǎnshǎo

abbey N 修道院 xiūdàoyuàn, 寺院 sìyuàn [M. WD 座 zuò]

abbreviate V 省略 shěnglüè, 缩略 suōlüè

abbreviation N 缩略语 suōlüèyǔ, 缩写 suōxiě

ABC (= American Broadcasting Corporation) ABBREV 美国广播公司 Měiguó guǎngbō gōngsī

abdomen N 腹部 fùbù, 肚子 dùzi

abduct V 劫持 jiéchí, 绑架 bǎngjià

aberration N 异常 yìcháng

abet V 唆使 suōshǐ, 教唆 jiàosuō

abhor V 厌恶 yàn'è, 憎恶 zēng'è

abhorrent ADJ 憎恶 zēng'è, 痛恨 tòng hèn

abide (PT & PP **abided/abode**) V (abide by) 遵守 zūnshǒu, 信守 xìnshǒu

abiding ADJ 永久的 yǒngjiǔ de, 持久的 chíjiǔ de

ability N 能力 nénglì, 才能 cáinéng ■ *Does she have the ability to do the job well?* 她有能力做好这件事吗? Tā yǒu nénglì zuòhǎo zhè jiàn shì ma?

abject ADJ 卑躬屈膝的 [+行为] bēigōng qūxī de [+xíngwéi], 低声下气的 [+ 道歉] dīshēng xiàqì de [+dàoqiàn]
abject poverty 赤贫 chìpín

ablaze ADJ 燃烧 ránshāo, 熊熊燃烧 xióngxióng ránshāo

able ADJ 能 néng, 能够 nénggòu

abnormal ADJ 不正常的 bú zhèngcháng de, 反常的 fǎncháng de

aboard ADV 在飞机/火车/轮船上 zài fēijī/huǒchē/lúnchuán shang, 上飞机/火车/轮船 shàng fēijī/huǒchē/lúnchuán

abode[1] N 住所 zhùsuǒ

abode[2] See **abide**

abolish V 废除 fèichú

Aborigine N (澳大利亚) 原住民 (Àodàlìyà) yuánzhùmín

abort V **1** 使 [+ 怀孕的妇女] 流产 shǐ [+huáiyùn de

fùnǚ] liúchǎn, 堕胎 duòtāi, 使堕胎 shǐ duòtāi
2 中止 [+行动/计划] zhōngzhǐ [+xíngdòng/jìhuà]

abortion N 堕胎 duòtāi, 人工流产 réngōng liúchǎn

abortive ADJ 流产的 liúchǎn de, 失败的 shībài de

abound V 大量存在 dàliàng cúnzài

about I PREP 关于 guānyú
How about/what about ...? ⋯, 怎么样 ⋯, zěnmeyàng, ⋯, 好不好? ..., hǎobuhǎo?
■ *How about dining out tonight?* 今天晚上出去吃饭, 好不好? Jīntiān wǎnshang chūqū chīfàn, hǎo bu hǎo?
II ADV 大约 dàyuē, 大概 dàgài
to be about to do sth 刚要 gāng yào, 正要 zhèngyào, 马上要 mǎshàng yào ■ *I was about to go out when the phone rang.* 我刚要出门, 电话铃响了。 Wǒ gāng yào chūmén, diànhuàlíng xiǎng le.

above I PREP **1** 在⋯上边 zài...shàngbian, 在⋯上面 zài...shàngmian
above all 首先 shǒuxiān, 最重要的 zuì zhòng yào de
2 超过 chāoguò
II ADV **1** 在上面 zài shàngmian
prices listed above 上面列出的价格 shàngmian lièchū de jiàgé
2 超过 chāoguò
families with above average incomes 超过平均收入的家庭 chāoguò píngjūn shōurù de jiātíng
III ADJ 上述的 shàngshù de

aboveboard ADJ 光明正大的 guāngmíng zhèngdà de

abrasive ADJ 生硬的 shēngyìng de, 鲁莽的 lǔmǎng de

abreast ADV 并排的 bìngpái de
to keep abreast of ... 了解⋯的最新情况 liǎojiě...de zuìxīn qíngkuàng

abridged ADJ 删节的 shānjié de, 节缩的 jié suō de

abroad ADV 到国外 dào guówài, 在国外 zài guówài

abrupt ADJ 突然的 tūrán de, 粗鲁的 [+态度] cūlǔ de [+tàidu]

abscess N 脓肿 nóngzhǒng

abscond V 携款潜逃 xiékuǎn qiántáo, 潜逃 qiántáo

absence N 不在 bú zài, 缺席 quēxí ■ *I did not notice his absence.* 我没有注意到他不在。 Wǒ méiyǒu zhùyìdào tā búzài.

absent ADJ 不在 búzài, 缺席 quēxí
absent-minded 心不在焉的 xīn bú zài yān de

absentee N 缺席者 quēxí zhě
absentee ballot 缺席投票 quēxítóupiào

absenteeism N 无故旷工（旷课）wúgù kuànggōng (kuàngkè)

absolute ADJ 绝对 juéduì, 完全 wánquán ■ *Do you believe in absolute truth?* 你相信绝对真理吗? Nǐ xiāngxìn juéduì zhēnlǐ ma?

absolve V 宣布无罪 xuānbù wúzuì

absorb V 吸收 xīshōu

absorbent ADJ 易吸水的 yì xīshuǐ de

absorbing ADJ 引人入胜的 yǐn rén rù shèng de

abstain V 1 放弃投票权 fàngqì tóupiào quán, 弃权 qìquán 2 避免 bìmiǎn, 戒除 jièchú
to abstain from sex before marriage 避免婚前 性生活 bìmiǎn hūnqián xìng shēnghuó

abstinence N 禁欲 jìnyù, 戒酒戒烟 jièjiǔ jièyān

abstract¹ ADJ 抽象的 chōuxiàng de

abstract² N（论文）摘要 (lùnwén) zhāiyào [M. WD 篇 piān]

absurd ADJ 荒谬 huāngmiù, 荒唐 huāngtang

abundance N 丰富 fēngfù, 充裕 chōngyù

abundant ADJ 丰富 fēngfù, 充沛 chōngpèi ■ *We have an abundant supply of food.* 我们的食品供应 很丰富。Wǒmen de shípǐn gōngyìng hěn fēngfù.

abundantly ADV 大量地 dàliàng de

abuse I N 滥用 lànyòng
drug/alchohol abuse 吸毒／酗酒（现象）xīdú/ xùjiǔ (xiànxiàng)
2 虐待 nüèdài ■ *Abuse of animals is quite common in that region.* 在那个地区，虐待动物 相当普遍。Zài nàge dìqū, nüèdài dòngwù xiāngdāng pǔbiàn. 3 谩骂 mànmà, 辱骂 rǔmà
II V 虐待 nüèdài
physical abuse 殴打 ōudǎ
verbal abuse 辱骂 rǔmà

abusive ADJ 虐待的 nüèdài de

abysmal ADJ 极坏的 jí huài de, 糟透的 zāotòu de

abyss N 1 深渊 shēnyuān 2 极其危险的境地 jíqí wēixiǎn de jìngdì

academic ADJ 学校的 xuéxiào de
academic degree 学位 xuéwèi
academic year 学年 xuénián

academy N 1 专科学院 zhuānkē xuéyuàn 2 研 究院 yánjiūyuàn, 学会 xuéhuì 3 私立学院 sīlì xuéyuàn
United States Military Academy at West Point 美国西点军事学院 Měiguó xīdiǎnjūnshì xuéyuàn

acccelerate V 加速 jiāsù, 使…加速 shǐ...jiāsù, 提前 tíqián, 使…提前 shǐ...tíqián

accelerator N 加速器 jiāsùqì, 油门 yóumén
to step on the accelerator 踩油门 cǎi yóumén

accent I N 口音 kǒuyīn
to speak Chinese with an English accent 讲 中文带有英语口音 jiǎng Zhōngwén dàiyǒu Yīngyǔ kǒuyīn
II V 强调 qiángdiào, 突出 tūchū

accept V 接受 jiēshòu ■ *We're happy to accept your invitation.* 我们非常高兴接受您的邀 请。Wǒmen fēicháng gāoxìng jiēshòu nín de yāoqǐng.

acceptable ADJ 可以接受的 kěyǐ jiēshòude, 还不 错的 hái búcuò de

acceptance N 接受 jiēshòu, 认可 rènkě

access I N 达到 dádào, 进入 jìnrù II V 1 获取 [+信 息] huòqǔ [+xìnxī] 2 进入 [+贮藏室] jìnrù [+zhùcángshì]
access time（计算机）读取（信息）时间 (jìsuànjī) dú qǔ (xìnxī) shíjiān

accessible ADJ 容易进入的 róngyì jìnrù de, 容易 得到的 róngyì dédào de

accessory N 1 装饰品 zhuāngshìpǐn [M. WD 件 jiàn], 附件 fùjiàn 2 从犯 cóngfàn, 帮凶 bāngxiōng

accident N 事故 shìgù [M. WD 件 jiàn/起 qǐ]
car accident 交通事故 jiāotōng shìgù
by accident 不是故意的 búshì gùyì de, 意外的 yìwài de

accidental ADJ 意外的 yìwài de, 偶然的 ǒurán de

accident-prone ADJ 容易造成事故的 róngyì zàochéng shìgù de, 很会闯祸的 hěn huì chuǎnghuò de

acclaim I V 称赞 chēngzàn, 叫好 jiàohǎo II N 称 赞 chēngzàn, 赞誉 zànyù

acclimatize V 使…适应 shǐ...shìyìng, 使…习惯 shǐ...xíguàn

accolade N 高度赞扬 gāodù zànyáng

accommodate V 1 提供住宿 tígōng zhùsù 2 适应 shìyìng, 迎合 yínghé ■ *We try hard to accommodate the needs of our guests.* 我们尽量 迎合客人的需要。Wǒmen jǐnliàng yínghé kèren de xūyào.

accommodating ADJ 愿意帮助人的 yuànyì bāngzhù rén de, 随和的 suíhe de

accommodation N 住宿 zhùsù, 住宿的地方 zhùsù de dìfang

accompaniment N（音乐）伴奏 (yīnyuè) bànzòu
with piano accompaniment 钢琴伴奏 gāngqín bànzòu

accompanist N（音乐）伴奏者 (yīnyuè) bànzòuzhě

accompany V 1 陪同 péitóng 2 为…伴奏 wéi... bànzòu
to accompany her on a trip to China 陪同她去 中国 péitóng tā qù Zhōngguó

accomplice N 帮凶 bāngxiōng, 同谋 tóngmóu

accomplished ADJ 很有才华的 hěn yǒu cáihuá de, 有造诣的 yǒu zàoyì de
an accomplished fact 既成事实 jìchéng shìshí

accomplishment N 1 成就 chéngjiù, 成绩 chéngjì 2 技能 jìnéng, 技巧 jìqiǎo
a high level of accomplishment in figure skat-

ing 非常高的花样滑冰技巧 fēicháng gāo de huāyàng huábīng jìqiǎo

accord I N **1** 符合 fúhé, 一致 yízhì **2** 协定 xiédìng [M. WD 项 xiàng]
of one's own accord 自愿地 zìyuànde
to reach an accord 达成协议 dáchéng xiéyì
II V 给与 jǐyǔ

accordance N (in accordance with) 与…一致 yǔ...yízhì, 根据 genjù
in accordance with his will 根据他的遗嘱 gēnjù tāde yízhǔ

according to PREP 根据 gēnjù, 按照 ànzhào

accordingly ADV 相应地 xiāngyìng de

accost V 走上去与…主动讲话 zǒushàng qù yǔ...zhǔdòng jiǎnghuà, 与…搭讪 yǔ...dāshàn

account I N **1** 叙述 xùshù, 描写 miáoxiě
to give an account of … 讲述 jiǎngshù
2 帐 zhàng, 账户 zhànghù, 账目 zhàngmù
accounts payable 应付账款 yìngfu zhàngkuǎn
accounts receivable 应收账款 yīngshōu zhàngkuǎn
checking account 活期账户 huóqī zhànghù
savings account 储蓄账户 chǔxù zhànghù
3 考虑 kǎolǜ, 想法 xiǎngfǎ
to take … into account/take account of 考虑 kǎolǜ ■ You should take account of the tight timeframe. 你应该考虑到时间很紧。Nǐ yīnggāi kǎolǜdào shíjiān hěn jǐn.
II V (to account for) 说明 shuōmíng, 解释 jiěshì ■ There's no accounting for taste. 青菜萝卜，各有所好。Qīngcài luóbo, gèyǒusuǒhào.

accountability N 负责 fùzé, 责任制 zérènzhì
police accountability to the public 警方对公众负责 jǐngfāng duì gōngzhòng fùzé

accountable ADJ 负有责任的 fùyǒu zérèn de

accountant N 会计 kuàijì, 会计师 kuàijìshī

accounting N 会计工作 kuàijì gōngzuò, 会计学 kuàijìxué

accreditation N 正式认可 zhèngshì rènkě, 授权 shòuquán

accredited ADJ 得到正式认可的 [+教师] dédào zhèngshì rènkě de [+jiàoshī], 有正式资格的 [+专业工作者] yǒu zhèngshì zīge de [+zhuānyè gōngzuòzhě]
an accredited accountant 有资格开业的会计师 yǒu zīgé kāiyè de kuàijìshī

accumulate V 积累 jīlěi, 集聚 jíjù

accuracy N 准确性 zhǔnquèxìng, 精确度 jīngquèdù

accurate ADJ 准确 zhǔnquè, 精确 jīngquè

accusation N 控告 kònggào, 指控 zhǐkòng

accuse V 控告 kònggào, 控诉 kòngsù
to accuse him of sex harassment 控告他性骚扰 kònggào tā xìngsāorǎo

accused N 被告 bèigào [M. WD 名 míng]

accustom V 使…习惯 shǐ...xíguàn

accustomed ADJ 习惯 xíguàn, 习惯于 xíguàn yú
be accustomed to a vegetarian diet 习惯于吃素食 xíguàn yú chīsù shí

ace I N **1** (扑克牌) A 牌 (pūkèpái) ēi pái **2** 王牌 wángpái, 高手 gāoshǒu
a tennis ace 网球高手 wǎngqiú gāoshǒu
II ADJ 第一流的 dìyīliú de, 棒极的 bàng jí de
an ace pitcher 王牌投球手 wángpái tóuqiú shǒu

acerbic ADJ 尖刻的 jiānkè de, 刻毒的 kèdú de

ache I N 疼 téng, 痛 tòng **II** V 疼 téng, 痛 tòng ■ I am aching all over. 我浑身疼。Wǒ húnshēn téng.

achieve V **1** 取得 [+平等地位] qǔdé [+píngděng dìwèi], 获得 huòdé **2** 实现 [+目标] shíxiàn [+mùbiāo]

achievement N 成就 chéngjiù, 成绩 chéngjì

acid N 酸 suān
acid cloud 酸云 suānyún
acid rain 酸雨 suānyǔ
an acid test 严峻的考验 yánjùn de kǎoyàn

acknowledge V **1** 承认 chéngrèn, 确认 quèrèn **2** 表示感谢 biǎoshì gǎnxiè, 鸣谢 míngxiè, 致谢 zhìxiè

acknowledgment N **1** 承认 chéngrèn, 确认 quèrèn **2** 感谢 gǎnxiè, 鸣谢 míngxiè
in acknowledgment of 确认 quèrèn, 表彰 biǎozhāng

acne N 粉刺 fěncì

acorn N 橡树的果子 xiàngshù de guǒzi, 橡果 xiàng guǒ

acoustic ADJ 声音的 shēngyīn de, 音响的 yīnxiǎng de

acoustics N **1** 音响效果 yīnxiǎng xiàoguǒ **2** 声学 shēngxué

acquaint V 认识 rènshi, 知晓 zhīxiǎo
to acquaint oneself with 了解 liǎojiě
to be acquainted with 认识 rènshi, 了解 liǎojiě

acquaintance N **1** 认识的人 rènshi de rén, 熟人 shúrén **2** 了解 liǎojiě, 认识 rènshi
to make sb's acquaintance 认识 rènshi, 结识 jiéshí

acquiesce V 默许 mòxǔ, 勉强同意 miǎnqiǎng tóngyì

acquire V 取得 qǔdé, 获得 huòdé

acquisition N **1** 获得 huòdé, 得到 dédào **2** 获得的东西 huòdé de dōngxi, 得到的东西 dédào de dōngxi
mergers and acquisitions 公司并购 gōngsī bìnggòu

acquit V 宣布无罪 xuānbù wúzuì

acquittal N 无罪宣判 wúzuì xuānpàn

acre N 英亩 yīngmǔ

acreage N 英亩数 yīngmǔ shù, 面积 miànjī

acrid ADJ **1** 刺鼻的 [+气味] cìbí de [+qìwèi] **2** 刻薄的 [+话] kèbó de [+huà]

acrimonious ADJ 充满敌意的 chōngmǎn díyì de, 激烈的 jīliè de

acrimony N 敌意 díyì, 互相仇视 hùxiāng chóushì

acrobat N 杂技演员 zájì yǎnyuán

acrobatics N 杂技 zájì

acronym N 首字母拼音词 shǒu zìmǔ pīnyīn cí

across I PREP **1** 过 guò, 穿过 chuānguo ■ *Can you swim across this river?* 你游泳过这条河吗? Nǐ yóuyǒng guò zhè tiáo hé ma? **2** 在···的对面 zài···de duìmiàn ■ *The bookstore is just across the street.* 书店就在马路对面。Shūdiàn jiù zài mǎlù duìmiàn. II ADV 过 guò, 穿过 chuānguo

act I v **1** [迅速+] 行动 [xùnsù+] xíngdòng **2** 演 [+主角] yǎn [+zhǔjué], 扮演 [+一个角色] bànyǎn [+yí ge juésè] **3** 装出 [+···的样子] zhuāngchū [+···de yàngzi], 假装 jiǎzhuāng ■ *He is just acting like a fool.* 他只是装得像傻瓜。Tā zhǐ shì zhuāngde xiàng shǎguā.

to act as 当 [+中间人] dāng [+zhōngjiānrén], 担任 dānrèn

II N **1** 行动 xíngdòng, 行为 xíngwéi ■ *She was caught in the act of shoplifting.* 她在商店偷窃时被抓获。Tā zài shāng diàn tōuqiè shí bèi zhuāhuò. **2** [通过+] 法令 [tōngguò+] fǎlìng

acting I ADJ 代理的 dàilǐ de

acting principal 代理校长 dàilǐ xiàozhǎng, 代校长 dài xiàozhǎng

II N 表演 biǎoyǎn

action N 行动 xíngdòng, 行为 xíngwéi ■ *We'll judge him by his actions.* 我们将根据他的行为来判断他。Wǒmen jiāng gēnjù tā de xíngwéi lái pànduàn tā.

Actions speak louder than words. 行动重于言辞。Xíngdòng zhòngyú yáncí.

to take action 采取行动 cǎiqǔ xíngdòng

active I ADJ 活跃 huóyuè, 积极 jījí II N 主动语态 zhǔdòng yǔtài

activist N 积极分子 jījí fènzǐ

activity N 活动 huódòng [M. WD 项 xiàng]

after-school activities 课外活动 kè wài huódòng

terrorist activities 恐怖主义活动 kǒngbù zhǔyì huódòng

actor N（男）演员 (nán) yǎnyuán

actress N（女）演员 (nǚ) yǎnyuán

actual ADJ 实际的 shíjì de, 真实的 zhēnshí de ■ *Things are much more complicated in actual life.* 在现实生活中，情况要复杂得多。Zài xiànshí shēnghuó zhōng, qíngkuàng yào fùzáde duō.

actuality N 真实 zhēnshí, 事实 shìshí

in actuality 事实上 shìshíshang, 实际上 shíjìshàng

actually ADV 事实上 shìshíshang, 其实 qíshí

acumen N 机敏 jīmǐn, 敏锐 mǐnruì

acupuncture N 针灸 zhēnjiǔ, 针灸疗法 zhēnjiǔ-liáofǎ

acute ADJ **1** 严重的 yánzhòng de **2** 急性的 jíxìng de

acute disease 急性病 jíxìngbìng

acute pain 剧烈疼痛 jùliè téngtòng

adamant ADJ 坚持 jiānchí, 坚决 jiānjué

Adam's apple N 喉结 hóujié

adapt v **1** 改变···以适应 gǎibiàn···yǐ shìyìng **2** 改编 [+小说] gǎibiān [+xiǎoshuō] ■ *This movie was adapted from a bestselling novel.* 这部电影是根据一本畅销小说改编的。Zhè bù diànyǐng shì gēnjù yìběn chàngxiāo xiǎoshuō gǎibiān de.

adaptable ADJ 能适应的 néng shìyìng de

adapter N 转接器 zhuǎnjiēqì, 插座 chāzuò

add v **1** 加 jiā **2** 补充 bǔchōng

addict N **1** 吸毒上瘾的人 xīdú shàngyǐn de rén **2** 上瘾的人 shàngyǐn de rén

cocaine addict 可卡因上瘾者 kěkǎyīn shàngyǐn zhě

computer addict 电脑迷 diànnǎo mí

addicted ADJ 上瘾的 xīdú shàngyǐn de

addicted to gambling 赌博上瘾的 dǔbó shàngyǐn de

addiction N 上瘾 shàngyǐn, 成瘾 chéngyǐn

drug addiction 毒瘾 dúyǐn

addictive ADJ 使人上瘾的 shǐrén shàngyǐn de

addition N 加 jiā, 加法 jiāfǎ

in addition 另外 lìngwài, 此外 cǐwài

in addition to···以外 chúle···yǐwài ■ *In addition to his full-time job, he moonlights as a translator.* 他除了全日工作以外，还兼职做翻译工作。Tā chúle quánrì gōngzuò yǐwài, hái jiānzhí zuò fānyì gōngzuò.

additional ADJ 额外的 éwàide, 附加的 fùjiāde

additive N 添加剂 tiānjiājì

address I N **1** 地址 dìzhǐ **2** 演说 yǎnshuō, 讲话 jiǎnghuà

to deliver an opening address 致开幕词 zhì kāimùcí

II v **1** (在邮件上) 写姓名地址 (zài yóujiàn shàng) xiě xìngmíng dizhǐ, 开信封 kāi xìnfēng **2** 讲演 yǎnjiǎng, 发表演说 fābiǎo yǎnshuō **3** 称呼 chēnghu

form of address 称呼方式 chēnghu fāngshì

adept I ADJ 擅长的 shàncháng de, 熟练的 shúliàn de II N 能手 néngshǒu, 内行 nèiháng

adequate ADJ 充分的 chōngfèn de, 足够的 zúgòu de

adhere v 黏附 niánfù

to adhere to 坚持 jiānchí

adherence N 坚持 jiānchí, 遵守 zūnshǒu

adherent N 信奉者 xìnfèngzhě

adhesion N 粘连 zhānlián, 黏附 niánfù

adhesive ADJ 有粘性的 yǒu zhānxìng de

adhesive tape 胶布 jiāobù, 胶带 jiāodài

d hoc ADJ 专门的 zhuānmén de, 特地 tèdì
an ad hoc committee 专门委员会 zhuānmén wěiyuánhuì

djacent ADJ 邻近的 línjìn de, 相连的 xiānglián de

djective N 形容词 xíngróngcí

djoining ADJ 相邻的 xiānglín de, 紧挨着的 jǐn'āizhe de

djourn V 暂停 zàntíng, 休会 xiūhuì

djudicate V 裁定 cáidìng, 评审 píngshěn

djunct N 附属物 fùshǔwù, 附件 fùjiàn

djust V 1 调整 tiáozhěng, 调节 tiáojié 2 适应 shìyìng
well-adjusted 身心健全的 shēnxīnjiànquán de, 能对付生活中的问题的 néng duìfu shēnghuó zhōngde wèntíde

djustment N 调整 tiáozhěng, 调节 tiáojié

d-lib V 即兴表演 jíxìng biǎoyǎn, 当场演说 dāngchǎng yǎnshuō

dminister V 1 管理 [+医院] guǎnlǐ [+yīyuàn], 治理 zhǐlǐ 2 执行 [+规定] zhíxíng [+guīdìng]

dministration N 1 管理 guǎnlǐ, 行政 xíngzhèng 2 政府 zhèngfǔ

dministrative ADJ 行政的 xíngzhèng de, 管理的 guǎnlǐ de
administrative assistant 行政助理 xíngzhèng zhùlǐ

dministrator N 行政管理人 xíngzhèng guǎnlǐ rén

dmirable ADJ 令人敬佩的 lìngrén jìng pèi de, 出色的 chūsè de

dmiral N 舰队司令 jiànduì sīlìng [M. WD 位 wèi], 海军上将 hǎijūn shàngjiàng [M. WD 位 wèi]

dmiration N 敬佩 jìngpèi, 佩服 pèifu

dmire V 1 敬佩 jìngpèi, 钦佩 qīnpèi, 佩服 pèifu 2 欣赏 [+美景] xīnshǎng [+měijǐng], 观赏 [+风景] guānshǎng [+fēngjǐng]
to admire the ocean view 观赏海景 guānshǎng hǎijǐng

dmissible ADJ 可接受的 kě jiēshòu de, 可采纳的 kě cǎinà de
admissible evidence 可接受的证词 kě jiēshòu dí zhèngcí

dmission N 1 承认 chéngrèn ■ With his admission of the error, we were quite ready to forgive him. 他承认了错误, 我们准备原谅他。Tā chéngrènle cuòwu, wǒmen zhǔnbèi yuánliàng tā. 2 门票 ménpiào
No admission 不准入内 bùzhǔn rùnèi

dmissions N 大学录取过程 dàxué lùqǔ guòchéng, 大学录取人数 dàxué lùqǔ rénshù

dmit V 1 承认 chéngrèn 2 允许加入 yǔnxǔ jiārù, 接纳 jiēnà
to be admitted to the country club 被接纳加入

乡村俱乐部 bèi jiēnà jiārù xiāngcūn jùlèbù
3 接收入医院 jiē shōu rù yīyuàn
to be admitted to the intensive care 送进医院特别护理部 sòngjìn yīyuàn tèbié hùlǐ bù

admittance N 进入 jìnrù
to gain admittance to Harvard 进入哈佛大学学习 jìnrù Hāfó Dàxué xuéxí, 被哈佛大学录取 bèi Hāfó Dàxué lùqǔ

admittedly ADV 应该承认 yīnggāi chéngrèn, 确实地 quèshíde

admonish V 劝告 quàngào, 告诫 gàojiè

admonition N 告诫 gàojiè, 警告 jǐnggào

adolescence N 青少年时期 qīng shàonián shíqī, 青春期 qīngchūnqī

adolescent I ADJ 青少年的 qīngshàonián de, 青春期的 qīngchūnqī de II N 青少年 qīngshàonián

adopt V 1 领养 lǐngyǎng 2 采用 cǎiyòng, 采纳 cǎinà

adoptive ADJ 领养的 lǐngyǎng de
an adoptive father 领养孩子的父亲 lǐngyǎng háizi do fùqin, 养父 yǎngfù

adorable ADJ 非常可爱的 fēicháng kě'ài de

adoration N 爱慕 àimù, 敬慕 jìngmù

adore V 爱慕 àimù, 敬慕 jìngmù

adorn V 装饰 zhuāngshì

adornment N 装饰品 zhuāngshìpǐn [M. WD 件 jiàn]

adrenaline N 1 肾上腺素 shènshàngxiànsù 2 强烈的兴奋 qiángliè de xīngfèn

adrift ADJ 漂流的 piāoliú de

adroit ADJ 1 灵巧的 [+手] líng qiǎo de [+shǒu] 2 口齿伶俐的 [+外交家] kǒuchǐ línglì de [+wàijiāojiā]

adulation N 恭维 gōngwei, 奉承 fèngcheng

adult I N 成年人 chéngniánrén, 成人 chéngrén ■ The movie is for adults only. 这部电影只适合成年人看。Zhè bù diànyǐng zhǐ shìhé chéngnián kàn. II ADJ 1 成年人的 chéngniánrén de, 成人的 chéngrén de 2 适合成年的 shìhé chéngnián de

adulterate V 掺假 chān jiǎ

adultery N 通奸 tōngjiān

advance I V 1 进展 jìnzhǎn, 发展 fāzhǎn ■ The world has advanced from the industrial age to an information age. 世界已经从工业时代进展到信息时代。Shijiè yǐjīng cóng gōngyè shídài jìnzhǎndào xìnxī shídài. 2 提出 [+计划、理论等] tíchū [+jìhuà, lǐlùn děng] 3 预支 [+工资、报酬等] yùzhī [gōngzī, bàochou děng] II N 1 预先 yùxiān
in advance 预先 yùxiān
2 进展 jìnzhǎn, 发展 fāzhǎn 3 预付款 yùfùkuǎn

advanced ADJ 1 先进的 [+技术] xiānjìn de [+jìshù] 2 高级(的)[+数学] gāojí (de) [+shùxué]

advances N 挑逗 tiǎodòu, 勾引 gōuyǐn

to make advances to sb 挑逗某人 tiǎodòu mǒurén, 对某人性骚扰 duì mǒurén xìngsāorǎo

advantage N 1 好处 hǎochù, 益处 yìchù 2 有利条件 yǒulì tiáojiàn ■ *It is an advantage to have a rich dad.* 有富爸爸是一个有利条件。 Yǒu fù bàba shì yí ge yǒulì tiáojiàn.
to have an advantage over 对…占有优势 duì… zhànyǒu yōushì
to take advantage of sb 占某人的便宜 zhàn mǒurén piányi
to take advantage of sth 利用某事 lìyòng mǒushì

advent N 出现 chūxiàn, 来临 láilín

adventure N 冒险 màoxiǎn ■ *Harry, an energetic young man, is always looking for adventures.* 哈里，一个精力充沛的小伙子，总是在寻找冒险。 Hālǐ, yí ge jīnglì chōngpèi de xiǎohuǒzi, zǒngshì zài xúnzhǎo màoxiǎn.
adventure tour 冒险旅游 màoxiǎn lǚyóu

adventurer N 冒险家 màoxiǎnjiā

adventurous ADJ 喜欢冒险的 xǐhuan màoxiǎn de, 有冒险精神的 yǒu màoxiǎn jīngshén de

adverb N 副词 fùcí

adversary N 敌手 díshǒu, 对手 duìshǒu

adverse ADJ 不利的 búlì de, 反面的 fǎnmiàn de

advertise V 1 做广告 zuò guǎnggào, 登广告 dēng guǎnggào 2 招聘 [+职员] zhāopìn [+zhíyuán]

advertisement N 广告 guǎnggào

advertising N 广告业 guǎnggàoyè
advertising agency 广告公司 guǎnggào gōngsī

advice N 劝告 quàngào, 意见 yìjiàn ■ *Let me give you a piece of advice.* 我劝你一句话。 Wǒ quàn nǐ yí jù huà.

advise V 1 劝 quàn ■ *The doctor advised him to give up smoking.* 医生劝他戒烟。 Yīshēng quàn tā jiè yān. 2 提供咨询 tígōng zīxún

adviser, advisor N 顾问 gùwèn [M. WD 位 wèi]

advisory ADJ 顾问的 gùwèn de, 咨询的 zīxún de
an advisory committee 顾问委员会 gùwèn wěiyuánhuì, 咨询委员会 zīxún wěiyuánhuì

advocate N, V 提倡 tíchàng, 主张 zhǔzhāng

aerial ADJ 从飞机上来的 cóng fēijī shànglái de
an aerial photograph 空中拍摄的照片 kōngzhōng pāishè de zhàopiàn

aerobic ADJ 增强心肺的 zēngqiáng xīnfèi de
aerobic exercise 有氧运动 yǒu yǎng yùndòng

aerobics N 有氧健身操 yǒu yǎng jiànshēncāo

aerodynamics N 空气动力学 kōngqì dònglìxué

aerosol N 喷雾罐 pēnwù guàn [M. WD 只 zhī]

aerospace ADJ 航空和航天工业 hángkōng hé hángtiān gōngyè

aesthetic ADJ 美学的 měixué de, 审美的 shěnměi de

aesthetics N 美学 měixué

afar ADV 从远方 cóng yuǎnfāng

affable ADJ 和蔼可亲的 hé'ǎi kěqīn de, 友好的 yǒuhǎo de

affair N 1 事 shì [M. WD 件 jiàn], 事情 shìqing [M. WD 件 jiàn], 事件 shìjiàn 2 事务 shìwù [M. WD 件 jiàn]
foreign affairs 外交事务 wàijiāo shìwù, 外事 wàishì
3 婚外恋 hūnwài liàn

affect V 1 影响 yǐngxiǎng 2 假装 jiǎzhuāng

affectation N 装模作样 zhuāngmú zuòyàng, 矫揉造作 jiǎoróu zàozuò

affected ADJ 做作的 zuòzuo de, 装出来的 zhuāngchū láide

affection N 爱 ài, 喜爱 xǐ'ài

affectionate ADJ 充满爱意的 chōngmǎn àiyì de

affidavit N 宣誓书 xuānshìshū, 法庭证词 fǎtíng zhèngcí

affiliate I N 附属机构 fùshǔ jīgòu II V 使附属 shǐ fùshǔ
an affiliated TV station to NBC 全国广播公司附属电视台 Quánguó Guǎngbō Gōngsī fùshǔ diànshìtái

affinity N 情投意合 qíngtóuyìhé, 生性喜好 shēngxìng xǐhào
affinity card/affinity credit card 爱心信用卡 àixīn xìnyòngkǎ

affirm V 确认 quèrèn, 断定 duàndìng

affirmative ADJ 肯定的 kěndìng de
an affirmative sentence 肯定句 kěndìng jù
affirmative action 积极措施 jījí cuòshī

affix V 使固定 shǐ gùdìng, 贴上 tiēshang

afflict V 使 [+病人] 经受痛苦 shǐ [+bìngrén] jīngshòu tòngkǔ, 折磨 zhémo
be afflicted with a disease 患上病 huànshang bìng

affliction N 痛苦 tòngkǔ, 折磨 zhémo

affluent ADJ 富裕的 fùyù de
affluent lifestyle 富裕的生活方式 fùyù de shēnghuó fāngshi

afford V 1 买得起 mǎideqǐ 2 …得起 …dé qǐ ■ *I can't afford to stay in a five-star hotel.* 我住不起五星级旅馆。 Wǒ zhùbuqǐ wǔxīngjí lǚguǎn.
cannot afford to offend sb 得罪不起某人 dézuì bùqǐ mǒurén

affordable ADJ 买得起的 mǎideqǐ de, 支付得起的 zhīfù dé qǐ de

affront N 侮辱性言行 wǔrǔ xìng yánxíng, 侮辱 wǔrǔ

afloat ADJ 资金周转良好的 zījīn zhōuzhuǎn liánghǎo de

afraid ADJ 1 怕 pà, 害怕 hàipà 2 恐怕 kǒngpà ■ *I'm afraid I can't help you.* 我恐怕帮不了你。 Wǒ kǒngpà bāngbuliǎo nǐ.

afresh ADV 重新 chóngxīn, 新 xīn

Africa N 非洲 Fēizhōu

African I ADJ 非洲的 Fēizhōu de II N 非洲人 Fēizhōu rén

African-American N 非洲裔美国人 Fēizhōuyì Měiguórén, 美国黑人 Měiguó hēirén

after I PREP, CONJ 在···以后 zài...yǐhòu ■ *After 6 p.m., you can reach me by cell phone.* 晚上六点以后你可以给我打手机。Wǎnshang liùdiǎn yǐhòu nǐ kěyǐ gěi wǒ dǎ shǒujī.
After you. 您先请。Nín xiān qǐng.
day after tomorrow 后天 hòutiān
after all 毕竟 bìjìng, 不管怎么说 bùguǎn zěnme shuō
II ADV 以后 yǐhòu
not long after 不久以后 bùjiǔ yǐhòu

after-effect N 后遗症 hòuyízhèng, 副作用 fùzuòyòng

afterlife N 来生 láishēng, 来世 láishì

aftermath N 后果 hòuguǒ, 余波 yúbō

afternoon N 下午 xiàwǔ

aftershave N 剃须后用的润肤油 tìxū hòu yòng de rùn fū yóu, 须后蜜 xūhòumì

aftertaste N 余味 yúwèi

afterthought N 事后的想法 shìhòu de xiǎngfǎ, 后来想起的事 hòulái xiǎngqǐ de shì

afterward, afterwards ADV 后来 hòulái

again ADV 又 yòu, 再 zài
Try it again! 再试一下! Zài shì yí xià!
again and again 一次又一次 yí cì yòu yí cì
now and again 常常 chángcháng

against PREP 反对 fǎnduì ■ *Many people in this region are against building another airport.* 这个地区许多人反对再建造一座飞机场。Zhè ge dìqū xǔduō rén fǎnduì zài jiànzào yí zuò fēijīchǎng.

age I N 1 年龄 niánlíng, 年纪 niánjì ■ *He is 14 years of age.* 他十四岁。Tā shísì suì.
at the age of 在···岁时 zài...suìshí ■ *My grandfather died at the age of 85.* 我的祖父在八十五岁时去世。Wǒ de zǔfù zài bāshí wǔ suì shí qùshì.
2 时代 shídài, 时期 shíqī
for ages 很长时间 hěn cháng shíjiān
II v 变老 biànlǎo

aged ADJ 年老的 niánlǎo de
the aged 老年人 lǎoniánrén

ageless ADJ 永不变老的 yǒngbú biànlǎo de, 永葆青春的 yǒngbǎoqīngchūn de

agency N （代理）公司 (dàilǐ) gōngsī
advertising agency 广告公司 guǎnggào gōngsī
dating agency 婚姻介绍所 hūnyīn jièshàosuǒ
employment agency 就业公司 jiùyè gōngsī, 职业介绍所 zhíyè jièshàosuǒ
travel agency 旅行社 lǚxíngshè

agenda N 1 会议议程 huìyì yìchéng 2 要做的事情 yào zuò de shìqing
high on the agenda 优先办的事情 yōuxiān

bàn de shìqing, 急需解决的问题 jíxū jiějué de wèntí
hidden agenda 隐秘的动机 yǐnmì de dòngjī, 不可告人的目的 bùkěgàorén de mùdì

agent N 1 代理人 dàilǐrén, 经纪人 jīngjìrén
real estate agent 房地产经纪商 fángdìchǎn jīngjì shāng
2 特工人员 tègōng rényuán
FBI agent 联邦调查局特工 liánbāng diàochájú tègōng

aggravate v 使恶化 shǐ èhuà, 加剧 jiājù

aggression N 侵略 qīnlüè

aggressive ADJ 1 侵略的 qīnlüè de 2 好斗的 hàodǒu de 3 有进取心的 yǒu jìnqǔxīn de, 冲劲十足的 chōng jìn shízú de

aggressor N 侵略者 qīnlüèzhě

aggrieved ADJ 深感委屈的 shēngǎn wěiqu de, 愤懑的 fènmèn de

aghast ADJ 吓呆了的 xiàdāile de, 大为震惊的 dàwéi zhènjīng de

agile ADJ 灵活的 línghuó de, 敏捷的 mǐnjié de

agitate v 煽动 shāndòng, 鼓动 gǔdòng

agitator N 鼓动者 gǔdòngzhě, 煽动者 shāndòngzhě

agnostic N 不可知论者 bùkězhīlùnzhě

ago ADV 前 qián, 以前 yǐqián

agonize v 痛苦 tòngkǔ, 苦恼 kǔnǎo
to agonize over sth 为 [+一项困难的决定] 苦恼 wéi [+yí xiàng kùnnan de juédìng] kǔnǎo, 难作决定 nán zuò juédìng

agonizing ADJ 极其痛苦的 jíqí tòngkǔ de, 极为苦恼的 jíwéi kǔnǎo de

agony N 剧烈的疼痛 jùliè de téngtòng, 痛苦 tòngkǔ
in agony 极其痛苦地 jíqí tòngkǔ de

agree v 1 同意 tóngyì 2 约定 yuēdìng, 决定 juédìng ■ *They agreed to disagree.* 他们决定各自保留不同意见。Tāmen juédìng gèzì bǎoliú bùtóngyì jiàn. 3 相符合 xiāngfú hé, 一致 yízhì
not to agree with sb 不对某人胃口 búduì mǒurén wèikǒu

agreeable ADJ 1 可以同意的 kěyǐ tóngyì de 2 讨人喜欢的 tǎorén xǐhuan de

agreement N 1 同意 tóngyì 2 协议 xiéyì

agriculture N 农业 nóngyè

ahead ADV 前面 qiánmian, 在前面 zài qiánmiàn ■ *Be prepared for bumpy roads ahead.* 准备好，前面道路不平。Zhǔnbèi hǎo, qiánmian dàolù bùpíng.
ahead of schedule 提前 tíqián

aid N, v 援助 yuánzhù, 帮助 bāngzhù ■ *We gave aid to the disaster area.* 我们援助受灾地区。Wǒmen yuánzhù shòuzāi dìqū.

aide N 助理人员 zhùlǐ rényuán, 助理 zhùlǐ, 助手 zhùshǒu

AIDS (= acquired immune deficiency syndrome) ABBREV 艾滋病 àizībìng
ailing ADJ 生病的 shēngbìng de
ailment N 小病 xiǎo bìng, 不舒服 bùshūfú
aim I v 1 打算 dǎsuan, 目标是 mù biāo shì 2 针对 zhēnduì 3 瞄准 miáozhǔn II N 目标 mùbiāo
  to take aim 瞄准 miáozhǔn
aimless ADJ 没有目标的 méiyǒu mùbiāo de, 没有目的的 méiyǒu mùdì de
ain't v 不 bù, 没有 méiyǒu
air I N 1 空气 kōngqì 2 空中 kōngzhōng, 天空 tiānkōng
  air crash 飞机坠落 fēijī zhuìluò
  air raid 空袭 kōngxí
  air strike 空中打击 kōngzhōng dǎjī, 空袭 kōngxí
  air time (广播电视) 播放时间 (guǎngbō diànshì) bōfàng shíjiān
  air travel 乘飞机旅行 chéngfēijī lǚxíng
  by air 坐飞机 zuò fēijī
  to be on air (电台) 正在广播 (diàntái) zhèng zài guǎngbō
II v 1 晾干 [+衣服] liànggān [+yīfu] 2 表达 [+意见] biǎodá [+yìjiàn]
airbag N 安全气囊 ānquán qìnáng
airbase N 空军基地 kōngjūn jīdì
airborne ADJ 1 在飞行中 zài fēixíng zhōng
  ■ Our plane is airborne now. 我们的飞机已经升空飞行。Wǒmende fēijī yǐjing shēngkōng fēixíng.
  2 空降的 kōngjiàng de
air conditioned ADJ 有空调装置的 yǒu kòng tiáo zhuāngzhì de
air conditioner N 空气调节器 kōngqì tiáojié qì, 空调器 kōngtiáoqì
air conditioning N 空调装置 kōngtiáo zhuāngzhì
airfare N 飞机票价 fēijī piàojià
airfield N (空军) 机场 (kōngjūn) jīchǎng
air force N 空军 kōngjūn
airhead N 笨蛋 bèndàn
airily ADV 轻率地 qīngshuài de, 轻浮地 qīngfú de
airless ADJ 空气不足的 kōngqì bùzú de, 不透气的 bútòuqì de
airline N 航空公司 hángkōng gōngsī [M. WD 家 jiā]
  Singapore Airlines 新加坡航空公司 Xīnjiāpō hángkōng gōngsī
  budget airline 廉价航空公司 liánjià hángkōng gōngsī
airliner N 班机 bānjī [M. WD 架 jià], 大型客机 dàxíng kèjī [M. WD 架 jià]
airmail N 航空邮件 hángkōng yóujiàn
airplane N 飞机 fēijī [M. WD 架 jià]
airport N 飞机场 fēijīchǎng [M. WD 座 zuò], 机场 jīchǎng [M. WD 座 zuò]
airspace N 领空 lǐngkōng
  Japanese airspace 日本领空 Rìběn lǐngkōng
airtight ADJ 密封的 mìfēng de

airwaves N 无线电波 wúxiàndiànbō
airy ADJ 通风良好的 tōngfēng liánghǎo de
aisle N 通道 tōngdào
  to walk down the aisle 结婚 jiéhūn
ajar ADJ (门) 微开的 (mén) wēi kāi de, 半开的 bàn kāi de
a.k.a. (= also known as) ABBREV 又名 yòumíng, 又叫 yòujiào
  Halsey, a.k.a. raging bull 海尔塞, 又名 "蛮牛" Hǎi'ěr sāi, yòumíng "mánniú"
akin ADJ 极为类似 jíwéi lèi sì
  akin to sth 和 (某物) 极为类似 hé (mǒu wù) jíwéi lèisì, 和 (某物) 十分相似 hé (mǒu wù) shífēn xiāngsì
à la carte ADJ (从菜单上) 点菜 (cóng càidān shàng) diǎncài
  to order à la carte 从菜单上点菜 cóng càidān shàng diǎncài
alacrity N 快捷 kuàijié
à la mode ADJ 加冰淇淋的 jiā bīngqílín de
alarm I N 1 警报 jǐngbào, 警报器 jǐngbàoqì 2 闹钟 nàozhōng 3 惊恐 jīngkǒng II v 警觉 jǐngjué
  alarm clock 闹钟 nàozhōng
  car alarm 汽车警报器 qìchē jǐngbàoqì
  false alarm 一场虚惊 yì cháng xūjīng
  to raise the alarm 发出警报 fāchū jǐngbào, 发出警告 fāchū jǐnggào
alarming ADJ 令人担忧的 lìng rén dānyōu de, 令人恐慌的 lìngrén kǒnghuāng de
alarmist ADJ 大惊小怪的 dàjīng xiǎoguài de, 危言耸听的 wēiyán sǒngtīng de
alas INTERJ 哎呀 āiyā
albino N 白化病病人 báihuàbìng bìngrén, 患白化病的动物 huàn báihuàbìng de dòngwù
album N 1 唱片 chàngpiàn [M. WD 张 zhāng], 音乐专辑 yīnyuè zhuānjí 2 照相簿 zhàoxiàngbù [M. WD 本 běn] 3 集邮册 jíyóucè [M. WD 本 běn]
alcohol N 酒 jiǔ, 酒精 jiǔjīng
  alcohol abuse 酗酒 xùjiǔ
alcoholic I ADJ 含有酒精的 hányǒu jiǔjīng de
  alcoholic beverage 含有酒精的饮料 hányǒu jiǔjīng de yǐnliào, 酒类 jiǔlèi
II N 酒鬼 jiǔguǐ, 酗酒者 xùjiǔzhě
alcoholism N 酒精中毒 jiǔjīng zhòngdú
alderman N 市政委员 shìzhèng wěiyuán, 市参议员 shì cānyìyuán
ale N 浓啤酒 nóngpíjiǔ, 麦芽酒 màiyá jiǔ
alert I ADJ 机敏的 jīmǐn de, 机警的 jījǐng de
II v 1 提醒 tíxǐng 2 发出警报 fāchū jǐngbào
III N 警report jǐngbào
  to be on the alert 保持警觉 bǎochí jǐngjué
algae N 藻 zǎo, 藻类 zǎolèi
algebra N 代数 dàishù
alias I ADV 又名 yòumíng, 又叫 yòujiào II N 化名 huàmíng, 假名 jiǎmíng

alibi N 不在犯罪现场的证明 búzài fànzuì xiànchǎng dízhèng míng [M. WD 份 fèn]

alien N **1** 外国人 wàiguórén, 侨民 qiáomín, (an illegal alien) 非法外侨 fēifǎ wàiqiáo **2** 外星人 wàixīngrén

alienate v **1** 离间 líjiàn, 使疏远 shǐ shūyuǎn **2** 转让 [+土地] zhuǎnràng [+tǔdì]

alight[1] ADJ 燃烧着的 ránshāozhe de

alight[2] v **1** 从 [+飞机／汽车上] 下来 cóng [+fēijī/qìchē shàng] xiàlai **2** [鸟+] 飞落 [niǎo+] fēi luò

align v **1** 与 [+大多数人] 一致 yǔ [+dàduōshù rén] yízhì **2** 使 [+车轮] 排成直线 shǐ [+chēlún] pái chéng zhíxiàn

alike I ADJ 相像 xiāngxiàng II ADV 同样 tóngyàng

alimony N (离婚) 赡养费 (líhūn) shànyǎngfèi [M. WD 笔 bǐ]

alive ADJ **1** 活着的 huózhāo de **2** 仍然存在的 réngrán cúnzài de
alive and well 活得好好的 huó dé hǎohǎode
to come alive 变得生动有趣 biàn dé shēngdòng yǒuqù
to be alive with 充满了… chōngmǎn le…

alkali N 碱 jiǎn

alkaline ADJ 含有碱的 hányǒu jiǎn de

all I ADJ 所有的 suǒyǒu de, 全部的 quánbù de II ADV 完全 wánquán ■ *I'm all for the plan.* 我完全赞成这个计划。Wǒ wánquán zànchéng zhè ge jìhuà. III PRON 全部 quánbù, 一切 yíqiè
all along 一直 yìzhí
all-around 全能的 quánnéng de
all right 行 xíng, 可以 kěyǐ
all the time 总是 zǒngshì, 老是 lǎoshi
at all 根本 gēnběn

Allah N 真主 Zhēnzhǔ, 安拉 Ānlā

all-American ADJ **1** 典型美国式的 diǎnxíng Měiguó shì de **2** 全美大学最佳运动员 quán Měi dàxué zuìjiā yùndòngyuán

allay v 减轻 jiǎnqīng
to allay suspicion 减轻怀疑 jiǎnqīng huáiyí

allegation N 指控 zhǐkòng
allegation of tax evasion 逃税的指控 táoshuì de zhǐkòng

allege v 指控 zhǐkòng, 声称 shēngchēng

alleged ADJ 被指控的 bèi zhǐkòng de, 有嫌疑的 yǒu xiányí de

allegiance N 效忠 xiàozhōng, 忠诚 zhōngchéng
to pledge allegiance to 向…宣誓效忠 xiàng… xuānshì xiàozhōng

allegory N 寓言 yùyán [M. WD 则 zé]

allergic ADJ 过敏的 guòmǐn de
an allergic reaction 过敏反应 guòmǐnfǎnyìng
to be allergic to 对…过敏 duì…guòmǐn

allergy N 过敏 guòmǐn, 过敏反应 guòmǐnfǎnyìng

alleviate v 缓解 huǎnjiě, 减轻 jiǎnqīng
to alleviate hardship for the rural poor 减轻

农村贫穷人口的艰难生活 jiǎnqīng nóngcūn pínqióng rénkǒu de jiānnán shēnghuó

alley N 小巷 xiǎoxiàng [M. WD 条 tiáo]

alliance N 联盟 liánméng, 同盟 tóngméng

allied ADJ **1** 结盟的 jiéméng de **2** 有关联的 yǒuguān lián de

alligator N (短吻) 鳄鱼 (duǎnwěn) èyú [M. WD 条 tiáo]

all-inclusive ADJ 全部包括的 quánbù bāokuò de, 费用全包的 fèiyòng quán bāo de

allocate v 分配 fēnpèi, 拨给 bōgěi
to allocate 200,000 dollars for a literacy program 拨给扫盲计划二十万美元 bō gěi sǎománg jìhuà èrshí wàn Měiyuán

allocation N **1** 分配 fēnpèi, 拨款 bōkuǎn **2** 配给量 pèijǐ liáng

allot v 分配 fēnpèi, 配给 pèijǐ
to allot 10 minutes for a quiz 安排十分钟做小测验 ānpái shífēn zhōng zuò xiǎo cèyàn

allow v 允许 yǔnxǔ, 准许 zhǔnxǔ ■ *You're not allowed to photocopy so many pages from a book.* 不允许从一本书中复印这么多页数。Bù yǔnxǔ cóng yì běn shū zhōng fùyìn zhème duō yèshù. Allow me! 让我来帮你! Ràng wǒ lái bāng nǐ!

allowance N **1** 限额 xiàn'é
baggage allowance 行李限重 xíngli xiàn zhòng **2** [住房+] 津贴 [zhùfáng+] jīntiē, [旅差+] 补助 [lǚchà+] bǔzhù

alloy N 合金 héjīn

allude v 暗指 ànzhǐ, 影射 yǐngshè

allure N 诱惑 yòuhuò, 魅力 mèilì, 吸引力 xīyǐnlì

allusion N **1** 暗指 ànzhǐ, 影射 yǐngshè **2** [文学+] 典故 [wénxué+] diǎngù

ally I N 盟国 méngguó, 盟友 méngyǒu II v 与…结盟 yǔ…jiéméng
to ally oneself with 与…结盟 yǔ…jiéméng, 与…联手 yǔ…liánshǒu

alma mater N 母校 mǔxiào

almanac N 历书 lìshū, 年鉴 niánjiàn

almighty ADJ 全能的 (上帝) quánnéng de (Shàngdì)
Almighty God 全能的上帝 quánnéng de Shàngdì

almond N 杏仁 xìngrén [M. WD 颗 kē]

almost ADV 几乎 jīhū, 差不多 chàbuduō

alms N 救济品 jiùjì pǐn, 施舍 shīshě

aloft ADV 在高处 zài gāo chù

alone ADJ 单独的 dāndú de, 孤独的 gūdú de
Leave me alone. 让我一个人待着。Ràng wǒ yí gè rén dāizhe. 别管我! Bié guǎn wǒ!
to go it alone 独自干 dúzì gàn, 单干 dāngàn

along PREP 沿着 yánzhe

alongside ADV **1** 在一起 zài yìqǐ **2** 靠着 kàozhe

aloof ADJ 冷淡的 lěngdàn de
to stay aloof from 远离 yuǎnlí, 不参与 bù cānyù

aloud ADV 大声地 dàshēng de

alphabet N 字母表 zìmǔ biǎo, 字母 zìmǔ

alphabetical ADJ 按照字母顺序的 ànzhào zìmǔ shùnxù de

already ADV 已经 yǐjīng

also ADV 也 yě ■ *He not only speaks Mandarin fluently, but also speaks Cantonese quite well.* 他不但普通话说得很流利，广东话也说得挺好。Tā búdàn Pǔtōnghuà shuóde hěn liúlì, Guǎngdōnghuà yě shuóde tǐng hǎo.

altar N 祭台 jìtái

altar boy 祭台助手 jìtái zhùshǒu

alter V 改 gǎi, 改变 gǎibiàn

alteration N 改变 gǎibiàn, 变动 biàndòng

alternate I V 轮流 lúnliú, 交替 jiāotì II ADJ 1 轮流的 lúnliú de, 交替的 jiāotì de 2 候补的 [+委员] hòubǔ de [+wěiyuán], 后备的 [+球员] hòubèi de [+qiúyuán]

alternative I ADJ 另一个 lìng yí ge, 可选择的 kě xuǎnzé de

alternative medicine 另类医药 lìnglèi yīyào II N 选择 ■ *You have no alternative in this case.* 这件事你没有选择余地。(→ 这件事你只能这么做。) Zhè jiàn shì nǐ méiyǒu xuǎnzé yúdì. (→ Zhè jiàn shì nǐ zhǐ néng zhème zuò.)

to have no alternative but ... 没有别的办法 méiyǒu biéde bànfǎ, 只能 zhǐ néng

although CONJ 虽然 suīrán

altitude N 高度 gāodù, 海拔 hǎibá

alto N 女低音 (歌唱家) nǚdīyīn (gēchàngjiā)

altogether ADV 一共 yígòng, 总共 zǒnggòng

altruism N 利他主义 lìtāzhǔyì

aluminum (AI) N 铝 lǚ

always ADV 总是 zǒngshì, 一直 yìzhí, 一向 yíxiàng ■ *He is always polite.* 他总是很有礼貌。Tā zǒngshì hěn yǒulǐmào.

am V See be

amalgamate V 合并 hébìng, 联合 liánhé

amass V 积聚 jījù, 积累 jīlěi

amateur I ADJ 业余的 yèyú de II N 1 业余爱好者 yèyú àihàozhě 2 生手 shēngshǒu

amaze V 使…十分惊奇 shǐ…shífēn jīngqí

amazed ADJ 惊奇的 jīngqí de, 感到惊奇的 gǎndào jīngqí de

amazement N 惊奇 jīngqí

amazing ADJ 令人惊奇的 lìngrén jīngqí de, 令人惊讶的 lìngrén jīngyà de

ambassador N 大使 dàshǐ [M. WD 位 wèi]

the Chinese ambassador to the U.S. 中国驻美国大使 Zhōngguó zhù Měiguó dàshǐ

ambiguity N 含义不清 hányì bùqīng

ambiguous ADJ 含义不清的 hányì bùqīng de, 模棱两可的 móléngliǎngkě de

ambition N 雄心 xióngxīn, 抱负 bàofù

ambitious ADJ 有雄心的 yǒu xióngxīn de, 有抱负的 yǒu bàofù de

ambivalent ADJ 内心矛盾的 nèixīn máodùn de

amble V 慢慢地走 mànmàn de zǒu

ambulance N 救护车 jiùhùchē [M. WD 辆 liàng]

ambush N, V 伏击 fújī

ameliorate V 改善 gǎishàn, 改进 gǎijìn

amen INTERJ 阿门 āmén

Amen to that. 同意 tóngyì, 赞成 zànchéng

amenable ADJ 愿意听从的 yuànyì tīngcóng de, 顺从的 shùncóng de

to be amenable to a compromise 愿意妥协 yuànyì tuǒxié

amend V 修正 xiūzhèng, 修改 xiūgǎi

amendment N 1 修正 xiūzhèng, 修改 xiūgǎi 2 修正案 xiūzhèng'àn

amends N 道歉 dàoqiàn, 赔偿 péicháng

to make amends 道歉 dàoqiàn, 赔偿 péicháng

amenities N 公益设施 gōngyì shèshī

American I ADJ 美国的 Měiguó de, 美洲的 Měizhōu de II N 美国人 Měiguórén

American Indian, Amerindian 美洲印第安人 Měizhōu Yìndì'ānrén

Americanism N 美式英语 Měishì Yīngyǔ, 美式英语的词语 Měishì Yīngyǔ de cíyǔ

Americanization N 美国化 Měiguó huà

Americas N (南北) 美洲 (Nán-Běi) Měizhōu

amiable ADJ 友好的 yǒuhǎo de, 亲切友好的 qīnqiè yǒuhǎo de

amicable ADJ 友好的 yǒuhǎo de, 和睦的 hémù de

an amicable out-of-court settlement 法庭外友好和解 fǎtíng wài yǒuhǎo héjiě

amid PREP 在…中间 zài…zhōngjiān

amiss ADJ 有差错的 yǒu chācuò de

to see something amiss 发现有差错 fāxiàn yǒu chācuò, 发现有问题 fāxiàn yǒu wèntí

ammunition N 弹药 dànyào

amnesia N 1 记忆丧失 jìyì sàngshī 2 健忘 jiànwàng, 健忘症 jiànwàngzhèng

amnesty N 赦免 shèmiǎn, 不予追究 bùyǔ zhuījiù

Amnesty International 国际大赦 guójì dàshè

among PREP 在…中间 zài…zhōngjiān

amoral ADJ 不道德的 bú dàodé de

amorous ADJ 色情的 sèqíng de, 男女情爱的 nánnǚ qíng'ài de

amorphous ADJ 不定形的 búdìngxíng de

amount N 数量 shùliàng

amphetamine N 安非他明 ānfēitāmíng

amphibian N 水陆两栖动物 shuǐlù liǎngqīdòngwù

amphibious ADJ 水陆两栖的 shuǐlù liǎngqī de, 水陆两用的 shuǐlùliǎngyòng de

amphitheater N 圆形露天剧场 yuánxíng lùtiānjùchǎng [M. WD 座 zuò], 圆形露天竞技场 yuánxíng lùtiān jìngjìchǎng [M. WD 座 zuò]

ample ADJ 充足的 chōngzú de

amplifier N 扩音器 kuòyīnqì, 扬声器 yángshēngqì

amplify v 放大 fàngdà

amputate v 切除 [+脚趾] qiēchú [+jiǎozhǐ], 截肢 jiézhī

amputee N 被截肢者 bèi jiézhī zhě

amuse v 使…快乐 shǐ…kuàilè, 让…高兴 ràng…gāoxìng

amusement N 娱乐 yúlè
amusement park 娱乐场 yúlè chǎng

amusing ADJ 好笑的 hǎoxiào de, 好玩的 hǎowán de ■ *I don't find the practical joke amusing.* 我觉得这个恶作剧没有什么好玩。Wǒ juéde zhè ge èzuòjù méiyǒu shénme hǎowán.

an See a

anachronism N 1 不合时代的人（事）bùhé shídài de rén (shì) 2 年代错乱 niándài cuòluàn

anal ADJ 1 肛门的 gāngmén de 2 吹毛求疵的 chuī máo qiú cī de

analgesic N 止痛药 zhǐtòngyào [M. WD 片 piàn/粒 lì]

analogous ADJ 类似的 lèisì de, 相似的 xiāngsì de

analogy N 类比 lèibǐ, 类似 lèisì

analysis N 分析 fēnxī ■ *They did a thorough analysis of the market.* 他们对市场情况作了彻底分析。Tāmen duì shìchǎng qíngkuàng zuòle chèdǐ fēnxī.

analyst N 分析员 fēnxī yuán
stock market analyst 股票市场分析员 gǔpiào shìchǎng fēnxī yuán

analytic, analytical ADJ 分析的 fēnxī de
analytic chemistry 分析化学 fēnxīhuàxué

analyze v 分析 fēnxī

anarchy N 混乱状态 hùnluàn zhuàngtài, 无政府状态 wúzhèngfǔ zhuàngtài

anatomy N 1 解剖 jiěpōu 2 解剖学 jiěpōuxué 3 解剖构造 jiěpōu gòuzào

ancestor N 1 祖先 zǔxiān, 祖宗 zǔzōng 2 原型 yuánxíng

ancestry N 祖先 zǔxiān, 祖宗 zǔzōng

anchor I N 1（船）锚 (chuán) máo 2 电视新闻节目主持人 diànshì xīnwén jiémù zhǔchírén 3 精神支柱 jīngshén zhīzhù II v 1 抛锚 pāomáo, 停船 tíngchuán 2 主持电视节目 zhǔchí diànshì jiémù 3 扎根于 zhāgēn yú 4 支持 zhīchí
anchorman 男电视节目主持人 nán diànshì jiémù zhǔchírén

anchorage N 船舶停泊处 chuánbó tíngbóchù, 锚地 máodì

ancient ADJ 古代的 gǔdài de

and CONJ 1 和 hé, 以及 yǐjí 2 然后 ránhòu 3 而且 érqiě ■ *The teacher assigned the homework last week, and she reminded us of this the day before yesterday.* 老师上星期布置了作业，而且前天还提醒过我们。Lǎoshī shàng xīngqī bùzhìle zuòyè, érqiě qiántiān hái tíxǐngguo wǒmen.

android N（似人的）机器人 (sì rén de) jīqìrén

anecdotal ADJ 趣闻轶事的 qùwén yìshi de

anecdote N 趣闻轶事 qùwén yìshi

anemia N 贫血 pínxuè, 贫血症 pínxuèzhèng

anesthesia N 1 麻醉 mázuì, 麻醉法 mázuìfǎ 2 麻醉状态 mázuì zhuàngtài

anesthetic N 麻醉剂 mázuìjì

anesthetist N 麻醉师 mázuìshī

anesthetize v 进行麻醉 jìnxíng mázuì

anew ADV 重新 chóngxīn
to start life anew 开始新生活 kāishǐ xīn shēnghuó

angel N 天使 tiānshǐ

anger N 愤怒 fènnù

angle N 角 jiǎo, 角度 jiǎodù

Anglican N 英国圣公会教徒 Yīngguó Shènggōnghuì jiàotú

angling N 钓鱼 diàoyú, 垂钓 chuídiào

angry ADJ 愤怒 fènnù, 生气 shēngqì

angst N 深切的忧虑 shēnqiè de yōulǜ

anguish N 极度痛苦 jídù tòngkǔ, 极度焦虑 jídù jiāolǜ

angular ADJ 1 骨瘦如柴的 [+老人] qǔ shòu rú chái de [+lǎorén] 2 有尖角的 [+图案] yǒu jiān jiǎo de [+tú'àn]

animal N 动物 dòngwù
party animal 喜欢参加社交聚会的人 xǐhuan cānjiā shèjiāo jùhuì de rén

animate I v 使 [+一幅画] 有生气 shǐ [+yì fú huà] yǒushēngqì II ADJ 有生命的 yǒushēng mìng de, 活的 huó de

animated ADJ 1 动画的 dònghuà de
an animated cartoon 动画片 dònghuàpiàn 2 活跃的 [+讨论] huóyuè de [+tǎolùn]

animation N 动画片制作 dònghuàpiàn zhìzuò

animosity N 仇恨 chóuhèn, 深深的敌意 shēnshēn de díyì

ankle N 踝 huái, 踝骨 huáigǔ

annals N 历史记载 lìshǐ jìzǎi

annex[1] v 并吞 bìngtūn, 兼并 jiānbìng

annex[2] N 附属建筑 fùshǔ jiànzhù

annihilate v 彻底消灭 chèdǐ xiāomiè, 彻底摧毁 chèdǐ cuīhuǐ

annihilation N 彻底消灭 chèdǐ xiāomiè, 彻底摧毁 chèdǐ cuīhuǐ

anniversary N [结婚+] 周年 [jiéhūn+] zhōunián, 纪念日 jìniànrì ■ *In 2006 we celebrated the 250th anniversary of the birth of the great Austrian musician Wolfgang Amadeus Mozart.* 在二〇〇六年，我们庆祝奥地利大音乐家莫扎特诞生二百五十周年。Zài èrlínglìngliù nián, wǒmen qìngzhù Àodìlì dà yīnyuèjiā Mòzhātè dànshēng èrbǎi wǔshí zhōunián.

announce v 宣布 xuānbù, 宣告 xuāngào

announcement N 告示 gàoshi, 启事 qǐshì
■ *The announcement of the new tax policy*

caused widespread concern. 新税收政策的宣布引起了广泛的关注。Xīn shuìshōu zhèngcè de xuānbù yǐnqǐle guǎngfàn de guānzhù.

birth announcement 出生启事 chūshēng qǐshì

wedding announcement 结婚启事 jiéhūn qǐshì

announcer N 播音员 bōyīnyuán

annoy V 使 [+人] 恼怒 shǐ [+rén] nǎonù, 使 [+人] 生气 shǐ [+rén] shēngqì ■ *She said that just to annoy me.* 她这么说就是要让我生气。Tā zhème shuō jiùshì yào ràng wǒ shēngqì.

annoyance N 恼怒 nǎonù, 生气 shēngqì

annoyed ADJ (感到) 恼怒 (gǎndào) nǎonù

annoying ADJ 使人恼怒的 shǐrén nǎonù de

annual I ADJ 每年的 měinián de, 年度的 [+全体会议] niándù de [+quántǐ huìyì] II N 一年生植物 yìniánshēng zhíwù

annuity N [优厚的+] 年金 [yōuhòu de+] niánjīn

annul V 解除 jiěchú, 废止 fèizhǐ

anomalous ADJ 异常的 yìcháng de, 反常的 fǎncháng de

anomaly N 异常 yìcháng, 反常 fǎncháng

anonymity N 匿名 nìmíng

anonymous ADJ 匿名的 nìmíng de

an anonymous phone call 匿名电话 nìmíng diànhuà

anorexia N 厌食症 yànshízhèng

anorexic ADJ 厌食的 yàn shí de

another PRON 1 又一 (个) yòu yí (ge), 再一 (个) zàiyí (ge) 2 另一 (个) lìng yí (ge), 别的 bié de

answer I V 1 回答 huídá ■ *I tried my best to answer his questions.* 我尽量回答他的问题。Wǒ jǐnliàng huídá tā de wèntí. 2 回应 huíyìng ■ *She thought her prayer had been answered.* 她认为她的祈祷得到了回应。Tā rènwéi tā de qídǎo dédàole huíyìng.

to answer a letter 回信 huíxìn

to answer the door 开门 kāimén

to answer the telephone 接电话 jiē diànhuà

II N 回答 huídá, 答案 dá'àn

answering machine 电话自动答录机 diànhuà zìdòng dá lù jī

answerable ADJ 必须承担责任的 bìxū chéngdān zérèn de, 对…负责的 duì…fùzé de

ant N 蚂蚁 mǎyǐ [M. WD 只 zhī]

antagonism N 敌对 díduì, 对抗 duìkàng

antagonist N 敌手 díshǒu, 对手 duìshǒu

antagonistic ADJ 对抗的 duìkàng de, 敌对的 díduì de

antagonize V 使…愤怒 shǐ…fènnù, 和…对抗 hé…duìkàng

Antarctic N 南极 Nánjí

Antarctica N 南极洲 Nánjízhōu, 南极大陆 Nánjí dàlù

ante N 赌注 dǔzhù

to up/raise the ante 增加赌注 zēngjiā dǔzhù

antecedent N 以前类似的事 yǐqián lèisì de shì [M. WD 件 jiàn], 前例 qiánlì

antechamber N [主人卧室的+] 前厅 [zhǔrén wòshì de+] qiántīng

antedate V 发生在…以前 fāshēng zài…yǐqián, 先于 xiānyú

antelope N 羚羊 língyáng [M. WD 只 zhī/头 tóu]

antenna N 天线 tiānxiàn

anteroom N 前室 qiánshì, 接待室 jiēdàishì

anthem N 赞歌 zàngē [M. WD 首 shǒu]

national anthem 国歌 guógē [M. WD 首 shǒu]

anthill N 蚁丘 yǐqiū

anthology N 选集 xuǎnjí

anthropology N 人类学 rénlèixué

antiaircraft ADJ 防空的 fángkōng de

antiaircraft missile 防空导弹 fángkōng dǎodàn

antibiotic N 抗生素 kàngshēngsù

antibody N 抗体 kàngtǐ

anticipate V 预期 yùqí, 预料 yùliào

anticipation N 预期 yùqí, 预料 yùliào

anticlimax N 远远没有预期好的情况 yuǎnyuǎn méiyǒu yùqí hǎode qíngkuàng, 令人扫兴的事 lìngrén sǎoxìng de shì

antics N 可笑的举动 kěxiào de jǔdòng

antidepressant N 抗忧郁药 kàngyōuyùyào

antidote N 解毒药 jiě dúyào

antifreeze N 防冻剂 fángdòngjì

antipathy N 强烈的反感 qiángliè de fǎngǎn

antiperspirant N 止汗剂 zhǐ hàn jì

antiquated ADJ 老式的 lǎoshì de, 过时的 guòshí de

antique N 古董 gǔdǒng, 古玩 gǔwán

antique dealer 古董商人 gǔdǒngshāng rén

antiquity N 1 古代 gǔdài 2 古建筑 gǔ jiànzhù, 文物 wénwù

anti-Semitism N 反犹太主义 fǎn yóutàizhǔyì

antiseptic N 消毒药品 xiāodúyào pǐn, 防腐剂 fángfǔjì

antisocial ADJ 1 反社会的 fǎn shèhuì de 2 不合群的 bùhé qún de

antithesis N 完全相反的人（事）wánquán xiāngfǎn de rén (shì)

antitrust ADJ 反垄断的 fǎn lǒngduàn de

antler N 鹿角 lùjiǎo [M. WD 只 zhī]

antonym N 反义词 fǎnyìcí

anus N 肛门 gāngmén

anvil N 铁砧 tiězhēn

anxiety N 焦虑 jiāolù

anxious ADJ 焦虑 jiāolù, 非常担忧 fēicháng dānyōu

any I ADJ 什么 shénme, 任何 rènhé II ADV 一点儿 yìdiǎnr ■ *I'm too tired to go any further.* 我太累了, 走不动了。Wǒ tài lèi le, zǒubudòng le. III PRON 哪个 nǎ ge, 哪些 nǎ xiē

anybody PRON 任何人 rènhénrén, 谁 shéi ■ *Has anybody seen my keys?* 谁看见我的钥匙了? Shéi kànjiàn wǒ de yàoshi le?

anyhow ADV 不管怎么 bùguǎn zěnme, 无论如何 wúlùn rúhé

anymore ADV 再 zài
not anymore 不再 búzài

anyone PRON 任何人 rènhé rén, 谁 shéi

anyplace ADV 任何地方 rènhé dìfang

anything PRON 任何事 rènhé shì, 什么事 shénme shì ■ *Is there anything I can do for you?* 能为你做什么事吗? Néng wèi nǐ zuò shénme shì ma?

anyway ADV 不管怎么说 bùguǎn zěnme shuō, 反正 fǎnzhèng

anywhere ADV 任何地方 rènhé dìfang, 无论哪里 wúlùn nǎlǐ ■ *I can meet you anywhere.* 我可以在任何地方和你见面。(→我在哪里跟你见面都行。) Wǒ kěyǐ zài rènhé dì fang hé nǐ jiànmiàn. (→Wǒ zài nǎlǐ gēn nǐ jiànmiàn dōu xíng.)

apart ADV 1 相隔 xiānggé 2 分开 fēnkāi, 隔离 gélí
apart from 除了 chúle

apartheid N (南非的)种族隔离制度 (Nánfēi de) zhǒngzú gélí zhìdù

apartment N 一套房间 yí tào fángjiān, 公寓 gōngyù [m. wo 套 tào]
apartment building 公寓大楼 gōngyù dàlóu
apartment complex 住宅小区 zhùzhái xiǎoqū

apathetic ADJ 不感兴趣的 bù gǎn xìngqù de, 冷淡的 lěngdàn de

apathy N 冷淡 lěngdàn, 麻木 mámù

ape I N 猿 yuán [m. wo 只 zhī] II v 模仿 mófǎng

aperitif N 开胃酒 kāiwèijiǔ

aperture N 孔 kǒng, 洞 dòng

apex N 顶点 dǐngdiǎn, 最高点 zuìgāo diǎn

aphorism N 警句 jǐngjù, 格言 géyán [m. wo 句 jù]

aphrodisiac N 激发性欲的药 jīfā xìngyù de yào, 春药 chūnyào

apiece ADV 每一个 měi yí gè, 每个 měige

aplomb N 自信 zìxìn, 自信力 zìxìn lì

apocalypse N 世界末日 shìjiè mòrì, 巨大灾难 jùdà zāinàn

apolitical ADJ 非政治的 fēi zhèngzhì de

apologetic ADJ 道歉的 dàoqiàn de, 有歉意的 yǒu qiànyì de

apologize v 道歉 dàoqiàn, 认错 rèncuò

apology N 道歉 dàoqiàn, 歉意 qiànyì

apoplexy N 中风 zhòngfēng

apostle N 耶稣基督的门徒 Yēsū Jīdū de méntú, 传道者 chuándào zhě

apostrophe N 撇号 piēhào (')

appall v 使…大为震惊 shǐ…dàwéi zhènjīng, 使…深感痛恨 shǐ…shēngǎn tònghèn
to be appalled 感到震惊 gǎndào zhènjīng, 感到极大的愤怒 gǎndào jídà de fènnù

appalling ADJ 1 坏极了 huài jíle, 糟糕透了 zāogāo tòu le 2 极其可怕 jíqí kěpà

apparatus N 器械 qìxiè, 设备 shèbèi

apparel N 服装 fúzhuāng, 服饰 fúshì

ready-to-wear apparel 现成时装 xiànchéng shízhuāng, 成衣 chéngyī

apparent ADJ 明显 míngxiǎn, 明白 míngbai

apparently ADV 明显地 míngxiǎn de, 显然地 xiǎnrán de

apparition N 鬼(魂) guǐ (hún)

appeal v 1 呼吁 hūyù, 请求 qǐngqiú 2 有吸引力 yǒu xīyǐnlì, 使…感兴趣 shǐ…gǎn xìngqu ■ *The idea of skiing in Switzerland appeals to me.* 去瑞士滑雪，对我很有吸引力。Qù Ruìshì huáxuě, duì wǒ hěn yǒu xīyǐnlì.

appealing ADJ 让人感动的 ràng rén gǎndòng de

appear v 1 看来 kànlái, 好像 hǎoxiàng ■ *She appeared to be worried.* 她好像很担心。Tā hǎoxiàng hěn dānxīn. 2 出现 chūxiàn

appearance N 1 外貌 wàimào 2 出现 chūxiàn ■ *The sudden appearance of two policemen in the bar made everyone uncomfortable.* 酒吧里突然出现两个警察，让大家感到不舒服。Jiǔbā lǐ tūrán chūxiàn liǎng ge jǐngchá, ràng dàjiā gǎndào bù shūfu.

appease v 平息 píngxī

append v 附上 fùshàng, 附加 fùjiā

appendage N 附加物 fùjiā wù

appendicitis N 阑尾炎 lánwěiyán, 盲肠炎 mángchángyán

appendix N 1 附录 fùlù 2 阑尾 lánwěi, 盲肠 mángcháng

appetite N 胃口 wèikǒu

appetizer N 开胃菜 kāiwèicài [m. wo 道 dào]

appetizing ADJ 开胃的 kāiwèi de

applaud v 鼓掌 gǔzhǎng

applause N 掌声 zhǎngshēng

apple N 苹果 píngguǒ [m. wo 只 zhī]
apple pie 苹果馅饼 píngguǒ xiànbǐng

appliance N 1 器具 qìjù 2 家用电器 jiāyòng diànqì

applicable ADJ 生效的 shēngxiào de, 有效的 yǒuxiào de

applicant N 申请人 shēnqǐngrén

application N 1 申请 shēnqǐng 2 申请书 shēnqǐngshū, 申请表 shēnqǐng biǎo

applied ADJ 应用的 yìngyòng de, 实用的 shíyòng de
allied chemistry 应用化学 yìngyònghuàxué

apply v 1 申请 [+工作／签证] shēnqǐng [+gōngzuò/qiānzhèng] 2 运用 [+新技术] yùnyòng [+xīn jìshù], 适用 shìyòng 3 涂 [+一层油漆] tú [+yì céng yóu qī]

appoint v 1 任命 rènmìng, 委派 wěipài 2 约定 yuēdìng, 指定 zhǐdìng

appointment N 1 (朋友的)约会 (péngyoude) yuēhuì [m. wo 次 cì] 2 (医生的)预约 yùyuē 3 (职务)任命 (zhíwù) rènmìng, 委任 wěirèn

apportion v 分配 fēnpèi, 分摊 fēntān

appraisal N 估价 gūjià, 鉴定 jiàndìng

appraise v 估价 gūjià, 鉴定 jiàndìng

appreciate v 1 感谢 gǎnxiè, 领情 lǐngqíng 2 理解 lǐjiě 3 [房产+] 增值 [fángchǎn+] zēngzhí

appreciation N 1 感谢 gǎnxiè 2 理解 lǐjiě, 欣赏 xīnshǎng 3 增值 zēngzhí

appreciative ADJ 1 感激的 gǎnji de 2 理解的 lǐjiě de

apprehend v 逮捕 dàibǔ, 拘捕 jūbǔ

apprehension N 1 逮捕 dàibǔ, 拘捕 jūbǔ 2 担忧 dānyōu

apprehensive ADJ 担忧的 dānyōu de, 忧虑的 yōulǜ de

apprentice I N 学徒 xuétú, 徒弟 túdi II v 当学徒 dāng xuétú

apprenticeship N 学徒期 xuétúqī

apprise v 正式通知 zhèngshì tōngzhī, 通告 tōnggào

approach I v 1 走近 zǒujìn, [新年+] 临近 [xīn-nián+] línjìn 2 接近 [+去年的水平] jiējìn [+qùnián de shuǐpíng] 3 与 [+政府部门] 交涉 yǔ [+zhèngfǔ bùmén] jiāoshè 4 处理 [+问题] chǔlǐ [+wèntí], 对付 duìfu II N 1 [教学+] 方法 [jiàoxué+] fāngfǎ 2 要求 yāoqiú, 请求 qǐngqiú 3 通道 tōngdào, 入口 rùkǒu 4 来临 láilín
to make approaches 主动接近 zhǔdòng jiējìn, 求爱 qiú'ài

approachable ADJ 1 可接近的 kě jiējìn de 2 可亲近的 kěqīn jìn de

approbation N 1 批准 pīzhǔn 2 称赞 chēngzàn

appropriate[1] ADJ 适合的 héshì de, 适合 shìhé

appropriate[2] v 1 [局长+] 挪用 [júzhǎng+] nuó yòng 2 [政府+] 拨款 [zhèngfǔ+] bōkuǎn

approval N 批准 pīzhǔn, 同意 tóngyì

approve v 1 批准 pīzhǔn
to approve of 赞成 zànchéng

approximate I ADJ 大约的 dàyuē de II v 近似 jìnsì, 接近 jiējìn

approximately ADV 大约 dàyuē

apricot N 杏 xìng [M. WD 只 zhī], 杏子 xìngzi [M. WD 只 zhī]

April N 四月 sìyuè

April Fool's Day N 愚人节 Yúrénjié

apron N 围裙 wéiqún [M. WD 条 tiáo]

apt ADJ 恰当的 qiàdàng de
apt to 容易…的 róngyì…de

aptitude N [学语言的+] 才能 [xuéyǔ yán de+] cáinéng, 能力 nénglì

aptitude test N 能力测验 nénglì cèyàn

aquarium N 水族馆 shuǐzúguǎn [M. WD 座 zuò]

Aquarius N 宝瓶宫 Bǎopínggōng

aquatic ADJ 水生的 shuǐshēng de
an aquatic product 水产品 shuǐchǎnpǐn

aqueduct N 高架渠 gāo jià qú [M. WD 道 dào/条 tiáo], 渡槽 dùcáo [M. WD 道 dào/条 tiáo]

Arabic I ADJ 阿拉伯的 Ālābó de

Arabic numeral 阿拉伯数字 Ālābó shùzì
II N 阿拉伯语 Ālābóyǔ

arable ADJ 可以耕种的 kěyǐ gēngzhòng de
arable land 可耕地 kěgēngdì

arbiter N 仲裁人 zhōng cáirén, 公断人 gōngduànrén

arbitrary ADJ 主观武断的 zhǔguān wǔduàn de
an arbitrary decision 主观武断的决定 zhǔguān wǔduàn de juédìng

arbitrate v 进行仲裁 jìnxíng zhòngcái, 作出公断 zuòchū gōngduàn

arbitration N 仲裁 zhòngcái, 公断 gōngduàn
to be settled by arbitration 通过仲裁得到解决 tōngguò zhòngcái dédào jiějué

arc N 弧线 húxiàn, 弧形 húxíng

arcade N 拱廊 gǒng láng [M. WD 条 tiáo]

arch I N 拱门 gǒngmén [M. WD 座 zuò], 拱顶 gǒngdǐng II v 使成弓形 shǐchéng gōngxíng, 拱起 gǒng qǐ

archaic ADJ 1 古老的 gǔlǎo de 2 古体的 gǔtǐ de, 不通用的 bù tōngyòng de
an archaic word 古词 gǔ cí, 古语 gǔyǔ

archbishop N 大主教 dàzhǔjiào

archeology, archaeology N 考古 kǎogǔ, 考古学 kǎogǔxué

archipelago N 群岛 qúndǎo

architect N 建筑师 jiànzhùshī
landscape architect 园林设计师 yuánlín shèjìshī

architecture N 建筑学 jiànzhùxué
marine architecture 造船学 zàochuánxué

archive N 档案 dàng'àn
archives 档案馆 dàng'ànguǎn

archway N 拱道 gǒngdào

Arctic N 北极 Běijí, 北极区 Běijíqū

ardent ADJ 热情的 [+支持] rèqíng de [+zhīchí], 热烈的 rèliè de

ardor N 热情 rèqíng, 激情 jīqíng

arduous ADJ 艰巨的 jiānjù de, 艰难的 jiānnán de

are See be

area N 1 地区 dìqū 2 面积 miànjī
area code 分区电话号码 fēnqū diànhuà hàomǎ

arena N 1 室内运动场 shìnèiyùndòng chǎng 2 (搏斗) 场所 (bódòu) chǎngsuǒ

arguable ADJ 1 有疑问的 yǒu yíwèn de 2 有论据的 yǒu lùnjù de

arguably ADV 可以说 kěyǐ shuō

argue v 争论 zhēnglùn

argument N 1 争论 zhēnglùn, 争吵 zhēngchǎo.
■ They reached an agreement without argument. 他们没有争论，取得了一致意见。Tāmen méiyǒu zhēnglùn, qǔdéle yízhì yìjiàn. 2 理由 lǐyóu, 论点 lùndiǎn

argumentative ADJ 1 爱争论的 ài zhēnglùn de 2 论证的 lùnzhèng de

aria N 咏叹调 yǒngtàndiào [M. WD 首 shǒu]

arid ADJ 1 干旱的 gānhàn de 2 枯燥乏味的 kūzào fáwèi de

Aries N 白羊宫 Báiyánggōng

arise (PT **arose**; PP **arisen**) v 1 起立 qǐlì 2 出现 chūxiàn 3 引起 yǐnqǐ

arisen See **arise**

aristocracy N 1 贵族 guìzú, 贵族集团 guìzú jítuán 2 贵族统治 guìzú tǒngzhì

aristocrat N 贵族 guìzú [M. WD 位 wèi]

arithmetic N 算术 suànshù

mental arithmetic 心算 xīnsuàn

arm I N 手臂 shǒubì [M. WD 条 tiáo] II v 给…武器 gěi…wǔqì, 武装 wǔzhuāng

armament N 1 武器 wǔqì [M. WD 件 jiàn] 2 (armaments) 军备 jūnbèi

armband N 袖章 xiùzhāng

armchair N 扶手椅 fúshǒuyǐ [M. WD 把 bǎ]

armed ADJ 有武器的 yǒu wǔqì de, 武装的 wǔzhuāng de

armed forces 武装部队 wǔzhuāng bùduì, 军队 jūnduì

armor N 1 铁甲 tiějiǎ, 装甲钢板 zhuāngjiǎ gāng bǎn 2 装甲兵 zhuāngjiǎbīng, 装甲部队 zhuāngjiǎ bùduì

armored division 装甲师 zhuāngjiǎshī

armory N 1 军械库 jūnxièkù [M. WD 座 zuò] 2 (信息+) 宝库 [xìnxī +] bǎokù

armpit N 腋窝 yèwō, 胳肢窝 gēzhīwō

arms N 武器 wǔqì

arms race 军备竞赛 jūnbèi jìngsài

to take up arms 拿起武器 náqǐ wǔqì, 准备战斗 zhǔnbèi zhàndòu

to be up in arms 强烈反对 qiángliè fǎnduì

army N 陆军 lùjūn, 军队 jūnduì

aroma N (香料的+) 芳香 [xiāngliào de+] fāngxiāng, (咖啡的+) 香气 [kāfēi de+] xiāngqì

aromatherapy N 芳香疗法 fāngxiāng liáofǎ

arose See **arise**

around I PREP 1 在…周围 zài…zhōuwéi, 围绕 wéirào 2 在…各地 zài…gèdì ■ *They traveled around the world after retirement.* 他们退休以后在世界各地旅游。Tāmen tuìxiū yǐhòu zài shìjiè gèdì lǚyóu. 3 大约 dàyuē II ADV 周围 zhōuwéi ■ *The thief looked around to see if anyone was watching him.* 小偷四周张望，看看有没有人在看着他。Xiǎotōu sìzhōu zhāngwàng, kànkan yǒu méiyǒu rén zài kànzhe tā.

arousal N 引起 yǐnqǐ, 激起 jīqǐ

arouse v 引起 yǐnqǐ, 激起 jīqǐ

arraign v 传讯 [+嫌疑犯] chuánxùn [+xiányífàn], 指控 zhǐkòng

arrange v 安排 [+会议] ānpái [+huìyì], 约定 yuēdìng 2 布置 [+陈列品] bùzhì [+chénlièpǐn], 排列 páiliè

arrangement N 1 安排 ānpái, 约定 yuēdìng 2 布置 bùzhì, 排列 páiliè

the art of floral arrangement 插花艺术 chāhuā yìshù

array I N 一系列 yíxìliè, 大量 dàliàng II v 部署 bùshǔ, 制定 zhìdìng

arrears N 1 积压 jīyā 2 应付欠款 yìngfu qiànkuǎn

in arrears 拖欠的 [+房租] tuōqiàn de [+fángzū]

arrest v 逮捕 dàibǔ ■ *He was arrested at a motel early this morning.* 今天清晨他在一家汽车旅馆里被逮捕。Jīntiān qīngchén tā zài yì jiā qìchē lǚguǎn lǐ bèi dàibǔ.

arrival N 到达 dàodá

arrive v 到达 dàodá, 抵达 dǐdá ■ *We arrived at the resort before dark.* 我们在天黑前抵达度假地。Wǒmen zài tiānhēi qián dǐdá dùjià dì.

arrogance N 傲慢 àomàn, 妄自尊大 wàng zì zūn dà

arrogant ADJ 傲慢的 àomàn de, 妄自尊大的 wàng zì zūn dà de

arrow N 箭头 jiàntóu

arsenal N 军火库 jūnhuǒkù [M. WD 座 zuò], 兵工厂 bīnggōngchǎng [M. WD 座 zuò]

arsenic (As) N 1 砷 shēn 2 砒霜 pīshuāng

arson N 放火 fànghuǒ, 纵火罪 zònghuǒ zuì

art N 艺术 yìshù, 美术 měishù

the arts 文艺 wényì

artery N 1 [人的+] 动脉 [rén de+] dòngmài 2 [交通+] 干线 [jiāotōng+] gànxiàn, 干道 gàndào

arthritis N 关节炎 guānjiéyán

article N 1 文章 wénzhāng [M. WD 篇 piān] 2 物件 wùjiàn ■ *An article of clothing was found at the crime scene.* 在犯罪现场发现一件衣物。Zài fànzuì xiànchǎng fāxiàn yí jiàn yīwù.

articulate I ADJ 表达力强的 biǎodálì qiáng de, 口才好的 kǒucái hǎode II v 清晰地说 qīngxī de shuō

artifact, artefact N 人工制品 réngōng zhìpǐn

artificial ADJ 人造的 rénzào de, 人工的 réngōng de

artificial intelligence 人工智能 réngōng zhìnéng

artificial respiration 人工呼吸 réngōng hūxī

artillery N 炮兵 pàobīng

artisan N 手艺人 shǒuyìrén

artist N 艺术家 yìshùjiā [M. WD 位 wèi] ■ *Very few artists are wealthy.* 只有很少的艺术家是富有的。Zhǐyǒu hěn shǎo de yìshùjiā shì fùyǒu de.

artistic ADJ 艺术的 yìshù de

artsy ADJ 美观而不实用的 měiguān ér bù shíyòng de

artwork N 艺术作品 yìshù zuòpǐn [M. WD 件 jiàn]

as I PREP 作为 zuòwéi ■ *As a parent, you are your children's guardian.* 作为家长，你是子女的监护人。Zuòwéi jiāzhǎng, nǐ shì zǐnǚ de jiānhùrén.

II CONJ 1 当 dāng, 在…的时候 zài…de shíhou

2 由于 yóuyú **III** ADV **1** 像…一样 xiàng…yíyàng ■ *In this area it may snow as early as September.* 这个地区最早九月就会下雪。Zhè ge dìqū zuìzǎo jiǔyuè jiù huì xiàxuě. **2** (as well) 也 yě

asbestos N 石棉 shímián

ascend V 上升 shàngshēng, 登高 dēnggāo

ascendancy N 支配地位 zhīpèi dìwèi, 优势 yōushì

to gain ascendancy over 胜过 shèngguò

ascent N 上升 shàngshēng, 登高 dēnggāo

ascertain V 确定 quèdìng, 查明 chámíng

ascetic ADJ 苦行的 kǔxíng de, 禁欲的 jìnyù de

ascribe V 把…归因于 bǎ…guīyīnyú

asexual ADJ 无性的 wúxìng de, 无性器官的 wúxìng qìguān de

asexual reproduction 无性繁殖 wúxìng fánzhí

ash N 灰 huī, 灰烬 huījìn

volcanic ashes 火山灰 huǒshānhuī

ashamed ADJ 惭愧 cánkuì, 羞愧 xiūkuì

ashen ADJ 灰白色的 [+脸色] huībáisè de [+liǎnsè], 苍白 cāngbái

ashore ADV 上岸 shàng'àn

ashtray N 烟灰缸 yānhuīgāng [M. WD 只 zhī]

Asia N 亚洲 Yàzhōu

Asian I N 亚洲人 Yàzhōurén II ADJ 亚洲 (的) Yàzhōu (de)

Asian-American N 亚裔美国人 Yàyì Měiguórén

aside I ADV 向边上 xiàng biānshàng, 在旁边 zài pángbiān II N 悄悄话 qiāoqiāohuà

ask V **1** 问 wèn **2** 请求 qǐngqiú, 请 qǐng ■ *He asked her to be more patient with him.* 他请求她更加耐心一点儿。Tā qǐngqiú tā gèngjiā nàixīn yìdiǎnr. **3** 邀请 yāoqǐng, 请 qǐng

to ask after 问候 wènhòu ■ *He always asks after my father whenever he sees me.* 他看到我，总是问候我的父亲。Tā kàndào wǒ, zǒngshì wènhòu wǒ de fùqin.

to ask the way 问路 wènlù

askance ADV 怀疑地 [+注视] huáiyí de [+zhùshì], 不满地 [+看] bùmǎn de [+kàn]

askew ADV 歪斜 wāixié

asleep ADJ 睡着 shuìzháo ■ *He is fast asleep.* 他睡得很熟。Tā shuìde hěn shóu.

to fall asleep 睡着 shuìzháo, 入睡 rùshuì

asparagus N 芦笋 lúsǔn

aspect N **1** 外表 wàibiǎo, 面貌 miànmào **2** 方面 fāngmiàn **3** 方向 fāngxiàng, 方位 fāngwèi

to study a problem from all aspects 全面地研究问题 quánmiàn de yánjiū wèntí

aspen N 杨 yáng, 杨树 yángshù [M. WD 棵 kē]

aspersion N 诽谤 fěibàng, 中伤 zhòngshāng

asphalt N 沥青 lìqīng, 柏油 bǎiyóu

aspiration N 志向 zhìxiàng, 抱负 bàofù

aspire V 追求 zhuīqiú, 渴望 kěwàng

aspirin N 阿司匹林 āsīpǐlín

ass N **1** 驴 lú [M. WD 头 tóu], 驴子 lúzi **2** 傻瓜 shǎguā **3** 屁股 pìgu

to get off your ass 别偷懒 bié tōulǎn

to make an ass of oneself 干傻事 gān shǎshì

assailant N 攻击者 gōngjīzhě

assassin N 暗杀者 àn shā zhě, 刺客 cìkè

assassinate V 暗杀 àn shā

assault N, V 攻击 gōngjī

sexual assault 强暴 qiángbào, 强奸 qiángjiān

assemble V **1** 集会 jíhuì **2** 收集 shōují **3** 装配 zhuāngpèi

assembly N **1** 集会 jíhuì

the freedom of assembly 集会自由 jíhuì zìyóu **2** 参加聚会的人 cānjiā jùhuì de rén **3** 装配 zhuāngpèi

assembly line 装配线 zhuāngpèixiàn

assent N 同意 tóngyì, 赞同 zàntóng

assert V 主张 zhǔzhāng, 坚称 jiānchēng

to assert oneself 坚持自己的权利 jiānchí zìjǐ de quánlì, 显示自己的地位 xiǎnshì zìjǐ de dìwèi

assertion N **1** 主张 zhǔzhāng **2** 断言 duànyán

assertive ADJ 过分自信的 guòfèn zìxìn de

assess V 测算 cèsuàn, 估价 gūjià

asset N **1** 资产 zīchǎn **2** 有价值的人 (或物) yǒu jiàzhí de rén (huò wù)

liquid assets 流动资金 liúdòng zījīn

asshole N **1** 屁眼 pìyǎn **2** 笨蛋 bèndàn

assign V **1** 分配 [+任务] fēnpèi [+rènwu] **2** 指派 zhǐpài

to assign sb to do sth 指派某人担任某职 zhǐpài mǒurén dānrèn mǒu zhí

assignment N 任务 rènwu [M. WD 项 xiàng]

homework assignment 作业 zuòyè

assimilate V 融入 róng rù, 同化 tónghuà

assimilation N 融入 róng rù, 同化 tónghuà

assist V 帮助 bāngzhù, 协助 xiézhù

assistance N 帮助 bāngzhù, 协助 xiézhù

assistant N 助理 zhùlǐ, 助理人员 zhùlǐ rényuán

sales assistant 店员 diànyuán, 售货员 shòuhuòyuán

assistant manager 副经理 fùjīnglǐ, 襄理 xiānglǐ

associate I V 联系 liánxì

to associate with sb 与某人交往 yǔ mǒurén jiāowǎng

II N **1** 伙伴 huǒbàn, 同事 tóngshì **2** 准学位获得者 zhǔn xuéwèi huòdézhě

Associate of Arts 准文学士 zhǔn wénxuéshì

III ADJ 副 fù, 准 zhǔn

associate member 准会员 zhǔn huìyuán

associate professor 副教授 fùjiàoshòu

association N 协会 xiéhuì, 社团 shètuán

assorted ADJ 各种各样的 gèzhǒng gèyàng de

assortment N 混合物 hùnhéwù, 什锦 shíjǐn

an assortment of desserts 什锦甜点 shíjǐn tiándiǎn

assume V 假定 jiǎdìng
   an assumed name 假名 jiǎmíng
assumption N 假设 jiǎshè, 假定 jiǎdìng
assurance N 自信 zìxìn
assure V 担保 dānbǎo, 保证 bǎozhèng
asterisk N 星号 xīnghào (*)
asteroid N 小行星 xiǎoxíngxīng
asthma N 哮喘病 xiàochuǎnbìng, 气喘 qìchuǎn
astonish V 使…吃惊 shǐ…chījīng
astonished ADJ 感到吃惊的 gǎndào chījīng de
astonishing ADJ 让人吃惊的 ràng rén chījīng de
astonishment N 惊讶 jīngyà
astound V 使…非常吃惊 shǐ…fēicháng chījīng
astounding ADJ 让人非常吃惊的 ràng rén
   fēicháng chījīng de
astray ADV 迷失 míshī
   to go astray 不务正业 bú wù zhèngyè
astride ADV 跨坐地 kuà zuò de
astringent ADJ 1 严厉的 [+批评] yánlì de [+pīpíng]
   2 止血的 zhǐxuè de
astrology N 占星术 zhānxīngshù
astronaut N 宇航员 yǔhángyuán
astronomical ADJ 1 天文学的 tiānwénxué de
   2 巨大的 [+数字] jùdà de [+shùzì], 天文数字的
   tiānwén shùzì de
astronomy N 天文学 tiānwénxué
astute ADJ 精明的 [+投资者] jīngmíng de
   [+tóuzīzhě]
asylum N 避难 bìnàn, 庇护 bìhù
   political asylum 政治避难 zhèngzhì bìnàn
at PREP 1 在…(地方) zài…(dìfang), 在…(时间)
   zài…(shíjiān) 2 对 duì, 向 xiàng ■ Don't yell
   at me! 别对我大声嚷嚷! Bié duì wǒ dàshēng
   rāngrang!
atheism N 无神论 wúshénlùn
atheist N 无神论者 wúshénlùnzhě
athletic ADJ 1 体育运动的 [+学校] tǐyù yùndòng
   de [+xuéxiào] 2 健壮的 [+青年], jiànzhuàng de
   [+qīngnián], 擅长体育的 shàncháng tǐyù de
athletics N 体育运动 tǐyù yùndòng
Atlantic Ocean N 大西洋 Dàxīyáng
atlas N 地图 dìtú [M. WD 张 zhāng], 地图册 dìtúcè
   [M. WD 本 běn]
ATM (= Automated Teller Machine) ABBREV 自动
   提款机 zìdòng tíkuǎnjī
atmosphere N 1 气氛 qìfen 2 大气 dàqì, 大气层
   dàqìcéng
atom N 原子 yuánzǐ
   atom bomb 原子弹 yuánzǐdàn
   atomic energy 原子能 yuánzǐnéng
atone V 赎罪 shúzuì, 弥补 [过失] míbǔ [+guòshī]
atrocious ADJ 坏极了的 huài jíle de, 糟透了的
   zāotòu le de
atrocity N 暴行 bàoxíng
attach V 附上 fùshang

   to be attached to 喜爱 xǐ'ài, 依恋 yīliàn
attaché N [大使馆的+] 随员 [dàshǐguǎn de+]
   suíyuán
   a military attaché (大使馆的) 武官 (dàshǐguǎn
   de) wǔguān
   attaché case 手提公文包 shǒutí gōngwénbāo
attachment N 附件 fùjiàn ■ Please send in your
   application form as an attachment to your e-mail.
   请把报名单以电子邮件附件寄上。Qǐng bǎ bàomíng
   dān yǐ diànzǐ yóujiàn fùjiàn jìshang.
attack I V 攻击 gōngjī II N 1 攻击 gōngjī 2 (疾病)
   发作 (jíbìng) fāzuò
   heart attack 心脏病发作 xīnzàngbìng fāzuò
attain V 实现 shíxiàn, 获得 huòdé
attempt I V 试图 shìtú, 想要 xiǎngyào ■ I attempted to contact them, but without success.
   我试图和他们联络，但是没有成功。Wǒ shìtú hé
   tāmen liánluò, dànshì méiyǒu chénggōng. II N 试
   图 shìtú
attend V 出席 chūxí, 参加 cānjiā
attendance N 出席 chūxí, 出席人数 chūxí rénshù
attendant N 服务员 fúwùyuán
   parking-lot attendant 停车场服务员 tíngchēchǎng fúwùyuán
attention N 注意 zhùyì
   to pay attention to 注意 zhùyì, 留意 liúyì
   ■ Nobody paid attention to his warning. 没有人留
   意他的警告。Méiyǒu rén liúyì tā de jǐnggào.
attentive ADJ 1 关注的 [+老师] guānzhù de
   [+lǎoshī] 2 周到的 [+服务] zhōudao de [+fúwù]
attest V 证明 zhèngmíng
attic N 阁楼 gélóu [M. WD 层 céng]
attire N 服装 fúzhuāng [M. WD 件 jiàn/套 tào]
attitude N 态度 tàidu, 心态 xīntài
attorney N 律师 lǜshī
   attorney general 首席检察官 shǒuxí jiǎncháguān [M. WD 位 wèi]
attract V 吸引 xīyǐn ■ The amusement park failed
   to attract large numbers of visitors. 游乐场没有
   能吸引大量游客。Yóulèchǎng méiyǒu néng xīyǐn
   dàliàng yóukè.
attraction N 吸引力 xīyǐnlì
   tourist attraction 旅游点 lǚyóudiǎn
attractive ADJ 有吸引力的 yǒu xīyǐnlì de, 漂亮的
   piàoliang de ■ It's an attractive idea! 这个主意很
   有吸引力! Zhè ge zhǔyì hěn yǒu xīyǐnlì!
attributable ADJ 可归因于 kě guīyīnyú
attribute I V (to attribute to) 归因于 guīyīnyú
   II N 特性 tèxìng, 品质 pǐnzhì
attributive ADJ 定语的 dìngyǔ de, 修饰的 xiūshì
   de
attrition N 1 消耗 [+战] xiāohào [+zhàn] 2 [公司
   的+] 自然减员 [gōngsī de+] zìrán jiǎnyuán
   natural attrition 自然缩减 zìrán suōjiǎn
attuned ADJ 适应的 shìyìng de

auburn N 红褐色, hóng hèsè

auction N, v 拍卖 pāimài
to put sth up for auction 把某物拿去拍卖 bǎ mǒuwù ná qù pāimài

auctioneer N 拍卖人 pāimài rén

audacious ADJ 大胆的 dàdǎn de, 鲁莽的 lǔmǎng de

audacity N 鲁莽 lǔmǎng, 大胆放肆 dàdǎn fàngsì

audible ADJ 听得见的 tīngdé jiàn de

audience N [+电影] 观众 [+diànyǐng] guānzhòng, [音乐会+] 听众 [+yīnyuèhuì+] tīngzhòng

audio N 音响的 yīnxiǎng de

audiotape N 录音磁带 lùyīn cídài

audiovisual ADJ 视听的 shìtīng de
audiovisual equipment 视听设备 shìtīng shèbèi

audit v, N 审计 shěnjì, 查账 cházhàng
to audit company accounts 审计公司账目 shěnjì gōngsī zhàngmù

audition N, v 试唱 shì chàng, 试演 shìyǎn
to audition for a musical 参加一处音乐剧的试演 cānjiā yíchù yīnyuè jù de shìyǎn

auditorium N 礼堂 lǐtáng

augment v 增加 zēngjiā, 扩大 kuòdà

August N 八月 bāyuè

aunt N 阿姨 āyí (mother's sister), 姑姑 gūgu (father's sister), 舅妈 jiùmā (maternal uncle's wife), 伯母 bómǔ (father's elder brother's wife), 婶婶 shěnshen (father's younger brother's wife)

aura N 气氛 qìfen, 氛围 fēnwéi

aural ADJ 听觉的 tīngjué de, 听力的 [+能力] tīnglì de [+nénglì]

auspices N 赞助 zànzhù
under the auspices of 由···赞助 yóu...zànzhù

auspicious ADJ 吉祥的 jíxiáng de, 吉利的 jílì de

austere ADJ **1** 严厉的 [+父亲] yánlì de [+fùqin] **2** 朴素的 [+生活] jiǎnpǔ de [+shēnghuó]

austerity N [+经济上] 紧缩 [+jīngjìshang] jǐnsuō, 节省 jiéshěng

Australia N 澳大利亚 Àodàlìyà

Australian I ADJ 澳大利亚的 Àodàlìyà de II N 澳大利亚人 Àodàlìyàrén

authentic ADJ **1** 正宗的 [+法国香槟酒] zhèngzōng de [+Fǎguó xiāngbīnjiǔ] **2** 原作的 yuánzuò de, 真的 zhēnde
an authentic painting of Piccaso 一幅毕加索的原画 yìfú Bìjiāsuǒ de yuánhuà

authenticate v **1** 鉴定···是真的 jiàndìng...shì zhēnde
to authenticate works of art 鉴定艺术品 jiàndìng yìshùpǐn
2 证实 zhèngshí

authenticity N 真实性 zhēnshíxìng

author N 作者 zuòzhě

authoritarian ADJ 专制独裁的 zhuānzhì dúcái de

authoritarianism N（政治）权威主义 (zhèngzhì) quánwēi zhǔyì

authoritative ADJ 权威性的 quánwēi xìng de

authority N 权威 quánwēi, 权力 quánlì
the authorities 当局 dāngjú

auto N 汽车 qìchē [M. WD 辆 liàng]
auto parts 汽车零件 qìchē língjiàn

autobiography N 自传 zìzhuàn [M. WD 篇 piān/本 běn]

autocracy N **1** 独裁 dúcái **2** 独裁政权 dúcái zhèngquán

autocratic ADJ 独裁的 dúcái de, 专制的 zhuānzhì de

autograph I N [名人的+] 签名 [míngrén de+] qiānmíng II v 签名 qiānmíng

automate v 使自动化 shǐ zìdònghuà

automatic I ADJ 自动的 zìdòng de, 自动化的 zìdònghuà de
automatic transmission 自动排档 zìdòng páidàng
II N 自动变速汽车 zìdòng biànsù qìchē

automation N 自动化 zìdònghuà

automobile N 汽车 qìchē [M. WD 辆 liàng]
automobile industry 汽车工业 qìchē gōngyè

automotive ADJ 与汽车有关的 yǔ qìchē yǒuguān de

autonomous ADJ 自治的 zìzhì de

autonomy N 自治 zìzhì

autopsy N 尸体检验 shītǐ jiǎnyàn

autumn N 秋天 qiūtian, 秋季 qiūjì

auxiliary I ADJ **1** 辅助的 fǔzhù de **2** 备用的 bèiyòng de II N 辅助人员 fǔzhù rényuán

avail v 有利于 yǒu lìyú
to avail oneself of 利用 lìyòng

available ADJ 能得到的 néng dédào de

avalanche N 雪崩 xuěbēng [M. WD 场 cháng]

avant-grade ADJ 前卫的 qiánwèi de, 先锋的 xiānfēng de

avarice N 贪婪 tānlán, 贪心 tānxīn

avenue N 大街 dà jiē, 街 jiē [M. WD 条 tiáo]
1600 Pennsylvania Avenue 宾西法尼亚大街 1600号 Bīnxīfǎníyà dàjiē 1600 hào

average I ADJ 平均 píngjūn, 通常 tōngcháng II N 平均数 píngjūnshù, 一般水平 yìbān shuǐpíng III v 平均是 píngjūn shì

averse ADJ 厌恶 yànwù, 很不喜欢 hěn bù xǐhuan

aversion N 厌恶 yànwù

avert v 避免 bìmiǎn, 防止 fángzhǐ

aviation N 避免 bìmiǎn, 防止 fángzhǐ

aviator N 飞行员 fēixíngyuán

avid ADJ 热心的 rèxīn de, 狂热的 kuángrè de

avocado N 鳄梨 èlí

avoid v 避免 bìmiǎn ■ She is trying to avoid her ex-husband. 她避免见到前夫。Tā bìmiǎn jiàndao qiánfū.

avow v 公开承认 gōngkāi chéngrèn, 声明 shēngmíng

avowed ADJ 公开的 gōngkāi de

awake I v (PT **awoke**; PP **awaken**) 叫醒 jiàoxǐng
II ADJ 醒着 xǐngzhe ■ *Is he awake or asleep?* 他醒着还是睡着了? Tā xǐngzhe háishi shuìzháo le?

awaken[1] v 1 叫醒 jiàoxǐng 2 唤醒 huànxǐng

awaken[2] See **awake**

awakening N 觉醒 juéxǐng

award I N 1 奖 jiǎng, 奖章 jiǎngzhāng [M. WD 枚 méi] 2 奖金 jiǎngjīn [M. WD 笔 bǐ]
Academy Award (美国电影艺术和科学学院) 学院奖 (Měiguó diànyǐng yìshù hé kēxué xuéyuàn) xuéyuàn jiǎng
II v 授奖 shòujiǎng, 颁奖 bānjiǎng

aware ADJ 意识到 yìshìdào, 知道 zhīdào

awareness N 意识 yìshi, 认识 rènshi

awash ADJ 充斥的 chōngchì de, 泛滥的 fànlàn de

away ADV 1 离开 líkāi
Go away! 走开! Zǒukāi! 滚! Gǔn!
2 不在(家、办公室) bú zài (jiā, bàngōngshì) ■ *I'll be away next week.* 我下星期不在。(→我下星期要外出。) Wǒ xià xīngqī bù zài. (→ Wǒ xià xīngqī yào wàichū.)
to put sth away 把…收起来 bǎ...shōuqǐlai

awe N 敬畏 jìngwèi, 畏惧 wèijù

awe-inspiring ADJ 令人敬畏的 lìngrén jìngwèi de

awesome ADJ 1 令人敬畏的 [+高山] lìngrén jìngwèi de [+gāoshān] 2 好极了 hǎo jí le

awful I ADJ 坏极了 huài jíle, 糟透了 zāotòu le
II ADV 1 糟糕透了 zāogāo tòu le 2 非常 fēicháng

awfully ADV 非常 fēicháng

awhile ADV 一会儿 yíhuìr

awkward ADJ 1 笨拙的 [+男孩] bènzhuō de [+nánhái], 不灵活 bùlínghuó 2 尴尬的 [+场面] gāngà de [+chǎngmiàn] ■ *The groom's absence created an awkward situation.* 新郎没来，造成尴尬局面。Xīnláng méi lái, zàochéng gāngà júmiàn.

awning N 遮蓬 zhēpéng, 雨蓬 yǔpéng

awoke See **awake**

awry ADJ 歪的 wāi de, 斜的 xié de
to go awry 出岔子 chūchàzi

ax I N 斧头 fǔtou [M. WD 把 bǎ]
to get the ax 解雇 jiěgù, 砍掉 kǎndiào
to have an ax to grind 抱有个人目的 bàoyǒu gèrén mùdì
II v 解雇 jiěgù, 砍掉 kǎndiào

axiom N 公理 gōnglǐ [M. WD 条 tiáo]

axiomatic ADJ 公理的 gōnglǐ de, 不言自明的 bù yán zì míng de

axis N 轴 zhóu, 轴线 zhóuxiàn

axle N 车轴 chēzhóu

aye INTERJ 是 shì, 赞成 zànchéng

B

babble v 1 [婴儿+] 牙牙学语 [yīng'ér+] yáyáxuéyǔ 2 [老太太+] 喋喋不休 [lǎotàitai+] diédié bùxiū

babe N 婴儿 yīng'ér

baby N 1 婴儿 yīng'ér, 小宝宝 xiǎobǎobao 2 (男子对心爱的女人) 宝贝 (nánzǐ duìxīn ài de nǚrén) bǎobèi
baby carriage 童车 tóngchē
baby talk 幼儿语 yòu'ér yǔ

baby boomer N 生育高峰期出生的人 shēngyù gāofēngqī chūshēng de rén, 1948–64年出生的人 1948–64 nián chūshēng de rén

babyish ADJ 婴儿似的 yīng'ér shìde, 孩子气的 háiziqì de

babysat See **babysit**

babysit (PT & PP **babysat**) v 照看小孩 zhàokàn xiǎohái

bachelor N 单身男子 dānshēn nánzǐ, 未婚男子 wèihūn nánzǐ
bachelor party 单身汉聚会 dānshēnhàn jùhuì
bachelor's degree 学士学位 xuéshì xuéwèi

back I N 背 bèi, 背部 bèibù II ADJ 背后 bèihòu, 后面 hòumian III ADV 1 后面 hòumian
Step back! 往后退! Wàng hòu tuì!
2 回 huí, 原处 yuánchù ■ *I'll be back soon.* 我马上回来。Wǒ mǎshàng huílai.
behind one's back 瞒着… mánzhe...
back and forth 来来回回 láilái huíhuí

backache N 腰酸背疼 yāosuān bèiténg

backbiting N 在背后说坏话 zài bèihòu shuō huàihuà

backbone N 1 脊柱 jǐzhù 2 骨干 gǔgàn

backbreaking ADJ 艰苦繁重的 [+体力劳动] jiānkǔ fánzhòng de [+ tǐlì láodòng]

backdate v 1 写上比实际时间早的日期 xiě shàng bǐ shíjì shíjiān zǎo de rìqī 2 追溯到 zhuīsù dào ■ *He backdated the check to last Friday.* 他在支票上写了上星期五的日期。Hā zài zhīpiào shàng xiě le shàngxīngqī wǔde rìqī.

backdrop N 背景 bèijǐng

backer N 支持者 zhīchízhě

backfire v 1 [汽车引擎+] 逆火 [qìchē yǐnqíng+] nìhuǒ 2 [计划+] 发生意外 [jìhuà+] fāshēng yìwài, 产生与预计相反的效果 chǎnshēng yǔ yùjì xiāngfǎn de xiàoguǒ

backgammon N 十五子棋 shíwǔ zi qí [M. WD 盘 pán/副 fù]

background N 背景 bèijǐng

backhanded ADJ 1 反手的 [+击球] fǎnshǒu de [+jīqiú] 2 讽刺挖苦的 [+赞扬] fěngcì wākǔ de [+zànyáng], 反话的 fǎnhuà de backing

a backhanded compliment 挖苦的恭维话 wāku de gōngweihuà

backing N 1 支持 zhīchí 2 后退 hòutuì

backlash N 反弹 fǎntán, 强烈反对 qiángliè fǎnduì

backlog N 积压（的工作）jīyā (de gōngzuò)
a backlog of criminal cases 积压的刑事案件 jīyā de xíngshì ànjiàn

backpack I N 背包 bēibāo [M. WD 只 zhī] II v 背着背包徒步旅行 bèizhe bēibāo túbù lǚxíng

backseat N 后座 hòu zuò
back seat driver 指手画脚乱指挥的人 zhǐshǒuhuàjiǎo luàn zhǐhuī de rén
to take a back seat 接受次要的地位 jiēshòu cìyào de dìwèi

backside N 屁股 pìgu

backspace N 退格键 tuì gé jiàn

backstage ADV 在后台 zàihòu tái, 往后台 wǎnghòu tái

back-to-back ADJ 一个接一个的 yí ge jiē yí ge de, 连续的 liánxù de

backtrack v 1 原路返回 yuánlù fǎnhuí 2 退缩 tuìsuō

backup N 1 备份 bèifèn, 备用品 bèiyòng pǐn
backup generator 备用发电机 bèiyòng fādiànjī 2 后备人员 hòubèi rényuán

backward I ADJ 1 向后的 xiànghòu de ■ He cast a backward glance before crossing the street. 他朝后看了一眼，穿过马路。Tā cháohòu kànle yìyǎn, chuānguo mǎlù. 2 落后的 [+地区] luòhòude [+dìqū] II ADV 向后 xiànghòu

backwater N 1 闭塞的地方 bìsè de dìfang 2 [小河的+] 死水 [xiǎo hé de+] sǐshuǐ

backwoods N 边远林区 biānyuǎn línqū

backyard N 后院 hòuyuàn

bacon N 咸肉 xiánròu
to bring home the bacon 挣钱养家 zhèngqián yǎngjiā

bacteria N 细菌 xìjūn

bacteriology N 细菌学 xìjūnxué [M. WD 位 wèi]

bad ADJ 1 坏 huài, 糟糕 zāogāo, 不行 bùxíng
That's too bad! 那太糟了! Nà tài zāo le!
to be bad at 不行 bùxíng, 不好 bùhǎo
to feel bad about 感到很不开心 gǎndào hěn bù kāixīn ■ She felt really bad about losing her temper. 她因为自己发脾气而感到很不开心。Tā yīnwèi zìjǐ fāpíqi ér gǎndào hěn bù kāixīn.
2 有害 yǒuhài

badge N 徽章 huīzhāng [M. WD 枚 méi]

badger N 獾 huān [M. WD 只 zhī]

badlands N 荒原 huāngyuán, 不毛之地 bùmáo zhī dì

badly ADV 1 很不好 hěn bùhǎo, 很糟 hěn zāo ■ He sang badly. 他唱歌唱得很糟。Tā chànggē changde hěn zāo. 2 极其 jíqí, 非常 fēicháng

badminton N 羽毛球运动 yǔmáoqiú yùndòng

badmouth v 说…坏话 shuō…huàihuà

baffle v 使…困惑 shǐ…kùnhuò, 难倒 nándǎo

baffled ADJ 被难住了 bèinàn zhù le, 感到困惑不解 gǎndào kùnhuò bùjiě

bag N 包 bāo, 袋 dài
bag lady 无家可归的女人 wú jiā kě guī de nǚrén
school bag 书包 shūbāo

bagel N 圆形硬面包 yuánxíng yìng miànbāo [M. WD 块 kuài]

bagful N 一袋的 yí dài de

baggage N 行李 xíngli [件 jiàn]
baggage car 火车的行李车 huǒchē de xínglichē
baggage room 行李寄存处 xíngli jìcúnchù

bail I N 保释金 bǎoshìjīn [M. WD 笔 bǐ]
to stand bail 交保释金 jiāobǎo shì jīn
to be released on bail 取保候审 qǔbǎo hòushěn II v 1 保释 bǎoshì 2 脱身 tuōshēn
to bail out 帮助 [+厂商] 脱离经济困境 bāngzhù [+chǎng shāng] tuōlí jīngjì kùnjìng

bait I N 诱饵 yòu'ěr
to take the bait 受诱惑上当 shòu yòuhuò shàngdàng II v 装上诱饵 zhuāngshàng yòu'ěr

bake v 烤 [+牛肉] kǎo [+niúròu], 烘 [+面包] hōng [+miànbāo]
bake sale 糕点义卖 gāodiǎn yìmài

baker N 面包师 miànbāoshī, 糕点师傅 gāodiǎn shīfu

bakery N 面包房 miànbāofáng

baking N 烘烤 hōngkǎo

balance I N 平衡 pínghéng
balance beam 平衡木 pínghéngmù
balance of international payments 国际收支平衡 guójì shōuzhī pínghéng
balance sheet 资产负债表 zīchǎn fùzhàibiǎo, 决算表 juésuànbiǎo II v 掂量 diānliang, 权衡 quánhéng

balanced ADJ 平衡的 pínghéng de, 均衡的 jūnhéng de
balanced diet 均衡饮食 jūnhéng yǐnshí

balcony N 阳台 yángtái

bald ADJ 秃的 tū de, 秃头的 [+男人] tūtóu de [+nánren]
bald eagle 秃鹰 tūyīng, 白头鹫 báitóu jiù

balding ADJ 脱发的 tuōfà de, 变秃的 biàn tū de

baleful ADJ 邪恶的 [+意图] xié'è de [+yìtú], 阴毒的 [+目光] yīndú de [+mùguāng]

ball¹ N [打+] 球 [dǎ+] qiú [M. WD 只 zhī]
ball game 球赛 qiúsài
ball park 球场 qiúchǎng

ball² N 舞会 wǔhuì [M. WD 次 cì/场 cháng]
to open the ball 带头跳第一场舞 dàitóu tiào dì yì cháng wǔ

ballad N 歌谣 gēyáo [M. WD 首 shǒu]

ballerina N 芭蕾舞女演员 bālěiwǔ nǚyǎnyuán

ballet N 芭蕾舞 bālěiwǔ

ballistic ADJ 弹道的 dàndào de

ballistics N 弹道学 dàndàoxué

balloon N 气球 qìqiú [M. WD 只 zhī]
hot air balloon 热气球 rèqìqiú

ballot N 选票 xuǎnpiào [M. WD 张 zhāng]
ballot box 投票箱 tóupiàoxiāng

ballpoint pen N 圆珠笔 yuánzhūbǐ [M. WD 支 zhī]

ballroom N 舞厅 wǔtīng
ballroom dancing 交谊舞 jiāoyìwǔ, 交际舞 jiāojìwǔ

balm N (镇痛) 油膏 (zhèntòng) yóugāo [M. WD 盒 hé]

balmy ADJ 温和的 [+天气] wēnhé de [+tiānqì], 柔和的 [+风] róuhe de [+fēng]

baloney N 胡扯 húchě, 鬼话 guǐhuà [M. WD 句 jù/篇 piān]

bamboo N 竹 zhú, 竹子 zhúzi [M. WD 根 gēn]

bamboozle v 欺骗 qīpiàn, 哄骗 hǒngpiàn

ban v 禁止 [+非法交易] jìnzhǐ [+fēifǎ jiāoyì]

banal ADJ 陈腐的 chénfǔ de, 乏味的 fáwèi de, 没有特色的 méiyǒu tèsè de

banana N 香蕉 xiāngjiāo [M. WD 根 gēn]

band I N 1 带子 dàizi [M. WD 条 tiáo]
rubber band 橡皮筋 xiàngpíjīn
2 群 qún
a band of wild dogs 一群野狗 yìqún yěgǒu
3 乐队 yuèduì
bandstand 乐池 yuèchí
II v 聚集 jùjí

bandage I N 绷带 bēngdài [M. WD 条 tiáo/卷 juàn] II v 用绷带包扎 yòng bēngdài bāozā

Band-Aid N 护创膏 hù chuàng gāo [M. WD 盒 hé]

bandit N 土匪 tǔfěi, 匪徒 fěitú

bandwagon N 1 乐队彩车 yuèduì cǎichē **2** 得势的一派 déshì de yípài
to jump on the bandwagon 投入得势的一派 tóurù déshì de yípài, 赶浪头 gǎn làngtou

bandy N 1 来回投掷 láihuí tóuzhì **2** 来回互答 láihuí hù dá

bane N 灾星 zāixīng, 祸根 huògēn
more of a bane than a boom 与其说是福音, 还不如说是祸根 yǔqí shuō shì fúyīn, hái bùrú shuō shì huògēn

bang I v 发出砰的一声 fāchū pēng de yìshēng II N 1 砰的一声 pēng de yìshēng **2** 一声巨响 yìshēng jùxiǎng

banish v 把 [+政治犯] 流放 bǎ [+zhèngzhìfàn] liúfàng

banister N [楼梯的+] 扶手 [lóutī de+] fúshou, 栏杆 lángān

banjo N 班卓琴 bān zhuó qín

bank¹ I N 1 银行 yínháng [M. WD 家 jiā]
bank account 银行账户 yínháng zhànghù
bank clerk 银行职员 yínháng zhíyuán

data bank 资料库 zīliàokù
II v 把钱存入银行 bǎ qián cún rù yínháng

bank² N 岸 àn, 河岸 hé'àn, 湖岸 hú'àn

banker N 银行家 yínhángjiā, 银行高级职员 yínháng gāojí zhíyuán [M. WD 位 wèi]

bankrupt ADJ 破产的 [+商人] pòchǎn de [+shāngrén]

bankruptcy N 1 破产 pòchǎn **2** 彻底失败 chèdǐ shībài

banner I N 旗 qí, 旗帜 qízhì [M. WD 面 miàn]
banner headline 通栏大标题 tōnglán dà biāotí
II ADJ 非常好的 fēicháng hǎo de

banquet N 宴会 yànhuì [M. WD 次 cì]

banter N 善意的取笑 shànyì de qǔxiào

baptism N 洗礼 xǐlǐ, 浸礼 jìnlǐ

Baptist N 浸礼会教友 Jìnlǐhuì jiàoyǒu

baptize v 行洗礼 xíng xǐlǐ

bar I N 1 酒吧 jiǔbā, 酒吧间 jiǔbājiān [M. WD 家 jiā] **2** 块 kuài
a bar of chocolate 一块巧克力 yí kuài qiǎokèlì
3 线条 xiàntiáo, 条纹 tiáowén
bar code 条形码 tiáoxíngmǎ
II v 阻挡 zǔdǎng

barbarian N 野蛮人 yěmánrén

barbaric ADJ 野蛮的 [+部落] yěmán de [+bùluò], 半开化的 bàn kāihuà de

barbecue (ABBREV BBQ) N 烧烤野餐 shāokǎo yěcān

barbed ADJ 有倒勾的 yǒu dǎo gōu de, 有倒刺的 yǒu dàocì de
barbed wire 有刺铁丝网 yǒucì tiěsīwǎng

barber N 理发师 lǐfàshī

bare I ADJ 赤裸 chìluǒ, 不穿衣服的 bù chuān yīfu de II v 露出 lòuchu

bareback ADJ [骑马+] 不用鞍具的 [qímǎ+] búyòng ānjù de

bare-bone ADJ 少到不能再少的 shǎo dào bùnéng zài shǎo de

bare-foot ADJ 赤脚的 chìjiǎo de

barely ADV 勉强 miǎnqiǎng ■ *He had barely enough money to buy a coach ticket.* 他勉强有钱买长途汽车票。Tā miǎnqiǎng yǒuqián mǎi chángtú qìchē piào.

barf v 呕吐 ǒutù

bargain I N 便宜货 piányihuò [M. WD 件 jiàn] II v 讨价还价 tǎojià huánjià

bargaining chip N 谈判的筹码 tánpàn de chóumǎ, 有利条件 yǒulì tiáojiàn

barge I N 大型平底船 dàxíng píngdǐchuán, 驳船 bóchuán [M. WD 艘 sōu] II v 冲撞 chōngzhuàng

baritone N 男中音 (歌唱家) nánzhōngyīn (gēchàngjiā)

bark¹ I v (狗) 叫 (gǒu) jiào, 汪汪叫 wāngwāng jiào II N 狗叫 gǒujiào, 狗叫声 gǒujiào shēng

barley N 大麦 dàmài

barn N 谷仓 gǔcāng, 粮仓 liángcāng [m. wd 座 zuò]

barnyard N 谷仓旁的场地 gǔcāng pángde chǎngdì

barometer N 气压表 qìyābiǎo, 气压计 qìyājì, 晴雨表 qíngyǔbiǎo

baroque ADJ 巴洛克风格 [+建筑/音乐] bāluòkè fēnggé [+jiànzhù/yīnyuè]

barracks N 营房 yíngfáng [m. wd 座 zuò]

barrage N 1 火力网 huǒlìwǎng 2 连珠炮似的问题 liánzhūpào shìde wèntí

barrel I N 桶 tǒng [m. wd 只 zhī] II v 装桶 zhuāng tǒng

barren ADJ 1 贫瘠的 [+土地] pínjí de [+tǔdì] 2 不 生育的 [+妇女] bù shēngyù de [+fùnǚ]
a barren mine 贫化矿 pínhuà kuàng

barrette N 条形发夹 tiáoxíng fàjiā [m. wd 只 zhī]

barricade I N 路障 lùzhàng, 街垒 jiēlěi II v 设置路 障 shèzhì lùzhàng

barrier N 屏障 píngzhàng, 障碍物 zhàng'àiwù

barring PREP 除了 [+意外情况] 以外 chú le [+yìwài qíngkuàng] yǐwài

barroom N 酒吧间 jiǔbajiān [m. wd 家 jiā]

bartender N 酒吧间服务员 jiǔbajiān fúwùyuán [m. wd 位 wèi]

barter I v 做易货贸易 zuò yìhuò màoyì, 以货易货 yǐ huò yì huò II N 易货贸易 yìhuò màoyì

base I N 1 底部 dǐbù, 基础 jīchǔ 2 基地 jīdì
military base 军事基地 jūnshì jīdì
II v 基于 jīyú, 以…为基础 yǐ…wéi jīchǔ

baseball N 棒球 bàngqiú

basement N 地下室 dìxiàshì [m. wd 间 jiān]

bash I v 打 dǎ, 痛打 tòngdǎ II N 猛击 měngjī

bashful ADJ 害羞的 [+女孩] hàixiū de [+nǚ hái]

bashing N 痛打 tòngdǎ, 猛击 měngjī

basic ADJ 基本的 [+问题] jīběn de [+wèntí]
■ Elementary schools teach basic skills, such as reading, writing and arithmetic. 小学教基本技能, 如阅读、写作和算术。 Xiǎoxué jiāo jīběn jìnéng, rú yuèdú, xiězuò hé suànshù.

basically ADV 基本上 jīběnshàng

basin N 1 盆 pén 2 水池 shuǐchí 3 盆地 péndì

basis N 基础 jīchǔ

bask v 晒太阳 shài tàiyáng

basket N 篮 lán, 篮子 lánzi [m. wd 只 zhī]
Don't put all your eggs in one basket. 不要把所 有的鸡蛋都放在一个篮子里。(→不要把一切希 望都寄托在一件事情上。) Bú yào bǎ suǒyǒu de jīdàn dōu fàng zài yí ge lánzi lǐ. (→Bú yào bǎ yíqiè xīwàng dōu jìtuō zài yí jiàn shìqing-shang.)

basketball N 篮球 lánqiú
basketball player 篮球运动员 lánqiú yùndòng-yuán
basketball court 篮球场 lánqiúchǎng

basketcase N 1 失去行动能力的人 shīqù xíng-dòng nénglì de rén 2 精神崩溃的人 jīngshén bēngkuì de rén

bass I N [音乐+] 低音 [yīnyuè+] dīyīn 2 男低音 nándīyīn II ADJ [音乐+] 低音的 [yīnyuè+] dīyīn de

bassoon N 巴松管 bāsōngguǎn, 低音管 dīyīnguǎn

bastard N 1 私生子 sīshēngzǐ 2 混蛋 húndàn, 王八蛋 wángbadàn

bat¹ N 蝙蝠 biānfú [m. wd 只 zhī]

bat² I N 球棒 qiúbàng [m. wd 根 gēn]
at bat 在 (棒球) 轮到击球 (bàngqiú) lúndào jīqiú II v 1 用棒击 yòng bàng jī 2 当 (棒球) 投球手 dāng (bàngqiú) tóuqiúshǒu

batch N [一+] 批 [yì+] pī, [一+] 捆 [yì+] kǔn

bated ADJ 抑制 yìzhì
with bated breath 屏息 bǐngxī, 不敢大声出气 búgǎn dàshēng chūqì

bath N 1 洗澡 xǐ zǎo 2 洗澡水 xǐ zǎo shuǐ [m. wd 盆 pén] ■ Will you run a bath for me, please. 给 我放好洗澡水, 好吗? Gěi wǒ fànghǎo xǐzǎo shuǐ, hǎoma?
Don't throw out the baby with the bathwater. 不要把婴儿连同洗澡水一起倒掉。Bú yào bǎ yīng'ér liántóng xǐzǎo shuǐ yìqǐ dàodiào. (→不要把珍贵的东西跟废物一起扔掉。Bú yào bǎ zhēnguì de dōngxi gēn fèiwù yìqǐ rēngdiào. Do not throw away precious things along with trash.)

bathe v 1 洗澡 xǐzǎo 2 沐浴 mùyù

bathing suit N 游泳衣 yóuyǒngyī [m. wd 件 jiàn]

bathrobe N 浴衣 yùyī [m. wd 件 jiàn]

bathroom N 浴室 yùshì, 洗澡间 xǐzǎojiān [m. wd 间 jiān]

bathtub N 浴缸 yùgāng

baton N 指挥棒 zhǐhuībàng [m. wd 根 gēn]

battalion N 营 yíng
battalion commander 营长 yíngzhǎng

batter I N [面粉、鸡蛋、牛奶调成的+] 面糊 [miànfěn, jīdàn, niúnǎi tiáo chéng de+] miànhu II v 连续猛打 liánxù měngdǎ

battered ADJ 破损的 pòsǔn de

battery N 电池 diànchí

battle N, v 战斗 zhàndòu, 斗争 dòuzhēng

battleground N 战场 zhànchǎng

battleship N 主力舰 zhǔlìjiàn, 战列舰 zhàn liè jiàn [m. wd 艘 sōu]

bawdy ADJ 猥亵的 [+笑话] wěixiè de [+xiàohua], 下流的 [+故事] xiàliú de [+gùshi]

bawl v 大地喊叫 cūyě de hǎnjiào, 咆哮 páoxiào

bay N 海湾 hǎiwān

bayonet N [枪上的+] 刺刀 [qiāng shàng de+] cìdāo

bazaar N 市场 shìchǎng, 集市 jíshì

B.C. (= Before Christ) ABBREV 公元前 gōngyuán-qián, 元前 yuán qian

be (am, are, is; PT was, were; PP been) [NEG is not/isn't; are not/aren't; was not/wasn't; were not/weren't] **I** v 1 (used with complement) 是 shì ■ *I'm American.* 我是美国人。Wǒ shì Měiguórén. ■ *She is my teacher.* 她是我的老师。Tā shì wǒ de lǎoshi. 2 (asking about time/age/location) ■ *How old is your son?* 你的孩子多大了？Nǐ de háizi duō dà le? ■ *What place is this?* 这个地方是什么地方？Zhè ge dìfāng shì shénme dìfāng? 3 (talking about daily occurrences) ■ *It is hot today.* 今天很热。Jīntiān hěn rè. 4 (exist, happen, etc) ■ *This is the happiest day in my life.* 这是我一生中最快乐的一天。Zhè shì wǒ yīshēng zhōng zuì kuàilè de yí tiān. 5 (price, cost) ■ *How much is that flower vase?* 那个花瓶多少钱？Nà ge huāpíng duōshao qián? **II** AUX v 1 (used with continuous tenses) ■ *I am thinking about my holiday plans.* 我在考虑假期的计划。Wǒ zài kǎolǜ jiàqī de jìhuà. 2 (with to-infinitive verbs) ■ *I have a feeling that something terrible is about to happen* 我有种感觉，有什么可怕的事正要发生了。Wǒ yǒu zhǒng gǎnjué, yǒu shénme kěpà de shì yào fāshēng le. 3 (with passive verbs) ■ *The windows of this office building are cleaned regularly by a professional company.* 这幢办公大楼的窗子由一家专业公司定期清洗。Zhè zhuàng bàngōng dàlóu de chuāngzi yóu yì jiā zhuānyè gōngsī dìngqī qīngxǐ. 4 (with question endings) ■ *Delicious, isn't it?* 真好吃，是不是？Zhēn hǎo chī, shìbúshì?

beach N 沙滩 shātān, 海滩 hǎitān
  beach ball 浮水气球 fúshuǐ qìqiú

beacon N 指路明灯 zhǐlùmíngdēng, 灯标 dēngbiāo
  radio beacon 无线电信标 wúxiàndiàn xìn biāo

bead N 珠子 zhūzi
  a string of beads 一串珠子 yíchuàn zhūzi

beady ADJ 又小又圆的 [+眼睛] yòu xiǎo yòu yuán de [+yǎnjing]

beagle N 小猎犬 xiǎo lièquǎn [M. WD 只 zhī/条 tiáo]

beak N 鸟嘴 niǎozuǐ

beaker N 1 烧杯 shāobēi 2 大酒杯 dà jiǔbēi

beam **I** N 1 (房) 梁 (fáng) liáng 2 光线 guāngxiàn 3 笑容 xiàoróng, 喜色 xǐsè
  with a beam of welcome 喜笑颜开地欢迎 xǐxiào yánkāi de huānyíng
  II v 1 发射出光芒 (或热量) fāshè chū guāngmáng (huò rèliàng) 2 喜笑颜开 xǐxiào yánkāi

bean N 豆 dòu [M. WD 棵 kē/粒 lì]
  coffee beans 咖啡豆 kāfēi dòu
  French beans 扁豆 biǎndòu
  soya beans 黄豆 huángdòu, 大豆 dàdòu
  full of beans 浑身是劲 húnshēnshìjìn
  to spill the beans 无意中泄露秘密 wúyìzhōng xièlòu mìmì

bear¹ (PT bore; PP borne) v 1 忍受 rěnshòu
  to bear with 容忍 róngrěn, 宽容 kuānróng 2 生 shēng, 产 chǎn, 结 (果) jié (guǒ)
  to bear out 证明 zhèngmíng, 证实 zhèngshí
  to bear a baby boy 生一个男孩 shēng yí ge nánhái 3 携带 xiédài

bear² N 熊 xióng [M. WD 头 tóu/只 zhī]
  bear market 熊市 xióng shì
  grizzly bear 大灰熊 dà huī xióng
  koala bear 树袋熊 shùdài xióng
  polar bear 北极熊 běijíxióng

bearable ADJ 可以忍受的 kěyǐ rěnshòu de

beard N 胡子 húzi, 胡须 húxū [M. WD 根 gēn/把 bǎ]

bearer N 1 携带者 xiédàizhě 2 抬棺人 tái guān rén

bearing N 举止 jǔzhǐ

bearish ADJ 1 像熊一样的 xiàng xióng yíyàng de, 粗鲁的 cūlǔ de, 笨拙的 bènzhuō de 2 熊市的 xióng shì de, 行情下跌的 hángqíng xiàdiē de

beast N 1 野兽 yěshòu, 畜牲 chùshēng 2 叫人讨厌的人 (或物) jiào rén tǎoyàn de rén (huò wù)

beat (PT beat; PP beaten) v 1 打败 dǎbài 2 打 dǎ
  Beat it! 滚开! Gǔnkāi

beaten See beat

beater N 搅拌器 jiǎobànqì
  egg beater 打蛋器 dǎdànqì

beat-up ADJ 破旧的 pòjiù de, 破破烂烂的 pòpò lànlàn de
  beat-up shoes 破旧的鞋子 pòjiù de xiézi

beaut N 极好的东西 (或人) jíhǎo de dōngxi (huò rén)

beautician N 美容师 měiróngshī

beautiful ADJ 美丽的 měilì de, 美的 měi de

beauty N 1 美 měi, 美丽 měilì ■ *Beauty is only skin deep.* 美色是肤浅的。Měisè shì fūqiǎn de. 2 美人 měirén 3 美丽的东西 měilì de dōngxi
  beauty salon 美容院 měiróngyuàn
  beauty spot ① 美人痣 měirénzhì ② 名胜 míngshèng, 风景点 fēngjǐng diǎn

beaver N 海狸 hǎilí [M. WD 只 zhī]

bebop N 一种爵士乐 yìzhǒng juéshìyuè

became See become

because CONJ 因为 yīnwèi

become (PT became; PP become) v 成为 chéngwéi, 变成 biànchéng ■ *The little boy has become a fine young man.* 小男孩变成了英俊小伙子。Xiǎo nánhái biànchéngle yīngjùn xiǎohuǒzi.

becoming ADJ 合适的 héshì de, 相配的 xiāngpèi de

bed **I** N 床 chuáng [M. WD 张 zhāng]
  to go to bed 上床睡觉 shàngchuáng shuìjiào
  to make the bed 铺床 pūchuáng
  II v 安置 ānzhì

bed and board

bed and board N 伙食和住宿 huǒshi hé zhùsù, 食宿 shísù

bedclothes N 床上用品 chuáng shàng yòngpǐn

bedlam N 吵吵闹闹的地方（或活动）chǎochǎo nàonào de dìfang (huò huódòng)

bedpan N [病人卧床时用的+] 便壶 [bìngrén wò-chuáng shí yòng de+] biànhú [M. WD 只 zhī]

bedraggled ADJ 凌乱不堪的 [+衣服和头发] língluànbùkān de [+yīfu hé tóufa]

bedridden ADJ [因生病或年老+] 卧床不起的 [yīn shēngbìng huò niánlǎo+] wòchuáng bùqǐ de

bedroom N 卧室 wòshì, 睡房 shuìfáng [M. WD 间 jiān]

bedside N 床边 chuáng biān
bedside lamp 床头灯 chuángtóudēng
bedside table 床头柜 chuángtóuguì

bedspread N 床罩 chuángzhào

bedtime N 睡觉时间 shuìjiào shíjiān ■ *It's way past your bedtime, Johnny.* 强尼，早过了你睡觉的时间了。Qiángní, zǎo guòle nǐ shuìjiào de shíjiān le.

bee N 蜜蜂 mìfēng [M. WD 只 zhī]
to have a bee in one's bonnet 老是想着一件事 lǎo shì xiǎngzhe yí jiàn shì

beef I N 牛肉 niúròu II v 发牢骚 fālāosāo

beefy ADJ 身材粗壮的 shēncái cūzhuàng de

beehive N 蜂窝 fēngwō

beeline N 直线 zhíxiàn [M. WD 条 tiáo/根 gēn]
to make a beeline for 朝…直奔过去 cháo… zhíbēn guòqù

beep v 发出嘟嘟声 fāchū dūdū shēng

beer N 啤酒 píjiǔ [M. WD 瓶 píng/罐 guàn/杯 bēi]
beer belly 啤酒肚 píjiǔ dù, 大肚子 dàdùzi
beer bust 啤酒宴会 píjiǔ yànhuì

beeswax N 蜂蜡 fēnglà

beet N 甜菜 tiáncài [M. WD 棵 kē]

beetle N 甲壳虫 jiǎqiàochóng [M. WD 只 zhī]

before CONJ, PREP 在…以前 zài…yǐqián ■ *Before they moved to New York, they used to live in small towns.* 他们在搬到纽约以前，一直住在小市镇。Tāmen zài bāndao Niǔyuē yǐqián, yìzhí zhù zài xiǎo shìzhèn. II ADV 以前 yǐqián

beforehand ADV 事先 shìxiān, 预先 yùxiān

befriend v 友好对待 yǒuhǎo duìdài

beg v 1 讨 tǎo, 乞讨 qǐtǎo 2 乞求 qǐqiú, 苦苦哀求 kǔkǔ āiqiú ■ *She begged him for forgiveness.* 她乞求他饶恕她。Tā qǐqiú tā ráoshù tā.
I beg your pardon. ① 对不起 duìbuqǐ ② 对不起，您说什么? Duìbuqǐ, nín shuō shénme?

began See begin

beggar N 乞丐 qǐgài, 叫花子 jiàohuāzi

begin (PT **began**; PP **begun**) v 开始 kāishǐ

beginning N 开始 kāishǐ, 开始的时候 kāishǐ de shíhou ■ *A good beginning is half the work done.* 良好的开端，就是成功了一半。Liánghǎo de kāiduān, jiù shì chénggōngle yíbàn.

begrudge v 不情愿 bùqíngyuàn, 不情愿给 bùqíngyuàn gěi

beguile v 欺骗 qīpiàn, 诱骗 yòupiàn

begun See begin

behalf N (in/on behalf of) 代表 dàibiǎo, 代表…的利益 dàibiǎo…de lìyì

behave v 举止 jǔzhǐ, 行为 xíngwéi
a well-behaved child 有礼貌的孩子 yǒulǐmàode háizi, 懂规矩的孩子 dǒng guīju de háizi
Behave yourself! 规矩点! Guīju diǎn!

behavior N 行为 xíngwéi, 举止 jǔzhǐ
to be on one's best behavior 行为规规矩矩 xíngwéi guīguī jūjū

beheld See behold

behind I PREP 1 在…后面 zài…hòumian 2 落后 luòhòu ■ *He is behind most of his classmates.* 他落后于大多数同学。Tā luòhòu yú dàduōshù tóngxué. 3 支持 zhīchí ■ *We're all behind you on this issue.* 在这个问题上我们都支持你。Zài zhè ge wèntíshang wǒmen dōu zhīchí nǐ. II ADV 在后面 zàihòumiàn
to leave behind 把…留在 bǎ…liú zài, 留下 liúxià
III N 臀部 túnbù

behold (PT & PP **beheld**) v 目睹 mùdǔ, 看到 kàndào

beige N 米黄色 mǐhuángsè

being N 1 存在 cúnzài
to come into being 开始存在 kāishǐ cúnzài, 形成 xíngchéng
for the time being 暂时 zànshí
2 生命 shēngmìng
human being N 人 rén, 人类 rénlèi

belated ADJ 被耽误的 bèi dānwù de, 迟到的 [+祝贺] chídào de [+zhùhè]

belch v 打嗝 dǎ gé

belie v 1 证明 [+他的话] 是虚假的 zhèngmíng [+tā de huà] shì xūjiǎ de, 揭穿 jiēchuān 2 给人错觉 gěi rén cuòjué

belief N 1 相信 xiāngxìn, 信心 xìnxīn 2（宗教）信仰 (zōngjiào) xìnyǎng ■ *It's a matter of belief; it works if you believe it.* 这是信不信的问题。信则灵。Zhè shì xìn bú xìn de wèntí. Xìn zé líng.

believable ADJ 可以相信的 kěyǐ xiāngxìn de

believe v 相信 xiāngxìn
Believe it or not! 信不信由你! Xìn bú xìn yóu nǐ!
to believe in 信任 xìnrèn, 信仰 xìnyǎng

believer N 信徒 xìntú

belittle v 轻视 qīngshì, 贬低 biǎndī

bell N 铃 líng, 钟 zhōng
bell bottoms 喇叭裤 lǎbakù [M. WD 条 tiáo]

belligerent ADJ 怒气冲冲准备打架的 nùqì chōng-chōng zhǔnbèi dǎjià de, 好斗的 hǎo dǒu de

bellow v [公牛+] 吼叫 [gōngniú+] hǒujiào

belly N 肚子 dùzi, 肚皮 dùpí

belly button 肚脐眼 dùqíyǎn

belong v 属于 shǔyú ■ *Who does this notebook computer belong to?* 这台笔记本电脑是谁的? Zhè tái bǐjìběn diànnǎo shì shéi de?

belongings N 个人物件 gèrén wùjiàn, 财物 cáiwù, 动产 dòngchǎn

beloved ADJ 亲爱的 qīn'ài de, 受到爱戴的 shòudào àidài de

below I PREP **1** 在…下面 zài…xiàmian **2** 在…以下 zài…yǐxià ■ *The lowest temperature here can be 10 degrees below zero.* 这里的最低气温可以到达零下十度。Zhèlǐ de zuì dī qìwēn kěyǐ dàodá língxià shí dù. **II** ADV 在下面 zài xiàmian

belt N 带 dài, 皮带 pídài [M. WD 条 tiáo]
seat (safety) belt 安全带 ānquándài
to hit below the belt 用不正当手段攻击 yòng búzhèngdāng shǒuduàn gōngjī
to tighten the belt 勒紧裤带 lēijǐnkùdài, 紧缩开支 jǐnsuō kāizhī

bemused ADJ 困惑不解的 kùnhuò bùjiě de

bench N 长椅 cháng yǐ, 长凳 chángdèng [M. WD 夵 tiáo/张 zhāng]

benchmark N 基准 jīzhǔn

bend I v (PT & PP **bent**) 弯曲 wānqū **II** N 弯曲形 wānqū xíng, [道路+] 转弯 [dàolù+] zhuǎn-wān ■ *There is a sharp bend in the road.* 路上有个急转弯。Lùshang yǒu ge jí zhuǎnwān.

beneath I PREP 在…下方 zài…xiàfāng **II** ADV 在下面 zàixià miàn

benediction N 祝福 zhùfú, 祝祷 zhùdǎo

benefactor N 捐助人 juānzhù rén, 赞助人 zànzhùrén

beneficial ADJ 有益的 yǒuyì de, 有利的 yǒulì de
to be beneficial to 对…有益 duì…yǒuyì, 对…有利 duì…yǒulì

beneficiary N 受益者 shòuyìzhě

benefit I v 对…有利 duì…yǒulì **II** N 利益 lìyì, 好处 hǎochu ■ *This scheme will bring benefits to the environment.* 这个计划会给环境带来好处。Zhè ge jìhuà huì gěi huánjìng dàilai hǎochu.
benefit of the doubt (在证据不足的情况下) 假定无罪 (zài zhèngjù bùzú de qíngkuàng xià) jiǎdìng wúzuì, 暂时相信 zànshí xiāngxìn

benevolent ADJ 仁慈的 réncí de, 善良的 shàn-liáng de

benign ADJ 仁爱的 rén'ài de
benign tumor 良性肿瘤 liángxìngzhǒngliú

bent¹ See **bend**

bent² I ADJ **1** 弯曲的 wānqū de **2** 决意的 juéyì de
to be bent on 一心一意要 yìxīn yíyì yào **II** N 爱好 àihào, 天生的才能 tiānshēng de cáinéng
a bent for music 音乐天赋 yīnyuè tiānfù

bequeath v 遗留给 yíliú gěi

bequest N 遗留 yíliú, 遗产 yíchǎn [M. WD 笔 bǐ]

a bequest of $ 750,000 一笔七十五万美元的遗产 yìbǐ qīshíwǔwàn Měiyuán de yíchǎn

berate v 训斥 xùnchì, 痛骂 tòngmà

bereaved I ADJ 丧失亲人的 sàngshī qīnrén de
a bereaved mother 失去孩子的母亲 shīqù háizi de mǔqin
II N 丧失亲人的人 sàngshī qīnrén de rén

bereft ADJ **1** 丧失了亲人的 sàngshī le qīnrén de **2** 缺乏的 quēfá de

beret N 贝雷帽 bèiléimào [M. WD 顶 dǐng]

berry N 浆果 jiāngguǒ

berserk ADJ 狂怒的 kuángnù de
to go berserk 变得狂怒 biàn de kuángnù, [气得+] 发疯 [qì dé+] fāfēng

berth N **1** 停泊位 tíngbó wèi, 锚地 máodì **2** 卧铺 wòpù

beset (PT & PP **beset**) v 不断困扰 búduàn kùnrǎo
to be beset with difficulties 困难重重 kùnnan chóngchóng

beside PREP 在…旁边 zài…pángbiān

besides I PREP 除了 chúle **II** ADV 而且 érqiě ■ *The new car is expensive, and besides, the style is not to my liking.* 这辆新车太贵了, 再说, 式样我也不喜欢。Zhè liàng xīn chē tài guì le, zàishuō, shìyàng wǒ yě bù xǐhuan.

besiege v 围困 wéikùn

best I ADJ 最好的 zuìhǎo de ■ *This is the best outcome.* 这样的结局最好。Zhèyàng de jiéjú zuìhǎo.
best man 男傧相 nánbīnxiàng
II ADV 最好地 zuìhǎo de
as best as one can 尽可能 jìnkěnéng
III N 最好的人 (或事) zuìhǎo de rén (huò shì)
to do one's best 尽力 jìnlì
All the best! 祝你万事如意! Zhù nǐ wànshì rúyì!

bestial ADJ 像禽兽一样的 [+行为] xiàng qínshòu yíyàng de [+xíngwéi], 极其残忍的 jíqí cánrěn de

bestow v 给予 jǐyǔ, 授予 [+名誉学位] shòuyǔ [+míngyù xuéwèi]

bestseller N 畅销书 chàngxiāoshū [M. WD 本 běn], 畅销货 chàngxiāohuò [M. WD 件 jiàn]

bet (PT & PP **bet**) v (打) 赌 (dǎ) dǔ

betray v 背叛 [+朋友] bèipàn [+péngyou]

betrayal N 背叛 bèipàn

better I ADJ 比较好 bǐjiào hǎo, 更好 gènghǎo
one's better half 妻子 (或丈夫) qīzi (huò zhàngfu)
Better late than never. 晚做比不做好。Wǎn zuò bǐ bú zuò hǎo.
II N 比较好的人 (或事) bǐjiào hǎode (rén huò shì)
a change for the better 好转 hǎozhuǎn
to get the better of 打败 dǎbài
III v 改进 gǎijìn

between I PREP 在…之间 zài…zhījiān **II** ADV 在中间 zài zhōngjiān

beverage N 饮料 [+茶、咖啡等] yǐnliào [+chá, kāfēi děng] [M. WD 杯 bēi]

beware V 谨防 [+骗子] jǐnfáng [+piànzi]
Beware of pickpockets. 谨防扒手。Jǐnfáng páshǒu.

bewilder V 使迷惑 shǐ míhuo, 使糊涂 shǐ hútu
feel bewildered 感到迷惑 gǎndào míhuo, 感到糊涂 gǎndào hútu

bewitch ADJ 施魔力 shī mólì, 使着迷 shǐzháo mí
bewitching smile 迷人的微笑 mírén de wēixiào

beyond I PREP 在 [+大墙以外] zài [+dà qiáng yǐwài]
II ADV 更远 gèng yuǎn, 再往前 zài wǎngqián

bias N 偏见 piānjiàn, 偏爱 piān'ài

biased ADJ 偏袒的 piāntǎn de, 有偏见的 yǒupiān jiàn de

bib N 围嘴 wéi zuǐ

Bible N 圣经 Shèngjīng [M. WD 本 běn]

bibliography N 书目 shūmù, 参考书目 cānkǎo shūmù [M. WD 份 fèn]

biceps N 二头肌 èrtóujī

bicker V 吵嘴 chǎozuǐ, 口角 kǒujué

bicycle I N 自行车 zìxíngchē [M. WD 辆 liàng]
II V 骑自行车 qí zìxíngchē

bid I N 1 出价 chūjià
a bid of $200 for the antique chair 出价两百元买一把古董椅子 chūjià liǎngbǎi yuán mǎi yì bǎ gǔdǒng yǐzi
2 投标 tóubiāo
bids for building a nuclear power plant 建造核电站的投标 jiànzào hédiànzhàn de tóubiāo
II V (PT & PP bid) 1 出价 chūjià
to bid $200 for the antique chair 出价两百元买一把古董椅子 chūjià liǎngbǎi yuán mǎi yì bǎ gǔdǒng yǐzi
2 叫牌 jiàopái

bidding N 出价 chūjià, 投标 tóubiāo
at the bidding of … 听…的吩咐 tīng…de fēnfù

bide V 等待 děngdài
to bide one's time 等待机会 děngdài jīhuì

biennial ADJ 两年一次的 liǎng nián yícì de

bifocals N 双光眼镜 shuāngguāng yǎnjìng [M. WD 副 fù]

big ADJ 大 dà
big mouth 多嘴多舌的人 duō zuǐ duō shé de rén
big name 大名鼎鼎的人 dàmíng dǐngdǐng de rén
big shot 大人物 dàrénwù
big ticket 昂贵的 ángguì de

bigamy N 重婚(罪) chónghūn (zuì)

Big Dipper N 北斗星 Běidǒuxīng

bighead N 妄自尊大的人 wàng zì zūn dà de rén

big-league ADJ 第一流水平的 [+球队] dìyìliú shuǐpíng de [+qiúduì]

bigot N 盲从的人 mángcóng de rén, 偏执的人 piānzhí de rén

bigoted ADJ 顽固不化的 [+老人] wángù bùhuà de [+lǎorén]

bigotry N 盲从 mángcóng, 偏见 piānjiàn

bigwig N 要人 yàorén

bike I N 自行车 qí zìxíngchē [M. WD 辆 liàng], 摩托车 qí mótuōchē [M. WD 辆 liàng] II V 骑自行车 qí zìxíngchē, 骑摩托车 qí mótuōchē

biker N 骑自行车的人 qí zìxíngchē de rén, 骑摩托车的人 qí mótuōchē de rén

bikini N 比基尼游泳服 Bǐjīní yóuyǒng fú [M. WD 件 jiàn], 三点式泳装 sāndiǎnshì yǒngzhuāng [M. WD 件 jiàn]

bilateral ADJ 双边的 shuāngbiān de

bile N 1 胆汁 dǎnzhī 2 坏脾气 huài píqì

bilingual ADJ 1 双语的 [+儿童] shuāngyǔ de [+értóng] 2 会两种语言的 huì liǎng zhǒng yǔyán de
a bilingual dictionary 双语词典 shuāngyǔ cídiǎn

bill I N 1 账单 zhàngdān [M. WD 张 zhāng]
to foot the bill 负担费用 fùdān fèiyòng, 付款 fùkuǎn
2 钞票 chāopiào [M. WD 张 zhāng] 3 法案 fǎ'àn, 议案 yì'àn
the Bill of Rights 人权法案 rénquán fǎ'àn
II V 给…帐单 gěi…zhàngdān

billboard N 广告牌 guǎnggàopái [M. WD 块 kuài]

billfold N 皮夹子 píjiāzi [M. WD 只 zhī], 钱包 qiánbāo [M. WD 只 zhī]

billiards N 桌球 zhuōqiú, 台球 táiqiú

billion N 十亿 shíyì

billow V 巨浪 jùlàng

bimonthly I ADJ 两个月一次的 liǎng gè yuè yícì de, 双月的 shuāngyuè de II N 双月刊 shuāngyuèkān

bin N 大箱子 dà xiāngzi

binary ADJ 由两部分组成的 yóu liǎng bù fēnzǔ chéng de, 双重的 shuāngchóng de

bind I V (PT & PP bound) 1 捆绑 [+受害人] kǔnbǎng [+shòuhàirén] 2 [条约+] 约束 [tiáoyuē+] yuēshù II N 困境 kùnjìng
in a bind 处于困境 chǔyú kùnjìng

binder N 1 装订机 zhuāngdìngjī 2 装订工 zhuāngdìng gōng 3 活页夹 huóyèjiā
four-ring binder 四眼活页夹 sì yǎn huóyèjiā

binding I ADJ 1 粘合的 zhānhé de 2 有约束力的 [+合同] yǒu yuēshùlì de [+hétong]
II N 1 [书的+] 封面 [shū de+] fēngmiàn 2 镶边 xiāngbiān

binge N 1 狂饮 kuángyǐn 2 狂热行为 kuángrè xíngwéi
shopping binge 疯狂大采购 fēngkuáng dà cǎigòu

bingo N 宾戈(游戏) bīngē (yóuxì)
Bingo! 你瞧! Nǐ qiáo! 嘿! Hēi!

binoculars N 望远镜 wàngyuǎnjìng [M. WD 副 fù]

biochemistry N 生物化学 shēngwù huàxué, 生化 shēnghuà

biodegradable ADJ 会自然分解的 huì zìrán fēnjiě de, 会腐烂的 huì fǔlàn de

biographer N 传记作者 zhuànjì zuòzhě

biography N 传记 zhuànjì [M. WD 本 běn]

biological ADJ 生物的 shēngwù de
biological warfare 生物战 shēngwùzhàn

biology N 生物学 shēngwùxué

biopic N 传记电影 zhuànjì diànyǐng [M. WD 部 bù], 传记片 zhuànjìpiàn [M. WD 部 bù]

biopsy N 活体组织检查 huótǐ zǔzhī jiǎnchá

biotechnology N 生物工程 shēngwù gōngchéng

bioterrorism N 生物恐怖主义（行为）shēngwù kǒngbùzhǔyì (xíngwéi)

bipartisan ADJ 两党的 liǎngdǎngde, 两党共同的 liǎngdǎng gòngtóng de

biped N 两足动物 liǎng zú dòngwù

biplane N 双翼飞机 shuāngyì fēijī [M. WD 架 jià]

birch N 白桦树 báihuàshù [M. WD 棵 kē]

bird N 鸟 niǎo [M. WD 只 zhī], 禽类 qínlèi
bird flu 禽流感 qínliúgǎn
bird of prey 猛禽 měngqín
bird's eye view 鸟瞰 niǎokàn
bird's nest 鸟巢 niǎocháo
to kill two birds with one stone 一举两得 yìjǔ liǎngdé

birth N 出生 chūshēng ■ *His wife gave birth to a girl baby last week.* 他的妻子上星期生了一个女孩。Tā de qīzi shàng xīngqī shēngle yí ge nǚhái.
birth certificate 出生证 chūshēng zhèng
birth control 计划生育 jìhuà shēngyù
date of birth 出生日期 chūshēng rìqī
place of birth 出生地 chūshēng dì

birthday N 生日 shēngrì

birthmark N 胎记 tāijì

birth rate N 出生率 chūshēnglǜ

biscuit N 1 烤饼 kǎobǐng [M. WD 块 kuài] 2 饼干 bǐnggān [M. WD 块 kuài/盒 hé]

bisect V 平分为二 píngfēn wéi èr

bisexual I ADJ 具有两性特征的 [+生物] jùyǒu liǎngxìng tèzhēng de [+shēngwù], 对男女两性都感兴趣的 duì nánnǚ liǎngxìng dōu gǎn xìngqu de II N 两性人 liǎngxìngrén, 具有两性特征的生物 jùyǒu liǎngxìng tèzhēng de shēngwù

bishop N 主教 zhǔjiào [M. WD 位 wèi]

bison N 野牛 yěniú [M. WD 头 tóu]

bit¹ N 一点儿 yìdiǎnr

bit² See **bite**

bitch N 1 母狗 mǔgǒu [M. WD 只 zhī] 2 坏女人 huài nǚrén
son of a bitch 狗养的 gǒuyǎngde
II V 发牢骚 fāláosāo

bitchy ADJ 恶毒的 èdú de, 讨厌的 tǎoyàn de

bite I V (PT **bit**; PP **bitten**) [虫子+] 咬 [chóngzi+] yǎo, [蚊子+] 叮 [wénzi+] dīng II N 咬 yǎo, 叮 dīng

bite-size ADJ 极小的 jíxiǎo de

biting ADJ 刺痛的 cìtòng de, 尖刻的 [+言词] jiānkè de [+yáncí]

bitten See **bite**

bitter ADJ 1 苦 kǔ
Good medicine tastes bitter. 良药苦口。Liáng yào kǔ kǒu
2 痛苦的 [+经历] tòngkǔ de [+jīnglì]
to the bitter end 坚持到最后 jiānchí dào zuìhòu

bittersweet ADJ 1 甜酸的 tián suān de 2 甜蜜而又辛酸的 [+爱情] tiánmì ér yòu xīnsuān de [+àiqíng], 有快乐也有痛苦的 yǒu kuàilè yě yǒu tòngkǔ de

biweekly ADJ 双周的 shuāng zhōu de

bizarre ADJ 奇怪的 [+现象] qíguài de [+xiànxiàng], 稀奇古怪的 xīqí gǔguài de

blab V 泄露秘密 xièlòu mìmì

black I ADJ 1 黑色的 hēisè de II N 黑色 hēisè
black coffee 不加糖的咖啡 bù jiā táng de kāfēi
black and white 黑白的 hēibái de ■ *Sometimes a black and white photo is more expressive than a color one.* 有时候黑白照片比彩色照片更有表现力。Yǒushíhou hēibái zhàopiàn bǐ cǎisè zhàopiàn gèng yǒu biǎoxiànlì.
III V (to black out) 昏倒 hūndǎo, 失去知觉 shīqù zhījué

blackberry N 1 黑莓 hēiméi 2 个人数字助手 gèrén shùzì zhùshǒu (See **PDA**)

blackbird N 黑鸫 hēidōng [M. WD 只 zhī]

blackboard N 黑板 hēibǎn [M. WD 块 kuài]

blacken V 1 变黑 biàn hēi 2 破坏 [+名誉] pòhuài [+míngyù]

blackhead N 黑头粉刺 hēitóu fěncì

blackjack N 二十一点（纸牌游戏）èrshí yì diǎn (zhǐpái yóuxì)

blacklist N 黑名单 hēimíngdān [M. WD 份 fèn/张 zhāng] II V 上黑名单 shàng hēimíngdān

blackmail N, V 讹诈 ézhà, 勒索 lèsuǒ

blackout N 1 灯火管制 dēnghuǒguǎnzhì 2 晕倒 yūndǎo

blacksmith N 铁匠 tiějiang

bladder N 膀胱 pángguāng

blade N 刀刃 dāorèn, 刀口 dāokǒu

blame I V 责怪 zéguài, 责备 zébèi ■ *He is not to blame for the accident.* 这次事故不应该责怪他。Zhè cì shìgù bù yīnggāi zéguài tā.
A bad workman blames his tools. 蹩脚工匠，责怪工具。Biéjiǎo gōngjiàng, zéguài gōngjù.
II N 责任 zérèn

blameless ADJ 无可指责的 wúkě zhǐzé de

blanch V 1 变白 biànbái 2 去皮 qùpí

bland ADJ 清淡的 [+食物] qīngdàn de [+shíwù], 无味的 [+汤] wúwèi de [+tāng]

blank I ADJ 空白的 [+支票] kòngbái de [+zhīpiào]
blank verse 无韵诗 wúyùnshī
II N 空白处 kòngbái chù, 空格 kònggé

blanket I N 毛毯 máotǎn [M. WD 条 tiáo], 毯子 tǎnzi [M. WD 条 tiáo] II ADJ 包括一切的 bāo kuò yíqiè de

blasé ADJ （享受过度而）感到厌倦的 [+富家子] (xiǎngshòu guòdù ér) gǎndào yànjuàn de [+fùjiāzǐ]

blasphemous ADJ 亵渎神明的 [+语言] xiè dú shénmíng de [+yǔyán], 出言不逊的 chūyán búxùn de

blasphemy N 亵渎神明 xiè dú shénmíng

blast I N 1 爆炸 bàozhà 2 强劲的风 qiángjìn de fēng
blast furnace 鼓风炉 gǔfēnglú
II V 爆破 bàopò

blasted ADJ 该死的 gāisǐ de

blast-off N 起飞 qǐfēi

blatant ADJ 公然的 gōngrán de

blaze I N 大火 dàhuǒ, 熊熊大火 xióngxióng dàhuǒ II V 熊熊燃烧 xióngxióng ránshāo

blazer N 茄克衫 jiākè shān [M. WD 件 jiàn], 运动服上衣 yùndòngfú shàngyī [M. WD 件 jiàn]

bleach I V 漂白 piǎobái, 变白 biànbái II N 漂白剂 piǎobáijì

bleak ADJ 阴冷的 [+天气] yīnlěng de [+tiānqì] 2 暗淡的 [+前途] àndàn de [+qiántú]

bleary ADJ （眼睛）红肿的 (yǎnjing) hóngzhǒng de, 视力模糊的 shìlì móhu de

bleat V （羊或小牛）叫 (yáng huò xiǎoniú) jiào

bled See **bleed**

bleed (PT & PP **bled**) V 流血 liúxuè

bleep I N （机器的）嘟嘟声 (jīqì de) dūdū shēng II V 发出嘟嘟声 fāchū dūdū shēng

blemish I N [声誉+] 污点 [shēngyù+] wūdiǎn, 瑕疵 xiácī II V 损害 [+性格] 的完美 sǔnhài [+xìnggé] de wánměi

blend I V 1 混合 hùnhé, 掺合 chānhé 2 调和 tiáohé II N 混合物 hùnhéwù

blender N 搅拌机 jiǎobànjī [M. WD 台 tái]

bless V 祝福 zhùfú, 保佑 bǎoyòu

blessed ADJ 有福的 yǒu fú de, 受到保佑的 shòudào bǎoyòu de

blessing N 1 祝福 zhùfú 2 批准 pīzhǔn, 允许 yǔnxǔ

blew See **blow**

blight I N 1 毁坏 huǐhuài 2 （植物）枯萎病 (zhíwù) kūwěi bìng II V 毁坏 huǐhuài, 折磨 zhémo

blind[1] ADJ 1 瞎的 xiā de, 看不见的 kànbujiàn de, 盲的 máng de
No one is more blind than those who refuse to see. 没有谁比拒绝看的人更瞎。Méiyǒu shéi bǐ jùjué kàn de rén gèngxiā.
blind date 与从未见过面的人约会 yǔ cóngwèi jiàn guò miàndī rén yuēhui, 初次约会 chūcì yuēhui
school for the blind 盲人学校 mángrén xuéxiào

blind[2] N 窗帘 chuānglián, 帘子 liánzi
Venetian blinds 百叶窗帘 bǎiyèchuānglián

blinders N （马的）眼罩 (mǎ de) yǎnzhào

blindfold I N 眼罩 yǎnzhào, 蒙眼布 méng yǎn bù II V 蒙住眼睛 méngzhùyǎnjing

blindside N 1 看不到的一面 kànbùdào de yímiàn 2 未加防备的方面 wèi jiā fángbèi de fāngmiàn

blindspot N 盲点 mángdiǎn

blink V 眨眼睛 zhǎyǎn jīng

blinkers N [马的+] 眼罩 [mǎ de+] yǎnzhào

blip I N [机器+] 哔哔声 [jīqì+] bìbì shēng II V 发出哔哔声 fāchū bìbì shēng

bliss N 极乐 jí lè, 至上的幸福 zhìshàng de xìngfú

blissful ADJ 快乐极了 kuàilè jíle, 无忧无虑的 wúyōu wúlǜ de

blister I N 水疱 shuǐpào II V 起水疱 qǐshuǐ pào

blithe ADJ 欢乐的 huānlè de

blitz N 1 闪电战 shǎndiànzhàn 2 突然的大规模袭击 tūrán de dàguīmó xíjī

blizzard N 暴风雪 bàofēngxuě [M. WD 场 cháng]

bloated ADJ 肿胀的 zhǒngzhàng de, 膨胀的 péngzhàng de

blob N 一滴 yìdī

bloc N 集团 jítuán

block I N 1 大块 dà kuài
a block of wood 一大块木头 yí dà kuài mùtou 2 街区 jiēqū II V 阻塞 zǔsè, 堵住 dǔzhù

blockade I N 封锁 fēngsuǒ II V 封锁 fēngsuǒ

blockage N 堵塞物 dǔsè wù

blockbuster N 1 大片 dàpiān [M. WD 部 bù] 2 成功的畅销书 chénggōng de chàngxiāoshū 3 了不起的人（或物）liǎobuqǐ de rén (huò wù)

blockhead N 傻瓜 shǎguā, 笨蛋 bèndàn

blog I N 互联网网页 hùliánwǎng wǎngyè II V 在互联网网页发表文章 zài hùliánwǎng wǎngyè fābiǎo wénzhāng ■ *My uncle blogs regularly.* 我的叔叔定期在互联网网页发表文章。Wǒ de shūshu dìngqī zài hùliánwǎng wǎngyè fābiǎo wénzhāng.

blogger N 博客 bókè, 在互联网网页发表文章的人 zài hùliánwǎng wǎngyè fābiǎo wénzhāng de rén

blond, blonde N 有金黄头发的人 yǒu jīnhuáng tóufa de rén, 金发女郎 jīnfà nǚláng

blood N 血 xuè [M. WD 滴 dī]
blood bank 血库 xuèkù
blood pressure 血压 xuèyā
blood type 血型 xuèxíng
blood vessel 血管 xuèguǎn

bloodshed N 流血 liúxuè

bloodshot ADJ 充血的 chōngxuè de, 带血丝的 dài xuèsī de

bloody ADJ **1** 带血的 dàixuè de **2** 残酷的 cánkù de

bloom I N 花朵 huāduǒ, 花 huā [M. WD 朵 duǒ] **II** V 开花 kāihuā

bloomers N （老式的）灯笼裤 (lǎoshì de) dēnglongkù [M. WD 条 tiáo]

blossom I N 花 huā, 花儿 huār [M. WD 朵 duǒ] **II** V 开花 kāihuā

blot I N 污迹 wūjì, 污点 wūdiǎn **II** V 留下污迹 liúxià wūjì

blotch N **1** 大片污迹 dàpiàn wūjì **2** （皮肤）红斑 (pífū) hóngbān

blotter N **1** 吸墨纸 xīmòzhǐ [M. WD 张 zhāng] **2** 记录簿 jìlùbù [M. WD 本 běn]

blotting paper N 吸墨纸 xīmòzhǐ [M. WD 张 zhāng]

blouse N 女式衬衫 nǚshì chènshān [M. WD 件 jiàn]

blow I V (PT blew; PP blown) 吹 chuī, 刮 guā
to blow one's nose 擤鼻涕 xǐng bítí
to blow one's own horn 自吹自擂 zìchuī zìléi
to blow sb a kiss 给…一个飞吻 gěi…yí ge fēiwěn
to blow the whistle on 揭发 jiēfā
II N **1** 吹 chuī, 吹动 chuīdòng **2** 重击 zhòngjī
to come to blows 打起来 dǎqǐlái
3 （心理上的）打击 (xīnlǐ shàng de) dǎjī
to deal sb a heavy blow 给某人打击 gěi mǒurén dǎjī

blow-by-blow ADJ 十分详细地 shífēn xiángxì de

blown See blow

blowout N **1** 轻而易举的胜利 qīng ér yìjǔ de shènglì **2** 盛大宴会 shèngdà yànhuì **3** （轮胎+）爆裂 [lúntāi+] bàoliè

blowtorch N 喷灯 pēndēng

blow-up N **1** 放大的照片 fàngdà de zhàopiàn **2** 突然发生的吵架 tūrán fāshēng de chǎojià

lubber[1] N [鲸鱼 / 人的+] 脂肪 [jīngyú/rén de+] zhīfáng

lubber[2] V （让人讨厌地）哇哇大哭 (ràng rén tǎoyàn de) wāwā dàkū

lue I ADJ **1** 蓝色的 [+天空] lánsè de [+tiānkōng]
blue chip 蓝筹股的 lánchóugǔ de, 稳赚的 wěn zhuàn de
2 色情的 sèqíng de **3** 悲观的 bēiguān de
II N **1** 蓝色 lánsè **2** 天空 tiānkōng, 海洋 hǎiyáng
out of the blue 突然的 tūrán de, 出人意料的 chūrén yìliào de

luebell N 兰花风铃草 lánhuā fēnglíngcǎo

lueberry N 蓝莓浆果 lán méi jiāngguǒ

luebird N 蓝色知更鸟 lánsè zhīgēngniǎo

lue-blood ADJ 血统高贵的 [+家族] xuètǒng gāoguì de [+jiāzú], 出生名门豪族的 chūshēng míngmén háozú de

lue-collar ADJ 蓝领阶层的 [+工人] lánlǐng jiēcéng de [+gōngrén]

luejay N 蓝背鲣鸟 lán bèi jiānniǎo [M. WD 只 zhī]

bluejeans N 牛仔裤 niúzǎikù [M. WD 条 tiáo]

blueprint N 蓝图 lántú [M. WD 幅 fú/张 zhāng]

blues N **1** 布鲁斯音乐 bùlǔsī yīnyuè **2** (the blues) 忧郁 yōuyù

bluff N, V 虚张声势 xūzhāng shēngshì, 吓唬 xiàhu

blunder I N 愚蠢的错误 yúchǔn de cuòwù, 重大的疏忽 zhòngdà de shūhu **II** V **1** 犯愚蠢的错误 fàn yúchǔn de cuòwu **2** 误入 wùrù

blunt I ADJ **1** 钝的 [+刀] dùn de [+dāo], 不锋利的 bù fēnglì de **2** 直言不讳的 [+话] zhíyán búhuì de [+huà], 毫不客气的 [+批评] háobú kèqi de [+pīpíng] **II** V **1** 使 [+剪刀] 变钝 shǐ [+jiǎndāo] biàndùn **2** 削弱 xuēruò

blur I N 一片模糊 yípiàn móhu **II** V 使 [+景象] 模糊 shǐ [+jǐngxiàng] móhu

blurb N [书的+] 内容提要 [shū de+] nèiróngtíyào

blurred ADJ 模糊的 [+记忆] móhu de [+jìyì]

blurt V 不假思索地说出来 bù jiǎ sīsuǒ de shuōchulai

blush I V [脸+] 红 [liǎn+] hóng **II** N 脸红 liǎnhóng

bluster I V [人+] 神气活现地叫嚷 [rén+] shénqi huóxiàn de jiàorǎng, 咆哮 páoxiào **II** N 夸夸其谈 kuākuā qí tán, 吹牛 chuīniú

blustery ADJ 狂风大作的 [+天气] kuángfēng dàzuò de [+tiānqì]

BO, B.O. (= body odor) ABBREV 体臭 tǐ chòu

boar N 公猪 gōngzhū [M. WD 头 tóu], 野猪 yězhū [M. WD 头 tóu]

board I N 木板 mùbǎn [M. WD 块 kuài]
bulletin board 布告牌 bùgàopái
2 董事会 dǒngshìhuì, 理事会 lǐshìhuì
chairman of the board （公司）董事长 (gōngsī) dǒngshìzhǎng
3 伙食 huǒshi, 伙食费 huǒshifèi
on board 上船（火车、飞机）shàngchuán (huǒchē, fēijī)
II V 登上 [+飞机 / 公共汽车 / 火车] dēngshàng [+fēijī/gōnggòng qìchē/huǒchē]

boarder N 寄宿生 jìsùshēng, 寄膳房客 jì shàn fángkè

boarding house N 寄宿公寓 jìsù gōngyù [M. WD 座 zuò]

boarding school N 寄宿学校 jìsùxuéxiào

boardwalk N 木板走道 mùbǎn zǒudào

boast I V 吹嘘 [+自己] chuīxū [+zìjǐ], 吹牛 chuīniú **II** N 吹嘘 chuīxū, 自吹 zìchuī

boastful ADJ 自吹自擂的 zìchuī zìléi de

boat N 船 chuán [M. WD 条 tiáo/艘 sōu], 小船 xiǎochuán [M. WD 条 tiáo/艘 sōu]
in the same boat 共患难 gòng huànnàn, 同舟共济 tóngzhōu gòngjì
to rock the boat 唱反调捣乱 chàng fǎndiào dǎoluàn
to row a boat 划船 huáchuán

bob V 上下摇动 shàngxià yáodòng

bobsled, bobsleigh N 大雪橇 dà xuěqiāo [M. WD 辆 liàng/架 jià]

bode V 预示 yùshì

bodice N 紧身胸衣 jǐnshēn xiōngyī [M. WD 件 jiàn]

bodily I ADJ 身体的 shēntǐ de, 肉体的 ròutǐ de II ADV 全体 quántǐ, 整个 zhěnggè

body N 1 身体 shēntǐ, 身躯 shēnqū
body language 体态语言 tǐtài yǔyán
2 (dead body) 尸体 shītǐ [M. WD 具 jù] 3 团体 tuántǐ 4 物体 wùtǐ [M. WD 件 jiàn]

bodyguard N 保镖 bǎobiāo, 警卫 jǐngwèi

body odor (ABBREV **BO, B.O.**) N 体臭 tǐ chòu, 狐臭 húchòu

bodywork N 车身修理 chēshēn xiūlǐ

bog N 沼泽 zhǎozé [M. WD 片 piàn]

bogeyman N 妖怪 yāoguài

boggle V 惊恐 jīngkǒng, 大为恐惧 dàwéi kǒngjù

bogus ADJ 假的 jiǎ de, 伪装的 wěizhuāng de

bohemian ADJ 放荡不羁的 fàngdàngbùjī de

boil V 1 [水+] 沸腾 [shuǐ+] fèiténg 2 烧开 [+水] shāokāi [+shuǐ] 3 煮 [+土豆] zhǔ [+tǔdòu]
boiled water 开水 kāishuǐ

boiler N 锅炉 guōlú

boiling ADJ 热到沸点 rè dào fèidiǎn, 沸腾 fèiténg

boiling point N 沸点 fèidiǎn

boisterous ADJ 吵吵闹闹的 chǎochǎo nàonào de

bold ADJ 勇敢的 yǒnggǎn de, 大胆的 dàdǎn de

bolster I V 增强 zēngqiáng, 支持 zhīchí II N 1 垫枕 diàn zhěn 2 垫木 diànmù [M. WD 段 duàn/块 kuài]

bolt I N 1 螺栓 luóshuān, 螺丝钉 luósīdīng 2 门拴 ménshuān, 窗拴 chuāng shuān II V 1 把…拴在一起 bǎ...shuān zài yìqǐ 2 [马+] 逃跑 [mǎ+] táopǎo 3 匆匆吞下 cōngcōng tūnxià III ADV 笔直 bǐzhí

bomb I N 炸弹 zhàdàn [M. WD 枚 méi] II V 1 轰炸 hōngzhà, [用炸弹+] 爆炸 [yòng zhàdàn+] bàozhà 2 失败 shībài

bombard V 1 对 [+敌人的阵地] 狂轰滥炸 duì [+dírén de zhèndì] kuánghōng lànzhà 2 对 [+市长] 提出一连串问题 duì [+shìzhǎng] tíchū yìliánchuàn wèntí

bombed ADJ 喝醉了(酒)hēzuìle (jiǔ)

bomber N 1 投放炸弹的人 tóufàng zhàdàn de rén 2 轰炸机 hōngzhàjī [M. WD 架 jià]

bombshell 1 N 惊人事件 jīngrén shìjiàn 2 炸弹 zhàdàn [M. WD 枚 méi]

bona fide ADJ 真正的 zhēnzhèng de, 真诚的 zhēnchéng de

bonanza N 1 财源 cáiyuán 2 繁荣兴旺 fánróng xīngwàng 3 富矿 fùkuàng [M. WD 座 zuò]

bond I N 1 债券 zhàiquàn
U.S. savings bond 美国储蓄债券 Měiguó chǔxù zhàiquàn
2 保释金 bǎoshìjīn 3 纽带 niǔdài, 联系 liánxì

II V 培养亲密关系 péiyǎng qīnmì guānxi

bondage N 1 奴役 núyì 2 束缚 shùfù

bonding N 亲密关系的形成 qīnmì guānxi de xíngchéng

bone I N 骨头 gǔtou [M. WD 根 gēn]
bone dry 干透的 gān tòu de
bone marrow 骨髓 gǔsuǐ
to make no bones about 对…毫无顾忌 duì…háo wú gùjì
to have a bone to pick with 对…有意见 duì…yǒu yìjiàn
to feel sth in one's bones 确信 quèxìn
II V 去掉 [+鸡] 的骨头 qùdiào [+jī] de gǔtou

bonfire N 篝火 gōuhuǒ, 营火 yínghuǒ

bonus N 奖金 jiǎngjīn, 红利 hónglì

bony ADJ 皮包骨头的 [+饥民] píbāo gútou de [+jīmín]

boo I V 发出嘘声 fāchū xū shēng, 向 [+演员] 喝倒彩 xiàng [+yǎnyuán] hèdàocǎi II N 嘘声 xūshēng

boob N 乳房 rǔfáng, 奶头 nǎitou

boo-boo N 犯傻 fànshǎ

booby prize N 倒数第一名奖 dàoshǔ dìyīmíng jiǎng

booby trap N 1 伪装地雷 wěizhuāng dìléi [M. WD 枚 méi] 2 恶作剧 èzuòjù

boogie man N 妖怪 yāoguài

book I N 1 书 shū, 图书 túshū [M. WD 本 běn] 2 本子 běnzi, 簿子 bùzi [M. WD 本 běn]
address book 地址簿 dìzhǐbù
notebook 笔记本 bǐjìběn
3 账本 zhàngběn, 账目 zhàngmù [M. WD 本 běn]
by the book 严格照章办事 yángé zhàozhāngbànshì
II V 预定 [+旅馆房间] yùdìng [+lǚguǎn fángjiān]

bookcase N 书橱 shūchú

bookmark N 书签 shūqiān [M. WD 张 zhāng]

bookshelf N 书架 shūjià

bookstore N 书店 shūdiàn [M. WD 家 jiā]

boom I N 1 [生意+] 兴隆 [shēngyì+] xīnglóng
boom times 繁荣时期 fánróng shíqī
boom town 兴旺发达的城市 xīngwàng fādá de chéngshì
2 隆隆声 lónglóng shēng II V 1 [生意+] 兴隆 [shēngyì+] xīnglóng, 兴旺 xīngwàng 2 发出隆隆声 fāchū lónglóng shēng

boomerang I N 回飞镖 huí fēibiāo II V 自作自受 zìzuò zìshòu

boon I N 带来极大好处的事物 dàilái jídà hǎochu de shìwù, 恩物 ēnwù

boondocks N 偏远的地方 piānyuǎn de dìfang

boor N 粗鲁的男子 cūlǔ de nánzǐ

boost I N 激励 jīlì, 鼓励 gǔlì II V 激励 [+士气] jīlì [+shìqì], 鼓励 gǔlì

booster N 1 增效药剂 zēng xiào yàojì 2 起鼓励作用的事物 qǐ gǔlì zuòyòng de shìwù moral booster 鼓励士气的事 gǔlì shìqì de shì **3** 助推器 zhùtuīqì

boot I N 靴子 xuēzi [M. WD zhī/双 shuāng]
boot camp 新兵训练营 xīnbīng xùnliàn yíng
II v **1** 使 [+电脑] 启动 shǐ [+diànnǎo] qǐdòng
2 赶走 [+捣乱的人] gǎnzǒu [+dǎoluàn de rén]

booth N **1** 小亭 xiǎo tíng
ticket booth 售票亭 shòupiào tíng
2 (餐馆)火车座 (cānguǎn) huǒchēzuò **3** 售货摊位 shòuhuò tānwèi

bootleg I ADJ 盗制的 dào zhì de, 走私的 zǒusī de **II** N 盗制 [+电脑软件等] dào zhì [+diànnǎo ruǎnjiàn děng]

bootlegging N 盗制或非法销售 [+电脑软件等] dào zhì huò fēifǎ xiāoshòu [+diànnǎo ruǎnjiàn děng]

bootstraps N 拔鞋带 bá xuē dài
to pull oneself up by one's bootstraps 自强不息 改善处境 zìqiáng bùxī gǎishàn chǔjìng

booty N 战利品 zhànlìpǐn [M. WD 件 jiàn]

booze I N 酒 jiǔ **II** v 豪饮 háoyǐn, 酗酒 xùjiǔ

bop I v 轻轻地拍 qīngqīng de pāi **II** N 轻拍 qīng pāi

border I N **1** 边儿 biānr **2** 国界 guójiè, 国境线 guójìngxiàn **II** v 与…接壤 yǔ…jiērǎng
to border on 接近 jiējìn

borderline I N 分界线 fēnjièxiàn [M. WD 道 dào/条 tiáo] **II** ADJ 几乎 jīhū

bore¹ See **bear¹**

bore² **I** v **1** 使…厌烦 shǐ…yànfán, 使…厌倦 shǐ…yànjuàn
to bore sb to death 使…厌烦得要死 shǐ…yànfán deyàosǐ
2 钻孔 zuānkǒng **II** N **1** 令人厌烦的人 [+或事] lìngrén yànfán de rén [+huò shì] **2** 口径 kǒujìng

bored ADJ 厌烦 yànfán, 厌倦 yànjuàn

boredom N 厌烦 yànfán, 厌倦 yànjuàn

boring ADJ 让人厌烦 ràng rén yànfán, 枯燥 kūzào ■ What a boring movie! 这部电影真枯燥! Zhè bù diànyǐng zhēn kūzào!

born ADJ 出生 chūshēng ■ I think some people are born leaders. 我认为，有的人天生就是有当领袖的才能。 Wǒ rènwéi, yǒude rén tiānshēng jiù shì yǒu dāng lǐngxiù de cáinéng.
be born with a silver spoon in one's mouth 生在富贵人家 shēng zài fùguì rénjiā

born-again ADJ 新近开始的 xīnjìn kāishǐ de
a born-again Christian 基督教再生教徒 Jīdūjiào zàishēng jiàotú
a born-again environmentalist 新近开始的环保主义者 xīn jìn kāishǐ de huánbǎo zhǔyìzhě

borne See **bear¹**

borough N (城市里的)区 (chéngshì lǐ de) qū

borrow v 借 jiè, 借用 jièyòng

borrower N 借款人 jièkuǎnrén

borrowing N **1** 借款 jièkuǎn [M. WD 项 xiàng/笔 bǐ], 贷款 dàikuǎn **2** 外来语 wàiláiyǔ
borrowing powers 借款限额 jièkuǎn xiàn'é

bosom N 胸部 xiōngbù
a bosom friend 心腹之交 xīnfù zhī jiāo, 知己朋友 zhījǐ péngyou

boss I N **1** 老板 lǎobǎn **2** 领袖 lǐngxiù [M. WD 位 wèi], 头目 tóumù
party boss 政党领袖 zhèngdǎng lǐngxiù
crime boss 犯罪分子头目 fànzuì fènzǐ tóumù
II v (to boss sb around) 对…发号施令 duì…fāhào shīlìng

botany N 植物学 zhíwù xué

botch v 把…搞糟 bǎ…gǎozāo

both I ADJ 两 liǎng ■ I will buy both books. 我这两本书都要买。 Wǒ zhè liǎng běn shū dōu yào mǎi.
II PRON 两个…都 liǎng ge…dōu
both … and … 既…又… jì…yòu… ■ He is both smart and kind. 他既聪明又仁慈。 Tā jì cōngmíng yòu réncí.

bother I v **1** 打搅 dǎjiǎo **2** 烦恼 fánnǎo, 发愁 fāchóu ■ What's bothering you? 你在为什么事发愁呢？ Nǐ zài wèishénme shì fāchóu ne? **3** 麻烦 máfan **II** N 麻烦 máfan
no bother 没关系 méi guānxi, 不费事 bú fèishì

bottle I N 瓶 píng [M. WD 只 zhī], 瓶子 píngzi
bottle opener 开瓶器 kāipíngqì
baby bottle 婴儿奶瓶 yīng'ér nǎipíng
II v 装瓶 zhuāng píng

bottled ADJ 瓶装的 píngzhuāng de

bottlefed See **bottlefeed**

bottlefeed (PT & PP **bottlefed**) v 人工喂养 réngōng wèiyǎng

bottleneck N **1** 瓶颈 píngjǐng, 瓶颈路段 píngjǐng lùduàn **2** 障碍 zhàng'ài

bottler N 装瓶工人／公司 zhuāng píng gōngrén/gōngsī

bottom I N 底 dǐ, 底部 dǐbù **2** 最后的位置 zuìhòu de wèizhì, 末尾 mòwěi ■ He is always at the bottom of the class. 他总是班上最差的。 Tā zǒngshì bānshang zuì chà de. **II** ADJ 最底下的 zuì dǐxia de, 最底层的 zuì dǐcéng de
bottom line ① 最基本的事实 zuì jīběn de shìshí ② 底线 dǐxiàn
III v (to bottom out) 降到最低点 jiàng dào zuì dīdiǎn

bottomless ADJ 无底的 wúdǐ de

bough N 主要的树叉 zhǔyào de shùchā [M. WD 条 tiáo]

bought See **buy**

boulder N 巨石 jù shí [M. WD 块 kuài]

boulevard N 林荫大道 lín yìn dàdào [M. WD 条 tiáo], 大道 dàdào [M. WD 条 tiáo]

bounce I v **1** 跳 tiào, 弹跳 tántiào **2** 退回 tuìhuí

to bounce back 恢复元气 huīfù yuánqì
II N **1** 跳 tiào, 弹跳 tántiào **2** 活力 huólì
bouncer N 门卫 ménwèi
bouncing ADJ 健壮的 jiànzhuàng de
bouncy ADJ **1** 弹性很足的 [+椅子] tánxìng hěn zú de [+yǐzi] **2** 精神饱满的 [+音乐] jīngshen bǎomǎn de [+yīnyuè], 快乐的 [+人] kuàilè de [+rén]
bound I ADJ **1** 肯定 kěndìng
be bound to 肯定会 kěndìng huì, 注定会 zhùdìng huì
2 有义务的 yǒu yìwù de **3** 装订好的 zhuāngdìng hǎode
a leather-bound volume 一本皮面书籍 yìběn pímiàn shūjí
II v 以…为界 yǐ…wéi jiè **III** N 界限 jièxiàn
■ *Out of bounds to foreigners.* 外国人不得入内。Wàiguórén bù děi rù nèi.
bound See bind
boundary N 分界线 fēnjièxiàn [M. WD 条 tiáo]
to push the boundary 开拓思路 kāituò sīlù
boundless ADJ 无限的 wúxiàn de
bountiful ADJ 充裕的 chōngyù de
bounty N 奖金 jiǎngjīn [M. WD 笔 bǐ], 悬赏金 xuánshǎng jīn [M. WD 笔 bǐ]
bouquet N 花束 huāshù
a bouquet of roses 一束玫瑰花 yíshù méiguìhuā
2 (酒)香 (jiǔ) xiāng
bourgeoisie N 中产阶级 zhōngchǎn jiějí, 资产阶级 zīchǎn jiějí
bout N [疾病+] 发作 [jíbìng+] fāzuò
boutique N 小精品店 xiǎo jīngpǐndiàn [M. WD 家 jiā]
bovine ADJ 牛的 niú de
bow I v **1** 鞠躬 [+谢幕] jūgōng [+xièmù] **2** 低头 [+祷告] dītóu [+dǎogào] **II** N **1** 鞠躬 jūgōng **2** 弓 gōng, 琴弓 qín gōng **3** 蝴蝶结 húdiéjié
bow tie 蝶形领结 diéxíng lǐngjié
bowel N 肠 cháng
to move bowels 解大便 jiě páidàbiàn, 大便 dàbiàn
bowl I N 碗 wǎn [M. WD 只 zhī]
fish bowl 鱼缸 yúgāng [M. WD 只 zhī]
II v 打保龄球 dǎ bǎolíngqiú
bow-legged ADJ 罗圈腿的 luóquāntuǐ de
bowling N 保龄球(运动)bǎolíngqiú (yùndòng)
bowling alley 保龄球馆 bǎolíngqiú guǎn
box I N 盒 hé, 箱 xiāng [M. WD 只 zhī] ■ *I need two big boxes for the books.* 我要两只大箱子装书。Wǒ yào liǎng zhī dà xiāngzi zhuāng shū.
P.O. Box 邮政信箱 yóuzhèngxìnxiāng
2 方框 fāngkuàng, 选项框 xuǎn xiàng kuàng
to check the box 在选项框内打勾 zài xuǎn xiàng kuàng nèi dǎ gōu
to think outside the box 想出新花招 xiǎngchū xīn huāzhāo

3 包厢 bāoxiāng **4** 电视机 diànshìjī [M. WD 台 tái]
box office 票房 piàofáng
II v 把…装入箱内 bǎ…zhuāngrù xiāng nèi **2** 与…比赛拳击 yǔ…bǐsài quánjī **3** 打…耳光 dǎ…ěrguāng
boxer N 拳击手 quánjīshǒu
boxer shorts (男用)平脚短裤 (nán yòng) píng jiǎo duǎnkù
boxing N 拳击 quánjī, 拳击运动 quánjī yùndòng
boy I N 男孩 nánhái
Boys will be boys! 男孩总是男孩!(= 总是会调皮捣蛋。)Nánhái zǒngshì nánhái! (= Zǒngshì huì tiáopídǎodàn.)
boyfriend 男朋友 nánpéngyou
Boy Scouts 童子军 tóngzǐjūn
2 儿子 érzi **3** 年轻人 niánqīngrén
II INTERJ 好家伙!
Oh boy! 啊呀! Āyā!
boycott I v 抵制 dǐzhì **II** N 抵制 dǐzhì
bozo N 傻瓜 shǎguā
bra N 胸罩 xiōngzhào
brace I v **1** 做好准备对付困难 zuò hǎo zhǔnbèi duìfu kùnnan **2** 加固 jiāgù, 支撑 zhī chēng **II** N 支撑物 zhīchēngwù
braces 矫正牙箍 jiǎozhèng yá gū
neck brace 颈托 jǐng tuō
bracelet N 手镯 shǒuzhuó [M. WD 只 zhī/副 fù]
bracing ADJ 令人心神清爽的 lìngrén xīnshén qīngshuǎng de, 清新的 qīngxīn de
bracket I N **1** 括号 kuòhào **2** 等级段 děngjíduàn, 组 zǔ
income bracket 收入等级 shōurù děngjí
II v **1** 把…放入括号内 bǎ…fàngrù kuòhào nèi **2** 把…放入同一等级段 bǎ…fàngrù tóngyī děngjí duàn
brackish ADJ 有点咸的 yǒudiǎn xián de
brag N 吹嘘 chuī xū
braggart N 吹牛大王 chuīniú dàwáng
braid I N **1** 发辫 fàbiàn [M. WD 条 tiáo], 辫子 biànzi [M. WD 条 tiáo] **2** 穗带 suì dài [M. WD 条 tiáo] **II** v **1** 编成辫子 biānchéng biànzi **2** 编成穗带 biānchéng suì dài
brain N **1** 脑 nǎo, 脑子 nǎozi
brain damage 脑损伤 nǎo sǔnshāng
2 脑力 nǎolì, 能力 nénglì
brain drain 人才外流 réncái wàiliú
brainchild N 脑力劳动的产物 nǎolì láodòng de chǎnwù, 独自想出来的东西 dúzì xiǎng chūlái de dōngxi
brainless ADJ 没有头脑的 méiyǒu tóunǎo de
brainstorming N [一群人+] 共同出主意 [yìqún rén+] gòngtóng chū zhǔyì, 群策群力 qún cè qún lì
brainwash v 洗脑 xǐnǎo
brainy ADJ 聪明的 cōngming de, 机敏的 jīmǐn de

braise v 用文火慢煮 yòng wénhuǒ màn zhǔ, 炖 dùn

brake I N 刹车 shāchē, 制动器 zhìdòngqì II v 踩刹车 cǎi shāchē

bran N 麦麸 màifū, 糠 kāng

branch I N 1 树枝 shùzhī [M. wD 条 tiáo] 2 分部 fēnbù 3 支流 zhīliú [M. wD 条 tiáo] II v 分支 fēnzhī, 分道 fēndào
to branch out 扩大领域 kuòdà lǐngyù

brand I N 牌子 páizi, 商标 shāngbiāo
brand name 商标名称 shāngbiāo míngchēng, 名牌 míngpái
II v 1 给…打上烙印 gěi…dǎshànglàoyìn 2 给…坏名声 gěi…huài míngshēng

brandish v 挥舞 huīwǔ

brand-new ADJ 崭新的 zhǎnxīn de

brandy N 白兰地 [+酒] báilándì [+jiǔ]

brash II ADJ 1 自以为是的 zìyǐwéishì de, 傲慢粗鲁的 àomàn cūlǔ de 2 刺耳的 cì'ěr de, 刺眼的 cìyǎn de

brass 1 N 1 黄铜 huángtóng 2 铜管乐器 tóngguǎnyuèqì
brass band 铜管乐队 tóngguǎn yuèduì
3 重要人物 zhòngyào rénwù [M. wD 位 wèi]

brasserie N（法式）小餐馆 (Fǎshì) xiǎo cānguǎn [M. wD 家 jiā]

brassy ADJ 1 黄铜的 huángtóng de 2 打扮艳丽举止粗俗的 [+女人] dǎban yànlì jǔzhǐ cūsú de [+nǚrén]

brat N 没有教养的小孩 méiyǒu jiàoyǎng de xiǎohái, 小坏蛋 xiǎo huàidàn

bravado N 虚张声势 xūzhāng shēngshì, 逞强的姿态 chěngqiáng de zītài

brave I ADJ 1 勇敢的 [+士兵] yǒnggǎn de [+shìbīng] 2 美好的 [+新世界] měihǎo de [+xīn shìjiè] II v 勇敢面对 yǒnggǎn miànduì

bravo INTERJ 好 hǎo, 妙 miào, 高 gāo

brawl N, v 打群架 dǎ qúnjià

bray v [驴+] 发出叫声 [lǘ+] fāchū jiàoshēng, [驴+] 叫 [lǘ+] jiào

brazen I ADJ 厚颜无耻的 hòuyán wúchǐ de
II v (to brazen it out) 厚着脸皮硬干 hòuzhe liǎnpí yìnggàn

brazier N 火盆 huǒpén [M. wD 只 zhī]

breach N 1 违反 wéifǎn
breach of security 违反安全规定 wéifǎn ānquán guīdìng
2 破裂 pòliè

bread N 面包 miànbāo [M. wD 片 piàn/块 kuài]

breadbasket N 产粮区 chǎnliángqū, 粮仓 liángcāng [M. wD 座 zuò]

breadcrumbs N 面包屑 miànbāoxiè

breaded ADJ 沾上面包屑的 zhānshang miànbāoxiè de

breadth N 宽度 kuāndù, 广度 guǎngdù

breadwinner N 挣钱养家的人 zhèngqián yǎngjiā de rén

break I v (PT **broke**; PP **broken**) 1 打破 dǎpò, 破损 pòsǔn ■ Who broke the fish bowl? 谁打破了鱼缸? Shéi dǎpòle yúgāng?
to break a record 打破纪录 dǎpò jìlù
2 摔坏 shuāi huài, 摔伤 shuāi shāng 3 摔断 shuāiduàn
to break down 出毛病 chūmáobing, 坏了 huàile ■ My car broke down. 我的车坏了。Wǒde chē huàile.
to break in/into 私自闯入 sīzì chuǎngrù
to break a promise 违背承诺 wéibèi chéngnuò, 食言 shíyán
to break a rule 犯规 fànguī
to break up 断绝来往 duànjué láiwǎng, 断交 duànjiāo
II N 1 [+谈话] 中断 [+tánhuà] zhōngduàn 2 [+午餐] 休息 [+wǔcān] xiūxi 3 骨折 gǔzhé 4 [+电影] 间歇 [+diànyǐng] jiānxiē

breakable ADJ 易破碎的 yì pòsuì de

breakage N 破损 pòsǔn

breakaway ADJ 分裂的 fēnliè de

breakdown N 失败 shībài, 破裂 pòliè

break-even ADJ 收支平衡的 shōuzhī pínghéng de

breakfast N 早饭 zǎofàn, 早餐 zǎocān

break-in N 非法闯入 fēifǎ chuǎngrù

breakneck ADJ 超高速的 chāogāosù de

breakthrough N 突破 tūpò

breakup N 破裂 pòliè, 分裂 fēnliè

breakwater N 防波堤 fángbōdī

breast 1 N 乳房 rǔfáng ■ She had one breast removed after being diagnosed with cancer. 她被诊断为乳房癌以后, 切除了乳房。Tā bèi zhěnduàn wéi rǔfángái yǐhòu, qiēchúle rǔfáng. 2 胸 xiōng, 胸部 xiōngbù

breastfed See **breastfeed**

breastfeed (PT & PP **breastfed**) v 用母乳喂养 yòng mǔrǔ wèiyǎng

breaststroke N 蛙式游泳 wāshì yóuyǒng, 蛙泳 wāyǒng

breath N 呼吸 hūxī
out of breath 喘不过气 chuǎnbúguò qì
to catch your breath 喘过气来 chuǎnguò qì lái
to hold your breath 屏住气 bǐngzhù qì
to take a deep breath 深吸一口气 shēn xī yì kǒu qì

breathable ADJ 透气性良好的 tòuqìxìng liánghǎo de

breathalyze v 做酒精检测 zuò jiǔjīng jiǎncè

Breathalyzer N 酒精检测仪 jiǔjīng jiǎncèyí

breathe v 呼吸 hūxī ■ The rescuer found the man still breathing. 抢救人员发现这个人还在呼吸。Qiǎngjiù rényuán fāxiàn zhè ge rén hái zài hūxī.

not to breathe a word 一句话也不说 yí jù huà yě bù shuō, 只字不露 zhǐzì bùlù
breathe in 吸气 xīqì
breathe out 呼气 hūqì

breathless ADJ 气喘吁吁的 qìchuǎn xūxū de
breathtaking ADJ 令人惊叹的 lìngrén jīngtàn de
breathy ADJ 带喘息声的 dài chuǎnxī shēng de
bred See **breed**
breeches N 马裤 mǎkù [M. WD 条 tiáo]
breed I N [动物的+] 品种 [dòngwù de+] pǐnzhǒng II v (PT & PP **bred**) 1 繁殖 [+名种狗] fánzhí [+míng zhǒng gǒu], 培育 péiyù ■ He makes a living breeding dogs. 他靠繁殖狗为生。Tā kào fánzhí gǒu wéishēng. 2 [动物+] 交配 [dòngwù+] jiāopèi 3 滋生 [+犯罪] zīshēng [+fànzuì], 引起 yǐnqǐ
breeder N 育种者 yùzhǒng zhě
breeding N 繁殖 fánzhí, 培育 péiyù
breeding ground 繁殖场 fánzhí chǎng, 孳生地 zīshēng dì
breeze I N 微风 wēifēng II v 飘然而来 piāorán érlái
breezy ADJ 1 有微风的 [+天气] yǒu wēifēng de [+tiānqì] 2 轻松自信的 [+青年] qīngsōng zìxìn de [+qīngnián], 快活的 kuàihuo de
brethren N 教友 jiàoyǒu
brevity N 简洁 jiǎnjié
brew I v 1 酿造 [+酒] niàngzào [+jiǔ] 2 冲泡 [+红茶] chōngpào [+hóngchá] 3 [麻烦的事+] 酝酿 [máfan de shì+] yùnniàng II N 1 啤酒 píjiǔ 2（酿造或冲泡的）饮料 (niàngzào huò chōngpào de) yǐnliào
home brew 家酿啤酒 jiāniàng píjiǔ
brewer N 啤酒公司 píjiǔ gōngsī [M. WD 家 jiā], 自酿啤酒者 zì niàng píjiǔ zhě
brewery N 啤酒厂 píjiǔchǎng [M. WD 家 jiā]
bribe I N 贿赂 huìlù
to take bribes 接受贿赂 jiēshòu huìlù, 受贿 shòuhuì
II v 贿赂 huìlù, 行贿 xínghuì
bribery N 贿赂的行为 huìlù de xíngwéi, 行贿 xínghuì, 受贿 shòuhuì
bric-a-brac N 小摆设 xiǎobǎishè [M. WD 件 jiàn]
brick I N 砖 zhuān [M. WD 块 kuài], 砖头 zhuāntóu [M. WD 块 kuài] II v 用砖砌 yòng zhuān qì
to brick off 用砖墙隔开 yòng zhuānqiáng gékāi
bricklayer N 砌砖工人 qìzhuān gōngrén, 泥瓦匠 níwǎjiàng
brickyard N 制砖厂 zhì zhuānchǎng [M. WD 家 jiā]
bridal ADJ 婚礼的 hūnlǐ de, 新娘的 xīnniáng de
bridal gown 婚纱 hūnshā
bride N 新娘 xīnniáng
bridegroom N 新郎 xīnláng
bridesmaid N 女傧相 nǚbīnxiàng
bridge I N 1 桥 qiáo [M. WD 座 zuò] 2 桥牌 qiáopái

II v 缩小 [+差异] suōxiǎo [+chāyì], 消除 [+分歧] xiāochú [+fēnqí]
bridle I N 马笼头 mǎlóngtóu II v 给马套上马笼头 gěi mǎ tàoshàng mǎlóngtóu
brief I ADJ 1 短暂的 duǎnzàn de 2 简洁的 jiǎnjié de, 简明的 jiǎnmíng de II N 1 简报 jiǎnbào, 摘要 zhāiyào 2 案情摘要 ànqíng zhāiyào, 诉讼要点 sùsòng yàodiǎn
to file a brief [+向法院] 提交诉讼 [+xiàng fǎyuàn] tíjiāo sùsòng
III v 向…介绍情况 xiàng…jièshào qíngkuàng
briefcase N 公事包 gōngshìbāo
briefing N 1 简要情况 jiǎnyào qíngkuàng 2 简报会 jiǎnbàohuì
briefs N 三角裤 sānjiǎokù [M. WD 条 tiáo]
brigade N 1（军队的）旅 (jūnduì de) lǚ 2 一队 yíduì, 一帮 yìbāng, 一群 yìqún
brigadier-general N 准将 zhǔnjiàng [M. WD 位 wèi]
bright ADJ 1 明亮的 míngliàng de 2 聪明的 cōngming de 3 欢快的 huānkuài de, 高兴的 gāoxìng de
brighten v 1 使 [+环境] 更美丽 shǐ [+huánjìng] gèng měilì 2 使 [+形势] 变得明亮 shǐ [+xíngshì] biàn de míngliàng
to brighten sb up 使某人高兴起来 shǐ mǒurén gāoxìng qǐlái
brights N 远光灯 yuǎn guāng dēng
brilliance N 1 [艺术家的+] 才华 [yìshùjiā de+] cáihuá 2 光亮 guāngliàng
brilliant ADJ 1 明亮的 [+灯光] míngliàng de [+dēngguāng], 光辉的 guānghuī de 2 才华洋溢的 [+艺术家] cáihuá yángyì de [+yìshùjiā] 3 绝妙的 [+主意] juémiào de [+zhǔyi]
brim I N 边缘 biānyuán, 边沿 biānyán, 边缘 biānyuán II v 充满 chōngmǎn, 洋溢 yángyì
to brim over ① [水池+] 满到溢出来 [shuǐchí+] mǎn dào yìchū lái ② 充满 [+信心] chōngmǎn [+xìnxīn]
brine N 浓盐水 nóng yánshuǐ
bring (PT & PP **brought**) v 1 带来 dàilai, 拿来 nálai 2 造成 zàochéng
to bring about 造成 zàochéng
not to bring oneself to do sth 不忍心（做某事）bù rěnxīn (zuò mǒushì)
to bring … to an end 使…结束 shǐ…jiéshù, 结束 jiéshù
to bring up 抚养 [+孩子] fǔyǎng [+háizi]
brink N 边缘 biānyuán
brisk ADJ 1 轻快的 [+步子] qīngkuài de [+bùzi] 2 兴隆的 [+生意] xīnglóng de [+shēngyì], 繁忙活跃的 fánmáng huóyuè de
bristle v 1 被激怒 bèi jīnù, 怒气冲冲 nùqì chōngchōng 2 [动物+] 毛发竖立 [dòngwù+] máofà shùlì
British I ADJ 英国的 Yīngguó de II N 英国人 Yīngguórén

brittle ADJ 脆的 cuì de, 易碎的 yì suìde

broach v 提出 tíchū, 提到 tídào

broad ADJ **1** 宽阔的 [+街道] kuānkuò de [+jiēdào], 宽的 kuān de **2** 简要的 [+说明] jiǎnyào de [+shuōmíng]

in broad daylight 大白天 dàbáitiān, 光天化日之下 guāngtiānhuàrì zhīxià

broadband N 宽带 kuāndài

broadcast I v (PT & PP **broadcast**) 广播 guǎngbō, 转播 zhuǎnbō II N 广播 guǎngbō

live broadcast 现场直播 xiànchǎng zhíbō

broadcaster N 播音员 bōyīnyuán

broadcasting N 广播 guǎngbō, 广播工作 guǎngbō gōngzuò

broaden v 扩大 kuòdà, 开拓 kāituò

broadly ADV 大体上 dàtǐshàng, 总体上 zǒngtǐ shàng

broadly speaking 大体上说 dàtǐshàng shuō

broadminded ADJ 心胸开阔的 xīnxiōngkāikuò de

broadside I ADV 侧面 cèmiàn II v 撞上…的侧面 zhuàngshàng...de cèmiàn

Broadway N (美国) 百老汇大街 (Měiguó) Bǎilǎohuì Dàjiē

brocade N 织锦 zhījǐn, 锦缎 jǐnduàn

broccoli N 花椰菜 huāyēcài [M. WD 棵 kē], 花茎甘蓝 huājīng gānlán [M. WD 棵 kē]

brochure N 小册子 xiǎocèzi [M. WD 本 běn]

brogue N **1** 厚底拷花皮鞋 hòudǐ kǎohuā pixie [M. WD 只 zhī/双 shuāng] **2** 浓重的地方口音 nóngzhòng de dìfang kǒuyīn

broil v 烤 kǎo, 烧烤 shāokǎo

broiler N 烤架 kǎojià

broke¹ ADJ 没有钱的 méiyǒu qián de, 身无分文的 shēn wú fēnwén de

to go broke 破产 pòchǎn

broke² See break

broken¹ See break

broken² ADJ **1** 破的 [+花瓶] pòde [+huāpíng], 破碎的 pòsuì de **2** 坏了的 [+沙发] huàile de [+shāfā] **3** 破裂的 [+婚姻] pòliè de [+hūnyīn]

broken-down ADJ 破旧的 pòjiù de

broken-hearted ADJ 心碎的 xīnsuì de

broker I N 经纪人 jīngjìrén, 掮客 qiánkè, 代理人 dàilǐrén II v 促成 cùchéng

to broker a deal 促成交易 cùchéng jiāoyì

brokerage N **1** 经纪业务 jīngjì yèwù **2** 经纪费 jīngjì fèi, 佣金 yòngjīn **3** 经纪行 jīngjìháng

bronchitis N 支气管炎 zhīqìguǎnyán

bronco N 野马 yěmǎ [M. WD 匹 pǐ]

bronze N 青铜 qīngtóng, 古铜 gǔtóng

bronze medal 铜牌 tóngpái

brooch N 胸针 xiōngzhēn [M. WD 枚 méi]

brood I v **1** 沉思 chénsī, 深思 shēnsī **2** 孵卵 fūluǎn II N 一窝 [+小鸟] yìwō [+xiǎoniǎo]

broom N 扫帚 sàozhou [M. WD 把 bǎ]

broomstick N 扫帚柄 sàozhoubǐng

broth N 汤 tāng [M. WD 碗 wǎn], 清汤 qīngtāng

brothel N 妓院 jìyuàn [M. WD 家 jiā]

brother N 兄弟 xiōngdì, 哥哥 gēge, 弟弟 dìdi

brotherhood N **1** 兄弟情谊 xiōngdì qíngyì, 手足之情 shǒuzú zhī qíng **2** (宗教) 兄弟会 (zōngjiào) xiōngdìhuì

brother-in-law N 大伯 dàbó (husband's elder brother), 小叔 xiǎoshū (husband's young brother), 内兄 nèixiōng (wife's elder brother), 内弟 nèidì (wife's younger brother), 姐夫 jiěfū (elder sister's husband), 妹夫 mèifū (younger sister's husband)

brotherly ADJ 兄弟情谊的 xiōngdì qíngyì de, 手足之情的 shǒuzú zhī qíng de

brought See bring

brow N 额 é, 额头 étóu

to knit one's brow 紧锁眉头 jǐnsuǒ méitóu, 愁眉不展 chóu méi bù zhǎn

browbeat (PT **browbeat**; PP **browbeaten**) v 对…吹胡子瞪眼睛 duì...chuīhúzi dèngyǎn jīng, 威逼 wēibī

browbeaten See browbeat

brown I ADJ 棕色的 zōngsè de, 咖啡色的 kāfēisè de II N 棕色 zōngsè, 咖啡色 kāfēisè

brownie N 果仁巧克力蛋糕 guǒ rén qiǎokèlì dàngāo

Brownies N 幼年女童子军 yòunián nǔtóngzǐjūn

brown-nose v 拍马屁 pāi mǎpì, 巴结 bājie

brownstone N 褐砂石 hèshāshí

browse v 随便翻阅 suíbiàn fānyuè, 浏览 liúlǎn

browser N 浏览器 liúlǎnqì

bruise I N 擦伤 cāshāng, 伤痕 shānghén II v 擦伤 cāshāng

brunch N 早午餐 zǎowǔcān

brunette N 深褐色头发的女子 shēn hèsè tóufa de nǔzǐ, 黑发女郎 hēi fā nǔláng

brunt N 重击 zhòngjī, 猛攻 měnggōng

to bear the brunt of 受到最猛烈的攻击 shòudàozuì měngliè de gōngjī, 首当其冲 shǒudāngqíchōng

brush I v 刷 shuā

to brush aside 不理会 bùlǐhuì

to brush up (on) 温习 wēnxí

II N **1** 刷子 shuāzi **2** 灌木林 guànmù lín, 丛林 cónglín

brush-off N 不理睬 bù lǐcǎi

to give sb the brush-off 让…碰一鼻子灰 ràng...pèng yì bízi huī

brusque ADJ 粗鲁的 cūlǔ de, 简慢的 jiǎnmàn de

Brussels sprout N 球芽甘蓝 qiúyá gānlán

brutal ADJ 野蛮的 yěmán de, 凶暴的 xiōngbào de

brutality N 野蛮 yěmán, 凶暴 xiōngbào

brutalize v **1** 野蛮凶暴地对待 yěmán xiōngbào de duìdài **2** 使…变得野蛮凶暴 shǐ...biàn de yěmán xiōngbào

brute I N **1** 野兽 yěshòu **2** 粗野汉子 cūyě hànzi, 凶残的人 xiōngcán de rén II ADJ 野蛮的 yěmán de

brute force 野蛮暴力 yěmán bàolì, 暴力 bàolì

brutish ADJ 没有人性的 méiyǒu rénxìng de, 兽性的 shòuxìng de

bubble I N 泡沫 pàomò, 气泡 qìpào
bubble gum 泡泡糖 pàopaotáng
II v 起泡 qǐpào, 冒泡 mào pào

bubbly I ADJ **1** 充满泡沫的 chōngmǎn pàomò de **2** 生气勃勃的 shēngqì bóbó de II N 香槟酒 xiāngbīnjiǔ

buck I N **1** 美元 Měiyuán, 钱 qián
to feel like a million bucks 感觉精神焕发 gǎnjué jīngshén huànfā
2 庄家标志 zhuāngjia biāozhì **3** 雄性动物 xióngxìng dòngwù II v **1** [马+] 弓背跃起 [mǎ+] gōngbèi yuèqǐ [汽车+] 颠簸行驶 [qìchē+] diānbǒ xíngshǐ **3** 反对 fǎnduì

bucket N 水桶 shuǐtǒng

buckle I N 扣子 kòuzi, 带扣 dàikòu II v **1** 系上扣子 jìshang kòuzi
Buckle up. 请系上安全带。Qǐng jìshang ānquándài.
2 腿软 tuǐ ruǎn, 站不直 zhàn bù zhí
to buckle under pressure 屈服压力 qūfú yālì **3** 弯曲变形 wānqū biànxíng

bud I N 花苞 huābāo, 芽 yá II v 长出花苞 zhǎng chū huābāo, 发芽 fāyá

Buddha N 佛陀 Fótuó, 菩萨 Púsà

Buddhism N 佛教 Fójiào

budding ADJ 崭露头角的 zhǎnlù tóujiǎo de, 开始发展的 kāishǐ fāzhǎn de

budge v **1** 移动 yídòng, 挪动 nuódong
not to budge an inch 一点儿都动不了 yìdiǎnr dōu dòngbuliǎo
2 改变注意 gǎibiàn zhùyì

budget I N 预算 yùsuàn II v **1** 计划用钱 jìhuà yòngqián, 省钱 shěngqián **2** 作预算 zuò yùsuàn, 编制预算 biānzhì yùsuàn **3** 精打细算 jīngdǎ xìsuàn III ADJ 经济的 jīngjì de, 便宜的 piányi de

buff I N **1** 爱好者 àihàozhě, 迷 mí
movie buff 电影迷 diànyǐngmí, 影迷 yǐngmí **2** 米黄色 mǐhuángsè II v 擦亮 cāliàng

buffalo N 牛 niú [M. WD 头 tóu], 水牛 shuǐniú [M. WD 头 tóu]

buffer N 缓冲物 huǎnchōngwù, 缓冲国 huǎnchōngguó, 缓冲储存器 huǎnchōng chǔcúnqì

buffet I N **1** 自助餐 zìzhùcān **2** 餐具柜 cānjù guì II v 冲击 chōngjī

buffoon N 丑角 chǒujué, 小丑 xiǎochǒu

buffoonery N 丑角表演 chǒujué biǎoyǎn, 丑角艺术 chǒujué yìshù

bug I N **1** 小虫子 xiǎo chóngzi

stomach bug 肚子不舒服 dùzi bùshūfú **2** 细菌 xìjūn, 病毒 bìngdú II v **1** 安装窃听器 ānzhuāng qiètīngqì, 窃听 qiètīng **2** 烦扰 fánrǎo

bugle N 军号 jūnhào [M. WD 把 bǎ]

build I v (PT & PP **built**) 建 jiàn, 建造 jiànzào
■ They plan to build a big house here. 他们计划在这里建造一幢大房子。Tāmen jìhuà zài zhèlǐ jiànzào yí zhuàng dà fángzi. II N 体格 tǐgé, 体形 tǐxíng

building N 建筑物 jiànzhùwù [M. WD 座 zuò]
building industry 建筑业 jiànzhùyè

building block N **1** 砌块 qìkuài **2** 基本要素 jīběn yàosù **3** 积木 jīmù [M. WD 块 kuài]

build-up N 增长 zēngzhǎng

built See **build**

built-in ADJ 内置的 nèizhì de, 内在的 nèizài de

built-up ADJ 盖了很多房子的 gàile hěn duō fángzi de

bulb N **1** 灯泡 dēngpào **2** 球茎 qiújīng

bulbous ADJ 球茎的 qiújīng de, 又肥又圆的 yòu féi yòu yuán de

bulge I N 膨胀 péngzhàng, 鼓出的地方 gǔ chū de dìfang II v 膨胀 péngzhàng, 鼓起 gǔqǐ

bulimia N 食欲过盛 shíyù guòshèng, 易饥症 yìjīzhèng

bulk N 大批 dàpī, 大量 dàliàng, 大宗 dàzōng
bulk buying 大量购买 dàliàng gòumǎi

bulky ADJ 体积大的 tǐjī dà de, 又大又重的 yòu dà yòu zhòng de

bull N **1** 公牛 gōngniú [M. WD 头 tóu] **2** 雄性动物 xióngxìng dòngwù

bulldog N 斗牛狗 dòuniú gǒu

bulldoze v [用推土机+] 推平 [yòng tuītǔjī+] tuī píng, [用推土机+] 推倒 [yòng tuītǔjī+] tuīdǎo

bulldozer N 推土机 tuītǔjī [M. WD 辆 liàng]

bullet N 子弹 zǐdàn [M. WD 枚 méi]
to bite the bullet 咬紧牙关忍受痛苦 yǎojǐn yáguān rěnshòu tòngkǔ, 忍痛 rěntòng

bulletin N 布告 bùgào, 公告 gōnggào

bulletin board N 布告牌 bùgàopái [M. WD 块 kuài]

bullfight, bullfighting N 斗牛 dòuniú

bullfighter N 斗牛士 dòuniúshì

bullhorn N 喇叭筒 lǎbatǒng, 扩音器 kuòyīnqì

bullion N 金 [或银+] 块 jīn [huò yín+] kuài, 金 [或银+] 条 jīn [+huò yín] tiáo

bullish ADJ **1** [股票市场+] 看涨的 [gǔpiào shìchǎng+] kànzhǎng de **2** 乐观自信的 [+投资者] lèguān zìxìn de [+tóuzīzhě]

bull market N 牛市 niú shì

bullpen N （棒球）投球区 [bàngqiú+] tóuqiú qū

bull's eye N 靶心 bǎxīn

bullshit INTERJ 狗屁 gǒupì, 胡说八道 húshuō bādà

bully I N 持强凌弱者 chíqiáng língruò zhě, 欺负人的恶棍 qīfù rén de ègùn II v 欺负 [+小同学] qīfù [+xiǎo tóngxué], 威吓 wēihè

bum I N 不务正业的人 bú wù zhèngyè de rén, 无用的人 wúyòng de rén II v 乞讨 qǐtǎo, 乞求 qǐqiú III ADJ 1 没有用处的 [+建议] méiyǒu yòng chù de [+jiànyì], 蹩脚货 biéjiǎohuò 2 受伤的 [+脚] shòushāng de [+jiǎo]

bumblebee N 大黄蜂 dàhuángfēng

bumbling ADJ 粗枝大叶的 cūzhīdàyè de, 一再出错的 yízài chūcuò de

bummed ADJ 难过的 nánguò de, 失望的 shīwàng de

bummer N 叫人扫兴的事 jiào rén sǎoxìng de shì

bump I v 1 撞 zhuàng, 碰 pèng 2 颠簸 diānbǒ II N 1 碰撞 pèngzhuàng 2 肿块 zhǒng kuài 3 凸起部分 tūqǐ bùfen

bumper I N 保险杠 bǎoxiǎngàng
bumper sticker（贴在汽车保险杠上的）小标语 (tiē zài qìchē bǎoxiǎngàng shàng de) xiǎo biāoyǔ
II ADJ 大量的 dàliàng de
bumper harvest 大丰收 dà fēngshōu

bumper-to-bumper ADV（汽车）一辆挨一辆 (qìchē) yíliàng ái yíliàng

bumpy ADJ 1 高低不平的 gāodī bùpíng de 2 颠簸的 diānbǒ de

bun N 小圆面包 xiǎo yuán miànbāo

bunch I N 束 shù, 串 chuàn
a bunch of flowers 一束花 yí shù huā
a bunch of keys 一串钥匙 yí chuàn yàoshi
II v 扎成一束 zhā chéng yí shù

bundle I N 1 一捆 yìkǔn, 一扎 yì zhā 2 包裹 bāoguǒ, 一包 yìbāo 3 捆绑销售的商品 kǔnbǎng xiāoshòu de shāngpǐn II v 捆绑销售 kǔnbǎng xiāoshòu

bungalow N 平房 píngfáng [M. WD 栋 dòng]

bungle v 搞糟 gǎozāo, 一再出错 yízài chūcuò

bunk I N 床铺 chuángpù, 铺位 pùwèi
bunk beds 双层床 shuāngcéngchuáng
II v（在别人家）过夜 (zài biéren jiā) guòyè

bunker N 掩体 yǎntǐ, 地堡 dìbǎo

bunny N 兔子 tùzi [M. WD 只 zhī]

buoy I N 浮标 fúbiāo, 航标 hángbiāo II v 1 鼓舞 [+士气] gǔwǔ [+shìqì], 振奋 [+精神] zhènfèn [+jīngshén] 2 维持 [+价格的高水平] wéichí [+jiàgé de gāoshuǐpíng]

buoyancy N 1 [轮船的+] 浮性 [lúnchuán de+] fúxìng, 浮力 fúlì 2 [新开公司的+] 乐观自信 [xīn kāi gōngsī de+] lèguān zìxìn 3 [市场+] 复苏力 [shìchǎng+] fùsūlì

buoyant ADJ 1 轻松愉快的 [+喜剧演员] qīngsōng yúkuài de [+xǐjù yǎnyuán], 充满自信的 chōngmǎn zìxìn de 2 欣欣向荣的 [+经济] xīnxīn xiàng róng de [+jīngjì] 3 有浮力的 [+泡沫塑料] yǒu fúlì de [+pàomò sùliào]

burden I N 负担 fùdān, 重担 zhòngdàn
burden of proof 举证责任 jǔ zhèng zérèn

II v 使…负担 shǐ…fùdān
to be burdened with 承受…的重负 chéng-shòu…de zhòngfù

bureau N 局 jú, 司 sī
the Federal Bureau of Investigation (FBI)（美国）联邦调查局 (Měiguó) Liánbāng Diàochájú

bureaucracy N 1 官僚制度 guānliáo zhìdù, 官僚主义 guānliáo zhǔyì 2 官僚集团 guānliáo jítuán

bureaucrat N 官僚 guānliáo

bureaucratic ADJ 官僚的 guānliáo de, 官僚主义的 guānliáo zhǔyì de

burgeoning ADJ 迅速增长的 xùnsù zēngzhǎng de

burger N 圆牛肉饼 yuán niúròubǐng

burglar N 破门盗窃者 pòmén dàoqiè zhě, 盗贼 dàozéi

burglarize v 破门盗窃 pòmén dàoqiè, 撬窃 qiào qiè

burglary N 破门盗窃罪 pòmén dàoqièzuì

burial N 埋葬 máizàng, 葬礼 zànglǐ

burly ADJ 高大粗壮的 gāodà cūzhuàng de, 魁梧的 kuíwú de

burn I v (PT & PP **burned**, **burnt**) 1 烧 shāo, 燃烧 ránshāo
to burn to the ground 烧成灰烬 shāo chéng huījìn
2 烧伤 shāoshāng 3 晒伤 shàishāng 4 照亮 zhàoliàng
to burn the midnight oil 熬夜工作 áoyè gōngzuò, 开夜车 kāiyèchē
to be burned out ① 精疲力尽 jīngpí lìjìn, 身心疲惫 shēnxīn píbèi ② 烧毁 shāohuǐ, 烧尽 shāo jìn ③ 使…非常气愤 shǐ…fēicháng qìfèn
5 复制 [+光碟] fùzhì [+guāngdié], 拷贝 kǎobèi
II N 烧伤 shāoshāng, 烫伤 tàngshāng

burner N 灶火头 zàohuo tóu, 火眼 huǒyǎn
to put sth on the back burner 推迟做某事 tuīchí zuò mǒushì, 暂时不考虑 zànshí bù kǎolǜ

burning ADJ 1 燃烧着的 ránshāo zhe de 2 感到发烫的 gǎndào fātàng de

burnish v 擦亮 cāliàng

burned, burnt See burn

burnt ADJ 烧焦的 shāojiāo de

burp v 打嗝 dǎ gé

burrow I v [动物+] 打洞 [dòngwù+] dǎ dòng II N 洞穴 dòngxué

bursar N 财务主管 cáiwù zhǔguǎn

burst I v (PT & PP **burst**) 1 爆裂 bàoliè
to burst out laughing/crying 突然大笑／大哭起来 tūrán dàxiào/dàkū qǐlái
to burst into tears 放声大哭 fàngshēng dàkū
2 闯 chuǎng, 闯入 chuǎngrù II N 破裂 pòliè, 爆裂 bàoliè

bury v 埋 mái, 埋葬 máizàng

bus I N 公共汽车 gōnggòng qìchē [M. WD 辆 liàng]

bus conductor 公共汽车售票员 gōnggòng qìchē shòupiàoyuán

bus driver 公共汽车驾驶员 gōnggòng qìchē jiàshǐyuán

bus lane 公交车辆专用道 gōngjiāo chēliàng zhuānyòngdào

bus stop 公共汽车站 gōnggòng qìchēzhàn

bus terminus 公共汽车总站 gōnggòng qìchē zǒngzhàn, 公共汽车终点站 gōnggòng qìchē zhōngdiǎnzhàn

II v **1** 用大客车运送 yòng dàkèchē yùnsòng **2** [餐馆里+] 收拾脏餐具 [cānguǎn lǐ+] shōushi zàng cānjù

busboy N 餐馆杂工 cānguǎn zágōng

bush N 灌木丛 guànmùcóng

bushed ADJ 精疲力尽的 jīngpí lìjìn de

bushel N （容量单位）蒲式耳 (róngliàng dānwèi) púshì'ěr (= 8 gallons/36.4 liters)

bushy ADJ [毛发+] 浓密的 [máofa+] nóngmì de

business N **1** 商业 shāngyè, 生意 shēngyì

business class [飞机+] 商务舱 [fēijī+] shāngwùcāng

2 商店 shāngdiàn [M. WD 家 jiā], 商行 shāng-háng [M. WD 家 jiā], 企业 qǐyè [M. WD 家 jiā]

business card 名片 míngpiàn [M. WD 张 zhāng]

business hours 营业时间 yíngyè shíjiān

Master of Business Administration (M.B.A.) 商业管理硕士 shāngyè guǎnlǐ shuòshì

3 工作 gōngzuò, 任务 rènwù

business lunch 工作午餐 gōngzuò wǔcān

business trip 出差 chūchāi

businessman, businesswoman N 商人 shāngrén

bust **I** v **1** 打破 dǎpò **2** [警察+] 指控 [jǐngchá+] zhǐkòng **3** 超支 chāozhī **II** N **1** 胸部 xiōngbù, 胸围 xiōngwéi **2** 半身塑像 bànshēn sùxiàng

buster N 小子 xiǎozǐ, 讨厌鬼 tǎoyànguǐ

bustle **I** v 忙乱 mángluàn, 奔忙 bēnmáng **II** N 忙乱 mángluàn, 喧闹 xuānnào

bustling ADJ 繁忙喧闹的 fánmáng xuānnào de

busy ADJ **1** 忙 máng, 繁忙 fánmáng **2** [电话+] 占线的 [diànhuà+] zhànxiàn de

busybody N 爱管闲事的人 ài guǎn xiánshì de rén

but **I** CONJ 但是 dànshì, 可是 kěshì **II** PREP 除了 chúle **III** ADV 仅仅 jǐnjǐn, 只不过 zhǐbúguò

butcher **I** N **1** 肉商 ròu shāng **2** 屠夫 túfū **II** v 屠宰 túzǎi

butler N 男管家 nánguǎnjiā

butt **I** N 屁股 pìgu **2** 烟头 yāntóu, 烟蒂 yāndì **3** 枪托 qiāngtuō **II** v 用头顶撞 yòngtou dǐngzhuàng

butter **I** N 黄油 huángyóu, 牛油 niúyóu **II** v 涂黄油 tú huángyóu

buttercup N 毛茛 máogèn

butterfingers N 抓不住东西的人 zhuā búzhù dōngxi de rén

butterfly N **1** 蝴蝶 húdié [M. WD 只 zhī] **2** 蝶泳 diéyǒng

buttermilk N 脱脂乳 tuōzhīrǔ

butterscotch N 奶油糖果 nǎiyóu tángguǒ

buttock N 屁股 pìgu

button **I** N **1** 纽扣 niǔkòu ■ *A button is missing on his shirt.* 他的衬衫有一颗纽扣掉了。Tā de chènshān yǒu yì kē niǔkòu diào le. **2** 按钮 ànniǔ **3** 胸针 xiōngzhēn [M. WD 枚 méi] **II** v 扣上纽扣 kòushang niǔkòu

buttonhole N 纽扣洞 niǔkòu dòng

buttress **I** N 扶壁 fú bì, 撑墙 chēng qiáng **II** v 支持 zhīchí

buxom ADJ 丰满健美的 [+女子] fēngmǎn jiànměi de [+nǚzǐ]

buy **I** v (PT & PP bought) **1** 买 mǎi ■ *He bought a new cell phone.* 他买了一个新手机。Tā mǎile yí ge xīn shǒujī. ■ *Have you bought the book the teacher recommended?* 你买到了老师推荐的书了吗？Nǐ mǎidaole lǎoshī tuījiàn de shū le ma?

to buy into 收购 shōugòu

to buy out 全部收购 quánbù shōugòu

to buy time 争取时间 zhēngqǔ shíjiān

2 相信 xiāngxìn, 接受 jiēshòu **II** N 购买 gòumǎ

to be a good buy 买得合算 mǎi dé hésuàn

buyer N 购买者 gòumǎizhě, 买主 mǎizhǔ

buyer's market 买方市场 mǎifāng shìchǎng

buyout N 全部收购 quánbù shōugòu

buzz **I** N 嗡嗡声 wēngwēng shēng **II** v 发出嗡嗡声 fāchū wēngwēng shēng

buzzer N 蜂鸣器 fēngmíngqì

buzzword N 术语 shùyǔ, 行话 hánghuà

by **I** PREP **1** 在…旁边 zài…pángbiān ■ *A man was standing by the hotel door.* 一名男子站在旅馆门口。Yì míng nánzǐ zhàn zài lǚguǎn ménkǒu. **2** 经过 jīngguò ■ *I walk by the store almost every day.* 我几乎每天走过这家商店。Wǒ jīhū měitiān zǒuguo zhè jiā shāngdiàn. **3** 在…以前 zài… yǐqián ■ *Please reply by the end of this week.* 请在本周末以前答复。Qǐng zài běn zhōumò yǐqián dáfù. **II** ADV 经过 jīngguò

by and large 大体上 dàtǐshàng, 大致 dàzhì

bye INTERJ 再见 zàijiàn

bygone ADJ 过去的 guòqù de, 以往的 yǐwǎng de

bygones N 过去的事 guòqù de shì

bylaw N [内部+] 章程 [nèibù+] zhāngchéng

byline N **1** 作者署名行 zuòzhě shǔmíng háng **2** 球门线 qiúménxiàn [M. WD 条 tiáo]

bypass **I** N **1** 旁道 pángdào **2** 心脏搭桥手术 xīnzàng dāqiáo shǒushù **II** v 绕过 ràoguò

by-product N 副产品 fùchǎnpǐn

bystander N 旁观者 pángguānzhě

byte N 字节 zìjié

byway N 偏僻小路 piānpì xiǎolù [M. WD 条 tiáo]

byword N 代名词 dàimíngcí

C

C (= Celsius, Centigrade) ABBREV 摄氏 shèshì
20° C 摄氏二十度 Shèshì èrshí dù

cab N 出租汽车 chūzū qìchē [M. WD 辆 liàng]
to hail a cab 叫出租汽车 jiào chūzū qìchē

cabaret N（夜总会或餐馆的）歌舞表演
(yèzǒnghuì huò cānguǎn de) gēwǔ biǎoyǎn

cabbage N 卷心菜 juǎnxīncài [M. WD 棵 kē]

cabbie, cabby N 出租汽车司机 chūzū qìchē sījī

cabin N 1 小木屋 xiǎo mùwū [M. WD 间 jiān/栋
dòng] 2 [轮船／飞机+] 客舱 [lún chuán/fēijī+]
kècāng [M. WD 间 jiān]

cabinet N 1 柜子 guìzi [M. WD 只 zhī]
display cabinet 陈列柜 chénlièguì
filing cabinet 档案柜 dàng'ànguì
2 [政府] 内阁 [zhèngfǔ] nèigé

cable N 1 电缆 diànlǎn [M. WD 条 tiáo]
cable car 电缆车 diànlǎnchē
2 有线电视 yǒuxiàn diànshì
cable television 有线电视 yǒuxiàn diànshì

cache N 隐藏物 yǐncángwù, 隐藏处 yǐncángchù

cachet N 声望 shēngwàng, 崇高的地位 chónggāo
de dìwèi

cackle v 1 [母鸡+] 咯咯叫 [mǔjī+] gēgē jiào 2 发
出刺耳的笑声 fāchū cì'ěr de xiàoshēng

cactus N 仙人掌 xiānrénzhǎng [M. WD 株 zhū]

caddy N（为高尔夫球手服务的）球童 (wéi
gāo'ěrfūqiú shǒu fúwù de) qiútóng

cadence N 1 [声调的+] 抑扬顿挫 [shēngdiào de+]
yìyáng dùncuò 2 韵律 yùnlǜ

cadet N（军官学校或警官学校）学生 (jūnguān
xuéxiào huò jǐngguān xuéxiào) xuésheng

cadre N 骨干队伍 gǔgànduìwǔ, 干部 gànbù

Caesarean N 剖腹产手术 pōufùchǎn shǒushù

café N 咖啡馆 kāfēiguǎn [M. WD 家 jiā]

cafeteria N 自助餐厅 zìzhù cāntīng [M. WD 家 jiā],
食堂 shítáng

caffeine N 咖啡因 kāfēiyīn

cage I N 笼子 lóngzi II v 放进笼子 fàngjìn lóngzi
to feel caged in 感到失去自由 gǎndào shīqù
zìyóu

cagey ADJ 说话十分谨慎的 shuōhuà shífēn
jǐnshèn de, 保守秘密的 bǎoshǒu mìmì de

cahoots N 同伙 tónghuǒ
to be in cahoots with 与…同伙 yǔ…tónghuǒ

cajole v 哄骗 hǒngpiàn

cake N 糕 gāo, 蛋糕 dàngāo
birthday cake 生日蛋糕 shēngrì dàngāo
wedding cake 结婚蛋糕 jiéhūn dàngāo
to bake a cake 烘蛋糕 hōng dàngāo
to be a piece of cake 轻而易举的事 qīng ér yì
jǔ de shì

to have your cake and eat it too 两者兼得
liǎngzhě jiān dé

calamitous ADJ 灾难的 zāinàn de, 灾难性的
zāinànxìng de

calamity N 灾难 zāinàn [M. WD 场 cháng], 灾祸
zāihuò [M. WD 场 cháng]

calcium N 钙 gài

calculate v 计算 jìsuàn

calculated ADJ 预料中的 yùliào zhòngdì, 预计的
yùjì de
calculated risk 预计的风险 yùjì de fēngxiǎn
be calculated to do sth 目的在于 mùdì zàiyú

calculating ADJ 很有心计的 hěn yǒuxīn jì de

calculation N 计算 jìsuàn, 估计 gūjì

calculator N 计算器 jìsuànqì

calculus N 微积分 wēijīfēn

calendar N 日历 rìlì

calf N 1 小牛 xiǎoniú 2 小腿 xiǎotuǐ

caliber N 1 [人的+] 才干能力 [rén de+] cáigàn
nénglì 2 [事物的+] 质量 [shìwù de+] zhìliàng

calibrate v 标定 [+刻度] biāodìng [+kèdù]

calibration N 刻度 kèdù

calico N 印花薄布 yìnhuā báo bù

call I v 1 打电话 dǎ diànhuà
to call back 回电话 huí diànhuà
to call collect 打对方付费的电话 dǎ duìfāng
fùfèi de diànhuà
2 叫 jiào, 喊 hǎn
to call for 要求 yāoqiú, 请求 qǐngqiú
to call off 取消 qǔxiāo ■ The meeting was called
off. 会议取消了。Huìyì qǔxiāo le.
3 把…叫作 bǎ…jiàozuo, 叫 jiào ■ What should
I call you? 我该叫你什么? (→我该怎么称呼你?)
Wǒ gāi jiào nǐ shénme? (→ Wǒ gāi zěnme
chēnghu nǐ?) 4 拜访 bàifǎng
to call on 拜访 bàifǎng
to call sb names 辱骂某人 rǔmà mǒurén
to call the shots 发号施令 fāhào shīlìng
II N 1 电话 diànhuà
call box 路边紧急救援电话 lùbiān jǐnjí qiúyuán
diànhuà
2 叫喊声 jiàohǎnshēng ■ I heard a call for help
in the dark alley. 我听到从漆黑的小巷传来求救
的叫喊声。Wǒ tīngdào cóng qīhēi de xiǎoxiàng
chuánlái qiújiù de jiàohǎnshēng. 3 拜访 bàifǎng
the call of nature 要小便 yào xiǎobiàn
to be on call 随叫随到 suíjiào suídào

caller N 打电话来的人 dǎ diànhuà láide rén
caller ID（电话）来电显示 (diànhuà) láidiàn
xiǎnshì

callgirl N 应召女郎 yìngzhào nǚláng, 妓女 jìnǚ

calligraphy N 书法（艺术）shūfǎ (yìshù)

call-in N 电话热线节目 diànhuà rèxiàn jiémù, 叫
应节目 kòuyìng jiémù

calling N 使命感 shǐmìnggǎn

callous ADJ 冷漠的 lěngmò de, 冷酷的 lěngkù de

callously ADV 冷漠地 lěngmò de, 冷酷地 lěngkù de

callousness N 冷漠 lěngmò, 冷酷 lěngkù

callus N [手脚上的+] 硬皮 [shǒujiǎo shàng de+] yìng pí, 老茧 lǎojiǎn

calm I ADJ 镇静的 zhènjìng de, 镇定的 zhèndìng de II v 使…镇静 shǐ…zhènjìng

calorie N 卡路里 kǎlùlǐ, 卡 kǎ

camaraderie N 同志情谊 tóngzhì qíngyì

camcorder N 便携式摄像机 biànxiéshì shèlù-xiàngjī [M. WD 只 zhī/台 tái]

came See come

camel N 骆驼 luòtuo [M. WD 只 zhī/头 tóu]

camellia N 山茶花 shānchāhuā [M. WD 朵 duǒ], 茶花 cháhuā [M. WD 朵 duǒ]

cameo N 1 浮雕宝石 fúdiāo bǎoshí 2 名演员客串的片段 míng yǎnyuán kèchuàn de piànduàn

camera N 照相机 zhàoxiàngjī [M. WD 只 zhī/台 tái]
digital camera 数码照相机 shùmǎ zhàoxiàngjī
surveillance camera 监控摄像机 jiānkòng shèxiàngjī

cameraman, camerawoman N 摄影师 shèyǐngshī

camouflage I N 1 伪装 wěizhuāng 2 迷彩服 mícǎifú II v 用伪装隐蔽 yòng wěizhuāng yǐnbì

camp I N 营 yíng, 营地 yíngdì
campfire 营火 yínghuǒ, 篝火 gōuhuǒ
campground 野营地 yěyíngdì
campsite 露营地 lùyíngdì
summer camp 夏令营 xiàlìngyíng
II v 露营 lùyíng

campaign I N [一系列的+] 活动/运动 [yíxìliè de+] huódòng/yùndòng II v 发起或参与（一系列的）活动、运动 fāqǐ huò cānyù (yíxìliè de) huódòng, yùndòng

camper N 1 露营者 lùyíng zhě 2 野营车 yěyíng chē [M. WD 辆 liàng]

campus N（大学）校园 (dàxué) xiàoyuán

can¹ MODAL V [NEG **cannot** ABBREV **can't** (PT **could**; NEG **could not** ABBREV **couldn't**)] 1 能 néng, 能够 nénggòu ■ *"Can you do the job?" "Yes, I can."* "你能做这个工作吗？" "能。" Nǐ néng zuò zhè ge gōngzuò ma? "Néng." 2 可以 kěyǐ ■ *You can leave.* 你可以走了。 Nǐ kěyǐ zǒu le.

can² I N 1 罐头 guàntou 2 桶 tǒng
can opener 开罐器 kāiguànqì
garbage can 垃圾桶 lājītǒng
II v 把（食物）装罐 bǎ (shíwù) zhuāngguàn

Canadian I ADJ 加拿大的 Jiānádà de II N 加拿大人 Jiānádàrén

canal N 运河 yùnhé [M. WD 条 tiáo], 水渠 shuǐqú [M. WD 条 tiáo]

canary N 金丝雀 jīnsīquè [M. WD 只 zhī]

cancel v 取消 qǔxiāo
to cancel out 抵消 dǐxiāo

cancellation N 取消 qǔxiāo, 作废 zuòfèi

cancer N 癌 ái, 癌症 áizhèng

Cancer N 巨蟹宫 Jùxiègōng

candidacy N 候选人资格 hòuxuǎnrén zīgé

candidate N 候选人 hòuxuǎnrén

candidly ADV 直言不讳地 zhíyán búhuì de, 坦率地 tǎnshuài de

candle N 蜡烛 làzhú [M. WD 支 zhī]
to burn the candle at both ends 起早摸黑地工作 qǐzǎomōhēi de gōngzuò

candlestick N 烛台 zhútái

candor N 坦率 tǎnshuài, 坦诚 tǎnchéng

candy N 糖果 tángguǒ

cane I N 拐杖 guǎizhàng [M. WD 根 gēn], 手杖 shǒuzhàng [M. WD 根 gēn] II v 用藤鞭抽打 yòng téngbiān chōudǎ

canine ADJ 犬类的 quǎn lèi de, 狗的 gǒu de
police canine unit 警犬小组 jǐngquǎn xiǎozǔ

canister N 方形圆顶罐桶 fāngxíng yuándǐng guàn tǒng, 罐 guàn, 桶 tǒng

canker N 口（角）疮 kǒu (jué) chuāng
canker sore 植物溃疡 zhíwù kuìyáng

cannabis N 大麻毒品 dàmá dúpǐn

canned ADJ 1 罐装的 guànzhuāng de
canned beef 罐装牛肉 guànzhuāng niúròu 2 预先录音的 [+笑声/音乐] yùxiān lùyīn de [xiàoshēng, yīnyuè]
canned laughter 预先录制的笑声 yùxiān lùzhì de xiàoshēng

cannery N 罐头食品厂 guàntoushípǐn chǎng [M. WD 家 jiā]

cannibal N 食人肉者 shí rénròu zhě

cannibalism N 食人 shí rén

cannibalistic ADJ 食人的 shí rén de

cannon N 大炮 dàpào [M. WD 门 mén], 加农炮 jiānóngpào [M. WD 门 mén]

canny ADJ 精明的 jīngmíng de, 不容易上当的 bù róngyì shàngdàng de

canoe N 独木舟 dúmùzhōu

canopy N 1 树冠 shùguān 2 顶罩 dǐng zhào

can't See can

cantankerous ADJ 脾气暴躁的 píqi bàozao de, 爱抱怨的 ài bàoyuàn de

canteen N 1 食堂 shítáng [M. WD 间 jiān], 行军水壶 xíngjūn shuǐhú

canter v（骑马）中速跑 (qímǎ) zhōng sù pǎo

Cantonese N 1 广东话 Guǎngdōnghuà 2 广东人 Guǎngdōng rén

canvas N 1 帆布 fānbù [M. WD 块 kuài] 2 油画布 yóuhuàbù, 油画 yóuhuà [M. WD 块 kuài]

canvass v 征求意见 zhēngqiú yìjiàn, 了解情况 liǎojiě qíngkuàng, 游说 yóushuì

canyon N 峡谷 xiágǔ

cap N 帽子 màozi [M. WD 顶 dǐng], 鸭舌帽 yāshémào [M. WD 顶 dǐng]

capability N 能力 nénglì, 才能 cáinéng

capable ADJ 能干的 nénggàn de, 有能力的 yǒu nénglì de

to be capable of 能够 nénggòu

capacity N 1 能力 nénglì ■ *This test is beyond the capacity of most students in my class.* 这个考试超出了我班上大多数同学的能力。 Zhè ge kǎoshì chāochūle wǒ bānshang dàduōshù tóngxué de nénglì. 2 容量 róngliàng

cape N 1 海角 hǎijiǎo 2 斗篷 dǒupéng [M. WD 件 jiàn], 披风 pīfēng [M. WD 件 jiàn]

caper I N 1 不法勾当 bùfǎ gòudang, 冒险举动 màoxiǎn jǔdòng 2 动作片 dòngzuò piàn II v 兴奋地跳跃 xīngfèn de tiàoyuè

Cape Verde N 佛德角 Fódé jiǎo

capillary N 毛细血管 máoxì xuèguǎn [M. WD 根 gēn]

capital I N 1 首都 shǒudū 2 资本 zīběn
capital assets 固定资产 gùdìng zīchǎn
II ADJ 1 大写的 dàxiě de
capital letter 大写字母 dàxiězìmǔ
2 死刑的 sǐxíng de
capital punishment 死刑 sǐxíng

capitalism N 资本主义 zīběnzhǔyì

capitalist I N 资本家 zīběnjiā II ADJ 资本主义的 zīběn zhǔyì de

capitalize v 1 提供资金 tígōng zījīn 2 大写 [+第一个字母] dàxiě [dìyīgè zìmǔ] 3 (to capitalize on) 利用 [+机会] lìyòng [+jīhuì]

Capitol N（美国）国会大厦 (Měiguó) Guóhuì dàshà
Capitol Hill（美国）国会山 (Měiguó) Guóhuìshān

capitulate v 屈服 qūfú, 投降 tóuxiáng

capitulation N 屈服 qūfú, 投降 tóuxiáng

cappuccino N 卡普奇诺咖啡 kǎpǔqínuò kāfēi

caprice N 任性多变 rènxìng duōbiàn

capricious ADJ 1 任性的 rèn xìng de 2 不合理的 bùhélǐ de

Capricorn N 摩羯宫 Mójiégōng

capsize v [船+] 倾覆 [chuán+] qīngfù, 翻船 fānchuán

capsule N 1 胶囊 jiāonáng [M. WD 粒 lì] 2 航天舱 hángtiāncāng [M. WD 间 jiān], 密封舱 mìfēngcāng [M. WD 间 jiān]

captain N 1 船长 chuánzhǎng, 机长 jīzhǎng 2（球队等）队长 (qiúduì děng) duìzhǎng
captain of industry 产业巨头 chǎnyè jùtóu

caption N 1 [图片+] 说明文字 [túpiàn+] shuōmíng wénzì 2 [电影/电视+] 字幕 [diànyǐng/diànshì+] zìmù

captivate v 迷住 mízhù, 吸引 xīyǐn

captivating ADJ 迷人的 mírén de, 非常吸引人的 fēicháng xīyǐnrén de

captive I ADJ 被关押的 bèi guānyā de
to take sb captive 关押某人 guānyā mǒurén
II N 囚徒 qiútú, 战俘 zhànfú

captivity N 囚禁 qiújìn, 关押 guānyā

captor N 捕捉者 bǔzhuōzhě

capture I v 1 捕获 [+罪犯] bǔhuò [+zuìfàn] 2 攻占 [+城市] gōngzhàn [chéngshì] 3 夺取 [+市场] duóqǔ [+shìchǎng], 赢得 yíngdé
to capture sb's imagination 唤起某人的想象 huànqǐ mǒurén de xiǎngxiàng
II N 捕获 bǔhuò

car N 汽车 qìchē [M. WD 辆 liàng]
car pool 合伙用车的人 héhuǒ yòng chē de rén
luxury car 豪华车 háohuáchē
sports car 赛车 sàichē
used car 二手车 èrshǒuchē, 旧车 jiùchē

carafe N 饮料瓶 yǐnliàopíng

caramel N 焦糖块 jiāotángkuài [M. WD 块 kuài]

carat N 克拉 kèlā

caravan N 长途旅行车队 chángtú lǚxíng chēduì

carbohydrate N 碳水化合物 tànshuǐ huàhéwù

carbon (C) N 碳 tàn
carbon copy 复写本 fùxiěběn
carbon dating 碳年代测定法 tàn niándài cèdìngfǎ
carbon dioxide 二氧化碳 èryǎng huàtàn
carbon monoxide 一氧化碳 yìyǎng huàtàn
carbon paper 复写纸 fùxiězhǐ
carbon footprint 消耗能源的纪录 xiāohào néngyuán de jìlù

carbonated ADJ 含有二氧化碳的 hányǒu èryǎnghuàtàn de

carburettor N（汽车）汽化器 (qìchē) qìhuàqì

carcass N（动物）尸体 (dòngwù) shītǐ

carcinogen N 致癌物质 zhì'ái wùzhì

carcinogenic ADJ 致癌的 zhì'ái de

card N 1 卡 kǎ [M. WD 张 zhāng], 卡片 kǎpiàn [M. WD 张 zhāng] 2 贺卡 hèkǎ 3 银行卡 yínhángkǎ 4 扑克牌 pūkèpái, 纸牌 zhǐpái
card table 牌桌 pái zhuō
card shark 靠作弊赢牌的人 kào zuòbì yíng pái de rén
birthday card 生日贺卡 shēngrì hèkǎ
business card 名片 míngpiàn
Christmas card 圣诞贺卡 shèngdàn hèkǎ
credit card 信用卡 xìnyòngkǎ
ID card 身份证 shēnfenzhèng
library card 借书证 jièshūzhèng
student ID card 学生证 xuéshengzhèng

cardboard N 硬纸板 yìngzhǐbǎn [M. WD 块 kuài/张 zhāng]

cardiac ADJ 心脏的 xīnzàng de
cardiac arrest 心脏停搏 xīnzàng tíng bó

cardigan N 对襟羊毛衫 duìjīn yángmáoshān [M. WD 件 jiàn]

cardinal I ADJ 基本的 jīběn de, 主要的 zhǔyào de
cardinal number 基数 jīshù
II N 枢机主教 Shūjī Zhǔjiào, 红衣主教 Hóngyī zhǔjiào

cardiograph N 心电图仪 xīndiàntúyí [M. WD 台 tái]

cardiology N 心脏病学 xīnzàngbìngxué

cardiovascular ADJ 心血管的 xīnxuèguǎn de

care I v 1 关心 guānxīn, 关怀 guānhuái 2 照顾 zhàogù, 照料 zhàoliào ■ *Who would care for you in case you are sick?* 你万一生病了，谁来照顾你呢？Nǐ wànyī shēngbìng le, shéi lái zhàogù nǐ ne? 3 喜欢 xǐhuan ■ *Would you care for some Italian food tonight?* 今天晚上我们吃意大利饭，你喜欢吗？Jīntiān wǎnshang wǒmen chī Yìdàlì fàn, nǐ xǐhuan ma? 4 在乎 zàihu II N 1 注意 zhùyì, 小心 xiǎoxīn
Handle with care! 小心轻放！Xiǎoxīn qīngfàng!
to take care of ① 照顾 zhàogù, 照料 zhàoliào ② 处理 chǔlǐ, 料理 liàolǐ
care package [寄给学生／军人的+] 食品包裹 [jìgěi xuéshēng/jūnrén de+] shípǐn bāoguǒ

careen v 歪歪扭扭地疾驶向前 wāiwāi niǔniǔ de jíshǐ xiàngqián

career I N [个人的+] 事业 [gèrén de+] shìyè
career counsellor 就业指导员 jiùyè zhǐdǎoyuán
II ADJ 职业的 zhíyè de, 专业的 zhuānyè de
career diplomat 职业外交官 zhíyè wàijiāoguān
career woman 职业妇女 zhíyè fùnǚ

carefree ADJ 无忧无虑 wúyōu wúlǜ

careful ADJ 小心的 xiǎoxīn de, 仔细的 zǐxì de
to be careful with money 花钱很谨慎 huāqián hěn jǐnshèn

caregiver N 照看儿童或病人的人 zhàokàn értóng huò bìngrén de rén

careless ADJ 粗心的 cūxīn de

caress v 爱抚 àifǔ, 抚摸 fǔmō

caretaker N 看管人 kānguǎn rén, 管理员 guǎnlǐyuán

cargo N 货物 huòwù

Caribbean ADJ 加勒比海的 Jiā lè bǐ hǎi de
Caribbean Sea 加勒比海 Jiālèbǐhǎi

caribou N 北美驯鹿 Běiměi xùnlù [M. WD 只 zhī/头 tóu]

caricature I N 1 漫画 mànhuà [M. WD 幅 fú] 2 讽刺画 fěngcìhuà 2 讽刺文章 fěngcì wénzhāng [M. WD 篇 piān] II v 把…画成漫画 bǎ…huà chéng mànhuà

caring ADJ 关心别人的 guānxīn biéren de, 关爱的 guān'ài de

carjacking N 劫持汽车 jiéchí qìchē

carnage N 大屠杀 dà túshā [M. WD 场 cháng]

carnal ADJ 肉欲的 ròuyù de, 肉体的 ròutǐ de

carnation N 麝香石竹 shèxiāng shízhú [M. WD 朵 duǒ/株 zhū], 康乃馨 kāngnǎixīn

carnival N 1 狂欢节 kuánghuānjié 2 流动游艺团 liúdòng yóuyìtuán

carnivore N 食肉动物 shíròu dòngwù

carnivorous ADJ 食肉的 shíròu de

carol N 圣诞颂歌 Shèngdàn sònggē

carouse v 狂饮作乐 kuángyǐn zuòlè

carousel N 旋转木马 xuánzhuǎn mùmǎ

carp¹ N 鲤鱼 lǐyú

carp² v 挑剔 tiāoti, 吹毛求疵 chuī máo qiú cī

carpenter N 木工 mùgōng, 木工师傅 mùgōng shīfu

carpentry N 木匠手艺 mùjiang shǒuyì, 木匠工作 mùjiang gōngzuò

carpet N 地毯 dìtǎn [M. WD 块 kuài]

carpeting N 地毯（的料子）dìtǎn (de liàozi)

carport N 停车棚 tíngchēpéng

carriage N 车厢 chēxiāng

carrier N 1 航空运输公司 hángkōng yùnshū gōngsī 2 航空母舰 hángkōngmǔjiàn 3 运送人 yùnsòngrén

carrot N 1 胡萝卜 húluóbo [M. WD 根 gēn] 2 许诺 xǔnuò
a carrot-and-stick approach 胡萝卜加大棒的方法 húluóbo jiā dàbàng de fāngfǎ

carry v 1 运送 yùnsòng 2 随身带 suíshēn dài, 携带 xiédài ■ *The photographer carries his camera wherever he goes.* 这位摄影师不论去哪儿总是带着照相机。Zhè wèi shèyǐngshī búlùn qù nǎr zǒngshì dàizhe zhàoxiàngjī.
to carry on 继续 jìxù
to carry out 实行 shíxíng, 进行 jìnxíng
to get/be carried away 激动得失去控制 jīdòng de shīqù kòngzhì

carryall N 大手提袋 dà shǒutídài

carry-on ADJ 随身带上飞机的 suíshēn dàishàng fēijī de

carsick ADJ 晕车的 yùnchē de

carsickness N 晕车 yùnchē

cart I N 推车 tuīchē
shopping cart 购物车 gòuwùchē
II v 搬运 bānyùn, 装运 zhuāngyùn

cartel N 卡特尔 kǎtè'ěr, 同业联盟 tóngyè liánméng

cartilage N 软骨组织 ruǎngǔ zǔzhī

cartography N 地图绘制 dìtú huìzhì

carton N 纸板箱 zhǐbǎnxiāng

cartoon N 1 漫画 mànhuà 2 (animated cartoon) 动画片 dònghuàpiàn

cartridge N 1 小盒子 xiǎohézi [M. WD 只 zhī] 2 子弹 zǐdàn [M. WD 颗 kē/枚 méi]
computer game cartridge 电脑游戏卡 diànnǎo yóuxìkǎ
ink cartridge （打印机）油墨盒 (dǎyìnjī) yóumò hé

cartwheel N 侧手翻 cèshǒufān

carve v 雕刻 diāokè

carving N 雕刻 (品) diāokè(pǐn)

cascade I N 小瀑布 xiǎopùbù [M. WD 条 tiáo] II v 瀑布一样地落下 pùbù yíyàng de luòxia

case N 1 事例 shìlì 2 （法律）案件 (fǎlù) ànjiàn 3 病例 bìnglì ■ *We haven't had a case of bird flu* *in this region.* 我们这个地区还没有禽流感病例。Wǒmen zhège dìqū hái méiyǒu qínliúgǎn bìnglì.

case study 个案研究 gè'àn yánjiū

in case 万一 wànyī

in any case 无论如何 wúlùn rúhé, 不管怎样 bùguǎn zěnyàng

in that case 既然那样 jìrán nàyàng ■ *You don't feel well today? In that case, you'd better stay at home.* 你今天不舒服？既然这样，最好待在家里。Nǐ jīntiān bùshūfú? Jìrán zhèyàng, zuìhǎo dàizài jiālì.

caseload N 工作量 gōngzuòliàng

cash I N 现金 xiànjīn II V 兑换现金 duìhuàn xiànjīn ■ *Could you please cash this check for me?* 能不能把这张支票兑换成现金? Néngbunéng bǎ zhè zhāng zhīpiào duìhuàn chéng xiànjīn?

cash cow 摇钱树 yáoqiánshù

cash crop 经济作物 jīngjì zuòwù

cash flow 现金流通 xiànjīn liútōng

cash on delivery 货到付款 huò dào fù kuǎn

cash register（商店里的）收银柜 (shāngdiàn lǐ de) shōuyínguì

cashew N 腰果 yāoguǒ [M. WD 粒 lì]

cashier N 出纳（员）chūnà (yuán)

cashmere N（山）羊绒 (shān) yángróng

cash-strapped ADJ 资金困难的 zījīn kùnnan de

casing N 套套 tào tào, 罩罩 zhào zhào

casino N 赌场 dǔchǎng

cask N（装酒的）木桶 (zhuāng jiǔ de) mùtǒng

casket N 1 棺材 guāncai 2 首饰盒 shǒushíhé

casserole N 1 砂锅 shāguō, 炖锅 dùnguō 2 砂锅菜 shāguōcài, 炖锅菜 dùnguōcài
beef casserole 砂锅牛肉 shāguō niúròu

cassette N 盒式磁带 hé shì cídài
cassette recorder 盒式磁带录音机 héshì cídài lùyīnjī
audio cassette 盒式录音带 héshì lùyīndài
video cassette 盒式录像带 héshì lùxiàngdài

cast I V (PT & PP cast) 1 投 tóu, 掷 zhì 2 清除 qīngchú, 扔掉 rēngdiào 3 投射 tóushè
to cast a vote 投票 tóupiào
to cast a shadow 投下阴影 tóuxià yīnyǐng
II N 1 全体演员 quántǐ yǎnyuán 2 人物 rénwù, 角色 juésè

castaway N [沉船后+] 漂流到荒岛的人 [chén-chuán hòu+] piāoliú dào huāngdǎo de rén

caste N（印度的）种姓制度 (Yìndù de) zhǒngxìng zhìdù

caster N 脚轮 jiǎolún

castigate V 严厉批评 yánlì pīpíng, 严惩 yánchéng

castigation N 严厉批评 yánlì pīpíng, 严惩 yánchéng

casting N 挑选演员 tiāoxuǎn yǎnyuán

cast-iron N 铸铁 zhùtiě, 生铁 shēngtiě

castle N 城堡 chéngbǎo [M. WD 座 zuò]

castoff N 丢弃的 [+衣服] diūqì de [+yīfu]

castrate V 阉割 yāngē

castration N 阉割 yāngē

casual ADJ 1 非正式的 fēizhèngshì de 2 随意的 suíyì de, 漫不经心的 màn bù jīngxīn de 3 不是经常的 bú shì jīngcháng de, 偶然的 ǒurán de
casual clothes 休闲服装 xiūxián fúzhuāng
a casual remark 随口说的一句话 suíkǒu shuōde yí jù huà
casual worker 临时工 línshígōng

casualty N 伤亡人员 shāngwáng rényuán, 伤亡人数 shāngwáng rénshù

cat N 猫 māo [M. WD 只 zhī]
like a cat on a hot tin roof 像热锅上的蚂蚁 xiàng règuōshàng de mǎyǐ

cataclysm N 大灾难 dàzāinàn, 剧变 jùbiàn

cataclysmic ADJ 剧变的 jùbiàn de

catalog N 1 商品目录 shāngpǐn mùlù [M. WD 份 fèn], 样品簿 yàngpǐnbù [M. WD 本 běn] 2 图书目录 túshūmùlù, 索引 suǒyǐn

catalysis N 催化作用 cuīhuà zuòyòng

catalyst N 1 催化剂 cuīhuàjì 2 促使巨变的人（或事）cùshǐ jùbiàn de rén (huò chì)

catamaran N 双体船 shuāngtǐchuán [M. WD 艘 sōu]

catapult I N 1 弹弓 dàngōng 2 飞机弹射器 fēijī tánshèqì II V 把…弹出去 bǎ...dàn chūqu

cataract N 白内障 báinèizhàng

catastrophe N 巨大灾难 jùdà zāinàn

catastrophic ADJ 灾难性的 zāinànxìng de

catch I V (PT & PP caught) 1 抓住 zhuāzhù, 抓获 zhuāhuò 2 赶上 gǎn shàng 3 感染上 gǎnrǎn shàng
to be caught up in sth 被卷入某事 bèijuǎn rù mǒu shì
to catch on 开始明白 kāishǐ míngbai
to catch one's breath 喘过气来 chuǎn guòqì lái, 喘气 chuǎnqì
to catch sb's eye 吸引某人的注意 xīyǐn mǒurén de zhùyì
to catch up (with) 追赶上 zhuī gǎn shàng
II N 1 抓住 zhuāzhù, 接到 jiēdào 2（隐藏的）问题 (yǐncáng de) wèntí, 隐患 yǐnhuàn 3 圈套 quāntào, 诡计 guǐjì 4 [海产的+] 捕获量 [hǎichǎn de+] bǔhuòliàng 5 [项链+] 扣子 [xiàngliàn+] kòuzi
catch phrase 流行语 liúxíng yǔ, 口头禅 kǒutóuchán

catcher N（棒球）接球手 (bàngqiú) jiēqiúshǒu

catching ADJ 传染性的 chuánrǎnxìng de

catchword N 口号 kǒuhào, 标语 biāoyǔ

catchy ADJ 朗朗上口的 lǎnglǎng shàngkǒu de, 顺口的 shùnkǒu de

catechism N（基督教的）教理问答 (Jīdūjiào de) jiàolǐ wèndá

categorical ADJ 明确的 míngquè de

categorically ADV 明确地 míngquè de, 断然地 duànrán de

categorize V 把…分类 bǎ…fēnlèi

category N 种类 zhǒnglèi, 类别 lèibié

cater V 提供饮食服务 tígōng yǐnshí fúwù, 办酒席 bànjiǔxí
to cater to/for 满足 [顾客+] 的需要 mǎnzú [gùkè+] de xūyào

catering N 提供饮食 tígōng yǐnshí, 承办酒席 chéngbàn jiǔxí
catering industry 饮食行业 yǐnshí hángyè

caterpillar N 毛虫 máochóng [M. WD 只 zhī/条 tiáo]

catfish N 鲶鱼 niányú [M. WD 条 tiáo]

cathedral N 大教堂 dàjiàotáng

Catholic N 天主教 Tiānzhǔjiào

catholic ADJ 广泛的 guǎngfàn de

catnap N 小睡 xiǎoshuì
to take catnaps 小睡一会儿 xiǎoshuì yíhuìr, 打盹儿 dǎdǔnr

catnip N 樟脑草 zhāngnǎocǎo

cattail N 香蒲 xiāngpú

cattle N 牛群 niúqún, 牛 niú

catty ADJ 恶毒的 èdú de, 歹毒的 dǎidú de

catwalk N (时装表演) 步行台 (shízhuāng biǎoyǎn) bùxíngtái, T 形台 tǐxíngtái

Caucasian N, ADJ 白种人 (的) báizhǒngrén (de)

caucus N 政党地区会议 zhèngdǎng dìqū huìyì

caught See **catch**

cauliflower N 花椰菜 huāyēcài [M. WD 颗 kē], 花菜 huācài [M. WD 颗 kē]

cause I N 1 原因 yuányīn, 理由 lǐyóu
with good cause 有充分理由 yǒu chōngfèn lǐyóu 2 事业 shìyè II V 因其 yīnqí, 造成 zàochéng

caustic ADJ 1 刻薄的 [+言词] kèbó de [+yáncí], 尖刻的 jiānkè de 2 腐蚀性的 [+物质] fǔshíxìng de [+wùzhì]

caution I N 谨慎 jǐnshèn II V 告诫 gàojiè, 提醒 tíxǐng

cautionary ADJ 警告的 jǐnggào de
a cautionary tale 有警示意义的事例 yǒu jǐngshì yìyì de shìlì

cautious ADJ 谨慎的 jǐnshèn de

cave¹ N 洞 dòng, 洞穴 dòngxué

cave² V (to cave in) 1 [煤矿+] 塌方 [méikuàng+] tāfāng 2 停止抵抗 tíngzhǐ dǐkàng, 屈从 qūcóng

caveman N (史前) 洞穴人 (shǐqián) dòngxué rén

cavern N 大山洞 dà shāndòng, 大洞穴 dà dòngxué

caviar N 鱼子酱 yúzǐjiàng

cavity N 1 蛀牙洞 zhùyá dòng 2 腔 qiāng, 洞 dòng

cavort V 欢腾 huānténg, 欢闹 huān nào

cc (= cubic centimeter) ABBREV 立方厘米 lìfānglímǐ

CCTV (= closed-circuit televison) ABBREV 闭路电视 bìlù diànshì

CD (= compact disk) ABBREV 光碟 guāngdié [M. WD 张 zhāng/盘 pán]

CD player 光碟播放机 guāngdié bōfàngjī, 激光唱机 jīguāng chàngjī

CD-ROM N 只读存储光盘 zhǐ dú cúnchǔ guāngpán

cease V 终止 zhōngzhǐ, 停止 tíngzhǐ

ceasefire N 停火 tínghuǒ

ceaseless ADJ 不停的 bùtíng de

cedar N 西洋杉 Xīyáng shān, 雪松 xuěsōng

cede V 割让 gēràng, 交出 jiāochū

ceiling N 1 天花板 tiānhuābǎn 2 上限 shàngxiàn

celebrate V 1 庆祝 [+新年] qìngzhù [+xīnnián] 2 赞美 [+大自然] zànměi [+dàzìrán], 颂扬 sòngyáng

celebrated ADJ 著名的 zhùmíng de, 闻名的 wénmíng de

celebration N 1 庆祝 qìngzhù 2 颂扬 sòngyáng

celebrity N 名人 míngrén

celery N 芹菜 qíncài

celestial ADJ 天上的 tiānshàng de, 天堂的 tiāntáng de

celibacy N 1 (因宗教而) 禁欲 (yīn zōngjiào ér) jìnyù 2 不结婚独居生活 bù jiéhūn dújū shēnghuó

celibate ADJ (因宗教而) 禁欲的 (yīn zōngjiào ér) jìnyù de

cell N 1 牢房 láofáng [M. WD 间 jiān] 2 细胞 xìbāo 3 电池 diànchí [M. WD 节 jié]

cellar N 地窖 dìjiào
wine cellar 酒窖 jiǔjiào, 储藏在地窖的酒 chǔcáng zài dìjiào de jiǔ

cellist N 大提琴演奏者 dàtíqín yǎnzòuzhě

cello N 大提琴 dàtíqín [M. WD 把 bǎ]

cellophane N 玻璃纸 bōlizhǐ [M. WD 张 zhāng]

cell phone N 手机 shǒujī, 移动电话 yídòng diànhuà

cellular ADJ 1 细胞的 xìbāo de 2 移动电话的 yídòng diànhuà de

cellular phone See **cell phone**

cellulite N 皮下脂肪 pí xià zhīfáng

celluloid N (早期) 电影的 (zǎoqī) diànyǐng de

cellulose N 纤维素 xiānwéisù

Celsius N See **C**

cement I N 1 水泥 shuǐní 2 胶合剂 jiāohéjì II V 1 涂上水泥 tú shàngshuǐ ní 2 巩固 gǒnggù

cemetery N 公墓 gōngmù, 墓地 mùdì

censor I V 审查 shěnchá II N 审查人员 shěnchá rényuán

censorship N 审查 shěnchá, 审查制度 shěnchá zhìdù

censure V 正式批评 zhèngshì pīpíng, 公开谴责 gōngkāi qiǎnzé

census N 人口普查 rénkǒu pǔchá

cent N [钱] 分 [qián] fēn

centennial, centenary N 一百周年 yìbǎi zhōunián, 一百周年纪念 yìbǎi zhōunián jìniàn

center N 中间 zhōngjiān, 中心 zhōngxīn
center of gravity 重心 zhòngxīn
shopping center 购物中心 gòuwù zhōngxīn

center field N（棒球）中外场 (bàngqiú) zhōng-wàichǎng

centerfold N（杂志中页的）裸女照片 (zázhì zhōng yè de) luǒnǚ zhàopiàn

centerpiece N 1 餐桌中央的装饰品 cānzhuō zhōngyāng de zhuāngshìpǐn 2 最重要的部分 zuì zhòngyào de bùfen

Centigrade N 摄氏 Shèshì

centimeter N 厘米 límǐ, 公分 gōngfēn

centipede N 百足虫 bǎizúchóng, 蜈蚣 wúgong

central ADJ 中心的 zhōngxīn de, 中央的 zhōngyāng de
(New York) Central Park（纽约）中央公园 (Niǔyuē) zhōngyāng gōngyuán
party central 聚会场所 jùhuì chǎngsuǒ

century N 世纪 shìjì

CEO (= Chief of Executive Officer) ABBREV 首席执行官 shǒuxí zhíxíngguān [M. WD 位 wèi], 总经理 zǒngjīnglǐ [M. WD 位 wèi]

ceramics N 陶瓷器（制作）táocíqì (zhìzuò)

cereal N 早餐谷物食品 zǎocān gǔwù shípǐn, 麦片 màipiàn

cerebral ADJ 1 大脑的 dànǎo de 2 需要大脑思考的 xūyào dànǎo sīkǎo de, 深奥的 shēn'ào de

ceremonial ADJ 礼仪的 lǐyí de, 典礼的 diǎnlǐ de

ceremony N 仪式 yíshì, 典礼 diǎnlǐ
marriage ceremony 结婚仪式 jiéhūn yíshì
master of ceremony 司仪 sīyí

certain ADJ 1 肯定的 kěndìng de ■ *I'm certain that we'll win the game.* 我肯定我们能赢这场比赛。Wǒ kěndìng wǒmen néng yíng zhè chǎng bǐsài. ■ *It's almost certain that he will be the new principal.* 他几乎肯定会当新校长。Tā jīhū kěndìng huì dāng xīn xiàozhǎng. 2 某个 mǒu ge, 某些 mǒuxiē ■ *In certain places in the world you have to bribe officials to get things done.* 在世界上某些地方你得贿赂官员才能办事。Zài shìjièshang mǒuxiē dìfang nǐ děi huìlù guānyuán cái néng bànshì.

certainly ADV 1 肯定 kěndìng 2 当然 dāngrán ■ *"Will you share your findings with me?" "Certainly!"* "你会让我分享你的发现吗？" "当然会！" "Nǐ huì ràng wǒ fēnxiǎng nǐ de fāxiàn ma?" "Dāngrán huì!"

certainty N 确定性 quèdìngxìng, 确定的事 quèdìng de shì
to say with (any) certainty 确切地说 quèqiè de shuō

certifiable ADJ 1 可以证明的 kěyǐ zhèngmíng de 2 可以通过的 kěyǐ tōngguò de

certificate N 证书 zhèngshū, 证明 zhèngmíng [M. WD 份 fèn/张 zhāng]
birth certificate 出生证 chūshēngzhèng

certificate of deposit 存款单 cúnkuǎndān
death certificate 死亡证 sǐwángzhèng
marriage certificate 结婚证 jiéhūnzhèng

certification N 证书 zhèngshū, 合格证 hégézhèng [M. WD 份 fèn/张 zhāng]

certified ADJ 1 完成专业培训的 wánchéng zhuānyè péixùn de, 合格的 hégé de
certified public accountant 合格的开业会计 hégé de kāiyè kuàijì, 执业会计 zhíyè kuàijì
2 被核准的 bèi hézhǔn de
certified check 保付支票 bǎofù zhīpiào
a certified copy 经鉴定核准的副本 jīng jiàndìng hézhǔn de fùběn
certified mail 挂号邮件 guàhào yóujiàn, 保送邮件 bǎosòng yóujiàn

certify V 正式证明 zhèngshì zhèngmíng

cervical ADJ 子宫颈的 zǐgōngjǐng de
cervical cancer 子宫颈癌 zǐgōngjǐng ái

cervix N 子宫颈 zǐgōngjǐng

cessation N 停止 tíngzhǐ, 中断 zhōngduàn

cesspool N 污秽的场所 wūhuì de chǎngsuǒ

chafe V 恼火 nǎohuǒ, 焦躁 jiāozào

chagrin I N 懊恼 àonǎo, 失望 shīwàng II V 使（某人）懊恼 shǐ (mǒurén) àonǎo, 使（某人）失望 shǐ (mǒurén) shīwàng
to be chagrined 感到气恼 gǎndào qìnǎo

chain I N 1 链条 liàntiáo [M. WD 根 gēn] 2 一系列 yíxìliè 3 连锁商店 liánsuǒshāngdiàn/餐馆 cānguǎn/旅馆 lǚguǎn II V 用链条栓住 yòng liàntiáo shuānzhù
chain letter 连锁信 liánsuǒ xìn
chain reaction 连锁反应 liánsuǒ fǎnyìng

chainsaw N 链锯 liànjù [M. WD 把 bǎ]

chainsmoke V 一支接一支地吸烟 yìzhī jiē yìzhī de xīyān

chainsmoker N 一支接一支地吸烟的人 yìzhī jiē yìzhī de xīyān de rén, 烟鬼 yānguǐ

chair N 椅子 yǐzi [M. WD 把 bǎ]
armchair 扶手椅 fúshǒuyǐ [M. WD 把 bǎ]
wheelchair 轮椅 lúnyǐ [M. WD 辆 liàng]

chairperson N 主席 zhǔxí [M. WD 位 wèi]
chairman of a company 公司董事长 gōngsī dǒngshìzhǎng

chalet N（瑞士）小屋 (Ruìshì) xiǎo wū [M. WD 栋 dòng/幢 zhuàng]

chalk I N 1 粉笔 fěnbǐ [M. WD 支 zhī] 2 白垩 bái'è II V 用粉笔写 yòng fěnbǐ xiě
to chalk up 获分 huò fēn

chalkboard N 黑板 hēibǎn [M. WD 块 kuài]

challenge I N 1 挑战 [+权威] tiǎozhàn [+quánwēi] 2 要求 [+做困难的事] yāoqiú [+zuò kùnnáo de shì] II N 1 挑战 tiǎozhàn, 挑战书 tiǎozhànshū 2 很难对付的人（或事）hěn nán duìfu de rén (huò shì) 3 质疑 zhìyí

chamber N 1 房间 fángjiān 2 室 shì, 腔 qiāng

chamber music 室内(音)乐 shìnèi (yīn) yuè

chamber of commerce 商会 shānghuì

chamber pot 夜壶 yèhú

chameleon N 1 变色蜥蜴 biànsè xīyì 2 见风使舵的人 jiàn fēng shǐ duò de rén, 变色龙 biànsèlóng

champagne N 香槟酒 xiāngbīnjiǔ [M. WD 杯 bēi/瓶 píng]

champion N 冠军 guànjūn [M. WD 位 wèi]

championship N 锦标赛 jǐnbiāosài [M. WD 场 chǎng/次 cì]

chance I N 1 机会 jīhuì

to take a chance, to take chances 冒险 màoxiǎn, 冒风险 mào fēngxiǎn

fat chance 不可能 bùkěnéng

by chance 偶然 ǒurán, 正巧 zhèngqiǎo

to leave nothing to chance 毫不疏忽 háobù shūhu

to stand a chance 有可能 yǒukěnéng

II v 1 冒险 màoxiǎn 2 碰巧 pèngqiǎo III ADJ 偶然的 ǒurán de

chancellor N 1 (某些大学的)校长 (mǒuxiē dàxué de) xiàozhǎng 2 (德国)总理 (Déguó) Zǒnglǐ

chancy ADJ 担风险的 dānfēngxiǎn de

chandelier N 枝形吊灯 zhīxíng diàodēng [M. WD 架 jià/盏 zhǎn]

change I v 1 变化 biànhuà 2 改变 gǎibiàn 3 换乘(火车、飞机等)huàn chéng (huǒchē、fēijī děng) II N 1 变化 biànhuà ■ Lots of changes have taken place in my hometown in the past few years. 我的故乡在过去几年发生了很多变化。Wǒ de gùxiāng zài guòqù jǐnián fāshēngle hěn duō biànhuà. 2 找头 zhǎotou ■ You may keep the change. 你不用给我找头了。Nǐ bú yòng gěi wǒ zhǎotou le. 3 零钱 língqián ■ I have no change on me. 我没有带零钱。Wǒ méiyǒu dài língqián. small change 零钱 língqián

a change of clothes 备换的衣服 bèi huàn de yīfu

changeable ADJ 常常变化的 chángcháng biànhuà de

changeover N 改变 gǎibiàn, 转型 zhuǎnxíng

channel I N 1 电视频道 diànshì píndào 2 海峡 hǎixiá 3 [供水+]管道 [gōngshuǐ+] guǎndào 4 [获取信息的+]途径 tújìng, 渠道 qúdào

to go through diplomatic channels 通过外交渠道 tōngguò wàijiāo qúdào

II v 把(金钱、精力)用于 bǎ (jīnqián, jīnglì) yòng yú

to channel resources into research and development 把资源用于开发研究 bǎ zīyuán yòng yú kāifā yánjiū

chant I v 1 反复地喊叫 fǎnfù de hǎnjiào 2 吟唱 [+宗教歌曲] yínchàng [+zōngjiào gēqǔ]

II N 1 一再重复的话 yízài fǎnfù dehuà 2 宗教歌曲 zōngjiào gēqǔ [M. WD 首 shǒu]

chaos N 混乱 hùnluàn, 无序状态 wú xù zhuàngtài

chaotic ADJ 极其混乱的 jíqí hùnluàn de, 紊乱不堪的 wěnluàn bùkān de

chapel N 小教堂 xiǎojiàotáng

wedding chapel 婚礼教堂 hūnlǐ jiàotáng

chaperone I N (未成年人在社交场合的)监护人 (wèi chéngnián rén zài shèjiāo chǎnghé de) jiānhùrén II v 当监护人 dāng jiānhùrén

chaplain N (军队、医院等地的)牧师 (jūnduì, yīyuàn děng dì de) mùshī

chapped ADJ 皲裂的 jūnliè de, 干燥的 gānzào de

chapter N 1 章 zhāng, 章节 zhāngjié 2 时期 shíqī, 事件 shìjiàn 3 分会 fēnhuì

char v 烧焦 shāojiāo

character N 1 [电影 / 小说+] 人物 / 角色 [diànyǐng/xiǎoshuō+] rénwù/juésè 2 性格 xìnggé ■ She has a complex character. 她的性格很复杂。Tā de xìnggé hěn fùzá. 3 特征 tèzhēng 4 书写符号 shūxiě fúhào

Chinese character 汉字 Hànzì

characteristic I N 特点 tèdiǎn, 特性 tèxìng II ADJ 独特的 dútè de, 显著的 xiǎnzhe de

characterize v 把…说成 bǎ…shuōchéng, 描绘…的特征 miáohuì…de tèzhēng

to characterize the economic situation as dire 把经济形势说成是极其糟糕的 bǎ jīngjì xíngshì shuōchéng shì jíqí zāogāo de

charade N 装模作样的把戏 zhuāngmú zuòyàng de bǎxì, 伪装 wěizhuāng

charades N 猜字游戏 cāizì yóuxì

charcoal N 炭 tàn, 木炭 mùtàn

charge I v 1 要价 yàojià 2 记账 jìzhàng 3 指控 zhǐkòng ■ He was charged with drink driving. 他被指控酒后驾驶。Tā bèi zhǐkòng jiǔhòu jiàshǐ. 4 猛冲 měngchōng II N 1 费用 fèiyòng ■ What is the charge for an international telephone call to Shanghai? 打国际长途电话到上海要多少钱? Dǎ guójì chángtú diànhuà dào Shànghǎi yào duōshǎo qián?

charge account 信用账户 xìnyòng zhànghù

charge card 记帐卡 jìzhàngkǎ

free of charge 免费 miǎnfèi

2 指控 zhǐkòng, 罪名 zuìmíng 3 负责 fùzé 4 突然猛冲 tūrán měngchōng 5 充电 chōngdiàn

charger N 充电器 chōngdiànqì

chariot N (古代)战车 (gǔdài) zhànchē [M. WD 辆 liàng]

charisma N 魅力 mèilì, 个人魅力 gèrén mèilì

charitable ADJ 1 慈善的 císhàn de, 慈善事业的 císhàn shìyè de 2 宽容的 kuānróng de, 同情的 tóngqíng de

charitably ADV 1 慈善地 císhàn de 2 宽容地 kuānróng de

charity N 1 慈善 císhàn, 慈善事业 císhàn shìyè
charity concert 为慈善事业募捐的音乐会 wéi císhàn shìyè mùjuān de yīnyuèhuì, 义演音乐会 yìyǎn yīnyuèhuì
2 施舍物 shīshě wù

charlatan N 冒充内行的骗子 màochōng nèiháng de piànzi

charm N 1 迷人之处 mírén zhī chù, 魅力 mèilì
2 装饰挂件 zhuāngshì guàjiàn [M. WD 件 jiàn]
lucky charm 护身符 hùshēnfú [M. WD 件 jiàn]

charmed ADJ 好像有魔法保护的 hǎoxiàng yǒu mófǎ bǎohù de, 幸运的 xìngyùn de
to lead a charmed life 生活一直很幸运 shēnghuó yìzhí hěn xìngyùn

charming ADJ 迷人的 mírén de, 可爱的 kě'ài de

charred ADJ 烧焦的 shāojiāo de

chart I N 图表 túbiǎo
pie chart 饼形分析图 bǐngxíng fēnxī tú
II v 1 记录 jìlù 2 制订计划 zhìdìng jìhuà

charter I N 1 [飞机／船只+] 包租 [fēijī/chuánzhǐ+] hānzū 2 纲领 gānglǐng
charter flight 包机旅行 bāojī lǚxíng
II v 包租 [+飞机／船只] bāozū [+fēijī/chuánzhī]

chase v 1 追 zhuī, 追赶 zhuīgǎn 2 追求 zhuīqiú
to chase down 找到 zhǎodào, 追捕到 zhuībǔdào

chasm N 1 深渊 shēnyuān 2 巨大的分歧 jùdà de fēnqí

chassis N (汽车) 底盘 (qìchē) dǐpán

chaste ADJ 贞洁的 zhēnjié de, 纯洁的 chúnjié de

chasten v 惩戒 chéngjiè, 使…接受教训 shǐ…jiēshòu jiàoxùn

chastise v 严厉斥责 yánlì chìzé

chastity N 贞洁 zhēnjié, 纯洁 chúnjié

chat I v 1 闲谈 xiántán, 聊天 liáotiān 2 网上聊天 wǎngshàng liáotiān II N 1 闲谈 xiántán, 聊天 liáotiān 2 网上聊天 wǎngshàng liáotiān
chat room 网上聊天室 wǎngshàng liáotiānshì

chateau N (法国的) 城堡 (Fǎguó de) chéngbǎo

chatter v 1 [人+] 唠叨 [ren+] láodao, 喋喋不休 diédié bùxiū 2 [猴子／鸟+] 鸣叫 [hóuzi/niǎo+] míngjiào 3 [牙齿+] 打战 [yáchǐ+] dǎzhàn

chatterbox N 喋喋不休的人 diédié bùxiū de rén

chatty ADJ 爱闲聊的 ài xiánliáo de

chauffeur I N (私人) 司机 (sīrén) sījī II v 当私人司机 dāng sīrén sījī
a chauffeured limousine 配有私人司机的豪华轿车 pèiyǒu sīrén sījī de háohuá jiàochē

chauvinism N 沙文主义 Shāwén zhǔyì
national chauvinism 民族沙文主义 mínzú Shāwén zhǔyì
male chauvinsim 大男子主义 dànánzǐ zhǔyì

chauvinist N 沙文主义者 Shāwén zhǔyìzhě

chauvinistic ADJ 沙文主义的 Shāwén zhǔyì de

cheap ADJ 1 便宜的 piányi de, 廉价的 liánjià de
2 劣质的 lièzhì de 3 不尊重的 bù zūnzhòng de
cheap remarks 不公平的批评 bùgōngpíng de pīpíng

cheapen v 使…降低身份 shǐ…jiàngdī shēnfen

cheapskate N 小气鬼 xiǎoqìguǐ

cheat I v 1 骗 piàn, 欺骗 qīpiàn 2 作弊 zuòbì
■ She was caught cheating on the exam. 她考试的时候作弊，被发现了。Tā kǎoshì de shíhou zuòbì, bèi fāxiàn le. II N 骗子 piànzi, 作弊者 zuòbìzhě

check I v 1 检查 jiǎnchá, 核对 héduì 2 托运 tuōyùn
to check in ① [在旅馆／医院+] 登记入住 [zài lǚguǎn/yīyuàn+] dēngjì rùzhù ② 办登机手续 bàn dēng fēijī shǒuxù ③ 打电话报平安 dǎ diànhuà bàopíng'ān
to check out ① [在旅馆／医院+] 结帐离开 [zài lǚguǎn/yīyuàn+] jiézhàng líkāi ② 从图书馆借书 cóng túshūguǎn jiè shū
3 核实 [+信息] héshí [+xìnxī] 4 检查 jiǎnchá
II N 1 检查 jiǎnchá, 核对 héduì
security check 安全检查 ānquán jiǎnchá
2 控制 kòngzhì, 抑制 yìzhì
checks and balances 制衡 zhìhéng, 制衡的制度 zhìhéng de zhìdù
3 支票 zhīpiào 4 [餐馆+] 账单 [cānguǎn+] zhàngdān

checkbook N 支票簿 zhīpiàobù [M. WD 本 běn]

checked ADJ 彩色方格图案的 cǎisè fānggé tú'àn de

checker N 1 (超市) 收银员 (chāoshì) shōuyínyuán 2 检查员 jiǎncháyuán
spelling checker (电脑) 拼写检查程序 (diànnǎo) pīnxiě jiǎnchá chéngxù

checkers N 西洋跳棋 Xīyáng tiàoqí

check-in N 1 [旅馆+] 入住手续 [lǚguǎn+] rùzhù shǒuxù 2 登机手续 dēngjī shǒuxù
check-in counter [旅馆+] 入住手续处 [lǚguǎn+] rùzhù shǒuxùchù, [机场+] 登机手续柜台 [jīchǎng+] dēngjī shǒuxùguìtái

checking account N 活期存款帐户 huóqī cúnkuǎn zhànghù

checklist N (核对用的) 清单 (héduì yòng de) qīngdān [M. WD 份 fèn]

checkout N 1 付款处 fùkuǎnchù, 收银台 shōuyíntái 2 [旅馆+] 退房时间 [lǚguǎn+] tuìfáng shíjiān

checkpoint N 检查站 jiǎncházhàn

check-up N 体格检查 tǐgé jiǎnchá

cheddar N 切德奶酪 qiēdé nǎilào

cheek N 面颊 miànjiá

cheekbone N 颧骨 quángǔ

cheer N, v 欢呼 huānhū ■ The birthday boy was given three cheers. 寿星受到三声欢呼。Shòuxing shòudào sānshēng huānhū.
to cheer ... on 为…加油 wéi…jiāyóu
to cheer up 振作起来 zhènzuòqǐlái, 高兴起来 gāoxìng qǐlái

Cheer up! 振作起来! Zhènzuòqǐlái! 高兴一点
儿! Gāoxìng yìdiǎnr!

cheerful ADJ 快活的 kuàihuo de, 令人愉快的
lìngrén yúkuài de

cheerleader N 1 [橄榄球+] 啦啦队员 [gǎnlǎnqiú+]
lālāduìyuán 2 鼓励者 gǔlì zhě

cheery ADJ 欢乐的 huānlè de

cheese N 奶酪 nǎilào
Say cheese! (照相时) 笑一笑! (zhàoxiàng shí)
Xiào yí xiào! 说 "茄子"! Shuo "qiézi"!

cheeseburger N 奶酪汉堡包 nǎilào hànbǎobāo

cheesecake N 奶酪蛋糕 nǎilào dàngāo [M. WD
块 kuài]

cheetah N 猎豹 lièbào [M. WD 头 tóu]

chef N 大厨师 dàchúshī [M. WD 位 wéi]
pastry chef 点心师傅 diǎnxīn shīfu

chemical I N 化学制品 huàxué zhìpǐn II ADJ 化学
的 huàxué de, 化工的 huàgōng de
chemical plant 化工厂 huàgōngchǎng
chemical engineer 化工工程师 huàgōng
gōngchéngshī
chemical weapon 化学武器 huàxué wǔqì

chemist N 化学家 huàxuéjiā

chemistry N 化学 huàxué

chemotherapy N 化学疗法 huàxué liáofǎ, 化疗
huàliáo

cherish V 珍视 zhēnshì

cherry N 樱桃 yīngtáo [M. WD 颗 kē/粒 lì]
cherry blossom 樱花 yīnghuā

cherub N 小天使 xiǎotiānshǐ

chess N 象棋 xiàngqí [M. WD 副 fù/盘 pán], 国际象
棋 guójì xiàngqí [M. WD 副 fù/盘 pán]

chest N 1 胸 xiōng, 胸口 xiōngkǒu 2 大箱子
dàxiāngzi
medicine chest 药品橱 yàopǐnchú
chest of drawers 五斗橱 wǔdǒuchú

chestnut N 栗子 lìzi [M. WD 粒 lì/颗 kē]

chew V 嚼 jiáo, 咀嚼 jǔjué
to chew on 深思 shēnsī
to chew out 严厉责备 yánlì zébèi

chewing gum N 口香糖 kǒuxiāngtáng [M. WD 块
kuài]

chewy ADJ 很难嚼碎的 hěn nán jiáosuì de

chic ADJ 时髦漂亮的 shímáo piàoliang de

Chicago N 芝加哥 Zhījiāgē

chick N 1 小鸡 xiǎojī [M. WD 只 zhī], 小鸟 xiǎoniǎo
[M. WD 只 zhī] 2 小妞 xiǎoniū

chicken I N 1 鸡 jī [M. WD 只 zhī]
chicken feed 很少的一点儿钱 hěn shǎo de yì
diǎnr qián, 九牛一毛 jiǔniú yìmáo
a chicken-and-egg situation 先有鸡还是先有蛋
的问题 xiān yǒu jī háishi xiān yǒu dàn de wèntí
2 鸡肉 jīròu II ADJ 胆小的 dǎnxiǎo de III V (to
chicken out) (因害怕而) 退缩 (yīn hàipà ér)
tuìsuō

chickenpox N 水痘 shuǐdòu

chide V 斥责 chìzé, 怒骂 nùmà

chief I ADJ 主要的 zhǔyào de
chief executive officer (CEO) 首席执行官
shǒuxí zhíxíngguān
the Chief Executive 美国总统 Měiguó zǒngtǒng
chief justice 首席法官 shǒuxí fǎguān
II N 主管 zhǔguǎn, 头儿 tóur
chief of staff 参谋长 cānmóuzhǎng
police chief 警长 jǐngzhǎng

chiefly ADV 主要 zhǔyào, 大部分 dàbùfen

chieftain N 酋长 qiúzhǎng [M. WD 位 wéi], 族长
zúzhǎng [M. WD 位 wéi]

chiffon N 雪纺绸 xuěfǎngchóu

chihuahua N 奇瓦瓦狗 Qíwǎwǎ gǒu [M. WD 只
zhī]

child N (PL **children**) 1 儿童 értóng, 孩子 háizi
2 子女 zǐnǚ, 孩子 háizi
child support 子女抚养费 zǐnǚ fǔyǎngfèi

childbearing N 生孩子 shēng háizi, 分娩 fēnmiǎn
childbearing age 育龄 yùlíng

childbirth N 分娩 fēnmiǎn, 生孩子 shēng háizi

childcare N 儿童照管 értóng zhàoguǎn
childcare center 儿童照管中心 értóng
zhàoguǎn zhōngxīn, 托儿所 tuō'érsuǒ

childhood N 童年 tóngnián

childish ADJ 孩子气的 háiziqì de, 幼稚的 yòuzhì
de

childless ADJ 无子女的 wú zǐnǚ de

childlike ADJ 孩子般的 háizi bān de, 天真的
tiānzhēn de

childproof ADJ 儿童不能开启的 értóng bù néng
kāiqǐ de, 对儿童无害的 duì értóng wúhài de

children See **child**

chili, chilli N 辣椒 làjiāo

chill I V 使…冷却 shǐ…lěngquè, 使…变冷 shǐ…
biàn lěng II N 1 寒意 hányì 2 害怕 hàipà, 胆战
心惊 dǎnzhàn xīnjīng III ADJ 非常冷的 fēicháng
lěng de

chilling ADJ 令人极其害怕的 lìngrén jíqí hàipà de,
令人毛骨悚然的 lìngrén máogǔ sǒngrán de

chilly ADJ 寒冷的 hánlěng de

chime I N 编钟 biānzhōng
wind chimes 风铃 fēnglíng
II V [钟+] 响 [zhōng+] xiǎng
to chime in 插话 [+表示赞同] chāhuà [+biǎoshì
zàntóng]

chimney N 烟囱 yāncōng

chimpanzee N 黑猩猩 hēixīngxīng [M. WD 只 zhī]

chin N 下巴 xiàba
chin up 引体向上 yǐntǐxiàngshàng
to take it on the chin 承受 [+不公正对待] chéngshòu [+bù gōngzhèng duìdài]

china N 瓷器 cíqì

China N 中国 Zhōngguó

Chinatown N 唐人街 Tángrénjiē, 华人区 Huárén qū

Chinese I ADJ 中国的 Zhōngguó de II N 1 中国人 Zhōngguórén 2 中文 Zhōngwén, 汉语 Hànyǔ, 华语 Huáyǔ

chink N 缝隙 fèngxì, 漏洞 lòudòng

chip I N 1 炸土豆条 zhá tǔdòutiáo, 炸薯条 zhá shǔtiáo 2 (计算机) 集成电路片 (jìsuànjī) jíchéng diànlù piàn 3 (碗) 豁口 (wǎn) huōkǒu, 缺口 quēkǒu 4 (赌场) 筹码 (dǔchǎng) chóumǎ II V (to chip in) 插嘴 chāzuǐ, 插话 chāhuà

chipmuck N 花鼠 huāshǔ [M. WD 只 zhī], 金花鼠 jīnhuā shǔ

chipper ADJ 轻松愉快的 qīngsōng yúkuài de, 活泼的 huópo de

chiropractor N 背部按摩师 bèibù ànmóshī

chirp V [鸟或昆虫+] 叫 [niǎo huò kūnchóng+] jiào, 唧唧喳喳地叫 jījīzhāzhā de jiào

chisel N 凿子 záozi [M. WD 把 bǎ], 凿刀 záo dāo [M. WD 把 bǎ] II V (用凿子) 凿 (yòng záozi) záo

chit N 借贷字据 jièdài zìjù [M. WD 张 zhāng], 欠账单 qiànzhàng dān [M. WD 张 zhāng]

chit-chat N 闲聊 xiánliáo

chivalrous ADJ 有骑士风度的 yǒu qíshì fēngdù de, 对女士仁慈有礼的 [+男子] duì nǚshì réncí yǒulǐ de [+nánzǐ]

chivalry N 骑士风度 qíshì fēngdù

chives N 细香葱 xìxiāngcōng

chlorinate V [在水中+] 加氯 [+消毒+] [zài shuǐ zhōng+] jiā lǜ [+xiāodú]

chlorine N 氯 lǜ, 氯气 lǜqì

chock-a-block ADJ 满满的 mǎnmǎn de, 爆满的 bàomǎn de

chock-full ADJ 装满的 zhuāngmǎn de, 塞满的 sāimǎn de

chocoholic, chocaholic N 特别爱吃巧克力的人 tèbié ài chī qiǎokèlì de rén

chocolate N 巧克力 qiǎokèlì
hot chocolate 热巧克力饮料 rè qiǎokèlì yǐnliào

chocolate chip N 巧克力片 qiǎokèlì piàn

choice I N 选择 xuǎnzé
by choice 自己选择的 zìjǐ xuǎnzé de, 自愿的 zìyuàn de
II ADJ 精选的 jīngxuǎn de, 优质的 yōuzhì de

choir N (教会) 唱诗班 (jiàohuì) chàngshībān, (学校) 合唱团 (xuéxiào) héchàngtuán

choke I V 1 使…窒息 shǐ…zhìxī 2 堵塞 dǔsè 3 (因激动) 说不出话来 (yīn jīdòng) shuōbuchū huà lái II N 1 窒息 zhìxī 2 阻门器 zǔ mén qì
choke collar (狗) 项圈 (gǒu) xiàngquān

cholera N 霍乱 huòluàn

cholesterol N 胆固醇 dǎngùchún

choose (PT chose; PP chosen) V 1 选择 xuǎnzé, 挑选 tiāoxuǎn 2 决定 juédìng

choosy ADJ 十分挑剔的 shífēn tiāoti de

chop I V 1 劈开 pī kāi, 切成小块 qiēchéng xiǎo kuài 2 砍 kǎn 3 削减 xuējiǎn
to chop down 砍倒 kǎn dǎo
II N 1 排骨 páigǔ
pork chop 猪排 zhūpái
2 劈 pī, 砍 kǎn
to get the chop 被解雇 bèi jiěgù

chopper N 直升飞机 zhíshēng fēijī [M. WD 架 jià]

chopping block N 案板 ànbǎn [M. WD 块 kuài]

choppy ADJ 波浪起伏的 bōlàng qǐfú de

chopsticks N 筷子 kuàizi [M. WD 根 gēn/双 shuāng]

choral ADJ (教会) 唱诗班的 (jiàohuì) chàngshībān de, (学校) 合唱团的 (xuéxiào) héchàngtuán de

chord N 和音 héyīn, 和弦 héxián
to strike a chord 引起共鸣 yǐnqǐ gòngmíng

chore N 1 家务杂事 jiāwu záshì 2 乏味的工作 fáwèi de gōngzuò, 烦人的杂事 fánrén de záshì

choreography N 舞蹈设计 wǔdǎo shèjì

chortle I V 咯咯地笑个不停 gēgē de xiào gè bùtíng II N 咯咯的笑声 gēgē de xiàoshēng

chorus N 1 合唱队 héchàngduì 2 合唱部分 héchàng bùfen
in chorus 齐声说 qíshēngshuō

chose See **choose**

chosen I V See **choose** II ADJ 被选中的 bèi xuǎnzhòng de
God's chosen people 上帝的子民 Shàngdì de zǐmín

chow I N 1 食物 shíwù 2 狮子狗 shīzigǒu II V (to chow down) 狼吞虎咽地吃 lángtūn hǔyān de chī

chowder N 浓汤 nóngtāng [M. WD 碗 wǎn]

Christ I N 基督 Jīdū, 耶稣 Yēsū II INTERJ 天哪 tiān na

christen V 为…行洗礼 wéi…xíng xǐlǐ

christening N 洗礼命名仪式 xǐlǐ mìngmíng yíshì

Christian N 基督教徒 Jīdū jiàotú

Christianity N 基督教 Jīdūjiào

Christian Science N 基督教科学派 Jīdūjiào Kēxuépài

Christmas N 圣诞节 Shèngdànjié
Christmas card 圣诞贺卡 Shèngdàn hèkǎ
Christmas carol 圣诞赞歌 Shèngdàn zàngē
Christmas Day 圣诞节 Shèngdànjié
Christmas eve 圣诞夜 Shèngdànyè, 平安夜 píng'ān yè
Christmas tree 圣诞树 Shèngdànshù

chrome N 铬合金 gè héjīn

chromosome N 染色体 rǎnsètǐ

chronic ADJ 1 慢性的 mànxìng de 2 长期的 chángqī de, 反复发作的 fǎnfù fāzuò de
a chronic gambler 赌棍 dǔgùn, 赌徒 dǔtú

chronically ADV 长期地 chángqī de

the chronically ill 长期患病的人 chángqī huàn-bìng de rén

chronicle I N 编年史 biān niánshǐ **II** v 记载入历史 jìzǎi rù lìshǐ

chronological ADJ 按照年代／时间顺序排列的 ànzhào niándài/shíjiān shùnxù páiliè de

chronologically ADV 按照年代／时间顺序排列地 ànzhào niándài/shíjiān shùnxù páiliè de

chronology N 大事年表 dàshì niánbiǎo [M. WD 份 fèn]

chrysanthemum N 菊花 júhuā [M. WD 朵 duǒ]

chubby ADJ 胖嘟嘟的 pàngdūdū de

chuck v 随手扔 suíshǒu rēng

chuckle I v 低声地笑 dīshēng de xiào **II** N 低声的笑 dīshēng de xiào, 暗笑 ànxiào

chug v 缓慢行驶 huǎnmàn xíngshǐ

chug-a-lug v 一口气喝完 yìkǒuqì hēwán

chump N 傻瓜 shǎguā

chunk N 一大块 yí dà kuài

chunky ADJ 大块的 dà kuài de

church N **1** 教会 jiàohuì **2** 教堂 jiàotáng

churlish ADJ 粗鲁的 cūlǔ de, 不友好的 bù yǒuhǎo de

churn v [胃里+] 剧烈搅动 [wèi lǐ+] jùliè jiǎodòng to churn up 剧烈翻腾 jùliè fānteng

chute N 滑运道 huáyùndào, 斜槽 xié zāo

CIA (= Central Intelligence Agency) ABBREV （美国）中央情报局 (Měiguó) Zhōngyāng Qíngbàojú

cider N 苹果汁 píngguǒzhī, 苹果酒 píngguǒjiǔ

cigar N 雪茄（烟）xuějiā (yān) [M. WD 支 zhī]

cigarette N 香烟 xiāngyān [M. WD 支 zhī] a pack of cigarettes 一包香烟 yì bāo xiāngyān

cinch I N **1** 一定会发生的事 yídìng huì fāshēng de shì, 非常容易做的事 fēicháng róngyì zuò de shì **2** 一定会做某事的人 yídìng huì zuò mǒu shì de rén **II** v **1** 确保 quèbǎo **2** 系紧带子 jì jǐn dàizi

cinder N 煤渣 méizhā, 炭渣 tànzhā

cinema N 电影院 diànyǐngyuàn [M. WD 座 zuò]

cinematography N 电影摄影艺术 diànyǐng shèyǐng yìshù

cinnamon N 肉桂 ròuguì

cipher, cypher N **1** 密码 mìmǎ **2** 无足轻重的人 wúzú qīngzhòng de rén

circa PREP 约 yuē, 大约 dàyuē

circle I N 圆圈 yuánquān to draw a circle 划圆圈 huà yuánquān **II** v 在…上画圆圈 zài…shàng huà yuánquān

circuit N **1** 电路 diànlù **2** 巡回演出（讲座、比赛等）xúnhuí yǎnchū (jiǎngzuò, bǐsài děng) circuit board 电路板 diànlùbǎn, 印刷电路 yìnshuā diànlù circuit breaker 断路器 duànlùqì circuit court 巡回法庭 xúnhuí fǎtíng

circuitous ADJ 迂回曲折的 yūhuí qūzhé de

circuitry N 电路系统 diànlù xìtǒng

circular¹ ADJ 圆（形）的 yuán (xíng) de circular saw 电动圆锯 diàndòng yuánjù

circular² N **1** 广告纸 guǎnggàozhǐ [M. WD 张 zhāng] **2** 通知 tōngzhī [M. WD 张 zhāng]

circulate v **1** 流通 liútōng **2** 流传 liúchuán

circulation N **1** 血液循环 xuèyè xúnhuán **2** 流通 liútōng

circumcise v **1** 切除包皮 qiēchú bāopí **2** 切除阴蒂 qiēchú yīndì

circumcision N **1** 包皮环切 bāopí huánqiē **2** 阴蒂切除 yīndì qiēchú

circumference N 周长 zhōucháng

circumscribe v 约束 yuēshù, 限制 xiànzhì

circumspect ADJ 谨慎 jǐnshèn, 考虑周到的 kǎolǜzhōudào de

circumstance N 情况 qíngkuàng, 处境 chǔjìng under no circumstances 绝不 juébù

circumstantial ADJ 间接的 jiànjiē de circumstantial evidence 间接证据 jiànjiē zhèngjù

circumvent v 回避 huíbì

circus N **1** 马戏团 mǎxìtuán, 马戏 mǎxì **2** 乱哄哄的场面 luànhōnghōng de chǎngmiàn

cirrhosis N 肝硬化 gānyìnghuà

cistern N 储水箱 chǔ shuǐxiāng

citation N **1** [法庭+] 传票 [fǎtíng+] chuánpiào **2** [违章停车+] 罚款单 [wéizhāng tíngchē+] fákuǎndān **3** 嘉奖状 jiājiǎngzhuàng **4** 引文 yǐnwén

cite v **1** 传讯 chuánxùn **2** 嘉奖 jiājiǎng **3** 引证 yǐnzhèng

citizen N **1** 公民 gōngmín citizen's arrest 公民逮捕 gōngmín dàibǔ citizens band 民用波段 mínyòng bōduàn **2** 市民 shìmín

citizenship N 公民身份 gōngmín shēnfen, 公民权 gōngmínquán

citrus ADJ 柑橘类水果 gānjú lèi shuǐguǒ

city N 城 chéng [M. WD 座 zuò], 城市 chéngshì [M. WD 座 zuò] city council 市政议会 shìzhèng yìhuì city hall 市政厅 shìzhèngtīng

civic ADJ **1** 公民的 gōngmín de **2** 市政的 shìzhèng de

civics N 公民课 gōngmín kè [M. WD 堂 táng/门 mén]

civil ADJ 公民的 gōngmín de, 民用的 mínyòng de civil engineering 土木工程 tǔmù gōngchéng civil lawsuit 民事案件 mínshì ànjiàn civil rights 公民权利 gōngmín quánlì civil servant 公务员 gōngwùyuán, 公仆 gōngpú civil service 政府文职部门 zhèngfǔ wénzhí bùmén

civilian N 平民 píngmín

civilization N 文明 wénmíng

civilize v 使…文明 shǐ…wénmíng
civilized ADJ 文明的 wénmíng de
clad ADJ 穿…衣服的 chuān…yīfu de
claim I v 1 认领 rènlǐng 2 声称 shēngchēng ∎ *He claimed to have taken this prize-winning photo.* 他声称是他拍了这张获奖照片。Tā shēngchēng shì tā pāile zhè zhāng huòjiǎng zhàopiàn. 3 索取 [+赔偿] suǒqǔ [+péicháng] II N 1 索赔 suǒpéi
claim form 索赔申请表 suǒpéi shēnqǐngbiǎo
2 声称 shēngchēng, 声明 shēngmíng 3 权利 quánlì
claimant N [索赔+] 申请人 [suǒpéi+] shēnqǐngrén
clairvoyant N 声称有超人洞察力的人 shēngchēng yǒu chāorén dòngchálì de rén
clam I N 1 蛤蜊 géli 2 沉默寡言的人 chénmò guǎyán de rén II v 闭口不言 bìkǒu bùyán
clamber v 攀登 pāndēng
clammy ADJ 湿冷的 shī lěng de, 粘糊糊的 niánhūhūde
clamor I N 1 吵嚷声 chǎo rǎng shēng 2 强烈要求 qiángliè yàoqiú II v 1 大声吵嚷 dàshēng chǎorǎng 2 大声疾呼 dàshēng jíhū
clamp I N 夹具 jiājù, 夹钳 jiāqián II v 夹紧 jiā jǐn
clampdown N 取缔 qǔdì, 严禁 yánjìn
clan N 1 大家族 dà jiāzú 2 宗族 zōngzú
clandestine ADJ 秘密的 mìmì de
clang v 发出叮当声 fāchū dīngdāngshēng
clank v 发出当啷声 fāchū dānglāngshēng
clap I v 拍手 pāishǒu, 鼓掌 gǔzhǎng II N 1 拍手声 pāishǒushēng, 鼓掌声 gǔzhǎngshēng 2 响声 xiǎngshēng
a clap of thunder 轰隆的雷声 hōnglōng de léishēng
clapboard N 护墙 hùqiáng [M. WD 道 dào/垛 duǒ]
clapper N 钟锤 zhōngchuí [M. WD 把 bǎ]
clarification N 澄清 chéngqīng
clarify v 澄清 chéngqīng
clarinet N 单簧管 dānhuángguǎn
clarity N 清楚明确 qīngchu míngquè
clash I v 1 发生冲突 fāshēng chōngtū 2 不相配 bù xiāngpèi II N 1 冲突 chōngtū 2 争论 zhēnglùn
clasp I N 1 钩子 gōuzi, 扣环 kòuhuán 2 紧握 jǐnwò II v 紧紧握住 jǐnjǐn wòzhù, 扣住 kòuzhù
class I N 1 [学校] 班 [xuéxiào] bān, 级 jí, 班级 bānjí 2 课 (程) kè (chéng) 3 阶级 jiējí
middle class 中产阶级 zhōngchǎn jiējí
4 等级 děngjí
to travel first class 乘头等舱飞机 (或轮船) chéng tóuděngcāng fēijī (huò lúnchuán)
II v 把…归类 bǎ…guīlèi
class action N 集体诉讼 jítǐ sùsòng
classic I ADJ 经典的 jīngdiǎn de, 典型的 diǎnxíng de
a classic case 典型实例 diǎnxíng shílì
II N 经典作品 jīngdiǎn zuòpǐn

classical ADJ [文学／艺术+] 经典的 [wénxué/yìshù+] jīngdiǎn de, 古典的 gǔdiǎn de
classical music 古典音乐 gǔdiǎn yīnyuè
classification N 1 分类 fēnlèi 2 类别 lèibié, 等级 děngjí
classified ADJ 1 分类的 fēnlèi de 2 保密的 bǎomì de, 机密的 jīmì de
classified ad 分类广告 fēnlèi guǎnggào
classify v 1 把…分类 bǎ…fēnlèi 2 把…列为 bǎ…lièwéi
classmate N 同班同学 tóngbān tóngxué, 同学 tóngxué
classroom N 教室 jiàoshì [M. WD 间 jiān], 课堂 kètáng [M. WD 间 jiān]
classwork N 课堂作业 kètáng zuòyè
classy ADJ 高档的 gāodàng de, 高级的 gāojí de
clatter I v 发出咔嗒声 fāchū kǎdā shēng II N 咔嗒声 kǎdā shēng
clause N 1 (法律) 条款 (fǎlǜ) tiáokuǎn 2 从句 cóngjù, 分句 fēnjù
claustrophobia N 幽闭恐惧症 yōubì kǒngjùzhēng
claw N 1 爪 zhuǎ, 鸟爪 niǎozhuǎ 2 起钉器 qǐdīngqì
clean I ADJ 1 干净的 gānjìng de, 清洁的 qīngjié de 2 守法的 (不吸毒、不带武器等) shǒufǎ de (bù xīdú, bù dài wǔqì děng) 3 公平的 gōngping de, 廉洁的 liánjié de
a clean bill of health 健康证明 jiànkāng zhèngmíng, (机器、建筑物等) 安全证明 (jīqì, jiànzhùwù děng) ānquán zhèngmíng
a clean government 廉洁的政府 liánjié de zhèngfǔ
to come clean 坦白认罪 tǎnbái rènzuì
II v 弄干净 nòng gānjìng III ADV 完全 (地) wánquán (de)
clean-cut ADV 整洁体面的 zhěngjié tǐmian de
cleaner N 清洁工 qīngjiégōng
cleaning N 清理 qīnglǐ, 清扫 qīngsǎo
cleanly ADV 利落地 lìluo de
cleanse v 清洗 qīngxǐ
cleanser N 清洗剂 qīngxǐjì
clean-shaven ADJ 胡子刮得很干净的 húzi guā de hěn gānjìng de
cleanup N 大扫除 dàsǎochú
clear I ADJ 1 清澈的 qīngchè de, 明亮的 míngliàng de 2 清楚的 qīngchu de, 明白的 míngbai de
II v 收拾干净 shōushi gānjìng
clearance N 1 许可 xǔkě
security clearance 安全审查 ānquán shěnchá
2 清理 qīnglǐ
clearance sale 清仓拍卖 qīngcāng pāimài
clear-cut ADJ 明显的 míngxiǎn de, 显著的 xiǎnzhù de
clear-headed ADJ 头脑清醒的 tóunǎo qīngxǐng de
clearing N (树林中) 小块空地 (shùlín zhōng) xiǎo kuài kòngdì

clearly

clearly ADV 1 清楚地 qīngchu de 2 明显地 míngxiǎn de, 显然地 xiǎnrán de

clear-sighted ADJ 有见识的 yǒu jiànshi de

cleat N 1 防滑鞋 fánghuáxié [M. WD 只 zhī/双 shuāng] 2 防滑条 fánghuátiáo [M. WD 条 tiáo]

cleavage N 1 分歧 fēnqí 2 乳沟 rǔgōu

cleaver N 剁肉刀 duòròudāo [M. WD 把 bǎ]

clef N 谱号 pǔhào

cleft N 1 裂缝 lièfèng [M. WD 条 tiáo] 2 凹痕 āohén

clemency N [对罪行+] 从宽处理 [duì zuìxíng+] cóngkuān chǔlǐ, 宽大 kuāndà

clench V 握紧拳头 wòjǐn quántou
to clench one's teeth 咬紧牙关 yǎojǐn yáguān

clergy N 神职人员 shénzhí rényuán

clergyman, clergywoman N 神职人员 shénzhí rényuán

clerical ADJ 1 神职人员的 shénzhí rényuán de 2 办事员的 bànshìyuán de, 文书的 wénshū de

clerk N 办事员 bànshìyuán, 职员 zhíyuán
file clerk 档案管理员 dàng'àn guǎnlǐ yuán

clever ADJ 聪明的 cōngming de

cliché N 1 老一套的话 lǎoyítào de huà, 陈词滥调 chéncí làndiào 2 陈腐的想法 chénfǔ de xiǎngfǎ, 老生常谈 lǎoshēng chángtán

click I V 1 发出咔嗒声 fāchū kǎdāshēng 2 （电脑鼠标）点击 (diànnǎo shǔbiāo) diǎnjī 3 突然明白 tūrán míngbai, 开窍 kāiqiào II N 咔嗒声 kǎdāshēng

client N 1 客户 kèhù, 顾客 gùkè 2 救济对象 jiùjì duìxiàng

cliff N 悬崖 xuányá

cliffhanger N 1 扣人心弦的结局 kòu rén xīnxián de jiéjú 2 扣人心弦的比赛 kòu rén xīnxián de bǐsài

climactic ADJ 高潮的 gāocháo de

climate N 1 [温带+] 气候 [wēndài+] qìhòu 2 [保守的+] 风气 [bǎoshǒu de+] fēngqì

climax I N 高潮 gāocháo II V 达到高潮 dádào gāocháo

climb V 1 攀登 pāndēng, 爬 pá ■ *It only took him less than one minute to climb to the top of the tree.* 他花了一分钟不到就爬到树顶。Tā huāle yì fēnzhōng búdào jiù pádao shù dǐng. 2 [价格+] 攀升 [jiàgé+] pānshēng, 上升 shàngshēng

climber N 1 登山运动员 dēngshān yùndòngyuán 2 攀缘植物 pānyuán zhíwù

climbing N 登山 dēngshān, 攀岩 pānyán

clinch V 最终赢得 zuìzhōng yíngdé
to clinch a deal 敲定交易 qiāodìng jiāoyì

clincher N 关键的事实论点／行动 guānjiàn de shìshí lùndiǎn/xíngdòng

cling (PT & PP **clung**) V 拼命地抓住 pīnmìng de zhuāzhù

clingy ADJ 过于依赖他人的 guòyú yīlài tārén de, 依赖性特强的 yīlàixìng tè qiáng de

clinic N 门诊所 ménzhěnsuǒ

clinical ADJ 1 临床的 [+试验] línchuáng de [+shìyàn] 2 诊所的 [+管理] zhěnsuǒ de [+guǎnlǐ] 3 绝对冷静的 [+观点] juéduì lěngjìng de [+guāndiǎn]

clinician N 临床医生 línchuáng yīshēng

clink V 发出叮当声 fāchū dīngdāng shēng
to clink their glasses 碰杯 pèngbēi

clip I N 1 回形针 huíxíngzhēn 2 夹子 jiāzi 3 电影(电视)片段 diànyǐng (diànshì) piànduàn II V 1 夹住 jiāzhù 2 剪下 [+报上的文章] jiǎn xià [+bàoshang de wénzhāng]

clipboard N 1 [电脑+] 剪贴板 [diànnǎo+] jiǎntiēbǎn 2 有夹子的书写板 yǒu jiāzi de shūxiě bǎn

clip-on ADJ 用夹子夹住的 yòng jiāzi jiāzhù de

clippers N 修剪器 xiūjiǎnqì

clipping N 剪报 jiǎnbào

clique N 小集团 xiǎojítuán

clitoris N 阴蒂 yīndì

cloak I N 1 披风 pīfēng [M. WD 件 jiàn] 2 幌子 huǎngzi, 掩盖 yǎngài
under the cloak of 打着…的幌子 dǎzhe...de huǎngzi
II V 掩盖 yǎngài

cloak-and-dagger ADJ 秘密的 [+间谍活动] mìmì de [+jiàndié huódòng]

cloakroom N 衣帽间 yīmàojiān

clobber V 猛揍 měng zòu, 狠打 hěn dǎ

clock I N 钟 zhōng [M. WD 座 zuò/只 zhī]
alarm clock 闹钟 nàozhōng
clock radio 收音机闹钟 shōuyīnjī nàozhōng
around the clock 日夜 rìyè
to set one's clock for 把闹钟开到… bǎ nàozhōng kāidào...
II V 记下…的速度／时间 jìxià...de sùdù/shíjiān
to clock in/out 打卡上班／下班 dǎkǎ shàngbān/xiàbān

clockwise ADJ, ADV 按顺时钟方向 àn shùn shízhōng fāngxiàng
anti-clockwise 按反时钟方向 àn fǎn shízhōng fāngxiàng

clockwork N 钟表机械 zhōngbiǎo jīxiè
like clockwork 准时地 zhǔnshí de, 有规律地 yǒuguīlǜ de

clog V 阻塞 zǔsè, 堵塞 dǔsè

clogs N 木拖鞋 mù tuōxié [M. WD 只 zhī/双 shuāng]

clone I N 1 无性繁殖 wúxìng fánzhí, 克隆 kèlóng 2 仿制机 fǎngzhì jī II V 1 使…无性繁殖 shǐ...wúxìng fánzhí, 克隆 kèlóng 2 盗用 [+手机号码] dàoyòng [+shǒujī hàomǎ]

close I ADJ 1 近 jìn, 接近 jiējìn
in close quarters [住得+] 很靠近 [zhù dé+] hěn kàojìn
2 亲密的 qīnmì de
a close friend 亲密的朋友 qīnmì de péngyou

II v **1** 关 guān, 关闭 guānbì **2** 结束 jiéshù
to close ranks 团结起来 tuánjié qǐlái
3 收盘 shōupán **III** ADV 接近地 jiējìn de
close by 在附近 zài fùjìn
IV N 结尾 jiéwěi
to come to a close 结束 jiéshù

closed ADJ **1** 仅限特定的人 [+会议] jǐn xiàn tèdìng
de rén [+huìyì]
a closed shop 只雇用工会会员的工厂 zhǐ
gùyòng gōnghuì huìyuán de gōngchǎng
behind closed doors 不公开地 bù gōngkāi de,
秘密地 mìmì de
2 关闭的 guānbì de, 封闭的 fēngbì de

closed circuit television See **CCTV**

close-knit ADJ 紧密连接的 jǐnmì liánjiē de

closely ADV **1** 密切地 [+关注] mìqiè de [+guān-
zhù], 严密地 yánmì de **2** 紧挨着 jǐn'āizhe, 紧接
着 jǐnjiēzhe

close-mouthed ADJ 守口如瓶的 shǒu kǒu rú
píng de

closet N 壁橱 bìchú
to be in the closet 否认自己是同性恋者 fǒurèn
zìjǐ shì tóngxìngliànzhě
to come out of the closet 承认自己是同性恋者
chéngrèn zìjǐ shì tóngxìngliànzhě

close-up N 特写照片 tèxiě zhàopiàn [M. WD 张
zhāng]

closure N **1** 关闭 guānbì **2** 封闭 fēngbì

clot I N (血、牛奶等) 凝块 (xuè、niúnǎi děng)
níngkuài **II** v (血、牛奶等) 凝结成块 (xuè、
niúnǎi děng) níngjié chéng kuài

cloth N 布料 bùliào, 毛料 máoliào

clothe v **1** 为…提供衣服 wéi…tígōng yīfu **2** 给…
穿衣 gěi…chuān yī

clothes N 衣服 yīfu [M. WD 件 jiàn]
work clothes 工作服 gōngzuòfú

clothesline N 晾衣绳 liàngyīshéng [M. WD 条 tiáo]

clothespin N 衣夹 yī jiā

clothing N 服装 fúzhuāng [M. WD 件 jiàn/套 tào]
■ Come December, everyone will be wearing
winter clothing. 到了十二月，人们都穿上了冬季服
装。Dàole shí'èr yuè, rénmen dōu chuānshangle
dōngjì fúzhuāng.

cloud I N 云 yún [M. WD 朵 duǒ]
under a cloud 受到猜疑 shòudào cāiyí
II v **1** 使…变得模糊不清 shǐ…biàn de móhu
bùqīng **2** 使…糊涂 shǐ…hútu **3** 使…蒙上阴影
shǐ…méng shàng yīnyǐng

cloudburst N 短暂的暴雨 duǎnzàn de bàoyǔ

cloudy ADJ **1** 多云的 duōyún de, 阴 yīn
a cloudy day 阴天 yīntiān
2 模糊的 móhu de

clout N [经济] 权势 [jīngjì+] quánshì, [政治+] 影
响力 [zhèngzhì+] yǐngxiǎnglì

clover N 三叶草 sānyècǎo, 苜蓿 mùxu

clown N **1** 小丑 xiǎochǒu, 丑角 chǒujué **2** 讨厌家
伙 tǎoyàn jiāhuo

club I N **1** 俱乐部 jùlèbù **2** (纸牌) 梅花 (zhǐpái)
méihuā **3** 大棒 dàbàng [M. WD 根 gēn] **II** v 用棍
棒打 yòng gùnbàng dǎ

clubhouse N **1** 俱乐部会所 jùlèbù huìsuǒ **2** (体育
场) 更衣室 (tǐyùchǎng) gēngyīshì

cluck v **1** [母鸡+] 发出咯咯声 [mǔjī+] fāchū gēgē
shēng **2** [人+] 发出啧啧声 [rén +] fāchū zézé
shēng

clue I N **1** 线索 xiànsuǒ [M. WD 条 tiáo]
to have no clue 一无所知 yìwúsuǒzhī
2 提示 tíshì **II** v 提供线索 tígōng xiànsuǒ

clump I N **1** 一簇树木 yí cù shùmù **2** 一块泥土 yí
kuài nítǔ **II** v 凝集成块 níngjí chéng kuài

clumsy ADJ **1** 笨拙的 [+男人] bènzhuō de [+nán-
ren] **2** 粗制滥造的 [+文章] cūzhì lànzào de
[+wénzhāng]

clung See **cling**

clunker N **1** 破旧的汽车／机器 pòjiù de qìchē/jīqì
2 彻底的失败 chèdǐ de shībài

clunky ADJ 笨重的 bènzhòng de

cluster I N 串 chuàn, 组 zǔ, 群 qún **II** v 成群
chéngqún

clutch I v 紧紧握住 jǐnjǐn wòzhù **II** N **1** (汽车)
离合器 (qìchē) líhéqì **2** 紧握 jǐnwò **3** 一小簇 yì
xiǎo cù

clutter I v 堆满 duīmǎn, 塞满 sāimǎn **II** N 杂乱无
章的东西 záluàn wúzhāng de dōngxi
free of clutter 没有杂乱无章的东西 méiyǒu
záluàn wú zhāng de dōngxi, 整洁 zhěngjié

cm (= centimeter) ABBREV 厘米 límǐ, 公分 gōngfēn

CNN (= Cable News Network) ABBREV (美国)
有线电视新闻网 (Měiguó) Yǒuxiàn Diànshì
Xīnwénwǎng

coach[1] I N 教练 jiàoliàn **II** v 辅导 fǔdǎo, 训练
xùnliàn

coach[2] I N **1** 长途汽车 chángtú qìchē [M. WD 辆
liàng] **2** (飞机) 经济舱 (fēijī) jīngjìcāng

coagulate v 使…凝结 shǐ…níngjié

coagulation N 凝结 níngjié, 凝固 nínggù

coal N 煤 méi [M. WD 块 kuài]
coal gas 煤气 méiqì
coal mine 煤矿 méikuàng
coal tar 煤焦油 méijiāoyóu

coalfield N 煤田 méitián

coalition N 联盟 liánméng, 同盟 tóngméng
coalition government 联合政府 liánhé zhèngfǔ

coarse ADJ **1** 粗糙的 [+衣料] cūcāo de [+yīliào]
2 粗俗的 [+语言] cūsú de [+yǔyán]

coarsen v **1** 使…变得粗糙 shǐ…biàn de cūcāo
2 使…变得粗俗 shǐ…biàn de cūsú

coast I N 海岸 hǎi'àn
Coast Guard (美国) 海岸警卫队 (Měiguó)
Hǎi'àn Jǐngwèiduì

coastal

II v（汽车或自行车）滑行 (qìchē huò zìxíngchē) huáxíng

coastal ADJ 近海的 jìnhǎi de, 沿海的 yánhǎi de

coaster N 1 杯垫 bēidiàn 2 沿海岸航行的船只 yánhǎi àn hángxíng de chuánzhī

coastline N 海岸线 hǎi'ànxiàn

coat I N 1 外衣 wàiyī [M. WD 件 jiàn], 大衣 dàyī [M. WD 件 jiàn] 2 上装 shàngzhuāng
coat hangar 衣架 yījià
coat of arms 纹章 wénzhāng, 盾徽 dùnhuī
coat rack 挂衣架 guàyījià
II v 涂一层 tú yìcéng

coax v 劝诱 quànyòu, 哄 hōng

cob N 玉米棒子芯 yùmǐ bàngzi xīn
corn on the cob 玉米棒子 yùmǐ bàngzi

cobbled ADJ 铺鹅卵石的 pū éluǎnshí de

cobbler N 1 水果馅饼 shuǐguǒ xiànbǐng 2 修鞋匠 xiūxiéjiàng

cobblestone N 鹅卵石 éluǎnshí [M. WD 块 kuài]

cobra N 眼镜蛇 yǎnjìngshé [M. WD 条 tiáo]

cobweb N 蜘蛛网 zhīzhūwǎng [M. WD 张 zhāng]

Coca-Cola N 可口可乐 Kěkǒukělè [M. WD 瓶 píng/杯 bēi/罐 guàn]

cocaine N 可卡因 kěkǎyīn

cock I N 1 公鸡 gōngjī [M. WD 只 zhī] 2 雄鸟 xióng niǎo [M. WD 只 zhī] 3 鸡巴 jība
cock-and-bull story 荒唐的故事/借口 huāngtang de gùshi/jièkǒu
II v 竖起 shùqǐ, 翘起 qiàoqǐ

cock-a-doodle-doo N 喔喔声 wōwōshēng

cockeyed ADJ 1 歪的 wāi de, 倾斜的 qīngxié de 2 荒谬的 huāngmiù de, 不切实际的 bù qiè shíjì de

cockpit N（飞机）驾驶舱 (fēijī) jiàshǐ cāng,（赛车）驾驶座 (sàichē) jiàshǐ zuò

cockroach N 蟑螂 zhānglǎng [M. WD 只 zhī]

cocksure ADJ 自以为是的 zì yǐwéi shì de

cocktail N 鸡尾酒 jīwěijiǔ
cocktail bar 鸡尾酒吧 jīwěijiǔ jiǔbā
cocktail dress 晚礼服 wǎnlǐfú [M. WD 套 tào]
cocktail lounge 酒吧间 jiǔbājiān
cocktail party 鸡尾酒会 jīwěi jiǔhuì
2 冷盘 lěngpán [M. WD 道 dào], 开胃菜
seafood cocktail 海鲜冷盘 hǎixiān lěngpán
3 危险的混合物 wēixiǎn de hùnhéwù
Molotov cocktail 莫洛托夫汽油弹 Mòluòtuōfū qìyóudàn

cocky ADJ 自高自大的 zìgāo zìdà de

cocoa N 可可粉 kěkěfěn

coconut N 椰子 yēzi [M. WD 只 zhī]

cocoon I N 1 蚕茧 cánjiǎn, 茧 jiǎn 2 舒适安全的地方 shūshì ānquán de dìfang **II** v 将…严密保护 jiāng…yánmì bǎohù

C.O.D (= cash on delivery, collect on delivery) ABBREV 货到付款 huòdàofùkuǎn

cod N 雪鱼 xuěyú [M. WD 条 tiáo]

code I N 1 编码 biānmǎ, 邮政编码 yóuzhèng biānmǎ 2（电脑）编码 (diànnǎo) biānmǎ 3 行为准则 xíngwéi zhǔnzé
code of conduct/ethics 行为准则 xíngwéi zhǔnzé
code of practice 行业准则 hángyè zhǔnzé
code word 代码 dàimǎ, 代称 dài chēng
II v 编码 biānmǎ

co-ed ADJ 男女同校的 nánnǚ tóngxiào de

coerce v 强迫 qiǎngpò, 迫使 pòshǐ

coercion N 强迫 qiǎngpò, 迫使 pòshǐ

coexist v（和平地）共存 (hépíng de) gòngcún

coexistence N 和平共存 hépíng gòngcún

coffee N 咖啡 kāfēi [M. WD 杯 bēi]
black coffee 不加牛奶的咖啡 bù jiā niúnǎi de kāfēi
instant coffee 速溶咖啡 sùróng kāfēi
coffee break 工间休息 gōngjiān xiūxi
coffee cake 咖啡糕 kāfēi gāo
coffee house 咖啡馆 kāfēiguǎn

coffee maker N 煮咖啡器 zhǔ kāfēi qì

coffin N 棺材 guāncai

cog N 齿轮 chǐlún

cogency N 说服力 shuōfúlì

cogent ADJ 令人信服的 lìngrén xìnfú de

cogently ADV 令人信服地 lìngrén xìnfú de

cognac N（干邑）白兰地 (gānyì) báilándì

cohabit v 未婚同居 wèihūn tóngjū

cohabitation N 未婚同居 wèihūn tóngjū

coherence N 1 条理性 tiáolǐxìng 2 凝聚力 níngjùlì

coherent ADJ 有条理的 yǒu tiáolǐ de

cohesion N 凝聚力 níngjùlì

coil I v (to coil up) 盘绕 pánrào, 缠绕 chánrào **II** N 1 [电路+] 线圈 [diànlù+] xiànquān 2 一圈 yìquān, 一卷 yí juàn

coin I N 硬币 yìngbì [M. WD 枚 méi] **II** v 创造 [+新词语] chuàngzào [+xīncíyǔ]

coincide v 1 同时发生 tóngshí fāshēng 2 一致 yízhì, 相符 xiāngfú

coincidence N 巧合 qiǎohé
by coincidence 碰巧 pèngqiǎo

coincidental ADJ 巧合的 qiǎohé de

coke N 焦炭 jiāotàn, 焦煤 jiāoméi

Coke See **Coca-cola**

cola N 可乐类饮料 kělè lèi yǐnliào

colander N 滤盆 lùpén

cold I ADJ 1 冷 lěng, 寒冷 hánlěng
cold sore 冻疮 dòngchuāng
cold war 冷战 lěngzhàn
2 冷漠的 lěngmò de, 不友好的 bù yǒuhǎo de **II** N 1 感冒 gǎnmào, 伤风 shāngfēng 2 寒冷 hánlěng

cold-blooded ADJ 1 冷酷的 [+人] lěngkù de [+rén], 毫不留情的 háobù liúqíng de 2 冷血的 [+动物] lěngxuè de [+dòngwù]

cold-hearted ADJ 铁石心肠的 tiěshí xīncháng de, 毫无同情心的 háowú tóngqíngxīn de

coldly ADV 冷漠地 lěngmò de, 冷淡地 lěngdàn de

coleslaw N 凉拌卷心菜丝 liángbàn juǎnxīncàisī

colic N 腹绞痛 fù jiǎotòng

collaborate V **1** 合作 hézuò **2** 与敌人合作 yǔ dírén hézuò, 通敌 tōngdí

collaboration N **1** 合作 hézuò **2** 通敌 tōngdí

collaborator N **1** 合作者 hézuòzhě **2** 通敌者 tōngdí zhě

collage N 拼贴画 pīntiēhuà

collapse I V **1** 突然倒下 tūrán dǎoxià, 倒塌 dǎotā **2** 崩溃 bēngkuì, 垮掉 kuǎdiào II N **1** 崩溃 bēngkuì, 垮掉 kuǎdiào **2** 倒塌 dǎotā **3** 昏倒 hūndǎo

collapsible ADJ 可折叠的 kě zhédié de
a collapsible chair 折叠椅 zhédiéyǐ

collar I N **1** 领子 lǐngzi, 衣领 yīlǐng **2** 颈圈 jǐngquān II V **1** (给动物) 戴颈圈 (gěi dòngwù) dài jǐngquān **2** 逮住 dàizhù, 抓捕 zhuābǔ

collarbone N 锁骨 suǒgǔ

collate V 校对 jiàoduì, 核对 héduì

collateral N 抵押品 dǐyāpǐn [M. WD 件 jiàn]

colleague N 同事 tóngshì

collect V **1** 收集 shōují **2** 聚集 jùjí

collected ADJ **1** 收集成的 [+作品] shōují chéng de [+zuòpǐn] **2** 镇定的 [+人] zhèndìng de [+rén], 不慌不忙的 bùhuāng bùmáng de

collectible, collectable N 有收藏价值的东西 yǒu shōucáng jiàzhí de dōngxi, 收藏品 shōucángpǐn [M. WD 件 jiàn]

collection N **1** 收藏 shōucáng **2** 捐款 juānkuǎn
■ *A collection will be taken at the end of the meeting.* 会后将要募捐。 Huì hòu jiāngyào mùjuān.

collective ADJ 集体的 jítǐ de, 共同的 gòngtóng de
collective bargaining 集体谈判 jítǐ tánpàn

collector N **1** 收款人 shōukuǎnrén, 检票员 jiǎnpiàoyuán **2** 收藏者 shōuzàngzhě, 收藏家 shōucángjiā

college N **1** 大学 dàxué [M. WD 所 suǒ/座 zuò]
college student 大学生 dàxuésheng
2 学院 xuéyuàn
college of the arts and humanities 人文艺术学院 rénwén yìshù xuéyuàn

collide V **1** 相撞 xiāngzhuàng
to collide head-on 迎面相撞 yíngmiàn xiāngzhuàng
2 冲突 chōngtū

collie N 克里牧羊犬 kè lǐ mùyángquǎn

collision N **1** [车辆+] 相撞 [chēliàng+] xiāngzhuàng **2** [两派+] 冲突 [liǎng pài+] chōngtū
on a collision course 有发生冲突的趋势 yǒu fāshēng chōngtū de qūshì

colloquial ADJ 口语的 kǒuyǔ de

colloquialism N 口语词语 kǒuyǔ cíyǔ, 口语体 kǒuyǔtǐ

collude V 勾结 gōujié, 共谋 gòngmóu

collusion N 勾结 gōujié, 共谋 gòngmóu

colon N **1** 结肠 jiécháng **2** 冒号 màohào (:)

colonel N 上校 shàngxiào [M. WD 位 wéi]

colonial ADJ 殖民的 zhímín de, 殖民时期的 zhímín shíqī de

colonialism N 殖民主义 zhímín zhǔyì

colonialist N 殖民主义者 zhímín zhǔyì zhě

colonize V 开拓…为殖民地 kāituò…wéi zhímín dì

colony N 殖民地 zhímíndì

color I N **1** 颜色 yánsè
color scheme 色彩设计 sècǎi shèjì
2 脸色 liǎnsè II V 给…涂上颜色 gěi…tú shàng yánsè, 上色 shàngsè III ADJ 彩色的 cǎisè de
color TV/movie 彩色电视／电影 cǎisè diànshì/diànyǐng

colorblind ADJ 色盲的 sèmáng de

color-coordinated ADJ 颜色协调的 yánsè xiétiáo de

colored ADJ 有 (颜) 色的 yǒu (yán) sè de

colorfast ADJ 不褪色的 bù tuìsè de

colorful ADJ **1** 色彩鲜艳的 [+服装] sècǎi xiānyàn de [+fúzhuāng] **2** 丰富多彩的 [+生活] fēngfù duōcǎi de [+shēnghuó], 生动有趣的 shēngdòng yǒuqù de

coloring N **1** 填色 tiánsè, 上色 shàngsè **2** 食用色素 shíyòngsèsù
coloring book 填色书 tiánsèshū

colorless ADJ 无色的 wúsè de, 无趣味的 wú qùwèi de, 没有生气的 méiyǒu shēngqì de

colossal ADJ 巨大的 jùdà de

colossus N 庞然大物 pángrán dàwù, 巨人 jùrén

colt N 小公马 xiǎo gōngmǎ [M. WD 匹 pǐ], 雄马驹 xióng mǎjū [M. WD 匹 pǐ]

column N **1** 圆柱 yuánzhù [M. WD 根 gēn], 柱子 zhùzi [M. WD 根 gēn] **2** (报纸) 专栏 (bàozhǐ) zhuānlán **3** (军事) 纵队 (jūnshì) zòngduì

columnist N 专栏作家 zhuānlán zuòjiā

coma N 昏迷 hūnmí
in a coma 处于昏迷状态 chù yú hūnmí zhuàngtài, 昏迷之中 hūnmí zhīzhōng

comatose ADJ **1** 昏迷的 [+病人] hūnmí de [+bìngrén] **2** 极其疲倦 jíqí píjuàn, 呆滞的 dāizhì de

comb I N 梳子 shūzi [M. WD 把 bǎ] **2** (公鸡的) 鸡冠 (gōngjī de) jīguān **3** 蜂巢 fēngcháo, 蜂房 fēngfáng II V 梳 shū, 梳理 shūlǐ

combat I N 战斗 zhàndòu
killed in combat 死于战斗 sǐ yú zhàndòu, 阵亡 zhènwáng
combat vehicle 战车 zhànchē
II V 与…作战 yǔ…zuòzhàn

combatant N 战斗人员 zhàndòu rényuán, 战士 zhànshì

combative ADJ 好斗的 hǎo dǒu de, 好争论的 hǎo zhēnglùn de

combination N **1** 联合 liánhé **2** 组合 zǔhé
a winning combination 成功的组合 chénggōng de zǔhé
combination lock 密码锁 mìmǎsuǒ
combine[1] v **1** 结合 jiéhé, 组合 zǔhé **2** 混合 hùnhé, 化合 huàhé
combine[2] N **1** 联合收割机 liánhé shōugējī [M. WD 台 tái] **2** 联合企业 liánhéqǐyè, 联合体 liánhétǐ
combust v 燃烧 ránshāo
combustible ADJ 易燃的 yìrán de, 可燃的 kěrán de
combustion N 燃烧 ránshāo
come (PT **came**; PP **come**) v 来 lái, 到来 dàolái
to come across 碰见 pèngjiàn, 遇到 yùdào
to come from 是 (…地方) 人 shì (…dìfang) rén ■ He comes from Shanghai. 他是上海人。Tā shì Shànghǎi rén.
come on! 快点儿! Kuài diǎnr! 行了! Xíngle!
comeback N 复活 fùhuó, 东山再起 dōngshān zài qǐ
comedian N 喜剧演员 xǐjù yǎnyuán, 谐星 xiéxīng
comedown N 失落 shīluò, 失势 shīshì
comedy N 喜剧 xǐjù
come-on N 勾引 gōuyǐn, 挑逗 tiǎodòu
comet N 彗星 huìxīng
comeuppance N 报应 bàoyìng, 惩罚 chéngfá
comfort I N **1** 安慰 ānwèi **2** 舒适 shūshì
in comfort 舒适 shūshì
3 (comforts, creature comforts) 使生活舒适的东西 shǐ shēnghuó shūshì de dōngxi II v 安慰 ānwèi ■ The mother comforted her crying baby. 母亲安慰哭泣的婴儿。Mǔqin ānwèi kūqì de yīng'ér.
comfortable ADJ **1** 舒服 shūfu, 舒适 shūshì **2** 自在 zìzài, 不拘束 bù jūshù ■ He didn't feel comfortable meeting his former girlfriend and her husband at the party. 他在聚会上遇到以前的女友和她丈夫, 感到很不自在。Tā zài jùhuìshang yùdào yǐqián de nǚyǒu hé tā zhàngfu, gǎndào hěn bú zìzài.
comforter N 被子 bèizi [M. WD 条 tiáo]
comfy ADJ 舒适的 shūshì de
comic I ADJ 滑稽的 huájī de
comic book 儿童连环画 értóng liánhuánhuà
comic strip 连环漫画 liánhuán mànhuà
II N **1** 喜剧演员 xǐjù yǎnyuán **2** 儿童连环画 értóng liánhuánhuà
comical ADJ 滑稽的 huájī de, 可笑的 kěxiào de
coming I N 到来 dàolái
coming and going 来来往往 láilái wǎngwǎng II ADJ 即将到来的 jíjiāng dàolái de
comma N 逗号 dòuhào (,)
command I v **1** 指挥 zhǐhuī **2** 命令 mìnglìng II N **1** 指挥 zhǐhuī **2** 命令 mìnglìng **3** 兵团 bīngtuán **4** 掌握 zhǎngwò, 运用能力 yùnyòng nénglì
to have a good command of Chinese 具有很好

的中文能力 jùyǒu hěn hǎode Zhōngwén nénglì
commandant N 司令官 sīlìngguān [M. WD 位 wéi/名 míng], 指挥官 zhǐhuīguān [M. WD 位 wéi/名 míng]
commandeer v 征用 zhēngyòng
commander N 司令 sīlìng [M. WD 位 wéi/名 míng], 司令员 sīlìngyuán [M. WD 位 wéi/名 míng]
commanding ADJ **1** 指挥的 [+军官] zhǐhuī de [+jūnguān] **2** 威严的 [+口气] wēiyán de [+kǒuqì] **3** 居高临下的 [+山峰] jūgāo línxià de [+shānfēng] **4** 遥遥领先的 yáoyáo lǐng xiān de
commandment N 戒律 jièlǜ
the Ten Commandments (圣经) 十戒 (Shèngjīng) shíjiè
commando N 突击队 tūjīduì, 特种部队 tèzhǒng bùduì
commemorate v 纪念 jìniàn
commemoration N 纪念 jìniàn
commemorative ADJ 纪念的 jìniàn de
commence v 开始 kāishǐ
commencement N **1** 开始 kāishǐ **2** 毕业典礼 bìyè diǎnlǐ
commend v 公开表扬 gōngkāi biǎoyáng, 赞扬 zànyáng
commendable ADJ 值得赞扬的 zhíde zànyáng de
commendation N 奖品 jiǎngpǐn, 荣誉 róngyù
commensurate ADJ 相称的 xiāngchèn de, 相应的 xiāngyìng de
comment I v 议论 yìlùn, 评论 pínglùn II N 议论 yìlùn, 评论 pínglùn ■ His sudden resignation caused much comment. 他突然辞职, 引起了很多议论。Tā túrán cízhí, yǐnqǐle hěn duō yìlùn.
commentary N [球赛的+] 现场解说 [qiúsài de+] xiànchǎng jiěshuō, [新闻的+] 实况报道 [xīnwén de+] shíkuàng bàodào
running commentary 现场评介 xiànchǎng píngjiè
commentator N 解说员 jiěshuōyuán
commerce N 商业 shāngyè, 商务 shāngwù
commercial I ADJ 商业的 shāngyè de
commercial break 广告时间 guǎnggào shíjiān II N 电视广告 diànshì guǎnggào
commercialism N 赢利第一 yínglì dìyī, 利润至上 lìrùn zhìshàng
commercialize v 商业化 shāngyèhuà
commiserate v 表示同情 biǎoshì tóngqíng
commission I N **1** [税务+] 委员会 [shuìwù+] wěiyuánhuì **2** [代理人+] 佣金 [dàilǐrén+] yòngjīn **3** [专门定做的+] 艺术品 [zhuānmén dìngzuò de] yìshùpǐn
in commission 仍在服役的 [+军舰] réng zài fúyì de [+jūnjiàn]
out of commission 不能使用的 bùnéng shǐyòng de

II v **1** 委托 [+制作艺术品] wěituō [+zhìzuò yìshùpǐn] **2** 授予军衔 shòuyǔ jūnxián
a commissioned officer (被授予军衔的)军官 (bèi shòuyǔ jūnxián de) jūnguān

commissioner N 负责长官 fùzé zhǎngguān

commit v **1** 保证 bǎozhèng, 承担 chéngdān
to commit oneself to 保证 bǎozhèng
2 付出 fùchū **3** 犯(罪/错误)fàn (zuì/cuòwù)
to committ a felony 犯重罪 fàn zhòngzuì

commitment N **1** 承诺 chéngnuò **2** 奉献 fèngxiàn, 敬业精神 jìngyè jīngshén

committed ADJ 献身的 xiànshēn de, 尽职的 jìnzhí de

committee N 委员会 wěiyuánhuì ■ *A special committee has been set up to solve the problem.* 成立了一个特殊委员会，来解决这个问题。Chénglìle yí ge tèshū wěiyuánhuì, lái jiějué zhè ge wèntí.

commodity N 商品 shāngpǐn

commodore N (美国)海军准将 (Měiguó) hǎijūn zhǔnjiàng

common ADJ **1** 共同的 gòngtóng de **2** 普通的 pǔtōng de ■ *She thinks herself above the common people.* 她认为自己高人一等。Tā rènwéi zìjǐ gāo rén yì děng.
to have something/much/nothing in common with 和…有些/有很多/没有共同点 hé… yǒuxiē/yǒu hěn duō/méiyǒu gòngtóngdiǎn
common sense 常识 chángshí
3 常见的 chángjiàn de
common cold 感冒 gǎnmào

common-law ADJ 普通法 pǔtōngfǎ
common-law marriage 事实婚姻 shìshí hūnyīn, 同居关系 tóngjū guānxi

commonly ADV 通常 tōngcháng, 一般 yìbān

commonplace ADJ 平常的 píngcháng de, 不足为奇的 bùzú wéi qí de

commonwealth N 联合体 liánhétǐ, 联邦 liánbāng
British Commonwealth (大)英联邦 (Dà) Yīng liánbāng

commotion N 吵闹 chǎonào, 混乱 hùnluàn

communal ADJ 公共的 gōnggòng de, 共用的 gòngyòng de

commune I N 公社 gōngshè II v 交流 jiāoliú

communicable ADJ 传染的 chuánrǎn de

communicate v **1** 沟通 gōutōng, 交流 jiāoliú
2 [痢疾+] 传染 [lìji+] chuánrǎn

communication N 沟通 gōutōng, 交流 jiāoliú
■ *The problem was caused by poor communication.* 问题是因为没有好好沟通引起的。Wèntí shì yīnwèi méiyǒu hǎohǎo gōutōng de yǐnqǐ de.

communications N **1** [现代+] 通讯手段 [xiàndài+] tōngxùn shǒuduàn **2** [学习+] 传媒学 [xuéxí+] chuánméixué

communicative ADJ 乐于沟通的 lèyú gōutōng de, 善于言谈的 shànyú yántán de

communion N **1** 情感思想交流 qínggǎn sīxiǎng jiāoliú **2** 圣餐仪式 Shèngcān yíshì
Holy Communion 圣餐仪式 Shèngcān yíshì

communique N 公报 gōngbào

communism N 共产主义 Gòngchǎn zhǔyì

communist N 共产主义者 Gòngchǎn zhǔyìzhě, 共产党党员 Gòngchǎndǎng dǎngyuán

community N **1** 社区 shèqū
community college 社区学院 shèqū xuéyuàn
community service 社区服务 shèqū fúwù
2 群体 qúntǐ, 公众 gōngzhòng
community property 夫妻共有财产 fūqī gòngyǒu cáichǎn

commute I v 远距离上下班 yuǎnjùlí shàngxiàbān II N (远距离)上下班的时间 (yuǎnjùlí) shàngxiàbān de shíjiān

commuter N 远距离上下班的人 yuǎnjùlí shàngxiàbān de rén

compact I ADJ 小而紧凑的 xiǎo ér jǐncòu de
a compact car 小型汽车 xiǎoxíng qìchē
compact disc, CD 光盘 guāngpán
II N **1** 小型汽车 xiǎoxíng qìchē [M. WD 辆 liàng]
2 化妆粉盒 huàzhuāng fěnhé III v 压紧 yā jǐn

companion N **1** 同伴 tóngbàn **2** [旅游+] 手册 [lǚyóu+] shǒucè

companionable ADJ 友善的 yǒushàn de

companionship ADJ 友伴 yǒubàn, 友好往来 yǒuhǎowǎnglái

company N **1** 公司 gōngsī [M. WD 家 jiā]
limited company 有限公司 yǒuxiàn gōngsī
listed company 上市公司 shàngshì gōngsī
2 交往 jiāowǎng, 陪伴 péibàn ■ *I'll stay and keep you company.* 我留下来陪你。Wǒ liúxiàlai péi nǐ. **3** 同伴 tóngbàn, 朋友 péngyou
to fall into bad company 交了坏朋友 jiāole huài péngyou
4 客人 kèren, 访客 fǎngkè
to expect company 等客人到来 děng kèren dàolái

comparable ADJ 类似的 lèisì de, 可相提并论的 kě xiāngtí bìnglùn de

comparative I ADJ **1** 相对的 xiāngduì de
comparative freedom 相对的自由 xiāngduì de zì yóu
2 (学术研究方面)比较的 (xuéshù yánjiū fāngmiàn) bǐjiào de
comparative literature 比较文学(研究)bǐjiào wénxué (yánjiū)
II N (形容词/副词的)比较级 (xíngróngcí/fùcí de) bǐjiàojí

compare v 比 bǐ, 比较 bǐjiào

comparison N 比较 bǐjiào ■ *This new equipment is much more energy efficient in comparison to the old one.* 与旧设备相比，新设备利用能源的效率高得多。Yǔ jiù shèbèi xiāngbǐ, xīn shèbèi lìyòng néngyuán de xiàolǜ gāode duō.

by comparison 相比之下 xiāngbǐ zhī xià

compartment N 1 分隔间 fēngé jiān
freezer compartment 冷冻格 lěngdòng gé
2（飞机/火车等）舱 (fēijī/huǒchē děng) cāng
first-class compartment 头等舱 tóuděngcāng

compartmentalize V 分成小间 fēnchéng
xiǎojiān, 划分 huàfēn

compass N 1 指南针 [+路] zhǐnánzhēn [+zhǐlù]
2 圆规 yuánguī

compassion N 强烈的同情心 qiángliè de
tóngqíngxīn

compassionate ADJ 有同情心的 yǒu tóngqíngxīn
de
compassionate leave 私事假 sīshìjià, 丧假
sāngjià

compatibility N 兼容性 jiānróngxìng

compatible I ADJ 兼容的 jiānróng de, 一致的
yīzhì de II N 兼容机 jiānróng jī

compatriot N 同胞 tóngbāo

compel V 强迫 qiángpò

compelling ADJ 令人不得不注意的 lìngrén
bùdébù zhùyì de, 极为有趣的 jíwéi yǒuqù de
a compelling reason 强烈的理由 qiángliè de
lǐyóu

compendium N 大全 dàquán

compensate V 1 赔偿 péicháng 2 弥补 míbǔ

compensation N 赔偿 péicháng [M. WD 笔 bǐ], 赔
偿金 péichángjīn [M. WD 笔 bǐ]

compete N 1 竞争 jìngzhēng 2 参加比赛 cānjiā
bǐsài

competence N 能力 nénglì

competent ADJ 有能力的 yǒu nénglì de, 能胜任的
néng shēngrèn de

competition N 1 竞争 jìngzhēng 2 比赛 bǐsài

competitive ADJ 有竞争力的 yǒu jìngzhēnglì de

competitor N 竞争者 jìngzhēngzhě, 参赛者
cānsàizhě

compilation N 汇编集 huìbiānjí

compile V 汇编 huìbiān, 编辑 biānjí

complacency N 自满 zìmǎn

complacent ADJ 自满的 zìmǎn de, 心满意足的 xīn
mǎnyì dé de

complain V 1 抱怨 bàoyuàn
I can't complain. 还算不错。Háisuàn bùcuò.
2 投诉 tóusù ■ A customer has complained to
the manager about her terrible service. 一位顾客
因为她服务太差而向经理投诉。Yí wèi gùkè yīnwèi
tā fúwù tài chà ér xiàng jīnglǐ tóusù.

complaint N 1 抱怨 bàoyuàn ■ We have no complaints about your school. 对你们学校我没什么
可抱怨的。Duì nǐmen xuéxiào wǒ méishénme
kě bàoyuàn de. 2 投诉 tóusù 3（病人的）主诉
(bìngrén de) zhǔsù

complement I N 1 补充物（或人）bǔchōng wù
(huò rén) 2 全数 quánshù II V 衬托 chèntuō

complementary ADJ 补充的 bǔchōng de

complete I ADJ 完的 wánquán de, 全部的
quánbù de II V 完成 wánchéng ■ We need
to complete the pilot project first. 我们得优先完成
试点工程。Wǒmen děi xiān wánchéng shìdiǎn
gōngchéng.

completely ADV 完全地 wánquán de, 彻底地
chèdǐ de

completion N 完成 wánchéng

complex I ADJ 复杂 fùzá II N 1 综合建筑群
zōnghé jiànzhùqún
movie complex 综合影剧院 zōnghé yǐngjùyuàn
2 情结 qíngjié
Electra complex 恋父情结 liànfù qíngjié
Oedipus compex 恋母情结 liànmǔ qíngjié

complexion N 面色 miànsè

complexity N 复杂性 fùzáxìng

compliance N 遵守 zūnshǒu, 服从 fúcóng

compliant ADJ 服从的 fúcóng de, 顺从的
shùncóng de

complicate V 使···复杂 shǐ...fùzá

complicated ADJ 复杂的 fùzá de

complication N 1 复杂性 fùzáxìng 2 并发症 bìng-
fāzhèng

complicity N 共谋 gòngmóu, 共犯 gòngfàn

compliment N, V 称赞 chēngzàn, 赞美 zànměi
■ Thank you for your compliment. 谢谢你的称
赞。Xièxie nǐde chēngzàn.
a backhanded (left-handed) compliment 挖苦
的恭维话 wāku de gōngweihuà

complimentary ADJ 1 称赞的 chēngzàn de 2 赠
送的 zèngsòng de, 免费的 miǎnfèi de

compliments N 问候 wènhòu, 致意 zhìyì

comply V 遵守 zūnshǒu, 服从 fúcóng

component N 组成部分 zǔchéng bùfen

compose V 1 组成 zǔchéng
to be composed of 由···组成 yóu...zǔchéng
■ That dictionary is composed of two parts: a
Chinese-English section and an English-Chinese
section. 那本词典由两个部分组成—汉英和英汉部
分。Nà běn cídiǎn yóu liǎng ge bùfen zǔchéng—
Hànyīng hé YīngHàn bùfen.
2 写 xiě, 谱写 pǔxiě

composed ADJ 平静的 píngjìng de

composer N 作曲者 zuòqǔzhě, 作曲家 zuòqǔjiā

composite I ADJ 拼合成的 pīnhéchéng de II N 混
合物 hùnhéwù

composition N 1 [化学成份+] 组成 [huàxué chéng-
fèn+] zǔchéng 2 [学生的+] 作文 [xuésheng
de+] zuòwén 3 [音乐+] 作品 [yīnyuè+] zuòpǐn

compost N 堆肥 duīféi

composure N 镇定 zhèndìng, 冷静 lěngjìng

compound I N 1 大院 dàyuàn, 场地 chǎngdì
2 化合物 huàhéwù, 混合物 hùnhéwù 3 复合词
fùhécí II V 1 使混合 shǐ hùnhé 2 使恶化 shǐ

èhuà **3** 计算复利 jìsuàn fùlì **III** ADJ **1** 复合的 fùhé de

a compound sentence 复合句 fùhéjù

2 重复的 chóngfù de

compound interest 复利 fùlì

comprehend v 理解 lǐjiě, 领悟 lǐngwù

comprehensible ADJ 容易理解的 róngyì lǐjiě de

comprehension N 理解 lǐjiě, 领悟 lǐngwù

comprehensive ADJ 综合的 zōnghé de, 全面的 quánmiàn de

compress v 压缩 yāsuō, 压紧 yā jǐn

compression N 压缩 yāsuō, 压紧 yā jǐn

comprise v 由…组成 yóu…zǔchéng

compromise I N 妥协 tuǒxié

to make compromises 让步 ràngbù

II v **1** 妥协 tuǒxié, 让步 ràngbù **2** 损害 sǔnhài

to compromise oneself 损害自己 sǔnhài zìjǐ, 损害自己的形象 sǔnhài zìjǐ de xíngxiàng

compromising ADJ 不光彩的 bùguāngcǎi de, 有失体面的 yǒu shī tǐmian de

compulsion N **1** 强烈冲动 qiángliè chōngdòng **2** 强迫 qiǎngpò

compulsive ADJ 有强烈冲动的 yǒu qiángliè chōngdòng de, 强迫性的 qiǎngpò xìng de

a compulsive gambler 赌博成性的人 dǔbó chéngxìng de rén

compulsory ADJ 必须做的 bìxū zuò de, 强迫性的 qiǎngpò xìng de

compulsory (school) subject 学校必修课目 xuéxiào bìxiūkè mù

compunction N 内疚 nèijiù, 后悔 hòuhuǐ

computation N 计算 jìsuàn, 计算的技能 jìsuàn de jìnéng

compute v 计算 jìsuàn

computer N 计算机 jìsuànjī [M. WD 台 tái], 电脑 diànnǎo [M. WD 台 tái]

computer game 电脑游戏 diànnǎo yóuxì

computer jockey 计算机编程高手 jìsuànjī biānchéng gāoshǒu

computer literate 会使用计算机的 huì shǐyòng jìsuànjī de

computerize v 电脑化 diànnǎohuà

computing N 计算机操作 jìsuànjī cāozuò

comrade N 同志 tóngzhì

con I v 欺骗 qīpiàn, 诈骗 zhàpiàn **II** N 欺骗 qīpiàn, 诈骗 zhàpiàn

con artist 骗子 piànzi

concave ADJ 凹面的 āomiàn de

a concave mirror 凹透镜 āotòujìng

conceal v 隐藏 yǐncáng

concealment N 隐藏 yǐncáng

concede v（勉强）承认（miǎnqiǎng）chéngrèn

conceit N 自负 zìfù, 骄傲 jiāo'ào

conceited ADJ 自负的 zìfù de, 自高自大的 zìgāo zìdà de

conceivable ADJ 可以想象的 kěyǐ xiǎngxiàng de

conceive v **1** 想象 [+状况] xiǎngxiàng [+zhuàngkuàng], 相信 xiāngxìn **2** 设想 [+新方法] shèxiǎng [+xīn fāngfǎ], 构想 gòuxiǎng **3** 怀胎 huáitāi

concentrate I v **1** 集中 jízhōng **2** 专心 zhuānxīn, 集中注意力 jízhōng zhùyìlì ■ *After learning the disturbing news, she found it difficult to concentrate in class.* 听到那个扰人的消息，她觉得上课的时候很难专心。Tīngdao nà ge rǎorén de xiāoxi, tā juéde shàngkè de shíhou hěn nán zhuānxīn.

II N 浓缩液 nóngsuōyè, 浓缩物 nóngsuōwù

concentrated ADJ **1** 浓缩的 [+水果汁] nóngsuō de [+shuǐguǒzhī] **2** 全神贯注的 quánshén guànzhù de

to make a concentrated effort 全力以赴地 quánlì yǐfù de

concentration N **1** 专心致志 zhuānxīn zhìzhì **2** 集中 jízhōng **3** 浓度 nóngdù

concentric ADJ 同心的 tóngxīn de

concept N 概念 gàiniàn, 观念 guānniàn

conception N **1** 概念 gàiniàn, 观念 guānniàn **2** 构想 gòuxiǎng **3** 怀胎 huáitāi

conceptual ADJ 概念的 gàiniàn de, 观念的 guānniàn de

concern I v **1** 和…有关系 hé…yǒu guānxi **2** 使…担心 shǐ…dānxīn ■ *What concerns many people is the rise in teenage mothers.* 使很多人担心的是少年母亲越来越多。Shǐ hěn duō rén dānxīn de shì shàonǎ mǔqin yuèláiyuè duō.

to be concerned with 关注 guānzhù, 担心 dānxīn

II N **1** 关心 guānxīn, 担心 dānxīn ■ *Global warming has caused growing concern.* 全球天气变暖，引起越来越大的关注。Quánqiú tiānqì biàn nuǎn, yǐnqǐ yuèláiyuè dà de guānzhù. **2** 关心的事 guānxīn de shì **3** 公司 gōngsī, 企业 qǐyè

concerned ADJ **1** 焦虑的 jiāolǜ de, 担心的 dānxīn de **2** 有关的 yǒuguān de

to be concerned for 关心 guānxīn, 挂念 guàniàn

as far as … is concerned 就…而言 jiù…éryán

concerning PREP 关于 guānyú

concert N 音乐会 yīnyuèhuì [M. WD 场 cháng]

concert grand 平台大钢琴 píngtái dàgāngqín

concert master 首席小提琴手 shǒuxí xiǎotíqínshǒu

in concert with 共同行动 gòngtóng xíngdòng

concerted ADJ 共同的 gòngtóng de, 一致的 yízhì de

concerto N 协奏曲 xiézòuqǔ [M. WD 首 shǒu]

concession N **1** 让步 ràngbù **2** 特许权 tèxǔquán

concession stand 小食品摊 xiǎo shípǐn tān

concierge N 旅馆服务台职员 lǚguǎn fúwùtái zhíyuán

conciliate v 调停 tiáotíng, 调解 tiáojiě
conciliation N 调停 tiáotíng, 调解 tiáojiě
conciliatory ADJ 和解的 héjiě de
concise ADJ 简明的 jiǎnmíng de, 简洁的 jiǎnjié de
conclude v 1 结束 jiéshù 2 下结论 xiàjiélùn, 得出结论 déchū jiélùn ■ *The police report concluded that this man was innocent.* 警察报告得出结论, 该人无罪。Jǐngchá bàogào déchū jiélùn, gāirén wúzuì.
conclusion N 1 结束 jiéshù, 结局 jiéjú 2 结论 jiélùn, 断言 duànyán
to jump to conclusions 轻易下结论 qīngyì xiàjiélùn
conclusive ADJ 确信无意的 quèxìn wúyì de, 毫无疑问的 háo wúyí wèn de
concoct v 1 编造 [+谎言] biānzào [+huǎngyán], 虚构 xūgòu 2 配制 [+食谱] pèizhì [+shípǔ], 拼凑 pīncòu
concoction N 调制品 tiáozhì pǐn
concourse N 大厅 dàtīng
concrete I N 混凝土 hùnníngtǔ II ADJ 1 混凝土的 [+大桥] hùnníngtǔ de [+dàqiáo] 2 具体的 [+计划] jùtǐ de [+jìhuà]
concur v 与⋯意见一致 yǔ⋯yìjiàn yízhì, 完全赞同 wánquán zàntóng
concurrence N 1 同意 tóngyì 2 同时发生 tóngshí fāshēng
concurrent ADJ 1 同意的 tóngyì de 2 同时发生的 tóngshí fāshēng de
concussion N 1 震荡 zhèndàng 2 脑震荡 nǎozhèndàng
condemn v 1 谴责 qiǎnzé 2 判刑 pànxíng 3 宣布为危房 xuānbù wéi wēifáng
condemnation N 谴责 qiǎnzé
condensation N 1 凝结 níngjié 2 水滴 shuǐdī 3 压缩 yāsuō
condense v 1 凝结 níngjié 2 压缩 yāsuō
condescend v 1 表现出高人一等 biǎoxiànchū gāo rén yì děng 2 屈尊 qūzūn
condescending ADJ 居高临下的 jūgāo línxià de, 带有优越感的 dàiyǒu yōuyuègǎn de
condiment N 调味品 tiáowèipǐn
condition I N 1 条件 tiáojiàn ■ *Conditions apply to this sale.* 这一销售, 附有一定条件。Zhè yì xiāoshòu, fùyǒu yídìng tiáojiàn. 2 情况 qíngkuàng, 条件 tiáojiàn 3 健康状况 jiànkāng zhuàngkuàng 4 疾病 jíbìng
a skin condition 皮肤病 pífūbìng
II v 1 使⋯习惯 shǐ⋯xíguàn, 使⋯适应 shǐ⋯shìyìng 2 支配 zhīpèi, 训练 xùnliàn
conditional ADJ 有条件的 yǒu tiáojiàn de
conditional upon 以⋯为前提 yǐ⋯wéi qiántí
conditioner N 护发素 hùfàsù
conditioning N 形成条件反射的过程 xíngchéng tiáojiàn fǎnshè de guòchéng

condolence N 吊唁 diàoyàn, 慰问 wèiwèn
condom N 避孕套 bìyùntào
condominium N 公寓 gōngyù [M. WD 套 tào], 公寓楼 gōngyù lóu [M. WD 幢 zhuàng/栋 dòng]
condone v 纵容 zòngróng, 宽容 kuānróng
conduce v 有助于 yǒuzhù yú
conducive ADJ 有助于的 yǒuzhù yú de
conduct I v 1 进行 jìnxíng 2 带领 dàilǐng 3 指挥 [+乐队] zhǐhuī [+yuèduì] 4 传导 [+电／热] chuán dǎo [+diàn/rè]
to conduct oneself 举止 jǔzhǐ, 表现 biǎoxiàn
II N 1 行为 xíngwéi, 举止 jǔzhǐ 2 经营 jīngyíng
conductive ADJ 导电(或热) 性能强的 dǎo diàn (huò rè) xìngnéng qiáng de
conductor N 1 [音乐+] 指挥 [yīnyuè+] zhǐhuī 2 [火车+] 列车员 [huǒchē+] lièchēyuán 3 导体 dǎotǐ
cone N 1 圆锥体 yuánzhuītǐ 2 冰淇淋蛋卷筒 bīngqílín dànjuǎntǒng 3 球果 qiúguǒ
confection N 糖果饼干 tángguǒ bǐnggān
confectioner N 糖果商 tángguǒ shāng
confederacy N (美国) 南部邦联 (Měiguó) nánbù bānglián
confederate I N 1 同谋 tóngmóu 2 (美国) 南部邦联的士兵 (Měiguó) nánbù bānglián de shì bīng II v 联盟 liánméng
confederation N 联盟 liánméng
confer v 1 [与顾问+] 商议 [yǔ gùwèn+] shāngyì 2 授予 [+奖章] shòuyǔ [+jiǎngzhāng]
conference N 会议 huìyì
confess v 坦白 tǎnbái, 承认 [+错误] chéngrèn [+cuòwù]
confession N 1 坦白 tǎnbái, 供认 gòngrèn 2 (天主教) 忏悔 (Tiānzhǔjiào) chànhuǐ
confetti N 彩色纸屑 cǎisè zhǐxiè
confidant, confidante N 知心密友 zhīxīn mìyǒu
confide v 吐露 [+私人秘密] tǔlù [+sīrén mìmì]
confidence N 信心 xìnxīn
to have confidence in 对⋯有信心 duì⋯yǒu xìnxīn
2 确信 quèxìn 3 信任感 xìnrèngǎn
confident ADJ 有信心的 yǒu xìnxīn de ■ *I'm confident of his ability.* 我对他的能力有信心。Wǒ duì tā de nénglì yǒu xìnxīn.
confidential ADJ 机密的 jīmì de
confidentiality N 机密 jīmì
breach of confidentiality 违反保密原则 wéifǎn bǎomì yuánzé
configuration N 1 外形 wàixíng 2 构造 gòuzào 3 (计算机) 配置 (jìsuànjī) pèizhì
configure v 1 (计算机) 配置 (jìsuànjī) pèizhì
confine v 1 监禁 [+嫌疑犯] jiānjìn [+xiányífàn], 关押 guānyā 2 控制 [+传染病] kòngzhì [+chuánrǎnbìng], 限制 xiànzhì
confined ADJ 狭小的 xiáxiǎo de

confinement N 1（产妇的）分娩期 (chǎnfù de) fēnmiǎn qī 2 监禁 jiānjìn, 关押 guānyā

confines N 范围 fànwéi
within the confines of 在…的范围内 zài…de fànwéinèi

confirm V 1 确定 quèdìng 2 证实 zhèngshí
neither confirm nor deny 既不证实, 也不否认 jì bú zhèngshí, yě bù fǒurèn, 不置可否 bú zhì kě fǒu

confirmation N 1 确定 quèdìng 2 证实 zhèngshí

confirmed ADJ 坚定的 jiāndìng de
a confirmed bachelor 坚定的单身汉 jiāndìng de dānshēnhàn, 决心打光棍的人 juéxīn dǎguānggùn de rén

confiscate V 没收 mòshōu, 把…充公 bǎ…chōnggōng

confiscation N 充公 chōnggōng, 没收 mòshōu

conflict I N 冲突 chōngtū, 矛盾 máodùn
conflict of interest 利益冲突 lìyì chōngtū
II V 冲突 chōngtū

conform V 1 保持一致 bǎochí yízhì 2 遵循 zūnxún

conformist I ADJ 墨守成规的 mòshǒu chéngguī de, 循规蹈矩的 xúnguī dǎojǔ de II N 墨守成规的人 mòshǒu chéngguī de rén

confound V 使…困惑 shǐ…kùnhuò, 使…惊讶 shǐ…jīngyà

confront V 1 面临 miànlín, 遭遇 zāoyù 2 面对 [+问题] miànduì [+wèntí], 对抗 duìkàng

confrontation N 对抗 duìkàng, 冲突 chōngtū

confuse V 使…糊涂 shǐ…hútu, 把…搞错 bǎ…gǎocuò ■ The instructions given in the manual confused many users. 这份使用说明书里的指令使很多人搞糊涂了。 Zhè fèn shǐyòng shuōmíngshū lǐ de zhǐlìng shǐ hěn duō rén gǎo hútu le.

confused ADJ 搞糊涂了 gǎo hútu le

confusing ADJ 使人糊涂的 shǐrén hútu de ■ I find the company policy extremely confusing. 我觉得公司的政策极其糊涂。 Wǒ juéde gōngsī de zhèngcè jíqí hútu.

confusion N 1 困惑 kùnhuò 2 混乱 hùnluàn

congeal V 凝结 níngjié

congenial ADJ 1 令人舒适轻松的 lìngrén shūshì qīngsōng de 2 和善的 héshàn de

congenital ADJ 1 先天的 xiāntiān de 2 天生的 tiānshēng de

congested ADJ 1 拥挤的 yōngjǐ de 2 堵塞的 dǔsè de

congestion N 1 [交通+] 拥挤 [jiāotōng+] yōngjǐ 2 [鼻子+] 堵塞 [bízi+] dǔsè

conglomerate N 1 大型企业集团 dàxíng qǐyè jítuán 2 混合体 hùnhé tǐ

conglomeration N 聚集体 jùjí tǐ

congratulate V 祝贺 zhùhè
to congratulate oneself 自我满足 zìwǒ mǎnzú, 自豪 zìháo

congratulations N 祝贺 zhùhè
Congratulations! 恭喜恭喜! Gōngxǐ gōngxǐ! 祝贺你(们)! Zhùhè nǐ (men)!

congregate V 聚集 jùjí, 聚合 jùhé

congregation N（教堂）会众 (jiàotáng) huìzhòng

Congregational ADJ 公理会的 Gōnglǐhuì de

congress N 1 代表大会 dàibiǎo dàhuì 2（美国）国会 (Měiguó) Guóhuì,（美国）国会众议院 (Měiguó) Guóhuì zhòngyìyuàn

congressman, congresswoman N（美国）国会议员 (Měiguó) Guóhuì Yìyuán,（美国）国会众议员 (Měiguó) Guóhuì zhòngyìyuán

conical, conic ADJ 圆锥形的 yuánzhuī xíng de

conifer N 针叶树 zhēnyèshù

conjecture N, V 猜测 cāicè

conjugal ADJ 婚姻的 hūnyīn de, 夫妻之间的 fūqī zhījiān de
conjugal visit 配偶探监同房 pèi ǒu tànjiān tóngfáng

conjunction N 1 结合 jiéhé, 连接 liánjiē
in conjunction with 与…结合起来 yǔ…jiéhéqǐlái
2 同时发生 tóngshí fāshēng 3 连接词 liánjiēcí

conjure V 变魔术 biàn móshù, 变出 biàn chū

conman N 骗子 piànzi

connect V 连接 liánjiē

connection N 1 关系 guānxi, 联系 liánxì 2 连接 liánjiē

connivance N 1 默许 mòxǔ 2 合谋 hémóu

connive V 默许 mòxǔ, 纵容 zòngróng
to connive to do sth 串通起来 chuàntōng qǐlái, 合谋 hémóu

connoisseur N 鉴赏家 jiànshǎngjiā

connotation N 隐含意义 yǐnhán yìyì

connote V 使人联想到 shǐrén liánxiǎng dào

conquer V 征服 zhēngfú

conquest N 征服 zhēngfú

conscience N 良心 liángxīn, 是非感 shìfēigǎn
a guilty conscience 负罪感 fùzuìgǎn

conscientious ADJ 认真的 rènzhēn de

conscious ADJ 感觉到的 gǎnjuédào de, 有感觉的 yǒu gǎnjué de ■ They were not conscious of the inherent danger. 他们没有意识到潜在的危险。 Tāmen méiyǒu yìshidao qiánzài de wēixiǎn.

consciousness N 知觉 zhījué, 感觉 gǎnjué
to lose consciousness 失去知觉 shīqù zhījué
to regain consciousness 恢复知觉 huīfù zhījué

conscript I V 征召 zhēngzhāo II N 应征入伍的士兵 yìngzhēngrùwǔ de shìbīng [M. WD 名 míng]

consecrate V 宣布…为神圣 xuānbù…wéi shénshèng

consecutive ADJ 连续的 liánxù de

consensus N 共识 gòngshí, 一致意见 yízhì yìjiàn

consent N, V 同意 tóngyì, 允许 yǔnxǔ

consequence N 后果 hòuguǒ

consequential ADJ **1** 意义重大的 yìyì zhòngdà de **2** 随后发生的 suíhòu fāshēng de

consequently ADV 因此 yīncǐ, 所以 suǒyǐ

conservation N 保护 bǎohù, 保存 bǎocún
wildlife conservation 野生动物保护 yěshēng dòngwù bǎohù

conservationist N 环境保护主义者 huánjìng bǎohù zhǔyì zhě, 关心环保的人 guānxīn huánbǎo de rén

conservatism N 保守的态度 bǎoshǒu de tàidu, 守旧 shǒujiù

conservative ADJ 保守的 bǎoshǒude ■ He becomes more and more conservative as he gets older. 他年纪越来越大，就变得越来越保守。Tā niánjì yuèláiyuè dà, jiù biànde yuèláiyuè bǎoshǒu.

conservator N **1** （法律）监护人 (fǎlǜ) jiānhùrén **2** （图书馆／博物馆）管理员 (túshūguǎn/ bówùguǎn) guǎnlǐyuán

conservatory N **1** 音乐学院 yīnyuè xuéyuàn **2** 温室 wēnshì

conserve V 保护 bǎohù, 保存 bǎocún

consider V **1** 考虑 kǎolǜ **2** 认为 rènwéi ■ I consider him blameless. 我认为他没有错。Wǒ rènwéi tā méiyǒu cuò.

considerable ADJ 相当多的 xiāngdāng duō de, 相当大的 xiāngdāng dà de

considerate ADJ 考虑周到的 kǎolǜ zhōudào de, 体贴的 tǐtiē de

consideration N **1** 考虑 kǎolǜ **2** 需要考虑的事 xūyào kǎolǜ de shì, 因素 yīnsù ■ There are financial considerations that must be taken into account. 有一些财务上的因素必须考虑进去。Yǒu yìxiē cáiwùshang de yīnsù bìxū kǎolǜ jìnqu. **3** 体谅 tǐliang

considered ADJ 经过深思熟虑的 jīngguò shēnsī shúlǜ de

considering PREP 考虑到 kǎolǜdào, 由于 yóuyú

consign V **1** 使…陷于 shǐ…xiànyú, 使…处于 shǐ… chǔyú **2** 运送 yùnsòng

consignment N **1** 运送 yùnsòng **2** 运送的货物 yùnsòng de huòwù

consist V 组成 zǔchéng
to consist in 在于 zàiyú
to consist of 由…组成 yóu…zǔchéng, 包括 bāokuò

consistency N 连贯性 liánguànxìng

consistent ADJ 一贯的 yíguàn de
consistent with 与…一致 yǔ…yízhì

consolation N 安慰 ānwèi
consolation prize 安慰奖 ānwèijiǎng

console I V 安慰 ānwèi II N 控制台 kòngzhìtái, 仪表板 yíbiǎobǎn

consolidate V **1** 合并 hébìng **2** 巩固 gǒnggù

consonant N 辅音 fǔyīn

consortium N 财团 cáituán

conspicuous ADJ 显眼的 xiǎnyǎn de, 引人注目的 yǐnrén zhùmù de

conspiracy N 阴谋 yīnmóu

conspirator N 参与阴谋的人 cānyù yīnmóu de rén, 密谋者 mìmóu zhě

conspiratorial ADJ 阴谋的 yīnmóu de, 秘密的 mìmì de

conspire V 搞阴谋 gǎo yīnmóu, 密谋 mìmóu

constant I ADJ 经常的 jīngcháng de, 不变的 búbiàn de II N 不变的事 búbiàn de shì, 常数 chángshù

constellation N 星座 xīngzuò

consternation N 惊慌失措 jīnghuāng shīcuò, 惊恐 jīngkǒng

constipation N 便秘 biànbì

constituency N **1** 选区 xuǎnqū **2** 支持者 zhīchízhě

constituent N 成分 chéngfèn

constitute V 组成 zǔchéng, 构成 gòuchéng

constitution N **1** [美国+] 宪法 [Měiguó+] xiànfǎ **2** [强壮的+] 体质 [qiángzhuàng de+] tǐzhì

constitutional ADJ **1** 宪法的 xiànfǎ de **2** 体质的 tǐzhì de

constrain V 约束 yuēshù, 限制 xiànzhì

constrained ADJ **1** 受到约束的 shòudào yuēshù de **2** 拘谨的 [+笑容] jūjǐn de [+xiàoróng]

constraint N 约束 yuēshù, 限制 xiànzhì

constrict V 压缩 yāsuō, 收紧 shōujǐn

construct V 建筑 jiànzhù, 建造 jiànzào

construction N 建造 jiànzào, 建设 jiànshè
construction paper 彩色厚纸 cǎisè hòuzhǐ

constructive ADJ 建设性的 jiànshèxìng de

construe V 理解为 lǐjiě wéi

consul N 领事 lǐngshì

consular ADJ 领事的 lǐngshì de

consulate N 领事馆 lǐngshìguǎn
the U.S. Consulate in Shanghai 美国驻上海领事馆 Měiguó zhù Shànghǎi lǐngshìguǎn, 上海美国领事馆 Shànghǎi Měiguó lǐngshìguǎn

consult V **1** 咨询 [+专家] zīxún [+zhuānjiā], 请教 qǐngjiào **2** [与同事+] 磋商 [yǔ tóngshì+] cuōshāng **3** 查阅 [+参考资料] cháyuè [+cānkǎo zīliào]

consultancy N 咨询公司 zīxún gōngsī

consultant N 顾问 gùwèn [M. WD 位 wéi]

consultation N **1** 咨询 zīxún **2** 磋商 cuōshāng **3** 查阅 cháyuè

consume V **1** 耗费 [+汽油] hàofèi [+qìyóu] **2** 吃喝 chīhē

consumer N 消费者 xiāofèizhě

consumerism N 消费主义 xiāofèi zhǔyì

consummate I ADJ **1** 技艺高超的 [+球员] jìyì gāochāo de [+qiúyuán] **2** 完美的 [+艺术作

品] wánměi de [+yìshù zuòpǐn], 无暇可击
的 wúxiá kě jī de ‖ v 1 使…圆满成功 shǐ…
yuánmǎn chénggōng 2 完婚 wánhūn, 做成夫
妻 zuòchéng fūqī

consumption N 1 消费量 xiāofèiliàng 2 消耗量
xiāohàoliàng 3 吃 chī, 喝 hē

contact I v 联系 liánxì ‖ N 1 联系 liánxì 2 接触
jiēchù 3 熟人 shúrén ■ *Do you have any contacts in that government department?* 你在那个
政府部门有熟人吗? Nǐ zài nà ge zhèngfǔ bùmén
yǒu shúrén ma?
  contact lens 隐形眼镜 yǐnxíng yǎnjìng
  to come into contact with 跟…发生联系 gēn…
  fāshēng liánxì
  to lose contact with 跟…失去联系 gēn…shīqù
  liánxì

contagious ADJ 接触传染的 jiēchù chuánrǎn de

contain v 1 容纳 róngnà, 包含 bāohán 2 克制
[+愤怒的情绪] kèzhì [+fènnù de qíngxù]

container N 1 容器 róngqì 2 集装箱 jízhuāngxiāng
  container port 集装箱货轮港口 jízhuāngxiāng
  huòlún gǎngkǒu
  container ship 集装箱货轮 jízhuāngxiāng
  huòlún
  container truck 集装箱卡车 jízhuāngxiāng kǎchē

containment N 控制 kòngzhì, 抑制 yìzhì

contaminate v 把…弄脏 bǎ…nòngzāng, 污染
wūrǎn, 毒害 dúhài

contamination N 污染 wūrǎn, 毒害 dúhài

contemplate v 打算 dǎsuan, 认真考虑 rènzhēn
kǎolǜ

contemplation N 思考 sīkǎo, 深思 shēnsī

contemporary I ADJ 1 当代的 dāngdài de 2 同
时代的 tóngshí dài de ‖ N 同时代的人 tóngshí
dài de rén

contempt N 蔑视 mièshì, 轻蔑 qīngmiè
  contempt of court 蔑视法庭 mièshì fǎtíng

contemptible ADJ 可蔑视的 kě mièshì de, 可耻
的 kěchǐ de

contemptuous ADJ 轻蔑的 qīngmiè de, 看不起的
kànbuqǐ de

contend v 竞争 jìngzhēng

contender N 竞争者 jìngzhēngzhě

content I N 1 内容 nèiróng 2 满足 mǎnzú
  to one's heart's content 尽情地 jìnqíng de
  ‖ ADJ 满足的 mǎnzú de, 满意的 mǎnyì de ‖ v
  使…满足 shǐ…mǎnzú

contented ADJ 心满意足的 xīnmǎn yìzú de

contention N 主张 zhǔzhāng, 论点 lùndiǎn

contentious ADJ 1 有争议的 yǒu zhēngyì de
2 喜欢争议的 xǐhuan zhēngyì de

contents N 内容 nèiróng
  table of contents 目录 mùlù

contest N, v 竞赛 jìngsài, 比赛 bǐsài

contestant N 竞争者 jìngzhēngzhě, 参赛者
cānsàizhě

context N 上下文 shàngxiàwén ■ *You can't quote
him out of context.* 你不能不顾上下文就引用他的
话。 Nǐ bùnéng búgù shàngxiàwén jiù yǐnyòng tā
de huà.
  to take sth out of context 断章取义 duànzhāng
  qǔyì

contiguous ADJ 相邻的 xiānglín de

continent N 洲 zhōu, 大陆 dàlù ■ *There are
seven continents in the world—Asia, Europe,
Africa, North America, South America, Oceania
and Antarctica.* 世界上有七大洲—亚洲、欧洲、
非洲、北美洲、南美洲和南极洲。 Shìjièshang
yǒu qī dà zhōu—Yàzhōu、Ōuzhōu、Fēizhōu、Běi
Měizhōu、Nán Měizhōu hé Nánjízhōu.

continental ADJ 大陆的 dàlù de
  continental breakfast 欧洲大陆式早餐 Ōuzhōu
  dàlù shì zǎocān

contingency N 意外事件 yìwài shìjiàn

contingent I ADJ 视将来情况而定的 shì jiānglái
qíngkuàng ér dìng do
  contingent upon 取决于… qǔjuéyú…
  ‖ N 特遣部队 tèqiǎnbùduì

continual ADJ 一再重复的 yízài chóngfù de, 没完
没了的 méiwán méiliǎo de

continuation N 继续 jìxù

continue v 继续 jìxù ■ *World population will continue to grow.* 世界人口将继续增长。 Shìjiè rénkǒu
jiāng jìxù zēngzhǎng.

continuing education N 继续教育 jìxù jiàoyù, 成
人教育 chéngrén jiàoyù

continuity N 连续 liánxù, 连续性 liánxùxìng

continuous ADJ 1 连续的 liánxù de 2 正在进行的
zhèngzài jìnxíng de
  the continuous form (动词)进行式 (dòngcí)
  jìnxíng shì

contort v 使…扭曲 shǐ…niǔqū

contour N 轮廓 lúnkuò, 外形 wàixíng

contraband N 走私货 zǒusīhuò [M. WD 件 jiàn/批 pī]

contraception N 避孕 bìyùn

contraceptive N 避孕药 bìyùnyào, 避孕用具
bìyùn yòngjù

contract I N 合同 hétong [M. WD 份 fèn]
  contract bridge 定约桥牌 dìngyuē qiáopái
  to bid/tender for a contract 为合同投标 wéi
  hétong tóubiāo
  to enter into a contract 签订合同 qiāndìng
  hétong
  to terminate a contract 终止合同 zhōngzhǐ
  hétong
  ‖ v 1 签订合同 qiāndìng hétong 2 紧缩 jǐnsuō
  3 感染 [+病] gǎnrǎn [+bìng]

contraction N 收缩 shōusuō, 缩小 suōxiǎo

contractor N 承包商 chéngbāoshāng

contractual ADJ 合同规定的 hétong guīdìng de

contradict v 与…相矛盾 yǔ…xiāng máodùn
to contradict oneself 自相矛盾 zìxiāng máodùn

contradiction N 矛盾 máodùn

contraption N（不好的）新发明 (bùhǎo de) xīn fāmíng

contrary I N 相反 xiāngfǎn
on the contrary 正相反 zhèngxiāngfǎn
II ADJ 相反的 xiāngfǎn de

contrast v, N 对比 duìbǐ ■ This book contrasts American culture with Chinese culture. 这本书对比了美国文化和中国文化。Zhè běn shū duìbǐle Měiguó wénhuà hé Zhōngguó wénhuà.
in contrast 相比之下 xiāngbǐ zhī xià

contravene v 相抵触 xiāngdǐ chù

contribute v 1 贡献 gòngxià 2 捐款 juānkuǎn 3 促成 cùchéng

contribution N 1 贡献 gòngxiàn ■ This scientist has made contributions to environmental protection. 这位科学家为环境保护作出了贡献。Zhè wèi kēxuéjiā wèi huánjìng bǎohù zuòchūle gòngxiàn.
2 [慈善事业+] 捐款 [císhàn shìyè+] juānkuǎn

contrite ADJ 认错的 rèncuò de, 痛悔的 tònghuǐ de

contrition N 认错 rèncuò, 痛悔 tònghuǐ

contrive v 1 设法 shèfǎ 2 创造出 chuàngzàochū 3 谋划 móuhuà

contrived ADJ 牵强的 qiānqiǎng de

control v, N 控制 kòngzhì
to control costs 控制成本 kòngzhì chéngběn
to control one's temper 控制自己的脾气 kòngzhì zìjǐ de píqi
to control the ball（球类比赛时）掌握控球权 (qiúlèi bǐsài shí) zhǎngwò kòngqiúquán
control key（计算机）控制键 (jìsuànjī) kòngzhìjiàn
control freak 控制狂 kòngzhìkuáng
control tower 控制塔 kòngzhìtǎ
quality control 质量检查 zhìliàng jiǎnchá

controller N 审计人员 shěnjì rényuán

controversial ADJ 有争议的 yǒu zhēngyì de

controversy N 争议 zhēngyì, 争论 zhēnglùn

convalesce v 疗养 liáoyǎng, 恢复健康 huīfù jiànkāng, 康复 kāngfù

convalescence N 康复期 kāngfù qī

convalescent I ADJ 康复的 kāngfù de II N 康复病人 kāngfù bìngrén

convene v 召集 zhàojí, 召开 zhàokāi

convenience N 方便 fāngbiàn
convenience food 方便食品 fāngbiàn shípǐn
convenience store 便民店 biànmíndiàn, 方便店 fāngbiàndiàn

convenient ADJ 方便的 fāngbiàn de, 便利的 biànlì de

convent N 女修道院 nǚxiūdàoyuàn

convention N 1 惯例 guànlì, 习俗 xísú 2 大会 dàhuì
the Republican Convention 共和党大会 Gònghédǎng dàhuì
3 公约 gōngyuē, 协定 xiédìng
the Geneva Convention 日内瓦公约 Rìnèiwǎ Gōngyuē

conventional ADJ 传统的 chuántǒng de, 常规的 chángguī de
conventional wisdom 普遍的看法 pǔbiàn de kànfa

converge v 聚集 jùjí, 汇集 huìjí

convergence N 聚集 jùjí, 汇集 huìjí

conversant ADJ 熟悉的 shúxī de, 有经验的 yǒu jīngyàn de

conversation N 会话 huìhuà, 谈话 tánhuà
a conversation piece 交谈的题材 jiāotán de tícái
to make conversation 没话找话说 méi huà zhǎo huà shuō

converse[1] v 交谈 jiāotán

converse[2] ADJ 相反的 xiāngfǎn de
the converse 相反情况 xiāngfǎn qíngkuàng

conversely ADV 正相反 zhèng xiāngfǎn, 另一方面 lìngyìfāngmiàn

conversion N 1 转换 zhuǎnhuàn, 转化 zhuǎnhuà 2 皈依 guīyī 3（橄榄球）附加得分 (gǎnlǎnqiú) fùjiā défēn

convert I v 1 转换 [+为美元] zhuǎnhuàn [+wéi Měiyuán], 转化 [+为能量] zhuǎnhuà [+wéi néngliàng] 2 使…皈依 [+基督教] shǐ…guīyī [+Jīdūjiào] 3 改变 gǎibiàn II N 改变信仰者 gǎibiàn xìnyǎngzhě

convertible I ADJ 1 可兑换的 [+货币] kěduìhuàn de [+huòbì] 2 可折叠的 [+的沙发] kě zhédié de [+de shāfā] II N 折蓬轿车 zhé péng jiàochē

convex ADJ 凸出的 tūchū de, 凸的 tū de

convey v 1 转达 chuándá 2 传送 chuánsòng
conveyor belt 传送带 chuánsòngdài

convict I v 被判有罪 bèi pàn yǒuzuì II N 囚犯 qiúfàn, 犯人 fànrén

conviction N 1 坚定的信仰 jiāndìng de xìnyǎng, 坚信 jiānxìn 2 有罪判决 yǒuzuì pànjué, 定罪 dìngzuì

convince v 使…相信 shǐ…xiāngxìn

convinced ADJ 相信 xiāngxìn, 确信 quèxìn

convincing ADJ 有说服力的 yǒu shuōfúlì de

convivial ADJ 友好的 yǒuhǎo de, 轻松愉快的 qīngsōng yúkuài de

convoluted ADJ 复杂的 fùzá de, 很难懂的 hěn nándǒng de

convoy N 车队 chēduì, 船队 chuánduì

convulse v 1 使…动乱 shǐ…dòngluàn 2 痉挛 jìngluán, 抽搐 chōuchù

convulsion N 1 痉挛 jìngluán, 抽搐 chōuchù 2 动乱 dòngluàn

coo v 1 [鸽子+] 咕咕叫 [gēzi+] gūgū jiào 2 [情人+] 轻声柔语 [qíngrén+] qīngshēng róuyǔ

cook I v 做饭 zuòfàn
to cook the book 做假账 zuò jiǎzhàng
II N 厨师 chúshī, 炊事员 chuīshìyuán

cookbook N 食谱 shípǔ, 烹饪书 pēngrèn shū

cooked ADJ 煮熟的 zhǔshú de
cooked breakfast 有煎肉煎蛋的早餐 yǒu jiān ròu jiān dàn de zǎocān

cookie N 1 甜饼干 tián bǐnggān 2 网络跟踪文件 wǎngluò gēnzōng wénjiàn

cool I ADJ 1 好 hǎo, 棒 bàng, 酷 kù ■ *Your new cell phone looks really cool!* 你的新手机看上去真棒! Nǐ de xīn shǒujī kànshangqu zhēn bàng! 2 凉 liáng, 凉快 liángkuai II v 变冷 biàn lěng, 冷下来 lěng xiàlai
Cool it! 别着急, 慢慢来。Bié zháojí, mànmàn-lái.
III N 冷静 lěngjìng
to keep one's cool 保持冷静 bǎochí lěngjìng
to lose one's cool 失去冷静 shīqù lěngjìng
IV ADV 冷静地 lěngjìng de
to play it cool 冷静对待 lěngjìng duìdài

cooler N 冷却器 lěngquèqì, 冰桶 bīngtǒng

coop I N 鸡笼 jīlóng II v (be cooped up) 被困在 bèi kùn zài, 被关在 bèi guān zài

cooperate v 合作 hézuò, 同心协力 tóngxīn xiélì

cooperation N 合作 hézuò, 同心协力 tóngxīn xiélì

cooperative I ADJ 合作的 hézuò de II N 1 合作社 hézuòshè 2 合作公寓 hézuò gōngyù

co-opt v 收买 shōumǎi, 拉拢 lālong 2 强占 qiángzhàn

coordinate I v 协调 xiétiáo II N 坐标 zuòbiāo

coordination N 协调 xiétiáo

coordinator N 协调人 xiétiáo rén

cop N 警察 jǐngchá

cope v 1 应付 yìngfu 2 处理 chǔlǐ

copier N 复印机 fùyìnjī [M. WD 台 tái]

co-pilot N (飞机) 副驾驶员 (fēijī) fùjiàshǐyuán

copious ADJ 丰富的 fēngfù de, 大量的 dàliàng de

copper (Cu) N 1 铜 tóng 2 红棕色 hóngzōngsè, 紫铜色 zǐtóngsè

copter N See helicopter

copulate v 交配 jiāopèi

copulation N 交配 jiāopèi

copy I v 1 复印 [+书] fùyìn [+shū], 复制 [+产品] fùzhì [+chǎnpǐn] 2 [用手+] 抄写 [yòng shǒu+] chāoxiě 3 模仿 mófǎng, 仿效 fǎngxiào II N 1 复印本 fùyìn běn, 副本 fùběn ■ *I'll give you a copy of his letter.* 我会给你他来信的副本。Wǒ huì gěi nǐ tā láixìn de fùběn. 2 本 běn, 册 cè 3 文字稿 wénzì gǎo

copycat N 只会模仿的人 zhǐ huì mófǎng de rén
a copycat crime 模仿性犯罪 mófǎng xìng fànzuì

copyright N 版权 bǎnquán ■ *By making pirated copies of the movie, they seriously breached copyright.* 他们复制这部电影的盗版, 严重侵犯了版权。Tāmen fùzhì zhè bù diànyǐng de dàobǎn, yánzhòng qīnfàn le bǎnquán.

copywriter N 广告撰稿人 guǎnggào zhuàngǎorén

coral N 珊瑚 shānhú

cord N 1 电线 diànxiàn 2 绳子 shéngzi

cordial ADJ 亲切的 qīnqiè de, 热忱的 rèchén de

cordiality N 亲切 qīnqiè, 热忱 rèchén

cordless ADJ 无绳的 wú shéng de
cordless telephone 无绳电话 wú shéng diànhuà

cordon I N 警戒线 jǐngjièxiàn II v (to cordon off) 设置警戒线 shèzhì jǐngjièxiàn, 封锁 fēngsuǒ

corduroy N 灯线绒 dēngxiàn róng

core I N 核 hé, 核心 héxīn II v 挖去 [+水果的] 核 wā qù [+shuǐguǒ de] hé

cork I N 软木 (塞) ruǎnmù (sāi) II v (用软木塞) 塞紧 (yòng ruǎnmùsāi) sāijǐn

corkscrew N 螺丝起子 luósīqǐzi, 瓶塞钻 píngsāi-zuān

corn N 1 玉米 yùmǐ
corn on the cob 玉米棒子 yùmǐ bàngzi 2 鸡眼 jīyǎn

cornbread N 玉米粉面包 yùmǐ fěnmiàn bāo

cornea N (眼睛) 角膜 (yǎnjing) jiǎomó

corned beef N 咸牛肉 xiánniúròu

corner I N 1 拐角 guǎijiǎo 2 角落 jiǎoluò 3 (足球的) 角球 (zúqiú de) jiǎoqiú II v 使…陷入绝境 shǐ…xiànrù juéjìng

cornerstone N 基石 jīshí

cornet N 短号 duǎnhào

cornflakes N 玉米片 yùmǐ piàn

cornflower N 向日葵 xiàngrìkuí

cornmeal N 玉米面 yùmǐmiàn, 玉米粉 yùmǐ fěn

cornstarch N 玉米淀粉 yùmǐ diànfěn, 勾芡粉 gōuqiàn fěn

corny ADJ 过时的 guòshí de, 老掉牙的 lǎodiàoyá de

coronary ADJ 心脏的 xīnzàng de

coronation N 加冕 jiāmiǎn, 加冕典礼 jiāmiǎn diǎnlǐ

coroner N 验尸官 yànshīguān

corporal I N 下士 xiàshì II ADJ 肉体的 ròutǐ de
corporal punishment 体罚 tǐfá

corporate ADJ 1 公司的 gōngsī de
corporate hospitality 公司招待客户 gōngsī zhāodài kèhù 2 团体的 tuántǐ de, 共同的 gòngtóng de

corporation N 大公司 dàgōng sī, 股份公司 gǔfèn gōngsī
multinational corporation (MNC) 跨国公司 kuàguógōngsī

corps N 1 军团 jūntuán 2 部队 bùduì

Marine Corps 海军陆战队 hǎijūn lùzhànduì

corpse N 尸体 shītǐ

corpulent ADJ 肥胖的 féipàng de

corral N 畜栏 chùlán

correct I ADJ 1 正确 zhèngquè, 对 duì 2 恰当的 qiàdàng de II v 纠正 jiūzhèng, 改正 gǎizhèng ■ *Correct me, if I'm wrong.* 如果我错了, 就纠正我。 Rúguǒ wǒ cuò le, jiù jiūzhèng wǒ. I stand corrected. 我承认有错。Wǒ chéngrèn yǒu cuò.

correction N 改正 gǎizhèng, 纠正 jiūzhèng correction fluid 改正液 gǎizhèngyè

corrective ADJ 改正的 gǎizhèng de, 纠正的 jiū zhèngde

correlate v 与…相关联 yǔ…xiāngguān lián

correlation N 相互关联 xiānghù guānlián

correspond v 1 与 … 相对应 yǔ…xiāngduì yìng 2 通信 tōngxìn

correspondence N 1 关系 guānxi, 对应 duìyìng 2 通信 tōngxìn 3 信件 xìnjiàn, 函件 hánjiàn correspondence course 函授课程 hánshòu kèchéng

correspondent N 1 记者 jìzhě a foreign correspondent 驻外记者 zhùwài jìzhě 2 通信者 tōngxìnzhě

corresponding ADJ 相应的 xiāngyìng de, 相关联的 xiāngguānlián de

corridor N 走廊 zǒuláng [M. WD 条 tiáo]

corroborate v 证实 zhèngshí

corroboration N 证实 zhèngshí

corroborative ADJ 提供证实的 tígōng zhèngshí de

corrode v 腐蚀 fǔshí, 侵蚀 qīnshí

corrosion N 腐蚀 fǔshí, 侵蚀 qīnshí

corrugated ADJ 瓦楞的 wǎléng de a corrugated iron roof 瓦楞铁制屋顶 wǎléng tiězhì wūdǐng

corrupt I ADJ 腐败的 fǔbài de, 道德败坏的 dàodé bàihuài de II v 使…腐败 shǐ…fǔbài, 使…道德败坏 shǐ…dàodé bàihuài

corruption N 腐败 fǔbài, 贪污 tānwū

cosmetic ADJ 1 化妆用的 huàzhuāng yòng de 2 表面的 biǎomiàn de, 装饰门面的 zhuāngshì ménmian de

cosmetician N 美容师 měiróng shī

cosmetics N 1 化妆品 huàzhuāngpǐn 2 装饰门面的东西 zhuāngshì ménmian de dōngxi

cosmic ADJ 1 宇宙的 yǔzhòu de 2 特大的 tèdà de

cosmonaut N 宇航员 yǔhángyuán

cosmopolitan ADJ 1 世界性的 shìjièxìng de 2 见多识广的 jiàn duō shí guǎng de

cosmos N 宇宙 yǔzhòu

cost I v (PT & PP cost) 花费 huāfèi, 花(多少钱) huā (duōshaoqián) II N 1 费用 fèiyòng, 成本 chéngběn ■ *We should try hard to reduce pro-*

duction costs. 我们应该努力降低生产成本。 Wǒmen yīnggāi nǔlì jiàngdī shēngchǎn chéngběn. cost of living 生活费用 shēnghuó fèiyòng 2 代价 dàijià at any cost/at all costs 不惜代价 bùxī dàijià

co-star I N 合演者 héyǎnzhě II v 合演 héyǎn

cost-effective ADJ 效益高的 xiàoyì gāo de

costly ADJ 昂贵的 ángguì de, 花很多钱的 huā hěn duō qián de

costume N (某一时期或某一地区的)服装 (mǒu yì shíqí huò mǒu yí dìqū de) fúzhuāng costume drama 古装戏 gǔzhuāngxì costume jewelry 人造首饰 rénzào shǒushi

cot N 轻便折叠床 qīngbiàn zhédiéchuáng

cottage N 小屋 xiǎo wū cottage cheese 农家奶酪 nóngjiā nǎilào

cotton N 棉花 miánhua

cottonwool N 棉白杨 mián báiyáng [M. WD 棵 kē]

couch N (长)沙发 (cháng) shā fā couch potato 老是坐在沙发上看电视的人 lǎoshi zuò zài shāfā shàng kàn diànshì de rén

cough N, v 咳嗽 késou cough drop 润喉糖 rùnhóutáng [M. WD 粒 lì] cough syrup 止咳糖浆 zhǐké tángjiāng

could MODEL v (PT of can) ■ *He said he could do that all by himself.* 他说他自己能做。Tā shuō tā zìjǐ néngzuo.

couldn't See can

council N (市)议会 (shì) yìhuì, 理事会 lǐshìhuì the Security Council of the U.N. 联合国安全理事会 Liánhéguó Ānquán Lǐshìhuì

councilman, councilwoman N 市政议员 shìzhèng yìyuán

counsel I N 1 辩护律师 biànhù lǜshī 2 法律顾问 fǎlǜ gùwèn 3 忠告 zhōnggào to keep one's own counsel 不透露自己的想法 bú tòulù zìjǐ de xiǎngfǎ II v 提供咨询 tígōng zīxún, 辅导 fǔdǎo

counseling N 咨询(服务) zīxún (fúwù)

counselor N 咨询人员 zīxún rényuán, 辅导人员 fǔdǎo rényuán

count I v 1 数 shǔ, 计数 jìshù Don't count your chickens before they are hatched. 蛋未孵出莫数小鸡。(→好事不要指望过早。) Dàn wèi fūchū mò shǔ xiǎojī. (→Hǎoshì bú yào zhǐwàng guòzǎo.) 2 算数 suànshù, 有效 yǒuxiào 3 很重要 hěn zhòng yào ■ *Everybody's opinion counts.* 每个人的意见都很重要。Měige rén de yìjiàn dōu hěn zhòngyào. to count on 指望 zhǐwàng, 依靠 yīkào to count out 不包括 bù bāokuò II N 1 总数 zǒngshù to keep count 记录 jìlù, 记录数字 jìlù shùzì to lose count 记不清数字 jìbuqīng shùzì

2 计量 jìliàng **3** 罪状 zuìzhuàng

countable ADJ 可数的 kěshù de

countdown N 倒计时 dǎojìshí

countenance N 面容 miànróng, 面部表情 miànbù biǎoqíng

counter I N **1** [商店+] 柜台 [shāngdiàn+] guìtái **2** [厨房+] 操作台 [chúfáng+] cāozuò tái under the counter 暗地里 àndìli **II** v 反驳 fǎnbó **III** ADV 相反 xiāngfǎn

counteract v 抵消 dǐxiāo

counterattack v, N 反击 fǎnjī, 反攻 fǎngōng

counterbalance I v 抵消 dǐxiāo **II** N 抵消 dǐxiāo

counterclockwise I ADJ 反时针方向的 fǎnshízhēn fāngxiàng de **II** ADV 反时针方向 fǎnshízhēn fāngxiàng

counterfeit I ADJ 伪造的 wěizào de a counterfeit bill 一张假钞票 yìzhāng jiǎ chāopiào, 一张假币 yìzhāng jiǎbì **II** v 伪造 wěizào

counterpart N 地位相当的人（或物）dìwèi xiāngdāng de rén (huò wù)

counterproductive ADJ 起反作用的 qǐ fǎnzuòyòng de, 效果适得其反的 xiàoguǒ shìdé qífǎn de

countersign v 联署 liánshǔ

countless ADJ 无数的 wúshù de

country N **1** 国家 guójiā **2** 乡下 xiāngxia ■ *They prefer to live out in the country.* 他们喜欢住在乡下。Tāmen xǐhuan zhù zài xiāngxia. country and western 乡间音乐与西部音乐 xiāngjiān yīnyuè yǔ xībù yīnyuè country club 乡村俱乐部 xiāngcūn jùlèbù

countryman N 同胞 tóngbāo

countryside N 乡下 xiāngxia, 农村 nóngcūn

county N 县 xiàn county fair 农村集市 nóngcūn jíshì

coup N **1** (军事) 政变 (jūnshì) zhèngbiàn **2** 成功 的行动 chénggōng de xíngdòng

couple I N **1** 一对夫妻 yíduì fūqī, 一对情人 yíduì qíngrén **2** 两个 liǎng ge, 两三个 liǎng sān ge **II** v 结合 jiéhé, 连接 liánjiē

coupon N 优惠券 yōuhuìquàn [M. WD 张 zhāng], 礼券 lǐquàn [M. WD 张 zhāng]

courage N 勇气 yǒngqì, 勇敢 yǒnggǎn

courageous ADJ 勇敢的 yǒnggǎn de, 有勇气的 yǒu yǒngqì de

courier N 信使 xìnshǐ [M. WD 名 míng]

course I N **1** 路程 lùchéng, 过程 guòchéng ■ *We should avoid changing the course of action.* 我们应该避免改变行动方向。Wǒmen yīnggāi bìmiǎn gǎibiàn xíngdòng fāngxiàng. **2** 课程 kèchéng **3** 道（菜）dào (cài) ■ *Now we're having our last course of the dinner—fruit.* 我们正在吃晚餐最后的一道—水果。Wǒmen zhèngzài chī wǎncān zuìhòu de yí dào—shuǐguǒ.

of course 当然 dāngrán **II** v 流 liú, 流动 liúdòng

court I N **1** 法庭 fǎtíng **2** 球场 qiú chǎng tennis court 网球场 wǎngqiú chǎng basketball court 篮球场 lánqiúchǎng **3** 宫廷 gōngtíng, 王室 wángshì **II** v 讨好 tǎohǎo, 追求 zhuīqiú

courteous ADJ 有礼貌的 yǒulǐmào de, 彬彬有礼 bīnbīn yǒulǐ

courtesy N 礼貌 lǐmào, 好意 hǎoyì courtesy of 承蒙…的好意 chéngméng…de hǎoyì courtesy bus 免费巴士 miǎnfèi bāshì courtesy call 礼节性拜访 lǐjiéxìng bàifǎng

courthouse N 法院 fǎyuàn

courtmartial N **1** 军事法庭 jūnshì fǎtíng **2** 军法审判 jūnfǎ shěnpàn

courtroom N 法庭 fǎtíng

courtship N 恋爱 liàn'ài, 恋爱期 liàn'àiqī

courtyard N 院子 yuànzi

cousin N 堂哥 táng gē (paternal uncle's son, older than yourself), 堂弟 tángdì (paternal uncle's son, younger than yourself), 堂姐 tángjiě (paternal uncle's daughter, older than yourself), 堂妹 tángmèi (paternal uncle's daughter, younger than yourself), 表哥 biǎogē (maternal uncle or aunt's son, paternal aunt's son, older than yourself), 表弟 biǎo dì (maternal uncle or aunt's son, paternal aunt's son, younger than yourself), 表姐 biǎo jiě (maternal uncle or aunt's daughter, paternal aunt's daughter, older than yourself), 表妹 biǎomèi (maternal uncle or aunt's daughter, paternal aunt's daughter, younger than yourself)

cove N 小海湾 xiǎo hǎiwān

covenant N 契约 qìyuē

cover I v **1** 盖 gài, 覆盖 fùgài to cover up 掩盖 yǎngài ■ *The company spokesperson tried to cover up the scandal.* 公司发言人试图掩盖这件丑闻。Gōngsī fāyánrén shìtú yǎngài zhè jiàn chǒuwén.

2 涉及 shèjí, 包括 bāokuò ■ *His talk covered the latest marketing techniques.* 他的讲话涉及了最新的销售技巧。Tā de jiǎnghuà shèjíle zuìxīn de xiāoshòu jìqiǎo. **3** 给…保险 gěi…bǎoxiǎn, 承保 chéngbǎo not to cover cosmetic surgery 不承保整容手术 bù chéngbǎo zhěngróng shǒushù **4** 有钱支付 yǒuqián zhīfù to cover all expenses 有钱支付所有的费用 yǒuqián zhīfù suǒyǒu de fèiyong **5** 走完 [+距离] zǒu wán [+jùlí] **II** N **1** 盖 gài, 盖子 gàizi **2** (书、杂志) 封面 (shū、zázhì) fēngmiàn **3** 掩护 yǎnhù **4** 保险范围 bǎoxiǎn fànwéi

cover charge 服务费 fúwùfèi
cover letter 附信 fù xìn

coverage N **1** 报道 bàodào, 新闻报道 xīnwén bàodào **2** 保险 bǎoxiǎn, 保险范围 bǎoxiǎn fànwéi

coveralls N（衣裤相连的）工作服 (yīkù xiānglián de) gōngzuòfú

covering N 覆盖物 fùgàiwù

covert ADJ 秘密的 mìmì de

cover-up N 隐瞒 yǐnmán

covet v 贪求 tānqiú, 对…垂涎三尺 duì…chuíxián sānchǐ

cow N **1** 母牛 mǔniú [M. WD 头 tóu] **2** 大型雌性哺乳动物 dàxíng cíxìng bǔrǔ dòngwù

coward N 胆小鬼 dǎnxiǎoguǐ, 懦夫 nuòfū

cowardice N 胆小 dǎnxiǎo, 怯懦 qiènuò

cowardly ADJ 胆小的 dǎnxiǎo de, 怯懦的 qiènuò de

cowboy N 牛仔 niúzǎi

cower v 畏缩 wèisuō, 蜷缩 quánsuō

cowgirl N 牧牛女工 mùniú nǚgōng

co-worker N 同事 tóngshì

coy ADJ **1** 装作害羞的 zhuāngzuò hàixiū de, 故作扭怩的 gùzuò niǔní de **2** 含糊其词的 hánhu qí cí de

coyote N 丛林狼 cónglínláng

coziness N 温暖舒适 wēnnuǎn shūshì

cozy ADJ 温暖舒适的 wēnnuǎn shūshì de

CPA (= Certified Public Accountant) ABBREV 注册会计师 zhùcè kuàijìshī

CPR (= cardiopulmonary resuscitation) ABBREV 人工呼吸抢救 réngōng hūxī qiǎngjiù

CPU (= Central Processing Unit) ABBREV（计算机）中央处理器 (jìsuànjī) zhōngyāng chǔlǐqì

crab N 蟹 xiè [M. WD 只 zhī]

crabby ADJ 暴躁的 bàozao de

crack I v **1** 破裂 pòliè **2** 精神崩溃 jīngshén bēngkuì, 崩溃 bēngkuì **3** [嗓音+] 变嘶哑 [sǎngyīn+] biàn sīyǎ **4** 破解 [+密码] pòjiě [+mìmǎ] II N **1** 裂缝 lièfèng **2** 强效可卡因 qiáng xiào kěkǎyīn III ADJ 第一流的 dìyīliú de

crackdown N 镇压 zhènyā, 取缔 qǔdì

cracked ADJ **1** 有裂缝的 yǒu lièfèng de **2** [嗓音+] 嘶哑的 [sǎngyīn+] sīyǎ de

cracker N 薄脆饼干 báo cuì bǐnggān, 梳打饼干 shūdǎ bǐnggān [M. WD 片 piàn/块 kuài]

crackle v 发出噼啪声 fāchū pīpāshēng

crackling N 噼啪声 pīpāshēng

crackpot I ADJ 古怪离奇的 gǔguài líqí de II N 有古怪离奇念头的人 yǒu gǔguài líqí niàntou de rén

cradle I N 摇篮 yáolán II v 小心翼翼地抱着 xiǎoxīn yìyì de bàozhe

craft N 手（工）艺 shǒu (gōng) yì

craftsman N 手工艺人 shǒugōngyìrén

craftsmanship N 手工艺技能 shǒugōngyì jìnéng

crafty ADJ 足智多谋的 zú zhì duō móu de, 狡猾的 jiǎohuá de

crag N 峭壁 qiàobì, 巨岩 jù yán

craggy ADJ 陡峭多石的 dǒuqiào duō shí de

cram v 把…塞进 bǎ…sāijìn **2**（考试前）死记硬背 (kǎoshì qián) sǐjì yìngbèi
to cram for a test 在考试前死记硬背 zài kǎoshì qián sǐjì yìngbèi

cramp I v **1** 痉挛 jìngluán, 抽筋 chōujīn **2** 约束 yuēshù, 限制 xiànzhì II N 痉挛 jìngluán, 抽筋 chōujīn

cramped ADJ 狭小的 xiáxiǎo de

cramps N [腹部+] 绞痛 [fùbù+] jiǎotòng, [妇女+] 经痛 [fùnǚ+] jīngtòng

cranberry N 越橘 yuèjú

crane I N **1** 起重机 qǐzhòngjī [M. WD 台 tái] **2** 鹤 hè, 仙鹤 xiānhè [M. WD 只 zhī] II v 伸长脖子看 shēncháng bózi kàn

cranium N 头颅 tóulú

crank I N 曲柄 qūbǐng II v（用曲柄）转动 (yòng qūbǐng) zhuàndòng

cranky ADJ 易怒的 yì nù de

crap N **1** 胡诌 húchē, 废话 fèihuà **2** 劣质品 lièzhìpǐn, 破玩意儿 pòwányìr **3** 粪便 fènbiàn

craps N 双骰子赌博游戏 shuāng tóuzi dǔbó yóuxì

crash I v **1** 撞 zhuàng, 碰撞 pèngzhuàng **2**（电脑）死机 (diànnǎo) sǐjī ■ *Damn it! The computer crashed again.* 糟糕! 电脑又死机了。Zāogāo! Diànnǎo yòu sǐjī le. **3** 猛撞发出巨响 měngzhuàng fāchū jùxiǎng **4** [股市+] 崩盘 [gǔshì+] bēngpán
to crash and burn 突然垮台 tūrán kuàtái
II N [飞机／火车+] 撞 [fēijī/huǒchē] xiāngzhuàng, 失事 shīshì
crash helmet 防护头盔 fánghù tóukuī
crash landing 强行着陆 qiángxíng zhuólù
III ADJ 快速的 kuàisù de
crash course 速成班 sùchéngbān
crash diet 快速减肥食谱 kuàisù jiǎnféi shípǔ

crass ADJ 粗鲁的 cūlǔ de, 令人厌恶的 lìngrén yàn è de

crate N 大装货箱 dà zhuānghuò xiāng

crater N **1** 火山口 huǒshānkǒu **2** 坑 kēng

crave v 渴望 kěwàng, 渴求 kěqiú

craving N 渴望 kěwàng

crawl I v **1** 爬 pá, 爬行 páxíng II v 缓慢移动 huǎnmàn yídòng
the crawl 自由式游泳 zìyóushì yóuyǒng, 自由泳 zìyóuyǒng

crayfish N 淡水螯虾 dànshuǐ áoxiā

crayon N 彩色蜡笔 cǎisè làbǐ

craze N 时尚 shíshàng, 热 rè
Chinese craze 学中文热 xué Zhōngwén rè

crazed ADJ 狂热的 kuángrè de

crazy ADJ **1** 疯 fēng, 发疯 fāfēng **2** 喜欢得要命 xǐhuan deyàomìng **3** 古怪的 gǔguài de crazy code 乱码 luànmǎ

creak I v 发出嘎吱嘎吱的声响 fāchū gāzhī gāzhī de shēngxiǎng II N 嘎吱嘎吱的声响 gāzhī gāzhī de shēngxiǎng

creaky ADJ 1 发出嘎吱嘎吱的声响的 fāchū gāzhī gāzhī de shēngxiǎng de 2 老旧的 lǎojiù de

cream N 1 奶油 nǎiyóu
cream cheese 奶油干酪 nǎiyóu gānlào
2 油膏 yóugāo
face cream 面霜 miànshuāng
sun cream 防晒油膏 fángshài yóugāo
the cream of the crop（一群人中的）精英 (yìqún rénzhōng de) jīngyīng, 佼佼者 jiǎojiǎozhě

creamer N 1 代用奶油 dàiyòng nǎiyóu 2 奶油壶 nǎiyóu hú

crease I N 皱褶 zhòuzhě, 折缝 zhé féng II v 使…起皱 shǐ…qǐzhòu

create v 1 创造 chuàngzào, 创建 chuàngjiàn 2 发明 fāmíng, 设计 shèjì

creation N 1 创造 chuàngzào 2 创造物 chuàngzào wù
the Creation（上帝）创世 (Shàngdì) chuàng-shì, 创造世界 chuàngzào shìjiè

creative ADJ 有创造性的 yǒu chuàngzàoxìng de

creativity N 创造性 chuàngzàoxìng

creator N 创作者 chuàngzuòzhě
the Creator 造物主 Zàowùzhǔ

creature N 动物（包括人）dòngwù (bāokuò rén)

credence N 信任 xìnrèn, 相信 xiāngxìn

credentials N 1 资格证书 zīge zhèngshū 2 资格 zīge, 能力 nénglì

credibility N 可信性 kěxìnxìng, 信赖 xìnlài

credible ADJ 可信的 kěxìn de, 可靠的 kěkào de

credit I N 1 信贷 xìndài, 借款 jièkuǎn ■ He bought a new car on credit. 他借款买新车。Tā jièkuǎn mǎi xīn chē.
credit limit 信贷限额 xìndài xiàn'é
credit rating 信用等级 xìnyòng děngjí
credit report 信用报告 xìnyòng bàogào
2 信誉 xìnyù, 声望 shēngwàng ■ She never got the credit she deserved. 她从来没有得到应有的声望。Tā cónglái méiyǒu dédào yīngyǒu de shēngwàng.
to do sb credit 使某人赢得声誉 shǐ mǒurén yíngdé shēngyù
to take credit 归功于己 guī gōng yú jǐ
3 带来荣誉／好名声的人（或事）dàilai róngyào/hǎo míngshēng de rén (huò shì) 4（大学）学分 (dàxué) xuéfēn II v 1 存入 [+钱] cúnrù [+qián] 2 归功于 guī gōng yú

creditable ADJ 值得赞扬的 zhíde zànyáng de

creditor N 债权人 zhàiquánrén

credo N 信条 xìntiáo, 教义 jiàoyì

credulous ADJ 轻信的 qīngxìn de

creed N 信条 xìntiáo, 信仰 xìnyǎng

creek N 小溪 xiǎoxī [M. WD 条 tiáo], 溪流 xīliú [M. WD 条 tiáo]

creep I v (PT & PP crept) 1 爬 pá, 爬行 páxíng 2 蔓生 mànshēng II N 讨厌的人 tǎoyàn de rén
to give sb the creeps 叫…毛骨悚然 jiào…máogǔ sǒngrán

cremate v 火化 huǒhuà, 火葬 huǒzàng

crematorium N 火葬场 huǒzàngchǎng

crépe N 绉纱 zhòushā, 绉绸 zhòuchóu
crepe paper 绉纸 zhòuzhǐ

crept See creep

crescendo N [声音+] 渐强 [shēngyīn+] jiàn qiáng

crescent N 新月 xīnyuè

crest N 1 山顶 shāndǐng, 浪峰 làngfēng 2 鸟冠 niǎoguān

crestfallen ADJ 沮丧的 jǔsàng de, 垂头丧气的 chuítóu sàngqì de

crevice N 裂缝 lièfèng, 缺口 quēkǒu

crew N 1（飞机）机组人员 (fēijī) jīzǔ rényuán, （轮船）船员 (lúnchuán) chuányuán 2 工作人员 gōngzuò rényuán
crew cut 板刷头 bānshuātou

crib N 婴儿床 yīng'ér chuáng

crick N 痛性痉挛 tòngxìng jìngluán

cricket N 1 蟋蟀 xīshuài 2 板球 bǎnqiú

crime N 罪 zuì, 罪行 zuìxíng
Crime does not pay. 犯罪是不值得的。Fànzuì shì bù zhíde de.

criminal I ADJ 犯罪的 fànzuì de II N 罪犯 zuìfàn
criminal law 刑法 xíngfǎ

crimson I N 深红色 shēnhóngsè II ADJ 深红色的 shēnhóngsè de

cringe v 1 退缩 tuìsuō 2 感到难堪 gǎndào nánkān

crinkle v 起皱 qǐzhòu

cripple I N 残疾人 cánjírén, 跛子 bǒzi II v 1 使…致残 shǐ…zhìcán 2 使…遭受重创 shǐ…zāoshòu zhòngchuāng

crisis N 危机 wēijī

crisp I ADJ 1 [食品+] 脆的 [shípǐn+] cuì de 2 易碎的 yì suì de 3 [天气+] 干冷的 [tiānqì+] gānlěng de II v 使…变脆 shǐ…biàn cuì

crispy ADJ 松脆的 sōngcuì de

crisscross v 1 往返 wǎngfǎn, 来回奔波 láihuí bēnbō 2 画交错的直线 huà jiāocuò de zhíxiàn, 纵横交错 zònghéng jiāocuò

criterion N (PL criteria) 标准 biāozhǔn

critic N 1 批评者 pīpíngzhě, 反对者 fǎnduìzhě 2 评论员 pínglùnyuán, 批评家 pīpíngjiā

critical ADJ 1 批判的 pīpàn de, 批评的 pīpíng de 2 关键的 guānjiàn de, 危险的 wēixiǎnde ■ The patient is still in a critical condition. 病人还处于危险期。Bìngrén hái chǔyú wēixiǎnqī.

criticism N 批评 pīpíng, 评论 pínglùn

criticize v 批评 pīpíng, 评论 pínglùn ■ The trade unions criticized the law as anti-labor. 工会批评这

critique

个法律是反工会的。Gonghuì pīpíng zhè ge fǎlǜ shì fǎn gōnghuì de.
critique N, V 评论 pínglùn
croak I V 1 用低沉沙哑的声音说 yòng dī chén shāyǎ de shēngyīn shuō 2 [青蛙+] 鸣叫 [qīngwā+] míngjiào II N 1 低沉沙哑的声音 dīchén shāyǎ de shēngyīn 2 (青蛙) 鸣叫 (qīngwā) míngjiào
crochet V 用钩针编结 yòng gōuzhēn biānjié
crock N 瓦罐 wǎguàn
　a crock of shit 胡说八道 húshuō bādào
crockery N 陶器 táoqì
crocodile N 鳄鱼 èyú [M. WD 条 tiáo]
　to shed crocodile tears 掉几滴鳄鱼的眼泪 diào jǐ dī èyú de yǎnlèi
crocus N 藏红花 zànghónghuā
croissant N 羊角面包 yángjiǎo miànbāo
crony N 亲密的朋友 qīnmì de péngyou
crook N 骗子 piànzi, 贼 zéi 2 弯曲 wānqū II V 1 使…弯曲 shǐ…wānqū 2 弯 wān, 勾 gōu
crooked ADJ 1 弯曲的 wānqū de 2 狡诈的 jiǎozhà de
croon V 轻柔地歌唱 (或说话) qīngróu de gēchàng (huò shuōhuà)
crop I N 1 庄稼 zhuāngjia, 农作物 nóngzuòwù 2 收成 shōucheng ■ *The farmers are expecting a bumper crop this year.* 农民们期待着丰收。Nóngmínmen qīdàizhe fēngshōu. 3 平头发型 píngtóu fàxíng, 短头发 duǎn tóu fà II V 剪断 [+头发] jiǎnduàn [+tóufa]
croquet N 门球 (游戏) ménqiú (yóuxì)
cross I N 1 十字架 shízìjià 2 十字形 shízì xíng, 叉 chā
　the Red Cross 红十字 Hóngshízì
　3 混合物 hùnhéwù, 杂交品种 zájiāo pǐnzhǒng II V 1 穿越 chuānyuè, 度过 dùguò 2 交叉 jiāochā
　to cross one's heart 在胸前画十字 zài xiōngqián huà shízì, 发誓 fāshì
　to cross one's fingers 但愿有好运 dànyuàn yǒu hǎoyùn
　3 杂交 zájiāo III ADJ 生气的 shēngqì de
crosscheck V 核对 héduì, 对证 duìzhèng
cross-country ADJ 越野的 yuèyě de
　cross-country running 越野赛跑 yuèyěsàipǎo
cross-cultural ADJ 跨文化的 kuà wénhuà de
cross-examine V 反复盘问 fǎnfù pánwèn
cross-eyed ADJ 内斜视的 nèixiéshì de, 斗鸡眼的 dòujīyǎn de
crossfire N 交叉火力 jiāochā huǒlì
crossing N 1 (铁路) 过道 (tiělù) guòdào 2 十字路口 shízì lùkǒu 3 跨海旅程 kuà hǎi lǚchéng
cross-legged ADV 盘腿而坐 pántuǐ ér zuò
cross-purposes N 相反目的 xiāngfǎn mùdì
　at cross purposes 相互矛盾 xiānghù máodùn

cross-reference N 相互参照 xiānghù cānzhào, 互见 hùjiàn
crossroads N 十字路口 shízì lùkǒu
cross-section N 1 横剖面 héngpōumiàn 2 一组有代表性的人 yìzǔ dàibiǎoxìng de rén
crosswalk N 人行横道 rénxíng héngdào
crossword N 纵横填字游戏 zònghéng tiánzì yóuxì
crotch N 胯部 kuàbù
crotchety ADJ 暴躁的 bàozao de
crouch V 蹲 (下) dūn (xià)
crow I N 1 乌鸦 wūyā [M. WD 只 zhī] 2 (公鸡) 鸣叫 (gōngjī) míngjiào II V (公鸡) 叫 [gōngjī+] jiào
crowbar N 铁撬棒 tiě qiàobàng [M. WD 根 gēn]
crowd I N 人群 rénqún, 一群人 yìqún rén II V 1 群集 qúnjí, 群聚 qúnjù 2 挤 jǐ, 推挤 tuījǐ 3 催 cuī, 催促 cuīcù
crowded ADJ 拥挤的 yōngjǐ de
crown I N 1 王冠 wángguān, 冕 miǎn 2 王国政府 wángguó zhèngfǔ 3 [牙齿+] 人造冠 [yáchǐ+] rénzào guān II V 1 为 [+国王] 加冕 wéi [+guówáng] jiāmiǎn 2 为…镶假牙冠 wéi…xiāng jiǎ yáguān 3 达到顶峰 dádào dǐngfēng
crowning ADJ 达到顶峰的 dádào dǐngfēng de
crown prince N 王储 wángchǔ [M. WD 位 wèi]
crown princess N 女王储 nǚwángchǔ [M. WD 位 wèi]
crucial ADJ 决定性的 juédìngxìng de, 关键的 guānjiàn de
crucifix N 有耶稣象的十字架 yǒu Yēsū xiàng de shízìjià
crucifixion N 耶稣被钉在十字架上 Yēsū bèi dīng zài shízìjià shàng, 耶稣受难 Yēsū shòunàn
crucify V 1 把…钉在十字架上 bǎ…dīng zài shízìjià shàng 2 当众狠狠指责 dāngzhòng hěnhěn zhǐzé
crud N 令人恶心的东西／人 lìngrén èxīn de dōngxi/rén
crude ADJ 1 粗俗的 [+语言] cūsú de [+yǔyán] 2 粗糙的 [+估计] cūcāo de [+gūjì] 3 未经提炼的 [+石油] wèijīng tíliàn de [+shíyóu]
　crude oil 原油 yuányóu
cruel ADJ 残酷 cánkù
cruelty N 1 残酷 cánkù 2 虐待 (的行为) nüèdài (de xíngwéi)
cruise I V 1 [船+] 巡游 [chuánchuán+] xúnyóu 2 [汽车+] 稳速行驶 [qìchē+] wěn sù xíngshǐ 3 (乘车) 兜风 (chéngchē) dōufēng II N 乘大游轮度假 chéng dà yóulún dùjià
　cruise ship 大游轮 dà yóulún [M. WD 艘 sōu]
cruiser N 巡洋舰 xúnyángjiàn [M. WD 艘 sōu]
crumb N 食物碎屑 shíwù suìxiè, 面包屑 miànbāo xiè
crumble V 1 把…弄成碎屑 bǎ…nòngchéng suìxiè 2 [建筑物+] 年久倒塌 [jiànzhùwù+] niánjiǔ dǎotā 3 瓦解 wǎjiě
crummy ADJ 劣质的 lièzhì de, 差劲的 chàjìn de

rumple v 1 把⋯弄皱 bǎ...nòng zhòu 2 晕倒 yūndǎo

crunch I v 1 发出嘎吱嘎吱的声响 fāchū gāzhī gāzhī de shēngxiǎng 2 嘎吱嘎吱地吃 gāzhī gāzhī de chī

to crunch the numbers 作大量计算 zuò dàliáng jìsuàn

II N 1 嘎吱嘎吱的声响 gāzhī gāzhī de shēngxiǎn 2 困境 kùnjìng, 危机 wēijī

credit crunch 信贷危机 xìndài wēijī

crunchy ADJ 脆脆的 cuìcuìde

crusade I N 1 改革运动 gǎigé yùndòng 2 十字军东征 Shízìjūn dōngzhēng II v 致力于改革 zhìlì yú gǎigé

crush I v 压碎 yāsuì, 粉碎 fěnsuì II N 迷恋 míliàn, 强烈的暗恋 qiángliè de ànliàn

to have a crush on 暗暗的迷恋上 àn'àn de míliàn shàng

crust N 1 面包皮 miànbāopí, 比萨饼皮 bǐsàbǐngpí 2 硬壳 yìngké

Earth's crust 地壳 dìqiào

crustacean N 甲壳纲动物 jiǎqiàogāng dòngwù

crusty ADJ 1 外皮脆的 wàipí cuì de 2 暴躁的 bàozao de

crutch N 拐杖 guǎizhàng

crux N 中心 zhōngxīn, 症结 zhēngjié

cry I v 1 喊叫 hǎnjiào ■ "Look ahead!" she cried. "看前面！" 她喊叫。"Kàn qiánmian!" tā hǎnjiào.

to cry out 大声高喊 dàshēng gāohǎn

to cry foul（大声）抗议 (dàshēng) kàngyì

to cry over spilled milk 作无益的悔恨 zuò wúyì de huǐhèn

to cry wolf ① 叫 "狼来了" jiào "láng lái le" ② 发假警报 fā jiǎ jǐngbào

2 哭 kū

to cry for help 大声呼救 dàshēng hūjiù

II N 1 叫喊（声）jiàohǎn (shēng) 2 哭（声）kū (shēng) 3（动物的）叫声 (dòngwù de) jiàoshēng

to be a far cry from 与⋯相差很远 yǔ...xiāngchà hěn yuǎn

crybaby N 1 爱哭的孩子 ài kū de háizi 2 爱发牢骚的人 àifā láosāo de rén

crypt N 教堂地下室 jiàotáng dìxiàshì

cryptic ADJ 神秘的 shénmì de, 难懂的 nándǒng de

crystal N 水晶 shuǐjīng

crystal ball 水晶球 shuǐjīngqiú

crystal clear 明白易懂的 míngbai yìdǒng de, 明摆着的 míngbǎizhe de

crystallize v 1 [盐+] 结晶 [yán+] jiéjīng 2 使 [+思路] 变得明朗清晰 shǐ [+sīlù] biàn de mínglǎng qīngxī

cub N 小熊 xiǎoxióng, 小老虎 xiǎolǎohǔ, 小狮子 xiǎoshīzi

cube I N 1 立方体 lìfāngtǐ

ice cube 冰块 bīngkuài

2 立方 lìfāng

the cube of (a number)（某数的）立方 (mǒu shù de) lìfāng

cubic ADJ 立方的 lìfāng de

cubic inch/feet/yard 立方英寸／英尺／码 lìfāng yīngcùn/yīngchǐ/mǎ

cubicle N 小隔间 xiǎo géjiān

Cub Scouts N 幼年童子军 yòunián tóngzǐjūn

cuckoo I N 杜鹃 dùjuān [M. WD 只 zhī], 布谷鸟 bùgǔniǎo [M. WD 只 zhī] II ADJ 疯了 fēng le, 痴颠 chī diān

cucumber N 黄瓜 huángguā [M. WD 条 tiáo/根 gēn]

cuddle I v 拥抱 yōngbào, 搂搂抱抱 lǒulǒubào-bào II N 拥抱 yōngbào

cuddly ADJ 让人想搂抱的 ràng rén xiǎng lǒubào de, 可爱的 kě'ài de

cue N 1 提示 tíshì

on cue 恰好这时候 qiàhǎo zhè shíhòu

to take one's cue from 学⋯的样 xué...de yàng, 仿效 fǎngxiào

2 球杆 qiú gǎn

cuff I N 袖口 xiùkǒu

off the cuff 未经考虑的 [+讲话] wèi jīng kǎolǜ de [+jiǎnghuà]

II v 给 [+犯人] 戴手铐 gěi [+fànrén] dài shǒukào

cuffs N 手铐 shǒukào [M. WD 副 fù]

cuisine N 1 烹饪法 pēngrènfǎ, 烹饪风味 pēngrèn fēng wèi 2 菜肴 càiyáo

cul-de-sac N 无尾巷 wúwěixiàng, 死胡同 sǐhútòng

culinary ADJ 烹饪的 pēngrèn de

cull I v 1 挑选 tiāoxuǎn, 选用 xuǎnyòng 2 宰杀 zǎishā II N 宰杀 zǎishā

culminate v 1 告终 gàozhōng, 结束 jiéshù 2 达到顶峰 dádào dǐngfēng

culmination N 顶峰 dǐngfēng, 结果 jiéguǒ

culpable ADJ 应负责任的 yìng fù zérèn de

culpable negligence 失职罪 shīzhízuì

culprit N 罪犯 zuìfàn, 有过失的人 yǒuguò shī de rén

cult N 1 异教 yìjiào, 邪教 xiéjiào 2 时尚观念 shíshàng guānniàn

cultivate v 1 耕作 gēngzuò 2 培育 péiyù, 培养 péiyǎng

cultivated ADJ 1 有教养的 yǒu jiàoyǎng de 2 养殖的 yǎngzhí de

cultural ADJ 文化的 wénhuà de

culture N 1 文化 wénhuà ■ I'm very interested in Chinese culture. 我对中国文化很感兴趣。Wǒ duì Zhōngguó wénhuà hěn gǎn xìngqu. 2 文明 wénmíng 3 细菌培养 xìjūn péiyǎng

cultured ADJ 文化修养很高的 wénhuà xiūyǎng hěn gāo de

cumbersome ADJ 运转不灵的 yùnzhuǎn bù líng de, 笨重的 bènzhòng de

cumulative ADJ 积累的 jīlěi de

cunning I ADJ 狡猾的 jiǎohuá de II N 狡猾 jiǎohuá

cunt N 阴道 yīndào

cup I N 1 杯子 bēizi 2 奖杯 jiǎngbēi II V 捧 pěng, 托 tuō

cupboard N 柜子 guìzi, 食柜 shíguì, 碗柜 wǎnguì

cupcake N 杯形蛋糕 bēixíng dàngāo

curable ADJ 可以医好的 kěyǐ yīhǎo de, 医得好的 yī dé hǎode

curator N [博物馆+] 馆长 [bówùguǎn+] guǎnzhǎng

curb I N 1 路沿 lù yán 2 抑制 yìzhì, 控制 kòngzhì II V 抑制 yìzhì, 控制 kòngzhì

curd N 凝乳 níngrǔ

curdle V 凝结 níngjié

cure I V 1 治愈 [+病] zhìyù [+病], 治好 zhìhǎo 2 烟熏 [+火腿] yānxūn [+huǒtuǐ], 腌制 yānzhì II N 1 治疗 zhìliáo 2 治愈 zhìyù, 治好 zhìhǎo

curfew N 宵禁 xiāojìn

curio N 古董 gǔdǒng [M. WD 件 jiàn], 古玩 gǔwán [M. WD 件 jiàn]

curiosity N 好奇心 hàoqíxīn

curious ADJ 1 好奇的 hàoqí de 2 奇怪 qíguài

curl I N 1 卷发 juǎnfà 2 卷曲的东西 juǎnqū de dōngxi II V 1 缠绕 chánrǎo 2 卷曲 juǎnqū, 卷发 juǎnfà

curler N 卷发夹子 juǎnfà jiāzi

curling iron N 烫发器 tàngfàqì

currant N 醋栗 cùlì

currency N 1 货币 huòbì 2 流通 liútōng

current I N 1 水流 shuǐliú 2 电流 diànliú
alternating current (AC) 交流电 jiāoliúdiàn
direct current (DC) 直流电 zhíliúdiàn
II ADJ 当前的 dāngqián de, 当今的 dāngjīn de
current events 时事 shíshì

curriculum N 课程 kèchéng

curriculum vitae (ABBREV CV) N（个人）简历 (gèrén) jiǎnlì, 履历 lǚlì

curry N 加哩（粉）jiālī (fěn)

curse V, N 1 骂 mà, 咒骂 zhòumà 2 诅咒 zǔzhòu

cursed ADJ 1 遭到咒的 zāo zǔzhòu de 2 受到折磨无法解脱的 shòudào zhémo wúfǎ jiětuō de

cursor N 光标 guāngbiāo

cursory ADJ 粗略的 cūlüè de, 草草了事的 cǎocǎo liǎoshì de

curt ADJ 简短而不礼貌的 jiǎnduǎn ér bù lǐmào de

curtail V 削减 xuējiǎn, 减少 jiǎnshǎo

curtailment N 削减 xuējiǎn, 减少 jiǎnshǎo

curtain N 窗帘 chuānglián ■ She drew the curtain and turned on the lights. 她拉上窗帘，打开灯。Tā lāshang chuānglián, dǎkāi dēng. 2 幕布 mùbù

curtsy, curtsey V 行屈膝礼 xíng qūxīlǐ

curve I N 曲线 qūxiàn, 弯曲 wānqū ■ There is a sharp curve in the road. 路上有一个急转弯。Lùshang yǒu yí ge jí zhuǎnwān. II V 弯曲 wānqū

cushion I N 垫子 diànzi, 靠垫 kàodiàn II V 缓冲 huǎnchōng

cuss V 咒骂 zhòumà

custard N 乳蛋糕 rǔ dàngāo

custodian N [大楼+] 管理员 [dàlóu+] guǎnlǐyuán

custody N 1 监护（权）jiānhù (quán) 2 拘留 jūliú
in custody 被拘留 bèi jūliú, 被监禁 bèi jiānjìn

custom I N 风俗 fēngsú II ADJ 定做的 dìngzuò de

customary ADJ 1 习俗的 xísú de 2 习惯性的 xíguànxìng de

customer N 顾客 gùkè

customize V 定做 dìngzuò, 定制 dìngzhì

customs N 海关 hǎiguān ■ You'll have to declare these goods when you go through customs. 你通过海关时，得申报这些东西。Nǐ tōngguo hǎiguān shí, děi shēnbào zhèxiē dōngxi.

cut I V (PT & PP cut) 1 切 qiē, 剪 jiǎn 2 划破 huápò 3 打断 dǎduàn 4 切牌 qiē pái
to cut corners 偷工减料 tōu gōng jiǎn liào
cut and dried 已成定局的 yǐ chéng dìngjú de
to cut and paste 剪贴 jiǎntiē
to cut sb short 打断 dǎduàn
II N 1 伤口 shāngkǒu 2 减少 jiǎnshǎo 3 剪头发 jiǎntóufà, 理发 lǐfà 4（服装的）款式 (fúzhuāng de) kuǎnshì, 式样 shìyàng

cutback N 削减 xuējiǎn

cute ADJ 可爱的 kě'ài de, 漂亮的 piàoliang de

cutlery N 餐具（刀叉等）cānjù (dāochā děng)

cutlet N 肉排 ròupái [M. WD 块 kuài]

cutoff N 截止点 jiézhǐ diǎn

cut-rate, cut-price ADJ 减价的 jiǎnjià de

cutter N 1 切割器具 qiēgēqì jù 2 小船艇 xiǎochuán tǐng

cut-throat ADJ 不择手段的 bù zé shǒuduàn de, 你死我活的 nǐsǐwǒhuó de

cutting I ADJ 1 尖刻的 jiānkè de 2 刺骨的 cìgǔ de
cutting board 案板 ànbǎn
at the cutting edge of 处于领先地位 chǔyú lǐngxiān dìwèi
II N 插枝 chāzhī

cyanide N 氰化物 qínghuàwù

cybercafe N 网吧 wǎngbā [M. WD 间 jiān]

cyberspace N 计算机空间 jìsuànjī kōngjiān, 网络空间 wǎngluò kōngjiān

cycle I N 1 周期 zhōuqī
life cycle 生命周期 shēngmìng zhōuqī
2 循环 xúnhuán
a vicious cycle 恶性循环 èxìng xúnhuán
II V 骑自行车 qí zìxíngchē

cyclic, cyclical ADJ 周期性的 zhōuqīxìng de

cyclist N 骑自行车的人 qí zìxíngchē de rén, 自行车运动员 zìxíngchē yùndòngyuán

yclone N 龙卷风 lóngjuǎnfēng [m. wb 场 cháng]

ylinder N 1 圆柱(体) yuánzhù (tǐ) 2 圆筒
yuántǒng, 圆罐 yuán guan
gas cylinder 煤气罐 méiqìguàn
3 气缸 qìgāng

ylindrical ADJ 圆柱体的 yuánzhùtǐ de

ymbal N 钹 bó, 铙钹 náobó

ynic N 认为人性恶的人 rènwéi rénxìng è de rén,
犬儒 quǎnrú

ynical ADJ 1 认为人性恶的 rènwéi rénxìng è de
2 不讲道德的 bù jiǎngdào dé de

ynicism N 人性恶论 rénxìng è lùn, 犬儒主义
Quǎnrúzhǔyì

yst N 囊肿 nángzhǒng

zar N 沙皇 shāhuáng

D

ab I N 1 少量 [+黄油] shǎoliàng [+huángyóu],
一点儿 yìdiǎnr 2 轻拍 qīng pāi II v 轻拍 qīng
pāi, 轻触 qīngchù

abble v 稍微涉足 shāowēi shèzú, 不很认真地做
bù hěn rènzhēn de zuò

ad, daddy N 爸爸 bàba, 爹爹 diēdie

affodil N 水仙花 shuǐxiānhuā [m. wb 朵 duǒ/株
zhū]

agger N 匕首 bǐshǒu [m. wb 把 bǎ], 短剑
duǎnjiàn [m. wb 把 bǎ]

aily ADJ, ADV 每天 měitiān, 每日 měirì

ainty ADJ 1 精致的 [+小点心] jīngzhì de [+xiǎo
diǎnxin] 2 优雅的 [+举止] yōuyǎ de [+jǔzhǐ]

airy N 牛奶场 niúnǎi chǎng
dairy product 乳制品 rǔzhìpǐn

aisy N 雏菊 chújú [m. wb 朵 duǒ/棵 kē]

ally v 浪费时间 làngfèi shíjiān, 磨蹭 móceng

almatian N 斑点狗 bāndiǎngǒu [m. wb 只 zhī/条
tiáo]

am N 水坝 shuǐbà [m. wb 座 zuò]

amage I N 损害 sǔnhài, 损伤 sǔnshāng
damages 损害赔偿金 sǔnhài péichángjīn
II v 损坏 sǔnhuài, 损害 sǔnhài ■ Years of
poor nutrition and lack of exercise damaged his
health. 多年的营养不良和缺乏运动损坏了他的
健康。Duōnián de yíngyǎng bùliáng hé quēfá
yùndòng sǔnhuàile tā de jiànkāng.

amn I ADJ 该死的 gāisǐ de II ADV 非常 fēicháng,
很 hěn
damn well 非常地 fēicháng de
III INTERJ 该死 gāisǐ, 天哪 tiānnǎ
Damn it! 该死的! Gāisǐ de!
Damn you! 你这个混蛋! Nǐ zhège húndàn! 混
蛋! Húndàn!

amnedest ADJ 最奇怪的 zuì qíguài de

to do one's damnedest 尽最大的努力 jìn zuìdà
de nǔlì

damning ADJ 极其不利的 jíqí búlì de

damp I ADJ 潮湿的 cháoshī de II v 使···削弱／减少
shǐ... xuēruò/jiǎnshǎo, 抑制 yìzhì
to damp one's interest 使兴趣减少 shǐ xìngqu
jiǎnshǎo

dampen v 1 使 [+一块布] 潮湿 shǐ [+yí kuài bù]
cháoshī 2 削弱 [+热情] xuēruò [+rèqíng] 3 使扫
兴 shǐ sǎoxìng

damper N 令人扫兴的人／事 lìngrén sǎoxìng de
rén/shì
to put a damper on 让人扫兴 ràng rén
sǎoxìng

damsel N 未婚少女 wèihūn shàonǚ

dance I v 1 跳舞 tiàowǔ 2 跳动 tiàodòng II N 1 舞
蹈 wǔdǎo 2 舞会 wǔhuì [m. wb 场 cháng]
school dances 学校舞会 xuéxiào wǔhuì
3 舞曲 wǔqǔ [m. wb 首 shǒu]

dancer N 舞蹈演员 wǔdǎo yǎnyuán

dandelion N 蒲公英 púgōngyīng

dandruff N 头皮屑 tóupíxiè

dandy ADJ 挺好的 tǐng hǎode

Dane N 丹麦人 Dānmàirén

danger N 危险 wēixiǎn ■ In hot summer months
there is danger of fire in this area. 在高温的夏季,
这个地区有火灾的危险。Zài gāowēn de xiàjì, zhè
ge dìqū yǒu huǒzāi de wēixiǎn.
in danger of 有危险 yǒu wēixiǎn, 处于危险之中
chǔyú wēixiǎn zhīzhōng
out of danger 脱离危险 tuōlí wēixiǎn

dangerous ADJ 危险的 wēixiǎn de

dangle v 挂着来回摆动 guàzhe láihuí bǎidòng,
悬吊 xuándiào

Danish I ADJ 丹麦的 Dānmài de, 丹麦语的
Dānmàiyǔ de, 丹麦人的 Dānmàirén de II N 丹
麦语 Dānmàiyǔ

dank ADJ 湿冷的 shīlěng de, 阴冷的 yīnlěng de

dapper ADJ 衣冠楚楚的 yīguān chǔchǔ de, 矮小
而精悍的 ǎixiǎo ér jīnghàn de

dare I v 1 敢 gǎn 2 激将 jījiàng, 挑战 tiǎozhàn
I dare you! 我谅你不敢! Wǒ liàng nǐ bù gǎn!
II N 挑战 tiǎozhàn

daredevil N 鲁莽大胆的人 lǔmǎng dàdàn de rén,
喜欢冒险的人 xǐhuan màoxiǎn de rén

daring I ADJ 大胆的 dàdǎn de II N 勇气 yǒngqì,
胆量 dǎnliàng

dark I ADJ 1 黑暗的 hēi'àn de, 黑色的 hēisè de
2 深颜色的 shēn yánsè de 3 邪恶的 [+势力]
xié'è de [+shìlì] 4 苦难的 [+岁月] kǔnàn de
[+suìyuè] II N 1 黑暗 hēi'àn
in the dark 完全不知道 wánquán bùzhīdào
2 天黑 tiānhēi ■ You must come back home
before dark. 你们必须在天黑前回家。Nǐmen bìxū
zài tiānhēi qián huíjiā.

darken v 使 [+前景] 变得暗淡 shǐ [+qiánjǐng] biàn de àndàn, 变暗 biàn àn

darkroom N 暗房 ànfáng, 暗室 ànshì

darling I ADJ 亲爱的 qīn'ài de II N 亲爱的（人）qīn'ài de (rén), 宝贝儿 bǎobèir

darn I v 缝补 féngbǔ II ADJ 该死的 gāisǐ de, 讨厌的 tǎoyàn de
Darn it！该死！Gāisǐ! 真倒霉！Zhēn dǎoméi! Darn you！你这个该死的! Nǐ zhège gāisǐ de! 你这个浑蛋! Nǐ zhège húndàn!
III ADV 非常 fēicháng

dart I N 镖 biāo, 飞镖 fēibiāo
darts 掷镖游戏 zhìbiāo yóuxì
II v 1 投掷 tóuzhì 2 猛冲 měngchōng

dash I v 猛冲 měngchōng, 疾奔 jí bēn
to dash sb's dream 使某人的希望落空 shǐ mǒurén de xīwàng luòkōng
II N 1 短跑 duǎnpǎo 2 破折号 pòzhéhào (—) 3 少量 shǎoliàng, 一点点 yìdiǎndiǎn
a dash of pepper 一点点胡椒 yìdiǎndiǎn hújiāo

dashboard N（汽车）仪表板 (qìchē) yíbiǎobǎn

data N 数据 shùjù, 资料 zīliào
data processing 数据处理 shùjù chǔlǐ

database, databank N 数据库 shùjùkù, 资料库 zīliàokù

date¹ I N 1 日期 rìqī
date of birth 出生日期 chūshēng rìqī
to date 至今 zhìjīn
out of date 过期了的 guòqíle de, 陈旧的 chénjiù de
2 约会 yuēhui
date rape 约会强奸 yuēhui qiángjiān
3 约会的对象 yuēhui de duìxiàng, 男／女朋友 nán/nǚ péngyou II v 1 写上日期 xiěshàng rìqī 2 和 [+一个女孩子] 约会 hé [+yí ge nǚháizi] yuēhuì 3 [科学家+] 鉴定…的年代 [kēxuéjiā+] jiàndìng...de niándài

date² N 海枣 hǎizǎo [M. WD 颗 kē], 枣子 zǎozi [M. WD 颗 kē]

dated ADJ 过时的 guòshí de

daub v 在…涂抹 zài...túmǒ

daughter N 女儿 nǚ'ér
daughter-in-law 媳妇 xífù, 儿媳 érxí

daunt v 使…胆怯 shǐ...dǎnqiè

daunting ADJ 使人胆怯的 shǐrén dǎnqiè de

davenport N 坐卧两用大沙发 zuò wò liǎngyòng dà shāfā, 沙发床 shāfāchuáng

dawdle ADJ 磨蹭 móceng

dawn I N 1 黎明 límíng, 天亮 tiānliàng 2 开端 kāiduān, 开始 kāishǐ II v 1 破晓 pòxiǎo, 天亮 tiānliàng 2 开始 kāishǐ
to dawn on 开始明白 kāishǐ míngbai, 想到 xiǎngdào

day N 1 天 tiān, 日 rì 2 白天 báitiān
day after day 一天又一天 yì tiān yòu yì tiān

day after tomorrow 后天 hòutiān
day before yesterday 前天 qiántiān
the other day 最近（有）一天 zuìjìn (yǒu) yì tiān

daybreak N 黎明 límíng

daycare N 日托 rìtuō
daycare center 托儿所 tuō'érsuǒ

daydream I v 做白日梦 zuò báirìmèng, 想入非非 xiǎng rù fēifēi II N 白日梦 báirìmèng

daylight N 1 日光 rìguāng 2 大白天 dàbáitiān
daylight saving time 夏令时间 xiàlìng shíjiān

daytime N 白天 báitiān, 日间 rìjiān

day-to-day ADJ 日常的 rìcháng de, 日复一日的 rì fù yí rì de

daze I v 使…发昏 shǐ...fāhūn II N 迷茫 mímáng, 迷乱 míluàn

dazed ADJ 迷茫的 mímáng de

dazzle v 使…惊讶 shǐ...jīngyà, 使…赞叹不已 shǐ...zàntàn bùyǐ

dazzling ADJ 令人赞叹不已的 lìng rén zàntàn bùyǐ de, 令人眼花缭乱的 lìng rén yǎnhuā liáoluàn de

deacon, deaconess N [基督教] 执事 [Jīdūjiào] zhíshì, [天主教] 助祭 [Tiānzhǔjiào] zhùjì

dead I ADJ 1 死的 sǐ de, 去世 qùshì 2 用完了 yòngwán le 3 死气沉沉的 sǐqì chénchén de
dead center 正中 zhèngzhōng
dead end 死胡同 sǐhútòng, 绝境 juéjìng
dead heat 不分胜负的比赛 bù fēn shèng fù de bǐsài
dead wood 没有用的人／东西 méiyǒu yòng de rén/dōngxi
II N 死人 sǐrén, 死者 sǐzhě
be dead against 完全反对 wánquán fǎnduì
III ADV 完全地 wánquán de

deadline N 截至时间 jiézhì shíjiān

deadlock N 僵局 jiāngjú

deadly I ADJ 致命的 zhìmìng de
a deadly enemy 不共戴天的仇敌 bú gòng dài tiān de chóudí
II ADV 极其 jíqí, 非常 fēicháng

deadpan ADJ 故作严肃的 gùzuò yánsù de

deaf ADJ 聋 lóng, 耳聋 ěrlóng
the deaf 耳聋的人 ěrlóng de rén
the deaf and mute 聋哑人 lóngyǎrén

deafening ADJ 震耳欲聋的 zhèn ěr yù lóng de

deal I N 1 交易 jiāoyì [M. WD 笔 bǐ], 买卖 mǎimai [M. WD 笔 bǐ]
It's a deal! 就这么讲定了! Jiù zhème jiǎngdìng le!
2 协议 xiéyì [M. WD 项 xiàng]
to strike a deal 达成协议 dáchéng xiéyì
3 对待 duìdài, 待遇 dàiyù
a great deal 大量 dàliàng
a rough deal 不公平待遇 bù gōngpíng dàiyù

ll v (PT & PP dealt) 1 做买卖 zuò mǎimai, 经营 jīngyíng 2 发牌 fā pái
to deal with 和…打交道 hé...dǎ jiāodào, 处理 chǔlǐ ■ *I've never dealt with such people.* 我从来没有和这样的人打过交道。 Wǒ cónglái méiyǒu hé zhèyàng de rén dǎguo jiāodào.

dealer N 1 经销商 jīngxiāoshāng, [毒品+] 贩子 [dúpǐn+] fànzi 2 [扑克牌+] 发牌人 [pūkèpái+] fāpáirén

dealership N 特许经销商店 tèxǔ jīngxiāo shāngdiàn

dealings N 商业活动 shāngyè huódòng, 交易 jiāoyì [M. WD 笔 bǐ]

dealt See **deal**

dean N（大学）学院院长（dàxué）xuéyuàn yuànzhǎng [M. WD 位 wèi], 学监 xuéjiān

dear I ADJ 1 亲爱的 qīn'ài de 2 珍贵的 zhēnguì de, 昂贵的 ángguì de II N 亲爱的（人）qīn'ài de (rén)
Oh dear! 天啊! Tiānna!

dearth N 稀少 xīshǎo

death N 死亡 sǐwáng, 去世 qùshi
(the angel of) Death 死神 Sǐshén
death penalty 死刑 sǐxíng
death row 死囚牢房 sǐqiú láofáng
death trap 死亡陷阱 sǐwáng xiànjǐng
Death Valley（美国）死亡谷 (Měiguó) Sǐwánggǔ

deathbed N 死亡时睡的床 sǐwáng shí shuì de chuáng
on one's deathbed 临死时 línsǐ shí, 临终时 línzhōng shí

debacle N 惨败 cǎnbài, 崩溃 bēngkuì

debase v 降低品质 jiàngdī pǐnzhì, 降低价值 jiàngdī jiàzhí

debate I v 1 辩论 biànlùn 2 反复考虑 fǎnfù kǎolǜ II N 1 辩论 biànlùn ■ *The conservatives have lost the debate over abortion.* 保守派在关于堕胎问题的辩论中失败。Bǎoshǒupài zài guānyú duòtāi wèntí de biànlùn zhōng shībài. 2 正式讨论 zhèngshì tǎolùn

debauched ADJ 堕落的 duòluò de, 道德败坏的 dàodé bàihuài de

debauchery N 放荡 fàngdàng, 纵情声色 zòngqíng shēngsè

debilitate v 使…虚弱 shǐ...xūruò

debilitating ADJ 导致虚弱的 dǎozhì xūruò de

debility N 虚弱 xūruò

debit I N 借项 jièxiàng II v 取款 qǔkuǎn
debit card 借记卡 jièjìkǎ

debonair ADJ 衣着入时的 yīzhuó rùshí de, 温文自信的 wēnwén zìxìn de

debrief v 听取汇报 tīngqǔ huìbào, 询问情况 xúnwèn qíngkuàng

debriefing N 听取汇报 tīngqǔ huìbào

debris N 碎片垃圾 suìpiàn lājī

debt N 债 zhài [M. WD 笔 bǐ], 债务 zhàiwù [M. WD 笔 bǐ]
to be in sb's debt 深欠某人的情 shēn qiàn mǒurén de qíng
to be in debt 欠债 qiànzhài
to pay off debts 还清债务 huánqīng zhàiwù

debtor N 债务人 zhàiwùrén

debug v 1 拆除窃听器 chāichú qiètīngqì 2 排除计算机程序中的错误 páichú jìsuànjī chéngxù zhòng de cuòwù 3 排除故障 páichúgùzhàng

debunk v 证明…是错误的 zhèngmíng...shì cuòwù de

debut N, v 首次登场 shǒucì dēngchǎng, 首次登台 shǒucì dēngtái

debutante N 初进社交界的女子 chū jìn shèjiāo jiè de nǚzǐ

decade N 十年 shí nián

decadence N 颓废 tuífèi, 堕落 duòluò

decadent ADJ 颓废的 tuífèi de, 堕落的 duòluò de

decaf N 去咖啡因的咖啡 qù kāfēiyīn de kāfēi

decaffeinated ADJ 脱去咖啡因的 [+茶/咖啡] tuōqù kāfēiyīn de [+chá/kāfēi]

decanter N 玻璃酒瓶 bōli jiǔ píng

decathlon N 十项全能运动 shíxiàng quánnéng yùndòng

decay I v 1 腐烂 fǔlàn 2 [文明+] 衰亡 [wénmíng+] shuāiwáng II N 1 腐烂 fǔlàn 2 衰亡 shuāiwáng ■ *The port has fallen into decay in the past decade.* 这个港口在过去十年中已经衰亡。Zhège gǎngkǒu zài guòqu shí nián zhōng yǐjīng shuāiwáng.

deceased I ADJ 已死亡的 yǐ sǐwáng de, 已故世的 yǐ gùshì de II N 死者 sǐzhě, 故亡者 gùwángzhě

deceit N 欺骗 qīpiàn

deceitful ADJ 欺骗的 qīpiàn de

deceive v 欺骗 qīpiàn
to deceive oneself 自欺欺人 zì qī qī rén

December N 十二月 shí'èryuè

decency N 起码的尊严 qǐmǎ de zūnyán, 体面 tǐmian
human decency 做人的起码标准 zuòrén de qǐmǎ biāozhǔn
to have the decency to 懂得起码的礼仪 dǒngde qǐmǎ de lǐyí

decent 1 ADJ 正派的 [+人] zhèngpài de [+rén], 体面的 tǐmian de 2 像样的 [+衣服] xiàngyàng de [+yīfu], 可以接受的 kěyǐ jiēshòu de

decentralization N 下放权力 xiàfàng quánlì

decentralize v 分散 fēnsàn, 下放权力 xiàfàng quánlì

deception N 欺骗 qīpiàn

deceptive ADJ 欺骗的 qīpiàn de, 欺诈的 qīzhà de

decibel N 分贝 fēnbèi

decide v 决定 juédìng ■ *He has decided not to*

decided

go to college. 他决定不上大学。Tā juédìng bú shàng dàxué.

decided ADJ 明显的 míngxiǎn de

deciduous ADJ 落叶的 luòyè de

decimal I ADJ 十进位的 shíjìnwèi de II N 小数 (比如 0.8, 0.45, 0.3536)

decimal point 小数点 xiǎoshùdiǎn

decimate v 大量毁灭 dàliàng huǐmiè

decipher v 破译 pòyì

decision N 决定 juédìng

decisive ADJ 1 决定性的 [+胜利] juédìngxìng de [+shènglì] 2 果断的 [+领导人] guǒduàn de [+lǐngdǎorén] 3 明确的 [+回答] míngquè de [+huídá]

deck I N 1 甲板 jiǎbǎn

deck chair 折叠躺椅 zhédié tǎngyǐ

2 露天木平台 lùtiān mù píngtái 3 一副 [+扑克牌] yífù [+pūkèpái] II v 装饰 zhuāngshì

declaration N 宣言 xuānyán, 声明 shēngmíng

declare v 1 宣布 xuānbù ■ Japan attacked Pearl Harbor in 1941 without declaring war on the U.S. 1941年日本没有向美国宣战就攻击珍珠港。Yāojiǔsìyāo nián Rìběn méiyǒu xiàng Měiguó xuānzhàn jiù gōngjī Zhēnzhū gǎng. 2 申报 shēnbào

decline I v 1 变小 biàn xiǎo, 变弱 biàn ruò, 衰弱 shuāiruò 2 拒绝 [+邀请] jùjué [+yāoqǐng] II N 消减 xiāojiǎn, 衰落 shuāiluò

decode v 解码 jiěmǎ

decoder N 解码器 jiěmǎ qì

decompose v 1 使···腐烂 shǐ...fǔlàn 2 分解 fēnjiě

décor N 装饰 zhuāngshì

decorate v 1 装饰 zhuāngshì 2 授予···勋章 shòuyǔ...xūnzhāng

a much decorated veteran 一位获得多枚勋章的老兵 yíwèi huòdé duō méi xūnzhāng de lǎobīng

decoration N 1 装饰 zhuāngshì, 装修 zhuāngxiū 2 装饰品 zhuāngshìpǐn 3 勋章 xūnzhāng [M. WD 枚 méi]

decorative ADJ 装饰的 zhuāngshì de

decorator N 室内设计师 shìnèi shèjì shī

decorous ADJ 得体的 détǐ de, 稳重的 wěnzhòng de

decorum N 有礼 yǒulǐ, 得体 détǐ

decoy I N 诱饵 yòu'ěr, 诱惑物 yòuhuò wù II v 诱骗 yòupiàn

decrease I v 减少 jiǎnshǎo, [数量+] 下降 [shù-liàng+] xiàjiàng II N 减少 jiǎnshǎo, (数量) 下降 (shùliàng) xiàjiàng

decree I N 法令 fǎlìng, 命令 mìnglìng II v 规定 guīdìng, 命令 mìnglìng

decrepit ADJ 破旧的 pòjiù de, 老朽的 lǎoxiǔ de

decriminalization N 合法化 héfǎhuà

decriminalize v 使···合法化 shǐ...héfǎhuà

decry v 公开反对 gōngkāi fǎnduì, 谴责 qiǎnzé

dedicate v 1 把···献给 bǎ...xiàngěi 2 以···命名 yǐ...mìngmíng

to dedicate oneself to 献身于 xiànshēn yú

dedicated ADJ 1 有献身精神的 yǒu xiànshēn jīngshén de, 敬业的 jìngyè de 2 致力于···的 zhìlì yú...de 3 专用的 zhuānyòng de

dedication N 献身精神 xiànshēn jīngshén, 奉献 fèngxiàn

deduce v 推断 tuīduàn, 推理 tuīlǐ

deduct v 扣除 kòuchú, 减去 jiǎnqù

deductible ADJ 可减免的 kě jiǎnmiǎn de

deduction N 1 扣除 kòuchú, 减去 jiǎnqù 2 推理 tuīlǐ, 演绎 yǎnyì

deed N 1 行为 xíngwéi, 事迹 shìjì 2 (房地产) 契约 (fángdìchǎn) qìyuē

in deed 事实上 shìshíshang, 确实 quèshí

deem v 认为 rènwéi, 看作 kànzuò

deep I ADJ 1 深涵深 shēn

deep freeze 深冻 shēndòng

deep sleep 沈睡 chénshuì, 酣睡 hānshuì

2 深刻 shēnkè, 深奥 shēn'ào 3 专心 zhuānxīn

deep in thought 沉思 chénsī

II ADV 深深地 shēnshēn de

deep down 内心深处 nèixīn shēnchù

deepen v 加深 jiāshēn, 加剧 jiājù

deep-fry v 油炸 yóuzhá, 油煎 yóujiān

deeply ADV 深深地 shēnshēn de

deep-seated, deep-rooted ADJ 根深蒂固的 gēnshēn dìgù de

deer N 鹿 lù [M. WD 只 zhī/头 tóu]

deface v 毁坏···的容貌 huǐhuài...de róngmào, 涂污 túwū

de facto ADJ 实际上的 shíjì shang de

defamation N 诋毁 dǐhuǐ, 中伤 zhòngshāng

defamatory ADJ 诋毁的 dǐhuǐ de, 中伤的 zhòngshāng de

defame v 破坏···的声誉 pòhuài...de shēngyù, 诋毁 dǐhuǐ

default I N 1 未履行 wèi lǚxíng 2 缺席 quēxí

by default 因对手缺席而赢 yīn duìshǒu quēxí ér yíng

3 缺乏 quēfá

in default of 因为没有 yīnwèi méiyǒu

4 默认 (值) mòrèn (zhí), 预设 (值) yùshè (zhí) II v 1 不履行 bùlǚxíng, 拖欠 tuōqiàn

to default on a loan 不还贷款 bù huán dàikuǎn

defeat I v 打败 dǎbài II N 失败 shībài, 输 shū

defeatism N 失败主义 shībài zhǔyì

defeatist I ADJ 失败主义的 shībài zhǔyì de II N 失败主义者 shībài zhǔyìzhě

defecate v (排) 大便 (pái) dàbiàn

defect I N 缺点 quēdiǎn, 缺陷 quēxiàn II v 背叛 bèipàn, 投敌 tóudí

defective ADJ 有缺陷的 yǒu quēxiàn de, 有毛病的 yǒu máobìng de

defend v 1 保卫 [+国土] bǎowèi [+guótǔ], 捍卫 hànwèi 2 为 [+被告] 辩护 wéi [+bèigào] biànhù 3 防守 fángshǒu

defendant N 被告 bèigào ■ *The defendant was charged with fraud.* 被告被指控舞弊。Bèigào bèi zhǐkòng wǔbì.

defense N 1 防御 fángyù, 抵御 dǐyù
self-defense 自卫 zìwèi ■ *I acted in self-defense.* 我是采取自卫行动。Wǒ shì cǎiqǔ zìwèi xíngdòng.
2 国防 guófáng
national defense 国防 guófáng

defenseless ADJ 无防卫能力的 wú fángwèi nénglì de

defensive ADJ 1 防御性的 fángyùxìng de 2 防备的 fángbèi de
on the defensive 采取守势的 cǎiqǔ shǒushì de, 防备的 fángbèi de
defensive driving 防御性驾驶 fángyùxìng jiàshǐ
3 防守的 fángshǒu de

defer v 1 推迟 tuīchí, 拖延 tuōyán 2 遵从 zūncóng, 顺从 shùncóng

deference N 尊重 zūnzhòng, 敬重 jìngzhòng

deferential ADJ 恭敬的 gōngjìng de

defiance N 对抗 duìkàng, 藐视 miǎoshì
in defiance of 不顾 búgù
in defiance of the government ban 不顾政府禁令 búgù zhèngfǔ jìnlìng

defiant ADJ 对抗的 duìkàng de, 藐视的 miǎoshì de

deficient ADJ 缺乏的 quēfá de, 不足的 bùzú de

deficit N 赤字 chìzì [M. WD 笔 bǐ], 亏损 kuīsǔn [M. WD 笔 bǐ]

defile v 污损 wūsǔn, 污染 wūrǎn

define v 1 给…下定义 gěi…xià dìngyì ■ *How do you define "self-defense" in the legal sense?* 怎么样在法学的意义上给 "自卫" 下定义？Zěnmeyàng zài fǎxué de yìyìshang gěi "zìwèi" xià dìngyì? 2 规定 guīdìng 3 标明…的界限 biāomíng…de jièxiàn

definite ADJ 1 确定的 quèdìng de, 明确的 míngquè de
definite article 定冠词 dìngguàncí
2 肯定的 kěndìng de, 一定的 yídìng de

definition N 1 定义 dìngyì 2 清晰度 qīngxīdù

definitive ADJ 1 权威的 [+著作] quánwēi de [+zhùzuò], 最可靠的 zuì kěkào de 2 最终的 [+判决] zuìzhōng de [+pànjué], 结论性的 jiélùn xìng de

deflate v 1 放掉 [+轮胎] 的气 fàngdiào [+lúntāi] de qì 2 使 [+人] 泄气 shǐ [+rén] xièqì 3 揭穿 [+论点] jiēchuān [+lùndiǎn]

deflation N 1 [轮胎+] 漏气 [lúntāi+] lòuqì 2 泄气 xièqì 3 通货紧缩 tōnghuò jǐnsuō

deflect v 使…转向 shǐ…zhuǎnxiàng
to deflect attention 转移注意力 zhuǎnyí zhùyìlì

deflection N 转向 zhuǎnxiàng, 偏离 piānlí

deform v 使…变形 shǐ…biànxíng

deformation N 变形 biànxíng

deformed ADJ 畸形的 jīxíng de

deformity N 畸形 jīxíng, 变形 biànxíng

defraud v 骗取 piànqǔ, 欺诈 qīzhà

defrost v 解冻 jiědòng

deft ADJ 熟练的 shúliàn de, 灵巧的 língqiǎo de

defunct ADJ 1 不再存在的 [+团体] búzài cúnzài de [+tuántǐ], 解散的 jiěsàn de 2 不再使用的 [+方法] búzài shǐyòng de [+fāngfǎ]

defuse v 缓解 huǎnjiě, 改善 gǎishàn

defy v 违抗 wéikàng, 蔑视 mièshì
to defy explanation 无法解释 wúfǎ jiěshì
to defy description 无法形容 wúfǎ xíngróng

degenerate I v 堕落 duòluò, 退化 tuìhuà II ADJ 堕落的 duòluò de, 败坏的 bàihuài de III N 堕落的人 duòluò de rén

degeneration N 退化 tuìhuà, 堕落 duòluò

degradation N 贬低 biǎndī, 侮辱 wǔrǔ

degrade v 贬低 biǎndī, 侮辱 wǔrǔ

degrading ADJ 有辱人格的 yǒu rǔ réngé de, 有失身份的 yǒu shīshēn fèn de

degree N 1 程度 chéngdù ■ *Teachers must be aware that their students may have different degrees of ability.* 教师必须明白，学生能力的程度是不一样的。Jiàoshī bìxū míngbai, xuésheng nénglì de chéngdù shì bù yíyàng de. 2 学位 xuéwèi 3 (气温等) 度 (qìwēn děng) dù

dehumanize v 使…丧失人性 shǐ…sàngshī rénxìng

dehydrate v 使…脱水 shǐ… tuōshuǐ, 使…干燥 shǐ…gānzào

dehydration N 脱水 tuōshuǐ

deign v 降低身份 jiàngdī shēnfen, 屈尊 qūzūn
to deign to do 降低身份 (做某事) jiàngdī shēnfen (zuò mǒu shì)

deity N 神 shén, 女神 nǚshén
the Deity 上帝 Shàngdì

déjà vu N 似曾相识 sì céng xiāngshí, 似曾经历 sì céng jīnglì

dejected ADJ 情绪低落的 qíngxù dīluò de, 忧郁的 yōuyù de

dejection N 情绪低落 qíngxù dīluò, 忧郁 yōuyù

delay I v 耽误 dānwù, 耽搁 dāngé II N 耽误 dānwù, 耽搁 dāngé
without delay 马上 mǎshàng, 立即 lìjí

delectable ADJ 美味的 měiwèi de, 香喷喷的 xiāngpēnpēn de

delegate I N 代表 dàibiǎo [M. WD 名 míng] II v 授权 shòuquán, 委托 wěituō

delegation N 1 代表团 dàibiǎotuán 2 授权 shòuquán, 委托 wěituō

delete v 删除 shānchú

deletion N 删除 shānchú

deli, delicatessen N 熟食店 shúshídiàn [M. WD 家 jiā]

deliberate I ADJ 1 故意的 gùyì de ■ *This is a deliberate lie!* 这是故意撒谎! Zhè shì gùyì sāhuǎng! 2 深思熟虑的 shēnsī shúlǜ de II v 仔细考虑 zǐxì kǎolǜ

deliberation N 1 仔细考虑 zǐxì kǎolǜ 2 谨慎 jǐnshèn, 从容 cóngróng

delicacy N 1 敏感 mǐngǎn, 谨慎 jǐnshèn 2 精美 jīngměi, 雅致 yǎzhì 3 美味佳肴 měiwèi jiāyáo

delicate ADJ 1 脆弱的 cuìruò de, 易碎的 yìsuì de 2 敏感的 mǐngǎn de, 微妙的 wēimiào de

delicious ADJ 好吃的 hǎochī de, 美味的 měiwèi de

delight I N 高兴 gāoxìng, 快乐 kuàilè II v 使…高兴 shǐ...gāoxìng, 使…快乐 shǐ...kuàilè

delightful ADJ 令人愉快的 lìng rén yúkuài de, 惹人喜爱的 rě rén xǐ'ài de

delineate v 描写 miáoxiě, 描绘 miáohuì

delinquency N 1 违法 wéifǎ, (青少年) 犯罪 (qīngshàonián) fànzuì juvenile delinquency 青少年犯罪 qīngshàonián fànzuì 2 拖欠款 tuō qiànkuǎn

delinquent I ADJ 1 违法的 wéifǎ de 2 拖欠不付的 tuōqiàn bú fù de II N 少年犯 shàoniánfàn

delirious ADJ 昏迷的 hūnmí de

deliver v 1 送交 sòngjiāo, 递交 dìjiāo 2 发表 fābiǎo 3 接生 jiēshēng ■ *The midwife has delivered countless babies in her career.* 这位助产士在她职业生涯中接生了无数的婴儿。Zhè wèi zhùchǎnshì zài tā zhíyè shēngyá zhōng jiēshēngle wúshù de yīng'ér.

delivery N 1 送交 sòngjiāo, 递交 dìjiāo 2 发表 fābiǎo 3 接生 jiēshēng, 分娩 fēnmiǎn

delta N 三角洲 sānjiǎozhōu

delude v 欺骗 qīpiàn, 哄骗 hǒngpiàn

deluge I N 1 大洪水 dàhóngshuǐ 2 大量涌来的东西 dàliàng yǒnglái de dōngxi II v 使…淹没 shǐ...yānmò to be deluged with applications 申请书大量涌来 shēnqǐngshū dàliàng yǒng lái

delusion N 错觉 cuòjué, 幻觉 huànjué

deluxe ADJ 豪华的 háohuá de, 优质的 yōuzhì de

delve v 探索 tànsuǒ, 钻研 zuānyán

demagogue N 煽动家 shāndòngjiā, 蛊惑人心的政客 gǔhuò rénxīn de zhèngkè

demagogic ADJ 煽动的 shāndòng de, 蛊惑的 gǔhuò de

demand I N 1 要求 yāoqiú 2 需求 xūqiú market demand 市场需求 shìchǎng xūqiú II v 要求 yāoqiú ■ *The management decided to meet the demands made by the union.* 管理层决定接受工会的要求。Guǎnlǐcéng juédìng jiēshòu gōnghuì de yāoqiú.

demanding ADJ 1 要求很高的 [+任务] yāoqiú hěn gāo de [+rènwu] 2 费力的 fèilì de 3 要求过高的 [+老板] yāoqiú guògāo de [+lǎobǎn], 苛求的 kēqiú de

demean v 降低…的身份 jiàngdī...de shēnfen, 贬低 biǎndī

demeaning ADJ 贬低的 biǎndī de, 侮辱的 wǔrǔ de

demeanor N 举止 jǔzhǐ, 风度 fēngdù

demented ADJ 疯狂的 fēngkuáng de, 变态的 biàntài de

dementia N 1 痴呆 chīdāi 2 精神错乱 jīngshén cuòluàn

demerit N 1 过失 guòshī, 过错 guòcuò 2 记过 jìguò

demise N 1 死亡 sǐwáng, 消亡 xiāowáng 2 终结 zhōngjié

demo N 1 样品 yàngpǐn 2 演示 yǎnshì

democracy N 1 民主 (制度) mínzhǔ (zhìdù) 2 民主国家 mínzhǔ guójiā

democrat N 主张民主的人 zhǔzhāng mínzhǔ de rén, 民主派 mínzhǔ pài Democrat (美国) 民主党人 (Měiguó) Mínzhǔdǎngrén

democratic ADJ 民主的 mínzhǔ de ■ *We should make decisions in a democratic way.* 我们应该以民主的方式作出决定。Wǒmen yīnggāi yǐ mínzhǔ de fāngshì zuòchū juédìng. Democratic Party (美国) 民主党 (Měiguó) Mínzhǔdǎng

demographic ADJ 人口的 rénkǒu de

demographics N 人口统计 (数据) rénkǒu tǒngjì (shùjù)

demography N 人口 (统计) 学 rénkǒu (tǒngjì) xué

demolish v 拆除 chāichú

demolition N 拆除 chāichú

demon N 1 魔鬼 móguǐ inner demon 心魔 xīnmó 2 高手 gāoshǒu, 技艺高超的人 jìyì gāochāo de rén

demonstrate v 1 显示 xiǎnshì 2 示范 shìfàn, 演示 yǎnshì ■ *The chemistry teacher demonstrated the experiment to the class.* 化学老师向全班演示实验。Huàxué lǎoshī xiàng quánbān yǎnshì shíyàn. demonstration program 演示程序 yǎnshì chéngxù

demonstrative ADJ 1 感情外露的 gǎnqíng wàilù de 2 示范的 [+教学] shìfàn de [+jiàoxué] demonstrative pronoun 指示代词 zhǐshìdàicí

demonstrator N 1 示范者 shìfànzhě, 演示者 yǎnshìzhě 2 示威游行者 shìwēi yóuxíngzhě

demoralize v 使…泄气 shǐ...xièqì

demote v 将…降职 jiāng...jiàngzhí

demur v 娴静的 xiánjìng de, 端庄的 duānzhuāng de

den N 1 (野生动物的) 窝 (yěshēng dòngwù de)

wō, 洞穴 dòngxué **2** 贼窝 zéiwō, 赌窟 dǔkū **3** 密室 mìshì

denial N **1** 否认 fǒurèn **2** 拒绝给予 jùjué jǐyǔ

denigrate v 贬低 biǎndī

denim N 粗斜面布 cū xiémiàn bù denims 牛仔裤 niúzǎikù [M. WD 条 tiáo]

denominate v 定价 dìngjià

denomination N **1** 面值 miànzhí **2** [宗教] 派别 [zōngjiào] pàibié

denounce v 指责 zhǐzé, 谴责 qiǎnzé

dense ADJ **1** 浓密的 nóngmì de, 稠密的 chóumì de **2** 密度大的 mìdù dà de **3** 难懂的 nándǒng de **4** 迟钝的 chídùn de, 愚蠢的 yúchǔn de

density N 密度 mìdù

dent I N **1** 凹痕 āohén **2** 减少 jiǎnshǎo, 减轻 jiǎnqīng II v **1** 使…产生凹痕 shǐ…chǎnshēng āohén **2** 损害 sǔnhài, 削弱 xuēruò to dent one's image 损害形象 sǔnhài xíngxiàng

dental ADJ 牙医的 yáyī de, 牙齿的 yáchǐ de dental floss 洁牙线 jiéyáxiàn

dentist N 牙科医生 yákē yīshēng

dentures N 假牙 jiǎyá [M. WD 副 fù]

denunciation N 谴责 qiǎnzé, 斥责 chìzé

deny v **1** 否认 fǒurèn ■ *He denies any wrongdoing.* 他否认做错任何事情。Tā fǒurèn zuòcuò rènhé shìqíng. **2** 拒绝 jùjué, 不给 bùgěi

deodorant N 除臭剂 chúchòujì

deodorize v 除臭 chúchòu

depart v **1** 离开 líkāi, 离去 líqù **2** 死亡 sǐwáng

department N **1** [政府+] 部门 [zhèngfǔ+] bùmén **2** [大学的+] 系 [dàxué de+] xì department store 百货商店 bǎihuò shāngdiàn

departure N **1** 离开 líkāi, 离去 líqù **2** 启程 qǐchéng, 上路 shànglù **3** 背离 bèilí

depend v **1** 依靠 yīkào ■ *The town depends on tourism.* 这个小城靠旅游业。Zhè ge xiǎo chéng yīkào lǚyóuyè. **2** 得看 děikàn It/That depends. 看情况 kàn qíngkuàng

dependable ADJ 可靠的 kěkào de

dependent I ADJ 依赖于 yīlàiyú, 有赖于 yǒulàiyú ■ *Your success is dependent on your hard work.* 你的成功有赖于努力工作。Nǐ de chénggōng yǒulàiyú nǔlì gōngzuò. a dependent child 要抚养的孩子 yào fǔyǎng de háizi II N 家属 jiāshǔ ■ *He has no debts and no dependents—he can spend all he earns.* 他没有债务，也没有家属——他能挣多少用多少。Tā méiyǒu zhàiwù, yě méiyǒu jiāshǔ—tā néng zhèng duōshǎo yòng duōshǎo. army dependents 军人家属 jūnrén jiāshǔ, 军属 jūnshǔ

depict v 描写 miáoxiě, 描绘 miáohuì

deplete v 减少 jiǎnshǎo, 损耗 sǔnhào

deplorable ADJ 极坏的 jí huài de, 应受谴责的 yìng shòu qiǎnzé de

deplore v **1** 强烈批评 qiángliè pīpíng **2** 深感惋惜 shēngǎn wǎnxī

deploy v 部署 bùshǔ

deport v 驱逐出境 qūzhú chūjìng

deposit I N **1** 首期付款 shǒuqī fùkuǎn, 定金 dìngjīn **2** 预付租金 yùfù zūjīn, 押金 yājīn **3** [银行+] 存款 [yínháng+] cúnkuǎn **4** 矿藏 kuàngcáng II v **1** 把…放在 bǎ…fàng zài **2** 存入 [+银行] cún rù [+ yínháng] **3** 沉淀 chéndiàn

depot N **1** 库存处 kùcún chù, 仓库 cāngkù **2** (小) 车站 (xiǎo) chēzhàn

depraved ADJ 道德彻底败坏的 dàodé chèdǐ bàihuài de, 腐败透顶的 fǔbài tòudǐng de

depravity N 彻底堕落 chèdǐ duòluò

depreciate v **1** [货币+] 贬值 [huòbì+] biǎnzhí **2** 贬低 [+价值] biǎndī [+jiàzhí]

depress v 使…忧郁 shǐ…yōuyù

depressant N 抑止药 yìzhǐ yào

depressed ADJ 忧郁 yōuyù, 感到忧郁 gǎndào yōuyù

depressing ADJ 令人忧愁的 lìng rén yōuchóu de

depression N **1** 忧郁 (症) yōuyù (zhèng) **2** 经济萧条 (期) jīngjì xiāotiáo (qī) the Depression (三十年代) 经济大萧条 (sānshí niándài) jīngjì Dàxiāotiáo **3** 低气压 dīqìyā **4** 低洼 (地) dīwā (dì)

depressive I ADJ 忧郁的 yōuyù de II N 忧郁症患者 yōuyùzhèng huànzhě

deprive v 剥夺 bōduó

deprived ADJ 贫困的 pínkùn de, 穷苦的 qióngkǔ de

depth N 深度 shēndù ■ *The depth of his knowledge of American history is amazing.* 他的美国历史知识的深度让人吃惊。Tā de Měiguó lìshǐ zhīshi de shēndù ràng rén chījīng.

deputy N 副 fù, 副手 fùshǒu

derail v **1** [火车+] 出轨 [huǒchē+] chūguǐ **2** 破坏 [+计划] pòhuài [+jìhuà]

deranged ADJ 精神错乱的 jīngshén cuòluàn de

derelict I ADJ **1** 破败的 [+建筑物] pòbài de [+jiànzhù wù], 废弃的 fèiqì de **2** 玩忽职守的 [+官员] wánhū zhíshǒu de [+guānyuán], 渎职的 dúzhí de II N 无家可归者 wújiākěguīzhě

deride v **1** 嘲笑 cháoxiào **2** 戏弄 xìnòng

derision N 嘲笑 cháoxiào

derisory ADJ 嘲笑的 cháoxiào de

derivation N 起源 qǐyuán, 出处 chūchù

derivative¹ N **1** 派生物 pàishēngwù, [语言] 派生词 [yǔyán] pàishēngcí **2** [化学] 提取物 [huàxué] tíqǔwù **3** [金融] 衍生投资 [jīnróng] yǎnshēng tóuzī

derivative² ADJ 非独创的 fēi dúchuàng de, 模仿的 mófǎng de

derive v **1** 获取 huòqǔ, 得到 dédào **2** 起源于 qǐyuán yú

dermatitis N 皮肤炎 pífūyán

dermatologist N 皮肤病医生 pífūbìng yīshēng, 皮肤病专家 pífūbìng zhuānjiā

dermatology N 皮肤病学 pífūbìngxué

derogatory ADJ 侮辱的 wǔrǔ de, 贬低的 biǎndī de

derrick N **1** 油井架 yóujǐngjià, 钻塔 zuàntǎ **2** (货轮) 吊杆起重机 (huò lún) diàogān qǐzhòngjī

descend v 下降 xiàjiàng, 下落 xiàluò
in descending order 从大到小排列 cóng dà dào xiǎo páiliè, 按降序排列 àn jiàngxù páiliè
to descend from 是…的后代 shì…de hòudài

descendant N 后代 hòudài, 后裔 hòuyì

descent N **1** 下降 xiàjiàng, 下落 xiàluò **2** 下坡路 xiàpōlù **3** 出身 chūshēn, 血统 xuètǒng

describe v 描写 miáoxiě, 描绘 miáohuì

description N 描写 miáoxiě, 描绘 miáohuì

descriptive ADJ 描写的 miáoxiě de, 描绘的 miáohuì de

desecrate v 亵渎 xièdú, 污辱 wūrǔ

desecration N 亵渎 xièdú

desegregate v 废除种族隔离制度 fèichú zhǒngzú gélí zhìdù

desegregation N 废除种族隔离制度 fèichú zhǒngzú gélí zhìdù

desensitize v 使…变得不敏感 shǐ…biàn de bù mǐngǎn, 使…习惯 shǐ…xíguàn

desert I N 沙漠 shāmò [M. WD 片 piàn] II v 离开 líkāi, 抛弃 pāoqì

deserve v 值得 zhíde ■ *You deserve some reward for all your hard work.* 你的辛勤劳动值得回报。Nǐ de xīnqín láodòng zhíde huíbào.

design N, v 设计 shèjì

designate v 指定 zhǐdìng, 指派 zhǐpài

designation N 指定 zhǐdìng, 指派 zhǐpài

designer I N 设计师 shèjìshī II ADJ 特别设计的 tèbié shèjì de
designer drug 化合迷幻药 huàhé míhuànyào

desirable ADJ 可取的 kěqǔ de, 称心的 chènxīn de ■ *It is desirable that the new principal should know a language other than English.* 新校长除了英语还懂别的语言, 就好了。Xīn xiàozhǎng chúle Yīngyǔ hái dǒng biéde yǔyán, jiù hǎo le.

desire I N 愿望 yuànwàng, 欲望 yùwàng II v 希望得到 xīwàng dédào, 欲求 yùqiú ■ *We all desire love and happiness.* 我们都希望得到爱和幸福。Wǒmen dōu xīwàng dédào ài hé xìngfú.

desist v 停止 tíngzhǐ

desk N **1** 办公桌 bàngōngzhuō [M. WD 只 zhī/张 zhāng], 写字台 xiězìtái [M. WD 只 zhī/张 zhāng] **2** 工作台 gōngzuòtái, 服务台 fúwùtái
front desk [旅馆] 前台 [lǚguǎn] qiántái
information desk 问事处 wènshìchù

desktop N **1** 桌面 zhuōmiàn **2** 桌上型电脑 zhuōshàngxíng diànnǎo
desktop publishing 桌面出版 zhuōmiàn chūbǎn

desolate ADJ 荒凉的 huāngliáng de

despair I N 绝望 juéwàng II v 感到绝望 gǎndào juéwàng

desperate ADJ **1** 不顾一切的 búgù yíqiè de, 拼命的 pīnmìng de **2** 非常想要的 fēicháng xiǎngyào de

desperation N 绝望 juéwàng, 不顾一切 búgù yíqiè

despicable ADJ 卑鄙的 bēibǐ de, 可鄙的 kěbǐ de

despise v 鄙视 bǐshì, 看不起 kànbuqǐ

despite PREP 尽管 jǐnguǎn

despondent ADJ 忧伤的 yōushāng de, 沮丧的 jǔsàng de

despot N 暴君 bàojūn

despotism N 暴政 bàozhèng

dessert N (饭后) 甜食 (fànhòu) tiánshí, 甜点心 tiándiǎnxin

destabilize v 使…不稳定 shǐ…bùwěndìng

destination N 目的地 mùdìdì, 终点 zhōngdiǎn

destined ADJ (命中) 注定的 (mìngzhōng) zhùdìng de

destiny N 命运 mìngyùn

destroy v 毁灭 huǐmiè, 破坏 pòhuài

destroyer N 驱逐舰 qūzhújiàn [M. WD 艘 sōu]

destruction N 毁灭 huǐmiè, 破坏 pòhuài ■ *The destruction of the rainforest is inevitable if logging continues.* 如果继续伐木, 雨林的毁灭就不可避免。Rúguǒ jìxù fámù, yǔlín de huǐmiè jiù bùkě bìmiǎn.

destructive ADJ 破坏性的 pòhuàixìng de

detach v 拆开 chāikāi, 脱落 tuōluò

detached ADJ 超然的 chāorán de, 客观的 kèguān de

detachment N **1** 超然 chāorán, 客观 kèguān **2** [军事] 小分队 [jūnshì] xiǎofēnduì

detail I N 细节 xìjié, 详情 xiángqíng
in detail 详细地 xiángxì de ■ *Can you explain this in detail?* 你能不能详细解释一下? Nǐ néngbunéng xiángxì jiěshì yíxià?
II v 详细叙述 xiángxì xùshù
to detail sb to do sth 派遣某人去做某事 pàiqiǎn mǒurén qù zuò mǒushì

detailed ADJ 详细的 xiángxì de

detain v **1** 拘留 jūliú, 扣留 kòuliú **2** 阻留 zǔliú

detect v 察觉 chájué, 发现 fāxiàn

detective N 侦探 zhēntàn

detector N 探测器 tàncèqì
metal detector 金属探测器 jīnshǔ tàncèqì
lie detector 测谎器 cèhuǎngqì
smoke detector 烟雾报警器 yānwù bàojǐng qì

détente N (国家关系的) 缓和 (guójiā guānxi de) huǎnhé

detention N 1 拘留 jūliú, 扣留 kòuliú 2 [学校] 课后留校 [xuéxiào] kè hòu liúxiào

deter v 制止 zhìzhǐ, 威慑 wēishè

detergent N 洗衣粉 xǐyīfěn, 洗涤精 xǐdíjīng

deteriorate v 越来越坏 yuèláiyuè huài, 恶化 èhuà

deterioration N 恶化 èhuà

determinate ADJ 严格控制的 yángé kòngzhì de

determination N 1 决心 juéxīn 2 [官方+] 决定 [guānfāng+] juédìng 3 [成份+] 测定 [chéngfèn+] cèdìng

determine v 1 下决心 xià juéxīn, 决定 juédìng 2 确定 quèdìng ■ *More studies are needed to determine the cause of the disease.* 还需要更多的研究来确定这种疾病的起因。Hái xūyào gèngduō de yánjiū lái quèdìng zhè zhǒng jíbìng de qǐyīn.

determined ADJ 下了决心的 xià le juéxīn de, 坚定的 jiāndìng de

determiner N 限定词 xiàndìngcí

deterrent N 威慑力 wēishèlì, 威慑手段 wēishè shǒuduàn

detest v 憎恨 zēnghèn, 嫌恶 xiánwù

dethrone v 把…赶下台 bǎ…gǎnxiàtái, 推翻 tuīfān

detonate v 引爆 yǐnbào

detonation N 引爆 yǐnbào, 爆炸 bàozhà

detonator N 引爆装置 yǐnbàozhuāngzhì, 雷管 léiguǎn

detour v 绕道 (而行) ràodào (ér xíng)

detox I N 戒酒治疗 jièjiǔ zhìliáo, 戒毒治疗 jièdú zhìliáo II v 戒酒治疗 jièjiǔ zhìliáo, 戒毒治疗 jièdú zhìliáo

detoxification N 排毒 páidú

detract v 贬损 biǎnsǔn, 诋毁 dǐhuǐ

detriment N 伤害 shānghài

detrimental ADJ 有害的 yǒuhài de

devalue v 贬值 biǎnzhí

devastate v 1 使…极其伤心 shǐ…jíqí shāngxīn, 使…垮掉 shǐ…kuǎdiào 2 摧毁 [+城市] cuīhuǐ [+chéngshì], 毁掉 huǐdiào

devastating ADJ 1 让人极其伤心的 [+消息] ràng rén jíqí shāngxīn de [+xiāoxi] 2 毁灭性的 [+打击] huǐmièxìng de [+dǎjī]

devastation N 摧毁 cuīhuǐ, 摧残 cuīcán

develop v 1 发展 fāzhǎn, 开发 kāifā 2 发育 fāyù ■ *The boy has developed into a fine young man.* 男孩发育成了英俊小伙子。Nánhái fāyù chéngle yīngjùn xiǎohuòzi. 3 开始出现 [+问题] kāishǐ chūxiàn [+wèití] 4 冲印 [+底片] chōngyìn [+dǐpiàn]

developed ADJ 1 发达的 [+国家] fādá de [+guójiā] 2 更严重的 [+危机] gèng yánzhòng de [+wēijī]

developer N (土地房产) 开发商 (tǔdì fángchǎn) kāifāshāng, (新产品) 开发者 (xīnchǎnpǐn) kāifāzhě

developing ADJ 发展中的 fāzhǎnzhōng de

development N 1 发展 fāzhǎn, 开发 kāifā a new housing development 新建住宅区 xīnjiàn zhùzháiqū 2 新情况 xīn qíngkuàng

deviant I ADJ 变态的 biàntài de II N 变态者 biàntàizhě

deviate I v 偏离 piānlí II ADJ 变态的 biàntài de

deviation N 偏差 piānchā, 异常 yìcháng

device N 1 设备 shèbèi, 设施 shèshī 2 [测试+] 装置 [cèshì+] zhuāngzhì 3 [通讯+] 手段 [tōngxùn+] shǒuduàn, 方法 fāngfǎ

devil N 1 魔鬼 móguǐ 2 家伙 jiāhuo lucky devil 幸运的家伙 xìngyùn de jiāhuo 3 调皮鬼 tiáopí guǐ

the devil …? 究竟…? jiūjìng…? 到底…? dàodǐ…?

to play the devil's advocate 故意唱反调 gùyì chàng fǎndiào

devilish ADJ 1 恶毒的 èdú de, 坏透了的 huàitòule de 2 淘气的 táoqì de, 调皮的 tiáopí de

devious ADJ 欺诈的 qīzhà de, 不老实的 bù lǎoshí de

devise v 设计出 shèjìchū, 想出 xiǎngchū

devoid ADJ 完全没有的 wánquán méiyǒu de, 毫无 háowú

devolution N 1 权力下放 quánlì xiàfàng 2 沦为 lúnwéi

devolve v 权力下放 quánlì xiàfàng

devote v 把…奉献给 bǎ…fèngxiàn gěi to devote oneself to 献身于 xiànshēn yú

devoted ADJ 忠诚的 zhōngchéng de, 挚爱的 zhì'ài de

devotee N 爱好者 àihàozhě, 仰慕者 yǎngmùzhě

devotion N 1 忠诚 zhōngchéng, 挚爱 zhì'ài 2 献身 xiànshēn, 奉献 fèngxiàn

devour v 1 狼吞虎咽地吃 lángtūn hǔyàn de chī 2 贪婪地阅读 tānlán de yuèdú 3 吞噬 tūnshì, 耗尽 hàojìn

devout ADJ 虔诚的 qiánchéng de

dew N 露水 lùshuǐ [m. wp 滴 dī]

dexterity N 灵巧 língqiǎo, 敏捷 mǐnjié

dexterous, dextrous ADJ 灵巧的 língqiǎo de, 敏捷的 mǐnjié de

diabetes N 糖尿病 tángniàobìng

diabetic I ADJ 糖尿病的 tángniàobìng de II N 糖尿病人 tángniàobìngrén

diabolical ADJ 恶魔似的 èmó shì de, 邪恶的 xié'è de

diagnose v 诊断 zhěnduàn

diagnosis N 诊断 zhěnduàn

diagonal I ADJ 1 斜的 xié de, 斜线的 xiéxiàn de 2 对角的 duìjiǎo de II N 斜线 xiéxiàn, 对角线 duìjiǎoxiàn

diagram N 图表 túbiǎo, 示意图 shìyìtú

dial I v 拨号 bō hào

dial tone 拨音号 bōyīnhào
II N 刻度盘 kèdùpán

dialect N 方言 fāngyán

dialogue, dialog N 对话 duìhuà
dialogue box 对话框 duìhuàkuàng

dialysis N（血液）透析 (xuèyè) tòuxī

diameter N 直径 zhíjìng

diametrically ADV (diametrically different) 截然相反的 jiérán xiāngfǎn de

diamond N 1 钻石 [+戒指] zuànshí [+jièzhi] 2 菱形 [+瓷砖] língxíng [+cízhuān] 3 [纸牌] 方块牌 [zhǐpái+] fāngkuàipái

diaper N 尿布 niàobù [M. WD 块 kuài]

diaphragm N 横膈膜 hénggémó

diarrhea N 腹泻 fùxiè

diary N 日记 rìjì [M. WD 本 běn], 日记簿 rìjìbù [M. WD 本 běn]

diaspora N 1（民族）大流散 (mínzú) dà liúsàn 2 移民社群 yímín shèqún

diatribe N 严厉谴责 yánlì qiǎnzé, 愤怒抨击 fènnù pēngjī

dice I N 1 骰子 shǎizi
to roll the dice 掷骰子 zhì shǎizi
2 小块食物 xiǎo kuài shíwù II v 把…食物切成小块 bǎ...shíwù qiēchéng xiǎo kuài

dicey ADJ 冒险的 màoxiǎn de, 不可靠的 bù kěkào de

dichotomy N 二分法 èrfēnfǎ

dick N 1 鸡巴 jība 2 笨蛋 bèndàn

dictaphone N 口述录音机 kǒushù lùyīnjī

dictate v 1 口授 kǒushòu 2 强制规定 qiángzhì guīdìng

dictation N 1 口授 kǒushòu 2 [学校] 听写练习 [xuéxiào] tīngxiě liànxí

dictator N 独裁者 dúcáizhě

dictatorial ADJ 独裁的 dúcái de, 专横的 zhuānhèng de

dictatorship N 独裁政府 dúcái zhèngfǔ, 专政 zhuānzhèng

diction N 用词 yòngcí, 措词 cuòcí

dictionary N 词典 cídiǎn [M. WD 本 běn], 字典 zìdiǎn [M. WD 本 běn]

did See **do**

didactic ADJ 说教的 shuōjiào de

didn't See **do**

die¹ v 1 死 sǐ, 去世 qùshì 2 [旧风俗+] 消失 [jiù fēngsú+] xiāoshī 3 [机器+] 停止运转 [jīqì+] tíngzhǐ yùnzhuǎn

die² N 1 金属模具 jīnshǔmó jù, 铸模 zhùmú 2 骰子 shǎizi ■ *The die is cast.* 木已成舟。Mùyǐchéngzhōu.

diehard ADJ 死硬的 sǐyìng de, 顽固的 wángù de

diesel N 柴油 cháiyóu
diesel engine 柴油发动机 cháiyóu fādòngjī, 柴油机 cháiyóujī

diet I N 1 日常食品 rìcháng shípǐn 2（规定）食谱 (guīdìng) shípǔ
to be on diet 按规定食谱饮食 àn guīdìng shípǔ yǐnshí, 控制饮食 kòngzhì yǐnshí
II v 节食 jiéshí, 控制饮食 kòngzhì yǐnshí

differ v 不同 bùtóng
Tastes differ. 各人口味不同。Gè rén kǒuwèi bùtóng. ■ *My ideas differ widely from yours.* 我的想法和你有很大不同。Wǒ de xiǎngfǎ hé nǐ yǒu hěn dà bùtóng.

difference N 1 不同的地方 bùtóng de dìfang, 分歧 fēnqí ■ *I noticed a real difference between their views.* 我注意到他们之间的观点确实不一样。Wǒ zhùyìdao tāmen zhījiān de guāndiǎn quèshí bù yíyàng. 2 差别 chābié, 差异 chāyì
to make a difference 产生影响 chǎnshēng yǐngxiǎng, 起作用 qǐzuòyòng ■ *What difference does it make if you don't buy this new car?* 你不买这辆新车又会有什么不同？Nǐ bù mǎi zhè liàng xīn chē yòu huì yǒu shénme bùtóng?
to make no difference 没有任何作用 méiyǒu rènhé zuòyòng

different ADJ 不同 bùtóng ■ *Her approach to this problem is different from ours.* 她对这个问题的处理方法和我们不同。Tā duì zhè ge wèntí de chǔlǐ fāngfǎ hé wǒmen bùtóng.

differential N 差别程度 chābié chéngdù

differentiate v 区别 qūbié, 辨别 biànbié

difficult ADJ 1 困难的 kùnnan de, 难的 nán de ■ *His lack of experience made it difficult for him to find a good job.* 他缺乏经验，使他很难找到工作。Tā quēfá jīngyàn, shǐ tā hěn nán zhǎodao gōngzuò. 2 难以对付的 [+人] nányǐ duìfu de [+rén]

difficulty N 困难 kùnnan, 难处 nánchu ■ *Chinese characters present a special difficulty to us.* 汉字是我们的特殊困难。Hànzì shì wǒmen de tèshū kùnnan.

diffuse I ADJ 1 分散的 fēnsàn de, 松散的 sōngsǎn de 2 啰嗦的 luōsuō de, 转弯抹角的 zhuǎnwān mòjiǎo de II v 1 分散 fēnsàn 2 减轻 jiǎnqīng, 减弱 jiǎnruò 3 使…扩散 shǐ...kuòsàn

dig I v (PT & PP **dug**) 1 挖 wā, 挖掘 wājué
to dig one's own grave 自掘坟墓 zìjuéfénmù 2 搜寻 sōuxún, 搜集 sōují
to dig into ① 开始使用 kāishǐ shǐyòng ② 插入 chārù
to dig up 挖掘出 wājué chū, 发现 fāxiàn
II N 1 讽刺 fěngcì, 挖苦 wākǔ 2（考古）发掘 (kǎogǔ) fājué

digest v 1 消化 xiāohuà **II** N 摘要 zhāiyào [M. WD 份 fèn/篇 piān], 文摘 wénzhāi [M. WD 份 fèn/篇 piān]
Reader's Digest 读者文摘 Dúzhě Wénzhāi

digestion N 消化 xiāohuà

digestive ADJ 消化的 xiāohuà de

digit N **1** (1 到 9) 数字 (1 dào 9) shùzì **2** 手指 shǒuzhǐ, 脚趾 jiǎozhǐ

digital ADJ 数字的 shùzì de, 数码的 shùmǎ de
digital camera 数码照相机 shùmǎ zhàoxiàngjī

digitize V 数字化 shùzìhuà

dignified ADJ 有尊严的 yǒuzūnyán de, 庄重的 zhuāngzhòng de

dignify V 使…有尊严 shǐ…yǒu zūnyán, 抬高…的身价 táigāo…de shēnjià

dignitary N 显贵 xiǎnguì [M. WD 位 wèi], 要人 yàorén [M. WD 位 wèi]

dignity N 尊严 zūnyán, 尊贵 zūnguì

digress V 离题 lítí, 跑题 pǎotí

digression N 离题 lítí, 跑题 pǎotí

dike N 堤坝 dībà, 堤 dī, 坝 bà

dilapidated ADJ 破烂的 pòlàn de, 快倒塌的 kuài dǎotā de

dilapidation N 破烂的状态 pòlàn de zhuàngtài

dilate V 扩大 kuòdà, 扩张 kuòzhāng

dilemma N 进退维谷的局面 jìn tuì wéi gǔ de júmiàn, 两难境地 liǎngnán jìngdì

diligence N 勤奋 qínfèn

diligent ADJ 勤奋的 qínfèn de

dilute I V **1** 稀释 xīshì, 冲淡 chōngdàn **2** 使…削弱 shǐ… xuēruò II ADJ 稀释的 xīshì de

dilution N 稀释 xīshì

dim ADJ 昏暗的 hūn'àn de, 模糊的 móhu de

dime N 一角钱 yì jiǎo qián, 一毛钱 yì máo qián
dime store 廉价小商品店 liánjià xiǎoshāngpǐn diàn
a dime a dozen 多得不值钱 duō dé bù zhíqián

dimension N **1** [三个+] 维度 [sānge+] wéidù **2** [新的+] 方面 [xīn de+] fāngmiàn **3** (dimensions) 尺寸 chǐcùn

dimensional ADJ 维度的 wéi dù de
three-dimensional 三维的 sānwéi de, 立体的 lìtǐ de

dimensions N [物体的+] 长高宽 [wùtǐ de+] cháng gāo kuān, 体积 tǐjī

diminish V **1** [人数+] 减少 [rénshù+] jiǎnshǎo, 减小 jiǎnxiǎo **2** 削弱 [+重要性] xuēruò [+zhòngyàoxìng], 降低 jiàngdī
diminishing returns 收益递减 shōuyì dìjiǎn

diminutive ADJ 个子矮小的 gèzi hěn ǎixiǎo de

dimple N 酒窝 jiǔwō

dim sum N 中国点心 Zhōngguó diǎnxin [M. WD 件 jiàn]

din N 嘈杂声 cáozáshēng, 喧闹声 xuānnàoshēng

dine V 进餐 jìncān, 吃饭 chīfàn
to dine out 外出用餐 wàichū yòngcān, 到饭店去吃饭 dào fàndiàn qù chīfàn

diner N 便宜的小饭馆 piányi de xiǎo fànguǎn [M. WD 家 jiā]

ding-dong N 铃声 língshēng, 叮当声 dīngdāngshēng

dinghy N 单桅小赛艇 dān wéi xiǎo sàitǐng [M. WD 艘 sōu]

dingy ADJ 肮脏破旧的 āngzāng pòjiù de

dining room N 餐厅 cāntīng, 饭厅 fàntīng

dinner N **1** 正餐 zhèngcān, 晚饭 wǎnfàn
■ *We often have animated conversations at the dinner table.* 我们在吃晚饭的时候常常谈得很活跃。Wǒmen zài chī wǎnfàn de shíhou chángcháng tánde hěn huóyuè. **2** 宴会 yànhuì, 晚宴 wǎnyàn
dinner jacket 男子夜礼服 nánzǐ yèlǐfú
dinner party 家宴 jiāyàn
dinner service [一套+] 西餐餐具 [yítào+] xīcān cānjù

dinnertime N 用餐时间 yòngcān shíjiān

dinosaur N 恐龙 kǒnglóng

dip I V **1** 浸 jìn, 蘸 zhàn ■ *Don't dip your bread in the soup.* 不要把面包浸在汤里。Búyào bǎ miànbāo jìn zài tānglǐ. **2** 下降 xiàjiàng, 降低 jiàngdī II N **1** 调味酱 tiáowèi jiàng **2** (短时间的) 游泳 (duǎn shíjiān de) yóuyǒng **3** 小量减少 xiǎoliàng jiǎnshǎo

diphtheria N 白喉 báihóu

diploma N 文凭 wénpíng [M. WD 张 zhāng/份 fèn], 毕业证书 bìyè zhèngshū [M. WD 张 zhāng/份 fèn]

diplomat N 外交官 wàijiāoguān [M. WD 位 wèi/名 míng]

diplomatic ADJ **1** 外交的 wàijiāo de **2** 世故练达的 shìgù liàndá de, 讲究策略的 jiǎngjiu cèlüè de

dipstick N 油量计 yóuliángjì

dire ADJ 极其严重的 jíqí yánzhòng de, 极糟的 jí zāo de

direct I ADJ **1** 直接的 zhíjiē de
direct current 直流电 zhíliúdiàn
direct deposit 直接存款付薪 zhíjiē cúnkuǎn fù xīn
2 坦率的 tǎnshuài de, 率直的 shuàizhí de II V **1** 针对 zhēnduì **2** 指挥 zhǐhuī, 指导 zhǐdǎo ■ *The Chief will direct the operation himself.* 头头要自己指挥这次行动。Tóutou yào zìjǐ zhǐhuī zhè cì xíngdòng. III ADV 直接 zhíjiē, 直接地 zhíjiē de ■ *I flew direct from New York to San Francisco.* 我从纽约直接飞到旧金山。Wǒ cóng Niǔyuē zhíjiē fēidào Jiùjīnshān.

direction N 方向 fāngxiàng ■ *We found that we were going in the wrong direction.* 我们发现走错路了。Wǒmen fāxiàn zǒucuò lù le.
directions 指路 zhǐ lù, 指明方向 zhǐmíng fāngxiàng
sense of direction 方向感 fāngxiànggǎn

directive N 指令 zhǐlìng, 指示 zhǐshì

director N **1** [公司] 董事 [gōngsī] dǒngshì [M. WD 位 wèi] ■ *Mr Smith is the new finance director of our company.* 史密斯先生是我们公司的新任财务董事。Shǐmìsī xiānsheng shì wǒmen gōngsī de xīnrèn cáiwù dǒngshì. **2**（电影）导演 (diànyǐng) dǎoyǎn [m. wᴅ 位 wèi]

directory N **1** 姓名地址录 xìngmíng dìzhǐ lù
telephone directory 电话号码簿 diànhuà hàomǎ bù
2（计算机）文档目录 (jìsuànjī) wéndàng mùlù

dirt N **1** 灰尘 huīchén, 尘土 chéntǔ ■ *His shoes were all covered with dirt.* 他的鞋上全是尘土。Tā de xiéshang quán shì chéntǔ.
dirt bike 轻型摩托车 qīngxíng mótuōchē
dirt cheap 极其便宜 jíqí piányi
dirt road 泥路 nílù
2 丑闻 chǒuwén
to dig up dirt on sb 发掘某人的丑闻 fājué mǒurén de chǒuwén

dirty ADJ **1** 肮脏 āngzāng ■ *Could you wash up the dirty dishes in the sink, please?* 请你洗一下水池里的脏盘子，好吗？Qǐng nǐ xǐ yíxià shuǐchílǐ de zāng pánzi, hǎoma? **2** 黄色的 huángsè de, 下流的 xiàliú de ■ *We were disgusted by his dirty jokes.* 他的黄色笑话，让我们感到讨厌。Tā de huángsè xiàohua, ràng wǒmen gǎndao tǎoyàn.
a dirty trick 卑鄙花招 bēibǐ huāzhāo, 下流手段 xiàliú shǒuduàn

disability N 残疾 cánjí, 残障 cánzhàng

disable V 使 [士兵+] 残疾 shǐ [shìbīng+] cánjí, 使 [系统+] 无法使用 shǐ [xìtǒng+] wúfǎ shǐyòng

disabled ADJ 残疾的 cánjí de, 残障的 cánzhàng de

disadvantage N 不利条件 búlì tiáojiàn, 缺陷 quēxiàn

disadvantaged ADJ **1** 处于不利地位的 chǔ yú búlì dìwèi de **2** 社会下层的 shèhuì xiàcéng de, 弱势的 ruòshì de

disagree V 不同意 bù tóngyì ■ *I disagree with your assessment of the situation.* 我不同意你对形势的看法。Wǒ bù tóngyì nǐ duì xíngshì de kànfa.

disagreeable ADJ 讨厌的 tǎoyàn de ■ *The lecturer has some disagreeable mannerisms.* 那位讲师有一些讨厌的习惯性动作。Nà wèi jiǎngshī yǒu yìxiē tǎoyàn de xíguànxìng dòngzuò.

disagreement N 意见不合 yìjiàn bùhé, 分歧 fēnqí

disallow V 不允许 bù yǔnxǔ, 驳回 bóhuí

disappear V **1** 消失 xiāoshī ■ *This species of frog could soon disappear forever.* 这种青蛙可能永远消失。Zhè zhǒng qīngwā kěnéng yǒngyuǎn xiāoshī. **2** 失踪 shīzōng, 丢失 diūshī

disappearance N **1** 消失 xiāoshī **2** 失踪 shīzōng, 丢失 diūshī

disappoint V 使…失望 shǐ…shīwàng

disappointed ADJ 失望的 shīwàng de

disappointing ADJ 令人失望的 lìng rén shīwàng de

disappointment N 失望 shīwàng, 扫兴（的事）sǎoxìng (de shì)

disapproval N 不赞成 bú zànchéng, 反对 fǎnduì

disapprove V 不赞成 bú zànchéng, 反对 fǎnduì

disarm V 解除武装 jiěchú wǔzhuāng

disarmament N 裁军 cáijūn

disarming ADJ 消除敌意的 xiāochú díyì de, 让人感到友好的 ràng rén gǎndào yǒuhǎo de

disarray N 混乱 hùnluàn

disaster N **1** 灾难 zāinàn, 灾害 zāihài **2** 彻底失败 chèdǐ shībài

disastrous ADJ 灾难性的 zāinànxìng de, 彻底失败的 chèdǐ shībài de

disavow V 否认 fǒurèn

disavowal N 否认 fǒurèn

disband V 解体 jiětǐ, 解散 jiěsàn

disbelief N 不相信 bù xiāngxìn, 怀疑 huáiyí

disbelieve V 不相信 bù xiāngxìn, 怀疑 huáiyí

disc See disk

discard I V **1** 扔掉 [+旧衣服] rēngdiào [+jiù yīfú] **2** 打出 [+扑克牌] dǎchū [+pūkèpái] II N **1** 扔掉的东西 rēngdiào de dōngxi, 废物 fèiwù **2** 打出的牌 dǎchū de pái, 废牌 fèi pái

discern V 觉察出 juécháchū, 辨明 biànmíng

discerning ADJ 有眼力的 yǒu yǎnlì de, 识别力很强的 shíbiélì hěn qiáng de

discharge I V **1** 准许…离开 zhǔnxǔ…líkāi
to be discharged from a hospital（病人）出院 (bìngrén) chūyuàn
to be discharged from the Army（军人）退役 (jūnrén) tuìyì
2 排放 [+污水] páifàng [+wūshuǐ]
to discharge polluted water 排放污水 páifàng wūshuǐ
3 履行 [+职责] lǚxíng [+zhízé] II N **1** 准许离开 zhǔnxǔ líkāi **2** 排放 páifàng

disciplinarian N 严格执行纪律者 yángé zhíxíng jìlǜ zhě

discipline I N **1** 纪律 jìlǜ **2** 处分 chǔfēn, 处罚 chǔfá
to face discipline 接受处分 jiēshòu chǔfēn
3 学科 xuékē
core disciplines 重点学科 zhòngdiǎn xuékē, 重点课程 zhòngdiǎn kèchéng
II V **1** 惩罚 chéngfá ■ *How do you discipline your children when they're behaving badly?* 你的孩子表现很不好时，你怎样惩罚他们? Nǐ de háizi biǎoxiàn hěn bù hǎo shí, nǐ zěnyàng chéngfá tāmen? **2** 管教 guǎnjiào

disclaim V 正式否认 zhèngshì fǒurèn

disclaimer N 免责声明 miǎnzé shēngmíng

disclose V 透露 tòulù

disclosure N 透露 tòulù

disco N 迪斯科舞（厅）dísīkēwǔ (tīng)

discotheque N 迪斯科舞厅 dísīkēwǔ tīng

discolor V（使…）褪色／变色 (shǐ…) tuìsè/biànsè

discoloration N 褪色 tuìsè

discomfort N **1** 不舒服 bùshūfú, 不适 búshì **2** 使人不舒服的东西 shǐrén bùshūfú de dōngxī

disconcert v 使…心烦意乱 shǐ...xīn fán yì luàn, 使…窘迫 shǐ...jiǒngpò

disconcerting ADJ 令人心烦意乱的 lìng rén xīn fán yì luàn de, 令人窘迫的 lìng rén jiǒngpò de

disconnected ADJ 无关联的 wú guānlián de, 断开的 duànkāi de

discontent ADJ 不满足的 bù mǎnzú de, 不满意 bù mǎnyì

discontinuation N 停止 tíngzhǐ, 中断 zhōngduàn

discontinue v 停止 tíngzhǐ, 中断 zhōngduàn

discord N 不和 bù hé, 不协调 bù xiétiáo

discount I N 折扣 zhékòu II v 1 [商品+] 打折扣 [shāngpǐn+] dǎ zhékòu, 削价 xuējià 2 不重视 [+某一可能性] búzhòngshì [+mǒu yì kěnéngxìng]

discourage v 1 使…丧失信心 shǐ...sàngshī xìnxīn, 使…灰心 shǐ...huīxīn

discouraged ADJ 灰心的 huīxīn de, 失去信心的 shīqù xìnxīn de

discouraging ADJ 令人丧气的 lìngrén sàngqì de, 令人灰心的 lìngrén huīxīn de

discourse N 1 [严肃的+] 交谈 [yánsù de+] jiāotán, 讨论 tǎolùn 2 [关于国际法的+] 论述 [guānyú guójìfǎ de+] lùnshù 3 [学术的+] 话语 [xuéshù de+] huàyǔ

discourteous ADJ 不礼貌的 bù lǐmào de, 失礼的 shīlǐ de

discourtesy N 失礼 shīlǐ

discover v 发现 fāxiàn ■ *Scientists have discovered a new plant species in the remote jungle.* 科学家在遥远的丛林里发现一个新的植物品种。Kēxuéjiā zài yáoyuǎn de cónglínlǐ fāxiàn yí ge xīn de zhíwù pǐnzhǒng.

discovery N 发现 fāxiàn

discredit I v 使…变得不可信 shǐ...biàn de bù kěxìn, 破坏…的信誉 pòhuài...de xìnyù II N 丧失信誉 sàngshī xìnyù

discreet ADJ 谨慎的 jǐnshèn de, 慎重的 shènzhòng de

discrepancy N 差异 chāyì, 不一致 bù yízhì

discretion N 谨慎 jǐnshèn, 慎重 shènzhòng

discriminate v 歧视 qíshì

discriminating ADJ 有识别能力的 yǒu shíbié nénglì de, 有鉴赏力的 yǒu jiànshǎnglì de

discrimination N 歧视 qíshì

discus N 铁饼 tiěbǐng
discus-throwing 掷铁饼 (运动) zhì tiěbǐng (yùndòng)

discuss v 讨论 tǎolùn, 商讨 shāngtǎo

discussion N 讨论 tǎolùn, 商讨 shāngtǎo

disdain N, v 蔑视 miǎoshì, 轻视 qīngshì

disdainful ADJ 蔑视的 miǎoshì de, 轻视的 qīngshì de

disease N 疾病 jíbìng [M. WD 种 zhǒng]

disembark v 下车 xià chē, 下飞机 xià fēijī, 下船 xià chuán

disenchanted ADJ 感到幻灭的 gǎndào huànmiè de, 失望的 shīwàng de

disenchantment N 幻灭 huànmiè, 失望 shīwàng

disenfranchised ADJ 被剥夺权力的 bèi bōduó quánlì de

disengage v 分离 fēnlí, 摆脱 bǎituō

disengagement N 分离 fēnlí, 摆脱 bǎituō

disentangle v 分清 fēnqīng, 梳理 shūlǐ

disfavor N 不喜欢 bù xǐhuan, 反感 fǎngǎn

disfigure v 毁坏…的容貌 huǐhuài...de róngmào

disfigurement N 毁容 huǐróng

disgrace I N 耻辱 chǐrǔ II v 使…蒙受耻辱 shǐ...méngshòuchǐrǔ, 给…丢脸 gěi...diūliǎn

disgruntled ADJ 不满的 bùmǎn de, 恼火的 nǎohuǒ de

disguise v, N 伪装 wěizhuāng

disgust v 使…厌恶 shǐ...yànwù, 使…极为反感 shǐ...jíwéi fǎngǎn ■ *His cruelty to the dog disgusts me.* 他对狗的残酷行为使我感到厌恶。Tā duì gǒu de cánkù xíngwéi shǐ wǒ gǎndào yànwù.

disgusted ADJ 感到厌恶的 gǎndào yànwù de

disgusting ADJ 使人厌恶的 shǐ rén yànwù de

dish I N 1 菜盘 càipán, 盘子 pánzi
dish rack 碗碟架 wǎndiéjià
dish towel 擦碗碟的干毛巾 cā wǎndié de gān máojīn

2 一盘菜 yì pán cài, 菜 cài ■ *She cooked us a delicious Mexican dish.* 她给我们做了一个美味的墨西哥菜。Tā gěi wǒmen zuòle yí ge měiwèi de Mòxīgē cài. 3 碟形天线 dié xíng tiānxiàn II v 1 (to dish out) 大量分发 dàliàng fēnfā
to dish out unwanted advice 随便提供别人不需要的建议 suíbiàn tígōng biéren bù xūyào de jiànyì

2 (to dish up) 上菜 shàngcài

dishearten v 使…沮丧 shǐ...jǔsàng, 使…灰心 shǐ...huīxīn

disheartened ADJ 沮丧的 jǔsàng de, 灰心的 huīxīn de

disheartening ADJ 令人沮丧的 lìng rén jǔsàng de, 令人灰心的 lìng rén huīxīn de

disheveled ADJ 衣衫凌乱的 yīshān língluàn de, 衣冠不整的 yīguānbùzhěng de

dishonest ADJ 不诚实的 bù chéngshí de, 不老实的 bù lǎoshí de

dishonesty N 不诚实的行为 bù chéngshí de xíngwéi, 欺诈 qīzhà

dishonor I N 耻辱 chǐrǔ II v 使…蒙羞 shǐ...méngxiū, 使…丢脸 shǐ...diūliǎn

dishonorable ADJ 不光彩的 bù guāngcǎi de

dishwasher N 洗碗机 xǐwǎnjī [M. WD 台 tái]

dishwashing detergent N 餐具洗涤剂 cānjù xǐdíjì

dishwashing liquid N 餐具洗涤精 cānjù xǐdíjīng

disillusion v 使…幻灭 shǐ...huànmiè, 使…醒悟 shǐ...xǐngwù

disillusionment N 幻灭 huànmiè, 醒悟 xǐngwù

disinclined ADJ 不愿意 bú yuànyì

disinfect v 给…消毒 gěi…xiāodú

disinfectant N 消毒 xiāodú

disinherit v 剥夺…的继承权 bōduó…de jìchéngquán

disintegrate v 使…分崩离析 shǐ…fēnbēng líxī, 使…瓦解 shǐ…wǎjiě

disintegration N 分崩离析 fēnbēng líxī, 瓦解 wǎjiě

disinterest N 无利益关系 wú lìyì guānxi, 无偏见 wú piānjiàn

disinterested ADJ 无利害关系的 wú lìhài guānxi de, 公正的 gōngzhèng de

disjointed ADJ 不连贯的 bù liánguàn de, 散乱的 sǎnluàn de

disk (disc) N 1 磁盘 cípán
  disk drive 磁盘驱动器 cípán qūdòng qì 2 圆盘 yuánpán

diskette N [计算机+] 软盘 [jìsuànjī+] ruǎnpán

dislike v, N 不喜欢 bù xǐhuan, 讨厌 tǎoyàn

dislocate v 脱位 tuōwèi

dislocation N 脱位 tuōwèi

dislodge v 把…移开 bǎ…yíkāi

disloyal ADJ 不忠诚的 bù zhōngchéng de, 不忠 bù zhōng

dismal ADJ 凄凉的 qīliáng de, 令人忧郁的 lìng rén yōuyù de

dismantle v 1 拆除 [+旧机器] chāichú [+jiù jīqì], 拆开 chāikāi 2 废除 [+旧制度] fèichú [+jiù zhìdù], 取消 qǔxiāo

dismay I N 1 惊恐 jīngkǒng 2 失望 shīwàng, 沮丧 jǔsàng II v 使…失望 shǐ…shīwàng, 使…担忧 shǐ…dānyōu

dismember v 肢解 zhījiě

dismiss v 1 解散 jiěsàn 2 解雇 jiěgù ■ He was dismissed from his job for falsifying his qualifications. 他因为伪造资格而被解雇。Tā yīnwèi wěizào zīgé ér bèi jiěgù. 3 不理会 bù lǐhuì, 不屑一顾 bú xiè yígù

dismissal N 1 解雇 jiěgù 2 不予理会 bùyù lǐhuì

dismissive ADJ 不予理会的 bùyù lǐhuì de

dismount v 1 下马 xià mǎ, 下车 xià chē 2 取下 qǔxià, 卸下 xièxià

disobedience N 不顺从 bú shùncóng, 不听话 bù tīnghuà

disobedient ADJ 不顺从的 bú shùncóng de, 不听话的 bù tīnghuà de

disobey v 不服从 bù fúcóng, 违抗 wéikàng

disorder N 1 混乱 hùnluàn
  to throw … into disorder 使…陷入混乱状态 shǐ…xiànrù hùnluàn zhuàngtài
  2 (身体) 失调 (shēntǐ) shītiáo, 紊乱 wěnluàn, 病 bìng
  digestive disorder 消化系统紊乱 xiāohuàxìtǒng wěnluàn, 消化系统疾病 xiāohuàxìtǒng jíbìng

mental disorder 精神病 jīngshénbìng
  3 (社会) 动乱 (shèhuì) dòngluàn, 骚乱 sāoluàn

disorderly ADJ 破坏公共秩序的 pòhuài gōnggòng zhìxù de, 扰乱治安的 rǎoluàn zhì'ān de

disorganize v 1 打乱 dǎluàn, 扰乱 rǎoluàn 2 使…瓦解 shǐ…wǎjiě

disorganized ADJ 计划不周的 jìhuà bùzhōu de, 毫无计划的 háowú jìhuà de

disoriented ADJ 1 迷失方向的 míshī fāngxiàng de 2 头脑混乱的 tóunǎo hùnluàn de

disown v 与…断绝关系 yǔ…duànjué guānxi

disparage v 说某人的坏话 shuō mǒurén de huàihuà, 贬低 biǎndī

disparate ADJ 完全不同的 wánquán bùtóng de, 不相干的 bùxiānggān de

disparity N 不公平 bùgōngpíng, 差异 chāyì

dispassionate ADJ 客观冷静的 kèguān lěngjìng de

dispatch I v 派遣 pàiqiǎn, 调遣 diàoqiǎn II N 1 派遣 pàiqiǎn, 调遣 diàoqiǎn 2 公文 gōngwén 3 [新闻+] 报道 [xīnwén+] bàodào
  with dispatch 迅速地 xùnsù de

dispel v 驱散 qūsàn, 消除 xiāochú

dispensary N 配药处 pèiyàochù, 药房 yàofáng [M. WD 家 jiā]

dispense v 发放 fāfàng, 分发 fēnfā
  to dispense medicine 配药 pèiyào
  to dispense with 省掉 shěngdiào, 不需要 bù xūyào

dispenser N 自动售货机 zìdòng shòuhuòjī

dispersal N 驱散 qūsàn, 散开 sànkāi

disperse v 驱散 qūsàn, 散开 sànkāi

dispirited ADJ 灰心丧气的 huīxīn sàngqì de

displace v 1 移动 yídòng 2 撤…的职 chè…de zhí 3 取代 qǔdài

displacement N 1 移动 yídòng 2 撤职 chèzhí 3 取代 qǔdài

display I v 1 陈列 chénliè, 展出 zhǎnchū 2 显示 xiǎnshì ■ He displayed no sign of emotion when he was told of his daughter's death. 他被告知女儿的死讯时，没有显示任何表情。Tā bèi gàozhī nǚ'ér de sǐ xùn shí, méiyǒu xiǎnshì rènhé biǎoqíng. II N 1 陈列 chénliè, 展出 zhǎnchū 2 显示 xiǎnshì, 炫耀 xuànyào

displease v 使…不高兴 shǐ…bù gāoxīng, 使…不满意 shǐ…bù mǎnyì

displeased ADJ 不高兴的 bù gāoxīng de, 不满意的 bù mǎnyì de

displeasure N 不悦 búyuè, 不满 bùmǎn

disposable ADJ 1 一次性的 yícìxìng de 2 可支配的 kě zhīpèi de
  disposable income 可支配收入 kězhīpèi shōurù

disposal N 处置 chǔzhì, 处理 chǔlǐ
  at sb's disposal 供某人使用 gōng mǒurén shǐyòng

dispose v 处置 chǔzhì, 处理 chǔlǐ

disposed ADJ 倾向于 qīngxiàng yú, 愿意的 yuànyì de

disposition N 1 [快乐的+] 性情 [kuàilè de+] xìngqíng, 性格 xìnggé 2 处置 [+个人财产] chǔzhì [+gèrén cáichǎn], 出让 chūràng 3 部署 [+军队] bùshǔ [+jūnduì] 4 倾向 [+妥协] qīngxiàng [+tuǒxié], 意向 yìxiàng

dispossess v 剥夺 [+财产] bōduó [+cáichǎn]

disproportionate ADJ 不成比例的 bù chéng bǐlì de, 不相称的 bùxiāngchèn de

disprove v 证明…是虚假的 zhèngmíng…shì xūjiǎ de, 反驳 fǎnbó

dispute I N 争端 zhēngduān, 争议 zhēngyì II v 1 对…提出异议 duì…tíchū yìyì 2 与…争论 yǔ…zhēnglùn

disqualification N 不合格 bùhégé, 不合适 bùhéshì

disqualify v 取消…的资格 qǔxiāo…de zīge

disregard I v 不顾 búgù, 忽视 hūshì II N 无视 wúshì, 忽视 hūshì

disrepair N 失修 shīxiū, 破旧 pòjiù

disreputable ADJ 名声不好的 míngshēng bùhǎo de, 声名狼藉的 shēngmíng lángjí de

disrepute N 坏名声 huài míngshēng

disrespect N 不尊重 bù zūnzhòng, 轻慢无礼 qīngmàn wúlí

disrespectful ADJ 不尊重的 bù zūnzhòng de, 轻慢无礼的 qīngmàn wúlí de

disrupt v 1 扰乱 rǎoluàn 2 中断 zhōngduàn

disruption N 1 扰乱 rǎoluàn 2 中断 zhōngduàn

disruptive ADJ 扰乱的 rǎoluàn de, 捣乱的 dǎoluàn de

dissatisfaction N 不满意 bù mǎnyì, 不满 bùmǎn

dissatisfied ADJ 感到不满意 gǎndào bù mǎnyì

dissect v 解剖 jiěpōu

disseminate v 散布 sànbù, 传播 chuánbō

dissemination N 散布 sànbù, 传播 chuánbō

dissension N 争执 zhēngzhí, 意见不一 yìjiàn bùyī

dissent I N 异议 yìyì II v 持有异议 chíyǒu yìyì

dissenter N 异议分子 yìyì fènzǐ

dissertation N（博士）论文 (bóshì) lùnwén [M. WD 篇 piān]

disservice N 损害 sǔnhài, 帮倒忙 bāngdàománg

dissident I ADJ 持不同政见的 chí bùtóng zhèngjiàn de II N 持不同政见者 chí bùtóng zhèngjiànzhě

dissimilar ADJ 很不相同的 hěn bù xiāngtóng de

dissimilarity N 差异 chāyì, 区别 qūbié

dissipate v 消散 xiāosàn, 消失 xiāoshī

dissociate v 分开 fēnkāi, 分离 fēnlí
to dissociate oneself from 断绝与…的关系 duànjué yǔ…de guānxi

dissociation N 分开 fēnkāi, 分离 fēnlí

dissolute ADJ 放荡的 fàngdàng de

dissolution N [婚约的+] 解除 [hūnyuē de+] jiěchú, 终结 zhōngjié

dissolve v 1 [固体+] 溶解 [gùtǐ+] róngjiě 2 解除 [+婚约] jiěchú [+hūnyuē]

dissuade v 劝阻 quànzǔ

distance N 距离 jùlí
long-distance runner 长跑运动员 chángpǎo yùndòngyuán
from a distance 从远处 cóng yuǎnchù
within walking distance 在可以步行去的距离内 zài kěyǐ bùxíng qù de jùlí nèi

distant ADJ 1 远距离的 yuǎnjùlí de, 遥远 yáoyuǎn 2 疏远的 shūyuǎn de, 冷淡 lěngdàn ■ He appeared distant and impersonal even to his children. 他就是对自己的孩子也很疏远、见外。Tā jiù shì duì zìjǐ de háizi yě hěn shūyuǎn, jiànwài.

distaste N 厌恶 yànwù, 反感 fǎngǎn

distasteful ADJ 令人厌恶的 lìng rén yànwù de, 令人反感的 lìng rén fǎngǎn de

distend v 使…膨胀 shǐ…péngzhàng, 使…肿胀 shǐ…zhǒngzhàng

distill v 1 蒸馏 zhēngliú 2 提炼 tíliàn

distillery N 酿酒厂 niàngjiǔchǎng, 酿酒者 niàngjiǔ zhě

distinct ADJ 明显的 míngxiǎn de, 清清楚楚的 qīngqīng chǔchǔ de

distinction N 1 区别 qūbié 2 殊荣 shūróng, 荣誉 róngyù ■ He achieved distinction in his research field. 他在研究领域获得了荣誉。Tā zài yánjiū lǐngyù huòdéle róngyù.

distinctive ADJ 与众不同的 yǔ zhòng bùtóng de, 特别的 tèbié de

distinguish v 区别 qūbié, 分别 fēnbié

distinguished ADJ 杰出的 jiéchū de, 卓越的 zhuóyuè de

distort v 1 歪曲 [+事实] wāiqū [+shìshí], 扭曲 niǔqū 2 使 [+形象] 失真 shǐ [xíngxiàng+] shīzhēn

distortion N 1 歪曲 wāiqū, 扭曲 niǔqū 2 变形 biànxíng

distract v 1 使…分心 shǐ…fēnxīn 2 使…心烦意乱 shǐ…xīn fán yì luàn

distracted ADJ 心烦意乱的 xīn fán yì luàn de, 心神不定的 xīnshén búdìng de

distress I N 1 （精神上的）痛苦 (jīngshén shàng de) tòngkǔ 2 贫困 pínkùn, 困苦 kùnkǔ
a distress signal 求救信号 qiújiù xìnhào
II v 使…痛苦 shǐ… tòngkǔ, 使…不安 shǐ…bù'ān

distressed ADJ 极其忧虑的 jíqí yōulù de, 十分苦恼的 shífēn kǔnǎo de

distribute v 分配 fēnpèi

distribution N 分配 fēnpèi

distributor N 1 分销商 fēnxiāoshāng 2 配电器 pèidiàn qì

district N 区 qū

shopping district 购物区 gòuwùqū

district attorney 地方检察官 dìfang jiǎncháguān

district court 地方法庭 dìfang fǎtíng

distrust N, V 不信任 bú xìnrèn, 猜疑 cāiyí

disturb V 1 打扰 dǎrǎo, 干扰 gānrǎo

a "Do Not Disturb" sign "请勿打扰" 的牌子 "qǐngwù dǎrǎo" de páizi

2 使…焦虑 shǐ…jiāolǜ, 使…烦恼 shǐ…fánnǎo

mentally disturbed 精神上不正常 jīngshén shàng bùzhèngcháng

disturbance N 1 干扰 [+日常生活] gānrǎo [+rìcháng shēnghuó], 扰乱 rǎoluàn 2 [种族+] 骚乱 [zhǒngzú+] sāoluàn, 动乱 dòngluàn

ditch I N 1 沟渠 gōu qú

drainage ditch 排水沟 páishuǐ gōu

II V 1 开沟渠 kāi gōuqú 2 丢弃 diūqì, 抛弃 pāoqì

dither V 1 犹豫 yóuyù 2 紧张 jǐnzhāng, 慌乱 huāngluàn

ditto N 同上 tóngshàng, 同前 tóngqián

I say ditto. (Ditto.) 我也一样。Wǒ yěyíyàng. 我也是。Wǒ yěshì.

ditty N 小诗 xiǎo shī

diva N 歌剧女主角 gējù nǚzhǔjué, 女歌唱家 nǚ gēchàngjiā

dive I V (PT dived, dove; PP dived) 1 跳水 tiàoshuǐ 2 潜水 qiánshuǐ 3 [飞机+] 俯冲 [fēijī+] fǔchōng II N 1 [股票+] 大幅度下降 [gǔpiào+] dàfúdù xiàjiàng 2 [飞机+] 俯冲 [fēijī+] fǔchōng 3 [守门员+] 扑过去 [shǒuményuán+] pūguòqù

dived See dive

diver N 潜水员 qiánshuǐyuán

diverge V 1 [意见+] 出现分歧 [yìjiàn+] chūxiàn fēnqí 2 [道路+] 分岔 [dàolù+] fēnchà, 分开 fēnkāi

divergence N 分歧 fēnqí, 差异 chāyì

divergent ADJ 分歧很大的 fēnqí hěn dà de, 很不相同的 hěn bù xiāngtóng de

diverse ADJ 多样化的 duōyànghuà de, 各种各样的 gèzhǒng gèyàng de

diversify V 多样化 duōyànghuà, 多元化 duōyuánhuà

diversion N 1 消遣 xiāoqiǎn, 娱乐 yúlè 2 转移 zhuǎnyí, 转向 zhuǎnxiàng 3 转移注意力的事物 zhuǎnyí zhùyìlì de shìwù

diversity N 多样性 duōyàngxìng, 多元状态 duōyuán zhuàngtài

divert V 转移 zhuǎnyí, 转向 zhuǎnxiàng

divide V 1 把…分为 bǎ…fēnwéi, 划分 huàfēn 2 除 chú, 以…除 yǐ chú 3 分配 fēnpèi

dividend N 股息 gǔxī, 红利 hónglì

divider N 1 [公路+] 中间隔离带 [gōnglù+] zhōngjiān gélídài 2 [档案+] 分隔卡 [dàng'àn+] fēngé kǎ

dividers 分线规 fēnxiànguī

divine¹ I ADJ 1 上帝的 Shàngdì de, 神圣的 shénshèng de

divine right 神授之权 shén shòu zhī quán

2 极好的 jíhǎo de, 极妙的 jí miào de

divine² V 发现 fāxiàn, 猜出 cāichū

diving N 潜水 qiánshuǐ

diving board 跳水板 tiàoshuǐbǎn

diving suit 潜水服 qiánshuǐ fú

divinity N 1 神性 shénxìng, 神力 shénlì 2 神学 shénxué

divisible ADJ 1 可分的 kě fēn de 2 可除尽的 kě chújìn de

division N 1 分开 fēnkāi, 划分 huàfēn

division of labor 分工 fēngōng

2 除 chú, 除法 chúfǎ 3 部门 bùmén 4 (体育)级 (tǐyù) jí, 级别 jíbié 5 (军队)师 (jūnduì) shī

air-borne division 空降师 kōngjiàng shī

divisive ADJ 造成不和的 zàochéng bùhé de, 导致分裂的 dǎozhì fēnliè de

divorce V, N 1 离婚 líhūn

divorce settlement 离婚协议 líhūn xiéyì

to file for divorce 提出离婚 tíchū líhūn

2 分开 fēnkāi, 分离 fēnlí

divorcee N 离婚女子 líhūn nǚzǐ

divulge V 泄露 xièlòu, 透露 tòulù

DIY (= do-it-yourself) ABBREV 自己动手做的 zìjǐ dòngshǒu zuò de

dizzy ADJ 头晕 tóuyūn, 眩晕 xuànyùn

DJ (= disc jockey) ABBREV 电台唱片节目主持人 diàntái chàngpiàn jiémù zhǔchírén, 舞厅唱片播放员 wǔtīng chàngpiàn bōfàng yuán

DNA (= deoxyribonucleic acid) ABBREV 脱氧核糖核酸 tuōyǎng hé táng hé suān

do [NEG do not ABBREV don't; 3rd person: does NEG does not ABBREV doesn't. PAST NEG did not ABBREV didn't] (PT did; PP done) V 1 做 zuò, 干 gàn ■ "What are you doing?" "Preparing for dinner." "你在做什么?" "准备晚饭。" "Nǐ zài zuò shénme?" "Zhǔnbèi wǎnfàn." 2 行 xíng, 可以 kěyǐ ■ "Can we go there on foot?" "No, it won't do." "我们可以走去吗?" "不行。" "Wǒmen kěyǐ zǒu qù ma?" "Bù xíng."

to do away with ① 摆脱 bǎituō ② 干掉 [+人] gàndiào [+rén], 杀死 shāsǐ

to do a favor 做好事 zuò hǎoshì, 帮忙 bāngmáng

to do a lot for 有利 yǒulì

to do one's hair/makeup 做头发/化妆 zuò tóufa/huàzhuāng

to do well by sb 善待某人 shàndài mǒurén

to do up ① 系上 [+纽扣] jìshang [+niǔkòu], 扣上 kòushang ② 装修 [+房屋] zhuāngxiū [+fángwū]

to do without 没有…也行 méiyǒu…yěxíng

to have nothing to do with 与…无关 yǔ… wúguān

to have something to do with 与…有关 yǔ… yǒuguān

docile ADJ 温顺的 wēnshùn de, 驯服的 xùnfú de

dock I N 1 码头 mǎtou, 船坞 chuánwù 2 [法庭] 被告席 [fǎtíng] bèigàoxí II v 1 进码头 jìn mǎtou 2 扣 [+工资] kòu [+gōngzī]

docket N 1 诉讼摘录 sùsòng zhāilù 2 议事日程 yìshì rìchéng 3 单据 dānjù

doctor I N 1 医生 yīshēng 2 博士 bóshì (= Dr.) Doctor of Philosophy (Ph.D.) 博士 bóshì II v 1 医治 [+伤口] yīzhì [+shāngkǒu] 2 伪造 [+文件] wěizào [+wénjiàn]

doctrine N 信条 xìntiáo, 主义 zhǔyì

docudrama N 文献影片 wénxiàn yǐngpiàn, 文献片 wénxiànpiàn

document I N 1 文件 wénjiàn 2 (计算机) 文件／文档 (jìsuànjī) wénjiàn/wéndàng II v 1 记录 jìlù 2 [事实+] 证明 [shìshí+] zhèngmíng

documentary N 纪录片 jìlùpiàn

documentation N 1 证明文件 zhèngmíng wénjiàn 2 搜集提供证明文件 sōují tígōng zhèngmíng wénjiàn

dodge I v 躲开 duǒkāi, 避开 bìkāi II N 1 逃避 táobì 2 托词 tuōcí, 脱身伎俩 tuōshēn jìliǎng

doe N 母鹿 mǔ lù [M. WD 只 zhī/头 tóu], 母兔 mǔ tù [M. WD 只 zhī]

does See do

doesn't See do

dog I N 1 狗 gǒu [M. WD 只 zhī/条 tiáo] 2 低劣的东西 dīliè de dōngxi, 蹩脚货 biéjiǎohuò dog-eat-dog 你死我活的 nǐ sǐ wǒ huó de dog collar 狗项圈 gǒu xiàngquān dog paddle 狗爬式游泳 gǒupáshì yóuyǒng dog tag (军人的) 身份牌 (jūnrén de) shēnfen pái to be dog-tired 累得要死 lèi deyàosǐ II v 追随 zhuīsuí, 跟踪 gēnzōng

dog-eared ADJ (书／文件) 折角的 (shū/wénjiàn) zhéjiǎo de, 卷边的 juǎnbiān de

dogged ADJ 顽强的 wánqiáng de, 不屈不挠的 bùqū bùnáo de

doggone, doggone it INTERJ 该死的 gāisǐ de, 去他妈的 qù tāmāde

doggy, doggie N 狗儿 gǒu ér

doggy bag N 剩菜袋 shèngcàidài

doghouse N 狗窝 gǒuwō

dogma N 教条 jiàotiáo

dogmatic ADJ 自以为是的 zì yǐwéi shì de, 武断的 wǔduàn de

do-gooder N (多管闲事的) 慈善家 (duōguǎn xiánshì de) císhànjiā

dogwood N 狗木树 gǒu mù shù [M. WD 棵 kē]

doing N 做的事 zuò de shì to be sb's own doing 自己干的坏事 zìjǐ gàn de huàishì

to take some doing 得花些功夫 děi huā xiē gōngfu

doldrums N 1 [经济+] 萧条 [jīngjì+] xiāotiáo, 低潮 dīcháo in the doldrums [经济+] 处在停滞状态 [jīngjì+] chǔzài tíngzhì zhuàngtài 2 情绪低落 qíngxù dīluò

dole I v (to dole out) 少量地发放 shǎoliàng de fāfàng II N 救济金 jiùjì jīn on the dole 领取救济金 lǐngqǔ jiùjìjīn

doleful ADJ 愁苦的 chóukǔ de, 哀伤的 āishāng de

doll I N 洋娃娃 yángwáwa, 玩偶 wán'ǒu II v (to doll up) 打扮得花枝招展 dǎban dé huāzhī zhāo zhǎn

dollar N 美元 Měiyuán, 元 yuán Australian dollar 澳元 Àoyuán Hong Kong dollar 港币 Gǎngbì Singaporean dollar 新加坡元 Xīnjiāpōyuán

dolphin N 海豚 hǎitún [M. WD 条 tiáo]

domain N 领域 lǐngyù, 领地 lǐngdì

dome N 圆屋顶 yuánwūdǐng, 穹顶 qióngdǐng

domestic ADJ 1 国内的 guónèi de 2 家庭内的 jiātíng nèi de

domesticate v 驯养 xùnyǎng

domesticated ADJ 家养的 jiāyǎng de

domesticity N 家庭生活 jiātíng shēnghuó, 天伦之乐 tiānlúnzhīlè

domicile N 住处 zhùchù

dominance N 优势 yōushì, 统治地位 tǒngzhì dìwèi

dominant ADJ 占优势的 zhàn yōushì de, 主要的 zhǔyào de

dominate v 支配 zhīpèi, 主导 zhǔdǎo

domineering ADJ 专横的 zhuānhèng de, 霸道的 bàdào de

dominion N 1 统治 (权) tǒngzhì (quán) 2 自治领 Zìzhìlǐng

domino N 多米诺骨牌 duōmǐnuògǔpái dominoes 多米诺骨牌游戏 duōmǐnuògǔpái yóuxì

donate v 捐赠 juānzèng, 赠送 zèngsòng

donation N 捐赠 juānzèng

done I See do II ADJ 1 做好了 zuòhǎo le 2 煮好了 zhǔ hǎole It's a done deal. 生米已经煮成熟饭。Shēngmǐ yǐjing zhǔ chéngshú fàn. 木已成舟。Mù yǐ chéng zhōu。

donkey N 驴 (子) lǘ (zi) [M. WD 头 tóu] donkey work 单调乏味的苦差事 dāndiào fáwèi de kǔchāishi

donor N 捐赠者 juānzèngzhě, 捐献者 juānxiàn-zhě

don't See do

donut N See doughnut

doodad N (什么) 小玩意儿 (shénme) xiǎowányìr

doodle

doodle v 乱涂乱写 luàn tú luànxiě

doom I N 1 毁灭 huǐmiè, 失败 shībài 2 (doom and gloom) 一片阴暗 yípiàn yīn'àn, 绝望 juéwàng II v 注定 [+失败／灭亡] zhùdìng [+shībài/mièwáng]
to doom to failure 注定失败 zhùdìng shībài

doomsday N 世界末日 shìjiè mòrì

door N 门 mén [M. WD 扇 shàn/道 dào]
back/front door 后门／前门 hòumén/qiánmén
door to door 挨门挨户 āiménāihù
next door 隔壁 gébì

doorbell N 门铃 ménlíng

doorknob N 球形门把手 qiúxíng ménbà shǒu

doorman N 门卫 ménwèi

doormat N 1 蹭鞋垫 cèngxiédiàn [M. WD 块 kuài] 2 任人欺负的人 rènrén qīfu de rén, 逆来顺受的人 nìlái shùnshòu de rén

doorstep N 门前台阶 mén qián tái jiē

doorway N 出入口 chūrùkǒu

dope I N 1 大麻 dàmá, 毒品 dúpǐn 2 傻瓜 shǎguā 3 内幕消息 nèimù xiāoxi II v 1 [运动员+] 服用兴奋剂 [yùndòngyuán+] fúyòng xīngfènjì 2 服用麻醉剂 fúyòng mázuìjì

dork N 傻瓜 shǎguā

dorm See **dormitory**

dormant ADJ 1 休眠的 [+火山] xiūmián de [+huǒshān], 冬眠的 [+灰熊] dōngmián de [+huī xióng] 2 暂时不用的 [+账户] zànshí bùyòng de [+zhànghù]

dormitory N [学生+] 宿舍 [xuésheng+] sùshè

DOS (= Disk Operating System) ABBREV 磁盘操作系统 cípán cāozuò xìtǒng

dosage N（药物的）剂量（yàowù de）jìliàng, 服用量 fúyòng liáng
recommended dosage（医生）嘱咐的剂量（yīshēng）zhǔfù de jìliàng

dose I N 1 剂量 jìliàng
a lethal dose of sedatives 致命的镇静药剂量 zhìmìng de zhènjìngyào jìliàng
2 一次剂量 yícì jìliàng, 一剂 yí jì
a dose of antibiotics 一剂抗菌素 yí jì kàngjūnsù
3 一回 yìhuí, 一点 yìdiǎn
a dose of reality 一点现实感 yìdiǎn xiànshígǎn
II v 给 [+病人] 服药 gěi [+bìngrén] fú yào

dossier N 档案 dàng'àn [M. WD 份 fèn/件 jiàn]

dot I N 小点儿 xiǎo diǎnr II v 加上点儿 jiāshang diǎnr
dot the i's and cross the t's 在字母"i"上加点儿, 在"t"上加横线 zài zìmǔ "i" shang jiādiǎnr, zài "t" shang jiā héngxiàn, 注意细节 zhùyì xìjié
dotted line 虚线 xūxiàn

dotage N 衰老 shuāilǎo

dot-com ADJ 与…网上公司有关的 yǔ…wǎngshàng gōngsī yǒuguān de

dote v 溺爱 nì'ài, 宠爱 chǒng'ài

double I ADJ 加倍的 jiābèi de
double bass 低音提琴 dīyīntíqín
double date 两对男女同时约会 liǎng duì nánnǚ tóngshí yuēhui
double feature 两部电影同时放映 liǎng bù diànyǐng tóngshí fàngyìng
double vision 叠影 diéyǐng, 复视 fù shì
double whammy 双重打击 shuāngchóng dǎjī, 祸不单行 huò bù dān xíng
2 双人的 shuāngrén de, 双重的 shuāngchóng de
double standard 双重标准 shuāngchóng biāozhǔn
II v 加倍 jiābèi III N 1 两倍 liǎngbèi, 双份 shuāngfèn 2 替身演员 tìshēnyǎnyuán IV ADV 双倍 shuāng bèi
to see double 看到叠影 kàndào diéyǐng

double-breasted ADJ 双排钮口的 shuāngpái niǔkǒu de

double-check v 一再检查 yízài jiǎnchá, 复查 fùchá

double-header N 一天连续两场棒球赛 yìtiān liánxù liǎngchǎng bàngqiúsài

double-park v 并排停放 bìngpái tíngfàng

double-spaced ADJ 双倍行距的 shuāng bèi hángjù de

double-talk N 含糊其词的话 hánhu qí cí dehuà

doublethink N 相互矛盾的想法 xiānghù máodùn de xiǎngfǎ

double-time I N 双倍工资 shuāng bèi gōngzī II ADV 以加倍的速度 yǐ jiābèi de sùdù, 尽可能快 jìnkěnéng kuài

doubly ADV 加倍地 jiābèi de

doubt I N 怀疑 huáiyí
reasonable doubt 合理疑点 hélǐ yídiǎn
without doubt 毫无疑问 háowú yíwèn
II v 怀疑 huáiyí, 不相信 bù xiāngxìn

doubtful ADJ 大有疑问的 dàyǒu yíwèn de, 不确定的 bú quèdìng de

doubtless ADV 无疑地 wúyí de

dough N 1 生面团 shēngmiàn tuán 2 钱 qián

doughnut, donut N 炸面圈 zhámiànquān, 多福饼 duōfúbǐng

dour ADJ 1 脸色阴郁的 liǎnsè yīnyù de, 毫无笑意的 háowú xiàoyì de 2 严厉的 yánlì de

douse v 1 泼水 pōshuǐ, 浇水 jiāoshuǐ 2 把…浸入水中 bǎ…jìnrù shuǐ zhōng 3 灭火 mièhuǒ

dove¹ N 1 鸽子 gēzi [M. WD 只 zhī] 2 鸽派人物 gēpài rénwù

dove² v See **dive**

dowdy ADJ（女子穿着）不时髦的（nǚzǐ chuānzhuó）bùshí máo de, 过时的 guòshíde, 土气的 tǔqìde

down I ADV 下 xià, 下面 xiàmiàn

down payment 首期付款 shǒuqī fùkuǎn, 定金 dìngjīn
II PREP 向下 xiàngxià ■ *He walked down the stairs.* 他走下楼梯。Tā zǒuxia lóutī. **III** v **1** 喝下 [+一大杯啤酒] hēxià [+yí dà bēi píjiǔ], 吞下 [+三个汉堡包] tūnxià [+sānge hànbǎobāo] **2** 击败 [+球队] jībài [+qiúduì], 打倒 dǎdǎo **IV** N 羽绒 yǔróng, 绒毛 róngmáo

down-and-out ADJ 穷愁潦倒的 qióngchóu liǎodǎo de, 穷困的 qióngkùn de

downcast ADJ 垂头丧气的 chuítóu sàngqì de, 沮丧的 jǔsàng de

downer N **1** 令人扫兴的人（或事）lìng rén sǎoxìng de rén (huò shì) **2** 镇静药 zhènjìngyào

downfall N 垮台 kuǎtái, 破产 pòchǎn

downgrade v **1** 降职 jiàng zhí **2** 减弱 jiǎnruò, 贬低 biǎndī

downhill I ADV 向山下 xiàng shān xià
to go downhill 走下坡路 zǒu xiàpōlù, 每况愈下 měi kuàng yù xià
II ADJ 下坡的 xiàpō de
to be all downhill 从此一帆风顺 cóngcǐ yìfān fēng shùn

download v 下载 xiàzài

downplay v 把…看得不重要 bǎ…kàn dé bú zhòngyào

downpour N 倾盆大雨 qīngpén dàyǔ [M. WD 场 cháng]

downright ADV 十足的 shízú de, 完全的 wánquán de

downriver ADV （在）下游 (zài) xiàyóu

downside N 不利方面 bùlì fāngmiàn

downsize v 精简裁员 jīngjiǎn cáiyuán

downspout N 水落管 shuǐluòguǎn [M. WD 条 tiáo], 排水管 páishuǐguǎn [M. WD 条 tiáo]

Down's syndrome N 唐氏综合征 tángshì zōnghézhēng

downstairs I ADV （在）楼下 (zài) lóuxià **II** ADJ 楼下的 lóuxià de

downstate ADJ, ADV [州的+] 南部地区 [zhōu de+] nánbù dìqū

downtime N 停机期间 tíngjī qījiān

down-to-earth ADJ 脚踏实地的 jiǎo tà shídì de, 实实在在的 shíshí zàizài de

downtown I N 市中心 shìzhōngxīn **II** ADJ, ADV 市中心的／地 shìzhōngxīn de

downtrodden ADJ 被践踏的 bèi jiàntà de, 受压迫的 shòuyā pò de

downturn N [经济+] 下滑期 [jīngjì+] xiàhuáqī, 衰退期 shuāituìqī

downward, downwards I ADV 向下 xiàngxià, 朝下 cháoxià **II** ADJ 向下的 xiàngxià de

downwind I ADV （在）下风 (zài) xiàfēng **II** ADJ 下风的 xiàfēng de

dowry N 嫁妆 jiàzhuang [M. WD 份 fèn]

doze v 打瞌睡 dǎ kēshuì
to doze off （不知不觉）打盹 (bùzhī bùjué) dǎ dǔn

dozen N 一打 yì dá, 十二（个）shí'èr (ge)
baker's dozen 一打加一个 yìdá jiā yíge, 十三个 shísān ge
dozens of 几十 jǐshí, 好多 hǎoduō

Dr. (= Doctor) ABBREV 博士 bóshì, 医生 yīshēng

drab ADJ **1** 单调乏味的 dāndiào fáwèi de **2** 暗淡的 àndàn de

draconian ADJ 严厉的 yánlì de, 严酷的 yánkù de

draft N **1** 草案 cǎo'àn
final draft 定稿 dìnggǎo
2 征兵制 zhēngbīngzhì
draft dodger 逃避兵役者 táobì bīngyì zhě
3 选拔（运动员）xuǎnbá (yùndòngyuán)
draft pick 选拔进职业队的运动员 xuǎnbá jìn zhíyè duì de yùndòngyuán
4 冷风 lěngfēng **5** 汇票 huìpiào **II** v **1** 起草 qǐcǎo **2** 征召（入伍）zhēngzhāo (rùwǔ) **3** 选拔 xuǎnbá, 挑选 tiāoxuǎn

draft beer N 散装啤酒 sǎnzhuāng píjiǔ

draftsman, draftwoman N **1** 绘图员 huìtú yuán, 制图员 zhìtúyuán **2** 法案起草人 fǎ'àn qǐcǎorén

drafty ADJ 透风的 tòufēng de

drag I v **1** 拖 tuō, 拉 lā, 拽 zhuài **II** N **1** 乏味的人（或事）fáwèi de rén (huò shì) **2** 累赘 léizhuì

dragon N 龙 lóng [M. WD 条 tiáo]

dragonfly N 蜻蜓 qīngtíng

drag race N 短程汽车赛 duǎnchéng qìchē sài

drain I v **1** 排水 páishuǐ **2** 使…精疲力尽 shǐ…jīngpí lìjìn **3** 喝完 hē wán **II** N 下水道 xiàshuǐdào [M. WD 条 tiáo], 下水管 xiàshuǐguǎn [M. WD 条 tiáo]
to be a drain on 对…消耗很大 duì…xiāohào hěn dà
down the drain 浪费掉 làngfèi diào, 一无收获 yìwú shōuhuò

drainage N **1** 排水 páishuǐ **2** 排水系统 páishuǐ xìtǒng

drain-board N 滴水板 dīshuǐ bǎn

drained ADJ 精疲力尽的 jīngpí lìjìn de

drama N 戏剧 xìjù
drama class 戏剧课 xìjù kè
drama group 戏剧小组 xìjù xiǎozǔ

dramatic ADJ **1** 戏剧的 xìjù de **2** 戏剧性的 xìjùxìng de, 惊人的 jīngrén de ■ *Since the beginning of the year dramatic changes have taken place in the economy.* 自从今年年初，经济发生了惊人的变化。Zìcóng jīnnián niánchū, jīngjì fāshēng le jīngrén de biànhuà.

dramatics N 夸张做作的举止 kuāzhāng zuòzuo de jǔzhǐ

dramatist N 剧作家 jùzuòjiā

dramatize v 把…改变成戏剧 bǎ…gǎibiànchéng xìjù

drank

drank See **drink**

drape v 披挂 pīguà, 披盖 pīgài

drapery N 1 厚窗帘 hòu chuānglián [M. WD 块 kuài] 2 打褶的布料 dǎzhě de bùliào

drapes N 厚窗帘 hòu chuānglián [M. WD 块 kuài]

drastic ADJ 激烈的 jīliè de, 严厉的 yánlì de

draw I v (PT **drew**; PP **drawn**) 1 画 huà
to draw a line in the sand 警告 jǐnggào
2 拉 lā, 拔 bá 3 吸引 [+注意力] xīyǐn [+zhùyìlì]
4 领取 [+救济金] lǐngqǔ [+jiùjìjīn] 5 抽签 chōuqiān II N 1 平局 píngjú 2 抽奖 chōujiǎng
3 具有吸引力的 (或地方) jùyǒu xīyǐnlì de (huò dìfāng)

drawback N 缺点 quēdiǎn

drawbridge N 吊桥 diàoqiáo [M. WD 座 zuò]

drawer N 抽屉 chōutì

drawing N 铅笔画 qiānbǐhuà [M. WD 幅 fú], 素描 sùmiáo [M. WD 幅 fú]
drawing board 制图板 zhìtúbǎn

drawl I v 拖长声调慢吞吞地说 tuōcháng shēngdiào màntūntūn de shuō II N 拖长声调慢吞吞说话 tuōcháng shēngdiào màntūntūn shuōhuà

drawn[1] ADJ 苍白憔悴的 cāngbái qiáocuì de

drawn[2] v See **draw**

drawn-out ADJ 冗长的 rǒngcháng de, 拖长的 tuōcháng de

dread N, v 惧怕 jùpà, 担忧 dānyōu

dreadful ADJ 可怕的 kěpà de, 令人担忧的 lìng rén dānyōu de

dreadlocks N 长发辫 cháng fàbiàn [M. WD 条 tiáo]

dream I N 1 梦 mèng, 梦境 mèngjìng 2 梦想 mèngxiǎng, 理想 lǐxiǎng
a dream house 理想的住宅 lǐxiǎng de zhùzhái
a dream come true 梦想成真 mèngxiǎng chéngzhēn
II v (PT & PP **dreamed**, **dreamt**) 做梦 zuòmèng
to dream up 虚构出 xūgòu chū

dreamed, dreamt See **dream**

dreamer N 空想家 kōngxiǎngjiā

dreamy ADJ 1 如梦的 [+感觉] rú mèng de [+gǎnjué], 梦幻的 mènghuàn de 2 爱幻想的 [+小女孩] ài huànxiǎng de [+xiǎonǚ hái]

dreary ADJ 1 乏味的 [+讲座] fáwèi de [+jiǎngzuò] 2 沉闷的 [+气氛] chénmèn de [+qìfen], 阴沉的 [+天气] yīnchén de [+tiānqì]

dredge v 挖掘 wājué, 疏浚 shūjùn

dredger N 挖掘机 wājuéjī

dregs N 渣滓 zhāzǐ

drench v 使…湿透 shǐ…shītòu

dress I N 女装 nǚzhuāng [M. WD 套 tào], 连衣裙 liányīqún [M. WD 件 jiàn] II v 1 穿衣服 chuān yīfú
to dress down ① 穿得比平时随便 chuān dé bǐ píng shí suíbiàn ② 训斥 xùnchì
to dress up 打扮 dǎban
2 包扎 [+伤口] bāozā [+shāngkǒu] 3 给 [+蔬菜] 加调料 gěi [+ shūcài] jiā tiáoliào III ADJ 1 正式 场合穿的 zhèngshì chǎnghé chuān de 2 服装 的 fúzhuāng de
dress code 服装要求 fúzhuāng yāoqiú
dress rehearsal 彩排 cǎipái

dresser N 1 梳妆台 shūzhuāngtái 2 穿着 [+时髦／邋遢] 的人 chuānzhuó [+shímáo/lāta] de rén

dressing N 1 穿衣 chuān yī 2 包扎用品 bāozā yòngpǐn, 敷料 fūliào 3 调料 tiáoliào
dressing gown 晨衣 chén yī
dressing room [剧院+] 化妆室 [jùyuàn+] huàzhuāngshì, [体育场+] 更衣室 [tǐyùchǎng+] gēngyīshì

dressmaker N [女装+] 裁缝 [nǚzhuāng+] cáifeng

dressy ADJ 时髦的 shímáo de, 漂亮的 piàoliang de

drew See **draw**

drib v 滴 dī, 点滴 diǎndī
in dribs and drabs 点点滴滴地 diǎndiǎn dīdìdì de, 零星地 língxīng de

dribble v 1 流 (口水) liú (kǒushuǐ), 淌 (口水) tǎng (kǒushuǐ) 2 运 (球) yùn (qiú)

drift I N 1 潮流 piāoliú, 流动 liúdòng 2 雪堆 xuě duī, 沙堆 shā duī II v 潮流 piāoliú, 流动 liúdòng
to drift apart [人和人+] 渐渐疏远 [rén hé rén+] jiànjiàn shūyuǎn

drifter N 漂泊者 piāobózhě, 流浪者 liúlàngzhě

driftwood N 漂流来的木头 piāoliú láide mùtou [M. WD 段 duàn]

drill I N 1 钻孔机 zuānkǒngjī 2 操练 cāoliàn 3 演习 yǎnxí
fire drill 消防演习 xiāofángyǎnxí
II v 1 钻孔 zuānkǒng 2 训练 xùnliàn, 操练 cāoliàn

drink I N 1 饮料 yǐnliào [M. WD 杯 bēi/份 fèn]
cold drink 冷饮 lěngyǐn
2 喝酒 hējiǔ, 酗酒 xùjiǔ II v (PT **drank**; PP **drunk**) 1 喝 hē 2 喝酒 hējiǔ, 酗酒 xùjiǔ

drinker N 饮酒者 yǐnjiǔzhě, 酒鬼 jiǔguǐ

drinking fountain N 喷泉式饮水器 pēnquán shì yǐnshuǐqì

drinking problem N 酗酒问题 xùjiǔ wèntí

drip I v 滴 dī, 滴下 dī xià II N 1 滴 dī, 滴水声 dīshuǐ shēng 2 静脉滴注器 jìngmài dīzhùqì
drip-feed 静脉滴注 jìngmài dī zhù

drip-dry ADJ 滴干 dī gān

drive I v (PT **drove**; PP **driven**) 1 驾驶 jiàshǐ, 开车 kāichē 2 用车送 yòngchē sòng ■ Can you drive me home? 可以开车送我回家吗？Kěyǐ kāichē sòng wǒ huíjiā ma? 3 赶 gǎn, 驱赶 qūgǎn II N 1 开车 kāichē, 乘车 chéngchē
to drive … crazy/nuts 逼得…发疯 bīdé… fāfēng, 逼得…受不了 bī dé…shòubuliǎo
2 本能要求 běnnéng yāoqiú
sex drive 性本能 xìng běnnéng, 性欲 xìngyù

364

3 运动 yùndòng

membership drive 发展新会员运动 fāzhǎn xīnhuì yuán yùndòng

4 干劲 gànjìn, 魄力 pòlì **5**（计算机）驱动器（jìsuànjī）qūdòngqì

drive-in ADJ 免下车的 miǎn xiàchē de

a drive-in restaurant 免下车餐馆 miǎn xiàchē cānguǎn

drivel N 胡说八道 húshuō bādào

driven[1] See **drink**

driven[2] ADJ 有进取心的 yǒu jìnqǔxín de

driver N 驾驶员 jiàshǐyuán, 司机 sījī

driver's license 驾驶执照 jiàshǐ zhízhào

driveway N（私人）车道（sīrén）chēdào [M. WD 条 tiáo]

drizzle I N 细雨 xìyǔ, 毛毛雨 máomaoyǔ II V 下细雨 xiàxì yǔ, 下毛毛雨 xià máomaoyǔ

droll ADJ 滑稽可笑的 gǔjī kěxiào de, 古里古怪的 gǔ lǐ gǔguài de

drone I V 发出嗡嗡声 fāchū wēngwēngshēng II N 1 嗡嗡声 wēngwēngshēng **2** 工蜂 gōngfēng, 雄蜂 xióngfēng **3** 无线电遥控设备 wúxiàndiàn yáokòng shèbèi, 无人驾驶飞机 wúrén jiàshǐ fēijī

drool I V 流口水 liú kǒushuǐ II N 口水 kǒushuǐ

droop V 低垂 dīchuí, 下垂 xiàchuí

drop I V 1 落下 luòxià **2** 下车 xiàchē ■ *"Where shall I drop you?"* "我在哪里让你下车?" "Wǒ zài nǎlǐ ràng nǐ xiàchē?" **3** 下降 xiàjiàng **4** 无意中／突然说出 wúyìzhōng/tūrán shuōchū

to drop a bomb 突然说出惊人消息 tūrán shuōchū jīngrén xiāoxi

to drop a hint 露口风 lù kǒufēng, 暗示 ànshì

5 将…除名 jiāng…chúmíng, 开除 kāichú

to drop anchor 抛锚 pāomáo

to drop the ball 失手犯错 shī shǒu fàn cuò

to drop by/in 顺道拜访 shùndào bàifǎng

to drop dead 突然死亡 huran shiwang

II N 1 水滴 shuǐdī

a drop in the bucket 杯水车薪 bēishuǐ chēxīn

eye/ear/nose drops 眼／耳朵／鼻药水 yǎn/ěrduo/bí yàoshuǐ

2 下降 xiàjiàng **3** 空投 kōng tóu

air drops of relief supplies 空投救济物资 kōng tóu jiùjì wùzī

dropout N 1 中途辍学的人 zhōngtú chuòxué de rén **2** 逃避社会者 táobì shèhuìzhě, 遁世者 dùnshìzhě

dropper N 滴管 dīguǎn

droppings N [鸟+] 屎 [niǎo+] shǐ, [动物+] 粪便 [dòngwù+] fènbiàn

drought N 干旱 gānhàn, 旱灾 hànzāi

drove[1] V See **drive**

drove[2] N 1 一群牲畜 yìqún shēngchù **2** 一大群人 yí dà qún rén

drown V 1 淹死 yānsǐ **2** 浸泡 jìnpào

drowsy ADJ 昏昏欲睡的 hūnhūn yùshuì de

drudge I N 做繁重无聊工作的人 zuò fánzhòng wúliáo gōngzuò de rén II V 做繁重无聊的工作 zuò fánzhòng wúliáo gōngzuò

drudgery N 繁重无聊的工作 fánzhòng wúliáo de gōngzuò, 苦工 kǔgōng

drug I N 1 毒品 dúpǐn

drug addict 吸毒者 xīdúzhě

drug dealing/trafficking 贩毒 fàndú

Drug Enforcement Administration（美国）麻醉药物强制管理局 (Měiguó) mázuì yàowù qiángzhì guǎnlǐjú

drug rehabilitation 吸毒康复 xīdú kāngfù, 戒毒 jiè dú

hard drugs 剧毒品 jùdúpǐn

to do drugs 吸毒 xīdú

2 药 yào, 药品 yàopǐn II V 1（用药）麻醉（yòngyào）mázuì **2** 投放麻醉药 tóufàng mázuìyào

drugstore N 1 杂货店 záhuòdiàn [M. WD 家 jiā] **2** 药店 yaodiàn [M. WD 家 jiā]

drum I N 1 鼓 gǔ [M. WD 面 miàn]

drum major 游行乐队的指挥 yóuxíng yuèduì de zhǐhuī

2 大油桶 dà yóutǒng II V [击+] 鼓 [jī+] gǔ

drummer N 鼓手 gǔshǒu

drumstick N 1 鸡腿 jītuǐ [M. WD 条 tiáo] **2** 鼓槌 gǔchuí [M. WD 根 gēn]

drunk I V See **drink** II ADJ 喝醉 hēzuì

drunk driver 酒后驾车的人 jiǔhòu jiàchē de rén

drunk driving, drink driving 酒后驾车 jiǔhòu jiàchē

III N 醉鬼 zuìguǐ, 酒鬼 jiǔguǐ

drunkard N 醉鬼 zuìguǐ, 酒鬼 jiǔguǐ

drunken ADJ 喝醉酒的 hēzuì jiǔ de

dry I ADJ 1 干 gān, 干燥 gānzào

dry clean 干洗 gānxǐ

dry cleaner 干洗店 gānxǐdiàn

dry goods ① 干货 gānhuò ② 纺织品 fǎngzhīpǐn

2 干 [+葡萄酒] gān [+pútaojiǔ] **3** 乏味的 [+课程] fáwèi de [+kèchéng] II V 使…变干 shǐ…biàn gān, 晒干 shàigān

dryer, drier N 烘干机 hōnggānjī [M. WD 台 tái]

dual ADJ 双重的 shuāngchóng de

dual nationality 双重国籍 shuāngchóng guójí

dub V 1 给…起绰号 gěi…qǐ chuòhào **2** [给电影+] 配音 [gěi diànyǐng+] pèiyīn

dubious ADJ 可疑的 kěyí de, 不可靠的 bùkěkào de

duchess N 女公爵 nǚgōngjué [M. WD 位 wéi], 公爵夫人 Gōngjué Fūrén [M. WD 位 wéi]

duck I N 1 鸭子 yāzi [M. WD 只 zhī] II V 1 低下头躲避 [+打过来的球] dīxià tóu duǒbì [+dǎguòlái de qiú], 弯腰躲避 wānyāo duǒbì, 闪开 shǎnkai

duckling N 小鸭子 xiǎo yāzi [M. WD 只 zhī]

duct N 管道 guǎndào [M. WD 条 tiáo/根 gēn]

dud ADJ 废物 fèiwù

dude N 男人 nánren

dude ranch 度假牧场 dùjià mùchǎng

due I ADJ 1 到期的 dàoqī de

due date ① 预产期 yùchǎnqī ② 最后期限 zuìhòu qīxiàn

2 应付的 yìngfu de

due process, due process of law 合法的诉讼程序 héfǎ de sùsòng chéngxù

due to 由于 yóuyú

II N 应有的权益 yīngyǒu de quányì

dues 会员费 huìyuánfèi

duel N 1 [体育运动+] 激烈的竞争 [tǐyù yùndòng+] jīliè de jìngzhēng 2 唇枪舌剑的争论 chúnqiāng shéjiàn de zhēnglùn

duet N 二重唱 èrchóngchàng, 二重奏 èrchóngzòu

duffel bag N 圆筒旅行袋 yuántǒng lǚxíngdài

dug See **dig**

dugout N 1 [棒球场边底的+] 休息棚 [bàngqiú cháng biān dǐ de +] xiūxipéng 2 独木舟 dúmùzhōu [M. WD 只 zhī]

duke N 公爵 Gōngjué [M. WD 位 wèi]

dull ADJ 1 沉闷的 [+电影] chénmèn de [+diànyǐng] 2 愚笨的 [+孩子] yúbèn de [+háizi] 3 钝的 [+刀] dùn de [+dāo] 4 隐约的 [+疼痛] yǐnyīn de [+téngtòng]

duly ADV 恰当地 qiàdàng de, 应当地 yīngdāng de

dumb I ADJ 1 愚蠢的 yúchǔn de 2 哑巴的 yǎba de II v 把…搞得过于简单 bǎ…gǎode guòyú jiǎndān

dumbbell N 哑铃 yǎlíng [M. WD 只 zhī/副 fù]

dumbfound v 使…惊呆 shǐ…jīng dāi

dumbfounded ADJ 惊讶得不知所措 jīngyà dé bù zhī suǒ cuò, 惊讶极了 jīngyà jíle

dummy I N 1 笨蛋 bèndàn 2 人体模型 réntǐ móxíng 3 仿制样品 fǎngzhì yàngpǐn II ADJ 仿真的 fǎngzhēn de, 假的 jiǎde

dump I v 1 丢掉 [+垃圾] diūdiào [+lājī], 丢弃 [+男朋友] diūqì [+nánpéngyou] 2 倾销 [+商品] qīngxiāo [+shāngpǐn], 倾倒 qīngdǎo 3 [电脑+] 转存 [+文件] [diànnǎo+] zhuǎncún [+wénjiàn]

II N 1 垃圾场 lājī chǎng 2 军需品临时堆放处 jūnxūpǐn línshí duīfàngchù

dumpster N 装垃圾的大铁桶 zhuāng lājī de dà tiětǒng

dump truck N 翻斗车 fāndǒuchē [M. WD 辆 liàng]

dunce N 迟钝的学生 chídùn de xuésheng, 愚笨的人 yúbèn de rén

dune N 沙丘 shāqiū

dung N 牛粪 niúfèn, [动物的+] 粪便 [dòngwù de+] fènbiàn

dungeon N 地牢 dìláo

dunk v 1 把 [+食物] 浸一下 bǎ [+shíwù] jìn yíxià 2 [篮球+] 扣篮 [lánqiú+] kòulán

duo N 两人表演 liǎng rénbiǎo yǎn

dupe I v 欺骗 qīpiàn, 哄骗 hǒngpiàn II N 受骗上当的人 shòupiàn shàngdàng de rén

duplex N 二连式住宅 èrliánshì zhùzhái

duplicate I N 复制品 fùzhìpǐn, 副本 fùběn

duplicate of a key 配制的钥匙 pèizhì de yàoshi

in duplicate 一设两份 yí shè liǎngfèn

II v 复制 fùzhì

duplicity N 欺诈 qīzhà

durable ADJ 耐用的 nàiyòng de

duration N 持续时间 chíxù shíjiān

duress N 胁迫 xiépò, 威逼 wēibī

during PREP 在…期间 zài…qījiān ■ He called during my absence and left a message on the phone. 我不在的时候，他打来电话，在电话上留了话。Wǒ bùzài de shíhou, tā dǎlai diànhuà, zài diànhuàshang liúle huà.

dusk N 黄昏时分 huánghūn shífèn

from dawn till dusk 从早到晚 cóng zǎo dào wǎn

dust I N 灰尘 huīchén

dust jacket [书+] 护封 [shū+] hùfēng

II v 1 擦去灰尘 cā qù huīchén 2 在…上撒 [+粉状物] zài…shàng sǎ [+fēnzhuàngwù]

duster N 掸子 dǎnzi [M. WD 把 bǎ], 抹布 mābù [M. WD 块 kuài]

dustpan N 簸箕 bòjī

dusty ADJ 满是灰尘的 mǎn shì huīchén de

Dutch I N 1 荷兰语 Hèlányǔ 2 荷兰人 Hèlánrén

II ADJ 荷兰的 hèlán de

to go Dutch 各付各的帐 gè fù gè de zhàng, 平摊费用 píng tān fèiyòng

dutiful ADJ 尽职的 jìnzhí de, 顺从的 shùncóng de

duty N 1 责任 zérèn, 义务 yìwù

sense of duty 责任感 zérènggǎn

garbage duty（日常）倒垃圾的工作 (rìcháng) dào lájī de gōngzuò

2 税 shuì

customs duty 关税 guānshuì

duty-free ADJ 免税 miǎnshuì

DVD (= digital video disk) ABBREV 数字视频光盘 shùzì shìpín guāngpán, DVD

dwarf I N 小矮人 xiǎo'àirén, 侏儒 zhūrú II v 使…显得微小 shǐ…xiǎnde wēixiǎo

dwell (PT & PP **dwelled, dwelt**) v 居住 jūzhù

to dwell on (sth) 老是想到 lǎoshì xiǎngdào, 说个没完 shuō gè méiwán

dwelled, dwelt See **dwell**

dweller N 居住在…的人／动物 jūzhù zài…de rén/dòngwù

dwindle v 越来越少 yuèláiyuè shǎo, 越来越小 yuèláiyuè xiǎo

dye I N 染料 rǎnliào II v 染 rǎn

dyed-in-the-wool ADJ 根深蒂固的 gēnshēn dìgù de, 十足的 shízú de

dynamic ADJ 精力充沛的 jīnglì chōngpèi de, 生气勃勃的 shēngqì bóbó de

dynamics N 动力学 dònglìxué, 力学 lìxué

dynamism N 动力 dònglì, 活力 huólì

dynamite I N 炸药 zhàyào II v（用炸药）炸毁 (yòng zhàyào) zhàhuǐ

dynamo N 1 直流发电机 zhíliú fādiànjī 2 精力充沛的人 jīnglì chōngpèi de rén 3 强大的动力 qiángdà de dònglì

dynasty N 朝代 cháodài, 王朝 wángcháo

dysentery N 痢疾 lìji

dysfunctional ADJ 1 违法正常规范的 wéifǎ zhèngcháng guīfàn de 2 有功能障碍的 yǒu gōngnéng zhàng'ài de

dyslexia N 诵读困难症 sòngdú kùnnan zhēng, 诵读困难 sòngdú kùnnan

E

each ADJ, PRON 各个 gè gè, 每 měi
each other 彼此 bǐcǐ, 互相 hùxiāng

eager ADJ 热切 rèqiè, 热衷 rèzhōng ■ *Children are often eager to show what they can do.* 小孩子常常热切地想显示自己的能力。Xiǎoháizi chángcháng rèqiède xiǎng xiǎnshì zìjǐ de nénglì.

eagle N 鹰 yīng [M. WD 只 zhī], 老鹰 lǎoyīng [M. WD 只 zhī]

eagle-eyed ADJ 目光锐利的 mùguāng ruìlì de

ear¹ N 1 耳 ěr, 耳朵 ěrduo 2 听觉 tīngjué, 听力 tīnglì
to be all ears 全神贯注地听 quánshén guànzhù de tīng
to be out on one's ears 被迫离开 bèipò líkāi
to go in one ear and out the other 一只耳朵进, 一只耳朵出 yì zhī ěrduo jìn, yì zhī ěrduǒ chū, 只当耳边风 zhǐdàng ěrbiānfēng
to have a good ear for languages 语言听力的能力很强 yǔyán tīnglì de nénglì hěn qiáng

ear² N [麦+] 穗 [mài+] suì

eardrum N 耳膜 ěrmó

earlobe N 耳垂 ěrchuí

early I ADJ 1 很早的 hěn zǎo de
The early bird catches the worm. 早起的鸟儿吃到虫。(→ 捷足先登。) Zǎoqǐ de niǎor chīdao chóng. (→ Jiézú xiāndēng.)
2 初期 chūqī ■ *It is still quite cold in early spring.* 早春时节还挺冷。Zǎochūn shíjié hái tǐng lěng.
II ADV 1 早 zǎo 2 早期 zǎoqī, 初期 chūqī ■ *He had a very hard time early in life.* 他早期生活很艰苦。Tā zǎoqī shēnghuó hěn jiānkǔ.

earmark I v 指定…作为专门款项 zhǐdìng…

作为 zuòwéi 专门款项 zhuānmén kuǎnxiàng II N 特征 tèzhēng, 标记 biāojì

earmuff N 耳套 ěrtào [M. WD 副 fù]

earn v 1 挣钱 zhèngqián, 赚钱 zhuànqián
earned income 劳动收入 láodòng shōurù, 工资 gōngzī
to earn a living 谋生 móushēng
to earn one's keep 做工换取食宿 zuògōng huànqǔ shísù
2 获得 huòdé, 赢得 yíngdé

earnest I ADJ 认真的 rènzhēn de II N 严肃认真 yánsù rènzhēn
in earnest 认真地 rènzhēn de

earnings N 工资 gōngzī, 薪水 xīnshui

earphones N 耳机 ěrjī [M. WD 副 fù]

earplugs N 耳塞 ěrsāi

earring N 耳环 ěrhuán [M. WD 副 fù]

earshot N 可听见的距离 kě tīngjiàn de jùlí
within earshot 在听得到的范围 zài tīngdé dào de fànwéi
out of earshot 在听不到的范围 zài tīngbùdào de fànwéi

earsplitting ADJ 震耳欲聋的 zhèn ěr yù lóng de

earth N 1 地球 dìqiú 2 泥土 nítǔ
what on earth 到底 dàodǐ, 究竟 jiūjìng ■ *Why on earth did he drink and drive?* 他到底为什么要酒后驾车? Tā dàodǐ wèishénme yào jiǔhòu jiàchē?
3 世界 shìjiè 4 大地 dàdì, 地面 dìmian
to come down to earth 回到现实 huídào xiànshí

earthly ADJ 世俗的 shìsú de, 尘世的 chénshì de
no earthly reason 毫无理由 háowú lǐyóu

earthquake N 地震 dìzhèn

earth-shattering ADJ 惊天动地的 jīngtiān dòngdì de

earthworm N 蚯蚓 qiūyǐn [M. WD 条 tiáo]

earthy ADJ 1 自然的 zìrán de, 朴实的 pǔshí de 2 泥土的 nítǔ de

ease I N 1（工作）容易 (gōngzuò) róngyì
ease of use 使用方便 shǐyòng fāngbiàn
2（生活）安逸 (shēnghuó) ānyì, 舒适 shūshì
at ease 无拘无束 wújū wúshù, 轻松自在 qīngsōng zìzài
ill at ease 不自在 bú zìzài
3（军事口令）稍息 (jūnshì kǒulìng) shāoxī
II v 减轻 [+工作负担] jiǎnqīng [+gōngzuò fùdān], 缓和 [+紧张局势] huǎnhé [+jǐnzhāng júshì]

easel N 画架 huàjià

easily ADV 1 容易地 róngyì de, 不费力地 bú fèilì de 2 明显地 míngxiǎn de, 没有疑问 méiyǒu yíwèn

east I N 东 dōng, 东面 dōngmiàn II ADJ 东的 dōng de, 东面 dōngmiàn III ADV 朝东 cháodōng, 向东 xiàngdōng
the East 东方 dōngfāng
the Middle East 中东 Zhōngdōng

eastbound ADJ 向东的 xiàng dōng de
Easter N 复活节 Fùhuójié
Easter Bunny 复活节兔子 Fùhuójié tùzi
Easter egg 复活节彩蛋 Fùhuójié cǎidàn
eastern ADJ 东面的 dōngmiànde, 东方的
dōngfāngde
Eastern Europe 东欧 Dōng'ōu
easternmost ADJ 最东面的 zuì dōngmiàn de
eastward ADJ 朝东面的 cháo dōngmiàn de
easy I ADJ 1 容易 róngyì
Easier said than done. 说说容易做起来难。
Shuōshuo róngyì zuòqilái nán.
to take it easy 别着急, 慢慢来。Bié zháojí,
mànmàn lái.
easy money 很容易赚的钱 hěn róngyì zhuàn
de qián, 来得容易的钱 láide róngyì de qián
2 轻松的 qīngsōng de, 方便的 fāngbiàn de
I'm easy. 我随便。Wǒ suíbiàn. 都可以。Dōu kěyǐ.
easy listening 休闲音乐 xiūxián yīnyuè
II ADV 放松 fàngsōng
easygoing ADJ 随和的 suíhe de, 心平气和的
xīnpíngqìhe de
eat (PT **ate**; PP **eaten**) V 吃 chī, 吃饭 chīfàn
eating disorder 饮食失调症 yǐnshí shītiáo zhēng
to eat one's heart out 嫉妒 jìdù, 难过 nánguò
to eat one's word 承认说错了话 chéngrèn
shuōcuò le huà
eaten See **eat**
eaves N 屋檐 wūyán
eavesdrop V 偷听 tōutīng, 窃听 qiètīng
ebb N, V 退潮 tuìcháo
ebb and flow 起伏 qǐfú, 涨落 zhǎngluò
to be at a low ebb 处于低潮 chǔyú dīcháo
to ebb away 衰退 shuāituì, 逐渐减少 zhújiàn
jiǎnshǎo
ebony I N 乌木 wūmù, 黑檀 hēitán II ADJ 乌黑的
wūhēi de
e-book N 电子书（籍）diànzǐ shū (jí)
ebullience N 欣喜 xīnxǐ
ebullient ADJ 兴高采烈的 xìnggāo cǎiliè de
e-business N 电子商务 diànzǐ shāngwù
eccentric I ADJ 怪诞的 guàidàn de II N 怪诞的人
guàidàn de rén, 怪人 guàirén
eccentricity N 怪诞 guàidàn
echo I N 1 回声 huíshēng, 回音 huíyīn 2（意见／
感情的）共鸣（yìjiàn/gǎnqíng de）gòngmíng
II V 1 发出回声 fāchū huíshēng, 回响 huíxiǎng
2 附和 fùhè, 重复 chóngfù
éclair N 巧克力酥卷 qiǎokèlì sūjuǎn
eclipse I N 日食 rìshí, 月食 yuèshí II V 1 遮蔽 [+日
光或月光] zhēbì [+rìguāng huò yuèguāng]
2 胜过 shèngguò
ecological ADJ 生态的 shēngtài de
ecologist N 生态学家 shēngtàixuéjiā
ecology N 生态（学）shēngtài (xué)

e-commerce N 电子商务 diànzǐ shāngwù, 电子商
业 diànzǐ shāngyè
economic ADJ 经济的 jīngjì de ■ *This region
enjoyed good economic growth last year.* 这个地
区去年经济增长良好。Zhè ge dìqū qùnián jīngjì
zēngzhǎng liánghǎo.
economical ADJ 节省的 jiéshěng de, 节俭的
jiéjiǎn de
economics N 1 经济学 jīngjìxué 2 经济意义 jīngjì
yìyì, 经济因素 jīngjì yīnsù
economist N 经济学家 jīngjìxuéjiā
economize V 节省 jiéshěng
economy I N 1 经济 jīngjì
market economy 市场经济 shìchǎng jīngjì
service-based economy 以服务行业为基础的经
济 yǐ fúwù hángyè wéi jīchǔ de jīngjì
2 节省 jiéshěng, 节约 jiéyuē ■ *It is not good
economy to buy shoddy goods.* 买劣质商品不是省
钱的好办法。Mǎi lièzhì shāngpǐn bú shì shěngqiá
de hǎo bànfǎ. II ADJ 便宜的 piányi de, 经济的
jīngjì de
economy class 经济舱 jīngjìcāng
economy pack 经济包 jīngjìbāo
ecosystem N 生态系统 shēngtài xìtǒng
ecstasy N 1 狂喜 kuángxǐ 2 摇头丸 yáotóuwán
ecumenical ADJ 支持基督教各教派大联合的
zhīchí Jīdūjiào gè jiàopài dà liánhé de
eczema N 湿疹 shīzhěn
eddy I N 漩涡 xuánwō II V 起漩涡 qǐ xuánwō
edge I N 1 边 biān, 边缘 biānyuán 2 优势 yōushì,
竞争力 jìngzhēnglì
to gain a competitive edge 获得竞争优势
huòdé jìngzhēng yōushì
II V 1 加边 jiā biān 2 慢慢移动 mànmàn yídòng
3 渐渐发展 jiànjiàn fāzhǎn
edgewise ADV 侧着 cèzhe, 斜着 xiézhe
edgy ADJ 紧张不安的 jǐnzhāng bù'ān de
edible ADJ 可以食用的 kěyǐ shíyòng de
edict N 法令 fǎlìng [M. WD 条 tiáo]
edification N 启示 qǐshì
edifice N 宏伟的建筑物 hóngwěi de jiànzhùwù
[M. WD 幢 zhuàng], 大楼 dàlóu [M. WD 幢 zhuàng]
edify V 教诲 jiàohuì, 开导 kāidǎo
edit V 编辑 biānjí
edition N 1 版本 bǎnběn 2 一集 yì jí, 一期 yìqī
first edition (of a book)（一本书的）第一版（yì
běn shū de）dìyībǎn
editor N 编辑 biānjí
editorial N 社论 shèlùn [M. WD 篇 piān]
educate V 教育 jiàoyù, 训练 xùnliàn
educated ADJ 受过教育的 shòuguo jiàoyù de, 有
知识的 yǒu zhīshi de ■ *She is an highly intelligen
and well-educated young woman.* 她是一位智力很
高、受过良好教育的年轻女子。Tā shì yí wèi zhìlì
hěn gāo、shòuguo liánghǎo jiàoyù de niánqīng nǚzǐ

ducation N 教育 jiàoyù

ducational ADJ 教育的 jiàoyù de, 有教育意义的 yǒu jiàoyù yìyì de

dutainment N 教育娱乐电影/电视节目/电脑软件 jiàoyù yúlè diànyǐng/diànshì jiémù/diànnǎo ruǎnjiàn

el N 鳗 mán [M. WD 条 tiáo], 鳗鱼 mányú [M. WD 条 tiáo]

erie ADJ 怪异而恐怖的 guàiyì ér kǒngbù de

ffect I N 效果 xiàoguǒ, 作用 zuòyòng ■ *Physical exercise has brought about a marked effect on his health.* 体育锻炼给他的健康带来明显效果。Tǐyù duànliàn gěi tā de jiànkāng dàilai míngxiǎn xiàoguǒ.

side effect (药品的)副作用 (yàopǐn de) fùzuòyòng

special effects (电影)特技 (diànyǐng) tèjì

to come into effect 生效 shēngxiào

II v 引起 yǐnqǐ, 造成 zàochéng

to effect immediate change 立即引起变化 lìjí yǐnqǐ biànhuà

ffective ADJ 有效的 yǒuxiào de

to be/become effective 生效 shēngxiào ■ *The new law will become effective on April 1st.* 新法律将在四月一日生效。Xīn fǎlǜ jiāng zài sìyuè yī rì shēngxiào.

ffects N 私人物品 sīrén wùpǐn [M. WD 件 jiàn]

ffeminate ADJ 女人气的 nǚrénqì de, 娘娘腔的 niángniangqiāng de

ffervescent ADJ 冒气泡的 mào qìpào de

fficiency N 效率 xiàolǜ

fficient ADJ 高效率的 gāoxiàolǜ de

ffigy N 模拟像 mónǐ xiàng

ffluent N 污水 wūshuǐ, 废液 fèiyè

ffort N 1 努力 nǔlì, 气力 qìlì 2 费力 fèilì, 痛苦的事 tòngkǔ de shì ■ *For him, every step was an effort.* 对他来说，每走一步都很费力。Duì tā láishuō, měi zǒu yíbù dōu hěn fèilì.

ffortless ADJ 不费力的 bú fèilì de

ffusive ADJ (过于)热情的 (guòyú) rèqíng de, 热情奔放的 rèqíng bēnfàng de

FL (= English as a Foreign Language) ABBREV 作为外语的英语(教学) zuòwéi wàiyǔ de Yīngyǔ (jiàoxué)

.g. (= for example) ABBREV 例如 lìrú

gg I N 1 蛋 dàn, 鸡蛋 jīdàn 2 卵 luǎn

egg cell 卵细胞 luǎnxìbāo

II v 怂恿 sǒngyǒng, 鼓动 gǔdòng

gghead N 学究 xuéjiū, 学问家 xuéwèn jiā

ggplant N 茄子 qiézi

ggshell N 蛋壳 dànké

go N 自我 zìwǒ

an ego trip 自我表现的行为 zìwǒ biǎoxiàn de xíngwéi

to have a big ego 自以为很了不起 zì yǐwéi hěn liǎobuqǐ

egoism See egotism

egotism N 自我主义 zìwǒ zhǔyì

egotistical ADJ 自高自大的 zìgāo zìdà de, 自负的 zìfù de

egregious ADJ 极坏的 jí huài de, 令人震惊的 lìng rén zhènjīng de

eight NUM 八 bā, 8

eighteen NUM 十八 shíbā, 18

eighteenth NUM 第十八 dì shíbā

eighth NUM 第八 dì bā

either I ADJ (of two) 任何一个 rènhé yí ge, 两个都 liǎng ge dōu II PRON (of two) 任何一个 rènhé yí ge ■ *You can write on either of the topics.* 你可以在两个题目中写任何一个。Nǐ kěyǐ zài liǎng ge tímù zhōng xiě rènhé yí ge. III ADV 也(不) yě (bù)

either … or … …或者… …huòzhě…, 不是…就是… bú shì…jiùshì…

ejaculate v 射精 shèjīng

eject v 弹出 dàn chū, 推出 tuīchū

eke v (to eke out) 勉强维持 (生计) miǎnqiǎng wéichí (shēngjì)

elaborate I ADJ 精心制作的 jīngxīn zhìzuò de, 精心设计的 jīngxīn shèjì de II v 详细说明 xiángxì shuōmíng

elapse v (时间)过去 (shíjiān) guòqù, 流逝 liúshì

elastic I ADJ 1 有弹性的 yǒu tánxìng de 2 有伸缩性的 [+计划] yǒu shēnsuōxìng de [+jìhuà] II N 橡皮圈 xiàngpíquān, 松紧带 sōngjǐndài

elasticity N 弹性 tánxìng

elated ADJ 欣喜的 xīnxǐ de

elation N 欣喜 xīnxǐ

elbow I N 1 肘 zhǒu, 肘部 zhǒu bù 2 衣服的肘部 yīfu de zhǒu bù II v 用肘挤开 yòng zhǒu jǐ kāi

elder I ADJ 年长的 niánzhǎng de

elder brother 哥哥 gēge

elder sister 姐姐 jiějie

II N 长者 zhǎngzhě, 长辈 zhǎngbèi

elderly ADJ 老年的 lǎonián de, 上了年纪的 shàngle niánjì de

elderly man/gentleman 老先生 lǎoxiānsheng

elderly woman/lady 老太太 lǎotàitai

elect I v 1 选举 [+国会议员] xuǎnjǔ [+guóhuì yìyuán]

president-elect 当选总统 dāngxuǎn zǒngtǒng

2 选择 xuǎnzé II ADJ 当选了的 dāngxuǎnle de

governer-elect 当选州长 dāngxuǎn zhōuzhǎng, 候任州长 hòurèn zhōuzhǎng

election N 选举 xuǎnjǔ ■ *It was the first time a free and fair election was held in that country.* 这是这个国家第一次举行自由而公正的选举。Zhè shì zhè ge guójiā dì yī cì jǔxíng zìyóu ér gōngzhèng de xuǎnjǔ.

elective I N 选修课 xuǎnxiūkè [M. WD 门 mén]

II ADJ 1 选举产生的 [+代表] xuǎnjǔ chǎnshēng

de [+dàibiǎo] **2** 选择性的 [+治疗] xuǎnzéxìng de [+zhìliáo], 非必需的 [+课程] fēi bìxū de [+kèchéng]

electoral ADJ 与选举有关的 yǔ xuǎnjǔ yǒuguān de
electoral college 总统选举团 zǒngtǒng xuǎnjǔ tuán

electorate N 全体选民 quántǐ xuǎnmín

electric ADJ **1** 电的 diàn de, 电器的 diànqì de
electric chair 电椅 diànyǐ
2 激动人心的 jīdòng rénxīn de

electrical ADJ 电的 diàn de, 电力的 diànlì de

electrician N 电工 diàngōng

electricity N **1** 电 diàn **2** 极其激动的情绪 jíqí jīdòng de qíngxù, 激情 jīqíng

electrify V 使 [+铁路系统] 电气化 shǐ [+tiělù xìtǒng] diànqìhuà, 供电 gōngdiàn **2** 使 [+听众] 万分激动 shǐ [+tīngzhòng] wànfēn jīdòng

electrocute V **1** 触电身亡 chùdiàn shēnwáng **2** 用电刑处死 yòng diànxíng chǔsǐ

electrode N 电极 diànjí

electrolysis N 电蚀除去毛发 diànshí chúqù máofà

electron N 电子 diànzǐ

electronic ADJ 电子的 diànzǐ de, 用电子操作的 yòng diànzǐ cāozuò de
electronic funds transfer 电子资金转账 diànzǐ zījīn zhuǎnzhàng

electronics N **1** [学习+] 电子学 [xuéxí+] diànzǐxué **2** [发展+] 电子工业 [fāzhǎn+] diànzǐ gōngyè **3** [购买+] 电子设备 [gòumǎi +] diànzǐ shèbèi

elegance N 优雅 yōuyǎ, 高雅 gāoyǎ

elegant ADJ 优雅的 yōuyǎ de, 高雅的 gāoyǎ de

elegy N 挽歌 wǎngē [M. WD 首 shǒu/曲 qū], 哀歌 āigē

element N **1** 元素 yuánsù [M. WD 种 zhǒng] **2** 因素 yīnsù, 成份 chéngfèn
to be in one's element 适得其所 shì dé qí suǒ
the elements 恶劣天气 èliè tiānqì

elemental ADJ 最基本的 zuì jīběn de

elementary ADJ **1** 初级的 chūjí de
elementary school 小学 xiǎoxué
2 基本的 jīběn de
an elementary right 基本的权利 jīběn de quánlì

elephant N 象 xiàng [M. WD 头 tóu], 大象 dàxiàng [M. WD 头 tóu]

elevate V 使···上升 shǐ···shàngshēng, 提升 tíshēng

elevated ADJ **1** 高出地面的 gāochū dìmiàn de
an elevated highway 高架公路 gāojià gōnglù
2 偏高的 piāngāo de

elevator N 电梯 diàntī [M. WD 部 bù], 升降机 shēngjiàngjī [M. WD 部 bù]

eleven NUM 十一 shíyī, 11

eleventh NUM 第十一 dì shíyī
at the eleventh hour 最后一刻 zuìhòu yíkè

elf N 小精灵 xiǎojīnglíng

elicit V 引出 yǐnchū, 套出 tàochū
to elicit a response 得到回应 dédào huíyìng

eligible ADJ 有资格的 yǒu zīgé de **2** 合适的 [+婚姻对象] héshì de [+hūnyīn duìxiàng]

eliminate V **1** 消除 [+分歧] xiāochú [+fēnqí], 消灭 xiāomiè **2** 淘汰 [+选手] táotài [+xuǎnshǒu]

elite I N 精英 jīngyīng II ADJ 精锐的 jīngruì de, 杰出的 jiéchū de
elite troops 精锐部队 jīngruì bùduì

elitism N 精英主义 jīngyīng zhǔyì

elitist ADJ 精英的 jīngyīng de

elixir N 灵丹妙药 língdān miàoyào

elk N 驼鹿 tuólù [M. WD 头 tóu], 麋 mí [M. WD 头 tóu]

ellipse N 椭圆 tuǒyuán

ellipsis N **1** 省略 shěnglüè **2** 省略号 shěnglüèhào (...)

elliptical ADJ 椭圆的 tuǒyuán de

elm N 榆树 yúshù [M. WD 棵 kē]

elongate V 使···变得瘦长 shǐ···biàn de shòucháng, 拉长 lācháng

elongated ADJ 瘦长的 shòucháng de

elope V 私奔 sībēn

eloquence N 雄辩 xióngbiàn, 好口才 hǎo kǒucái

eloquent ADJ 雄辩的 xióngbiàn de, 口才极好的 kǒucái jíhǎo de

else ADV 别的 biéde, 其他的 qítā de

elsewhere ADV 别的地方 biéde dìfang, 其他地方 qítā dìfang ■ Sorry, we don't have this brand. Please look elsewhere. 对不起，我们没有这种牌子。请上别的地方看看。Duìbuqǐ, wǒmen méiyǒu zhè zhǒng páizi. Qǐng shàng biéde dìfang kànkan.

elucidate V 阐明 chǎnmíng, 解释清楚 jiěshì qīngchu

elude V 逃避 táobì, 躲避 duǒbì

elusive ADJ **1** 很难捕捉的 [+猎物] hěn nán bǔzhuō de [+lièwù] **2** 难以说清的 [+词义] nányǐ shuōqīng de [+cíyì]

emaciated ADJ 消瘦的 xiāoshòu de, 憔悴的 qiáocuì de

email, e-mail (= electronic mail) I ABBREV 电子邮件 diànzǐ yóujiàn, 伊妹儿 yī mèir
e-mail address 电子邮件地址 diànzǐ yóujiàn dìzhǐ
II V 给···发电子邮件 gěi···fā diànzǐ yóujiàn

emanate V 来自 láizì, 发自 fāzì

emancipate V 解放 jiěfàng

emancipated ADJ 解放了的 jiěfàngle de

embalm V 做防腐处理 zuò fángfǔ chǔlǐ

embankment N 堤岸 dī'àn [M. WD 条 tiáo], 堤围 dīwéi [M. WD 条 tiáo]

embargo N, V 禁运 jìnyùn

embark V **1** 上飞机 shàng fēijī, 上船 shàng chuán **2** 出发 chūfā, 启程 qǐchéng

to embark on sth 开始做某事 kāishǐ zuò mǒushì
embarrass v 使…难堪 shǐ … nánkān, 使…难为情
shǐ…nánwéiqíng
embarrassed ADJ 难为情 nánwéiqíng, 尴尬 gāngà
embassy N 大使馆 dàshǐguǎn
the American embassy in Beijing 美国驻北京大
使馆 Měiguó zhù Běijīng dàshǐguǎn
embattled ADJ 1 被 (敌人) 包围的 bèi (dírén) bāowéi de 2 困难重重的 kùnnan chóngchóng de
embed v 1 插入 chārù 2 深植 shēn zhí
embellish v 1 装饰 zhuāngshì, 修饰 xiūshì 2 给
[+故事] 添枝加叶 gěi [gùshi+] tiān zhī jiā yè
ember N 余烬 yújìn
embezzle v 贪污 tānwū, 侵吞 qīntūn
embezzler N 贪污犯 tānwūfàn, 侵吞公款的人
qīntūn gōngkuǎn de rén
embittered ADJ 怨恨的 yuànhèn de, 怨愤的
yuànfèn de
emblazon v 印 yìn, 印上 yìn shàng
emblem N 标志 biāozhì, 象征 xiàngzhēng
embodiment N 化身 huàshēn, 体现 tǐxiàn
embody v 1 体现 tǐxiàn 2 包涵 bāokuò
emboss v 用浮雕图案装饰 yòng fúdiāo tú'àn
zhuāngshì
embrace v 1 拥抱 [+朋友] yōngbào [+péngyou]
2 采纳 [+建议] cǎinà [+jiànyì], 接受 jiēshòu
embroider v 1 绣 xiù, 刺绣 cìxiù 2 给 [+故事] 添油
加醋 gěi [+gùshi] tiān yóu jiā cù
embroiled ADJ 被卷入 bèi juǎnrù
embryo N 胚胎 pēitāi
embryonic ADJ 处于萌芽阶段的 chǔyú méngyá
jiēduàn de, 刚起步的 gāng qǐbù de
emcee (ABBREV **mc**) N 司仪 sīyí
emerald N 翡翠 fěicuì, 绿宝石 lǜbǎoshí
emerge v 显露 xiǎnlù, 出现 chūxiàn
emergency N 紧急情况 jǐnjí qíngkuàng
emergency landing 紧急降落 jǐnjí jiàngluò
emergency medical technician (EMT) 急救医师
jíjiù yīshī
emergency room (ER) 急救室 jíjiùshì, 急诊室
jízhěnshì
emergency services 紧急应变部门 jǐnjí yìngbiàn
bùmén
emergent ADJ 新出现的 xīn chūxiàn de
emeritus ADJ 荣誉的 róngyù de
professor emeritus 荣誉退休教授 róngyù tuìxiū
jiàoshòu
emigrant N (移居外国的) 移民 (yíjū wàiguó de)
yímín
emigrate v (向外) 移民 (xiàngwài) yímín
eminent ADJ 著名的 zhùmíng de, 杰出的 jiéchū
de
eminent domain (美国) 政府征用土地权
(Měiguó) zhèngfǔ zhēngyòng tǔdì quán
emirate N (阿拉伯) 酋长国 (Ālābó) qiúzhǎngguó

emissary N 使者 shǐzhě, 特使 tèshǐ
emission N 排气 páiqì, 排放物 páifàng wù
emit v 发出 fāchū
e-money N 电子货币 diànzǐ huòbì
emotion N 感情 gǎnqíng
emotional ADJ 1 感情的 gǎnqíng de
emotional quotient (EQ) 情商 qíngshāng
2 情绪激动的 [+球赛观众] qíngxù jīdòng de
[+qiúsài guānzhòng], 感情用事的 gǎnqíng
yòngshì de
emotive ADJ 使人激动的 shǐ rén jīdòng de
empathize v 有同感 yǒu tónggǎn
empathy N 同感 tónggǎn
emperor N 皇帝 huángdì [M. WD 位 wéi]
emphasis N 1 重点 zhòngdiǎn 2 重要性 zhòngyàoxìng
to give/place emphasis on 重视 zhòngshì, 强调
qiángdiào
emphasize v 强调 qiángdiào ■ Our teacher
emphasizes the importance of daily practice of
the language. 我们的老师强调每天练习语言的重
要性。Wǒmen de lǎoshī qiángdiào měitiān liànxí
yǔyán de zhòngyàoxìng.
emphatic ADJ 强调的 qiángdiào de, 着重的
zhuózhòng de
emphysema N 肺气肿 fèiqìzhǒng
empire N 帝国 dìguó
empirical ADJ 经验的 jīngyàn de, 实验的 shíyàn
de
employ v 1 雇用 gùyòng, 聘用 pìnyòng 2 使用
shǐyòng ■ Computers are now extensively employed in film-making. 现在在电影制作中广泛使用
电脑。Xiànzài zài diànyǐng zhìzuò zhōng guǎngfàn
shǐyòng diànnǎo.
employee N 雇员 gùyuán
employer N 雇主 gùzhǔ
employment N 1 就业 jiùyè ■ Is full employment
an achievable goal? 全部就业是一个能到达的
目标吗？Quánbù jiùyè shì yí ge néng dàodá de
mùbiāo ma? 2 使用 shǐyòng
emporium N 大百货商场 dà bǎihuò shāngchǎng
empower v 给…权力 gěi…quánlì, 使…有权 shǐ…
yǒuquán
empress N 女皇 nǚhuáng [M. WD 位 wéi], 皇后
Huánghòu [M. WD 位 wéi]
emptiness N 1 空虚 (的感觉) kōngxū (de
gǎnjué) 2 空旷 kōngkuàng
empty ADJ 1 空 kōng, 空的 kōng de 2 空洞的
kōngdòng de, 空虚的 kōngxū de ■ The mayor's
speech is nothing but empty words. 市长演讲只是
一些空话。Shìzhǎng yǎnjiǎng zhǐ shì yìxiē kōnghuà.
empty-handed ADJ 两手空空的 liǎngshǒu
kōngkōng de, 一无所获的 yīwú suǒ huò de
emulate v 1 仿效 fǎngxiào, 模仿 mófǎng 2 仿真
fǎngzhēn

enable v 使…能够 shǐ…nénggòu

enact v 制定 [+法规] zhìdìng [+fǎguī]

enamel N 1 搪瓷 tángcí 2 珐琅质 fàlángzhì

enamored ADJ 迷恋 míliàn, 喜爱 xǐ'ài

encase v 包住 bāozhù

enchanted ADJ 1 被施了魔法的 [+镜子] bèi shī le mófǎ de [+jìngzi] 2 陶醉的 [+情人] táozuì de [+qíngrén]

enchanting ADJ 令人陶醉的 lìng rén táozuì de

encircle v 围绕 wéirào, 环绕 huánrào

enclave N 聚居地 jùjūdì

enclose v 1 附上 fùshang ■ *Enclosed please find a check for $100.* 现附上一百元支票。Xiàn fùshang yì bǎi yuán zhīpiào. 2 围住 wéizhù

enclosure N 1 围场 wéichǎng, 圈地 quāndì 2 (信中) 附件 (xìnzhōng) fùjiàn

encompass v 1 包括 bāokuò, 包含 bāohán 2 围绕 wéirào, 围住 wéizhù

encore I N 加演的节目 jiā yǎn de jiémù II INTERJ 再来一个 zài lái yí gè

encounter I v (意外) 遇到 (yìwài) yùdào II N 相遇 xiāngyù, 遭遇 zāoyù
a close encounter 近距离遭遇 jìnjùlí zāoyù

encourage v 鼓励 gǔlì, 支持 zhīchí

encouraging ADJ 令人鼓舞的 lìngrén gǔwǔ de, 鼓舞人心的 gǔwǔ rénxīn de

encroach v 侵占 qīnzhàn, 蚕食 cánshí

encrusted ADJ 覆盖着硬壳的 fùgài qiáng yìngké de

encrypt v 给 [+计算机] 加密 gěi [+jìsuànjī] jiāmì

encumber v 阻碍 zǔ'ài, 妨碍 fáng'ài

encumbrance N 阻碍 zǔ'ài, 妨碍 fáng'ài

encyclopedia N 百科全书 bǎikē quánshū

end I N 1 尽头 jìntóu
end zone 球门区 qiúménqū
2 结局 jiéjú, 结束 jiéshù 3 目的 mùdì ■ *The end justifies the means.* 只要达到目的, 可以不择手段。Zhǐyào dádào mùdì, kěyǐ bù zé shǒuduàn.
to make ends meet 收支相抵 shōuzhī xiāngdǐ
II v 结束 jiéshù
All's well that ends well. 结果好才是一切都好。Jiéguǒ hǎo cái shì yíqiè dōu hǎo.

endanger v 使…处于危险 shǐ…chǔyú wēixiǎn, 危及 wēijí
an endangered species 濒危物种 bīnwēi wùzhǒng

endear v 使…受欢迎 shǐ…shòu huānyíng

endearing ADJ 惹人喜爱的 rě rén xǐ'ài de

endearment N 亲爱的言行 shì ài de yánxíng
a term of endearment 爱称 àichēng

endeavor I N 努力 nǔlì, 行动 xíngdòng
human endeavor 人类活动 rénlèi huódòng
II v 努力 nǔlì

endemic ADJ 地方性的 [+疾病] dìfāngxìng de [+jibing]

ending N 结局 jiéjú, 结尾 jiéwěi

endless ADJ 没完没了的 méiwán méiliǎo de, 无休止的 wú xiūzhǐ de

endorse v 1 赞同 [+行动计划] zàntóng [+xíngdòng jìhuà], 支持 zhīchí 2 背书 [+支票] bèishū [+zhīpiào] 3 为 [+产品] 代言 wèi [+chǎnpǐn] dàiyán
be endowed with 天赋 [+以才能] tiānfù [+yǐ cáinéng], 赋予 fùyǔ

endowment N 1 捐助 juānzhù, 捐助物 juānzhùwù 2 (音乐+) 天赋 [yīnyuè+] tiānfù

endurance N 忍耐力 rěnnàilì, 耐力 nàilì

endure v 1 忍耐 rěnnài, 忍受 rěn shòu 2 持续 (下去) chíxù (xiàqù)

enduring ADJ 持久的 chíjiǔ de

enemy N 敌人 dírén ■ *With friends like that, who needs enemies?* 有那样的朋友, 还需要敌人吗？Yǒu nàyàng de péngyou, hái xūyào dírén ma?
arch enemy 头号敌人 tóuhào dírén, 大敌 dàdí

energetic ADJ 精力充沛的 jīnglì chōngpèi de

energy N 1 精力 jīnglì, 活力 huólì 2 能 néng, 能量 néngliàng
solar/atomic energy 太阳/原子能 tàiyáng/yuánzǐnéng

enforce v (强制) 执行 (qiángzhì) zhíxíng, 实施 shíshī

enforcer N 1 执法者 zhífǎzhě 2 "打手" 球员 "dǎshou" qiúyuán

enfranchise v 给予选举权 jǐyǔ xuǎnjǔ quán

engage v 1 聘用 pìnyòng 2 吸引 [+兴趣] xīyǐn [+xìqu] 3 与 [+敌军] 交战 yǔ [+díjūn] jiāozhàn

engaged ADJ 1 订了婚的 dìngle hūn de ■ *Jane's got engaged to a naval officer.* 珍妮和一位海军军官订了婚。Zhēnnī hé yíwèi hǎijūn jūnguān dìngle hūn. 2 (电话) 占线 (diànhuà) zhànxiàn

engagement N 1 订婚 dìnghūn
engagement ring 订婚戒指 dìnghūn jièzhǐ
2 约会 yuēhui
a previous engagement 已经订好的约会 yǐjing dìnghǎode yuēhui
3 (军队) 交战 (jūnduì) jiāozhàn

engaging ADJ 迷人的 mírén de, 动人的 dòngrén de

engender v 引起 yǐnqǐ, 导致 dǎozhì

engine N 1 引擎 yǐnqíng, 发动机 fādòngjī 2 机车 jīchē
fire engine 消防车 xiāofángchē

engineer N 1 工程师 gōngchéngshī
civil/electronics/software engineer 土木/电子/软件工程师 tǔmù/diànzǐ/ruǎnjiàn gōngchéngshī
2 轮机员 lúnjīyuán, 火车司机 huǒchē sījī

engineering N 工程 gōngchéng, 工程师行业 gōngchéngshī hángyè

hydraulic engineering 水利工程 shuǐlì gōngchéng

electrical engineering 电机工程 diànjī gōngchéng

English I N **1** 英语 Yīngyǔ **2** 英格兰人 Yīnggélánrén, 英国人 Yīngguórén
American English 美式英语 Měishì Yīngyǔ
British English 英式英语 Yīngshì Yīngyǔ
II ADJ **1** 英格兰的 Yīnggélán de, 英国的 Yīngguó de **2** 英语的 Yīngyǔ de

engrave v 雕刻 diāokè
be engraved on one's mind 铭刻在脑中 míngkè zài nǎo zhōng

engraving N 雕版印刷品 diāobǎn yìnshuāpǐn

engrossed ADJ 全神贯注的 quánshén guànzhù de

engrossing ADJ 引人入胜的 yǐn rén rù shèng de

engulf v 吞没 tūnmò

enhance v 提高 tígāo, 改进 gǎijìn

enigma N 神秘的人／事物 shénmì de rén/shìwù

enjoy v **1** 喜爱 xǐ'ài **2** 享受 xiǎngshòu ■ *As a member of the club, you'll enjoy many privileges.* 作为俱乐部成员你享受很多特权。Zuòwéi jùlèbù chéngyuán nǐ xiǎngshòu hěn duō tèquán.
to enjoy oneself 开心 kāixīn, 过得很愉快 guòde hěn yúkuài

enjoyable ADJ 愉快的 yúkuài de, 开心的 kāixīn de ■ *We had an enjoyable walk in the woods.* 我们在树林里散步，很愉快。Wǒmen zài shùlín lǐ sànbù, hěn yúkuài.

enjoyment N **1** 喜爱 xǐ'ài **2** 享乐 xiǎnglè, 享受 xiǎngshòu

enlarge v 放大 fàngdà, 增大 zēngdà

enlargement N **1** 放大 fàngdà, 增大 zēngdà **2** 放大的照片 fàngdà de zhàopiàn

enlarger N（照片）放大机 (zhàopiàn) fàngdàjī [M. WD 台 tái]

enlighten v 启迪 qǐdí, 开导 kāidǎo

enlightened ADJ 开明的 kāimíng de, 明智的 míngzhì de

enlightening ADJ 启迪的 qǐdí de, 使人明白的 shǐrén míngbai de

enlightenment N **1** 启迪 qǐdí, 启蒙 qǐméng
the Enlightenment（欧洲）启蒙运动 (Ōuzhōu) qǐméng yùndòng
2（佛教）觉悟 (Fójiào) juéwù, 般若 bōrě

enlist v **1** 请求（帮助）qǐngqiú (bāngzhù) **2** 参加（军队）cānjiā (jūnduì)

enliven v 使…生动有趣 shǐ…shēngdòng yǒuqù

en masse ADV 全体 quántǐ, 整体 zhěngtǐ

enmity N 敌意 díyì, 仇恨 chóuhèn

enormity N **1** 艰巨性 jiānjù xìng **2** 严重性 yánzhòngxìng

enormous ADJ 巨大的 jùdà de

enough I PRON 足够 zúgòu **II** ADV 足够 zúgòu, 够 gòu

enrage v 使…大怒 shǐ…dà nù, 激怒 jīnù

enraged ADJ 激怒的 jīnù de, 大怒的 dà nù de

enrich v **1** 使 [+文化生活] 丰富 shǐ [+wénhuà shēnghuó] fēngfù **2** 强化 qiánghuà **3** 使…富裕 shǐ…fùyù

enroll v 招收 [+学生] zhāoshōu [+xuésheng]

enrollment N 入学 rùxué, 注册 zhùcè

en route ADV 在路上 zài lùshang, 沿途 yántú

ensemble N **1** 小乐队 xiǎo yuèduì **2** 成套的东西 chéngtào de dōngxi

enshrine v 珍藏 zhēncáng, 铭记 míngjì

ensign N **1**（美国）海军少尉 (Měiguó) hǎijūn shàowèi **2** 舰旗 jiàn qí [M. WD 面 miàn]

enslave v 奴役 núyì

ensue v（接着）发生 (jiēzhe) fāshēng

ensure v 确保 quèbǎo, 担保 dānbǎo

entail v 需要 xūyào

entangle v 使…卷入 shǐ…juǎnrù

entanglement N 卷入 juǎnrù, 纠纷 jiūfēn

enter v **1** 进入 jìnrù ■ *Please knock before you enter.* 请先敲门，再进入。Qǐng xiān qiāomén, zài jìnrù. **2** 加入 jiārù, 参加 cānjiā **3**（在计算机里）输入 [+信息] (zài jìsuànjī lǐ) shūrù [+xìnxī]

enterprise N **1** 企业 qǐyè **2** 家 jiā **3** 开创精神 kāichuàng jīngshén, 创业能力 chuàngyè nénglì

enterprising ADJ 富有创业精神的 fùyǒu chuàngyè jīngshén de

entertain v **1** 使…高兴 shǐ…gāoxìng ■ *The children were thoroughly entertained by the circus.* 马戏团让孩子们高兴极了。Mǎxìtuán ràng háizimen gāoxìng jíle. **2** 招待 zhāodài **3** 抱有（想法）bàoyǒu (xiǎngfǎ)

entertainer N 演艺人员 yǎnyì rényuán, 表演者 biǎoyǎnzhě

entertaining ADJ 逗趣的 dòuqù de

entertainment N **1** 娱乐 yúlè, 文娱节目 wényú jiémù **2** 招待 zhāodài
entertainment center 娱乐中心 yúlè zhōngxīn
entertainment cost 招待费 zhāodàifèi

enthrall v 使…入迷 shǐ…rùmí, 迷住 mízhù

enthralling ADJ 使人入迷的 shǐrén rùmí de, 非常有趣的 fēicháng yǒuqù de

enthuse v 热情高涨 rèqíng gāozhǎng

enthusiasm N **1** 热情 rèqíng **2** 极大的兴趣 jídà de xìngqu

enthusiast N 爱好者 àihàozhě

enthusiastic ADJ 热情的 rèqíng de

entice v 诱惑 yòuhuò, 引诱 yǐnyòu

enticing ADJ 有诱惑力的 yǒu yòuhuòlì de, 迷人的 mírén de

entire ADJ 全部的 quánbù de, 整个 zhěnggè

entirely ADV 全部 quánbù ■ *He devoted his life entirely to the well-being of his family.* 他把一生都献给家人的福利。Tā bǎ yìshēng dōu xiàngěi jiārén de fúlì.

entirety N 全部 quánbù, 整个 zhěnggè
entitle V 1 使…有权 shǐ…yǒuquán 2 给…题名 gěi…tímíng
entitled ADJ 1 有权利的 yǒuquánlì de 2 书 (电影, 戏) 名叫 shū (diànyǐng, xì) míng jiào
■ *Have you read the book entitled "Uncle Tom's Cabin"?* 你读过一本书名叫《汤姆叔叔的小屋》的书吗? Nǐ dúguo yì běn shūmíng jiào "Tāngmǔ shūshu de xiǎo wū" de shū ma?
entitlement N 权利 quánlì, 资格 zīge
entitlement to compensation 获得赔偿的权利 huòdé péicháng de quánlì
entity N 实体 shítǐ
entomologist N 昆虫学家 kūnchóngxuéjiā
entomology N 昆虫学 kūnchóngxué
entourage N 随行人员 suíxíng rényuán
entrails N 内脏 nèizàng, 肠子 chángzi
entrance N 1 入口 rùkǒu 2 进入 jìnrù
entranced ADJ 着迷的 zháomí de
entrant N 参赛者 cānsàizhě
entrap V 使…陷入圈套 shǐ…xiànrùquāntào, 诱骗 yòupiàn
entrapment N 诱骗 yòupiàn, 诱捕 yòubǔ
entreat V 恳求 kěnqiú
entrée N 1 主菜 zhǔcài 2 进入权 jìnrù quán, 进入许可 jìnrù xǔkě
entrenched ADJ 根深蒂固的 gēnshēn dìgù de, 不可动摇的 bùkě dòngyáo de
entrepreneur N 企业家 qǐyèjiā
entrepreneurial ADJ 有创业精神的 yǒu chuàngyè jīngshén de
entrust V 委托 wěituō
entry N 1 进入 jìnrù
entry point 入境口 rùjìngkǒu
No Unauthorized Entry 非公莫入 fēigōng mòrù 2 入口 rùkǒu, 进入通道 jìnrù tōngdào 3 (词典) 词条 (cídiǎn) cí tiáo, 条目 tiáomù 4 参赛作品 cānsài zuòpǐn
entwined ADJ 交错在一起的 jiāocuò zài yìqǐ de, 密切有关的 mìqiè yǒuguān de
enumerate V 列举 lièjǔ
enunciate V 清晰地发音吐字 qīngxī de fāyīn tǔzì
envelop V 包住 bāozhù, 裹住 guǒ zhù
envelope N 信封 xìnfēng
stamped addressed envelope 贴好邮票写好地址的回信信封 tiēhǎo yóupiào xiěhǎo dìzhǐ de huíxìn xìnfēng
postpaid envelope 邮资已付的信封 yóuzī yǐfù de xìnfēng
enviable ADJ 叫人羡慕的 jiào rén xiànmù de
envious ADJ 羡慕的 xiànmù de, 妒忌的 dùjì de
environment N 环境 huánjìng ■ *The government has not done enough to protect the environment.* 政府在环境保护方面做得不够。Zhèngfǔ zài huánjìng bǎohù fāngmiàn zuò de bú gòu.

natural environment 自然环境 zìrán huánjìng
pollution of the environment 环境污染 huánjìng wūrǎn
environmental ADJ 环境的 huánjìng de
environmentalist N 环保主义者 huánbǎo zhǔyìzhě
environs N 周围 zhōuwéi
envisage V 展望 zhǎnwàng, 想像 xiǎngxiàng
envision V 设想 shèxiǎng, 想像 xiǎngxiàng
envoy N 使者 shǐzhě [M. WD 位 wéi], 外交官 wàijiāoguān [M. WD 位 wéi]
envy I V 羡慕 xiànmù, 嫉妒 jídù II N 1 羡慕 xiànmù, 嫉妒 jídù 2 被人羡慕的东西 bèi rén xiànmù de dōngxi
the envy of the world 人人都羡慕的东西／事物 rénrén dōu xiànmù de dōngxi/shìwù
enzyme N 酶 méi
epaulet N 肩章 jiānzhāng
ephemeral ADJ 短暂的 duǎnzàn de, 瞬息的 shùnxī de
epic I N 史诗 shǐshī, 史诗般的电影 (或小说) shǐshī bān de diànyǐng (huò xiǎoshuō) II ADJ 1 史诗的 shǐshī de 2 英雄的 yīngxióng de, 宏伟的 hóngwěi de
epicenter N (地震) 中心 (dìzhèn) zhōngxīn, 震中 zhènzhōng
epidemic N 流行病 liúxíngbìng [M. WD 种 zhǒng], 传染病 chuánrǎnbìng [M. WD 种 zhǒng]
epigram N 警句 jǐngjù
epilepsy N 癫痫 diānxián, 羊痫疯 yángxiánfēng
epileptic I ADJ 癫痫的 diānxián de II N 癫痫病人 diānxián bìngrén
epilogue N 1 结尾 jiéwěi, 终场 zhōngchǎng 2 结束语 jiéshùyǔ
Episcopal Church N 圣公会 Shènggōnghuì
Episcopalian ADJ 圣公会教徒 Shènggōnghuì jiàotú
episode N 1 (连续剧) 一集 (liánxùjù) yì jí 2 一段经历 yíduàn jīnglì
epistle N 书信 shūxìn, 信 xìn
epitaph N 墓志铭 mùzhìmíng
epithet N 1 [污辱性的+] 描写词语 [wūrǔxìng de+] miáoxiě cíyǔ 2 绰号 chuòhào, 别名 biémíng
epitome N 典范 diǎnfàn
epitomize V 成为…的典范 chéngwéi…de diǎnfàn, 象征 xiàngzhēng
epoch N 时代 shídài, 纪元 jìyuán
EQ (= emotional quotient) ABBREV 情绪智商 qíngxù zhìshāng, 情商 qíngshāng
equal I ADJ 1 平等 píngděng 2 等于 děngyú ■ *Ten percent of his monthly income is equal to 580 dollars.* 他月收入的百分之十等于五百八十元。Tā yuè shōurù de bǎifēnzhī shí děngyú wǔ bǎi bāshí yuán
equal sign 等号 děnghào (=)
II V 等于 děngyú ■ *2 plus 3 equals 5.* 二加三等于五。Èr jiā sān děngyú wǔ.

equality N 平等 píngděng

equalize v 使…平等 shǐ…píngděng, 使…相等 shǐ…xiāngděng

equally ADV 平等地 píngděng de, 相同地 xiāngtóng de

equanimity N 镇静 zhènjìng, 镇定 zhèndìng

equate v 平等看待 píngděng kàndài

equation N 等式 děngshì

equator N 赤道 chìdào

equestrian ADJ 骑马的 qímǎ de, 马术的 mǎshù de

equilateral ADJ 等边的 děngbiān de

equilibrium N 均衡 jūnhéng, 平衡 pínghéng

equine ADJ 马的 mǎ de

equinox N 春分 chūnfēn, 秋分 qiūfēn, 昼夜平分时 zhòuyè píngfēn shí

equip v 装备 zhuāngbèi, 配备 pèibèi
well-equipped 设施齐全的 shèshī qíquán de, 装备良好的 zhuāngbèi liánghǎo de

equipment N 设备 shèbèi, 装备 zhuāngbèi

equitable ADJ 公平的 gōngpíng de, 公正的 gōngzhèng de

equity N 1 公平 gōngpíng, 公正 gōngzhèng 2 [房产的+] 财产净值 [fángchǎn de+] cáichǎn jìngzhí

equivalent I ADJ 等值的 děngzhí de, 相等的 xiāngděng de II N 等价物 děngjiàwù, 对应物 duìyìngwù

equivocal ADJ 含糊的 hánhu de, 模棱两可的 móléng liǎngkě de

era N 时代 shídài, 年代 niándài

eradicate v 根除 gēnchú, 彻底消灭 chèdǐ xiāomiè

erase v 消除 xiāochú, 抹去 mǒqù

eraser N 1 橡皮 xiàngpí [M. WD 块 kuài] 2 黑板擦 hēibǎn cā [M. WD 块 kuài]

erect I ADJ 笔直的 bǐzhí de, 垂直的 chuízhí de II v 建立 [+纪念碑] jiànlì [+jìniànbēi], 建造 jiànzào

erection N 1 建立 jiànlì, 建造 jiànzào 2 [阴茎+] 勃起 (阴茎+) bóqǐ

erode v 1 侵蚀 [+土壤] qīnshí [+tǔrǎng] 2 削弱 [+权力] xuēruò [+quánlì]

erosion N 1 [土壤受到+] 侵蚀 [tǔrǎng shòudào+] qīnshí 2 [权力的+] 削弱 [quánlì de+] xuēruò

erotic ADJ 色情的 sèqíng de, 性的 xìng de

eroticism N 色情 sèqíng, 肉欲 ròuyù

err v 犯错误 fàn cuòwu
to err on the side of caution 宁可犯错, 也要谨慎。Nìngkě fàncuò, yě yào jǐnshèn.
To err is human, to forgive divine. 犯错是人, 宽恕是神。Fàncuò shì rén, kuānshù shì shén.

errand N 差事 chāishi, 跑腿儿 pǎotuǐr
to send sb on an errand 派某人去办一件事 pài mǒurén qù bàn yí jiàn shì

errant ADJ 迷途的 mítú de, 错误的 cuòwù de

errata N 勘误表 kānwùbiǎo [M. WD 张 zhāng/份 fèn]

erratic ADJ 不稳定的 bùwěndìng de, 不可捉摸的 bùkě zhuōmō de

erroneous ADJ 错误的 cuòwù de

error N 1 错误 cuòwù 2 谬误 miùwù ■ He has made an error in processing the data. 他在处理数据时犯了一个错误。Tā zài chǔlǐ shùjù shí fànle yí ge cuòwù.

erudite ADJ 博学的 bóxué de, 知识渊博的 zhīshi yuānbó de

erupt v (火山) 爆发 (huǒshān) bàofā

escalate v 1 升级 shēngjí 2 升高 shēnggāo

escalator N 自动扶梯 zìdòng fútī [M. WD 部 bù]

escapade N 1 刺激行为 cìjī xíngwéi 2 越轨行为 yuèguǐ xíngwéi

escape I v 1 逃离 táolí, 逃避 táobì
to escape one's attention 逃避某人的注意 táobì mǒurén de zhùyì
2 记不起 [+某人的姓名] jì bùqǐ [mǒurén de xìngmíng] II N 逃离 táolí, 逃避 táobì ■ They made their escape at night. 他们在夜间逃离。Tāmen zài yèjiān táolí.

escapism N 逃避现实 táobì xiànshí

eschew v 回避 huíbì, 躲避 duǒbì

escort I v 1 押送 [+犯人] yāsòng [+fànrén], 护送 hùsòng 2 为 [+旅游者] 导游陪同 wéi [+lǚyóuzhě] dǎoyóu péitóng II N 1 护卫者 hùwèizhě 2 妓女 jìnǚ
male escort 男妓 nánjì

Eskimo N 爱斯基摩人 Àisījīmórén

esophagus N 食管 shíguǎn

esoteric ADJ 深奥的 shēn'ào de

especially ADV 特别 tèbié, 尤其 yóuqí

espionage N 间谍活动 jiàndié huódòng

espouse v 信奉 xìnfèng, 支持 zhīchí

espresso N 蒸馏咖啡 zhēngliú kāfēi

essay N 文章 wénzhāng, 论说文 lùnshuōwén, 散文 sǎnwén

essence N 1 要素 yàosù, 本质 běnzhì
Time is of the essence. 时间是至关重要的。Shíjiān shì zhìguān zhòngyào de.
2 精油 jīngyóu, 精 jīng
vanilla essence 香草精 xiāngcǎojīng

essential I ADJ 必不可少的 bì bùkěshǎo de, 必要的 bìyào de ■ It is essential that our top man in Beijing speak Chinese. 我们在北京的最高级人员要会说中文, 这是必要的。Wǒmen zài Běijīng de zuìgāojí rényuán yào huì shuō Zhōngwén, zhè shì bìyào de. II N 必需品 bìxūpǐn
the essentials 要点 yàodiǎn
essentials of Chinese grammar 汉语语法要点 Hànyǔ yǔfǎ yàodiǎn

establish v 成立 chénglì, 建立 jiànlì

establishment N 1 成立 chénglì, 建立 jiànlì
■ The increase in road accidents has led to the establishment of a committee to investigate road

safety. 交通事故不断增加，导致了道路安全调查委员会的成立。Jiāotōng shìgù búduàn zēngjiā, dǎozhìle dàolù ānquán diàochá wěiyuánhuì de chénglì. **2** 机构 jīgòu, 组织 zǔzhī
the Establishment 当权者 dàngquánzhě

estate N **1** 地产 dìchǎn, 房地产 fángdìchǎn **2** 遗产 yíchǎn
estate tax 遗产税 yíchǎnshuì

esteem N, V 尊重 zūnzhòng, 尊敬 zūnjìng
to hold sb in esteem 对某人很尊敬 duì mǒurén hěn zūnjìng

esthetic See **aesthetic**

estimable ADJ 值得尊敬的 zhídé zūnjìng de

estimate V, N 估计 gūjì ■ *An official estimate suggests that these security measures will cost airline companies 12 million dollars a year.* 一项官方估计提示，这些保安措施将每年花费航空公司一千二百万。Yí xiàng guānfāng gūjì tíshì, zhèxiē bǎo'ān cuòshī jiāng měinián huāfèi hángkōng gōngsī yì qiān èr bǎi wàn.

estimation N 估计 gūjì
in sb's estimation 根据某人的估计 gēnjù mǒurén de gūjì

estranged ADJ **1** 分居的（夫妻）fēnjū de (fūqī) **2** 不再联系的（亲友）búzài liánxì de (qīnyǒu)

estrogen N 雌激素 cí jīsù

estuary N 河流入海口 héliú rǔhǎikǒu, 河口 hékǒu

et al ADV 以及其他人 yǐjí qítārén, 等人 děng rén

etc (= etcetera) ABBREV 等等 děngděng

etch V 蚀刻 shíkè

eternal ADJ 永恒的 yǒnghéng de, 永远的 yǒngyuǎn de

eternity N **1** 永恒 yǒnghéng, 永远 yǒngyuǎn **2** 来生 láishēng, 来世 láishì

ether N（乙）醚（yǐ）mí

ethereal ADJ 飘逸的 piāoyì de, 超凡的 chāofán de

ethic N 伦理 lúnlǐ, 道德体系 dàodé tǐxì

ethical ADJ 伦理的 lúnlǐ de

ethics N **1** 道德规范 dàodé guīfàn **2** 伦理学 lúnlǐxué

ethnic ADJ 种族的 zhǒngzú de, 民族的 mínzú de
ethnic minority 少数民族群体 shǎoshù mínzú qúntǐ
an ethnic slur 侮辱少数民族的诽谤 wūrǔ shǎoshù mínzú de fěibàng

ethos N 精神特质 jīngshén tèzhì

etiquette N 礼仪 lǐyí

etymology N 词源 cíyuán, 词源学 cíyuánxué

EU (= the European Union) ABBREV 欧洲联盟 Ōuzhōu Liánméng

eulogize V 赞美 zànměi, 歌颂 gēsòng

eulogy N 颂词 sòngcí [M. WD 篇 piān]

eunuch N 太监 tàijiān

euphemism N 委婉语 wěiwǎnyǔ

euphemistic ADJ 委婉的 wěiwǎn de

euphoria N 异常兴奋 yìcháng xīngfèn, 无名欣喜 wúmíng xīnxǐ

euro N 欧元 Ōuyuán

Europe N 欧洲 Ōuzhōu

European I ADJ 欧洲的 Ōuzhōu de **II** N 欧洲人 Ōuzhōurén

euthanasia N 安乐死 ānlèsǐ

evacuate V 撤离 chè lí

evacuee N 撤离者 chèlízhě

evade V 回避 huíbì, 避开 bìkāi

evaluate V 评估 pínggū, 评价 píngjià

evangelical ADJ 福音传道的 fúyīn chuándào de

evangelist N 福音传道者 fúyīn chuándàozhě

evaporate V **1**［气体+］挥发［qìtǐ+］huīfā, 蒸发 zhēngfā **2**［人+］消失［rén+］xiāoshī

evasion N 回避 huíbì, 避开 bìkāi

evasive ADJ 推脱的 tuītuō de, 回避的 huíbì de

eve N 前一天 qián yìtiān, 前夜 qiányè

even 1 ADJ 平的 píng de, 平坦的 píngtǎn de **2** 平衡的 pínghéng de, 均恒的 jūnhéng de ■ *The chemicals must be stored at an even temperature.* 这些化学品必须恒温储藏。Zhèxiē huàxuépǐn bìxū héngwēn chǔcáng.
even number 偶数 ǒushù
II ADV 甚至 shènzhì ■ *He is so busy that he even has to work on Sundays.* 他忙得甚至星期天都得工作。Tā mángde shènzhì xīngqītiān dōu děi gōngzuò. **III** V **1** 使…平坦 shǐ…píngtǎn **2** 使…平衡 shǐ…pínghéng
to even out 使…相等 shǐ…xiāngděng

even-handed ADJ 公平的 gōngping de, 不偏不倚的 bù piān bù yǐ de

evening N 晚上 wǎnshang, 傍晚 bàngwǎn
evening dress, evening wear 夜礼服 yèlǐfú
evening gown 女子夜礼服 nǚzǐ yèlǐfú

evenly ADV 均匀地 jūnyún de

event N 事件 shìjiàn
in any event 不管怎样 bùguǎn zěnyàng
in the event of 万一 wànyī **2** 活动 huódòng **3**（体育）项目（tǐyù）xiàngmù ■ *The 100 meter dash event attracted a large crowd of spectators.* 一百公尺短跑比赛吸引了一大群观众。Yì bǎi gōngchǐ duǎnpǎo bǐsài xīyǐnle yí dà qún guānzhòng.

eventful ADJ 发生很多事情的 fāshēng hěn duō shìqing de, 多事之秋 duōshì zhī qiū

eventual ADJ 最终的 zuìzhōng de

eventuality N 可能发生的事情 kěnéng fāshēng de shìqing, 可能产生的恶果 kěnéng chǎnshēng de èguǒ

eventually ADV 终于 zhōngyú ■ *The journey was difficult, but we eventually reached the destination.* 路程很艰难，但是我们终于到达了目的地。Lùchéng hěn jiānnán, dànshì wǒmen zhōngyú dàodále mùdìdì.

ever ADV **1** 一直 yìzhí ■ *Nothing ever happens in*

this small town. 在这座小镇，从来没有发生过什么事件。Zài zhè zuò xiǎo zhèn, cónglái méiyǒu fāshēngguo shénme shìjiàn. **2** 在任何时候 zài rènhé shíhou

evergreen I ADJ 常青的 chángqīng de, 常绿的 chánglǜ de **II** N 常青树 chángqīngshù [M. WD 棵 kē]

everlasting ADJ 永恒的 yǒnghéng de, 永久的 yǒng jiǔ de

every ADJ 每 měi, 每个 měi ge ■ You are advised to change your PIN every six months. 建议您每六个月更换一个人密码。Jiànyì nín měi liù ge yuè gēnghuàn gèrén mìmǎ.

everybody (= everyone)

everyday ADJ 每天的 měitiān de, 日常的 rìcháng de

everyone PRON 每个人 měige rén, 人人 rénrén, 大家 dàjiā ■ Everyone likes a bargain. 人人都喜欢买便宜货。Rénrén dōu xǐhuan mǎi piányi huò.

everyplace ADV 各地 gèdì

everything PRON 每件事 měi jiàn shì, 一切 yíqiè

everywhere ADV 每个地方 měi ge dìfang, 到处 dàochù ■ They're so inseparable that they go everywhere together. 他们形影不离，到哪儿都在一块儿。Tāmen xíngyǐng bùlí, dào nǎr dōu zài yíkuàir.

evict v (依法)驱逐 (yīfǎ) qūzhú, 赶出 gǎnchū

eviction N 驱逐(房客) qūzhú (fángkè)

evidence N **1** 证据 zhèngjù ■ Do you have any evidence to support your assertion? 你有没有证据支持你的断言？Nǐ yǒu méiyǒu zhèngjù zhīchí nǐ de duànyán? **2** 证词 zhèngcí

evident ADJ 明显的 míngxiǎn de

evil I N 邪恶 xié'è
the lesser of two evils 两害相比较轻者 liǎng hài xiāngbǐ jiào qīng zhě
II ADJ **1** 邪恶的 xié'è de **2** 恶魔的 èmó de, 恶魔似的 èmó shìde
evil spirit 恶鬼 èguǐ

evocative ADJ 唤起 huànqǐ, 引起 yǐnqǐ

evoke v 唤起 huànqǐ, 引起 yǐnqǐ

evolution N 进化(论) jìnhuà (lùn)

evolutionary ADJ **1** 进化(论)的 jìnhuà (lùn) de **2** 演变的 yǎnbiàn de

evolve v 逐步演变 zhúbù yǎnbiàn

ewe N 母羊 mǔyáng [M. WD 头 tóu]

exacerbate v 使…恶化 shǐ…èhuà

exacerbation N 恶化 èhuà

exact ADJ 确切的 quèqiè de, 精确的 jīngquè de

exactly ADV **1** 完全地 wánquán de, 精确地 jīngquè de **2** 正是 zhèngshì ■ This is exactly what I've been looking for. 这正是我一直想要的。Zhè zhèngshì wǒ yìzhí xiǎngyào de. **3** 正是这样 zhèng shì zhèyàng, 确实如此 quèshí rúcǐ

exaggerate v 夸大 kuādà, 夸张 kuāzhāng

exaggerated ADJ 夸大的 kuādà de, 夸张的 kuāzhāng de

exaggeration N 夸大 kuādà, 夸张 kuāzhāng

exalt v 赞扬 zànyáng, 歌颂 gēsòng

exam N **1** 考试 kǎoshì [M. WD 次 cì/场 cháng] ■ She did poorly in the final exams. 她期终考试考得很差。Tā qīzhōng kǎoshì kǎode hěn chà. **2** (医学)检查 (yīxué) jiǎnchá

examination N **1** 检查 jiǎnchá [M. WD 次 cì], 检验 jiǎnyàn [M. WD 次 cì] ■ Pilots must have a thorough medical examination every six months. 飞行员必须每六个月做一次彻底的身体检查。Fēixíngyuán bìxū měi liù ge yuè zuò yí cì chèdǐ de shēntǐ jiǎnchá. **2** 考试 kǎoshì [M. WD 次 cì/场 cháng]

examine v 检查 jiǎnchá, 检验 jiǎnyàn

example N **1** 例子 lìzi ■ Can you give me an example of climate change? 你能不能举一个气候变化的例子？Nǐ néngbunéng jǔ yí ge qìhòu biànhuà de lìzi?
for example 例如 lìrú
2 榜样 bǎngyàng, 范例 fànlì ■ They follow Mother Teresa's example and work among the poor and the sick. 他们学习特丽萨嬷嬷的榜样，在穷人、病人中服务。Tāmen xuéxí Tèlìsà mómo de bǎngyàng, zài qióngrén, bìngrén zhōng fúwù.

exasperate v 使…恼怒 shǐ…nǎonù

exasperated ADJ 恼怒的 nǎonù de

exasperating ADJ 让人恼怒的 ràng rén nǎonù de

excavate v 发掘 fājué, 挖掘 wājué

exceed v 超出 chāochū, 超过 chāoguò

exceedingly ADV 极其 jíqí, 非常 fēicháng

excel v **1** 优于 yōuyú, 胜过 shèngguò **2** 擅长 shàncháng

excellence N 卓越 zhuóyuè, 优秀 yōuxiù

excellent ADJ 优秀 yōuxiù, 杰出的 jiéchū de

except I PREP **1** 除了 chúle, 除了…以外 chúle…yǐwài ■ The zoo is open every day except Christmas Day. 动物园除了圣诞节每天开放。Dòngwùyuán chúle Shèngdànjié měitiān kāifàng. **2** 只是 zhǐ shì ■ This is a very good movie, except for the seemingly abrupt ending. 这部电影很好，只是结尾显得太仓促了。Zhè bù diànyǐng hěn hǎo, zhǐ shì jiéwěi xiǎnde tài cāngcù le. **II** v 除去 chúqù, 除掉 chúdiào

exception N 例外 lìwài ■ Most of the girls don't like science and math, but Jill is an exception. 大多数女孩不喜欢科学和数学，但是吉尔是个例外。Dàduōshu nǚhair bù xǐhuan kēxué he shùxué, dànshì Jiér shì ge lìwài.

exceptional ADJ **1** 杰出的 jiéchū de, 出类拔萃的 chūlèi bácuì de **2** 例外的 lìwài de, 特殊的 tèshū de

excerpt N 摘录 zhāilù [M. WD 段 duàn/篇 piān], 节录 jiélù [M. WD 段 duàn/篇 piān]

excess I N 过分 guòfèn, 过量 guòliàng

in excess of 超过 chāoguò

II ADJ 多余的 duōyú de, 额外的 éwài de

excess baggage 超重行李 chāozhòng xíngli

excesses N 过激行为 guòjī xíngwéi, (不必要的) 暴力 (bú bìyào de) bàolì

excessive ADJ 过分的 guòfèn de, 过度的 guòdù de

exchange I N **1** 交换 jiāohuàn, 兑换 duìhuàn

■ *She gave him free English lessons in exchange for piano lessons.* 她免费教他英文，来交换他的钢琴课。Tā miǎnfèi jiào tā Yīngwén, lái jiāohuàn tā de gāngqín kè.

exchange rate 兑换率 duìhuànlǜ

exchange student 交换学生 jiāohuàn xuésheng

2 交易所 jiāoyìsuǒ

New York Stock Exchange (NYSE) 纽约证券交易所 Niǔyuē zhèngquàn jiāoyìsuǒ

II v 交换 jiāohuàn

excise I N (特种)消费税 (tèzhǒng) xiāofèishuì, 国内货物税 guónèi huòwùshuì **II** v 除去 chúqù, 切除 qiēchú

excitable ADJ 容易激动的 róngyì jīdòng de

excite v 使激动 shǐ jīdòng ■ *Don't excite yourself. Keep calm.* 别让自己激动。保持镇静。Bié ràng zìjǐ jīdòng. Bǎochí zhènjìng.

excited ADJ 激动 jīdòng, 兴奋的 xīngfèn de

excitement N 激动 jīdòng, 兴奋 xīngfèn ■ *She could hardly conceal her excitement when she was awarded the scholarship.* 她得了奖学金，几乎不能掩饰激动。Tā déle jiǎngxué jīn, jīhū bù néng yǎnshì jīdòng.

exciting ADJ 令人激动地 lìng rén jīdòng de

exclaim v 叫喊 jiàohǎn, 呼叫 hūjiào

exclamation N 叫喊声 jiàohǎn shēng, 呼叫声 hūjiàoshēng

exclamation point 感叹号 gǎntànhào (!)

exclude v **1** 不包括 bù bāokuò **2** 排除 [+可能性] páichú [+kěnéngxìng]

excluding PREP 不包括 bù bāokuò, 除了 chúle

exclusive ADJ **1** 独家的 [+采访] dújiā de [+cǎifǎng], 专门的 zhuānmén de **2** 难以进入的 [+俱乐部] nányǐ jìnrù de [+jùlèbù] **3** 昂贵的 [+餐厅] ángguì de [+cāntīng]

excommunicate v 开除 [+出教会] kāichú [+chū jiàohuì], 逐出教门 zhúchū jiàomén

excrement N 粪便 fènbiàn

excrete v 排泄 páixiè

excruciating ADJ 剧烈疼痛的 jùliè téngtòng de, 疼痛得难以忍受的 téngtòng de nányǐ rěnshòu de

excursion N 短途旅游 duǎntú lǚyóu

excusable ADJ 可以原谅的 kěyǐ yuánliàng de

excuse I v **1** 原谅 yuánliàng

Excuse me 对不起 duìbuqǐ ■ *Excuse me, I didn't mean it.* 对不起，我不是这个意思。Duìbuqǐ, wǒ bú shì zhè ge yìsi.

2 为···辩解 wèi...biànjiě **II** N 理由 lǐyóu, 借口 jièkǒu

execute v **1** 执行 zhíxíng, 实施 shíshī **2** 处以死刑 chù yǐ sǐxíng, 处死 chǔsǐ

execution N **1** 执行 zhíxíng, 实施 shíshī **2** 处死 chǔsǐ

executioner N 死刑执行人 sǐxíng zhíxíng rén

executive I N 高级管理人员 gāojí guǎnlǐ rényuán ■ *This luxury home belongs to an executive of a multinational corporation.* 这幢豪宅属于一位跨国公司的高级管理人员。Zhè zhuàng háozhái shǔyú yí wèi kuàguó gōngsī de gāojí guǎnlǐ rényuán.

the Executive (政府)行政部门 (zhèngfǔ) xíngzhèng bùmén

II ADJ 执行的 zhíxíng de

executor N 遗嘱执行人 yízhǔ zhíxíngrén

exemplary ADJ 可以作为好榜样的 kěyǐ zuòwéi hǎo bǎngyàng de, 楷模的 kǎimó de

exemplify v 是···的典型例子 shì...de diǎnxíng lìzi

exempt I ADJ 被免除的 bèi miǎnchú de

exempt from taxation 免于缴税 miǎnyú jiǎoshuì

II v 免除 miǎnchú

exemption N **1** 免除 miǎnchú **2** 免税额 miǎnshuìé

exercise I N **1** (体育)锻炼 (tǐyù) duànliàn

exercise bike 健身脚踏车 jiànshēn jiǎotàchē

2 体操 tǐcāo, 健身操 jiànshēncāo **3** 练习 liànxí ■ *The teacher gives her students exercises to do every day.* 老师每天给学生规定练习。Lǎoshī měitiān gěi xuésheng guīdìng liànxí.

4 活动 huódòng

a futile exercise 没有效果的活动 méiyǒu xiàoguǒ de huódòng, 徒劳之举 túláo zhī jǔ

5 (军事)演习 (jūnshì) yǎnxí

a joint naval exercise 联合海军演习 liánhé hǎijūn yǎnxí

II v **1** (体育)锻炼 (tǐyù) duànliàn **2** 运用 [+权力] yùnyòng [+quánlì], 行使 xíngshǐ

exert v 施加 shījiā

to exert oneself 努力 nǔlì, 卖力 màilì

exertion N **1** 运用 yùnyòng **2** 用力 yònglì, 努力 nǔlì

exhale v 呼气 hūqì

exhaust I v **1** 使···精疲力尽 shǐ...jīngpí lìjìn **2** 用尽 yòngjìn **II** N **1** (汽车)废气 (qìchē) fèiqì **2** 排气管 páiqìguǎn, 排气系统 páiqì xìtǒng

exhausted ADJ 精疲力尽的 jīngpí lìjìn de, 累极了的 lèi jíle de

exhaustion N **1** 精疲力尽 jīngpí lìjìn **2** 耗尽 hàojìn, 用完 yòngwán

exhaustive ADJ 彻底的 chèdǐ de

exhibit I v **1** 展览 zhǎnlǎn, 展示 zhǎnshì **2** 显示 xiǎnshì, 展示 zhǎnshì **II** N **1** 展览品 zhǎnlǎnpǐn [M. WD 件 jiàn] ■ *Sorry, the exhibits are not for* sale. 对不起，展览品不出售。Duìbuqǐ, zhǎnlǎnpǐn bù chūshòu. **2** (法庭上的) 证物 (fǎtíng shàng de) zhèngwù [M. WD 件 jiàn]

exhibition N 展览 zhǎnlǎn, 展览会 zhǎnlǎnhuì an exhibition of temper 大发脾气 dà fā píqi to make an exhibition of oneself 出洋相 chūyángxiàng, 出丑 chūchǒu

exhibitionism N 风头主义 fēngtóu zhǔyì, 表现狂 biǎoxiànkuáng

exhilarated ADJ 兴高采烈的 xìnggāo cǎiliè de

exhilarating ADJ 让人极其兴奋的 ràng rén jíqí xīngfèn de

exhort V 恳请 kěnqǐng, 劝告 quàngào

exhortation N 规劝 guīquàn, 劝谕 quànyù

exhume V 掘出 (尸体) juéchū (shītǐ)

exile I V 流放 liúfàng, 放逐 fàngzhú II N **1** 流放 liúfàng, 流亡 liúwáng **2** 流放者 liúfàngzhě a political exile 政治流放者 zhèngzhì liúfàngzhě in exile 流放中 liúfàng zhōng

exist V 存在 cúnzài, 有 yǒu ■ Does life exist on Mars? 火星上存在生命吗? Huǒxīngshang cúnzài shēngmìng ma?

existence N **1** 存在 cúnzài **2** 生存 shēngcún ■ The continued existence of many species is under threat. 许多物种的继续生存受到威胁。Xǔduō wùzhǒng de jìxù shēngcún shòudào wēixié.

exit I N **1** 出口 chūkǒu, 出口处 chūkǒuchù **2** 离去 líqù, 退场 tuìchǎng to make a hasty exit 匆忙离去 cōngmáng líqù II V **1** 离开 líkāi **2** 退出 tuìchū

exodus N (大批人) 离开 (dàpī rén) líkāi

exonerate V 免除 (指控) miǎnchú (zhǐkòng)

exorbitant ADJ [价格+] 过高的 [jiàgé+] guògāo de, 昂贵的 ángguì de

exorcise, exorcize V **1** 忘却 wàngquè, 忘掉 wàngdiào **2** 驱除 qūchú, 消除 xiāochú

exotic ADJ 异国情调的 yìguó qíngdiào de, 异国的 yìguó de

expand V 变大 biàn dà, 扩张 kuòzhāng

expanse N 广阔的空间 guǎngkuò de kōngjiān

expansion N 变大 biàn dà, 扩张 kuòzhāng

expansive ADJ **1** 广阔的 [+草甸] guǎngkuò de [+màitián] **2** 扩张的 [+野心] kuòzhāng de [+yěxīn] **3** 开朗健谈的 [+朋友] kāiláng jiàntán de [+péngyou]

expatriate N 居住在外国的人 jūzhù zài wàiguó de rén, 侨民 qiáomín

expect V **1** 期待 qīdài, 指望 zhǐwàng ■ Do you really expect me to believe you? 你真的指望我相信你? Nǐ zhēn de zhǐwàng wǒ xiàngxìn nǐ? **2** [女子+] 怀孕 [nǚzǐ+] huáiyùn

expectancy N 期待 qīdài, 期望 qīwàng

expectant ADJ **1** 期待的 qīdài de, 期望的 qīwàng de **2** 怀孕的 huáiyùn de

an expectant mother 快要当母亲的人 kuàiyào dāng mǔqin de rén, 孕妇 yùnfù

expectation N 期待 qīdài, 期望 qīwàng ■ They have unrealistic expectations of their children. 他们对孩子的期待脱离实际。Tāmen duì háizi de qīdài tuōlí shíjì.
contrary to expectation 出乎意料 chūhū yìliào

expediency N 不讲原则只求效果的做法 bù jiǎng yuánzé zhǐ qiú xiàoguǒ de zuòfǎ, 权宜之计 quányí zhī jì

expedient I ADJ 权宜之计的 quányí zhī jì de, 应急的 yìngjí de II N 应急办法 yìngjí bànfǎ

expedite V 加快 jiākuài, 促进 cùjìn

expedition N 探险 (队) tànxiǎ (duì), 考察 (队) kǎochá (duì)

expel V **1** 驱逐 qūzhú, 开除 kāichú **2** 排出 [+气体] páichū [+qìtǐ]

expend V 花费 huāfèi

expendable ADJ 可有可无的 kěyǒu kěwú de, 不必保留的 búbì bǎoliú de

expenditure N 花费 huāfèi, 费用 fèiyòng

expense N 费用 fèiyòng [M. WD 笔 bǐ], 花费 huāfèi expenses 业务费用 yèwù fèiyòng, 差旅交际费 chāilǚ jiāojìfèi expense account 报销账单 bàoxiāo zhàngdān at the expense of 以…为代价 yǐ…wéi dàijià ■ He achieved his career aspiration at the expense of his health. 他以健康为代价，实现了事业上的雄心。Tā yǐ jiànkāng wéi dàijià, shíxiànle shìyèshang de xióngxīn.

expensive ADJ 昂贵的 ángguì de

experience I N **1** 经历 jīnglì ■ This movie is based on his personal experiences. 这部电影基于他的亲身经历。Zhè bù diànyǐng jīyú tā de qīnshēn jīnglì. **2** 经验 jīngyàn ■ He has not had any experience in this type of work. 他对这类工作没有任何经验。Tā duì zhè lèi gōngzuò méiyǒu rènhé jīngyàn.
Experience is the better teacher. 经验是最好的老师。Jīngyàn shì zuì hǎo de lǎoshī.
II V 经历 jīnglì, 体验 tǐyàn

experienced ADJ 有经验的 yǒu jīngyàn de

experiment I N 实验 shíyàn [M. WD 项 xiàng/次 cì], 试验 shìyàn [M. WD 项 xiàng/次 cì] ■ The scientist is carrying out a pioneering experiment in his laboratory. 这位科学家正在试验室进行一项开创性试验。Zhè wèi kēxuéjiā zhèngzài shìyànshì jìnxíng yí xiàng kāichuàngxìng shìyàn. II V 实验 shíyàn, 试验 shìyàn

experimental ADJ 实验的 shíyàn de, 试验的 shìyàn de

expert I N 专家 zhuānjiā [M. WD 位 wéi], 行家 hángjiā [M. WD 位 wéi] ■ The committee will consult a panel of experts before making the final decision. 委员会要在做出最终决定以前咨询一个

专家组。Wěiyuánhuì yào zài zuòchū zuìzhōng juédìng yǐqián zīxún yí ge zhuānjiāzǔ. **II** ADJ 专家的 zhuānjiā de, 内行的 nèiháng de
expert advice 专家意见 zhuānjiā yìjiàn
expert system（计算机）专家系统 (jìsuànjī) zhuānjiā xìtǒng

expertise N 专业知识 zhuānyè zhīshi

expiration N 过期失效 guòqī shīxiào
expiration date 失效日期 shīxiào rìqī

expire V 过期 guòqī, 到期 dàoqī

explain V **1** 解释 jiěshì **2** 说明 shuōmíng, 给出原因 gěichū yuányīn

explanation N 解释 jiěshì ■ They offered a convincing explanation for the late arrival of our order. 他们对我们订货晚到一事作了令人信服的解释。Tāmen duì wǒmen dìnghuò wǎndào yí shì zuòle lìng rén xìnfú de jiěshì.

explanatory ADJ 解释的 jiěshì de, 说明的 shuōmíng de

expletive N 骂人的话 màrén dehuà [M. WD 句 jù], 粗话 cūhuà [M. WD 句 jù]

explicable ADJ 容易理解的 róngyì lǐjiě de

explicit ADJ **1** 清楚的 qīngchu de, 直截了当的 zhíjiéliǎodàng de **2**（色情描写）露骨的 (sèqíng miáoxiě) lùgǔ de

explode V 爆炸 bàozhà

exploit¹ N 英勇行为 yīngyǒng xíngwéi, 壮举 zhuàngjǔ

exploit² V **1** 剥削 [+雇员] bōxuē [+gùyuán] **2** 利用 [+资源] lìyòng [+zīyuán], 开发 kāifā

exploitation N **1** 剥削 bōxuē
exploitation of child labor 剥削童工 bōxuē tónggōng
2 利用 lìyòng

explore V **1** 探索 tànsuǒ ■ Geologists are exploring for oil in this region. 地质学家在这个地区探索石油。Dìzhìxuéjiā zài zhège dìqū tànsuǒ shíyóu. **2** 仔细研究 zǐxì yánjiū, 考察 kǎochá ■ His proposal sounds interesting and is worth exploring in some detail. 他的提案听来很有意思，值得做一些仔细研究。Tā de tí'àn tīnglai hěn yǒuyìsi, zhíde zuò yìxiē zǐxì yánjiū.

explorer N 探险者 tànxiǎnzhě, 探险家 tànxiǎnjiā

explosion N 爆炸 bàozhà [M. WD 次 cì] **2** 急剧增长 jíjù zēngzhǎng
population explosion 人口急剧增长 rénkǒu jíjù zēngzhǎng, 人口爆炸 rénkǒu bàozhà

explosive I ADJ **1** 会爆炸的 huì bàozhà de **2** 爆炸性的 bàozhàxìng de **II** N 炸药 zhàyào

exponent N 倡导者 chàngdǎozhě, 拥护者 yōnghùzhě

export I V 出口 chūkǒu **II** N 出口（商品）chūkǒu (shāngpǐn)

expose V **1** 暴露 bàolù ■ You should not expose your skin to the summer sun. 你不应该把皮肤暴

露在夏日的阳光下。Nǐ bù yīnggāi bǎ pífū bàolù zài xiàrì de yángguāng xià. **2** 揭露 jiēlù ■ The sacked accountant threatened to expose the company's tax evasion to the police. 被解雇的会计师威胁要向警方揭露公司的逃税行为。Bèi jiègù de kuàijìshī wēixié yào xiàng jǐngfāng jiēlù gōngsī de táoshuì xíngwéi.

exposé N 揭露阴暗面的作品 jiēlù yīn'ànmiàn de zuòpǐn, 曝光揭秘的作品 bàoguāng jiēmì de zuòpǐn

exposed ADJ 暴露在外的 bàolù zàiwài de

exposition N **1** 详细讲解 xiángxì jiǎngjiě **2** 展览会 zhǎnlǎnhuì, 博览会 bólǎnhuì

exposure N **1** 暴露 bàolù **2** 揭露 jiēlù **3** 曝光（量）bàoguāng (liáng)
exposure meter（摄影用）曝光表 (shèyǐng yòng) bàoguāngbiǎo

express¹ V 表示 biǎoshì, 表达 biǎodá ■ I can't express fully how grateful I am for your help. 我无法充分表达对你的帮助的谢意。Wǒ wúfǎ chōngfèn biǎodá duì nǐ de bāngzhù de xièyì.
to express oneself 表达自己的意思／观点 biǎodá zìjǐ de yìsi/guāndiǎn

express² I ADJ 快速的 kuàisù de, 高速的 gāosù de
Express Mail Delivery Service (EMD) 特快专递 tèkuài zhuān dì
II N **1** 特快邮递 tèkuài yóudì **2** 特快火车 tèkuài huǒchē [M. WD 列 liè]

expression N **1** 表达法 biǎodáfǎ, 习惯用语 xíguàn yòngyǔ **2** 表情 biǎoqíng **3** 表达意见／感情 biǎodá yìjiàn/gǎnqíng ■ He did not know how to give expression to his frustration. 他不知道怎么样表达自己的挫折感。Tā bù zhīdào zěnmeyàng biǎodá zìjǐ de cuòzhégǎn.

expressionless ADJ 面无表情的 miàn wú biǎoqíng de

expressive ADJ 富于表现力的 fùyú biǎoxiànlì de, 充满感情的 chōngmǎn gǎnqíng de

expressly ADV **1** 明确地 míngquè de **2** 特意地 tèyì de

expressway N 快速干道 kuàisù gàndào

expropriate V 征用 zhēngyòng, 没收 mòshōu

expulsion N **1** 开除 kāichú, 驱逐 qūzhú **2** 排出 páichū

exquisite ADJ 精美的 jīngměi de, 精致的 jīngzhì de

extemporaneous ADJ 不作准备的 bú zuò zhǔnbèi de, 即兴的 jíxìng de
an extemporaneous piano performance 即兴钢琴演奏 jíxìng gāngqín yǎnzòu

extend V **1** 伸 shēn, 伸展 shēnzhǎn **2** 延长 yáncháng
extended family 扩大式家庭 kuòdà shì jiātíng, 大家庭 dàjiātíng
3 提供 [+帮助] tígōng [+bāngzhù]

extension N 1 (电话) 分机 (diànhuà) fēnjī, (电话) 分机号码 (diànhuà) fēnjī hàomǎ 2 延期 yánqī 3 扩展 kuòzhǎn, 扩大 kuòdà
extension cord 电线延长线 diànxiàn yán-chángxiàn
4 (大学) 附设部 (dàxué) fùshèbù

extensive ADJ 1 广泛的 guǎngfàn de 2 大范围的 dà fànwéi de, 广大的 guǎngdà de

extent N 1 程度 chéngdù ■ *We do not yet know the extent of the damage caused by the cyclone.* 我们不知道龙卷风造成的损害达到什么程度。Wǒmen bù zhīdào lóngjuǎnfēng zàochéng de sǔnhài dádào shénme chéngdù.
to a certain/some extent 在一定程度上 zài yídìng chéngdùshang
2 范围 fànwéi

exterior I ADJ 外面的 wàimiàn de, 外部来的 wàibù láide II N 外部 wàibù, 外面 wàimiàn

external ADJ 外部的 wàibù de
(of medicine) for external use 外用药 wài-yòngyào

extinct ADJ 1 灭绝的 mièjué de, 灭种的 mièzhǒng de 2 熄灭了的 xīmièle de

extinction N 1 灭绝 mièjué, 灭种 mièzhǒng on the brink of extinction 频临灭绝 pínlín mièjué 2 熄灭 xīmiè, 消灭 xiāomiè

extinguish V 灭灭 mièmiè, 消灭 xiāomiè

extinguisher, fire extinguisher N 灭火器 mièhuǒqì

extol V 高度赞扬 gāodù zànyáng

extort V 敲诈勒索 qiāozhà lèsuǒ

extortion N 敲诈勒索 qiāozhà lèsuǒ

extortionate ADJ 敲诈性的 qiāozhàxìng de, 过高的 guògāo de

extra I ADJ 附加的 fùjiā de II ADV 特别 tèbié, 非常 fēicháng ■ *This wine is of extra fine quality.* 这种酒质量特别好。Zhè zhǒng jiǔ zhìliàng tèbié hǎo. III N 1 外加的东西 (如付款) wàijiā de dōngxi (rú fùkuǎn) ■ *There are no hidden extras to this price.* 这个价格以外没有隐含的附加付款。Zhè ge jiàgé yǐwài méiyǒu yǐnhán de wàijiā fùkuǎn. 2 (报纸) 号外 (hàozhǐ) hàowài [M. WD 份 fèn] 3 (电影) 临时演员 (diànyǐng) línshí yǎnyuán

extract I V 1 拔出 bá chū, 取出 qǔchū 2 提炼 tíliàn, 采掘 cǎijué 3 设法取得 shèfǎ qǔdé II N 1 提炼物 tíliànwù, 浓缩物 nóngsuōwù 2 摘录 zhāilù [M. WD 段 duàn/篇 piān], 选段 xuǎnduàn [M. WD 段 duàn/篇 piān]

extraction N 1 提炼 tíliàn 2 血统 xuètǒng, 出身 chūshēn
a family of Italian extraction 一个意大利血统的家庭 yí ge Yìdàlì xuètǒng de jiātíng

extracurricular ADJ 课外的 kèwài de
extracurricular activities 课外活动 kèwài huódòng

extradite V 引渡 yǐndù

extraneous ADJ 不相关的 bù xiāngguān de, 无足轻重的 wúzú qīngzhòng de

extraordinary ADJ 1 非凡的 fēifán de, 极其出色的 jíqí chūsè de 2 很特别的 hěn tèbié de

extrapolate V 推断 tuīduàn

extraterrestrial I ADJ 外星的 wàixīng de II N 外星生物 wàixīng shēngwù, 外星人 wàixīngrén

extravagant ADJ 奢侈豪华的 shēchǐ háohuá de, 挥霍无度的 huī huò wúdù de

extreme I ADJ 1 极端 jíduān, 极其 jíqí 2 极限的 jíxiàn de, 尽头的 jìntóu de II N 极端 jíduān ■ *Love and hate are extremes.* 爱和恨是两个极端。Ài hé hèn shì liǎng ge jíduān.

extremely ADV 极其 jíqí ■ *It is extremely annoying to miss a flight.* 没赶上飞机, 让人极其恼火。Méi gǎnshang fēijī, ràngrén jíqí nǎohuǒ.

extremism N 极端主义 jíduānzhǔyì

extremist N 极端分子 jíduān fènzi

extremities N 四肢 sìzhī, 手脚 shǒujiǎo

extremity N 极端 jíduān, 末端 mòduān

extricate V 解救 jiějiù

extrovert N 性格外向的人 xìnggé wàixiàng de rén

exuberance N 朝气 zhāoqì, 活力 huólì

exuberant ADJ 朝气蓬勃的 zhāoqì péngbó de, 精力旺盛的 jīnglì wàngshèng de

exude V 1 表现出 biǎoxiànchū 2 渗透出 shèntòuchū

exult V 欢欣鼓舞 huānxīn gǔwǔ

eye N 1 眼睛 yǎnjing 2 眼力 yǎnlì, 眼光 yǎnguāng
to have an eye for sth 对某事物有鉴赏能力 duì mǒu shìwù yǒu jiànshǎng nénglì
an eye for an eye, a tooth for a tooth 以眼还眼, 以牙还牙 yǐ yǎn huǎn yǎn, yǐ yá huǎn yá

eyeball N 眼球 yǎnqiú

eyebrow N 眉毛 méimao [M. WD 条 tiáo]
to raise one's eyebrows 表示惊讶/反对 biǎoshì jīngyà/fǎnduì

eye-catching ADJ 醒目 xǐngmù, 令人注目的 lìng rén zhùmù de

eyelash N 眼睫毛 yǎnjiémáo

eyelid N 眼皮 yǎnpí, 眼睑 yǎnjiǎn

eye-opener N 使人大开眼界的事 shǐ rén dà kāi yǎnjiè de shì

eyeshadow N 眼影 yǎnyǐng

eyesight N 视力 shìlì

eyesore N 刺眼的东西 cìyǎn de dōngxi, 难看的事物 nánkàn de shìwù

eyewitness N 目击者 mùjīzhě ■ *There was no eyewitness to this crime.* 这桩犯罪案件没有目击人。Zhè zhuāng fànzuì ànjiàn méiyǒu mùjīrén.

F

fable N 寓言（故事）yùyán (gùshi)

fabric N 布料 bùliào [M. WD 块 kuài]，织品 zhīpǐn [M. WD 件 jiàn]

fabricate V 1 编造 [+故事] biānzào [+gùshi]，捏造 niēzào 2 制造 [+部件] zhìzào [+bùjiàn]

fabrication N 编造的信息 biānzào díxīn xī，谎言 huǎngyán

fabulous ADJ 1 极好的 jíhǎo de，好得不得了 hǎo dé bùdéliǎo 2 巨大的 jùdà de，大得惊人的 dà dé jīngrén de

façade N 1 表面 biǎomiàn，外表 wàibiǎo 2（建筑物的）正面 (jiànzhùwù de) zhèngmiàn

face I N 1 脸 liǎn，面孔 miànkǒng 2 表面 biǎomiàn face value 表面价值 biǎomiàn jiàzhí ■ This stamp with the face value of 10 cents can easily grab 1,000 dollars at an auction. 这枚面值十美分的邮票可以轻而易举地拍卖到一千元。Zhè méi miànzhí shí měifēn de yóupiào kěyǐ qīngéryìjǔ de pāimài dào yì qiān yuán.
to lose face 丢脸 diūliǎn，丢面子 diū miànzi
to pull a long face 拉长脸 lācháng liǎn，一脸不高兴的表情 yì liǎn bù gāoxīng de biǎoqíng
II v 1 面临 [+挑战] miànlín [+ tiǎozhàn]，面对 miànduì 2 正视 [+现实] zhèngshì [+xiànshí]
to face the music 接受批评 jiēshòu pīpíng
to face up to 勇敢正视 [+困难的处境] yǒnggǎn zhèngshì [+kùnnan de chǔjìng]

Facebook N（网络通信）脸谱 (wǎngluò tōngxìn) liǎnpǔ

faceless ADJ 不受重视的 bú shòu zhòngshì de，没有趣味的 méiyǒu qùwèi de

facelift N 1 面部拉皮手术 miànbù lāpí shǒushù 2 [建筑物+] 翻新 [jiànzhùwù+] fānxīn

facet N 1 方面 fāngmiàn 2（宝石的）琢面 (bǎoshí de) zhuómiàn

facetious ADJ 乱开玩笑的 luàn kāiwánxiào de，想逗人笑的 xiǎng dòurén xiào de

facial I ADJ 脸部的 liǎnbù de II N 面部美容 miànbù měiróng

facile ADJ 1 肤浅的 fūqiǎn de，浅薄的 qiǎnbó de 2 过于容易的 guòyú róngyì de 3 未经认真考虑的 wèijīng rènzhēn kǎolǜ de，随便的 suíbiàn de

facilitate V 使…容易 shǐ…róngyì，便于 biànyú

facility N 1 设施 shèshī 2 才能 cáinéng ■ I believe you have great facility for learning languages. 我相信你有很好的语言学习才能。Wǒ xiāngxìn nǐ yǒu hěn hǎo de yǔyán xuéxí cáinéng.

facsimile N 1 [文件+] 复制品 [wénjiàn+] fùzhìpǐn，[名画+] 摹本 [míng huà+] móběn 2 传真 chuánzhēn

fact N 事实 shìshí ■ No one can deny the fact that the world has become a more dangerous place after 9/11. 没有人能否认这个事实："九一一" 以后世界更危险了。Méiyǒu rén néng fǒurèn zhè ge shìshí: "jiǔ yāo yāo" yǐhòu shìjiè gèng wēixiǎn le.
a fact of life 现实 xiànshí
the facts of life 性知识 xìng zhīshi
in fact, as a matter of fact 事实上 shìshíshang

faction N 派别 pàibié，派系 pàixì

factitious ADJ 虚假的 xūjiǎ de，做作的 zuòzuo de

factor N 因素 yīnsù

factory N 工厂 gōngchǎng [M. WD 家 jiā/座 zuò]

factual ADJ 事实的 shìshí de，基于事实的 jīyú shìshí de

faculty N 1 全体教师 quántǐ jiàoshī，师资 shīzī 2 天生的能力 tiānshēng de nénglì
the mental faculty 大脑功能 dànǎo gōngnéng，思维能力 sīwéi nénglì

fad N 短暂的时髦 duǎnzàn de shímáo，一时的风尚 yìshí de fēngshàng

fade V 1 [记忆+] 逐渐消失 [jìyì+] zhújiàn xiāoshī 2 [颜色+] 褪色 [yánsè+] tuìsè

Fahrenheit (ABBREV F) N 华氏温度 huáshì wēndù 45° F 华氏42度 huáshì sìshíèr dù

fail I v 1 [努力+] 失败 [nǔlì+] shībài ■ The business venture failed completely. 这项商业冒险活动彻底失败了。Zhè xiàng shāngyè màoxiǎn huódòng chèdǐ shībài le. 2 没有能 méiyǒu néng，未能 wèi néng ■ I failed to persuade him to work harder. 我没有能说服他工作更努力些。Wǒ méiyǒu néng shuōfú tā gōngzuò gèng nǔlì xiē. 3 [考试+] 不及格 [kǎoshì+] bùjígé [车乇+] 失灵 [shāchē+] shīlíng 5 [机器／人体器官+] 出毛病 [jīqì/réntǐ qìguān+] chūmáobìng，失灵 shīlíng failing health 越来越差的健康情况 yuèláiyuè chà de jiànkāng qíngkuàng
6 [生意+] 倒闭 [shēngyì+] dǎobì 7 使 [+人] 失望 shǐ [+rén] shīwàng II N (without fail) 必定 bìdìng，一定 yídìng

failing I N 缺点 quēdiǎn，弱点 ruòdiǎn II PREP 如果不行 rúguǒ bùxíng

failsafe ADJ 1 配有安全保障装置的 pèiyǒu ānquán bǎozhàng zhuāngzhì de 2 万无一失的 wànwú yìshī de

failure N 1 失败 shībài，倒闭 dǎobì ■ All his efforts ended in failure. 他的一切努力都以失败告终。Tā de yíqiè nǔlì dōu yǐ shībài gàozhōng. 2 没有能 méiyǒu néng 3 [考试+] 不及格 [kǎoshì+] bùjígé 4 失灵 shīlíng 5 失败者 shībàizhě

faint I ADJ 微弱的 wēiruòde II v 晕倒 yūndǎo ■ At the sight of her badly wounded son, the poor woman fainted. 可怜的女人看到身负重伤的儿子就晕倒了。Kělián de nǚrén kàndào shēnfù zhòngshāng de érzi jiù yūndǎo le. III N 昏厥 hūnjué

fair I ADJ 1 公正的 gōngzhèng de ■ Every teacher tries hard to be fair when grading exams. 每一个

教师在评判考试卷子时都尽力做到公正。Měi yí wèi jiàoshī zài píngpàn kǎoshì juǎnzi shí dōu jìnlì zuòdao gōngzhèng. **2** 中等水平的 zhōngděng shuǐpíng de **3** 金黄的(头发) jīnhuáng de (tóufa), 白皙的(肤色) báixī de (fūsè) **4** 晴朗的(天气) qínglǎng de (tiānqì) **II** ADV 公正地 gōngzhèng de, 公平地 gōngpíng de
fair and square 正大光明地 zhèngdà guāngmíng de
play fair 公平办事 gōngping bànshì
III N **1** 集市 jíshì **2** 交易会 jiāoyìhuì
job fair 职业招聘会 zhíyè zhāopìnhuì
trade fair 商品交易会 shāngpǐn jiāoyìhuì
3 博览会 bólǎnhuì
book fair 图书博览会 túshū bólǎnhuì

fairground N 露天游乐场 lùtiān yóulèchǎng, 露天集市 lùtiān jíshì

fairly ADV **1** 公正地 gōngzhèng de **2** 相当地 xiāngdāng de, 还不错 hái búcuò ■ *Laura is very proud of her tennis skill, but I think she plays only fairly well.* 劳拉对自己的网球技术很骄傲, 但我看她只是打得还不错而已。Láolā duì zìjǐ de wǎngqiú jìshù hěn jiāo'ào, dàn wǒ kàn tā zhǐshì dǎde hái bùcuò éryǐ.

fairy N 小仙子 xiǎoxiānzǐ, 小精灵 xiǎojīnglíng
fairy tale 童话 tónghuà, 童话故事 tónghuà gùshi

fait accompli N 既成事实 jìchéng shìshí

faith N **1** 极其信任 jíqí xìnrèn **2** 信仰 xìnyǎng ■ *In spite of her personal tragedies she still has faith in God.* 尽管个人悲剧, 她还是信仰上帝。Jǐnguǎn gèrén bēijù, tā háishi xìnyǎng Shàngdì. **3** 宗教 zōngjiào

faithful ADJ **1** 忠诚的 zhōngchéng de ■ *My grandfather was entirely faithful to grandma all his life.* 我的祖父对祖母终身忠诚。Wǒ de zǔfù duì zǔmǔ zhōngshēn zhōngchéng. **2** 准确可靠的 [+翻译] zhǔnquè kěkào de [+ fānyì]

faithless ADJ 不守信义的 bù shǒu xìnyì de, 不可依赖的 bùkě yīlài de

fake I N **1** 假货 jiǎhuò **2** 假冒者 jiǎmàozhě **II** ADJ 伪造的 wěizào de, 假冒的 jiǎmào de
a fake artwork 假冒艺术品 jiǎmào yìshùpǐn
III v 假装 jiǎzhuāng, 伪装 wěizhuāng
to fake one's signature 伪造某人的签名 wěizào mǒurén de qiānmíng

falcon N 猎鹰 lièyīng [M. WD 只 zhī]

fall[1] I N **1** 跌倒 diēdǎo, 摔倒 shuāidǎo **2** 下降 xiàjiàng, 下跌 xiàdiē ■ *Experts predict a big fall in house prices.* 专家预测房产价格要大跌。Zhuānjiā yùcè fángchǎn jiàgé yào dà diē.
fall guy 替罪羊 tìzuìyáng
3 降雨量 jiàngyǔliàng **II** v (PT fell; PP fallen)
1 跌倒 diēdǎo, 摔倒 shuāidǎo ■ *The old man stumbled and almost fell.* 老人绊了一下, 差点儿

跌倒。Lǎorén bànle yí xià, chàdiǎnr diēdǎo. **2** 下降 xiàjiàng, 落下 luòxià
to fall in love 爱上 àishang
to fall short (of) 缺少 quēshǎo, 缺乏 quēfá
to fall off 减少 jiǎnshǎo, 降低 jiàngdī
to fall through 未能成功 wèi néng chénggōng, 失败 shībài

fall[2] N 秋季 qiūjì, 秋天 qiūtiān

fallacious ADJ 谬误的 miùwù de, 错误的 cuòwù de

fallacy N 谬论 miùlùn, 错误的看法 cuòwù de kànfa

fallen v See fall[1]

fallible ADJ 会出错的 huì chūcuò de, 难免犯错误的 nánmiǎn fàn cuòwù de

fallout N **1** [核爆炸后的+] 放射性尘埃 [hébàozhà hòu de+] fàngshèxìng chén'āi **2** [金融危机的+] 不良后果 [jīnróng wēijī de+] bùliáng hòuguǒ

fallow ADJ **1** 休耕的 [+土地] xiūgēng de [+tǔdì] **2** 休闲的 [+人] xiūxián de [+rén]

falls N 瀑布 pùbù [M. WD 条 tiáo]

false ADJ **1** 错误的 cuòwù de ■ *Say if the following answers are true or false.* 说说下面的回答是对是错。Shuōshuo xiàmiàn de huídá shì duì shì cuò.
a false step 失足 shīzú, 出错 chūcuò
2 假的 jiǎ de, 虚假的 xūjiǎ de
false teeth 假牙 jiǎyá
under false pretenses 以欺诈手段 yǐ qīzhà shǒuduàn
3 虚伪的 xūwěi de
false alarm 一场虚惊 yì cháng xūjīng

falsehood N 谎言 huǎngyán

falsetto N 假声唱法 jiǎshēng chàngfǎ, 假声 jiǎshēng

falsify v 伪造 wěizào, 篡改 cuàngǎi

falter v **1** [勇气+] 变弱 [yǒngqì+] biàn ruò **2** [经济+] 衰退 [jīngjì+] shuāituì **3** 支支吾吾地说 zhīzhī wūwū de shuō

fame N 名气 míngqì, 名声 míngshēng

famed ADJ 有名的 yǒumíng de

familiar ADJ **1** 熟悉的 shúxī de, 精通的 jīngtōng de
to be familiar with 对…熟悉 duì…shúxī ■ *I'm thoroughly familiar with this part of the city.* 我对城市这个地区完全熟悉。Wǒ duì chéngshì zhè ge dìqū wánquán shúxī.
2 随便的 suíbiàn de, 亲切的 qīnqiè de

familiarity N **1** 熟悉 shúxī, 精通 jīngtōng **2** 亲切 qīnqiè

familiarize v 熟悉 shúxī

family N **1** 家 jiā, 家庭 jiātíng
family name 姓 xìng ■ *What is your family name?* 你姓什么? (→您贵姓?) Nǐ xìng shénme? (→Nín guìxìng?)
family room 家庭娱乐室 jiātíng yúlèshì
family tree 家谱图 jiāpǔtú

famine

single-parent family 单亲家庭 dānqīn jiātíng
2 年幼的子女 niányòu de zǐnǚ, 孩子 háizi
family planning 计划生育 jìhuà shēngyù
3 亲人 qīnrén, 家人 jiārén
immediate family 直系亲族 zhíxì qīnzú ■ *Only the immediate family knows this secret.* 只有直系亲族知道这个秘密。Zhǐyǒu zhíxì qīnzú zhīdào zhè ge mìmì.
4 (动物／植物）科 (dòngwù/zhíwù) kē, (语言）语族 (yǔyán) yǔzú ■ *English and German belong to the same language family.* 英语和德语属于同一个语族。Yīngyǔ hé Déyǔ shǔyú tóngyíge yǔzú.

famine N 饥荒 jīhuang

famished ADJ 饥饿的 jī'è de

famous ADJ 有名的 yǒumíng de, 著名的 zhùmíng de
to be famous for 因…而出名 yīn…ér chūmíng

fan¹ I N **1** 扇子 shànzi [m. wd 把 bǎ] II v 扇 shàn, 扇动 shāndòng
to fan out 呈扇形散开 chéng shànxíng sànkāi

fan² N 热情崇拜者 rèqíng chóngbàizhě, …迷 …mí, 粉丝 fěnsī
fan club 追星俱乐部 zhuī xīng jùlèbù, 影迷会 yǐngmí huì
football fan 足球迷 zúqiúmí
movie fan 电影迷 diànyǐngmí, 影迷 yǐngmí

fanatic N 狂热分子 kuángrè fènzi

fanatical ADJ 狂热的 kuángrè de

fanaticism N 狂热 kuángrè

fanciful ADJ **1** 花哨的 [+装饰] huāshao de [+zhuāngshì] **2** 空想的 [+念头] kōngxiǎng de [+niàntou]

fancy I ADJ **1** 豪华的 [+汽车] háohuá de [+qìchē], 新潮的 xīncháo de **2** 优质的 [+乳制品] yōuzhì de [+rǔzhìpǐn] **3** 高难度的 [+舞蹈动作] gāonándù de [+wǔdǎo dòngzuò] II N **1** 喜爱 xǐ'ài
to take a fancy to sb 喜欢上某人 xǐhuan shàng mǒurén
2 想象力 xiǎngxiànglì
a flight of fancy 幻想 huànxiǎng
III v **1** 以为 yǐwéi, 错认为 cuò rènwéi
to fancy oneself 自以为 zì yǐwéi, 自认为是 zì rènwéi shì
2 喜爱 xǐ'ài

fanfare N **1** 嘹亮的小号声 liáoliàng de xiǎohào shēng **2** 大张声势 dà zhāng shēngshì

fang N (动物）尖牙 (dòngwù) jiānyá [m. wd 颗 kē]

fanny N 屁股 pìgǔ
fanny pack 腰包 yāobāo

fantasize v 幻想 huànxiǎng

fantastic ADJ **1** 好极了 hǎo jí le, 太妙了 tài miào le **2** 荒诞的 huāngdàn de, 古怪的 gǔguài de

fantasy N 幻想 huànxiǎng

FAQ (= frequently asked questions) ABBREV 常问问题 chángwèn wèntí

far I ADV **1** 远 yuǎn, 遥远 yáoyuǎn ■ *We hadn't gone far before a snowstorm began.* 我们没有走很远，暴风雪就开始了。Wǒmen méiyǒu zǒu hěn yuǎn, bàofēngxuě jiù kāishǐ le. **2** 远比…得多 yuǎn bǐ…de duō ■ *Prevention is far more important than finding a cure.* 预防比治疗重要得多。Yùfáng bǐ zhìliáo zhòngyào de duō. II ADJ 远 yuǎn, 遥远 yáoyuǎn
to be a far cry from 相差很远 xiāngchà hěn yuǎn ■ *The new job is a far cry from what I expected.* 这份新工作和我期望的相差很远。Zhè fèn xīn gōngzuò hé wǒ qīwàng de xiāngchà hěn yuǎn.
so far 到目前为止 dào mùqián wéizhǐ

faraway ADJ 遥远的 yáoyuǎn de

farce N 闹剧 nàojù

fare¹ N **1** [飞机、火车和长途汽车+] 票价 [fēijī, huǒchē hé chángtú qìchē+] piàojià **2** 出租汽车乘客 chūzū qìchē chéngkè **3** 膳食 shànshí, 食物 shíwù

fare² v 进展 jìnzhǎn
to fare well/badly 情况很好／很坏 qíngkuàng hěn hǎo/hěn huài

(the) Far East N 远东 Yuǎndōng

farewell N 告别 gàobié
farewell party 告别聚会 gàobié jùhuì, 告别宴会 gàobié yànhuì

far-fetched ADJ 牵强附会的 qiānqiǎngfùhuì de ■ *I think this metaphor is far-fetched.* 我觉得这个比喻牵强附会。Wǒ juéde zhè ge bǐyù qiānqiǎngfùhuì.

far-flung ADJ 远在四方的 yuǎn zài sìfāng de

farm I N 农场 nóngchǎng II v 经营农场 jīngyíng nóngchǎng, 务农 wùnóng

farmer N 农场主 nóngchǎngzhǔ

farmhand N 农场工人 nóngchǎng gōngrén

farming N 务农 wùnóng

farmyard N 农家院落 nóngjiā yuànluo

far-off ADJ 偏远的 piānyuǎn de

far-out ADJ 远离的 yuǎnlí de

far-reaching ADJ 深远的 shēnyuǎn de

far-sighted ADJ 目光远大的 mùguāngyuǎndà de

fart v 放屁 fàngpì

fascinate v 强烈地吸引 qiángliè de xīyǐn, 迷住 mízhu

fascinating ADJ 让人着迷的 ràng rén zháomí de

fascination N **1** 着迷 zháomí, 迷恋 míliàn **2** 极大的吸引力 jídà de xīyǐnlì

fascism N 法西斯主义 fǎxīsī zhǔyì

fascist N 法西斯分子 fǎxīsī fènzi II ADJ 法西斯的 fǎxīsī de

fashion I N **1** 流行式样 liúxíng shìyàng, 风尚 fēngshàng **2** 时装 shízhuāng ■ *Her dream is to become a fashion designer.* 她的梦想是成为一名

384

名时装设计师。Tā de mèngxiǎng shì chéngwéi yì míng shízhuāng shèjìshī.

fashion show 时装表演 shízhuāng biǎoyǎn
II v **1** 制作 zhìzuò **2** 塑造 sùzào, 形成 xíngchéng

fashionable ADJ 流行的 liúxíng de, 时髦的 shímáo de

fast¹ I ADJ 快 kuài, 迅速 xùnsù
fast food 快餐 kuàicān
II ADV **1** 快 kuài, 迅速 xùnsù ■ *The child learns fast.* 这个孩子学得很快。Zhè ge hái xué de hěn kuài.
to fast forward 快进 kuài jìn
2 紧紧地 jǐnjǐn de
Not so fast! 慢点! Màn diǎn! 仔细点! Zǐxì diǎn! ■ *Not so fast! You've got to wait for your turn.* 别这么着急，还没有轮到你呢。Bié zhème zháojí, hái méiyǒu lúndao nǐ ne.
fast asleep 熟睡 shúshuì

fast² I v 禁食 jìnshí, 斋戒 zhāijiè
the fast day 禁食日 jìnshí rì
II N 禁食（期）jìnshí (qī), 斋戒 zhāijiè

fasten v 系上 [+安全带] jìshang [+ānquán dài], 关紧（门/窗）guānjǐn (mén/chuāng)
to fasten one's attention on sth 把注意力集中在某事 bǎ zhùyìlì jízhōng zài mǒushì
to fasten blame on sb（错误地）责怪某人 (cuòwù de) zéguài mǒurén

fastener, fastening N 扣件 kòujiàn, 扣紧物 kòujǐn wù

fastidious ADJ 过分讲究的 guòfènjiǎngjiū de, 挑剔的 tiāoti de

fat I ADJ 胖 pàng ■ *She is in mortal fear of getting fat.* 她怕胖，怕得要死。Tā pà pàng, pà de yàosǐ.
fat farm 减肥营 jiǎnféiyíng
II N 脂肪 zhīfáng, 肥肉 féiròu ■ *She cut off all the fat from the chicken before cooking it.* 她在煮鸡前把鸡油全都割掉。Tā zài zhǔ jī qián bǎ jīyóu quándōu gēdiao.

fatal ADJ **1** 致命的 [+错误] zhìmìng de [+cuòwù] **2** 毁灭性的 [+打击] huǐmièxìng de [+dǎjī], 灾难性的 zāinànxìng de

fatalism N 宿命论 sùmìnglùn

fatalistic ADJ 宿命论的 sùmìnglùn de

fatality N 死亡（事件）sǐwáng (shìjiàn)

fate N 命运 mìngyùn

fated ADJ 命中注定的 mìngzhōng zhùdìng de

fateful ADJ 灾难性的 zāinànxìng de

fat-free ADJ 无脂肪的 wú zhīfáng de

father N **1** 父亲 fùqin
father-in-law 岳父 yuèfù (wife's father), 公公 gōnggong (husband's father)
2 …之父 …zhī fù, 开创者 kāichuàngzhě
the father of one's country 国父 guófù
3（天主教）神父 (Tiānzhǔjiào) shénfu
fathers 祖先 zǔxiān

father figure 父亲般的人物 fùqin bān de rénwù,（崇敬的）长者 (chóngjìng de) zhǎngzhě

fatherly ADJ 父亲（般）的 fùqin (bān) de

Father's Day N 父亲节 fùqinjié

fathom I v 彻底了解 chèdǐ liǎojiě, 完全看清楚 wánquán kàn qīngchǔ **II** N（测水深的）英寻 (cè shuǐshēn de) yīngxún

fatigue N 疲劳 píláo, 疲倦 píjuàn

fatigues N 宽松军装 kuānsōng jūnzhuāng

fatten v 使…长肥 shǐ…zhǎng féi, 喂肥 wèiféi

fattening ADJ 使人发胖的 shǐrén fāpàng de

fatty ADJ **1** 高脂肪的 gāo zhīfáng de **2** 肥胖的 féipàng de

fatuous ADJ 愚昧的 yúmèi de, 昏庸的 hūnyōng de

faucet N 水龙头 shuǐlóngtóu, 开关者 kāiguānzhě

fault N **1** 过错 guòcuò **2** 缺点 quēdiǎn
to find fault with 挑剔毛病 tiāoti máobing **3**（地表的）断层 (dìbiǎo de) duàncéng

faulty ADJ **1** 有毛病的 yǒu máobing de **2** 有缺点的 yǒu quēdiǎn de ■ *I can understand him though his pronunciation is faulty.* 虽然他发音有缺点，我还是能听得懂。Suīrán tā fāyīn yǒu quēdiǎn, wǒ háishi néng tīngdedǒng.

fauna N 动物（群）dòngwù (qún)

favor I N **1** 善意的行为 shànyì de xíngwéi ■ *Can I ask you a favor?* 可以请你帮个忙吗？Kěyǐ qǐng nǐ bāng ge máng ma? **2** 赞成 zànchéng, 支持 zhīchí
in favor of 赞成 zànchéng, 同意 tóngyì
to find favor with sb 受到某人的喜爱 shòudào mǒurén de xǐ'ài
to curry favor with 奉承讨好 fèngcheng tǎohǎo, 拍马屁 pāi mǎpì
II v **1** 赞同 [+计划] zàntóng [+jìhuà], 支持 zhīchí **2** 偏爱 [+人] piān'ài [+rén]
the most favored nation 最惠国（待遇）zuìhuìguó (dàiyù)

favorable ADJ **1** 有利的 yǒulì de ■ *The human resources manager wrote a favorable report on his work.* 人力资源经理对他的工作写了一份有利的报告。Rénlì zīyuán jīnglǐ duì tā de gōngzuò xiěle yí fèn yǒulì de bàogào. **2** 优惠的 yōuhuì de
favorable financing terms 优惠的融资条件 yōuhuì de róngzī tiáojiàn
3 给人好印象的 gěi rén hǎo yìnxiàng de
to make a favorable impression 给人留下好印象 gěi rén liúxia hǎo yìnxiàng

favorite I ADJ 最喜爱的 zuì xǐ'ài de **II** N **1** 最喜爱的人（或东西）zuì xǐ'ài de rén (huò dōngxi), 宠儿 chǒng'ér **2** 最有希望获胜的人 zuì yǒu xīwàng huòshèng de rén

fawn¹ v 巴结 bājie, 讨好 tǎohǎo

fawn² N **1** 幼鹿 yòu lù [M. WD 头 tóu] **2** 浅黄褐色 qiǎnhuáng hèsè

fax I (= fascimile) ABBREV 传真 chuánzhēn, 电传

diànchuán **II** v 电传 diànchuán ■ *He faxed his diagram to the boss.* 他把图表电传给老板。Tā bǎ túbiǎo diànchuán gěi lǎobǎn.

fax machine 传真机 chuánzhēnjī

faze v 使…窘迫 shǐ…jiǒngpò, 使…感到困扰 shǐ… gǎndào kùnrǎo

fazed ADJ 窘迫的 jiǒngpò de, 不知所措的 bù zhī suǒ cuò de

FBI (= the Federal Bureau of Investigation) ABBREV（美国）联邦调查局 (Měiguó) Liánbāng Diàochájú

fear I v 1 怕 pà, 惧怕 jùpà, 恐惧 kǒngpà 2 担忧 dānyōu ■ *They really fear that their daughter is on drugs.* 他们真的担忧女儿吸毒。Tāmen zhēn de dānyōu nǚ'ér xīdú. II N 怕 pà, 惧怕 jùpà

fearful ADJ 担心的 dānxīn de, 惧怕的 jùpà de

fearless ADJ 无畏的 wúwèi de, 无所惧怕的 wú suǒ jùpà de

fearlessness N 无畏 wúwèi

fearsome ADJ 极其可怕的 jíqí kěpà de, 吓人的 xiàrén de

feasibility N 可行 kěxíng, 可行性 kěxíngxìng feasibility study/report 可行性研究／报告 kěxíngxìng yánjiū/bàogào

feasible ADJ 可行的 kěxíng de, 办得到的 bàndédào de

feast I N 宴会 yànhuì, 盛宴 shèngyàn II v 大吃大喝 dàchī dàhē, 尽情饱餐 jìnqíng bǎocān
to feast one's eye on 欣赏 [+美景／美色] xīnshǎng [+měijǐng/měisè]

feat N 事迹 shìjì

feather I N 羽毛 yǔmáo [M. WD 根 gēn]
Birds of a feather flock together. 物以类聚，人以群分。Wù yǐ lèi jù, rén yǐ qún fēn.
II v 长羽毛 zhǎng yǔmáo
to feather one's nest（通过不正当手段）致富 (tōngguò bú zhèngdāng shǒuduàn) zhìfù, 敛财 liǎncái

feathery ADJ 羽毛状的 yǔmáozhuàng de

feature I N 1 特征 tèzhēng 2 容貌 róngmào 3（报纸杂志）特写报道 (bàozhǐ zázhì) tèxiě bàodào,（电视）特别报道 (diànshì) tèbié bàodào 4 故事片（电影）gùshìpiàn (diànyǐng)
II v 1 由…主演 yóu…zhǔyǎn
a blockbuster movie featuring Kate Winslet 一部由凯特·温斯莱主演的大片 yí bù yóu Kǎitè·Wēnsīlái zhǔyǎn de dàpiān
2 成为…的特色 chéngwéi…de tèsè 3 特别推介（商品）tèbié tuījiè (shāngpǐn)

February N 二月 èryuè

feces N 粪便 fènbiàn

fed v See feed

Fed (= the Federal Reserve System) ABBREV（美国）联邦储备系统 (Měiguó) Liánbāng Chǔbèi xìtǒng

federal ADJ 联邦政府的 liánbāng zhèngfǔ de, 联邦的 liánbāng de

federalism N 联邦主义 liánbāng zhǔyì

federation N 联盟 liánméng, 联合会 liánhéhuì

fed up ADJ 厌烦的 yànfán de, 受够了的 shòu gòu le de

fee N 费 fèi, 费用 fèiyòng
annual fee 年费 niánfèi
consultancy fee 咨询费 zīxúnfèi
legal fee 律师费 lǜshīfèi
monthly fee 月费 yuèfèi

feeble ADJ 微弱的 wēiruò de, 菲薄的 fěibó de

feeble-minded ADJ 思维不清的 sīwéi bùqīng de, 弱智的 ruòzhì de

feed I v (PT & PP fed) 喂 wèi II N 1（动物）饲料 (dòngwù) sìliào
chicken feed 鸡饲料 jī sìliào
2 燃料输送管 ránliào shūsòng guǎn, 进料管 jìnliào guǎn

feedback N 反馈 fǎnkuì

feedbag N 饲料袋 sìliàodài

feeding N 喂奶 wèinǎi

feel I v (PT & PP felt) 1 感觉 gǎnjué ■ *She feels very tired after a day's work.* 工作一天以后她感觉非常累。Gōngzuò yì tiān yǐhòu tā gǎnjué fēicháng lèi. 2 感到 gǎndao ■ *I feel that he is an honest man.* 我感到他是个老实人。Wǒ gǎndao tā shì ge lǎoshi rén. 3 摸 mō, 抚摸 fǔmō
to feel like 觉得 juéde, 感到 gǎndao
to feel for 同情 tóngqíng ■ *She is pretty unhappy about failing her math test. I really do feel for her.* 她数学测验不及格，很不高兴。我真的非常同情她。Tā shùxué cèyàn bù jígé, hěn bù gāoxìng. Wǒ zhēn de fēicháng tóngqíng tā.
II N 感觉 gǎnjué, 感受 gǎnshòu
to get a feel for sth 对某事有感受 duì mǒushì yǒu gǎn shòu, 对某事有所了解 duì mǒushì yǒusuǒ liǎojiě
to get the feel of sth 适应某事物 shìyìng mǒushìwù

feeler N 1 试探 shìtàn 2 [昆虫的+] 触须 [kūnchóng de+] chùxū, 触角 chùjiǎo
to put out feelers 进行试探 jìnxíng shìtàn

feeling N 1 感情 gǎnqíng 2 感觉 gǎnjué ■ *It was a good feeling to have passed all the exams.* 所有的考试都通过了，这种感觉真好。Suǒyǒu de kǎoshì dōu tōngguo le, zhè zhǒng gǎnjué zhēn hǎo.
to hurt sb's feelings 伤害感情 shānghài gǎnqíng
a bad feeling 反感 fǎngǎn
with feeling 带着深情 dàizhe shēnqíng
to put one's feelings into words 用语言表达感情 yòngyǔ yán biǎodá gǎnqíng
3 预感 yùgǎn
to have a feeling that … 有…的预感 yǒu…de yùgǎn

feign v 假装 jiǎzhuāng, 装出 zhuāngchū

feint I v (拳击) 佯攻 (quánjī) yánggōng, 虚晃一拳 xū huǎng yì quán II N (拳击) 佯攻 (quánjī) yánggōng, 虚晃 xū huǎng

feisty ADJ 1 精力充沛的 jīnglì chōngpèi de 2 勇于争辩的 yǒngyú zhēngbiàn de, 好斗的 hǎodǒu de

feline I ADJ 猫科的 māo kē de, 猫的 māo de II N 猫科动物 māo kē dòngwù, 猫 māo [M. WD 只 zhī]

fell¹ v See **fall¹**

fell² v 砍伐 (树木) kǎnfá (shùmù)

fellow N 1 人 rén, 男人 nánren 2 研究生奖学金获得者 yánjiūshēng jiǎngxuéjīn huòdézhě, 学者 xuézhě 3 [学会的+] 会员 [xuéhuì de+] huìyuán

fellowship N 1 研究生奖学金 yánjiūshēng jiǎngxuéjīn 2 (基督教) 团契 (Jīdūjiào) tuánqì 3 友情 yǒuqíng

felon N 重罪犯 zhòngzuì fàn

felony N 重罪 zhòngzuì

felt¹ v See **feel**

felt² N 毛毡 máozhān

  felt tip pen 毡头笔 zhān tóu bǐ

female I ADJ 1 (动物/鸟类) 雌的 (dòngwù/niǎolèi) cí de, 母的 mǔ de ■ *A female tiger is much more ferocious than a male one.* 母虎比雄虎凶猛得多。Mǔ hǔ bǐ xióng hǔ xiōngměngde duō. 2 (人) 女的 (rén) nǚ de, 女性的 nǚxìng de II N 1 女人 nǚrén, 女子 nǚzǐ 2 雌性动物 cíxìng dòngwù, 母动物 mǔ dòngwù

feminine ADJ 女性的 nǚxìng de

femininity N 女性气质 nǚxìng qìzhì, 女性特征 nǚxìng tèzhēng

feminism N 女权主义 nǚquánzhǔyì

feminist N 女权主义者 nǚquánzhǔyì zhě

fence I N 栅栏 zhàlan, 篱笆 líba

  Good fences make good neighbors. 栅栏牢, 邻居好。Zhàlan láo, línjú hǎo.

  II v 1 用栅栏 (篱笆) 围起来 yòng zhàlan (líba) wéi qǐlái 2 击剑 jījiàn

fencing N 击剑 (运动) jījiàn (yùndòng)

fend v 抵挡 dǐdǎng

  to fend for oneself 独立谋生 dúlì móushēng, 照料自己 zhàoliào zìjǐ

fender N 挡泥板 dǎngníbǎn, 翼板 yì bǎn

ferment I v 发酵 fājiào II N 骚动 sāodòng, 动乱 dòngluàn

fern N 蕨类植物 juélèizhíwù

ferocious ADJ 凶猛的 xiōngměng de, 狂暴的 kuángbào de

ferocity N 凶猛 xiōngměng, 凶暴 xiōngbào

ferret I v 搜查找出 sōuchá zhǎochū II N 雪貂 xuě diāo [M. WD 只 zhī]

ferris wheel N 大转轮 dà zhuǎnlún, 摩天轮 mótiānlún

ferrous ADJ 含铁的 hán tiě de, 铁的 tiě de

ferry I N 渡轮 dùlún [M. WD 艘 sōu] II v (用渡轮、直升飞机等) 运送 (yòng dùlún, zhíshēng fēijī děng) yùnsòng, 摆渡 bǎidù

fertile ADJ 1 肥沃的 [+土地] féiwò de [+tǔdì] 2 能生育的 [+妇女] néng shēngyù de [+fùnǚ] 3 丰富的 [+想象力] fēngfù de [+xiǎngxiànglì]

fertilizer N 肥料 féiliào

fervent ADJ 强烈的 qiángliè de, 真诚的 zhēnchéng de

fervor N 激情 jīqíng, 热情 rèqíng

fester v 1 [关系+] 越来越糟 [guānxi +] yuèláiyuè zāo, 恶化 èhuà 2 [伤口+] 溃烂 [shāngkǒu+] kuìlàn 3 [垃圾+] 腐烂发臭 [lājī+] fǔlàn fāchòu

festival N 节 jié, 节日 jiérì

festive ADJ 喜庆的 xǐqìng de, 节日的 jiérì de

festivities N 庆祝活动 qìngzhù huódòng, 庆典 qìngdiǎn

festoon v 用彩带和彩旗装饰 yòng cǎidài hé cǎiqí zhuāngshì, 结彩 jiécǎi

fetal ADJ 胎儿的 tāi'ér de

  a fetal position 胎儿的姿势 tāi'ér de zīshì, 胎位 tāiwèi

fetch v 1 拿来 nálái, 接来 jiēlái 2 卖到 màidào

fete I v 致敬 zhìjìng II N 庆祝活动 qìngzhù huódòng

fetid ADJ 恶臭的 èchòu de

fetish N 迷恋 míliàn, 恋物癖 liànwùpǐ

  foot fetish 恋脚癖 liànjiǎopǐ

  to make a fetish of 迷恋 míliàn, 盲目崇拜 mángmù chóngbài

fetter v 束缚 shùfù

fetters N 束缚 shùfù, 桎梏 zhìgù

fetus N 胎儿 tāi'ér, 胚胎 pēitāi

feud N 长期的纠纷 chángqī de jiūfēn, 怨仇 yuànchóu

feudal ADJ 封建 (制度) 的 fēngjiàn (zhìdù) de

feudalism N 封建主义 fēngjiàn zhǔyì

fever N 1 发烧 fāshāo 2 狂热 kuángrè, 极度兴奋 jídù xīngfèn

feverish ADJ 1 发烧的 fāshāo de 2 极度兴奋的 jídù xīngfèn de

few I ADJ 很少 hěn shǎo, 不多 bù duō ■ *Few people understand Einstein's theory of relativity.* 很少人懂爱因斯坦的相对论。Hěn shǎo rén dǒng Àiyīnsītǎn de xiāngduìlùn. II PRON 一些 yìxiē, 不多 bù duō

  a few 有些 yǒuxiē

fiancé N 未婚夫 wèihūnfū

fiancée N 未婚妻 wèihūnqī

fiasco N 惨败 cǎnbài, 大败 dàbài

fiat N 法令 fǎlìng, 命令 mìnglìng

fib I N 无关紧要的谎言 wúguān jǐnyào de huǎngyán, 小谎话 xiǎo huǎnghuà II v 撒小谎 sā xiǎo huǎng

fiber N 纤维 xiānwéi
    fiber optics 光纤通讯 guāngxiāntōngxùn
fiberglass N 纤维玻璃 xiānwéi bōli
fibrous ADJ 多纤维的 duō xiānwéi de
fickle ADJ 经常变化的 jīngcháng biànhuà de, 变化无常的 biànhuàwúcháng de
fiction N 小说 xiǎoshuō [M. WD 本 běn], 虚构作品 xūgòu zuòpǐn [M. WD 本 běn]
fictional ADJ 小说的 xiǎoshuō de
fictionalize v 把…编成小说（或电影）bǎ…biān chéng xiǎoshuō (huò diànyǐng)
fictitious ADJ 虚构的 xūgòu de
fiddle I v 1 [手指+] 拨弄 [shǒuzhǐ+] bōnong 2 拉小提琴 lā xiǎotíqín II N 小提琴 xiǎotíqín [M. WD 把 bǎ]
fiddler N 小提琴手 xiǎotíqínshǒu
fidelity N 1 [夫妻之间+] 忠贞 [fūqī zhījiān+] zhōngzhēn, 忠诚 zhōngchéng 2 [音响设备+] 保真（度）[yīnxiǎng shèbèi+] bǎozhēn (dù)
fidget v 手脚不停地动 shǒujiǎo bùtíngde dòng, 坐立不安 zuòlì bù'ān
fidgety ADJ 坐立不安的 zuòlì bù'ān de, 烦躁不安的 fánzào bù'ān de
field I N 1 田 tián [M. WD 片 piàn], 农田 nóngtián [M. WD 片 piàn], 田地 chǎngdì [M. WD 块 kuài]
    field day ① 体育活动日 tǐyù huódòng rì ② 大显身手的时机 dàxiǎn shēnshǒu de shíjī
    football field 足球场 zúqiúchǎng
    field event 田赛项目 tiánsài xiàngmù
    field glasses 望远镜 wàngyuǎnjìng
    field goal（橄榄球）球踢过球门横木 (gǎnlǎnqiú) qiú tī guò qiúmén héngmù
    field hockey 曲棍球 qūgùnqiú
    field house 室内运动场 shìnèiyùndòngchǎng
    field test 现场试验 xiànchǎng shìyàn
    field trip（学生）实地考察 (xuésheng) shídì kǎochá
    magnetic field 磁场 cíchǎng
    II v 1 回答（难题）huídá (nántí) 2 接球 jiē qiú
fielder N（棒球）守场员 (bàngqiú) shǒuchǎngyuán
fieldwork N 实地考察 shídì kǎochá, 野外调查 yěwài diàochá
fiend N 恶魔 èmó
    dope fiend 吸毒者 xīdúzhě
    sex fiend 色情狂 sèqíngkuáng
fiendish ADJ 恶魔似的 èmó shìde, 极其可怕的 jíqí kěpà de
fierce ADJ 1 凶猛 xiōngměng 2 激烈 jīliè ■ *Bidders have to engage in fierce competition to win the contract.* 投标者为了赢得合同必须进行激烈竞争。Tóubiāozhě wèile yíngdé hétong bìxū jìnxíng jīliè jìngzhēng.
fiery ADJ 1 燃烧的 ránshāo de, 着火的 zháohuǒ de 2 火辣辣的 huǒlàlà de, 火热的 huǒrè de

3 激情燃烧的 jīqíng ránshāo de
fiesta N 1 节日 jiérì, 喜庆日 xǐqìngrì 2 宗教节日 zōngjiào jiérì
fifteen NUM 十五 shíwǔ, 15
fifth NUM 第五 dì wǔ
fifty NUM 五十 wǔshí, 50
fifty-fifty I ADJ 平分的 píngfēn de, 一半的 yíbàn de II ADV 一半对一半 yíbàn duì yíbàn, 对半 duìbàn
fig N 无花果 wúhuāguǒ
fight I v (PT & PP fought) 1 战斗 zhàndòu 2 打架 dǎjià, 争吵 zhēngchǎo 3 奋斗 fèndòu ■ *It is time to fight against ignorance and intolerance.* 到了与无知和无宽容精神作斗争的时候了。Dàole yǔ wúzhī hé wú kuānróng jīngshén zuò dòuzhēng de shíhou le. II N 1 打架 dǎjià 2 吵架 chǎojià, 争吵 zhēngchǎo
fighter N 1 [自由+] 斗士 [zìyóu+] dòushì 2 [职业+] 拳击手 [zhíyè+] quánjīshǒu 3 [空军+] 战斗机 [kōngjūn+] zhàndòujī [M. WD 架 jià]
figment N 凭空想象出来的事物 píngkōng xiǎngxiàng chūlái de shìwù
    a figment of one's imagination 凭空想象出来的事物 píngkōng xiǎngxiàng chūlái de shìwù
figurative ADJ 比喻的 bǐyù de
figure I N 1 身材 shēncái 2 数字 shùzì ■ *According to official figures, the unemployment rate is the highest in 10 years.* 根据官方数字，失业率是十年内最高的。Gēnjù guānfāng shùzì, shīyèlǜ shì shí nián nèi zuì gāo de. 3 人物 rénwù [M. WD 位 wéi], 人士 rénshì [M. WD 位 wéi] II v 1 崭露头角 zhǎnlù tóujiǎo 2 计算 jìsuàn
figurehead N 有名无实的领袖 yǒu míng wú shí de lǐngxiù
figure of speech N 比喻 bǐyù
figure skating N 花样滑冰 huāyàng huábīng
filch v 小偷小摸 xiǎotōu xiǎomō
file I N 1 档案 dàng'àn ■ *The government keeps secret files on terrorist suspects.* 政府有恐怖主义嫌疑犯的秘密档案。Zhèngfǔ yǒu kǒngbù zhǔyì xiányífàn de mìmì dàng'àn. 2 档案计算机 dàng'àn (jìsuànjī), 文件 wénjiàn
    file cabinet 文件柜 wénjiànguì
    back-up file 储备文件 chǔbèi wénjiàn ■ *Don't forget to create a back-up file.* 别忘了做一个储备文件。Bié wàngle zuò yí ge chǔbèi wénjiàn. 3 锉刀 cuòdāo
    nail file 指甲刀 zhǐjiadāo
    II v 1 正式立案 zhèngshì lì'àn
    to file a divorce 正式提出离婚 zhèngshì tíchū líhūn
    2 (to file away) 把…存档 bǎ…cúndàng 3 锉（平）cuò (píng)
filet, fillet N（去骨的）肉片／鱼片 (qù gǔ de) ròupiàn/yúpiàn
filibuster v（美国国会）以冗长演说阻止议事

(Měiguó Guóhuì) yǐ rǒngcháng yǎnshuō zǔzhǐ yìshì

filigree N 金银丝饰品 jīnyínsī shìpǐn [M. WD 件 jiàn]

filing N 存档 cúndàng, 归档 guīdàng

fill I V 装满 zhuāngmǎn, 倒满 dàomǎn
to fill out a form 填表 tiánbiǎo
II N 充分 chōngfèn, 足够 zúgòu
to eat one's fill 吃得饱饱的 chī dé bǎobǎo de, 吃得心满意足 chī dé xīnmǎn yìzú

filling I N 1 [补牙的+] 填料 [bǔ yá de+] tiánliào, 填补物 tiánbǔ wù 2 [食品+] 馅心 [shípǐn+] xiàn xīn, 馅 xiàn II ADJ 使人吃得饱饱的 shǐ rén chī dé bǎobǎo de

filly N 小母马 xiǎo mǔmǎ [M. WD 匹 pǐ]

film I N 1 胶卷 jiāojuǎn [M. WD 卷 juǎn] 2 电影 diànyǐng [M. WD 部 bù] ■ I hope someday I'll be able to attend the famous Cannes Film Festival. 我希望有朝一日能出席康城电影节。Wǒ xīwàng yǒuzhāoyírì néng chūxí Kāngchéng diànyǐngjié. 3 薄膜 bómó, 薄层 báo céng II V 拍摄 pāishè

filmmaker N 电影导演 diànyǐng dǎoyǎn, 电影制片人 diànyǐng zhìpiànrén

filmstrip N 幻灯片 huàndēngpiàn [M. WD 张 zhāng]

filter I N 1 过滤器 guòlǜqì, 漏斗 lòudǒu 2 (照相机) 滤色镜 (zhàoxiàngjī) lǜsèjìng II V 过滤 guòlǜ

filth N 脏东西 zàng dōngxi, 污秽 wūhuì

filthy ADJ 极其肮脏 jíqí āngzāng, 污秽不堪 wūhuìbùkān

fin N 1 鱼鳍 yúqí 2 (飞机) 垂直尾翼 (fēijī) chuízhí wěiyì
shark's fin soup 鱼翅汤 yúchìtāng

finagle V 要手段搞到手 shuǎ shǒuduàn gǎodào shǒu

final I ADJ 最终的 zuìzhōng de, 最后的 zuìhòu de II N 1 期终考试 qīzhōng kǎoshì, 大考 dàkǎo 2 决赛 juésài

finale N [歌剧+] 最后一幕 [gējù+] zuìhòu yímù, [交响乐+] 终曲 [jiāoxiǎngyuè+] zhōngqǔ

finalist N 决赛选手 juésài xuǎnshǒu

finality N 定局 dìngjú, 不可改变 bùkě gǎi biàn

finalize V 最后定下 zuìhòu dìngxià, 确定 quèdìng

finally ADV 终于 zhōngyú, 最终 zuìzhōng

finance I N 1 财务 cáiwù, 财政 cáizhèng ■ How do you plan your finances for your retirement? 你是怎样为退休计划你的财务的? Nǐ shì zěnyàng wèi tuìxiū jìhuà nǐ de cáiwù de?
corporate finance 公司财政 gōngsī cáizhèng 2 金融 jīnróng
finance company 金融公司 jīnróng gōngsī, 信贷公司 xìndài gōngsī
finance institution 金融机构 jīnróng jīgòu 3 款项 kuǎnxiàng, 钱 qián ■ The school needs to obtain additional finances for the renovation of its gym. 学校需要取得额外款项来修复体育

馆。Xuéxiào xūyào qǔdé éwài kuǎnxiàng lái xiūfù tǐyùguǎn. II V 为…提供资金 wéi…tígōng zījīn, 出资 chūzī

finances N 1 (公司+) 资金 [gōngsī+] zījīn 2 财务管理 cáiwù guǎnlǐ

financial ADJ 财务的 cáiwù de ■ The company is in deep financial difficulties. 公司财务困难重重。Gōngsī cáiwù kùnnan chóngchóng.
financial aid 助学金 zhùxuéjīn [M. WD 份 fèn/笔 bǐ], 助学贷款 zhùxué dàikuǎn [M. WD 份 fèn/笔 bǐ]

financier N 金融家 jīnróngjiā [M. WD 位 wèi]

financing N 筹集的资金 chóují de zījīn, 融资 róngzī

finch N 雀科鸟类 què kē niǎolèi, 雀 què [M. WD 只 zhī]

find I V (PT & PP found) 1 找到 zhǎodao 2 发现 fāxiàn ■ Prof Brown found it necessary to explain some of the basic concepts again. 布朗教授发现需要把一些基本概念再解释一遍。Bùlǎng jiàoshòu fāxiàn xūyào bǎ yìxiē jīběn gàiniàn zài jiěshì yí biàn.
to find out 发现 fāxiàn
3 觉得 juéde ■ I didn't find his jokes funny at all. 我觉得他讲的笑话一点儿也不好笑。Wǒ juéde tā jiǎngde xiàohua yìdiǎnr yě bù hǎoxiào. II N 被发现的东西 bèi fāxiàn de dōngxi
an archeological find 考古发现 kǎogǔ fāxiàn, 出土文物 chū tǔ wénwù

finding N 1 调查 (研究) 结果 diàochá (yánjiū) jiéguǒ ■ The latest research findings will be published next month. 最新研究结果将在下个月公布。Zuìxīn yánjiū jiéguǒ jiāng zài xià ge yuè gōngbù. 2 发现 fāxiàn ■ The wisdom of his words takes finding. 他话中的智慧，要想一想才会发现。Tā huà zhōng de zhìhui, yào xiǎngyixiǎng cái huì fāxiàn.

fine[1] ADJ 1 美好的 měihǎo de, 极好的 jíhǎo de 2 晴朗的 [+天气] qínglǎng de [+tiānqì] 3 健康的 [+身体] jiànkāng de [+shēntǐ], 身体好的 shēntǐ hǎo de ■ "How are you?" "I'm fine." "你好吗?" "挺好。" "Nǐ hǎo ma?" "Tǐng hǎo." 4 细微的 xìwēi de
a fine line 极细微的差别 jí xìwēi de chābié
fine print 细则 xìzé
not to put too fine a point on 说得不客气一点 shuó de bú kèqi yìdiǎn

fine[2] I V 对…罚款 duì…fákuǎn
to be fined for speeding 因超速驾车而被罚款 yīn chāosù jiàchē ér bèi fákuǎn
II N 罚款 fákuǎn, 罚金 fájīn ■ He got a heavy fine for driving without a license. 他因为无照驾车受到重罚。Tā yīnwéi wúzhào jiàchē shòudao zhòngfá.

fine arts N 艺术 (美术、音乐等) yìshù (měishù、yīnyuè děng)

finely

finely ADV **1** 细小地 xìxiǎo de **2** 精确地 jīngquè de

finesse I N 技巧 jìqiǎo II v 巧妙而略带欺骗性地处理 qiǎomiào ér lüè dài qīpiànxìng de chǔlǐ

finger I N 手指 shǒuzhǐ
index finger 食指 shízhǐ
middle finger 中指 zhōngzhǐ
ring finger 无名指 wúmíngzhǐ
small finger 小指 xiǎozhǐ
II v 用手指触摸 yòng shǒuzhǐ chùmō

fingernail N 指甲 zhǐjia

fingerprint N 指纹 zhǐwén

fingertip N 指尖 zhǐjiān
to have sth at one's fingertips 随时可供使用 suíshí kěgōng shǐyòng

finicky ADJ 爱挑剔的 ài tiāoti de

finish I v **1** 结束 jiéshù **2** 完成 wánchéng, …完…wán **3** 获得名次 huòdé míngcì II N **1** 结果 jiéguǒ **2** 光洁度 guāngjiédù
finish line 终点线 zhōngdiǎnxiàn

finite ADJ 有限制的 yǒuxiàn zhì de, 有限的 yǒuxiàn de

fir N 冷杉 lěngshān [M. WD 棵 kē]

fire I N **1** 火 huǒ
to catch fire 着火 zháohuǒ
2 火灾 huǒzāi [M. WD 场 cháng] ■ "Fire! Fire!" "着火了！着火了！" "Zháohuǒ le! Zháohuǒ le!"
fire alarm 火警报警器 huǒjǐng bàojǐngqì
fire brigade 义务消防队 yìwù xiāofángduì
fire department 消防队 xiāofángduì
fire engine 消防车 xiāofángchē, 救火车 jiùhuǒchē
fire extinguisher 灭火器 mièhuǒqì
fire drill 防火演习 fánghuǒ yǎnxí
fire fighter 消防员 xiāofángyuán
fire hydrant 消防龙头 xiāofánglóngtóu
to open fire 开枪 kāiqiāng
II v **1** 开枪 kāiqiāng **2** 解雇 jiěgù **3** 使…激动 shǐ…jīdòng, 激励 jīlì

firearm N 枪支 qiāngzhī

firebrand N 煽动暴乱者 shāndòng bàoluàn zhě

firecracker N 爆竹 bàozhú, 鞭炮 biānpào

firefly N 萤火虫 yínghuǒchóng [M. WD 只 zhī]

fireplace N 壁炉 bìlú

fireproof ADJ 防火的 fánghuǒ de, 耐火的 nàihuǒ de

fireside N 炉边 lúbiān

firewall N 防火墙 fánghuǒqiáng [M. WD 道 dào]

firewood N 木柴 mùchái

fireworks N 焰火 yànhuǒ

firing line N 火线 huǒxiàn, 前线 qiánxiàn
to be on the firing line 处在受到攻击的地位 chǔzài shòudào gōngjī de dìwèi, 首当其冲 shǒudāngqíchōng

firing squad N 行刑队 xíngxíngduì

firm I ADJ **1** 坚固的 jiāngù de, 结实的 jiēshi de ■ I prefer a firm mattress. 我喜欢结实的床垫。Wǒ xǐhuan jiēshi de chuángdiàn. **2** 坚定的 jiāndìng de ■ Our biology teacher is a firm believer in the theory of evolution. 我们的生物老师坚定地相信进化论。Wǒmen de shēngwù lǎoshī jiāndìng de xiāngxìn jìnhuàlùn. II N 商行 shāngháng [M. WD 家 jiā], 事务所 shìwùsuǒ, 公司 gōngsī [M. WD 家 jiā]
law firm 法律事务所 fǎlǜ shìwùsuǒ

first I PRON, ADJ 第一 dìyī, 最早 zuìzǎo ■ He is always the first to come and the last to leave. 他总是第一个来，最后一个走。Tā zǒngshì dìyī ge lái, zuìhòu yí ge zǒu.
first aid 急救 jíjiù
first base (baseball) 第一垒 dìyī lěi
first class 头等舱 tóuděngcāng, 第一类邮件 dìyī lèi yóujiàn
first lady 第一夫人 dìyī fūrén, 总统夫人 zǒngtǒng fūrén
first mate 大副 dàfù
first name 名字 míngzì, 名 míng
first person 第一人称 dìyī rénchēng
first rate 第一流的 dìyīliú de, 一流的 yīliú de
first things first 重要的事先做 zhòngyào de shì xiān zuò
love at first sight 一见钟情 yíjiàn zhōngqíng
II ADV 第一 dìyī, 首先 shǒuxiān
at first 起先 qǐ xiān, 刚开始 gāng kāishǐ
first of all 首先 shǒuxiān ■ First of all, let's define these terms. 首先让我们给这些术语下个定义。Shǒuxiān ràng wǒmen gěi zhèxiē shùyǔ xià ge dìngyì.

firsthand ADJ, ADV 第一手 dìyīshǒu

firstly ADV 第一 dìyī, 首先 shǒuxiān

fiscal ADJ 财政的 cáizhèng de
fiscal year 财务年度 cáiwù niándù, 会计年度 kuàijì niándù

fish I N 鱼 yú [M. WD 条 tiáo] II v 捕鱼 bǔyú, 钓鱼 diàoyú

fishbowl N 玻璃鱼缸 bōli yúgāng

fisherman N 钓鱼者 diàoyúzhě, 渔民 yúmín

fishery N 渔场 yúchǎng

fishing N 钓鱼 diàoyú, 捕鱼 bǔyú
fishing rod 钓鱼竿 diàoyúgān

fishnet N 鱼网 yúwǎng [M. WD 张 zhāng], 网眼袜子 wǎngyǎn wàzi [M. WD 只 zhī/双 shuāng]

fishtail v 摆尾行驶 bǎiwěi xíngshǐ, 摆尾飞行 bǎiwěi fēixíng

fishy ADJ **1** 鱼腥气的 yú xīngqi de **2** 可疑的 kěyí de ■ There's something fishy going on. 事情有些可疑。Shìqíng yǒuxiē kěyí.

fission N（原子）裂变（yuánzǐ）lièbiàn

fissure N 裂缝 lièfèng

fist N 拳头 quántou, 拳 quán

fit I ADJ **1** 合适 héshì ■ Do as you see fit. 你看怎么

合适就怎么办。（→你看着办。）Nǐ kàn zěnme héshì jiù zěnme bàn. (→Nǐ kànzhe bàn.) **2** 健康 jiànkāng, 身体好 shēntǐ hǎo **II** v **1** (PT & PP **fit**, **fitted**) 合身 héshēn ■ *I can hardly find clothes to fit me.* 我很难找到合身的衣服。Wǒ hěn nán zhǎodao héshēn de yīfu. **2** 适合 [+心意] shìhé [+xīnyì] **3** 安装 [+家具] ānzhuāng [+jiājù], 组装 zǔzhuāng **III** N **1** 发脾气 fāpíqi
to throw a fit 大发脾气 dàfā píqi
2（病或强烈感情）发作 (bìng huò qiángliè gǎnqíng) fāzuò
fits of laughter 一阵阵大笑 yí zhèn zhèn dàxiào
3 (a good fit) 适合 shìhé

fitful ADJ 一阵阵的 yízhèn zhèn de

fitness N 健康 jiànkāng, 身体好 shēntǐ hǎo

fitted ADJ **1** 定做的 dìngzuò de **2** 配备 pèibèi

fitting I ADJ 合适的 héshì de, 恰当的 qiàdàng de **II** N **1** 试穿 shìchuān
fitting room 试衣间 shìyījiān
2 装置 zhuāngzhì

five NUM 五 wǔ, 5

fix I v **1** 修理 xiūlǐ **2** 准备 zhǔnbèi
to fix a meal 准备一顿饭 zhǔnbèi yídùn fàn, 做饭 zuòfàn
3 确定 quèdìng ■ *Have you fixed a day to invite them to dinner?* 你确定了请他们来吃饭的日子吗？Nǐ quèdìngle qǐng tāmen lái chīfàn de rìzi ma? **4** 操纵 [+比赛] cāozòng [+bǐsài] **II** N **1** 困境 kùnjìng
to be in a fix 处于困境 chǔyú kùnjìng
2 毒品 dúpǐn, 上瘾的东西 shàngyǐn de dōngxi
coffee fix 不得不喝的咖啡 bùdébù hē de kāfēi
3 受到非法操纵的事 shòudào fēifǎ cāozòng de shì

fixation N 过分的兴趣 guòfèn de xìngqu, 偏爱 piān'ài

fixed ADJ 固定的 gùdìng de
to have fixed ideas 抱有固执的想法 bàoyǒu gùzhí de xiǎngfǎ

fixedly ADV 固定地 gùdìng de, 专注地 zhuānzhù de

fixture N **1** 固定装置 gùdìng zhuāngzhì **2** 一直在的东西／节目 yìzhí zài de dōngxi/jiémù, 不会离去的东西 bú huì líqù de dōngxi

fizz N [饮料的+] 泡沫 [yǐnliào de+] pàomò

fizzle v 最终失败 zuìzhōng shībài

fjord N 峡湾 xiáwān

flab N 松弛的赘肉 sōngchí de zhuìròu

flabbergasted ADJ 大吃一惊的 dàchīyìjīng de

flabby 1 松弛的(肌肉) sōngchí de (jīròu) **2** 无力的(争辩) wúlì de (zhēngbiàn)

flaccid ADJ 软弱的 ruǎnruò de, 松软的 sōngruǎn de

flag I N 旗 qí [M. WD 面 miàn], 旗子 qízi [M. WD 面 miàn] **II** v **1** 标出 [+重要部分] biāo chū [+zhòngyào bùfen], 标志 biāozhì **2** [经济+]
变得疲软 [+jīngjì] biàn de píruǎn **3** (to flag down) 招手要 [+出租汽车] 停下 zhāoshǒu yào [+chūzū qìchē] tíng xià

flagpole N 旗杆 qígān [M. WD 根 gēn]

flagrant ADJ 明目张胆的 míngmù zhāngdǎn de, 公然的 gōngrán de

flagship N **1** 旗舰 qíjiàn [M. WD 艘 sōu] **2** 标志性／最佳产品 biāozhìxìng/zuìjiā chǎnpǐn

flagstone N 石板 shíbǎn

flail v 挥动 [+手臂或腿] huīdòng [+shǒubì huò tuǐ]

flair N 天赋 tiānfù, 天分 tiānfèn

flak N 强烈的批评 qiángliè de pīpíng

flake I N **1** 小薄片 xiǎo báopiàn **2** 健忘而古怪的人 jiànwàng ér gǔguài de rén **II** v **1** 碎成小片 suì chéng xiǎopiàn **2** 剥落 bōluò

flamboyant ADJ **1** 炫耀的 xuànyào de, 卖弄的 màinong de **2**（色彩）艳丽的 (sècǎi) yànlì de

flame I N **1** 火 huǒ, 火焰 huǒyàn **2** 欲火 yùhuǒ, 情欲 qíngyù
old flame 往日情人 wǎngrì qíngrén
II v 变成火红色 biànchéng huǒhóngsè

flaming ADJ **1** 熊熊燃烧的 [+大火] xióngxióng ránshāo de [+dàhuǒ] **2** 火红的 [+落日] huǒhóng de [+luòrì], 光亮的 guāngliàng de

flamingo N 火烈鸟 huǒlièniǎo [M. WD 只 zhī]

flammable ADJ 易燃的 yìrán de

flank I N 侧翼 cèyì, 侧面 cèmiàn **II** v 在…的侧翼 zài...de cèyì
to be flanked by 两边有 liǎngbiān yǒu, 两边是 liǎngbiān shì

flannel N 法兰绒 fǎlánróng

flap I v **1** [鸟+] 拍动 [+翅膀] [niǎo+] pāi dòng [+chìbǎng] **2** [旗+] 呼啦啦地拍动 [qí+] hūlālā de pāi dòng **II** N **1**（信封）封盖口 (xìnfēng) fēng gài kǒu **2** 激动不安 jīdòng bù'ān, 慌乱 huāngluàn

flare I v [火+] 突然烧旺 [huǒ+] tūrán shāo wàng
to flare up 突然大怒 tūrán dà nù, 突然狂暴起来 tūrán kuángbào qǐlái
II N 闪光信号 shǎnguāng xìnhào, 闪光灯 shǎnguāngdēng

flare-up N 突然爆发 tūrán bàofā

flash I v **1** 闪光 shǎnguāng ■ *Lightning flashed and then there was a boom of thunder.* 一道闪电，接着雷声隆隆。Yí dào shǎndiàn, jiēzhe léishēng lónglóng. **2** 迅速传送 [+消息] xùnsù chuánsòng [+xiāoxi] **3** [汽车+] 飞驰 [qìchē+] fēichí **II** N 闪光 shǎnguāng [M. WD 道 dào]

flashback N **1** [小说+] 倒叙 [xiǎoshuō+] dàoxù **2** 往事突然重现 wǎngshì tūrán chóngxiàn

flashcard N 识图卡 shítúkǎ, 识字卡 shízìkǎ

flasher N 露阴狂 lùyīnkuáng

flashlight N 电筒 diàntǒng, 手电筒 shǒudiàntǒng

flashy ADJ 俗艳的 súyàn de

flask N **1** 扁酒瓶 biǎn jiǔpíng **2** 烧瓶 shāopíng

flat I ADJ **1** 平坦 píngtǎn **2** 没有气的 [+轮胎／球等] méiyǒu qì de [+lúntāi/qiú děng] **3** 走了气的 [+饮料] zǒu le qì de [+yǐnliào] **4** 偏低的 [+音乐] piāndī de [+yīnyuè] **5** 萧条的 [+经济] xiāotiáo de [+jīngjì], 不景气的 bùjǐngqì de **6** 固定的 [+价格] gùdìng de [+jiàgé] **7**（音乐）降半音 (yīnyuè) jiàng bànyīn
E flat 降 E 调 jiàng E tiáo
II N **1** 漏气的轮胎 lòuqì de lúntāi, 瘪胎 biě tāi **2** 降半音符号 jiàng bànyīn fúhào (♩) **III** ADV **1** 平坦地 píngtǎn de **2** (to fall flat) [笑话+] 不好笑 [xiàohua+] bùhǎo xiào, 完全失败 wánquán shībài

flatly ADV **1** 断然地 [+拒绝] duànrán de [+jùjué] **2** 平淡地 [+回答] píngdàn de [+huídá]

flats N 平跟女鞋 píng gēn nǚxié [M. WD 只 zhī/双 shuāng]

flatten V 把…弄平 bǎ…nòng píng

flatter V **1** 恭维 gōngwei, 讨好 tǎohǎo **2** 胜过 [+真人] shèngguò [+zhēnrén] ■ *This photo flatters her.* 这张照片比她本人好看。Zhè zhāng zhàopiàn bǐ tā běnrén hǎokàn.

flatterer N 恭维者 gōngweizhě, 拍马屁的人 pāi mǎpì de rén

flattery N 恭维 gōngwei, 奉承 fèngcheng

flatulence N [胃肠+] 气涨的 [wèicháng+] qì zhǎng de

flaunt V 炫耀 xuànyào, 夸耀 kuāyào

flavor I N **1** [冰淇淋的+] 味道 [bīngqilín de+] wèidao, 味 wèi **2** [地中海的+] 风味 [Dìzhōnghǎi de+] fēngwèi, 情调 qíngdiào **II** V 对…加味 duì…jiā wèi

flavored ADJ 加味的 jiā wèi de

flavoring N 调味品 tiáowèipǐn

flaw N 缺陷 quēxiàn, 缺点 quēdiǎn

flawed ADJ 有缺陷的 yǒu quēxiàn de, 错误的 cuòwù de

flawless ADJ 没有缺点的 méiyǒu quēdiǎn de, 无瑕的 wúxiá de, 完美的 wánměi de

flax N 亚麻 yàmá

flea N 跳蚤 tiàozǎo [M. WD 只 zhī]
flea collar 驱蚤项圈 qū zǎo xiàngquān
flea market 旧货市场 jiùhuò shìchǎng

fleabag N 肮脏的低级旅馆 āngzāng de dī jí lǚguǎn

fleck N 斑点 bāndiǎn

flecked ADJ 有斑点的 yǒu bāndiǎn de

fled V See flee

fledgling I ADJ 新生的 xīnshēng de **II** N（刚学飞的）小鸟 (gāng xué fēi de) xiǎoniǎo

flee (PT & PP **fled**) V 逃走 táozǒu, 逃掉 táodiào

fleece I N 羊毛 yángmáo, 羊皮 yángpí [M. WD 张 zhāng] **II** V 向 [+用户] 过多收费 xiàng [+yònghù] guòduō shōufèi, 榨取 zhàqǔ

fleet N 舰队 jiànduì, 船队 chuánduì,（汽）车队 (qì) chēduì

fleeting ADJ 极其短暂的 jíqí duǎnzàn de

flesh I N 肉 ròu
one's own flesh and blood 亲骨肉 qīngǔròu, 亲人 qīnrén
II V 使…长肉 shǐ…zhǎngròu
to flesh out 使…更生动 shǐ…gèng shēngdòng, 使…更丰富 shǐ…gèng fēngfù

fleshy ADJ 肉体的 ròutǐ de, 肉欲的 ròuyù de

flew V See fly¹

flex V 收紧 (肌肉) shōujǐn (jīròu)
to flex one's muscle 展示实力 zhǎnshì shílì

flexibility N 灵活性 línghuóxìng

flexible ADJ **1** 灵活的 [+安排] línghuó de [+ānpái], 有弹性的 yǒu tánxìng de **2** 易弯曲的 [+材料] yì wānqū de [+cáiliào], 柔软的 róuruǎn de

flextime N 弹性工作时间 tánxìng gōngzuò shíjiān

flick I V 弹去 tán qù, 弹 tán **II** N **1** 弹 tán **2** 动作片 dòngzuò piàn

flicker I V **1** [火+] 闪烁 [huǒ+] shǎnshuò **2** [表情+] 闪现 [biǎoqíng+] shǎnxiàn **II** N 闪烁 shǎnshuò

flier, flyer N **1** 广告纸 guǎnggàozhǐ [M. WD 张 zhāng] **2** 飞行员 fēixíngyuán [M. WD 名 míng]

flight N **1** 飞行 fēixíng **2** 航班 hángbān
flight attendant 空中服务员 kōngzhōng fúwùyuán
flight deck 驾驶舱 jiàshǐcāng
night flight 夜间飞行 yèjiān fēixíng
non-stop flight 直航 zhíháng
3 一段楼梯 yí duàn lóutī **4** 逃跑 táopǎo

flightless ADJ 不会飞的 bú huì fēi de

flighty ADJ 反复无常的 fǎnfù wúcháng de, 见异思迁的 jiàn yì sī qiān de

filmsy ADJ **1** 轻薄的 [+衣服] qīngbáo de [+yīfu+] **2** 不牢固的 [房屋／设备+] bù láogù de [fángwū/shèbèi+], 简陋 jiǎnlòu de **3** 不可靠的 [论点+] bùkěkào de [lùndiǎn+]

flinch V 退缩 tuìsuō **2** 回避 huíbì

fling I V (PT & PP **flung**) 抛 [+球] pāo [+qiú], 扔 rēng
to fling oneself 扑 pū, 冲 chōng
II N 一时的放纵 yìshí de fàngzòng, 一段风流情 yí duàn fēngliúqíng

flint N 火石 huǒshí [M. WD 块 kuài]

flip I V **1** 翻转 fānzhuǎn, 翻过来 fānguolái **2** 旋转 xuánzhuǎn
to flip out 突然大发脾气 tūrán dàfā píqi
to flip for 喜欢上 xǐhuanshàng, 爱上 àishang
to flip a coin 抛硬币（来决定）pāo yìngbì (lái juédìng)
II N 筋斗 jīndǒu, 空翻 kōngfān
a backward flip 后空翻 hòukōngfān
(decided by) a flip of the coin 由抛硬币来决定 yóu pāo yìngbì lái juédìng
III ADJ 轻率的 qīngshuài de

flip-flop N **1** 后空翻 hòukōngfān **2** 轻率改变 qīngshuài gǎibiàn

flippant ADJ 轻率的 qīngshuài de, 轻佻的 qīngtiāo de

flipper N（游泳用）鸭脚板 (yóuyǒng yòng) yājiǎobǎn

flip side N 不好的方面 bùhǎo de fāngmiàn

flirt I v 调情 tiáoqíng
to flirt with (an idea) 有点儿想 yǒudiǎnr xiǎng
to flirt with (a danger) 轻率地对待 qīngshuài de duìdài
II N 调情者 tiáoqíngzhě

flirtation N **1** 调情 tiáoqíng **2** 一时的兴趣 yìshí de xìngqu

flirtatious ADJ 爱调情的 ài tiáoqíng de

float I v **1** 漂浮 piāofú **2** 飘 piāo, 飘浮 piāofú
■ *Some colorful balloons were floating across the sky.* 几只彩色气球在天空飘浮。Jǐ zhī cǎisè qìqiú zài tiānkōng piāofú. **3** 提出（建议）tíchū (jiànyì) **4** 浮动（货币）fúdòng (huòbì) II N **1** 花车 huāchē **2** 备用零钱 bèiyòng língqián

flock I N 一群鸟 yì qún niǎo, 一群羊 yì qún yáng II v 成群结队地前往 chéngqún jiéduì de qiánwǎng

flog v **1** 鞭打 biāndǎ, 棒打 bàngdǎ **2** 出售 chūshòu, 卖 mài

flogging N 鞭打 biāndǎ, 棒打 bàngdǎ

flood I N 淹没 yānmò II N 洪水 hóngshuǐ, 水灾 shuǐzāi

floodgate N 防洪闸 fánghóng zhá

floodlight N 泛光灯 fànguāngdēng, 探照灯 tànzhàodēng [M. WD 台 tái]

floodlit ADJ 泛光灯照明的 fànguāngdēng zhàomíng de

floor I N **1** 地板 dìbǎn
floor lamp 落地台灯 luòdì táidēng
2（楼房）层 (lóufáng) céng, 楼 lóu
floor plan 楼层平面图 lóucéng píngmiàntú
to take the floor（在重要会议上）开始发言 (zài zhòngyào huìyì shàng) kāishǐ fāyán,（在舞会上）率先跳舞 (zài wǔhuì shàng) shuàixiān tiàowǔ

floorboard N 木地板 mù dìbǎn

flooring N 铺地面的材料 pūdì miàndī cáiliào

floozy N 淫荡的女人 yíndàng de nǚrén, 荡妇 dàngfù

flop I v **1** 猛然坐下／躺下／倒下 měngrán zuòxià/tǎngxià/dǎoxià **2** 彻底失败 chèdǐ shībài, 砸锅 záguō **3**（鸟／鱼+）扑腾 [niǎo/yú+] pūténg II N **1** 重重落下 chóngchóng luòxià, 重摔 zhòng shuāi **2** 失败 shībài, 砸锅 záguō

flophouse N 廉价低档旅馆 liánjià dīdàng lǚguǎn

floppy ADJ 松软垂下的 sōngruǎn chuíxià de

floppy disk, floppy N 软盘 ruǎnpán

flora N 植物（群）zhíwù (qún)

floral ADJ 用花装饰的 yòng huā zhuāngshì de, 花的 huā de

florid ADJ 花哨的 huāshao de

florist N 花店店主 huādiàn diànzhǔ

floss I N 洁牙线 jiéyáxiàn [M. WD 根 gēn] II v 使用洁牙线 shǐyòng jiéyáxiàn

flotation N **1** 漂浮 piāofú
flotation ring 救生圈 jiùshēngquān
2 首次发行 shǒucì fāxíng

flotilla N 小舰队 xiǎo jiànduì, 小船队 xiǎochuán duì

flotsam N **1**（水面上）漂浮垃圾 (shuǐmiàn shàng) piāofú lājī **2** 废物 fèiwù

flounder[1] v **1** 遇到大困难 yùdào dà kùnnan **2** 艰难地行走 jiānnán de xíngzǒu

flounder[2] N 鲆鱼 píng yú [M. WD 条 tiáo], 鲆鱼肉 píngyúròu

flour N 面粉 miànfěn

flourish I v 兴旺繁荣 xīngwàng fánróng II N 华丽的词藻 huálì de cízǎo, 不必要的装饰 bú bìyào de zhuāngshì
with a flourish 用专狂的动作 yòng kuāzhāng de dòngzuò

flout v 公然无视 gōngrán wúshì, 违背 wéibèi

flow v, N 流 liú, 流动 liúdòng
to go with the flow 随大流 suí dàliú, 随遇而安 suí yù ér ān
to go against the flow 反潮流 fǎn cháoliú
flow chart, flow diagram 流程图 liúchéngtú

flower I N 花 huā, 花儿 huār II v 开花 kāihuā

flowerbed N 花圃 huāpǔ

flowerpot N 花盆 huāpén

flowery ADJ **1** 用花装饰的 [+图案] yòng huā zhuāngshì de [+tú'àn] **2** 华丽的 [+文体] huálì de [+wéntǐ], 花哨的 huāshao de

flown v See fly[1]

flu (= influenza) N 流感 liúgǎn, 流行性感冒 liúxíngxìng gǎnmào

fluctuate v 上下波动的 shàngxià bōdòng de, 波动的 bōdòng de

fluctuation N 波动 bōdòng

flue N 烟道 yāndào

fluency N 流利 liúlì

fluent ADJ 流利的 liúlì de ■ *When will I become a fluent speaker of Chinese?* 我什么时候能流利地说中文？Wǒ shénme shíhòu néng liúlì de shuō Zhōngwén?

fluently ADV 流利地 liúlì de

fluff I N 蓬松毛 péngsōng máo, 线团 xiàntuán II v **1** 把…而松 bǎ…pāi sōng **2** 起毛 qǐmáo

fluffy ADJ 毛茸茸的 máoróngróng de

fluid I N 流体 liútǐ, 流质 liúzhì
fluid ounce 液益司 yè àngsī
II ADJ **1** 流动的 liúdòng de **2** 优雅流畅的 [+演奏] yōuyǎ liúchàng de [+yǎnzòu]

fluids N 体液 tǐyè

fluke N 侥幸 jiǎoxìng

flung v See fling

flunk v 不及格 bù jígé, 没有通过 méiyǒu tōngguò

flunky, flunkey N **1** 勤杂工 qínzágōng **2** 马屁精 mǎpìjīng

fluorescent ADJ 荧光的 yíngguāng de
fluorescent light 日光灯 rìguāngdēng

fluoride N 氟化物 fúhuàwù

flurry N 一阵忙乱 yí zhèn mángluàn, 慌乱 huāngluàn

flush I v **1** 水冲 shuǐ chōng, 冲洗 chōngxǐ **2** [脸+] 发红 [liǎn+] fāhóng II N **1** 水冲 shuǐ chōng, 冲洗 chōngxǐ **2** 一阵 (情绪) yízhèn (qíngxù) a flush of pride 一阵自豪感 yízhèn zìháogǎn III ADV 齐平地 qí píngde

flushed ADJ 脸红的 liǎnhóng de
flushed with excitement 激动得脸色通红 jīdòng dé liǎnsè tōnghóng

flustered ADJ 紧张慌乱的 jǐnzhāng huāngluàn de

flute N 长笛 chángdí, 笛 dí

flutist, flautist N 吹笛的人 chuī dí de rén, 笛手 chuīshǒu

flutter I v **1** 拍打 [+翅膀] pāi dǎ [+chìbǎng] **2** [旗+] 飘动 [qí+] piāodòng **3** [心+] 快速跳动 [xīn+] kuàisù tiàodòng II N 拍打 pāida, 飘动 piāodòng

flux N 流动 liúdòng
in a flux 不断变化中 búduàn biànhuà zhōng

fly¹ v (PT flew; PP flown) **1** 飞 fēi, 飞翔 fēixiáng **2** 飞 fēi, 飞行 fēixíng **3** 驾驶飞机 jiàshǐ fēijī

fly² N (PL flies) 苍蝇 cāngying **2** (裤子) 拉锁盖 lāsuǒ gài, 拉链 lāliàn

fly-by-night ADJ 靠不住的 kàobúzhù de, 长不了的 chángbùliǎo de

flying I N 乘飞机 chéngfēijī, 飞行 fēixíng II ADJ 能飞的 néng fēi de
flying saucer 飞碟 fēidié
with flying colors 大大成功地 dàdà chénggōng de
to get off to a flying start 有良好的开端 yǒu liánghǎo de kāiduān, 打响第一炮 dǎxiǎng dìyī pào

flyswatter N 苍蝇拍 cāngying pāi

FM (= frequency modulation) ABBREV 调频 tiáopín

foal N 马驹 mǎjū [M. WD 匹 pǐ], 幼马 yòu mǎ [M. WD 匹 pǐ]

foam I N 泡沫 pàomò [M. WD 块 kuài]
foam rubber 海绵橡胶 hǎimián xiàngjiāo
II v 起泡沫 qǐ pàomò

fob v (to fob sth off) 用欺骗手段把某物处理掉 yòng qīpiàn shǒuduàn bǎ mǒuwù chǔlǐdiào

focal point N 焦点 jiāodiǎn, 重点 zhòngdiǎn

focus I N **1** 重点 zhòngdiǎn **2** 焦点 jiāodiǎn, 焦距 jiāojù II v 把重点放在 bǎ zhòngdiǎn fàng zài ■ *People tend to focus on their own interests.* 人们往往注重自身的利益。Rénmen wǎngwǎng zhùzhòng zìshēn de lìyì.
out of focus 焦距不对 jiāojù bú duì, 模糊 móhu ■ *In this photo, your child is out focus.* 在这张照片上你孩子很模糊。Zài zhè zhāng zhàopiànshang nǐ háizi hěn móhu.

fodder N **1** 饲料 sìliào **2** 素材 sùcái

foe N 仇敌 chóudí, 敌人 dírén

fog I N 雾 wù II v 蒙上水汽 méng shàng shuǐqì

fogbound ADJ 因大雾而受阻的 yīn dà wù ér shòuzǔ de

fogey, fogy N 守旧的人 shǒujiù de rén, 老顽固 lǎowángu

foggy ADJ 多雾的 duō wù de, 有雾的 yǒu wù de

foghorn N 大雾天警告船只的汽笛声 dà wù tiān jǐnggào chuánzhǐ de qìdíshēng, 雾笛 wùdí

foible N 弱点 ruòdiǎn

foil I N **1** 铂纸 bózhǐ, 锡纸 xīzhǐ **2** 陪衬物 péichènwù, 陪衬 péichèn II v 挫败 cuòbài

foist v 把…强加于 bǎ…qiángjiā yú
to foist sth on sb 把某物强加给某人 bǎ mǒuwù qiángjiā gěi mǒurén

fold I v **1** 折叠 zhédié
folding bed 折叠床 zhédiéchuáng
to fold one's arms 交叉双臂 jiāochā shuāngbì **2** [公司+] 倒闭 [gōngsī+] dǎobì II N 折叠的部分 zhédié de bùfen, 褶 zhě

folder N 文件夹 wénjiàn jiā

foliage N 树叶 shùyè [M. WD 片 piàn], 叶子 yèzi

folk ADJ 民间的 mínjiān de
folk music 民间音乐 mínjiān yīnyuè
folk remedy 民间疗法 mínjiān liáofǎ

folklore N 民俗学 mínsúxué, 民俗 mínsú

folks N 人们 rénmen
Hi, folks! 各位, 大家好! Gèwèi, dàjiā hǎo!
country folks 乡下人 xiāngxiarén
townsfolks 城里人 chénglǐrén **2** (one's folks) 父母 fùmǔ, 家里人 jiālirén

folksy ADJ 随和的 suíhe de, 友好的 yǒuhǎo de

follow v **1** 跟着 gēnzhe, 跟随 gēnsuí **2** 接着发生 jiēzhe fāshēng **3** 遵循 zūnxún ■ *I followed the instructions in the manual very carefully.* 我仔细地遵循使用手册上的指令。Wǒ zǐxì de zūnxún shǐyòng shǒucèshang de zhǐlìng. **4** 留意 [+形势的发展] liúyì [+xíngshì de fāzhǎn], 关注 guānzhù **5** 领会 [+别人的话] lǐnghuì [+biérén dehuà], 听懂 tīngdǒng

follower N 追随者 zhuīsuízhě, 支持者 zhīchízhě

following I ADJ 下一个 xià yí ge, 下列 xiàliè II N (一群) 追随者 (yìqún) zhuīsuízhě, (一群) 支持者 (yìqún) zhīchízhě
the following 下列 xiàliè III PREP 在…以后 zài…yǐhòu, 由于 yóuyú

follow-up I ADJ 后续的 hòuxù de **II** N 后续行动 hòuxù xíngdòng, 随访 suífǎng

folly N 荒唐事 huāngtangshì, 蠢事 chǔnshì

foment v 挑起 tiǎoqǐ, 引发 yǐnfā

fond ADJ **1** 喜爱的 xǐ'ài de ■ *Nina is fond of all her grandchildren.* 尼娜喜爱她所有的孙子孙女。Nínà xǐ'ài tā suǒyǒu de sūnzi sūnnǚ. **2** 痴心的 chīxīn de a fond hope 痴心妄想 chīxīn wàngxiǎng

fondle v 爱抚 àifǔ, 抚弄 fǔnòng

fondly ADV 深情地 shēnqíng de
to fondly believe 天真地以为 tiānzhēn de yǐwéi

font N 字形 zìxíng, 字体 zìtǐ

food N 食物 shíwù, 食品 shípǐn ■ *I love food, delicious food.* 我喜欢吃，吃美味的食物。Wǒ xǐhuan chī, chī měiwèi de shíwù.

food bank 食品救济站 shípǐn jiùjìzhàn
food chain 食物链 shíwùliàn
food poisoning 食物中毒 shíwù zhòngdú
food processor 食品加工器 shípǐn jiāgōngqì
food stamp 免费食品券 miǎnfèi shípǐnquàn
baby food 婴儿食品 yīng'ér shípǐn
health food 保健食品 bǎojiàn shípǐn
food for thought 需要认真考虑的事 xūyào rènzhēn kǎolǜ de shì ■ *Her tragic experiences gave us food for thought.* 她的悲惨经历让我们认真思考一些事。Tā de bēicǎn jīnglì ràng wǒmen rènzhēn sīkǎo yìxiē shì.

fool I N 傻瓜 shǎguā, 笨蛋 bèndàn **II** v 欺骗 qīpiàn, 哄骗 hǒngpiàn

foolhardy ADJ 鲁莽而又愚蠢的 lǔmǎng ér yòu yúchǔn de, 傻大胆 shǎ dàdǎn

foolish ADJ 傻的 shǎ de, 愚蠢的 yúchǔn de

foolproof ADJ 万无一失的 wànwúyìshī de, 不会出毛病的 bú huì chūmáobing de

foot I N 足 zú, 脚 jiǎo [M. WD 只 zhī]
foot locker 床脚柜 chuángjiǎoguì
II v (to foot the bill) 付款 fùkuǎn, 付账 fùzhàng

footage N 镜头 jìngtóu, 一组镜头 yìzǔ jìngtóu

football N **1** (美国) 橄榄球 (Měiguó) gǎnlǎnqiú, 美式足球 Měishì zúqiú **2** 足球 zúqiú

footbridge N 步行桥 bùxíngqiáo [M. WD 座 zuò]

footfall N 脚步声 jiǎobùshēng

foothill N 山麓 shānlù [M. WD 座 zuò], 小山 xiǎo shān [M. WD 座 zuò]

foothold N 立足点 lìzúdiǎn, 稳固的地位 wěngù de dìwèi

footing N **1** 状况 zhuàngkuàng, 基础 jīchǔ
on an equal footing 以平等的地位 yǐ píngděng de dìwèi
2 站稳 zhànwěn
to lose one's footing 没有站稳 méiyǒu zhànwěn, 站不稳 zhàn bùwěn

footlights N 脚灯 jiǎodēng

footloose ADJ 无牵无挂的 wúqiān wúguà de, 随心所欲的 suí xīn suǒ yù de

footloose and fancy-free 无牵无挂的 wúqiān wúguà de, 随心所欲的 suí xīn suǒ yù de

footnote N 脚注 jiǎozhù

footpath N 小路 xiǎolù [M. WD 条 tiáo]

footprint N 脚印 jiǎoyìn, 足迹 zújì

footrest N 搁脚架 gēijiǎojià

footsie N (在桌下) 碰脚调情 (zài zhuō xià) pèng jiǎo tiáoqíng, 勾搭 gōuda

footstep N 脚步声 jiǎobùshēng, 脚印 jiǎoyìn

footstool N 搁脚凳 gējiǎodèng [M. WD 只 zhī]

footwear N 鞋类 xié lèi

footwork N **1** [拳击手的+] 步法 [quánjīshǒu de+] bùfǎ **2** [外交+] 手腕 [wàijiāo+] shǒuwàn

for I PREP **1** 为 wèi, 为了 wèile ■ *One for all, all for one.* 我为人人，人人为我。Wǒ wèi rénrén, rénrén wèi wǒ. ■ *What did you do that for?* 你为什么那么做？Nǐ wèishénme nàme zuò? **2** 花 (钱) huā (qián), 以…为代价 yǐ…wéi dàijià
for all I know 我真的不知道 wǒ zhēnde bù zhīdào
for now 目前 mùqián, 暂时 zànshí
for rent 招租 zhāozū
for sale 出售 chūshòu
3 支持 zhīchí **II** CONJ 因为 yīnwèi, 由于 yóuyú ■ *You can sleep in late tomorrow, for it's Sunday.* 你明天可以睡懒觉，因为是星期天。Nǐ míngtiān kěyǐ shuìlǎnjiào, yīnwèi shì xīngqītiān.

forage v 搜索 sōusuǒ, 寻找 xúnzhǎo

foray N **1** 短暂的尝试 duǎnzàn de chángshì **2** 突袭 tūxí

forbade, forbid v See **forbid**

forbear (PT **forbore**; PP **forborne**) v 忍耐 rěnnài

forbearance N 忍耐宽容 rěnnài kuānróng, 自制 zìzhì

forbid (PT **forbade, forbid**; PP **forbidden**) v 禁止 jìnzhǐ

forbidden I ADJ 被禁止的 bèi jìnzhǐ de
forbidden fruit 禁果 jìnguǒ
II v See **forbid**

forbidding ADJ 让人害怕的 ràng rén hàipà de, 可怕的 kěpà de

forbore, forborne v See **forbear**

force I N **1** 力 lì, 力量 lìliang ■ *We do certain things by force of habit, e.g. brushing teeth before going to bed.* 我们做某些事是出于习惯势力，象在睡前刷牙。Wǒmen zuò mǒuxiē shì shì chūyú xíguàn shìlì, xiàng zài shuì qián shuāyá.
(armed) forces 武装力量 wǔzhuāng lìliàng, 军队 jūnduì
II v 强迫 qiǎngpò

forced ADJ **1** 强迫的 [+纪律] qiǎngpò de [+jìlǜ] **2** 勉强的 [+笑] miǎnqiǎng de [+xiào]

forcefeed v See **forcefeed**

forcefeed (PT & PP **forcefed**) v 强迫…进食 qiǎngpò…jìnshí, 强喂 qiáng wèi

forceful ADJ 有说服力的 yǒu shuōfúlì de

forceps N 钳子 qiánzi, 镊子 nièzi
forcibly ADV 强行地 qiángxíng de
ford I N 浅滩 qiǎntān, 渡口 dùkǒu II v 涉水过河 shèshuǐ guòhé
fore I N 前面 qiánmian
to come to the fore 开始显著 kāishǐ xiǎnzhe, 开始变得重要 kāishǐ biànde zhòngyào II ADJ 前部的 qiánbù de
forearm N 前臂 qiánbì
forebear N 祖先 zǔxiān, 祖宗 zǔzōng
foreboding N 不祥的预感 bùxiáng de yùgǎn
forecast I v (PT & PP **forecast**) 预报 yùbào II N 预报 yùbào
forecaster N 气象预报员 qìxiàng yùbàoyuán
foreclose v [银行+] 收回房产 [yínháng+] shōuhuí fángchǎn
foreclosure N（银行）收回房产 (yínháng+) shōuhuí fángchǎn
forefathers N 前辈 qiánbèi, 祖先 zǔxiān
forefinger N 食指 shízhǐ
forefront N 前列 qiánliè, 前沿 qiányán
foregone conclusion N 意料中的结果 yìliào zhòngde jiéguǒ
foreground N 1 [相片或图画+] 近景 [xiàngpiàn huò túhuà+] jìnjǐng 2 重要地位 zhòngyào dìwèi
forehead N 额 é, 前额 qián é
foreign ADJ 外国的 wàiguó de
foreign exchange 外汇 wàihuì
foreign policy 外交政策 wàijiāo zhèngcè
foreign trade 对外贸易 duìwài màoyì
a foreign body (in the eye)（眼睛中的）异物 (yǎnjing zhōng de) yìwù
to be foreign to sb 对某人来说very陌生的 duì mǒurén láishuō hěn mòshēng de
foreleg N（动物）前腿 (dòngwù) qiántuǐ [M. WD 条 tiáo]
forelock N 前发 qiánfà, 刘海 liúhǎi
foreman N 工头 gōngtóu, 工长 gōngzhǎng
foremost ADJ 1 首要的 shǒuyào de, 最重要的 zuì zhòngyào de
first and foremost 首先 shǒuxiān 2 最杰出的 [+科学家] zuì jiéchū de [+kēxuéjiā], 屈指首一的 qūzhǐ shǒu yī de
forensic ADJ 法庭的 fǎtíng de, 法医的 fǎyī de
forensic medicine 法医（学）fǎyī (xué)
foreplay N 前戏 qián xì, 性爱抚 xìng'ài fǔ
forerunner N 先驱 xiānqū, 前身 qiánshēn
foresaw v See foresee
foresee (PT **foresaw**; PP **foreseen**) v 预知 yùzhī
foreseeable ADJ 在可见的未来 zài kějiànde wèilái, 可以预见的 kěyǐ yùjiàn de
foreseen v See foresee
foreshadow v 预示 yùshì
foresight N 先见之明 xiānjiàn zhī míng, 远见 yuǎnjiàn

foreskin N 包皮 bāopí
forest N 森林 sēnlín [M. WD 片 piàn]
forest ranger 林警 lín jǐng, 管林人 guǎnlínrén
forestall v 预先阻止 yùxiān zǔzhǐ
forestry N（森）林学 (sēn) línxué, 林业 línyè
foretaste N 预兆 yùzhào, 预示 yùshì
foretell (PT & PP **foretold**) v 预言 yùyán
forethought N 事先的考虑 shìxiān de kǎolǜ, 筹划 chóuhuà
foretold v See foretell
forever ADV 永远 yǒngyuǎn, 很长时间 hěn cháng shíjiān ■ They have been arguing forever. 他俩一直在争论不休。Tā liǎ yìzhí zài zhēnglùn bùxiū.
forewarn v 事先警告 shìxiān jǐnggào, 预警 yùjǐng
forewoman N 女工头 nǚgōng tóu, 女工长 nǚgōng cháng
foreword N 前言 qiányán
forfeit I v 丧失 sàngshī, 失去 shīqù II N（作为惩罚）丧失的东西 (zuòwéi chéngfá) sàngshī de dōngxi, 没收物 mòshōu wù
forgave v See forgive
forge I v 1 伪造 [+文件] wěizào [+wénjiàn] 2 建立 [+关系] jiànlì [+guānxi] 3 锻造 [+剑] duànzào [+jiàn] II N 1 锻铁炉 duàntiělú, 锻造车间 duànzào chējiān 2 铁匠铺 tiějiangpù
forger N 伪造者 wěizàozhě
forgery N 1 伪造罪 wěizàozuì, 伪造 wěizào 2 伪造品（伪造文件、赝品画、伪币等）wěizàopǐn (wěizào wénjiàn, yīng pǐnhuà, wěibì děng)
forget (PT **forgot**; PP **forgotten**) v 忘记 wàngjì
forgetful ADJ 健忘的 jiànwàng de, 记性很差的 jìxìng hěn chà de
forget-me-not N 勿忘我草 wù wàng wǒ cǎo
forgive (PT **forgave**; PP **forgiven**) v 原谅 yuánliàng, 宽恕 kuānshù ■ I forgave him for his carelessness. 我原谅他粗心。Wǒ yuánliàng tā cūxīn.
to forgive and forget 宽恕并且遗忘（→不念旧恶）kuānshù bìngqiě yíwàng (→bú niàn jiù'è)
forgiven v See forgive
forgiving ADJ 1 宽容的 [+人] kuānróng de [+rén] 2 容许出错的 róngxǔ chūcuò de
forgo [also **forego**] (PT **forwent**; PP **forgone**) v 放弃 fàngqì
forgone v See forgo
forgot, forgotten v See forget
fork I N 1 叉 chā [M. WD 把 bǎ], 叉子 chāzi [M. WD 把 bǎ] 2 岔路 chàlù, 岔口 chàkǒu II v 1 用叉子 yòng chāzi 2 分岔 fēn chà 3 (to fork over/out/up) 付出（钱）fùchū (qian)
forked ADJ 分叉的 fēn chā de
forklift N 叉车 cháchē [M. WD 辆 liàng], 铲车 chǎnchē [M. WD 辆 liàng]
forlorn ADJ 孤独凄凉的的 gūdú qīliáng de
form I N 1 形式 xíngshì, 状态 zhuàngtài ■ The

school will not tolerate bullying in any shape or form. 学校不会容忍任何形式的欺负人的行为。Xuéxiào bú huì róngrěn rènhé xíngshìde qīfùrén de xíngwéi. **2** 表格 biǎogé [M. WD 张 zhāng/份 fèn] **3** [运动员的+] 竞技状态 [yùndòngyuán de+] jìngjì zhuàngtài **II** v 形成 xíngchéng, 组成 zǔchéng

formal I ADJ **1** 正式 zhèngshì ■ *The wording sounds too formal for the occasion.* 对这样的场合来说，这么用词听起来太正式了。Duì zhèyàng de chǎnghé láishuō, zhème yòngcí tīngqilai tài zhèngshì le. **2** 正规 zhèngguī **II** N **1** 正式的 [+邀请] zhèngshì de [+yāoqǐng] **2** 正规的 [+教育] zhèngguī de [+jiàoyù]

formality N **1** (必同的) 手续 (bì bàn de) shǒuxù **2** [婚礼上的+] 礼节 [hūnlǐ shàng de+] lǐjié

formalize v 使⋯确定下来 shǐ...quèdìng xiàlai

format I N 格式 géshi, 样式 yàngshì **II** v 把⋯格式化 bǎ...géshi huà

formation N **1** 形成 xíngchéng, 组成 zǔchéng **2** [士兵的+] 列队 [shìbīng de+] lièduì

formative ADJ 促使形成的 cùshǐ xíngchéng de formative years 人格形成的时期 réngé xíngchéng de shíqī

former I ADJ 以前的 yǐqián de, 前 qián ■ *A former superior court judge will lead the investigation.* 一位前最高法庭法官将领导这项调查。Yí wèi qián zuìgāo fǎtíng fǎguān jiāng lǐngdǎo zhè xiàng diàochá. **II** N 前者 qiánzhě

formerly ADV 以前 yǐqián

formidable ADJ 令人生畏的 lìng rén shēng wèi de, 很厉害的 hěn lìhai de

formless ADJ 不成形的 bù chéngxíng de, 无定形的 wú dìngxíng de

formula N **1** 方案 fāng'àn ■ *He believes he's found a formula for happiness.* 他相信自己找到了得到幸福的方案。Tā xiāngxìn zìjǐ zhǎodào le dédào xìngfú de fāng'àn. **2** 方程式 fāngchéngshì, 公式 gōngshì **3** 配方 pèifāng

formulate v **1** 制定 [+计划、规则等] zhìdìng [+jìhuà, guīzé děng] **2** 配制 [+化工产品] pèizhì [+huàgōng chǎnpǐn] **3** 清晰表达 [+想法] qīngxī biǎodá [+xiǎngfǎ]

fornicate v 通奸 tōngjiān

forsake (PT forsook; PP forsaken) v 放弃 fàngqì, 遗弃 fàngqì

forswear (PT forswore; PP forsworn) v 发誓放弃 fāshì fàngqì

fort N 要塞 yàosài, 堡垒 bǎolěi

forte N 专长 zhuāncháng, 强项 qiángxiàng

forth ADV 向前 xiàngqián

forthcoming ADJ **1** 即将来到的 [+事件] jíjiāng láidào de [+shìjiàn] **2** 愿意提供的 yuànyì tígōng de

forthright ADJ 坦率的 tǎnshuài de, 直言不讳的 zhíyán búhuì de

fortieth NUM 第四十 dìsìshí

fortification N 加强 jiāqiáng
fortifications 防御工事 fángyù gōngshì

fortify v **1** 设防于 shèfáng yú **2** 加强 jiāqiáng, 激励 jīlì **3** 强化（食品）qiánghuà (shípǐn)

fortitude N 坚韧的精神 jiānrèn de jīngshén, 毅力 yìlì

fortnight N 两个星期 liǎng gè xīngqī, 双周 shuāng zhōu

fortress N 堡垒 bǎolěi [M. WD 座 zuò], 要塞 yàosài [M. WD 座 zuò]

fortuitous ADJ 凑巧的 còuqiǎo de, 正巧的 zhèngqiǎo de

fortunate ADJ 幸运的 xìngyùn de

fortune N **1** 一大笔钱 yí dàbǐ qián, 财富 cáifù
to make a fortune 赚一大笔钱 zhuàn yí dàbǐ qián, 发财 fācái
2 运气 yùnqi, 命运 mìngyùn
fortune cookie 幸运小饼 xìngyùn xiǎo bǐng
fortune teller 算命的人 suànmìngde rén, 算命先生 suànmìng xiānsheng
to tell one's fortunes 算命 suànmìng

forty NUM 四十 sìshí, 40

forum N 论坛 lùntán

forward I [also forwards] ADV 向前 xiàngqián ■ *He leaned forward to whisper into her ear.* 他俯身向前，跟她耳语。Tā fǔshēn xiàngqián, gēn tā ěryǔ. **II** ADJ **1** 向前的 xiàngqián de, 在前部的 zàiqián bù de **2** 预先的 yùxiān de, 前瞻性的 qiánzhānxìng de **III** v 转交 zhuǎnjiāo, 转寄 zhuǎnjì **IV** N 前锋 qiánfēng

forwarding address N 转递地址 zhuǎndì dìzhǐ

forward-looking, forward-thinking ADJ 前瞻性的 qiánzhānxìng de, 前瞻的 qián zhān de

forwent v See forgo

fossil N 化石 huàshí
fossil fuel 矿物燃料 kuàngwù ránliào

fossilize v 形成化石 xíngchéng huàshí

foster I v **1** 促进 cùjìn, 助长 zhùzhǎng **2** 照管（孩子）zhàoguǎn (háizi) **II** ADJ 收养的 shōuyǎng de, 寄养的 jìyǎng de

fought v See fight

foul I v **1** 犯规 fànguī **2** 污染 wūrǎn, 弄脏 nòngzāng
to foul up 把⋯搞得一团糟 bǎ...gǎode yìtuánzāo **II** N（体育比赛）犯规 (tǐyù bǐsài) fànguī **III** ADJ **1** 又脏又臭的 [+气味] yòu zàng yòu chòu de [+qìwèi] **2** 肮脏的 [+空气] āngzāng de [+kōngqì] **3** 恶劣的 [+天气] èliè de [+tiānqì]
foul language 粗话 cūhuà, 脏话 zānghuà
foul play 违法行为 wéifǎ xíngwéi
in a foul mood 心情很坏 xīnqíng hěn huài

found¹ v See find

found² (PT & PP founded) v 建立 jiànlì, 创建 chuàngjiàn

foundation N 1 基础 jīchǔ ■ *Christianity provided the foundation for Western civilization.* 基督教为西方文明提供了基础。Jīdūjiào wèi xīfāng wénmíng tígōngle jīchǔ. 2 基金会 jījīn huì 3 地基 dìjī, 房基 fángjī

founder¹ N 创立人 chuànglìrén, 创始者 chuàngbànzhě

founder² v 1 [船只+] 沉没 [chuánzhī+] chénmò 2 [生意+] 垮掉 [shēngyì+] kuǎdiào

founding father N 创始人 chuàngshǐrén
the Founding Fathers（美国）开国元勋 (Měiguó) kāiguó yuánxūn

foundry N 铸造车间 zhùzào chējiān, 铸造厂 zhùzàochǎng

fountain N 喷泉 pēnquán, 喷泉池 pēnquánchí
fountain pen 自来水笔 zìláishuǐbǐ, 钢笔 gāngbǐ

four NUM 四 sì, 4

fourteen NUM 十四 shísì, 14

fourteenth NUM 第十四 dì shísì

fourth NUM 第四 dì sì

(the) Fourth of July N 美国独立纪念日 Měiguó dúlì jìniànrì

fowl N 家禽 jiāqín

fox N 狐狸 húli [M. WD 只 zhī]

foxtrot N 狐步舞（曲）húbùwǔ (qū)

foxy ADJ 1 狡猾的 jiǎohuá de 2 性感的 [+女人] xìnggǎn de [+nǚrén]

foyer N 休息厅 xiūxītīng [M. WD 间 jiān], 大堂 dàtáng [M. WD 间 jiān]

fracas N 喧闹的斗殴 xuānnào de dòu'ōu

fraction I N 1 极小的部分 jíxiǎo de bùfen, 非常少 fēicháng shǎo 2 小于一的数目 xiǎoyú yí de shùmù, 分数（如 ¼, ⅜）fēnshù (rú ¼, ⅜)

fractional ADJ 1 少量的 shǎoliàng de 2 小数的 xiǎoshù de

fractious ADJ 暴躁的 bàozao de

fracture I v 1 [骨+] 断裂 [gǔ+] duànliè 2 [组织+] 出现裂痕 [zǔzhī+] chūxiàn lièhén II N 1 骨折 gǔzhé 2 裂缝 lièfèng

fragile ADJ 1 易碎的 [+花瓶] yì suìde [+huāpíng], 易损坏的 yì sǔnhuài de
Fragile! Handle With Care. 易碎物品，小心轻放。Yì suì wùpǐn, xiǎoxīnqīngfàng.
2 虚弱的 [+身体] xūruò de [+shēntǐ], 脆弱的 cuìruò de

fragment N 1 [玻璃／金属+] 碎片 [bōli/jīnshǔ+] suìpiàn 2 [谈话的+] 片断 [tán huà de+] piànduàn

fragmentary ADJ 1 碎片的 suìpiàn de 2 片断的 piànduàn de

fragmented ADJ 分裂的 fēnliè de, 支离破碎的 zhīlí pòsuì de

fragrance N 香味 xiāngwèi, 香气 xiāngqì, 芬芳 fēnfāng

fragrant ADJ 香的 xiāng de, 芬芳的 fēnfāng de

frail ADJ 柔弱的 róuruò de

frailty N 柔弱 róuruò, 弱点 ruòdiǎn

frame I N 1 镜框 jìngkuàng 2 框架 kuàngjià
frame of mind 思想状况 sīxiǎng zhuàngkuàng
II v 1 给 [+一幅画] 装框 gěi [+yìfú huà] zhuāng kuàng 2 陷害 [+无辜者] xiànhài [+wúgūzhě] 3 仔细考虑 [+答复] zǐxì kǎolǜ [+dáfù]

frames N 眼镜框 yǎnjìngkuàng [M. WD 副 fù]

frame-up N 阴谋陷害 yīnmóu xiànhài, 陷害 xiànhài

framework N 1 框架 kuàngjià 2 [法律的+] 体系 [fǎlǜ de+] tǐxì

franchise N 1 特许经营 tèxǔ jīngyíng 2 特许经营店 tèxǔ jīngyíngdiàn, 专卖店 zhuānmàidiàn [M. WD 家 jiā]

frank¹ ADJ 坦率的 tǎnshuài de, 坦诚的 tǎnchéng de

frank² v（在信封上）加盖 "邮资已付" (zài xìnfēng shàng) jiāgài "yóuzī yǐfù"

frankfurter N 熏肉香肠 xūnròu xiāngcháng [M. WD 根 gēn]

frantic ADJ 1 惊恐的 jīngkǒng de, 情绪失控的 qíngxù shīkòng de 2 紧张纷乱的 jǐnzhāng fēnluàn de

frat (member of a fraternity) N 男生联谊会会员 nánshēng liányìhuì huìyuán

fraternal ADJ 兄弟般的 xiōngdìbān de, 亲如手足的 qīn rú shǒuzú de

fraternity N 1 男生联谊会 nánshēng liányìhuì 2 情谊 qíngyì, 博爱 bó'ài

fraud N 1 诈骗 zhàpiàn, 欺骗 qīpiàn 2 骗子 piànzi

fraudulent ADJ 欺诈的 qīzhà de, 舞弊的 wǔbì de

fraught ADJ 充满的 chōngmǎn de
fraught with problems 问题成堆的 wèntí chéngduī de

fray¹ v 1 磨损 mósǔn, 磨破 mópò 2 [神经+] 紧张 [shénjīng+] jǐnzhāng
frayed nerves 紧张的神经 jǐnzhāng de shénjīng

fray² N 1 争论 zhēnglùn, 争吵 zhēngchǎo 2 打架 dǎjià, 斗殴 dòu'ōu

freak I N 1 怪人 guàirén, 怪物 guàiwu 2 狂热爱好者 kuángrè àihàozhě
control freak 喜欢控制别人的人 xǐhuan kòngzhì biéren de rén, 支配欲极强的人 zhīpèiyù jíqiáng de rén
II v 突然大怒 tūrán dà nù, 突然失态 tūrán shī tài III ADJ 奇怪的 qíguài de, 离奇的 líqí de
a freak accident 离奇的事故 líqí de shìgù

freaky ADJ 古怪吓人的 gǔguài xiàrén de

freckle N 雀斑 quèbān

free I ADJ 1 自由的 zìyóude ■ *You're free to choose the holiday destination – Paris or Venice.* 你可以随意挑选度假地—巴黎，或者威尼斯。Nǐ kěyǐ suíyì tiāoxuǎn dùjià dì–Bālí, huòzhě Wēinísī.
free market 自由市场 zìyóu shìchǎng
free thinker 思想自由的人 sīxiǎng zìyóu de rén
free throw 罚球 fáqiú

free will 自由意志 zìyóu yìzhì
2 免费的 miǎnfèi de **3** 有空的 yǒukòng de **II** v
1 释放 shìfàng ■ *He was freed after new evidence proved his innocence.* 他在新证据证明他无罪以后获释。Tā zài xīn zhèngjù zhèngmíng tā wúzuì yǐhòu huòshì. **2** 解救 jiějiù **III** ADV 免费地 miǎnfèi de
feel free 随意 suíyì ■ *Feel free to take a copy.* 请随意取。Qǐng suíyì qǔ.

freebie, freebee N 免费小礼品 miǎnfèi xiǎo lǐpǐn

freedom N 自由 zìyóu **2** 免受 miǎnshòu
freedom from fear 免受恐惧 miǎnshòu kǒngjù

free-for-all N **1** 七嘴八舌的争吵 qīzuǐ bāshé de zhēngchǎo **2** 混战 hùnzhàn

freehand ADJ 徒手画的 túshǒu huà de

freelance I ADJ 自由职业的 zìyóu zhíyède
freelance translator 个体翻译工作者 gètǐ fānyì gōngzuòzhě
II v 从事自由职业 cóngshì zìyóu zhíyè

freelancer N 自由职业者 zìyóu zhíyèzhě

freeload v 吃白食 chī báishí, 白吃白拿 bái chī bái ná

freely ADV 自由自在地 zìyóu zìzài de, 自如地 zìrú de

freeway N 高速公路 gāosù gōnglù [M. WD 条 tiáo]

freewheeling ADJ 无拘无束的 wújū wúshù de

freeze I v (PT **froze**; PP **frozen**) **1** 冻结 dòngjié, 结冰 jiébīng **2** 极冷 jí lěng **II** N **1** 冻结 dòngjié **2** 寒流 hánliú

freeze-dried ADJ 快速冷冻干燥的 kuàisù lěngdòng gānzào de

freezer N 冷藏箱 lěngcángxiāng

freezing N 冰点 bīngdiǎn
freezing point 冰点 bīngdiǎn
below/above freezing point 零度以下／以上 língdù yǐxià/ yǐshàng

freight I N 货物 huòwù
freight train（火车）货车（huǒchē）huòchē
II v 运输 yùnshū

freighter N 货轮 huòlún [M. WD 艘 sōu]

French I ADJ 法国的 Fǎguó de
French bread 法式长条面包 Fǎshì cháng tiáo miànbāo
French fry 炸土豆条 zhá tǔdòutiáo
French toast 法式炸面包片 Fǎshì zhá miànbāopiàn
2 法国人的 Fǎguórén de **II** N **1** 法语 Fǎyǔ **2** 法国人 Fǎguórén

frenetic ADJ 疯狂的 fēngkuáng de, 狂乱的 kuángluàn de

frenzied ADJ 狂热的 kuángrè de

frenzy N 狂热 kuángrè

frequency N **1** 频率 pínlǜ **2** 发生的次数 fāshēng de cìshù

frequent ADJ 频繁的 pínfán de

frequent flier 经常乘坐飞机的旅客 jīngcháng chéngzuò fēijī de lǚkè

frequently ADV 频繁 pínfán ■ *Lately she has frequently been absent from school.* 最近她频繁旷课。Zuìjìn tā pínfán kuàngkè.

fresh ADJ **1** 新的 [+东西] xīn de [+dōngxi] **2** 新鲜的 [+水果] xīnxian de [+de shuǐguǒ] **3** 冷冷的 [+风] lěnglěng de [+fēng] **4** 精神饱满的 [+人] jīngshen bǎomǎn de [+rén]
to make a fresh start 从新开始 cóng xīn kāishǐ ■ *After heated quarrels, the couple decided to make a fresh start.* 经过激烈争吵，这对夫妻决定从新开始。Jīngguò jīliè zhēngchǎo, zhè duì fūqī juédìng cóng xīn kāishǐ.

freshen v 使…干净清新 shǐ…gānjìng qīngxīn

freshman N（高中或大学）一年级学生 (gāozhōng huò dàxué) yìniánjí xuésheng

freshwater ADJ 淡水 dànshuǐ

fret v 烦恼 fánnǎo, 发愁 fāchóu

fretful ADJ 烦躁的 fánzào de, 发牢骚的 fāláosāo de

friction N 摩擦 mócā, 倾轧 qīngyá

Friday N 星期五 xīngqīwǔ, 周五 zhōuwǔ

fridge N 冰箱 bīngxiāng [M. WD 台 tái]

friend N 朋友 péngyou
A friend in need is a friend indeed. 患难见真交。Huànnàn jiàn zhēn jiāo.
to make friends (with)（和…）交朋友 (hé…) jiāo péngyǒu

friendly ADJ 友好的 yǒuhǎo de ■ *We have been very friendly to the new neighbors.* 我们对新邻居很友好。Wǒmen duì xīn línjū hěn yǒuhǎo.
user-friendly 方便使用者的 fāngbiàn shǐyòngzhě de

friendship N 友谊 yǒuyì

fries N (French fries) 炸薯条 zhá shǔtiáo, 炸土豆条 zhá tǔdòutiáo

frigate N 护航舰 hùhángjiàn [M. WD 艘 sōu]

fright N 惊吓 jīngxià

frighten v 惊吓 jīngxià, 使害怕 shǐ hàipà

frightening ADJ 可怕的 kěpà de

frigid ADJ **1** 寒冷的 lěngdàn de **2**（女子）性冷淡的 (nǚzǐ) xìng lěngdàn de **3** 严寒的 yánhán de

frill N **1** 不必要的额外物品 bú bìyào de éwài wùpǐn **2** 饰边 shìbiān

fringe N **1** 边缘 biānyuán, 边缘组织 biānyuán zǔzhī **2** 流苏 liúsū, 缘饰 yuánshì
fringe benefit 附加福利 fùjiā fúlì, 额外津贴 éwài jīntiē

Frisbee N 飞盘 fēipán, 飞碟 fēidié

frisk v **1** 对 [+旅客] 搜身 duì [+lǚkè] sōushēn, 安全检查 ānquán jiǎnchá **2** [小狗+] 欢蹦乱跳 [xiǎo gǒu+] huānbèngluàntiào

fritter I N 油炸馅饼 yóuzhá xiànbǐng [M. WD 块 kuài] **II** v 浪费 làngfèi, 挥霍 huīhuò

fritz N 故障 gùzhàng

to be on the fritz 出故障 chū gùzhàng

frivolity N 轻浮 qīngfú, 轻佻 qīngtiāo

frivolous ADJ 极不严肃的 jí bù yánsù de, 轻率的 qīngshuài de

fro ADV 向后 xiànghòu

to and fro 来来回回的 láilái huíhuí de

frog N 蛙 wā [M. WD 只 zhī], 青蛙 qīngwā [M. WD 只 zhī]

frolic I v 欢快地玩耍 huānkuài de wánshuǎ II N 嬉闹 xǐ'nào

from PREP 1 从 cóng ■ *I lived in Canada from 1998 to 2002.* 我从一九九八年到二零零二年住在加拿大。Wǒ cóng yāojiǔjiǔbā nián dào èrlínglíng'èr nián zhù zài Jiānádà. 2 是…人 shì…rén, 来自 láizì ■ *Our Chinese teacher is from Taipei.* 我们的中文老师是台北人。Wǒmen de Zhōngwén lǎoshī shì Táiběirén.

from now on 从现在开始 cóng xiànzài kāishǐ

3 离… lí…, 距… jù….

front I ADJ 前面的 qiánmian de, 前方的 qiánfāng de ■ *I prefer a front seat on the plane.* 我喜欢飞机的前座。Wǒ xǐhuan fēijī de qián zuò. II N 1 前面 qiánmian, 正面 zhèngmiàn

in front of 在…前面 zài…qiánmian

2 外表 wàibiǎo, 装出来的样子 zhuāngchū láide yàngzi

to put on a brave front 装出勇敢的样子 zhuāngchū yǒnggǎn de yàngzi

3 领域 lǐngyù, 活动 huódòng

frontage N 正面 zhèngmiàn

frontal ADJ 正面的 zhèngmiàn de

frontier N 前沿 qiányán, 前线 qiánxiàn

front man N 出面人 chūmiàn rén, 代言人 dàiyánrén

frontrunner N 领先者 lǐngxiān zhě

frost I N 1 霜 shuāng 2 冰冻的天气 bīngdòng de tiānqì, 严寒 yánhán II v 1 结霜 jié shuāng 2 撒上糖霜 sā shàng tángshuāng

frostbite N 冻伤 dòngshāng

froth I N 1 沫 mò, 白沫 báimò 2 空谈 kōngtán, 美好的空想 měihǎo de kōngxiǎng II v 起泡沫 qǐpào mò, 冒白沫 mào báimò

to be frothing at the mouth 气得发昏 qì dé fāhūn

frothy ADJ 1 泡沫多的 pàomò duō de 2 空洞的 kōngdòng de, 肤浅的 fūqiǎn de

frown v 皱眉头 zhòu méitou

to frown upon 对…很不赞成 duì…hěn bú zànchéng

froze v See freeze

frozen I ADJ 1 冷冻的 lěngdòng de ■ *I picked up some frozen food from the supermarket.* 我从超级市场买了些冷冻食品。Wǒ cóng chāojí shìchǎng mǎile xiē lěngdòng shípǐn. 2 [人+] 冷极了 [rén+]

冷 jíle, 冻坏了 dòng huài le ■ *I'm frozen.* 我冷极了。Wǒ lěng jíle. II v See freeze

frugal ADJ 节俭的 jiéjiǎn de

fruit N 1 水果 shuǐguǒ 2 成果 chéngguǒ ■ *He can now enjoy the fruits of his labor.* 他现在可以享受劳动成果了。Tā xiànzài kěyǐ xiǎngshòu láodòng chéngguǒ le.

fruit tree 果树 guǒshù

to bear fruit 结果 jiéguǒ

fruitcake N 水果蛋糕 shuǐguǒ dàngāo

fruitful ADJ 富有成果的 fùyǒu chéngguǒ de

fruition N 实现 shíxiàn, 成功 chénggōng

fruitless ADJ 没有结果的 méiyǒu jiéguǒ de, 无效的 wúxiào de

fruity ADJ 有水果味的 yǒu shuǐguǒ wèi de

frustrate v 1 使…恼怒 shǐ…nǎonù 2 挫败 cuòbài, 阻挠 zǔnáo

frustrated ADJ 气恼的 qìnǎo de, 沮丧的 jǔsàng de

frustrating ADJ 让人恼怒的 ràng rén nǎonù de

frustration N 恼怒 nǎonù, 沮丧 jǔsàng

fry v (油) 煎 (yóu) jiān, 炸 zhá, 炒 chǎo

to deep-fry 油炸 yóuzhá

to shallow-fry 炒 chǎo

fry-pan, frying pan N 平底煎锅 píngdǐ jiānguō

fuck v 性交 xìngjiāo

Fuck off! 滚你的蛋! Gǔn nǐde dàn!

to fuck up 把…弄糟 bǎ…nòngzāo

fudge I N 乳脂软糖 rǔzhī ruǎntáng [M. WD 块 kuài] II v 回避 huíbì, 搪塞 tángsè

fuel I N 燃料 ránliào ■ *They fueled up their car before heading for the mountains.* 他们进山前给汽车加满了燃料。Tāmen jìn shān qián gěi qìchē jiāmǎnle ránliào. 2 刺激 cìjī, 促进 cùjìn

fugitive N 逃犯 táofàn, 逃亡者 táowángzhě

fulcrum N 支点 zhīdiǎn

fulfill v 1 实现 shíxiàn, 达到 dádào 2 满足 mǎnzú

to fulfill oneself 实现自己的潜能 shíxiàn zìjǐ de qiánnéng, 充分发挥自己的才能 chōngfèn fāhuī zìjǐ de cáinéng

fulfilled ADJ 满足的 mǎnzú de, 有成就感的 yǒu chéng jiùgǎn de

fulfilling ADJ 给人成就感的 gěi rén chéngjiùgǎn de, 使人满意的 shǐ rén mǎnyì de

full I ADJ 1 满的 mǎn de, 充满的 chōngmǎn de ■ *The hotel is full; there is no vacancy.* 旅馆满了，没有空房了。Lǚguǎn mǎn le, méiyǒu kòng fáng le.

full house [电影院+] 客满 [diànyǐngyuàn+] kèmǎn

full moon 满月 mǎnyuè

2 饱了 bǎo le, 吃饱了 chībǎo le ■ *I'm full. Thanks.* 吃饱了，谢谢。Chībǎo le, xièxie.

on a full stomach 刚吃饱 gāng chībǎo

3 整整的 zhěngzhěng de, 全部的 quánbù de

full speed 全速 quánsù

II ADV 正好 zhènghǎo, 直接地 zhíjiē de
to know full well 完全明白 wánquán míngbai
III N (in full) 全部地 quánbù de, 一点不少的 yìdiǎn bùshǎo de

full-blown ADJ 充分发展了的 chōngfèn fāzhǎn le de, 成熟的 chéngshú de

full-fledged ADJ 1 羽毛长好的 [+鸟] yǔmáo zhǎnghǎo de [+niǎo] 2 经过全面训练的 [+教师] jīngguò quánmiàn xùnliàn de [+jiàoshī], 成熟的 chéngshú de

full-grown ADJ 发育成熟的 fāyù chéngshú de

full-length ADJ 1 羽毛长好的 [+鸟] yǔmáo cháng hǎode [+niǎo] 2 经过全面训练的 [+教师] jīngguò quánmiàn xùnliàn de [+jiàoshī], 成熟的 chéngshú de

full-scale ADJ 全面的 quánmiàn de, 最大限度的 zuìdà xiàndù de

full-time ADJ, ADV 全日（的／地）quánrì (de)

fully ADV 完全的 wánquán de, 十分 shífēn

fumble I v 1 摸索 mōsuo, 乱摸 luànmō 2 接球不稳 jiēqiú bùwěn, 失球 shī qiú II N 失球 shī qiú

fume v [一言不发地+] 牛气 [yìyán bù fā de+] shēngqì, 怒火中烧 nùhuǒ zhōng shāo

fumes N 难闻的气味 nánwén de qìwèi

fumigate v 烟熏 yānxūn

fun I N 乐趣 lèqù, 欢乐 huānlè ■ Have fun! 好好玩吧! Hǎohǎo wán ba!
for fun 取乐 qǔlè ■ He sang in the choir, just for fun. 他参加唱诗班，只是为了好玩。Tā cānjiā chàngshībān, zhǐshì wèile hǎowán.
to make fun of 嘲笑 cháoxiào
II ADJ 1 好玩的 hǎowán de, 让人快乐的 ràng rén kuàilè de 2 好玩儿的 hǎowánr de, 逗笑的 dòuxiào de ■ He wore a fun hat and made everyone laugh. 他戴了一顶好玩儿的帽子，逗得大家哈哈笑。Tā dàile yì dǐng hǎowánr de màozi, dòude dàjiā hāhā xiào.

function I N 1 功能 gōngnéng 2 函数 hánshù II v 起作用 qǐ zuòyòng, 运转 yùnzhuǎn
function key（计算机）功能键 (jìsuànjī) gōngnéngjiàn

functional ADJ 1 实用的 shíyòng de 2 正常运转的 zhèngcháng yùnzhuǎn de

fund I N 1 专款 zhuānkuǎn 2 资金 zījīn, 钱 qián II v 拨款 bō kuǎn, 资助 zīzhù ■ The new road system will be funded by the federal government. 新道路系统将由联邦政府拨款建造。Xīn dàolù xìtǒng jiāng yóu liánbāng zhèngfǔ bō kuǎn jiànzào.

fundamental I ADJ 基本的 jīběn de, 根本的 gēnběn de II N 基本原理 jīběn yuánlǐ

fundamentalism N 原教旨主义 yuánjiāozhǐzhǔyì

fundamentalist I N 原教旨主义者 yuánjiāozhǐ zhǔyìzhě II ADJ 原教旨主义的 yuánjiāozhǐ zhǔyì de

funding N 1 拨款 bō kuǎn, 出资 chūzī 2 专款 zhuānkuǎn

fund-raising ADJ 募款 mù kuǎn, 筹款 chóu kuǎn

funeral N 葬礼 zànglǐ ■ The funeral will be held on Monday morning at the local church. 葬礼将于星期一上午在当地教堂举行。Zànglǐ jiāng yú xīngqīyī shàngwǔ zài dāngdì jiàotáng jǔxíng.
funeral home 殡仪馆 bìnyíguǎn

fungus N 真菌 zhēnjūn

funk N 1 乡土爵士音乐 xiāngtǔ juéshì yīnyuè 2 体臭 tǐ chòu 3 (in a blue funk) 恐慌地 kǒnghuāng de, 惊恐地 jīngkǒng de

funky ADJ 1 时髦的 shímáo de, 有趣的 yǒuqù de 2 臭烘烘的 chòuhōnghōng de, 脏兮兮的 zàngxīxī de

funnel I N 漏斗 lòudǒu, 烟囱 yāncōng II v 1 [水+] 流经漏斗 [shuǐ+] liú jīng lòudǒu 2 汇集 [+钱] huìjí [+qián]

funnies N 漫画专栏 mànhuà zhuānlán

funny ADJ 1 好笑的 hǎoxiào de, 可笑的 kěxiào de 2 奇怪的 qíguài de ■ That's funny—I left my book here just a moment ago and now it's gone. 好奇怪—我刚才把书放在这里，现在不见了。Hǎo qíguài—wǒ gāngcái bǎ shū fàng zài zhèlǐ, xiànzài bújiàn le.

fur N 毛皮 máopí

furious ADJ 1 狂怒的 kuángnù de 2 强烈的 [+攻击] qiángliè de [+gōngjī]

furl v 卷起 juǎnqǐ, 折起 zhéqǐ

furlong N 俳ulong xiūjiǎ

furlough N 休假 xiūjià

furnace N 熔炉 rónglú, 火炉 huǒlú

furnish v 1 为…配备家具 wéi…pèi bèi jiājù 2 提供 tígōng

furnished ADJ 有家具的 yǒu jiājù de

furnishings N 家具 jiājù, 室内陈设 shìnèi chén-shè

furniture N 家具 jiājù

furor, furore N 公众的愤怒 gōngzhòng de fènnù

furrow I N 1 犁沟 lígōu [M. WD 道 dào] 2 皱纹 zhòuwén [M. WD 道 dào] II v 1 开沟槽 kāi gōucáo 2 起皱纹 qǐ zhòuwén

furry ADJ 毛茸茸的 máoróngróng de

further I ADV 1 进一步 jìnyíbù ■ I don't have anything further to say. 我没有进一步的话要说了。Wǒ méiyǒu jìnyíbù de huà yào shuō le. 2 更远地 gèng yuǎn de 3 而且 érqiě II ADJ 进一步的 jìnyíbù de ■ Further investigation is needed before the case is closed. 需要进一步调查，才能结案。Xūyào jìnyíbù diàochá, cái néng jié'àn. III v 促进 cùjìn, 推进 tuījìn

furthermore ADV 而且 érqiě, 不仅如此 bù jǐn rúcǐ

furthest ADJ, ADV 最远的／地 zuì yuǎn de

furtive ADJ 偷偷的 tōutōu de, 鬼鬼祟祟的 guǐguǐ suìsuì de

fury N 狂怒 kuángnù, 暴怒 bàonù

fuse I N **1** [电表+] 保险丝 [diànbiǎo+] bǎoxiǎnsī
2 [炸弹的+] 定时引信 [zhàdàn de+] dìngshí
yǐnxìn
to have a short fuse 容易发火 róngyì fāhuǒ,
脾气急躁 píqi jízào
II v **1** 熔合 rónghé **2** 使…结合 shǐ…jiéhé
fuse-box N 保险丝盒 bǎoxiǎnsīhé
fuselage N 飞机机身 fēijī jīshēn
fusion N 熔合 rónghé, 融合 rónghé
fusion jazz 融合爵士乐 rónghé juéshìyuè
fuss I N 不必要的激动 bú bìyào de jīdòng, 无事
生非 wúshì shēngfēi
to kick up a fuss 因为小事而大吵大闹 yīnwèi
xiǎoshì ér dàchǎo dànào
to make a fuss over 过分注意 guòfèn zhùyì,
过分照顾 guòfèn zhàogù
II v **1** 局促不安 júcù bù'ān **2** 过分讲究 guòfèn
jiǎngjiū
to fuss over 过分地照料 guòfèn de zhào liào
fussy ADJ 过分讲究的 guòfèn jiǎngjiū de, 挑剔
的 tiāoti de
futile ADJ 无用的 wúyòng de
futility N 徒劳 túláo
futon N 蒲团 pútuán
future I N 将来 jiānglái, 未来 wèilái **2** 前途 qiántú
II ADJ 将来的 jiānglái de, 未来的 wèilái de
■ *The poor woman knows practically nothing
about her future husband.* 这个可怜的女人对她未
来的丈夫几乎一无所知。Zhè ge kělián de nǚrén
duì tā wèilái de zhàngfu jīhū yìwú suǒzhī.
futuristic ADJ 未来主义的 wèiláizhǔyì de
fuzz N 茸毛 róngmáo, 细毛 xìmáo
fuzzy ADJ **1** 模糊的 móhu de **2** 不清楚的
bùqīngchu de
fuzzy logic 模糊逻辑 móhu luóji
FYI (= for your information) ABBREV 仅供参考 jǐn
gōng cānkǎo

G

gab v 喋喋不休 diédié bùxiū, 闲扯 xiánchě
gable N 三角墙 sānjiǎo qiáng
gadget N 小玩意儿 xiǎowányìr
gaffe N 说错话 shuōcuò huà, 失言 shīyán
gag[1] **I** v **1** 作呕 zuò'ǒu, 想吐 xiǎng tǔ **2** 用布塞
住嘴 yòng bù sāizhù zuǐ **3** 不让 [+人] 说话 bú
ràng [+rén] shuōhuà, 压制言论自由 yāzhì
yánlùn zìyóu **II** v 塞住嘴的布 sāizhù zuǐ de bù
gag[2] N 笑话 xiàohua
gaggle N **1** 一群鹅 yì qún é **2** 一群喧闹的人 yì
qún xuānnào de rén
gaiety N 欢乐 huānlè
gaily ADV 色彩鲜艳的 sècǎi xiānyàn de

gain I v **1** 获得 huòdé, 赢得 yíngdé **2** 增加
zēngjiā
to gain on 渐渐赶上 jiànjiàn gǎnshàng
II N **1** 增进 zēngjìn, 增加 zēngjiā
One man's gain is another man's loss. 有人得,
便有人失。Yǒurén dé, biàn yǒurén shī.
2 获利 huòlì, 收益 shōuyì
gait N 步伐 bùfá
gal N 女孩 nǚhái
gala N 盛会 shènghuì [M. WD 次 cì], 欢庆
huānqìng [M. WD 次 cì]
galactic ADJ 星系的 xīngxì de
galaxy N 星系 xīngxì
gale N 大风 dàfēng, 八级大风 bā jí dàfēng
gall N 厚脸皮 hòu liǎnpí
to have the gall to … 竟然有脸皮… jìngrán yǒu
liǎnpí…
gallant ADJ **1** 英勇的 yīngyǒng de **2** (对女子) 献
殷勤的 (duì nǚzǐ) xiàn yīnqín de
gallantry N 英勇 yīngyǒng
gall bladder N 胆囊 dǎnnáng
gallery N **1** 画廊 huàláng **2** 美术馆 měishùguǎn
art gallery 艺术馆 yìshùguǎn
3 楼座 lóuzuò
galley N 船上的厨房 chuánshàng de chúfáng
gallivant v 游逛 yóuguàng
gallon N 加仑 jiālún ■ *The SUV has a 15 gallon
tank.* 这辆越野车的油箱可加十五加仑油。Zhè
liàng yuèyěchē de yóuxiāng kě jiā shíwǔ jiālún yóu
gallop I v [马+] 飞奔 [mǎ+] fēibēn **II** N [马的+] 飞
奔 [mǎ de+] fēibēn
galloping ADJ 飞速增长的 fēisù zēngzhǎng de,
迅速发展的 xùnsù fāzhǎn de
gallows N 绞刑架 jiǎoxíngjià
galore ADJ 大量的 dàliàng de
galoshes N 橡胶套鞋 xiàngjiāo tàoxié [M. WD 双
shuāng]
galvanize v 激起 jīqǐ, 激励 jīlì
gambit N 策略 cèlüè, 手段 shǒuduàn
gamble I v 赌博 dǔbó, 冒险 màoxiǎn **II** N 赌博
dǔbó, 冒险 (的做法) màoxiǎn (de zuòfǎ)
to take a gamble 冒一下险 mào yíxià xiǎn
gambler N 赌徒 dǔtú
gambling N 赌博 dǔbó
game N **1** 游戏 yóuxì
game plan (体育比赛) 策略 (tǐyù bǐsài) cèlüè
game show (电视) 有奖比赛节目 (diànshì) yǒu
jiǎng bǐsài jiémù
to play games 玩花招 wán huāzhāo ■ *Stop
playing games with me and pay your bill!* 别跟我玩
花招, 付款吧! Bié gēn wǒ wán huāzhāo, fù kuǎn
ba!
to be just a game 仅仅是一场游戏 jǐnjǐn shì yì
cháng yóuxì
2 (球赛) 局 (qiúsài) jú, 盘 pán **3** 猎物 lièwù

games N 运动会 yùndònghuì
  the Olympic Games 奥林匹克运动会 Àolínpǐkè Yùndònghuì

gamut N 所有的 suǒyǒu de, 全部的 quánbù de

gander N 公鹅 gōng é [м. wᴅ 只 zhī/头 tóu]

gang I N 帮 bāng, 帮派 bāngpài II v 结帮 jié bāng
  to gang up on 合伙对付 héhuǒ duìfu

gangland N 黑社会 hēi shèhuì

gangling ADJ 又高又瘦动作笨拙的 yòu gāo yòu shòu dòngzuò bènzhuō de

gangplank N 跳板 tiàobǎn, 步桥 bùqiáo [м. wᴅ 块 kuài]

gangrene N 坏疽 huàijū

gangster N 犯罪团伙成员 fànzuì tuánhuǒ chéngyuán, 匪徒 fěitú

gangway N 大跳板 dà tiàobǎn, 大步桥 dà bùqiáo

gap I N 1 空隙 kòngxì, 间隔 jiàngé 2 差距 chājù, 差别 chābié

gape v 目瞪口呆地看 mùdèng kǒudāi de kàn

gaping ADJ 张开的 zhāngkāi de, 敞开的 chǎngkāi de

garage I N 1 车库 chēkù [м. wᴅ 间 jiān]
  garage sale 旧物大甩卖 jiùwù dàshuǎimài 2 修车行 xiū chē háng [м. wᴅ 家 jiā]

garb N 服装 fúzhuāng, 制服 zhìfú [м. wᴅ 件 jiàn/套 tào]

garbage N 1 垃圾 lājī
  garbage can 垃圾桶 lājītǒng
  garbage disposal 厨房垃圾处理机 chúfáng lājī chǔlǐjī
  garbage truck 垃圾车 lājīchē
2 废话 fèihuà, 愚蠢的念头 yúchǔn de niàntou

garbled ADJ 含混不清的 hánhùn bùqīng de

garden N 1 花园 huāyuán 2 菜园 càiyuán
  garden center 花木商店 huāmù shāngdiàn

gardener N 园艺工人 yuányì gōngrén, 花匠 huājiàng

gardening N 园艺 yuányì

gardens N 植物园 zhíwùyuán [м. wᴅ 座 zuò]
  botanical gardens 植物园 zhíwùyuán

gargantuan ADJ 巨大的 jùdà de, 特大的 tèdà de

gargle v 漱口 shùkǒu, 漱喉 shù hóu
  to gargle with salt water 用盐水漱口 yòng yánshuǐ shùkǒu

gargoyle N 滴水嘴 dīshuǐzuǐ

garish ADJ 过于艳丽的 guòyú yànlì de

garland N 花环 huāhuán

garlic N 大蒜 dàsuàn
  a clove of garlic 一个蒜瓣 yí ge suànbàn

garment N 服装 fúzhuāng [м. wᴅ 件 jiàn/套 tào]

garnet N 石榴石 shíliúshí, 石榴红色 shíliúhóng sè

garnish I v 给…加上配菜 gěi…jiāshàng pèicài
II N 配菜 pèicài, 装饰菜 zhuāngshì cài

garret N 阁楼 gélóu, 顶楼 dǐnglóu

garrison N 卫戍部队 wèishù bùduì

garrulous ADJ 说个不完的 shuō gè bù wán de, 絮絮叨叨的 xùxu dāodāo de

garter N 吊带 diàodài
  garter snake 束带蛇 shùdài shé

gas I N 1 (gasoline) 汽油 qìyóu
  the gas (gas pedal) 油门 yóumén ■ *He put his foot on the gas and the car sped on.* 他踩下油门，汽车快速向前。Tā cǎixia yóumén, qìchē kuàisù xiàng qián.
  gas guzzler 耗油厉害的车 hàoyóu lìhai de chē, 油老虎 yóu lǎohǔ
  gas station 加油站 jiāyóuzhàn
2 气体 qìtǐ ■ *Can you believe that water is made of two gases, Hydrogen and Oxygen?* 你能相信吗，水是两种气体—氢气和氧气—组成的？ Nǐ néng xiāngxìn ma, shuǐ shì liǎng zhǒng qìtǐ—qīngqì hé yǎngqì—zǔchéng de? 3 煤气 méiqì
  gas mask 防毒面具 fángdú miànjù
  gas stove 煤气灶 méiqì zào
II v 用毒气杀死 yòng dúqì shā sǐ, 毒死 dúsǐ

gaseous ADJ 气体的 qìtǐ de, 气态的 qìtài de

gash N 又深又长的切口 yòu shēn yòu cháng de qiēkǒu, 伤口 shāngkǒu

gasket N 橡皮垫圈 xiàngpí diànquān, 密封垫 mìfēng diàn

gasoline N 汽油 qìyóu

gasp I v（大口）喘气 (dà kǒu) chuǎnqì
  to gasp for air 呼吸急促 hūxī jícù
II N 喘气 chuǎnqì, 深呼吸 shēn hūxī

gassy ADJ [肠胃+] 胀气的 [chángwèi+] zhàngqì de

gastric ADJ 胃的 wèi de
  gastric ulcer 胃溃疡 wèikuìyáng

gastronomic ADJ 美食的 měishí de
  a gastronomic tour 美食之旅 měishí zhī lǚ

gasworks N 煤气厂 méiqìchǎng [м. wᴅ 家 jiā]

gate N 大门 dàmén [м. wᴅ 扇 shàn/道 dào]

gatecrash v 不请自来 bù qǐng zì lái

gatecrasher N 不请自来的人 bù qǐng zì lái de rén

gated community N 封闭式住宅小区 fēngbìshì zhùzhái xiǎoqū

gateway N 出入口 chūrùkǒu, 入门 rùmén

gather v 1 聚集 jùjí, 集合 jíhé ■ *A crowd of fans gathered at the rear door, hoping to get a glimpse of the movie star.* 一群戏迷聚集在后门，希望能一睹明星的风采。Yì qún xìmí jùjí zài hòumén, xīwàng néng yì dǔ míngxīng de fēngcǎi. 2 收集 shōují
  to gather up 收拾起 shōushiqǐ

gathered N 有褶裥的 yǒu zhějiǎn de

gathering N 集会 jíhuì

gaudy ADJ 俗丽的 súlì de, 花哨的 huāshao de

gauge I N 测量仪器 cèliáng yíqì, 表 biǎo
  tire-pressure gauge（汽车）轮胎气压表 (qìchē) lúntāi qìyābiǎo

II v **1** 测量 cèliáng **2** 估计 gūjì, 判定 pàndìng
  to gauge public opinions 对社会舆论作出估计
  duì shèhuì yúlùn zuòchū gūjì
gaunt ADJ 憔悴的 qiáocuì de, 瘦削的 shòuxuē de
gauntlet N 夹道鞭刑 jiádào biānxíng
  to run the gauntlet 受到攻击 shòudào gōngjī,
  经受困难 jīngshòu kùnnan
  to throw down the gauntlet 挑战 tiǎozhàn
gauze N 纱布 shābù
gave v See **give**
gawk v 呆呆地看 dāidāide kàn, 傻看 shǎ kàn
gawky ADJ 笨手笨脚的 bènshǒu bènjiǎo de
gay I ADJ **1** 同性恋的 tóngxìngliàn de **2** 快活的
  kuàihuo de **II** N 男同性恋者 nán tóngxìngliànzhě
gaze v, N 凝视 níngshì, 注视 zhùshì
gazebo N 凉亭 liángtíng [M. WD 座 zuò]
gazelle N 瞪羚 dènglíng [M. WD 只 zhī/头 tóu]
gazette N **1** 报纸 bàozhǐ [M. WD 张 zhāng/份 fèn]
  2 杂志 zázhì [M. WD 本 běn]
gear I N **1** (汽车) 排挡 (qìchē) páidǎng
  to change gears 换挡 huàn dǎng
  2 设备 shèbèi, 工具 gōngjù **II** v 调整 tiáozhěng
  to be geared to 使适合 shǐ shìhé
  to be geared up 准备好 zhǔnbèi hǎo
gearbox N 变速箱 biànsùxiāng
gearshift N 换挡杆 huàndǎnggǎn
GED (= General Equivalency Diploma; general
  educational development) ABBREV 通用(中等
  教育)同等学历文凭 tōngyòng (zhōngděng
  jiàoyù) tóngděng xuélì wénpíng
gee INTERJ 哎呀 āiyā, 哇 wā
geek N 怪人 guàirén, 怪家伙 guài jiāhuo
geese See **goose**
geezer N 老头子 lǎotóuzi
geisha N 日本艺妓 Rìběn yìjì
gel I N 冻胶 dòngjiāo
  hair gel 发胶 fàjiāo
  II v 涂发胶 tú fàjiāo
gelatin N 骨胶 gǔjiāo
gem N 宝石 bǎoshí [M. WD 颗 kē/粒 lì/块 kuài]
Gemini N 双子宫(星座) shuāngzǐgōng (xīngzuò)
gender N 性别 xìngbié
gene N 基因 jīyīn
genealogy N 家谱 jiāpǔ [M. WD 本 běn], 家谱图
  jiāpǔtú [M. WD 张 zhāng]
general ADJ **1** 大致的 dàzhì de
  in general 一般来说 yì bān láishuō
  2 普遍的 pǔbiàn de ■ Educators have noticed
  a general lowering of academic standards in
  schools. 教育家们注意到中小学教学水准的普遍下
  降。Jiàoyùjiāmen zhùyìdao zhōngxiǎoxué jiàoxué
  shuǐzhǔn de pǔbiàn xiàjiàng.
  general store 杂货店 záhuòdiàn
  the general public 公众 gōngzhòng
  3 总 zǒng ■ He is general manager of the chain

stores. 他是这些连锁店的总经理。Tā shì zhèxiē
liánsuǒdiàn de zǒngjīnglǐ.
  a general election 大选 dàxuǎn
  II N 将军 jiāngjūn [M. WD 位 wéi]
generality N 笼统的话 lǒngtǒng de huà [M. WD 句
  jù], 泛泛而谈 fànfàn ér tán
generalization N 概括 gàikuò, 归纳 guīnà
  to make sweeping generalizations 笼统地概括
  lǒngtǒng de gàikuò
generalize v **1** 概括分类 gàikuò fēnlèi **2** 笼统地表
  达 lǒngtǒng de biǎodá
generally ADV **1** 普遍地 pǔbiàn de **2** 一般(地)来
  说 yì bān (de) láishuō
generate v 产生 chǎnshēng, 引起 yǐnqǐ ■ Tourism is expected to generate $10 million a year for
this city. 期待旅游业能每年为这个城市带来一千
万元。Qīdài lǚyóu yè néng měi nián wèi zhè ge
chéngshì dàilai yì qiānwàn yuán.
generation N **1** 代 dài, 世代 shìdài ■ The José
family has lived in Arizona for five generations. 何
塞一家在亚利桑那居住了五代了。Hésāi yì jiā zài
Yàlìsāngnà jūzhùle wǔ dài le.
  generation gap 代沟 dàigōu
  2 产生 chǎnshēng ■ The generation of electricity
from solar energy has a bright future. 太阳能发电前
途光明。Tàiyáng néng fādiàn qiántú guāngmíng.
generator N 发电机 fādiànjī [M. WD 台 tái/部 bù]
generic ADJ **1** 没有注册商标的 [+商品] méiyǒu
  zhùcè shāngbiāo de [+shāngpǐn] **2** 通用的 [+称
  呼] tōngyòng de [+chēnghu], 泛指的 fànzhǐ de
generosity N 慷慨 kāngkǎi
generous ADJ 慷慨 kāngkǎi, 大方 dàfang
genesis N 起源 qǐyuán, 开端 kāiduān
  Genesis (圣经) 创世纪 (Shèngjīng) chuàngshìjì
genetic ADJ 基因的 jīyīn de
  genetic engineering 基因工程 jīyīn gōngchéng
  genetic fingerprint 基因图谱 jīyīn túpǔ, 遗传指
  纹 yíchuán zhǐwén
geneticist N 遗传学家 yíchuánxuéjiā
genetics N 遗传学 yíchuánxué
genial ADJ 和蔼可亲的 hé'ǎi kěqīn de
genie N 妖怪 yāoguài
genital ADJ 生殖器的 shēngzhíqì de
genitals N 外生殖器 wàishēngzhíqì
genius N 天才 (人物) tiāncái (rénwù), 天赋 tiānfù
  a stroke of genius 天才之举 tiāncái zhī jǔ
genocide N 种族灭绝 zhǒngzú mièjué
genome N 基因组 jīyīnzǔ
  human genome 人类基因组 rénlèi jīyīnzǔ
genre N (文学艺术的) 种类 (wénxué yìshù de)
  zhǒnglèi, 类型 lèixíng
genteel ADJ **1** 彬彬有礼的 bīnbīn yǒulǐ de **2** 雅致
  的 yǎzhi de
gentile N (对犹太人而言的) 异教徒 (duì Yóutàirén
  éryán de) yìjiàotú, 非犹太人 fēi Yóutàirén

gentle ADJ 温和 wēnhé, 温柔 wēnróu

gentleman N **1** 先生 xiānsheng ■ *Ladies and gentlemen, boys and girls, ...* 女士们、先生们、小朋友们, … Nǚshìmen、xiānshengmen、xiǎopéngyǒumen,... **2** 君子 jūnzǐ, 绅士 shēnshì

gently ADV 温和地 wēnhé de, 轻柔地 qīngróu de

gentrification N 提高地区的档次 tígāo dìqū de dàngcì

gentry N 上流社会人士 shàngliú shèhuì rénshì

genuflect V 屈膝跪拜 qūxī guìbài

genuine ADJ 真诚的 zhēnchéng de, 真正的 zhēnzhèng de

genus N (生物) 属 (shēngwù) shǔ

geographical ADJ 地理的 dìlǐ de

geography N **1** 地理 (学) dìlǐ (xué)
economic geography 经济地理学 jīngjì dìlǐxué
physical geography 自然地理学 zìrán dìlǐxué
2 地理情况 dìlǐ qíngkuàng

geological ADJ 地质的 dìzhì de, 地质学的 dìzhìxué de

geologist N 地质学家 dìzhìxuéjiā

geology N 地质学 dìzhìxué

geometric ADJ 几何学的 jǐhéxué de

geometry N 几何 (学) jǐhé (xué)

geranium N 天竺葵 tiānzhúkuí

geriatric ADJ 老年医学的 lǎoniányīxué de

geriatrics N 老年医学 lǎoniányīxué

germ N 细菌 xìjūn

German I ADJ 德国的 Déguó de
German shepherd 德国牧羊犬 Déguó mùyáng quán
II N **1** 德国人 Déguórén **2** 德语 Déyǔ

germinate V **1** 发芽 fāyá, 使…发芽 shǐ…fāyá **2** 开始产生 kāishǐ chǎnshēng, 萌发 méngfā

gerrymander V 不公正地重划选区 bù gōngzhèng de chónghuà xuǎnqū

gerund N 动名词 dòngmíngcí

gestation N **1** 怀孕 (期) huáiyùn (qī) **2** [新技术的+] 形成 [xīn jìshù de+] xíngchéng, 形成期 xíngchéng qī

gesticulate V 做手势 zuò shǒushì

gesture I N **1** [表示欢迎的+] 手势 [biǎoshì huānyíng de+] shǒushì **2** [友好的+] 姿势 [yǒuhǎo de+] zīshì, 表示 biǎoshì II V 打手势 dǎ shǒushì

get (PT got; PP gotten) V **1** 得到 dédào, 买到 mǎidào ■ *Can you get me something to drink?* 能给我点喝的吗? Néng gěi wǒ diǎn hē de ma? **2** 变得 biànde ■ *I really got mad at her.* 我真的对她生气极了。Wǒ zhēn de duì tā shēngqì jíle. **3** 到达 dàodá **4** 使得 shǐde, 让 ràng ■ *I can't get this machine to work properly today.* 我今天无法使这台机器正常工作。Wǒ jīntiān wú fǎ shǐ zhè tái jīqì zhèngcháng gōngzuò.
to get across 把意思表达清楚 bǎ yìsi biǎodá qīngchu
to get along with 相处 xiāngchǔ

to get away with 不受惩罚 bú shòu chéngfá

to get by 勉强维持 miǎnqiǎng wéichí ■ *The old couple got by on their meager pension.* 这对老夫妻靠微薄的养老金勉强维持。Zhè duì lǎo fūqī kào wēibó de yǎnglǎojīn miǎnqiǎng wéichí.

to get up 起床 qǐchuáng

to get going 离开 líkāi, 走 zǒu

to get to do 有机会 yǒu jīhuì

to get the phone/door 接电话/开门 jiē diànhuà/kāi mén

getaway N **1** [周末+] 旅游 [zhōumò+] lǚyóu **2** 逃跑 táopǎo
a getaway car [犯罪分子+] 准备逃跑的汽车 [fànzuì fènzi+] zhǔnbèi táopǎo de qìchē

get-together N 联欢 liánhuān, 联欢会 liánhuānhuì

getup N 奇装异服 qízhuāng yìfú

get-up-and-go N 干劲 gànjìn, 雄心 xióngxīn

geyser N 间隙喷泉 jiànxì pēnquán

ghastly ADJ 极其糟糕的 jíqí zāogāo de, 极其可怕的 jíqí kěpà de

ghetto N 贫民区 pínmínqū, 贫民窟 pínmínkū

ghost N 鬼 guǐ, 鬼魂 guǐhún
ghost town 废弃的城镇 fèiqì de chéngzhèn
ghost writer 代笔人 dàibǐrén

ghoul N 食尸鬼 shíshīguǐ

GI (= Government Issue) ABBREV (美国) 士兵 (Měiguó) shìbīng

giant I N **1** 巨人 jùrén **2** [工业界+] 重要人物 [gōngyèjiè+] zhòngyào rénwù, 巨头 jùtóu, [流行音乐+] 巨星 [liúxíng yīnyuè+] jùxīng II ADJ 巨大的 jùdà de, 特大的 tèdà de

gibberish N 胡言乱语 húyán luànyǔ

giblets N (家禽) 内脏 (jiāqín) nèizàng

giddy ADJ **1** 快活的 kuàihuo de, 开心得忘乎所以的 kāixīn dé wàng hū suǒyǐ de
be giddy with successes 因成功而冲昏头脑 yīn chénggōng ér chōnghūn tóunǎo **2** 眩晕的 xuànyùn de

gift N **1** 礼物 lǐwù [M. WD 件 jiàn/份 fèn]
gift certificate 购物礼券 gòuwù lǐquàn
gift wrap 礼品包装纸 lǐpǐn bāozhuāngzhǐ **2** 天生的才能 tiānshēng de cáinéng ■ *Eugene sure has a gift for languages.* 尤金确实在语言方面有天生的才能。Yóujīn quèshí zài yǔyán fāngmiàn yǒu tiānshēng de cáinéng.

gifted ADJ 天才的 tiāncái de
a special class for gifted children 天才儿童特别班 tiāncái értóng tèbiébān

gig N 演奏会 yǎnzòu huì, (音乐) 演出 (yīnyuè) yǎnchū

gigabyte N 千兆字节 qiānzhào zìjié

gigantic ADJ 巨大的 jùdà de

giggle V 咯咯地笑 gēgē de xiào, 傻乎乎地笑 shǎhūhū de xiào

gild

gild v 给…镀金 gěi…dùjīn
to gild the lily 画蛇添足 huà shé tiān zú

gill N 鱼鳃 yúsāi

gilt I ADJ 镀金的 dùjīn de
gilt-edged 金边的 jīnbiān de
II N 1 镀金层 dùjīncéng 2 金边股票 jīnbiān
gǔpiào

gimmick N 花招 huāzhāo
advertising gimmicks 广告花招 guǎnggào
huāzhāo

gimmicky ADJ 耍花招的 shuǎ huāzhāo de

gin N 杜松子酒 Dùsōngzǐjiǔ

ginger N 姜 jiāng, 生姜 shēngjiāng
ginger ale 姜味汽水 jiāng wèi qìshuǐ

gingerbread N 姜饼 jiāngbǐng

gingerly ADV 小心翼翼地 xiǎoxīn yìyì de

giraffe N 长颈鹿 chángjǐnglù [M. WD 头 tóu]

girder N 大梁 dàliáng

girdle N 紧身褡 jǐnshēn dā

girl N 1 女孩 nǚhái ■ *Little girls are usually more sensible than little boys.* 小女孩通常比小男孩懂事。Xiǎo nǚhái tōngcháng bǐ xiǎo nánhái dǒngshì.
girlfriend 女朋友 nǚpéngyou
Girl Scouts 女童子军 nǚ tóngzǐjūn
2 女儿 nǚ'ér ■ *Their girl is now a college student.* 他们的女儿现在是大学生了。Tāmen de nǚ'ér xiànzài shì dàxuésheng le.

girlhood N 少女时期 shàonǚ shíqī, 少女时代 shàonǚ shídài

girth N 围长 wéicháng, (人的) 腰围 (rén de) yāowéi

gist N 主要内容 zhǔyào nèiróng, 要点 yàodiǎn

give (PT **gave**; PP **given**) v 1 给 gěi, 给与 jǐyǔ
2 举行 jǔxíng ■ *They gave a dinner party to celebrate the birth of their first child.* 他们举行宴会，庆祝第一个孩子的诞生。Tāmen jǔxíng yànhuì, qìngzhù dìyī ge háizi de dànshēng.
to give away 赠送 zèngsòng
to give up 放弃 fàngqì

give-and-take ADJ 互相忍让 hùxiāng rěnràng

giveaway I N 1 赠送 zèngsòng, 捐赠 juānzèng
holiday giveaway 假日捐赠 jiàrì juānzèng
2 赠送的东西 zèngsòng de dōngxi, 赠品 zèngpǐn II ADJ 等于是送的 děngyú shì sòng de, 极其便宜的 jíqí piányi de

given I v See give II ADJ 任何特定的 rènhé tèdìng de
at any given time 在任何 (特定的) 时间 zàirènhé (tèdìng de) shíjiān
III PREP 考虑到 kǎolǜdào IV N 基本事实 jīběn shìshí, 肯定的事实 kěndìng de shìshí ■ *That's a given.* 这是肯定的。Zhè shì kěndìng de.
given name 名字 míngzi

glacial ADJ 1 冰川的 bīngchuān de, 冰的 bīng de 2 冷冰冰的 (表情) lěngbīngbīng de (biǎoqíng)

glacier N 冰川 bīngchuān

glad ADJ 高兴 gāoxìng

gladiator N 角斗士 juédòushì

gladly ADV 1 高兴地 gāoxìngde 2 乐意地 lèyì de

glamor N 迷人的诱惑 mírén de yòuhuò, 魅力 mèilì
glamor girl 时髦迷人的姑娘 shímáo mírén de gūniang, 时尚女郎 shíshàng nǚláng

glamorize v 使…充满诱惑力 shǐ…chōngmǎn yòuhuòlì, 美化 měihuà

glamorous ADJ 迷人的 mírén de, 有诱惑力的 yǒu yòuhuòlì de

glance v, N 看一下 kàn yíxià, 看一眼 kàn yìyǎn ■ *I glanced at my watch, hoping the visitor would soon leave.* 我看了一眼手表, 希望来访者快点走。Wǒ kàn le yìyǎn shǒubiǎo, xīwàng láifǎngzhě kuài diǎn zǒu.

gland N 腺 xiàn
sweat gland 汗腺 hànxiàn

glandular ADJ 腺的 xiàn de
glandular fever 腺热 xiàn rè

glare v 1 愤怒地注视 fènnù de zhùshì 2 [玻璃窗+] 发出强光 [bōlichuāng+] fāchū qiáng guāng

glaring ADJ 1 怒视的 nùshì de 2 刺眼的 [+阳光] cìyǎn de [+yángguāng] 3 明显的 [+错误] míngxiǎn de [+cuòwù]

glass N 1 玻璃杯 bōli bēi [M. WD 只 zhī] 2 玻璃 bōli [M. WD 块 kuài]

glass ceiling N 无形的限制 wúxíng de xiànzhì

glassed-in ADJ 玻璃围成的 bōli wéi chéng de

glasses N 眼镜 yǎnjìng [M. WD 副 fù]
sunglasses 太阳眼镜 tàiyáng yǎnjìng

glassware N 玻璃器皿 bōli qìmǐn [M. WD 件 jiàn]

glassy ADJ 光亮的 guāngliàng de, 光滑的 guānghuá de

glaze I v 1 [目光+] 呆滞 [mùguāng+] dāizhì 2 上釉 shàngyòu II N 釉 yòu

gleam I v 1 [玻璃+] 闪光 [bōli+] shǎnguāng 2 闪现 shǎnxiàn II v 1 [玻璃+] 闪光 [bōli+] shǎnguāng 2 闪现 [+表情] shǎnxiàn [+biǎoqíng]

glean v 搜集 sōují

glee N 欣喜 xīnxǐ, 兴奋 xīngfèn

glen N 峡谷 xiágǔ, 幽谷 yōugǔ

glib ADJ 1 油嘴滑舌的 [+节目主持人] yóuzuǐ huáshé de [+jiémù zhǔchírén] 2 草率的 [+结论] cǎoshuài de [+jiélùn]

glide v 滑行 huáxíng

glider N 滑翔机 huáxiángjī [M. WD 架 jià]

gliding N 滑翔 (运动) huáxiáng (yùndòng)

glimmer I N 微光 wēiguāng
a glimmer of hope 一线希望 yí xiàn xīwàng
II v 发出微光 fāchū wēiguāng

glimpse I N 1 一眼 yìyǎn, 一瞥 yìpiē 2 短暂的经历 duǎnzàn de jīnglì II v 1 瞥见 piējiàn 2 突然领悟 tūrán lǐngwù, 顿悟 dùnwù

lint I v 闪闪发光 shǎnshǎn fāguāng, 闪烁 shǎnshuò **II** N 闪光 shǎnguāng

listen v 闪闪发光 shǎnshǎn fāguāng, 闪闪发亮 shǎnshǎn fāliàng

litch N 故障 gùzhàng, 差错 chācuò
computer glitch 电脑故障 diànnǎo gùzhàng

litter I v 闪光 shǎnguāng, 闪烁 shǎnshuò **II** N **1** 闪光 shǎnguāng, 闪烁 shǎnshuò **2** 诱惑（力）yòuhuò (lì)

loat v 得意洋洋 déyì yángyáng
to gloat over sb's misfortune 因别人的不幸而得意 yīn biérén de búxìng ér déyì, 幸灾乐祸 xìngzāi lèhuò

lobal ADJ 全地球的 quán dìqiú de, 世界范围的 shìjièfànwéide
global warming 全球变暖 quánqiú biànnuǎn

lobalization N [经济的] 全球化 [jīngji de+] quánqiúhuà

lobe N **1** 地球 dìqiú
from every corner of the globe 世界各地的 shìjiè gèdì de
2 地球仪 dìqiúyí

lobular ADJ 球形的 qiúxíng de, 水珠形的 shuǐzhū xíng de

lobule N 水滴 shuǐdī, 水珠 shuǐzhū

loom N **1** 幽暗 yōu'àn, 昏暗 hūn'àn **2** 忧伤 yōushāng

loomy ADJ **1** 阴暗的 [+房间] yīn'àn de [+fángjiān] **2** 悲观的 bēiguān de

lorified ADJ 被美化的 bèi měihuà de

lorify v **1** 赞美 [+上帝] zànměi [+Shàngdì] **2** 颂扬 [+冒险精神] sòngyáng [+màoxiǎn jīngshén], 吹捧 chuīpěng

lorious ADJ 光荣的 guāngróng de, 荣耀的 róngyào de, 辉煌的 huīhuáng de

lory N 光荣 guāngróng, 荣耀 róngyào, 辉煌 huīhuáng
one's former glory 昔日的辉煌 xīrì de huīhuáng

loss I N **1** [银器+] 光泽 [yínqì+] guāngzé, 光亮 guāngliàng **2** [古诗+] 注释 [gǔshī+] zhùshì, 注解 zhùjiě **II** v 加注释 jiāzhù shì

lossary N 词汇表 cíhuìbiǎo, 难词表 náncíbiǎo

lossy ADJ 有光泽的 yǒuguāng zé de
glossy paper 上光纸 shàngguāng zhǐ

love N 手套 shǒutào [M. WD 只 zhī/副 fù]
glove compartment （汽车）贮藏柜 (qìchē) zhùcáng guì

low v **1** 发出光亮 fāchū guāngliàng
to glow with happiness 因幸福而容光焕发 yīn xìngfú ér róngguāng huànfā
2 [脸部+] 发热 [liǎn bù+] fārè **II** N **1** 光亮 guāngliàng, 发热 fārè **2** 脸上（健康）的光泽 liǎnshàng (jiànkāng) de guāngzé **3** （美好的）感觉 (měihǎo de) gǎnjué

a glow of pride 自豪的感觉 zìháo de gǎnjué

glower v 怒目而视 nùmù ér shì, 怒视 nùshì

glowing ADJ 热烈赞扬的 rèliè zànyáng de, 好话连篇的 hǎohuà liánpiān de
glowing recommendation 热烈赞扬的推荐（信）rèliè zànyáng de tuījiàn (xìn)

glowworm N 萤火虫 yínghuǒchóng [M. WD 只 zhī]

glucose N 葡萄糖（糖浆）pútaotáng (tángjiāng)

glue I N 胶 jiāo, 胶水 jiāoshuǐ **II** v 粘贴 zhān tiē, 胶合 jiāohé

glum ADJ 闷闷不乐的 mènmèn bú lè de, 沉闷的 chénmèn de

glut N 供应过剩 gōngyìng guòshèng

glutton N 嘴馋的人 zuǐchán de rén, 馋嘴鬼 chánzuǐguǐ

gluttony N 贪吃贪喝 tān chī tān hē, 暴食暴饮 bào shí bào yǐn

glycerin N 甘油 gānyóu

GM (= genetically modified) ABBREV 转基因 zhuǎnjīyīn
GM food 转基因食物 zhuǎnjīyīn shíwù

gnarled ADJ **1** 多瘤多节的 [+树] duō liú duōjié de [+shù], 扭曲的 niǔqū de **2** 粗糙的 [+手] cūzào de [+shǒu]

gnash v 咬牙 yǎoyá
to gnash one's teeth 咬牙切齿 yǎo yá qiē chǐ

gnat N 叮人的小虫 dīng rén de xiǎo chóng [M. WD 只 zhī]

gnaw v **1** 啃 kěn, 咬 yǎo **2** 折磨 zhémo, 使…精神痛苦 shǐ…jīngshen tòngkǔ

gnawing ADJ 折磨人的 zhémo rén de, 令人痛苦的 lìng rén tòngkǔ de

gnome N 土地神 Tǔdìshén

GNP (= Gross National Product) ABBREV 国民生产总值 guómín shēngchǎn zǒngzhí

go I v (PT went; PP gone) **1** 去 qù, 到…去 dào… qù **2** 离去 líqu, 离开 líkāi
to be going to do 要 yào, 会 huì ■ *I'm not going to bend over backwards to please her.* 我不会曲意讨好她。Wǒ bú huì qǔyì tǎohǎo tā
Go away! 走开! zǒukāi ■ *Go away! Leave me alone.* 走开，别管我。Zǒukāi, bié guǎn wǒ.
to go back 回到 huídao
to go for a walk/drive 散步/开车兜风 sànbù/kāichē dōufēng
to go on ① 继续 jìxù ② 发生 fāshēng ■ *What's going on down there?* 那里发生什么事了? Nàlǐ fāshēng shénme shì le?
to go out 出去玩 chūqu wán
to go shopping/camping/swimming 去购物/去野营/去游泳 qù gòuwù/qù yěyíng/qù yóuyǒng **II** N 尝试 chángshì
to make a go of sth 试图 shìtú, 使 [+生意] 成功 shǐ [+shēng yì] chénggōng
to give sth a go 尝试做某事 chángshì zuò mǒushì

goad v 驱使 qūshǐ, 激励 jīlì

go-ahead I N 准许 zhǔnxǔ, 许可 xǔkě
to give sb the go-ahead 给予准许 jǐyǔ zhǔnxǔ
to get the go-ahead 得到批准 dédào pīzhǔn
II ADJ 领先的 lǐngxiān de
a go-ahead touchdown 使球队领先的触地得分 shǐ qiúduì lǐngxiān de chù dì défēn

goal N 1 目标 mùbiāo 2 球门 qiúmén
to score a goal 踢(打)进一球 tī (dǎ) jìn yì qiú

goalkeeper N 守门员 shǒuményuán

goalpost N 球门柱 qiúménzhù [M. WD 根 gēn]

goat N 山羊 shānyáng [M. WD 只 zhī/头 tóu]

goatee N (山羊) 胡子 (shānyáng) húzi

gobble v 狼吞虎咽 lángtūn hǔyàn

gobbledygook N 冗长难懂又无聊的文字 rǒngcháng nándǒng yòu wúliáo de wénzì, 官样文章 guānyàng wénzhāng

go-between N 中间人 zhōngjiānrén

goblet N 高脚杯 gāojiǎobēi [M. WD 只 zhī]

goblin N 调皮的小妖精 tiáopí de xiǎoyāojing

go-cart N 单座赛车 dān zuò sàichē [M. WD 辆 liàng]

God N 上帝 Shàngdì, 老天 Lǎotiān
God helps those who help themselves. 天助自助者。Tiān zhù zì zhù zhě.

god N 神 shén, 神仙 shénxian [M. WD 位 wèi]

god-awful ADJ 糟透了的 zāotòu le de

godchild N 教子 jiàozǐ, 教女 jiàonǚ

goddammit INTERJ 该死 gāisǐ, 他妈的 tāmāde

goddamn ADJ 该死的 gāisǐ de

goddess N 女神 nǚshén [M. WD 位 wéi]

godfather N 教父 jiàofù

god-fearing ADJ 敬畏上帝的 jìngwèi Shàngdì de

god-forsaken ADJ 荒凉的 huāngliáng de, 鬼也不到的 guǐ yě bú dào de

godless ADJ 不敬上帝的 bújìng Shàngdì de, 不信神的 bú xìn shén de

godlike ADJ 神圣的 shénshèng de, 如同神明的 rútóng shénmíng de

godly ADJ 虔诚的 qiánchéng de

godmother N 教母 jiàomǔ

godparent N 教父 jiàofù, 教母 jiàomǔ

godsend N 飞来的好运 fēiláide hǎoyùn, 意外的惊喜 yìwài de jīngxǐ

gofer N 勤杂工 qínzágōng, 跑腿儿的 pǎotuǐr de

go-getter N 有进取心的人 yǒu jìnqǔxīn de rén

goggle-eyed ADJ 瞪大眼睛的 dèng dà yǎnjing de, 极其惊讶的 jíqí jīngyà de

goggles N 防风眼镜 fángfēng yǎnjìng [M. WD 副 fù], 护目镜 hùmùjìng [M. WD 副 fù]

going I N 1 离去 líqù 2 进展 jìnzhǎn
rough going 进展艰难 jìnzhǎn jiānnán
II ADJ 通行的 tōngxíng de
going rate 通行的价格 tōngxíng de jiàgé, 时价 shíjià

going-over N 仔细的检查 zǐxì de jiǎnchá

goings-on N (不寻常的) 事件 (bù xúncháng de) shìjiàn

gold I N 金 (子) jīn (zi), 黄金 huángjīn
All that glitters is not gold. 闪光的不都是金子。Shǎnguāng de bù dōu shì jīnzi.
II ADJ 金子的 jīnzi de ■ She bought herself a gold necklace. 她给自己买了一条金项链。Tā gěi zìjǐ mǎile yì tiáo jīn xiàngliàn.
gold digger 靠色相骗取钱财的女人 kào sèxiāng piànqǔ qiáncái de nǚrén
gold medal 金质奖章 jīnzhì jiǎngzhāng, 金牌 jīnpái
gold standard 金本位 jīnběnwèi
2 金黄色的 jīn huáng sè de

golden ADJ 1 金子的 jīnzi de, 金色的 jīnsè de 2 极好的 jíhǎo de, 宝贵的 bǎoguì de
a golden age 黄金时代 huángjīn shídài
a golden handshake 优厚的退休金 yōuhòu de tuìxiūjīn, 一大笔离职费 yí dàbǐ lízhí fèi
a golden opportunity 非常难得的机会 fēicháng nándé de jīhuì

goldfish N 金鱼 jīnyú [M. WD 条 tiáo]
goldfish bowl 金鱼缸 jīnyúgāng

goldmine N 1 金矿 jīnkuàng [M. WD 座 zuò] 2 财源 cáiyuán, 宝库 bǎokù

golf N 高尔夫球 gāo'ěrfūqiú
golf course 高尔夫球场 gāo'ěrfūqiúchǎng

gondola N 1 [意大利威尼斯的+] 平底船 [Yìdàlì Wēinísī de+] píngdǐchuán 2 [风景点+] (电) 缆车 [fēngjǐng diǎn+] diànlǎnchē, 缆车 lǎnchē

gone v See go

goner N 快完蛋的人 kuài wándàn de rén

gong N 锣 luó [M. WD 面 miàn]

gonorrhea N 淋病 línbìng

good I ADJ 1 好的 hǎo de, 优良的 yōuliáng de ■ It's good to see you. 见到你, 太好了。Jiàndào nǐ, tài hǎo le. 2 守规矩的 shǒu guīju de, 乖的 guāi de ■ Dear Santa, I've been a good boy this year. 亲爱的圣诞老人, 我今年很乖。Qīn'ài de Shèngdàn Lǎorén, wǒ jīnnián hěn guāi. 3 愉快的 yúkuài de
Have a good holiday! 祝你假期愉快! Zhù nǐ jiàqī yúkuài!
4 有益健康的 yǒuyì jiànkāng de
to be good for sb 对某人的健康有益 duì mǒurén de jiànkāng yǒuyì
II N 1 好处 hǎochu, 利益 lìyì 2 善 shàn, 道德 dàodé
to do good 有好处 yǒu hǎochù
be good at 擅长于 shàncháng yú, 善于 shàngy
as good as 跟……一样 gēn……yíyàng
for good 永远 yǒngyuǎn ■ She is leaving for good. 她永远离开了。(→她一去不返。) Tā yǒngyuǎn líkāi le. (→Tā yí qù bù fǎn.)
good morning 早上好 zǎoshang hǎo

good afternoon 下午好 xiàwǔ hǎo
good evening 晚上好 wǎnshang hǎo
good night 晚安 wǎn'ān
goodbye 再见 zàijiàn
good-for-nothing N 一无用处的人 yìwú yòngchu de rén, 懒人 lǎn rén
good-humored ADJ 快活友好的 kuàihuo yǒuhǎo de
good-looking ADJ 好看的 [+人] hǎokàn de [+rén], 漂亮的 piàoliang de
good-natured ADJ 性情温和的 xìngqíng wēnhé de
goodness N 1 善 shàn, 善良 shànliáng 2 食物中最有营养的部分 shíwù zhōng zuì yǒu yíngyǎng de bùfen
goods N 货物 huòwù, 商品 shāngpǐn
dry goods 纺织品 fǎngzhī pǐn
electrical goods 电器用品 diànqì yòngpǐn
goodwill N 善意 shànyì, 友善 yǒushàn
goody, goodie N 好吃的东西 hǎochī de dōngxi
goody-goody N 伪君子 wěijūnzǐ, 装乖的孩子 zhuāng guāi de háizi
goof I v 出错 chūcuò, 搞错 gǎocuò II N 愚蠢的错误 yúchǔn de cuòwù
goofy ADJ 傻乎乎的 shǎhūhū de
goon N 1 打手 dǎshou, 暴徒 bàotú 2 傻瓜 shǎguā, 蠢货 chǔnhuò
goose (PL geese) N 鹅 é [M. WD 只 zhī]
wild goose 大雁 dàyàn
goose-bumps N 鸡皮疙瘩 jīpí gēda
GOP (= Grand Old Party) ABBREV (美国) 共和党 (Měiguó) Gònghédǎng
gorge I N 峡谷 xiágǔ II v 狼吞虎咽 lángtūn hǔyàn
to gorge oneself on sth 狼吞虎咽地吃某物 lángtūn hǔyàn de chī mǒuwù
gorgeous ADJ 极好的 jíhǎo de, 好极了的 hǎo jíle de
gorilla N 大猩猩 dàxīngxing [M. WD 只 zhī]
gory ADJ 暴力的 bàolì de
gosh INTERJ 啊呀 āyā
gosling N 小鹅 xiǎo é
gospel N 1 (圣经) 福音 (Shèngjīng) Fúyīn 2 信条 xìntiáo 3 福音音乐 Fúyīn yīnyuè
gospel truth 绝对真实的事 juéduì zhēnshí de shì
gossip I N 1 流言蜚语 liúyán fēiyǔ, 道听途说的话 dàotīng túshuō de huà 2 喜欢谈论别人私生活的人 xǐhuan tánlùn biéren sīshēnghuó de rén
gossip mill 制造流言蜚语的人 zhìzào liúyán fēiyǔ de rén
II v 说别人的闲话 shuō biéren de xiánhuà, 传播流言蜚语 chuánbō liúyán fēiyǔ
got v See get
gotcha INTERJ 1 抓住了 zhuāzhù le 2 我赢了 wǒ yíng le

gotten v See get
gouge v 凿 (孔) záo (kǒng)
goulash N 辣椒炖肉 làjiāo dùnròu
gourd N 葫芦 húlu
gourmet I N 美食家 měishíjiā II ADJ 美食的 měishí de
a gourmet restaurant 美食餐厅 měishí cāntīng, 高级饭店 gāojí fàndiàn
gout N 痛风 (病) tòngfēng (bìng)
govern v 1 治理 zhìlǐ, 管辖 guǎnxiá 2 控制 kòngzhì, 支配 zhīpèi
governess N 家庭女教师 jiātíng nǚ jiàoshī
government N 1 政府 zhèngfǔ 2 治理 zhìlǐ
governmental ADJ 政府的 zhèngfǔ de
governor N 1 (美国) 州长 (Měiguó) Zhōuzhǎng 2 总督 Zǒngdū
governorship N 州长／总督的职位 Zhōuzhǎng／Zǒngdū de zhíwèi
gown N 1 女夜礼服 nǚ yèlǐfú [M. WD 件 jiàn] 2 (医院／实验室) 白大褂 (yīyuàn/shíyànshì) báidàguà
GP (= general practitioner) ABBREV 普通医生 pǔtōng yīshēng, 全科医生 quánkē yīshēng
GPA (= grade point average) ABBREV 平均积分点 píngjūn jīfēndiǎn
GPS (= global positioning system) ABBREV 1 全球定位系统 quánqiú dìngwèi xìtǒng 2 导航器 dǎohángqì
grab v, N 抓住 zhuāzhu ■ The police grabbed the criminal before he committed another crime. 警察在罪犯再次犯罪之前抓住了他。 Jǐngchá zài zuìfàn zài cì fànzuì zhīqián zhuāzhule tā.
to grab a chance 抓住机会 zhuāzhù jīhuì
to be up for grabs 大家都可以争取 dàjiā dōu kěyǐ zhēngqǔ
grace N 1 优雅 yōuyǎ 2 宽限 kuānxiàn
grace period 宽限期 kuānxiànqī
3 感恩祷告 gǎn'ēn dǎogào
to say grace 做感恩祷告 zuò gǎn'ēn dǎogào
to have the grace to 有…的气量 yǒu…de qìliàng, 有…的雅量 yǒu…de yǎliàng
graceful ADJ 1 优雅的 yōuyǎ de, 优美的 yōuměi de 2 得体的 détǐ de, 礼貌的 lǐmào de ■ He corrected my mistake in a graceful way. 他以得体的方式纠正了我的错误。 Tā yǐ fēicháng détǐ de fāngshì jiūzhèngle wǒ de cuòwù.
gracious ADJ 1 仁慈的 réncí de, 和善的 héshàn de 2 奢华的 (生活) shēhuá de (shēnghuó)
gradation N 渐变 jiànbiàn, 层次 céngcì, 等级 děngjí
grade I N 1 年级 niánjí
grade school 小学 xiǎoxué
2 等级 děngjí 3 分数 fēnshù II v 评分 píngfēn
gradient N 坡度 pōdù, 倾斜度 qīngxié dù
gradual ADJ 逐渐 zhújiàn, 渐渐 jiànbiàn

ENGLISH-CHINESE

■ *Grandpa is aware of the gradual decline of his own health.* 爷爷知道自己的健康正逐渐恶化。Yéye zhīdào zìjǐ de jiànkāng zhèngzhújiàn èhuà.

gradually ADV 逐渐地 zhújiàn de, 渐渐地 jiànjiàn de

graduate I N 毕业生 bìyèshēng II V 毕业 bìyè III ADJ 研究生的 yánjiūshēng de
graduate school 研究生院 yánjiūshēng yuàn
graduate student 研究生 yánjiūshēng

graduated ADJ 分级的 fēnjí de

graduation N 1 毕业 bìyè 2 毕业典礼 bìyè diǎnlǐ

graffiti N 乱涂乱画 luàn tú luàn huà, 涂鸦 túyā

graft I N 1 以权谋私 yǐ quán móu sī, 贪污 tānwū 2 (枝条) 嫁接 (zhītiáo) jiàjiē 3 (皮肤) 移植 (pífū) yízhí II V 1 嫁接 [+枝条] jiàjiē [+zhītiáo] 2 移植 [+皮肤] yízhí [+pífū]

grain N 1 谷物 gǔwù, 粮食 liángshi 2 (木头) 纹理 (mùtou) wénlǐ 3 颗粒 kēlì
a grain of truth 一点道理 yìdiǎn dàoli

grainy ADJ 1 模糊的 [+照片] móhu de [+zhàopiàn] 2 粗糙的 cūcāo de

gram N 克 kè

grammar N 1 语法 yǔfǎ ■ *If you are a serious student of a language, you must study its grammar.* 你如果想认真地学够一门语言，就必须学习它的语法。Nǐ rúguǒ xiǎng rènzhēn de xuéhǎo yì mén yǔyán, jiù bìxū xuéxí tā de yǔfǎ. 2 语法书 yǔfǎ shū [M. WD 本 běn]

grammatical ADJ 语法的 yǔfǎ de

grand ADJ 1 雄伟的 xióngwěi de 2 宏大的 hóngdà de ■ *He has a grand plan for his son.* 他为儿子制定了宏大计划。Tā wèi érzi zhìdìngle hóngdà jihuà.
grand jury 大陪审团 dàpéishěntuán
grand piano 大钢琴 dàgāngqín
grand prix 国际汽车大赛 guójì qìchē dàsài
grand slam (棒球) 全垒打 (bàngqiú) quánlěidǎ, (桥牌) 大满贯 (qiáopái) dà mǎnguàn

grandchild N 孙子 sūnzi (one's son's son), 孙女 sūnnǚ (one's son's daughter), 外孙 wàisūn (one's daughter's son), 外孙女 wàisūnnǚ (one's daughter's daughter)

granddad N 爷爷 yéye (paternal grandpa), 外公 wàigōng (maternal grandpa)

granddaughter N 孙女 sūnnǚ (one's son's daughter), 外孙女 wàisūnnǚ (one's daughter's daughter)

grandeur N 宏伟壮丽 hóngwěi zhuànglì

grandfather N 祖父 zǔfù (paternal grandfather), 外祖父 wàizǔfù (maternal grandfather)
grandfather clock 落地式自鸣钟 luòdìshì zìmíngzhōng

grandiose ADJ 华而不实的 huā ér bù shí de

grandma N 奶奶 nǎinai (paternal grandma), 姥姥 lǎolao (maternal grandma)

grandmother N 祖母 zǔmǔ (paternal grandmother), 外祖母 wàizǔmǔ (maternal grandmother)

grandpa N See grandad

grandparent N 祖父母 zǔfùmǔ (paternal grandparents), 外祖父母 wàizǔfùmǔ (maternal grandparents)

grandson N 孙子 sūnzi (one's son's son), 外孙 wàisūn (one's daughter's son)

grandstand N 大看台 dà kàntái

granite N 花岗岩 huāgǎngyán [M. WD 块 kuài]

granny N See grandma

granola N 格兰诺拉麦片 Gélánnuòlā màipiàn

grant I V 1 同意 tóngyì, 准许 zhǔnxǔ 2 承认 [+事实] chéngrèn [+shìshí] II N 拨款 bō kuǎn, 经费 jīngfèi
to take for granted 想当然 xiǎngdāngrán

granulated ADJ 砂状的 shā zhuàng de

granule N 小颗粒 xiǎo kēlì
instant coffee granule 速溶咖啡精 sùróng kāfēijīng

grape N 葡萄 pútao [M. WD 颗 kē/串 chuàn]

grapefruit N 西柚 xīyòu, 葡萄柚 pútaoyòu

grapevine N 葡萄 (藤) pútao (téng)
to hear about sth on the grapevine 从传闻中听到 cóng chuánwén zhōng tīngdào, 听到小道新闻 tīngdào xiǎodào xīnwén

graph N 图表 túbiǎo [M. WD 张 zhāng] ■ *He produced a graph showing global warming over the past five decades.* 他出示图表，显示过去五十年中全球气温上升的情况。Tā chūshì túbiǎo, xiǎnshì guòqù wǔshí nián zhōng quánqiú qìwēn shàngshēng de qíngkuàng.
bar graph 条形图 tiáoxíngtú
line graph 曲线图 qūxiàntú
pie graph 饼形分析图 bǐngxíng fēnxītú

graphic I ADJ 1 绘图的 huìtú de, 印刷的 yìnshuā de 2 详细的 [+报导] xiángxì de [+bàodǎo] 3 色情下流的 [+描述] sèqíng xiàliú de [+miáoshù]
graphic design 图像设计 túxiàng shèjì
II N (graphics) 图表 túbiǎo [M. WD 张 zhāng], 图像 túxiàng [M. WD 张 zhāng]

graphite N 石墨 shímò

grapple V 1 扭打 niǔdǎ 2 努力对付 [+困境] nǔlì duìfu [+kùnjìng], 设法解决 [+难题] shèfǎjiějué [+nántí]

grasp I V 1 抓牢 zhuā láo, 抓紧 zhuājǐn 2 完全理解 [+一个概念] wánquán lǐjiě [+yí ge gàiniàn] II N 1 理解 [+能力] lǐjiě [+nénglì] 2 达到 dádào, 到手 dàoshǒu

grasping ADJ 贪财的 tāncái de

grass N 草 cǎo [M. WD 颗 kē], 青草 qīngcǎo
grass roots 草根阶层 cǎogēn jiēcéng, 基层 jīcéng
The grass is always greener on the other side. 别人的情况总是比自己好。Biéren de

410

qíngkuàng zǒngshì bǐ zìjǐ hǎo. 家花哪有野花
香。Jiāhuā nǎyǒu yěhuā xiāng. 外国的月亮比较
圆。Wàiguó de yuèliàng bǐjiào yuán.

grasshopper N 蚱蜢 zhàměng [M. wᴅ 只 zhī],
蝗虫 huángchóng [M. wᴅ 只 zhī]

grassland N 草原 cǎoyuán

grassy ᴀᴅᴊ 长满草的 zhǎngmǎn cǎo de

grate I v 磨碎 mósuì, 发出刺耳的声音 fāchū cì'ěr
de shēngyīn II N 铁栅 tiězhà

grateful ᴀᴅᴊ 感谢 gǎnxiè, 感恩 gǎn'ēn

grater N 磨碎器 mósuì qì

gratification N 满足 mǎnzú
instant gratification 立即满足 lìjí mǎnzú

gratify v 满足 mǎnzú, 使⋯满意 shǐ...mǎnyì

gratifying ᴀᴅᴊ 令人满足的 lìngrén mǎnzú de

grating I N 铁栅 tiězhà II ᴀᴅᴊ 刺耳的 cì'ěr de

gratis ᴀᴅᴊ, ᴀᴅᴠ 免费的 miǎnfèi de, 免费 miǎnfèi

gratitude N 感激 (之情) gǎnjī (zhī qíng), 谢意 xièyì

gratuitous ᴀᴅᴊ 无缘无故的 wúyuán wúgù de

gratuity N 小费 xiǎofèi [M. wᴅ 笔 bǐ/份 fèn]

grave[1] N 墓 mù, 坟墓 fénmù, 坟 fén

grave[2] ᴀᴅᴊ 严重的 yánzhòng de ■ *The situation is
grave.* 情况很严重。Qíngkuàng hěn yánzhòng.

gravel N 碎石子 suì shízǐ

gravelly ᴀᴅᴊ 1 碎石子的 suì shízǐ de 2 低哑的
[+声音] dīyǎ de [+shēngyīn]

graveside N 坟墓边 fénmù biān

gravestone N 墓碑 mùbēi [M. wᴅ 块 kuài]

graveyard N 墓地 mùdì

gravitate v 吸引 xīyǐn

gravitation N 引力 yǐnlì

gravity N 地心引力 dìxīn yǐnlì, 重力 zhònglì

gravy N 肉汁 ròu zhī

gray I ᴀᴅᴊ 灰色的 huīsè de II N 灰色 huīsè
gray matter 大脑 dànǎo, 智力 zhìlì
III v 变成灰色 biànchéng huīsè

graze v 1 [动物+] 吃草 [dòngwù+] chī cǎo, 放牧
fàngmù 2 擦破 cāpò, 擦伤 cāshāng

grease I N 1 油脂 yóuzhī 2 润滑油 rùnhuáyóu
II v 给⋯涂上油 gěi...tú shàngyóu
to grease sb's palm 向某人行贿 xiàng mǒurén
xínghuì

greasy ᴀᴅᴊ 1 油脂很多的 yóuzhī hěn duō de
2 油腻腻的 yóunìnì de
a greasy spoon 破旧肮脏的小饭馆 pòjiù
āngzāng de xiǎo fànguǎn

great ᴀᴅᴊ 1 大的 dà de 2 极好的 jíhǎo de ■ *This
software is great for graphics.* 这个软件制图棒极
了。Zhè ge ruǎnjiàn zhìtú bàng jíle. 3 伟大 wěidà
a great many 很多 hěn duō

greatly ᴀᴅᴠ 非常 fēicháng, 大大的 dàdà de

greed N 贪心 tānxīn, 贪婪 tānlán

greedy ᴀᴅᴊ 1 贪吃 tānchī, 嘴馋 zuǐchán 2 贪心的
tānxīn de

Greek I ᴀᴅᴊ 希腊的 Xīlà de II N 1 希腊人 Xīlàrén

2 希腊语 Xīlàyǔ
It's all Greek to me. 我对此一窍不通。Wǒ duì cǐ
yíqiào bùtōng.

green I ᴀᴅᴊ 1 绿色的 lǜsè de 2 环境 (保护) 的
huánjìng (bǎohù) 3 年轻而没有经验的 niánqīng er méiyǒu jingyan de 4 (脸色) 苍白的
(liǎnsè) cāngbái de II N 1 绿 (色) lǜ (sè)
■ *The color green symbolizes nature.* 绿色标志大
自然。Lǜsè biāozhì dàzìrán.
green card 绿卡 lǜkǎ
2 草地 cǎodì, 草场 cǎochǎng
bowling green 草地滚木球场 cǎodì gǔnmù-
qiúchǎng

greenback N 美元 Měiyuán

greenhouse N 温室 wēnshì
greenhouse effect 温室效应 wēnshì xiàoyìng

greens N 绿色阔叶蔬菜 lǜsè kuò yè shūcài

greet v 1 问好 wènhǎo, 打招呼 dǎ zhāohu 2 欢
迎 huānyíng ■ *The hotel greets guests with a
free plate of fruit in their room.* 旅馆在客房里放
一盘免费水果来欢迎旅客。Lǚguǎn zài kèfáng lǐ fàng
yì pán miǎnfèi shuǐguǒ lái huānyíng lǚkè.

greeting N 1 问候 wènhòu, 问好 wènhǎo 2 祝贺
zhùhè
greeting card (祝) 贺卡 (zhù) hè kǎ

gregarious ᴀᴅᴊ 合群的 héqún de, 喜爱交际的
xǐ'ài jiāojì de

gremlin N (闯祸) 小妖精 (chuǎnghuò) xiǎoyāojing

grenade N 手榴弹 shǒuliúdàn [M. wᴅ 枚 méi]

grew v See grow

grey See gray

greyhound N 1 灰狗 huīgǒu [M. wᴅ 只 zhī/条
tiáo] 2 (美国) 灰狗长途汽车 (Měiguó) huīgǒu
chángtú qìchē

grid N 1 电力网 diànlìwǎng 2 方格图案 fānggé
tú'àn 3 (地图) 坐标方格 (dìtú) zuòbiāo fānggé

griddle N 平底锅 píngdǐguō

gridiron N 1 橄榄球球场 gǎnlǎnqiú qiúchǎng
2 烤架 kǎojià

gridlock N 1 僵局 jiāngjú, (工作) 停顿 (gōngzuò)
tíngdùn 2 交通堵塞 jiāotōng dǔsè

grief N 悲伤 bēishāng, 悲哀 bēi'āi

grievance N 委屈 wěiqu, 抱怨 bàoyuàn

grieve v 使⋯非常难过 shǐ...fēicháng nánguò,
使⋯感到悲痛 shǐ...gǎndào bēitòng ■ *It grieves
me to see you in such a situation.* 看到你现在的处
境，我非常难过。Kàndào nǐ xiànzài de chǔjìng,
wǒ fēicháng nánguò.

grievous ᴀᴅᴊ 严重的 yánzhòng de

grill I v 烤 kǎo, 烧烤 shāokǎo II N 1 烧烤架
shāokǎojià 2 烧烤餐厅 shāokǎo cāntīng

grim ᴀᴅᴊ 1 令人担忧的 [+前景] lìng rén dānyōu
de [+qiánjǐng] 2 严肃的 [+法官] yánsù de
[+fǎguān] 3 严峻的 yánjùn de

grimace v 1 (开玩笑) 扮鬼脸 (kāiwánxiào)

bàn guǐliǎn **2**（因疼痛／厌恶）扭曲了脸（yīn téngtòng/yànwù）niǔqūle liǎn

grime N（一层）油腻（yìcéng）yóunì

grimy ADJ 油腻的 yóunì de

grin I v 咧开嘴笑 liě kāi zuǐ xiào
to grin and bear it 苦笑忍受 kǔxiào rěnshòu
to grin from ear to ear 笑得合不拢嘴 xiào dé hébulǒng zuǐ
II v 咧开嘴笑 liě kāi zuǐ xiào

grind I v (PT & PP **ground**) **1** 碾碎 [+咖啡豆] niǎnsuì [+kāfēi dòu] **2** 绞碎 [+肉] jiǎo suì [+ròu] **3** 磨 [+刀] mó [+dāo] II N 苦工 kǔgōng

grinder N 碾磨机 niǎnmójī

grinding ADJ 折磨人的 zhémo rén de
grinding poverty 折磨人的贫穷 zhémo rén de pínqióng

grindstone N 磨刀石 módāoshí [M. WD 块 kuài]

grip I N **1** 紧握 jǐnwò **2** 牢牢控制 láoláo kòngzhì
to get a grip on oneself 控制住自己的感情 kòngzhì zhù zìjǐ de gǎnqíng
to get to grips with 真正懂得并且能应付 zhēnzhèng dǒngde bìngqiě néng yìngfu **3** 控制（力）kòngzhì (lì)
to lose one's grip 失去控制 shīqù kòngzhì **4** 理解力 lǐjiělì **5** 夹子 jiāzi II v **1** 紧紧地握住 jǐnjǐn de wòzhù **2** 引起…注意 yǐnqǐ...zhùyì

gripe I v 发牢骚 fā láosāo, 抱怨 bàoyuàn II N 牢骚 láosāo, 抱怨的小事 bàoyuàn de xiǎoshì

gripping ADJ 扣人心弦的 kòu rén xīnxián de

grisly ADJ 恐怖的 kǒngbù de

gristle N (肉) 软骨 (ròu) ruǎngǔ

grit I N **1** 沙粒 shālì **2** 决心和勇气 juéxīn hé yǒngqì II v 磨轧 móyà
to grit one's teeth 咬紧牙关 yǎojǐn yáguān

grizzly bear N（大）灰熊（dà）huīxióng [M. WD 只 zhī/头 tóu]

groan v 痛苦呻吟 tòngkǔ shēnyín

grocer N 食品杂货店老板（或店员）shípǐn záhuò diàn lǎobǎn (huò diànyuán)

grocery store N 食品杂货店 shípǐn záhuò diàn

groggy ADJ **1** [头脑+] 昏沉沉的 [tóunǎo+] hūnchénchén de **2** [四肢+] 无力的 [sìzhī+] wúlì de

groin N 腹股沟 fùgǔgōu

groom I v **1** 穿戴打扮 chuāndài dǎban
a well-groomed young man 穿戴打扮得整整齐齐的年轻人 chuāndài dǎban dé zhěngzhěng qíqí de niánqīngrén
2 [动物+] 梳理皮毛 [dòngwù+] shūlǐ pímáo **3** 培养 [+接班人] péiyǎng [+jiēbānrén], 培训 péixùn II N **1** 新郎 xīnláng **2** 马夫 mǎfū

groove N **1** 凹槽 āocáo [M. WD 道 dào] **2** 正常状态 zhèngcháng zhuàngtài
to get back in the groove 重新进入正常状态 chóngxīn jìnrù zhèngcháng zhuàngtài

groovy ADJ 时髦的 shímáo de, 流行的 liúxíng de

grope v [在黑暗中+] 摸索 [zài hēi'àn zhōng+] mōsuo

gross I ADJ **1** 总的 zǒngde
gross national product 国民生产总值 guómín shēngchǎn zǒngzhí
gross weight 毛重 máozhòng
2 恶心的 èxīn de **3** 恶劣的 èliè de, 极坏的 jí huài de II v **1** 总利润 zǒng lìrùn **2** 税前工资 shuì qián gōngzī

grotesque ADJ 怪诞的 guàidàn de, 荒唐的 huāngtang de

grotto N 石窟 shíkū

grouch I N 牢骚不断的人 láosāo búduàn de rén, 愤愤不平的人 fènfèn bùpíng de rén II v 愤愤地发牢骚 fènfèn de fāláosāo

grouchy ADJ（因为疲劳）心情很糟（yīnwéi píláo）xīnqíng hěn zāo

ground[1] I N **1** 地 dì, 地面 dìmiàn
ground crew (机场) 地勤人员 (jīchǎng) dìqín rényuán
sports ground 体育场 tǐyù chǎng, 操场 cāo chǎng
to get off the ground 开始正常运转 kāishǐ zhèngcháng yùnzhuǎn
to gain ground 取得优势 qǔdé yōushì, 渐渐取胜 jiànjiàn qǔshèng
to stand one's ground 坚持立场 jiānchí lìchǎng, 坚持己见 jiānchí jǐjiàn
2 意见 yìjiàn, 立场 lìchǎng
to give ground (in an argument)（在争论中）让步 (zài zhēnglùn zhōng) ràngbù
II v **1** (飞机) 停止飞行 (fēijī) tíngzhǐ fēixíng **2** 不准（小孩）做喜欢做的事 bùzhǔn (xiǎohái) zuò xǐhuan zuò de shì

ground[2] I v See **grind** II ADJ 碾碎的 niǎnsuì de, 磨细的 mó xì de
ground coffee 磨细的咖啡 móxì de kāfēi
ground beef 牛肉饼 niúròubǐng

ground-breaking ADJ 开创性的 kāichuàng xìng de

groundhog N 土拨鼠 tǔbōshǔ [M. WD 只 zhī]
Groundhog Day 土拨鼠日（二月二日）tǔbōshǔ rì (èryuè'èr rì)

groundless ADJ 没有根据的 méiyǒu gēnjù de

ground rule N 基本规则 jīběn guīzé [M. WD 条 tiáo]

groundswell N **1** 大海浪 dà hǎilàng **2** 高涨 gāozhǎng

groundwork N 基础 jīchǔ

group I N **1** 组 zǔ, 小组 xiǎozǔ **2** 群 qún
group therapy 集体心理治疗 jítǐ xīnlǐ zhìliáo
3 集团 jítuán ■ *The newspaper group controlled a number of national and local newspapers.* 这家报业集团控制几家全国和地方的报纸。Zhè jiā bàoyè jítuán kòngzhì jǐ jiā quánguó hé dìfang de

bàozhǐ. **II** v 1 聚集成一组 jùjí chéng yìzǔ
2 分组 fēnzǔ

grouping N 同类人/事 tónglèi rén/shì

rouse N, v 抱怨 bàoyuàn

rove N 小树林 xiǎoshù lín

grovel v 卑躬屈膝 bēigōng qūxī, 点头哈腰 diǎn tóu hā yāo

grow (PT grew; PP grown) v 1 增长 zēngzhǎng 2 生长 shēngzhǎng ■ *Any plant grows well here.* 这里什么植物都生长良好。Zhèlǐ shénme zhíwù dōu shēngzhǎng liánghǎo.

Grow up! 快快长大! (→ 别这么幼稚!) Kuàikuài zhǎng dà! (→ Bié zhème yòuzhì!) 3 变得 biànde

grower N 种植者 zhòngzhízhě, 种植公司 zhòng-zhí gōngsī [M. WD 家 jiā]

growing pains N 1 发育期痛 fāyùqī tong 2 发展时期的困难 fāzhǎn shíqī de kùnnan

growl v 1 怒气冲冲地说话 nùqì chōngchōng de shuōhuà 2 [狗+] 低声吼叫 [gǒu+] dīshēng hǒujiào

grown v See **grow**

grown-up I N 成人 chéngrén II ADJ 成年的 chéngnián de, 成熟的 chéngshú de

growth N 1 增长 zēngzhǎng 2 生长 shēngzhǎng 3 肿瘤 zhǒngliú, 赘生物 zhuìshēngwù

grub I N 1 食物 shíwù 2 蛆 qū [M. WD 条 tiáo] II v 1 翻找 fān zhǎo, 寻找 xúnzhǎo 2 乞讨 qǐtǎo, 要 yào

grubby ADJ 肮脏的 [+衣服] āngzāng de [+yīfu], 不干净的 bùgān jìng de 2 卑鄙的 bēibǐ de

grudge I N 怨恨 yuànhèn
to bear a grudge against sb 对某人有怨恨 duì mǒurén yǒu yuànhèn
to hold grudges 记住怨恨 jìzhù yuànhèn, 记仇 jìchóu
II v 勉强 [+做] miǎnqiǎng [+zuò]

grudging ADJ 勉强的 miǎnqiǎng de

gruel N 燕麦粥 yànmài zhōu, 麦片粥 màipiànzhōu

grueling ADJ 令人精疲力竭的 lìng rén jīngpí lìjié de

gruesome ADJ 恐怖的 kǒngbù de, 可怕的 kěpà de

gruff ADJ 生硬的 shēngyìng de, 不耐烦的 búnàifán de

grumble v 发牢骚 fāláosāo

grumpy ADJ 脾气不好又爱发牢骚的 píqi bù hǎo yòu àifā láosāo de

grunge N 1 颓废音乐 tuífèi yīnyuè 2 邋遢时尚的时装潮流 lātā shíshàng de shízhuāng cháoliú

grungy ADJ 肮脏发臭的 āngzāng fāchòu de

grunt I v [猪+] 咕噜咕噜叫 [zhū+] gūlū gūlū jiào 2 嘟哝 dūnong, 嘟哝地说 dūnong de shuō II N 嘟哝 dūnong, 嘟哝声 dūnong shēng

G-string N 丁字裤 dīngzì kù [M. WD 条 tiáo]

guarantee I v 1 保证 bǎozhèng, 担保 dānbǎo

2 保修 bǎoxiū II N 保证 bǎozhèng 2 保修单 bǎoxiū dān 3 担保 dānbǎo
loan guarantee 贷款担保 dàikuǎn dānbǎo

guarantor N 担保人 dānbǎorén

guaranty N (法律) 担保 (fǎlǜ) dānbǎo

guard I N 1 保安 (人员) bǎo'ān (rényuán) 2 (篮球、橄榄球) 后卫 (lánqiú, gǎnlǎnqiú) hòuwèi II v 1 保卫 bǎowèi, 守护 shǒuhù ■ *Important government buildings are all guarded by heavily armed troops.* 重要的政府大楼都有重兵把守。Zhòngyào de zhèngfǔ dàlóu dōu yǒu zhòngbīng bǎshǒu. 2 (体育) 防守 (tǐyù) fángshǒu

guarded ADJ 谨慎的 jǐnshèn de, 提防的 dīfang de

guardian N 1 监护人 jiānhùrén 2 保卫者 bǎowèizhě
guardian angel 守护天使 shǒuhù tiānshǐ

guardianship N 监护人身份 jiānhùrén shēnfen

guardrail N 护栏 hùlán [M. WD 道 dào/条 tiáo]

gubernatorial ADJ 州长的 zhōuzhǎng de

guerrilla N 游击队员 yóujīduìyuán
guerrilla warfare 游击战 yóujīzhàn

guess I v 1 猜 cāi, 猜想 cāixiǎng 2 认为 rènwéi, 想 xiǎng II N 猜想 cāixiǎng, 猜测 cāicè
anybody's guess 谁都不知道 shéi dōu bù zhīdào ■ *Your guess is as good as mine.* 你不知道，我也不知道。Nǐ bù zhīdào, wǒ yě bù zhīdào.

guesstimate N 大致的估计 dàzhì de gūjì

guesswork N 猜测 cāicè

guest N 客人 kèren, 宾客 bīnkè [M. WD 位 wèi] 2 特邀演员 tèyāo yǎnyuán 3 房客 fángkè

guff N 胡说八道 húshuō bādào

guffaw N, v 哈哈大笑 hāha dàxiào

guidance N 引导 yǐndǎo, 指导 zhǐdǎo
guidance counselor 咨询顾问 zīxún gùwèn, 辅导员 fǔdǎoyuán

guide I N 1 向导 xiàngdǎo 2 指南 zhǐnán [M. WD 本 běn] ■ *The retired banker is going to write a guide for first-time investors.* 退休银行家要写一本首次投资指南。Tuìxiū yínhángjiā yào xiě yì běn shǒucì tóuzī zhǐnán. 3 手册 shǒucè, 指南 zhǐnán II v 1 引导 yǐndǎo 2 指导 zhǐdǎo

guidebook N 旅行指南 lǚxíng shǒucè

guidelines N 指导方针 zhǐdǎo fāngzhēn

guild N 同业公会 tóngyègōnghuì, 行会 hánghuì

guile N 诡计 guǐjì, 欺骗 qīpiàn
by guile and skill 连蒙带骗 lián méng dài piàn

guileless ADJ 诚实的 chéngshí de, 不玩花招的 bù wán huāzhāo de

guillotine N 断头台 duàntóutái

guilt N 1 有罪 yǒuzuì, 犯罪 fànzuì 2 内疚 nèijiū, 羞愧 xiūkuì

guilt-ridden ADJ 有负罪感的 yǒu fùzuìgǎn de, 内疚的 nèijiù de

guilty ADJ 有罪的 yǒuzuì de

guinea pig N 1 豚鼠 túnshǔ [m. wd 只 zhī] 2 当试验品的人 dāng shìyànpǐn de rén
guise N 伪装 wěizhuāng, 外表 wàibiǎo
guitar N 吉他 jítā [m. wd 把 bǎ]
guitarist N 吉他琴手 jítāqínshǒu
gulf N 1 海湾 hǎiwān
the Gulf of Mexico 墨西哥湾 Mòxīgē wān
the Persian Gulf 波斯湾 Bōsī wān
2 重大分歧 zhòngdà fēnqí, 鸿沟 hónggōu
gull N 海鸥 hǎi'ōu [m. wd 只 zhī/头 tóu]
gullible ADJ 容易受骗的 róngyì shòupiàn de, 轻信的 qīngxìn de
gully N 冲沟 chōnggōu [m. wd 条 tiáo], 隘谷 àigǔ
gulp I v 1 很快地吞下 hěn kuài de tūnxià 2 大口吸气 dà kǒu xīqì II N 吞咽 tūnyàn
gum I N 1 口香糖 kǒuxiāngtáng [m. wd 块 kuài]
chewing gum 口香糖 kǒuxiāngtáng
2 牙龈 yáyín, 牙床 yáchuáng
bleeding gum 牙龈出血 yáyín chūxuè
3 树胶 shùjiāo II v (用树胶) 粘合 (yòng shùjiāo) zhānhé
gumbo N 秋葵汤 qiūkuítāng
gumdrop N 橡皮糖 xiàngpítáng
gumption N 魄力 pòlì, 精明 jīngmíng
gun I N 1 枪 qiāng [m. wd 支 zhī], 炮 páo [m. wd 门 mén] 2 喷射器 pēnshèqì II v 加速 jiāsù, 猛踩油门 měng cǎi yóumén
gunboat N 炮舰 pàojiàn [m. wd 艘 sōu]
gunfire N 炮火 pàohuǒ
gung-ho ADJ 非常热切的 fēicháng rèqiè de, 狂热的 kuángrè de
gunman N 持枪歹徒 chíqiāng dǎitú
gunner N 炮手 pàoshǒu
gunpoint N 枪口 qiāngkǒu
at gunpoint 在枪口威逼下 zài qiāngkǒu wēibī xià
gunpowder N 火药 huǒyào
gunshot N 1 (枪炮) 射击 (qiāngpào) shèjī 2 枪声 qiāngpàoshēng
gurgle I v [水+] 潺潺地流 [shuǐ+] chánchán de liú II N 潺潺流水声 chánchán liúshuǐshēng
guru N 大师 dàshī, 权威 quánwēi
gush I v 1 大量喷出 dàliàng pēn chū, 涌出 yǒngchu 2 滔滔不绝地说 tāotāo bùjué de shuō II N 大量喷出的液体 dàliàng pēnchū de yètǐ
gusher N 1 喷油井 pēnyóujǐng [m. wd 口 kǒu] 2 滔滔不绝地说话的人 tāotāo bùjué de shuōhuà de rén
gust I N 一阵狂风 yízhèn kuángfēng, 一阵大雪 yízhèn dàxuě II v [风+] 劲吹 [fēng+] jìngchuī
gusto N 热情 rèqíng
with gusto 兴致勃勃地 xìngzhìbóbó de
gut ADJ 直觉的 zhíjué de, 本能的 běnnéng de
gut feeling 强烈的直觉 qiángliè de zhíjué
gut reaction 本能的反应 běnnéng de fǎnyìng
guts I N 1 内脏 nèizàng, 肠胃 chángwèi

a pain in one's guts 肚子痛 dùzi tòng
2 勇气 yǒngqì
to have guts (to do sth) 有勇气做某事 yǒu yǒngqì (zuò mǒushì)
II v 彻底烧毁 chèdǐ shāohuǐ
gutter N 1 (路边) 排水沟 (lùbiān) páishuǐgōu [m. wd 条 tiáo] 2 (屋檐) 雨水槽 (wūyán) yǔshuǐcáo [m. wd 条 tiáo]
guttural ADJ 发自喉中的 fāzì hóuzhòng de, 低沉的 dīchén de
guy N (青年) 男人 (qīngnián) nánren
you guys 大家 dàjiā, 各位 gèwèi
guzzle v 1 大吃大喝 dàchī dàhē, 狂饮 kuángyǐn 2 大量耗油 dàliàng hàoyóu
gym N 健身房 jiànshēnfáng [m. wd 座 zuò], 体育馆 tǐyùguǎn [m. wd 座 zuò]
gymnasium N See gym
gymnast N 体操运动员 tǐcāo yùndòngyuán
gymnastics N 体操 (运动) tǐcāo (yùndòng)
gynecologist N 妇科医生 fùkē yīshēng
gynecology N 妇科 fùkē
gypsy N 吉卜赛人 Jípǔsàirén
gyrate v 快速旋转 kuàisù xuánzhuǎn
gyroscope, gyro N 回转仪 huízhuǎnyí

H

habit N 1 习惯 xíguàn 2 坏习惯 huài xíguàn, 毒瘾 dúyǐn
to break the habit 戒掉坏习惯 jiè diào huài xíguàn, 戒掉毒瘾 jiè diào dúyǐn
habitable ADJ 可以住人的 kěyǐ zhù rén de, 适于居住的 shìyú jūzhù de
habitat N 栖息地 qīxīdì, 居住地 jūzhùdì
habitation N 居住 jūzhù
habitual ADJ 习惯 (性) 的 xíguàn (xìng) de
hack¹ I v 1 乱砍 luàn kǎn, 乱劈 luàn pī 2 非法侵入 [+他人的计算机系统] fēi fǎ qīnrù [+tārén de jìsuànjī xìtǒng]
hack² I N 1 低级文人 dījí wénrén, 雇佣文人 gùyōng wénrén 2 老马 lǎo mǎ 3 出租车 chūzūchē, 出租车司机 chūzūchē sījī
hacker N 黑客 hēikè, 电脑迷 diànnǎo mí
hackneyed ADJ 陈词滥调的 chéncí làndiào de, 陈腐的 chénfǔ de
hacksaw N 钢锯 gāngjù
had v See have
hag N 丑陋的老太婆 chǒulòu de lǎotàipó, 母夜叉 mǔyèchā
haggard ADJ (面容) 憔悴的 (miànróng) qiáocuì de
haggle v 争吵 zhēngchǎo, 讨价还价 tǎojià huánjià

to haggle over prices 讨价还价 tǎojià huánjià

ha ha INTERJ 哈哈 hāha

hail¹ V **1** 大声招呼 dàshēng zhāohu, 叫 jiào **2** 赞扬 zànyáng, 称赞 chēngzàn

hail² I N 冰雹 bīngbáo II V 下冰雹 xià bīngbáo

hailstone N 雹（子）báo (zi)

hailstorm N 雹暴 báobào [M. WD 场 cháng]

hair N **1** 毛 máo [M. WD 根 gēn], 毛发 máofà [M. WD 根 gēn] **2** 头发 tóufa

to split hair 吹毛求疵 chuī máo qiú cī

hairbrush N 发刷 fāshuā [M. WD 把 bǎ]

haircut N 理发 lǐfà ■ *He has a haircut every fortnight.* 他每两个星期理一次发。Tā měi liǎng ge xīngqī lǐ yí cì fà.

hairdo N **1**（女子）发型 (nǚzǐ) fàxíng **2** 做头发 zuò tóufa

hairdresser N 理发师 lǐfàshī

hairdryer N 吹风机 chuīfēngjī, 干发机 gānfàjī

hairline N 发际线 fàjì xiàn

hairnet N 发网 fàwǎng

hair-raising ADJ 使人发毛耸立的 shǐrén fàmáo sǒnglì de, 万分惊险的 wànfēn jīngxiǎn de

hairsplitting N 吹毛求疵 chuī máo qiú cī

hairspray N 喷发胶 pēnfàjiāo

hairstyle N 发型 fàxíng

hairy ADJ 多毛的 duō máo de, 毛茸茸的 máoróngróng de

halcyon ADJ 美好的 měihǎo de

halcyon years 太平盛世 tàipíng shèngshì

hale ADJ 老当益壮的 lǎodāng yìzhuàng de

half I NUM 半 bàn, 一半 yí bàn

half time 半场休息 bàn chàng xiūxi

II N 半 bàn, 一半 yí bàn

half-and-half 一半一半的 yíbàn yíbàn de, 稀奶油 xīnǎiyóu

III ADV 部分 bùfen, 一半 yí bàn ■ *Do you see the glass as half full or half empty?* 你看这玻璃杯是一半满，还是一半空？Nǐ kàn zhè bōlibēi shì yí bàn mǎn, háishi yí bàn kōng? IV ADJ 一半 yíbàn

half-assed ADJ **1** 马马虎虎的 mǎma hūhū de, 敷衍了事的 fūyan liǎoshì de **2** 愚蠢的 yúchǔn de

half-baked ADJ 不成熟的 bù chéngshú de

half-brother N 同父／异母兄弟 tóng fù/yì mǔ xiōngdì

half-hearted ADJ 半心半意的 bànxīnbànyì de

half-mast N 降半旗 jiàngbànqí

to fly at half-mast 降半旗 jiàngbànqí

half-sister N 同父／异母姐妹 tóng fù/yì mǔ jiěmèi

half-time N（球类比赛）中场休息 (qiúlèi bǐsài) zhōngchàng xiūxi

half-truth N 半真半假的鬼话 bànzhēn bànjiǎ de guǐhuà

halfway ADV 半路 bànlù, 中间 zhōngjiān ■ *Halfway to the concert they found they had left the admission tickets at home.* 他们在去音乐会的

半路上才发现入场券忘在家里了。Tāmen zài qù yīnyuèhuì de bànlùshang cái fāxiàn rùchǎngquàn wàng zài jiālǐ le.

hall N **1** 走廊 zǒuláng, 过道 guòdào **2** 大厅 dàtīng, 堂 táng ■ *Lincoln Memorial is perhaps the best-known memorial hall in the world.* 林肯纪念堂或许是世界上最著名的纪念堂。Línkěn jìniàntáng huòxǔ shì shìjièshang zuìzhùmíng de jìniàntáng. **3**（大学生）宿舍楼 (dàxuéshēng) sùshè lóu

hallelujah INTERJ 哈利路亚 Hālìlùyà, 赞美上帝 zànměi Shàngdì, 感谢上帝 gǎnxiè Shàngdì

hallmark N 特征 tèzhēng, 标志 biāozhì

to bear the hallmark of sth 带有某事物的特征 dàiyǒu mǒushìwù de tèzhēng

Hall of Fame N **1** 体育明星榜 tǐyù míngxīngbǎng **2** 名人纪念馆 míngrén jìniànguǎn [M. WD 座 zuò]

hallowed ADJ 神圣的 shénshèng de

Halloween N 万圣节（十月三十一日夜晚）Wànshèngjié (shíyuè sānshíyī rì yèwǎn)

hallucinate V 产生幻觉／幻视／幻听 chǎnshēng huànjué/huànshì/huàntīng

hallucination N 幻觉／幻视／幻听 huànjué/huànshì/huàntīng

hallucinogen N 会产生幻觉的药物 huì chǎnshēng huànjué de yàowù, 致幻剂 zhìhuànjì

hallway N 门厅 méntīng, 走廊 zǒuláng

halo N 光轮 guānglún, 光圈 guāngquān

halt V, N 停止 tíngzhǐ

halting ADJ 断断续续的 duànduàn xùxù de, 犹犹豫豫的 yóuyóu yùyù de

halve V **1** 把…一分为二 bǎ…yìfēn wéi èr, 对半分 duìbàn fēn **2** 把…减半 bǎ…jiǎnbàn

ham I N **1** 火腿 huǒtuǐ **2** 表演过火的演员 biǎoyǎn guòhuǒ de yǎnyuán **3** 业余无线电爱好者 yèyú wúxiàndiàn àihàozhě

ham radio 业余无线电台 yèyú wúxiàndiàntái

II V 表演过火 biǎoyǎn guòhuǒ, 夸张地表演 kuāzhāng de biǎoyǎn

hamburger N **1** 汉堡牛肉饼 hànbǎo niúròubǐng, 汉堡包 hànbǎobāo **2** 碎牛肉 suìniúròu

hamlet N 小村庄 xiǎo cūnzhuāng, 小村子 xiǎo cūnzi

hammer I N 锤子 chuízi [M. WD 把 bǎ], 榔头 lángtou [M. WD 把 bǎ] II V 反复敲打 fǎnfù qiāoda

hammock N 吊床 diàochuáng [M. WD 张 zhāng]

hamper I V 阻碍 zǔ'ài, 妨碍 fáng'ài II N 大篮子 dà lánzi

picnic hamper 野餐食品篮 yěcān shípǐn lán

hamster N 金仓鼠 jīn cāngshǔ [M. WD 只 zhī]

hamstring¹ N 腘绳肌腱 guóshéng jījiàn

hamstring² (PT & PP **hamstrung**) V 使…受挫 shǐ…shòucuò, 阻扰 zǔrǎo

hamstrung V See **hamstring²**

hand I N **1** 手 shǒu [M. WD 只 zhī/双 shuāng]
hand luggage 手提行李 shǒutí xínglǐ
on the one hand … on the other hand 一方面
…另一方面 yì fāngmiàn…lìng yì fāngmiàn
■ On the one hand you should help her, but on
the other hand you shouldn't do everything for her.
你一方面应该帮助她，另一方面也不应该什么事
都给她做好。Nǐ yì fāngmiàn yīnggāi bāngzhu tā,
lìng yì fāngmiàn yě bù yīnggāi shénme shì dōu
gěi tā zuòhǎo.
by hand 手工的 shǒugōng de
to shake hands with 和…握手 hé…wòshǒu
2 帮助 bāngzhu ■ Can you give me a hand with
these books? 你能帮我搬这些书吗？ Nǐ néng bāng
wǒ bān zhèxiē shū ma? **3** （钟）指针 （zhōng）
zhǐzhēn **4** 手上的牌 shǒushang de pái **II** v 交
jiāo, 递 dì

handbag N 手提包 shǒutíbāo, 坤包 kūnbāo
handbook N 手册 shǒucè [M. WD 本 běn], 指南
zhǐnán [M. WD 本 běn]
handcuff I N 手铐 shǒukào [M. WD 副 fù] **II** v 给…
戴上手铐 gěi…dàishàng shǒukào
handful N 一把 yì bǎ
handgun N 手枪 shǒuqiāng
handicap N 不利条件 búlì tiáojiàn, 障碍 zhàng'ài
handicapped ADJ 有生理缺陷的 yǒu shēnglǐ
quēxiàn de, 残障的 cánzhàng de
the handicapped 残障人士 cánzhàng rénshì
handiwork N **1** 所做的事 suǒ zuò de shì **2** 手工
shǒugōng, 手工艺品 shǒugōngyìpǐn
handkerchief N 手帕 shǒupà [M. WD 块 kuài]
handle I N 把 bǎ, 柄 bǐng, 把手 bǎshǒu **II** v **1** 拿
ná, 抓 zhuā, 摆弄 bǎinòng
Handle with care. 小心轻放。Xiǎoxīn qīng fàng.
2 管理 guǎnlǐ, 控制 kòngzhì ■ Only my dad
knows how to handle this dog. 只有我爸爸知道怎
样控制这条狗。Zhǐ yǒu wǒ bàba zhīdào zěnyàng
kòngzhì zhè tiáo gǒu. **3** 处理 chǔlǐ, 对付 duìfu
handlebars N 把手 bǎshǒu
handler N **1** 搬运工 bānyùn gōng **2** （动物）驯练
员 （dòngwù）xùnliànyuán
handmade ADJ 手工制作的 shǒugōng zhìzuò de
hand-me-down N （从哥哥姐姐那里传下来的）旧
衣服 （cóng gēge jiějie nàli chuánxiálái de）
jiù yīfú
handout N **1** 救济款 jiùjìkuǎn [M. WD 笔 bǐ], 救济
物资 jiùjì wùzī [M. WD 批 pī] **2** 讲义 jiǎngyì
[M. WD 份 fèn], 材料 cáiliào [M. WD 份 fèn]
handpicked ADJ 精心挑选的 jīngxīn tiāoxuǎn de,
亲自挑选的 qīnzì tiāoxuǎn de
handshake N 握手 wòshǒu
hands off INTERJ 别碰 bié pèng ■ Hands off, that's
mine! 别碰，那是我的！ Bié pèng, nà shì wǒde!
handsome ADJ **1** 英俊的 [+男子] yīngjùn de
[+nánzǐ] **2** 健美的 [+女子] jiànměi de [+nǚzǐ]

3 出手大方的 [+礼物、捐助] chūshǒu dàfāng de
[+lǐwù, juānzhù], 慷慨的 kāngkǎi de
hands-on ADJ 实际操作的 shíjì cāozuò de, (计算
机) 上机的 (jìsuànjī) shàngjī de
hands-on computer training 计算机操作训练
jìsuànjī cāozuò xùnliàn
handstand N 双手倒立 shuāngshǒu dàolì
hands up INTERJ 举起手来 jǔqǐ shǒulái
handwriting N **1** 书写 shūxiě, 手写 shǒuxiě **2** 书
法 shūfǎ
handy ADJ **1** 方便的 fāngbiàn de **2** 在手边的 zài
shǒubiān de **3** 手巧的 shǒuqiǎo de
handyman N 手巧的人 shǒuqiǎo de rén, 善于做
零星修理的人 shànyú zuò língxīng xiūlǐ de rén
hang¹ (PT & PP hung) v 挂 guà, 悬挂 xuánguà
to hang about 闲荡 xiándàng
to hang in there 坚持下去 jiānchí xiàqù, 挺住
tǐng zhù
to hang on 等一会 děng yíhuì ■ Hang on half
a minute—I'm nearly ready. 等一会—我差不多好
了。Děng yíhuì—wǒ chàbuduō hǎo le.
to hang up 挂断 (电话) guàduàn (diànhuà)
hang² v (PT & PP hanged) **1** 吊死 diàosǐ **2** 处以绞
刑 chǔyǐjiǎoxíng
hang³ N v (to get the hang of) 掌握 zhǎngwò, 了解
liǎojiě
hangar N 飞机库 fēijīkù [M. WD 座 zuò]
hanger N 衣架 yījià
hanger-on N 跟随者 gēnsuízhě, 追随者 zhuīsuízhě
hang glider N 悬挂式滑翔机 xuánguàshì
huáxiángjī [M. WD 架 jià]
hanging N 绞刑 jiǎoxíng
hangings N 帘子 liánzi
hangman N 字母猜字游戏 zìmǔ cāizì yóuxì
hangout N 常去的地方 cháng qù de dìfang, 聚
集地 jùjí dì
hangover N 酗酒后第二天感到不适 xùjiǔ hòu
dì'èrtiān gǎndào búshì, 宿醉 sùzuì
a hangover from sth 遗留的问题 yíliú de wèntí,
后遗症 hòuyízhèng
hangup N 烦恼 fánnǎo, 焦虑 jiāolǜ, 心理障碍
xīnlǐ zhàng'ài
hanker v 渴望 kěwàng, 追求 zhuīqiú
hankering N 渴望 kěwàng, 追求 zhuīqiú
hankie, hanky N 手帕 shǒupà [M. WD 块 kuài]
hanky-panky N **1** 骗局 piànjú **2** 调情 tiáoqíng
haphazard ADJ 杂乱无章的 záluàn wúzhāng de,
毫无计划的 háowú jìhuà de
hapless ADJ 倒霉的 dǎoméi de
happen v **1** 发生 fāshēng **2** 碰巧 pèngqiǎo ■ She
happened to be at home when the burglar broke
into the house. 窃贼破门而入时，她碰巧在家。
Qièzéi pò mén ér rù shí, tā pèngqiǎo zài jiā.
happening¹ ADJ 时髦的 shímáo de, 流行的
liúxíng de

happening² N 发生的事情 fāshēng de shìqing
happily ADV 1 幸福地 xìngfú de ■ *They lived happily ever after.* 从此以后，他们生活得很幸福。Cóng cǐ yǐhòu, tāmen shēnghuóde hěn xìngfú. 2 高兴地 gāoxìng de ■ *Children played happily in the park.* 孩子们在公园里高兴地玩。Háizimen zài gōngyuán lǐ gāoxìng de wán. 3 幸运地 xìngyùn de, 幸好 xìnghǎo
happiness N 幸福 xìngfú, 快乐 kuàilè
happy ADJ 1 幸福的 xìngfú de 2 高兴的 gāoxìng de ■ *We'll be happy to give you a loan.* 我们将很高兴给你们贷款。Wǒmen jiāng hěn gāoxìng gěi nǐmen dàikuǎn. 3 满意的 mǎnyì de ■ *We're happy with your service.* 我们对你们的服务很满意。Wǒmen duì nǐmen de fúwù hěn mǎnyì.
Happy birthday to you! 祝你生日快乐! Zhù nǐ shēngri kuàilè!
Happy New Year! 新年快乐! Xīnnián kuàilè! 新年好! Xīnniánhǎo!
happy-go-lucky ADJ 乐天知命的 lè tiān zhī mìng de, 无忧无虑的 wúyōu wúlǜ de
happy hour N 快乐时光 kuàilè shíguāng, 优惠时段 yōuhuì shíduàn
harangue V 1 做长篇演说 zuò chángpiān yǎnshuō 2 滔滔不绝地训斥 tāotāo bùjué de xùnchì
harass V 骚扰 sāorǎo
harassment N 骚扰 sāorǎo, 侵扰 qīnrǎo
harbor N 港 gǎng, 港湾 gǎngwān
hard I ADJ 1 硬 yìng, 坚硬 jiānyìng ■ *I do like a firm mattress, but this one is way too hard.* 我确实喜欢坚实的床垫，但是这个实在太硬了。Wǒ quèshí xǐhuan jiānshí de chuángdiàn, dànshì zhè ge shízài tài yìng le.
hard hat 安全帽 ānquánmào
2 艰难的 jiānnán de 3 苛刻的 kēkè de
to be hard on 对…很苛刻 duì…hěn kēkè
II ADV 1 努力地 nǔlì de ■ *He works hard to support his family.* 他努力工作，养活家人。Tā nǔlì gōngzuò, yǎnghuo jiārén. 2 艰难地 jiānnán de 3 严重地 yánzhòng de ■ *It rained hard last night.* 昨晚下大雨。Zuóyè xià dàyǔ.
hard-and-fast ADJ 固定不变的 gùdìng búbiàn de
hard and fast rules 严格的规定 yángé de guīdìng
hardball N (to play hardball) 采取强硬手段 cǎiqǔ qiángyìng shǒuduàn
hard-boiled ADJ 1 [蛋+] 煮得老的 [dàn+] zhǔ dé lǎo de 2 不露声色的 bú lù shēngsè de, 精明老练的 jīngmíng lǎoliàn de
hard cash N 现钞 xiànchāo [M. WD 笔 bǐ], 现金 xiànjīn [M. WD 笔 bǐ]
hard copy N 打印文本 dǎyìn wénběn [M. WD 份 fèn]
hardcore ADJ 1 顽固不化的 wángù búhuà de 2 露骨的 lùgǔ de

hardcore pornography 赤裸裸的色情作品 chìluǒluǒ de sèqíng zuòpǐn
hard currency N 硬通货 yìngtōnghuò
hard disk, hard disk drive N (计算机) 硬盘 (jìsuànjī) yìngpán
hard drugs N 烈性毒品 lièxìng dúpǐn
harden V 1 (使…) 变硬 (shǐ)…biàn yìng 2 (使)…更强硬 (shǐ)…gèng qiángyìng 3 使…冷酷无情 shǐ…lěngkù wúqíng
hard-headed ADJ 1 心肠很硬的 xīncháng hěn yìng de, 没有同情心的 méiyǒu tóngqíngxīn de 2 讲究实际的 jiǎngjiu shíjì de, 头脑清醒的 tóunǎo qīngxǐng de
hard-hitting ADJ 激烈的 [+批评] jīliè de [+pīpíng]
hardline ADJ 强硬路线的 qiángyìng lùxiàn de
hardliner N 强硬派 qiángyìngpài
hardly ADV 1 刚刚 gānggāng, 仅仅 jǐnjǐn ■ *She had hardly begun to cook when her children came back, hungry as wolves.* 她刚刚开始做饭，孩子们就回家了，一个个像饿狼。Tā gānggāng kāishǐ zuòfàn, háizimen jiù huíjiā le, yígège xiàng èláng. 2 几乎不 jīhū bù 3 一点也不 yìdiǎn yě bù, 根本不 gēnběn bù
hard-nosed ADJ 无动于衷的 wúdòng yú zhōng de, 不妥协的 bù tuǒxié de
hard of hearing ADJ 听觉不好的 tīngjué bùhǎo de, 有听力障碍的 yǒu tīnglì zhàng'ài de
hard-pressed ADJ 困难重重的 kùnnan chóngchóng de, 窘迫的 jiǒngpò de
hard rock N 硬摇滚乐 yìng yáogǔnyuè
hard sell N 强行推销 qiángxíng tuīxiāo
hardship N 艰难 jiānnán, 苦难 kǔnàn
hard-up ADJ 缺钱的 quē qián de, 钱很紧的 qián hěn jǐn de
hardware N 1 (计算机) 硬件 (jìsuànjī) yìngjiàn 2 机器设备 jīqì shèbèi 3 军事装备 jūnshì zhuāngbèi 4 五金制品 wǔjīn zhìpǐn
hardwood N 硬木 yìngmù
hard-working ADJ 努力工作的 nǔlì gōngzuò de, 勤奋的 qínfèn de
hardy ADJ 能吃苦耐劳的 néng chīkǔ nàiláo de, 坚强的 jiānqiáng de
hare N 野兔 yětù [M. WD 只 zhī]
harebrained ADJ 轻率浮躁的 qīngshuài fúzào de, 愚蠢的 yúchǔn de
harelip N 兔唇 tùchún
harem N 1 (伊斯兰国家) 妻妾 (Yīsīlán guójiā) qīqiè 2 后宫 hòugōng
hark V 仔细听 zǐxì tīng, 倾听 qīngtīng
to hark back to 使人 (回) 想起 shǐrén (huí) xiǎng qǐ
harlot N 妓女 jìnǚ, 婊子 biǎozi
harm I N 坏处 huàichu, 损害 sǔnhài ■ *Taking too much vitamins can do more harm than good.* 服用太多的维他命只有坏处，没有好处。Fúyòng

ENGLISH-CHINESE

tài duō de wéitāmìng zhǐ yǒu huàichu, méiyǒu hǎochu.

No harm done. 没关系。Méiguānxi.

II v 损害 sǔnhài, 伤害 shānghài ■ *High interest rates have harmed the economy.* 高利率损害了经济。Gāo lìlǜ sǔnhàile jīngjì.

harmful ADJ 有害的 yǒuhài de

harmless ADJ **1** 无害的 [+动物] wúhài de [+dòngwù] **2** 无恶意的 [+玩笑] wú èyì de [+wánxiào]

harmonica N 口琴 kǒuqín [M. WD 只 zhī]

harmonious ADJ 和谐的 héxié de, 融洽的 róngqià de

harmony N **1** 和谐 héxié, 融洽 róngqià **2** (音乐) 和声 (yīnyuè) héshēng

harness I N **1** (马的)挽具 (mǎ de) wǎnjù, 马具 mǎjù **2** (人的)保险带 (rén de) bǎoxiǎndài **II** v 治理利用 zhìlǐ lìyòng

harp I N 竖琴 shùqín **II** v (to harp on) 唠唠叨叨地说 láoláo dāodāo de shuō, 没完没了地说 méiwán méiliǎo de shuō

harpoon N 捕鲸叉 bǔjīngchā [M. WD 把 bǎ]

harpsichord N 拨弦古钢琴 bōxiángǔgāngqín

harrowing ADJ 令人难受的 lìng rén nánshòu de, 令人痛苦的 lìng rén tòngkǔ de

harsh ADJ **1** 苛刻的 kēkè de, 严厉的 yánlì de **2** 严苛的 yánkù de, 严酷的 yánkù de ■ *I'm afraid this plant won't survive the harsh winter here.* 恐怕这种花受不起这里严酷的冬季。Kǒngpà zhè zhǒng huā jīngshòu bu qǐ zhèlǐ yánkù de dōngjì.

harvest I N **1** 收获 shōuhuò **2** 收获量 shōuhuòliàng, 收成 shōucheng

to reap a bumper harvest 获得丰收 huòdé fēngshōu

II v 收获 shōuhuò

has v See have

has-been N 风光不再的人 fēngguāng bú zài de rén, 过气的人 guòqì de rén

hash N **1** 肉末土豆泥 ròumò tǔdòuní **2** 大麻毒品 dàmá dúpǐn

hash browns N 煎土豆饼 jiān tǔdòubǐng [M. WD 块 kuài]

hasn't See have

hassle I N **1** 麻烦 máfan **II** v 一再打扰 yízài dǎrǎo, 骚扰 sāorǎo

haste N 匆忙 cōngmáng

More haste, less speed. 越是匆忙越是慢。(→欲速则不达。) Yuè shì cōngmáng yuè shì màn. (→Yù sù zé bù dá.)

hasten v 加快 jiākuài, 加速 jiāsù

hasty ADJ 仓促的 cāngcù de, 匆忙的 cōngmáng de

hat N 帽子 màozi [M. WD 顶 dǐng]

hats off to sb 向某人致敬 xiàng mǒurén zhìjìng

hatch I v **1** [蛋+] 孵化 [dàn+] fūhuà **2** 策划出 [+计划、秘密] cèhuà chū [+jìhuà, mìmì] **II** N (船、

飞机)舱口,舱门 (chuan, fēijī) cāngkǒu, cāng mén

hatchback N 两舱门式汽车 liǎng cāngmén shì qìchē [M. WD 辆 liàng]

hatchet N (短柄)小斧头 (duǎn bǐng) xiǎo fǔtou [M. WD 把 bǎ]

hate I v **1** 非常不喜欢 fēicháng bù xǐhuan, 讨厌 tǎoyàn **2** (憎)恨 (zèng) hèn **II** v 仇恨 chóuhèn

hateful ADJ **1** 充满仇恨的 chōngmǎn chóuhèn de **2** 可憎的 kězēng de, 讨厌的 tǎoyàn de

hatred N 恨 hèn, 仇恨 chóuhèn ■ *They were accused of stirring racial hatred.* 他们被控煽动种族仇恨。Tāmen bèi kòng shāndòng zhǒngzú chóuhèn.

haughty ADJ 傲慢的 àomàn de, 目中无人的 mùzhōng wú rén de

haul I v 搬运 bānyùn, 拉 lā, 拖 tuō

to haul off 硬拖 yìng tuō, 抓捕 zhuābǔ

II N **1** 时期 shíqī, 距离 jùlí

long haul 长途 chángtú, 很长的距离 hěn cháng de jùlí

over the long/short haul 长/短期 cháng/ duǎnqī

2 大量赃物 dàliàng zāngwù, 大量走私物品 dàliàng zǒusī wùpǐn

haunches N 后腿 hòutuǐ

sb's haunches 腿臀部 tuǐtúnbù

haunt I v **1** [鬼魂+] 出没 [guǐhún+] chūmò **2** [烦人的事+] 纠缠 [fánrén de shì+] jiūchán, 烦扰 fánrǎo **II** N 经常去的地方 jīngcháng qù de dìfang

haunted ADJ 有鬼的 yǒuguǐ de, 闹鬼的 nàoguǐ de

haunting ADJ 萦绕于心的 yíngrào yú xīn de, 难以忘怀的 nányǐ wànghuái de

have [NEG **have not** ABBREV **haven't**; 3rd person: **has**; NEG **has not** ABBREV **hasn't**] (PT & PP **had**) I v **1** 有 yǒu, 拥有 yōngyǒu ■ *How much money do you have on you?* 你身上有多少钱？Nǐ shēnshang yǒu duōshǎoqián?

to have time 有空 yǒu kòng, 有时间 yǒu shíjiān ■ *I don't have time to go to the movies with you today.* 我今天没有空跟你一块儿去看电影。Wǒ jīntiān méiyǒu kōng gēn nǐ yíkuàir qù kàn diànyǐng.

2 有 yǒu, 具有 jùyǒu **3** 吃 chī, 喝 hē ■ *Come and have a beer with us.* 来跟我们一起喝杯啤酒。Lái gēn wǒmen yìqǐ hē bēi píjiǔ. **4** 生病 shēngbìng

to have a bad cold 感冒 gǎnmào

II AUX V

to have (got) to 得 děi, 不得不 bùdebù ■ *You've got to be more careful next time.* 下次你得小心一点。Xiàcì nǐ děi xiǎoxīn yìdiǎn.

had better 最好 zuìhǎo, 还是 háishi ■ *You'd better save more money before buying the house.*

418

你最好多多积些钱再买房子。Nǐ zuìhǎo duō jī xiē qián zài mǎi fángzi.

haven N 安全地带 ānquán dìdài, 避难所 bìnànsuǒ

have-nots N (the have-nots) 穷人 qióngrén

haven't See **have**

haves N (the haves) 富人 fùrén

have to, has to V 得 děi, 必须 bìxū

havoc N 巨大的破坏 jùdà de pòhuài, 浩劫 hàojié

hawk¹ N **1** 鹰 yīng [M. WD 只 zhī], 老鹰 lǎoyīng [M. WD 只 zhī] **2** 鹰派人物 yīngpài rénwù, 强硬派 qiángyìngpài

hawk² N 叫卖 jiàomài, 兜售 dōushòu

hawker N (叫卖的) 小贩 (jiàomài de) xiǎofàn

hay N 干草 gāncǎo, 牧草 mùcǎo
Make hay while the sun shines. 趁天晴的时候，打晒干草。(→ 趁热打铁。) Chèn tiān qíng de shíhou, dǎ shài gāncǎo. (→Chèn rè dǎ tiě.)
hay fever 枯草热 kūcǎorè, 花粉病 huāfěnbìng

haystack N 干草堆 gāncǎoduī

haywire ADJ 乱糟糟的 luànzāozāo de
to go haywire 出错 chūcuò, 乱套 luàntào

hazard I N 危险 wēixiǎn, 隐患 yǐnhuàn
hazard lights (汽车) 危险警示灯 (qìchē) wēixiǎn jǐngshì dēng
hazard pay 危险工种岗位补贴 wēixiǎn gōngzhǒng gǎngwèi bǔtiē
occupational hazard 职业危险 zhíyè wēixiǎn **II** V 猜测 cāicè

hazardous ADJ 危险的 wēixiǎn de

haze N 烟雾 yānwù, 雾气 wùqì

hazel I N 榛树 zhēn shù [M. WD 棵 kē] **II** ADJ 淡褐色的 dànhèsè de

hazelnut N 榛子 zhēnzi [M. WD 颗 kē]

hazy ADJ **1** 雾蒙蒙的 [+天空] wù méngméng de [+tiānkōng] **2** 模糊的 [+印象] móhu de [+yìnxiàng]

H-bomb N 氢弹 qīngdàn [M. WD 枚 méi]

he PRON 他 tā

head I N **1** 头 tóu, 头部 tóubù
head count 数人头 shù réntóu
head start 先起步的优势 xiān qǐbù de yōushì, 有利的开端 yǒulì de kāiduān
2 领导人 lǐngdǎorén, 长 zhǎng, 头头 tóutou
head of state 国家元首 guójiā yuánshǒu
head waiter 服务员领班 fúwùyuán lǐngbān
3 头脑 tóunǎo, 智力 zhìlì
to use one's head 动脑子 dòng nǎozi
II V **1** 带领 dàilǐng, 率领 shuàilǐng ■ The delegation will be headed by the Secretary of Commerce. 代表团将由商务部长率领。Dàibiǎotuán jiāng yóu Shāngwù bùzhǎng shuàilǐng. **2** 朝…行进 cháo…xíngjìn ■ The stolen car headed east. 被窃的汽车朝东开去。Bèi qiè de qìchē cháo dōng kāiqu. **3** 用头顶球 yòngtou dǐng qiú

headache N 头疼 tóuténg, 头痛 tóutòng

headband N 束发带 shùfàdài, 扎头带 zhātóudài

headfirst ADV **1** 头朝前地 tóu cháoqián de **2** 轻率地 qīngshuài de, 鲁莽地 lǔmǎng de

headgear N 帽子 màozi [M. WD 顶 dǐng], 头饰 tóushì

headhunter N **1** 割取敌人头颅作为战利品的部落 gē qǔ dírén tóulú zuòwéi zhànlìpǐn de bùluò **2** 物色人才的人 wùsè réncái de rén

heading N 标题 biāotí

headland N 海岬 hǎijiǎ

headlight N (汽车) 前灯 (qìchē) qiándēng, 车头灯 chētóudēng

headline N **1** (报纸的) 标题 (bàozhǐ de) biāotí [M. WD 条 tiáo] **2** (社会上的) 热门话题 (shèhuìshang de) rèmén huàtí
to make the headline 成为热门话题 chéngwéi rèmén huàtí
3 新闻提要 xīnwén tíyào

headlong ADV **1** 头朝前地 tóu cháoqián de **2** 轻率地 qīngshuài de
to rush headlong into 轻率地 [+做某事] qīngshuài de [+zuò mǒushì]

headmaster, headmistress N (私立学校) 校长 (sīlì xuéxiào) xiàozhǎng

head-on ADV 迎面 yíngmiàn
to meet head-on 迎面相撞 yíngmiàn xiāngzhuàng

head-phones N 耳机 ěrjī [M. WD 副 fù]

headquarters N **1** (军队) 司令部 (jūnduì) sīlìngbù **2** (公司) 总部 (gōngsī) zǒngbù

headrest N 头靠 tóukào, 头垫 tóudiàn

headroom N 头顶空间 tóudǐng kōngjiān

headstone N 墓碑 mùbēi [M. WD 块 kuài]

headstrong ADJ 固执的 gùzhí de, 任性的 rènxìng de

head-to-head ADJ, ADV 直接 (的／地) [+竞争] zhíjiē (de) [+jìngzhēng], 正面 (的／地) zhèngmiàn (de)

headway N 进展 jìnzhǎn
to make headway 取得进展 qǔdé jìnzhǎn

headwind N 顶头风 dǐngtóu fēng, 顶风 dǐngfēng

heady ADJ 使人兴奋得忘乎所以的 shǐ rén xīngfèn dé wàng hū suǒyǐ de, 令人陶醉的 lìng rén táozuì de

heal V 愈合 yùhé, 治愈 zhìyù

health N 健康 (情况) jiànkāng (qíngkuàng)
health care 保健 bǎojiàn
health club 保健俱乐部 bǎojiàn jùlèbù

healthful ADJ 有利于健康的 yǒulì yú jiànkāng de

healthy ADJ **1** 健康的 jiànkāng de ■ A healthy body harbors a sound mind. 健康的身体才有健全的心灵。Jiànkāng de shēntǐ cái yǒu jiànquán de xīnlíng. **2** 对健康有利的 duì jiànkāng yǒulì de

heap I N 堆 duī ■ There is a heap of old magazines

in the corner. 角落里有一堆旧杂志。Jiǎoluo lǐ yǒu yì duī jiù zázhì. **II** v 堆积 duījī, 堆放 duīfàng

hear (PT & PP **heard**) v 1 听 tīng, 听到 tīngdao
■ *He listened hard but couldn't hear anything.*
他极力倾听，但是什么都听不到。Tā jílì qīngtīng, dànshì shénme dōu tīngbudào.
hard of hearing See **hard**
to hear from sb 得到关于某人的消息 dédào guānyú mǒurén de xiāoxi, 收到某人的来信/电邮 shōudào mǒurén de láixìn/diànyóu
to hear of 听说的 tīngshuōde
2 [法庭+] 审理 [fǎtíng+] shěnlǐ
to hear a case 审理一件案子 shěnlǐ yí jiàn ànzi

heard v See **hear**

hearing N 1 听觉 tīngjué, 听力 tīnglì 2 听证会 tīngzhènghuì
hearing aid 助听器 zhùtīngqì
hearing impaired 有听力障碍的 yǒu tīnglì zhàng'ài de

hearsay N 传闻 chuánwén, 道听途说 dàotīng túshuō

hearse N 灵车 língchē [M. WD 辆 liàng]

heart N 1 心 xīn, 心脏 xīnzàng 2 心 xīn, 心地 xīndì, 心情 xīnqíng ■ *With a broken heart, she watched him go.* 她伤心地看他走了。Tā shāngxīn de kàn tā zǒu le.
heart attack 心脏病发作 xīnzàngbìng fāzuò
heart disease 心脏病 xīnzàngbìng
heart failure 心力衰竭 xīnlì shuāijié ■ *He died of heart failure at the age of 87.* 他死于心力衰竭，终年八十七岁。Tā sǐ yú xīnlì shuāijié, zhōngnián bāshíqī suì.

heartache N 痛心 tòngxīn, 极其悲痛 jíqí bēitòng

heartbeat N 心跳 xīntiào

heartbreak N 伤心 shāngxīn, 心碎 xīnsuì

heartbreaking ADJ 令人心碎的 lìng rén xīnsuì de

heartbroken ADJ 心碎的 xīnsuì de, 极其悲痛的 jíqí bēitòng de

heartburn N 胃炎热 wèizhìrè, 烧心 shāoxīn

heartened ADJ 受到鼓舞的 shòudào gǔwǔ de, 振奋的 zhènfèn de

heartfelt ADJ 衷心的 zhōngxīn de

hearth N 壁炉边 bìlú biān

heartily ADV 1 开怀地 [+大笑] kāihuái de [+dà-xiào] 2 完全地 [+同意] wánquán de [tóngyì]

heartland N 心脏地区 xīnzàng dìqū, 腹地 fùdì

heartless ADJ 没有心肝的 méiyǒu xīngān de, 残酷的 cánkù de

heartrending ADJ 让人极其同情的 ràng rén jíqí tóngqíng de, 让人心酸的 ràng rén xīn suān de

heartstrings N 心弦 xīnxián, 内心深处 nèixīn shēnchù
to pull at sb's heartstrings 触动心弦 chùdòng xīnxián, 深深打动人心 shēnshēn dǎdòng rénxīn

heart-throb N 年轻人迷恋的明星 niánqīngrén míliàn de míngxīng

heart-to-heart N 坦诚的谈话 tǎnchéng de tánhuà, 谈心 tánxīn ■ *Maybe I should have a heart-to-heart with him.* 我或许应该跟他谈一次心。Wǒ huòxǔ yīnggāi gēn tā tán yí cì xīn.

heartwarming ADJ 暖人心的 nuǎn rénxīn de

hearty ADJ 1 热情友好的 [+欢迎] rèqíng yǒuhǎo de [huānyíng] 2 丰盛的 [+晚餐] fēngshèng de [+wǎncān]

heat I N 1 热 rè, 热量 rèliàng ■ *The fireplace did not give out much heat.* 壁炉没有发出多少热量。Bìlú méiyǒu fāchū duōshǎo rèliàng. 2 高温天气 gāowēn tiānqì
heat wave 高温期 gāowēnqī, 热浪 rèlàng
II v 变暖 biàn nuǎn, 变热 biàn rè ■ *Heating this office building is very costly.* 给这幢办公大楼供暖，非常花钱。Gěi zhè zhuàng bàngōng dàlóu gòng nuǎn, fēicháng huāqián.
to heat up 热一下 rè yíxià

heated ADJ 1 加热的 [+游泳池] jiārè de [+yóu-yǒngchí] 2 有暖气的 [+房间] yǒu nuǎnqì de [+fángjiān] 3 激烈的 [+争论] jīliè de [+zhēnglùn]
heated swimming-pool 温水游泳池 wēnshuǐ yóuyǒngchí

heater N 加热器 jiārèqì [M. WD 台 tái], 暖气 nuǎnq

heathen N 异教徒 yìjiàotú

heave I v (PT & PP **heaved, hove**) 1 用力拉 yònglì lā, 用力高举 yònglì gāojǔ 2 剧烈起伏 jùliè qǐfú 3 呕吐 ǒutù
to heave a sigh of relief 放心地舒了一口气 fàngxīn de shū le yì kǒu qì
II N 1 用力拉 yònglì lā, 用力高举 yònglì gāojǔ 2 呕吐 ǒutù

heaven N 1 天堂 tiāntáng, 老天爷 lǎotiānyé ■ *That was the will of the Heaven.* 那是老天爷的意旨。Nà shì lǎotiānyé de yìzhǐ. 2 极好的情况 jí hǎo de qíngkuàng, 美好乐园 měihǎo lèyuán
Good Heavens! 老天爷啊! Lǎotiānyé a!

heavenly ADJ 1 上天的 shàngtiān de 2 极好的 jíhǎo de
heavenly body 天体 tiāntǐ

heavily ADV 1 大量地 [+喝水] dàliàng de [+hēshuǐ] 2 重重地 [+喘息] zhòngzhòng de [+chuǎnxī]

heavy ADJ 1 重 zhòng, 沉重 chénzhòng
heavy industry 重工业 zhònggōngyè
heavy metal 重金属 zhòngjīnshǔ
2 很大的 hěn dà de, 很多的 hěn duō de ■ *At rush hour we always have very heavy traffic.* 在这个高峰时间交通总是非常繁忙。Zài zhè ge gāo-fēng shíjiān jiāotōng zǒngshì fēicháng fánmáng. 3 繁忙的 fánmáng de, 忙碌的 mánglù de
a heavy day at the office 办公室里繁忙的一天 bàngōngshì lǐ fánmáng de yìtiān

4 难消化的食物 nán xiāohuà de shíwù

heavy-duty ADJ **1** 耐用的 [+材料] nàiyòng de [+cáiliào] **2** 重型的 [+机器] zhòngxíng de [+jīqì] **3** 认认真真的 [+谈话] rèn rènzhēn zhēnde [+tánhuà]

heavy-handed ADJ 粗暴的 cūbào de, 高压的 gāo yā de

heavyweight N **1** （体育）重量级选手 (tǐyù) zhòngliàngjí xuǎnshǒu **2** 重量级人物 zhòngliàngjí rénwù

Hebrew N **1** 希伯来人 Xībóláirén **2** 希伯来语 Xībóláiyǔ

heckle V （在公众集会上）打断 [+发言] (zài gōngzhòng jíhuì shàng) dǎduàn [+fāyán], 呛声 qiāngshēng

heckler N 在公众集会上打断发言的人 zài gōngzhòng jíhuì shàng dǎduàn fāyán de rén, 呛声者 qiāng shēng zhě

heckling N （在公众集会上）打断发言 (zài gōngzhòng jíhuì shàng) dǎduàn fāyán

hectare N 公顷（10,000平方公尺）gōngqǐng (10,000 píngfāng gōngchǐ)

hectic ADJ 忙乱的 mángluàn de

hedge I N **1** 树篱 shùlí **2** 预防措施 yùfáng cuòshī II V **1** 回避 [+问题] huíbì [+wèntí] **2** 预防 [+风险] yùfáng [+fēngxiǎn]

to hedge one's bets 多处下（赌）注 duō chù xià (dǔ) zhù, 脚踩两条船 jiǎo cǎi liǎng tiáo chuan

hedgehog N 刺猬 cìwei

hedonism N 享乐主义 xiǎnglèzhǔyì

hedonist N 享乐主义者 xiǎnglèzhǔyìzhě

heed I V 听 tīng, 听取 tīngqǔ II N 注意 zhùyì, 考虑 kǎolǜ

to take heed of, to pay heed to 认真考虑 rènzhēn kǎolǜ

heedless ADJ 不注意 búzhùyì, 掉以轻心 diàoyǐqīngxīn

heel N **1** 脚跟 jiǎogēn **2** 鞋后跟 xié hòugēn

hefty ADJ **1** 大块头的 [+人] dàkuàitóu de [+rén] **2** 巨额的 [+金钱] jù'é de [+jīnqián] **3** 很高的 [+价钱] hěn gāo de [+jiàqian]

height N 高度 gāodù

heighten V 增加 zēngjiā, 增强 zēngqiáng

heights N 高地 gāodì [M. WD 块 kuài]

heinous ADJ **1** 极其邪恶的 jíqí xié'è de **2** 糟透了的 zāotòu le de

heir N 财产继承人 cáichǎn jìchéngrén

heiress N 女财产继承人 nǚ cáichǎn jìchéngrén

heirloom N 传家宝 chuánjiābǎo [M. WD 件 jiàn]

heist N 抢劫（商店或银行）qiǎngjié (shāngdiàn huò yínháng)

held V See hold

helicopter N 直升飞机 zhíshēng fēijī [M. WD 架 jià]

heliport N 直升飞机机场 zhíshēng fēijī jīchǎng

helium (He) N 氦 hài

hell N **1** 地狱 dìyù **2** 极坏的情况 jí huài de qíng-kuàng

to raise hell 大声吵闹 dàshēng chǎonào

hello INTERJ **1** 你好 nǐhǎo

to say hello 问好 wènhǎo

2 （打电话时）喂 (dǎ diànhuà shí) wèi ■ "Hel-lo?" "Hello, is Laura Smith there?" "喂？" "喂，劳拉·史密斯在吗？" "Wéi?" "Wéi, Láolā·Shǐmìsī zài ma?"

helm N 舵 duò, 舵柄 duòbǐng

helmet N 头盔 tóukuī [M. WD 顶 dǐng], 安全帽 ānquánmào [M. WD 顶 dǐng]

help I V 帮 bāng, 帮助 bāngzhu, 帮忙 bāngmáng

can't help (doing) 忍不住 rěnbuzhù, 禁不住 jīnbuzhù

II N **1** 帮助 bāngzhu **2** 佣人 yōngrén, 帮手 bāngshǒu

helper N 帮手 bāngshǒu, 助手 zhùshǒu

helpful ADJ 有帮助的 yǒubāngzhu de

helping[1] N 一份（食品／菜）yí fèn (shípǐn/cài)

helping[2] ADJ 帮助的 bāngzhù de

a helping hand 帮助 bāngzhù, 援助 yuánzhù

helpless ADJ **1** 无助的 wúzhù de, 束手无策的 shùshǒu wú cè de **2** 情不自禁的 qíng bù zìjīn de

helter-skelter ADV 杂乱无章地 záluàn wúzhāng de, 手忙脚乱地 shǒumáng jiǎoluàn de

hem I N （衣服）边 (yīfu) biān, 折边 zhé biān II V 缝边 féng biān

hemisphere N 半球 bànqiú

the northern hemisphere 北半球 Běibànqiú

hemline N （衣服的）下摆 (yīfu de) xiàbǎi

hemlock N 毒芹 dú qín

hemoglobin N 血红蛋白 xuèhóng dànbái

hemophilia N 血友病 xuèyǒubìng

hemophiliac N 血友病人 xuèyǒubìng rén

hemorrhage N （体内）大出血 (tǐnèi) dàchūxiě

hemorrhoids N 痔 zhì, 痔疮 zhì chuāng

hemp N 大麻 dàmá

hen N 母鸡 mǔjī [M. WD 只 zhī]

hence ADV 因而 yīn'ér, 因此 yīncǐ

henceforth, henceforward ADV 从今以后 cóngjīn yǐhòu, 从此以后 cóngcǐ yǐhòu

henchman N 亲信 qīnxìn, 喽啰 lóuluo

hepatitis N 肝炎 gānyán

her I ADJ 她的 tāde II PRON 她 tā

herald V 预示 yùshì

herb N **1** （调味）香草 (tiáowèi) xiāngcǎo **2** 药草 yàocǎo

herbal ADJ 香草的 xiāngcǎo de, 药草的 yàocǎo de

herbivore N 食草类动物 shícǎo lèi dòngwù

herd I N 一群 [+牛] yìqún [+niú] II V 把 [+人群] 集中在一起 bǎ [+rénqún] jízhōng zài yìqǐ

here ADV 这里 zhèlǐ, 这儿 zhèr ■ It's half an hour's drive from here to the airport. 从这里到机场开车

要半小时。Cóng zhèlǐ dào jīchǎng kāichē yào bàn xiǎoshí.

hereabouts ADV 附近 fùjìn

hereafter ADV 今后 jīnhòu
the hereafter 来世 láishì

hereby ADV 特此 tècǐ, 兹 zī

hereditary ADJ 遗传的 yíchuán de

heredity N 遗传 yíchuán

herein ADV 在此处 zài cǐchù, 在此情况下 zài cǐ qíngkuàng xià

heresy N 异教 yìjiào, 邪说 xiéshuō

heretic N 异教徒 yìjiàotú

herewith ADV 附上 fùshàng, 随函附上 suí hán fùshàng

heritage N 1 遗产 yíchǎn 2 传统 chuántǒng

hermetically ADV 密封地 mìfēng de

hermit N 隐士 yǐnshì, 遁世者 dùnshìzhě

hernia N 疝 shàn, 疝气 shànqì

hero N 1 英雄 yīngxióng [M. WD 位 wèi], 勇士 yǒngshì [M. WD 位 wèi]
a national hero 民族英雄 mínzú yīngxióng
2 (电影/小说) 男主角 (diànyǐng/xiǎoshuō) nán zhǔjué, 男主人公 nán zhǔréngōng

heroic ADJ 英雄的 yīngxióng de, 英勇的 yīngyǒng de

heroics N 英雄行为 yīngxióng xíngwéi, 豪言壮语 háoyán zhuàngyǔ

heroin N 海洛因 hǎiluòyīn

heroine N 女英雄 nǚyīngxióng [M. WD 位 wèi], 女勇士 nǚ yǒngshì [M. WD 位 wèi]

heroism N 英勇 yīngyǒng, 英雄的言行 yīngxióng de yánxíng

heron N 鹭 lù [M. WD 只 zhī]

herpes N 疱疹 pàozhěn

herring N 鲱鱼 fēiyú [M. WD 条 tiáo]
a red herring 转移他人注意力的小事 zhuǎnyí tārén zhùyìlì de xiǎoshì

hers PRON 她的 tāde

herself PRON 她自己 tā zìjǐ, 她亲自 tā qīnzì

hesitant ADJ 犹豫的 yóuyù de, 举棋不定的 jǔqí bùdìng de

hesitate V 犹豫 yóuyù, 拿不定主意 ná bùdìng zhǔyi

hesitation N 犹豫 yóuyù, 迟疑 chíyí

heterogeneous ADJ 混杂的 hùnzá de

heterosexual I ADJ 异性恋的 yìxìngliàn de II N 异性恋者 yìxìngliànzhě

heterosexuality N 异性恋 yìxìngliàn

hew V (PT **hewed**; PP **hewed, hewn**) 砍 kǎn, 劈 pī

hexagon N 六角形 liùjiǎoxíng, 六边形 liùbiānxíng

hexagonal ADJ 六角形的 liùjiǎoxíng de, 六边形的 liùbiānxíng de

hey INTERJ 喂 wèi, 嘿 hēi

heyday N 全盛时期 quánshèng shíqī

hi INTERJ 你好 nǐ hǎo

hiatus N 间断 jiànduàn, 停顿 tíngdùn

hibernate V 冬眠 dōngmián

hibernation N 冬眠 dōngmián

hiccup, hiccough I N 1 呃逆 ènì, 打嗝 dǎ gé 2 小问题 xiǎo wèntí II V 打呃 dǎ'è, 打嗝 dǎ gé

hick N 乡巴佬 xiāngbālǎo

hickey N 吻痕 wěnhén

hickory N 1 山核桃树 shānhétao shù 2 山核桃木 shānhétao mù

hid V See hide¹

hidden I V See hide¹ II ADJ 隐藏的 yǐncáng de

hide¹ (PT **hid**; PP **hidden**) V 1 隐蔽 yǐnbì, 隐藏 yǐncáng 2 躲 duǒ, 躲藏 duǒcáng
hide and seek 捉迷藏游戏 zhuōmícáng yóuxì

hide² N (动物) 皮 pí

hideaway N 躲藏地 duǒcángdì

hideous ADJ 难看极了 nánkàn jíle, 丑陋不堪 chǒulòu bùkān

hideout N 躲藏地 duǒcángdì, 藏匿 cángnì

hiding N 1 躲藏 duǒcáng, 藏匿 cángnì
to go into hiding 躲藏起来 duǒcáng qǐ lái, 藏匿 cángnì
2 痛打 tòngdǎ
to give sb a hiding 痛打某人 tòngdǎ mǒurén, 把某人痛打一顿 bǎ mǒurén tòngdǎ yídùn

hierarchical ADJ 等级的 děngjí de

hierarchy N 等级 děngjí, 等级制度 děngjí zhìdù

hieroglyphics N 象形文字 xiàngxíng wénzì

hi-fi (= high fidelity) ABBREV 高保真 [+音响设备] gāobǎozhēn [+yīnxiǎng shèbèi]

high I ADJ 1 高 gāo ■ People in high places are sometimes out of touch with reality. 身居高位的人有时候会脱离实际。Shēn jū gāo wèi de rén yǒushíhou huì tuōlí shíjì. 2 高层的 gāocéng de, 重要的 zhòngyào de 3 中期的 zhōngqī de, 最重要的时期 zuì zhòngyào de shíqī 4 (吸毒后) 极度兴奋的 (xīdú hòu) jídù xīngfèn de
high school 中学 zhōngxué
junior high school 初级中学 chūjí zhōngxué, 初中 chūzhōng
senior high school 高级中学 gāojízhōngxué, 高中 gāozhōng
II ADV 高 gāo ■ A line of wild geese are flying high in the sky. 一行大雁正在空中高飞。Yì háng dàyàn zhèngzài kōng zhōng gāo fēi.
to look/search high and low 到处寻找 dàochù xúnzhǎo
III N 1 最高点 zuìgāodiǎn 2 (吸毒后的) 极度兴奋 (xīdú hòu de) jídù xīngfèn

highbrow ADJ (趣味) 高雅的 (qùwèi) gāoyǎ de, 修养很高的 xiūyǎng hěn gāo de

high-class ADJ 高档的 gāodàng de, 优质的 yōuzhì de

higher education N 高等教育 gāoděng jiàoyù

high-grade ADJ 优质的 yōuzhì de

high-handed ADJ 专横的 zhuānhèng de, 盛气凌人的 shèngqì líng rén de

high-heel N 高跟鞋 gāogēnxié [M. WD 双 shuāng]

high jinks, hi jinks N 狂欢作乐 kuánghuān zuòlè

high jump N 跳高（运动）tiàogāo (yùndòng)

highlands N 高原 gāoyuán

high-level ADJ 高层的 gāocéng de

highlight I v **1** 使…突出 shǐ...tūchū **2**（在计算机上）突出显示 (zài jìsuànjī shàng) tūchū xiǎnshì, 标示 biāoshì II N **1** 最重要的部份 zuì zhòngyào de bùfen **2**（照片上的）强光部分 (zhàopiàn shàng de) qiáng guāng bùfen

highlighter N 亮光笔 liàngguāngbǐ [M. WD 支 zhī]

highly ADV **1** 高度地 gāodù de **2** 极其 jíqí
to speak highly of 称赞 chēngzàn

high-minded ADJ 高尚的 gāoshàng de

Highness N 殿下 Diànxià

high-pitched ADJ 高音的 gāoyīn de, 尖声的 jiānshēng de

high-powered ADJ **1** 大功率的 [+卡车] dàgōnglǜ de [+kǎchē] **2** 实力雄厚的 [+公司] shílì xiónghòu de [+gōngsī]

high-pressure ADJ 高气压的 gāoqìyā de, 高压的 gāoyā de

high-profile ADJ（故意）引人注目的 (gùyì) yǐn rén zhùmù de, 高调的 gāodiào de

high-rise N 高层建筑 gāocéng jiànzhù, 高楼 gāolóu [M. WD 幢 zhuàng]

high roller N 下大赌注的人 xià dà dǔzhù de rén, 挥金如土的人 huī jīn rú tǔ de rén

high-spirited ADJ 活泼的 huópo de, 生气勃勃的 shēngqì bóbó de

high-strung ADJ 易激动的 yì jīdòng de, 敏感的 mǐngǎn de

high-tech ADJ 高科技的 gāokējì de

high tide N 高潮 gāocháo

highway N 公路 gōnglù

hijack v **1** 劫持 [+飞机/船] jiéchí [+fēijī/chuán] **2** 把持 [+组织] bǎchí [+zǔzhī]

hijacker N 劫持者 jiéchízhě

hijacking N 劫持行为 jiéchí xíngwéi, 劫持案件 jiéchí ànjiàn

hike I N **1** 徒步旅行 túbù lǚxíng, 远足 yuǎnzú
on a long hike in the hills 在山间长途徒步旅行 zài shān jiān chángtú túbù lǚxíng
2 [价格+] 大幅度上升 [jiàgé+] dàfúdù shàngshēng
a hike in food prices 食品价格大幅度上升 shípǐn jiàgé dàfúdù shàngshēng
II v **1** 徒步旅行 túbù lǚxíng, 远足 yuǎnzú **2** [价格+] 大幅度上升 [jiàgé+] dàfúdù shàngshēng

hilarious ADJ 极好笑的 jí hǎoxiào de, 极搞笑的 jí gǎoxiào de

hilarity N 欢笑 huānxiào

hill N（小）山 (xiǎo) shān

hillbilly N 山里的乡巴佬 shān lǐ de xiāngbalǎo

hillside N 山坡 shānpō

hilly ADJ 多山（丘）的 duōshān (qiū) de

hilt N 刀把 dāobǎ
to the hilt 最大极限 zuìdà jíxiàn

him PRON 他 tā

himself PRON 他自己 tā zìjǐ, 他亲自 tā qīnzì
by himself 他自己一个人 tā zìjǐ yí ge rén

hind ADJ 后面的 hòumian de
the hind leg（动物）后腿 (dòngwù) hòutuǐ

hinder v 阻碍 zǔ'ài

Hindi N 印地语 Yìndìyǔ

hindquarters N（动物）后腿 (dòngwù) hòutuǐ

hindrance N 妨碍 fáng'ài
without let or hindrance 毫无障碍的 háowú zhàng'ài de, 畅通无阻的 chàngtōng wúzǔ de

hindsight N 后见之明 hòu jiàn zhī míng, 事后聪明 shìhòu cōngming
with the benefit of hindsight 依靠后见之明 yīkào hòu jiàn zhī míng

Hindu N 印度教教徒 Yìndùjiào jiàotú

Hinduism N 印度教 Yìndùjiào

hinge I N 铰链 jiǎoliàn II v (to hinge on/upon) 取决于 qǔjuéyú

hint I N **1** 暗示 ànshì, 提示 tíshì **2** 一点儿 yìdiǎnr, 细微 xìwēi II v 暗示 ànshì, 提示 tíshì

hinterland N 内地 nèidì, 偏远地区 piānyuǎn dìqū

hip[1] N 臀部 túnbù

hip[2] ADJ 赶时髦的 gǎnshímáo de

hippie, hippy N 嬉皮士 xīpíshì

hippopotamus, hippo N 河马 hémǎ

hire I v **1** 雇用 gùyòng, 聘任 pìnrèn **2** 租用 zūyòng, 租赁 zūlìn II v 出租 chūzū, 租用 zūyòng
a sex-for-hire business 色情服务公司 sèqíng fúwù gōngsī

his ADJ, PRON 他的 tāde

Hispanic I ADJ 西班牙语或葡萄牙语国家的 Xībānyáyǔ huò Pútaoyáyǔ guójiā de, 拉丁美洲的 Lādīngměizhōu de II N 拉丁美洲人 Lādīngměizhōurén

hiss I v **1** 发出嘶嘶声 fāchū sī sī shēng **2** 发嘘声反对 fā xū shēng fǎnduì II N 嘶嘶声 sīsīshēng

historian N 历史学家 lìshǐ xuéjiā, 研究历史的人 yánjiū lìshǐ de rén

historic ADJ 有历史意义的 yǒu lìshǐ yìyì de, 历史性的 lìshǐxìng de

historical ADJ 历史的 lìshǐ de

history N **1** 历史 lìshǐ ■ Many young people are quite ignorant of their country's history. 很多年轻人对自己国家的历史很无知。Hěn duō niánqīngrén duì zìjǐ guójiā de lìshǐ hěn wúzhī.
to make history 创造历史 chuàngzào lìshǐ **2** 发展史 fāzhǎnshǐ

histrionics N 装腔作势 zhuāngqiāng zuòshì

hit I v (PT & PP **hit**) **1** 打 dǎ ■ In some countries it *is illegal for a parent to hit a child.* 在有些国家父母打孩子是非法的。Zài yǒuxiē guójiā fùmǔ dǎ háizi shì fēifǎ de. **2** 碰 pèng, 撞 zhuàng **II** N **1** 打击 dǎjī ■ *The boxer made a clever hit.* 拳击手打出妙拳。Quánjīshǒu dǎchū miào quán. **2** 走红的人／事 zǒuhóng de rén/shì, 成功 chénggōng ■ *The song was a big hit.* 这首歌大为成功。Zhè shǒu gē dà wéi chénggōng.

hit-and-miss, hit-or-miss ADJ 无计划的 wú jìhuà de, 靠运气的 kào yùnqi de

hit-and-run ADJ **1** 肇事后逃逸 zhàoshì hòu táoyì **2** 打了就跑的 dǎ le jiù pǎo de

hitch[1] v 搭顺风车 dā shùnfēng chē
to hitch a ride 搭一段顺风车 dā yí duàn shùnfēng chē

hitch[2] N 故障 gùzhàng
without a hitch 顺利地 shùnlì de

hitchhike v See hitch[1]

hither and thither ADV 这里那里 zhèli nàli, 到处 dàochù

hitherto ADV 迄今 qìjīn, 至今 zhìjīn

hit man N 职业杀手 zhíyè shāshǒu

HIV (= human immunodeficiency virus) ABBREV 人体免疫缺损病毒 réntǐ miǎnyì quēsǔn bìngdú, 艾滋病病毒 àizībìng bìngdú
HIV positive 艾滋病病毒检测呈阳性 àizībìng bìngdú jiǎncè chéng yángxìng

hive N 蜂巢 fēngcháo, 蜂房 fēngfáng

hoard I v 储藏 chǔcáng, 囤积 túnjī **II** N 储藏物资 chǔcáng wùzī, 囤积物资 túnjī wùzī
a secret hoard of treasure 秘密的宝物储藏 mìmì de bǎowù chǔcáng

hoarse ADJ 哑 yǎ, 嘶哑 sīyǎ
to shout oneself hoarse 大声喊叫得嗓子嘶哑 dàshēng hǎnjiào dé sǎngzi sīyǎ

hoax I N 骗局 piànjú
to play a hoax 设置骗局 shèzhì piànjú **II** v 欺骗 qīpiàn, 作弄 zuònòng

hobble v 一瘸一拐地走 yì liú yì guǎi de zǒu, 跛行 bǒxíng

hobby N 嗜好 shìhào, (业余)爱好 (yèyú) àihào

hobnob v 与比自己地位高的人亲密交谈 yǔ bǐ zìjǐ dìwèi gāo de rén qīnmì jiāotán, 高攀 gāopān

hobo N 流浪汉 liúlànghàn

hock[1] N 债 zhài, 债务 zhàiwù
in hock ① 负债 fùzhài ② 被典当 bèi diǎndàng, 被抵押 bèi dǐyā **II** v 典当 diǎndàng, 抵押 dǐyā

hockey N 冰球(运动) bīngqiú (yùndòng)

hodgepodge N 大杂烩 dàzáhuì

hoe I N 锄头 chútou [M. WD 把 bǎ] **II** v 锄(地) chú (dì)

hog I N **1** 猪 zhū [M. WD 头 tóu] **2** 贪吃的人 tānchī de rén, 贪婪的人 tānlán de rén **II** v 独占 dúzhàn, 不分享 bù fēnxiǎng

ho-hum ADJ 沉闷乏味的 chénmèn fáwèi de

hoist I v 升起 shēngqǐ, 吊起 diào qǐ **II** N 起重机 qǐzhòngjī

hokey ADJ 娇柔造作的 jiāoróu zàozuo de, 可笑的 kěxiào de

hold I v (PT & PP held) **1** 拿 ná, 握 wò ■ *He held his daughter's hand tightly while crossing the street.* 他穿马路的时候，紧紧握住女儿的手。Tā chuān mǎlù de shíhou, jǐnjǐn wòzhù nǚ'ér de shǒu. **2** 抱 bào, 抱住 bàozhù **3** 扶 fú, 扶住 fúzhu **4** 可容纳 kě róngnà **5** 举行 jǔxíng ■ *The annual general meeting will be held next Monday.* 年会将在下周一举行。Niánhuì jiāng zài xià zhōuyī jǔxíng. **6** 担任 dānrèn
to hold on 等等 děngděng, 等一等 děngyiděng ■ *Hold on a minute, I'll be right back.* 稍等一会，我马上回来。Shāo děng yíhuì, wǒ mǎshàng huílai.
to hold one's breath 屏住气 píngzhu qì **II** N 拿住 názhu, 抓住 zhuāzhu ■ *The rescuers told him to take hold of the rope.* 救助人员叫他握住绳子。Jiùzhù rényuán jiào tā wòzhù shéngzi.
to get hold of 得到 dédao, 弄到 nòngdao

holder N **1** (信用卡/护照) 持有人 (xìnyòngkǎ/hùzhào) chíyǒurén **2** 容器 róngqì

holding N 拥有的财产 yōngyǒu de cáichǎn
holding company 控股公司 kònggǔ gōngsī

holdover N 残余 cányú, 残留物 cánliúwù

holdup N 持枪抢劫 chíqiāng qiǎngjié

hole I N **1** 洞 dòng **2** (野兽的)洞穴 (yěshòu de) dòngxué **3** (高尔夫球)球洞 (gāo'ěrfūqiú) qiú dòng **II** v **1** 打(高尔夫球)入洞 dǎ (gāo'ěrfūqiú) rù dòng **2** (to hole up) 躲藏 duǒcáng, 藏匿 cángnì

holiday N 假日 jiàrì, 假期 jiàqī
holiday season 年末假日期间 niánmò jiàrì qījiān
national holiday 国家法定假日 guójiā fǎdìng jiàrì
summer holiday 暑假 shǔjià
winter holiday 寒假 hánjià

holiness N 神圣的 shénshèng de
Your Holiness (对教皇的尊称)陛下 (duì Jiàohuáng de zūnchēng) bìxià, 圣座 shèng zuò

holistic ADJ 整体的 zhěngtǐ de
holistic medicine 整体医学 zhěngtǐ yīxué

holler v, N 大叫大嚷 dàjiào dàrǎng

hollow I ADJ **1** 空心的 kōngxīn de ■ *The tree, though hollow, still sprouts new leaves every spring.* 这棵树虽然空心了，到春天还是长出新叶。Zhè kē shù suīrán kōngxīn le, dào chūntiān háishì zhǎngchū xīn yè. **2** 空洞的 kōngdòng de **II** N 小山谷 xiǎo shāngǔ

holly N 冬青树 dōngqīng shù [M. WD 棵 kē]

Hollywood N 好莱坞 Hǎoláiwù, 美国电影业 Měiguó diànyǐngyè

holocaust N 大屠杀 dà túshā

hologram N 全息图 quánxītú [M. WD 张 zhāng/幅 fú]

holster N 手枪皮套 shǒuqiāng pítào

holy ADJ 神的 shén de, 神圣的 shénshèng de
Holy Bible 圣经 Shèngjīng

homage N 崇敬 chóngjìng, 敬意 jìngyì

home I N 1 家 jiā, 家庭 jiātíng, 家宅 jiāzhái
Home, sweet home. 家, 甜蜜的家。Jiā, tiánmì de jiā.
home office 家庭办公室 jiātíng bàngōngshì
home town 家乡 jiāxiāng
home team 本地队 běndì duì
to feel at home 感到在家一样 gǎndào zài jiā yíyàng
to make yourself at home 别客气, 请随意。Biékèqi, qǐng suíyì.
2 国内 guónèi 3 (养老) 院 (yǎnglǎo) yuàn
children's home 孤儿院 gū'éryuàn, 儿童福利院 értóng fúlìyuàn
II ADV 在家 zài jiā ■ He goes home immediately after work. 他下班后立即回家。Tā xiàbān hòu lìjí huíjiā. III ADJ 家里的 jiālide, 家用的 jiāyòng de
home computer 家用电脑 jiāyòng diànnǎo
home cooking 家常饭菜 jiācháng fàncài
IV V (to home in on) 对准 duìzhǔn

homecoming N 返乡 fǎnxiāng
homecoming dance 校友返校日舞会 xiàoyǒu fǎnxiàorì wǔhuì, 校友日 Xiàoyǒu rì

homeland N 国土 guótǔ, 祖国 zǔguó

homeless ADJ 无家可归的 wú jiā kě guī de
■ Many homeless people spend their nights at New York Central Station. 许多无家可归者在纽约中央车站过夜。Xǔduō wújiākěguīzhě zài Niǔyuē zhōngyāng chēzhàn guò yè.
the homeless 无家可归者 wújiākěguīzhě

homely ADJ 1 相貌平平的 [+人] xiàngmào píng-píng de [+rén] 2 简单的 [+饭菜] jiǎndān de [+fàncài]

homemade ADJ 家里做的 jiāli zuò de, 自制的 zìzhì de

homemaker N 家庭主妇 jiātíng zhǔfù

homeopathy N 顺势疗法 shùnshì liáofǎ

homepage N (网址) 主页 (wǎngzhǐ) zhǔyè

homer N (棒球) 本垒打 (bàngqiú) běnlěidǎ

homeroom N (学校) 年级教室 (xuéxiào) niánjí jiàoshì

home run N (棒球) 本垒打 (bàngqiú) běnlěidǎ

homesick ADJ 想家的 xiǎngjiā de, 思乡的 sīxiāng de

homesickness N 思乡 (病) sīxiāng (bìng)

homestead N 农庄 nóngzhuāng, 庄园 zhuāng-yuán

homeward ADJ, ADV 向家 (的／地) xiàng jiā (de)

homework N 家庭作业 jiātíng zuòyè, 功课 gōngkè

homey I ADJ 象家里一样的 xiàng jiāli yíyàng de, 舒适自在的 shūshì zìzài de II N 老乡 lǎoxiāng, 同乡 tóngxiāng

homicidal ADJ 有杀人倾向的 yǒu shārén qīngxiàng de

homicide N 1 杀人的 shārén de, 谋杀的 móushā de 2 (警察局) 凶杀科 (jǐngchájú) xiōngshākē

homogeneous ADJ 同一的 tóngyī de

homogenize V 使…同一 shǐ…tóngyī, 使…统一 shǐ…tǒngyī

homonym N 同音同形异义词 tóngyīn tóngxíng yìyìcí

homophobia N 对同性恋的厌恶 duì tóngxìngliàn de yànwù

homophone N 同音异义词 tóngyīn yìyìcí

homosexual I ADJ 同性恋的 tóngxìngliàn de II N 同性恋者 tóngxìngliànzhě

homosexuality N 同性恋 tóngxìngliàn

honcho N 头儿 tóur, 负责人 fùzérén

hone V 磨练 móliàn, 提高 [+能力] tígāo [+nénglì]

honest ADJ 诚实的 chéngshí de, 老实的 lǎoshi de

honestly ADV 1 诚实地 chéngshí de, 老实地 lǎoshi de 2 实在 shízài, 确实 quèshí

honesty N 诚实 chéngshí, 老实 lǎoshi ■ I believe honesty is the best policy. 我相信诚实是最好的方针。Wǒ xiàngxìn chéngshí shì zuìhǎo de fāngzhēn.

honey N 1 蜜 mì, 蜂蜜 fēngmì 2 亲爱的 qīn'ài de, 心肝宝贝儿 xīngān bǎobèir

honeycomb N 蜂巢 fēngcháo, 蜂窝 fēngwō

honeymoon N 蜜月 mìyuè

honeysuckle N 忍冬 rěndōng, 忍冬花 rěndōnghuā

honk I V 按 (汽车) 喇叭 àn (qìchē) lǎba II N (汽车) 喇叭声 (qìchē) lǎbashēng

honor I N 1 光荣 guāngróng, 荣幸 róngxìng ■ It's an honor to meet you. 和你见面很荣幸。Hé nǐ jiànmiàn hěn róngxìng. 2 荣誉 róngyù 3 高尚品德 gāoshàng pǐndé
Your Honor 法官大人 fǎguān dàren
II V 1 向…致敬 xiàng…zhìjìng 2 兑现 duìxiàn, 实现 shíxiàn
in honor of 为 wèi, 为了 wèile ■ The City Council gave a luncheon in honor of the retiring mayor. 市政府为退休市长举行午餐会。Shìzhèngfǔ wèi tuìxiū shìzhǎng jǔxíng wǔcānhuì.

honorable ADJ 品德高尚的 pǐndé gāoshàng de, 值得尊敬的 zhíde zūnjìng de

honorary ADJ 1 荣誉的 róngyù de
an honorary citizen 荣誉公民 róngyù gōngmín
2 名誉的 míngyù de
honorary doctorate 名誉博士学位 míngyù bóshì xuéwèi

honor roll N 优等生名单 yōuděngshēng míngdān, 光荣榜 guāngróngbǎng

honors N 大学荣誉学位课程 dàxué róngyù xuéwèi kèchéng

to graduate with honors 以优等成绩毕业 yǐ yōuděng chéngjì bìyè

hood N **1** 风帽 fēngmào **2** (汽车) 发动机罩盖 (qìchē) fādòngjī zhàogài

hooded ADJ 带风帽的 dài fēngmào de

hoodlum N 恶棍 ègùn, 坏小子 huàixiǎozi

hoodwink V 哄骗 hǒngpiàn

hoof (PL **hoofs/hooves**) N 蹄 (子) tí (zi)

hook I N 钩子 gōuzi
coat hook 衣钩 yīgōu
II V 钩住 gōu zhu ■ *Oh, my shirt was hooked on something.* 啊呀，我的衬衣给什么东西钩住了。Āyā, wǒ de chènyī gěi shénme dōngxī gōuzhu le.

hooked ADJ **1** 钩状的 gōu zhuàng de **2** 成瘾的 chéngyǐn de
be hooked on computer games 对电脑游戏上瘾 duì diànnǎo yóuxì shàngyǐn, 着迷于电脑游戏 zháomí yú diànnǎo yóuxì

hooker N 妓女 jìnǚ

hooky N 逃学 táoxué

hooligan N 流氓 liúmáng, 恶棍 ègùn

hoop N 圈 quān, 环 huán

hoops N 篮球运动 lánqiú yùndòng
to shoot hoops 打篮球 dǎ lánqiú

hooray INTERJ 好啊 hǎo ā, 太好了 tài hǎo le

hoot I N 嘘声 xūshēng, 嘲笑 cháoxiào II V 发出嘘声 fāchū xūshēng, 嘲笑 cháoxiào

hop I V 蹦 bèng, 蹦跳 bèngtiào II N 蹦 bèng, 蹦跳 bèngtiào
a hop, skip and a jump 极短的距离 jí duǎn de jùlí, 很近 hěn jìn

hops N 啤酒花 píjiǔhuā

hope I V 希望 xīwàng II N **1** 希望 xīwàng ■ *They all cherish the hope that their dear grandma will have a speedy recovery.* 他们都满怀希望，亲爱的祖母会很快康复。Tāmen dōu mǎnhuái xīwàng, qīn'ài de zǔmǔ huì hěn kuài kāngfù. **2** 寄予希望的人／事 jìyù xīwàng de rén/shì

hopeful ADJ 有希望的 yǒu xīwàng de

hopefully ADV **1** 如果一切顺利 rúguǒ yíqiè shùnlì, 很有可能 hěn yǒu kěnéng **2** 充满希望的 chōngmǎn xīwàng de

hopeless ADJ **1** 没有希望的 méiyǒu xīwàng de, 无救的 wú jiù de
a hopeless case 无药可救的病人 wú yào kě jiù de bìngrén, 毫无办法的情况 háowú bànfǎ de qíngkuàng
2 糟透了 zāotòule

hopelessly ADV **1** 毫无办法 háowú bànfǎ, 处于绝境 chǔyú juéjìng **2** 不能自拔的 bù néng zì bá de

hopscotch N (儿童游戏) 跳房子 (értóng yóuxì) tiào fángzi

horde N 一大群 [+旅游者] yí dà qún [+lǚyóuzhě]

horizon N 地平线 dìpíngxiàn

horizons N 视野 shìyě, 范围 fànwéi

to open new horizons 开拓新天地 kāituò xīn tiāndì

horizontal ADJ 水平的 shuǐpíng de, 横向的 héngxiàng de
horizontal axis 横轴 héngzhóu

hormone N 荷尔蒙 hé'ěrméng, 激素 jīsù
growth hormone 生长激素 shēngzhǎng jīsù

horn N **1** 喇叭 lǎba **2** (动物的) 角 (dòngwù de) jiǎo

hornet N 大黄蜂 dàhuángfēng [M. WD 只 zhī]

horny ADJ 性兴奋的 xìng xīngfèn de, 欲火中烧的 yùhuǒ zhōng shāo de

horoscope N 星相算命 xīngxiàng suànmìng

horrendous ADJ 骇人的 hài rén de, 可怕的 kěpà de

horrible ADJ **1** 可怕的 kěpà de **2** 糟透了的 zāo tòule de, 极讨厌的 jí tǎoyàn de

horrid ADJ 极其糟糕的 jíqí zāogāo de

horrific ADJ 吓人的 xià rén de, 恐怖的 kǒngbù de

horrified ADJ 深感恐惧的 shēngǎn kǒngjù de

horrify V 使…感到恐怖 shǐ...gǎndào kǒngbù, 吓坏 xiàhuài

horrifying ADJ 极其恐怖的 jíqí kǒngbù de, 可怕极了 kěpà jíle

horror N **1** 恐怖 kǒngbù **2** 恐怖的事 kǒngbù de shì
to one's horror 使某人大为恐慌 shǐ mǒurén dàwéi kǒnghuāng
horror movie 恐怖片 kǒngbùpiàn

hors d'oeuvre N 开胃菜 kāiwèicài, 开胃小吃 kāiwèi xiǎochī

horse N 马 mǎ [M. WD 匹 pǐ]

horse around V 胡闹 húnào, 打闹 dǎ nào

horseback N 马背 mǎbèi
horseback riding 骑马 qímǎ

horseplay N 打闹 dǎnào

horsepower N 马力 mǎlì [M. WD 匹 pǐ]

horseshoe N 马蹄铁 mǎtítiě, 马掌 mǎzhǎng

horticulture N 园艺 (学) yuányì (xué)

hose I N **1** 水管 shuǐguǎn **2** 连裤袜 liánkùwà [M. WD 双 shuāng] II V **1** (用水管) 冲 (yòng shuǐguǎn) chōng **2** 欺骗 qīpiàn

hosiery N 袜类 wà lèi

hospice N 临终医院 línzhōng yīyuàn, 安养院 ānyǎng yuàn

hospitable ADJ **1** 好客的 [+人] hàokè de [+rén] **2** 适宜的 [+条件] shìyí de [+tiáojiàn]

hospital N 医院 yīyuàn
to be admitted to the hospital 住进医院 zhù jìn yīyuàn, 住院 zhùyuàn
to be discharged from the hospital 出院 chūyuàn

hospitality N 好客 hàokè
hospitality industry 旅馆服务业 lǚguǎn fúwùyè

hospitalize V 住医院 zhùyīyuàn, 住院 zhùyuàn ■ *Two accident victims are still hospitalized.* 两名事故受害者还住在医院里。Liǎng míng shìgù shòuhàizhě hái zhù zài yīyuàn lǐ.

host¹ I N (F **hostess**) **1** 主人／女主人 zhǔrén／nǚzhǔrén ■ *Mrs. Brown is a perfect hostess.* 布朗太太待客十分周到。Bùlǎng tàitai dàikè shífēn zhōudao. **2** (电视) 节目主持人 (diànshì) jiémù zhǔchírén **3** (活动) 东道主 (huódòng) dōngdàozhǔ, (国际活动) 东道国 (guójì huódòng) dōngdàoguó ■ *The host club did everything possible to make the tournament a success.* 东道主俱乐部尽一切努力使这次锦标赛成功。Dōngdàozhǔ jùlèbù jìn yíqiè nǔlì shǐ zhècì jǐnbiāosài chénggōng. II v **1** 主持 zhǔchí **2** 举办 jǔbàn ■ *A couple of cities are keen to host this event.* 有几个城市对举办这个活动极感兴趣。Yǒu jǐ ge chéngshì duì jǔbàn zhè ge huódòng jí gǎnxīngqù.

host² N (a host of) 许多 xǔduō

hostage N 人质 rénzhì
to hold sb hostage 把某人扣作人质 bǎ mǒurén kòu zuò rénzhì

hostel N 旅舍 lǚshè
Youth Hostel 青年旅舍 qīngnián lǚshè

hostile ADJ 敌对的 díduì de, 抱有敌意的 bàoyǒu díyì de
a hostile takeover 恶意接管 èyì jiēguǎn

hostilities N 战斗 zhàndòu, 战事 zhànshì

hostility N 敌意 díyì

hot ADJ **1** 热 rè ■ *I was so hot that I perspired all over.* 我热得浑身出汗。Wǒ rè de húnshēn chūhàn.
hot air balloon 热气球 rèqìqiú
hot dog 热狗 règǒu, 长香肠 cháng xiāngcháng
hot plate 平板电炉 píngbǎn diànlú
hot potato 棘手的问题 jíshǒu de wèntí
hot seat 困难的处境 kùnnan de chǔjìng
2 辣的 (食物) là de (shíwù) **3** 暴躁的 bàozao de
a hot temper 暴躁的脾气 bàozao de píqi
4 色情的 sèqíng de

hotbed N 温床 wēnchuáng

hotcake N 煎饼 jiānbing
to sell like hotcakes 非常畅销 fēicháng chàngxiāo

hotel N 旅馆 lǚguǎn, 酒店 jiǔdiàn

hothead N 性急冲动的人 xìngjí chōngdòng de rén

hotheaded ADJ 头脑发热的 tóunǎo fārè de, 性急冲动的 xìngjí chōngdòng de

hotline N 热线 rèxiàn

hotly ADV **1** 强烈地 qiángliè de **2** 紧紧地 jǐnjǐn de

hotshot N 自信的成功者 zìxìn de chénggōngzhě

hotspot N (电脑网页) 热点 (diànnǎo wǎngyè) rèdiǎn

hot-tempered ADJ 脾气暴躁的 píqi bàozao de

hot-water bottle N 热水袋 rèshuǐ dài

hot-wire v 强行起动 (汽车) qiángxíng qǐdòng (qìchē)

hound I v 骚扰 sāorǎo, 追住不放 zhuī zhù bù fang II N 狗 gǒu, 猎狗 liègǒu

hour N 小时 xiǎoshí, 钟头 zhōngtóu
opening hours (商店／银行) 营业时间 (shāngdiàn/yínháng) yíngyè shíjiān, (图书馆／博物馆) 开放时间 (túshūguǎn/bówùguǎn) kāifàng shíjiān ■ *The public library's opening hours are from 10.00 a.m. till 8.00 p.m.* 公共图书馆的开放时间是上午十点到晚上八点。Gōnggòng túshūguǎn de kāifàng shíjiān shì shàngwǔ shí diǎn dào wǎnshang bā diǎn.
visiting hours (医院) 探视时间 (yīyuàn) tànshì shíjiān
after hours 下班后 xiàbān hòu

hourglass N 沙漏 shālòu
an hourglass figure 细腰身材 xìyāo shēncái

hourly ADJ, ADV **1** 每一小时的 měi yì xiǎoshí de **2** 按小时计算的 àn xiǎoshí jìsuàn de

house I N **1** 住宅 zhùzhái, 房子 fángzi
the White House 白宫 Báigōng
house arrest 软禁 ruǎnjìn
2 议院 yìyuàn
the House (美国) 众议院 (Měiguó) Zhòngyìyuàn
3 公司 gōngsī
printing house 印刷所 yìnshuāsuǒ
publishing house 出版社 chūbǎnshè
4 剧院 jùyuàn
opera house 歌剧院 gējùyuàn
II v 为…提供住房 wéi…tígōng zhùfáng

houseboat N 船屋 chuánwū

housebound ADJ 只能待在家里的 zhǐ néng dài zài jiālide

housebroken ADJ (宠物) 不在屋内便溺的 (chǒngwù) búzài wūnèi biànniào de

household N 家庭 jiātíng, 户 hù
head of a household 户主 hùzhǔ

housekeeper N **1** 管家 guǎnjiā **2** [旅馆的+] 清洁工 [lǚguǎn de+] qīngjiégōng

housekeeping N 家务管理 jiāwù guǎnlǐ

House of Representatives N (美国) 众议院 (Měiguó) Zhòngyìyuàn

houseplant N 室内盆栽植物 shìnèi pénzāi zhíwù

house-sit v 看管房屋 kānguǎn fángwū

house-sitter N 看管房屋的人 kānguǎn fángwū de rén

housewares N 家庭用品 jiātíng yòngpǐn

housewarming N 庆祝乔迁的聚会 qìngzhù qiáoqiān de jùhuì

housewife N 家庭主妇 jiātíng zhǔfù

housework N 家务事 jiāwushì

housing N 住房 zhùfáng
public housing 政府为低收入家庭提供的住房 zhèngfǔ wéi dī shōurù jiātíng tígōng de zhùfáng, 公房 gōngfáng

hover v 盘旋 pánxuán

hovercraft N 气垫船 qìdiànchuán [M. WD 艘 sōu]

how ADV **1** 怎样 zěnyàng, 怎么样 zěnmeyàng ■ *I don't know how to say it in Chinese.* 我不知道这个在中文里怎么说? Wǒ bù zhīdào zhè ge zài Zhōngwén lǐ zěnme shuō? **2** 多 duō, 多么 duōme ■ *How much did you pay for the used car?* 这辆二手车你花了多少钱? Zhè liàng èrshǒuchē nǐ huāle duōshǎoqián?

howdy INTERJ 你好 nǐhǎo

however I ADV **1** 不管怎么样 bùguǎn zěnmeyàng, 无论如何 wúlùn rúhé **2** 然而 rán'ér, 但是 dànshì ■ *I felt unwell yesterday morning, however I still went to work.* 昨天早上我感到不舒服, 但还是去上班了。Zuótiān zǎoshang wǒ gǎndao bù shūfu, dàn háishì qù shàngbān le. **II** CONJ 不管怎么样 bùguǎn zěnmeyàng, 无论如何 wúlùn rúhé

howl v **1** [动物+] 嚎叫 [dòngwù+] háojiào **2** 吼叫 hǒujiào, [人+] 象动物一样嚎叫 [rén+] xiàng dòngwù yíyàng háojiào

to howl with laughter 狂笑 kuángxiào

HQ (= headquarters) ABBREV (军队) 司令部 (jūnduì) sīlìngbù, (公司) 总部 (gōngsī) zǒngbù

HR (= human resources) ABBREV 人力资源 (管理) rénlìzīyuán (guǎnlǐ), 人事 (管理) rénshì (guǎnlǐ)

HTML (= Hypertext Markup Language) ABBREV (计算机) 超文本标记语言 (jìsuànjī) chāowénběn biāojì yǔyán

hub N 中心 zhōngxīn, 枢纽 shūniǔ

from hub to tire 从头到尾 cóng tóu dào wěi, 完全地 wánquán de

hubbub N 噪杂的人声 zàozá de rénshēng

huddle I v 挤作一团 jǐ zuò yì tuán

to huddle around 围着 wéizhe

II N 挤在一起的人 jǐ zài yìqǐ de rén

hue N 色调 sèdiào, 色度 sèdù

huff I v 气喘吁吁 qìchuǎn xūxū **II** N 气吁吁 qì xūxū

in a huff 怒气冲冲 nùqì chōngchōng

huffy ADJ 怒气冲冲的 nùqì chōngchōng de

hug v, N 拥抱 yōngbào

huge ADJ 巨大的 jùdà de, 极大的 jídà de ■ *The dinosaur was a huge animal.* 恐龙是种巨大的动物。Kǒnglóng shì zhǒng jùdà de dòngwù.

hulk N 废弃的飞机／轮船／火车 fèiqì de fēijī/lúnchuán/huǒchē

hull N **1** 船体 chuántǐ **2** 谷壳 gǔké, 豆荚 dòujiá

hullabaloo N 激烈的批评 jīliè de pīpíng

hum I v **1** 哼 [+歌/曲子] hēng [+gē/qǔzi] **2** 活跃 huóyuè, 忙碌 mánglù **II** N **1** 哼歌声 hēnggēshēng **2** 嗡嗡声 wēngwēngshēng

human I ADJ 人的 rén de, 人类的 rénlèi de

To err is human; to forgive, divine. 犯错误是人性, 饶恕错误是神性。Fàn cuòwu shì rénxìng, ráoshù cuòwu shì shénxìng.

human race 人类 rénlèi

human rights 人权 rénquán

II N 人 rén

human nature 人性 rénxìng, 人的本性 rén de běnxìng

humane ADJ 人道的 réndào de, 仁慈的 réncí de

humanism N 人本主义 rénběn zhǔyì, 人文主义 rénwénzhǔyì

humanist N 人本主义者 rénběn zhǔyìzhě, 人文主义者 rénwén zhǔyìzhě

humanitarian I ADJ 人道主义的 réndào zhǔyì de **II** N 人道主义者 réndào zhǔyìzhě

humanitarianism N 人道主义 réndàozhǔyì, 博爱精神 bó'ài jīngshén

humanities N 人文学科 rénwén xuékē

humanity N **1** 人类 rénlèi **2** 博爱 bó'ài, 仁慈 réncí

humanize v 使…人性化 shǐ…rénxìnghuà

humankind N 人类 rénlèi

humanly ADV 人的 rén de

humanly possible 尽最大努力 jìn zuì dà nǔlì

humble I ADJ **1** 谦恭的 qiāngōng de, 谦虚的 qiānxū de **2** 卑微的 [+出身] bēiwēi de [+chūshēn] II v 使…卑谦 shǐ…bēiqiān

humdrum ADJ 单调乏味的 dāndiào fáwèi de

humid ADJ 潮湿的 cháoshī de, 湿气很重的 shīqì hěn zhòng de

humidifier N 增湿器 zēngshī qì [M. WD 台 tái]

humidify v 使…湿润 shǐ…shīrùn

humidity N 湿度 shīdù

humiliate v 羞辱 xiūrǔ, 使…丢脸 shǐ…diūliǎn, 使…蒙羞 shǐ…méngxiū

humiliation N 羞辱 xiūrǔ

humility N 谦虚 qiānxū, 谦恭 qiāngōng

humor N 幽默 yōumò, 诙谐 huīxié

sense of humor 幽默感 yōumògǎn

humorist N 幽默作家 yōumò zuòjiā

humorless ADJ 没有幽默感的 méiyǒu yōumògǎn de, 一本正经的 yì běn zhèngjīng de

humorous ADJ 幽默的 yōumò de ■ *The author is able to see the humorous side of a situation.* 作者能够看到事物幽默的一面。Zuòzhě nénggou kàndao shìwù yōumò de yí miàn.

hump N **1** 圆形隆起物 yuánxíng lóngqǐ wù **2** 驼峰 tuófēng

hunch I N 预感 yùgǎn **II** v 弓起 [+背] gōng qǐ [+bèi]

hunchback N 驼背的人 tuóbèi de rén, 驼背 tuóbèi

hundred NUM 百 bǎi, 一百 yì bǎi

hundredweight N 美担 (= 100磅/45.36公斤) měidàn (= 100 bàng/45.36 gōng jīn)

hung v See hang¹

hung jury 未能取得一致意见的陪审团 wèi néng qǔdé yízhì yìjiàn de péishěntuán hung up 担忧的 dānyōu de

hunger I N **1** 饥饿 jī'è

hunger strike 绝食 juéshí

2 渴求 kěqiú

hunger for knowledge 对知识的渴求 duì zhīshi de kěqiú

II V (to hunger for) 渴求 kěqiú

to hunger for recognition 渴求获得他人的认可 kěqiú huòdé tārén de rènkě

hung over ADJ 宿醉 sùzuì

hungry ADJ 饿长, 饥饿的 jī'è de

to go hungry 挨饿 ái'è

hunk N 身材魁梧的人 shēncái kuíwú de rén, 性感的男子 xìnggǎn de nánzǐ

hunt I V **1** 打猎 dǎliè **2** 寻找 xúnzhǎo, 搜索 sōusuǒ
■ *I've hunted for my keys everywhere, but I can't find them.* 我到处找钥匙, 还是找不到。Wǒ dàochù zhǎo yàoshi, háishì zhǎobùdào. **II** N 寻找 xúnzhǎo

hunter N 猎人 lièrén

hunting N 打猎 dǎliè, 猎取 lièqǔ

hunting grounds 狩猎场 shòulièchǎng

bargain hunting 寻找便宜货 xúnzhǎo piányihuò

hurdle I N **1** [法律+] 障碍 [fǎlǜ+] zhàng'ài **2** [赛跑的+] 拦架 [sàipǎo de+] lánjià **II** V 跨越 [+拦架] kuàyuè [+lánjià]

hurl V 投掷 tóuzhì, 扔 rēng

hurricane N 飓风 jùfēng

hurried ADJ 匆忙的 cōngmáng de

hurry I V **1** 匆忙地做 cōngmáng de zuò **2** 催促 cuīcù ■ *Every morning she hurries the kids up so they won't be late for school.* 她每天早上都催促孩子快一点, 可以不迟到。Tā měitiān zǎoshang dōu cuīcù háizi kuài yìdiǎn, kěyǐ bù chídào. **II** N 匆忙 cōngmáng ■ *I'm not in any hurry.* 我一点儿也不着急。Wǒ yìdiǎn yě bù zháojí.

Hurry up! 快! Kuài!

hurt I V (PT & PP **hurt**) **1** 伤害 shānghài **2** 感到疼痛 gǎndao téngtòng ■ *Her feet hurt after she had stood there for so long.* 她站了这么久, 脚都疼了。Tā zhànle zhème jiǔ, jiǎo dōu téng le. **II** N (感情) 伤害 (gǎnqíng) shānghài

hurtful ADJ 伤害人的 shānghài rén de, 使人痛苦的 shǐrén tòngkǔ de

hurtle V 猛冲 měngchōng

husband N 丈夫 zhàngfu

hush I V 使…安静 shǐ…ānjìng

to hush up 保密 bǎomì, 秘而不宣 mì ér bù xuān

II N (重大事件前的) 沉默 (zhòngdà shìjiàn qián de) chénmò

hushed ADJ 寂静的 jìjìng de

hush-hush ADJ 秘密的 mìmì de

husk N (谷物) 外皮 (gǔwù) wàipí, 壳 ké

husky I ADJ **1** [嗓子+] 沙哑的 [sǎngzi+] shāyǎ de **2** 高大健壮的 [+男子] gāodà jiànzhuàng de [+nánzǐ] **II** N 爱斯基摩犬 Àisījīmó quǎn

hustle I V 乱推 luàn tuī, 混乱 hùnluàn **II** N 忙碌 mánglù

hustle and bustle 忙碌喧闹 mánglù xuānnào

hustler N 妓女 jìnǚ

hut N 小棚屋 xiǎo péngwū [M. WD 间 jiān]

hutch N 兔笼 tù lóng

hybrid N **1** 杂交品种 zájiāo pǐnzhǒng, 杂种 zázhǒng **2** 混合物 hùnhéwù

hybrid car 油电两用车 yóu diàn liǎngyòng chē

hydrant N 消防笼头 xiāofáng lóngtou, 消防栓 xiāofáng shuān

hydraulic ADJ 水压的 shuǐyā de, 水力的 shuǐlì de

hydraulics N 水压系统 shuǐyā xìtǒng

hydroelectric ADJ 水力发电的 shuǐlì fādiàn de

hydrogen (H) N 氢 (气) qīng (qì)

hydrogen bomb N See **H-bomb**

hydroplane V 水上飞机 shuǐshàng fēijī [M. WD 架 jià]

hyena N 鬣狗 lièqǒu [M. WD 只 zhī]

hygiene N (个人) 卫生 (gèrén) wèishēng

hygienic ADJ (个人) 卫生的 (gèrén) wèishēng de

hymn N 赞美诗 zànměishī, 颂歌 sònggē

hype N, V [媒体的+] 大肆炒作 [méitǐ de+] dàsì chǎozuò

hyped up ADJ 兴奋的 xīngfèn de, 激动的 jīdòng de

hyper I ADJ 过于兴奋的 guòyú xīngfèn de, 非常激动的 fēicháng jīdòng de **II** SUFFIX 过分的 guòfèn de, 过度的 guòdù de

hyperactive ADJ 过于活跃的 [+儿童] guòyú huóyuè de [+értóng], 多动的 duōdòng de

hyperactivity N (儿童) 多动症 (értóng) duōdòngzhèng

hyperbole N 夸张 kuāzhāng, 夸张法 kuāzhāngfǎ

hyperlink N 超链接 chāo liànjiē

hypersensitive ADJ 过敏的 guòmǐn de

hypertension N 高血压 gāoxuèyā

hyphen N 连接号 liánjiēhào (-)

hyphenate V (用连接号) 连接 (yòng liánjiēhào) liánjiē

hyphenated ADJ (用连接号) 连接起来的 (yòng liánjiēhào) liánjiē qǐlái de

hypnosis N 催眠 (状态) cuīmián (zhuàngtài)

hypnotic ADJ 催眠的 cuīmián de

hypnotism N 催眠状态 cuīmián zhuàngtài

hypnotist N 催眠师 cuīmiánshī

hypnotize V 对…催眠术 duì…cuīmiánshù

hypochondria N 过分担心健康 guòfèn dānxīn jiànkāng

hypochondriac N 过分担心健康的人 guòfèn dānxīn jiànkāng de rén, 无病呻吟者 wú bìng shēnyínzhě

hypocrisy N 伪善 wěishàn

hypocrite N 伪善者 wěishànzhě, 伪君子 wěijūnzǐ

hypodermic N 皮下注射针头 pí xià zhùshè zhēntóu

hypothermia N 体温过低 tǐwēn guò dī, 寒冷 hánlěng

hypothesis N 假设 jiǎshè

hypothesize V 提出假设 tíchū jiǎshè

hypothetical ADJ 假设的 jiǎshè de

hysterectomy N 子宫切除术 zǐgōng qiēchúshù

hysteria N 1 狂热 kuángrè, 狂热情绪 kuángrè qíngxù 2 歇斯底里 xiēsīdǐlǐ, 癔病 yìbìng

hysterical ADJ 狂热的 kuángrè de, 歇斯底里的 xiēsīdǐlǐ de

hysterics N 歇斯底里 xiēsīdǐlǐ

to go into hysterics 控制不了感情 kòngzhì bùliǎo gǎnqíng, 歇斯底里发作 xiēsīdǐlǐ fāzuò

I

I PRON 我 wǒ ■ *My wife and I are happy to accept your invitation.* 我和妻子很高兴接受您的邀请。Wǒ hé qīzi hěn gāoxìng jiēshòu nín de yāoqǐng.

ice N 冰 bīng

ice cream 冰淇淋 bīngqílín

ice cube 冰块 bīngkuài

ice hockey 冰球（运动）bīngqiú (yùndòng)

ice pack 冰袋 bīngdài

iceberg N 冰山 bīngshān

the tip of the iceberg 冰山的一角 bīngshān de yìjiǎo

ice skate I V 溜冰 liūbīng II N 溜冰鞋 liūbīng xié [M. WD 只 zhī/双 shuāng]

icicle N 冰柱 bīngzhù, 冰凌 bīnglíng

icing N 糖霜 tángshuāng

icky ADJ 让人恶心的 ràng rén èxīn de, 极讨厌的 jí tǎoyàn de

icon N 1 崇拜的偶像 chóngbài de ǒuxiàng 2（计算机的）图标 (jìsuànjī de) túbiāo

icy ADJ 1 冰冷的 bīnglěng de 2 结冰的 jiébīng de 3 冷淡的 [+态度] lěngdàn de [+tàidu], 极不友好的 jí bùyǒuhǎo de

ID I (= identity, identification) ABBREV 1 个人身份 gèrén shēnfen 2 身份证明 shēnfenzhèng míng

ID card, identity card 身份证 shēnfenzhèng II V 辨认 [+罪犯] biànrèn [+zuìfàn]

idea N 1 主意 zhǔyi 2 认识 rènshi ■ *His novels give you a good idea of life in 18th-century England.* 他的小说使你很好认识十八世纪英国的生活。Tā de xiǎoshuō shǐ nǐ hěn hǎo rènshi shíbā shìjì Yīngguó de shēnghuó. 3 想法 xiǎngfǎ

I don't have the slightest idea who did it. 我一点儿也不知道是谁干的。Wǒ yìdiǎnr yě bù zhīdào shì shéi gàn de.

ideal I N 理想 lǐxiǎng II ADJ 理想的 lǐxiǎng de, 最合适的 zuì héshì de

idealism N 理想主义 lǐxiǎngzhǔyì

idealistic ADJ 理想主义的 lǐxiǎngzhǔyì de

idealization N 理想化 lǐxiǎng huà

idealize V 把…理想化 bǎ...lǐxiǎng huà

idealized ADJ 理想化了的 lǐxiǎng huà le de

identical ADJ 完全相同的 wánquán xiāngtóng de, 同一的 tóngyī de

identifiable ADJ 可以识别的 kěyǐ shíbié de, 可以辨认的 kěyǐ biànrèn de

identification N 1 辨认 biànrèn, 识别 shíbié 2 身份（证明）shēnfen (zhèngmíng)

identify V 确认 quèrèn, 认出来 rènchūlai

identity N 1 身份 shēnfen 2 个性 gèxìng,（自身的）特征 (zìshēn de) tèzhēng

identity crisis 失去自身特征的危险 shīqù zìshēn tèzhēng de wēixiǎn 3 同一性 tóngyīxìng

ideology N 意识形态 yìshíxíngtài

idiocy N 极度愚蠢的 jídù yúchǔn de

idiom N 1 成语 chéngyǔ ■ *The Chinese language has a large number of four-character idioms in its vocabulary.* 中文词汇里有大量四个字的成语。Zhōngwén cíhuì lǐ yǒu dàliàng sì ge zì de chéngyǔ. 2 习惯用语 xíguàn yòngyǔ

idiomatic ADJ 1 地道的 [+中文] dìdao de [+Zhōngwén] 2 成语的 chéngyǔ de, 习惯用语的 xíguàn yòngyǔ de

idiosyncrasy N 特性 tèxìng

idiot N 白痴 báichī, 大笨蛋 dà bèndàn

idiotic ADJ 极其愚蠢的 jíqí yúchǔn de, 白痴一样的 báichī yíyàng de

idle I ADJ 1 闲置不用的 [+设备] xiánzhì búyòng de [+shèbèi] 2 没有意义的 [+话] méiyǒu yìyì de [+huà] 3 懒惰的 lǎnduò de, 闲散的 xiánsǎn de

the idle rich 富贵闲人 fùguì xiánrén II V 1 使 [+设备] 闲置 shǐ [+shèbèi] xián zhì 2 [发动机+] 空转 [fādòngjī+] kōngzhuàn

idol N 偶像 ǒuxiàng

idolatry N 偶像崇拜 ǒuxiàng chóngbài, 过分崇拜 guòfèn chóngbài

idolize V 极为崇拜 jíwéi chóngbài

idyllic ADJ 恬静宜人的 tiánjìng yírén de

if I CONJ 1 如果 rúguǒ, 要是 yàoshi ■ *Do it well, if it's worth doing.* 如果这件事值得做，就好好做。Rúguǒ zhè jiàn shì zhíde zuò, jiù hǎohǎo zuò. 2 是否 shìfǒu, 是不是 shìbushì, 会不会 huì bù huì

even if 即使 jíshǐ ■ *He will buy the new car, even if he has to get a loan.* 他即使借钱，也要买新车。Tā jíshǐ jiè qián, yě yào mǎi xīn chē.

only if 只有 zhǐyǒu, 只要 zhǐyào

if I were you 要是我是你的话 yàoshi wǒ shì nǐ de huà ■ *If I were you, I wouldn't marry that man.* 要是我是你的话，就不会跟那个男人结婚。

Yàoshi wǒ shì nǐ de huà, jiù bú huì gēn nà ge nánrén jiéhūn.

II N 可能 kěnéng, 可能性 kěnéngxìng ■ *No ifs, ands, or buts.* 别找任何借口。Bié zhǎo rènhé jièkǒu.

iffy ADJ 不确定的 bú quèdìng de

igloo N（爱斯基摩人）圆顶小屋 (Àisījīmórén) yuándǐng xiǎo wū

ignite v 1 点燃 [+炸药] diǎnrán [+zhàyào] 2 激发 [+热情] jīfā [+rèqíng]

ignition N（汽车）点火装置 (qìchē) diǎnhuǒ zhuāngzhì, 点火开关 diǎnhuǒ kāiguān

ignition key（汽车）启动钥匙 (qìchē) qǐdòng yàoshi

ignoble ADJ 卑鄙的 bēibǐ de, 不光彩的 bù guāngcǎi de

ignominious ADJ 极不光彩的 jí bù guāngcǎi de, 耻辱的 chǐrǔ de

ignorance N 无知 wúzhī ■ *Prejudice comes from ignorance.* 偏见来自无知。Piānjiàn láizì wúzhī.

ignorant ADJ 无知的 wúzhī de, 一点也不知道的 yìdiǎn yě bù zhīdào de

ignore v 不理睬 bù lǐcǎi

ill I ADJ 1 生病 shēngbìng 2 坏的 huài de, 有害的 yǒuhài de

ill effects 有害效果 yǒuhài xiàoguǒ, 不良反应 bùliáng fǎnyìng

3 (ill at ease) 不自在 bú zìzài, 紧张的 jǐnzhāng de **II** ADV 不好地 bù hǎo de **III** N 伤害 shānghài, 坏运 èyùn

ill-advised ADJ 不明智的 bùmíngzhì de

illegal I ADJ 非法的 fēifǎ de, 违法的 wéifǎ de

■ *It goes without saying that it is illegal to use drugs.* 使用毒品当然是非法的。Shǐyòng dúpǐn dāngrán shì fēifǎ de. **II** N 非法移民 fēifǎ yímín, 非法滞留者 fēifǎ zhìliúzhě

illegible ADJ 难以辨认的 [+字迹] nányǐ biànrèn de [+zìjī]

illegitimacy N 非法 fēifǎ

illegitimate ADJ 1 私生的 sī shēng de, 非婚生的 fēi hūn shēng de

an illegitimate child 私生子 sīshēngzǐ

2 非法的 fēifǎ de

ill-equipped ADJ 装备不良的 zhuāngbèi bù liáng de, 没有很好准备的 méiyǒu hěn hǎo zhǔnbèi de

ill-fated ADJ 倒霉的 dǎoméi de, 注定失败的 zhùdìng shībài de

illicit ADJ 1 违法的 wéifǎ de 2 社会不容的 shèhuì bù róng de

illiteracy N 不识字 bù shízì, 文盲 wénmáng

illiterate ADJ 不识字的 bù shízì de, 文盲的 wénmáng de

ill-mannered ADJ 不礼貌的 bù lǐmào de, 粗鲁的 cūlǔ de

illness N 病 bìng

illogical ADJ 不合逻辑的 bù hé luójí de, 不合道理的 bùhé dàoli de

ill-treat v 虐待 nüèdài

ill-treatment N 虐待 nüèdài

illuminate v 1 照亮 [+房间] zhàoliàng [+fángjiān] 2 阐明 [+道理] chǎnmíng [+dàoli]

illumination N 照亮 zhàoliàng, 阐明 chǎnmíng

illusion N 幻觉 huànjué, 幻想 huànxiǎng

optical illusion 视错觉 shìcuòjué

illusory ADJ 虚构的 xūgòu de, 虚假的 xūjiǎ de

illustrate v 1 举例子解释 jǔ lìzi jiěshì, 举例子说明 jǔ lìzi shuōmíng 2 画插图 huà chātú

illustration N 1 图示 túshì, 图解 tújiě 2 插图 chātú [M. WD 张 zhāng] 3 说明 shuōmíng

illustrator N 插图画家 chātú huàjiā

illustrious ADJ 杰出的 jiéchū de, 著名的 zhùmíng de

image N 1 形象 xíngxiàng 2 印象 yìnxiàng, 图像 túxiàng

imaginable ADJ 可以想象的 kěyǐ xiǎngxiàng de

imaginary ADJ 想像的 xiǎngxiàng de ■ *I think her fear was just imaginary.* 我认为她的恐惧是想像出来的。Wǒ rènwéi tā de kǒngjù shì xiǎngxiàng chūlai de.

imagination N 想像力 xiǎngxiànglì

imaginative ADJ 想像力丰富的 xiǎngxiànglì fēngfù de

imagine v 1 想像 xiǎngxiàng 2 设想 shèxiǎng

imbalance N 不平衡 bù pínghéng

imbecile I N 笨人 bènrén, 蠢货 chǔnhuò **II** ADJ 愚蠢透顶的 yúchǔn tòudǐng de

imbibe v 喝 [+酒] hē [+jiǔ]

imbue v 使…充满 shǐ…chōngmǎn

imitate v 1 模仿 mófǎng, 仿效 fǎngxiào 2 模拟 mónǐ

imitation I N 1 模仿 mófǎng, 仿效 fǎngxiào 2 仿制品 fǎngzhìpǐn, 伪造品 wěizàopǐn ■ *Of course that Ming vase is an imitation—how can I afford a genuine one?* 那只明代花瓶当然是仿制品—我怎么买得起真的呢？Nà zhī Míngdài huāpíng dāngrán shì fǎngzhìpǐn—wǒ zěnme mǎideqǐ zhēnde ne? **II** ADJ 仿造的 fǎngzào de, 人造的 rénzào de

imitation leather 人造（皮）革 rénzào (pí) gé

imitative ADJ 模仿的 mófǎng de, 仿效的 fǎngxiào de

imitator N 模仿者 mófǎngzhě, 仿效者 fǎngxiàozhě

immaculate ADJ 1 完美的 wánměi de, 无瑕可击的 wúxiá kějī de 2 十分清洁整齐的 shífēn qīngjié zhěngqí de

immaterial ADJ 1 无关紧要的 wúguān jǐnyào de 2 非实体的 fēi shítǐ de

immature ADJ 1 不成熟的 bù chéngshú de 2 未充分发育的 wéi chōngfèn fāyù de

immaturity N 不成熟 bù chéngshú, 发育不全 fāyù bù quán

immediacy N 紧迫性 jǐnpò xìng, 即刻 jíkè

immediate ADJ 1 立即的 lìjí de, 即刻的 jíkè de 2 当前的 dāngqián de, 目前的 mùqián de 3 直接的 zhíjiē de

the immediate future 最近 zuìjìn ■ *I don't have a plan to travel to Europe in the immediate future.* 我最近没有计划去欧洲。Wǒ zuìjìn méiyǒu jìhuà qù Ōuzhōu.

one's immediate family 直系亲属 zhíxì qīnshǔ

immediately ADV 立即 lìjí, 即刻 jíkè

immense ADJ 巨大的 jùdà de, 宏大的 hóngdà de

immerse V 浸没 jìnmò, 沉浸 chénjìn

to immerse oneself in 潜心于 qiánxīn yú

immersion N 1 [黄豆] 沉浸 [huángdòu+] chénjìn 2 专注 [+政治活动] zhuānzhù [+zhèngzhì huódòng] 3 沉浸式外语教学法 chénjìnshì wàiyǔ jiàoxuéfǎ

immigrant N 移民 (问题) yímín (wèntí) ■ *The restaurant was fined for employing illegal immigrants.* 这家餐馆因为雇佣非法移民而被罚款。Zhè jiā cānguǎn yīnwèi gùyòng fēifǎ yímín ér bèi fákuǎn.

immigrate V 移民 yímín, 移民到… yímín dào… ■ *The Chen family immigrated to America over 20 years ago.* 陈家在二十年前移民到美国。Chén jiā zài èrshí nián qián yímín dào Měiguó.

immigration N 移民 (问题) yímín (wèntí)

imminent ADJ 即刻会发生的 jíkè huì fāshēng de

immobile ADJ 固定的 gùdìng de, 动弹不得的 dòngtanbùdé de

immobilize V 固定 gùdìng, 使…不能动 shǐ… bùnéng dòng

immoral ADJ 不道德的 bú dàodé de

immortal I ADJ 1 不会死的 bú huì sǐ de, 长生不老的 chángshēngbùlǎo de 2 不朽的 [+功绩] bùxiǔ de [+gōngjì] II N 长生不老者 chángshēngbùlǎozhě, 仙人 xiānrén

immovable ADJ 1 不能移动的 bùnéng yídòng de, 固定的 gùdìng de 2 不可动摇的 bùkě dòngyáo de, 十分坚定的 shífēn jiāndìng de

immune ADJ 1 有免疫力的 yǒu miǎnyìlì de 2 不受影响的 bú shòu yǐngxiǎng de

immune system 免疫系统 miǎnyì xìtǒng

immunity N 免疫 miǎnyì, 免疫性 miǎnyìxìng

immunize V 使…免疫 shǐ…miǎnyì

immutable ADJ 不能改变的 bùnéng gǎibiàn de, 永恒的 yǒnghéng de

imp N 1 小鬼 xiǎoguǐ 2 小淘气 xiǎo táoqì

impact I N 1 影响 yǐngxiǎng 2 冲击 chōngjī, 撞击 zhuàngjī ■ *The impact of the crash made the car a crumpled wreck.* 撞车产生的冲击把车变成一堆扭曲的废铁。Zhuàngchē chǎnshēng de chōngjī bǎ chē biànchéng yì duī niǔqū de fèitiě. II V 产生 (重大) 影响 chǎnshēng (zhòngdà) yǐngxiǎng

impair V 损害 sǔnhài, 削弱 xuēruò

impaired ADJ 受损的 shòusǔn de

impairment N 损害 sǔnhài, 削弱 xuēruò

impale V 刺穿 cìchuān

impart V 1 传授 chuánshòu 2 给予 jǐyǔ, 赋予 fùyǔ

impartial ADJ 不偏不倚的 bùpiān bùyǐ de, 公正的 gōngzhèng de

impartiality N 公正 gōngzhèng

impassable ADJ 不能通过的 bùnéng tōngguò de

impasse N 僵局 jiāngjú

impassioned ADJ 热情的 rèqíng de, 激情的 jīqíng de

impassive ADJ 冷淡的 lěngdàn de

impatience N 没有耐心 méiyǒu nàixīn, 不耐烦 búnàifán

impatient ADJ 没有耐心的 méiyǒu nàixīn de, 不耐烦的 búnàifán de

impeach V 弹劾 tánhé, 控告 kònggào

impeachment N 弹劾 tánhé, 控告 kònggào

impeccable ADJ 无瑕可击的 wúxiákějī de, 完美的 wánměi de

impede V 妨碍 fáng'ài, 迟缓 chíhuǎn

impediment N 1 残疾 cánjí 2 妨碍 fáng'ài

impel V 促使 cùshǐ, 驱使 qūshǐ

impending ADJ 即将发生的 jíjiāng fāshēng de, 即将来临的 jí jiāng láilín de

impenetrabe ADJ 1 不能进入的 bùnéng jìnrù de 2 不能理解的 [+文章] bù néng lǐjiě de [+wénzhāng], 费解的 fèijiě de

imperative I ADJ 绝对必要的 juéduì bìyào de, 紧迫的 jǐnpò de II N 1 当务之急 dāngwù zhī jí 2 (语法) 祈使语气 (yǔfǎ) qíshǐ yǔqì

imperceptible ADJ 难以察觉到 nányǐ chájué dào

imperfect I ADJ 不完美的 bù wánměi de II N (语法) 未完成时态 (yǔfǎ) wèi wánchéng shítài

imperfection N 不完美性 bù wánměi xìng

imperial ADJ 帝国的 dìguó de, 皇帝的 huángdì de

imperialism N 帝国主义 dìguó zhǔyì

imperialist N 帝国主义者 dìguó zhǔyìzhě

imperil V 使…陷于危险境地 shǐ…xiànyú wēixiǎn jìngde

impersonal ADJ 1 无人情味的 wúrén qíngwèi de, 冷漠的 lěngmò de 2 (语法) 无人称的 (yǔfǎ) wúrénchēng de

impersonate V 冒充 màochōng

impersonator N 1 冒充者 [+行骗] màochōngzhě [+xíngpiàn] 2 [滑稽+] 模仿者 [gǔjī+] mófǎngzhě

impertinent ADJ 没有礼貌的 méiyǒu lǐmào de, 粗鲁的 cūlǔ de

impervious ADJ 1 不能渗透的 [+材料] bùnéng shèntòu de [+cáiliào] 2 [对批评+] 无动于衷的 [duì pīpíng+] wúdòng yú zhōng de

impetuous ADJ 冲动的 chōngdòng de

impetus N 1 动力 dònglì, 冲力 chōnglì 2 推动 tuīdòng, 促进 cùjìn

impinge on v 影响到 yǐngxiǎng dào

impish ADJ 顽皮的 wánpí de

implacable ADJ 难以满足的 nányǐ mǎnzú de, 难以平息的 nányǐ píngxī de

implant I v 移植 yízhí, 注入 zhùrù II N (手术) 植入物(手术) zhírùwù

implausible ADJ 难以置信的 nányǐ zhìxìn de

implement I v 执行 zhíxíng, 实施 shíshī II N 工具 gōngjù, 用具 yòngjù

implementation N 实施 shíshī, 实行 shíxíng

implicate v 使…受牵连 shǐ...shòu qiānlián

implication N 1 含义 hányì, 暗示 ànshì 2 牵连 qiānlián

implicit ADJ 1 隐含的 yǐnhán de, 暗指的 ànzhǐ de 2 (implicit trust) 绝对信任 juéduì xìnrèn

implode v (使…)内爆 (shǐ...) nèi bào

implore v 恳求 kěnqiú, 哀求 āiqiú

imply v 意味着 yìwèizhe, 暗示 ànshì ■ *I don't think her silence implies agreement.* 我想她的沉默并不意味着同意。Wǒ xiǎng tā de chénmò bìng bú yìwèizhe tóngyì.

impolite ADJ 不礼貌的 bù lǐmào de

import I v 进口 jìnkǒu II N 进口货 jìnkǒuhuò import duty 进口税 jìnkǒushuì

importance N 重要性 zhòngyàoxìng to attach importance to 重视 zhòngshì

important ADJ 重要的 zhòngyào de ■ *It is important that workplaces should be smoke-free.* 工作场所不准抽烟,这是很重要的。Gōngzuò chángsuǒ bù zhǔn chōuyān, zhè shì hěn zhòngyào de.

importation N 1 [商品+] 进口 [shāngpǐn+] jìnkǒu, 输入 shūrù 2 [新技术+] 引进 [xīn jìshù+] yǐnjìn

impose v 强加 qiángjiā ■ *Parents shouldn't impose their values on their children.* 家长不应该把自己的价值观强加给子女。Jiāzhǎng bù yīnggāi bǎ zìjǐ de jiàzhíguān qiángjiā gěi zǐnǚ. to impose tax [政府+] 征税 [zhèngfǔ+] zhēngshuì

imposing ADJ 壮观的 zhuàngguān de, 宏伟的 hóngwěi de

imposition N 1 强加于人的事 qiángjiā yú rén de shì, 不合理的要求 bùhélǐ de yāoqiú 2 实施 [+法令] shíshī [+fǎlìng]

impossible ADJ 1 不可能的 bù kěnéng de 2 极难对付的 jínán duìfù de

imposter N 冒充的人 màochōng de rén, 冒牌货 màopáihuò

impotence N 1 阳痿 yángwěi 2 无能为力 wú néng wéilì de

impotent ADJ 1 无性交能力的 wú xìngjiāo nénglì de, 阳痿的 yángwěi de 2 无能为力的 wú néng wéilì de

impound v 扣押 kòuyā, 扣留 kòuliú

impoverished ADJ 非常贫困的 fēicháng pínkùn de

impractical 1 不恰当的 bú qiàdàng de 2 不会应付实际问题的 [+人] bú huì yìngfu shíjì wèntí de [+rén]

impracticality N 不实际(性) bùshí jì (xìng)

imprecise ADJ 不精确 bù jīngquè

imprecision N 不精确(性) bù jīngquè (xìng)

impregnable ADJ 1 无法攻克的 [+堡垒] wúfǎ gōngkè de [+bǎolěi] 2 无懈可击的 [+论点] wúxiè kějī de [+lùndiǎn]

impress v 1 给人好印象 gěi rén hǎo yìnxiàng, 使人敬佩 shǐ rén jìngpèi 2 使…牢记 shǐ...láojì to impress the urgency of environmental protection on the public 使公众牢记环境保护的迫切性 shǐ gōngzhòng láojì huánjìng bǎohù de pòqièxìng 3 压印 yā yìn, 盖印 gài yìn

impression N 1 印象 yìnxiàng to make an impression on 给人印象 gěi rén yìnxiàng ■ *He made a good impression on his fiancée's parents.* 他给未婚妻的父母留下了好印象。Tā gěi wèihūnqī de fùmǔ liúxiale hǎo yìnxiàng. 2 印记 yìnjì, 印痕 yìnhén

impressionable ADJ 易受影响的 yì shòu yǐngxiǎng de

impressionistic ADJ 凭主观印象的 píng zhǔguān yìnxiàng de

impressive ADJ 给人良好印象的 gěi rén liánghǎo yìnxiàng de

imprint I N 印证 yìnzhèng II v 在…加印 zài...jiā yìn

imprison v 监禁 jiānjìn, 把…投进监狱 bǎ...tóu jìn jiānyù

imprisonment N 监禁 jiānjìn

improbable ADJ 1 不大可能的 [+事件] búdà kěnéng de [+shìjiàn] 2 出人意料的 [+搭档] chūrén yìliào de [+dādàng], 不可思议的 bùkěsīyì de

impromptu I ADJ 即兴的 [+表演] jíxìng de [+biǎoyǎn], 即席的 [+演说] jíxí de [+yǎnshuō] II ADV 即兴 jíxìng, 即席 jíxí

improper ADJ 不妥当 bù tuǒdāng, 不合适 bù héshì

impropriety N 不妥 bù tuǒ, 不合适 bù héshì

improve v 改善 gǎishàn, 改进 gǎijìn ■ *As her health improved, so did her mood.* 随着她健康的改善,情绪也变好了。Suízhe tā jiànkāng de gǎishàn, qíngxù yě biàn hǎo le.

improvement N 改进 gǎijìn, 改善 gǎishàn

improvise v 现编 xiàn biān, 临时凑出 línshí còuchū

impudence N 冒失 màoshi, 厚颜 hòuyán

impudent ADJ 冒失的 màoshi de, 厚颜的 hòuyán de

impulse N 1 冲动 chōngdòng

impulse buying 一时冲动下的购买 yìshí chōngdòng xià de gòumǎi **2** 电脉冲 diànmàichōng, 神经冲动 shénjīng chōngdòng

impulsive ADJ 冲动的 chōngdòng de

impunity N (with impunity) 不受惩罚 bú shòu chéngfá

impure ADJ 不纯的 bù chún de

impurity N **1** 不纯 bùchún **2** 杂质 zázhì

in I PREP **1** 在…里 zài...lǐ **2** 在…之内 zài...zhīnèi, 在…期间 zài...qījiān ■ *The work was done in a week.* 这件工作在一个星期里做好了。Zhè jiàn gōngzuò zài yí ge xīngqī lǐ zuòhǎo le. **3** 在…以后 zài...yǐhòu ■ *Summer will be here in a month.* 夏天将在一个月以后来临。Xiàtiān jiāng zài yí ge yuè yǐhòu láilín. **4** 在…方面 zài...fāngmiàn ■ *Human beings have made rapid advances in science and technology.* 人类在科学技术方面取得迅速进展。Rénlèi zài kēxué jìshù fāngmiàn qǔdé xùnsù jìnzhǎn. II ADV **1** 进 jìn, 入 rù **2** 在 [+家/办公室] zài [+jiā/bàngōngshì]

inability N 不能 bù néng, 无力 wú lì

inaccessible ADJ **1** 难达到的 nán dádào de **2** 得不到的 dé búdào de, 买不起的 mǎibuqǐ de

inaccuracy N 不准确 bù zhǔnquè

inaccurate ADJ 不准确 bù zhǔnquè

inaction N 无行动 wú xíngdòng, 无所作为 wú suǒ zuòwéi

inadequacy N 不足 bù zú, 欠缺 qiànquē

inadequate ADJ 不足的 bù zú de, 欠缺的 qiànquē de

inadmissible ADJ （法律）不可接受的 (fǎlǜ) bùkě jiēshòu de

inadvertent ADJ 因疏忽而造成的 yīn shūhu ér zàochéng de, 粗心大意的 cūxīn dàyì de

inadvisable ADJ 不明智的 bù míngzhì de, 不可取的 bùkě qǔ de

inalienable ADJ 不可剥夺的 bùkě bōduó de

inane ADJ 极其愚蠢的 jíqí yúchǔn de, 无聊的 wúliáo de

inanimate ADJ 无生命的 wú shēngmìng de

inappropriate ADJ 不合适的 bù héshì de, 不恰当的 bù qiàdàng de

inarticulate ADJ 不能表达自己的 bùnéng biǎodá zìjǐ de, 说不清楚的 shuō bùqīngchu de

inasmuch as CONJ 由于 yóuyú, 因为 yīnwèi

inaudible ADJ 听不见的 tīngbujiàn de

inaugural ADJ **1** 就职的 jiùzhí de an inaugural speech 就职演说 jiùzhí yǎnshuō **2** 首次的 shǒucì de inaugural show 首次演出 shǒucì yǎnchū

inaugurate v **1** [为州长+] 举行就职典礼 [wéi Zhōuzhǎng+] jǔxíng jiùzhí diǎnlǐ **2** [为大楼+] 举行落成典礼 [wéi dàlóu+] jǔxíng luòchéngdiǎnlǐ

inauguration N 就职典礼 jiùzhí diǎnlǐ

inauspicious ADJ 不吉利的 bù jílì de, 不祥的 bùxiáng de

in-betweeen ADJ 介于两者之间的 jièyú liǎngzhě zhījiān de

inborn ADJ 天生的 [+能力] tiānshēng de [+nénglì]

inbred ADJ **1** 天生的 [+偏见] tiānshēng de [+piānjiàn] **2** 近亲繁殖的 jìnqīn fánzhí de

inbreeding N 近亲繁殖 jìnqīn fánzhí

incalculable ADJ 数不清的 shǔbuqīng de, 无法估量的 wúfǎ gūliang de

incandescence N 炽热 chìrè, 白炽 báichì

incandescent ADJ 炽热的 chìrè de, 白炽的 báichì de

incantation N 咒语 zhòuyǔ

incapable ADJ 不能（的）bùnéng (de), 不会（的）bú huì (de)

incapacitate v **1** 使 [+人] 失去能力 shǐ [+rén] shīqù nénglì **2** 使 [+系统] 不能正常运转 shǐ [+xìtǒng] bùnéng zhèngcháng yùnzhuǎn

incapacity N 无能力 wúnéng lì

incarcerate v 监禁 jiānjìn, 幽禁 yōujìn

incarnate ADJ 成为…的化身 chéngwéi...de huàshēn

incarnation N 化身 huàshēn, 体现 tǐxiàn the Incarnation 上帝化身为基督 Shàngdì huàshēn wéi Jīdū

incendiary ADJ **1** 燃烧的 [+炸弹] ránshāo de [+zhàdàn] **2** 极具煽动性的 [+演说] jí jù shāndòngxìng de [+yǎnshuō]

incense¹ N 香 xiāng, 焚香 fénxiāng

incense² v 激怒 jīnù

incentive N 激励 jīlì, 鼓励 gǔlì

inception N 开创 kāichuàng

incessant ADJ 不停的 bù tíng de, 没完没了的 méiwán méiliǎo de

incest N 乱伦 luànlún

incestuous ADJ 乱伦的 luànlún de

inch I N 英寸 yīngcùn inch by inch 慢慢地 mànmàn de, 一点一点地 yìdiǎn yìdiǎn de II v 慢慢地移动 mànmàn de yídòng

incidence N 发生率 fāshēnglǜ

incident N 事件 shìjiàn

incidental ADJ **1** 偶然的 ǒurán de **2** 次要的 cìyào de, 附带的 fùdài de incidental fees 杂费 záfèi

incidentally ADV **1** 偶然地 ǒurán de **2** 顺便提一下 shùnbiàn tí yíxià

incinerate v 烧毁 shāohuǐ

incinerator v 焚化炉 fénhuàlú

incipient ADJ 刚开始的 gāng kāishǐ de

incise v 刻（上）kè (shàng)

incision N **1** 切入 qièrù, 切开 qiēkāi **2** 切口 qièkǒu

incisive ADJ 切中要害的 qièzhòng yàohài de, 直截了当的 zhíjiéliǎodàng de

incisor N 门齿 ménchǐ [M. WD 颗 kē], 门牙 ményá [M. WD 颗 kē]

incite V 煽动 shāndòng, 鼓动 gǔdòng

inclination N 1 [妥协的+] 意向 [tuǒxié de+] yìxiàng 2 [逃避灾害的+] 倾向 [táobì zāihài de+] qīngxiàng 3 斜坡 xiépō

incline I V 1 （使…）倾向于 [+反抗] (shǐ…) qīngxiàng yú [+fǎnkàng] 2 （使…）倾斜 (shǐ…) qīngxié II N 斜坡 xiépō

inclined ADJ 倾向于…的 qīngxiàng yú…de

include V 包括 bāokuò

including PREP 包括 bāokuò ■ *We paid $1,000 for the 7-day tour, including all meals.* 我们为这七天的旅游付了一千元，这包括所有的餐食。Wǒmen wèi zhè qī tiān de lǚyóu fùle yì qiān yuán, zhè bāokuò suǒyǒu de cānshí.

inclusion N 包括 bāokuò, 包含 bāohán

inclusive ADJ 包括在内的 bāokuò zàinèi de

incognito ADV 隐瞒身份的 yǐnmán shēnfen de, 微服 wēifú

incoherent ADJ 没有条理的 méiyǒu tiáolǐ de, 杂乱无章的 záluàn wúzhāng de

income N 收入 shōurù

income tax 收入税 shōurùshuì

incoming ADJ 1 进来的 [+电子邮件] jìnlai de [+diànzi yóujiàn] 2 新当选的 [+国会议员] xīn dāngxuǎn de [+Guóhuì Yìyuán]

incommunicado ADJ, ADV 不得与外界联系 bùde yǔ wàijiè liánxì

incomparable ADJ 无可比拟的 wúkě bǐnǐ de

incompatible ADJ 1 不兼容的 [+软件] bù jiānróng de [+ruǎnjiàn] 2 不相容的 [+言论] bù xiāngróng de [+yánlùn] 3 合不来的 [+姐妹] hébùlái de [+jiěmèi]

incompetence N 不胜任 bú shèngrèn, 不称职 bú chènzhí

incompetent ADJ 不能胜任的 bùnéng shēngrèn de, 不称职的 bú chènzhí de

incomplete ADJ 不完整的 bù wánzhěng de, 不完全的 bù wánquán de

incomprehensible ADJ 不可理解的 bùkě lǐjiě de

inconceivable ADJ 不能想象的 bùnéng xiǎngxiàng de, 不可思议的 bùkě sīyì de

inconclusive ADJ 非结论性的 fēi jiélùnxìng de, 无结论的 wú jiélùn de

incongruity N 不协调 bù xiétiáo

incongruous ADJ 不协调的 bù xiétiáo de

inconsequential ADJ 不重要的 bú zhòngyào de

inconsiderate ADJ 不为他人考虑的 bú wèi tārén kǎolǜ de

inconsistency N 自相矛盾 zìxiāng máodùn, 前后不一 qiánhòu bùyī

inconsistent ADJ 前后不一的 qiánhòu bùyī de, 自相矛盾的 zìxiāng máodùn de

inconsolable ADJ 悲伤得无法安慰的 bēishāng de wúfǎ ānwèi de

inconspicuous ADJ 不显眼的 bù xiǎnyǎn de

incontinence N （大小便）失禁 (dàxiǎobiàn) shījìn

incontinent ADJ （大小便）失禁的 (dàxiǎobiàn) shījìn de

incontrovertible ADJ 无可否认的 wúkě fǒurèn de

inconvenience I N 不便之处 búbiàn zhīchù, 麻烦 máfan II V 带来不便 dàilái búbiàn, 造成麻烦 zàochéng máfan

inconvenient ADJ 不方便的 bù fāngbiàn de, 麻烦的 máfan de

incorporate V 吸收 xīshōu, 包容 bāoróng

incorporated (ABBREV Inc) ADJ 股份有限公司 gǔfèn yǒuxiàn gōngsī

incorrect ADJ 不正确的 bú zhèngquè de, 错误的 cuòwù de

incorrigible ADJ 不可救药的 bù kě jiùyào de

incorruptible ADJ 刚正清廉的 gāngzhèng qīnglián de

increase I V 增长 zēngzhǎng, 增加 zēngjiā II N 增加 zēngjiā, 增长 zēngzhǎng

incredible ADJ （令人）难以置信的 (lìng rén) nányǐ zhìxìn de

incredulity N 不相信 bù xiāngxìn

incredulous ADJ 不相信的 bù xiāngxìn de, 怀疑的 huáiyí de

increment N 增长 zēngzhǎng

incremental ADJ 逐步增长的 zhúbù zēngzhǎng de

incriminate V 显示 [+嫌疑犯] 有罪 xiǎnshì [+xiányífàn] yǒuzuì, 牵连 qiānlián

incrimination N 牵连 qiānlián

incriminatory ADJ 使人显得有罪的 shǐrén xiǎnde yǒuzuì de

incubate V 孵化 fūhuà

incubator N 1 孵化器 fūhuàqì 2 （早产）婴儿保育箱 (zǎochǎn) yīng'ér bǎoyùxiāng

inculcate V 反复灌输 fǎnfù guànshū, 一再教诲 yízài jiàohuì

incumbent I ADJ 现任的 xiànrèn de II N 现任者 xiànrènzhě

incur V 引起 yǐnqǐ, 导致 dǎozhì

incurable ADJ 无法治愈的 wúfǎ zhìyù de, 不可医治的 bùkě yīzhì de

incursion N 突袭 tūxí, 侵犯 qīnfàn

indebted ADJ [对朋友的帮助+] 十分感激的 [duì péngyou de bāngzhù+] shífēn gǎnjī de

indebtedness N 感激 gǎnjī

indecency N 猥亵（行为）wěixiè (xíngwéi)

indecent ADJ 1 下流的 [+言语] xiàliú de [+yányǔ] 2 离谱的 [+价格] lípǔ de [+jiàgé], 完全不能接受的 wánquán bùnéng jiēshòu de

indecision N 犹豫（不决）yóuyù (bù jué)

indecisive ADJ 1 犹豫（不决）的 yóuyù (bù jué) de 2 结果不明确的 jiéguǒ bù míngquè de

indeed ADV 确实 quèshí, 的确 díquè ■ *That was indeed a remarkable achievement.* 这确实是了不起的成就。Zhè quèshí shì liǎobuqǐ de chéngjiù.

indefensible ADJ 不可原谅的 bùkě yuánliàng de, 无法辩解的 wúfǎ biànjiě de

indefinable ADJ 难以名状的 nányǐ míngzhuàng de, 难以解释的 nányǐ jiěshì de

indefinite ADJ 不确定的 bú quèdìng de, 不定的 bú dìng de

indelible ADJ 不可磨灭的 bù kě mómiè de

indelicate ADJ 不文雅的 bù wényǎ de, 粗鲁的 cūlǔ de

indemnify V 保障赔偿 bǎozhàng péicháng

indemnity N 1 (损失) 保障 (sǔnshī) bǎozhàng 2 赔偿金 péichángjīn, 赔款 péikuǎn

indent V 缩格 (书写) suō gé (shūxiě)

indentation N 1 (行首) 空格 (hángshǒu) kònggé 2 凹口 āokǒu

independence N 独立 dúlì
Independence Day (Fourth of July) (美国) 独立日 (七月四日) (Měiguó) dúlì rì (qīyuè sìrì)

independent ADJ 独立的 dúlì de, 不需帮助 bù xū bāngzhù de ■ *My grandma, in spite of her old age and declining health, is fiercely independent.* 我的奶奶虽然年纪大了，身体越来越差，但是极其独立。Wǒ de nǎinai suīrán niánjì dà le, shēntǐ yuèláiyuè chà, dànshì jíqí dúlì.

in-depth ADJ 深入的 shēnrù de

indescribable ADJ 难以形容的 nányǐ xíngróng de, 难以描绘的 nányǐ miáohuì de

indestructible ADJ 不可摧毁的 bùkě cuīhuǐ de

indeterminacy N 不确定 (性) bú quèdìng(xìng)

indeterminate ADJ 不确定的 bú quèdìng de

index I N (PL **indices**) 1 (图书) 索引 (túshū) suǒyǐn 2 (股票) 指数 (gǔpiào) zhǐshù 3 标指 biāozhǐ
index card 索引卡片 suǒyǐn kǎpiàn
index finger 食指 shízhǐ
II V 编索引 biān suǒyǐn

Indian I ADJ 1 印度的 Yìndù de
Indian Ocean 印度洋 Yìndùyáng
Indian summer 初秋的晴朗天气 chūqiū de qínglǎng tiānqì
2 印第安人的 Yìndì'ānrén de II N 1 印度人 Yìndùrén 2 印第安人 Yìndì'ānrén
American Indian 美洲印第安人 Měizhōu Yìndì'ānrén

indicate V 1 显示 xiǎnshì, 指示 zhǐshì 2 表示 biǎoshì, 示意 shìyì ■ *The principal has indicated that he may retire soon.* 校长表示过他可能不久就退休。Xiàozhǎng biǎoshìguo tā kěnéng bùjiǔ jiù tuìxiū.

indication N 显示 xiǎnshì, 表示 biǎoshì

indicative ADJ (indicative of) 表明 biǎomíng, 显示 xiǎnshì

indicator N 1 指示 zhǐshì, 指示器 zhǐshìqì 2 指针 zhǐzhēn

indices N See index

indict V 控告 kònggào, 起诉 qǐsù
to be indicted for a crime 被控犯罪 bèikòng fànzuì

indictable ADJ 可以控告的 kěyǐ kònggào de

indictment N 控告 kònggào, 起诉 qǐsù
under indictment 受到起诉 shòudào qǐsù

indifference N 漠不关心 mò bù guānxīn, 无所谓 wúsuǒwèi

indifferent ADJ 漠不关心的 mò bù guānxīn de, 无所谓的 wúsuǒwèi de

indigenous ADJ 土生土长的 tǔshēng tǔzhǎng de, 土著的 tǔzhù de

indigestible ADJ 1 难消化的 [+食物] nán xiāohuà de [+shíwù] 2 难以理解的 [+数据] nányǐ lǐjiě de [+shùjù]

indigestion N 消化不良的 xiāohuà bùliáng de

indignant ADJ 愤慨的 fènkǎi de, 气愤的 qìfèn de

indignation N 愤慨 fènkǎi, 气愤 qìfèn

indignity N 侮辱 wǔrǔ, 轻侮 qīngwǔ

indirect ADJ 间接的 jiànjiē de
indirect object 间接宾语 jiànjiē bīnyǔ
indirect speech 间接引语 jiànjiē yǐnyǔ

indiscreet ADJ 不谨慎的 bù jǐnshèn de, 言行失检的 yánxíng shī jiǎn de

indiscretion N 不谨慎 bù jǐnshèn, 言行失检 yánxíng shī jiǎn

indiscriminate ADJ 不加区别的 bù jiā qūbié de, 不分青红皂白的 bù fēn qīng hóng zào bái de

indispensable ADJ 不可缺少的 bùkě quēshǎo de, 必需的 bìxū de

indisputable ADJ 不容置疑的 bùróng zhìyí de, 完全正确的 wánquán zhèngquè de

indistinct ADJ 模糊不清的 móhu bùqīng de

indistinguishable ADJ 很难区分的 hěn nán qūfēn de, 难以辨别的 nányǐ biànbié de

individual I ADJ 个别的 gèbié de, 个人的 gèrén de II N 个人 gèrén ■ *The rights and obligations of the individual should be well defined.* 个人的权利和义务需要很好界定。Gèrén de quánlì hé yìwù xūyào hěn hǎo jièdìng.

individualism N 个人主义 gèrén zhǔyì, 重视个人权益自由 zhòngshì gèrén quányì zìyóu

individualist N 按照个人意愿行事的人 ànzhào gèrén yìyuàn xíngshì de rén, 特立独行的人 tèlì dúxíng de rén

individuality N 个性 gèxìng, 特性 tèxìng

individually ADV 个别地 gèbié de, 一个一个地 yígeyíge de

indivisible ADJ 不可分割的 bùkě fēn'gē de

indoctrinate V 向…灌输思想 xiàng...guànshū sīxiǎng

indoctrination N 灌输思想 guànshū sīxiǎng

indolence N 懒惰 lǎnduò
indolent ADJ 懒惰的 lǎnduò de
indomitable ADJ 不屈不挠的 bù qū bù náo de
indoor ADJ 室内的 shìnèi de
indoors ADV 室内 shìnèi, 房子里 fángzi lǐ
induce V 1 劝诱 quànyòu, 诱导 yòudǎo 2 [药物+] 诱发 [yàowù+] yòufā, 引产 yǐnchǎn
inducement N 劝诱 quànyòu, 诱导 yòudǎo
induct V 1 使…就职 shǐ…jiùzhí 2 吸纳…为会员 xīnà…wéi huìyuán
induction N 1 就职 jiùzhí 2 归纳法 guīnàfǎ
indulge V 1 让…尽情享受 ràng…jǐnqíng xiǎngshòu 2 满足 [+欲望] mǎnzú [+yùwàng], 放纵 fàngzòng
indulgence N 1 纵容 zòngróng 2 嗜好 shìhào, 迷恋 (的事物) míliàn (de shìwù)
indulgent ADJ 放纵的 fàngzòng de, 沉溺的 chénnì de
industrial ADJ 工业的 gōngyè de
industrial accident 工伤事故 gōngshāng shìgù
industrial action 罢工 bàgōng, 怠工 dàigōng
industrial park 工业园 gōngyèyuán
industrialist N 工业家 gōngyèjiā, 企业家 qǐyèjiā [M. WD 位 wèi]
industrialization N 工业化 gōngyèhuà
industrialize V (使…) 工业化 (shǐ…) gōngyèhuà
industrious ADJ 勤劳的 qínláo de
industry N 1 工业 gōngyè 2 行业 hángyè, 产业 chǎnyè ■ Tourism is the key industry for this state. 旅游业是这个州的关键产业。Lǚyóuyè shì zhè ge zhōu de guānjiàn chǎnyè.
inedible ADJ 不可食用的 bùkě shíyòng de
ineffective ADJ 无效果的 wú xiàoguǒ de
ineffectual ADJ 无能的 wú néng de, 没有效果的 méiyǒu xiàoguǒ de
inefficiency N 低效率 dī xiàolǜ, 低效 dīxiào
inefficient ADJ 效率低下的 xiàolǜ dīxiàde
inelegant ADJ 不雅致的 bù yǎzhi de, 不雅的 bù yǎ de
ineligibility N 无资格 wú zīge
ineligible ADJ 无资格的 wú zīge de
inept ADJ 没有技能的 méiyǒu jìnéng de, 笨拙的 bènzhuō de
ineptitude N 没有技能 (的状态) méiyǒu jìnéng (de zhuàngtài)
inequality N 不平等 bù píngděng
inequity N 不公正 bù gōngzhèng, 不公平 (现象) bùgōngpíng (xiànxiàng)
inert ADJ 1 惰性的 [+气体] duòxìng de [+qìtǐ] 2 迟缓的 [+行动] chíhuǎn de [+xíngdòng]
inertia N 惰性 duòxìng, 惯性 guànxìng
inescapable ADJ 不可避免的 bùkě bìmiǎn de
inessential ADJ 非必需的 fēi bìxū de, 可有可无的 kěyǒu kěwú de
inestimable ADJ (多得) 难以估计的 (duō dé) nányǐ gūjì de

inevitability N 必然 (性) bìrán (xìng)
inevitable ADJ 不可避免的 bùkě bìmiǎn de, 必然的 bìrán de
inexact ADJ 不精确的 bù jīngquè de
inexcusable ADJ 不可原谅的 bùkě yuánliàng de
inexhaustible ADJ 取之不尽的 qǔ zhī bú jìn de, 无穷无尽的 wúqióng wújìn de
inexorable ADJ 不可阻挡的 bùkě zǔdǎng de, 无法停止的 wúfǎ tíngzhǐ de
inexpensive ADJ 不贵的 bú guì de, 便宜的 piányi de
inexperience N 无经验 wú jīngyàn, 缺乏经验 quēfá jīngyàn
inexperienced ADJ 没有经验的 méiyǒu jīngyàn de, 缺乏经验的 quēfá jīngyàn de
inexplicable ADJ 无法解释的 wúfǎ jiěshì de
inextricable ADJ 不可分割的 bùkě fēngē de, 密不可分的 mìbùkěfēn de
infallibility N 永不犯错 yǒng bú fàncuò, 永远正确 yǒngyuǎn zhèngquè
infallible ADJ 不犯错的 bú fàncuò de, 永远正确的 yǒngyuǎn zhèngquè de
infamous ADJ 臭名昭彰的 chòumíng zhāozhāng de
infamy N 臭名昭彰 chòumíng zhāozhāng
infancy N 1 婴儿期 yīng'érqī 2 初期 chūqī, 早期 zǎoqī
infant N 婴儿 yīng'ér, 幼儿 yòu'ér
infantile ADJ 1 婴幼儿的 yīngyòu'ér de 2 幼稚的 yòuzhì de
infantry N 步兵部队 bùbīng bùduì
infatuated ADJ 痴迷的 chīmí de, 迷恋的 míliàn de
infatuation N 痴迷 chīmí, 迷恋 míliàn
infect V 1 传染 chuánrǎn, 感染 gǎnrǎn ■ Scientists fear that this virus will eventually infect humans. 科学家们恐惧，这一病毒终将传染给人类。Kēxuéjiāmen kǒngjù, zhè yí bìngdú zhōng jiāng chuánrǎn gěi rénlèi. 2 影响 [+别人的情绪] yǐngxiǎng [+biéren de qíngxù]
infection N 感染 gǎnrǎn
infectious ADJ 传染的 chuánrǎn de, 感染的 gǎnrǎn de
infer V 推断 tuīduàn, 推定 tuīdìng
inference N 推断 tuīduàn, 推论 tuīlùn
inferior I ADJ 次等的 cìděng de, 低劣的 dīliè de II N 下属 xiàshǔ, 部下 bùxià
inferno N 1 炼狱 liànyù, 地狱 dìyù 2 猛烈燃烧的大火 měngliè ránshāo de dàhuǒ
infertile ADJ 1 无生育能力的 [+夫妻] wú shēngyù nénglì de [+fūqī] 2 贫瘠的 [+土地] pínjí de [+tǔdì]
infertility N 1 不育症 búyùzhèng 2 (土地) 贫瘠 (tǔdì) pínjí
infest V [昆虫／老鼠+] 成群 [kūnchóng/lǎoshu+] chéngqún

infidel N 异教徒 yìjiàotú

infidelity N 通奸 tōngjiān, (夫妻) 不贞 (fūqī) bùzhēn

infield N (棒球场) 内场 (bàngqiúchǎng) nèichǎng

infielder N (棒球) 内场手 (bàngqiú) nèichǎngshǒu

infighting N 内讧 nèihòng, 窝里斗 wōlǐdòu

infiltrate V 渗透 shèntòu, 打入 [+内部] dǎrù [+nèibù]

infiltrator N 渗透者 shèntòuzhě

infinite ADJ 无限止的 wú xiànzhǐ de, 无限的 wú xiàn de

infinitesimal ADJ 极小的 jí xiǎo de, 极其细微的 jíqí xìwēi de

infinitive N 动词不定式 dòngcí búdìngshì, 动词的原形 dòngcí de yuánxíng

infinity N 无限 (的空间) wúxiàn (de kōngjiān)

infirm ADJ 体弱多病的 tǐruò duōbìng de, 年老体弱的 niánlǎo tǐruò de

infirmary N 医务室 yīwùshì, 医院 yīyuàn [M. WD 座 zuò]

infirmity N 1 体弱多病 tǐruò duōbìng 2 疾病 jíbìng

inflame V 1 激怒 [+人] jīnù [+rén] 2 加剧 [+紧张局势] jiājù [+jǐnzhāng júshì]

inflamed ADJ 发炎的 fāyán de, 红肿的 hóngzhǒng de

inflammable ADJ 1 易燃的 [+材料] yìrán de [+cáiliào] 2 易怒的 [+人] yì nù de [+rén]

inflammation N 1 发炎 fāyán 2 炎症 yánzhèng

inflammatory ADJ 1 引发炎症的 yǐnfā yánzhèng de 2 煽动性的 shāndòng xìng de

inflatable ADJ 充气的 chōngqì de

inflate V 1 给…充气 gěi...chōngqì 2 使 [+人] 自高自大 shǐ [+rén] zìgāo zìdà 3 使 [+价格] 上升 shǐ [+jiàgé] shàngshēng

inflated ADJ 1 充了气的 [+救生衣] chōngle qì de [+jiùshēngyī] 2 过高的 [+价格] guògāo de [+jiàgé], 通货膨胀的 tōnghuò péngzhàng de 3 夸大的 [+数据] kuādà de [+shùjù], 言过其实的 yán guò qí shí de

inflation N 通货膨胀 tōnghuò péngzhàng

inflationary ADJ 引起通货膨胀的 yǐnqǐ tōnghuò péngzhàng de

inflexibility N 僵硬 jiāngyìng

inflexible ADJ 不灵活的 bùlínghuó de, 不可更改的 bùkě gēnggǎi de

inflict V 使…遭受 shǐ...zāoshòu

influence N, V 影响 yǐngxiǎng ■ *Uncle Mark is a good influence on all of us.* 马克舅舅对我们大家都有好影响。Mǎkè jiùjiu duì wǒmen dàjiā dōu yǒu hǎo yǐngxiǎng.

influential ADJ 有影响力的 yǒu yǐngxiǎnglì de

influenza (= flu) N 流行性感冒 liúxíngxìng gǎnmào, 流感 liúgǎn

influx N 大量涌入 dàliàng yǒngrù

infomercial N 商品信息专题电视片 shāngpǐn xìnxī zhuāntí diànshìpiàn

inform V 1 通知 tōngzhī 2 (to inform on sb) 告发 gàofā, 举报 jǔbào

informal ADJ 非正式的 fēi zhèngshì de, 随和友好的 suíhé yǒuhǎo de

informant N 提供信息的人 tígōng xìnxī de rén, 告密者 gàomìzhě

information N 信息 xìnxī, 情报 qíngbào
information center 信息中心 xìnxī zhōngxīn, 问讯处 wènxùnchù
information retrieval (计算机) 信息检索 (jìsuànjī) xìnxī jiǎnsuǒ
information science 信息科学 xìnxī kēxué
information superhighway 信息高速公路 xìnxī gāosù gōnglù
information technology (IT) 信息技术 xìnxī jìshù

informative ADJ 提供大量信息的 tígōng dàliàng xìnxī de, 内容丰富的 nèiróng fēngfù de

informed ADJ 1 见多识广的 [+人] jiàn duō shí guǎng de [+rén]
well-informed 消息灵通的 xiāoxi língtōng de
2 有根据的 [+决定／选择] yǒu gēnjù de [+juédìng/xuǎnzé]

informer N 告密者 gàomìzhě

infotainment N 信息娱乐节目 xìnxī yúlè jiémù

infrared ADJ 红外线的 hóngwàixiàn de
an infrared camera 红外线照相机 hóngwàixiàn zhàoxiàngjī

infrastructure N 基础设施 jīchǔ shèshī, 基础结构 jīchǔ jiégòu

infrequent ADJ 不是经常的 bú shì jīngcháng de, 不常见的 bù chángjiàn de

infringe V 违反 wéifǎn, 侵犯 qīnfàn

infringement N 违反 wéifǎn, 侵犯 qīnfàn

infuriate V 使…大怒 shǐ...dà nù, 激怒 jīnù

infuriating ADJ 让人极为愤怒的 ràng rén jíwéi fènnù de

infuse V 1 向 [+儿童] 灌输思想 xiàng [+értóng] guànshū sīxiǎng 2 冲泡 [+茶叶] chōngpào [+cháyè], 泡茶 pào chá

infusion N 1 灌输思想 guànshū sīxiǎng 2 冲泡茶叶 chōngpào cháyè, 泡茶 pàochá

ingenious ADJ 巧妙的 qiǎomiào de, 机灵的 jīling de

ingenuity N 发明才能 fāmíng cáinéng, 心灵手巧 xīnlíng shǒuqiǎo

ingest V 摄取 [+食物] shèqǔ [+shíwù]

ingot N (金／银) 锭 (jīn/yín) dìng

ingrained ADJ 根深蒂固的 gēnshēn dìgù de, 顽固的 wángù de

ingratiate V 讨好 tǎohǎo
to ingratiate oneself with 讨好 tǎohǎo, 取得欢心 qǔdé...huānxīn

ngratiating ADJ 讨好的 tǎohǎo de, 逢迎的 féngyíng de

ngratitude N 忘恩负义 wàng ēn fù yì, 不知领情 bùzhī lǐngqíng

ngredient N （食品／药品的）成份 (shípǐn/yàopǐn de) chéngfèn [M. WD 种 zhǒng]

nhabit V 居住 jūzhù

nhabitable ADJ 可以居住的 kěyǐ jūzhù de

nhabitant N 居民 jūmín, 居住者 jūzhùzhě

nhale V 吸入 xīrù

nhaler N 吸入器 xīrùqì

nherent ADJ 内在的 nèi zài de, 与生俱来的 yǔ shēng jù lái de

nherit V 继承 jìchéng ■ Barbara inherited the antique furniture from her paternal grandmother. 芭芭拉从祖母手上继承了这些古董家具。Bābālā cóng zǔmǔ shǒushang jìchéngle zhè xiē gǔdǒng jiājù.

nheritance N 遗产 yíchǎn

nhibit V 抑制 yìzhì, 制约 zhìyuē

nhospitable ADJ 不适合居住的 bú shìhé jūzhù de, 恶劣的 èliè de

n-house ADJ, ADV 内部的 nèibù de
an in-house magazine [公司+] 内部杂志 [gōngsī+] nèibù zázhì

nhuman ADJ 无人性的 wú rénxìng de

nhumane ADJ 不人道的 bù réndào de, 残忍的 cánrěn de

nhumanity N 无人性的行为 wú rénxìng de xíngwéi

nimitable ADJ 无可仿效的 wúkě fǎngxiào de, 无与伦比的 wú yǔ lúnbǐ de

nitial I ADJ 起初的 qǐchū de, 开始的 kāishǐ de II N 名字的首字母 míngzi de shǒu zìmǔ III V 签上姓名的首字母 qiānshang xìngmíng de shǒu zìmǔ

nitiate I V 1 开始 kāishǐ, 发动 fādòng 2 吸收 [+新会员] xīshōu [+xīnhuì yuán] II N 新入会的人 xīn rùhuì de rén, 新成员 xīn chéngyuán

nitiative N 1 行动 xíngdòng ■ The government has introduced a new initiative to combat the drug problem. 政府已采取新行动来与毒品作斗争。Zhèngfǔ yǐ cǎiqǔ xīn xíngdòng lái yǔ dúpǐn zuò dòuzhēng. 2 主动性 zhǔdòngxìng, 积极性 jījíxìng

nject V 1 注射 [+针剂] zhùshè [+zhēnjì] 2 投入 [+资金] tóurù [+zījīn]

njection N 1 注射 [+针剂] zhùshè [+zhēnjì] 2 投入 [+资金] tóurù [+zījīn]

njunction N （法院的）禁令 (fǎyuàn de) jìnlìng

njure V 损伤 sǔnshāng, 伤害 shānghài

njury N 损伤 sǔnshāng, 伤害 shānghài

njustice N 不公正（行为／待遇）bù gōngzhèng (xíngwéi/dàiyù)

nk N 墨 mò, 油墨 yóumò, 墨水 mòshuǐ

ink cartridge 油墨盒 yóumòhé

inkjet printer N 喷墨打印机 pēn mò dǎyìnjī [M. WD 台 tái]

inkling N 模糊的想法 móhu de xiǎngfǎ
to have no Inkling 一点也不知道 yìdiǎn yě bù zhīdào, 毫无所知 háowú suǒzhī

inlaid ADJ 镶嵌着…的 xiāngqiànzhe...de

inland I ADJ 内陆的 nèilù de II ADV 在内陆 zài nèilù

in-laws N 姻亲 yīnqīn
brother-in-law 内兄 nèixiōng (wife's elder brother), 内弟 nèidì (wife's younger brother), 大伯子 dàbǎizi (husband's elder brother), 小叔子 xiǎoshūzi (husband's younger brother), 姐夫 jiěfu (elder sister's husband), 妹夫 (younger sister's husband) mèifū, 连襟 liánjīn (wife's sister's husband)
father-in-law 岳父 yuèfù (wife's father), 公公 gōnggong (husband's father)
mother-in-law 岳母 yuèmǔ (wife's mother), 婆婆 pópo (husband's mother)
sister-in-law 嫂子 sǎozi (elder brother's wife), 弟媳 dìxí (younger brother's wife), 姑子 gūzi (husband's sister), 姨子 yízi (wife's sister), 妯娌 zhóuli (husband's brother's wife)

inlay N 镶嵌物 xiāngqiàn wù

inlet N 小海湾 xiǎo hǎiwān

inmate N 1 （监狱）囚犯 (jiānyù) qiúfàn 2 （医院）病人 (yīyuàn) bìngrén

inn N 小旅店 xiǎo lǚdiàn [M. WD 家 jiā]

innate ADJ 天生的 tiānshēng de, 固有的 gùyǒu de

inner ADJ 里面的 lǐmian de, 内部的 nèibù de
inner ear 内耳 nèi'ěr
inner circle 核心集团 héxīn jítuán, 小圈子 xiǎoquānzi
inner city （一般穷人居住的）市中心 (yìbān qióngrén jūzhù de) shìzhōngxīn, 旧城区 jiù chéngqū
inner tube 内胎 nèitāi

innermost ADJ 内心深处 nèixīn shēnchù

innings N （棒球比赛）一局 (bàngqiú bǐsài) yìjú

innkeeper N （小）旅店老板 (xiǎo) lǚdiàn lǎobǎn

innocence N 1 清白无辜 qīngbái wúgū 2 （儿童的）天真无邪 (értóng de) tiānzhēn wúxié

innocent ADJ 1 清白无辜的 qīngbái wúgū de ■ The prisoner insisted to his last day that he was innocent of the crime. 囚犯到生命最后一天仍然坚持自己没有犯罪。Qiúfàn dào shēngmìng zuìhòu yìtiān réngrán jiānchí zìjǐ méiyǒu fànzuì. 2 天真无邪的 tiānzhēn wúxié de

innocuous ADJ 没有危险的 méiyǒu wēixiǎn de, 没有恶意的 méiyǒu èyì de, 无害的 wúhài de

innovate V 革新 géxīn, 创新 chuàngxīn

innovation N 革新 géxīn, 创新 chuàngxīn

innovative ADJ 创新的 chuàngxīn de

innovator N 革新者 géxīnzhě, 创新者 chuàngxīnzhě

innuendo N 影射 yǐngshè, 暗示 ànshì

innumerable ADJ 无数的 wúshù de

inoculate v 给…接种（疫苗）gěi…jiēzhòng (yìmiáo), 不合时宜 bùhé shíyí de

inoculation N 接种疫苗 jiēzhòng yìmiáo

inoffensive ADJ 不触犯人的 bú chùfàn rén de, 不得罪人的 bù dézuì rén de

inopportune ADJ 不合适的 bù héshì de

inordinate ADJ 过度的 guòdù de, 极度的 jídù de

inorganic ADJ 无机的 wújī de

inpatient N 住院病人 zhùyuàn bìngrén

input I N 1（输入计算机的）信息 (shūrù jìsuànjī de) xìnxī 2（资金／建议的）投入 (zījīn/jiànyì de) tóurù II v (PT & PP input) 输入 [+信息] shūrù [+xìnxī]

inquest N 询问 xúnwèn, 审讯 shěnxùn

inquire v 询问 xúnwèn, 查询 cháxún

inquiring ADJ 1 追根究底的 zhuī gēn jiū dǐ de 2 有疑问的 yǒu yíwèn de

inquiry N 询问 xúnwèn, 查询 cháxún

inquisition N 宗教法规 zōngjiào fǎguī

inquisitive ADJ 爱追根究底的 ài zhuī gēn jiū dǐ de, 好奇的 hàoqí de

inroads N 突然袭击 tūrán xíjī
to make inroads 侵占 qīnzhàn, 消耗 xiāohào

ins and outs N 详情细节 xiángqíng xìjié

insane ADJ 精神错乱的 jīngshén cuòluàn de, 发疯的 fāfēng de

insanity N 1 精神错乱 jīngshén cuòluàn 2 愚蠢至极（的行为）yúchǔn zhìjí (de xíngwéi)

insatiable ADJ 不满足的 bù mǎnzú de, 贪得无厌的 tāndé wúyàn de

inscribe v 雕刻 diāokè, 题字 tízì

inscrutable ADJ 不可理解的 bùkě lǐjiě de, 神秘的 shénmì de

insect N 昆虫 kūnchóng, 虫子 chóngzi

insecticide N 灭虫剂 mièchóngjì

insecure ADJ 1 不安全感的 [+职业] wú ānquángǎn de [+zhíyè] 2 缺乏自信的 [+人] quēfá zìxìn de [+rén]

insecurity N 1 无安全感 wú ānquángǎn 2 缺乏自信 quēfá zìxìn

inseminate v 使 [+动物] 受精 shǐ [+dòngwù] shòujīng, 使 [+人] 怀孕 shǐ [+rén] huáiyùn

insemination N 授精 shòujīng

insensible ADJ 1 (insensible of) 没有意识到的 méiyǒu yìshìdào de 2 (insensible to) 对…没有感觉 duì…méiyǒu gǎnjué

insensitive ADJ 不敏感的 bù mǐngǎn de, 麻木的 mámù de

inseparable ADJ 形影不离的 [+朋友] xíngyǐng bùlí de [+péngyou], 亲密无间的 qīnmì wújiān de

insert I v 插入 chārù, 加进 jiājìn II N 1 插页广告 chāyè guǎnggào 2 插入物 chārùwù

inset N 附图 fùtú, 附加资料 fùjiā zīliào

inside I PREP 在…里面 zài…lǐmian II ADV 里面 lǐmian, 在里面 zài lǐmian III N 里面 lǐmian IV ADJ 里面的 lǐmian de, 内部的 nèibù de

insider N 内部人 nèibùrén, 圈内人 quānnèirén
insider trading 内线交易 nèixiàn jiāoyì

insidious ADJ 暗藏的 àncáng de, 暗中为害的 ànzhōng wéi hài de

insight N 1 洞察力 dòngchálì, 眼光 yǎnguāng 2 顿悟 dùnwù

insignia N 1 军衔肩章 jūnxián jiānzhāng 2（团体）标志 (tuántǐ) biāozhì

insignificance N 无重大意义 wú zhòngdà yìyì, 无足轻重 wúzú qīngzhòng

insignificant ADJ 无重大意义的 wú zhòngdà yìyì de, 不重要的 bú zhòngyào de

insincere ADJ 不诚恳的 bù chéngkěn de, 虚伪的 xūwěi de

insincerity N 虚伪 xūwěi

insinuate v 暗示 ànshì

insinuation N 暗示 ànshì

insipid ADJ 淡而无味的 dàn ér wúwèi de, 无味的 wúwèi de

insist v 坚持 jiānchí, 一定要 yídìng yào

insistence N 坚持 jiānchí ■ He dropped his earlie insistence. 他放弃了先前的坚持。Tā fàngqìle xiānqián de jiānchí.

insistent ADJ 坚持的 jiānchí de

insolence N 傲慢无礼 àomàn wúlǐ

insolent ADJ 傲慢无礼的 àomàn wúlǐ de

insoluble ADJ 1 无法解决的 [+难题] wúfǎ jiějué de [+nántí] 2 不溶解 [+于水] 的 bùróngjiě [+yú shuǐ] de

insolvency N 无还债能力 wú huánzhài nénglì, 破产 pòchǎn

insolvent ADJ 无还债能力的 wú huánzhài nénglì de, 破产的 pòchǎn de

insomnia N 失眠（症）shīmián (zhèng)

insomniac N 失眠症患者 shīmiánzhèng huànzh

inspect v 1 仔细检查 zǐxì jiǎnchá 2 视察 [+分公司 shìchá [+fēngōngsī]

inspection N 1 仔细检查 zǐxì jiǎnchá 2 视察 shìchá

inspector N 视察员 shìcháyuán, 巡视员 xúnshìyuán

inspiration N 灵感 línggǎn, 启示 qǐshì

inspirational ADJ 给人启示的 gěi rén qǐshì de, 舞人心的 gǔwǔ rénxīn de

inspire v 鼓舞 gǔwǔ, 激励 jīlì

instability N 不稳定 bù wěndìng

install v 1 安装 ānzhuāng 2 任命 rènmìng, 使…就职 shǐ…jiùzhí

installation N 1 安装 ānzhuāng 2 装置 zhuāngzhì, 设备 shèbèi 3 [军事+] 设施 [jūnshì+] shès

installment N 1 分期付款（额）fēnqī fùkuǎn (é) 2 [电视连续剧+] 集 [diànshì liánxùjù+] jí

instance N 事例 shìlì, 例子 lìzi ■ *In most instances customers don't complain about poor service; they just won't come back.* 在大多数情况下，顾客不会抱怨服务不好；他们就是不再来了。Zài dàduōshù qíngkuàng xià, gùkè bù huì bàoyuàn fúwù bù hǎo; tāmen jiùshì búzài lái le.
for instance 例如 lìrú, 比如 bǐrú

instant I ADJ 立即的 lìjí de, 即刻的 jíkè de
instant coffee 速溶咖啡 sùróng kāfēi
instant noodle 速泡面 sùpàomiàn
instant replay 及时重放 jíshí chóngfàng
II N 片刻 piànkè
in an instant 一下子 yíxiàzi, 顷刻之间 qǐngkè zhī jiān

instantaneous ADJ 即将的 jíjiāng de, 立即的 lìjí de

instantly ADV 立即 lìjí, 马上 mǎshàng

instead ADV 代替 dàitì ■ *I'm not too well today, let's go out tomorrow instead.* 我今天不大舒服，我们明天出去吧。Wǒ jīntiān búdà shūfu, wǒmen míngtiān chūqu ba.
instead of 而不是 ér búshì

instep N 脚背 jiǎobèi

instigate v 煽动 shāndòng, 挑动 tiǎodòng

instigation N 煽动 shāndòng, 挑动 tiǎodòng

instigator N 煽动者 shāndòngzhě, 煽风点火的人 shānfēng diǎnhuǒ de rén

instill v 长期灌输 chángqī guànshū

instinct N 本能 běnnéng, 天性 tiānxìng ■ *Is maternal love a human instinct?* 母爱是人类的本能吗？Mǔ'ài shì rénlèi de běnnéng ma?

institute I N 院 yuàn, 学院 xuéyuàn, 研究院 yánjiūyuàn
research institute 科学研究院 kēxué yánjiū yuàn
Massachusetts Institute of Technology (MIT) 麻省理工学院 Máshěng Lǐgōng Xuéyuàn
II v 制定 zhìdìng, 开创 kāichuàng

institution N 1 机构 jīgòu
an institution of higher education 高等院校 gāoděng yuànxiào, 大学 dàxué
2 制度 zhìdù, 规章制度 guīzhāng zhìdù

institutionalized ADJ 1 把…送进精神病院／养老院 bǎ…sòngjìn jīngshén bìngyuàn／yǎnglǎoyuàn 2 把…制度化 bǎ…zhìdùhuà

instruct v 1 指令 zhǐlìng, 指示 zhǐshì 2 教 jiāo, 传授 chuánshòu

instruction N 1 指令 zhǐlìng, 指示 zhǐshì
instruction manual 使用／维修手册 shǐyòng／wéixiū shǒucè
2 教 jiāo, 教授 jiāoshòu

instructive ADJ 有教育意义的 yǒu jiàoyù yìyì de, 提供知识的 tígōng zhīshi de

instructor N 教员 jiàoyuán [M. WD 位 wèi], 教练 jiàoliàn, 指导者 zhǐdǎozhě

instrument N 1 器具 qìjù, 器械 qìxiè
instrument panel 仪表板 yíbiǎobǎn
2 乐器 yuèqì ■ *Do you play an instrument?* 你会什么乐器？Nǐ huì shénme yuèqì ma?

instrumental ADJ 1 乐器的 yuèqì de 2 起重要作用的 qǐ zhòngyào zuòyòng de

insubordinate ADJ 不服从的 bù fúcóng de, 不听话的 bù tīnghuà de

insubordination N 拒不服从（的行为）jù bùfúcóng (de xíngwéi), 违抗命令 wéikàng mìnglìng

insubstantial ADJ 1 证据不足的 [+论点] zhèngjù bùzú de [+lùndiǎn] 2 虚幻的 xūhuàn de

insufferable ADJ 难以忍受的 nányǐ rěnshòu de

insufficient ADJ 不足的 bùzú de, 不够的 búgòu de

insular ADJ 1 岛屿的 dǎoyǔ de 2 闭塞保守的 bìsè bǎoshǒu de

insulate v 使…绝缘／隔热／隔音 shǐ…juéyuán／gérè／géyīn

insulation N 绝缘／隔热／隔音材料 juéyuán／gérè／géyīn cáiliào

insulin N 胰岛素 yídǎosù

insult N, v 侮辱 wǔrǔ ■ *Fans of the two teams shouted insults at each other.* 两队球迷相互辱骂。Liǎng duì qiúmí xiānghù rǔmà.

insurance N 1 保险 bǎoxiǎn 2 保险业 bǎoxiǎn yè
car insurance 汽车保险 qìchē bǎoxiǎn
contents insurance 家庭财产保险 jiātíng cáichǎn bǎoxiǎn
health insurance 医疗保险 yīliáo bǎoxiǎn
house insurance 房产保险 fángchǎn bǎoxiǎn
life insurance 人寿保险 rénshòu bǎoxiǎn

insure v 1 投保 tóubǎo 2 确保 quèbǎo ■ *They save every cent to insure that their children will be able to go to university.* 他们省下每一分钱，确保孩子们能上大学。Tāmen shěngxia měi yì fēn qián, quèbǎo háizi men néng shàng dàxué.

insurgency N 起义 qǐyì, 叛乱 pànluàn

insurgent N 起义者 qǐyìzhě, 叛乱分子 pànluàn fènzi

insurmountable ADJ 不可逾越的 bùkě yúyuè de, 不可克服的 bùkě kèfú de

insurrection N 起义 qǐyì, 暴动 bàodòng

insurrectionist N 起义者 qǐyìzhě, 暴动者 bàodòngzhě

intact ADJ 未被损伤的 wèi bèi sǔnshāng de, 完美无缺的 wánměi wúquē de

intake N 吸入（量）xīrù (liáng)

intangible ADJ 1 难以捉摸的 [+气氛] nányǐ zhuōmō de [+qìfen] 2 无形的 [+价值] wúxíng de [+jiàzhí]

integer N 整数 zhěngshù

integral ADJ 构成整体的 gòuchéng zhěngtǐ de

integrate v 1 使…结合 shǐ…jiéhé 2 使…融合 shǐ…rónghé

integrated ADJ 综合的 zōnghéde, 协调的 xiétiáo de

integrity N 1 诚信 chéngxìn, 正直 zhèngzhí
moral integrity 高尚的道德 gāoshàng de dàodé
2 完整 wánzhěng
territorial integrity（国家）领土完整（guójiā）lǐngtǔ wánzhěng

intelligence N 1 智力 zhìlì
intelligence quotient (IQ) 智商 zhìshāng
artificial intelligence 人工智能 réngōng zhìnéng
2 情报 qíngbào, 谍报 diébào
the Central Intelligence Agency (CIA)（美国）中央情报局（Měiguó）Zhōngyāng Qíngbàojú

intelligent ADJ 智力很高的 zhìlì hěn gāo de, 聪明的 cōngming de
intelligent life 智能生命 zhìnéng shēngmìng
intelligent terminal（计算机）智能终端（jìsuànjī）zhìnéng zhōngduān

intelligible ADJ 可以理解的 kěyǐ lǐjiě de, 明白易懂的 míngbai yìdǒng de

intend V 打算 dǎsuàn, 意图 yìtú

intense 1 强烈的 qiángliè de, 剧烈的 jùliè de 2 过于认真的 [+人] guòyú rènzhēn de [+rén]

intensify V 加强 jiāqiáng, 加剧 jiājù

intensity N 强度 qiángdù

intensive ADJ 深入的 shēnrù de, 彻底的 chèdǐ de

intent I N 目的意图 mùdì yìtú
for all intents and purposes 实际上 shíjìshàng
agreement of intent 意向书 yìxiàngshū
II ADJ (intent on (doing sth)) 决意（做某事）juéyì (zuòmǒushì)

intention N 打算 dǎsuàn, 意图 yìtú ■ What was their real intention? 他们的真实意图是什么? Tāmen de zhēnshí yìtú shì shénme?

intentional ADJ 故意的 gùyì de

intently ADV 全神贯注地 quánshén guànzhù de

inter V 埋葬 máizàng

interact V 互相起作用 hùxiāng qǐ zuòyòng, 互动 hùdòng

interaction N 互相影响 hùxiāng yǐngxiǎng, 互动 hùdòng

interactive ADJ 1 互相起作用的 hùxiāng qǐ zuòyòng de, 互相影响的 hùxiāng yǐngxiǎng de 2（人和计算机）互动的 (rén hé jìsuànjī) hùdòng de

intercede V 代为请求 dàiwéi qǐngqiú, 为…说情 wéi…shuōqíng

intercept V 拦截 lánjié, 截住 jiézhù

interception N 拦截 lánjié

intercession N 求情 qiúqíng, 说情 shuōqíng

interchange I N 1 交换 jiāohuàn, 互换 hùhuàn 2（公路上的）立体交叉道（gōnglù shàng de）lìtǐ jiāochādào II V 互换 hùhuàn, 互相替换 hùxiāng tìhuan

interchangeable ADJ 可以互换的 kěyǐ hùhuàn de

intercom N 内部通讯系统 nèibù tōngxùn xìtǒng, 对讲系统 duìjiǎng xìtǒng

intercontinental ADJ 洲际的 zhōujì de, 跨洲的 kuà zhōu de

intercourse N 1 性交 xìngjiāo 2 [感情的+] 沟通 [gǎnqíng de+] gōutōng, 交流 jiāoliú

interdependence N 相互依赖 xiānghù yīlài

interdependent ADJ 相互依赖的 xiānghù yīlài de

interest N 1 兴趣 xìngqu 2 利益 lìyì, 好处 hǎochu ■ Every country is entitled to safeguarding its national interests. 每个国家都有权保护自己的国家利益。Měi ge guójiā dōu yǒu quán bǎohù zìjǐ de guójiā lìyì. 3 利息 lìxī ■ The interest rate on our mortgage has risen from 7% to 10% in the past 12 months. 我们房屋贷款的利息在过去十二个月里从百分之七上升到百分之十。Wǒmen fángwū dàikuǎn de lìxī zài guòqù shí'èr ge yuè lǐ cóng bǎifēnzhī qī shàngshēngdao bǎifēnzhī shí.

interested ADJ 1 对…感兴趣 duì…gǎn xìngqu 2 有关系的 yǒu guānxi de
an interested party（利益）相关的一方 (lìyì) xiāngguān de yìfāng

interesting ADJ 有趣 yǒuqù, 有意思 yǒu yìsi

interface N 1（计算机）接口（jìsuànjī）jiēkǒu, 接口程序 jiēkǒu chéngxù 2 相互影响 xiānghù yǐngxiǎng

interfere V 干涉 gānshè, 干预 gānyù

interference N 干涉 gānshè, 干预 gānyù

interim I ADJ 临时的 línshí de II N (in the interim) 在此期间 zài cǐ qījiān

interior I N 1 内部 nèibù, 里面 lǐmian 2 室内 shìnèi II ADJ 内部的 nèibù de
interior design 室内装饰 shìnèi zhuāngshì

interject V 突然插话 tūrán chāhuà

interjection N 1 插话 chāhuà 2 感叹词 gǎntàncí

interlock V 使…连锁 shǐ…liánsuǒ, 使…连接 shǐ…liánjiē

interloper N 擅自闯入者 shànzì chuǎngrù zhě, 不速之客 búsù zhī kè

interlude N 插曲 chāqǔ, 间歇 jiànxiē

intermarriage N 通婚 tōnghūn

intermarry V 通婚 tōnghūn

intermediary I N 1 调解人 tiáojiěrén, 中间人 zhōngjiānrén 2 代表 dàibiǎo, 代理人 dàilǐrén II ADJ 1 中间的 zhōngjiān de 2 调解人的 tiáojiěrénde, 中间人的 zhōngjiānrén de

intermediate ADJ 中等的 zhōngděng de, 中间的 zhōngjiān de

interminable ADJ 冗长乏味的 rǒngcháng fáwèi de

intermission N 幕间休息 mùjiān xiūxi

intermittent ADJ 断断续续的 duànduàn xùxù de, 间歇的 jiànxiē de

intern N 实习医生 shíxí yīshēng, 实习人员 shíxí rényuán

intern² v 拘留 jūliú, 关押 guānyā
internal ADJ 1 内部 nèibù 2 国内 guónèi
internal medicine 内科 nèikē, 内科医学 nèikē yīxué
Internal Revenue Service (IRS) 税务局 shuìwùjú
international ADJ 国际的 guójì de ■ *The United Nations Organization is the most important international body in the world.* 联合国是世界上最重要的国际组织。Liánhéguó shì shìjièshang zuì zhòngyào de guójì zǔzhī.
Internet N 互联网 hùliánwǎng, 英特网 yīngtèwǎng ■ *Has your company registered an Internet domain name?* 你们公司登记了互联网网址了吗？Nǐmen gōngsī dēngjìle hùliánwǎng wǎngzhǐ le ma?
Internet service provider (ISP) 互联网服务提供者 hùliánwǎng fúwù tígōng zhě
Internet café 网吧 wǎngbā
Internet chat room 聊天室 liáotiānshì
internist N 内科医生 nèikē yīshēng
internship N 实习（期间）shíxí (qījiān)
interpersonal ADJ 人际的 rénjì de
interplanetary ADJ 星球之间的 xīngqiú zhījiān de, 球际的 qiú jì de
interplay N 相互作用 xiānghù zuòyòng
interpose v（使…）插入 (shǐ...) chārù
interpret v 1 翻译 fānyì, 当口译 dāng kǒuyì 2 解释 jiěshì ■ *The Supreme Court has the right to interpret the Constitution.* 最高法院有权解释宪法。Zuìgāo fǎyuàn yǒu quán jiěshì xiànfǎ.
interpretation N 解释 jiěshì, 说明 shuōmíng ■ *This new theory puts a different interpretation on such behaviors.* 这个新理论对这种行为做出了不同的解释。Zhè ge xīn lǐlùn duì zhè zhǒng xíngwéi zuòchūle bù tóng de jiěshì.
interpreter N 口译 kǒuyì, 译员 yìyuán
interracial ADJ 种族之间的 zhǒngzú zhījiān de
interrogate v 审讯 shěnxùn, 询问 xúnwèn
interrogation N 审讯 shěnxùn
interrogator N 审讯人员 shěnxùn rényuán
interrupt v 打断 dǎduàn ■ *The mayor's speech was interrupted by questions from the floor.* 市长的演说被来自观众席的问题打断。Shìzhǎng de yǎnshuō bèi láizì guānzhòngxí de wèntí dǎduàn.
intersect v 相交 xiāngjiāo, 交叉 jiāochā
intersection N 交叉口 jiāochākǒu, 交点 jiāodiǎn
intersession N 学期之间的假期 xuéqī zhījiān de jiàqī, 年中假期 niánzhōng jiàqī
intersperse v 散布 sànbù, 点缀 diǎnzhui
interstate I ADJ（美国）州际（的）(Měiguó) zhōujì (de) II N（美国）州际公路 (Měiguó) zhōujì gōnglù
intertwined ADJ 1 缠绕在一起的 chánrào zài yìqǐ de 2 紧密相关的 jǐnmì xiāngguān de
interval N 间歇 jiànxiē

at regular intervals 定期 dìngqī
intervene v 1 介入 jièrù, 干预 gānyù 2 阻扰 zǔrǎo, 阻碍 zǔ'ài
intervening ADJ（两个年份）之间的 (liǎng gè niánfèn) zhījiān de
intervention N 介入 jièrù, 干预 gānyù
interview N, v 1 采访 cǎifǎng ■ *The Secretary of State granted an interview to a journalist from the BBC.* 国务卿同意英国广播公司的记者采访他。Guówùqīng tóngyì Yīngguó Guǎngbō Gōngsī de jìzhě cǎifǎng tā. 2 面试 miànshì, 面谈 miàntán ■ *The chairman himself interviewed several candidates.* 董事长亲自面试了几位候选人。Dǒngshìzhǎng qīnzì miànshìle jǐ wèi hòuxuǎnrén.
job interview 求职面试 qiúzhí miànshì
interviewee N 1 被采访者 bèi cǎifǎngzhě 2 接受面试的人 jiēshòu miànshì de rén
interviewer N 1 采访者 cǎifǎngzhě 2 主持面试者 zhǔchí miànshì zhě
interweave v (PT **interwove**; PP **interwoven**) 交织（在一起）jiāozhī (zài yìqǐ)
intestinal ADJ 肠道的 chángdào de, 肠内的 cháng nèi de
intestine N 肠 cháng, 肠道 chángdào
large intestine 大肠 dàcháng
small intestine 小肠 xiǎocháng
intimacy N 1 亲密 qīnmì 2 性行为 xìng xíngwéi
intimacies 亲昵的言语行为 qīnnì de yányu xíngwéi
intimate ADJ 1 亲密的 qīnmì de 2 私人的 sīrén de, 隐私的 yǐnsī de
be intimate with sb 和某人发生性关系 hé mǒurén fāshēng xìng guānxi
intimation N 先兆 xiānzhào, 预兆 yùzhào
intimidate v 恫吓 dònghè, 威胁 wēixié
intimidation N 恫吓 dònghè, 威胁 wēixié
into PREP 进入 jìnrù, 到里面 dào lǐmian ■ *As soon as he went into the laboratory he smelled a pungent smell.* 他一进实验室，就闻到刺鼻的气味。Tā yí jìn shíyànshì, jiù wéndao cìbí de qìwèi.
intolerable ADJ 无法忍受的 wúfǎ rěnshòu de, 无法容忍的 wúfǎ róngrěn de
intolerance N 不容忍 bù róngrěn
intolerant ADJ 1 不能包容的 bùnéng bāoróng de, 心胸狭窄的 xīnxiōng xiázhǎi de 2 不能忍受的 bùnéng rěnróng de, 过敏的 guòmǐn de
lactose intolerant 对乳制品过敏的 duì rǔzhìpǐn guòmǐn de
intonation N 语调 yǔdiào
intoxicated ADJ 1 喝醉酒的 hēzuì jiǔ de 2 陶醉 táozuì, 冲昏头脑的 chōnghūn tóunǎo de
intoxication N 醉酒 zuìjiǔ
intractable ADJ 难解决的 nán jiějué de, 棘手的 jíshǒu de
intramural ADJ 校内的 xiào nèi de

intransigent ADJ 不让步的 bú ràngbù de, 不讲理的 bù jiǎnglǐ de

intransitive verb N 不及物动词 bùjíwù dòngcí

intravenous ADJ 静脉内的 jìngmài nèi de intravenous drug 静脉注射的药物 jìngmài zhùshè de yàowù

intrepid ADJ 勇敢的 yǒnggǎn de, 无畏的 wúwèi de

intricacy N 复杂 fùzá intricacies 复杂的细节 fùzá de xìjié

intricate ADJ 错综复杂的 cuòzōng fùzá de

intrigue I v 1 引起…的兴趣 / 好奇心 yǐnqǐ…de xìngqu/hàoqíxīn 2 策划阴谋 cèhuà yīnmóu II N 阴谋 yīnmóu, 密谋 mìmóu

intriguing ADJ 引人入胜的 yǐn rén rù shèng de

intrinsic ADJ 固有的 gùyǒu de, 内在的 nèizài de

introduce v 1 介绍 jièshào 2 引进 yǐnjìn ■ *This government has introduced a new immigration policy.* 这个政府引进了新的移民政策。Zhè ge zhèngfǔ yǐnjìnle xīn de yímín zhèngcè. 3 引导 yǐndǎo, 让…首次接触 ràng…shǒucì jiēchù ■ *It is Mr Wang, my Chinese teacher, who introduced me to Chinese chess.* 是王先生，我的中文老师，让我首次接触中国象棋。Shì Wáng xiānsheng, wǒ de Zhōngwén lǎoshī, ràng wǒ shǒucì jiēchù Zhōngguó xiàngqí.

introduction N 1 介绍 jièshào 2 引进 yǐnjìn 3 引论 yǐnlùn, 入门 rùmén "An Introduction to Sociology"《社会学引论》"Shèhuìxué Yǐnlùn"

introductory ADJ 入门的 rùmén de, 引言的 yǐnyán de an introductory course 入门课 rùmén kè an introductory essay 引言 yǐnyán

introspection N 反省 fǎnxǐng

introspective ADJ 反省的 fǎnxǐng de

introvert N 性格内向的人 xìnggé nèixiàng de rén

introverted ADJ 性格内向的 xìnggé nèixiàng de, 不爱交际的 bú ài jiāojì de

intrude v 侵扰 qīnrǎo, 侵入 qīnrù

intruder N 入侵者 rùqīnzhě

intrusion N 侵入 qīnrù, 侵扰 qīnrǎo

intrusive ADJ 侵扰的 qīnrǎo de, 打扰的 dǎrǎo de

intuition N 直觉 zhíjué

intuitive ADJ 直觉的 zhíjué de

inundate v 淹没 yānmò, 泛滥 fànlàn be inundated with [+letters] 收到大量 [+来信] shōudào dàliàng [+láixìn]

inundation N 泛滥 fànlàn

invade v 侵入 qīnrù, 侵略 qīnlüè

invader N 入侵者 rùqīnzhě, 侵略者 qīnlüèzhě

invalid I ADJ 1 无效的 [+合同] wúxiào de [+hétong] 2 站不住脚的 [+理由] zhànbuzhù jiǎo de [+lǐyóu] II N（慢性）病人（mànxìng）bìngrén

invalidate v 1 使 [+身份证] 无效 shǐ [+shēnfen-zhèng] wúxiào 2 证明 [+论点] 是错误的 zhèng-míng [+lùndiǎn] shì cuòwù de

invalidity N 无效 wúxiào

invaluable ADJ 不变的 wújià de, 极其宝贵的 jíqí bǎoguì de

invariable ADJ 不变的 búbiàn de, 一直的 yìzhí de

invasion N 侵入 qīnrù, 侵略 qīnlüè

invent v 1 发明 fāmíng 2 编造 [+谎言] biānzào [+huǎngyán], 捏造 niēzào

invention 1 发明（物）fāmíng（wù）2 编造 biānzào, 捏造 niēzào

inventive ADJ 善于发明的 shànyú fāmíng de, 有创造性的 yǒu chuàngzàoxìng de

inventor N 发明者 fāmíngzhě

inventory N 清单 qīngdān, 详细目录 xiángxì mùlù to take inventory 列出清单 lièchū qīngdān, 盘点（存货）pándiǎn（cúnhuò）

inverse N, ADJ 相反（的）xiāngfǎn de in inverse proportion to 与…成反比例 yǔ…chéng fǎnbǐlì

invert v 使…倒置 shǐ…dàozhì

invest v 1（商业）投资（shāngyè）tóuzī ■ *My grandma wouldn't invest directly in the stock market.* 我的奶奶不愿意直接投资股票市场。Wǒ de nǎinai bú yuànyì zhíjiē tóuzī gǔpiào shìchǎng. 2 投入 [+时间 / 金钱] tóurù [+shíjiān/jīnqián]

investigate v 调查 diàochá ■ *The police are investigating the cause of the fire.* 警方正在调查火灾的原因。Jǐngfāng zhèngzài diàochá huǒzāi de yuányīn.

investigation N 调查 diàochá ■ *A thorough investigation has revealed a dark secret.* 一场彻底的调查揭露了罪恶的秘密。Yì cháng chèdǐ de diàochá jiēlùle zuì'è de mìmì.

investment v 投资 tóuzī

inveterate ADJ 根深蒂固的 gēnshēn dìgù de, 难改的 nán gǎi de

invigorate v 使…生气勃勃 shǐ…shēngqì bóbó, 使…精力充沛 shǐ…jīnglì chōngpèi

invincible ADJ 不可战胜的 bùkě zhànshèng de, 不可征服的 bùkě zhēngfú de

invisibility N 隐形 yǐnxíng

invisible ADJ 看不见的 kànbujiàn de, 隐形的 yǐnxíng de

invitation N 1 邀请 yāoqǐng 2 请帖 qǐngtiě, 请柬 qǐngjiǎn ■ *Mary has sent out dozens of invitations to her birthday party.* 玛丽发出了几十份生日聚会邀请。Mǎlì fāchū le jǐ shí fèn shēngrì jùhuì yāoqǐng.

invite I v 1 邀请 yāoqǐng 2 招致 [+批评] zhāozhì [+pīpíng], 引起 yǐnqǐ II N 邀请 yāoqǐng

inviting ADJ 吸引人的 xīyǐnrén de, 诱人的 yòurén de

invoice I N 发货 / 工作清单 fāhuò/gōngzuò qīngdān [M. WD 张 zhāng/份 fèn] II v 发出发货 / 工作清单 fāchū fāhuò/gōngzuò qīngdān

invoke v 诉诉 [+法律] zhūsù [+fǎlǜ], 实施 shíshī

involuntary ADJ 不受意识控制的 bú shòu yìshi kòngzhì de, 不自觉的 bú zìjué de

involve v 1 涉及 shèjí ■ *This fraud case involves some local politicians and businessmen.* 这个舞弊案件涉及一些当地的政客和商人。Zhè ge wǔbì ànjiàn shèjí yìxiē dāngdì de zhèngkè hé shāngrén. **2** 需要 xūyào ■ *Working as a sales representative involves lots of travel.* 担任销售代表需要经常旅行。Dānrèn xiāoshòu dàibiǎo xūyào jīngcháng lǚxíng.

involved ADJ 与…有关的 yǔ...yǒuguān de

involvement N 涉及 shèjí, 牵连 qiānlián

inward ADJ **1** 内心的 nèixīn de **2** 向内的 xiàng nèi de

iodine (I) N 碘 diǎn

ion N 离子 lízǐ

iota N 极少量 jí shǎoliàng
not one iota 一点也不/没有 yìdiǎn yě bù/méiyǒu

IOU (= I owe you) ABBREV 借条 jiètiáo [M. WD 张 zhāng]

IQ (= Intelligence Quotient) ABBREV 智商 zhìshāng

irascible ADJ 脾气暴躁的 píqi bàozao de, 脾气很坏的 píqí hěn huài de

irate ADJ 极为愤怒的 jíwéi fènnù de

iridescence N 彩虹色 cǎihóngsè

iridescent ADJ 变色的 biànsè de, 彩虹色的 cǎihóngsè de

iris N **1** 虹膜 hóngmó **2** 鸢尾属植物 yuānwěishǔ zhíwù

Irish I ADJ 爱尔兰的 Ài'ěrlán de **II** N **1** 爱尔兰人 Ài'ěrlánrén **2** 爱尔兰语 Ài'ěrlányǔ

irk v 使…恼怒 shǐ...nǎonù, 使…气恼 shǐ...qìnǎo

irksome ADJ 让人烦恼的 rang rén fánnǎode, 恼人的 nǎorén de

iron I N **1** 铁 tiě ■ *Red meat is rich in iron.* 牛羊肉含有丰富的铁质。Niúyángròu hányǒu fēngfùde tiězhì. **2** 熨斗 yùndǒu
ironing board 熨衣板 yùnyībǎn
Strike while the iron is hot. 趁热打铁。Chèn rè dǎ tiě.
II ADJ 铁的 tiě de **III** v 熨烫 [+衣服] yùntàng [+yīfu]

ironic ADJ 有讽刺意味的 yǒu fěngcì yìwèi de

irony N 讽刺 fěngcì

irrational ADJ 不合理的 bù hélí de

irrationality N 不合理 bù hélí

irreconcilable ADJ 不可调和的 bùkě tiáohe de, 不相容的 bù xiāngróng de

irrefutable ADJ 无可辩驳的 wúkě biànbó de

irregular ADJ **1** 不规则的 bù guīzé de **2** 不定时的 bú dìngshí de
irregular verb（英语）不规则动词 (Yīngyǔ) bùguīzé dòngcí

irregular heart beats 心率不齐 xīnlǜ bù qí

irregularity N **1** 不规则 bùguīzé **2** 违规行为 wéiguī xíngwéi, 违规 wéiguī

irrelevance N 不相关 bù xiāngguān, 无关 wúguān

irrelevant ADJ 不相关的 bù xiāngguān de, 无关的 wúguān de

irreparable ADJ 无法弥补的 wúfǎ míbǔ de

irreplaceable ADJ 不可代替的 bùkě dàitì de, 独一无二的 dúyī wú'èr de

irreproachable ADJ 无可指责的 wúkě zhǐzé de, 没有过失的 méiyǒu guòshī de

irresistible ADJ 无法抗拒的 wúfǎ kàngjù de

irrespective of PREP 不管 bùguǎn, 不顾 búgù

irresponsible ADJ 不负责任的 bú fù zérèn de, 没有责任心的 méiyǒu zérènxīn de

irreverence N 不敬 bújìng, 不恭 bùgōng

irreverent ADJ 不尊敬的 bù zūnjìng de, 不谦恭的 bù qiāngōng de

irreversible ADJ 不可逆转的 bùkě nìzhuǎn de, 不可挽回的 bùkě wǎnhuí de

irrevocable ADJ 不可更改的 bùkě gēnggǎi de, 不可取消的 bùkě qǔxiāo de

irrigate v 灌溉 guàngài

irrigation N 灌溉 guàngài

irritable ADJ **1** 易怒的 [+老人] yì nù de [+lǎorén] **2** 疼痛的 [+伤口] téngtòng de [+shāngkǒu]

irritant N **1** 让人恼火的事 ràng rén nǎohuǒ de shì **2** 刺激物 cìjīwù

irritate v **1** 使 [+人] 恼怒 shǐ [+rén] nǎonù **2** 使 [+伤口] 发炎 shǐ [+shāngkǒu] fāyán **3** 使…疼痛 shǐ...téngtòng

irritation N **1** 恼火 nǎohuǒ, 恼怒 nǎonù **2** 让人恼火的事 ràng rén nǎohuǒ de shì **3** 疼痛 téngtòng, 发炎 fāyán

IRS ABBREV See **Internal Revenue Service**

is See be

Islam N 伊斯兰 Yīsīlán, 伊斯兰教 Yīsīlánjiào

island N 岛 dǎo

islander N 岛上的居民 dǎo shàng de jūmín, 岛民 dǎomín

isle N 岛 dǎo

isolate v **1** 隔离 [+病人] gélí [+bìngrén] **2** 分离 [+物质] fēnlí [+wùzhì] **3** 孤立 [+敌人] gūlì [+dírén]

isolated ADJ **1** 孤立的 gūlì de **2** 孤零零的 gūlínglíng de
an isolated incident 孤立的事件 gūlì de shìjiàn
an isolated island（大洋中）一个孤零零的小岛 (dàyáng zhōng) yí ge gūlínglíng de xiǎodǎo

isolation N 隔离 gélí
isolation ward 隔离病房 gélíbìngfáng

ISP (= Internet service provider) ABBREV See **Internet**

issue I N **1** 有争论的问题 yǒu zhēnglùn de wèntí,

问题 wèntí ■ *There are a number of issues that need further discussion.* 有一些问题需要进一步讨论。Yǒu yìxiē wèntí xūyào jìnyíbù tǎolùn. **2**（杂志）期 (zázhì) qī

to take issue with 不同意 bù tóngyì, 有争议 yǒu zhēngyì

II v 1 发表 [+声明] fābiǎo [+shēngmíng] **2** 发行 [+邮票] fāxíng [+yóupiào] **3** 分发 [+枪支] fēnfā [+qiāngzhī]

IT (= information technology) ABBREV See **information**

it PRON 它 tā

Italian I ADJ 意大利的 Yìdàlì de **II** N **1** 意大利语 Yìdàlìyǔ **2** 意大利人 Yìdàlìrén

italicize v 用斜体字写 yòng xiétǐzì xiě

italics N 斜体字 xiétǐzì

itch I v 痒 yǎng, 发痒 fāyǎng **II** N **1** 痒 yǎng, 发痒 fāyǎng **2** 渴望 kěwàng

item N **1** 项目 xiàngmù, 条目 tiáomù ■ *The first item on the agenda is recruitment of new members.* 议事日程的第一项是吸收新会员。Yìshì rìchéng de dìyī xiàng shì xīshōu xīn huìyuán. **2** 一条新闻 yì tiáo xīnwén

itemize v 一项一项地记下 yí xiàng yí xiàng de jìxià, 分项记载 fēnxiàng jìzǎi

itemized ADJ 逐项分列的 zhúxiàng fēnliè de

itinerant ADJ 流动的 liúdòng de

itinerant circus 流动马戏团 liúdòng mǎxìtuán

itinerary N 旅行日程表 lǚxíng rìchéngbiǎo

to plan an itinerary 计划旅行日程 jìhuà lǚxíng rìchéng

its ADJ 它的 tā de

itself PRON 它自己 tā zìjǐ

IV (= intravenous) ABBREV 静脉滴注 jìngmài dī zhù

ivory N **1** 象牙 xiàngyá

ivory tower 象牙塔 xiàngyá tǎ

the ivories 钢琴键 gāngqín jiàn

2 象牙色 xiàngyá sè

ivy N 常青藤 chángqīng téng [M. WD 颗 kē/条 tiáo]

Ivy League（美国）常青藤联盟大学 (Měiguó) chángqīng téng liánméng dàxué

J

jab I v 1 刺 cì, 猛击 měngjī **2** 打针 dǎzhēn, 注射 zhùshè **II** N 批评（的话）pīpíng (de huà), 责备（的话）zébèi (de huà)

to take a jab at 抨击 pēngjī

jabber v 激动地说 jīdòng de shuō

jack I N **1** 起重器 qǐzhòng qì, 千斤顶 qiānjīndǐng **2**（纸牌）杰克牌 (zhǐpái) jiékè pái, J 牌 J pái **II** v (to jack up)（用起重器）顶起 [+重物] (yòng qǐzhòngqì) dǐng qǐ [+zhòngwù]

jackal N 豺 chái, 胡狼 húláng [M. WD 只 zhī/条 tiáo]

jackass N 讨厌的蠢货 tǎoyàn de chǔnhuò

jacket N **1** 上衣 shàngyī [M. WD 件 jiàn], 夹克衫 jiākèshān [M. WD 件 jiàn] **2** 护封 hùfēng, 书套 shūtào **3** 保护罩 bǎohùzhào

jackhammer N 风钻 fēngzuān

jack-in-the-box N 玩偶盒 wán'ǒuhé

jack-knife N 折刀 zhédāo [M. WD 把 bǎ] **II** v 弯曲 wānqū

jack-of-all-trades N 博而不精的人 bó ér bù jīng de rén, 万事通 wànshìtōng

jack-o-lantern N 南瓜灯笼 nánguā dēnglong

jackpot N 一大笔钱 yí dà bǐ qián

to hit the jackpot ① 赢得大奖 yíngdé dàjiǎng, 中头彩 zhòng tóucǎi ②（突然）交上好运 (tūrán) jiāo shàng hǎoyùn

jade N 玉 yù, 碧玉 bìyù, 翡翠 fěicuì

jaded ADJ 厌倦的 yànjuàn de, 没有激情的 méiyǒu jīqíng de

jagged ADJ 锯齿状 jùchǐzhuàng

jaguar N 美洲豹 Měizhōubào [M. WD 只 zhī]

jail I N **1** 监狱 jiānyù **2** 看守所 kānshǒusuǒ **II** v 监禁 jiānjìn

jailor, jailer N 监狱看守 jiānyù kānshǒu

jam I N **1** 果酱 guǒjiàng **2** 交通堵塞 jiāotōng dǔsè **II** v **1** [车辆+] 堵塞 [chēliàng+] dǔsè **2** 把…塞进 bǎ…sāijìn

to jam on the brakes 猛踩刹车 měng cǎi shāchē

jamboree N **1** 童子军大会 tóngzǐjūn dàhuì **2** 喧闹的大会 xuānnào de dàhuì

jammed ADJ **1** 挤满 [+人] 的 jǐmǎn [+rén] de **2** 塞满 [+东西] 的 sāimǎn [+dōngxi] de **3** 卡住的 [+锁] qiǎzhù de [+suǒ]

jam-packed ADJ **1** 挤满 [+人] 的 jǐmǎn [+rén] de **2** 塞满 [+东西] 的 sāimǎn [+dōngxi] de

jam session N（爵士乐/摇滚乐）即兴演奏会 (juéshìyuè/yáogǔnyuè) jíxìng yǎnzòu huì

Jane Doe N 某女 mǒu nǚ, 一名女性 yì míng nǚxìng

jangle I v（使金属）发出丁零当啷声 (shǐ jīnshǔ) fāchū dīnglíng dānglāng shēng **II** N 刺耳的金属当啷声 cì'ěr de jīnshǔ dānglāngshēng

janitor N（照管房屋的）工人 (zhàoguǎn fángwū de) gōngrén, 工友 gōngyǒu

school janitor 校工 xiàogōng

January N 一月 yīyuè ■ *January 1st is the New Year's Day.* 一月一日是元旦。Yīyuè yīrì shì Yuándàn.

Japanese I ADJ 日本的 Rìběn de **II** N **1** 日语 Rìyǔ **2** 日本人 Rìběnrén

jar I N 广口瓶 guǎngkǒupíng, 罐子 guànzi **II** v **1** 使…烦乱 shǐ…fánluàn **2** 碰伤 pèngshāng

jargon N 行话 hánghuà, 专门术语 zhuānmén shùyǔ

jaundice N 黄疸病 huángdǎnbìng

jaundiced ADJ **1** 患黄疸病的 huàn huángdǎnbìng de **2** 有偏见的 yǒu piānjiàn de

jaunt N 短途旅游 duǎntú lǚyóu

javelin N 标枪 biāoqiāng
javelin 掷标枪（运动）zhì biāoqiāng (yùndòng), 标枪投掷（运动）biāoqiāng tóuzhì (yùndòng)

jaw N **1** 颌 gé, 上下颌 shàng xià gé **2** 下巴 xiàba

jaws N **1**（猛兽的）嘴（měngshòu de）zuǐ **2** 钳口 qiánkǒu
jaws of death 生死关头 shēngsǐ guāntóu

jaywalking N 乱穿马路 luàn chuān mǎlù

jazz I N 爵士（音）乐 juéshì (yīn) yuè II V (to jazz up) 使…更有吸引力 shǐ...gèng yǒu xīyǐnlì

jazzed ADJ 兴奋的 xīngfèn de

jazzy ADJ **1** 鲜艳的 xiānyàn de **2** 爵士风格的 juéshì fēnggé de

jealous ADJ 妒嫉的 dùjì de

jealousy N 妒嫉（的行为）dùjì (de xíngwéi) ■ *His promotion caused jealousy among his colleagues.* 他的提升在同事中引起了妒嫉。Tā de tíshēng zài tóngshì zhōng yǐnqǐle dùjì.

jeans N 牛仔裤 niúzǎikù [M. WD 条 tiáo]

jeep N 吉普车 jípǔchē [M. WD 辆 liàng]

jeer I V 嘲笑 cháoxiào, 哄笑 hōngxiào II N 嘲笑 cháoxiào

jeez INTERJ 哎呀 āiyā

jelly N 果酱 guǒjiàng, 果冻 guǒdòng

jellyfish N 海蜇 hǎizhé, 水母 shuǐmǔ

jeopardize V 使…陷入危险境地 shǐ...xiànrù wēixiǎn jìngdì

jeopardy N 危险（的境地）wēixiǎn (de jìngdì)
in jeopardy 处于险境 chǔyú xiǎnjìng

jerk¹ I V 猛地一动 měng de yídòng II N 猛拉 měng lā

jerk² N 蠢人 chǔnrén, 鲁莽的人 lǔmǎng de rén

jerky¹ ADJ 忽动忽停的 hūdòng hūtíng de, 晃动的 huàngdòng de

jerky² ADJ 熏肉条 xūnròutiáo, 肉干 ròugān

jersey N **1** 运动衫 yùndòngshān [M. WD 件 jiàn] **2** 针织弹力衫 zhēnzhī tánlì shān [M. WD 件 jiàn]

jest I N 笑话 xiàohua, 俏皮话 qiàopihuà
in jest 开玩笑地 kāiwánxiào de
II V 说笑话 shuō xiàohua, 开玩笑 kāi wánxiào

jester N（宫廷）小丑（gōngtíng）xiǎochǒu, 弄臣 nòngchén

Jesus (Jesus Christ) N 耶稣（基督）Yēsū (Jīdū)

jet I N **1** 喷气式飞机 pēnqìshì fēijī [M. WD 架 jià]
jet engine 喷气发动机 pēnqì fādòngjī
jet lag 时差反应 shíchā fǎnyìng
jet set 常乘飞机的富人 cháng chéng fēijī de fùrén
jet stream 高空急流 gāokōng jíliú
2 喷射流 pēnshèliú **3** 黑玉 hēi yù II V **1** 乘喷气式飞机 chéng pēnqìshì fēijī **2** 喷射 pēnshè

jetblack ADJ 乌黑的 wūhēi de

jettison V 丢弃 diūqì, 摆脱 bǎituō

jetty N **1** 小码头 xiǎo mǎtou **2** 防波堤 fángbōdī

Jew N 犹太人 Yóutàirén

jewel N 珠宝 zhūbǎo, 宝石 bǎoshí
jewel box 首饰盒 shǒushihé

jeweler N 珠宝商 zhūbǎoshāng
jeweler's 珠宝商店 zhūbǎo shāngdiàn, 首饰店 shǒushidiàn

jewelry N 珠宝 zhūbǎo, 首饰 shǒushi ■ *A wedding ring is more than a piece of jewelry.* 结婚戒指不仅仅是一件首饰。Jiéhūn jièzhǐ bù jǐnjǐn shì yí jiàn shǒushi.

Jewish ADJ 犹太人的 Yóutàirén de, 犹太的 Yóutài de

jibe¹ N, V 挖苦 wāku, 嘲弄 cháonòng

jibe² V 相一致 xiāng yízhì, 符合 fúhé

jig N 吉格舞（曲）jí gé wǔ (qū)

jiggle V（使…）快速移动（shǐ...）kuàisù yídòng

jigsaw puzzle N 拼图（玩具）pīn tú (wánjù)

jihad N（伊斯兰教）圣战（Yīsīlánjiào）shèngzhàn

jilt V 突然抛弃情人 tūrán pāoqì qíngrén, 突然断交 tūrán duànjiāo

jingle I V（使…）发出叮当的声响（shǐ...）fāchū dīngdāng de shēngxiǎng II N **1** 叮当声 dīngdāng shēng [M. WD 阵 zhèn] **2** 短歌 duǎn gē [M. WD 首 shǒu]

jinx N **1** 不详的人 bùxiángde rén, 不详的事 bùxiángde shì **2** 倒霉的时期 dǎoméi de shíqī

jinxed ADJ 倒霉的 dǎoméi de, 交恶运的 jiāo èyùn de

jitters N 紧张不安 jǐnzhāng bù'ān, 焦虑 jiāolǜ

jittery ADJ 紧张不安的 jǐnzhāng bù'ān de, 焦虑的 jiāolǜ de

jive I N 摇摆舞 yáobǎiwǔ II V 跳摇摆舞 tiào yáobǎiwǔ

job N **1** 职业 zhíyè, 工作 gōngzuò
job description 工作职责范围 gōngzuò zhízé fànwéi
job hunting 寻找工作 xúnzhǎo gōngzuò
job security 工作保障 gōngzuò bǎozhàng
2 职责 zhízé, 任务 rènwu ■ *It is Mr Brown's job as school janitor to lock the gate in the evening.* 晚上给大门上锁是学校工友布朗先生的职责。Wǎnshang gěi dàmén shàngsuǒ shì xuéxiào gōngyǒu Bùlǎng xiānsheng de zhízé.
to do a good job 做得好 zuò de hǎo
an insider job 内部作案 nèibù zuò'àn, 监守自盗 jiānshǒu zì dào

jobless ADJ 没有工作的 méiyǒu gōngzuò de, 失业的 shīyè de

jockey I N 赛马骑师 sàimǎ qíshī II V **1**〔赛马骑师+〕骑马〔sàimǎ qíshī+〕qímǎ **2** 激烈争夺 [+职位] jīliè zhēngduó [+zhíwèi]

jockstrap N 下体护身 xiàtǐ hùshēn, 护裆 hù dàng

jocular ADJ 爱说笑的 ài shuōxiào de
jog I v 1 慢长跑 màn chángpǎo, 跑步 pǎobù
2 轻碰 qīngpèng, 轻推 qīng tuī
to jog sb's memory 唤起某人的记忆 huànqǐ mǒurén de jìyì
II N 1 慢长跑 màn chángpǎo, 慢跑 mànpǎo
2 轻碰 qīngpèng, 轻推 qīng tuī
jogger N 慢跑健身者 màn pǎo jiànshēnzhě
jogging N 健身慢跑 jiànshēn mànpǎo
john N 1 厕所 cèsuǒ 2 嫖客 piáokè
John Doe N 某男 mǒu nán, 一名男性 yì míng nánxìng
join v 1 参加 cānjiā 2 跟⋯⋯一起 gēn...yìqǐ
■ We're going out for lunch. Why don't you join us? 我们出去吃中饭。干吗不跟我们一块儿去呢? Wǒmen chūqù chī zhōngfàn. Gànmá bù gēn wǒmen yíkuàir qù ne? 3 连接 liánjiē, 结合 jiéhé
joint I ADJ 联合的 liánhé de, 联名的 liánmíng de ■ The house is under joint ownership of the couple. 住房是夫妻联名所有的。Zhùfáng shì fūqī liánmíng suǒyǒu de.
joint bank account 联名银行账户 liánmíng yínháng zhànghù
Joint Chiefs of Staff (美国)参谋长联席会议 (Měiguó) cānmóuzhǎng liánxí huìyì
II N 1 关节 guānjié ■ He suffers from stiff joints. 他的关节不灵活。Tā de guānjié bù línghuó. 2 结合部 jiéhébù, 连接处 liánjiēchù 3 (含有大麻的)香烟 (hányǒu dàmá de) xiāngyān 4 酒吧 jiǔbā, 饭店 fàndiàn
jointly ADV 联合地 liánhé de
joint venture N 合资企业 hézī qǐyè [M. WD 家 jiā]
joke I N 1 笑话 xiàohua, 玩笑 wánxiào
to play a practical joke 搞恶作剧 gǎo èzuòjù
II v 说笑话 shuō xiàohua
joker N 1 小丑 xiǎochǒu 2 (纸牌)百搭牌 (zhǐpái) bǎidà pái [M. WD 张 zhāng]
jokingly ADV 开玩笑地 kāi wánxiào de, 不是一本正经地 bú shì yìběnzhèngjīng de
jolly ADJ 高兴的 gāoxìng de, 快活的 kuàihuo de
jolt I N (突然的)震动 (tūrán de) zhèndòng
II v 使⋯⋯震动 shǐ...zhèndòng
jostle v 推挤 tuǐjǐ, 拥挤 yōngjǐ
jot v (草草)记下 (cǎocǎo) jìxià
journal N 1 报刊 bàokān, 期刊 qīkān 2 日志 rìzhì, 日记 rìjì
journalism N 新闻事业 xīnwén shìyè, 新闻工作 xīnwén gōngzuò
journalist N (新闻)记者 (xīnwén) jìzhě
journey I N (长途)旅行 (chángtú) lǚxíng ■ A Chinese proverb goes that a journey of a 1,000 miles starts with one step. 中国有一句谚语说,"千里之行, 始于足下。" Zhōngguó yǒu yí jù yànyǔ shuō, "Qiānlǐ zhī xíng, shǐ yú zúxià." II v 旅行 lǚxíng

jovial ADJ 快活友善的 kuàihuo yǒushàn de, 快快乐乐的 kuàikuài lèlè de
jowls N 下颌 xiàgé
joy N 1 极大的快乐 jídà de kuàilè, 欢愉 huānyú 2 欢愉的事 huānyú de shì
joyful ADJ 快乐的 kuàilè de, 令人欢愉 lìng rén huānyú de
joyous ADJ 欢乐的 huānlè de
joyriding N 偷车兜风 tōu chē dōufēn
joystick N (电脑游戏/飞机)操纵杆 (diànnǎo yóuxì/fēijī) cāozònggǎn
jubilant ADJ 兴高采烈的 xìnggāo cǎiliè de, 狂欢的 kuánghuān de
jubilation N 欢乐 huānlè, 狂欢 kuánghuān
jubilee N (25/50)周年纪念日 (èrshíwǔ/wǔshí) zhōunián jìniàn rì
Judaism N 犹太教 Yóutàijiào, 犹太文化 Yóutài wénhuà
Judas N 犹大 Yóudà, 叛徒 pàntú
judge I N 1 法官 fǎguān [M. WD 位 wèi] 2 裁判 cáipàn [M. WD 位 wèi] ■ The judge of the gymnastic event was less than fair. 这位体操裁判不够公正。Zhè wèi tǐcāo cáipàn bú gòu gōngzhèng. 3 (对某事有/没有)判断能力的人 (duì mǒushì yǒu/méiyǒu) pànduàn nénglì de rén
a good judge of character 能识人的人 néng shí rén de rén
II v 1 判断 pànduàn ■ You should not judge people by the way they dress. 不应该以衣衫取人。Bù yīnggāi yǐ yīshān qǔrén. 2 审判 [+案件] shěnpàn [+ànjiàn], 审理 shěnlǐ
judgment N 1 判断(力) pànduàn (lì) ■ I have every confidence in your judgment. 我完全信任你的判断。Wǒ wánquán xìnrèn nǐ de pànduàn.
poor judgment 判断错误 pànduàn cuòwù
2 判决 pànjué
judgmental ADJ 爱批评他人的 ài pīpíng tārén de, 评头品足 píng tóu pǐn zú
Judgment Day N (基督教)最后审判日 (Jīdūjiào) zuìhòu shěnpàn rì
judicial ADJ 法庭的 fǎtíng de
judicial branch 司法部门的 sīfǎ bùmén de
judiciary N 司法部门 sīfǎ bùmén
judicious ADJ 审慎的 shěnshèn de, 明智的 míngzhì de
judo N 柔道 róudào
jug N (水)壶 (shuǐ) hú
juggle v 1 杂耍 záshuǎ 2 应付 [+很多工作] yìngfu [+hěn duō gōngzuò] 3 玩弄 [+数字] wánnòng [+shùzì]
juggler N 杂耍演员 záshuǎ yǎnyuán
jugular N 颈静脉 jǐngjìngmài
to go for the jugular 激烈攻击 jīliè gōngjī
juice I N 1 果汁 guǒzhī, 菜汁 càizhī 2 肉汁 ròuzhī
II v 榨(果汁) zhà (guǒzhī)

juicy ADJ 多汁的 duō zhī de, 多液的 duō yè de

juke box N 投币自动唱机 tóu bì zìdòng chàngjī [M. WD 台 tái]

July N 七月 qīyuè

jumble I N 杂乱的一堆 záluàn de yìduī II V 使…杂乱 shǐ…záluàn

jumbo ADJ 特大(号)的 tèdà (hào) de
jumbo jet 巨型喷气式客机 jùxíng pēnqìshì kèjī

jump I V 1 跳 tiào, 跳跃 tiàoyuè ▪ *It was a horrible sight to see people jumping out of windows during the fire.* 在大火中人们跳出窗口，这真是可怕的景象。Zài dàhuǒ zhōng rénmen tiàochu chuāngkǒu, zhè zhēn shì kěpà de jǐngxiàng. 2 猛增 měngzēng, 暴涨 bàozhǎng II N 1 跳 tiào, 跳跃 tiàoyuè
jump rope 跳绳 tiàoshéng
2 猛增 měngzēng, 暴涨 bàozhǎng

jumper N 1 无袖连衣裙 wú xiù liányīqún 2 (篮球) 跳投 (lánqiú) tiàotóu
jumper cable 启动连线 qǐdòng liánxiàn

jump-start V 1 (用启动连线) 发动 [+汽车] (yòng qǐdòng liánxiàn) fādòng [+qìchē] 2 帮助启动 [+项目] bāngzhù qǐdòng [+xiàngmù], 推动 tuīdòng

jumpsuit N 女式连衫裤 nǚshì liánshānkù [M. WD 套 tào]

jumpy ADJ 心惊肉跳的 xīn jīng ròu tiào de

junction N 交叉(口) jiāochā (kǒu)

juncture N (特定)时刻 (tèdìng) shíkè, 当口 dāngkǒu

June N 六月 liùyuè

jungle N 丛林 cónglín

junior I ADJ 地位较低的 dìwèi jiào dī de
junior college 两年制专科学院 liǎngniánzhì zhuānkē xuéyuàn
junior high school 初级中学 chūjí zhōngxué, 初中 chūzhōng
II N 1 (中学/大学) 三年级学生 (zhōngxué/dàxué) sānniánjí xuésheng
be two/three/four years one's junior 比某人小两/三/四岁 bǐ mǒurén xiǎo liǎng/sān/sì suì 2 年纪较小的人 niánjì jiàoxiǎo de rén ▪ *His wife is 10 years his junior.* 他的妻子比他小十岁。Tā de qīzi bǐ tā xiǎo shí suì.

junk I N 1 垃圾货 lājīhuò, 无用的旧东西 wúyòng de jiù dōngxī
junk bond 垃圾股票 lājī gǔpiào
junk food 垃圾食品 lājī shípǐn
junk mail 垃圾邮件 lājī yóujiàn
2 中国式帆船 Zhōngguóshì fānchuán II V 废弃 fèiqì

junket N 公费旅游 gōngfèi lǚyóu

junta N 军政府 jūnzhèngfǔ

Jupiter N 木星 Mùxīng

jurisdiction N 管辖(权) guǎnxiá (quán), 司法 (权) sīfǎ (quán)

juror N 陪审团成员 péishěntuán chéngyuán

jury N 1 陪审团 péishěntuán
The jury is still out. 还没有定论。Hái méiyǒu dìnglùn.
foreman of the jury 陪审团团长 péishěntuán tuánzhǎng
member of the jury 陪审员 péishěnyuán
2 (比赛) 评判委员会 (bǐsài) píngpàn wěiyuánhuì

just[1] ADV 1 正是 zhèng shì
just then 正在那时 zhèngzài nàshí
2 正要 zhèng yào, 刚要 gāng yào 3 仅仅 jǐnjǐn, 只是 zhǐ shì ▪ *I just want to remind you of this.* 我只是想提醒你这件事。Wǒ zhǐ shì xiǎng tíxǐng nǐ zhè jiàn shì. 4 刚才 gāngcái, 刚刚 gānggāng

just[2] ADJ 公正的 gōngzhèng de ▪ *It was a just punishment to sentence him to five-year imprisonment.* 判他五年徒刑，是公正的惩罚。Pàn tā wǔ nián túxíng, shì gōngzhèng de chéngfá.

justice N 1 公正 gōngzhèng, 正义 zhèngyì 2 司法 sīfǎ ▪ *Do you believe in the justice system of this country?* 你信任这个国家的司法制度吗？Nǐ xìnrèn zhè ge guójiā de sīfǎ zhìdù ma? 3 法官 fǎguān [M. WD 位 wèi]
Justice of the Peace 太平绅士 tàipíng shēnshì

justifiable ADJ 情有可原 qíng yǒu kěyuán

justification N (正当)理由 (zhèngdàng) lǐyóu

justified ADJ 有(正当)理由的 yǒu (zhèngdàng) lǐyóu de, 有道理的 yǒudào lǐ de

justify V 证明…有理由 zhèngmíng…yǒu lǐyóu, 证明…合理 zhèngmíng…hélǐ

jut V 突出 tūchū, 伸出 shēnchū

juvenile I ADJ 1 青少年的 qīngshàonián de
juvenile delinquent 青少年罪犯 qīngshàonián zuìfàn
2 幼稚的 yòuzhì de, 不成熟的 bù chéngshú de II N 青少年 qīngshàonián

juxtapose V 把…放在一起 bǎ…fàng zài yīqǐ, 并列 bìngliè

juxtaposition N (把不同的东西)并列 (bǎ bùtóng de dōngxi) bìngliè

K

kabob, kebab N 烤肉串 kǎoròuchuàn

kaleidoscope N 1 万花筒 wànhuātǒng 2 千变万化 qiānbiàn wànhuà, 多姿多彩 duōzī duōcǎi

kangaroo N 袋鼠 dàishǔ

kaput ADJ 坏了的 huàile de

karaoke N 卡拉OK kǎlā OK

karat [British **carat**] N 开 kāi, K
22 karat 22 开(黄金) 22 kāi (huángjīn), 22 K (黄金) 22 K (huángjīn)

karate N 空手道 kōngshǒudào

karma N 因果报应 yīnguǒ bàoyìng, 命运 mìngyùn

kayak N 小艇 xiǎotǐng [M. WD 艘 sōu]

keel I N (to stay on an even keel) 保持平稳 bǎochí píngwěn II v (to keel over) 翻倒 fāndǎo, 倒下 dǎoxià

keen ADJ 1 热切的 rèqiè de, 非常希望的 fēicháng xīwàng de 2 敏捷的 [+头脑] mǐnjié de [+tóunǎo] 3 敏锐的 [+眼力] mǐnruì de [yǎnlì]

keenly ADV 敏锐地 mǐnruì de, 强烈地 qiánglìè de

keep I v (PT & PP **kept**) 1 保有 bǎoyǒu, 留下 liúxià ■ *Keep the change.* 留下找头。（→不用 找了。）Liúxià zhǎotou. (→Bú yòng zhǎo le.)
to keep a diary 记日记 jì rìjì
to keep one's promise 实现诺言 shíxiàn nuòyán ■ *Be slow to make a promise, but once you've made it, keep it.* 不要轻易许诺，但是一旦 承诺，就要做到。Bú yào qīngyì xǔnuò, dànshì yídàn chéngnuò, jiù yào zuòdào.
2 留住 liúzhù, 保留 bǎoliú 3 一直 yìzhí, 老是 lǎoshi ■ *Why do you keep asking me the same question?* 你为什么老是问我同样的问题？Nǐ wèishénme lǎoshi wèn wǒ tóngyàng de wèntí? ■ *Don't keep grumbling.* 别老是抱怨。Bié lǎoshi bàoyuàn.
to keep ... from doing ... 不让…做… búràng... zuò...
to keep up 继续 jìxù, 保持 bǎochí
to keep up with 跟上 gēnshang ■ *It is not easy to keep up with the rapid changes of technology.* 要跟上迅速变化的技术，不是容易的。Yào gēnshang xùnsù biànhuà de jìshù, bú shì róngyì de.
Keep Out! 不准入内! Bùzhǔn rùnèi!
to keep fit 保持健康 bǎochí jiànkāng
II N 生活费 shēnghuófèi
to earn one's keep 养活自己 yǎnghuo zìjǐ, 谋生 móushēng

keeper N 1 (动物) 饲养员 (dòngwù) sìyǎngyuán 2 (财产) 管理者 (cáichǎn) guǎnlǐzhě

keeping N 保持 bǎochí
in keeping with 与…一致 yǔ...yízhì

keepsake N 纪念品 jìniànpǐn

keg N 大 (啤酒) 圆桶 dà (píjiǔ) yuántǒng

kennel N 1 狗窝 gǒuwō 2 养狗场 yǎnggǒucháng

kept See **keep**

kernel N 1 果仁 guǒ rén, 果核 guǒhé 2 要点 yàodiǎn
kernel of truth 主要事实 zhǔyào shìshí, 要点 yàodiǎn

kerosene N 煤油 méiyóu

ketchup N 番茄酱 fānqiéjiàng

kettle N 水壶 shuǐhú

key I N 1 钥匙 yàoshi

key ring 钥匙圈 yàoshiquān
spare key 备用钥匙 bèiyòng yàoshi
skeleton key 万能钥匙 wànnéng yàoshi
2 键 jiàn ■ *Hit these keys to log off your computer.* 要关计算机，按这几个键。Yào guān jìsuànjī, àn zhè jǐ ge jiàn. 3 关键 guānjiàn ■ *The key to successful language learning is constant practice.* 成功地学好语言的关键是经常练习。Chénggōng de xuéhǎo yǔyán de guānjiàn shì jīngcháng liànxí. 4 (练习题／考题的) 答案 (liànxítí/kǎotí de) dá'àn II ADJ 关键的 guānjiàn de, 至关重要 的 zhìguān zhòngyào de III v 1 (to key in) 把 [+信息] 输入电脑 bǎ [+xìnxī] shūrù diànnǎo 2 (to key a car) 用钥匙划伤车 yòng yàoshi huáshāng chē

keyboard I N 键盘 jiànpán
keyboard skill 打字技术 dǎzì jìshù
II v 用键盘 (将信息) 输入电脑 yòng jiànpán (jiāng xìnxī) shūrù diànnǎo

keyed up ADJ 神经紧张的 shénjīng jǐnzhāng de

keyhole N 锁眼 suǒyǎn

keynote ADJ 主旨的 zhǔzhǐ de, 主题的 zhǔtí de
keynote speech 主题发言 zhǔtí fāyán, 主要发 言 zhǔyào fāyán

kg (= kilogram) ABBREV 千克 qiānkè, 公斤 gōngjīn

khaki N 1 卡其黄 kǎqí huáng 2 卡其布 kǎqíbù

khakis N 卡其布裤子 kǎqíbù kùzi [M. WD 条 tiáo]

KFC (= Kentucky Fried Chicken) ABBREV 肯德基烤 鸡店 Kěndéjī kǎojī diàn

kick v, N 踢 tī
to kick in [药物+] 开始生效 [yàowù+] kāishǐ shēngxiào
to kick off 开球 kāiqiú, [球赛+] 开始 [qiúsài+] kāishǐ
kick boxing 跆拳道 táiquándào
to get a kick out of sth 从某事得到乐趣 cóng mǒushì dédào lèqù

kickback N 回扣 huíkòu

kickoff N 开球 kāiqiú, 比赛开始 bǐsài kāishǐ

kick-start I N 1 脚踏启动器 jiǎotà qǐdòngqì 2 启动 qǐdòng, 促进 cùjìn II v 1 发动 [+摩托车] fādòng [+mótuōchē] 2 启动 [+经济] qǐdòng [+jīngjì], 刺激 cìjī

kid I N 1 小孩子 xiǎo háizi 2 小山羊 xiǎo shānyáng II v 哄骗 hǒngpiàn, 开玩笑 kāi wán- xiào, 说着玩 shuōzhe wán
just kidding 只是开个玩笑 zhǐ shì kāi gè wán- xiào ■ *Quit kidding.* 别开玩笑。（→说正经的。）Bié kāi wánxiào. (→Shuō zhèngjing de.)
III ADJ 幼小的 yòuxiǎo de
one's kid brother/sister 小弟弟／小妹妹 xiǎodìdi/xiǎomèimei

kiddo N 小家伙 xiǎojiāhuo

kidnap I v 绑架 bǎngjià ■ *A billionaire's daughter has been kidnapped by a gang.* 一名亿万富翁的

女儿被一伙黑帮绑架了。Yì míng yìwàn fùwēng de nǚ'ér bèi yì huǒ hēi bāng bǎngjià le. **II** N 绑架 bǎngjià

kidnapper N 绑匪 bǎngfěi, 绑架的罪犯 bǎngjià de zuìfàn

kidnapping N 绑架 bǎngjià, 劫持 jiéchí

kidney N 肾 (脏) shèn (zàng)
kidney bean 四季豆 sìjìdòu, 芸豆 yúndòu

kill v **1** 杀死 shāsǐ ■ *Smoking kills.* 吸烟致死。Xīyān zhìsǐ.
to kill time 消磨时间 xiāomó shíjiān
to kill two birds with one stone 一石二鸟 yì shí èr niǎo, 一箭双雕 yíjiàn shuāngdiāo, 一举两得 yì jǔ liǎng dé
2 终止 [+疼痛] zhōngzhǐ [+téngtòng] **3** 对 [+人] 极为生气 duì [+rén] jíwéi shēngqì **II** N **1** 捕杀 bǔshā **2** 被捕杀的动物 bèibǔ shā de dòngwù

killer I N 杀手 shāshǒu
killer whale 杀人鲸 shārénjīng, 虎鲸 hǔjīng, 逆载鲸 nìjǐ jīng
II ADJ 好得要命的 hǎo de yàomìng de, 极好的 jíhǎo de

killing I N **1** 谋杀 móushā
to make a killing 一下子赚大钱 yíxiàzi zhuàn dàqián
II ADJ 要命的
a killing workload 要人命的工作量 yào rénmìng de gōngzuòliàng, 累死人的工作量 lèisǐ rén de gōngzuòliàng

killjoy N 令人扫兴的人 lìng rén sǎoxìng de rén

kiln N 窑 yáo

kilobyte N 千字节 qiān zìjié

kilogram N 公斤 gōngjīn

kilometer N 公里 gōnglǐ

kilowatt N 千瓦 qiānwǎ

kilt N 苏格兰男子传统短裙 Sūgélán nánzǐ chuántǒng duǎnqún

kimono N (日本) 和服 (Rìběn) héfú

kin N 家人 jiārén, 亲属 qīnshǔ
next of kin (最亲近的) 亲属 (zuì qīnjìn de) qīnshǔ

kind I N 种 zhǒng, 种类 zhǒnglèi **II** ADJ 好心的 hǎoxīn de, 和蔼的 hé'ǎi de ■ *You're so kind.* 你真的太好了。Nǐ zhēnde tài hǎo le.
kind of 有点儿 yǒudiǎnr ■ *I'm kind of confused.* 我有点被搞糊涂了。Wǒ yǒudiǎnr bèi gǎo hútu le.

kindergarten N 幼儿园 yòu'éryuán [M. WD 座 zuò]

kind-hearted ADJ 好心的 hǎoxīn de, 仁慈的 réncí de

kindle v **1** 点燃 diǎnrán **2** 激起 jīqǐ

kindly ADV **1** 好心地 hǎoxīn de, 仁慈地 réncí de
to put it kindly 往好里说 wǎng hǎo lǐ shuō
2 请 qǐng, 能不能 néngbunéng ■ *Would you kindly …?* 请…, Qǐng…?

kindness N 好意 hǎoyì, 仁慈 réncí

kindred I N 亲属 (关系) qīnshǔ (guānxi) **II** ADJ 同样的 tóngyàng de
kindred spirit 心投意合的人 xīn tóu yìhé de rén

kinfolk N 家人 jiārén, 亲属 qīnshǔ

king N **1** 国王 guówáng **2** (纸牌) 老 K 牌 (zhǐpái) lǎo K pái

kingdom N **1** 王国 wángguó
the United Kingdom of Great Britain and Northern Ireland 大不列颠及北爱尔兰联合王国 Dàbùlièdiān jí Běi Ài'ěrlán Liánhé Wángguó
the Kingdom of God 天国 Tiānguó
2 界 jiè
the animal kingdom 动物界 dòngwùjiè

kingfisher N 翠鸟 cuìniǎo

kingpin N 头目 tóumù, 领袖 lǐngxiù

king-size ADJ 特大号的 tèdàhào de

kink N **1** 纽结 niǔjié **2** 障碍 zhàng'ài

kinky ADJ 变态的 biàntài de

kiosk N 小商亭 xiǎo shāngtíng [M. WD 座 zuò]

kiss v, N 吻 wěn, 亲吻 qīnwěn ■ *Granddad kissed me on the forehead.* 爷爷亲吻了我的额头。Yéye qīnwěnle wǒ de étóu.
to kiss sb's ass 拍马屁 pāi mǎpì
to kiss sth goodbye 失去获得某事的机会 shīqùhuòdé mǒushì de jīhuì
the kiss of death 死亡之吻 sǐwáng zhī wěn, 带来灾难的事 dàilái zāinàn de shì

kit N 成套工具 chéngtào gōngjù
repair kit 修理用的成套工具 xiūlǐ yòng de chéngtào gōngjù

kitchen N 厨房 chúfáng ■ *Their kitchen is not big, but is well-equipped.* 他们的厨房不大，但是设备很好。Tāmen de chúfáng bú dà, dànshì shèbèi hěn hǎo.

kite N 风筝 fēngzheng

kitsch N 俗气的装饰 súqi de zhuāngshì

kitten N 小猫 xiǎomāo

kiwi N **1** 几维鸟 jǐ wéi niǎo, 鹬鸵鸟 yùtuó niǎo **2** 新西兰人 Xīnxīlánrén
kiwi fruit 猕猴桃 míhóutáo

kleptomaniac N 有偷窃癖的人 yǒu tōuqièpǐ de rén, 偷窃狂 tōuqiè kuáng

km (= kilometer, kilometre) ABBREV 千米 qiānmǐ, 公里 gōnglǐ

knack N 天生的本领 tiānshēng de běnlǐng

knapsack N 大背包 dà bēibāo

knead v 揉 [+面团] róu [+miàntuán], 揉捏 [+背部] róu niē [+bèibù]

knee N 膝 xī, 膝盖 xīgài ■ *He sat his baby daughter on his knees and began to play with her.* 他把女儿放在膝上，开始跟她玩。Tā bǎ nǚ'ér fàng zài xīshang, kāishǐ gēn tā wán.
to bring sb to his/her knees 使某人屈服 shǐ mǒurén qūfú
on one's knees 跪着 guìzhe

knee-cap N 膝盖骨 xīgàigǔ

knee-deep ADJ 齐膝高的 qí xī gāo de

knee-jerk ADJ 本能的 běnnéng de, 本能反应的 běnnéng fǎnyìng de

kneel v (PT & PP **knelt**, **kneeled**) 跪 guì, 跪下 guìxia ■ *She kneeled down to pull weeds from the flowerbed.* 她跪下拔花圃的杂草。Tā guìxia bá huāpǔ de zácǎo.

knelt See **kneel**

knew See **know**

knickers N 灯笼裤 dēnglongkù [M. WD 条 tiáo]

knick-knack N 小摆设 xiǎobǎishè

knife I N (PL **knives**) 刀 dāo [M. WD 把 bǎ]
carving knife 切肉刀 qiēròudāo
kitchen knife 菜刀 càidāo
paper knife 裁纸刀 cáizhǐdāo
II v 用刀扎 yòng dāo zhā

knight I N 1 (古代欧洲) 骑士 (gǔdài Ōuzhōu) qíshì 2 (英国) 爵士 (Yīngguó) juéshì II v 封…为爵士 fēng…wéi juéshì

knighthood N 爵士头衔 juéshì tóuxián

knit I v (PT & PP **knit**, **knitted**) 1 编结 biānjié 2 紧密地结合 jǐnmì de jiéhé II N 编结 (品／服装) biānjié (pǐn/fúzhuāng)

knitting needle N 编结针 biānjiézhēn

knob N 球形把手 qiúxíng bǎshǒu

knobby ADJ 似球形把手的 sì qiúxíng bǎshǒu de

knock I v 1 敲 (打) qiāo (dǎ) ■ *Someone is knocking at the door.* 有人在敲门。Yǒurén zài qiāomén.
to knock against 撞到 zhuàngdào
to knock down 碰倒 pèngdǎo, 打到 dǎdào
to knock off 下班 xiàbān
2 批评 pīpíng ■ *Don't knock it until you've tried it.* 没试过就别乱批评。Méi shì guò jiù bié luàn pīpíng. II N 1 敲击声 qiāojī shēng 2 倒霉的事 dǎoméi de shì
to have a few hard knocks in one's life 生活中遇到一些倒霉事 shēnghuó zhōng yùdào yìxiē dǎoméi shì

knocker N 门环 ménhuán

knockout N 1 击倒 jī dǎo 2 极具魅力的人 jí jù mèilì de rén
knockout pills 麻醉剂 mázuìjì, 蒙汗药 ménghànyào
knockout punch 把对手打倒在地的一拳 bǎ duìshǒu dǎdǎo zài dì de yì quán

knoll N 小土丘 xiǎo tǔqiū

knot I N 1 (绳) 结 (shéng) jié 2 紧张 (感) jǐnzhāng (gǎn)
to feel the knots in one's stomach 感到非常紧张 gǎndào fēicháng jǐnzhāng, 心揪得紧紧地 xīn jiū dé jǐnjǐn de
II v 把…打成结 bǎ…dǎchéng jié, 打结 dǎjié

knotty ADJ 棘手的 jíshǒu de

know I v (PT **knew**; PP **known**) 1 知道 zhīdào ■ *You don't know how lucky you are.* 你不知道自己多么幸运。Nǐ bù zhīdào zìjǐ duōme xìngyùn. 2 认识 rènshi, 结识 jiéshí ■ *We've known each other since childhood.* 我们从小认识。Wǒmen cóngxiǎo rènshi. 3 精通 jīngtōng, 熟悉 shúxī II N 知晓 zhīxiǎo
in the know 知晓内情 zhīxiǎo nèiqíng

know-how N 知识 zhīshi, 技术 jìshù

knowing ADJ 会意的 huìyì de, 心照不宣的 xīnzhào bù xuān de

knowingly ADV 1 心照不宣地 xīnzhào bù xuān de 2 故意地 gùyìde, 明知故犯地 míngzhī gùfàn de

know-it-all N 自以为无所不知的 zì yǐwéi wúsuǒ bù zhī de

knowledge N 1 知识 zhīshi ■ *Your knowledge of Chinese culture is impressive.* 你的中国文化知识很了不起。Nǐ de Zhōngguó wénhuà zhīshi hěn liǎobuqǐ. 2 知道 zhīdào, 理解 lǐjiě
to the best of my knowledge 就我所知 jiù wǒ suǒ zhī
3 学问 xuéwèn

knowledgeable ADJ 知识丰富的 zhīshí fēngfù de

known[1] v See **know**

known[2] ADJ 大家知道的 dàjiā zhīdào de, 知名的 zhīmíng de

knuckle I N 指节 zhǐjié II v (to knuckle under) 屈服 qūfú, 认输 rènshū

knucklehead N 傻乎乎的人 shǎhūhū de rén

koala (bear) n (澳洲) 树袋熊 (Àozhōu) shùdàixióng

Koran N 古兰经 Gǔlánjīng, 可兰经 Kělánjīng

Korean I ADJ 韩国的 Hánguó de, 朝鲜的 Cháoxiān de II N 1 韩语 Hányǔ, 朝鲜语 Cháoxiānyǔ 2 韩国人 Hánguórén, 朝鲜人 Cháoxiānrén

kosher ADJ 符合犹太教规定的 fúhé Yóutàijiào guīdìng de

kowtow v 1 磕头 kētóu, 叩头 kòutóu 2 卑躬屈膝 bēigōngqūxī, 唯命是从 wéi mìng shì cóng

Kremlin N (俄国) 克里姆林宫 (Éguó) Kèlǐmǔlíngōng, 俄国政府 Éguó zhèngfǔ

kudos N 威望 wēiwàng, 荣誉 róngyù

kung fu N (中国) 功夫 (Zhōngguó) gōngfu

L

label I N 标签 biāoqiān, 标记 biāojì ■ *Read the information on the label before you buy any foodstuff.* 在购买食品前，要先读一下标签上的说明。Zài gòumǎi shípǐn qián, yào xiān dú yíxià biāoqiān shang de shuōmíng. II v 加标记 jiā biāojì, 加标签 jiā biāoqiān ■ *These folders should be labeled since they look alike.* 这些文

件袋看来都一样，所以应该加上标记。Zhè xiē wénjiàndài kànlai dōu yíyàng, suǒyǐ yīnggāi jiāshang biāojì.

labor I N **1** 劳动 láodòng **2** 劳工 láogōng, 工人 gōngrén
labor camp 劳改营 láogǎiyíng
Labor Day 劳动节 Láodòngjié
labor union 工会 gōnghuì
manual/physical labor 体力劳动 tǐlì láodòng
skilled labor 技术工人 jìshù gōngrén
3 分娩（期）fēnmiǎn (qī) ■ *She's been in labor for an hour, I'm afraid it's a difficult labor.* 她已经分娩了一个小时了，恐怕是难产。Tā yǐjing fēnmiǎnle yí ge xiǎoshí le, kǒngpà shì nánchǎn. **II** v 劳动 láodòng, 劳作 láozuò

laboratory N 实验室 shíyànshì

laborer N 体力劳动者 tǐlì láodòngzhě

laborious ADJ 缓慢而吃力的 huǎnmàn ér chīlì de

Labrador N 拉布拉多猎犬 Lābùlāduō lièquǎn [M. WD 只 zhī/条 tiáo]

labyrinth N 迷宫 mígōng, 曲径 qūjìng

lace I N **1** 网眼织物 wǎngyǎn zhīwù **2** 鞋带 xiédài [M. WD 根 gēn/副 fù] **II** v 用带子束紧 yòng dàizi shùjǐn
to lace up 系上 jìshang

lacerate v 划破（皮肉）huápò (pínnòu)

laceration N 划破 huápò, 撕裂 sīliè

lack I v 缺乏 quēfá **II** N 缺乏 quēfá, 短缺 duǎnquē ■ *There is a severe lack of skilled labor.* 现在技术工人严重缺乏。Xiànzài jìshù gōngrén yánzhòng quēfá.

lackadaisical ADJ 无精打采的 wújīng dǎcǎi de, 懒散的 lǎnsǎn de

lacking ADJ 缺乏 quēfá

lackluster ADJ 平平淡淡的 píngpíng dàndàn de, 毫不吸引人的 háo bù xīyǐnrén de

laconic ADJ 精炼的 jīngliàn de, 简洁的 jiǎnjié de

lacquer N 漆 qī

lacquerware N 漆器 qīqì

lacy ADJ 网眼织物的 wǎngyǎn zhīwù de

lad N 小伙子 xiǎohuǒzi, 男孩 nánhái

ladder N **1** 梯子 tīzi **2** 阶梯 jiētī
the corporate ladder 公司的阶梯 gōngsī de jiētī

laden ADJ 满载的 mǎnzǎi de, 装满的 zhuāngmǎn de

ladies' room N 女厕所 nǚcèsuǒ

ladle I N 长柄勺 chángbǐngsháo [M. WD 把 bǎ], 勺资 sháozi **II** v（用长柄勺）盛 [+汤] (yòng chángbǐngsháo) shèng [+tāng]

lady (PL **ladies**) N **1** 女士 nǚshì, 小姐 xiǎojiě ■ *The lady on the phone was not very helpful.* 听电话的小姐没有给我多大帮助。Tīng diànhuà de xiǎojiě méiyǒu gěi wǒ duōdà bāngzhù.
First Lady 总统夫人 zǒngtǒng fūrén
2 女子 nǚzǐ, 女人 nǚrén

ladybug N 瓢虫 piáochóng [M. WD 只 zhī]

ladylike ADJ 贵妇人似的 guìfùrén sì de

lag I v 落后 luòhòu
to lag behind 落后于 luòhòu yu, 比…落后 bǐ... luòhòu
II N 间歇 jiànxiē
jet lag 飞行时差综合症 fēixíng shíchā zōnghézhèng, 时差反应 shíchāfǎnyìng

lager N 淡啤酒 dàn píjiǔ

lagoon N 泻湖 xièhú, 环礁湖 huánjiāo hú

laid See **lay**[1]

laidback ADJ 悠闲自在的 yōuxián zìzài de

lain See **lie**[1]

lair N **1** 藏身地 cángshēndì **2** 兽穴 shòuxuè

laissez-faire N 自由放任的经济政策 zìyóu fàngrèn de jīngjì zhèngcè, 不干预主义 bù gānyù zhǔyì

lake N 湖 hú, 湖泊 húpō

lakefront N 临湖平地 lín hú píngdì

lakeside N 湖畔 húpàn, 湖滨 húbīn

lama N 喇嘛 Lǎma,（藏传佛教的）僧侣 (cángchuán Fójiào de) sēnglǚ

lamb I N **1** 羊肉 yángròu ■ *Can we get New Zealand lamb at the supermarket here?* 这里的超市里能买到新西兰羊肉吗？Zhèlǐ de chāoshì lǐ néng mǎidao Xīnxīlán yángròu ma? **2** 小羊 xiǎo yáng, 羊羔 yánggāo
roast lamb 烤羊肉 kǎo yángròu
II v 生产羊羔 shēngchǎn yánggāo
lambing season 羊羔出生的季节 yánggāo chūshēng de jìjié

lame ADJ **1** 跛的 bǒ de, 瘸的 qué de
a lame duck 跛足鸭 bǒzúyā, 任期将满的总统 rènqī jiāng mǎn de zǒngtǒng
2 处于困境的 [+人] chǔyú kùnjìng de [+rén]
a lame duck president 任期将满（无所作为）的总统 rènqī jiāng mǎn (wú suǒ zuòwéi) de zǒngtǒng

lament I v **1** 悲悼 bēitào, 哀悼 āidào **2** 抱怨 baoyuan **II** N 挽歌 wǎngē [M. WD 首 shǒu/曲 qū], 哀乐 āiyuè

lamentable ADJ 令人深深惋惜的 lìng rén shēnshēn wǎnxī de

laminate v 层压板 céngyābǎn

laminated ADJ 塑料薄膜覆盖的 sùliào bómó fùgài de, 烫塑的 tàng sù de

lamp N 灯 dēng
desk/table lamp 台灯 táidēng
floor lamp 落地台灯 luòdì táidēng
street lamp 街灯 jiēdēng

lampoon I v 讽刺 fěngcì, 挖苦 wāku **II** N 讽刺文 fěngcì wén, 讽刺画 fěngcì huà

lampshade N 灯罩 dēngzhào

lance N 长矛 cháng máo

land I N **1** 土地 tǔdì

land of milk and honey 乳蜜之乡 rǔmì zhī
xiāng, 鱼米之乡 yúmǐ zhī xiāng
2 国土 guótǔ, 国家 guójiā **II** v **1** [飞机+] 着陆
[fēijī+] zhuólù ■ *Our flight will land in London
at 1 p.m. local time.* 我们的飞机在当地时间下
午一点到达伦敦。Wǒmen de fēijī zài dāngdì
shíjiān yìdiǎn dàodá Lúndūn. **2** [军队+] 登陆
[jūnduì+] dēnglù

landfill N 垃圾场 lājī chǎng

landing N **1** （飞机）着陆 (fēijī) zhuólù,（船）登陆
(chuán) dēnglù **2** 楼梯平台 lóutī píngtái
landing gear （着陆）起落架 (zhuólù) qǐluòjià
landing pad 直升飞机起落场 zhíshēng fēijī
qǐluò chǎng
landing strip 简易跑道 jiǎnyì pǎodào

landlady N 女房东 nǚ fángdōng

landlocked ADJ 内陆的 nèilù de, 无海岸线的 wú
hǎi'ànxiàn de

landlord ADJ 房东 fángdōng

landmark N 地标 dìbiāo

landowner N 土地拥有者 tǔdì yōngyǒuzhě, 地
主 dìzhǔ

landscape I N 风景 fēngjǐng, 景色 jǐngsè **II** v
对…进行景观美化 duì…jìnxíng jǐngguān
měihuà

landslide N **1** 山崩 shānbēng, 塌方 tāfāng **2** （选
举）压倒性胜利 (xuǎnjǔ) yādǎoxìng shènglì

lane N **1** 巷 xiàng, 小街 xiǎo jiē [M. wD 条 tiáo]
2 车道 chēdào
the fast lane 快车道 kuàichēdào

language N **1** 语言 yǔyán
foreign language 外国语 wàiguóyǔ, 外语 wàiyǔ
strong language 强硬的语言 qiángyìng de
yǔyán
language student 语言学生 yǔyán xuésheng
language teacher 语言老师 yǔyán lǎoshī
2 计算机语言 jìsuànjī yǔyán
a programming language 程序语言 chéngxù
yǔyán
3 粗话 cūhuà, 骂人话 màrénhuà ■ *Watch your
language!* 注意你的语言！（→说话要规矩点！别
说脏话！) Zhùyì nǐde yǔyán!（→Shuō huà guīju
diǎn! Bié shuō zānghuà!)

languid ADJ 懒洋洋的 lǎnyāngyāng de, 慢吞吞的
màntūntūn de

languish v **1** 没有进展 méiyǒu jìnzhǎn **2** 受煎熬
shòu jiān'áo

languorous ADJ 无精打采的 wújīng dǎcǎi de, 沉
闷的 chénmèn de

lanky ADJ 又高又瘦的 yòu gāo yòu shòu de

lantern N 灯笼 dēnglong

lap¹ I N **1** 腿 tuǐ, 膝 xī ■ *The cat likes to sit on my
lap.* 猫很喜欢坐在我腿上。Māo hěn xǐhuan zuò
zài wǒ tuǐshang. **2** （跑道的）一圈 (pǎodào de)
yìquan

in the lap of luxury 养尊处优 yǎngzūn chǔyōu

lap² v 轻轻拍打 qīngqīng pāida
to lap up （动物）舔饮 (dòngwù) tiǎn yǐn

lapel N 翻领 fānlǐng

lapse I N **1** 疏忽 shūhu, 失误 shīwù
memory lapse 暂时失忆 zànshí shī yì
2 （时间）流逝 (shíjiān) liúshì **3** （一时的）
下降 (yìshí de) xiàjiàng **II** v **1** [保险+] 终止
[bǎoxiǎn+] zhōngzhǐ, 失效 shīxiào **2** 渐渐结束
jiànjiàn jiéshù

laptop N 笔记本电脑 bǐjìběn diànnǎo [M. wD 台
tái], 膝上电脑 xīshang diànnǎo [M. wD 台 tái]

larceny N 偷窃罪 tōuqièzuì, 盗窃罪 dàoqièzuì

larch N 落叶松 luòyèsōng

lard N 猪油 zhūyóu

large ADJ **1** 大 dà **2** （身材）高大的 (shēncái)
gāodà de
be at large 在逃 zàitáo, 未被抓到 wèi bèi zhuā
dào

largely ADV 主要地 zhǔyào de ■ *This band is
popular largely in English-speaking countries.* 这
个乐队主要在英语国家受欢迎。Zhè ge yuèduì
zhǔyào zài Yīngyǔ guójiā shòu huānyíng.

large-scale ADJ 大规模的 dàguīmó de

lark N **1** 云雀 yúnquè [M. wD 只 zhī] **2** 玩乐 wánlè
for a lark 为了玩乐 wèile wánlè, 为了消遣 wèile
xiāoqiǎn

larva N 幼虫 yòuchóng

laryngitis N 喉炎 hóuyán

larynx N 喉 hóu

lascivious ADJ 好色的 hàosè de, 淫荡的 yíndàng
de

laser N 激光（器）jīguāng (qì)
laser printer 激光打印机 jīguāng dǎyìnjī

lash I v **1** 鞭打 [+犯人] biāndǎ [+fànrén] **2** 捆绑 [+
行李] kǔnbǎng [+xíngli] **3** 抨击 [+政客] pēngjī
[+zhèngkè]
to lash out 猛烈抨击 měngliè pēngjī
II N 鞭子 biānzi [M. wD 条 tiáo]

lasso I N **1** 套索 tàosuǒ **II** v 用套索套捕 （牛马）yòng
tàosuǒ tào bǔ (niúmǎ)

last I ADJ **1** 最后的 zuìhòu de ■ *The last time I
saw him he was working in a computer store.* 我最
后一次见到他时，他正在一家电脑商店工作。Wǒ
zuìhòu yí cì jiàndao tā shí, tā zhèngzài yì jiā
diànnǎo shāngdiàn gōngzuò.
last name 姓 xìng ■ *I only know he is Jason,
and I don't know his last name.* 我只知道他叫
贾森，不知道他姓什么。Wǒ zhǐ zhīdào tā jiào
Jiǎsēn, bù zhīdào tā xìng shénme.
2 上一个 shàng yí ge **3** 最不合适的 zuì bù
héshì de, 最不可能的 zuì bù kěnéng de
■ *I thought Jason was the last person she would
marry, but she did!* 我以为她最不可能嫁给贾森，
但是她就是嫁了！Wǒ yǐwéi tā zuì bù kěnéng

jiā gěi Jiǎsēn, dànshì tā jiùshì jià le! **II** ADV 最后 zuìhòu **III** V **1** 持续 chíxù ■ *Her first marriage lasted only eight months.* 她的第一次婚姻只持续了八个月。Tā de dìyī cì hūnyīn zhǐ chíxùle bā ge yuè. **2** [钱+] 够用 [qián+] gòuyòng **IV** N **1** 最后一个 zuìhòu yí ge **2** (at long last) 终于 zhōngyú, 总算 zǒngsuàn

last-ditch ADJ 最后的 zuìhòu de
a last-ditch effect 最后的努力 zuìhòu de nǔlì

lasting ADJ 持久的 chíjiǔ de, 耐久的 nàijiǔ de

lastly ADV 最后 zuìhòu

latch I N 门闩 ménshuān, 窗闩 chuāng shuān **II** V (用门闩／窗闩) 闩上 (yòng ménshuān／chuāng shuān) shuānshang

late I ADJ **1** 迟到 chídào **2** 晚 wǎn ■ *He had a very late lunch today.* 他今天中饭吃得很晚。Tā jīntiān zhōngfàn chīde hěn wǎn. **3** 已故的 yǐ gù de
his late grandfather 他已故的祖父 tā yǐ gù de zǔfù
II ADV 比通常晚 bǐ tōngcháng wǎn
Better late than never. 迟做比不做好。Chí zuò bǐ bú zuò hǎo. 晚来比不来好。Wǎnlái bǐ bùlái hǎo.

lately ADV 最近 zuìjìn, 近来 jìnlái ■ *Have you been to a dentist lately?* 你最近去看过牙医吗？Nǐ zuìjìn qù kànguo yáyī ma?

latent ADJ 潜在的 qiánzài de

later I ADV 后来 hòulái, 以后 yǐhòu ■ *See you later.* 回头见。Huítóujiàn. 再见。Zàijiàn. **II** ADJ 较晚的 jiào wǎn de, 以后的 yǐhòu de

lateral ADJ 侧面的 cèmiàn de, 侧的 cè de

latest ADJ 最后的 zuìhòu de, 最新的 zuì xīn de
at the latest 最迟 zuì chí, 最晚 zuì wǎn

latex N 胶乳 jiāorǔ

lather I N 肥皂泡沫 féizào pàomò **II** V **1** 起泡沫 qǐ pàomò **2** 用皂沫涂 yòng zào mò tú

Latin I ADJ 拉丁国家的 Lādīng guójiā de, 拉丁的 Lādīng de
Latin America 拉丁美洲 Lādīng Měizhōu
II N **1** 拉丁语 Lādīngyǔ **2** 拉丁美洲人 Lādīng Měizhōu rén

Latino N (美国) 拉丁美洲裔男人 (Měiguó) Lādīng Měizhōu yì nánren

latitude N 纬度 wěidù

latrine N 户外厕所 hùwài cèsuǒ

latter I N 后者 hòuzhě **II** ADJ **1** 后者的 hòuzhě de **2** 后期的 hòuqī de, 末期的 mòqī de

lattice N 格子图案／结构 gézi tú'àn/jiégòu

laudable ADJ 值得赞美的 zhíde zànměi de

laugh I V 大笑 dàxiào
to laugh at 取笑 qǔxiào ■ *Please don't laugh at me; I'm just learning the language.* 请不要笑我；我正在学这种语言。Qǐng bú yào qǔxiào wǒ; wǒ zhèngzài xué zhè zhǒng yǔyán.
to burst out laughing 大笑起来 dàxiào qǐlai

II N 笑 (声) xiào (shēng)
to get a laugh out of sth 从做某事得到很多乐趣 cóng zuò mǒushì dédào hěn duō lèqù

laughing stock N 笑柄 xiàobǐng

laughter N **1** 笑 xiào, 大笑 dàxiào ■ *Laughter is the best medicine, according to my doctor.* 按照我的医生的说法，大笑是最好的药品。Ànzhào wǒ de yīshēng de shuōfǎ, dàxiào shì zuìhǎo de yàopǐn. **2** 笑声 xiàoshēng

launch I V **1** 发动 [+运动] fādòng [+yùndòng] **2** 发射 [+航天飞机] fāshè [+hángtiān fēijī] **3** 投入 [+市场] tóurù [+shìchǎng] **4** 发行 [+新书] fāxíng [+xīnshū] **II** N **1** 发射 fāshè, 发出 fāchū
launch pad 发射场 fāshèchǎng
2 汽艇 qìtǐng

launder V **1** 洗 (黑) 钱 xǐ (hēi) qián **2** 洗熨 (衣服) xǐ yùn (yīfu)

laundromat N 自助洗衣房 zìzhù xǐyīfáng [M. WD 家 jiā]

laundry N **1** 洗衣房 xǐyīfáng, 洗衣店 xǐyīdiàn **2** 要洗的衣服 yào xǐ de yīfu, 洗好的衣服 xǐ hǎo de yīfu

laureate N 奖章获得者 jiǎngzhāng huòdézhě [M. WD 位 wèi]
Nobel laureate 诺贝尔奖获得者 Nuòbèi'ěr jiǎng huòdézhě

laurel N 桂冠 guìguān [M. WD 顶 dǐng]

lava N 岩浆 yánjiāng

lavatory N 厕所 cèsuǒ, 洗手间 xǐshǒujiān

lavender N 薰衣草 xūnyīcǎo
lavender water 薰衣草香水 xūnyīcǎo xiāngshuǐ

lavish I ADJ 铺张的 pūzhāng de, 豪华的 háohuá de **II** V 过份慷慨地给予 guòfèn kāngkǎi de gěiyú
to lavish praise on sb 对某人大加赞扬 duì mǒurén dà jiā zànyáng

law N **1** 法律 fǎlǜ, 法规 fǎguī ■ *It is against the law to drive while drunk.* 酒后驾车是违法的。Jiǔ hòu jiàchē shì wéifǎ de.
law and order 法律和秩序 fǎlǜ hé zhìxù, 法治 fǎzhì
tax law 税务法 shuìwù fǎ
to break the law 犯法 fànfǎ
2 法学 fǎxué, 法律业务 fǎlǜ yèwù
law firm 法律事务所 fǎlǜ shìwùsuǒ
law school 法学院 fǎxuéyuàn
3 规律 fǎlǜ, 法则 fǎzé
law of the jungle 丛林法则 cónglín fǎzé, 弱肉强食的法则 ruòròu qiángshí de fǎzé
4 (体育) 规则 (tǐyù) guīzé

law-abiding ADJ 奉守法律的 fèng shǒu fǎlǜ de, 守法的 shǒufǎ de

lawful ADJ 合法的 héfǎ de

lawless ADJ 不守法的 bù shǒufǎ de

lawn N 草坪 cǎopíng [M. WD 片 piàn], 草地 cǎodì [M. WD 片 piàn] lawn mower 割草机 gēcǎojī

lawn tennis 草地网球（运动）cǎodì wǎngqiú (yùndòng)

lawsuit N 法律案件 fǎlǜ ànjiàn, 诉讼 sùsòng

lawyer N 律师 lǜshī

criminal lawyer 刑事律师 xíngshì lǜshī

lax ADJ 松懈的 sōngxiè de, 马虎的 mǎhu de

laxative N 通便药 tōngbiàn yào, 泻药 xièyào

laxity N 松懈 sōngxiè, 松弛 sōngchí

lay¹ (PT & PP **laid**) v **1** 放 fàng, 放置 fàngzhì **2** 铺 pū, 铺设 pūshè **3** 产卵 chǎnluǎn, 下蛋 xiàdàn ■ *Every year sea turtles lay eggs on this remote beach.* 每年海龟都在这片遥远的海滩下蛋。Měinián hǎiguī dōu zài zhè piàn yáoyuǎn de hǎitān xiàdàn.

to lay off 解雇 jiěgù ■ *Many people were laid off in this mining town.* 在这个矿区很多人被解雇。Zài zhè ge kuàngqū hěn duō rén bèi jiěgù.

lay² ADJ **1** 不担任神职的 bù dānrèn shénzhí de, 世俗的 shìsú de **2** 非专业的 fēi zhuānyè de, 外行的 wàiháng de

lay³ v See **lie¹**

lay⁴ N (the lay of the land)（当前的）形势 (dāngqián de) xíngshì, 现状 xiànzhuàng

layaway N 分期预付购物 fēnqī yùfù gòuwù

layer I N 层 céng II v 把…堆成层 bǎ…duī chéng céng

layman N 外行 wàiháng, 门外汉 ménwàihàn

lay-off N 解雇 jiěgù

layout N **1** 版面设计 bǎnmiànshèjì, 版式 bǎnshì **2** [花园的+] 布局 [huāyuán de+] bùjú

layover N 中途停留 zhōngtútíngliú

layperson N 普通信徒 pǔtōng xìntú, 门外汉 ménwàihàn

laze v 懒散地生活 lǎnsǎn de shēnghuó

lazy ADJ **1** 懒惰 lǎnduò ■ *If you weren't so lazy, your room wouldn't be so disorderly.* 要是你不是这么懒惰，你的房间就不会这么乱。Yàoshì nǐ bú shì zhème lǎnduò, nǐ de fángjiān jiù bú huì zhème luàn. **2** 使人懒洋洋的 shǐrén lǎnyāngyāng de **3** 慢吞吞的 màntūntūn de

lead¹ I v (PT & PP **led**) **1** 带领 dàilǐng ■ *You can lead a horse to water, but you can't force it to drink.* 你可以把马牵到水边，但是不能强迫马喝水。Nǐ kěyǐ bǎ mǎ qiāndao shuǐ biān, dànshì bù néng qiǎngpò mǎ hēshuǐ.

to lead to 导致 dǎozhì, 造成 zàochéng ■ *Global warming leads to a rise in sea level.* 全球变暖导致海面上升。Quánqiú biàn nuǎn dǎozhì hǎimiàn shàngshēng.

2 领导 lǐngdǎo ■ *The research project will be led by a world-class biologist.* 这个研究项目将由一位世界级的生物学家领导。Zhè ge yánjiū xiàngmù jiāng yóu yí wèi shìjiè jí de shēngwùxuéjiā lǐngdǎo. **3** 领先 lǐngxiān **4** 生活 shēnghuó, 过 guò ■ *Af-*

ter retirement, the former governor led a peaceful life. 这位前州长在退休以后过着平静的生活。Zhè wèi qián Zhōuzhǎng zài tuìxiū yǐhòu guòzhe píngjìng de shēnghuó. **5** 使 shǐ, 导致 dǎozhì **6** 通向 tōngxiàng, 通达 tōngdá II N **1** 领先 lǐngxiān, 领先地位 lǐngxiān dìwèi

to follow sb's lead 仿效某人 fǎngxiào mǒurén **2** 线索 xiànsuǒ ■ *The detective followed every possible lead.* 侦探跟踪每一个线索。Zhēntàn gēnzōng měi yí ge xiànsuǒ. **3**（电影）主角 (diànyǐng) zhǔjué

lead² (Pb) N 铅 qiān, 铅笔芯 qiānbǐxīn

a lead foot 喜欢开快车的人 xǐhuan kāi kuàichē de rén

leader N 领袖 lǐngxiù [M. WD 位 wèi], 领导人 lǐngdǎorén [M. WD 位 wèi] ■ *This company is a world leader in the development of renewable energy.* 这家公司在全世界开发再生能源方面处于领先地位。Zhè jiā gōngsī zài quánshìjiè kāifā zàishēng néngyuán fāngmiàn chǔyú lǐngxiān dìwèi.

leadership N 领导（地位）lǐngdǎo (dìwèi)

leading ADJ 主要的 zhǔyào de ■ *France is one of the leading European countries in wine production.* 法国是主要的欧洲产酒国家之一。Fǎguó shì zhǔyào de Ōuzhōu chǎn jiǔ guójiā zhīyī.

a leading question 诱导性问题 yòudǎo xìng wèntí

leading role 主角 zhǔjué

leaf I N (PL **leaves**) **1** 叶子 yèzi **2**（一）页（书）(yí) yè (shū) II v (to leave through) 翻阅 [+书] fānyuè [+shū]

leaflet N 传单 chuándān [M. WD 张 zhāng/份 fèn]

leafy ADJ **1** 绿树成荫的 [+住宅区] lǜ shù chéngyìn de [+zhùzháiqū] **2** 多叶的 [+蔬菜] duōyè de [+shūcài]

league N 联盟 liánméng, 联合会 liánhéhuì

the National Basketball League （美国）全国篮球联合会 (Měiguó) quánguó lánqiú liánhéhuì

leak I N **1** 漏洞 lòudòng, 裂缝 lièfèng II v **1** 漏 lòu **2** 泄露 [+秘密] xièlòu [+mìmì]

to leak out [消息+] 泄漏出去 [xiāoxi+] xièlòu chūqu

leakage N **1** 漏出 lòuchū, 渗出 shènchū **2** 泄漏 xièlòu, 泄露 xièlòu

leaky ADJ 漏的 lòu de, 有漏洞的 yǒu lòudòng de

lean¹ v (PT & PP **leaned**, **leant**) 靠 kào, 前（后）倾 qián (hòu) qīng

lean² ADJ **1** 瘦 shòu, 瘦而健康 shòu ér jiànkāng ■ *His lean athletic body is the envy of many of his classmates.* 他精瘦的运动员的体格引起班上很多人羡慕。Tā jīngshòu de yùndòngyuán de tǐgé yǐnqǐ bānshang hěn duō rén xiànmù. **2** 瘦 [+肉] shòu [+ròu], 脂肪很少的 zhīfáng hěn shǎo de ■ *She eats only lean meat.* 她只吃瘦肉。Tā zhǐ chī shòuròu.

leaning N 倾向 qīngxiàng, 偏好 piānhǎo

leap I v (PT & PP **leaped, leapt**) 跳 tiào, 跳跃 tiàoyuè

to leap at 抓住 [+机会] zhuāzhù [+jīhuì]

II N 跳跃 tiàoyuè

by leaps and bounds 突飞猛进 tūfēi měngjìn

leapfrog I N 跳背游戏 tiào bèi yóuxì, 跳山羊 tiào shānyáng II v 跳越 tiào yuè

leap year N 闰年 rùnnián

learn v (PT & PP **learned/learnt**) **1** 学 xué, 学会 xuéhuì **2** 获悉 huòxī, 听说 tīngshuō ■ *I learned of the news only yesterday.* 我昨天才获悉这个消息。Wǒ zuótiān cái huòxī zhè ge xiāoxi. **3** 记住 jìzhù

to learn one's lesson 记住教训 jìzhu jiàoxun, 吸取教训 xīqǔ jiàoxun ■ *I hope you've learned your lesson from this experience.* 我希望你从这个经历吸取教训。Wǒ xīwàng nǐ cóng zhè ge jīnglì xīqǔ jiàoxun.

learned I v See **learn** II ADJ 有学问的 yǒu xuéwèn de, 博学的 bóxué de

learning N **1** 学问 xuéwèn, 知识 zhīshi

a man of learning 一位很有学问的人 yíwèi hěn yǒu xuéwèn de rén

2 学习 xuéxí

learning disability 学习障碍 xuéxí zhàng'ài

lease I N 租约 zūyuē, 租契 zūqì

a one-year lease on an apartment 为期一年的公寓租约 wéiqī yìnián de gōngyù zūyuē

II v **1** 出租 chūzū **2** 租用 zūyòng

leaseback N 售后回租 shòuhòu huí zū

leasehold N（长期）租赁契约（chángqī）zūlìn qìyuē

leash N 绳子 shéngzi [M. WD 条 tiáo]

(dog) on a leash（狗）用绳子牵住（gǒu）yòng shéngzi qiān zhù

least I ADJ 最少的 zuì shǎo de, 最小的 zuì xiǎo de

at least 至少 zhìshǎo ■ *The new luxury car cost him at least $100,000.* 这辆新车花了他至少十万元。Zhè liàng xīn chē huāle tā zhìshǎo shí wàn yuán.

II ADV 最少 zuì shǎo, 最小 zuì xiǎo ■ *In my experience, big things often happen when you least expect it.* 在我的经历中，重大的事情往往在你以最不可能发生的时候来到。Zài wǒ de jīnglì zhōng, zhòngdà de shìqíng wǎngwǎng zài nǐ yǐwéi zuì bù kěnéng fāshēng de shíhou láidào.

leather N 皮（革）pí（gé）

leathery ADJ 象皮革一样的 xiàng pígé yíyàng de, 粗糙的 cūcāo de

leave I v (PT & PP **left**) **1** 离开 líkāi ■ *After their youngest daughter left home, the house seemed so empty.* 他们的小女儿离家以后，家里显得空荡荡的。Tāmen de xiǎonǚ'ér líjiā yǐhòu, jiāli xiǎnde kōngdàngdàng de. **2** 留下 liúxià ■ *Will you leave a message?* 你要留口信吗？Nǐ yào liú kǒuxìn ma?

left-luggage office 行李保管处 xíngli bǎoguǎn chù

to leave sb alone 不打搅某人 bù dǎjiǎo mǒurén ■ *We'd better leave her alone and let her cry for a while.* 我们最好别打搅她，让她哭一会儿。Wǒmen zuìhǎo bié dǎjiǎo tā, ràng tā kū yíhuìr.

to leave sth alone 不动某物 bú dòng mǒuwù

II N 假 jià, 假期 jiàqī

leave of absence 获准休假 huòzhǔn xiūjià

maternity leave 产假 chǎnjià

sick leave 病假 bìngjià

leaven N **1** 酵母 jiàomǔ **2** 使事物变得有趣的小事 shǐ shìwù biàn de yǒuqù de xiǎoshì II v 使…变得有趣 shǐ…biàn de yǒuqù

leavening N 酵母 jiàomǔ

leavening agent 酵母 jiàomǔ

lecherous ADJ 好色的 hàosè de

lectern N 斜面讲桌 xiémiàn jiǎngzhuō

lecture I N 1 讲座 jiǎngzuò, 讲课 jiǎngkè ■ *Prof Kerry will deliver a series of lectures on Islam.* 克里教授将做一系列关于伊斯兰教的讲座。Kèlǐ jiàoshòu jiāng zuò yíxìliè guānyú Yīsīlánjiào de jiǎngzuò. II v 1 讲课 jiǎngkè, 做讲座 zuò jiǎngzuò 2 教训 jiàoxun ■ *Stop lecturing me!* 别教训我了！Bié jiàoxun wǒ le!

lecturer N 讲师 jiǎngshī

a senior lecturer 高级讲师 gāojí jiǎngshī

led See **lead**[1]

ledger N 分类帐 fēnlèizhàng, 账本 zhàngběn

leech N **1** 蚂蟥 mǎhuáng [M. WD 条 tiáo] **2** 榨取他人钱财的人 zhàqǔ tārén qiáncái de rén, 吸血鬼 xīxuèguǐ

leek N 韭葱 jiǔcōng

leer I v 色迷迷地看 sèmímí de kàn II N 色迷迷的眼神 sèmímí de yǎnshén

leery ADJ 不信任的 bú xìnrèn de, 怀有戒心的 huáiyǒu jièxīn de

leeway N 自由行事的余地 zìyóu xíngshì de yúdì

left[1] I N 左 zuǒ, 左边 zuǒbiān

left field 左外场 zuǒ wàichǎng

II ADJ, ADV 左的 zuǒ de, 左边 zuǒbiān ■ *He uses his left hand to do most things: he is a left-handed person.* 他大多数事情都是用左手做；他是个左撇子。Tā dàduōshù shìqing dōu shì yòng zuǒshǒu zuò; tā shì ge zuǒpiězi.

the left 左派 zuǒpài

left[2] See **leave**

left-hand ADJ 左边的 zuǒbiān de

left-handed ADJ 用左手的 yòng zuǒshǒu de, 左撇子的 zuǒpiězi de

leftovers N 剩菜 shèngcài

leftwing ADJ 左翼 zuǒyì

leg N **1** 腿 tuǐ, 大腿 dàtuǐ **2** 一段（旅程）yí duàn（lǚchéng）

legacy N 1 遗留下来的情况 yíliú xiàlai de qíng-kuàng 2 遗产 yíchǎn

legal ADJ 1 法律的 fǎlǜ de 2 合法的 héfǎ de
■ *What is the legal age for drinking in your country?* 在你们国家合法饮酒年龄是几岁？Zài nǐmen guójiā héfǎ yǐnjiǔ niánlíng shì jǐsuì?

legality N 合法（性）héfǎ (xìng)

legalization N 合法化 héfǎhuà

legalize V 使…合法 shǐ…héfǎ

legend N 1 传说 chuánshuō, 传奇 chuánqí 2 传奇性人物 chuánqí xìng rénwù 3 （图片）说明 (túpiàn) shuōmíng, 图例 túlì

legendary ADJ 1 传奇的 chuánqí de 2 著名的 zhùmíng de, 大名鼎鼎的 dàmíng dǐngdǐng de

leggings N 绑腿 bǎngtuǐ [M. WD 条 tiáo]

leggy ADJ 腿长的 tuǐ cháng de

legible ADJ 可以认读的 kěyǐ rèn dú de

legion N 1 一大批人 yí dàpī rén, 很多人 hěn duō rén 2 （古罗马）军团 (gǔ Luómǎ) jūntuán

legislate V 制定法律 zhìdìng fǎlǜ, 立法 lìfǎ

legislation N 立法 lìfǎ

legislative ADJ 立法的 lìfǎ de

legislator N 立法者 lìfǎzhě

legislature N 立法机构 lìfǎ jīgòu

legit ADJ 符合规则的 fúhé guīzé de, 守法的 shǒufǎ de

legitimacy N 合法（性）héfǎ (xìng)

legitimate ADJ 1 合法的 héfǎ de 2 正当的 zhèngdàng de
a legitimate reason 正当的理由 zhèngdàng de lǐyóu
a legitimate child 合法婚姻所生的子女 héfǎ hūnyīn suǒ shēngde zǐnǚ, 婚生子 hūn shēngzǐ

leisure N 休闲 xiūxián
at one's leisure 有空时 yǒukòng shí

leisurely I ADJ 从容的 cóngróng de, 悠闲的 yōuxián de II ADV 从容地 cóngróng de, 悠闲地 yōuxián de

lemon N 柠檬 níngméng

lemonade N 柠檬汽水 níngméng qìshuǐ

lend (PT & PP lent) V 借给 jiè gěi, 借出 jiè chū

length N 1 长度 chángdù 2 时间（长度）shíjiān (chángdù)
at length ① 长时间地 chángshíjiān de ② 最终 zuìzhōng, 最后 zuìhòu

lengthen V 把…加长 bǎ…jiā cháng

lengthwise ADV 纵向地 zòngxiàng de

lengthy ADJ 1 冗长的 [+报告] rǒngcháng de [+bàogào], 过于详细的 guòyú xiángxì de 2 漫长的 [+等待] màncháng de [+děngdài]

lenient ADJ 宽大的 kuāndà de, 仁慈的 réncí de

lens N 1 （照相机）镜头 (zhàoxiàngjī) jìngtóu [M. WD 片 piàn] 2 （眼镜）镜片 (yǎnjìng) jìngpiàn [M. WD 片 piàn]
contact lens 隐形眼镜 yǐnxíng yǎnjìng

lent V See **lend**

Lent N （基督教）大斋期 (Jīdūjiào) dàzhāiqī

lentil N 小扁豆 xiǎobiǎndòu [M. WD 粒 lì]

Leo N 狮子宫座 Shīzigōngzuò

leopard N 豹 bào [M. WD 只 zhī/头 tóu]

leper N 麻风病人 máfēng bìngrén

leprosy N 麻风病 máfēngbìng

lesbian N, ADJ 女同性恋者 nǚ tóngxìngliànzhě

less I PRON, ADJ 较少的 jiào shǎo de, 较小的 jiào xiǎo de, 不那么 bú nàme ■ *Her new job has less pay, but is less stressful.* 她的新工作工资较少，但是也不那么紧张。Tā de xīn gōngzuò gōngzī jiào shǎo, dànshì yě bú nàme jǐnzhāng. II ADV 较少 jiào shǎo, 不那么 bú nàme ■ *I do hope she will care less about money.* 我真的希望她不那么在乎钱。Wǒ zhēn de xīwàng tā bú nàme zàihu qián.

lessee N 承租人 chéngzū rén, 租户 zūhù

lessen V 使…减少 shǐ…jiǎnshǎo

lesser ADJ 次要的 cìyào de, 较小的 jiào xiǎo de

lesson N 1 课 kè, 课程 kèchéng ■ *I'm taking Taichi lessons.* 我在上太极拳课。Wǒ zài shàng tàijíquán kè. 2 教训 jiàoxun
to learn a lesson See **learn**
to teach sb a lesson See **teach**

lest CONJ 以免 yǐmiǎn, 免得 miǎnde
Lest We Forget. 永志不忘。Yǒng zhì bú wàng.

let V (PT & PP let) 让 ràng, 允许 yǔnxǔ ■ *Father did not let Tom drive his car.* 父亲不让汤姆开他的车。Fùqin bú ràng Tāngmǔ kāi tā de chē.
to let go (of) 放开 fàngkāi, 放掉 fàngdiao ■ *Joanne let go of the kitten before it scratched her.* 乔安娜在小猫还没有抓她以前把它放了。Qiáo'ānnà zài xiǎomāo hái méiyǒu zhuā tā yǐqián bǎ tā fàng le.
let alone 更不用说 gèng bú yòng shuō

letdown N 失望 shīwàng, 令人失望的事 lìng rén shīwàng de shì

lethal ADJ 致命的 zhìmìng de

lethargic ADJ 无精打采的 wújīng dǎcǎi de, 懒洋洋的 lǎnyāngyāng de

lethargy N 无精打采 wújīng dǎcǎi, 倦怠 juàndài

letter N 1 信 xìn ■ *These days people seldom write letters; they send each other emails.* 现在人们不大写信了；人们互相送电子邮件。Xiànzài rénmen búdà xiěxìn le; rénmen hùxiāng sòng diànzǐ yóujiàn. 2 字母 zìmǔ
to the letter 不折不扣地 bù zhé bú kòu de, 精确地 jīngquè de

letterhead N 印有台头的信纸 yìn yǒu tái tóu de xìnzhǐ

lettuce N 生菜 shēngcài, 莴苣 wōjù

letup N 减弱 jiǎnruò, 松懈 sōngxiè

leukemia N 白血病 báixuèbìng

levee N 防洪提 fánghóngtí

level I ADJ 平的 píng de, 平坦的 píngtǎn de
■ *Make sure the ground is absolutely level before you start the game.* 在比赛开始前，要确保地面是平坦的。Zài bǐsài kāishǐ qián, yào quèbǎo dìmiàn shì píngtǎn de. **II** N 1 水平线 shuǐpíngxiàn
■ *Rising sea level may submerge these tiny islands before long.* 海平面升高，可能不要很长时间就会淹没这些小岛。Hǎi píngmiàn shēng gāo, kěnéng bú yào hěn cháng shíjiān jiù huì yānmò zhèxiē xiǎo dǎo. **2** 水平 shuǐpíng
basic/beginner's level 初级水平 chūjí shuǐpíng
advanced level 高级水平 gāojí shuǐpíng
III v 1 把 [+地面] 弄平 bǎ [+dìmiàn] nòng píng, 使…平坦 shǐ...píngtǎn **2** 推倒 [+房屋] tuīdǎo [+fángwū]
to level accusation (提出) 指控 (tíchū) zhǐkòng

leveler N 使人人平等的事 shǐ rénrén píngděng de shì
Death is the great leveler. 死亡，让人人平等。Sǐwáng, ràng rénrén píngděng. (→ 人无论贵贱，都不免一死。Rén wúlùn guìjiàn, dōu bùmiǎn yì sǐ.)

level-headed ADJ (头脑) 冷静 (tóunǎo) lěngjìng, 稳健的 wěnjiàn de

lever I N 1 杠杆 gànggǎn, 操纵杆 cāozònggǎn **2** 手段 shǒuduàn **II** v (用杠杆) 撬动 (yòng gànggǎn) qiàodòng

leverage I N 1 杠杆作用 gànggǎn zuòyòng **2** 影响 yǐngxiǎng, 力量 lìliang **3** 借贷经营 jièdài jīngyíng **II** v 借贷经营 jièdài jīngyíng

levitate v (使…) 浮在空中 (shǐ...) fú zài kōngzhōng

levitation N 漂浮空中 piāofú kōngzhōng

levity N 轻松 qīngsōng, 活跃 huóyuè

levy I v 征税 zhēngshuì **II** N 税 (款) shuì (kuǎn), 征 (款) zhēng (kuǎn)

lewd ADJ 好色的 hàosè de, 淫荡的 yíndàng de

lexical ADJ 词汇的 cíhuì de

lexicon N 词汇 cíhuì

liability N 1 责任 zérèn, 义务 yìwù **2** 累赘 léizhuì, 不利因素 búlì yīnsù **3** (liabilities) 债务 zhàiwù, 负债 fùzhài

liable ADJ 1 很可能会 hěn kěnéng huì [+犯错误] [+fàn cuòwù], 很容易遭受 hěn róngyì zāoshòu [+攻击] [+gōngjī] **2** 应负责的 yìng fùzé de
liable for taxes 应缴税的 yìng jiǎoshuì de

liaise v 联络 liánluò, 联系 liánxì

liaison N 1 联络 liánluò
liaison officer 联络官 liánluòguān
2 (男女之间) 私通 (nánnǚ zhījiān) sītōng

liar N 说谎的人 shuōhuǎng de rén
You liar! 你这个坏蛋说谎! Nǐ zhè ge huàidàn shuōhuǎng!

libel I N 诽谤 fěibàng
libel suit 诽谤诉讼 fěibàng sùsòng

II v 诽谤 fěibàng, 说…的坏话 shuō...de huàihuà

libelous ADJ 诽谤的 fěibàng de, 中伤的 zhòngshāng de

liberal I ADJ 宽容的 kuānróng de, 开明的 kāimíng de
liberal arts 文科 wénkē
II N 宽容大度的人 kuānróng dàdù de rén, 自由派 zìyóu pài ■ *Some liberals become conservatives when they get old.* 有些自由派年纪大了就变成了保守派。Yǒuxiē zìyóu pài niánjì dàle jiù biànchéngle bǎoshǒu pài.

liberalism N 自由主义 zìyóu zhǔyì

liberalize v 1 使…自由化 shǐ...zìyóuhuà **2** 放宽 fàngkuān

liberally ADV 大量地 dàliàng de

liberate v 解放 jiěfàng, 解救 jiějiù

liberated ADJ 思想解放的 sīxiǎng jiěfàng de, 不受约束的 bú shòu yuēshù de

liberation N 解放 jiěfàng, 解救 jiějiù

liberator N 解放者 jiěfàngzhě

libertarian N 自由意志论者 zìyóu yìzhì lùnzhě

liberty N 自由 zìyóu, 自由权 zìyóuquán ■ *The French Revolution of 1789 raised the slogan of "Liberty, Equality and Fraternity".* 一七八九年的法国革命提出了"自由、平等、博爱"的口号。Yāoqībājiǔ nián de Fǎguó gémìng tíchūle "zìyóu, píngděng, bó'ài" de kǒuhào.

libido N 性欲 xìngyù

Libra N 天秤 (星) 座 tiānchèng (xīng) zuò, 天秤宫 tiānchènggōng

librarian N 图书馆馆长 túshūguǎn guǎnzhǎng, 图书馆管理人员 túshūguǎn guǎnlǐ rényuán

library N 图书馆 túshūguǎn, 图书室 túshūshì

lice See louse

license I N 执照 zhízhào, 许可证 xǔkězhèng
driver's license 汽车驾驶执照 qìchē jiàshǐ zhízhào, 汽车驾驶证 qìchē jiàshǐzhèng
gun license 持枪许可证 chíqiāng xǔkězhèng
license plate 汽车执照牌 qìchē zhízhàopái
II v 许可 xǔkě, 准许 zhǔnxǔ

lichen N 地衣 dìyī

lick I v 1 舔 tiǎn
to lick one's lips 舔唇 tiǎn chún, 热切期望 rèqiè qīwàng
2 打败 dǎbài **II** N 1 舔 tiǎn **2** 少量 shǎoliàng

licking N 1 痛打 tòngdǎ **2** 失败 shībài, 失利 shīlì

licorice N 甘草糖果 gāncǎo tángguǒ

lid N 盖 (子) gài (zi) ■ *Where is the lid for this saucepan?* 这个锅的盖子呢? Zhè ge guō de gàizi ne?

lie¹ I v (PT **lay**; PP **lain**) **1** 躺 tǎng
to lie down 躺下 tǎngxia
to lie low 躲藏 duǒcáng, 隐蔽起来 yǐnbì qǐlái
2 在于 zàiyú ■ *Good health lies in regular*

exercises. 健康在于经常锻炼。Jiànkāng zàiyú jīngcháng duànliàn. **3** 位于 wèiyú

lie² I v **1** 说谎 shuōhuǎng ■ *Honesty is the best policy, so don't lie to people.* 诚实是最好的政策，所以不要对人说谎。Chéngshí shì zuì hǎo de zhèngcè, suǒyǐ bú yào duì rén shuōhuǎng. II N 谎言 huǎngyán ■ *It's a lie!* 撒谎! Sāhuǎng!
  lie detector 测谎器 cèhuǎngqì

lien N 扣押权 kòuyāquán

lieu N (in lieu of) 代替 dàitì

lieutenant N (陆军／海军陆战队) 中尉 (lùjūn/hǎijūn lùzhànduì) zhōngwèi, (海军／空军) 上尉 (hǎijūn/kōngjūn) shàngwèi

life (PL **lives**) N **1** 生命 shēngmìng
  life buoy 救生圈 jiùshēngquān
  life cycle 生命周期 shēngmìng zhōuqī
  life insurance 人寿保险 rénshòu bǎoxiǎn
  life jacket 救生衣 jiùshēngyī
  life support system 生命维持器械 shēngmìng wéichí qìxiè
2 生活 shēnghuó ■ *They lived a peaceful and comfortable life in the countryside.* 他们在乡间过着平静而舒适的生活。Tāmen zài xiāngjiān guòzhe píngjìng ér shūshì de shēnghuó. **3** 一生 yìshēng, 寿命 shòumìng
  life expectancy 平均寿命 píngjūn shòumìng
  early life (人生的) 早期 (rénshēng de) zǎoqī, 早年 zǎonián
  all one's life 终生 zhōngshēng, 终身 zhōngshēn
4 无期徒刑 wúqī túxíng, 终身监禁 zhōngshēn jiānjìn
  life sentence 无期徒刑 wúqī túxíng, 终身禁监 zhōngshēn jìnjiān

lifeboat N 救生艇 jiùshēngtǐng [M. WD 艘 sōu]

lifeguard N 救生员 jiùshēngyuán

lifeless ADJ **1** 死的 sǐde **2** 无生气的 wú shēngqì de, 无活力的 wú huólì de, 无生命的 wú shēngmìng de

lifelike ADJ 生动逼真的 shēngdòng bīzhēn de, 栩栩如生的 xǔxǔ rú shēng de

lifeline N 生命线 shēngmìngxiàn, 命脉 mìngmài

lifelong ADJ 终生的 zhōngshēng de

lifesaver N 救星 jiùxīng

life-size, life-sized ADJ 与真人一样大小的 yǔ zhēnrén yíyàng dàxiǎo de

lifestyle N 生活方式 shēnghuó fāngshì ■ *I don't think her income could support her lifestyle.* 我想她的收入无法支撑她的生活方式。Wǒ xiǎng tā de shōurù wúfǎ zhīchēng tā de shēnghuó fāngshì.

life-threatening ADJ 危及生命的 wēijí shēngmìng de

lifetime N 一生 yìshēng, 终生 zhōngshēng

lift I v **1** 抬起 táiqǐ, 举起 jǔqǐ **2** 提高 [+水平] tígāo [+shuǐpíng], 增加 zēngjiā

to lift one's spirits 提高某人的情绪 tígāo mǒurén de qíngxù
3 解除 [+禁令] jiěchú [+jìnlìng], 撤销 chèxiāo II N **1** 升降机 shēngjiàngjī [M. WD 台 tái] **2** (to give sb a lift) 让某人搭便车 ràng mǒurén dābiàn chē, 使某人搭便车 shǐ mǒurén jīngshén zhènzuò

lift-off N [火箭+] 发射 [huǒjiàn+] fāshè

ligament N 韧带 rèndài

light¹ I N **1** 光 guāng, 光线 guāngxiàn ■ *The light is too poor to read by.* 光线太差，不能阅读。Guāngxiàn tài chà, bù néng yuèdú.
  light year 光年 guāngnián
2 灯光 dēngguāng **3** 灯 dēng, 电灯 diàndēng [M. WD 盏 zhǎn]
  light bulb 灯泡 dēngpào, 电灯泡 diàn dēngpào
II v (PT & PP **lit, lighted**) **1** 点燃 diǎnrán **2** 照亮 zhàoliàng ■ *The fireworks lit up the night sky.* 烟火照亮了夜空。Yānhuǒ zhàoliàngle yèkōng.

light² ADJ **1** 轻的 qīng de ■ *The box is light and she lifts it up easily.* 盒子很轻，她很容易地举了起来。Hézi hěn qīng, tā hěn róngyì de jǔle qǐlai.
  light-fingered ① 有偷窃习惯的 yǒu tōuqiè xíguàn de ② (弹奏乐器) 手指灵巧的 (tánzòu yuèqì) shǒuzhǐ língqiǎo de
2 (衣服等) 轻便的 qīngbiàn de, 薄的 bó de **3** 淡颜色的 dàn yánsè de
  light brown eyes 浅棕色的眼睛 qiǎn zōngsè de yǎnjing

lighten v **1** 减轻 [+工作] jiǎnqīng [+gōngzuò] **2** [天色+] 变亮 [tiānsè+] biàn liàng

lighter N 打火机 dǎhuǒjī

light-headed ADJ **1** 晕眩的 yūnxuàn de **2** 头脑不清的 tóunǎo bù qīng de, 步履不稳的 bùlǚ bù wěn de

light-hearted ADJ 轻松愉快的 qīngsōng yúkuài de, 无忧无虑的 wúyōu wúlǜ de

lighthouse N 灯塔 dēngtǎ [M. WD 座 zuò]

lighting N 照明 (灯) zhàomíng (dēng)

lightly ADV **1** 轻轻地 qīngqīng de **2** 少量地 shǎoliàng de

lightning I N 闪电 shǎndiàn [M. WD 道 dào] II ADJ 闪电般的 shǎndiàn bān de
  at lightning speed 以闪电般的速度 yǐ shǎndiàn bān de sùdù

lights-out N 熄灯时间 xīdēng shíjiān

lightweight I N **1** (体育) 轻量级 (tǐyù) qīngliàngjí **2** 没有分量的人 méiyǒu fènliàng de rén, 微不足道的人 wēi bù zú dào de rén II ADJ **1** 轻薄的 [+机器] qīngbáo de [+jīqì] **2** 轻薄的 [+衣服] qīngbó de [+yīfu] **3** 浅薄的 [+书籍] qiǎnbó de [+shūjí]

likable ADJ 惹人喜爱的 rě rén xǐ'ài de

like¹ I v **1** 喜欢 xǐhuan ■ *She likes Harry a lot, but she doesn't love him.* 她挺喜欢哈里，但是并不爱

他。Tā tǐng xǐhuan Hālǐ, dànshì bìng bú ài tā.
2 喜好 xǐhào
would like 想要 xiǎngyào ■ *How do you like that?* 你觉得这个怎么样？Nǐ juéde zhège zěnmeyàng?
II N **1** 喜欢的事 xǐhuan de shì
sb's likes and dislikes 某人喜欢和不喜欢的事 mǒurén xǐhuan hé bù xǐhuan de shì
2 像…的事 xiàng…de shì
… **and the like** 以及诸如此类的事 yǐjí zhū rú cǐlèi de shì
the likes of sb 像某人这种人 xiàng mǒurén zhè zhǒng rén
like² **I** PREP 像…一样 xiàng…yíyàng **II** CONJ 就像 jiù xiàng
like I said 就像我说过的（那样）jiù xiàng wǒ shuō guò de (nà yàng)
like³ ADJ 相似的 xiāngsì de, 相像的 xiāngxiàng de
likelihood N 可能（性）kěnéng (xìng)
in all likelihood 极有可能 jí yǒu kěnéng
likely **I** ADJ 很可能的 hěn kěnéng de **II** ADV 很可能 hěn kěnéng ■ *I would very likely have done the same as you did.* 我很可能像你一样，也这样做。Wǒ hěn kěnéng xiàng nǐ yíyàng, yě zhèyàng zuò.
like-minded ADJ 想法差不多的 xiǎngfǎ chàbuduōde
liken v 把…比作 bǎ…bǐzuò
likeness N **1** 相像 xiāngxiàng, 相似 xiāngsì **2** 画像 huàxiàng [M. WD 幅 fú], 照片 zhàopiàn [M. WD 张 zhāng]
likewise ADV 同样地 tóngyàng de
liking N 喜欢 xǐhuan, 爱好 àihào
to have a liking for 喜欢 xǐhuan
to take a liking to sb 喜欢上某人 xǐhuan shang mǒurén
lilac N **1** 丁香树 dīngxiāng shù **2** 淡紫色 dànzǐ sè
lilt N 抑扬顿挫的声音 yìyáng dùncuò de shēngyīn
lily N 百合花 bǎihéhuā
limb N **1**（树）主干 (shù) zhǔgàn [M. WD 根 gēn] **2**（四）肢 (sì) zhī, 臂 bì [M. WD 条 tiáo]
be out on a limb 处于孤立无援的境地 chǔyú gūlì wúyuán de jìngdì
limbo N (be in limbo) 处于不确定的状态 chǔyú bú quèdìng de zhuàngtài
lime N **1** 石灰 shíhuī **2** 酸橙树 suānchéng shù [M. WD 棵 kē]
limelight N 公众关注的中心 gōngzhòng guānzhù de zhōngxīn
to seek the limelight 爱出风头 ài chū fēngtou
limerick N 打油诗 dǎyóushī [M. WD 首 shǒu]
limit **I** N **1** 限度 xiàndù ■ *There is a limit to how much we're able to spend on the holiday.* 我们度假能花多少钱，是有限度的。Wǒmen dùjià néng huā duōshǎo qián, shì yǒu xiàndù de.

within limits 在合理的范围内 zài hélǐ de fànwéinèi
speed limit 最高车速 zuì gāo chēsù
2 边缘 biānyuán ■ *They asked the real estate agent to find them an apartment within the city limits.* 他们要房产经纪人为他们在市区范围内找一套公寓。Tāmen yào fángchǎn jīngjìrén wèi tāmen zài shìqū fànwéi nèi zhǎo yí tào gōngyù.
off limit 不准入内 bù zhǔn rù nèi
II v 限制 xiànzhì
limitation N 限制 xiànzhì
limited ADJ **1** 有限的 yǒuxiàn de **2** 受到限制的 shòudào xiànzhì de
limousine N 大型豪华轿车 dàxíng háohuá jiàochē [M. WD 辆 liàng]
limp **I** ADJ 软绵绵的 ruǎnmiánmián de, 无力的 wúlì de **II** v 一瘸一拐地走 yì qué yì guǎi de zǒu **III** N 一瘸一拐地走 yìqué yìguǎi de zǒu, 跛行 bǒxíng
linchpin, lynchpin N 关键人物 guānjiàn rénwù, 关键的事 guānjiàn de shì
line **I** N **1** 线 xiàn [M. WD 条 tiáo/道 dào] **2** 排队 páiduì ■ *I stood in line for half an hour before reaching my airline's checking-in desk.* 我排了半小时队才到航空公司的登机处。Wǒ páile bàn xiǎoshí duì cái dào hángkōng gōngsī de dēngjīchù. **3** 皱纹 zhòuwén [M. WD 条 tiáo/道 dào] **4** 电话线 diànhuàxiàn
online 联网 liánwǎng, 上网 shàngwǎng
5 态度 tàidu, 立场 lìchǎng
to take a hard line on sth 对某事采取强硬立场 duì mǒushì cǎiqǔ qiángyìng lìchǎng
6（书页上的）行 (shūyè shàng de) háng **II** v 排成一行 pái chéng yì háng
finish line 终点线 zhōngdiǎnxiàn
lineage N **1** 行数 xíng shù **2** 血统 xuètǒng, 家系 jiāxì
linear ADJ **1** 线条的 xiàntiáo de
linear diagram 线条图 xiàntiáotú
2 线性的 xiànxìng de
linear thinking 线性思维 xiànxìng sīwéi
3 长度的 chángdù de
linear measurements 长度测量 chángdù cèliáng
linebacker N（美式橄榄球）中后卫 (Měishì gǎnlǎnqiú) zhōnghòuwèi
lined ADJ **1** 印有线条的 [+纸] yìn yǒu xiàntiáo de [+zhǐ] **2** 有衬里的 [+上衣] yǒu chènlǐ de [+shàngyī]
linen N 家用纺织品（床单、台布、内衣等）jiāyòng fǎngzhīpǐn (chuángdān, táibù, nèiyī děng)
liner¹ N 客轮 kèlún [M. WD 艘 sōu]
cruise liner 游轮 yóulún
liner² N 衬里 chènlǐ, 衬垫 chèndiàn
liner notes（激光唱盘）说明文字 (jīguāng chàngpán) shuōmíng wénzì

linesman N 1 （橄榄球）锋线球员 (gǎnlǎnqiú) fēngxiàn qiúyuán 2 （铁路）养路工 (tiělù) yǎnglùgōng

line-up N 1 （球类比赛）运动员阵容 (qiúlèi bǐsài) yùndòngyuán zhènróng 2 （演出）全体演员 (yǎnchū) quántǐ yǎnyuán 3 （电视）一系列节目 (diànshì) yíxìliè jiémù

linger v [人+] 逗留不离去 [rén+] dòuliú bù líqù, [事+] 持续 [shì+] chíxù

lingerie N （女子）内衣裤 (nǚzǐ) nèiyīkù

lingering ADJ 持续的 chíxù de, 拖延的 tuōyán de

lingo N 隐语 yǐnyǔ, 行话 hánghuà

lingua franca N （国际）通用语 (guójì) tōngyòngyǔ

linguist N 1 语言学家 yǔyánxuéjiā 2 通晓多国语言的人 tōngxiǎo duōguó yǔyán de rén

linguistic ADJ 语言的 yǔyán de, 语言学的 yǔyánxué de

linguistics N 语言学 yǔyánxué

liniment N 涂剂 tújì, 搽剂 chájì

lining N （衣服）衬里 (yīfu) chènlǐ

link I v 1 连接 liánjiē ■ This airline links almost all state capitals to New York. 这家航空公司把几乎所有的州首府和纽约连接起来。Zhè jiā hángkōng gōngsī bǎ jīhū suǒyǒu de zhōu shǒufǔ hé Niǔyuē liánjiē qǐlai. 2 与…有关 yǔ…yǒuguān ■ This terrorist attack has been linked to an extreme religious group abroad. 这个恐怖分子攻击与外国极端宗教组织有关。Zhè ge kǒngbù fènzǐ gōngjī yǔ wàiguó jíduān zōngjiào zǔzhī yǒuguān. II N 1 关系 guānxi, 联系 liánxì

to link up 连接（电脑）liánjiē (diànnǎo) 2 （计算机）链接 (jìsuànjī) liànjiē 3 环节 huánjié

a weak link (in sth) （某事中的）薄弱环节 (mǒushì zhòngde) bóruò huánjié

linkage N 1 连接系列 liánjiē xìliè 2 关联原则 guānlián yuánzé

linking verb N 连系动词 liánxì dòngcí

linoleum N 油地毡 yóudìzhān

lint N 棉绒 miánróng

lion N (F **lioness**) 狮子 shīzi [M. WD 只 zhǐ/头 tóu] the lion's share 最大的份额 zuì dà de fèn'é

lip N 嘴唇 zuǐchún

lip gloss 亮彩唇膏 liàng cǎi chúngāo

lip synch 假唱 jiǎ chàng

to keep one's lips sealed 守口如瓶 shǒu kǒu rú píng

to pay lip service 只说好话没有行动 zhǐ shuō hǎohuà méiyǒu xíngdòng, 口惠而实不至 kǒu huì ér shí bù zhì

lip-read v 唇读 chúndú, 观察对方的唇形（来猜测语意）guānchá duìfāng de chún xíng (lái cāicè yǔyì)

lip-reading N 唇读 chúndú

lipstick N 唇膏 chúngāo, 口红 kǒuhóng

liquefy v （使…）液化 (shǐ…) yèhuà

liqueur N 利口酒 lìkǒu jiǔ

liquid I N 液体 yètǐ ■ I prefer to use liquid soap, not bar soap. 我喜欢用液体香皂，不喜欢用固体香皂。Wǒ xǐhuan yòng yètǐ xiāngzào, bù xǐhuan yòng gùtǐ xiāngzào. II ADJ 1 液体的 yètǐ de 2 很容易变成现金的 hěn róngyì biànchéng xiànjīn de

liquid assets 流动资金 liúdòng zījīn

liquidate v 停业清理 tíngyè qīnglǐ, 清算（破产企业）qīngsuàn (pòchǎn qǐyè)

liquidation N 停业清理 tíngyè qīnglǐ

liquor N 烈性酒 lièxìng jiǔ

liquor store 酒店 jiǔdiàn

list I N 1 单子 dānzi [M. WD 份 fèn/张 zhāng], 清单 qīngdān [M. WD 份 fèn/张 zhāng] 2 目录 mùlù

list price （厂商的）定价 (chǎngshāng de) dìngjià

shopping list 购物单 gòuwùdān

II v 列出 lièchū

listen v 1 听 tīng 2 （你）听着 (nǐ) tīngzhe ■ Listen, this is my last offer. Take it or leave it. 听着，这是我最后的条件。你要么接受，要么就算了。Tīngzhe, zhè shì wǒ zuìhòu de tiáojiàn. Nǐ yàome jiēshòu, yàome jiù suàn le.

to listen in 偷听 tōutīng

to listen up 注意听 zhùyì tīng

listener N 听者 tīngzhě, 听众 tīngzhòng

listing N （清单上的）一项 (qīngdān shàng de) yí xiàng

listings 活动内容时间表 huódòng nèiróng shíjiānbiǎo

listless ADJ 无精打采的 wújīng dǎcǎi de, 懒洋洋的 lǎnyāngyāng de

lit See light¹

litany N 1 （基督教）应答祈祷 (Jīdūjiào) yìngdá qídǎo 2 冗长的话 rǒngcháng de huà

lite ADJ 低度的 dī dù de, 低脂肪的 dī zhīfáng de

lite beer 淡啤酒 dàn píjiǔ

liter N 公升 gōngshēng ■ One gallon equals about four liters. 一加仑大约等于四公升。Yì jiālún dàyuē děngyú sì gōngshēng.

literacy N 有读写能力 yǒu dú xiě nénglì

literal ADJ 字面上的 zìmiàn shàng de, 逐字的 zhúzì de

a literal translation 逐字的翻译 zhúzì de fānyì

literally ADV 1 按照字面 ànzhào zìmiàn 2 确实 quèshí, 简直 jiǎnzhí

to take … literally 照字面理解 zhào zìmiàn lǐjiě

literary ADJ 文学的 wénxué de

literate ADJ 能读会写的 néng dú huì xiě de, 识字的 shízì de

literature N 1 文学 wénxué 2 文献资料 wénxiàn zīliào

medical literature 医学文献 yīxué wénxiàn

ithe ADJ 柔软灵活的 róuruǎn línghuó de

itigate v 提出诉讼 tíchū sùsòng, 打官司 dǎ guānsi

itigation N 诉讼 sùsòng [M. WD 项 xiàng/件 jiàn]

itmus test 1 试金石 shìjīnshí, 检验 jiǎnyàn **2** 石蕊测试 shíruǐ cèshì

itter¹ I N 垃圾 lājī

litter bag 垃圾袋 lājīdài

II v 乱扔垃圾 luànrēng lājī

itter² N 一窝（幼兽）yìwō (yòu shòu)

a litter of puppies 一窝小狗 yìwō xiǎogǒu

itterbug N 乱扔垃圾的人 luànrēng lājī de rén

ittle I ADJ **1** 小 xiǎo **2** 年幼的 niányòu de, 小 xiǎo **3** 不多的 bù duō de, 很少的 hěn shǎo de ■ *I need a little help to move the furniture.* 我需要有人帮我搬一下家具。Wǒ xūyào yǒurén bāng wǒ bān yíxià jiājù. **II** ADV 稍许一点儿 shāoxǔ yìdiǎnr ■ *This artist was little known in his time.* 这位艺术家生前鲜为人知。Zhè wèi yìshùjiā shēngqián xiǎn wéi rén zhī.

a little 一点儿 yì diǎnr ■ *I'd like to have a little more cake, not too much, please.* 我想再吃一点儿蛋糕，不要太多，行吗？Wǒ xiǎng zài chī yìdiǎnr dàngāo, búyào tài duō, xíng ma?

a little while 一会儿 yíhuìr

little by little 一点一点地 yì diǎnr yìdiǎnr de

Little League N 儿童棒球联合会 Értóng bàngqiú liánhéhuì

iturgical ADJ 礼拜仪式的 lǐbài yíshì de

iturgy N **1** 礼拜仪式 lǐbài yíshì **2** 祈祷书 qídǎoshū

live I v **1** 活 huó, 生活 shēnghuó ■ *All his life he lived simply and honestly.* 他一生都简朴诚实。Tā yì shēng dōu jiǎnpǔ chéngshí.

to live and let live 自己活，也让别人活。Zìjǐ huó, yě ràng biéren huó.

to live off 靠…为生 kào...wéishēng ■ *He lives off the money his parents left him.* 他靠父母留下的钱为生。Tā kào fùmǔ liúxia de qián wéishēng. **2** 居住 jūzhù, 住 zhù ■ *She still lives with her parents.* 她还和父母一起住。Tā hái hé fùmǔ yìqǐ zhù.

to live together 同居 tóngjū

II ADJ **1** 现场 xiànchǎng ■ *The café has live music every Friday and Saturday nights.* 这家咖啡馆每星期五、星期六晚上有现场音乐演出。Zhè jiā kāfēiguǎn měi xīngqīwǔ, xīngqīliù wǎnshang yǒu xiànchǎng yīnyuè yǎnchū. **2** 活着的 huózhào de

an experiment on live animals 活体动物实验 huótǐ dòngwù shíyàn

ivelihood N 生计 shēngjì ■ *My father earned his livelihood by teaching.* 我的父亲靠教书谋生。Wǒ de fùqin kào jiāoshū móushēng.

ively ADJ 活跃的 huóyuè de, 活泼的 huópo de

liven v（使…）活跃起来 (shǐ...) huóyuè qǐlái, （使…）更有趣 (shǐ...) gèng yǒuqù

liver N 肝（脏）gān (zàng)

lives N, PL See life

livestock N 牲畜 shēngchù, 家畜 jiāchù

livid ADJ **1** 气得脸色铁青的 qì dé liǎnsè tiěqīng de, 大怒的 dà nù de **2** 铅灰色的 qiān huīsè de

living I ADJ **1** 活的 huó de ■ *He is one of our greatest living Jazz musicians.* 他是我们在世的最伟大的爵士音乐家之一。Tā shì wǒmen zàishì de zuì wěidà de juéshì yīnyuèjiā zhīyī.

the living 活着的人 huózhe de rén, 生者 shēngzhě

2 在使用的 zài shǐyòng de

living room 起居室 qǐjūshì, 客厅 kètīng

living standard 生活水平 shēnghuó shuǐpíng ■ *Many people feel their living standard is falling.* 很多人觉得生活水平在下降。Hěn duō rén juéde shēnghuó shuǐpíng zài xiàjiàng.

II N 生计 shēngjì

to make a living 谋生 móushēng

lizard N 蜥蜴 xīyì [M. WD 只 zhī]

llama N 美洲驼 Měizhōutuó [M. WD 头 tóu]

load I N **1** 一大批 yí dà pī, 大量 dàliàng ■ *A ship carrying a full load of tourists sailed into the harbor.* 一艘载满游客的轮船驶进海港。Yì sōu zàimǎn yóukè de lúnchuán shǐjìn hǎigǎng. **2**（一车）运载物（yì chē）yùnzài wù

a truck/boat/coach load of 一卡车/一船/一旅游车 yì kǎchē/yì chuán/yì lǚyóuchē

3（沉重的）负担 (chénzhòng de) fùdān **4** 附加费 fù jiāfèi **II** v **1** 装载 zhuāngzài **2** 给（枪）上子弹 gěi (qiāng) shàng zǐdàn

loaded ADJ **1** 装着货物的 [+卡车] zhuāngzhe huòwù de [+kǎchē] **2** 装有子弹的 [+枪] zhuāngyǒu zǐdàn de [+qiāng] **3**（棒球）满垒的 (bàngqiú) mǎnlěi de **4** 话中有话的 [+问题] huà zhōng yǒu huà de [+wèntí]

a loaded question 别有用心的问题 biéyǒu yòngxīn de wèntí

5 富有的 fùyǒu de, 有钱的 yǒuqián de

loaf¹（PL loaves）N 大面包 dà miànbāo

loaf² 游手好闲 yóu shǒu hào xián, 虚度光阴 xūdù guāngyīn

loafer N **1** 游手好闲者 yóu shǒu hào xián zhě **2** 平跟船鞋 pínggēn chuánxié [M. WD 双 shuāng]

loan I N **1** 借出物 jièchūwù **2** 借款 jièkuǎn, 笔 bǐ, 贷款 dàikuǎn [M. WD 笔 bǐ] ■ *He asked me for a loan again.* 他又向我借钱。Tā yòu xiàng wǒ jiè qián.

loan shark N 放高利贷者 fàng gāolìdài zhě

II v 借出 jièchū ■ *Can you loan me $100 until Thursday?* 你能借我一百块吗？我星期四还。Nǐ néng jiè wǒ yì bǎi kuài ma? Wǒ xīngqīsì huán.

on loan 借来的 jièlái de ■ *This tent is on loan from a friend of mine.* 这个帐篷是我从朋友那里借来的。Zhè ge zhàngpeng shì wǒ cóng péngyou nàlǐ jièlái de.

loanword N 外来语 wàiláiyǔ, 借译词 jièyìcí

loath, loth ADJ 厌恶 yànwù, 不愿意 bú yuànyì

loathe V 厌恶 yànwù, 憎恨 zēnghèn

loathing N 厌恶 yànwù, 强烈的反感 qiángliè de fǎngǎn

loathsome ADJ 令人厌恶的 lìng rén yànwù de

loaves See **loaf¹**

lobby I N 1 大厅 dàtīng, 大堂 dàtáng 2 (美国国会的) 游说团 (Měiguó Guóhuì de) yóushuìtuán a powerful environmental lobby 强大的环保游说团 qiángdà de huánbǎo yóushuìtuán II V (美国政治) 游说 (Měiguó zhèngzhì) yóushuì

lobe N 1 耳垂 ěrchuí 2 (脑) 叶 (nǎo) yè, (肺) 叶 (fèi) yè

lobster N 龙虾 lóngxiā [M. WD 只 zhī]

local I ADJ 1 当地的 dāngdì de, 本地的 běndì de ■ *Local calls are free so long as you pay for the line.* 只要你付线路费, 本地电话就是免费的。Zhǐ yào nǐ fù xiànlùfèi, běndì diànhuà jiù shì miǎnfèi de. 2 局部的 júbù de ■ *The doctor has not decided whether a local or general anesthetic is needed for this operation.* 医生还没有决定这个手术用局部还是全身麻醉。Yīshēng hái méiyǒu juédìng zhè ge shǒushù yòng júbù háishì quánshēn mázuì. II N 当地人 dāngdì rén

locale N 地点 dìdiǎn, 现场 xiànchǎng

locality N 地区 dìqū

localize V 使…局部化 shǐ…júbùhuà

locally ADV 在当地 zài dāngdì, 在本地 zài běndì

locate V 1 找到 zhǎodao 2 设在 shè zài to be located in/at 位于 wèi yú, 坐落在 zuòluò zài ■ *The restaurant is located in a shopping mall.* 这家餐馆坐落在一个购物中心。Zhè jiā cānguǎn zuòluò zài yí ge gòuwù zhōngxīn.

location N 位置 wèizhi ■ *I don't think this is a suitable location for a nursing home.* 我想这个地方养老院不合适。Wǒ xiǎng zhè ge dìfang jiàn yǎnglǎoyuàn bù héshì.

lock I N 1 锁 suǒ combination lock 号码锁 hàomǎsuǒ 2 水闸 shuǐzhá, 船闸 chuánzhá lock, stock and barrel 全部 quánbù 3 一绺 (头发) yì liǔ (tóufa) II V 锁 suǒ, 锁上 suǒshang to lock sb up 把某人监禁起来 bǎ mǒurén jiānjìn qǐlái, 把某人关起来 bǎ mǒurén guān qǐlái to lock sth up 把某物锁起来 bǎ mǒuwù suǒqǐlái

locker N 存放柜 cúnfàngguì [M. WD 只 zhī] locker room 衣物间 yīwùjiān, 更衣室 gēngyīshì

locket N 盒式项链坠物 héshì xiàngliàn zhuìwù

locksmith N 锁匠 suǒjiang, 修锁工人 xiū suǒ gōngrén

locomotive N 火车头 huǒchētóu, 机车 jīchē [M. WD 台 tái]

locust N 蝗虫 huángchóng

lodge I V 1 租住 zū zhù, 寄宿 jìsù 2 供…寄宿 gōng…jìsù 3 卡在 qiǎ zài, 卡住 qiǎ zhù 4 提出 [+抗议] tíchū [+kàngyì] II N 1 小屋 xiǎo wū 2 地方分会 dìfang fēnhuì

lodging N 住宿的地方 zhùsù de dìfang, 寄宿处 jìsùchù

loft N 阁楼 gélóu

lofty ADJ 1 崇高的 [+理想] chónggāo de [+lǐxiǎng] 2 高傲的 [+人] gāo'ào de [+rén], 傲慢的 àomàn de

log I N 1 木材 mùcái, 木块 mùkuài 2 飞行日记 fēixíng rìjì [M. WD 本 běn], 航海日记 hánghǎi rìjì [M. WD 本 běn] II V 1 砍伐 (树木) kǎnfá (shùmù) 2 正式记录 zhèngshì jìlù 3 工作了 (若干时间) gōngzuò le (ruògān shíjiān) log cabin 原木小屋 yuánmù xiǎowū to log in/on (计算机) 进入系统 (jìsuànjī) jìnrù xìtǒng to log out/off (计算机) 退出系统 (jìsuànjī) tuìchū xìtǒng

loggerheads N (at loggerheads with sb) 与某人不和 yǔ mǒurén bùhé, 同某人争吵 tóng mǒurén zhēngchǎo

logging N 伐木 (业) fámù (yè)

logic N 逻辑 (学) luójí (xué)

logical ADJ 合乎逻辑的 hé hū luójí de

logistics N 组织安排工作 zǔzhī ānpái gōngzuò, 后勤 (工作) hòuqín (gōngzuò)

logjam N 无法进展的局面 wúfǎ jìnzhǎn de júmiàn, 僵局 jiāngjú

logo N 标志 biāozhì, 标识 biāoshì

loincloth N 腰布 yāobù [M. WD 块 kuài]

loins N 腰部 yāobu

loiter V 游荡 yóudàng, 闲逛 xiánguàng

loitering N 游荡 yóudàng, 徘徊 páihuái

loll V 懒洋洋地坐/躺 lǎnyāngyāng de zuò/tǎng

lollipop N 棒糖 bàngtáng [M. WD 根 gēn/块 kuài]

lone ADJ 孤独的 gūdú de, 仅有的 jǐnyǒu de

lonely ADJ 1 寂寞的 jìmò de, 孤独的 gūdú de 2 荒无人迹的 huāng wú rénjì de

loner N 独来独往的人 dú lái dú wǎng de rén

lonesome ADJ 孤独的 gūdú de, 孤寂的 gūjì de

long¹ I ADJ 长 cháng long johns 长内裤 cháng nèikù long jump 跳远 (运动) tiàoyuǎn (yùndòng) long shot 可能性不大的事 kěnéngxìng bùdà de shì, 玄乎的事 xuánhu de shì II ADV 长时间 cháng shíjiān ■ *Were you there long?* 你在那里待了很久吗? Nǐ zài nàlǐ dàile hěn jiǔ ma?

long before/after 在…很久以前／以后 zài…hěn jiǔ yǐqián/yǐhòu ■ *My parents came to this city long before I was born.* 我父母在我出生很久以前就到这个城市来了。Wǒ fùmǔ zài wǒ chūshēng hěn jiǔ yǐqián jiù dào zhè ge chéngshì lái le.

for long 很久 hěn jiǔ

as long as 只要 zhǐ yào ■ *I can give you a loan as long as you pay me back in three months.* 你如果在三个月之内还我，我就可以借给你钱。Nǐ rúguǒ zài sān ge yuè zhīnèi huán wǒ, wǒ jiù kěyǐ jiè gěi nǐ qián.

no longer 不再 bú zài

III N (the long and short of it) 主要是 zhǔyào shì, 关键是 guānjiàn shì

long² v 渴望 kěwàng, 盼望 pànwang

a longed-for reunion 盼望已久的团聚 pànwàng yǐjiǔ de tuánjù

long-distance ADJ 长途的 chángtú de

long-distance call 长途电话 chángtú diànhuà

long-distance driver 长途卡车司机 chángtú kǎchē sījī

long-distance runner 长跑运动员 chángpǎo yùndòngyuán

long-drawn-out ADJ 拖得太长的 tuō dé tài cháng de, 冗长的 rǒngcháng de

longevity N 长寿 chángshòu

longhand N 普通手写 pǔtōng shǒuxiě

longing N 渴望 kěwàng

a longing for friendship 对友谊的渴望 duì yǒuyì de kěwàng

longitude N 径度 jìngdù

longitude 30° east 东经30度 dōngjīng sānshí dù

longitudinal ADJ 长时间的 cháng shíjiān de, 历时的 lìshí de

long-lasting ADJ 1 长久的 chángjiǔ de, 耐用的 nàiyòng de 2 纵向的 zòngxiàng de, 经度的 jīngdù de

long-lived ADJ 长期存在的 chángqī cúnzài de, 长寿的 chángshòu de

long-lost ADJ 丢失很久的 diūshī hěn jiǔ de, 久未见面的 jiǔwèi jiànmiàn de

long-range ADJ 1 远程的 yuǎnchéng de, 远距离的 yuǎnjùlí de 2 长期的 chángqī de

long-running ADJ 持续很长时间的 chíxù hěn chángshíjiān de

longshoreman N 码头工人 mǎtou gōngrén

long-standing ADJ 长期（存在）的 chángqī (cúnzài) de

long-suffering ADJ 长期忍受的 chángqī rěnshòu de

long-term ADJ 长期的 chángqī de

longtime ADJ 长久的 chángjiǔ de

long-winded ADJ 絮絮叨叨的 xùxù dāodao de

look I v 1 看 kàn, 瞧 qiáo

to look after 照顾 zhàogu, 照料 zhàoliao

to look down upon 看不起 kànbuqǐ ■ *That snob looks down upon people with low incomes.* 那个势利鬼看不起低收入的人。Nà ge shìlìguǐ kànbuqǐ dī shōurù de rén.

to look forward to 期待 qīdài, 盼 pàn ■ *Johnny is looking forward to Christmas.* 强尼期待圣诞节。Qiángní qīdài Shèngdànjié.

to look up 查 chá, 查阅 cháyuè ■ *Would you please teach me how to look up a word in a Chinese dictionary?* 你能不能教我怎样在中文词典上查词？Nǐ néngbunéng jiāo wǒ zěnyàng zài Zhōngwén cídiǎnshang chá cí?

2 寻找 xúnzhǎo 3 看上去 kànshangqu ■ *He looks as if he's going to cry.* 他看上去要哭了。Tā kànshangqu yào kū le. II v 看 kàn ■ *Will you have a look at this photo?* 你看一看这张照片，好吗？Nǐ kànyíkàn zhè zhāng zhàopiàn, hǎoma?

2 表情 biǎoqíng

lookalike N 长得极像某名人的人 zhǎngde jí xiàng mǒu míngrén de rén

lookout N 岗哨 gǎngshào, 了望台 liàowàngtái

to be on the lookout for 监视 jiānshì

loom I v 1 隐隐出现 yǐnyǐn chūxiàn 2 临近 línjìn II N 织布机 zhībùjī [M. WD 架 jià]

loony ADJ 怪异的 guàiyì de, 愚蠢的 yúchǔn de

loop I N 1 环形 huánxíng 2 圈 quān, 环 huán

to be out of the loop 圈外人 quānwàirén II v 把…绕成圈 bǎ…ràochéng quān

loophole N 漏洞 lòudòng, 空子 kòngzi

loose ADJ 1 松 sōng, 松开 sōngkāi 2 宽松的（衣服）kuānsōng de (yīfu) ■ *I like to wear loose clothes.* 我喜欢穿宽松的衣服。Wǒ xǐhuan chuān kuānsōng de yīfu. 3 不精确的 bù jīngquè de, 粗略的 cūlüè

a loose translation 粗略的译文 cūlüè de yìwén

loose-leaf ADJ 活页的 huóyè de

loosen v（使…）变松（shǐ…）biàn sōng, 松开 sōngkāi

loot I v 抢劫 qiǎngjié, 掠夺 lüèduó II N 1 赃物 zāngwù 2 战利品 zhànlìpǐn 3 钱财 qiáncái

lop v 砍掉 kǎndiào

lopsided ADJ 歪斜的 wāixié de, 倾斜的 qīngxié de

Lord N 上帝 Shàngdì, 耶稣 Yēsū

lord N 1（英国）贵族（Yīngguó）guìzú 2 主人 zhǔrén

lose (PT & PP lost) v 1 丢失 [+钱包] diūshī [+qiánbāo], 失去 [+工作] shīqù [+gōngzuò]

to lose one's way 迷路 mílù

to lose heart 丧失信心 sàngshī xìnxīn

2 输 [+比赛] shū [+bǐsài]

loser N 1 失败者 shībàizhě 2 倒霉蛋 dǎoméidàn

loss N 1 丧失 sàngshī ■ *The loss of her grandson was too much a blow to the old woman.* 老妇人丧失了孙子，这个打击太大，她忍受不了。Lǎo fùrén sàngshīle sūnzi, zhè ge dǎjī tàidà, tā rěnshòubuliǎo. **2** 损失 sǔnshī ■ *Her departure is a great loss to the school.* 她的离去是学校的损失。Tāde líqù shì xuéxiào de sǔnshī. **3**（商业）亏损 (shāngyè) kuīsǔn

lost I ADJ **1** 丢失的 [+宠物] diūshī de [+chǒngwù] **2** 迷路的 [+旅行者] mílù de [+lǚxíngzhě] **3** 浪费掉的 [+时间] làngfèi diào de [+shíjiān]
II v See lose

lost-and-found N 失物招领处 shīwù zhāolǐngchù

lot I PRON, ADJ **1** (a lot of, lots of) 很多 hěn duō, 许多 xǔduō ■ *They spend lots of money on overseas holidays.* 他们在海外度假上花了很多的钱。Tāmen zài hǎiwài dùjiàshang huāle hěn duō de qián. **2** 很多 hěn duō
to have a lot on one's plate 有很多事情要处理 yǒu hěn duō shìqing yào chǔlǐ, 有很多难题要解决 yǒu hěn duō nántí yào jiějué
II ADV 多 duō, 得多 dé duō ■ *I feel a lot better.* 我感到好多了。Wǒ gǎndào hǎo duō le. **III** N **1** 一块地 yí kuài dì **2** 一块空地 yí kuài kòngdì **3** 命运 mìngyùn, 运气 yùnqi
to draw lots 抽签 chōuqiān
to throw in your lot with sb 与某人共命运 yǔ mǒurén gòng mìngyùn
3 一批人 yìpī rén, 一群人 yìqún rén

lotion N **1** 护肤液 hùfūyè **2** 药液 yàoyè

lottery N 彩票 cǎipiào, 乐透 lètòu

loud ADJ **1** 响 xiǎng, 大声 dàshēng **2** 色彩过分鲜艳的 sècǎi guòfèn xiānyàn de, 刺眼的 cìyǎn de

loudly ADV 大声地 dàshēng de ■ *"Help! Help!" the drowning man cried out loudly.* "救命！""救命！"落水的男子大声喊叫。"Jiùmìng! Jiùmìng!" luòshuǐ de nánzǐ dàshēng hǎnjiào.

loud-mouth N 夸夸其谈的人 kuākuā qí tán de rén, 言语粗俗的人 yányǔ cūsú de rén

loudspeaker N 扩音器 kuòyīnqì, 扬声器 yángshēngqì

lounge I N（旅馆）休息室 (lǚguǎn) xiūxishì,（机场）候机大厅 (jīchǎng) hòujī dàtīng
lounge chair 躺椅 tǎngyǐ
II v 懒洋洋地坐 lǎnyāngyāng de zuò, 懒洋洋地站 ǎnyāngyāng de zhàn

louse I N (PL **lice**) 虱子 shīzi **II** v (to louse up) 把…弄糟 bǎ...nòngzāo

lousy ADJ 糟透了的 zāotòule de

lovable ADJ 让人喜爱的 ràng rén xǐ'ài de, 可爱的 kě'ài de

love I v **1** 喜爱 xǐ'ài **2** 爱 ài, 心爱 xīn'ài ■ *She loves her husband dearly.* 她深深地爱丈夫。Tā shēnshēn de ài zhàngfu. **II** N **1** 爱 ài ■ *Some people say the love of money is the root of all evil.* 有人说，爱钱是万恶之源。Yǒurén shuō, ài qián shì wàn'è zhī yuán. **2** 爱情 àiqíng

love affair 恋爱关系 liàn'ài guānxi

love seat 双人小沙发 shuāngrén xiǎo shāfā

love triangle 三角恋爱 sānjiǎo liàn'ài

lovely ADJ **1** 可爱的 kě'ài de ■ *Who can say no to such a lovely little girl?* 谁忍心对这么可爱的小姑娘说不？Shéi rěnxīn duì zhème kě'ài de xiǎogūniang shuō bù? **2** 美妙的 měimiào de, 极好的 jíhǎo de ■ *Oh, what lovely music!* 啊，这音乐真美妙！A, zhè yīnyuè zhēn měimiào!

lover N 情人 qíngrén **2** 爱好者 àihàozhě

lovesick ADJ 害相思病的 hài xiāngsībìng de

loving ADJ 表示爱的 biǎoshì ài de, 爱的 ài de

low ADJ **1** 低 dī **2** 低下的 dīxià de ■ *The price of the product is low, but the quality isn't.* 这个产品的价格低，质量可不低。Zhè ge chǎnpǐn de jiàgé dī, zhìliàng kě bù dī.

lowbrow ADJ 低俗的 dīsú de, 庸俗的 yōngsú de

low-cal ADJ 低热量的 dī rèliáng de

lowdown[1] N 最重要的信息 zuì zhòngyào de xìnxī

lowdown[2] ADJ 卑劣的 bēiliè de, 低下的 dīxià de

low-end ADJ 低档的 dīdàng de, 廉价的 liánjià de

lower I v 降低 jiàngdī ■ *Please lower your voice.* 请小点儿声。Qǐng xiǎo diǎnr shēng. **II** ADJ 较低的 jiào dī de

lowercase N 小写字体 xiǎoxiě zìtǐ

lowfat ADJ 低脂肪的 dī zhīfáng de

low-key ADJ 低调的 dīdiào de

low-life ADJ 人类渣滓 rénlèi zhāzǐ, 败类 bàilèi

lowly ADJ 低微的 dīwēi de, 低下的 dīxià de

lowlying ADJ 高出海面不多的 gāochū hǎimiàn bù duō de

loyal ADJ 忠诚的 zhōngchéng de

loyalty N 忠诚 zhōngchéng, 忠心 zhōngxīn ■ *Can I count on your loyalty?* 我可以依赖你的忠诚吗？Wǒ kěyǐ yīlài nǐ de zhōngchéng ma?

lozenge N 糖锭 tángdìng
cough lozenge 止咳糖 zhǐkétáng

LSD ABBREV（一种）迷幻药 (yìzhǒng) míhuànyào

lube N 加滑润剂 jiā huárùnjì
a lube job 给汽车加滑润油的活儿 gěi qìchē jiā huárùnyóu de huór

lubricant N 滑润剂 huárùnjì

lubricate v 给…加润滑剂 gěi...jiā rùnhuájì

lubrication N 加滑润剂 jiā huárùnjì

lucid ADJ **1** 神志清楚的 shénzhì qīngchu de **2** 表达清楚的 biǎodá qīngchu de

luck N 运气 yùnqi, 运道 yùndào ■ *Even with a university degree, you still need luck to get a good job.* 你即使有大学学位，还要靠运气好才能找到好工作。Nǐ jíshǐ yǒu dàxué xuéwèi, hái yào kào yùnqi hǎo cái néng zhǎodao hǎo gōngzuò.
Good luck! 祝您好运! Zhù nín hǎo yùn!
Just my luck! 都怪我运气不好! Dōu guài wǒ yùnqi bù hǎo!

lucky ADJ 幸运的 xìngyùn de

lucrative ADJ 赚大钱的 zhuàn dàqián de, 利润丰厚的 lìrùn fēnghòu de

ludicrous ADJ 可笑的 kěxiào de, 荒唐的 huāngtang de

lug V 艰难地拖 jiānnán de tuō

luggage N 行李 xíngli [M. WD 件 jiàn]

lugubrious ADJ 悲伤的 bēishāng de

lukewarm ADJ 1 温吞的 [+水] wēntun de [+shuǐ] 2 冷淡的 [+态度] lěngdàn de [+tàidu]

lull I V 使…平静下来 shǐ…píngjìng xiàlai II N 间歇 jiànxiē

lullaby N 摇篮曲 yáolánqǔ, 催眠曲 cuīmiánqǔ

lumbago N 腰肌劳损 yāojī láosǔn, 腰痛 yāotòng

lumber I N 木材 mùcái II V 1 伐木制成木材 fámù zhìchéng mùcái 2 缓慢笨拙地移动 huǎnmàn bènzhuō de yídòng

lumberjack N 伐木工人 fámù gōngrén

luminary N 名人 míngrén, 杰出人物 jiéchū rénwù

luminous ADJ 1 发光的 fā guāng de 2 色彩亮丽的 sècǎi liànglì de

lump I N 块 kuài, 肿块 zhǒng kuài
lump sum 一次性付款 yícìxìng fùkuǎn
to have a lump in one's throat 感到哽咽 gǎndào gěngyè
II V 把…混在一起 bǎ…hùn zài yìqǐ

lumpy ADJ 有团块的 yǒu tuánkuài de, 疙疙瘩瘩的 gēgedada de

lunacy N 疯狂 fēngkuáng, 精神错乱 jīngshén cuòluàn

lunar ADJ 月(亮)的 yuè (liàng) de

lunatic I ADJ 精神错乱的 jīngshén cuòluàn de, 疯的 fēng de II N 精神病患者 jīngshénbìng huànzhě, 疯子 fēngzi

lunch I N 午餐 wǔcān, 午饭 wǔfàn II V 吃午饭 chī wǔfàn, 进午餐 jìn wǔcān

luncheon N (正式)午餐 (zhèngshì) wǔcān

lunchtime N 午餐时间 wǔcān shíjiān, 午休 wǔxiū

lung N 肺 fèi
lung function 肺功能 fèi gōngnéng

lunge V, N 猛冲 měngchōng, 猛扑 měngpū

lurch¹ V 跌跌撞撞 diēdiē zhuàngzhuàng

lurch² N 1 晃动 huàngdòng 2 踉跄 liàngqiàng
to leave sb in the lurch 使某人处于困境而不顾 shǐ mǒurén chǔyú kùnjìng ér bú gù

lure V 引诱 yǐnyòu, 诱惑 yòuhuò

lurid ADJ 骇人听闻的 hàirén tīngwén de, 充满性和暴力的 chōngmǎn xìng hé bàolì de

lurk V 潜伏 qiánfú

luscious ADJ 美味的 měiwèi de

lush ADJ 茂盛的 màoshèng de

lust I N 强烈的性欲 qiángliè de xìngyù II V 1 强烈渴求发生性关系 qiángliè kěqiú fāshēng xìng guānxi de 2 热烈追求 rèliè zhuīqiú, 贪恋 tānliàn

luster N 光彩 guāngcǎi, 光耀 guāngyào

lustrous ADJ 有光泽的 yǒu guāngzé de

lusty ADJ 健壮的 jiànzhuàng de, 精力充沛的 jīnglì chōngpèi de

Lutheran I ADJ 路德会的 Lùdéhuì de II N 路德会教友 Lùdéhuì jiàoyǒu

luxuriant ADJ 茂盛的 màoshèng de, 茂密的 màomì de

luxuriate V 尽情享受 jǐnqíng xiǎngshòu

luxurious ADJ 奢侈的 shēchǐ de, 豪华的 háohuá de

luxury N 1 奢侈 shēchǐ, 豪华 háohuá ■ She's led a life of luxury since her childhood. 她从小过着奢侈的生活。Tā cóngxiǎo guòzhe shēchǐ de shēnghuó. 2 奢侈品 shēchǐpǐn
luxury hotel 豪华旅馆 háohuá lǚguǎn

lymph N 淋巴 línbā

lymphoma N 淋巴肿瘤 línbā zhǒngliú

lynch V 用私刑处死 yòng sīxíng chǔsǐ

lyric I N 抒情诗 shūqíngshī [M. WD 首 shǒu] II ADJ 抒情的 [+歌声] shūqíng de [+gēshēng]

lyrical ADJ 抒情(诗)的 shūqíng (shī) de

lyricist N 歌词作者 gēcí zuòzhě

M

M.A. (= Master of Arts) ABBREV 文学硕士(学位) wénxué shuòshì (xuéwèi)

ma N 妈 mā, 妈妈 māma

ma'am N 夫人 fūrén, 太太 tàitai

macabre ADJ 与死亡有关的 yǔ sǐwáng yǒuguān de, 恐怖的 kǒngbù de

macaroni N 通心面 tōngxīnmiàn, 通心粉 tōngxīnfěn

machete N 大砍刀 dà kǎndāo [M. WD 把 bǎ]

machine I N 机器 jīqì [M. WD 台 tái]
machine gun 机关枪 jīguānqiāng
sewing machine 缝纫机 féngrènjī
washing machine 洗衣机 xǐyījī
office machine 办公用机器 bàngōng yòng jīqì
II V 用机器加工 yòng jīqì jiāgōng

machine-readable ADJ 计算机可读的 jìsuànjī kě dú de

machinery N 机械 qìxiè, 机器 jīqì

machinist N 机器操作工 jīqì cāozuògōng

macho ADJ 有男子汉气概的 yǒu nánzǐhàn qìgài de, 有阳刚气的 yǒu yánggāng qì de

mackerel N 鲭鱼 qīng yú [M. WD 条 tiáo]

macrocosm N 宏观世界 hóngguān shìjiè

mad ADJ 1 发疯 fāfēng 2 十分生气 shífēn shēngqì, 气得要命 qìde yàomìng 3 极其愚蠢 jíqí yúchǔn ■ What a mad thing to do! 这件事做得多么愚蠢! Zhè jiàn shì zuò de duōme yúchǔn! like mad 极快地 jí kuài de, 拼命地 pīnmìng de ■ *These boy racers drive like mad.* 这些男孩车手开起汽车来不要命。Zhè xiē nánhái chēshǒu kāiqǐ qìchē lai bú yào mìng.

mad cow disease 疯牛病 fēngniúbìng

madam N 太太 tàitai, 夫人 fūrén

maddening ADJ 让人极为恼火的 ràng rén jíwéi nǎohuǒ de

made See **make**

madhouse N 很多人闹哄哄的地方 hěn duō rén nàohōnghōng de dìfang, 疯人院 fēngrényuàn

madly ADV 发疯似地 fāfēng shìde
be madly in love with sb 发疯似地爱上某人 fāfēng sì de àishang mǒurén, 爱某人爱得要命 ài mǒurén ài deyàomìng

madman N 狂人 kuángrén, 疯子 fēngzi

madness N 精神错乱 jīngshén cuòluàn, 疯狂 fēngkuáng

Madonna N 圣母玛丽亚 Shèngmǔ Mǎlìyà

maelstrom N 混乱的局面 hùnluàn de júmiàn, 大动乱 dà dòngluàn

maestro N（音乐）大师（yīnyuè）dàshī [M. WD 位 wèi]

mafia N 黑手党 hēishǒudǎng

magazine N 1 杂志 zázhì, 期刊 qīkān 2 子弹夹 zǐdànjiā, 弹盒 dànhé 3 弹药库 dànyàokù, 军火库 jūnhuǒkù 4 胶卷盒 jiāojuǎnhé

magenta N 洋红色 yánghóngsè

maggot N 蛆 qū [M. WD 条 tiáo]

magic I N 魔术 móshù, 戏法 xìfǎ
to work like magic 取得神奇的效果 qǔdé shénqí de xiàoguǒ
II ADJ 魔术的 móshù de, 有魔力的 yǒu mólì de
a magic number 一个神奇的数字 yí ge shénqí de shùzì
magic touch 神奇本领 shénqí běnlǐng

magical ADJ 1 有魔力的 yǒu mólì de 2 奇异的 qíyì de, 迷人的 mírén de

magician N 魔术师 móshùshī, 变戏法的人 biànxìfǎ de rén

magistrate N 地方法官 dìfang fǎguān [M. WD 位 wèi]

magnanimity N 宽宏 kuānhóng, 慷慨 kāngkǎi

magnanimous ADJ 宽宏大量的 kuānhóng dàliàng de

magnate N 巨头 jùtóu, 大亨 dàhēng

magnesium (Mg) N 镁 měi

magnet N 1 磁铁 cítiě [M. WD 块 kuài], 磁石 císhí [M. WD 块 kuài] 2 特别有吸引力的人／地方 tèbié yǒu xīyǐnlì de rén/dìfang

magnetic ADJ 磁性的 cíxìng de

magnetism N 1 磁性 cíxìng 2 魅力 mèilì

magnification N 放大（率）fàngdà (lǜ)

magnificence N 宏伟壮丽 hóngwěi zhuànglì

magnificent ADJ 宏伟壮丽的 hóngwěi zhuànglì de, 宏大的 hóngdà de

magnify V 放大 fàng dà
a magnifying glass 放大镜 fàngdàjìng

magnitude N 1 重大 zhòngdà 2 [地震+] 度 [dìzhèn+] dù
an earthquake of magnitude six 六级地震 liù jí dìzhèn

magnolia N 木兰 mùlán, 玉兰 yùlán

magpie N 喜鹊 xǐque [M. WD 只 zhī]

mahjong, mahjongg N 麻将（牌）májiàng (pái)
to play mahjong 打麻将 dǎ májiàng

mahogany N 桃花心木 táohuāxīnmù, 红木 hóngmù

maid N 女佣人 nǚ yōngrén, 清洁女工 qīngjié nǚgōng

maiden N 少女 shàonǚ
maiden name 女子婚前的姓 nǚzǐ hūnqián de xìng

maid of honor N 首席女傧相 shǒuxí nǚbīnxiàng

mail I N 1 邮件 yóujiàn ■ *When does the mail arrive every day?* 每天邮件什么时候到？Měitiān yóujiàn shénme shíhou dào? 2 邮政 yóuzhèng
II V 邮寄 yóujì
mail order 邮购 yóugòu ■ *Have you bought anything from www.amazon.com by mail order?* 你从www.amazon.com邮购过什么东西吗？Nǐ cóng www.amazon.com yóugòuguo shénme dōngxī ma?

mailbox N 信箱 xìnxiāng, 邮箱 yóuxiāng

maildrop N 1 邮政地址 yóuzhèng dìzhǐ 2（设在邮局的）私人信箱 (shèzài yóujú de) sīrén xìnxiāng

mailing list N 1 邮寄名单 yóujì míngdān 2（计算机）邮件列表 (jìsuànjī) yóujiàn lièbiǎo

mailman N 邮递员 yóudìyuán

maim V 使…残废 shǐ...cánfèi

main I ADJ 主要的 zhǔyào de ■ *My main concern is to make sure this mistake is not repeated.* 我主要关心的是确保这样的错误不再犯。Wǒ zhǔyào guānxīn de shì quèbǎo zhèyàng de cuòwù búzài chóng fàn.
main course 主菜 zhǔcài
the main thing 最重要的事 zuì zhòngyào de shì
II N（水／煤气）总管道 (shuǐ/méiqì) zǒngguǎndào, 干线电缆 gànxiàn diànlǎn

mainframe N（大型计算机）主机 (dàxíng jìsuànjī) zhǔjī

mainland N 大陆 dàlù, 本土 běntǔ

mainly ADV 主要（地）zhǔyào (de), 大部分（地）dàbùfen (de)

mainstay N 支柱 zhīzhù, 骨干 gǔgàn

mainstream N, ADJ 主流（的）zhǔliú (de)

maintain V 1 保养 bǎoyǎng, 维修 wéixiū ■ *I maintain my car every half a year.* 我每半年维修一次汽车。Wǒ měi bànnián wéixiū yí cì qìchē.

2 保持 bǎochí, 维持 wéichí

maintenance N **1** 维护 wéixiū, 保养 bǎoyǎng
 2 保持 bǎochí, 维持 wéichí

majestic ADJ 雄伟的 xióngwěi de, 庄严的 zhuāngyán de

majesty N 雄伟 xióngwěi, 庄严 zhuāngyán
 Your Majesty 国王陛下 guówáng bìxià, 皇帝陛下 huángdì bìxià

major I ADJ 重要的 zhòngyào de, 主要的 zhǔyào de II N **1** 大学主修科目 dàxué zhǔxiū kēmù **2** 主修某专业的学生 zhǔxiū mǒu zhuānyè de xuésheng ■ *Her boyfriend is an Information Science major.* 她的男朋友主修信息科学。Tā de nánpéngyou zhǔxiū xìnxī kēxué. **3** (军队) 少校 (jūn duì) shàoxiào III v 主修 zhǔxiū ■ *I'm majoring in Chinese.* 我主修中文。Wǒ zhǔxiū Zhōngwén.

majority N 多数 duōshù ■ *The majority of people are right-handed.* 多数人是用右手的。Duōshù rén shì yòng yòushǒu de.
 the overwhelming majority 绝大多数 juédà duōshù
 the silent majority 沉默的大多数 chénmò de dàduōshù

Major league N (美国) 职业棒球大联盟 (Měiguó) Zhíyè bàngqiú dà liánméng

make I v (PT & PP **made**) **1** 做 zuò, 制造 zhìzào
 be made of 是……做的 shì...zuò de
 Made in China 中国制造 Zhōngguó zhìzào
 2 使 shǐ, 让 ràng, 使得 shǐde ■ *What made you decide to major in journalism?* 是什么使你决定主修新闻？Shì shénme shǐ nǐ juédìng zhǔxiū xīnwén? **3** 挣 (钱) zhèng (qián) **4** 成为 chéngwéi ■ *I'm sure my sister will make a good teacher.* 我肯定姐姐能成为一名好老师。Wǒ kěndìng jiějie néng chéngwéi yì míng hǎo lǎoshī.
 to make a difference 起作用 qǐ zuòyòng
 ■ *The maintenance of the machine made a difference in its performance.* 机器维修了，在功能上起作用了。(→机器维修以后，工作起来果然不一样。) Jīqì wéixiū le, zài gōngnéngshang qǐ zuòyòng le. (→Jīqì wéixiū yǐhòu, gōngzuò qǐlai guǒrán bù yíyàng.)
 to make the bed 铺床 pūchuáng
 to make out 弄清 nòngqīng ■ *Can you make out what the old man is saying?* 你能听出那位老人在说什么吗？Nǐ néng tīngchū nà wèi lǎorén zài shuō shénme ma?
 to make up 构成 gòuchéng ■ *Women make up 70% of the teaching staff in the school.* 妇女构成这所学校百分之七十的师资。(→这所学校师资的百分之七十是女子。) Fùnǚ gòuchéng zhè suǒ xuéxiào bǎifēnzhī qīshí de shīzī. (→Zhè suǒ xuéxiào shīzī de bǎifēnzhī qīshí shì nǚzǐ.)
 to make ends meet 收支相抵 shōuzhī xiāngdǐ
 II N 牌子 páizi, 品牌 pǐnpái

make-believe ADJ 虚假的 xūjiǎ de, 假的 jiǎ de

maker N 制造商 zhìzàoshāng, 生产厂 shēngchǎnchǎng
 decision maker 决策人 juécèrén
 popcorn maker 爆玉米花机 bàoyùmǐhuājī

makeshift ADJ 临时的 línshí de

makeup N 化妆品 huàzhuāngpǐn, 化妆用品 huàzhuāng yòngpǐn

making N 制造 zhìzào, 制作 zhì zuò
 (a tragedy) of one's own making 自己一手造成的 (悲剧) zìjǐ yīshǒu zàochéng de (bēijù)

makings N 要素 yàosù, 素质 sùzhì
 to have the makings of an entrepreneur 具备企业家的素质 jùbèi qǐyèjiā de sùzhì

malady N **1** 疾病 jíbìng **2** 弊端 bìduān, 通病 tōngbìng
 the malady of the welfare state (社会) 福利制度的弊端 (shèhuì) fúlì zhìdù de bìduān

malaise N **1** 烦躁不安的情绪 fánzào bù'ān de qíngxù **2** 心神不定 xīnshén búdìng

malaria N 疟疾 nüèji

male I ADJ **1** 雄 (性) 的 xióng (xìng) de **2** 男性的 nánxìng de II N 雄性动物 xióngxìng dòngwù, 男人 nánren ■ *The detectives believe the criminal must be a male, in his 30s.* 侦探相信，罪犯一定是男性、三十多岁。Zhēntàn xiāngxìn, zuìfàn yídìng shì nánxìng, sānshí duō suì.
 male chauvinist 大男子主义 dànánzǐ zhǔyì

malevolent ADJ 恶意的 èyì de

malformation N 畸形 (的器官) jīxíng (de qìguān)

malfunction I N 故障 gùzhàng, 失灵 shīlíng II v 不能正常运转 bùnéng zhèngcháng yùnzhuǎn

malice N 恶意 èyì, 害人的意图 hàirén de yìtú

malicious ADJ 恶意的 èyì de, 恶毒的 èdú de

malign I v 诽谤 fěibàng, 中伤 zhòngshāng II ADJ 有害的 yǒuhài de

malignant ADJ **1** 恶性的 èxìng de
 a malignant tumor 恶性肿瘤 èxìng zhǒngliú
 2 恶意的 èyì de, 邪恶的 xié'è de

mall N 购物中心 gòuwù zhōngxīn

mallard N 绿头鸭 lǜtóuyā

malleable ADJ **1** 可锻造的 [+金属] kě duànzào de [+jīnshǔ] **2** 易受影响的 [+人] yì shòu yǐngxiǎng de [+rén]

mallet N **1** 木槌 mùchuí [M. WD 根 gēn] **2** 长柄球棍 chángbǐng qiúgùn [M. WD 根 gēn]

malnourished ADJ 营养不良的 yíngyǎng bùliáng de

malnutrition N 营养不良 yíngyǎng bùliáng

malpractice N 玩忽职守 wánhū zhíshǒu

malt N **1** 麦芽 màiyá **2** 麦乳精 (饮料) màirǔjīng (yǐnliào)

maltreat v 虐待 nüèdài

maltreatment N 虐待 nüèdài

mama

mama N 妈妈 māma

mammal N 哺乳动物 bǔrǔ dòngwù

mammogram N 乳房X光照片 rǔfáng X guāng zhàopiàn

mammoth ADJ 巨大的 jùdà de

man I N (PL **men**) **1** 男人 nánren, 男子 nánzǐ **2** 人 rén, 人类 rénlèi ■ *Man will never stop exploring the frontier.* 人类不会停止探索新天地。 Rénlèi bú huì tíngzhǐ tànsuǒ xīn tiāndǐ. **II** v 使用 shǐyòng, 操纵 cāozòng **III** INTERJ 啊呀 āyā, 嘿 hēi

manacle I N 镣铐 liàokào, 手铐 shǒukào, 脚镣 jiǎoliáo **II** v **1** 给 [+人] 上手铐/脚镣 gěi [+rén] shàng shǒukào/jiǎoliáo **2** 束缚 shùfù

manage v **1** 设法 shèfǎ, 做成 zuòchéng **2** 经营 jīngyíng ■ *My father has managed this factory for 12 years.* 我父亲经营这家工厂十二年了。Wǒ fùqin jīngyíng zhè jiā gōngchǎng shí'èr nián le. **3** 管理 guǎnlǐ ■ *He is very good at managing his money.* 他很会管钱。Tā hěn huì guǎn qián.

manageable ADJ 容易对付的 róngyì duìfu de, 容易处理的 róngyì chǔlǐ de

management N **1** 管理 guǎnlǐ, 经营 jīngyíng asset management 资产管理 zīchǎn guǎnlǐ database management 数据库管理 shùjùkù guǎnlǐ

system management 系统管理 xìtǒng guǎnlǐ **2** 管理人员 guǎnlǐ rényuán, 资方 zīfāng

manager N 经理 jīnglǐ

managerial ADJ 管理的 guǎnlǐ de, 经营的 jīngyíng de

Mandarin N (中国) 普通话 (Zhōngguó) Pǔtōnghuà, 国语 guóyǔ, 华语 Huáyǔ

mandate I N **1** 授权 shòuquán **2** 托管权 tuōguǎnquán, 受托管的国家 shòutuōguǎn de guójiā **3** 训令 xùnlìng **II** v **1** 指示 zhǐshì, 指令 zhǐlìng **2** 授权 shòuquán, 委任 wěirèn

mandatory ADJ 法定的 fǎdìng de, 强制性的 qiángzhìxìng de

mane N 鬃毛 zōngmáo

maneuver I N **1** 熟练的动作 shúliàn de dòngzuò **2** 花招 huāzhāo, 巧计 qiǎojì **II** v 熟练地操作 shúliàn de cāozuò, 巧妙地移动 qiǎomiào de yídòng

room to maneuver 回旋的余地 huíxuán de yúdì

maneuvers 军事演习 jūnshì yǎnxí joint maneuvers 联合军事演习 liánhé jūnshì yǎnxí

maneuverable ADJ 灵活的 línghuó de

manger N (牲畜) 食槽 (shēngchù) shícáo

mangle v **1** 伤害 shānghài **2** 弄糟 nòngzāo, 糟蹋 zāota

mango N 芒果 (树) mángguǒ (shù)

mangrove N 红树 hóngshù [M. WD 棵 kē]

manhandle v 粗暴地推 [+人] cūbào de tuī [+rén], 粗暴地对待 cūbào de duìdài

manhole N 检修孔 jiǎnxiūkǒng, 进人孔 jìnrénkǒng

manhood N **1** 男子气概 nánzǐ qìgài **2** (男子) 成年 (nánzǐ) chéngnián

manhunt N 搜捕 sōubǔ, 追捕 zhuībǔ

mania N **1** 狂热 kuángrè **2** 躁狂症 zàokuángzhèng

maniac N 疯子 fēngzi, 迷 mí computer maniac 电脑迷 diànnǎomí, 电脑发烧友 diànnǎo fāshāoyǒu

maniacal ADJ 疯狂的 fēngkuáng de

manic ADJ 焦躁的 jiāozào de, 十分激动的 shífēn jīdòng de

manicure N, v 修指甲 xiū zhǐjia

manicurist N 修指甲的美容师 xiū zhǐjia de měiróngshī

manifest I v 表现 biǎoxiàn, 表露 biǎolù **II** ADJ 明显的 míngxiǎn de, 显著的 xiǎnzhe de

manifestation N 明显迹象 míngxiǎn jìxiàng

manifesto N 宣言 xuānyán [M. WD 份 fèn], 声明 shēngmíng

manifold I ADJ 多方面的 duōfāngmiàn de, 各种各样的 gèzhǒng gèyàng de **II** N (发动机的) 歧管 (fādòngjī de) qíguǎn

manila envelope N 牛皮纸信封 niúpízhǐ xìnfēng

manipulate v **1** 操纵 cāozòng, 影响 yǐngxiǎng **2** 处理 [+国家] chǔlǐ [+guójiā]

manipulative ADJ **1** 善于操纵他人的 shànyú cāozòng tārén de **2** 推拿正骨法的 tuīná zhènggǔfǎ de

manipulator N 善于操纵他人的人 shànyú cāozòng tārén de rén

mankind N 人类 rénlèi

manly ADJ 有男子汉气概的 yǒu nánzǐhàn qìgài de, 阳刚气的 yánggāngqì de

man-made ADJ 人造的 rénzào de, 人工的 réngōng de

mannequin, manikin N 人体模型 réntǐ móxíng, 橱窗模特儿 chúchuāng mótèr

manner N **1** 方式 fāngshì, 方法 fāngfǎ **2** 态度 tàidu, 仪态 yítài

mannered ADJ 做作的 zuòzuo de, 娇柔造作的 jiāoróu zàozuo de

mannerism N (言谈举止的) 习惯性动作 (yántán jǔzhǐ de) xíguànxìng dòngzuò, 习性 xíxìng

manners N 礼貌 lǐmào

mannish ADJ 像男人一样的 [+女子] xiàng nánren yíyàng de [+nǚzǐ]

manor N 庄园大宅 zhuāngyuán dàzhái [M. WD 座 zuò]

manpower N 劳动力 láodònglì, 人力 rénlì

mansion N 大宅 dàzhái, 大厦 dàshà

manslaughter N 过失杀人 guòshī shārén

mantel, mantelpiece N 壁炉架 bìlújià

mantle N 1 披风 pīfēng, 斗篷 dǒupéng [M. WD 件 jiàn]

to inherit sb's mantle 继承某人的衣钵 jìchéng mǒurén de yībó

2 一层 yìcéng

a mantle of snow 一层积雪 yìcéng jīxuě

mantra N 1 一再重复的名言 yízài chóngfù de míngyán **2** 祷文 dǎowén

manual I ADJ 体力的 tǐlì de, 手工的 shǒugōng de **2** N 使用说明 shǐyòng shuōmíng, 使用手册 shǐyòng shǒucè

manual labor 体力劳动 tǐlì láodòng, 体力活 tǐlìhuó

manufacture I V 制造 zhìzào ■ *Japan manufactures some of the world's most popular cars.* 日本生产了世界上几种最流行的汽车。Rìběn shēngchǎnle shìjièshang jǐ zhǒng zuì liúxíng de qìchē. II N 1 制造 zhìzào **2** 制造品 zhìzàopǐn, 产品 chǎnpǐn

manufacturing industry 制造业 zhìzàoyè

manufacturer N 制造商 zhìzàoshāng, 制造厂商 zhìzào chǎngshāng

manufacturing N 制造业 zhìzàoyè

manure N 粪肥 fènféi

manuscript N 手稿 shǒugǎo, 原稿 yuángǎo

many ADJ 很多 hěn duō, 许多 xǔduō

map I N 地图 dìtú ■ *Can you find me a street map of Boston?* 你能帮我找到一张波士顿街道地图吗? Nǐ néng bāng wǒ zhǎodao yì zhāng Bōshìdùn jiēdào dìtú ma? II V 绘制地图 huìzhì dìtú **2** 策划 cèhuà, 筹划 chóuhuà

maple N 枫树 fēngshù [M. WD 棵 kē]

mar V 损坏 sǔnhuài, 把...弄脏 bǎ...nòngzāng

marathon I N 马拉松赛跑 mǎlāsōng sàipǎo II ADJ 马拉松式的 mǎlāsōng shì de, 长时间的 cháng shíjiān de

marauding ADJ 侵扰的 qīnrǎo de, 四处抢杀的 sìchù qiǎng shā de

marble N 1 大理石 dàlǐshí **2** 弹子 dànzi, 玻璃弹子 bōli dànzi

game of marbles 弹子游戏 dànzi yóuxì

March N 三月 sānyuè

march I V 齐步行进 qíbù xíngjìn, 行军 xíngjūn

marching band 军乐队 jūnyuèduì

II N 1 [军队+] 行军 [jūn duì+] xíngjūn **2** 示威游行 shìwēi yóuxíng **3** 进行曲 jìnxíngqǔ

Mardi Gras N (巴西)狂欢节 (Bāxī) Kuánghuānjié

mare N 母马 mǔ mǎ [M. WD 匹 pǐ]

margarine N 人造黄油 rénzào huángyóu

margin N 1 页边空白的 yèbiān kòngbái de **2** 差数 chāshù

by a wide margin 以很大的差数 yǐ hěn dà de chāshù

3 利润 lìrùn

pre-tax margin 税前利润 shuì qián lìrùn

4 边缘 biānyuán

to live on the margins of society 生活在社会边缘 shēnghuó zài shèhuì biānyuán

marginal ADJ 1 极小的 jíxiǎo de, 可以忽略不计的 kěyǐ hūlüè bújì de **2** 边缘的 biānyuán de

marijuana N 大麻(烟) dàmá (yān)

marina N 1 小港湾 xiǎo gǎngwān **2** 游艇停泊港 yóutǐng tíngbógǎng

marinade N 混合调味酱 hùnhé tiáowèijiàng

marinate V 把 [+鱼] 浸在调味酱里 bǎ [+yú] jìn zài tiáowèijiàng lǐ

marine ADJ 1 海洋的 hǎiyáng de **2** 海运的 hǎiyùn de

mariner N 海员 hǎiyuán, 水手 shuǐshǒu

Marines, the Marine Corps N (美国)海军陆战队 (Měiguó) Hǎijūn lùzhànduì

marionette N 牵线木偶 qiānxiàn mù'ǒu

marital ADJ 婚姻的 hūnyīn de

marital status 婚姻状况 hūnyīn zhuàngkuàng

maritime ADJ 海事的 hǎishì de, 船舶的 chuánbó de

mark I N 1 痕迹 hénjì, 污斑 wūbān ■ *How did you get that dirty mark on your shirt?* 你衬衫上怎么有那块污斑? Nǐ chènshānshang zěnme yǒu nà kuài wūbān? **2** 记号 jìhào

On your mark, get set, go! 各就各位，预备，起! Gè jiù gè wèi, yùbèi, qǐ!

punctuation mark 标点符号 biāodiǎn fúhào

3 (学生的)分数 (xuéshéng de) fēnshù

II V 1 做记号 zuò jìhào, 写着 xiězhe ■ *The envelope was marked "private and confidential".* 信封上写着"私人机密"。Xìnfēngshang xiězhe "sīrén jīmì".

to mark down 降低价格 jiàngdī jiàgé

to mark up 提高价格 tígāo jiàgé ■ *It's not the time to mark up the goods.* 现在不是提高价格的时机。Xiànzài bú shì tígāo jiàgé de shíjī.

2 纪念 jìniàn ■ *To mark its 100th anniversary, the company will throw a grand dinner party.* 为了纪念成立一百周年，公司将举行盛大宴会。Wèile jìniàn chénglì yì bǎi zhōunián, gōngsī jiāng jǔxíng shèngdà yànhuì.

markdown N 减价 jiǎnjià

marked ADJ 明显的 míngxiǎn de, 显著的 xiǎnzhù de

marker N 1 标志 biāozhì **2** 记号笔 jìhàobǐ [M. WD 支 zhī]

market I N 市场 shìchǎng

market maker 证券交易商 zhèngquàn jiāoyìshāng

market price 市场价格 shìchǎng jiàgé, 时价 shíjià

market share 市场占有率 shìchǎng zhànyǒulǜ

buyer's market 买方市场 mǎifāng shìchǎng
seller's market 卖方市场 màifāng shìchǎng
II v 推销 tuīxiāo ■ *This new electronic gadget has been successfully marketed in East Asia.* 这个新电子玩意儿在东亚推销得很成功。Zhè ge xīn diànzǐ wányìr zài Dōngyà tuīxiāode hěn chénggōng.
marketable ADJ 有销路的 yǒu xiāolù de, 符合市场需求的 fúhé shìchǎng xūqiú de
marketing N 营销 yíngxiāo, 推销 tuīxiāo
marketplace N **1** 商业销售活动 shāngyè xiāoshòu huódòng **2**（露天）市场 (lùtiān) shìchǎng
marking N **1** 识别标志 shíbié biāozhì **2** 斑点 bāndiǎn
marksman N 神枪手 shénqiāngshǒu
markup N 提价幅度 tíjià fúdù
marmalade N 柑橘果酱 gānjú guǒjiàng
maroon v 将…遗弃在荒野 jiāng...yíqì zài huāngyě
marquee N 大帐篷 dà zhàngpéng [M. WD 顶 dǐng]
marriage N 婚姻 hūnyīn ■ *She will contemplate marriage only after finding her Mr Right.* 她在找到如意郎君以后，才会考虑婚姻。Tā zài zhǎodao rúyì lángjūn yǐhòu, cái huì kǎolǜ hūnyīn.
married ADJ 结了婚的 jiéle hūn de, 已婚的 yǐhūn de ■ *She is happily married with three children.* 她婚姻幸福，并已有三个孩子。Tā hūnyīn xìngfú, bìng yǐ yǒu sān ge háizi.
marrow N **1** 骨髓 gǔsuǐ
bone marrow transplant 骨髓移植 gǔsuǐ yízhí
2 最深处 zuì shēnchù, 骨子里 gǔzilǐ
to know sb to the marrow 透彻地了解某人 tòuchè de liǎojiě mǒurén
marry v **1** 结婚 jiéhūn ■ *He was married to his high school sweetheart.* 他和中学时的情人结婚。Tā hé zhōngxué shí de qíngrén jiéhūn. **2** 为…主持婚礼 wéi...zhǔchí hūnlǐ
Mars N 火星 huǒxīng
marsh N 沼泽地 zhǎozédì
marshal I N **1**（美国）联邦政府执法官 (Měiguó) liánbāng zhèngfǔ zhífǎguān **2**（美国）消防局长 (Měiguó) xiāofáng júzhǎng **3**（游行）总指挥 (yóuxíng) zǒngzhǐhuī **4**（军队）元帅 (jūnduì) yuánshuài
grand marshal 大司仪 dà sīyí
II v 组织 zǔzhī
to marshal one's arguments 整理自己的论点 zhěnglǐ zìjǐ de lùndiǎn
marshmallow N 棉花糖 miánhuātáng
marsupial N 有袋动物 yǒudài dòngwù
martial ADJ 军事的 jūnshì de, 打斗的 dǎdòu de
martial arts 武术 wǔshù, 功夫 gōngfu
martial law 军事管制 jūnshì guǎnzhì, 戒严 jièyán

Martian N 火星人 huǒxīng rén
Martin Luther King Day N 马丁路德金纪念日 Mǎdīnglùdéjīn jìniànrì
martyr I N 烈士 lièshì, 殉道者 xùndàozhě [M. WD 位 wèi] **II** ADJ (be martyred) 成为烈士 chéngwéi lièshì, 成为殉道者 chéngwéi xùndàozhě
martyrdom N 殉道 xùndào
marvel I N 奇迹 qíjì **II** v 对…感到惊讶 duì... gǎndào jīngyà, 惊叹 jīngtàn
marvelous ADJ 绝妙的 juémiào de, 极好的 jí hǎo de
Marxism N 马克思主义 Mǎkèsī zhǔyì
Marxist N 马克思主义者 Mǎkèsī zhǔyìzhě
mascot N 吉祥物 jíxiángwù
masculine ADJ 男性的 nánxìng de, 有男性特征的 yǒu nánxìng tèzhēngde
masculinity N 男性特征 nánxìng tèzhēng, 阳刚气 yánggāngqì
mash I v 把…捣烂 bǎ...dǎolàn
mashed patato 土豆泥 tǔdòuní
II N 糊状物 húzhuàngwù
mask I N **1** 面具 miànjù, 假面具 jiǎ miànjù **2** 面罩 miànzhào, 口罩 kǒuzhào **II** v 掩饰 yǎnshì, 掩盖 yǎngài
masked ADJ 蒙面的 méngmiàn de
masochism N（性）受虐狂 (xìng) shòunüèkuáng
mason N 砖瓦匠 zhuānwǎjiàng
Mason N 共济会会员 gòngjìhuì huìyuán
masonry N **1** 砖石 zhuānshí **2** 砖石建筑技术 zhuānshí jiànzhù jìshù
masquerade I N **1** 假面舞会 jiǎmiàn wǔhuì **2** 伪装 wěizhuāng **II** v 伪装 wěizhuāng, 假装 jiǎzhuāng
mass I N **1** 大量 dàliàng, 大批 dàpī ■ *The newspaper editor received masses of letters from angry readers.* 报纸编辑收到大批愤怒读者的来信。Bàozhǐ biānjí shōudao dàpī fènnù dúzhě de láixìn.
the masses 群众 qúnzhòng
2 质量 zhìliàng **II** ADJ 大量的 dàliàng de
mass media 大众传播媒介 dàzhòng chuánbō méijiè
mass murderer 谋杀多人的凶手 móushā duō rén de xiōngshǒu
mass production 大量生产 dàliàng shēngchǎn, 大规模生产 dàguīmó shēngchǎn
III v 集中 jízhōng
Mass N（天主教）弥撒 (Tiānzhǔjiào) mísa, 弥撒曲 mísaqǔ
massacre I N 大屠杀 dà túshā **II** v 屠杀 túshā
massage I N 按摩 ànmó, 推拿 tuīná ■ *The doctor recommended massage to ease the pain.* 医生建议做按摩，来减轻疼痛。Yīshēng jiànyì zuò ànmó lái jiǎnqīng téngtòng.
massage parlor 按摩院 ànmóyuàn, 妓院 jìyuàn

II v 给…按摩/推拿 gěi…ànmó/tuīná

masseur N（男）按摩师 (nán) ànmóshī

masseuse N（女）按摩师 (nǚ) ànmóshī

massive ADJ **1** 又大又重的 [+大门] yòu dà yòu zhòng de [+dàmén]，厚重的 hòuzhòng de **2** 巨大的 jùdà de

mass-produce v 大批量生产 dà pīliàng shēngchǎn

mast N 桅杆 wéigān [M. WD 根 gēn]

master **I** N **1** 主人 zhǔrén

master of ceremonies 司仪 sīyí

2 大师 dàshī **3** 硕士 shuòshì

Master of Arts 文学硕士（学位）wénxué shuòshì (xuéwèi)

Master of Science 理科硕士（学位）lǐkē shuòshì (xuéwèi)

master's degree, master's 硕士学位 shuòshì xuéwèi

II v 精通 jīngtōng ■ *I can't say I've mastered Chinese.* 我不能说自己精通中文。Wǒ bù néng shuō zìjǐ jīngtōng Zhōngwén. **III** ADJ **1** 技艺精湛的 jìyì jīngzhàn de

master chef 技艺精湛的大厨师 jìyì jīngzhàn de dàchúshī

2 原始的 yuánshǐ de，最重要的 zuì zhòngyào de

master key 万能钥匙 wànnéng yàoshi

masterful ADJ **1** 能控制的 néng kòngzhì de，能驾驭的 néng jiàyù de **2** 技艺高超的 jìyì gāochāo de

mastermind **I** N 出谋划策者 chūmóu huàcè zhě，幕后策划者 mùhòu cèhuà zhě **II** v 出谋划策 chūmóu huàcè

masterpiece N 杰作 jiézuò，名作 míngzuò [M. WD 部 bù/幅 fú]

mastery N **1** 精通 jīngtōng，掌握 zhǎngwò **2** 控制（权）kòngzhì (quán)

masturbate v 手淫 shǒuyín，自慰 zìwèi

mat N 席子 xízi [M. WD 张 zhāng]，垫子 diànzi [M. WD 块 kuài]

matador N 斗牛士 dòuniúshì

match[1] N 火柴 huǒchái

match[2] **I** N **1** 比赛 bǐsài **2** 相配的东西 xiāngpèi de dōngxi ■ *Those shoes are really not a good match for the dress.* 这双鞋和衣服不相配。Zhè shuāng xié hé yīfu bù xiāngpèi.

a perfect match 完全相配的人 wánquán xiāngpèi de rén，天作之合 tiānzuò zhī hé

3 对手 duìshǒu

to be no match for sb 不是某人的对手 bú shì mǒurén de duìshǒu

II v 相配 xiāngpèi

matchbook N 纸夹火柴 zhǐjiā huǒchái

matchbox N 火柴盒 huǒcháihé

matching ADJ 相配的 xiāngpèi de

matchless ADJ 无与伦比的 wú yǔ lúnbǐ de，举世无双的 jǔshì wúshuāng de

match-maker N 媒人 méiren

mate **I** N **1** 伙伴 huǒbàn **2**（动物）交配对象 (dòngwù) jiāopèi duìxiàng **II** v（动物）交配 (dòngwù) jiāopèi

material **I** N **1** 布料 bùliào，料子 liàozi **2** 材料 cáiliào

raw materials 原材料 yuáncáiliào

building materials 建筑材料 jiànzhù cáiliào

II ADJ **1** 物质上的 wùzhì shàng de

material comforts 物质享受 wùzhì xiǎngshòu

2（法律上）至关重要的 (fǎlǜshàng) zhìguān zhòngyào de

material evidence 重要证据 zhòngyào zhèngjù

materialism N 唯物主义 wéiwù zhǔyì，实利主义 shílì zhǔyì

materialistic ADJ 实利主义的 shílì zhǔyì de

materialize v **1** [计划+] 实现 [jìhuà+] shíxiàn **2** 出现 chūxiàn

maternal ADJ **1** 母亲的 mǔqin de，母性的 mǔxìng de **2** 母亲方面的 mǔqin fāngmiàn de

maternal grandmother 外祖母 wàizǔmǔ

maternity ADJ 孕妇的 yùnfù

maternity leave 产假 chǎnjià

maternity ward 产科病房 chǎnkē bìngfáng

math N 数学 shùxué

mathematical ADJ 数学的 shùxué de

mathematician N 数学家 shùxuéjiā

mathematics N 数学 shùxué

matinee N 下午场 xiàwǔchǎng，日间演出 rìjiān yǎnchū

matriarch N 女家长 nǚ jiāzhǎng [M. WD 位 wèi]，女族长 nǚ zúzhǎng [M. WD 位 wèi]

matriarchal ADJ 女子统治的 nǚzǐ tǒngzhì de，母系的 mǔxì de

a matriarchal society 母系社会 mǔxì shèhuì

matriarchy N 母系社会 mǔxì shèhuì，母系制 mǔxìzhì

matriculate v 注册入学 zhùcè rùxué

matriculation N 注册入学 zhùcè rùxué

matrimonial ADJ 婚姻的 hūnyīn de

matrimony N 婚姻 hūnyīn

matron N **1** 中年已婚的妇女 zhōngnián yǐhūn de fùnǚ **2** 女总管 nǚ zǒngguǎn

matronly ADJ 中年妇女的 zhōngnián fùnǚ de，发福的 fāfú de

matte, mat ADJ 无光泽的 wú guāngzé de

matted ADJ 缠结在一起的 chánjié zài yìqǐ de

matter **I** N **1** 事情 shìqing，事件 shìjiàn **2** 问题 wèntí ■ *A major earthquake in this region is not a matter of if but a matter of when.* 在这个地区，问题不是会不会发生大地震，而是什么时候发生。Zài zhè ge dìqū, wèntí bú shì huìbuhuì fāshēng dà dìzhèn, ér shì shénme shíhou fāshēng. **3** 情况 qíngkuàng ■ *It didn't help matters that* *he wasn't able to speak the local language.* 因为他不会说当地的语言，情况就更糟。Yīnwèi tā bú huì shuō dāngdì de yǔyán, qíngkuàng jiù gēng zāo. **4** 物质 wùzhì **II** v 重要 zhòngyào, 有关系 yǒu guānxi

It doesn't matter. 没有关系。méiyǒu guānxi.

matter-of-fact ADJ 就事论事的 jiùshì lùnshì de, 不动感情的 búdòng gǎnqíng de

matting N 编织用的材料 biānzhī yòng de cáiliào

mattress N 床垫 chuángdiàn

mature I ADJ **1** 成熟的 chéngshú de **2** 到期的 [+存款] dàoqī de [+cúnkuǎn] **II** v **1** (变得)成熟 (biàn de) chéngshú **2** [存款+] 到期 [cúnkuǎn+] dàoqī

maturity N **1** 成熟 chéngshú **2** 到期 dàoqī

maudlin ADJ **1** 哭哭啼啼的 [+人] kūkū títí de [+rén] **2** 伤感而可笑的 [+歌曲] shānggǎn ér kěxiào de [+gēqǔ]

maul v 撕破皮肉 sīpò pírou, 伤害 shānghài

mausoleum N 陵墓 língmù

mauve N, ADJ 淡紫色(的) dànzǐsè (de)

maverick N 独立思考的人 dúlì sīkǎo de rén, 自行其事的人 zìxíng qí shì de rén

mawkish ADJ 自作多情的 zìzuò duōqíng de, 过分动感情的 guòfèn dòng gǎnqíng de

max I N 最大限度 zuì dà xiàndù **II** v (to max out) 用得精光 yòng dé jīngguāng

maxim N 格言 géyán

maximize v 把…增加到最大限度 bǎ…zēngjiā dào zuì dà xiàndù

maximum N **1** 最大量 zuì dà liáng **2** ADJ 最大的 zuì dà de, 最多的 zuì duō de

May N 五月 wǔyuè

may [NEG **may not**] MODAL V (PT **might**) **1** 可能 kěnéng ■ *It may rain tonight.* 今晚可能下雨。Jīnwǎn kěnéng xiàyǔ. **2** 可以 kěyǐ

maybe ADV 或许 huòxǔ, 大概 dàgài ■ *Maybe someone at the information desk can help you.* 问讯台或许有人能帮助你。Wènxùntái huòxǔ yǒurén néng bāngzhu nǐ.

May Day N (五一) 劳动节 (Wǔyī) Láodòngjié

mayday N 求救信号 qiújiù xìnhào

mayhem N 极为混乱的局面 jíwéi hùnluàn de júmiàn

mayonnaise N 蛋黄酱 dànhuángjiàng

mayor N 市长 shìzhǎng [M. WD 位 wèi]

maze N 迷宫 mígōng

M.B.A , MBA (= Master of Business Administration) ABBREV See **master**

MC (= Master of Ceremonies) ABBREV 司仪 sīyí

McCoy N (the real McCoy) 真货 zhēnhuò, 货真价实的东西 huò zhēn jià shí de dōngxi

M.D. (= Doctor of Medicine) ABBREV 医学博士 yīxué bóshì

me PRON 我 wǒ

meadow N 草地 cǎodì, 牧场 mùchǎng

meager ADJ 极少的 jí shǎo de, 微薄的 wēibó de

meal N **1** (一顿)饭 (yí dùn) fàn **2** (谷物的)粗磨粉 (gǔwù de) cū mòfěn

mealtime N 吃饭时间 chīfàn shíjiān, 开饭时间 kāifàn shíjiān

mealy-mouthed ADJ (说话)转弯抹角的 (shuōhuà) zhuǎnwān mòjiǎo de

mean¹ (PT & PP **meant**) v **1** 意思是 yìsi shì ■ *The word "polyglot" means "knowing many languages".* "polyglot" 这个词的意思是 "懂多种语言" 。"polyglot" 这个词的意思是 "dǒng duō zhǒng yǔyán". **2** 有意 yǒuyì ■ *Sorry, I didn't mean it.* 对不起，我不是有意的。Duìbuqǐ, wǒ bú shì yǒuyì de. **3** 意味着 yìwèizhe

mean² ADJ **1** 卑鄙的 bēibǐ de **2** 刻薄的 kèbó de, 小气的 xiǎoqi de

a no mean player 一个出色的运动员 yí ge chūsè de yùndòngyuán

mean³ N (the mean) 平均数 píngjūnshù

meander v **1** [河水+] 弯弯曲曲地流 [héshuǐ+] wānwān qūqū de liú **2** [人+] 荡来荡去 [rén+] dànglái dàngqù **3** [谈话+] 东拉西扯 [tánhuà+] dōnglā xīchě

meaning N 意思 yìsi ■ *I know the meanings of all these words, but I don't know the meaning of the sentence.* 这些词的意思我都知道，但是句子的意思我不明白。Zhèxiē cí de yìsi wǒ dōu zhīdào, dànshì jùzi de yìsi wǒ bù míngbai. **2** 意义 yìyì

meaningful ADJ 有意义的 yǒu yìyì de, 有意思的 yǒu yìsi de

meaningless ADJ 毫无意义的 háowú yìyì de, 没有价值的 méiyǒu jiàzhí de

means N **1** 手段 shǒuduàn, 方法 fāngfǎ ■ *She will try to get what she wants by all means, legal or illegal.* 她想要的，就会用一切手段来取得，不管是合法还是非法的。Tā xiǎng yào de, jiù huì yòng yíqiè shǒuduàn lái qǔdé, bùguǎn shì héfǎ háishi fēifǎ de. **2** 收入 shōurù, 财产 cáichǎn

by all means 当然 dāngrán

by no means 一点都不 yìdiǎn dōu bù ■ *She by no means dislikes him; in fact she is quite fond of him.* 她一点都不厌恶他；事实上她挺喜爱他。Tā yìdiǎn dōu bú yàn'è tā; shìshíshang tā tǐng xǐ'ài tā

means test 经济状况调查 jīngjì zhuàngkuàng diàochá

to live beyond one's means 花费超过收入 huāfèi chāoguò shōurù, 透支 tòuzhī

meant See **mean¹**

meantime N (in the meantime) 与此同时 yǔ cǐ tóngshí

meanwhile ADV 同时 tóngshí

measles N 麻疹 mázhěn

German measles 风疹 fēngzhěn

measly ADJ 少得可怜的 shǎo dé kělián de

measurable ADJ 可测量的 kě cèliáng de

measure I N **1** 措施 cuòshī ■ *The government has taken measures to reduce fuel consumption.* 政府已经采取措施减少燃料消耗。Zhèngfǔ yǐjīng cǎiqǔ cuòshī jiǎnshǎo ránliào xiāohào.
half measures（效果不佳的）折中办法 (xiàoguǒ bùjiā de) zhézhōng bànfǎ，将就措施 jiāngjiu cuòshī
2 量具 liángjù，量器 liáng qì
tape measure（钢）卷尺 (gāng) juǎnchǐ，软尺 ruǎnchǐ
in large/some measure 在很大／某种程度上 zài hěn dà/mǒuzhǒng chéngdù shàng
II V 量 liáng，测量 cèliáng

measured ADJ 深思熟虑的 shēnsī shúlǜ de，稳妥的 wěntuǒ de

measurement N **1** 度量 dùliàng **2** 长度 chángdù，宽度 kuāndù
the metric system of measurement 公制度量衡 gōngzhì dùliànghéng

meat N（食用的）肉 (shíyòng de) ròu

meatball N 肉丸 ròu wán

meatloaf N 肉糕 ròu gāo [M. WD 块 kuài]

meaty ADJ **1** 肉很多的 ròu hěn duō de **2** 重大的 zhòngdà de

Mecca N **1**（沙地阿拉伯）麦加 (Shādì Ālābó) Màijiā **2** 朝圣地 cháoshèngdì，众人向往的地方 zhòngrén xiàngwǎng de dìfang

mechanic N 汽车修理工 qìchē xiūlǐgōng，机械工 jīxiè gōng

mechanical ADJ **1** 机械（方面）的 jīxiè (fāngmiàn) de，机械操纵的 jīxiè cāozòng de
mechanical failure 机械故障 jīxiè gùzhàng
2 机械的 [+回答] jīxiè de [+huídá]，不加思索的 bù jiā sīsuǒ de

mechanics N **1** 力学 lìxué **2** 工作的方法 gōngzuò de fāngfǎ，技术细节 jìshù xìjié

mechanism N 机械装置 jīxiè zhuāngzhì **2** 机制 jīzhì，机构 jīgòu
survival mechanism 求生手段 qiúshēng shǒuduàn

mechanize V 把…机械化 bǎ...jīxièhuà

mechanized ADJ 机械化的 jīxièhuà de

medal N 奖牌 jiǎngpái，奖章 jiǎngzhāng
gold medal 金牌 jīnpái

medalist N 奖牌获得者 jiǎngpái huòdézhě

medallion N 圆形挂饰 yuánxíng guàshì

meddle V 干预 gānyù，管闲事 guǎn xiánshì

meddler N 多管闲事的人 duō guǎn xiánshì de rén

meddlesome ADJ 爱管闲事的 ài guǎn xiánshì de

media N（新闻）媒体 (xīnwén) méitǐ ■ *The media had a field day over the scandal.* 媒体因为这件丑闻而忙碌兴奋了一阵。Méitǐ yīnwèi zhè jiàn chǒuwén ér mánglù xīngfènle yí zhèn.
mass media 大众媒体 dàzhòng méitǐ

median I N **1**（道路）中间安全带 (dàolù) zhōngjiān ānquándài **2**（统计）中位数 (tǒngjì) zhōngwèishù **II** ADJ 中间的 zhōngjiān de，中位的 zhōngwèi de
the median price 中位价 zhōngwèijià

mediate V 调解 tiáojiě，调停 tiáoting

mediation N 调解 tiáojiě，调停 tiáoting

mediator N 调解员 tiáojiě yuán

Medicaid N（美国）医疗补助制度 (Měiguó) yīliáo bǔzhù zhìdù

medical ADJ **1** 医学的 yīxué de，医疗的 yīliáo de ■ *She was rushed to the hospital for medical treatment.* 她被赶送到医院接受治疗。Tā bèi gǎnsòngdao yīyuàn jiēshòu zhìliáo.
medical certificate 疾病证明 jíbìng zhèngmíng
medical school 医学院 yīxuéyuàn
medical checkup 体格检查 tǐgé jiǎnchá
2 内科的 nèikē de

Medicare N（美国）老年人医疗保健制度 (Měiguó) lǎoniánrén yīliáo bǎojiàn zhìdù

medicated ADJ 含有药物的 hányǒu yàowù de

medication N 药物 yàowù

medicinal ADJ 药用的 yàoyòng de，药的 yào de

medicine N **1** 药 yào，医药 yīyào ■ *Remember to take your medicine.* 记住吃药。Jìzhu chīyào.
Good medicine tastes bitter. 良药苦口。Liáng-yào kǔkǒu.
2 医学 yīxué，医药 yīyào ■ *She is very interested in traditional Chinese medicine.* 她对传统中医非常感兴趣。Tā duì chuántǒng Zhōngyī fēicháng gǎnxìngqu.

medieval ADJ 中世纪的 Zhōngshìjì de

mediocre ADJ 平庸的 píngyōng de，一般的 yìbān de

mediocrity N 平庸 píngyōng

meditate V 沉思 chénsī，打坐 dǎzuò

meditation N 沉思 chénsī，打坐 dǎzuò

meditative ADJ 沉思的 chénsī de

Mediterranean ADJ 地中海的 Dìzhōnghǎi de
the Mediterranean 地中海 Dìzhōnghǎi

medium I ADJ 中等的 zhōngděng de，中号的 zhōnghào de
medium rare 半熟的 bàn shóu de
II N **1** 传播媒介 chuánbō méijiè **2** 方法 fāngfǎ，手段 shǒuduàn

medium-sized, medium-size ADJ 中号的 zhōnghào de

medley N **1**（音乐）组合曲 (yīnyuè) zǔhéqū，组曲 zǔqǔ **2**（游泳）混合接力赛 (yóuyǒng) hùnhé jiēlìsài **3**（食品）大拼盘 (shípǐn) dà pīnpán

meek ADJ 温顺的 wēnshùn de

meet I V (PT & PP met) **1** 会见 huìjiàn，见面 jiàn-miàn **2** 接见 jiē jiē，迎接 yíngjiē **3** 满足 [+需要] mǎnzú [+xūyào]，符合 [+要求] fúhé [+yāoqiú] **II** N（运动）会 (yùndòng) huì

meeting N 会 huì, 会议 huìyì
  meeting house 聚会所 jùhuìsuǒ
mega ADJ 百万倍 bǎiwànbèi
megabyte N (计算机)兆字节 (jìsuànjī) zhàozìjié
megalomania N 妄自尊大 wàngzì zūn dà
megalomaniac N, ADJ 自大狂 zìdàkuáng, 妄自尊大的人 wàngzì zūn dà de rén
megaphone N 喇叭筒 lǎbatǒng
megastore N 超大型商店 chāo dàxíng shāngdiàn
megaton N 百万吨(级) bǎiwàndūn (jí)
melancholy I ADJ 忧郁的 yōuyù de II N 忧郁症 yōuyùzhèng
melee N 混乱局面 hùnluàn júmiàn
mellow I ADJ **1** 温和平静的 [+心情] wēnhé píngjìng de **2** 友善随和的 [+人] yǒushàn suíhe de **3** 圆润悦耳的 [+声音] yuánrùn yuè'ěr de **4** 醇和的 [+酒] chúnhé de [+jiǔ] II v **1** 使…变得温和平静 shǐ... biàn de wēnhé píngjìng **2** 使 [+颜色] 变得柔和 shǐ [+yánsè] biàn de róuhe
melodic ADJ 旋律优美的 xuánlǜ yōuměi de
melodious ADJ 悦耳动听的 yuè'ěr dòngtīng de
melodrama N **1** 情节剧 qíngjiéjù [M. WD 出 chū/部 bù] **2** 戏剧化的局面 xìjùhuà de júmiàn
melodramatic ADJ **1** 情节剧的 qíngjiéjù de **2** 吵吵闹闹的 chǎochǎo nàonào de, 夸张的 kuāzhāng de
melody N **1** 主旋律 zhǔxuánlǜ, 主调 zhǔdiào **2** 曲调 qǔdiào
melon N 瓜 guā
melt v 融化 rónghuà ■ *The cake was so good it melted in my mouth.* 蛋糕做得好极了，进嘴就化了。Dàngāo zuòde hǎo jíle, jìn zuǐ jiù huà le.
meltdown N 崩溃 bēngkuì, 彻底瘫痪 chèdǐ tānhuàn
  financial meltdown 金融崩溃 jīnróng bēngkuì
melting point N 熔点 róngdiǎn
melting pot N (民族)大熔炉 (mínzú) dàrónglú
member N 成员 chéngyuán, 会员 huìyuán
  life member 终身会员 zhōngshēn huìyuán
membership N **1** 会员资格 huìyuán zīgé **2** 全体会员 quántǐ huìyuán
  membership fee 会员费 huìyuánfèi
membrane N (薄)膜 (bó) mó, 膜状物 mózhuàngwù
memento N 纪念品 jìniànpǐn
memo, memorandum N 公务便条 gōngwù biàntiáo [M. WD 张 zhāng/份 fèn], 备忘录 bèiwànglù
memoirs N 回忆录 huíyìlù [M. WD 本 běn]
memorabilia N (与某人或某事物有关的)收藏纪念品 (yǔ mǒurén huò mǒu shìwù yǒuguān de) shōucáng jìniànpǐn
memorable ADJ 值得纪念的 zhíde jìniàn de, 难忘的 nánwàng de

memorial I ADJ 悼念的 dàoniàn de, 纪念(死者)的 jìniàn (sǐzhě) de
  memorial service 追悼仪式 zhuīdào yíshì
  II N 纪念碑 jìniànbēi
  Memorial Day 阵亡将士纪念日 zhènwáng jiàngshì jìniànrì
memorize v 记住 jìzhu
memory N **1** 记忆力 jìyìlì ■ *His memory is not as good as it used to be.* 他的记忆力不如以前了。Tā de jìyìlì bùrú yǐqián le. **2** 记忆 jìyì
  in memory of 纪念 jìniàn
men See **man**
menace I N **1** 威胁 wēixié, 恫吓 dònghè **2** 危险人物 wēixiǎn rénwù II v 威胁 wēixié, 恫吓 dònghè
menacing ADJ **1** 威吓的 wēihè de **2** 凶兆的 xiōngzhào de
menagerie N **1** 一批野生动物 yìpī yěshēng dòngwù **2** 一帮形形色色的人 yìbāng xíngxíng sèsè de rén
mend v **1** 缝补 féngbǔ, 修补 xiūbǔ
  to mend one's ways 改过自新 gǎiguò zìxīn
  to mend fences 恢复良好关系 huīfù liánghǎo guānxi, 消释前嫌 xiāoshì qiánxián
  2 [骨头+] 愈合 [gǔtou+] yùhé
menial ADJ 不需要技能的 bù xūyào jìnéng de, 枯燥的 kūzào de
  a menial job 低档工作 dīdàng gōngzuò, 粗活 cūhuó
meningitis N 脑膜炎 nǎomóyán
menopause N (女子)更年期 (nǚzǐ) gēngniánqī, 绝经 juéjīng
menstrual ADJ 月经的 yuèjīng de
  menstrual period 月经期 yuèjīng qī
menstruate v [妇女+] 来月经 [fùnǚ+] lái yuèjīng, 行经 xíngjīng
mental ADJ **1** 精神的 jīngshén de, 智力的 zhìlì de ■ *He is eighteen years old but has a mental age of ten.* 他今年十八岁，但是智力年龄只有十岁。Tā jīnnián shíbā suì, dànshì zhìlì niánlíng zhǐ yǒu shí suì. **2** 精神病的 jīngshénbìng de
  mental health 精神医学 jīngshén yīxué
  mental hospital 精神病院 jīngshén bìngyuàn
  mental illness/disorder 精神病 jīngshénbìng
mentality N 心态 xīntài
mentally handicapped ADJ 有智力缺陷的 yǒu zhìlì quēxiàn de, 弱智的 ruòzhì de
menthol N 薄荷脑 bòhenǎo
mention I v 提到 tídào ■ *Did I hear my name mentioned?* 有人提到我吗? Yǒu rén tídao wǒ ma? II N 提及 tíjí
mentor N 导师 dǎoshī [M. WD 位 wèi]
menu N 菜单 càidān, 菜谱 càipǔ
meow N 猫叫声 māo jiàoshēng
mercenary I N 雇佣兵 gùyōngbīng II ADJ 只是

为钱的 zhǐ shì wéi qián de, 唯利是图的 wéi lì shì tú de

merchandise N 商品 shāngpǐn, 货物 huòwù

merchant I N 商人 shāngrén, 批发商 pīfāshāng **II** ADJ 商业的 shāngyè de
the merchant marine 商船 (队) shāngchuán (duì)

mercifully ADV 幸运地 xìngyùn de, 幸亏 xìngkuī

mercury (Hg) N 汞 gǒng, 水银 shuǐyín
the mercury 室外温度 shìwài wēndù

Mercury N 水星 Shuǐxīng

mercy N 仁慈 réncí, 宽恕 kuānshù
at the mercy of sb 听任某人摆布 tīngrèn mǒurén bǎibù
a mercy mission 救援任务 jiùyuán rènwu

mercy-killing N 安乐死 ānlèsǐ

mere ADJ 只不过 zhǐbúguò, 仅仅 jǐnjǐn

merely ADV 仅仅 jǐnjǐn, 只不过 zhǐbúguò ■ *I merely asked for a sample.* 我仅仅要了一个样品。 Wǒ jǐnjǐn yàole yí ge yàngpǐn.

merge V **1** 合并 hébìng, 融合 rónghé **2** [车辆+] 会合 [chēliàng+] huìhé

merger N （公司）合并 (gōngsī) hébìng

meridian N 子午线 zǐwǔxiàn

meringue N 蛋白酥 dànbáisū [M. WD 块 kuài]

merit I N 优点 yōudiǎn, 长处 chángchù **II** V 值得 zhíde, 应得 yīngdé

meritocracy N 精英管理/统治 jīngyīng guǎnlǐ/ tǒngzhì

mermaid N 美人鱼 měirényú

merry ADJ 快乐的 kuàilè de
Merry Christmas! 圣诞快乐! Shèngdàn kuàilè!

merry-go-round N 旋转木马 xuánzhuǎn mùmǎ

mesh I N **1** 网状物 wǎngzhuàng wù **2** 混合物 hùnhéwù **II** V 把…相配 bǎ…xiāngpèi

mesmerize V 迷住 mízhù

mess¹ I N **1** 脏乱的状态 zāngluàn de zhuàngtài **2** 一团糟 yì tuán zāo ■ *You've made a mess of the job.* 你把这件事弄得一团糟了。 Nǐ bǎ zhè jiàn shì nòngde yì tuán zāo le. **II** V **1** (to mess around) 鬼混 guǐhùn **2** (to mess up) 弄糟 nòngzāo

mess² N 军人食堂 jūnrén shítáng
mess hall 军人食堂 jūnrén shítáng

message N **1** 信息 xìnxī, 口信 kǒuxìn, 短信 duǎnxìn
to get the message 得到了信息 dédaole xìnxī, 明白了意思 míngbaile yìsi
2 启示 qǐshì, 主题 zhǔtí ■ *The movie has a clear message: Good will triumph over evil.* 这部电影有个明确的主题：善良将战胜邪恶。 Zhè bù diànyǐng yǒu ge míngquè de zhǔtí: shànliáng jiāng zhànshèng xié'è.

messenger N 信使 xìnshǐ, 传递信息的人 chuándì xìnxī de rén

messiah N **1** 救世主 Jiùshìzhǔ, 救星 jiùxīng

2 （基督教）耶稣基督 (Jīdūjiào) Yēsū Jīdū

3 （犹太教）弥赛亚 (Yóutàijiào) Mísàiyà

Messrs. See **Mr.**

messy ADJ **1** 脏乱 zāngluàn **2** 极其复杂麻烦 jíqí fùzá máfan ■ *Every divorce case is messy.* 每一个离婚案都是极其复杂麻烦的。 Měi yí ge líhūn àn dōu shì jíqí fùzá máfan de.

met See **meet**

metabolism N 新陈代谢 xīn chén dài xiè

metal N **1** 金属 jīnshǔ ■ *Gold, silver, iron and copper are all metals.* 金、银、铁、铜，都是金属。 Jīn, yín, tiě, tóng, dōu shì jīnshǔ.
metal detector 金属探测器 jīnshǔ tàncèqì
precious metal 贵金属 guìjīnshǔ
2 重金属摇滚乐 zhòngjīnshǔ yáogǔnyuè

metallic ADJ 金属 (般) 的 jīnshǔ (bān) de

metallurgy N 冶金学 yějīnxué

metamorphosis N （彻底的）变化 (chèdǐ de) biànhuà

metaphor N 比喻 bǐyù, 隐喻 yǐnyù

metaphorical ADJ 比喻的 bǐyù de, 隐喻的 yǐnyù de

metaphysics N 形而上学 xíng'érshàngxué

mete V (to mete out) 给予 [+惩罚] jǐyǔ [+chéngfá]

meteor N 流星 liúxīng [M. WD 颗 kē]

meteoric ADJ **1** 流星 (似) 的 liúxīng (sì) de **2** 突发而迅速的 tūfā ér xùnsù de

meteorite N 小流星 xiǎo liúxīng, 陨石 yǔnshí

meteorologist N 气象学家 qìxiàngxuéjiā, 天气预报员 tiānqì yùbàoyuán

meteorology N 气象学 qìxiàngxué

meter N **1** 公尺 gōngchǐ, 米 mǐ **2** 仪表 yíbiǎo
electricity meter 电表 diànbiǎo
gas meter 煤气表 méiqìbiǎo
parking meter 停车计时表 tíngchē jìshíbiǎo
water meter 水表 shuǐbiǎo

methane N 甲烷 jiǎwán, 沼气 zhǎoqì

method N **1** 方法 fāngfǎ ■ *What is your method of payment?* 你用什么方法付款？ Nǐ yòng shénme fāngfǎ fù kuǎn? **2** 条理 tiáolǐ, 秩序 zhìxù

methodical ADJ 有条理的 yǒu tiáolǐ de, 井井有条的 jǐngjǐng yǒutiáo de

Methodist N 通道宗信徒 dùndàozōng xìntú

methodological ADJ 方法论的 fāngfǎlùn de

methodology N 方法论 fāngfǎlùn, 一整套方法 yìzhěngtào fāngfǎ

meticulous ADJ 注意细节的 zhùyì xìjié de, 十分谨慎的 shífēn jǐnshèn de

metric ADJ 公制的 gōngzhì de, 十进制的 shíjìnzhì de
metric system 公制 gōngzhì, 十进制 shíjìnzhì

metro N 地下铁路系统 dìxià tiělù xìtǒng

metropolis N 大城市 dà chéngshì, 大都会 dà dūhuì

metropolitan ADJ 大城市的 dà chéngshì de, 大都会的 dà dūhuì de

mettle N 勇气 yǒngqì, 毅力 yìlì

Mexican I ADJ 墨西哥的 Mòxīgēde **II** N **1** 墨西哥语 Mòxīgēyǔ **2** 墨西哥人 Mòxīgērén

mezzanine N **1** 夹层楼 jiācénglóu, 夹楼 jiālóu **2**（剧院）底层楼厅的前面几排（jùyuàn）dǐcéng lóu tīng de qiánmian jǐ pái

mice See **mouse**

microbe N 微生物 wēishēngwù

microbiologist N 微生物学家 wēishēngwùxuéjiā

microbiology N 微生物学 wēishēngwùxué

microchip N 微晶片 wēijīngpiàn [M. WD 块 kuài], 微芯片 wēixìnpiàn [M. WD 块 kuài]

microcomputer N 微型电脑 wēixíng diànnǎo, 微机 wēijī

microcosm N 微观世界 wēiguān shìjiè, 缩影 suōyǐng

microfiche N 微缩胶片 wēisuō jiāopiàn

microfilm N 微缩胶卷 wēisuō jiāojuǎn

microorganism N 微生物 wēishēngwù

microphone (ABBREV **mike**) N 扩音器 kuòyīnqì, 麦克风 màikèfēng

microprocessor N（计算机）微处理器（jìsuànjī）wēichǔlǐqì

microscope N 显微镜 xiǎnwēijìng [M. WD 台 tái/架 jià]

microscopic ADJ 微小的 wēixiǎo de, 显微镜的 xiǎnwēijìng de

microwave (stove) N 微波炉 wēibōlú

midair N 空中 kōngzhōng

midday N 中午 zhōngwǔ, 午间 wǔjiān

middle I N 中间 zhōngjiān, 中部 zhōngbù ■ *A couple of runners collapsed in the middle of the marathon.* 有几个跑步者在马拉松赛跑中途倒地了。Yǒu jǐ ge pǎobùzhě zài mǎlāsōng sàipǎo zhōngtú dǎodǐ le. **II** ADJ 中间的 zhōngjiān de
Middle Ages 中世纪（年代）Zhōngshìjì（niándài）
Middle America ①（美国）中部地区（Měiguó）zhōngbù dìqū ② 美国中产阶级 Měiguó zhōngchǎnjiējí
middle class 中产阶级 zhōngchǎn jiējí
Middle East 中东（地区）Zhōngdōng（dìqū）
middle finger 中指 zhōng zhǐ
middle name 中名 zhōng míng
middle school（美国）初级中学（Měiguó）chūjí zhōngxué, 初中 chūzhōng

middle-aged N 中年 zhōngnián

middleman N 中间人 zhōngjiānrén, 中间商 zhōngjiānshāng

middle-of-the-road ADJ 中间路线的 zhōngjiān lùxiàn de, 温和的 wēnhé de

midget N 矮人 ǎirén, 矮子 ǎizi

midlife crisis N 中年危机 zhōngnián wēijī

midnight N 午夜 wǔyè, 半夜 bànyè

midriff N 腹部 fùbù

midst N (in the midst) 在…中间 zài...zhōngjiān

midterm N **1** 期中考试 qīzhōng kǎoshì **2**（官员任职的）中期（guānyuán rènzhí de）zhōngqī

midway ADJ, ADV 中途（的）zhōngtú (de)

midweek ADJ, ADV 在一周中 zài yìzhōu zhōng

Midwest N（美国）中西部（Měiguó）zhōngxī bù

midwife N 助产士 zhùchǎnshì, 接生员 jiēshēngyuán

miffed ADJ 有点恼火的 yǒudiǎn nǎohuǒ de

might[1] [NEG **might not**] MODAL V **1** 可能 kěnéng, 或许 huòxǔ ■ *I might be wrong, but he did say something about tomorrow.* 我可能错了，不过他确实提到明天。Wǒ kěnéng cuò le, búguò tā quèshí tídao míngtiān. **2** 可以 kěyǐ **3** 不妨 bùfāng
might as well 还是 háishi, 还不如 hái bùrú ■ *You might as well go now.* 你还是现在就走吧。Nǐ háishi xiànzài jiù zǒu ba.

might[2] N 威力 wēilì, 力量 lìliang
Might is right. 强权即公理。Qiángquán jí gōnglǐ.

mighty ADJ **1** 极其强大的 jíqí qiángdà de **2** 巨大的 jùdà de, 庞大的 pángdà de

migraine N 偏头痛 piāntóutòng

migrant N **1**（经济）移民（jīngjì）yímín **2** 候鸟 hòuniǎo, 迁徙动物 qiānxǐ dòngwù

migrate V **1** 移居 yíjū, 移民 yímín **2** 迁徙 qiānxǐ

migration N 移居 yíjū, 迁移 qiānyí

migratory ADJ 移居的 yíjū de, 迁都的 qiāndū de

mike See **microphone**

mild ADJ **1** 温和的 wēnhé de, 轻微的 qīngwēi de **2** 淡的（味道）dàn de (wèidao)

mildew N 霉（菌）méi (jùn)

mile N 英里 yīnglǐ

mileage N **1** 行车里程 xíngchē lǐchéng **2** 利益 lìyì, 好处 hǎochu

milestone N 里程碑 lǐchéngbēi [M. WD 块 kuài]

milieu N 生活环境 shēnghuó huánjìng

militant I ADJ 激进的 jījìn de **II** N 战斗人员 zhàndòurényuán

militarism N 军国主义 jūnguó zhǔyì

militaristic ADJ 军国主义的 jūnguó zhǔyì de

military I ADJ 军事的 jūnshì de ■ *Using military means should be the last resort.* 使用军事手段应该是最后的办法。Shǐyòng jūnshì shǒuduàn yīnggāi shì zuìhòu de bànfǎ. **II** N 军队 jūnduì

militate V (to militate against) 阻止 zǔzhǐ, 妨碍 fáng'ài

militia N 民兵 mínbīng

milk I N **1** 奶 nǎi ■ *Mother's milk is the best food for babies.* 母奶是婴儿最好的食物。Mǔnǎi shì yīng'ér zuì hǎo de shíwù. **2** 牛奶 niúnǎi
milkman 送牛奶的工人 sòng niúnǎi de gōngrén

milk powder 奶粉 nǎifěn
milk shake 泡沫牛奶 pàomò niúnǎi, 奶昔 nǎixī
3 乳液 rǔyè **II** v **1** 挤奶 jǐnǎi **2** 榨取 zhàqǔ
milky ADJ **1** 多奶的 duō nǎi de **2** 乳白色的 rǔbáisè de

Milky Way N 银河 Yínhé
mill N **1**（工）厂（gōng）chǎng **2** 磨粉机 mòfěnjī
cotton mill 棉纺织厂 miánfǎngzhīchǎng
steel mill 钢铁厂 gāngtiěchǎng
II v **1** 将 [+谷物] 磨碎 jiāng [+gǔwù] mósuì
2 (to mill around) 来回乱转 láihuí luàn zhuǎn

millennial ADJ（一）千年的 (yì) qiānnián de
millennium N（一）千年 (yì) qiānnián
millet N 小米 xiǎomǐ [M. WD 颗 kē/粒 lì]
milligram N 毫克 háokè
milliliter N 毫升 háoshēng
millimeter N 毫米 háomǐ
millinery N 帽类 màolèi
million NUM 百万 bǎiwàn
millions 数百万的 shù bǎiwàn de, 很多的 hěn duō de
millionaire N 百万富翁 bǎiwàn fùwēng
mime I N **1** 哑剧 yǎjù **2** 做手势（来表达意思）zuò shǒushì (lái biǎodá yìsi) **II** v 演哑剧 yǎn yǎjù
mimic I v 模仿（他人）mófǎng (tārén) **II** N 滑稽模仿表演 gǔjī mófǎng biǎoyǎn
mince v **1** 把 [+食物] 剁碎 bǎ [+shíwù] duòsuì **2** 吞吞吐吐地说话 tūntūn tǔtǔ de shuōhuà
not to mince one's words 直截了当地说 zhíjié liǎodàng de shuō
mincemeat N 百果馅 bǎiguǒxiàn
to make mincemeat of sb 彻底打败某人 chèdǐ dǎbài mǒurén
mind I N **1** 头脑 tóunǎo, 心智 xīnzhì **2** 心思 xīnsi, 主意 zhǔyi ■ *Are you quite sure in your own mind what you really want?* 你心里确实明白想要什么吗? Nǐ xīnlǐ quèshí míngbai xiǎng yào shénme ma?
to change one's mind 改变主意 gǎibiàn zhǔyì
to make up one's mind 打定主意 dǎdìng zhǔyi, 决定 juédìng
to keep/bear in mind 记住 jìzhu ■ *I will keep your wishes in mind.* 我会记住你的愿望。Wǒ huì jìzhu nǐ de yuànwang.
II v **1** 在意 zàiyì ■ *I don't mind doing overtime, so long as I'm paid for it.* 我不在意加班, 只要付我钱。Wǒ bú zàiyì jiābān, zhǐyào fù wǒ qián. **2** 注意 zhùyì, 留神 liúshén **3** 照看 zhàokān, 管理 guǎnlǐ
mind-boggling ADJ 难以想象的 nányǐ xiǎngxiàng de
mindful ADJ 留意的 liúyì de, 记住的 jìzhu de
mindless ADJ **1** 不动脑子的 búdòng nǎozi de **2** 没有脑子的 méiyǒu nǎozi de, 愚笨的 yúbèn de

mine¹ PRON 我的 wǒ de ■ *No, this is not my laptop; mine is a Dell.* 这不是我的笔记本电脑, 我的是戴尔牌的。Zhè bú shì wǒ de bǐjìběn diànnǎo, wǒ de shì Dàiěr pái de.
mine² I N 矿 kuàng ■ *It's no longer profitable to work this mine.* 再开采这个矿, 已经无利可图了。Zài kāicǎi zhè ge kuàng, yǐjīng wú lì kě tú le.
coal mine 煤矿 méikuàng
gold mine 金矿 jīnkuàng
II v 开矿 kāikuàng, 采矿 cǎikuàng
minefield N 布雷区 bùléiqū
miner N 矿工 kuànggōng
mineral N 矿物质 kuàngwùzhì
mineral water 矿泉水 kuàngquánshuǐ
minesweeper N 扫雷艇 sǎoléitǐng [M. WD 艘 sōu]
mingle v（使…）混合（shǐ…）hùnhé
mini ADJ 小型的 xiǎoxíng de
miniature I ADJ 微型的 wēixíng de
miniature golf 小型高尔夫球场 xiǎoxíng gāo'ěrfū qiúchǎng
II N **1** 微型复制品 wēixíng fùzhìpǐn **2** 袖珍画像 xiùzhēn huàxiàng
minimal ADJ 极小的 jí xiǎo de, 极少的 jí shǎo de
minimize v 把…降低到最小限度 bǎ…jiàngdī dào zuì xiǎo xiàndù
minimum I N 最小量 zuì xiǎo liáng, 最低限度 zuì dī xiàndù **II** ADJ 最小 zuì xiǎo, 最少 zuì shǎo
minimum wage 最低工资 zuì dī gōngzī
mining N 采矿（业）cǎikuàng (yè)
miniseries N（电视）连续短片 (diànshì) liánxù duǎnpiàn
miniskirt N 超短裙 chāoduǎnqún [M. WD 条 tiáo]
minister I N **1** 部长 bùzhǎng **2** 牧师 mùshi ■ *The new minister of the local Presbyterian church is a young man with an angelic face.* 当地长老会教堂的新牧师是一位长着天使般面容的年轻人。Dāngdì zhǎnglǎohuì jiàotáng de xīn mùshī shì yí wèi zhǎngzhe tiānshǐbān miànróng de niánqīng rén.
II v **1** 当牧师 dāng mùshi **2** (to minister to) 帮助 bāngzhù
ministerial ADJ 部长的 bùzhǎng de, 牧师的 mùshi de
ministry N **1**（政府）部 (zhèngfǔ) bù ■ *The Chinese Ministry of Foreign Affairs issued an important statement yesterday.* 中国外交部昨天发表了重要声明。Zhōngguó Wàijiāobù zuótiān fābiǎole zhòngyào shēngmíng. **2** 牧师的职责 mùshī de zhízé
minivan N 小型客车 xiǎoxíng kèchē [M. WD 辆 liàng], 面包车 miànbāochē [M. WD 辆 liàng]
mink N 水貂（皮）shuǐdiāo (pí)
minor I ADJ 次要的 cìyào de, 不很重要的 bú hěn zhòngyào de **II** N 未成年人 wèi chéngnián-rén **III** v 副修 fùxiū ■ *Helen majors in political science and minors in Arabic.* 海伦主修政治学,

副修阿拉伯文。Hǎilún zhǔxiū Zhèngzhìxué, fùxiū Ālābówén.

minority N 少数 shǎoshù

Minor league N（美国）职业棒球小联盟 (Měiguó) Zhíyè bàngqiú xiǎo liánméng

minstrel N 歌手 gēshǒu

mint¹ I v **1** 创造（新词）chuàngzào (xīncí) **2** 授予学位 shòuyǔ xuéwèi

a newly minted graduate 一位新获得学位的大学毕业生 yíwèi xīn huòdé xuéwèi de dàxué bìyèshēng

II N 铸币厂 zhùbìchǎng [M. WD 座 zuò]

to make a mint 赚一大笔钱 zhuàn yí dà bǐ qián

III ADJ (in mint condition) 崭新的 zhǎnxīn de

mint² N 薄荷 bòhe, 薄荷糖 bòhetáng [M. WD 块 kuài]

minty ADJ 有薄荷味的 yǒu bòhe wèi de

minus I v PREP **1** 减去 jiǎnqù ■ *20 minus 4 is 16.* 20减去4等于16。Èrshí jiǎnqù sì děngyú shíliù.

2 少了 shǎole, 缺少 quēshǎo **II** N **1** 减号 jiǎnhào, 负号 fùhào

minus sign 减号 jiǎnhào, 负号 fùhào (−)

2 缺点 quēdiǎn **III** ADJ **1** 零下 língxià

minus 10° 零下十度 língxià shí dù (−10°)

2（学校分数）减 (xuéxiào fēnshù) jiǎn

B minus B减 B jiǎn (B−)

minuscule ADJ 极其微小的 jíqí wēixiǎo de

minute¹ N 分 fēn, 分钟 fēnzhōng

at the last minute 最后一刻 zuì hòu yí kè ■ *She decided to go with me at the last minute.* 她在最后一刻决定和我一起去。Tā zài zuì hòu yí kè juédìng hé wǒ yìqǐ qù.

at any minute 随时 suíshí, 马上 mǎshàng

minute² ADJ 极小的 jíxiǎo de, 微小的 wēixiǎo de

minutes N（会议）记录 (huìyì) jìlù

to keep minutes 做（会议）记录 zuò (huìyì) jìlù

miracle N 奇迹 qíjì ■ *It's a miracle that he survived the accident!* 他经过那次事故而没有死，真是奇迹！Tā jīngguò nà cì shìgù ér méiyǒu sǐ, zhēnshì qíjì!

miraculous ADJ 奇迹般的 qíjì bān de, 神奇的 shénqí de

mirage N 海市蜃楼 hǎishì shènlóu

mire I N **1** 泥潭 nítán **2** 困境 kùnjìng **II** v **1** 使…陷入泥潭 shǐ…xiànrù nítán **2** 使…陷入困境 shǐ…xiànrù kùnjìng

mirror I N 镜子 jìngzi

mirror image ① 非常相像的事物 fēicháng xiāngxiàng de shìwù ② 完全相反的事物 wánquán xiāngfǎn de shìwù

rearview mirror 后视镜 hòushì jìng

II v 与…完全一样 yǔ…wánquán yíyàng

mirth N 欢乐 huānlè

misadventure N 灾祸 zāihuò, 不幸 búxìng

misapprehension N 误会 wùhuì, 误解 wùjiě

misappropriate v 挪用 nuóyòng, 盗用 dàoyòng

misappropriation N 挪用 nuóyòng, 盗用 dàoyòng

misbehave v 行为不端 xíngwéi bùduān, 做坏事 zuò huàishì

miscalculate v **1** 误算 [+开支] wù suàn [+kāizhī] **2** 错误估计 [+形势] cuòwù gūjì [+xíngshì], 错误判断 cuòwù pànduàn

miscalculation N **1** 误算 wù suàn **2** 错误估计 cuòwù gūjì, 错误判断 cuòwù pànduàn

miscarriage N 流产 liúchǎn, 小产 xiǎochǎn

miscarry v 流产 liúchǎn, 小产 xiǎochǎn

miscellaneous ADJ 各种各样的 gèzhǒng gèyàng de, 混杂的 hùnzá de

miscellaneous expenses 杂费 záfèi

mischief N 调皮捣乱 tiáopí dǎoluàn

mischievous ADJ 调皮捣乱的 tiáopí dǎoluàn de

misconception N 错误想法 cuòwù xiǎngfǎ, 误解 wùjiě

misconduct N 行为不端 xíngwéi bùduān

misconstrue v 误解 wùjiě

misdeed N 错误行为 cuòwù xíngwéi, 违法行为 wéifǎ xíngwéi

misdemeanor N 轻罪 qīngzuì

misdirect v **1** 错误地使用 cuòwù de shǐyòng **2** 把…送错地方 bǎ…sòngcuò dìfang

miser N 守财奴 shǒucáinú, 小气鬼 xiǎoqìguǐ

miserable ADJ 悲惨的 bēicǎn de

miserly ADJ **1** 吝啬 lìnsè, 小气的 xiǎoqì de **2** 少得可怜的 shǎo dé kělián de

misery N 苦难 kǔnàn, 痛苦 tòngkǔ

misfit N 格格不入的人 gégé búrù de rén, 不适应环境的人 bú shìyìng huánjìng de rén

misfortune N 不幸 búxìng

misgiving N 疑虑 yílù, 担忧 dānyōu

misguided ADJ 事与愿违的 shì yǔ yuàn wéi de, 帮倒忙的 bāngdàománg de

mishandle v 对…处理不当 duì…chǔlǐ búdàng

mishap N 小过失 xiǎo guòshī, 小事故 xiǎo shìgù

misinform v 向…提供错误信息 xiàng…tígōng cuòwù xìnxī

misinterpret v 曲解 qūjiě, 误解 wùjiě

misjudge v 错误判断 cuòwù pànduàn, 误判 wùpàn

mislaid See **mislay**

mislay (PT & PP **mislaid**) v 忘记把 [钥匙+] 放在哪里 wàngjì bǎ [yàoshi+] fàng zài nǎli

mislead (PT & PP **misled**) v 误导 wùdǎo

misleading ADJ 误导的 wùdǎo de

misled See **mislead**

mismanage v 管理不善 guǎnlǐ búshàn, 错误处置 cuòwù chǔzhì

mismanagement N 管理不善 guǎnlǐ bú shàn, 处置失当 chǔzhì shīdàng

mismatch N 错误的搭配 cuòwù de dāpèi

mismatched ADJ 不成对的 bù chéngduì de

mismatched gloves 不成对的手套 bù chéngduì de shǒutào

misnomer N 错误的名称 cuòwù de míngchēng

misogynist N 憎恨女性的人 zēnghèn nǚxìng de rén

misogyny N 对女性的憎恨 duì nǚxìng de zēnghèn, 厌女症 yànnǚzhēng

misplace v 错放 cuò fàng

misplaced ADJ 错给的 cuò gěi de, 不应该给予的 bù yīnggāi jǐyǔ de

misprint N 印刷错误 yìnshuā cuòwù

misquote v 错误地使用 cuòwù de shǐyòng, 错误地引述 cuòwù de yǐnshù

misread (PT & PP **misread**) v **1** 错误地判断 cuòwù de pánduàn **2** 读错 dú cuò

misrepresent v（故意）错误地描述 (gùyì) cuòwù de miáoshù

miss¹ I v **1** 错过 cuòguò ■ *If you miss this chance, there may not be a second chance.* 如果你错过这次机会，可能不会有第二次机会了。Rúguǒ nǐ cuòguò zhè cì jīhuì, kěnéng bú huì yǒu dì'èr cì jīhuì le. **2** 想念 xiǎngniàn, 怀念 huáiniàn II N 失误 shīwù

A miss is as good as a mile. 因小失误失败，终究也是失败。Yīn xiǎo shīwù shībài, zhōngjiū yě shì shībài.

miss² N 小姐 xiǎojiě

misshapen ADJ 畸形的 jīxíng de, 变形的 biànxíng de

missile N 导弹 dǎodàn [M. WD 枚 méi]

missing ADJ **1** 失踪的 shīzōng de
a missing person 失踪者 shīzōngzhě
2 丢失的 diūshī de, 找不到的 zhǎobudào de
a missing document 一份丢失的文件 yí fèn diūshī de wénjiàn
3 缺少的 quēshǎo de, 漏掉的 lòudiào de
missing link 缺少的一环 quēshǎo de yì huán

mission N **1** 使命 shǐmìng ■ *Their mission was to bring relief supplies to the villages.* 他们的使命是把救济物资运到村庄。Tāmen de shǐmìng shì bǎ jiùjì wùzī yùndao cūnzhuāng. **2** 代表团 dàibiǎotuán **3** 传教 chuánjiào, 布道 bùdào

missionary N 传教士 chuánjiàoshì

misspell v (PT & PP **misspelled**, **misspelt**) 拼错 pīn cuò

misspelling N 拼写错误 pīnxiě cuòwù

misspend (PT & PP **misspent**) v 使用不当 shǐyòng bùdang, 滥用 lànyòng

misspent v See misspend

misstep N 失误 shīwù, 失策 shīcè

mist I N 雾气 wùqì, 水蒸气 shuǐzhēngqì ■ *The woods are shrouded in a thick mist.* 树林笼罩在浓雾中。Shùlín lǒngzhào zài nóng wù zhōng.
II v 蒙上雾气 méng shàng wùqì ■ *When I drink coffee, my glasses mist over.* 我喝咖啡时，眼镜蒙

上了雾气。Wǒ hē kāfēi shí, yǎnjìng méngshàngle wùqì.

mistake I N 错误 cuòwù, 过失 guòshī II v (PT **mistook**; PP **mistaken**) **1** 误会 wùhui, 误解 wùjiě **2** 把…误认为 bǎ…wùrènwéi

mistaken I v See mistake II ADJ 弄错的 nòngcuò de

mister See Mr.

mistletoe N 槲寄生 hújìshēng

mistook See mistake

mistreat v 虐待 nüèdài

mistreatment N 虐待 nüèdài

mistress N **1** 情妇 qíngfù **2** 女主人 nǚzhǔren

mistrial N 无效审判 wúxiào shěnpàn

mistrust N, v 不信任 bú xìnrèn

mistrustful ADJ 不信任的 bú xìnrèn de

misty ADJ 有雾的 yǒu wù de, 多雾的 duō wù de

misunderstand v 误解 wùjiě, 误会 wùhuì

misunderstanding N 误解 wùjiě, 误会 wùhuì

misuse I v **1** 用错 yòngcuò **2** 滥用 [+公款] lànyòng [+gōngkuǎn] II N **1** 错用 cuòyòng **2** 滥用 lànyòng

mite¹ N 螨 mǎn, 螨虫 mǎnchóng

mite² N (a mite of) 有点儿 yǒudiǎnr

mitigate v 减少 jiǎnshǎo, 减轻 jiǎnqīng

mitigation N 减少 jiǎnshǎo, 减轻 jiǎnqīng

mitt N 防护手套 fánghù shǒutào [M. WD 副 fù]
boxing mitt 拳击手套 quánjī shǒutào

mitten N 连指手套 lián zhǐ shǒutào [M. WD 只 zhī/副 fù]

mix I v **1** 混合 hùnhé **2** 和 [+不很熟的人] 交往 hé [+bù hěn shú de rén] jiāowǎng
to mix up 弄混 nòng hùn, 混淆 hùnxiáo
II N 混合（物）hùnhé (wù)

mixed ADJ 混合的 hùnhé de
mixed marriage 异族通婚 yìzú tōnghūn, 异教通婚 yìjiào tōnghūn

mixer N（食物）搅拌器 (shíwù) jiǎobànqì

mixture N 混合物 hùnhéwù ■ *Have you prepared the cake mixture?* 你拌好了做蛋糕的面团了吗？ Nǐ bànhǎole zuò dàngāo de miàntuán le ma?

mix-up N 乱中出错 luàn zhōng chū cuò, 错误 cuòwù

moan I v **1** 呻吟 shēnyín **2** 抱怨 bàoyuàn II N **1** 呻吟（声）shēnyín (shēng) **2** 怨声 yuàn shēng

moat N 护城河 hùchénghé

mob I N（一群）暴民 (yìqún) bàomín II v 围住 wéizhù

mobile ADJ 移动的 yídòng de, 流动的 liúdòng de
mobile clinic 流动诊所 liúdòng zhěnsuǒ
mobile home 流动住房 liúdòng zhùfáng
mobile phone 移动电话 yídòng diànhuà, 手机 shǒujī

mobility N 流动性 liúdòngxìng
upward mobility 提升（社会）地位 tíshēng (shèhuì) dìwèi

mobilization

mobilization N 动员 dòngyuán
mobilize v 动员 dòngyuán, 调动 diàodòng
mobster N 犯罪集团成员 fànzuì jítuán chéng-yuán, 暴徒 bàotú
mock I v 嘲笑 cháoxiào, 嘲弄 cháonòng II ADJ 1 模拟的 mónǐ de
a mock trial 模拟审判 mónǐ shěnpàn
2 装出来的 zhuāngchūlái de, 假装的 jiǎzhuāng de
mock indignation 装作愤怒的样子 zhuāngzuò fènnù de yàngzi
mockery N 1 无用的东西 wúyòng de dōngxi
to make a mockery of 使…变得无用 shǐ…biàn de wúyòng
2 嘲弄 cháonòng
mockingbird N 嘲鸫(鸟) cháodōng (niǎo) [M. WD 只 zhī]
modal verb N 情态动词 qíngtài dòngcí
mode N 方式 fāngshì, 模式 móshì
model I N 1 模特儿 mótèr 2 模型 móxíng 3 型号 xínghào ■ The new model proved very popular. 这种新型号很受欢迎。Zhè zhǒng xīn xínghào hěn shòu huānyíng. 4 榜样 bǎngyàng ■ The princi-pal praised him as a model of service and dedica-tion. 校长赞扬他是服务和献身的榜样。Xiàozhǎng zànyáng tā shì fúwù hé xiànshēn de bǎngyàng.
II ADJ 1 模范的 mófàn de, 楷模的 kǎimó de
a model student 模范学生 mófàn xuésheng
2 模型(的) móxíng (de)
model train 火车模型 huǒchē móxíng
III v 1 当模特儿 dāng mótèr 2 以…为榜样 yǐ…wéi bǎngyàng
to model oneself after sb 以某人为榜样 yǐ mǒurén wéi bǎngyàng
be modeled on sth 仿照某物 fǎngzhào mǒuwù
modeling N 1 模特儿的工作 mótèr de gōngzuò 2 模型制作 móxíng zhìzuò
modem N 调制调解器 tiáozhì tiáojiěqì
moderate I ADJ 适度的 shìdù de, 不偏激的 bù piānjī de II v 1 主持 [+辩论会] zhǔchí [+biàn-lùnhuì] 2 调解 [+争执] tiáojiě [+zhēngzhí] 3 使 [+观点] 和缓 shǐ [+guāndiǎn] héhuǎn III N 温和派(人士)wēnhépài (rénshì)
moderation N 1 缓和 huǎnhé 2 节制 jiézhì, 不过分 bú guòfēn
in moderation 适度地 shìdù de, 有节制地 yǒu jiézhì de
moderator N 1 主持人 zhǔchírén 2 调解人 tiáojiě rén
modern ADJ 1 现代的 xiàndài de 2 现代化的 xiàndàihuà de ■ This modern building does not match the surrounding classic architecture. 这幢现代化大楼和周围的古典建筑不相配。Zhè zhuàng xiàndàihuà dàlóu hé zhōuwéi de gǔdiǎn jiànzhù bù xiāngpèi. 3 新式的 xīnshì de, 时髦的 shímáo de

modernization N 现代化 xiàndàihuà
modernize v 使…现代化 shǐ…xiàndàihuà
modest ADJ 1 谦虚的 qiānxū de 2 朴素的 pǔsù, 不起眼的 bù qǐyǎn de
modesty N 谦虚 qiānxū
modicum N 少量 shǎoliàng, 一点 yìdiǎn
modification N 修改 xiūgǎi, 调节 tiáo jié
modifier N 修饰语 xiūshìyǔ
modify v 修改 xiūgǎi, 调节 tiáojié
modular ADJ 模块化的 mókuàihuà de
modulate v 调节 tiáojié, 调整 tiáozhěng
modulation N 调节 tiáojié, 调整 tiáozhěng
module N 1 单元 dānyuán, 部件 bùjiàn 2 (计算机软件) 模块 (jìsuànjī ruǎnjiàn) mókuài 3 (宇宙飞船) 分离舱 (yǔzhòu fēichuán) fēnlícāng
mohair N 马海毛绒 mǎhǎimáoróng
Mohammed N 穆罕默德(伊斯兰教领袖)Mùhǎnmòdé (Yīsīlánjiào lǐngxiù)
moist ADJ 湿润的 shīrùn de, 潮湿的 cháoshī de
moisten v 使…湿润 shǐ…shīrùn
moisture N 湿气 shīqì, 水汽 shuǐqì
moisturizer N 润肤膏 rùnfūgāo
molar N 臼齿 jiùchǐ [M. WD 颗 kē], 磨牙 móyá
molasses N 糖浆 tángjiāng
mold¹ N 1 模具 mújù, 模式 móshì
to break the mold 打破模式 dǎpò móshì
2 类型 lèixíng, 气质 qìzhì
the mold of a typical businessman 典型商人的气质 diǎnxíng shāngrén de qìzhì
3 霉(菌)méi (jùn)
mold² v 1 用模具制作 [+蛋糕] yòng mújù zhìzuò [+dàngāo] 2 塑造 [+青年人] sùzào [+qīng-niánrén]
molder v 腐烂 fǔlàn, 烂掉 làndiào
molding N 1 模制件 mózhìjiàn 2 装饰线条 zhuāngshì xiàntiáo
moldy ADJ 发霉的 fāméi de
mole N 1 (色素) 痣 (sèsù) zhì 2 内奸 nèijiān, 奸细 jiānxì 3 鼹鼠 yǎnshǔ
molecule N 分子 fènzǐ
molest v (性) 骚扰 (xìng) sāorǎo, 猥亵 wěixiè
mollify v 安抚 ānfǔ, 平息怒气 píngxī nùqì
molt v [动物+] 蜕皮 [dòngwù+] tuìpí, [鸟+] 换羽 [niǎo+] huànyǔ
molten ADJ 熔化的 rónghuà de
mom N 妈妈 māma
moment N 1 片刻 piànkè, 一会儿 yíhuìr 2 那时 nàshí, 正在那时 zhèngzài nàshí ■ At that mo-ment, his cell phone rang. 正在那时，他的手机铃响了。Zhèngzài nàshí, tā de shǒujī líng xiǎng le. 3 时机 shíjī ■ This is not the right moment to ask for a raise. 现在是要求加薪的好时机。Zhè bú shì yāoqiú jiāxīn de hǎo shíjī.
for the moment 暂时 zànshí
momentary ADJ 一时的 yìshí de, 片刻的 piànkè de

momentous ADJ 重大的 zhòngdà de, 重要的 zhòngyào de

momentum N 势头 shìtóu, 动力 dònglì

mommy N 妈咪 māmī

monarch N 君主 jūnzhǔ, 国王／女王 guówáng/nǚwáng

monarchy N 君主政体 jūnzhǔ zhèngtǐ

monastery N 修道院 xiūdàoyuàn [M. WD 座 zuò], 寺院 sìyuàn [M. WD 座 zuò]

Monday N 星期一 xīngqīyī, 周一 zhōuyī

monetary ADJ 货币的 huòbì de, 金融的 jīnróng de

money N 钱 qián, 金钱 jīnqián
Money makes the world turn. 有钱能使鬼推磨。Yǒu qián néng shǐ guǐ tuī mò. (→*If you have money you can make the devil push your mill stone.*)
money market 货币市场 huòbì shìchǎng
money order 汇票 huìpiào, 汇款单 huìkuǎndān

mongrel N 杂种狗 zázhǒng gǒu [M. WD 只 zhī/条 tiáo]

moniker N 绰号 chuòhào, 名号 mínghào

monitor I N 1 (机算计) 显示器 (jīsuànjì) xiǎnshìqì [M. WD 台 tái] 2 (安全) 监视器 (ānquán) jiānshìqì, 监护器 jiānhùqì 3 (学校) 班长 (xuéxiào) bānzhǎng, 级长 jízhǎng II V 1 监视 jiānshì, 监听 jiāntīng

monk N 修道士 xiūdào shì, 僧侣 sēnglǚ
Buddhist monk 和尚 héshang

monkey I N 猴 (子) hóu (zi) ■ *The monkeys in the zoo attract many children.* 动物园里的猴子吸引很多孩子。Dòngwùyuán lǐ de hóuzi xīyǐn hěn duō háizi. II V (to monkey around) 打闹 dǎnào, 捣蛋 dǎodàn

monkey wrench N 活动扳手 huódòngbānshǒu [M. WD 把 bǎ]

mono N 1 单声道音响系统 dān shēng dào yīnxiǎng xìtǒng 2 腺热 xiàn rè

monochrome ADJ 单色的 dānsè de, 黑白的 hēibái de

monogamy N 一夫一妻制 yìfūyìqīzhì

monogram N 字母组合图案 zìmǔ zǔ hé tú'àn

monolithic ADJ 1 宏伟的 [+大楼] hóngwěi de [+dàlóu] 2 庞大的 [+组织] pángdà de [+zǔzhī]

monologue N 独白 dúbái [M. WD 篇 piān]

monopolistic ADJ 垄断的 lǒngduàn de

monopolize V 垄断 lǒngduàn, 独占 dúzhàn

monopoly N 1 垄断 (权) lǒngduàn (quán) 2 垄断企业 lǒngduàn qǐyè

monorail N 单轨铁道 dānguǐ tiědào [M. WD 条 tiáo]

monosyllable N 单音节 dānyīnjié

monotone N 单调 dāndiào, 单调的声音 dāndiào de shēngyīn

monotonous ADJ 单调的 dāndiào de, 乏味的 fáwèi de

monsoon N 雨季 yǔjì

monster N 巨大的怪物 jùdà de guàiwu, 魔鬼 móguǐ

monstrosity N 巨大丑陋的东西 jùdà chǒulòu de dōngxi

monstrous ADJ 1 极大的 jídà de 2 极坏的 jí huài de

montage N 剪辑 jiǎnjí, 蒙太奇 Méngtàiqí

month N 月 yuè, 月份 yuèfen

monthly I ADJ 每月的 měiyuè de, 每月一次的 měi yuè yícì de II ADV 每月 měi yuè ■ *Are you paid monthly or fortnightly?* 你是每月还是每两周发工资？Nǐ shì měi yuè háishi měi liǎng zhōu fā gōngzī? III N 月刊 yuèkān

monument N 纪念碑 jìniànbēi

monumental ADJ 1 伟大的 wěidà de, 不朽的 bùxiǔ dé 2 巨大的 jùdà de

moo N 牛哞声 niú mōu shēng, 哞 mōu

mooch V 乞讨 qǐtǎo, 讨 tǎo

mood N 1 情绪 qíngxu, 心情 xīnqíng
in no mood to do sth 不想做某事 bù xiǎng zuò mǒushì
2 不好的心情 bù hǎo de xīnqíng
to be in a mood 心情不好 xīnqíng bù hǎo, 暗暗生气 àn'àn shēngqì

moody ADJ 情绪多变的 qíngxù duōbiàn de, 喜怒无常的 xǐnù wúcháng de

moon N 1 月 yuè, 月亮 yuèliang 2 月球 yuèqiú

moonbeam N 月光 yuèguāng [M. WD 道 dào]

moonless ADJ 没有月亮的 méiyǒu yuèliang de

moonlight I N 月光 yuèguāng II V 从事第二职业 cóngshì dì'èr zhíyè, 兼职 jiānzhí

moonlighter N 从事第二职业的人 cóngshì dì'èr zhíyè de rén

moor[1] V 停泊 tíngbó

moor[2] N 荒野 huāngyě

mooring N 1 停泊地 tíngbódì 2 系泊用具 xìbó yòngjù

moose N (PL **moose**) 麋 mí, 驼鹿 tuólù [M. WD 头 tóu]

moot ADJ 1 没有结论的 méiyǒu jiélùn de
a moot point 还有争议的事 háiyǒu zhēngyì de shì
2 不会再发生的 búhuì zài fāshēng de, 不再重要的 búzài zhòngyào de

mop I N 1 拖把 tuōbǎ 2 蓬乱的头发 péngluàn de tóufa II V (用拖把) 拖地板 (yòng tuōbǎ) tuō dìbǎn

mope V 闷闷不乐 mènmèn búlè

moped N 机动自行车 jīdòng zìxíngchē [M. WD 辆 liàng]

moral I ADJ 1 道德的 dàodé de ■ *You shouldn't always avoid moral judgment.* 你不应该总是回避道德判断。Nǐ bù yīnggāi zǒngshì huíbì dàodé pànduàn. 2 有道德的 yǒu dàodé de II N 教育意义 jiàoyù yìyì, 寓意 yùyì

morale N 士气 shìqì, 斗志 dòuzhì
moralistic ADJ 道德说教的 dàodé shuōjiào de
morality N 道德（观）dàodé (guān), 道德水准 dàodé shuǐzhǔn
moralize V 说教 shuōjiào, 训导 xùndǎo
morals N 道德（准则）dàodé (zhǔnzé)
 loose morals 低下的道德准则 dīxià de dàodé zhǔnzé, 放荡的品行 fàngdàng de pǐnxíng
morass N **1** 困境 kùnjìng **2** 沼泽（地）zhǎozé (dì)
moratorium N 暂停 zàntíng
morbid ADJ **1** 病态的 bìngtài de, 不健康的 bú jiànkāng de **2** 疾病的 jíbìng de
more I ADJ 更多的 gèngduō de, 比较多的 bǐjiào duō de ■ *I need more time to do the homework.* 我需要更多的时间来做作业。Wǒ xūyào gèngduō de shíjiān lái zuò zuòyè. II PRON 更多的（东西）gèngduō de (dōngxi) ■ *I want to learn more about the colleges before I make the final decision.* 我想对这些大学有更多了解，再作最后决定。Wǒ xiǎng duì zhèxiē dàxué yǒu gèngduō liǎojiě, zài zuò zuìhòu juédìng. III ADV 更 gèng, 比较 bǐjiào
 more and more 越来越（多）yuèláiyuè (duō) ■ *His political views are more and more radicalized.* 他的政治观点越来越激进了。Tāde zhèngzhì guāndiǎn yuèláiyuè jīn le.
 the more ... the more 越…越 yuè...yuè
 not any more 不再 búzài
moreover ADV 而且 érqiě, 此外 cǐwài
mores N 习俗 xísú
morgue N 停尸房 tíng shī fáng, 太平间 tàipíngjiān
Mormon I N 摩门教徒 Mómén jiào tú II ADJ 摩门教的 Móménjiào de
Mormonism N 摩门教 Móménjiào
morning N **1** 上午 shàngwǔ (from 6.00 a.m. to 12 noon) **2** 早上 zǎoshang (from 6.00 a.m.–8.00 a.m.)
 morning glory 牵牛花 qiānniúhuā [M. WD 朵 duǒ/棵 kē]
moron N 白痴 báichī, 蠢货 chǔnhuò
morose ADJ 阴郁的 yīnyù de, 闷闷不乐的 mènmèn bú lè de
morph V 变形 biànxíng, 改变 gǎibiàn
morphine N 吗啡 mǎfēi
morphing N （计算机）图象渐变 (jìsuànjī) tú-xiàng jiànbiàn
Morse code N 莫尔斯密码 Mò'ěrsī mìmǎ
morsel N 一点儿食物 yìdiǎnr shíwù
mortal I ADJ **1** 不会长生不老的 bú huì chángshēngbùlǎo de, 会死亡的 huì sǐwáng de **2** 致命的 [+打击] zhìmìng de [+dǎjī]
 mortal sin 弥天大罪 mítiān dàzuì
 3 极度的 [+恐惧] jídù de [+kǒngjù] II N 凡人 fánrén, 普通人 pǔtōngrén

mortality N **1** 死亡率 sǐwánglǜ **2** 终有一死 zhōng yǒu yì sǐ
mortar N **1** 迫击炮 pǎijīpào [M. WD 门 mén] **2** 砂浆 shā jiāng **3** 研钵 yánbō, 臼 jiù
mortarboard N 学位帽 xuéwèimào [M. WD 顶 dǐng]
mortgage I N 抵押货款 dǐyā huòkuǎn, 按揭 ànjiē II V 抵押 dǐyā
mortician N 丧葬承办人 sāngzàng chéngbàn rén, 殡仪馆工作人员 bìnyíguǎn gōngzuò rényuán
mortify V 使…难堪 shǐ...nánkān
mortuary N 停尸房 tíngshīfáng, 太平间 tàipíngjiān
mosaic N 马赛克 mǎsàikè, 镶嵌图案 xiāngqiàn tú'àn
mosey V 闲逛 xiánguàng
Moslem N See Muslim
mosque N 清真寺 qīngzhēnsì [M. WD 座 zuò]
mosquito N 蚊子 wénzi [M. WD 只 zhī]
moss N 苔藓 táixiǎn
mossy ADJ 有苔藓的 yǒu táixiǎn de
most I ADJ 大多数 dàduōshù ■ *Most people at least try to lead a moral life.* 大多数人至少试图过有道德的生活。Dàduōshù rén zhìshǎo shìtú guò yǒudàodé de shēnghuó. II PRON 大多数 dàduōshù ■ *It rained for most of the day yesterday.* 昨天大多时间都在下雨。Zuótiān dàduō shíjiān dōu zài xiàyǔ. III ADV 最 zuì ■ *Of all my friends, Jack is the most successful.* 在我的朋友中，杰克是最成功的。Zài wǒ de péngyou zhōng, Jiékè shì zuì chénggōng de.
 most of all 最重要的 zuì zhòngyào de
mostly ADV 大部分 dàbùfen, 通常 tōngcháng
motel N 汽车旅馆 qìchē lǚguǎn [M. WD 家 jiā]
moth N 飞蛾 fēié [M. WD 只 zhī]
mothball I N 樟脑丸 zhāngnǎowán [M. WD 粒 lì] II V **1** 长期关闭 [+工厂] chángqī guānbì [+gōngchǎng] **2** 把 [+计划] 束之高阁 bǎ [+jìhuà] shù zhī gāogé
moth-eaten ADJ 虫咬（坏）的 chóng yǎo (huài) de
mother I N **1** 母亲 mǔqin, 妈妈 māma
 Mother Earth 大地母亲 dàdì mǔqin
 Mother Nature 大自然 dàzìrán
 teenage mother 少女母亲 shàonǚ mǔqin
 2 起源 qǐyuán, 根源 gēnyuán
 Necessity is mother of invention. 需要是发明之母。Xūyào shì fāmíng zhī mǔ.
 3 范例 fànlì, 最好/最坏的事例 zuì hǎo/zuì huài de shìlì
 the mother of battles 最激烈的战斗 zuì jīliè de zhàndòu
 II V 像母亲一样照管 [+他人] xiàng mǔqin yíyàng zhàoguǎn [+tārén]
motherboard N （计算机）主板 (jìsuànjī) zhǔbǎn
motherfucker N 混蛋 húndàn, 不要脸的东西 búyàoliǎn de dōngxi

motherhood N 母性 mǔxìng

mother-in-law N 岳母 yuèmǔ (one's wife's mother), 婆婆 pópo (one's husband's mother)

motherly ADJ 向母亲一样的 xiàng mǔqin yíyàng de, 慈母般的 címǔ bān de

mother-of-pearl N 珍珠母 zhēnzhūmǔ [M. WD 颗 kē]

Mother's Day N 母亲节 Mǔqinjié

motif N **1** 主题 zhǔtí **2** 图案 tú'àn

motion I N **1** 运动 yùndòng, 移动 yídòng
motion picture 电影 diànyǐng
to go through the motion 装装样子 zhuāng zhuāng yàngzi
2 动议 dòngyì, 提议 tíyì ■ *His motion was debated and passed at the board meeting.* 他的动议在董事会上经过辩论通过。Tā de dòngyì zài dǒngshìhuìshang jīngguò biànlùn tōngguò. II v 做手势 zuò shǒushì, 示意 shìyì

motionless ADJ 不动的 búdòng de, 静止的 jìngzhǐ de

motivate V 激励 jīlì, 激发 jīfā

motivated ADJ 有动机的 yǒu dòngjī de

motivation N 动机 dòngjī, 原因 yuányīn

motive N 动机 dòngjī, 原因 yuányīn

motley ADJ 形形色色的 xíngxíng sèsè de

motor I N 发动机 fādòngjī, 马达 mǎdá II ADJ 机动车辆的 jīdòng chēliàng de
motor home 旅宿汽车 lǚsù qìchē, 房车 fáng chē
motor vehicle 机动车辆 jīdòng chēliàng

motorbike N 摩托车 mótuōchē [M. WD 辆 liàng]

motorcade N 车队 chēduì

motorcycle N （大型）摩托车 (dàxíng) mótuōchē [M. WD 辆 liàng]

motorist N 开汽车的人 kāi qìchē de rén, 驾车人 jiàchē rén

motorized ADJ 装发动机的 zhuāng fādòngjī de, 机动的 jīdòng de

mottled ADJ 杂色的 zásè de, 斑驳的 bānbó de

motto N 座右铭 zuòyòumíng, 格言 géyán

mound N **1** 土堆 tǔduī, 土丘 tǔqiū **2** 堆 duī

mount[1] v **1** 骑上 qíshang, 跨上 kuàshang
Royal Canadian Mounted Police 加拿大皇家骑警 Jiānádà Huángjiā Qíjǐng
2 增长 zēngzhǎng, 上升 shàngshēng **3** 裱贴 [+图画] biǎotiē [+túhuà]

mount[2] N 山 shān, 峰 fēng

mountain N **1** 山 shān, 山岳 shānyuè
to make a mountain out of a molehill 小题大做 xiǎo tí dà zuò
mountain bike 山地车 shāndìchē
2 (mountains of) 大量的 dàliàng de, 一大堆的 yídàduī de

mountaineering N 登山（运动）dēngshān (yùndòng)

mountainous ADJ 多山的 duōshān de

mountainside N 山坡 shānpō

mountaintop N 山顶 shāndǐng

Mountie, Mounty N 加拿大皇家骑警 Jiānádà Huángjiā Qíjǐng

mounting ADJ 日益增长的 rìyì zēngzhǎng de

mourn V 哀悼 āidào

mourner N 参加葬礼者 cānjiā zànglǐ zhě

mournful ADJ 悲痛的 bēitòng de, 哀伤的 āishāng de

mourning N **1** 哀悼 āidào, 悲痛 bēitòng **2** 丧服 sāngfú [M. WD 件 jiàn]

mouse (PL **mice**) N **1** （老）鼠 (lǎo) shǔ **2** (also PL **mouses**)（计算机）鼠标 (jìsuànjī) shǔbiāo
Mickey Mouse 米老鼠 Mǐlǎoshǔ

mousse N 奶油冻 nǎiyóudòng

mousy ADJ **1** 安静害羞的 [+女孩] ānjìng hàixiū de [+nǚhái] **2** 灰褐色的 huīhèsè de

mouth I N **1** 嘴 zuǐ, 嘴巴 zuǐba **2** 口状物 kǒu zhuàng wù
mouth of a river 河口 hékǒu, 入海口 rùhǎikǒu
II v **1** 不出声地说 bù chūshēng de shuō **2** 言不由衷地说 [+动听的好话] yán bù yóuzhōng de shuō [+dòngtīng de hǎohuà]

mouthful N **1** 一口（食物／饮料）yìkǒu (shíwù/yǐnliào) **2** 满口 mǎnkǒu **3** 长而拗口的词 cháng ér àokǒu de cí

mouthpiece N **1** 代言人 dàiyánrén, 喉舌 hóushé **2** （电话）送话口 (diànhuà) sònghuàkǒu **3** （乐器）吹口 (yuèqì) chuīkǒu

mouthwash N 漱口药水 shùkǒu yàoshuǐ

mouth-watering ADJ 令人馋言欲滴的 lìng rén chányán yù dī de, 诱人的 yòurén de

movable ADJ 活动的 huódòng de

move I v **1** 动 dòng, 移动 yídòng **2** 迁移 qiānyí, 搬家 bānjiā ■ *The Smiths have moved to Oklahoma.* 史密斯一家搬到俄克拉何马州去了。Shǐmìsī yì jiā bāndào Ékèlāhémǎ zhōu qù le. **3** 感动 gǎndòng **4** （会议上）提出动议 (huìyìshang) tíchū dòngyì, 提议 tíyì II N **1** 动 dòng, 移动 yídòng ■ *One false move, and you're a dead man!* 你敢乱动，就要你命！Nǐ gǎn luàndòng, jiù yào nǐ mìng! **2** 迁移 qiānyí, 搬家 bānjiā **3** 行动 xíngdòng

movement N **1** 动 dòng, 动静 dòngjìng **2** 运动 yùndòng

mover N **1** 搬运工人 bānyùn gōngrén **2** 有势力的人 yǒu shìlì de rén
a mover and shaker 权势人物 quánshì rénwù
a prime mover 倡导者 chàngdǎozhě

movie N 电影 diànyǐng
movie star 电影明星 diànyǐng míngxīng
movie theater See **(the) movies**

(the) movies N 电影院 diànyǐngyuàn [M. WD 座 zuò/家 jiā]

moving ADJ **1** 感动人的 gǎndòng rén de, 感人至深的 gǎnrén zhì shēn de **2** 移动的 yídòng de moving van 搬家卡车 bānjiā kǎchē

mow (PT mowed; PP mown, mowed) V 割草 gē cǎo

mower N 割草机 gēcǎojī [M. WD 台 tái]

Mr. (= mister PL Messrs) ABBREV 先生 xiānsheng

Mrs. (= missis/missus) ABBREV 太太 tàitai

Ms. N 女士 nǚshì

MTV (= Music Television) ABBREV 音乐电视公司 yīnyuè diànshì gōngsī

much I ADJ 很多 hěn duō ■ Did you have much difficulty finding your way here? 你找到这里困难吗? Nǐ zhǎodào zhèlǐ kùnnan ma? II PRON 很多 hěn duō III ADV 很 hěn, 非常 fēicháng how much ① 多么地 duōme de ② 多少钱 duōshao qián, 多少 duōshao too much 太多 tài duō ■ Sometimes you talk too much. 你有时候话太多。Nǐ yǒushíhou huà tài duō.

muck N 污物 wūwù, 污秽 wūhuì

muckracking N 搜集/发表（名人的）丑闻 sōují/fābiǎo (míngrén de) chǒuwén

mucous ADJ 粘液的 niányède

mucus N 粘液 niányè

mud N（烂）泥 (làn) ní

muddle I V (to muddle along) 混日子 hùnrìzi, 得过且过 dé guò qiě guò II N 混乱 hùnluàn

muddy I ADJ 1 沾泥的 zhānní de 2 泥泞的 nínìng de ■ We really need a SUV for such a muddy road. 开这样泥泞的路，我们确实需要越野车。Kāi zhèyàng nínìng de lù, wǒmen quèshí xūyào yuèyěchē. II V 使…沾上污泥 shǐ…zhānshang wūní

mudslide N 泥石流 níshíliú

muff V 把…弄错 bǎ…nòngcuò

muffin N 小面包圈 xiǎo miànbāoquān, 小甜饼 xiǎo tiánbǐng

muffle V 1 使 [+声音] 减弱 shǐ [+shēngyīn] jiǎnruò 2 把…包起来 bǎ…bāo qǐlái, 裹住 guǒzhù

muffled ADJ 听不清的（声音）tīngbuqīng de (shēngyīn)

muffler N 1 消音器 xiāoyīnqì 2 厚围巾 hòu wéijīn

mug¹ N 大杯子 dà bēizi, 茶缸 chágāng

mug² V（行凶）抢劫 (xíngxiōng) qiǎngjié

mugger N（行凶）抢劫犯 (xíngxiōng) qiǎngjiéfàn

muggy ADJ 闷热的 mēnrè de, 湿热的 shīrè de

mugshot N（罪犯的）面部照片 (zuìfàn de) miànbù zhàopiàn

mulatto N（黑人与白人的）混血儿 (hēirén yǔ báirén de) hùnxuè'ér

mulch I N 腐叶 fǔ yè II V 用腐叶覆盖 yòng fǔ yè fùgài

mule N 1 骡子 luózi [M. WD 头 tóu] as stubborn as a mule 顽固的人 wángù de rén, 固执的人 gùzhí de rén 2 被雇用来夹带毒品的人 bèi gùyòng lái jiādài

dúpǐn de rén, 毒品走私犯 dúpǐn zǒusī fàn

mull V 1 在 [+葡萄酒] 内放糖和香料后加热 zài [+pútaojiǔ] nèi fàng táng hé xiāngliào hòu jiārè 2 (to mull over) 反复思考 [+问题] fǎnfù sīkǎo [+wèntí]

mullah N 毛拉 máolā [M. WD 位 wèi]

multicolored ADJ 有不同色彩的 yǒu bùtóng sècǎi de

multicultural ADJ 多元文化的 duōyuán wénhuà de

multiculturalism N 多元文化主义 duōyuán wénhuà zhǔyì

multilateral ADJ 多方的 duōfāng de, 多边的 duōbiān de, 多国的 duōguó de multilateral negotiation 多边谈判 duōbiān tánpàn

multimedia N, ADJ 多媒体（的）duōméitǐ (de)

multinational I ADJ 跨国的 kuàguó de, 多国的 duōguó de multinational manufacturer 跨国制造商 kuàguó zhìzàoshāng II N 跨国公司 kuàguó gōngsī

multiple¹ ADJ 多个的 duōge de, 多种的 duōzhǒng de multiple choice 选择题 xuǎnzétí

multiple² N 倍数 bèishù

multiplex N 多放映厅电影院 duō fàngyìngtīng diànyǐngyuàn [M. WD 座 zuò]

multiplication N 乘法（运算）chéngfǎ (yùnsuàn)

multiplicity N 多样（性）duōyàng (xìng)

multiply V 1 乘 chéng 2 增多 zēngduō

multipurpose ADJ 多用途的 duōyòngtú de

multiracial ADJ 多种族的 duōzhǒngzú de

multitude N 大量 dàliàng, 大批 dàpī the multitude 大众 dàzhòng, 民众 mínzhòng

mum I N (mum's the word) 别讲给人家听 bié jiǎng gěi rénjiā tīng II ADJ 沉默的 chénmò de to keep mum 守口如瓶 shǒu kǒu rú píng

mumble V 含糊地说 hánhu de shuō

mumbo-jumbo N 晦涩难懂的东西 huìsè nándǒng de dōngxi

mummy N 木乃伊 mùnǎiyī [M. WD 具 jù]

mumps N 腮腺炎 sāixiànyán

munch V（用力）嚼 (yònglì) jiáo

munchies N 零食 língshí, 小吃 xiǎochī to have the munchies 感到饥饿 gǎndào jī'è

mundane ADJ 平淡乏味的 píngdàn fáwèi de, 平凡无奇的 píngfán wú qí de

municipal ADJ 市（政府）的 shì (zhèngfǔ) de

municipality N（自治）市 (zìzhì) shì, 市政府 shìzhèngfǔ

munitions N 军火 jūnhuǒ, 军需品 jūnxūpǐn

mural N 壁画 bìhuà [M. WD 幅 fú]

murder I N 谋杀 móushā, 谋杀案 móushā'àn II V 谋杀 móushā

murderous ADJ 可能杀人的 kěnéng shārén de, 凶残的 xiōngcán de

murky ADJ **1** 见不到的 [+水] jiànbúdào dì de [+shuǐ] **2** 复杂难懂的 [+问题] fùzá nándǒng de [+wèntí]

murmur I v **1** 轻柔低语 qīngróu dīyǔ II N **1** 低语声 dīyǔ shēng **2** (心脏) 杂音 (xīnzàng) záyīn **3** 悄悄抱怨 qiāoqiāo bàoyuàn

a murmur of opposition 轻轻的反对声 qīngqīng de fǎnduìshēng

without a murmur 毫无怨言 háowú yuànyán

muscle N 肌肉 jīròu

muscular ADJ 肌肉发达的 jīròu fādá de

muse v 默默思考 mòmò sīkǎo

museum N 博物馆 bówùguǎn ■ This museum is famous for its collection of Chinese ceramics. 这家博物馆因收藏中国瓷器而著名。Zhè jiā bówùguǎn yīn shōucáng Zhōngguó cíqì ér zhùmíng.

mush N 烂糊状的东西 lànhu zhuàng de dōngxi

mushroom I N 蘑菇 mógu II v 快速成长 kuàisù chéngzhǎng

mushy ADJ **1** 软乎乎的 [+香蕉] ruǎn hū hū de [+xiāngjiāo] **2** 过于多情的 guòyú duōqíng de

music N 音乐 yīnyuè, 乐曲 yuèqǔ

to face the music 受责备 shòu zébèi

musical I ADJ **1** 音乐的 yīnyuè de ■ Where can I rent musical instruments? 我在哪里可以租到乐器？Wǒ zài nǎlǐ kěyǐ zūdao yuèqì? **2** 有音乐天赋的 yǒu yīnyuè tiānfù de II N 音乐喜剧 yīnyuè xǐjù ■ I enjoy watching musicals, whether it's a play or movie. 我喜欢观看音乐喜剧，不管是戏，还是电影。Wǒ xǐhuan guānkàn yīnyuè xǐjù, bùguǎn shì xì, háishí diànyǐng.

musician N 音乐家 yīnyuèjiā [M. WD 位 wèi]

musing N 沉思 chénsī, 思索 sīsuǒ

musk N 麝香 shèxiāng

Muslim N, ADJ 穆斯林 (的) Mùsīlín (de), 伊斯兰教信徒 (的) Yīsīlán jiào xìntú (de)

muss v 弄乱 nòngluàn

mussel N 贻贝 yíbèi, 壳菜 qiàocài, 淡菜 dàncài

must I [NEG must not ABBREV **mustn't**] MODAL v **1** 必须 bìxū **2** 一定 yídìng, 想必 xiǎngbì ■ You've been driving for three hours; you must be tired. 你开了三小时车，一定累了。Nǐ kāile sān xiǎoshí chē, yídìng lèi le. II N 必不可少的东西 bì bùkě shǎo de dōngxi, 必须做的事 bìxū zuò de shì

mustache, moustache N 小胡子 xiǎo húzi

mustang N 小野马 xiǎo yěmǎ [M. WD 匹 pǐ]

mustard N 芥末 (酱) jièmo (jiàng)

muster v 召集 zhàojí, 集合 jíhé

to muster up courage 鼓足勇气 gǔzú yǒngqì

musty ADJ 发霉的 fāméi de, 发出霉味的 fāchū méi wèi de

mutable ADJ 可变的 kěbiàn de

mutate v (动植物) 变异 (dòngzhíwù) biànyì

mutation N (动植物) 变异 (dòngzhíwù) biànyì

mute I ADJ **1** 不会说话的 bú huì shuōhuà de, 哑的 yǎ de **2** 不说话的 bù shuō huà de, 默不作声的 mòbú zuòshēng de II N 哑巴 yǎba III v 使 [+声音] 减弱 shǐ [+shēngyīn] jiǎnruo, 使 [+声音] 消失 shǐ [+shēngyīn] xiāoshì

mutilate v 使…伤残 shǐ...shāngcán, 肢解 zhījiě

mutilation N 使人伤残的 shǐrén shāngcán de, 肢解 zhījiě

mutinous ADJ 反叛的 fǎnpàn de, 拼命的 pīnmìng de

mutiny N 反叛 fǎnpàn, 兵变 bīngbiàn [M. WD 次 cì/场 cháng]

mutt N 杂种狗 zázhǒng gǒu

mutter I v 嘀咕 dígu, 咕哝 gūnong II N 嘀咕声 dígushēng

mutton N 羊肉 yángròu

mutual ADJ 相互的 xiānghù de, 彼此的 bǐcǐ de, 共同的 gòngtóng de

mutual fund 单位投资 dānwèi tóuzī, 共同基金 gòngtóng jījīn

muzzle I N **1** (动物的) 口鼻部 (dòngwù de) kǒubíbù **2** (狗的) 口套 (gǒu de) kǒutào **3** (枪) 口 (qiāng) kǒu, (炮) 口 (páo) kǒu II v **1** 不让…说话 búràng...shuōhuà **2** 给狗戴口套 gěi gǒu dài kǒutào

my ADJ 我的 wǒde

myopia N **1** 近视 jìnshi **2** 目光短浅 mùguāng duǎnqiǎn

myopic ADJ **1** 近视的 jìnshi de **2** 目光短浅的 mùguāng duǎnqiǎn de

myriad I N (a myriad of) 无数的 wúshù de II ADJ 无数的 wúshù de

myself PRON 我自己 wǒ zìjǐ ■ I've got only myself to blame. 我只能怪自己。Wǒ zhǐ néng guài zìjǐ.

mysterious ADJ 神秘的 shénmì de, 不可思议的 bùkě sīyì de ■ Mysterious events keep occurring in the ancient monastery. 在这座古老的修道院神秘的事情一再发生。Zài zhè zuò gǔlǎo de xiūdàoyuàn shénmì de shìqíng yízài fāshēng.

mystery N 神秘的事物 shénmì de shìwù, 无法解释的事 wúfǎ jiěshì de shì

mystic, mystical ADJ 神秘 (主义) 的 shénmì (zhǔyì) de

mystic N 神秘主义者 shénmì zhǔyì zhě

mysticism N 神秘主义 shénmì zhǔyì

mystique N 神秘 (性) shénmì (xìng)

myth N **1** 神话 (故事) shénhuà (gùshi) **2** 无根据的说法 wú gēnjù de shuōfa

mythical ADJ 神话 (故事) 的 shénhuà (gùshi) de

mythological ADJ 神话 (学) 的 shénhuà (xué) de

mythology N 神话 (学) shénhuà (xué)

N

nab v 当场抓获 dāngchǎng zhuāhuò

nag I v 1 不停地指责／抱怨 bùtíngde zhǐzé/bàoyuàn, 唠叨 láodao 2 困扰 kùnrǎo II N 1 爱唠叨的人 ài láodao de rén 2 (老) 马 (lǎo) mǎ

nagging ADJ 不断困扰人的 búduàn kùnrǎo rén de, 烦人的 fánrén de

nail I N 1 钉 dīng, 钉子 dīngzi 2 指甲 zhǐjia, 趾甲 zhǐjiǎ

　nail file 指甲锉 zhǐjiacuò

　nail polish 指甲油 zhǐjiayóu

　II v 1 用钉子钉住 yòng dīngzi dìngzhù 2 抓住 zhuā zhù, 逮住 dài zhù

　to nail sb/sth down 最终确定 zuìzhōng quèdìng, 终于获得 zhōngyú huòdé

nailbrush N 指甲刷 zhǐjiashuā [M. WD 把 bǎ]

naive ADJ 天真的 tiānzhēn de, 幼稚的 yòuzhì de

naked ADJ 裸体的 luǒtǐ de

　the naked eye 肉眼 ròuyǎn

　naked truth 明显的事实 míngxiǎn de shìshí

name I N 1 名字 míngzi, 姓名 xìngmíng

　name tag 姓名牌 xìngmíngpái

　2 名称 míngchēng 3 名声 míngshēng, 声誉 shēngyù ■ Our school enjoys a very good name. 我们学校享有很好的声誉。Wǒmen xuéxiào xiǎngyǒu hěn hǎo de shēngyù.

　in the name of 以…的名义 yǐ…de míngyì

　the name of the game 最重要的东西 zuì zhòngyào de dōngxi

　II v 1 取名 qǔmíng, 命名 mìngmíng ■ They named their new-born baby after their grandfather. 他们以他们祖父的名字命名新生儿。Tāmen yǐ tāmen zǔfù de míngzi mìngmíng xīnshēng'ér. 2 说出名字 shuōchū míngzi

　to name your price 出个价 chū gè jià, 你说要多少钱 nǐ shuō yào duōshaoqián

name-calling N 骂人 màrén, 辱骂 rǔmà

name-drop v 提及名人来抬高自己 tíjí míngrén lái táigāo zìjǐ

nameless ADJ 1 不便提及的 búbiàn tíjí de 2 无名的 wúmíng de, 未名的 wèi míng de 3 不知其名的 bùzhī qí míng de

namely ADV 也就是说 yě jiù shì shuō, 即 jí

namesake N 同名的人 tóngmíng de rén

nanny N 保姆 bǎomǔ

nano technology N 纳米技术 nàmǐjìshù

nap I N (白天) 小睡 (báitiān) xiǎoshuì II v 在 (白天) 小睡 zài (báitiān) xiǎoshuì

napalm N 凝固汽油 nínggù qìyóu

nape N 颈背 jǐngbèi, 后颈 hòujǐng

napkin N 1 餐巾 cānjīn [M. WD 块 kuài] 2 餐巾纸 cānjīnzhǐ [M. WD 张 zhāng]

narc I N 缉毒警察 jīdú jǐngchá II v (向警方) 告密 (xiàng jǐngfāng) gàomì

narcissism N 自恋 zì liàn, 自我欣赏 zìwǒ xīnshǎng

narcissist N 自恋者 zìliànzhě, 极度我自欣赏的人 jídù zìwǒ xīnshǎng de rén

narcissistic ADJ 自恋的 zì liàn de

narcissus N 水仙花 shuǐxiānhuā [M. WD 朵 duǒ/棵 kē]

narcotic I N 麻醉剂 mázuìjì II ADJ 1 麻醉剂的 mázuìjì de 2 毒品的 dúpǐn de

　narcotic addiction 毒瘾 dúyǐn

narrate v 叙述 xùshù, 讲述 jiǎngshù

narration N 1 叙述 xùshù 2 解说 jiěshuō

narrative N 故事 gùshi, 叙事 xùshì

narrator N 叙述者 xùshùzhě, 解说人 jiěshuōrén

narrow I ADJ 1 窄 zhǎi, 狭窄 xiázhǎi 2 心胸狭小的 xīnxiōng xiáxiǎo de, 狭隘的 xiá'ài de ■ She has a narrow mind and lacks sympathy for people of other social classes. 她心胸狭小，对其他社会阶层的人缺乏同情。Tā xīnxiōng xiáxiǎo, duì qítā shèhuì jiēcéng de rén quēfá tóngqíng. 3 微弱的 wēiruò de, 有限的 yǒuxiàn de

　a narrow majority 微弱多数 wēiruò duōshù

　II v (使…) 变窄 (shǐ…) biàn zhǎi

　to narrow down 缩小范围 suōxiǎo fànwéi, 缩小差距 suōxiǎo chājù

narrow-minded ADJ (思想) 不开放的 (sīxiǎng) bù kāifàng de, 保守的 bǎoshǒu de

nasal ADJ 1 鼻 (子) 的 bí (zi) de 2 鼻音的 bíyīn de

nasty ADJ 1 让人厌恶的 ràng rén yànwù de 2 恶劣的 èliè de ■ What a nasty thing to say! 这话说得多么恶劣！Zhè huà shuōde duōme èliè!

nation N 1 国家 guójiā 2 民族 mínzú

　the Chinese nation 中华民族 Zhōnghuá Mínzú

national I ADJ 1 国家的 guójiā de, 民族的 mínzú de ■ What is the impact of globalization on national boundaries? 全球化对国家界限有什么影响？Quánqiúhuà duì guójiā jièxiàn yǒu shénme yǐngxiǎng? 2 国有的 guóyǒu de, 国立的 guólì de

　national anthem 国歌 guógē

　national debt 国债 guózhài

　the National Guard (美国) 国民警卫队 (Měiguó) guómín jǐngwèi duì

　national monument 国家保护单位 guójiā bǎohù dānwèi

　national park 国家公园 guójiā gōngyuán

　National University of Singapore 新加坡国立大学 Xīnjiāpō Guólì Dàxué

　II N 国民 guómín, 公民 gōngmín

　Chinese national 一名中国公民 yì míng Zhōngguó gōngmín

nationalism N 民族主义 mínzú zhǔyì

nationalist I ADJ 民族主义的 mínzú zhǔyì de II N 民族主义者 mínzú zhǔyìzhě

nationalistic ADJ (狭隘) 民族主义的 (xiá'ài)

mínzú zhǔyì de, 民族主义情绪的 mínzú zhǔyì qíngxù de

nationality N 国籍 guójí

American nationality 美国国籍 Měiguó guójí

dual nationality 双重国籍 shuāngchóng guójí

nationalize V 将…国有化 jiāng…guóyǒuhuà

nationally ADV 全国 quánguó, 全民族 quánmín zú

nationwide ADJ 全国范围（的）quánguó fànwéi (de), 全国性的 quánguó xìng de

native I ADJ 1 出生地的 chūshēngdì de ■ *His native language is Spanish.* 他的母语是西班牙文。Tā de mǔyǔ shì Xībānyá wén. 2 当地的 dāngdì de, 土生的 tǔshēng de II N 1 本国人 běnguó rén ■ *Our Chinese teacher is a native of Northern China.* 我们的中文老师是中国北方人。Wǒmen de Zhōngwén lǎoshī shì Zhōngguó Běifāng rén.

a Native American 美国印第安人 Měiguó Yìndì'ān rén

2 当地土生的动／植物 dāngdì tǔshēng de dòng/zhíwù

Nativity, nativity N 耶稣降生 Yēsū jiàngshēng

a Nativity play 叙述耶稣降生的短剧 xùshù Yēsū jiàngshēng de duǎn jù

NATO (= North Atlantic Treaty Organization) ABBREV 北大西洋公约组织 Běidàxīyáng Gōngyuē zǔzhī

natural I ADJ 1 自然的 zìrán de, 天然的 tiānrán de

natural gas 天然气 tiānránqì

natural history 博物学 bówùxué

natural resources 自然资源 zìrán zīyuán

natural selection 自然淘汰 zìrántáotài, 天择 tiānzé

2 本能的 běnnéng de, 本性的 běnxìng de 3 天生的 tiānshēng de ■ *Louis Armstrong was a natural musician.* 路易斯·阿姆斯特朗是一位天生的音乐家。Lùyìsī·Āmǔsītèlǎng shì yí wèi tiānshēng de yīnyuèjiā. II N 天生具有某种才能的人 tiānshēng jùyǒu mǒuzhǒng cáinéng de rén, 天才 tiāncái

naturalist N 博物学家 bówùxuéjiā

naturalization N 归化 guīhuà

naturalize V 使…归化 shǐ…guīhuà, 使…入国籍 shǐ…rù guójí

naturally ADV 1 自然地 zìrán de 2 天生（地）tiānshēng (de) 3 大大方方地 dàdà fāngfāng de

nature N 1 大自然 dà zìrán 2 本性 běnxìng, 天性 tiānxìng ■ *It's children's nature to be curious.* 好奇是儿童的天性。Hàoqí shì értóng de tiānxìng.

nature reserve 自然保留地 zìrán bǎoliúdì

naught N 零 líng

to come to naught 毫无结果 háo wú jiéguǒ, 泡汤 pàotāng

naughty ADJ 调皮捣蛋的（小孩）tiáopí dǎodàn de (xiǎohái)

nausea N 呕吐感 ǒutùgǎn, 恶心 èxīn

nauseate V 使…恶心 shǐ…èxīn, 使…想吐 shǐ…xiǎng tù

nauseous ADJ 想呕吐的 xiǎng ǒutù de, 感到恶心的 gǎndào èxīn de

nauseating ADJ 让人呕吐的 ràng rén ǒutù de, 令人作呕的 lìngrén zuò'ǒu de

nautical ADJ 船舶的 chuánbó de, 航海的 hánghǎi de

nautical mile 海哩 hǎi li

naval N 海军的 hǎi jūn de

nave N （教堂的）中堂 (jiàotáng de) zhōngtáng

navel N 肚脐 dùqí

navigable ADJ 可通航的 kě tōngháng de

navigate V 1 航行 hángxíng, 导航 dǎoháng 2 找对方向 zhǎo duì fāngxiàng

navigation N 航行(学) hángxíng (xué), 航海术 hánghǎi shù, 航空(术) hángkōng (shù)

navigational ADJ 航行的 hángxíng de, 航海的 hánghǎi de, 海空的 hǎikōng de

navigator N 领航员 lǐnghángyuán

navy N 海军 hǎijūn

navy blue 海军蓝 hǎijūn lán

near I ADJ 1 近的 jìn de, 不远的 bùyuǎn de

in the near future 在不久的将来 zài bùjiǔ de jiānglái

2 近似 jìnsì, 相似 xiāngsì ■ *The English translation is quite near to its Chinese original.* 英文译本和中文原文很相近。Yīngwén yìběn hé Zhōngwén yuánwén hěn xiāngjìn. II ADV 近 jìn ■ *The kids got more and more excited as Christmas drew near.* 圣诞节越来越近，孩子们也越来越兴奋了。Shèngdànjié yuèláiyuè jìn, háizimen yě yuèláiyuè xīngfèn le. III PREP 离…近 lí…jìn ■ *I don't want to live near a nuclear power plant.* 我不想住得离核电站很近。Wǒ bù xiǎng zhùde lí hédiànzhàn hěn jìn. IV V 接近 jiējìn, 靠近 kàojìn

nearby ADV 附近的 fùjìn de

nearly ADV 很接近地 hěn jiējìn de, 几乎 jīhū ■ *We're nearly there.* 我们很接近那里了。(→我们快到了。) Wǒmen hěn jiējìn nàlǐ le. (→Wǒmen kuài dào le.)

nearsighted ADJ 近视的 jìnshì de

nearsightedness N 近视 jìnshì

neat ADJ 1 整齐的 zhěngqí de 2 爱整洁的 ài zhěngjié de 3 挺好的 tǐng hǎo de ■ *For $5,000 he bought a neat car.* 他花五千块钱买了一辆挺好的汽车。Tā huā wǔ qiān kuài qián mǎile yì liàng tǐng hǎo de qìchē. 4 （不加冰／水的）纯酒 (bù jiā bīng/shuǐ de) chúnjiǔ

necessarily ADV 必然（地）bìrán (de)

not necessarily 不一定 bù yídìng, 未必 wèibì ■ *More money does not necessarily make you happier.* 钱多不一定使你幸福。Qián duō bù yídìng shǐ nǐ xìngfú.

necessary ADJ **1** 必需的 bìxū de ■ *Co-operation from the public is necessary for the police.* 对警方来说，公众的合作是必需的。Duì jǐngfāng láishuō, gōngzhòng de hézuò shì bìxū de. **2** 有必要的 yǒu bìyào de

necessitate v 使…成为必需 shǐ…chéngwéi bìxū

necessity N 必要的东西 bìyào de dōngxi ■ *A computer with a language kit is a necessity for compiling this dictionary.* 对编写这部词典来说，一台带有语言工具的电脑是必要的。Duì biānxiě zhè bù cídiǎn láishuō, yìtái dàiyǒu yǔyán gōngjù de diànnǎo shì bìyào de.

neck I N **1** 颈 jǐng, 头颈 tóujǐng

neck and neck 不相上下 bù xiāng shàng xià **2** 瓶颈 píngjǐng II v 拥抱亲吻 yōngbào qīnwěn, 热吻 rèwěn

necklace N 项链 xiàngliàn [M. WD 条 tiáo/根 gēn]

neckline N 领口 lǐngkǒu

necktie N 领带 lǐngdài [M. WD 条 tiáo/根 gēn]

nectar N **1** 浓果汁 nóng guǒzhī **2** 花蜜 huāmì

nectarine N **1** 油桃 yóutáo **2** 油桃树 yóutáo shù [M. WD 棵 kē]

née ADJ (女子的)婚前姓 (nǚzǐ de) hūnqián xìng

need I v 需要 xūyào, 有必要 yǒu bìyào ■ *What do you need to take with you on a camping trip?* 去露营需要带些什么? Qù lùyíng xūyào dài xiē shénme? II N 需要 xūyào ■ *There's a need for further research on this subject.* 这个问题需要进一步研究。Zhè ge wèntí jí xūyào jìnyíbù yánjiū. A friend in need is a friend indeed. 患难中的朋友才是真正的朋友。(→患难见真交。) Kùnnan zhòng de péngyou cái shì zhēnzhèng de péngyou (→Huànnàn jiàn zhēn jiāo. *Adversity shows up a true friend.*)

needs 基本需要 jīběn xūyào

needle I N 针 zhēn, 指针 zhǐzhēn, 注射针 zhùshèzhēn II v 刺激 cìjī, 激怒 jīnù

needless ADJ 不必要的 búbìyào de

needless to say 不用说 búyòng shuō, 当然 dāngrán

needlework N **1** 缝纫 féngrèn, 刺绣 cìxiù **2** 针线活 zhēnxianhuó

needy ADJ 贫困的 pínkùn de, 缺食少衣的 quē shí shǎo yī de

negate v **1** 否定 fǒudìng, 否认 fǒurèn **2** 取消 [+决定] qǔxiāo [+juédìng]

negation N 否定 fǒudìng, 取消 qǔxiāo

negative ADJ **1** 消极的 xiāojí de ■ *Rising oil prices will have a negative impact on the economy.* 油价上升对经济有消极影响。Yóujià shàngshēng duì jīngjì yǒu xiāojí yǐngxiǎng. **2** 否定的 fǒudìng de **3** (化验)阴性的 (huàyàn) yīnxìng de ■ *Much to his relief, the results of his HIV test were nega-*

tive. 他的HIV检查结果是阴性的，使他很宽慰。Tā de HIV jiǎnchá jiéguǒ shì yīnxìng de, shǐ tā hěn kuānwèi.

neglect I v 忽略 hūlüè, 不重视 bú zhòngshì ■ *For too long has he neglected his health; now he has to face the consequences.* 他长期以来一直忽略健康，现在不得不面对后果了. Tā chángqī yǐlái yìzhí hūlüè jiànkāng, xiànzài bùdébù miànduì hòuguǒ le. II N 忽视 hūshì, 忽略 hūlüè

neglect of duty 玩忽职守 wánhū zhíshǒu

neglectful ADJ 疏忽(大意)的 shūhu (dàyì) de

negligee, negligé N (女式)薄料内衣 (nǚ shì) báoliào nèiyī

negligence N 疏忽大意 shūhu dàyì, 玩忽职守 wánhū zhíshǒu

negligent ADJ 疏忽大意的 shūhu dàyì de, 玩忽职守的 wánhū zhíshǒu de

negligible ADJ 可忽视的 kě hūshì de, 微不足道的 wēi bùzú dào de

negotiable ADJ **1** 可谈判的 kě tánpàn de, 可协商的 kě xiéshāng de **2** 可通行的 kě tōngxíng de

negotiate v 谈判 tánpàn

negotiation N 谈判 tánpàn ■ *Differences should be resolved through negotiation, not confrontation.* 应该通过谈判，而不是对抗，来解决分歧。Yīnggāi tōngguò tánpàn, ér bùshì duìkàng, lái jiějué fēnqí.

Negro N 黑人 hēirén

neigh I v (马)嘶(叫) sī II N 马嘶声 mǎsīshēng

neighbor N **1** 邻居 línjū **2** 旁边的人 pángbiān de rén

neighborhood N 邻近地区 línjìn dìqū, 地段 dìduàn

in the neighborhood of 大约 dàyuē, 约为 yuē wéi

neighboring ADJ 相邻的 xiānglín de, 邻近的 línjìn de

neighborly ADJ (邻居之间)友好的 (línjū zhījiān) yǒuhǎo de, 睦邻的 mùlín de

neither I PRON (两/二者)都不 (liǎng /èrzhě) dōu bù ■ *Neither of us speaks Japanese.* 我们俩都不会说日语。Wǒmen liǎ dōu bú huì shuō Rìyǔ. II ADV 也不 yě bù ■ *"I don't like the new math teacher." "Neither do I."* "我不喜欢新来的数学老师。" "我也不喜欢。" "Wǒ bù xǐhuan xīnlái de shùxué lǎoshī. "Wǒ yě bù xǐhuan."

neither … nor 既不…也不 jì bù…yě bù, …和…都不 …hé…dōu bù ■ *Neither his father nor his mother knows about his drug problem.* 他的父亲、母亲都不知道他的吸毒问题。Tā de fùqin、mǔqin dōu bú zhīdào tā de xīdú wèntí.

neon (Ne) N 氖 nǎi

neon light 霓虹灯 níhóngdēng

nephew N 侄子 zhízi (brother's son), 外甥 wàisheng (sister's son)

nepotism N 裙带关系 qúndài guānxi

Neptune N 海王星 Hǎiwángxīng

nerd N 书呆子 shūdāizi

computer nerd 电脑迷 diànnǎo mí

nerve N 1 胆量 dǎnliàng, 勇气 yǒngqì 2 (厚)脸皮 (hòu) liǎnpí ■ *What nerve he has to ask for another loan!* 他竟然有脸皮再要借钱。Tā jìngrán yǒu liǎnpí zài yào jiè qián. 3 神经 shénjīng

nerve-racking ADJ 让人心烦(意乱)的 ràng rén xīnfán (yì luàn) de

nerves N 焦虑紧张 jiāolǜ jǐnzhāng

nervous ADJ 紧张 jǐnzhāng, 不自在 bú zìzài

a nervous breakdown 精神崩溃 jīngshén bēngkuì

the nervous system 神经系统 shénjīng xìtǒng

nest I N 1 鸟巢 niǎocháo, 鸟窝 niǎowō 2 (小动物的)窝 (xiǎo dòngwù de) wō, 穴 xué

nest egg 积蓄 jīxù

II v 筑巢 zhù cháo

nestle v 偎依 wēiyī

nestling N 幼鸟 yòuniǎo, 雏鸟 chúniǎo

net[1] N 网 wǎng

net[2] I v 1 净赚 [+一大笔钱] jìngzhuàn [+yí dàbǐ qián] 2 获得 huòdé, 获取 huòqǔ II ADJ 净的 jìng de ■ *Last year their business earned a net profit of $200,000.* 去年他们的生意赚了净利润二十万元。Qùnián tāmen de shēngyì zhuànle jìng lìrùn èrshí wàn yuán.

net income 净收入 jìngshōurù

net result 最终结果 zuìzhōng jiéguǒ

net weight 净重 jìngzhòng

netting N 网 wǎng, 网状物 wǎngsang wù

nettle I N 荨麻 qiánmá II v 惹恼 rěnǎo

network I N 1 系统 xìtǒng, 网 wǎng ■ *All the TV networks covered the trial in detail.* 所有的电视系统都详尽报道了这次审判。Suǒyǒu de diànshì xìtǒng dōu xiángjìn bàodàole zhè cì shěnpàn. 2 (计算机)网络 (jìsuànjī) wǎngluò II v 1 使 [+计算机] 联网 shǐ [+jìsuànjī] liánwǎng 2 联络的 liánluò de, 接触 jiēchù

networking N (同行间)联络 (tóngháng jiān) liánluò

neurology N 神经(病)学 shénjīng (bìng) xué

neurosis N 神经官能症 shénjīng guānnéngzhèng

neurotic I N 神经官能症(患者)shénjīng guānnéngzhèng (huànzhě) II ADJ 神经质的 shénjīngzhì de, 神经过敏的 shénjīng guòmǐn de

neuter I v 阉割 [+雄性动物] yāngē [+xióngxìng dòngwù] II ADJ 1 中性的 zhōngxìng de 2 无生殖器的 [+动物] wú shēngzhíqì de [+dòngwù]

neutral I ADJ 1 中立的 [+国家] zhōnglì de [+guójiā] 2 素淡的 [+颜色] sùdàn de [+yánsè] 3 中性的 [+词语] zhōngxìng de [+cíyǔ] II N 1 中立国 zhōnglìguó, 中立人士 zhōnglì rénshì 2 素淡的颜色 sùdàn de yánsè 3 (汽车)空档位置 (qìchē) kōngdàng wèizhì

neutrality N 中立(地位)zhōnglì (dìwèi)

neutralize v 1 使…[+国家] 中立 shǐ… [+guójiā] zhōnglì 2 使 [+毒药] 无效 shǐ [+dúyào] wúxiào

neutron N 中子 zhōngzǐ

never ADV 从不 cóng bù, 永远不 yǒngyuǎn bù ■ *Never, ever, lie to me!* 永远不要对我撒谎! Yǒngyuǎn bú yào duì wǒ sāhuǎng!

nevertheless ADV 尽管如此 jǐnguǎn rúcǐ, 然而 rán'ér

new ADJ 1 新 xīn, 新的 xīn de

New Age 新时代 xīnshídài

New World 新大陆(南北美洲)Xīndàlù (nánběi Měizhōu)

New Year 新年 xīnnián

New Year's Day 元旦 Yuándàn

New Year's Eve 除夕 chúxī

2 不熟悉的 bùshú xī de

newborn I N 新生儿 xīnshēng'ér II ADJ 新生的 xīnshēng de

newcomer N 新来的人 xīnlái de rén, 新手 xīnshǒu

newfangled ADJ 新花样的 xīn huāyàng de

newly ADV 新近(地)xīnjìn (de)

newlyweds N 新婚夫妇 xīnhūn fūfù

news N 1 消息 xiāoxi

No news is good news. 没有消息就是好消息。Méiyǒu xiāoxi jiù shì hǎo xiāoxi.

2 新闻 xīnwén 3 新闻节目 xīnwén jiémù ■ *The first thing he does in the morning is watch the news.* 他每天早上第一件事就是看新闻节目。Tā měitiān zǎoshang dìyī jiàn shì jiù shì kàn xīnwén jiémù.

news agency 新闻通讯社 xīnwéntōngxùn shè

news bulletin 新闻简讯 xīnwén jiǎnxùn

newscast N (电视)新闻报导 (diànshì) xīnwén bàodào

newscaster N (电视)新闻播报员 (diànshì) xīnwén bōbàoyuán

newsletter N 简讯 jiǎnxùn

newspaper N 报 bào, 报纸 bàozhǐ

newsprint N 新闻纸 xīnwénzhǐ, 白报纸 báibàozhǐ

newsstand N 报摊 bàotān, 卖报摊 mài bàotān

newsy ADJ 新闻很多的 [+来信] xīnwén hěn duō de [+láixìn]

New Testament N (圣经)新约全书 (Shèngjīng) Xīnyuē quán shū

next I ADJ 1 下 xià, 下一个 xià yí ge

next day 下一天 xià yì tiān, 第二天 dì'èr tiān

next door 隔壁 gébì

next week 下星期 xià xīngqī, 下周 xià zhōu

next month 下个月 xià ge yuè

next time 下次 xià cì, 下一次 xià yí cì ■ *Please come earlier next time.* 下次请来得早一点。Xiàcì qǐng láide zǎo yì diǎn.

next year 明年 míngnián

2 隔壁的 [+房间] gébì de [+fángjiān] **II** ADV 接着 jiēzhe, 接下来 jiēxiàlái **III** PRON 下一个 xià yí ge
next of kin 最近的亲属 zuìjìn de qīnshǔ

NFL (= National Football League) ABBREV（美国）全国橄榄球联盟 (Měiguó) Quánguó gǎnlǎnqiú liánméng

NHL (= National Hockey League) ABBREV（美国）全国曲棍球联盟 (Měiguó) Quánguó qūgùnqiú liánméng

nib N 笔尖 bǐjiān

nibble I v 一点一点地吃 yìdiǎn yìdiǎn de chī, 啃 kěn **II** N 一小口 yì xiǎokǒu

nice ADJ **1** 好 hǎo, 令人愉快的 lìng rén yúkuài de ■ We had a nice time at the party. 我们在聚会上很愉快。Wǒmen zài jùhuìshang hěn yúkuài. **2** 友好 yǒuhǎo, 和善 héshàn ■ Be nice to your grandma! 对你奶奶要好一点！Duì nǐ nǎinai yào hǎo yì diǎn! **3** 正派的 zhèngpài de

nice-looking ADJ 好看的 hǎokàn de, 漂亮的 piàoliang de

nicely ADV 很好地 hěnhǎo de, 让人满意地 ràng rén mǎnyì de

nicety N **1** 细节 xìjié
legal niceties 法律细节 fǎlǜ xìjié
2 细微的区别 xìwēi de qūbié

niche N **1** 特定的市场 tèdìng de shìchǎng **2** 正好合适的工作 zhènghǎo héshì de gōngzuò **3** 壁龛 bìkān

nick[1] N (in the nick of time) 正在这当口 zhèngzài zhè dāngkǒu

nick[2] I N 小切口 xiǎo qièkǒu **II** v 留下小切口 liúxia xiǎo qièkǒu

nickel N（美国）五分钱硬币 (Měiguó) wǔfēnqián yìngbì

nickel-and-dime ADJ 小规模的 xiǎoguīmó de, 小打小闹 xiǎo dǎ xiǎo nào de

nickname N 绰号 chuòhào, 外号 wàihào

nicotine N 尼古丁 nígǔdīng

niece N 侄女 zhínǚ (brother's daughter), 外甥女 wàishengnǚ (sister's daughter)

night N 夜 yè, 夜晚 yèwǎn
night and day, day and night 日日夜夜 rìrì yèyè
night club 夜总会 yèzǒnghuì
night owl 喜欢熬夜的人 xǐhuan áoyè de rén, 夜猫子 yèmāozi
night school 夜校 yèxiào

nightgown N 睡袍 shuìpáo

nightfall N 天黑时分 tiānhēi shífèn, 傍晚 bàngwǎn

nightingale N 夜莺 yèyīng

nightlife N 夜生活 yèshēnghuó, 夜间娱乐 yèjiān yúlè

nightly ADJ, ADV 每晚（的）měi wǎn (de), 每夜（的）měi yè (de)

nightmare N **1** 恶梦 èmèng **2** 极其可怕的经历 jíqí kěpà de jīnglì

nightmarish ADJ 恶梦般的 èmèng bān de

nightstand, night table N 床头柜 chuángtóuguì

nighttime N 夜间 yèjiān

nil N 无 wú, 零 líng
virtually nil 几乎为零 jīhū wéi líng

nimble ADJ 敏捷的 mǐnjié de, 灵敏的 língmǐn de

nine NUM 九 jiǔ, 9 ■ She has a nine-to-five job. 她的工作是从九点到五点。Tā de gōngzuò shì cóng jiǔ diǎn dào wǔ diǎn.

nineteen NUM 十九 shíjiǔ, 19

nineteenth NUM 第十九 dì shíjiǔ

ninety NUM 九十 jiǔshí, 90

ninth NUM 第九 dìjiǔ

nip I v **1**（轻轻地）啃咬 (qīngqīng de) kěn yǎo **2** 掐断 [+花朵] qiāduàn [+huāduǒ]
to nip sth in the bud 消灭在萌芽状态 xiāomiè zài méngyá zhuàngtài
3 冻伤 dòngshāng **II** N（轻）咬 (qīng) yǎo, （轻）啃 (qīng) kěn
nip and tuck 两种可能性都有 liǎng zhǒng kěnéngxìng dōu yǒu, 胜负难分 shèngfù nánfēn

nipple N **1** 乳头 rǔtóu **2** 橡皮奶嘴 xiàngpí nǎizuǐ

nippy ADJ 冷飕飕的 lěngsōusōu de

nitpicking N 过分挑剔的 guòfèn tiāoti de, 鸡蛋里挑骨头 jīdàn lǐ tiāo gútou

nitrogen (N) N 氮 dàn

nitty-gritty N 实质性部份 shízhìxìng bùfen

nitwit N 笨人 bènrén

no I ADV 不 bù, 不是 bú shì, 没有 méiyǒu ■ "Are you an American?" "No, I'm not. I'm a Canadian." "你是美国人吗？" "不是，我是加拿大人。" "Nǐ shì Měiguó rén ma?" "Bú shì, wǒ shì Jiānádà rén."
no good 没有好处 méiyǒu hǎochu
no more/less than 不多于／少于 bùduō yú/ shǎoyú
II ADJ 没有 méiyǒu ■ No words can express my gratitude. 没有言词可以表达我的谢意。Méiyǒu yáncí kěyǐ biǎodá wǒ de xièyì.
in no time 马上 mǎshàng
III N 拒绝 jùjué, 不 bù

nobility N 贵族（阶级）guìzú (jiējí)

noble I ADJ **1** 高尚的 gāoshàng de **2** 贵族的 guìzú de **II** N 贵族 guìzú [M. WD 位 wèi]

nobleman, noblewoman N 贵族 guìzú [M. WD 位 wèi]

nobody I PRON 没有人 méiyǒu rén ■ There was nobody at home that afternoon. 那天下午家里没有人。Nà tiān xiàwǔ jiālǐ méiyǒu rén. **II** N 无足轻重的人 wúzú qīngzhòng de rén, 小人物 xiǎorénwù

no-brainer N 不用动脑筋的事 búyòng dòng nǎo jìng de shì, 十分简单的事 shífēn jiǎndān de shì

nocturnal ADJ 夜间（活动）的 yèjiān (huódòng) de

nod v **1** 点头 diǎntóu **2** (to nod off) 打瞌睡 dǎkēshuì

node N 1 (计算机系统的)终端计算机 (jìsuànjī xìtǒng de) zhōngduān jìsuànjī 2 交点 jiāodiǎn
lymph node 淋巴结 línbājié

no-fault ADJ 不考虑是谁造成过失的 bùkǎolǜ shì shéi zàochéng guòshī de
a no-fault car insurance 不计过失的汽车保险 bújì guòshī de qìchē bǎoxiǎn
a no-fault divorce 无过失离婚 wú guòshī líhūn

no-frills ADJ 无花俏的 wú huāqiào de, 最基本的 zuì jīběn de

noise N 噪音 zàoyīn ■ *The machines at the construction site made a terrible noise.* 建筑工地上的机器噪音很大。Jiànzhù gōngdìshang de jīqì zàoyīn hěn dà.

noiselessly ADV 无声无息地 wúshēng wúxī de, 静悄悄地 jìngqiāoqiāo de

noisy ADJ 吵闹的 chǎonào de, 嘈杂的 cáozá de

nomad N 1 游牧者 yóumùzhě 2 经常搬家／换工作的人 jīngcháng bānjiā/huàngōng zuò de rén, 经常到处旅行的人 jīngcháng dàochù lǚxíng de rén

nomadic ADJ 游牧(部落)的 yóumù (bùluò) de

no-man's land N 无人地带 wúréndìdài

nomenclature N 命名法 mìngmíngfǎ

nominal ADJ 1 名义上的 míngyìshàng de 2 名词(性)的 míngcí (xìng) de
a nominal phrase 名词(性)词组 míngcí (xìng) cízǔ
3 象征性的 xiàngzhēngxìng de, 极少的 jí shǎo de
a nominal fee 象征性收费 xiàngzhēngxìng shōufèi

nominate V 1 提名 tímíng 2 任命 rènmìng

nomination N 1 提名 tímíng 2 任命 rènmìng

nominee N 被提名者 bèi tímíng zhě

nonaggression N 互不侵犯的 wúbù qīn fàn de

nonalcoholic ADJ 不含酒精的 bù hán jiǔjīng de

nonchalant ADJ 毫不在意的 háobú zàiyì de, 若无其事的 ruòwú qí shì de

noncombatant N 非战斗人员 fēi zhàndòu rényuán

noncommittal ADJ 不做承诺的 bú zuò chéngnuò de, 不明确表态的 bù míngquè biǎotài de

non-dairy ADJ 不含奶的 bù hán nǎi de

nondescript ADJ 难以描绘的 nányí miáohuì de, 平淡无奇的 píngdàn wúqí de

none I PRON 一个也没有 yí ge yě méiyǒu ■ *The old couple has four children—none stays in their hometown.* 老夫妻有四个儿女——一个也没有留在家乡。Lǎo fūqī yǒu sì ge érnǚ—yí ge yě méiyǒu liú zài jiāxiāng.
none other than 正是 zhèng shì, 恰恰是 qiàqià shì
II ADV 一点也没有 yìdiǎn yě méiyǒu
none the better 一点也没有更好 yìdiǎn yě méiyǒu gèng hǎo

none too happy 一点也不高兴 yìdiǎn yě bù gāoxìng

nonentity N 无名之辈 wúmíng zhī bèi

nonetheless ADV 尽管如此 jǐnguǎn rúcǐ, 然而 rán'ér, 但是 dànshì

non-event N 无关紧要的 wúguān jǐnyào de

nonexistent ADJ 不存在的 bù cúnzài de

nonfat ADJ 不含脂肪的 bù hán zhīfáng de, 脱脂的 tuōzhī de

nonfiction N 非小说类书籍 fēi xiǎoshuō lèi shūjí

nonintervention N 不干涉 bù gānshè

non-negotiable ADJ 1 没有商量余地的 [+安排] méiyǒu shāngliang yúdì de [+ānpái] 2 不可转让的 [+支票] bùkě zhuǎnràng de [+zhīpiào]

no-no N 不准干的事 bùzhǔn gàn de shì, 不许可的事 bù xǔkě de shì

no-nonsense ADJ 务实的 wùshí de, 实用的 shíyòng de

nonpayment N 无力支付 wúlì zhīfù

nonplussed ADJ 惊奇得无以对答的 jīngqí de wúyǐ duìdá de, 不知所措的 bù zhī suǒ cuò de

nonprofit ADJ 非盈利(性)的 fēi yínglì (xìng) de

nonproliferation N 防止核／化学武器扩散 fángzhǐ hé/huàxué wǔqì kuòsàn

non-refundable ADJ 不可退款的 bùkě tuìkuǎn de

non-renewable ADJ 不可再生的 bùkě zàishēng de

non-resident N 非本国／本地居民 fēi běnguó/běndì jūmín

nonsense N 1 胡说 húshuō, 荒唐念头 huāngtang niàntou ■ *"I'm not going to the interview." "Nonsense! You've got to go."* "我不去面试了。" "胡说! 你非得去不可。" "Wǒ bú qù miànshì le." "Húshuō! Nǐ fēiděi qù bùkě." 2 胡闹 húnào, 胡作非为 húzuò fēiwéi

nonsensical ADJ 没有意义的 méiyǒu yìyì de, 荒谬的 huāngmiù de

non sequitur N 1 不符合前提的推论 bù fúhé qiántí de tuīlùn 2 前后不一致的叙述 qiánhòu bù yīzhì de xùshù

nonsmoker N 不吸烟的人 bù xīyān de rén

nonsmoking ADJ 禁烟的 jìnyān de

nonstandard ADJ 不标准的 bù biāozhǔn de

nonstick ADJ 不沾食物的 bù zhān shíwù de

nonstop ADJ, ADV 不停顿(的)bù tíngdùn (de), 直达的 zhídá de

nonverbal ADJ 不用言语表达的 bú yòng yányǔ biǎodá de

nonviolence N 非暴力行为 fēibàolì xíngwéi

nonviolent ADJ 非暴力的 fēibàolì de

noodle N 面 miàn
noodle soup 汤面 tāngmiàn
fried noodle 炒面 chǎomiàn

nook N (房间的)角落 (fángjiān de) jiǎoluò

noon N 正午 zhèngwǔ, 中午 zhōngwǔ

no one PRON 没有人 méiyǒu rén ■ *No one knew who she was.* 没有人知道她是谁。Méiyǒu rén zhīdào tā shì shéi.

noose N 绳套 shéngtào, 绞索 jiǎosuǒ

nope ADV 不 bù, 不是 bú shì

nor ADV 也不 yě bù ■ *She did not do well last year, nor do I think she will do any better this year.* 她去年干得不好, 我看今年也不会干得好一点。Tā qùnián gàn de bù hǎo, wǒkàn jīnnián yě bú huì gàn de hǎo yìdiǎn.

norm N 规范 guīfàn, 标准 biāozhǔn

normal I ADJ 正常的 zhèngcháng de II N 正常水平 zhèngcháng shuǐpíng

normality N 正常状态 zhèngcháng zhuàngtài

normalization N 正常化 zhèngchánghuà

normalize v 使…正常化 shǐ…zhèngchánghuà

normally ADV 正常 zhèngcháng, 正常地 zhèngcháng de

north I N 北 běi, 北面 běimiàn II ADJ 北面的 běimiàn de, 朝北的 cháo běi de
North America 北美 Běiměi, 北美洲 Běiměi zhōu
North American ① 北美洲的 Běiměi zhōu de ② 北美洲人 Běiměi zhōu rén
the North Pole 北极 Běijí
III ADV（朝）北（cháo）běi

northbound ADJ 往北的 wǎng běi de, 北行的 běi xíng de

northeast I N 1 东北（方向）dōngběi（fāngxiàng）2 东北（地区）dōngběi（dìqū）II ADJ 1 在东北（地区）的 zài dōngběi（dìqū）de 2 来自东北（地区）的 láizì dōngběi（dìqū de）III ADV 朝东北（方向）cháo dōngběi（fāngxiàng）

northerly ADJ 在北部的 zài běibù de, 朝北部的 cháo běibù de
the northerly 北面吹来的风 běimiàn chuī láide fēng, 北风 běifēng
in a northerly direction 朝北的方向 cháo běi de fāngxiàng, 往北 wǎng běi

northern ADJ 北方的 běifāng de ■ *She speaks Chinese with a northern accent.* 她的中文带有北方口音。Tā de Zhōngwén dàiyǒu běifāng kǒuyīn.
the northern hemisphere 北半球 Běi bànqiú

northerner, Northerner N 北方人 Běifāngrén

Northern Lights N 北极光 Běijíguāng

northernmost ADJ 最北面的 zuì běimiàn de

northward ADJ, ADV 往北（的）wǎng běi (de)

northwest I N 1 西北（方向）xīběi（fāngxiàng）2 西北（地区）xīběi（dìqū）II ADJ 1 在西北（地区）的 zài xīběi（dìqū）de 2 来自西北（地区）的 láizì xīběi（dìqū）de III ADV 朝西北（方向）cháo xīběi（fāngxiàng）

nose I N 鼻子 bízi
to have a runny nose 流鼻涕 liú bíti
nose job 鼻子整形（手术）bízi zhěngxíng（shǒushù）

II v (to nose around) 四处查看 sìchù chákàn, (to nose forward) [车辆+] 缓慢前行 [chēliàng+] huǎnmàn qiánxíng

nosebleed N 鼻出血 bíchūxuè

nosedive I N 1（飞机）俯冲（fēijī）fǔchōng 2（股票）猛跌（gǔpiào）měngdiē II v 1 [飞机+] 突然俯冲 [fēijī+] tūrán fǔchōng 2（股票）猛跌（gǔpiào）měngdiē

no-show N 预定而没来的人 yùdìng ér méi láide rén

nostalgia N 怀旧（情绪）huáijiù（qíngxù）

nostalgic ADJ 怀旧的 huáijiù de

nostril N 鼻孔 bíkǒng

nosy, nosey ADJ 爱打听别人隐私的 ài dǎting biéren yǐnsī de

not ADV 不 bù ■ *The use of cell phones is not allowed in the library.* 图书馆里不准使用手机。Túshūguǎn lǐ bù zhǔn shǐyòng shǒujī.
not at all 一点也不 yì diǎn yě bù, 根本不 gēnběn bù
not only … but also 不但…而且… bùdàn…érqiě…

notable I ADJ 值得注意的 zhíde zhùyì de, 显著的 xiǎnzhe de II N 著名人物 zhùmíng rénwù, 名人 míngrén

notarize v 对…进行公证 duì…jìnxíng gōngzhèng, 公证 gōngzhèng

notary public, notary N 公证人员 gōngzhèng rényuán

notation N 1（一套）符号（yítào）fúhào 2 标志法 biāozhìfǎ

notch I N 1（V字形）切口（V zìxíng）qiēkǒu, 凹口 āo kǒu 2 等级 děngjí II v 1 刻（V字形）切口 kè（V zìxíng）qiēkǒu 2 (to notch up) 赢得 [+胜利] yíngdé [+shènglì]

note I N 1 笔记 bǐjì
to make notes 做笔记 zuò bǐjì
to take notes 纪录 jìlù ■ *She took detailed notes of her father's medication.* 她对父亲用药的情况作详细的记录。Tā duì fùqin yòng yào de qíngkuàng zuò xiángxì de jìlù.
to make a mental note of 记在心里 jì zài xīnlǐ ■ *He made a mental note to send her a birthday card next week.* 他在心里记住, 下星期要给她寄一张生日贺卡。Tā zài xīnlǐ jìzhu, xià xīngqī yào gěi tā jì yì zhāng shēngrì hèkǎ.
2 便条 biàntiáo [M. WD 张 zhāng] 3 注解 zhùjiě [M. WD 条 tiáo] ■ *He studied this book very carefully, reading every note in it.* 他仔仔细细地学习了这本书, 把每一个注解都读过了。Tā zǐzǐ xìxì de xuéxíle zhè běn shū, bǎ měi yí ge zhùjiě dōu dúguo le. 4 纸币 zhǐbì [M. WD 张 zhāng], 钞票 chāopiào [M. WD 张 zhāng] 5 音调 yīndiào, 音符 yīnfú
a high/low note 高／低音 gāo/dīyīn

II v 1 注意 zhùyì 2 指出 zhǐchū

notebook N 笔记(本)bǐjì (běn) [M. WD 本 běn]

noted ADJ 知名的 zhīmíng de

notepaper N 便条纸 biàntiáo zhǐ [M. WD 张 zhāng], 信纸 xìnzhǐ [M. WD 张 zhāng]

noteworthy ADJ 值得注意的 zhíde zhùyì de

nothing PRON 没有什么 méiyǒu shénme, 没有什么东西 méiyǒu shénme dōngxi
nothing but 只不过 zhǐbuguò, 仅仅是 jǐnjǐn shì
nothing less than 完全是 wánquán shì
to have nothing to lose 不会有损失 bú huì yǒu sǔnshī

notice I N 1 布告 bùgào, 通知 tōngzhī ■ *Employees must give the management a month's notice before leaving the job.* 雇员必须在离职前一个月通知主管人员。Gùyuán bìxū zài lízhí qián yí ge yuè tōngzhī zhǔguǎn rényuán. **2** (to give notice) 提出离职／辞职 tíchū lízhí/cízhí II v 注意到 zhùyìdao
to take no notice of 不理会 bù lǐhuì ■ *Take no notice of what she said; she was just jealous.* 别理会她说的话；她只是嫉妒。Bié lǐhuì tā shuō de huà; tā zhǐ shì jídu.

noticeable ADJ 看得到的 kàndédào de, 显著的 xiǎnzhe de

notification N 通知 tōngzhī

notify v 通知 tōngzhī

notion N 概念 gàiniàn, 观念 guānniàn

notoriety N 臭名远扬 chòumíng yuǎn yáng, 坏名声 huàimíng shēng

notorious ADJ 臭名远扬的 chòumíng yuǎn yáng de, 有坏名声的 yǒu huài míngshēng de

notwithstanding PREP 尽管 jǐnguǎn

nougat N 牛轧糖 niúgáitáng [M. WD 块 kuài]

noun N 名词 míngcí

nourish v 1 给…营养 gěi...yíngyǎng, 滋养 zīyǎng **2** 怀有 [+感情] huáiyǒu [+gǎnqíng]

nourishing ADJ 有营养的 yǒu yíngyǎng de, 滋养的 zīyǎng de

nourishment N 营养 yíngyǎng

novel[1] N 小说 xiǎoshuō [M. WD 篇 piān/部 bù]

novel[2] ADJ 新的 xīn de, 新奇的 xīnqí de

novelist N 小说家 xiǎoshuōjiā, 小说作者 xiǎoshuō zuòzhě

novelty N 1 新奇 xīnqí 2 新鲜玩意儿 xīnxian wányìr

November N 十一月 shíyīyuè

novice N 新手 xīnshǒu, 初学者 chūxuézhě

now I ADV 1 现在 xiànzài 2 立刻 lìkè, 马上 mǎshàng
by now (到)现在 (dào) xiànzài ■ *Father should have arrived in Beijing by now.* 父亲现在应该到达北京了。Fùqin xiànzài yīnggāi dàodá Běijīng le.
for now 目前 mùqián, 暂时 zànshí

from now on 从现在起 cóng xiànzài qǐ ■ *From now on, please use my new e-mail address.* 请从现在起使用我的电子邮件地址。Qǐng cóng xiànzài qǐ shǐyòng wǒ xīn de diànzǐ yóujiàn dìzhǐ.
not now 现在不行 xiànzài bùxíng
right now 马上 mǎshàng, 就是现在 jiùshì xiànzài II CONJ (now that) 既然 jìrán

nowadays ADV 现今 xiànjīn, 如今 rújīn

nowhere ADV 没有(什么)地方 méiyǒu (shénme) dìfang, 无处 wúchù
to get nowhere 毫无进展 háowú jìnzhǎn ■ *He was getting nowhere with job hunting until he met an old classmate.* 他在遇到一位老同学之前，找工作毫无进展。Tā zài yùdao yí wèi lǎo tóngxué zhīqián, zhǎo gōngzuò háowú jìnzhǎn.

noxious ADJ 有毒的 yǒudú de, 有害的 yǒuhài de

nozzle N 喷嘴 pēnzuǐ

nuance N 细微差异 xìwēi chāyì

nuclear ADJ 原子核的 yuánzǐhé de, 核子的 hézǐ de
nuclear disarmament 核裁军 hécáijūn
nuclear energy 核能 héněng
nuclear family 核心家庭 héxīn jiātíng
nuclear power 核电 hédiàn
nuclear power plant 核电站 hédiànzhàn
nuclear reaction 核反应 héfǎnyìng
nuclear reactor 核反应堆 héfǎnyìngduī
nuclear weapon 核武器 hé wǔqì

nucleus N 1 核子 hézǐ 2 细胞核 xìbāohé 3 核心(人物)héxīn (rénwù)

nude I ADJ 裸体的 luǒtǐ de II N 裸体画 luǒtǐhuà, 人体雕塑 réntǐ diāosù

nudge v 1 用(肘)轻推 yòng (zhǒu) qīng tuī
to nudge one's way 往前挤 wǎngqián jǐ 2 劝说 quànshuō, 鼓励 gǔlì

nudist I N 裸体主义者 luǒtǐ zhǔyìzhě II ADJ 裸体的 luǒtǐde
nudist camp 裸体营 luǒtǐyíng, 天体营 tiāntǐyíng

nudity N 裸体 luǒtǐ

nugget N 1 小(天然)金块 xiǎo (tiānrán) jīnkuài 2 (食物)小块 (shíwù) xiǎo kuài 3 有重大价值的东西 yǒu zhòngdà jiàzhí de dōngxi
a nugget of information 有重大价值的信息 yǒu zhòngdà jiàzhí de xìnxī

nuisance N 讨厌鬼 tǎoyànguǐ, 讨厌的事 tǎoyàn de shì
to make a nuisance of oneself 做令人讨厌的事 zuò lìng rén tǎoyàn de shì

nuke I N 核武器 hé wǔqì II v 用核武器攻击 yòng hé wǔqì gōngjī

null ADJ 无效的 wúxiào de
null and void 无效的 wúxiào de
null result 零效果 líng xiàoguǒ

nullify v 宣布…(在法律上)无效 xuānbù...(zài fǎlǜshàng) wúxiào

numb I ADJ 麻木的 mámù de, 失去感觉的 shīqù

495

gǎnjué de **II** v 使…麻木 shǐ…mámù, 使…失去
感觉 shǐ…shīqù gǎnjué
number I n **1** 数字 shùzì ■ *Sudoku is a number
game.* "数独" 是一种数字游戏。"Shùdú" shì yì
zhǒng shùzì yóuxì. **2** 数目 shùmù, 号码 hàomǎ
number crunching 做数字工作 zuò shùzì
gōngzuò, 运算 yùnsuàn
3 数量 shùliàng
number one 第一 dìyī, 最好的 zuìhǎo de
II v **1** 给…编号 gěi…biānhào
to number the pages 编页码 biān yèmǎ
2 总共 zǒnggòng, 共计 gòngjì
The days are numbered. 不会很久了。Bú huì
hěn jiǔ le. 快完蛋了。Kuài wándàn le.
numbness n 麻木 mámù
numeral n 数词 shùcí
numerate adj 懂算术的 dǒng suànshù de, 会简
单计算的 huì jiǎndān jìsuàn de
numerical adj 数字上的 shùzì shàng de, 数量上
的 shùliàng shàng de
numerous adj 众多的 zhòngduō de, 数量很多的
shùliàng hěn duō de
nun n 修女 xiūnǚ
Buddhist nun 尼姑 nígū
nuptial adj 婚姻的 hūnyīn de, 婚礼的 hūnlǐ de
nuptial vows 婚姻誓言 hūnyīn shìyán
pre-nuptial agreement 婚前契约 hūnqián qìyuē
nuptials n 婚礼 hūnlǐ [m. wd 次 cì/场 cháng]
nurse I n 护士 hùshi
a registered nurse 注册护士 zhùcè hùshi
II v **1** 护理 [+病人] hùlǐ [+bìngrén] **2** 给 [+婴儿]
喂奶 gěi [+yīng'ér] wèinǎi **3** 心中充满 [+仇恨]
xīnzhōng chōngmǎn [+chóuhèn]
nursery n **1** 托儿所 tuō'érsuǒ
nursery rhyme 童谣的 tóngyáo, 儿歌 érgē
nursery school 幼儿园 yòu'éryuán
2 苗圃 miáopǔ
nursing n 护理 hùlǐ
nursing home 养老院 yǎnglǎoyuàn
nurture v, n 培育 péiyù, 培养 péiyǎng
nut n **1** 坚果 jiānguǒ, 干果 gānguǒ **2** 螺母 luómǔ,
螺帽 luómào **3** 怪人 guàirén
soccer nut 足球迷 zúqiúmí
a hard nut to crack 棘手的问题 jíshǒu de wèntí
a tough nut 难对付的人 nán duìfu de rén
nutcracker n 胡桃夹子 hútáo jiāzi
nutrient n 营养 yíngyǎng, 滋养 zīyǎng
nutrition n 营养 yíngyǎng
nutritious adj 营养丰富的 yíngyǎng fēngfù de
nuts adj 发疯的 fāfēng de, 发狂的 fākuáng de
to go nuts 气得发疯 qìde fāfēng
nutshell n (in a nutshell) 用一句话来说 yòng yí
jù huà láishuō, 一言以蔽之 yì yán yǐ bì zhī
nutty adj **1** 古怪的 gǔguài de, 发疯的 fāfēng de
2 有坚果味的 yǒu jiānguǒ wèi de

nuzzle v（用鼻子）触碰（yòng bízi）chùpèng
nylon n 尼龙 nílóng
nylons n 尼龙长袜 nílóng chángwà [m. wd 双
shuāng], 连裤袜 liánkùwà [m. wd 条 tiáo]
nymph n 仙女 xiānnǚ
nymphomania n（女子）性欲旺盛（nǚzǐ）xìngyù
wàngshèng
nymphomaniac n 女色情狂 nǚ sèqíngkuáng

oaf n（男）傻瓜（nán）shǎguā, 笨蛋 bèndàn
oak n **1** 橡树 xiàngshù [m. wd 棵 kē] **2** 橡木 xiàng
mù
oar n 桨 jiāng
oasis n 绿洲 lǜzhōu
oath n **1** 誓言 shìyán
to take/swear an oath 宣誓 xuānshì ■ *The
witness took an oath before giving his testimony.*
证人在作证前先宣誓。Zhèngrén zài zuòzhèng
qián xiān xuānshì.
to take the oath of office 宣誓就职 xuānshì
jiùzhí
2 咒骂 zhòumà, 诅咒 zǔzhòu
oatmeal n 燕麦片 yànmàipiàn
oats n 燕麦 yànmài
to sow wild oats（年轻时）生活放荡（niánqīng
shí）shēnghuó fàngdàng
obedience n 服从 fúcóng, 顺从 shùncóng
obedient adj 顺从的 shùncóng de, 听话的
tīnghuà de
obese adj（过度）肥胖的（guòdù）féipàng de
obesity n 过度肥胖 guòdù féipàng, 肥胖症
féipàng zhèng
obey v 服从 fúcóng ■ *Every citizen should obey
the law.* 每一个公民都应该服从法律。Měi yí ge
gōngmín dōu yīnggāi fúcóng fǎlǜ.
obituary n 讣告 fùgào [m. wd 份 fèn]
object I n **1** 物体 wùtǐ, 东西 dōngxi
Unidentified Flying Object (UFO) 不明飞行物
bù míng fēixíngwù
2 目的 mùdì, 目标 mùbiāo **3**（语法）宾语（yǔfǎ）
bīnyǔ ■ *In the sentence "I study Chinese", the
word "Chinese" is the object.* 在 "I study Chinese" 这句话中, "Chinese" 是宾语。Zài "I
study Chinese" zhè jù huà zhōng, "Chinese" shì
bīnyǔ. **II** v 反对 fǎnduì
objection n 反对 fǎnduì, 厌恶 yànwù ■ *She
has a strong objection to abortion.* 她强烈反对堕
胎。Tā qiángliè fǎnduì duòtāi.
objectionable adj 令人厌恶的 lìng rén yànwù
de
objective I n 目标 mùbiāo, 目的 mùdì ■ *Her*

sole objective in life is to be a Hollywood star. 她生活中的唯一目标是当一个好莱坞电影明星。Tā shēnghuó zhōng de wéiyī mùbiāo shì dāng yí ge Hǎoláiwù diànyǐng míngxīng. II ADJ 客观的 kèguān de, 真实的 zhēnshí de

objectivity N 客观(性)kèguān (xìng), 公正(性)gōngzhèng (xìng)

obligate v 使…负义务 shǐ…fù yìwù

obligation N 义务 yìwù, 职责 zhízé

obligatory ADJ 必须做的 bìxū zuò de, 强制性的 qiángzhìxìng de

oblige v **1** 迫使 pòshǐ **2** 应请求(做)yìng qǐngqiú (zuò)
to feel obliged to do sth 感到有义务做某事 gǎndào yǒu yìwù zuò mǒushì
much obliged 非常感谢 fēicháng gǎnxiè

obliging ADJ 乐意助人的 lèyì zhù rén de

oblique ADJ **1** 间接的 jiànjiē de **2** 斜的 xié de, 倾斜的 qīngxié de

obliterate v **1** 抹掉 [+记忆] mǒdiào [+jìyì] **2** 毁灭 [+罪证] huǐmiè [+zuìzhèng] **3** 遮蔽 zhēbì

oblivion N 忘却 wàngquè, 遗忘 yíwàng

oblivious ADJ 未注意到的 wèi zhùyì dào de, 未察觉的 wèi chájué de

oblong ADJ, N 长方形(的)chángfāngxíng (de), 椭圆形(的)tuǒyuánxíng (de)

obnoxious ADJ 讨厌的 tǎoyàn de, 极坏的 jí huài de

oboe N 双簧管 shuānghuángguǎn

obscene ADJ 淫秽的 yínhuì de, 下流的 xiàliú de

obscenity N 淫秽/下流(的语言/行为)yínhuì/xiàliú (de yǔyán/xíngwéi)

obscure I ADJ **1** 不出名的 bù chūmíng de, 不为人知的 bù wéi rén zhī de **2** 难以理解的 nányǐ lǐjiě de, 晦涩的 huìsè de II v 使…难以理解 shǐ…nányǐ lǐjiě, 混淆 hùnxiáo

obscurity N **1** 默默无闻 mòmò wú wén **2** 费解(的事)fèijiě (de shì)

observable ADJ 可观察到的 kěguān chá dào de, 可看到的 kěkàn dào de

observance N **1** 遵守 zūnshǒu, 奉行 fèngxíng **2** 庆祝 qìngzhù

observant ADJ 观察能力很强的 guānchá nénglì hěn qiáng de

observation N **1** 观察 guānchá **2** 言论 yánlùn, 评论 pínglùn ■ *Grandpa made some witty observations about life.* 爷爷对生活发表了一些风趣的评论。Yéye duì shēnghuó fābiǎole yìxiē fēngqù de pínglùn.

observatory N 天文台 tiānwéntái [M. WD 座 zuò], 气象台 qìxiàngtái [M. WD 座 zuò]

observe v **1** 观察 guānchá, 注意到 zhùyìdao **2** 纪念 [+节日] jìniàn [+jiérì], 庆祝 qìngzhù

observer N 观察者 guāncházhě, 观察员 guāncháyuán

obsessed ADJ 老是想着的 lǎoshi xiǎngzhe de, 痴迷 chīmí

obsession N 着迷 zháomí, 强迫性思维 qiǎngpò-xìng sīwéi

obsessive ADJ 缠住不放的 chánzhù bú fàng de, 强迫性的 qiǎngpòxìng de

obsolescence N 过时 guòshí, 废弃 fèiqì

obsolescent ADJ 即将过时的 jíjiāng guòshí de, 逐步废弃的 zhúbù fèiqì de

obsolete ADJ 过时的 guòshí de, 废弃的 fèiqì de

obstacle N 障碍(物)zhàng'ài (wù)

obstetrician N 产科医生 chǎnkē yīshēng

obstetrics N 产科(学)chǎnkē (xué)

obstinacy N 固执 gùzhí, 顽固 wángù

obstinate ADJ 固执的 gùzhí de, 顽固的 wángù de

obstruct v **1** 阻碍 zǔ'ài, 妨碍 fáng'ài ■ *He was arrested for obstructing a police officer in the course of his duty.* 他因妨碍警官执行公务而被捕。Tā yīn fáng'ài jǐngguān zhíxíng gōngwù ér bèibǔ. **2** 堵塞 [+交通] dǔsè [+jiāotōng]

obstruction N **1** 堵塞(物)dǔsè (wù), 梗塞 gěngsè **2** 阻扰 zǔráo

obtain v 获得 huòdé, 取得 qǔdé

obtainable ADJ 能得到的 néng dédào de

obtrude v 强行闯入 qiángxíng chuǎngrù

obtrusive ADJ 过分突出的 guòfèn tūchū de, 太显眼的 tài xiǎnyǎn de

obtuse ADJ **1** 愚笨的 yúbèn de **2**（数学）钝角(shùxué) dùnjiǎo
an obtuse triangle 钝角三角形 dùnjiǎo sānjiǎoxíng

obverse N 对立面 duìlìmiàn, 相反的事物 xiāngfǎn de shìwù

obvious ADJ 明显的 míngxiǎn de ■ *Wasn't it obvious from the start that he was trying to cover up something?* 他想掩盖什么事，这不是从一开始就很明显的吗？Tā xiǎng yǎngài shénme shì, zhè bú shì cóng yì kāishǐ jiù hěn míngxiǎn de ma?

obviously ADV 明显(地)míngxiǎn (de)

occasion N **1** 场合 chǎnghé, 时刻 shíkè **2** 特殊的事件 tèshū de shìjiàn, 喜庆的场合 xǐqìng de chǎnghé ■ *What is the occasion for this party?* 举行这次聚会是为了庆祝什么事件？Jǔxíng zhè cì jùhuì shì wèile qìngzhù shénme shìjiàn?

occasional ADJ 偶尔的 ǒu'ěr de

occasionally ADV 偶然地 ǒurán de, 有时候 yǒushíhou

occult I N 神秘行为 shénmì xíngwéi, 魔法 mófǎ II ADJ 神秘的 shénmì de, 奥秘的 àomì de

occupancy N 占用(期)zhànyòng (qī), 占有(期)zhànyǒu (qī)

occupant N 居住者 jūzhùzhě, 住户 zhùhù

occupation N **1** 占领 zhànlǐng, 占据 zhànjù **2** 职业 zhíyè

occupational ADJ 职业的 zhíyè de
occupational therapy 职业治疗 zhíyè zhìliáo

occupy v 1 占据 zhànjù, 占用 zhànyòng ■ *The lavatory is occupied.* 洗手间有人使用。Xǐshǒujiān yǒu rén shǐyòng. 2 (军事) 占领 (jūnshì) zhànlǐng

occur v 1 发生 fāshēng ■ *This disease first occurred in Africa.* 这种疾病首先在非洲发生。Zhè zhǒng jíbìng shǒuxiān zài Fēizhōu fāshēng.
2 想到 xiǎngdao, 想起 xiǎngqǐ ■ *The idea has never occurred to me.* 我从来没有这个想法。Wǒ cónglái méiyǒu zhè ge xiǎngfǎ.

occurrence N 发生 (的事) fāshēng (de shì), 出现 chūxiàn

ocean N 洋 yáng, 海洋 hǎiyáng

oceanographer N 海洋学工作者 hǎiyángxué gōngzuòzhě, 海洋学家 hǎiyángxuéjiā

oceanography N 海洋学 hǎiyángxué

o'clock ADV 点钟 diǎnzhōng, 点 diǎn ■ *It's ten o'clock.* 现在是十点钟。Xiànzài shì shí diǎnzhōng.

octagon N 八角形 bājiǎoxíng, 八边形 bābiānxíng

October N 十月 shíyuè ■ *Leaves change color in late October.* 树叶在十月转色。Shùyè zài shíyuè zhuǎn sè.

octopus N 章鱼 zhāngyú

OD (= overdose) ABBREV 服用过量毒品 fúyòng guòliàng dúpǐn

odd ADJ 1 古怪的 gǔguàide, 奇特的 qítè de
an odd ball 举止古怪的人 jǔzhǐ qíguàide rén
the odd man out 与众不同的人 yǔ zhòng bù tóng de rén
2 奇数的 jīshù de ■ *1, 3, 5, 7, etc. are odd numbers.* 一、三、五、七等等，都是奇数。Yī、sān、wǔ、qī děngděng, dōu shì jīshù. 3 偶尔的 ǒu'ěr de, 零星的 língxīng de 4 多一点 duō yìdiǎn
20-odd 二十多个 èrshí duō gè

oddity N 1 古怪 (的人) gǔguài (de rén) 2 奇特 (的事) qítè (de shì)

oddly ADV 1 古怪地 qíguài de, 古怪地 gǔguài de 2 奇怪的是 qíguài de shì, 古怪的是 gǔguài de shì

oddments N 零头 língtóu, 碎屑 suìxiè

odds N 可能 (性) kěnéng (xìng)
against all odds 尽管困难重重 jǐnguǎn kùnnan chóngchóng
be at odds with 与…不合 yǔ…bùhé
odds and ends 零星杂物 língxīng záwù

ode N 颂歌 sònggē, 颂曲 sòng qū

odious ADJ 丑恶的 chǒu'è de, 可憎的 kězēng de

odometer N (汽车) 里程计 (qìchē) lǐchéng jì

odor N 气味 qìwèi

odorless ADJ 无气味的 wú qìwèi de

odyssey N 漫长艰难的旅程 màncháng jiānnán de lǚchéng

of PREP 1 …的 …de ■ *Students of this school all study a foreign language.* 这所学校的学生都学外语。Zhè suǒ xuéxiào de xuésheng dōu xué wàiyǔ. ■ *The President of the United States of America is the commander-in-chief of all armed forces of the country.* 美利坚合众国总统是国家所有武装力量的最高司令。Měilìjiān Hézhòngguó zǒngtǒng shì guójiā suǒyǒu wǔzhuāng lìliàng de zuìgāo sīlìng. 2 来自 láizì
a sage of the East 一位来自东方的圣贤 yíwèi láizì dōngfāng de shèngxián

off I ADV 1 取消 qǔxiāo ■ *The match is off owing to bad weather.* 由于天气不好比赛取消了。Yóuyú tiānqì bù hǎo bǐsài qǔxiāo le. 2 除掉 chúdiao, 减去 jiǎnqu ■ *You get 10% off if you pay by cash.* 如果付现金，可获百分之十的折扣。Rúguǒ fù xiànjīn, kě huò bǎifēnzhī shí de zhékòu. 3 离 lí, 离去 líqù II PREP 1 离去 líqù ■ *Employees are reminded to turn off their computers during the lunch break.* 雇员被提示，在午间休息时要关掉电脑。Gùyuán bèi tíshì, zài wǔjiān xiūxi shí yào guāndiao diànnǎo. 2 附近 fùjìn ■ *The shopping mall is just off the main road.* 购物中心就在大路附近。Gòuwù zhōngxīn jiù zài dàlù fùjìn.

offbeat ADJ 不寻常的 bùxúncháng de, 不落俗套的 búluò sútào de

offcolor ADJ 下流的 xiàliú de, 黄色的 huángsè de

offend v 冒犯 màofàn, 触怒 chùnù

offender N 违法者 wéifǎzhě, 罪犯 zuìfàn
first-time offender 初犯 (罪犯) chūfàn (zuìfàn)

offense N 1 违法行为 wéifǎ xíngwéi, 犯法 fànfǎ ■ *Speeding is the most common offense motorists commit.* 超速是驾车人最普遍的违法行为。Chāosù shì jiàchērén zuì pǔbiàn de wéifǎ xíngwéi. 2 伤害 shānghài, 伤感情 shānghài gǎnqíng
No offense. 请不要见怪。Qǐng bú yào jiànguài. ■ *No offense, but your figures don't add up.* 请不要见怪，不过你的数字不对。Qǐng bú yào jiànguài, búguò nǐde shùzì bú duì.

offensive ADJ 冒犯的 màofàn de, 很不礼貌的 hěn bù lǐmào de ■ *This hand gesture is offensive in many cultures.* 这个手势在很多文化里都是很不礼貌的。Zhè ge shǒushì zài hěn duō wénhuà lǐ dōu shì hěn bù lǐmào de.

offer I v 1 提供 tígōng ■ *In addition to a high salary, the company offers him a car and an apartment in New York.* 公司除了高薪以外，还为他提供汽车和在纽约的公寓。Gōngsī chúle gāoxīn yǐwài, hái wèi tā tígōng qìchē hé zài Niǔyuē de gōngyù. 2 出价 chūjià, 报价 bàojià 3 表示愿意提供 biǎoshì yuànyì tígōng II N 1 (提供帮助的) 建议 (tígōng bāngzhu de) jiànyì ■ *I don't understand why they refused our offer to help.* 我不明白，他们为什么拒绝我们提供帮助的建议。Wǒ bù míngbai, tāmen wèishénme jùjué wǒmen tígōng bāngzhu de jiànyì. 2 出价 chūjià

offering N 1 赠品 zèngpǐn, 献金 xiànjīn 2 提供的东西 tígōng de dōngxi

offhand ADJ, ADV 1 不假思索的 bù jiǎ sīsuǒ de, 脱口而出的 tuōkǒu ér chū de 2 漫不经心的 màn bù jīngxīn de

office N 1 办公室 bàngōng shì, 办公大楼 bàngōng dàlóu 2 办事处 bànshì chù ■ *Their company will set up an office in Shanghai next month.* 他们的公司下个月要在上海设立办事处。Tāmen de gōngsī xià ge yuè yào zài Shànghǎi shèlì bànshì chù.
office building 办公大楼 bàngōng dàlóu, 写字楼 xiězì lóu

officer N 1 军官 jūnguān ■ *The commanding officer of the submarine enjoys the trust and loyalty of his men.* 这艘潜水艇的司令官得到士兵的信任和忠诚。Zhè sōu qiánshuǐtǐng de sīlìngguān dédào shìbīng de xìnrèn hé zhōngchéng. 2 警官 jǐngguān ■ *He was arrested by two plainclothes officers at the airport.* 他在机场被两名便衣警官逮捕。Tā zài jīchǎng bèi liǎng míng biànyī jǐngguān dàibǔ. 3（政府）官员 (zhèngfǔ) guānyuán 4（公司）高级职员 (gōngsī) gāojí zhíyuán

official I ADJ 官方的 guānfāng de, 正式的 zhèngshì de II N 官员 guānyuán ■ *A senior official from the Ministry of Commerce came to investigate the scandal.* 商业部一名高级官员来调查这件丑闻。Shāngyèbù yì míng gāojí guānyuán lái diàochá zhè jiàn chǒuwén.

officialdom N（全体）官僚 (quántǐ) guānliáo

officially ADV 正式地 zhèngshì de, 公开地 gōngkāi de

officiate V 行使正式的职责 xíngshǐ zhèngshì de zhízé

offing N (be in the offing) 即将发生的 jíjiāng fāshēng de

offline ADV 不联网地 (jìsuàn jī) bùliánwǎng de, 脱机（地）tuōjī (de)
to work offline 脱机工作 tuōjī gōngzuò

offpeak ADJ 非高峰（时间）的 fēi gāofēng (shíjiān) de
offpeak hours 非高峰时间 fēi gāofēng shíjiān

off-ramp N 出口坡道 chūkǒu pōdào

offset (PT & PP offset) V 1 补偿 bǔcháng, 弥补 míbǔ 2 衬托 chèntuō

offshoot N 分支 fēnzhī

offshore ADJ, ADV 1 在近海的 zài jìnhǎi de
offshore drilling 近海钻探 jìnhǎi zuāntàn 2 境外的 jìngwài de, 海外的 hǎiwài de
offshore investment 海外投资 hǎiwài tóuzī

offspring N 子孙后代 zǐsūn hòudài

off-the-record ADJ 不公开发表的 bù gōngkāi fābiǎo de, 私下的 sīxià de

off-the-wall ADJ 有些不同寻常的 yǒuxiē bùtóng xúncháng de

often ADV 经常 jīngcháng, 常常 chángcháng

ogle V（色迷迷地）盯着看 (sèmímí de) dīngzhe kàn

ogre N 吃人妖魔 chīrén yāomó

ohm N 欧姆 Ōumǔ

oil I N 1 油 yóu ■ *The mechanic applied some oil to the machine to lubricate it.* 机修工给机器上些油，使它滑润。Jīxiūgōng gěi jīqì shàng xiē yóu, shǐ tā huárùn. 2 石油 shíyóu
oil field 油田 yóutián
oil painting 油画 yóuhuà
oil rig 采油架 cǎiyóujià
oil slick 浮油 fúyóu
oil well 油井 yóujǐng
peanut oil 花生油 huāshēngyóu
olive oil 橄榄油 gǎnlǎnyóu
deep sea fish oil 深海鱼油 shēnhǎiyúyóu II V 加滑润油 jiā huárùnyóu, 上油 shàng yóu

oiled ADJ 涂了油的 tú le yóu de

oily ADJ 含油的 [+鱼] hán yóu de [+yú], 油质的 [+头发] yóuzhì de [+tóufa], 油滑的 [+人] yóuhuá de [+rén]

ointment N 油膏 yóugāo, 软膏 ruǎngāo

OK I ADJ 1 好 hǎo, 不错 búcuò ■ *I think I did OK in the interview.* 我想我面试还不错。Wǒ xiǎng wǒ miànshì hái búcuò. 2 行 xíng, 可以 kěyǐ ■ *Is it OK if I don't come tomorrow?* 我明天不来，行吗? Wǒ míngtiān bù lái, xíng ma? II V 同意 tóngyì, 批准 pīzhǔn III INTERJ 好 hǎo, 好吧 hǎo ba ■ *OK, I'll let you try.* 好吧，你来试试吧。Hǎo ba, nǐ lái shìshi ba.

old ADJ 1 老 lǎo, 上了年纪的 shàngle niánjì de ■ *Both her parents are very old and in poor health.* 她的父母都很老了，身体都不好。Tā de fùmǔ dōu hěn lǎo le, shēntǐ dōu bù hǎo.
old age 老年（时期）lǎonián (shíqī)
old timer 老资格的人 lǎozīgé de rén, 老前辈 lǎoqiánbèi
2 旧 jiù ■ *Anyone wants these old books? Help yourself.* 谁要这些旧书? 自己拿吧。Shéi yào zhèxiē jiùshū? Zìjǐ ná ba. 3 熟悉的 shúxī de, 有深交的 yǒu shēnjiāo de
old boy network（男）校友关系网 (nán) xiàoyǒu guānxiwǎng
old flame 老情人 lǎoqíngrén
old friend 老朋友 lǎopéngyou

olden ADJ (in olden days) 过去 guòqù, 往昔 wǎngxī

old-fashioned ADJ 老式的 lǎoshì de, 守旧的 shǒujiù de

oldie N 1 名人 míngrén 2 旧物 jiùwù

Old Testament N（圣经）旧约书 (Shèngjīng) Jiùyuēshū

olive N 橄榄 gǎnlǎn [M. WD 颗 kē]
to offer an olive branch 表示和解 biǎoshì héjiě

Olympic Games N 奥林匹克运动会 Àolínpǐkè Yùndònghuì

omelet, omelette N 煎蛋卷 jiāndànjuǎn

omen N 预兆 yùzhào, 兆头 zhàotou

ominous ADJ 不吉利的 bù jílì de, 不祥的 bùxiáng de

omission N 省略（的东西）shěnglüè (de dōngxi), 遗漏 yílòu

omit V 省略 shěnglüè, 排除 páichú

omnipotence N 全能 quánnéng, 无所不能 wúsuǒbùnéng

omnipotent ADJ 全能的 quánnéng de

omniscience N 全知 quánzhī

omniscient ADJ 全知的 quán zhī de, 无所不知的 wúsuǒbùzhī de

omnivorous ADJ 杂食的 [+动物] zá shí de [+dòngwù]

on I PREP **1** 在…上 zài...shang ■ *Can I find our town on this map?* 在这张地图上能找到我们的小城吗？ Zài zhè zhāng dìtúshang néng zhǎodao wǒmen de xiǎo chéng ma? **2** 在 zài ■ *I'm leaving for Seattle on Friday.* 我星期五去西雅图。 Wǒ xīngqīwǔ qù Xīyàtú. **3** 关于 guānyú II ADV **1** 继续 jìxù, …下去 …xiaqu ■ *She walked on until she reached the river.* 她一直走，直到河边。 Tā yìzhí zǒu, zhídào hébiān. **2** 穿着 chuānzhe, 戴着 dàizhe **3** 接通 jiētōng

to turn/switch on 开（灯，电视机，etc.）kāi (dēng, diànshìjī, etc.)

to get on 乘 chéng

to go on 继续 [+说／做] jìxù [+shuō/zuò]

once I ADV **1** 一次 yí cì

once more 再一次 zài yí cì, 又一次 yòu yí cì ■ *He tried once more, but still had no luck.* 他又试了一次，还是不行。 Tā yòu shìle yí cì, háishì bù xíng.

at once ① 马上 mǎshàng ② 同时 tóngshí ■ *Do not drive and talk on the phone all at once.* 不要在开车的同时打电话。 Bú yào zài kāichē de tóngshí dǎ diànhuà.

once in a while 偶尔 ǒu'ěr

2 曾经 céngjīng

once upon the time 从前 cóngqián

II CONJ 一旦 yī, 一旦 yídàn ■ *Once you've started the engine, you should concentrate on driving.* 你一发动引擎，就应该集中注意力驾车。 Nǐ yì fādòng yǐnqíng, jiù yīnggāi jízhōng zhùyìlì jià chē.

once-over N 大致一看 dàzhì yíkàn

to give sb/sth the once-over 对某人／某事粗略地打量一下 duì mǒurén/mǒushì cūlüè de dǎliang yíxià

oncoming ADJ 迎面而来的 yíngmiàn érlái de

one I NUM **1** 一 yī II PRON 一个 yí ge ■ *No, I don't want this one; I want that one.* 不，我不要这个，我要那个。 Bù, wǒ bú yào zhè ge, wǒ yào nà ge.

one by one 一个接着一个 yí ge jiēzhe yíge

one another 相互 xiānghù, 彼此 bǐcǐ

one-liner N 俏皮话 qiàopíhuà

one-of-a-kind ADJ 独一无二的 dúyī wú èr de

onerous ADJ 繁重的（工作）fánzhòng de (gōngzuò), 艰巨的（任务）jiānjù de (rènwu)

oneself PRON 自己 zìjǐ, 自身 zìshēn

one-sided ADJ 片面的 piànmiàn de, 不公正的 bù gōngzhèng de

onetime ADJ **1** 从前的 cóngqián de **2** 一次性的 yícìxìng de, 只发生一次的 zhǐ fāshēng yícì de

one-to-one ADJ **1** 一对一的 [+讨论] yīduìyī de [+tǎolùn] **2** 一比一的 [+兑换率] yībǐyī de [+duìhuànlǜ]

one-track mind N 只想一件事的头脑 zhǐ xiǎng yí jiàn shì de tóunǎo, 老是想着一件事的脑子 lǎoshì xiǎngzhe yí jiàn shì de nǎozi

one-upmanship N 胜人一筹 shèng rén yì chóu

one-way ADJ 单（方）向的 dān (fāng) xiàng de

a one-way street 单行（街）道 dānxíng (jiē) dào

ongoing ADJ 持续的 chíxù de

onion N 洋葱 yángcōng

online ADJ, ADV 联网的 liánwǎng de, 联线的 liánxiàn de

onlooker N 旁观者 pángguānzhě

only I ADV 只 zhǐ, 只有 zhǐyǒu, 只是 zhǐ shì ■ *Don't get mad with me; I was only telling you the truth.* 别对我发这么大火，我只是对你说说真话。 Bié duì wǒ fā zhème dà huǒ, wǒ zhǐ shì duì nǐ shuōshuo zhēn huà. II ADJ 唯一的 wéiyī de

an only child 独生子女 dúshēng zǐnǚ

III CONJ 只是 zhǐ shì, 但是 dànshì

on-ramp N 进入坡道 jìnrù pōdào

onrush N 向前猛冲 xiàngqián měngchōng

onset N 开始 kāishǐ

onslaught N 强攻 qiánggōng

onto PREP 到…上 dào...shang, 在…上 zài...shang ■ *It's amazing how the boys got onto the roof.* 这些男孩是怎么上屋顶的，真是奇怪。 Zhèxiē nánhái shì zěnme shàng wūdǐng de, zhēn shì qíguài.

onus N 责任 zérèn

onward ADV, ADJ 向前（方）的／地 xiàngqián (fāng) de

oodles N 大量 dàliàng, 许多 xǔduō

oops INTERJ 啊呀 āyā

ooze I V 慢慢流出 mànmàn liúchū, 渗出 shènchū II N **1** 慢慢流动 mànmàn liúdòng **2** 淤泥 yūní

opal N 蛋白石 dànbáishí, 澳宝 àobǎo

opaque ADJ **1** 不透明的 [+玻璃] bú tòumíng de [+bōli] **2** 难懂的 [+文字] nándǒng de [+wénzì]

open I ADJ **1** 开（着）的 kāi (zhe) de, 打开的 dǎkāi de **2** 营业中的 yíngyè zhōng de ■ *Is the bank open on Saturday mornings?* 银行在星期六上午营业吗？ Yínháng zài xīngqīliù shàngwǔ yíngyè ma? **3** 开放的 kāifàng de

open house 开放日 kāifàngrì

an open plan 公开计划 gōngkāi jìhuà

open season 捕猎开放季节 bǔliè kāifàng jìjié
4 公开的 gōngkāi de
an open letter 公开信 gōngkāixìn
an open secret 公开的秘密 gōngkāi de mìmì
5 还没有结论的 hái méiyǒu jiélùn de, 还没有决定的 hái méiyǒu juédìng de
to keep an open mind 不匆忙下结论 bù cōngmáng xià jiélùn
II v 1 开 kāi, 打开 dǎkāi ■ Can you open the can for me, John? 约翰，你帮我打开这个罐头，好吗？Yuēhàn, nǐ bāng wǒ dǎkāi zhè ge guàntou, hǎo ma? 2 开始营业 kāishǐ yíngyè, 开门 kāimén 3 开放 kāifàng
to open fire 开火 kāihuǒ ■ The young police officer opened fire in panic. 年轻的警官在慌乱中开枪。Niánqīng de jǐngguān zài huāngluàn zhōng kāi qiāng.

open-air ADJ 露天的 lùtiān de ■ Everybody enjoyed the open-air concert. 人人都喜欢这个露天音乐会。Rénrén dōu xǐhuan zhè ge lùtiān yīnyuèhuì.

open-heart surgery N 心脏（直视）手术 xīnzàng (zhíshì) shǒushù

open-and-shut case N 很容易解决的问题 hěn róngyì jiějué de wèntí

open-ended ADJ 1 无限期的 wúxiànqī de 2 无明确答案的 [+问题] wú míngquè dá'àn de [+wèntí]

opener N 1 开启 [瓶／罐子的] 工具 kāiqǐ [píng/guànzi de] gōngjù 2（体育比赛）开局（tǐyù bǐsài）kāijú
for openers 首先 shǒuxiān

opening I N 1 [新店+] 开张 [xīndiàn+] kāizhāng 2 [新公司+] 开业 [xīn gōngsī+] kāiyè 3 [职位的+] 空缺 [zhíwèi de+] kòngquē 4 通道 tōngdào [M. WD 条 tiáo] 5 孔 kǒng, 洞 dòng II ADJ 首次的 shǒucì de

open-minded ADJ 思想开放的 sīxiǎng kāifàng de ■ Our principal is open-minded about the new teaching methods. 我们的校长能够接受新的教学方法。Wǒmen de xiàozhǎng nénggou jiēshòu xīn de jiàoxué fāngfǎ.

open-mindedness N（思想）开通（sīxiǎng）kāitōng, 开明 kāimíng

openness N 1 坦诚 tǎn chéng 2 开明 kāimíng, 思想（开通）sīxiǎng（kāitōng）

opera N 歌剧 gējù
Peking opera 京剧 Jīngjù, 京戏 Jīngxì

operable ADJ 可动手术的 kě dòng shǒushù de

operate v 1 操纵 cāozòng, 操作 cāozuò ■ The whole system is operated by a computer. 整个系统是由电脑操纵的。Zhěng ge xìtǒng shì yóu diànnǎo cāozòng de. 2 运行 yùnxíng, 运转 yùnzhuǎn 3 动手术 dòng shǒushù

operating system N（计算机）操作系统（jìsuànjī）cāozuò xìtǒng

operation N 1 手术 shǒushù [M. WD 次 cì] ■ Helen will have an operation to remove her tonsils. 海伦要动手术切除扁桃腺。Hǎilún yào dòng shǒushù qiēchú biǎntáoxiàn. 2 行动 xíngdòng ■ The relief operation was funded by charities. 这个救济行动是由慈善组织出资的。Zhè ge jiùjì xíngdòng shì yóu císhàn zǔzhī chūzī de. 3 运转 yùnzhuǎn

operational ADJ 可以使用的 kěyǐ shǐyòng de

operative I ADJ 1 起作用的 qǐ zuòyòng de 2 关键的 guānjiàn de
the operative word 最重要的词 zuì zhòngyào de cí
II N 1 特工 tègōng, 间谍 jiàndié 2 操作工 cāozuògōng, 技工 jìgōng

operator N 操作工 cāozuògōng, 操作员 cāozuòyuán,（电话）接线员（diànhuà）jiēxiànyuán
computer operator 电脑操作员 diànnǎo cāozuòyuán
sewing-machine operator 缝纫机操作工 féngrènjī cāozuògōng

ophthalmologist N 眼科医生 yǎnkē yīshēng

ophthalmology N 眼科（学）yǎnkē（xué）

opinion N 1 意见 yìjiàn, 看法 kànfǎ ■ What's your opinion on the fight against terrorism? 你对反恐怖主义，有什么看法？Nǐ duì fǎn kǒngbù zhǔyì, yǒu shénme kànfǎ? 2 舆论 yúlùn, 公众看法 gōngzhòng kànfa
public opinion 舆论 yúlùn, 民意 mínyì
to have a high/low opinion of 对…评价很高/不高 duì…píngjià hěn gāo/bù gāo ■ The board has a high opinion of the new CEO. 董事会对新总经理评价很高。Dǒngshìhuì duì xīn zǒngjīnglǐ píngjià hěn gāo.
opinion poll 民意调查 mínyì diàochá

opinionated ADJ 自以为是的 zì yǐwéi shì de, 固执的 gùzhí de

opium N 鸦片 yāpiàn

opponent N 反对者 fǎnduìzhě, 对手 duìshǒu

opportune ADJ 1 合适的 [+时刻] héshì de [+shíkè] 2 及时的 [+行动] jíshí de [+xíngdòng]

opportunism N（不讲原则的）机会主义（bù jiǎng yuánzé de）jīhuì zhǔyì, 投机（行为）tóujī（xíngwéi）

opportunist N（不讲原则的）机会主义者（bù jiǎng yuánzé de）jīhuìzhǔyìzhě

opportunistic ADJ（不讲原则的）机会主义的（bù jiǎng yuánzé de）jīhuìzhǔyì de

opportunity N 机会 jīhuì ■ I haven't yet had an opportunity to talk to her. 我还没有机会和她谈话。Wǒ hái méiyǒu jīhuì hé tā tánhuà.
Opportunity knocks at the door only once. 机不可失，时不再来。Jī bù kě shī, shí bú zài lái. (→ The opportunity shouldn't be missed and this occasion will not come again.)

oppose v 1 反对 fǎnduì ■ Environmentalists

strongly oppose logging the rain forests. 环境保护主义者强烈反对在雨林伐木。Huánjìng bǎohù zhǔyìzhě qiángliè fǎnduì zài yǔlín fámù. **2** 对抗 duìkàng

opposed ADJ 反对的 fǎnduì de

opposing ADJ 对立的 duìlì de, 对抗的 duìkàng de

opposite I ADJ 相对的 xiāngduì de, 对面的 duìmiàn de ■ *China lies on the opposite side of the Pacific.* 中国位于太平洋的对岸。Zhōngguó wèiyú Tàipíngyáng de duì'àn. **II** N 相反的事物 xiāngfǎn de shìwù ■ *I thought quite the opposite.* 我还以为情况正好相反呢。Wǒ hái yǐwéi qíngkuàng zhènghǎo xiāngfǎn ne. **III** PREP, ADV 在…对面的 zài...duìmiàn de

opposition N 1 反对 fǎnduì 2 (体育比赛) 竞争对手 (tǐyù bǐsài) jìngzhēng duìshǒu 3 (the Opposition) 反对党 fǎnduìdǎng

oppress v 1 压迫 yāpò 2 使…感到压抑 shǐ... gǎndào yāyì

oppressed ADJ 1 受压迫的 shòu yāpò de 2 受压抑的 shòu yāyì de

oppression N 压迫 yāpò, 压制 yāzhì

oppressive ADJ 1 暴虐的 [+统治] bàonüè de [+tǒngzhì], 不公平的 bùgōngpíng de 2 压抑的 [+气氛] yāyì de [+qìfen] 3 闷热的 [+天气] mēnrè de [+tiānqì]

oppressor N 压迫者 yāpòzhě

opt v 选择 xuǎnzé
to opt for 挑选 tiāoxuǎn
to opt out 决定 (不做某事) juédìng (bú zuò mǒushì), 逃避 táobì

optic ADJ 眼睛的 yǎnjing de, 视觉的 shìjué de

optical ADJ 1 光学的 guāngxué de
optical fiber 光学纤维 guāngxué xiānwéi
2 视觉的 shìjué de
optical illusion 视错觉 shì cuòjué

optician N 眼镜 (制造) 商 yǎnjìng (zhìzào) shāng

optimism N 乐观主义 lèguān zhǔyì

optimist N 乐观主义者 lèguān zhǔyìzhě

optimistic ADJ 乐观的 lèguān de

optimize v 使…最优化 shǐ...zuì yōuhuà, 使…最有效 shǐ...zuì yǒuxiào

optimum ADJ 最优的 zuì yōu de, 最佳的 zuì jiā de
an optimum condition 最佳条件 zuì jiā tiáo-jiàn

option N 选择 xuǎnzé, 选择权 xuǎnzéquán ■ *I don't have much of an option in this matter, do I?* 关于这件事，我没有太多的选择，不是吗？Guānyú zhè jiàn shì, wǒ méiyǒu tài duō de xuǎnzé, bú shì ma?

optional ADJ 可选择的 kě xuǎnzé de, 非强迫的 fēi qiǎngpò de

optometrist N 验光师 yànguāngshī

opulence N 豪华 háohuá, 奢侈 shēchǐ

opulent ADJ 豪华的 háohuá de, 奢侈的 shēchǐ de

or CONJ **1** 或者 huòzhě ■ *Your father or mother must come to the parents meeting.* 你的父亲，或者母亲，必须出席家长会。Nǐ de fùqin, huòzhě mǔqin, bìxū chūxí jiāzhǎnghuì. **2** 还是 háishì ■ *Would you like vanilla or chocolate ice cream?* 你要香草冰淇淋，还是巧克力冰淇淋？Nǐ yào xiāngcǎo bīngqílín, háishì qiǎokèlì bīngqílín? **3** (要) 不然 (yào) bùrán, 否则 fǒuzé ■ *Save your important files every day, or you may lose them.* 你要每天储存重要的文件，要不然可能会丢失。Nǐ yào měitiān chǔcún zhòngyào de wénjiàn, yàobùrán kěnéng huì diūshī.

oral I ADJ **1** 口头的 kǒutóu de **2** 口腔的 kǒuqiāng de
oral examination 口试 kǒushì
oral contraceptive 口服避孕药 kǒufú bìyùnyào
II N 口试 kǒushì

orange N **1** 橙子 chéngzi, 橘子 júzi
orange juice 橘子汁 júzizhí
2 橙黄色 chénghuángsè, 橘红色 júhóngsè

orang-utang N 红毛猩猩 hóngmáo xīngxing [M. WD 只 zhī]

orator N 演说家 yǎnshuō jiā

oratory N **1** 演说技巧 yǎnshuō jìqiǎo **2** 雄辩的口才 xióngbiàn de kǒucái

orbit I N **1** 轨道 guǐdào **2** 范围 fànwéi **II** v 环绕 [+轨道] huánrào [+guǐdào] 运行 yùnxíng

orchard N 果园 guǒyuán

orchestra N 管弦乐队 (guǎnxián) yuèduì
orchestra pit 乐池 yuèchí
symphony orchestra 交响乐队 jiāoxiǎng yuèduì

orchestral ADJ 管弦乐队的 (guǎnxián) yuèduì de

orchestrate v (秘密地) 组织策划 (mìmì de) zǔzhī cèhuà

orchestration N 精心策划 jīngxīn cèhuà

orchid N 兰花 lánhuā [M. WD 株 zhū/朵 duǒ]

ordain v 任命…为牧师 rènmìng...wéi mùshi, 授予…神职 shòuyǔ...shénzhí

ordeal N 痛苦经历 tòngkǔ jīnglì, 艰难过程 jiānnán guòchéng

order I N **1** 顺序 shùnxù ■ *The manager asked his secretary to put the files in order.* 经理要秘书按顺序整理好档案。Jīnglǐ yào mìshū àn shùnxù zhěnglǐhǎo dàng'àn. **2** 秩序 zhìxù ■ *The new teacher found it difficult to keep his class in order.* 新老师觉得很难维持课堂秩序。Xīn lǎoshī juéde hěn nán wéichí kètáng zhìxù.
law and order 法律与秩序 fǎlǜ yǔ zhìxù
3 订单 dìngdān, 订货 dìnghuò **4** 命令 mìnglìng ■ *The police chief gave the order to raid the house.* 警长下达命令突击那幢房子。Jǐngzhǎng xiàdá mìnglìng tūjī nà zhuàng fángzi. **II** v **1** 点菜 diǎn cài **2** 订购 dìnggòu ■ *The bookstore can order the book for you, if you like.* 你要的话，书

店可以为你订购那本书。Nǐ yào de huà, shūdiàn kěyǐ wèi nǐ dìnggòu nà běn shū. **3** 命令 mìnglìng, 嘱咐 zhǔfù

in order to 为了 wèile

orderly I ADJ 有条理的 yǒu tiáolǐ de, 守秩序的 shǒu zhìxù de **II** N（医院）勤杂工 (yīyuàn) qínzágōng

ordinal I ADJ 顺序的 shùnxù de
ordinal number 序数（词）xùshù (cí)
II N 序数 xùshù

ordinance N 法令 fǎlìng, 法规 fǎguī

ordinarily ADV 通常（来说）tōngcháng (láishuō)

ordinary ADJ 普通的 pǔtōng de, 平常的 píngcháng de

ordination N 授予神职 shòuyǔ shénzhí

ore N 矿石 kuàngshí

organ N **1** 器官 qìguān ■ *The boy received an organ transplant.* 男孩做了器官移植手术。Nánhái zuòle qìguān yízhí shǒushù. **2** 风琴 fēngqín

organic ADJ **1** 有机的 yǒujī de, 生物的 shēngwù de
organic vegetables 有机蔬菜 yǒujī shūcài
2（人体）器官的 (réntǐ) qìguān de
organic disorder 器官性疾病 qìguān xìng jíbìng

organism N 有机体 yǒujītǐ, 生物 shēngwù

organist N 管风琴手 guǎnfēngqínshǒu

organization N 组织 zǔzhī
non-governmental organization (NGO) 非政府组织 fēizhèngfǔ zǔzhī

organizational ADJ 组织的 zǔzhī de

organize V 组织 zǔzhī, 安排 ānpái ■ *The school is organizing a trip to China.* 学校在组织去中国的旅行。Xuéxiào zài zǔzhī qù Zhōngguó de lǚxíng.

organized ADJ 有组织的 yǒu zǔzhī de
organized crime 有组织犯罪 yǒu zǔzhī fànzuì, 集团犯罪 jítuán fànzuì
2（时间）安排得好的 (shíjiān) ānpái de hěn hǎode, 有条有理的 yǒutiáo yǒulǐ de

organizer N 组织者 zǔzhīzhě

orgasm N 性高潮 xìng gāocháo

orgy N 纵欲狂欢 zòngyù kuánghuān

orient V 定（方）位 dìng (fāng) wèi
to orient oneself 确定自己的位置 quèdìng zìjǐ de wèizhì
to be oriented towards 将…作为主要目的 jiāng…zuòwéi zhǔyào mùdì

Orient N 东方 dōngfāng

Oriental ADJ 东方的 dōngfāng de

orientation N **1** 目标 mùbiāo, 目的 mùdì **2** 倾向 qīngxiàng **3**（让新来者）熟悉情况 (ràng xīnláizhě) shúxī qíngkuàng
orientation week（大学）新生入学周 (dàxué) xīnshēng rùxué zhōu

origin N **1** 起源 qǐyuán, 来历 láilì ■ *Many American place names have Indian origin, e.g. Massa-*

chusetts. 很多美国地名起源于印第安语，例如"马萨诸塞州"。Hěn duō Měiguó dìmíng qǐyuán yú Yìndì'ān yǔ, lìrú "Mǎsàzhūsāi zhōu".
country of origin（产品）原产国 (chǎnpǐn) yuánchǎn guó
2 出身 chūshēn,（家庭）背景 (jiātíng) bèijǐng

original ADJ 原始的 yuánshǐ de, 最初的 zuìchū de ■ *We had to abandon our original plan as it was too expensive.* 我们不得不放弃最初的计划，因为花费太大。Wǒmen bùdébù fàngqì zuìchū de jìhuà, yīnwèi huāfèi tài dà. **2** 新颖的 xīnyǐng de, 有创见的 yǒu chuàngjiàn de

originality N 独创（性）dúchuàng (xìng), 创造力 chuàngzàolì

originally ADV 起初 qǐchū, 原先 yuánxiān

originate V 起源（于）qǐyuán (yú), 起始（于）qǐshǐ (yú)

oriole N 金黄鹂 jīn huánglí [M. WD 只 zhī]

ornament I N 装饰物 zhuāngshì wù **II** V 点缀 diǎnzhui

ornamental ADJ 装饰的 zhuāngshì de

ornate ADJ 装饰华丽的 zhuāngshì huálì de, 装饰过分的 zhuāngshì guòfèn de

ornery ADJ 脾气很坏的 píqi hěn huài de, 叛逆的 pànnì de

ornithologist N 鸟类学家 niǎolèixuéjiā

ornithology N 鸟类学 niǎolèixué

orphan I N 孤儿 gū'ér **II** V (be orphaned) 成为孤儿 chéngwéi gū'ér

orphanage N 孤儿院 gū'éryuàn

orthodox ADJ 正统的 zhèngtǒng de

Orthodox Church N 东正教（会）Dōngzhèngjiào (huì)

orthopedics N 矫形外科 jiǎoxíng wàikē

Oscar N 奥斯卡金像奖 Àosīkǎ jīnxiàngjiǎng

oscillate V **1** 来回摆动 láihuí bǎidòng, 振荡 zhèndàng **2** 反复改变 fǎnfù gǎibiàn

ostentation N 卖弄 màinong

ostentatious ADJ 讲究排场的 jiǎngjiu páichǎng de, 铺张的 pūzhāng de

ostracism N 排斥 páichì, 抵制 dǐzhì

ostracize V 排斥 páichì, 抵制 dǐzhì

ostrich N 鸵鸟 tuóniǎo [M. WD 只 zhī]

other I ADJ 其他的 qítā de, 另外的 lìngwài de ■ *Only Jonathan plays soccer: all the other boys play football.* 只有乔纳森踢足球，其他的男孩都打橄榄球。Zhǐyǒu Qiáonàsēn tī zúqiú, qítā de nánhái dōu dǎ gǎnlǎn qiú.
the other day 不久前一天 bù jiǔ qián yì tiān
every other day/week/year, etc. 每隔一天／一星期／一年 měi gé yì tiān/yì xīngqī/yì nián, 每两天／两周／两年一次 měi liǎng tiān/liǎng zhōu/liǎng nián yí cì
in other words 也就是说 yě jiù shì shuō, 换句话说 huàn jù huà shuō

II PRON 另一个 lìng yí ge ■ *They have two houses—one for living and the other as an investment.* 他们有两处房产——一处自己住，另一处是投资。Tāmen yǒu liǎng chù fángchǎn—yí chù zìjǐ zhù, lìng yí chù shì tóuzī.

otherwise I CONJ 不然 bùrán, 否则 fǒuzé ■ *You must pass all exams, otherwise no college will accept you.* 你必须通过所有的考试，否则没有大学会录取你。Nǐ bìxū tōngguò suǒyǒu de kǎoshì, fǒuzé méiyǒu dàxué huì lùqǔ nǐ. **II** ADV 不同 bù tóng, 不同地 bù tóng de

otter N 水獭 shuǐtǎ [M. WD 只 zhī]

ouch INTERJ 哎哟 āiyō, 疼啊 téng a

ought to [NEG **ought not to**] MODAL V 应该 yīnggāi, 该 gāi ■ *You ought to leave now if you're going to catch the train.* 你如果要赶火车，现在该走了。Nǐ rúguǒ yào gǎn huǒchē, xiànzài gāi zǒu le.

ounce N 盎司 àngsī, （英）两 (yīng) liǎng (= 28.35 克 kè)

our PRON 我们的 wǒmen de ■ *We love our country dearly.* 我们热爱我们的国家。Wǒmen rè'ài wǒmen de guójiā.

ours PRON 我们的 wǒmen de

ourselves PRON （我们）自己 (wǒmen) zìjǐ ■ *We're all grown-ups and can take care of ourselves.* 我们都是成人了，能够照顾自己。Wǒmen dōu shì chéngrén le, nénggou zhàogù zìjǐ.

oust V 把…赶走 bǎ…gǎnzǒu

ouster N 赶走 gǎnzǒu, 撤职 chèzhí

out ADV **1** 外面 wàimian, 不在（家／办公室）búzài (jiā/bàngōngshì) ■ *Mr Clark is out now. Would you like to leave a message?* 克拉克先生外出了。要留口信吗? Kèlākè xiānsheng wàichū le. Yào liú kǒuxìn ma? Get out! 出去! 滚出去! Chūqu! Gǔnchūqu! **2** 有差错的 yǒu chācuò de ■ *These statistics are way out!* 这些统计数字差得太远了! Zhè xiē tǒngjì shùzìchàde tài yuǎn le! **3** 不可能 bù kěnéng

outage N 断供期 duàngòngqī power outage 停电期间 tíngdiànqījiān

outbreak N 爆发 bàofā, 突发 tūfā epidemic outbreak 流行病突发 liúxíngbìng tūfā

outburst N 突然大发脾气 tūrán dàfā píqi, （强烈情绪的）爆发 (qiángliè qíngxù de) bàofā

outcast N 被遗弃的人 bèi yíqì de rén

outcome N 结果 jiéguǒ ■ *They're waiting for the outcome of the general election.* 他们在等大选的结果。Tāmen zài děng dàxuǎn de jiéguǒ.

outdated ADJ 过时的 guòshí de, 老式的 lǎoshì de

outdoors ADV 户外 hùwài

outer ADJ 外面的 wàimian de, 远离中心的 yuǎnlí zhōngxīn de outer space 外层空间 wàicéng kōngjiān

outgoing ADJ 外向的 wàixiàng de, 开朗的 kāilǎng de

outing N 远足 yuǎnzú, 短途旅行 duǎntú lǚxíng

outlet N **1** 电源插座 diànyuán chāzuò **2** 零售商店 língshòushāng diàn, 经销点 jīngxiāo diǎn **3** 通风口 tōngfēngkǒu, 排水道 páishuǐdào **4** 发泄（强烈感情）的方法 fāxiè (qiángliè gǎnqíng) de fāngfǎ

outline I N **1** 提纲 tígāng ■ *Here is an outline of our business plan.* 这是我们商业计划的提纲。Zhè shì wǒmen shāngyè jìhuà de tígāng. **2** 轮廓 lúnkuò, 外形 wàixíng **II** V 扼要说明 èyào shuōmíng

outlive V 活得比…长 huó dé bǐ…cháng to outlive one's usefulness 不再有用 búzài yǒuyòng, 失去功效 shīqù gōngxiào

outlying ADJ 边远的 biānyuǎn de, 外围的 wàiwéi de

out of PREP **1** 从…里出来 cóng…lǐ chūlai ■ *He's been out of the country for years.* 他在国外多年了。Tā zài guówài duō nián le. **2** 用完 yòngwán **3** 出于 chūyú out of curiosity 出于好奇心 chū yú hàoqí xīn out of bounds ①（球类运动）球出界 (qiúlèiyùndòng) qiú chūjiè ② 不准入内 bùzhǔn rùnèi Out of Bounds to Foreigners. 外国人不准入内。Wàiguórén Bùzhǔn Rùnèi. out of touch 脱离现实 tuōlí xiànshí, 不了解现实情况 bùliǎojiě xiànshí qíngkuàng out of work 失业 shīyè

out-of-date ADJ 过时的 guòshí de, 陈旧的 chénjiù de

out-of-state ADJ （美国）外州的 (Měiguó) wài zhōu de

out-of-the-way ADJ 偏远的 piānyuǎn de

outpatient N 门诊病人 ménzhěn bìngrén

outperform V 做得比…好 zuòde bǐ…hǎo, 胜过 shèngguò

outpost N 边缘军事哨所 biānyuán jūnshì shàosuǒ, 边缘贸易点 biānyuán màoyìdiǎn

outpouring N **1** 大量涌现 dàliàng yǒngxiàn **2** 强烈感情的表达 qiángliè gǎnqíng de biǎodá

output N （出）产量 (chū) chǎnliàng ■ *The factory plans to increase output by 10%.* 工厂计划增加产量百分之十。Gōngchǎng jìhuà zēngjiā chǎnliàng bǎifēnzhī shí.

outrage I N 震怒 zhènnù, 极大的愤慨 jídà de fènkǎi **II** V 使…震怒 shǐ…zhènnù

outrageous ADJ **1** 令人震怒的 [+行为] lìngrén zhènnù de [+xíngwéi] **2** 极不合理的 [+价格] jí bùhélǐ de [+jiàgé], 离谱的 lípǔ de

outreach N 扩大服务 kuòdà fúwù

outright ADJ **1** 彻底的 chèdǐ de **2** 毫不掩饰的 háobù yǎnshì de **II** ADV **1** 彻底地 chèdǐ de **2** 不掩饰地 bù yǎnshì de **3** 立刻 lìkè, 立即 lìjí

outrun V 跑得比…快 pǎo de bǐ…kuài, 超过 chāoguò

outset N 开头 kāitóu, 开始 kāishǐ

outshine v 使…黯然失色 shǐ...ànrán shīsè, 优于 yōuyú

outside I ADV（在）外面 (zài) wàimiàn ■ *Leave your dog outside, please.* 请把你的狗留在外面。Qǐng bǎ nǐ de gǒu liú zài wàimian. II ADJ 外面的 wàimiàn de, 室外的 shìwài de ■ the outside world 外面的世界 wàimiàn de shìjiè, 外界 wàijiè III PREP 在…外面 zài...màimian ■ *They live outside of the city.* 他们住在城外。Tāmen zhù zài chéngwài. IV N 外面 wàimiàn

outsider N（局）外人 (jú) wàirén

outskirts N 远郊 yuǎnjiāo, 郊区 jiāoqū

outsmart v 比…精明 bǐ...jīngmíng

outsourcing N 将工作外包 jiāng gōngzuò wàibāo, 从外部采购（部件）cóng wàibù cǎigòu (bùjiàn)

outspoken ADJ 直言不讳的 zhíyán búhuì de, 坦率的 tǎnshuài de

outstanding ADJ 杰出的 jiéchū de, 出色的 chūsè de

outstretched ADJ 张开的 zhāngkāi de, 伸展的 shēnzhǎn de

outstrip v 在数量上超过 zài shùliàng shàng chāoguò, 多于 duōyú

outward ADJ, ADV 向外（的/地）xiàngwài (de)、外面（的/地）wàimiàn (de)

outwardly ADV 在外表上 zàiwài biǎo shàng

outweigh v 超过 chāoguò

outwit v 智胜 zhì shèng

oval ADJ 椭圆形 tuǒyuánxíng

ovary N 卵巢 luǎncháo

ovation N（热烈）鼓掌 (rèliè) gǔzhǎng

oven N 烘箱 hōngxiāng, 烤炉 kǎolú

over I ADV 1 倒下 dǎoxià
to fall over 摔倒 shuāidǎo, 倒下 dǎoxià
2 在 zài, 到 dào
over there 在那里 zài nàli
3 翻转 fānzhuǎn
to turn over 翻过来 fānguolái
4 (Over!) 完毕! Wánbì! 完了! Wán lol
II ADJ 结束 jiéshù, 完了 wánle III PREP 1 在…上方 zài...shàngfāng ■ *A hot-air balloon flew over the town.* 一只热气球飞过小镇。Yì zhī rè qìqiú fēiguo xiǎo zhèn. 2 覆盖在… fùgài zài... ■ *She put her hand over her mouth to cover a yawn.* 她用手捂住口，悄悄打个哈欠。Tā yòng shǒu wǔzhu kǒu, qiāoqiāo dǎ ge hāqian. 3 在…之上 zài...zhīshàng, 超过 chāoguò

overall I ADJ 一切的 yíqiè de II ADV 总之 zǒngzhī, 总共 zǒnggòng ■ *Overall, I would say the project was a huge success.* 总之，我想说，这个工程是个巨大的成功。Zǒngzhī, wǒ xiǎng shuō, zhè ge gōngchéng shì ge jùdà de chénggōng.

overalls N 背带工装裤 bēidài gōngzhuāngkù [M. WD 条 tiáo]

overbearing ADJ 专横 zhuānhèng

overboard ADV (to fall overboard)（从船上）掉入水中 (cóng chuánshàng) diào rù shuǐ zhōng
to go overboard 做得太过分 zuòde tài guòfēn

overburdened ADJ 负担过重的 fùdān guòzhòng de

overcast ADJ（天空）多云的 (tiānkōng) duōyún de

overcharge v 1 多收…的钱 duō shōu...de qián, 要价太高 yàojià tàigāo 2 使…充电过度 shǐ...chōngdiàn guòdù

overcoat N 大衣 dàyī [M. WD 件 jiàn]

overcome v 1 克服 [+障碍] kèfú [+zhàng'ài] 2 使…失去知觉 shǐ...shīqù zhījué

overcompensate v 对…过多赔偿 duì...guòduō péicháng

overcrowded ADJ 太拥挤 tài yōngjǐ, 人太多 rén tài duō

overdo v 做得过火 zuòde guòhuǒ, 做得过份 zuòde guòfèn

overdone ADJ 煮得太久的 [+菜] zhǔ dé tài jiǔ de [+cài]

overdose I N 1 药物过量 yàowù guòliàng, 过量服用 guòliàng fúyòng 2 过量 guòliàng, 过分喜爱 guòfèn xǐ'ài II v 用药过量 yòngyào guòliàng

overdraft N 透支（额）tòuzhī (é)

overdraw v（存款账户）透支 (cúnkuǎn zhànghù) tòuzhī

overdue ADJ 1 过期不付的 [+借款] guòqī bùfu de [+jièkuǎn] 2 过期不还的 [+图书] guòqī bù huán de [+túshū] 3 过期不交的 [+作业] guòqī bù jiāo de [+zuòyè]

overeat v 吃得过多 chī dé guòduō

overestimate v 过高估计 guògāo gūjì

overextend v (to overextend oneself) 消费超过财力 xiāofèi chāoguò cáilì, 超前消费 chāoqián xiāofèi

overflow I v 溢出 yìchū, 漫过 mànguò II N 1 泛滥 fànlàn, 溢流 yìliú 2 溢流管 yìliú guǎn [M. WD 条 tiáo] 3 无法容纳的人（或物）wúfǎ róngnà de rén (huò wù)

overgrown ADJ 长满 zhǎngmǎn

overhang v 悬在…上方 xuán zài...shàngfāng

overhaul v 1 彻底检修 [+排水系统] chèdǐ jiǎnxiū [+gōngshuǐ xìtǒng] 2 对 [+税收制度] 全面改革 duì [+shuìshōu zhìdù] quánmiàn gǎigé

overhead¹ ADJ, ADV 在头顶（的/地）zài tóudǐng (de), 在空中（的/地）zài kōngzhōng (de)
overhead projector（高射）投影仪 (gāo shè) tóuyǐngyí

overhead² N 1 行政管理费用 xíngzhèng guǎnlǐfèi yòng, 管理成本 guǎnlǐ chéngběn 2 透明胶片 tòumíng jiāopiàn [M. WD 张 zhāng]

overhear v 无意中听到 wúyìzhōng tīngdào

overjoyed ADJ 非常高兴的 fēicháng gāoxìng de

overkill N 1 过度杀伤 guòdù shāshāng 2 过分行为 guòfèn xíngwéi

overland ADJ, ADV 经陆路 (的/地) jīng lùlù (de)

overlap I v 部份重叠 bùfen chóngdié II N 重叠 (的部份) chóngdié (de bùfen)

overload I v 1 使 [+卡车] 超重装载 shǐ [+kǎchē] chāozhòng zhuāngzài 2 使 [+电器设备] 超负荷 shǐ [+diànqì shèbèi] chāofùhè II N 1 超重装载 chāozhòng zhuāngzài 2 (电器设备) 超负荷 (diànqì shèbèi) chāofùhè

overlook v 1 俯瞰 fǔkàn, 俯视 fǔshì ■ *Their luxury apartment in New York overlooks Central Park.* 他们在纽约的豪华公寓俯视中央公园。Tāmen zài Niǔyuē de háohuá gōngyù fǔshì Zhōngyāng Gōngyuán. 2 忽视 hūshì, 忽略 hūlüè 3 不计较 bújì jiào, 原谅 yuánliàng

overly ADV (太) 过于 (tài) guòyú
not overly 不太 bútài

overnight I ADJ 在一夜间 zài yíyè jiān
an overnight flight 整夜飞行 zhěngyè fēixíng
an overnight success 一举成功 yìjǔ chénggōng II ADV (一) 夜间 (yí) yèjiān

overpass N 天桥 tiānqiáo [M. WD 座 zuò], 立交桥 lìjiāoqiáo [M. WD 座 zuò]

overpopulated ADJ 人口过多的 rénkǒu guòduō de

overpopulation N 人口过多 rénkǒu guòduō

overpower v 制服 zhìfú

overpowering ADJ 不可抗拒的 bùkě kàngjù de, 强烈的 qiángliè de

overpriced ADJ 定价太高的 dìngjià tàigāo de

overrated ADJ 评价过高的 píngjià guògāo de

overreact v 对…反应过度 duì…fǎnyìng guòdù

overreaction N 过火反应 guòhuǒ fǎnyìng

override v 1 推翻 [+以前的决定] tuīfān [+yǐqián de juédìng] 2 改变 [+自动程序] gǎibiàn [+zìdòng chéngxù] 3 比…更重要 bǐ…gèng zhòngyào

overriding ADJ 首要的 shǒuyào de

overrule v 否决 fǒujué, 推翻 tuīfān
Objection overruled. 反对无效。Fǎnduì wúxiào.

overrun[1] v 1 [植物+] 蔓延 [zhíwù+] mànyán 2 [河水+] 溢出 [héshuǐ+] yìchū, 泛滥 fànlàn

overrun[2] N 超支 chāozhī

overseas ADJ, ADV 海外的 hǎiwài de, 国外的 guówài de

oversee v 监督 jiāndū, 监管 jiānguǎn

overshadow v 给…蒙上阴影 gěi…méng shàng yīnyǐng 2 使相形见绌 shǐ…xiāngxíng jiànchù

overshoot v 1 错过 [+目的地] cuòguò [+mùdìdì] 2 超出 [+预算] chāochū [+yùsuàn]

oversight N 疏忽 shūhu, 失误 shīwù

oversimplification N 过分简单 (化) guòfèn jiǎndān (huà)

oversimplify v 使…过于简单 shǐ…guòyú jiǎndān

oversleep v 睡过头 shuìguotóu

overstate v 夸大 kuādà, 夸张 kuāzhāng

overt ADJ 公开的 gōngkāi de

overtake v 1 领先 lǐngxiān, 超过 chāoguò 2 突然降临 tūrán jiànglín

over-the-counter ADJ 非处方的 (药) fēi chǔfāng de (yào)

overthrow v 推翻 tuīfān, 打倒 dǎdǎo

overtime N 1 加班时间 jiābān shíjiān 2 加班费 jiābānfèi 3 (体育比赛) 加时 (tǐyù bǐsài) jiā shí

overture N 1 序曲 xùqǔ 2 主动表示 (友好) zhǔdòng biǎoshì (yǒuhǎo)
to make overtures to sb 向某人示好 xiàng mǒurén shìhǎo

overturn v 推翻 tuīfān, 否决 fǒujué

overview N 概况 gàikuàng, 概述 gàishù

overweight ADJ (体重) 超重 (tǐzhòng) chāozhòng

overwhelm v 压倒 yādǎo, 彻底打败 chèdǐ dǎbài

overwhelming ADJ 1 压倒的 yādǎo de 2 不可抗拒的 bùkě kàngjù de
an overwhelming majority 压倒多数 yādǎo duōshù, 绝对多数 juéduì duōshù

overwork v (使…) 工作过度 (shǐ…) gōngzuò guòdù

overwrought ADJ 神经非常紧张的 shénjīng fēicháng jǐnzhāng de, 极其焦虑的 jíqí jiāolǜ de

owe v 1 欠 qiàn ■ *He owes me $500.* 他欠我五百元。Tā qiàn wǒ wǔ bǎi yuán.
to owe sb a favor 欠某人人情 qiàn mǒurén rénqíng
2 (应该) 把…归功于 (yīnggāi) bǎ…guīgōng yú ■ *He owed his success to perseverance.* 他应该把成功归功于坚持不懈。Tā yīnggāi bǎ chénggōng guīgōng yú jiānchí bù xiè.

owing to PREP 由于 yóuyú ■ *Many flights were delayed owing to the nasty weather.* 由于这种恶劣天气，很多航班都延期了。Yóuyú zhè zhǒng èliè tiānqì, hěn duō hángbān dōu yánqī le.

owl N 猫头鹰 māotóuyīng [M. WD 只 zhī]

own I v 拥有 yōngyǒu ■ *We do not own this apartment; we're renting it.* 我们并不拥有这套公寓，我们是租用的。Wǒmen bìng bù yōngyǒu zhè tào gōngyù, wǒmen shì zūyòng de. II ADJ, PRON 自己的 zìjǐ de ■ *She makes her own clothes.* 她自己做衣服。Tā zìjǐ zuò yīfú.

owner N 物主 wùzhǔ, 业主 yèzhǔ

ox N 公牛 gōngniú [M. WD 头 tóu]

oxide N 氧化物 yǎnghuàwù

oxidize v 氧化 yǎnghuà

oxygen N 氧气 yǎngqì

oyster N 牡蛎 mǔlì, 生蚝 shēng háo

ozone N 臭氧 chòuyǎng
ozone layer 臭氧层 chòuyǎngcéng

P

ENGLISH-CHINESE

paint

pace I N 1 速度 sùdù
to keep pace with 与…保持同样的速度 yǔ… bǎochí tóngyàng de sùdù
to speed up the pace 加快速度 jiākuài sùdù
2 (一) 步 (yí) bù
to step a pace 走一步 zǒu yíbù
II v 1 慢步走 mànbù zǒu, 踱步 duó bù
to pace the floor 在房间里走来走去 zài fángjiān lǐ zǒulái zǒuqù, 在房间里踱步 zài fángjiān lǐ duó bù
2 为…定速 wéi…dìngsù

pacemaker N (心脏) 起搏器 (xīnzàng) qǐ bó qì

pacesetter N 1 带头人 dàitóurén, (体育) 领跑人 (tǐyù) lǐng pǎo rén 2 榜样 bǎngyàng

Pacific Ocean N 太平洋 Tàipíngyáng

Pacific Rim N 环太平洋国家 huán Tàipíngyáng guójiā

pacifier N 1 镇静剂 zhènjìngjì 2 橡皮奶嘴 xiàngpí nǎizuǐ

pacifism N 和平主义 hépíngzhǔyì

pacify v 1 使…平静 (下来) shǐ…píngjìng (xiàlai) 2 平定 píngdìng

pack I N 1 包 bāo, 盒 hé, 副 fù 2 群 qún
a pack of cigarettes 一包香烟 yì bāo xiāngyān
a pack of gum 一盒口香糖 yì hé kǒuxiāngtáng
a pack of wolves 一群狼 yì qún láng
II v 1 把…装进 [+箱子] bǎ…zhuāngjìn [+xiāngzi] 2 把…包装好 bǎ…bāozhuāng hǎo 3 [人+] 挤进 [+rén] jǐjìn
to pack up ① 收拾行李 shōushi xíngli ② 停止工作 tíngzhǐ gōngzuò, 收工 shōugōng
to pack one's bags 卷铺盖走人 juǎn pūgai zǒurén

package I N 1 包裹 bāoguǒ 2 套 tào ■ The new government will introduce a package of reforms. 新政府将引进一整套改革。Xīn zhèngfǔ jiāng yǐnjìn yì zhěngtào gǎigé.
package deal 一揽子交易 yì lǎn zi jiāoyì
package tour 配套旅游 pèitào lǚyóu
II v 1 把 [+东西] 打包 bǎ [+dōngxi] dǎbāo 2 对 [+人] 进行包装 duì [+rén] jìnxíng bāozhuāng

packaging N 包装材料 bāozhuāng cáiliào

packed ADJ 非常拥挤的 fēicháng yōngjǐ de
packed to the roof 挤得水泄不通 jǐ dé shuǐxièbùtōng

packer N 打包工 dǎbāo gōng

packet N 1 一小包 yì xiǎobāo, 一小袋 yì xiǎo dài 2 (计算机) 信息包 (jìsuànjī) xìnxībāo

packing N 打包 dǎbāo, 装箱 zhuāngxiāng
packing case 装货大木箱 zhuānghuò dàmù xiāng

pad I N 1 拍纸簿 pāizhǐbù [M. WD 本 běn]
note pad 记事本 jìshìběn
2 护垫 hùdiàn [M. WD 块 kuài]
knee pad 护膝 hùxī
3 (妇女用的) 卫生巾 (fùnǚ yòng de) wèishēngjīn 4 (导弹) 发射台 (dǎodàn) fāshètái 5 (直升飞机) 停机坪 (zhíshēng fēijī) tíngjīpíng 6 (动物的) 爪垫 (dòngwù de) zhuǎdiàn II v 1 (用软物) 填塞 (yòng ruǎn wù) tiánsāi 2 虚报 [+费用] xūbào [+fèiyòng] 3 放轻脚步走 fàngqīng jiǎobù zǒu

padding N 1 垫衬材料 diàn chèn cáiliào 2 (书中) 凑幅的内容 (shū zhōng) còu piānfu de nèiróng

paddle I N 短桨 duǎn jiāng [M. WD 把 bǎ] II v 用桨划 yòng jiāng huà

paddy, rice paddy N 水稻田 shuǐdào tián [M. WD 块 kuài]

padlock I N 挂锁 guàsuǒ [M. WD 把 bǎ] II v (用挂锁) 锁上 (yòng guàsuǒ) suǒshang

padre N (随军) 牧师 (suíjūn) mùshi [M. WD 名 míng/位 wèi]

pagan N, ADJ 异教 (徒) yìjiào (tú)

page I N 页 yè II v 1 (用扩音器) 唤人 (yòng kuòyīnqì) huàn rén 2 翻页 fān yè
to page through 很快地翻阅 hěn kuài de fānyuè

pageant N 1 盛装游行 shèngzhuāng yóuxíng 2 (选美) 表演 (xuǎn měi) biǎoyǎn

pageantry N 盛大庆典 shèngdà qìngdiǎn

pager N 寻呼机 xúnhūjī

pagoda N (宝) 塔 (bǎo) tǎ [M. WD 座 zuò]

paid See **pay**

pail N 提桶 títǒng

pain N 疼痛 téngtòng, 痛苦 tòngkǔ ■ The doctor gave him an injection to relieve his pain. 医生给他打了一针解痛。Yīshēng gěi tā dǎle yì zhēn jiě tòng.
to be a pain (in the neck) 极其讨厌 jíqí tǎoyàn

pained ADJ (感情) 受到伤害的 (gǎnqíng) shòudào shānghài de, (感到) 痛苦的 (gǎndào) tòngkǔ de

painful ADJ 1 疼痛的 téngtòng de 2 (令人) 痛苦的 [+事] (lìngrén) tòngkǔ de [+shì] ■ The memory of his failed marriage is still painful to him. 回想起失败的婚姻，他仍然很痛苦。Huíxiǎngqǐ shībài de hūnyīn, tā réngrán hěn tòngkǔ.
a painful experience 痛苦经历 tòngkǔ jīnglì
a painful decision (令人) 痛苦的决定 (lìng rén) tòngkǔ de juédìng

painkiller N 止痛药 zhǐtòngyào

painless ADJ 1 无痛的 wú tòng de 2 不费力的 bú fèilì de

pains N 尽力 (去做某事) jìnlì (qù zuò mǒushì)

painstaking ADJ 仔细的 zǐxì de, 精心的 jīngxīn de

paint I N 漆 qī, 油漆 yóuqī
paint thinner 油漆稀释液 yóuqī xīshì yè

507

II v **1** 漆 qī, 油漆 yóuqī ■ *He has painted his room yellow.* 他把房间漆成黄色。Tā bǎ fángjiān qīchéng huángsè. **2** (用油彩) 画 (yòng yóucǎi) huà, 绘画 huìhuà ■ *Who painted this landscape?* 这幅风景画是谁画的？Zhè fú fēngjǐng huà shì shéi huà de?
Wet paint. 油漆未干。Yóuqī wèi gān.

paintbrush N **1** 漆刷 qī shuā, 油漆刷子 yóuqī shuāzi [m. wd 把 bǎ] **2** 画笔 huàbǐ [m. wd 支 zhī]

painter N **1** 画家 huàjiā **2** 油漆工 yóuqīgōng

painting N 绘画作品 huìhuà zuòpǐn, (图) 画 (tú) huà ■ *Several paintings were stolen from the museum.* 好几幅绘画作品从博物馆偷走了。Hǎojǐ fú huìhuà zuòpǐn cóng bówùguǎn tōuzǒu le.

pair I N 双 shuāng, 副 fù, 对 duì
a pair of shoes 一双鞋子 yì shuāng xiézi
a pair of gloves 一副手套 yí fù shǒutào
a pair of scissors 一把剪刀 yì bǎ jiǎndāo
a pair of spectacles 一副眼镜 yí fù yǎnjìng
a pair of pants 一条裤子 yì tiáokùzi
a pair of dancers 一对舞伴 yí duì wǔbàn
II v 和某人配成一对 he mǒurén pèichéng yíduì

pajamas N 睡衣睡裤 shuìyī shuìkù [m. wd 套 tào]

pal N 好朋友 hǎo péngyou

palace N **1** 王宫 wánggōng, 皇宫 huánggōng, 宫殿 gōngdiàn **2** (像王宫一样的) 豪华大宅 (xiàng wánggōng yíyàng de) háohuá dàzhái

palatable ADJ **1** 美味可口的 měiwèi kěkǒu de **2** 合心意的 hé xīnyì de, 可以接受的 kěyǐ jiēshòu de

palate N 味觉 wèijué

palatial ADJ 象宫殿似的 xiàng gōngdiàn sìde, 豪华的 háohuá de

pale I ADJ **1** 苍白的 cāngbái de ■ *She turned pale when she heard the terrible news.* 她听到这个可怕的消息，脸色变得刷白。Tā tīngdao zhè ge kěpà de xiāoxi, liǎnsè biàndé shuābái. **2** 浅淡的 qiǎndàn de **II** v 使…相形失色 shǐ… xiāngxíngshīsè **III** N (beyond the pale) 出格的 [+行为] chūgé de [+xíngwéi], 无法接受的 wúfǎ jiēshòu de

paleontologist N 古生物学家 gǔshēngwùxuéjiā

paleontology N 古生物学 gǔshēngwùxué

palette N 调色板 tiáosèbǎn [m. wd 块 kuài]

palimony N 分居赔偿金 fēnjū péichángjīn

pall I N **1** (一层) 烟幕 (yìcéng) yānmù
to cast a pall over sth 给某事蒙上阴影 gěi mǒushì méng shàng yīnyǐng
2 棺罩 guān zhào **II** v 渐渐失去吸引力 jiànjiàn shīqù xīyǐnlì

pallbearer N 抬棺者 tái guān zhě, 护柩者 hù jiù zhě

pallet N 货板 huòbǎn, 托盘 tuōpán

pallid ADJ 苍白的 cāngbái de, 无血色的 wú xuèsè de

pallor N 苍白 cāngbái

palm I N **1** 手掌 shǒuzhǎng, 手心 shǒuxīn
palm reader 看手相的人 kàn shǒuxiàng de rén
palm top 掌上电脑 zhǎngshàng diànnǎo
to read sb's palm 看手相 kàn shǒuxiàng
2 (palm tree) 棕榈树 zōnglǘshù [m. wd 棵 kē]
II v (to palm sth off) 哄骗人接受假货 hǒngpiàn rén jiēshòu jiǎhuò

Palm Sunday N (基督教) 棕榈主日 (Jīdūjiào) zōnglǘ zhǔrì

palpable ADJ 可以感觉到的 kěyǐ gǎnjué dào de, 明显的 míngxiǎn de

palpitate v (心脏) 跳动过速 (xīnzàng) tiàodòng guòsù, 不规则跳动 bùguīzé tiàodòng

palpitations N 心悸 xīnjì, 心动过速 xīndòng guòsù, 心律不齐 xīnlǜ bù qí

paltry ADJ 太少的 tài shǎo de, 微不足道的 wēi bùzú dào de

pamper v 娇惯 jiāoguàn, 娇养 jiāoyǎng

pamphlet N 小册子 xiǎocèzi

pan I N **1** 锅 guō, 平底锅 píngdǐguō ■ *They bought a set of non-sticking pans.* 他们买了一套不粘锅。Tāmen mǎile yí tào bùzhānguō.
frying pan 煎锅 jiān guō
broiler pan 烤盆 kǎo pán
roasting pan 烤盘 kǎo pán
saucepan 长柄锅 chángbǐng guō
2 浅盘 qiánpán, 淘金盘 táojīn pán **II** v **1** 严厉批评 [+电影] yánlì pīpíng [+diànyǐng] **2** [摄影机+] 摇动拍摄 [shèyǐngjī+] yáodòng pāishè **3** (金等) 淘 (jīn děng) táo
to pan out [事件+] 进展 [shìjiàn+] jìnzhǎn

panacea N 万灵药 wànlíngyào

panache N 潇洒自如 xiāosǎ zìrú

pancake N 圆煎饼 yuán jiānbǐng [m. wd 块 kuài]

pancreas N 胰 (腺) yí (xiàn)

panda N 熊猫 xióngmāo
giant panda 大熊猫 dàxióngmāo

pandemic N (广泛流传的) 流行病 (guǎngfàn liúchuán de) liúxíngbìng

pandemonium N 大混乱 dà hùnluàn

pander v 迎合 yínghé, 讨好 tǎohǎo

pane N (窗子) 玻璃 (chuāngzi) bōli [m. wd 块 kuài]

panel¹ N 专家小组 zhuānjiā xiǎozǔ, 委员会 wěiyuánhuì

panel² N **1** 护墙板 hù qiáng bǎn [m. wd 块 kuài], 镶板 xiāngbǎn [m. wd 块 kuài] **2** 仪表板 yíbiǎobǎn [m. wd 块 kuài], 操纵台 cāozòng tái **II** v 铺设护墙板 pūshè hùqiángbǎn
room paneled with walnut wood 铺设桃木护墙板的房间 pūshè táomù hùqiángbǎn de fángjiān

panelist N 专家小组成员 zhuānjiā xiǎozǔ chéngyuán

pang N 剧痛 jùtòng

panhandle v 乞讨 qǐtǎo, 行乞 xíngqǐ

panhandler N 乞丐 qǐgài, 叫花子 jiàohuāzi

panic I N 惊慌 jīnghuāng, 惊恐 jīngkǒng
panic-stricken 惊慌失措 jīnghuāng shīcuò
II v (使…)惊慌 (shǐ...) jīnghuāng

panic-stricken ADJ 惊慌失措的 jīnghuāng shīcuò de

panorama N 1 全景 quánjǐng 2 概述 gàishù

panoramic ADJ 全景的 quánjǐng de

pansy N 三色紫罗兰 sānsè zǐluólán

pant v 气喘 qìchuǎn

pantheism N 泛神论 Fànshénlùn

panther N 黑豹 hēibào [M. WD 只 zhī]

panties N（女子）内裤 (nǚzǐ) nèikù [M. WD 条 tiáo]

pantomime N 哑剧 yǎjù [M. WD 出 chū]

pantry N 食物储藏室 shíwù chǔcángshì

pants N 裤子 kùzi

pantsuit N（女式）裤套装 (nǚ shì) kù tàozhuāng [M. WD 套 tào]

pantyhose N（女式）连裤袜 (nǚ shì) liánkùwà [M. WD 双 shuāng]

pantyliner N 卫生护垫 wèishēng hùdiàn

papa N 爸爸 bàba

papacy N 教皇的职权 Jiàohuáng de zhíquán

paper I N 1 纸 zhǐ ■ *Could you give me some blank paper?* 能不能给我一些空白的纸张？ Néngbunéng gěi wǒ yìxiē kòngbái de zhǐzhāng?
paper clip 回形针 huíxíngzhēn
2 报纸 bàozhǐ
paper boy/girl 送报的男孩／女孩 sòng bào de nánhái/nǚhái
3 （学校课程）文章 (xuéxiào kèchéng) wénzhāng 4 论文 lùnwén ■ *Prof Johnson will deliver a paper on global warming at the conference.* 约翰逊教授将在研讨会上宣读关于全球变暖的论文。Yuēhànxùn jiàoshòu jiāng zài yántǎohuìshang xuāndú guānyú quánqiú biànnuǎn de lùnwén. 5 证件 zhèngjiàn, 文件 wénjiàn II v 用纸糊 yòng zhǐ hú
to paper over a problem 掩盖问题 yǎngài wèntí

paperback N 简装本 jiǎnzhuāng běn

papers N 个人文件 gèrén wénjiàn

paperweight N 镇纸 zhènzhǐ [M. WD 块 kuài]

paperwork N 文书工作 wénshū gōngzuò

par N 1 水平 shuǐpíng, 标准 biāozhǔn
below par ① 在（一般）水平之下 zài (yìbān) shuǐpíng zhī xià ② 身体欠佳 shēntǐ qiànjiā
on a par with 与…水平相同 yǔ...shuǐpíng xiāngtóng
2 （高尔夫球）标准杆数 (gāo'ěrfūqiú) biāozhǔn gǎn shù

parable N 寓言故事 yùyán gùshi

parachute I N 降落伞 jiàngluò sǎn II v [军人+] 跳伞 [jūnrén+] tiàosǎn 2 空投 [+救济物资] kōngtóu [+jiùjì wùzī]

parade N 庆祝游行 qìngzhù yóuxíng
New York's Village Halloween Parade 纽约万圣节大游行 Niǔyuē wàn shèng jié dà yóuxíng

paradigm N 1 思维方式 sīwéi fāngshì 2 做事模式 zuòshì móshì 3 范例 fànlì

paradise N 天堂 tiāntáng, 乐园 lèyuán

paradox N 1 似乎自相矛盾的情况 sìhu zìxiāng máodùn de qíngkuàng 2 是非而是的隽语 shìfei ér shi de juànyǔ

paradoxical ADJ 似乎自相矛盾的 sìhu zìxiāng máodùn de

paraffin N 石蜡 shílà

paragon N（完美的）典范 (wánměi de) diǎnfàn

paragraph N（文章中的）段 (wénzhāng zhòngde) duàn, 段落 duànluò

parakeet N 长尾小鹦鹉 cháng wěi xiǎo yīngwǔ [M. WD 只 zhī]

paralegal N 律师助手 lǜshī zhùshǒu

parallel I N 1 平行线 píngxíng xiàn 2 相同的人或情况 xiāngtóng de rén huò qíngkuàng II ADJ 1 平行的 píngxíng de ■ *The railway runs parallel to the river for about 20 miles.* 铁路线和那条河平行大约二十英里。Tiělù xiàn hé nà tiáo hé píngxíng dàyuē èrshí yīnglǐ. 2 相同的 xiāngtóng de ■ *The solicitor spent the whole afternoon in the legal library to search for a parallel case.* 律师在法律图书室花了一个下午，寻找一个相同的案例。Lǜshī zài fǎlǜ túshūshì huāle yí ge xiàwǔ, xúnzhǎo yí ge xiāngtóng de ànlì. III v 与…相似 yǔ...xiāngsì

paralysis N 瘫痪 tānhuàn

paralytic I ADJ 瘫痪的 tānhuàn de II N 瘫痪病人 tānhuàn bìngrén

paramedic N 辅助医务人员 fǔzhù yīwù rényuán, 护理人员 hùlǐ rényuán

parameter N 界限 jièxiàn, 范围 fànwéi

paramilitary I ADJ 准军事的 zhǔn jūnshì de II N 准军事人员 zhǔn jūnshì rényuán

paramount ADJ 最重要的 zuì zhòngyào de, 高于一切的 gāoyú yíqiè de

paranoia N 1 多疑症 duōyí zhèng 2 偏执狂 piānzhíkuáng

paranoid ADJ 1 多疑的 duōyí de, 疑神疑鬼的 yíshén yíguǐ de 2 偏执狂的 piānzhíkuáng de

paranormal ADJ 超自然的 chāozìrán de, 神秘的 shénmì de

paraphernalia N 随身物品 suíshēn wùpǐn

paraphrase I v 对…释义 duì...shìyì, 改述 gǎi shù II N 释义 shìyì, 改述 gǎi shù

paraplegic N 半身不遂者 bànshēn bùsuí zhě

parasite N 寄生虫 jìshēngchóng

parasitic ADJ 寄生的 jìshēng de

parasol N 太阳伞 tàiyáng sǎn [M. WD 把 bǎ]

paratrooper N 空降部队 kōngjiàng bùduì, 伞兵 sǎnbīng

parcel I N **1** 邮包 yóubāo, 包裹 bāoguǒ **2** 一块
（土地）yí kuài (tǔdì)
parcel post（美国）包裹邮递系统 (Měiguó)
bāoguǒ yóudì xìtǒng
II V (to parcel out) 把…分成小部份 bǎ…
fēnchéng xiǎo bùfen

parched ADJ 极其干旱的 jíqí gānhàn de, 干枯的
gānkū de

parchment N 羊皮纸 yángpízhǐ [M. WD 张 zhāng]

pardon I V **1** 宽恕 kuānshù, 原谅 yuánliàng **2** 赦
免 [+犯人] shèmiǎn [+fànrén]
pardon me 对不起 duìbuqǐ
Pardon? 请再说一遍。Qǐng zàishuō yí biàn.
II N 赦免令 shèmiǎnlìng

pardonable ADJ 可原谅的 kěyuán liàng de

pare V **1** 削减 xuējiǎn, 减少 jiǎnshǎo **2** 削皮 xiāopí

parent N 父亲或母亲 fùqīn huò mǔqīn ■ Jack
and Michelle have recently become parents. 杰
克和密歇尔最近当爸爸妈妈了。Jiékè hé Mìxiē'ěr
zuìjìn dāng bàba māma le.

parentage N 出身 chūshēn, 身世 shēnshì

parental ADJ 父母的 fùmǔ de
parental guidance 父母的指导 fùmǔ de zhǐdǎo

parenthesis N 括号 yuánkuòhào [( )]

parenthood N 父母的身份 fùmǔ de shēnfen

parish N（基督教）教区 (Jīdūjiào) jiàoqū

parishioner N 教区居民 jiàoqū jūmín

parity N（报酬）相同 (bàochou) xiāngtóng, 同等
tóngděng

park I N **1** 公园 gōngyuán **2**（天然）公园
(tiānrán) gōngyuán
national park 国家公园 guójiā gōngyuán
amusement park 娱乐场 yúlè cháng, 乐园 lèyuán
ball park 棒球场 bàngqiú chǎng
car park 停车场 tíngchē chǎng
science park 科学园区 kēxué yuánqū, 新科技开
发区 xīnkē jì kāifāqū
II V **1** 停车 tíngchē ■ Is it OK if I park here? 我能
在这里停车吗？Wǒ néng zài zhèlǐ tíngchē ma?
park and ride 换车通勤 huànchē tōngqín
2 停放 tíngfàng

parka N（带帽的）风雪大衣 (dài mào de)
fēngxuě dàyī

parking N 停车 tíngchē
parking ticket 违章停车罚款 wéizhāng tíngchē
fákuǎn
parking lot 停车场 tíngchēchǎng
parking meter 停车计费收费表 tíngchē jìshù
shōufèi biǎo

parkway N 林荫大道 línyìn dàdào

parliament N 国会 Guóhuì

parliamentary ADJ 议会的 yìhuì de, 国会的
Guóhuì de

parlor N 商店 shāngdiàn
beauty parlor 美容院 měiróngyuàn

dental parlor 牙科诊所 yákē zhěnsuǒ
funeral parlor 殡仪馆 bìnyíguǎn
icecream parlor 冰淇凌店 bīngqílín diàn

parochial ADJ **1** 教区的 jiàoqū de **2** 狭隘的 xiá'ài
de

parody I N（滑稽）模仿 (huájī) mófǎng **II** V [滑稽
地+] 模仿 [huájīde+] mófǎng

parole I N 假释 jiǎshì **II** V 准许假释 zhǔnxǔ jiǎshì

parquet N 镶木地板 xiāngmù dìbǎn

parrot N 鹦鹉 yīngwǔ [M. WD 只 zhī]

parsley N 西芹 xīqín

parsnip N 欧洲萝卜 Ōuzhōu luóbo

part I N **1** 部分 bùfen **2** 零件 língjiàn ■ Do you
sell parts for GM cars? 你们出售通用汽车的零件
吗？Nǐmen chūshòu Tōngyòng qìchē de língjiàn
ma? **3** 角色 juésè
to play a part (in) 扮演角色 bànyǎn juésè, 起
到作用 qǐdào zuòyòng
to take part (in) 参加 cānjiā ■ The teacher encouraged everyone to take part in the discussion.
老师鼓励每一个人都参加讨论。Lǎoshī gǔlì měi yí
ge rén dōu cānjiā tǎolùn.
II V **1**（使）…分开 (shǐ)…fēnkāi **2** [与朋友+] 分手
[yǔ péngyou+] fēnshǒu

partial ADJ 部分的 bùfen de
be partial to 偏袒 piāntǎn, 偏爱 piān'ài

partiality N 偏袒 piāntǎn, 不公正 bù gōngzhèng

participant N 参加者 cānjiāzhě, 参与者 cānyùzhě

participate V 参加 cānjiā, 参与 cānyù

participation N 参加 cānjiā, 参与 cānyù

participle N 分词 fēncí
past participle 过去分词 guòqùfēncí
present participle 现在分词 xiànzàifēncí

particle N **1** 微粒 wēilì **2**（原子中的）粒子 (yuánzǐ
zhòng de) lìzi

particular I ADJ 特别的 tèbié de, 特殊的 tèshū
de ■ In this particular case, we may need to
waive the rules. 对这个特殊情况，我们可能要放
弃规定。Duì zhè ge tèshū qíngkuàng, wǒmen
kěnéng yào fàngqì guīdìng. **II** N (in particular) 特
别（地）tèbié (de), 尤其 yóuqí

particularly ADV 特别 tèbié ■ This Chinese
restaurant serves good food; their roast duck is
particularly good. 这家中菜馆的菜很好，特别是烤
鸭。Zhè jiā Zhōngcài guǎn de cài hěn hǎo, tèbié
shì kǎoyā.

particulars N 细节 xìjié, 详情 xiángqíng

parting I N 分离 fēnlí, 离别 líbié **II** ADJ 临别（时）的
línbié (shí) de
parting shot 临别时的攻击 línbié shí de gōngjī

partisan ADJ 热烈支持某一党派的 rèliè zhīchí
mǒu yì dǎngpài de

partition I N **1**（国家的）分裂 (guójiā de) fēnliè
2 隔墙 géqiáng **II** V 分割 fēngē, 分开 fēnkāi

partly ADV 部分 bùfen, 部分地 bùfen de ■ It was

partly my fault. 一部分是我的错。Yí bùfen shì wǒ de cuò.

partner N 1 合伙人 héhuǒrén 2 搭档 dādàng ■ *They've been partners at bridge for many years.* 他们两人搭档打桥牌已经好几年了。Tāmen liǎng rén dādàng dǎ qiáopái yǐjīng hǎojǐ nián le. 3 性伴侣 xìng bànlǚ, 配偶 pèi'ǒu 4 舞伴 wǔbàn

partnership N 合伙（关系）héhuǒ (guānxi), 合作（关系）hézuò (guānxi)

part of speech N 词性 cíxìng, 词类 cílèi

partridge N 鹧鸪 zhègū [M. WD 只 zhī]

part-time ADJ, ADV 兼职（的/地）jiānzhí (de), 部分时间的 bùfen shíjiān de

partway ADV 1（在）途中 (zài) túzhōng 2 一段时间后 yí duàn shíjiān hòu

party I N 1 派对 pàiduì, 聚会 jùhuì, 社交聚会 shèjiāo jùhuì
birthday party 生日庆祝会 shēngri qìngzhù huì
dinner party 宴会 yànhuì
garden party 游园会 yóuyuán huì
2（政）党 (zhèng) dǎng 3 小组 xiǎozǔ ■ *The search party returned to the base, empty-handed.* 搜索小组空手回到基地。Sōusuǒ xiǎozǔ kōngshǒu huídào jīdì. II v 尽情吃喝玩乐 jìnqíng chīhē wánlè

pass I v 1 通过 tōngguò, 经过 jīngguò ■ *The jungle was so dense that the explorers could hardly pass.* 丛林很密，探险者几乎无法通过。Cónglín hěn mì, tànxiǎn zhě jīhū wúfǎ tōngguò. 2 走过 zǒuguo 3 传 chuán, 递 dì, 传递 chuándì 4 过去 guòqu ■ *Two weeks passed and there was still no news about the missing girl.* 两个星期过去了，还没有失踪女孩的消息。Liǎng ge xīngqī guòqu le, hái méiyǒu shīzōng nǚhái de xiāoxi. 5 通过 [+考试] tōngguò [+kǎoshì],（考试）及格 (kǎoshì) jígé
to pass away 去世 qùshì
to pass for 冒充 màochōng ■ *With a pair of thick glasses and a deep voice, young Alec could pass for a teacher.* 小艾力克戴了一副厚眼镜，说话嗓门很粗，可以冒充老师。Xiǎo Àilìkè dàile yí fù hòu yǎnjìng, shuōhuà sǎngmén hěn cū, kěyǐ màochōng lǎoshī.
to pass out 昏厥 hūnjué, 晕倒 yūndǎo
II v 1 传 chuán, 传递 chuándì ■ *The forward got a long pass to score.* 前锋接到一个长传，投篮得分。Qiánfēng jiēdào yí ge chángchuán, tóulán défēn. 2 通行证 tōngxíng zhèng 3（考试）及格 (kǎoshì) jígé 4 山口 shānkǒu

passable ADJ 过得去的 guòdequ de, 还可以的 hái kěyǐ de

passage N 1 通道 tōngdào 2 通过 tōngguò ■ *Passage of heavy trucks over this bridge is forbidden.* 重型卡车不准通过这座桥。Zhòngxíng kǎchē bù zhǔn tōngguò zhè zuò qiáo. 3（书/乐曲）一段 (shū/yuèqǔ) yí duàn 4（时间的）流逝 (shíjiān de) liúshì

passageway N（狭窄的）通道 (xiázhǎi de) tōngdào [M. WD 条 tiáo]

passbook N（银行）存折 (yínháng) cúnzhé [M. WD 本 běn]

passé ADJ 过时的 guòshí de, 老式的 lǎoshì de

passenger N 乘客 chéngkè
passenger seat（汽车）驾驶员旁边的座位 (qìchē) jiàshǐyuán pángbiān de zuòwèi

passerby N 过路人 guòlùrén

passing I ADJ 1 经过的 [+车辆] jīngguò de [+chēliàng] 2 一时的 [+兴趣] yìshí de [+xìngqu] II N 1 终止 zhōngzhǐ, 消失 xiāoshī
passing of time 时间的流逝 shíjiān de liúshì 2 去世 qùshì, 过世 guòshì 3 (in passing) 顺便提到 shùnbiàn tídào

passion N 激情 jīqíng, 热爱 rè'ài

passionate ADJ 感情强烈的 gǎnqíng qiángliè de, 充满激情的 chōngmǎn jīqíng de

passive I ADJ 被动的 bèidòng de
passive smoking 被动抽烟 bèidòng chōuyān
II N 被动式 bèidòngshì

passport N 护照 hùzhào

password N 口令 kǒulìng, 通行字 tōngxíng zì

past I ADJ 过去的 guòqu de ■ *In the past few weeks shares prices have been on a roller coaster.* 过去几周里，股票价格大起大落。Guòqu jǐ zhōu lǐ, gǔpiào jiàgé dà qǐ dà luò. II N 过去 guòqù III PREP 1 晚于 wǎn yú, 在… 以后 zài...yǐhòu ■ *He is past 70, but he still plays basketball.* 他七十多岁了，但还是打篮球。Tā qīshí duō suì le, dàn hái shì dǎ lánqiú. 2 远于 yuǎn yú, 过了… guòle... ■ *The farm is 15 miles past the railway.* 那个农场在过了铁路十五英里的地方。Nà ge nóngchǎng zài guòle tiělù shíwǔ yīnglǐ de dìfang. 3 经过 jīngguò 4 (past caring) 不在乎 búzàihu

paste I N 1 浆糊 jiànghu, 糨糊 jiànghu 2 糊状物 húzhuàng wù 3 [鱼+] 酱 [yú+] jiàng
wallpaper paste 贴墙纸的浆糊 tiē qiángzhǐ de jiànghu
II v 1（用糨糊）粘帖 (yòng jiànghu) zhān tiē 2（计算机）粘帖 (jìsuànjī) zhān tiē

pastel I N 1 彩色粉笔 cǎisè fěnbǐ [M. WD 支 zhī], 蜡笔 làbǐ 2 彩色粉笔画 cǎisè fěnbǐhuà [M. WD 幅 fú] II ADJ 浅 [+颜色] qiǎn [+yánsè], 淡 dàn

pasteurization N 灭菌 mièjūn, 消毒 xiāodú

pasteurize v 灭菌 mièjūn, 消毒 xiāodú

pastime N 消遣 xiāoqiǎn, 娱乐 yúlè

pastor N 牧师 mùshi

pastoral ADJ 1 牧师的 mùshi de 2 田园风光的 tiányuán fēngguāng de, 乡村生活的 xiāngcūn shēnghuó de

(the) past perfect N 过去完成时态 guòqù wánchéng shítài

pastry N 1 油酥面团 yóu sū miàntuán 2 油酥点心 yóu sū diǎnxin [M. WD 块 kuài/件 jiàn] (the) past tense

(the) past tense N 过去式 guòqù shì, 过去时态 guòqù shítài

pasture N 牧场 mùchǎng

pasty I ADJ 苍白的 cāngbái de II N （肉等的）馅饼 (ròu děng de) xiànbǐng

pat I v 轻轻地拍 qīngqīng de pāi
to pat sb on the back 赞扬某人 zànyáng mǒurén
II N 1 轻拍 qīng pāi 2 （黄油等）小块 (huángyóu děng) xiǎokuài
a pat on the back 赞扬 zànyáng
III ADJ 脱口而出的 [+回答] tuōkǒu ér chū de [+huídá]

patch I N 1 （衣服上的）补丁 (yīfu shàng de) bǔdīng 2 （计算机）程序补丁 (jìsuànjī) chéngxù bǔdīng 3 膏药 gāoyao 4 小块土地 xiǎo kuài tǔdì II v 1 缝补 [+衣服] féngbǔ [+yīfu] 2 (to patch up) 修补 [+关系] xiūbǔ [+guānxi], 解决分歧 jiějué [+fēnqí]

patchwork N 拼布工艺（品）pīn bù gōngyì (pǐn)

patchy ADJ 1 局部零星的 [+阵雨] júbù língxīng de [+zhènyǔ] 2 零碎的 [+知识] língsuì de [+zhīshi]

paté N 肉酱 ròujiàng, 鱼酱 yú jiàng

patent I N 专利（权）zhuānlì (quán) II v 取得专利（权）qǔdé zhuānlì (quán) III ADJ 明显的 míngxiǎn de
a patent lie 明显的谎言 míngxiǎn de huǎngyán

patent leather N 漆皮 qīpí
patent leather shoes 漆皮皮鞋 qīpí píxié

patently ADV 显然地 xiǎnrán de

paternal ADJ 1 父亲的 fùqin de 2 父权的 fùquán de

paternalism N 父权主义 fùquánzhǔyì, 家长式统治 jiāzhǎng shì tǒngzhì

paternalistic ADJ 父权主义的 fùquánzhǔyì de, 家长式的 jiāzhǎng shì de

paternity N 父亲的身份 fùqin de shēnfen
paternity leave 陪产假 péi chǎnjià

path N 小路 xiǎolù, 道路 dàolù

pathetic ADJ 1 可怜的 kělián de 2 没用的 méiyòng de

pathological ADJ 1 病态的 bìngtài de, 无法控制的 wúfǎ kòngzhì de
a pathological liar 无法不撒谎的人 wúfǎ bù sāhuǎng de rén, 说谎成性的人 shuōhuǎng chéngxìng de rén
2 病理（学）的 bìnglǐ (xué) de

pathology N 病理（学）bìnglǐ (xué)

pathos N 引起怜悯的因素 yǐnqǐ liánmǐn de yīnsù, 感伤力 gǎnshāng lì

pathway N 途径 tújìng

patience N 耐心 nàixīn, 忍耐心 rěn nài xīn ■ The salesman eventually ran out of patience with that difficult customer. 售货员终于对那个难缠的顾客失去了耐心。Shòuhuò yuán zhōngyú duì nà ge nánchán de gùkè shīqùle nàixīn.

patient I ADJ 耐心的 nàixīn de II N 病人 bìngrén ■ The patient complained of a nagging stomachache. 病人诉说肚子隐隐地痛。Bìngrén sùshuō dùzi yǐnyǐn de tòng.

patio N 露天平台 lùtiān píngtái

patriarch N （男）家长 (nán) jiāzhǎng, 族长 zúzhǎng, 受尊敬的长者 shòu zūnjìng de zhǎngzhě

patriarchal ADJ 父权制的 fùquánzhì de

patriarchy N 父权制 fùquánzhì, 男性统治 nánxìng tǒngzhì

patricide N 弑父（罪）shì fù (zuì), 杀父罪 shā fù zuì

patrimony N 1 （祖传）遗产 (zǔchuán) yíchǎn 2 国家资源 guójiā zīyuán, 国宝 guóbǎo

patriot N 爱国者 àiguózhě

patriotic ADJ 爱国（主义）的 àiguó (zhǔyì) de

patriotism N 爱国主义 àiguózhǔyì

patrol I N 1 巡逻 xúnluó, 巡查 xúnchá 2 巡逻兵 xúnluó bīng, 巡逻队 xúnluóduì II v 巡逻 xúnluó, 巡查 xúnchá

patrolman N 巡警 xúnjǐng, 巡逻（保安）人员 xúnluó (bǎo'ān) rényuán

patron N 1 赞助人 zànzhùrén, 资助人 zīzhù rén 2 顾客 gùkè

patronage N 1 赞助 zànzhù, 资助 zīzhù 2 任命权 rènmìng quán

patronize v 1 以高人一筹的姿态对待 [+人] yǐ gāorén yì chóu de zītài duìdài [+rén] 2 光顾 [+饭店] guānggù [+fàndiàn]

patter I N 1 急速的轻拍声 jísù de qīng pāi shēng, 啪嗒啪嗒声 pādā pādā shēng 2 顺口溜 shùnkǒuliū II v 发出急速的轻拍声 fāchū jísù de qīng pāi shēng, 发出啪嗒啪嗒的声音 fāchū pādā pādā de shēngyīn

pattern I N 1 图案 tú'àn, 花样 huāyàng 2 模式 móshì, 方式 fāngshì II v 模仿 mófǎng, 仿效 fǎngxiào

patterned ADJ 有图案装饰的 yǒu tú'àn zhuāngshì de

patty N 肉饼 ròubǐng [m. wd 块 kuài]

paucity N 贫乏 pínfá, 贫困 pínkùn

paunch N （男人的）大肚子 (nánren de) dàdùzi, 啤酒桶肚子 píjiǔtǒng dùzi

pauper N 贫民 pínmín, 穷人 qióngrén

pause N, v 暂停 zàntíng, 停顿 tíngdùn ■ The children paused to pick raspberries along the trail. 孩子们在小路上停下采复盆子。Háizimen zài xiǎolùshang tíngxia cǎi fùpénzi.

pave v 铺（路）pū (lù)
to pave the way for sb/sth 为某人／某事铺设道路 wéi mǒurén/mǒushì pūshè dàolù, 为某事做准备 wéi mǒushì zhǔnbèi

pavement N 1 铺好的路面 pū hǎode lùmiàn 2 人行道 rénxíngdào

pavilion N **1** 展览馆 zhǎnlǎnguǎn **2** 亭子 tíngzi
paw I N (动物的)爪子 (dòngwù de) zhuǎzi II v **1** 用爪子抓 yòng zhuǎzi zhuā **2** 对 [+青年女子] 动手动脚 duì [+qīngnián nǚzǐ] dòngshǒu dòngjiǎo
pawn I N **1** (象棋)兵 (xiàngqí) bīng, 卒 zú **2** (被利用的)棋子 (bèi lìyòng de) qízǐ II v 典当 diǎndàng, 抵押 dǐyā
pawnbroker N 当铺老板 dàngpùlǎobǎn
pawnshop N 当铺 dàngpù
pay I v (PT & PP **paid**) 付 [+钱] fù [+qián], 付钱 (给某人) fùqián (gěi mǒurén)
　to pay attention to 注意 zhùyì, 关注 guānzhù
　to pay back 还(债) huán (zhài) ■ I'll pay you back next month. 我下个月还你钱。Wǒ xià ge yuè huán nǐ qián.
　to pay for 受惩罚 shòu chéngfá ■ Bruce had a car accident—he paid for his reckless driving. 布鲁斯出车祸了—他开车莽撞受到了惩罚。Bùlǔsī chū chēhuò le—tā kāichē mǎngzhuàng shòudàole chéngfá.
　to pay off ① 还清(债) huánqīng (zhài) ② 获得成功 huòdé chénggōng, 产生利润 chǎnshēng lìrùn
II N 工资 gōngzī, 报酬 bàochou
payable ADJ 应付的 yìngfu de
　(a check) payable to sb 应付给某人(的支票) yìngfu gěi mǒurén (de zhīpiào)
paycheck N 工资支票 gōngzī zhīpiào, 薪酬 xīnchóu
payday N 发薪日 fāxīnrì
payee N 收款人 shōukuǎnrén, 受款人 shòukuǎnrén
payload N (有效)载重量 (yǒuxiào) zàizhòngliàng
payment N 付款 fùkuǎn
payoff N 得益 déyì, 收益 shōuyì
pay phone N 公用电话 gōngyòng diànhuà
payroll N 发薪员工名单 fāxīn yuángōng míngdān
　be on the payroll (of a company) 是(一家公司的)雇员 shì (yì jiā gōngsī de) gùyuán
pay-TV N 收费电视(频道) shōufèi diànshì (píndào)
PBS (= Public Broadcasting System) ABBREV 公共广播公司 gōnggòng guǎngbō gōngsī
PC (= personal computer) ABBREV 个人电脑 gèrén diànnǎo [M. WD 台 tái]
PC (= politically correct) ABBREV 政治正确的 zhèngzhì zhèngquè de
PDA (= personal digital assistant) ABBREV 个人数字助手 gèrén shùzì zhùshǒu
pea N 豌豆 wāndòu [M. WD 粒 lì]
peace N **1** 和平 hépíng ■ Everybody wants peace; the question is on what condition. 人人想要和平；问题是什么样条件下的和平。Rénrén xiǎngyào

hépíng; wèntí shì shénmeyàng tiáojiànxia de hépíng. **2** 安静 ānjìng, 宁静 níngjìng ■ The peace of the summer afternoon was broken by a thunderstorm. 夏日午后的宁静被一场雷雨打破。Xiàrì wǔhòu de níngjìng bèi yì cháng léiyǔ dǎpò.
　to make peace with sb 和某人和解 hé mǒurén héjiě
peaceable ADJ 温和的 wēnhé de, 不爱争吵的 bú àizhēng chǎo de
Peace Corps N (美国)和平队 (Měiguó) Hépíngduì
peaceful ADJ **1** 和平的 hépíng de ■ Countries should seek peaceful co-existence. 各个国家应该追求和平共处。Gège guójiā yīnggāi zhuīqiú hépíng gòngchǔ. **2** 安静的 ānjìng de, 宁静的 níngjìng de
peacekeeping forces N (联合国)维持和平部队 (Liánhéguó) wéichí hépíng bùduì
peacemaker N 调停人 tiáotíngrén
peacetime N 和平时期 hépíng shíqī
peach N 桃树 táoshù [M. WD 棵 kē], 桃子 táozi
peacock N 孔雀 kǒngquè [M. WD 只 zhī]
peak I N 顶峰 dǐngfēng, 最高点 zuìgāodiǎn II v 达到顶峰 dádào dǐngfēng III ADJ 最高的 zuìgāo de
peal N 响亮的声音 xiǎngliàng de shēngyīn
　a peal of thunder 一阵雷声 yízhèn léishēng
　peals of laughter 一阵阵笑声 yízhèn zhèn xiàoshēng
peanut N 花生(米) huāshēng (mǐ) [M. WD 颗 kē]
　peanut butter 花生酱 huāshēngjiàng
peanuts N 很少的钱 hěn shǎo de qián
pear N 梨树 líshù [M. WD 棵 kē], 梨 lí
pearl N **1** 珍珠 zhēnzhū
　pearl necklace 一串珍珠项链 yíchuàn zhēnzhū xiàngliàn
2 珍珠色 zhēnzhū sè
peasant N 农民 nóngmín
peat N 泥炭 nítàn, 泥灰 níhuī
pebble N 卵石 luǎnshí [M. WD 块 kuài], 小圆石 xiǎo yuánshí [M. WD 块 kuài]
pecan N 山核桃树 shānhétao shù [M. WD 棵 kē], 山核桃 shānhétao [M. WD 颗 kē]
peck I v [鸟+] 啄 [niǎo+] zhuó **2** [情人+] 轻吻 [qíngrén+] qīng wěn II N **1** (鸟)啄 (niǎo) zhuó **2** 轻吻 qīng wěn
pecking order N (社群中的)等级 (shèqún zhōng de) děngjí
peculiar ADJ 怪异的 guàiyì de, 奇特的 qítè de
peculiarity N **1** 独特(性) dútè (xìng) **2** 奇异的东西 qíyì de dōngxi
pedagogical ADJ 教学上的 jiàoxué shàng de
pedagogy N 教学(法) jiàoxué (fǎ)
pedal I N 踏板 tàbǎn II v 踩踏板 cǎi tàbǎn
pedantic ADJ 学究似的 xuéjiū shìde, 书呆子气的 shūdāizi qì de

peddle v 兜售 dōushòu

pedestal N 基座 jīzuò
to place sb on a pedestal 偶像崇拜某人 ǒuxiàng chóngbài mǒurén

pedestrian I N 行人 xíngrén, 步行者 bùxíngzhě
II ADJ 1 行人的 xíngrén de
pedestrian crossing 行人横道线 xíngrén-héngdào xiàn
2 平淡无奇的 píngdàn wúqí de

pediatrician N 儿科医生 érkēyīshēng

pediatrics N 儿科 (学) érkē (xué)

pedicure N 修脚 xiūjiǎo

pedigree I N 血统 xuètǒng, 谱系 pǔxì II ADJ 纯种的 chúnzhǒng de

pee v, N 撒尿 sāniào, 小便 xiǎobiàn

peek I v 偷看 tōukàn II N 偷看 (一眼) tōukàn (yìyǎn)

peel I v 削/剥 [水果+] 皮 xiāo/bō [+shuǐguǒ] pí, [油漆+] 剥落 [yóuqī+] bōluò II N 果皮 guǒpí

peelings N (削/剥下的) 皮 (xiāo/bō xiàde) pí

peep N, v 偷看 tōukàn, 窥视 kuīshì

peephole N 窥视孔 kuīshìkǒng

peeping Tom N 喜欢偷看的人 xǐhuan tōukàn de rén, 窥视狂 kuīshìkuáng

peer¹ N 1 同龄 (或地位) 相同的人 tónglíng (huò dìwèi) xiāngtóng de rén, 同龄人 tónglíngrén, 同事 tóngshì, 同伴 tóngbàn
peer pressure 同辈人的压力 tóngbèi rén de yālì
2 (英国) 贵族 (Yīngguó) guìzú

peer² v 盯着看 dīngzhe kàn, 凝视 níngshì

peerless ADJ 无与伦比的 wú yǔ lúnbǐ de

peeve N 令人恼火的事 lìngrén nǎohuǒ de shì

peg I N 1 挂衣钩 guàyīgōu 2 (小提琴) 弦轴 (xiǎotíqín) xiánzhóu II v 把…固定在 (某一水平) bǎ...gùdìng zài (mǒu yì shuǐpíng)

pejorative ADJ 贬义的 biǎnyì de, 贬损的 biǎnsǔn de

Pekingese, Pekinese N 哈巴狗 hǎbagǒu [M. WD 只 zhī]

pelican N 鹈鹕 tíhú [M. WD 只 zhī]

pellet N 小硬球 xiǎo yìngqiú

pelt I v 连续投掷 liánxù tóuzhì, 扔 rēng II N 兽皮 shòupí [M. WD 张 zhāng]

pelvis N 骨盆 gǔpén

pen¹ I N 笔 bǐ
The pen is mightier than the sword. 文事胜武功。Wénshì shèng wǔgōng.
ball pen 圆珠笔 yuánzhūbǐ
fountain pen 钢笔 gāngbǐ
pen name 笔名 bǐmíng
pen pal 笔友 bǐyǒu
II v (用笔) 写 (yòngbǐ) xiě

pen² N (关养家畜的) 栏/圈 (guān yǎngjiā chū de) lán/quān

penal ADJ 刑罚的 xíng zuì de
penal code 刑法典 xíngfǎ diǎn
penal colony 罪犯流放地 zuìfàn liúfàng dì

penalize v 惩罚 chéngfá, 处罚 chǔfá

penalty N 惩罚 chéngfá, 处罚 chǔfá

penance N 自我惩罚 zìwǒ chéngfá, 忏悔 chànhuǐ

penchart N 嗜好 shìhào, 爱好 àihào

pencil N 铅笔 qiānbǐ
pencil drawing 铅笔画 qiānbǐ huà
pencil sharpener 削铅笔刀 xiāo qiānbǐ dāo, 削铅笔器 xiāo qiānbǐ qì

pendant N 挂件 guà jiàn, 垂饰 chuí shì

pending I PREP 当…时 dāng...shí, 直到 zhídào
II ADJ 1 未定的 wèidìng de 2 即将发生的 jíjiāng fāshēng de

pendulum N 钟摆 zhōngbǎi

penetrate v 1 进入 jìnrù, 打进 dǎjìn 2 穿透 chuāntòu, 渗透 shèntòu

penetrating ADJ 1 有深度的 [+见解] yǒu shēndù de [+jiànjiě], 有洞察力的 yǒu dòngchálì de 2 刺耳的 [+尖叫] cì'ěr de [+jiānjiào]

penguin N 企鹅 qǐ'é [M. WD 只 zhī/头 tóu]

penicillin N 青霉素 qīngméisù, 盘尼西林 pánníxīlín

peninsula N 半岛 bàndǎo

peninsular ADJ 半岛的 bàndǎo de

penis N 阴茎 yīnjīng

penitence N 忏悔 chànhuǐ, 悔过 huǐguò

penitent ADJ 忏悔的 chànhuǐ de, 悔过的 huǐguò de

penitentiary N 监狱 jiānyù [M. WD 座 zuò]

penknife N 小折刀 xiǎozhédāo

pennant N 三角旗 sānjiǎoqí [M. WD 面 miàn]

penniless ADJ 身无分文的 shēn wúfèn wén de, 一贫如洗的 yìpín rú xǐ de

penny N (英国/加拿大) 一分钱 (Yīngguó/Jiānádà) yì fēn qián

pension¹ N 养老金 yǎnglǎo jīn, 退休金 tuìxiū jīn
pension fund 退休基金 tuìxiū jījīn

pension² N (法国的) 旅舍 (Fǎguó de) lǚshè

pensioner N 领取养老金的人 lǐngqǔ yǎnglǎojīn de rén, 老年人 lǎoniánrén

pensive ADJ 忧伤的 yōushāng de

pentagon N 五边形 wǔbiānxíng

Pentagon N (美国) 五角大楼 (Měiguó) Wǔjiǎo Dàlóu

Pentecostal I ADJ 五旬节派教会的 wǔxúnjiépài jiàohuì de
Pentecostal churches 五旬节派教会 wǔxúnjiépài jiàohuì
II N 五旬节派教会教友 wǔxúnjiépài jiàohuì jiàoyǒu

penthouse N 楼顶公寓 lóudǐng gōngyù [M. WD 套 tào]

pent-up ADJ 郁结的 yùjié de

penury N 贫穷 pínqióng, 贫困·pínkùn

peon N 劳工 láogōng, 苦工 kǔgōng

people I N 人 rén, 人们 rénmen
the people 人民 rénmín ■ *Abraham Lincoln wished to establish in America a government of the people, by the people and for the people.* 亚伯拉罕·林肯希望在美国建立一个民有、民治、民享的政府。Yàbólāhǎn·Línkěn xīwàng zài Měiguó jiànlì yí ge mínyǒu, mínzhì, mínxiǎng de zhèngfǔ.
II v (be peopled with) 充满 chōng mǎn, 挤满 jǐmǎn
(the) People' Republic of China (PRC) N 中华人民共和国 Zhōnghuá Rénmín Gònghéguó

pep I v 使…充满活力 shǐ...chōngmǎn huólì
II N 活力 huólì, 精力 jīnglì
pep rally 动员大会 dòngyuán dàhuì
pep talk 鼓动士气的讲话 gǔdòng shìqì de jiǎnghuà, 打气的讲话 dǎqì de jiǎnghuà

pepper I N 胡椒粉 hújiāofěn, 辣椒粉 làjiāofěn
II v 1 撒胡椒粉 sā hújiāofěn 2 使 [+讲话] 有趣 shǐ [+jiǎnghuà] yǒuqù

peppermint N 薄荷 bòhe

pepperoni N (意大利) 辣味香肠 (Yìdàlì) làwèi xiāngcháng

Pepsi N 百事可乐 Bǎishì Kělè

per PREP 每 měi ■ *This hybrid car gets 50 miles per gallon of gasoline.* 这种油电两用汽车每五十英里耗油一加仑。Zhè zhǒng yóudiàn liǎngyòng qìchē měi wǔshí yīnglǐ hào yóu yì jiālún.

per capita ADJ, ADV 人均(的) rénjūn (de)

perceive v 1 察觉 chájué, 注意到 zhùyìdào 2 认为 rènwéi

percent (%) ADJ 百分之… bǎifēnzhī...

percentage N 百分比 bǎifēnbǐ

perceptible ADJ 可以察觉到的 kěyǐ chájué dào de

perception N 1 察觉 chájué 2 认为 rènwéi

perch I N 1 (鸟) 栖息处 (niǎo) qīxī chù 2 (观看的) 高处 (guānkàn de) gāo chù II v 1 [鸟+] 栖息 [niǎo+] qīxī 2 (be perched on) 位于 wèiyú

percolate v 用渗滤壶煮 (咖啡) yòng shènlǜ hú zhǔ (kāfēi)

percussion N 1 打击乐器 dǎjīyuèqì 2 撞击声 zhuàngjī shēng

peremptory ADJ 专横的 zhuānhèng de, 霸道的 bàdào de

perennial I ADJ 长期的 chángqī de, 多年的 duōnián de II N 多年生植物 duōniánshēng zhíwù

perfect I ADJ 完美的 wánměi de, 尽善尽美的 jìnshàn jìnměi de ■ *Nobody is perfect.* 没有人是完美的。(→金无足赤，人无完人。) Méiyǒu rén shì wánměi de. (→Jīn wú zúchì, rén wú wánrén. *As no gold is 100% pure, no man is perfect.*) Practice makes perfect. 熟能生巧。Shú néng shēng qiǎo. (→*Long experience produces skill.*)
II v 使…完美 shǐ...wánměi

perfection N 完美 wánměi, 完善 wánshàn

perfectionist N 完美主义者 wánměizhǔyì zhě

perfectly ADV 完美地 wánměi de, 完全 wánquán, 十分 shífēn

perforated ADJ 有齿孔的 yǒu chǐkǒng de

perform v 1 表演 biǎoyǎn, 演出 yǎnchū 2 做 zuò, 履行 lǚxíng ■ *The surgeon and his team are performing a delicate eye operation.* 外科医生和他的小组正在做一个精细的眼科手术。Wàikē yīshēng hé tā de xiǎozǔ zhèngzài zuò yí ge jīngxì de yǎnkē shǒushù.

performance N 1 演出 yǎnchū, 表演 biǎoyǎn 2 (工作) 表现 (gōngzuò) biǎoxiàn ■ *In December the management will review the performance of every staff member.* 管理人员将在十二月评估每个职工的表现。Guǎnlǐ rényuán jiāng zài shí'èr yuè pínggū měi ge zhígōng de biǎoxiàn.

performer N 表演者 biǎoyǎnzhě, 演出者 yǎnchūzhě

performing arts N 表演艺术 biǎoyǎn yìshù

perfume I N 香水 xiāngshuǐ II v 使…充满香气 shǐ...chōngmǎn xiāngqì

perfunctory ADJ 敷衍 (了事) fūyǎn (liǎoshì) de, 草率的 cǎoshuài de

perhaps ADV 或许 huòxǔ, 大概 dàgài

peril N 危险 wēixiǎn

perilous ADJ 危险的 wēixiǎn de, 险要的 xiǎnyào de

perimeter N 四周 sìzhōu, 周围 zhōuwéi

period I N 1 一段时间 yí duàn shíjiān, 时期 shíqī ■ *After the war there was a period of peace and prosperity.* 战后有一段和平繁荣的时期。Zhànhòu yǒu yí duàn hépíng fánróng de shíqí. 2 (在学校) 一节课 (zài xuéxiào) yì jié kè, 一堂课 yì táng kè 3 句号 jùhào ■ *While we use a dot as a period when writing English, the period for Chinese is a tiny circle.* 我们用写英文的时候，用一个点作为句号，而中文的句号是一个小圆圈。Wǒmen xiě Yīngwén de shíhou, yòng yí ge diǎn zuòwéi jùhào, ér Zhōngwén de jùhào shì yí ge xiǎo yuánquān. ■ *Period! No more discussion!* 就是这样，不用再说了。Jiùshì zhèyàng, bú yòng zài shuō le. 4 月经 yuèjīng II ADJ 特定历史时期的 tèdìng lìshǐ shíqí de
a period piece 历史戏剧／电影

periodic, periodical ADJ 定期的 dìngqī de

periodical N 期刊 qīkān [m. wɒ 本 běn], 杂志 zázhì [m. wɒ 本 běn]

periodically ADV 定期(地) dìngqī (de)

periodic table N (元素) 周期表 (yuánsù) zhōuqībiǎo

peripheral I ADJ 1 边缘的 biānyuán de, 外围的 wàiwéi de 2 次要的 cìyào de II N (计算机) 外围设备 (jìsuànjī) wàiwéi shèbèi

periphery N 边缘 biānyuán

periscope N 潜望镜 qiánwàngjìng [m. wɒ 台 tái]

perish v 1 死亡 sǐwáng 2 消亡 xiāowáng 3 [水果+] 腐烂 [shuǐguǒ+] fǔlàn

perishable ADJ [食物+] 易腐烂的 [shíwù+] yì fǔlàn de

perjure v 作伪证 zuò wěizhèng

perjury N 伪证（罪）wěizhèng (zuì)

perk I N 特殊福利 tèshū fúlì, 特权 tèquán II v 振作（起来）zhènzuò (qǐlái)

perky ADJ 自信而快活的 zìxìn ér kuàihuo de, 生气勃勃的 shēngqì bóbó de

perm N, v 烫发 tàngfà

permanence N 永久（性）yǒngjiǔ (xìng), 持久（性）chíjiǔ (xìng)

permanent ADJ 永久的 yǒngjiǔ de, 持久的 chíjiǔ de

permeate v 充满 chōngmǎn, 弥漫 mímàn

permissible ADJ 允许的 yǔnxǔ de, 许可的 xǔkě de

permission N 许可 xǔkě, 准许 zhǔnxǔ

permissive ADJ 放纵的 fàngzòng de, 宽容的 kuānróng de

permit I v 许可 xǔkě, 准许 zhǔnxǔ II N 许可（证）xǔkě (zhèng)

permutation N 排列 páiliè, 组合 zǔhé

pernicious ADJ 恶毒的 èdú de, 极有害的 jí yǒuhài de

perpendicular ADJ 垂直的 chuízhí de, 直立的 zhílì de

perpetrate v 犯（罪）fàn (zuì), 做（错事）zuò (cuò shì)

perpetrator N 犯罪者 fànzuìzhě, 作恶者 zuò'èzhě

perpetual ADJ 永恒的 yǒnghéng de, 持续不变的 chíxù búbiàn de

perpetuate v 使 [+坏事] 永远存在下去 shǐ [+huàishì] yǒngyuǎn cúnzài xiàqu

perplex v 使…困惑 shǐ...kùnhuò

perplexity N 困惑 kùnhuò, 茫然 mángrán

perquisite N See perk I (N)

per se ADV 本身 běnshēn, 就其本身而言 jiù qí běnshēn éryán

persecute v 迫害 pòhài

persecution N 迫害 pòhài
persecution complex 受迫害妄想症 shòupò hài wàngxiǎng zhēng

persecutor N 迫害者 pòhàizhě

perseverance N 坚韧（精神）jiānrèn (jīngshén)

persevere v 锲而不舍 qiè ér bù shě, 坚持不懈 jiānchí bú xiè

persist v 1 坚持 jiānchí, 执意 zhíyì 2 [坏天气+] 持续 [huài tiānqì+] chíxù

persistence N 坚持 jiānchí

persistent ADJ 1 坚持的 jiānchí de, 执意的 zhíyì de 2 持续的 [+大雨] chíxù de [+dàyǔ]

person N 人 rén
in person 亲自 qīnzì

persona N 表面人格 biǎomiàn réngé

personable ADJ 美貌而有风度的 měimào ér yǒu fēngdù de

personal ADJ 1 个人的 gèrén de, 私人的 sīrén de
personal belongings 个人物件 gèrén wùjiàn, 私人财物 sīrén cáiwù
personal computer 个人电脑 gèrén diànnǎo
personal hygiene 个人卫生 gèrén wèishēng
personal organizer 掌上电脑 zhǎngshàng diànnǎo
personal pronoun 人称代词 rénchēng dàicí
personal stereo 小型音响 xiǎoxíng yīnxiǎng, 随身听 suíshēn tīng
personal trainer 私人健身教练 sīrén jiànshēn jiàoliàn
2 人身攻击的 rénshēn gōngjī de, 批评个人的 pīpíng gèrénde ■ It's nothing personal—I just don't agree with your views. 我不是要批评你—我只是不同意你的观点。Wǒ bú shì yào pīpíng nǐ—wǒ zhǐ shì bù tóngyì nǐ de guāndiǎn.

personality N 1 个性 gèxìng, 性格 xìnggé 2 [电视+] 名人 [diànshì+] míngrén

personalize v 1 印上姓名 yìn shàng xìngmíng 2 个性化 gèxìng huà

personally ADV 就个人而言 jiù gèrén éryán

personals N（报纸上）个人信息栏 (bàozhǐ shàng) gèrén xìnxīlán

personification N 化身 huàshēn

personify v 是…的典范 shì...diǎnfàn

personnel N 1 全体员工 quántǐ yuángōng 2 人事部门 rénshì bùmén

perspective N 1 [看问题的+] 视角 [kàn wèntí de+] shìjiǎo, 观点 guāndiǎn
to keep … in perspective 正确认识 zhèngquè rènshi
2 透视画法 tòushì huàfǎ

perspiration N 汗水 hànshuǐ

perspire v 出汗 chūhàn, 流汗 liúhàn

persuade v 1 说服 shuōfú, 劝服 quànfú 2 使…相信 shǐ...xiāngxìn

persuasion N 说服 shuōfú, 劝服 quànfú

persuasive ADJ 有说服力的 yǒu shuōfúlì de

pert ADJ 1 活泼可爱的 [+女孩] huópo kě'ài de [+nǚhái] 2 调皮的 [+回答] tiáopí de [+huídá]

pertain v 与…直接有关 yǔ...zhíjiē yǒuguān

pertinent ADJ 直接有关的 zhíjiē yǒuguān de

perturbed ADJ 感到不安的 gǎndào bù'ān de, 烦恼的 fánnǎo de

peruse v 阅读 yuèdú

pervade v 弥漫 mímàn, 遍及 biànjí

pervasive ADJ 普遍的 pǔbiàn de, 无处不在的 wúchù búzài de

perverse ADJ 不合常理的 bùhé chánglǐ de, 乖张的 guāizhāng de

perversion N 1（性）变态 (xìng) biàntài 2 歪曲 wāiqū

pervert I v 使…变坏 shǐ…biànhuài, 破坏 pòhuài
II N 性变态者 xìng biàntàizhě
perverted ADJ 变态的 biàntài de, 荒谬的
huāngmiù de
pesky ADJ 令人讨厌的 lìngrén tǎoyàn de
pessimism N 悲观主义 bēiguānzhǔyì
pessimist N 悲观主义者 bēiguānzhǔyìzhě
pessimistic ADJ 悲观(主义)的 bēiguān (zhǔyì) de
pest N 有害动物 yǒuhài dòngwù [M. WD 只 zhī],
害虫 hàichóng [M. WD 只 zhī], 害鸟 hàiniǎo
[M. WD 只 zhī]
pester v 不断烦扰 búduàn fánrǎo, 纠缠 jiūchán
pesticide N 灭虫剂 miè chóng jì
pet I N 宠物 chǒngwù ■ *She keeps a piglet as
her pet.* 她养了一头小猪当宠物。Tā yǎngle yì tóu
xiǎozhū dāng chǒngwù.
pet name 小名 xiǎomíng, 昵称 nìchēng
pet store 宠物商店 chǒngwù shāngdiàn
II v 抚弄 fǔnòng, 摸 [+宠物] mō [+chǒngwù]
III ADJ 特别喜爱的 tèbié xǐ'ài de
petal N 花瓣 huābàn [M. WD 片 piàn]
peter v (to peter out) 逐渐减少 zhújiàn jiǎnshǎo
petite ADJ 娇小的 jiāoxiǎo de
petition I v 请愿 qǐngyuàn, 请求 qǐngqiú **II** N 请愿
(书) qǐngyuàn (shū)
petrified ADJ 惊呆了的 jīng dāi le de, 吓呆的
xiàdāi de
petrified wood 石化木 shíhuà mù
petrochemical N 石(油)化(学) shí (yóu) huà
(xué)
petroleum N 石油 shíyóu
petty ADJ 琐碎的 suǒsuì de, 小的 xiǎode
petty cash 小额现金 xiǎo'é xiànjīn
petty crime 轻罪 qīngzuì
petty officer N (海军)军士 (hǎijūn) jūnshì
[M. WD 名 míng]
petulant ADJ 随意发脾气的 suíyì fāpíqi de, 任性
暴躁的 rènxìng bàozao de
pew N (教堂)长木椅 (jiàotáng) cháng mù yǐ [M.
WD 排 pái/张 zhāng]
PG (= parental guidance) ADJ 在家长指导下观看
(的电影) zài jiā zhǎng zhǐdǎo xià guānkàn
(de diànyǐng)
phallic ADJ 阴茎的 yīnjīng de
phallus N 男性生殖器 nánxìng shēngzhíqì, 阴
茎 yīnjīng
phantom N **1** 幽灵 yōulíng, 鬼魂 guǐhún **2** 幻影
huànyǐng
pharmaceutical ADJ 制药(工业) zhìyào (gōngyè)
pharmacist N 药剂师 yàojìshī
pharmacologist N 药理学家 yàolǐxué jiā
pharmacology N 药理学 yàolǐxué
pharmacy N 药店 yàodiàn, 药房 yàofáng
Pharoah N 法老(古埃及统治者) Fǎlǎo (gǔ Āijí
tǒngzhìzhě)

phase I N 阶段 jiēduàn, 时期 shíqī **II** v (to phrase
in) 逐步实行 zhúbù shíxíng
to phase out 逐步停止 zhúbù tíngzhǐ
Ph.D. N 博士(学位) bóshì (xuéwèi)
pheasant N 雉 zhì (M. WD 只 zhī), 野鸡 yějī
phenomenal ADJ 非凡的 fēifán de, 不同寻常的
bùtóng xúncháng de
phenomenon N **1** 现象 xiànxiàng **2** 奇迹 qíjì, 奇
人 qírén
philanderer N 玩弄女性的人 wánnòng nǚxìng de
rén, 放荡公子 fàngdàng gōngzǐ
philandering N, ADJ 玩弄女性 wánnòng nǚxìng,
风流放荡 fēngliú fàngdàng
philanthropist N 慈善家 císhànjiā
philistine N 不懂文学艺术的人 bùdǒng wénxué
yìshù de rén, 没有教养的人 méiyǒu jiàoyǎng
de rén
philosopher N 哲学家 zhéxuéjiā
philosophical ADJ **1** 哲学的 zhéxué de **2** 想得开
的 xiǎng dé kāi de, 豁达的 huòdá de
philosophy N 哲学 zhéxué
phlegm N 痰 tán
phlegmatic ADJ 不会激动的 bú huì jīdòng de, 冷
漠的 lěngmò de
phobia N 恐惧 kǒngjù
phoenix N 凤凰 fènghuáng [M. WD 只 zhī]
phone I N 电话(机) diànhuà (jī)
phone booth (共用)电话亭 (gòngyòng) diàn-
huàtíng
phone number 电话号码 diànhuà hàomǎ
cordless phone 移动电话 yídòng diànhuà
to be on the phone 在打电话 zàidǎ diànhuà
II v 打电话 dǎ diànhuà ■ *I'll phone the doctor to
find out the test result.* 我要给医生打电话，了解
检查结果。Wǒ yào gěi yīshēng dǎ diànhuà, liǎojiě
jiánchá jiéguǒ.
phonetic ADJ 语音的 yǔyīn de
phonetics N 语音学 yǔyīnxué
phony, phoney I ADJ **1** 假冒 [+产品] 的 jiǎmào
[+chǎnpǐn] de **2** 假装的 [+友好] jiǎzhuāng
de [+yǒuhǎo], 虚伪的 xūwěi de **II** N 伪造品
wěizàopǐn, 虚假的东西 xūjiǎ de dōngxi
phosphorescence N 磷光 línguāng
phosphorescent ADJ 发磷光的 fā línguāng de
phosphorus (P) N 磷 lín
photo N 照片 zhàopiàn, 象片 xiàng piàn
photo finish ① 摄影定胜负 shèyìng dìng
shèngfù ② 难分胜负的比赛 nánfēn shèngfù de
bǐsài
photocopier N 复印机 fùyìnjī [M. WD 台 tái]
photocopy I N 复印件 fùyìnjiàn, 影印件 yǐngyìn
II v 复印 fùyìn, 影印 yǐngyìn
photogenic ADJ 上镜(头)的 shàng jìng (tóu)
de, 上相的 shàngxiàng de
photograph N 照片 zhàopiàn

photographer N 摄影师 shèyǐngshī, 摄影家 shèyìng jiā

photographic ADJ 摄影的 shèyǐng de

photography N 摄影 (术) shèyǐng (shù)

photosynthesis N 光合作用 guānghé zuòyòng

phrasal verb N 短语动词 duǎnyǔ dòngcí

phrase I N 1 短语 duǎnyǔ, 词组 cízǔ 2 警句 jǐngjù, 隽语 juànyǔ ■ *"Equal pay for equal work" is a phrase trade unions often use.* "同工同酬" 是工会经常使用的警句。"Tónggōng tóngchóu" shì gōnghuì jīngcháng shǐyòng de jǐngjù. II v (用词语) 表达 (yòngcí yǔ) biǎodá

phrasing N 1 措词 cuòcí, 选词 xuǎn cí 2 乐句划分 yuèjù huàfēn

physical I ADJ 1 身体的 shēntǐ de ■ *His problem is physical, not mental.* 他是身体有问题，不是精神有问题。Tā shì shēntǐ yǒu wèntí, bú shì jīngshén yǒu wèntí. 2 物质的 wùzhì de ■ *The police have so far not got any physical evidence of his crime.* 警方目前还没有掌握他犯罪的物质证据。Jǐngfāng mùqián hái méiyǒu zhǎngwò tā fànzuì de wùzhì zhèngjù.

physical education (PE) 体育 tǐyù

physical examination/checkup 体格检查 tǐgé jiǎnchá

physical therapy 物理疗法 wùlǐliáofǎ, 理疗 lǐliáo II N 体格检查 tǐgé jiǎnchá

physician N (内科) 医生 (nèikē) yīshēng [M. WD 位 wèi]

physicist N 物理学家 wùlǐxuéjiā [M. WD 位 wèi]

physics N 物理 (学) wùlǐ (xué)

physiology N 1 生理学 shēnglǐxué 2 生理 (机能) shēnglǐ (jīnéng)

physiotherapy N 物理疗法 wùlǐliáofǎ, 理疗 lǐliáo

physique N 体格 tǐgé

pi (π) N 圆周率 yuánzhōulǜ (= 3.1416)

pianist N 钢琴演奏者 gāngqín yǎnzòuzhě, 钢琴家 gāngqínjiā [M. WD 位 wèi]

piano N 钢琴 gāngqín [M. WD 架 jià]

piccolo N 短笛 duǎndí [M. WD 支 zhī]

pick I v 1 挑选 tiāoxuǎn 2 采 cǎi, 采集 cǎijí ■ *Some farmers hire illegal immigrants to pick fruit.* 有些农民雇佣非法移民来采摘水果。Yǒuxiē nóngmín gùyòng fēifǎ yímín lái cǎizhāi shuǐguǒ. 3 挖 wā, 剔 tī

to pick one's nose 挖鼻孔 wā bíkǒng

to pick up ① (使) 站起来 (shǐ) zhànqǐlai ■ *Pick yourself up, Tom!* 汤姆，自己站起来! Tāngmǔ, zìjǐ zhànqǐlai! ② 拣起来 jiǎnqǐlai, 收拾起 shōushiqǐ ③ 好转 hǎozhuǎn ■ *Sales will pick up in November.* 到十一月销售会好转的。Dào shíyī yuè xiāoshòu huì hǎozhuǎn de. ④ (开汽车) 接人 (kāi qìchē) jiē rén ⑤ 结识 jiéshí, 搭上 dāshang ■ *He picked up a young woman at the bar on Friday night.* 他星期五晚上在酒吧搭上了一个青年

女子。Tā xīngqīwǔ wǎnshang zài jiǔbā dāshangle yí ge qīngnián nǚzǐ.

to pick on 找…的岔子 zhǎo…de chàzi ■ *Why are you always picking on me?* 你为什么老是找我的岔子? Nǐ wèishénme lǎoshi zhǎo wǒ de chàzi?

to pick and choose 挑挑拣拣 tiāotiāo jiǎnjiǎn II N 1 挑选 tiāoxuǎn 2 最好的 zuìhǎo de, 精华 jīnghuá

pickax N 镐 gǎo, 鹤嘴锄 hèzuǐchú [M. WD 把 bǎ]

picket I N 1 抗议者 kàngyìzhě 2 (罢工) 纠察队 (bàgōng) jiūcháduì

picket line 纠察线 jiūcháxiàn

II v 1 抗议示威 kàngyì shìwēi 2 [罢工工人+] 设置纠察队 [bàgōng gōngrén+] shèzhì jiūcháduì

pickings N 可挑选的东西 kě tiāoxuǎn de dōngxi

pickle I N 1 酸黄瓜 suānhuánggua 2 腌菜 yāncài II v 腌制 [+黄瓜] yānzhì [+huánggua]

pick-me-up N 兴奋饮料 xīngfèn yǐnliào, 兴奋药物 xīngfèn yàowù

pickpocket N 扒手 páshǒu, 贼 zéi

Beware of pickpockets. 谨防扒手。Jǐnfáng páshǒu.

pickup I N 1 敞篷小货车 chǎngpéng xiǎo huòchē [M. WD 辆 liàng] 2 增加 zēngjiā, 提高 tígāo 3 提取的时间 tíqǔ de shíjiān II ADJ 临时拼凑的 [+游戏／比赛] línshí pīncòu de [+yóuxì/bǐsài]

picky ADJ 挑剔的 tiāoti de

picnic I N 1 野餐 yěcān 2 轻松愉快的事 qīngsōng yúkuài de shì II v 举行野餐 jǔxíng yěcān

pictorial I ADJ 有图片的 yǒu túpiàn de II N 画报 huàbào [M. WD 本 běn]

picture N 1 画 huà, 图画 túhuà

picture book 图画书 túhuà shū [M. WD 本 běn] 2 照片 zhàopiàn [M. WD 张 zhāng] ■ *He took many pictures of his daughter's birthday party.* 他在女儿的生日聚会上拍了很多照片。Tā zài nǚ'ér de shēngrì jùhuìshang pāile hěn duō zhàopiàn. 3 情景 qíngjǐng ■ *The movie gives a vivid picture of the Civil War.* 这部电影生动地体现了美国南北战争的情景。Zhè bù diànyǐng shēngdòng de tǐxiànle Měiguó Nán-Běi zhànzhēng de qíngjǐng. 4 [电视+] 图像 [diànshì+] túxiàng

picturesque ADJ 风景如画的 fēngjǐng rú huà de

piddling ADJ 琐碎的 suǒsuì de, 微不足道的 wēi bùzú dào de

pidgin N 混杂语言 hùnzá yǔyán, 洋泾浜 yáng-jīngbāng

pie N 馅饼 xiànbǐng [M. WD 块 kuài]

as easy as pie 极容易 jí róngyì

pie in the sky 空中楼阁 kōngzhōng lóugé

pot pie 菜肉馅饼 càiròuxiànbǐng

piece I N 1 块 kuài, 份 fèn, 片 piàn ■ *She gave every child a big piece of the cake.* 她给每个孩子一大块蛋糕。Tā gěi měi ge háizi yí dà kuài dàngāo. 2 件 jiàn, 条 tiáo a piece of advice 一个忠告 yí ge zhōnggào

a piece of information 一条信息 yì tiáo xìnxī

a piece of news 一条新闻 yì tiáo xīnwén

a piece of paper 一张纸 yì zhāng zhǐ

to go to pieces 精神崩溃 jīngshén bēngkuì ■ *After the disappearance of their daughter, the couple almost went to pieces.* 女儿失踪以后，这对夫妻几乎精神崩溃了。Nǚ'ér shīzōng yǐhòu, zhè duì fūqī jīhū jīngshén bēngkuì le.

to smash/tear to pieces 砸／撕得粉碎 zá/sīde fěnsuì

to be a piece of cake 容易极了 róngyì jíle, 轻而易举 qīng ér yì jǔ ■ *Taking care of a small child is not a piece of cake.* 照看小孩可不是轻而易举的事。Zhàokàn xiǎohái kě bú shì qīng ér yì jǔ de shì.

II v (to piece together) [把细节+] 拼合起来 [bǎxì jié+] pīnhé qǐlái

piecemeal ADJ, ADV 一步一步（的）yíbù yíbù (de), 逐步（的）zhúbù (de)

piecework N 计件工作 jìjiàn gōngzuò

pie chart N 圆形统计图 yuánxíng tǒngjìtú

pier N 1（突堤）码头 (tū dī) mǎtou 2 桥墩 qiáodūn

pierce V 刺穿 cì chuān

pierced ears 耳朵穿孔的 ěrduo chuānkǒng de

piercing ADJ 1 刺耳的 [+声音] cì'ěr de [+shēngyīn], 尖利的 jiānlì de 2 锐利的 [+眼光] ruìlì de [+yǎnguāng]

piety N 虔诚的 qiánchéng de

pig I N 1 猪 zhū [M. WD 头 tóu] 2 贪吃的人 tānchī de rén, 肮脏的人 āngzāng de rén II v (to pig out) 大吃（大喝）dà chī (dà hē)

pigeon N 鸽子 gēzi [M. WD 只 zhī]

pigeonhole I N 信件格 xìnjiàn gé, 文件格 wénjiàn gé II v 把 [人+] 不公平地归类 bǎ [rén+] bùgōngpíng de guīlèi

pigeon-toed ADJ 内八字的 nèi bāzì de

piggy N 小猪 xiǎo zhū [M. WD 头 tóu]

piggy bank 储蓄罐 chǔxù guàn

piggyback ride N 骑在别人背上 qí zài biéren bēishàng

pigheaded ADJ 固执的 gùzhí de, 顽固的 wángù de

piglet N 小猪 xiǎo zhū, 猪崽 zhūzǎi

pigment N 1（天然）色素 (tiānrán) sèsù 2 颜料 yánliào

pigmentation N 天然颜色 tiānrán yánsè

pigpen, pigsty N 1 猪圈 zhūjuàn, 猪栏 zhūlán 2 极其肮脏凌乱的地方 jíqí āngzāng língluàn de dìfang

pigtail N 发辫 fàbiàn [M. WD 条 tiáo], 辫子 biànzi [M. WD 条 tiáo]

pike N 1 收费高速公路 shōufèi gāosù gōnglù [M. WD 条 tiáo] 2 狗鱼 gǒuyú [M. WD 条 tiáo] 3 长矛 chángmáo

pile I N 1（一大）堆 (yí dà) duī 2 大量 dàliàng, 许多 xǔduō ■ *After a week's absence from the office, I found a pile of mail in my inbox.* 我一个星期没有上班，发现电子邮件的邮箱里有很多很多的邮件。Wǒ yí ge xīngqī méiyǒu shàngbān, fāxiàn diànzǐ yóujiàn de yóuxiāng lǐ yǒu hěn duō hěn duō de yóujiàn. 3 桩（子）zhuāng (zi) II v 堆起来 duīqǐlái

piles See **hemorrhoids**

pile-up N 多车相撞（事故）duō chē xiāngzhuàng (shìgù)

pilfer V 偷窃 [+不太值钱的东西] tōuqiè [+bútài zhíqián de dōngxi], 小偷小摸 xiǎotōu xiǎomō

pilgrim N 朝圣者 cháoshèngzhě

pilgrimage N 朝圣 cháoshèng

piling N 房柱 fáng zhù [M. WD 根 gēn],（桥）墩 (qiáo) dūn

pill N 药片 yàopiàn [M. WD 片 piàn]

the pill 口服避孕药 kǒufú bìyùnyào [M. WD 片 piàn]

pillar N 房柱 fángzhù [M. WD 根 gēn], 柱子 zhùzi [M. WD 根 gēn]

pillion N 摩托车后座 mótuōchē hòuzuò

to ride pillion 骑在摩托车后座 qí zài mótuōchē hòuzuò

pillow N 枕头 zhěntou

pillow case 枕头套 zhěntoutào

pilot I N 1（飞机）驾驶员 (fēijī) jiàshǐyuán, 飞行员 fēixíng yuán 2 领港员 lǐnggǎngyuán II v 驾驶（飞机）jiàshǐ (fēijī) III ADJ 试验性的 shìyànxìng de, 试点的 shìdiǎn de

pilot project 试验项目 shìyàn xiàngmù ■ *Our school will launch a pilot project for the new curriculum.* 我们学校将开始新课程的试验项目。Wǒmen xuéxiào jiāng kāishǐ xīn kèchéng de shìyàn xiàngmù.

pilot light ①（煤气灶）常燃火苗 (méiqìzào) cháng ránhuǒ miáo ②（显示通电的）指示灯 (xiǎnshì tōngdiàn de) zhǐshìdēng

pimp N 拉皮条的男子 lāpítiáo de nánzǐ

pimple N 粉刺 fěncì

PIN (= personal identity number) ABBREV 个人密码 gèrén mìmǎ ■ *Do not tell your PIN to anybody!* 别把你的个人密码告诉任何人。Bié bǎ nǐ de gèrén mìmǎ gàosu rènhé rén.

pin I N 1 大头针 dàtóuzhēn, 别针 biézhēn

safety pin 安全别针 ānquán biézhēn, 别针 biézhēn 2 饰针 shìzhēn

rolling pin 擀面杖 gǎnmiàn zhàng

tie pin 领带扣针 lǐngdài kòuzhēn 3（保龄球）球柱 (bǎolíngqiú) qiúzhù

II v 1 把…固定住 bǎ…gùdìng zhù

to pin down 使…明确表态 shǐ…míngquè biǎotài, 使…详细说明 shǐ…xiángxì shuōmíng 2 (to pin one's hope on sb/sth) 把希望寄托在

某人／某事上 bǎ xīwàng jìtuō zài mǒurén/ mǒushì shàng

pinball N 弹球游戏 tánqiú yóuxì

pincer N 螯 áo

pincers N 钳子 qiánzi [M. WD 把 bǎ]

pinch I v 1 掐 qiā, 拧 nǐng, 夹 jiā 2 偷 tōu, 顺手牵羊 shùnshǒu qiān yáng II N 掐 qiā, 拧 nǐng, 夹 jiā

pinch of salt 一撮盐 yì cuō yán

to take sth with a pinch of salt 对（某事）心存怀疑 duì (mǒushì) xīn cún huáiyí

pinched ADJ 1 资金不足的 zījīn bùzúde, 拮据的 jiéjū de 2 消瘦的 xiāoshòu de

pinch-hit v（棒球比赛中）替补击球 (bàngqiú bǐsài zhōng) tìbǔ jīqiú

pincushion N 针垫 zhēndiàn

pine[1] N 松树 sōngshù [M. WD 棵 kē]

pine cone 松果 sōngguǒ, 松球 sōngqiú

pine needle 松针 sōngzhēn

pine[2] v (to pine for sb) 苦苦思念某人 kǔkǔ sīniàn mǒurén

pineapple N 菠萝 bōluó, 凤梨 fènglí

ping N 砰的一声 pēng de yì shēng

ping-pong N 乒乓球（运动）pīngpāngqiú (yùndòng)

pinion v 剪去 [+鸟的] 飞羽 jiǎn qù [+niǎo de] fēiyǔ

pink I ADJ 粉红的 fěnhóng de, 淡红的 dànhóng de, 浅红的 qiǎnhóng de II N 粉红 fěnhóng, 淡红 dànhóng, 浅红 qiǎnhóng

pink slip ① 汽车所有权证明 qìchē suǒyǒuquán zhèngmíng ② 解雇通知书 jiěgù tōngzhīshū

pinnacle N 1 顶点 dǐngdiǎn, 顶峰 dǐngfēng 2（教堂的）顶尖 (jiàotáng de) dǐngjiān

pinpoint N 极小的点 jíxiǎo de diǎn

with pinpoint accuracy 极其精确 jíqí jīngquè II v 精确地说出 jīngquè de shuōchū

pinprick N（用针刺出来的）小孔 (yòng zhēncì chūlái de) xiǎokǒng

pins and needles N 发麻 fāmá, 针刺感 zhēncì gǎn

on pins and needles 坐立不安 zuòlì bù'ān

pinstripe N 细条纹 xìtiao wén

pinstriped ADJ 有细条纹的 yǒu xì tiáowén de

a pinstriped suit 一套条纹西服 yítào tiáowén xīfú

pint N 品脱 pǐntuō (= 0.4732 liter)

pinup N 性感美女图 xìnggǎn měinǚtú [M. WD 张 zhāng]

pioneer I N 先锋 xiānfēng, 先驱 xiānqū [M. WD 位 wéi] II v 开创 kāichuàng, 当先驱 dāngxiān qū

pious ADJ 虔诚的 qiánchéng de

pip N 1 [苹果的+] 籽 [píngguǒ de+] zǐ, 种子 zhǒngzi 2（骰子的）点 (tóuzi de) diǎn

pipe I N 1 管道 guǎndào 2 烟斗 yāndǒu ■ Very few people smoke a pipe these days. 现在很少人抽烟斗。Xiànzài hěn shǎo rén chōu yāndǒu.

pipe dream 白日梦 báirìmèng

sewer pipe 污水管 wūshuǐ guǎn

II v 1 用管道运输 yòng guǎndàoyùnshū 2 吹奏（管乐器）chuīzòu (guǎnyuèqì)

pipeline N 管道 guǎndào

in the pipeline [计划+] 正在进行中 [jìhuà+] zhèngzài jìnxíngzhōng

piping I N 管道系统 guǎndào xìtǒng II ADV (piping hot) 非常烫的 fēicháng tàng de

pipsqueak N 无足轻重的小人物 wúzú qīngzhòng de xiǎorénwù

piquant ADJ 1 辛辣开胃的 [+食物] xīnlà kāiwèi de [+shíwù] 2 有趣的 [+故事] yǒuqù de [+gùshi], 激动人心的 jīdòng rénxīn de

pique I v 1 激起 [+好奇心] jīqǐ [+hàoqíxīn] 2 使…生气 shǐ…shēngqì II N 激怒 jīnù

in a fit of pique 一怒之下 yí nù zhīxià

piracy N 1 海盗（行为）hǎidào (xíngwéi) 2（出版物）非法翻印 (chūbǎnwù) fēifǎ fānyìn,（电子产品）非法复制 (diànzǐ chǎnpǐn) fēifǎ fùzhì, 盗版 dàobǎn

pirate I N 1 盗版者 dàobǎn zhě, 偷盗版权的人 tōudào bǎnquán de rén 2 海盗 hǎidào II v 盗版 dàobǎn, 偷盗版权 tōudào bǎnquán

pirated edition 盗版本 dàobǎn běn

pirated DVD 盗版的DVD dàobǎn de DVD

Pisces N 双鱼宫 shuāngyú gōng

piss v, N 撒尿 sāniào

pissed, pissed off ADJ 恼火的 nǎohuǒ de, 失望的 shīwàng de

pistol N 手枪 shǒuqiāng [M. WD 把 bǎ]

piston N 活塞 huósāi

pit I N 1 坑 kēng, 大坑 dà kēng 2 矿井 kuàngjǐng 3 麻点 mádiǎn 4（水果）硬核 (shuǐguǒ) yìng hé

cherry pit 樱桃核 yīngtáo hé

II v 1 去核 qù hé 2 留下伤痕 liúxia shānghén

pit bull N 比特犬 bǐtè quǎn, 凶猛的狗 xiōngměng de gǒu

pitch I v 1（棒球）当投手 (bàngqiú) dāng tóushǒu ■ Jim will pitch for his team for the first time tomorrow. 杰姆明天要第一次当投手。Jiémǔ míngtiān yào dìyī cì dāng tóushǒu. 2 定调 dìngdiào, 定音 dìngyīn ■ The song is pitched too high for me. 这首歌音调太高，我唱不上去。Zhè shǒu gē yīndiào tài gāo, wǒ chàng bú shàngqù. 3 (to pitch a tent) 搭帐篷 dā zhàngpéng II N 1（棒球）投球 (bàngqiú) tóuqiú 2 音调 yīndiào 3 沥青 lìqīng

pitch black 漆黑 qīhēi

pitcher N 1（茶）壶 (chá) hú 2（棒球）投手 (bàngqiú) tóushǒu

pitchfork N 干草叉 gāncǎochā [M. WD 把 bǎ]

piteous ADJ 让人怜悯的 ràng rén liánmǐn de

pitfall N 陷井 xiànjǐng, 隐患 yǐnhuàn

pitiful ADJ 1 可怜的 kělián de 2 很糟糕的 hěn zāogāo de, 蹩脚的 biéjiǎo de

pitiless ADJ 没有怜悯心的 méiyǒu liánmǐn xīn de, 冷酷的 lěngkù de

pit-stop N（赛车中的）停车加油维修时间 (sàichē zhòngde) tíngchē jiāyóu wéixiū shíjiān
to make a pit-stop（长途驾车旅行中）中途停车休息 (chángtú jiàchē lǚxíngzhōng) zhōngtú tíngchē xiūxi

pittance N 少得可怜的钱 shǎo dé kělián de qián

pity I N 1 怜悯 liánmǐn, 可怜 kělián ■ She was full of pity for the orphan. 她对这个孤儿充满了怜悯。Tā duì zhè ge gū'ér chōngmǎnle liánmǐn. 2 可惜 kěxī, 遗憾 yíhàn II v 怜悯 liánmǐn, 同情 tóngqíng

pivot I N 1 支点 zhīdiǎn, 支轴 zhī zhóu 2 关键（人物或事情）guānjiàn (rénwù huò shìqing), 中心 zhōngxīn II v（在支轴上）移动 (zài zhī zhóu shàng) yídòng

pivotal ADJ 关键的 guānjiàn de, 至关重要的 zhìguān zhòngyào de

pixel N 像素 xiàngsù, 像点 xiàng diǎn

pixie N 小妖怪 xiǎo yāoguài, 小精灵 xiǎo jīnglíng

pizza N 比萨饼 bǐsà bǐng, 意大利馅饼 Yìdàlì xiànbǐng
Pizza Hut 必胜客 Bìshèngkè, 比萨饼店 bǐsà bǐngdiàn

placard N 1 标语牌 biāoyǔpái, 广告牌 guǎnggàopái [m. wd 块 kuài] 2 布告 bùgào, 招贴 zhāotiē [m. wd 张 zhāng]

placate v 使…平息 shǐ…píngxī, 安抚 ānfǔ

placatory ADJ 安抚性的 ānfǔ xìng de

place I N 1 地方 dìfang 2 地位 dìwèi, 身份 shēnfen ■ He often drops hints that he knows people in high places. 他常常暗示，认识地位很高的人。Tā chángcháng ànshì, rènshi dìwèi hěn gāo de rén. 3 场合 chǎnghé ■ To be in the right places with the right people—that is what she always tries to do. 在适当的场合，和适当的人在一起——她总是极力这么做。Zài shìdàng de chǎnghé, hé shìdàng de rén zàiyìqǐ—tā zǒngshì jílì zhème zuò. 4 位子 wèizi ■ Will you please keep me a place in the auditorium? I'll be there in a minute. 你在礼堂里给我留个位子，好不好？我一会儿就到。Nǐ zài lǐtáng lǐ gěi wǒ liú ge wèizi, hǎobuhǎo? Wǒ yíhuìr jiù dào. II v 1 把…放在 bǎ…fàng zài, 使…处于 shǐ…chǔyú 2 确定价格／年代 quèdìng jiàgé/niándài
to place a call 打电话 dǎ diànhuà
to place an order 下订单 xià dìngdān
to take place 发生 fāshēng ■ No one knows exactly what took place that night. 没有人确切地知道那天夜里发生了什么。Méiyǒurén quèqiè de

zhīdào nàtiān yèlǐ fāshēngle shénme.

placebo N 1（做药物试验用的）无效对照剂 (zuò yàowù shìyànyòng de) wúxiào duìzhàojì 2 安慰剂 ānwèijì

placement N 1 安置 ānzhì 2 放置 fàngzhì, 布置 bùzhì

placenta N 胎盘 tāipán

placid ADJ 平静的 píngjìng de, 宁静的 níngjìng de

plagiarism N 剽窃（行为）piāoqiè (xíngwéi), 抄袭（行为）chāoxí (xíngwéi)

plagiarist N 剽窃者 piāoqièzhě, 抄袭者 chāoxízhě

plagiarize v 剽窃 piāoqiè, 抄袭 chāoxí

plague I N 1 瘟疫 wēnyì 2 鼠疫 shǔyì 3 祸害 huòhai, 麻烦 máfan II v 困扰 kùnrǎo, 烦扰 fánrǎo

plaid N（布料的）彩格图案 (bùliào de) cǎi gé tú'àn

plain I ADJ 1 明白的 míngbai de, 明显的 míngxiǎn de 2 简单的 jiǎndān de, 朴素的 pǔsù de ■ I find her all the more attractive when she wears that plain white dress. 她穿了那条朴素的白裙子，我觉得更漂亮。Tā chuānle nà tiáo pǔsù de báqúnzi, wǒ juéde gèng piàoliang. 3 坦率的 [+话] tǎnshuài de [+huà]
plain truth 坦率的事实 tǎnshuài de shìshí, 老实话 lǎoshi huà
II N 平原 píngyuán

plainclothes ADJ 穿便衣的 [+警察] chuān biànyī de [+jǐngchá]

plainly ADV 1 清楚地 qīngchu de, 明显地 míngxiǎn de 2 坦率地 [+说话] tǎnshuài de [+shuōhuà] 3 朴素地 [+穿衣] pǔsù de [+chuān yī]

plaintiff N 原告 yuángào, 起诉人 qǐsùrén

plaintive ADJ 哀伤的 āishāng de

plan I N 1 计划 jìhuà, 规划 guīhuà 2 平面图 píngmiàntú 3 示意图 shìyìtú II v 计划 jìhuà, 订计划 dìng jìhuà ■ We should plan our overseas holiday carefully. 我们应该仔细计划我们的海外旅游。Wǒmen yīnggāi zǐxì jìhuà wǒmen de hǎiwài lǚyóu.

plane I N 1 飞机 fēijī 2 平面 píngmiàn
plane geometry 平面几何 píngmiàn jǐhé 3 刨子 bàozi [m. wd 把 bǎ] II ADJ 平面的 píngmiàn de III v 用刨子刨平 yòng bàozi bàopíng

planet N 行星 xíngxīng

planetarium N 天文馆 tiānwénguǎn [m. wd 座 zuò], 太空馆 tàikōng guǎn [m. wd 座 zuò]

plank N 厚木板 hòu mùbǎn [m. wd 块 kuài/条 tiáo]

plankton N 浮游生物 fúyóushēngwù

planner N 规划者 guīhuàzhě, 策划者 cèhuàzhě

planning N 计划 jìhuà, 规划 guīhuà
family planning 计划生育 jìhuà shēngyù

plant I N 1 植物 zhíwù, 作物 zuòwù ■ This botanical garden boasts of some rare plants. 这座植

物园拥有一些稀有植物。Zhè zuò zhíwù yuán yōngyǒu yìxiē xīyǒu zhíwù. 2 花 huā, 花草 huācǎo 3 厂 chǎng, 工厂设备 gōngchǎng shèbèi 4 栽赃物 zāizāng wù 5 间谍 jiàndié II v 1 种 zhǒng, 种植 zhòngzhí ■ *A forestry company will plant pine trees on the mountain slopes here.* 一家森林公司将在这里的山坡上植松树。Yī jiā sēnlín gōngsī jiāng zài zhèlǐ de shānpōshang zhí sōngshù. 2 安插 [+间谍] ānchā [+jiàndié]

plantation N 1 庄园 zhuāngyuán 2 种植园 zhòngzhíyuán

planter N 1 种植者 zhòngzhí zhě 2 种植机 zhòngzhí jī [M. WD 台 tái] 3 花盆 huāpén [M. WD 只 zhǐ]

plaque N 1 （金属或石料的）饰板 (jīnshǔ huò shíliào de) shì bǎn 2 牙斑 yá bān

plasma N 1 血浆 xuèjiāng 2 等离子体 děnglí zǐtǐ

plaster I N 1 灰泥 huīní 2 熟石膏 shúshígāo
plaster cast 石膏绷带 shígāo bēngdài, 石膏夹 shígāo jiā
3 橡皮膏 xiàngpígāo II v 1 抹石灰 mǒ shíhuī 2 在…上厚厚地涂抹 zài...shàng hòu hòu de túmǒ

plastered ADJ 喝得烂醉的 hē dé lànzuì de

plastic I N 塑料 sùliào
plastic surgery 整容外科 zhěngróng wàikē, 整容手术 zhěngróng shǒushù
II ADJ 做作的 [+笑容] zuòzuo de [+xiàoróng], 不自然的 bú zìrán de

plasticity N 可塑性 kěsùxìng

plate N 1 盘子 pánzi, 碟子 diézi 2 （镀金／银的）金属 (dùjīn/yín de) jīnshǔ, 镀金／银的器皿 dùjīn/yín de qìmǐn 3 假牙 jiǎyá, 牙齿校正器 yáchǐ jiàozhèngqì

plateau I N 1 高原 gāoyuán 2 稳定时期 wěndìng shíqī II v 进入稳定时期 jìnrù wěndìng shíqī

plated ADJ 镀 [+金银] 的 dù [+jīn/yín] de

platelet N 血小板 xuèxiǎobǎn

platform N 1 讲台 jiǎngtái, 舞台 wǔtái 2 （火车站）站台 (huǒchēzhàn) zhàntái, 月台 yuètái 3 （钻井）平台 (zuànjǐng) píngtái 4 （政党）纲领 (zhèngdǎng) gānglǐng

plating N 金属镀层 jīnshǔ dùcéng

platinum (Pt) N 铂 bó, 白金 báijīn

platitude N 老生常谈 lǎoshēng chángtán, 陈词滥调 chéncí làndiào

platonic ADJ 柏拉图式的 Bólātú shì de, 纯精神恋爱的 chún jīngshén liàn'ài de

platoon N （军队）排 (jūnduì) pái

platter N 大盘子 dà pánzi
seafood platter 海鲜大拼盘 hǎixiān dà pīnpán

platypus N 鸭嘴兽 yāzuǐshòu [M. WD 只 zhǐ]

plaudits N 赞扬 zànyáng, 颂扬 sòngyáng

plausible ADJ 似有道理的 sìyǒu dàolǐ de, 可信的 kě xìn de

play I v 1 玩 wán, 玩耍 wánshuǎ ■ *Tommy is playing with the dog—both are having a really swell time!* 汤米在玩狗—人和狗都玩得可高兴了！Tāngmǐ zàiwán gǒu—rén hé gǒu dōu wánde kě gāoxìng le! 2 比赛 bǐsài ■ *In the 2006 Football World Cup final, France played against Italy.* 二〇〇六年世界足球杯决赛时，法国队对意大利队。Èr líng líng liù nián shìjiè zúqiú bēi juésài shí, Fǎguó duì duì Yìdàlì duì. 3 打 (球) dǎ (qiú), 下 (棋) xià (qí) 4 演奏 yǎnzòu, 弹 dàn, 拉 lā 5 演 yǎn, 表演 biǎoyǎn II N 1 游戏 yóuxì
All work and no play makes Jack a dull boy. 整天工作不会玩，使杰克呆头呆脑。Zhěngtiān gōngzuò bú huì wán, shǐ Jiékè dāitóu dāinǎo. 2 戏剧 xìjù, 剧本 jùběn ■ *Shakespeare's plays are some of the best literature ever written.* 莎士比亚的剧本是有史以来最好的文学。Shāshìbǐyà de jùběn shì yǒushǐ yǐlái zuìhǎo de wénxué.
to play a part/role ① 扮演…的角色 bànyǎn…de juésè ② 起…的作用 qǐ…de zuòyòng
to play a trick/jokes on 恶作剧 èzuòjù
to play with fire 玩火 wánhuǒ, 冒险 màoxiǎn
■ *If you don't want to play with fire, you shouldn't touch those shares.* 如果你不想冒险，就别碰那些股票。Rúguǒ nǐ bù xiǎng màoxiǎn, jiù bié pèng nàxiē gǔpiào.
play on words 双关语 shuāngguānyǔ ■ *"Pre-arranged marriage pre-paired people for the future" is an example of a play on words.* "Pre-arranged marriage pre-paired people for the future" 是双关语。"Pre-arranged marriage pre-paired people for the future" shì shuāngguānyǔ.

play-acting v 装作一本正经的 zhuāngzuò yì běn zhèngjīng de, 假装 jiǎzhuāng

playboy N 花花公子 huāhuā gōngzi

play-by-play ADJ (play-by-play commentary) （体育）比赛实况报导 (tǐyù) bǐsài shíkuàng bàodào
a play-by-play man （体育）比赛实况播音员 (tǐyù) bǐsài shíkuàng bōyīnyuán

Play-Doh N （彩色）橡皮泥 (cǎisè) xiàngpíní [M. WD 块 kuài]

player N 1 球员 qiúyuán, 选手球员 xuǎnshǒu qiúyuán, 选手 xuǎnshǒu 2 （事件）参与者 (shìjiàn) cānyùzhě 3 （乐器）演奏者 (yuèqì) yǎnzòuzhě 4 (a CD player) 激光唱机 jīguāngchàngjī

playful ADJ 开玩笑的 kāiwánxiào de, 轻快的 qīngkuài de

playground N 操场 cāochǎng, 游戏场 yóuxìchǎng

playhouse N 戏院 xìyuàn, 剧场 jùchǎng

playing card N 扑克牌 pūkèpái, 纸牌 zhǐpái [M. WD 副 fù]

playmate N 1 玩伴 wán bàn, 游戏伙伴 yóuxì huǒbàn 2 性玩乐伙伴 xìng wánlè huǒbàn

playoff N 总决赛 zǒng juésài

playroom N 游戏室 yóuxì shì

plaything N 1 玩具 wánjù 2 玩物 wánwù, 玩弄的对象 wánnòng de duìxiàng

playwright N 剧作家 jùzuòjiā [M. WD 位 wèi]

plaza N 1 广场 guǎngchǎng, 市场 shìchǎng 2 购物区 gòuwù qū

plea N 1 悬求 kěnqiú, 请求 qǐngqiú 2 (法庭上) 申诉 (fǎtíng shàng) shēnsù

plea-bargain N 辩诉交易 biànsù jiāoyì, 认罪求情 rènzuì qiúqíng

plead (PT & PP **pled/pleaded**) V 1 悬求 kěnqiú, 央求 yāngqiú 2 争辩 zhēngbiàn, 解释 jiěshì 3 (to plead guilty/ not guilty) (法庭上) 承认 / 不承认有罪 (fǎtíng shàng) chéngrèn/bùchéngrèn yǒuzuì

pleasant ADJ (使人) 愉快的 (shǐrén) yúkuài de, 可心的 kěxīn de ■ *She was attracted by his pleasant voice over the phone.* 她被他电话里悦耳的嗓音吸引。Tā bèi tā diànhuà lǐ yuè'ě rde sǎngyīn xīyǐn.

pleasantry N 客套话 kètàohuà, 寒暄 hánxuān

please I INTERJ 请 qǐng ■ *"Would you like to try this wine?" "Yes, please."* "您要尝尝这种酒吗?""要的,谢谢。""Nín yào chángchang zhè zhǒng jiǔ ma?" "Yào de, xièxie." II V 使…愉快 shǐ…yúkuài, 使…满意 shǐ…mǎnyì

pleased ADJ 愉快的 yúkuài de, 满意的 mǎnyì de

pleasurable ADJ 愉快的 yúkuài de

pleasure N 1 愉快 yúkuài, 满足 mǎnzú 2 乐事 lèshì ■ *It gives me much pleasure to introduce to you our new deputy principal.* 我很高兴地向大家介绍我们的新副校长。Wǒ hěn gāoxìng de xiàng dàjiā jièshào wǒmen de xīn fù xiàozhǎng. 3 令人愉快的事 lìng rén yúkuài de shì, 乐事 lèshì

pleat I N 褶(子) zhě (zi) II V 打褶(子) dǎzhě (zi)

pleated ADJ 有褶的 yǒu zhě de

plebiscite N 公民投票(制度) gōngmín tóupiào (zhìdù)

pled See plead

pledge I N 1 誓言 shìyán, 保证 bǎozhèng

a pledge of love 爱情誓约 àiqíng shìyuē

2 抵押品 dǐyāpǐn II V 1 发誓 fāshì, 保证 bǎozhèng 2 宣誓加入 xuānshì jiārù

Pledge of Allegiance N (美国) 效忠美国誓言 (Měiguó) xiàozhōng Měiguó shìyán

plentiful ADJ 丰富的 fēngfù de, 富饶的 fùráo de

plenty I PRON 充裕 chōngyù, 绰绰有余 chuòchuò yǒuyú II ADV 绰绰有余 chuòchuò yǒuyú ■ *There's plenty more toys for all the children.* 每个孩子都有玩具, 还绰绰有余。Měi ge háizi dōu yǒu wánjù, hái chuòchuò yǒuyú.

plethora N (a plethora of) 过多的 guòduō de, 许多 xǔduō

pliable, pliant ADJ 1 柔韧的 [+材料] róurèn de

[+cáiliào], 柔软的 róuruǎn de 2 柔顺的 [+人] róushùn de [+rén], 易受影响的 yì shòu yǐngxiǎng de

pliers N 钳子 qiánzi [M. WD 把 bǎ]

plight N 困境 kùnjìng, 悲惨的境地 bēicǎn de jìngde

plod V 1 缓慢而沉重地走 huǎnmàn ér chénzhòng de zǒu 2 做辛苦而单调的工作 zuò xīnkǔ ér dāndiào de gōngzuò

plodding ADJ 缓慢的 huǎnmàn de, 艰难的 jiānnán de

plop I V 1 扑通一声落下 pūtōng yì shēng luòxia 2 随便地扔 suíbiàn de rēng II N 扑通声 pūtōng shēng

plot¹ I N 1 情节 qíngjié

The plot thickens. 情况变得复杂起来。Qíngkuàng biàn de fùzá qǐlái. 2 阴谋 yīnmóu, 秘密计划 mìmì jìhuà II V 密谋 mìmóu, 策划 cèhuà

plot² I N (小块) 土地 (xiǎo kuài) tǔdì II V 标绘出…的位置 biāohuì chū…de wèizhì

plow, plough I N 犁 lí [M. WD 把 bǎ] II V 1 犁 [+地] lí [+dì], 耕 [+地] gēng [+dì] 2 用雪犁清除雪 yòng xuělí qīngchú xuě

to plow on 继续努力 jìxù nǔlì

ploy N 计谋 jìmóu, 手段 shǒuduàn

pluck I V 1 拔 [+鸡毛] bá [+jīmáo] 2 弹 [+琴弦] dàn [+qínxián] 3 拉 lā 4 采 [+花] cǎi [+huā] II N 勇气 yǒngqì, 胆量 dǎnliàng

plug I N 1 插头 chātóu

to pull the plug 中断 (资助) zhōngduàn (zīzhù) 2 (浴缸) 塞子 (yùgāng) sāizi 3 (汽车) 火花塞 (qìchē) huǒhuāsāi II V 1 堵塞 dǔsè 2 填补 tiánbǔ 3 插入插头 chārù chātóu, 接通电源 jiētōng diàn yuán

plum I N (plum tree) 李(子) 树 lǐ (zi) shù [M. WD 棵 kē] II ADJ (a plum job) 人人想要的好职位 rénrén xiǎngyào de hǎo zhíwèi, 美差 měichāi

plumage N 鸟的彩色羽毛 niǎo de cǎisè yǔmáo

plumber N 水暖工 shuǐnuǎngōng, 管子工 guǎnzigōng

plumbing N 1 水暖管道 (设备) shuǐnuǎn guǎndào (shèbèi) 2 水暖工的工作 shuǐnuǎngōng de gōngzuò

plume N 1 (鲜艳的长) 羽毛 (xiānyàn de cháng) yǔmáo 2 一缕 [+烟雾] yì lǚ [+yānwù]

plummet V 急剧跌落 jíjù diēluò

plump I ADJ 胖乎乎的 pànghūhū de, 丰满的 fēngmǎn de II V 1 使…胖起来 shǐ…pàng qǐlái 2 把 [+枕头] 拍得松软 bǎ [+zhěntou] pāi dé sōngruǎn

plunder I V 掠夺 lüèduó, 抢劫 qiǎngjié II N 1 掠夺 lüèduó, 抢劫 qiǎngjié 2 战利品 zhànlìpǐn

plunge I V 突然冲下 tūrán chōng xià, 突然撞 tūrán zhuàng II N 冲 chōng, 暴跌 bàodiē

to take the plunge 决定冒险 juédìng màoxiǎn

plunger

plunger N 活塞 huósāi, 柱塞 zhùsāi

plunk V 乱扔 luànrēng

to plunk down 花很多钱 huā hěn duō qián

(the) pluperfect N 过去完成时态 guòqù wánchéng shítài

plural N, ADJ 复数 fùshù ■ *The plural of "mouse" is "mice" and the plural of "deer" is "deer."* "Mouse" 的复数是 "mice"，而 "deer" 的复数是 "deer"。"Mouse" de fùshù shì "mice", ér "deer" de fùshù shì "deer".

plurality N 得票（数）dépiào (shù)

plus I PREP 加 jiā II CONJ 再加上 zài jiāshang, 而且 érqiě ■ *He earns a six-figure salary, plus his parents have left him some properties.* 他的工资是六位数的，再加上他父母又留给他一些产业。Tā de gōngzī shì liù wèi shù de, zài jiāshang tā fùmǔ yòu liúgěi tā yìxiē chǎnyè. III ADJ 多于 duōyú ■ *The highest temperature today is 60° F plus.* 今天的最高气温高于华氏六十度。Jīntiān de zuìgāo qìwēn gāoyú huáshì liùshí dù.

(school grades) A/B/C plus A／B／C 加（A+／B+／C+）A/B/C jiā

plus sign 加号 jiāhào (+)

IV N 有利因素 yǒulì yīnsù, 优点 yōudiǎn ■ *The highest temperature today is 60° F plus.* 今

pluses and minuses 有利和不利因素 yǒulì hé búlì yīnsù, 利弊 lìbì

plush ADJ 豪华舒适的 háohuá shūshì de

Pluto N 冥王（星）Míngwáng (xīng)

plutocracy N 富豪统治的（国家）fùháo tǒngzhì (de guójiā)

plutonium (Pu) N 钚 bù

ply I N 1（胶合板）层 (jiāohébǎn) céng,（卫生纸）层 (wèishēngzhǐ) céng, 绳（股）shéng (gǔ) 2 两层卫生纸 liǎngcéng wèishēngzhǐ II V [船+] 定期航行 [chuán+] dìngqī hángxíng

to ply one's trade 从事自己的行当 cóngshì zìjǐ de hángdang

plywood N 胶合板 jiāo báibǎn [M. WD 块 kuài]

pneumatic ADJ 用压缩空气推动的 yòng yāsuōkōngqì tuīdòng de

pneumonia N 肺炎 fèiyán

poach V 1 偷猎 [+大象] tōu liè [+dàxiàng] 2 挖走 [+球员] wā zǒu [+qiúyuán] 3 煮 [+鸡蛋] zhǔ [+jīdàn]

poacher N 偷猎者 tōu lièzhě

P.O. Box N 邮政信箱 yóuzhèngxìnxiāng

pocket I N 1 口袋 kǒudài

pocket change 零钱 língqián

pocket knife 小折刀 xiǎozhédāo

pocket money 零花钱 línghuāqián

2 财力 cáilì, 收益 shōuyì

out of one's own pocket 自掏腰包 zì tāo yāobāo

3 小片地区 xiǎopiàn dìqū

pockets of shower 小片地区有阵雨 xiǎopiàn dìqū yǒu zhènyǔ

II V 1 放进口袋 fàngjìn kǒudài 2 侵吞 qīntūn

pocket, pocket-sized ADJ 袖珍的 xiùzhēn de

pocketbook N 小笔记本 xiǎo bǐjìběn

pocketful N 一袋 yídài

pockmark N 麻点 mádiǎn

pod N 豆荚 dòujiá

podiatrist N 足病医生 zúbìng yīshēng

podiatry N 足病 zúbìng

podium N（讲）台 (jiǎng) tái,（演出）台 (yǎnchū) tái

poem N 诗 shī [M. WD 首 shǒu], 诗歌 shīgē [M. WD 首 shǒu]

poet N 诗人 shīrén

poetic ADJ 诗歌的 shīgē de, 有诗意的 yǒu shīyì de

poetic justice 应得的惩罚 yīngdé de chéngfá, 恶有恶报 èrén bì yǒu èbào

poetic license 诗的破格 shī de pògé

poetry N 诗歌 shīgē ■ *It is a sign of the times that few people read poetry and even fewer write poetry.* 现在很少人读诗歌，写诗的人就更少，这是时代的特征。Xiànzài hěn shǎo rén dú shīgē, xiěshī de rén jiù gēngshǎo, zhè shì shídài de tèzhēng.

poignancy N 哀伤 āishāng, 惋惜 wǎnxī

poignant ADJ 令人哀伤的 lìngrén āishāng de, 令人惋惜的 lìngrén wǎnxī de

point I N 1 点 diǎn ■ *"The suspect was found speeding that night." "That's a very interesting point."* "有人那天晚上发现嫌疑犯超速驾车。" "这一点十分有意思。" "Yǒurén nàtiān wǎnshang fāxiàn xiányífàn chāosù jiàchē." "Zhè yì diǎn shífēn yǒuyìsi."

point of view 看法 kànfa, 视角 shìjiǎo

strong point 长处 chángchu

weak point 弱点 ruòdiǎn

up to a point 在一定程度上 zài yídìng chéngdùshang

to make a point of 特地 tèdì, 很重视 hěn zhòngshì ■ *He makes a point of saving all important emails for three months.* 他特地把所有重要的电子邮件都保存三个月。Tā tèdì bǎ suǒyǒu zhòngyào de diànzǐ yóujiàn dōu bǎocún sān ge yuè.

2 要点 yàodiǎn, 关键 guānjiàn

point man 重要骨干 zhòngyào gǔgàn, 负责人 fùzérén

3 道理 dàolǐ, 价值 jiàzhí 4 时刻 shíkè ■ *At this point I can't give you a definite answer.* 眼下我不能给你确切的回答。Yǎnxià wǒ bù néng gěi nǐ quèqiè de huídá. 5（小数）点 (xiǎoshù)diǎn ■ *The Dow Jones index rose 20 points to 11,239.* 道琼指数上升二十个点，到达一万一千两百三十九点。Dàoqióng zhǐshù shàngshēng èrshí ge diǎn, dàodá yí wàn yì qiān liǎng bǎi sānshí jiǔ diǎn.

6（比赛得）分(bǐsài dé) fēn II V 指 zhǐ, 对 duì ■ *"Out!" the angry host said, pointing at the*

door. "出去！" 愤怒的主人指着门说。"Chūqu!" fènnù de zhǔrén zhǐzhe mén shuō.
to point out 指出 zhǐchū

pointblank ADV 1 近距离 [+射击] jìnjùlí [+shèjī] 2 直截了当地 [+拒绝] zhíjiéliǎodàng de [+jùjué], 断然 duànrán

pointed ADJ 1 尖的 [+指甲] jiān de [+zhǐjiǎ] 2 锐利的 [+批评] ruìlì de [+pīpíng], 尖刻的 jiānkè de

pointer N 1 指示棒 zhǐshì bàng 2（仪器的）指针（yíqì de）zhǐzhēn 3（计算机）鼠标箭头（jìsuànjī）shǔbiāo jiàntóu 4 指示猎犬 zhǐshì lièquǎn [M. WD 只 zhǐ/条 tiáo]

pointless ADJ 没有意义的 méiyǒu yìyì de
pointy ADJ 尖的 jiānde

poise I N 沉着 chénzhuó, 自信 zìxìn II v 使…平衡 shǐ…pínghéng

poised ADJ 1 作好准备的 zuò hǎo zhǔnbèi de 2 沉着自信的 chénzhuó zìxìn de

poison I N 毒 dú, 毒药 dúyào
One man's meat is another man's poison. 一个人的肉食是另一个人毒药。（→各人的口味爱好不同。）Yí ge rén de ròushí shì lìng yí ge rén dúyào.（→Gèrén de kǒuwèi àihào bù tóng.）II v 放毒 fàngdú

poisoning I N 1 中毒 zhòngdú
food poisoning 食物中毒 shíwù zhòngdú
2 投毒 tóudú

poisonous ADJ 有毒的 yǒudú de ■ *Globefish is poisonous but it is an expensive delicacy in Japan.* 豚鱼有毒，但是在日本是昂贵的美食。Túnyú yǒudú, dànshì zài Rìběn shì ángguìde měishí.

poke I v 伸入 [+头] shēnrù [+tóu], 插入 chārù 2 刺入 cìrù, 戳进 chuōjìn
to poke fun at 取笑 qǔxiào
to poke one's nose into sth 多管闲事 duōguǎn xiánshì
II N 戳 chuō, 捅 tǒng
to take a poke at sb 打某人 dǎ mǒurén, 批评某人 pīpíng mǒurén

poker N 1 拨火棒 bōhuǒ bàng [M. WD 根 gēn] 2 打 [+扑克牌] dǎ [+pūkèpái]

poker-faced ADJ 不露表情的 búlù biǎoqíng de, 不动声色的 búdòng shēngsè de

polar ADJ 北极的 Běijí de, 南极的 Nánjí de
polar bear 北极熊 Běijíxióng

polarity N 截然相反 jiérán xiāngfǎn
polarize v 使…两极化 shǐ…liǎngjíhuà

Polaroid N 1 一次成象照相机 yícì chéngxiàng zhàoxiàngjī [M. WD 台 tái] 2 一次成象图片 yícì chéngxiàng túpiàn [M. WD 张 zhāng]

Pole N 波兰人 Bōlánrén

pole N 1 杆 gǎn [M. WD 根 gēn], 杆子 gānzi [M. WD 根 gēn], 竿 gān [M. WD 根 gēn]
fishing pole 鱼竿 yúgān

2 极 jí, 南极 Nánjí, 北极 Běijí
the North Pole 北极 Běijí
the South Pole 南极 Nánjí
3 电极 diànjí, 磁极 cíjí
be poles apart 截然相反 jiérán xiāngfǎn, 完全不同 wánquán bùtóng

polemic N 大辩论 dàbiànlùn, 论战 lùnzhàn [M. WD 场 cháng]

polemical ADJ 辩论的 biànlùn de, 论战的 lùnzhàn de

police I N 警察 jǐngchá, 警方 jǐngfāng ■ *The police chased the suspect for miles until he pulled over.* 警察追赶嫌疑犯好多英里，嫌疑犯才把车停在路边。Jǐngchá zhuīgǎn xiányífàn hǎoduō yīnglǐ, xiányífàn cái bǎ chē tíng zài lùbiān.
police department 警察局 jǐngchájú
police force 警察部队 jǐngchá bùduì
police officer 警察 jǐngchá
police state 警察国家 jǐngchá guójiā
police station 派出所 pàichūsuǒ, 警察分局 jǐngchá fēnjú
II v 监督 jiāndū, 监察 jiānchá

policeman N 警察 jǐngchá, 男警察 nán jǐngchá
policewoman N 女警察 nǚ jǐngchá

policy N 1 政策 zhèngcè ■ *Does the government have a clear policy on marijuana?* 政府对大麻有明确的政策吗？Zhèngfǔ duì dàmá yǒu míngquè de zhèngcè ma? 2 保险单 bǎoxiǎn dān, 保险 bǎoxiǎn

polio N 小儿麻痹症 xiǎo'ér mábìzhèng

Polish I ADJ 波兰的 Bōlán de, 波兰人的 Bōlánrén de, 波兰语的 Bōlányǔ de II N 波兰语 Bōlányǔ

polish v 1 擦亮 [+银器] cāliàng [+yínqì], 磨光 [+地板] móguāng [+dìbǎn] 2 修改 [+文章] xiūgǎi [+wénzhāng], 润色 rùnsè
to polish up ① 擦亮 cāliàng ②（进修）提高（jìnxiū）tígāo

polished ADJ 1 擦亮的 cāliàng de, 磨光的 móguāng de 2 优美的 yōuměi de, 文雅的 wényǎ de

polite ADJ 有礼貌的 yǒulǐmào de ■ *When he complimented the Chinese girl on her good English, she replied with a polite smile.* 当他恭维这个中国女孩英文说得好时，她有礼貌地笑笑。Dāng tā gōngwéi zhè ge Zhōngguó nǚhái Yīngwén shuóde hǎo shí, tā yǒulǐmào de xiàoxiào.

political ADJ 政治的 zhèngzhì de ■ *The political situation in that Latin American country is, to say the least, volatile.* 那个拉丁美洲国家的政治局势，至少应该说是动荡不定。Nà ge Lādīng Měizhōu guójiā de zhèngzhì júshì, zhìshǎo yīnggāi shuō shì dòngdàng bùdìng.
political prisoner 政治犯 zhèngzhìfàn

politically correct ADJ 政治正确的 zhèngzhì zhèngquè de

politician N 政客 zhèngkè, 政治领袖 zhèngzhì lǐngxiù

politicize v 使…政治化 shǐ…zhèngzhì huà, 使…卷入政治 shǐ…juǎnrù zhèngzhì

politics N 1 政治 zhèngzhì 2 权术 quánshù, 勾心斗角 gōuxīn dòujiǎo ■ *Office politics will inevitably get in the way of getting work done.* 办公室里勾心斗角是肯定会影响工作的。Bàngōngshì lǐ gōuxīn dòujiǎo shì kěndìng huì yǐngxiǎng gōngzuò de. 3 政治学 zhèngzhìxué

polka N 波尔卡舞曲 Bō'ěrkǎwǔ qū [M. WD 首 shǒu]

poll I N 1 民意调查 mínyì diàochá, 民意测验 mínyì cèyàn 2 选举 xuǎnjǔ II v 对…进行民意调查 duì…jìnxíng mínyì diàochá

pollen N 花粉 huāfěn
pollen count 花粉量 huāfěn liáng

pollinate v 给 [+果树] 授花粉 gěi [+guǒshù] shòu huāfěn

polling place, polling station N 投票站 tóupiàozhàn

pollster N 民意调查者 mínyì diàocházhě

pollutant N 污染物 wūrǎnwù

pollute v 污染 wūrǎn, 弄脏 nòngzāng

pollution N 污染 wūrǎn

polo N 马球（运动）mǎqiú (yùndòng)
polo shirt 马球衫 mǎqiúshān

polyester N 涤纶 dílún

polygamist N 有几个妻子的男子 yǒu jǐge qīzi de nánzǐ

polygamous ADJ 一夫多妻的 yìfūduōqī de

polygamy N 一夫多妻制 yìfūduōqī zhì

polygon N 多边形 duōbiānxíng, 多角形 duōjiǎoxíng

polygraph N 测谎器 cèhuǎngqì [M. WD 台 tái]

polymer N 聚合物 jùhéwù

polytechnic N 综合性理工学院 zōnghéxìng lǐgōng xuéyuàn, 工艺专科学校 gōngyì zhuānkē xuéxiào

polyunsaturated fat N 不饱和脂肪 bù bǎohé zhīfáng

pomegranate N 石榴 shíliu

pomp N 盛大的仪式 shèngdà de yíshì, 盛典 shèngdiǎn

pompom N 小绒球 xiǎo róngqiú

pomposity N 自命不凡 zìmìng bùfán, 大摆架子 dà bǎi jiàzi

pompous ADJ 自命不凡的 zìmìng bùfán de, 爱摆架子的 ài bǎi jiàzi de

poncho N 披风 pīfēng, 斗篷 dǒupéng [M. WD 件 jiàn]

pond N 池塘 chítáng

ponder v 郑重考虑 zhèngzhòng kǎolǜ, 深思 shēnsī

ponderous ADJ 1 笨拙的 [+行动] bènzhuō de [+xíngdòng] 2 严肃而乏味的 [+说教] yánsù ér fáwèi de [+shuōjiào]

pontiff N（天主教）教皇 (Tiānzhǔjiào) Jiàohuáng

pontificate v 自以为是地夸夸其谈 zìyǐwéishì de kuākuāqítán

pontoon N 浮舟 fúzhōu

pony N 小种马 xiǎo zhǒngmǎ

ponytail N 马尾辫 mǎwěi biàn [M. WD 条 tiáo/根 gēn]

pooch N 狗 gǒu [M. WD 只 zhī/条 tiáo]

poodle N 长毛狗 chángmáogǒu [M. WD 只 zhī/条 tiáo]

pooh-pooh v 嗤之以鼻 chī zhī yǐ bí

pool I N 1 池 chí, 水池 shuǐ chí 2 游泳池 yóuyǒng chí 3 台球 táiqiú
pool hall 台球厅 táiqiú tīng
pool table 台球桌 táiqiú zhuō
to play pool 打台球 dǎ táiqiú
4 公用物 gōngyòng wù 5 备用人员 bèiyòng rényuán II v 集中使用 jízhōng shǐyòng

poop I N 大便 dàbiàn II v 拉大便 lādà biàn

poor ADJ 1 穷 qióng, 贫穷 pínqióng 2 不好的 bù hǎo de ■ *Attendance at the church is poor.* 上教堂的人很少。Shàng jiàotáng de rén hěn shǎo. 3 差的 chà de, 蹩脚的 biéjiǎo de ■ *No one wants to play with him, as he is a poor loser.* 没有人想跟他玩，因为他输不起的。Méiyǒurén xiǎng gēn tā wán, yīnwèi tā shūbuqǐ de.
to be in poor health 身体不好 shēntǐ bù hǎo
the poor 穷人 qióngrén

poorly ADV 很差（地）hěn chà (de)

pop¹ I v 1 发出噼啪的声音 fāchū pī pā de shēngyīn 2 爆 [+玉米花] bào [+yùmǐhuā] 3 蹦出 bèng chū 4 很快地来（或去）hěn kuài de lái (huò qù) II N 1 劈啪声 pīpā shēng 2 汽水 qìshuǐ, 啤酒 píjiǔ

pop² N 流行音乐 liúxíng yīnyuè
pop concert 流行音乐会 liúxíng yīnyuè huì

pop³ N 爸爸 bàba

popcorn N 爆玉米花 bào yùmǐhuā

Pope N（天主教）教皇 (Tiānzhǔjiào) Jiàohuáng [M. WD 位 wèi]

poplar N 杨树 yángshù [M. WD 棵 kē]

poppy N 罂粟 yīngsù

populace N 民众 mínzhòng

popular ADJ 1 很受欢迎的 hěn shòu huānyíng de 2 流行的 liúxíng de ■ *What's hot in popular culture now?* 眼下流行文化中最热门的什么？Yǎnxià liúxíng wénhuà zhōng zuìrèmén de shénme? 3 大众的 dàzhòng de

popularity N 1 流行 liúxíng 2 受欢迎 shòu huānyíng

popularize v 使…流行 shǐ…liúxíng, 使…普及 shǐ…pǔjí

popularly ADV 大众（地）dàzhòng (de)
popularly priced 定价适中 dìngjià shìzhōng

populate v (be populated by) 居住着 jūzhùzhe
densely populated 人口稠密的 [+地区] rénkǒu chóumì de [+dìqū]

thinly populated 人口稀少的 [+地区] rénkǒu xīshǎo de [+dìqū]

population N **1** 人口 rénkǒu **2** (动物的)数量 (dòngwù de) shùliàng ■ *Thanks to conservation efforts, the population of this endangered bird has doubled in the past five years.* 由于致力于环保，这种濒临灭绝的鸟类的数量在过去五年里增加了一倍。Yóuyú zhìlì yú huánbǎo, zhè zhǒng bīnlín mièjué de niǎolèi de shùliàng zài guòqù wǔ nián lǐ zēngjiāle yí bèi.

populous ADJ 人口众多的 rénkǒu zhòngduō de

porcelain N 瓷器 cíqì
an expensive porcelain dinner set 一套昂贵的瓷器餐具 yítào ángguì de cíqì cānjù

porch N 门廊 ménláng

porcupine N 豪猪 háozhū [M. WD 只 zhī/头 tóu]

pore¹ N 毛孔 máokǒng

pore² v (to pore over) 长时间仔细阅读 chángshíjiān zǐxì yuèdú

pork N 猪肉 zhūròu

pornographer N 色情作品的制作者 sèqíng zuòpǐn de zhìzuòzhě

pornography N 色情作品 sèqíng zuòpǐn, 黄色电影/杂志 huángsèdiànyǐng/zázhì

porous ADJ 多孔的 duōkǒng de, 水能渗透的 shuǐnéng shèntòu de

porridge N (燕麦)粥 (yànmài) zhōu

port N **1** 港 gǎng, 港口 gǎngkǒu **2** (计算机)插口 (jìsuànjī) chākǒu **3** (船舶/飞机)左舷 (chuánbó/fēijī) zuǒxián **4** (葡萄牙)波尔图葡萄酒 (Pútaoyá) bō ěr tú pútaojiǔ

portable I ADJ **1** 手提式的 shǒutíshì de, 便携式的 biànxiéshì de
a portable toilet 流动厕所 liúdòng cèsuǒ
2 (计算机)可兼容 [+程序] (jìsuànjī) kě jiānróng [+chéngxù] II N 手提式电器 shǒutíshì diànqì

portal N **1** (互联网)门户网站 (hùliánwǎng) ménhù wǎngzhàn **2** 大门 dàmén [M. WD 座 zuò]

portend v 预示 [+大灾难] yùshì [+dàzāinàn]

portent N 预兆 yùzhào, 迹象 jìxiàng

porter N **1** (行李)搬运工 (xíngli) bānyùn gōng **2** (大楼)修理工 (dàlóu) xiūlǐ gōng, 清洁工 qīngjiégōng **3** (旅馆)守门人 (lǚguǎn) shǒumén rén

portfolio N **1** 公事包 gōngshìbāo **2** (个人)投资组合 (gèrén) tóuzī zǔhé
investment portfolio 投资组合 tóuzī zǔhé
3 (政府高级官员的)职责范围 (zhèngfǔ gāojí guānyuán de) zhízé fànwéi

porthole N (飞机/船)舷窗 (fēijī/chuán) xiánchuāng

portico N (有柱子的)门廊 (yǒu zhùzi de) ménláng

portion I N **1** (一)部分 (yí) bùfen **2** 一份(食物) yí fèn (shíwù)
double portion of chips 两份炸土豆条 liǎngfèn zhátǔdòutiáo
II v (to portion out) 把…分成几份 bǎ…fēnchéng jǐ fèn, 分 fēn

portly ADJ 胖的 pàng de, 发福的 fāfú de

portrait N 肖像 xiàoxiàng [M. WD 幅 fú]

portraiture N 肖像画艺术 xiàoxiànghuà yìshù

portray v **1** 描绘 miáohuì, 描述 miáoshù **2** 扮演 [+角色] bànyǎn [+juésè]

portrayal N **1** 描绘 miáohuì, 描述 miáoshù **2** 扮演 bànyǎn

Portuguese I ADJ 葡萄牙的 Pútaoyá de, 葡萄牙人的 Pútaoyárén de, 葡萄牙语 Pútaoyáyǔ II N **1** 葡萄牙语 Pútaoyáyǔ **2** 葡萄牙人 Pútaoyárén

pose I v **1** 摆姿势(拍照或画像) bǎi zīshì (pāizhào huò huàxiàng)
to pose as 冒充 màochōng
2 引起 [+问题] yǐnqǐ [+wèntí], 导致 dǎozhì II N **1** 姿势 zīshì **2** 装腔作势的举止 zhuāngqiāng zuòshì de jǔzhǐ

poseur N 装腔作势的人 zhuāngqiāng zuòshì de rén

posh ADJ 高档的 gāodàng de, 豪华的 háohuá de

position N **1** 位置 wèizhì ■ *From her position at the window, she had a good view of the garden.* 从她在窗口的位置，可以清楚地看到花园。Cóng tā zài chuāngkǒu de wèizhì, kěyǐ qīngchu de kàndao huāyuán. **2** 姿势 zīshì **3** 地位 dìwèi ■ *People in a position of authority should have high ethical standards.* 占据高位的人应该有较高的道德标准。Zhànjù gāowèi de rén yīnggāi yǒu jiàogāo de dàodé biāozhǔn. **4** 职务 zhíwù **5** 立场 lìchǎng

positive ADJ **1** 肯定的 kěndìng de, 无疑的 wúyí de ■ *I'm absolutely positive that this was the man who attacked me.* 我完全肯定他就是攻击我的男子。Wǒ wánquán kěndìng tā jiù shì gōngjī wǒ de nánzǐ. **2** 积极的 jījí de ■ *Our teaching staff is very positive in dealing with children's learning difficulties.* 我们的老师在对付学生学习困难时采取非常积极的态度。Wǒmen de lǎoshī zài duifu xuéshēng xuéxí kùnnan shí cǎiqǔ fēicháng jījí de tàidu. **3** 阳性的 yángxìng de ■ *The tests proved positive.* 化验结果是阳性的。Huàyàn jiéguǒ shì yángxìng de.

positively ADV **1** 确实(地) quèshí (de), 无疑(地) wúyí (de) **2** 积极地 jījí de, 正面地 zhèng-miàn de, 肯定地 kěndìng de

posse N (a posse of) 一群 yìqún, 一大帮 yí dàbāng

possess v **1** 拥有 chíyǒu, 拥有 yōngyǒu **2** 控制 kòngzhì, 支配 zhīpèi

possessed ADJ 中邪的 zhòngxié de, 鬼迷心窍的 guǐmíxīnqiào de

possession N **1** 拥有 yōngyǒu, 持有 chíyǒu ■ *He has in his possession an extremely valuable rare* *stamp.* 他拥有一枚极其珍贵的稀有邮票。Tā yōng-yǒu yì méi jíqí zhēnguì de xīyǒu yóupiào. **2** 财产 cáichǎn

possessive I ADJ **1** 占有欲很强的 zhànyǒu yù hěn qiáng de **2** (语法) 所有格的 (yǔfǎ) suǒyǒugé de **II** N 所有格 (形式) suǒyǒugé (xíngshì)

possibility N **1** 可能性 kěnéng xìng ■ *The possibility of becoming a millionaire never occurred to me.* 我从来没有想过有可能成为百万富翁。Wǒ cónglái méiyǒu xiǎngguo yǒukěnéng chéngwéi bǎi wàn fùwēng. **2** 可能的事 kěnéng de shì

possible ADJ 可能的 kěnéng de ■ *Snow is possible, but unlikely at this time of year.* 这个时候下雪是可能的, 但是可能性不大。Zhège shíhou xiàxuě shì kěnéng de, dànshì kěnéng xìng bú dà.

possibly ADV 可能 kěnéng, 也许 yěxǔ

possum N 负鼠 fùshǔ [M. WD 只 zhī], 袋貂 dàidiāo [M. WD 只 zhī]

post I N **1** 柱子 zhùzi ■ *The fence post is crooked.* 围栏的柱子有点弯曲。Wéizhà de zhùzi yǒudiǎn wānqū. **2** 要职 yàozhí, 重要的位置 zhòngyào de wèizhì **3** (British) 邮件 yóujiàn

post office 邮政局 yóuzhèngjú

post office box 邮箱 yóuxiāng, 信箱 xìnxiāng **II** v 贴公告 tiē gōnggào, 通告 tōnggào ■ *A warning sign "Beware of Dogs" has been posted on the gate.* 一块警告牌 "小心护家狗" 贴在大门上。Yí kuài jǐnggào pái "xiǎoxīn hù jiā gǒu" tiē zài dàménshang.

Post no bills. 请勿张贴。Qǐn gwù zhāngtiē.

postage N 邮资 yóuzī

postal ADJ 邮政的 yóuzhèng de

postal service 邮政 yóuzhèng

postcard N 明信片 míngxìnpiàn [M. WD 张 zhāng]

postdate v (在支票上) 写比实际晚的日期 (zài zhīpiào shàng) xiě bǐ shíjì wǎn de rìqī

postdoctoral ADJ 博士后的 bóshìhòu de

poster N 海报 hǎibào, 广告画 guǎnggàohuà

posterior N 臀部 túnbù, 屁股 pìgu

posterity N 子孙后代 zǐsūn hòudài

postgraduate I ADJ 研究生的 yánjiūshēng de, 硕士 (或博士) 的 shuòshì (huò bóshì) de **II** N 硕士 (或博士) 研究生 shuòshì (huò bóshì) yánjiūshēng

posthumous ADJ 死后发生的 sǐhòu fāshēng de a posthumous son 遗腹子 yífùzǐ

posthumously ADV 死后 sǐhòu

Post-it N 便条粘帖纸 biàntiáo zhāntiē zhǐ [M. WD 张 zhāng]

postman N 邮递员 yóudìyuán

postmark N 邮戳 yóuchuō

postmaster N 邮政局长 yóuzhèngjúzhǎng

postmortem, postmortem examination N **1** 尸体检验 shītǐ jiǎnyàn **2** (对失败的) 事后检讨 (duì shībài de) shìhòu jiǎntǎo

postnatal ADJ 产后的 chǎnhòu de, 分娩的 fēnmiǎn de

postnatal depression 产后忧郁 (症) chǎnhòu yōuyù (zhēng)

postpone v 把…延期 bǎ…yánqī, 推迟 tuīchí

postponement N 延期 yánqī

postscript (ABBREV **P.S.**) N 附笔 fùbǐ, 又及 yòují

postulate v, N 假定 jiǎdìng, 假设 jiǎshè

posture N **1** 仪态 yítài **2** 立场 lìchǎng, 姿态 zītài

pot I N **1** 锅 guō, 壶 hú

pots and pans 锅碗瓢盆 guō wǎn piáo pén

coffee pot 咖啡壶 kāfēi hú

tea pot 茶壶 chá hú

2 花盆 huāpén **3** 大麻 dàmá **II** v 把植物移植到花盆里 bǎ zhíwù yízhí dào huāpén lǐ

potassium (**K**) N 钾 jiǎ

potato N 土豆 tǔdòu, 马铃薯 mǎlíngshǔ

potato chip N (炸) 土豆片 (zhá) tǔdòupiàn

potbelly N 大肚子 dàdùzi, 啤酒桶肚子 píjiǔtǒng dùzi

potency N **1** [药物+] 效力 [yàowù+] xiàolì, 效能 xiàonéng **2** [男子的+] 性能力 [nánzǐ de+] xìngnénglì

potent ADJ **1** 有效的 [+药] yǒuxiào de [+yào] **2** 强有力的 [+武器] qiángyǒulì de [+wǔqì] **3** 有性能力的 [+男子] yǒu xìngnénglì de [+nánzǐ]

potential I ADJ 潜在的 qiánzài de ■ *This ambiguous clause in the contract is a potential source of dispute.* 合同里这一条模糊不清的条款有可能引起争端。Hétong lǐ zhè yì tiáo móhú bù qīng de tiáokuǎn yǒukěnéng yǐnqǐ zhēngduān. **II** N 潜力 qiánlì ■ *The boy has enormous potential as a football player.* 这个男孩具有当足球运动员的巨大潜力。Zhè ge nánhái jùyǒu dāng zúqiú yùndòngyuán de jùdà qiánlì.

potentiality N 潜力 qiánlì, 可能性 kěnéngxìng

potentially ADV 有可能 yǒu kěnéng, 可能 kěnéng

pothead N 吸大麻的人 xī dàmá de rén

potholder N 防烫厚布垫 fáng tàng hòu bù diàn [M. WD 块 kuài]

pothole N (路面) 凹坑 (lùmiàn) āokēng

potion N 药水 yàoshuǐ

love potion 春药 chūnyào, 发情药水 fāqíng yào shuǐ

potluck (potluck dinner/lunch) N 自带菜肴的聚餐 zì dài càiyáo de jùcān, 百乐餐 bǎi lè cān

potpourri N **1** 百花香 bǎihuāxiāng **2** (音乐或文学) 集锦 (yīnyuè huò wénxué) jíjǐn

pottery N 陶器 táoqì

potty N (小孩用的) 便盆 (xiǎohái yòng de) biànpén

pouch N 小袋 (子) xiǎo dài (zi)

poultry N 家禽 jiāqín

pounce v 突然猛扑 tūrán měngpū, 突然袭击 tūrán xíjī

pound I N **1** 磅 bàng **2** (英) 镑 (Yīng) bàng (£)

pound cake 重油重糖蛋糕 zhòngyóu zhòng táng dàngāo

II v 1 连续猛击 liánxù měngjī 2 [心脏+] 剧烈跳动 [xīnzàng+] jùliè tiàodòng

pour v 1 倒 dǎo, 倾倒 qīngdǎo ■ Shall I pour you some coffee? 要不要我给你倒一些咖啡? Yàobuyào wǒ gěi nǐ dǎo yìxiē kāfēi? 2 下倾盆大雨 xià qīngpén dàyǔ

It never rains but it pours. 要么不下雨, 一下就 大雨倾盆。(→ 祸不单行。) Yàome bú xiàyǔ, yí xià jiù dàyǔ qīngpén. (→Huò bù dān xíng. Misfortunes never come singly.)

poverty N 贫穷 pínqióng

the poverty line 贫困线 pínkùnxiàn

poverty-stricken ADJ 极其贫穷的 jíqí pínqióng de

P.O.W (= prisoner of war) ABBREV 战俘 zhànfú

P.O.W. camp 战俘营 zhànfúyíng

powder I N 粉末 fěnmò

powder room（女用）卫生间 (nǚ yòng) wèishēngjiān

II v 给 [+皮肤] 涂粉 gěi [+pífū] túfěn

powdery ADJ 1 粉状的 fěnzhuàng de 2 涂粉的 túfěn de

power I N 1 权力 quánlì, 力量 lìliang ■ Schools do not have the power to search students for drugs or firearms. 学校没有权力对学生搜身, 找出毒 品或枪支。 Xuéxiào méiyǒu quánlì duì xuésheng sōushēn, zhǎochū dúpǐn huò qiāngzhī.

power base 权力基础 quánlìjīchǔ

power of attorney（法律）代理权 (fǎlǜ) dàilǐ quán 2 政治权力 zhèngzhì quánlì, 政权 zhèngquán 3 电力 diànlì ■ The snowstorm caused widespread power failure. 这场暴风雪造成大面积停 电。 Zhè cháng bàofēngxuě zàochéng dàmiànjī tíng diàn.

power plant 发电站 fādiàn zhàn

power tool 电动工具 diàndònggōngjù

powerboat N 摩托赛艇 mótuō sàitǐng [M. WD 艘 sōu]

powerful ADJ 1 强有力的 qiángyǒulì de ■ The new model SUV is equipped with a powerful engine. 这种新型越野车装备强有力的发动机。 Zhè zhǒng xīnxíng yuèyěchē zhuāngbèi qiángyǒulìde fādòngjī. 2 权力大的 quánlì dà de, 强大的 qiángdà de

powerless ADJ 无权的 wúquán de, 无势力的 wú shìlì de

powerline N 输电线（路）shūdiànxiàn (lù)

powwow N 会议 huìyì, 讨论 tǎolùn

practicable ADJ 行得通的 xíngdetōng de, 可行 的 kěxíng de

practical ADJ 1 实践的 shíjiàn de, 实际的 shíjì de ■ She has a lot of practical experience in nursing. 她在护理方面有丰富的实践经验。 Tā zài hùlǐ fāngmian yǒu fēngfù de shíjiàn jīngyàn. 2 实

用的 shíyòng de 3 讲究实际的 jiǎngjiu shíjì de ■ Be practical and do not buy that fancy car. 讲究实际一点吧, 别买那辆花哨的车。 Jiǎngjiu shíjì yì diǎn ba, bié mǎi nà liàng huāshào de chē.

practical joke 恶作剧 èzuòjù

practicality N 1 可行性 kěxíngxìng 2 实际（情况） shíjì (qíngkuàng)

practically ADV 1 讲究实际地 jiǎngjiu shíjì de 2 几乎 jīhū, 差不多 chàbuduō

practice I N 1 实践 shíjiàn, 实际 shíjì ■ Has anyone put this theory into practice? 有人实践过这条 理论吗? Yǒurén shíjiànguo zhè tiáo lǐlùn ma? 2 练习 liànxí ■ Spoken Chinese requires lots of practice. 中文口语需要多多练习。 Zhōngwén kǒuyǔ xūyào duōduō liànxí. 3 常规 chángguī 4（医生）诊所 (yīshēng) zhěnsuǒ,（律师）事务 所 (lǜshī) shìwùsuǒ II v (British practise) 1 练 习 liànxí ■ She often practices her Chinese on Meiying. 她常常和梅英练习中文。 Tā chángcháng hé Méiyīng liànxí Zhōngwén. 2 执业 zhíyè, 当医 生 dāng yīshēng, 当律师 dāng lǜshī

practiced ADJ 经验丰富的 jīngyàn fēngfù de, 老 练的 lǎoliàn de

practicing ADJ 1 开业的 kāiyè de

practicing lawyer 开业律师 kāiyè lǜshī 2 遵循教义的 [+宗教徒] zūnxún jiàoyì de [+zōngjiàotú]

practitioner N 1 开业者 kāiyè zhě, 从业者 cóngyèzhě

medical practitioner 开业医生 kāiyè yīshēng 2 实践者 shíjiànzhě

pragmatic ADJ 讲究实用的 jiǎngjiu shíyòng de, 务实的 wùshí de

pragmatism N 实用主义 shíyòngzhǔyì

prairie N 草原 cǎoyuán

prairie dog 草原犬鼠 cǎoyuán quǎnshǔ

praise v 1 表扬 biǎoyáng, 赞扬 zànyáng ■ Children need to be praised when they do good things. 孩子做了好事, 就需要表扬。 Háizi zuòle hǎo shì, jiù xūyào biǎoyáng

praiseworthy ADJ 值得赞扬的 zhíde zànyáng de

prance v 昂首阔步 ángshǒu kuòbù

prank N 恶作剧 èzuòjù

prankster N 恶作剧者 èzuòjùzhě

prattle N 絮絮叨叨地说 xùxu dāodāo de shuō

prawn N 大虾 dàxiā [M. WD 只 zhī]

pray v 祈祷 qídǎo, 祷告 dǎogào

prayer N 祈祷 qídǎo, 祷告 dǎogào ■ Your prayer will be answered. 上帝会回应你的祈祷 的。 Shàngdì huì huíyìng nǐ de qídǎo de.

preach v 1 布道 bùdào, 宣扬 xuānyáng 2 说教 shuōjiào

preacher N 讲道者 jiǎngdàozhě, 说教的人 shuōjiào de rén

preachy ADJ 爱说教的 ài shuōjiào de

preamble N 前言 qiányán, 序言 xùyán

prearranged ADJ 预先安排好的 yùxiān ānpái hǎo de

precarious ADJ 不稳定的 bùwěndìng de, 有危险的 yǒu wēixiǎn de

precaution N 预防 (措施) yùfáng (cuòshī)

precautionary ADJ 预防 (性) 的 yùfáng (xìng) de

precede V 在…前发生 zài...qián fāshēng

precedence N (to take precedence over) 优先于 yōuxiān yú

precedent N 先例 xiānlì, 判例 pànlì
  to break a precedent 打破惯例 dǎpò guànlì
  to set a precedent 开创先例 kāichuàng xiānlì

preceding ADJ 前面的 qiánmian de

precept N 准则 zhǔnzé

precinct N 1 分区 fēnqū 2 警察分局 jǐngchá fēnjú 3 周围地区 zhōuwéi dìqū

precious I ADJ 珍贵的 zhēnguì de
  precious metal 贵金属 guìjīnshǔ
  precious stone 宝石 bǎoshí
  II ADV (precious little) 非常少 fēicháng shǎo

precipice N 悬崖 xuányá

precipitate I V 迅速导致 xùnsù dǎozhì, 加速 jiāsù II ADJ 仓促的 cāngcù de, 贸然的 màorán de III N 沉淀物 chéndiànwù

precipitation N 1 降雨 (或雪) jiàngyǔ (huò xuě), 降雨 (或雪) 量 jiàngyǔ (huò xuě) liáng 2 沉淀 chéndiàn 3 仓促 cāngcù

precipitous ADJ 突然的 tūrán de

précis N 摘要 zhāiyào

precise ADJ 精确的 jīngquè de, 精密的 jīngmì de

precisely ADV 1 精确地 jīngquè de 2 恰好 qiàhǎo, 正巧是 zhèngqiǎo shì

precision N 精密 jīngmì, 精确 jīngquè
  precison tool 精密工具 jīngmì gōngjù

preclude V 使…不能 shǐ...bùnéng, 防止 fángzhǐ

precocious ADJ 早熟的 zǎoshú de, 智力超常的 zhìlì chāocháng de

preconceived ADJ 预先形成的 yùxiān xíngchéng de

preconception N 先入为主的偏见 xiān rù wéi zhǔ de piānjiàn

precondition N 先决条件 xiānjué tiáojiàn, 前提 qiántí

precursor N 前身 qiánshēn

predate V 先于…发生 xiānyú...fāshēng

predator N 1 捕食其他动物的动物 bǔshí qítā dòngwù de dòngwù 2 掠夺者 lüèduózhě, 损人利己的人 sǔnrén lìjǐ de rén

predatory ADJ 1 捕食其他动物的 bǔshí qítā dòngwù de 2 掠夺性的 lüèduó xìng de

predecessor N 前任 qiánrèn, 前辈 qiánbèi

predestination N 宿命论 sùmìnglùn

predestined ADJ 命中注定 (的) mìngzhōng zhùdìng (de)

predetermined ADJ 预先确定 (的) yùxiān quèdìng (de)

predicament N 困境 kùnjìng

predicate N (语法) 谓语 (yǔfǎ) wèiyǔ

predict V 预言 yùyán, 预测 yùcè

prediction N 预言 yùyán, 预测 yùcè

predilection N 偏爱 piān'ài

predisposed ADJ 1 有…倾向的 yǒu...qīngxiàng de 2 易患 [+高血压] de yìhuàn [+gāoxuèyā] de

predominance N 优势 yōushì

predominant ADJ 占优势的 zhàn yōushì de

predominantly ADV 绝大多数 (地) juédà duōshù (de)

predominate V 占主要地位 zhàn zhǔyào dìwèi

preeminent ADJ 卓越的 zhuóyuè de, 杰出的 jiéchū de

preempt V 先发制人以阻止 [+敌人的进攻] xiānfāzhìrén yǐ zǔzhǐ [+dírén de jìngōng]

preemptive ADJ 先发制人的 xiānfāzhìrén de

preen V [鸟+] 整理羽毛 [niǎo +] zhěnglǐ yǔmáo
  to preen oneself [人+] 精心打扮 [rén+] jīngxīn dǎban

pre-existing ADJ 早先就存在的 zǎoxiān jiù cúnzài de

prefabricated ADJ 预制的 yùzhì de

preface I N 序言 xùyán, 前言 qiányán II V 以…作为开始 yǐ...zuòwéi kāishǐ

prefer V 更喜欢 gèngxǐhuan, 比较喜欢 bǐjiào xǐhuan ■ *We can have steak or fish for the main course. Which would you prefer?* 我们主菜可以吃肉排, 或者鱼; 你喜欢哪一样? Wǒmen zhǔcài kěyǐ chī ròupái, huòzhě yú; nǐ xǐhuan nǎ yí yàng?

preferable ADJ 更可取的 gèng kěqǔ de, 更好 gènghǎo

preferably ADV 更可取 (地) gèng kěqǔ (de), 最好 zuìhǎo

preference N 偏爱 piān'ài
  in preference to sth 不要某事 búyào mǒu shì

preferential ADJ 优惠的 yōuhuì de, 优待的 yōudài de

prefix N 前缀 qiánzhuì

pregnancy N 怀孕 (期) huáiyùn (qī)

pregnant ADJ 1 怀孕的 huáiyùn de ■ *Ellen is three months pregnant and is already suffering from discomfort.* 艾伦怀孕三个月, 已经不舒服了。Àilún huáiyùn sān ge yuè, yǐjing bù shūfú le. 2 富有含义的 fùyǒu hányì de, 意味深长的 yìwèi shēncháng de
  a pregnant pause 意味深长的停顿 yìwèi shēncháng de tíngdùn

preheat V 预热 yùrè

prehistoric ADJ 史前的 shǐqián de

prehistory N 史前时期 shǐqián shíqī

prejudge V 过早判断 guòzǎo pànduàn

prejudice I N 偏见 piānjiàn, 成见 chéngjiàn

II v 使…有偏见 shǐ…yǒu piānjiàn, 使…有成见 shǐ…yǒu chéngjiàn

prejudicial ADJ 不利的 búlì de

preliminary I ADJ 初步的 chūbù de, 起始的 qǐshǐ de II N (preliminaries) 初步行动 chūbù xíngdòng, 筹备工作 chóubèi gōngzuò

prelude N (戏剧) 序幕 (xìjù) xùmù, (音乐) 序曲 (yīnyuè) xùqǔ [M. WD 首 shǒu]

premarital ADJ 婚前的 hūnqián de
premarital sex 婚前性行为 hūnqián xìng xíngwéi

premature ADJ 过早的 guòzǎo de, 不成熟的 bùchéngshú de
premature death 早逝 zǎoshì, [儿童+] 夭折 [értóng+] yāozhé, [中年人+] 英年早逝 [zhōngniánrén+] yīngnián zǎoshì

premeditated ADJ 预谋的 yùmóu de

premeditation N 预谋 yùmóu

premenstrual ADJ 月经前的 yuèjīng qián de

premier I N 总理 zǒnglǐ II ADJ 最好的 zuìhǎo de, 首要的 shǒuyào de

première N (电影) 首映 (diànyǐng) shǒuyìng, (戏剧) 首演 (xìjù) shǒuyǎn, (电视连续剧) 首播 (diànshì liánxùjù) shǒubō

premise N 前提 qiántí

premises N 房屋连土地 fángwū lián tǔdì, 场所 chǎngsuǒ

premium N 1 保险费 bǎoxiǎnfèi 2 优质汽油 yōuzhì qìyóu
at a premium 紧缺 jǐnquē
to place a premium on sth 高度重视某事 gāodù zhòngshì mǒushì

premonition N 预感 yùgǎn

premonitory ADJ 给予警告的 jǐyǔ jǐnggào de, 预兆的 yùzhào de

prenatal ADJ 产前的 chǎnqián de, 孕期的 yùnqī de

preoccupation N 全神贯注 quánshén guànzhù, 入神 rùshén

preoccupied ADJ 全神贯注的 quánshén guànzhù de, 入神的 rùshén de

preoccupy v 使…全神贯注 shǐ…quánshén guànzhù, 使…入神 shǐ…rùshén

preordained ADJ 命中注定的 mìngzhōng zhùdìng de

prepaid ADJ 预付的 yùfù de
prepaid envelope 邮资已付的信封 yóuzīyǐfù de xìnfēng

preparation N 准备 zhǔnbèi
to make preparations for 准备 zhǔnbèi, 为…作准备 wèi…zuò zhǔnbèi

preparatory ADJ 预备的 yùbèi de, 准备的 zhǔnbèi de
preparatory school (prep school) 私立预备学校 sīlì yùbèi xuéxiào

prepare v 准备 zhǔnbèi

prepared ADJ 1 有准备的 yǒu zhǔnbèi de, 做好准备的 zuò hǎo zhǔnbèi de ■ *"Be prepared!" the boy scouts shouted in chorus.* "时刻准备着！" 童子军齐声喊叫。"Shíkè zhǔnbèizhe!" tóngzǐjūn qíshēng hǎnjiào.
be prepared for the worst 做最坏打算 zuò zuì huài dǎsuan
2 愿意的 yuànyì de

preparedness N 有准备 (的状态) yǒu zhǔnbèi (de zhuàngtài)

preponderance N 优势 yōushì, 多数 duōshù

preposition N 介词 jiècí, 前置词 qiánzhìcí

preposterous ADJ 荒诞的 huāngdàn de, 完全不合理的 wánquán bùhélǐ de

preppy ADJ 私立学校学生的 sīlì xuéxiào xuésheng de

preregister v 预先登记 yùxiān dēngjì, 预先注册 yùxiān zhùcè

preregistration N 预先登记 yùxiān dēngjì, 预先注册 yùxiān zhùcè

prerequisite N 先决条件 xiānjué tiáojiàn, 必备条件 bìbèi tiáojiàn

prerogative N 特权 tèquán

presage v 预示 yùshì, 预告 yùgào

Presbyterian N 长老会教徒 Zhǎnglǎohuì jiàotú

preschool N 学前班 xué qián bān, 幼儿园 yòu'éryuán

prescribe v 1 [医生+] 嘱咐 (使用) 开处方 [yīshēng+] zhǔfù (shǐyòng) kāi chǔfāng 2 规定 guīdìng, 指定 zhǐdìng

prescription N 处方 chǔfāng [M. WD 份 fèn/张 zhāng], 药方 yàofāng [M. WD 份 fèn/张 zhāng]

prescriptive ADJ 规定的 guīdìng de, 指定的 zhǐdìng de

presence N 1 在场 zàichǎng, 出席 chūxí 2 风采气势 fēngcǎi qìshì

present[1] I ADJ 1 在场的 zàichǎng de, 出席的 chūxí de ■ *There were about 80 people present at the wedding.* 大约有八十个人参加了婚礼。Dàyuē yǒu bāshí ge rén cānjiāle hūnlǐ. 2 目前的 mùqián de, 现在的 xiànzài de
present participle 现在分词 xiànzài fēncí
present perfect 现在完成时态 xiànzài wánchéng shítài
(the) present tense 现在时态 xiànzài shítài
II N 现在 xiànzài, 目前 mùqián

present[2] I N 礼物 lǐwù, 礼品 lǐpǐn II v 1 给予 [+礼物] jǐyǔ [+lǐwù], 赠与 zèngyǔ 2 提出 [+论文] tíchū [+lùnwén], 宣布 xuānbù 3 上演 [+戏剧] shàngyǎn [+xìjù], 演出 yǎnchū

presentable ADJ 拿得出手的 nádéchūshǒu de, 体面的 tǐmiàn de

presentation N 1 报告 bàogào, 陈述 chénshù
to give a presentation on the new project 介绍新产品 jièshào xīnchǎnpǐn

2 授予 shòuyǔ, 颁发 bānfā
presentation ceremony 授奖仪式 shòujiǎng yíshì
3 (a presentation copy) 赠阅本 zèngyuèběn
present-day ADJ 今日的 jīnrì de, 现今的 xiànjīn de
presently ADV 立即 lìjí, 即刻 jíkè
preservation N 保护 bǎohù, 维护 wéihù
preservative N 防腐剂 fángfǔjì
preserve I V 1 维护 wéihù, 保护 bǎohù ■ *The local authorities are doing a remarkable job in preserving this 18th century house.* 地方当局在保护这座十八世纪建筑方面做得很出色。Dìfāng dāngjú zài bǎohù zhè zuò shíbā shìjì jiànzhù fāngmian zuòde hěn chūsè. II N 1 自然保护区 zìrán bǎohùqū
2 独占的地盘 dúzhàn de dìpán **3** 果酱 guǒjiàng
preside V 主持 zhǔchí, 负责 fùzé
presidency N 总统的职位 zǒngtǒng de zhíwèi, 大学校长的职位 dàxué xiàozhǎng de zhíwèi
president N 总统 zǒngtǒng, 大学校长 dàxué xiàozhǎng, 主席 zhǔxí
    president of a university 大学校长 dàxué xiàozhǎng
    president of a bank 银行行长 yínháng hángzhǎng
    president of a club 俱乐部主任 jùlèbù zhǔrèn
    president of a company 公司董事长 gōngsī dǒngshìzhǎng
    president of a trade union 工会主席 gōnghuì zhǔxí
    U.S. President 美国总统 Měiguó zǒngtǒng
president-elect N 当选总统 dāngxuǎn zǒngtǒng
presidential ADJ 总统的 zǒngtǒng de
    presidential suite（旅馆的）总统套房 (lǚguǎn de) zǒngtǒng tàofáng
President's Day N（美国）总统日 (Měiguó) zǒngtǒng rì (the 3rd Monday of February)
press I N 1 新闻界 xīnwén jiè
    press agent 新闻代理人 xīnwén dàilǐrén
    press conference 记者招待会 jìzhě zhāodàihuì
    press corps 记者团 jìzhě tuán
    press release 新闻稿 xīnwéngǎo
2 出版社 chūbǎnshè ■ *The family owns a small press specializing in Christian books.* 这个家庭拥有一家小出版社，专门出版基督教书籍。Zhè ge jiātíng yōngyǒu yì jiā xiǎo chūbǎn shè, zhuānmén chūbǎn Jīdūjiào shūjí. II V 1 按 àn ■ *Press F11 for a full screen.* 按F11键，得到全屏幕。Àn F11 jiàn, dédào quán píngmù. **2** 熨烫 [+衬衫] yùn tàng [+chènshān], 烫平 tàngpíng **3** 压平 yāpíng, 压碎 yāsuì **4** 催促 cuīcù, 力劝 lìquàn
5 (to press charges) 提出诉讼 tíchū sùsòng
pressed ADJ (be pressed for time/money) 时间／资金紧张 shíjiān/zījīn jǐnzhāng
pressing ADJ 紧迫的 jǐnpò de
pressure I N 1 压力 yālì **2**（大）气压 (dà) qìyā

pressure cooker 压力锅 yālì guō
    II V 对…施加压力 duì…shījiā yālì
pressured ADJ 感觉有压力的 gǎnjué yǒu yālì de
pressure group N 压力集团 yālì jítuán
pressurized ADJ 加压的 jiāyā de, 增压的 zēngyā de
prestige N 威望 wēiwàng, 声望 shēngwàng
prestigious ADJ 有声望的 yǒushēng wàng de, 威望很高的 wēiwàng hěn gāo de
presumably ADV 可能 kěnéng, 大概 dàgài, 据推测 jù tuīcè
presume V 猜想 cāixiǎng, 认为 rènwéi, 推测 tuīcè
presumption N 假定 jiǎdìng, 推定 tuīdìng
presumptuous ADJ 自以为是的 zì yǐwéi shì de, 冒失的 màoshi de
presuppose V 预先假设 yùxiān jiǎshè, 预设 yù shè
pretend I V 假装 jiǎzhuāng ■ *Stop pretending!* 别装模作样了！Bié zhuāng mú zuò yàng le! II ADJ 假装的 jiǎzhuāng de, 假想的 jiǎxiǎng de
pretense N 假装 jiǎzhuāng, 伪称 wěichēng
    under false pretense 以虚假的借口 yǐ xūjiǎ de jièkǒu
    under the pretense of 以…为借口 yǐ…wéi jièkǒu, 借口 jièkǒu
pretension N 虚荣 xūróng, 自负 zìfù
pretentious ADJ 装腔作势的 zhuāngqiāng zuòshì de, 矫饰的 jiǎoshì de
pretext N 借口 jièkǒu, 托词 tuōcí
    under the pretext that 以…为借口 yǐ…wéi jièkǒu
pretty I ADJ 漂亮的 piàoliang de, 可爱的 kě'ài de
    II ADV 相当 xiāngdāng ■ *His financial situation is pretty awful.* 他的财务情况相当糟。Tā de cáiwù qíngkuàng xiāngdāng zāo.
pretzel N 椒盐饼干 jiāoyán bǐnggān [M. WD 块 kuài]
prevail V 1 占优势 zhàn yōushì, 占上风 zhàn shàngfēng **2** 盛行 shèngxíng, 流行 liúxíng
prevailing ADJ 流行的 liúxíng de, 普遍的 pǔbiàn de
prevalence N 流行的程度 liúxíng de chéngdù
prevalent ADJ 盛行的 shèngxíng de, 流行的 liúxíng de
prevent V 防止 fángzhǐ, 阻止 zǔzhǐ ■ *The police successfully prevented a terrorist attack.* 警察成功地阻止了一起恐怖攻击事件。Jǐngchá chénggōng de zǔzhǐle yì qǐ kǒngbù gōngjī shìjiàn.
prevention N 防止 fángzhǐ, 阻止 zǔzhǐ
    Prevention is better than cure. 预防胜于治疗。Yùfáng shèngyú zhìliáo.
preventive ADJ 预防（性）的 yùfáng (xìng) de, 防备的 fángbèi de
preview N（电影）预映 (diànyǐng) yù yìng,（戏剧）预演 (xìjù) yùyǎn

previous ADJ 前一个 qián yí ge, 上一个 shàng yí ge ■ *The previous manager made a mess of things.* 前经理把事情弄得一团糟。Qián jīnglǐ bǎ shìqing nòngde yìtuánzāo.

previously ADV 以前 yǐqián, 先前 xiānqián

prewar ADJ, ADV 战前（的）zhànqián (de)

prey I N 被捕食的动物 bèi bǔshí de dòngwù, 猎物 lièwù

beast of prey 食肉猛兽 shí ròu měngshòu

to fall prey to 成为…的牺牲品 chéngwéi…de xīshēngpǐn

II v (to prey on) 伤害 shānghài

price I N 1 价格 jiàgé, 价钱 jiàqian 2 代价 dàijià ■ *Age is a high price to pay for maturity.* 年老是成熟的昂贵代价。Niánlǎo shì chéngshú de ángguì dàijià.

the asking price 要价 yàojià ■ *The asking price for the notebook computer is $950, but I paid $800 for it.* 这个笔记本电脑要价九百五十元，我付了八百元。Zhè ge bǐjìběn diànnǎo yàojià jiǔ bǎi wǔshí yuán, wǒ fùle bā bǎi yuán.

at a price 以代价 yǐ dàijià ■ *Regular exercises are a small price to pay for keeping fit.* 经常锻炼是为保持健康付出的小小代价。Jīngcháng duànliàn shì wèi bǎochí jiànkāng fùchū de xiǎoxiǎo dàijià.

at any price 不惜代价 bù xī dàijià ■ *He is determined to move up the corporate ladder at any price.* 他决定不惜代价攀登企业的台阶。Tā juédìng bù xī dàijià pāndēng qǐyè de táijiē.

II v 给…定价 / 标价 gěi…dìngjià/biāojià

priceless ADJ 无价的 wújià de, 价值极高的 jiàzhí jí gāo de

pricey, pricy ADJ（价格）昂贵的 (jiàgé) ánguì de

prick I v 1（刺）破 (cì) pò,（扎）穿 (zhā) chuān 2 刺痛 cìtòng

to prick up one's ears 竖起耳朵听 shùqǐ ěrduo tīng

II N 1 刺孔 cìkǒng 2 刺痛 cìtòng

prickle I N 1 皮刺 pí cì 2 刺痛（感）cìtòng (gǎn)

II v 刺痛 cìtòng

prickly ADJ 1 多刺的 [+玫瑰] duō cì de [+méigui] 2 引起刺痛的 yǐnqǐ cìtòng de 3 棘手的 [+事] jíshǒu de [+shì]

pride N 骄傲 jiāo'ào, 自傲 zì'ào ■ *I don't want your money; I have my pride.* 我不要你的钱，我有自尊心。Wǒ bú yào nǐ de qián, wǒ yǒu zìzūnxīn.

priest N 神甫 shénfu, 教士 jiàoshì

priesthood N 神职人员的职位 shénzhí rényuán de zhíwèi, 神职 shénzhí

prim ADJ 古板的 gǔbǎn de, 一本正经的 yì běn zhèngjīng de

primacy N 首位 shǒuwèi, 首要 shǒuyào

prima donna N 1 首席女歌唱家 shǒuxí nǚ gēchàngjiā 2 妄自尊大的人 wàng zì zūn dà de rén

primal ADJ 原始的 yuánshǐ de, 基本的 jīběn de

primarily ADV 主要地 zhǔyào de

primary I ADJ 1 首要的 shǒuyào de, 第一的 dìyī de ■ *It is of primary importance to have constant practice if you want to improve your Spoken Chinese.* 你如果想改进中文口语，最重要的是经常练习。Nǐ rúguǒ xiǎng gǎijìn Zhōngwén kǒuyǔ, zuìzhòngyào de shì jīngcháng liànxí. 2 最初的 zuìchū de, 基本的 jīběn de

primary care 基础保健 jīchǔ bǎojiàn

primary color 原色 yuánsè, 基色 jīsè

primary school 小学 xiǎoxué

II N（美国总统候选人的）初选 (Měiguó zǒngtǒng hòuxuǎnrén de) chūxuǎn

primate N 灵长目动物 língzhǎngmù dòngwù

prime I ADJ 最重要的 zhòngyào de, 最好的 zuìhǎo de

prime minister 首相 shǒuxiàng, 总理 zǒnglǐ

prime number 质数 zhìshù

prime time 黄金时段 huángjīn shíduàn

II N 盛年 shèngnián, 鼎盛年华 dǐngshèng niánhuá III v (to be primed) 准备好 zhǔnbèi hǎo, 做好准备 zuòhǎo zhǔnbèi

primer N 1 底漆 dǐqī 2 入门指南（书）rùmén zhǐnán (shū)

primeval ADJ 1 太初的 tàichū de, 太古的 tàigǔ de 2 远古的 yuǎngǔ de, 原始的 yuánshǐ de

primitive ADJ 原始的 yuánshǐ de ■ *Cannibalism was practiced in some primitive societies.* 某些原始社会有吃人的习俗。Mǒuxiē yuánshǐ shèhuì yǒu chīrén de xísú.

primordial ADJ 太古的 tàigǔ de, 太初的 tàichū de

primp v 梳妆打扮 shūzhuāngdǎbàn

primrose N 1 报春花 bàochūnhuā [M. WD 朵 duǒ] 2 淡黄色 dànhuángsè

prince N 王子 wángzǐ, 亲王 qīnwáng

princely ADJ 1 王子的 wángzǐ de, 亲王的 qīnwáng de 2 慷慨的 kāngkǎi de, 大度的 dàdù de

a princely sum 一笔巨款 yìbǐ jùkuǎn

princess N 公主 gōngzhǔ, 王妃 wángfēi

principal I ADJ 主要的 zhǔyào de ■ *The principal aim of the program is to reduce poverty in the region.* 这项计划的主要目标是减少地区的贫穷现象。Zhè xiàng jìhuà de zhǔyào mùbiāo shì jiǎnshǎo dìqū de pínqióng xiànxiàng. II N 1 校长 xiàozhǎng, 院长 yuànzhǎng 2 本金 běnjīn, 资本 zīběn

principality N 公国 gōngguó

principally ADV 主要地 zhǔyào de

principle N 1 原则 yuánzé ■ *I agree with you in principle.* 我原则上同意你。Wǒ yuánzéshang tóngyì nǐ. 2 原理 yuánlǐ ■ *I don't even understand the basic principles of corporate accountancy.* 我甚至不懂公司会计学的基本原理。（→我对公司会计学一窍不通。）Wǒ shènzhì bù dǒng gōngsī kuàijìxué de jīběn yuánlǐ. (→Wǒ duì gōngsī kuàijìxué yí qiào bù tōng.)

principled ADJ 有原则的 yǒu yuánzé de, 坚持原则的 jiānchí yuánzé de

print I v 印 yìn, 印刷 yìnshuā ■ *This beautiful art book was printed in China.* 这本漂亮的艺术书是在中国印刷的。Zhè běn piàoliang de yìshù shū shì zài Zhōngguó yìnshuā de.

to print money 大量印发钞票 dàliàng yìnfā chāopiào

2 用印刷体书写 yòngyìn shuā tǐ shūxiě II N **1** 印刷字体 yìnshuā zìtǐ ■ *The print is too small for old people to read.* 这种印刷字体太小，老年人看不清。Zhè zhǒng yìnshuā zìtǐ tài xiǎo, lǎoniánrén kànbuqīng.

the fine print 小号印刷体 xiǎohào yìnshuātǐ, 文件的细节 wénjiàn de xìjié ■ *Be sure to read and understand the fine print in a document before signing it.* 在文件上签字以前，一定要看懂小号印刷体印的细节。Zài wénjiànshang qiānzì yǐqián, yídìng yào kàndǒng xiǎohào yìnshuātǐ yìn de xìjié.

in print [书+] 买得到 [shū+] mǎidedào

out of print 印刷 (书) 绝版 juébǎn (shū), 买不到的书 mǎibudào de shū

2 印刷品 yìnshuāpǐn

printed matter（邮寄的）印刷品 (yóujì de) yìnshuāpǐn

print media 报刊（媒体）bàokān (méitǐ)

3（印出来的）照片 (yìnchū láide) zhàopiàn, 电影拷贝 diànyǐng kǎobèi **4** 印记 yìnjì, 印痕 yìnhén

printer N **1**（计算机）打印机 (jìsuànjī) dǎyìnjī [M. WD 台 tái] **2** 印刷工人 yìnshuāgōngrén

printing N **1** 印刷（技术）yìnshuā (jìshù) **2**（书的一次）印刷 (shū de yícì) yìnshuā

printing press N 印刷机 yìnshuājī [M. WD 台 tái]

printout N（计算机）打印出来的材料 (jìsuànjī) dǎyìn chūlái de cáiliào [M. WD 份 fèn]

prior ADJ 事先的 shìxiān de, 以前的 yǐqián de

prior conviction 犯罪前科 fànzuì qiánkē

prior warning 事先警告 shìxiān jǐnggào

prior to sth 在某事之前 zài mǒushì zhī qián

prioritize v 确定…先后顺序 quèdìng…xiānhòu shùnxù

priority N **1** 最重要的事 zuìzhòngyào de shì, 首先要做的事 shǒuxiān yào zuò de shì ■ *I'll make it my priority to pass all the exams.* 我要把通过考试作为我最重要的事。Wǒ yào bǎ tōngguò kǎoshì zuòwéi wǒ zuìzhòngyào de shì.

to get one's priorities right 按照轻重缓急办事 ànzhào qīng zhòng huǎn jí bànshì ■ *The first principle of time management is to get your priorities right.* 时间管理的第一条原则是按照轻重缓急办事。Shíjiān guǎnlǐ de dìyī tiáo yuánzé shì ànzhào qīng zhòng huǎn jí bànshì.

to get one's priorities wrong 不按照轻重缓急办事 bú ànzhào qīng zhòng huǎn jí bànshì

to give priority to 把…作为重点 bǎ…zuòwéi zhòngdiǎn, 优先办理 yōuxiān bànlǐ

2 优先（权）yōuxiān (quán)

to have priority over 享有优先权 xiǎngyǒu yōuxiānquán ■ *What makes you think you have priority over me?* 你凭什么要优先于我？Nǐ píng shénme yào yōuxiān yú wǒ?

prism N 棱镜 léngjìng

prison N 监狱 jiānyù [M. WD 座 zuò]

prisoner N 犯人 fànrén, 囚犯 qiúfàn

prisoner of conscience 政治犯 zhèngzhìfàn, 良心犯 liángxīn fàn

prissy ADJ 谨小慎微的 jǐn xiǎo shènwēi de, 一板一眼的 yìbǎnyìyǎn de

pristine ADJ 崭新的 zhǎnxīn de, 一尘不染的 yì chén bù rǎn de

privacy N 隐私（权）yǐnsī (quán)

private I ADJ **1** 私人的 sīrén de ■ *These are my private papers—you've no right to look at them!* 这些是我的私人文件—你没有权力看them! Zhèxiē shì wǒ de sīrén wénjiàn—nǐ méiyǒu quánlì kàn!

private investigator 私家侦探 sījiā zhēntàn

private parts 生殖器 shēngzhíqì, 私处 sīchù

2 私立的 sīlì de, 私营的 sīyíng de ■ *This private school is very expensive.* 这所私立学校很贵。Zhè suǒ sīlì xuéxiào hěn guì.

private enterprise 私营企业制 sīyíng qǐyè zhì

II N (in private) 私下（地）sīxia (de), 秘密地 mìmì de

privatize v 将…私有化 jiāng…sīyǒuhuà

privilege N 特权 tèquán, 特殊的荣幸 tèshū de róngxìng

privileged ADJ 享有特权的 xiǎngyǒu tèquán de

privy I ADJ (privy to) 了解 [+内情] 的 liǎojiě [+nèiqíng] de II N 厕所 cèsuǒ

prize I N 奖 jiǎng, 奖赏 jiǎngshǎng, 奖品 jiǎngpǐn II v 十分珍视 shífēn zhēnshì, 高度重视 gāodù zhòngshì III ADJ 优等的 yōuděng de, 获奖的 huòjiǎng de

prizefight N 职业拳击赛 zhíyè quánjī sài

pro N 专业人员 zhuānyè rényuán, 职业运动员 zhíyè yùndòngyuán

to go pro 成为职业运动员 chéngwéi zhíyè yùndòngyuán

probability N **1** 可能性 kěnéngxìng

in all probability 极有可能 jí yǒu kěnéng

2 概率 gàilǜ

probable ADJ 很可能的 hěn kěnéng de

probably ADV 很有可能（地）hěn yǒu kěnéng (de) ■ *Scientists say the polar bear will probably be extinct in 30 years.* 科学家说，北极熊很有可能在三十年内灭绝。Kēxuéjiā shuō, Běijí xióng hěn yǒukěnéng zài sānshí nián nèi mièjué.

probation N 1 （罪犯）缓刑 (zuìfàn) huǎnxíng 2 （雇员）试用期 (gùyuán) shìyòngqī 3 （雇员）留任察用期 (gùyuán) liúrèn chá yòng qī probation officer 缓刑监督官 huǎnxíng jiāndū guān

probe I v 调查 diàochá II N 1 （彻底）调查 (chèdǐ) diàochá 2 航天探测器 hángtiān tàncèqì

problem N 1 难题 nántí, 困难 kùnnan ■ *I've had a problem with the computer—it often crashes.* 我的电脑出问题了—老是死机。Wǒ de diànnǎo chūwèntí le—lǎo shì sǐjī. 2 问题 wèntí 3 题目 tímù ■ *This math problem is really difficult.* 这道数学题真难。Zhè dào shùxué tí zhēn nán. No problem. ① 没问题。Méi wèntí. ■ *"Can I use your dictionary?" "Sure, no problem."* "我可以用你的词典吗？" "没问题。" "Wǒ kěyǐ yòng nǐ de cídiǎn ma?" "Méi wèntí." ② 没什么 méishénme ■ *"I'm sorry to have kept you waiting." "No problem."* "对不起，让你等了。" "没什么。" "Duìbuqǐ, ràng nǐ děng le." "Méishénme."

problematic ADJ 有很多难题的 yǒu hěn duō nántí de, 很难对付的 hěn nán duìfu de

procedure N 1 程序 chéngxù, 步骤 bùzhòu 2 （特殊的）外科手术 (tèshū de) wàikē shǒushù

proceed v 1 （继续）进行 (jìxù) jìnxíng, 进行下去 jìnxíng xiàqu 2 行进 xíngjìn, 前进 qiánjìn

proceedings N 1 [刑事+] 诉讼 [xíngshì+] sùsòng 2 会议记录 huìyì jìlù

proceeds N 收入 shōurù, 收益 shōuyì

process I N 1 过程 guòchéng ■ *We're in the process of selling our house.* 我们正在出售我们的住房。Wǒmen zhèngzài chūshòu wǒmen de zhùfáng. 2 工艺流程 gōngyìliúchéng II v 1 加工 [+食品] jiāgōng [+shípǐn] 2 处理 [+数据] chǔlǐ [+shùjù]

procession N 1 游行队伍 yóuxíng duìwǔ, 车队 chēduì 2 一系列（事件）yíxìliè (shìjiàn)

processor N （计算机）信息处理器 (jìsuànjī) xìnxī chǔlǐqì word processor 文字处理器 wénzì chǔlǐqì

proclamation N 公告 gōnggào, 宣言 xuānyán

procrastinate v 耽搁 dānge, 拖延 tuōyán

procrastination N 耽搁 dānge, 拖延 tuōyán

procreate v 生育（后代）shēngyù (hòudài)

procreation N 生育（后代）shēngyù (hòudài)

procure v 获取 huòqǔ, 采购 cǎigòu

procurement N 获取 huòqǔ, 采购 cǎigòu

prod v, N 1 激励 jīlì, 促使 cùshǐ 2 戳 chuō, 捅 tǒng

prodigal I ADJ 挥霍浪费的 huīhuòlàngfèi de II N 挥霍浪费的人 huīhuòlàngfèi de rén

prodigious ADJ 大得惊人的 dà de jīngrén de

prodigy N 奇才 qícái, 神童 shéntóng

produce I v 1 生产 shēngchǎn ■ *The factory is producing a new line of shoes.* 这家工厂在生产一系列新鞋。Zhè jiā gōngchǎng zài shēngchǎn yí xìliè xīn xié. 2 出产 chūchǎn 3 出示 [+文件] chūshì [+wénjiàn] 4 制作电影/电视节目 zhìzuò diànyǐng/diànshì jiémù II N 蔬菜水果 shūcài shuǐguǒ, 农产品 nóngchǎnpǐn

producer N 1 生产者 shēngchǎnzhě, 制造厂商 zhìzào chǎng shāng 2 （电影/电视/广播）制片人 (diànyǐng/diànshì/guǎngbō) zhìpiànrén

product N 1 产品 chǎnpǐn, 制品 zhìpǐn ■ *New Zealand is well-known for its quality dairy products.* 新西兰因高质量的乳制品而闻名。Xīnxīlán yīn gāo zhìliàng de rǔzhìpǐn ér wénmíng. 2 结果 jiéguǒ, 产物 chǎnwù 3 （数学）乘积 (shùxué) chéngjī

production N 1 生产 shēngchǎn ■ *Production of hybrid cars is expected to increase dramatically.* 人们预料，油电两用车的生产将大大增加。Rénmen yùliào, yóu diàn liǎng yòng chē de shēngchǎn jiāng dàdà zēngjiā. 2 电影作品 diànyǐng zuòpǐn, 戏剧作品 xìjù zuòpǐn

productive ADJ 1 多产的 duō chǎn de 2 富有成效的 fùyǒuchóngxiào de 3 生产性 [+设备] 的 shēngchǎnxìng [+shèbèi] de

productivity N 生产（效）率 shēngchǎn (xiào) lǜ

profane ADJ 1 亵渎（神灵）的 xièdú (shénlíng) de 2 下流的 [+语言] xiàliú de [+yǔyán]

profanity N 亵渎的语言 xièdú de yǔyán, 下流话 xiàliúhuà

profess v 1 自称 zìchēng, 谎称 huǎngchēng 2 公开表明 gōngkāi biǎomíng

profession N 1 专业 zhuānyè, 职业 zhíyè ■ *She is a clinical psychologist by profession.* 她的专业是临床心理学家。Tā de zhuānyè shì línchuáng xīnlǐxuéjiā. 2 [所有的+] 专业人士 [suǒyǒu de+] zhuānyè rénshì 3 公开表白 gōngkāi biǎobái

professional I ADJ 专业的 zhuānyè de ■ *Professional athletes make tons of money.* 专业运动员大把大把地赚钱。Zhuānyè yùndòngyuán dàbǎ dàbǎ de zhuànqián. II N 专业人士 zhuānyè rénshì

professionalism N 专业精神 zhuānyè jīngshén, 精益求精的态度 jīng yì qiú jīng de tàidu

professor N 教授 jiàoshòu, 大学教师 dàxué jiàoshī

proffer v （正式）提出 [+道歉] (zhèngshì) tíchū [+dàoqiàn]

proficiency N 精通 jīngtōng, 熟练 shúliàn, proficiency in Chinese 中文水平 Zhōngwén shuǐpíng, 精通中文 jīngtōng Zhōngwén

proficient ADJ 精通的 jīngtōng de, 熟练的 shúliàn de be proficient in a language 精通一门言语 jīngtōng yìmén yǔyán

profile N 1 （人头部的）侧面 (réntóu bù de) cèmiàn 2 （人物）简介 (rénwù) jiǎnjiè to keep a high/low profile 保持高/低姿态 bǎochí gāo/dī zītài

profit I N **1** 利润 lìrùn ■ *I sold my house and actually made a profit.* 我卖了房子，实际上赚了钱。Wǒ màile fángzi, shíjìshang zhuànle qián.
profit margin 利润率 lìrùnlǜ
profit sharing 分享利润 fēnxiǎng lìrùn, 分红制 fēnhóngzhì
gross profit 毛利 máolì
net profit 净利润 jìng lìrùn, 纯利润 chún lìrùn **2** 利益 lìyì, 好处 hǎochu **II** v **1** 对…有益 duì… yǒuyì, 对…有利 duì…yǒulì **2** 获利 huòlì
profitability N 获利（程度）huòlì (chéngdù)
profitable ADJ 可获利的 kě huò lì de, 盈利的 yínglì de
profiteer N 牟取非法暴利者 móuqǔ fēifǎ bàolì zhě, 奸商 jiānshāng
profiteering N 牟取非法暴利（的行为）móuqǔ fēifǎ bàolì (de xíngwéi)
profligate ADJ 挥霍浪费的 huīhuòlàngfèi de
profound ADJ **1** 深刻的 shēnkè de, 深远的 shēnyuǎn de **2** 知识渊博的 zhīshi yuānbó de
profoundity N 深刻 shēnkè, 深度 shēndù
profuse ADJ 大量的 dàliàng de, 极其丰富的 jíqí fēngfù de
profusion N 大量 dàliàng, 充沛 chōngpèi
progeny N **1** 后代 hòudài **2** 后续的事 hòuxù de shì
prognosis N 预后 yùhòu, 预测 yùcè
program N **1**（电视／演出）节目 (diànshì/yǎnchū) jiémù **2**（电脑）程序 (diànnǎo) chéngxù ■ *This program allows you to edit digital photos.* 这个电脑程序使你可以编辑数码照片。Zhè ge diànnǎo chéngxù shǐ nǐ kěyǐ biānjí shùmǎ zhàopiàn. **3** 课程 kèchéng ■ *The teachers are encouraged to enroll in an IT training program.* 老师们被鼓励参加信息技术训练课程。Lǎoshīmen bèi gǔlì cānjiā xìnxī jìshù xùnliàn kèchéng. **4** 方案 fāng'àn, 计划 jìhuà ■ *Greenpeace is going to launch a program to save dolphins.* 绿色和平要开展一项拯救海豚的计划。Lǜsè hépíng yào kāizhǎn yí xiàng zhěngjiù hǎitún de jìhuà.
programmer N（计算机）程序编写员 (jìsuànjī) chéngxù biānxiěyuán
programming N **1**（计算机）程序编写 (jìsuànjī) chéngxù biānxiě **2**（电视／广播）节目 (diànshì/guǎngbō) jiémù
progress I N **1** 进步 jìnbù **2** 进展 jìnzhǎn **II** v **1**（工作+）进展 [gōngzuò+] jìnzhǎn **2** [人+] 缓慢行进 [rén+] huǎnmàn xíngjìn
progression N 进展 jìnzhǎn **2** 移动 yídòng, 行进 xíngjìn
progressive I ADJ 进步的 jìnbù de **II** N 进步人士 jìnbùrénshì [M. WD 位 wèi]
prohibit v 禁止 jìnzhǐ
prohibitive ADJ **1** 禁止（性）的 jìnzhǐ (xìng) de **2** 高得负担不起的 [+价格] gāo de fùdān bùqǐ de [+jiàgé]

project I N **1** 项目 xiàngmù ■ *This research project is funded by the state government.* 这个研究项目是州政府资助的。Zhè ge yánjiū xiàngmù shì zhōu zhèngfǔ zīzhù de. **2** 课题 kètí, 作业 zuòyè **II** v **1** 预计 yùjì, 推测 tuīcè **2** 放映（电影）fàngyìng (diànyǐng) **3** 作投影图 zuò tóuyǐngtú
projectile N 投掷物 tóuzhì wù, 发射物 fāshè wù
projection N **1** 预测 yùcè, 推断 tuīduàn **2** 凹出物 āo chū wù **3** 投影 tóuyǐng, 投射 tóushè
projectionist N 电影放映员 diànyǐng fàngyìngyuán
projector N 幻灯机 huàndēngjī, 电影放映机 diànyǐng fàngyìngjī
proletarian ADJ 无产阶级的 wúchǎnjiējí de
proletariat N 无产阶级 wúchǎnjiējí
proliferate v 扩散 kuòsàn
proliferation N 扩散 kuòsàn
a prohibition on the proliferation of nuclear weapons 禁止核武器扩散 jìnzhǐ héwǔqì kuòsàn
prolific ADJ 多产的 [+作家] duō chǎn de [+zuòjiā]
prologue N（戏剧）序幕 (xìjù) xùmù,（叙事诗）序诗 (xùshìshī) xù shī,（书）序言 (shū) xùyán
prolong v 延长 yáncháng, 拉长 lācháng
prolonged ADJ 持续很久的 chíxù hěn jiǔ de, 长时间的 chángshíjiān de
prom N（高中生的）学年舞会 (gāozhōngsheng de) xuénián wǔhuì, 嘉年华会 jiānián huáhuì
senior prom（中学生）毕业舞会 (zhōngxuésheng) bìyè wǔhuì
promenade N 海滨散步道 hǎibīn sànbù dào
prominence N **1** 突出 tūchū, 显著 xiǎnzhe **2** 杰出 jiéchū
to gain prominence 开始闻名 kāishǐ wénmíng
prominent ADJ **1** 显著的 xiǎnzhe de **2** 杰出的 jiéchū de
promiscuous ADJ 淫乱的 yínluàn de, 滥交的 lànjiāo de
promise v, N 承诺 chéngnuò, 答应 dāying ■ *He's promised his children that he would take them to the zoo this weekend.* 他答应孩子这个周末带他们去动物园。Tā dāying háizi zhè ge zhōumò dài tāmen qù dòngwù yuán.
promising ADJ 大有前途的 dàyǒu qiántú de, 大有希望的 dàyǒu xīwàng de
promo N 广告短片 guǎnggào duǎnpiàn
promontory N 海角 hǎijiǎo
promote v **1** 促进 cùjìn **2** 促销 cùxiāo **3** 提升 tíshēng, 晋升 jìnshēng ■ *She was promoted to professorship after the publication of her third book.* 她在第三本书出版后被提升为教授。Tā zài dìsān běn shū chūbǎn hòu bèi tíshēngwéi jiàoshòu.
promoter N **1** [绿色生活方式+] 倡导者 [lǜsè shēnghuó fāngshì+] chàngdǎozhě **2** [音乐会+] 主办者 [yīnyuèhuì+] zhǔbànzhě

promotion N **1** 提升 tíshēng, 晋升 jìnshēng **2** 促进 cùjìn ■ *We work for the promotion of social progress.* 我们为促进社会进步而努力。Wǒmen wèi cùjìn shèhuì jìnbù ér nǔlì. **3** 促销 cùxiāo, 推销 tuīxiāo

promotional V 促销的 cùxiāo de
promotional tour 巡回促销 xúnhuí cùxiāo

prompt¹ ADJ 及时的 jíshí de, 迅速的 xùnsù de

prompt² I V 促使 cùshǐ, 引起 yǐnqǐ II N **1** (计算机) 提示 (jìsuànjī) tíshì **2** (给演员的) 提词 (gěi yǎnyuán de) tící

prompter N 提词员 tícíyuán

prone ADJ 倾向于…的 qīngxiàng yú...de, 容易…的 róngyì...de
prone to accidents 容易发生事故的 róngyì fāshēng shìgù de

pronoun N (语法) 代词 (yǔfǎ) dàicí

pronounce V **1** 发音 fāyīn ■ *How do you pronounce this word?* 这个词怎么发音？Zhè ge cí zěnme fāyīn? **2** 宣告 xuāngào

pronounced ADJ 明显的 míngxiǎn de

pronouncement N 公告 gōnggào, 声明 shēngmíng

pronto ADV 马上 mǎshàng, 立刻 lìkè

pronunciation N 发音 fāyīn ■ *Pronunciation is very important in learning a foreign language.* 学习外语，发音很重要。Xuéxí wàiyǔ, fāyīn hěn zhòngyào.

proof¹ N 证明 zhèngmíng, 证据 zhèngjù ■ *Do you have any proof that she started the malicious rumor?* 你有没有证据，是她造了这个恶毒的谣言？Nǐ yǒu méiyǒu zhèngjù, shì tā zàole zhè ge èdú de yáoyán?

proof² ADJ 能抵挡…的 néng dǐdǎng...de, 防防 fángfáng, 抗 kàng
bulletproof 防弹的 fángdàn de
earthquake-proof 抗地震的 kàng dìzhèn de

proofread V 校对 jiàoduì

proofreader N 校对员 jiàoduìyuán

prop I V 支撑 zhīchēng, 支持 zhīchí II N **1** 支撑物 zhīchēng wù **2** 小道具 xiǎo dàojù

propaganda N 宣传 xuānchuán

propagate V **1** 繁殖 [+植物] fánzhí [+zhíwù] **2** 传播 [+信仰] chuánbō [+xìnyǎng]

propel V 推进 tuījìn, 推动 tuīdòng

propeller N 螺旋桨 luóxuánjiǎng, 推进器 tuījìnqì

propensity N 习性 xíxìng, 倾向 (性) qīngxiàng (xìng)

proper ADJ **1** 适当的 shìdàng de, 恰当的 qiàdàng de ■ *You should follow the proper procedure.* 你应该按照正确的程序去做。Nǐ yīnggāi ànzhào zhèngquè de chéngxù qù zuò. **2** 符合礼仪的 fúhé lǐyí de, 正派的 zhèngpài de
proper noun, proper name (语法) 专有名词 (yǔfǎ) zhuānyǒu míngcí

properly ADV 适当地 shìdàng de

property N **1** 财产 cáichǎn [M. WD 笔 bǐ] **2** 房地产 fángdìchǎn, 产业 chǎnyè ■ *He owns expensive properties in prime locations.* 他在最好的地段拥有昂贵的房地产。Tā zài zuìhǎode dìduàn yōngyǒu ángguì de fángdìchǎn.
intellectual property 知识产权 zhīshi chǎnquán
lost property office 失物招领处 shīwù zhāolǐng chù
stolen property 赃物 zāngwù
3 性质 xìngzhì, 特性 tèxìng

prophecy N (宗教的) 预言 (zōngjiào de) yùyán

prophesy V 预言 yùyán, 预示 yùshì

prophet N **1** (宗教的) 先知 (zōngjiào de) xiānzhī **2** (新观念的) 倡导者 (xīn guānniàn de) chàngdǎozhě

prophetic ADJ 正确预见的 zhèngquè yùjiàn de, 有预见的 yǒu yùjiàn de

propitious ADJ 吉利的 jílì de, 最佳的 zuìjiā de

proponent N 支持者 zhīchízhě, 提倡者 tíchàngzhě

proportion N **1** 比例 bǐlì ■ *The proportion of passes to failures in the exam is 9 to 1.* 这次考试及格与不及格之比是九比一。Zhè cì kǎoshì jígé yǔ bù jígé zhībǐ shì jiǔ bǐ yī. **2** 部分 bùfen
in proportion to sth 按照与某物的比例 ànzhào yǔ mǒu wù de bǐlì

proportional ADJ 成比例的 chéngbǐlì de

proposal N **1** 提议 tíyì ■ *The proposal was shot down when the boss considered the cost.* 老板考虑到费用，就取消了提议。Lǎobǎn kǎolǜdào fèiyòng, jiù qǔxiāole tíyì. **2** 求婚 qiúhūn ■ *She accepted his proposal happily.* 她喜滋滋地接受了他的求婚。Tā xǐzīzī de jiēshòule tā de qiúhūn.

propose V **1** 提议 tíyì ■ *I propose a toast to the health of all present.* 我提议为大家的健康干杯。Wǒ tíyì wèi dàjiā de jiànkāng gānbēi. **2** 求婚 qiúhūn ■ *He's still divided about whether he should propose to her.* 要不要向她求婚，他还举棋不定。Yàobuyào xiàng tā qiúhūn, tā hái jǔ qí bù dìng. **3** 打算 dǎsuan

proposition I N **1** 观点 guāndiǎn, 见解 jiànjiě **2** [商业+] 提议 [shāngyè+] tíyì, 建议 jiànyì II V 提出发生性关系 tíchū fāshēng xìng guānxi

proprietary ADJ **1** 专卖的 [+产品] zhuānmài de [+chǎnpǐn] **2** 属于自己的 [+感觉] shǔyú zìjǐ de [+gǎnjué]
proprietary information (公司) 内部信息 (gōngsī) nèibù xìnxī

proprietor N 拥有者 yōngyǒuzhě, 老板 lǎobǎn

propriety N 得体的行为 détǐ de xíngwéi, 规范 (的言行) guīfàn (de yánxíng)

propulsion N 推进力 tuījìnlì, 推进器 tuījìnqì

pro rata ADJ 按比例计算的 [+报酬] àn bǐlì jìsuàn de [+bàochou]

prosaic ADJ 平淡乏味的 píngdàn fáwèi de
proscribe V 禁止 jìnzhǐ, 取缔 qǔdì
proscription N 禁止 jìnzhǐ, 取缔 qǔdì
prose N 散文 sǎnwén [M. WD 篇 piān]
　prose poem 散文诗 sǎnwénshī
prosecute V 起诉 qǐsù, 检控 jiǎnkòng
prosecution N 1 起诉 qǐsù, 检控 jiǎnkòng 2 检控
　方 jiǎnkòng fāng, 原告（律师）yuángào (lǜshī)
prosecutor N 检控官 jiǎnkòng guān, 起诉人
　qǐsùrén
proselytize V 说服 [+人] 入教 shuōfú [+rén] rùjiào
prospect I N 1 前景 qiánjǐng
　in prospect 可能即将发生 kěnéng jíjiāng
　fāshēng
　2 会成功的人 huì chénggōng de rén II V 勘探
　kāntàn, 勘察 kānchá
prospective ADJ 可能的 kěnéng de, 预期的 yùqī
　de
prospectus N 1 [简况+] 小册子 [jiǎnkuàng+]
　xiǎocèzi 2 [投资+] 计划书 [tóuzī+] jìhuà shū
prosper V 兴旺 xīngwàng, 成功 chénggōng
prosperity N 兴旺 xīngwàng, 繁荣 fánróng
prosperous ADJ 兴旺的 xīngwàng de, 繁荣的
　fánróng de ■ *The region became prosperous af-*
　ter a huge oil field was discovered there. 在发现大
　油田以后，这个地区兴旺起来。Zài fāxiàn dàyóu
　tián yǐhòu, zhège dìqū xīngwàng qǐlái.
prosthesis N 假肢 jiǎzhī, 假牙 jiǎyá
prostitute I N 1 妓女 jìnǚ II V 出卖 [+自己的才能]
　chūmài [+zìjǐ de cáinéng], 滥用 lànyòng
　to prostitute oneself 卖淫 màiyín, 出卖自己
　chūmài zìjǐ
prostitution N 1 娼妓业 chāngjì yè 2 滥用
　lànyòng
prostrate I ADJ 俯卧的 fǔwò de, 卧倒在地的
　wòdǎo zài dì de, [被悲伤+] 压垮的 [bèi bēi-
　shāng+] yā kuǎ de, 一蹶不振的 yì jué bú
　zhèn de II V (to prostrate oneself) 拜倒 bàidǎo
　be prostrate 一蹶不振 yì jué bú zhèn, 压垮的
　yā kuǎ de
protagonist N 1 [电影+] 主要人物 [diànyǐng+]
　zhǔyào rénwù, 主角 zhǔjué 2 提倡者 tíchàng-
　zhě, 支持者 zhīchízhě
protect V 保护 bǎohù, 保卫 bǎowèi
protection N 保护 bǎohù, 保卫 bǎowèi
protective ADJ 保护（性）的 bǎohù (xìng) de
　protective custody 保护性拘留 bǎohùxìng jūliú
protégé N 被保护人 bèi bǎohùrén, 门生
　ménshēng
protein N 蛋白质 dànbáizhì
protest V, N 抗议 kàngyì
Protestant I ADJ（基督教）新教的 (Jīdūjiào)
　Xīnjiào de II N（基督教）新教徒 (Jīdūjiào)
　Xīnjiàotú
Protestantism N（基督教）新教 (Jīdūjiào) Xīnjiào

protocol N 1 礼仪 lǐyí 2 协议 xiéyì, 协定 xiédìng
proton N 质子 zhìzǐ
prototype N 原型 yuánxíng, 典范 diǎnfàn
protracted ADJ 持久的 chíjiǔ de, 长久的 chángjiǔ
　de
protractor N 量角器 liángjiǎoqì
protrude V 伸出 shēnchū, 凸出 tūchū
protruding ADJ 凸出的 tūchū de
protrusion N 凸出（物）tūchū (wù)
proud ADJ 骄傲的 jiāo'ào de, 自傲的 zì'ào de
　■ *The self-made millionaire is very proud of his*
　achievement. 这个白手起家的百万富翁对自己的
　成就非常自傲。Zhè ge báishǒu qǐjiā de bǎiwàn
　fùwēng duì zìjǐ de chéngjiù fēicháng zì'ào.
prove V (PT **proved**; PP **proved**, **proven**) 证明
　zhèngmíng
proven ADJ 被证实的 bèi zhèngshí de
proverb N 谚语 yànyǔ
proverbial ADJ 大名鼎鼎的 dàmíng dǐngdǐng de
　the proverbial sth 常言中的 cháng yánzhòng
　de
provide V 提供 tígòng, 供给 gōngjǐ ■ *The church*
　provides meals to the homeless here every Tues-
　day night. 每星期二晚上教会为这里的无家可归者
　提供一顿饭。Měi xīngqī'èr wǎnshàng jiàohuì wèi
　zhèlǐ de wújiā kěguī zhě tígòng yí dùn fàn.
　to provide for 养活 yǎnghuo ■ *He has to pro-*
　vide for a large family with his meager wages. 他
　要以微薄的工资养活大家庭。Tā yào yǐ wēibó de
　gōngzī yǎnghuo dà jiātíng.
provided (that) CONJ 如果 rúguǒ, 假设 jiǎshè
　■ *You'll be awarded a generous scholarship pro-*
　vided that you pass all the exams with As. 你如果
　门门课都得A，就可以获得一份优厚的奖学金。Nǐ
　rúguǒ ménmén kè dōu dé A, jiù kěyǐ huòdé yí fèn
　yōuhòu de jiǎngxuéjīn.
providence N 天意 tiānyì, 天命 tiānmìng
providential ADJ 象天意安排的 xiàng tiānyì
　ānpái de, 正巧的 zhèngqiǎo de
provider N 供应者 gōngyīngzhě
providing CONJ 如果 rúguǒ, 假设 jiǎshè
province N 1 [中国的+] 省 [Zhōngguó de+] shěng
　Sichuan Province of China 中国四川省
　Zhōngguó Sìchuānshěng
　2 [知识的+] 领域 [zhīshi de+] lǐngyù, 范围
　fànwéi
provincial I ADJ 1 省的 shěng de, 行政的
　xíngzhèng de
　the provincial government of Sichuan 四川省政
　府 Sìchuānshěng zhèngfǔ
　2 狭隘的 xiá'ài de, 守旧的 shǒujiù de II N 外
　省人 wàishěngrén, 来自小地方的人 láizì xiǎo
　dìfang de rén
provision N 1 提供 tígòng, 供应 gōngyìng 2 条款
　tiáokuǎn, 规定 guīdìng

provisional ADJ 临时的 línshí de, 暂时的 zànshí de

provisions N 粮食 liángshi, 食物 shíwù

proviso N 附加条件 fùjiā tiáojiàn, 前提 qiántí

provocation N 挑衅 (行为) tiǎoxìn (xíngwéi)

provocative ADJ 1 挑衅 (性) 的 tiǎoxìn (xìng) de 2 十分性感的 shífēn xìnggǎn de, 挑逗性的 tiǎodòu xìng de

provoke V 激怒 jīnù, 激起 jīqǐ

provost N (大学) 教务长 (dàxué) jiàowùzhǎng

prow N 船头 chuántóu

prowess N 高超的技艺 gāochāo de jìyì

prowl I V 来回行走 láihuí xíngzǒu, 巡逻 xúnluó II N (on the prowl) 四处寻觅 sìchù xúnmì, 流窜 liúcuàn

prowler N 流窜伺机作案者 liúcuàn sìjī zuò'àn zhě

proximity N 邻近 línjìn, 靠近 kàojìn

proxy N 代理人 dàilǐrén
   proxy vote 委托投票 wěituō tóupiào
   by proxy 委托他人代理 wěituō tārén dàilǐ

prude N (在性方面) 过分拘谨的人 (zài xìng fāngmiàn) guòfèn jūjǐnde rén

prudence N 谨慎 jǐnshèn, 理性 lǐxìng

prudent ADJ 慎重的 shènzhòng de, 理性的 lǐxìng de

prudish ADJ (在性方面) 一本正经的 (的) (zài xìng fāngmiàn) yìběnzhèngjīng (de)

prune¹ V (to prune back) 1 修剪 [+树枝] xiūjiǎn [+shùzhī] 2 剪除 jiǎnchú, 除去 chúqù

prune² N 西梅干 xī méi gān

prurience N 淫荡 yíndàng, 好色 hàosè

prurient ADJ 好色的 hàosè de, 淫荡的 yíndàng de

pry V 1 撬开 qiàokāi 2 打听 [+别人的隐私] dǎtīng [+biéren de yǐnsī]
   prying eyes 窥视者 kuīshìzhě

psalm N 圣歌 shènggē [M. WD 首 shǒu], 赞美诗 zànměishī [M. WD 首 shǒu]

pseudonym N 笔名 bǐmíng

psych V (to psych out) 吓住 [+对手] xiàzhù [+duìshǒu]

psyche N 心灵 xīnlíng, 灵魂 línghún

psyched ADJ 作好心理准备 zuò hǎo xīnlǐ zhǔnbèi

psychedelic ADJ 引起迷幻的 [+药物] yǐn qǐ míhuàn de [+yàowù]

psychiatrist N 精神病医生 jīngshénbìng yīshēng

psychiatry N 精神病学 jīngshénbìngxué

psychic I ADJ 通灵的 tōnglíng de, 超自然的 chāo zìrán de
   psychic prediction 通灵预言 tōnglíng yùyán II N 通灵的人 tōnglíng de rén, 有特异功能的人 yǒu tèyì gōngnéng de rén

psycho N 精神病人 jīngshénbìngrén, 变态人格者 biàntài réngé zhě

psychoanalysis N 精神分析 (治疗法) jīngshén fēnxī (zhìliáofǎ)

psychoanalyst N 精神分析医生 jīngshén fēnxī yīshēng

psychoanalyze V 对…进行精神分析 duì…jìnxíng jīngshén fēnxī, 用精神分析法治疗 yòng jīngshén fēnxīfǎ zhìliáo

psychological ADJ 心理学的 xīnlǐxué de, 心理上的 xīnlǐ shàng de

psychologist N 心理学家 xīnlǐxuéjiā

psychology N 心理 (学) xīnlǐ (xué)

psychopath N 精神病患者 jīngshénbìng huànzhě, 严重精神变态者 yánzhòng jīngshén biàntàizhě

psychosis N 精神病 jīngshénbìng

psychosomatic ADJ 有精神引起的 [+疾病] yóu jīngshén yǐn qǐ de [+jíbìng], 身心的 shēnxīn de

psychotherapist N 心理治疗医生 xīnlǐzhìliáo yīshēng

psychotherapy N 心理治疗法 xīnlǐzhìliáo fǎ

psychotic I ADJ 精神病的 jīngshénbìng de II N 精神病患者 jīngshénbìng huànzhě

pub N 酒吧 jiǔbā

puberty N 青春期 qīngchūnqī

pubescent ADJ 处于青春期的 chǔyú qīngchūnqī de

pubic ADJ 阴部的 yīnbù de
   pubic hair 阴毛 yīnmáo

public I N 公众 gōngzhòng, 大众 dàzhòng ■ *The library is open to the public every day except public holidays.* 除了公共假日，图书馆每天向公众开放。Chúle gōnggòng jiàrì, túshūguǎn měitiān xiàng gōngzhòng kāifàng.
   in public 在公众场合 zài gōngzhòng chǎnghé ■ *To use a cell phone in public, though a common practice, may still make people feel uncomfortable.* 虽然在公众场合使用手机是很普遍的，但是仍然使人感觉不舒服。Suīrán zài gōngzhòng chǎnghé shǐyòng shǒujī shì hěn pǔbiàn de, dànshì réngrán shǐ rén gǎnjué bù shūfú.
   II ADJ 1 公共的 gōnggòng de, 公用的 gōngyòng de
   public access 公众进入权 gōngzhòng jìnrù quán
   public address (PA) system 扩音系统 kuòyīn xìtǒng
   public assistance 政府补助 zhèngfǔ bǔzhù
   public defender 公设辩护律师 gōngshè biànhù lǜshī
   public housing 政府住房 zhèngfǔ zhùfáng
   public relations 公共关系 gōnggòng guānxì, 公关 gōngguān
   public school 公立学校 gōnglì xuéxiào, (英国) 私立学校 (Yīngguó) sīlì xuéxiào
   2 公开的 gōngkāi de
   to go public 公开 gōngkāi, 公布于众 gōngbù yú zhòng

publication N 出版 chūbǎn ■ *The publication of this book made her rich and famous.* 这本书的出版使她名利双收。Zhè běn shū de chūbǎn shǐ tā míng lì shuāng shōu. 2 出版物 chūbǎn wù, 书刊报章 shūkān bàozhāng

publicist N 广告员 guǎnggào yuán, 公关人员 gōngguān rényuán

publicity N 公共关注 gōnggòng guānzhù, 宣传 xuānchuán

good/bad publicity 有利的／不利的宣传 yǒulì de/búlì de xuānchuán

publicity campaign 宣传活动 xuānchuán huódòng

publicize v 传播 chuánbō, 公开 gōngkāi

publicly ADV 公开 gōngkāi ■ *The politician denounced his colleagues publicly and created a scandal.* 这个政客公开谴责同僚，引起一场丑闻。Zhè ge zhèngkè gōngkāi qiǎnzé tóngliáo, yǐnqǐ yì chǎng chǒuwén.

publish v 出版 chūbǎn

publisher N 出版人 chūbǎnrén, 出版商 chūbǎnshāng, 出版公司 chūbǎn gōngsī

publishing N 出版事业 chūbǎn shìyè, 出版界 chūbǎnjiè

puck N 冰球 bīngqiú

pucker v 撅起嘴 juē qǐ zuǐ

pudding N 布丁 bùdīng, 甜食 tiánshí

puddle N 水坑 shuǐkēng, 小水潭 xiǎoshui tán

pudgy ADJ 肥胖的 féipàng de

puerile ADJ 傻乎乎的 shǎhūhū de, 孩子气的 háiziqì de

puff I v 1 (吸烟时) 喷烟 (xīyān shí) pēn yān 2 [烟囱+] 冒烟 [yāncōng+] màoyān 3 喘粗气 chuǎn cū qì II N 吸 (烟) xī (yān)

puffy ADJ [眼睛+] 肿大的 [yǎnjing+] zhǒngdà de

pugnacious ADJ 爱争吵的 àizhēng chǎo de, 好斗的 hǎo dǒu de

puke I v 呕吐 ǒutù II N 呕吐物 ǒutù wù

pull I v 1 拉 lā ■ *Little Jimmy likes to pull the cat's tail.* 小杰姆喜欢拉猫儿的尾巴。Xiǎo Jiémǔ xǐhuan lā māo de wěiba. 2 拖 tuō, 牵 qiān 3 拔 bá ■ *He had to have his decayed tooth pulled yesterday.* 昨天他不得不把蛀牙拔掉。Zuótiān tā bùdebù bǎ zhùyá bádiao.

to pull one's leg 戏弄 xìnòng, 对…说假话 duì…shuō jiǎhuà

to pull one's weight 尽力, 做好本份工作 jìnlì, zuòhǎo běnfèn gōngzuò

to pull over [汽车+] 停在路边 [qìchē+] tíng zài lùbiān

II N 1 拉 lā, 拖 tuō, 牵 qiān 2 拉绳 lā shéng 3 吸引力 xīyǐnlì

pulley N 滑轮 huálún

pullout N 1 撤离 chèlí 2 插页 chāyè

pullover N 套头毛衣 tàotóu máoyī

pull-up N 引体向上 yǐn tǐ xiàng shàng

pulmonary ADJ 肺的 fèi de

pulp I N 1 果肉 guǒròu 2 纸浆 zhǐjiāng II v 把…捣成浆 bǎ…dǎo chéng jiāng III ADJ 低俗的 dīsú de

pulp fiction 低俗小说 dīsú xiǎoshuō

pulpit N (教堂中的) 讲坛 (jiàotáng zhòng de) jiǎngtán, 布道坛 bùdàotán

pulsate v 有规律的振动 yǒuguīlǜ de zhèndòng

pulsation N (心脏) 搏动 (xīnzàng) bódòng, (脉) 跳动 (mài) tiàodòng

pulse I N 1 脉搏 màibó 2 [光波+] 脉冲 [guāngbō+] màichōng 3 [社会+] 动向 [shèhuì+] dòngxiàng, 走向 zǒuxiàng 4 (音乐) 拍子 (yīnyuè) pāizi, 节奏 jiézòu II v 1 [心脏+] 搏动 [xīnzàng+] bódòng 2 [机器+] 振动 [jīqì+] zhèndòng

pulverization N 粉末化 fěnmò huà

pulverize v 把…磨成粉末 bǎ…mó chéng fěnmò

puma N 美洲狮 měizhōushī [m. wp 只 zhǐ/头 tóu]

pumice N 浮石 fúshí [m. wp 块 kuài]

pummel v [拳头+] 连续捶打 [quántou+] liánxù chuídǎ

pump I N 1 抽水机 chōushuǐ jī, 泵 bèng 2 打气筒 dǎqì tǒng II v 1 抽水 chōushuǐ 2 打气 dǎqì ■ *The tire was flat so I pumped it up.* 轮胎瘪了, 我就打气。Lúntāi biě le, wǒ jiù dǎqì.

pumpkin N 南瓜 nánguā [m. wp 只 zhǐ]

pun N 双关语 shuāngguānyǔ, 一语双关 yìyǔ shuāngguān

punch¹ I v 1 用拳猛击 yòng quán měngjī 2 按 [+键] àn [+jiàn] 3 打洞 dǎdòng

to punch in (上班) 打卡 (shàngbān) dǎkǎ

to punch out (下班) 打卡 (xiàbān) dǎkǎ

II N 1 (用拳) 猛击 (yòng quán) měngjī 2 穿孔机 chuānkǒngjī

punch² N 潘趣酒 pānquùjiǔ, 混合饮料 hùnhé yǐnliào

punching bag N (拳击练习用的) 吊袋 (quánjī liànxí yòng de) diào dài

punch line N 抛出笑料的妙语 pāochū xiàoliào de miàoyǔ

punctuate v 1 加标点符号 jiā biāodiǎn fúhào 2 (be punctuated by) 不时被打断 bùshí bèi dǎdan

punctuation N 标点符号 (用法) biāodiǎn fúhào (yòngfǎ)

punctuation mark 标点符号 biāodiǎn fúhào

puncture I N (轮胎的) 穿孔 (lúntāi de) chuānkǒng II v 扎穿 [+轮胎] zhā chuān [+lúntāi]

pundit N 权威 quánwēi, 专家 zhuānjiā

pungent ADJ 1 刺鼻的 [+气味] cìbí de [+qìwèi] 2 辛辣的 [+文章] xīnlà de [+wénzhāng]

punish v 罚 fá, 惩罚 chéngfá ■ *Those who break the law must be punished.* 犯法者, 必须受到惩罚。Fànfǎ zhě, bìxū shòudao chéngfá.

punishable ADJ 会受到惩罚的 huì shòudào

chéngfá de, 应受到惩罚的 yìng shòudào chéngfá de

punishable by/with life imprisonment 会受到终身监禁 huì shòudào zhōngshēn jiānjìn

punishing ADJ 极其累人的 jíqí lèirén de, 繁重不堪的 fánzhòng bùkān de

punishment N 惩罚 chéngfá, 处罚 chǔfá

punitive ADJ 惩罚(性)的 chéngfá (xìng) de

punk N 朋克 péng kè, 小流氓 xiǎo liúmáng
punk rock 朋克摇滚乐 péng kè yáogǔnyuè
punk rocker 朋克摇滚乐迷 péng kè yáogǔnyuèmí

punt I N 1 悬空长球 xuánkōng cháng qiú 2 方头平底船 fāngtóu píngdǐchuán [M. WD 艘 sōu] II v 1 踢悬空长球 tī xuánkōng cháng qiú 2 乘方头平底船 chéng fāngtóu píngdǐchuán

puny ADJ 1 瘦小的 [+孩子] shòuxiǎo de [+háizi] 2 微薄的 [+利润] wēibó de [+lìrùn]

pup N 小狗 xiǎogǒu [M. WD 只 zhī]

pupil[1] N 小学生 xiǎo xuésheng

pupil[2] N 瞳孔 tóngkǒng

puppet N 1 木偶 mù ǒu 2 傀儡 kuǐlěi

puppeteer N 玩木偶的人 wán mù'ǒu de rén, 木偶艺人 mù'ǒu yìrén

puppy N 小狗 xiǎogǒu [M. WD 只 zhī]
puppy love 少男少女的恋情 shàonán shàonǚ de liànqíng, 早恋 zǎoliàn

purchase I v 购买 gòumǎi II N 购买到的物品 gòumǎi dào de wùpǐn

pure ADJ 纯的 chún de, 纯净的 chúnjìng de
■ *This trout stream has some of the purest water in this area.* 这条鳟鱼小溪里的水是这个地区最纯净的。Zhè tiáo zūnyú xiǎoxī lǐ de shuǐ shì zhè ge dìqū zuìchúnjìng de.

puree N (番茄+)酱 [fānqié+] jiàng, 糊 hú

purely ADV 纯粹(地)chúncuì (de), 完全(地)wánquán (de)

purgatory N 炼狱 liànyù, 遭受极大苦难的地方 zāoshòu jídà kǔnàn de dìfang

purge I v 清洗 [+政敌] qīngxǐ [+zhèngdí], 清除 qīngchú II N 清洗(行动)qīngxǐ (xíngdòng)

purification N 净化 jìnghuà

purify v 使…纯净 shǐ…chúnjìng, 净化 jìnghuà

purist N 力求纯正的人士 lìqiú chúnzhèng de rénshì, 纯正主义者 chúnzhèng zhǔyìzhě

Puritan N 清教徒 Qīngjiàotú

puritan N 道德上很严格的人 dàodé shàng hěn yángé de rén

puritanical ADJ 清教徒式的 Qīngjiàotú shì de

purity N 纯洁(度)chúnjié (dù), 纯度 chúndù

purple I N 紫色 zǐsè II ADJ 紫色的 zǐsè de

purport I v 据说 jùshuō, 声称 shēngchēng
II N 大意 dàyì

purpose N 目的 mùdì ■ *To put it bluntly, the primary, if not the only, purpose of most businesses is to make money.* 坦率地说，大多数商家的主要目的，如果不是唯一目的，就是赚钱。Tǎnshuài de shuō, dàduōshù shāngjiā de zhǔyào mùdì, rúguǒ bú shì wéiyī mùdì, jiù shì zhuànqián.
on purpose 故意 gùyì (de)
to no purpose 毫无成果 háowú chéngguǒ
accidentally on purpose 明明是故意却装作无意 míngmíng shì gùyì què zhuāngzuò wúyì

purposeful ADJ 1 有明确目的的 yǒu míngquè mùdì de 2 坚定的 jiāndìng de, 果断的 guǒduàn de

purposely ADV 故意(地)gùyì (de)

purr I v 1 [猫+] 发出呼噜声 [māo+] fāchū hūlushēng 2 [人+] 轻柔地说 [rén+] qīngróu de shuō II N 轻柔的说话声 qīngróu de shuōhuàshēng

purse I N 1 (女用)钱包 (nǚ yòng) qiánbāo, 手提包 shǒutíbāo 2 资金 zījīn
public purse 政府资金 zhèngfǔ zījīn
to control the purse string 控制财权 kòngzhì cáiquán, 掌管钱财 zhǎngguǎn qiáncái
II v (to purse one's lips) 撅起嘴巴 juē qǐ zuǐba

purser N (各轮船的)事务长 (kèlún de) shìwùzhǎng

pursue v 1 追求 [+财富] zhuīqiú [+cáifù] 2 追赶 [+小偷] zhuīgǎn [+xiǎotōu] 3 从事 cóngshì, 继续 jìxù

pursuit N 1 追求 zhuīqiú 2 追赶 zhuīgǎn

purvey v 供应 [+商品] gōngyìng [+shāngpǐn], 提供 [+信息] tígōng [+xìnxī]

purveyor N 供应商 gōngyìngshāng, 提供者 tígōngzhě

pus N 脓 nóng

push v 1 推 tuī 2 按 àn 3 推动 tuīdòng, 逼迫 bīpò ■ *He was pushed into the language class by his parents.* 他是被父母推着来上语言班的。Tā shì bèi fùmǔ tuīzhe lái shàng yǔyán bān de. 4 贩卖 fànmài
to push around 摆布 bǎibù ■ *I won't allow anyone to push me around.* 我不允许任何人摆布我。Wǒ bù yǔnxǔ rènhé rén bǎibù wǒ.
to push on 继续前进 jìxù qiánjìn
to push up 提高价格 tígāo jiàgé
II N 1 推 tuī ■ *I gave Tommy a push and he fell into the pool.* 我推了汤姆一把，他就掉下水去了。Wǒ tuīle Tāngmǔ yì bǎ, tā jiù diàoxia shuǐ qù le. 2 试图 shìtú

pusher N 毒品贩子 dúpǐn fànzi

pushover N 很容易被说服的人 hěn róngyì bèi shuōfú de rén, 容易被影响的人 róngyì bèi yǐngxiǎng de rén

push-up N 俯卧撑 fǔwòchēng

pushy ADJ 咄咄逼人的 duōduō bīrén de

pussycat N 1 猫咪 māomī [M. WD 只 zhī] 2 温和的好人 wēnhé de hǎorén

pussyfoot v 畏首畏尾 wèi shǒu wèi wěi, 犹豫不决 yóuyù bù jué

put

put v (PT & PPT **put**) **1** 放 fàng, 放置 fàngzhì **2** 写 xiě, 写下 xiěxia ■ *She put her signature to the will only after reading it very carefully.* 她仔细读了一遍以后，才在遗嘱上签字。Tā zǐxì dúle yí biàn yǐhòu, cái zài yízhǔshang qiānzì. **3** 表达 biǎodá ■ *How should I put it?* 我该怎么说呢？Wǒ gāi zěnme shuō ne? **4** 使 shǐ ■ *The news put me in a bad mood.* 这个消息让我心情很坏。Zhè ge xiāoxi ràng wǒ xīnqíng hěn huài.

to put aside 储蓄 chǔxù ■ *It's a good idea to put aside some money for a rainy day.* 储蓄一些钱以防万一，是个好主意。Cúxù yìxiē qián yǐ fáng wànyī, shì ge hǎo zhúyi.

to put away 放回去 fàng huíqu

to put down 羞辱 xiūrǔ ■ *He resented at being put down by the young teacher in class.* 他对那个年轻老师在上课时羞辱他，感到恼怒。Tā duì nà ge niánqīng lǎoshī zài shàngkè shí xiūrǔ tā, gǎndào nǎonù.

to put forward 提出 tíchū ■ *May I put forward a proposal?* 我可以提一个提议吗？Wǒ kěyǐ tí yí ge tíyì ma?

to put on ① 穿上 [+衣服／鞋子] chuānshang [+yīfu/xiézi] ② 增加 [+体重] zēngjiā [+tǐzhòng] ③ 放 [+音乐] fàng [+yīnyuè] ■ *Let's put on some music.* 我们放些音乐吧。Wǒmen fàng xiē yīnyuè ba.

to put out 扑灭 [+火] pūmiè [+huǒ] ■ *The fire was finally put out.* 火终于扑灭了。Huǒ zhōngyú pūmiè le.

(to feel) put out 感到有点恼火 gǎndào yǒudiǎn nǎohuǒ

putrefy v 腐烂 fǔlàn

putrid ADJ 腐臭的 fǔchòu de

putt I v 轻轻地打 [+高尔夫球] qīngqīngde dǎ [+gāo'ěrfūqiú], 推 [+高尔夫球] tuī [+gāo'ěrfūqiú] II N 轻击 qīng jī, 推（高尔夫）球 tuī (gāo'ěrfū) qiú

putty N 油灰 yóuhuī

put upon ADJ (to feel put upon) 感到被人占了便宜 gǎndào bèi rénzhànle piányi

puzzle I N **1** 智力游戏 zhìlì yóuxì

crossword puzzle 纵横填字游戏 zònghéng tiánzìyóuxì

jigsaw puzzle 拼图游戏 pīn tú yóuxì

2 不可理解的事 bùkě lǐjiě de shì ■ *Her sudden departure is still a puzzle to me.* 我还是不明白她为什么突然离去。Wǒ háishi bù míngbai tā wèishénme tūrán líqù. II v **1** 使…困惑 shǐ… kùnhuò, 把…弄糊涂 bǎ…nònghú tú ■ *The teachers were puzzled by his very poor performance in the exams.* 他考得非常不好，使老师们很困惑。Tā kǎo dé fēicháng bùhǎo, shǐ lǎoshīmen hěn kùnhuò. **2** 苦思冥想 kǔsī míngxiǎng

puzzled ADJ 困惑的 kùnhuò de

pygmy N 非常矮小的人 fēicháng ǎixiǎo de rén, 侏儒 zhūrú

pylon N **1** 高压电线架 gāoyādiàn xiàn jià **2** 圆锥形路障 yuánzhuī xíng lùzhàng

pyramid N 金字塔 jīnzìtǎ, 金字塔形物 jīnzìtǎxíng wù

pyre N 火葬柴堆 huǒzàng chái duī

python N（大）蟒蛇 (dà) mǎngshé [M. WD 条 tiáo]

Q

quack¹ I v [鸭子+] 嘎嘎叫 [yāzi+] gāgā jiào
II N [鸭子+] 嘎嘎叫声 [yāzi+] gāgā jiàoshēng

quack² N 冒牌医生 màopáiyīshēng, 庸医 yōngyī

quad ABBREV See **quadrangle**, **quadruplet**

quadrangle N 四边形 sìbiānxíng, 四角形 sìjiǎoxíng

quadrant N 四分之一圆 sì fēn zhī yī yuán

quadraphonic ADJ 四声道（的）sìshēng dào (de)

quadrilateral N 四边形 sìbiānxíng

quadriplegic I N 四肢瘫痪者 sìzhī tānhuàn zhě
II ADJ 四肢瘫痪的 sìzhī tānhuàn de

quadruped N 四足动物 sìzú dòngwù

quadruple I v 增加到四倍 zēngjiā dào sìbèi, 增加三倍 zēngjiā sānbèi, 翻两番 fān liǎng fān
II ADJ 四倍的 sìbèi de

quadruplet N 四胞胎之一 sìbāotāi zhī yī

quagmire N **1** 泥潭 nítán **2**（难以脱身的）困境 (nán yī tuīshēn de) kùnjìng

quail¹ N 鹌鹑 ānchún [M. WD 只 zhī]

quail² v 发抖 fādǒu, 害怕 hàipà

quaint ADJ 古色古香的 gǔsè gǔxiāng de, 奇特的 qítè de

quake I v **1** [人+] 颤抖 [rén+] chàndǒu, 哆嗦 duōsuo **2** [大地+] 震动 [dàdì+] zhèndòng II N 地震 dìzhèn

Quaker N（基督教）贵格会 (Jīdūjiào) Guìgéhuì, 公谊会 gōngyìhuì

qualification N 资格 zīgé, 资格证明 zīgé zhèngmíng

qualified ADJ **1** 合格的 hégé de **2** 有保留的 [+同意] yǒu bǎoliú de [+tóngyì]

qualify v 获得资格 huòdé zīgé ■ *She won't qualify for teaching until next year.* 她明年才获得教师资格。Tā míngnián cái huòdé jiàoshī zīgé.

qualitative ADJ 质量（上）的 zhìliàng (shàng) de, 性质的 xìngzhì de

qualitiative analysis 定性分析 dìngxìng fēnxī

quality I N **1** 品质 pǐnzhì ■ *Many teachers believe that Robert has leadership qualities.* 很多老师相信罗伯特有领袖品质。Hěn duō lǎoshī xiāngxìn Luóbótè yǒu lǐngxiù pǐnzhì. **2** 质量 zhìliàng
II ADJ 优质的 yōuzhì de, 高质量的 gāo zhìliàng de ■ *The furniture maker only uses quality*

timber. 这家家具制造商只采用优质木材。Zhè jiā jiājù zhìzàoshāng zhǐ cǎiyòng yōuzhì mùcái.

quality control 质量管理 zhìliàng guǎnlǐ

quality time 宝贵时光 bǎoguì shíguāng

qualm N 疑虑 yílǜ, 不安 bù'ān

quandary N （不知所措的）困境 (bù zhī suǒ cuò de) kùnjìng

quantifiable ADJ 可以量化的 kěyǐ liànghuà de

quantifier N （语法）数量词 (yǔfǎ) shùliàngcí

quantify V 用数字测定 yòng shùzì cèdìng, 量化 liànghuà

quantitative ADJ 数量（上）的 shùliàng (shàng) de

quantitative analysis 定量分析 dìngliàng fēnxī

quantity N 数量 shùliàng

in quantity 大量 dàliàng, 大批 dàpī

quantum N 量子 liàngzǐ

quantum leap 突飞猛进 tūfēi měngjìn, 飞跃 fēiyuè

quarantine I N 隔离检疫（期）gélí jiǎnyì (qī) II V 对…隔离检疫 duì…gélí jiǎnyì

quark N 夸克 kuākè

quarrel N, V 争吵 zhēngchǎo, 吵架 chǎojià

quarrelsome ADJ 爱争吵的 ài zhēngchǎo de

quarry I N 1 采石场 cǎishíchǎng 2 猎场 lièchǎng II V 采石 cǎishí

quart N 夸脱 kuātuō (= 0.9463 liter)

quarter I N 1 四分之一 sì fēn zhī yī ■ *Roughly a quarter of Canadians speak French.* 大约有四分之一的加拿大人说法语。Dàyuē yǒu sì fēnzhī yī de Jiānádà rén shuō fǎyǔ. 2 一刻钟 yí kè zhōng ■ *It's a quarter to one now; I'll have lunch at a quarter after.* 现在是一点差一刻，我在一点一刻吃中饭。Xiànzài shì yì diǎn chà yí kè, wǒ zài yì diǎn yí kè chī zhōngfàn. 3 季度 jìdù 4 （大学的）学季 (dàxué de) xué jì 5 25分的硬币 èrshíwǔ fēn de yìngbì II ADJ 四分之一的 sì fēn zhī yī de III V 1 把…分成四份 bǎ…fēnchéng sì fèn 2 提供食宿 tígōng shísù

quarterback N 1 （美式足球）枢纽前卫 (Měishì zúqiú) shūniǔ qiánwèi, 四分卫 sì fēn wèi 2 组织者 zǔzhīzhě, 指挥者 zhǐhuīzhě

quarterfinal N 四分之一决赛 sì fēn zhī yī juésài

quarterly I ADJ, ADV 一年四次的 yìnián sìcì de, 季度的 jìdù de II N 季刊（杂志）jìkān (zázhì)

quarters N 居住的地方 jūzhù de dìfang, 住处 zhùchù

servants' quarters 佣人睡房 yōngrén shuìfáng

quartet N 四重唱（小组）sìchóngchàng (xiǎozǔ), 四重奏（乐队）sìchóngzòu (yuèduì)

string quartet 弦乐四重奏乐队 xiányuè sìchóngzòu yuèduì

quartz N 石英 shíyīng

quasar N 类星体 lèixīngtǐ

quash V 1 平息 [+骚乱] píngxī [+sāoluàn], 镇压

zhènyā 2 撤销 [+上诉] chèxiāo [+shàngsù], 废除 fèichú

quaver I V 1 颤抖 chàndǒu 2 用颤抖的声音说 yòng chàndǒu de shēngyīn shuō II N 颤抖 chàndǒu, 颤音 chànyīn

quay N 码头 mǎtou

queasy ADJ （感到）恶心的 (gǎndào) èxīn de, 想呕吐 xiǎng ǒutù

queen N 女王 nǚwáng, 王后 wánghòu

queen bee 蜂后 fēng hòu

queen-size ADJ 大号的 [+床] dàhào de [+chuáng]

queer I ADJ 1 怪怪的 guài guài de, 奇怪的 qíguài de 2 同性恋的 tóngxìngliàn de, 双性恋的 shuāngxìngliàn de, 变性恋的 biànxìng liàn de II N 同性恋者 tóngxìngliànzhě

quell V 镇压 zhènyā, 平息 píngxī

quench V (to quench one's thirst) 解渴 jiěkě, (to quench a fire) 灭火 mièhuǒ

querulous ADJ 爱发牢骚的 ài fāláoshào de, 老是抱怨的 lǎoshi bàoyuàn de

query I N 疑问 yíwèn, 问题 wèntí II V 1 提出疑问 tíchū yíwèn 2 询问 xúnwèn

quest N, V 追求 zhuīqiú, 探求 tànqiú

question I N 1 问题 wèntí ■ *Do you have any questions?* 你有什么问题吗？Nǐ yǒu shénme wèntí ma?

question mark 问号 wènhào (?)

2 考题 kǎotí ■ *There's a typo error in Question 5.* 第五个问题有一个打印错误。Dìwǔ ge wèntí yǒu yí ge dǎyìn cuòwù.

without question 肯定无疑 kěndìng wúyí ■ *The cheap imports are without question a challenge to local industry.* 廉价进口货对当地工业肯定是一个挑战。Liánjià jìnkǒu huò duì dāngdì gōngyè kěndìng shì yí ge tiǎozhàn.

out of the question 绝对不可能 juéduì bù kěnéng

(It's a) good question! 问得好！我也不知道。Wènde hǎo! Wǒ yě bù zhīdào. ■ *"What should be done to ensure both economic development and environmental conservation?" "It's a good question!"* "应该怎么样确保经济发展和环境保护？" "问得好，但是我也不知道。" Yīnggāi zěnmeyàng quèbǎo jīngjì fāzhǎn hé huánjìng bǎohù?" Wènde hǎo, dànshì wǒ yě bù zhīdào." II V 1 [警察+] 审问 [jǐngchá+] shěnwèn 2 怀疑 huáiyí, 质疑 zhìyí ■ *I question the accuracy of these figures.* 我怀疑这些数字的准确性。Wǒ huáiyí zhèxiē shùzì de zhǔnquè xìng.

questionable ADJ 1 有问题的 [+结论] yǒu wèntí de [+jiélùn], 不能确定的 bùnéng quèdìng de 2 不诚实的 [+交易] bù chéngshí de [+jiāoyì]

questioning ADJ 询问的 xúnwèn de

questionnaire N 问卷 wènjuàn, 调查表 diàochábiǎo [M. WD 份 fèn]

queue I N 1（计算机）队列 (jìsuànjī) duìliè
print queue 打印队列 dǎyìn duìliè
2 排队 páiduì II v 排队 páiduì

quibble I v（为小事）争吵 (wéi xiǎoshì) zhēngchǎo II N 有一点不满意 yǒu yìdiǎn bù mǎnyì

quiche N 蛋奶火腿馅饼 dàn nǎi huǒtuǐ xiànbǐng [M. WD 块 kuài]

quick I ADJ 1 快的 kuài de, 迅速的 xùnsù de
■ *The subway is quicker than buses.* 乘地铁比乘公共汽车快。Chéng dìtiě bǐ chéng gōnggòng qìchē kuài. 2 聪明的 cōngming de, 灵活的 línghuó de
quick study 学得很快的聪明人 xué dehěn kuài de cōngmingrén
3 性急的 jíxìng de II ADV 快快（地）kuài kuài (de), 迅速（地）xùnsù (de)

quicken v（使…）加快 (shǐ...) jiā kuài

quickie I ADJ 又快又容易的 yòu kuài yòu róngyì de II N 又快又容易做的事 yòu kuài yòu róngyì zuò de shì

quickly ADV 快 kuài, 迅速 xùnsù

quicksand N 流沙 liúshā

quick-tempered ADJ 脾气急躁的 píqì jízào, 性急的 xìngjí de

quick-witted ADJ 敏捷的 mínjié de, 对答如流的 duìdá rú liú de

quid pro quo N 交换（物）jiāohuàn (wù)

quiescent ADJ（暂时）静止的 (zànshí) jìngzhǐ de

quiet I ADJ 1 安静的 ānjìng de ■ *Please keep quiet.* 请保持安静。Qǐng bǎochí ānjìng. 2 清淡的 qīngdàn de ■ *Business is quiet on Mondays.* 星期一生意很清淡。Xīngqīyī shēngyì hěn qīngdàn. II N 平静 píngjìng

quill N 羽毛管 yǔmáo guǎn
quill pen 羽毛笔 yǔmáo bǐ

quilt N 被子 bèizi [M. WD 条 tiáo]
patchwork quilt 百衲被 bǎinà bèi

quilted ADJ 夹（层）的 jiā (céng) de

quinine N 奎宁 kuíníng, 金鸡纳霜 jīnjīnàshuāng

quintessence N 典范 diǎnfàn

quintessential ADJ 典型的 diǎnxíng de, 典范的 diǎnfàn de

quintet N 五重唱（小组）wǔchóngchàng (xiǎozǔ), 五重奏（乐队）wǔchóngzòu (yuèduì)

quintuplet N 五胞胎之一 wǔbāotāi zhī yī

quip I v 说俏皮话 shuō qiàopihuà II N 俏皮话 qiàopihuà

quirk N 1 古怪的行为 gǔguài de xíngwéi, 怪癖 guàipǐ 2 古怪的巧事 gǔguài de qiǎoshì, 奇合 qíhé

quirky ADJ 离奇古怪的 líqí gǔguài de

quit v (PT & PP **quit**) 1 辞去 [+工作] cíqù [+gōngzuò], 离开 líkāi 2 停止 [+抽烟] tíngzhǐ [+chōuyān], 不再 búzài

quite ADV 相当 xiāngdāng
not quite 不完全 bù wánquán, 不｜分不

shífēn ■ *I'm not quite sure if he can do the job well.* 我不完全肯定他能做好这件事。Wǒ bù wánquán kěndìng tā néng zuòhǎo zhè jiàn shì.

quits ADJ (to call it quits) 停止（做某事）tíngzhǐ (zuò mǒu shì), 结束 jiéshù

quitter N 打退堂鼓的人 dǎ tuìtánggǔ de rén, 半途而废的人 bàntú ér fèi de rén

quiver N 微微发抖 wēiwēi fādǒu, 颤抖 chàndǒu

quixotic ADJ 唐吉珂德似的 tángjíkēdé shìde, 浪漫而空想的 làngmàn ér kōngxiǎng de

quiz I N 小测验 xiǎo cèyàn II v 1 查问 cháwèn 2 给 [+学生] 做小测验 gěi [+xuésheng] zuò xiǎocèyàn

quizzical ADJ 疑问的 yíwèn de, 好奇的 hàoqí de

quorum N（会议的）法定人数 (huìyì de) fǎdìng rénshù

quota N 配额 pèi'é, 定量 dìngliàng

quotable ADJ 值得引用的 zhíde yǐnyòng de

quotation N 1 引言 yǐnyán 2 报价 bàojià
quotation marks 引号 yǐnhào (" ")

quote I v 1 引用…的话 yǐnyòng...de huà 2 报价 bàojià II N 引言 yǐnyán

quotient N（数学）商（数）(shùxué) shāng (shù)
intelligence quotient (IQ) 智商 zhìshāng

Quran N See Koran

qwerty ADJ (a qwerty keyboard) 标准键盘 biāozhǔn jiànpán

R

rabbi N（犹太教的）教士 (Yóutàijiào de) jiàoshì, 拉比 lābǐ

rabbit N 兔（子）tù (zi) [M. WD 只 zhī]

rabble N（一群）暴民 (yìqún) bàomín,（一帮）痞子 (yìbāng) pǐzi

rabid ADJ 1 患狂犬病的 huàn kuángquǎnbìng de 2 过激狂热的 guòjī kuángrè de

rabies N 狂犬病 kuángquǎn bìng

raccoon N 浣熊 huànxióng [M. WD 头 tóu]

race[1] I N（跑步、游泳等）比赛 (pǎobù、yóuyǒng děng) bǐsài II v 1 参加 [+赛车] 比赛 cānjiā [+sàichē] bǐsài ■ *Hundreds of cyclists race in the "Tour de France" every year.* 每年几百名自行车运动员在"法国之旅"中赛车。Měi nián jǐ bǎi míng zìxíngchē yùndòngyuán zài "Fǎguó zhī lǚ" zhōng sài chē. 2 飞快地奔跑 fēikuài de bēnpǎo

race[2] N 种族 zhǒngzú ■ *People should be treated with respect regardless of race and religion.* 人们不分种族和宗教都应得到尊重。Rénmen bù fēn zhǒngzú hé zōngjiào dōu yīng dédào zūnzhòng.
race relations 种族关系 zhǒngzú guānxi

race-course, racetrack N 赛道 sàidào [M. WD 条 tiáo]

racial ADJ 种族的 zhǒngzú de
  racial discrimination 种族歧视 zhǒngzú qíshì
racing N 赛车／马／跑 sàichē/mǎ/pǎo
racism N 种族主义 zhǒngzú zhǔyì
racist I 种族主义的 zhǒngzúzhǔyì de II N 种族分子 zhǒngzú fènzi
rack I N 架子 jiàzi
  dish rack 盘碟架 pándié jià
  luggage rack 行李架 xínglijià
  roof rack 车顶架 chēdǐng jià
  wine rack 酒瓶架 jiǔ píng jià
  II v (to rack one's brains) 绞尽脑汁 jiǎojìn nǎozhī
racket N 1 吵闹 chǎonào 2 非法勾当 fēifǎ gòudang 3 球拍 qiúpāi
racketeer N 干非法勾当的人 gàn fēifǎ gòudang de rén
racketeering N 非法勾当（如敲诈、勒索、诈骗）fēifǎ gòudang (rú qiāozhà, lèsuǒ, zhàpiàn)
racquet N 球拍 qiúpāi
racy ADJ 带有性挑逗的 dàiyǒu xìng tiǎodòu de, 有趣味的 yǒuqù wèi de
radar N 雷达 léidá
radial ADJ 辐射状的 fúshè zhuàng de
  radiant tire 辐射状轮胎 fúshè zhuàng lúntāi
radiance N 1 喜气洋洋 xǐqì yángyáng, 容光焕发 róngguāng huànfā 2 光辉 guānghuī
radiant ADJ 1 喜气洋洋的 xǐqì yángyáng de, 容光焕发的 róngguāng huànfā de 2 光辉的 guānghuī de, 灿烂的 cànlàn de
radiate v 1 发射出 [+光辉] fāshè chū [+guānghuī] 2 显示出 xiǎnshì chū
radiation N 辐射 fúshè
  radiation sickness 放射病 fàngshèbìng
radiator N 1 （汽车的）散热器 (qìchē de) sànrèqì 2 （房屋的）暖气装置 (fángwū de) nuǎnqì zhuāngzhì
radical I ADJ 1 根本的 [+改变] gēnběn de [+gǎibiàn], 彻底的 chèdǐ de 2 激进的 [+政治主张] jījìn de [+zhèngzhì zhǔzhāng], 极端的 jíduān de II N 激进分子 jījìn fènzi
radicalism N 激进主义 jījìnzhǔyì
radio I N 1 收音机 shōuyīnjī, 无线电 wúxiàndiàn 2 无线电收发设备 wúxiàndiàn shōufā shèbèi 3 广播事业 guǎngbō shìyè II v 用无线电发送信息 yòng wúxiàndiàn fāsòng xìnxī
radioactive ADJ 有发射性的 [+材料] yǒu fāshè xìng de [+cáiliào]
radiologist N 放射科医生 fàngshèkē yīshēng
radiology N 放射（医）学 fàngshè (yī) xué
radiotherapy N 放射治疗 fàngshèzhìliáo
radish N 小萝卜 xiǎoluóbo
radium (Ra) N 镭 léi
radius N （圆的）半径 (yuán de) bànjìng
radon (Rn) N 氡 dōng

raffle I N 抽奖 chōujiǎng II v (to raffle off) 以…为奖品 yǐ…wéi jiǎngpǐn
raft N 木筏 mùfá, 橡皮筏 xiàngpífá [M. WD 艘 sōu]
rafter N 1 乘筏的人 chéng fá de rén 2 椽子 chuánzi
rafting N 漂流（运动）piāoliú (yùndòng)
rag I N 1 抹布 mābù 2 （低质量的）报纸 (dī zhìliàng de) bàozhǐ, 小报 xiǎobào 3 See ragtime
  rag doll 布娃娃 bùwáwa
  II v (to rag on) 戏弄 xìnòng
ragamuffin N 穿得破烂的小孩 chuān dé pòlàn de xiǎohái
ragbag N (a ragbag of sth) 杂乱无章的东西 záluàn wúzhāng de dōngxi, 七零八碎的事物 qīlíng bāsuì de shìwù
rage I N 大怒 dà nù
  to fly into a rage 突然大发脾气 tūrán dà fā píqi
  II v 1 激烈地进行 jīliè de jìnxíng 2 对…大发脾气 duì…dà fā píqi
ragged, raggedy ADJ 1 破烂的 [+衣服] pòlàn de [+yīfu], 衣衫褴褛的 yīshān lánlǚ de 2 不完美的 [+表演] bù wánměi de [+biǎoyǎn]
ragtag ADJ 1 乱哄哄的 luànhōnghōng de, 杂乱的 záluàn de 2 肮脏的 āngzāng de
ragtime N 雷格泰姆（音乐／舞蹈）léigétàimǔ (yīnyuè/wǔdǎo)
rah-rah I ADJ 太会叫好的 tài huì jiàohǎo de II INTERJ 好！好！hǎo! hǎo!
raid I v 1 袭击 xíjī, 突袭 tūxí 2 [警察+] 突袭搜捕 [jǐngchá+] tūxí sōubǔ II N 1 袭击 xíjī, 突袭 tūxí 2 （警察）突袭搜捕 (jǐngchá) tūxí sōubǔ 3 挪用 [+资金] nuóyòng [+zījīn]
rail¹ I N 1 栏杆 lángān, 扶手 fúshou 2 铁轨 tiěguǐ
  by rail 乘火车（旅行）chénghuǒchē (lǚxíng)
rail² v 声讨 shēngtǎo
railing N 栏杆 lángān, 扶手 fúshou
railroad¹ N 铁路 tiělù, 铁道 tiědào
railroad² v 强迫 qiǎngpò, 强行 qiángxíng
railway N See railroad¹
rain I N 雨 yǔ, 雨水 yǔshuǐ ■ We were caught in the rain. 我们赶上下雨了。Wǒmen gǎnshang xiàyǔ la. II v 下雨 xiàyǔ
  rain forest 雨林 yǔlín
rainbow N 虹 hóng, 彩虹 cǎihóng
rain check N 1 近期兑现的优惠券 jìnqī duìxiàn de yōuhuì quàn 2 （体育）近期比赛入场券 (tǐyù) jìnqī bǐsài rùchǎngquàn [M. WD 张 zhāng]
  to take a rain check 改日再做某事 gǎirì zài zuò mǒu shì
raincoat N 雨衣 yǔyī [M. WD 件 jiàn]
raindrop N 雨点 yǔdiǎn
rainfall N 降雨量 jiàngyǔliàng
rains N （热带的）雨季 (rèdài de) yǔjì
rainstorm N 暴雨 bàoyǔ [M. WD 场 cháng]
rainwater N 雨水 yǔshuǐ

rainy ADJ 多雨的 duō yǔ de, 经常下雨的 jīngcháng xiàyǔ de
to save for a rainy day 存钱以备不时之需 cúnqián yǐbèi bùshízhīxū

raise I v **1** 举起 jǔqǐ, 升起 shēngqǐ, 抬起 táiqǐ ■ *Every morning the flag is raised at school.* 每天早上，国旗在学校升起。Měitiān zǎoshang, guóqí zài xuéxiào shēngqǐ. **2** 提高 tígāo ■ *Don't raise your voice at me, son.* 小子，别对我大声嚷嚷。Xiǎozi, bié duì wǒ dàshēng rāngrang. **3** 饲养 sìyǎng **4** 提出 [+问题] tíchū [+wèntí] II N 加薪 jiā xīn ■ *It's not a good time to ask for a raise.* 现在不是要求加薪的好时机。Xiànzài bú shì yāoqiú jiā xīn de hǎo shíjī.
to raise hell/Cain 大吵大闹 dà chǎo dà nào ■ *He raised hell when he found his car damaged.* 他发现汽车被弄坏了，大吵大闹。Tā fāxiàn qìchē bèi nònghuài le, dà chǎo dà nào.

raison d'être N 存在的理由 cúnzài de lǐyóu

rake I N 耙子 pázi [M. WD 把 bǎ] II v 用耙子耙 yòng pázi bà
to rake leaves 把落叶耙在一起 bǎ luòyè bà zài yìqǐ

rally I N **1** 大型 [+抗议] 集会 dàxíng [+kàngyì] jíhuì **2** 汽车拉力赛 qìchē lālìsài **3** [股票+] 反弹 [gǔpiào+] fǎntán, 重新振作 chóngxīn zhènzuò II v **1** 集合 jíhé **2** 重新振作 chóngxīn zhènzuò, 反弹 fǎntán

rallying cry N (有号召力的) 战斗口号 (yǒu hàozhàolì de) zhàndòu kǒuhào

rallying point N 凝聚力 níngjùlì

RAM (= Random Access Memory) ABBREV （计算机）随机存取存储器 (jìsuànjī) suíjī cúnqǔ cúnchǔqì

ram I v 猛撞 měngzhuàng II N 公羊 gōngyáng [M. WD 头 tóu]

Ramadan N （伊斯兰教）斋月 (Yīsīlánjiào) zhāiyuè

ramble v, N **1** 漫步 mànbù, 闲逛 xiánguàng **2** 漫谈 màntán, 没有边际的说很多话 méiyǒu biānjì de shuō hěn duō huà

rambling ADJ **1** 漫无边际的 [+文章] màn wú biānjì de [+wénzhāng] **2** 杂乱无章的 [+建筑] záluàn wúzhāng de [+jiànzhù]

rambunctious ADJ 吵吵闹闹的 chǎochǎo nàonào de

ramification N 意料不到的后果 yìliào búdào de hòuguǒ

ramp N （出入高速公路的）坡道 (chūrù gāosù gōnglù de) pōdào

rampage v, N 横冲直撞 héngchōng zhízhuàng
to go on a rampage 骚乱 sāoluàn, 闹事 nàoshì

rampant ADJ 猖獗的 chāngjué de, 失控的 shīkòng de

ramshackle ADJ 破烂的 pòlàn de

ran See **run**

ranch N 大牧场 dà mùchǎng, 大农场 dà nóngchǎng
ranch house 牧场式住房 mùchǎngshì zhùfáng

rancher N 牧场主 mùchǎng zhǔ, 农场主 nóngchǎng zhǔ

ranching N 经营农场 jīngyíng nóngchǎng, 经营牧场 jīngyíng mùchǎng

rancid ADJ 变味的 [+黄油] biànwèi de [+huángyóu], 不新鲜的 bù xīnxian de

rancor N 怨恨 yuànhèn, 深仇 shēn chóu

rancorous ADJ 充满怨恨的 chōngmǎn yuànhèn de

random I ADJ 随意的 suíyì de, 任意的 rènyì de
random sample 随机抽样 suíjī chōuyàng II N (at random) 随机（地）suíjī (de), 任意（地）rènyì (de)

rang See **ring**

range I N **1** 系列 xìliè ■ *Come to our store and see the new range of furniture from Italy.* 请到我们店来，看看意大利来的新家具系列。Qǐng dào wǒmen diàn lái, kànkan Yìdàlì lái de xīn jiājù xìliè. **2** 范围 fànwéi **3** 幅度 fúdù ■ *What is the salary range for an associate professor in your university?* 你们大学副教授的工资幅度是多少？Nǐmen dàxué fù jiàoshòu de gōngzī fúdù shì duōshǎo? **4** 距离 jùlí II v **1** 范围在…和…之间 fànwéi zài…hé…zhījiān **2** 涉及 shèjí **3** 排列 páiliè

ranger N **1** 护林员 hùlínyuán, 管理员 guǎnlǐyuán **2** 巡逻骑警 xúnluó qíjǐng

rank I N **1** 级别 jíbié, 军阶 jūnjiē **2** 社会阶层 shèhuì jiēcéng, 身份 shēnfen II v 分成等级 fēnchéng děngjí, 排名 páimíng ■ *Every year this magazine ranks American universities and colleges.* 每年这家杂志都为美国大学排名。Měi nián zhè jiā zázhì dōu wèi Měiguó dàxué páimíng. III ADJ **1** 十足的 shízú de, 完全的 wánquán de **2** 难闻的 nánwén de

rank and file N 普通成员 pǔtōng chéngyuán

ranking I N 排名 páimíng, 名次 míngcì II ADJ 级别最高的 jíbiézuìgāo de, 高级的 [+官员] gāojí de [+guānyuán]

rankle v 使…十分恼火 shǐ…shífēn nǎohuǒ

ransack v **1** 彻底搜查 chèdǐ sōuchá **2** 洗劫 xǐjié

ransom N （绑票）赎金 (bǎngpiào) shújīn II v 付赎金救人 fù shújīn jiù rén

rant v 怒气冲冲地叫嚷 nùqì chōngchōng de jiàorǎng

rap I N **1** 轻敲 qīngqiāo **2** 指控 zhǐkòng
drunk driving rap 酒后驾车的指控 jiǔhòu jiàchē de zhǐkòng
3 （音乐）说唱乐 (yīnyuè) shuōchàngyuè II v **1** 轻敲 qīngqiāo
to rap sb on the knuckles 轻轻地批评某人 qīngqīng de pīpíng mǒurén

2 气愤地指责 qìfèn de zhǐzé 3 念出说唱乐的歌词 niàn chū shuōchàng yuè de gēcí

rape V, N 强奸 qiángjiān, 强暴 qiángbào
date rape 约会强奸 yuēhuì qiángjiān

rapid ADJ 迅速的 xùnsù de ■ *Rapid economic development requires more and more energy supply.* 迅速的经济发展需要越来越多的能源供应。Xùnsù de jīngjì fāzhǎn xūyào yuèláiyuè duō de néngyuán gōngyìng.
rapid heartbeats 心动过速 xīndòng guòsù

rapidly ADV 迅速(地)xùnsù (de)

rapids N 激流 jīliú

rapist N 强奸犯 qiángjiānfàn

rapport N 融洽关系 róngqià guānxi
to establish a rapport with sb 与某人建立融洽关系 yǔ mǒurén jiànlì róngqià guānxi

rapprochement N [两国+] 关系重新缓和 [liǎngguó+] guānxi chóngxīn huǎnhé

rapt ADJ 出神的 chūshén de, 全神贯注的 quánshén guànzhù de
with rapt attention 全神贯注地 quánshén guànzhù de

rapture N 狂喜 kuángxǐ

rapturous ADJ 狂喜的 kuángxǐde

rare ADJ 1 稀有的 xīyǒu de, 难得的 nándé de ■ *A white Christmas is rare in the Southern Hemisphere.* 下雪的圣诞节在南半球是很难得的。Xiàxuě de Shèngdàn jié zài nánbànqiú shì hěn nándé de. 2 半熟的 bàn shóu de ■ *No, I don't like my steak well-done; I like it rare.* 不，我不喜欢牛排煮得太老，我喜欢半熟的。Bù, wǒ bù xīhuan niúpái zhǔde tài lǎo, wǒ xǐhuan bàn shóu de.

rarely ADV 很少(发生)hěn shǎo (fāshēng)

raring ADJ 急切的 jíqiè de, 渴望的 kěwàng de

rarity N 1 珍贵的东西 zhēnguì de dōngxi, 稀有的宝物 xīyǒu de bǎowù 2 不常发生的事 bù cháng fāshēng de shì

rascal N 恶棍 èqùn, 无赖 wúlài

rash I ADJ 急躁的 jízào de, 草率的 cǎoshuài de II N 皮疹 pízhěn
to break out in a rash 起疹子 qǐ zhěnzi, 发出疹子 fāchū zhěnzi

rasp V 发出刺耳的声音 fāchū cì'ěr de shēngyīn II N 1 粗哑刺耳的声音 cūyǎ cì'ěr de shēngyīn 2 粗锉刀 cūcuòdāo

raspberry N 山莓 shānméi, 悬钩子 xuángōuzi

rat I N (老)鼠(lǎo) shǔ [M. WD 只 zhī]
rat race 无休止的竞争 wú xiūzhǐ de jìngzhēng, 相互倾轧 xiānghù qīngzhá II V (背信弃义地)告密 (bèixìn qìyì de) gàomì

rate N 1 率 lǜ, 比率 bǐlǜ 2 费用 fèiyòng, 价格 jiàgé 3 速度 sùdù ■ *He reads at the rate of 250 words per minute.* 他的阅读速度是一分钟二百五十个词。Tā de yuèdú sùdù shì yì fēnzhōng èr bǎi wǔshí ge cí.

first-rate 一等 yì děng, 第一流 dìyī liú
at any rate 不管怎么说 bùguǎn zěnme shuō, 无论如何 wúlùn rú hé

rather ADV 相当 xiāngdāng ■ *I've done rather badly in the exam.* 我考试考得相当差。Wǒ kǎoshì kǎode xiāngdāng chà.
rather than 不 bù, 不是 bú shì ■ *I'll stay at home rather than go out with them.* 我要呆在家里，不跟他们一起出去。Wǒ yào dāi zài jiālǐ, bù gēn tāmen yìqǐ chūqu.
rather too 未免 wèimiǎn ■ *This punishment is rather too harsh.* 这个惩罚未免太严厉了。Zhè ge chéngfá wèimiǎn tài yánlì le.
would rather 宁愿 nìngyuàn

ratification N 正式签署 zhèngshì qiānshǔ, 批准 pīzhǔn

ratify V 正式签署 [+条约] zhèngshì qiānshǔ [+tiáoyuē], 批准 pīzhǔn

rating N 1 等级 děngjí, 率 lǜ 2 (电影的)级别 (diànyǐng de) jíbié
approval rating 支持率 zhīchílǜ
credit rating 信用等级 xìnyòng děngjí

ratings N (电影/电视)收视率 (diànyǐng/diànshì) shōushìlǜ

ratio N 比(例)bǐ (lì), 比率 bǐlǜ

ration I N 配给(量)pèijǐ (liáng) II V 定量供应 dìngliàng gōngyìng, 实行配给 shíxíng pèijǐ

rationale N 原因 yuányīn, 依据 yījù

rationalize V 1 合理的解释 hélǐ de jièshì 2 合理化 hélǐhuà

rationalization N 合理化 hélǐhuà

rationing N 配给 pèijǐ, 定量供应 dìngliàng gōngyìng

rations N (每日的)口粮配给 (měirì de) kǒuliáng pèijǐ

rattle I V 1 使…咯咯震动 shǐ...gēgē zhèndòng 2 使…神经紧张 shǐ...shénjīng jǐnzhāng II N 1 咯咯的声音 gēgē de shēngyīn 2 拨浪鼓(玩具)bōlanggǔ (wánjù)

rattlesnake N 响尾蛇 xiǎngwěishé [M. WD 条 tiáo]

raucous ADJ 1 嘈杂的 [+人群] zàozá de [+rénqún] 2 沙哑的 [+声音] shāyǎ de [+shēngyīn]

raunchy ADJ 色情的 sèqíng de, 下流的 xiàliú de

ravage V 严重摧毁 yánzhòng cuīhuǐ, 毁坏 huǐhuài

ravages N (破坏性)后果 (pòhuàixìng) hòuguǒ

rave I V 胡言乱语 húyán luànyǔ
to rave about 赞赏 zànshǎng
to rant and rave 大叫大嚷 dàjiào dàrǎng, 大骂 dàmà
II ADJ 赞扬的 zànyáng de
rave review 热烈好评 rèliè hǎopíng
III N 狂欢聚会 kuánghuān jùhuì

raven N 渡鸦 dùyā [M. WD 只 zhī]

ravenous ADJ 极饿的 jí'è de, 饿的 è de

ravine N 深谷 shēngǔ, 峡谷 xiágǔ

raving ADJ 胡言乱语的 húyán luànyǔ de
raving success 巨大成功 jùdà chénggōng
ravings N 胡言乱语 húyán luànyǔ, 疯话 fēnghuà
ravish V 1 使…陶醉 shǐ...táozuì 2 强奸 qiángjiān
ravishing ADJ 令人心醉的 lìngrén xīnzuì de, 十分
美丽的 shífēn měilì de
raw ADJ 1 生的 [+食物] shēng de [+shíwù]
raw materials 原材料 yuán cáiliào
2 不成熟的 [+人] bùchéngshú de [+rén], 没有
经验的 méiyǒu jīngyàn de
a raw recruit 新兵 xīnbīng
3 阴冷的 [+天气] yīnlěng de [+tiānqì]
ray N 光线 guāngxiàn
a ray of hope 一线希望 yí xiàn xīwàng
ray gun 光束枪 guāngshùqiāng, 激光枪
jīguāng qiāng
rayon N 人造丝 rénzàosī
raze V 把…夷为平地 bǎ...yí wéi píngdì
razor N 剃刀 tìdāo [M. WD 把 bǎ], 剃胡刀 tì hú dāo
[M. WD 把 bǎ]
razor blade N 刀片 dāopiàn
razz V 嘲笑 cháoxiào
re PREP 关于 guānyú
reach I V 1 到达 dàodá ■ Police reached the crime
scene in 25 minutes. 警察在二十五分钟内到达犯罪
现场。Jǐngchá zài èrshíwǔ fēnzhōng nèi dàodá fànzuì xiànchǎng. 2 够得着 gòudezháo ■ The child
stood on tiptoes, but still couldn't reach the cooker
jar. 小孩踮起脚，但还是够不着饼干罐头。Xiǎohái
diǎnqǐjiǎo, dàn háishi gòubuzháo bǐnggān guàntou.
3 伸手拿 shēnshǒu ná 4 和…联系 hé...liánxì II N
1 河段 héduàn
the upper/lower reaches (of a river) (河流)上
游/下游 (héliú) shàngyóu/xiàyóu
2 可能得到 kěnéng dédào ■ She believes that
the scholarship is within her reach. 她相信能得到
奖学金。Tā xiāngxìn néng dédào jiǎngxuéjīn.
beyond the reach of sb 某人不可能得到
mǒurén bù kěnéng dédào
out of/beyond (one's) reach ① 在手伸不到的
地方 zài shǒu shēnbudào de dìfang ■ Keep
the medicines out of the reach of children. 把药
放在孩子拿不到的地方。Bǎ yào fàng zài háizi
nábúdàode dìfang. ② 买不起 mǎibuqǐ
within (one's) reach ① 在手伸得到的地方 zài
shǒu shēndedào de dìfang, 在可以达到的地
方 zài kěyǐ dádào de dìfang ■ My apartment is
within easy reach of a supermarket. 我的公寓离超
市很近。Wǒ de gōngyù lí chāoshì hěn jìn. ② 买得
起 mǎideqǐ
react V 反应 fǎnyìng
to react against 反对 fǎnduì, 反抗 fǎnkàng
reaction N 1 反应 fǎnyìng, 反响 fǎnxiǎng ■ His
anti-immigration speech provoked angry reactions
in some ethnic communities. 他的反移民演说在一

些种族社区里激起愤怒的反应。Tā de fǎn yímín
yǎnshuō zài yìxiē zhǒngzú shèqū lǐ jīqǐ fènnù de
fǎnyìng. 2 药物反应 yàowù fǎnyìng, 生理反
应 shēnglǐ fǎnyìng ■ I know a man who has a
strong reaction to peanuts. 我知道一个人对花生有
生理反应。Wǒ zhīdào yí ge rén duì huāshēng yǒu
shēnglǐ fǎnyìng.
reactionary I ADJ 反动的 fǎndòng de II N 反动派
fǎndòngpài, 反动份子 fǎndòng fènzi
reactive ADJ 反应(性的) fǎnyìng (xìng) de
reactor N (核)反应堆 (hé) fǎnyìngduī
read (PT & PP **read**) V 1 读 dú, 阅读 yuèdú, 看得
懂 kàndedǒng 2 读到 dúdao, 看到 kàndào
■ I've read that a new medicine has been
invented to cure Alzheimer's disease. 我读到一
篇文章 (or 一条消息)，说已经发明出治疗老年
性痴呆症的药物了。Wǒ dúdao yì piān wénzhāng
(or yì tiáo xiāoxi), shuō yǐjīng fāmíngchū zhìliáo
lǎoniánxìng chīdāizhèng de yàowù le.
to read between the lines 仔细读 (找出言外之
意) zǐxì dú (zhǎochū yán wài zhī yì) ■ If you
read between the lines, you'll see she's not totally
against your proposal. 如果你仔细读，就会发现她
并不是完全不同意你的提议。Rúguǒ nǐ zǐxì dú, jiù
huì fāxiàn tā bìng bú shì wánquán bù tóngyì nǐ de
tíyì.
readable ADJ (读起来)有趣的 (dú qǐlái) yǒuqù
de, 易读的 yì dú de
reader N 1 读者 dúzhě 2 读书的人 dúshū de rén
3 读本 dúběn [M. WD 本 běn], 读物 dúwù [M. WD
本 běn]
readership N 读者(群) dúzhě (qún)
readily ADV 1 容易地 róngyì de 2 乐意地 lèyì de
readiness N 1 愿意 yuànyì, 情愿 qíngyuàn 2 准备
好 zhǔnbèi hǎo, 准备就绪 zhǔnbèi jiùxù
reading N 1 阅读 yuèdú ■ He enjoys reading and
playing soccer. 他喜欢阅读和踢英式足球。Tā
xǐhuan yuèdú hé tī Yīngshì zúqiú. 2 阅读材料
yuèdú cáiliào ■ The teacher assigned us a lot of
reading. 老师布置很多阅读材料要我们看。Lǎoshī
bùzhì hěn duō yuèdú cáiliào yào wǒmen kàn. 3 理
解 lǐjiě, 解释 jiěshì
reading room N 阅览室 yuèlǎn shì
readjust V 重新适应 chóngxīn shìyìng, 调整适应
tiáozhěng shìyìng
read-only memory See ROM
readout N (计算机)信息读出 (jìsuànjī) xìnxī dú
chū
ready ADJ 准备好 zhǔnbèihǎo ■ Dinner's ready!
饭做好了！Fàn zuòhǎo le!
(Get) ready, (get) set, go! 各就各位，预备，起!
Gè jiù gè wèi, yùbèi, qǐ!
ready-made ADJ 现成的 xiànchéng de
ready-to-wear 现成的(服装) xiànchéng de
(fúzhuāng)

real I ADJ 真正的 zhēnzhèng de, 真实的 zhēnshí de ■ *You can't meet such people in real life.* 在真实生活里你不会遇到这样的人。Zài zhēnshí shēnghuó lǐ nǐ bú huì yùdao zhèyàng de rén. **II** ADV 确实 quèshí, 实在 shízài ■ *That test is real hard.* 那次考试确实很难。Nà cì kǎoshì quèshí hěn nán.

real estate N 房地产 fángdìchǎn
real estate agency 房地产公司 fángdìchǎn gōngsī
real estate agent 房地产经纪人 fángdìchǎn jīngjìrén

realism N 现实主义 xiànshízhǔyì

realist N 现实主义者 xiànshízhǔyì zhě

realistic ADJ 现实(主义)的 xiànshí (zhǔyì) de, 讲究实际的 jiǎngjiu shíjì de

realistically ADV 现实(主义)地 xiànshí (zhǔyì) de, 讲究实际地 jiǎngjiu shíjì de

reality N 现实 xiànshí, 真实情况 zhēnshí qíngkuàng
reality show 写实节目 xiěshí jiémù, 真人秀 zhēnrén xiù

realization N **1** 意识 yìshi, 领悟 lǐngwù **2** 实现 shíxiàn, 达到 dádào

realize V **1** 意识到 yìshidao, 了解 liǎojiě **2** 实现 shíxiàn ■ *He has realized his ambitions and is proud of it.* 他实现了自己的抱负，感到很自傲。Tā shíxiànle zìjǐ bàofù, gǎndao hěn zì'ào.

really ADV 真正地 zhēnzhèng de, 真地 zhēn de ■ *"Martha gave birth to a baby boy." "Really? When?"* "玛莎生了个男孩。" "真的吗？什么时候生的？" "Mǎshā shēngle ge nánhái." "Zhēn de ma? Shénme shíhòu shēng de?"
not really 不太 bú tài ■ *"Was the band's performance good?" "Not really."* "乐队的演出好吗？" "不太好。" Yuèduì de yǎnchū hǎo ma? "Bú tài hǎo."

realm N 领域 lǐngyù, 范围 fànwéi

real-time ADJ (计算机)即时处理的 (jìsuànjī) jíshí chǔlǐ de

realtor N 房地产经纪人 fángdìchǎn jīngjìrén

realty N 房地产 fángdìchǎn

ream N **1** 令 lìng (= 500 张纸 zhāngzhǐ) **2** 大量 (文字材料) dàliàng (wénzì cáiliào)

reap V 获得 huòdé
You reap what you sow. 种瓜得瓜，种豆得豆。Zhòng guā dé guā, zhòng dòu dé dòu.

rear¹ I N **1** 后面 hòumian, 背面 bèimiàn
to bring up the rear 处在最后的地位 chǔzài zuìhòu de dìwèi
2 臀部 túnbù **II** ADJ 后面的 hòumian de
rear door 后门 hòumén **II** ADJ 后面的 hòumian de

rear² V **1** 养育 [+孩子] yǎngyù [+háizi], 抚养 fǔyǎng **2** 饲养 [+家畜] sìyǎng [+jiāchù] **3** [动物+] 用后腿直立 [dòngwù+] yòng hòutuǐ zhílì **4** (to rear its ugly head) [丑闻+] 出现 [chǒuwén+] chūxiàn, 冒头 màotóu

rearrange V 重新安排 chóngxīn ānpái

rearrangement N 重新安排 chóngxīn ānpái

rearview mirror N 后视镜 hòushìjìng

rearward ADV 在后面 zàihòu miàn

reason I N **1** 原因 yuányīn, 理由 lǐyóu **2** 理性 lǐxìng, 道理 dàolǐ **3** 思考 sīkǎo ■ *Only man has the ability to reason.* 只有人类具有思考的能力。Zhǐ yǒu rénlèi jùyǒu sīkǎo de nénglì. **2** 推论 tuīlùn ■ *The detective reasoned that the crime must have been committed by an insider.* 侦探推论，一定是内部人作的案。Zhēntàn tuīlùn, yídìng shì nèibù rén zuò de àn.

reasonable ADJ **1** 讲道理的 jiǎng dàolǐ de ■ *No reasonable person will impose such harsh punishment.* 没有一个讲道理的人会强加这么严酷的惩罚。Méiyǒu yí ge jiǎng dàolǐ de rén huì qiángjiā zhème yánkù de chéngfá. **2** 符合情理的 fúhé qínglǐ de

reasonably ADV **1** 相当(地) xiāngdāng (de) **2** 合情合理(地) héqíng hélǐ (de), 按照情理 ànzhào qínglǐ
reasonably priced 价格合理的 jiàgé hélǐ de

reasoned ADJ 经过慎重考虑的 jīngguò shènzhòng kǎolǜ de, 理智的 lǐzhì de

reasoning N **1** 推理 tuīlǐ **2** 道理 dàolǐ

reassurance N 安慰 ānwèi

reassure V 使…放心 shǐ…fàngxīn, 消除疑虑 xiāochú yílǜ

reassuring ADJ 让人放心的 ràng rén fàngxīn de, 安慰的 ānwèi de

rebate N (部分)退款 (bùfen) tuìkuǎn, 回扣 huíkòu

rebel I N 造反者 zàofǎnzhě, 反叛 fǎnpàn **II** V 造反 zàofǎn, 反叛 fǎnpàn

rebellion N 叛乱 pànluàn

rebellious ADJ 反抗的 fǎnkàng de, 反叛的 fǎnpàn de

rebirth N **1** 重生 chóngshēng, 再生 zàishēng **2** 复兴 fùxìng

reboot V 重新启动 (计算机) chóngxīn qǐdòng (jìsuànjī)

rebound I V **1** [球+] 弹回 [qiú+] tánhuí **2** [价格+] 回升 [jiàgé I] huíshēng, 反弹 fǎntán **II** N (on the rebound) **1** [球+] 在弹回 [qiú+] zài tánhuí **2** [事情+] 正有起色 [shìqing+] zhèng yǒuqǐse
on the rebound 因失恋而情绪低落时 yīn shīliàn ér qíngxù dīluò shí

rebuff N, V 回绝 huíjué, 拒绝 jùjué

rebuild V 重建 chóngjiàn, 恢复 huīfù

rebuke I V 指责 zhǐzé, 斥责 chìzé **II** N 指责 zhǐzé

rebut V 驳斥 bóchì, 反驳 fǎnbó

rebuttal N 驳斥 bóchì, 反驳 fǎnbó

recalcitrance N 桀骜不驯 jié'ào búxùn

recalcitrant ADJ 不听话的 [+小孩] bù tīnghuà de [+xiǎohái], 难管的 nán guǎn de

recall I V **1** 想起 xiǎngqǐ **2** 回想 huíxiǎng, 回忆

huíyì ■ *Try to recall what happened that evening.* 尽量回想一下那天晚上发生了什么。 Jìnliàng huíxiǎng yí xià nà tiān wǎnshang fāshēngle shénme. **3** [制造厂商+] 收回 [+产品] [zhìzào chǎngshāng+] shōuhuí [+chǎnpǐn] **4** 召回 [+大使] zhàohuí [+dàshǐ] **5**（在计算机上）重新调出信息 (zài jìsuànjī shàng) chóngxīn tiáo chū xìnxī **II** N **1** 记忆（力）jìyì (lì) **2**（对官员的）罢免 (duì guānyuán de) bàmiǎn **3**（商品）收回令 (shāngpǐn) shōuhuílíng·

recant v 公开宣布放弃 [+以前的观点] gōngkāi xuānbù fàngqì [+yǐqián de guāndiǎn]

recap, recapitulate v 重新说一下内容简要 chóngxīn shuō yíxià nèiróng jiǎnyào, 复习 fùxí

recapitalize v 给 [+公司] 再投资 gěi [+gōngsī] zàitóuzī

recapture v **1** 重新抓获 [+逃犯] chóngxīn zhuāhuò [+táofàn] **2** 再现 [+历史时期] zàixiàn [+lìshǐ shíqī]

recede v **1** 渐渐消失 jiànjiàn xiāoshī **2** [洪水+] 退去 [hóngshuǐ+] tuìqù

receipt N 收据 shōujù, 收条 shōutiáo

receive v **1** 收到 shōudao **2** 得到 dédao, 受到 shòudao ■ *After his promotion he received congratulations from his colleagues.* 他提升以后，收到同事们的祝贺。Tā tíshēng yǐhòu, shōudao tóngshìmen de zhùhè.

receiver N **1**（电话）听筒 (diànhuà) tīngtǒng **2** 破产企业管理人 pòchǎn qǐyè guǎnlǐ rén **3** 买卖赃物者 mǎimai zāngwùzhě **4**（电子信号）接收机 (diànzǐ xìnhào) jiēshōujī **5**（橄榄球）接球手 (gǎnlǎnqiú) jiēqiúshǒu

receivership N 破产管理 pòchǎn guǎnlǐ

recent ADJ 近来的 jìnlái de

recently ADV 近来 jìnlái, 最近 zuìjìn

receptacle N 容器 róngqì

reception N **1** 招待会 zhāodàihuì, 宴会 yànhuì wedding reception 婚宴 hūn yàn **2** 接待 jiēdài, 欢迎 huānyíng reception desk（旅馆的）接待处 (lǚguǎn de) jiēdài chù, 登记台 dēngjì tái **3**（电视机的）收视质量 (diànshìjī de) shōushì zhìliàng,（收音机的）接收性能 (shōuyīnjī de) jiēshōu xìngnéng poor reception（电视）收视质量很差 (diànshì) shōushì zhìliàng hěn chà

receptionist N 接待员 jiēdài yuán

receptive ADJ 乐于接受的 lèyú jiēshòu de

recess N 中途休息时间 zhōngtú xiūxi shíjiān, 休会 xiūhuì

recession N（经济）衰退（期）(jīngjì) shuāituì (qī)

recharge v **1** 给 [+电池] 充电 gěi [+diànchí] chōngdiàn **2** 使⋯恢复精力 shǐ⋯huīfù jīnglì

rechargeable ADJ 可充电的 [+电池] kě chōngdiàn de [+diànchí]

recipe N 烹饪法 pēngrèn fǎ, 菜谱 càipǔ

recipient N 领受者 lǐngshòu zhě, 得奖人 déjiǎngrén

reciprocal ADJ 互相的 hùxiāng de, 互惠的 hùhuì de

reciprocate v 报答 bàodá, 给以回报 gěiyǐ huíbào

recital N（音乐）演奏会 (yīnyuè) yǎnzòu huì,（诗歌）朗诵会 (shīgē) lǎngsòng huì

recitation N 背诵 bèisòng

recite v 朗诵 lǎngsòng, 背诵 bèisòng

reckless ADJ 不考虑后果的 bù kǎolǜ hòuguǒ de, 鲁莽的 lǔmǎng de

reckon v **1** 估计 gūjì **2** 看作 kànzuò, 认为 rènwéi to reckon with 认真对付 rènzhēn duìfu

reckoning N **1** 估计 gūjì, 估算 gūsuàn **2** (a day of reckoning) 算总帐的日子 suàn zǒngzhàng de rìzi, 报应的那一天 bàoyìng de nà yì tiān

reclaim v **1** 回收 [+有用材料] huíshōu [+yǒuyòng cáiliào] **2** 收回 [+部分税款] shōuhuí [+bùfen shuìkuǎn] **3** 开垦 [+土地] kāikěn [+tǔdì]

recline v 躺 tǎng

recluse N 隐居者 yǐnjūzhě, 隐士 yǐnshì

reclusive ADJ 隐居的 yǐnjū de

recognition N **1** 认出 rènchū **2** 认识到 rènshidào, 接受 jiēshòu **3** 承认 chéngrèn **4** 表彰 biǎozhāng, 赞扬 zànyáng

recognizable ADJ 能认出来的 néng rènchū láide

recognize v **1** 认出 rènchū, 辨认出 biànrènchū ■ *No one recognized this language until Eugene had a look and declared it to be Tibetan.* 没有人能辨认出这种语言，直到尤金看了一眼，宣布那是西藏文。Méiyǒu rén néng biànrènchū zhè zhǒng yǔyán, zhídào Yóujīn kànle yì yǎn, xuānbù nà shì Xīzàng wén. **2** 认识到 rènshidao ■ *The principal recognized that some teachers' workloads were too heavy.* 校长认识到，有些老师的工作量太重了。Xiàozhǎng rènshidao, yǒuxiē lǎoshī de gōngzuòliàng tài zhòng le. **3** 承认 chéngrèn, 公认 gōngrèn **4** 表彰 biǎozhāng, 赞扬 zànyáng

recoil I v **1**（因厌恶）退避 (yīn yànwù) tuìbì **2** [枪炮+] 反冲 [qiāngpào+] fǎnchōng **II** N 反冲 fǎnchōng, 后座力 hòuzuòlì

recollect v 努力回想 nǔlì huíxiǎng, 记起 jìqǐ

recollection N **1** 想起 xiǎngqǐ **2** 记忆 jìyì, 回忆 huíyì

recommend v **1** 推荐 tuījiàn, 介绍 jièshào **2** 建议 jiànyì

recommendation N **1** 推荐 tuījiàn, 介绍 jièshào **2**（正式）建议 (zhèngshì) jiànyì, 意见 yìjiàn

recompense N, v 补偿 bǔcháng, 赔偿 péicháng

reconcile v 使⋯重归于好 shǐ⋯chóng guīyú hǎo, 调和 tiáohé

reconciliation N 重归于好 chóng guīyú hǎo, 调和 tiáohé, 和解 héjiě spirit of reconciliation 和解的精神 héjiě de jīngshén

recondition v 修复 [+旧机器] xiūfù [+jiù jīqì]

reconnaissance N 侦察 zhēnchá
aerial reconnaissance 空中侦察 kōngzhōng zhēnchá
reconnaissance aircraft 侦察机 zhēnchájī

reconnoiter v 侦察 zhēnchá

reconsider v 重新考虑 chóngxīn kǎolǜ

reconsideration N 重新考虑 chóngxīn kǎolǜ

reconstitute v 重组 chóngzǔ, 重建 chóngjiàn

reconstruct v **1** 再现 [+某一事件] zàixiàn [+mǒuyí shìjiàn] **2** 重建 chóngjiàn

reconstruction I N **1** 重建 chóngjiàn **2** 重现 chóngxiàn **3** 修复手术 xiūfù shǒushù

record I N **1** 记录 jìlù ■ *There is no record of her being baptized at this church.* 在这个教堂里没有她洗礼的记录。Zài zhè ge jiàotáng lǐ méiyǒu tā xíng xǐlǐ de jìlù. **2** 最高记录 zuìgāo jìlù ■ *There was a record number of applicants for the college.* 那所大学的报名人数创下最高记录。Nà suǒ dàxué de bàomíng rénshù chuàng xia zuìgāo jìlù. **3** 唱片 chàngpiàn [M. WD 张 zhāng]
to break a record 打破记录 dǎpò jìlù
record player 唱机 chàngjī
III v 记录下来 jìlùxiàlai
off the record 不得发表的 bù dé fābiǎo de

record-breaking ADJ 破记录的 pò jìlù de

recorder N 录音机 lùyīnjī [M. WD 台 tái], 摄象机 shèxiàngjī

recording N 录音 lùyīn, 录象 lùxiàng

recount v 叙述 xùshù, 描述 miáoshù

re-count N 重新计算选票 chóngxīn jìsuàn xuǎnpiào

recoup v 偿还 chánghuán, 补偿 bǔcháng

recourse N 求助 (的对象) qiúzhù (de duìxiàng)
without recourse to sth 得不到某事物的帮助 dé búdào mǒushìwù de bāngzhù

recover v **1** 康复 kāngfù **2** 恢复 huīfù ■ *It will take some time for the economy to recover.* 经济恢复需要一些时间。Jīngjì huīfù xūyào yìxiē shíjiān. **3** 找回 zhǎohuí

recovery N **1** 恢复健康 huīfù jiànkāng, 康复 kāngfù **2** [经济+] 复苏 [jīngjì+] fùsū **3** 重新获得 chóngxīn huòdé, [失物的+] 复得 [shīwù de+] fùdé

recreate v 重建 chóngjiàn, 重演 chóngyǎn

recreation N 消遣 xiāoqiǎn, 娱乐 yúlè

recrimination N 互相指责 hùxiāng zhǐzé

recruit I v 吸收新成员 xīshōu xīn chéngyuán, 招募 zhāomù II N 新成员 xīn chéngyuán, 新兵 xīn bīng

rectal ADJ 直肠的 zhícháng de

rectangle N 长方形 chángfāngxíng, 矩形 jǔxíng

rectangular ADJ 长方形的 chángfāngxíng de

rectify v 纠正 jiūzhèng, 矫正 jiǎozhèng

rector N **1** (基督教) 教区长 (Jīdūjiào)

jiàoqūzhǎng **2** 学院院长 xuéyuàn yuànzhǎng

rectum N 直肠 zhícháng

recuperate v [病人+] 康复 [bìngrén+] kāngfù, 复原 fùyuán

recuperation N 康复 kāngfù

recur v 复发 fùfā, 重现 chóngxiàn

recyclable ADJ 可回收利用的 kě huíshōu lìyòng de

recycle v 回收利用 huíshōu lìyòng

red N, ADJ 红 (的) hóng (de), 红色 (的) hóngsè (de)
red carpet 红地毯 hóng dìtǎn, (对贵宾的) 隆重接待 (duì guìbīn de) róngzhòng jiēdài
Red Crescent 红新月 Hóng xīnyuè
Red Cross 红十字 Hóng shízì
red meat 牛羊肉 niúyángròu

red-blooded ADJ 血气方刚的 xuèqì fāng gāng de

redden v (使…) 变红 (shǐ…) biàn hóng

redeem v **1** 补救 bǔjiù, 补偿 bǔcháng
to redeem oneself 挽回声誉 wǎnhuí shēngyù
a redeeming feature 可以起弥补作用的特点 kěyǐ qǐ míbǔ zuòyòng de tèdiǎn **2** 赎回 [+抵押物] shúhuí [+dǐyāwù]

redeemable ADJ 可以补救的 kěyǐ bǔjiù de

redemption I N **1** 补救 bǔjiù, 挽救 wǎnjiù
to be past redemption 不可挽回的 bùkě wǎnhuí de, 不可救药的 bù kě jiùyào de **2** 兑换 (现款) duìhuàn (xiànkuǎn)

redevelop v 重新开放 chóngxīn kāifā, 重建 chóngjiàn

redevelopment N 重新开放 chóngxīn kāifā, 重建 chóngjiàn

red-eye N 夜间航班 yèjiān hángbān

red-handed ADJ (to catch sb red-handed) 当场抓获某人 dāngchǎng zhuāhuò mǒurén

redhead N 红头发的人 hóng tóufa de rén

red-herring N 转移注意力的事情 zhuǎnyí zhùyìlì de shìqing

redhot ADJ **1** 炽热的 [+金属] chìrè de [+jīnshǔ] **2** 火热的 [+爱情] huǒrè de [+àiqíng] **3** 令人万分激动的 [+故事] lìng rén wànfēn jīdòng de [+gùshì]

redirect v 使…改变方向 shǐ…gǎibiàn fāngxiàng

red-light district N 红灯区 hóngdēngqū

redneck N 没有文化思想保守的乡巴佬 méiyǒu wénhuà sīxiǎng bǎoshǒu de xiāngbalǎo

redo v 重做 zhòng zuò

redouble v (to redouble one's efforts) 加倍努力 jiābèi nǔlì

redress I v 修正 xiūzhèng, 纠正 jiūzhèng II N 赔偿 péicháng

reduce v 减少 jiǎnshǎo, 降低 jiàngdī ■ *The doctor recommended that he reduce his weight by 40 pounds.* 医生建议他减肥四十磅。Yīshēng jiànyì tā jiǎnféi sìshí bàng.

reduction N 减少 jiǎnshǎo, 降低 jiàngdī ■ *The*

reduction of costs improved the company's profitability. 降低成本改善了公司的盈利状况。Jiàngdī chéngběn gǎishànle gōngsī de yínglì zhuàngkuàng.

redundancy N 1 多余(的东西) duōyú (de dōngxi) 2 解雇(员工) jiěgù (yuángōng) redundancy compensation 解雇补偿 jiěgù bǔcháng
redundancy notice 解雇通知 jiěgù tōngzhī

redundant ADJ 1 多余的 duōyú de, 重复的 chóngfù de 2 被解雇的 bèi jiěgù de, 失业的 shīyè de

redwood N 红杉(树) hóngshān (shù) [M. WD 棵 kē]

reed N 芦苇 lúwěi

re-educate V 再教育 zài jiàoyù, 重新教育 chóngxīn jiàoyù

re-education N 再教育 zài jiàoyù, 重新教育 chóngxīn jiàoyù

reef N 礁(石) jiāo (shí)

reek I V 发出臭味 fāchū chòuwèi II N 臭味 chòuwèi

reel I N 一卷(线) yī juàn (xiàn), 一盘(电影片) yìpán (diànyǐngpiàn) II V 1 摇摇晃晃地走 yáoyán huǎnghuǎng de zǒu 2 慌乱 huāngluàn, 眩晕 xuànyùn

reelect V 重选 zhòngxuǎn

reelection N 重新选举 chóngxīn xuǎnjǔ

re-enact V 重演 chóngyǎn, 再现 zàixiàn

reenactment V 重演 chóngyǎn, 再现 zàixiàn

reentry N 再次进入 zàicì jìnrù, 重返 chóngfǎn

refer V 1 指 zhǐ, 针对 zhēnduì ■ *When I made the criticism, I was not referring to you.* 我批评时，不是指你。Wǒ pīpíng shí, bú shì zhǐ nǐ. 2 提到 tídao 3 查阅 cháyuè 4 转交 zhuǎnjiāo ■ *Her family doctor referred her to a heart specialist.* 她的家庭医生把她转到心脏专家那里。Tā de jiātíng yīshēng bǎ tā zhuǎndào xīnzàng zhuānjiā nàlǐ.

referee N 1 (体育比赛) 裁判(员) (tǐyù bǐsài) cáipàn (yuán) 2 (学术论文) 审阅人 (xuéshù lùnwén) shěnyuè rén 3 (纠纷) 调停人 (jiūfēn) tiáotíngrén

reference N 1 提到 tídao ■ *All her friends avoid making any references to her son who died in a car accident.* 她所有的朋友都回避提到她的儿子，他死于车祸。Tā suǒyǒu de péngyou dōu huíbì tídao tā de érzi, tā sǐ yú chēhuò. 2 注 zhù, 附注 fùzhù ■ *If you quote somebody, you must give reference to the original source.* 你如果引用谁的话，一定要注明出处。Nǐ rúguǒ yǐnyòng shéi de huà, yídìng yào zhùmíng chūchù. 3 证明 zhèngmíng, 介绍信 jièshào xìn 4 参考 cānkǎo reference book 参考书 cānkǎo shū
reference library 参考书图书馆 cānkǎoshū túshūguǎn

referendum N 全民投票 quánmín tóupiào, 公民直接投票 gōngmín zhíjiē tóupiào

refill¹ V 1 再注满 zài zhù mǎn 2 再斟满一杯 zài zhēnmǎn yìbēi

refill² N 新添制 xīn tiān zhì
refill for a ballpoint pen 圆珠笔笔芯 yuánzhūbǐ bǐxīn

refinance V 重新安排财务/债务 chóngxīn ānpái cáiwù/zhàiwù

refine V 1 提炼 [+石油] tíliàn [+shíyóu] 2 逐步改进 zhúbù gǎijìn

refined ADJ 1 提炼过的 tíliàn guò de, 精炼的 jīngliàn de 2 高雅的 [+古典音乐爱好者] gāoyǎ de [+gǔdiǎn yīnyuè àihàozhě] 3 [精确的+] 测量方法 [jīngquè de+] cèliáng fāngfǎ

refinement N 1 精炼 jīngliàn; 提纯 tíchún 2 高雅 gāoyǎ, 有修养 yǒu xiūyǎng 3 改进 gǎijìn, 补充 bǔchōng

refinery N 提炼厂 tíliàn chǎng
oil refinery 炼油厂 liànyóuchǎng

refinish V 再抛光 [+家具] zài pāoguāng [+jiājù]

reflect V 1 反映 fǎnyìng 2 思考 sīkǎo ■ *The convict spent a lot of time in his cell reflecting on his past life.* 这个囚犯在监牢里花很多时间思考他过去的生活。Zhè ge qiúfàn zài jiānláo lǐ huā hěn duō shíjiān sīkǎo tā guòqù de shēnghuó. 3 反射 fǎnshè

reflection N 1 倒影 dàoyǐng
one's reflection in the mirror 镜子里的自己 jìngzi lǐ de zìjǐ
2 思考 sīkǎo
upon reflection 经过思考 jīngguò sīkǎo
3 反映 fǎnyìng
reflection of sb's intelligence 反映出某人的智力 fǎnyìng chū mǒurén de zhìlì
4 反射 fǎnshè
light reflection 光线的反射 guāngxiàn de fǎnshè

reflective ADJ 1 沉思的 chénsī de 2 反光的 fǎnguāng de

reflector N 1 反光板 fǎnguāng bǎn 2 反射镜 fǎnshèjìng

reflex N (生理) 反射 (shēnglǐ) fǎnshè
reflex action 反射动作 fǎnshè dòngzuò, 本能反应 běnnéng fǎnyìng

reform V, N 改革 gǎigé, 改进 gǎijìn ■ *Some people fear that the new government will introduce radical reforms in the social welfare system.* 有人恐怕新政府将在社会福利发面引进激烈的改革。Yǒurén kǒngpà xīn zhèngfǔ jiāng zài shèhuì fúlì fāmian yǐnjìn jīliè de gǎigé. ■ *He has reformed his ways and is now a "born-again" Christian.* 他洗心革面，成了一位"再生"基督教徒。Tā xǐxīn gémiàn, chéngle yí wèi "zàishēng" Jīdū jiàotú.

reform school 少年管教所 shàonián guǎnjiàosuǒ

reformation N 改革 gǎigé, 改进 gǎijìn

reformer N 改革者 gǎigézhě, 改良者 gǎiliángzhě

refrain[1] V 克制 kèzhì, 抑制 yìzhì
to refrain from laughing 克制住不笑 kèzhì zhù bú xiào, 忍住不笑 rěnzhù bú xiào

refrain[2] N 1 副歌 fùgē 2 一再重复的话 yízài chóngfù de huà

refresh V 1 使…恢复精力 shǐ…huīfù jīnglì
to refresh one's memory 唤起记忆 huànqǐ jìyì
2 更新 [+计算机信息] gēngxīn [+jìsuànjī xìnxī]

refresher course N 进修课程 jìnxiū kèchéng [M. WD 门 mén]

refreshing ADJ 清新的 qīngxīn de, 提神的 tíshén de

refreshments N 点心饮料 diǎnxin yǐnliào

refrigerate V 冷冻 [+食物] lěngdòng [+shíwù]

refrigeration N 冷冻 lěngdòng, 冷藏 lěngcáng

refrigerator N 冰箱 bīngxiāng, 电冰箱 diàn bīngxiāng

refuel V 1 给…加燃料 gěi…jiā ránliào 2 使 [+感情] 更强烈 shǐ [+gǎnqíng] gèng qiángliè, 重新点燃 chóngxīn diǎnrán

refuge N 避难所 bìnànsuǒ, 庇护所 bìhùsuǒ

refugee N 难民 nànmín

refund I N 退款 tuìkuǎn [M. WD 笔 bǐ] II V 退款 tuìkuǎn, 退票 tuìpiào

refurbish V 翻修 fānxiū

refurbishment N 翻修 fānxiū

refusal N 拒绝 jùjué

refuse[1] V 拒绝 jùjué

refuse[2] N 废物 fèiwù, 垃圾 lājī

refute V 驳斥 bóchì, 反驳 fǎnbó

regain V 收回 shōuhuí, 恢复 huīfù

regal ADJ 帝王般的 dìwáng bān de

regalia N（典礼时的）盛装 (diǎnlǐ shí de) shèngzhuāng

regard I V 把…看作 bǎ…kànzuo II N 1 尊重 zūnzhòng ■ I have great regard for his judgment. 我非常尊重他的判断。Wǒ fēicháng zūnzhòng tā de pànduàn. 2 关心 guānxīn, 关注 guānzhù
in this/that regard 关于这/那方面 guānyú zhè/nà fāngmiàn
with regard to 关于 guānyú
without regard to 不考虑 bùkǎolǜ, 不管 bùguǎn

regarding PREP 关于 guānyú

regardless ADV 不管 bùguǎn, 不顾 búgù

regards N 问候 wènhòu, 致意 zhìyì ■ Please give my regards to your father. 请向您父亲问候。Qǐng xiàng nín fùqin wènhòu.

regatta N 划船比赛 huáchuán bǐsài, 赛船会 sàichuán huì

regenerate V 再生 zàishēng, 恢复 huīfù

regent N 摄政者 shèzhèngzhě
prince regent 摄政王 Shèzhèngwáng

regime N 政权 zhèngquán, 政府 zhèngfǔ

regimen N 养生之道 yǎngshēng zhī dào

regiment N（军队）团 (jūnduì) tuán
regiment commander 团长 tuánzhǎng

regimented ADJ 严格控制的 yángé kòngzhì de

region N 地区 dìqū, 区域 qūyù

regional ADJ 地区的 dìqū de, 区域性的 qūyùxìng de

register I V 1 注册 zhùcè 2 登记 dēngjì ■ You'd better register with the embassy when you're in a foreign country. 你到了外国，最好在大使馆登记一下。Nǐ dàole wàiguó, zuìhǎo zài dàshǐguǎn dēngjì yí xià. II N 登记簿 dēngjì bù
cash register 收银机 shōuyínjī

registered mail N 保价信 bǎojiàxìn [M. WD 封 fēng]

registered nurse N 注册护士 zhùcè hùshi

registered voter N 登记了的选民 dēngjì le de xuǎnmín

registrar N（大学）教务长 (dàxué) jiàowùzhǎng

registration N 1（大学）注册 (dàxué) zhùcè 2 登记 dēngjì
voter registration 选民登记 xuǎnmín dēngjì 3 机动车登记证 jīdòngchē dēngjìzhèng

registry N 1 登记 dēngjì, 注册 zhùcè
bridal registry 新婚礼品单 xīnhūn lǐpǐn dān 2 登记处 dēngjìchù

regress V 倒退 dàotuì, 退化 tuìhuà

regret N, V 懊悔 àohuǐ, 遗憾 yíhàn

regretful ADJ 懊悔的 àohuǐ de, 遗憾的 yíhàn de

regrettable ADJ 让人懊悔的 ràng rén àohuǐ de, 令人遗憾的 lìngrén yíhàn de

regroup V 重新编组 chóngxīn biānzǔ, 重组 chóngzǔ

regular I ADJ 1 正常的 zhèngcháng de ■ He was relieved to learn that his pulse and heartbeat were regular. 他听说自己的脉搏和心跳正常，放下了心。Tā tīngshuō zìjǐ de màibó hé xīntiào zhèngcháng, fàngxiale xīn. 2 常规的 chángguī de 3 有规则的 yǒu guīzé de, 整齐的 zhěngqí de ■ He has regular features but is not really handsome. 他五官端正，但不能算英俊。Tā wǔguān duānzhèng, dàn bù néng suàn yīngjùn. II N 1 常客 chángkè, 老主顾 lǎozhǔgu 2 正规兵 zhèngguī bīng

regulate V 1 [通过规章来+] 管理 [tōngguò guīzhāng lái+] guǎnlǐ, 控制 kòngzhì 2 调整 [+机器] tiáozhěng [+jīqì], 校准 jiàozhǔn

regulation N 1 规章 guīzhāng, 规定 guīdìng, 条例 tiáolì
building regulations 营造规章 yíngzào guīzhāng
safety regulations 安全条例 ānquán tiáolì 2 管理 guǎnlǐ, 控制 kòngzhì

financial regulation 金融管理 jīnróng guǎnlǐ

regulatory ADJ 管理的 guǎnlǐ de

regurgitate v 1 吐出已吞咽的食物 tùchū yǐ tūnyàn de shíwù, 回翻 huí fān 2 不加思索地重复 [+别人的话] bù jiā sīsuǒ de chóngfù [+biérende huà]

rehab N (吸毒者的) 康复治疗 (xīdúzhě de) kāngfù zhìliáo

rehab center 康复中心 kāngfù zhōngxīn, 戒毒所 jièdúsuǒ

rehabilitate v 1 使…恢复正常生活 shǐ…huīfù zhèngcháng shēnghuó 2 恢复…的名誉 huīfù…de míngyù, 平反 píngfǎn

rehash I v 用新方式重复 (旧内容) yòng xīn fāngshì chóngfù (jiù nèiróng), 用新瓶装旧酒 yòng xīnpíng zhuāng jiùjiǔ II N 新瓶装旧酒 xīnpíng zhuāng jiùjiǔ

rehearsal N 排练 páiliàn, 排演 páiyǎn

dress rehearsal 彩排 cǎipái

rehearse v 排练 páiliàn, 排演 páiyǎn

reign I N 统治 (时期) tǒngzhì (shíqī)

reign of terror 恐怖统治 kǒngbùtǒngzhì

II v 1 统治 [+一个王国] tǒngzhì [+yí ge wángguó] 2 占支配地位 zhàn zhīpèi dìwèi

the reigning champion 当今冠军 dāngjīn guànjūn

reimburse v 付还 fùhuán, 偿还 chánghuán

to reimburse sb for travel expenses 给某人报销旅差费 gěi mǒurén bàoxiāo lǚchāifèi

to be reimbursed for travel expenses 报销旅差费 bàoxiāo lǚchāifèi

rein I N 缰绳 jiāngshéng [M. WD 条 tiáo]

to give sb free rein 给予某人行动的自由 jǐyǔ mǒurén xíngdòng de zìyóu

II v (to rein in) 加强管理／控制 jiāqiáng guǎnlǐ/kòngzhì

reincarnate v 再生 zàishēng, 转世 zhuǎnshì

reincarnation N 再生 zàishēng, 转世 zhuǎnshì

reindeer N 驯鹿 xùnlù [M. WD 头 tóu]

reinforce v 加强 jiāqiáng, 增强 zēngqiáng

reinforcement N 加强 jiāqiáng, 增强 zēngqiáng

reinforcements N 增援部队 zēngyuánbùduì

reinstate v 1 使…恢复原职 shǐ…huīfù yuánzhí 2 恢复 (原来的) 制度／规章 huīfù (yuánlái de) zhìdù/guīzhāng

reinvent v (在现有基础上) 重新制定 (zài xiànyǒu jīchǔ shàng) chóngxīn zhìdìng

to reinvent oneself 改变自我 gǎibiàn zìwǒ, 改头换面 gǎitóu huànmiàn

to reinvent the wheel 做别人早已做过的事 zuò biérén zǎoyǐ zuò guò de shì, 浪费精力 làngfèi jīnglì

reissue I v 重新发行 chóngxīn fāxíng, 重印 chóngyìn II N 重新发行的唱片 chóngxīn fāxíng de chàngpiàn, 重印的书刊 chóngyìn de shūkān

reiterate N 反复地讲 fǎnfù de jiǎng, 重申 chóngshēn

reiteration N 重申 chóngshēn

reject I v 1 拒绝 jùjué, 不赞同 bú zàntóng 2 拒绝接受 jùjué jiēshòu, 丢弃 diūqì II N 退货 tuìhuò, 残次产品 cáncì chǎnpǐn

rejoice N 欢欣 huānxīn, 欣喜 xīnxǐ

rejoicing N 欢庆 huānqìng

rejoin v 1 重新加入 [+组织] chóngxīn jiārù [+zǔzhī], 重返 chóngfǎn 2 回答 huídá

rejoinder N 巧妙地回答 qiǎomiào de huídá

rejuvenate v 1 使 [+人] 变得年轻 shǐ [+rén] biàn de niánqīng, 使…恢复活力 shǐ…huīfù huólì 2 重振 [+地区] chóngzhèn [+dìqū]

rekindle v 重新激起 [+兴趣] chóngxīn jīqǐ [+xìngqu]

relapse N (旧病／坏习惯) 复发 (jiùbìng/huài xíguàn) fùfā, 故态复萌 gùtàifùméng

relate v 1 联系起来 liánxiqǐlai ■ I find it difficult to relate cause and effect in this case. 在这件事中，我很难把原因和结果联系起来。Zài zhè jiàn shì zhōng, wǒ hěn nán bǎ yuányīn hé jiéguǒ liánxiqǐlai. 2 理解 lǐjiě ■ Bill is sometimes so crazy that I can't relate to him anymore. 比尔有时候疯疯颠颠的，我无法再理解他了。Bǐ'ěr yǒushíhou fēngdiāndiān de, wǒ wú fǎ zài lǐjiě tā le. 3 讲述 jiǎngshù

related ADJ 1 与…有关的 yǔ…yǒuguān de ■ Road accidents related to fatigue are on the rise. 与疲劳有关的交通事故在上升。Yǔ píláo yǒuguān de jiāotōng shìgù zàishàngshēng. 2 与…是亲戚 yǔ…shì qīnqi

relation N 1 关系 guānxi ■ No one can deny the relation between low family income and poor performance at school. 没有人可以否认家庭收入低下与在学校表现不佳之间的关系。Méiyǒu rén kěyǐ fǒurèn jiātíng shōurù dīxià yǔ zài xuéxiào biǎoxiàn bù jiā zhījiān de guānxi. 2 亲戚 qīnqi

relationship N 1 关系 guānxi 2 情人关系 qíngrén guānxi, 夫妻关系 fūqī guānxi

relative I ADJ 相对的 xiāngduì de ■ Many people fled the war zone to relative safety. 很多人逃离战区，到相对比较安全的地方。Hěn duō rén táolí zhàn qū, dào xiāngduì bǐjiào ānquán de dìfang. II N 亲戚 qīnqi ■ We have relatives in Arizona. 我们在亚利桑那有几个亲戚。Wǒmen zài Yàlìsāngnà yǒu jǐ ge qīnqi.

relatively ADV 相对 (地) xiāngduì (de), 比较 (地) bǐjiào (de)

relatively speaking 相对来说 xiāngduì láishuō

relativity N 相对性 xiāngduìxìng

relax v 放松 fàngsōng ■ Breathe slowly and deeply, and relax your muscles. 缓慢地深呼吸，肌肉放松。Huǎnmàn de shēn hūxī, jīròu fàngsōng.

relaxation N 1 松弛 sōngchí

relaxation therapy 松弛疗法 sōngchí liáofǎ

2 休闲 xiūxián, 消遣 xiāoqiǎn

relaxed ADJ 1 轻松的 qīngsōng de 2 舒适的 shūshì de

relay I v 传达 chuándá, 传递 chuándí II N 1 接力赛跑 jiēlìsàipǎo 2 转播设备 zhuǎnbō shèbèi

release I v 1 释放 shìfàng 2 放开 fàngkai ■ *He released the handbrake and started the engine.* 他放开手闸，发动引擎。Tā fàngkai shǒuzhá, fādòng yǐnqíng. 3 发行 [+电影] fāxíng [+diàn-yǐng] II N 释放 shìfàng

relegate v 贬低 biǎndī

to relegate sb to 把某人降低到… bǎ mǒurén jiàngdī dào...

relent v 变得温和 / 宽容 biàn de wēnhé / kuānróng, 不再坚持 búzài jiānchí

relentless ADJ 无情的 wúqíng de, 严厉的 yánlì de

relevance N 关系 guānxi

relevant ADJ 有关的 yǒuguān de, 相关的 xiāngguān de

reliable ADJ 可靠的 kěkào de, 可依赖的 kě yīlài de ■ *I don't want a luxury car, but I do need a reliable car.* 我不要豪华的汽车，但是我确实需要一辆可靠的车。Wǒ bú yào háohuá de qìchē, dànshì wǒ quèshí xūyào yí liàng kěkào de chē.

reliance N 依赖 yīlài, 依靠 yīkào

reliant ADJ 依赖于 yīlàiyú

relic N 遗迹 yíjī, 遗物 yíwù

relief[1] N 1 不再担忧 bú zài dānyōu ■ *Much to my relief, no one was hurt in the accident.* 没有在事故中受伤，使我不再担忧。Méiyǒu zài shìgù zhōng shòushāng, shǐ wǒ bú zài dānyōu. 2 解痛 jiětòng ■ *The drug gives temporary relief from pain.* 这种药暂时解痛。Zhè zhǒng yào zànshí jiětòng. 3 救济物资 jiùjì wùzī

relief[2] N 浮雕 fúdiāo

relief map 地势图 dìshìtú, 地形图 dìxíngtú

relieve v 1 减轻 jiǎnqīng 2 替换 tìhuan

to relieve oneself 大小便 dàxiǎobiàn

to relieve sb of duties/a post 解除某人的职务 / 职位 jiěchú mǒurén de zhíwù/zhíwèi

relieved ADJ 宽慰的 kuānwèi de, 不再担心的 búzài dānxīn de

religion N 宗教 zōngjiào ■ *Christianity, Islam and Buddhism are three great religions of the world.* 基督教、伊斯兰教和佛教是世界上三大宗教。Jīdūjiào、Yīsīlánjiào hé Fójiào shì shìjièshang sān dà zōngjiào.

religious ADJ 1 宗教的 zōngjiào de ■ *Solemnity is the hallmark of religious services.* 庄严是宗教仪式的共同特点。Zhuāngyán shì zōngjiào yíshì de gòngtóng tèdiǎn. 2 相信宗教的 xiāngxìn zōngjiào de, 虔诚的 qiánchéng de

religiously ADV 1 与宗教有关 yǔ zōngjiào yǒuguān 2 十分认真（地）shífēn rènzhēn (de), 一丝不苟（地）yìsī bùgǒu (de)

relinquish v 放弃 fàngqì, 交出 jiāochū

relish I v 享受 xiǎngshòu, 真心喜欢 zhēnxīn xǐhuan II N 1 调味品 tiáowèipǐn 2 享受 xiǎngshòu, 喜欢 xǐhuan

relive v 重温 chóngwēn, 回忆 huíyì

relocate v 重新安置 chóngxīn ānzhì, 迁移 qiānyí

relocation N 迁移 qiānyí, 安置 ānzhì

reluctance N 不情愿 bùqíngyuàn, 勉强 miǎnqiǎng

reluctant ADJ 不情愿 bù qíngyuàn, 勉强 miǎnqiǎng

rely v 1 依靠 yīkào, 依赖 yīlài ■ *The modern world relies heavily on oil.* 现代世界深地依赖石油。Xiàndài shìjiè shēnshēn de yīlài shíyóu. 2 信赖 xìnlài, 信任 xìnrèn

remain v 1 仍然是 réngrán shì, 还是 hái shì 2 仍然存在 réngrán cúnzài, 还在 hái zài ■ *The house where Shakespeare was born remains and attracts visitors from all over the world.* 莎士比亚出生的故居还在，吸引世界各地的参观者。Shāshìbǐyà chūshēng de gùjū hái zài, xīyǐn shìjiè gèdì de cānguānzhě. 3 留下 liúxia, 剩下 shèngxia

remainder N 剩余部份 shèngyú bùfen, 余数 yúshù

remaining ADJ 剩下的 shèngxia de, 留下的 liúxia de

remains N 1 遗址废墟 yízhǐ fèixū 2 遗体 yítǐ

Roman remains 罗马时代的遗址 Luómǎ shídài de yízhǐ

remark I N [一句+] 话 [yí jù+] huà, 评论 pínglùn ■ *It is inappropriate to make such personal remarks at the meeting.* 在会上说这种涉及个人隐私的话，是不恰当的。Zài huìshang shuō zhè zhǒng shèjí gèrén yǐnsī de huà, shì bú qiàdàng de. II v 说 shuō, 评论 pínglùn

remarkable ADJ 不寻常的 bù xúncháng de, 了不起的 liǎobuqǐ de ■ *Anyone who speaks many languages is remarkable.* 任何会说好几种语言的人都挺了不起。Rènhé huì shuō hǎojǐ zhǒng yǔyán de rén dōu tǐng liǎobuqǐ.

remarriage N 再婚 zàihūn

remarry v 再婚 zàihūn, 再娶 zàiqǔ, 再嫁 zàijià

remedial ADJ 1 补救的 bǔjiù de, 治疗的 zhìliáo de

remedial action 补救措施 bǔjiù cuòshī 2 补习的 bǔxí de

remedial English class 英文补习班 Yīngwén bǔxíbān

remedy I N 1 补救办法 bǔjiù bànfǎ 2 药物 yàowù, 治疗 zhìliáo

herbal remedy 草药治疗 cǎoyào zhìliáo II v 补救 bǔjiù, 改善 gǎishàn

remember v 1 记住 jìzhu, 记得 jìde ■ *Remember to send Mary an e-card today!* 别忘了给玛丽送一张电子贺卡！Bié wàngle gěi Mǎlì sòng diànzǐ hèkǎ! 2 悼念 [+死者] dàoniàn [+sǐzhě], 纪念 jìniàn 3 给…送礼物 gěi...sònglǐ wù

remind v 提醒 tíxǐng, 使…想起 shǐ…xiǎngqǐ
■ *This old watch often reminds me of my grandfather.* 这块旧表使我想起祖父。Zhè kuài jiù biǎo shǐ wǒ xiǎngqǐ zǔfù.

reminder N 1 提醒（物）tíxǐng (wù)
a friendly reminder.友好的提醒 yǒuhǎo de tíxǐng 2 让人回忆过去的东西 ràng rén huíyì guòqù de dōngxi
a reminder of her high school days 让她回想起中学时代的东西 ràng tā huíxiǎng qǐ zhōngxué shídài de dōngxi

reminisce v 缅怀往事 miǎnhuái wǎngshì, 追忆往事 zhuīyì wǎngshì

reminiscences N 回忆（录）huíyì (lù)

reminiscent ADJ 令人回想过去的 lìngrén huíxiǎng guòqù de

remiss ADJ 玩忽职守的 wánhū zhíshǒu de, 失误的 shīwù de

remission N 1 减轻（时期）jiǎnqīng (shíqī), 缓解（期）huǎnjiě (qī) 2 减免刑期 jiǎnmiǎn xíngqī

remit v 汇款 huìkuǎn

remittance N 汇款（额）huìkuǎn (é)

remnant N 剩余物 shèngyú wù, 残余 cányú

remodel v 整修 zhěngxiū, 重新塑造 chóngxīn sùzào

remonstrate v 抗议 kàngyì

remorse N 悔恨 huǐhèn, 深深的内疚 shēnshēn de nèijiù

remorseful ADJ 悔恨的 huǐhèn de, 极其内疚的 jíqí nèijiù de

remorseless ADJ 毫无悔意的 háowú huǐ yì de

remote ADJ 1 遥远的 yáoyuǎn de
remote control 遥控器 yáokòng qì
2 冷淡的 lěngdàn de, 漠不关心的 mò bù guānxīn de 3 微小的 wēixiǎo de
remote chance 微小的机会 wēixiǎo de jīhuì

remove v 1 拿掉 nádiao, 移开 yíkāi ■ *Please remove your car or it will be towed away.* 请把你的车开走，不然就要被拖走。Qǐng bǎ nǐ de chē kāizǒu, bùrán jiù yào bèi tuōzǒu. 2 排除 páichú ■ *The threat of an all-out war cannot be removed by one ceasefire after another.* 一次又一次的停火不会排除全面战争的威胁。Yí cì yòu yí cì de tínghuǒ bú huì páichú quánmiàn zhànzhēng de wēixié. 3 免职 miǎnzhí

remunerate v 酬劳 chóuláo

remuneration N 酬金 chóujīn

Renaissance N（欧洲）文艺复兴 (Ōuzhōu) Wényì Fùxīng

renal ADJ 肾脏的 shènzàng de

rename v 重新命名 chóngxīn mìngmíng, 更名 gēngmíng

render v 1 使…成为 shǐ…chéngwéi
to render sth obsolete 使某物过时 shǐ mǒuwù guòshí

2 给予 jǐyǔ, 提供 tígōng
services rendered 提供的服务 tígōng de fúwù

rendering N 1 表现（方式）biǎoxiàn (fāngshì) 2 透视圈 tòushì quān

rendezvous I N 1 相会 xiānghuì, 约会 yuēhuì 2 约会地点 yuēhuì dìdiǎn II v 相会 xiānghuì, 会合 huìhé

rendition N 1 表演 biǎoyǎn, 演奏 yǎnzòu 2 翻译 fānyì, 译文 yìwén

renegade I N 叛徒 pàntú, 变节者 biànjiézhě
II ADJ 变节的 biànjié de, 背叛的 bèipàn de

renege v 违背 wéibèi
to renege on a promise 违背诺言 wéibèi nuòyán

renew v 1 延长 yáncháng, 延期 yánqī
to renew a book (从图书馆) 续借图书 (cóng túshūguǎn) xùjiè túshū
2 恢复 [+关系] huīfù [+guānxi]

renewable ADJ 1 可再生的 kě zàishēng de
renewable energy 可再生能源 kězàishēng néngyuán
2 可延期的 kě yánqī de, 可延续的 kě yánxù de

renewal N 延长 yáncháng, 延期 yánqī

renewed ADJ 重新开始的 chóngxīn kāishǐ de

renounce v（正式）放弃 (zhèngshì) fàngqì, 抛弃 pāoqì

renovate v 修复 xiūfù, 装修 zhuāngxiū

renovation N 修复 xiūfù, 装修 zhuāngxiū

renowned ADJ 著名的 zhùmíng de, 有名望的 yǒu míngwàng de

rent I v 1 租借 zūjiè, 租用 zūyòng ■ *They rented a camper and vacationed the entire summer in the Yellow Stone National Park.* 他们租了一辆野营车，整个夏天都在黄石国家公园度假。Tāmen zūle yí liàng yěyíng chē, zhěngge xiàtiān dōu zài Huángshí guójiā gōngyuán dùjià. 2 出租 chūzū ■ *Mr Bell makes a living by renting out small apartments to students.* 倍尔先生以出租小公寓给学生为生。Bèi'ěr xiānsheng yǐ chūzū xiǎo gōngyù gěi xuésheng wéi shēng. II N 租金 zūjīn, 房租 fángzū

rental I N 1 租借（物）zūjiè (wù), 租赁（物）zūlìn (wù) 2 租金 zūjīn II ADJ 供出租的 gòngchū zū de, 租来的 zū láide

renunciation N（正式）放弃 (zhèngshì) fàngqì, 抛弃 pāoqì

reorder v 1 重新订购 chóngxīn dìnggòu 2 重新安排 chóngxīn ānpái
to reorder one's priorities 重新安排轻重缓急 chóngxīn ānpái qīngzhònghuǎnjí

reorganize v 改组 gǎizǔ, 改编 gǎibiān

rep[1] (= representative) ABBREV 1 代表 dàibiǎo 2 推销员 tuīxiāoyuán

rep[2] (= reputation) ABBREV 名声 míngshēng

repair I v 修 xiū, 修理 xiūlǐ II N 1 修理 xiūlǐ,

缮 xiūshàn 2 (in good repair) [房屋+] 情况良好 [fángwū+] qíngkuàng liánghǎo

reparation N 赔偿 péicháng, 赔款 péikuǎn

repatriate v 遣送…回国 qiǎnsòng…huíguó, 遣返 qiǎnfǎn

repatriation N 遣返（回国）qiǎnfǎn (huíguó)

repay v 1 付还 fùhuán, 偿还 chánghuán 2 报答 bàodá

repayment N 1 付还 fùhuán, 偿还 chánghuán 2 还款（额）huánkuǎn (é) 3 报答 bàodá

repeal v 废除 fèichú, 取消 qǔxiāo

repeat I v 1 重复 chóngfù ■ Sorry, could you please repeat what you said? 对不起，请你把刚才说的话再说一遍。Duìbùqǐ, qǐng nǐ bǎ gāngcái shuō de huà zài shuō yí biàn.
to repeat oneself 重复自己说过的话 chóngfù zìjǐ shuō guò dehuà
2 重播 [+电视节目] chóngbō [+diànshì jiémù] II N 1 重现的事 chóngxiàn de shì 2 重播的（电视）节目 chóngbō de (diànshì) jiémù
repeat customer 回头客 huítóukè

repeated ADJ 反复的 fǎnfù de, 再三的 zàisān de

repeatedly ADV 反复地 fǎnfù de

repel v 1 使…厌恶 shǐ…yànwù, 使…强烈反感 shǐ…qiángliè fǎngǎn 2 驱除 qūchú, 驱走 qūzǒu

repellent I N 除虫剂 chúchóngjì
mosquito repellent 驱蚊剂 qūwénjì
II ADJ 令人厌恶的 lìngrén yànwù de, 令人反感的 lìng rén fǎngǎn de

repent v 忏悔 chànhuǐ, 懊悔 àohuǐ

repentance N 忏悔 chànhuǐ, 懊悔 àohuǐ

repentant ADJ 忏悔的 chànhuǐ de, 懊悔的 àohuǐ de

repercussion N 反响 fǎnxiǎng, 持续的影响 chíxù de yǐngxiǎng

repertoire N 1 (剧团/演员的) 全部剧目 (jùtuán/yǎnyuán de) quánbù jùmù 2 (某人的) 全部技能 (mǒurén de) quánbù jìnéng

repertory N 1 轮流演出的剧目 lúnliú yǎnchū de jiémù 2 See **repertoire**

repetitious ADJ (一再) 重复的 (yízài) chóngfù de

repetitive ADJ 重复的 chóngfù de

rephrase v 重新措词 chóngxīn cuòcí, 换个说法 huàn gè shuōfa

replace v 1 替代 tìdài, 替换 tìhuan 2 放回 fànghuí ■ Please check if you've replaced the receiver. 请看一下电话听筒放回去了吗？Qǐng kàn yíxià diànhuà tīngtǒng fànghuíqu le ma?

replacement N 接替 jiētì, 替代（物）tìdài (wù)
kneel replacement 膝部置换手术 xībù zhìhuàn shǒushù

replay v, N 1 重播 [+电视节目] chóngbō [+diànshì jiémù] 2 重新比赛 chóngxīn bǐsài

replenish v 再装满 zài zhuāngmǎn, 补充 bǔchōng

replete ADJ 充足的 chōngzú de, 充裕的 chōngyù de

replica N 复制品 fùzhìpǐn

replicate v 复制 fùzhì, 重做 zhòngzuò

replication N 复制 fùzhì, 重做 zhòngzuò

reply I v 回答 huídá, 回复 huífù II N 回答 huídá, 答复 dáfù ■ The company made no reply to my complaint. 公司没有回答我的抱怨。Gōngsī méiyǒu huídá wǒ de bàoyuàn.

report I N 报告 bàogào ■ Their representative in Beijing sends periodic reports to the headquarters. 他们在北京的代表周期性地向总部报告。Tāmen zài Běijīng de dàibiǎo zhōuqīxìng de xiàng zǒngbù bàogào.
report card (学生) 成绩报告单 (xuésheng) chéngjì bàogàodān
II v 报告 bàogào ■ When you see anything suspicious, report it to the police immediately. 看到可疑情况，立即报告警察。Kàndao kěyí qíngkuàng, lìjí bàogào jǐngchá.

reported speech N 间接引语 jiànjiē yǐnyǔ

reportedly ADV 据报导 jù bàodǎo

reporter N 记者 jìzhě

repose N, v 1 休息 xiūxi 2 安置 ānzhì

repository N 1 仓库 cāngkù 2 知识渊博的人/书 zhīshí yuānbó de rén/shū

repossess v 收回 shōuhuí

reprehensible ADJ 应受谴责的 yìng shòu qiǎnzé de

represent v 1 代表 dàibiǎo 2 象征 xiàngzhēng, 是…的象征 shì…de xiàngzhēng ■ The bald eagle represents the U.S.A. 秃鹰是美国的象征。Tūyīng shì Měiguóde xiàngzhēng.

representation N 代表 dàibiǎo ■ I believe there should be student representation in the consultative committee. 我相信在协商委员会里应该有学生的代表。Wǒ xiāngxìn zài xiéshāng wěiyuánhuì lǐ yīnggāi yǒu xuésheng de dàibiǎo.

representative I N 代表 dàibiǎo ■ Dr. Harrison doesn't have time to see drug company representatives today. 哈里森医生今天没有时间会见医药公司代表。Hālǐsēn yīshēng jīntiān méiyǒu shíjiān huìjiàn yīyào gōngsī dàibiǎo. II ADJ 有代表性的 yǒu dàibiǎoxìng de

repress v 抑制 [+感情／冲动] yìzhì [+gǎnqíng/chōngdòng], 克制 kèzhì 2 镇压 [+抗议者] zhènyā [+kàngyìzhě]

repressed ADJ 受压抑的 shòu yāyì de

repression N 1 压抑 yāyì, 克制 kèzhì 2 镇压 zhènyā

repressive ADJ 1 压抑的 yāyì de 2 残酷 cánkù de

reprieve N 1 缓解 huǎnjiě, 缓行 huǎnxíng 2 死刑撤销令 sǐxíng chèxiāo lìng

reprimand v, N 谴责 qiǎnzé, 斥责 chìzé

reprint I v 重印 chóngyìn, 再版 zàibǎn **II** N 重印书 chóngyìn shū

reprisal N 报复（行动）bàofu (xíngdòng)

reprise N, v 重演 chóngyǎn, 重奏 chóngzòu

reproach v, N 责备 zébèi, 责怪 zéguài
beyond reproach 无可非议 wúkě fēiyì, 完全 wánquán

reproduce v 1 [生物+] 繁殖 [shēngwù+] fánzhí 2 复制 [+艺术品] fùzhì [+yìshùpǐn]

reproduction N 1 繁殖 fánzhí, 生殖 shēngzhí 2 复制（品）fùzhì (pǐn)
reproduction furniture 仿古家具 fǎnggǔ jiājù

reproductive ADJ 繁殖的 fánzhí de, 生殖的 shēngzhí de

reprove v 责备 zébèi, 指责 zhǐzé

reptile N 爬行动物 páxíng dòngwù

republic N 共和国 gònghéguó

republican I ADJ（美国）支持共和党的 (Měiguó) zhīchí Gònghédǎng de **II** N 1（美国）共和党支持者 (Měiguó) Gònghédǎng zhīchízhě 2 共和（国／政体）的 gònghé (guó/zhèngtǐ) de

Republican Party N（美国）共和党 (Měiguó) Gònghédǎng

repudiate v 1 驳斥 bóchì, 否认 fǒurèn 2 拒绝（接受）jùjué (jiēshòu)

repudiation N 1 驳斥 bóchì 2 拒绝（接受）jùjué (jiēshòu)

repugnance N 强烈的反感 qiángliè de fǎngǎn, 极其厌恶 jíqí yànwù

repugnant ADJ 强烈反感的 qiángliè fǎngǎn de, 极其厌恶的 jíqí yànwù de

repulse v 1 使…强烈反感 shǐ...qiángliè fǎngǎn, 使…极其厌恶 shǐ...jíqí yànwù 2 击退 jītuì, 打退 dǎtuì

repulsion N 1 强烈反感 qiángliè fǎngǎn, 厌恶 yànwù 2 排斥（力）páichì (lì)

repulsive ADJ 令人强烈反感的 lìngrén qiángliè fǎngǎn de, 令人厌恶的 lìng rén yànwù de

reputable ADJ 声誉良好的 shēngyù liánghǎo de, 有信誉的 yǒu xìnyù de

reputation N 名声 míngshēng, 名望 míngwàng

repute N 名声 míngshēng, 名望 míngwàng

reputed ADJ 普遍认为 pǔbiàn rènwéi

reputedly ADV 据说 jùshuō

request I N 请求 qǐngqiú, 要求 yāoqiú ■ The branch manager has made a request for more staff. 分公司经理要求增加员工。Fēngōngsī jīnglǐ yāoqiú zēngjiā yuángōng. **II** v 请求, 请求 qǐngqiú

requiem N 1 安魂弥撒 ānhún mísa 2 安魂曲 ānhún qū

require v 1 需要 xūyào 2 要求 yāoqiú ■ Motorists are required to report a road accident as soon as possible. 要求驾车人尽快报告交通事故。Yāoqiú jiàchē rén jǐnkuài bàogào jiāotōng shìgù.

requirement N 1 必需的事物 bìxū de shìwù 2 规定的条件 guīdìng de tiáojiàn ■ This computer meets your requirements exactly. 这台计算机完全符合你规定的条件。Zhè tái jìsuànjī wánquán fúhé nǐ guīdìng de tiáojiàn.

requisite I ADJ 必要的 bìyào de, 必需的 bìxū de **II** N 必需的事物 bìxū de shìwù

requisition I N 征用（令）zhēngyòng (lìng) **II** v 征用 zhēngyòng

reroute v 改变路线 gǎibiàn lùxiàn

rerun I N 重演的电影 chóngyǎn de diànyǐng, 重播的电视／广播节目 chóngbō de diànshì/guǎngbō jiémù **II** v 重演 [+电影] chóngyǎn [+diànyǐng], 重播 [+电视／广播节目] chóngbō [+diànshì/guǎngbō jiémù]

rescind v 废除 fèichú, 取消 qǔxiāo

rescue v N 救援 jiùyuán, 营救 yíngjiù
rescue team 救援队 jiùyuán duì, 营救人员 yíngjiù rényuán

research I v 研究 yánjiū, 调查 diàochá ■ The sociologist is researching single parenthood in rural areas. 这位社会科学家正在研究农村地区的单亲现象。Zhè wèi shèhuì kēxuéjiā zhèngzài yánjiū nóngcūn dìqū de dānqīn xiànxiàng. **II** N 研究 yánjiū
research and development (R & D) 研究和开发 yánjiū he kāifā

resemblance N（外表的）相似（wàibiǎo de）xiāngsì, 相像 xiāngxiàng
to bear a resemblance to sb 长的很像某人 zhǎng de hěn xiàng mǒurén

resemble v 象 xiàng, 与…相似 yǔ...xiāngsì

resent v 怨恨 yuànhèn, 愤愤不平 fènfèn bùpíng

resentful ADJ 怨恨的 yuànhèn de, 十分不满的 shífēn bùmǎn de

resentment N 怨恨 yuànhèn, 愤懑 fènmèn

reservation N 1 保留 bǎoliú, 预订 yùdìng
to make a reservation 预订 [+机票／旅馆房间] yùdìng [+jīpiào/lǚguǎn fángjiān] 2 疑问 yíwèn
to express reservation 表示怀疑 biǎoshì huáiyí 3 印第安人保留地 Yìndì'ānrén bǎoliúdì

reserve I v 保留 bǎoliú, 预订 yùdìng
to reserve the right (to do sth) 保留（做某事的）权利 bǎoliú (zuò mǒushì de) quánlì **II** N 1 储备（金）chǔbèi (jīn)
in reserve 备用 bèiyòng 2 拘谨寡言 jūjǐn guǎyán
to drop one's reserve 不再矜持 búzài jīnchí 3（野生动物）保护区 (yěshēng dòngwù) bǎohùqū 4 后备部队 hòubèibùduì

reserved ADJ 1 预订的 yùdìng de 2 矜持的 jīnchí de, 拘谨寡言的 jūjǐn guǎyán de

reservoir N 1 水库 shuǐkù [M. WD 座 zuò] 2 储藏 chǔcáng
vast reservoir of information on the Internet 互

联网上大量的信息 hùliánwǎng shàng dàliàng díxìn xī

reshuffle N, V 调整 tiáozhěng, 改组 gǎizǔ

reside V 居住 jūzhù

residence N 1 居住 jūzhù
permanent residence 永久居住（权）yǒngjiǔ jūzhù (quán)
2 寓所 yùsuǒ [M. WD 座 zuò]
private residence 私人住宅 sīrén zhùzhái, 私寓 sī yù
official residence 官邸 guāndǐ

residency N 1 （医生）住院实习（期）(yīshēng) zhùyuàn shíxí (qī) 2 永久居住权 yǒngjiǔ jūzhù quán

resident I N 1 居民 jūmín 2 住院（实习）医生 zhùyuàn (shíxí) yīshēng II ADJ 居住的 jūzhù de
resident artist in a university 大学常驻艺术家 dàxué chángzhù yìshùjiā

residential ADJ 住宅区的 zhùzháiqū de
a leafy residential area 树木成荫的住宅区 shùmù chéngyìn de zhùzháiqū

residual ADJ 残余的 cányú de, 剩余的 shèngyú de

residue N 残留（物）cánliú (wù), 剩余（物）shèngyú (wù)

resign V 1 辞职 cízhí 2 (to resign oneself to sth) 无可奈何地接受某事 wúkě nàihé de jiēshòu mǒushì

resignation N 1 辞职 cízhí 2 顺从 shùncóng, 无可奈何地接受 wúkě nàihé de jiēshòu

resigned ADJ 1 无可奈何的 wúkě nàihé de 2 屈从的 qūcóng de, 顺从的 shùncóng de

resilience N 复苏的能力 fùsū de nénglì, 弹性 tánxìng

resin N （合成）树脂 (héchéng) shùzhī

resist V 1 抵抗 [+攻击] dǐkàng [+gōngjī], 抵制 dǐzhì 2 忍住 [+冲动] rěnzhù [+chōngdòng], 顶住 dǐngzhù
to resist temptation 顶住诱惑 dǐngzhù yòuhuò

resistance N 1 抵抗 dǐkàng, 抗拒 kàngjù 2 （身体的）抵抗力 (shēntǐ de) dǐkànglì

resistant ADJ 1 抵抗的 dǐkàng de 2 有抵抗力的 yǒu dǐkànglì de

resolute ADJ 坚决的 jiānjué de, 坚定的 jiāndìng de

resolution N 1 决议 juéyì
U.N. resolution 联合国的一项决议 Liánhéguó de yí xiàng juéyì
2 决定 juédìng, 决心 juéxīn
New Year's Resolutions 新年决心 xīnnián juéxīn
3 解决（办法）jiějué (bànfǎ)
successful resolution of the financial crisis 金融危机的成功解决 jīnróng wēijī de chénggōng jiějué

resolve I V 1 决定 juédìng, 下决心 xià juéxīn 2 解决 [+难题] jiějué [+nántí] II N 决心 juéxīn
unyielding resolve 不可动摇的决心 bùkě dòngyáo de juéxīn

resonance N 1 嘹亮 liáoliàng, 洪亮 hóngliàng 2 共鸣 gòngmíng 3 共振 gòngzhèn

resonant ADJ 洪亮的 hóngliàng de, 回荡的 huídàng de

resonate V 1 回荡 huídàng 2 产生共鸣／共振 chǎnshēng gòngmíng/gòngzhèn

resort[1] I N 手段 shǒuduàn
the last resort 最后一招 zuìhòu yìzhāo
II V 求助于 qiúzhù yú, 诉诸 sùzhū
to resort to law 求助于法律 qiúzhù yú fǎlǜ, 诉诸法律 sùzhū fǎlǜ

resort[2] N 度假地 dùjiàdì
resort hotel 度假酒店 dùjià jiǔdiàn
summer resort 避暑地 bìshǔdì

resound V 回荡 huídàng, 回响 huíxiǎng

resounding ADJ 极响亮的 jí xiǎngliàng de, 洪亮的 hóngliàng de

resource N 1 资源 zīyuán
natural resources 自然资源 zìrán zīyuán
■ *Australia is rich in natural resources.* 澳大利亚有丰富的自然资源。Àodàlìyà yǒu fēngfù de zìrán zīyuán.
2 资料 zīliào, 信息资源 xìnxī zīyuán

resourceful ADJ 办法很多的 bànfǎ hěn duō de, 足智多谋的 zúzhì duōmóu de

respect I N 1 尊敬 zūnjìng ■ *Dr. Williams is respected for his superb diagnostic skills.* 威廉士医生因有高超的诊断技术而受到尊敬。Wēiliánshì yīshēng yīn yǒu gāochāo de zhěnduàn jìshù ér shòudao zūnjìng.
to pay last respects 向死者告别 xiàng sǐzhě gàobié
2 尊重 zūnzhòng 3 方面 fāngmian ■ *Your essay is unsatisfactory in many respects.* 你的文章在很多方面不能令人满意。Nǐ de wénzhāng zài hěn duō fāngmian bù néng lìngrén mǎnyì. II V 1 尊敬 zūnjìng ■ *I respect him for his moral courage.* 我尊敬他的道德勇气。Wǒ zūnjìng tā de dàodé yǒngqì. 2 尊重 zūnzhòng

respectability N 体面 tǐmian, 可敬 kějìng

respectable ADJ 1 体面的 [+外表] tǐmian de [+wàibiǎo] 2 正派的 [+行为] zhèngpài de [+xíngwéi] 3 还过得去的 [+成绩] hái guòdequ de [+chéngjì]

respected ADJ 受尊敬的 shòu zūnjìng de

respectful ADJ 恭敬的 gōngjìng de, 彬彬有礼的 bīnbīn yǒulǐ de

respective ADJ 各自的 gèzì de

respectively ADV 各自 gèzì

respiration N 呼吸 hūxī

respirator N 人工呼吸器 réngōng hūxīqì

respiratory ADJ 呼吸（道）的 hūxī (dào) de

respite N 暂停 zàntíng, 暂缓 zànhuǎn

resplendent ADJ 华丽的 huálì de, 辉煌的 huīhuáng de

respond V 1 反应 fǎnyìng ■ *He responded to her request with a dismissive note.* 他对她的请求的反应，是一张口气轻蔑的便条。Tā duì tā de qǐngqiú de fǎnyìng, shì yì zhāng kǒuqì qīngmiè de biàntiáo. **2** 回答 huídá, 答复 dáfù

response N 反应 fǎnyìng

responsibility N 1 责任 zérèn ■ *Willy has taken responsibility for the fundraising event.* 威利负责这项筹款活动。Wēilì fùzé zhè xiàng chóukuǎn huódòng. **2** 职责 zhízé ■ *It is the responsibility of parents to train their children about morality.* 在道德方面训练子女，是家长的职责。Zài dàodé fāngmiàn xùnliàn zǐnǚ, shì jiāzhǎng de zhízé.

responsible ADJ 1 负有责任的 fùyǒu zérèn de **2** 有责任心的 yǒu zérènxīn de ■ *Can we find a responsible man to take care of the equipment?* 能找到一个有责任心的人照管设备吗？Néng zhǎodao yí ge yǒu zérènxīn de rén zhàoguǎn shèbèi ma? **3** 负责的 fùzé de ■ *The vice president of the company is responsible for research and development.* 公司副总经理负责研究和开发。Gōngsī fù zǒngjīnglǐ fùzé yánjiū hé kāifā. to hold ... responsible 要…负责任 yào...fù zérèn ■ *Parents hold the school responsible for the safety of their children.* 家长要学校对孩子的安全负责任。Jiāzhǎng yào xuéxiào duì háizi de ānquán fù zérèn.

responsibly ADV 负责地 fùzé de, 妥善地 tuǒshàn de

responsive ADJ 1 反应快的 fǎnyìng kuài de, 机敏的 jīmǐn de be responsive to treatment 容易治疗的 róngyì zhìliáo de **2** 同情的 tóngqíng de, 响应的 xiǎngyìng de

rest[1] N 剩下的东西 shèngxia de dōngxi, 其余 qíyú ■ *She counted the rest of her money and found it to be less than $50.* 她数了数剩下的钱，发现只有五十块不到了。Tā shùle shù shèngxia de qián, fāxiàn zhǐ yǒu wǔshí kuài bú dào le.

rest[2] I N 休息 xiūxi ■ *A man deserves a good rest after a day's honest work.* 一个人老老实实工作一天之后，理应得到好好休息。Yí ge rén lǎolǎoshíshí gōngzuò yì tiān zhīhòu, lǐyīng dédao hǎohǎo xiūxi. rest home 疗养所 liáoyǎngsuǒ II V 1 休息 xiūxi rest assured 放心 fàngxīn **2** [死者+] 长眠 [sǐzhě+] chángmián Rest in Peace (RIP) 安息 ānxī **3** (to rest upon) 依赖于 yīlàiyú, 依据 yījù

restate V 重申 chóngshēn, 换一种方式说 huàn yìzhǒng fāngshì shuō

restaurant N 饭店 fàndiàn [M. WD 家 jiā], 餐馆 cānguǎn [M. WD 家 jiā]

restful ADJ 使人心情平静的 shǐrén xīnqíng píngjìng de, 悠闲的 yōuxián de

restitution N 赔偿 péicháng

restive ADJ 不安宁的 bù ānníng de, 难控制的 nán kòngzhì de

restless ADJ 烦躁的 fánzao de, 静不下来的 jìng bú xià lái de

restoration N 1 恢复 huīfù **2** 修复 xiūfù

restore V 1 恢复 [+信心] huīfù [+xìnxīn], 回复 huífù **2** 修复 [+家具] xiūfù [+jiājù]

restrain V 1 克制 kèzhì, 控制 kòngzhì **2** 制服 [+罪犯] zhìfú [+zuìfàn]

restrained ADJ 克制的 kèzhì de, 冷静的 lěngjìng de

restraint N 1 克制 kèzhì, 抑制 yìzhì **2** 限制 xiànzhì, 约束 yuēshù

restrict V 限制 xiànzhì ■ *Parents should restrict what their children have access to on the computer.* 家长应该限制孩子在电脑上能看到的东西。Jiāzhǎng yīnggāi xiànzhì háizi zài diànnǎoshang néng kàndao de dōngxi.

restricted ADJ 1 受限制的 shòu xiànzhì de **2** 内部的 nèibù de, 不准外传的 bù zhǔn wàichuán de restricted document 内部文件 nèibù wénjiàn

restriction N 限制 xiànzhì to impose restrictions 加以限制 jiāyǐ xiànzhì to lift restrictions 解除限制 jiěchú xiànzhì

restrictive ADJ 限制(性)的 xiànzhì (xìng) de

restroom N 洗手间 xǐshǒujiān

restructure V 改组 gǎizǔ, 调整 [+组织] tiáozhěng [+zǔzhī]

result I N 1 结果 jiéguǒ as a result of 由于 yóuyú ■ *As a result of the doctor's negligence, the boy had to have his leg amputated.* 由于医生的疏忽，男孩只能锯掉一条腿。Yóuyú yīshēng de shūhu, nánhái zhǐ néng jùdiao yì tiáo tuǐ. **2** 效果 xiàoguǒ, 成果 chéngguǒ **3** 成绩 chéngjì 业绩 yèjì II V 发生 fāshēng to result from 起因于 qǐyīn yú, 是由于 shì yóuyú ■ *The increased sales resulted from a successful promotion.* 销售增加是由于促销成功。Xiāoshòu zēngjiā shì yóuyú cùxiāo chénggōng. to result in 造成了 zàochéng le

resultant ADJ 因而发生的 yīn'ér fāshēng de, 作为后果的 zuòwéi hòuguǒ de

resume V 重新开始 chóngxīn kāishǐ, 继续 jìxù to resume one's position 恢复原职 huīfù yuánzhí

résumé N 个人简历 gèrén jiǎnlì, 履历 lǚlì ■ *Do you update your résumé regularly?* 你定期更新个人简历吗？Nǐ dìngqī gēngxīn gèrén jiǎnlì ma?

resurface v **1** 重新出现 chóngxīn chūxiàn, 重现 chóngxiàn **2** 重铺路面 chóng pūlù miàn

resurgence N 重新流行 chóngxīn liúxíng, 死灰复燃 sǐhuī fùrán

resurgent ADJ 重新流行的 chóngxīn liúxíng de

resurrect v 复活 fùhuó, 恢复 huīfù

resurrection N 复活 fùhuó, 恢复 huīfù

resuscitate v 抢救 qiǎngjiù, (使…)恢复呼吸 (shǐ…) huīfù hūxī
Do not resuscitate. 不要抢救。Búyào qiǎngjiù.

resuscitation N 抢救 qiǎngjiù

retail I N 零售 língshòu
a chain of retail stores 零售连锁店 língshòu liánsuǒdiàn
II ADV 以零售价(格)yǐ língshòujià (gé) III v 零售 língshòu, 零卖 língmài

retailer N 零售商 língshòushāng, 零售(商)店 língshòu (shāng) diàn

retain v **1** 保留 bǎoliú **2** 记住 jìzhù **3** 付定金聘请 [+律师] fùdìng jīn pìnqǐng [+lǜshī]

retainer N 预付聘请费 yùfù pìnqǐng fèi, 律师费 lǜshī fèi

retake v 收复 shōufù, 夺回 duóhuí

retaliate v 报复 bàofu, 反击 fǎnjī

retaliation N 报复 bàofu, 反击 fǎnjī

retard I v 使…迟缓 shǐ…chíhuǎn, 阻碍 zǔ'ài II N 笨蛋 bèndàn

retarded ADJ 智力发展迟缓的 zhìlì fāzhǎn chíhuǎn de, 弱智的 ruòzhì de

retch v 恶心 èxīn, 作呕 zuò'ǒu

retention N 保留 bǎoliú, 留住 liúzhù

rethink v 重新考虑 chóngxīn kǎolǜ, 反思 fǎnsī

reticence N 沉默寡言 chénmò guǎyán

reticent ADJ 沉默的 chénmò de, 不爱说话的 bú ài shuōhuà de

retina N 视网膜 shìwǎngmó

retinue N (一大批)随从 (yí dàpī) suícóng, 随行人员 suíxíng rényuán

retire v **1** 退休 tuìxiū **2** 退出(体坛)tuì chū (tǐtán)

retiree N 退休者 tuìxiūzhě

retirement N 退休 tuìxiū, 退休生活 tuìxiū shēnghuó
retirement community (退休)老人社区 (tuìxiū) lǎorén shèqū
retirement home (退休)老人福利院 (tuìxiū) lǎorén fúlìyuàn

retort v, N 反驳 fǎnbó, 回嘴 huízuǐ

retract v **1** 正式收回 [+说过的话] zhèngshì shōuhuí [+shuōguòde huà] **2** 缩回 suōhuí

retractable ADJ 可收缩的 kě shōusuō de

retraction N 正式收回 zhèngshì shōuhuí, 撤回 chèhuí

retread N **1** 翻新的轮胎 fānxīn de lúntāi **2** 翻版 fānbǎn

retreat I v **1** [军队+]撤退 [jūnduì+] chètuì **2** [撤回+]承诺 [chèhuí+] chéngnuò **3** 往后退 wǎnghòu tuì II N **1** (军队)撤退 (jūnduì) chètuì **2** (承诺的)撤回 (chéngnuò de) chèhuí **3** 后退 hòutuì **4** 休养地 xiūyǎng dì

retrial N 重新审理 chóngxīn shěnlǐ, 重审 chóngshěn

retribution N 惩罚 chéngfá, 报应 bàoyìng

retrieve v **1** 收回 shōuhuí, 找到 zhǎodào **2** (计算机)检索 (jìsuànjī) jiǎnsuǒ

retriever N (能找回猎物的)猎犬 (néng zhǎohuí lièwù de) lièquǎn

retroactive ADJ 有追溯效力的 yǒu zhuīsù xiàolì de

retrospect N 回顾 huígù, 回想 huíxiǎng

retrospective ADJ 回顾的 huígù de

retry v 重新审理 [+案件] chóngxīn shěnlǐ [+ànjiàn], 重审 chóngshěn

return I v **1** 回 huí, 返回 fǎnhuí **2** 还 huán, 归还 guīhuán ■ *If you can't return the books by the due date, you can renew them.* 如果你到期不能还书, 可以续借。Rúguǒ nǐ dàoqī bù néng huán chū, kěyǐ xù jiè. **3** 回报 huíbào, 报答 bàodá II N **1** 返回 fǎnhuí ■ *On her return home from Africa she found the weather unbearably cold.* 她从非洲回来, 觉得天气冷得受不了。Tā cóng Fēizhōu huílai, juéde tiānqì lěng de shòubuliǎo. **2** 归还 guīhuán **3** 恢复 huīfù **4** 往返票 wǎngfǎn piào **5** (投资的)回报 (tóuzī de) huíbào, 利润 lìrùn ■ *He prayed to God for a big return from his investment.* 他祈求上帝, 让他在这项投资中得到好回报。Tā qíqiú Shàngdì, ràng tā zài zhè xiàng tóuzī zhōng dédào hǎo huíbào.

returnable ADJ **1** 必须归回的 [+文件] bìxū guīhuí de [+wénjiàn] **2** 可以收回的 [+瓶子] kěyǐ shōuhuí de [+píngzi]

reunion N **1** 团聚 tuánjù **2** (校友)聚会 (xiàoyǒu) jùhuì

reunite v (使…)再联合 (shǐ…) zài liánhé, (使…)重聚 (shǐ…) chóngjù
be reunited with sb 与某人团聚 yǔ mǒurén tuánjù

rev I N 旋转一周 xuánzhuǎn yìzhōu, 一转 yì zhuǎn II v (to rev up) 加快转速 jiākuài zhuànsù

revaluation N **1** (货币)升值 (huòbì) shēngzhí **2** 重新估价 chóngxīn gūjià

revalue v **1** 使 [+货币]升值 shǐ [+huòbì] shēngzhí **2** 重新估价 chóngxīn gūjià

revamp v 更新改造 gēngxīn, 修改 xiūgǎi

reveal v **1** 显露 xiǎnlù, 露出来 lòuchulai ■ *I think dressing in a way that reveals the navel is bad taste.* 我认为穿衣服时露出肚脐, 品味很差。Wǒ rènwéi chuān yīfú shí lòuchu dùqí, pǐnwèi hěn chà. **2** 透露 tòulù, 揭露 jiēlù ■ *Should the doctor reveal the truth to him?* 医生应该向病人透露真

情吗? Yīshēng yīnggāi xiàng bìngrén tòulù zhēn qíng ma?

revealing ADJ **1** 揭露性的 [+书／文章] jiēlùxìng de [+shū/wénzhāng] **2** 暴露的 [+衣服] bàolù de [+yīfu]

revel v **1** 狂欢 kuánghuān **2** (to revel in) 陶醉于 táozuì yú

revelation N **1** 揭露 jiēlù **2** 揭露出来的事 jiēlù chūlái de shì **3** (上帝的) 启示 (Shàngdì de) qǐshì

reveler N 狂欢者 kuánghuānzhě, 寻欢作乐的人 xúnhuān zuòlè de rén

revelry N 狂欢 kuánghuān, 寻欢作乐 xúnhuān zuòlè

revenge I N 报仇 bàochóu, 复仇 fùchóu
II v (为…) 报仇 (wéi…) bàochóu
be revenged on sb 向某人报仇 xiàng mǒurén bàochóu
to revenge sb 为某人报仇 wéi mǒurén bàochóu

revenue N 收入 shōurù ■ Tax revenues have decreased because of property devaluation. 因为房产贬值, 税收减少了。Yīnwèi fángchǎn biǎn zhí, shuìshōu jiǎnshǎo le.

reverberate v 回响 huíxiǎng, 回荡 huídàng

reverberation N 回响 huíxiǎng, 回荡 huídàng

revere v 尊敬 zūnjìng, 崇敬 chóngjìng

reverence N 尊敬 zūnjìng, 崇敬 chóngjìng

Reverend N 牧师 mùshi

reverent ADJ 恭敬的 gōngjìng de, 虔诚的 qiánchéng de

reverie N 幻想 huànxiǎng, 梦想 mèngxiǎng

reversal N 倒转 dàozhuǎn, 逆转 nìzhuǎn
reversal of fortune 时运倒转 shíyùn dàozhuǎn, 交恶运 jiāo èyùn

reverse I v **1** [汽车+] 倒退 [qìchē+] dàotuì **2** 颠倒 [+顺序] diāndǎo [+shùnxù] **3** 取消 [+原判] qǔxiāo [+yuánpàn]
to reverse a ruling 取消裁决 qǔxiāo cáijué
II N **1** [硬币的+] 背面 [yìngbì de+] bèimiàn **2** [工作中的+] 挫折 [gōngzuò zhòngde+] cuòzhé, 恶运 èyùn **3** (汽车的) 倒车挡 (qìchē de) dàochēdǎng
to put the car into reverse 把车挂上倒车挡 bǎchē guàshang dàochēdǎng
III ADJ 背面的 bèimiàn de, 反面的 fǎnmiàn de
reverse side (of a form) (表格的) 背面 biǎogé de bèimiàn
reverse discrimination 逆向歧视 nìxiàng qíshì

revert v 回复 [+到以前的情况] huífù [+dào yǐqián de qíngkuàng]

review I N **1** 复查 fùchá, 检查 jiǎnchá **2** 评论 pínglùn II v **1** 复查 fùchá, 检查 jiǎnchá ■ The professor reviewed his notes before lecturing. 教授在讲课前又看了一下笔记。Jiàoshòu zài jiǎngkè

qián yòu kànle yíxià bǐjì. **2** 写评论 xiě pínglùn ■ Her first novel was favorably reviewed. 她的第一部小说受到了很好的评论。Tā de dìyī bù xiǎoshuō shòudaole hěn hǎo de pínglùn. **3** 复习功课 fùxí gōngkè ■ Tonight most of the students will be reviewing their lessons for tomorrow's exam. 今天晚上大多数学生将复习功课, 准备明天的考试。Jīntiān wǎnshang dàduōshù xuésheng jiāng fùxí gōngkè, zhǔnbèi míngtiān de kǎoshì.

reviewer N 评论家 pínglùnjiā

revile v 辱骂 rǔmà, 漫骂 mànmà

revise v **1** 修订 xiūdìng, 改正 gǎizhèng **2** 复习 (功课) fùxí (gōngkè)

revision N 修订 xiūdìng, 修正 xiūzhèng

revitalize v 使…重获活力 shǐ…zhòng huò huólì, 使…新生 shǐ…xīnshēng

revival N 复兴 fùxīng, 再生 zàishēng

revive v **1** (使…) 苏醒 (shǐ…) sūxǐng **2** 再次流行 zàicì liúxíng, 恢复 huīfù

revoke v 吊销 [+执照] diàoxiāo [+zhízhào], 废除 fèichú

revolt N, v 反叛 fǎnpàn, 起义 qǐyì

revolting ADJ 令人厌恶的 lìngrén yànwù de, 令人作呕的 lìngrén zuò'ǒu de

revolution N **1** 革命 gémìng ■ The American Revolution was one of the pivotal events in world history. 美国独立革命是世界历史上最关键的事件之一。Měiguó dúlì gémìng shì shìjiè lìshǐshang zuìguānjiàn de shìjiàn zhī yī. **2** 重大变革 zhòngdà biàngé, 重大突变 zhòngdà tūbiàn

revolutionary I ADJ 革命 (性的) gémìng (xìng) de II N 革命者 gémìngzhě

revolutionize v 使…发生革命 (性) 变化 shǐ…fāshēng gémìng (xìng) biànhuà

revolve v **1** (使…) 旋转 (shǐ…) xuánzhuǎn **2** (to revolve around) 围绕 wéirào

revolver N 左轮手枪 zuǒlúnshǒuqiāng [m. wd 把 bǎ]

revolving ADJ 旋转的 xuánzhuǎn de

revue N (时事讽刺) 歌舞表演 (shíshì fěngcì) gēwǔ biǎoyǎn

revulsion N 厌恶 yànwù, 憎恨 zēnghèn

revved up ADJ 兴奋的 xīngfèn de, 激动的 jīdòng de

reward I N 报偿 bàocháng [m. wd 份 fèn], 报酬 bàochou [m. wd 份 fèn] II v 报偿 bàocháng, 报酬 bàochou, 奖赏 jiǎngshǎng ■ Students' efforts should be properly rewarded. 学生作出的努力应该好好奖赏。Xuésheng zuòchū de nǔlì yīnggāi hǎohāo jiǎngshǎng.

rewind (PT & PP **rewound**) v 倒回 dǎo huí

rewire v 更换路线 gēnghuàn lùxiàn

reword v 换个说法 huàn gè shuōfa

rework v 改编 gǎibiān

rewrite v 重写 zhòng xiě, 改写 gǎixiě

rhapsody N 1 狂想曲 kuángxiǎngqǔ [M. WD 首 shǒu] 2 赞美 zànměi

rhetoric N 1 华丽词藻 huálì cízǎo 2 修辞学 xiūcíxué

rhetorical ADJ 修辞的 xiūcí de
a rhetorical question 修辞性疑问句 xiūcíxìng yíwènjù

rheumatic ADJ 风湿病的 fēngshībìngde
rheumatic fever 风湿热 fēngshīrè

rheumatism N 风湿病 fēngshībìng

rhinoceros, rhino N 犀牛 xīniú [M. WD 头 tóu]

rhododendron N 杜鹃花 dùjuānhuā [M. WD 株 zhū/朵 duǒ]

rhubarb N 大黄 dàihuáng

rhyme I N 1 韵 yùn, 韵脚 yùnjiǎo 2 同韵词 tóngyùncí ■ *Can you think of a rhyme for "picnic"?* 你能想到一个词和 "picnic" 押韵吗? Nǐ néng xiǎngdào yí ge cí hé "picnic" yāyùn ma? II v 押韵 yāyùn

rhythm N 节奏 jiézòu

rhythmic ADJ 有节奏的 yǒu jiézòu de

rib I N 1 肋骨 lèigǔ
rib cage 胸腔 xiōngqiāng
2 肋条肉 lèitiáo ròu [M. WD 块 kuài] II v 跟…开玩笑 gēn...kāi wánxiào

ribald ADJ 粗俗的 cūsú de, 下流的 xiàliú de

ribbon N 丝带 sīdài [M. WD 条 tiáo], 缎带 duàndài [M. WD 条 tiáo]

rice N 1 米饭 mǐfàn 2 米 mǐ, 稻米 dàomǐ ■ *Rice is probably the most widely eaten grain in the world.* 稻米很可能是世界上食用最广的谷物。Dàomǐ hěn kěnéng shì shìjièshang shíyòng zuì guǎng de gǔwù.
rice paddy (水) 稻田 (shuǐ) dào tián

rich ADJ 1 富 fù, 富有的 fùyǒu de ■ *She has a rich dad.* 她有一个富爸爸。Tā yǒu yí ge fù bàba.
2 富有 fùyǒu, 有丰富的 yǒu fēngfù de ■ *You should eat food rich in iron.* 你应该多吃富有铁质的食物。Nǐ yīnggāi duō chī fùyǒu tiězhì de shíwù.

riches N 财富 cáifù

richly ADV 1 富贵地 fùguì de, 华丽地 huálì de
richly colored 色彩鲜艳的 sècǎi xiānyàn de
richly flavored 味道浓郁的 wèidao nóngyù de
2 大量地 dàliàng de

rickets N 佝偻病 gōulóubìng

rickety ADJ 1 快要散架的 [+椅子] kuàiyào sǎnjià de [+yǐzi] 2 摇摇晃晃的 yáoyáo huǎnghuǎng de

rickshaw N 人力车 rénlìchē, 黄包车 huángbāochē

ricochet v 弹飞 dàn fēi, 反弹 fǎntán

rid v (PT & PP **rid**) 摆脱 bǎituō ■ *We've tried every means to rid the house of mice.* 我们试了种种办法清除房子里的老鼠。Wǒmen shìle zhǒngzhǒng bànfǎ qīngchú fángzi lǐ de lǎoshǔ.

to get rid of 摆脱 bǎituō, 清除 qīngchú

riddance N (good riddance) 终于滚蛋了 zhōngyú gǔndàn le, 走得好 zǒu de hǎo

riddle N 1 谜(语) mí (yǔ) 2 奥秘 àomì

riddled ADJ 1 充满…的 chōngmǎn...de 2 到处是小洞的 dàochù shì xiǎodòng de

ride I v (PT **rode**; PP **ridden**) 1 骑 [+马/自行车] qí [+mǎ/zìxíngchē] 2 乘坐 [+火车] chéngzuò [+huǒchē] II N 乘 [+汽车/火车/摩托车] chéng [+qìchē/huǒchē/mótuōchē] ■ *Can you give me a ride to the airport?* 你可以开车送我去机场吗? Nǐ kěyǐ kāi chē sòng wǒ qù jīchǎng ma?
to take sb for a ride 欺骗某人 qīpiàn mǒurén

rider N 骑马/自行车的人 qí mǎ/zìxíngchē de rén

ridge N 山脊 shānjǐ

ridicule N, v 嘲笑 cháoxiào, 取笑 qǔxiào

ridiculous ADJ 可笑的 kěxiào de, 荒唐的 huāngtáng de

riding N 骑马 qímǎ

rife ADJ 流行的 liúxíng de, 普遍存在的 pǔbiàn cúnzài de

rifle[1] N 枪 qiāng, 步枪 bùqiāng

rifle[2] v 翻遍 [+抽屉] fān biàn [+chōutì]

rift N 1 裂缝 lièfèng 2 分裂 fēnliè, 分歧 fēnqí

rig I v 1 操纵 [+选举] cāozòng [+xuǎnjǔ] 2 给(船)配备绳索帆具 gěi (chuan) pèibèi shéngsuǒ fānjù II N (石油) 钻井架 (shíyóu) zuān jǐngjià

rigging N 帆缆 fānlǎn, 帆具 fānjù

right I ADJ 正确的 zhèngquè de, 对的 duì de ■ *"Is this the DVD you were looking for?" "Right, that's it."* "你就在找这张DVD吗?" "对。" "Nǐ jiù zài zhǎo zhè zhāng DVD ma?" "Duì." 2 恰当的 qiàdàng de, 适当的 shìdàng de 3 右面的 yòumian de
right field (棒球) 右外场 (bàngqiú) yòu wàichǎng
II ADV 1 就 jiù, 正 zhèng ■ *The CD was right under his nose all the time.* 那张光碟就一直在他鼻子底下。Nà zhāng guāngdié jiù yìzhí zài tā bízi díxià. 2 正确地 zhèngquè de, 对 duì ■ *Have I guessed it right?* 我猜对了吗? Wǒ cāiduì le ma? 3 右面 yòumian III N 1 正确 zhèngquè, 正当 zhèngdàng ■ *Don't underestimate children's ability to tell the difference between right and wrong.* 不要低估儿童辨别是非的能力。Bú yào dīgū értóng biànbié shìfēi de nénglì. 2 权利 quánlì 3 右 yòu, 右面 yòumian IV v (to right a wrong) 纠正错误 jiūzhèng cuòwù

right-angled ADJ 直角的 zhíjiǎo de

righteous ADJ 正义的 zhèngyì de
righteous anger 义愤 yìfèn

righteousness N 正义 zhèngyì

rightful N 合法的 héfǎ de, 公正的 gōngzhèng de
a rightful owner 合法主人 héfǎ zhǔrén

563

right-hand

right-hand ADJ 右边的 yòubian de, 右侧的 yòucè de

rightly ADV 正确地 zhèngquè de, 有道理的 yǒudào lǐ de

right of way N 先行权 xiānxíng quán

rights N 特许使用权 tèxǔ shǐyòngquán
property rights (法定)房产使用权 (fǎdìng) fángchǎn shǐyòngquán

right-wing N, ADJ (政治)右翼(的)(zhèngzhì) yòuyì (de)
right-wing politician 右翼政客 yòuyì zhèngkè

rigid ADJ **1** 严格的 [+方法] yángé de [+fāngfǎ] **2** 僵硬的 [+观点] jiāngyìng de [+guāndiǎn]

rigidity N 严格 yángé, 僵硬 jiāngyìng

rigmarole N 繁琐费时的手续 fánsuǒ fèishí de shǒuxù, 繁文缛节 fánwén rùjié

rigor N 严谨 yánjǐn

rigorous ADJ 严谨的 yánjǐn de, 严格的 yángé de

rile V 激怒 jīnù

rim I N 边缘 biānyuán II V 环绕 huánrào

rind N (水果的)厚皮 (shuǐguǒ de) hòu pí

ring¹ I N **1** 戒指 jièzhi ■ *A wedding ring is more than a piece of jewelery.* 结婚戒指不仅仅是一件首饰。Jiéhūn jièzhi bù jǐnjǐn shì yí jiàn shǒushi. ring finger 无名指 wúmíngzhǐ
2 环 huán, 圆圈 yuánquān ■ *The Olympics symbol is five rings in different colors.* 奥林匹克的标志是不同颜色的五个环。Àolínpǐkè de biāozhì shì bù tóng yánsè de wǔ ge huán. key ring 钥匙环 yàoshihuán
3 拳击/摔跤台 quánjī/shuāijiāo tái
to retire from the ring 退出拳击运动 tuìchū quánjī yùndòng
4 犯罪团伙 fànzuì tuánhuǒ

ring² I N **1** 铃声 língshēng ■ *Did you hear a ring at the door?* 你听到门铃了吗？Nǐ tīngdao ménlíng le ma?
to have a familiar ring 听起来耳熟 tīngqilai ěrshú
2 语气 yǔqì
to have a ring of truth 听起来像真的 tīngqilai xiàng zhēnde
II V (PT **rang**; PP **rung**) **1** 按电铃 àn diànlíng, 打铃 dǎlíng **2** [铃+]响 [líng+] xiǎng
to ring a bell 听起来耳熟 tīngqilai ěrshú ■ *Does the name James Dolittle ring a bell?* 詹姆士·杜利特尔这个名字你听起来耳熟吗？Zhānmǔshì·Dùlìtè'ěr zhè ge míngzì nǐ tīngqilai ěrshú ma?

ringleader N (匪帮)头目 (fěibāng) tóumù

ringside N 台边区 tái biānqū
ringside seat 台边区前排座位 tái biān qū qiánpáizuòwèi

ringworm N (头)癣 (tóu) xuǎn

rink N 溜冰场 liūbīngchǎng, 旱冰场 hànbīngchǎng

rinky-dink ADJ 低廉劣质的 dīlián lièzhì de

rinse I V 冲洗 chōngxǐ II N **1** 冲洗 chōngxǐ **2** 染发剂 rǎnfà jì

riot I N **1** 骚乱 sāoluàn, 暴乱 bàoluàn
riot police 防暴警察 fángbào jǐngchá
a riot of color 色彩绚丽 sècǎi xuànlì
II V 骚乱 sāoluàn, 闹事 nàoshì

rioting N 骚乱 sāoluàn, 暴乱 bàoluàn

riotous ADJ 狂暴的 kuángbào de, 放纵的 fàngzòng de

RIP (= "Rest in Peace") ABBREV 安息 ānxī

rip I V 撕裂 sīliè
to rip into 不公平的猛烈抨击 bùgōngpíng de měngliè pēngjī
to rip sb off 欺诈 qīzhà, 多收钱 duō shōuqián
II N 裂缝 lièfèng, 裂口 lièkǒu

ripcord N (降落伞的)开伞索 (jiàngluòsǎn de) kāi sǎn suǒ

ripe ADJ 成熟的 chéngshú de ■ *The time is ripe for a structural reform of the finance sector.* 对财政部门进行结构性改革的时机已经成熟。Duì cáizhèng bùmén jìnxíng jiégòuxìng gǎigé de shíjī yǐjīng chéngshú.

ripen V (使…)成熟 (shǐ…) chéngshú

ripoff N **1** 要价不合理的商品 yàojià bù hélǐ de shāngpǐn, 宰人的东西 zǎiren de dōngxi **2** (音像)盗版 (yīnxiàng) dàobǎn

ripple I V 泛起微波 fàn qǐ wēibō II N 微波细浪 wēibō xì làng
a ripple of laughter 一阵笑声 yízhèn xiàoshēng
ripple effect 连锁反应 liánsuǒ fǎnyìng

rip-roaring ADJ, ADV 喧闹的 xuānnào de, 热闹的 rènao de

rise I V (PT **rose**; PP **risen**) **1** 上涨 shàngzhǎng, 增加 zēngjiā **2** [太阳+]升起 [tàiyáng+] shēngqǐ **3** [社会地位+]上升 [shèhuì dìwèi+] shàngshēng **4** 起床 qǐchuáng ■ *Early to bed, and early to rise makes you healthy, wealthy and wise.* 早睡早起，使你健康、富有、智慧。Zǎo shuì zǎo qǐ, shǐ nǐ jiànkāng、fùyǒu、zhìhuì. ■ *All rise.* 全体起立。Quántǐ qǐlì.
to rise to one's feet 站起来 zhànqǐlai
II N 增加 zēngjiā ■ *Experts attribute the rise in racial discrimination cases to the worsening economy.* 专家们把种族歧视案件的增加归罪于经济情况恶化。Zhuānjiāmen bǎ zhǒngzú qíshì ànjiàn de zēngjiā guīzuìyú jīngjì qíngkuàng èhuà.
to give rise to 引起 yǐnqǐ

riser N (early/late riser) 早起/晚起的人 zǎoqǐ/wǎnqǐ de rén

risk I N 风险 fēngxiǎn ■ *Have you taken into consideration the risk of failure?* 你有没有考虑过失败的风险？Nǐ yǒuméiyǒu kǎolǜguo shībài de fēngxiǎn?
risk-free 没有风险的 méiyǒu fēngxiǎn de
at your own risk 风险自负 fēngxiǎn zìfù

to run the risk of ... 冒...的险 mào...de xiǎn
■ *By making this criticism he ran the risking of offending his supervisor.* 他提出这个批评，冒着得罪上司的风险。Tā tíchū zhè ge pīpíng, màozhe dézuì shàngsī de fēngxiǎn.
to take a risk 冒险 màoxiǎn
II v 冒险 màoxiǎn ■ *He risked his life to save an old woman from the fire.* 他冒着生命危险把一位老太太从大火中救出来。Tā màozhe shēngmìng wēixiǎn bǎ yí wèi lǎotàitai cóng dàhuǒ zhōng jiùchūlai.

riskiness N 冒险（性）màoxiǎn (xìng), 冒险的程度 màoxiǎn de chéngdù

risky ADJ 冒险的 màoxiǎn de

risqué ADJ 粗俗的 cūsú de, 色情的 sèqíng de

rite N 仪式 yíshì, 礼仪 lǐyí

ritual I N 1 仪式 yíshì, 礼仪 lǐyí, 惯例 guànlì, 老程式 lǎo chéngshì **II** ADJ 仪式的 yíshì de, 礼仪的 lǐyí de

ritzy ADJ 豪华时髦的 háohuá shímáo de

rival I N （竞争）对手 (jìngzhēng) duìshǒu **II** v 可与...相匹敌 kě yǔ...xiāng pǐdí, 与...旗鼓相当 yǔ...qígǔxiāngdāng

rivalry N 竞争 jìngzhēng, 争斗 zhēngdòu
gang rivalry 帮派争斗 bāngpài zhēngdòu

river N 河 hé, 江 jiāng

riverbed N 河床 héchuáng

riverside N 河边 hébiān

rivet I N 铆钉 mǎodīng [M. WD 枚 méi] **II** v 1 用铆钉固定 yòng mǎodīng gùdìng 2 吸引 [+注意] xīyǐn [+zhùyì]

riveting ADJ 十分吸引人的 shífēn xīyǐn rén de, 极其精彩的 jíqí jīngcǎi de

roach N 1 (= cockroach) 蟑螂 zhāngláng 2 （大麻烟的）烟蒂 (dàmáyān de) yāndì

road N 道路 dàolù [M. WD 条 tiáo], 公路 gōnglù [M. WD 条 tiáo] ■ *You must reduce speed on residential roads.* 在住宅区的街道上你要减速。Zài zhùzhái qū de jiēdàoshang nǐ děi jiǎnsù.
main road 主要街道 zhǔyào jiēdào
side/back road 小路 xiǎolù
road test 道路试车 dàolù shìchē
road trip 长途驾车旅行 chángtú jiàchē lǚxíng

roadblock N 路障 lùzhàng

roadhouse N （公路旁的）饭店 (gōnglù pángde) fàndiàn

roadkill N 公路上被压死的动物 gōnglù shàng bèi yā sǐde dòngwù

roadside N 路边 lùbiān, 路旁 lùpáng

roadway N 车行道 chēxíngdào [M. WD 条 tiáo]

roadworthy ADJ 可以行驶的 kěyǐ xíngshǐ de, 可上路的 kěyǐ shànglù de

roam v 漫步 mànbù, 闲逛 xiánguàng

roaming N 漫游 mànyóu

roar v, N [动物+] 吼叫 [dòngwù+] hǒujiào, 咆哮 páoxiào

roast I v 烤 kǎo, 烘 hōng **II** N 1 烤肉 kǎoròu 2 露天烧烤聚会 lùtiān shāokǎo jùhuì **III** ADJ 烤好的 kǎo hǎode
roast beef 烤牛肉 kǎoniúròu

rob v 抢 qiǎng, 抢劫 qiǎngjié ■ *What? Someone's robbed the HSBC in New York?* 什么？有人抢了纽约的汇丰银行？Shénme? Yǒurén qiǎngle Niǔyuē de Huìfēng yínháng?

robber N 强盗 qiángdào, 抢劫犯 qiǎngjié fàn

robbery N 抢劫 qiǎngjié

robe N 1 [法官的+] 长袍 [fǎguān de+] chángpáo 2 睡袍 shuìpáo [M. WD 件 jiàn]

robin N 知更鸟 zhīgēngniǎo [M. WD 只 zhī]

robot N 机器人 jīqì rén

robotics N 机器人制造及运用研究 jīqìrén zhìzào jí yùnyòng yánjiū, 机器人学 jīqìrénxué

robust ADJ 1 健壮的 [+人] jiànzhuàng de [+rén] 2 健全的 [+组织] jiànquán de [+zǔzhī] 3 坚固的 [+房屋] jiāngù de [+fángwū]

rock[1] N 石头 shítou [M. WD 块 kuài], 岩石 yánshí

rock[2] I v 1 摇动 yáodòng
The hand that rocks the cradle rules the world. 摇动摇篮的手统治世界。Yáodòng yáolán de shǒu tǒngzhì shìjiè.
2 剧烈震动 jùliè zhèndòng **II** N 摇滚音乐 yáogǔn yīnyuè
rock 'n' roll 摇滚乐 yáogǔnyuè

rock bottom I N 谷底 gǔdǐ **II** ADJ 最低的 zuìdī de
rock bottom prices 最低价 zuìdījià, 跳楼价 tiàolóu jià
to hit rock bottom 达到最坏的境况 dádào zuì huài de jìngkuàng, 陷入谷底 xiànrù gǔdǐ

rocker N 1 摇椅 yáoyǐ [M. WD 把 bǎ] 2 摇滚乐手 yáogǔnyuè shǒu [M. WD 名 míng]

rocket I N 火箭 huǒjiàn ■ *The launch of the rockets drew condemnation from all over the world.* 火箭的发射引起全世界的谴责。Huǒjiàn de fāshè yǐnqǐ quán shìjiè de qiǎnzé.
rocket scientist 火箭专家 huǒjiàn zhuānjiā, 极其聪明博学的人 jíqí cōngming bóxué de rén
II v 迅速上升 xùnsù shàngshēng, 猛增 měngzēng

rocking chair N 摇椅 yáoyǐ [M. WD 把 bǎ]

rocking horse N 摇动木马 yáodòng mùmǎ

rocky ADJ 1 多岩石的 duō yánshí de 2 困难重重的 kùnnan chóngchóng de

Rocky Mountains N （美国）洛矶山脉 (Měiguó) Luòjī shānmài

rod N 杆 gǎn, 棍 gùn ■ *The rod bent in half as the shark tried to get away from the fisherman.* 当鲨鱼试图逃离时，鱼杆一折为二。Dāng shāyú shìtú táolí shí, yúgān yì zhé wéi èr.

rodent N 啮齿动物 nièchǐ dòngwù, 老鼠 lǎoshu, 松鼠 sōngshǔ

rodeo N 牛仔竞技表演 niúzǎi jìngjì biǎoyǎn

roe N 鱼籽 yúzǐ

rogue¹ ADJ 不守规矩的 bù shǒu guīju de, 制造麻烦的 zhìzào máfan de

rogue² N 恶棍 èguùn, 坏蛋 huàidàn

roguish ADJ 淘气的 táoqì de, 调皮的 tiáopí de

role N 1 作用 zuòyòng ■ *His PhD thesis is on the role of technological advances in globalization.* 他的博士论文是技术进步在全球化中的作用。Tā de bóshì lùnwén shì jìshù jìnbù zài quánqiúhuà zhōng de zuòyòng. 2 角色 juésè

leading role 主要人物 zhǔyào rénwù, 主角 zhǔjué

a role model 榜样 bǎngyàng, 楷模 kǎimó ■ *Our Chinese teacher, Miss Clark, an American who speaks fluent Chinese, is a role model for us all.* 我们的中文老师克拉克小姐说一口流利的中文，是我们的好榜样。Wǒmen de Zhōngwén lǎoshī Kèlākè xiǎojiě shuō yì kǒu liúlìde Zhōngwén, shì wǒmen de hǎo bǎngyàng.

role-play N 角色扮演 juésè bànyǎn

roll I v 1 滚 gǔn, 滚动 gǔndòng 2 转动 zhuàndòng ■ *He has a habit of rolling a pencil between his fingers when he is thinking.* 他在动脑筋的时候，习惯把铅笔夹在手指中间转动。Tā zài dòng nǎojīn de shíhou, xíguàn bǎ qiānbǐ jiā zài shǒuzhǐ zhōng zhuàndòng. 3 卷起 juǎnqǐ ■ *The child rolled himself up in the rug.* 孩子把自己卷在毯子里。Háizi bǎ zìjǐ juàn zài tǎnzi lǐ. 4 轧平 yàpíng ■ *She is rolling the dough and getting ready to make some pastries.* 她在擀面，准备做小甜饼。Tā zài gǎnmiàn, zhǔnbèi zuò xiǎo tiánbǐng. II N 1 卷 juàn ■ *The engineer put a roll of blueprints on the shelf.* 工程师把一卷蓝图放在书架上。Gōngchéngshī bǎ yí juàn lántú fàng zài shūjiàshang. 2 名单 míngdān

roll call 点名 diǎnmíng

3 小圆面包 xiǎo yuán miànbāo

roller N 1 滚筒 gǔntǒng 2 卷发卷 juǎnfà jiā

roller coaster N 过山车 guòshānchē, 云霄飞车 yúnxiāo fēi chē

roller skate I N 旱冰鞋 hànbīngxié II v 溜旱冰 liū hànbīng

roller skating N 溜旱冰 liū hànbīng

rollicking ADJ 热闹的 rènao de, 喧闹的 xuānnào de

rolling ADJ 连绵起伏的 liánmiánqǐfú de

rolling-pin N 擀面棍 gǎnmiàn gùn [M. WD 根 gēn]

roly-poly ADJ 圆圆胖胖的 yuányuán pàngpàng de

ROM (= Read-Only Memory) ABBREV（计算机）只读存储器 (jìsuànjī) zhǐ dú cúnchǔ qì

Roman Catholic N 罗马天主教会 Luómǎ Tiānzhǔ jiàohuì

Roman numeral N 罗马数字 Luómǎ shùzì

romantic I ADJ 浪漫的 làngmàn de II N 1 浪漫的人 làngmàn de rén, 爱幻想的人 ài huànxiǎng de rén 2 浪漫主义者 làngmànzhǔyìzhě

romanticize v 把…浪漫化 bǎ…làngmàn huà

romp I v 追跑打闹 zhuī pǎo dǎnào II N 嬉闹 xīnào, 玩耍 wánshuǎ

roof I N 屋顶 wūdǐng, 车顶 chēdǐng

a roof over one's head 栖身之地 qīshēn zhī dì

under one roof 住在同一所房子 zhù zài tóng yì suǒ fángzi

II v 盖屋顶 gài wūdǐng

tile-roofed 瓦屋顶 wǎwū dǐng

roofing N 盖层面材料 gàicéng miàn cáiliào

roofrack N（汽车）车顶（行李）架 (qìchē) chēdǐng (xíngli) jià

rooftop N 屋顶 wūdǐng

rookie N 新队员 xīn duìyuán, 新人 xīnrén

room N 1 房间 fángjiān 2 空间 kōngjiān ■ *There's no room for a piano in the sitting room.* 在会客室里没有放钢琴的地方了。Zài huìkèshì lǐ méiyǒu fàng gāngqín de dìfang le. 3 余地 yúdì

room and board 供应住宿和膳食 gōngyìng zhùsù hé shànshí

room service 客房（用餐）服务 kèfáng (yòngcān) fúwù

to room with sb 和某人同住一室 hé mǒurén tóng zhù yí shì

roommate N 室友 shì yǒu

roomy ADJ 宽敞的 kuānchang de

roost I N（鸟的）栖息处 (niǎo de) qīxī chù, 鸟窝 niǎowō, 鸟巢 niǎocháo II v [鸟+] 栖息 [niǎo+] qīxī

has come home to roost 来报应 láibào yìng

rooster N 公鸡 gōngjī, 雄鸡 xióngjī [M. WD 只 zhī]

root I N 1 根 gēn, 根子 gēnzi 2（家族的）根 (jiāzú de) gēn, 老根 lǎo gēn ■ *Meilin's grandfather went back to China to trace their roots.* 梅琳的祖父回中国寻根。Méilín de zǔfù huí Zhōngguó xún gēn.

root beer 根汁汽水 gēn zhī qìshuǐ

3 根源 gēnyuán ■ *The English and German languages share a common root.* 英语和德语有共同的根源。Yīngyǔ hé Déyǔ yǒu gòngtóng de gēnyuán. II v [植物+] 生根 [zhíwù+] shēnggēn

rootless ADJ 无根的 wú gēn de, 无归属感的 wú guīshǔ gǎn de

rope I N 绳 shéng, 绳子 shéngzi, 绳索 shéngsuǒ II v 用绳子捆绑 yòng shéngzi kǔnbǎng

ropes N (be on the ropes) 处境危险 chǔjìng wēixiǎn

rosary N 念珠 niànzhū

rose¹ N 1 玫瑰 méiguì, 玫瑰花 méiguihuā 2 粉红色 fěnhóngsè

rose² v See rise

Rosh Hashanah N（犹太人的）新年 (Yóutàirén de) xīnnián, 岁首节 suìshǒu jié

roster N 名单 míngdān, 值勤表 zhíqín biǎo

duty roster 值勤表 zhíqín biǎo, 值日表 zhírìbiǎo

rostrum N 讲台 jiǎngtái

rosy ADJ **1** 玫瑰色的 méiguìsè de, 粉红色的 fěnhóngsè de **2** 美好的 měihǎo de, 充满希望的 chōngmǎn xīwàng de

rot I v 烂 làn, 腐烂 fǔlàn II N **1** 腐烂（的过程）fǔlàn (de guòchéng) **2**（制度的）腐败 (zhìdù de) fǔbài

rotary ADJ 旋转的 xuánzhuǎn de

Rotary Club N 扶轮社 Fúlúnshè

rotate v **1**（使…）旋转 (shǐ...) xuánzhuǎn, （使…）转动 (shǐ...) zhuàndòng **2** 轮换 lúnhuàn, 轮流 lúnliú

rotation N **1** 选转 xuánzhuǎn **2** 轮换 lúnhuàn

ROTC (= Reserve Officers' Training Corp) AB-BREV（美国）后备军官训练团 hòubèijūn guān xùnliàn tuán

rote N 死记硬背 sǐjì yìngbèi

rote learning 死记硬背的学习方法 sǐjì yìngbèi de xuéxí fāngfǎ

rotisserie N 旋转式烤肉架 xuánzhuǎnshì kǎoròu jià

rotor N 转动件 zhuàndòng jiàn, 转子 zhuànzǐ

rotten ADJ **1** 腐烂的 fǔlàn de, 变质的 biànzhì de **2** 糟透的 zāotòu de

rotund ADJ 圆胖的 yuán pàng de

rotunda N 圆形建筑物 yuánxíng jiànzhù wù

rouge N 胭脂 yānzhi

rough I ADJ **1** 高低不平的 gāodī bù píng de **2** 粗暴的 cūbào de ■ *Nancy hates rough sports; she watches American football only to please her boyfriend.* 南茜厌恶粗暴的体育，她看美式足球只是为了让男朋友高兴。Nánxī yànwù cūbào de tǐyù, tā kàn Měishì zúqiú zhǐ shì wèile ràng nánpéngyou gāoxìng. **3** 粗略的 cūlüè de ■ *Can you give me a rough translation of this Chinese story?* 你能粗略地翻译一下这个中文故事吗？Nǐ néng cūlüè de fānyì yí xiàzhège Zhōngwén gùshi ma? II v (to rough it out) 过艰苦的生活 guò jiānkǔ de shēnghuó, (rough sb up) 殴打某人 ōudǎ mǒurén III N **1**（高尔夫球场的）深草区 (gāo'ěrfū qiúchǎng de) shēn cǎo qū **2** 草图 cǎotú, 略图 lüètú

to take the rough with the smooth 既能享受也能吃苦 jì néng xiǎngshòu yě néng chīkǔ, 能屈能伸 néng shēn néng qū

IV ADV 粗野（地）cūyě (de)

roughage N（食物中的）粗纤维 (shíwù zhòngde) cūxiānwéi

rough-and-tumble ADJ（很多人）残酷竞争的 (hěn duō rén) cánkù jìngzhēng de

roughhouse v 打闹游戏、殴斗 ōudòu

roughly ADV 大致上 dàzhìshàng, 大约 dàyuē

roughneck N **1** 油井工人 yóujǐng gōngrén **2** 脾气暴躁的人 píqì bàozao de rén

roughshod ADJ (to run roughshod over sth) 粗暴对待某事物 cūbào duìdài mǒushìwù

roulette N 轮盘赌 lúnpándǔ

round I ADJ **1** 圆的 yuán de **2** 整数的 zhěngshù de ■ *How much is the day's takings, in round figures?* 今天进账多少钱？给我一个整数。Jīntiān jìn zhàng duōshǎo qián? Gěi wǒ yí ge zhěngshù. **3** 来回的 láihuí de, 往返的 wǎngfǎn de II N **1** 一系列（事件）yíxìliè (shìjiàn)

the next round of talks 下一轮会谈 xià yì lún huìtán

2（比赛的）一轮 (bǐsài de) yìlún, 一局 yìjú, 一场 yìcháng **3** 巡诊 xún fǎng,（医生的）定期出诊 (yīshēng de) dìngqī chūzhěn

a mailman's rounds 邮递员的定时递信 yóudìyuán de dìngqī dìxìn

4 一发（子弹）yìfā (zǐdàn), 一次（射击）yícì (shèjī) III v 环绕 huánrào

to round sth off 圆满结束 yuánmǎn jiéshù

to round sb up 聚拢 jùlǒng

IV ADV 旋转（地）xuánzhuǎn (de)

round about 大约 dàyuē

V PREP 围绕 wéirào

roundabout ADJ 拐弯抹角的 guǎiwan mójiǎo de

round-the-clock ADJ 日夜的 rìyè de, 二十四小时的 èrshísì xiǎoshí de

round-trip ADJ 往返的 wǎngfǎn de

rouse v **1** 唤醒 huànxǐng **2** 振奋 zhènfèn, 激励 jīlì **3** 引起…的兴趣 yǐnqǐ...de xìngqu

rousing ADJ 激励人的 jīlì rén de

rout v, N 彻底击败 chèdǐ jībài, 溃败 kuìbài

route I N **1** 路线 lùxiàn **2** 航线 hángxiàn, 行车路线 xíngchē lùxiàn

bus route 公共汽车路线 gōnggòng qìchē lùxiàn

3 [做事的+] 方法 [zuòshì de+] fāngfǎ **4** 公路 gōnglù

route 68 68号公路 68 hào gōnglù

II v 按特定路线传送 àn tèdìng lùxiàn chuánsòng

routine I N 常规 chángguī, 例行公事 lìxíng gōngshì

daily routine 每天的例行公事 měitiān de lìxíng gōngshì

II ADJ 惯例的 guànlì de, 例行的 lìxíng de

roving ADJ (a roving reporter) 巡回（记者）xúnhuí (jìzhě)

row¹ I N 排 pái ■ *My ticket says that I'm in row 12, seat 5 of row 12.* 我的票是十二排，十二排五座。Wǒ de piào shì shí'èr pái, shí'èr pái wǔ zuò. II v 划 huá, 划船 huáchuán

in a row 连续 liánxù ■ *It rained three days in a row.* 连续下了三天雨。Liánxù xiàle sān tiān yǔ.

row² I N, v（大声）吵架 (dàshēng) chǎojià

rowboat N 划艇 huátǐng [M. WD 艘 sōu]

rowdy ADJ 吵吵闹闹的 chǎochǎo nàonào de, 粗野的 cūyě de

rowing N 划船（运动）huáchuán (yùndòng)

royal N, ADJ 王室（的）wáng shì (de), 皇家（的）, huángjiā (de)

royalty N 1 版税 bǎnshuì, 稿费 gǎofèi
a royalty of 7% for each copy sold 每出售一本得稿费7% měi chūshòu yìběn dé gǎofèi 7% 2 王室成员 wángshì chéngyuán, 皇族成员 huángzú chéngyuán

RSVP (= Repondez s'il vous plaît) ABBREV 敬请赐复 jìngqǐng cì fù

rub I v 擦 cā, 摩擦 mócā ■ *Don't rub your eyes; use eye drops.* 别擦眼睛—用眼药水。Bié cā yǎnjing—yòng yǎn yàoshuǐ.
to rub sb the wrong way 惹怒某人 rěnù mǒurén
to rub salt into a wound 雪上加霜 xuě shàng jiā shuāng
II N 擦 cā, 摩擦 mócā
the rub 问题 wèntí, 难题 nántí

rubber N 橡皮 xiàngpí
rubber band 橡皮筋 xiàngpíjīn

rubberneck v （好奇地）东张西望 (hàoqí de) dōngzhāng xīwàng

rubber-stamp v 不经考虑就批准 bùjīng kǎolǜ jiù pīzhǔn

rubbery ADJ 橡皮似的 xiàngpí shìde

rubbish I N 1 胡说八道 húshuō bādào, 废话 fèihuà 2 垃圾 lājī II v 把…说得一无所是 bǎ…shuó de yìwú suǒ shì

rubble N 瓦砾 wǎlì

rubdown N 1 按摩 ànmó 2 摩平 mópíng

ruby N 红宝石 hóngbǎoshí [M. WD 颗 kē]

rudder N （方向）舵 (fāngxiàng) duò

ruddy ADJ [脸色+] 红润的 [liǎnsè+] hóngrùn de, 气色很好的 qìsè hěn hǎo de

rude ADJ 粗鲁的 cūlǔ de, 无礼的 wúlǐ de
a rude awakening 突然发觉 tūrán fājué

rudimentary ADJ 基本的 jīběn de, 初浅的 chūqiǎn de

rudiments N 基础（部分）jīchǔ (bùfen)

rue v 后悔 hòuhuǐ, 懊悔 àohuǐ

rueful ADJ 后悔的 hòuhuǐ de, 懊悔的 àohuǐ de

ruffle I v 把…弄乱 bǎ…nòngluàn
to ruffle sb's feathers 使别人不快 shǐ biéren búkuài
II N （衣服的）褶边 (yīfu de) zhě biān

rug N 小地毯 xiǎo dìtǎn [M. WD 块 kuài]

rugby N （英式）橄榄球 (Yīngshì) gǎnlǎnqiú

rugged ADJ 1 高低不平的 [+地形] gāodī bùpíng de [+dìxíng], 崎岖的 qíqū de 2 坚固的 [+汽车] jiāngù de [+qìchē], 结实的 jiēshi de 3 粗犷的 [+容貌] cūguǎng de [+róngmào] 4 自信的 [+人] zìxìn de [+rén]
rugged individualism 自信而粗犷的个人主义 zìxìn ér cūguǎng de gèrénzhǔyì

ruin I v 毁 huǐ, 毁坏 huǐhuài ■ *The birthday party was ruined when the dog knocked over the birthday cake.* 狗打翻了生日蛋糕，毁了这个生日聚会。Gǒu dǎfānle shēngri dàngāo, huǐle zhè ge shēngri jùhuì. 2 使…破产 shǐ… pòchǎn II N 毁坏 huǐhuài
ruins 废墟 fèixū ■ *Every day busloads of tourists come to see the ruins of the 12th-century abbey.* 每天一车一车的旅游者来参观这座十二世纪修道院的废墟。Měitiān yì chē yì chē de lǚyóuzhě lái cānguān zhè zuò shí'èr shìjì xiūdàoyuàn de fèixū.

ruinous ADJ 毁灭性的 huǐmièxìng de

rule I N 1 规则 guīzé 2 统治 tǒngzhì, 执政 zhízhèng ■ *America is a country based on the rule of law.* 美国是个基于法治的国家。Měiguó shì ge jīyú fǎzhì de guójiā. II v 统治 tǒngzhì, 执政 zhízhèng ■ *Kings and queens still rule some countries.* 在有些国家还是国王、女王统治。Zài yǒuxiē guójiā hái shì Guówáng、Nǚwáng tǒngzhì. 2 [法庭+] 裁决 [fǎtíng+] cáijué
as a rule 通常 tōngcháng

ruled ADJ 有平行线的 [+纸] yǒu píngxíngxiàn de [+zhǐ]

ruler N 1 统治者 tǒngzhìzhě ■ *The king was considered a benevolent ruler.* 这位国王被认为是明君。Zhè wèi Guówáng bèi rènwéi shì míngjūn. 2 尺 chǐ [M. WD 把 bǎ]

ruling I N （法庭的）裁决 (fǎtíng de) cáijué, 裁定 cáidìng II ADJ 执政的 zhízhèng de

rum N 朗姆酒 Lǎngmǔjiǔ

rumble I v 1 发出轰隆声 fāchū hōnglōng shēng 2 [肚子饿得+] 咕咕叫 [dùzi è dé+] gūgū jiào II N 轰隆声 hōnglōng shēng

ruminate v 1 长时间沉思 chángshíjiān chénsī 2 [动物的+] 反刍 [dòngwù de+] fǎnchú

rummage v 翻找 fānzhǎo
rummage sale 旧物义卖 jiùwù yìmài

rumor N 谣传 yáochuán, 谣言 yáoyán

rumored ADJ 谣传的 yáochuán de, 据传的 jùchuán de

rump N 臀部 túnbù

rumple v 把…弄皱 bǎ…nòng zhòu

run I v (PT ran; PP run) 1 跑 pǎo, 奔跑 bēnpǎo ■ *You have to run to catch the bus.* 你要赶汽车，就得奔跑了。Nǐ yào gǎn qìchē, jiù děi bēnpǎo le. 2 管理 guǎnlǐ 3 行驶 xíngchí ■ *Does Greyhound run on Christmas day?* 灰狗长途汽车圣诞节也跑吗？Huīgǒu chángtú qìchē Shèngdànjié yě pǎo ma? 4 运行 yùnxíng ■ *The New York subway runs 24/7.* 纽约地铁一天二十四小时、一星期七天运行。Niǔyuē dìtiě yì tiān èrshísì xiǎoshí, yì xīngqī qī tiān yùnxíng. 5 流 liú, 流淌 liútǎng 6 竞选 jìngxuǎn
to run across/to run into 遇见 yùjiàn
to run after ① 追 zhuī ② 追求 zhuīqiú ■ *The young businessman is running after his boss' daughter.* 这个年轻的商人在追求他老板的女儿。

Zhè ge niánqīng de shāngrén zài zhuīqiú tā lǎobǎn de nǚ'ér.

to run out of 用完 yòngwán

to run through 快快检查 kuàikuài jiǎnchá **II N 1** 跑步 pǎobù

to do sth on the run 边跑边做事 biān pǎo biān zuòshì, 急急匆匆 jíjí cōngcōng

to be on the run 东藏西躲 dōngcángxīduǒ **2** 竞选 jìngxuǎn **3** 挤兑(银行) jǐduì (yínxíng), 抛售 (货币) pāoshòu (huòbì) **4** (棒球比赛)一分 (bàngqiú bǐsài) yìfēn

runaround N (to give sb the runaround) 搪塞 tángsè, 敷衍 fūyǎn

runaway I N 离家出走的儿童 líjiā chūzǒu de értóng **II** ADJ **1** 离家出走的 líjiā chūzǒu de **2** 失控的 [+车辆] shīkòng de [+chēliàng]

a runaway success 迅速的成功 xùnsù de chénggōng

run-down[1] ADJ **1** 破旧的 [+房屋] pòjiù de [+fángwū] **2** 虚弱的 [+人] xūruò de [+rén]

run-down[2] N 简报 jiǎnbào, 要点 yàodiǎn

rung[1] See ring (v)

rung[2] N **1** (梯子的)横档 (tīzi de) héngdàng **2** (社会)等级 (shèhuì) děngjí, 地位 dìwèi

run-in N 争吵 zhēngchǎo

runner N **1** 参加赛跑的人 cānjiā sàipǎo de rén

marathon runner 马拉松赛跑选手 mǎlāsōng sàipǎo xuǎnshǒu

2 雪橇滑板 xuěqiāo huábǎn **3** (a drug runner) 走私毒品的人 zǒusī dúpǐn de rén

runner-up N 亚军 yàjūn, 第二名 dì'èrmíng

running N **1** 跑步 pǎobù, 赛跑 sàipǎo

running commentary 现场实况报道 xiànchǎng shíkuàng bàodào

running mate 竞选伙伴 jìngxuǎnhuǒbàn

running shorts 运动短裤 yùndòng duǎnkù

running water 自来水 zìláishuǐ

in running order (机器)运行正常 (jīqì) yùnxíng zhèngcháng

2 经营 jīngyíng, 管理 guǎnlǐ

runny ADJ 流鼻涕眼泪的 liú bíti yǎnlèi de

run-of-the-mill ADJ 极普通的 jí pǔtōng de, 很一般的 hěn yìbān de

run-up N (跳高时的)助跑 (tiàogāo shí de) zhùpǎo

the run-up to sth 某事件的前奏 mǒu shìjiàn de qiánzòu

runway N (机场)跑道 (jīchǎng) pǎodào [M. WD 条 tiáo]

rupture I N 破裂 pòliè **II** V (使⋯) 破裂 (shǐ...) pòliè

rural ADJ 农村的 nóngcūn de

ruse N 诡计 guǐjì

rush I V **1** 匆匆来去 cōngcōng láiqù ■ *During a fire alarm, it's not a good idea to rush down the stairs.* 发生火警时，冲下楼梯不是一个好办法。Fāshēng huǒ jǐng shí, chōngxia lóutī bú shì yí ge hǎo bànfǎ. **2** 催促 cuīcù **II** N **1** 匆忙 cōngmáng, 赶紧 gǎnjǐn **2** 繁忙时期 fánmáng shíqī

the Christmas rush 圣诞节前的购物忙季 Shèngdànjié qián de gòuwù mángjì

rush hour (交通)高峰时间 (jiāotōng) gāofēng shíjiān

Russian I ADJ 俄国的 Éguóde, 俄国人的 Éguórén de, 俄语的 Éyǔ de **II** N **1** 俄国人 Éguórén **2** 俄语 Éyǔ

rust I N **1** 铁锈 tiěxiù **2** (植物的)锈病 (zhíwù de) xiùbìng **II** V (使⋯) 生锈 (shǐ...) shēngxiù

rustic ADJ 乡村(风味)的 xiāngcūn (fēngwèi) de

rustle I V (使⋯) 沙沙作响 (shǐ...) shāshā zuòxiǎng **II** N 沙沙声 shāshā shēng

rustler N 偷牲畜的贼 tōu shēngchù de zéi

rustproof ADJ 防锈的 fángxiù de

rusty ADJ **1** 生锈的 shēngxiù de **2** 荒废的 huāngfèi de, 生疏的 shēngshū de

rut N 车辙 chēzhé

be stuck in a rut 刻板而乏味地生活 kèbǎn ér fáwèi de shēnghuó, 没有新意 méiyǒu xīnyì

ruthless ADJ 无情的 wúqíng de, 冷酷的 lěngkù de

ruthlessness N 无情 wúqíng, 冷酷 lěngkù

rye N 裸麦 luǒmài

S

Sabbath N 安息日 Ānxīrì

sabbatical N (大学教师)学术休假 (dàxué jiàoshī) xuéshù xiūjià

saber N **1** 佩剑 pèijiàn [M. WD 把 bǎ], 花剑 huājiàn [M. WD 把 bǎ] **2** 军刀 jūndāo, 马刀 mǎdāo

sable N **1** 貂皮 diāopí [M. WD 张 zhāng] **2** 貂 diāo [M. WD 只 zhī]

sabotage V, N (蓄意)破坏 (xùyì) pòhuài

sac N (动植物的)囊 (dòngzhíwù de) nāng

saccharin N 糖精 tángjīng

saccharine ADJ **1** 过分甜蜜的 guòfèn tiánmì de **2** 自作多情的 zìzuò duōqíng de, 肉麻的 ròumá de

sachet N 香袋 xiāngdài

sack[1] N **1** 大厚纸袋 dà hòu zhǐdài **2** 麻袋 mádài [M. WD 只 zhī], 粗衣袋 cū yīdài [M. WD 只 zhī]

sack[2] V **1** (橄榄球)擒抱 [+四分卫] (gǎnlǎnqiú) qín bào [+sì fēn wèi] **2** 解雇 [+工人] jiěgù [+gōngrén] **3** [军队+] 洗劫 [jūnduì+] xǐjié **4** (to sack out) 上床睡觉 shàngchuáng shuìjiào

sacrament N (基督教)圣餐 (Jīdūjiào) Shèngcān, 圣事 Shèngshì

sacred ADJ **1** 神圣的 shénshèng de ■ *Hardly*

anything seems sacred anymore. 似乎没有什么东西是神圣的了。Sìhu méiyǒu shénme dōngxī shì shénshèng de le. **2** 神的 shén de, 宗教的 zōngjiào de
sacred cow 神圣的信条 shénshèngde xìntiáo

sacrifice I v 牺牲 [+自己的利益] xīshēng [+zìjǐ de lìyì], 放弃 fàngqì II N 牺牲 xīshēn
the ultimate supreme sacrifice 牺牲自己的生命 xīshēng zìjǐ de shēngmìng, 捐躯 juānqū

sacrilege N 亵渎神明（的行为）xièdú shénmíng (de xíngwéi) **2** 不敬（行为）bújìng (xíngwéi)

sacrosanct ADJ 神圣不可侵犯的 shénshèng bùkě qīnfàn de, 不可亵渎的 bùkě xièdú de

sad ADJ 悲哀的 bēi'āi de, 难过的 nánguò de, 伤心的 shāngxīn de

sadden v 使…伤心 shǐ…shāngxīn

saddle I N 1 马鞍 mǎ'ān 2（自行车／摩托车）车座（zìxíngchē/mótuōchē) chēzuò II v 装马鞍 zhuāng mǎ'ān

saddlebag N 1（马）鞍囊 (mǎ) ānnáng 2（自行车／摩托车车座后的）工具袋 (zìxíngchē/mótuōchē chēzuò hòu de) gōngjùdài, 挂包 guàbāo

sadism N 虐待狂 nüèdàikuáng, 性虐待 xìngnüèdài

sadist N 虐待狂（人）nüèdàikuáng (rén)

sadistic ADJ 虐待狂的 nüèdàikuáng de

sadly ADV 1 伤心地 shāngxīn de 2 很可惜 hěn kěxī, 说来伤心 shuōlái shāngxīn

safari N 非洲野外观兽旅行 Fēizhōu yěwài guānshòu lǚxíng

safe I ADJ 安全的 ānquán de, 保险的 bǎoxiǎn de ■ It's not safe going out at night in the downtown area. 夜里去市中心不安全。Yèlǐ qù shì zhōngxīn bù ānquán.
to be on the safe side 为了安全（起见）wèile ānquán (qǐjiàn)
to be in safe hands 被妥善照顾着 bèi tuǒshàn zhàogùzhe
safe sex 安全性交 ānquánxìng jiāo
II N 保险箱 bǎoxiǎnxiāng, 保险柜 bǎoxiǎngguì

safe-deposit box N（银行）保险箱 (yínháng) bǎoxiǎn xiāng

safeguard I N 保护（性）措施 bǎohù (xìng) cuòshī, 安全措施 ānquán cuòshī II v 保护 bǎohù, 保卫 bǎowèi

safekeeping N 妥善保管 tuǒshàn bǎoguǎn
for safekeeping 以便妥善保管 yǐbiàn tuǒshàn bǎoguǎn

safety N 安全 ānquán ■ More and more people are concerned about safety on the subway. 越来越多的人关注地铁的安全。Yuèláiyuè duō de rén guānzhù dìtiě de ānquán.
Safety first. 安全第一。Ānquán dìyī.
safety belt 安全带 ānquándài

safety pin 别针 biézhēn
safety valve 安全阀 ānquánfá

sag v 1 [肌肉+] 下垂 [jīròu+] xiàchuí, 下陷 xiàxiàn 2 [价格+] 下跌 [jiàgé+] xiàdiē, 下降 xiàjiàng

saga N 长篇家族史 chángpiān jiāzú shǐ [M. WD 篇 piān/本 běn]

sage I N 圣人 shèngrén, 哲人 zhérén II ADJ 贤明的 xiánmíng de, 明智的 míngzhì de

Sagittarius N 人马星座 rénmǎ xīngzuò, 人马宫 rénmǎ gōng

said I v See say II ADJ 上述的 shàngshù de

sail I N 1 帆 fān [M. WD 张 zhāng] 2 起航 qǐháng ■ The ship set sail at noon and headed into the open sea. 船儿中午扬帆，向大海驶去。Chuán'r zhōngwǔ yángfān, xiàng dàhǎi shǐqu. II v 航行 hángxíng

sailboat N 帆船 fānchuán [M. WD 艘 sōu]

sailing N 1 帆船运动 fānchuán yùndòng 2 启程时间 qǐchéng shíjiān, 航班 hángbān
smooth sailing 一帆风顺 yì fān fēng shùn

sailor N 水手 shuǐshǒu, 海员 hǎiyuán

saint N 1 圣人 shèngrén
Saint Peter 圣徒彼得 shèngtú Bǐdé, 圣彼得 shèng Bǐdé
2 道德高尚的人 dàodé gāoshàng de rén, 仁慈的人 réncí de rén, 大好人 dà hǎorén

sake N (for the sake of sb/sth) 为了某人／某事 wèile mǒurén/mǒushì

salable, saleable ADJ 可以出售的 kěyǐ chūshòu de

salad N 凉拌菜沙律 liángbàncài shālǜ, 色拉 sèlā
salad bar 凉拌菜自助柜 liángbàncài zìzhùguì
salad dressing 凉拌菜调味酱 liángbàncài tiáowèi jiàng

salami N 萨拉米香肠 Sàlā mǐ xiāngcháng

salaried ADJ 领薪金的 lǐng xīnjīn de

salary N 工资 gōngzī, 薪水 xīnshui

sale N 1 卖 mài, 出售 chūshòu ■ Sale of alcohol to underage people is illegal. 向未成年人出售酒类是非法的。Xiàng wèichéngnián rén chūshòu jiǔlèi shì fēifǎ de. **2** 减价出售 jiǎnjià chūshòu
clearance sale 清仓大拍卖 qīngcāng dà pāimài
for sale 供出售 gòngchūshòu
going-out-of-business sale 关门大拍卖 guānmén dà pāimài
on sale ① 在出售 zài chūshòu, 在上市 zài shàngshì ② 在减价出售 zài jiǎnjià chūshòu ■ All the books in the store are on sale, with a discount of up to 50% on the marked items. 店里所有的书都减价出售，最多的在标价上打对折。Diàn lǐ suǒyǒu de shū dōu jiǎnjià chūshòu, zuìduō de zài biāojiàshang dǎ duìzhé.

sales N 销售额量 xiāoshòu'é liàng ■ Sales were down last month. 上个月销售量减少了。Shàng ge yuè xiāoshòuliàng jiǎnshǎo le.

sales clerk 售货员 shòuhuòyuán

sales representative 销售代表 xiāoshòu dàibiǎo

sales slip (receipt) 购物发票 gòuwù fāpiào

sales tax 销售税 xiāoshòushuì

salesperson N 推销员 tuīxiāoyuán, 售货员 shòuhuòyuán

salience N 显著 xiǎnzhe, 明显 míngxiǎn

salient ADJ 显著的 xiǎnzhe de, 明显的 míngxiǎn de

saline I ADJ（含）盐的（hán）yán de II N 生理盐水 shēnglǐ yánshuǐ

saliva N 口水 kǒushuǐ, 唾沫 tuòmò

salivate V 流口水 liú kǒushuǐ, 垂涎（三尺）chuíxián (sānchǐ)

sallow ADJ 灰黄色的 huīhuáng sè de

salmon N 鲑鱼 guīyú [M. WD 条 tiáo], 大马哈鱼 dàmǎhǎyú [M. WD 条 tiáo]

salon N 院 yuàn, 厅 tīng, 店 diàn

beauty salon 美容厅 měiróngtīng

bridal salon 婚纱店 hūnshādiàn

hairdressing salon 美发厅 měi fā tīng, 发廊 fàláng

saloon N 1 客厅 kètīng 2 酒吧 jiǔbā

salsa N 1 辣沙司 là shāsī 2 萨尔萨舞（曲）Sà'ěrsà wǔ (qū)

salt N 盐 yán ■ The dish needs a little bit of salt. 这个菜要放一点儿盐。Zhè ge cài yào fàng yì diǎnr yán.

salt fish 咸鱼 xián yú

salt pork 腌肉 yān ròu

salt shaker 盐瓶 yánpíng

the salt of the earth 平凡而诚实的好人 píngfán ér chéngshí de hǎorén, 社会中坚力量 shèhuì zhōngjiān lìliàng

to take sth with a pinch of salt 不完全相信某事 bù wánquán xiāngxìn mǒushì

saltwater N 海水 hǎishuǐ, 咸水 xiánshuǐ

salty ADJ 1 咸（的）xián（de）2 粗俗的 cūsú de

salutation N 称呼（语）chēnghu (yǔ)

salute I V 1 向…敬礼 xiàng...jìnglǐ, 行军礼 xíngjūn lǐ 2 赞扬 zànyáng II N 敬礼 jìnglǐ, 致敬 zhìjìng

salvage I V 1 抢救 qiǎngjiù 2 挽救 wǎnjiù, 挽回 wǎnhuí II N 1 抢救 qiǎngjiù, 救援 jiùyuán 2 抢救出来的东西 qiǎngjiù chūlái de dōngxi

salvation N（基督教）拯救（Jīdūjiào）zhěngjiù, 挽救 wǎnjiù

Salvation Army（基督教）救世军（Jīdūjiào）Jiùshìjūn

salve I N 1 宽慰 kuānwèi, 缓解 huǎnjiě 2（解痛）软膏（jiětòng）ruǎngāo II V (to salve one's conscience) 使良心得到宽慰 shǐ liángxīn dédào kuānwèi

salvo N（大炮）齐放（dàpào）qífàng

Samaritan N 助人为乐者 zhù rén wéi lè zhě

same I ADJ 相同的 xiāngtóng de, 同样的 tóngyàng de ■ I moved to another part of town but I have the same phone number. 我搬到城里另一个区了，但是电话号码没有变。Wǒ bāndao chénglǐ lìng yí ge qū le, dànshì diànhuà hàomǎ méiyǒu biàn.

at the same time 同时 tóngshí

same difference 都一样 dōu yíyàng ■ "Would you like a smoked salmon sandwich or a bacon and egg sandwich?" "Same difference." "您要吃薰鲑鱼三明治，还是咸肉鸡蛋三明治？" "都一样。" "Nín yào chī xūn guīyú sānmíngzhì, háishì xiánròu jīdàn sānmíngzhì?" "Dōu yí yàng."

II PRON 同样的人／物 tóngyàng de rén/wù

sameness N 相同性 xiāngtóngxìng, 千篇一律 qiānpiān yílǜ

sample I N 样品 yàngpǐn II V 试 shì, 试用 shìyòng

random sample 抽样 chōuyàng ■ The survey covers a random sample of 1,000 women between 25 and 45. 这项调查涉及一千名年龄在二十五到四十五之间的妇女。Zhè xiàng diàochá shèjí yì qiān míng niánlíng zài èrshíwǔ dào sìshíwǔ zhījiān de fùnǚ.

sampling N 抽样调查 chōuyàng diàochá

samurai N（古代日本的）武士（gǔdài Rìběn de）wǔshì

sanatorium, sanitorium N 疗养院 liáoyǎngyuàn

sanctify V 1 使…神圣化 shǐ...shénshèng huà 2 认可 rènkě

sanctimonious ADJ 假装高尚的 jiǎzhuāng gāoshàng de, 冠冕堂皇的 guānmiǎn tánghuáng de

sanction I N (sanctions) 批准 pīzhǔn, 认可 rènkě

to break sanctions 打破制裁 dǎpò zhìcái

to impose sanctions on 对…实施制裁 duì... shíshī zhìcái

to lift sanctions 取消制裁 qǔxiāo zhìcái

II V 1 制裁 zhìcái 2 批准 pīzhǔn, 许可 xǔkě

sanctity N 神圣（性）shénshèng (xìng)

sanctuary N 1 避难所 bìnànsuǒ, 庇护所 bìhùsuǒ

to give sanctuary to 提供避难（所）tígōng bìnàn (suǒ)

to seek sanctuary 寻求庇护 xúnqiú bìhù

2（动物）保护区（dòngwù）bǎohùqū

wildlife sanctuary 野生动物保护区 yěshēng dòngwù bǎohùqū

sanctum N（机）密室（jī）mìshì

sand I N 沙 shā

sand dune 沙丘 shāqiū

II V 磨光 móguāng

sandal N 凉鞋 liángxié [M. WD 只 zhī/双 shuāng]

sandbag I N 沙包 shābāo, 沙袋 shādài II V 用沙包堵 yòng shābāo dǔ

sandbank N 沙坝 shābà

sandbox N 沙箱 shāxiāng, 沙坑 shākēng

sandcastle N（在海滩堆成的）沙堡（zài hǎitān duī chéng de）shābǎo

sandpaper I N **1** 砂纸 shāzhǐ, 沙皮纸 shāpí zhǐ
II v 用砂纸打磨 yòng shāzhǐ dǎmó
sandstone N 砂岩 shāyán
sandstorm N 沙 (尘) 暴 shā (chén) bào
sandwich I N **1** 夹心面包 jiāxīn miànbāo, 三明治
sānmíngzhì
club sandwich 大三明治 dà sānmíngzhì
II v (be sandwiched between) 被夹在…中间 bèi
jiā zài...zhōngjiān
sandy ADJ **1** 被沙覆盖的 bèi shā fùgài de **2** 浅黄
色的 qiǎnhuángsè de
sane ADJ 头脑清醒的 tóunǎo qīngxǐng de, 明智
的 míngzhì de
sang See **sing**
sanguine ADJ 乐观的 lèguān de, 充满自信的
chōngmǎn zìxìn de
sanitary ADJ (清洁) 卫生的 (qīngjié) wèishēng
de, 有利健康的 yǒulì jiànkāng de
sanitary napkin 卫生巾 wèishēngjīn
sanitation N 公共卫生 gōnggòng wèishēng
sanitation worker 拉圾工 lājī gōng
sanitize v **1** 净化 [+语言] jìnghuà [+yǔyán] **2** 对…
消毒 duì...xiāodú
sanity N 明智 míngzhì, 理智 lǐzhì
sank See **sink**
Santa Claus N 圣诞老人 Shèngdàn Lǎorén
sap I N (植物的) 液 (zhíwù de) yè, 汁 zhī **II** v 使
…伤元气 shǐ...shāng yuánqì, 消耗 xiāohào
sapling N 幼树 yòushù [M. WD 棵 kē]
sapphire N 蓝宝石 lánbǎoshí [M. WD 块 kuài], 蓝
宝石色 lánbǎoshí sè
sappy ADJ **1** 多液的 [+植物] duō yè de [+zhíwù]
2 多情得傻乎乎的 duōqíng de shǎhūhū de
sarcasm N 挖苦 wāku, 刻薄的讽刺 kèbóde
fēngcì
sarcastic ADJ 挖苦的 wāku de, 刻薄讽刺的 kèbó
fēngcì de
sardine N (罐头) 沙丁鱼 (guàntou) shādīngyú
be packed like sardines 拥挤不堪 yōngjǐ bùkān
sardonic ADJ 嘲讽的 cháofěng de
sari N (印度女子穿的) 莎丽服 (Yìndù nǚzǐ chuān
de) shālìfú [M. WD 件 jiàn]
SASE (= self-addressed stamped envelope) AB-
BREV (写好回信地址贴有邮票的) 回信信封 (xiě
hǎo huíxìn dìzhǐ tiē yǒu yóupiào de) huíxìn
xìnfēng
sash N **1** 宽腰带 kuān yāodài [M. WD 条 tiáo] **2** 绶
带 shòudài [M. WD 条 tiáo]
sass N, v 对…粗鲁无理 duì...cūlǔ wúlǐ
sassy ADJ 粗鲁无礼的 cūlǔ wúlǐ de
sat See **sit**
Satan N 魔鬼 móguǐ, 撒旦 Sādàn
satanic ADJ **1** 崇拜魔鬼的 chóngbài móguǐ de
2 恶魔般的 èmó bān de, 邪恶的 xié'è de
Satanism N 魔鬼崇拜 móguǐ chóngbài

satellite N 卫星 wèixīng
satellite dish 卫星电视碟形天线 wèixīng diànshì diéxíng tiānxìng
satellite television 卫星电视 wèixīng diànshì,
卫视 wèi shì
satin N 缎 (子) duàn (zi)
satiny ADJ 光滑柔软的 guānghuá róuruǎn de, 绸
缎似的 chóuduàn shìde
satire N 讽刺 (作品) fěngcì (zuòpǐn)
satirist N 讽刺作家 fěngcì zuòjiā
satirize v 讽刺 fěngcì
satisfaction N 满意 mǎnyì
satisfactory ADJ 令人满意的 lìngrén mǎnyì de
satisfied ADJ (感到) 满意的 (gǎndào) mǎnyìde
a satisified customer 满意的顾客 mǎnyì de gùkè
satisfy v **1** 使…满意 shǐ...mǎnyì ■ Nothing satis-
fies him—he's always grumbling. 没有什么东西
能使他满意—他一天到晚抱怨。Méiyǒu shénme
dōngxī néng shǐ tā mǎnyì—tā yì tiān dào wǎn
bàoyuàn. **2** 使…满足 shǐ...mǎnzú ■ If my
answers can't satisfy your curiosity, try to get
more information on the Internet. 如果我的回答
不能满足你的好奇心，试试在因特网上获取更
多的信息。Rúguǒ wǒ de huídá bù néng mǎnzú
nǐde hàoqíxīn, shìshi zài Yīntèwǎng shang huòqǔ
gèngduō de xìnxī.
satisfying ADJ 令人满意的 lìngrén mǎnyì de
saturate v **1** (使…) 浸湿 (shǐ...) jìnshī **2** (使…)
充满 (shǐ...) chōngmǎn, 饱和 bǎohé
saturated ADJ **1** 浸透了的 jìntòu le de **2** 饱和的
bǎohé de
saturated fat 饱和脂肪 bǎohézhīfáng
saturation N **1** 浸透 jìntòu **2** 饱和 bǎohé
saturation advertising 密集广告 mìjí guǎnggào
Saturday N 星期六 xīngqīliù
Saturn N 土星 Tǔxīng
sauce N 酱 jiàng, 调味汁 tiáowèizhī, 沙士 shāshì
tomato sauce 番茄酱 fānqiéjiàng
saucepan N (有柄) 平底锅 (yǒu bǐng) píngdǐguō
saucer N 茶托 chátuō, 茶碟 chádié
saucy ADJ 色情的 sèqíng de, 无礼的 wúlǐ de, 有
趣的 yǒuqù de
sauna N **1** 蒸气浴 zhēngqìyù, 桑那浴 sāngnàyù
2 蒸气浴室 zhēngqì yùshì, 桑那浴室 sāngnà
yùshì
saunter N, v 慢慢踱步 mànmàn duóbù, 慢慢地走
mànmàn de zǒu
sausage N 香肠 xiāngcháng
sauté v 快炒 [+素菜] kuài chǎo [+sùcài]
savage I ADJ 野蛮的 yěmán de **II** N 野蛮人
yěmánrén
savagery N 野蛮 (性) yěmán (xìng)
save I v **1** (拯) 救 (zhěng) jiù **2** 存 (钱) cún
(qián), 储蓄 chǔxù ■ I'm trying to save up for a
holiday in China. 我在为到中国去度假存钱。Wǒ zài

ΒΑΝΜΑΣΚΑ

wèi dào Zhōngguóquó dùjià cúnqián. **3** 省 shěng, 节
省 jiéshěng ■ *Walking to work saves me money
on gasoline.* 步行去上班为我省下汽油钱。Bùxíngqu
shàngbān wèi wǒ shěngxia qìyóu qián.

A penny saved is a penny earned. 省下一分钱,
就是多赚一分钱。Shěngxia yì fēn qián, jiù shì
duō zhuàn yì fēn qián.

4 (电脑) 存盘 (diànnǎo) cún pán, 储存 chǔcún
to save face 保全面子 bǎoquán miànzi
II N (守门员) 救球 (shǒuményuán) jiù qiú
III PREP 除了 chúle

saver N 节省的方法／装置 jiéshěng de fāngfǎ/
zhuāngzhì

savings N **1** 储蓄 chǔxù, 存款 cúnkuǎn **2** 省下的
钱 shěngxia de qián ■ *You can have 10% savings if you pay cash.* 你如果付现金, 可以省百分之
十的钱。Nǐ rúguǒ fù xiànjīn, kěyǐ shěng bǎifēnzhī
shí de qián.

savings account 储蓄账户 chǔxù zhànghù
savings bank 储蓄银行 chǔxù yínháng

savior N 救世主 Jiùshìzhǔ, 救星 jiùxīng

savor N **1** 好味道 hǎo wèidao **2** [生活的+] 乐趣
[shēnghuó+] de lèqù

savory ADJ 美味的 měiwèi de, 鲜美的 xiānměi
de **II** N 香薄荷 xiāng bòhe

savvy **I** N (丰富的) 知识 (fēngfù de) zhīshi
II ADJ 知识丰富的 zhīshífēngfù de

saw¹ V See see

saw² **I** N 锯 (子) jù (zi) [M. WD 把 bǎ] **II** V (PT
sawed, PP **sawn, sawed**) (用锯子) 锯 (yòng
jùzi) jù

sawdust N (锯) 木屑 (jù) mù xiè

sawmill N 锯木厂 jùmùchǎng [M. WD 家 jiā]

saxophone N 萨克斯管 sàkèsīguǎn

say **I** V (PT & PP **said**) **1** 说 shuō ■ *Confucius says:
"Human beings are all similar in nature while they
are widely different in practices and customs."* 孔
夫子说: "性相近也, 习相远也。" Kǒngfūzǐ shuō:
"Xìng xiàng jìn yě, xí xiāng yuǎn yě."

they say 据说 jùshuō

that is to say 也就是说 yě jiù shì shuō ■ *China
is the most populous country in the world; that is
to say Chinese is the most popular language.* 中国
是世界上人口最多的国家, 也就是说中国话是使用
者最多的语言。Zhōngguó shì shìjièshang rénkǒu
zuìduō de guójiā, yě jiù shì shuō Zhōngguóhuà
shì shǐyòng zhě zuìduō de yǔyán.

having said that 尽管如此 jǐnguǎn rúcǐ, 不过
búguò ■ *The boss is very strict; having said that,
he is quite fair.* 这个老板很严格, 尽管如此, 他还
是公正的。Zhè ge lǎobǎn hěn yángé, jǐnguǎn rúcǐ,
tā hái shì gōngzhèng de.

2 说明 shuōmíng, 表达 biǎodá **II** N 说话的权利
shuōhuà de quánlì, 发言权 fāyánquán

saying N 俗话 súhuà [M. WD 句 jù]

scab N **1** 破坏罢工的人 pòhuài bàgōng de rén,
工贼 gōngzéi **2** (伤) 痂 (shāng) jiā

scads N 大量 dàliàng, 大批 dàpī

scaffold N **1** 脚手架 jiǎoshǒujià **2** 升降吊架
shēngjiàng diàojià, 吊篮 diào lán **3** 绞刑架
jiǎoxíng jià

scaffolding N 搭脚手架的材料 dā jiǎoshǒujià de
cáiliào

scald **I** V **1** 烫伤 tàngshāng **2** 把…加热到接近
沸点 bǎ…jiārè dào jiējìn fèidiǎn **II** N 烫伤
tàngshāng

scalding ADJ 滚烫的 gǔntàng de

scale¹ **I** N **1** 规模 guīmó **2** 级别 jíbié, 等级 děngjí
■ *"On a scale from 1 to 10, how would you rate
this computer game?"* "从一到十, 你给这个电脑
游戏几分?" "Cóng yī dào shí, nǐ gěi zhè ge
diànnǎo yóuxì jǐ fēn?" **II** V (to scale sth back/down)
缩小某事的规模 suōxiǎo mǒushì de guīmó

scale² **I** N (鱼) 鳞 (yú) lín **II** V 刮鱼鳞 guāyúlín

scale³ V 攀登 (山峰) pāndēng (shānfēng)

scales N 秤 chèng ■ *She bought bathroom scales
to monitor her weight.* 她为了监督自己的体重,
买了一个体重秤。Tā wèile jiāndū zìjǐ de tǐzhòng,
mǎi le yí ge tǐzhòng chèng.

scallop N 扇贝 shànbèi

scalp N 头皮 tóupí **II** V 倒卖 dǎomài

scalpel N 手术刀 shǒushùdāo [M. WD 把 bǎ], 解刨
刀 jiě bàodāo [M. WD 把 bǎ]

scaly ADJ 有鳞的 yǒu lín de

scam N 骗局 piànjú, 诈骗 (行为) zhàpiàn (xíngwéi)

scamper V 跳跳蹦蹦 tiào tiào bèng bèng

scan **I** V **1** 浏览 [+报纸标题] liúlǎn [+bàozhǐ biāotí]
2 迅速地查找 xùnsù de cházhǎo **3** [用扫描器+]
扫描 [yòng sǎomiáoqì+] sǎomiáo **II** N 扫描检
查 sǎomiáo jiǎnchá
brain scan 大脑扫描 dànǎo sǎomiáo
ultrasound scan 超声波扫描 (检查)
chāoshēngbō sǎomiáo (jiǎnchá)

scandal N 丑闻 chǒuwén

scandalize V 使…震惊 shǐ…zhènjīng, 引起…的公
愤 yǐnqǐ…de gōngfèn

scandalous ADJ 丑恶无耻的 chǒu'è wúchǐ de, 令
人发指的 lìngrén fàzhǐ de

scanner N 扫描装置 sǎomiáo zhuāngzhì [M. WD
台 tái], 扫描仪 sǎomiáo yí [M. WD 台 tái]

scant ADJ 不足的 bùzú de, 少量的 shǎoliàng de

scapegoat N 替罪羊 tìzuìyáng

scar **I** N 伤疤 shāngbā, 疤痕 bāhén **II** V (be
scarred with) 留下…的伤疤 liúxia…de shāngbā

scarce ADJ 稀有的 xīyǒu de, 缺乏的 quēfá de

scarcely ADV **1** 几乎不 jīhūbù, 几乎没有 jīhū
méiyǒu **2** 刚刚 gānggāng

scarcity N 短缺 duǎnquē, 不足 bùzú

scare **I** V 惊吓 jīngxià ■ *I was scared driving home*

last night because of all the lightning and thundering. 我昨天夜里开车回家一路上闪电雷鸣，把我吓坏了。Wǒ zuótiān yèlǐ kāichē huíjiā yílùshang shǎndiàn léimíng, bǎ wǒ xiàhuai le. **II N** 惊吓 jīngxià ■ *What a scare you gave me!* 你把我吓了一跳！Nǐ bǎ wǒ xiàle yí tiào!

scarecrow N 稻草人 dàocǎorén

scarf N 围巾 wéijīn [**M. WD** 条 tiáo], 头巾 tóujīn [**M. WD** 条 tiáo]

scarlet ADJ, N 猩红色 xīnghóngsè, 绯红色 fēihóng sè

scary ADJ 吓人的 xiàrén de, 恐怖的 kǒngbù de

scathing ADJ 极其严厉的 jíqí yánlì de, 尖刻的 jiānkè de

scatter V 1 散开 sànkai 2 撒 sā

scatterbrained ADJ 心不在焉的 xīnbúzàiyān de, 疏忽的 shūhu de

scavenge V 1 [动物+] 吃别的动物吃剩的东西 [dòngwù+] chī biéde dòngwù chī shèng de dōngxi, 吃腐肉 chī fǔròu 2 [人+] 在垃圾中寻食 [rén+] zài lājī zhōng xún shí

scenario N 1 可能发生的情况 kěnéng fāshēng de qíngkuàng

the worst scenario 最坏的情况 zuì huài de qíngkuàng

2（电影）脚本 (diànyǐng) jiǎoběn

scene N 1（戏剧的）场 (xìjù de) chǎng, 场景 chǎngjǐng ■ *This war movie has some heartbreaking scenes.* 这部战争影片有几个令人心碎的场景。Zhè bù zhànzhēng yǐngpiàn yǒu jǐ ge lìng rén xīn suì de chǎngjǐng. 2 景色 jǐngsè ■ *After their son's birthday party, the sitting room was a scene of disorder.* 儿子的生日聚会后，客厅里一片凌乱。Érzi de shēngri jùhuì hòu, kètīng lǐ yí piàn língluàn. 3 现场 xiànchǎng 4 (to make a scene) 大吵大闹 dà chǎo dà nào, 大发脾气 dà fā píqi

behind the scenes 幕后 mùhòu ■ *Diplomats work feverishly behind the scenes to avoid a war.* 外交官在幕后紧张活动，以避免一场战争。Wàijiāoguān zài mùhòu jǐnzhāng huódòng, yǐ bìmiǎn yì cháng zhànzhēng.

scenery N 1 自然景色 zìrán jǐngsè 2（舞台）布景 (wǔtái) bùjǐng

scenic ADJ 景色优美的 jǐngsè yōuměi de

scent I N 1 气味 qìwèi, 气息 qìxī

to throw sb off the scent 使某人失去线索 shǐ mǒurén shīqù xiànsuǒ

2 香味 xiāngwèi, 芳香 fāngxiāng **II V** 1 散布香味 sànbù xiāngwèi 2 [动物+] 嗅出 [dòngwù+] xiù chū

scented ADJ 有香味的 yǒu xiāngwèi de

scepter N（国王／女王的）权杖 (guówáng/ nǚwáng de) quánzhàng

schedule I N 1（火车/汽车）时刻表 (huǒchē/ qìchē) shíkèbiǎo 2（工作）日程表 (gōngzuò)

rìchéng biǎo

ahead of schedule 提前 tíqián

II V 安排在（某一时间）ānpái zài (mǒu yìshíjiān)

scheduled flight 定期航班 dìngqī hángbān

scheme I N 1 方案 fāng'àn, 计划 jìhuà 2 诡计 guǐjì, 阴谋 yīnmóu ■ *He always seems to have a new scheme to make money.* 他好像总有赚钱的诡计。Tā hǎoxiàng zǒng yǒu zhuànqián de guǐjì. **II V** 策划 cèhuà, 阴谋 yīnmóu

schism N 分裂 fēnliè

schizophrenia N 精神分裂症 jīngshén fēnlièzhèng

schmaltzy ADJ 伤感的 [+音乐] shānggǎn de [+yīnyuè]

schmooze V 闲聊 xiánliáo, 敷衍 fūyan

schmuck N 笨蛋 bèndàn

scholar N 学者 xuézhě [**M. WD** 位 wèi]

scholarly ADJ 学术的 xuéshù de

scholarship N 1 奖学金 jiǎngxuéjīn [**M. WD** 笔 bǐ] 2 学术研究 xuéshù yánjiū, 学问 xuéwèn

scholastic ADJ 教学的 jiàoxué de, 学术的 xuéshù de

school N 1 [中、小+] 学校 [zhōng、 xiǎo+] xuéxiào

elementary school/primary school 小学 xiǎoxué

high school 中学 zhōngxué

junior high school 初级中学 chūjí zhōngxué, 初中 chūzhōng

senior high school 高级中学 gāojí zhōngxué, 高中 gāozhōng

after school 课外 kèwài

to be in school 在学校（上课）zài xuéxiào

■ *She checked and replied to e-mails while her children were in school.* 孩子在学校里的时候，她检查、回答电子邮件。Háizi zài xuéxiào lǐ de shíhou, tā jiǎnchá、 huídá diànzǐ yóujiàn.

to go to school 上学 shàngxué

2 [大学+] 院、系 [dàxué+] yuàn、 xì ■ *He has applied to Harvard School of Medicine.* 他已经在哈佛大学医学院报名了。Tā yǐjīng zài Hāfó dàxué Yīxuéyuàn bàomíng le.

graduate school 研究生院 yánjiūshēng yuàn

3（鱼）群 qún ■ *Eugene could see schools of fish swimming in the clear river.* 尤金可以看到一群群鱼儿在清澈的河水中游者。Yóujīn kěyǐ kàndao yì qún qún yúr zài qīngchè de héshuǐ zhōng yóuzhe. **II V** 训练 xùnliàn, 教育 jiàoyù

schooling N 学校教育 xuéxiào jiàoyù

schooner N 1 双桅帆船 shuāng wéi fānchuán 2 大啤酒杯 dà píjiǔ bēi

science N 1 科学 kēxué

science fiction See **sci-fi**

pure science 纯科学 chún kēxué

social science 社会科学 shèhuì kēxué

2 自然科学 zìrán kēxué, 理科 lǐkē ■ *This univer-*

sity has an excellent college of arts and science. 这所大学拥有一个极好的文理学院。Zhè suǒ dàxué yōngyǒu yí ge jí hǎo de wénlǐ xuéyuàn.

science park 科学园区 kēxué yuánqū, 新科技开发区 xīn kējì kāifāqū

applied science 应用科学 yìngyòng kēxué

natural science 自然科学 zìrán kēxué

scientific ADJ 科学的 kēxué de ■ *That theory does not sound so scientific to me.* 这个理论我听起来不是很科学。Zhè ge lǐlùn wǒ tīngqilai bú shì hěn kēxué.

scientist N 科学家 kēxuéjiā, 科学工作者 kēxué gōngzuòzhě

scientology N 科学论 (教会) kēxué lùn (jiàohuì)

sci-fi (= science fiction) ABBREV 科学幻想小说 kēxué huànxiǎng xiǎoshuō

scintillating ADJ 闪烁发光的 shǎnshuò fāguāng de

scissors N 剪刀 jiǎndāo

scoff v 嘲笑 cháoxiào

scold v 训斥 xùnchì, 斥责 chìzé

scone N 司康烤饼 sī kāng kǎobǐng

scoop I N 1 (冰淇淋) 勺 (bīngqílín) sháo, 球形勺 qiúxíng sháo 2 独家抢先报导 dújiā qiǎngxiān bàodǎo II v 1 用勺铲起 yòng sháo chǎn qǐ 2 抢先报导 qiǎngxiān bàodǎo

scooter I N 1 小型摩托车 xiǎoxíng mótuō chē 2 踏板车 tàbǎn chē

scope I N 1 范围 fànwéi

to extend the scope of 扩大…的范围 kuòdà… de fànwéi

2 (发挥才能的) 机会 (fāhuī cáinéng de) jīhuì

scope for creativity 发挥创造性的机会 fāhuī chuàngzàoxìng de jīhuì

II v (to scope out) 了解 liǎojiě, 查明 chámíng

scorch I v 1 (使…) 烤焦 (shǐ…) kǎojiāo 2 烫伤 [+人] tàngshāng [+rén] II N 烤焦 kǎojiāo, 枯萎 kūwěi

scorcher N 大热天 dà rètiān

scorching ADJ 太阳火辣辣的 tàiyáng huǒlàlà de, 极热的 jí rè de

score I N 1 比分 bǐfēn, 得分 défēn

tō keep score 记分 jìfēn

to settle a score 报仇 bàochóu, 算旧账 suàn jiùzhàng

2 分数 fēnshù 3 乐谱 yuèpǔ 4 二十 èrshí

scores of 许多 xǔduō, 大量 dàliàng

II v 1 得分 défēn

to score ponts 得分 défēn, 赢得好感 yíngdé hǎogǎn

2 获得成功 huòdé chénggōng

scoreboard N 记分牌 jìfēnpái

scorecard N 记分卡 jìfēn kǎ [M. WD 张 zhāng]

scorer N 1 (体育比赛的) 记分员 (tǐyù bǐsài de) jìfēnyuán 2 得分的运动员 défēn de yùndòngyuán

scorn N, v 鄙视 bǐshì, 蔑视 mièshì

scorpion N 蝎子 xiēzi

Scotch N (苏格兰) 威士忌酒 (Sūgélán) wēishìjì jiǔ

scotch v 制止 zhìzhǐ, 阻止 zǔzhǐ

scot-free ADV (to get off scot-free) 逃脱惩罚 táotuō chéngfá

Scotland N 苏格兰 Sūgélán

Scotsman N 苏格兰 (男) 人 Sūgélán (nán) rén

Scotswoman N 苏格兰 (女) 人 Sūgélán (nǚ) rén

Scottish ADJ 苏格兰的 Sūgélán de, 苏格兰人的 Sūgélán rén de

scoundrel N 恶棍 ègùn, 无赖 wúlài

scour v 1 擦亮 [+餐具] cāliàng [+cānjù] 2 彻底搜查 [+地方] chèdǐ sōuchá [+dìfang]

scourge I N 大祸害 dàhuòhai, 灾星 zāixīng II v 使…遭受巨大灾难 shǐ…zāoshòu jùdà zāinàn

scout I N 侦察兵 zhēnchábīng 2 童子军 tóngzǐjūn

Boy Scouts 男童子军 nán tóngzǐjūn

Girl Scouts 女童子军 nǚ tóngzǐjūn

talent scout 物色新秀者 wùsè xīnxiù zhě

II v 1 侦察 zhēnchá

to scout for 物色新秀 wùsè xīnxiù

2 寻找 xúnzhǎo

scowl I N 愤怒的表情 fènnù de biǎoqíng II v 愤怒地看 fènnù de kàn, 怒视 nùshì

Scrabble N 纵横拼字游戏 zònghéng pīnzì yóuxì

scrabble v 翻找 fānzhǎo

scraggly ADJ 凌乱的 língluàn de, 散乱的 sànluàn de

scram v 逃离 táo lí, 跑开 pǎokāi

scramble I v 1 争夺 zhēngduó, 争抢 zhēngqiǎng

to scramble for front seats 争夺前排的座位 zhēngduó qiánpái de zuòwèi

2 仓促行动 cāngcù xíngdòng

to scramble to safety 仓促逃离到安全地带 cāngcù táolí dào ānquán dìdài

scrambled egg 炒蛋 chǎodàn

3 (美式橄榄球) 持球抢跑 (Měishì gǎnlǎnqiú) chí qiú qiǎng pǎo

II N 1 争夺 zhēngduó 2 乱忙 luànmáng

scrap I N 1 废料 fèiliào, 废品 fèipǐn

scrap metal 金属废料 jīnshǔ fèiliào

2 吃剩的食物 chī shèng de shíwù

table scraps 剩菜 shèngcài

3 小纸片 xiǎo zhǐpiàn, 碎布片 suìbù piàn

II v 1 把…当废料处理 bǎ…dāng fèiliào chǔlǐ

2 放弃 fàngqì 3 争吵 zhēngchǎo

scrapbook N 剪贴簿 jiǎntiēbù [M. WD 本 běn]

scrape I v 1 刮 guā

to scrape sth away 把某物刮掉 bǎ mǒuwù guādiào

to scrape sth clean 把某物刮干净 bǎ mǒuwù guā gānjìng

2 摩擦 mócā, 擦伤 cāshāng

to scrape by 勉强度日 miǎnqiǎng dùrì

to scrape through 勉强通过 miǎnqiǎng tōngguò

3 [金属+] 发出刮擦声 [jīnshǔ+] fāchū guācāshēng **II** **N 1** 擦伤 cāshāng **2** 困境 kùnjìng

scraper N 刮漆刀 guāqīdāo [M. WD 把 bǎ]

scrappy ADJ 敢作敢为的 gǎn zuò gǎn wèi de

scratch **I** v **1** 搔 [+皮肤] sāo [+pífū]

to scratch the surface 触及（问题的）表面 chùjí (wèntí de) biǎomiàn

to scratch one's head 大伤脑筋 dà shāng nǎojīn

2 [猫+] 抓 [māo+] zhuā, 划伤 huá shāng **II** N 刮痕 guāhén, 划痕 huàhén

from scratch 从零开始 cóng líng kāishǐ

scratch paper 单面草稿纸 dānmiàn cǎogǎozhǐ

scratchy ADJ **1** 扎人的 zhārén de **2** 低沉沙哑的 [+嗓音] dīchén shǎyǎ de [+sǎngyīn] **3** 疼痛的 [+喉咙] téngtòng de [+hóulóng]

scrawl **I** v 潦草地写 liǎocǎo de xiě **II** N 潦草写成的东西 liǎocǎo xiě chéng de dōngxi, 潦草的笔迹 liǎocǎo de bǐjì

scrawny ADJ 瘦弱的 shòuruò de

scream **I** v **1** 尖叫 jiānjiào, 大声呼喊 dàshēng hūhǎn **II** N 尖叫声 jiānjiào shēng

be a scream 非常滑稽的人／事 fēicháng huájī de rén/shì

screech **I** v [车轮+] 发出刺耳声 [chēlún+] fāchū cì'ěr shēng,

to screech to a halt [汽车+] 突然刹车停下 [qìchē+] tūrán shāchē tíng xià **II** N（车轮的）刺耳声 (chēlún de) cì'ěr shēng

screen **I** N **1** 屏幕 píngmù

screen saver（计算机）屏幕保护程序 (jìsuànjī) píngmù bǎohù chéngxù

2 纱窗 shāchuāng ■ *Don't be surprised to find mosquitoes in the house—the screen door is full of holes.* 屋子里有蚊子不奇怪，纱窗全是洞。Wūzi lǐ yǒu wénzi bù qíguài, shāchuāng quán shì dòng. **3** 屏风 píngfēng **II** v **1** 检查 jiǎnchá, 审查 shěnchá

to be screened for breast cancer 作乳房癌检查 zuò rǔfáng ái jiǎnchá

2 隐蔽 yǐnbì, 遮蔽 zhēbì

screenplay N（电影／电视）剧本 (diànyǐng/diànshì) jùběn

screenwriter N（电影／电视）剧本作者 (diànyǐng/diànshì) jùběn zuòzhě

screw **I** N 螺丝钉 luósī dīng

to have a screw loose 头脑出了问题 tóunǎo chūle wèntí, 有点儿怪 yǒudiǎnr guài, 古怪 gǔguài ■ *He collects all sorts of junk—he must have a screw loose.* 他什么样的垃圾都收集—肯定头脑出了问题。Tā shénme yàng de lājī dōu shōují—kěndìng tóunǎo chūle wèntí.

II v **1** 用螺丝钉钉上 yòng luósī dīng dìngshang

2 拧上 nǐngshang, 拧紧 nǐngjǐn ■ *Don't forget to screw the lid back on the jar.* 别忘了把瓶盖子拧上。Bié wàngle bǎ píng gàizi nǐngshang.

to screw up 搞糟 gǎozāo ■ *I'm giving you an easy assignment, so don't screw it up.* 我给你一件容易的事做，所以别弄糟了。Wǒ gěi nǐ yí jiàn róngyì de shì zuò, suǒyǐ bié nòngzāo le.

screwball N 古怪的人 gǔguài de rén

screwball comedy 荒诞喜剧 huāngdàn xǐjù

screw-driver N 螺丝刀 luósīdāo

screwed up ADJ **1** 弄糟的 [+计划] nòngzāo de [+jìhuà] **2** 焦躁的 [+人] jiāozào de [+rén]

screwy ADJ 古怪的 gǔguài de, 荒谬的 huāngmiù de

scribble **I** v **1** 潦草的写 liǎocǎo de xiě **2** 乱涂乱画 luàn tú luàn huà **II** N 乱涂乱写 luàn tú luànxiě

script **I** N **1** 演讲稿 yǎnjiǎnggǎo **2** 电影剧本 diànyǐng jùběn **3** 笔迹 bǐjì, 手迹 shǒujì

to read from a script 照稿子念 zhào gǎozi niàn **II** v **1** 写 [+演讲稿／剧本] xiě [+yǎnjiǎnggǎo/jùběn] **2** 精心策划 jīngxīn cèhuà

scripted ADJ **1** 预先写好的 [+演讲] yùxiān xiě hǎo de [+yǎnjiǎng], 照稿宣读的 zhào gǎo xuāndú de **2** 刻意安排的 [+事件] kèyì ānpái de [+shìjiàn]

scriptural ADJ 圣书的 shèngshū de, 圣典的 shèngdiǎn de

scripture N **1** 基督教圣经 Jīdūjiào Shèngjīng **2**（宗教）经文 (zōngjiào) jīngwén, 圣书 shèngshū

scriptwriter N（电影／电视）剧作家 (diànyǐng/diànshì) jùzuòjiā

scroll **I** N 纸卷 zhǐ juàn, 卷轴 juànzhóu **II** v（在计算机显示器上）上下滚动 (zài jìsuànjī xiǎnshìqì shàng) shàngxià gǔndòng

scrooge N 守财奴 shǒucáinú, 吝啬鬼 lìnsèguǐ

scrotum N 阴囊 yīnnáng

scrounge v 索要 suǒyào, 索讨 suǒtǎo

scrub¹ v, N 擦洗 cāxǐ, 刷洗 shuāxǐ

scrub² N 矮树丛 ǎishùcóng, 灌木丛 guànmù cóng

scruffy ADJ 邋遢的 lātā de, 肮脏的 āngzāng de

scrumptious ADJ 美味的 měiwèi de

scrunch v 把…揉成一团 bǎ...róu chéng yì tuán

scruple N 顾忌 gùjì, 顾虑 gùlù

scrupulous ADJ **1** 诚实公正的 chéngshí gōngzhèng de, 讲良心道德的 jiǎng liángxīn dàodé de **2** 细微认真的 xìwēi rènzhēn de, 一丝不苟的 yìsī bùgǒu de

scrutinize v 仔细检查 zǐxì jiǎnchá, 细查 xìchá

scrutiny N 仔细检查 zǐxì jiǎnchá, 细查 xìchá

scuba-diving N 斯库巴潜泳 sīkùbā qiányǒng

scuff v 使…磨损 shǐ...mósǔn

scuffle v, N 扭打 niǔdǎ

sculptor N 雕塑家 diāosùjiā, 雕刻家 diāokèjiā

sculpture **I** N 雕塑 diāosù, 雕塑作品 diāosù zuòpǐn **II** v 雕塑 diāosù

sculptured ADJ 有雕塑装饰的 yǒu diāosù zhuāngshì de

scum N 1 浮渣 fúzhā 2 人渣 rén zhā, 人类渣滓 rénlèi zhāzǐ

scumbag N 人渣 rén zhā, 人类渣滓 rénlèi zhāzǐ

scurrilous ADJ 辱骂的 rǔmà de

scurry N, V 小步急跑 xiǎobù jí pǎo

scurvy N 坏血病 huàixuèbìng

scuttle V 1 破坏 pòhuài, 力阻 lìzǔ 2 小步疾行 xiǎobù jíxíng

scythe N 长柄大镰刀 cháng bǐng dàliándāo

sea N (大) 海 (dà) hǎi
sea level 海平面 hǎi píng miàn
sea plane 海上飞机 hǎi shàng fēijī

seabed N 海床 hǎichuáng, 海底 hǎidǐ

seafaring ADJ 航海的 hánghǎi de

seafood N 海鲜 hǎixiān

seagull N 海鸥 hǎi'ōu [M. WD 只 zhī]

seahorse N 海马 hǎimǎ [M. WD 只 zhī]

seal¹ N 海豹 hǎibào [M. WD 头 tóu]

seal² V 封闭 fēngbì ■ *Police sealed off the area after a shooting incident.* 发生枪击事件以后，警方封闭了这一地区。Fāshēng qiāngjī shìjiàn yǐhòu, jǐngfāng fēngbìle zhè yí dìqū.
to seal a deal 确保达成交易 quèbǎo dáchéng jiāoyì

seal³ N 印章 yìnzhāng, 图章 túzhāng

sealed ADJ 1 密封的 [+信封] mìfēng de [+xìnfēng] 2 保密的 [+文件] bǎomì de [+wénjiàn]

sealion N 海狮 hǎishī [M. WD 头 tóu]

seam N 1 缝 fèng, 线缝 xiànfèng 2 (煤) 矿层 (méi)kuàng céng

seaman N 海员 hǎiyuán

seamanship N 航海技能 hánghǎi jìnéng, 航海术 hánghǎishù

seamless ADJ 1 无缝的 wú fèng de 2 连贯的 liánguàn de

seamstress N 女裁缝 nǚ cáifeng, 女缝纫工 nǚ féngrèngōng

seamy ADJ 丑陋的 chǒulòu de
the seamy side 阴暗面 yīn'ànmiàn

sear V 烧焦 shāojiāo, 烧烤 shāokǎo

search N, V 寻找 xúnzhǎo, 搜索 sōusuǒ ■ *Two weeks later, the police called off the search for the missing girl.* 两星期以后，警方放弃了对失踪女孩的搜索。Liǎng xīngqī yǐhòu, jǐngfāng fàngqìle duì shīzōng nǚhái de sōusuǒ. ■ *What are you searching for?* 你在找什么呀？Nǐ zài zhǎo shénme ya?
search and rescue 搜索营救 sōusuǒ yíngjiù
search engine 搜索引擎 sōusuǒ yǐnqíng
search party 搜索队 sōusuǒ duì
search warrant 搜索证 sōusuǒ zhèng
Search me! 我不知道! Wǒ bù zhīdào!

searching ADJ 探究的 tànjiū de
searching inquiry 彻底的调查 chèdǐ de diàochá

searchlight N 探照灯 tànzhàodēng [M. WD 台 tái]

searing ADJ 1 灼热的 [+天气] zhuórè de [+tiānqì], 炽热的 chìrè de 2 严苛的 [+语言] yánkē de [+yǔyán]

seashell N 海贝壳 hǎibèiké

seashore N 海岸 hǎi'àn, 海滩 hǎitān

seasick ADJ 晕船的 yùnchuán de

seaside ADJ 海边的 hǎibiān de, 海滨的 hǎibīn de

season¹ N 1 季节 jìjié ■ *In most parts of America there are four distinct seasons: spring, summer, fall and winter.* 美国大部分地方四季分明：春季、夏季、秋季和冬季。Měiguó dà bùfen dìfang sìjì fēnmíng: chūnjì, xiàjì, qiūjì hé dōngjì. 2 时令 shílìng 3 时期 shíqī
season ticket 季票 jìpiào

season² V 给 [+食物] 加调料 gěi [+shíwù] jiā tiáoliào

seasonable ADJ 符合时令的 fúhé shílìng de

seasonal ADJ 季节性的 jìjiéxìng de

seasoned ADJ 1 有经验的 [+水手] yǒu jīngyàn de [+shuǐshǒu] 2 调好味的 [+食物] tiáo hǎo wèi de [+shíwù]

seasoning N 调味品 tiáowèipǐn

seat I N 1 座位 zuòwèi
seat belt 安全带 ānquándài
aisle seat 靠过道的座位 kào guòdào de zuòwèi
passenger seat 副驾驶员座位 fùjiàshǐyuán zuòwèi, 驾驶员旁边的座位 jiàshǐyuán pángbiān de zuòwèi
window seat 靠窗口的座位 kào chuāngkǒu de zuòwèi
2 席位 xíwèi
a seat on the committee 委员会中的一个席位 wěiyuánhuì zhòng de yí ge xíwèi, 委员会成员 wěiyuánhuì chéngyuán
II V 1 坐 zuò 2 坐得下 zuòdexia ■ *Our school gym can seat 2,000 people.* 我们学校的体育馆坐得下两千个人。Wǒmen xuéxiào de tǐyùguǎn zuòdexia liǎng qiān ge rén.

seating N 1 全部座位 quánbù zuòwèi 2 座位安排 zuòwèi ānpái

seaweed N 海草 hǎicǎo, 海藻 hǎizǎo

sec N (just a sec) 等一会儿 děng yíhuìr

secede V (to secede from) 退出 [+某组织] tuìchū [+mǒu zǔzhī], 脱离 [+某国而独立] tuōlí [+mǒu guó ér dúlì]

secession N 退出 [+某组织] tuìchū [+mǒu zǔzhī], 脱离 [+某国而独立] tuōlí [+mǒu guó ér dúlì]

secluded ADJ 僻静的 pìjìng de, 僻远的 pìyuǎn de

seclusion N 隐居 yǐnjū

second¹ I ADJ 1 第二 dì'èr ■ *Jim is the second child in the family.* 杰姆是家里第二个孩子。Jiémǔ shì jiālǐ dì'èr ge háizi.
second base（棒球的）二垒 (bàngqiú de) èr lěi

second class mail 二类邮件 èr lèi yóujiàn
second nature 第二天性 dì'èrtiān xìng
second person 第二人称 dì èr rénchēng
second sight 预见（力）yùjiàn (lì)
2 另一个 lìng yí ge, 再一次 zàiyícì
second chance/opinion 再一次机会 zàiyícì
jīhuì, 另一种意见 lìngyì zhǒng yìjiàn
II ADV 第二 dì'èr, 其次 qícì **III** v 附议 fùyì, 支
持 zhīchí ■ *I second the motion.* 我支持这项动
议。Wǒ zhīchí zhè xiàng dòngyì. 我附议一项动
议。Wǒ fùyì yī xiàng dòngyì.
second² N **1** 秒 miǎo **2** 片刻 piànkè ■ *A hum-
mingbird flutters its wings over 100 times per second.* 蜂鸟每秒钟振动翅膀一百次以上。Fēngniǎo
měi miǎozhōng zhèndòng chìbǎng yì bǎi cì
yǐshàng.
in a second 极快地 jí kuài de, 瞬间 shùnjiān
secondary ADJ **1** 第二位的 dì'èr wèi de, 次要的
cìyào de
secondary school 中等学校 zhōngděng xuéxiào, 中学 zhōngxué
2 继发性的 jìfāxìng de
secondary infection 继发性感染 jì fā xìnggǎn
rǎn
second-class ADJ 二等的 èrděng de
second-class citizen 二等公民 èrděng gōngmín
second-class ticket 二等票 èrděng piào
second-degree ADJ (second-degree murder) 二级
谋杀 èrjí móushā
second-guess v **1** 事后批评 shìhòu pīpíng **2** 猜测
cāicè, 预测 yùcè
secondhand I N 二手货 èrshǒu huò, 旧货 jiù huò
II ADJ 二手的 èrshǒu de
secondhand store 旧货店 jiùhuòdiàn
secondly ADV 第二 dì'èr, 其次 qícì
second-rate ADJ 次等的 cìděng de
seconds N **1** 第二份（饭菜）dì èr fèn (fàncài)
2 次品（服装）cìpǐn (fúzhuāng)
secrecy N 保密 bǎomì ■ *The testing of the new
airplane was conducted in secrecy.* 新飞机的测试
是保密的。Xīn fēijī de cèshì shì bǎomì de.
secret I N 秘密 mìmì
to keep a secret 保守秘密 bǎoshǒu mìmì
II ADJ 秘密（的）mìmì (de), 隐蔽的 yǐnbì de
■ *The newspaper had got hold of a secret
document, but wasn't sure if it would be legal to
publish it.* 这家报社获得了一份秘密文件，但是
不知道该是不是合法。Zhè jiā bàoshè huòdéle
yí fèn mìmì wénjiàn, dànshì bù zhīdào fābiǎo
shìbushì héfǎ.
secret agent 特工 tègōng, 特务 tèwu
secret service 特工处 tègōng chù, 特工部门
tègōng bùmén
to keep sth secret from sb 对某人隐瞒某事 duì
mǒurén yǐnmán mǒushì

secretarial ADJ 秘书的 mìshū de
secretariat N 秘书处 mìshūchù
the U.N. Secretariat 联合国秘书处 Liánhéguó
Mìshūchù
secretary N **1** 秘书 mìshu **2**（美国）部长 bùzhǎng
(U.S.) Secretary of State（美国）国务卿
（Měiguó）Guówùqīng
secrete v 分泌 fēnmì
secretion N 分泌 fēnmì
secretive ADJ 严守秘密的 yánshǒu mìmì de, 守口
如瓶的 shǒu kǒu rú píng de
sect N 派别 pàibié,（宗教）教派 (zōngjiào)
jiàopài
sectarian ADJ 教派（之间）的 jiàopài (zhījiān) de
sectarian conflict 教派（之间的）冲突 jiàopài
(zhījiān de) chōngtū
section N **1** 部分 bùfen, 段 duàn **2** 部门
bùmén ■ *Dr. Jones heads the financial section
of the company.* 琼斯博士是公司财务部门的主
管。Qióngsī bóshì shì gōngsī cáiwù bùmén de
zhǔguǎn. **3**（报纸）栏目 (bàozhǐ) lánmù
sector N 部门 bùmén, 领域 lìngyù ■ *My father left
government service and now works for the private
sector.* 我的父亲从政府部门离职，现在在私营部
门工作。Wǒ de fùqin cóng zhèngfǔ bùmén lízhí,
xiànzài zài sīyíng bùmén gōngzuò.
secular ADJ 世俗的 shìsú de, 非宗教的 fēi
zōngjiào de
secure I ADJ **1** 安全的 ānquán de, 没有风险
的 méiyǒu fēngxiǎn de **2** 牢固的 láogù de,
绝对安全的 juéduì ānquán de **II** v **1** 固定
住 gùdìngzhu ■ *Make sure all the doors and
windows are secured before the storm comes.* 在
风暴来临之前，要确保门窗都固定住。Zài fēngbào
láilín zhīqián, yào quèbǎo ménchuāng dōu
gùdìngzhu. **2** 获得 huòdé, 得到 dédào **3** 保护
bǎohù, 使…免于攻击 shǐ…miǎnyú gōngjī
security N **1** 安全 ānquán ■ *The President gives
priority to national security.* 总统把国家安全放
在第一位。Zǒngtǒng bǎ guójiā ānquán fàng zài
dìyī wèi. **2** 保障 bǎozhàng ■ *What is your social
security number?* 你的社会保障号码是多少？Nǐ
de shèhuì bǎozhàng hàomǎ shì duōshǎo? **3** 抵押
品 dǐyā pǐn
security check 安（全）检（查）ān (quán) jiǎn
(chá)
security clearance 安全审查 ānquán shěnchá
security deposit (租房) 押金 (zū fáng) yājīn
security forces 保安部队 bǎo'ān bùduì, 安全部
队 ānquán bùduì
security guard 保安人员 bǎo'ān rényuán
social security 社会保障 shèhuì bǎozhàng
sedan N 小轿车 xiǎojiàochē [M. WD 辆 liàng]
sedate ADJ 庄重的 zhuāngzhòng de, 严肃的
yánsù de

sedated ADJ 服用了镇静剂的 fúyòngle zhènjìngjì de

sedative N 镇静剂 zhènjìngjì

sedentary ADJ 1 坐着的 zuòzhe de, 很少活动的 hěn shǎo huódòng de 2 定居的 dìngjū de, 不迁移的 bù qiānyí de

sedentary population 固定人口 gùdìng rénkǒu

sediment N 沉淀 (物) chéndiàn (wù)

sedimentary ADJ 沉积的 chénjī de

sedition N 煽动推翻政府 (罪) shāndòng tuīfān zhèngfǔ (zuì), 造反 zàofǎn

seditious ADJ 煽动推翻政府的 shāndòng tuīfān zhèngfǔ de

seduce V 勾引 gōuyǐn, 引诱 yǐnyòu

seduction N 勾引 gōuyǐn, 引诱 yǐnyòu

seductive ADJ (性感) 诱人的 (xìnggǎn) yòurén de, 富有性感诱惑力的 fùyòu xìnggǎn yòuhuòlì de

seductress N 勾引男人的女人 gōuyǐn nánren de nǚrén

see (PT **saw**; PP **seen**) V 1 看到 kàndao ■ Did you see what happened? 发生的事，你看到了吗? Fāshēng de shì, nǐ kàndao le ma? 2 理解 lǐjiě, 明白 míngbai

Oh, I see. 啊，我明白了。A, wǒ míngbai le. I don't see why not. 没有什么不以。Méiyǒu shénme bù kěyǐ. ■ "Can we have pizza for dinner tonight?" "I don't see why not." "我们今天晚上吃比萨饼，好不好?". "我看没有什么不可以。" "Wǒmen jīntiān wǎnshang chī bǐsà bǐng, hǎobuhǎo?" "Wǒ kàn méiyǒu shénme bù kěyǐ." 3 看望 kànwàng 4 会面 huìmiàn 5 想 xiǎng ■ "How much more money do we need to save for a new car?" "Let me see." "我们买新车还要储蓄多少钱?" "让我想一想。" "Wǒmen mǎi xīn chē hái yào chǔxù duōshǎo qián?" "Ràng wǒ xiǎng yì xiǎng."

seed I N 1 (植物的) 种子 (zhíwù de) zhǒngzi 2 (水果／蔬菜的) 籽 (shuǐguǒ/shūcài de) zǐ 3 (体育比赛) 种子选手 (tǐyù bǐsài) zhǒngzi xuǎnshǒu, 种子队 zhǒngziduì II V 1 播种 bōzhòng 2 去掉籽 qùdiào zǐ 3 挑选为种子选手 tiāoxuǎn wéi zhǒngzi xuǎnshǒu

seedless ADJ 无籽的 wú zǐ de

a seedless watermelon 无籽西瓜 wú zǐ xīguā

seedling N 幼苗 yòumiáo, 秧苗 yāngmiáo

seedy ADJ 肮脏下流的 āngzāng xiàliú de

seek V (PT & PP **sought**) 谋求 móuqiú, 寻求 xúnqiú

to seek one's fortune 离家寻求成功和财富 líjiā xúnqiú chénggōng hé cáifù

seem V 看来 kànlai, 似乎 sìhū

seeming ADJ 表面上的 biǎomiànshàng de, 似乎…的 sìhu…de

seemingly ADV 看上去 kànshangqu, 看来 kànlái, 看样子 kànyàngzi

seen See **see**

seep V 渗漏 shènlòu

seepage N 渗漏 shènlòu

seesaw I N 跷跷板 qiāoqiāobǎn II V 时上时下 (地动) shí shàng shíxià (de dòng)

seethe V 1 发怒 fānù, 怒火中烧 nùhuǒzhōngshāo

to seethe with jealousy 妒火中烧 dùhuǒ zhōngshāo, 因妒嫉而愤怒 yīn dùjí ér fènnù 2 到处都是 dàochù dōu shì

to seethe with ants 到处都是蚂蚁 dàochù dōu shì mǎyǐ, 满是蚂蚁 mǎn shì mǎyǐ

see-through ADJ 透明的 tòumíng de

segment N 1 部份 bùfen 2 线段 xiànduàn 3 片 piàn, 节 jié

segmented ADJ 分段的 fēnduàn de, 分节的 fēnjié de

segregate V 分离 fēnlí, 隔离 gélí

segregated ADJ 分离的 fēnlí de, 隔离的 gélí de

segregation N 分离 fēnlí, 隔离 gélí

seismic ADJ 地震的 dìzhèn de

seismograph N 地震仪 dìzhènyí [M. WD 台 tái/架 jià]

seismologist N 地震学家 dìzhènxuéjiā

seismology N 地震学 dìzhènxué

seize V 1 一把抓住 yì bǎ zhuāzhu, 紧紧抓住 jǐnjǐn zhuāzhu, 夺过 duóguo ■ The thief seized my bag and ran off. 小偷一把夺过我的包，奔走了。Xiǎotōu yì bǎ duóguo wǒ de bāo, bēnzǒu le. 2 扣押 kòuyā, 没收 mòshōu ■ Customs officers seized a large amount of drugs yesterday. 海关官员昨天扣押了大量毒品。Hǎiguān guānyuán zuótiān kòuyāle dàliàng dúpǐn.

seizure N 1 没收 mòshōu

drug seizure 没收毒品 mòshōu dúpǐn 2 (疾病的) 突然发作 (jíbìng de) tūrán fāzuò, 昏厥 hūnjué

seldom ADV 不常常 bù chángcháng, 很少 hěn shǎo

select I V 选择 xuǎnzé, 选拔 xuǎnbá ■ With so many highly qualified applicants, it is really difficult to select the right person. 有这么多高水准的合格的求职者，真的很难选出最合适的人。Yǒu zhème duō gāo shuǐzhǔn de hégé de qiúzhízhě, zhēn de hěn nán xuǎnchū zuìhéshì de rén. II ADJ 1 精心挑选出来的 jīngxīn tiāoxuǎn chūlái de 2 少数人专用的 shǎoshùrén zhuānyòng de

selection N 1 选择 xuǎnzé, 选拔 xuǎnbá 2 挑选出来的人或物 tiāoxuǎn chūlai de rén huò wù

selective ADJ 1 有选择的 [+记忆] yǒu xuǎnzé de [+jìyì] 2 认真挑选的 [+顾客] rènzhēn tiāoxuǎn de [+gùkè]

self N 自我 zìwǒ, 自己 zìjǐ

self-absorbed ADJ 自顾自的 zìgùzìde

self-appointed ADJ 自封的 zìfēng de, 自以为是…的 zì yǐwéi shì…de

self-assurance N 十足的自信 shízú de zìxìn

self-assured ADJ 十分自信的 shífēn zìxìn de

self-centered ADJ 自我中心的 zìwǒ zhōngxīn de

self-confident ADJ 自信的 zìxìn de

self-conscious ADJ 怕羞的 pà xiū de, 不自然的 bú zìrán de

self-control N 自我控制 zì wǒ kòngzhì, 自制力 zìzhìlì

self-defeating ADJ 效果适得其反的 xiàoguǒ shì dé qí fǎn de

self-defense N 自卫 zìwèi

self-denial N 克己苦行 kèjǐ kǔxíng, 自我牺牲 zìwǒ xīshēng

self-destructive ADJ 自我毁灭的 zìwǒ huǐmiè de

self-discipline N 自我约束 zìwǒ yuēshù, 自律 zìlǜ

self-employed ADJ 拥有自己的生意的 yōngyǒu zìjǐ de shēngyì de, 个体经营的 gètǐ jīngyíng de

self-esteem N 自尊(心) zìzūn (xīn)

self-evident ADJ 显而易见的 xiǎn'éryìjiàn de, 不言而喻的 bùyán'éryù de

self-explanatory ADJ 无需解释的 wúxū jiěshì de

self-fulfilling prophecy N 自我应验的预言 zìwǒ yìngyàn de yùyán, 咒语成真 zhòuyǔ chéng zhēn

self-help N 自助 zìzhù, 自救 zìjiù

self-image N 自我形象 zìwǒ xíngxiàng

self-important ADJ 妄自尊大 wàng zì zūn dà, 自负的 zìfù de

self-improvement N 自我改进 zìwǒ gǎijìn

self-indulgence N 放纵 fàngzòng

self-indulgent ADJ 放纵自己的 fàngzòng zìjǐ de

self-inflicted ADJ 自作自受的 zìzuò zìshòu de

self-interest N 自我利益 zìwǒ lìyì, 自私自利 zìsī zìlì
be motivated by pure self-interest 纯粹出于自私自利的动机 chúncuì chūyú zìsī zìlì de dòngjī

selfish ADJ 自私的 zìsī de ■ This selfish man won't be a good husband. 这个自私的人不可能当一个好丈夫。Zhè ge zìsī de rén bù kěnéng dāng yí ge hǎo zhàngfu.

selfless ADJ 无私的 wúsī de

self-made ADJ 白手起家而成功的 báishǒu qǐjiā ér chénggōng de
self-made millionaire 白手起家的百万富翁 báishǒu qǐjiā de bǎiwàn fùwēng

self-pity N 自怜 zì lián
tears of self-pity 自怜的眼泪 zì lián de yǎnlèi

self-portrait N 自画像 zìhuàxiàng

self-possessed ADJ 镇定的 zhèndìng de

self-preservation N 自我保护 zìwǒ bǎohù

self-reliance N 自力更生 zìlì gēngshēng

self-reliant ADJ 自力更生的 zìlì gēngshēng de, 依靠自己的 yīkào zìjǐ de

self-respect N 自尊 zìzūn
to keep one's self-respect 保持自尊 bǎozhí zìzūn

self-respecting ADJ 有自尊心的 yǒu zìzūnxīn de

self-restraint N 自我克制的 zìwǒ kèzhì de

self-righteous ADJ 自命道德高人一等的 zìmìng dàodé gāo rén yì děng de

self-sacrifice N 自我牺牲 zìwǒ xīshēng

self-seeking ADJ 追逐私利的 zhuīzhú sīlì de

self-service ADJ 自助式的 zìzhù shì de

self-serving ADJ 只为谋私利的 zhǐ wèi móu sīlì de

self-styled ADJ 自封的 zìfēng de

self-sufficiency N 自给自足 zìjǐ zìzú

self-sufficient ADJ 自给自足的 zìjǐ zìzú de

self-supporting ADJ 自食其力的 zìshí qílì de

sell V (PT & PP **sold**) **1** 卖 mài, 出售 chūshòu **2** 销售 xiāoshòu ■ Our products sell in over 30 countries. 我们的产品在三十多个国家销售。Wǒmen de chǎnpǐn zài sānshí duō ge guójiā xiāoshòu. **3** 兜售 dōushòu, 推销 tuīxiāo ■ Don't you even try to sell me this crazy idea! 你要向我兜售这个怪念头，想都别想！Nǐ yào xiàng wǒ dōushòu zhè ge guài niàntou, xiǎng dōu bié xiǎng!

selling point N 卖点 màidiǎn

sellout N **1** 门票售完的比赛／演出 ménpiào shòu wán de bǐsài/yǎnchū **2** 背信弃义者 bèixìn qìyì zhě, 叛徒 pàntú

semantic ADJ 语义(上)的 yǔyì (shàng) de, 词义(上)的 cíyì (shàng) de

semantics N **1** 语义 yǔyì **2** 语义学 yǔyìxué

semblance N 相似的情况／事物 xiāngsì de qíngkuàng/shìwù

semen N 精液 jīngyè

semester N 学期 xuéqī

semicircle N 半圆 bànyuán

semicolon N 分号 fēnhào

semiconductor N 半导体 bàndǎotǐ

semifinal N 半决赛 bànjuésài

seminal ADJ 开创性的 kāichuàngxìng de, 对后来者有巨大影响的 duì hòuláizhě yǒu jùdà yǐngxiǎng de

seminar N 讨论课 tǎolùnkè, 研讨会 yántǎohuì

seminary N 神学院 shénxuéyuàn

semiprecious ADJ 次贵重的 [+宝石] cì guìzhòng de [+bǎoshí]

Semitic ADJ **1** 闪米特人的 Shǎnmǐtérén de, 闪米特语的 Shǎnmǐtéyǔ de **2** 犹太人的 Yóutàirén de

senate N **1** 参议院 cānyìyuàn **2** (某些大学的)校董会 (mǒuxiē dàxué de) xiàodǒnghuì

senator N 参议员 cānyìyuán

send V (PT & PP **sent**) V **1** 寄 jì, 发 fā ■ She has sent out job applications to a dozen companies. 她向十几家公司寄去了求职申请。Tā xiàng shíjǐ jiā gōngsī jìqùle qiúzhí shēnqǐng. **2** 送 sòng ■ They sent their son to a private school in California. 他们送儿子上加州的一所私立学校。Tāmen sòng érzi shàng Jiāzhōu de yì suǒ sīlì xuéxiào. **3** 派 pài, 派遣 pàiqiǎn

to send for 要求⋯来 yāoqiú...lái, 请 qǐng
send-off N 欢送会 huānsònghuì
senile ADJ 年老糊涂的 niánlǎo hútu de
senility N 年老糊涂 niánlǎo hútu
senior I ADJ 1 年长的 niánzhǎng de ■ *My brother Paul is three years my senior.* 我哥哥保罗比我大三岁。 Wǒ gēge Bǎoluó bǐ wǒ dà sān suì.
senior citizen 老年人 lǎoniánrén, 长者 zhǎngzhě
2 资深的 zīshēn de ■ *A senior official met them to hear their complaint.* 一位资深官员会见他们，听了他们的抱怨。 Yíwèi zīshēn guānyuán huìjiàn tāmen, tīngle tāmende bàoyuàn. II N 高中毕业班学生 gāozhōng bìyèbān xuésheng
senior high school 高（级）中（学）gāo (jí) zhōng (xué)
seniority N 高年资 gāonián zī, 资历 zīlì
sensation N 1 感觉 gǎnjué 2 轰动 hōngdòng ■ *The documentary caused a sensation.* 那部纪录片造成了轰动。 Nà bù jìlùpiàn zàochéngle hōngdòng.
sensational ADJ 1 引起轰动的 [+消息] yǐnqǐ hōngdòng de [+xiāoxi], 耸人听闻的 sǒngrén tīngwén de 2 令人激动的 [+演出] lìngrén jīdòng de [+yǎnchū]
sensationalism N 哗众取宠（的手法）huázhòng qǔchǒng (de shǒufǎ), 一味追求轰动效应 yíwèi zhuīqiú hōngdòng xiàoyìng
sensationalize V 把 [+一条新闻] 渲染得耸人听闻 bǎ [+yì tiáo xīnwén] xuànrǎn dé sǒngrén tīngwén
sense I N 1 感觉 gǎnjué ■ *The five senses are the senses of sight, hearing, taste, smell and touch.* 五种感官是视觉、听觉、味觉、嗅觉和触觉。 Wǔ zhǒng gǎnguān shì shìjué, tīngjué, wèijué, xiùjué hé chùjué.
sense of humor/shame/guilt 幽默感／羞耻感／负罪感 yōumògǎn/xiūchǐgǎn/fùzuìgǎn
2 理解 lǐjiě, 领悟 lǐngwù ■ *He won't admit that he has a poor sense of direction.* 他不愿意承认方向感很差。 Tā bú yuànyì chéngrèn fāngxiàng gǎn hěn chà. **3** 词义 cíyì, 意义 yìyì ■ *This word is not used in a literal sense.* 这个词不是用在字面意思上。 Zhè ge cí bú shì yòng zài zìmiàn yìsishang. II V 感觉到 gǎnjuédào
to make sense 有道理 yǒudàolǐ ■ *His angry response made no sense whatsoever.* 他愤怒的反应没有什么道理。 Tā fènnù de fǎnyìng méiyǒu shénme dàolǐ.
in a sense 在一定意义上 zài yídìng yìyìshang
senseless ADJ 1 无知觉的 wú zhījué de 2 没有意义的 méiyǒu yìyì de
senses N 理智 lǐzhì ■ *She must have lost her senses.* 她准是疯了。 Tā zhǔn shì fēng le.
sensibility N 感觉 gǎnjué, 感受（力）gǎnshòu (lì)
sensible ADJ 明白事理的 míngbai shìlǐ de, 懂事的 dǒngshì de

sensitive ADJ 1 敏感的 mǐngǎn de ■ *Some people are very sensitive to the smell of cigarettes.* 有些人对香烟气味非常敏感。 Yǒuxiē rén duì xiāngyān qìwèi fēicháng mǐngǎn. 2 能理解的 néng lǐjiě de, 体贴的 tǐtiē de 3 需小心处理的 xū xiǎoxīn chǔlǐ de, 机密的 jīmì de
commercially sensitive 商业机密的 shāngyè jīmì de
4 对⋯很灵敏的 duì...hěn língmǐn de
light-sensitive 对光敏感的 duìguāng mǐngǎn de
sensor N 传感器 chuángǎnqì
sensory ADJ 感官的 gǎnguān de
sensual ADJ 肉欲的 ròuyù de, 性感的 xìnggǎn de
sensuous ADJ 给感官快感的 gěi gǎnguān kuàigǎn de, 赏心悦目的 shǎngxīn yuèmù de
sent See send
sentence I N 1 句子 jùzi ■ *I know the words in the sentence, but I can't understand this sentence.* 这个句子里的词我都认识，但是句子的意思我不明白。 Zhè ge jùzi lǐ de cí wǒ dōu rènshi, dànshì jùzi de yìsi wǒ bù míngbai. 2 判决 pànjué ■ *The judge will pronounce sentence on the convicted tomorrow.* 法官明天对罪犯判决。 Fǎguān míngtiān duì zuìfàn pànjué. II V 判决 pànjué, 判处 pànchǔ
sentiment N 意见 yìjiàn, 态度 tàidu
public sentiment 公众的情绪 gōngzhòng de qíngxù
sentimental ADJ 1 自作多情的 zìzuò duōqíng de, 多愁善感 duōchóu shàngǎn 2 感情上的 gǎnqíng shàng de
sentimental value 感情价值 gǎnqíng jiàzhí
sentimentality N 多愁善感 duōchóu shàngǎn
sentry N 哨兵 shàobīng, 卫兵 wèibīng
separable ADJ 可以分开的 kěyǐ fēnkāi de
separate I ADJ 1 分开的 fēnkāi de 2 不相关的 bù xiāngguān de II V 1 分开 fēnkai, 分离 fēnlí ■ *This difficult assignment will separate gifted students from others.* 这个难度很大的作业将把有天赋的学生和其他学生分开。 Zhè ge nándù hěn dà de zuòyè jiāng bǎ yǒu tiānfù de xuésheng hé qítā xuésheng fēnkai.
to separate the men from the boys 把强者和弱者区分开来 bǎ qiángzhě hé ruòzhě qūfēn kāilái, 把勇敢者和胆怯者区分开来 bǎ yǒnggǎnzhě hé dǎnqièzhě qūfēn kāilái
to separate the sheep from the goats 区分好人和坏人 qūfēn hǎorén hé huàirén
2 [夫妻+] 分居 [fūqī] fēnjū
separated ADJ 分居的 [+夫妻] fēnjū de [+fūqī]
separation N 1 分开 fēnkāi ■ *Early separation of an infant from the mother is not desirable.* 很早就把婴儿和母亲分开是不好的。 Hěn zǎo jiù bǎ yīng'ér hé mǔqin fēnkaī shì bù hǎo de. **2** 分居 fēnjū
sepsis N 脓毒症 nóngdúzhēng

September N 九月 jiǔyuè
sequel N 续集 xùjí, 后续 hòuxù
sequence N 顺序 shùnxù
sequencing N 编排顺序 biānpái shùnxù
sequential ADJ 顺序的 shùnxù de, 连续的 liánxù de
sequin N 闪光塑料小圆片 shǎnguāng sùliào xiǎo yuánpiàn [M. WD 片 piàn]
sequoia N 红杉 hóngshān
serenade I N 小夜曲 xiǎoyèqǔ II V 对…唱／奏小夜曲 duì…chàng/zòu xiǎoyèqǔ
serendipity N 发现珍奇事物的天生本领 fāxiàn zhēnqí shìwù de tiānshēng běnlǐng
serene ADJ 安详的 ānxiáng de, 安宁的 ānníng de
sergeant N 军士 jūnshì, 巡佐 xúnzuǒ
serial I ADJ 1 一系列的 yíxìliè de
serial killer 系列杀人犯 xìliè shārénfàn, 连环杀手 liánhuán shāshǒu
2（按）顺序（安排）的 (àn) shùnxù (ānpái) de
serial number 顺序编号 shùnxù biānhào
II N 电视连续剧 diànshì liánxùjù, 报刊连载小说 bàokān liánzǎi xiǎoshuō
series N 1 一系列 yíxìliè ■ Dr Baker will give a series of public lectures on Islam. 贝克博士将作一系列关于伊斯兰教的公众讲座。Bèikè bóshì jiāng zuò yíxìliè guānyú Yīsīlánjiào de gōngzhòng jiǎngzuò. 2 连续剧 liánxùjù ■ The popular TV series will soon be on cable. 这套很受欢迎的电视连续剧将在有线电视频道播放。Zhè tào hěn shòu huānyíng de diànshì liánxùjù jiāng zài yǒuxiàn diànshì píndào bōfàng.
serious ADJ 1 严重的 yánzhòng de, 重大的 zhòngdà de 2 严肃的 yánsù de ■ Mr Wilkinson seems serious, but he enjoys a good joke. 威尔金森先生看起来很严肃，但是他喜欢说笑话。Wēi'ěrjīnsēn xiānsheng kànqilai hěn yánsù, dànshì tā xǐhuan shuō xiàohuà. 3 认真的 rènzhēn de ■ You can't be serious! 你不可能是认真的！（→别开玩笑！）Nǐ bù kěnéng shì rènzhēn de! (→ Bié kāi wánxiào!)
seriously ADV 1 严重（地）yánzhòng (de) 2 严肃（地）yánsù (de) 3 严格（地）yángé (de)
to take sb seriously 把某人当作值得尊重的人 bǎ mǒurén dāngzuò zhíde zūnzhòng de rén
to take oneself seriously 觉得自己了不起 juéde zìjǐ liǎobuqǐ
4 认真（地）rènzhēn (de) ■ You all know I like to joke around, but seriously, I do plan to get married one of these days. 大家知道我喜欢说笑话，不过说真的，我打算最近结婚。Dàjiā zhīdào wǒ xǐhuan shuō xiàohuà, búguò shuō zhēn de, wǒ dǎsuàn zuìjìn jiéhūn.
sermon N （基督教的）布道 (Jīdūjiào de) bùdào, 讲道 jiǎngdào
serpent N （大）蛇 (dà) shé [M. WD 条 tiáo]

serrated ADJ 有锯齿的 yǒu jùchǐ de
serum N 免疫血清 miǎnyì xuèqīng
servant N 佣人 yōngrén, 仆人 púrén
serve I V 1 为…服务 wéi...fúwù, 接待 jiēdài ■ Are you being served? 有人招呼你了吗？Yǒu rén zhāohu nǐ le ma? 2 服役 fúyì, 当兵 dāngbīng ■ He served in the army for 10 years. 他在部队里服役十年。Tā zài bùduì lǐ fúyì shí nián. 3 提供食品 tígōng shípǐn 4 用作 yòngzuo ■ The kitchen also serves as a dining area. 厨房也用作吃饭的地方。Chúfáng yě yòngzuo chīfàn de dìfang. 5 发球 fā qiú
it serves … right 活该 huógāi ■ I'm sorry that Mike failed the exam, but it served him right for not doing his studies. 迈克考试不及格，我很难过，不过他不学习，也是活该。Màikè kǎoshì bù jígé, wǒ hěn nánguò, búguò tā bù xuéxí, yě shì huógāi.
II V （网球／排球）发球 (wǎngqiú/páiqiú) fāqiú
server N 1（计算机）服务器 (jìsuànjī) fúwù qì 2 发球者 fāqiú zhě 3（饭店）服务员 (fàndiàn) fúwùyuán, 侍者 shìzhě
service I N 1 服务 fúwù
service charge 服务费 fúwùfèi, 小费 xiǎofèi
service door （工作人员）专用门 (gōngzuò rényuán) zhuānyòng mén
service station （汽车）加油站 (qìchē) jiāyóuzhàn
service industry 服务业 fúwùyè, 第三产业 dìsān chǎnyè
2 任职 rènzhí ■ After 30 years service in the company, Mr. Clifford retired last month. 克里福德先生在公司服务三十年以后，于上个月退休了。Kèlǐfúdé xiānsheng zài gōngsī fúwù sānshí nián yǐhòu, yú shàng ge yuè tuìxiū le. 3 宗教仪式 zōngjiào yíshì 4 效力 xiàolì ■ I'm happy to be of service, sir. 先生，我很高兴为您效力。Xiānsheng, wǒ hěn gāoxìng wéi nín xiàolì. II V 1 维修 wéixiū, 保养 bǎoyǎng 2 支付利息 zhīfù lìxī
public services 公用事业 gōngyòng shìyè
serviceable ADJ 1 可以使用的 [+设备] kěyǐ shǐyòng de [+shèbèi] 2 还可以的 [+食物] hái kěyǐ de [+shíwù]
serviceman N 军人 jūnrén
services N (the services) 军队 jūnduì, 武装部队 wǔzhuāng bùduì
servicewoman N （女）军人 (nǚ) jūnrén
servile ADJ 完全屈从的 wánquán qūcóng de, 奴颜婢膝的 núyánbìxī de
serving N 一份食物 yí fèn shíwù
five servings of fruit and vegetable every day 每天五份水果蔬菜 měitiān wǔ fèn shuǐguǒ shūcài
servitude N 奴役 núyì, 劳役 láoyì
session N 1（一段）时间 (yí duàn) shíjiān 2 开庭 kāitíng ■ The court is still in session. 还在开庭。Hái zàikāitíng. 3 学期 xuéqī

to be in session 正在开会 zhèngzài kāihuì, 正在开庭 zhèngzài kāitíng

set I v (PT & PP set) **1** 摆 bǎi, 摆放 bǎifàng ■ *Dinner will be ready soon. Will you please set the table?* 很快就要吃饭了，你摆一摆碗筷，好不好? Hěn kuài jiù yào chīfàn le, nǐ bǎiyibǎi wǎnkuài, hǎobuhǎo? **2** 调 tiáo, 调整 tiáozhěng **3** 建立 jiànlì, 创造 chuàngzào ■ *This sentencing set a dangerous precedent for future cases.* 这个判决为以后的案件创造了一个危险的先例。Zhè ge pànjué wèi yǐhòu de ànjiàn chuàngzàole yí ge wēixiǎn de xiānlì.

to set a record 创造纪录 chuàngzào jìlù

to set an example 树立榜样 shùlì bǎngyàng ■ *My father set me a good example in being punctual.* 我父亲在准时方面为我树立了一个好榜样。Wǒ fùqin zài zhǔnshí fāngmian wèi wǒ shùlìle yí ge hǎo bǎngyàng.

4 (日) 落 (rì) luò ■ *In summer the sun sets at 9.00 p.m. in this part of America.* 在美国这一地区，夏天晚上九点太阳才落山。Zài Měiguó zhè yí dìqū, xiàtiān wǎnshang jiǔ diǎn tàiyáng cái luòshān.

to set aside 省下 shěngxia, 留下 liúxia

to set out 出发 chūfā, 动身 dòngshēn

to set up ① 成立 chénglì ② 准备好使用 zhǔnbèihǎo shǐyòng, 安装 ānzhuāng ■ *David is helping his grandmother set up her computer.* 戴维在帮他祖母安装电脑。Dàiwéi zài bāng tā zǔmǔ ānzhuāng diànnǎo. ③ 竖立 shùlì

II N **1** 一套 yí tào, 一付 yí fù ■ *She gave her husband a set of golf clubs on his birthday.* 她在丈夫生日时送给他一套高尔夫球棒。Tā zài zhàngfu shēngrì shí sòng gěi tā yí tào gāo'ěrfūqiú bàng. **2** 电视机 diànshìjī, 收音机 shōuyīnjī **3** (电影/电视) 拍摄场 (diànyǐng/diànshì) pāishèchǎng, 戏剧布景 (xìjù) bùjǐng **4** (球赛) 一盘 (qiúsài) yìpán **5** 一组 (乐曲) yìzǔ (yuèqǔ)

setback N 挫折 cuòzhé

setter N **1** 蹲伏猎犬 dūnfú lièquǎn **2** 制定者 zhìdìngzhě

example-setter 树立榜样的人 shùlì bǎngyàng de rén

setting N **1** 环境 huánjìng ■ *The private kindergarten is in a peaceful setting of a residential area.* 这座私人幼儿园坐落在一个住宅区的安静环境之中。Zhè zuò sīrén yòu'éryuán zuòluò zài yí ge zhùzháiqū de ānjìng huánjìng zhīzhōng. **2** 背景 bèijǐng ■ *The setting of the movie is a small Midwest town in the 50's.* 这部电影的背景是五十年代中西部的一个小城。Zhè bù diànyǐng de bèijǐng shì wǔshí niándài zhōngxī bù de yí ge xiǎo chéng. **3** 定位档 dìngwèidàng

settle v **1** 定居 dìngjū **2** 安顿 āndùn ■ *Eric settled himself down on the couch to watch a baseball game.* 埃力克舒舒服服地躺在沙发上看垒球比赛。Āilìkè shūshūfúfú de tǎng zài shāfāshang kàn lěiqiú bǐsài. **3** 解决 [+争端] jiějué [+zhēngduān] ■ *International disputes should be settled through negotiations.* 国际争端应该通过谈判解决。Guójì zhēngduān yīnggāi tōngguò tánpàn jiějué.

to settle out of court 法庭外和解 fǎtíng wài héjiě

4 偿还 chánghuán, 结清 jiéqīng

settled ADJ **1** 不可能改变的 bùkěnéng gǎibiàn de **2** 安定的 [+生活] āndìngde [+shēnghuó], 舒适的 shūshì de

settlement N **1** [和解+] 协议 [héjiě+] xiéyì ■ *A settlement was reached between the judge and lawyers.* 法官和律师之间达成了协议。Fǎguān hé lǜshī zhījiān dáchéngle xiéyì. **2** 结账 jiézhàng, 偿还 chánghuán ■ *He transferred $8,000 to her bank account as a settlement of the debt.* 他把八千元转到她的账户，偿还债务。Tā bǎ bā qiān yuán zhuǎndao tā de zhànghù, chánghuán zhàiwù. **3** 定居 dìngjū

settler N 定居者 dìngjuzhě, 移民 yímín

set-up N **1** 安排 ānpái, 布局 bùjú **2** (计算机系统的) 调试 (jìsuànjī xìtǒng de) tiáoshì, 装配 zhuāngpèi **3** 全套设备 quántào shèbèi **4** 圈套 quāntào, 陷阱 xiànjǐng

seven NUM 七 qī, 7

seventeen NUM 十七 shíqī, 17

seventh NUM 第七 dìqī

Seventh Day Adventist I ADJ 基督教复临安息会的 Jīdūjiào fùlín ānxī huì de **II** N 基督教复临安息会教友 Jīdūjiào fùlín ānxī huì jiàoyǒu

seventy NUM 七十 qīshí, 70

sever v **1** 切断 qiēduàn

a severed finger 断指 duàn zhǐ

2 断绝 [+关系] duànjué [+guānxi]

several I ADJ 几个 jǐ ge, 一些 yìxiē ■ *Several customers have complained about his bad service.* 有几位顾客抱怨他服务不好。Yǒu jǐ wèi gùkè bàoyuàn tā fúwù bù hǎo. **II** PRON 几个 jǐ ge, 一些 yìxiē ■ *Several of our students have gone to the Ivy League universities.* 我们有几个学生上常青藤联合会名牌大学了。Wǒmen yǒu jǐ ge xuésheng shàng chángqíngténg liánhéhuì míngpái dàxué le.

severance pay N 解雇费 jiěgù fèi, 离职金 lízhí jīn

severe ADJ **1** 严厉的 yánlì de ■ *She thinks her husband is too severe with their son.* 她觉得丈夫对孩子太严厉。Tā juéde zhàngfu duì háizi tài yánlì. **2** 剧烈的 jùliè de ■ *The storm was so severe that power was knocked out for hours.* 风暴十分剧烈，以至于停电了好几小时。Fēngbào shífēn jùliè, yǐzhìyú tíngdiànle hǎojǐ xiǎoshí.

sew (PT sewed; PP sewn) v 缝 féng, 缝纫 féngrèn

sewage N (下水道的) 污水 (xiàshuǐdào de) wūshuǐ

sewer N 下水道 xiàshuǐdào, 阴沟 yīngōu

sewn See **sew**

sex N **1** 性别 xìngbié ■ *"Can you tell which sex the puppy is?" "I think it's male."* "你知道这条小狗是雌的，还是雄的？""我想是雄的。" "Nǐ zhīdào zhè tiáo xiǎogǒu shì cí de, háishi xióng de?" "Wǒ xiǎng shì xióng de." **2** 性行为 xìng xíngwéi, 性交 xìngjiāo ■ *Many young people pledge not to have sex until marriage.* 许多青年人发誓，在婚前不发生性关系。Xǔduō qīngnián rén fāshì, zài hūn qián bù fāshēng xìng guānxi.

sex education 性教育 xìng jiàoyù

opposite sex 异性 yìxìng

sexism N 性别歧视 xìngbié qíshì

sexist I ADJ 性别歧视的 xìngbié qíshì de, 歧视妇女的 qíshì fùnǚ de II N 性别歧视者 xìngbié qíshì zhě, 歧视妇女的人 qíshì fùnǚ de rén

sex symbol N 性感偶像 xìnggǎn ǒuxiàng

sexual ADJ 1 性别的 xìngbié de ■ *Sexual equality has been achieved in many workplaces.* 在很多工作场所性别平等已经实现了。Zài hěn duō gōngzuò chǎngsuǒ xìngbié píngděng yǐjing shíxiàn le. **2** 性交的 xìngjiāo de

sexual assault 性侵犯 xìng qīnfàn, 强奸 qiángjiān

sexual desire 性欲 xìngyù

sexual harassment 性骚扰 xìng sāorǎo

sexual intercourse 性交 xìngjiāo

sexual transmitted diseases (STDs) 性传播疾病 xìng chuánbō jíbìng

sexuality N 性欲 xìngyù, 性行为 xìng xíngwéi

sexy ADJ 性感的 xìnggǎn de, 引起性欲的 yǐnqǐ xìngyù de

shabby ADJ 1 破旧的 [+城区] pòjiù de [+chéngqū], 寒酸的 [+衣服] hánsuān de [+yīfu] **2** 不公平的 [+对待] bù gōngping de [+duìdài]

shack I N 简陋的小屋 jiǎnlòu de xiǎo wū, 棚屋 péngwū [M. WD 间 jiān] II v (to shack up with sb) 与某人同居 yǔ mǒurén tóngjū

shackle I N 1 镣铐 liàokào [M. WD 副 fù] **2** 枷锁 jiāsuǒ, 桎梏 zhìgù

the shackle of the family 家庭的桎梏 jiātíng de zhìgù

II v **1** 给⋯带上镣铐 gěi⋯dàishang liàokào **2** 束缚 shùfù

shade I N 1 荫 yìn, 背阴 bèiyīn ■ *Even in the shade, the temperature is still 100° F.* 即使在背阴处，温度仍是华氏一百度。Jíshǐ zài bèiyīn chù, wēndù réng shì huáshì yì bǎi dù. **2** （色彩的）浓淡 (sècǎi de) nóngdàn

a warm shade 暖色 nuǎnsè

3 细微差别 xìwēi chābié

shades of opinions 各种不同意见 gè zhǒng bùtóng yìjiàn

4 灯罩 dēngzhào II v 为⋯遮阳 wéi⋯zhēyáng

shades N 百叶窗 bǎiyèchuāng [M. WD 扇 shàn], 遮阳窗帘 zhēyáng chuānglián [M. WD 幅 fú]

shadow I N 影子 yǐngzi, 阴影 yīnyǐng

beyond/without a shadow of doubt 毫无疑问 háowú yíwèn

II v 跟踪 gēnzōng, 盯梢 dīngshāo

shadowy ADJ 1 多阴影的 duō yīnyǐng de, 模糊的 móhu de **2** 神秘的 shénmì de

shady ADJ 1 遮阳的 zhēyáng de, 背阴的 bèiyīn de

shady courtyard 背阴的院子 bèiyīn de yuànzi

2 不正当的 búzhèngdāng de, 可疑的 kěyí de

a shady deal 一项可疑的交易 yí xiàng kěyí de jiāoyì

shaft N 1 竖井 shùjǐng

elevator shaft 电梯竖井 diàntī shùjǐng

2 (a shaft of sunshine) 一道阳光 yídào yángguāng

shaggy ADJ （毛发）又长又乱的 (máofà) yòu cháng yòu luàn de

shake I v (PT **shook**; PP **shaken**) **1** 摇动 yáodòng ■ *Shake the bottle before taking the medicine.* 服药前先摇动药瓶。Fú yào qián xiān yáodòng yàopíng.

to shake hands with 和⋯握手 hé⋯wòshǒu

to shake one's fist 挥动拳头 huīdòng quántou

to shake one's head 摇头 yáotóu

2 [人+] 发抖 [rén+] fādǒu, 打颤 dǎchàn ■ *He was shaking with cold when he climbed out of the pool.* 他从游泳池爬上来，冷得直发抖。Tā cóng yóuyǒngchí páshanglai, lěng de zhí fàdǒu. **3** 动摇 [+信心] dòngyáo [+xìnxīn] II N 1 摇动 yáodòng, 摇晃 yáohuang **2** 泡沫牛奶 pàomò niúnǎi, 奶昔 nǎixī

shakedown N 1 敲诈勒索 qiāozhà lèsuǒ **2** 彻底搜查 chèdǐ sōuchá

shaken See **shake**

shakeup N 改组 gǎizǔ

a major shakeup of the company 公司的大改组 gōngsī de dà gǎizǔ

shaky ADJ 1 摇晃的 [+椅子] yáohuang de [+yǐzi] **2** 不牢靠的 [+知识] bù láokào de [+zhīshi] **3** 颤抖的 [+声音] chàndǒu de [+shēngyīn]

shall MODAL V (PT **should**) **1** 必须 bìxū, 应当 yīngdāng **2** 一定会 yídìng huì **3** 要不要 yàobuyào Shall I ...? 要不要我⋯? Yàobuyào wǒ...? We shall see. 我们再看看吧。Wǒmen zài kàn kàn ba.

shallot N 青葱 qīngcōng [M. WD 根 gēn]

shallow ADJ 1 浅 qiǎn **2** 肤浅 fūqiǎn ■ *I find his argument shallow.* 我觉得他的论点很肤浅。Wǒ juéde tā de lùndiǎn hěn fūqiǎn.

sham I N 1 虚假 xūjiǎ **2** 骗局 piànjú, 假象 jiǎxiàng **3** 假冒者 jiǎmào zhě II ADJ 虚假的 xūjiǎ de

a sham marriage 虚假的婚姻 xūjiǎ de hūnyīn, 假结婚 jiǎ jiéhūn

shambles N (in a shambles) 彻底失败 chèdǐ shībài, 一团糟 yìtuánzāo

shame I N 1 羞耻 xiūchǐ, 耻辱 chǐrǔ ■ *Didn't he feel shame for having told a lie?* 他撒了谎，就不感到羞耻吗? Tā sāle huǎng, jiù bù gǎndao xiūchǐ ma? **2** 可惜 kěxī ■ *What a shame our home team hasn't won a game this year!* 我们的主队今年一场球也没有赢，真可惜! Wǒmen de zhǔduì jīnnián yì cháng qiú yě méiyǒu yíng, zhēn kěxī! Shame on you! 你真丢脸! Nǐ zhēn diūliǎn!

II V 使…感到羞愧 shǐ…gǎndào xiūkuì

shamefaced ADJ 面有愧色的 miànyǒukuìsè de, 羞愧的 xiūkuì de

shameful ADJ 可耻的 [+行为] kěchǐ de [+xíngwéi]

shameless ADJ 无耻的 [+人] wúchǐ de [+rén]

shampoo I N 洗发精 xǐfà jīng, 香波 xiāngbō

II V (用洗发精) 洗头发 (yòng xǐfàjīng) xǐtóufa

shamrock N 三叶草 sānyècǎo

shanty N 简陋的小屋 jiǎnlòu de xiǎowū, 棚屋 péngwū

shantytown N 棚户区 pénghùqū, 贫民区 pínmínqū

shape I N 1 形状 xíngzhuàng 2 状态 zhuàngtài, 情况 qíngkuàng

in shape 身体健康 shēntǐ jiànkāng ■ *I jog every day to keep in shape.* 我每天跑步，保持身体健康。Wǒ měitiān pǎobù, bǎochí shēntǐ jiànkāng.

II V 1 形成 xíngchéng 2 使…成形 shǐ…chéngxíng

shaped ADJ 有…形状的 yǒu…xíngzhuàng de

shapely ADJ 样子好看的 yàngzi hǎokàn de

share I V 1 分享 fēnxiǎng, 合用 héyòng ■ *I will share my last dollar with her.* 我会和她分享最后一块钱。Wǒ huì hé tā fēnxiǎng zuìhòu yí kuài qián. **2** 共有 gòngyǒu II N 1 个人的份儿 gèrén de fènr ■ *Jimmy took his share of the cake and left the kitchen.* 杰米拿了他的那份蛋糕，离开了厨房。Jiémǐ nále tā de nà fèn dàngāo, líkāile chúfáng. **2** 股 gǔ, 股份 gǔfèn [M. WD 份 fèn]

shark N 鲨鱼 shāyú [M. WD 条 tiáo]

sharp ADJ 1 锐利的 [+刀子] ruìlì de [+dāozi], 锋利的 fēnglì de 2 尖锐的 [+批评] jiānruì de [+pīpíng] ■ *She made the sharp criticism out of a deep concern for your well-being.* 她是出于对你的利益的深切关心才做这个尖锐批评的。Tā shì chūyú duì nǐ de lìyì de shēnqiè guānxīn cái zuò zhè ge jiānruì pīpíng de. **3** 急剧的 [+上升] jíjù de [+shàngshēng] **4** 敏锐的 [+头脑] mǐnruì de [+tóunǎo]

as sharp as a tack 头脑机敏 tóunǎo jīmǐn **5** 剧烈的 [+疼痛] jùliè de [+téngtòng]

sharp pain 剧痛 jùtòng

sharpen V 1 使 [+刀子] 锋利 shǐ [+dāozi] fēnglì **2** 使 [+照片] 清晰 shǐ [+zhàopiàn] qīngxī

sharpener N 磨刀器 módāo qì, 卷笔刀 juǎnbǐdāo

shatter V 1 使 [+玻璃] 粉碎 shǐ [+bōli] fěnsuì **2** 使 [+希望] 破灭 shǐ [+xīwàng] pòmiè

shatterproof ADJ 防碎的 fángsuì de

shave V, N 刮胡子 guā húzi, 剃须 tìxū

a close shave 侥幸脱险 jiǎoxìng tuōxiǎn

shaver N (电动) 剃刀 (diàndòng) tìdāo

shavings N 刨片 páo piàn

shawl N 披肩大围巾 pījiān dà wéijīn [M. WD 条 tiáo]

she PRON 她 tā

sheaf (PL **sheaves**) N (一) 叠 (纸) (yì) dié (zhǐ)

shear (PT **sheared**; PP **shorn**) V 1 给羊剪毛 gěi yáng jiǎnmáo, 剪羊毛 jiǎnyángmáo **2** 剪断 jiǎnduàn, 砍掉 kǎndiào

shears N 园艺大剪刀 yuányì dà jiǎndāo [M. WD 把 bǎ]

sheath N 1 (刀) 套 (dāo) tào, (剑) 鞘 (jiàn) qiào **2** (女子) 紧身衣 (nǚzǐ) jǐnshēnyī [M. WD 件 jiàn]

sheathe V 包覆起来 bāofù qǐlái

shed¹ N 小库房 xiǎo kùfáng, 工具房 gōngjùfáng [M. WD 间 jiān]

shed² (PT & PP **shed**) **1** 摆脱 bǎituō, 去掉 qùdiào

to shed hairs 掉毛 diào máo

2 流出 liúchū

to shed blood 流血 liú xiè

to shed tears 流泪 liú lèi

3 [灯+] 发光 [dēng+] fāguāng

sheen N 一层光泽 yì céng guāngzé

sheep (PL **sheep**) N 羊 yáng [M. WD 只 zhī/头 tóu], 绵羊 miányáng

a flock of sheep 一群羊 yì qún yáng

sheep dog 牧羊犬 mùyángquǎn

sheepish ADJ 窘困的 jiǒngkùn de, 腼腆的 miǎntian de

sheer ADJ 1 十足的 shízú de, 纯粹的 chúncuì de

sheer folly 纯粹是愚蠢 chúncuì shì yúchǔn

sheer luck 完全是运气 wánquán shì yùnqi **2** 陡峭的 [+悬崖] dǒuqiào de [+xuányá] **3** 极薄的 jí báo de, 几乎透明的 jīhū tòumíng de

sheet N 1 床单 chuángdān **2** 一张 yì zhāng

sheik, sheikh N (阿拉伯) 酋长 (Ālābó) qiúzhǎng, 王子 wángzǐ

shelf (PL **shelves**) N 搁板 gēbǎn, 搁架 gējià ■ *There are many books on Chinese history on the top shelf.* 在最高一层搁板上有许多关于中国历史的书。Zài zuìgāo yì céng gēbǎn shang yǒu xǔduō guānyú Zhōngguó lìshǐ de shū.

shell N 1 壳 ké, 外壳 wàiké, 甲 jiǎ ■ *The turtle started to poke its head out of its shell.* 乌龟开始把头从龟壳里探出来。Wūguī kāishǐ bǎ tóu cóng guīké lǐ tànchūlai. **2** 贝壳 bèiké **3** 子弹 zǐdàn, 炮弹 pàodàn

shellfish N 贝类 (动物) bèilèi (dòngwù)

shelter I N 1 遮蔽 zhēbì ■ *Many people took shelter from the shower in the mall.* 许多人在商场避雨。Xǔduō rén zài shāngchǎng bì yǔ. **2** 遮蔽所

sheltered

zhēbì suǒ, 避难的地方 bìnàn de dìfang ■ *Local churches provide food and shelter for the homeless.* 当地的教堂为无家可归者提供食物和住所。Dāngdì de jiàotáng wèi wú jiā kě guī zhě tígōng shíwù hé zhùsuǒ. II v 1 遮蔽 zhēbì, 挡住 dǎngzhu 2 窝藏 wōcáng ■ *She was sentenced to a six-month prison term for sheltering her fugitive brother.* 她因为窝藏她的逃犯兄弟而被判六个月徒刑。Tā yīnwèi wōcáng tā de táofàn xiōngdì ér bèi pàn liù ge yuè túxíng.

sheltered ADJ 1 避开风雨的 bìkāi fēngyǔ de 2 备受庇护的 bèishòu bìhù de
a sheltered childhood 备受庇护的童年 bèishòu bìhù de tóngnián

shelve v 1 搁置 [+计划] gēzhì [+jìhuà] 2 将 [+商品] 放在货架上 jiāng [+shāngpǐn] fàng zài huò jià shàng

shenanigans N 捣鬼 dǎoguǐ, 恶作剧 èzuòjù

shepherd I N 牧羊人 mùyángrén II v 带领 [+一群人] dàilǐng [+yìqún rén]

sheriff N（美国）民选的县治安官 (Měiguó) mínxuǎn de xiàn zhì'ānguān

sherry N 雪莉酒 xuělìjiǔ

shh INTERJ 嘘 xū

shield N 盾 dùn, 盾牌 dùnpái

shift I N 1 变化 biànhuà 2 [早 / 晚+] 班 [zǎo/wǎn+] bān
day shift 白天班 báitiān bān, 日班 rìbān
night shift 夜班 yèbān
II v 1 变化 biànhuà 2 转移 zhuǎnyí, 转换 zhuǎnhuàn
to shift the responsibility 转嫁责任 zhuǎnjià zérèn

shiftless ADJ 不求上进的 bù qiú shàngjìn de, 得过且过的 déguò qiěguò de

shifty ADJ 狡猾的 [+人] jiǎohuá de [+rén], 贼眼溜溜的zéiyǎn liūliū de

shimmer v 闪闪发微光 shǎnshǎn fā wēiguāng

shin N 肋部 lèibù, 小腿 xiǎotuǐ

shine I v (PT & PP **shone**) 1 照（耀）zhào (yào) 2 照射 zhàoshè ■ *Hey, don't shine your flashlight in my face!* 喂, 不要用手电筒照我! Wèi, bú yào yòng shǒudiàntǒng zhào wǒ! 3 (PT & PP **shined**) 擦亮 cāliàng II N 1 光泽 guāngzé, 光亮 guāngliàng 2 擦亮 cāliàng

shingle N 1 木瓦 mù wǎ [M. WD 片 piàn], 墙面板 qiángmiàn bǎn [M. WD 块 kuài] 2（海滩上的）卵石 (hǎitān shàng de) luǎnshí

shingles N 带状疱疹 dàizhuàng pàozhěn

shining ADJ 光辉的 guānghuī de, 杰出的 jiéchū de
shining example 光辉榜样 guānghuī bǎngyàng

shiny ADJ 光滑发亮的 guānghuá fāliàng de

ship I N 船 chuán, 舰 jiàn II v 运送 yùnsòng, 发出 fāchū

shipload N（船舶）运载量／载人数 (chuánbó) yùnzàiliàng/zàirén shù
a shipload of grain 一船的谷物 yì chuán de gǔwù

shipment N 1 一批货物 yì pī huòwù
a shipment of drugs 一批毒品 yìpī dúpǐn 2 运送 yùnsòng
illegal shipment of weapons 非法运送武器 fēifǎ yùnsòng wǔqì

shipping N 船舶 chuánbó, 船运 chuányùn
shipping clerk 船运公司办事员 chuányùn gōngsī bànshìyuán
shipping and handling fees（货物）运发费 (huòwù) yùn fā fèi

shipwreck I N 1 船只失事 chuánzhī shīshì, 海难 hǎinàn 2 失事船只 shīshì chuánzhī [M. WD 艘 sōu] II v [船+] 沉没 [chuán+] chénmò

shipyard N 造船厂 zàochuán chǎng [M. WD 家 jiā]

shirk v 逃避 [+责任] táobì [+zérèn]

shirt N 衬衫 chènshān ■ *Do you know how to iron a shirt?* 你会熨烫衬衫吗? Nǐ huì yùntàng chènshān ma?

shirtsleeves N 衬衫袖子 chènshān xiùzi
in shirtsleeves 只穿衬衫 zhǐ chuān chènshān

shit N 1 粪便 fènbiàn, 大便 dàbiàn
Oh, shit! 啊呀, 坏了! Āyā, huàile!
2 呸, 放屁! Pēi, fàngpì!
to give sb shit 侮辱某人 wǔrǔ mǒurén
to feel like shit 感到很不舒服 gǎndào hěn bù shūfú, 感到浑身不对劲 gǎndào húnshēn búduìjìn

shiver N, v 发抖 fādǒu
to shiver with cold 冷得发抖 lěng de fādǒu

shoal N 1 一大群鱼 yí dà qún yú 2 浅滩 qiǎntān

shock I N 1 震惊 zhènjīng ■ *The news of the terrorist attack was a terrible shock to all of us.* 关于恐怖主义分子袭击的消息, 使我们大受震惊。Guānyú kǒngbù zhǔyì fènzǐ xíjī de xiāoxi, shǐ wǒmen dà shòu zhènjīng. 2 震动 zhèndòng, 冲击 chōngjī
shock absorber 减震器 jiǎnzhènqì
shock wave 冲击波 chōngjībō, 强烈反应 qiángliè fǎnyìng
3 休克 xiūkè ■ *The road accident victim is still in shock.* 交通事故受害者还在休克中。Jiāotōng shìgù shòuhàizhě háizài xiūkè zhōng.
shock therapy 休克疗法 xiūkè liáofǎ
II v 震惊 zhènjīng ■ *I was shocked to hear that the company had gone bankrupt.* 听说公司破产了, 我很震惊。Tīngshuō gōngsī pòchǎn le, wǒ hěn zhènjīng.
cultural shock 文化冲击 wénhuà chōngjī

shocking ADJ 令人震惊的 lìngrén zhènjīng de

shod v 1 See shoe II v 2 穿着…鞋子的 chuānzhuó…xiézi de

shoddy ADJ **1** 粗制滥造的 [+商品] cūzhì lànzào de [+shāngpǐn], 劣质的 lièzhì de **2** 不公正的 bù gōngzhèng de

shoe I N 鞋 xié, 鞋子 xiézi ■ *What size shoes do you wear?* 你穿什么尺码的鞋? Nǐ chuān shénme chǐmǎ de xié?
ballet shoes 芭蕾舞鞋 bālěiwǔxié
high-heeled shoes 高跟鞋 gāogēnxié
sports shoes 运动鞋 yùndòngxié
tennis shoes 网球鞋 wǎngqiúxié
walking shoes 步行鞋 bùxíngxié
If the shoe fits, (wear it.) 既然说得对, 就接受吧。Rúguǒ shuōde duì, jiù jiēshòu ba. ■ *"Are you saying I'm a wimp?" "If the shoe fits, ..."* "你说我是没用的人?" "如果说得不错, …。" "Nǐ shuō wǒ shì méiyòng de rén?" "Rúguǒ shuó de bú cuò,...."
II V (PT & PP shod) 给 (马) 钉铁蹄 gěi (mǎ) dīng tiětí

shoehorn N 鞋拔 xiébá

shoelace N 鞋带 xiédài [M. WD 根 gēn/副 fù]

shoestring N 鞋带 xiédài [M. WD 根 gēn/副 fù]
a shoestring budget 微薄的预算 wēibó de yùsuàn
on a shoestring 精打细算 jīngdǎ xìsuàn

shone See **shine**

shoo I INTERJ 嘘 xū II V (to shoo sb away) 把某人赶走 bǎ mǒurén gǎnzǒu

shoo-in N 会轻易得胜的人 huì qīngyì déshèng de rén

shook See **shake**

shook-up ADJ 心烦意乱的 xīn fán yì luàn de

shoot¹ I V (PT & PP shot) **1** 开枪 kāiqiāng, 射击 shèjī
to shoot on sight 见人就开枪 jiàn rén jiù kāiqiāng
2 拍摄 (照片/电影/电视片) pāishè (zhàopiàn/diànyǐng/diànshì piàn) ■ *The movie was shot in New Zealand.* 这部电影是在新西兰拍的。Zhè bù diànyǐng shì zài Xīnxīlán pāi de. **3** 投 [+篮] tóu [+lán], 射 [+门] shè [+mén] ■ *Paul shot the ball into the goal and won the only point.* 保罗射门进球, 得了唯一的一分。Bǎoluó shèmén jìn qiú, déle wéiyī de yì fēn.
to shoot the breeze 聊天 liáotiān, 侃大山 kǎn dàshān
to shoot your mouth off 到处乱说 dàochù luànshuō ■ *I warn you: don't shoot your mouth off about my divorce.* 我警告你: 别到处乱说我离婚的事。Wǒ jǐnggào nǐ: bié dàochù luànshuō wǒ líhūn de shì.
II N **1** (照片/电影/电视片) 拍摄 (zhàopiàn/diànyǐng/diànshì piàn) pāishè **2** 打猎 dǎliè

shoot² N 芽 yá, 苗 miáo

shooting N 枪击 qiāngjī

shooting star N 流星 liúxīng [M. WD 颗 kē]

shop I N **1** 店 diàn [M. WD 家 jiā], 店铺 diànpù [M. WD 家 jiā] **2** 工场 gōngchǎng [M. WD 间 jiān], 车间 chējiān **3** 工艺课 gōngyìkè, 手工课 shǒugōngkè ■ *I took shop in high school and enjoyed it.* 我在中学的时候上了工艺课, 很喜欢。Wǒ zài zhōngxué de shíhou shàngle gōngyì kè, hěn xǐhuan. II V 购物 gòuwù, 买东西 mǎi dōngxi

shoplift V 偷窃商品 tōuqiè shāngpǐn

shoplifter N 偷商店货物的人 tōu shāngdiàn huòwù de rén

shoplifting N 商店货物扒窃 shāngdiàn huòwù páqiè

shopping N 购物 gòuwù
shipping cart 购物推车 gòuwù tuīchē
shopping mall 购物中心 gòuwù zhōngxīn, 商场 shāngchǎng
shopping plaza 购物广场 gòuwù guǎngchǎng
shopping spree 尽情采购 jìnqíng cǎigòu
to go shopping 上街买东西 shàngjiē mǎi dōngxi, 上街采购 shàngjiē cǎigòu

shore I N 岸边 ànbian, 海岸 hǎi'àn, 湖畔 húpàn II V (to shore up) 支撑 zhīchēng

shorn See **shear**

short I ADJ **1** 短 duǎn
short circuit 短路 duǎnlù
short cut 近路 jìnlù, 捷径 jiéjìng
short story 短篇小说 duǎnpiān xiǎoshuō
short wave 短波 duǎnbō
2 矮 ǎi, 矮小 ǎixiǎo ■ *Some historical giants were short men, such as Napoleon and Deng Xiaoping.* 有些历史巨人很矮小, 像拿破仑、邓小平。Yǒuxiē lìshǐ jùrén hěn ǎixiǎo, xiàng Nápólún、Dèng Xiǎopíng. **3** 不够 bú gòu, 缺乏 quēfá
in short supply 很缺乏 hěn quēfá ■ *Bilingual talents are in short supply.* 双语人材很缺乏。Shuāngyǔ réncái hěn quēfá.
to be short with 对…很粗暴无礼 duì...hěn cūbào wúlǐ, 简慢 jiǎnmàn ■ *Sorry I was so short with you—I was really in a hurry then.* 对不起, 刚才太粗暴无礼, 我实在很匆忙。Duìbuqǐ, gāngcái tài cūbào wúlǐ, wǒ shízài hěn cōngmáng.
II V 使 [+电器] 短路 shǐ [+diànqì] duǎnlù
III N (in short) 简单地说 jiǎndān de shuō IV ADV **1** (short of) 除非 chúfēi, 要不是 yàobùshi **2** (to stop short of) 差一点 chàyìdiǎn, 险些 xiǎnxiē **3** (to cut short) 突然中断 tūrán zhōngduàn, 打断 dǎduàn

shortage N 短缺 duǎnquē

shortbread N 黄油甜酥饼 huángyóu tiánsūbǐng

short-change V 少给找头 shǎo gěi zhǎotou, 欺诈 qīzhà

shortcoming N 缺点 quēdiǎn

shorten V 缩短 suōduǎn ■ *Doctors try hard to shorten the waiting time for surgery in public* *hospitals.* 医生们努力缩短在公共医院做手术的等候时间。Yīshēngmen nǔlì suōduǎn zài gōnggòng yīyuàn zuò shǒushù de děnghòu shíjiān.

shortening N 起酥油 qǐsūyóu

shortfall N 差额 chā'é, 不足之数 bùzú zhī shù

shorthand N 速记（法）sùjì (fǎ)

shorthanded ADJ 人手不够的 rénshǒu búgòu de

shortlist V 准备决选名单 zhǔnbèi juéxuǎn míngdān

be shortlisted 进入决赛 jìnrù juésài

short-lived ADJ 短暂的 duǎnzàn de

shortly ADV **1** 不久 bù jiǔ **2** 不耐烦地 bú nàifán de

short-range ADJ **1** 短程的 duǎnchéng de **2** 短期的 duǎnqī de, 近期的 jìnqī de

a short-range plan 近期计划 jìnqī jìhuà

shorts N 短裤 duǎnkù [M. WD 条 tiáo]

short-sighted ADJ **1** 近视的 [+眼睛] jìnshi de [+yǎnjīng] **2** 短视的 [+政策] duǎnshì de [+zhèngcè]

short-term ADJ 短期的 duǎnqī de

short-term lease 短期租赁 duǎnqī zūlìn

shot I V See **shoot** II N **1** 射击 shèjī ■ *Her shots missed the target.* 她的射击都没有命中。Tā de shèjī dōu méiyǒu mìngzhòng. **2** 注射 zhùshè **3** 镜头 jìngtóu ■ *He got some great shots of his daughter in the ballet performance.* 他拍了几张很好的女儿在芭蕾舞演出时的照片。Tā pāile jǐ zhāng hěn hǎo de nǚ'ér zài bālěiwǔ yǎnchū shí de zhàopiàn.

shot in the arm 兴奋剂 xīngfènjì, 令人鼓舞的事 lìngrén gǔwǔ de shì ■ *The extra funding was a much-needed shot in the arm for the research project.* 这笔额外拨款对这项科研项目来说是十分需要的兴奋剂。Zhè bǐ éwài bōkuǎn duì zhè xiàng kēyán xiàngmù láishuō shì shífēn xūyào de xīngfènjì.

shotgun N 猎枪 lièqiāng [M. WD 支 zhī/把 bǎ]

shotgun wedding（因女方已怀孕）不得不举行的婚礼 (yīn nǚfāng yǐ huáiyùn) bùdebù jǔxíng de hūnlǐ, 奉子成婚 fèng zi chénghūn

shot put N 推铅球（运动）tuīqiānqiú (yùndòng)

should [NEG **should not** ABBREV **shouldn't**] MODAL V **1** 应该 yīnggāi ■ *You should have told me sooner.* 你应该早点告诉我的。Nǐ yīnggāi zǎodiǎn gàosu wǒ de. **2** 可能 kěnéng ■ *He should be home now.* 他现在可能回家了。Tā xiànzài kěnéng huíjiā le.

shoulder I N 肩膀 jiānbǎng ■ *Nathan injured his shoulder playing soccer.* 内森踢足球时伤了肩膀。Nèisēn tī zúqiú shí shāngle jiānbǎng.

shoulder bag 挎包 kuàbāo, 肩背包 jiānbēi bāo shoulder blade 肩胛骨 jiānjiǎgǔ

to shrug one's shoulder 耸肩膀 sǒng jiānbǎng II V 承担 [+责任] chéngdān [+zérèn]

shout V, N 喊 hǎn, 喊叫 hǎnjiào

to shout at 对…嚷嚷 duì…rāngrang ■ *She told the children to shut up when they began to shout at each other.* 孩子开始相互嚷嚷，她叫他们闭嘴。Háizi kāishǐ xiānghù rāngrang, tā jiào tāmen bìzuǐ.

shove N, V 推 tuī

push and shove 你推我挤 nǐtuīwǒjǐ

shovel I N 铁锹 tiěqiāo [M. WD 把 bǎ], 铲子 chǎnzi [M. WD 把 bǎ] II V 用铲子铲起 yòng chǎnzi chǎn qǐ

show I V (PT **showed**; PP **shown**) **1** 显示 xiǎnshì ■ *Bill's school report shows that he has made good progress.* 比尔的成绩报告单显示他大有进步。Bǐ'ěr de chéngjì bàogào dān xiǎnshì tā dà yǒu jìnbù. **2** 给…看 gěi…kàn **3** 放 fàng, 放映 fàngyìng II N **1** 演出 yǎnchū ■ *The show starts at 8 p.m.* 演出晚上八点开始。Yǎnchū wǎnshang bā diǎn kāishǐ. **2** 节目 jiémù **3** 展览 zhǎnlǎn ■ *The annual flower show attracts visitors from neighboring states.* 每年一度的花卉展览吸引了邻州来的参观者。Měi nián yí dù de huāhuì zhǎnlǎn xīyǐnle lín zhōu lái de cānguānzhě.

to be on show 展览中 zhǎnlǎn zhōng, 展出中 zhǎnchū zhōng

4 表面的样子 biǎomiàn de yàngzi ■ *His public support of the workers was nothing but a show.* 他在公众场合对工人的支持只是做做样子。Tā zài gōngzhòng chǎnghé duì gōngrén de zhīchí zhǐ shì zuòzuò yàngzi.

show business 演艺界 yǎnyìjiè

to show ... around 带领…参观 dàilíng…cānguān ■ *Thank you very much for showing us around the campus.* 谢谢你带领我们参观你们的学校。Xièxie nǐ dàilíng wǒmen cānguān nǐmen de xuéxiào.

to show off 显示 xiǎnshì, 卖弄 màinong

to show up 来 lái, 出席 chūxí ■ *The party was a disaster – only a couple of guests showed up.* 这次聚会完全失败—只有两三个人来。Zhè cì jùhuì wánquán shībài—zhǐyǒu liǎng sān ge rén lái.

show and tell N 展示与讲述课 zhǎnshì yǔ jiǎngshù kè

showcase I N [新产品+] 展示 [xīnchǎnpǐn+] zhǎnshì, 陈列 chénliè II V 展示 [+新产品] zhǎnshì [+xīn chǎnpǐn]

showdown N 摊牌 tānpái, 决战 juézhàn

shower I N **1** 阵雨 zhènyǔ **2** 淋浴（间）línyù (jiān)

shower cap 淋浴帽 línyùmào

shower gel 浴液 yù yè

3 (baby shower) 产前送礼会 chǎnqián sònglǐ huì, (bridal shower) 结婚送礼会 jiéhūn sònglǐ huì II V **1** 洗淋浴 xǐ línyù **2** 洒落 sǎluò **3** 大量地给 dàliàng de gěi

to shower sb with praise 对某人赞扬有加 duì mǒurén zànyáng yǒu jiā

showery ADJ 多阵雨的 duō zhènyǔ de

showgirl N 歌舞女演员 gēwǔ nǚyǎnyuán

showing N 1（电影）放映 (diànyǐng) fàngyìng
a private showing 内部放映 nèibù fàngyìng
2（艺术品）展览 (yìshùpǐn) zhǎnlǎn 3 表现
biǎoxiàn
a disappointing showing 令人失望的表现
lìngrén shīwàng de biǎoxiàn

showman N 演员 yǎnyuán, 艺人 yìrén

showmanship N 1 表演技巧 biǎoyǎn jìqiǎo
2（政客）作秀 (zhèngkè) zuòxiù

shown See **show**

show-off N 喜欢卖弄自己的人 xǐhuan màinong
zìjǐ de rén

showpiece N 公开展示的东西 gōngkāi zhǎnshì
de dōngxi, 样板 yàngbǎn

showroom N 陈列厅 chénlièﾂtīng

showtime N 开演时间 kāiyǎn shíjiān
It's showtime! 演出现在开始了! Yǎnchū xiànzài
kāishǐ le!

showy ADJ 花哨的 huāshao de

shrank See **shrink**

shrapnel N 弹片 dànpiàn [M. WD 片 piàn]

shred I N 细条 xìtiáo, 碎片 suìpiàn
to tear sth to shreds 把某物撕成碎片 bǎ
mǒuwù sī chéng suìpiàn
II v 1 把 [+文件] 切碎 bǎ [+wénjiàn] qiēsuì
2 把 [+食物] 切成碎片 bǎ [+shíwù] qiēchéng
suìpiàn

shredder N 碎纸机 suìzhǐjī

shrewd ADJ 精明的 jīngmíng de, 判断正确的
pànduàn zhèngquè de

shriek N, v 尖叫 jiānjiào, 尖声喊叫 jiānshēng
hǎnjiào
a shriek of terror 恐怖的尖叫声 kǒngbù de
jiānjiào shēng

shrill ADJ 尖叫的 jiānjiào de

shrimp N 小虾 xiǎoxiā

shrine N 圣坛 shèng tán, 圣地 shèngdì

shrink[1]（PT **shrank**; PP **shrunk**）v 缩缩 suō, 缩小
suōxiǎo
to shrink from 逃避 táobì

shrink[2] 精神病医生 jīngshénbìng yīshēng

shrinkwrap N 收缩性薄膜 shōusuōxìng bómó

shrivel, shrivel up v（使…）收缩 (shǐ...)
shōusuō,（使…）干瘪 (shǐ...) gānbiě

shroud I N 1 覆盖（物）fùgài (wù), 遮蔽（物）
zhēbì (wù)
in a shroud of secrecy 在完全秘密之中 zài wánquán mìmì zhī zhōng
2（包）尸布 (bāo) shī bù II v 覆盖 fùgài, 遮蔽
zhēbì

shrub N 灌木 guànmù [M. WD 棵 kē]

shrubbery N 灌木丛 guànmù cóng

shrug I v 耸肩 sǒngjiān
to shrug off 不予重视 bùyú zhòngshì, 不加理会
bù jiā lǐhuì

II N 耸肩 sǒngjiān

shrunk See **shrink**

shrunken ADJ 干瘪的 gānbiě de

shudder v 发抖 fādǒu, 颤抖 chàndǒu

shuffle I v 1 拖着脚走 tuōzhe jiǎo zǒu, 蹒跚
pánshān 2 洗牌 xǐpái 3 调动 [+人员] diàodòng
[+rényuán] II N 1 拖着脚走路 tuōzhe jiǎo
zǒulù, 蹒跚 pánshān 2 洗牌 xǐpái 3（人员）调动
(rényuán) diàodòng

shun v 躲避 duǒbì, 躲开 duǒkāi

shunt I v 1 使 [电／血液+] 分流 shǐ [diàn/xuèyè]
fēnliú 2 把 [+人] 转移到 bǎ [+rén] zhuǎnyí dào
II N 旁路 pánglù, 旁通道 pángtōng dào

shush v 示意保持安静 shìyì bǎochí ānjìng, 叫人
别作声 jiào rén bié zuòshēng

shut I v（PT & PP **shut**）关上 guānshang ■ Please
shut the door. The AC is on. 请把门关上，空调开
着呢。Qǐng bǎ mén guānshang, kōngtiáo kāizhe
ne.
to shut down 关门 guānmén, 停止营业（生产）
tíngzhǐ yíngyè (shēngchǎn)
to shut up 闭嘴 bìzuǐ ■ Just shut up; I've had
enough. 闭嘴，我听够了。Bìzuǐ, wǒ tīnggou le.
II ADJ 关好的 guānhǎo de

shutdown N 关闭 guānbì, 停业 tíngyè

shut-eye N (to get some shut-eye) 闭一会眼睛 bì
yíhuì yǎnjing, 睡一会 shuì yíhuì

shut-in N 不能外出的人 bùnéng wàichū de rén

shutter N 1（照相机）快门 (zhàoxiàngjī) kuài-
mén 2 百叶窗 bǎiyèchuāng [M. WD 扇 shàn]

shuttle I N 1 来回往返的汽车／飞机 láihuí wǎngfǎn
de qìchē/fēijī 2（织布机）梭子 (zhībùjī) suōzi
shuttle diplomacy 穿梭外交 chuānsuō wàijiāo
II v 穿梭往返 chuānsuō wǎngfǎn

shuttle-cock N 羽毛球 yǔmáoqiú

shy I ADJ 1 害羞的 hàixiū de ■ Even at 20, he is
still shy around girls. 即使二十岁了，他在女孩子
面前还是害羞。Jíshí èrshí suì le, tā zài nǚháizi
miànqián hái shì hàixiū. 2 (shy of sth) 没有达
到 méiyǒu dádào II v (to shy away from) 避开
bìkāi, 回避 huíbì

shyster N 奸诈的人 jiānzhà de rén

sibling N 兄弟姐妹 xiōngdi jiěmèi
sibling rivalry 兄弟姐妹之间的竞争 xiōngdi
jiěmèi zhījiān de jìngzhēng

sic ADV 原文如此 yuánwén rú cǐ

sick I ADJ 1 病了 bìng le, 生病了 shēngbìng le
sick leave 病假 bìngjià
sick pay 病假工资 bìngjià gōngzī
2 恶心 ěxīn, 呕吐 ǒutù ■ The boat ride made him
terribly sick. 乘船让他感到恶心难受。Chéngchuán
ràng tā gǎndao ěxīn nánshòu. 3 厌倦 yànjuàn
■ I'm really sick and tired of his grumbling. 他老
是唠唠叨叨地抱怨，我实在听厌了。Tā lǎoshì lāolāo
dāodāo bàoyuàn, wǒ shízài tīngyàn le.

sickbay

to make ... sick 叫…感到厌恶 jiào...gǎndao yànwù, 叫…感到愤慨 jiào...gǎndao fènkǎi **II** N (the sick) 病人 bìngrén

sickbay N 病房 bìngfáng [M. WD 间 jiān]

sickbed N 病床 bìngchuáng [M. WD 张 zhāng]

sicken v 1 使…厌恶 shǐ...yànwù 2 (使…) 生病 (shǐ...) shēngbìng

sickening ADJ 令人厌恶的 lìng rén yànwù de, 令人作呕的 lìng rén zuò'ǒu de

sickle N 镰刀 liándāo [M. WD 把 bǎ]

sickly ADJ 1 体弱多病的 [+人] tǐruò duōbìng de [+rén] 2 难闻的 [+气味] nánwén de [+qìwèi]

sickness N 病 bìng, 疾病 jíbìng

side I N 1 部分 bùfen, 部位 bùwèi, 面 miàn 2 身边 shēnbiān, 身旁 shēnpáng ■ *Come and sit by my side.* 来，坐到我旁边来。Lái, zuò dào wǒ pángbiān lái. 3 面 miàn, 侧面 cèmiàn 4 边 biān ■ *They set up a fruit stand by the side of the road.* 他们在路边摆设水果摊。Tāmen zài lùbiān bǎishè shuǐguǒ tān. 5 一方 yì fāng ■ *There are faults on both sides.* 双方都有错。Shuāngfāng dōu yǒu cuò. **II** ADJ 旁边的 pángbiān de, 侧面的 cèmiàn de

a side street 小巷 xiǎoxiàng, 小路 xiǎolù

side dish 配菜 pèicài

side effect 副作用 fù zuòyòng

side order 另点的小菜 lìng diǎn de xiǎocài **III** v (to side against) 站在…的对立面 zhàn zài...de duìlìmiàn

to side with 站在…的一面 zhàn zài...de yímiàn, 支持 zhīchí

sideboard N 餐具柜 cānjù guì

sideburns N 脸腮胡子 liǎnsāi húzi

sidecar N (摩托车的) 边车 (mótuōchē de) biānchē

sidekick N 助手 zhùshǒu

sideline I N 副业 fùyè

on the sideline 旁观 pángguān, 采取观望态度 cǎiqǔ guānwàng tàidu **II** v 不让 [+运动员] 参加比赛 búràng [+yùndòng-yuán] cānjiā bǐsài

sidelong ADJ (a sidelong glance) 斜着眼睛看 xiézhe yǎnjing kàn, 偷看 tōukàn

sideshow N 1 主场外的游乐节目 zhǔchǎng wài de yóulè jiémù 2 次要事件 cìyào shìjiàn

sidestep v 避开 bìkāi, 回避 huíbì

sidetrack v 1 使…离题 shǐ...lítí 2 拖延 tuōyán

sidewalk N 人行道 rénxíngdào [M. WD 条 tiáo]

sideways ADV 向一边 (地) xiàng yìbiān (de)

siding N 1 墙板 qiáng bǎn [M. WD 块 kuài], 壁板 bìbǎn [M. WD 块 kuài] 2 (铁道) 岔轨 (tiědào) páng guǐ, 侧线 cèxiàn

sidle v 悄悄走近 qiāoqiāo zǒujìn

siege N 包围 bāowéi, 围困 wéikùn

to be under siege ① 被包围 bèibāo wéi ② 受到围攻 shòudào wéigōng

siesta N 午睡 wǔshuì

sieve I N (筛) 子 (shāi) zi, 漏勺 lòusháo **II** v (用筛子) 筛 (yòng shāizi) shāi

sift v 1 筛 [+面粉] shāi [+miànfěn], 过滤 guòlǜ 2 详细检查 xiángxì jiǎnchá

sigh v 叹气 tànqì, 舒了口气 shū le kǒuqì ■ *Mom sighed with relief when Jimmy came back home, safe and sound.* 杰米安全回家，妈妈放心地舒了一口气。Jiémí ānquán huíjiā, māma fàngxīn de shū le yìkǒuqì. **II** N 叹气 tànqì

sight N 1 视觉 shìjué ■ *The old man has lost the sight of one eye.* 老人一只眼失明了。Lǎorén yì zhī yǎn shīmíng le. 2 看到 kàndao 3 景象 jǐngxiàng ■ *Welcome to the sights of Singapore!* 欢迎来新加坡观光。Huānyíng lái Xīnjiāpō guānguāng.

out of sight 不看见 bú kànjiàn

out of sight, out of mind 不看见，不想到。(→眼不见，心不烦。) Bú kànjiàn, bù xiǎng dào. (→Yǎn bú jiàn, xīn bù fán.)

sighted ADJ 有视力的 yǒu shìlì de, 能看见的 néng kànjian de

sighting N 看到 kàndào, 目击 mùjī

UFO sighting 目击不明飞行物 mùjī bùmíng fēixíngwù

sightings of the fugitive 多次看到逃犯 duōcì kàndào táofàn

sightless ADJ 失明的 shīmíng de

sightread v 随看随奏 [+乐曲] suí kàn suí zòu [+yuèqǔ], 随看随唱 [+歌曲] suí kàn suí chàng [+gēqǔ]

sightseeing N 观光 guānguāng, 游览 yóulǎn

sign I N 1 符号 fúhào ■ *"Do you know what this sign ">" means?"* "你知道 ">" 这个符号是什么意思吗？" "Nǐ zhīdào ">" zhè ge fúhào shì shénme yìsi ma?" 2 标志 biāozhì 3 招牌 zhāopai 4 手势 shǒushì ■ *The man in the car in front gave us a sign to pass him.* 我们前面车里的人向我们打手势，让我们超过去。Wǒmen qiánmian chēlǐ de rén xiàng wǒmen dǎ shǒushì, ràng wǒmen chāoguoqu. 5 迹象 jìxiàng ■ *There is no sign of an immediate cessation of hostilities.* 没有立即停止冲突的迹象。Méiyǒu lìjí tíngzhǐ chōngtū de jìxiàng. **II** v 1 签字 qiānzì 2 打手势 dǎ shǒushì, 示意 shìyì

to sign for 签收 qiānshōu

to sign up ① 聘用 pìnyòng ■ *A multinational corporation signed him up even before he left college.* 他大学还没有毕业，一家跨国公司就聘用他了。Tā dàxué hái méiyǒu bìyè, yì jiā kuàguó gōngsī jiù pìnyòng tā le. ② 报名参加 bàomíng cānjiā

signal I N 信号 xìnhào ■ *When I give the signal, press the button.* 我给你信号，你就按铃。Wǒ gěi nǐ xìnhào, nǐ jiù àn líng. **II** v 1 打手势示意 dǎ shǒushì shìyì ■ *The policeman raised his hand*

and signaled to the motorist to stop. 警察举起手，要驾车人停下。Jǐngchá jǔqǐ shǒu, yào jiàchē rén tíngxià. **2** 标志 biāozhì ■ *This state visit signaled the beginning of a new relationship between the two countries.* 这次国事访问标志两国新关系的开始。Zhè cì guóshì fǎngwèn biāozhì liǎng guó xīn guānxi de kāishǐ. **3** 明确表示 míngquè biǎoshì **III** ADJ *(a signal success)* 巨大的成功 jùdà de chénggōng

signatory N 签署者 qiānshǔzhě, 签约国 qiānyuē guó

signature I N **1** 签字 qiānzì, 签名 qiānmíng
an illegible signature 无法辨认的签名 wúfǎ biànrèn de qiānmíng
to collect signatures 收集签名 shōují qiānmíng **2** 特征 tèzhēng, 标志 biāozhì **II** ADJ 标志性的 biāozhìxìng de, 特有的 tèyǒu de

significance N 意义 yìyì

significant ADJ 有重大意义的 yǒu zhòngdà yìyì de ■ *That law proved to be significant to the legal system of the state.* 那项法律被证明对州法律制度有重大意义。Nà xiàng fǎlǜ bèi zhèngmíng duì zhōu fǎlǜ yǒu zhòngdà yìyì.
significant other 最重要的那位（丈夫／妻子，男朋友／女朋友）zuì zhòngyàode nà wèi (zhàngfu/qīzi, nánpéngyou/nǚpéngyou)

signify V 标志 biāozhì, 意味 yìwèi

signing N 签字 qiānzì, 签署 qiānshǔ
signing ceremony 签字仪式 qiānzì yíshì

sign language N 手（势）语 shǒu (shì) yǔ

signpost N 路标 lùbiāo, 指示牌 zhǐshì pái

silence N **1** 寂静 jìjìng ■ *The silence of the night was broken by peals of thunder.* 夜的寂静被阵阵雷声打破。Yè de jìjìng bèi zhènzhèn léishēng dǎpò. **2** 沉默 chénmò
Speech is silver, and silence is golden 言语是银，沉默是金。Yányǔ shì yín, chénmò shì jīn.

silencer N 消音器 xiāoshēngqì

silent ADJ **1** 寂静的 jìjìng de ■ *The street was deserted and silent.* 街上没有人，一片寂静。Jiēshang méiyǒu rén, yí piàn jìjìng. **2** 沉默的 chénmò de, 一言不发的 yì yán bù fā de ■ *She was silent for a few months before I got an e-mail from her.* 她沉默了几个月，我才收到她一份电子邮件。Tā chénmòle jǐ ge yuè, wǒ cái shōudao tā yí fèn diànzǐ yóujiàn.
(the) silent majority 沉默的大多数 chénmò de dàduōshù
silent partner 不参与经营的合伙人 bù cānyù jīngyíng de héhuǒrén

silhouette I N 侧面影像 cèmiàn yǐngxiàng, 黑色轮廓画象 hēisè lúnkuò huàxiàng **II** V 现出黑色轮廓 xiànchū hēisè lúnkuò

silicon (Sì) N 硅 guī
Silicon Valley 硅谷 Guīgǔ

silk N 丝绸 sīchóu, 绸缎 chóuduàn

silken ADJ **1** 丝绸做的 sīchóu zuò de **2** 光泽柔滑的 guāngzé róuhuá de

silkworm N 蚕 cán

silky ADJ 丝绸般的 sīchóu bān de, 光泽柔滑的 guāngzé róuhuá de

sill N 窗台 chuāngtái

silly ADJ 愚蠢的 yúchǔn de, 傻的 shǎ de ■ *He made one silly mistake and there was no end to his troubles.* 他犯了一个愚蠢的错误，就麻烦不断。Tā fànle yí ge yúchǔn de cuòwù, jiù máfan bú duàn.

silt I N 淤泥 yūní, 泥沙 níshā **II** V (to silt up) 淤塞 yūsè

silver I N **1** 银 yín, 银器 yínqì **2** 银（白）色 yín (bái) sè **II** ADJ 银制的 yínzhì de, 银质的 yínzhì de
silver anniversary 银婚（纪念日）yínhūn (jìniànrì), 结婚二十五周年 jiéhūn èrshíwǔ zhōunián
silver medal 银牌 yínpái
silver plate 镀银器皿 dùyín qìmǐn
silver plated ADJ 镀银的 dùyín de

silversmith N 银匠 yínjiàng

silverware N 银器 yínqì ■ *Her parents sold all their silverware to pay for her college education.* 她的父母卖掉了所有的银器供她上大学。Tāde fùmǔ màidiaole suǒyǒu de yínqì gòng tā shàng dàxué.

similar ADJ 相似的 xiāngshì de ■ *His family background is similar to mine.* 他的家庭背景和我很相像。Tā de jiātíng bèijǐng hé wǒ hěn xiāngxiàng.

similarity N 相似 xiāngsì, 相似性 xiāngsì xìng ■ *Discuss the similarities and differences between the two business plans.* 请你们讨论一下这两个商业计划的相似和不同点。Qǐng nǐmen tǎolùn yí xià zhè liǎng ge shāngyè jìhuà de xiāngsì hé bù tóng diǎn.

similarly ADV 同样（地）tóngyàng (de), 相似（地）xiāngsì (de)

simile N 明喻 míngyù

simmer I V **1** （用文火）慢慢煮 (yòng wénhuǒ) mànmàn zhǔ, 炖 dùn **2** （冲突）渐渐激化 (chōngtū) jiànjiàn jīhuà **II** N （用文火）慢慢煮 (yòng wénhuǒ) mànmàn zhǔ, 炖 dùn

simper V 傻笑 shǎxiào

simple ADJ **1** 简单的 jiǎndān de ■ *If you say it in simple Chinese, I can understand you.* 如果你说简单的中文，我就听得懂。Rúguǒ nǐ shuō jiǎndān de Zhōngwén, wǒ jiù tīngde dǒng. **2** 简朴的 jiǎnpǔ de
simple fracture 单纯性骨折 dānchún xìng gǔzhé
simple interest 单利 dānlì

simple-minded ADJ 头脑简单的 tóunǎo jiǎndān de

simplicity N 简单容易 jiǎndān róngyì

simplify v 简化 jiǎnhuà ■ *The process has been much simplified.* 这个过程被简化了。Zhè ge guòchéng bèi jiǎnhuà le.
simplified (Chinese) character 简体字 jiǎntǐzì

simply ADV 1 仅仅 jǐnjǐn, 只是 zhǐ shì ■ *He took the job simply because it was the only one available.* 他拿了那份工作，仅仅因为当时只有那一份工作。Tā nále nà fèn gōngzuò, jǐnjǐn yīnwèi dāngshí zhǐ yǒu nà yí fèn gōngzuò. 2 简直 jiǎnzhí ■ *I simply can't understand how you wrecked the car.* 我简直不明白，你是怎么样把车毁成这个样子的。Wǒ jiǎnzhí bù míngbai, nǐ shì zěnme yàng bǎ chē huǐchéng zhè ge yàngzi de. 3 简单地 jiǎndān de 4 简朴地 jiǎnpǔ de

simulate v 模拟 mónǐ, 模仿 mófǎng

simulation N 模拟 mónǐ, 模仿 mófǎng
simulation exercise 模拟练习 mónǐ liànxí
computer simulation 计算机模拟 jìsuànjī mónǐ

simultaneous ADJ 同时（发生）tóngshí (fāshēng)
simultaneous interpreter 同声传译译员 tóngshēng chuányì yìyuán

sin I N 罪 zuì, 罪孽 zuìniè II v 违犯教规 wéifàn jiàoguī, 犯罪 fànzuì

since I CONJ 1 自从 zìcóng ■ *Philip has been wearing glasses since he was 15.* 菲利浦从十五岁就开始戴眼镜。Fēilìpǔ cóng shíwǔ suì jiù kāishǐ dài yǎnjìng. 2 因为 yīnwèi, 由于 yóuyú ■ *Dad is sleeping in since it's Saturday.* 爸爸在睡懒觉，因为今天是星期六。Bàba zài shuìlǎnjiào, yīnwèi jīntiān shì xīngqīliù. II PREP 自从 zìcóng ■ *We haven't had much rain since spring.* 自从春季以来，没有下过什么雨。Zìcóng chūnjì yǐlái, méiyǒu xiàguo shénme yǔ. III ADV 自从那以后 zìcóng nà yǐhòu, 后来 hòulái ■ *I met him last Christmas and haven't heard from him since.* 我在上个圣诞节和他见过面，以后就一直没有听到他的消息。Wǒ zài shàngge Shèngdànjié hé tā jiàn guò miàn, yǐhòu jiù yìzhí méiyǒu tīngdào tāde xiāoxi.

sincere ADJ 真诚的 zhēnchéng de ■ *My best friend Ralph is a sincere and honest man.* 我最好的朋友拉尔夫是一个真诚老实的人。Wǒ zuìhǎo de péngyou Lā'ěrfū shì yí ge zhēnchéng lǎoshi de rén.

sincerely ADV 真诚地 zhēnchéng de
Sincerely Yours 您诚挚的 nín zhēnchéng de, 你的 nǐde

sincerity N 真诚 zhēnchéng, 诚挚 chéngzhì
in all sincerity 十分真诚地 shífēn zhēnchéng de

sinew N 腱 jiàn, 力量 lìliang

sinewy ADJ 肌肉发达的 jīròu fādá de

sinful ADJ 有罪（过）的 yǒuzuì (guò) de, 极不应该的 jí bù yīnggāi de

sing (PT **sang**; PP **sung**) v 唱 chàng, 唱歌 chànggē ■ *She is singing the baby to sleep.* 她唱着歌给孩子催眠。Tā chàngzhe gē gěi háizi cuīmián.
to sing along 跟着…一起唱 gēnzhe…yìqǐ chàng
to sing sb's praises 高度赞扬某人 gāodù zànyáng mǒurén

Singapore N 新加坡 Xīnjiāpō

Singaporean I ADJ 新加坡的 Xīnjiāpō de II N 新加坡人 Xīnjiāpōrén

singe v 烧焦 shāojiāo

singer N 歌手 gēshǒu, 歌唱家 gēchàngjiā [M. WD 名 míng/位 wèi]
pop singer 流行歌手 liúxíng gēshǒu

single I ADJ 1 一 yī, 唯一的 wéiyī de ■ *They won by a single point.* 他们赢了一分。(→他们以一分领先。) Tāmen yíngle yì fēn. (→Tāmen yǐ yì fēn lǐngxiān.) 2 单人的 dānrén de ■ *Can I reserve one single room and one double room?* 我能不能订一间单人房、一间双人房？Wǒ néngbunéng dìng yì jiān dānrénfáng, yì jiān shuāngrénfáng? single file 一路纵排 yílù zòng pái, 单行 dānxíng 3 单身（的）dānshēn (de) ■ *George stayed single his entire life.* 乔治一辈子都是单身。Qiáozhì yí bèizi dōu shì dānshēn. II v (to single out) 挑选出 tiāoxuǎn chū

single-breasted ADJ 单排纽扣的（上衣）dānpái niǔkòu de (shàngyī) [M. WD 件 jiàn]

single-handed ADJ 单枪匹马的 dānqiāng pǐmǎ de, 独自一人的 dúzì yìrén de

single-minded ADJ 一心一意 yì xīn yí yì

singles N 1 单身汉 dānshēnhàn, 未婚女子 wèihūn nǚzǐ 2 单打比赛 dāndǎbǐsài

singly ADV 单个地 dān gè de, 一个一个地 yí ge yí ge de

singsong N 反复起伏的语调 fǎnfù qǐfú de yǔdiào

singular I ADJ 1 （语法）单数的 (yǔfǎ) dānshù de 2 唯一的 wéiyī de, 独一的 dúyī de 3 异常的 [+才能] yìcháng de [+cáinéng], 非凡的 fēifán de II N （语法）单数 (yǔfǎ) dānshù

singularly ADV 异常地 yìcháng de, 非凡地 fēifán de

sinister ADJ 邪恶的 xié'è de, 阴险的 yīnxiǎn de

sink[1] (PT **sank**; PP **sunk**) v 1 [石头+] 下沉 [shítou+] xiàchén ■ *The rock sank to the bottom of the pond.* 岩石沉到池塘底。Yánshí chéndào chítáng dǐ. 2 [价格+] 下降 [jiàgé+] xiàjiàng, 减少 jiǎnshǎo
to sink into despair 陷入绝望之中 xiànrù juéwàng zhīzhōng
to sink or swim 沉浮 chénfú, 自找生路 zìzhǎo shēnglù
3 挖 [+井] wā [+jǐng]

sink[2] N 洗脸盆 xǐliǎnpén, 洗涤池 xǐdí chí

sinner N 有罪过的人 yǒu zuìguò de rén, 罪人 zuìrén

sinus N 鼻窦 bídòu

sip I v 小口喝 xiǎokǒu hē, 啜 chuò, 抿 mǐn II N 一小口 [+酒] yì xiǎokǒu [+jiǔ]

siphon I N 虹吸管 hóngxīguǎn II v 1 用虹吸管吸出 yòng hóngxīguǎn xīchū 2 (非法) 抽调 [+资金] (fēifǎ) chōudiào [+zījīn]

sir N 先生 xiānsheng ■ *May I take your order, sir?* 先生，可以请您点菜了吗？Xiānsheng, kěyǐ qǐng nín diǎncài le ma?

sire v 生殖 shēngzhí, 繁殖 fánzhí

siren N 气筒 qìtǒng, 警报器 jǐngbàoqì air-raid siren 空袭警报 kōngxí jǐngbào

sirloin, sirloin steak N 牛里脊肉 niú lǐji ròu

sissy I N 女孩子气的男孩 nǔháizi qì de nánhái, 娘娘腔的男孩 niángniangqiāng de nánhái II ADJ 女孩子气的 nǔháizi qì de, 娘娘腔的 niángniangqiāng de

sister N 1 姐姐 jiějie, 妹妹 mèimei, 姐妹 jiěmèi ■ *My sister Agnes and I went to the art exhibit together.* 我和我的姐妹阿格尼丝一起去看艺术展览。Wǒ hé wǒ de jiěmèi Āgénísī yìqǐ qù kàn yìshù zhǎnlǎn.
sister city 姐妹城市 jiěmèi chéngshì ■ *San Francisco and Shanghai are sister cities.* 旧金山和上海是姐妹城市。Jiùjīnshān hé Shanghǎi shì jiěmèi chéngshì.
2 修女 xiūnǚ

sisterhood N 1 姐妹情谊 jiěmèi qíngyì 2 妇女宗教团契 fùnǔ zōngjiào tuánqì

sister-in-law N 嫂嫂 sǎosao (elder brother's wife), 弟媳 dìmèi (younger brother's wife), 小姨 xiǎoyí (wife's sister), 小姑 xiǎogū (husband's sister)

sit (PT & PP sat) v 1 坐 zuò
to sit back 放松休息 fàngsōng xiūxi ■ *At the holiday resort all you have to do is sit back and be pampered.* 在这个度假胜地，你要做的就是完全放松、让人侍候。Zài zhè ge dùjià shèngdì, nǐ yào zuò de jiù shì wánquán fàngsōng, ràng rén shìhòu.
to sit up and take notice 开始关注 kāishǐ guānzhù, 警觉起来 jǐngjué qǐlái
2 [国会+] 开会 [guóhuì+] kāihuì
to sit on 是委员会成员 shì wěiyuánhuì chéngyuán

sitcom See **situation comedy**

sit-down ADJ 有服务员侍候的 [+餐馆] yǒufú wùyuán shìhòu de [+cānguǎn], 非自助餐的 fēi zìzhùcān de

site I N 地方 dìfang, 地点 dìdiǎn
on site 在现场 zài xiànchǎng
camp site 露营地 lùyíngdì
construction/building site 建筑工地 jiànzhù gōngdì, 工地 gōngdì
II v (be sited) 位于 wèiyú

sit-in N 静坐示威 jìngzuò shìwēi

sitter N (babysitter) (替人照看孩子的) 保姆 (tìrén zhàokàn háizi de) bǎomǔ

sitting N 1 (分批用餐的) 一批 (fēnpī yòngcān de) yìpī 2 (in one sitting) 一口气 yìkǒuqì
a sitting duck 容易击中的目标 róngyì jīzhòng de mùbiāo

situated ADJ 位于 wèiyú, 座落在 zuòluò zài

situation N 1 形势 xíngshì ■ *The present international situation is, to say the least, volatile.* 目前的国际形势说得最好也是变幻不定。Mùqián de guójì xíngshì shuóde zuìhǎo yě shì biànhuàn bú dìng.
2 处境 hǔjìng, 状况 zhuàngkuàng

situation comedy (ABBREV sitcom) N 情景喜剧 qíngjǐng xǐjù

sit-up N 仰卧起坐 yǎng wò qǐ zuò

six NUM 六 liù, 6

six-pack N 六罐/瓶装 liù guàn/píng zhuāng, 半打瓶 bàndá píng

sixteen NUM 十六 shíliù, 16

sixth NUM 第六 dìliù

sixty NUM 六十 liùshí, 60

sizable ADJ 相当大 /多的 xiāngdāng dà/duō de

size N 1 大小 dàxiǎo, 体积 tǐjī, 分量 fènliàng ■ *Good things come in small sizes.* 好东西，小分量。(→好东西份量都不大。) Hǎo dōngxi, xiǎo fènliàng. (→ Hǎo dōngxi fènliáng dōu bú dà.)
2 多少 duōshǎo, 数目 shùmù ■ *The bank branch seldom receives a deposit of that size.* 这家银行分行很少收到这么大的一笔存款。Zhè jiā yínháng fēnháng hěn shǎo shōudao zhème dà de yì bǐ cúnkuǎn. 3 尺码 chǐmǎ

sizzle I v [在煎锅里+] 发出嘶嘶声 [zài jiānguō lǐ] fā chū sīsī shēng II N 嘶嘶声 sīsī shēng

skate I v 溜冰 liūbīng I N (ice skate) 滑冰鞋 huábīng xié [M. WD 双 shuāng], 溜冰鞋 liūbīng xié [M. WD 双 shuāng]
roller skate 旱冰鞋 hànbīng xié

skateboard N 滑板 huábǎn

skater N 溜冰者 liūbīng zhě, 滑冰者 huábīng zhě

skeleton N 骨架 gǔjià, 骨骼 gǔgé
skeleton key 万能钥匙 wànnéng yàoshi
skeleton service 最基本的服务 zuì jīběn de fúwù
skeleton staff 必不可少的工作人员 bì bùkěshǎo de gōngzuò rényuán

skeptic N 怀疑论者 huáiyílùnzhě

skeptical ADJ 持怀疑态度的 chí huáiyí tàidu de, 不相信的 bù xiāngxìn de

skepticism N 怀疑态度 huáiyí tàidu, 怀疑论 huáiyílùn

sketch I N 1 素描 sùmiáo, 速写 sùxiě 2 滑稽短剧 gǔjī duǎnjù [M. WD 出 chū] II v 画速写 huà sùxiě, 画素描 huà sùmiáo

sketchy ADJ 粗略的 cūlüè de

skew v 歪曲的 wāiqū de, 曲解 qūjiě

skewer I N 烤肉叉 kǎoròuchā [M. WD 把 bǎ]

II v (用烤肉叉) 把 [+食物] 串起来 (yòng kǎoròuchā) bǎ [+shíwù] chuànqǐlái

ski I v 滑雪 huáxuě II N 滑雪板 huáxuě bǎn [M. WD 副 fù]

skid I v [汽车+] 滑向一边 [qìchē+] huá xiàng yìbiān, 打滑 dǎhuá II N (车辆) 打滑 (chēliàng) dǎhuá
skid marks (汽车) 打滑痕迹 (qìchē) dǎhuá hénjì
to hit the skids 突然恶化 tūrán èhuà

skier N 滑雪者 huáxuězhě

skies N 天空 tiānkōng

skill N 技能 jìnéng, 技巧 jìqiǎo

skilled ADJ 有技巧的 yǒu jìqiǎo de
skilled worker 技术工人 jìshù gōngrén

skillet N 长柄平底煎锅 chángbǐng píngdǐ jiānguō

skillful ADJ 高技能的 gāo jìnéng de, 有技巧的 yǒu jìqiǎo de, 熟练的 shúliàn de ■ The skillful skater gave a dazzling performance. 技巧很高的溜冰运动员作了一场令人眼花缭乱的表演。Jìqiǎo hěn gāo de liūbīng yùndòngyuán zuòle yì cháng lìngrén yǎnhuā liáoluàn de biǎoyǎn.

skim v 1 从液体表面撇去浮物 cóng yètǐ biǎomiàn piē qù fúwù 2 浏览 [+报纸标题] liúlǎn [+bàozhǐ biāotí]
skim milk 脱脂牛奶 tuōzhī niúnǎi

skimp v 舍不得花钱／时间 shěbudé huāqián/shíjiān

skimpy ADJ 1 太短的 [+裙子] tài duǎn de [+qúnzi], 过于暴露的 guòyú bàolù de 2 过分节省的 guòfèn jiéshěng de

skin I N 1 皮肤 pífū ■ One should never be discriminated against because of the color of one's skin. 一个人不应该因为是肤色而受歧视。Yí ge rén bù yīnggāi yīnwèi fūsè ér shòu qíshì. 2 [动物／水果+] 皮 [dòngwù/shuǐguǒ+] pí ■ Don't throw the banana skin on the footpath—someone might slip on it. 不要把香蕉皮扔在走道上，可能有人会滑倒。Bú yào bǎ xiāngjiāopí rēng zài zǒudàoshang, kěnéng yǒurén huì huádǎo.
to be skin and bone 皮包骨 pí bāo gǔ, 骨瘦如柴 gǔ shòu rú chái
to have thick skin 脸皮厚 liǎnpí hòu
II v 剥去…的皮 bāoqù...de pí, 去皮 qùpí

skin-deep ADJ 肤浅的 fūqiǎn de

skinflint N 小气鬼 xiǎoqi guǐ

skinhead N 光头党 guāngtóu dǎng

skinny ADJ 瘦得皮包骨头的 shòu dé pí bāo gútou de
skinny dipping 裸 (体) (游) 泳 luǒ (tǐ) (yóu) yǒng

skin-tight ADJ 紧身的 jǐnshēn de

skip I v 1 轻快得跳 qīngkuài dé tiào, 蹦跳 bèngtiào
to skip rope 跳绳 tiàoshéng
2 匆匆离开 cōngcōng líkāi

to skip town 逃离出城 táolí chūchéng
to skip a year 跳级 tiàojí
3 不做 bú zuò, 跳过 tiàoguò
to skip breakfast 不吃早饭 bù chī zǎo fàn
II N 轻跳 qīng tiào, 蹦跳 bèngtiào

skipper I N 1 船长 chuánzhǎng [M. WD 位 wèi] 2 运动队队长 yùndòngduì duìzhǎng II v 当船长／运动队队长 dāng chuánzhǎng/yùndòngduì duìzhǎng

skirmish N 小规模冲突 xiǎoguīmó chōngtū

skirt I N 裙子 qúnzi II v 1 沿着…边缘行走 yánzhe...biānyuán xíngzǒu 2 绕过 [+敏感话题] ràoguò [+mǐngǎn huàtí]

skit N 滑稽短剧 gǔjī duǎnjù, 讽刺短文 fěngcì duǎnwén

skittish ADJ 1 [马+] 容易受惊的 [mǎ+] róngyì shòujīng de 2 [人+] 小心翼翼的 [rén+] xiǎoxīn yìyì de

skulk v 躲躲闪闪 duǒduǒ shǎnshǎn, 鬼鬼祟祟 guǐguǐ suìsuì

skull N 头颅 tóulú

skullcap N (牧师／犹太男子戴的) 圆便帽 (mùshi/Yóutài nánzǐ dài de) yuán biànmào

skunk N 臭鼬 chòuyòu [M. WD 只 zhī], 黄鼠狼 huángshǔláng [M. WD 只 zhī]

sky (PL **skies**) N 天空 tiānkōng ■ For this remarkable young man's career, the sky's the limit. 这位杰出的年轻人前途无量。Zhè wèi jiéchū de niánqīng rén qiántú wú liàng.

skydiver N 跳伞运动员 tiàosǎn yùndòngyuán

skydiving N 跳伞 (运动) tiàosǎn (yùndòng)

sky-high ADJ 极高的 [+价格] jí gāo de [+jiàgé]

skylark N 云雀 yúnquè [M. WD 只 zhī]

skylight N 天窗 tiānchuāng [M. WD 扇 shàn]

skyline N (空中) 轮廓线 (kōngzhōng) lúnkuòxiàn

skyrocket v 猛升 měng shēng, 剧增 jùzēng

skyscraper N 摩天大楼 mótiān dàlóu [M. WD 幢 zhuàng/座 zuò]

slab N 厚板 hòubǎn, 平板 píngbǎn [M. WD 块 kuài]
a slab of beef 一大块牛肉 yí dà kuài niúròu

slack I ADJ 1 [生意+] 清淡的 [shēngyì+] qīngdàn de, 萧条的 xiāotiáo de 2 [纪律+] 松懈的 [jìlǜ+] sōngxiè de, 马虎的 mǎhu de 3 [绳子+] 松的 [shéngzi+] sōng de II N 1 多余的资金／能力 duōyú de zījīn/nénglì 2 松弛 (部份) sōngchí (bùfen)
to take up the slack 接替 jiētì, 补足 bǔzú
III v 松劲 sōngjìn, 松懈 sōngxiè

slacken, slacken off v (使…) 放慢／变弱 (shǐ...) fàng màn/biàn ruò

slacks N 便装裤 biànzhuāng kù [M. WD 条 tiáo]

slag N 炉渣 lúzhā [M. WD 块 kuài], 矿渣 kuàngzhā [M. WD 块 kuài]

slain See **slay**

slake v 满足 mǎnzú

to slake your thirst 解渴 jiěkě

to slake a desire 满足欲望 mǎnzú yùwàng

slam I v 1 使劲关门 shǐjìn guānmén 2 砰地放下 pēng de fàngxià

to slam on the brakes 猛踩刹车 měng cǎi shāchē

II N 碰的一声 pèng de yì shēng

slander N, v 诽谤 fěibàng, 诋毁 dǐhuǐ

slanderous ADJ 诽谤的 fěibàng de, 诋毁的 dǐhuǐ de

slang N 俚语 lǐyǔ

slant I v 倾斜 qīngxié, 斜穿 xiéchuān II N 1 斜面 xiémiàn, 斜线 xiéxiàn 2 有偏向性的观点 yǒupiān xiàngxìng de guāndiǎn

slap I V 用巴掌打 yòng bāzhang dǎ, 掴 [+耳光] guāi [+ěrguāng]

to slap sb on the back 赞扬恭贺某人 zànyáng gōnghè mǒurén

to slap sb on the face 打某人一巴掌 dǎ mǒurén yì bāzhǎng, 掴耳光 guāi ěrguāng

II N 一巴掌 yì bāzhǎng, (一记)耳光 (yí jì) ěrguāng

slapdash ADJ 草草仓促的 [+工作] cāngcù de [+gōngzuò]

slapstick N 滑稽打闹喜剧 huájī dǎnào xǐjù [M. WD 出 chū]

slash I v 1 猛砍 měngkǎn 2 大幅度削减 dàfúdù xuējiǎn II N 1 猛砍 měngkǎn 2 斜线号 xiéxiànhào (/)

slat N 薄板条 báobǎntiáo

slate[1] N 1 板岩 bǎnyán [M. WD 块 kuài], 板石 bǎnshí [M. WD 块 kuài]

a clean slate 清白的历史 qīng bái de lìshǐ, 无不良记录 wúbù liáng jìlù

2 候选人名单 hòuxuǎnrén míngdān

slate[2] v 预定 yùdìng, 预计 yùjì

slather v 给 [+面包] 涂上厚厚的一层 [+花生酱] gěi [+miànbāo] túshàng hòuhòude yìcéng [huāshēngjiàng]

slaughter v, N 屠宰 túzǎi, 屠杀 túshā

slaughterhouse N 屠宰场 túzǎichǎng

slave I N 1 奴隶 núlì 2 完全受摆布的人 wánquán shòu bǎibù de rén ■ Some young people are really slaves to electronic gadgets. 有些年轻人真的成了电子玩意儿的奴隶。Yǒuxiē niánqīngrén zhēn de chéngle diànzǐ wányìr de núlì. II v 苦干 kǔ gān, 拼命工作 pīnmìng gōngzuò ■ I've been slaving for days over this report. 我连续几天埋头苦干写这份报告。Wǒ liánxù jǐ tiān mái tóu kǔ gàn xiě zhè fèn bàogào.

slave driver 奴隶监工 núlì jiāngōng, 驱使别人拼命工作的人 qūshǐ biéren pīnmìng gōngzuò de rén

slavery N 奴役 núyì

slavish ADJ 奴性的 núxìng de

slay (PT **slew**; PP **slain**) v 杀死 shāsǐ, 谋杀 móushā

sleazy ADJ 低级庸俗的 dījí yōngsú de

sled N 雪橇 xuěqiāo

sledge hammer N 大锤 dàchuí

sleek ADJ 1 线条流畅优美的 [+轿车] xiàntiáo liúchàng yōuměi de [+jiàochē] 2 光滑的 [+毛皮] guānghuá de [+máopí]

sleep I v (PT & PP **slept**) 睡 shuì, 睡觉 shuìjiào

to sleep around 乱搞性关系 luàn gǎo xìng guānxi

to sleep in 睡懒觉 shuìlǎnjiào ■ Dad slept in until 11.00 last Saturday. 爸爸上星期六睡到十一点钟才起来。Bàba shàng xīngqīliù shuì dào shíyī diǎnzhōng cái qǐlai.

to sleep over 在别人家过夜 zài biéren jiā guò yè

to lose sleep over … 因为…而睡不着觉 yīnwèi…ér shuìbuzháo jiào ■ I won't lose sleep over this matter. 我不会因为这件事儿睡不着觉。Wǒ bú huì yīnwèi zhè jiàn shìr shuìbuzháo jiào.

II N 睡眠 shuìmián

sleep deprivation 睡眠不足 shuìmián bùzú, 缺乏睡眠 quēfá shuìmián

sleeper N 1 (a heavy/light sleeper) 睡得很深/很浅的人 shuì dehěn shēn/hěn qiǎn de rén 2 火车卧铺车厢 huǒchē wòpù chēxiāng 3 儿童睡衣 értóng shuìyī

sleeping bag N 睡袋 shuìdài

sleeping pill N 安眠药 ānmiányào

sleepless ADJ 不眠的 bù mián de, 睡不着觉的 shuì bù zháo jiào de

sleepless night 不眠之夜 bù mián zhī yè

sleepwalk v 梦游 mèngyóu

sleepwalker N 梦游者 mèngyóuzhě

sleepwalking N 梦游 mèngyóu

sleepy ADJ 瞌睡的 kēshuì de, 困倦的 kùnjuàn de

sleepyhead N 想睡觉的人 xiǎng shuìjiào de rén, 瞌睡虫 kēshuìchóng

sleet N 雨夹雪 yǔjiāxuě [M. WD 场 cháng]

sleeve N 衣袖 yīxiù, 袖子 xiùzi

sleeveless ADJ 无袖的 wú xiù de

sleigh N 雪橇 xuěqiāo

sleight of hand N 1 (魔术师的)巧妙花招 (móshùshī de) qiǎomiào huāzhāo 2 [欺骗的+] 花招 [qīpiàn de+] huāzhāo, 手法 shǒufǎ

slender ADJ 苗条的 miáotiao de, 纤细的 xiānxì de

slept See **sleep**

sleuth N 侦探 zhēntàn

slew[1] 1 See **slay** 2 [汽车+] 突然急转弯 [qìchē+] tūrán jí zhuǎnwān

slew[2] N 大量 dàliàng

slice I N 1 一(薄)片 yì (báo) piàn

a slice of lemon 一片柠檬 yípiàn níngméng

2 一部分 yí bùfen

slick

a slice of life 生活的一个片断 shēnghuó de yí ge piànduàn

a slice of profits 利润的一部分 lìrùn de yí bùfen

II v 把…切成薄片 bǎ…qiēchéng bópiàn

slick I ADJ 1 油滑的 [+推销员] yóuhuá de [+tuīxiāoyuán] 2 华丽而无意义的 [+演出] huálì ér wúyìyì de [+yǎnchū] **II** N 1（路面／水面上的）浮油 (lùmiàn/shuǐmiàn shàng de) fúyóu 2 优质光纸印刷的精美杂志 yōuzhì guāngzhǐ yìnshuā de jīngměi zázhì **III** v 用油把头发梳得光滑发亮 yòng yóu bǎ tóufa shū dé guānghuá fāliàng

slid See **slide**

slide I v (PT & PP **slid**) 1 滑 huá ■ The children screamed with delight as they were sliding down the icy slope. 孩子们从冰坡上滑下来，快活地尖叫。Háizimen cóng bīngpōshàng huáxiàlai, kuàihuo de jiānjiào. 2 下滑 xiàhuá，下降 xiàjiàng 3 越来越坏 yuèláiyuè huài，每况愈下 měi kuàng yù xià ■ After his wife's death, the old man slid into depression. 老伴去世以后，老人的健康每况愈下。Lǎobàn qùshì yǐhòu, lǎorén de jiànkāng měi kuàng yù xià. **II** N 1 滑梯 huátī 2 幻灯片 huàndēngpiàn [M. WD 张 zhāng/套 tào] ■ Our geography teacher gave a slide show on the African savannah. 我们的地理老师放了非洲草原的幻灯片。Wǒmen de dìlǐ lǎoshī fàngle Fēizhōu cǎoyuán de huàndēngpiàn.

slide projector 幻灯机 huàndēngjī

3 下滑 xiàhuá，下降 xiàjiàng 4 崩落 bēngluò ■ Heavy rainfall has caused landslides in the hills. 大雨在山区造成土崩。Dàyǔ zài shānqū zàochéng tǔbēng.

sliding door N 拉门 lāmén [M. WD 道 dào]，滑动门 huádòng mén [M. WD 道 dào]

sliding scale N 浮动计算法 fúdòng jìsuàn fǎ

slight I ADJ 轻微的 qīngwēi de，微小的 wēixiǎo de **II** v 怠慢 dàimàn，轻视 qīngshì

slightly ADV 稍 shāo，稍微 shāowēi ■ The prices in this store are slightly higher than in other stores. 这家商店的价格比其他商店稍贵贵一点儿。Zhè jiā shāngdiàn de jiàgé bǐ qítā shāngdiàn shāowēi guì yìdiǎnr.

slim I ADJ 1 苗条的 miáotiao de，修长的 xiūcháng de 2 微小的 wēixiǎo de

slim chance 微小的机会 wēixiǎo de jīhuì

3 薄的 [+本子] báo de [+běnzi] **II** v 使…减少 shǐ…jiǎnshǎo

slime N 黏液 niányè，黏糊糊的东西 niánhūhūde dōngxi

slimy ADJ 黏糊糊的 niánhūhūde

sling I v (PT & PP **slung**) 投 tóu，掷 zhì，抛 pāo **II** N 吊带 diàodài，吊索 diàosuǒ

slings and arrows 恶意攻击 èyìgōngjī

slingshot N 弹弓 dàngōng

slink (PT & PP **slunk**) v 悄悄溜走 qiāoqiāo liūzǒu

slip I v 1 滑 huá，滑动 huádòng ■ Many people slipped and fell on the icy stairs. 很多人在结冰的台阶上滑倒。Hěn duō rén zài jiébīng de táijiēshang huádǎo. 2 溜 liū，偷偷走动 tōutōu zǒudòng ■ A couple of students slipped out during the lecture. 有两个学生在上课时溜走了。Yǒu liǎng sān ge xuésheng zài shàngkè shí liūzǒu le. 3 下降 xiàjiàng ■ Regulars to the bar complain that the standards have slipped under the new management. 酒吧的老主顾抱怨，自从来了新经理，水准下降了。Jiǔbā de lǎo zhǔgu bàoyuàn, zìcóng láile xīn jīnglǐ, shuǐzhǔn xiàjiàng le. **II** N 1 一小张纸 yì xiǎo zhāng zhǐ 2 失误 shīwù

a slip of the pen 笔误 bǐwù

a slip of the tongue 口误 kǒuwù

slipknot N 活结 huójié

slipper N 拖鞋 tuōxié [M. WD 只 zhī/双 shuāng]

slippery ADJ 1 滑的 huá de，光滑的 guānghuá de 2 油滑的 yóuhuá de，狡猾的 jiǎohuá de

slipshod ADJ 不认真的 bú rènzhēn de，马虎的 mǎhu de

slip-up N 失误 shīwù，疏忽 shūhu

slit I v (PT & PP **slit**) 切开 qiēkāi，撕开 sīkāi **II** N 狭长的口子 xiácháng de kǒuzi，裂缝 lièfèng

slither v 弯弯曲曲地滑动 wānwān qūqū dé huádòng

sliver N 碎片 suìpiàn，一小片 yì xiǎo piàn

slob N 懒惰而肮脏的人 lǎnduò ér āngzāng de rén，粗鲁无礼的人 cūlǔ wúlǐ de rén

slobber v 流口水 liú kǒushuǐ

slog I v 1 艰难地走 jiānnán de zǒu 2 辛苦地工作 xīnkǔ de gōngzuò **II** N 漫长而艰巨的事 màncháng ér jiānjù de shì

slogan N 标语 biāoyǔ，口号 kǒuhào

slop I v [水+] 晃荡溢出 [shuǐ+] huàngdang yìchū **II** N 泔脚 gānjiǎo

slope I N 斜面 xiémiàn，山坡 shānpō **II** v 倾斜 qīngxié

sloppy ADJ 马虎的 mǎhu de，草率的 cǎoshuài de

slosh v 使 [+液体] 晃荡 shǐ [+yètǐ] huàngdang

sloshed ADJ 喝醉的 hēzuì de

slot I N 1 狭缝 xiáféng，投物口 tóu wù kǒu 2 固定时间 gùdìng shíjiān，固定位置 gùdìng wèizhì

parking slot 停车位 tíngchēwèi

II v 把…插入狭缝 bǎ…chārù xiáféng

sloth N 1 树懒 shùlǎn [M. WD 只 zhī] 2 懒惰 lǎnduò

slothful ADJ 懒惰的 lǎnduò de

slot machine N 投币式赌博机 tóubìshì dǔbójī，吃角子老虎（机）chī jiǎozi lǎohǔ (jī)

slouch I v 无精打采地坐／站／走 wújīng dǎcǎi de zuò/zhàn/zǒu **II** N 无精打采 wújīng dǎcǎi

be no slouch at sth 善于做某事 shànyú zuò mǒushì

slough[1] N 泥沼 nízhǎo，泥潭 nítán

slough² v (to slough off) **1** 脱皮 tuōpí **2** 摆脱 [+不好的名声] bǎituō [+bùhǎo de míngshēng]

slovenly ADJ 不整洁的 bùzhěng jié de, 邋遢的 lāta de

slow I ADJ **1** 慢 màn, 缓慢 huǎnmàn ■ *They're making slow but steady progress.* 他们正在缓慢而稳步地向前进。Tāmen zhèngzài huǎnmàn ér wěnbù de xiàng qiánjìn.
the slow lane 慢车道 mànchē dào
2 愚笨的 [+人] yúbèn de [+rén]
be slow on the uptake 领会很慢的 lǐnghuì hěn màn de, 迟钝的 chídùn de
3 清淡的 [+生意] qīngdàn de [+shēngyì] II v 减慢 jiǎnmàn III ADV 慢慢(地) mànmàn (de)

slowdown N **1** 放慢 fàngmàn
a slowdown in social life 社交活动放慢 shèjiāohuódòng fàngmàn
2 (工人) 怠工 (gōngrén) dàigōng

slowly ADV 慢 màn, 慢慢地 mànmān de

slowpoke N 做事慢吞吞的人 zuòshì màntūntūn de rén

slow-witted ADJ 愚笨的 yúbèn de, 迟钝的 chídùn de

sludge N 污泥 wūní, 污物 wūwù

slug I N **1** 鼻涕虫 bítìchóng [M. WD 条 tiáo], 蛞蝓 kuòyú [M. WD 条 tiáo] **2** 少量(烈性酒) shǎoliàng (lièxìngjiǔ) II v 用拳头打 yòng quántou dǎ
to slug it out 狠狠地打架 hěnhěn de dǎjià, 拼个输赢 pīn ge shūyíng

sluggish ADJ 缓慢的 huǎnmàn de, 无力的 wúlì de

sluice I N 水闸 shuǐzhá, 水门 shuǐmén II v 冲洗 chōngxǐ

slum I N 贫民窟 pínmínkū II v 过苦日子 guò kǔrìzi

slumber I N 深睡 shēn shuì, 睡眠 shuìmián II v 睡得很深 shuì dehěn shēn, 睡觉 shuìjiào

slump I v **1** [价格+] 暴跌 [jiàgé+] bàodiē, 急剧下降 jíjù xiàjiàng **2** [人+] 突然倒下 [rén+] tūrán dǎoxià II N **1** 暴跌 bàodiē, 猛降 měng jiàng
2 衰落 shuāiluò, 衰退 shuāituì

slung See **sling**

slunk See **slink**

slur I v **1** 含糊不清地说话 hánhu bùqīng de shuōhuà **2** 污蔑 wūmiè, 诋毁 dǐhuǐ II N 污蔑 wūmiè, 诋毁 dǐhuǐ
racist slur 种族主义的诋毁 zhǒngzúzhǔyì de dǐhuǐ

slurp v 咕嘟咕嘟地喝 gūdū gūdū de hē

slush N **1** 半融的雪 bàn róng de xuě, 雪水 xuěshuǐ **2** (加碎冰的)冷饮 (jiā suì bīng de) lěngyǐn
slush fund 行贿资金 xínghuì zījīn

slut N 浪荡女人 làngdàng nǚrén, 荡妇 dàngfù

sly ADJ 狡猾的 jiǎohuá de, 滑头的 huátóu de

smack I v **1** (用手掌) 拍打 (yòng shǒuzhǎng) pāida **2** (to smack of) 有点…的味道 yǒudiǎn…

de wèidao II N **1** 拍打 pāida **2** (to give sb a smack on the lip) 给某人一个响吻 gěi mǒurén yí ge xiǎng wěn

small I ADJ **1** 小(的) xiǎo (de) ■ *Rhode Island is the smallest state in the U.S.A.* 罗得岛是美国最小的州。Luódé Dǎo shì Měiguó zuì xiǎo de zhōu.
small change 零钱 língqián
small claims court 小额索赔法庭 xiǎo'é suǒpéi fǎtíng
small fry 小人物 xiǎorénwù
small hours 凌晨(时分) língchén (shífèn)
small matter 小事 xiǎoshì, 不重要的事 bú zhòngyào de shì
small potatoes 小人物 xiǎorénwù
small talk 闲聊 xiánliáo, 寒暄 hánxuān
2 年幼的 niányòu de **3** 少量的 shǎoliàng de
a small fortune 一大笔钱 yí dà bǐ qián ■ *Their month-long holiday in Europe must have cost them a small fortune.* 他们在欧洲度假一个月，肯定花了一大笔钱。Tāmen zài Ōuzhōu dùjià yí ge yuè, kěndìng huāle yí dà bǐ qián.
II N (the small of the back) 腰 yāo, 腰部 yāobù

small-minded ADJ 气量小的 qìliàngxiǎo de, 心胸狭窄的 xīnxiōng xiázhǎi de

smallpox N 天花 tiānhuā

small-scale ADJ 小规模的 xiǎoguīmó de, 小型的 xiǎoxíng de

small-time ADJ 不重要的 bú zhòngyào de
small-time conman 小骗子 xiǎo piànzi

smart¹ ADJ **1** 聪明的 cōngming de, 敏捷的 mǐnjié de
the smart money [投资+] 高明人士 [tóuzī+] gāomíngrénshì
2 耍小聪明的 shuǎ xiǎocōngming de
smart aleck 自作聪明的人 zìzuò cōngmíng de rén, 喜欢耍嘴皮子的人 xǐhuan shuǎ zuǐpízi de rén

smart² v 感到难过 gǎndào nánguò

smash I v **1** 打破 [+玻璃] dǎpò [+bōli], 打碎 dǎsuì **2** 打破 [+体育记录] dǎpò [+tǐyù jìlù] **3** [汽车+] 猛撞 [qìchē+] měngzhuàng **4** 捣毁 [+犯罪集团] dǎohuǐ [+fànzuì jítuán] **5** (网球) 扣球 (wǎngqiú) kòuqiú, 杀球 shāqiú II N **1** 破碎声 pòsuì shēng, 碰撞声 pèngzhuàng shēng
2 获得巨大成功的新书／新剧 huòdé jùdà chénggōng de xīnshū/xīnjù
smash hit 大获成功的新书／新剧 dà huò chénggōng de xīnshū/xīnjù

smashed ADJ **1** 喝得烂醉的 hē dé lànzuì de **2** (吸毒后) 药性发作的 (xīdú hòu) yàoxìng fāzuò de

smattering N 一点点 yìdiǎndiǎn

smear I v **1** 涂抹 túmǒ **2** 弄脏 nòngzāng **3** 污蔑 wūmiè, 诽谤 fěibàng II N **1** 污斑 wū bān, 油迹 yóujì **2** 污蔑 wūmiè, 诽谤 fěibàng
smear campaign 诽谤活动 fěibàng huódòng

smell

smell I N 1 气味 qìwèi 2 嗅觉 xiùjué II v 1 闻 wén, 闻出 wénchū

I smell a rat. 我闻到老鼠的气味。(→我觉得有可疑的地方。) Wǒ wéndao lǎoshǔ de qìwèi. (→Wǒ juéde yǒu kěyí de dìfang.)

2 闻起来 wénqǐlai ■ *These roses smell wonderful.* 这些玫瑰花闻起来香极了。Zhèxiē méiguì huā wénqǐlai xiāng jíle.

smelly ADJ 臭的 chòu de, 发出臭味的 fāchū chòuwèi de

smelt v 熔炼 róngliàn, 提炼 tíliàn

smidgen N 一点点 yìdiǎndiǎn

smile v, N 笑 xiào, 微笑 wēixiào

to be all smiles 笑容满面 xiàoróng mǎnmiàn, 满面春风 mǎnmiàn chūnfēng

to smile to oneself 暗暗地笑 àn àn de xiào

smirk N, v 不怀好意地笑 bù huái hǎoyì de xiào, 得意地笑 déyì de xiào

smith N 1 铁匠 tiějiang 2 工匠 gōngjiàng

smithereens N 碎片 suìpiàn

smitten ADJ (be smitten with sb) 对某人一见钟情 duì mǒurén yíjiàn zhōngqíng, 深深爱上某人 shēnshēn àishang mǒurén

smock N 工作服 gōngzuòfú [M. WD 件 jiàn]

smog N 烟雾 yānwù

smoke I N 烟 yān ■ *Where there's smoke, there's fire.* 有烟必有火。Yǒu yān bì yǒu huǒ. (→无风不起浪。Wú fēng bù qǐ làng. Where there is no wind, there is no wave.) II v 1 吸烟 xī yān 2 冒烟 màoyān ■ *This fireplace smokes badly.* 这个壁炉冒烟太多。Zhè ge bìlú mào yān tài duō.

smoker N 吸烟者 xīyānzhě

smokescreen N 1 烟幕 yānmù 2 障眼法 zhàngyǎnfǎ, 伪装 wěizhuāng

smokestack N 大烟囱 dà yāncōng

smoking gun N 真凭实据 zhēnpíng shíjù

smoky ADJ 烟雾弥漫的 yānwù mímàn de

smolder v 没有火焰地燃烧 méiyǒu huǒyàn de ránshāo, 焖烧 mèn shāo

smooch I v 亲密接吻 qīnmì jiēwěn II N 亲密的接吻 qīnmì de jiēwěn

smooth I ADJ 1 平坦的 píngtǎn de, 光滑的 guānghuá de ■ *The baby's skin is so smooth to the touch.* 婴儿的皮肤摸上去真光滑。Yīng'ér de pífū mōshàngqu zhēn guānghuá. 2 糊状的 hú zhuàng de, 无颗粒的 wú kēlì de 3 圆滑的 yuánhuá de ■ *He's a smooth talker, so watch out what you agree to.* 他说话油嘴滑舌，你答应什么要小心点。Tā shuōhuà yóuzuǐhuáshé, nǐ dāying shénme yào xiǎoxīn diǎnr. 4 顺利的 shùnlì de, 一帆风顺的 yì fān fēng shùn de II v 1 把...弄平 bǎ...nòng píng

to smooth the way 铺平道路 pūpíngdàolù

2 涂抹 [+油膏] túmǒ [+yóugāo]

smorgasbord N (品种丰富的) 自助餐 (pǐnzhǒng fēngfù de) zìzhùcān

a smorgasbord of 各式各样的 gèshì gèyàng de, 种类繁多的 zhǒnglèi fánduō de

smother v 1 使...窒息 shǐ...zhìxī, 闷死 mènsi 2 覆盖 fùgài

SMS (= Short Message Service) ABBREV 短信服务 duǎnxìn fúwù

smudge I N 污斑 wūbān, 污渍 wūzì II v 把...弄脏 bǎ...nòngzāng, 留下污斑 liúxia wū bān

smug ADJ 自鸣得意的 zìmíng déyì de, 自我满意的 zìwǒ mǎnyì de

smuggle v 走私 zǒusī, 偷运 tōuyùn

smuggler N 走私者 zǒusīzhě

smuggling N 走私 (活动) zǒusī (huódòng)

smut N 淫秽图书/画片 yínhuì túshū/huàpiàn

snack N 点心 diǎnxin, 小吃 xiǎochī

snack bar 小吃店 xiǎochīdiàn, 点心铺 diǎnxin pū

snafu N 连出故障 lián chū gùzhàng, 一团糟 yìtuánzāo

snag I N 小故障 xiǎogù zhàng, 意外情况 yìwài qíngkuàng

to hit a snag 出了点故障 chū le diǎn gùzhàng

II v 1 钩破 gōu pò, 撕破 sīpò 2 抓住 zhuāzhù 3 引起注意 yǐnqǐ zhùyì

snail N 蜗牛 wōniú

snake N 蛇 shé [M. WD 条 tiáo]

snake oil 蛇油 shé yóu, (骗人的) 万灵良药 (piànrén de) wàn líng liángyào

snakebite N 毒蛇咬伤 dúshé yǎoshāng

snap I v 1 [树枝+] 啪的一声折断 [shùzhī+] pā de yì shēng shéduàn 2 [人+] 厉声地说 [rén+] lìshēng de shuō 3 [人+] 精神崩溃 [rén+] jīngshén bēngkuì 4 [狗+] 猛咬 [gǒu+] měng yǎo 5 拍快照 pāi kuàizhào

to snap one's fingers 打响指 dǎxiǎng zhǐ

to snap out of it 别再伤心 bié zài shāngxīn, 振作起来 zhènzuòqǐlai

II v 1 (突然折断发出的) 啪的一声 (tūrán shéduàn fāchū de) pā de yì shēng 2 轻而易举的事 qīng ér yìjǔ de shì III ADJ 仓促的 cāngcù de, 草率的 cǎoshuài de

snappy ADJ 1 时髦漂亮的 [+时装] shímáo piàoliang de [+shízhuāng] 2 活泼有趣的 [+语言] huópo yǒuqù de [+yǔyán]

snapshot N 快照 kuàizhào, 生活照 shēnghuó zhào

snare I N 1 (捕捉动物的) 罗网 (bǔzhuō dòngwù de) luówǎng, 陷阱 xiànjǐng 2 (让人上当的) 圈套 (ràng rén shàngdàng de) quāntào II v 1 捕捉 (动物) bǔzhuō (dòngwù) 2 诱 (人) 中圈套 yòu (rén) zhòng quāntào

snarl I v 1 [动物+] 呲牙咆哮 [dòngwù+] zī yá páoxiào 2 [人+] 愤怒地高叫 [rén+] fènnù de gāo jiào, 怒吼 nùhǒu 3 使 [+交通] 堵塞 shǐ [+jiāotōng] dǔsè

to get snarled up 变得一团糟 biàn de yìtuánzāo

snarl-up N 混乱局面 hùnluàn júmiàn, 僵局 jiāngjú

snatch I v 1 抢走 [+钱包] qiǎng zǒu [+qiánbāo], 夺走 duó zǒu 2 抓住 [+机会] zhuāzhù [+jīhuì] II N 片断 piànduàn

in snatches 断断续续地 duànduàn xùxù de

snazzy ADJ 漂亮的 piàoliang de, 光彩夺目的 guāngcǎi duómù de

sneak I v 1 偷偷地走 tōutōu de zǒu, 偷偷摸摸地行动 tōutōu mōmō de xíngdòng 2 偷运 [+毒品] tōuyùn [+dúpǐn]

to sneak a glance 偷偷地看一眼 tōutōu de kàn yìyǎn

II N 偷偷摸摸的人 tōutōu mōmō de rén

a sneak preview (电影) 内部预映 (diànyǐng) nèibù yù yìng

sneakers N 胶底运动鞋 jiāo dǐ yùndòngxié

sneaking ADJ 暗暗的 àn'àn de

a sneaking suspicion 暗自怀疑 ànzì huáiyí

sneaky ADJ 偷偷摸摸的 tōutōu mōmō de

sneer v, N 冷笑 lěngxiào, 讥笑 jīxiào

sneeze v, N (打) 喷嚏 (dǎ) pēntì

snicker N, v 暗自发笑 ànzì fāxiào, 暗笑 ànxiào

sniff N, v (出声地) 闻 (chūshēng de) wén, 嗅 xiù

to sniff at 对…嗤之以鼻 duì...chī zhī yǐ bí, 不屑一顾 búxiè yígù

sniffle v 反复地抽鼻子 fǎnfù de chōu bízi

sniffles N 反复抽鼻子 fǎnfù chōu bízi

to have the sniffles 患轻感冒 huàn qīng gǎnmào

snip v, N 快速剪 kuàisù jiǎn, 剪断 jiǎnduàn

snipe v 1 打冷枪 dǎlěngqiāng, 狙击 jūjī 2 指责 zhǐzé, 攻击 gōngjī

sniper N 狙击手 jūjīshǒu

snippet N (音乐/消息) 片断 (yīnyuè/xiāoxi) piànduàn

snitch v 1 告密 gàomì, 告发 gàofā 2 偷窃 tōuqiè, 小偷小摸 xiǎotōu xiǎomō

sniveling ADJ 抽泣 chōuqì, 哭诉 kūsù

snob N 1 势利小人 shìlìxiǎorén

snob appeal (商品) 对势利顾客的吸引力 (shāngpǐn) duì shìlì gùkè de xīyǐnlì 2 自命不凡的人 zìmìng bùfán de rén

wine snob 自以为很会品酒的人 zìyǐwéi hěn huì pǐn jiǔ de rén

snobbery N 势利 shìlì

snobbish, snobby ADJ 势利的 shìlì de

snooker N 斯诺克式台球 Sīnuòkè shì táiqiú

snoop N, v 打听 [+别人的隐私] dǎtīng [+biéren de] yǐnsī, 窥探 kuītàn

snooty ADJ 目中无人的 mùzhōng wúrén de, 妄自尊大的 wàng zì zūn dà de

snooze v, N 打盹 dǎ dǔn, 小睡 xiǎoshuì

snore N, v 打鼾 dǎ hān, 打呼噜 dǎ hūlu

snorkel I N 1 (潜水) 呼吸管 (qiánshuǐ) hūxī guǎn 2 (潜水艇) 通气管 (qiánshuǐtǐng) tōngqì guǎn

II v 用呼吸管潜泳 yòng hūxī guǎn qiányǒng

snort v 哼鼻子 hēng bízi, 哼着鼻子说话 hēngzhe bízi shuōhuà

to snort at 对…嗤之以鼻 duì...chī zhī yǐ bí

snot N 鼻涕 bíti

snotty ADJ 自以为了不起的 zìyǐwéi liǎobuqǐ de

snout N (猪) 鼻子 (zhū) bízi

snow I N 雪 xuě II v 下雪 xiàxuě

snow tire 雪地防滑轮胎 xuědì fánghuá lúntāi

snowball I N 雪球 xuěqiú

snowball effect 滚雪球效应 gǔnxuěqiú xiàoyìng II v (像滚雪球一样) 迅猛增长/发展 (xiàng gǔnxuěqiú yíyàng) xùnměng zēngzhǎng/fāzhǎn

snowbound ADJ 被积雪困住的 bèi jīxuě kùnzhù de

snowdrift N 雪堆 xuěduī

snowed under ADV (工作) 多得没法完成 (gōngzuò) duō de méi fǎ wánchéng ■ *The teacher is snowed under grading homework assignments.* 这位老师的作业多得改不完。Zhè wèi lǎoshī de zuòyè duō de gǎibuwán.

snowfall N 降雪 jiàngxuě, 降雪量 jiàngxuě liàng

snowflake N 雪花 xuěhuā

snowman N 雪人 xuěrén

snowplow N 扫雪车 sǎoxuěchē [M. WD 辆 liàng]

snowshoe N 雪鞋 xuě xié [M. WD 双 shuāng]

snowstorm N 暴风雪 bàofēngxuě

snow-white ADJ 雪白 xuěbái

snowy ADJ 1 下雪的 xiàxuě de, 多雪的 duō xuě de 2 雪白的 xuěbái de

snub v, N 冷落 lěngluò, 怠慢 dàimàn

snuff I v 1 掐灭 [+蜡烛] qiāmiè [+làzhú] 2 扼杀 èshā, 杀死 shāsǐ II N 鼻烟 bíyān

snug ADJ 1 温暖舒适的 [+家] wēnnuǎn shūshì de [+jiā] 2 安乐舒服的 [+人] ānlè shūfu de [+rén]

snuggle, snuggle up v 偎依 wēiyī, 蜷缩 quánsuō

so I ADV 1 这么 zhème, 那么 nàme, 如此 rúcǐ ■ *The shopping mall is always so crowded.* 购物中心总是这么拥挤。Gòuwù zhōngxīn zǒngshì zhème yōngjǐ. 2 这样 zhèyàng ■ *I don't think so.* 我想不是这样。Wǒ xiǎng bú shì zhèyàng. II CONJ 所以 suǒyǐ

so as to 以便于 yǐbiànyú, 这样 zhèyàng ■ *He sat by the door so as to be able to slip out if the lecture was boring.* 他坐在门口，以便于讲课枯燥就溜走。Tā zuò zài ménkǒu, yǐbiànyú jiǎngkè kūzào jiù liūzǒu.

so ... as to 如此地…以至于 rúcǐ de...yǐzhìyú ■ *She was so weak as to have difficulty speaking.* 她虚弱得说话都有困难。Tā xūruò de shuōhuà dōu yǒu kùnnan.

so that 以便于 yǐbiànyú, 这样 zhèyàng

so ... that 如此地… rúcǐ de..., 以至于… yǐzhìyú..., 得 de ■ *The assignment was so difficult that no one could do it.* 这个作业难得没有人会做。Zhè ge zuòyè nánde méiyǒu rén huì zuò.

… or so …左右 …zuǒyòu
and so on 等等 děngděng, 什么的 shénme de
soak N, v 浸 jìn, 浸透 jìntòu
soaking ADJ 湿透的 shītòu de, 湿淋淋的 shīlínlín de
so-and-so N 某某人 mǒumǒu rén, 某某事 mǒumǒu shì
soap N 肥皂 féizào [M. WD 块 kuài]
a bar of soap 一块肥皂 yí kuài féizào
liquid soap 液体肥皂 yètǐ féizào
soap opera 肥皂剧 féizàojù
soar v 1 急剧上升 jíjù shàngshēng ■ *Fuel prices soared when war broke out in the Middle East.* 当中东爆发战争，燃料价格急剧上升。Dāng Zhōngdōng bàofā zhànzhēng, ránliào jiàgé jíjù shàngshēng. 2 高飞 gāo fēi
S.O.B (= son of a bitch) ABBREV 狗养的 gǒuyǎng-de
sob v 哭泣 kūqì, 抽泣 chōuqì
sob story (骗人眼泪的)伤感故事 (piànrén yǎnlèi de) shānggǎn gùshi
sober I ADJ 1 清醒的 qīngxǐng de 2 严肃的 yánsù de, 朴素的 pǔsù de II v (to sober up) 使 [+醉酒者] 清醒过来 shǐ [+zuìjiǔ zhě] qīngxǐng guòlai
soccer N (英式)足球 (Yīngshì) zúqiú
sociable ADJ 好交际的 hào jiāojì de, 喜欢与人交往的 xǐhuan yǔ rén jiāowǎng de
social ADJ 1 社会的 shèhuì de ■ *Duncan is keenly interested in social issues and that's why he wants to study sociology in college.* 邓肯对社会问题极感兴趣，所以他要在大学里学社会学。Dèngkěn duì shèhuì wèntí jí gǎn xīngqù, suǒyǐ tā yào zài dàxué lǐ xué shèhuì xué.
social science 社会科学 shèhuì kēxué
social studies 社会科学课程 shèhuì kēxué kèchéng
social work 社会福利工作 shèhuì fúlì gōngzuò, 社工 shègōng
social worker 社会福利工作者 shèhuì fúlì gōngzuòzhě, 社工 shègōng
2 社交的 shèjiāo de ■ *Do you have an active social life?* 你的社交生活丰富吗? Nǐ de shèjiāo shēnghuó fēngfù ma?
social climber 试图向上爬的人 shìtú xiàngshàng pá de rén
social drinking 在交际场合饮酒 zài jiāojì chǎnghé yǐnjiǔ
socialism N 社会主义 shèhuìzhǔyì
socialist I N 社会主义者 shèhuìzhǔyìzhě II ADJ 社会主义的 shèhuìzhǔyì de
socialite N 社交界名人 shèjiāojiè míngrén
socialize v 社交 shèjiāo, 搞社交活动 gǎo shèjiāo huódòng
society N 1 社会 shèhuì ■ *America is a democratic society.* 美国是一个民主社会。Měiguó shì yí ge mínzhǔ shèhuì. 2 社交界 shèjiāo jiè 3 社 shè, 协会 xiéhuì, 社团 shètuán
socioeconomic ADJ 社会经济的 shèhuì jīngjì de
sociologist N 社会学家 shèhuìxuéjiā
sociology N 社会学 shèhuìxué
sociopath N 反社会者 fǎn shèhuìzhě
sock¹ N 袜子 wàzi [M. WD 只 zhī, 双 shuāng], 短袜子 duǎn wàzi [M. WD 只 zhī, 双 shuāng]
sock² v 猛击 měngjī, 狠打 hěn dǎ
socket N 1 (电源)插座 (diànyuán) chāzuò
floor socket 地面插座 dìmiàn chāzuò
headphone socket 耳机插座 ěrjī chāzuò
wall socket 墙上插座 qiáng shàng chāzuò
2 眼窝 yǎnwō
sod N 草皮 cǎopí
soda N 苏打 sūdá
soda icecream 冰淇淋苏打 bīngqílín sūdá
soda pop 汽水 qìshuǐ
soda water 苏打水 sūdáshuǐ
sodden ADJ 湿淋淋的 shīlínlín de
sodium (Na) N 钠 nà
sofa N 沙发 shāfā [M. WD 张 zhāng]
soft ADJ 1 柔软的 róuruǎn de ■ *This little kitten is so soft and cuddly.* 小猫儿这么柔软，真想抱抱它。Xiǎomāor zhème róuruǎn, zhēn xiǎng bàobao tā. 2 轻声的 qīngshēng de 3 软心肠的 ruǎn xīncháng de
soft drinks 软饮料 ruǎnyǐnliào
soft sell 软性推销 ruǎnxìng tuīxiāo
soft touch 容易受骗上当的人 róngyì shòupiàn shàngdàng de rén, 软果子 ruǎnguǒzi
softball N 垒球 lěiqiú
soft-boiled ADJ 煮得半熟的 zhǔ dé bàn shóu de, 溏心的 tángxīn de
soften v 1 软化 ruǎnhuà 2 缓和 huǎnhé, 减少 jiǎnshǎo
to soften the impact 减弱冲击 jiǎnruò chōngjī
softhearted ADJ 软心肠的 ruǎn xīncháng de, 好心的 hǎoxīn de
soft-pedal v 淡化 dànhuà
soft-spoken ADJ 说话轻柔的 shuōhuà qīngróu de
software N 软件 ruǎnjiàn ■ *Which software do you recommend for computer security?* 你推荐哪一个电脑安全软件? Nǐ tuījiàn nǎ yí ge diànnǎo ānquán ruǎnjiàn?
anti-virus software 防(电脑)病毒软件 fáng (diànnǎo) bìngdú ruǎnjiàn
soggy ADJ 湿透的 shītòu de, 浸水的 jìnshuǐ de
soil I N 1 土壤 tǔrǎng, 泥土 nítǔ
one's native soil 某人的故土 mǒurén de gùtǔ
II v 弄脏 nòngzāng, 玷污 diànwū
sojourn N 短暂居住 duǎnzàn jūzhù, 暂住 zànzhù
solace N 慰籍 wèijí, 安慰 ānwèi
solar ADJ 太阳的 tàiyáng de ■ *More and more*

new houses have installed a solar energy system.
越来越多的新住宅装了太阳能系统。Yuèláiyuè duō
de xīn zhùzhái zhuāngle tàiyángnéng xìtǒng.
solar cell 太阳能电池 tàiyángnéng diànchí
solar eclipse 日蚀 rìshí
solar panel 太阳能电池板 tàiyángnéng diànchí
bǎn
solar system 太阳系 tàiyángxì
sold See sell
soldier I N 军人 jūnrén, 士兵 shìbīng
soldier of fortune 雇佣兵 gùyōngbīng
II v (to soldier on) 坚持下去 jiānchí xiàqu
sold-out ADJ 满座的 mǎnzuò de
sole¹ N 1 脚底 jiǎodǐ 2 鞋底 xiédǐ 3 鳎鱼 tǎyú
[M. WD 条 tiáo]
sole² ADJ 唯一的 wéiyī de, 独有的 dúyǒu de
sole authorship 独享著作权 dúxiǎng zhù-
zuòquán
solely ADV 唯一地 wéiyī de, 独有地 dúyǒu de
solemn ADJ 严肃庄重的 yánsù zhuāngzhòng de
a solemn ceremony 庄重的仪式 zhuāngzhòng
de yíshì
a solemn promise 严肃的承诺 yánsù de
chéngnuò
solemnity N 严肃庄重 yánsù zhuāngzhòng
solicit v 1 请求 [+募捐] qǐngqiú [+mùjuān], 征
求 [+意见] zhēngqiú [+yìjiàn] 2 推销 [+商品]
tuīxiāo [+shāngpǐn] 3 [妓女+] 拉客 [jìnǚ+]
lākè
solicitor N 1 推销员 tuīxiāoyuán, 揽客 qiánkè
■ *The sign on the door reads, "No Solicitors".* 门
上的牌子说：“谢绝推销。” Ménshang de páizi
shuō: "xièjué tuīxiāo." 2 法务官 fǎwùguān
■ *The city government will consult the solicitor on
this case.* 市政府要为这件案子咨询法务官。Shì
zhèngfǔ yào wèi zhè jiàn ànzi zīxún fǎwùguān.
3（英国）初级律师 (Yīngguó) chūjí lǜshī
solicitor general （美国）司法部副部长 (Měiguó)
Sīfǎbù fùbùzhǎng
solicitous ADJ 关怀的 guānhuái de, 关心的
guānxīn de
solid I ADJ 1 固体的 gùtǐ de, 坚固的 jiāngù de
2 结实的 jiēshi de 3 牢靠的 láokào de, 可靠
的 kěkào de ■ *She has most of her money
invested in a solid business firm.* 她大部分钱都
投资在一家可靠的商业公司里。Tā dà bufen qián
dōu tóuzī zài yì jiā kěkào de shāngyè gōngsī lǐ.
II N 固体 gùtǐ ■ *When the temperature drops to
below zero, water turns into a solid, i.e. ice.* 当气
温下降到零度以下，水就变成固体，也就是变成
冰。Dāng qìwēn xiàjiàng dào língdù yǐxià, shuǐ jiù
biànchéng gùtǐ, yě jiù shì biànchéng bīng.
solidarity N 团结一致 tuánjié yízhì
solidify v 1（使…）变成固体 (shǐ…) biànchéng
gùtǐ 2 巩固 gǒnggù, 加强 jiāqiáng

solids N 固体食物 gùtǐ shíwù
solid-state ADJ 1 固态体的 gùtàitǐ de
solid-state physics 固态体物理 (学) gùtàitǐ wùlǐ
(xué)
2 全晶体管的 [+电子设备] quán jīngtǐguǎn de
[+diànzǐ shèbèi]
soliloquy N 独白 dúbái
solitaire N 1 独粒宝石 dú lì bǎoshí
diamond solitaire 独立钻石 dú lì zuànshí
2 单人纸牌游戏 dānrén zhǐpái yóuxì
solitary ADJ 单一的 dānyī de, 单独的 dāndú de
solitary confinement 单独监禁 dāndú jiānjin,
禁闭 jìnbì
solitude N 孤独 gūdú, 单独 dāndú
in solitude 独自 (地) dúzì (de)
solo I ADJ, ADV 单人的 [+表演] dānrén de
[+biǎoyǎn]
to play solo 做单人表演 zuò dānrén biǎoyǎn,
单人飞行 dānrén fēixíng
II N 1 独奏曲 dúzòu qū, 独唱曲 dúchàng qū
2 独奏 dúzòu, 独唱 dúchàng, 单人 (飞行) 表演
dānrén (fēixíng) biǎoyǎn
violin solo 小提琴独奏 (曲) xiǎotíqín dúzòu (qū)
solo flight 单人飞行 dānrén fēixíng
soloist N 独奏者 dúzòu zhě, 独唱者 dúchàngzhě
solstice N (summer solstice) 夏至 xiàzhì, (winter
solstice) 冬至 dōngzhì
soluble ADJ 1 可溶解的 [+固体] kěróngjiě de
[+gùtǐ] 2 可解决的 [+问题] kě jiějué de [+wèntí]
solution N 1 解决 jiějué, 解决办法 jiějué bànfǎ
2 解答 jiědá, 答案 dá'àn ■ *Grandpa was so
delighted to find the solution to the sudoku puzzle.*
爷爷解答出了"数独"难题，开心极了。Yéye
jiědáchūle "shùdú" nántí, kāixīn jíle. 3 溶液
róngyè, 溶解 róngjiě
solve v 1 解决 jiějué ■ *At the dinner table
everybody offered his idea of how to solve the
problems of the world.* 在饭桌上，人人提出解决
世界问题的办法。Zài fànzhuōshang, rénrén tíchū
jiějué shìjiè wèntí de bànfǎ. 2 解答 jiědá
solvent¹ N 溶剂 róngjì
solvent² ADJ 有偿付能力的 yǒucháng fù nónglì de
somber ADJ 1 阴沉的 [+天空] yīnchén de [+tiān-
kōng] 2 严峻的 [+表情] yánjùn de [+biǎoqíng]
some I ADJ 有些 yǒuxiē, 一些 yìxiē ■ *Some people would do anything to realize their ambitions.*
有的人为了实现抱负，什么事都会做。Yǒu de rén
wèile shíxiàn bàofù, shénme shì dōu huì zuò.
II ADV 大约 dàyuē ■ *Some 100 people attended
the funeral of the former mayor.* 大约一百个人参
加了前市长的葬礼。Dàyuē yì bǎi ge rén cānjiāle
qián shìzhǎng de zànglǐ. **III** PRON 一些 yìxiē
somebody See someone
someday ADV 总有一天 zǒng yǒu yìtiān, 有朝一日
yǒuzhāo yí rì

somehow ADV **1** 总得 zǒngděi ■ *We must find new sources of energy somehow.* 我们总得找到新能源。Wǒmen zǒngděi zhǎodao xīn néngyuán. **2** 不知怎么搞的 bù zhī zěnme gǎo de, 不知怎样的 bùzhī zěnyàng de

someone, somebody PRON 有人 yǒurén, 某人 mǒurén ■ *Dr. Jones, someone is here to see you.* 琼斯医生，有人来看你。Qióngsī yīshēng, yǒurén lái kàn nǐ.

someone else 另一个人 lìng yí ge rén

someplace ADV 某个地方 mǒu gè dìfang

somersault I N 翻跟斗 fāngēndou, 筋斗 jīndǒu II V 翻跟斗 fāngēndou, 前／后滚翻 qián／hòu gǔnfān

something PRON 有东西 yǒu dōngxi, 有事情 yǒu shìqing, 某物 mǒuwù, 某事 mǒushì

something like 就好像 jiù hǎoxiàng, 大约 dàyuē ■ *The company earned something like a million dollars last year.* 这家公司去年赚了大约一百万。Zhè jiā gōngsī qùnián zhuànle dàyuē yì bǎi wàn.

to have something to do with 和…有关系 hé… yǒu guānxi ■ *The document had something to do with the new salary scale.* 这个文件和新的工资级别有关。Zhè ge wénjiàn hé xīn de gōngzī jíbié yǒuguān.

sometime I ADV 在某一个时候 zài mǒu yí ge shíhou

sometime before night 午夜前某个时候 wǔyè qián mǒu gè shíhou

II ADJ 偶尔的 ǒu'ěr de

sometimes ADV 有时候 yǒushíhou ■ *My friend Peggy, who is working in Shanghai, sometimes sends me e-mails.* 我的朋友佩其正在上海工作，有时候发电子邮件给我。Wǒde péngyou Pèijī zhèngzài Shànghǎi gōngzuò, yǒushíhou fā diànzi yóujiàn gěi wǒ.

somewhat ADV 有点儿 yǒudiǎnr

somewhere ADV 什么地方 shénme dìfang, 某地 mǒudì

son N **1** 儿子 érzi

the Son 圣子 Shèngzǐ, 耶稣基督 Yēsū Jīdū **2** 孩子 háizi, 小伙子 xiǎohuǒzi

sonata N 奏鸣曲 zòumíngqǔ [M. WD 首 shǒu]

song N 歌 gē [M. WD 首 shǒu], 歌曲 gēqǔ [M. WD 首 shǒu]

sonic ADJ 声音的 shēngyīn de, 声波的 shēngbō de

sonic boom 声震 shēng zhèn

son-in-law N 女婿 nǚxu

sonnet N 十四行诗 shísìhángshī [M. WD 首 shǒu]

sonorous ADJ 洪亮的 [+声音] hóngliàng de [+shēngyīn]

soon ADV 不久 bù jiǔ, 很快 hěn kuài ■ *I hope he comes home soon since I'm beginning to worry about him.* 我希望他马上回家，因为我开始为他担心了。Wǒ xīwàng tā mǎshàng huíjiā, yīnwèi wǒ kāishǐ wèi tā dānxīn le.

as soon as … 一…就… yī…jiù… ■ *As soon as he arrives in Shanghai, he will call Mr Li.* 他一到上海，就打电话给李先生。Tā yí dào Shànghǎi, jiù dǎ diànhuà gěi Lǐ xiānsheng.

soot N 烟灰 yānhuī, 煤灰 méihuī

soothe V 使 [+某人] 平静 shǐ [+mǒurén] píngjìng, 抚慰 fǔwèi

soothing ADJ 柔和平静的 róuhe píngjìng de, 抚慰人心的 fǔwèi rénxīn de

sop V (to sop up) 抹干 mǒ gān, 吸干 xīgān

sophisticated ADJ **1** 经历丰富的 [+人] jīnglì fēngfù de [+rén], 老练的 lǎoliàn de **2** 精密的 [+仪表] jīngmì de [+yíbiǎo], 尖端的 [+技术] jiānduān de [+jìshù]

sophistication N **1** 经历丰富 jīnglì fēngfù **2** 精密尖端 jīngmì jiānduān

sophomore N（高中或大学）二年级学生 (gāozhōng huò dàxué) èr niánjí xuésheng

sophomoric ADJ 幼稚的 yòuzhì de, 肤浅的 fūqiǎn de

soporific ADJ 使人昏昏欲睡的 shǐrén hūnhūn yùshuì de, 催眠的 cuīmián de

sopping ADJ 湿透的 shītòu de

soprano N 女高音（歌手）nǚgāoyīn (gēshǒu)

sorbet N 冰糕 bīnggāo

sorcerer N 魔法师 mófǎ shī, 巫师 wūshī

sorceress N 女魔法师 nǚ mófǎshī, 女巫师 nǚ wūshī

sorcery N 巫术 wūshù, 魔法 mófǎ

sordid ADJ **1** 肮脏的 [+地方] āngzāng de [+dìfang] **2** 卑鄙的 [+行为] bēibǐ de [+xíngwéi], 下流的 xiàliú de

sore I ADJ 酸痛 suāntòng ■ *My arm is still sore from playing tennis yesterday.* 我昨天打了网球，今天胳膊还酸痛。Wǒ zuótiān dǎle wǎngqiú, jīntiān gēbo hái suāntòng. II N **1** 疤 bā **2** 伤痛处 shāngtòng chù

sorely ADV 极其严重（地）jíqí yánzhòng (de)

sorority N（美国）大学女生联谊会 (Měiguó) dàxué nǚshēng liányìhuì

sorrow N 悲伤 bēishāng, 悲痛 bēitòng

sorry ADJ **1** 对不起 duìbuqǐ ■ *I forgot all about calling you yesterday. Sorry about that.* 我昨天忘了要给你打电话，对不起。Wǒ zuótiān wàngle yào gěi nǐ dǎ diànhuà, duìbuqǐ. **2** 难过 nánguò ■ *We're sorry to learn that Miss Grey is leaving us for another job.* 我们听说格雷小姐另有高就，要离开我们，都很难过。Wǒmen tīngshuō Géléi xiǎojiě lìng yǒu gāo jiù, yào líkai wǒmen, dōu hěn nánguò. **3** 遗憾 yíhàn **4** 惭愧 cánkuì

sort I N **1** (sort of) 有点儿 yǒudiǎnr **2** 种（类）zhǒng (lèi) **3**（计算机操作）分类 (jìsuànjī cāozuò) fēnlèi, 排序 páixù II V 将…分类 jiāng…fēnlèi

to sort out 整理 zhěnglǐ

to sort through 查找 cházhǎo

SOS N 紧急求救信号 jǐnjí qiújiù xìnhào

so-so ADJ, ADV 一般性的 yìbānxìng de, 不好也不坏 bùhǎo yě búhuài

soufflé N 蛋奶酥 dànnǎisū

sought See **seek**

sought-after ADJ 很受欢迎的 hěn shòu huānyíng de, 吃香的 chīxiāng de

soul N **1** 灵魂 línghún ■ *Christians believe in the immortality of the soul.* 基督教徒相信灵魂不朽。Jīdūjiàotú xiāngxìn línghún bù xiǔ.
soul mate 知己 zhījǐ, 心灵之交 xīnlíng zhī jiāo
soul music 灵歌 línggē, 灵曲 língqū
2 人 rén ■ *She is such a lovely soul that everyone enjoys her company.* 她是个很可爱的人，人人都喜欢跟她在一起。Tā shì ge hěn kě'ài de rén, rénrén dōu xǐhuan gēn tā dāi zài yìqǐ. **3** 精神 jīngshén, 特质 tèzhì

soulful ADJ 深情而伤感的 shēnqíng ér shānggǎn de

soulless ADJ 无情无义的 wúqíngwúyì de

soul-searching N 深刻反省 shēnkè fǎnxǐng, 自我解剖 zìwǒ jiěpōu

sound I N 声音 shēngyīn
by the sound of it 听起来 tīngqǐlai, 看来 kànlai
sound barrier 声障 shēngzhàng
sound bite 政客的录音片断 zhèngkè de lùyīn piàn duàn
sound effects 音响效果 yīnxiǎng xiàoguǒ
II V 听起来 tīngqǐlai, 似乎 sìhū ■ *This pension scheme sounds too good to be true.* 这个养老金计划听起来太好了，不可能是真的。Zhè ge yǎnglǎojīn jìhuà tīngqǐlai tài hǎo le, bù kěnéng shì zhēn de.
to sound sb out 探听某人的意见 tàntīng mǒurén de yìjiàn
Sounds good. 好啊 hǎo a ■ *"Do you want to play a game of chess with me?" "Sounds good."* "想不想和我下一盘棋？" "好啊。" "Xiǎngbuxiǎng hé wǒ xià yì pán qí?" "Hǎo a."
III ADJ **1** 健全的 jiànquán de ■ *A sound body harbors a sound mind.* 健全的身体才有健全的心灵。Jiànquán de shēntǐ cái yǒu jiànquán de xīnlíng. **2** 合理的 hélǐ de IV ADV (sound asleep) 睡得很熟 shuì dehěn shú

sounding board N 被征询意见的人 bèi zhēngxún yìjiàn de rén

soundly ADV **1** 深沉地 [+睡眠] shēnchén de [+shuìmián] **2** 彻底地 [+打败] chèdǐ de [+dǎbài]

soundproof ADJ 隔音的 géyīn de

soundtrack N 电影配乐 diànyǐng pèiyuè

soup N 汤 tāng, 羹 gēng
soup kitchen 救济穷人的流动厨房 jiùjì qióngrén de liúdòng chúfáng

souped-up ADJ 增强了马力的 [+汽车] zēngqiáng le mǎlì de [+qìchē]

sour I ADJ **1** 酸 suān ■ *Max hates sour apples.* 马克斯讨厌酸苹果。Mǎkèsī tǎoyàn suān píngguǒ.
sour cream 酸奶油 suān nǎiyóu
sour grapes 酸葡萄（心态）suān pútao (xīntài) **2** 坏脾气的 huài píqi de ■ *After that tragic experience he became a disillusioned, sour man.* 那次悲剧性的经历以后，他成了一个理想破灭、脾气很坏的人。Nà cì bēijù xìng de jīnglì yǐhòu, tā chéngle yí ge lǐxiǎng pòmiè、píqi hěn huài de rén. II V 变坏 biàn huài ■ *Their relationship began to sour after they moved in together.* 他们俩搬到一块儿住以后，关系开始变坏了。Tāmen liǎ bān dào yíkuàir zhù yǐhòu, guānxi kāishǐ biàn huài le.

source N 来源 láiyuán ■ *Oranges are a good source of vitamin C.* 橘子是维生素C的好来源。Júzi shì wéishēngsù C de hǎo láiyuán.
source code（计算机）源代码 (jìsuànjī) yuán dàimǎ
source language（翻译的）起始语 (fānyì de) qǐshǐ yǔ, 译出语 yìchū yǔ

sourdough N 酵头 jiàotóu

south I N **1** 南面 nánmian **2** (the South) 南方 nánfāng II ADJ 南面的 nánmian de
South America 南美洲 Nán Měizhōu
South Pacific 南太平洋 Nán Tàipíngyáng
the South Pole 南极 Nánjí
III ADV 在南面 zài nánmian
to go south 变坏 biànhuài, 恶化 èhuà

southbound ADJ 朝南的 cháonán de

southeast N 东南 dōngnán

southeastern ADJ 东南的 dōngnán de

southerly ADJ （在）南方的 (zài) nánfāng de
southerly wind 南风 nánfēng

southern ADJ 南的 nán de, 南部 nánbù de ■ *If you live in southern Texas, consider learning Spanish.* 你如果住在南得克萨斯州，可以考虑学西班牙语。Nǐ rúguǒ zhù zài nán Dékèsàsī zhōu, kěyǐ kǎolǜ xué Xībānyáyǔ.
the southern hemisphere 南半球 nánbànqiú

southerner N 南方人 nánfāngrén, 南部人 nánbù rén

southernmost ADJ 最南面的 zuì nánmian de

southward ADJ, ADV 向南（的）xiàng nán (de)

southwest N 西南 xīnán

southwestern ADJ 西南的 xīnán de

souvenir N 纪念品 jìniànpǐn [M. WD 件 jiàn]

sovereign I ADJ 享有独立主权的 xiǎngyǒu dúlì zhǔquán de II N 君主 jūnzhǔ, 国王 guówáng, 女王 nǚwáng

sow¹ (PT **sowed**; PP **sowed**, **sown**) V 播（种）bō (zhǒng)
to sow one's wild oats（年轻时）放荡不羁 (niánqīng shí) fàngdàng bùjī, 到处拈花惹草 dàochù niānhuā rě cǎo

sow² N 母猪 mǔzhū [M. WD 头 tóu]

sown

sown See **sow**[1]

soy, soya N 黄豆 huángdòu [M. WD 粒 lì/颗 kē], 大
豆 dàdòu [M. WD 粒 lì/颗 kē]
soy bean 黄豆 huángdòu, 大豆 dàdòu
soy milk 豆浆 dòujiāng
soy sauce 酱油 jiàngyóu

spa N 1 矿泉疗养地 kuàngquán liáoyǎngdì 2 按
摩浴缸 ànmó yùgāng 3 水疗 shuǐliáo

space N 1 空白 kòngbái 2 空地 kòngdì, 地方
dìfang 3 空间 kōngjiān ■ The exploration of
outer space is costly but necessary. 探索外层空
间, 花费昂贵, 但是很有必要。 Tànsuǒ wàicéng
kōngjiān, huāfèi ángguì, dànshì hěn yǒu bìyào.

space-age ADJ 太空时代的 tàikōng shídài de, 高
度现代化的 gāodù xiàndàihuà de
space-age laboratory 高度现代化的实验室
gāodù xiàndàihuà de shíyànshì

spacecraft/spaceship/space shuttle N 宇宙飞船
yǔzhòu fēichuán, 航天器 hángtiānqì

spaced-out ADJ 迷迷糊糊的 mími húhu de, 头脑
不清楚的 tóunǎo bùqīngchu de

spaceship N 太空船 tàikōngchuán

spacey, spacy ADJ 迷迷糊糊的 mími huhu de, 头
脑不清楚的 tóunǎo bùqīngchu de

spacious ADJ 宽敞的 kuānchang de, 宽阔的
kuānkuò de

spade N 1 (纸牌/扑克牌) 黑桃 (zhǐpái/pūkèpái)
hēitáo 2 铲 chǎn, 铲子 chǎnzi [M. WD 把 bǎ]
Call a spade a spade. 是什么就说什么。(→直
言不讳。) Shì shénme jiù shuō shénme.
(→Zhíyán bú huì.)

spaghetti N (意大利) 细面条 (Yìdàlì) xìmiàntiáo

span I N 1 期间 qījiān 2 持续时间 chíxù shíjiān
sb's life span 某人的寿命 mǒurén de shòumìng
attention span 注意力持续的时间 zhùyìlì chíxù
de shíjiān
3 跨距 kuàjù, 全长 quáncháng II v 1 [大桥+]
跨越 [dà qiáo+] kuàyuè 2 [事件+] 持续
[shìjiàn+] chíxù

spangle N (服装的) 金属饰片 (fúzhuāng de)
jīnshǔ shìpiàn

Spanish I ADJ 西班牙的 Xībānyá de, 西班牙人的
Xībānyárén de, 西班牙语的 Xībānyáyǔ de II N
1 西班牙人 Xībānyárén 2 西班牙语 Xībānyáyǔ

spank v 1 打 (小孩) 屁股 dǎ (xiǎohái) pìgu 2 击
败 jībài

spanking N 打 (小孩) 屁股 dǎ (xiǎohái) pìgu

spar v 1 (拳击手之间) 练拳 (quánjīshǒu zhījiān)
liànquán 2 争论 zhēnglùn

spare I ADJ 1 备用的 bèiyòng de ■ We have a
spare room for guests. 我们有一间备用客房。
Wǒmen yǒu yì jiān bèiyòng kèfáng.
spare change 多余的硬币 duōyú de yìngbì
spare key 备用钥匙 bèiyòng yàoshi
spare wheel 备用轮胎 bèiyòng lúntāi

2 空闲的 kòngxián de II v 1 使…免受 shǐ...
miǎnshòu
to spare sb the trouble 使某人免受麻烦 shǐ
mǒurén miǎnshòu máfan
to spare sb's feelings 使某人免于难受 shǐ
mǒurén miǎnyú nánshòu
2 不伤害 bù shānghài
Spare me. 饶了我吧。Ráo le wǒ ba.
3 不使用 bù shǐyòng, 节省 jiéshěng
to spare no expenses 不节省任何费用 bù jiéshěng rènhé fèiyòng, 不惜工本 bùxī gōngběn
III N 备用品 bèiyòngpǐn

sparingly ADV 节省地 jiéshěng de, 有节制地
yǒujié zhì de

spark I N 1 火花 huǒhuā, 火星 huǒxīng
spark plug 火花塞 huǒhuāsāi
2 (麻烦的) 起因 (máfan de) qǐyīn 3 才智 cáizhì,
活力 huólì II v 1 引起 [+麻烦] yǐnqǐ [+máfan], 导
致 dǎozhì 2 迸发火花 bèngfā huǒhuā

sparkle I v 1 闪闪发亮 shǎnshǎn fāliàng, 闪光
shǎnguāng II N 1 闪亮 shǎnliàng, 闪光 shǎnguāng 2 兴致 xìngzhì

sparkler N 烟花棒 yānhuā bàng

sparrow N 麻雀 máquè [M. WD 只 zhī]

sparse ADJ 稀少的 xīshǎo de

sparsely ADV 稀疏地 xīshǎo de
sparsely populated 人烟稀少的 rényān xīshǎo
de

spartan ADJ 简朴的 jiǎnpǔ de, 清苦的 qīngkǔ de

spasm N 痉挛 jìngluán, 抽筋 chōujīn
a spasm of coughing 一阵猛烈的咳嗽 yízhèn
měngliè de késou

spasmodic ADJ 1 痉挛的 jìngluán de, 抽搐的
chōuchù de 2 断断续续的 duànduàn xùxù de

spastic I ADJ 极其笨拙的 jíqí bènzhuō de, 极易激
动的 jí yì jīdòng de II N 患大脑麻痹的人 huàn
dànǎo mábì de rén

spat[1] N 口角 kǒujué, 拌嘴 bànzuǐ

spat[2] v See spit

spate N (a spate of sth) 多起 [+事故] duō qǐ
[+shìgù], 大量 dàliàng
a spate of H1N1 cases 多起猪流感病例 duǒqǐ
zhū liúgǎn bìnglì

spatial ADJ 关于空间的 guānyú kōngjiān de

spatter v 溅 jiàn, 洒 sǎ

spatula N 铲子 chǎnzi [M. WD 把 bǎ], 刮刀 guādāo
[M. WD 把 bǎ]

spawn I v 1 [鱼+] 大量产卵 [yú+] dàliàng
chǎnluǎn 2 酿成 [+危机] niàngchéng [+wēijī]
II N 成团的鱼卵 chéngtuán de yúluǎn

spay v 切除 (动物的) 卵巢 qiēchú (dòngwù de)
luǎncháo

speak (PT spoke; PP spoken) v 1 说 shuō ■ Do
you speak Chinese? 你会说中文吗? Nǐ huì shuō
Zhōngwén ma? 2 说话 shuōhuà ■ Bruce didn't

begin to speak until he was three. 布鲁斯到三岁才开始说话。Bùlǔsī dào sān suì cái kāishǐ shuōhuà. **3** 演讲 yǎnjiǎng, 演说 yǎnshuō

generally speaking 一般来说 yìbān láishuō ■ *Generally speaking, girls have more aptitude for languages than boys.* 一般来说, 女孩子学语言的能力比男孩子强。Yìbān láishuō, nǚháizi xué yǔyán de nénglì bǐ nánháizi qiáng.

to speak out 公开发表议论 gōngkāi fābiǎo yìlùn, 公开抗议 gōngkāi kàngyì

to speak up 说得大声一点儿 shuō de dàshēng yìdiǎnr ■ *I can't hear you; could you please speak up?* 我听不清楚, 能不能说得大声一点儿? Wǒ tīngbuqīngchu, néngbunéng shuōde dàshēng yìdiǎnr?

speaker N **1** 演讲者 yǎnjiǎngzhě **2** 说某种语言的人 shuō mǒu zhǒng yǔyán de rén ■ *If you're a fluent Chinese speaker, you'll have a much better chance of getting the job.* 如果你能流利地说中文, 得到这份工作的机会就大得多。Rúguǒ nǐ néng liúlì de shuō Zhōngwén, dédào zhè fèn gōngzuò de jīhuì jiù dà de duō. **3** 扬声器 yángshēngqì, 喇叭 lǎba

spear I N 矛 máo [M. WD 根 gēn/把 bǎ], 梭标 suō biāo [M. WD 把 bǎ] II V **1** 用矛刺 yòng máo cì **2** 用叉子叉起 yòng chāzi chā qǐ

spearhead V 当…的先锋 dāng…de xiānfēng, 为…带头 wéi…dàitóu

special I ADJ 特别的 tèbié de, 特殊的 tèshū de ■ *Is there anything special you'd like to do for this year's birthday, dear?* 亲爱的, 你今年的生日想做些什么特别的事吗? Qīn'ài de, nǐ jīnnián de shēngri xiǎng zuò xiē shénme tèbié de shì ma?

special education 特殊教育 tèshū jiàoyù ■ *Special education teachers need to be all the more caring and patient.* 特殊教育的老师需要更有爱心和耐心。Tèshū jiàoyù de lǎoshi xuyào gèngyǒu àixīn hé nàixīn.

special effects 特技效果 tèjì xiàoguǒ II N **1** 特价 tèjià, 特别便宜的商品 tèbié piànyi de shāngpǐn **2** 特别节目 tèbié jiémù

specialist N 专科医生 zhuānkē yīshēng, 专门工作者 zhuānmén gōngzuòzhě

specialization N 专业分工 zhuānyèfēngōng

specialize V 专门研究 [+中国经济] zhuānmén yánjiū [+Zhōngguó jīngjì], 专门从事 [+体育用品销售] zhuānmén cóngshì [+tǐyù yòngpǐn xiāoshòu]

specialized ADJ 专门训练的 zhuānmén xùnliàn de, 专门的 zhuānmén de

specially ADV 专门地 zhuānmén de, 特地 tèdì

specialty N **1** 专业 zhuānyè, 专长 zhuāncháng **2** 特色菜 tèsècài, 特色食品 tèsè shípǐn

species N 种 zhǒng, 物种 wùzhǒng

specific ADJ 特定的 tèdìng de, 明确的 míngquè

de ■ *What is the specific equipment you need for doing this job?* 你做这个工作需要什么特定的设备? Nǐ zuò zhè ge gōngzuò xūyào shénme tèdìng de shèbèi?

specific gravity 比重 bǐzhòng

specification N 规格说明 guīgé shuōmíng, 明细规则 míngxì guīzé

job specifications 职务详细说明 zhíwù xiángxì shuōmíng

technical specifications 技术指标说明 jìshù zhǐbiāo shuōmíng

specifics N 细节 xìjié, 详情 xiángqíng

specify V 详细说明 xiángxì shuōmíng, 明确规定 míngquè guīdìng

specimen N 抽样 chōuyàng, 样本 yàngběn

specious ADJ 似是而非的 sìshì'érfēi de

speck N 小斑点 xiǎo bāndiǎn, 污点 wūdiǎn

speckle N 小斑点 xiǎo bāndiǎn

spectacle N **1** 景象 jǐngxiàng **2** 不寻常的事 bùxúncháng de shì, 奇事 qíshì

to make a spectacle of yourself 丢人现眼 diūrén xiànyǎn, 出洋相 chūyángxiàng

spectacles N See **glasses**

spectacular I ADJ 壮观的 [+场面] zhuàngguān de [+chǎngmiàn], 宏伟的 hóngwěi de II N 壮观的场面 zhuàngguān de chǎngmiàn

spectator N 观众 guānzhòng, 观看者 guānkànzhě

spectator sport 观赏性体育项目 guānshǎng xìngtǐ yù xiàngmù

specter N 鬼魂 guǐhún, 幽灵 yōulíng

spectrum N **1** 光谱 guāngpǔ, 谱 pǔ **2** 一系列 yíxìliè

a spectrum of opinion 一系列意见 yíxìliè yìjiàn

speculate V **1** 推测 tuīcè, 思考 sīkǎo **2** 做投机生意 zuò tóujī shēngyì

speculation N **1** 推测 tuīcè **2** (商业) 投机 (shangyè) tóujī

speculator N 投机商人 tóujī shāngrén, 投机者 tóujīzhě

speculative ADJ **1** 推测的 tuīcè de **2** 投机的 tóujī de

sped See **speed**

speech N **1** 演说 yǎnshuō **2** 说话的能力 shuōhuà de nénglì

freedom of speech 言论自由 yánlùn zìyóu

speechless ADJ 说不出话的 shuōbuchū huà de, 哑口无言的 yǎkǒu wúyán de

speechwriter N 演讲稿撰写人 yǎnjiǎnggǎo zhuànxiěrén

speed I N 速度 sùdù

speed limit 最高限速 zuìgāo xiànsù

speed skating 速度滑冰 sùdù huábīng

II V (PT & PP sped) **1** 快速行进 kuài sù xíngjìn **2** (to speed up) 使…加快速度 shǐ…jiākuài sùdù **3** 超速驾驶 chāosù jiàshǐ

speedboat N 快艇 kuàitǐng [M. WD 艘 sōu]

speeding N（驾车）超速（jiàchē）chāosù

speedometer N（汽车的）速度表（qìchē de）sùdùbiǎo

speedy ADJ 快速的 kuàisù de, 及时的 jíshí de
speedy recovery 早日康复 zǎorì kāngfù

spell¹ (PT & PP **spelled**, **spelt**) V 1 拼写 pīnxiě
■ *How do you spell your last name?* 你的姓怎么拼写？Nǐde xìng zěnme pīnxiě? 2 造成 zàochéng ■ *This boy's antisocial behavior will surely spell trouble for his future.* 这个男孩的反社会行为肯定会为他的将来造成危害。Zhè ge nánhái de fǎn shèhuì xíngwéi kěndìng huì wèi tā de jiānglái zàochéng wēihài.

spell² N 1 一段（短暂的）时间 yí duàn (duǎnzàn de) shíjiān
a spell of unemployment 一段失业的时间 yí duàn shīyè de shíjiān
2 魔咒 mózhòu, 魔法 mófǎ

spellbound ADJ 入迷的 rùmí de, 被迷惑的 bèi míhuo de

spelling N 拼写 pīnxiě
spelling bee（单词）拼写比赛 (dāncí) pīnxiě bǐsài

sped See speed

spend (PT & PP **spent**) V 花 [+钱／时间] huā [+qián/shíjiān], 消耗 xiāohào
to spend the night with sb 与某人一起过夜 yǔ mǒurén yìqǐ guòyè, 与某人一夜情 yǔ mǒurén yíyèqíng

spending N 开支 kāizhī, 开销 kāixiao

spendthrift N 浪费金钱的人 làngfèi jīnqián de rén, 挥霍者 huīhuòzhě

spent I V See spend II ADJ 用过的 yòng guò de, 失效的 shīxiào de
to be a spent force 已丧失权力的 yǐ sàngshī quánlì de, 过气的 guòqì de

sperm N 精子 jīngzǐ

spew V 1 大量排出 [+有毒气体] dàliàng páichū [+yǒudú qìtǐ] 2 大肆宣扬 [+有害思想] dàsì xuānyáng [+yǒuhài sīxiǎng]

sphere N 1 球 qiú, 球体 qiútǐ 2 范围 fànwéi, 领域 lǐngyù
sphere of influence 势力范围 shìlì fànwéi

spherical ADJ 球体的 qiútǐ de, 球形的 qiúxíng de

sphinx N（埃及）狮身人面像 (Āijí) shīshēn rénmiànxiàng

spice I N 香料 xiāngliào
herbs and spices 芳草和香料 fāngcǎo hé xiāngliào
II V 给 [+食物] 添加香料 gěi [+shíwù] tiānjiā xiāngliào

spick-and-span ADJ 干干净净的 gāngān jìngjìng de, 一尘不染的 yì chén bù rǎn de

spicy ADJ 1 加了香料的 jiāle xiāngliào de 2 辣的 là de, 辣味的 làwèi de 3 色情的 sèqíng de, 下流的 xiàliú de

spider N 蜘蛛 zhīzhū

spidery ADJ 蜘蛛网似的 [+字迹] zhīzhūwǎng shìde [+zìjī]

spiel N 喋喋不休推销商品的话 diédié bùxiū tuīxiāo shāngpǐn de huà

spiffy ADJ 整洁漂亮的 [+服装] zhěngjié piàoliang de [+fúzhuāng]

spike I N（金属的）钉状物 (jīnshǔ de) dīng zhuàng wù, 尖铁 jiān tiě II V 1 刺进 cì jìn, 插入 chārù 2 大幅度上升 dàfúdù shàngshēng
to spike with 搀进 [+毒药／烈酒] chānjìn [+dúyào/lièjiǔ]

spikes N 钉鞋 dīngxié [M. WD 双 shuāng]

spill (PT & PP **spilled**, **spilt**) I V（使…）溢出 (shǐ...) yìchū,（使…）溅落 (shǐ...) jiànluò II N 溢出 yìchū
oil spill 石油泄漏 shíyóu xièlòu

spilt See spill

spin I V (PT & PP **spun**) 1 旋转 xuánzhuǎn ■ *The child screamed with delight as his father spun him around.* 爸爸拉着孩子的手抡圈儿，孩子开心得直叫。Bàba lāzhe háizi de shǒu lūn quānr, háizi kāixīnde zhí jiào. 2 编造故事 biānzào gùshi
■ *Philip spun a tale about him beating off a mugger.* 菲利普编造了一个他打退抢劫犯的故事。Fēilìpǔ biānzàole yí ge tā dǎtuì qiǎngjiéfàn de gùshi.
spin doctor 舆论导向专家 yúlùn dǎoxiàng zhuānjiā, 公关顾问 gōngguān gùwèn 3 纺线 fǎngxiàn II N 1 旋转 xuánzhuǎn, 旋球 xuán qiú ■ *The bowler added some spin to the ball.* 投球手打了一个旋球。Tóuqiúshǒu dǎle yí ge xuánqiú. 2 兜风 dōufēng
to spin a tale/yarn 编造故事 biānzào gùshi

spinach N 菠菜 bōcài [M. WD 棵 kē]

spinal ADJ 脊椎的 jǐzhuī de, 脊髓的 jǐsuǐ de
spinal cord 脊髓 jǐsuǐ

spindly ADJ 细长纤弱的 xìcháng xiānruò de

spine N 脊椎 jǐzhuī, 脊柱 jǐzhù

spineless ADJ 没有骨气的 méiyǒu gǔqì de, 懦弱的 nuòruò de

spinning wheel N 手纺车 shǒufǎngchē [M. WD 架 jià/部 bù]

spin-off N 1 子公司 zǐgōngsī, 成立子公司 chénglì zǐgōngsī 2 派生电视节目 pàishēng diànshì jiémù

spinster N 大龄未婚女子 dàlíng wèihūn nǚzǐ, 老处女 lǎochǔnǚ

spiral I N 1 螺旋形 luóxuánxíng, 螺丝 luósī 2 螺旋形过程 luóxuánxíng guòchéng
downward spiral 螺旋形下降 luóxuánxíng xiàjiàng
II V 螺旋形上升／下降 luóxuánxíng shàngshēng/xiàjiàng
to spiral out of control 不断恶化以至于失去控制 búduàn èhuà yǐzhìyú shīqù kòngzhì

spire N [教堂+] 尖顶 [jiàotáng+] jiāndǐng, 塔顶 tǎdǐng

spirit N 1 精神 jīngshén ■ *A series of personal tragedies did not beat her spirit.* 一系列的个人悲剧没有挫败她的精神。Yí xìliè de gèrén bēijù méiyǒu cuòbài tā de jīngshén.
team spirit 团队精神 tuánduì jīngshén
2 情绪 qíngxù
in high spirits 情绪很高 qíngxù hěn gāo
in low spirits 情绪低落 qíngxù dīluò
3 精灵 jīnglíng, 灵魂 línghún, 鬼魂 guǐhún

spirited ADJ 精神饱满的 jīngshén bǎomǎn dc, 充满活力的 chōngmǎn huólì de

spirits N 烈性酒 lièxìngjiǔ

spiritual I ADJ 精神（上）的 jīngshén (shàng) de, 心灵的 xīnlíng de II N 灵歌 línggē

spit I N 1 口水 kǒushuǐ, 唾液 tuòyè **2** 烤肉叉 kǎoròu chā [m. wd 把 bǎ] II v (PT & PP **spat**)
1 吐 (掉) tǔ (diào)
to spit up blood 吐血 tǔ xiě
2 吐口水 tǔkǒu shuǐ, 吐痰 tǔtán

spite I N 恶意 èyì ■ *He made that offensive remark out of spite.* 他说这句冲撞的话，是出于恶意。Tā shuō zhè jù chōngzhuàng de huà, shì chūyú èyì.
in spite of 尽管 jǐnguǎn
II v 故意…使恼火 gùyì… shǐ nǎohuǒ, 存心捉弄 cúnxīn zhuōnòng

spiteful ADJ 出于恶意的 chūyú èyì de, 存心捣乱的 cúnxīn dǎoluàn de

splash I v 溅 jiàn, 泼 pō
to splash around 啪嗒啪嗒地趟水 pādā pādā de tàng shuǐ
II N （水的）溅泼声 (shuǐ de) jiàn pō shēng
to make a splash 引起公众的注意 yǐnqǐ gōngzhòng de zhùyì, 大出风头 dà chū fēngtou

splashy ADJ 鲜艳的 xiānyàn de, 引人注目的 yǐnrén zhùmù de

splat N 啪嗒声 pādā shēng

splatter v （使…）溅满 (shǐ…) jiàn mǎn
a wall splattered with blood 溅满鲜血的墙 jiàn mǎn xiānxuè de qiáng

splendid ADJ 1 出色的 [+成绩] chūsè de [+chéngjì], 极好的 jíhǎo de **2** 壮丽的 [+景色] zhuànglì de [+jǐngsè]

splendor N 壮丽 zhuànglì, 光辉 guānghuī

splint N （外科用）夹板 (wàikē yòng) jiābǎn

splinter I N （金属／木头）碎片 (jīnshǔ/mùtou) suìpiàn, 木刺 mùcì
splinter group 分裂出来的小派别 fēnliè chūlái de xiǎo pàibié
II v 1 使 [+木头] 裂成碎片 shǐ [+mùtou] liè chéng suìpiàn **2** [团体+] 分裂 [tuántǐ+] fēnliè

split I v (PT & PP **split**) **1** 分开 fēnkāi, 分成 fēnchéng
to split a bill 分摊费用 fēntān fèiyòng

2 裂开 lièkai
to split sth three/four ways 把某物分成三／四份 bǎ mǒuwù fēnchéng sān/sì fèn
to split up [夫妻+] 离婚 [fūqī+] líhūn, [朋友+] 断交 [péngyou+] duànjiāo
II N 1 裂口 lièkǒu, 裂缝 lièfèng **2** （团体的）分裂 (tuántǐ de) fēnliè, 分歧 fēnqí **3** 差别 chābié, 差异 chāyì **4** (a split second) 一刹那 yíchànà, 顷刻 qǐngkè **5** (split level) 错层式的 [+房间] cuòcéngshì de [+fángjiān]

splitting ADJ (splitting headache) 头痛欲裂的 tóutòng yùliè de

splurge N, v 任意挥霍（金钱）rènyì huīhuò (jīnqián), 乱花钱 luànhuāqián

splutter v See **sputter**

spoil (PT & PP **spoiled, spoilt**) v 1 弄坏 nònghuài, 毁掉 huǐdiao ■ *The power failure spoiled their dinner party.* 停电毁了他们的宴请。Tíngdiàn huǐle tāmen de yànqíng. **2** 宠坏 chǒnghuài **3** [食物+] 变质 [shíwù+] biànzhì, 变坏 biànhuài

spoils N 战利品 zhànlìpǐn, 赃物 zāngwù

spoilsport N 破坏别人兴趣的人 pòhuài biérén xìngqu de rén, 扫兴者 sǎoxìngzhě

spoilt ADJ 宠坏的 [+小孩] chǒnghuài de [+xiǎohái], 惯坏的 guànhuài de
spoilt rotten 完全被宠坏了 wánquán bèi chǒnghuài le

spoke¹ v See **speak**

spoke² N （自行车）轮辐 (zìxíngchē) lúnzhóu [m. wd 条 tiáo/根 gēn]

spoken¹ See **speak**

spoken² ADJ 口语的 kǒuyǔ de

spokesman N 发言人 fāyánrén

spokeswoman N （女）发言人 (nǚ) fāyánrén

sponge I N 海绵 hǎimián
sponge cake 海绵（状）蛋糕 hǎimián (zhuàng) dàngao, 松蛋糕 sōng dàngāo
II v 1 （用海绵或毛巾）擦洗 (yòng hǎimián huò máojīn) cāxǐ **2** (to sponge on/off) 依赖 [+父母] 生活 yīlài [+fùmǔ] shēnghuó, 揩 [+朋友的] 油 kāi [+péngyou de] yóu

spongy ADJ 海绵似的 hǎimián shìde, 松软多孔的 sōngruǎn duōkǒng de

sponsor I N 1 （活动）赞助人 (huódòng de) zànzhùrén **2** （申请资格的）担保人 (shēnqǐng zīge de) dānbǎorén, 保证人 bǎozhèngrén **3** （法案的）提案人 (fǎ'àn de) tí'àn rén, 发起人 fāqǐrén II v 1 赞助 [+募捐活动] zànzhù [+mùjuān huódòng] **2** 为 [+某人] 做担保 wéi [+mǒurén] zuò dānbǎo **3** 提议 [+法案] tíyì [+fǎ'àn]

sponsorship N 1 赞助 zànzhù **2** 担保 dānbǎo **3** 倡议 chàngyì

spontaneity N 自发（性）zìfā (xìng)

spontaneous ADJ 自发的 zìfā de, 自动的 zìdòng de

spoof N 滑稽模仿（作品）gǔjī mófǎng (zuòpǐn)

spook I N 1 鬼 guǐ, 鬼魂 guǐhún 2 暗探 àntàn II v 惊吓 jīngxià, 惊唬 jīnghǔ

spooky ADJ 阴森吓人的 yīnsēn xiàrén de, 象有鬼的 xiàng yǒuguǐ de

spool N 卷轴 juànzhóu

spoon I N 勺 sháo, 匙子 chízi
be born with a silver spoon in one's mouth 生在富贵人家 shēng zài fùguì rénjiā ■ Charles was born with a silver spoon in his mouth. 查尔斯出生在富贵人家。Chá'ěrsī chūshēng zài fùguì rénjiā.
II v（用勺子）舀 (yòng sháozi) yǎo

spoonfed See **spoonfeed**

spoonfeed (PT & PP **spoonfed**) v 1 用匙子喂 [+婴儿] yòng chízi wèi [+yīng'ér] 2 对 [+学生] 作填鸭式灌输 duì [+xuésheng] zuò tiányāshì guànshū

spoonful N 一匙（糖）yí chí (táng)

sporadic ADJ 零星的 língxīng de, 断断续续的 duànduàn xùxù de

sport I N 1 体育 tǐyù, 体育活动 tǐyù huódòng ■ Carl is very good at sports. 卡尔体育很棒。Kǎ'ěr tǐyù hěn bàng.
sports car 跑车 pǎochē
sports center 体育运动中心 tǐyù yùndòng zhōngxīn
sports club 体育俱乐部 tǐyù jùlèbù
sports pages 体育版 tǐyù bǎn
2 娱乐 yúlè, 玩乐 wánlè
for sport 为了娱乐 wèile yúlè, 为了好玩 wèile hàowán
3 热情开朗的人 rèqíng kāilǎng de rén
a good sport 开得起玩笑的人 kāidéqǐ wánxiào de rén, 输得起的人 shūdéqǐ de rén
II v 炫耀 xuànyào, 卖弄 màinong

sporting ADJ（有关）体育运动的 (yǒuguān) tǐyù yùndòng de
sporting chance 相当大的机会 xiāngdāng dà de jīhuì, 公平的机会 gōngping de jīhuì
sporting goods 体育用品 tǐyùyòngpǐn
sporting life 户外运动生活 hùwài yùndòng shēnghuó

sportscast N 体育比赛的电视转播 tǐyù bǐsài de diànshì zhuǎnbō

sportsman N 运动员 yùndòngyuán

sportsmanlike ADJ 有体育道德的 yǒu tǐyù dàodé de, 有良好体育风尚的 yǒu liánghǎo tǐyùfēngshàng de

sportsmanship N 体育道德 tǐyù dàodé, 良好的体育风尚 liánghǎo de tǐyù fēngshàng

sportswear N 运动服装 yùndòngfúzhuāng, 休闲服装 xiūxiánfú zhuāng

sportswoman N 女运动员 nǚ yùndòngyuán

sporty ADJ 漂亮花哨的 piàoliang huāshao de

spot I N 1 地点 dìdiǎn, 地方 dìfang
on the spot 当场 dāngchǎng ■ After seeing their factory, the buyer placed an order on the spot. 采购员在看了他们的工厂后，当场下了订单。Cǎigòuyuán zài kànle tāmede gōngchǎng hòu, dāngchǎng xiàle dìngdān.
spot check 抽样检查 chōuyàng jiǎnchá
2 斑点 bāndiǎn
A leopard never changes its spots. 豹不会改变斑点。Bào bú huì gǎibiàn bāndiǎn. (→ 本性难移。Běnxìng nán yí. It is difficult to change one's nature.)
II v 1 认出 rènchū, 发现 fāxiàn 2 让 [+对方] ràng [+duìfāng] III ADJ 现货的 xiànhuò de, 现付的 xiànfù de
spot sale 现货现金销售 xiànhuò xiànjīn xiāoshòu

spotless ADJ 一尘不染的 yì chén bù rǎn de

spotlight I N 1 聚光灯 jùguāngdēng 2（公众的）瞩目 (gōngzhòng de) zhǔmù, 高度的关注 gāodù de guānzhù II v 使…突出 shǐ…tūchū

spotty ADJ 1 有斑点的 yǒu bāndiǎn de 2 有好有坏的 yǒu hǎo yǒu huài de 3 时有时无的 shí yǒu shí wú de, 断断续续的 duànduàn xùxù de

spouse N 配偶 pèi'ǒu

spout I N 1 喷管 pēnguǎn 2（茶壶）嘴 (cháhú) zuǐ 3 水柱 shuǐzhù II v 1 [液体+] 喷出 [yètǐ+] pēn chū, 喷涌 pēnyǒng 2 [人+] 滔滔不绝的说话 [rén+] tāotāo bùjué de shuōhuà, 口若悬河 kǒu ruò xuánhé

sprain I v 扭伤 [+关节] niǔshāng [+guānjié] II N 扭伤 niǔshāng

sprang See **spring**¹

sprawl I v 1 [人+] 伸开手脚躺／坐 [rén+] shēnkāi shǒujiǎo tǎng/zuò 2 [植物+] 蔓生 [zhíwù+] mànshēng II N 1 伸开四肢的躺／坐姿势 shēnkāi sìzhī de tǎng/zuò zīshì 2 杂乱无章的房屋建筑 záluàn wúzhāng de fángwū jiànzhù
urban sprawl 杂乱无章的市镇扩展 záluàn wúzhāng de shìzhèn kuòzhǎn

spray I v 喷 pēn, 喷洒 pēnsǎ II N 喷雾剂 pēnwù jì, 喷雾液体 pēnwù yètǐ
spray gun 喷枪 pēnqiāng
spray paint 喷漆 pēnqī
body spray 香水喷雾 xiāngshuǐ pēnwù
fly spray 灭蝇喷雾剂 miè yíng pēnwùjì
hair spray 定发型喷雾 dìng fàxíng pēnwù

spread (PT & PP **spread**) v 1 铺开 pūkāi, 摊开 tānkāi
to spread oneself thin 工作太多无法应付 gōngzuò tài duō wúfǎ yìngfù, 摊子铺得太大 tānzi pū dé tàidà
to spread one's wings 开始独立生活 kāishǐ dúlì shēnghuó
2 传开 chuánkāi, 传播 chuánbō ■ Mosquitoes spread diseases. 蚊子传播疾病。Wénzi

chuánbō jíbìng. **3** 涂 tú ■ *Sally spread jam on the slice of bread.* 赛莉在面包上涂果酱。Sàilì zài miànbāoshang tú guǒjiàng.

spreadsheet N 空白表格程序 kòngbái biǎogé chéngxù

spree N 狂欢 kuánghuān, 尽情作乐 jìnqíng zuòlè buying/drinking/crime spree 大肆采购／狂饮／疯狂犯罪作案 dàsì cǎigòu/kuángyǐn/fēngkuáng fànzuì zuò'àn

sprig N 小树枝 xiǎo shùzhī [M. WD 根 gēn]

spring[1] I v (PT **sprang**; PP **sprung**) 跳跃 tiàoyuè ■ *He sprang up from his chair and ran to answer the door.* 他从椅子上跳起来，跑去开门。Tā cóng yǐzishang tiàoqǐlai, pǎoqu kāi mén. to spring a surprise 出其不意 chū qí bùyì II N 弹簧 tánhuáng

spring[2] N 春天 chūntiān ■ *Most people welcome the arrival of spring.* 大多数人都欢迎春天来临。Dàduōshù rén dōu huānyíng chūntiān láilín.

spring[3] N 泉水 quánshuǐ, 泉源 quán yuán hot spring 温泉 wēnquán

springboard N（跳水）跳板 (tiàoshuǐ) tiàobǎn [M. WD 块 kuài],（体操）踏板 (tǐcāo) tàbǎn [M. WD 块 kuài]

springbreak N（学校）春假 (xuéxiào) chūnjià

springtime N 春天 chūntiān, 春季 chūnjì

springy ADJ 有弹性的 yǒu tánxìng de

sprinkle I v **1** 洒 [+香水] sǎ [+xiāngshuǐ], 撒 [+花瓣] sā [+huābàn] **2** 下小雨 xià xiǎoyǔ **3** 以 [+俏皮话] 点缀 [+演讲] yǐ [+qiàopíhuà] diǎnzhuì [+yǎnjiǎng] II N（食物）碎屑 (shíwù) suìxiè **2** 小雨 xiǎoyǔ

sprinkler N 洒水器 sǎshuǐqì

sprint I v 快速短跑 kuàisù duǎnpǎo, 冲刺 chōngcì II N 短跑（比赛）duǎnpǎo (bǐsài), 冲刺 chōngcì 100-meter sprint 一百公尺短跑 yì bǎi gōngchǐ duǎnpǎo

sprout I v **1** [树+] 发芽 [shù+] fāyá **2** [突然+] 长出头发 [tūrán+] zhǎng chū tóufa **3** [新城镇+] 大量涌现 [xīn chéngzhèn+] dàliàng yǒngxiàn II N **1** 新芽 xīn yá, 嫩芽 nènyá **2** 豆芽 dòuyá bean sprout 豆芽 dòuyá

spruce[1] v (to spruce up) 收拾整理 shōushi zhěnglǐ, 美化 měihuà

spruce[2] N 云杉 yúnshān [M. WD 棵 kē]

sprung See **spring**[1]

spry ADJ 充满活力的 [+老人] chōngmǎn huólì de [+lǎorén]

spud N 土豆 tǔdòu, 马铃薯 mǎlíngshǔ

spun See **spin**

spunk N 胆量 dǎnliàng, 勇气 yǒngqì

spunky ADJ 胆大的 dǎndà de, 勇敢的 yǒnggǎn de

spur I N **1** 马刺 mǎcì, 靴刺 xuēcì **2** 刺激 cìjī, 激励 jīlì

on the spur of the moment 一时冲动之下 yì shí chōngdòng zhīxià II v 刺激 cìjī, 促使 cùshǐ

spurious ADJ **1** 虚假的 [+态度] xūjiǎ de [+tàidu], 虚伪的 xūwěi de **2** 谬误的 [+论点] miùwù de [+lùndiǎn], 不能成立的 bùnéngchénglì de

spurn v（轻蔑地）拒绝 (qīngmiè de) jùjué, 唾弃 tuòqì

spurt I v [火焰+] 喷出 [huǒyàn+] pēn chū, 迸发 bèngfā II N 喷出 pēnchū, 迸发 bèngfā

sputter v **1** [引擎+] 发出噼啪的声音 [yǐnqíng+] fāchū pī pā de shēngyīn **2** [人+] 结结巴巴地说 [rén+] jiējie bābā de shuō to sputter along [工作+] 进行得很不顺利 [gōngzuò+] jìnxíng de hěn bú shùnlì

spy I N 间谍 jiàndié, 密探 mìtàn II v **1** 从事间谍活动 cóngshì jiàndié huódòng **2** (to spy on) 暗中监视 ànzhōng jiānshì

squabble v（因小事）吵嘴 (yīn xiǎoshì) chǎozuǐ, 发生口角 fāshēng kǒujué

squad N **1**（军队的）班 (jūnduì de) bān, 小队 xiǎoduì **2**（警察的）特别行动队 (jǐngchá de) tèbié xíngdòng duì riot squad 防暴小组 fángbào xiǎozǔ **3**（体育）运动队 (tǐyù) yùndòngduì squad car 执勤警车 zhíqín jǐngchē

squadron N **1** 飞行中队 fēixíng zhōngduì **2**（海军）分遣舰队 (hǎijūn) fēnqiǎn jiànduì

squalid ADJ **1** 肮脏的 [+地方] āngzāng de [+dìfang], 污秽的 wūhuì de **2** 不道德的 [+行为] búdàodé de [+xíngwéi], 龌龊的 wòchuò de

squall N（一阵）狂风 (yí zhèn) kuángfēng

squalor N 肮脏 āngzāng, 污秽 wūhuì

squander v 挥霍 huīhuò, 浪费 làngfèi

square I N **1** 广场 guǎngchǎng **2** 正方形 zhèngfāngxíng **3** 平方 píngfāng square dance 方形舞 fāngxíng wǔ II ADJ **1** 正方形的 zhèngfāngxíng de **2** 平方的 píngfāng de square foot/meter 平方英尺／公尺 píngfāng yīngchǐ/gōngchǐ square root 平方根 píngfānggēn a square deal 公平交易 gōngpíng jiāoyì to eat a square meal 好好地吃一顿 hǎohǎo de chī yí dùn to be back to square one 从头开始 cóng tóu kāishǐ III v 自乘 zìchéng, 成为平方 chéngwéi píngfāng to square an account 还清人情（债）huánqīng rénqíng (zhài) to square the circle 做不可能做到的事 zuò bù kěnéng zuòdào de shì

squarely ADV **1** 完全地 wánquán de, 毫不含糊地 háobù hánhu de **2** 精确地 jīngquè de, 直接地 zhíjiē de squash¹

squash¹ N **1** 壁球 bìqiú, 墙网球 qiáng wǎngqiú **2** 南瓜 nánguā, 西葫芦 xīhúlu

squash² V **1** 压扁 yābiǎn, 压碎 yāsuì **2** 塞进 sāijìn, 挤 jǐ

squat I V **1** 蹲 dūn
to squat down 蹲下来 dūnxià lái
2 擅自占用 [+旧房] shànzì zhànyòng [+jiùfáng] II N 蹲 dūn III ADJ 矮胖的 ǎipàng de

squeak I V 发出尖厉短促的叫声 fāchū jiānlì duǎncù de jiàoshēng, 吱吱作响 zhīzhī zuòxiǎng II N 吱吱的响声 zhīzhī de xiǎngshēng

squeaky ADJ 吱吱作响的 zhīzhī zuòxiǎng de
squeaky clean ① 光洁的 guāngjié de ② 品行端正的 pǐnxíng duānzhèng de

squeal I V **1** 发出长而尖锐的声音 fāchū cháng ér jiānruì de shēngxiǎng **2** (to squeal over sb) 举报某人 jǔbào mǒurén II N 长而尖锐的声音 cháng ér jiānruì de shēngxiǎng
squeal of brakes 急刹车的声音 jíshāchē de shēngxiǎng

squeamish ADJ 容易感到恶心的 róngyì gǎndào èxīn de, 神经质的 shénjīngzhì de

squeeze I V 挤 jǐ, 挤压 jǐyā ■ I had to squeeze in my lunch break between two classes today. 我今天得在两课的中间挤出时间来吃午饭。Wǒ jīntiān děi zài liǎng kè de zhōngjiān jǐchū shíjiān lái chī wǔfàn.
to squeeze past 挤过去 jǐ guòqù
to squeeze sth out of sb 从某人口中逼出信息 cóng mǒurén kǒuzhōng bī chū xìnxī II N **1** 拥挤 yōngjǐ **2** (财务) 困难 (cáiwù) kùnnan, 拮据 jiéjū
to put the squeeze on sb 逼迫某人 bīpò mǒurén
squeeze play 施加压力 shījiā yālì

squelch I V **1** 吱吱作响 zhīzhī gēge zuòxiǎng **2** 消除 [+想法 / 说法] xiāochú [+xiǎngfǎ/shuōfa] II N 吱吱咯咯的声音 zhīzhī gēgē de shēngyīn

squid N 鱿鱼 yóuyú, 乌贼 (鱼) wūzéi (yú)

squiggle N 扭曲的短线 niǔqū de duǎn xiàn

squint I V 眯着眼睛看 mízhe yǎnjing kàn II N **1** 眯着眼睛 mízhe yǎnjing **2** 斜视 (症) xiéshì (zhēng)

squire N (中世纪欧洲的) 骑士的随从 (Zhōngshìjì Ōuzhōu de) qíshì de suícóng

squirm I V **1** 扭动 (身体) niǔdòng (shēntǐ) **2** 感到尴尬 gǎndào gāngà, 局促不安 júcù bù'ān II N 扭动 (身体) niǔdòng (shēntǐ)

squirrel N 松鼠 sōngshǔ [M. WD 只 zhī]

squirt I V 喷射 pēnshè, 喷出 pēnchū, 射出 shèchū II N 喷射出来的东西 pēnshè chūlái de dōngxi

squishy ADJ **1** 软软的 ruǎnruǎn de **2** 可榨汁的 kě zhà zhī de

stab I V 用刀刺 [+人] yòng dāo cì [+rén], 捅 tǒng
to be stabbed to death 被刺身亡 bèicì shēnwáng
to stab sb in the back 背后说某人的坏话 bèihòu shuō mǒurén de huàihuà II N (刀) 刺 (dāo) cì, 捅 tǒng
stab on the back 背后中伤 bèihòu zhòngshāng, 背叛 bèipàn

stabbing I N 利器伤人 (罪) lìqì shāng rén (zuì) II ADJ 刀割似的 [+疼痛] dāo gē shìde [+téngtòng], 一阵剧痛的 yí zhèn jùtòng de

stability N 稳定 wěndìng

stabilize V (使…) 稳定 (shǐ…) wěndìng

stable¹ ADJ **1** 稳定的 [+社会] wěndìng de [+shèhuì], 安定的 āndìng de **2** 稳重的 [+人] wěnzhòng de [+rén], 平静的 píngjìng de

stable² N 马厩 mǎjiù, 养马场 yǎngmǎchǎng

stack I N **1** 一叠 yì dié, 一堆 yì duī
a stack of shoe boxes 一叠鞋盒 yì dié xié hé **2** 高烟囱 gāo yāncōng **3** 计算机临时资料存储 jìsuànjī línshí zīliào cúnchǔ II N 堆放 duīfàng
to stack up 相比较 xiāng bǐjiào, 比高低 bǐ gāodī

stacks N (图书馆) 书库 (túshūgān) shūkù

stadium N 体育场 tǐyù chǎng, 运动场 yùndòngchǎng

staff¹ I N 职工 zhígōng, 雇员 gùyuán II V 配备员工 pèibèi yuángōng
fully staffed 员工配备齐全 yuángōng pèibèi qíquán
short staffed 员工配备不足 yuángōng pèibèi bù zú

staff² **1** 拐杖 guǎizhàng **2** 五线谱 wǔxiànpǔ

staffer N 工作人员 gōngzuò rényuán, 职员 zhíyuán

stag N 成年雄鹿 chéngnián xióng lù
stag party 男人聚会 nánren jùhuì

stage I N **1** 阶段 jiēduàn ■ The doctor diagnosed him to be in an advanced stage of lung cancer. 医生诊断他已是肺癌晚期。Yīshēng zhěnduàn tā yǐ shì fèi'ái wǎnqī. **2** 舞台 wǔtái
stage fright 怯场 qièchǎng, 临上场时的胆怯 lín shàngchǎng shí de dǎnqiè
to go on stage 登台演出 dēngtái yǎnchū, 成为演员 chéngwéi yǎnyuán
to take the center stage 成为公众注意的焦点 chéngwéi gōngzhòng zhùyì de jiāodiǎn II V **1** 举行 jǔxíng, 举办 jǔbàn
to stage a comeback 复出 fùchū, 复辟 fùbì **2** 上演 shàngyǎn

stagecoach N (公用) 马车 gōngyòng mǎchē [M. WD 辆 liàng]

stage-manager N 舞台监督 wǔtáijiāndū

stagger I V **1** 摇摇晃晃地走 yáoyáo huànghuàng de zǒu **2** 使 [+人] 震惊 shǐ [+rén] zhènjīng II N 摇晃 yáohuang, 蹒跚 pánshān

staggering ADJ 令人震惊的 lìngrén zhènjīng de

staging N 演出 yǎnchū, 上演 shàngyǎn

stagnant ADJ **1** 不流动的 [+水] bù liúdòng de [+shuǐ] **2** 不发展的 bù fāzhǎn de, 停滞的 tíngzhì de

stagnate v 停滞 tíngzhì, 不发展 bù fāzhǎn

stagnation N 停滞 tíngzhì, 停顿 tíngdùn

staid ADJ 老派的 lǎopài de, 枯燥的 kūzào de

stain I N 污点 wūdiǎn, 污斑 wūbān II v 沾污 zhānwū, 弄脏 nòngzāng

stained glass 彩色玻璃 cǎisè bōli

stainless steel N 不锈钢 búxiùgāng

staircase, stairway N 楼梯 lóutī

stairs N 楼梯 lóutī ■ *In the event of fire, everyone must use the stairs to go downstairs.* 万一发生 火灾，大家必须使用楼梯下楼。Wànyī fāshēng huǒzāi, dàjiā bìxū shǐyòng lóutī xiàlóu.

stake I N **1** 尖桩 jiān zhuāng, 桩子 zhuāngzi **2** 赌 注 dǔzhù, 投资 tóuzī

to be at stake 处于危险境地 chǔyú wēixiǎn jìngdì

to have a stake in 有股份的 yǒu gǔfèn de, 有利 害关系 yǒu lìhài guānxi

II v 用 [+家产] 去赌博 yòng [+jiāchǎn] qù dǔbó, 拿 [+生命] 去冒险 ná [+shēngmìng] qù màoxiǎn

to stake a claim 声称拥有所有权 shēngchēng yōngyǒu suǒyǒuquán

to stake sth out 对某处进行监视 duì mǒuchù jìnxíng jiānshì

stakeholder N **1** 股份持有人 gǔfèn chíyǒurén **2** 利益相关者 lìyì xiāngguānzhě **3** (临时) 财产 保管人 (línshí) cáichǎn bǎoguǎnrén

stakeout N (警察) 秘密监视 (jǐngchá) mìmì jiānshì

stale ADJ **1** 不新鲜的 [+食物] bù xīnxian de [+shíwù] **2** 乏味的 [+生活] fáwèi de [+shēnghuó]

stalemate N 僵局 jiāngjú, 僵持 jiāngchí **2** (象 棋) 和棋 (xiàngqí) héqí

stalk¹ N (植物的) 茎 (zhíwù de) jīng, 杆 gǎn

stalk² v 跟踪的 gēnzōng, 纠缠骚扰 jiūchán sāorǎo

stalker N 跟踪者 gēnzōngzhě, 纠缠骚扰的人 jiūchán sāorǎo de rén

stall I N **1** 摊 tān, 摊子 tānzi **2** (引擎) 停止运转 (yǐnqíng) tíngzhǐ yùnzhuǎn, 熄火 xīhuǒ **3** 停滞 (状态) tíngzhì (zhuàngtài) II v **1** [飞机发动机+] 停止运转 [fēijī fādòngjī+] tíngzhǐ yùnzhuǎn, 熄火 xīhuǒ **2** 停滞不前 tíngzhì bùqián, 停顿 tíngdùn **3** 故意拖延 gùyì tuōyán

to stall for time 拖延时间 tuōyán shíjiān, 观望 不前 guānwàng bù qián

stallion N 种马 zhǒngmǎ

stalwart ADJ 强壮的 qiángzhuàng de

stalwart supporter 忠实有力的支持者 zhōngshí yǒulì de zhīchízhě

stamina N 耐力 nàilì, 毅力 yìlì

stammer N, v 结结巴巴地说 jiējiēbābā de shuō, 口吃 kǒuchī

stamp I N **1** 邮票 yóupiào ■ *My grandpa used to collect stamps.* 我爷爷过去集邮。Wǒ yéye guòqù jíyóu.

stamp album 集邮簿 jíyóubù

commemorative stamp 纪念邮票 jìniàn yóupiào **2** 印记 yìnjì ■ *His passport has got a Chinese entry stamp on it.* 他的护照上有入境中国的印记。Hā de hùzhàoshang yǒu rùjìng Zhōngguó de yìnjì. II v **1** 在…盖印 zài...gàiyìn **2** 跺脚 duòjiǎo ■ *It was so cold they stamped the ground to keep warm.* 天冷得他们直跺脚取暖。Tiān lěng de tāmen zhí duòjiǎo qǔnuǎn. **3** 跺 (脚) duò (jiǎo), 顿 (足) dùn (zú)

stampede I v **1** [人群+] 争先恐后地奔跑 [rénqún+] zhēngxiān kǒnghòu de bēnpǎo, 蜂拥 fēngyōng **2** [动物+] 奔逃 [dòngwù+] bēntáo II N **1** (动物的) 四处奔逃 (dòngwù de) sìchù bēntáo **2** (人群的) 奔跑 (rénqún de) bēnpǎo

stance N 立场 lìchǎng, 姿态 zītài

to adopt a neutral stance 采取中立的立场 cǎiqǔ zhōnglì de lìchǎng

stand I v (PT & PP **stood**) **1** 站 zhàn, 站立 zhànlì ■ *Everyone stood up when the U.S. President entered the room.* 美国总统进入房间时，大家起 立。Měiguó zǒngtǒng jìnrù fángjiān shí, dàjiā qǐlì. **2** 忍受 rěnshòu **3** 经受 jīngshòu

to stand by ① 坚持 jiānchí ■ *I'll stand by my principles, whatever the cost.* 我要不惜代价坚持 原则。Wǒ yào bù xī dàijià jiānchí yuánzé. ② 支持 zhīchí ③ 待命 dàimìng

to stand out 突出 tūchū ■ *Peter stands out in the class as the most mature boy.* 彼得在班上很突 出，因为他是最成熟的男孩。Bǐdé zài bānshang hěn tūchū, yīnwèi tā shì zuì chéngshú de nánhái.

to stand up for 维护 wéihù

II N **1** 架子 jiàzi

newspaper stand 报纸架 bàozhǐ jià **2** 摊位 tānwèi, 售货摊 shòuhuò tān

exhibition stand 展示摊位 zhǎnshì tānwèi **3** 立场 lìchǎng, 态度 tàidu

to take a stand against 明确表示反对 míngquè biǎoshì fǎnduì **4** (the stand) 证人席 zhèngrénxí

stand-alone ADJ 独立的 [+计算机] dúlì de [+jìsuànjī]

standard I N **1** 标准 biāozhǔn ■ *A restaurant has to meet certain health standards to stay in business.* 餐馆必须符合一定的卫生标准，才能 营业。Cānguǎn bìxū fúhé yídìng de wèishēng biāozhǔn, cái néng yíngyè. **2** 水准 shuǐzhǔn

standard of living 生活水准 shēnghuó shuǐzhǔn **3** 手动档汽车 shǒudòngdàng qìchē [M. WD 辆

liàng] **4** 旗帜 qízhì [M. WD 面 miàn] **II** ADJ **1** 标准的 biāozhǔn de **2** 普通的 pǔtōng de, 正常的 zhèngcháng de

standard-bearer N **1** 旗手 qíshǒu **2** 领袖 lǐngxiù, 倡导人 chàngdǎorén

standard-issue N 标准配发的 [+军队装备] biāozhǔn pèifā de [+jūnduì zhuāngbèi]

standardize V 使…标准化 shǐ…biāozhǔnhuà

standby N **1** 备用品 bèiyòng pǐn **2**（乘客）等候退票（chéngkè）děnghòu tuìpiào passenger on standby 等候退票的乘客 děnghòu tuìpiào de chéngkè on standby 随时待命 suíshí dàimìng

stand-in N 替身 tìshēn, 替代者 tìdàizhě

standing **I** ADJ 长期有效的 chángqī yǒuxiào de, 常设的 chángshè de standing order 长期订单 chángqī dìngdān standing joke 经常性笑料 jīngchángxìng xiàoliào **II** N 地位 dìwèi, 等级 děngjí

standoff N（战斗中的）僵持局面（zhàndòu zhòngde）jiāngchí júmiàn

standout N（相貌／表现）突出的人（xiàngmào/biǎoxiàn）tūchū de rén

standpoint N 立足点 lìzúdiǎn, 立场 lìchǎng

standstill N 静止 jìngzhǐ, 停顿 tíngdùn at a standstill 处于停顿状态 chǔyú tíngdùn zhuàngtài

standup ADJ **1** 单人说笑表演 dānrén shuōxiào biǎoyǎn, 单口相声 dānkǒu xiàngsheng **2** 竖立的 shùlì de

stank See **stink**

stanza N（诗的）节（shī de）jié

staple **I** N **1** 订书钉 dìngshūdīng **2** 主要食物 zhǔyào shíwù, 主食 zhǔshí **3** 常见的人／事 chángjiàn de rén/shì **II** V 用订书钉订住 yòng dìngshūdīng dìng zhù **III** ADJ 主要的 zhǔyào de, 最重要的 zuì zhòngyào de

stapler N 订书机 dìngshūjī

star **I** N **1** 星 xīng star sign 星座 xīngzuò **2** 星级 xīngjí ■ I can't afford to stay in a five-star hotel. 我住不起五星级旅馆。Wǒ zhùbuqǐ wǔxīngjí lǚguǎn. **3** 明星 míngxīng **II** V 由…主演 yóu…zhǔyǎn, 主演 zhǔyǎn, 担任主角 dānrèn zhǔjué ■ Who'll star in this screen adaptation of "The Twelfth Night"? 谁将在这部由《第十二夜》改编的电影中担任主角？Shéi jiāng zài zhè bù yóu "Dì shí'èr yè" gǎibiān de diànyǐng zhōng dānrèn zhǔjué?

starboard N（船的）右舷（chuán de）yòuxián, 右侧 yòucè

Starbucks N 星巴克咖啡馆 xīngbākè kāfēiguǎn

starch **I** N **1** 淀粉 diànfěn **2** 含淀粉的食物 hán diànfěn de shíwù **3** 浆粉 jiāngfěn **II** V 用浆粉上浆 yòng jiāngfěn shàng jiāng

starchy ADJ 含有大量淀粉的 hányǒu dàliàng diànfěn de

stardom N（电影／体育）明星的地位（diànyǐng/tǐyù）míngxīng de dìwèi to rise to stardom 成名 chéngmíng, 走红 zǒuhóng

stare **I** V 盯着看 dīngzhe kàn, 注视 zhùshì ■ Stop staring at me! 别盯着看看！Bié dīngzhe wǒ kàn! to stare sb in the face ① 明摆在某人面前 míng bǎi zài mǒurén miànqián ②[灾难+]不可避免 [zāinàn+] bùkě bìmiǎn **II** N 盯视 dīngshì, 凝视 níngshì

starfish N 海星 hǎixīng

stark **I** ADJ **1** 荒凉的 [+景色] huāngliáng de [+jǐngsè] **2** 明显的 míngxiǎn de in stark contrast 形成明显的对照 xíngchéng míngxiǎn de duìzhào **II** ADV 完全地 wánquán de stark naked 赤裸的 chìluǒ de, 一丝不挂的 yì sī bú guà de

starlet N 演配角的年轻女演员 yǎn pèijué de niánqīng nǚyǎnyuán, 二流女演员 èrliú nǚyǎnyuán

starlight N 星光 xīngguāng

starling N 椋鸟 liángniǎo [M. WD 只 zhī]

starlit ADJ 星光闪烁的 [+夜空] xīngguāng shǎnshuò de [+yèkōng]

starry ADJ 满天星斗的 mǎntiān xīngdǒu de

starry-eyed ADJ 充满幻想的 chōngmǎn huànxiǎng de, 不讲究实际的 bù jiǎngjiu shíjì de

Stars and Stripes N（美国）星条旗（Měiguó）xīngtiáoqí [M. WD 面 miàn], 美国国旗 Měiguó guóqí

Star-Spangled Banner N（美国）星条旗之歌（Měiguó）xīngtiáoqí zhī gē, 美国国歌 Měiguó guógē

star-studded ADJ 明星云集的 [+社交聚会] míngxīng yúnjí de [+shèjiāo jùhuì]

start **I** V 开始 kāishǐ to start a family 开始生儿育女 kāishǐ shēng'ér yùnǔ, 生第一个孩子 shēng dìyīgè háizi to start from scratch 从头开始 cóngtóu kāishǐ, 零起点 líng qǐdiǎn **2** 出发 chūfā ■ Do we have to start out so early tomorrow? 明天我们非得这么早出发吗？Míngtiān wǒmen fēiděi zhème zǎo chūfā ma? **3** 发动 fādòng ■ He couldn't start his car this morning. 今天早上他发动不起汽车。Jīntiān zǎoshang tā fādòng bùqǐ qìchē. **4** 创建 chuàngjiàn **II** N **1** 开始部分 kāishǐ bùfen **2** 起点 qǐdiǎn, 起跑线 qǐpǎoxiàn at the start 在起跑线上 zài qǐpǎoxiàn shàng **3** 惊吓 jīngxià to give sb a start 让某人吓一跳 ràng mǒurén xià yí tiào

starter N **1** 起动装置 qǐdòng zhuāngzhì **2** 第一道

菜 dìyī dào cài 3 起跑发令员 qǐpǎo fālìngyuán
4（球队）首批上场队员 (qiúduì) shǒupī
shàngchǎng duìyuán
for starters 首先 shǒuxiān

starting lineup N 开赛阵容 kāisài zhènróng

startle v 惊吓 jīngxià, 吓…一跳 xià…yí tiào
■ Hiding behind the door, the boy was ready
to startle his sister. 男孩躲在们背后，准备吓妹
妹。Nánhái duǒ zài mén bèihòu, zhǔnbèi xià
mèimei.

start-up I ADJ 新创的 [+企业] xīnchuàng de [+qǐyè]
start-up budget 创业资金 chuàngyè zījīn
II N 新创办的小企业 xīn chuàngbàn de xiǎo
qǐyè

starvation N 饥饿 jī'è

starve v 饿 è, 饿极了 è jíle
starved to death 饿死 èsǐ

stash I v 藏匿 cángnì, 隐藏 yǐncáng II N 隐藏的东
西 yǐncáng de dōngxi

state I N 1 状态 zhuàngtài, 情况 qíngkuàng
State of the Union（美国总统的）国情咨文
(Měiguó zǒngtǒng de) Guóqíng Zīwén
2（美国）州 (Měiguó) zhōu,（印度）邦 (Yìndù)
bāng
state university 州立大学 zhōulì dàxué
3 国家 guójiā
head of state 国家元首 guójiā yuánshǒu
State Department（美国）国务院 (Měiguó)
Guówùyuàn
Secretary of State（美国）国务卿 (Měiguó)
guówùqīng
II v 声明 shēngmíng, 发表声明 fābiǎo shēngmíng ■ She stated that she had never visited
that house. 她声明从来没有去过那幢房子。Tā
shēngmíng cónglái méiyǒu qùguo nà zhuàng
fángzi.

stately ADJ 1 堂皇的 tánghuáng de, 宏大的
hóngdà de 2 庄严的 zhuāngyán de

statement N 声明 shēngmíng [M. WD 份 fèn]
bank statement 银行帐单 yínháng zhàngdān
■ The bank statement seems to have an error.
银行帐单上好像有一个错误。Yínháng zhàng-
dānshang hǎoxiàng yǒu yí ge cuòwù.
financial statement 财务报表 cáiwù bàobiǎo
sworn statement 宣誓证词 xuānshì zhèngcí

state-of-the-art ADJ 最先进的 zuì xiān jìn de, 最
高水平的 zuìgāo shuǐpíng de, 最新的 zuì xīn de

States N (the States) 美国 Měiguó

statesman N 政治家 zhèngzhìjiā [M. WD 位 wèi]

statesmanlike ADJ 1 政治家似的 zhèngzhìjiā
shìde 2 有政治家风度的 yǒu zhèngzhìjiā
fēngdù de

stateswoman N 女政治家 nǚ zhèngzhìjiā [M. WD
位 wèi]

static I ADJ 静止的 jìngzhǐ de, 不变的 búbiàn de

II N 1 静电干扰 jìngdiàn gānrǎo 2 负面的议论
fùmiàn de yìlùn

station I N 1 站 zhàn, 车站 chēzhàn
station wagon 客货两用汽车 kèhuò liǎngyòng
qìchē
police station 派出所 pàichūsuǒ, 警察局
jǐngchájú
2 无线电台 wúxiàndiàntái, 电视台/频道 diàn-
shìtái/píndào II v 部署 bùshǔ, 驻扎 zhùzhá

stationary ADJ 静止的 jìngzhǐ de, 不动的 bú dòng
de

stationery N 1 文具 wénjù 2 信纸 xìnzhǐ [M. WD
张 zhāng]

statistic N 1 统计数字 tǒngjì shùzì 2 数据 shùjù,
统计资料 tǒngjì zīliào

statistical ADJ 统计学的 tǒngjìxué de, 统计业的
tǒngjì yè de

statistician N 统计工作者 tǒngjì gōngzuòzhě, 统
计学家 tǒngjìxuéjiā

statistics N 统计（学）tǒngjì（xué）

statue N 雕像 diāoxiàng, 塑像 sùxiàng
the Statue of Liberty（纽约）自由女神象
(Niǔyuē) zìyóu nǚshén xiàng

stature N 1 身材 shēncái 2 声望 shēngwàng, 地
位 dìwèi
a scientist of international stature 一位有国际
声望的科学家 yí wèi yǒu guójì shēngwàng de
kēxuéjiā

status N 1 地位 dìwèi ■ We have to face the fact
that wealth gives one high social status. 我们得
面对这个事实：财富提高社会地位。Wǒmen děi
miànduì zhè ge shìshí: cáifù tígāo shèhuì dìwèi.
2 状况 zhuàngkuàng ■ The Commerce Department provided the media with statistics on the
status of the economy. 商业部向媒体提供有关经
济状况的统计数字。Shāngyèbù xiàng méitǐ tígōng
yǒuguān jīngjì zhuàngkuàng de tǒngjì shùzì.
status quo 现状 xiànzhuàng

statute N 法令 fǎlìng, 法规 fǎguī
statute law 成文法 chéngwénfǎ

statutory ADJ（根据）法令的 (gēnjù) fǎlìng de
statutory rape 法定强奸罪 fǎdìng qiángjiānzuì

staunch[1] ADJ 坚定忠实的 jiāndìng zhōngshí de

staunch[2], stanch v 止住 [+血] zhǐzhù [+xuè]

stave[1] (PT & PP stove, staved) v (to stave off) 避
开 bìkāi, 阻挡 zǔdǎng

stave[2] N 五线谱 wǔxiànpǔ

stay I v 1 待 dài, 待在 dài zài
to stay in bed 卧床 wòchuáng
to stay put 留在原地 liú zài yuándì, 不动 bú
dòng ■ As the company is in endless trouble,
shall I stay put or start looking elsewhere? 公司麻
烦不断，我该留在公司呢，还是另找工作? Gōngsī
máfan bú duàn, wǒ gāi liú zài gōngsī ne, háishì
lìng zhǎo gōngzuò?

to stay up 很晚还不睡 hěn wǎn hái bú shuì, 熬夜 áoyè

2 住 zhù, 住在 zhù zài **3** 保持 bǎochí, 持续 chíxù ■ *Inflation stayed below 4% in the first two quarters.* 在今年头两个季度，通货膨胀保持在百分之四以下。Zài jīnnián tóu liǎng ge jìdù, tōnghuò péngzhàng bǎochí zài bǎifēnzhī sì yǐxià. **II** N **1** 逗留 dòuliú, 停留 tíngliú **2** 停止 tíngzhǐ, 推迟 tuīchí

steadfast ADJ **1** 坚定的 jiāndìng de **2** 忠诚的 zhōngchéng de

steady I ADJ **1** 稳的 wěn de, 平稳的 píngwěn de **2** 稳重的 wěnzhòng de, 可靠的 kěkào de **3** 均匀的 jūnyún de **II** v **1** (使⋯)稳定 (shǐ⋯) wěndìng **2** (使⋯)镇定 (shǐ⋯) zhèndìng

to steady one's nerves 使自己的心情平静下来 shǐ zìjǐ de xīnqíng píngjìng xiàlai

to steady oneself 站稳 zhànwěn

III ADV (to go steady with sb) 与某人确定恋爱关系 yǔ mǒurén quèdìng liàn'ài guānxi ■ *Jeremy and Sandra have been going steady for quite a while.* 杰里米和桑德拉保持情人关系已经多时了。Jiélǐmǐ hé Sāngdélā bǎochí qíngrén guānxi yǐjīng duō shí le.

steak N (牛)肉排 (niú) ròupái, 鱼排 yúpái

salmon steak 三文鱼鱼排 sānwényú yúpái

steal I v (PT **stole**; PP **stolen**) 偷 tōu, 偷窃 tōuqiè

to steal a march on sb 抢在某人面前 qiǎng zài mǒurén miànqián

to steal the show 抢出风头 qiǎng chū fēngtou

II N **1** (棒球)偷垒 (bàngqiú) tōulěi **2** 便宜货 piányihuò

stealth N **1** 悄声秘密行动 qiǎoshēng mìmì xíngdòng **2** 隐形系统 yǐnxíng xìtǒng

stealth aircraft 隐形飞机 yǐnxíng fēijī

stealthy ADJ 偷偷摸摸的 tōutōu mōmō de, 悄悄的 qiāoqiāo de

steam I N 蒸汽 zhēngqì

to blow off steam 发泄怒火 fāxiè nùhuǒ, 渲泄多余的精力 xuānxiè duōyú de jīnglì

to run out of steam 精疲力尽 jīngpí lìjìn

II v **1** 蒸 [+食物] zhēng [+shíwù] **2** 散发蒸汽 sànfā zhēngqì, 冒热气 mào rèqì

steamroll v 大败 [+对手] dàbài [+duìshǒu]

steamroller N 蒸汽压路机 zhēngqì yālùjī [M. WD 台 tái]

steamy ADJ **1** 充满水蒸汽的 [+更衣室] chōngmǎnshuǐ zhēngqì de [gēngyīshì] **2** 色情的 sèqíng de

steel I N 钢 gāng, 钢材 gāngcái ■ *The auto industry uses a tremendous amount of steel to produce cars.* 汽车工业用大量钢材。Qìchē gōngyè yòng dàliàng gāngcái.

steel wool 钢丝绒 gāngsīróng

II v (to steel oneself for) 坚强起来 jiānqiáng qǐlái

steely ADJ 钢铁般坚定的 gāngtiě bān jiāndìng de

steep I ADJ 陡 dǒu, 陡峭的 dǒuqiào de **II** v **1** 浸泡 jìnpào **2** (to be steeped in) 根植于(传统) gēnzhí yú (chuántǒng), 深陷在(争斗中) shēn xiàn zài (zhēngdòu zhōng)

steeple N (教堂)尖塔 (jiàotáng) jiān tǎ

steer v **1** 驾驶 [+汽车] jiàshǐ [+qìchē] **2** 引导 [+人] yǐndǎo [+rén]

to steer clear of sb/sth 避开某人／某事 bìkāi mǒurén/mǒushì

to steer a middle course 走中间道路 zǒu zhōngjiāndàolù

steering N (汽车／船舶的)操纵装置 (qìchē/chuánbó de) cāozòng zhuāngzhì

steering committee 程序委员会 chéngxù wěiyuánhuì

steering wheel 方向盘 fāngxiàngpán

stellar ADJ 光彩夺目的 guāngcǎi duómù de, 出色的 chūsè de

stem I N 茎 jīng ■ *When the roses finish flowering in fall, cut back all the stems.* 在秋季玫瑰花结束花期时，就把花茎都剪去。Zài qiūjì méiguìhuā jiéshù huāqī shí, jiù bǎ huājīng dōu jiǎnqu.

stem cell 干细胞 gànxìbāo

II v 遏制 èzhì ■ *Will the federal government be able to stem the flow of illegal drugs?* 联邦政府有能力遏制非法药物的流动吗？Liánbāng zhèngfǔ yǒu nénglì èzhì fēifǎ yàowù de liúrù ma?

to stem from 是由于 shì yóuyú, 起源于 qǐyuán yú ■ *Her high credit card debt stems from her addiction to shopping.* 她在信用卡上债台高筑，是由于她购物上瘾了。Tā zài xìnyòngkǎshang zhàitái gāo zhù, shì yóuyú tā gòuwù shàngyǐn le.

stench N **1** 恶臭 èchòu **2** 恶劣的社会风气 èliè de shèhuì fēngqì

stench of corruption 腐败的气息 fǔbài de qìxī

stenographer N 速记打字员 sùjì dǎzìyuán

stenography N 速记(法) sùjì (fǎ)

step I N **1** 脚步(声) jiǎobù (shēng) **2** 一步 yí bù ■ *Your decision is a step in the right direction.* 你的决定是朝正确方向走出了一步。Nǐ de juédìng shì cháo zhèngquè fāngxiàng zǒuchūle yí bù. **3** 台阶 táijiē **II** v **1** 走 zǒu ■ *Onlookers stepped back to let the policemen through.* 旁观者后退，让警察通过。Pángguānzhě hòutuì, ràng jǐngchá tōngguò. **2** 踩 cǎi

to step on one's toes 惹怒 rěnù, 触犯 chùfàn ■ *He was even not aware that he had stepped on his boss' toes.* 他已经惹怒了老板，还不知道。Tā yǐjīng rěnùle lǎobǎn, hái bù zhīdào.

to step up 加强 jiāqiáng

stepbrother N 同父异母／同母异父的兄弟 tóng fù yì mǔ/tóng mǔ yì fù de xiōngdi

step-by-step ADJ 一步步(的) yíbù bù (de)

stepchild N 继子／继女 jìzǐ/jìnǚ

stepdaughter N 继女 jìnǚ

stepfather N 继父 jìfù

stepladder N 活梯 huótī

stepmother N 继母 jìmǔ

stepped-up ADJ 加快的 jiākuài de, 加强的 jiāqiáng de

stepping-stone N 1 垫脚石 diànjiǎoshí [M. WD 块 kuài] 2 (事业发展中的) 阶梯 (shìyè fāzhǎnzhōng de) jiētī

stepsister N 同父异母/同母异父的姐妹 tóng fù yì mǔ/tóng mǔ yì fù de jiěmèi

stepson N 继子 jìzǐ

stereo N 立体声音响设备 lìtǐshēng yīnxiǎng shèbèi

stereotype I N 固定的模式 gùdìng de móshì, 老一套 lǎoyítào II v 1 把…模式化 bǎ…móshì huà 2 对…产生成见 duì…chǎnshēng chéngjiàn

stereotypical ADJ 模式化的 móshì huà de, 固定不变的 gùdìng búbiàn de

sterile ADJ 1 无菌的 wújūn de, 消过毒的 xiāoguòdú de 2 不能生育/结果的 bùnéng shēngyù/jiéguǒ de

sterilization N 1 消毒 xiāodú 2 绝育 juéyù

sterilize v 1 消毒 xiāodú, 灭菌 mièjūn 2 使…失去生殖能力 shǐ…shīqù shēngzhí nénglì, 对…做绝育手术 duì…zuòjué yù shǒushù

sterling ADJ 优秀的 yōuxiù de, 极有价值的 jí yǒu jiàzhí de

sterling work 杰出的工作 jiéchū de gōngzuò

sterling silver N 标准纯银 biāozhǔn chúnyín

stern I ADJ 严厉的 yánlì de, 苛刻的 kēkè de II N 船尾 chuánwěi

steroid N 类固醇 lèigùchún

stethoscope N 听诊器 tīngzhěnqì

stew I v 炖 dùn, 煨 wēi, 焖 mèn

to stew in one's own juice 自作自受 zìzuò zìshòu

II N 炖菜 dùncài

be in a stew 焦急的 jiāojí de, 困惑的 kùnhuò de

steward N 1 (轮船/飞机上的) 男乘务员 (lúnchuán/fēijī shàng de) nán chéngwùyuán 2 (公共资产的) 守护人 (gōnggòng zīchǎn de) shǒuhù rén 3 伙食管理人 huǒshi guǎnlǐ rén

stewardess N (轮船/飞机上的) 女乘务员 (lúnchuán/fēijī shàng de) nǚ chéngwùyuán

stick I v (PT & PP stuck) 1 粘 zhān, 粘住 zhānzhu ■ *You're not allowed to stick posters here.* 你不能在这里贴布告。 Nǐ bù néng zài zhèlǐ tiē bùgào. 2 插入 chārù 3 卡住 qiǎzhu ■ *Gosh, the zipper is stuck!* 啊呀, 拉链卡住了! Āyā, lāliàn qiǎzhu le!

to stick out 伸出 shēnchū ■ *It's dangerous to stick your head out of the car window.* 头伸出车窗是很危险的。 Tóu shēnchū chē chuāng shì hěn wēixiǎn de.

to stick to 坚持 jiānchí, 还是 hái shì

II N 1 小树枝 xiǎo shùzhī [M. WD 根 gēn] 2 棍 gùn [M. WD 根 gēn], 棒 bàng [M. WD 根 gēn]

walking stick 拐杖 guǎizhàng

3 条状物 tiáozhuàngwù

a stick of gum 一条口香糖 yìtiáo kǒuxiāngtáng

stickball N 棍球 (运动) gùnqiú (yùndòng)

sticker N (粘帖) 标签 (zhāntiē) biāoqiān [M. WD 张 zhāng]

sticker price 标(签)价 biāo (qiān) jià

stick-in-the-mud N 顽固守旧者 wángù shǒujiùzhě, 保守者 bǎoshǒuzhě

stickler N (a stickler for rules/details/protocols) 十分注重规则/细节/礼节的人 shífēn zhùzhòng guīzé/xìjié/lǐjié de rén

(the) sticks N 远离城市的地方 yuǎnlí chéngshì de dìfang

sticky ADJ 1 粘的 nián de 2 不愉快的 bù yúkuài de, 麻烦的 máfan de ■ *It's easy to get into a sticky situation if you're dating more than one person.* 你同时和两个人谈恋爱, 很容易造成不愉快的局面。 Nǐ tóngshí hé liǎng ge rén tán liàn'ài, hěn róngyì zàochéng bù yúkuài de júmiàn.

stiff I ADJ 1 激烈的 jīliè de ■ *He got the job through stiff competition.* 他通过激烈的竞争才得到这份工作。 Tā tōngguò jīliè de jìngzhēng cái dédào zhè fèn gōngzuò. 2 硬 yìng, 坚硬的 jiānyìng de 3 不灵便的 bù língbiàn de, 疼痛的 téngtòng de

stiff drink 烈酒 lièjiǔ

II ADV 非常 fēicháng, 极其 jíqí

be bored stiff 厌烦得要死 yànfán de yàosǐ, 无聊得要命 wúliáo de yàomìng

III v 不付小费 bú fù xiǎofèi

stiffen v 1 使…变硬 shǐ…biàn yìng 2 突然生气/不友好 tūrán shēngqì/bùyǒuhǎo 3 (使…) 更严厉/强硬 (shǐ…) gèng yánlì/qiángyìng

to stiffen up [肌肉+] 僵硬 [jīròu+] jiāngyìng

stiff-necked ADJ 傲慢的 àomàn de, 倔强的 juéjiàng de

stifle v 1 使 [+人] 窒息 shǐ [+rén] zhìxī 2 抑制 yìzhì, 强忍住 qiáng rěnzhù

stigma N 羞耻 xiūchǐ, 丢脸的感觉 diūliǎn de gǎnjué

stigmatize v 使 [+人] 感到羞耻 shǐ [+rén] gǎndào xiūchǐ

still¹ ADV 仍然 réngrán, 还是 hái shì ■ *After eight years, Dan is still working on his PhD thesis.* 八年以后, 丹现在还在做博士论文。 Bā nián yǐhòu, Dān xiànzài háizài zuò bóshì lùnwén. 2 更加 gèngjiā

still² I ADJ 静止的 jìngzhǐ de

Still water run deep. 静水流深。 Jìngshuǐ liú shēn.

still life 静物画 jìngwùhuà

II N 1 寂静 jìjìng 2 剧照 jùzhào 3 蒸馏器 zhēngliúqì

stillbirth

stillbirth N 死产 sǐchǎn
stillborn ADJ **1** 死胎的 [+产儿] sǐtāi de [+chǎn'ér]
2 夭折的 [+计划] yāozhé de [+jìhuà]
stilted ADJ 生硬呆板的 shēngyìng dāibǎn de
stilts N 高跷 gāoqiāo [M. WD 付 fù]
stimulant N 兴奋剂 xīngfènjì
stimulate V 刺激 cìjī, 促进 cùjìn
stimulating ADJ 使人振奋的/有精神的 shǐrén
  zhènfèn de/yǒu jīngshén de
stimulation N 刺激 cìjī
stimulus N 刺激(物) cìjī (wù), 促进(因素) cùjìn
  (yīnsù)
sting I V (PT & PP **stung**) **1** [蚊子+] 叮 [wénzi+]
  dīng, [蜜蜂+] 刺 [mìfēng+] cì **2** 感到刺痛
  gǎndao cìtòng ■ My eyes are stinging from the
  smoke. 我的眼睛被烟刺痛。Wǒ de yǎnjing bèi
  yān cìtòng. II N **1** 刺痛 cìtòng, 剧痛 jùtòng ■ I
  felt the sharp sting of soap in my eyes. 肥皂水进了
  眼睛, 我感到刺痛。Féizàoshuǐ jìnle yǎnjing, wǒ
  gǎndao cìtòng. **2** 圈套 quāntào
  a sting operation (警察)诱捕行动 (jǐngchá)
  yòubǔ xíngdòng
stinger N (昆虫的)刺 (kūnchóng de) cì
stinginess N 小气 xiǎoqi, 吝啬 lìnsè
stingray N 刺魟 cìhóng [M. WD 条 tiáo]
stingy ADJ **1** 小气的 [+人] xiǎoqi de [+rén], 吝啬
  的 lìnsè de **2** 极少的 [+食物] jí shǎo de [+shíwù]
stink I V (PT **stank**; PP **stunk**) **1** 发臭 fā chòu, 有
  臭味的 yǒu chòuwèi de **2** 糟透了 zāotòu le
  to stink up the place 表现极差 biǎoxiàn jíchà
  II N 恶臭 èchòu
  to cause a stink 强烈抗议 qiángliè kàngyì
stinker N **1** 讨厌的人 tǎoyàn de rén **2** 糟透的电
  影/书/比赛 zāotòu de diànyǐng/shū/bǐsài
stinking ADJ **1** 发出恶臭的 fāchū èchòu de **2** 糟透
  的 zāotòu de
  stinking drunk 酩酊大醉 mǐngdǐng dàzuì, 烂醉
  如泥 lànzuì rúní
stint I N 期限 qīxiàn, 任期 rènqī II V 限制 xiànzhì,
  少量提供 shǎoliàng tígōng
stipend N (学生的)助学金 (xuésheng de)
  zhùxuéjīn, (牧师的)生活费 (mùshi de)
  shēnghuófèi, 薪金 xīnjīn
stipulate V 规定 guīdìng, 约定 yuēdìng
stipulation N **1** 规定 guīdìng, 约定 yuēdìng **2** 条
  款 tiáokuǎn
stir I V **1** 搅拌 jiǎobàn **2** 激发 [+感情] jīfā
  [+gǎnqíng] **3** [风+] 吹动 [fēng+] chuīdòng
  to stir things up 挑起事端 tiǎoqǐ shìduān
  II N **1** 骚动 sāodòng, 激动 jīdòng **2** 搅拌 jiǎobàn
stir-fry I V 快炒 [+菜] kuài chǎo [+cài] II N 快炒
  kuàichǎo
stitch I N (缝)一针 (féng) yì zhēn II V 缝 féng,
  缝合 fénghé
  A stitch in time saves nine. 及时缝一针, 免得

缝十针。(→小洞不补, 大洞吃苦。) Jíshí féng yì
zhēn, miǎnde féng shí zhēn. (→Xiǎo dòng
bù bǔ, dà dòng chī kǔ. If you don't mend a
small hole, you will suffer from a big hole.)
stitches N (in stitches) 忍不住大笑 rěnbuzhù
  dàxiào
stock I N **1** 存货 cúnhuò, 库存 kùcún ■ Your
  order can be supplied from stock. 你订的货可以
  从库存中提供。Nǐ dìng de huò kěyǐ cóng kùcún
  zhōng tígōng.
  in stock 有现货 yǒu xiànhuò
  out of stock 没有现货 méiyǒu xiànhuò, 脱销
  tuōxiāo ■ Sorry, but that model of truck is out
  of stock. 对不起, 这种型号的卡车没有现货。
  Duìbuqǐ, zhè zhǒng xínghào de kǎchē méiyǒu
  xiànhuò.
  to take stock ① 盘点(货物) pán diǎn (huòwù)
  ② 检讨 jiǎntǎo
  2 股份 gǔfèn, 股票 gǔpiào
  stock certificate 股权证 gǔquánzhèng
  stock exchange 股票交易所 gǔpiào jiāoyìsuǒ
  stock market 股票市场 gǔpiào shìchǎng, 股市
  gǔshì
  3 汤汁 tāngzhī ■ Stewing mushrooms in chicken
  stock is a good way to prepare them. 在原汁鸡
  汤里炖蘑菇, 是做蘑菇菜的好方法。Zài yuán
  zhī jītāng lǐ dùn mógu, shì zuò mógu cài de hǎo
  fāngfǎ. **4** 牲畜 shēngchù II V 备货 bèihuò, 储存
  chǔcún
  to stock up 备货 bèihuò ■ Stores are stocking
  up for Christmas. 商店正在为圣诞节备货。
  Shāngdiàn zhèngzài wèi Shèngdànjié bèihuò.
stockade N 栏 péng lán [M. WD 道 dào], 防御工事
  fángyù gōngshì
stockbroker N 证券/股票经纪人 zhèngquàn/
  gǔpiào jīngjìrén
stockbroking N 证券/股票买卖 zhèngquàn/
  gǔpiào mǎimai
stockholder N 股票持有人 gǔpiào chíyǒurén,
  股东 gǔdōng
stocking N 长筒袜 chángtǒngwà
stockpile I N 贮存的大量物资/武器 zhùcún de
  dàliàng wùzī/wǔqì II V 贮存 zhùcún, 囤积 túnjī
stock-still ADV 一动不动地 yídòng bú dòng de,
  完全静止地 wánquán jìngzhǐ de
stocky ADJ 身子矮而结实的 shēnzi ǎi ér jiēshí de,
  矮胖的 ǎipàng de
stockyard N 牲畜围栏 shēngchù wéilán
stodgy ADJ 古板乏味的 gǔbǎn fáwèi de
stoic, stoical ADJ 刻苦耐劳的 kèkǔnàiláo de,
  坚忍的 jiānrěn de
stoke V **1** 给 [+炉子] 添加燃料 gěi [+lúzi] tiānjiā
  ránliào **2** 使 [+情绪] 加剧 shǐ [+qíngxù] jiājù,
  给 [+纠纷] 火上加油 gěi [+jiūfēn] huǒshàng
  jiāyóu

stoked ADJ 非常兴奋的 fēicháng xīngfèn de

stole See **steal**

stolen See **steal**

stolid ADJ 不激动的 bù jīdòng de, 无动于衷的 wúdòng yú zhōng de

stomach I N 肚子 dùzi, 胃 wèi

to turn one's stomach 使人恶心 shǐrén èxīn

II v 忍受 rěnshòu, 接受 jiēshòu

stomachache N 肚子痛 dùzi tòng, 胃痛 wèitòng

stomp v 重重地踩 zhòngzhòng de cǎi

stone I N 石(头) shí (tóu) [M. WD 块 kuài], 石块 shíkuài

precious stone 宝石 bǎoshí

a stone's throw 近在咫尺 jìn zài zhǐchǐ, 离得很近 líde hěnjìn

II v 向⋯扔石头 xiàng...rēng shítou

stoned ADJ (服毒后) 极度兴奋 (fúdú hòu) jídù xīngfèn

stone-deaf ADJ 完全聋的 wánquán lóng de

stonewall v 拒不回答 jù bù huídá

stoneware N 粗陶器 cū táoqì

stonewashed ADJ 石洗的 [+牛仔裤] shí xǐ de [+niúzǎikù]

stony ADJ 1 多石的 duō shí de 2 冷冰冰的 lěngbīngbīng de, 毫无同情心的 háowú tóngqíngxīn de

stood See **stand**

stool N 凳子 dèngzi

stoop I v 弯腰 wānyāo, 俯身 fǔshēn

to stoop to doing sth 道德堕落到做某事 dàodé duòluò dào zuò mǒushì

a stooped old woman 驼背老太太 tuóbèi lǎotàitai

II N 驼背 tuóbèi

to walk with a stoop 驮着背走路 tuózhe bèi zǒulù

stop I v 1 停 tíng, 停住 tíngzhu ■ Traffic stops at the red light. 车辆在红灯前停下。Chēliàng zài hóngdēng qián tíngxia. 2 阻止 zǔzhǐ ■ No one can stop her from going out with that man. 没有人能阻止她和那个男人出去玩。Méiyǒurén néng zǔzhǐ tā hé nà ge nánren chūqu wán.

to stop at nothing 不择手段 bù zé shǒuduàn

to stop short of doing sth 差一点做某事 chàyìdiǎn zuò mǒushì

stop press 最新消息 zuìxīn xiāoxi

Stop the presses! 有惊人新闻! Yǒu jīngrén xīnwén!

to stop by 串门儿 chuànménr ■ She often stops by for a chat. 她常来串门儿聊天。Tā cháng lái chuànménr liáotiān.

Stop thief! 抓小偷! Zhuā xiǎotōu!

II N 1 停止 tíngzhǐ

to put a stop on a check 通知银行不兑现支票 tōngzhī yínháng bú duìxiàn zhīpiào

2 停车站 tíngchēzhàn

stopgap N 临时替代的人 línshí tìdài de rén

stoplight N 红绿灯 hónglǜdēng, 交通灯 jiāotōngdēng

stopover N 中途停留 zhōngtútíngliú

stoppage N 1 停工 tínggōng, 罢工 bàgōng 2 停止 tíng zhǐ, 中止 zhōngzhǐ 3 堵塞物 dǔsèwù

stopper N 瓶塞 píngsāi

stopwatch N 秒表 miǎobiǎo

storage N 贮藏 zhùcáng, 储藏 chǔcáng

storage capacity (汽车行李箱) 贮存空间 (qìchē xínglǐxiāng) zhùcún kōngjiān

store[1] N 店 diàn, 商店 shāngdiàn ■ I'm going to the store to get some milk. 我去小店买牛奶。Wǒ qù xiǎodiàn mǎi niúnǎi.

department store 百货商店 bǎihuò shāngdiàn

store[2] I N 贮藏 zhùcáng, 储藏 chǔcáng ■ They have stores of firewood for the winter. 他们储藏了很多木柴过冬。Tāmen chǔcángle hěn duō mùchái guò dōng.

in store 快要发生 kuài yào fāshēng

II v 贮藏 zhùcáng, 储存 chǔcún

storehouse N 仓库 cāngkù [M. WD 座 zuò], 宝库 bǎokù [M. WD 座 zuò]

storehouse of information 信息宝库 xìnxī bǎokù

storekeeper N 店主 diànzhǔ

storeroom N 贮藏室 zhùcángshì [M. WD 间 jiān]

stork N 鹳 guàn [M. WD 只 zhī]

storm N 1 风暴 fēngbào, 暴风雨 bàofēng yǔ 2 风潮 fēngcháo, 浪潮 làngcháo ■ The new law created a storm of protest. 新法律引起抗议浪潮。Xīn fǎlǜ yǐnqǐ kàngyì làngcháo.

storm cloud ① 暴风云 bàofēngyún ② 凶兆 xiōngzhào

sand storm 沙(尘)暴 shā (chén) bào

snow storm 暴风雪 bàofēngxuě

stormy ADJ 1 暴风雨/雪的 bàofēngyǔ/xuě de 2 动荡的 dòngdàng de, 多风波的 duō fēngbō de

story[1] N 1 故事 gùshi ■ The child knows many stories from the Bible. 这个孩子知道许多圣经故事。Zhè ge háizi zhīdào xǔduō Shèngjīng gùshi. it's a long story 说来话长 shuō lái huà cháng

to make a long story short 长话短说 chánghuà duǎnshuō

2 新闻 xīnwén [M. WD 条 tiáo], 新闻报道 xīnwén bàodào [M. WD 条 tiáo]

story[2] N 层 céng, 层楼 cénglóu ■ The tallest building in Taipei has 101 stories. 台北最高的大楼有一百零一层。Táiběi zuì gāo de dàlóu yǒu yìbǎi líng yī céng.

a three-story (three-storied) house 一幢三层楼的房子 yí zhuàng sān céng lóu de fángzi

storyteller N 讲故事的人 jiǎng gùshi de rén, 说书人 shuōshū rén

stout I ADJ **1** 粗壮的 cūzhuàng de, 结实的 jiēshi de **2** 坚定勇敢的 jiāndìng yǒnggǎn de **II** N 烈性黑啤酒 lièxìng hēipíjiǔ

stove N 炉子 lúzi, 炉灶 lúzào ■ *Mom is making jam on the stove.* 妈妈在炉子上做果酱。Māma zài lúzishang zuò guǒjiàng.

stow, stow away V 仔细收藏 zǐxì shōucáng

stowaway N 无票偷乘的人 wú piào tōu chéng de rén, 偷渡者 tōudùzhě

straddle V **1** 跨坐 [+在自行车上] kuà zuò [+zài zìxíngchē shàng] **2** 横跨 [+两地] héngkuà [+liǎng dì]

straggle V **1** [一队人+] 散乱地行进 [yí duì rén+] sànluàn de xíngjìn **2** [一个人+] 掉队 [yí ge rén+] diàoduì

straight I ADJ **1** 直的 zhí de **2** 正的 zhèng de, 端正的 duānzhèng de ■ *Is my tie straight?* 我的领带戴正了吗? Wǒ de lǐngdài dàizhèng le ma? **3** 连续的 liánxù de ■ *He sometimes has to work 14 straight hours.* 他有时候要连续工作十四个小时。Tā yǒushíhou yào liánxù gōngzuò shísì ge xiǎoshí. **4** 正直的 zhèngzhí de, 诚实的 chéngshí de
straight shooter 正直的人 zhèngzhí de rén
to get straight A's 考试全部得 "优" kǎoshì quánbù dé "A"
to keep a straight face 板着脸 bǎnzheliǎn
II ADV **1** 直接 zhíjiē, 马上 mǎshàng **2** 直截了当地 zhíjié liǎodàng de, 坦率地 tǎnshuài de ■ *I'll come straight to the point—your performance is not satisfactory.* 我直截了当地说吧—你的工作表现不能令人满意。Wǒ zhíjié liǎodàng de shuō ba—nǐ de gōngzuò biǎoxiàn bù néng lìngrén mǎnyì.
to get straight 正确地理解 zhèngquè de lǐjiě, 搞清楚 gǎo qīngchu
to think straight 有条理地思考 yǒu tiáolǐ de sīkǎo
III N **1** 异性恋者 yìxìngliànzhě **2** (the straight and narrow) 循规蹈矩的生活方式 xúnguī dǎojǔ de shēnghuó fāngshì

straighten V 把…弄直 bǎ…nòng zhí
to straighten up 挺直身子 tǐngzhí shēnzi
to straighten sb out 使某人变好 shǐ mǒurén biàn hǎo
to straighten sth out 理清某事 lǐ qīng mǒushì

straightforward ADJ **1** 坦率地 tǎnshuài de, 坦诚的 tǎnchéng de **2** 简单明了的 jiǎndān míngliǎo de

strain¹ N **1** 拉力 lālì, 张力 zhānglì **2** 压力 yālì, 焦虑 jiāolǜ
under a lot of strain 承受很大压力 chéngshòu hěn dà yālì
3 负担 fùdān, 困难 kùnnan
to put a strain on sb 给某人带来负担 gěi mǒurén dàilái fùdān
4 品种 pǐnzhǒng, 类型 lèixíng

a new strain of virus 一种新病毒 yí zhǒng xīn bìngdú

strain² V **1** 竭力 [+去做某事] jiélì [+qù zuò mǒushì], 全力以赴 quánlì yǐfù
to strain every nerve 竭尽全力 jiéjìn quánlì **2** 拉伤 [+肌肉] lā shāng [+jīròu], 扭伤 niǔshāng **3** 使 [+关系] 紧张 shǐ [+guānxi] jǐnzhāng, 严重损伤 yánzhòng sǔnshāng

strained ADJ **1** 不自然的 [+气氛] bú zìrán de [+qìfen], 紧张的 jǐnzhāng de **2** 身心疲惫的 shēnxīn píbèi de

strainer N 过滤器 guòlǜqì

strait N 海峡 hǎixiá
the Straits of Taiwan 台湾海峡 Táiwān hǎixiá **2** (in dire straits) 处于非常困难的境地 chǔyú fēicháng kùnnan de jìngdì

straitjacket N 约束 yuēshù, 限度 xiàndù

strand N **1** 一股 (绳／线) yì gǔ (shéng/xiàn) **2** (故事的) 线索 (gùshi de) xiànsuǒ **II** V **1** 使 [+人] 滞留 shǐ [+rén] zhìliú **2** 使 [+人] 处于困境 shǐ [+rén] chǔyú kùnjìng

stranded ADJ 被困 (在) bèi kùn (zài), 滞留 zhìliú

strange ADJ **1** 奇怪 qíguài, 不寻常的 bù xúncháng de **2** 陌生 (的) [+人] mòshēng (de) [+rén]
to feel strange 觉得不对劲 juéde bú duìjìn

stranger N 陌生人 mòshēng rén

strangle V **1** 勒死 lēisǐ, 绞死 jiǎosǐ **2** 严重阻碍 yánzhòng zǔ'ài

stranglehold N 有力的控制 yǒulì de kòngzhì
to break the stranglehold of sth 打破某事的束缚 dǎpò mǒushì de shùfù

strangulation N 勒死 lēisǐ, 窒息而死 zhìxì ér sǐ

strap I N **1** 带 (子) dài (zi) [M. WD 根 gēn/条 tiáo] **II** V 用带子束住 yòng dàizi shù zhù, 捆扎 kǔnzā

strapless ADJ (a strapless dress) 露肩连衣裙 lù jiān liányīqún [M. WD 带 dài]

strapped ADJ 没有多少钱的 méiyǒu duōshao qián de

strapping ADJ 高大健壮的 [+青年人] gāodà jiànzhuàng de [+qīngniánrén]

stratagem N 计谋 jìmóu, 花招 huāzhāo

strategic ADJ 战略上 (的) zhànlüè shàng (de), 策略上 (的) cèlüè shàng (de)
strategice weapon 战略武器 zhānglüè wǔqì

strategy N 策略 cèlüè ■ *The government has employed an effective strategy to achieve its objective.* 政府采取了有效策略以达到目的。Zhèngfǔ cǎiqǔle yǒuxiào cèlüè yǐ dádào mùdì. **2** 战略 (部署) zhànlüè (bùshǔ)

stratified ADJ 等级化的 [+社会] děngjíhuà de [+shèhuì]

stratosphere N 平流层 píngliúcéng, 极高的水平 jí gāo de shuǐpíng

stratum N **1** (社会) 阶层 (shèhuì) jiēcéng **2** 岩层 yáncéng

straw N **1** （喝饮料的）吸管 (hē yǐnliào de) xīguǎn [M. WD 根 gēn] **2** 麦秆 màigǎn [M. WD 根 gēn], 稻草 dàocǎo [M. WD 根 gēn]
straw hat 草帽 cǎomào
straw man 稻草人 dàocǎorén, 不堪一击的对手 bùkān yì jī de duìshǒu
straw poll 非正式投票 fēi zhèngshì tóupiào, 民意测验 mínyì cèyàn

strawberry N 草莓 cǎoméi

stray I v 走入岔道 zǒu rù chàdào, 迷路 mílù **2** 偏离话题 piānlí huàtí II ADJ 迷路的 mílù de, 走失的 zǒushī de
a stray dog 流浪狗 liúlànggǒu
III N 走失的动物 zǒushī de dòngwù

streak I N **1** 条纹 tiáowén **2** 个性特征 gèxìng tèzhēng, 特色 tèsè
streak of adventurism 爱好冒险的个性特征 àihào màoxiǎn de gèxìng tèzhēng
3 一阵 yí zhèn, 一般时间 yì bān shíjiān
on a winning/losing streak 连续获胜／失利的时期 liánxù huòshèng/shīlì de shíqī
II v **1** 在……上加条纹 zài…shàng jiā tiáowén **2** 飞快地跑 fēikuài de pǎo

stream I N 小河 xiǎo hé [M. WD 条 tiáo], 溪流 xīliú [M. WD 条 tiáo]
streams of consciousness 意识流 yìshíliú
II v 奔流 bēnliú, 流动 liúdòng

streamer N 彩色纸带 cǎisè zhǐdài [M. WD 条 tiáo]

streamline v 使 [+企业] 效力更高 shǐ [+qǐyè] xiàolì gènggāo

street N 街 jiē, 街道 jiēdào [M. WD 条 tiáo] ■ What's the name of this street? 这条街叫什么名字？ Zhè tiáo jiē jiào shénme míngzi?
street light 街灯 jiēdēng
street musician 街头音乐家 jiētóu yīnyuèjiā
street smarts 在城市社会底层生存的能力 zài chéngshì shèhuì dǐcéng shēngcún de nénglì
street value [毒品的+] 街头黑市价值 [dúpǐn de+] jiētóu hēishì jiàzhí

streetcar N 电车 diànchē

streetwise ADJ 善于在城市街头生存的 shànyú zài chéngshì jiētóu shēngcún de, 老于世故的 lǎoyú shìgù de

strength N **1** 力（量）lì (liang) **2** 勇气 yǒngqì **3** 势力 shìlì ■ There is strength in numbers. 人多势力大。 Rén duō shìlì dà. **4** 强点 qiángdiǎn, 长处 chángchu

strengthen v 加强 jiāqiáng, 增强 zēngqiáng
to strengthen one's hand 增加某人的实力 zēngjiā mǒurén de shílì

strenuous ADJ **1** 艰苦繁重的 jiānkǔ fánzhòng de **2** 强烈的 qiángliè de

strep throat N 脓毒性喉炎 nóngdúxìng hóuyán

stress I N **1** 忧虑 yōulù, 精神压力 jīngshén yālì ■ Soldiers in battleground are under great stress. 在战场上的士兵精神压力很大。 Zài zhànchǎng-shang de shìbīng jīngshén yālì hěn dà. **2** 强调 qiángdiào, 注重 zhùzhòng
to lay stress on sth 强调某事 qiángdiào mǒushì, 注重某事 zhùzhòng mǒushì
3 重力 zhònglì, 应力 yìnglì **4** 重音 zhòngyīn, 重读 chóngdú II v **1** 强调 qiángdiào, 着重 zhuózhòng **2** 重读 zhòngdú

stressed ADJ **1** 焦虑紧张的 jiāolù jǐnzhāng de **2** 受力的 [+金属] shòu lì de [+jīnshǔ] **3** 重读的 zhòngdú de

stressful ADJ 很紧张的 hěn jǐnzhāng de, 压力很大的 yālì hěn dà de

stretch v **1** 拉长 lācháng, 撑大 chēngdà **2** 伸展 shēnzhǎn, 绵延 miányán **3** 伸懒腰 shēn lǎnyāo ■ The cat stretched after its nap. 猫儿小睡醒来，伸了个懒腰。 Māo xiǎoshuì xǐnglai, shēnle ge lǎnyāo.

stretcher N 担架 dānjià [M. WD 副 fù]

stricken ADJ 受到打击的 shòudào dǎjī de, 受灾的 [+地区] shòuzāi de [+dìqū], 受苦的 [+人] shòukǔ de [+ren]
a poverty-stricken area 贫困地区 pínkùn dìqū

strict ADJ 严格 yángé ■ His parents are very strict—no TV on school nights. 他的父母很严格—上课的日子晚上不准看电视。 Tā de fùmǔ hěn yángé—shàngkè de rìzi wǎnshang bù zhǔn kàn diànshì.
a strict vegetarian 严格的素食（主义）者 yángé de sùshí (zhǔyì) zhě
in the strict sense 严格地说 yángé de shuō

strictly ADV 完全地 wánquán de, 确切地 quèqiè de

stride I v (PT **strode**) 大踏步走 dàtàbù zǒu II N 大步 dàbù, 阔步 kuòbù
to make great strides 取得巨大进步 qǔdé jùdà jìnbù
to take sth in strides 坦然对待某事 tǎnrán duìdài mǒushì, 冷静处理某事 lěngjìng chǔlǐ mǒushì

strident ADJ **1** 坚定有力的 jiāndìng yǒulì de, 强烈的 qiángliè de **2** 刺耳的 cì'ěr de, 尖声的 jiān shēng de

strife N 争斗 zhēngdòu, 冲突 chōngtū

strike I v (PT & PP **struck**) **1** 打（击）dǎ (jī) **2** 罢工 bàgōng ■ Bus drivers are threatening to strike. 公共汽车司机威胁说要罢工。 Gōnggòng qìchē sījī wēixié shuō yào bàgōng. **3** 袭击 xíjī ■ Hardly had the people recovered from the last hurricane, another one struck the area. 人们还没有从上次飓风恢复过来，另一场飓风又袭击了该地区。 Rénmen hái méiyǒu cóng shàngcì jùfēng huīfù guòlai, lìng yì chǎng jùfēng yòu xíjīle gāi dìqū. **4** 突然想起 tūrán xiǎngqǐ **5** 显得 xiǎnde
to strike a deal 达成交易 dáchéng jiāoyì ■ I struck a deal with Dad—he would allow me to use the car on Friday evening if I would wash it on

Saturday. 我跟爸爸达成交易—如果我在星期六洗车, 他就让我星期五晚上用汽车。Wǒ gēn bàba dáchéng jiāoyì—rúguǒ wǒ zài xīngqīliù xǐ chē, tā jiù ràng wǒ xīngqīwǔ wǎnshang yòng qìchē.

to strike up a conversation 开始交谈 kāishǐ jiāotán, 搭讪 dāshàn

II N 1 罢工 bàgōng

strike pay 罢工津贴 bàgōng jīntiē

to go on strike 参加罢工 cānjiā bàgōng, 举行罢工 jǔxíng bàgōng

2 军事打击 jūnshì dǎjī, 空袭 kōngxí

pre-emptive strike 先发制人的军事打击 xiān fā zhì rén de jūnshì dǎjī

3 (保龄球) 一击全中 (bǎolíngqiú) yì jī quán zhòng

strikebreaker N 破坏罢工者 pòhuài bàgōngzhě

striker N 罢工者 bàgōngzhě

striking ADJ 1 惊人的 jīngrén de, 显著的 xiǎnzhù de 2 相貌出众的 [+人] xiàngmào chūzhòng de [+rén], 极具魅力的 jí jù mèilì de

string I N 1 线 xiàn 2 一连串 yì liánchuàn, 一系列 yí xìliè 3 附加条件 fùjiā tiáojiàn

no strings attached 不带任何附加条件 bú dài rènhé fùjiā tiáojiàn

4 (乐器的) 弦 (yuèqì de) xián

string instrument 弦乐器 xiányuèqì

II v (PT & PP strung) 1 (用线) 串起来 (yòng xiàn) chuàn qǐlái 2 悬挂起 xuánguàqǐ 3 给乐器装弦 gěi yuèqì zhuāng xián

string bean N 四季豆 sìjìdòu, 红花菜豆 hónghuā càidòu

stringent ADJ 严格的 yángé de, 苛刻的 kēkè de

strings N (乐队) 弦乐部 (yuèduì) xiányuèbù

stringy ADJ 1 纤维多的 [+食物] xiānwéi duō de [+shíwù] 2 极瘦的 jí shòu de

strip¹ v 1 脱去 [+衣服] tuōqù [+yīfu]

strip club 脱衣舞夜总会 tuōyīwǔ yèzǒnghuì

to be stripped to the waist 光着上身的 guāngzhe shàngshēn de

2 剥夺 [+权利] bōduó [+quánlì] 3 剥掉 [+树皮] bōdiào [+shùpí]

strip² N 1 一条 yìtiáo

a strip of bacon 一条咸肉 yìtiáo xiánròu

to cut sth into strips 把某物剪成长条 bǎ mǒuwù jiǎn chéng chángtiáo

2 商业街 shāngyèjiē 3 连环漫画 liánhuán mànhuà

stripe N 条纹 tiáowén, 线条 xiàntiáo

(people) of all stripes 各种各样的 (人) gèzhǒng gèyàng de (rén)

striped ADJ 有彩色条纹的 yǒu cǎisè tiáowén de

stripper N 脱衣舞女 tuōyīwǔ wǔnǚ

striptease N 脱衣舞表演 tuōyīwǔ biǎoyǎn

strive (PT strove; PP striven) v 努力奋斗 nǔlì fèndòu

striven See **strive**

strode See **stride**

stroke I N 1 中风 zhòngfēng, 血管破裂 xuèguǎn pòliè 2 (体育运动的) 击球 (tǐyù yùndòngde) 3 (写字) 一笔 (xiě zì) yì bǐ, (画画) 一画 (huà huà) yí huà 4 (钟) 一响 (zhōng) yì xiǎng

a stroke of luck 意外的好运 yìwài de hǎoyùn

a stroke of genius 天才之作 tiāncái zhī zuò

II v 1 击球 jīqiú 2 轻轻抚摸 qīngqīng fǔmō 3 讨好 tǎohǎo

stroll N, v 散步 sànbù, 闲逛 xiánguàng

stroller N 手推婴儿车 shǒutuī yīng'érchē [M. WD 辆 liàng]

strong ADJ 1 强有力的 qiáng yǒulì de, 气力大的 qìlì dà de 2 强大的 qiángdà de ■ *That country is developing a strong navy.* 那个国家在发展强大的海军。Nà ge guójiā zài fāzhǎn qiángdà de hǎijūn. 3 强烈的 qiángliè de 4 浓的 nóng de ■ *I like my coffee strong.* 我喜欢咖啡浓一点儿。Wǒ xǐhuan kāfēi nóng yìdiǎnr.

strong-arm ADJ 强制性的 qiángzhìxìng de

a strong-arm method 强制的方法 qiángzhì de fāngfǎ

strongbox N 保险箱 bǎoxiǎnxiāng, 保险柜 bǎoxiǎnguì

stronghold N 据点 jùdiǎn, 大本营 dàběnyíng

strongly ADV 强烈地 qiángliè de

strongman N 强人 qiángrén, 铁腕人物 tiěwàn rénwù

strong-willed ADJ 意志坚强的 yìzhì jiānqiáng de

strove See **strive**

struck See **strike**

structural ADJ 结构 (性) 的 jiégòu (xìng) de

structural overproduction 结构性生产过剩 jiégòuxìng shēngchǎn guòshèng

structure I N 1 结构 jiégòu ■ *The social structure of the country has undergone major changes in the past decade.* 在过去十年这个国家的社会结构发生了重大变化。Zài guòqù shí nián zhè ge guójiā de shèhuì jiégòu fāshēngle zhòngdà biànhuà. 2 条理 (性) tiáolǐ (xìng) **II** v 组织安排 [+系统] zǔzhī ānpái [+xìtǒng]

highly-structured 精心安排的 jīngxīn ānpái de

struggle I v 1 尽力 jìnlì, 努力 nǔlì ■ *My parents struggled their whole life to make a living.* 我的父母为谋生努力了一辈子。Wǒ de fùmǔ wèi móushēng nǔlìle yíbèizi. 2 搏斗 bódòu, 打斗 dǎdòu 3 作斗争 zuò dòuzhēng ■ *We must struggle for a better world.* 我们必须为更美好的世界作斗争。Wǒmen bìxū wèi gèng měihǎo de shìjiè zuò dòuzhēng. **II** N 奋斗 fèndòu

strum v 弹奏 [+吉他] tánzòu [+jítā]

strung See **string**

strung-out ADJ 1 极度焦虑的 jídù jiāolǜ de 2 有毒瘾的 yǒu dúyǐn de

strut I v 趾高气扬地走 zhǐgāo qìyáng de zǒu
to strut one's stuff 卖弄自己 màinong zìjǐ, 大显身手 dàxiǎn shēnshǒu
II N **1** 趾高气扬的步伐 zhǐgāo qìyáng de bùfá **2** 支柱 zhīzhù [M. WD 根 gēn], 撑杆 chēnggǎn [M. WD 根 gēn]

stub I N **1** 香烟头 xiāngyāntóu, 铅笔头 qiānbǐtóu **2** 支票存根 zhīpiào cúngēn **II** v (to stub ... out) 熄灭（烟头）xīmiè (yāntóu)

stubble N **1** 胡子茬儿 húzichár, 短髭 duǎnzī **2** 残枝 cán zhī, 茬 chá

stubborn ADJ **1** 顽固的 wángù de, 固执的 gùzhí de **2** 顽强的 [+抵抗] wánqiáng de [+dǐkàng]

stubby ADJ 粗短的 cūduǎn de

stucco N 灰泥 huīní

stuck¹ v See stick **II** ADJ 卡住了的 qiǎzhùle de, 动不了的 dòngbuliǎo de
to be stuck in traffic 遇到交通堵塞 yùdào jiāotōng dǔsè
to be stuck with sth 无法摆脱某事 wúfǎ bǎituō mǒushì
to be stuck on sb 迷恋上某人 míliàn shàng mǒurén

stuck-up ADJ 自命不凡的 zìmìng bùfán de, 傲慢的 àomàn de

stud¹ N **1** 种马 zhǒngmǎ [M. WD 匹 pǐ], 种畜 zhǒngchù **2** 性感男子 xìnggǎn nánzǐ

stud² N 饰钉 shìdīng

studded ADJ 镶满…的 xiāng mǎn...de

student N 学生 xuésheng
student body 全体学生 quántǐ xuésheng
student council, student government 学生自治会 xuésheng zìzhìhuì
student loan 助学货款 zhùxué huòkuǎn
student teaching 教学实习 jiàoxué shíxí
student union 学生活动大楼 xuésheng huódòng dàlóu

studied ADJ 装模作样的 zhuāngmú zuòyàng de, 故意的 gùyì de

studies N 学科 xuékē
business studies 商科 shāngkē, 商业课程 shāngyè kèchéng
religious studies 宗教研究 zōngjiào yánjiū

studio N **1** 艺术家工作室 yìshùjiā gōngzuòshì ■ *The sculptor works long hours in his studio.* 雕塑家在工作室长时间工作。Diāosùjiā zài gōngzuòshì cháng shíjiān gōngzuò. **2** 照相馆 zhàoxiàngguǎn **3** 电影/电视制片厂 diànyǐng/diànshì zhìpiànchǎng
studio apartment 单间公寓 dān jiān gōngyù

studious ADJ **1** 勤奋好学的 [+学生] qínfèn hǎoxué de [+xuésheng] **2** 细致认真的 [+工作] xìzhì rènzhēn de [+gōngzuò]

study I v **1** 学习 xuéxí ■ *"What did you study in college?" "I studied economics."* "你在大学是学什么的？" "学经济的。" "Nǐ zài dàxué shì xué shénme de?" "Xué jīngjì de." **2** 研究 yánjiū ■ *Jenny spent quite a few years on the African savannah studying animal behavior.* 詹妮在非洲草原好几年，研究动物行为。Zhānnī zài Fēizhōu cǎoyuán hǎojǐ nián, yánjiū dòngwù xíngwéi. **3** 仔细观察 zǐxì guānchá **II** N **1** 学习 xuéxí ■ *Mr Rusk started a bible study group last year.* 腊斯克先生去年建立了一个圣经学习小组。Làsīkè xiānsheng qùnián jiànlìle yí ge Shèngjīng xuéxí xiǎozǔ. **2** 研究 yánjiū **3** 学 xué, 学科 xuékē ■ *Are you interested in religious studies?* 你对宗教感兴趣吗? Nǐ duì zōngjiàoxué gǎn xìngqu ma? **4** 书房 shūfáng, 研究室 yánjiūshì

stuff I N 东西 dōngxi **II** v 塞满 sāimǎn ■ *She stuffed some clothes into a suitcase and left.* 她把一些衣服塞进皮箱，就走了。Tā bǎ yìxiē yīfu sāijin píxiāng, jiù zǒu le.
to be stuffed 吃饱了 chībǎo le, 吃不下了 chībuxià le

stuffed-up ADJ 鼻子塞住的 bízi sāizhù de

stuffing N 馅 xiàn, 填料 tiánliào

stuffy ADJ **1** 空气不流通的 kōngqì bù liútōng de, 闷的 mèn de **2** 一本正经的 yì běn zhèngjing de

stumble v **1** 绊脚 bànjiǎo **2** 绊跤 bànjiāo **3** 说错 shuōcuò, 结结巴巴地说 jiējie bābā de shuō
to stumble on 偶然碰到 ǒurán pèngdào

stumbling block N 绊脚石 bànjiǎoshí [M. WD 块 kuài], 障碍物 zhàng'àiwù

stump I N **1** 树桩 shùzhuāng, 树墩 shùdūn **2** 残余部分 cányú bùfen **II** v 把…难住 bǎ...nánzhù
to get sb stumped 把某人 nánzhù mǒurén

stun v **1** 使…大吃一惊 shǐ...dàchīyìjīng **2** 使…失去知觉 shǐ...shīqù zhījué
stun gun 眩晕枪 xuànyùn qiāng

stung See sting

stunk See stink

stunning ADJ **1** 令人吃惊的 lìngrén chījīng de **2** 美得惊人的 měide jīngrén de, 极漂亮的 jí piàoliang de

stunt I N **1** （电影）特技动作 (diànyǐng) tèjì dòngzuò **2** （政治）花招 (zhèngzhì) huāzhāo
publicity stunt 公关花招 gōngguān huāzhāo
to pull a stunt 令人难堪的蠢事 lìngrén nánkān de chǔnshì
II v 抑制 yìzhì, 阻遏 zǔ'ài

stuntman N 特技替身演员 tèjì tìshēn yǎnyuán

stupefied ADJ 目瞪口呆的 mùdèng kǒudāi de

stupefying ADJ 令人目瞪口呆的 lìngrén mùdèng kǒudāi de

stupendous ADJ 巨大的 jùdà de, 了不起的 liǎobuqǐ de

stupid ADJ 愚蠢的 yúchǔn de

stupor N 昏迷的 hūnmí de, 不省人事的 bùxǐng rénshì de

sturdy

to drink oneself to a stupor 喝得昏昏沉沉 hē dé hūnhūn chénchén

sturdy ADJ **1** 结实的 [+家具] jiēshi de [+jiājù], 坚固的 jiāngù de **2** 健壮的 [+人] jiànzhuàng de [+rén]

stutter V 结结巴巴地说 jiējiebābā de shuō, 口吃 kǒuchī

sty¹ N 猪圈 zhūjuàn

sty² N 麦粒肿 màilìzhǒng, 睑腺炎 jiǎnxiànyán

style I N **1** 风格 fēnggé **2** 款式 kuǎnshì, 式样 shìyàng II V 设计 [+发型] shèjì [+fàxíng]
to style oneself as 自称是 zìchēng shì, 以…自居 yǐ...zìjū

styling N (演奏/演说)风格 (yǎnzòu/yǎnshuō) fēnggé

styling brush N (造型)发刷 (zàoxíng) fàshuā [M. WD 把 bǎ]

stylish ADJ 时髦的 shímáo de, 漂亮的 piàoliang de

stylist N 发型师 fàxíngshī

stylistic ADJ 风格上的 fēnggé shàng de, 文体上的 wéntǐ shàng de

stylized ADJ 有独特风格的 yǒu dútè fēnggé de

stymie V 阻碍 zǔ'ài, 妨碍 fáng'ài

Styrofoam N (聚苯乙烯)泡沫塑料 (jùběnyǐxī) pàomò sùliào

suave ADJ 温文尔雅的 wēnwén ěryǎ de

sub¹ (= submarine) ABBREV **1** 潜艇 qiántǐng [M. WD 艘 sōu] **2** 潜艇型三明治 qiántǐngxíng sānmíngzhì

sub² ABBREV **1** (= substitute teacher) 代课老师 dàikè lǎoshī **2** 替补队员 tìbǔ duìyuán

subcommittee N (委员会下设的)小组 (wěiyuánhuì xiàshè de) xiǎozǔ

subconscious I N 潜意识 qiányìshí, 下意识 xiàyìshí II ADJ 潜意识的 qiányìshí de, 下意识的 xiàyìshí de

subcontinent N 次大陆 cìdàlù
the South Asian subcontinent 南亚次大陆 Nányà Cìdàlù

subculture N 亚文化(群) yà wénhuà (qún)

subdivide V 细分 xì fēn, 把…再分 bǎ...zàifēn

subdivision N **1** 分支 fēnzhī **2** (建造住宅的)一块土地 (jiànzào zhùzhái de) yí kuài tǔdì

subdue V **1** 制服 zhìfú, 镇压 zhènyā **2** 控制 kòngzhì, 抑制 yìzhì

subdued ADJ **1** 稳重安静的 [+人] wěnzhòng ānjìng de [+rén] **2** 沉闷的 [+气氛] chénmèn de [+qìfen] **3** 柔和的 [+灯光] róuhe de [+dēngguāng]

subject I N **1** 题目 tímù, 主题 zhǔtí **2** 课 kè, 科目 kēmù **3** (语法)主语 (yǔfǎ) zhǔyǔ ■ *In the sentence "I love Lucy," "I" is the subject.* 在 "I love Lucy" 这句话里，"I" 是主语。Zài "I love Lucy" zhè jù huà lǐ, "I" shì zhǔyǔ. **4** 实验对象 shíyàn

duìxiàng II ADJ (subject to) **1** 受…约束 shòu... yuēshù **2** 有待于… yǒudàiyú...
subject to approval 有待于批准 yǒudàiyú pīzhǔn
subject to change 可能改变 kěnéng gǎibiàn
subject to the law [人+] 受法律约束 [rén+] shòu fǎlǜ yuēshù
III V 使…遭受 shǐ...zāoshòu
to subject him to police investigation 使他受到警方调查 shǐ tā shòudào jǐngfāng diàochá

subjective ADJ 主观(上)的 zhǔguān (shàng) de

subjugate V 征服 zhēngfú, 降服 xiángfú

subjugation N 征服 zhēngfú, 降服 xiángfú

subjunctive N (语法中的)虚拟语气 (yǔfǎ zhòng de) xūnǐ yǔqì

sublet V 转租 zhuǎnzū, 分租 fēnzū

sublime I ADJ 令人赞叹的 lìngrén zàntàn de, 至高无上的 zhìgāo wúshàng de II N 崇高 chónggāo, 至高无上 zhìgāo wúshàng

subliminal ADJ 潜意识的 qiányìshí de, 下意识的 xiàyìshí de

submarine N 潜水艇 qiánshuǐtǐng [M. WD 艘 sōu]

submerged ADJ 在水面下的 zài shuǐmiàn xià de

submersion N 淹没 yānmò, 浸没 jìnmò

submission N **1** 顺从 shùncóng, 屈从 qūcóng
to force sb to submission 强迫某人顺从 qiǎngpò mǒurén shùncóng **2** 提交 tíjiāo, 呈送 chéngsòng

submissive ADJ 顺从的 shùncóng de, 屈从的 qūcóng de

submit V **1** 呈送 [+文件] chéngsòng [+wénjiàn], 提交 tíjiāo **2** 服从 [+规定] fúcóng [+guīdìng], 顺从 shùncóng

subordinate I V 使…从属于 shǐ...cóngshǔ yú
to subordinate the needs of the individual to those of the state 使个人需求从属于国家需求 shǐ gèrén xūqiú cóngshǔ yú guójiā xūqiú
II ADJ 从属的 cóngshǔ de, 次要的 cìyào de
subordinate clause 从句 cóngjù
III N 下属 xiàshǔ, 下级 xiàjí, 部下 bùxià

subpoena I N (法庭上的)传票 (fǎtíng shàng de) chuánpiào II V [法庭+] 发出传票 [fǎtíng+] fāchū chuánpiào

subscribe, subscribe to V **1** 订阅 [+报刊] dìngyuè [+bàokān] **2** [为某项服务+] 定期付款 [wéi mǒu xiàng fúwù+] dìngqī fùkuǎn **3** 赞同 [+观点] zàntóng [+guāndiǎn]

subscriber N 订户 dìnghù

subscription N 订阅(费) dìngyuè (fèi), 用户费 yònghùfèi

subsequent ADJ 随后的 suíhòu de

subservient ADJ 恭顺的 gōngshùn de, 奉承的 fèngcheng de

subside V **1** 逐渐减弱 zhújiàn jiǎnruò, 平息 píngxī **2** [土地+] 下沉 [tǔdì+] xiàchén **3** [大水+] 退落 [dàshuǐ+] tuìluò

subsidiary I N 子公司 zǐgōngsī [M. WD 家 jiā]
II ADJ 附属的 fùshǔ de, 补充的 bǔchōng de
subsidize V 补贴 bǔtiē, 补助 bǔzhù
subsidy N 补贴 bǔtiē
government subsidy to agriculture 政府对农业
的补贴 zhèngfǔ duì nóngyè de bǔtiē
subsist V 维持生存 wéichí shēngcún
subsistence N **1** 维持生存 wéichí shēngcún **2** 仅
够活命的粮食／钱 jǐngòu huómìng de liángshi/
qián
subsistence wage 仅够活命的工资 jǐn gòu
huómìng de gōngzī
substance N **1** 物质 wùzhì **2** 实质内容 shízhì
nèiróng ■ His long essay, written in academic
English, lacks substance. 他的这篇用学术英文
写的长文，缺乏实质内容。Tā de zhè piān yòng
xuéshù Yīngwén xiě de cháng wén, quēfá shízhì
nèiróng.
substance abuse 药物滥用 yàowù lànyòng
man of substance 有家产的人 yǒu jiāchǎn de
rén, 富人 fùrén
substandard ADJ 低标准的 dī biāozhǔn de, 次等
的 cìděng de
substantial ADJ **1** 相当大的 xiāngdāng dà de, 可
观的 kěguān de
substantial meal 丰盛的一餐 fēngshèng de
yīcān
2 有权势的 yǒu quánshì de, 有影响的 yǒu
yǐngxiǎng de
substantiate V 证实 zhèngshí, 证明 zhèngmíng
substitute V 替代 tìdài **II** N 替代者 tìdàizhě, 代用
品 dàiyòngpǐn
substitute teacher 代课老师 dàikè lǎoshī
subterfuge N 花招 huāzhāo, 诡计 guǐjì
subterranean ADJ 地下的 dìxia de
subtitles N **1** （电影）字幕 (diànyǐng) zìmù **2** （文
章／书籍）副标题 (wénzhāng/shūjí) fùbiāotí
subtle ADJ 微妙的 wēimiào de, 细微的 xìwēi de
subtlety N 微妙（之处）wēimiào (zhī chù)
subtract V 减（去）jiǎn (qù), 扣除 kòuchú ■ Here
is your money I owe you subtracting, of course,
the amount you owed me. 这儿是我欠你的钱，当
然减掉了你欠我的那一笔。Zhèr shì wǒ qiàn nǐ de
qián, dāngrán jiǎndiaole nǐ qiàn wǒ de nà yì bǐ.
suburb N 郊区 jiāoqū
the suburbs 郊区 jiāoqū, 城郊 chéngjiāo
suburban ADJ 郊区的 jiāoqū de
suburbia N 郊区 jiāoqū, 城郊住宅区 chéngjiāo
zhùzháiqū
subversive I ADJ 颠覆性的 diānfùxìng de **II** N 颠
覆分子 diānfù fènzi
subvert V 颠覆 diānfù
subway N 地铁 dìtiě [M. WD 条 tiáo], 地下铁路
dìxià tiělù [M. WD 条 tiáo]
succeed V **1** 成功 chénggōng ■ If you don't suc-

ceed at first, try and try again. 如果第一次不成
功，那就一次次试下去。Rúguǒ dìyī cì bù chéng-
gōng, nà jiù yí cìcì shìxiàqu. **2** 继承 jìchéng
succeeding ADJ 随后的 suíhòu de, 接着的 jiēzhe
de
success N **1** 成功 chénggōng
I wish you success! 祝你成功! Zhù nǐ chénggōng!
2 成功人物 chénggōng rénwù, 成功的事
chénggōng de shì
successful ADJ 成功的 chénggōng de
succession N **1** 连续 liánxù
in succession 接连（地）jiēlián (de)
2 一连串 yìliánchuàn
a succession of 一连串的 yìliánchuàn de
successive ADJ 连续的 liánxù de, 接连的 jiēlián
de
successor N 继承者 jìchéngzhě
succinct ADJ 简炼的 jiǎnliàn de, 简要的 jiǎnyào de
succor N 救济 jiùjì, 求助 qiúzhù
succulence N 多汁 duōzhī
succulent ADJ 多汁水的 [+水果] duō zhīshui de
[+shuǐguǒ]
succumb V 屈服 qūfú, 屈从 qūcóng
such I ADJ 这样的 zhèyàng de, 如此的 rúcǐ de
■ He is not such a fool as he seems to be. 他并不
像看起来那么傻。Tā bìng bú xiàng kànqǐlai nàme
shǎ. **II** PRON 这个 zhè ge ■ She is a sympathetic
teacher and has always been regarded as such by
her students. 她是一位对学生很有同情心的老师，
学生们也这么认为。Tā shì yí wèi duì xuésheng
hěn yǒu tóngqíngxīn de lǎoshī, xuéshēngmen yě
zhème rènwéi.
such as 就像 jiù xiàng, 比如 bǐrú
such-and-such 这样那样 zhèyàng nàyàng
suck N, V 吸 xī, 吮吸 shǔnxī
It sucks … …真不舒服 …zhēn bù shūfu ■ It
really sucks when it rains the whole day. 整天下
雨，真不舒服。Zhěngtiān xiàyǔ, zhēn bù shūfu.
sucker N **1** 容易上当的傻瓜 róngyì shàngdàng
de shǎguā
to be a sucker to sth 偏爱某事物 piān'ài
mǒushìwù
2 （动物的）吸盘 (dòngwù de) xīpán
suckling N **1** 乳儿 rǔ'ér **2** 乳畜 rǔchù
suckling pig 乳猪 rǔzhū
suction N 吸 xī, 抽吸 chōuxī
suction pump 真空泵 zhēnkōngbèng [M. WD 台
tái]
sudden ADJ 突然 tūrán ■ Why did the chairman
make the sudden decision to inspect the branch
in Beijing? 董事长为什么突然决定视察北京分
公司？Dǒngshìzhǎng wèishénme tūrán juédìng
shìchá Běijīng fēngōngsī?
sudden death 加分加时决定胜负 jiā fēn jiā shí
juédìng shèngfù

suddenly ADV 突然 tūrán

suds N 1 肥皂泡沫 féizàopào mò 2 啤酒 píjiǔ

sue V 控告 kònggào ■ *The company sued its chief accountant for embezzlement.* 公司控告会计主任盗用资金。Gōngsī kònggào kuàijì zhǔrèn dàoyòng zījīn.

suede N 绒面皮革 róngmiàn pígé, 软皮革 ruǎn pígé

suffer V 1 遭受 zāoshòu 2 患 [+病] huàn [+bìng] ■ *He has been suffering from insomnia for a long time.* 他患失眠已经很长时间了。Tā huàn shīmián yǐjīng hěn cháng shíjiān le. 3 变坏 biànhuài

suffice V 足够的 zúgòu de, 能满足的 néng mǎnzú de

suffice it to say 只要说…就(足)够了 zhǐyào shuō...jiù (zú) gòu le

sufficient ADJ 足够的 zúgòu de ■ *Ten dollars a week for allowance should be sufficient for children.* 一个星期十块零花钱，对孩子来说应该是足够了。Yí ge xīngqī shí kuài línghuā qián, duì háizi láishuō yīnggāi shì zúgòu le.

suffix N 后缀 hòuzhuì

suffocate V 使 [+人] 窒息而死 shǐ [+rén] zhìxī ér sǐ, 闷死 mènsǐ

suffocation N 窒息 zhìxī

suffrage N 选举权 xuǎnjǔquán, 投票权 tóupiàoquán

sugar N 糖 táng, 食糖 shítáng ■ *Are any of the sugar substitutes really safe?* 那些代用糖真的很安全吗？Nàxiē dàiyòng táng zhēn de hěn ānquán ma?

sugar cube 方糖 fāngtáng

sugar maple 糖槭 tángqì

sugarcane N 甘蔗 gānzhe [M. WD 根 gēn]

sugarcoated ADJ 1 包有糖衣的 bāo yǒu tángyī de 2 美化的 měihuà de

suggest V 1 建议 jiànyì ■ *The guidance counselor suggested that he apply to a community college.* 学校辅导员建议他报考社区学院。Xuéxiào fǔdǎoyuán jiànyì tā bàokǎo shèqū xuéyuàn. 2 暗示 ànshì

suggestible ADJ 易受影响的 yì shòu yǐngxiǎng de

suggestion N 1 建议 jiànyì ■ *May I offer a suggestion to break their monopoly of the industry?* 我可以提一个建议来打破他们的行业垄断吗？Wǒ kěyǐ tí yí ge jiànyì lái dǎpò tāmen de hángyè lǒngduàn ma? 2 暗示 ànshì

suggestive ADJ 1 暗示的 ànshì de

suggestive of sth 使人联想起某物 shǐrén liánxiǎng qǐ mǒuwù

2 性挑逗的 xìng tiǎodòu de

suicidal ADJ 有自杀倾向的 yǒu zìshā qīngxiàng de

suicide N 自杀 zìshā

to attempt suicide 试图自杀 shìtú zìshā, 自杀(未遂) zìshā (wèisuì)

to commit suicide 自杀(身亡) zìshā (shēnwáng)

suit¹ N 1 一套服装 yí tào fúzhuāng 2 同花色的纸牌 tóng huāsè de zhǐpái

a suit of hearts 一组红桃牌 yìzǔ hóngtáopái

3 (= lawsuit) 诉讼 sùsòng

to file suit against sb 对某人提出诉讼 duì mǒurén tíchū sùsòng

suit² V 适合 shìhé ■ *The early morning flight will suit me very well.* 清晨的这个航班对我很合适。Qīngchén de zhè ge hángbān duì wǒ hěn héshì. Suit yourself. 随便你。Suíbiàn nǐ. ■ *"I'd rather stay at home tonight." "Suit yourself."* "今天晚上我宁愿留在家里。""随便你。""Jīntiān wǎnshang wǒ nìngyuàn liú zài jiālǐ." "Suíbiàn nǐ."

suitable ADJ 合适的 héshì de, 适宜的 shìyí de

suitcase N 手提箱 shǒutíxiāng, 皮箱 píxiāng

suite N 1 一套房间 yí tào fángjiān, 套房 tàofáng

bridal suite (旅馆) 新婚套房 (lǚguǎn) xīnhūn tàofáng

2 一套家具 yí tào jiājù

bedroom suite 一套卧室家具 yí tào wòshì jiājù

3 (音乐) 组曲 (yīnyuè) zǔqǔ

suitor N 求婚者 qiúhūnzhě, 求婚男子 qiúhūn nánzǐ

sulfur, sulphur (S) N 硫 liú

sulfuric acid N 硫酸 liúsuān

sulk V 生闷气 shēng mènqì

sulky ADJ 生闷气的 shēng mènqì de, 愠怒的 yùnnù de

sullen ADJ 面带怒容的 miàn dài nùróng de, 生气的 shēngqì de

sultan N 苏丹 Sūdān [M. WD 位 wèi]

sultry ADJ 1 闷热的 [+天气] mēnrè de [+tiānqì] 2 性感迷人的 [+女子] xìnggǎn mírén de [+nǚzǐ]

sum N 1 一笔(钱) yì bǐ (qián) ■ *A large sum of cash was found under the mattress after the death of the old man.* 老人死后，在床垫下发现一大笔现金。Lǎorén sǐ hòu, zài chuángdiànxia fāxiàn yí dà bǐ xiànjīn. 2 总数 zǒngshù ■ *The sum of 7 and 9 is 16.* 七加九得十六。Qī jiā jiǔ dé shíliù. II V (to sum up) 总结 zǒngjié, 概括 gàikuò

summarize V 总结 zǒngjié

summary I N 总结 zǒngjié, 摘要 zhāiyào II ADJ 1 总结性(的) zǒngjié xìng (de), 概括(性)的 gàikuò (xìng) de 2 立即的 lìjí de

summary execution 立即处决 lìjí chǔjué

summer N 夏天 xiàtiān, 夏季 xiàjì

summer camp 夏令营 xiàlìngyíng

summer home 避暑别墅 bìshǔ biéshù

summer school 暑期班 shǔqībān ■ *What courses are you going to take for summer school?* 你在暑期班上什么课？Nǐ zài shǔqībān shàng shénme kè?

summer vacation 暑期 shǔqī, 暑假 shǔjià

summertime N 夏天 xiàtiān, 夏令季节 xiàlìng jìjié

summon V 1 传唤 chuánhuàn
to summon the police 叫警察来 jiào jǐngchá lái, 报警 bàojǐng
2 鼓起 [勇气] gǔqǐ [+yǒngqì], 振作 [+精神] zhènzuò [+jīngshén]
to summon up courage 鼓足勇气 gǔzú yǒngqì

summons N (法庭的) 传票 (fǎtíng de) chuánpiào

sumptuous ADJ 豪华的 háohuá de, 奢华的 shēhuá de

sun I N 太阳 tàiyáng II V 晒太阳 shài tàiyáng

sunbathe V 沐日光浴 mù rìguāngyù

sunbathing N 日光浴 rìguāngyù

sunblock N 防晒油／霜 fángshàiyóu/shuāng [M. WD 瓶 píng/盒 hé]

sunburn N 晒伤 shàishāng

sundae N 圣代冰淇淋 shèngdài bīngqílín

Sunday N 星期日 xīngqīrì, 星期天 xīngqītiān

sundial N 日晷 rìguǐ, 日规 rìguī

sundown N 日落 (时) rìluò (shí)

sundries N 杂物 záwù, 杂项 záxiàng

sundry ADJ 杂七杂八的 záqīzábā de, 各种各样的 gèzhǒng gèyàng de

sunflower N 向日葵 xiàngrìkuí [M. WD 朵 duǒ]

sung See **sing**

sunglasses N 太阳眼镜 tàiyáng yǎnjìng, 遮阳镜 zhēyángjìng

sunk See **sink**[1]

sunken ADJ 1 沉没的 [+船只] chénmò de [+chuánzhī] 2 凹陷的 [+双眼] āoxiàn de [+shuāngyǎn] 3 低于周围的 dī yú zhōuwéi de
a sunken living room 低于地面的客厅 dī yú dìmiàn de kètīng

sunlight N 日光 rìguāng

sunlit ADJ 阳光照耀的 yángguāng zhàoyào de

sunny ADJ 阳光充足的 yángguāng chōngzú de

sunrise N 日出 (时分) rìchū (shífēn)

sunroof N 活动车顶 huódòng chēdǐng

sunset N 日落 (时分) rìluò (shífèn)

sunshine N 阳光 yángguāng, 日照 rìzhào

sunstroke N 中暑 zhòngshǔ

suntan N 太阳晒黑的皮肤 tàiyáng shàihēi de pífū

super ADJ 好极了 hǎo jíle

superb ADJ 好极了 hǎo jíle, 最好的 zuì hǎo de

Super Bowl N (美国橄榄球) 超级比赛 (Měiguó gǎnlǎnqiú) chāojí bǐsài

supercilious ADJ 傲慢的 àomàn de, 目中无人的 mùzhōng wúrén de

superficial ADJ 表面 (上) 的 biǎomiàn (shàng) de, 肤浅的 fūqiǎn de

superfluous ADJ 多余的 duōyú de, 不必要的 bú bìyào de

superhighway N (超级) 高速公路 (chāojí) gāosù gōnglù

superhuman ADJ 超过常人的 chāoguò chángrén de, 超人的 chāorén de

superintendent N 1 主管人 zhǔguǎn rén, 总监 zǒngjiān
superintendent of schools (美国) 地区教育局长 (Měiguó) dìqū jiàoyùjú zhǎng
2 (大楼) 管理员 (dàlóu) guǎnlǐyuán

superior I ADJ 优越的 yōuyuè
to act superior 摆出比别人优越的架子 bǎichū bǐ biéren yōuyuè de jiàzi
to be superior to 比…优越 bǐ…yōuyuè
2 优质的 [+材料] yōuzhì de [+cáiliào], 高超的 gāochāo de 3 上级的 shàngjí de
superior officer 上级军官 shàngjí jūnguān
II N 上级 shàngjí, 上司 shàngsi

superiority N 优越 yōuyuè, 优秀 yōuxiù
sense of superiority 优越感 yōuyuègǎn

superlative I ADJ 1 最好的 zuì hǎo de 2 (形容词／副词) 最高级的 (xíngróngcí/fùcí) zuìgāojí de II N (形容词／副词) 最高级形式 (xíngróngcí/fùcí) zuì gāojí xíngshì

supermarket N 超级市场 chāojí shìchǎng, 超市 chāoshì

supernatural I ADJ 超自然的 chāozìrán de II N 超自然事物／力量 chāozìrán shìwù/lìliang

superpower N 超级大国 chāojí dàguó

supersede V 替代 tìdài, 取代 qǔdài

supersonic ADJ 超音速的 chāoyīnsù de
supersonic jet 超音速喷气式飞机 chāoyīnsù pēnqìshì fēijī

superstar N 超级明星 chāojí míngxīng

superstition N 迷信 míxìn

superstitious ADJ 迷信的 míxìn de

superstore N 超级商场 chāojí shāngchǎng

superstructure N 1 (建筑物) 上部结构 (jiànzhùwù) shàngbù jiégòu 2 (社会) 上层建筑 (shèhuì) shàngcéng jiànzhù

supervise V 监督指导 jiāndū zhǐdǎo

supervision N 指导 zhǐdǎo, 监督 jiāndū

supervisor N 1 (大学研究生) 导师 (dàxué yánjiūshēng) dǎoshī 2 (工程) 监督 (gōngchéng) jiāndū

supervisory ADJ 监督的 jiāndū de, 督导的 dūdǎo de

supper N 晚饭 wǎnfàn, 晚餐 wǎncān
supper club 小型夜总会 xiǎoxíng yèzǒnghuì

supple ADJ 柔软的 róuruǎn de, 柔韧的 róurèn de

supplement I V 补充 bǔchōng, 增补 zēngbǔ II N 补充 (物) bǔchōng (wù), 增补 (物) zēngbǔ (wù)

supplementary ADJ 补充的 bǔchōng de, 增补的 zēngbǔ de

supplier N 供应商 gōngyìngshāng

supplies N 1 供应品 gōngyìngpǐn
medical supplies 医疗用品 yīliáo yòngpǐn

2 供应量 gōngyìngliáng

supply N, V 供给 gōngjǐ, 供应 gōngyìng ■ *Some developing countries have an abundant supply of labor.* 有些发展中国家可以提供大量的劳动力。Yǒuxiē fāzhǎnzhōng guójiā kěyǐ tígōng dàliàng de láodònglì.
electricity supply 电力供应 diànlì gōngyìng
supply and demand 供求（关系）gōngqiú (guānxi)

support I V **1** 支持 zhīchí **2** 养活 yǎnghuo ■ *Tom pays alimony to support his three children living with their mother.* 汤姆付赡养费来养活和前妻住在一起的三个孩子。Tāngmǔ fù shànyǎng fèi lái yǎnghuo hé qiánqī zhù zài yìqǐ de sān ge háizi. **3** 维持 wéichí II N **1** 支持 zhīchí **2** 支撑物 zhīchēng wù

supporter N 支持者 zhīchízhě, 拥护者 yōnghùzhě

supportive ADJ 支持的 zhīchí de, 给予帮助的 jǐyǔ bāngzhù de

suppose V **1** 认为 rènwéi, 想 xiǎng **2** 料想 liàoxiǎng, 预期 yùqī
be supposed to 应该 yīnggāi

supposedly ADV 据说 jùshuō, 一般认为 yì bān rènwéi

supposing CONJ 假设 jiǎshè, 假定 jiǎdìng

supposition N 假定 jiǎdìng, 推测 tuīcè

suppress V **1** 抑制 [+发展] yìzhì [+fāzhǎn], 阻止 zǔzhǐ **2** 镇压 [+叛乱] zhènyā [+pànluàn], 压制 yāzhì **3** 封锁 [+信息] fēngsuǒ [+xìnxī]

supremacy N 最高地位 zuìgāo dìwèi
to challenge male supremacy 挑战男性至上 tiǎozhàn nánxìng zhìshàng

supreme ADJ 最高的 zuìgāo de
Supreme Court 最高法院 zuìgāo fǎyuàn

surcharge N 附加费 fùjiāfèi, 额外收费 éwài shōufèi
to levy a surcharge for excess baggage 对过重行李收取附加费 duì guòzhòng xíngli shōuqǔ fùjiāfèi

sure I ADJ **1** 肯定 kěndìng **2** 有把握 yǒu bǎwò ■ *She is sure of having a place in one of the Ivy League colleges.* 她有把握能在常春藤联盟大学有一席之地。Tā yǒu bǎwò néng zài Chángchūnténg Liánméng dàxué yǒu yī xí zhī dì.
a sure thing ① 当然 dāngrán ② 能有把握的事 néng yǒu bǎwò de shì
to be sure of oneself 很自信 hěn zìxìn ■ *He is always so sure of himself that sometimes he appears smug.* 他总是这么自信，有时候显得自以为是。Tā zǒngshì zhème zìxìn, yǒushíhou xiǎnde zì yǐ wéi shì.
to make sure (that) 确保 quèbǎo, 保证 bǎozhèng
II ADV 肯定（地）kěndìng (de), 当然 dāngrán
sure enough 果然 guǒrán, 果真 guǒzhēn

surefire ADJ 肯定能取胜的 kěndìng néng qǔshèng de

a surefire way 肯定能成功的办法 kěndìng néng chénggōng de bànfǎ

surely ADV 肯定地 kěndìng de, 无疑 wúyí ■ *This is surely your best chance.* 这无疑是你最好的机会。Zhè wúyí shì nǐ zuì hǎo de jīhuì.

surf V 冲浪 chōnglàng **2** 浏览 liúlǎn

surface I N 表面 biǎomiàn II V 浮出表面 fúchū biǎomiàn, 突然出现 tūrán chūxiàn

surfboard N 冲浪板 chōnglàngbǎn [M. WD 块 kuài]

surge I V **1** [水+] 汹涌而来 [shuǐ+] xiōngyǒng érlái **2** [人群+] 蜂涌向前 [rénqún+] fēngyǒng ér qián **3** （感情）涌起（gǎnqíng）yǒngqǐ **4** （电流）浪涌（diàn liú）làng yǒng II N **1** （水）汹涌（shuǐ）xiōngyǒng **2** （人群）拥挤（rénqún）fēngyǒng **3** （感情）涌起（gǎnqíng）yǒngqǐ **4** 电涌 diànyǒng

surgeon N 外科医生 wàikē yīshēng
brain sugeon 脑外科医生 nǎo wàikē yīshēng
dental surgeon 口腔外科医生 kǒuqiāng wàikē yīshēng

surgery N **1** 外科（手术）wàikē (shǒushù)
major surgery 大手术 dàshǒushù
plastic surgery 整形外科（手术）zhěngxíng wàikē (shǒushù)
2 外科学 wàikēxué **3** 手术室 shǒushùshì

surgical ADJ **1** 外科手术的 wàikē shǒushù de **2** 外科手术式的 wàikē shǒushù shì de, 精确的 jīngquè de

surly ADJ 脾气粗暴的 píqi cūbào de, 很不友好的 hěn bù yǒuhǎo de

surmise V 推测 tuīcè, 猜测 cāicè

surmount V 克服 [+障碍] kèfú [+zhàng'ài]

surname N 姓（氏）xìng (shì)

surpass V 超过 chāoguò, 超越 chāoyuè

surplus I N 剩余（额）shèngyú (é), 多余（量）duōyú (liáng)
budget surplus 预算盈余 yùsuàn yíngyú
trade surplus 贸易顺差 màoyì shùnchā
II ADJ 剩余的 shèngyú de, 多余的 duōyú de
surplus stock 多余的库存 duōyú de kùcún

surprise I N 惊奇 jīngqí ■ *The birthday party is supposed to be a surprise, so keep your lips sealed.* 这个生日聚会应该是个惊奇，所以要守口如瓶。Zhè ge shēngri jùhuì yīnggāi shì ge jīngqí, suǒyǐ yào shǒu kǒu rú píng. II V 使…惊奇 shǐ… jīngqí

surprised ADJ （感到）惊奇的（gǎndào）jīngqí de

surprising ADJ 令人（感到）惊奇的 lìngrén (gǎndào) jīngqí de

surreal ADJ 超现实的 chāoxiànshí de, 不象真实的 bú xiàng zhēnshí de

surrealistic ADJ 超现实的 chāoxiànshí de, 离奇的 líqí de

surrénder I V **1** 投降 tóuxiáng **2** 放弃 [+权利] fàngqì [+quánlì] II N 投降 tóuxiáng unconditional surrender 无条件投降 wútiáojiàn tóuxiáng

surreptitious ADJ 秘密的 mìmì de

surreptitiously ADV 偷偷（地）tōutōu (de), 秘密地 mìmì de

surrogate I ADJ 替代的 tìdài de
surrogate mother 替不育者生育的妇女 tì búyùzhě shēngyù de fùnǚ, 替身母亲 tìshēn mǔqin **II** N 1 替身 tìshēn 2 替身母亲 tìshēn mǔqin

surround v 围 wéi, 围住 wéizhù ■ *A high fence surrounded the entire property.* 高高的围墙围住了这整个房产。Gāo gāo de wéiqiáng wéizhule zhè zhěnggè fángchǎn.

surrounding ADJ 周围的 zhōuwéi de, 四周的 sìzhōu de

surroundings N 环境 huánjìng

surveillance N 监视 jiānshì
surveillance camera 监视摄像机 jiānshì shèxiàngjī
CCTV surveillance 闭路电视监视系统 bìlù diànshì jiānshì xìtǒng
2（军事）侦察（jūnshì）zhēnchá
surveillance mission 军事侦察任务 jūnshì zhēnchá rènwu
aerial surveillance 空中侦察 kōngzhōng zhēnchá

survey I v 1 调查 diàochá, 做（社会）调查 zuò (shèhuì) diàochá ■ *Most people surveyed agree that the law should be changed.* 被调查的大多数人都同意denovo法律必须修改。Bèi diàochá de dàduōshù rén dōu tóngyì zhè tiáo fǎlǜ bìxū xiūgǎi. 2 概括论述 gàikuò lùnshù ■ *This report surveys the climate changes in the Arctic.* 这份报告概括论述了北极的气候变化。Zhè fèn bàogào gàikuòlùnshùle Běijí de qìhòu biànhuà. 3 勘测 kāncè 4 检查 jiǎnchá **II** N 1（社会）调查（shèhuì）diàochá
survey respondent 调查回音者 diàochá huíyīnzhě
doorstep survey 登门调查 dēngmén diàochá
2 勘测 kāncè 3 概论 gàilùn, 概述 gàishù
survey course 概论课 gàilùnkè

surveyor N（土地）测量员（tǔdì）cèliángyuán, 勘测员 kāncèyuán

survival N 生存 shēngcún, 存活 cúnhuó
survival kit 救生包 jiùshēngbāo
survival of the fittest 适者生存 shìzhě shēngcún

survive v 1 幸存 xìngcún, 生存下来 shēngcún xialai
the only surviving member of the family 那个家庭中唯一还活着的成员 nàge jiātíng zhōng wéiyī hái huózhe de chéngyuán
2 活得比…长 huóde bǐ...cháng, 遗留下 yíliú xià ■ *Mrs. Jones survived her husband by 15 years.* 琼斯太太比她丈夫多活十五年。Qióngsī tàitai bǐ tā zhàngfu duō huó shíwǔ nián.

survivor N 1 幸存者 xìngcúnzhě, 生还者 shēnghuánzhě 2 善于在逆境中求存者 shànyú zài nìjìng zhōng qiúcúnzhě

susceptible ADJ 1 容易被感染的 róngyì bèi gǎnrǎn de, 容易生…病的 róngyì shēng...bìng de
be susceptible to depression 容易得忧郁症 róngyì dé yōuyùzhèng
2 容易受影响的 róngyì shòu yǐngxiǎng de
be susceptible to suggestions 容易受暗示影响的 róngyì shòu ànshì yǐngxiǎng de
a highly susceptible girl 一个极易受影响的女孩 yí ge jí yì shòu yǐngxiǎng de nǚhái

suspect I v 疑心 yíxīn, 认为 rènwéi ■ *I suspect that he's been lying.* 我疑心他在撒谎。Wǒ yíxīn tā zài sāhuǎng. **II** N 嫌疑犯 xiányífàn **III** ADJ 可疑的 kěyí de, 不可信的 bùkě xìn de

suspend v 1 暂停 zàntíng 2 勒令停学 lèlìng tíngxué 3 悬挂 xuánguà, 吊 diào

suspenders N（裤子的）吊带（kùzi de）diàodài [M. WD 副 fù]

suspense N（故事的）悬念（gùshi de）xuánniàn
to keep sb in suspense 让人提心吊胆的 ràng rén tíxīn diàodǎn de

suspension N 1 暂停 zàntíng, 中止 zhōngzhǐ 2 停学 tíngxué, 暂时除名 zànshí chúmíng 3 悬架 xuán jià, 减震系统 jiǎnzhèn xìtǒng
suspension bridge 悬索桥 xuánsuǒqiáo

suspicion N 怀疑 huáiyí ■ *He was arrested on suspicion of murder.* 他因谋杀嫌疑被捕。Tā yīn móushā xiányí bèibǔ.

suspicious ADJ 1 怀疑 huáiyí, 有疑心的 yǒu yíxīn de ■ *I was increasingly suspicious of her intentions.* 我对她的动机越来越怀疑。Wǒ duì tāde dòngjī yuèláiyuè huáiyí. 2 使人怀疑的 shǐrén huáiyí de

sustain v 1 维持 [+生命] wéichí [+shēngmìng] 2 遭受 [+打击] zāoshòu [+dǎjī] 3 [法官+] 同意 [fǎguān+] tóngyì
objection sustained（法庭上）反对有效（fǎtíng shàng）fǎnduì yǒuxiào

sustainable ADJ 能continued的 néng chíxù de, 能保持的 néng bǎochí de
sustainable development 叫持续性（经济）发展 kěchíxù xìng (jīngjì) fāzhǎn

sustenance N 食物 shíwù, 营养 yíngyǎng

svelte ADJ 身材修长的 shēncái xiūcháng de

swab I N 棉花球 miánhuāqiú, 药签 yàoqiān **II** v 清洗 qīngxǐ
to swab out 清洗伤口 qīngxǐ shāngkǒu

swagger I v（神气活现）大摇大摆地走（shénqi huóxiàn）dàyáo dàbǎi de zǒu **II** N 神气活现的样子 shénqi huóxiàn de yàngzi, 狂妄自大 kuángwàng zìdà

swallow¹ I v 吞咽 [+食物] tūnyàn [+shíwù], 咽 yān

to swallow up 耗尽 hàojìn, 用完 yòngwán
2 压住 [+感情] yāzhù [+gǎnqíng]
to swallow one's pride 忍受屈辱 rěnshòu qūrǔ
II N 吞咽 tūnyàn

swallow² N 燕子 yànzi [M. WD 只 zhī]

swam See **swim**

swamp I N 沼泽（地）zhǎozé (dì) **II** V **1** 淹没
yānmò **2** 使 [+人] 陷入 shǐ [+rén] xiànrù
to be swamped with problems 陷入难题之中
xiànrù nántí zhīzhōng

swan N 天鹅 tiān'é [M. WD 只 zhī]

swanky ADJ 十分时髦奢侈的 shífēn shímáo
shēchǐ de

swap I V 交换 jiāohuàn, 交易 jiāoyì
to swap stories with sb 和某人相互讲述自己
的经历 hé mǒurén xiānghù jiǎngshù zìjǐ de
jīnglì
II N 交换 jiāohuàn, 交易 jiāoyì
swap meet 旧货交易市场 jiùhuò jiāoyì shìchǎng

swarm I V **1** [昆虫+] 成群 [kūnchóng+] chéngqún
2 [人群+] 蜂拥 [rénqún+] fēngyōng, 成群结队
地移动 chéngqún jiéduì de yídòng **II** N 一群 (昆
虫／人）yìqún (kūnchóng/rén)

swarthy ADJ 皮肤黝黑的 pífū yǒuhēi de

swat V 重重地拍 zhòngzhòng de pāi, 重拍 zhòng
pāi

swatch N 布样 bùyàng

SWAT (= Special Weapons and Tactics Team)
ABBREV 特警队 tèjǐngduì

sway I V **1** （使…）摆动（shǐ…）bǎidòng **2** 影响
yǐngxiǎng, 左右 zuǒyòu
be swayed by public opinions 受舆论的影响
shòu yúlùn de yǐngxiǎng
II N **1** 摆动 bǎidòng, 摇摆 yáobǎi **2** 影响（力）
yǐngxiǎng (lì), 支配 zhīpèi

swear (PT **swore**; PP **sworn**) V **1** 骂脏话 mà
zānghuà, 诅咒 zǔzhòu
to swear like a sailor 破口大骂 pòkǒu dàmà
2 宣誓 xuānshì, 保证 bǎozhèng ■ In court
witnesses are asked to swear to tell the truth, the
whole truth and nothing but the truth. 在法庭，
证人要宣誓 "说出真相、说出全部真相、只说真
相。" Zài fǎtíng, zhèngrén yào xuānshì "Shuōchū
zhēnxiàng, shuōchū quánbù zhēnxiàng, zhǐ shuō
zhēnxiàng."
to swear sb to secrecy 要某人发誓保守秘密 yào
mǒurén fāshì bǎoshǒu mìmì

sweat I N 汗 hàn, 汗水 hànshuǐ
no sweat 一点儿也不难 yìdiǎnr yě bù nán
II V **1** 出汗 chūhàn, 流汗 liúhàn ■ The heat was
unbearable and everyone was sweating. 热得叫人
受不了，人人都在出汗。Rède jiào rén shòubuliǎo,
rénrén dōu zàichūhàn. **2** 努力工作 nǔlì gōngzuò
3 焦虑 jiāolǜ, 担心 dānxīn
to sweat blood 拼命工作 pīnmìng gōngzuò

Don't sweat the small stuff. 别为小事操心。Bié
wéi xiǎoshì cāoxīn.

sweater N 毛线衫 máoxiànshān, 套衫 tàoshān

sweatshirt N 棉毛衫 miánmáoshān [M. WD 件
jiàn], 运动衫 yùndòngshān [M. WD 件 jiàn]

sweatshop N 血汗工厂 xuèhàn gōngchǎng
[M. WD 家 jiā]

sweaty ADJ **1** 汗水湿透的 [+衣衫] hànshuǐ shītòu
de [+yīshān] **2** 使人出汗的 [+工作] shǐrén
chūhàn de [+gōngzuò], 劳累的 láolèi de

sweep I V (PT & PP **swept**) **1** 扫 sǎo, 打扫 [+房间]
dǎsǎo [+fángjiān] ■ Amy, will you please sweep
the kitchen floor? 艾米，你把厨房地板扫一扫吧。
Àimǐ, nǐ bǎ chúfáng dìbǎn sǎoyìsǎo ba. **2** [风暴+] 扫
过 [fēngbào+] sǎo guò, 掠过 lüèguò **3** [谣言+]
流行 [yáoyán+] liúxíng, 风行 fēngxíng **4** [政党+]
大获全胜 [zhèngdǎng+] dà huò quánshèng
II N 扫动 sǎo dòng, 挥动 huīdòng
to make a sweep 大面积搜查 dàmiànjī sōuchá

sweeping ADJ **1** 范围广的 fànwéi guǎng de, 影响
大的 yǐngxiǎng dà de
sweeping changes 影响深远的变化 yǐngxiǎng
shēnyuǎn de biànhuà
2 笼统的 lǒngtǒng de
sweeping generalization 一概而论 yígài ér lùn

sweepstakes N 抽奖 chōujiǎng

sweet ADJ **1** 甜 tián ■ This cake is too sweet. 这个
蛋糕太甜了。Zhè ge dàngāo tài tián le.
sweet popato 番薯 fānshǔ, 红薯 hóngshǔ
to have a sweet tooth 喜欢吃甜食 xǐhuan chī
tiánshí
2 香的 xiāng de, 芬香的 fēnxiāng de ■ A rose,
by any other name, smells just as sweet. 无论叫
什么名字，玫瑰总是芬香的。Wúlùn jiào shénme
míngzi, méiguì zǒngshì fēnxiāng de. **3** 动听的
dòngtīng de, 悦耳的 yuè'ěr de **4** 温柔的
wēnróu de

sweeten V **1** （使…）变甜（shǐ…）biàn tián **2** 使…
更有吸引力 shǐ…gèng yǒu xīyǐnlì

sweetener N **1** 甜味调料 tián wèi tiáoliào **2** 笼络
人心的东西 lǒngluò rénxīn de dōngxi

sweetheart N 甜心 tiánxīn, 亲爱的 qīn'ài de, 情
人 qíngrén

sweetie N 亲爱的 qīn'ài de, 小心肝儿 xiǎoxīngānr

sweets N 糖果 tángguǒ

swell¹ I V (PT **swelled**; PP **swollen**, **swelled**)
肿 zhǒng, 红肿 hóngzhǒng **2** [河水+] 上
涨 [héshuǐ+] shàngzhǎng **3** [数量+] 增大
[shùliàng+] zēngdà **4** 使…鼓起 shǐ…gǔqǐ
to swell with pride 得意洋洋 déyì yángyáng
II N **1** 浪涛 làngtāo, 浪涌 làngyǒng
heavy swells 大浪 dà làng
2 （音量）增强（yīnliàng）zēngqiáng **3** 膨胀
péngzhàng

swell² ADJ 棒极了 bàng jíle

swelling N 肿块 zhǒngkuài, 肿胀 zhǒngzhàng

sweltering ADJ 酷热难忍的 kùrè nánrěn de

swept See **sweep**

swerve N, v 突然转向一边 tūrán zhuǎnxiàng yì biān

swift ADJ 迅速的 xùnsù de, 立刻的 lìkè de

swig I v 大口痛饮 dà kǒu tòngyǐn II N 大口饮 dà kǒu yǐn
to take a few swigs 喝了几大口 hēle jǐ dà kǒu

swill I v 大口喝 dà kǒu hē, 痛饮 tòngyǐn II N 泔脚 饲料 gānjiǎo sìliào

swim I v 1 (PT **swam**; PP **swum**) 游泳 yóuyǒng 2（头脑）发晕 (tóunǎo) fāyūn, 眩晕 xuànyùn II N 游泳 yóuyǒng

swimming pool N 游泳池 yóuyǒngchí

swimsuit N 游泳衣 yóuyǒngyī [M. WD 件 jiàn]

swindle I v 诈骗 zhàpiàn, 骗取 piànqǔ II N 诈骗 zhàpiàn, 骗局 piànjú

swindler N 诈骗犯 zhàpiànfàn, 骗子 piànzi

swine N 1 猪 zhū [M. WD 头 tóu] 2 令人讨厌的人 lìng rén tǎoyàn de rén, 混蛋 húndàn

swing I v (PT & PP **swung**) 1（使…）摆动 (shǐ...) bǎidòng,（使…）摇摆 (shǐ...) yáobǎi 2（使…）旋转 (shǐ...) xuánzhuǎn,（使…）拐弯 (shǐ...) guǎiwān 3 [想法+] 转变 [xiǎngfǎ+] zhuǎnbiàn II N 1 秋千 qiūqiān
to play on the swings 荡秋千 dàng qiūqiān
2 挥动 huīdòng, 挥舞 huīwǔ 3 转变 zhuǎnbiàn, 改变 gǎibiàn
to be in the swing of things 全力投入 quánlì tóurù

swinging ADJ 令人兴奋的 lìngrén xīngfèn de
the swinging 60s 自由放纵的（二十世纪）六十 年代 zìyóu fàngzòng de (èrshí shìjì) liùshí niándài

swipe I v 1 猛击 měngjī 2 偷窃 tōuqiè 3 刷 [+卡] shuā [+kǎ] II N 1 猛烈抨击 měngliè pēngjī, 公开批评 gōngkāi pīpíng 2 猛击 měngjī 3 (a swipe card) 刷卡 shuān kǎ
swipe card deposits 刷卡存款 shuākǎ cúnkuǎn

Swiss I ADJ 瑞士的 Ruìshì de II N 瑞士人 Ruìshìrén

switch I v 1 改 gǎi, 改变 gǎibiàn 2 交换位置 jiāohuàn wèizhi
to switch off 关（灯／电视机／收音机）guān (dēng/diànshìjī/shōuyīnjī)
to switch on 开（灯／电视机／收音机）kāi (dēng/diànshìjī/shōuyīnjī)
II N 开关 kāiguān ■ Where is the switch? 开关在 哪里？Kāiguān zài nǎlǐ?

switchboard N 电话交换台 diànhuà jiāohuàntái
switchboard operator 交换机接线员 jiāohuàntái jiēxiànyuán

swivel I v 旋转 xuánzhuǎn II N 旋转 xuánzhuǎn
swivel chair 转椅 zhuànyǐ

swollen I v See **swell** II ADJ 1 肿起来的 zhǒng qǐlái de 2 上涨的 [+水] shàngzhǎng de [+shuǐ]

swoon v 欣喜若狂 xīnxǐ ruò kuáng

swoop v 向下猛冲 xiàngxià měngchōng

sword N 剑 jiàn [M. WD 把 bǎ], 刀 dāo [M. WD 把 bǎ]

swordfish N 剑鱼 jiànyú [M. WD 条 tiáo]

sworn I v See **swear** II ADJ (sworn enemies) 死 敌 sǐdí
sworn testimony 宣誓后作出的证词 xuānshì hòuzuò chū dízhèng cí

swum See **swim**

swung See **swing**

sycamore N 美国梧桐树 Měiguó wútóng shù, 悬 铃木 xuánlíngmù

sycophant N 拍马屁的人 pāi mǎpì de rén, 马屁 精 mǎpìjīng

syllable N 音节 yīnjié ■ "How many syllables does the word 'syllable' have?" "Three." "'Syllable' 这个词里有几个音节？" "三个。" "'Syllable' zhège cí lǐ yǒu jǐge yīnjié?" "Sān ge."

syllabus N 教学大纲 jiàoxué dàgāng

symbol N 1 象征 xiàngzhēng, 标志 biāozhì 2 符号 fúhào, 记号 jìhao

symbolic ADJ 象征性的 xiàngzhēngxìng de
a symbolic gesture 象征性姿态 xiàngzhēngxìng zītài
be symbolic of sth 是某事物的象征 shì mǒushìwù de xiàngzhēng, 象征某事物 xiàngzhēng mǒushìwù

symbolism N 象征主义 xiàngzhēngzhǔyì

symbolize v 象征（着）xiàngzhēng (zhe), 是…的 象征 shì...de xiàngzhēng

symmetric, symmetrical ADJ 对称的 duìchèn de

symmetry N 对称 duìchèn

sympathetic ADJ 1 同情的 tóngqíng de ■ We were enormously sympathetic when the tsunami hit South Asia. 当海啸袭击南亚，我们都极为同 情。Dāng hǎixiào xíjī Nányà, wǒmen dōu jíwéi tóngqíng. 2 赞同的 zàntóng de, 支持的 zhīchí de
to offer sb a sympathetic ear 同情地倾听某人诉 说 tóngqíng de qīngtíng mǒurén sùshuō

sympathize v 1（表白）同情 (biǎobái) tóngqíng, 怜悯 liánmǐn 2 赞同 zàntóng, 支持 zhīchí

sympathy N 同情 tóngqíng, 同情心 tóngqíngxīn
to play on one's sympathy 利用某人的同情心 lìyòng mǒurén de tóngqíngxīn

symphony N 交响乐 jiāoxiǎngyuè
Beethoven's symphony No 9 贝多芬的第九交响 曲 Bèiduōfēn de dì jiǔ jiāoxiǎngqǔ
symphony orchestra 交响乐团 jiāoxiǎng yuètuán

symptom N 1 症状 zhèngzhuàng 2（严重问题的）征兆 (yánzhòng wèntí de) zhèngzhào

synagogue N 犹太教堂 Yóutài jiàotáng [M. WD 座 zuò]

sync N (in sync) 同步（的）tóngbù (de), 协调（的）xiétiáo (de)

synchronization N 同步（化）tóngbù (huà)

synchronize V 使···同步 shǐ...tóngbù
to synchronize the sound track with the picture 使（电影的）声响与画面同步 shǐ (diànyǐng de) yīnxiǎng yǔ huàmiàn tóngbù
synchronized swimming 花样游泳 huāyàng yóuyǒng

syndicate N 辛迪加 xīndíjiā, 大财团 dà cáituán
banking syndicate 银行集团 yínháng jítuán

syndrome N 综合症 zōnghézhēng
Down's Syndrome 唐氏综合症 táng shì zōnghézhèng

synod N 教会领袖会议 jiàohuì lǐngxiù huìyì

synonym N 同义词 tóngyìcí, 近义词 jìnyìcí

synonymous ADJ **1** 同义的 tóngyì de, 近义的 jìnyì de **2** 相同的 xiāngtóng de, 近似的 jìnsì de

synopsis N 提要 tíyào, 梗概 gěng gài

syntax N（语法学中的）句法 (yǔfǎxué zhòng de) jùfǎ,（计算机语言的）句法规则 (jìsuànjī yǔyán de) jùfǎ guīzé, 语法 yǔfǎ

synthesis N **1** 综合（体）zōnghé (tǐ) **2** 综合 zōnghé, 合成 héchéng

synthesize V 合成 héchéng, 综合 zōnghé

synthesizer N 音响合成器 yīnxiǎng héchéngqì
speech synthesizer 言语合成器 yányǔ héchéngqì

synthetic ADJ 合成的 héchéng de, 人造的 rénzào de
synthetic material 合成材料 héchéng cáiliào

syphilis N 梅毒 méidú

syringe N **1** 注射器 zhùshèqì, 针筒 zhēntǒng **2** 洗涤器 xǐdíqì, 灌肠器 guànchángqì

syrup N 糖浆 tángjiāng

system N **1** 体系 tǐxì ■ When the air-conditioning system failed, the manager had to let his staff go home. 空调系统坏了，经理只好让职工回家。Kōngtiáo xìtǒng huài le, jīnglǐ zhǐhǎo ràng zhígōng huíjiā. **2** 制度 zhìdù

systematic ADJ 系统的 xìtǒng de, 有条理的 yǒu tiáolǐ de

T

tab I N **1** 标签 biāoqiān, 布条 bùtiáo
to keep tabs on 密切注视 mìqiè zhùshì **2** 账单 zhàngdān [M. WD 份 fèn]
to pick up the tab（代人）付账 (dài rén) fùzhàng **3**（计算机键盘）跳格键 (jìsuànjī jiànpán) tiàogéjiàn **4**（铁罐容器）拉环 (tiě guàn róngqì) lāhuán II V **1**（计算机）使用跳格键 (jìsuànjī) shǐyòng tiàogéjiàn **2** 选中 xuǎnzhòng, 选上 xuǎnshàng

tabby N 斑猫 bānmāo [M. WD 只 zhī]

tabernacle N 教堂 jiàotáng [M. WD 座 zuò], 礼拜堂 lǐbàitáng [M. WD 座 zuò]

table I N **1** 桌子 zhuōzi
table tennis 乒乓球 pīngpāngqiú
dining table 餐桌 cānzhuō
to clear the table 收掉餐具 shōudiao cānjù
to set the table（在餐桌上）摆上餐具 (zài cānzhuōshang) bǎishang cānjù
2 表格 biǎogé ■ The researcher showed population growth in a statistical table. 研究人员用统计表格显示人口增长。Yánjiū rényuán yòng tǒngjì biǎogé xiǎnshì rénkǒu zēngzhǎng.
multiplication table 乘法表 chéngfǎbiǎo, 九九表 jiǔjiǔbiǎo
table of contents 目录 mùlù
II V 搁置 gēzhì

tablecloth N 台布 táibù [M. WD 块 kuài], 桌布 zhuōbù [M. WD 块 kuài]

tablespoon N 大汤匙 dà tāngchí [M. WD 把 bǎ]

tablespoonful ADJ 满满一大汤匙的 mǎnmǎn yí dà tāngchí de

tablet N **1** 药片 yàopiàn [M. WD 片 piàn] **2** 石匾 shí biān [M. WD 块 kuài], 金属匾 jīnshǔbiān

tabloid N 通俗小报 tōngsú xiǎobào [M. WD 份 fèn]

taboo N 禁忌 jìnjì, 忌讳 jìhuì

tabular ADJ 表格的 biǎogé de

tabulate V 把 [+数字] 用表格列出 bǎ [+shùzì] yòng biǎogé lièchū

tabulation N 制表格 zhìbiǎo gé

tacit ADJ 心照不宣的 xīnzhào bù xuān de, 有默契的 yǒu mòqì de
tacit agreement 默契 mòqì

taciturn ADJ 沉默寡言的 chénmò guǎyán de

tack¹ I N **1** 图钉 túdīng **2** 平头钉 píngtóudīng **3** 方法 fāngfǎ, 思路 sīlù II V 用图钉/平头钉把···钉住 yòng túdīng/píngtóudīng bǎ...dìngzhù

tack² I N **1**（帆船的）航行方向 (fānchuán de) hángxíng fāngxiàng **2**（帆船）改变航行方向 (fānchuán) gǎibiàn hángxíng fāngxiàng II V [帆船+] 改变航行方向 [fānchuán+] gǎibiàn hángxíng fāngxiàng

tackle I V **1** 处理 chǔlǐ, 对付 duìfu **2** [橄榄球+] 阻挡 [gǎnlǎnqiú+] zǔdǎng, 抱截 bàojié II N **1**（橄榄球中的）阻挡 (gǎnlǎnqiú zhòng de) zǔdǎng, 抱截 bàojié **2** 运动器具 yùndòng qìjù, 钓具 diàojù

tacky ADJ **1** 俗气的 súqi de, 不雅的 bù yǎ de **2** 有点粘糊糊的 yǒudiǎn niányhūhū de

tact N 机敏圆滑 jīmǐn yuánhuá, 待人的技巧 dàirén de jìqiǎo

tactful ADJ 讲究策略的 jiǎngjiu cèlüè de, 得体的 détǐ de ■ David was tactful enough not to say anything on the issue. 戴维很讲究策略，他在这个问题上一言不发。Dàiwéi hěn jiǎngjiu cèlüè, tā zài zhè ge wèntíshang yì yán bù fā.

tactic N 手法 shǒufǎ, 策略 cèlüè

tactical ADJ **1** 策略(上)的 cèlüè (shàng) de **2** 战术(性)的 zhànshù (xìng) de

tactical retreat 战术性撤退 zhànshùxìng chètuì

tactics N 战术谋略 zhànshù móulüè

delaying tactics 拖延战术 tuōyán zhànshù

tadpole N 蝌蚪 kēdǒu

taffy N 太妃糖 tàifēitáng [M. WD 块 kuài], 乳脂糖 rǔzhītáng [M. WD 块 kuài]

tag¹ I N **1** 标签 biāoqiān

name tag 姓名标签 xìngmíng biāoqiān

price tag 价格标签 jiàgé biāoqiān

2 (错误的) 称呼 (cuòwù de) chēnghu **3** (绳子／鞋带的) 金属包头 (shéngzi/xiédài de) jīnshǔ bāotóu II v **1** 给…贴上标签 gěi... tiēshang biāoqiān **2** 给 [+人] 取绰号 gěi [+rén] qǔ chuòhào, 把 [+人] 看成 bǎ [+rén] kànchéng

be tagged as a cheat 被看成是骗子 bèi kànchéng shì piànzi

tag² I N 抓人游戏 zhuārén yóuxì II v (在游戏中) 抓到 [+人] (zài yóuxì zhōng) zhuā dào [+rén]

tail I N **1** 尾巴 wěiba **2** 结尾部分 jiéwěi bùfen ■ *I did not understand the lecture until the tail end.* 我直到结尾部分才听懂了讲座。Wǒ zhídào jiéwěi bùfen cái tīngdǒngle jiǎngzuò. II v 跟踪 gēnzōng ■ *The actress sensed someone was tailing her.* 女演员感觉到有人在跟踪她。Nǚ yǎnyuán gǎnjuédao yǒu rén zài gēnzōng tā.

to tail off 变小／变弱直至消失 biàn xiǎo/biàn ruò zhízhì xiāoshī

tailcoat N 燕尾服 yànwěifú [M. WD 件 jiàn]

tailgate I v [驾车人+] 开车紧盯着前面的车 [jiàchērén+] kāichē jǐndīngzhe qiánmian de chē II N (汽车的) 后门 (qìchē de) hòumén

taillight N (汽车) 尾灯 (qìchē) wěidēng

tailor N 裁缝 cáifeng, 裁缝师傅 cáifeng shīfu

tailoring N 裁缝手艺 cáifeng shǒuyì, 裁缝业 cáifengyè

tailor-made ADJ **1** 裁缝特制的 [+服装] cáifeng tèzhì de [+fúzhuāng] **2** 量体定做的 liáng tǐ dìngzuò de, 正合适的 zhèng héshì de

tailpipe N (汽车) 排气管 (qìchē) páiqìguǎn

tails N See tailcoat

tailspin N 失控状态 shīkòng zhuàngtài

to send ... into a tailspin 使…陷入失控状态 shǐ...xiànrù shīkòng zhuàngtài

taint v **1** 沾污 [+名声] zhānwū [+míngshēng], 败坏 bàihuài

tainted money 不干净的钱 bù gānjìng de qián **2** 在食品中添加有毒物质 zài shípǐn zhōng tiānjiā yǒudú wùzhì

tainted milk powder (有) 毒奶粉 (yǒu) dú nǎifěn

Taiwanese I ADJ 台湾的 Táiwān de, 台湾人的 Táiwānrén de II N 台湾人 Táiwānrén

take I v (PT **took**; PP **taken**) **1** 带 dài, 送 sòng **2** 拿 ná, 握 wò ■ *He took the school report from his son and began to read it.* 他从儿子手上拿来成绩报告单, 看起来。Tā cóng érzi shǒushang nálai chéngjì bàogàodān, kànqilai. **3** 带走 dàizǒu, 拿走 názǒu ■ *The burglar took almost everything valuable from their home.* 撬窃贼几乎把家中值钱的东西都拿走了。Qiàoqièzéi jīhū bǎ jiā zhōng zhíqián de dōngxi dōu názǒu le. **4** 花费 huāfèi ■ *It took the search team two days to find the missing tourist.* 搜索队花了两天找到了失踪的旅游者。Sōusuǒduì huāle liǎng tiān zhǎodaole shīzōng de lǚyóuzhě. **5** 接受 jiēshòu, 领取 lǐngqǔ **6** 承受 chéngshòu ■ *She couldn't take the loss of their only child.* 她无法承受失去独生子的现实。Tā wúfǎ chéngshòu shīqu dúshēngzǐ de xiànshí.

to take after (跟父亲或母亲) 很象 (gēn fùqin huò mǔqin) hěn xiàng

to take it for granted 认为理所当然而不重视 rènwéi lǐ suǒ dāngrán ér bú zhòngshì, 不以为然 bù yǐ wéi rán ■ *Some children just take their parents for granted.* 有些孩子认为父母就是应该对他们好的。Yǒuxiē háizi rènwéi fùmǔ jiùshì yīnggāi duì tāmen hǎo de.

to take off (飞机) 起飞 (fēijī) qǐfēi

to take ... out on 拿…出气 ná...chūqì ■ *Why are you taking it out on the poor dog?* 你干吗拿可怜的狗出气？Nǐ gànmá ná kělián de gǒu chūqì?

to take to 马上产生好感 mǎshàng chǎnshēng hǎo gǎn

to take up 开始 (工作、从事) kāishǐ (gōngzuò, cóngshì) ■ *The new finance director will take up her duties next month.* 新财务主任将在下个月开始工作。Xīn cáiwù zhǔrèn jiāng zài xià ge yuè kāishǐ gōngzuò.

II N **1** 营业额 yíngyè'é, 进账 jìnzhàng **2** 看法 kànfǎ, 观点 guāndiǎn **3** 拍摄 (电影／电视镜头) pāishè (diànyǐng/diànshì jìngtóu)

take-home pay N 实发工资 shí fā gōngzī, 净薪 jìngxīn

taken See take

takeoff N **1** (飞机) 起飞 (fēijī) qǐfēi, 升空 shēngkōng **2** 滑稽模仿 huájī mófǎng

take-out N 外卖食品 wàimài shípǐn

takeover N (公司的) 购股兼并 (gōngsī de) gòugǔ jiānbìng, 接管 jiēguǎn

talcum powder N 滑石粉 huáshífěn

tale N 故事 gùshi ■ *Fairy tales are appealing even to adults.* 童话故事即使对成人也有吸引力。Tónghuà gùshi jíshǐ duì chéngrén yě yǒu xīyǐnlì. **2** (可能是编造的) 经历 (kěnéng shì biānzào de) jīnglì

talent N **1** 特殊才能 tèshū cáinéng, 天才 tiāncái **2** 有特殊才能的人 yǒu tèshū cáinéng de rén, 天才 tiāncái ■ *The coach has a keen eye for* talented

spotting talent. 这位教练有眼光发现天才。Zhè wèi jiàoliàn yǒu yǎnguāng fāxiàn tiāncái.

talented ADJ 才能出众的 cáinéng chūzhòng de, 有天赋的 yǒu tiānfù de

talisman N 护身符 hùshēnfú, 辟邪物 bìxié wù

talk I v 1 谈话 tánhuà, 讲话 jiǎnghuà ■ *Jim, we need to talk.* 杰姆，我们得谈谈。Jiémǔ, wǒmen děi tántan. 2 谈论 tánlùn ■ *People have begun to talk about the CEO's affair with his secretary.* 人们开始谈论总经理和秘书的婚外情。Rénmen kāishǐ tánlùn zǒngjīnglǐ hé mìshū de hūnwàiqíng.

to talk down to sb 居高临下地对…谈话 jūgāo línxià de duì...tánhuà ■ *Some voters felt they were being talked down to by the candidate.* 一些选民觉得候选人居高临下地对他们说话。Yìxiē xuǎnmín juéde hòuxuǎnrén jūgāo línxià de duì tāmen shuōhuà.

to talk ... into 说服…做 shuōfú...zuò

to talk ... out of 说服…不做 shuōfú...bú zuò ■ *I tried to talk her out of buying that necklace.* 我试图说服她别买那条项链。Wǒ shìtú shuōfú tā bié mǎi nà tiáo xiàngliàn.

to talk over 讨论 tǎolùn, 商量 shāngliang

II N 1 谈话 tánhuà ■ *He had a long talk with his son about his plan after graduating from high school.* 他和儿子关于中学毕业后的打算长谈了一次。Tā he érzi guānyú zhōngxué bìyè hòu de dǎsuan chángtánle yí cì.

talk show（电视／广播的）访谈节目 (diànshì/guǎngbō de) fǎngtán jiémù

2 会谈 huìtán, 交谈 jiāotán 3 谣传 yáochuán

talkative ADJ 喜欢说话的 xǐhuan shuōhuà de, 多嘴的 duōzuǐ de

talking book N 有声读物 yǒushēng dúwù

talks N 正式会谈 zhèngshì huìtán, 谈判 tánpàn

tall ADJ 高 gāo

a tall order 很难办到的事 hěn nán bàndao de shì ■ *That's a tall order. I'm not sure if I can do it.* 这件事很难办到，我不肯定能不能办到。Zhè jiàn shì hěn nán bàndao, wǒ bù kěndìng néngbunéng bàndao.

tally I N 1 账目 zhàngmù [M. WD 本 běn], 流水帐 liúshuǐzhàng [M. WD 本 běn] 2（体育比赛）记分 (tǐyù bǐsài) jìfēn

to keep a tally 记录 jìlù

II v 1 计算 [+得分／得票数] jìsuàn [+défēn/dépiàoshù] 2 与…一致 yǔ...yízhì, 相符合 xiāngfú hé

talon N（鸟的）利爪 (niǎo de) lìzhuǎ

tambourine N 铃鼓 língqǔ, 手鼓 shǒugǔ

tame I ADJ 1 驯服的 xùnfú de, 温顺的 wēnshùn de 2 平淡无味的 píngdàn wú wèi de II v 1 驯服 xùnfú, 驯化 xùnhuà 2 制服 zhìfú, 抑制 yìzhì

tamper v (to tamper with) 瞎摆弄 xiā bǎinòng,（擅自）改动 (shànzì) gǎidòng

tampon N 月经棉塞 yuèjīng miánsāi

tan I ADJ 1 晒黑的 [+皮肤] shàihēi de [+pífū] 2 棕黄色的 zōnghuáng sè de II N 1（太阳晒的）棕褐肤色 (tàiyáng shài de) zōng hè fūsè 2 棕黄色 zōnghuáng sè III v 晒黑 [+皮肤] shàihēi [+pífū]

tandem N 1 双人脚踏车 shuāngrén jiǎotàchē 2（两人）协同工作 (liǎng rén) xiétóng gōngzuò

in tandem with 同时 tóngshí, 同期 tóngqī

tang N 强烈的味道／气味 qiángliè de wèidao/qìwèi

tangent N（几何）切线 (jǐhé) qiēxiàn, 正切 zhèngqiē

to go off on a tangent 突然改变话题／做法 tūrán gǎibiàn huàtí/zuòfǎ

tangerine N 橘子 júzi, 红橘 hóngjú

tangible N 1 有形的 yǒuxíng de, 可触摸到的 kě chùmō dào de

tangible asset 有形资产 yǒuxíngzīchǎn

2 确实的 quèshí de

tangible proof 确实的证据 quèshí de zhèngjù

tangle I N 1 乱线团 luàn xiàntuán, 乱成一团的头发 luànchéng yì tuán de tóufa 2 纷乱 fēnluàn, 混乱 hùnluàn

to get into a tangle 搞得一团糟 gǎode yìtuánzāo

II v 1 扭打 niǔdǎ, 打架 dǎjià 2（使…）乱成一团 (shǐ...) luànchéng yìtuán

tangled, tangled up ADJ 1 缠绕在一起的 [+电线] chánráo zài yìqǐ de [+diànxiàn] 2 纷乱复杂的 [+局势] fēnluàn fùzá de [+júshì]

tango I N 探戈舞（曲）tàngēwǔ (qū) II v 跳探戈舞 tiào tàngēwǔ ■ *It takes two to tango.* 一个巴掌拍不响。Yí ge bāzhang pāibuxiǎng.

tank N 1（水／油）箱 (shuǐ/yóu) xiāng 2 坦克（车）tǎnkè (chē) [M. WD 辆 liàng] ■ *The tank was a formidable weapon in World War I.* 坦克在第一次世界大战时是可怕的武器。Tǎnkè zài Dìyī cì Shìjiè Dàzhàn shí shì kěpà de wǔqì.

tankard N 大金属酒杯 dà jīnshǔ jiǔbēi

tanker N 油轮 yóulún [M. WD 艘 sōu], 油罐车 yóuguànchē [M. WD 辆 liàng]

tantalizing ADJ 诱人的 yòurén de, 逗引人的 dòuyǐn rén de

tantamount ADJ (be tantamount to) 相当于 xiāngdāngyú

tantrum N 突发脾气 tūfā píqi

to throw a tantrum [无缘无故地+] 大发脾气 [wúyuán wúgù de+] dà fā píqi

Taoism N 道家 Dàojiā, 道教 Dàojiào

tap¹ I N 1（水）龙头 (shuǐ) lóngtóu

tap water 自来水 zìláishuǐ

on tap 取自酒桶的 [+啤酒] qǔzì jiǔtǒng de [+píjiǔ], 现成的 xiànchéng de

2 电话窃听器 diànhuà qiètīngqì II v 1 窃听

(电话) qiètīng (diànhuà) **2** 从酒桶取酒 cóng jiǔtǒng qǔ jiǔ **3** 利用 lìyòng, 开发 kāifā

tap² I v 轻轻地敲击 qīngqīng de qiāojī
tap dancing 踢踏舞 tītàwǔ
II N 轻踏 qīng tà, 轻拍 qīng pāi, 轻叩 qīng kòu
tap on the shoulder 拍一下肩膀 pāi yíxià jiānbǎng

tape I N **1** 磁带 cídài, 录音带 lùyīndài [M. WD 盘 pán], 录像带 lùxiàngdài [M. WD 盘 pán]
tape recorder 磁带录音机 cídài lùyīnjī
2 胶带 jiāodài ■ *She sealed the envelope with tape.* 她用胶带封上信封。Tā yòng jiāodài fēngshang xìnfēng.
tape measure 卷尺 juǎnchǐ, 软尺 ruǎnchǐ
II v **1** 录音 lùyīn, 录像 lùxiàng ■ *The suspect's confession was taped at the police station.* 嫌疑犯的口供都在警察局录下来了。Xiányífàn de kǒugòng dōu zài jǐngchájú lùxialai le.
blank tape 空白磁带 kòngbái cídài
red tape 繁琐的公事程序 fánsuǒ de gōngshì chéngxù
2 (用胶带) 扎起来 (yòng jiāodài) zhā qǐlái

taper I N 细长的蜡烛 xìcháng de làzhú [M. WD 根 gēn] II v **1** 渐渐变细 jiànjiàn biàn xì **2** 渐渐终止 jiànjiàn zhōngzhǐ
tapering fingers 尖尖的手指 jiān cháng de shǒuzhǐ

tapestry N 挂毯 guàtǎn [M. WD 块 kuài], 壁毯 bìtǎn [M. WD 块 kuài]

tapeworm N 绦虫 tāochóng

tar I N **1** 柏油 bǎiyóu, 沥青 lìqīng **2** (烟草中的) 焦油 (yāncǎo zhōngde) jiāoyóu II v 用沥青铺路 yòng lìqīng pūlù

tardy ADJ 缓慢的 huǎnmàn de, 迟缓的 chíhuǎn de

target I N 目标 mùbiāo ■ *Any place, from a vegetable market to army barracks, could be the target of terrorist attacks.* 任何地方，从菜市场到军营，都可能是恐怖分子攻击的目标。Rènhé dìfang, cóng càishìchǎng dào jūnyíng, dōu kěnéng shì kǒngbùfènzǐ gōngjī de mùbiāo. **2** 对象 duìxiàng **3** 指标 zhǐbiāo II v 以…为目标 yǐ…wéi mùbiāo ■ *Commercials for toys are shamelessly targeting small children.* 玩具广告公然以小孩子为目标。Wánjù guǎnggào gōngrán yǐ xiǎoháizi wéi mùbiāo.

tariff N **1** 关税 guānshuì **2** 收费表 shōufèibiāo **3** 价目表 jiàmùbiāo

tarmac N (机场) 跑道 (jīchǎng) pǎodào [M. WD 条 tiáo]

tarnish v **1** 沾污 [+名誉] zhānwū [+míngyù], 使 [+名声] 蒙羞 shǐ [+míngshēng] méngxiū
tarnished honor 蒙上污点的荣耀 méngshàng wūdiǎn de róngyào
2 使 [+金属] 失去光泽 shǐ [+jīnshǔ] shīqù guāngzé

taro N 芋头 yùtou

tarp, tarpaulin N 防水 (帆) 布 fángshuǐ (fān) bù

tart I ADJ **1** 微酸的 [+味道] wēi suān de [+wèidao] **2** 尖刻的 [+回答] jiānkè de [+huídá] II N **1** 水果馅饼 shuǐguǒ xiànbǐng **2** 荡妇 dàngfù

tartan N (苏格兰) 格子花呢 (图案) (Sūgélán) gézihuāní (tú'àn)

tartar N 牙垢 yágòu, 牙石 yáshí

task N 任务 rènwu ■ *To raise $250,000 for renovating our gym is no easy task.* 要募款二十五万来修缮体育馆，可不是容易的事。Yào mùkuǎn èrshíwǔwàn lái xiūshàn tǐyùguǎn, kě bú shì róngyì de shì.
to take … to task 指责 zhǐzé, 责备 zébèi

task force N 特遣部队 tèqiǎn bùduì, 特别行动队 tèbié xíngdòngduì

tassel N 流苏 liúsū, 缨 yīng

taste I N **1** 味道 wèidao ■ *I don't like the taste of this cheese.* 我不喜欢这种奶酪的味道。Wǒ bù xǐhuan zhè zhǒng nǎilào de wèidao. **2** 尝试 chángshì ■ *She had a taste of the wine and found it very good.* 她尝了一口酒，觉得好极了。Tā chángle yì kǒu jiǔ, juéde hǎo jíle. **3** 口味 kǒuwèi II v **1** 尝出 (味道) chángchū (wèidao) **2** 有…的味道 yǒu…de wèidao ■ *Dishes in a Shanghai restaurant may taste a bit too sweet for you.* 上海菜馆的菜对你来说可能太甜了一点。Shànghǎi càiguǎn de cài duì nǐ láishuō kěnéng tài tián le yìdiǎn.
in good taste 得体 détǐ, 优雅 yōuyǎ ■ *The commercials for this company are usually in good taste.* 这家公司做的广告一般很得体。Zhè jiā gōngsī zuò de guǎnggào yìbān hěn détǐ.
in bad taste 粗俗 cūsú

tasteful ADJ (品味) 高雅的 (pǐnwèi) gāoyǎ de

tasteless ADJ **1** 没有味道的 [+食物] méiyǒu wèidao de [+shíwù] **2** 格调低的 [+电视节目] gédiào dī de [+diànshì jiémù], 无聊的 wúliáo de

taster N 试味专家 shì wèi zhuānjiā
wine taster 品酒师 pǐnjiǔshī

tasty ADJ 美味可口的 měiwèi kěkǒu de

tattered ADJ 破烂的 [+衣服] pòlàn de [+yīfu]

tatters N 破烂衣服 pòlàn yīfu
in tatters ① [穿得+] 破破烂烂 [chuān dé+] pòpòlànlàn ② 问题百出的 [+计划] wèntí bǎichū de [+jìhuà]

tattle v [小孩+] 向父母 / 老师告状 [xiǎohái+] xiàng fùmǔ/lǎoshī gàozhuàng, 打小报告 dǎ xiǎobàogào

tattletale N 打小报告的人 dǎ xiǎobàogào de rén, 搬弄是非者 bānnòngshìfēi zhě

tattoo¹ I N 纹身 wénshēn, 刺青 cìqīng
tattoo artist 纹身师 wénshēnshī
II v 刺花纹 cì huāwén, 纹身 wén shēn

tattoo² N 连续击鼓 liánxù jīgǔ, (英国) 军乐表演 (Yīngguó) jūnyuè biǎoyǎn taught

taught See **teach**

taunt N, V 嘲弄 cháonòng, 嘲笑 cháoxiào

Taurus N 金牛宫 jīnniúgōng

taut ADJ **1** 拉紧的 [+绳子] lājǐn de [+shéngzi], 绷紧的 bēngjǐn de **2** 忧愁的 [+表情] yōuchóu de [+biǎoqíng]

tavern N 酒馆 jiǔguǎn [M. WD 家 jiā]

tawdry ADJ **1** 不值钱的 [+货物] bù zhíqián de [+huòwù], 廉价的 liánjià de **2** 无耻的 [+行为] wúchǐ de [+xíngwéi]

tawny ADJ 黄褐色的 huánghèsè de

tax I N 税 shuì, 税收 shuìshōu ■ *Why is the agency for collecting taxes called Internal Revenue Service?* 为什么收税的机构叫做 "国内收入服务"？ Wèishénme shōushuì de jīgòu jiàozuo "Guónèi Shōurù Fúwù"? II V **1** 征税 zhēngshuì, 收税 shōushuì ■ *In that country, income above 100,000 dollars is taxed at 45%.* 在那个国家，十万元以上的收入要收税百分之四十五。Zài nà ge guójiā, shíwànyuán yǐshàng de shōurù yào shōushuì bǎifēnzhī sìshíwǔ. **2** 耗尽 hàojìn ■ *The three overnight fires taxed the resources of the fire brigade.* 夜间的三场火灾耗尽了消防队的人力物力。Yèjiān de sān cháng huǒzāi hàojìnle xiāofángduì de rénlì wùlì.

tax break 减税优惠 jiǎn shuì yōuhuì

tax cut 减税 jiǎn shuì

tax dodge（合法或非法的）避税 (héfǎ huò fēifǎ de) bì shuì

tax evasion（非法）逃税 (fēifǎ) táo shuì

tax haven 避税天堂 bìshuì tiāntáng

tax return 报税单 bàoshuìdān

tax year 税务年度 shuìwù niándù

income tax 个人所得税 gèrén suǒdéshuì

taxation N 税收 shuìshōu, 征税 zhēngshuì

tax-exempt ADJ 免税的 miǎnshuì de

taxi[1] N 出租汽车 chūzū qìchē

taxi driver 出租汽车司机 chūzū qìchē sījī

taxi stand 出租汽车候客地 chūzū qìchē hòukèdì

taxi[2] V [飞机+] 滑行 [fēijī+] huáxíng

taxidermy N 动物标本制作（术）dòngwù biāoběn zhìzuò (shù)

taxiway N（跑道）滑行道 (pǎodào) huáxíng dào

taxpayer N 纳税人 nàshuìrén

tea N 茶 chá ■ *"What is your favorite kind of tea?" "Oolong."* "你最喜欢哪一种茶？" "乌龙茶。" *"Nǐ zuìxǐhuan nǎ yì zhǒng chá?" "Wūlóngchá."*

tea bag 茶袋 chádài

tea party 茶（话）会 chá (huà) huì

black tea 红茶 hóngchá

green tea 绿茶 lǜchá

jasmine tea 茉莉花茶 mòlì huāchá, 花茶 huāchá

teach (PT & PP **taught**) V **1** 教 jiāo, 教会 jiāohuì **2** 教训 jiàoxun

to teach … a lesson 给……一个教训 gěi…yí ge jiàoxun ■ *"Mom, the dog snapped at me when I pulled on its tail." "That should teach you a lesson."* "妈，我拉狗的尾巴，狗就要咬我。" "这应该给你一个教训。" *"Mā, wǒ lā gǒu de wěiba, gǒu jiù yào yǎo wǒ." "Zhè yīnggāi gěi nǐ yí ge jiàoxun.*

teaching N 教学（工作）jiàoxué (gōngzuò)

student teaching 教学实习 jiàoxué shíxí

teacup N 茶杯 chábēi

teak N 柚木 yóumù

tea leaf N 茶叶 cháyè [M. WD 片 piàn]

team N **1** 队 duì, 团队 tuánduì ■ *Mack has been selected for the school basketball team.* 马克被选为学校篮球队队员了。Mǎkè bèi xuǎnwéi xuéxiào lánqiúduì duìyuán le.

team player 善于与人合作者 shànyú yǔ rén hézuò zhě, 好伙伴 hǎo huǒbàn

team spirit 团队精神 tuánduì jīngshén **2** 组 zǔ II V (to team up with) 与…结成一队 yǔ… jiéchéng yíduì, 与…合作 yǔ…hézuò

teammate N 队友 duìyǒu

teamwork N 合作（精神）hézuò (jīngshén), 协作（能力）xiézuò (nénglì)

teapot N 茶壶 cháhú [M. WD 把 bǎ]

tear[1] N 眼泪 yǎnlèi ■ *Her face was covered with tears when her Barbie doll lost an arm.* 芭比娃娃的手臂断了，她哭得满脸泪痕。Bābǐ wáwa de shǒubì duàn le, tā kūde mǎnliǎn lèihén.

in tears 在哭 zài kū

to burst into tears 放声大哭 fàngshēng dàkū

to shed tears 流泪 liúlèi

tear[2] I V (PT **tore**; PP **torn**) 撕 sī, 撕开 sīkai

can't tear oneself away 舍不得离开 shěbudé líkāi II N [衣服上的+] 破洞 [yīfu shàng de+] pòdòng

tease I V **1** 逗弄 dòunong, 取笑 qǔxiào **2** 戏弄 xìnòng, 惹怒 rěnù II N **1** 逗弄 dòunong, 戏弄 xìnòng **2** 喜欢逗弄的人 xǐhuan dòunong de rén **3** 性挑逗者 xìng tiǎodòu zhě, 风骚女人 fēngsāo nǚrén

teaspoon N 茶匙 cháchí [M. WD 把 bǎ], 小调羹 xiǎo tiáogēng [M. WD 把 bǎ]

teat N（动物的）奶头 (dòngwù de) nǎitou

technical ADJ **1** 技术的 jìshù de ■ *He has had high-level technical training and is well qualified for the job.* 他受到过高级技术训练，担任这个工作完全合格。Tā shòudaoguo gāojí jìshù xùnliàn, dānrèn zhè ge gōngzuò wánquán hégé. **2** 很专业的 hěn zhuānyè de

technicality N 技术细节 jìshù xìjié, 程序细节 chéngxù xìjié

to release somebody on a technicality 出于程序细节的原因而释放某人 chūyú chéngxù xìjié de yuányīn ér shìfàng mǒurén

technically ADV **1** 从技术/程序细节上说 cóng jìshù/chéngxù xìjié shàng shuō **2** 技巧上的 jìqiǎo shàng de

technician N 技术员 jìshùyuán, 技师 jìshī
  computer technician 电脑技术员 diànnǎo
  jìshùyuán

technique N 技巧 jìqiǎo, 技能 jìnéng
  standard sales techniques 标准的销售技巧
  biāozhǔn de xiāoshòu jìqiǎo

technologically ADV 从技术上说 chong jìshù
  shang shuō

technologist N 技术专家 jìshù zhuānjiā

technology N 技术 jìshù, 科技 kējì
  a sophisticated digital technology 尖端的数码
  技术 jiānduān de shùmǎ jìshù

teddy bear N 玩具熊 wánjùxióng

tedious ADJ 冗长的 rǒngcháng de, 沉闷的 chénmèn de

tedium N 冗长 rǒngcháng, 沉闷 chénmèn

tee N（高尔夫球）发球区域 (gāo'ěrfūqiú) fāqiú
  qūyù

tee shirt N See **T-shirt**

teem V 到处都是 dàochù dōu shì, 充满 chōngmǎn
  a pond teeming with fish 有很多鱼的池塘 yǒu
  hěnduō yú de chítáng

teen N See **teenager**

teenage ADJ 青少年的 qīngshàonián de
  teenage mother 少女母亲 shàonǔ mǔqin
  teenage problem 青少年问题 qīngshàonián
  wèntí

teenager N 青少年 qīngshàonián

teens N 青少年时期 qīng shàonián shíqī, 十几岁
  的年龄 shí jǐ suì de niánlíng

teeter V 站立不稳 zhànlì bùwěn, 摇摇欲坠
  yáoyáo yù zhuì
  to be teething on the brink of 处在…的边缘
  chǔzài…de biānyuán

teethe V [婴儿+] 长乳牙 [yīng'ér+] zhǎng rǔyá

teetotaler N 不喝酒的人 bù hējiǔ de rén

telecommunications N 电信 diànxìn

telecommuter N 在家上班者 zài jiā shàngbān-
  zhě, 远距离工作者 yuǎnjùlí gōngzuòzhě

teleconference N 电话会议 diànhuà huìyì

telegram N 电报 diànbào, 电文 diànwén

telegraph N（老式）电报 (lǎoshì) diànbào, 电报
  机 diànbàojī

telepathy N 心灵感应（术）xīnlíng gǎnyìng (shù),
  遥感 yáogǎn

telephone I N 电话（机）diànhuà (jī)
  telephone directory/book 电话簿 diànhuà bù
  cordless telephone 无线电话 wúxiàn diànhuà
  international telephone call 国际长途电话 guójì
  chángtú diànhuà
  to make/return a telephone call 打/回电话 dǎ/
  huí diànhuà
  II V 打电话给 dǎ diànhuà gěi

telephoto lens N 长焦距镜头 chángjiāojù
  jìngtóu, 远摄镜头 yuǎnshè jìngtóu

telescope I N 望远镜 wàngyuǎnjìng II V 1（象望
  远镜一样）伸缩 (xiàng wàngyuǎnjìng yíyàng)
  shēnsuō 2 缩短 suōduǎn

telethon N 马拉松式电视募捐节目 mǎlāsōngshì
  diànshì mùjuān jiémù

televise V 在电视上播放 zài diànshìshàng bōfàng

television, TV I N 电视（机）diànshì (jī) ■ *Hundreds of millions of people watched the opening
  ceremony of the Olympics on live television.* 几亿
  观众观看奥林匹克运动会开幕式电视实况转播。Jǐ
  yì guānzhòng guānkàn Àolínpǐkè Yùndònghuì
  kāimùshì diànshì shíkuàng zhuǎnbō.
  television program 电视节目 diànshì jiémù
  television producer 电视节目制作 diànshì jiémù
  zhìzuòrén
  digital television 数码电视 shùmǎ diànshì

telex N 打字电报 dàzidiànbào, 电传 diànchuán

tell (PT & PP **told**) V 1 告诉 gàosu 2 讲 jiǎng,
  讲述 jiǎngshù ■ *On the long journey to Yellow
  Stone, we told each other stories and jokes to
  kill time.* 在开往黄石公园的漫长旅途中，我们彼此
  讲故事、讲笑话，消磨时间。Zài kāiwǎng Huángshí Gōngyuán de màncháng lǚtú zhōng, wǒmen
  bǐcǐ jiǎng gùshi, jiǎng xiàohua, xiāomó shíjiān.
  3 吐露 tǔlù, 泄密 xièmì 4 判断 pànduàn ■ *I
  can't tell whether their offer to cooperate is
  sincere or not.* 我无法判断，他们提出合作是不
  是真心。Wǒ wú fǎ pànduàn, tāmen tíchū hézuò
  shìbushì zhēnxīn.
  to tell … from … 分辨 fēnbiàn, 区分 qūfēn
  to tell off 责骂 zémà ■ *The boy got told off for
  not doing his share of household chores.* 男孩因为
  不做份内的家务活而受到责骂。Nánhái yīnwèi bú
  zuò fènnèi de jiāwùhuó ér shòudao zémà.
  to tell on 告发 gàofā ■ *Marianne caught her
  brother visiting porn sites and told on him.* 玛丽安
  抓到弟弟在看色情网站，就告发了。Mǎlī'ān zhuā-
  dao dìdi zàikàn sèqíng wǎngzhàn, jiù gàofā le.
  to tell the truth 说真的 shuō zhēn de ■ *To tell
  the truth, I never liked him very much.* 说真的，
  我从来没有喜欢过他。Shuō zhēn de, wǒ cónglái
  méiyǒu xǐhuanguo tā.

teller N 出纳（员）chūnà (yuán)

telling ADJ 有力的 yǒulì de, 意义重大的 yìyì
  zhòngdà de

telling-off N 责骂 zémà, 训斥 xùnchì

telltale ADJ 泄露秘密的 xièlòu mìmì de, 露馅的
  lòu xiàn de

temp I N 临时雇员 línshí gùyuán, 临时工作 línshí
  gōngzuò II V 当临时雇员 dāng línshí gùyuán

temper I N 1 坏脾气 huài píqi ■ *You really need to
  learn to control your temper.* 你真应该学会控制自
  己的坏脾气。Nǐ zhēn yīnggāi xuéhuì kòngzhì zìjǐ
  de huài píqi. 2 恶劣心情 èliè xīnqíng
  to have a hot temper 脾气暴躁 píqi bàozào

to keep one's temper 忍住不发脾气 rěnzhù bù fā píqì ■ He struggled to keep his temper. 他极力忍住不发脾气。 Tā jílì rěnzhù bù fā píqì.

to lose one's temper 发脾气 fā píqì

temperament N 气质 qìzhì, 性情 xìngqíng sanguine temperament 热情乐观的气质 rèqíng lèguān de qìzhì

temperamental ADJ **1** 喜怒无常的 [+人] xǐnù wúcháng de [+rén] **2** 性能不稳定的 [+机器] xìngnéng bù wěndìng de [+jīqì]

temperance N **1** 禁酒 jìnjiǔ, 戒酒 jièjiǔ **2** 自己克制 zìjǐ kèzhì

temperate ADJ **1** 有节制的 yǒu jiézhì de **2** 温和的 wēnhé de
temperate climate 温带气候 wēndài qìhòu
temperate zone 温带 wēndài

temperature N **1** 气温 qìwēn, 温度 wēndù ■ Scientists warn that if the temperature rises by 5°C, the earth will reach the tipping point. 科学家们警告，如果气温上升摄氏五度，地球就到达倾斜点。 Kēxuéjiāmen jǐnggào, rúguǒ qìwēn shàngshēng Shèshì wǔ dù, dìqiú jiù dàodá qīngxiédiǎn.
constant temperature 恒温 héngwēn **2** 体温 tǐwēn, 温度 wēndù ■ Normal body temperature is 37°C. 正常体温是摄氏三十七度。 Zhèngcháng tǐwēn shì Shèshì sānshíqī dù.
to have a temperature 发烧 fāshāo
to take one's temperature 量体温 liáng tǐwēn

tempest N 暴风雨 bàofēngyǔ
a tempest in a teacup 茶壶里的风暴 cháhú lǐ de fēngbào, 小题大作 xiǎo tí dàzuò

tempestuous ADJ **1** 暴风雨般的 [+时代] bàofēngyǔ bān de [+shídài] **2** 风暴骤起的 [+关系] fēngbào diéqǐ de [+guānxi], 大起大落的 dàqǐ dàluò de

template N （计算机文件编写的）模板 (jìsuànjī wénjiàn biānxiě de) múbǎn

temple¹ N 庙（宇）miào (yǔ)

temple² N 太阳穴 tàiyángxué

temporary ADJ 暂时的 zànshí de, 临时的 línshí de

tempt v 引诱 yǐnyòu, 吸引 xīyǐn
to tempt fate 冒生命危险 mào shēngmìng wēixiǎn, 玩命 wánmìng

temptation N **1** 诱惑 yòuhuò **2** 有极大诱惑力的东西 yǒu jídà yòuhuòlì de dōngxi
to resist/succumb to the temptation 经受/经不起诱惑 jīngshòu/jīngbuqǐ yòuhuò

tempting ADJ 十分诱人的 shífēn yòurén de, 及吸引人的 jí xīyǐnrén de

ten NUM 十 shí, 10
the Ten Commandments 十诫 Shíjiè

tenancy N **1** 租用期 zūyòngqī **2** 租用权 zūyòngquán

tenant N 房客 fángkè, 租用人 zūyòngrén

tend v **1** 倾向于 qīngxiàngyú, 往往 wǎngwǎng **2** 照料 zhàoliào ■ David tends his father's bar over the weekend to earn pocket money. 戴维在周末照料父亲的酒吧来赚一些零花钱。 Dàiwéi zài zhōumò zhàoliào fùqin de jiǔbā lái zhuàn yìxiē línghuāqián.

tendency N 趋向 qūxiàng, 趋势 qūshì ■ Nina has a tendency to flirt when boys are around. 有男孩子在，妮娜往往会卖弄风情。 Yǒu nánháizi zài, Nīnà wǎngwǎng huì màinong fēngqíng. **2** 习性 xíxìng, 倾向 qīngxiàng
suicidal tendency 自杀倾向 zìshā qīngxiàng

tender¹ ADJ **1** 温柔的 [+态度] wēnróu de [+tàidu], 体贴的 tǐtiē de **2** 嫩的 [+食物] nèn de [+shíwù] **3** 疼痛的 [+身体] téngtòng de [+shēntǐ]

tender² v 提出 tíchū, 呈交 chéngjiāo

tenet N 基本信念 jīběn xìnniàn, 信条 xìntiáo

tennis N 网球运动 wǎngqiú yùndòng
tennis shoes 网球鞋 wǎngqiúxié

tenor N 男高音（歌手）nángāoyīn (gēshǒu)

tense¹ **I** ADJ **1** 紧张的 [+情绪] jǐnzhāng de [+qíngxù] **2** 绷紧的 [+肌肉] bēngjǐn de [+jīròu], 僵直的 jiāngzhí de **II** v （使…）紧张 (shǐ...) jǐnzhāng, （使…）绷紧 (shǐ...) bēngjǐn
to be tensed up 极其紧张的 jíqí jǐnzhāng de

tense² （语法）时态 (yǔfǎ) shítài
present/past/future tense 现在/过去/将来时态 xiànzài/guòqù/jiānglái shítài

tension N **1** 紧张（局势/心情）jǐnzhāng (júshì/xīnqíng) **2** （肌肉）绷紧 (jīròu) bēngjǐn **3** （绳子）拉紧 (shéngzi) lājǐn

tent N 帐蓬 zhàngpéng

tentacle N **1** （海洋动物的）触须 (hǎiyáng dòngwù de) chùxū, 触角 chùjiǎo **2** 影响力 yǐngxiǎnglì

tentative ADJ 暂时的 zànshí de, 试探性的 shìtànxìng de
to make a tentative offer 提出试探性报价 tíchū shìtànxìng bàojià

tenth NUM 第十 dìshí

tenuous ADJ 不确定的 búquèdìng de
a tenuous relationship 脆弱的（人际）关系 cuìruò de (rénjì) guānxi

tenure N **1** （教师）终身任职 (jiàoshī) zhōngshēn rènzhí **2** （重要职位的）任期 (zhòngyào zhíwèi de) rènqī

tepid ADJ 冷漠的 lěngmò de, 不感兴趣的 bù gǎn xìngqù de

term **I** N **1** 术语 shùyǔ ■ Few would understand what these scientific terms mean. 很少人懂这些科学术语是什么意思。 Hěn shǎo rén dǒng zhèxiē kēxué shùyǔ shì shénme yìsi. **2** 任期 rènqī
in the long/short term 长期/短期 chángqī/duǎnqī ■ No one has a clue as to what impact globalization will have on the world in the long

term. 没有人知道全球化对世界有什么长期的影响。Méiyǒu rén zhīdào quánqiúhuà duì shìjiè yǒu shénme chángqī de yǐngxiǎng.

3 (政府官员的) 任期 (zhèngfǔ guānyuán de) rènqī 4 (犯人) 服刑期限 (fànrén) fúxíng qīxiàn

5 (学校) 学期 (xuéxiào) xuéqī

term paper 学期论文 xuéqī lùnwén

II v 把…称作 bǎ…chēng zuò

terminal I N 1 飞机候机大楼 fēijī hòujī dàlóu, 公共汽车总站 gōnggòng qìchē zǒngzhàn 2 (计算机) 终端 (jìsuànjī) zhōngduān **II** ADJ 1 不活的 bù huó de

terminal disease 绝症 juézhèng

2 越来越坏的 yuèláiyuè huài de, 没有希望的 méiyǒu xīwàng de

terminal decline 最终的没落 zuìzhōng de mòluò

3 终端的 zhōngduān de

terminal adaptor 终端适配器 zhōngduān shìpèiqì

terminate v 终止 zhōngzhǐ, 结束 jiéshù

termination N 终止 zhōngzhǐ, 结束 jiéshù

terminology N 术语 shùyǔ, 专门用语 zhuānmén yòngyǔ

terminus N (公共汽车 / 火车) 终点站 (gōnggòng qìchē/huǒchē) zhōngdiǎnzhàn

termite N 白蚁 báiyǐ

terms N 条款 tiáokuǎn

in terms of 在…方面 zài…fāngmian, 就…而言 jiù…éryán ■ *In terms of population China is the largest country in the world.* 就人口而言, 中国是世界上最大的国家。Jiù rénkǒu éryán, Zhōngguó shì shìjièshang zuì dà de guójiā.

in no uncertain terms 明确无误地 míngquè wúwù de

to be on good/bad terms with 和…关系好 / 坏 hé…guānxi hǎo/huài

to come to terms with 接受现实 jiēshòu xiànshí ■ *How does one come to terms with a death in the family?* 怎么样才能接受家人死亡的现实呢? Zěnmeyàng cái néng jiēshòu jiārén sǐwáng de xiànshí ne?

terrace N 1 露天平台 lùtiān píngtái 2 梯田 tītián

terracotta N 赤陶 (土) chìtáo (tǔ)

terracotta warriors 兵马俑 bīngmǎyǒng

terrain N 地形 dìxíng, 地势 dìshì

terrestrial ADJ 地球的 dìqiú de, 陆栖的 lù qī de

terrible ADJ 1 可怕的 kěpà de 2 极其坏的 jíqí huài de, 糟透了的 zāotòu le de

terribly ADV 非常 fēicháng, 极其 jíqí

terrier N 小猎犬 xiǎo lièquǎn

terrific ADJ 1 好极的 hǎo jí de, 棒极的 bàng jí de 2 极大的 jídà de

terrifically ADV 1 极好 (地) jíhǎo (de), 非常棒 fēicháng bàng 2 极其 jíqí, 非常 fēicháng

terrify v 使 [+人] 恐惧 shǐ [+rén] kǒngjù

terrifying ADJ 令人恐惧的 lìngrén kǒngjù de, 极其可怕的 jíqí kěpà de

territorial ADJ 领土的 lǐngtǔ de

territorial airspace 领空 lǐngkōng

territorial waters 领海 lǐnghǎi

territory N 1 领土 lǐngtǔ 2 领域 lǐngyù

unknown territory 未知的 (知识) 领域 wèizhī de (zhīshi) lǐngyù

3 地区 dìqū

sales territory 销售地区 xiāoshòu dìqū

terror N 1 恐怖 kǒngbù ■ *The big dog next door wreaks terror on the entire neighborhood.* 邻居的大狗给街坊造成恐怖。Línjū de dà gǒu gěi jiēfang zàochéng kǒngbù. 2 恐怖活动 kǒngbù huódòng 3 让人感到恐怖的人 / 事 ràng rén gǎndào kǒngbù de rén/shì

terrorism N 恐怖主义 kǒngbù zhǔyì

terrorist I N 恐怖分子 kǒngbùfènzǐ **II** ADJ 恐怖主义的 kǒngbùzhǔyì de, 恐怖活动的 kǒngbù huódòng de

terrorize v 恐吓 kǒnghè, 使 [+人] 恐怖 shǐ [+rén] kǒngbù

terrycloth N 毛布巾 máobù jīn

terse ADJ 简短的 jiǎnduǎn de, 三言两语的 sānyán liǎngyǔ de

tertiary ADJ 第三级的 dì sān jí de

TESL (= the Teaching of English as a Second Language) ABBREV 作为第二语言的英语教学 zuòwéi dì'èr yǔyán de Yīngyǔ jiàoxué

TESOL (= the Teaching of English to Speakers of Other Languages) ABBREV 作为外语的英语教学 zuòwéi wàiyǔ de Yīngyǔ jiàoxué

test I N 1 测验 cèyàn [M. WD 次 cì] 2 测试 cèshì [M. WD 次 cì] ■ *He failed his driver's test again.* 他又没有考到驾驶执照。Tā yòu méiyǒu kǎodao jiàshǐ zhízhào.

test case (法律) 判例案件 (fǎlǜ) pànlì ànjiàn

test drive (买车前的) 试车 (mǎi chēqián de) shìchē

test pilot (新飞机) 试飞驾驶员 (xīn fēijī) shìfēi jiàshǐyuán

test tube 试管 shìguǎn

3 考验 kǎoyàn [M. WD 次 cì] ■ *His sudden loss of the job has put their relationship to the test.* 他突然失业, 使他们的关系受到了考验。Tā tūrán shīyè, shǐ tāmen de guānxi shòudaole kǎoyàn.

II v 1 测试 cèshì 2 考验 kǎoyàn ■ *The child's chronic illness really tested his parents' endurance.* 孩子得了慢性病, 对家长真是个忍耐的考验。Háizi déle mànxìngbìng, duì jiāzhǎng zhēnshì ge rěnnài de kǎoyàn.

testament N (正式的) 证明 (zhèngshì de) zhèngmíng

testicle N 睾丸 gāowán

testify v **1** (在法庭上) 作证 (zài fǎtíng shàng) zuòzhèng **2** 证实 zhèngshí, 证明 zhèngmíng

testimonial N **1** 证明书 zhèngmíngshū [M. WD 份 fèn], 推荐信 tuījiànxìn [M. WD 份 fèn] **2** 赞誉 zànyù, 表扬 biǎoyáng

testimony N **1** (法庭) 证词 (fǎtíng) zhèngcí **2** 证明 zhèngmíng, 证据 zhèngjù

testy ADJ 烦躁不安的 fánzào bù'ān de

tetanus N 破伤风 pòshāngfēng

tether N 系绳 xì shéng, 系链 xì liàn
at the end of one's tether 山穷水尽 shān qióng shuǐ jìn, 一筹莫展 yìchóu mòzhǎn

text I N **1** 课文 kèwén [M. WD 篇 piān] **2** 文本 wénběn [M. WD 篇 piān] ■ Do you have the text of the Minister of Foreign Affairs' speech? 你有外交部长演说的文本吗？Nǐ yǒu wàijiāobùzhǎng yǎnshuō de wénběn ma? **3** 短信 duǎnxìn II v 发短信 fā duǎnxìn ■ She is texting Rita to ask her a question in today's homework. 她在给丽塔发短信，问她今天作业中的一个问题。Tā zài gěi Lìtǎ fā duǎnxìn, wèn tā jīntiān zuòyè zhōng de yí ge wèntí.

textbook I N 课本 kèběn, 教科书 jiàokēshū II ADJ 规范的 guīfàn de, 典型的 diǎnxíng de
a textbook case 典型病例 diǎnxíng bìnglì, 典型 (法律) 案例 diǎnxíng (fǎlǜ) ànlì

textile N 纺织品 fǎngzhīpǐn
textile industry 纺织工业 fǎngzhī gōngyè

textual ADJ 文本的 wénběn de, 原文的 yuánwén de
textual analysis 文本分析 wénběn fēnxī

texture N **1** (材料的) 质地 (cáiliào de) zhìdì, 手感 shǒugǎn **2** (饮食的) 口感 (yǐnshí de) kǒugǎn

textured ADJ **1** 质地粗糙的 [+衣料] zhìdì cūcāo de [+yīliào] **2** 结构丰富的 [+故事] jiégòu fēngfù de [+gùshì]

than CONJ 比 bǐ ■ She likes Italian food more than American food. 她喜欢意大利食品胜于美国食品。Tā xǐhuan Yìdàlì shípǐn shèngyú Měiguó shípǐn.

thank v 谢 xiè, 感谢 gǎnxiè

thankful ADJ 很感谢 hěn gǎnxiè, 感激的 gǎnjī de ■ I'm very thankful for his advice. 我非常感谢他的忠告。Wǒ fēicháng gǎnxiè tā de zhōnggào.

thankless ADJ 出力不讨好的 chūlì bù tǎohǎo de

thanks I INTERJ 谢谢 xièxie ■ Thanks for showing me around the school. 谢谢你带我参观你们学校。Xièxie nǐ dài wǒ cānguān nǐmen xuéxiào. II N 道谢的话／做法 dàoxiè dehuà/zuòfǎ
letter of thanks 感谢信 gǎnxièxìn
thanks to 由于 yóuyú

Thanksgiving N 感恩节 Gǎn'ēn jié

that (PL **those**) I ADJ 那 nà ■ That topic caused much discussion. 那个题目引起很多讨论。Nà ge tímù yǐnqǐ hěn duō tǎolùn. II PRON 那 nà, 那个 nà ge ■ That's the car I want to buy. 那就是我想买的汽车。Nà jiù shì wǒ xiǎng mǎi de qìchē. III CONJ

(used to introduce a clause) ■ I understand that the membership fee is due today. 我明白今天要交会员费。Wǒ míngbai jīntiān yào jiāo huìyuán fèi. IV ADV 那么 nàme ■ He's not that stupid. 他没有那么蠢。Tā méiyǒu nàme chǔn.

thatch N **1** 茅草 máocǎo **2** 茅草屋顶 máocǎo wūdǐng

thatched ADJ 用茅草覆盖的 yòng máocǎo fùgài de

thaw I v **1** [冰雪+] 融化 [bīngxuě+] rónghuà **2** [食品+] 解冻 [shípǐn+] jiědòng **3** [态度+] 变得温和 [tàidu+] biàn de wēnhé II N **1** 冰雪融化 (的时期) bīngxuě rónghuà (de shíqí) **2** [关系+] 缓和 [guānxi de+] huǎnhé, 解冻 jiědòng

the ART 这 zhè, 那 nà ■ I ordered a book from an Internet bookstore last week. The book came this morning. 我上星期在网页上订购了一本书。这本书今天上午到了。Wǒ shàng xīngqī zài wǎngyèshang dìnggòule yì běn shū. Zhè běn shū jīntiān shàngwǔ dào le.
the hottest day in a year 一年中最热的一天 yìnián zhōng zuì rè de yìtiān

theater N **1** 戏剧 (事业) xìjù (shìyè), 剧作 jùzuò a career in the theater 戏剧生涯 xìjù shēngyá classic theater 古典戏剧 gǔdiǎn xìjù
2 剧院 jùyuàn, 剧场 jùchǎng, 电影院 diànyǐngyuàn

theatergoer N 常上剧院的人 cháng shàng jùyuàn de rén, 戏迷 xìmí

theatrical ADJ **1** 戏剧的 xìjù de
theatrical troupe 剧团 jùtuán
2 剧院的 jùyuàn de **3** 戏剧性的 xìjùxìng de, 夸张的 kuāzhāng de

theatrics N 戏剧性举止 xìjùxìng jǔzhǐ, 夸张的举止 kuāzhāng de jǔzhǐ

theft N 盗窃 (罪) dàoqiè (zuì)

their ADJ, PRON 他们的 tāmen de, 她们 tāmen de, 它们的 tāmen de

theirs PRON 他们的 tāmen de, 她们的 tāmen de, 它们的 tāmen de ■ This is my dog, not theirs. 这是我的狗，不是他们的狗。Zhè shì wǒ de gǒu, bú shì tāmen de gǒu.

them PRON 他们 tāmen, 她们 tāmen, 它们 tāmen

theme N **1** 主题 zhǔtí
theme park 主题乐园 zhǔtí lèyuán
theme song 主题歌 zhǔtígē
2 风格 fēnggé, 格调 gédiào **3** (音乐的) 主旋律 (yīnyuè de) zhǔxuánlǜ, 主调 zhǔdiào

themselves PRON 他们自己 tāmen zìjǐ, 她们自己 tāmen zìjǐ, 它们自己 tāmen zìjǐ
by themselves 独自地 dúzì de
in themselves 就本身而言 jiù běnshēn éryán

then I ADV **1** 那时候 nà shíhou ■ I didn't know then what was in store for me. 我那时候不知道会发生什么。Wǒ nà shíhou bù zhīdào huì fāshēng shénme.

back then 往昔 wǎngxī

then and only then 只有在那种情况下 zhǐyǒu zài nà zhǒng qíngkuàng xià

2 然后 ránhòu ■ *I'll finish my homework and then watch the DVD with you.* 我先做完功课，然后跟你一起看DVD。Wǒ xiān zuòwán gōngkè, ránhòu gēn nǐ yìqǐ kàn DVD. **II** ADJ 那时的 nàshí de

the then government 那时的政府 nàshí de zhèngfǔ

theologian N 神学家 shénxuéjiā, 神学研究者 shénxué yánjiūzhě

theological ADJ 神学的 shénxué de

theology N 神学 shénxué, 宗教信仰 zōngjiào xìnyǎng

theorem N（数学）定理 (shùxué) dìnglǐ

theoretical ADJ 理论（上）的 lǐlùn (shàng) de

theoretically ADV **1** 从理论上讲 cóng lǐlùnshang jiǎng **2** 按道理讲 àn dàoli jiǎng

theorist, theoretician N 理论家 lǐlùnjiā

theorize V 提出理论 tíchū lǐlùn, 推论 tuīlùn

theory N **1** 理论 lǐlùn, 学说 xuéshuō

in theory 从理论上讲 cóng lǐlùnshang jiǎng
■ *In theory globalization should bring about a win-win situation for all countries.* 从理论上讲，全球化应该给所有的国家带来双赢的局面。Cóng lǐlùnshang jiǎng, quánqiúhuà yīnggāi gěi suǒyǒu de guójiā dàilai shuāngyíng de júmiàn.

Darwin's theory of evolution 达尔文的进化论（学说）Dá'ěrwén de jìnhuàlùn (xuéshuō)

2 假设 jiǎshè, 推测 tuīcè

therapeutic ADJ **1** 治疗的 zhìliáo de **2** 使人镇静的 shǐrén zhènjìng de

therapy N **1**（治）疗法 (zhì) liáofǎ

alternative therapy 另类疗法 lìnglèi liáofǎ

2 心理治疗 xīnlǐ zhìliáo

relaxation therapy 放松疗法 fàngsōng liáofǎ

there I PRON (there + to be) 有 yǒu ■ *There are a few points that need to be clarified.* 有几点需要澄清。Yǒu jǐ diǎn xūyào chéngqīng. **II** ADV 那里 nàlǐ ■ *It was almost dark when we got there.* 我们到达那里时，天快黑了。Wǒmen dàodá nàlǐ shí, tiān kuài hēi le. ■ *Is anyone there?* 有人吗？Yǒu rén ma?

thereabouts ADV 大约 dàyuē, 左右 zuǒyòu

thereafter ADV 从此以后 cóngcǐ yǐhòu, 此后 cǐhòu

thereby ADV 从而 cóng'ér, 因而 yīn'ér

therefore ADV 因此 yīncǐ, 所以 suǒyǐ ■ *I'll be coming home late tonight; therefore, don't lock the front door.* 今天晚上我要晚回来，所以前门不要锁上。Jīntiān wǎnshang wǒ yào wǎn huílai, suǒyǐ qiánmén bú yào suǒshang.

therein ADV 于此 yúcǐ, 缘此 yuán cǐ

thereupon ADV 随即 suíjí, 随后 suíhòu

thermal ADJ **1** 热 rè

thermal energy 热能 rènéng

2 保暖的 bǎonuǎn de, 保温的 bǎowēn de

thermal springs 温泉 wēnquán

thermal underwear 保暖内衣 bǎonuǎn nèiyī

thermometer N 温度计 wēndù jì, 体温计 tǐwēn jì

thermonuclear ADJ 热核的 rèhé de

Thermos, Thermos bottle N 热水瓶 rèshuǐpíng

thermostat N 恒温器 héngwēnqì

thesaurus N 分类词典 fēnlèi cídiǎn, 分类词汇大全 fēnlèi cíhuì dàquán [m. wd 本 běn]

these PRON, PL 这些 zhèxiē ■ *These books are outdated.* 这些书已经过时了。Zhèxiē shū yǐjīng guòshí le.

they PRON **1** 他们 tāmen, 她们 tāmen, 它们 tāmen ■ *I have many friends here. They're all baseball fans.* 我在这里有很多朋友，他们都是垒球迷。Wǒ zài zhèlǐ yǒu hěn duō péngyou, tāmen dōu shì lěiqiúmí. **2** 那些人 nàxiē rén, 人们 rénmen

they say 很多人说 hěn duō rén shuō, 据说 jùshuō

thick ADJ **1** 厚 hòu **2** 粗 cū ■ *She needs thick needles for this knitting wool.* 打这种毛线，她需要粗的毛线针。Dǎ zhè zhǒng máoxiàn, tā xūyào cū de máoxiànzhēn. **3** 浓 nóng

thick soup 浓汤 nóngtāng

thicken V 使…变厚/粗/浓 shǐ…biàn hòu/cū/nóng

thickener N 增稠剂 zēngchóujì

thicket N 灌木丛 guànmùcóng

thick-headed ADJ 非常愚笨的 fēicháng yúbèn de

thickness N 厚度 hòudù, 浓度 nóngdù

thickset ADJ 粗壮结实的 cūzhuàng jiēshi de

thick-skinned ADJ 厚脸皮的 hòuliǎnpí de, 经得起批评的 jīngdeqǐ pīpíng de

thief N 贼 zéi, 窃贼 qièzéi ■ *Stop thief!* 抓贼！Zhuā zéi! 抓小偷！Zhuā xiǎotōu!

thievery N 偷窃行为 tōuqiè xíngwéi

thieving ADJ（从事）偷窃的 (cóngshì) tōuqiè de

thigh N 大腿 dàtuǐ [m. wd 条 tiáo]

thimble N 顶针 dǐngzhēn, 针箍 zhēngū

thin I ADJ **1** 瘦 shòu ■ *How do you stay so thin?* 你怎么一直这么瘦？Nǐ zěnme yìzhí zhème shòu? **2** 薄 báo

thin crust pizza 我喜欢薄底比萨饼。Wǒ xǐhuan báo de bǐsà bǐng.

3 细 xì ■ *He used some thin wire to fix the parts.* 他用了细的金属丝来固定部件。Tā yòngle hěn xì de jīnshǔsī lái gùdìng bùjiàn. **4** 稀 xī ■ *The invalid can only eat thin porridge.* 病人只能吃稀粥。Bìngrén zhǐ néng chī xīzhōu. **II** V **1** [头发+] 变得稀少 [tóufa+] biàn de xīshǎo **2** [液体+] 稀释 [yètǐ+] xīshì

to thin the ranks 使（人员）减少 shǐ (rényuán) jiǎnshǎo

III ADV (to cut sth too thin) 把某物切得太薄 bǎ mǒuwù qiē dé tài báo

thing N **1** 东西 dōngxi **2** 事情 shìqing ■ *He has his own way of doing things.* 他做事情有自己的一套办法。Tā zuò shìqing yǒu zìjǐ de yí tào bànfǎ.

not to know a thing about 一无所知 yì wú suǒ zhī ■ *He doesn't know a thing about Chinese history.* 他对中国历史一无所知。Tā duì Zhōngguó lìshǐ yì wú suǒ zhī.

to do one's own thing 做自己喜欢做的事 zuò zìjǐ xǐhuan zuò de shì, 按照自己的意志办 ànzhào zìjǐ de yìzhì bàn

thingamajig N 那个什么人 nàge shénme rén, 那个什么东西 nàge shénme dōngxī

that white thingamajig 那个白的什么东西 nàge bái de shénme dōngxī

things N **1** 情况 qíngkuàng, 形势 xíngshì ■ *How are things going?* 情况怎么样? Qíngkuàng zěnmeyàng?

all things considered 考虑到所有的情况 kǎolǜdào suǒyǒu de qíngkuàng

2 东西 dōngxi, 物品 wùpǐn

think I V **1** (PT & PP thought) 想 xiǎng ■ *Think before you act.* 行动以前，要想一想。Xíngdòng yǐqián, yào xiǎngyixiǎng.

to think … over 慎重考虑 shènzhòng kǎolǜ

to think … up 想出 xiǎngchū ■ *I can't think up any excuse for not going to his birthday party.* 我想不出什么借口，可以不去参加他的生日聚会。Wǒ xiǎngbuchū shénme jièkǒu, kěyǐ bú qù cānjiā tā de shēngrì jùhuì.

2 认为 rènwéi ■ *She didn't think he was serious about their relationship.* 她认为他对他俩的关系并不很认真。Tā rènwéi tā duì tā liǎ de guānxi bìng bù hěn rènzhēn.

to think poorly of 对…评价不高 duì…píngjià bù gāo ■ *It's sad that many local people think poorly of their own town.* 很多当地人对自己的小城评价不高，这是让人伤心的。Hěn duō dāngdì rén duì zìjǐ de xiǎo chéng píngjià bù gāo, zhè shì ràng rén shāngxīn de.

to think the world of 对…评价非常高 duì…píngjià fēicháng gāo

3 考虑 kǎolǜ ■ *I'll think about it and let you know soon.* 我要考虑一下，很快就会告诉你。Wǒ yào kǎolǜ yíxià, hěn kuài jiù huì gàosu nǐ. **II** N 思考 sīkǎo, 考虑 kǎolǜ

thinking I N 想法 xiǎngfǎ, 态度 tàidu

to one's way of thinking 按照某人的想法 ànzhào mǒurén de xiǎngfǎ

II ADJ 有思想的 yǒu sīxiǎng de, 思考的 sīkǎo de

to put on one's thinking cap 开始思考 kāishǐ sīkǎo

think tank N 思想库 sīxiǎngkù, 智囊团 zhìnáng-tuán

thinly ADV 很薄地 hěn báo de, 稀疏地 xīshū de

thinly disguised 很容易看穿的 hěn róngyì kànchuān de

thinly staffed 人员短缺的 rényuán duǎnquē de

third NUM 第三 dìsān

third party [法律+] 第三方 [fǎlǜ+] dì sān fāng, 第三者 dìsānzhě

third person 第三人称 dìsān rénchēng

third rate 三流的 [+货色] sān liú de [+huòsè], 下等的 xiàděng de

(the) Third World N 第三世界 Dìsān Shìjiè

third-degree burn N 三度烧伤 sāndù shāoshāng

thirst I N **1** (口) 渴 (kǒu) kě **2** 渴望 kěwàng

a thirst for power 对权力的渴望 duì quánlì de kěwàng

II V (to thirst for/after) 渴望 kěwàng, 渴求 kěqiú

thirsty ADJ 口渴的 kǒukě de

thirsty for power 渴望权力 kěwàng quánlì

thirteen NUM 十三 shísān, 13

thirty NUM 三十 sānshí, 30

this (PL these) I ADJ 这 zhè ■ *This house has been on the market for six months.* 这幢房子在市场上求售已经六个月了。Zhè zhuàng fángzi zài shìchǎngshang qiúshòu yǐjīng liù ge yuè le. **II** PRON 这 zhè, 这个 zhè ge ■ *Dad, this is Warwick. Warwick, this is my Dad.* 爸爸，这是沃立克。沃立克，这是我爸爸。Bàba, zhè shì Wòlìkè. Wòlìkè, zhè shì wǒ bàba.

thongs N 人字凉鞋 rénzì liángxié

thorn N (植物的) 刺 (zhíwù de) cì

a thorn in one's side 肉中刺 ròuzhōngcì, 眼中钉 yǎnzhōngdīng

thorny ADJ **1** 多刺的 [+植物] duō cì de [+zhíwù] **2** 棘手的 [+问题] jíshǒu de [+wèntí]

thorough ADJ **1** 彻底的 chèdǐ de, 全面的 quánmiàn de **2** 仔细的 zǐxì de, 细致的 xìzhi de

thoroughbred N 纯种马 chúnzhǒngmǎ [M. WD 匹 pǐ]

thoroughfare N 大道 dàdào [M. WD 条 tiáo], 大路 dàlù [M. WD 条 tiáo]

thoroughly ADV 完全地 wánquán de, 彻底地 chèdǐ de

those ADJ, PRON 那些 nàxiē ■ *I remember my childhood well—ah, those were the days.* 我的童年记得很清楚—啊，那些日子多好。Wǒ de tóngnián jìde hěn qīngchu—A, nàxiē rìzi duō hǎo.

though I CONJ 虽然 suīrán **II** ADV 不过 búguò, 然而 rán'ér ■ *I think this is her e-mail address—I'll check it, though.* 我想这是她的电子邮件地址—不过我还要查一查。Wǒ xiǎng zhè shì tā de diànzǐ yóujiàn dìzhǐ—búguò wǒ hái yào cháchá.

as though 好像 hǎoxiàng, 似乎 shìhū

thought I V See think **II** N **1** 想法 xiǎngfǎ, 看法 kànfǎ ■ *What are your thoughts on the current situation in the Middle East?* 你对目前的中东局势

有什么看法? Nǐ duì mùqián de Zhōngdōng júshì yǒu shénme kànfǎ?

just a thought 只是不成熟的想法 zhǐshì bù chéngshú de xiǎngfǎ ■ *Shall we go to Spain for holiday? Just a thought.* 我们去西班牙度假, 好吗? 只是不成熟的想法。Wǒmen qù Xībānyá dùjià, hǎo ma? Zhǐshì bù chéngshú de xiǎngfǎ.

2 思考 sīkǎo

on second thought 经过重新考虑 jīngguò chóngxīn kǎolǜ

3 想到 xiǎngdao ■ *The mere thought of a toad is repulsive to her.* 就是想到癞蛤蟆, 她也感到恶心。Jiù shì xiǎngdao làihámá, tā yě gǎndao ěxīn.

thoughtful ADJ **1** 周到的 zhōudao de, 体谅的 tǐliang de **2** 沉思的 chénsī de, 深思的 shēnsī de ■ *He looked thoughtful for a while before answering the question.* 他看上去沉思了一会儿, 才回答这个问题。Tā kànshangqu chénsīle yíhuìr, cái huídá zhè ge wèntí.

thoughtless ADJ **1** 未经思考的 [+做法] wèijīng sīkǎo de [+zuòfǎ], 轻率的 qīngshuài de **2** 不体谅他人的 [+人] bù tǐliang tārén de [+rén]

thousand NUM 千 qiān ■ *This school has over 1,000 students.* 这个学校有一千多名学生。Zhè ge xuéxiào yǒu yì qiān duō míng xuésheng.

thrash V **1** 痛打 [+人] tòngdǎ [+rén] **2** 打败 [+对手] dǎbài [+duìshǒu] **3** 猛烈动作 měngliè dòngzuò

to thrash sth out 商讨某事并找出解决办法 shāngtǎo mǒushì bìng zhǎochū jiějué bànfǎ

thrashing N (一顿) 痛打 (yí dùn) tòngdǎ

thread I N **1** (细) 线 (xì) xiàn

embroidery thread 刺绣线 cìxiùxiàn

sewing thread 缝衣线 féngyīxiàn

2 思路 sīlù, 头绪 tóuxù ■ *The speaker lost his thread of thought minutes after he began to talk.* 发言的人说了几分钟就跑题了。Fāyán de rén shuōle jǐ fēnzhōng jiù pǎotí le. **3** 一丝 yìsī, 一点儿 yìdiǎnr

thread of human decency 做人最起码的道德标准 zuòrén zuì qǐmǎ de dàodé biāozhǔn

II V **1** 穿线 chuān xiàn **2** (用线) 把…串起来 (yòng xiàn) bǎ...chuàn qǐlái

threadbare ADJ **1** 破旧的 [+衣服] pòjiù de [+yīfu] **2** 陈旧的 [+借口] chénjiù de [+jièkǒu], 老掉牙的 lǎodiàoyá de

threat N 威胁 wēixié, 恐吓 kǒnghè

bomb threat 炸弹恐吓 zhàdàn kǒnghè

an empty threat 虚张声势的恐吓 xūzhāng shēngshì de kǒnghè

threaten V **1** 威胁 wēixié ■ *She threatened to file for a divorce if he got drunk again.* 她威胁说, 如果他再喝醉, 就提出离婚。Tā wēixié shuō, rúguǒ tā zài hēzuì, jiù tíchū líhūn. **2** 似乎会 sìhū huì ■ *Bad weather threatened to close down the flower show for the weekend.* 坏天气似乎会关闭

周末的花展。Huài tiānqì sìhū huì guānbì zhōumò de huāzhǎn.

threatening ADJ 威胁 (性) 的 wēixié (xìng) de

three NUM 三 sān, 3

three-dimensional ADJ 三维的 sānwéi de, 立体的 lìtǐ de

thresh V 打谷子 dǎgǔzi, 脱粒 tuōlì

thresher N 打谷机 dǎgǔjī, 脱粒机 tuōlìjī

threshold N **1** 门槛 ménkǎn **2** 下限 xiàxiàn

on the threshold of sth 处在某事物的开端 chǔzài mǒushìwù de kāiduān

to reach a critical threshold 达到关键的界限 dádào guānjiàn de jièxiàn

threw See **throw**

thrift N 节省 jiéshěng, 节俭 jiéjiǎn

thrift shop (慈善机构的) 廉价旧货店 (císhàn jīgòu de) liánjià jiùhuòdiàn

thrifty ADJ 节省的 jiéshěng de, 节俭的 jiéjiǎn de

thrill I N **1** (强烈的) 激动 (qiángliè de) jīdòng, 狂喜 kuángxǐ **2** 引起激动的事 yǐnqǐ jīdòng de shì II V 使 [+人] 极为激动 shǐ [+rén] jíwéi jīdòng, 使 [+人] 狂喜 chǐ [+rén] kuángxǐ

thrilled ADJ 深感激动的 shēngǎn jīdòng de, 极其兴奋的 jíqí xīngfèn de

thriller N 惊险电影/小说 jīngxiǎn diànyǐng/xiǎoshuō

thrive (PT **thrived**, **throve**; PP **thrived**, **thriven**) V 兴旺 xīngwàng, 茁壮成长 zhuózhuàng chéngzhǎng

thriving ADJ 兴旺发达的 xīngwàng fādá de

throat N 喉咙 hóulóng, 嗓子 sǎngzi

to clear one's throat 清一下嗓子 qīng yíxià sǎngzi

to have a sore throat 嗓子疼 sǎngzi téng

throaty ADJ 声音沙哑的 shēngyīn shāyǎ de, 声音低沉的 shēngyīn dīchén de

throb I V **1** [心脏+] 跳动 [xīnzàng+] tiàodòng, 搏动 bódòng **2** [音乐+] 节奏强烈地振动 [yīnyuè+] jiézòu qiángliè de zhèndòng II N 跳动 tiàodòng, 振动 zhèndòng

throes N (in the throes of) 正处于困境之中 zhèng chǔyú kùnjìng zhīzhōng

throne N **1** 王位 wángwèi, 皇位 huángwèi, 宝座 bǎozuò **2** 王权 wángquán, 皇权 huángquán, 君权 jūnquán

throng I N 人群 rénqún II V [人群+] 聚集 [rénqún+] jùjí

throttle I V **1** 掐死 qiāsǐ, 勒死 lēisǐ **2** 扼杀 èshā, 压制 yāzhì II N (汽车) 油门 (qìchē) yóumén, 节流阀 jiéliúfá

full throttle 全速地 quánsù de

through I PREP **1** 通过 tōngguò ■ *The police believe that the criminal got in through the window.* 警察相信, 罪犯是从窗户进入房子的。Jǐngchá xiāngxìn, zuìfàn shì cóng chuānghu jìnrù fángzi de.

2 直到 zhídao **3** 由于 yóuyú ■ *The terrible accident happened through a human error.* 那个可怕的事故是由于人为的错误而发生的。Nàge kěpà de shìgù shì yóuyú rénwéi de cuòwù ér fāshēng de. **II** ADJ **1** 完了 wán le, 用完了 yòngwán le ■ *I'm through with the computer now if you still need it.* 我用完电脑了，你要用可以用。Wǒ yòngwán diànnǎo le, nǐ yào yòng kěyǐ yòng. **2** 恋爱关系结束了 liàn'ài guānxi jiéshù le, 吹了 chuī le

to read/think ... through 从头到尾仔细地读 cóng tóu dào wěi zǐxì de dú, 想 xiǎng

throughout PREP 在…所有的地方/时候 zài… suǒyǒu de defang/shíhou ■ *The marketing manager was frantically busy throughout the promotion campaign.* 在整个促销期间，销售经理忙得不可开交。Zài zhěng ge cùxiāo qījiān, xiāoshòu jīnglǐ máng de bù kě kāi jiāo.

throw I v (PT **threw**; PP **thrown**) **1** 扔 rēng, 投 tóu ■ *The boy threw a stick for his dog to retrieve.* 男孩扔出树枝，让狗衔回来。Nánhái rēngchū shùzhī, ràng gǒu xiánhuílai.

to throw away 抛弃 pāoqì, 丢掉 diūdiao

2 猛力地推 měnglì de tuī **3** 使…震惊 shǐ… zhènjīng

to throw caution to the wind 不顾一切风险 búgù yíqiè fēngxiǎn

to throw a tantrum 大发脾气 dàfā píqi

II N 投掷的距离 tóuzhì de jùlí

throw rug 小毯子 xiǎotǎnzi

throwaway ADJ **1** 一次性的 [+商品] yícìxìng de [+shāngpǐn]

throwaway camera 一次性相机 yícìxìng xiàngjī **2** 即兴的 jíxìng de, 不加考虑的 bù jiā kǎolǜ de

a throwaway comment 脱口而出的评语 tuōkǒu ér chū de píngyǔ

throwback N 复旧（现象）fùjiù (xiànxiàng), 返祖（现象）fǎnzǔ (xiànxiàng)

thrown See **throw**

thrust I v (PT & PP **thrust**) **1** 猛推 měng tuī, 猛塞 měng sāi **2** 刺 cì, 戳 chuō **II** N **1** 猛推 měng tuī, 猛塞 měng sāi **2** （发动机的）推力 (fādòngjī de) tuīlì **3** （讲话的）要点 (jiǎnghuà de) yàodiǎn, 主旨 zhǔzhǐ

thruway N （付费）高速公路 (fùfèi) gāosù gōnglù

thud I N 重物碰击发出的声音 zhòngwù pèngjī fāchū de shēngyīn, 砰的一声 pēng de yì shēng **II** v 砰的一声碰击 pēng de yì shēng pèngjī

thug N 暴徒 bàotú

thumb N （大）拇指 (dà) mǔzhǐ

to give the thumbs up 称赞 chēngzàn ■ *I gave him the thumbs up for his bold proposal.* 我称赞他大胆的提议。Wǒ chēngzàn tā dàdàn de tíyì.

thumbnail I ADJ 简略的 [+描述] jiǎnlüè de [+miáoshù] **II** N 拇指甲 mǔzhǐjiǎ

thumbtack N 图钉 túdīng

thump I v **1** 发出重击声 fāchū zhòngjīshēng **2** 心怦怦跳动 xīn pēngpēng tiàodòng **II** N 重击声 zhòngjīshēng

thunder I N **1** 雷 léi **2** 轰隆声 hōnglōng shēng

a clap of thunder 一阵雷声 yí zhèn léishēng **II** v 打雷 dǎléi **2** 轰隆隆地经过 hōnglōnglōng de jīngguò

thunderbolt N **1** 电闪雷鸣 diànshǎn léimíng **2** 晴天霹雷的事件 qíngtiān pīléi de shìjiàn

thunderclap N （打）雷声 (dǎ) léishēng

thundercloud N 雷雨云 léiyǔyún

thunderous ADJ 雷鸣般的 léimíng bān de

thunderstorm N 雷雨 léiyǔ, 雷电雨 léidiànyǔ

Thursday N 星期四 xīngqísì, 周四 zhōusì

thus ADV 因此 yīncǐ, 结果是 jiéguǒ shì ■ *Many large users increased their stock, thus pushing up the prices.* 许多大客户增加存货，因此抬高了价格。Xǔduō dà kèhù zēngjiā cúnhuò, yīncǐ táigāole jiàgé.

thus far 到目前为止 dào mùqián wéi zhǐ, 迄今为止 qì jīn wéi zhǐ

thwart v 阻扰 zǔrǎo, 阻碍 zǔ'ài

thyroid, thyroid gland N 甲状腺 jiǎzhuàngxiàn

tic N （面部肌肉）抽搐 (miànbù jīròu) chōuchù

tick I N **1** （钟表的）滴答声 (zhōngbiǎo de) dīdāshēng **2** （股票价）微小变动 (gǔpiàojià) wēixiǎo biàndòng **3** 打勾的记号 dǎ gōu de jìhao (√) **II** v **1** [钟表+] 滴答滴答响 [zhōngbiǎo+] dīdā dīdā xiǎng

to tick away [时间+] 一点一点过去 [shíjiān+] yìdiǎn yìdiǎn guòqù

What makes him tick? 是什么在左右他? Shì shénme zài zuǒyòu tā? 他是受什么影响的? Tā shì shòu shénme yǐngxiǎng de?

2 做打勾 (√) 的记号 zuò dǎ gōu de jìhao

ticket I N **1** 票（子）piào (zi) [M. WD 张 zhāng], 入场券 rùchǎngquàn [M. WD 张 zhāng]

ticket booth 售票亭 shòupiàotíng

ticket office 售票处 shòupiàochù

ticket window 售票窗口 shòupiào chuāngkǒu

2 （交通违章）罚款通知 (jiāotōng wéizhāng) fákuǎn tōngzhī [M. WD 张 zhāng], 罚单 fádān [M. WD 张 zhāng]

parking ticket 违章停车罚单 wéizhāng tíngchē fádān

speeding ticket 超速驾车罚单 chāosù jiàchē fádān

3 价格标签 jiàgé biāoqiān **4** （美国大选时）政党候选人名单 (Měiguó dàxuǎn shí) zhèngdǎng hòuxuǎnrén míngdān **■** 罚单 qiē...fádān

tickle I v **1** 搔 [+人] 痒 sāo [+rén] yǎng **2** 使…开心 shǐ...kāixīn **II** N [嗓子+] 发痒 [sǎngzi+] fāyǎng

ticklish ADJ **1** 怕痒的 pàyǎng de **2** 需小心对待的 [+问题] xū xiǎoxīn duìdài de [+wèntí]

tidal ADJ 潮汐的 cháoxì de, 潮水的 cháoshuǐ de

tidal wave 海啸 hǎixiào, 浪潮 làngcháo

tidbit N 少量的精美食品 shǎoliàng de jīngměi shípǐn

tide I N **1** 潮 cháo, 潮汐 cháoxùn ■ *A rising tide lifts every ship.* 水涨船高。Shuǐ zhǎng chuán gāo. **2** (社会)潮流 (shèhuì) cháoliú

to swim against the tide 逆潮流而动 nì cháoliú ér dòng

II v (to tide over) 渡过难关 dùguò nánguān

tidewater N 潮水 cháoshuǐ

tidings N 消息 xiāoxi

great tidings 喜讯 xǐxùn

tidy ADJ 整齐的 zhěngqí de, 整洁的 zhěngjié de

a tidy sum 一大笔钱 yí dà bǐ qián

tie I v **1** 系 xì, 结 jié ■ *Can your kid tie shoelaces?* 你们的孩子会结鞋带了吗? Nǐmen de háizi huì jié xiédài le ma?

to tie up ① 捆绑 kǔnbǎng ② 使停顿 shǐ tíngdùn, 耽搁 dānge ■ *The heavy fog tied up rush hour traffic.* 浓雾在高峰期间使交通停顿。Nóng wù zài gāofēng qījiān shǐ jiāotōng tíngdùn. ③ 非常繁忙 fēicháng fánmáng

2 打成平局 dǎchéng píngjú ■ *The two teams tied with each other.* 两队打成平局。Liǎng duì dǎchéng píngjú. II N **1** 领带 lǐngdài **2** 平局 píngjú ■ *The race was declared a tie.* 宣布竞赛为平局。Xuānbù jìngsài wéi píngjú.

to end in a tie 打成平局 dǎ chéng píngjú

tiebreaker N (平局以后的)决胜分/决胜局/决胜题 (píngjú yǐhòu de) juéshèng fēn/juéshèngjú/juéshèng tí

tier N **1** 一排(梯形座位) yì pái (tīxíng zuòwèi) **2** 层次 céngcì, 等级 děngjí

tiff N 口角 kǒujué, 小争吵 xiǎo zhēngchǎo

tiger N (老)虎 (lǎo) hǔ [M. WD 只 zhī]

tight I ADJ **1** 紧 jǐn ■ *The jeans are too tight to be comfortable.* 牛仔裤太紧了,不能可舒服的。Niúzǎikù tài jǐn le, bù kěnéng shūfu de. **2** 严密 yánmì ■ *When the governor visited the school, the security was really tight.* 州长访问学校时,保安十分严密。Zhōuzhǎng fǎngwèn xuéxiào shí, bǎo'ān shífēn yánmì. **3** 小气的 xiǎoqi de ■ *He is very tight with his money.* 他花钱很小气。Tā huāqián hěn xiǎoqi. **4** 紧张的 jǐnzhāng de II ADV 紧紧地 jǐnjǐn de

hold tight 抓紧 zhuājǐn

tighten v **1** (使…)变紧 (shǐ…) biàn jǐn

to tighten one's belt 勒紧裤腰带 lēijǐn kùyāodài, 紧缩开支 jǐnsuō kāizhī

to tighten a screw 拧紧螺钉 níngjǐn luódīng

to tighten violin strings 绷紧小提琴琴弦 bēngjǐn xiǎotíqín qínxián

2 加紧 jiājǐn, 加强 jiāqiáng

to tighten one's hold on sth 加强对某事的控制 jiāqiáng duì mǒushì de kòngzhì

tightfisted ADJ 用钱小气的 yòngqián xiǎoqi de

tightrope N (杂技表演的)钢丝 (zájì biǎoyǎn de) gāngsī

to walk a tightrope 走钢丝 zǒugāngsī

tights N (女用)连裤袜 (nǚ yòng) liánkùwà [M. WD 双 shuāng]

tightwad N 吝啬鬼 lìnsèguǐ, 小气鬼 xiǎoqiguǐ

tile I N **1** (屋顶的)瓦(片)(wūdǐng de) wǎ (piàn) [M. WD 块 kuài] **2** (铺地的)瓷砖 (pūdì de) cízhuān [M. WD 块 kuài] II v 铺设瓦片 pūshè wǎpiàn

till¹ CONJ, PREP See until

till² N 钱柜 qiánguì, 钱箱 qiánxiāng

till³ v 耕 [+地] gēng [+dì], 种 [+田] zhòng [+tián]

tiller N 耕地者 gēngdìzhě, 种田人 zhòngtiánrén

tilt I v (使…)倾斜 (shǐ…) qīngxié II N **1** 倾斜 qīngxié, 偏向 piānxiàng **2** (at full tilt) 全速地 quánsù de

timber N 木材 mùcái, 原木 yuánmù

timberland N 林地 líndì, 人造森林 rénzào sēnlín

timbre N 音色 yīnsè, 音质 yīnzhì

time I N **1** 时间 shíjiān

Time and tide wait for no man. 时不我待。Shí bù wǒ dài.

time bomb 定时炸弹 dìngshí zhàdàn

time card 考勤卡 kǎoqín kǎ

time capsule 时代文物密封罐 shídài wénwù mìfēngguàn

time clock 考勤钟 kǎoqínzhōng

time limit 时限 shíxiàn, 期限 qīxiàn

time off 休假 xiūjià, 放假 fàngjià

time out (体育比赛中)暂停 (tǐyù bǐsài zhōng) zàntíng, (惩罚儿童的)禁闭时间 (chéngfá értóng de) jìnbì shíjiān

time zone 时区 shíqū

2 次 cì ■ *It's my treat this time.* 这次我请客。Zhè cì wǒ qǐngkè.

at the same time 同时 tóngshí

for the time being 暂时 zànshí, 目前 mùqián ■ *Kelly is staying with her aunt for the time being.* 凯莉暂时和姨妈住在一起。Kǎilì zànshí hé yímā zhù zài yìqǐ.

in no time 马上 mǎshàng, 很快 hěn kuài ■ *Dinner will be ready in no time.* 晚饭马上好了。Wǎnfàn mǎshàng hǎo le.

on time 准时 zhǔnshí ■ *Be sure to hand in your assignments on time.* 一定要准时交作业。Yídìng yào zhǔnshí jiāo zuòyè.

to do time 在监狱服役 zài jiānyù fúyì, 吃官司 chī guānsi

to have a good time 过得很愉快 guòde hěn yúkuài

time and a half 一点五倍工资 yīdiǎnwǔ bèi gōngzī

II v **1** 安排…的时间 ānpái…de shíjiān **2** 记录…的时间 jìlù…de shíjiān time-consuming

time-consuming ADJ 花费很多时间的 huāfèi hěn duō shíjiān de, 耗时的 hào shí de

time-honored ADJ 历史悠久的 lìshǐ yōujiǔ de, 古老的 gǔlǎo de

time-keeper N（体育比赛的）计时员 (tǐyù bǐsài de) jìshíyuán

timeless ADJ 永远不会过时的 yǒngyuǎn bú huì guòshí de, 万古常新的 wàngǔ cháng xīn de

timely ADJ 及时的 jíshí de, 适时的 shìshí de

timer N 定时器 dìngshíqì
part-timer 兼职人员 jiānzhí rényuán
full-timer 全职人员 quánzhí rényuán

times PREP 乘以 chéngyǐ ■ *3 times 2 equals 6.* 三乘以二等于六。Sān chéng yǐ èr děngyú liù.

timetable N 1（火车／长途汽车）时刻表 (huǒchē/chángtú qìchē) shíkèbiǎo 2（活动）日程表 (huódòng) rìchéngbiǎo

timid ADJ 胆小的 dǎnxiǎo de, 胆怯的 dǎnqiè de

timidity N 胆怯 dǎnqiè

timing N 时间的选择 shíjiān de xuǎnzé
perfect timing 时间选得完美 shíjiān xuǎn dé wánměi

tin N 1 锡 xī 2 铁罐 tiěguàn, 金属盒子 jīnshǔ hézi

tinder N 火绒 huǒróng, 引火物 yǐnhuǒwù

tinderbox N 1 火绒盒 huǒrónghé 2 危险的局面 wēixiǎn de júmiàn, 火药桶 huǒyàotǒng

tinfoil N 锡纸 xīzhǐ [M. WD 张 zhāng]

tinge I N 1 淡淡的色彩 dàndàn de sècǎi 2 些微的感情 xiēwēi de gǎnqíng
tinge of regret 稍许有些悔意 shāoxǔ yǒuxiē huǐyì II v 1 淡淡地着色 dàndàn de zhuó sè 2 使…稍带 [+感情] shǐ...shāo dài [+gǎnqíng]
a voice tinged with regret 稍带悔意的口吻 shāo dài huǐyì de kǒuwěn

tingle I v 1 感到刺痛 gǎndào cìtòng 2 感到兴奋 gǎndào xīngfèn II N 刺痛感 cìtòng gǎn

tinker v 马马虎虎地修理 mǎma hūhū de xiūlǐ, 稍稍对付一下 shāoshāo duìfu yíxià

tinkle I v 发出叮当当声 fāchū dīngdāngshēng, 叮当叮当响 dīngdāng dīngdāng xiǎng II N 叮当声 dīngdāngshēng

tinny ADJ 尖细刺耳的 [+声音] jiānxì cì'ěr de [+shēngyīn]

tinsel N 1（装饰用的）闪光纸 (zhuāngshì yòng de) shǎnguāngzhǐ [M. WD 张 zhāng] 2 花哨无用的东西 huāshao wúyòng de dōngxi

tint I N 1（淡）颜色 (dàn) yánsè 2 染发剂 rǎnfàjì II v 给 [+头发] 染色 gěi [+tóufa] rǎnsè

tiny ADJ 微小的 wēixiǎo de ■ *A giant oak tree comes from a tiny acorn.* 高大的橡树来自微小的橡树果实。Gāodà de xiàngshù láizì wēixiǎo de xiàngshù guǒshí.

tip¹ I N 小费 xiǎofèi II v 付小费 fù xiǎofèi ■ *Have you tipped the taxi driver?* 你付给出租汽车司机小费了吗？Nǐ fùgěi chūzū qìchē sījī xiǎofèi le ma?

tip² I N 1 提示 tíshì ■ *She gave him some tips on how to make good coffee.* 她给他一些提示怎么样煮咖啡。Tā gěi tā yìxiē tíshì zěnmeyàng zhǔ kāfēi. 2 秘密情报 mìmì qíngbào II v 透露情报 tòulù qíngbào
to tip sb off sth 向某人通风报信 xiàng mǒurén tōngfēng bàoxìn

tip³ I N 顶端 dǐngduān
tip of an iceberg 冰山的一角 bīngshān de yìjiǎo
on the tip of one's tongue 就在嘴边（可是记不起）jiù zài zuǐbiān (kěshì jìbuqǐ) II v（使…）倾斜 (shǐ...) qīngxié,（使…）倒下 (shǐ...) dǎoxià

tip-off N 1 提示 tíshì, 暗示 ànshì 2（警察的）告发 (jǐngchá de) gàofā, 通风报信 tōngfēng bàoxìn 3（篮球比赛）开球 (lánqiú bǐsài) kāiqiú

tipper N 给小费的人 gěi xiǎofèi de rén
a generous tipper 付小费很大方的人 fù xiǎofèi hěn dàfang de rén

tipster N 出卖情报的人 chūmài qíngbào de rén, 告密者 gàomìzhě

tipsy ADJ 稍微有点醉的 shāowēi yǒudiǎn zuì de

tiptoe I N 脚尖 jiǎojiān II v 踮着脚走 diànzhe jiǎo zǒu, 悄悄地走 qiāoqiāo de zǒu

tirade N 长篇抨击性讲话 chángpiān pēngjīxìng jiǎnghuà

tire, tyre N [汽车+] 轮胎 [qìchē+] lúntāi

tired ADJ 1 累 lèi, 疲倦的 píjuàn de 2 厌倦的 yànjuàn de ■ *Don't you get tired of listening to the same music over and over again?* 这同样的音乐，你听了又听，不觉得厌倦吗？Zhè tóngyàng de yīnyuè, nǐ tīngle yòu tīng, bù juéde yànjuàn ma?

tireless ADJ（孜孜）不倦的 (zīzī) bújuàn de, 不知疲倦的 bù zhī píjuàn de

tiresome ADJ 烦人的 fánrén de, 令人厌烦的 lìngrén yànfán de

tiring ADJ 令人疲劳的 lìngrén píláo de, 令人疲倦的 lìngrén píjuàn de

tissue N 1（动／植物）组织 (dòng/zhíwù) zǔzhī
muscle tissue 肌肉组织 jīròuzǔzhī 2 纸巾 zhǐjīn [M. WD 张 zhāng], 面巾纸 miànjīnzhǐ [M. WD 张 zhāng] 3（包装）薄纸 (bāozhuāng) báozhǐ [M. WD 张 zhāng]

tit N（女人的）乳房 (nǚrén de) rǔfáng

titan, Titan N 1（希腊神话中的）大力士 (Xīlà shénhuà zhōng de) dàlìshì, 巨人 jùrén 2 泰斗 tàidǒu, 大师 dàshī

titanic ADJ 力大无穷的 lìdà wúqióng de, 巨大的 jùdà de

tit-for-tat ADJ 针锋相对的 zhēnfēng xiāngduì de, 以牙还牙的 yǐ yá huán yá de

tithe N 什一税 shíyíshuì, 什一费 shíyífèi

titillate v 使…兴奋的 shǐ...xīngfèn de,（性）挑逗 (xìng) tiǎodòu

title I N 1 书名 shūmíng, 题目 tímù ■ *The book*

has an interesting title. 这本书的书名很有趣。Zhè běn shū de shūmíng hěn yǒuqu.

title page 书名页 shūmíngyè

title role 剧名角色 jùmíng juésè

2 称号 chēnghào, 头衔 tóuxián **3** 所有权 suǒyǒuquán

title deed 产权证 chǎnquánzhèng, 房契 fángqì

titled ADJ 有贵族称号的 yǒu guìzú chēnghào de

titter v 窃笑 qièxiào, 傻笑 shǎxiào

tizzy N (in a tizzy) 心慌意乱的 xīn huāng yì luàn de

to¹ marker of verb infinitive

to² PREP **1** 往 wǎng, 向 xiàng, 到 dào

to walk to town 走到城里 zǒudào chéngli

2 (达) 到 (dá) dào

toad N (癞) 蛤蟆 (lài) háma [M. WD 只 zhī], 蟾蜍 chánchú [M. WD 只 zhī]

toady I N 马屁精 mǎpìjīng II v 拍马屁 pāi mǎpì, 奉承 fèngchéng

to and fro ADV 来来往往地 láilai wǎngwǎng de

to pace to and fro 走来走去 zǒulái zǒuqù

toast¹ I N 烤面包 kǎomiànbāo II v 烤 烤 kǎo, 烘 hōng

toast² I N 祝酒 zhùjiǔ ■ *I'd like to propose a toast to our generous host and hostess.* 我愿建议为我们慷慨的主人干杯! Wǒ yuàn jiànyì wèi wǒmen kāngkǎi de zhǔrén gānbēi! II v 为…举杯祝酒 wéi…jǔbēi zhùjiǔ

toaster N 烤面包器 kǎomiànbāoqì

toasty ADJ 暖洋洋的 nuǎnyángyáng de, 暖烘烘的 nuǎnhōnghōng de

tobacco N 烟草 yāncǎo, 烟叶 yānyè

tobacconist N 烟草商 yāncǎoshāng, 烟店老板 yāndiàn lǎobǎn

toboggan I N 平底木雪橇 píng dǐ mù xuěqiāo II v 坐平底木雪橇 zuò píng dǐ mù xuěqiāo

today N, ADV 今天 jīntiān ■ *China today is vastly different from China in the past.* 当今中国和过去大不一样。Dāngjīn Zhōngguó hé guòqù dà bù yíyàng.

toddle v [幼儿+] 蹒跚学走路 [yòu'ér+] pánshān xué zǒulù

toddler N 刚学走路的小孩 gāng xué zǒulù de xiǎohái

to-do list N 行动时刻表 xíngdòng shíkèbiǎo [M. WD 张 zhāng]

toe N 脚趾 jiǎozhǐ

TOEFL (= Test of English as a Foreign Language) ABBREV 托福考试 tuōfú kǎoshì

toehold N 立脚点 lìjiǎodiǎn

to get a toehold in sth 在某事中取得了立脚点 zài mǒushì zhōng qǔdé le lìjiǎodiǎn

toenail N 脚趾甲 jiǎozhǐjiǎ

toe-to-toe ADJ (to go toe-to-toe with sb) 与某人激烈对抗 yǔ mǒurén jīliè duìkàng

toffee N 太妃糖 tàifēitáng

tofu N 豆腐 dòufu

together I ADV 一起 yìqǐ, 一块儿 yíkuàir ■ *This glue should hold the two boards together.* 这种胶水应该能把这两块木板粘在一起。Zhè zhǒng jiāoshuǐ yīnggāi néng bǎ zhè liǎng kuài mùbǎn zhān zài yìqǐ. II ADJ 思路清晰的 sīlù qīngxī de, 有条有理的 yǒu tiáo yǒu lǐ de

togetherness N 友爱团结 yǒu'ài tuánjié

toggle N (计算机) 切换键 (jìsuànjī) qiēhuànjiàn

toil I v **1** 辛苦工作 xīnkǔ gōngzuò, 日夜劳作 rìyè láozuò **2** 吃力地行走 chīlì de xíngzǒu II N 劳作 láozuò, 苦干 kǔgàn

toilet N 便缸 biàngāng, 厕所 cèsuǒ

to flush the toilet 冲洗马桶 chōngxǐ mǎtǒng

toilet paper 卫生纸 wèishēngzhǐ [M. WD 张 zhāng], 手纸 shǒuzhǐ [M. WD 张 zhāng]

toilet water 花露水 huālùshuǐ

toiletries N 梳洗用具 shūxǐ yòngjù

token I N **1** 象征 xiàngzhēng, 标志 biāozhì **2** 代币 dàibì

subway token 地铁代币 dìtiě dàibì

token of appreciation 感谢的象征 gǎnxiè de xiàngzhēng

II ADJ 象征性的 xiàngzhēngxìng de

a token compromise 象征性妥协 xiàngzhēngxìng tuǒxié

tokenism N 表面文章 biǎomiàn wénzhāng, 装点门面 zhuāngdiǎn ménmian

told See tell

tolerable ADJ 过得去 guòdequ, 尚可接受的 shàngkě jiēshòu de

tolerance N 宽容 kuānróng, 容忍 róngrěn

religious tolerance 宗教宽容 zōngjiào kuānróng, 容忍不同的宗教 róngrěn bùtóng de zōngjiào

tolerant ADJ **1** 宽容的 kuānróng de, 容忍的 róngrěn de **2** 能忍耐的 [+植物] néng rěnnài de [+zhíwù]

tolerate v 容忍 róngrěn, 容许 róngxǔ

toll¹ I N N **1** 伤亡人数 shāngwáng rénshù **2** 道路使用费 dàolù shǐyòngfèi, 通行费 tōngxíngfèi

toll booth 道路收费处 dàolù shōufèichù, 公路收费处 gōnglù shōufèichù

toll² I N 钟声 zhōngshēng II v 敲 (丧) 钟 qiāo (sāngzhōng)

toll-bridge N 收费桥 shōufèiqiáo [M. WD 座 zuò]

toll-free ADJ 免费的 [+电话] miǎnfèi de [+diànhuà]

tollgate N (公路) 收费站 (gōnglù) shōufèizhàn

tomato N 番茄 fānqié, 西红柿 xīhóngshì

tomato sauce 番茄酱 fānqiéjiàng

tomb N 坟 fén, 坟墓 fénmù

tomboy N 假小子 jiǎxiǎozi, 野丫头 yěyātou

tombstone N 墓碑 mùbēi [M. WD 块 kuài]

tomcat N 公猫 gōng māo

tome N 大本厚书 dà běn hòu shū

tomfoolery N 愚蠢行为 yúchǔn xíngwéi

tomorrow N, ADV 明天 míngtiān ■ *Tomorrow will be Friday.* 明天是星期五。Míngtiān shì xīngqīwǔ. ■ *I'm going fishing tomorrow. Want to join me?* 我明天去钓鱼，一块儿去吗？Wǒ míngtiān qù diàoyú, yíkuàir qù ma?

ton N 吨 dūn
tons of 大量的 dàliàng de

tone I N 1 语气 yǔqì, 腔调 qiāngdiào 2 主调 zhǔdiào, 调子 diàozi ■ *The general tone of the report is rather optimistic.* 报告的主调很乐观。Bàogào de zhǔdiào hěn lèguān. 3 色调 sèdiào, 色度 sèdù 4 电话信号 diànhuà xìnhào
an engaged tone 占线信号 zhànxiàn xìnhào
5（肌肉）结实程度 (jīròu) jiēshi chéngdù II v 使 [+肌肤] 健康 shǐ [+ jīfū] jiànkāng
to tone down ① 使颜色柔和 shǐ yánsè róuhé ② 使语气缓和 shǐ yǔqì huǎnhé

tone-deaf ADJ 不能辨别不同音的 bùnéng biànbié bùtóng yīn de

toner N 墨粉 mòfěn

tongs N 夹子 jiāzi, 镊子 nièzi

tongue I N 1 舌头 shétou
tongue twister 绕口令 ràokǒulìng
2 语言 yǔyán
mother tongue 母语 mǔyǔ ■ *He speaks perfect English, though his mother tongue is Spanish.* 虽然他的母语是西班牙语，他的英语说得很完美。Suīrán tā de mǔyǔ shì Xībānyáyǔ, tā de Yīngyǔ shuōde hěn wánměi.
a slip of the tongue 口误 kǒuwù

tongue-in-check ADV 开玩笑的 kāi wánxiào de, 说了玩的 shuō le wán de

tongue-lashing N 破口大骂 pòkǒu dàmà, 狠狠训斥 hěnhěn xùnchì

tongue-tied ADJ 张口结舌的 zhāngkǒu jiéshé de, 说不出话的 shuōbuchū huà de

tonic I N 1（滋）补品 (zī) bǔpǐn, 强身剂 qiángshēnjì
tonic water 奎宁水 kuíníngshuǐ
2 有利于身心健康的事 yǒulì yú shēnxīn jiànkāng de shì II ADJ 1 强身滋补的 qiángshēn zībǔ de 2 有利的 yǒulì de
a tonic effect 很有利的效果 hěn yǒulì de xiàoguǒ

tonight N, ADV 今天晚上 jīntiān wǎnshang, 今天夜里 jīntiān yèlǐ ■ *Is there anything interesting in tonight's TV program?* 今天晚上的电视节目有什么有趣的内容吗？Jīntiān wǎnshang de diànshì jiémù yǒu shénme yǒuqù de nèiróng ma?

tonnage N 1 总吨数 zǒngdūnshù 2（船只的）吨位 (chuánzhǐ de) dūnwèi

tonsil N 扁桃体 biǎntáotǐ, 扁桃腺 biǎntáoxiàn
to remove the tonsil 切除扁桃体 qiēchú biǎntáotǐ

tonsillitis N 扁桃体炎 biǎntáotǐyán, 扁桃腺炎 biǎntáoxiànyán

too¹ ADV 也 yě ■ *May I come too?* 我也可以来吗？Wǒ yě kěyǐ lái ma?

too² ADV 太 tài ■ *This test is too difficult for most of the students.* 对大多数学生来说，这次测验太难。Duì dàduōshù xuésheng láishuō, zhè cì cèyàn tài nán.

took See take

tool I N 工具 gōngjù
tool box 工具箱 gōngjùxiāng
tool kit 工具包 gōngjù bāo
tool shed 工具房 gōngjùfáng
II v (to tool up) 装备 zhuāngbèi

toot I v 按 [+汽车喇叭] àn [+qìchē lǎba]
to toot one's own horn 吹捧自己 chuīpěng zìjǐ, 自夸 zìkuā
II N 汽车喇叭声 qìchē lǎbashēng

tooth (PL **teeth**) N 牙齿 yáchǐ [M. WD 颗 kē] ■ *Her dentist told her to brush her teeth at least twice a day.* 牙医要她每天至少刷两次牙。Yáyī yào tā měitiān zhìshǎo shuā liǎng cì yá.
to fight tooth and nail 尽极大努力 jìn jídà nǔlì
to have a sweet tooth 喜欢吃甜的东西 xǐhuan chī tián de dōngxi
to give teeth to … 使 [+规定] 有效力 shǐ [+guīdìng] yǒu xiàolì

toothache N 牙疼 yáténg, 牙痛 yátòng

toothbrush N 牙刷 yáshuā [M. WD 把 bǎ]

toothpaste N 牙膏 yágāo [M. WD 管 guǎn]

toothpick N 牙签 yáqiān [M. WD 根 gēn]

top¹ I N 1 顶 dǐng, 顶部 dǐngbù ■ *We climbed to the top of the hill and admired the view of the valley.* 我们爬上山顶，欣赏山谷的景色。Wǒmen páshang shāndǐng, xīnshǎng shāngǔ de jǐngsè.
2 [台+] 面 [tái+] miàn, [桌+] 面 [zhuō+] miàn ■ *I don't like a table with a glass top.* 我不喜欢玻璃台面的桌子。Wǒ bù xǐhuan bōli táimiàn de zhuōzi. 3 最高地位 zuìgāo dìwèi, 顶峰 dǐngfēng
top dog 大人物 dàrénwù
4 [女子+] 上衣 [nǚzǐ+] shàngyī II ADJ 最高的 zuìgāo de, 顶级的 dǐngjí de ■ *A top scientist was appointed to head the research team.* 一位顶级科学家被任命领导这个科研组。Yí wèi dǐngjí kēxuéjiā bèi rènmìng lǐngdǎo zhè ge kēyánzǔ.
III v 超过 chāoguo, 胜过 shèngguo
on top of ① 除了…以外 chúle…yǐwài ② 能对付 néng duìfu, 能控制 néng kòngzhì ■ *I'm on top of the problem.* 我能对付这个问题。Wǒ néng duìfu zhè ge wèntí.

top² N 陀螺 tuóluó

top-heavy ADJ 1 上重下轻的 shàng zhòng xià qīng de 2 管理人员太多的 guǎnlǐ rényuán tài duō de, 将多兵少的 jiāng duō bīng shǎo de

topic N 话题 huàtí, 题目 tímù

topical ADJ 热门（话题）的 rèmén (huàtí) de

topless ADJ 不穿上衣的 [+女子] bù chuān shàngyī de [+nǚzǐ], 袒胸的 tǎnxiōng de

topmost ADJ 最上面的 zuì shàngmian de, 最高的 zuì gāo de

topnotch ADJ 第一流的 dìyīliú de, 最杰出的 zuì jiéchū de

topography N 1 地貌（学）dìmào (xué), 地形 dìxíng 2（国家的）概貌 (guójiā de) gàimào, 概况 gàikuàng

topping N（加在食品上的）配料 (jiā zài shípǐnshang de) pèiliào

topple V 推翻 tuīfān, 使…倒塌 shǐ...dǎotā

top-secret ADJ 绝密的 juémì de

topsoil N 表土层 biǎotǔcéng, 耕作层 gēngzuò-céng

topsy-turvy ADJ 1 乱七八糟的 [+房间] luànqībāzāo de [+fángjiān], 凌乱不堪的 língluàn bùkān de 2 有好有坏的 [+工作] yǒu hǎo yǒu huài de [+gōngzuò]

top-up card N 加款使用卡 jiā kuǎn shǐyòngkǎ [M. WD 张 zhāng]

torch I N 火炬 huǒjù, 火把 huǒbǎ II V 点燃 diǎnrán

tore See **tear²**

torment I N 折磨 zhémo, 痛苦 tòngkǔ II V 折磨 zhémo, 使 [+人] 痛苦 shǐ [+rén] tòngkǔ

torn See **tear²**

tornado N 龙卷风 lóngjuǎnfēng

to be hit by a tornado 受到龙卷风的袭击 shòudào lóngjuǎnfēng de xíjī

torpedo I N 鱼雷 yúléi [M. WD 枚 méi] II V 1 用鱼雷袭击 yòng yúléi xíjī 2 破坏 pòhuài

torque N（发动机的）扭矩 (fādòngjī de) niǔjǔ

torrent N 激流 jīliú

a torrent of criticism 接连不断的抨击 jiēlián búduàn de pēngjī

torrid ADJ 1 热烈的 [+情爱] rèliè de [+qíng'ài], 炽热的 zhìrè de 2 灼热的 [+天气] zhuórè de [+tiānqì]

torso N 人体躯干 réntǐ qūgàn

tort N 民事案件 mínshì ànjiàn

tortilla N（墨西哥）薄玉米饼 (Mòxīgē) báo yùmǐbǐng [M. WD 片 piàn]

tortoise N（乌）龟 (wū) guī

tortuous ADJ 1 曲折的 qūzhé de, 弯弯曲曲的 wān-wān qūqū de 2 错综复杂的 cuòzōng fùzá de

torture I N 酷刑 kùxíng, 刑讯 xíngxùn II V 1 对…施酷刑 duì...shī kùxíng

to torture sb to death 对某人实行酷刑致死 duì mǒurén shíxíng kùxíng zhìsǐ

2 折磨 zhémo

toss I V 1 扔 rēng, 掷 zhì

to toss out 扔掉 rēngdiào, 丢弃 diūqì

2 使…动荡 shǐ...dòngdàng

to toss and turn（在床上）翻来复去 (zài chuángshang) fānlái fùqù

3 掷硬币（以作决定）zhì yìngbì (yǐ zuò juédìng) II N (coin toss) 掷硬币以决定 zhì yìngbì yǐ juédìng

toss-up N 还没有决定的事 hái méiyǒu juédìng de shì, 未见分晓的事 wèi jiàn fēnxiǎo de shì

tot N 小娃娃 xiǎowáwá

total I ADJ 总的 zǒng de, 全部的 quánbù de II N 总数 zǒngshù III V 总数为 zǒngshù wéi, 共计 gòngjì

totalitarian ADJ 极权主义的 jíquánzhǔyì de

totality N 整体 zhěngtǐ, 全部 quánbù

totally ADV 完全 wánquán

tote V 随身带 suíshēn dài

tote bag N 大袋子 dà dàizi

totem N 图腾 túténg

totem pole 图腾柱 túténg zhù

totter V 1 摇摇晃晃 yáoyáo huànghuàng 2 摇摇欲坠 yáoyáo yù zhuì

to totter toward collapse 走向崩溃 zǒuxiàng bēngkuì

touch I V 1 触 chù, 接触 jiēchù ■ *Don't touch the switch with wet fingers.* 不要用湿手接触开关。Bú yào yòng shī shǒu jiēchù kāiguān. 2 碰 pèng, 碰到 pèngdao 3 感动 gǎndòng ■ *I was deeply touched by her story.* 她的故事使我深受感动。Tā de gùshi shǐ wǒ shēn shòu gǎndòng.

to touch on/upon 涉及 shèjí, 谈到 tándao

touch wood 老天保佑 lǎotiān bǎoyòu

II N 1 碰 pèng, 触 chù, 接触 jiēchù ■ *She felt the touch of his hand.* 她感觉到他的手在碰她。Tā gǎnjuédao tā de shǒu zài pèng tā.

touch screen 触摸式显示屏 chùmō shì xiǎnshìpíng

to lose touch 失去联系 shīqù liánxi

to stay in touch 保持联系 bǎochí liánxi ■ *My brother stays in touch with his army buddies.* 我的哥哥还和军队中的战友保持联系。Wǒ de gēge hái he jūnduì zhōng de zhànyǒu bǎochí liánxi.

2 手法 shǒufǎ, 风格 fēnggé 3 (a touch) 有点儿 yǒudiǎnr

touch-and-go ADJ 风险极大的 fēngxiǎn jídà de, 极其危险的 jíqí wēixiǎn de

touchdown N 1（飞机）降落 (fēijī) jiàngluò 2（橄榄球）触地得分 (gǎnlǎnqiú) chù dì dé fēn

touched ADJ 受感动的 shòu gǎndòng de, 感激的 gǎnjī de

touchstone N 试金石 shìjīnshí, 检验标准 jiǎnyàn biāozhǔn

touchy ADJ 1 十分敏感的 [+人] shífēn mǐngǎn de [+rén] 2 微妙的 [+问题] wēimiào de [+wèntí]

tough I ADJ 1 坚韧的 [+材料] jiānrèn de [+cáiliào] 2 坚强的 [+人] jiānqiáng de [+rén], 耐劳的

nàiláo de **3** 棘手的 [+问题] jíshǒu de [+wèntí], 困难的 kùnnan de

tough love 严厉的爱 yánlì de ài, 严格要求的真爱 yángé yāoqiú de zhēn ài

II v (to tough it out) 渡过（难关）dùguò (nánguān), 挺过来 tǐngguòlai

toughen, toughen up v 使坚韧/坚强 shǐ jiānrèn/jiānqiáng

toupee N 假发 jiǎfà

tour I N **1** 旅游 lǚyóu, 旅行 lǚxíng ■ *The bus tour of Paris would have been better if the traffic had not been so bad.* 如果交通情况不那么坏，在巴黎的客车旅游会更好。Rúguǒ jiāotōng qíngkuàng bú nàme huài, zài Bālí de kèchē lǚyóu huì gèng hǎo. **2** 参观 cānguān ■ *Our class went on a tour of the nearby college last week.* 我们年级上星期去附近的大学参观。Wǒmen niánjí shàng xīngqī qù fùjìn de dàxué cānguān. **II** v 旅游 lǚyóu, 旅行 lǚxíng

guided tour 有导游的旅游 yǒu dǎoyóu de lǚyóu

package tour 一揽子旅游 yìlǎnzi lǚyóu

tourism N 旅游业 lǚyóuyè

tourist I N 旅游者 lǚyóuzhě ■ *Tourists like to take pictures at this historic site.* 旅游者喜欢在这个历史名胜地拍照。Lǚyóuzhě xǐhuan zài zhè ge lìshǐ míngshèng dì pāizhào. **II** ADJ 旅游（者/行业）的 lǚyóu (zhě/hángyè) de

tourist agency 旅游社 lǚyóushè

tourist attraction 旅游胜地 lǚyóu shèngdì

tourist class（飞机/轮船）经济舱 (fēijī/lúnchuán) jīngjìcāng

tourist trap 旅游者陷阱 lǚyóuzhě xiànjǐng

tournament N 锦标赛 jǐnbiāosài

tourniquet N 止血带 zhǐxuèdài [M. WD 条 tiáo]

tousled ADJ 蓬乱的 [+头发] péngluàn de [+tóufa]

tout v **1** 赞扬 zànyáng, 推崇 tuīchóng **2** 推销 [+商品] tuīxiāo [+shāngpǐn], 兜售 dōushòu

tow v, N 拖 tuō, 牵引 qiānyǐn

tow truck 托运车 tuōyùn chē

in tow 紧跟在后面 jǐngēn zàihòu miàn

toward, towards PREP **1** 朝着 cháozhe, 向着 xiàngzhe ■ *When I got out the car, my dog came running towards me.* 我下车时，狗朝我跑来。Wǒ xiàchē shí, gǒu cháo wǒ pǎolai. **2** 对 duì, 对于 duìyú ■ *She is friendly towards her colleagues.* 她对同事很友好。Tā duì tóngshì hěn yǒuhǎo. **3** 接近 jiējìn ■ *Towards the end of his life the writer became more withdrawn and had few friends.* 在晚年，这位作家变得更内向，没有多少朋友。Zài wǎnnián, zhè wèi zuòjiā biànde gèng nèixiàng, méiyǒu duōshǎo péngyou.

towaway zone N 禁止停车区（违章则拖走车）jìnzhǐ tíngchē qū (wéizhāng zé tuō zǒu chē)

towel I N 毛巾 máojīn

bath towel 浴巾 yùjīn

face towel 面巾 miànjīn, 手巾 shǒujīn

II v (to towel off/down) 用毛巾擦干 yòng máojīn cāgān

tower I N 高塔 gāo tǎ [M. WD 座 zuò] ■ *The church has a medieval bell tower.* 教堂有一座中世纪的钟塔。Jiàotáng yǒu yí zuò Zhōngshìjì de zhōng tǎ.

tower model 塔式计算机 tǎ shì jìsuànjī

observation tower 了望塔 liáowàngtǎ

TV tower 电视塔 diànshìtǎ

II v 高于 gāoyú ■ *The skyscraper towers over all the other buildings in town.* 摩天大楼高于城里所有其他的建筑。Mótiān dàlóu gāoyú chénglǐ suǒyǒu qítā de jiànzhù.

towering ADJ **1** 高耸的 [+树] gāosǒng de [+shù] **2** 杰出的 [+人物] jiéchū de [+rénwù]

town N **1** 镇 zhèn, 小城 xiǎo chéng

town council 镇议会 zhèn yìhuì, 市议会 shì yìhuì

town hall 市政厅 shìzhèngtīng

2 闹市区 nàoshìqū

to go into town 到市区去 dào shìqū qù, 进城 jìn chéng

townhouse N 连栋房屋 liándòng fángwū, 排屋 pái wū

township N 镇 zhèn, 镇区 zhèn qū

townspeople, townsfolk N 城镇居民 chéngzhèn jūmín

toxic ADJ 有毒的 yǒudú de

toxic waste 有毒垃圾 yǒudú lājī

toxicilogy N 毒物学 dúwùxué, 毒理学 dúlǐxué

toxicity N 毒性 dúxìng

toxin N 毒素 dúsù

toy I N 玩具 wánjù, 小玩意儿 xiǎowányìr ■ *Even a toy gun is not permitted on airplanes.* 甚至玩具手枪都不准带上飞机。Shènzhì wánjù shǒuqiāng dōu bù zhǔn dàishang fēijī. **II** v (to toy with) 不很认真地考虑 bù hěn rènzhēn de kǎolǜ **III** ADJ 极小的 jíxiǎo de, 迷你型的 mínǐxíng de

trace I v **1** 追踪 zhuīzōng ■ *The police have traced the criminal to Florida.* 警方追踪罪犯到佛罗里达。Jǐngfāng zhuīzōng zuìfàn dào Fóluólǐdá. **2** 追寻…的根源 zhuīxún...de gēnyuán **II** N **1** 踪迹 zōngjì ■ *The girl disappeared without a trace.* 女孩消失得无影无踪。Nǚhái xiāoshīde wú yǐng wú zōng. **2** 微量 wēiliàng

trace element 微量元素 wēiliàng yuánsù

tracer N 曳光弹 yèguāngdàn [M. WD 发 fā]

trachea N 气管 qìguǎn

track I N **1** 轨迹 guǐjì, 轨道 guǐdào

track record 业绩记录 yèjì jìlù, 过去的表现 guòqù de biǎoxiàn

to be on the right track 走上正轨 zǒushàng zhèngguǐ

to keep/lose track of sth 保持/失去与某人的联系 bǎochí/shīqù yǔ mǒurén de liánxì

2 跑道 pǎodào, 径赛（长跑、短跑，等）jìngsài (chángpǎo, duǎnpǎo, děng)
track and field (events) 田径赛（项目）tiánjìngsài (xiàngmù)
3 小路 xiǎolù [м. wᴅ 条 tiáo], 小道 xiǎodào
II v 1 追踪 zhuīzōng, 跟踪 gēnzōng
to track sb down 追踪到某人 zhuīzōng dào mǒurén
2 记录 [+某人的表现] jìlù [+mǒurén de biǎoxiàn]

tract N 1 （人体的）系统 (réntǐ de) xìtǒng
the digestive tract 消化系统 xiāohuàxìtǒng
2 一大片（土地）yí dàpiān (tǔdì) **3** [宣扬宗教的+] 小册子[xuānyáng zōngjiào de+] xiǎocèzi

traction N 1 附着摩擦力 fùzhuó mócālì **2** 牵引 (手)术 qiānyǐn (shǒu) shù **3** （车辆）牵引力 (chēliàng) qiānyǐnlì

tractor N 拖拉机 tuōlājī [м. wᴅ 台 tái], 拖车牵引车 tuōchē qiānyǐnchē [м. wᴅ 辆 liàng]

trade I N 1 贸易 màoyì, 生意 shēngyì ■ *The mission of the delegation is to promote trade.* 代表团 的使命是促进贸易。Dàibiǎotuán de shǐmìng shì cùjìn màoyì.
trade deficit 贸易赤字 màoyì chìzì
trade fair 交易会 jiāoyìhuì
arms trade 军火生意 jūnhuǒ shēngyì
2 手艺 shǒuyì, 职业 zhíyè
to learn a trade 学一门手艺 xué yìmén shǒuyì
3 行业 hángyè
trade union 工会 gōnghuì
II v 1 从事贸易 cóngshì màoyì, 做买卖 zuò mǎimai ■ *The firm has abundant experience in trading with Asian countries.* 这家商行和亚洲国 家做买卖有丰富的经验。Zhè jiā shānghán hé Yàzhōu guójiā zuò mǎimai yǒu fēngfù de jīngyàn.
2 交换 jiāohuàn ■ *This is my dream job; I wouldn't trade it for anything.* 这是我的理想工作， 我不会拿它来换任何东西。Zhè shì wǒ de lǐxiǎng gōngzuò, wǒ bú huì ná tā lái huàn rènhé dōngxi.

trade-in N 作价贴换交易 zuòjià tiēhuàn jiāoyì
trademark N 商标 shāngbiāo
trade-off N 权衡得失 quánhéng déshī
trader N 商人 shāngrén, 经商者 jīngshāngzhě
tradition N 传统 chuántǒng, 惯例 guànlì ■ *It is a tradition in many countries to exchange gifts on Christmas Day.* 在很多国家，圣诞节时交换礼物是 一个传统。Zài hěn duō guójiā, Shèngdànjié shí jiāohuàn lǐwù shì yí ge chuántǒng.
to break with tradition 打破惯例 dǎpò guànlì, 与传统决裂 yǔ chuántǒng juéliè

traditional ADJ 传统的 chuántǒng de
traditionalist N 传统主义者 chuántǒngzhǔyìzhě, 热爱传统的人 rè'ài chuántǒng de rén
traffic I N 1 来往车辆 láiwǎng chēliàng, 交通 jiāotōng ■ *On that morning the traffic was heavy as usual.* 那天早上，交通和往常一样繁忙。Nà tiān zǎoshang, jiāotōng hé wǎngcháng yíyàng fánmáng.
traffic jam 交通堵塞 jiāotōng dǔsè
traffic lights 红绿灯 hónglǜdēng, 交通灯 jiāotōngdēng
light/heavy traffic 很少／很多车辆 hěn shǎo/ hěn duō chēliàng
2 交通运输 jiāotōng yùnshū
air traffic control 空中交通管制 kōngzhōng jiāotōng guǎnzhì
3 非法交易 fēifǎ jiāoyì **II v** 非法交易 fēifǎ jiāoyì

trafficking N 非法贩卖 fēifǎ fànmài
arms trafficking 贩卖武器 fànmài wǔqì
drug trafficking 贩卖毒品 fànmài dúpǐn

tragedy N 1 悲剧 bēijù **2** 悲剧性事件 bēijùxìng shìjiàn, 惨剧 cǎnjù **3** 不幸（事件）búxìng (shìjiàn)

tragic ADJ 悲剧性的 bēijùxìng de, 极其不幸的 jíqí búxìng de

tragicomedy N 悲喜剧 bēixǐjù

trail I v 1 跟在后面 gēn zài hòumiàn, 尾随 wěisuí, 跟踪 gēnzōng **2** 落后于 luòhòu yú
to trail off（声音）逐渐变小 (shēngyīn) zhújiàn biàn xiǎo
II N 1 小路 xiǎolù, 小径 xiǎojìng **2** 足迹 zújì, 痕 迹 hénjì
a trail of blood 一长条血迹 yì cháng tiáo xuèjī
to be on the trail of 跟踪 gēnzōng

trailblazer N 开路先锋 kāilù xiānfēng, 创始人 chuàngshǐrén

trailer N 1 挂车 guàchē [м. wᴅ 辆 liàng], 拖车 tuōchē [м. wᴅ 辆 liàng] **2** （拖在汽车后的）活动 房屋 (tuō zài qìchē hòu de) huódòng fángwū **3** （电影）新片预告 (diànyǐng) xīn piàn yùgào
trailer park 活动房车停车场 huódòng fángchē tíngchēchǎng

train I N 1 火车 huǒchē, 列车 lièchē **2** 一连串 yìliánchuàn, 一系列 yíxìliè
train of events 一系列事件 yíxìliè shìjiàn
one's train of thought 思路 sīlù
II v 1 训练 xùnliàn ■ *The athletes trained hard for the Olympic Games.* 运动员们为奥林匹克运 动会刻苦训练。Yùndòngyuánmen wèi Àolínpǐkè Yùndònghuì kèkǔ xùnliàn. **2** 把 [+镜头] 对准 bǎ [+jìngtóu] duìzhǔn, 把 [+枪口] 瞄准 bǎ [+qiāngkǒu] miáozhǔn

trainee N 培训生 péixùnshēng, 实习生 shíxíshēng
teacher trainee 实习教师 shíxí jiàoshī

training N 训练 xùnliàn, 培训 péixùn ■ *All employees have to take security training once a year.* 所有的雇员每年都要参加一次安全训练。Suǒyǒu de gùyuán měi nián dōu yào cānjiā yí cì ānquán xùnliàn.

trait N 特征 tèzhēng, 品性 pǐnxìng
genetic trait 遗传特性 yíchuán tèxìng

national trait 民族特性 mínzú tèxìng, 国民性 guómínxìng

traitor N 叛徒 pàntú, 卖国贼 màiguózéi

trajectory N（抛物）轨道 (pāo wù) guǐdào, 抛物线 pāowùxiàn

tram N 1 有轨电车 yǒuguǐ diànchē [M. WD 辆 liàng] 2（上山）缆车 (shàngshān) lǎnchē [M. WD 辆 liàng]

tramp I N 1 流浪汉 liúlànghàn, 游民 yóumín 2 荡妇 dàngfù, 淫妇 yínfù 3 沉重的脚步声 chénzhòng de jiǎobùshēng 4 长途跋涉 chángtú báshè II v 脚步沉重地走 jiǎobù chénzhòng de zǒu

trample v 1 践踏 jiàntà, 踩坏 cǎi huài 2 无视 [+他人的权利] wúshì [+tārén de quánlì], 蔑视 mièshì

trampoline N 蹦床 bèngchuáng, 弹床 dàn chuáng

trance N 恍惚（状态）huǎnghū (zhuàngtài)
in a trance 走神 zǒu shén, 发呆 fādāi

tranquil ADJ 宁静的 níngjìng de, 平静的 píngjìng de

tranquilizer N 镇静剂 zhènjìngjì, 安定药 āndìngyào

transact v 做生意 zuò shēngyì, 买卖 mǎimai

transaction N 1 交易 jiāoyì, 生意 shēngyì
online transaction 网上交易 wǎngshàng jiāoyì 2 办理 bànlǐ, 处理 chǔlǐ

transatlantic ADJ 横跨大西洋的 héngkuà Dàxīyáng de, 欧美之间的 Ōu-Měi zhījiān de

transcend v 超越 chāoyuè, 超出 chāochū

transcendental ADJ 超越人类知识经验的 chāoyuè rénlèi zhīshi jīngyàn de

transcontinental ADJ 横跨大陆的 héngkuà dàlù de
transcontinental railroad 横贯大陆的铁路 héngguàn dàlù de tiělù

transcribe v 1 逐字记录 zhúzì jìlù 2 用音标记下 yòng yīnbiāo jìxià 3 改编 [+乐曲] gǎibiān [+yuèqǔ]

transcript N 1 文字记录 wénzì jìlù 2（大学）学生成绩单 (dàxué) xuésheng chéngjìdān [M. WD 份 fèn]

transcription N 1 记录 jìlù, 标音 biāoyīn 2 抄本 chāoběn [M. WD 份 fèn], 副本 fùběn [M. WD 份 fèn]

transfer I v 1 转学 zhuǎnxué 2 调动 diàodòng ■ He was transferred from the company headquarters to the Beijing branch. 他从公司总部调动到北京分公司。Tā cóng gōngsī zǒngbù diàodòngdao Běijīng fēngōngsī. 3 转账 zhuǎnzhàng, 转让 zhuǎnràng II N 1 调动 diàodòng 2 转账 zhuǎnzhàng 3（权力/财产的）转移 (quánlì/cáichǎn de) zhuǎnyí 4（可移印的）图案 (kě yíyìn de) tú'àn

transfixed ADJ 吓呆的 xiàdāi de, 惊呆的 jīngdāi de

transform v（使…）完全改变 (shǐ…) wánquán gǎibiàn,（使…）变形 (shǐ…) biànxíng

transfomation N 转变 zhuǎnbiàn, 改变 gǎibiàn
social transformation 社会变革 shèhuì biàngé

transfomer N 变压器 biànyāqì [M. WD 台 tái]

transfusion N 1 输血 shūxuè 2 注入资金 zhùrù zījīn

transgress v 违反 [+道德标准] wéifǎn [+dàodé biāozhǔn], 违背 wéibèi

transgression N 违反 wéifǎn, 违背 wéibèi

transient I ADJ 1 流动性的 [+人口] liúdòngxìng de [+rénkǒu] 2 短暂的 [+幸福] duǎnzàn de [+xìngfú] II N 流动人口 liúdòng rénkǒu, 旅馆住客 lǚguǎn zhùkè

transistor N 晶体管 jīngtǐguǎn
transistor radio 晶体管收音机 jīngtǐguǎn shōuyīnjī

transit N 运送 yùnsòng, 运输 yùnshū
transit camp 中转站 zhōngzhuǎnzhàn

transition N 过渡 guòdù, 转变 zhuǎnbiàn
peaceful transition 和平过渡 hépíng guòdù, 和平演变 hépíng yǎnbiàn

transitional ADJ 过渡的 guòdù de
transitional period 过渡阶段 guòdù jiēduàn

transitive verb N（语法）及物动词 (yǔfǎ) jíwù dòngcí

transitory ADJ 短暂的 duǎnzàn de, 一时的 yìshí de

translate v 翻译 fānyì ■ Could you please translate this letter into Chinese? 请你把这封信翻译成中文，好吗？Qǐng nǐ bǎ zhè fēng xìn fānyìchéng Zhōngwén, hǎo ma?
to translate into 转化为 zhuǎnhuà wéi

translation N 1 翻译（作品）fānyì (zuòpǐn)
lost in translation [含义+] 在翻译过程中丢失 [hányì+] zài fānyì guòchéng zhōng diūshī 2 转化 zhuǎnhuà

translator N（翻）译者 (fān) yìzhě, 翻译家 fānyìjiā

translucence N 半透明（状态）bàn tòumíng (zhuàngtài)

translucent ADJ 半透明的 bàn tòumíng de

transmission N 1（汽车）传动装置 (qìchē) chuándòng zhuāngzhì, 变速器 biànsùqì
auto transmission 自动变速器 zìdòng biànsùqì, 自动排挡 zìdòng páidǎng
manual transmission 手动变速器 shǒudòng biànsùqì, 手动排挡 shǒudòng páidǎng 2（电视/电台）节目播放 (diànshì/diàntái) jiémù bōfàng 3（信号）播送 (xìnhào) bōsòng

transmit v 1 播送 bōsòng, 播放 bōfàng 2 传递 chuándì, 传播 chuánbō

transmitter N（电视/电台信号）发射机 (diànshì/diàntái xìnhào) fāshèjī

transparency N 1 幻灯片 huàndēngpiàn 2 透明（性）tòumíng (xìng)

transparent ADJ **1** 透明的 tòumíng de **2** 含义清晰的 hányì qīngxī de

transpire V [事件+] 发生 [shìjiàn+] fāshēng it transpires that 透露出 tòulù chū, 人们得知 rénmen dézhī

transplant I V 移植 yízhí II N **1** 移植 yízhí heart transplant 心脏移植 xīnzàng yízhí **2** 搬迁者 bānqiānzhě

transport V 运输 yùnshū, 运送 yùnsòng

transportation N 交通 jiāotōng, 交通运输 jiāotōng yùnshū ■ With gas prices going up and up, public transportation is becoming more attractive. 由于油价一涨再涨, 公共交通就更有吸引力。Yóuyú yóujià yì zhǎng zài zhǎng, gōnggòng jiāotōng jiù gēng yǒu xīyǐnlì.

transpose V 调换 diàohuàn, 变换 biànhuàn

transsexual N 变性人 biànxìngrén

transvestite N 爱穿异性服装的人 ài chuān yìxìng fúzhuāng de rén

trap I N **1** 捕动物的器具 bǔ dòngwù de qìjù **2** 困境 kùnjìng ■ He was caught in the trap of an unhappy marriage. 他陷入了不幸婚姻的困境。Tā xiànrùle bú xìng hūnyīn de kùnjìng. II V **1** 使…困在 shǐ...kùn zài ■ Five people were trapped in the elevator when it broke down. 电梯坏了, 五个人被困在里面。Diàntī huài le, wǔ ge rén bèi kùn zài lǐmian. **2** 使…落入圈套 shǐ...luòrù quāntào, 诱骗 yòupiàn
trap door (天花板/地板的) 活门 (tiānhuābǎn/dìbǎn de) huómén

trapeze N (杂技表演) 高空秋千 (zájì biǎoyǎn) gāokōng qiūqiān

trapper N 设陷阱捕猎者 shè xiànjǐng bǔlièzhě

trappings N (标志地位级别的) 服饰 (biāozhì dìwèi jíbié de) fúshì

trash I N **1** 垃圾货 lājīhuò
trash bag 垃圾袋 lājīdài
trash can 垃圾桶 lājītǒng
to talk trash 说污辱性的话 shuō wūrǔxìng de huà
2 一钱不值的东西/人 yì qián bù zhí de dōngxi/rén II V **1** 把…说得一钱不值 bǎ... shuó de yì qián bù zhí, 抨击 pēngjī **2** 损坏 sǔnhuài

trashy ADJ 垃圾般的 lājī bān de, 一钱不值的 yì qián bù zhí de

trauma N 痛苦经历 tòngkǔ jīnglì
emotional trauma 精神创伤 jīngshén chuāngshāng

traumatic ADJ 痛苦的 tòngkǔ de, 造成精神创伤的 zàochéng jīngshén chuāngshāng de
a traumatic experience 痛苦的经历 tòngkǔ de jīnglì

traumatize V 使…受到精神创伤 shǐ...shòudào jīngshén chuāngshāng, 使…痛苦 shǐ...tòngkǔ

travel I V **1** 旅行 lǚxíng **2** 传(递) chuán (dì)

■ Light travels at an astonishing speed. 光以惊人的速度传递。Guāng yǐ jīngrén de sùdù chuándì. II N 旅行 lǚxíng
travel agency 旅行社 lǚxíngshè
travel alarm clock 旅行闹钟 lǚxíng nàozhōng

traveler N 旅行者 lǚxíngzhě, 旅客 lǚkè
traveler's check 旅行支票 lǚxíng zhīpiào

traverse V 横越 héngyuè, 穿过 chuānguò

travesty N 嘲弄 cháonòng, 歪曲 wāiqū

trawl N **1** 拖网 tuōwǎng [M. WD 张 zhāng] **2** 搜寻 sōuxún, 查找 cházhǎo

trawler N 拖网渔轮 tuōwǎng yúlún [M. WD 艘 sōu]

tray N 托盘 tuōpán

treacherous ADJ **1** 阴险的 [+人] yīnxiǎn de [+rén], 背信弃义的 bèixìn qìyì de **2** (暗藏) 危险的 [+天气] (àncáng) wēixiǎn de [+tiānqì]

treachery N 背叛(行为) bèipàn (xíngwéi), 背信弃义 bèi xìn qì yì

tread (PT **trod**; PP **trodden**) I V 轻轻地踩踏 qīngqīng de cǎità
to tread carefully 做事十分小心 zuòshì shífēn xiǎoxin, 言行谨慎 yánxing jǐnshèn II N **1** 轻轻的脚步(声) qīngqīng de jiǎobù (shēng) **2** 轮胎花纹 lúntāi huāwén

treadmill N **1** 踏步机 tàbùjī **2** 单调枯燥的生活/工作 dāndiào kūzào de shēnghuó/gōngzuò

treason N 叛国罪 pànguózuì, 通敌罪 tōngdízuì
high treason 严重叛国罪 yánzhòng pànguózuì

treasure I N **1** 珍宝 zhēnbǎo, 宝藏 bǎozàng
treasure house 宝库 bǎokù
family treasure 传家宝 chuánjiābǎo
2 宝贵的人 zhēnguì de rén II V 珍藏 zhēncáng, 珍惜 zhēnxī

treasurer N 财务主管 cáiwù zhǔguǎn, 司库 sīkù

treat I V **1** 对待 duìdài ■ He is believed to treat his parents badly. 据说他对待父母不好。Jùshuō tā duìdài fùmǔ bù hǎo. **2** 款待 kuǎndài, 请客 qǐngkè **3** 治疗 zhìliáo ■ Over a dozen people were treated for food poisoning over the weekend. 周末医治了十来个食物中毒的病人。Zhōumò yīzhìle shílái ge shíwù zhòngdú de bìngrén. II N **1** 难得的好东西 nándé de hǎo dōngxi ■ Roast duck? What a treat! 烤鸭? 真棒! Kǎoyā? Zhēn bàng! **2** 请客 qǐngkè

treatable ADJ 可医治的 kě yīzhì de

treatise N 专题论文 zhuāntí lùnwén [M. WD 篇 piān]

treatment N **1** 治疗 zhìliáo **2** 对待 duìdài ■ In some countries foreigners get special treatment. 在有些国家外国人得到特殊的对待。Zài yǒuxiē guójiā wàiguó rén dédao tèshū de duìdài.

treaty N 条约 tiáoyuē ■ The two countries signed a non-aggression treaty. 两国签订了互不侵犯条约。Liǎngguó qiāndìngle hù bù qīnfàn tiáoyuē.

treble¹ N (音乐的) 最高音部 (yīnyuè de) zuì gāo yīnbù

treble²

treble² v 成为三倍 chéngwéi sānbèi, 增加两倍 zēngjiā liǎngbèi

tree N 树 (木) shù (mù), 乔木 qiáomù ■ *Ronny tied his hammock to two trees.* 罗尼把吊床结在两棵树上。Luóní bǎ diàochuáng jié zài liǎng kē shùshang.

not to see the wood for the trees 见树不见林 jiàn shù bú jiàn lín

treehouse 树上小屋 shù shàng xiǎo wū

tree surgery 树木修整 (术) shùmù xiūzhěng (shù)

treetop N 树梢 shùshāo

tree-trunk N 树干 shùgàn

trek I v 长途艰苦跋涉 chángtú jiānkǔ báshè
II N See **trekking**

trekking N 长途跋涉 chángtú báshè

trellis N 攀缘植物架 pānyuánzhíwùjià

tremble N, v 发抖 fādǒu, 颤抖 chàndǒu

tremendous ADJ 巨大的 jùdà de, 非常的 fēicháng de

tremor N 1 (大地的) 轻微震动 (dàdì de) qīngwēi zhèndòng 2 (人体的) 颤抖 (réntǐ) chàndǒu, 发抖 fādǒu

trench N 1 地沟 dìgōu [M. WD 条 tiáo], 壕沟 háogōu [M. WD 条 tiáo] 2 战壕 zhànháo [M. WD 条 tiáo]
trench coat 长雨衣 cháng yǔyī, 风衣 fēngyī

trenchant ADJ 尖刻的 jiānkè de, 直言不讳的 zhíyán búhuì de

trend N 趋势 qūshì, 趋向 qūxiàng

trendsetter N 开创新潮流的人 kāichuàng xīn cháoliú de rén

trendy ADJ 新潮的 xīncháo de

trepidation N 恐惧不安 kǒngjùbù'ān

trespass v 非法进入 [+私人土地] fēifǎ jìnrù [+sīrén tǔdì]

trespasser N 擅自进入者 shànzì jìnrùzhě

trespassing N 非法进入私人土地 fēifǎ jìnrù sīrén tǔdì

trial N 1 审判 shěnpàn, 审理 shěnlǐ 2 试验 shìyàn ■ *The clinical trial of the new drug was successful.* 新药的临床试验很成功。Xīn yào de línchuáng shìyàn hěn chénggōng. 3 试用 shìyòng ■ *I was employed for a trial period before a contract was offered.* 我先被试用了一段时间，才拿到合同。Wǒ xiān bèi shìyòngle yí duàn shíjiān, cái nádao hétong.
trial and error 反复试验 fǎnfù shìyàn
trial balloon 试探汽球 shìtàn qìqiú, 试探性言行 shìtànxìng yánxíng
trial run (办法) 试行 (bànfǎ) shìxíng, (飞机) 试航 (fēijī) shìháng, (汽车) 试开 (qìchē) shìkāi

triangle N 三角 (形) sānjiǎo (xíng)

triangular ADJ 三角 (形) 的 sānjiǎo (xíng) de

tribe N 部落 bùluò ■ *The anthropologist did field work among a tribe In Papua New Guinea.* 这位人类学家在巴布亚新几内亚的一个部落里作实地调查。Zhè wèi rénlèixuéjiā zài Bābùyà Xīnjǐnèiyà de yí ge bùluò lǐ zuò shídì diàochá.

tribulation N 苦难 kǔnàn, 艰难 jiānnán

tribunal N 特别法庭 tèbié fǎtíng

tributary N 支流 zhīliú [M. WD 条 tiáo]

tribute N 1 颂词 sòngcí 2 礼品 lǐpǐn [M. WD 件 jiàn]
to pay last tribute to (向遗体) 告别 (xiàng yítǐ) gàobié

triceps N (手臂上) 三头肌 (shǒubì shàng) sāntóujī

trick I N 1 花招 huāzhāo
dirty trick 卑鄙伎俩 bēibǐ jìliǎng
to play tricks on 戏弄 xìnòng
2 诀窍 juéqiào ■ *There's no trick to it—practice makes perfect.* 没有什么诀窍—熟能生巧。Méiyǒu shénme juéqiào—shú néng shēng qiǎo.
trick of the trade 行业的绝招 hángyè de juézhāo
3 戏法 xìfǎ, 魔术 móshù II v 欺骗 qīpiàn ■ *I don't want to trick you.* 我不想欺骗你。Wǒ bù xiǎng qīpiàn nǐ.
trick or treat 不给好东西吃，就捣乱 bù gěi hǎo dōngxi chī, jiù dǎoluàn

trickery N 耍花招 shuǎ huāzhāo, 欺骗 qīpiàn

trickle I v 一滴一滴地流 yì dī yì dī de liú, 细流 xìliú II N 细流 xìliú

trickle-down effect N 滴水效应 dīshuǐ xiàoyìng

trickster N 骗子 piànzi

tricky ADJ 1 不容易对付的 bù róngyì duìfu de 2 诡计多端的 guǐjì duō duān de

tricycle N (小孩的) 三轮自行车 (xiǎohái de) sānlún zìxíngchē

trident N 三叉戟 sānchājǐ

tried ADJ (tried and tested) 经过反复证明的 jīngguò fǎnfù zhèngmíng de

trifle I N 1 无价值的东西 wú jiàzhí de dōngxi, 小事 xiǎoshì
a trifle 有点儿 yǒudiǎnr
2 蛋糕甜食 dàngāo tiánshí II v (to trifle with) 小看 xiǎokàn, 轻慢 qīngmàn

trigger I N 1 (枪) 扳机 (qiāng) bānjī 2 引发 (问题的) 因素 yǐnfā (wèntí de) yīnsù, 导火线 dǎohuǒxiàn II v (to trigger off) 引发 yǐnfā, 引起 yǐnqǐ

trigger-happy ADJ 随便开枪的 [+警察] suíbiàn kāiqiāng de [+jǐngchá]

trigonometry N (数学中的) 三角 (学) (shùxué zhōngde) sānjiǎo (xué)

trike N See **tricycle**

trilateral ADJ 三边的 sān biān de, 三方的 sān fāng de

trillion NUM (一) 万亿 (yí) wàn yì

trilogy N (小说/电影) 三部曲 (xiǎoshuō/diànyǐng) sānbùqǔ

trim I v **1** 修剪 [+胡子] xiūjiǎn [+húzi] **2** 削减 [+预算] xuējiǎn [+yùsuàn] **II** ADJ **1** 整洁的 [+小花园] zhěngjié de [+xiǎohuāyuán] **2** 苗条的 [+女子] miáotiao de [+nǚzǐ], 修长的 xiūcháng de **III** N **1** 修剪 xiūjiǎn **2** 镶边 (装饰) xiāngbiān (zhuāngshì)

trimmings N **1** 配菜 pèicài **2** 细小的装饰 xìxiǎo de zhuāngshì

trinket N 小饰品 xiǎo shìpǐn, 不值钱的小玩物 bùzhí qián de xiǎo wánwù

trio N 三重唱／奏 sānchóngchàng/zòu

trip N **1** [短途+] 旅行 [duǎntú+] lǚxíng business trip 出公差 chū gōngchāi **2** (服毒品后的) 幻觉 (fú dúpǐn hòu de) huàn-jué **3** 绊倒 bàndǎo **II** v **1** 绊倒 bàndǎo to trip sb up ① 使某人绊倒 bǎ mǒurén bàndǎo ② 使某人犯错 shǐ mǒurén fàncuò **2** 轻快地走路 qīngkuài de zǒulù

tripe N **1** 牛／猪肚 niú/zhūdǔ **2** 胡言乱说的东西 húbiān luànshuō de dōngxi, 废话 fèihuà

triple I ADJ 有三部分的 yǒu sān bù fēn de, 三个人的 sānge rén de triple digits 三位数 sānwèishù triple jump (运动) sānjítiào (yùndòng) triple play (棒球) 三重杀 (bàngqiú) sānchóngshā **II** v 使…成为三倍 shǐ…chéngwéi sānbèi, 使…增加两倍 shǐ…zēngjiā liǎngbèi

triplet N 三胞胎中的一个 sānbāotāi zhōng de yí ge

triplets N 三胞胎 sānbāotāi

triplicate N (in triplicate) 一设三份的 yí shè sān fèn de

tripod N 三脚架 sānjiǎojià

trite ADJ 老一套的 lǎoyítào de, 陈腐的 chénfǔ de

triumph I N 胜利 shènglì, 成就 chéngjiù, 成功 chénggōng a triumph over adversary 战胜逆境取得的成功 zhànshèng nìjìng qǔdé de chénggōng **II** v 战胜 zhànshèng, 获胜 huòshèng

triumphal ADJ 庆功的 qìng gōng de, 凯旋的 kǎixuán de a triumphal parade 庆功大游行 qìng gōng dà yóuxíng

triumphant ADJ 胜利的 shènglì de, 成功的 chénggōng de

trivia N 琐碎的小事 suǒsuì de xiǎoshì, 细节 xìjié

trivial ADJ 微不足道的 wēi bù zú dào de, 不值一提的 bùzhí yì tí de

trod See **tread**

trodden See **tread**

troll N (北欧传说中的) 妖精 (Běi'ōu chuán shuō zhōngde) yāojing

trolley N (有轨) 电车 (yǒu guǐ) diànchē [M. WD 辆 liàng]

trolley car 有轨电车 yǒuguǐ diànchē

trolleybus N 无轨电车 wúguǐ diànchē [M. WD 辆 liàng]

trombone N 长号 chánghào [M. WD 把 bǎ]

troop I N (troops) 部队 bùduì, 军队 jūnduì troops deployment 调遣部队 diàoqiǎn bùduì combat troops 战斗部队 zhàndòu bùduì crack troops 精锐部队 jīngruì bùduì regular troops 正规部队 zhèngguībùduì **II** v 成群结队地走 chéngqún jiéduì de zǒu

trooper N (美国) 州警察 (Měiguó) zhōu jǐngchá

trophy N 奖杯 jiǎngbēi, 奖牌 jiǎngpái trophy cabinet 奖杯／奖牌陈列柜 jiǎngbēi/jiǎngpái chénlièguì **2** 战利品 zhànlìpǐn

tropical ADJ 热带的 rèdài de ■ The mango is a tropical fruit. 芒果是热带水果。Mángguǒ shì rèdài shuǐguǒ.

tropics N 热带 (地区) rèdài (dìqū)

trot v **1** [马+] 小跑 [mǎ+] xiǎopǎo **2** [人+] 慢跑 [rén+] màn pǎo

trouble I N **1** 麻烦 máfan, 烦恼 fánnǎo ■ This dish is a lot of trouble to prepare. 这道菜做起来很烦。Zhè dào cài zuòqilai hěn máfan. **2** 病 bìng, 病痛 bìngtòng ■ He's had back trouble since he worked on the farm. 他自从在农场劳动以来，就有腰背疼的毛病。Tā zìcóng zài nóngchǎng láodòng yǐlái, jiù yǒu yāobèi téng de máobing. **II** v 麻烦 máfan ■ I'm sorry to have troubled you. 对不起，麻烦你了。Duìbuqǐ, máfan nǐ le. to be asking for trouble 自找麻烦 zì zhǎo máfan to be in trouble 遇到麻烦 yùdào máfan

troubled ADJ 忧虑的 yōulǜ de, 担忧的 dānyōu de

troublemaker N 捣蛋鬼 dǎodàn guǐ, 捣蛋分子 dǎodàn fènzi

troubleshooter N 调解人 tiáojiěrén, 解决难题的人 jiějué nántí de rén

troubleshooting N 调解 tiáojiě, 解决难题 jiějué nántí

troublesome ADJ (引起) 麻烦的 (yǐnqǐ) máfan de, 讨厌的 tǎoyàn de

trouble spot N 麻烦地带 máfan dìdài, 多事之地 duōshì zhī dì

trough N **1** 食槽 shícáo, 水槽 shuǐcáo **2** 山谷 shāngǔ, 浪谷 lànggǔ **3** 低谷 (期) dīgǔ (qī), 萧条期 xiāotiáoqī from peak to trough 从高峰到低谷 cóng gāofēng dào dīgǔ

trounce v 以高分打败 yǐ gāofēn dǎbài

troupe N 歌舞团 gēwǔtuán, 剧团 jùtuán

trousers N 裤子 kùzi [M. WD 条 tiáo]

trout N 鳟鱼 zūnyú [M. WD 条 tiáo]

truancy N 逃学 táoxué

truant I ADJ 逃学的 táoxué de **II** N 逃学的学生 táoxué de xuésheng truce

truce N 停战（协定）tíngzhàn (xiédìng), 休战 xiūzhàn

truck I N 1 卡车 kǎchē [M. WD 辆 liàng]
truck driver 卡车司机 kǎchē sījī
truck stop（路旁廉价）饭店 (lùpáng liánjià) fàndiàn
baggage truck 垃圾车 lājīchē
delivery truck 送货车 sònghuòchē
pickup truck 敞篷小货车 chǎngpéng xiǎohuòchē
2 手推车 shǒutuīchē [M. WD 辆 liàng] 3 (have no truck with) 不与…来往 bù yǔ…láiwǎng, 不与…打交道 bù yǔ…dǎ jiāodao II v 用卡车装运 yòng kǎchē zhuāngyùn

trucking N 货车运输业 huòchē yùnshūyè

truckload N 一货车货物 yí huòchē huòwù, 货车装载量 (huòchē) zhuāngzàiliàng

truculent ADJ 好斗的 hǎo dǒu de, 易怒的 yì nù de

trudge I v 吃力地走 chīlì de zǒu, 艰难地走 jiānnán de zǒu II N 长途跋涉 chángtú báshè

true I ADJ 1 真的 zhēn de, 真实的 zhēnshí de
■ "Is it true that Cindy and Rafael are dating?" "Yes, it's true." "辛蒂和拉菲尔在谈恋爱，这是真的吗？" "是真的。" "Xīndì hé Lāfēi'ěr zài tánliàn'ài, zhè shì zhēn de ma?" "Shì zhēnde."
2 真诚的 zhēnchéng de
true to one's word 信守诺言 xìnshǒu nuòyán, 说到做到 shuōdào zuòdào
true to one's principle 忠实于原则 zhōngshí yú yuánzé, 遵循自己的原则 zūnxún zìjǐ de yuánzé
to come true 实现 shíxiàn ■ His dream came true when he was appointed coach of the basketball team at his alma mater. 他被任命为母校的篮球队教练，梦想成真了。Tā bèi rènmìngwéi mǔxiào de lánqiúduì jiàoliàn, mèngxiǎng chéng zhēn le.
II N (out of true) 不正 bú zhèng, 不直 bù zhí

true-false ADJ (a true-false question) 是非题 shìfēití, 正误题 zhèngwùtí

true-life ADJ 以事实为依据的 yǐ shìshí wéi yījù de, 真实的 zhēnshí de

truffle N 1 巧克力软糖 qiǎokèlì ruǎntáng [M. WD 块 kuài] 2 块菌 kuàijūn

truism N 不言自明的道理 bù yán zì míng de dàoli

truly ADV 1 真实地 zhēnshí de, 确实 quèshí 2 准确地 zhǔnquè de
really and truly 千真万确（地）qiānzhēn wànquè (de)

trump I N 王牌 wángpái, 将牌 jiàngpái II v 1 打出王牌 dǎchū wángpái 2 胜过 shèngguò

trumped-up ADJ 捏造的 [+罪名] niēzào de [+zuìmíng]

trumpet I N 喇叭 lǎba [M. WD 把 bǎ], 小号 xiǎohào [M. WD 把 bǎ] II v 自吹自擂的 zìchuī zìléi de, 自我吹嘘 zìwǒ chuīxū

truncated ADJ 缩短了的 suōduǎnle de

trunk N 1 树干 shùgàn [M. WD 根 gēn] 2 大箱子 dà xiāngzi [M. WD 只 zhī] 3 （人体）躯干 (réntǐ) qūgàn 4 大象鼻子 dàxiàng bízi, 象鼻 xiàngbí

trunks (swimming trunks) 男式游泳裤 nánshì yóuyǒngkù [M. WD 条 tiáo]

trust I v 信任 xìnrèn ■ On every U.S. coin and bill are printed the words "In God We Trust". 美国的钱币上都写着 "我们信任上帝"。Zài Měiguó de qiánbìshang dōu xiězhe "wǒmen xìnrèn Shàngdì". II N 1 信任 xìnrèn 2 信托 xìntuō, 信托基金 xìntuō jījīn ■ Her wealthy parents have set up a trust for her. 她富有的父母已经为她建立了信托基金。Tā fùyǒu de fùmǔ yǐjīng wèi tā jiànlìle xìntuō jījīn.

trustee N 1 受托人 shòutuōrén 2 理事会成员 lǐshìhuì chéngyuán, 理事 lǐshì

trusting ADJ 容易信任别人的 róngyì xìnrèn biéren de, 轻信的 qīngxìn de

trustworthy ADJ 值得信赖的 zhíde xìnlài de, 可以信托的 kěyǐ xìntuō de

truth N 1 真相 zhēnxiàng, 真话 zhēnhuà ■ Please tell me the truth. Did you borrow my iPod? 你对我说真话，有没有借我的iPod？Nǐ duì wǒ shuō zhēnhuà, yǒuméiyǒu jiè wǒ de iPod? 2 真理 zhēnlǐ
to tell the truth 说真的 shuō zhēn de

truthful ADJ 诚实的 chéngshí de, 说真话的 shuō zhēnhuà de

try I v 1 试 shì, 试图 shìtú ■ Please try to be here on time. 请尽量准时到。Qǐng jǐnliàng zhǔnshí dào. 2 审问 shěnwèn ■ The computer wizard was tried for hacking. 这个电脑鬼才因为非法进入他人电脑而受审。Zhège diànnǎo guǐcái yīnwèi fēifǎ jìnrù tārén diànnǎo ér shòushěn. II N 试 shì, 尝试 chángshì ■ On the third try, the pole vaulter made a clean jump. 撑杆运动员第三次试跳时轻松地跃过栏杆。Chēnggān yùndòngyuán dìsān cì shì tiào shí qīngsōng de yuèguo lángān.
to try … on 试穿 shìchuān
to try … out 测试 cèshì ■ It's best to try out the drug on animals first. 最好先在动物身上测试这种药。Zuìhǎo xiān zài dòngwù shēnshang cèshì zhè zhǒng yào.
to try one's luck 碰碰运气 pèngpeng yùnqi

trying ADJ 使人厌烦的 shǐrén yànfán de, 恼人的 nǎorén de

tryout N 1 （运动员的）选拔 (yùndòngyuán de) xuǎnbá 2 （文艺节目）试演 (wényì jiémù) shìyǎn

Tsar N （俄国）沙皇 (Éguó) Shāhuáng

T-shirt N T恤衫 tīxùshān [M. WD 件 jiàn], 短袖运动衫 duǎnxiù yùndòngshān [M. WD 件 jiàn]

tub N 浴缸 yùgāng, 澡盆 zǎopén

tuba N 大号 dàhào

tubby ADJ 矮胖的 ǎipàng de

tube N 管 guǎn, 管道 guǎndào
  tube of toothpaste 一管牙膏 yì guǎn yágāo
  test tube 试管 shìguǎn
  to go down the tubes 被毁掉 bèi huǐdiào
tuberculosis N 结核病 jiéhébìng, 肺结核 fèijiéhé
tubing N 管道 guǎndào, 管子 guǎnzi
tubular ADJ 管状的 guǎnzhuàng de, 用管子制作
  的 yòng guǎnzǐ zhìzuò de
tuck I v 1 把 [+衣服] 塞进 bǎ [+yīfu] sāi jìn
  to tuck one's shirt in 把衬衣下摆塞进去 bǎ
  chènyī xiàbǎi sāijìnqu
  to tuck sb in 给某人掖被子 gěi mǒurén yè bèizi
  2 收藏 shōucáng, 藏起来 cángqǐlái II N 1 (衣服
  的) 缝褶 (yīfu de) féngzhe 2 小整容手术 xiǎo
  zhěngróng shǒushù
  tummy tuck 腹部整平手术 fùbù zhěngpíng
  shǒushù
Tuesday N 星期二 xīngqī'èr, 周二 zhōu'èr
tug I v 拉 lā, 拖 tuō
  to tug at one's heartstrings 触动某人的心
  chùdòng mǒurén de xīn
  II N 1 猛拉 měng lā, 拖 tuō 2 感情上的触动
  gǎnqíng shàng de chùdòng 3 (tugboat) 拖船
  tuōchuán [M. WD 艘 sōu]
tug-of-war N 拔河 (比赛) báhé (bǐsài)
tuition N 1 学费 xuéfèi 2 教学 jiàoxué
tulip N 郁金香 (花) yùjīnxiāng (huā) [M. WD 朵
  duǒ/棵 kē]
tumble I v 1 倒下 dǎoxià, 跌倒 diēdǎo 2 [价格+]
  猛跌 [jiàgé+] měngdiē II N (从高处) 倒下
  (cóng gāochù) dǎoxià, 跌倒 diēdǎo
tumbledown ADJ 摇摆欲坠的 yáobǎi yù zhuì de
tumbler N 无柄玻璃杯 wú bǐng bōlibēi
tummy N 肚子 dùzi
tumor N 肿瘤 zhǒngliú
  benign tumor 良性肿瘤 liángxìng zhǒngliú
  malignant tumor 恶性肿瘤 èxìng zhǒngliú
tumult N 1 (一大群人的) 混乱场面 (yídàqún rén
  de) hùnluàn chǎngmiàn 2 烦乱的情绪 fánluàn
  de qíngxù
tumultuous ADJ 极其混乱的 jíqí hùnluàn de, 乱
  哄哄的 luànhōnghōng de
tuna N 金枪鱼 jīnqiāngyú [M. WD 条 tiáo]
tundra N 冻土带 dòngtǔdài, 冻原 dòngyuán
tune I N 曲调 qǔdiào ■ That song has a beautiful
  tune. 那首歌的曲调很美。Nà shǒu gē de qǔdiào
  hěn měi.
  out of tune 走调 zǒu diào
  to change one's tune 改变言论 gǎibiàn yánlùn ■ The politician changed his tune after his
  meeting with the President. 这个政客和总统会见
  以后, 改变了论调。Zhè ge zhèngkè hé zǒngtǒng
  huìjiàn yǐhòu, gǎibiànle lùndiào.
  II v 1 调音 tiáoyīn 2 调整 [+机器] tiáozhěng
  [+jīqì] ■ The engine needs tuning. 发动机要调整

一下。Fādòngjī yào tiáozhěng yíxià. 3 调整频道
  tiáozhěng píndào
tuner N 1 (钢琴) 调音师 (gāngqín) tiáoyīnshī
  2 (电视/收音机) 调谐器 (diànshìjī/shōuyīnjī)
  tiáoxiéqì
tune-up N (发动机的) 调试 (fādòngjī de) tiáoshì
tunic N 长袍 chángpáo [M. WD 件 jiàn]
tunnel I N 1 隧道 suìdào [M. WD 条 tiáo] 2 地道
  dìdao [M. WD 条 tiáo]
  tunnel vision 管状视 guǎnzhuàngshì, 狭隘的眼
  光 xiá'ài de yǎnguāng
  II v 挖掘隧道/地道 wājué suìdào/dìdao
turbine N 涡轮机 wōlúnjī [M. WD 台 tái]
turbulence N 1 强气流 qiángqìliú, 湍急水流
  tuānjí shuǐliú 2 骚乱 sāoluàn, 骚动 sāodòng
turbulent ADJ 骚乱的 sāoluàn de, 动乱的
  dòngluàn de
turf N 1 (人工) 草皮 (réngōng) cǎopí 2 (自己的)
  地盘 (zìjǐ de) dìpán
  turf war [帮派间的+] 地盘争夺战 [bāngpài jiān
  de+] dìpán zhēngduózhàn
turgid ADJ 1 枯燥难懂的 kūzào nándǒng de 2 肿
  胀的 zhǒngzhàng de
turkey N 1 火鸡 huǒjī [M. WD 只 zhī] 2 失败的电
  影/剧作 shībài de diànyǐng/jùzuò
turmoil N 混乱 (状态) hùnluàn (zhuàngtài), 动
  乱 dòngluàn
turn I v 1 转 zhuǎn, 转向 zhuǎnxiàng 2 拐 guǎi,
  打弯 dǎwān 3 变 biàn, 变为 biànwéi ■ Wait
  till the lights turn green. 要等到绿灯才能走。Yào
  děngdao lǜdēng cái néng zǒu. 4 翻 fān ■ Children, turn your books to page 35. 孩子们, 把书翻
  到三十五页。Háizimen, bǎ shū fāndao sānshíwǔ
  yè.
  to turn off 关掉 guāndiao, 关上 guānshang
  to turn on 打开 dǎkāi
  II N 1 轮到 lúndao 2 转动 zhuàndòng 3 转弯
  zhuǎnwān ■ The road took a sudden turn to the
  left. 道路突然向左转弯。Dàolù tūrán xiàng zuǒ
  zhuǎnwān.
  to do a good turn 帮助人 bāngzhu rén, 做好事
  zuò hǎoshì
  4 变化 biànhuà
  to take a turn for the better/worse 好转/恶化
  hǎozhuǎn/èhuà
turnabout N 一百八十度大转弯 yìbǎi bāshí dù dà
  zhuǎnwān, 彻底改变 chèdǐ gǎibiàn
turnaround N 好转 hǎozhuǎn, 脱离困境 tuōlí
  kùnjìng
turncoat N 叛徒 pàntú, 变节者 biànjiézhě
turning point N 转折点 zhuǎnzhédiǎn
turnip N 白萝卜 báiluóbo [M. WD 根 gēn]
turnkey ADJ 可立即使用的 [+计算机软件] kě lìjí
  shǐyòng de [+jìsuànjī ruǎnjiàn]
turnoff N 1 岔路 chàlù [M. WD 条 tiáo], 支路 zhīlù

[M. WD 条 tiáo] **2** 使人丧失兴趣的事 shǐrén sàngshī xìngqù de shì

turnout N 出席人数 chūxí rénshù, 投票人数 tóupiào rénshù
a high/low voter turnout 选民投票人数多／少 xuǎnmín tóupiào rénshù duō/shǎo

turnover N **1** 人员流动（率）rényuán liúdòng (lǜ) **2** 现金流动 xiànjīn liúdòng **3** 小馅饼 xiǎo xiànbǐng [M. WD 块 kuài]

turnpike N 付费高速公路 fùfèi gāosù gōnglù [M. WD 条 tiáo]

turntable N **1** （唱机的）唱盘 (chàngjī de) chàng-pán **2** （微波炉的）转盘 (wēibōlú de) zhuànpán

turpentine N 松节油 sōngjiéyóu

turquoise N **1** 绿松石 lǜsōngshí [M. WD 块 kuài] **2** 绿松石色 lǜsōngshísè, 绿蓝色 lùlánsè

turret N 小塔楼 xiǎo tǎlóu [M. WD 座 zuò]

turtle N 海龟 hǎiguī [M. WD 只 zhī], 乌龟 wūguī

turtleneck N 高翻领（毛衣／衬衣）gāo fānlǐng (máoyī/chènyī) [M. WD 件 jiàn]

tusk N 象牙 xiàngyá, 獠牙 liáoyá

tussle N, v 扭打 niǔdǎ, 争斗 zhēngdòu

tutor N 私人教师 sīrén jiàoshī, 家庭教师 jiātíng jiàoshī **II** v 给…当私人教师 gěi…dāng sīrén jiàoshī, 辅导 fǔdǎo

tutorial **I** N 辅导课 fǔdǎokè **II** ADJ 辅导的 fǔdǎo de

tuxedo N 男式无尾礼服 nánshì wú wěi lǐfú

TV ABBREV See **television**

TV dinner N 电视便餐 diànshì biàncān

twang **I** N **1** 鼻音 bíyīn **2** 拨（琴）弦的嗡嗡声 bō (qín) xián de wēngwēng shēng **II** v **1** 用鼻音说话 yòng bíyīn shuōhuà **2** [琴弦+] 发出嗡嗡声 [qínxián+] fāchū wēngwēng shēng

tweak v **1** 捏 [+鼻子] niē [+bízi] **2** 对 [+句子] 作小修改 duì [+jùzi] zuò xiǎo xiūgǎi

tweed N 粗花呢 cūhuāní

tweezers N 镊子 nièzi [M. WD 副 fù]

twelfth NUM 第十二 dì shí'èr

twelve NUM 十二 shí'èr, 12

twenty NUM 二十 èrshí, 20

twenty-one NUM 二十一点（纸牌游戏）èrshí yī diǎn (zhǐpái yóuxì)

twice ADV **1** 两次 liǎng cì, 两遍 liǎng biàn
Once bitten, twice shy. 一朝被蛇咬，三年怕井绳。Yì zhāo bèi shé yǎo, sān nián pà jǐngshéng. (→ Once bitten by a snake, one fears a well rope for the next three years.)
2 两倍 liǎng bèi

twiddle v 抚弄 fǔnòng, 把玩 bǎxì
to twiddle one's thumbs 互绕大拇指 hù rào dàmuzhǐ, 闲得无聊 xián dé wúliáo

twig N （小）树枝 (xiǎo) shùzhī [M. WD 根 gēn]

twilight N **1** 暮色 mùsè, 黄昏时分 huánghūn shífèn **2** （人生）晚年 (rénshēng) wǎnnián
twilight world 阴暗世界 yīn'àn shìjiè

twin **I** N 双胞胎中的一个 shuāngbāotāi zhōng de yí ge
fraternal twin 异卵双胞胎 yì luǎn shuāngbāotāi
identical twin 同卵双胞胎 tóng luǎn shuāngbāotāi
II ADJ 孪生的 luánshēng de
twin brother/sister 孪生兄弟／姐妹 luánshēng xiōngdì/jiěmèi
twin bed 双人床 shuāngrénchuáng

twine **I** N 双股线 shuānggǔxiàn **II** v 缠绕 chánrǎo, 盘绕 pánrào

twinge N 突然的刺痛 tūrán de cìtòng
a twinge of guilt 一阵内疚 yí zhèn nèijiù

twinkle v, N [灯光+] 闪烁 [dēngguāng+] shǎnshuò, 闪耀 shǎnyào

twirl v （使…）旋转 (shǐ…) xuánzhuǎn, （使…）转动 (shǐ…) zhuǎndòng

twist **I** v **1** 扭（转）niǔ (zhuǎn), 拧 nǐng
to twist one's ankle 扭伤脚踝 niǔshāng jiǎohuái
to twist one's arm 把某人的手臂反扭到背后 bǎ mǒurén de shǒubì fǎn niǔ dào bèihòu, 向某人施加压力 xiàng mǒurén shījiā yālì
to twist and turn [道路+] 弯弯曲曲 [dàolù+] wānwān qūqū
2 转动 [+瓶盖] zhuàndòng [+pínggài] **3** 曲解 [+语言] qūjiě [+yǔyán] **II** N **1** 意外情况 yìwài qíngkuàng **2** 缠绕的形状 chánrǎo de xíngzhuàng **3** 扭摆舞 niǔbǎiwǔ **4** 扭（转）niǔ (zhuǎn), 拧 nǐng

twisted ADJ **1** 扭曲的 niǔqū de **2** 反常的 fǎncháng de, 变态的 biàntài de

twister N 龙卷风 lóngjuǎnfēng

twitch N, v [肌肉+] 抽搐 [jīròu+] chōuchù, 抽动 chōudòng

twitter v **1** [鸟+] 吱吱叫 [niǎo+] zhīzhījiào **2** （网络通讯）推特 (wǎngluò tōngxùn) tuītè

two NUM 二 èr, 两 liǎng
It takes two to tango. 要两个人才能跳探戈舞。Yào liǎng ge rén cái néng tiào tàngē wǔ. (一只碗不响，两只碗叮当。Yì zhī wǎn bù xiǎng, liǎng zhī wǎn dīngdāng. → While a bowl produces no sound, two bowls may make a lot of noise.)

two-bit ADJ 一钱不值的 yì qián bù zhí de, 微不足道的 wēi bù zú dào de

two-dimensional ADJ 二维的 èrwéi de, 平面的 píngmiàn de

two-faced ADJ 两面派的 liǎngmiànpài de, 两面三刀的 liǎngmiàn sāndāo de

two-piece ADJ 两件套的 [+服装] liǎng jiàn tào de [+fúzhuāng]

twosome N 一对搭档 yíduì dādàng

two-time v 偷情 tōuqíng

two-tone ADJ 双色的 [+服装／家具] shuāngsè de [+fúzhuāng/jiājù]

two-way ADJ 双向的 shuāngxiàng de
two-way trade 双向贸易 shuāngxiàng màoyì

tycoon N （工商）巨头 (gōngshāng) jùtóu

type I N **1** 类型 lèixíng
blood type 血型 xuèxíng
2 印刷字体 yìnshuā zìtǐ **3** （印刷用的）活字 (yìnshuā yòng de) huózì **II** v 用打字机／电脑打字 yòng dǎzìjī/diànnǎo dǎzì

typeface N （印刷用的）字体 (yìnshuā yòng de) zìtǐ

typewriter N 打字机 dǎzìjī [M. wD 台 tái/架 jià]

typewritten ADJ 用打字机打出来的 yòng dǎzìjī dǎchulai de

typhoid, typhoid fever N 伤寒 shānghán

typhoon N 台风 táifēng

typhus N 斑疹伤寒 bānzhěnshānghán

typical ADJ **1** 典型的 diǎnxíng de **2** 一贯如此的 yí guàn rúcǐ de ■ *"Chloe forgot to turn off the computer last night." "Typical!"* "科洛昨天晚上忘了关电脑。" "她一贯如此！" "Kēluò zuótiān wǎnshang wàngle guān diànnǎo." "Tā yí guàn rúcǐ!"

typically ADV **1** 典型地 diǎnxíng de **2** 一向 yíxiàng, 向来 xiànglái

typify v 是…的典型 shì…de diǎnxíng, 成为…的典型 chéngwéi…de diǎnxíng

typing N 打字（工作）dǎzì (gōngzuò)

typist N 打字员 dǎzìyuán

typo N 排列／打字错误 páiliè/dǎzì cuòwù

tyrannical ADJ 暴政的 bàozhèng de, 专横的 zhuānhèng de

tyranny N **1** 暴政 bàozhèng, 专制统治 zhuānzhì tǒngzhì **2** 专横 zhuānhèng, 暴虐 bàonüè

tyrant N 暴君 bàojūn

U

ubiquitous ADJ 到处都是的 dàochù dōu shì de, 无处不在的 wúchù bú zài de

udder N （母牛／母羊的）乳房 (mǔniú/mǔyáng de) rǔfáng

UFO (= Unidentified Flying Object) ABBREV 不明飞行物 bù míng fēixíng wù

ugh INTERJ 哎呀 āiya

ugly ADJ **1** 难看的 nánkàn de, 丑陋的 chǒulòu de **2** 险恶的 xiǎn'è de ■ *A fight broke out and things got pretty ugly.* 爆发了打斗，情况很险恶。Bàofāle dǎdòu, qíngkuàng hěn xiǎn'è.

uh INTERJ 嗯 ńg

UHF (= Ultra-High Frequency) ABBREV 超高频 chāogāopín

ulterior ADJ 隐秘 yǐnmì, 别有用心的 biè yǒu yòngxīn de

an ulterior motive 不可告人的动机 bùkě gàorén de dòngjī

ultimate I ADJ **1** 最终的 [+目标] zuì zhōng de [+mùbiāo] **2** 最大的 [+责任] zuì dà de [+zérèn] **II** N 极端 jíduān

the ultimate in bad taste 品味差到极点 pǐnwèi chàdào jídiǎn

ultimately ADV 最终 zuìzhōng, 终于 zhōngyú

ultimatum N 最后通牒 zuìhòu tōngdié [M. wD 份 fèn]

ultrasonic ADJ 超声波的 chāoshēngbō de

ultraviolet ADJ 紫外线的 zǐwàixiàn de

umbilical cord N 脐带 qídài

umbrage N (to take umbrage) 生气 shēngqì, 感到愤怒 gǎndào fènnù

umbrella N （雨）伞 (yǔ) sǎn [M. wD 把 bǎ]

umpire N 裁判（员）cáipàn (yuán)

umpteenth ADJ 第无数次的 dì wúsùcì de, 数不清的 sǔ bù qīng de

U.N. (= the United Nations) ABBREV 联合国 Liánhéguó

U.N.O. (= the United Nations Organization) ABBREV 联合国组织 Liánhéguó zǔzhī

unabashed ADJ 毫不掩饰的 háobù yǎnshì de, 公开宣扬的 gōngkāi xuānyáng de

unabated ADJ 不减弱的 bù jiǎnruò de, 保持势头的 bǎochí shìtóu de

unable ADJ 不能 bù néng

unabridged ADJ 未删节的 wèi shānjié de, 全文的 quánwén de

unacceptable ADJ 不可接受的 bù kě jiēshòu de, 不能容忍的 bùnéng róngrěn de

unaccountable ADJ **1** 无法解释的 [+现象] wúfǎ jiěshì de [+xiànxiàng], 不能理解的 bù néng lǐjiě de **2** 独断独行的 [+官员] dúduàn dúxíng de [+guānyuán]

unacknowledged ADJ 未受注意的 wèi shòu zhùyì de, 未被承认的 wèi bèi chéngrèn de

unadulterated ADJ 纯粹的 chúncuì de, 完全的 wánquán de

unaffected ADJ **1** 不受影响的 bú shòu yǐngxiǎng de **2** 不装腔作势的 bù zhuāngqiāng zuòshì de, 自然的 zìrán de

unaided ADJ 没有外来帮助的 méiyǒu wàilái bāngzhù de, 独立的 dúlì de

un-American ADJ 非美国（方式）的 fēi Měiguó (fāngshì) de

un-American activities 非美活动 fēi Měi huódòng

unanimous ADJ 一致的 yízhì de, 全体的 quántǐ de

unannounced ADJ 没有料想到的 méiyǒu liàoxiǎngdào de, 意外的 yìwài de

unanswered ADJ 未答复的 wèi dáfù de, 未回复的 wèi huífù de

unassuming ADJ 朴实无华的 pǔshí wúhuá de, 不摆架子的 bù bǎijiàzi de

unattached ADJ **1** 没有（恋爱）对象的 [+青年] méiyǒu (liàn'ài) duìxiàng de [+qīngnián] **2** 独立式的 [+车库] dúlì shì de [+chēkù]

unattended ADJ 无人照看的 wúrén zhàokàn de, 无人负责的 wúrén fùzé de

unauthorized ADJ 未经授权的 wèijīng shòuquán de, 未经批准的 wèijīng pīzhǔn de

unavailable ADJ 得不到的 débudào de, 买不到的 mǎibudào de

unavoidable ADJ 不可避免的 bùkě bìmiǎn de

unaware ADJ 未察觉到的 wèi chájuédào de

unawares ADV 不知不觉地 bùzhī bùjué de, 无意中 wúyìzhōng

to catch sb unawares 让某人措手不及 ràng mǒurén cuòshǒu bù jí

unbalanced ADJ **1** 不平衡的 bù pínghéng de unbalanced budget 收支不平衡（的预算）shōuzhī bù pínghéng (de yùsuàn) **2** 不公允的 [+论点] bù gōngyǔn de [+lùndiǎn] **3** 错乱失常的 [+精神状态] cuòluàn shīcháng de [+jīngshén zhuàngtài]

unbearable ADJ 无法忍受的 wúfǎ rěnshòu de, 不可容忍的 bùkě róngrěn de

unblemished ADJ 清白的 qīngbái de, 无污点的 wú wūdiǎn de

unbounded ADJ 无边无际的 wúbiān wújì de, 无限的 wúxiàn de

uncalled-for ADJ 不适当的 bú shìdāng de, 不必要的 bú bìyào de

uncanny ADJ 不可思议的 bùkě sīyì de, 离奇的 líqí de

uncertain ADJ 不确定的 bú quèdìng de, 不能决定的 bùnéng juédìng de

unclaimed ADJ 无人认领的 wúrén rènlǐng de, 无人领取的 wúrén lǐngqǔ de unclaimed luggage 无主行李 wúzhǔ xíngli

uncle N 伯父 bófù (father's elder brother), 叔父 shūfù (father's younger brother), 舅父 jiùfù (mother's brother), 姑父 gūfù (father's sister's husband), 姨夫 yífù (mother's sister's husband)

Uncle Sam N 山姆大叔（美国政府）Shānmǔ Dàshū (Měiguó zhèngfǔ)

Uncle Tom N 对白人过分热情的（美国）黑人 duì báirén guòfèn rèqíng de (Měiguó) hēirén

uncompromising ADJ 不妥协的 bù tuǒxié de, 不让步的 bú ràng bù de

unconditional ADJ 无条件的 wú tiáojiàn de unconditional love 无条件的爱 wú tiáojiàn de ài

unconfirmed ADJ 未经证实的 wèijīng zhèngshí de

unconscionable ADJ 不讲良心的 bù jiǎng liángxīn de, 不道德的 bú dàodé de

unconstitutional ADJ 不符合宪法（精神）的 bù fúhé xiànfǎ (jīngshén) de, 违宪的 wéixiàn de

unconventional ADJ 非常规的 fēi chángguī de, 不合习俗的 bù hé xísú de

uncountable ADJ（语法）不可数的 (yǔfǎ) bùkěshù de uncountable noun 不可数名词 bùkěshù míngcí

uncouth ADJ 没有教养的 méiyǒu jiàoyǎng de, 粗鲁的 cūlǔ de

uncover V **1** 揭开…盖子/覆盖物 jiēkāi…gàizi/fùgàiwù **2** 发现 fāxiàn

uncut ADJ 未剪辑的 wèi jiǎnjí de, 未删节的 wèi shānjié de

undaunted ADJ 不退缩的 bú tuìsuō de, 大无畏的 dàwúwèi de

undecided ADJ 尚未决定的 shàngwèi juédìng de, 犹豫不决的 yóuyù bùjué de

undeniable ADJ 不可否认的 bùkě fǒurèn de

under I PREP **1** 在…下面 zài…xiàmian, 到…下面 dào…xiàmian **2** 少于 shǎoyú, 低于 dī yú **3** 根据 [+法律] gēnjù [+fǎlǜ]

under construction/discussion 在建设/讨论之中 zài jiànshè/tǎolùn zhī zhōng

II ADV 下面 xiàmian, 以下 yǐxià ■ *Children of 12 and under must be accompanied by an adult.* 十二岁和十二岁以下的儿童必须有成人陪同。Shí'èr suì hé shí'èr suì yǐxià de értóng bìxū yǒu chéngrén péitóng.

underachiever N 未充分发挥能力的者 wèi chōngfèn fāhuī nénglì zhě, 成绩不理想者 chéngjì bù lǐxiǎng zhě

underage ADJ 未成年的 wèi chéngnián de

undercharge V 对…少要价 duì…shǎo yàojià

underclass N 下层社会 xiàcéng shèhuì, 贫穷阶层 pínqióng jiēcéng

undercover ADJ 暗中进行的 ànzhōng jìnxíng de, 秘密的 mìmì de to go undercover 暗中地 ànzhōng de, 暗暗地 àn'àn de

undercurrent N 潜伏的情绪 qiánfú de qíngxù, 隐患 yǐnhuàn

undercut V **1** 削减 [+价格]（与同行竞争）xuējiǎn [+jiàgé]（yǔ tóngháng jìngzhēng）, 削价抢生意 xuējià qiǎng shēngyì **2** 削弱 [+声誉] xuēruò [+shēngyì], 破坏 pòhuài

underdog N 竞争中处于劣势者 jìngzhēng zhōng chǔyú lièshì zhě, 被欺压者 bèiqīyāzhě

underestimate V 低估 dīgū

undergo V 经受 jīngshòu, 经历 jīnglì

undergraduate N 大学本科生 dàxué běnkēshēng

underground ADJ **1** 在地下的 zài dìxià de underground cellar 地下酒窖 dìxià jiǔjiào **2** 地下的 dìxià de an underground terrorist organization 地下恐怖组织 dìxia kǒngbù zǔzhī

undergrowth N（大树下的）灌木丛 (dàshùxià de) guànmùcóng

underhanded ADJ 偷偷摸摸的 tōutōu mōmō de, 不光明正大的 bù guāngmíng zhèngdà de

underline v 1 在…下划线 zài…xià huàxiàn ■ *The teacher underlined all the misspelled words in his essay.* 老师在他文章里所有拼错的词下面划了线。Lǎoshī zài tā wénzhāng lǐ suǒyǒu pīncuò de cí xiàmiàn huàle xiàn. 2 突出 tūchū

underlying ADJ 根本的 gēnběn de, 基本的 jīběn de

undermine v 逐渐削弱 zhújiàn xuēruò, 损害 sǔnhài

underneath PREP, ADV 在…下面 zài…xiàmian

undernourished ADJ 营养不良的 yíngyǎng bùliáng de

underpants N 内裤 nèikù, 衬裤 chènkù

underpass N 地下通道 dìxià tōngdào [M. WD 条 tiáo]

underpay v 付…过低的工资 fù…guòdī de gōngzī

underpin v 支持 zhīchí, 加固 jiāgù

underprivileged ADJ 贫困的 pínkùn de, 下层社会的 xiàchén shèhuì de

underrated ADJ 被低估的 bèi dīgū de, 被看轻的 bèi kànqīng de

underscore v 强调 qiángdiào, 着重 zhuózhòng

undershirt N 汗背心 hànbèixīn [M. WD 件 jiàn], 汗衫 hànshān [M. WD 件 jiàn]

underside N 底部 dǐbù, 下面 xiàmian

undersigned ADJ (the undersigned) 签名人 qiānmíngrén

undersized ADJ (尺寸) 偏小的 (chǐcùn) piān xiǎo de

understaffed ADJ 工作人员不足的 gōngzuò rényuán bù zú de, 人手不够的 rénshǒu bùgòu de

understand (PT & PP **understood**) v 1 理解 lǐjiě, 懂得 dǒngde ■ *Few people really understand Einstein's theory of relativity.* 很少人真正理解爱因斯坦的相对论。Hěn shǎo rén zhēnzhèng lǐjiě Àiyīnsītǎn de xiāngduìlùn. 2 了解 liǎojiě, 知道 zhīdào

understandable ADJ 可以理解的 kěyǐ lǐjiě de

understanding I N 1 理解 lǐjiě, 理解力 lǐjiělì 2 体谅 tǐliàng, 谅解 liàngjiě

to come to an understanding 达成谅解 dáchéng liàngjiě ■ *They've come to an understanding on how the payments will be made.* 他们在怎样付款的问题上达成了谅解。Tāmen zài zěnyàng fù kuǎn de wèntíshang dáchéngle liàngjiě.

II ADJ 通情达理的 tōng qíng dá lǐ de ■ *You're lucky to have such understanding parents.* 你有这么通情达理的父母真是很幸运。Nǐ yǒu zhème tōng qíng dá lǐ de fùmǔ zhēn shì hěn xìngyùn.

understate v 没有充分表达 méiyǒu chōngfèn biǎodá, 淡化 dànhuà

understated ADJ 不夸张的 bù kuāzhāng de, 有节制的 yǒu jiézhì de

understatement N 保守的说法 bǎoshǒu de shuōfa, 不夸张的说法 bù kuāzhāng de shuōfa

understood See **understand**

understudy N 预备演员 yùbèi yǎnyuán, 替身 tìshēn

undertake v 承担 chéngdān ■ *John is already very busy, but he agreed to undertake the new task at the request of his boss.* 约翰已经很忙了，但是应老板的请求，他同意承担新工作。Yuēhàn yǐjīng hěn máng le, dànshì yìng lǎobǎn de qǐngqiú, tā tóngyì chéngdān xīn gōngzuò.

undertaker N 丧葬承办人 sāngzàng chéngbànrén

undertaking N 重大任务 zhòngdà rènwu, 事业 shìyè

undertone N 1 潜在的感情 qiánzài de gǎnqíng, 隐含的意思 yǐnhán de yìsi 2 低声 dīshēng

underwater ADJ, ADV 水下 (的) shuǐxià (de)

underwear N 内衣 nèiyī, 内裤 nèikù ■ *My mother bought me new underwear for my birthday. How embarrassing!* 妈妈给我买了新的内衣裤做生日礼物，真不好意思！Māma gěi wǒ mǎile xīn de nèiyīkù zuò shēngri lǐwù, zhēn bù hǎo yìsi!

underweight ADJ 重量不足的 zhòngliàng bù zú de, 体重不足的 tǐzhòng bù zú de

underworld N 1 黑社会 hēishèhuì 2 地狱 dìyù, 阴界 yīnjiè

underwrite v 1 负担…的费用 fùdān…de fèiyòng to underwrite an environmental project 负担一个环保项目的费用 fùdān yíge huánbǎo xiàngmù de fèiyòng
2 为…保险 wèi…bǎoxiǎn

undesirable I ADJ 会造成损害的 huì zàochéng sǔnhài de, 不良的 bùliáng de II N (undesirables) 不良分子 bùliángfènzǐ

undeveloped ADJ 未开发的 wéi kāifā de, 不发达的 bù fādá de

undisclosed ADJ 不公开的 bù gōngkāi de, 秘密的 mìmì de

undisguised ADJ 公开的 gōngkāi de, 不加掩饰的 bù jiā yǎnshì de

undisturbed ADJ 不受干扰的 bú shòu gānrǎo de, 未改变的 wèi gǎibiàn de

undivided ADJ 未分割的 wèi fēngē de, 不分开的 bù fēnkāi de
undivided attention 全神贯注 quánshén guànzhù
undivided loyalty 忠心耿耿 zhōngxīn gěnggěng
undivided support 全力支持 quánlì zhīchí

undo v 1 解开 jiěkāi, 打开 dǎkāi 2 消除 xiāochú ■ *Sometimes you can't go back and undo the damage you've done.* 有时候你无法回过头去消除已经造成的伤害。Yǒushíhou nǐ wúfǎ huíguò tóu qù xiāochú yǐjīng zàochéng de shānghài.

undoing N (sb's undoing) 某人的垮台／失败 mǒurén de kuǎtái/shībài

659

undressed ADJ 不穿衣服的 bù chuān yīfú de, 裸体的 luǒtǐ de

undue ADJ 不应有的 bù yīngyǒu de, 过分的 guòfèn de

unduly ADV 过分地 guòfèn de, 不适当地 bú shìdāng de

undying ADJ 不灭的 bú miè de, 永恒的 yǒnghéng de

unearth V 1 挖掘 [+地下文物] wājué [+dìxia wénwù] 2 发现 [+真相] fāxiàn [+zhēnxiàng], 披露 pīlù

unearthly ADJ 奇异的 qíyì de, 不自然的 bú zìrán de

uneasy ADJ 1 忧虑不安的 yōulù bù'ān de 2 不安定的 bù'āndìng de, 不稳定的 bù wěndìng de
an uneasy truce 靠不住的休战 kàobuzhù de xiūzhàn

uneducated ADJ 未受教育的 wèi shòu jiàoyù de

unemployed ADJ 失业的 shīyè de ■ The unemployed teacher wrote fantasy novels, which became runaway bestsellers. 这位失业教师写神怪小说，这些小说一下成了畅销书。 Zhè wèi shīyè jiàoshī xiě shénguài xiǎoshuō, zhèxiē xiǎoshuō yíxià chéngle chàngxiāoshū.

unemployment N 1 失业 shīyè
unemployment benefits 失业救济金 shīyè jiùjìjīn
2 失业救济金 shīyè jiùjì jīn
on unemployment 领取失业救济金 lǐngqǔ shīyè jiùjìjīn

unequal ADJ 1 不平等的 bù píngděng de 2 不胜任的 bú shèng rèn de
be unequal to the task 不能胜任这项任务 bùnéng shēngrèn zhè xiàng rènwu

unequivocal ADJ 明确的 míngquè de, 毫不含糊的 háobù hánhu de

unerring ADJ 不会出错的 bú huì chūcuò de, 永远正确的 yǒngyuǎn zhèngquè de

unethical ADJ 违反道德标准的 wéifǎn dàodé biāozhǔn de, 不道德的 bú dàodé de

uneven ADJ 1 不平坦的 [+道路] bù píngtǎn de [+dàolù] 2 水平不一的 shuǐpíng bùyī de, 有好有坏的 yǒu hǎo yǒu huài de
of uneven equality 质量有好有坏的 zhìliàng yǒu hǎo yǒu huài de

unexpected ADJ 没想到的 méi xiǎngdào de, 意外的 yìwài de
an unexpected visitor 意外的客人 yìwài de kèren, 不速之客 búsù zhī kè

unfailing ADJ 始终如一的 shǐzhōng rúyī de, 经久不衰的 jīngjiǔ bù shuāi de

unfair ADJ 不公平的 bù gōngpíng de, 不公正的 bù gōngzhèng de
unfair competition 不公平竞争 bù gōngpíng jìngzhēng

unfaithful ADJ 对 [+妻子] 不忠的人 duì [+qīzi] bù zhōng de rén, 有外遇的 yǒu wàiyù de

unfaltering ADJ 坚定不移的 jiāndìng bùyí de

unfamiliar ADJ 不熟悉的 bù shúxī de, 陌生的 mòshēng de

unfasten V 解开 [+扣子] jiěkāi [+kòuzi]

unfavorable ADJ 1 不适宜的 bú shìyí de 2 不支持的 bù zhīchí de, 反对的 fǎnduì de

unfeeling ADJ 无情的 wúqíng de, 冷漠的 lěngmò de

unfettered ADJ 自由自在的 zìyóu zìzài de

unfinished ADJ 未完成的 wèi wánchéng de

unfit ADJ 1 不适合的 bú shìhé de
unfit for human inhabitation 不适合人类居住的 bú shìhé rénlèi jūzhù de
2 身体不好的 shēntǐ bùhǎo de

unfold V [情节+] 展开 [qíngjié+] zhǎnkāi, 渐渐出现 jiànjiàn chūxiàn

unforeseen ADJ 未预料到的 wèi yùliàodào de

unforgettable ADJ 忘不了的 wàngbuliǎo de, 难忘的 nánwàng de

unfortunate ADJ 1 倒霉的 dǎoméi de 2 不恰当的 bú qiàdàng de ■ The young man's unfortunate remark left a bad impression on his girlfriend's parents. 年轻人不恰当的话，给他女朋友的父母留下了坏印象。 Niánqīngrén bú qiàdàng de huà, gěi tā nǚpéngyou de fùmǔ liúxiale huài yìnxiàng.

unfortunately ADV 不幸 búxìng

unfounded ADJ 没有事实根据的 méiyǒu shìshí gēnjù de, 编造的 biānzào de

unfurl V 打开 [+旗帜] dǎkāi [+qízhì], 扬起 [+风帆] yáng qǐ [+fēngfān]

ungainly ADJ 笨拙的 [+动机] bènzhuō de [+dòngjī], 难看的 nánkàn de

unhappy ADJ 1 不愉快的 bù yúkuài de ■ Her parents' divorce made her childhood quite unhappy. 她的父母离婚，使她的童年很不愉快。 Tā fùmǔ líhūn, shǐ tā de tóngnián hěn bù yúkuài. 2 不满(意)的 bù mǎn (yì) de

unheard-of ADJ 前所未闻的 qiánsuǒ wèi wén de, 空前的 kōngqián de

unholy ADJ 1 不神圣的 bù shénshèng de
unholy alliance 邪恶同盟 xié'è tóngméng
2 不合理的 bù hélǐ de

UNICEF (= the United Nations International Children's Fund) ABBREV 联合国儿童基金会 Liánhéguó értóng jījīnhuì

unicorn N 独角兽 dújiǎoshòu

unidentified ADJ 身份不明的 shēnfen bùmíng de

uniform¹ N 制服 zhìfú

uniform² ADJ 一律的 yílù de, 一致的 yízhì de

unify V 1 (使…)统一 (shǐ…) tǒngyī 2 融合 rónghé, 结合 jiéhé

unilateral ADJ 单方(面)的 dānfāng (miàn) de

uninstall v 卸载 [+计算机软件] xièzài [+jìsuànjī ruǎnjiàn]

uninsured ADJ 无保险的 wú bǎoxiǎn de

unintelligible ADJ 无法理解的 wúfǎ lǐjiě de, 难懂的 nán dǒng de

uninterested ADJ 不感兴趣的 bù gǎn xìngqù de, 没有兴趣的 méiyǒu xìngqu de

union N 1 工会 gōnghuì 2 联合 liánhé ■ The union of the two parties is only a matter of time. 这两个党的联合只是时间问题。Zhè liǎng ge dǎng de liánhé zhǐ shì shíjiān wèntí.

unique ADJ 独特的 dútè de, 独一无二的 dú yī wú èr de ■ This is a rare, but not unique case. 这是一个少见的、但不是独特的事例。Zhè shì yí ge shǎo jiàn de、dàn bú shì dútè de shìlì.

unisex ADJ 不分男女的 bù fēn nánnǚ de, 男女皆宜的 nánnǚ jiē yí de

unison N (in unison) 1 一致 (地) yízhì (de) 2 齐声 (地) qíshēng (de)

unit N 1 单位 dānwèi 2 单元 dānyuán ■ The apartment house has 24 units. 这幢公寓大楼有二十四个单元。Zhè zhuàng gōngyù dàlóu yǒu èrshísì ge dānyuán. 3 部件 bùjiàn ■ The central processing unit (CPU) is the brain of a computer. 中心处理器是计算机的头脑。Zhōngxīn chǔlǐqì shì jìsuànjī de tóunǎo. 4 小组 xiǎozǔ

unite v 联合 liánhé, 使…团结 shǐ...tuánjié to be united in marriage 结成夫妻 jiéchéng fūqī, 结婚 jiéhūn

united ADJ 团结的 tuánjié de, 意见一致的 yìjiàn yízhì de ■ Your father and I are united in not allowing you to date until you're 16. 你父亲和我意见一致，都不允许你在十六岁以前谈恋爱。Nǐ fùqin hé wǒ yìjiàn yízhì, dōu bù yǔnxǔ nǐ zài shíliù suì yǐqián tánliàn'ài.

(the) United Kingdom (U.K.) N 联合王国 Liánhé Wángguó, 英国 Yīngguó the United Kingdom of Great Britain and Northern Ireland 大不列颠及北爱尔兰联合王国 Dàbùlièdiān jí Běi Ài'ěrlán Liánhé Wángguó

(the) United States (U.S.) N 美国 Měiguó the United States of America 美利坚合众国 Měilìjiān Hézhòngguó

unity N 团结 tuánjié, 统一 tǒngyī

universal ADJ 普遍的 pǔbiàn de, 全体的 quántǐ de ■ Maternal love is universal in the animal kingdom. 在动物王国，母爱是普遍性的。Zài dòngwù wángguó, mǔ'ài shì pǔbiànxìng de. universal values 普世价值 pǔ shì jiàzhí

universe N 宇宙 yǔzhòu

university N 大学 dàxué

unjust ADJ 不公平的 bù gōngpíng de, 不公正的 bù gōngzhèng de

unjustified ADJ 没有道理的 méiyǒu dàoli de, 不合理的 bù hélǐ de

unkempt ADJ 凌乱的 língluàn de [+头发] [+tóufa]

unknowingly ADV 不知道地 bù zhīdào de, 不知情的 bù zhīqíng de

unknown ADJ 未知的 wèizhī de, 不知道的 bù zhīdào de ■ The number of people who drowned in the ferry accident is still unknown. 在轮渡事故中淹死的人数，还不知道。Zài lúndù shìgù zhōng yānsǐ de rénshù, hái bù zhīdào. an unknown quantity 未知数 wèizhīshù, 让人捉摸不透的人 ràng rén zhuōmo bú tòu de rén

unleaded I ADJ 不含铅的 bù hán qiān de II N 无铅汽油 wúqiānqìyóu

unleash v 释放 shìfàng, 发泄 fāxiè

unless CONJ 除非 chúfēi ■ I plan to take you to the ball game tonight unless you've got other important things to do. 我计划今天晚上带你去看球赛，除非你有别的重要事情做。Wǒ jìhuà jīntiān wǎnshang dài nǐ qù kàn qiúsài, chúfēi nǐ yǒu biéde zhòngyào shìqing zuò.

unlike I PREP 不像 bú xiàng II ADJ 不相像的 bù xiāngxiàng de, 不一样的 bù yíyàng de

unlikely ADJ 不太可能 (是真) 的 bú tài kěnéng (shì zhēn) de

unlisted ADJ 未登记的 wèi dēngjì de, 未编入电话簿的 wèi biānrù diànhuàbù de

unload v 1 卸 (下) xiè (xia) 2 推卸 [+责任] tuīxiè [+zérèn], 摆脱 bǎituō 3 抛售 [+商品／股票] pāoshòu [+shāngpǐn/gǔpiào]

unlock v 开 (锁) kāi (suǒ)

unloose v 松开 sōngkāi, 解开 jiěkāi

unmarked ADJ 无标志的 wú biāozhì de an unmarked police car 无标志的警车 wú biāozhì de jǐngchē

unmistakable ADJ 不会弄错的 bú huì nòngcuò de, 显而易见的 xiǎn'éryìjiàn de

unmitigated ADJ 十足的 shízú de, 完全的 wánquán de unmitigated failure 完全彻底的失败 wánquán chèdǐ de shībài

unnamed ADJ 不知其名的 bùzhī qí míng de, 未提姓名的 wèi tí xìngmíng de

unnerve v 使…丧失勇气 shǐ...sàngshī yǒngqì, 使…忐忑不安的 shǐ...tǎntè bù'ān de

unobtrusive ADJ 不显眼的 bù xiǎnyǎn de, 不引人注目的 bù yǐnrén zhùmù de

unoccupied ADJ 未被占用的 wèi bèi zhànyòng de, 空着的 kòngzhe de

unorthodox ADJ 非正统的 fēi zhèngtǒng de

unpack v 1 打开 [+行李] dǎkāi [+xíngli] 2 对 [+电脑信息] 解包 duì [+diànnǎo xìnxī] jiě bāo

unpaid ADJ 未支付的 wèi zhīfù de

unpalatable ADJ 1 吃不下去的 [+食物] chībuxiàqù de [+shíwù], 难吃的 nánchī de 2 难以接受的 [+事实] nányǐ jiēshòu de [+shìshí], 讨厌的 tǎoyàn de

unplug v 拔去…的插头 bá qù...de chātóu

unprecedented ADJ 无先例的 wú xiānlì de, 空前的 kōngqián de

unpredictable ADJ 不可预测的 bùkě yùcè de, 捉摸不定的 zhuōmo bú dìng de

unprepossessing ADJ 不起眼的 bù qǐyǎn de, 不引人注目的 bù yǐnrén zhùmù de

unpretentious ADJ 不装腔作势的 bù zhuāngqiāng zuòshì de, 朴实的 pǔshí de

unprincipled ADJ 不讲原则的 bù jiǎng yuánzé de, 肆无忌惮的 sìwú jìdàn de

unqualified ADJ 不合格的 bù hégé de

unquestionable ADJ 不成问题的 bùchéng wèntí de, 毋庸置疑的 wúyōng zhìyí de

unravel v 1 把…弄清楚 bǎ...nòngqīngchǔ, 解释清楚 jiěshì qīngchu 2 [关系+] 破裂 [guānxi+] pòliè, 失败 shībài

unreadable ADJ 1 读不下去的 dú bú xiàqu de, 难读懂的 nán dú dǒng de 2 字迹潦草的 zìjī liǎocǎo de, 难辨认的 nán biànrèn de

unrealistic ADJ 不现实的 bú xiànshí de, 不切实际的 bú qiè shíjì de

unreasonable ADJ 不合理的 bù hélǐ de, 不公平的 bù gōngpíng de

unreasoning ADJ 缺乏理智的 quēfá lǐzhì de, 冲动的 chōngdòng de

unrecoverable ADJ 无法回收的 wúfǎ huíshōu de, 损失的 sǔnshī de

unrelated ADJ 1 不相关的 bù xiāngguān de 2 没有亲戚关系的 méiyǒu qīnqi guānxi de

unrelenting ADJ 不停歇的 bù tíngxiē de, 持续的 chíxù de

unrequited ADJ (unrequited love) 单相思 dānxiāngsī, 单恋 dānliàn

unreserved ADJ 毫无保留的 háowú bǎoliú de, 完全的 wánquán de

unresponsive ADJ 1 无反应的 wú fǎnyìng de be unresponsive to medical treatment 医治无效 yīzhì wú xiào
2 不作回应的 bú zuò huíyìng de, 冷淡的 lěngdàn de

unrest N 不安定 bù'āndìng, 动乱 dòngluàn

unrestrained ADJ 无拘束的 wú jūshù de, 放纵的 fàngzòng de

unrivaled ADJ 无敌的 wúdí de, 无与伦比的 wú yǔ lúnbǐ de

unruly ADJ 任性的 rènxìng de, 不受管束的 bú shòu guǎnshù de

unsaid ADJ (better left unsaid) [有些话+] 最好不要说出来 [yǒuxiē huà+] zuìhǎo bú yào shuōchulai

unsavory ADJ 可厌的 kěyàn de, 可憎的 kězēng de

unscathed ADJ 不受伤害的 bú shòu shānghài de

unscrew v 旋开 [+罐头盖] xuánkāi [+guàntougài], 拧开 nǐngkai

unscrupulous ADJ 不择手段的 bù zé shǒuduàn de, 不讲道理的 bù jiǎng dàoli de

unseasonable ADV 不合时令 bù hé shílìng, 反常地 fǎncháng de

unseat v 使 [+人] 离职／下台 shǐ [+rén] lízhí/ xiàtái

unseemly ADJ 不得体的 bù détǐ de, 不体面的 bù tǐmiàn de

unsettle v 使 [+人] 心绪不定 shǐ [+rén] xīnxù búdìng, 扰乱 [+人心] rǎoluàn [+rénxīn]

unsightly ADJ 不好看的 bù hǎokàn de, 难看的 nánkàn de

unskilled ADJ 非技术性的 fēi jìshùxìng de, 非熟练的 fēi shúliàn de

unsophisticated ADJ 1 不老练的 [+人] bù lǎoliàn de [+rén], 天真朴素的 tiānzhēn pǔsù de 2 不复杂的 [+工具] bú fùzá de [+gōngjù], 简单的 jiǎndān de

unspeakable ADJ 坏得无法形容的 huài dé wúfǎ xíngróng de, 说不出口的 shuōbuchū kǒu de

unspecified ADJ 未说明的 wèi shuōmíng de

unstoppable ADJ 不可阻挡的 bùkě zǔdǎng de, 一帆风顺的 yìfānfēngshùn de

unsung ADJ (unsung heroes) 默默无闻的英雄 mòmò wúwén de yīngxióng

unsustainable ADJ 不可持续的 bùkě chíxù de, 难以为继的 nányǐ wéijì de

unswerving ADJ 坚定不移的 jiāndìng búyí de

untapped ADJ 未开发利用的 wèi kāifā lìyòng de

untenable ADJ 难以维持的 nányǐ wéichí de, 难以继续的 nányǐ jìxù de

unthinkable ADJ 不可思议的 bùkě sīyì de, 难以信的 nányǐ zhìxìn de

untie v 解开 [+结] jiěkāi [+jié]

until CONJ, PREP 直到 zhídào ■ *Mom didn't go to bed until all her children came back.* 妈妈直到孩子们都回家了才睡觉。Māma zhídao háizimen dōu huíjiāle cái shuìjiào.

untimely ADJ 不适时的 bú shìshí de untimely death 过早死亡 guòzǎo sǐwáng

untiring ADJ 不知疲倦的 bùzhī píjuàn de, 坚持不懈的 jiānchí bú xiè de

untold ADJ 无数的 wúshù de, 无法估量的 wúfǎ gūliang de

untouchable ADJ 1 碰不得的 pèngbude de, 不可冒犯的 bùkě màofàn de 2 不可接触的 [+贱民] bùkě jiēchù de [+jiànmín]

untoward ADJ 异常的 yìcháng de, 意外的 yìwài de

unused[1] ADJ 未用过的 wèi yòngguo de

unused[2] ADJ 不习惯的 bù xíguàn de

unusual ADJ 不正常的 bú zhèngcháng de, 罕见的 hǎn jiàn de

unusually ADV 异常地 yìcháng de, 不同寻常地 bùtóng xúncháng de

unveil v 1 透露 tòulù, 宣布 xuānbù 2 揭幕 jiēmù

unwieldy ADJ **1** 无法搬动的 [+大钢琴] wúfǎ bāndòng de [+dàgāngqín] **2** 难以操作／控制的 [+系统] nányǐ cāozuò/kòngzhì de [+xìtǒng]

unwind V 放纵 fàngzòng, 松弛 sōngchí

unwittingly ADV 不知不觉（地）bùzhī bùjué (de), 无意中 wúyìzhōng

unwritten ADJ 不成文的 bùchéng wén de

unyielding ADJ 不屈从的 bù qūcóng de, 顽固的 wángù de

unzip V **1** 拉开拉链 lākāi lāliàn **2** 给（电脑文件）解压缩 gěi (diànnǎo wénjiàn) jiě yāsuō

up I ADV **1** 向上 xiàng shàng, 起来 qǐlai ■ *Many kids shot up their hands, eager to answer the question.* 许多孩子高高举起手，急切地想回答问题。Xǔduō háizi gāogāo jǔqǐ shǒu, jíqiè de xiǎng huídá wèntí. **2** 朝北面 cháo běimian, 在北面 zài běimian **3** 朝，向 cháo, xiàng ■ *A stranger came up to me in the street to ask me for directions.* 一个陌生人在街上走到我面前问路。Yí ge mòshēng rén zài jiēshang zǒudao wǒ miànqián wèn lù. **4** 增加 zēngjiā **5** 完 wán ■ *He ate up the whole chicken.* 他把一只鸡都吃完了。Tā bǎ yì zhī jī dōu chīwán le. **II** ADJ 醒着 xǐngzhe ■ *When the clock stuck midnight, I was still up.* 午夜钟响，我还醒着。Wǔyè zhōng xiǎng, wǒ hái xǐngzhe. **III** PREP 向上 xiàng shàng

up to ① 多达 duō dá ■ *The typhoon killed or injured up to 40 people.* 这场台风使多达四十人伤亡。Zhè chǎng táifēng shǐ duō dá sìshí rén shāngwáng. ② 能胜任 néng shèngrèn It's up to you 由你决定 yóu nǐ juédìng **IV** N (ups and downs) 有好有坏的经历 yǒu hǎo yǒu huài de jīnglì, 苦乐 kǔlè, 盛衰 shèngshuāi

up-and-coming ADJ 前途无量的 qiántú wúliàng de, 大有希望的 dàyǒu xīwàng de

upbeat ADJ 乐观的 lèguān de, 快乐的 kuàilè de

upbringing N [家庭+] 教养 [jiātíng+] jiàoyǎng

upchuck V 呕吐 ǒutù

upcoming ADJ 即将来临的 jíjiāng láilín de

update V 更新 gēngxīn

to update sb on sth 为某人提供有关某事的最新情况 wéi mǒurén tígōng yǒuguān mǒushì de zuìxīn qíngkuàng

upend V 倒放 dàofàng, 颠倒 diāndǎo

upfront ADJ **1** 坦率的 tǎnshuài de, 不吞吞吐吐的 bù tūntūn tǔtǔ de **2** (upfront fees) 马上要付的费用 mǎshàng yào fù de fèiyòng

upgrade V 升级 shēngjí, 升级换代 shēngjí huàndài ■ *These computers need upgrading.* 这些计算机要升级换代了。Zhèxiē jìsuànjī yào shēngjí huàndài le.

upheaval N 剧变 jùbiàn, 巨变 jùbiàn

uphill ADJ **1** 上坡的 shàngpō de, 上山的 shàngshān de **2** 艰难的 jiānnán de, 充满阻力的 chōngmǎn zǔlì de

uphold V **1** 坚持 [+原则] jiānchí [+yuánzé], 维护 wéihù **2** 维持 [+原来的决定] wéichí [+yuánlái de juédìng], 认可 rènkě

upholster V 为 [+椅子] 加上垫子／套子 wéi [+yǐzi] jiāshàng diànzi/tàozi

upholstery N [椅子的+] 垫料 [yǐzi de+] diànliào

upkeep N 保养 bǎoyǎng, 维修 wéixiū

uplifting ADJ 令人情绪高涨的 lìngrén qíngxù gāozhǎng de

upon PREP 在…上 zài…shàng

upper ADJ 上面的 shàngmian de, 较高的 jiào gāo de

to gain the upper hand 占上风 zhàn shàngfēng, 处于有利地位 chǔyú yǒulì dìwèi ■ *The labor union has got the upper hand in the dispute.* 工会在争端中占了上风。Gōnghuì zài zhēngduān zhōng zhànle shàngfēng.

upper case 大写（字母）dàxiě (zìmǔ)

upper class 上层社会 shàngcéng shèhuì

uppermost ADJ **1** 最高的 zuì gāo de **2** 最重要的 zuì zhòngyào de

be uppermost in one's mind 某人心目中最重要的 mǒurén xīnmùzhōng zuì zhòngyào de

uppity ADJ 傲慢的 àomàn de, 盛气凌人的 shèngqì língrén de

upright ADJ **1** 笔直的 bǐzhí de, 挺直的 tǐngzhí de ■ *The war veteran tried to stand upright at the ceremony.* 老兵在典礼上尽力站得笔直。Lǎobīng zài diǎnlǐshang jìnlì zhànde bǐzhí. **2** 正直的 zhèngzhí de ■ *Jerry is an upright and bright boy from a fine family.* 杰里是个出生于好家庭的正直聪明的男孩子。Jiélǐ shì ge chūshēng yú hǎo jiātíng de zhèngzhí cōngmíng de nánháizi.

uprising N 起义 qǐyì, 暴动 bàodòng

upriver ADV 向上游 xiàng shàngyóu

uproar N 喧闹 xuānnào, 吵闹 chǎonào

uproot V **1** 把 [+植物] 连根拔起 bǎ [+zhíwù] lián gēn bá qǐ **2** 使 [+家庭] 迁居 shǐ [+jiātíng] qiānjū

upscale ADJ 高档的 gāodàng de, 高层次的 gāocéngcì de

upset I V (PT & PP **upset**) **1** 打翻 [+一杯水] dǎfān [+yìbēi shuǐ] **2** 打乱 [+计划] dǎluàn [+jìhuà] **3** 使…心烦意乱 shǐ…xīn fán yì luàn, 不安 bù'ān ■ *Don't upset yourself—everything is under control.* 不要心烦—一切正常。Bú yào xīnfán—yíqiè zhèngcháng. **II** ADJ **1** 心烦的 xīnfán de, 心情烦乱的 xīnqíng fánluàn de **2** 不舒服的 bù shūfú de

to have an upset stomach 肚子痛 dùzi tòng, 肠胃不适 chángwèi búshì

III N 意外失败 yìwài shībài

upshot N 结果 jiéguǒ, 结局 jiéjú

upside down ADJ, ADV 上下颠倒（的）shàngxià diāndǎo (de), 翻转过来（的）fānzhuǎn guòlai (de) (de) ■ *That picture is upside down!* 这幅画挂倒了！Zhè fú huà guà dǎo le!

upstage I v 抢…的风头 qiǎng…de fēngtou II ADV 朝着舞台后方 cháozhe wǔtái hòufāng

upstairs I ADV 在楼上 zài lóushang, 往楼上 wǎng lóushàng II ADJ 楼上的 lóushàng de upstairs bedroom 楼上的卧室 lóushàng de wòshì

upstart N 暴发户 bàofāhù, 蹿红的 cuānhóng de

upstate ADJ （一个州的）北部地区 (yí ge zhōu de) běibù dìqū

upstream ADV 向上游 xiàng shàngyóu

upsurge N 急剧上升 jíjù shàngshēng, 剧增 jùzēng

upswing N 改进 gǎijìn, 起色 qǐsè

uptake N 1 领会 lǐnghuì, 理解 lǐjiě slow/quick on the uptake 领会慢／快 lǐnghuì màn/kuài
2 （养料的）摄取 (yǎngliào de) shèqǔ

uptight ADJ 1 保守拘谨的 bǎoshǒu jūjǐn de 2 紧张不安的 jǐnzhāng bù'ān de, 愤怒的 fènnù de

up-to-date ADJ 最新的 zuì xīn de ■ *This is an up-to-date dictionary.* 这是一本最新的词典。Zhè shì yì běn zuì xīn de cídiǎn.

upward ADJ, ADV 向上 xiàngshàng upward to 超过 chāoguo ■ *He earns upward to about 100 grand a year.* 他一年挣十万多元。Tā yìnián zhèng shíwàn duō yuán.

Uranus N 天王星 Tiānwángxīng

urban ADJ 城市的 chéngshì de, 市区的 shìqū de ■ *Reducing urban unemployment is high on the agenda of the new state government.* 减少城市失业现象是州政府重点考虑的问题。Jiǎnshǎo chéngshì shīyè xiànxiàng shì zhōu zhèngfǔ zhòngdiǎn kǎolǜ de wèntí.

urbane ADJ 温文尔雅的 wēnwén ěr yǎ de, 彬彬有礼的 bīnbīn yǒulǐ de

urchin N 小顽童 xiǎo wántóng

urge I v 催促 cuīcù, 促使 cùshǐ II N 冲动 chōngdòng
to repress sexual urges 抑制性冲动 yìzhì xìng chōngdòng

urgent ADJ 紧迫的 jǐnpò de, 紧急的 jǐnjí de

urinal N 小便池 xiǎobiànchí

urinate v 小便 xiǎobiàn, 解手 jiěshǒu

urine N 尿 niào, 小便 xiǎobiàn

URL (= Uniform Resource Locator) ABBREV 因特网址 yīntèwǎngzhǐ

urn N 1 （骨灰）瓮 (gǔhuī) wèng 2 大茶壶 dà cháhú

us PRON 我们 wǒmen

(the) U.S.(A.) See (the) United States (of America)

use v, N 1 （使）用 (shǐ) yòng 2 消耗 xiāohào, 耗费 hàofèi ■ *Leave that account alone—it's money for use in an emergency.* 别动那个账户—那是出现紧急情况时用的钱。Bié dòng nàge zhànghù—nà shì chūxiàn jǐnjí qíngkuàng shí yòng de qián.

used ADJ 旧的 jiù de, 二手的 èrshǒu de ■ *Used cars depreciate fast.* 旧车贬值很快。Jiùchē biǎnzhí hěn kuài.

used to[1] MODAL v 过去 guòqu ■ *Todd used to drive to work but he takes the bus now because of the cost of fuel.* 托德过去开车上班，现在因为油价太贵改乘公共汽车了。Tuōdé guòqu kāichē shàngbān, xiànzài yīnwèi yóujià tài guì gǎichéng gōnggòng qìchē le.

used to[2] ADJ 习惯 xíguàn, 对…习惯 duì…xíguàn

useful ADJ 有用的 yǒuyòng de ■ *Few things are more useful than a good dictionary.* 没有多少东西比一本好词典更有用。Méiyǒu duōshǎo dōngxi bǐ yì běn hǎo cídiǎn gèng yǒuyòng.

useless ADJ 无用的 wúyòng de, 没有用的 méiyǒu yòng de ■ *It's useless to cry over spilt milk.* 牛奶倒翻了，再哭也没有用。Niúnǎi dǎofān le, zài kū yě méiyǒu yòng. (→ 木已成舟。Mù yǐ chéng zhōu. *The tree has been made into a boat.*)

user N 使用者 shǐyòngzhě, 使用人 shǐyòngrén

user-friendly ADJ 容易使用的 róngyì shǐyòng de, 易操作的 yì cāozuò de

username N 使用人姓名 shǐyòngrén xìngmíng

usher I v 引领 yǐnlǐng, 引 yǐn, 领 lǐng II N [电影院+] 引座员 [diànyǐngyuàn+] yǐnzuòyuán, 引宾员 yǐnbīnyuán

usual ADJ 通常的 tōngcháng de ■ *He came home later than usual yesterday.* 他昨天比通常晚回家。Tā zuótiān bǐ tōngcháng wǎn huíjiā.

usually ADV 通常 tōngcháng, 平常 píngcháng ■ *Gordon usually goes to the gym three times a week.* 戈登通常一星期去三次健身房。Gēdēng tōngcháng yì xīngqí qù sān cì jiànshēnfáng.

usurp v 篡夺 cuànduó, （非法）夺取 (fēifǎ) duóqǔ

utensil N 用具 yòngjù, 器皿 qìmǐn

uterus N 子宫 zǐgōng

utilitarian ADJ 实用的 shíyòng de, 功利的 gōnglì de

utilities N 水电煤（气）服务 shuǐdiàn méi (qì) fúwù, 公共事业 gōnggòng shìyè

utilize v 利用 lìyòng

utmost ADJ 极端的 jíduān de with utmost care 极其小心地 jíqí xiǎoxīn de

utopia N 乌托邦 Wūtuōbāng, 理想世界 lǐxiǎng shìjiè

utter I ADJ 完全的 wánquán de, 彻头彻尾的 chètóu chèwěi de utter chaos 一片混乱 yípiàn hùnluàn
II v 说出 shuōchū, 讲 jiǎng

U-turn N 1 180度大转弯 yìbǎi bāshí dù dà zhuǎnwān 2 彻底改变 chèdǐ gǎibiàn

V

vacancy N **1** 空缺的职位 kòngquē de zhíwèi ■ *Sorry, but we don't have any vacancies at present.* 对不起，我们目前没有空缺的职位。Duìbuqǐ, wǒmen mùqián méiyǒu kòngquē de zhíwèi. **2**（旅馆的）空房 (lǚguǎn de) kōngfáng no vacancies 客满 kèmǎn

vacant ADJ **1** 未占用的 [+房间] wèi zhànyòng de [+fángjiān], 空着的 kòngzhe de a vacant lot（城市里的）空地 (chéngshì lǐ de) kòngdì **2** 空缺的 [+职位] kòngquē de [+zhíwèi] **3** 茫然的 mángrán de, 若有所思的 ruò yǒu suǒsī de

vacate V **1** 空出 [+房间] kòng chū [+fángjiān], 搬离 bānlí **2** 离开 [+职位] líkāi [+zhíwèi]

vacation N 假期 jiàqí

vaccinate V 注射疫苗 zhùshè yìmiáo

vaccination N 疫苗接种 yìmiáo jiēzhòng vaccination against tetanus 预防破伤风的疫苗接种 yùfáng pòshāngfēng de yìmiáo jiēzhòng

vaccine N 疫苗 yìmiáo measles vaccine 麻疹疫苗 mázhěn yìmiáo

vacillate V 犹豫不决 yóuyù bùjué, 拿不定主意 nábùdìng zhǔyi

vacuum I N **1** 真空 zhēnkōng **2**（真空）吸尘器 (zhēnkōng) xīchénqì vacuum cleaner 真空吸尘器 zhēnkōng xīchénqì II V **1**（用真空吸尘器）吸尘 (yòng zhēnkōng xīchénqì) xī chén ■ *Have you vacuumed the car seats?* 你用吸尘器打扫了车座了吗? Nǐ yòng xīchénqì dǎsǎole chēzuò le ma?

vacuum-packed ADJ 真空包装的 zhēnkōng bāozhuāng de

vagina N 阴道 yīndào

vagrant N 流浪汉 liúlànghàn, 游民 yóumín

vague ADJ **1** 含糊的 hánhu de, 不清楚的 bù qīngchu de **2** 模模糊糊的 mómó huhú de

vain ADJ **1** 白费的 báifèi de, 无目的的 wú mùdì de in vain 徒劳 túláo **2** 自视过高的 zìshì guògāo de, 自负的 zìfù de

valentine N 情人节贺卡 qíngrénjié hèkǎ, 情人卡 qíngrénkǎ [M. WD 张 zhāng]

Valentine's Day N 情人节 qíngrénjié (February 14th)

valet N **1** 男佣人 nán yōngrén **2**（旅馆）男服务员 (lǚguǎn) nán fúwùyuán valet parking（旅馆）代客停车服务 (lǚguǎn) dàikè tíngchē fúwù

valiant ADJ 勇敢的 yǒnggǎn de, 英勇的 yīngyǒng de

valid ADJ **1** 有 [+法律] 效力的 yǒu [+fǎlǜ+] xiàolì de ■ *This contract is not valid owing to some technical errors.* 由于某些技术性的错误，这份合同没有法律效力。Yóuyú mǒuxiē jìshùxìng de cuòwù, zhè fèn hétong méiyǒu fǎlǜ xiàolì. **2** 正当的 [+理由] zhèngdàng de [+lǐyóu], 合理的 hélǐ de

validate V **1** 使…生效 shǐ...shēngxiào **2** 证实 zhèngshí

validity N **1** 正当性 zhèngdàngxìng, 合理性 hélǐxìng **2** 有效性 yǒuxiàoxìng

valley N 山谷 shāngǔ

valor N 勇气 yǒngqì, 英勇 yīngyǒng

valuable ADJ **1** 非常有价值的 fēicháng yǒu jiàzhí de, 贵重的 guìzhòng de ■ *You can get valuable information on the internet for free.* 你可以免费从因特网获取有价值的信息。Nǐ kěyǐ miǎnfèi cóng Yīntèwǎng huòqǔ yǒu jiàzhí de xìnxī. **2** 宝贵的 bǎoguì de, 珍贵的 zhēnguì de

valuables N 贵重物品 guìzhòng wùpǐn

valuation N 估价 gūjià market valuation 市场价值 shìchǎng jiàzhí, 市值 shì zhí

value I N 价值 jiàzhí ■ *The value of the American dollar has been declining.* 美元的价值一直在下跌。Měiyuán de jiàzhí yīzhí zài xiàdiē. value-added tax 增值税 zēngzhíshuì practiced value 使用价值 shǐyòngjià zhí sentimental value 感情价值 gǎnqíng jiàzhí ■ *That ring has sentimental value for her.* 那枚戒指对她有感情上的价值。Nà méi jièzhi duì tā yǒu gǎnqíngshang de jiàzhí. II V **1** 珍视 zhēnshì **2** 估价 gūjià

values N 价值观（念）jiàzhí guān (niàn) ■ *Do you have any shared values in your family?* 你们家庭中有共同的价值观吗? Nǐmen jiātíng zhōng yǒu gòngtóng de jiàzhíguān ma?

valve N **1** 阀 fá, 活门 huómén safety valve 安全阀 ānquánfá **2**（心脏）瓣膜 (xīnzàng) bànmó

vampire N 吸血鬼 xīxuèguǐ

van N **1** 小型货车 xiǎoxíng huòchē [M. WD 辆 liàng] **2** 小客车 xiǎokèchē, 面包车 miànbāochē [M. WD 辆 liàng]

vandal N 故意破坏财物者 gùyì pòhuài cáiwù zhě, 破坏公物者 pòhuài gōngwù zhě

vandalism N 破坏 pòhuài, 破坏行为 pòhuài xíngwéi

vandalize V 故意破坏 [+公共财物] gùyì pòhuài [+gōnggòng cáiwù]

vanguard N 先锋 xiānfēng, 前卫 qiánwèi

vanilla N 香草 xiāngcǎo, 香草味 xiāngcǎowèi vanilla icecream 香草冰淇淋 xiāngcǎo bīngqilín

vanish V 消失 xiāoshī, 不见 bújiàn

vanity N 虚荣 xūróng, 虚荣心 xūróng xīn

vanquish V 征服 zhēngfú, 击败 jībài

vantage point N **1** 有利位置 yǒulì wèizhi **2** 立场 lìchǎng, 观点 guāndiǎn

vapor N（水）蒸汽 (shuǐ) zhēngqì

vaporize V（使…）蒸发 (shǐ...) zhēngfā, 汽化 qìhuà

variable I ADJ **1** 多变的 duōbiàn de **2** 情况不一样的 qíngkuàng bù yíyàng de, 变化的 biànhuà de II N **1** 可变因素 kěbiàn yīnsù **2**（数学）变量 (shùxué) biànliàng

variant ADJ, N 变体 biàntǐ, 变种 biànzhǒng

variation N 变化 biànhuà, 不同 bù tóng

varicose veins N（腿部）静脉曲张 (tuǐ bù) jìngmài qūzhāng

varied ADJ 各种各样的 gèzhǒng gèyàng de, 形形色色的 xíngxíng sèsè de

variety N 品种 pǐnzhǒng ■ *Several varieties of apple are grown in this state.* 这个州里种植着几个不同品种的苹果。Zhè ge zhōu lǐ zhòngzhí jǐ ge bù tóng pǐnzhǒng de píngguǒ.

a variety of 各种 gè zhǒng, 种种 zhǒngzhǒng

variety show 综艺表演 zōngyì biǎoyǎn

various ADJ 不同的 bù tóng de

varnish I N **1** 清漆 qīngqī, 罩光漆 zhàoguāngqī II V 涂上清漆 tú shàng qīngqī

vary V 不同 bù tóng, 变化 biànhuà ■ *Temperature varies with the season.* 气温因季节而不同。Qìwēn yīn jìjié ér bù tóng.

varying ADJ 不同的 bù tóng de, 有差异的 yǒu chāyì de

vase N 花瓶 huāpíng

Ming vase 中国明代的花瓶 Zhōngguó Míngdài de huāpíng

vasectomy N 输精管切除术 shūjīngguǎn qiēchúshù

vast ADJ 巨大的 jùdà de

vast majority 绝大多数 juédàduōshù

vastly ADV 非常 fēicháng, 极其 jíqí

VAT (= value-added tax) ABBREV See **value**

vat N 大（水）缸 dà (shuǐ) gāng

vault¹ N **1**（银行）保险库 (yínháng) bǎoxiǎnkù **2**（地下）墓穴 (dìxià) mùxué [M. WD 座 zuò]

vault² V **1** 跳跃 tiàoyuè, 跳过 tiàoguò **2** 跃升 yuèshēng

pole vault 撑竿跳 chēnggāntiào

V chip N V形芯片 V xíng xìnpiàn

VCR (= video cassette recorder) ABBREV 录像机 lùxiàngjī

veal N 小牛肉 xiǎoniúròu

vegetable N 蔬菜 shūcài ■ *Doctors tell us to eat lots of vegetables.* 医生要我们多吃蔬菜。Yīshēng yào wǒmen duō chī shūcài.

vegetarian N 素食主义者 sùshízhǔyìzhě

vegetarianism N 素食主义 sùshízhǔyì

vegetation N 植被 zhíbèi, 草木 cǎomù

vehement ADJ 强烈的 qiángliè de, 激烈的 jīliè de

vehicle N **1** 车辆 chēliàng **2** 媒介 méijiè, 表达工具 biǎodá gōngjù

veil I N **1** 面纱 miànshā [M. WD 块 kuài]

bridal veil 新娘面纱 xīnniáng miànshā

2 烟幕 yānmù **3** (the veil)（伊斯兰国家妇女）戴面纱的制度 (Yīsīlánguójiā fùnǚ) dài miànshā de zhìdù II V 遮上面纱 zhēshàng miànshā

veiled ADJ 隐蔽的 yǐnbì de, 含蓄的 hánxù de

veiled threat 含蓄的威胁 hánxù de wēixié

vein N **1** [人体的+] 静脉 [réntǐ de+] jìngmài [M. WD 条 tiáo]

jugular vein 颈静脉 jǐng jìngmài

2 [叶子的+] 叶脉 [yèzi de+] yèmài **3** [石头的+] 纹路 [shítou de+] wénlù **4** 矿脉 kuàngmài

velocity N 速度 sùdù

the velocity of light 光速 guāngsù

velvet N 天鹅绒 tiān'éróng, 丝绒 sīróng

vendetta N **1** 报复 bàofu

personal/political vendetta 个人／政治报复 gèrén/zhèngzhì bàofu

2 世仇 shìchóu, 血仇 xuèchóu

vending machine N 自动售货机 zìdòng shòuhuòjī

vendor N **1**（街头）小贩 (jiētóu) xiǎofàn **2** 推销商 tuīxiāoshāng **3** 卖主 màizhǔ

veneer N **1** 贴板 tiēbǎn [M. WD 块 kuài], 镶板 xiāngbǎn [M. WD 块 kuài]

walnut veneer 桃木镶板 táomù xiāngbǎn

2 假象 jiǎxiàng, 虚饰 xūshì

a veneer of kindness 和善的假象 héshàn de jiǎxiàng

venerable ADJ 德高望重的 dégāo wàngzhòng de, 深受尊敬的 shēnshòu zūnjìng de

venerate V 崇敬 chóngjìng, 敬重 jìngzhòng

Venetian blind N 百叶窗帘 bǎiyèchuānglián

vengeance N 报仇 bàochóu, 复仇 fùchóu

with a vengeance 变本加厉地 biànběn jiālì de, 过度地 guòdù de

vengeful ADJ 怀有复仇心的 huáiyǒu fùchóuxīn de, 报仇的 bàochóu de

venison N 鹿肉 lùròu

venom N **1** 毒液 dúyè **2** 极度憎恨 jídù zēnghèn

vent I N **1** 通风孔 tōngfēngkǒng

to give vent to 发泄 [+怒火] fāxiè [+nùhuǒ]

II V 发泄 fāxiè, 发牢骚 fāláosāo

to vent one's spleen 发泄怒火 fāxiè nùhuǒ

ventilate V **1**（使…）通风 (shǐ...) tōngfēng **2** 发表 [+意见] fābiǎo [+yìjiàn]

ventilator N **1** 通风装置 tōngfēngzhuāngzhì **2** 人工呼吸机 réngōng hūxījī

ventriloquism N 口技 kǒujì

ventriloquist N 口技表演者 kǒujì biǎoyǎnzhě, 口技演员 kǒujì yǎnyuán

venture I N **1** 风险 fēngxiǎn, 冒险 màoxiǎn **2** 风险投资 fēngxiǎn tóuzī, 商业投资 shāngyè tóuzī

venture capital 风险资本 fēngxiǎn zīběn

joint venture 合资企业 hézī qǐyè

II V **1** 冒（风）险 mào (fēng) xiǎn **2** 敢于 gǎnyú

Nothing ventured, nothing gained. 不入虎穴, 焉得虎子? Bú rù hǔxué, yāndé hǔzǐ? (→ 不冒险进入虎穴, 怎能抓到小老虎? Bú màoxiǎn jìnrù hǔxué, zěn néng zhuā dào xiǎo lǎohǔ? If you don't venture into a tiger's den, how can you catch a tiger cub?)

venue N (举办)地点 (jǔbàn) dìdiǎn, 会址 huìzhǐ

Venus N 1 金星 Jīnxīng 2 维纳斯 (爱情女神) Wéinàsī (àiqíng nǚshén)

veranda N 游廊 yóuláng [M. WD 条 tiáo], 走廊 zǒuláng [M. WD 条 tiáo]

verb N 动词 dòngcí

verbal ADJ 1 口头的 kǒutóu de
verbal agreement 口头协定 kǒutóu xiédìng 2 语言的 yǔyán de, 词语的 yáncí de
verbal skill 语言技能 yǔyán jìnéng

verbatim ADJ, ADV 逐字 (的／地) zhúzì (de)
to quote sb verbatim 逐字引用某人的话 zhúzì yǐnyòng mǒurén de huà

verbose ADJ 话太多的 huà tài duō de, 啰嗦的 luōsuō de

verdict N (法庭) 裁决 (fǎtíng) cáijué, 判决 pànjué
a guilty verdict 有罪裁定 yǒuzuì cáidìng

verge I N 边缘 biānyuán
on the verge of bankruptcy 濒于破财的边缘 bīnyú pòcái de biānyuán
II v (to verge on) 接近 jiējìn, 几乎 jīhū
to verge on the impossible 几乎不可能 jīhū bù kěnéng

verification N 核实 héshí, 证实 zhèngshí

verify v 核实 héshí, 证实 zhèngshí

veritable ADJ 真正的 zhēnzhèng de, 名副其实的 míngfù qíshí de

vermin N 1 害虫 hàichóng, 害兽 hàishòu 2 害人精 hàirénjīng, 坏蛋 huàidàn

vernacular ADJ, N 本地语 běndìyǔ, 方言 fāngyán, 土话 tǔhuà

versatile ADJ 1 多才多艺的 [+人] duōcái duōyì de [+rén], 多面手的 duōmiànshǒu de 2 用途广泛的 [+工具] yòngtúguǎngfàn de [+gōngjù], 万能的 wànnéng de

verse N 1 诗 shī, 韵文 yùnwén 2 一节 (歌词) yìjié (gēcí)

versed ADJ (be versed in) 精通 jīngtōng, 对…造诣很深 duì…zàoyì hěn shēn

version N 1 版本 bǎn 2 说法 shuōfǎ ■ Witnesses gave different versions of how the accident took place. 关于事故是怎样发生的, 目击者有不同的说法。 Guānyú shìgù shì zěnyàng fāshēng de, mùjīzhě yǒu bù tóng de shuōfǎ.

versus PREP 1 (体育比赛／法律诉讼)…对… (tǐyù bǐsài/fǎlǜ sùsòng)…duì… 2 与…相比 yǔ… xiāngbǐ, 与…相对 yǔ…xiāngduì

vertebra N 脊椎 jǐzhuī [M. WD 块 kuài], 椎骨 zhuīgǔ [M. WD 块 kuài]

vertical I ADJ 垂直的 chuízhí de II N 垂直线 chuízhíxiàn

vertigo N (登高而产生的)眩晕 (dēnggāo ér chǎnshēng de) xuànyùn, 头晕 tóuyūn

verve N 活力 huólì, 生机 shēngjī

very I ADV 非常 fēicháng II ADJ 正是 zhèng shì, 实在的 shízài de ■ Joshua's big smile was the very reason Amy decided to marry him. 正是乔舒亚的开朗笑容, 使艾米决定嫁给他。 Zhèngshì Qiáoshūyà de kāilǎng xiàoróng, shǐ Àimǐ juédìng jià gěi tā.

vessel N 1 航船 hángchuán, 艘 sōu 2 容器 róngqì 3 血管 xuèguǎn, 脉管 màiguǎn

vest N 1 内衣背心 nèiyī bèixīn [M. WD 件 jiàn]
bulletproof vest 防弹背心 fángdàn bèixīn 2 马甲 mǎjiǎ [M. WD 件 jiàn]

vested interest N 既得利益 jìdé lìyì
vested interests 既得利益集团 jìdé lìyì jítuán

vestibule N 门厅 méntīng, 前厅 qiántīng

vestige N 痕迹 hénjì, 遗迹 yíjì

vet I N 1 (= veterinarian) 兽医 shòuyī 2 (= veteran) 老兵 lǎobīng II v (政治) 审查 (zhèngzhì) chǎnchá
vetting procedure (政治) 审查程序 (zhèngzhì) shěnchá chéngxù

veteran N 老兵 lǎobīng, 老手 lǎoshǒu

veterinarian N 兽医 shòuyī

veterinary ADJ 兽医的 shòuyī de
veterinary medicine 兽医 (学) shòuyī (xué)

veto I v 否决 fǒujué, 反对 fǎnduì II N 否决 (权) fǒujué (quán)
veto power 否决权 fǒujuéquán

vex v 使…恼怒 shǐ…nǎonù

VHF (= very high frequency) ABBREV 甚高频 shèngāopín

via PREP 经过 jīngguo ■ You can get downtown either via the tunnel or via the suspension bridge. 你可以经过地道, 或者经过悬索桥达到市中心。 Nǐ kěyǐ jīngguo dìdào, huòzhě jīngguo xuánsuǒqiáo dádào shì zhōngxīn.

viability N 可行性 kěxíngxìng

viable ADJ 1 切实可行的 qièshí kěxíng de 2 能存活的 néng cúnhuó de

viaduct N 高架桥 gāojiàqiáo

Viagra N 伟哥 (壮阳药) Wěigē (zhuàngyángyào)

vial N 小 (药) 瓶 xiǎo (yào) píng

vibe N 感觉 gǎnjué, 感应 gǎnyìng

vibrant ADJ 1 令人兴奋的 lìngrén xīngfèn de, 充满活力的 chōngmǎn huólì de 2 鲜艳明亮的 [+色彩] xiānyàn míngliàng de [+sècǎi]

vibrate v (使…) 颤动 (shǐ…) chàndòng, (使…) 震动 (shǐ…) zhèndòng

vibration N 1 颤动 chàndòng, 震动 zhèndòng 2 感应 gǎnyìng, 共鸣 gòngmíng
high-frequency vibration 高频振荡 gāopín zhèndàng

vicar N（教区）牧师 (jiàoqū) mùshi

vicarious ADJ 间接感受的 jiànjiē gǎnshòu de, 如同身临其境的 rútóng shēn lín qí jìng de

vice¹ I N 1 犯罪（活动）fànzuì (huódòng), 邪恶（行为）xié'è (xíngwéi)
vice squad 警察打击犯罪小组 jǐngchá dǎjī fànzuì xiǎozǔ
2 劣根性 lièegēnxìng,（本性的）邪恶 (běnxìng de) xié'è

vice² ADJ 副 fù
vice admiral 海军中将 hǎijūn zhōngjiàng
vice president 副总统 fùzǒngtǒng, 副总裁 fùzǒngcái

vice versa ADV 反过来也是这样 fǎnguòlái yě shì zhèyàng, 反之亦然 fǎn zhī yì rán

vicinity N 1 附近 fùjìn
in the vicinity of the school 学校附近 xuéxiào fùjìn
2 左右 zuǒyòu
in the vicinity of 7,000 years 七千年左右 qīqiān nián zuǒyòu

vicious ADJ 恶毒的 èdú de, 凶险的 xiōngxiǎn de
vicious circle 恶性循环 èxìng xúnhuán

victim N 受害人 shòuhài rén ■ *His uncle was a victim of the terrorist attacks on 9/11.* 他的叔父是"九一一"恐怖主义攻击的受害人。Tā de shūfù shì "jiǔ yāo yāo" kǒngbù zhǔyì gōngjī de shòuhàirén.

victimize V 不公正地对待 bù gōngzhèng de duìdài, 迫害 pòhài

victor N 获胜者 huòshèngzhě, 胜利者 shènglìzhě
runaway victor 遥遥领先的获胜者 yáoyáo lǐng xiān de huòshèngzhě

victorious ADJ 获胜的 huòshèng de, 胜利的 shènglì de

victory N 胜利 shènglì, 赢 yíng

video I N 录像 lùxiàng
music video 音乐录像 yīnyuè lùxiàng
II ADJ 电视的 diànshì de, 视频的 shìpín de
video camera 摄像机 shèxiàngjī
video conference 电视会议 diànshì huìyì
video game 电子游戏 diànzǐ yóuxì

videotape I N 录像带 lùxiàngdài II V 把 [+电影] 录在录像带上 bǎ [+diànyǐng] lù zài lùxiàngdài shàng

vie V 竞争 jìngzhēng, 角逐 juézhú

view I N 1 观点 guāndiǎn, 看法 kànfǎ ■ *What are your views on capital punishment?* 你对死刑有什么看法？Nǐ duì sǐxíng yǒu shénme kànfǎ?
2 景色 jǐngsè II V 考虑 kǎolǜ ■ *Let's view the situation objectively.* 让我们客观地考虑形势。Ràng wǒmen kèguān de kǎolǜ xíngshì.
in view of 由于 yóuyú, 考虑到 kǎolǜdào

viewer N 电视观众 diànshì guānzhòng, 电视观看者 diànshì guānkànzhě

viewfinder N（照相机）取景器 (zhàoxiàngjī) qǔjǐngqì

vigil N 1 守夜 shǒuyè, 陪夜 péi yè 2（夜间）静坐抗议 (yè jiān) jìngzuò kàngyì

vigilance N 警惕（心）jǐngtì (xīn), 警戒 jǐngjiè

vigilant ADJ（保持）警惕的 (bǎochí) jǐngtì de

vigilante N（公民）自发维持治安者 (gōngmín) zìfā wéichí zhì'ān zhě,（公民）治安行动者 (gōngmín) zhì'ān xíngdòngzhě

vigor N 活力 huólì, 精力 jīnglì

vigorous ADJ 充满精力的 chōngmǎn jīnglì de, 精力充沛的 jīnglì chōngpèi de

vile ADJ 令人讨厌的 lìngrén tǎoyàn de, 坏透了的 huàitòule de

vilify V 污蔑 wūmiè, 中伤 zhòngshāng

villa N（乡间）别墅 (xiāngjiān) biéshù [M. WD 幢 zhuàng]

village N 村 cūn, 村庄 cūnzhuāng ■ *Most families in the village are related by blood.* 村里大多数人家都有血缘关系。Cūnlǐ dàduōshù rénjiā dōu yǒu xuèyuán guānxi.

villager N 村民 cūnmín

villain N 1 坏人 huàirén, 罪犯 zuìfàn 2（电影/小说中的）反面人物 (diànyǐng/xiǎoshuō zhōngde) fǎnmiànrénwù, 反派角色 fǎnpài juésè

villainy N 罪行 zuìxíng, 堕落 duòluò

vindicate V 为…辩白 wéi...biànbái, 证明…清白 zhèngmíng...qīngbái

vindictive ADJ 有报复心的 yǒu bàofu xīn de, 怀恨在心的 huáihèn zài xīn de

vine N 1 藤本植物 téngběn zhíwù 2 葡萄（藤）pútáo (téng) [M. WD 棵 kē]

vinegar N 醋 cù

vineyard N 葡萄园 pútaoyuán

vintage I ADJ 1 优质的 [+酒] yōuzhì de [+jiǔ]
vintage wine 特定年代出产的佳酿酒 tèdìng niándài chūchǎn de jiāniàngjiǔ
2 老式的 [+汽车] lǎoshì de [+qìchē], 珍藏的 zhēncáng de
vintage car 古董车 gǔdǒngchē, 珍藏老式车 zhēncáng lǎoshìchē
II N 酒的酿造年份 jiǔ de niàngzào niánfèn

vinyl N 乙烯基 yǐxījī
vinyl flooring 乙烯基铺地材料 yǐxījī pūdì cáiliào

viola N 中提琴 zhōngtíqín [M. WD 把 bǎ]

violate V 1 违反 wéifǎn, 违背 wéibèi 2 强奸 [+妇女] qiángjiān [+fùnǚ]

violation N 1 违反 wéifǎn, 违背 wéibèi 2 侵犯 qīnfàn, 侵害 qīnhài

violator N 违反者 wéifǎnzhě, 违规者 wéiguīzhě

violence N 1 暴力（行为）bàolì (xíngwéi) ■ *This movie contains too much violence and should be restricted to viewers over 18.* 这部电影暴力镜头太多，应该限制在十八岁以上的人才能看。Zhè bù diànyǐng bōli jìngtóu tài duō, yīnggāi xiànzhì zài shíbā suì yǐshàng de rén cái néng kàn.

domestic violence 家庭暴力 (行为) jiātíng bàolì (xíngwéi)

2 强大的破坏力量 qiángdà de pòhuàilì liáng

violent ADJ **1** 暴力的 bàolì de **2** 强烈的 qiángliè de ■ *The fishing boat capsized in a violent storm.* 渔船在一次强烈的风暴中倾覆。Yúchuán zài yí cì qiángliè de fēngbào zhōng qīngfù.

a violent earthquake 强地震 qiáng dìzhèn

violet N **1** 紫罗兰 zǐluólán **2** 紫罗兰色 zǐluólánsè

violin N 小提琴 xiǎotíqín [M. wD 把 bǎ]

violinist N 小提琴手 xiǎotíqínshǒu

VIP (= very important person) ABBREV 大人物 dàrénwù, 贵宾 guìbīn [M. wD 位 wèi]

viper N 小毒蛇 xiǎo dúshé [M. wD 条 tiáo]

viral ADJ 病毒 (性) 的 bìngdú (xìng) de, 病毒引起的 bìngdú yǐnqǐ de

virgin N **1** 处女 chǔnǚ, 贞女 zhēnnǚ **2** 未开发的 wèi kāifā de

virgin land 未开发的处女地 wèi kāifā de chǔnǚdì

virginity N 处女状态 chǔnǚ zhuàngtài, 童真 tóngzhēn

Virgin Mary N 贞女玛丽亚 zhēnnǚ Mǎlìyà

Virgo N 处女宫 (座) Chùnǚgōng (zuò)

virile ADJ 充满阳刚气的 chōngmǎn yánggāngqì de, 有男子气概的 yǒu nánzǐ qìgài de

virtual ADJ **1** 爱交际的 ài jiāojì de, 事实上的 shìshíshang de **2** (电脑中) 虚拟的 (diànnǎo zhōng) xūnǐ de, 非真实世界的 fēi zhēnshí shìjiè de

virtual reality 虚拟现实 xūnǐ xiànshí

virtually ADV **1** 实质上 shízhìshàng, 实际上 shíjìshàng **2** 几乎 jīhū, 差不多 chàbuduō **3** 虚拟地 xūnǐ de

virtue N **1** 美德 měidé **2** 优点 yōudiǎn, 优越性 yōuyuèxìng

by virtue of sth 凭借 píngjiè, 由于 yóuyú

to make a virtue of necessity 很愿意地做不得不做的事 hěn yuànyì de zuò bùdebù zuò de shì

virtuoso N (音乐) 名家 (yīnyuè) míngjiā, 高手 gāoshǒu

a virtuoso performance 名家表演 míngjiā biǎoyǎn

virtuous ADJ (品德) 高尚的 (pǐndé) gāoshàng de, 善良的 shànliáng de

virulent ADJ **1** 剧毒的 jùdú de, 迅速致死的 xùnsù zhìsǐ de **2** 刻毒的 kèdú de, 恶毒的 èdú de

virus N 病毒 bìngdú

visa N 签证 qiānzhèng

entry visa 入境签证 rùjìng qiānzhèng

exit visa 离境签证 líjìng qiānzhèng

student's visa 学生签证 xuésheng qiānzhèng

transit visa 过境签证 guòjìng qiānzhèng

tourist visa 旅游签证 lǚyóu qiānzhèng

work visa 工作签证 gōngzuò qiānzhèng

visage N 脸 liǎn, 面容 miànróng

vis-à-vis PREP 与…相比 yǔ…xiāngbǐ

vise N 老虎钳 lǎohǔqián [M. wD 把 bǎ]

visibility N 能见度 néngjiàndù, 视程 shìchéng

visible ADJ 能看得见的 néng kàndejiàn de, 可见的 kějiànde

vision N **1** 视力 shìlì ■ *Children with poor vision are seated in the front rows.* 视力不好的孩子坐在前排。Shìlì bù hǎo de háizi zuò zài qiánpái. **2** 幻想 huànxiǎng **3** 远见 yuǎnjiàn ■ *Now our country desperately needs a statesman of great vision, but where is he?* 我们的国家现在需要有远见的政治家，可是他在哪里呢？Wǒmen de guójiā xiànzài xūyào yǒu yuǎnjiàn de zhèngzhìjiā, kěshì tā zài nǎlǐ ne?

visionary ADJ 有远见的 yǒu yuǎnjiàn de, 有眼光的 yǒu yǎnguāng de

visit I v **1** 看望 kànwàng **2** 参观 cānguān, 访问 fǎngwèn II N **1** 看望 kànwàng, 拜访 bàifǎng **2** 访问 fǎngwèn, 参观 cānguān ■ *They're preparing for a visit to China.* 他们在准备访问中国。Tāmen zài zhǔnbèi fǎngwèn Zhōngguó.

visitation N **1** 访问 fǎngwèn **2** 探视 (权) tànshì (quán)

visitor N **1** 访问者 fǎngwènzhě, 访客 fǎngkè **2** 参观者 cānguānzhě ■ *Visitors to this art gallery are advised that photography is not allowed.* 这座艺术馆的参观者被告知：不准摄影。Zhè zuò yìshùguǎn de cānguānzhě bèi gàozhī: bù zhǔn shèyǐng.

visor N **1** 帽舌 màoshé **2** (汽车的) 遮阳板 (qìchē de) zhēyángbǎn

vista N 远景 yuǎnjǐng, 展望 zhǎnwàng

visual ADJ 视觉的 shìjué de, 视力的 shìlì de

visual aid 直观教具 zhíguān jiàojù

visual arts 视觉艺术 shìjué yìshù

visualize v 想象 xiǎngxiàng, 设想 shèxiǎng

vital ADJ **1** 至关重要的 zhìguān zhòngyào de **2** 生命的 shēngmìng de

vital signs 生命特征 shēngmìng tèzhēng

vital statistics 人口动态统计 rénkǒu dòngtài tǒngjì

vitality N 活力 huólì, 生命力 shēngmìnglì

vitally ADV 极大地 jídà de

vitamin N 维生素 wéishēngsù, 维他命 wéitāmìng

viticulture N 葡萄栽培术 pútao zāipéi shù, 葡萄园管理 pútaoyuán guǎnlǐ

vitriol N 刻毒的话 kèdú dehuà, 尖刻的讽刺 jiānkè de fěngcì

vitriolic ADJ 刻毒的 kèdú de, 尖刻的 jiānkè de

vivacious ADJ 活泼的 huópo de, 快活的 kuàihuo de

vivid ADJ **1** 生动的 [+描写] shēngdòng de [+miáoxiě], 逼真的 bīzhēn de **2** 鲜艳明亮的 [+色彩] xiānyàn míngliàng de [+sècǎi] vivid imagination 丰富的想象力 fēngfù de xiǎngxiànglì

vivisection N 动物活体解剖 dòngwù huótǐ jiěpōu

VJ (= video jockey) ABBREV 电视音乐节目主持人 diànshì yīnyuè jiémù zhǔchírén

V-neck N 鸡心领 jīxīnlǐng
V-neck sweater 鸡心领羊毛衫 jīxīnlǐng yángmáoshān

VOA (= Voice of America) ABBREV 美国之音 Měiguó zhī yīn

vocabulary N 1 词汇 cíhuì 2 专业词汇 zhuānyè cíhuì, 术语 shùyǔ
business vocabulary 商业词汇 shāngyè cíhuì

vocal I ADJ 1 嗓音的 sǎngyīn de
vocal cords 声带 shēngdài
vocal music 声乐 shēngyuè
2 直言不讳的 zhíyán búhuì de
a vocal critic 直言不讳的批评者 zhíyán búhuì de pīpíngzhě
II N 歌唱 gēchàng, 歌咏 gēyǒng

vocalist N 歌手 gēshǒu, 演唱者 yǎnchàngzhě

vocation N 1 职业 zhíyè, 工作 gōngzuò
sense of vocation 敬业精神 jìngyè jīngshén
2 神召 shén zhào, (宗教) 使命感 (zōngjiào) shǐmìnggǎn

vocational ADJ 职业训练的 zhíyè xùnliàn de
vocational school 职业学校 zhíyè xuéxiào

vociferous ADJ 大声的 dàshēng de, 强烈表达的 qiángliè biǎodá de

vogue N 时尚 shíshàng, 风行 fēngxíng
a vogue word 流行语 liúxíngyǔ

voice I N 1 说话声 shuōhuàshēng, 声音 shēngyīn 2 嗓子 sǎngzi, 嗓音 sǎngyīn ■ *Opal has a good singing voice.* 奥帕尔唱歌的嗓音很好听。Àopà'ěr chànggē de sǎngyīn hěn hǎotīng.
to raise one's voice 提高嗓音 tígāo sǎngyīn
voice mail 语音信箱 yǔyīn xìnxiāng
3 发言权 fāyánquán
to give voice to sth 对某事发表意见 duì mǒushì fābiǎo yìjiàn

Voice of America N See VOA

void I ADJ 无效的 wúxiào de
null and void (法律上) 无效的 (fǎlǜshàng) wúxiào de
be void of 毫无 háowú
II N 空虚感 kōngxūgǎn, 空白 kòngbái
to fill the void 填补空虚感 tiánbǔ kōngxūgǎn
III v 使 [+协议] 无效 shǐ [+xiéyì] wúxiào, 使…作废 shǐ...zuòfèi

volatile ADJ 不确定的 bú quèdìng de, 动荡不定的 dòngdàng búdìng de

volcano N 火山 huǒshān [M. WD 座 zuò]
active/dormant volcano 活 / 死火山 huó/sǐ huǒshān

volition N 意志 (力) yìzhì (lì)

of one's own volition 自愿地 zìyuàn de

volley N 1 [炮弹 / 子弹+] 齐射 [pàodàn/zǐdàn+] qíshè 2 一连串 [+质问 / 批评] yìliánchuàn (zhìwèn/pīpíng) 3 (球类比赛中的) 拦击 (qiúlèi bǐsài zhòng de) lánjī, 截踢 jiétī

volleyball N 排球 (运动) páiqiú (yùndòng)

volt N 伏特 fútè

voltage N 电压 diànyā

voluble ADJ 健谈的 jiàntán de, 滔滔不绝的 tāotāo bù jué de

volume N 1 音量 yīnliàng 2 容量 róngliàng 3 (书籍) 册 (shūjí) cè ■ *Volume 3 of the encyclopedia is missing.* 这套百科全书的第三册不见了。Zhè tào bǎikē quánshū de dìsān cè bú jiàn le.

voluminous ADJ 1 篇幅很长的 piānfu hěn cháng de 2 容量大的 róngliàng dà de

voluntary ADJ 自愿的 zìyuàn de, 志愿的 zhìyuàn de

volunteer I N 志愿人员 zhìyuàn rényuán, 义工 yìgōng
Red Cross volunteer 红十字会义工 Hóngshízìhuì yìgōng
II v 自愿 zìyuàn, 自告奋勇 zìgào fènyǒng

voluptuous ADJ 丰满的 fēngmǎn de, 丰乳肥臀的 fēng rǔ féi tún de

vomit I v 呕吐 ǒutù, 吐出 tùchū II N 呕吐物 ǒutùwù

voodoo N 伏都教 fúdūjiào
voodoo doll 巫毒娃娃 wūdú wáwa

voracious ADJ 1 食量很大的 shíliàng hěn dà de, 贪吃的 tānchī de 2 求知欲旺盛的 qiúzhīyù wàngshèng de

vortex N 漩涡 xuánwō, 旋风 xuànfēng

vote I N 表决 biǎojué, 投票 tóupiào
the vote 得票总数 dépiào zǒngshù
vote of confidence 信任投票 xìnrèn tóupiào
vote of no confidence 不信任投票 bú xìnrèn tóupiào
II v 1 投票 tóupiào ■ *Many of my friends will be eligible to vote for the first time this year.* 我很多朋友将在今年第一次有资格投票。Wǒ hěn duō péngyou jiāng zài jīnnián dìyī cì yǒu zīgé tóupiào.
voting booth 投票站 tóupiàozhàn
2 评选 píngxuǎn
be voted the best program 被评选为最佳节目 bèi píngxuǎn wéi zuìjiā jiémù
to vote with one's feet 退席表示反对 tuìxí biǎoshì fǎnduì

voter N 选民 xuǎnmín, 投票人 tóupiàorén

vouch v (to vouch for) 为…担保 wéi...dānbǎo, 保证 bǎozhèng

voucher N 1 代金券 dàijīnquàn, 凭证 píngzhèng
gift voucher 礼券 lǐquàn
2 收据 shōujù, 收条 shōutiáo

vow I N 誓言 shìyán

marriage vows 结婚誓言 jiéhūn shìyán, 婚誓 hūnshì

II v 发誓 fāshì, 起誓 qǐshì

vowel N 元音 yuányīn

voyage I N 航行 hángxíng

Bon Voyage! 旅途愉快! Lǚtú yúkuài!

II v 航海 hánghǎi, 航行 hángxíng

voyeur N **1** 窥淫狂 kuīyínkuáng **2** 特别喜欢窥视他人隐私的人 tèbié xǐhuan kuīshì tārén yǐnsī de rén

vs ABBREV See versus

vulcanology N 火山学 huǒshānxué

vulgar ADJ 低俗的 dīsú de, 粗俗的 cūsú de

vulnerable ADJ **1** 脆弱的 cuìruò de, 敏感的 mǐngǎn de **2** 易受攻击的 yìshòu gōngjī de

be vulnerable to terrorist attacks 很容易受到恐怖活动攻击的 hěn róngyì shòudào kǒngbù huódòng gōngjī de

vulture N 秃鹫 tūjiù [M. WD 只 zhī]

W

wacko N 怪人 guàirén, 疯子 fēngzi

wacky ADJ 疯疯癫癫的 fēngfeng diāndiān de, 古怪的 gǔguài de

wad N 一叠 yì dié

a wad of money 一叠钱 yì dié qián

waddle v（像鸭子一样）摇摇摆摆地走 (xiàng yāzi yíyàng) yáoyáo bǎibǎi de zǒu

wade v 涉（水）shè (shuǐ), 蹚（水）tāng (shuǐ)

wafer N **1** 华夫饼干 huáfū bǐnggān [M. WD 块 kuài], 威化饼干 wēihuà bǐnggān [M. WD 块 kuài] **2**（宗教）圣饼 (zōngjiào) shèngbǐng [M. WD 块 kuài]

waffle N 蛋奶烘饼 dànnǎi hōngbǐng

waft v [气味／音乐声+] 飘荡 [qìwèi/yīnyuè shēng] piāodàng

wag v **1** [狗+] 摇尾巴 [gǒu+] yáo wěibā **2** [人+] 摇手指 [rén+] yáo shǒuzhǐ

wage[1] N 工资 gōngzī ■ Hourly wages are higher in New York than in Alabama, I believe. 我相信，纽约的每小时工资比阿拉巴马的高。Wǒ xiāngxìn, Niǔyuē de měi xiǎoshí gōngzī bǐ Ālābāmǎ de gāo.

wage earner 挣钱的人 zhèngqián de rén

wage freeze 工资冻结 gōngzī dòngjié

minimum wage（法定）最低工资 (fǎdìng) zuì dī gōngzī

wage[2] v 发动 fādòng

wager I v 打赌 dǎ dǔ, 下赌注 xià dǔzhù **II** N 打赌 dǎ dǔ, 赌注 dǔzhù

wagon N **1** 客货两用车 kèhuò liǎngyòngchē [M. WD 辆 liàng] **2**（老式）马拉货车 (lǎoshì)

mǎlā huòchē [M. WD 辆 liàng]

wail I v **1** [人+] 大声哭叫 [rén+] dàshēng kūjiào, 嚎啕大哭 háotáo dàkū **2** [警报器+] 呼啸 [jǐngbàoqì+] hūxiào **II** N **1** 大哭声 dàkūshēng **2** 呼啸声 hūxiàoshēng

waist N 腰 yāo

waistline 腰围 yāowéi

wait I v **1** 等 děng, 等候 děnghou

to wait up 不睡觉等候 bú shuìjiào děnghou ■ I'll be very late tonight, don't bother waiting up for me. 我今天很晚才回家，不必不睡觉等我。Wǒ jīntiān hěn wǎn cái huí jiā, bú bì bú shuìjiào děng wǒ.

2 (to wait on) 服侍 fúshi, 伺候 cìhou **II** N 等候 děnghòu

waiter N [饭店+] 服务员 [fàndiàn+] fúwùyuán

waiting list N [医院+] 等候者名单 [yīyuàn+] děnghòuzhě míngdān

waiting room N 候诊室 hòuzhěnshì, 候车室 hòuchēshì

waitress N（饭店）女服务员 (fàndiàn) nǚ fúwùyuán

waive v 放弃 [+权利] fàngqì [+quánlì], 取消 [+规定] qǔxiāo [+guīdìng]

waiver N 弃权声明书 qìquán shēngmíng shū

wake[1] **I** v (PT woke; PP woken) **1** 醒 xǐng **2** 叫醒 jiàoxǐng ■ His wife woke him up since he was having nightmares. 他在做恶梦，妻子叫醒了他。Tā zài zuò èmèng, qīzi jiàoxǐngle tā. **II** N 守灵 shǒulíng

wake[2] N **1** 船的尾波 chuán de wěi bō, 航迹 hángjì **2** (in the wake of) 紧接着 jǐnjiēzhe, 在…以后 zài...yǐhòu

wakeful ADJ 不能入眠的 bùnéng rùmián de, 醒着的 xǐngzhe de

waken v **1** 醒（来）xǐng (lái) **2** 叫醒 jiàoxǐng, 唤醒 huànxǐng

to waken at the baby's cry 听到婴儿哭而醒来 tīngdào yīng'ér kū ér xǐnglái

wake-up call N **1** 叫醒电话 jiàoxǐng diànhuà **2** 警钟 jǐngzhōng, 警示 jǐngshì

waking ADJ 醒着的 xǐngzhe de

waking hours 醒着的时间 xǐngzhe de shíjiān

walk I v 走 zǒu, 步行 bùxíng ■ Little Timmy learned to walk when he was 10 months old. 小提米十个月的时候学走路。Xiǎo Tímǐ shí ge yuè de shíhou xué zǒulù.

to walk the dog 溜狗 liūgǒu

to walk away 不负责任地离开 bú fù zérèn de líkāi

II N **1** 走 zǒu, 行走 xíngzǒu **2** 步行路径 bùxíng lùjìng ■ This national park has some beautiful walks. 这座国家公园有几条很美的步行路径。Zhè zuò guójiā gōngyuán yǒu jǐ tiáo hěn měi de bùxíng lùjìng.

to go for/take a walk 散步 sànbù

walkie-talkie N 步话机 bùhuàjī, 无线电对讲机 wúxiàndiàn duìjiǎngjī

walk-in ADJ (a walk-in wardrobe/closet) 步入式衣柜／壁柜 bùrù shì yīguì/bìguì

walking papers N 辞退书 cítuìshū [M. WD 份 fèn], 解雇通知单 jiěgù tōngzhīdān [M. WD 份 fèn/张 zhāng]

walking stick N 拐杖 guǎizhàng [M. WD 根 gēn], 手杖 shǒuzhàng [M. WD 根 gēn]

walk-on N 未获体育奖学金的大学体育队队员 wèi huò tǐyù jiǎngxuéjīn de dàxué tǐyù duì duìyuán

walk-on part 跑龙套的角色 pǎo lóngtào de juésè

walkover N 轻而易举的胜利 qīng ér yìjǔ de shènglì

walk-up N 无电梯的大楼 wú diàntī de dàlóu

walkway N 人行通道 rénxíng tōngdào, 有遮走道 yǒu zhē zǒudào

wall I N 墙 qiáng ■ *Talking to him is like talking to a wall—you won't get anywhere.* 对他讲话就像对墙讲话一样—根本没用。Duì tā jiǎnghuà jiù xiàng duì qiáng jiǎnghuà yíyàng—gēnběn méiyòng.

the Great Wall (of China)（中国）长城 (Zhōngguó) Chángchéng

II v 1 (to wall … in) 用墙围起来 yòng qiáng wéi qǐlái 2 (to wall … up) 用砖堵上 yòng zhuān dǔ shàng

wallaby N 澳洲沙袋鼠 Àozhōu shādàishǔ

wallet N 皮夹 píjiā, 钱包 qiánbāo

a fat wallet（钱装得）鼓鼓的皮夹 (qián zhuāng dé) gǔgǔ de píjiā

wallow v 1 [动物+] 快乐地打滚 [dòngwù+] kuàilè de dǎgǔn 2 (to wallow in self-pity) 沉溺于自怜 chénnì yú zìlián

wallpaper I N 墙纸 qiángzhǐ, 壁纸 bìzhǐ II v 给 [+房间] 贴墙纸 gěi [+fángjiān] tiē qiángzhǐ

Wall Street N 1（纽约）华尔街 (Niǔyuē) Huá'ěrjiē 2 美国金融界 Měiguó jīnróngjiè

walnut N 核桃 hétao [M. WD 颗 kē], 胡桃 hútáo [M. WD 颗 kē]

walrus N 海象 hǎixiàng [M. WD 头 tóu]

waltz I N 华尔兹舞（曲）huá'ěrzīwǔ (qū), 圆舞（曲）yuánwǔ (qū) II v 跳华尔兹舞 tiào huá'ěrzīwǔ

wan ADJ 苍白的 [+脸色] cāngbái de [+liǎnsè], 憔悴的 qiáocuì de

wand N 魔杖 mózhàng [M. WD 根 gēn]

wander v 1 游荡 yóudàng, 漫游 mànyóu ■ *When Jack plays hooky, he just wanders around shopping malls and streets.* 杰克逃学的时候，就在商场和大街上游荡。Jiékè táoxué de shíhou, jiù zài shāngchǎng hé dàjiēshang yóudàng.

to wander off 走开 zǒukāi, 走散 zǒusàn

2 偏离话题 piānlí huàtí, 离题 lítí 3 思想不集中 sīxiǎng bù jízhōng, 走神 zǒushén

wanderings N（走走停停的）漫游 (zǒuzou tíngtíng de) mànyóu

wanderlust N 旅游癖 lǚyóupǐ, 游山玩水的强烈欲望 yóushān wánshuǐ de qiángliè yùwàng

wane I v 1 衰败 shuāibài, 没落 mòluò 2 [月亮+] 缺／亏 [yuèliang+] quē/kuī II N 衰败 shuāibài, 没落 mòluò

on the wane 正在衰落 zhèngzài shuāiluò

wangle v 哄骗 hǒngpiàn

to wangle sth out of sb 从某人那里用巧计得到某物 cóng mǒurén nàli yòng qiǎojì dédào mǒuwù

to wangle one's way out of 设法脱身 shèfǎ tuōshēn

want I v 1 要 yào, 想 xiǎng, 想要 xiǎngyào 2 缺乏 quēfá II N 需要但缺乏的事物 xūyào dàn quēfá de shìwù

for want of sth 由于缺乏某事物 yóuyú quēfá mǒushìwù

for want of anything better 只因为没有更好的 zhǐ yīnwéi méiyǒu gèng hǎo de

for want of a better word 因为没有更好的词语 yīnwèi méiyǒu gèng hǎo de cíyǔ

want ad N（报纸上）分类广告 (bàozhǐ shàng) fēnlèi guǎnggào

wanted ADJ 被警方追捕的 bèi jǐngfāng zhuībǔ de ■ *You're wanted on the phone.* 有人找你打电话。Yǒu rén zhǎo nǐ de diànhuà.

wanting ADJ 不够好的 bùgòu hǎode, 有待改进的 yǒudài gǎijìn de

wanton ADJ 肆意的 sìyì de, 胡乱的 húluàn de

a wanton killing 滥杀 lànshā

war N 1 战争 zhànzhēng 2 斗争 dòuzhēng, 竞争 jìngzhēng

war bride 战时新娘 zhànshí xīnniáng

war crime 战争罪行 zhànzhēng zuìxíng

war criminal 战犯 zhànfàn

war zone 战区 zhànqū

to declare war on 向…宣战 xiàng…xuānzhàn

to wage war on 与…作战 yǔ…zuòzhàn

warble v [鸟+] 啭鸣 zhuànmíng, 象鸟一样歌唱 xiàng niǎo yíyàng gēchàng

ward I N 1 病房 bìngfáng

maternity/surgical ward（妇）产科／外科病房 (fù) chǎnkē/wàikēbìngfáng

2 被监护人 bèi jiānhùrén 3（城市中的）选区 (chéngshì zhòngde) xuǎnqū II v (to ward off) 防止 fángzhǐ

warden N 1 监护人 jiānhùrén, 管理员 guǎnlǐyuán

warden of an old people's home 养老院管理员 yǎnglǎoyuàn guǎnlǐyuán

2 监督人员 jiāndū rényuán

traffic warden 交通执勤人员 jiāotōng zhíqín rényuán
3 监狱长 jiānyùzhǎng
wardrobe N **1** 大衣柜 dàyīguì, 衣橱 yīchú **2**（个人所有的）衣服 (gèrén suǒyǒu de) yīfu ■ *Her extensive wardrobe is the envy of her friends.* 她衣物极多，是朋友们羡慕的事。Tā yīwù jí duō, shì péngyoumen xiànmù de shì. **3**（剧团）戏装管理部 (jùtuán) xìzhuāng guǎnlǐ bù
warehouse N 货栈 huòzhàn, 仓库 cāngkù
wares N（不在商店出售的）货物 (búzài shāngdiàn chūshòu de) huòwù, 商品 shāngpǐn
warfare N 战争 zhànzhēng
　conventional warfare 常规战争 chángguī zhànzhēng
　guerrila warfare 游击战 yóujīzhàn
　nuclear warfare 核战争 hézhànzhēng
warhead N（导弹）弹头 (dǎodàn) dàntóu
warlike ADJ 好战的 hàozhàn de, 善战的 shànzhàn de
warm I ADJ **1** 温暖的 wēnnuǎn de ■ *Everyone seems to enjoy the warm weather of May.* 几乎人人都喜欢五月的温暖天气。Jīhū rénrén dōu xǐhuan wǔyuè de wēnnuǎn tiānqì. **2** 热情友好的 rèqíng yǒuhǎo de ■ *The flight attendant greeted me with a warm smile as I entered the airplane.* 我走进机舱时，空中小姐向我热情友好地微笑。Wǒ zǒujìn jīcāng shí, kōngzhōng xiǎojiě xiàng wǒ rèqíng yǒuhǎo de wēixiào. II V 使…温暖 shǐ…wēnnuǎn, 使…暖和 shǐ…nuǎnhuo
　to warm up to sb 对某人产生好感 duì mǒurén chǎnshēng hǎogǎn, 喜欢上某人 xǐhuan shàng mǒurén
warm-blooded ADJ 温血的 [+动物] wēnxuè de [+dòngwù], 恒温的 héngwēn de
warm-hearted ADJ 热心（肠）的 rèxīn (cháng) de, 热情的 rèqíng de
warmonger N 战争贩子 zhànzhēng fànzi
warmth N **1** 温暖 wēnnuǎn, 暖和 nuǎnhuo **2** 热情友好 rèqíng yǒuhǎo
warn V 警告 jǐnggào, 提醒 tíxǐng ■ *Tourists are warned not to walk alone in the city center after nightfall.* 旅游者被警告，天黑以后不要在市中心单独行走。Lǚyóuzhě bèi jǐnggào, tiānhēi yǐhòu bú yào zài shìzhōngxīn dāndú xíngzǒu.
　To be warned is to be prepared. 受到警告，就是让你做好准备。Shòudao jǐnggào, jiùshì ràng nǐ zuòhǎo zhǔnbèi.
warning N 警告 jǐnggào, 提醒 tíxǐng ■ *I got a warning message on my computer but couldn't figure out what I was doing wrong.* 我在计算机上得到一个"警告"，但想不出我错在哪里。Wǒ zài jìsuànjīshang dédao yí ge "jǐnggào", dàn xiǎngbuchū wǒ cuò zài nǎlǐ.
warp I N 弯曲 wānqū, 变形 biànxíng II V **1**（使…）

变形 (shǐ…) biànxíng **2**（使…）反常 (shǐ…) fǎncháng, 扭曲 niǔqū
warrant I N **1** 令 lìng, 证 zhèng
　arrest warrant 逮捕证 dàibǔzhèng
　death warrant 死刑令 sǐxíng lìng
　search warrant 搜查证 sōucházhèng
2 充分理由 chōngfèn lǐyóu II V 提供充分理由 tígōng chōngfèn lǐyóu, 成为…的理由 chéngwéi…de lǐyóu
warranty N 保修单 bǎoxiūdān, 产品质量保证书 chǎnpǐn zhìliàng bǎozhèngshū
warren N 野兔窝 yětùwō
warrior N 战士 zhànshì, 斗士 dòushì
warship N 军舰 jūnjiàn [M. WD 艘 sōu], 战舰 zhànjiàn [M. WD 艘 sōu]
wartime N 战争时期 zhànzhēng shíqī, 战时 zhànshí
wary ADJ 小心翼翼的 xiǎoxīn yìyì de, 戒备的 jièbèi de
was See **be**
wash I V **1** 洗 xǐ ■ *Wash your hands before eating.* 吃东西前要洗手。Chī dōngxi qián yào xǐ shǒu.
　to wash one's hands of 与…脱离关系 yǔ…tuōlí guānxi, 不再参与 búzài cānyù
2 站得住脚 zhàn dé zhù jiǎo ■ *His explanation won't wash (with me).* 他的解释（在我看来）站不住脚。Tā de jiěshì (zài wǒ kàn lái) zhànbuzhùjiǎo. II N **1** 洗 xǐ, 洗涤 xǐdí **2** 正在洗的衣服 zhèngzài xǐ de yīfu
　to do the wash 洗衣服 xǐyī fú
3 洗涤剂 xǐdíjì
　face wash 洗面乳 xǐmiànrǔ
　mouth wash 漱口（药）水 shùkǒu (yào) shuǐ
washable ADJ 可洗的 kě xǐ de, 耐洗的 nàixǐ de
washcloth N（洗脸）毛巾 (xǐliǎn) máojīn [M. WD 块 kuài]
washed-out ADJ 褪色的 tuìsè de, 变白的 biànbái de
washed up ADJ 没有前途的 méiyǒu qiántú de, 彻底失败的 chèdǐ shībài de
washer, washing machine N 洗衣机 xǐyījī
washing N 洗好的衣服 xǐ hǎode yīfu
　to hang the washing out to dry 把洗好的衣服挂出去晒干 bǎ xǐhǎo de yīfu guàchūqu shàigān
washroom N 洗手间 xǐshǒujiān, 厕所 cèsuǒ
wasp N 黄蜂 huángfēng
wastage N 耗费（量）hào fèi (liáng), 浪费 làngfèi
waste I V 浪费 làngfèi
　Waste not, want not. 不浪费，就不会缺乏。Bú làngfèi, jiù bú huì quēfá.
II N **1** 浪费 làngfèi **2** 废料 fèiliào, 垃圾 lājī ■ *The local government has strict regulations on the disposal of hazardous waste.* 地方政府对清除有害废料有严格的规章。Dìfāng zhèngfǔ duì qīngchú yǒuhài fèiliào yǒu yángé de guīzhāng.
　waste water 废水 fèishuǐ

3 荒地 huāngdì, 不毛之地 bùmáo zhī dì
III ADJ 废弃的 fèiqì de, 废物的 fèiwù de
waste tank 大垃圾箱 dà lājīxiāng

wasteful ADJ 浪费的 làngfèi de, 糟蹋的 zāota de

waste(paper) basket N 废纸篓 fèizhǐlǒu

watch I V **1** 看 kàn, 注视 zhùshì **2** 观看 guānkàn
3 注意 zhùyì ■ *Watch your tongue!* 你说话注意点! Nǐ shuōhuà zhùyì diǎnr! **II** N **1** 表 biǎo, 手表 shǒubiǎo
to watch out 留意 liúyì, 小心 xiǎoxīn ■ *Watch out! There's a car coming!* 小心! 有汽车! Xiǎoxīn! Yǒu qìchē!
2 关注 guānzhù, 注意 zhùyì
to keep a close watch on sb/sth 密切注意某人／某事 mìqiè zhùyì mǒurén/mǒushì
3 留意 liúyì
be on the watch for sth 留意某事 liúyì mǒushì

watchdog N **1** 监督者 jiāndūzhě **2** 看门狗 kānméngǒu

watchful ADJ 提防的 dīfang de, 警戒的 jǐngjiè de

watchmaker N 钟表匠 zhōngbiǎojiàng

watchman N 守卫 shǒuwèi, 守门人 shǒuménrén

watchword N 口号 kǒuhào, 标语 biāoyǔ

water I N 水 shuǐ ■ *You should drink a lot of water in hot weather.* 你在热天应该多喝水。Nǐ zài rètiān yīnggāi duō hē shuǐ.
water bottle 水瓶 shuǐpíng, 水壶 shuǐhú
water main 总水管道 zǒng shuǐguǎn dào
water polo 水球 (运动) shuǐqiú (yùndòng)
water shed 分水岭 fēnshuǐlǐng
water sports 水上运动 shuǐshàng yùndòng
drinking water 饮用水 yǐnyòngshuǐ
fresh water 淡水 dànshuǐ
running water 自来水 zìláishuǐ
II V **1** 浇水 jiāoshuǐ ■ *These flowers need watering.* 这些花需要浇水了。Zhèxiē huā xūyào jiāoshuǐ le. **2** 流口水 liú kǒushuǐ ■ *The sight of the dishes made my mouth water.* 看到这些菜肴我不禁流口水了。Kàndào zhè xiē càiyáo wǒ bùjīn liú kǒushuǐ le. **3** [眼睛+] 流泪 [yǎnjing+] liú lèi **4** 给 [动物+] 饮水 gěi [dòngwù+] yǐn shuǐ

watercolor N **1** 水彩画 shuǐcǎihuà [M. WD 幅 fú]
2 水彩颜料 shuǐcǎi yánliào

waterfall N 瀑布 pùbù

waterfront N 河／湖／海滨 hé/hú/hǎibīn

waterhole N **1** (动物饮水的) 水坑 (dòngwù yǐn shuǐ de) shuǐkēng **2** (常去的) 酒吧 (cháng qù de) jiǔbā

watering can N 洒水壶 sǎshuǐhú

watermark N **1** (纸上的) 水印 (zhǐ shàng de) shuǐyìn **2** 水位标志 shuǐwèi biāozhì

watermelon N 西瓜 xīguā

waters N 水域 shuǐyù, 领海 lǐnghǎi

watertight ADJ **1** 不透水的 bútòushuǐ de
a watertight compartment 水密舱 shuǐmìcāng

2 周密的 zhōumì de, 毫无破绽的 háowú pòzhàn de
a watertight argument 无懈可击的论点 wúxiè kějī de lùndiǎn

waterway N 水路 shuǐlù [M. WD 条 tiáo], 航道 hángdào [M. WD 条 tiáo]

waterworks N 供水系统 gōngshuǐ xìtǒng
to turn on the waterworks (为了别人的同情) 哭起来 (wèile biéren de tóngqíng) kūqǐlái

watery ADJ 含水过多的 hánshuǐ guòduō de, 味淡的 wèidàn de

watt N 瓦(特) wǎ (tè)

wave I V **1** 挥手 huī shǒu, 招手 zhāo shǒu
to wave goodbye to 向⋯告别 xiàng...gàobié
to wave ... down 挥手示意⋯停车 huī shǒu shìyì...tíngchē
to wave ... off 挥手示意要⋯走开 huī shǒu shìyì yào...zǒukāi
2 挥动 huīdòng **II** N **1** 浪 làng, 波浪 bōlàng **2** 光波 guāngbō, 声波 shēngbō, 无线电波 wúxiàn diànbō
long/medium/short waves (无线电) 长／中／短波 (wúxiàndiàn) cháng/zhōng/duǎnbō
3 高潮 gāocháo, 骤增 zhòuzēng
crime wave 犯罪高峰 fànzuì gāofēng, 犯罪浪潮 fànzuì làngcháo
4 攻击波 gōngjībō
waves of soldiers 一波一波的士兵 yì bō yì bō de shìbīng

waveband N (无线电) 波段 (wúxiàndiàn) bōduàn

wavelength N (无线电) 波长 (wúxiàndiàn) bōcháng

waver V **1** 动摇 dòngyáo, 犹豫 yóuyù **2** 摇摆 yáobǎi

wavy ADJ **1** 波浪形的 bōlàngxíng de **2** 卷曲的 [+头发] juǎnqū de [+tóufa]

wax¹ I N **1** 蜡 là
wax paper 蜡纸 làzhǐ
2 耳垢 ěrgòu **II** V **1** 给 [+地板] 上蜡 gěi [+dìbǎn] shàng là **2** (to wax eloquent/poetic) 滔滔不绝地说／诗情十足地说 tāotāo bùjué de shuō/shīqíng shízú de shuō

wax² V [月亮+] 渐渐变圆 [yuèliang+] jiànjiàn biàn yuán

waxworks N 蜡像 làxiàng

way N **1** 路 lù, 道路 dàolù ■ *Could you tell me the way to the gas station?* 能告诉我去加油站的路吗? (→能告诉我去加油站怎么走吗？) Néng gàosu wǒ qù jiāyóuzhàn de lù ma? (→Néng gàosu wǒ qù jiāyóuzhàn zěnme zǒu ma?) **2** 边 biān, 面 miàn ■ *Everyone, please step this way.* 请各位走这一边。Qǐng gè wèi zǒu zhè yì biān. **3** 办法 bànfǎ, 方法 fāngfǎ **4** 作风 zuòfēng, 态度 tàidu ■ *The way she talks drives me nuts.* 她说话的样子，让我受不了了。Tā shuōhuà de yàngzi, ràng wǒ shòubuliǎo le.

way of life 生活方式 shēnghuó fāngshì
to go out of one's way 特地 tèdì ■ *Phyllis
went out of her way to prepare a big meal for
her husband.* 菲莉斯特地为丈夫作了一顿丰盛
的饭菜。Fēilìsī tèdì wèi zhàngfu zuòle yí dùn
fēngshèng de fàncài.

to have one's way 如愿以偿 rú yuàn yǐ cháng
■ *At home Ray always has his way; that's why
he's such a spoilt brat.* 瑞在家里总是能如愿以偿,
怪不得成了一个被宠坏的坏小子。Ruì zài jiāli
zǒngshì néng rú yuàn yǐ cháng, guàibude chéngle
yí ge bèi chǒnghuài de huài xiǎozi.

to make way 让路 rànglù

waylay (PT & PP **waylaid**) V 1 (为了讲话) 路上
拦住 [+人] (wèile jiǎnghuà) lùshang lánzhù
[+rén] 2 拦路抢劫 lánlù qiǎngjié

way-out ADJ 新奇古怪的 xīnqí gǔguài de, 时髦的
shímáo de

wayside N 路边 lùbiān

wayward ADJ 走入歧路的 zǒurù qílù de, 行为不良
的 xíngwéi bùliáng de

WC (= water closet) ABBREV 厕所 cèsuǒ

we PRON 我们 wǒmen

weak ADJ 1 虚弱的 xūruò de ■ *Recovering from
a long illness, my dad is still very weak.* 我父亲久
病后正在康复, 身体还很虚弱。Wǒ fùqin jiǔ bìng
hòu zhèngzài kāngfù, shēntǐ hái hěn xūruò. 2 软
弱的 ruǎnruò de
to be weak in 在…方面很弱 zài...fāngmian
hěn ruò ■ *This report is weak in details.* 这份报
告在细节方面比较弱。Zhè fèn bàogào zài xìjié
fāngmian bǐjiào ruò.

weaken V (使…) 变弱 (shǐ...) biàn ruò, 弱化
ruòhuà
to weaken sb's determination 动摇某人的决心
dòngyáo mǒurén de juéxīn

weak-kneed ADJ 懦弱的 nuòruò de, 胆怯的
dǎnqiè de

weakling N 身体虚弱的人 shēntǐ xūruò de rén,
没有力气的人 méiyǒu lìqi de rén

weakness N 1 虚弱 xūruò, 软弱 ruǎnruò
physical weakness 身体虚弱 shēntǐ xūruò
2 弱点 ruòdiǎn, 缺点 quēdiǎn
strengths and weaknesses 强项和弱点 qiángxiàng hé ruòdiǎn, 长处和缺点 chángchu hé
quēdiǎn
3 偏爱的人／东西 piān'ài de rén/dōngxi
to have a weakness for chocolate 偏爱巧克力
piān'ài qiǎokèlì, 嗜好吃巧克力 shìhào chī
qiǎokèlì

wealth N 1 财富 cáifù ■ *Alan and his siblings have
squandered all the wealth their father worked so
hard to accumulate.* 阿伦和他的兄弟姐妹挥霍光
了他们的父亲辛辛苦苦工作积累起来的财富。Ālún
hé tā de xiōngdì jiěmèi huīhuò guāngle tāmen de

fùqin xīnxīn kǔkǔ gōngzuò jīlěiqǐlai de cáifù. 2 大
量 dàliàng
a wealth of information 大量信息 dàliàng xìnxī

wealthy ADJ 富有的 fùyǒu de
the wealthy 富人 fùrén

wean V 1 使 [+婴儿] 断奶 shǐ [+yīng'ér] duànnǎi
2 使 [+人] 戒掉 [+坏习惯] shǐ [+rén] jièdiào
[+huài xíguàn]
to gradually wean him off the drugs 使他逐步
戒掉毒品 shǐ tā zhúbù jièdiào dúpǐn

weapon N 1 武器 wǔqì
weapons of mass destruction (WMD) 大规模杀
伤武器 dà guīmó shāshāng wǔqì
2 手段 shǒuduàn
secret weapon 秘密武器 mìmì wǔqì, 秘而不宣
的手段 mì'érbùxuān de shǒuduàn

wear I V (PT **wore**; PP **worn**) 1 穿 chuān ■ *She
never wears jeans.* 她从来不穿牛仔裤。Tā cónglái
bù chuān niúzǎikù. 2 戴 dài ■ *He noticed that
she wore a wedding ring.* 他注意到她戴了一枚结
婚戒指。Tā zhùyìdao tā dàile yì méi jiéhūn jièzhǐ.
to wear one's heart on one's sleeve 公开表露
真实感情 gōngkāi biǎolù zhēnshí gǎnqíng
3 磨损 mósǔn
to wear sb out 使某人非常劳累 shǐ mǒurén
fēicháng láolèi
to wear sth out 把某事物用坏 bǎ mǒushìwù
yòng huài
II N 1 服装 fúzhuāng
casual/men's/women's/children's wear 便装／
男子服装／女子服装／儿童服装 biànzhuāng/
nánzǐ fúzhuāng/nǚzǐ fúzhuāng/értóng
fúzhuāng
2 磨损 mósǔn
wear and tear (长期使用引起的) 磨损 (chángqī
shǐyòng yǐnqǐ de) mósǔn ■ *Damage caused
by wear and tear is normally not covered by insurance.* 因磨损造成的毁坏, 保险公司一般不赔。Yīn
mósǔn zàochéng de huǐhuài, bǎoxiǎn gōngsī
yìbān bù péi.

wearing ADJ 1 消耗性的 xiāohàoxìng de, 损耗
的 sǔnhào de 2 让人疲倦／厌烦的 ràng rén
píjuàn/yànfán de

wearisome ADJ 让人疲倦／厌烦的 ràng rén
píjuàn/yànfán de

weary I ADJ 精疲力尽的 jīngpí lìjìn de II V 使 [+人]
厌倦 shǐ [+rén] yànjuàn

weasel I N 1 黄鼠狼 huángshǔláng, 鼬 yòu 2 滑
头骗子 huátóu piànzi
weasel word 滑头话 huátóuhuà
II V 狡猾地逃避责任 jiǎohuá de táobì zérèn

weather I N 天气 tiānqì ■ *The weather is very
changeable in England.* 英国的天气非常多变。
Yīngguó de tiānqì fēicháng duō biàn.
weather bureau 气象局 qìxiàngjú

weather forecast 天气预报 tiānqì yùbào

weather pattern 天气形势 tiānqì xíngshì

weather station 气象站 qìxiàngzhàn

under the weather 身体不舒服 shēntǐ bù shūfú **II** v 经受住 [+风暴] jīngshòu zhù [+fēngbào]

weather-beaten ADJ 饱经风霜的 bǎojīng fēngshuāng de, 经受日晒雨淋的 jīngshòu rìshàiyǔlín de

weathercock N 风信鸡 fēngxìn jī, 风标 fēngbiāo

weatherman N 气象预报员 qìxiàng yùbàoyuán

weave I v 1 (PT **wove**; PP **woven**) 1 织 [+布] zhī [+bù] ■ *People on this island are clever at weaving mats and baskets.* 这个岛上的人在编席、编篮子方面很聪敏。Zhè ge dǎoshang de rén zài biān xí、biān lánzi fāngmian hěn cōngmǐn. **2** 编造 biānzào, 编织 biānzhī **3** (PT & PP **weaved**) 穿插行进 chuānchā xíngjìn **II** N 编织(法) biānzhī (fǎ)

weaver N 织工 zhīgōng, 编织者 biānzhīzhě

web N 1 网 wǎng ■ *It's indeed amazing how spiders weave their intricate webs.* 蜘蛛能编织复杂的网，实在奇妙。Zhīzhū néng biānzhī fùzá de wǎng, shízài qímiào.

web of deceit 错综复杂的骗局 cuòzōng fùzá de piànjú

2 (= World Wide Web) 互联网 hùliánwǎng

web browser 互联网浏览器 hùliánwǎng liúlǎnqì

web page 网页 wǎngyè

3 (鸭子的) 蹼 (yāzi de) pǔ

webbed ADJ (趾间) 有蹼的 (zhǐ jiān) yǒu pǔ de

web-footed ADJ 有蹼足的 yǒu pǔzú de

website N 网址 wǎngzhǐ ■ *Can you give us some websites for learning Chinese?* 你能告诉我们一些学中文的网址吗？Nǐ néng gàosu wǒmen yìxiē xué Zhōngwén de wǎngzhǐ ma?

wed v 1 结婚 jiéhūn **2** (be wedded to) 拘泥于 jūnì yú

wedding N 婚礼 hūnlǐ ■ *They've invited about 100 guests to their wedding.* 他们邀请了一百多位宾客参加婚礼。Tāmen yāoqǐngle yìbǎi duō wèi bīnkè cānjiā hūnlǐ.

wedding anniversary 结婚周年纪念日 jiéhūn zhōunián jìniànrì

wedding gown 婚礼长裙 hūnlǐ chángqún, 婚纱 hūn shā

wedding ring 结婚戒指 jiéhūn jièzhǐ

church wedding 在教堂里举行的婚礼 zài jiàotáng lǐ jǔxíng de hūnlǐ

wedge I N 楔子 xiēzi, 楔形物 xiēxíngwù

to drive a wedge between ... and ... 在…和…之间挑拨离间 zài...hé...zhījiān tiǎobō líjiàn **II** v 把…挤入 bǎ...jǐrù

to wedge a door open 在门下塞东西使它开着 zài ménxià sāi dōngxi shǐ tā kāizhe

wedlock N 已婚状态 yǐhūn zhuàngtài, 婚姻 hūnyīn

Wednesday N 星期三 xīngqīsān, 周三 zhōusān

wee ADJ 一丁点儿 yìdīngdiǎnr

a wee bit 有点儿 yǒudiǎnr

the wee hours 凌晨 língchén, 半夜一两点钟 bànyè yì liǎng diǎnzhōng

weed I N 1 野草 yěcǎo, 杂草 zácǎo **2** 大麻烟 dàmáyān **II** v 除草 chú cǎo

to weed out 排除 páichú, 淘汰 táotài

weedy ADJ 1 杂草丛生的 [+园子] zácǎo cóngshēng de [+yuánzi] **2** 身高而瘦弱的 shēn gāo ér shòuruò de

week N 周 zhōu, 星期 xīngqī

weekday N 工作日 (星期一到星期五) gōngzuòrì (xīngqīyī dào xīngqīwǔ)

weekend N 周末 zhōumò ■ *Have a relaxing weekend!* 祝你周末过得悠闲！Zhù nǐ zhōumò guòde yōuxián!

weekend retreat 周末休养地 zhōumò xiūyǎngdì

long weekend 长周末 cháng zhōumò

weekly I ADJ 每周的 měi zhōu de, 每星期的 měi xīngqī de ■ *The town newspaper comes out weekly.* 小镇的报纸每周出一次。Xiǎo zhèn de bàozhǐ měizhōu chū yí cì. **II** N 周报 zhōubào [M. WD 期/本 qī/běn], 周刊 zhōukān [M. WD 期/本 qī/běn]

weeknight N 工作日夜晚 gōngzuòrì yèwǎn

weep (PT & PP **wept**) v 流泪 liú lèi, 哭 kū

to weep copiously 泪如雨下 lèi rú yǔ xià

to weep and wail 嚎啕大哭 háotáo dàkū

weigh v 1 称重量 chēng zhòngliàng ■ *How much do you weigh?* 你体重多少？Nǐ tǐzhòng duōshǎo? **2** 仔细考虑 zǐxì kǎolǜ

to weigh sth against sb 权衡比较 quánhéng bǐjiào

to weigh one's words 推敲用词 tuīqiāo yòng cí

to weigh anchor 起锚 qǐ máo, 启程 qǐ chéng

weight I N 1 重量 zhòngliàng **2** 体重 tǐzhòng ■ *She would do anything to lose weight.* 只要能减轻体重，她什么都愿意做。Zhǐ yào néng jiǎnqīng tǐzhòng, tā shénme dōu yuànyì zuò.

to gain weight 增加体重 zēngjiā tǐzhòng

3 负担 fùdān, 重担 zhòngdàn **4** 重要性 zhòngyàoxìng, 影响 yǐngxiǎng

to carry much weight behind sth 很有影响 hěn yǒu yǐngxiǎng

to throw one's weight behind sth 利用某人的影响支持做某事 lìyòng mǒurén de yǐngxiǎng zhīchí zuò mǒushì

5 (锻炼用的) 杠铃 (duànliàn yòng de) gànglíng [M. WD 副 fù] **II** v 加重量 jiā zhòngliáng

weightless ADJ 失重的 shīzhòng de

weighty ADJ 重要的 zhòngyào de, 重大的 zhòngdà de

weir N 鱼梁 yúliáng

weird ADJ 怪异的 guàiyì de, 古怪的 gǔguài de

welcome I ADJ 受欢迎的 shòu huānyíng de
■ *The rain is welcome after weeks of dry weather.* 几星期的干旱天气以后，这场雨很受欢迎。Jǐ xīngqī de gānhàn tiānqì yǐhòu, zhè cháng yǔ hěn shòu huānyíng. II V 欢迎 huānyíng ■ *Families and friends gathered at the airport to welcome the soldiers back home.* 家人和朋友聚集在机场欢迎军人回家。Jiārén hé péngyou jùjí zài jīchǎng huānyíng jūnrén huíjiā. III N 欢迎 huānyíng
IV INTERJ 欢迎 huānyíng
Welcome to Boston! 欢迎您来波士顿! Huānyíng nín lái Bōshìdùn!
Welcome home! 欢迎你回家了! Huānyíng nǐ huíjiā!

weld I V 1 焊接 hànjiē, 熔接 róngjiē 2 团结 tuánjié, 拧成一股绳 níngchéng yì gǔ shéng II N 焊接点 hànjiēdiǎn

welder N (电)焊工 (diàn) hàngōng

welfare N 1 福利 fúlì, 福祉 fúzhǐ 2 福利救济金 fúlì jiùjìjīn ■ *Many families in this neighborhood are on welfare.* 这个地区很多家庭领福利救济金。Zhè ge dìqū hěn duō jiātíng lǐng fúlì jiùjìjīn.
welfare state 福利国家 fúlì guójiā, 福利制度 fúlì zhìdù

well¹ I ADV 1 好 hǎo ■ *Bill plays the saxophone well.* 比尔萨克斯管吹得很好。Bǐ'ěr sàkèsīguǎn chuīde hěn hǎo.
Well done! 干得好! Gàn de hǎo! 好样的! Hǎo yàng de!
2 相当地 xiāngdāng de, 很 hěn ■ *She came back home well after midnight—who had she been with?* 她午夜过了很久才回家—她和谁待在一起呢? Tā wǔyè guòle hěn jiǔ cái huíjiā—tā hé shéi dài zài yìqǐ ne? 3 彻底地 chèdǐ de, 完全地 wánquán de II ADJ 身体好 shēntǐ hǎo, 健康 jiànkāng
III INTERJ 好吧 hǎo ba ■ *Well, it's a deal.* 好吧，就这么说定了。Hǎo ba, jiù zhème shuōdìng le.
2 唉 ài ■ *Well, it can't be helped.* 唉，没办法。Ài, méi bànfǎ. 3 嗯 ńg ■ *Well, let me think about it.* 嗯，让我想想。Ńg, ràng wǒ xiǎngxiǎng.
as well as 也 yě ■ *He speaks Chinese as well as several European languages.* 他会说几种欧洲语言，也会说中文。Tā huì shuō jǐ zhǒng Ōuzhōu yǔyán, yě huì shuō Zhōngwén.
might as well 不妨 bùfáng

well² I N 井 jǐng II V (to well up) 流出 liúchū

well-advised ADJ (确实)应该 (quèshí) yīnggāi ■ *You're well-advised to quit smoking.* 你确实应该戒烟。Nǐ quèshí yīnggāi jiè yān.

well-balanced ADJ 1 均衡的 jūnhéng de
well-balanced diet 营养成份均衡的饮食 yíngyǎng chéngfèn jūnhéng de yǐnshí
2 (头脑)清醒的 [+人] (tóunǎo) qīngxǐng de [+rén], 高度理智的 gāodù lǐzhì de

well-being N 感觉良好 gǎnjué liánghǎo, 健康 jiànkāng, 幸福 xìngfú

wellbred ADJ 有教养的 yǒu jiàoyǎng de, 修养好的 xiūyǎng hǎo de

well-done ADJ 煮得熟透 zhǔde shútòu ■ *I'd like my steak well-done.* 我要牛排煎得透一点。Wǒ yào niúpái jiān de tòu yìdiǎnr.

well-earned ADJ 依靠辛勤工作挣来的 yīkào xīnqín gōngzuò zhènglái de, 理应得到的 lǐyìng dédào de

well-groomed ADJ 衣着整齐/讲究的 yīzhuó zhěngqí/jiǎngjiu de

well-grounded ADJ 1 有确凿证据的 [+想法] yǒu quèzáo zhèngjù de [+xiǎngfǎ] 2 训练有素的 [+人] xùnliàn yǒusù de [+rén]

well-informed ADJ 消息灵通的 xiāoxi língtōng de, 对…知识渊博的 duì…zhīshi yuānbó de

well-intentioned, well-meaning ADJ 出于好意的 chūyú hǎoyì de, 好心的 hǎoxīn de

well-known ADJ 著名的 zhùmíng de

well-meaning ADJ 本意良好的 běnyì liánghǎo de

well-off ADJ 富有的 fùyǒu de

well-read ADJ 熟读得很多的 shú dú de hěn duō de, 知识面很广的 zhīshìmiàn hěn guǎng de

well-spoken ADJ 善于辞令的 shànyú cílíng de

well-thought-of ADJ 受到好评的 shòudào hǎopíng de, 受欢迎的 shòu huānyíng de

well-timed ADJ 时机合适的 shíjī héshì de, 及时的 jíshí de

well-to-do ADJ 富有的 fùyǒu de, 有相当地位的 yǒu xiāngdāng dìwèi de

well-wisher N 表示良好祝愿的人 biǎoshì liánghǎo zhùyuàn de rén, 祝福者 zhùfúzhě

well-worn ADJ 穿旧的 chuān jiùde, 用得过多的 yòng de guòduō de
a well-worn excuse 用得太多的借口 yòng de tài duō de jièkǒu

Welsh ADJ, N 威尔士语 Wēi'ěrshìyǔ, 威尔士人 Wēi'ěrshìrén

welt N 1 (被虫咬后的)肿块 (bèi chóng yǎo hòu de) zhǒngkuài 2 (被打后的)伤痕 (bèi dǎ hòu de) shānghén

welter N (a welter of sth) 一大堆乱七八糟的东西/事情 yídàduī luànqī bāzāo de dōngxi/shìqing

wench N 姑娘 gūniang, 少妇 shàofù

went See go

wept See weep

were See be

werewolf N 会变成狼的人 huì biànchéng láng de rén, 狼人 lángrén

west I N 西(面) xī (miàn) ■ *The Pacific Ocean lies to the west of America.* 太平洋在美国西面。Tàipíngyáng zài Měiguó xīmiàn. II ADJ 西 xī, 西面的 xīmiàn ■ *The West Bank refers to the territory west of the Jordan River in the Middle*

East. "西岸" 是指中东约旦河以西的领土。"Xī'àn"
shì zhǐ Zhōngdōng Yuēdàn hé yǐ xī de lǐngtǔ.
the West 西方 Xīfāng
2 来自西面的 láizì xīmiàn de **III** ADV 朝西 cháo
xī, 向西 xiàng xī

westbound ADJ 向西行驶的 xiàng xī xíngshǐ de,
往西的 wǎng xī de

westerly ADV, ADJ 在西方 (地／的) zài xīfāng (de),
向西方 (的) xiàng xīfāng (de)
westerly wind 西风 xīfēng

western I ADJ **1** 西面的 xīmiàn de, 西部的 xībù
de ■ *The western part of the island is covered
with forests.* 岛的西部为森林覆盖。Dǎo de xībù
wéi sēnlín fùgài. **2** 西方的 xīfāng de **II** N 西部电
影 xībù diànyǐng ■ *He likes to watch westerns.*
他喜欢看西部电影。Tā xǐhuan kàn xībù diànyǐng.
western United States 美国西部 Měiguó xībù

Westerner N 西方人 Xīfāngrén

West Indies N 西印度群岛 Xīyìndù Qúndǎo

westward ADJ, ADV 朝西方地／向 cháo xīfāng de

wet I ADJ **1** 湿的 shī de, 潮湿的 cháoshī de ■ *He
was caught in the downpour and came home
dripping wet.* 他遇到了倾盆大雨，回家时全身湿透
了。Tā yùdào le qīngpén dàyǔ, huíjiā shí quánshēn
shītòu le. **2** 下雨的 xiàyǔ de
Wet paint. 油漆未干。Yóuqī wèi gān.
II v **1** 把…弄湿 bǎ...nòngshī **2** (to wet oneself)
尿裤 niào kù, 小便失禁 xiǎobiàn shījìn

whack I v 猛击 měngjī, 重创 zhòngchuāng **II** N 重
击声 zhòngjī shēng
out of whack [机器+] 不正常运转 [jīqì+] bú
zhèngcháng yùnzhuǎn, 坏了 huàile

whale N 鲸 (鱼) jīng (yú)

whaling N 捕鲸 (业) bǔjīng (yè)

wharf N 码头 mǎtou, 停泊处 tíngbóchù

what PRON **1** 什么 shénme ■ *This is not what I
want.* 这不是我要的。Zhè bú shì wǒ yào de. **2** 多
么 duōme ■ *What a beautiful day!* 多么美好的一
天！Duōme měihǎo de yìtiān!

whatever I PRON **1** 任何…的事物 rènhé...de
shìwù, 随便什么 suíbiàn shénme ■ *Her father
gave her whatever she asked.* 她要什么，她父
亲就给什么。Tā yào shénme, tā fùqin jiù gěi
shénme. (→她父亲对她百求百应。Tā fùqin duì
tā bǎi qiú bǎi yìng.) **2** 无论如何 wúlùn rúhé, 不
管什么 bùguǎn shénme **II** ADJ 任何的 rènhé de

wheat N 小麦 xiǎomài, 麦子 màizi ■ *Wheat and
rice are the two major types of grain in the world.*
小麦和大米是世界上两种主要的谷物。Xiǎomài hé
dàmǐ shì shìjièshang liǎng zhǒng zhǔyào de gǔwù.
wheat flour 面粉 miànfěn
whole wheat (bread) 全麦面包 quánmài
miànbāo

wheedle v 哄骗 hǒngpiàn, 甜言蜜语地骗取
tiányán mìyǔ de piànqǔ

wheel I N **1** 轮子 lúnzi, 车轮 chēlún ■ *Those who
can't afford wheels must hitch a ride.* 买不起汽车
的人只能搭便车。Mǎibuqǐ qìchē de rén zhǐ néng
dā biànchē. **2** 方向盘 fāngxiàng pán ■ *Getting
behind the wheel of a car while drinking is a big
no-no.* 一边喝酒一边开车，绝对不行。Yì biān hē
jiǔ yì biān kāi chē, juéduì bù xíng.
II v **1** 用 [+轮椅] 运送 yòng [+lúnyǐ] yùnsòng
2 突然转过身来 tūrán zhuǎn guò shēn lái
to wheel and deal 玩弄花招 wánnòng
huāzhāo, 投机取巧 tóujī qǔqiǎo

wheelbarrow N 独轮 (推) 车 dúlún (tuī) chē
[M. WD 辆 liàng]

wheelchair N 轮椅 lúnyǐ

wheeze I v 发出呼哧呼哧的声音 fāchū hūchīhūchī de shēngyīn, 气喘吁吁 qìchuǎn xūxū
II N 呼哧呼哧的声音 hūchīhūchī de shēngyīn

wheezy ADJ 气喘吁吁的 qìchuǎn xūxū de

when I ADV **1** 什么时候 shénme shíhou ■ *When
are you coming home today?* 你今天什么时候回
家？Nǐ jīntiān shénme shíhou huíjiā? **2** 那时候
nàshíhou **II** CONJ 当…的时候 dāng...de shíhou,
…的时候 ...de shíhou ■ *When I arrived in
Shanghai, my Chinese friends were waiting for me
in the terminal.* 我到上海时，我的中国朋友在机
场等我。Wǒ dào Shànghǎi shí, wǒ de Zhōngguó
péngyou zài jīchǎng děng wǒ.

whence ADV 从那里 cóng nàli

whenever I CONJ **1** 每当 měidāng **2** 无论什么时
候 wúlùn shénme shíhòu **II** ADV 无论什么时候
wúlùn shénme shíhòu

where I ADV **1** 什么地方 shénme dìfang, 哪里 nǎlǐ
2 在那里 zài nàlǐ ■ *This is the school where,
20 years ago, I met your mother, the captain of
the cheerleaders.* 就是在这座学校，我二十年前
遇到你的母亲，她当时是啦啦队队长。Jiùshì zài
zhè zuò xuéxiào, wǒ èrshí nián qián yùdao nǐ de
mǔqin, tā dāngshí shì lālāduì duìzhǎng. **II** CONJ 但
是 dànshì, 而 ér

whereabouts I N 去向 qùxiàng, 下落 xiàluò
the whereabouts of the missing girl 失踪女孩的
下落 shīzōng nǚhái de xiàluò
II ADV 哪个地方 nǎge dìfang

whereas CONJ 而 ér, 然而 rán'ér

whereby ADV 由此 yóucǐ, 借以 jièyǐ

wherein ADV 在那里 zài nàli, 在那方面 zài nà
fāngmiàn

whereof ADV 关于那个 guānyú nàge

whereupon CONJ 即刻 jíkè, 马上 mǎshàng

wherever ADV 无论在哪里 wúlùn zài nǎli, 不论何
处 búlùn héchù ■ *He took his dog wherever he
went.* 他不论去哪里都带着狗。Tā búlùn qù nǎli
dōu dàizhe gǒu.
wherever possible 要是有可能 yàoshi yǒu
kěnéng, 只要有可能 zhǐyào yǒu kěnéng

wherewithal N (the wherewithal to do sth) 做某事的钱 zuò mǒushì de qián

whet V (to whet one's appetite) 激起某人的兴趣 jīqǐ mǒurén de xìngqù, 吊起某人的胃口 diàoqǐ mǒurén de wèikǒu

whether CONJ …还是 …háishì, …是不是 …shìbushì

whew INTERJ 哎呀 āiyā

which I PRON, ADJ 1 哪（个）nǎ (ge) ■ Which instrument do you play in music class? 你在音乐课上玩什么乐器？Nǐ zài yīnyuèkèshang wán shénme yuèqì? II CONJ …的那个／那些 …de nàge/nàxiē ■ This is the computer which I bought last week. 这是我上星期买的电脑。Zhè shì wǒ shàngxīngqī mǎi de diànnǎo.

whichever ADJ, PRON 不论哪个 búlùn nǎge, 不论哪里 búlùn nǎli

whiff N 1 气味 qìwèi, 味儿 wèir 2 有一点儿 yǒu yìdiǎnr, 极少的 jí shǎo de
whiff of danger 有一点儿危险 yǒu yìdiǎnr wēixiǎn

while I CONJ 1 同时 tóngshí ■ While the children are growing up, their parents are getting old. 孩子们在长大，同时他们的父母在变老。Háizimen zài zhǎngdà, tóngshí tāmen de fùmǔ zài biàn lǎo. 2 虽然 suīrán ■ While the job could be very demanding, the pay is really good. 虽然工作有时候要求很高，工资真的不错。Suīrán gōngzuò yǒushíhou yāoqiú hěn gāo, gōngzī zhēnde búcuò. 3 但是 dànshì, 而 ér ■ My mother likes quiet places while my dad likes crowds. 我母亲喜欢安静的地方，而我父亲喜欢人多。Wǒ mǔqin xǐhuan ānjìng de dìfang, ér wǒ fùqin xǐhuan rén duō II N 一会儿 yíhuìr
all the while 一直 yìzhí, 始终 shǐzhōng
for a while 曾经 céngjīng, 有一段时间 yǒu yí duàn shíjiān
III V (to while away the hours) 消磨时间 xiāomó shíjiān

whim N 一时的兴致 yìshí de xìngzhì, 一时的想法 yìshí de xiǎngfǎ
at the whim of sb 由于某人一时的念头 yóuyú mǒurén yìshí de niàntou
on a whim 一时兴起 yìshí xīngqǐ

whimper I V 呜咽 wūyè, 抽泣 chōuqì II N 呜咽声 wūyèshēng, 抽泣声 chuòqìshēng
with a whimper 平淡地 píngdàn de [+结束] [+jiéshù]
with hardly a whimper 一声不响地 yì shēng bù xiǎng de

whimsical ADJ 离奇古怪的 líqí gǔguài de, 异想天开的 yìxiǎng tiānkāi de

whimsy N 离奇古怪 líqí gǔguài, 稀奇 xīqí

whine I V 1 哀叫 āijiào, 哭哭啼啼 kūkū títí 2 机器的隆隆声 jīqì de lónglóng shēng II N 1 哀叫声 āijiàoshēng 2 隆隆声 lónglóngshēng

whip I N 1 鞭子 biānzi [M. WD 条 tiáo] 2 政党的纪律督导员 zhèngdǎng de jìlǜ dūdǎoyuán II V 1 鞭打 biāndǎ 2 搅打 [+奶油] 使变稠 jiǎodǎ [+nǎiyóu] shǐ biàn chóu 3 迅速行进 xùnsù xíngjìn to whip up 煽动起 shāndòngqǐ, 激起 jīqǐ

whipping N 鞭刑 biānxíng, 鞭笞 biānchī
whipping cream 搅奶油 guànnǎiyóu

whirl V 1 (使…) 迅速旋转 (shǐ….) xùnsù xuánzhuǎn 2 [头+] 眩晕 [tóu+] xuànyùn

whirlpool N 1 漩涡 xuánwō 2 漩涡式浴缸 xuánwōshì yùgāng

whirlwind N 旋风 xuànfēng, 龙卷风 lóngjuǎnfēng
whirlwind tour 旋风式旅行 xuánfēngshì lǚxíng

whisk I V 搅拌 jiǎobàn
to whisk away 将 [+人] 迅速带走 jiāng [+rén] xùnsù dàizǒu
II N 搅拌器 jiǎobànqì

whisker N 1 (男人的) 连鬓胡子 (nánren de) liánbìn húzi, 髯 rán 2 (猫／老虎的) 须 (māo/lǎohǔ de) xū [M. WD 根 yēn]

whisky N 威士忌 (酒) wēishìjì (jiǔ)

whisper I V 耳语 ěryǔ, 说悄悄话 shuō qiāoqiāohuà II N 耳语 ěryǔ, 悄悄话 qiāoqiāohuà ■ Why on earth are you speaking in a whisper? Speak up! 你到底为什么说话声音这么轻？说大声点！Nǐ dàodǐ wèishénme shuōhuà shēngyīn zhème qīng? Shuō dàshēng diǎn!

whist N 惠斯特纸牌游戏 huìsītè zhǐpái yóuxì

whistle I V 1 吹口哨 chuī kǒushào 2 吹哨子 chuī shàozi II N 哨子 shàozi

whistle-blower N (内部) 告发者 (nèibù) gàofāzhě, 揭露 (公司／机构) 内部非法行为的人 jiēlù (gōngsī/jīgòu) nèibù fēifǎ xíngwéi de rén

whistle-stop N (火车) 小站 (huǒchē) xiǎo zhàn, 小镇 xiǎo zhèn
whistle-stop tour 沿途逗留很多地方的旅行 yántú dòuliú hěn duō dìfang de lǚxíng

white I ADJ 1 白色的 báisè de
white blood cell 白血球 báixuèqiú
white bread 白面包 bái miànbāo
white Christmas 下雪的圣诞节 xiàxuě de Shèngdànjié
white elephant 贵重而无用的东西 guìzhòng ér wúyòng de dōngxi
white pages 白页电话簿 báiyè diànhuàbù
white paper 白皮书 báipíshū
white pollution 噪音污染 zàoyīn wūrǎn
white slavery 拐卖妇女到异国卖淫 guǎimài fùnǔ dào yìguó màiyín
white trash 白人垃圾 báirén lājī, 贫穷无知的白人 pínqióng wúzhī de báirén
2 白种人的 báizhǒngrén de

white supremacy 白种人优越感 báizhǒngrén yōuyuègǎn

II N 1 白（颜）色 bái (yán) sè
White House（美国）白宫 (Měiguó) Báigōng
white lie 善意的谎言 shànyì de huǎngyán
2 白人 báirén, 白种人 báizhǒngrén 3 眼白 yǎnbái 4 蛋白 dànbái 5 白（葡萄）酒 bái (pútao) jiǔ

whiteboard N 白板 báibǎn [M. WD 块 kuài]

white-collar ADJ 白领阶层的 báilǐng jiēcéng de ■ Sam is very proud that all his adult children are white collar workers. 山姆的孩子都是白领，他为此骄傲。Shānmǔ de háizi dōu shì báilǐng, tā wèi cǐ jiāo'ào.

white-collar crime 白领罪行 báilǐng zuìxíng

whiten V（使…）变白 (shǐ…) biànbái

whitepepper N 白胡椒粉 bái hújiāofěn

whitewash I V 1 用石灰水粉刷 [+墙壁] yòng shíhuīshuǐ fěnshuā [+qiángbì] 2 掩饰 [+真相] yǎnshì [+zhēnxiàng], 粉饰 fěnshì **II** N 1 石灰水 shíhuīshuǐ 2 掩饰真相 yǎnshì zhēnxiàng, 遮掩丑闻 zhēyǎn chǒuwén

whither CONJ, ADV 向何处去 xiàng héchù qù

whittle V（使…）逐渐减少 (shǐ…) zhújiàn jiǎnshǎo
to whittle away 削弱 xuēruò, 减弱 jiǎnruò

whiz[1] V 飕飕飞驰 sōusōu fēichí

whiz[2] N 1 奇才 qícái, 高手 gāoshǒu
whiz kid 神童 shéntóng
2 (to take a whiz) 撒尿 sāniào

WHO (= World Health Organization) ABBREV 世界卫生组织 Shìjiè Wèishēng Zǔzhī

who I PRON 谁 shéi ■ I would like to know who borrowed my laptop computer. 我想知道谁借走了我的笔记本电脑。Wǒ xiǎng zhīdào shéi jièzǒule wǒ de bǐjìběn diànnǎo.
who's who of sth 某一方面的名人大全 mǒu yì fāngmiàn de míngrén dàquán, 某一方面所有的名人 mǒu yì fāngmiàn suǒyǒu de míngrén **II** CONJ …的那个/那些人 …de nàge/nàxiē rén ■ The book was written by a journalist who worked in China for five years. 这本书是一位在中国工作了五年的新闻记者写的。Zhè běn shū shì yíwèi zài Zhōngguó gōngzuòle wǔ nián de xīnwén jìzhě xiě de.

whoever PRON 无论谁 wúlùn shéi, 不管什么人 bùguǎn shénmerén

whole I ADJ 1 整个的 zhěng ge de, 全部的 quánbù de
in the whole wide world 全世界 quán shìjiè, 这个世界上 zhège shìjiè shàng
to go the whole log 全力以赴 quánlì yǐfù
2 完整的 wánzhěng de
whole mushroom 完整的蘑菇 wánzhěng de mógu, 整个蘑菇 zhěnggè mógu

II N 整体 zhěngtǐ, 全部 quánbù ■ The whole is bigger than a part. 整体大于部分。Zhěngtǐ dàyú bùfen.

wholegrain bread 全谷面包 quángǔ miànbāo
on the whole 总的来说 zǒng de lái shuō, 整体上 zhěngtǐ shàng

whole-hearted ADJ 全心全意的 quánxīn quányì de, 全力以赴的 quánlì yǐfù de

wholesale I N 批发 pīfā **II** ADJ 批发的 pīfā de ■ The company buys its supplies wholesale. 公司以批发的方式采购用品。Gōngsī yǐ pīfā de fāngshì cǎigòu yòngpǐn.
wholesale price 批发价 pīfājià

wholesaler N 批发商 pīfāshāng, 批发公司 pīfā gōngsī

wholesome ADJ 1 有利于健康的 yǒulì yú jiànkāng de 2 有益于道德的 yǒuyì yú dàodé de

wholly ADV 完全（地）wánquán (de), 彻底（地）chèdǐ (de)

whom PRON 谁 shéi ■ Whom may I ask are you talking about? 我可以问一下你们在谈谁吗？Wǒ kěyǐ wèn yí xià nǐmen zài tán shéi ma?

whore N 妓女 jìnǚ, 婊子 biǎozi

whose ADJ, PRON 谁的 shéi de ■ Whose car is parked out front? I don't recognize it. 谁的车停在外面了？我认不出来。Shéi de chē tíng zài wàimian le? Wǒ rènbuchūlái.

why I ADV 为什么 wèishénme ■ Why are you often late for work? 你为什么上班经常迟到？Nǐ wèishénme shàngbān jīngcháng chídào? **II** N (the whys and wherefores) 原因 yuányīn, 理由 lǐyóu

wick N 蜡烛芯 làzhúxīn [M. WD 根 gēn]

wicked ADJ 1 不讲道德的 bù jiǎng dàodé de, 有坏心思的 yǒu huài xīnsī de 2 淘气的 táoqì de, 调皮的 tiáopí de

wicker I N 干枝条 gān zhītiáo [M. WD 根 gēn], 藤条 téngtiáo [M. WD 根 gēn] **II** ADJ 干枝条编的 gān zhītiáo biān de, 藤条编的 téngtiáo biān de
wicker chair 枝编椅子 zhī biān yǐzi

wide ADJ 1 宽的 kuān de, 宽阔的 kuānkuò de ■ The wide river becomes a mere stream in winter. 在冬天，这条宽阔的河会变成涓涓小溪。Zài dōngtiān, zhè tiáo kuānkuò de hé huì biànchéng juānjuān xiǎoxī. 2 广泛的 guǎngfàn de, 范围很大的 fànwéi hěn dà de
a wide variety 品种多样 pǐnzhǒng duōyàng
3 远离的 yuǎnlí de
wide off the mark 远离目标 yuǎnlí mùbiāo, 离目标很远 lí mùbiāo hěn yuǎn

widely ADV 广泛地 guǎngfàn de, 普遍地 pǔbiàn de

widen V 1（使…）变宽 (shǐ…) biàn kuān, [眼睛+] 睁大 [yǎnjing+] zhēngdà 2（使…）增大 (shǐ…) zēngdà ■ The gap between the rich and the *poor has widened in the past decade.* 过去十年内贫富差距增大了。Guòqù shíniánnèi pín fù chājù zēngdà le.

widespread ADJ 广泛的 guǎngfàn de, 分布很广的 fēnbù hěn guǎng de
the widespread use of the cellphone 手机的广泛使用 shǒujī de guǎngfàn shǐyòng

widow N 寡妇 guǎfu, 遗孀 yíshuāng

widowed ADJ 守寡的 shǒuguǎ de

widower N 鳏夫 guānfū

width N 宽度 kuāndù ■ *The timber floor is available in various widths.* 可以供应不同宽度的地板。Kěyǐ gōngyìng bùtóng kuāndù de dìbǎn.

wield V 1 挥动 huīdòng [+工具] huīdòng [+gōngjù], 挥舞 huīwǔ 2 施展 [+影响／权力] shīzhǎn [+yǐngxiǎng/quánlì]

wife N 妻子 qīzi, 太太 tàitai ■ *His wife has just given birth to a daughter.* 他妻子刚生了一个女儿。Tā qīzi gāng shēngle yí ge nǚ'ér.

wig N 假(头)发 jiǎ (tóu) fà

wiggle V 扭动 niǔdòng, 摆动 bǎidòng

wild I ADJ 1 野的 yě de, 野生的 yěshēng de 2 感情奔放的 gǎnqíng bēnfàng de, 不受拘束的 bú shòu jūshù de ■ *The audience was wild with delight when the pop star walked down the stage and blew kisses here and there.* 当流行歌星走下舞台, 四处飞吻时, 观众欣喜得发狂。Dāng liúxíng gēxīng zǒuxia wǔtái, sìchù fēiwěn shí, guānzhòng xīnxǐ de fākuáng.
to be wild about 对…狂热 duì…kuángrè
3 不同寻常的 bù tóng xúncháng de ■ *"Their son is 13 and is already studying at Harvard." "That's wild."* "他们的儿子十三岁, 已经在哈佛读书了。""真不同寻常。" "Tāmen de érzi shísān suì, yǐjīng zài Hāfó dúshū le." "Zhēn bù tóng xúncháng."
wild card 不定因素 búdìng yīnsù, 捉摸不定的人／事 zhuōmo bú dìng de rén/shì
wild guess 乱猜 luàncāi, 瞎猜 xiācāi
the Wild West (19世纪美国)西部 (19 shìjì Měiguó) xībù, 西大荒 xīdàhuāng
4 荒野的 huāngyě de, 荒芜的 huāngwú de
II N (the wilds) 荒无人烟的地方 huāngwú rényān de dìfang, 荒原 huāngyuán

wildcat I N 野猫 yěmāo [M. WD 只 zhī] II ADJ 冒险的 màoxiǎn de, 靠不住的 kàobuzhù de
wildcat strike (未经工会批准的)自发罢工 (wèijīng gōnghuì pīzhǔn de) zìfā bàgōng

wilderness N 荒无人烟的地方 huāngwú rényān de dìfang, 荒原 huāngyuán

wildfire N 野火 yěhuǒ, 凶猛的(森林)大火 xiōngměng de (sēnlín) dàhuǒ

wildfowl N 野禽 yěqín

wild-goose chase N 白费力气的努力 báifèi lìqì de nǔlì

wildlife N 野生动物 yěshēng dòngwù

wildly ADV 疯狂地 fēngkuáng de

wiles N 花言巧语 huāyánqiǎoyǔ, 巧计 qiǎojì

will I MODAL V (PT **would**) [NEG **will not** ABBREV **won't**] 1 会 huì, 将要 jiāngyào ■ *I'm sure your performance will be a great success.* 我肯定, 你们的演出会非常成功。Wǒ kěndìng, nǐmen de yǎnchū huì fēicháng chénggōng. 2 愿 yuàn, 愿意 yuànyì II N 1 意志 yìzhì ■ *He overcame all the difficulties with the strength of will.* 他以意志力克服了所有的困难。Tā yǐ yìzhìlì kèfúle suǒyǒu de kùnnan.
Where there is a will, there is a way. 有志者事竟成。Yǒuzhìzhě shì jìng chéng.
2 遗嘱 yízhǔ

willful ADJ 任性的 rènxìng de, 一意孤行的 yíyì gūxíng de

willing ADJ 愿意 yuànyì ■ *Are you willing to take on this new task?* 你愿意接受这个新任务吗？Nǐ yuànyì jiēshòu zhè ge xīn rènwù ma?

willow N 柳(树) liǔ (shù) [M. WD 棵 kē]

willowy ADJ 高挑苗条的 gāotiǎo miáotiáo de, 婀娜的 ēnuóde

willpower N 意志力 yìzhìlì, 克制力 kèzhìlì

willy-nilly ADV 随意(地) suíyì (de), 乱七八糟 (地) luànqī bāzāo (de)

wily ADJ 狡猾的 jiǎohuá de, 会玩花招的 huì wán huāzhāo de

wimp N 1 懦弱的人 nuòruò de rén, 无用的人 wúyòng de rén 2 瘦弱的人 shòuruò de rén

win I V (PT & PP **won**) 赢(得) yíng (dé) 2 获得 huòdé, 取得 qǔdé
to win sb's heart 获得某人的爱情 huòdé mǒurén de àiqíng
II N (体育比赛)获胜 (tǐyù bǐsài) huòshèng, 赢 yíng

wince V, N 皱眉头 zhòu méitou, 倒吸一口气 dǎo xī yì kǒu qì
to wince at 感到不自在 gǎndào bú zìzài

winch I N 绞车 jiǎochē [M. WD 辆 liàng], 吊车 diàochē [M. WD 辆 liàng] II V (用吊车)提起来 (yòng diàochē) tíqǐ lái

wind¹ N 风 fēng ■ *A strong wind has been blowing since early morning.* 从早晨起, 一直刮着大风。Cóng zǎochén qǐ, yìzhí guāzhe dà fēng.
the wind of change 变革的趋势 biàngé de qūshì
wind chime 风铃 fēnglíng
wind turbine 风力发电机 fēnglì fādiànjī
head wind 顶风 dǐng fēng
tail wind 顺风 shùn fēng
to get wind of 听到…的风声 tīngdào…de fēngshēng
to take the wind out of sb's sails 使某人丧失信心 shǐ mǒurén sàngshī xìnxīn

681

wind²

wind² (PT & PP **wound**) v 1 缠绕 chánrào 2 给 [+钟表] 上发条 gěi [+zhōngbiǎo] shàng fātiáo
to wind down（使…）平静下来 (shǐ…) píngjìng xiàlai
to wind up（以…）告终 (yǐ…) gàozhōng, 结束 jiéshù
3 曲折 qūzhé, 逶迤 wēiyí

windbag N 喋喋不休的人 diédié bùxiū de rén

windbreak N 防风墙／林 fángfēng qiáng/lín

windbreaker N 风衣 fēngyī [M. WD 件 jiàn]

windfall N 意外之财 yìwàizhīcái, 意外收益 yìwài shōuyì

winding ADJ 曲曲弯弯的 qūqū wānwān de

wind instrument N 管乐器 guǎnyuèqì

windmill N 风车 fēngchē [M. WD 座 zuò]

window N 1 窗子 chuāngzi, 窗户 chuānghu 2 橱窗 chúchuāng
window dressing ① (商店) 橱窗布置 (shāngdiàn) chūchuāng bùzhi ② 装饰门面 zhuāngshì ménmian, 弄虚作假 nòngxū zuòjiǎ
window shopping 浏览商店橱窗 liúlǎn shāngdiàn chúchuāng, 逛街 guàngjiē ■ *Window shopping is a major pastime for some city girls.* 对有些城市姑娘来说，浏览商店橱窗是主要的消遣活动。Duì yǒuxiē chéngshì gūniang láishuō, liúlǎn shāngdiàn chúchuāng shì zhǔyào de xiāoqiǎn huódòng.
3 (计算机) 窗口 (jìsuànjī) chuāngkǒu ■ *You'd better close a couple of windows.* 你最好关闭几个窗口。Nǐ zuìhǎo guānbì jǐ ge chuāngkǒu.

windowpane N 窗玻璃 chuāng bōli [M. WD 块 kuài]

windpipe N 气管 qìguǎn

windshield N (汽车／摩托车) 挡风玻璃 (qìchē/mótuōchē) dǎngfēng bōli, 挡风窗 dǎngfēngchuāng
windshield wiper 雨刷 yǔshuā

windsock N 风向标 fēngxiàngbiāo, 风向袋 fēngxiàngdài

windswept ADJ 1 强风席卷的 [+平原] qiángfēng xíjuǎn de [+píngyuán] 2 被风吹乱的 [+头发] bèi fēng chuī luàn de [+tóufa]

windy ADJ 风大的 fēng dà de, 多风的 duō fēng de

wine N 酒 jiǔ, 葡萄酒 pútaojiǔ
wine bar 酒巴 jiǔbā
wine cellar 酒窖 jiǔjiào
wine tasting 品酒 pǐn jiǔ
wine vinegar 酒醋 jiǔ cù

wing I N 1 翅膀 chìbǎng 2 ■ *The wild duck flapped its wings and flew off.* 野鸭拍拍翅膀，飞走了。Yěyā pāipāi chìbǎng, fēizǒu le. **2** (飞机) 机翼 (fēijī) jīyì **3** (大楼) 侧翼 (dàlóu) cèyì, 侧厅 cè tīng **4** (党政中的) 派系 (zhèngdǎng zhòngde) pàixì

left/right wing 左／右翼 zuǒ/yòuyì
to take sb under one's wing 保护某人 bǎohù mǒurén
to take wings 开始起飞 kāishǐ qǐfēi, 很快发展壮大 hěn kuài fāzhǎn zhuàngdà
II v 1 飞行 fēixíng, 飞翔 fēixiáng **2** (to wing it) 临时凑成 línshí còuchéng

wings N (舞台的) 侧面 (wǔtái de) cèmiàn

wingspan N 翼幅 yìfú

wink v, N 1 眨眼 (示意) zhǎyǎn (shìyì)
to wink at 睁一眼闭一眼 zhēng yì yǎn bì yì yǎn, 假装没有看到 jiǎzhuāng méiyǒu kàndào
not to sleep a wink 一点都没有睡着 yìdiǎn dōu méiyǒu shuìzháo
2 [灯光+] 闪烁 [dēngguāng+] shǎnshuò

winner N 1 获胜者 huòshèngzhě 2 获奖者 huòjiǎngzhě ■ *The winner of last night's jackpot was an elderly woman in a nursing home.* 获得昨天夜里彩票头奖的是一位在养老院的老太太。Huòdé zuótiān yèlǐ cǎipiào tóujiǎng de shì yí wèi zài yǎnglǎoyuàn de lǎotàitai.

winning ADJ 1 获胜的 huòshèng de
winning score 获胜的得分 huòshèng de défēn
winning team 获胜的 (球) 队 huòshèng de (qiú) duì
2 赢得好感的 yíngdé hǎo gǎn de, 迷人的 mírén de
a winning smile 迷人的微笑 mírén de wēixiào

winnings N 赢得的钱 yíngdé de qián [M. WD 笔 bǐ]

winnow v 筛选 shāixuǎn
to winnow out 剔去 tīqù, 去掉 qùdiào

wino N 醉鬼 zuìguǐ, 酒鬼 jiǔguǐ

winsome ADJ 赢得人心的 yíngdé rénxīn de, 令人喜欢的 lìngrénxǐhuan de

winter I N 冬天 dōngtiān, 冬季 dōngjì ■ *We had an unusually mild winter last year.* 去年的冬天出奇地暖和。Qùnián de dōngtiān chūqí de nuǎnhuo.
Winter Olympics 冬季奥林匹克运动会 Dōngjì Àolínpǐkè Yùndònghuì
winter solstice 冬至 dōngzhì
II v 过冬 (天) guòdōng (tiān)

wintergreen N 冬青树 dōngqīngshù [M. WD 棵 kē]

wintertime N 冬天 dōngtiān, 冬季 dōngjì

wintry ADJ 寒冬似的 hándōng shìde, 冬天的 dōngtiān de

wipe I v 擦 cā, 揩 kāi
to wipe the floor with sb 彻底打败某人 chèdǐ dǎbài mǒurén
to wipe the slate clean 把以往一笔勾销 bǎ yǐwǎng yì bǐ gōuxiāo, 忘掉过去 (的不愉快) wàngdiào guòqù (de bù yúkuài)
II N 1 擦 cā, 揩 kāi 2 (一次性) 抹布 (yícìxìng) mābù

wiper N See **windshield**

wire I N 1 金属线 jīnshǔxiàn, 铅丝 qiānsī ■ *Prison-*

ers are kept behind barbed wire. 囚犯被关在铅丝
网后面。Qiúfàn bèi guān zài qiānsīwǎng hòumian.
2 电线 diànxiàn ■ *A tree fell and knocked the
utility wire onto the street.* 一棵树倒下，把
电线打倒在街上。Yì kē shù dǎoxia, bǎ diànxiàn
dǎdǎo zài jiēshang.

wire transfer 电子转账 diànzǐ zhuǎnzhàng
II v **1** 接电线 jiē diànxiàn, 接通电源 jiētōng
diànyuán ■ *Is the new computer wired up correctly?* 新电脑接线接对了吗？Xīn diànnǎo jiēxiàn
jiēduì le ma? **2** 电汇（钱）diànhuì (qián)
to get wired up 极其兴奋 jíqí xīngfèn ■ *Fred
always gets wired up just before going to a heavy
metal concert.* 佛雷德去听重金属摇滚音乐会前总
是极其兴奋。Fóléidé qù tīng zhòngjīnshǔ yáogǔn
yīnyuèhuì qián zǒngshì jíqí xīngfèn.

wiretap v （在电话线上）搭线窃听 (zài diànhuàxiàn shàng) dāxiàn qiètīng

wiring N （供电）线路 (gōngdiàn) xiànlù

wiry ADJ **1** 瘦而结实的（人）shòu ér jiēshi de (rén)
2 硬而卷曲的（头发）yìng ér juǎnqū (de tóufa)

wisdom N 智慧 zhìhuì
wit and wisdom 风趣的智慧 fēngqù de zhìhui
with the wisdom of hindsight 以事后之明 yǐ
shìhòu zhī míng, 当事后诸葛亮 dāng shìhòu
Zhūgé Liàng (→ *to be as wise as the legendary
Zhuge Liang*)

wisdom tooth N 智牙 zhìyá [M. WD 颗 kē], 智齿
zhìchǐ [M. WD 颗 kē]

wise I ADJ 明智的 míngzhì de, 智慧的 zhìhuì
de ■ *It was very wise of you to start saving as
soon as you had an income.* 你一有收入就开始
储蓄，这是很明智的。Nǐ yì yǒu shōurù jiù kāishǐ
chǔxù, zhè shì hěn míngzhì de.
wise guy 自作聪明的讨厌家伙 zì zuò cōngming
de tǎoyàn jiāhuo
II v (to wise up) 明白过来 míngbai guòlai, 醒悟
xǐngwù

wisecrack I N 俏皮话 qiàopíhuà, 风凉话
fēngliánghuà **II** v 说俏皮话 shuō qiàopíhuà

wish I v **1** 想要 xiǎngyào ■ *Be realistic, you know
you can't always get what you wish for.* 现实一点，
你知道不可能总是想要什么就得到什么的。Xiànshí
yìdiǎn, nǐ zhīdào bù kěnéng zǒngshì xiǎngyào
shénme jiù dédao shénme de. **2** 但愿 dànyuàn
■ *I wish I had listened to your advice.* 但愿我听
了你的忠告。Dànyuàn wǒ tīngle wǒ de zhōnggào.
(→ 要是我听了你的忠告，该多好啊！Yàoshì wǒ
tīngle nǐ de zhōnggào, gāi duō hǎo a!) **3** 祝 zhù,
祝愿 zhùyuàn **II** N 愿望 yuànwàng ■ *If you had
only one wish, what would you wish for?* 假如只有
一个愿望，你的愿望是什么？Jiǎrú zhǐ yǒu yí ge
yuànwàng, nǐ de yuànwàng shì shénme?

wishbone N 如愿骨 rúyuàngǔ, （鸡的）叉骨 (jī
de) chāgǔ

wishful thinking N 一厢情愿（的想法）yìxiāng
qíngyuàn (de xiǎngfǎ), 如意算盘 rúyì suànpán

wishywashy ADJ **1** 优柔寡断的 yōuróuguǎduàn
de **2** 淡的 [+颜色] dàn de [+yánsè]

wisp N 一小把 yì xiǎo bǎ, 一缕 yì lǚ
a wisp of hair 一缕头发 yì lǚ tóufa
a wisp of smoke 一缕轻烟 yì lǚ qīngyān

wistful ADJ 渴望的 kěwàng de, 忧愁的 yōuchóu
de

wit N **1** 风趣 fēngqù
quick wit 急智 jízhì, 风趣迅速应对的能力
fēngqù xùnsù yìngduì de nénglì
2 说话风趣的人 shuōhuà fēngqù de rén **3** 机智
jīzhì
to be at one's wit's end 束手无策 shùshǒu wú
cè, 一点办法都没有了 yìdiǎn bànfǎ dōu méiyǒu
le
to gather one's wits 镇定下来 zhèndìng xiàlai,
别慌张 bié huāngzhāng

witch N 巫婆 wūpó, 妖婆 yāopó

witchcraft N 巫术 wūshù, 妖法 yāofǎ

witchdoctor N 巫医 wūyī

witch-hunt N 迫害 pòhài

with PREP **1** 和…在一起 hé…zài yìqǐ ■ *Rena has
gone to the movies with her friends.* 丽娜和朋友们
一起去看电影了。Lìnà hé péngyoumen yìqǐ qù kàn
diànyǐng le. **2** 有 yǒu, 具有 jùyǒu **2** *A person
with common sense wouldn't have made that remark.* 有常识的人是不会说这种话的。Yǒu cháng-
shí de rén shì bú huì shuō zhè zhǒng huà de. **3** 带
dài, 带有 dàiyǒu **4** 在…一边 zài…yì biān

withdraw v **1** 撤回 chèhuí, 收回 shōuhuí **2** 提取
（钱）tíqǔ (qián) **3** 撤退 chètuì ■ *The invading
troops withdrew from the country.* 入侵部队从该国
撤退了。Rùqīn bùduì cóng gāiguó chètuì le.
4 退出 [+比赛] tuìchū [+bǐsài]

withdrawal N **1** 提款（额）tíkuǎn (é) **2** （军队）撤
退 (jūnduì) chètuì **3** 退出 tuìchū **4** 戒毒 jiè dú,
脱瘾 tuō yǐn

withdrawn ADJ 不与人交往的 bù yǔ rén
jiāowǎng de, 沉默寡言的 chénmò guǎyán de

wither v 枯萎 kūwěi, 干枯 gānkū
to wither and die 渐渐衰弱直至死亡 jiànjiàn
shuāiruò zhízhì sǐwáng

withering ADJ 咄咄逼人的 duōduō bīrén de, 尖刻
的 jiānkè de

withhold v 拒绝给予 jùjué jǐyǔ
to withhold evidence from the police 对警方隐
瞒证据 duì jǐngfāng yǐnmán zhèngjù

withholding tax N 预扣税款 yù kòu shuìkuǎn

within PREP, ADV 在…之内 zài…zhīnèi ■ *You
should live within your income.* 你应该量入为
出。Nǐ yīnggāi liàng rù wéi chū.
from within 在内部 zài nèibù ■ *The problem*

can be handled from within. 这个问题可以在内部解决。Zhè ge wèntí kěyǐ zài nèibù jiějué.

without PREP 没有 méiyǒu ■ *I can't translate this article without a good dictionary.* 我没有一本好词典就不能翻译这篇文章。Wǒ méiyǒu yì běn hǎo cídiǎn jiù bù néng fānyì zhè piān wénzhāng.

without a doubt 毫无疑问 háo wú yíwèn

without fail 一定 yídìng ■ *When I make a promise, I will fulfill it without fail.* 我作出承诺，就一定实现。Wǒ zuòchū chéngnuò, jiù yídìng shíxiàn.

withstand v 经受(住) jīngshòu (zhù), 忍耐 rěnnài to withstand the test of time 经受了时间的考验 jīngshòule shíjiān de kǎoyàn

witness I N 证人 zhèngrén, 见证人 jiànzhèngrén witness stand 证人席 zhèngrénxí to bear witness to 证明 zhèngmíng ■ *The computer breakdown bears witness to the necessity of constantly upgrading the system.* 计算机故障证明，系统经常升级是必要的。Jìsuànjī gùzhàng zhèngmíng, xìtǒng jīngcháng shēngjí shì bìyào de.

II v (亲眼)目睹 (qīnyǎn) mùdǔ, 亲历 qīnlì

witticism N 妙语 miàoyǔ, 俏皮话 qiàopihuà

witty ADJ 风趣的 fēngqù de, 妙趣横生的 miàoqù héngshēng de

wizard N 奇才 qícái, 怪才 guài cái computer wizard 电脑奇才 diànnǎo qícái

wizened ADJ 干瘪的 gānbiě de, 干瘦的 gānshòu de

wobble v 摇晃 yáohuang, 抖动 dǒudòng

wobbly ADJ 摇摆的 yáobǎi de, 颤动的 chàndòng de

woe N 灾难 zāinàn, 痛苦 tòngkǔ

woebegone ADJ 愁苦的 chóukǔ de, 愁眉苦脸的 chóuméi kǔliǎn de

woeful ADJ 糟透的 zāotòu de, 极坏的 jí huài de

wok N (中国式的)炒菜锅 (Zhōngguó shì de) chǎocàiguō

woke See **wake**¹

woken See **wake**¹

wolf (PL **wolves**) I N 狼 láng [M. WD 条 tiáo/只 zhī] II v (to wolf down) 狼吞虎咽 lángtūn hǔyàn, 狼吞虎咽地吃 lángtūn hǔyàn de chī

woman (PL **women**) N 女人 nǚrén, 妇女 fùnǚ ■ *Women are playing an ever more important role in politics.* 妇女正在政治上起越来越重要的作用。Fùnǚ zhèngzài zhèngzhìshang qǐ yuèláiyuè zhòngyào de zuòyòng.

womanhood N 1 成年女子(状态) chéngnián nǚzǐ (zhuàngtài) 2 (全体)妇女 (quántǐ) fùnǚ

womanish ADJ 女人腔的 nǚrénqiāng de, 娘娘腔的 niángniangqiāng de

womanize v 玩弄女性 wánnòng nǚxìng

womanizer N 玩弄女性的人 wánnòng nǚxìng de rén, 好色鬼 hàosèguǐ

womankind N 女性 nǚxìng

womanly ADJ 有女性特征的 yǒu nǚxìng tèzhēng de, 有女人气质的 yǒu nǚrén qìzhì de

womb N 子宫 zǐgōng

womenfolk N 全体妇女 quántǐ fùnǚ

won See **win**

wonder I v 1 想知道 xiǎng zhīdào, 疑惑 yíhuò ■ *I wonder who did it.* 我很想知道是谁干的。Wǒ hěn xiǎng zhīdào shì shéi gàn de. 2 怀疑 huáiyí, 不相信 bù xiāngxìn 3 请问 qǐngwèn ■ *I was wondering if I could leave an hour earlier today, sir.* 请问，先生，我今天可不可早一小时走? Qǐngwèn, xiānsheng, wǒ jīntiān kěbùkě zǎo yī xiǎoshí zǒu? II N 1 惊奇 jīngqí 2 奇迹 qíjī the Seven Wonders of the World 世界七大奇迹 shìjiè qī dà qíjī seven days/nineteen days wonder 不能维持的好事 bùnéng wéichí de hǎoshì, 昙花一现 tánhuā yíxiàn III ADJ 奇异的 qíyì de, 效果特好的 xiàoguǒ tè hǎo de

wonderful ADJ 1 极好的 jí hǎo de, 极妙的 jí miào de ■ *It's simply wonderful!* 简直妙极了! Jiǎnzhí miào jíle! 2 精彩的 jīngcǎi de ■ *Their performance was so wonderful that I went two days in a row to see it.* 他们的演出精彩极了，我连续两天去看。Tāmen de yǎnchū jīngcǎi jíle, wǒ liánxù liǎng tiān qù kàn.

won't See **will**

woo v 追求 zhuīqiú, 讨好 tǎohǎo

wood N 木(头) mù (tou) ■ *In Canada people chop wood during the fall in preparation for the long cold winter.* 在加拿大，人们在秋天砍木柴，准备过漫长而寒冷的冬季。Zài Jiānádà, rénmen zài qiūtian kǎn mùchái, zhǔnbèi guò màncháng ér hánlěng de dōngjì.

woodcutter N 伐木工人 fámù gōngrén, 伐木者 fámùzhě

wooded ADJ 长满树木的 zhǎngmǎn shùmù de, 树木茂盛的 shùmù màoshèng de

wooden ADJ 1 木头的 mùtou de, 木制的 mùzhì de 2 呆板的 [+人] dāibǎn de [+rén], 木纳的 [+人] mù nà de [+rén]

woodpecker N 啄木鸟 zhuómùniǎo [M. WD 只 zhī]

woods N 树林 shùlín, 林地 líndì not out of the woods 还没有脱离困境 hái méiyǒu tuōlí kùnjìng

woodwind N 木管乐器 mùguǎn yuèqì

woodwork N 木建部份 mùjiàn bùfen

woodworm N 蛀木虫 zhùmùchóng [M. WD 条 tiáo]

woody ADJ 木质的 mùzhì de, 木头的 mùtou de

woof INTERJ 狗汪汪叫 gǒu wāngwāng jiào

wool N 羊毛 yángmáo ■ *This suit is made of pure wool.* 这套服装是纯羊毛的。Zhè tào fúzhuāng shì chún yángmáo de.

wool carpet 羊毛地毯 yángmáodìtǎn
to pull the wool over sb's eyes 蒙骗某人 mēngpiàn mǒurén

woolen ADJ 羊毛的 yángmáo de, 呢绒的 níróng de

woolens N 针织毛衣 zhēnzhī máoyī, 毛料衣服 máoliào yīfu

woolly ADJ 象羊毛一样的 xiàng yángmáo yíyàng de

woolly-headed ADJ 头脑混乱的 tóunǎo hùnluàn de, 糊涂的 hútu de

woozy ADJ 虚弱的 xūruò de, 眩晕的 xuànyùn de

word I N 1 词 cí, 词语 cíyǔ, 字 zì ■ *New words are coined to refer to new things in life.* 新词创造出来指称生活中的新事物。Xīn cí chuàngzào chūlai zhǐchēng shēnghuó zhōng de xīn shìwù.
word processor (计算机)文字处理软件 (jìsuànjī) wénzì chǔlǐ ruǎnjiàn
2 话 huà, 话语 huàyǔ
swear/dirty word 脏话 zānghuà, 骂人话 màrénhuà
to have the final word 最后决定 zuìhòu juédìng, 拍板 pāibǎn ■ *Of course, the boss will have the final word.* 当然，老板会做最后的决定。Dāngrán, lǎobǎn huì zuò zuìhòu de juédìng.
to put in a good word for 为…说好话 wèi… shuō hǎohuà
to take one's word for it 相信…的话 xiāngxìn… de huà ■ *You don't have to take my word for it—ask the others.* 你不必相信我—可以问问别人。Nǐ bú bì xiāngxìn wǒ—kěyǐ wènwen biéren.
3 谈话 tánhuà ■ *May I have a word with you?* 可以跟你谈谈吗？Kěyǐ gēn nǐ tántan ma? 4 消息 xiāoxi 5 承诺 chéngnuò, 保证 bǎozhèng
a man of his word 讲信用的人 jiǎng xìnyòng de rén
on my word 以名誉担保 yǐ míngyù dānbǎo
II v 斟词酌句地表达 zhēn cí zhuó jù de biǎodá

wording N 措词用语 cuòcí yòngyǔ

wordy ADJ 话太多的 huà tài duō de, 唠叨的 láodao de

wore See **wear**

work I v 1 工作 gōngzuò ■ *Elton works in a government agency.* 埃尔顿在政府部门工作。Āi'ěrdùn zài zhèngfǔ bùmén gōngzuò. 2 运转 yùnzhuǎn ■ *This photocopier is not working properly this morning.* 这台复印机今天上午运转不正常。Zhè tái fùyìnjī jīntiān shàngwǔ yùnzhuǎn bú zhèngcháng.
to work out 算出来 suànchūlai
3 行得通 xíngdetōng ■ *We have to reschedule the meeting at 3; does it work for you?* 我们得把会议改到三点钟，你行吗？Wǒmen děi bǎ huìyì gǎidao sān diǎnzhōng, nǐ xíng ma? II N 1 工作 gōngzuò, 职业 zhíyè ■ *It pays to hire a profes-*

sional to do the work. 请一位专业人士来做这项工作是划得来的。Qǐng yí wèi zhuānyè rénshì lái zuò zhè xiàng gōngzuò shì huádelái de.
work clothes 工作服 gōngzuòfú
2 著作 zhùzuò, 作品 zuòpǐn

workaholic N 工作狂 gōngzuòkuáng

workbench N 工作台 gōngzuòtái

workday N 工作日 gōngzuòrì

worked up ADJ 激动不安的 jīdòng bù'ān de

worker N 工人 gōngrén, 工作者 gōngzuòzhě ■ *Workers are working overtime to fill the order.* 工人们在加班赶订单。Gōngrénmen zài jiābān gǎn dìngdān.

workforce N 劳动人口 láodòng rénkǒu, 劳动力 láodònglì

working ADJ 1 劳动的 láodòng de, 工作的 gōngzuò de
working class 工人阶级 gōngrén jiējí
working girl 年轻职业妇女 niánqīng zhíyè fùnǚ, 妓女 jìnǚ
working group, working party 特别工作组 tèbié gōngzuòzǔ, 专题调查委员会 zhuāntí diàochá wěiyuánhuì
2 为了工作的 wèile gōngzuò de
working breakfast/lunch 工作早餐/午餐 gōngzuò zǎocān/wǔcān
a working definition 可以使用的定义 kěyǐ shǐyòng de dìngyì
a working knowledge of 能对付工作的 néng duìfu gōngzuò de, 足够的 zúgòu de

workings N (组织/系统的)运行方式 (zǔzhī/xìtǒng de) yùnxíng fāngshì

workload N 工作量 gōngzuòliàng

workman N 工匠 gōngjiàng, 工人 gōngrén

workmanship N 工艺 gōngyì, 手艺 shǒuyì

workout N 锻炼(时间) duànliàn (shíjiān), (赛前)训练 (sài qián) xùnliàn

workplace N 工作场所 gōngzuò chǎngsuǒ

workroom N 工作室 gōngzuòshì, 工作坊 gōngzuò fāng

works N 工厂 gōngchǎng ■ *The steel works is the major employer in this town.* 这家钢厂是这个镇上主要雇主。Zhè jiā gāngchǎng shì zhè ge zhènshang zhǔyào gùzhǔ.

worksheet N 活页练习题 huóyè liànxítí, 工作单 gōngzuòdān

workshop N 车间 chējiān, 工场 gōngchǎng

workstation N 工作区 gōngzuòqū

workstudy N 半工半读 bàngōng bàndú, 勤工俭学 qíngōng jiǎnxué

world N 1 世界 shìjiè
the Third World 第三世界 Dìsān Shìjiè
in the world ① 世界上 shìjièshang ② 到底 dàodǐ ■ *Where in the world have you been? I haven't seen you for ages.* 你到底去哪儿了？ 这

么长时间没见到你了。Nǐ dàodǐ qù nǎr le? Zhème cháng shíjiān méi jiàndao nǐ le.

2 领域 lǐngyù, 界界 jièjiè

financial world 金融界 jīnróngjiè

3 人类（社会）rénlèi (shèhuì)

way of the world 世故人情 shìgù rénqíng

world-class ADJ 世界一流水平的 shìjiè yìliú shuǐpíng de, 世界级的 shìjièjí de

world-class artist 世界级艺术家 shìjièjí yìshùjiā

worldly ADJ **1** 老于世故的 lǎoyú shìgùde, 社会经验丰富的 shèhuì jīngyàn fēngfù de **2** 世俗的 shìsú de, 尘世间的 chénshì jiān de

all the worldly possessions 某人的全部家当 mǒurén de quánbù jiādang

worldly-wise ADJ 处事圆滑老到的 chǔshì yuánhuá lǎodào de

World Series N 世界职业棒球竞标赛 Shìjiè Zhíyè Bàngqiú Jìngbiāosài

worldwide ADJ 世界范围的 shìjiè fànwéide, 全世界的 quánshìjiè de

World Wide Web (ABBREV WWW) N 互联网 hùliánwǎng

worm I N **1** 蠕虫 rúchóng [M. WD 条 tiáo] **2** 寄生虫 jìshēngchóng [M. WD 条 tiáo] II V 象虫子一样蠕动 xiàng chóngzi yíyàng rúdòng

to worm one's way into sb's confidence 渐渐骗取某人的信任 jiànjiàn piànqǔ mǒurén de xìnrèn

worn[1] See **wear**

worn[2] ADJ **1** 用得很破旧的 yòng de hěn pòjiù de, 破损的 pòsǔn de **2** 疲倦的 píjuàn de

worn-out ADJ **1** 穿破了的 [+衣服] chuānpò le de [+yīfu] **2** 精疲力竭的 [+人] jīngpí lìjié de [+rén]

worried ADJ 担心的 dānxīn de, 担忧的 dānyōu de

worry I V 担忧 dānyōu, 担心 dānxīn ■ *She'd worried herself sick about her son's drug problem.* 她儿子的吸毒问题让她很担忧。Tā érzi de xīdú wèntí ràng tā hěn dānyōu. II N **1** 担忧 dānyōu, 忧愁 yōuchóu ■ *Their daughter's obesity caused them much worry.* 他们女儿的肥胖症让他们很担忧。Tāmen nǚ'ér de féipàngzhēng ràng tāmen hěn dānyōu. **2** 让人担忧的事 ràng rén dānyōu de shì

worrying ADJ 令人担忧的 lìngrén dānyōu de

worrywart N（总是）忧心忡忡的人 (zǒngshì) yōuxīn chōngchōng de rén

worse I ADJ, ADV 比较坏 bǐjiào huài, 更坏 gèng huài ■ *What is worse—a bad marriage or an awful job?* 婚姻不理想，职业很糟糕—两者哪个更坏？Hūnyīn bù lǐxiǎng, zhíyè hěn zāogāo—liǎngzhě nǎ ge gèng huài?

to go from bad to worse 越来越坏 yuèláiyuè huài, 越来越糟 yuèláiyuè zāo ■ *His behavior went from bad to worse, and his parents were summoned for a meeting with the principal.* 他的行为越来越坏，家长被请来和校长见面。Tā de

xíngwéi yuèláiyuè huài, jiāzhǎng bèi qǐnglái hé xiàozhǎng jiànmiàn.

II N 更坏的事 gèng huài de shì

to take a turn for the worse 变得更坏 biàn de gèng huài, 恶化 èhuà

worsen V 更坏 gèng huài, 恶化 èhuà

worship I N **1** 敬奉上帝／神 jìngfèng Shàngdì/shén

house of worship 敬奉上帝／神的场所 jìngfèng Shàngdì/shén de chǎngsuǒ,（佛教）庙宇 (Fójiào) miàoyǔ,（基督教）教堂 (Jīdūjiào) jiàotáng,（穆斯林）清真寺 (Mùsīlín) qīngzhēnsì **2** 崇拜 chóngbài II V **1** 敬奉 [+上帝] jìngfèng [+Shàngdì], 拜 [+神] bài [+shén] **2** 崇拜 [+人] chóngbài [+rén], 敬仰 jìngyǎng

worshipper N 敬神者 jìngshénzhě, 信徒 xìntú

worst I ADJ, ADV 最坏 zuì huài

at worst 最坏 zuì huài, 最坏的情况 zuì huài de qíngkuàng ■ *At worst he could lose his job.* 最坏的情况是他丢掉饭碗。Zuì huài de qíngkuàng shì tā diūdiao fànwǎn.

II N 最坏的人／事 zuì huài de rén/shì

when/if worst comes to worst 万一发生最坏的情况 wànyī fāshēng zuì huài de qíngkuàng ■ *If worst comes to worst, they'll have to sell their family home.* 万一发生最坏的情况，他们得卖掉家宅。Wànyī fāshēng zuì huài de qíngkuàng, tāmen děi màidiao jiāzhái.

worsted N 精纺毛料 jīngfǎng máoliào

worth I ADJ 值得 zhídé

An ounce of prevention is worth a pound of cure. 一两预防值得一磅治疗。(→预防为主。) Yì liǎng yùfáng zhídé yí bàng zhìliáo. (→Yùfáng wéi zhǔ.)

II N 价值 jiàzhí ■ *His real worth was not appreciated in the company until he resigned.* 他的真正价值在公司里一直没有被认识到，直到他辞职。Tā de zhēnzhèng jiàzhí zài gōngsī lǐ yìzhí méiyǒu bèi rènshidao, zhídào tā cízhí. (→他辞职以后，公司才认识到他的真正价值。Tā cízhí yǐhòu, gōngsī cái rènshidao tā de zhēnzhèng jiàzhí.)

worthless ADJ 没有价值的 méiyǒu jiàzhí de, 没用的 méi yòng de

worthwhile ADJ 值得花时间／金钱／精力 zhídé huā shíjiān/jīnqián/jīnglì, 合算的 hésuàn de

worthy ADJ 值得尊敬的 zhídé zūnjìng de

be worthy of consideration 值得考虑的 zhídé kǎolǜ de

would MODEL V (PT of **will**) [NEG **would not** ABBREV **wouldn't**] ■ *She promised that she would call me.* 她答应给我打电话。Tā dāyìng gěi wǒ dǎ diànhuà.

wound[1] I N 伤 shāng, 伤口 shāngkǒu ■ *The dog's bite resulted in a painful wound.* 狗咬造成了疼痛的伤口。Gǒuyǎo zàochéngle téngtòng de

shāngkǒu. **II** v 1 使…受伤 shǐ…shòushāng
■ *Several people were wounded when the car bomb went off, but luckily no one was killed.* 汽车炸弹爆炸时，好几个人受伤了，幸运的是，没有人被炸死。Qìchē zhàdàn bàozhà shí, hǎo jǐ gè rén shòushāng le, xìngyùn de shì, méiyǒu rén bèi zhàsǐ. **2** 伤害 shānghài

wound² v See **wind²**

wove See **weave**

woven See **weave**

wow I INTERJ 哇 wā, 呀 yā **II** v 使…称赞 shǐ…chēngzàn

wrangle v, N 争吵 zhēngchǎo, 吵架 chǎojià

wrap I v 1 裹 bāo, 包裹 bāoguǒ
to wrap up 结束 jiéshù
II N 1 塑料保鲜膜 sùliào bǎoxiān mó 2 披肩 pījiān 3 三明治卷 sānmíngzhì juàn

wrapper N 包装纸 bāozhuāngzhǐ

wrapping N 包装材料 bāozhuāng cáiliào

wrath N 愤怒 fènnù, 震怒 zhènnù

wrathful ADJ 愤怒的 fènnù de, 大怒的 dà nù de

wreak v (to wreak havoc) 造成巨大破坏 zào-chéng jùdà pòhuài
to wreak vengeance on sb 对某人狠狠报复 duì mǒurén hěnhěn bàofu

wreath N 花环 huāhuán, 花圈 huāquān

wreck I v 1 毁坏 huǐhuài, 毁掉 huǐdiào **II** N 1 毁坏 huǐhuài, 破灭 pòmiè 2 失事船只/飞机的残骸 shīshì chuánzhī/fēijī de cánhái 3 快要精神崩溃的人 kuàiyào jīngshén bēngkuì de rén

wreckage N 1 毁坏 huǐhuài, 破坏 pòhuài 2 飞机/船只/建筑物被毁后的残骸 fēijī/chuánzhī/jiànzhùwù bèi huǐ hòu de cánhái

wrench I v 1 挣脱 zhèngtuō 2 扭伤 niǔshāng **II** N 1 扳手 bānshǒu [M. WD 把 bǎ]
to throw a wrench in sth 对某事捣乱 duì mǒushì dǎoluàn, 破坏某事 pòhuài mǒushì
2 悲痛 bēitòng, 悲伤 bēishāng **3** 扭伤 niǔshāng

wrest v 1 抢夺 qiǎngduó, 猛拧 měng nǐng 2 夺取 duóqǔ, 夺得 duódé

wrestle v 摔跤 shuāijiāo, 扭打 niǔdǎ
to wrestle with ① 与…扭打 yǔ…niǔdǎ ② 费劲得撺 fèijìn dé hān

wrestler N 摔跤运动员 shuāijiāo yùndòngyuán

wrestling N 摔跤（运动）shuāijiāo (yùndòng)

wretch N 讨厌鬼 tǎoyànguǐ, 淘气鬼 táoqìguǐ
poor wretch 可怜的人 kělián de rén

wriggle v 蠕动 rúdòng, 扭动 niǔdòng
to wriggle out of sth 找借口逃避 zhǎo jièkǒu táobì, 找借口脱身 zhǎo jièkǒu tuōshēn

wring (PT & PP **wrung**) v 把…拧干 bǎ…nínggān
to wring one's hands 搓着手（表示焦虑）cuōzhe shǒu (biǎoshì jiāolǜ)
to wring sb's neck 对某人发烦恼 duì mǒurén fā fánnǎo

wringer N (to go through the wringer) 吃尽苦头 chījìn kǔtóu

wrinkle I N 1 （皮肤的）皱纹 (pífu de) zhòuwén 2 （衣服）皱褶 (yīfu) zhòu zhě
to iron out the wrinkles 解决一些小问题 jiějué yìxiē xiǎo wèntí
II v 起皱纹 qǐ zhòuwén
to wrinkle one's nose 皱起鼻子 zhòu qǐ bízi

wrist N 手腕 shǒuwàn

wristband N 护腕 hùwàn, 腕带 wàndài

wristwatch N 手表 shǒubiǎo [M. WD 块 kuài/只 zhī]

writ I N （法院的）令状 (fǎyuàn de) lìngzhuàng
II v (writ large) 明显的 míngxiǎn de, 显而易见的 xiǎn'éryìjiàn de

write v (PT **wrote**; PP **written**) **1** 写 xiě ■ *Prof Laird wrote a glowing reference for Andrew, his star pupil.* 莱尔德教授给得意门生安德鲁写了一封热烈称赞的推荐信。Lái'ěrdé jiàoshòu gěi déyì ménshēng Āndélǔ xiěle yì fēng rèliè chēngzàn de tuījiànxìn. **2** 写信 xiě xìn
to write off 注销 [+账] zhùxiāo [+huài zhàng], 一笔勾销 yì bǐ gòuxiāo ■ *The bank has to write off bad debts every year.* 银行每年都要注销坏账。Yínháng měi nián dōu yào zhùxiāo huàizhàng.
3 开 [+支票] kāi [+zhīpiào]
to write out 详细写出 [+清单] xiángxì xiěchū [+qīngdān]

write-off N 注销 zhùxiāo, 勾销 gōuxiāo

writer N 1 作家 zuòjiā 2 会写作的人 huì xiězuò de rén ■ *To be a good writer, you need to write every day.* 要写得好，就得天天写。Yào xiěde hǎo, jiù děi tiāntiān xiě.

write-up N （报纸的）评论文章 (bàozhǐ de) pínglùn wénzhāng

writhe v 扭动 niǔdòng
to writhe in pain 痛得打滚 tòng de dǎgǔn

writing N 1 书写 shūxiě, 写作 xiězuò ■ *The importance of reading and writing cannot be overemphasized.* 阅读和书写的重要性，再强调也不过分。Yuèdú hé shūxiě de zhòngyàoxìng, zài qiángdiào yě bú guòfèn. **2** 笔迹 bǐjì ■ *His writing on the answer sheet was hardly legible.* 他在答卷上的笔迹几乎辨认不出来。Tā zài dájuànshang de bǐjì jīhū biànrèn bùchūlai. **3** 著作 zhùzuò
■ *Charles Dickens' writings are full of sympathy for the poor.* 查尔斯·狄更斯的著作充满了对穷人的同情。Chá'ěrsī·Dígèngsī de zhùzuò chōngmǎnle duì qióngrén de tóngqíng.

written I See **write II** ADJ 书面（的）shūmiàn (de)

wrong I ADJ 1 错的 cuò de, 错误的 cuòwù de
■ *The car went the wrong way down the freeway.* 汽车在超级公路上朝错误的方向开去。Qìchē zài chāojí gōnglùshang cháo cuòwù de fāngxiàng kāiqu. **2** 不合适的 bùhéshì de

to be on the wrong track 思路不对 sīlù bú duì, 路子不对 lùzi bú duì

to get on the wrong side of sb 冒犯某人 màofàn mǒurén

II ADV 错 cuò ■ *Don't get me wrong—I'm not criticizing you.* 别搞错我的意思—我不是在批评你。Bié gǎocuò wǒ de yìsi—wǒ bú shì zài pīpíng nǐ.

to go wrong 出错 chūcuò, 弄错 nòngcuò

III N **1** 错误 cuòwù ■ *I wonder if they know the difference between right and wrong.* 我不明白，他们知道不知道正确和错误之间的区别。Wǒ bù míngbai, tāmen zhīdàobuzhīdào zhèngquè hé cuòwù zhījiān de qūbié. (→ 我不明白，他们会不会分辨是非。Wǒ bù míngbai, tāmen huìbuhuì fēnbiàn shìfei.)

to be in the wrong 犯错误 fàn cuòwu

2 冤屈 yuānqū **IV** V **3** 不公正地对待 bù gōngzhèng de duìdài, 冤枉 yuānwang

wrongdoer N 做错事的人 zuòcuò shì de rén, 违法者 wéifǎzhě

wrongdoing N 违法的事 wéifǎ de shì, 错事 cuò shì

wrongful ADJ 不公正的 bù gōngzhèng de, 非法的 fēifǎ de

a wrongful death 由他人非法造成的死亡 yóu tārén fēifǎ zàochéng de sǐwáng

wrote See **write**

wrought iron N 锻铁 duàntiě, 熟铁 shútiě

wrung See **wring**

wry ADJ 嘲笑的 cháoxiào de, 露出怪相的 lòuchu guàixiàng de

a wry smile 嘲弄的微笑 cháonòng de wēixiào, 苦笑 kǔxiào

WTO (= World Trade Organization) ABBREV 世界贸易组织 Shìjiè Màoyì Zǔzhī

www see **World Wide Web**

X

X-chromosome N X染色体 X rǎnsètǐ

xenophobia N 排外情绪 páiwài qíngxù, 恐外症 kǒng wàizhèng

xerox I N（静电）复印（件）(jìngdiàn) fùyìn (jiàn) **II** v（用复印机）复印 (yòng fùyìnjī) fùyìn

X-mas N See **Christmas**

X-ray I N X射线 X shèxiàn, X光 X guāng, X 光检查 X guāng jiǎnchá ■ *Luckily, the X-ray revealed no broken bone.* 很幸运，X光检查没有发现骨折。Hěn xìngyùn, X guāng jiǎnchá méiyǒu fāxiàn gǔzhé. **II** v 用X射线检查 yòng X shèxiàn jiǎnchá

xylophone N 木琴 mùqín [M. WD 台 tái]

Y

yacht N 游艇 yóutǐng [M. WD 艘 sōu], 大型帆船 dàxíng fānchuán [M. WD 艘 sōu]

yachting N 驾驶游艇 jiàshǐ yóutǐng, 帆船比赛 fānchuán bǐsài

yahoo I N 粗鄙的人 cūbǐ de rén **II** INTERJ 好哇 hǎo wā

yam N 山药 shānyao

yank v 使劲拉 shǐjìn lā, 猛扯 měng chě

Yankee N **1** 美国佬 Měiguólǎo **2**（美国）北方佬 (Měiguó) běifānglǎo

yap v **1** [小狗+] 乱叫 [xiǎogǒu+] luànjiào, 狂吠 kuángfèi **2** 哇啦哇啦地乱叫 wālā wālā de luànjiào

yard N **1** 院子 yuànzi ■ *There is a flowerbed in the front yard and a swing set in the back yard.* 前院有花圃，后院有秋千架。Qiányuàn yǒu huāpǔ, hòuyuàn yǒu qiūqiān jià. **2** 码 mǎ (= 3 feet)

yard sale（在家院子里）旧货贱卖 (zài jiā yuànzi lǐ) jiùhuò jiànmài

yard stick 衡量标准 héngliáng biāozhǔn, 评判尺度 píngpàn chǐdù

yarn N **1** 奇闻轶事 qíwén yìshì, 夸张的冒险故事 kuāzhāng de màoxiǎn gùshi **2** 纱线 shāxiàn

yawn I N 哈欠 hāqian ■ *The cat let out a big yawn as it woke from its afternoon nap.* 猫儿午睡醒来，打了一个长长的哈欠。Māor wǔshuì xǐnglái, dǎ le yí ge chángcháng de hāqian. **II** v **1** 打哈欠 dǎ hāqian **2** 产生差距 chǎnshēng chājù

a yawning gap 巨大差距 jùdà chājù

Y-chromosome N Y染色体 Y rǎnsètǐ

year N **1** 年 nián **2** 岁 suì

academic/school year 学年 xuénián ■ *The academic year starts in September.* 学年在九月开始。Xuénián zài jiǔyuè kāishǐ.

all year round 一年到头 yì nián dào tóu, 终年 zhōngnián ■ *This eccentric man wears a red baseball cap all the year round.* 这个怪人一年到头戴着一顶红色的棒球帽。Zhè ge guàirén yì nián dào tóu dàizhe yì dǐng hóngsè de bàngqiúmào.

year after year 一年又一年 yì nián yòu yì nián

never in a million years 绝不可能 juébù kěnéng, 肯定不会 kěndìng bú huì

yearbook N 年鉴 niánjiàn [M. WD 本 běn]

yearling N（一两岁的）小动物 (yì liǎng suì de) xiǎo dòngwù, 幼马 yòumǎ [M. WD 匹 pǐ]

yearly ADJ 每年的 měi nián de, 年度的 niándù de ■ *The general assembly of the club meets yearly, usually in May.* 俱乐部全体会议每年开一次，通常在五月。Jùlèbù quántǐ huìyì měi nián kāi yí cì, tōngcháng zài wǔyuè.

yeast N 酵母 jiàomǔ, 发酵物 fājiàowù

yell I v 叫嚷 jiàorǎng, 喊叫 hǎnjiào ■ *Don't yell*

at me. 别对我大声嚷嚷。Bié duì wǒ dàshēng rāngrang. **II** N 啦啦队的喊叫声 lālāduì de hǎnjiàoshēng
a yell of protest 抗议声 kàngyìshēng

yellow I ADJ 黄色的 huángsè de ■ *The yellow curtains make the dining room bright and lively.* 黄色的窗帘使餐厅明亮而充满生气。Huángsè de chuānglián shǐ cāntīng míngliàng ér chōngmǎn shēngqì. **II** N 黄色 huángsè
Yellow Pages 黄页 huángyè, 商业电话簿 shāngyè diànhuàbù
III v 变黄 biàn huáng

yelp v 尖叫 jiānjiào, 喊叫 hǎnjiào

yen[1] N 日元 Rìyuán

yen[2] N 渴望 kěwàng, 热望 rèwàng

yep N See **yes**

yes INTERJ 是 shì, 是的 shì de ■ *"Don't you like Chinese food?" "Yes, I do."* "你喜欢中国菜吗？""喜欢。""Nǐ xǐhuan Zhōngguócài ma?" "Xǐhuan."

yesterday ADV, N 昨天 zuótiān ■ *He didn't come to work yesterday.* 他昨天没有来上班。Tā zuótiān méiyǒu lái shàngbān.
yesterday's news 昨日新闻 zuórì xīnwén, 旧闻 jiùwén

yet I ADV 还 hái, 仍然 réngrán ■ *I haven't caught any fish yet. How about you?* 我还没有钓到鱼，你呢？Wǒ hái méiyǒu diàodao yú, nǐ ne? **II** CONJ 可是 kěshì, 然而 rán'ér ■ *His story is very unlikely, yet it may well be true.* 他的故事不大会发生，然而很有可能是真的。Tā de gùshi bú dà huì fāshēng, rán'ér hěn yǒukěnéng shì zhēnde.

yew N 紫杉树 zǐshānshù [M. WD 棵 kē]

Yiddish N 依地语 yīdìyǔ

yield I v 1 产生 [+结果] chǎnshēng [+jiéguǒ] 2 出产 [+农产品] chūchǎn [+nóngchǎnpǐn] 3 (被迫) 交出 [+权利] (bèipò) jiāochū [+quán-lì] 4 屈从 [+压力] qūcóng [+yālì], 服从 fúcóng
to yield to traffic on the right 给右边的车辆让道 gěi yòubian de chēliàng ràngdào
II N 收益 shōuyì, 产量 chǎnliàng

yippee INTERJ 好哇 hǎo wā, 太好了! Tài hǎo le!

YMCA (= Young Men's Christian Association) ABBREV 基督教青年会 Jīdūjiào Qīngniánhuì

yodel I N 岳得尔唱法 yuèdéěr chàngfǎ, 岳得尔曲调 yuèdéěr qǔdiào II v 用岳得尔唱法歌唱 yòng yuèdéěr chàngfǎ gēchàng

yoga N 瑜伽 (法) yújiā (fǎ)

yogurt N 酸奶 suānnǎi

yoke N 1 牛轭 niú'è 2 束缚 shùfù
yoke of tradition 传统的束缚 chuántǒng de shùfù

yokel N 土包子 tǔbāozi, 乡巴佬 xiāngbalǎo

yolk N 蛋黄 dànhuáng

yonder ADV 那边 nàbian, 远方 yuǎnfāng

you PRON 你 nǐ, 您 nín, 你们 nǐmen ■ *You said you knew the way.* 你说你认得路的。Nǐ shuō nǐ rènde lù de. ■ *I didn't expect you would all come at the same time.* 我没有想到你们都同来。Wǒ méiyǒu xiǎngdao nǐmen dōu tóngshí lái.

young I ADJ 1 幼年的 yòunián de ■ *To me, a young elephant is the cutest thing in the world.* 对我来说，幼象是世界上最可爱的东西。Duì wǒ láishuō, yòu xiàng shì shìjièshang zuì kě'ài de dōngxi. 2 年轻的 niánqīng de ■ *"Is a man in his early thirties still young?" "It depends."* "一个三十多岁的人还年轻吗？""这要看起来。""Yí ge sānshíduō suì de rén hái niánqīng ma?" "Zhè yào kànqǐlai."
young at heart 人老心不老 rén lǎo xīn bù lǎo
II N 1 年轻人 niánqīngrén 2 仔 zǎi, 雏 chú

youngster N 孩子 háizi, 年轻人 niánqīngrén

your ADJ 你的 nǐ de, 您的 nín de, 你们的 nǐmen de ■ *Your effort is much appreciated.* 我很欣赏你们的努力。Wǒ hěn xīnshǎng nǐmen de nǔlì.

yours PRON 你的 nǐde, 您的 nín de, 你们的 nǐmen de ■ *Sorry, that's not yours, that's mine.* 对不起，这不是您的，是我的。Duìbuqǐ, zhè bú shì nín de, shì wǒ de.

yourself PRON 你自己 nǐ zìjǐ, 您自己 nín zìjǐ

yourselves PRON 你们自己 nǐmen zìjǐ ■ *You should try to resolve your differences by yourselves.* 你们应该自己设法消除分歧。Nǐmen yīnggāi zìjǐ shèfǎ xiāochú fēnqí.

youth N 1 青年时代 qīngnián shídài ■ *In his youth he lived an active and exciting life.* 他在青年时代，过着活跃而令人兴奋的生活。Tā zài qīngnián shídài, guòzhe huóyuè ér lìngrén xīngfèn de shēnghuó. 2 青春 qīngchūn ■ *Is there such a thing as the fountain of youth?* 世界上有青春泉吗？Shìjièshang yǒu qīngchūn quán ma? (→ 世界上有喝了让人长生不老的泉水吗？Shìjièshang yǒu hēle ràng rén cháng shēng bù lǎo de quánshuǐ ma?) 3 青年 qīngnián ■ *In what ways are the youth of today different from their parents?* 今天的青年和他们的父辈在哪些方面不同？Jīntiān de qīngnián hé tāmen de fùbèi zài nǎ xiē fāngmian bù tóng?

youthful ADJ 1 年轻人的 niánqīngrén de 2 富有青春活力的 fùyǒu qīngchūn huólì de

yowl v, N 大声惨叫 dàshēng cǎnjiào

yo-yo N 1 游游拉线盘 yóuyóu lāxiànpán 2 笨蛋 bèndàn, 傻瓜 shǎguā

yuck INTERJ 呸 pēi, 恶心 èxīn

Yule N 圣诞节 Shèngdànjié

yum INTERJ 好味道 hǎo wèidao, 好吃 hǎochī

yummy ADJ 好吃的 hǎochī de, 好味道的 hǎo wèidao de

yuppie N 雅皮士 yāpíshì

YWCA (= Young Women's Christian Association) ABBREV 基督教女青年会 Jīdūjiào Nǚqīngniánhuì

Z, z

zany ADJ 滑稽可笑的 huáji kěxiào de

zap V 1 用电波攻击 yòng diànbō gōngjī, 摧毁 cuīhuǐ 2 (计算机) 速递信息 (jìsuànjī) sùde xìnxī 3 用遥控器转换电视频道 yòng yáokòngqì zhuǎnhuàn diànshì píndào

zeal N 热情 rèqíng, 热忱 rèchén

zealot N 狂热分子 kuángrè fènzi

zebra N 斑马 bānmǎ [M. WD 匹 pǐ]

Zen N 禅宗 chánzōng

zenith N 顶点 dǐngdiǎn, 顶峰 dǐngfēng

zephyr N 微风 wēifēng, 和风 héfēng

zero I NUM 零 líng ■ *"How much money do you have?" "Zero dollars. I'm broke."* "你有多少钱？" "零，我现在身无分文。" "Nǐ yǒu duōshǎo qián?" "Líng, wǒ xiànzài shēn wú fēn wén."
zero growth 零增长 líng zēngzhǎng
zero hour 开始时刻 kāishǐ shíkè
II V (to zero in on sb/sth) 把注意力集中在某人／某事 bǎ zhùyìlì jízhōng zài mǒurén/mǒushì

zest N 热情 rèqíng, 热心 rèxīn

Zeus N 宙斯 (希腊神话中的众神之王) Zhòusī (Xīlà shénhuà zhōng de zhòngshén zhī wáng)

zigzag I N 之字形 zhīzìxíng, Z字形 Z zìxíng II V 曲折行进 qūzhé xíngjìn

zillion N 极大的数目 jídà de shùmù

zinc (Zn) N 锌 xīn

zip V 拉 (拉链) lā (lāliàn)
to zip sth open/close 把某物的拉链拉开／拉上 bǎ mǒuwù de lāliàn lā kāi/lā shàng
Zip your lip! 闭嘴! Bì zuǐ! 别作声! Bié zuòshēng!

zip code N 邮政编号 yóuzhèng biānhào ■ *The town with the lowest zip code in the U.S. seems to be Agawam, Massachusetts, 01001. Well, isn't it interesting!* 美国城镇中最小的邮政编号是马萨诸塞州的阿格瓦姆，01001，挺有趣的，是吗？Měiguó chéngzhèn zhōng zuì xiǎo de yóuzhèng biānhào shì Mǎsàzhūsàizhōu de Āgéwǎmǔ, líng-yāo-líng-líng-yāo, tǐng yǒuqù de, shì ma?

zip file N (计算机) 压缩文件 (jìsuànjī) yāsuō wénjiàn

zip gun N 自制手枪 zìzhì shǒuqiāng [M. WD 把 bǎ]

zipper N 拉链 lāliàn [M. WD 条 tiáo]

zodiac N 黄道带 huángdàodài, 黄道十二宫图 huángdào shí'èr gōngtú
Chinese Zodiac 属相 shǔxiang, 生肖 shēngxiào

zombie N 1 还魂尸 huánhúnshī 2 行动缓慢思维迟钝的人 xíngdòng huǎnmàn sīwéi chídùn de rén

zone N 区域 qūyù, 地带 dìdài

zoning N 划分区域 huàfēn qūyù, 分区布局 fēnqū bùjú

zoo N 动物园 dòngwùyuán ■ *The local zoo's star attraction is Lolly the polar bear cub.* 当地动物园的大明星是小北极熊洛利。Dāngdì dòngwùyuán de dà míngxīng shì xiǎo běijíxióng Luòlì.

zookeeper N 动物园饲养员 dòngwùyuán sìyǎngyuán

zoology N 动物学 dòngwùxué

zoom V 1 [汽车+] 飞速行进 [qìchē+] fēisù xíngjìn, 疾驶 jíshǐ 2 [股票+] 陡升 [gǔpiào+] dǒushēng, 猛增 měngzēng
to zoom in/out 把镜头拉近／推远 bǎ jìngtóu lājìn/tuī yuǎn

zoom lens N 可变焦距镜头 kěbiàn jiāojù jìngtóu

zucchini N 小胡瓜 xiǎohúguā [M. WD 根 gēn]

zygote N 受精卵 shòujīngluǎn

zzz N 呼呼 (的鼾声) hūhū (de hānshēng)

AS A CITY ON A HILL

DISCARD

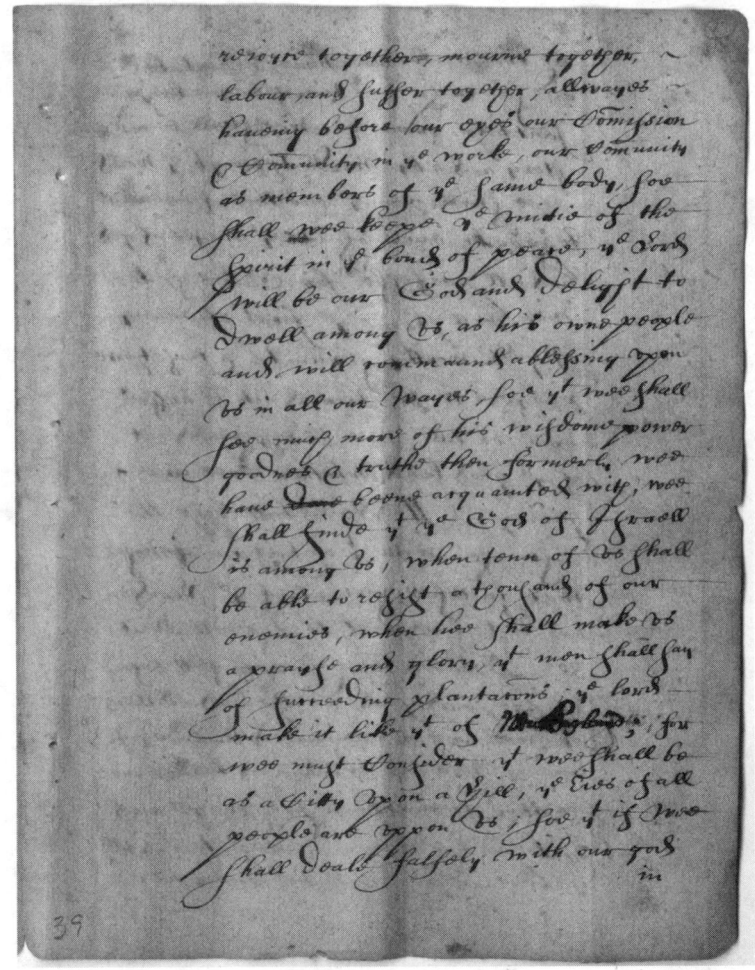

Figure 1. John Winthrop, "A Modell of Christian Charity," p. 39: "for wee must consider that wee shall be as a citty upon a hill, the eies of all people are uppon us; soe that if wee shall deale falsely with our god . . ." can be made out in the last four lines.

John Winthrop, "A Model of Christian Charity," 1630; from BV Winthrop, John; image #79597d, New-York Historical Society.

AS A CITY ON A HILL

The Story of America's Most
Famous Lay Sermon

Daniel T. Rodgers

PRINCETON UNIVERSITY PRESS
Princeton and Oxford

Copyright © 2018 by Princeton University Press

Published by Princeton University Press
41 William Street, Princeton, New Jersey 08540
6 Oxford Street, Woodstock, Oxfordshire OX20 1TR

press.princeton.edu

All Rights Reserved

LCCN 2018942281
ISBN 968-0-691-18159-2

British Library Cataloging-in-Publication Data is available

Editorial: Brigitta van Rheinberg and Amanda Peery
Production Editorial: Debbie Tegarden
Jacket design: Emily Weigel
Jacket image: "A modell of [Chris]tian charity: Written on board [the] *Arbella,* on [the]
Atlantic Ocean," John Winthrop, 1630. Courtesy of the New-York Historical Society
Production: Jacquie Poirier
Publicity: James Schneider

This book has been composed in Adobe Caslon Pro and Arno Pro

Printed on acid-free paper. ∞

Printed in the United States of America

10 9 8 7 6 5 4 3 2 1

To the memory of four of my teachers:

William G. McLoughlin
George W. Morgan
Edmund S. Morgan
C. Vann Woodward

Contents

PART III   ICON

AS A CITY ON A HILL

"The Most Famous Lay Sermon in All of American History"

F OR THE LAST SIXTY YEARS, a story has been told about the origins of America. Like many historical stories, it is told as a parable: deep and timeless continuities flow out of the specifics of time and place. It is an uplifting story and a haunting one. And it is at least half wrong.

The setting is a vessel in mid-passage on the Atlantic Ocean. The year is 1630. Fast-forward another decade and a half, and a revolution among those passengers' countrymen would turn the political and religious order of absolutist England upside down. But the voyagers aboard the *Arbella* were seeking out a new place of settlement in part because they did not believe such a striking break in human affairs was possible. Balancing hope against despair, they were headed instead for North America.

Somewhere in that mid-ocean passage, their elected governor, John Winthrop, confident and commanding in his presence, rose to deliver an address in which he outlined the purpose of their undertaking. "A Model of Christian Charity" Winthrop's text would come to be titled. A "lay sermon," historians since the middle of the

twentieth century have called it: "the most famous lay sermon in all
of American history."[1] In it Winthrop confirmed these new Americans' commitment to a new life of obedience, love, and mutual affections. He reminded them that they sailed not on their own whim or
private ambitions but under a covenant with God: a commission as
clear as God's covenant with biblical Israel. Their responsibilities to
each other were intense, and the risks of failure were, literally, terrifying. But in return, Winthrop offered a promise. If they should keep
true to their purposes they would not only overcome the hardships
the future held for them in New England. The eyes of all people would
be upon them. They would be made "a praise and glory." And they
would be "as a city upon a hill" to the world.

This story of John Winthrop's "Model of Christian Charity" has been
repeated over and over in the history books and in the civic creed of
Americans. It has been celebrated not only for its elements of drama—
dangerous ocean passage, inspired words, and exalted sense of
purpose—but as the origin story of the nation that the United States
was to become. Ronald Reagan made a sentence-long extract from
Winthrop's Model—"we shall be as a city upon a hill; the eyes of all
people are upon us"—into the signature line of his presidency.
Preached to a "little band of settlers" crowded onto the "tiny ship"
bearing them across the Atlantic, as Reagan saw the event in his mind's
eye, the Model set the vision to which "our people always have held
fast . . . since our first days as a nation"—that they were destined from
their origins to be a beacon of hope and liberty to the world, a model
to all nations. "It was right here, in the waters around us, where the
American experiment began," Barack Obama told the graduating class
at the University of Massachusetts at Boston in 2006 in the same vein.
It was right here that the earliest settlers "dreamed of building a City
upon a Hill . . . and the world watched waiting to see if this improbable idea called America would succeed."[2]

This origin story is so familiar that it barely seems to invite question. Virtually no modern high school or college textbook on American history or the American political tradition fails to mention Winthrop's words or impress upon students their enduring importance. "A Model of Christian Charity" has been heralded as the nation's "point of departure," as the "founding text in American political rhetoric," and the key script in the "founding moment" of American civic republicanism.[3] "City on a hill" is now an instantly recognizable phrase in the vernacular of American nationalism. Thousands of other lay sermons preached in a future United States would outstrip the original circulation of "A Model of Christian Charity." But Winthrop's Model is the statement that we have made foundational to "the idea called America." "In relation to the principal theme of the American mind," the immensely influential Harvard historian Perry Miller declared in 1954, "Winthrop stands at the beginning of our consciousness."[4]

There are powerful reasons behind these judgments. The sense of national mission that marks American civic-political culture, its confidence, and its fervent sense of exception from the lot of all other nations: From what source could these have flowed except from that first, origin moment, when a sense of acting on a special covenant with God became fused with the experience of America? Winthrop's "we shall be as a city upon a hill" seems to hold in its grasp what the future would bring for the United States: its magnet status for a world of immigrants, its economic ascendancy, and its rise to world leadership. The nation's moralism, its Wilsonian idealism, the endurance of its religious cultures, and its certainty that it had been granted a unique and special part in the unrolling of human history all seem presaged in Winthrop's text. Critics see less attractive traits of American national culture embedded there as well: the self-righteousness with which the Americans would roll across the continent and project their power throughout the world as if they and God were working hand in hand to expand the special promises of America. All this has been traced to the Puritan origins of America and the mission statement that John Winthrop wrote for it.

No serious observer claims that "A Model of Christian Charity" holds *all* the elements of the nation the United States would become. There would be trial and error in the American future and furious contention as well. But since the middle of the twentieth century Winthrop's Model has seemed to hold in embryo the nation's most powerful and distinctive threads. To begin at the American beginning is to begin with a text in its mid-oceanic setting, just before its words and its promise to be a "city upon a hill" would begin to be etched on the land.

Most of this is a modern invention and much of it is wrong. None of those who voyaged with John Winthrop to the Puritan settlement in New England left any record that they heard Winthrop's words in mid-passage. Most likely "A Model of Christian Charity" was never delivered as a sermon at all. Although copies of Winthrop's text circulated in England during his lifetime, by the end of the seventeenth century they had all literally vanished from memory. One of those long-forgotten copies was discovered in a bundle of old sermons and documents of New England history in 1809, but it was not put into print until 1838. And then it lapsed from sight again almost as completely. An occasional nineteenth-century historian mentioned Winthrop's "Model of Christian Charity," but most did not and none pulled it—or its "city upon a hill" line—out of the mass of other colonial American documents as especially important. Through the 1970s mention of "A Model of Christian Charity" was a hit-or-miss affair in standard histories of the United States. It was only in the decade of the 1980s, three hundred and fifty years after its writing, that the incongruously parallel work of a conservative Cold War president, Ronald Reagan, and a radical, immigrant literary scholar, Sacvan

Bercovitch, combined to make Winthrop's text and metaphor famous. "A Model of Christian Charity" is old, but its foundational status is a twentieth-century invention.

The meanings we now grasp for so eagerly in Winthrop's words are largely twentieth-century inventions as well. John Winthrop never doubted that he and his fellow New England Puritans sailed under the seal of a covenant with God. Of nothing was he more confident than that they had a key part to play in God's scheme of history. But in its own time, the call to greatness in Winthrop's "city upon a hill" line was vastly overshadowed by its reminder of the settlement project's immense vulnerability. Caution saturated his "city upon a hill" metaphor. It did not promise these incipient Americans that they were destined to be a radiant light to the world but that they would need to work out their ambitions under the world's most intense, critical scrutiny. The core theme that laced the Model's words together, from its opening statement of the mutual relations between rich and poor to its fervent closing peroration, was not nationalistic but local and intense: an insistence on love and the obligations of social solidarity that would be often sharply at odds with what capitalist America would become.

The conventional story of Winthrop's "city on a hill" text is wrong in still other ways. Its current status as a founding statement of American "exceptionalism" to the contrary, almost none of the themes that circulated through Winthrop's text were unique to the nation that would become the United States. Dreams of founding a new and purer Israel circulated all across the early modern Atlantic. During the long nineteenth-century era of economic and imperial expansion, conviction that a nation's people had been uniquely commissioned to lead God's forces of good and civilization played a bedrock role in patriotic cultures far beyond the United States. Even the idea that nations owed their essential character to a foundational moment, to a timeless and enduring origin statement, is far less unique to the United States than is typically acknowledged.

Most conspicuously of all, the phrase "city on a hill" was itself a borrowing, a repurposing for Winthrop's occasion of the one of the Bible's most familiar metaphors, which was to be repurposed hundreds of times again, in and far beyond the United States. The importance of Winthrop's "Model of Christian Charity" is not that it broached ideas and themes exceptional to the history of the United States but that it was, from the beginning, so deeply enmeshed in the world around it.

Above all, to read Winthrop's "city upon a hill" seriously we need to disentangle ourselves from the lure of simple origin stories. Texts live in and through time. A certain kind of nationalism recoils against that assumption. It strains to fix the nation to a foundational moment or proposition or text as if the *idea* of the nation—whatever its actual missteps or temporary disruptions—could be held exempt from history itself. But no words or text can be insulated from time. Their occasions change, the possibilities others see in them change, sometimes radically. Every subsequent use is by necessity a rewriting, a reinvention for new hopes, new conditions, and new contentions. To take a key historical text seriously is not to shove these afterlives aside as a debris of misreadings. It is not merely to sketch a history of "reception," "circulation," or "influence," important as these themes may be. Texts endure only through their continuous reappropriation for inescapably shifting times and purposes.

The point is true of every document a nation holds sacred. The Declaration of Independence whose words reverberate through American culture now is not the Declaration of 1776. It is not the radically different Declaration that Thomas Jefferson's political allies fashioned, taking his "all men are created equal" line out of the sidebar place it occupied in his original text and turning it into a political slogan. Nor is it the yet more sweeping Declaration that antislavery activists would make from a slaveholder's words or rights activists would construct in the twentieth century. Into our own day the Declaration of Independence has been simultaneously an object of veneration and a site for fierce, vitally important contention over the shapes and forms of justice. The "living Constitution" is, by the same token, not simply a phrase for loose constructionists. Even before its adoption, the U.S. Constitution was being reworked, its silences fleshed out, its ambiguities debated, and its elasticities contended for. Reinvention of their core texts is part of the work that nations do. There is potential chaos in this, of course. But without it there can hardly be any serious public life at all.

Pushing back against the origin myths that have obscured it, this book tells the story of the lives of a text that many twentieth-century Americans would construct to be foundational to the "idea" of America. It is a story of disappearance and revival, long absence and neglect, and successive modern reinventions.

Part I, "Text," reconstructs the meanings of Winthrop's words and metaphors in his own seventeenth-century setting. It begins with the occasion of Winthrop's writing and the key terms he injected into "A Model of Christian Charity"—city upon a hill, chosen people, covenant, charity, and history. Set against the background of an Atlantic culture filled with model cities on a hill, scores of them more prominent in their time than New England, Winthrop's phrases take on much less triumphant meanings than the standard *Arbella* story has it. "Charity" was the Model's most important keyword. For Winthrop, it meant that the rule of love and mutual obligation must take precedence above mere calculus of price and market return whenever the public weal is at risk. From what occasion did that startling premise arise and how was it worked out in the day-to-day practice of economic life?

In part II, "Nation," a second phase of the story of "A Model of Christian Charity" begins. In the late eighteenth and nineteenth centuries the text itself was all but forgotten. But as nationalism swept across Europe and the Americas, some of the themes that had lodged

a century earlier in Winthrop's text sprang into circulation all the more
vigorously. Patriotic cultures fanned desires for origin stories and
foundational texts. Empires were constructed on new convictions of
divine-historical destiny. Critics turned the chosen people idea into
a tool of dissent. African Americans carried the "city upon a hill"
metaphor to the new black republic of Liberia. On the dying fields
of World War I, where part II concludes, these globally circulating
reverberations of the covenant idea played themselves out in a key of
high tragedy.

Finally, in part III, "Icon," Winthrop's "Model of Christian Charity" and its "city upon a hill" phrase finally slips into the place that
modern nationalism had already made for it: as an invented foundation
for the new world colossus that the United States had become. Cold
War American writers made the Model into the defining document
we now take it to be. They did that in part by canonizing it and in
part by unexpectedly remaking Winthrop's New England Puritans,
whose reputation had long been buried under the burdens of their
religious intolerance and labyrinthine theology, as the nation's true
"Founders." Then, in the 1980s, Winthrop's text suddenly swept from
the domains of the scholars into the White House and the rhetorical
center of modern American politics. No presidents before Ronald
Reagan had used the phrase "city on a hill" to define the very character of the American nation and its place in the world. After Reagan,
virtually no serious political figure could escape the obligation to
quote it.

But the Model's story had not reached an end. Social scientists
attached a new term—exceptionalism—to Winthrop's text, even as the
exceptional post–World War II character of the United States was
visibly eroding beneath them. Evangelical Protestants struggled to decide if the America to which they were so deeply attached and yet
with which they were so deeply in quarrel was properly called a city
on a hill. And in 2016, the nation elected to the presidency a man who
did not like the phrase at all—who, turning the Model on its head,

made not America's shining example but rather the nation's manifold "disasters" his signature trope.

Through these shifts and turns in uses and meaning, the career of Winthrop's text runs as a skein of threads through the American past. A forgotten document would arc, much later, toward iconic status. A biblical image would become a metaphor for a settlement project, a free-floating cliché, an element in the transnationally circulating vocabulary of civic patriotism, a statement of high Cold War purpose, and the creedal foundation of a truly "exceptional" nation. Even in Winthrop's day, his "Model of Christian Charity" carried no single, stable message. "The American point of departure" would be what people would make of it. Braiding together three centuries of making and remaking, this book tells the story of a text that we think we know so well that we barely know it all it.

PART I

Text

CHAPTER I

Writing "A Model of Christian Charity"

F OR ALL THE HISTORICAL WEIGHT that has been placed
on John Winthrop's "A Model of Christian Charity," the text
itself carries an unexpectedly modest, even mysterious appearance.
No special rotunda exhibits it. Winthrop's "city upon a hill" statement
does not rise out of an underground vault each morning for display,
honored by flags and guarded by soldiers, as the Declaration of Independence did in the years of the high Cold War. The only surviving
copy is housed in the New-York Historical Society in a small archival
box, barely five by seven inches. Bound as a pamphlet, it is the
seventeenth-century version of a slim modern paperback.

At first glance, Winthrop's words seem barely touched by history's passage. The National Archives' copy of the Declaration of Independence, its ink faded with age, is now an almost completely illegible ghost of the parchment that its endorsers once signed. By
contrast, "A Model of Christian Charity," although almost a century
and a half older, initially seems immune from change. The Model's
words flow over the pages in confident lines of loops and flourishes.
The letters *s* and *f* blossom into extravagant swirls of form. The *p*'s
shoot down below the line of text like daggers. The word *the* is con-
densed into a special symbol of its own, like a character in a modern

text message. No special emphasis marks off its "city upon a hill" line, tucked into a sentence three pages from the end; but the *h* in *hill* soars and dives like an elegant bird in flight. All seems certain and dependable.

But a second glance disrupts that first impression. Marks of time and alteration, in fact, lie all over the manuscript. None of this lettering is Winthrop's own work. His handwriting was much less fluid than this and far harder to read. This is a copyist's output: a product of the system of "scribal publication" through which hand-copied editions of a seventeenth-century text were moved into circulation without the costly intermediation of a printing press.[1] How many copies this or other copyists made or how widely they were distributed we will never know, just as we will never know what Winthrop's original looked like. All these have disappeared. This is the only seventeenth-century version of the Model that has survived into our day.

The copyist's pen moves confidently across the page but then, suddenly, you see the copymaker stumble. There are places where, working too fast, the copyist left something out and came back with a caret mark to insert it. On one page most of a line is crossed out and corrected as if the copyist had momentarily mistaken his place or let her attention slip. A later hand corrects a word. Most striking of all, a whole word was washed out from the sentence just before the "city upon a hill" line. If we hold fast to our purposes, the text reads, the Lord "shall make us a praise and glory, that men shall say of succeeding plantations, the Lord make it like that of New England." But "New England," inked in by a much cruder hand, was written over top of something else. What had been blotted out so determinedly as to leave only the faintest traces? A set of scans reveal that the original word had been "Massachusetts." Why did the alteration matter so much to whoever came along later to make it? Why the hurried corrections? Why the text's blank spaces, as if the original's words, even then, could not be fully deciphered? Why the nagging mysteries?

Coming in search of origins and certainty, you find everything—text, identities, keywords, and meanings—in motion.

Motion, of course, shaped every aspect of the composition of "A Model of Christian Charity." The English in the early seventeenth century were a restlessly mobile people. London in the early modern era swelled with uprooted countryfolk. Scots and English migrants swarmed by the scores of thousands into Ireland. Across the course of the seventeenth century almost four hundred thousand English and Scots emigrants would embark for the new settlements of British North America, half of them headed for the mainland, half for the West Indies. John Winthrop's Massachusetts Bay Company took shape within this larger pattern of displacement. The Massachusetts colony was not the first deliberately planned English settlement in North America, but with almost a thousand voyagers under sail in 1630 under the moral and financial sponsorship of its godly Puritan organizers, it was the largest to date and the best organized. Over the next decade, another ten to twenty thousand English folk would follow them to raise new churches and villages and work to plow out new farms from the resistant soils of New England.[2] There would be social and political turmoil to come, too, before John Winthrop's dream of "a due form of government both civil and ecclesiastical" would be solidified.

Still, within this swirl of motion, what place did this text occupy? When and for what purposes was it written or spoken? What was its setting? We see the famous story in our mind's eye: the ship, the piously gathered people, and their collective assent to the mission that their governor, John Winthrop, spelled out for them. In our inner ear, we already hear the repercussions echoing through the centuries. We see the story of America begin. But urgently as these images press on a reader's mind, the copyist's text gives no hint of them.

The absence is striking. "Christian Charitie / A Modell hereof," the text is headed. As it was originally copied out, it carried no author, date, or context. We know that the Model was in circulation among English Puritans as early as 1635, when a friend of Winthrop's eldest son asked for a copy of "the Model of Charity" along with a half dozen other documents from the Massachusetts colony's founding.[3] We know the authorship of the "Model of Christian Charity," too, for there are enough traces from Winthrop's earlier writings to make us certain that the Model was his own work, even if it originally circulated anonymously. But for the occasion for its writing we have only the word of a second, later document, a cover sheet written in a different, much cruder hand than the copyist's.

It was the cover sheet writer who added, "Written on Board the Arrabella on the Atlantick Ocean By the Honorable John Winthrop Esq. In His passage with the great Company of Religious people of which he was the Governor, from the Island of Greate Brittaine to New-England in the North America. Anno 1630." And when this did not seem sufficient, it was the cover sheet writer who went back later in parentheses and interlining to stress that these were "Christian Tribes" of which Winthrop was the "Brave leader and famous" governor. Though it is now bound into the copyist's text, the original pamphlet did not carry this cover page. A bit of wax, the seventeenth-century equivalent of a paper clip, Ted O'Reilly, head of the Manuscript Department at the New-York Historical Society explains, stained the first page. But there is no corresponding stain on the cover sheet. The cover sheet identifying the authorship of the now "famous" Winthrop, placing the composition of the Model in the Atlantic Ocean and setting the scene that has become all but inextricable from the Model's story was the work—if not the fiction—of a later time.[4]

The first historians to take John Winthrop's "A Model of Christian Charity" seriously did not pause to question this setting of the Model's composition. Knowing what they were looking for, they found it in the cover sheet writer's "on the Atlantick Ocean" assertion. As Perry Miller, the leading mid-twentieth century scholar of New England

Puritanism, taught generations of historians to read it, "A Model of Christian Charity" was a mission statement for the society that Winthrop and his fellow voyagers would build in their new world. It stood at a doorway between mental frames, at the threshold of a new consciousness that was no longer English but on its way to becoming American. The shores of a new historical destiny lay right over the horizon. Where else could it have been written and assented to but on the open, yet undefined space of the sea: "in the broad Atlantic, halfway between the Old World and the New, [where] nothing was settled"?[5]

Others writing after Miller would draw this origin scene even more vividly and push it still closer to the moment of American arrival. One of Ronald Reagan's early speechwriters envisioned the Model delivered on the "tiny deck of the Arabella off the coast of Massachusetts" where a little band strained to hear, against "the stormy seas raging around them," what their new life had in store for them.[6] In the leading textbook account of American religious history, Jon Butler and his coauthors set the Model literally at the moment of the Winthrop fleet's entry into their new world, preached while the *Arbella* lay at anchor off the Massachusetts coast, just before its passengers disembarked into their new tasks and new identities.[7]

More recently historians have grown skeptical of the literal truth of the Model's "on the Atlantic ocean" setting. John Winthrop began writing his *Journal*, from which so much of what we know about Puritan New England derives, when he boarded the *Arbella* in the English Channel in late March 1630. Sketchy though Winthrop's subsequent entries were, he made them faithfully virtually every day. He noted the sighting of a spouting whale and the case of a maidservant who drank so much "strong water" that she almost died. He noted days in which sermons were preached and other days when both minister and people were too sick for any sermons.[8] But no hint of "A Model of Christian Charity" appears in any of Winthrop's seaboard entries. The Model's text is not wholly consistent in its allusions to time and place, but its reference to the sufferings experienced by some of our forefathers "here in England," historians now object, is hard to square with composition in the mid-Atlantic, much less just off the shores of New England.[9]

But even those who push the Model's composition point back to England, just prior to the emigrants' departure, have a hard time envisioning it as anything other than a publicly witnessed threshold utterance: the moment when, figuratively speaking, Winthrop's company of New England–bound Puritans walked through the door to the America that the Model framed for them. John Winthrop's most distinguished modern biographer candidly invents such a setting. Winthrop preached the Model, Francis Bremer writes, under the Gothic roof of the Holy Rood Church in Southampton, England, rising to do so right on the heels of John Cotton's much more widely distributed farewell sermon—though Bremer admits there is no hard evidence that any such gathering took place there, much less that Winthrop had any such part in it.[10]

In all these imagined settings, whether on the sea or in sight or smell of oceans, "A Model of Christian Charity" marked a moment of social identity's remaking. Its imagined setting, its "city upon a hill" line, and its message of a new-made people mirrored and reinforced each other. A people gather to hear a text, to embrace their mission in history, as some of their descendants would gather, almost a century and a half later, to hear a public reading of the Declaration of Independence. It is as close to a foundational scene as early American history possesses.

So runs the myth. But, in fact, by the time of the *Arbella*'s sailing "A Model of Christian Charity" had already been months in composition. Parts of it had been framed in Winthrop's mind during the fall and winter of 1629–30, well before the New England Puritans' departure in March—before it was even certain that there would be a departure at all. The Model was not written all of a piece at the doorway to America. Different audiences had heard different pieces of it. Most of Winthrop's fellow passengers to Massachusetts Bay almost certainly never heard it all. Modern readers yearn for it to lead us back to an origin point in the American experiment. But its words were not shaped in a single sitting, either at the English seaport of Southampton or in a liminal Atlantic.

Evidence for the serial process by which the words and themes of "A Model of Christian Charity" came to Winthrop lies right in the text itself. The copyist's determination not to waste paper on section breaks and section headings does not disguise the fact that the Model falls into four clearly distinct segments, only one of which looks explicitly toward America. The first and shortest of the Model's parts is its opening premise, whose utter, uncompromising certainty almost inevitably jars on modern ears: "God almighty in his most holy and wise providence hath so disposed of the condition of mankind, as in all times some must be rich, some poor, some high and eminent in power and dignity, others mean and in subjection." From that unchangeable fact of human inequality, charity descends. The Model's second part outlines the practice of that charity, drawing out of a cluster of biblical examples the demanding rules that a godly community must observe in lending, loan forgiveness, and generosity both in normal times and in times of peril. The third and longest part explains the engine of that charity: the love and sympathy that binds each one to others.

It is in its fourth part that the Model shifts abruptly in tone and language to apply these rules of heart and practice to the project at hand. As a covenanted people in a new land, where subordination of "all private respects" to "the care of the public" will be all the more required, the emigrants will live under a stricter charge of unity and love than they had ever practiced before in England. The burden of their special covenant with God swells into prominence. The voyagers' responsibilities are fearsome. They will stand, above the common lot of mankind "as a city upon a hill." "The eyes of all people are upon us."

In the last part of the Model, Winthrop's imagination leapt ahead to the settlement that he and his fellow colonizers would struggle to create. But the first three parts of the Model had already congealed in Winthrop's mind months before the voyage to New England began.

When John Winthrop wrote in the Model's opening sentence that society was so disposed that "some must be rich, some poor," he was writing as much from personal experience as from abstract social theory. That he himself belonged to the "high and eminent" fraction of humankind was beyond question. His grandfather had been a successful London clothing merchant who rose to become a master of the city's Clothworkers' Guild and, from there, had made his way into the English gentry by investing in manor properties in East Anglia. In his mid-twenties John assumed possession of his family's landholdings at Groton, England, together with its tenants and servants, its church, and the responsibilities of presiding over the manor court that went with it. He studied at Cambridge's Trinity College and at one of the Inns of Court in London. He would bring as many as eight servants with him to Massachusetts in 1630. Sometime before departure, he posed for an elegant oil portrait, his face framed by a high ruffed collar, his hand holding a silk glove.[11]

The great majority of those caught up in the currents of the new Protestant piety that swept over England in the 1610s and 1620s came from much humbler backgrounds than Winthrop. Small farmers, agricultural leaseholders, artisans, servants, and their wives and children formed the bulk of the English folk who would emigrate to New England in the 1630s. Some were drawn by promoters' promises of abundant soils and fisheries. Some were recruited for their artisan skills. Many came through family and kinship ties. Those who set the dominant tone of the emigration yearned most of all for a more pious and godly community: its churches restored to what they imagined to be Christianity's original practices, purged of the novelties of Catholic invention, and its mores purged of lawlessness and corruption.

Within these ranks, Winthrop knew that he was among those whom God had designated for power and dignity. And except for some sharp, humbling occasions, his fellow New Englanders did too. They returned Winthrop to the Massachusetts governorship by annual election twelve times from 1630 to his death in 1649.

Still, among the originators of the Massachusetts venture there were far wealthier figures than the country gentleman John Winthrop. At the social pinnacle of those who enlisted in the Puritan movement were merchants and titled aristocrats whose plans and ventures spread far beyond New England. Matthew Craddock, who preceded Winthrop as head of the Massachusetts Bay Company, had substantial investments not only in the Massachusetts project but in the Levant Company's trading operations in the Near East, the East India Company's trade with India, and the tobacco trade with the West Indies; he was to play a leading role in Parliament at the opening of the Puritan Revolution. Another Puritan grandee, the Earl of Warwick, who had been instrumental in obtaining the charter for New England, had deep investments in the East India Company and in colonization ventures in Bermuda, Virginia, and along the Nicaragua coast. He owned a fleet of West Indies–based privateering ships that regularly harassed Spain's Atlantic trading routes. All these ventures of colonization, commerce, and empire were, in his and others' minds, part of a common front against the power of global Catholicism.

Winthrop's advantage to the Massachusetts Bay Company was that, with his more modest land holdings and investments, he was willing to put all at risk and join the emigrant fleet himself. Winthrop's election to governorship of the Massachusetts Bay Company coincided with the most momentous decision the company would make: to replace the standard model of an emigrant venture governed by its London-based officers with a chartered company located in North America itself. But recruiting almost a thousand emigrants and restructuring the company's finances to match its new ambitions was an immense undertaking. Winthrop's first task as governor while still in England was to oversee a long and tortuous series of negotiations between those who had pledged to emigrate and those who had invested heavily in shares of the project but, choosing to stay behind in England, were about to forfeit any direct say over the course of the colony. Without an agreement among the company shareholders to forgive a part of their initial investments and relinquish control over the rest, the Massachusetts project was merely a pipe dream, a paper design without the financial means for its realization.

In the records of Winthrop's drawn-out efforts to conciliate both sides in the fall and winter of 1629–30 we see, written in his own hand, the same distinctive ideas and phrases that would frame the first three parts of his "Model of Christian Charity." Agreement of the major investors to forego a speedy return on their investments was the hinge of the compromise the company would reach. In early December, addressing a meeting of the company's governing body in London, Winthrop argued eloquently for the investors' concession.

"What rule must we observe in lending?" the Model was soon to ask; if it be a matter of "necessity," then "thou must lend him, *though there be danger of losing it*" (italics added). In his address to the company in December, Winthrop had urged the same point in virtually the same terms: "Why should we forbeare our money so long, etc. Answer: You have given it to God, and made such a protestation, as *if God's glory and the welfare of the plantation should require it, you would not only lend it, but lose it*."[12]

And all for what purpose?

That we "*might be all knit more nearly together in the bond of brotherly affection*," the Model declared. That "*we might be knit together in a most firm bond of love and friendship*," Winthrop had pleaded in his December address.[13]

Still more, "the eyes of all people" was already on Winthrop's mind. "*The eyes of all people are upon us*," the Model declares. "Consider your reputation, *the eyes of all the godly are upon you*," Winthrop had urged the nonemigrating investors in December. "What can you do more honorable for this city, and the Gospel which you profess, than to deny your own profit, that we may say Londoners can be willing to lose that the Gospel, etc."[14]

Structure, syntax, and phrases—the rules of lending, the knitted bonds of love and affection, the critical eyes of the godly and of the world—all moved intact from Winthrop's December plea to the company's investors into "A Model of Christian Charity." If this were not sufficient to show the extent to which the Model's major themes were already written in Winthrop's mind in the winter of 1629–30, an additional scrap of evidence leads in the same direction. On a back page of Winthrop's journal, written upside down as if Winthrop had turned the book over before he began his day-to-day entries the next spring, the *Journal's* modern editor, Richard Dunn, noticed a cryptic list of scriptural references. Though no date for the list is given, its setting is clearly the winter of 1629–30, for it is followed by notes of commercial transactions for hiring and provisioning the company's flagship that Winthrop concluded in November and December. All but one of the scriptural passages Winthrop listed there enjoined the faithful to generosity in loans and in giving, which was the primary issue on Winthrop's mind during the investors' controversy in December. Four of those passages were incorporated directly into the Model's text.[15]

Read "A Model of Christian Charity" closely, push aside our assumptions of what it must have announced and the setting in which it therefore must have announced it, and the dramatic scene of its mid-Atlantic conception evaporates. The bulk of the Model came to Winthrop as an inspiration neither at sea aboard the *Arbella* nor in a Southampton church but months earlier, amidst the commercial tensions of a London business meeting.

The last part of the Model, as even a casual reader recognizes, strikes a significantly different tone from the sections that precede it. The first three sections work out a series of static problems. What purpose did God have in making some rich and many others poor? What rules must those with means follow in giving and lending? What is the nature of the love that knits both parts together? In the last section of the Model, its subjects are now, suddenly, a people in passage. The idea of a covenant with God, rehearsed in hundreds of Protestant sermons since Calvin helped inject it into the core of Reformation theology in Geneva, becomes a special commission that the New Englanders will take with them across the seas. Moses's words as he stood in sight of the Jordan River become the emigrant Puritans' words for their own journey to a new land.

The preacherly tone intensifies: "Whatsoever we did, or ought to have done, when we lived in England, the same must we do, and more also, where we go," Winthrop urged. "We must delight in each other, make others conditions our own, rejoice together, mourn together, labor and suffer together, always having before our eyes our commission and community in the work, our community as members of the same body." If we succeed in this, God will make us "a praise and glory." And if we fail, "we shall shame the faces of many of God's worthy servants, and cause their prayers to be turned into curses upon us til we be consumed out of the good land whither we are a going."

It is this section of "A Model of Christian Charity" that seems to cry out for a public setting. In our mind's eye we see the Massachusetts-bound emigrants, clustered on a ship's deck or crowded into a church's pews, gathered around their orator-governor to confirm the heavy commission they have undertaken. Ten years earlier a much smaller band of Pilgrims had, in fact, met in such a way aboard ship, the adult men putting their hands to the document we now know as the Mayflower Compact when it became clear that they were about to be set ashore where they had no legal patent to settle and no legal right to establish a self-governing community. But did the New

England Puritans gather in any similar way around the last part of Winthrop's Model? As the Model's themes and elements were assembled in Winthrop's mind over these months, did its full text ever have a public hearing or a public setting?

The setting that comes most quickly to mind is the sermon. A "sermon" was what Perry Miller called the Model: a collective public affirmation of the errand that was to bring this fragment of Puritan England to America. That is the way collections of the key texts in American history almost universally describe the Model now. As befits the seriousness of the occasion, Winthrop stands, literally or figuratively, in the pulpit with the New England emigrants arrayed before him.

Sermons were certainly the most common occasions for public oratory that most people encountered in early seventeenth-century England. Puritans heard a lot of them: two each Sunday, another each Wednesday evening, others on fast days and, in New England, on election days as well. Yearning for holy preaching, the Massachusetts-bound voyagers might have gathered before Winthrop in that spirit.

But by early seventeenth-century Puritan understandings, "A Model of Christian Charity" was not literally a sermon. By 1630 the forms of a sermon had been carefully set down by the leading English Puritan preachers. A Puritan sermon came in sections clearly enough punctuated that listeners could outline them, as Winthrop himself did in his notes on the sermons he heard in England. Some of those structures of reasons, objections, answers, and applications Winthrop would incorporate into the Model. But most important of all, Puritan preachers began by specifying and expounding on a specific biblical text.[16] "Opening" a verse of scripture, the preachers called it. This was not a matter of aesthetics. Even more than others shaped by the Reformation, English Puritans were people of the Book. Their religious culture developed in tandem with the early modern print revolution, which for the first time poured vernacular translations of the

Bible into the hands of lay readers. Moral homilies read from the pulpit were a fixture of the established English church. But in the eyes of those drawn to the Puritan revival of piety, the point of a true sermon was not to state a moral truism but to explicate God's own authentic word. To launch that enterprise from any other ground than from an explicit text in the Bible itself would have been to fall headfirst into the pit of mere humanism.[17]

Yet "A Model of Christian Charity" opened with, and took its very frame from, a text that had no direct source in the Bible. Winthrop knew the Bible's books intimately. Early in his adulthood he had aspired briefly to the ministry. He studded his written texts, the Model included, with scriptural references. He preached himself from time to time as well, as other laymen did in early modern Puritan circles when there was a temporary shortage of properly installed ministers. The opening text of the Model—"God almighty in his most holy and wise providence hath so disposed of the condition of mankind, as in all times some must be rich, some poor, some high and eminent in power and dignity, others mean and in subjection"—reiterated a commonplace of early seventeenth-century English commentary on society and morals. But an exposition of a text that was not drawn directly from the Bible, whatever it might have been, was not what Puritans gathered to hear as a sermon.

There is a second problem with the "sermon" designation. If it was beyond the realm of possibilities for a Puritan preacher to draw his text from any source other than the Bible, it was almost equally beyond the bounds of Puritan practice to read one's sermon from a written text. A few preachers did, of course, but the sermon guides were explicit in their criticism of the practice. Effective preaching, they insisted, must speak immediately to the souls and hearts of listeners, not issue from a dry text. Although some Puritan ministers went to great lengths to memorize their sermons, much more common was preaching from notes where careful preparation and the preacher's spontaneously inspired voice could work together. The great majority of the printed sermons that are preserved from the early seventeenth century were based on sermon notes, either as the preacher offered them to a London printer or as one of his church members transcribed what she or he heard into notes to be reworked and expanded in a copyist's or printer's shop before being sent into circulation. It was an efficient process. But it means that almost none of the extant early seventeenth-century sermons are verbatim transcriptions of the preacher's actual words.[18] In the Model's case, this leaves us in a quandary. If Winthrop read the text of "A Model of Christian Charity" word for carefully chosen word, it was a failure for a sacred setting. If he delivered it as a sermon was expected to be delivered, we have only an approximate record of what he actually said.

But the greatest difficulty with the conventional image of the Model's public setting is one of size and scale. The *Mayflower* brought a little over a hundred Pilgrims across the Atlantic in a boat so small that it was barely seaworthy. The Puritan emigrants of 1630, by contrast, sailed in sixteen different ships. Altogether almost a thousand persons, drawn from over twenty different counties in England, set out under the Massachusetts Bay Company's auspices in 1630. Most sailed from Southampton, but migrants recruited from the West Country sailed separately from Plymouth. Arriving in Massachusetts where water supplies were scarce and disease a fearful threat, the New England Puritans dispersed again almost immediately. It is possible to imagine that Winthrop delivered the Model orally to some group of those bound for New England; but it impossible that the majority could have heard it.

Where does this leave the riddle of the Model's setting? Perhaps the Model was indeed delivered on board the *Arbella*. The ship carried the most prominent of the colony's initial settlers. Perhaps disputes had arisen among them or between them and their poorer fellow passengers, and Winthrop rose to meet the occasion with words drawn from a conflict that had taken place months earlier. Perhaps instead

Winthrop delivered an oral version of the text that we know as "A Model of Christian Charity" to a larger assembly of emigrants and others at Southampton, not as a sermon but as a lecture or discourse. In that case an outline of Winthrop's words might well have been noted down by one of his listeners and sent to London for expansion and copying. We would not need then to imagine emigrants who hated the dry, reading preacher listening to their own governor reading to them with his head in his text. Still, it makes the link between spoken and copied word much less firm than we imagine it to be. And even then those who sailed with the "Western fleet" would not have heard it.

But it is worth taking seriously the possibility that the cover sheet author's verb choice was right after all. "Written" on board the Arabella, the cover sheet had it: not "preached" or "spoken." The first historians to notice the Model did not call it a "sermon." To them it was a "homily," a "treatise," a "booklet." A "tract" was Samuel Eliot Morison's term at the Model's republication in 1916. The assumption that it was orally delivered is a mid-twentieth-century invention and perhaps a misleading one.[19]

Certainly the notion of a people gathered together at the brink of collectively assuming new identities as Americans is a fiction. Identity reconstruction was not the work of a moment. For the English who became New Englanders the process of supplanting old habits and self-understandings with new ones was a long and gradual one.[20] Some of the emigrants never accomplished it. Some two hundred of those who embarked on the New England–bound ships in 1630 returned to England before the year was out, discouraged by the quality of the land and the first months' devastating course of disease.[21] Many more returned in the 1640s.

Appealing though the scene may be of a people collected within the range of their governor's voice, there is even better reason to suspect that the text we know was not delivered at a public occasion at all. Winthrop's days before sailing were consumed with practical arrangements. But the week during which the *Arbella* lay off the English coast waiting for favorable winds and the next two months of ocean crossing gave Winthrop time he had not possessed once the hectic preparations for departure began. Did he spend some of those long hours and days at sea writing up from his own notes a compound of the arguments he had used during the tense weeks of negotiation over the expedition's finances, together with the things he had felt or had said on the eve of embarking?

Winthrop was an experienced writer who valued the written word. Two of his texts lodged quickly in the canon of Puritan writings: his treatise on arbitrary government and his "little speech" on liberty. Both were devised in a series of versions over time. Winthrop wrote up his thoughts on arbitrary government first as a "model," then "drew it up more at large," only to find that his opponents had circulated a copy of it anonymously before he could present it properly.[22] His little speech on liberty began as an extemporaneous address to the General Court that he subsequently revised as a "memorial" for entry into his journal. Something of the same serial process of creation might have shaped "A Model of Christian Charity." Perhaps to satisfy his own mind Winthrop gathered together his thoughts about the Massachusetts venture that had been taking form since December, wrote them out in a legible copy, and sent them back to his contacts in England late that summer, as we know he sent a bundle of other writings.[23] It would not diminish the importance of the text to Winthrop himself to admit the possibility that his fellow emigrants may never have heard the Model as we now know it.

What we can know for sure from reading the text—reading rather than weaving stories around it—is that the Model's words and themes took shape not all at once but over a span of months. They recorded not a sharp moment of clarified consciousness at a threshold to the New World, not the birth of "the idea of America," but Winthrop's response to a succession of closely packed events. From the beginning, like the copyist's text, they were words in motion.

In the course of those events the Model swept up not one motif and meaning but a cargo load of them, collected over time. The Model carried deep scars from the investors' battles. It carried an accountant's language of debt and the rules for loan forgiveness. It incorporated the language of love that early Puritan communities thought foreign to the formalistic churches' rote and ritual and that they fostered so intensely in their own congregations. It carried a yearning for obedience—for lives that would "keep his [God's] commandments and his ordinance and his laws"—and a sense of forward propulsion into a space where that obedience might be more possible to achieve. It was a text saturated with biblical language. It carried a powerful sense of collective identity and covenant bonds, language that came right to the brink of identifying Winthrop's company with the chosen people of God. It was a document of multiple intentions and multiple sources, long before those who revived it poured their own meanings into it or appropriated it for new purposes. This much we know, even if we cannot know with certainty the setting of its composition or who might have read or heard it.

In modern times we have taken "A Model of Christian Charity" as a statement of hope—which it was. Should we hold true to our part of the covenant, Winthrop's Model promises, "we shall find that the God of Israel is among us, when ten of us shall be able to resist a thousand of our enemies, when he shall make us a praise and glory, that men shall say of succeeding plantations, the Lord make it like that of Massachusetts." In the late twentieth century, that was the way Americans preferred to read it. But hope was not its only theme. In all its accreted baggage, the Model carried broad veins of doubt and caution as well.

CHAPTER 2

"We Shall Be as a City upon a Hill"

DOUBT DOES NOT FIT the standard picture of New England's Puritans. Dogmatism came easily to them. They shared a zeal for contention and a powerful streak of intolerance. Contemporaries mocked them not for their uncertainty but for their rigidity and self-righteousness. Worried that they lived like the biblical Israelites in the "fleshpots" of their own English Egypt, the leaders of the New England project yearned for stricter social mores and tighter church discipline.[1] They banished their most vocal dissenters without remorse. In portraits made of John Winthrop during his lifetime, with his steeply arched eyebrows and tightly compressed mouth, a viewer would be hard pressed to find any sign of doubt.

The line that most readers know best from "A Model of Christian Charity" has come to radiate an indomitable sense of confidence. "We shall be as a city upon a hill; the eyes of all people are upon us," Winthrop wrote as he neared the Model's climax. This was the line that was to hold Ronald Reagan's attention so vividly. A "shining" city on a hill, Reagan came to reimagine it. "In my mind," his speechwriter Peggy Noonan had Reagan say as he left the White House in 1989, Winthrop's city on a hill was "a tall, proud city built on rocks stronger than oceans, windswept, God-blessed, and teeming with people of all kinds living in harmony and peace." On her "granite ridge," her light "steady" no matter how fierce the storm, that city, America, remained steadfast. It was "still a beacon, still a magnet for all who must have freedom, for all the pilgrims from all the lost places who are hurtling through the darkness, toward home."[2]

In terms like these, "as a city on a hill" has morphed from a reference to the aspirations of the New England Puritans to a characterization of the American mission itself. A nation that in time would rivet the eyes of all people, that would claim a manifest destiny to subdue the continent and reform the world, seemed already formed in Winthrop's imagination before it began. "As a city upon a hill" contains all that most Americans now know about "A Model of Christian Charity" because it seems, prophetically, to contain all that was to come afterward.

In fact, the decision Winthrop's contemporaries made to leave their home country for North America was as steeped in doubt as in ambition. Uncertainty hung over it. And uncertainty hung over the "city on a hill" phrase as well.

A mixture of motives impelled Winthrop and his contemporaries to uproot themselves for North America. As early modern European settlements went, the Winthrop expedition was more homogenous than most. The Virginia settlement began with a hodgepodge of mutually jealous adventurers: gentlemen's sons, soldiers of fortune, artisans, youths, and laborers. Among those who boarded the *Mayflower* for Plymouth in 1620, only half were Pilgrims, subscribers to the small dissenting church that had already tried exile in Holland. The other half were "strangers," many with private interests of their own. In the Massachusetts Bay Company settlement there were strangers too, servants and indentured men who came in the employ of the company or of one of the wealthier Puritans, though they did not call the tune in the face of the leadership's passion for control. In time there would also be slaves, captured in warfare with the native peoples or African-born slaves purchased on commercial voyages to the Caribbean. Recruitment in England was regionally concentrated yet organizationally diffuse. Many of the emigrants of the 1630s came in kinship clusters or networks with a compelling preacher at their center; others were isolates drawn by word of mouth or by the company's recruitment literature. No single purpose drew them all. Still, the motives of those who formed the core of the Massachusetts Bay project can be mapped with some certainty, along with the place of the "city on a hill" motif within them.[3]

From the first, there were both publicly announced motives and privately confided ones. Converting the native peoples of the continent to Christianity was a particularly loudly advertised goal, though in practice, except for John Eliot, very few of the New England Puritans pursued it seriously. Forming a bulwark against the Catholics, Jesuits, and their armies of "antichrist" whom the English feared were about to sweep the whole continent into their possession was another prominent theme in the public arguments for emigration—though New England was much too far away from any of the territories of Spanish America to make these more than abstract talking points. The abundance of the land and sea was a third theme, heavily underscored in the company's recruitment materials. Salmon, cod, lobsters, eels, fowl, deer, fur, the cutting of masts and timber, the making of iron, fields ripe for hemp and flax, all lay waiting for settlers, it was claimed, in a cornucopia of plenty. Some certainly believed that; perhaps many hoped as much.[4]

The private reasons, however, were more agonizing and filled with doubt. The most striking remnant of these early decision-making documents is the lengthy, hand-copied "General Observations for the Plantation of New England" that circulated among the leading settlement organizers in the winter of 1629–30. Arguments and objections, followed by answers and more objections, pressed on one another. Would it not be a great wrong to strip the church and country of so many of its best people? Was it lawful to take the land that

other sons of Adam possessed as their own? Was there a clear biblical
warrant for the undertaking? Had it not gone badly with other, similar ventures, even where the soil and climate were more promising
than in New England?[5]

The last point was a weighty one. The mortality rate at the first
Virginia settlement effort had been devastating. Out of the 105 members of that expedition who arrived in the summer of 1607, only
thirty-eight were still alive in January.[6] The death rate among those
who sailed with Winthrop in 1630, while less severe, would prove
daunting enough. Some two hundred of the first year's voyagers to
Massachusetts were to die, mainly from malnutrition and disease, before their initial winter was over.[7] Despite the leadership's reassurances to themselves that there was land enough for all, and that the
natives, in any case, did not hold proper title to any of it, the New Englanders would find themselves savagely prosecuting war with one
of their native trade rivals before the decade was out. On all these
grounds, there were ample reasons for doubt.

Many of the counterarguments in favor of the New England project were themselves tinged with pessimism. Particularly prominent
was the burden of economic distress that had overwhelmed England
in the 1620s. Poor harvests and a collapse in the woolen export trade
on which the economy of East Anglia depended produced ripple effects all through the regions from which the emigration to New
England would draw. Towns reported an alarming rise in the numbers of poor and vagrant workers, far beyond what their reserved food
stocks could sustain. Even after the worst of the crisis had passed at
the decade's end, the depression's effects persisted. "Many of our
people perish for want of sustenance and employment, many others
live miserably," John Winthrop wrote explaining his decision to join
the emigration project in the fall of 1629. "The whole land of the kingdom as it is reckoned is scarce sufficient to give employment to one
half of the people: all our towns complain of the burden of poor
people and strive by all means to rid any such as they have, and to keep

off such as would come to them."[8] "This land grows weary of its inhabitants," the authors of the "Reasons to be Considered, and Objections and Answers" urged in the same vein; "all towns complain of the burden of their poor."[9] Wishing the Winthrop fleet's emigrants farewell, John Cotton offered a highly qualified assurance that "when the hive of the commonwealth is so full that tradesmen cannot live one by another but eat up one another" there was ample moral ground to leave.[10]

Winthrop's own lot was not so hard, but he, too, felt the pinch of the economic depression of the 1620s. He had a family of eight children to support on a manor that, already shrunken by division among his three adult sons, seemed to him less and less capable of bearing the costs of his household. His sons were adrift; the second of them has just squandered money in a tobacco investment in Barbados. Winthrop himself had once thought of striking out for Ireland to see if he could do better by joining the settlement of other English emigrants there. Now when an opportunity opened to leave, he felt he could not refuse it. "When a man is to wade through a deep water, there is required tallness, and if he finds it past his depth, and God open a gap another way, he may take it," he wrote.[11] More adequate "tallness" in a time of economic distress was part of the new world's promise.

In the colonists' minds, however, hard economic times could not be isolated from what many feared was England's still more terrifying fall from God's favor. Every sign of decay—the overpopulation of the countryside so that "the land groaneth under her inhabitants," the "spectacles of misery in all our streets," and the burdens of poor relief—pointed not merely to a vicious turn of the economic cycle. They were the outward marks of God's growing anger at England.[12] So were the outbreaks of plague in the English cities and the military defeats of England's Protestant allies in Bohemia, Denmark, and the German Palatinate. So were the intemperance in display and consumption at home, dishonesty and corruption in the trades, and the "licentious government" of the schools and seminaries.[13] God was leaving England, Thomas Hooker wrote on the eve of his own departure to the Netherlands in 1631. "God is packing up his Gospel, because none will buy his wares." When the fires of God's wrath at his disobedient nation should pour out upon England, Hooker warned, the Turks and infidels "shall have a cooler summer parlor in Hell than you."[14]

In the face of impending catastrophe, New England offered an escape. Who could know, but that God had carved out a small place of safety there for his godly remnant? Wrestling with the decision to stay or to leave in the spring of 1629, Winthrop wrote his wife, Margaret: "I am verily persuaded, God will bring some heavy affliction upon this land, and that speedily." But "if the Lord seeth it will be good for us, he will provide a shelter and a hiding place for us and ours as a Zoar for Lott, Sarephtah for his prophet, etc."[15] Richard Mather, the first in a family line of illustrious New England ministers, likened the move to New England to Noah, to Lot, and to the "woman" in Revelation who is given wings to fly into the wilderness "for a time" to safety.[16] To uproot oneself for New England, for many of the leaders of the expedition, was not to move *to* America but to flee *from* England, to escape the train of disasters they thought was about to overrun their home country.

Setting an ocean between themselves and England in itself promised no safety from God's wrath, even if Winthrop might have imagined for a moment huddling out of God's punishing notice in New England. God's eyes were all-seeing for orthodox Puritans; the vials of his wrath knew no continental boundaries. The shelter that escape to New England offered in its leading figures' minds was the chance to organize their worship and churches in what they imagined to be their original form and purity. They hoped to live within God's true ordinances, out from under the heavy hand and Catholic tendencies of the established English church and its bishops. They did not come for religious liberty in the sense we now understand it. They

did not come to innovate. They had come, John Cotton, the strictest
of them, wrote, to escape from innovation, to be "freed from the bondage of . . . human inventions."[17] If God's punishing hand was to pass
over New England, it would be because there, uncorrupted, his laws
would rule private and public affairs with particular visibility.

These impulses added up to no simple, unified rationale for emigration. Winthrop himself cycled through more than one of them:
anxiety about his private fortunes, fear of God's anger at a morally and
spiritually decaying England, the need for men of stature to take a
hand in the project if its success were to be insured, and the quest for
shelter in the impending providential storm.

Within this tangle of statements of motive and mission, these pleas
for money and recruits, these questions, doubts, and reassurances,
what place did a sense of being set as a beacon to the world occupy?
The idea stands out, heavily underlined in our mind's eye, in the
closing pages of "A Model of Christian Charity": "For we must consider that we shall be as a city upon a hill; the eyes of all people are
upon us." No other scrap of Puritan rhetoric has been quoted more
often in modern times than this. No other has been invested with
such heavy sense of meaning. But scour the surviving texts from the
first years of the New England settlement and you will be extremely
hard pressed to find it mentioned again. Winthrop never used the
"city upon a hill" phrase in any of his other surviving writings, private or public, before or after 1630. None of the others who emigrated in the 1630s cited the phrase among their motives for leaving
England. Not until 1646, when the eyes of Protestants everywhere
were glued not to the remote Puritan outpost in Massachusetts
but to the momentous events of a tumultuous civil war between a
Catholic-leaning king and a Puritan-dominated Parliament in
England, did a New England writer use the phrase again.[18]

There was nothing remote about the words themselves. The origins of Winthrop's "city upon a hill" phrase lay at the very heart of

biblical Christianity, engraved in the Sermon on the Mount that Jesus had delivered early in his preaching. In the book of Matthew's retelling of that sermon, it opened with a series of blessings: on the meek, the merciful, the peacemakers, the pure in heart, and the seekers of righteousness. From there Jesus's words pivoted suddenly to a note of caution. Though they would have their ultimate reward in heaven, those who followed him would find themselves on earth reviled and persecuted. And then the sermon pivoted again to reassurances. Scorned and mocked though they might be, they should rejoice and be glad. "Ye are the salt of the earth." "Ye are the light of the world. A city that is set on an hill cannot be hid." And finally: encouragement. "Neither do men light a candle and put it under a bushel, but on a candlestick, and it giveth light unto all that are in the house. Let your light so shine before men, that they may see your good works, and glorify your Father which is in heaven."[19] The long list of injunctions that forms the heart of the Sermon on the Mount immediately followed. But to the first Christian generation, outcasts in a hostile world, the motifs that saturated the "city on a hill" phrase were the themes of encouragement and comfort.

In the centuries of commentary on the Matthew text that were to follow, the "ye" in the sermon went through many metamorphoses. To most of the term's explicators, it was the church itself that stood as a city on a hill. In the polemical contests of the Reformation, Roman Catholicism's defenders would underline that institutional claim. The church of St. Peter had been from Christendom's beginning the publicly visible, earthly manifestation of the City of God, Catholic writers insisted. Rather than take refuge in man's mercurial, private conscience, the true Catholic Church had remained prominently, continuously visible to all.[20]

Puritan writers countered that the "city on a hill" stood not for the church of the popes but for the community of the godly and, above all, for the godly ministry. William Perkins, the most prominent of the English Puritan theologians, was explicit in this regard. The "ye" of the Sermon on the Mount applied to believers generally, but most particularly to the clergy who were the direct descendants of the disciples at Jesus's feet.[21] Calvin had made the same point concerning the ministry: "The eyes of all are turned upon them as upon a beacon."[22] "True ministers are like a *light that shineth to all the house*," the English Puritan theologian Richard Baxter wrote later in the century: they are *"like a City on a Hill that cannot be hid."*[23]

Other uses joined these in the phrase's circulation through Protestant England. Sometimes particularly pious places were singled out. Colchester, England, was described in the early years of the English Reformation as "like unto a city upon a hill, or as a candle upon a candlestick" for "the earnest profession of the Gospel" there. Rye was described in the 1650s as "as a city set on an hill."[24] John Milton wrote of England itself in 1641 as "holding up, as from a hill," a "light to all Christendom."[25]

A word of caution often accompanied Reformation uses of the "city on a hill" phrase. In his *Exposition on Christ's Sermon on the Mount*, Perkins took pains to warn ministers that the simile was not given to them as title of praise "but to make them acquainted with their hard condition" of prominence and exposure. In consequence of their "great and weighty calling" they could not escape being a "spectacle to all the world."[26] Lay believers bore the same double burden of honor and exposure. "Men will take notice of you, as they do of a City seated upon a Hill; if your Lives are not according to the rules of my Gospel, your Christianity, and Discipleship will soon be seen through, and you will quickly betray your *Hypocrisy*," Anthony Horneck preached on the Matthew text.[27]

But in the case of "A Model of Christian Charity," the move from glorification to warning is vastly more abrupt and the stakes of failure vastly larger. The Model gives its "city upon a hill" phrase only a sentence's pause before the voice of admonition breaks in. In one of the many jump cuts from the New to the Old Testament that occur

throughout the Model, Matthew's text is almost immediately interrupted by the harsh, terrifying warnings of the prophets. Pairing
the lines of the Model with the texts they paraphrased illustrates the
point vividly.

"For we must consider that we shall be as a city upon a hill."	*"Ye are the light of the world. A city that is set on an hill cannot be hid."* Matt. 5:14 (Geneva Bible)
"The eyes of all people are upon us, so that if we shall deal falsely with our God in this work we have undertaken, and so cause him to withdraw his present help from us, we shall be made a story and a byword through the world."	*"Then will I pluck them up by the roots out of my land which I have given them; and this house, which I have sanctified for my name, will I cast out of my sight, and will make it to be a proverb and a byword among all nations."* 2 Chron. 7:20 (King James Version)
"We shall open the mouths of enemies to speak evil of the ways of God and all professors for God's sake. We shall shame the faces of many of God's worthy servants and cause their prayers to be turned into curses upon us til we be consumed out of the good land whither we are a going."	*"When ye shall transgress the covenant of the Lord your God, which he commanded you, and shall go and serve other gods, and bow yourselves to them; then shall the wrath of the Lord wax hot against you, and ye shall perish quickly out of the good land which he hath given you."* Josh. 23:16 (Geneva Bible)

The Model's swerve from words of encouragement to visions of
shame and disaster was less head-spinning to those steeped, like Winthrop and the New England ministerial elite, in the ineradicable sinfulness of human nature than it might now seem. Exaltation of one's
place in history and in the world was an invitation to moral collapse.
Adam's expulsion from Eden, Lucifer's fall from heaven—tropes
deeply etched in Puritan consciousness—witnessed as much. Imagining that the Puritan colony in New England might actually realize

an image of perfection could not be unlinked from the anxiety of terrible failure.

But there was something more immediate than the anxieties of pride at work in the Model's reversals too: a sense that the project of emigration was a deeply precarious one, not only for those who undertook it but for those who remained behind. Launched under the scrutiny of the Puritan movement's English critics, every misstep of the Puritan experiment in New England was sure to be magnified. Its errors would bear down in shame not only on its organizers but on every English Puritan. Its mistakes would become proverbs and stories: bywords in the mouths of their enemies. The "city upon a hill" image, as it steered Winthrop's pen through these juxtapositions, was no mountaintop of faith, immune to time. Everything was conditional. In the Sermon on the Mount, "light" surrounds the "city on a hill" phrase. "Ye are the light of the world. . . . Neither do men light a candle, and put it under a bushel, but on a candlestick; and it giveth light unto all that are in the house." Winthrop's mind had run right up to those words of exaltation, but the candlestick and light motifs occur nowhere in the Model. The Model's "city upon a hill" was, before any of these, a place of exposure.

Winthrop's sense of living under the critical eyes of the world may have been heightened by his place at the head of the New England venture, but it was not his alone. In early 1632, John Winthrop Jr.'s friend Edward Howes wrote of his distress at hearing of the excessively cruel punishments that the magistrate John Endecott had imposed for scandalous speeches in Salem, Massachusetts. "If you endeavor in all mildness to do god's work, he will preserve you from all the enemies of his truth," Howes cautioned. But if not "there are here a thousand eyes watching over you to pick a hole in your coats."[28] William Fiennes, a prominent early backer of the Massachusetts Bay Company, cautioned John Cotton that he had heard more than he wished of its "rents and divisions." "It behooveth you in that place who are a city set upon a hill to use all means to prevent his [the devil's] slights and subtleties."[29] Much later at the seventeenth century's end, a bawdy, anti-Puritan dictionary of English slang listed among the synonyms of "eminence"—"to be conspicuous, as a City set on a Hill cannot be hid."[30]

It was the lot of the Puritans, and to some extent their desire as well, to live under the gaze of critics. The very name Puritan was a term of criticism that others imposed on them in critique of their excessive scrupulousness; they would have liked to have gone down in history simply as the "godly."[31] What Winthrop was reminding himself was that the New England venture might not provide a "hiding place" at all. It offered the emigrants no invulnerable refuge from their critics. It offered no refuge from their own self-scrutiny either, whose severity was to pour out from New England pulpits for the rest of the century in distress at the colony's failures and backslidings. Finally, flight from England offered no respite from the judging gaze of God. To be as a city on a hill was to live, permanently and inescapably, in the conditional tense.

Cutting the "city upon a hill" phrase down to size does not bring the motives with which the Massachusetts emigrants began their North Atlantic venture into any simple order. No people start out to live under what they imagine to be the purified ordinances of God without a prominent streak of pride—if not pride in their ability to hold themselves up to the task then, at least, pride in their ability to have discerned, better than others, what those rules required. Were the New Englanders to make good on their pledges to their God and keep his commandments and his laws, Winthrop would write in the sentences immediately preceding the Model's "city upon a hill" line, "the Lord will be our God and delight to dwell among us as his own people and will command a blessing upon us in all our ways." He will strengthen our arms against our enemies. He "shall make us a praise and glory, that men shall say of succeeding plantations, the Lord make it like that of Massachusetts." Succeeding *plantations*, Winthrop wrote, not nations: a model for future Puritan colonies. But in the context of 1630 that was ambition enough for a place in divine and human history.

There were other ways in which the New England Puritans would give their cosmic confidence more expansive expression. But in 1630, confidence and doubt, visions of new world righteousness and vivid fear that if they slipped in their part, God's anger could as easily break out in their new world hiding place as in decaying England—all these swirled together in the emigrant generation's decisions and within Winthrop's Model.

They would not *construct* a city upon a hill in North America, in Winthrop's words. They would *be* as a city upon a hill, whether they willed it or not. Repurposing the Matthew image, Winthrop drew from it a hauntingly sober moral. The eyes of all people would not be cast in simple wonder. The gaze of the Puritans' religious and political enemies in England would be on them. The eyes of God would be unrelenting. Their own consciences would be under self-examination. Out of this sense of nakedness the New England Puritans would strike out cruelly at their dissenters; their preachers would compulsively compile their sins and elaborate their faults. But they would also launch a project more open to self-criticism, even to a certain humility, than most in history's annals.

It is perhaps impossible now to put the "city upon a hill" line back into the place it occupied in Winthrop's mind. A passing trope, a fleeting biblical extract among the dozens of others that scaffold the Model, it would never occur in his writings again. But to pull it into relief, nonetheless, is not to see the sense of radiance or invulnerability that later Americans would inject into the phrase. It was a phrase for a people living under a relentless sense of scrutiny.

CHAPTER 3

A Chosen People

"**A**S A CITY UPON A HILL**"** was a line filled with ambiguity and anxiety. For a clearer measure of the pride that runs through "A Model of Christian Charity," we must go back a dozen sentences earlier. "Thus stands the cause between God and us," Winthrop had written there, as the Model moved from its opening themes to their application to the project at hand. God will expect more of us than before and more from us than from others; he will be all the more angry at our failings—all "in regard of the more near bond of marriage between him and us, wherein he hath taken us to be his after a most strict and peculiar manner."

"Taken us to be his" was no casual expression. It radiated confidence. Unlike Winthrop's onetime use of the "city upon a hill" motif, his sense of a people bound in a special relationship with God saturated the Model as it was to saturate New England preaching for a century and more to come. Like Saul on the eve of his destruction of the Amalekites, God has given us a "special commission," Winthrop wrote. "We are entered into covenant with him for this work." "We have taken out a commission," which by bringing us safely across the ocean God will "seal" and "ratify" and to which he will hold us strictly to account.

To be as a city upon a hill was a condition from which there was no escape. To act on a *commission* from God, by contrast, was a choice:

an act of the imagination weighted with self-importance. In claiming God's "seal" on their work, the Model transfigured the New Englanders' voyage from a flight to safety, as Winthrop had described it to his wife that spring, to an undertaking on God's behalf. It was to conceive of that decision as fulfilling a covenant between themselves and their God. Holding the biblical parallels close to their hearts, it was to imagine themselves as stepping into the Old Testament part of God's first chosen people. No other text from New England's first decade ran the theme of pride as close to the limits of what a godly people could imagine. And yet here, too, the edge of anxiety could not be held out of sight.

Ideas of contract and covenant were commonplace in early modern England. The great trading companies were products of contract, the Massachusetts Bay Company among them. Winthrop's legal work had immersed him in a culture of contract. English Puritans had sealed their churches by a mutual pledge among their members when they could do so without attracting the hostility of their bishops. They would apply the covenant model even more thoroughly in New England. They formed their churches by mutual covenants. They chose their ministers and other public authorities by consent, joining in a covenant with each other to serve and to obey.[1] In constructing the project for New England, Winthrop wrote in the Model, the New Englanders had drawn up the "articles" of their own intentions and pledged to hold each other to those obligations. Ladders of infinitely graded authority and status ascending from peasant to king controlled the symbolic system of orthodox England. The Puritans, by contrast, were people of contract.

But in the social contracts that seventeenth-century Puritans made with each other, God was an essential partner. New England magistrates ruled by a three-part covenant, Winthrop would later write, between the colony's freemen, the magistrates they elected, and the God whose laws they were pledged to serve. Similarly, in the covenant with which the emigrants had embarked on their project to New England, though the voyagers had drawn up their own terms, ultimately God was the empowering party. Obedience would be the rent that the emigrants would owe their divine "landlord," as John Cotton put it.[2] Joining mutually with one another, they had offered up to God the articles of their contract and received it back as their "sealed" commission.

Biblical history offered the New Englanders a wealth of examples. God's contract with Adam lay at their root, along with Adam's example of the wages of disobedience. But the stories that riveted early modern Puritan imaginations most strongly were the stories of the Israelites: the people whom God had chosen as his own, to bind in a covenant of law and obedience apart from all other people of the world. Their travails, their struggles to keep up their end of the bargain and never-ending failures to do so, their pride, their lamentations, their sense of chosenness and their fears of abandonment lay at the very heart of the Puritan leadership's understanding of history and themselves.

The Puritans' sense of living within the terms of their Bible's Old Testament flowed in part from the high drama of its stories, broadcast now to every pious reader. But it was framed, even more, by a distinctive way of thinking about history and time. An idea of human history as in constant motion, propelled ceaselessly toward the new and unexpected, was not the world in which Winthrop's contemporaries lived. They thought of historical time as a succession of already prefigured events, as a plot whose broad outlines had already been written in God's mind and intentions. That was what Puritans meant by the "designs of providence." In this reading of time and circumstances, every occurrence carried the marks of divine intention. A military victory or battlefield defeat, a stroke of good material fortune or a crippling loss, a plague or a recovery: however obscure their grounds might initially appear, all issued in one way or another from a larger cosmic purpose. Within this providentialist understanding of history, there were no accidents. Thus when a particularly profane sailor on the *Arbella* died or when Winthrop heard that a mouse had eaten through an Anglican prayer book but stopped gnawing when it reached the Gospels, he could be sure that God's hand was at work.[3]

For those who worked within the circles of John Calvin's massive influence on Reformation ways of thinking, as the English Puritans did, there was still more. The Bible, as they understood it, prefigured itself. The events of the Old Testament preenacted the events of the New; events of the present day had their prefigurements in both. To live within this sense of time, as Winthrop injected it into the Model, was to live within a nearly endless array of historical analogies.

The technical name for this way of relating the Old and New Testaments was "typology." It offered Bible-learned Protestants a technique for mapping the authority of the Hebrew and Christian scriptures onto each other as "types" and "antitypes" of the same divine script and intention. Jesus's forty days of purification in the wilderness was the antitype of the Israelites' forty years of wandering in the desert. Jonah's emergence intact from the belly of a whale was the type of the resurrected Christ, rising from the tomb and the belly of the world to heaven.[4] Typology was a way of joining the disparate books of the Bible into a single whole. When the same habits of analogical reasoning moved out into the secular world, its mappings of worldly events onto those events' biblical foreshadowings were less exact. It would be more accurate to call this worldly application of typological reasoning a way of "thinking in biblical time." But whatever we choose to call it, its impact on the experience of figures like Winthrop was foundational.

Every event for those who lived in biblical time had its scriptural analogue. Straining to parse out their right to occupy the land of New England's native inhabitants, the designers of the Massachusetts Bay project could barely get started on the question without appealing to analogies between themselves and the position of Abraham among the Sodomites, Joshua's incursion on the Canaanites' land, or Jacob's bargain with Laban.[5] To fly from a place of persecution to one of safety and potential future service: Was that not analogous to Joseph's flight from Judea or the flight of the "woman" in the book of Revelation into the wilderness?[6] When the French Catholic royal governor of Acadia showed up unexpectedly and alarmingly in Boston in 1643 with his forty troops and accompanying friars, Winthrop's journal shows a man desperately turning over the possible biblical analogues—Jehoshaphat's entertainment of Ahazia, Josiah's aid to the king of Babylon, Solomon's presents to the queen of Sheba, and so on—to help discern the analogy that would show what the colony's response should be.[7]

Within this context it was all but impossible to doubt that the chosen people of biblical Israel had their analogues somewhere in the modern world. The orthodox Christian interpretation held that all of Christendom was now the fulfillment of God's election of ancient Israel. But in a world of rising nationalisms, it was hard for persons immersed in Bible-reading cultures to resist the idea that old Israel called out for a new Israel like itself. English nationalists were particularly possessed by the new Israel theme. Assertion that God had "tied himself to this whole nation" was "a commonplace of commonplaces," the historian Michael McGiffert writes of early modern English literature. The late sixteenth-century English author and playwright John Lyly felt no blasphemy in praising God for taking special care of England "as of a new Israel, his chosen and peculiar people." At the coronation of William and Mary, England's new sovereigns were assured that "it may be affirmed without any arrogant preferring our own Nation to others, or any partiality for ourselves, in imagining that we are God's favorite People; that within this last Age . . . we have had such a Series of Deliverances, as perhaps cannot be matched in History, since that of the Israelites coming out of Egypt."[8] The same analogies saturated the language of Dutch nationalism. Dutch Calvinist preachers thanked God that you "have dealt kindly with us, even as you have led the Children of Israel from their Babylonian prison. . . . You brought us dry-footed even as the people of yore, with Moses and with Joshua, were brought to their Promised Land."[9]

Acts of colony making, too, found themselves wrapped in biblical analogies. After reading about the prospect of English settlement in Newfoundland, the Rev. Richard Eburne wrote with inspired delight in 1624, "I do thereby after a sort, as blessed Moses from Mount Nebo . . . view and behold with the eyes of my mind those goodly countries which there God doth offer to give unto us and to our seed."[10] An advocate for the colonization of the Georgia coast could not resist pointing out that it lay on the same latitude as "that promised Canaan, which was pointed out by God's own choice, to bless the labors of a favorite people."[11] If the natives should resist, another colonization advocate advised, the English should do as the Israelites had done in Canaan and expel them, for "every example in the scripture is a precept."[12] Moses searching out for more favorable lands for settlement, like Joshua's conquest of Canaan, were to those living in biblical time, transportable events—precedent and authorization for the Europeans who were now beginning to swarm into the new world.

All these were analogies and consciously held so. Press them too closely to literal truth, and one slid over the brink into blasphemy. For seventeenth-century Christian believers, there had been only one explicitly chosen people. Only the people of Moses had received their tablets of laws directly from God; only one nation had heard God's voice in a burning bush or been led by a pillar of fire. All the other peoples who claimed a parallel place in providential history had to make do with similarities. The line between likeness and outright identity was thin but important.

Indeed, a few of Winthrop's contemporaries denied the parallels with biblical Israel altogether. There were no new, chosen nations of

God in the modern world, Roger Williams, for one, objected: "The pattern of the national church of Israel was a non-such, unimitable by any civil state" in any of the nations of the present day.[13] The Plymouth colony's organizer, Robert Cushman, made the same point: "Neither is there any land or possession now, like unto the possession which the Jews had in *Canaan*. . . . We are in all places strangers and Pilgrims, travelers, and sojourners . . . our home is no where, but in the heavens."[14]

But most pressed their analogies with God's first chosen people right up to the breaking point. That number included John Winthrop. In the Model he did not explicitly declare that the New England Puritans were "chosen" by God for their part. Nowhere did he claim direct succession to the place of the biblical Israelites. Seventy-two years later, the most learned of the Boston ministers, Cotton Mather, would style Winthrop as New England's "Nehemiah," rebuilder of Jerusalem's temple.[15] But Winthrop himself never styled his New England a new Jerusalem or a New World Canaan.

Winthrop did something else in the last pages of the Model: a claiming of the Bible's words as his people's own that was, in its own way, far more remarkable. In the first sections of the Model, Winthrop's scriptural citations ranged widely through the Bible's Old and New Testaments, with Paul's injunctions to charity as their most frequent single source. But in the last pages on the "application" of these precepts to the project at hand, parallels with the chosen people of the Old Testament rushed into Winthrop's mind and imagination. Saul's failure to live up to the terms of the commission God had given him came to mind. So did God's double-edged promise to Amos: "You only have I known of all the families of the earth, therefore I will punish you for all your iniquities."[16] If the New Englanders should keep the terms of their covenant, Winthrop wrote, "we shall find that the God of Israel is among us." But if they failed, as the Bible's chosen people

had failed so often, God would make them know the price of disobedience: "We shall be made a story and a byword through the world."

The words and structure of that line were virtually a literal appropriation from Deuteronomy. There an angry Moses had warned
his people that if they should defy God's commandments yet again
they would be cursed in their lands and bodies; they would be assailed
with inflammation, pestilence, and mildews; rain would fall on them
as powder and dust; locusts would consume their trees and crops;
"and thou shalt become an astonishment, a proverb, and a byword
among all nations whither the Lord shall lead thee."[17]

In the last three pages of the Model there is hardly a sentence that
does not literally repeat or paraphrase, like this one, an Old Testament
original. If Winthrop did not have all of these committed to memory,
he surely had a Bible close at hand as he reached the Model's climax. Its final peroration comes almost word for word from Deuteronomy's record of Moses's words to his people before they were finally to cross to their promised land beyond the banks of the River
Jordan: "Behold, I have set before thee this day life and good, death
and evil."

Almost word for word, but not quite. Into the biblical text Winthrop added phrases and substitutions that possessed the text for the
New England Puritans even before they came close to possessing
their promised land. Moses had commanded his people to keep the
laws and commandments. Reiterating the Model's central theme,
Winthrop added another injunction: "*to love one another.*" Moses had
cautioned his people not to be seduced by other gods; Winthrop
raised the stakes by warning his people not to be seduced either by
other gods or by "*our pleasures and profits.*" If they fell grievously short,
Moses had warned his people that they would "surely perish . . . in the
land whither thou passeth over Jordan to possess it." Winthrop warned
they would "surely perish out of the good land whither we pass over
this vast sea to possess it."[18]

The Jordan River's transmutation into the Atlantic Ocean, casual as it may seem now, was no minor slip of the tongue. It was as if a minor player in a theater company had stepped forward to declaim Henry V's lines, editing them so that the alteration better fit his character. The Puritans believed in the sacredness of words. Above all they treasured the biblical word. They distrusted wordplay and they despised the flowery, metaphorical preaching of their non-Calvinist rivals. All this makes the conscious word-slippage in the Model all the more remarkable. Winthrop did not announce there that the Puritans were the heirs to the exclusive relationship with God that Moses's people had held. Close as he was to come in later moments, he never made that claim explicitly. God might hold multiple commissions, after all, and dwell simultaneously with many peoples. In "A Model of Christian Charity" Winthrop did something else that was, in its own way, just as hubristic. Letting the distinction between the emigrants to New England and the children of Abraham all but dissolve, he appropriated the words of the Bible's chosen people as the Puritans' own. He borrowed their speech. He voiced the part.

In all these ways, pride saturated the Model's closing section. But doubts and questions could not be left behind. For where, exactly, was the New Englanders' new Israel? The question is rarely asked, as if the answer were self-evident: in America itself. But in the early years of the New England venture that was anything but clear.

"Be not unmindful of our Jerusalem at home," John Cotton had preached to the departing Winthrop fleet.[19] Cotton's own heart, for the moment, was still in England, but the plea was not merely a personal one. The issue of England's place among the chosen people went to the core of the first New England generation's identity problem. They were leaving England, Thomas Hooker preached in defense of emigration, because God had given up on England: "God is going. His glory is departed from England." But that God had first chosen England as his special people was inextricable from the theme that

God's patience was being exhausted. Hooker's progressive verbs ("God is packing up his Gospel"), like Winthrop's (God is "turning" the "bitter cup of tribulation" on us in England), spoke to a God who had still not rescinded England as his first choice among modern nations.[20] In their formal statement of farewell to their English brethren, Winthrop and the project's leaders professed themselves "a Church springing out of your own bowels," a "weak colony from yourselves" like one of the small, distant churches Paul had planted. "Such hope and part as we have obtained in the common salvation, we have received in her [England's] bosom, and sucked from her breasts."[21]

It was safer to leave, of course, with assertions of common love than with a cleaner break. In other contexts, different terms would be more useful. Defending their invasion of Native Americans' land, the New Englanders seized on analogies with Canaan. Had not Joshua fought his way into the promised land? Had not God decimated the Canaanites with a plague, precisely like the plague that was decimating the Native American population around them?[22] Yet in still other contexts, the language of place shifted once more. New England Puritans dotted the land with settlements whose names looked back to those they left behind in England (Boston, Dorchester, Cambridge, Lynn, Weymouth), but they did not found any Canaans until the eighteenth century.

And other terms were much less prideful. "Our Macedonia," Thomas Dudley called New England in 1630; worse, the emigrants were "almost as the Egyptians" given the terrible death rate of the colony's first year.[23] Often New England writers described their land as a "wilderness"—though rarely did they mean by "wilderness" the place of purification and atonement through which Moses had led his people. Theirs was a "wilderness, where there are nothing but wild beasts and beastlike men," Winthrop wrote at a low point in the colony's fortunes.[24] "A rude and unsubdued wilderness," Richard Mather characterized Massachusetts.[25] A place of "nothing but care and temptations."[26] In terms like these, the New England Puritans stressed not their central place in providential history but their distance from it. Writing in dismay at the prospect of a revocation of the Massachusetts Bay Company's charter in 1646, the Massachusetts magistrates reminded the Commissioners for Foreign Plantations of the immense labor the New Englanders had expended in raising "these poor infant plantations" in "this remote part of the world." They hoped their arguments would prevail even if they could only plead their case as "such poor rustics as a wilderness can breed up."[27]

Every reference of this sort was a reference with a purpose. It was more strategic in petitioning the authorities at home for the New Englanders to present themselves as poor rustics than as founders of a new Israel. Winthrop came closest to equating the Massachusetts colony with God's promised land when others disparaged or threatened to desert it. When the Puritan magnate Lord Saye and Sele undertook to divert English emigrants from New England to the rival venture in the West Indies in which Saye and Sele was deeply invested, Winthrop could barely contain his anger. "How evident it was," he wrote Saye and Sele, "that God had chosen this country to plant his people in, and therefore how displeasing it would be to the Lord, and dangerous to himself, to hinder this work."[28] Saye and Sele wrote back in kind to warn Winthrop that he was verging on blasphemy by "misapply[ing] scriptures in this manner . . . by assuming . . . that there is the like call from God for your going to that part of America and fixing there, that there was for the Israelites going to the land of promise and fixing there" when good reason showed that there were better grounds for moving elsewhere. "I will grant you that God is with you, that you are glorious churches," but what grounds in scripture was there to resist the conclusion that, now that they had been carried to safety in their wilderness and "sheltered by a gracious providence" until their strength and numbers increased, they should not now move to a place of better soil and less bitter coldness where they "might do more service" than in the remote place in which they now found themselves?[29]

Winthrop's counterthrust of biblical references has not been preserved. But he took his revenge in his journal by noting that one of those who left Massachusetts for the West Indies had all his hay burned by his discontented servants and that Lord Saye and Sele and his company had ultimately lost more than 60,000 pounds on their investment when a Spanish fleet overran their colony.[30] Another scoffer, Winthrop reported with satisfaction, lost both his freedom and his fortune when, deserting Massachusetts to return home to England, he was seized as a slave by Turkish sailors.[31]

The New Englanders were as like as any others to the new Israelites of their times; at the same time they were a "people poor and contemptible" in their remote and distant wilderness. Theirs was a central act in divine and human history; theirs was an act among many in a church that was "universal without respect of countries" or "places."[32] That God was with them, those who stayed in New England did not doubt. But where else might he be? Jerusalem was also at home in England, John Cotton had reminded them. The boundaries of the territory they imagined God to have claimed for his own people were in constantly unsettled motion.

All of these issues of geographical place and stability, in conscious play in the writings of the first New England generation, muddled the analogy with God's chosen people that Winthrop's echoes of Mosaic language seemed to make so plain. Still more, if place was less certain than we have been led to expect, so was the question of time and permanence. For if God chose a place and a people, could he unchoose them? Was the act of making a chosen people irrevocable?

This was not an abstract question for the New Englanders. And their answer this time was unequivocal. They were leaving England because, having been elected by God as his own, the land's mounting sins were driving God to abandon it. In the scriptural type that was biblical Israel, God had scourged and plagued and scolded his people, but he never got around to cutting them off fully. If there was no ease in being a chosen people, in Old Testament history there was at least a stubborn fixity in it. For the chosen people living in the modern antitype of biblical Israel, by contrast, there was only conditionality. God stayed as long as his covenant was kept. Break it, and he would choose another, better people.

God could "cast off a People, and unchurch a Nation," Connecticut's founder Thomas Hooker preached. He could sue out "a bill of divorcement." He could reduce his Jerusalems to rubble and leave his Protestant churches on the continent strewn with bodies of the dead. He could say, "Ye are not my people."[33] Somewhat less harrowingly, he could remove the candlesticks from those he had once chosen. This was what Concord's minister Peter Bulkeley meant by his reference to a city upon a hill in 1646. Having pledged to be "a special people, an only people" so that there "were none like thee in all the earth," neglect of the New Englanders' covenant with God would bring all the more severe consequences. Take heed that God should not "remove thy candlestick out of the midst of thee," Bulkeley wrote, that "being now as a City upon a hill, which many seek unto, thou be left like a Beacon on the top of a mountain, desolate and forsaken."[34]

This acute sense of the conditionality of God's promises ran as an abiding thread through Puritan preaching. God planted, John Cotton preached; but an angry and disappointed God could "root you out again."[35] Winthrop underscored the point in the Model: play falsely with God and "we shall be made a story and a byword through the world." We shall "open the mouths of enemies," their curses shall turn against us, and we will be "consumed out of the good land whither we are a going."

None of this should be taken to dismiss the force of the chosen people theme in "A Model of Christian Charity." Winthrop's seizure of

Moses's lines for the New Englanders' purposes has to go down among the striking acts of the English Reformation. His appropriation of the language of God's chosen people, his repurposing of the scriptural text for the New Englanders' own circumstances, his reading of God's providential hand in every detail of their venture, his confidence that he could pierce the analogies between modern and biblical time: these were all audacious acts. Roger Williams quailed at the hubris he saw in them.

But in our certainty that we can read all the rest of the modern American nation in the closing section of the Model, we have not read it nearly as seriously as we should. To fold the history of biblical Israel into the history of New England was striking enough. But nothing in that act clarified exactly where the territory of a chosen people, now spread across an ocean, might lie. Nothing guaranteed its permanence. Nothing assured its future. Conditionality, not assurance, governed the modern life of a chosen people.

And Winthrop's colony was not alone. There were chosen peoples and sacred projects, bigger and still more confident than New England of their place in God's plan for history, all over the early modern Atlantic world.

CHAPTER 4

New England in a World of Holy Experiments

THE IMPULSE TO SET UP A NEW, purer society as an example to a misshapen world is a dream as old as humankind. Folklores have reverberated with the theme. All religious revitalization movements have been touched by it, including the Puritans'. The standing obstacle to the work of constructing new model worlds is not the limits of mind but space enough—geographical, cultural, and political—to allow the work of imagination to be put into practice. The sudden expansion of European ambitions across the Atlantic Ocean in the century and a half before the writing of "A Model of Christian Charity" was, in that regard, a transformative event. It did not inaugurate the dream of building cities on a hill for humankind to emulate. But it accelerated that impulse and scattered its products far from the remote shores of New England.

The Europeans' "discovery" of the Americas, as it is still conventionally called, does not do justice to the immense consequences of one continent's people's sudden intrusion on another. Within a generation of Christopher Columbus's first voyage, awareness that Europeans had stumbled on a hemisphere as vast as the one they thought they had already mapped and understood worked a profound impact on European consciousness. As the environmental historian Donald Worster writes, it was as if a "second earth" had floated in from outer space to embrace and suddenly double the world the Europeans knew.[1] The shock changed everything they understood about the limits of material possibilities. A radically new belief in the inexhaustible resources of the earth rushed in with profound and lasting consequences. So, still more, did a sense of the possibilities of power. For the early modern nations with seagoing capacity and experience, the dimensions across which economic and political domination could be projected expanded dramatically. The conceivable bounds of conquest, extraction, exploitation, and trade multiplied overnight. Empires were to be made in the "second earth." Populations, both slave and free, were set in global motion on a scale unknown before.

Consciousness of the sudden arrival of a second earth changed religious and historical imaginations as well. If the Americas quickly evolved into a site of war and devastating disease, gold and resource extraction, forced labor and imperial rivalry, the new American hemisphere offered an outlet for spiritual ambitions as well. The Americas became a screen for the projection of European longings: for biblical prophecies, millennial visions, utopian experiments, and models of social perfection. There had been cities on a hill in Europe before: holy undertakings, as their founders imagined them, closer to the social templates that God had mandated than the world had yet seen. But after 1492 the scale of those ambitions dramatically expanded.[2]

Reset within this context, Winthrop's Model reads differently than it does within a carefully trimmed ensemble of U.S.-focused texts or the nationalist formulas of political oratory. In an Atlantic world saturated with spiritual visions, rife with projected biblical analogues, and dotted with godly experiments, what is most striking is not the audacity of the New England project but how much more common its impulse was than exceptionalist American history has portrayed it—and how much more distant from the attention of the world it lay than the prouder and more visible Zions elsewhere.

In this cascade of holy experiments, the Spanish seized the promise of the second earth first. For the first two centuries after Columbus's landfall, the preponderance of power was theirs. Appropriating the continents' main sources of human and material wealth early, they were soon extracting resources from the Americas on a scale virtually no empire had enjoyed before them. Greed, cruelty, and violence shaped those processes from the very beginning. Gold, sugar, and slaves were packed aboard the ships sailing to and from Spanish America, along with armies of mercenary soldiers and imperial administrators.

But partly because of their amazement at Spain's providential turn of fortune, annalists of the Spanish conquest almost immediately saturated it with scriptural and prophetic meaning. Like the New England elite over a century later, they could barely understand the new hemisphere outside the types and prophecies of the Bible. For some, the Americas were the new Canaan that had been promised to God's chosen people. For others, they held out hopes of fallen man's return to paradise. Still others imagined the Americas were destined to be the site of the world's last, apocalyptic battle between the forces of God and Satan at the terrifying end of which New Jerusalem might descend from the heavens into its midst.[3] Through speculative analogies like these, John Phelan writes, Spanish publicists enveloped their overseas empire with a "huge corpus of political-ecclesiastical theory."[4]

Columbus was one of the first to see holy visions in the New World. He was a man whose mind was drenched with gold fever, though never solely for riches' sake. "In carrying out the enterprise of the Indies, I was served neither by reason, nor by mathematics, nor by world map; simply, what Isaiah said was fulfilled," he would later (and only partly disingenuously) justify his work.[5] With the riches he hoped would flow from the Americas, Columbus urged, the

crusaders' dream of conquering Jerusalem could at last succeed and
the millennium brought that much closer at hand. When that first
vision failed, Columbus imagined on his last voyage an even more
startling one: that he had seen off the coast of the Americas the waters
of paradise itself, flowing from Eden's gates into the sea.

"To venture into the attitudinal dimensions" of Columbus's life,
Leonard Sweet wrote years ago, "is to take a medieval journey into
mysticisms, dreams, visions, poetry, monasticism, crusading ideology,
prophecies, messianic illusions, apocalypticism, and millennialism."[6]
Modern scholars would add heavy doses of economic ambition, technological skill, and Renaissance rationality to that jumble as well.
But they were not Columbus's alone. Sacred and secular ambitions
swirled together in mixtures whose ingredients circulated across the
hemispheres.

The Franciscan friars, who first arrived in 1524, were particularly
fervent carriers of biblical ambitions into the Americas. Like the English Puritans a century later, they lived in a world of scriptural analogies and providential anticipations, where sacred and human history
flowed interchangeably into each other. The Americas gave them an
extraordinary new field of ambition. Encountering an unexpected
hemisphere of persons outside the bounds of Christian faith, early
Franciscan missionaries swelled with visions of a mass conversion of
the continent's native peoples, at whose climax the rush to sacred
end-time would surely begin. At their high point, the Franciscans
claimed to be converting forty thousand persons a week in the "new
Canaan" of America. "Oh Mexico! . . . Your fame will rightly fly
abroad," the Franciscans' most ardent publicist enthused. "Then you
were a Babylon, full of confusion and evil; now you are another
Jerusalem, mother of provinces and kingdoms."[7]

Others dreamed of rebuilding the physical outlines of Jerusalem
in the Americas. The Spanish conquerors planted four-square, grid-
ded cities across their New World empire, in part because their
rectilinear order made land easier to survey, allot, and defend, but

also because, in the minds of many Spanish American city designers, their checkerboard layouts were thought to mirror the biblical "type" of Moses's army's encampments in the wilderness. With similar analogues in mind, the most ambitious of the Spanish American church builders took their plans from models that they imagined replicated, with pious precision, the scale and proportions of the temple Ezekiel had envisioned for Jerusalem itself.[8]

This sense of anticipating or recapitulating sacred history was not an alternative vision to the greed and enormously destructive violence that these same conquerors brought to the Americas. All it took to condone massive violence against the natives was a slip of the imagination so that the native people, who were the continent's most puzzling anomaly since the Bible writers seemed to have so little inkling of them, could shift from being potential Christian converts to rebel tribes that had been tossed out of God's covenant, or, worse, devils: armies of Satan whom it was a glory and a pleasure to murder. Even William Bradford of the Pilgrim settlement at Plymouth, far less full of providential self-confidence than Winthrop, could write of the massacre of four hundred Pequod natives, burned, slain with swords, or hacked to pieces: "It was a fearful sight to see them thus frying in the fire . . . horrible was the stink and scent thereof; but the victory seemed a sweet sacrifice, and they [the Pilgrims] gave the praise thereof to God, who had wrought so wonderfully for them."[9] There was nothing inherently gentle in imagining oneself in the vanguard of sacred time and space. What was all but inescapable was the colonizers' sense of acting a pivotal part in providential history, where the sacred and the secular melded into one.

Along with visions of holy place and time came ambitions to construct model societies in miniature: templates for a better world. These experiments in godly social engineering found their niche in the peripheries of Spanish America rather than its urban centers, its silver-mining cores, or its great agricultural *encomiendas*—just as the

New England Puritans found their niche on an outer edge of the British Atlantic. But the seriousness of these ambitions to set a new pattern for human society cannot be discounted. A particularly well-documented case was the work of Vasco de Quiroga, bishop of Michoacán in sixteenth-century Mexico. A prominent figure in the judiciary establishment in New Spain who had read Thomas More's *Utopia*, de Quiroga set out to construct Utopia's real-world analogues with Native American inhabitants. Communally owned property, rotation between farm and urban labor, simple clothing, and a limited form of representative government formed its ingredients. The still more famous Dominican defender of Native Americans against Spanish American slave raiders, Bartolomé de las Casas, constructed a similar venture in what is now present-day Guatemala in the mid-sixteenth century. First burning the existing native dwellings and sacred sites to cleanse the way, he replaced them with a plan far closer to a holy ideal than the straggling villages that would characterize New England until the eighteenth century: church and community buildings, straight streets, and central plaza looking straight up to the heavens.[10]

The most famous of these New World Zions was the work of the Jesuits in seventeenth- and eighteenth-century Paraguay. Begun almost contemporaneously with the Puritan settlement of New England, the Jesuit missionaries constructed a network of some thirty precisely planned villages for Native American converts. The "Guarani republic," some of its admirers called it. The Jesuit missions were laid out, all on the same model, on a grid with a church and huge public plaza at their center. Within them, their Native American inhabitants were not only to be converted to Christianity but disciplined to European-style civilization. Mills, granaries, butcher shops, foundries, and common fields for the production of livestock, cotton, wool, and tea undergirded their economies. Hospitals, printing presses, and schools for trade education and literacy reeducated bodies and minds. Discipline was intensive and inescapable. Drummers awakened the mission populations each morning. Medical aides checked each household every day for signs of sickness. Daily attendance at Mass was mandatory. Sunday afternoons were punctuated by dances, games, theatrical performances, or a parade.[11]

The scale of the Jesuits' project in Paraguay was as striking as the elaborate cords of discipline it wrapped around its inhabitants. The largest of the missions held a population one and a half times the size of Boston in the 1680s. All told 140,000 persons, six times the total population of New England at the time of Winthrop's death, lived in one of the Paraguay missions at the system's height. Their central churches grew increasingly grand and ornate, covered with gold leaf and ornament, the largest capable of holding up to six thousand persons. Except for the Guarani language, which the Jesuit administrators assiduously preserved, the project was premised on a deliberate destruction of Native American culture. At the same time, it offered highly vulnerable native populations ("this nation of Israel," one of the mission superintendents called them) a refuge from the slavers and labor-greedy *encomenderos* who preyed on them.[12]

The Jesuits did not advertise their Guarani settlements with the phrase "cities on a hill." But like las Casas and de Quiroga they advertised their sacred and moral ambitions far more aggressively than the New England Puritans. Voltaire knew and wrote admiringly of them. So did other prominent writers of the day.[13] Ultimately the Spanish Crown's expulsion of the Jesuits from Spanish America in 1767 broke the system the Paraguay missionaries had labored to create. But in terms of reputation, they were the most prominent examples of the impulse to create new world models of piety and virtue that John Winthrop's day contained.

There was a second godly experiment much better known in New England and even more visible to the early modern world. That was the Dutch Republic, the most gloriously successful combination of wealth, power, and Calvinist-Puritan piety that the seventeenth century afforded. The Massachusetts colony paled in comparison.

The Dutch Republic was not a New World entity, but the New World was key to its fortunes. Dutch merchants drew their wealth from the sea, tapping the long-distance trade of Asia and the Americas. By the end of the seventeenth century, the commercial ship tonnage owned by Dutch investors exceeded that of all of its European competitors combined.[14] Dutch vessels reached out to India, China, Africa, the West Indies, and Brazil carrying spices, sugar, slaves, and other trade goods. In turn, the riches that poured into the Netherlands from these enterprises underwrote one of the most striking flowerings of art, science, and learning in early modern Europe.

The Dutch bourgeoisie built not only a world of wealth and culture but one of the most open societies in Europe. In a world where monarchy was the nearly unbroken rule, mid-seventeenth century Holland was a republic. Although Catholics still suffered church and civil liabilities under the United Provinces' proudly Protestant civic culture, the Dutch Republic came closer to a working model of religious toleration in the early seventeenth century than any other major power of its day. The New England partisan Edward Johnson might deride the Dutch confusion of sects and churches as a "hods-podge, the great mingle-mangle of Religion," but Holland's openness to religious nonconformity made it a magnet for Protestant dissenters.[15] The Pilgrims' flight to New England after their unhappy stay in Holland in 1607–1620 was an exception to the larger pattern. During a single six-month period in 1637, twice as many English emigrants left the port of Yarmouth, the principal doorway from Puritan-dominated East Anglia, for the Netherlands as left for New England.[16]

And nowhere else, in either the old hemisphere or the new, did the Calvinistic language of a chosen people in covenant with their God reverberate so strongly. "Every Sunday (at least) a cascade of rhetoric would crash down from the pulpit, invoking the destiny of the Hebrews as though the congregation were itself a tribe of Israel," the chronicler of the Dutch Republic's golden age Simon Schama writes. God had brought them out of their captivity to the Spanish Crown, "even as the people of yore, with Moses and with Joshua, were brought to their Promised land . . . even as you have led the Children of Israel from their Babylonian prison." Now to the world the Dutch Republic offered a model. "Lines dividing history and scripture dissolved as the meaning of Dutch independence and power was attributed to the providential selection of a new people to be as a light unto the nations," Schama writes.[17] Ordeal, exodus, and redemption: the covenantal promise of a chosen people and the providential blessings of wealth, power, and civilization—these were the themes of seventeenth-century Dutch republican culture, broadcast loudly and unabashedly to the world.

Like most such experiments, the Dutch experiment in godly republicanism was not ultimately to last. Caught up in war and the imperial rivalries that its prominence on the global stage made all but inescapable, the United Provinces found itself saddled with an imposed, de facto monarch in the 1670s and saw its wealth and power slip in the decades afterward. But in Winthrop's generation of the early seventeenth century, the Calvinist Netherlands was the most luminous and important Protestant "city on a hill" in the early modern world. On a continent riddled with privilege, intolerance, and violence, Schama writes, "the Dutch Republic was the Great Seventeenth-Century Exception."[18]

Still nearer at hand by the end of the seventeenth century was William Penn's "holy experiment" three hundred miles to the south of Boston. Fond as Quakers were of the "city on a hill" motif in their own writing as a constant reminder to themselves that their faith should be a model to others, Penn did not use the phrase in his advertisements for his colony along the Delaware River. Nor did he employ the New Jerusalem motif. But that Penn hoped that from his design

would emerge not only a refuge for his fellow Quakers but a more perfect society than the world had ever seen brought to practical realization before was not in doubt. Penn's hope for his colony was
nothing less than that there, as he put it, "an example may be set up
to the nations" of the world.[19]

At its material base Pennsylvania was an economic venture. Dependent on recouping his costs through land sales, Penn dispatched
agents throughout Britain, Ireland, and the Protestant German states
to find hard-working husbandmen and craftsmen seeking the "improvement of their own happiness." Fertile soil and "sober and free
men," Penn promised, would together produce a diffused general
wealth unknown anywhere in Europe. To England, Pennsylvania offered an advantage as well, Penn urged, as a safety valve against the
influx of country folk into the already swarming English cities. None
of the other colony founders worked in an idiom of market rationality as direct as Penn's.[20]

But the model-society theme was as fully present in Penn's project as in the gilded churches of Jesuit Paraguay. By the colony's founding in the 1680s, the religious radicalism of Quakerism's early days
had begun to wane. The zeal for disruption that had landed Penn in
an English jail for open-air preaching and that sealed Mary Dyer's
hanging in Boston in 1660 for defiance of the authorities had begun
to give way to a more ordered imperative of inner self-control. A
peaceable, tolerant beacon to a strife-ridden world was the Penn colony's promise. Pennsylvania's holiness was not to be measured in
religious orthodoxy but its fostering of a more "brotherly" way of life
than any society had realized before it. Nowhere else in greater Britain and its empire were the ideals we now associate with the promise
of contemporary America as strongly or clearly pronounced as in
Penn's colony: self-government, economic self-advancement, the
rewards of hard work and honest trade, eagerness for new immigrants,
truthfulness in commerce, fair dealings with the native peoples,
widely diffused education, and religious toleration.

It was Penn's vision, not Winthrop's, that carried the promise of British America to its most ardent European admirers. Voltaire knew of Penn's work and wrote glowingly of it as a "new spectacle to the world."[21] Popular versions of that same reputation made Pennsylvania a magnet for the economically ambitious and for religious nonconformists throughout northern Europe. Where New England's inmigration flows stagnated after 1640, Pennsylvania swelled with immigrants. Between 1700 and 1760, the colony's population grew at a rate four and a half times that of Massachusetts.[22] Not even the Dutch Republic opened the gates of religious and ethnic toleration wider than did Penn's Pennsylvania.

The bourgeois society that the Quaker merchant elite erected on Penn's initial plan was not to everyone's taste. Although armored by their plain dress, plain manners, and not-so-plain sense of moral superiority, the Quakers' ability to set the moral and political tone of their colony proved, in the end, insufficient. Class and ethnic divisions opened up in eighteenth-century Pennsylvania as they did elsewhere. Penn himself soon lost control of his colony and, ultimately, his fortune in the manipulations of some of those around him. Still, however imperfectly realized, Penn's vision of the moral possibilities of America cast a light far broader through the eighteenth century than any of the other English-speaking outposts in the Atlantic world.

Between these models of piety there were profound differences. Early seventeenth-century Franciscans saw their mission as hastening history to its divinely appointed end. However much they looked backward to Canaan and Jerusalem they were, still more, agents of the millennium. The Jesuit creators of the Guarani republic understood their core mission differently. Skeptical of the Franciscans' theater of mass conversion, they saw their part in history's providential design as the painstaking reshaping of the bodies and souls of others. The Dutch made their republic into a glorious advertisement of the material and cultural rewards that God could give his specially chosen people. Quaker Pennsylvania was an experiment in precisely the premise that John Winthrop had set out to refute in the opening line of "A Model of Christian Charity": that God had intended a far greater equality between peoples than humans had tried yet. The New England Puritan elite projected its sense of mission, above all, inward: into management of its people's own inner weaknesses. Keeping the ordinances of faith and church practice as God had commanded them was, in New England's first half century, the ministerial and magisterial elite's overriding task. What these ventures held in common was hope that they stood on the rim of new sacred and human possibilities, that they might offer the world a new template for religious and social life.

There were good reasons for the New England Puritans to be more guarded in their self-advertisement than other builders of new Zions in the Americas. Presiding over an anomaly in English law and church order, the leaders of the Massachusetts colony could not escape the fear that conspicuousness might be their downfall. They had jury-rigged a commercial company charter into a grant of self-government. They had rewritten long-standing English liberties. Radically remaking the governance of their churches to give their congregations roles that in England only bishops wielded, it was all the more important for them to insist that they had not actually broken with the English church at all. Too much advertisement of their separate way risked having all this pulled out from under them. Better to carry themselves circumspectly than to flaunt their innovations too boldly, particularly in the first, fragile decades of the Massachusetts venture.

Still, read in these contexts, the words Winthrop chose for the Model take on a sharply qualified meaning. New England might set the pattern for "succeeding plantations," as the Model put it, but not, as the phrase tacitly admitted, a pattern for the world. The eyes of all people would be upon the New England Puritans' project, but less in admiration than in skeptical anticipation of its missteps. The God at whose call they were undertaking their venture was, at the same time, the God whose power to punish, to make them a story and a byword, could never be expelled from mind.

Pride, too, undergirded the New England experiment. The New Englanders were the people of Exodus and Isaiah as well as persons in search of a sheltered cove in a world at storm. But in an era of holy visions and on a continent dotted with chosen peoples' cities upon a hill, there is no missing the relative modesty of the Model's claims. In a new world full of social-religious ambitions, the Model offered an American Zion not more bold—as American histories typically portray it—but more timid and inward-looking than many.

CHAPTER 5

Left All Alone in America

IN 1640, TEN YEARS AFTER Boston's founding, a new wave of enthusiasm flooded in on Puritans in Old and New England. Winthrop's "Model of Christian Charity" had reflected a mood of deep discouragement about England's future. A new monarch openly hostile to further Protestant innovations, a new bishop of London determined to force dissenting clergy into line, and a steady reimposition of Catholic liturgical practices into the churches had made "godly" Protestants less and less confident that the Reformation could be sustained in England. To persons of this persuasion, New England in the 1630s had offered a double refuge: shelter from the growing pressure on religious dissidents in England, and, still more, a hiding place from the terrible punishments they were sure that God would rain down on England in fury at his once chosen people.

Then in the 1640s the circumstances in which the Model had been written dramatically changed. In England, the Puritans' sense of despair suddenly lifted. Charles I, forced to call a Parliament to raise funds to suppress resistance in Scotland, suddenly found himself overwhelmed by rebellion at home. Within a year, Parliament had clapped the Puritans' chief nemesis, Archbishop Laud, in the Tower of London. Outright civil war broke out between rival armies of the Crown, the English Parliament, and the Scots. The underground debates of the 1630s over the proper organization of the church and liturgy erupted into open, continuous, and searching dispute. By 1646 the office of bishop had been abolished outright. Charles I, his military forces routed and his own attempt at escape foiled, was tried for treason in early 1649. Within a month he had followed Laud under the executioner's axe.

For the next eleven years a godly commonwealth ruled in England. The Puritan-dominated Parliament seized the reins of power first and then, when it faltered, lost them to the Puritan-dominated army, led by its military hero and the nation's Protector, Oliver Cromwell. Prayer-book-reading ministers were rooted out of their offices. A corps of major-generals was dispatched to try to bring English popular culture to heel by suppressing drunkenness, idleness, gambling, cock-fighting, unlicensed alehouse keeping, and every form of Sabbath breaking. A rhetoric of providential destiny now reverberated with a force unmatched in colonial Boston from English pulpits. "If a stranger ask, what news in England?," Thomas Coleman preached to the Westminster Assembly of ministers in 1643, "why the best news that ever was, God had established Sion . . . and as for his people, there is a new world with them."[1] Cromwell a decade later described England in the same way: "A People that are to God as 'the apple of His eye' . . . a People under His safety and protection. . . . You have of this no parallel; no, not in all the world."[2]

A new and purified Israel seemed close at hand in England with ambitions that eclipsed anything that Winthrop's New Englanders had dreamed of. Cromwell's military forces crushed Catholic Ireland and launched an ambitious attack on Catholic Spain's trade routes through the West Indies. And then it all fell apart in war and factionalism. A new king was installed; the old church forms were restored. The "godly" abandoned their bid to dictate the terms of English politics and popular culture and much of their ambition to do so. But for twenty years the drama of the English Revolution riveted the attention of Protestants everywhere.

Under the impact of these events, New England slipped, by contrast, almost completely into irrelevance. A sense of acting a specially chosen part in history had pervaded Winthrop's Model. He had written with certainty of his people's special commission from God for the work they were undertaking. He had allowed himself to come right to the brink of conflating their history with the history of biblical Israel. He had sensed the "eyes of all people" upon them. But now the eyes of the world were elsewhere. In a world of revolutionary ambitions, New England had become by the 1660s a backwater. Even the efforts of its elite to hold firm the bounds of religious orthodoxy were increasingly out of step with the New Englanders' closest allies in England.

And yet one would have barely discerned the region's shifts in status from the tropes of self-importance that swelled into prominence in the pulpit literature of late seventeenth-century New England. The biblical analogies that the Model had implied now poured as certainties from the New England pulpits. Talk of a New Israel in their midst slipped into more and more of the ministers' texts. The irony of the rhetoric of a chosen people illuminating the world now linked so strongly with Winthrop and his "Model of Christian Charity" was that it flourished not when the New England project was new. It blossomed most exuberantly when the region found itself most isolated from the world.

A sense that New England's fate was intertwined with the international fate of Reformed Protestantism had marked the colony's elite from the beginning. In the 1630s English friends kept John Winthrop's eldest son steadily supplied with news as the armies of rival Catholic and Protestant powers maneuvered across continental Europe. The Massachusetts General Court declared a day of public thanksgiving in 1632 to celebrate the Swedish army's success in bringing relief to the embattled Protestants in Germany and the

Palatinate. A general fast was held in early 1637 in public sorrow for the "miserable estate" of the German Protestants and a thanksgiving day in September to give thanks that their military situation had improved.[3] International reports flowed into New England through a constant stream of exiles.[4]

But none of this compared with the dramatic consequences of the convening of the English Parliament in 1640. The first and most disruptive result was the almost immediate cessation of the flow of new immigrants to New England. At a minimum, some eleven thousand English folk had emigrated to New England in the 1630s. Less than half that number came in the 1640s and even fewer in the 1650s.[5] In the New England port towns, whose economies had essentially been sustained by the new money for supplies and land that a steady stream of newcomers provided, disruption of in-migration triggered a quick and severe economic depression. Cash and credit dried up. Prices soared.

More striking still was the backflow of migration to England. Some of those who left New England for home were pushed by the economic hardships of the 1640s. But the surge of returning emigrants after the surrender of the king in 1646 points to a different cause: a sense that there was now more room for personal and political ambition in England than in its New English outpost. Susan Moore, who has studied the question most closely, has estimated that perhaps one out of every five New Englanders pulled up stakes for England between 1640 and 1660. Among the ministerial and merchant elite the proportions were even higher. One in three of the ministers who had sailed to New England in the 1630s returned home in the 1640s and 1650s. Of the nine graduates of Harvard College's first class of 1642, seven soon made their way to England. Out of the Harvard class of 1647, all but one left for England.[6]

Some of these back migrants leapt quickly into prominent roles in the English Revolution. Hugh Peter, one of the original investors in the Massachusetts colonization venture and minister at Salem, vaulted to influence as a charismatic army chaplain and a member of Cromwell's inner circle. Sir Henry Vane, who had replaced Winthrop for a year as the Massachusetts Bay colony's governor, quickly emerged as a leading figure in the Puritan-dominated Parliament. Three other former New Englanders served in the revolutionary Parliaments. At least ten former New Englanders earned the rank of major or higher in the parliamentary armies. One of Winthrop's own sons, who had sailed with his father on the *Arbella*, rose to the rank of colonel.[7]

Winthrop bemoaned the desertions. "Ask thy conscience," he pleaded in his journal in 1642, "if thou wouldst have plucked up thy stakes, and brought thy family 3000 miles, if thou hadst expected that all, or most, would have forsaken thee there. Ask again, what liberty thou hast towards others . . . for if one may go, another may, and so the greater part, and so church and commonwealth may be left destitute in a wilderness, exposed to misery and reproach, and all for thy ease and pleasure."[8] But even Winthrop did not deny that the main stage of providential drama had moved to England. When his son Stephen wrote that he felt "a clear providence" for staying in England where he had "found a way of Advancing God's Kingdom," his father did not rebut him.[9]

As far as most English Puritans were concerned, there was no question of the relative importance of New England and newest England. The dramatic shrinkage of new arrivals was material proof of that. Oliver Cromwell, for his part, thought the New England venture had been rendered wholly useless by the turn of events. It had been from the beginning mistakenly sited, he thought, in a place too cold, too barren, and, most importantly, too far from the front lines of the Protestant-Catholic struggle for domination. He tried hard to persuade New England's leading ministers to turn their ambitions, instead, to Ireland where there was a far more important people to subdue and colony to plant. For the rest, Cromwell would have had them move to the West Indies where there were richer crops to bring

out of the soil and where a Puritan colony, astride the trade routes
funneling the wealth of Spanish America into the supply of Catholic
armies in Europe, could be an effective base for harassment and
interception.[10]

We should not be surprised that many stayed behind. They had lands
and established livelihoods in New England. The abrupt and unan-
ticipated spinoff of events in revolutionary England was disturbing
to many. War was never far from hand. Even at its height the English
Puritans' efforts to discipline unruly English popular culture never enjoyed more than localized success.[11] If an orderly society was one's
first priority, its realization was much closer in New England, where
the structures of authority remained intact, than in England. England
after 1640 was for risk-takers. The conservative course was to stay
in America.

Still we might expect the New Englanders to have bombarded
their English brethren with advice. "A Model of Christian Charity"
seemed to have promised as much. Winthrop's generation had
amassed a decade of practical experience in the organization of church
and state polity. Fresh from the expulsion of their latest dissenters,
their leadership was not wanting in its sense of righteousness. In one
of the most famous essays ever written about the New England Puritans, the historian Perry Miller argued that ambition to remake
England in its image had been the key impulse behind the New
England project from the beginning.

In their secret heart, Miller wrote in his influential essay "Errand
into the Wilderness" in 1952, Winthrop and his colleagues knew that
theirs was "an essential maneuver in the drama of Christendom." Their
New England was not merely a place of regroupment and refuge.

> The Bay Company was not a battered remnant of suffering Sepa-
> ratists thrown up on a rocky shore; it was an organized task force
> of Christians, executing a flank attack on the corruptions of Chris-

tendom. These Puritans did not flee to America; they went in order to work out that complete reformation which was not yet accomplished in England and Europe, but which would quickly be accomplished if only the saints back there had a working model to guide them. . . . This was the large unspoken assumption in the errand of 1630: if the conscious intention were realized, not only would a federated Jehovah bless the new land, but He would bring back these temporary colonials to govern England.[12]

Most of the evidence for an "errand" this grand was the work of Miller's imagination, but it was true that New England's leading ministers initially hoped that they might advise and shape the course of the events in England. They dispatched letters, treatises, and sermons. They offered rafts of public prayers. They held official fast days for England's sake. They quarreled heatedly in print with English Puritan advocates of alternative forms of church order to theirs. In 1641, on the receipt of news of the imprisonment of Archbishop Laud ("our great enemy"), the Massachusetts General Court ordered that a three-person delegation of ministers and merchants be sent to England to congratulate it on the "happy success" of events there, to plead the reasons why the colony had fallen so badly behind in its debt payments, and to offer any advice "as it should be required, for the settling the right form of church discipline there."[13]

Through the first half of the 1640s, there is good evidence that many English Puritans were willing to look to New England for advice. In 1642 thirty-nine members of Parliament wrote to urge New England's three leading ministers to come over to help influence the framing of English church governance on New English lines. Although none of them ultimately made the journey, in the pages of English pamphlets and sermons the New England model was extensively scrutinized.[14] But if New Englanders had hoped to remake England on their own model, they did not sustain that ambition long. In the revolutionary Parliament of the 1640s, the Presbyterian party had far more supporters than did advocates of New England-style congregational autonomy. The invited New England preachers pressed the congregationalist case in writing but, sensing themselves badly outnumbered, they were reluctant to enter in person into a contest over church organization that they thought they could only lose.

Compounding the New Englanders' growing sense of isolation was the still more vexed question of the allowable limits of religious dissent. At the Puritan Revolution's outset, toleration was not its object. The project was to purify and reorganize the English church, not to let it splinter into pieces. But the very intensity of the political-spiritual struggle was not easily held in bounds. By the end of the 1640s, the "godly" were spinning off a bewildering variety of dissenting sects: baptists and anabaptists, Quakers who thought the clergy superfluous to the inner light of faith, ranters, Fifth Monarchy believers in an impending apocalypse, and more. Punishment was their lot. But within the army, where the New Englanders had their strongest allies on the church organization question, a grudging sense that a broad-tent Protestant alliance was a political necessity—perhaps even, within limits, a concession to conscience—gathered increasing strength. In 1650 Parliament acknowledged that there might be plural religious communities within each parish. In the Instrument of Government that established the Protectorate in 1653, all those "such as profess faith in God by Jesus Christ" were to be protected "in the profession of the Faith and the exercise of their religion." Catholics and blasphemers stood outside that tent. Mass imprisonment of Quakers for defiance of authority persisted. Still, modest though it was, a measure of tolerance for religious pluralism had arrived in Puritan England.[15]

The New England elite resisted. By 1645 Winthrop was already complaining in his journal about the margins of toleration that the latest books from England were defending. In the English pamphlet wars, Roger Williams held up the Massachusetts magistrates to shame for their harsh and rigid treatment of dissenters. But the "vast liberty" of the churches coming into practice in England, as Winthrop called it, did not sit well with the Model's purposes of establishing an obedient and conforming society.[16] In this collision of goals, the New Englanders' possibilities of influence quickly narrowed. In 1648, at the invitation of some of their congregationalist English allies, the New England churches sent over a systematic statement of their principles of church and state organization, prefaced by the hope that "the example of such poor outcasts as ourselves, might prevail if not with all ... yet with some or other of our brethren in England."[17] They could not have been terribly surprised that it did not.

Isolated and criticized, those who stayed behind in New England tacitly surrendered whatever hope they might have had to turn the course of English history. Prayers and fastings would be their "deadly" battle weapons, Taunton's minister William Hooke advised as early as 1645. "I know that we [in New England] are little dreamt of at this time in any part of Christendom," Hooke acknowledged, but they would wait like "bands of soldiers lying in ambush here under the fern and brushet of the Wilderness," wielding swords invisible to the eye.[18]

Nowhere in these exchanges did the New England Puritans claim that they had an exclusive and especially chosen place in God's designs that was bigger and more important than England's or that of Protestant Europe generally. Nowhere did they argue that preservation of the New England way was the fulcrum on which the political and religious fate of a tumult-filled world would turn. In 1648, distressed by the growing calls for toleration, Thomas Shepard wondered if God was about "to remove the Candlesticks" from the old England and transfer them to the new. Shepard's colleague in the New England ministry, Nathaniel Ward, wrote with more typical modesty that the New Englanders' place in the English struggle was to abide "beyond *Jordan*" and send over their "Armies of prayers" to God— and presumably to those closer to Canaan than themselves.[19] The New Englanders conceived themselves within—not detached—

from the life struggles of international Protestantism. But at a moment in the providential drama fraught with so much destiny, they had barely a foothold on the main historical stage.

With the revival of the monarchy in 1660, visions of a new Zion in England collapsed. The deflation of Puritan ambitions in England, however, brought no corresponding revival to their New English offshoot. The 1660s brought a momentary return of earlier levels of in-migration to New England; but for the next ten decades after that the net migration into New England was negative. Ambitious English emigrants streamed by the hundreds of thousands into Ireland, the West Indian sugar and slave islands, and the colonies of the Southern mainland. But New England essentially disappeared from their horizon of possibilities.[20]

New England's cherished autonomy eroded as well as the restored monarchy slowly brought New English law into conformity with English law and procedures. Though persecution of dissenters initially increased in England with the Restoration in 1660, in time pressure from a changing England overwhelmed what the founding New England generation had taken to be the essential core of its mission: to establish by its collective, undivided will, as Winthrop had put it, "a due form of government both civil and ecclesiastical." The new charter imposed by the Crown on the Massachusetts colony in 1691 ended the monopoly that church members had held since 1630 on the liberty to vote in colony-wide elections. It extended liberty of conscience to all Christians—"Papists" excluded. Over the resistance of the ministerial and magisterial elite, a limited form of religious toleration had found its way into Winthrop's covenanted community.

But insularity nonetheless remained New England's more prominent feature. Later, in the eighteenth century, New England merchants, extending their trading routes across the seas, were to knit New England back into the Atlantic world of commerce and market culture. In the late seventeenth century, however, closed in on its own peculiar political and religious order, far from the immigration routes that were each decade bringing more and more European migrants into North America, New England's marginal place in the world could not be missed even by its most articulate defenders.

And yet one would barely have gathered as much from the words of pride and compensation that poured from New England's late seventeenth-century preachers. For it was in this age of New England's isolation and obscurity that the "city on a hill" and New Israel motifs flourished most exuberantly. The terms were common enough in the language of biblical Protestantism. Typological thinking encouraged them. Looking back on New England's own history, Edward Johnson in 1654 had written of Winthrop's generation as "lights upon a hill, more obvious than the highest mountain in the world." But it was after 1660 that the terms came into their own in New England. "Let us remember (I do beseech you) that the Eyes of the World are now upon us more than ever," Increase Mather preached in 1680. "The eyes of the whole *Christian world*" are upon you; yea what is more, the eyes of *God*," Cambridge's minister, Jonathan Mitchell, extended the theme. "God forbid that, after New England has shined twenty years and more, like a light upon an hill, it should at last go out," overwhelmed by greed, trade, and blasphemy, John Norton warned.[21]

Talk of a New English "Israel" rose even more strongly in volume. "Just as God had assigned Canaan to the children of Israel," Urian Oakes maintained in 1673, so "this Wilderness was the place which God decreed to make a Canaan to you." "Here the Lord hath caused as it were *New Jerusalem* to come down from Heaven; he dwells in this place," Increase Mather assured his listeners. New England stands "in like circumstances before the Lord as Jerusalem then did: A parallel people with them, both in respect of privilege and provocation, profession and prevarication," Samuel Wakeman preached in an election-day sermon in Hartford, Connecticut, in 1685.[22]

Wakeman's last words—"provocation" and "prevarication"—were not casual add-ons. There was hardly a reference to the "New English Israel" that did not begin by tightening up the parallel between the new and old Israels as closely as possible only to drive the moral home all the more insistently: the punishments that God had poured out on his first chosen people were surely to consume New England unless its people reformed thoroughly and quickly. "That faithful City" of Jerusalem "became a harlot," Wakeman plunged ahead in his simile. And so, if our revolt from God continues, will we. "What is Jerusalem at this day, but a Miserable Town, in which there are no inhabitants but Infidels and Idolaters?" Increase Mather warned. "If the Glory has been removed from Jerusalem . . . [and] if from so many places of Europe? Is it not possible that it may be removed from New-England also?"[23]

In sermons like these, the point of emphasis in the covenant relationship was not its glory but its special demands—and the special fierceness with which failure on a chosen people's part would be punished. A covenant with God was "a covenant with conditions." "We are under a divine probation," Increase Mather preached. If a people did not return to him, "the Lord can easily remove the candlestick." Or "break" it.[24] The price of New England's special place was its special vulnerability. The greater the visibility, the greater the shame of its lapses into sin and irreligion.

Historians of New England have called this form of sermonizing the "Jeremiad." Repetition made its forms utterly familiar. New England's likeness to a new Israel ("Was there ever a place so like unto a new Jerusalem as New England hath been?")[25] and its special place in the eyes of the world opened into an agonizingly long catalogue of the sins that beset it on every side before the preachers called their people back, for one last chance, from scourge and destruction. The Jeremiad was not only the ministers' platform for reaffirming ethical and theological doctrine. It was not only their response to the devastating impact of renewed native warfare in the 1670s. It was their disciplinary instrument, their tool of popular control, the wrecking hook with which they tried, season in and season out in late seventeenth-century New England, to haul their people out of the sloughs of sin and into compliance with the increasingly isolated political and religious ordinances of New England.

Within the Jeremiad, the New England preachers' hopes for New England's enduring importance and their recognition of its practical obscurity hung in an increasingly delicate balance. "You have been as a City upon a hill (though in a remote and obscure Wilderness)," Urian Oakes preached on election day in Boston in 1673. Guided as by a pillar of cloud and fire, New Englanders had come to a place both prominent and obscure: remote from that "dear Nation [i.e., England] of which you are a part" as England had become embroiled in "distractions," war, and "alterations." In these "Chambers of Secrecy and Safety . . . in this place of Retirement and Hiding," you have endeavored to keep the purity of the faith from error, from excess liberty, and the "abomination" of toleration. We in New England have exhibited nothing less than "a little model of the Kingdom of Christ upon Earth," Oakes told his listeners.[26] But that was not a boast of influence. New England's exemplary task in the contest for God's kingdom was to keep itself apart. It was to mind its own purity lest its candle, too, go out in the gale of destruction that might yet come.

Oakes's most prominent successor in the third generation of New England preachers, Cotton Mather, shows the strain of these circumstances most acutely. The most highly educated man in his New England, an avid reader of science and contemporary English learning, Cotton Mather knew more acutely than any of his fellow preachers the marginal place of his culture in the larger world of ideas and Protestant culture. Among his hundreds of books and pamphlets, his history of New England stands out for the way he threaded the term "New English Israel" so densely through it. In his portraits New England's founders were the typological twins of biblical Israel's patriarchs. Winthrop was New England's Nehemiah, Edward Hopkins was its Solomon, Theophilus Eaton and John Davenport were as Moses and Aaron to the New Haven colony. The Pilgrims had "as plain a command of Heaven" to leave for New England "as ever their father Abraham had for his leaving the Caldean territories."[27] Evidences of divine providence, as abundant as the children of biblical Israel had ever enjoyed, marked virtually every one of Cotton Mather's pages.

But Cotton Mather could not write a history of "New-English-Israel" without stirring in an almost equally vivid strain of apology. "This little Israel," he called his people: inhabitants of "poor little New-England." He wrote for English readers situated in "the best Island of the universe" to tell them of "wonders" that had occurred on the edges of the Protestant world. He brought news from "the American strand," from "the utmost parts of the earth," from an "Indian Wilderness," from "that little country NEW-ENGLAND," from a country that might have already fulfilled the purpose it was planted for and now, its foundations "shaking," might "come to nothing" more. Perhaps all that remained would be the memories that he hoped his history might preserve.[28]

Cotton Mather's *Magnalia Christi Americana* was, for the moment, the resting place of the language of destiny that Winthrop had written into "A Model of Christian Charity." The sense of living in biblical types and time endured. References to a new Israel in America had become more frequent and overt. By Cotton Mather's generation, some New England writers had begun to hope that just before the world's great scourging a literal New Jerusalem might be let down from heaven in their midst. But millennial images of the world's end were an evasion of the New Englanders' increasingly isolated present. In truth, those who had stayed in New England had missed their moment to make a difference. They had kept themselves on the sidelines of history—closer to the purity of the first Christians, as they imagined it, but farther from the sight of any but themselves.

For those who stayed behind, reassurance that they still mattered, that they still stood, somehow, as a "city on a hill," had become a ritual of compensation. They yearned for the attention of their God; they hoped for his corrective punishment. They wielded the obligations of a visible people as a scourge against their countrymen who, they worried more and more, might be growing "sermon proof."[29] But in sober fact, they now found themselves alone in America. They talked still of their hope to be a beacon to the world. But by the end of the century, no one was watching.

CHAPTER 6

Love Is a Bond or Ligament

AD HE LIVED INTO THE 1660s, John Winthrop would probably have been disappointed by the newly marginal place of his colony on the larger Atlantic scene. But he might not have been surprised. Influence had not been foremost on Winthrop's mind as he drafted "A Model of Christian Charity." That he yearned to find his proper place in the course of providential history was patently clear. His writings on the eve of departure are filled with concern to read God's intentions in history. He longed to decipher God's plan for England, for Reformed churches all across Europe, and for the remnant that was putting in motion a voyage of escape across the Atlantic. But that he intended by sailing west to change England and the world requires a reading of the Model's words that they do not sustain. Even the theme of a chosen people freighted with the awful responsibility of their covenant with God sweeps into the Model only at its very end.

For readers who have been taught to anticipate the theme of mission as the great, overarching motif of "A Model of Christian Charity," this displacement of the expected point until the text's very end still comes as a shock. Nowhere in the Model's first thirty pages is the idea of an errand into destiny anywhere anticipated. From Winthrop's opening sentence until the "application of this discourse to the present design," nine pages from the end, the Model's theme is the right ordering of social and economic relationships. Eager to get on to the

Puritans' sense of their world-historical task, modern editors routinely cut out the first three-quarters of the Model in their abridgments, as if the text had arrived at its proper destination only after an extraordinary digression on inequality, charity, and love.

But Winthrop was not an indirect writer. He wrote for occasions: to lay out with care his reasons for joining the New England venture in the summer of 1629, for example, or to refute the contentions of the religious dissenters who so profoundly shook the political and social unity of the Massachusetts Bay colony in 1636–37.[1] His celebrated speech to the General Court on the true bounds of liberty and authority went straight to its point: rulers might be chosen by the people but their authority had "the image of God eminently stamped upon it."[2] The rest was an elaboration of that opening premise. If mission and destiny were the key themes of the Model, why the long detour to get to the heart of the matter?

The answer lies not in the Model but in the preconceptions with which we have surrounded it in modern times. Too sure of the providentialist section as the essential motif and rhetorical climax of the text, we have plucked out only one of the core themes it carried. There was a second text within "A Model of Christian Charity," as close to Winthrop's heart and intentions as the covenant idea. Its controlling theme was not mission or pride. Its theme was love. Its journey was not across space but across social relations.

There was nothing hidden about Winthrop's "second" text. "Christian Charitie / A Modell hereof" the seventeenth-century copyist headed the first page in a bold and clear hand. We know from Henry Jessey's request for a copy of the Massachusetts colony's "Model of Charity" in 1635 that the title was part of the original text, not a later addition.[3] To take the Model seriously, we must refocus our attention from an "America" to come to something more immediately at hand: the idea and practice of charity in a society where some were rich in power, dignity, and wealth and others were poor.

The term "model" in Winthrop's text held more than one meaning in the seventeenth century. A model might be a smaller-scale
embodiment of a thing, in the way that an architect's model was a
miniature of a building, or a child the model of its father. A model
might be an especially perfect example to be imitated, in the way
that an especially well-made contrivance might forge the standard
for later designs. Seventeenth-century English print shops published
reams of "models" for the better ordering of church government,
poor relief, customs collection, governments, and the like. Oliver
Cromwell's "New Modelled Army," organized on a new pattern of
professional soldiery, was a particularly prominent linkage of the term
with the English Puritans' zeal for social invention.

But "model" could mean something else: a condensation, the
marrow and principle of the thing being outlined. This was John
Yates's meaning of the term in his *Modell of Divinitie* of 1622 and the
meaning behind James Harrington's "models" of his conception of a
radically more egalitarian society.[4] Winthrop would use the term
"model" in exactly that fashion himself in 1645, noting that he had
first tendered his thesis about arbitrary government "in a model" to
the colony's deputies and then later "drew it up more at large" in a
written copy afterward.[5] In this sense, "Christian Charity / A Model
hereof" was a digest—not a mission statement for a colony but a
summation of all that Winthrop was sure must lie at the kernel of
charity.

In Winthrop's mind, as his opening sentence made clear, charity
was rooted not in human likenesses but in the intractable inequality
of persons. The world's contrasts between rich and poor, between
those with power and those in subjection, Winthrop explained in the
Model's opening paragraphs, flowed first from God's delight in diversity. Secondly, inequality gave God all the more occasions to show
his hand, by restraining the greed of those with wealth and moderating the resentments of the poor. But most importantly, inequality
insured that "every man might have need of others," that through

acts of charity "they might be all knit more nearly together in the bonds of brotherly affection."

In practice, Winthrop went on to elaborate, charity followed rules. There was a law of justice and a law of mercy; there was a law of nature and a law of the gospel. None of these were easy to fulfill. To follow Winthrop through the Model's densely packed scriptural quotations is to be led into the most demanding injunctions of the Puritans' Bible. The laws of debt-forgiveness laid down by Moses, the scolding of the angry Hebrew prophets, and some of the most uncompromisingly antimaterialist lines of Jesus's parables—"A Model of Christian Charity" drew them all together in a pattern that allowed for little relaxation. What rule shall a man observe in giving to another who stood in need? As much as his prudence and abundance afforded but in extraordinary times far more; as much as he can, even to his own discomfort. What rule must we observe in lending? By way of commerce, as much as one might prudently expect to be repaid, but by the law of mercy, as much as one's brethren may need, even at the risk that the loans would never return. And in cases of a "community of peril," all of this "but with [still] more enlargement towards others and less respect towards ourselves and our own right."

These were familiar sentiments to the biblically literate. For righteousness to return to the people of Israel, they must break every yoke and let the oppressed go free, Isaiah had warned with a prophet's moral thunder. They must deal out their bread to the hungry. Only when they had done all that, when they had brought the wandering poor into their houses and clothed their nakedness, would finally "thy light break forth as the morning." Mosaic law had expressed the point more concisely: "If one of thy brethren with thee be poor . . . thou shalt open thine hand unto him, and shalt surely lend him sufficient for his need."[6] The New Testament writers put the same words in Jesus's mouth: "From him that would borrow of thee turn not away." From the letter of Saint John: "He who hath this world's goods, and seeth his brother have need, and shutteth up his compassion from him, how dwelleth the love of God in him?"[7]

Centuries of biblical gloss and compromise, however, had softened most of the passages toward which Winthrop's mind ran. Excessive charity might be imprudent. It might risk the well-being of one's own family; it might not take sufficient heed of the misfortunes one might face in the future. Better than through an extravagant gift, charity's obligations might be satisfied with a tithe or with a coin in the alms box. Lending might be divided into prudent commerce and the outright grinding of the poor, for staying clear of the sin of usury was no necessary call to lend soft-headedly, to throw money where repayment was at risk. Interrupting his discourse with objections and answers in the dialectic Puritans knew so well, Winthrop acknowledged all of this only to sweep moderation and prudence aside. When practiced according to the law of justice, charity might be corralled in relatively modest bounds. But when practiced according to the law of mercy, the most striking mark of charity, as Winthrop modeled it, lay in its ultimately uncompromising demands.

If the rules of charity were demanding, as the Model outlined them, the "affections" that powered its practice were more demanding still. For charity, the Model went on to make clear, did not run by mere law or the force of its own habits. Just as a clock had a main wheel, a prime mover that set all its hands and gears in common motion, so charity had a power that sustained it. And that was love. In Winthrop's vocabulary, love was not a private, individual feeling. Love was the "ligament" of the social body. It was the "sensibleness and sympathy of each others conditions [that] will necessarily infuse into each part a native desire and endeavor to strengthen, defend, preserve and comfort the other." In the central section of the Model, the language of sentiment pours out of Winthrop's description of the good society, knitted together not only by mutual benefit but by love itself.

Love, Winthrop wrote, was the bond between Jonathan and David within which an injury to one could not be told from an injury to the other. Love was like the mutual nourishment and pleasure of the mouth and the body in which there was no advantage or gain but "a most equal and sweet kind of commerce." Love was the bond that made a mother recognize herself in her child, or Eve find her being in Adam, so that should they be separated "she is still looking towards the place where she left her beloved. If she hear it groan, she is with it presently. If she find it sad and disconsolate, she sighs and mourns with it." The bonds of love overcame the awful estrangement that Adam's disobedience had brought into the world: the propensity to "love and seek himself only." Love meant the rebirth of the "sociable nature" of the soul.

Here at the inner heart of the Model, before any hint of mission across space was broached, was a description of the first voyage it heralded: not an ocean passage but a passage from self to others. In its course, love would create a new "habit in a soul," from which would "naturally" flow the power to fulfill even the most demanding rules of charity.

Generations of historians have sought to cushion the force of these passages by suggesting how ordinary and expected they were in their day. "None of this would have sounded exceptional to Winthrop's audience," Winthrop's most closely informed biographer writes. The significance of the Model "lies in its typicality, its commonplace culling together of basic Puritan and early modern beliefs," a particularly acute, recent study of Puritan sympathy contends.[8]

But that is not the case. It is true that virtually none of the ideas and phrases, the yearnings and injunctions that Winthrop injected into the Model, were distinctive to him, nor did he mean them to be. That God had ordered the universe so that some would be rich and others in need, "some are in high degree, some in low, some kings and

princes, some inferiors and subjects, priests and laymen, masters and
servants, fathers and children, husbands and wives, rich and poor,"
so that "there be some order among us" (as John Calvin put it) and
so that they might have more need of each other, was a commonplace
of early modern social thought. So was the need to "tear from our inward parts this most deadly pestilence . . . of love of self," as Calvin
remonstrated his beleaguered community in Geneva, so that we all
"should be embraced in one feeling of love." [9]

Practical ventures of peril sparked similar sentiments. Thirty years
ago Edmund Morgan pointed out the parallel between Winthrop's language and a different set of stock injunctions that early modern European expedition commanders often gave their crew and company as
they launched into the unknown. Thus Sebastian Cabot instructed his
officers in 1553 to "be so knit and accorded in unitie, love, conformity,
and obedience in every degree on all sides, that no dissention, variance,
or contention may rise or spring betwixt them and the mariners of this
companie."[10] Thus Sir Thomas Smith, on the eve of his diplomatic mission to Russia in 1603, urged those who accompanied him to "love and
delight in each other," especially in time of distress.[11]

Like so many other texts of its time, the Model was a work of re-
combinations, a sampler of phrases already many times reused. But
that did not make it a commonplace document or make its phrases
and argument banal. Winthrop was not setting the tone for a short-
term venture like Cabot or Smith. Most important, the Model did not
rush past the day-to-day practices of charity to focus its audience's attention on the still more perfect love that was the love of God. That
was the expected structure of a religious meditation on love in Winthrop's time and culture. The ultimate destination of virtually every
early modern sermon on charity was faith itself. The great Puritan
theologian William Ames, elaborating on the Sermon on the Mount,
described the innermost core of charity as "a virtue whereby we love
God as the chief good."[12] In Jonathan Edwards's fourteen sermons in
Charity and Its Fruits in 1738, the spiritual linkages of love between

God and his human creatures subsumed every worldly act. "If a man possessed the richest kingdom, and should give all, If a wealthy prince should make himself a poor beggar" and, giving all his goods away, clothe himself in rags, but did so without sufficient faith and sincerity, Edwards preached, it would not be charity.[13] Without faith, none of this would bring pleasure to God.

In contrast, the Model's last section does not swirl up to the love of God. It swings back, earthward, to the "work" at hand. The task on which the New England emigrants were setting out—to seek a place of cohabitation and consortship under a due form of government both civil and ecclesiastical—was "extraordinary," Winthrop warned. It could not succeed by the "usual, ordinary means." Self-regard would not suffice. "In cases such as this, the care of the public must oversway all private respects." For even the strongest claims to private property—to our "particular estates"—"cannot subsist in the ruin of the public." The covenant into which the New Englanders had entered, the covenant that they could only break at the risk of God's fury, was not separate from the practices and affections of charity. For their extraordinary work to succeed, confidence, even faith, would not be enough. It demanded a social ethic as well.

> We must be knit together in this work as one man. We must entertain each other in brotherly affection. We must be willing to abridge ourselves of our superfluities for the supply of others necessities. We must uphold a familiar commerce together in all meekness, gentleness, patience and liberality [i.e., generosity]. We must delight in each other, make others conditions our own, rejoice together, mourn together, labor and suffer together, always having before our eyes our commission and community in the work, our community as members of the same body.

"A Model of Christian Charity" envisioned not one voyage but two: the first a journey beyond egotism, the second a journey across space. In the last pages of the Model, its two texts merge. The voyage to America and the voyage into mutual sympathy turn out to be one and the same.

Winthrop's Model was only one of the many statements of intention that English Puritans wrote or circulated in the late 1620s and 1630s. The covenant that the leaders of the New England–bound emigrants forged on the eve of their Atlantic voyage was a covenant to purge the rituals of the English Protestant church of all that they found so noxious and corrupt. Theirs was a mission of escape from the ills and destruction about to overtake England. It was an extravagant act of imagining themselves stepping into the place of God's first chosen people. It was a commercial venture: the work of an investment company and its shareholders.

There was a codicil, too, to Winthrop's account of charity, which partially mitigated the Model's running critique of economic individualism, a concession that cannot be discounted. That the strongest injunctions to charity and love applied "especially" to those within "the household of faith" his biblical quotations left no doubt. Lawyer though he was, Winthrop did not clearly parse out his rules of giving and lending between those concerning the "brethren" of the church and all others. It would not take long, however, for distinctions between insiders and outsiders to intensify as the settlement grew.

But if we read "A Model of Christian Charity" without putting the demands of charity at its inner heart, we miss the assumptions within which all the rest of it was held in place. Much later, a Cold War generation of readers would see the Model as a call to destiny and greatness. Others would read it as mapping a flight to freedom. Those later lives of Winthrop's Model cannot be dismissed. But the Model of 1630 began with themes of obligation. It ended with obligations.

For in New England, too, some would be rich and some poor, some (like Winthrop himself) high in power and eminence, others lowly, mean, and in subjection. The Puritans never imagined escaping that core condition of humankind. But if we take seriously the task Winthrop outlined in 1630, a central test of the success of the colony was not going to be measured in its global influence. It was going to be worked out not only in the realms of faith and governance but on the grounds of economic practice. It was going to be seen in the ways the New England–bound emigrants would deal with the culture of markets and self-interest that they could not escape bringing with them to their city on a hill.

Moralizing the Market Economy

WAS AMERICA BORN CAPITALIST? it is often asked. Ever since Max Weber proposed a causal relationship between early Protestants' longing for order and rational control and the spirit of modern capitalism, the question has consumed the attention of generations of sociologists and historians. Weber's ideal types were too abstract, it is now clear. The careful accounting and control of the self that the Puritans so conspicuously valued was only one of the cultural traits on which capitalist economies have thrived. Others, like the risk-taking and labor exploitation on which the tobacco and slave economy of early Virginia was founded, could be successfully capital-generative as well. Capitalism's identifying features lie as much in its institutions of trade, property law, and labor as in the inner ethos that captured Weber's imagination.

Measured in these ways, there can be no doubt that Puritan New England was a by-product of capitalism in its expansive, early modern phase. Winthrop's settlement arose within one of the great commercial empires of the early modern world. Unlike the Spanish conquest a century earlier, in which arms, expropriation of easily obtained wealth, and missionary zeal took the vanguard roles, the English colonization of the Americas was a merchants' endeavor. Trading corporations—the

Virginia Company, the Massachusetts Bay Company, the Providence Island Company, the Plymouth Company—undertook the work of settlement throughout British America, capitalized by investors' purchase of their joint stock.[1]

Economic transactions saturated the daily life of Winthrop's New England as well. Private property in land was relatively easily sold and purchased. Production was primarily for markets: local markets for most New England farmers, long-distance markets in timber, fish, and grain for others. Debt, too, left its mark all across these money-scarce economies. Debt cases pervade the early records of the Massachusetts General Court, just as they saturated early modern English society, etching the economy with complex lines of trust, reputation, and obligation. The rules of lending, repayment, and loan forgiveness that Winthrop outlined in the long second section of his "Model of Christian Charity" were, in the context of New England's everyday economic life, anything but abstract.[2]

Finally, the world the New England Puritans made was not only a world of trade and commerce but a world in which wealth was a sign of value. Wealthier men like Winthrop played a vastly outsized role in public affairs in the Massachusetts colony. Land distribution was sharply skewed in favor of the wealthy as well. A society without ranks and order, as the Model made clear, was no dream of the New England Puritans.

And yet, deep as their immersion in market institutions and presumptions was, early New England Puritans did not accept market morals whole. "A Model of Christian Charity" itself was born at a moment of high tension between commercial interests and social ends, when an investors' quarrel over risk and lending had threatened to undo the Massachusetts settlement project before it had truly begun. Disputes over buying and selling erupted aboard the ships during the ocean voyage, and they did not go away thereafter. The concerns with self-love that Winthrop poured into his model of charity spilled over into every aspect of colonial New England life. To the extent that the

Model stands at one of the foundation points of the American story, Winthrop's concern to establish the proper place of markets within the moral imperatives of charity must be recognized to stand there, just as prominently, too.[3]

Matters of price and commerce weighed heavily on John Winthrop in the winter and spring of 1629–30 as many of the key phrases that he would rework in "A Model of Christian Charity" began to crystallize in his mind. Recruited as the Massachusetts Bay Company's governor in late October as the head of a yet-unfunded expedition scheduled to sail on the first of March, he was immediately sucked into a whirlwind of business concerns. There were emigrants to be recruited if the project was to realize its envisioned scale. There were ministers who had to be persuaded to leave their settled parishes for a church order that was, as yet, anything but clearly defined. Artisans of many different sorts were needed. There were persons of wealth to recruit as well. There were ships to be hired and stocked with the beer, water, biscuits, and dried meat that the ocean voyage would require. Arrangements for the sale of his own lands had to be made.

"Our business comes so fast upon us here" in London, Winthrop found himself apologizing to his wife Margaret all through the winter, that he could scarcely predict when the occasions for the trips home that he longed for would arise. "In regard of business, which so take up my time and thoughts," he wrote, he could not express his love "so largely to thee as I was wont to do." He had six more letters to write that evening, he apologized to his "most sweet wife" on another occasion.[4]

The most pressing point of business was the challenge of finding adequate capital for the enterprise. Like all the other English colonization ventures in the Americas, the Massachusetts Bay Company was organized as an investment corporation. Merchants with wealth and a special degree of tolerance for risk, both for God's sake and for their own, had invested sums on which they anticipated return. For the first two years after its organization in 1628, the company had managed the work of a small community of settlers at Salem, supplying them with clothing, tools, provisions, arms, and the services of a resident governor, minister, and doctor, in expectation that trade in fish, timber, and beaver skins would repay their investments and allow the settlement to prosper.

But the first two years' trial had not been a success. By the time that serious consideration began of reorganizing the company as a self-governing colony in New England, managed by its emigrants rather than its London-based investors, its capital stock was deeply in debt. Some of the supplies and cattle sent over had miscarried. Many of the servants (transported at extraordinary charge, a company report complained) had not proved as useful as expected. Trade had not been as profitable as expected. Not all those who had pledged to participate in the share offerings had actually done so. Altogether, an accounting in late 1629 concluded, fully one-third of the initial capital had been lost. The company's governor alone was owed 1,200 pounds; other primary investors were in similar straits. Before the seat of the company's government could move to New England, separating its English investors from the management of their investments, some sort of reckoning would have to be made.[5]

To read the minutes of the company's meetings through the fall and winter of 1629–30 is to find oneself tugged into a deeply contentious debate over what the initial investors were owed and how those debts might be made whole. A "labyrinth," Winthrop would call it, that "infolded" them all. "The further we waded, the more difficulties we encountered."[6] Committees appointed to represent the interest of the company's initial investors and the interest of those intending to emigrate wrote up position papers and debated at length. Tickets were sent to those who had fallen behind in their stock subscriptions imploring them to send their payments in. Panels of ministers were recruited as arbiters.

Finally, with the matter at a standstill, three options were placed before the company's members. The first was that every shareholder agree to double his original investment—a fantastical scheme, given the risks, that was quickly rejected. The second was that the company fold up its affairs, selling off all its property, distributing what it could realize among its shareholders, and essentially abandoning the colony project. The third proposal was more realistic than the other two, but to many individual investors it was much more painful. It proposed that the capital stock of the company be reorganized, that the value of all existing shares be written down by two-thirds, and that a smaller group of undertakers assume control, pledging to pay the original shareholders back on their now sharply reduced value at the end of seven years. Without that debt forgiveness, without some act of self-sacrifice, the settlement venture would not move forward.

The matter was judged too weighty for an immediate decision. Three trusted ministers were summoned to the next meeting to help bring clarity to the deliberations. Finally on December 1, after "long debate," the write-down of the shareholders' stock values was approved.[7] There would be more contentions and modifications before the fleet sailed in March. Land grants were authorized to help defray some of the losses of the original investors; wrangles over the claims of particularly aggrieved shareholders were given over to arbitration after yet another "large discussion" in the company as a whole. But the agreement of December 1 was the turning point, when the investors agreed to forgive a significant part of the sums they had pledged for the sake of the larger good.

It fell to Winthrop, as the company's new governor, to introduce the compromise proposal and, with it, the key phrases he would use again at the core of "A Model of Christian Charity." He knew the debt-satisfaction proposal would "startle" some of those present, as Moses himself (Winthrop said) had sometimes been startled by things proposed to him. But he urged the reluctant investors that in sacrificing their claims to full repayment they would reenact, in modern time, the part that God himself had taken when he had fed and clothed the people of Israel as they journeyed into Canaan. You are the "root" of this project, the "family" from which it was derived, Winthrop urged. You are "the City, the greatest Church, etc." The emigrants were only a "hopeful plantation." But with this sacrifice on the investors' part, the two would be "knit together in a most firm bond of love" and "affection."

You have already given your money to God, Winthrop counseled the company's members in his December 1 address. Of what advantage would it be to haggle over 100 pence or 50 pounds? For the sake of God's glory and the plantation's welfare, you should be ready "not only [to] lend it, but lose it." And then came the line that Winthrop would rework just after the "city upon a hill" sentence in "A Model of Christian Charity": "Consider your reputation, the eyes of all the godly are upon you, what can you do more honorable for this City, and the Gospel which you profess, than to deny your own profit, that we may say Londoners can be willing to lose that the Gospel etc."[8]

This pattern of reuses from Winthrop's appeal to the colony's investors gives no clear-cut answer as to when Winthrop found the time for the Model's final composition, but it leaves no doubt about the moral issue that initially stood at its center. Whatever else the Model would become, its initial occasion was commerce and, more pointedly, the pyramids of debt and obligation that a market economy opened up. Triggered by a deeply fraught meeting in London, its subject was the labyrinth where commerce and morality cut across, blurred, and confronted each other.

Winthrop's fellow voyagers carried all these concerns with markets and morals, self-interest and the public good, directly into their new settlement. They absorbed the energy of the colony from the beginning. The prices men began to ask for labor were a particularly tender issue. From the beginning, the colony's governing bodies followed their fluctuations with concern. Alarmed that carpenters, sawyers, bricklayers, and thatchers were taking advantage of the first summer's building boom by inflating their wage expectations, the colony's General Court ordered a ceiling on house builders' charges in August 1630; it set them free again the next March, only to reimpose a maximum price per board on sawyers again in September. When wages surged once more in the fall of 1633, the General Court imposed a general scale of wages on artisans, agricultural workers, and common laborers before letting this, too, lapse when the demand for labor subsided.[9]

Unexpected fluctuations in the prices of goods brought a similar response. Price legislation was a repeated reaction to sharp swings from the norm. Corn and beer were subject to price controls from time to time. In 1638 a committee of twenty-nine of the colony's leading figures was tasked with sorting out the general problem of "oppression" in wages and prices, though it failed to bring in the report it had been mandated to make. A more pointed order in 1640, when the emigration stream from England suddenly came to a halt and cash dried up in response, decreed that corn, wheat, and rye might pass as money at specified rates until accustomed conditions returned. In the meantime, when debts were to be satisfied, their no longer realistic nominal values would be subject to third-party arbitration, lest "a great part of the people in the country be undone."[10]

The arrival of ships with goods to sell, like the arrival of new emigrants with shelter and goods to contract for, added to the economic instability. In the general clamor of purchasers, prices inevitably shot far beyond their norms. At one point the General Court proposed that ship masters be required to lie at anchor until their goods were inspected and put up for sale to the local authorities as they were "judged to be useful for the country" before the rest were offered to the public.[11] At yet another point, one of the colony's prominent ministers raised the capital to purchase the entire provision load of an incoming ship for resale to the towns and thereby circumvent excessive profit-taking.[12] John White, the prominent Puritan minister at

Dorchester, urged Winthrop to make the practice general.[13] Even though resistance from the merchants and ship masters frustrated most of these proposals, public concern with unfairly inflated prices persisted.

The notion that each good had a "just price"—a value divorced from the commercial relations in which it was embedded—was rarely enunciated in these debates. Even John Cotton, the most prominent of the early settlement's clergy, thought the issue was not the abstract value of the thing but the sale of a good "above the current price, i.e. such price as is usual in the time and place."[14] But distortion of the customary price by uneven market power or distress posed a deep and pressing concern. A General Court decision on the proper rules for appraising cattle in 1641 made it clear that value was not to be judged by the "market price" by "which some are forced by urgent necessity to sell a beast for." The source of a cow's value lay in the expected return from the milk or calves she might produce minus the cost of hay "etc."[15] To charge more than that in the face of one party's necessity or weaker market power, as we might now put it, was not exchange but "oppression" and "extortion." "Covetousness" and "self-love," Winthrop fumed in his journal, were being allowed to rule the terms of trade.[16]

Buying, selling, and lending that trespassed into self-love were hardly distant matters for Winthrop. The second year of settlement was not over before Winthrop accused his deputy governor, Thomas Dudley, of "oppressing usury" by selling seven and a half bushels of corn to some of his poorer co-settlers in exchange for ten bushels to be received after the fall harvest.[17] Three years later, Winthrop himself was accused of mixing up his own goods and profits with the commodities he had received as governor from the common stock. Winthrop successfully defended his accounts, but in 1638 the General Court was still lamenting "novelties, oppression, atheism, excess, superfluity, idleness, contempt of authority, and troubles in other parts to be remembered."[18]

The most celebrated case of commercial oppression in the early years of the Puritan colony was that of Robert Keayne. A London merchant tailor who had settled in the new colony as a general trader in 1635, Keayne was not a man whom many of his Boston neighbors liked. He was a prodigiously pious Puritan. At his death he left behind not only the copious records of a lifetime of sermon note-taking but also his own four "great writing books" intended as an exposition of the whole of the Bible and its prophecies. He also left behind a considerable fortune, made in commercial trades of all sorts that many thought skirted the edge of oppression.

Indeed in 1639 Keayne was formally charged in court with overpricing, taking a 50 percent markup on one sale and a 75 percent markup on another.[19] He had not done more than others, Keayne protested. He had never forced a purchaser to pay more than she or he agreed to. If he had sometimes set off losses he faced on some trades by higher margins on others, if he had bought the button or bridle in question himself for far less than he sold it for, was that not the custom of trade? Was selling 6 penny nails for 8 pennies a pound "such a crying and oppressing sin" that he should have been censored by the Boston church and fined the stupendous sum of 200 pounds by the General Court?

Winthrop took the side of leniency toward Keayne. Because some others had done as much as he did and because, "though much labor had been bestowed upon it," the General Court had not been able to construct a clear and certain rule on the matter, an admonition against covetousness would have been the wiser course, Winthrop thought.[20] But Winthrop meticulously recorded the rules of commerce that John Cotton laid out in the public sermon that Cotton preached in the immediate aftermath of Keayne's trial. A person must not sell above the customary price; that is, "such a price as is usual in the time and place," Cotton admonished. If there were no specific regulation against it, merchants could raise their prices in the face of scarcity, Cotton admitted, for scarcity must necessarily come from the providence of God. But if a merchant faced losses due to his own clumsiness in trade, or because he had not turned a profit on other transactions, he could not charge beyond an item's current worth without stepping over the line from a shrewd bargain into usury. That "a man might sell as dear as he can, and buy as cheap as he can"—the maxim that would become fixed centuries later in the idea of efficient, self-balancing markets—was a "false principle."[21] Adam's sin, his temptation "to love and seek himself only," as Winthrop put it in "A Model of Christian Charity," cast its shadow all across the Puritans' efforts to deal with the practical ethics of their economic life.

Facilitated by men like Robert Keayne, commercial exchange formed a vital part of early New England economic life. Buying, selling, and lending were everyday actions. Puritans did not resist these. But deep as their immersion in market institutions and presumptions was, they did not accept market morals whole. They refused to accept that trade should run along any natural course it took, that voluntary exchange was always an ethical act regardless of the power relations that stood behind it. By fixing prices and then, when the results disappointed, setting them free again; by looking to custom to unknot questions of price and excessive profit-taking; by exhorting their fellows against usury and oppression; and by scapegoating an unpopular trader like Keayne, they kept up a running quarrel with the market relations in which they lived.

Over the course of the seventeenth century, these efforts to set moral bounds on economic relations weakened.[22] Suits against economic oppression grew rarer in New England courts in the second half of that century. Looking farther outward for markets, Boston's merchants immersed themselves more and more deeply in the Atlantic economy. Many proved highly successful overseas traders, whose ships fanned out across the North American coast, the Caribbean Islands, Africa, and Europe carrying goods and, in time, highly profitable cargos of human slaves.[23] Boston's learned ministers gradually softened their censorship of money lent purely for a contracted amount of interest without any productive object at its base. By the nineteenth century, to those outside New England, the term "Yankee" was more likely to denote an especially shrewd and clever trader than an honest and socially minded one.

But, attenuated though they were, the injunctions against covetousness and economic oppression did not wholly disappear. Nor, hemmed in and qualified though they became, did the demands of charity that had preoccupied Winthrop in 1630. To read "A Model of Christian Charity" seriously is to see it as rooted in an effort to enlist the power of capital in a venture for which profit, alone, was not incentive enough. It is to find self-interest in constant tension with the demands of the larger social good. It is to find oneself in a culture in which market relations, though they impinged on every aspect of life, were not to be fully trusted.

Finally, it is to see within the lines of Winthrop's Model not only early New England's familiar characters, its merchants and farmers, ministers and church members, but others: the poor who lived among them.

CHAPTER 8

The Poor and the Boundaries of Obligation

W E KNOW THE TRIALS of Robert Keayne as intimately as we do because he himself could not stop thinking about them. Fourteen years after his conviction, a wealthy man once more, Keayne began a will whose writing was ultimately to consume five obsessive months and occupy 158 pages in the county court records. Over and over the details of his transactions Keayne went, repeating and refuting the charges of those who had cried out against him, defending his trade practices as nothing other than what was common "in every shop and warehouse." Had offering gold buttons at the price he asked amounted to "such a heinous sin"? Or marking up the cost of a bridle as steeply as he had? Had following the customs of the trade warranted the "deep and sharp censure that was laid upon me"? "Out of the grief and trouble of my heart" he defended his acts, still rankling at the shame his towns-folk had imposed on him.[1]

Now at the end of his life, not out of a guilty conscience but to show that the clamor against him had never been warranted, he gave away a munificent bundle of public bequests. Out of an estate he valued at 4,000 pounds, he willed 300 pounds for the erection of a new

town house for Boston where the courts and ministers might meet,
a library might be housed, the town's supply of arms might be stored,
a new water conduit might be run, and where country folk bringing
goods to sell might rest and store their stock against the weather. He
willed another 10 pounds to improve the equipment of the artillery
company. He provided for his widow and family. And finally he willed
the income from 100 pounds to be spent on the Boston poor: for assistance to the poor of his church, for the education of the ablest and
most "hopeful" of the town's poor children, and the provisioning of
a town granary where a common stock might be stored against emer-
gencies and where the "poorer sort" might purchase grain at cost
during times of need. He had not made significant charitable gifts before, he admitted. But he would now, and the poor of Boston would
receive a significant fraction of it.[2]

The poor do not occupy a prominent place in most popular histories of America. They live on the margins of the stories of success
and enterprise we like to tell about American society and culture. But
they were not the least invisible in their time. Traces of the life struggles of the poor run all through the early New England town records.
"A Model of Christian Charity" announced their presence in its very
first sentence. If rules for lending gave the Model its propulsive force,
Winthrop left no doubt that the poor, the needy, and those in distress
held a special claim on a community dedicated to the godly life. "Curse"
he who "shutteth his ears from hearing the cry of the poor," reads the
Model. "If thy brother be in want and thou canst help him, thou
needst not make doubt what thou shouldst do; if thou lovest God
thou must help him."

The mission to America, as it took shape in Winthrop's mind
in early 1630, would not only require a passage from self-love to an
ethic of social affection. It would not only call into question accustomed rules of commerce. Their voyage would force them to confront a still deeper knot of social ethics: what the fortunate owed to

those who struggled to construct their lives under the burdens of poverty.

That the world had too many poor, early modern Puritans were certain. They "swarmed" over England. "Why do we meet so many wandering ghosts in shape of men?" Winthrop himself wrote on the eve of his decision to cast in his lot with the Massachusetts Bay Company venture. Why "so many spectacles of misery in all our streets, our houses full of victuals and our entries of hunger-starved Christians?"[3] Those who emigrated to New England were eager to leave behind the roving beggars of the English countryside and the squalor of London's streets and alleys—portents, as they interpreted the signs, of God's coming fury. They saw no true charity in the medieval Christian church's sanctification of holy alms and barefoot friars. A coin dropped in a beggar's hand was a wasted gesture, not an act of piety.

Still, they could not abandon the poor in their moral imaginations. The telltale mark of Puritan policy was the poor's "improvement." Their temptation to idleness needed to be scrubbed out of them. Their beggary needed to be curbed. Their inner self-discipline needed to be radically strengthened. To this end, the poor in the "godly cities" whose administration Puritans and Puritan sympathizers began to control in early seventeenth-century England formed the objects of some of the most ambitious programs of social discipline and management to be found in the early modern world. In Puritan strongholds like Dorchester and Norwich, poor vagabond children were swept into the cities' new municipal workhouses; beggary was banned; vagrant men without work or means were whipped out of town. Overseers of the poor went house to house to assess the needs and moral conditions of poor families. In some notable instances those who accepted parish or public relief were "badged" with initials sewn in their clothing so that their status would be visible to all.[4]

But hand in hand with tighter regimes of social discipline, Puritan reformers simultaneously embraced broader and more systematic obligations of public support. The mandate of the Elizabethan Poor Laws of 1597 and 1601 that each English town and parish support its resident poor through public tax funds came only slowly into practice. By 1660, thirty years after the Winthrop fleet's sailing, only a third of all English parishes are estimated to have regularly raised taxes for relief of the poor.[5] But in the permeation of the idea of a public responsibility toward the poor, the "godly cities" of early seventeenth-century England took the lead. Workhouses and schools were established to shelter as well as to discipline the poor. Public granaries distributed food stocks at cost to the poor in times of dearth. In slack times the well-to-do were urged to grant interest-free loans to poor artisans who could not afford to purchase stock to employ themselves.

The most notable of the English Puritan urban strongholds in this regard was Dorchester where, in the wake of a disastrous town fire in 1613, a civic revival swept through the town. A new hospital was constructed where poor children could be catechized and set to work; a municipal fuel house was established to sell fuel below cost to the poor; prices of basic goods were regulated in times of shortage; special collections were solicited for the support of both the local poor and distant causes. To help finance this outburst of civic provision, the city established a municipal brew house whose ale profits were plowed back into the town's poor relief efforts. In addition, Dorchester's leading preacher, John White, boasted that the town had doubled its poor law tax levies.[6]

If this combination of ambitious institution building, poor relief taxation, and heavy-handed moral reform seems to our modern temperaments a mash-up of contradictory impulses, it did not seem so to its architects. To rid these English "cities on a hill" of Sabbath breaking, begging, and swearing, to pipe them with better water supplies, to inspect their households, to provide public support for their poor, and set the idle and abandoned to work: all this was of a piece. The "voracious appetites" of these godly civic reformers, as historian Paul Slack termed it, embraced a full-scale assault on traditional, hard-drinking, riotous popular culture as the quid pro quo for more systematic, sustained support of the needy poor.[7]

All these enterprises were ultimately fragile. During the Puritan Revolution, a newly established London Corporation for the Poor undertook a systematic survey of the city's needy, built a string of new workhouses for poor children and youth, and provided employment to up to a thousand adults, many in their own homes, only to see their effort to eradicate traditional poverty collapse in the strains of civil war.[8] And yet, its fragility and harshness notwithstanding, the moral impulse behind this early modern welfare state should not be dismissed out of hand.

English Puritan reformers made a central place for the poor—in all their need and unruliness—within the bounds of their moral imagination. Dorchester's John White himself reminded Winthrop of the point in a letter in which White chided New Englanders for failing to provide for a public storehouse from which "needful" goods could be reasonably purchased and, instead, letting shop-keeping grow so quickly among them. "The good which ought to be respected is Bonum publicum not Privatum Commodum. . . . I would fain know what the General [i.e., the common good of all] shall gain by making half a dozen rich by pinching more than so many thousands."[9]

With their unusually young population, New Englanders did not immediately face the questions of poverty that "A Model of Christian Charity" posed in the abstract and that absorbed their "godly" counterparts in England. The issue barely comes up in the early records of the colony's General Court. In 1640, the General Court granted thirty bushels of corn to Thomas Buckmaster, "being in distress." In 1646, it exempted "such as are poor, by sickness, lameness, or other infirmity" from colony-wide taxation. The same year, the

General Court remitted the fines levied on five Hingham men provided they could prove to an impartial observer that they were
poor.[10]

At the local level, however, where responsibility for the poor soon
descended, the record of activity is much denser. Though the English
Poor Laws did not formally apply in the Massachusetts Bay colony
until the 1690s, New England's emigrants brought with them from
the colony's beginning the principle of local responsibility to care for
those in distress. The towns' forms of assistance varied. Elaborate
poor relief regimes on the scale of London or Dorchester involved
capital expenses far too great for early New England towns. Even
almshouses were rare until the eighteenth century. Instead, New
England towns chose simpler forms of relief. Abatement of taxes for
poorer town residents was a common practice. Destitute families
might be granted permission to cut wood from the town's common
lands. At other times towns authorized direct grants of grain or firewood or called for voluntary contributions to help relieve a family in
distress.[11] In 1653 the town of Dorchester, Massachusetts, paid Good-
man Mosely 12 shillings for attending to "old Bartholmy" at his time
of sickness. In 1679 the town distributed a bequest specifically designated to assist the town's poor among its sixteen neediest families.[12]

Families played a central role in these matters. Poverty meant
both the breakup of poor families and the public use of other families as a means of relief. Parents who bore more children than the
town's selectmen thought they could afford were an object of particularly assiduous scrutiny. Their newborn children were regularly
apprenticed out to other families, the town paying the expenses for
the first few years until the child could become an economic asset
to its surrogate family. In the cases of deepest need, the town put
the care of its impoverished in the hands of another household to
board and feed in return for a set rate of payments from the town's
treasury.

The total amount spent in all these ways is not easy to measure. By one estimate, Boston in the late 1640s spent only a little over 5 percent of its total budget on poor relief, not counting tax abatements. But as New England's population aged, the cost of maintaining the towns' poor increased. A sharply higher estimate for Watertown in 1661 put poor relief expenses at 20–30 percent of the town's budget. By 1700 Boston was spending perhaps a quarter of its budget on poor relief.[13] With rising expenditures, pressures for cost controls increased. Watertown in 1727 publicly solicited bids from householders offering to take in poor children at lowest cost to the town, an early instance of the pauper "auctions" that became notorious in New England in the early nineteenth century.[14] But grudging as it often was, public, tax-supported responsibility for the poor was a fixture of New England town life.

None of these measures of relief made the life of the poor easy. We can see this poignantly in the case of Dorchester, Massachusetts, where an unusually complete record of the town meetings survives for the 1660s and 1670s. Certain figures cycled through them, persons whom their neighbors certainly knew well. Robert Stiles showed up in the town records first in 1671 to answer for the idleness of himself and his wife and to be publicly shamed for not having "improved their time to the advantage of their family." And yet, two years later the town granted Stiles 20 shillings of corn "for his present relief" and, not long afterward, another pound for the same ends. In 1673, the town ordered Stiles to "dispose" of one of his children, although it is not clear that he did so. In 1678 Stiles was in trouble once more for failing to improve his time and ordered again "to look out for a place for one of his children at least," or else the selectmen would do it, as they finally did three years later.[15] Frances Bale, ordered to dispose of two of his children whom the selectmen judged he could not afford, demurred because his wife was not willing to do so. The "selectmen persuaded him to persuade his wife to it."[16] Still, men like Stiles and Bale could not simply be brushed aside. Both were among the recipients of the bequest for the poor the Dorchester selectmen received in 1679.[17] Joseph Birch was admonished for failing to come to church and, on another occasion, put in the stocks for egregious drunkenness, but he was nonetheless granted the town's liberty to cut trees in the common woods or swamps to "make coals for his calling."[18]

Frances Bacon's was a harder case. "Being destitute of a habitation," she threw herself and her young child on the town's charity in 1674. In response, the Dorchester selectmen ordered that a list be drawn up of families that might take her and her child into their households in return for the town's payment of 3 shillings a week, plus a little more for bedding and clothing. For the next eight years at least, Frances Bacon was passed from one family to another. Thomas Modesley took her for a while, Nicholas Clap for a five-week stretch, Captain Foster for two weeks. William Sumner "tabled" her for a time. In 1676 her child was apprenticed to James Foster, who promised support and employment until the child reached age twenty-one. In the meantime expenses for "keeping Frances," sometimes for six weeks, more often for two, dot the town's accounts record. The last mention of her name in the town meeting records that survive was a payment to Daniel Preston of 13 shillings "for killing a wolf and for francis."[19]

No one would call this generous. Impossible as it is to enter Frances's thoughts across this wide an expanse of time, it would be hard to imagine that her mind was settled, or even grateful. But she found herself wrapped in a deeply stubborn sense of charity nonetheless. An unmarried mother, without relations or friends to take her in but with settlement rights in the town, the townspeople did not slough her off. Like Robert Stiles, she was one of *their* poor. Her distress—however grudgingly relieved—was their public responsibility. The Dorchester townsfolk certainly did not love Frances Bacon, as Winthrop's "Model of Christian Charity" might seem to have required. But the Model's injunctions to relieve those in need found in her case, nonetheless, real, practical traction.

Beyond each town's borders, however, the rules of obligation changed abruptly. To cross from one town to another was to traverse a massive ethical and legal boundary. In law and practice, the corollary of each New England town's responsibility for its poor was its release from responsibility for any of the poor who belonged elsewhere. Fear that this line might be violated by an invasion of outsiders who might end up throwing themselves on the town's poor relief expenses was a fierce preoccupation of New England town life. Towns required permission for newcomers to settle in their midst. Those who did not attend to that formality could expect to receive legal notice that they would be ineligible for any relief or legal "settlement" rights from the town. "Warning out" notices, these were called, often followed by orders of outright expulsion. Persons without a trade, laborers on temporary employment, poorer folk generally, and pregnant women about to bear a child whose birth in the town might give it settlement rights were particularly acute objects of towns' suspicion. They were not only "strangers" to the town but objects of potentially heavy burden on the town's tax rate.

Warning out notices regularly punctuated the Dorchester, Massachusetts, town records. In 1670 the selectmen warned Henry Merrifield, whose married daughter had been living with him for about a week, that he must either get a notice from her own town that it had assumed full responsibility for her, or send her away. When the Merrifield family ultimately demurred, stating "that she was their daughter and [they] could not turn her out of door this winter time," the town ordered him to do so anyway. In another case, when Mercy Chubb, being pregnant, left her husband to move back in with her birth family, "contrary to good order and hazarding of a charge upon the town," as the record put it, she was ordered be gone within six or eight days.[20] Like the charity of other New England towns, Dorchester's sense of its "own" and its poor relief responsibilities stopped abruptly at its village edge.

In eighteenth-century Rhode Island, as Ruth Herndon has shown, expulsion of strangers who might be a charge on the towns' poor rates was even more systemic and harrowingly thorough. Neighbors who sensed a family's need or illness typically filed the complaint that triggered warning out orders. Visible signs of strangerhood had the same effect. Blacks, Indians, and mulattoes were far more likely to be warned out in early eighteenth-century Rhode Island than persons of European descent. More women than men were warned out, particularly women who might give birth to a child within the town's limits. In one case a whole family was removed because one of its daughters had become visibly pregnant. In another, the town officials were in the very act of removal when the woman they had seized fell into labor.[21]

The rule of responsibility only for the poor relief of those legally "settled" in the town was an English import. Still, the practice of locally limited responsibility was carried out in colonial New England with particular intensity. The towns shouldered their local obligations seriously but kept the horizons of responsibility strictly limited. They practiced a public charity that was, at one and the same time, intrusive, strong-willed, exacting, and fiercely bounded.

By the end of the eighteenth century, as labor mobility increased and town populations grew, new poor relief practices arose that exaggerated these earlier tensions. Boarding out the poor to neighboring families became a less and less adequate means of relief in the region's larger towns. Workhouses on the English model began to supplant family-based support. There, New England poor reformers hoped, by living within the structured discipline of an institution and laboring regularly at a repetitive task—spinning, weaving, or, more typically, picking strands from castoff rope for reuse as oakum caulking—those unable to support themselves could be more efficiently housed, more gainfully employed, and, in theory, morally remade.[22]

Boston had built a municipal workhouse by 1738. By the 1780s it formed part of a cluster of welfare institutions on the edge of the built-up city: a municipal almshouse for the infirm and elderly poor, a bridewell for the punishment of minor criminals, a municipal granary where the poor could purchase grain below the prices that storekeepers asked, and the workhouse. Isolation, discipline, and habit-instilling labor were the reciprocal obligations Boston's poor now gave in return for public support.[23]

The cruelties that were to overcome the poorhouses by the nineteenth century have been abundantly documented. But it is too easy to read the movement from boarding-out to institutionalization as simply a callous abandonment of the principles of charity that Winthrop had tried so hard to lay out. The idea of making over the character of the poor on more disciplined, work-capable lines, however flawed in practice, was not a small moral ideal.

In Philadelphia, the new civic vision of poor relief had its most ambitious trial. There, in 1766, the city's Quaker merchants persuaded the legislature to take management of the city's poor away from its public overseers and place it under their own elite direction. A nonprofit association would set the city's poor tax rate and direct the use of its proceeds. To that end, the newly formed contributors' corporation undertook to build and staff the largest and most carefully administered Almshouse and House of Employment that the colonies had seen. Inmates were sorted out by gender, race, and estimates of their moral ability and set to a steady regime of work, reflection, and religious instruction, all with the hope of making new persons of them. The "Bettering House," it was dubbed, in reflection of the scope of the Quaker merchants' ambition. If its managers had had their way, they would have cut off every other form of public poor support in the city to funnel the poor through its door and reformatory influences. That project ultimately proved too large and too costly for them to manage. By 1788 the merchants had given the task of poor relief management back to the city, but not before they had built at the city's edge the largest and one of the most architecturally impressive buildings in English North America. Wealthy Philadelphians visited the Bettering House's gardens; travelers took note of it in their diaries.[24]

Boston's elite did not act on quite the same scale. But when the property around the city's charitable institutions began rapidly to gentrify in the 1790s, the city government undertook the construction of a new and larger institution at a more distant unbuilt edge of the city. For its design they commissioned the young Charles Bulfinch, already New England's most celebrated architect. With the Massachusetts and Connecticut State Houses, churches, banks, and elegant Boston town houses to his credit, Bulfinch was a master of Federal-era elegance. When it was completed in 1801, his New Almshouse dwarfed every other building in the city. Three stories high and 270 feet long, its commanding feature was a dramatically tall central pavilion, its windows outlined in marble and topped by a broad marble pediment. High brick walls and a large ornamented gate encircled the Almshouse grounds. As in the case of Philadelphia's Bettering House, this was public charity made not only efficient but visible, proud, and monumental.[25]

The mixed messages in these new expressions of civic charity cannot be unspooled along any single thread. They isolated the poor behind their new institutional walls. They extracted the recipients of public poor relief from the temptations of the city but also from the bonds of family. They set them at the city's margins. In hopes of cutting the mounting costs of more promiscuous forms of relief, they imposed far stricter regimes of moral and physical discipline than the poor in colonial America had ever experienced before. They hoped for far more moral reformation than had been expected before. But they also broadcast—with whatever mixture of vanity and self-importance—the public and moral benevolence of their builders. The same structures that stored the poor away celebrated the obligations of rich and poor, each to the other.

Had Winthrop's concept of charity been broader? Did a sense of boundaries not run through his own text as well? Winthrop never specified that only those in good moral and religious standing deserved the love and sacrifice of others. Until "there be no poor with thee," he wrote, the obligations of charity persisted. But the Model's stress on care for one's "brethren" in distress, on the need to do good to all but "especially to the household of faith," suggests an implicit sense of limits. Winthrop wrote the Model with those in mind who intended to sail for New England and whose financial sacrifice that enterprise required. The ethical community in his imagination was essentially homogenous. The diversity of opinions that so quickly erupted in New England caught him by alarm. That a population in need might emerge outside the fold of church membership he most likely did not anticipate. The "we" of his "we shall be as a city upon a hill" was partial, not universal. His "we" was not, in any meaning of the term, "America." Winthrop's community of the godly was both intense and, in a literal sense, parochial.

The "we" that emerged in social and political practice in early New England was, in some ways, broader than the "we" of Winthrop's text. It reached out to the poor without regard to their full membership in the church. It gave, however harshly or begrudgingly, to backsliders and the reprobate as well as to the pious. It secularized the imperative of charity and made the welfare of the poor a legal, civic, tax-supported obligation. Like the monumental almshouses on Boston's and Philadelphia's outer edges, the practice of early New England charity kept the poor at a distance. But it had not yet given way before the full-scale economization of economic life and contempt for the indigent that would sweep through the nation in the nineteenth century.

Nor had John Winthrop's Model itself made its peace with market individualism. Winthrop's "we" was fervent: "We must love brotherly without dissimulation. We must love one another with a pure heart fervently. . . . We must not look only on our own things, but also on the things of our brethren." If Winthrop's sense of the social whole did not stretch as far as we might like, the Model's economic message was clear: market price and ordinary market relations would not suffice for a moral community. The kernel of "charity," as he turned it over in his mind in 1630, lay precisely in that lesson.

But no text remains stable. When after centuries of neglect "A Model of Christian Charity" was plucked out of Winthrop's context to be reimagined as something quite different—as a founding document for the nation itself—the moral question Winthrop had placed at the core of his text would no longer be the part of the Model that mattered.

PART II

Nation

CHAPTER 9

Inventing Foundations

THE DISTANCE FROM PHILADELPHIA'S Bettering House in July 1776 to the building we now know as Independence Hall was barely three-quarters of a mile. To imagine it, you have to whisk the modern city out of your mind's eye. Setting off from the Bettering House across the rural buffer that separated the morally quarantined poor from the city that supported them, your walk would have started out through open fields and farmsteads. Abutting the Bettering House's grounds you might have paused to admire a second monumental institution of the city's philanthropic elite, the Pennsylvania Hospital for the free care of the city's sick poor. Reaching Sixth Street where the commercial city began, you would have passed yet a third charitable institution, the Loganian Library, the gift of one of William Penn's secretaries who had devoted a part of his merchant-made fortune to accruing one of the largest book collections in British North America. Although it did not turn out quite as James Logan had originally hoped, he had intended to bequeath his collection for public use, free to any ambitious reader who wanted to use it. Finally, swinging around the corner of Chestnut Street you would have come up on the Pennsylvania State House, known in our day as Independence Hall. In all, the walk would have taken you less than fifteen minutes.[1]

But in historical distance, that journey would have taken you from a cultural-political world whose links to Winthrop's "Model of Christian Charity" were still discernible to a world in which he would have been radically out of place. In Philadelphia's great charitable institutions, Winthrop would have recognized the bonds of assistance between unequals whose importance his Model had so insistently underscored. When Winthrop wrote that "we shall be as a city upon a hill," the "we" in his mind was a people held together by their acts of common faith and mutual obligation. However quickly dissension would shake its covenant claims, the society Winthrop's Model envisioned was, at root, a consensual rather than a legal-political one: a voluntary company of "godly" English Protestants in search of a place of settlement, purity, obedience, and exile.

The "we" that was under construction in Independence Hall in June and July of 1776 was part of an altogether different global experiment in nation making. "*We* hold these truths to be self-evident," the Declaration of Independence boldly announced. The agent of that new collective purpose was not simply the delegates who signed the document. It was not a cluster of refugees on an unfamiliar shore. It was a political entity that Winthrop and his peers had never remotely anticipated: a newly invented nation.

Ultimately, conscription into that nationalist project would change everything about the ways in which "A Model of Christian Charity" was read and understood. Nation making fostered a new search for foundations: for texts and founders who could be imagined to stand at the very beginning point of a nation's history. It encouraged a radical foreshortening of time so that a nation's origins and future could be imagined as seamlessly connected. It held out a special place for each nation in the designs of providence and of history; it imbued nations with missions that far exceeded their borders and their mere self-interest. It was in this context that "A Model of Christian Charity" would, much later, be rediscovered and remade, and that its status as a foundational text in the American civic canon—indeed its foundational place in the story of the nation itself—would be invented and broadcast.

It is routinely suggested that Winthrop's words impressed their mark all across the emergent culture of American nationalism: that the providential themes he articulated in his last pages poured into the new nation to articulate its deepest, inchoate ambitions. But that misreads the history of both the text and the nation. For three centuries after its writing, except for scattered references to its charity theme, "A Model of Christian Charity" lay out of sight, virtually invisible as a cultural reference point. Its "we" was almost never identified with the ideas of nation swelling in volume around it. Most attempts to identify direct echoes of Winthrop's words in documents written before the twentieth century are false sightings, in which phrases that Winthrop had lifted directly from the Bible or nationalist tropes constructed independently of Winthrop's uses are mistaken for evidence of the Model's influence.

"Chosen people," "city on a hill," "manifest destiny," and "mission" to the world: all across the world's new nationalist cultures, key phrases the Model is said to have set in motion proliferated. Fueled by desires to wrap nations in language grander than that of mere contrivances, they were passed from one nation to another in circuits that swept both through and far beyond the United States. This transnational production of cultures of patriotism should not startle us. Paradoxical as it may seem, nationalism was an international project. Reworking borrowed material, nationalism's articulators across Europe and the Americas filled the political air with variations on claims to special destiny and visibility. Ultimately those claims would absorb "A Model of Christian Charity" in their embrace. When Winthrop's words finally came into general circulation in the second half of the twentieth century, they would be read in the light of assumptions and desires that the constructors of the idea of the nation had prearticulated for them.

As in Winthrop's day, moreover, the formula of a chosen people, set as a city upon a hill, could not be held within any single meaning. With a twist of setting, the words could be turned from celebration into dissent. They could become critical. They could be carried elsewhere for replanting to an alternative nation, farther from the sins of the one in which they originated. They could be hurled like grenades across the most savage fields of war.

Following some of these instances of reappropriated words and ideas, partial resemblances, and radically proliferating employments will almost never bring us directly to Winthrop's text until the twentieth century. But if "A Model of Christian Charity" all but vanishes from center stage during the long nineteenth, its larger story does not. The era's burgeoning culture of nationalism, filled with new hungers for identities, history, and foundations: this, too, braids into the lives of Winthrop's city upon a hill.

For those who live within the claims of nations now, it takes some effort to imagine their novelty when they burst onto the scene. The architects of modern nationalism were not only inventors of new devices for governance; they were fashioners of a new form of political identity, underwritten by the new rituals, historical myths, and practices of belonging. The more loosely constructed polities that preceded them in Europe and its empires were, in comparison, patchworks of authorities, customs, laws, and regions. Stitched together by dynastic alliances, accretion, or conquest, they rarely tried to impose a uniform law or political culture across their quilts of difference. Loyalties were typically local or regional. Winthrop's Massachusetts Bay colony had been part of a distended empire of this sort: a patchwork of allied states, globally dispersed "plantations," voluntary ventures like Penn's and the New England colonies, and quasi-public commercial companies on the East India Company model.

Although one can find premonitions of modern forms of nationalism in the seventeenth century, it was not until the last decades of the eighteenth century that a new figure, the citizen, loyal in the first instance not to a locale or a distant crown but to the nation, stepped out of the French and American Revolutions onto the political stage.[2] States that succeeded in joining their citizens into new phalanxes of loyalty turned out to be political entities of extraordinary power. Late eighteenth- and nineteenth-century nations learned to tax, to legislate, to conscript, to punish, and to wage war still more energetically than the realms they displaced.

But to make all this possible, nations needed to enlist the allegiance of their subjects in deliberately new ways. It was not enough simply to burnish older bonds of ethnic or social affinity. "More than a sentiment," David Bell writes, "nationalism is a political program, which has as its goal not merely to praise, or defend, or strengthen a nation, but actively to construct one [by] casting its human raw material into a fundamentally new form."[3] If nations were to succeed, their leaders had to will their citizens into a new collective sense of themselves, their history, and their solidarity.

Construction of the new nationalist cultures of the late eighteenth and nineteenth centuries was no easy task. Nations often failed. They split apart into fragments; they collapsed in civil war; counterrevolutionary backlash overwhelmed them; they fell prey to stronger powers greedy for expansion; they sank into global insignificance. In the breakaway nations of Latin America that emerged out of the implosion of the Spanish empire, the strains of nation making were particularly pronounced as coups and countercoups, war and rebellion, civil uprisings and the militias' dissolution into the private forces of rival caudillos kept much of the region in turmoil for decades.[4] In the United States, too, the success of the nationalist project was a much less certain thing than the dominant line of American history books commonly acknowledges. Neither the formal declaration of independence nor the ensuring war immediately knitted the peoples of British America together. The revolutionary armies had difficulty recruiting; militias often refused to fight beyond their home grounds. Slaves fled by the thousands across the patriot lines to the freedom the British authorities promised them. Backcountry Southern whites, divided by long-standing grievances from their wealthier seaboard cousins, often chose the loyalist cause. In Philadelphia, as elsewhere, many of the elite sided with the familiar British order rather than with the rough crowds and their haranguers in the streets.[5]

Caught in pressures like these, proponents of the new nationalisms everywhere intensified their efforts to shore up their popular foundations. Symbols proliferated to condense the newly imagined nations into tangible forms. Consciously engineered "technologies" of modern nationalism circulated between the new regimes. By the 1790s the red Phrygian cap and red cockade of the French Revolutionaries had become badges of identity for American nationalists, too, who feared their revolution was being hijacked by forces of reaction. Liberty trees and liberty poles became ubiquitous parts of the nationalist landscape. National anthems on the British model of 1740 gathered popularity; Southern Confederates would enthusiastically take up "La Marseillaise" as their own in 1861. Heroes were singled out for honor, or dragged out of obscurity, or invented altogether. In the United States, George Washington was recast as the new American nation's patriotic saint. The French poured their sense of nation into the figure of Marianne and the goddess of liberty.[6]

In this invented riot of symbols and practices, history held a particularly important place. Ancient traditions were exhumed, generalized, or created anew to bind nations to deep, imagined pasts. Scots authors reinvented the Highland kilt as if it ran back to the beginnings of Scottish history. French nationalists donned the costumes of republican Rome. Folklorists found a German *Volk* far older and more foundational than the new German nation. Southern Confederates invented a Norman heritage for themselves, radically different from the overbearing Anglo-Saxonism of Northern Unionists. Historical pageants re-created dramatic versions of the past. Schoolbooks broadcast narratives of patriotic history. Historical societies spread to collect, honor, and valorize the texts that would give nations a sense of depth and lineage.[7] Through means such as these, Mona Ozouf writes, the "the new social bond was made to be manifest, eternal, and untouchable."[8]

Integral to all these projects was a reconstruction of time. The older logic of typological history in which Winthrop's "Model of Christian Charity" had been immersed did not wholly disappear. To live within the tropes of Old Testament time, to believe that contemporary history unfolded on patterns prefigured in the Bible, to read the signs of the moment through a screen of preset analogies— all this persisted in the new era of nation making. Even patriotic phrase makers who had themselves shaken off the core of Christian beliefs knew the rhetorical utility of biblically prefigured history. Thus Deist Tom Paine could liken George III to the Pharaoh of the book of Exodus. Thus Benjamin Franklin's proposed design for the Great Seal of the new nation could show the Red Sea's waters engulfing the Egyptian army. Jefferson's Great Seal design would have depicted the Israelites being led through the wilderness by a cloud and pillar of fire. Providentialist readings of contemporary events endured. So did the Jeremiad's explanation of each national setback as God's punishment of a morally inadequate people.[9]

But increasingly these ways of reading time and history were displaced by others. One powerful axis of nationalist time leapt forward to the promises of the future. One can hardly begin to read through the patriotic literature of the American Revolution without being struck by the force of the future tense. America had hardly been born but that it was bent on future glory, the Fourth of July orators insisted. Its liberty, the virtue of its citizens, the genius of its commerce and agriculture, and the sheer size of its territory all surely destined it to be one of the great powers of the world. "It may seem presumptuous for us, who are a nation of but yesterday, to arrogate to ourselves the merit of having enlightened mankind in the art of government," David Ramsey declared in an Independence Day oration in Charleston, South Carolina, in 1794. But where else, he went on, were rights so fully secured and happiness so widely diffused? Where else were a nation's people so orderly, peaceable, and virtuous? "To what height of national greatness may we not aspire?" he continued. A "golden age" was around the corner, Samuel Stillman urged in the same vein in Boston in 1789, when American "science, arts, industry, religion, freedom, and public happiness, shall exalt her to the most distinguished eminence among the nations of the world." John L. O'Sullivan was to put it more tersely in 1839: America was "the great nation of futurity."[10]

A second axis of nationalist time, especially prominent in invented nations like the United States, celebrated the nation's heroic break with the past. Destruction of the symbols of the ancien régime—the street crowds' toppling of statues and trampling of coats of arms; the cartoonists' and pamphleteers' vicious libeling of former rulers—were not only acts of political defiance. They were assertions that the new nation had shattered history's chains and encagements: that time itself was starting anew. "The birthday of a new world is at hand," Tom Paine urged Americans in 1776—if only they would cut their ties with a rotten and tyrannical king and seize the new world's promise. Asserting that time's restart had already begun, the Jacobin Convention declared in 1793 that henceforth the beginning year of the French Revolution would be known as Year I.

But a nation suspended only in predictions of future greatness or a moment of radical break with the past could not fully command the affections of those on whose loyalty it depended. Consciously or half-consciously, the architects of nationalism were driven not only to pronounce their nation's novelty but, just as urgently, to disguise it. Whether in the case of the scattered British settlements in North America, or the political patchworks of late nineteenth-century Italy and Germany, the legitimacy of new nations was made to rest, in part, on a sense that they had always existed. Traditions and texts invented for particular occasions were taken out of time as if their roots ran back to the unchanging foundations of the nation itself.

An early example of the effort to enshrine written words with meanings that could transcend their contingency-strewn, politically fraught, and hasty circumstances was the exhuming of the Magna Carta as the very foundation stone of English liberty. A royal concession that had been all but forgotten by the fifteenth century, the Magna Carta was revived in the seventeenth century by parliamentary opponents of the Stuart kings, who inserted it into British nationalist tradition as if it had been, all along, the keystone of England's "ancient constitution."[11] The French did the same after 1848 with the slogan of the modern French nation, "Liberté, Egalité, Fraternité." *Liberté* and *égalité* had been quickly codified during the Revolution. But the word *fraternité* had carried too many associations with Jacobin social radicalism for conservatives and centrists (who much preferred "order" or "property") to accept until decades later—but then to present it as if it had been the nation's birth cry from its beginnings.[12]

This was to be the way the Declaration of Independence was absorbed into the history of the American nation as well. It was not at the beginning a timeless text. Once its purpose of declaring independence to the nation and the world had been accomplished, the historian Pauline Maier writes, the Declaration of Independence was "all but forgotten." When the text came back into currency in the 1790s it was as a partisan document: a polarizing manifesto in a newly polarized political culture. Democratic-Republican Party rallies made the Declaration of Independence's reading the centerpiece of their Independence Day celebrations, all the more enthusiastically once the hand in its authorship of Thomas Jefferson, their party hero, became more publicly known. Federalist newspaper editors, by contrast, deemed its philosophically central sentence ("We hold these truths to be self-evident . . .") too abstract, too French, and too alien to American circumstances. Federalist newspaper editors disdained to print it in their Independence Day issues; Federalist rally organizers almost never read it. Not until the tensions of the first party system eased a half century after independence did the "sacralization" of the Declaration of Independence begin.[13]

Nations needed to promise newness; they needed to display their break with a senescent past. But to manufacture the citizens' consciousness that nationalist loyalty depended upon, they needed to appear to be timeless as well. The past needed to be reinjected into the present. If the nation did not possess foundational documents—and, in sober fact, few did—the impulse to invent them or to remake others for that purpose ran too hard to dismiss. As Drew Faust writes of Confederate nationalism, the new nations' proponents everywhere worked hard to help their citizens see that "their new departure was, in reality, no departure at all."[14] In this service history needed to be folded over upon itself.

This reworking of history would in time fundamentally remake the meaning of Winthrop's "Model of Christian Charity." In the twentieth century the Model would not only be enshrined in the canon of American foundational texts, it would be reimagined as having been there all along. The historical distance between past and present would be foreshortened. Winthrop's words would be made to seem, like the Magna Carta, impervious to time.

CHAPTER 10

Mobile Metaphors of Nationalism

F OR THE MOMENT, however, the silence that enveloped Winthrop's words was profound. A single reference to "A Model of Christian Charity" survives from the seventeenth century. The Model's next sighting, after a gap of almost two centuries, dates from 1809. Almost thirty years later it was given its first printing. Exactly where the text had been in the interim years—how many copies in handwritten circulation had been lost to fire or decay or disinterest—we will never know. All we do know is that the text now preserved in the New-York Historical Society somehow ended up in a cache of family papers possessed by John Winthrop's great-great-grandson and New York City merchant Francis Bayard Winthrop in 1809.

Francis Bayard Winthrop received them from one eldest son to another in the way most intergenerational property was transferred in the seventeenth, eighteenth, and nineteenth centuries. Historical documents were conventionally treated as family possessions in that era, passed on as inheritances, sometimes intact, in many cases parceled out among family heirs. Only rarely were they made accessible to others. John Winthrop's journal, the indispensable source on which every history of early New England depends, had been one of the

earliest American manuscripts to escape this private property vortex. Loaned out by his descendants from time to time, Winthrop's
journal temporarily ended up in the hands of Connecticut's governor
Jonathan Trumbull in the late eighteenth century. Catching wind of
Trumbull's copy, the young Noah Webster, whose flood of American
spellers, grammars, histories, dictionaries, and readers was to impress
so strong a nationalist signature on the early republic's culture, arranged for a Connecticut printer to bring out an edition in 1790.[1]
But this was an exception. Most historical manuscripts were routinely
squirreled away among a family's treasures only to be turned up by
chance and accident.

An alternative to the custom of private property in historical texts
in the early nineteenth century was the newly invented historical society. The nation's first was organized by Boston's ministerial-merchant
elite in 1791 as a repository where books and manuscripts that might
"conduce to mark the genius, delineate the manners, and trace the
progress of society in the United States" could be preserved from private ignorance and neglect. Begun as a small, select association akin
to a subscription library, the Massachusetts Historical Society within
a year had begun printing collections of the most accessible of its documents for broader circulation.[2]

Francis Bayard Winthrop's brother, Thomas Lindall Winthrop—
Boston merchant, bibliophile, and insatiable institution-joiner—
became an early supporter of the historical society movement. By the
end of his life, he could boast not only of his past presidency of the
Massachusetts Historical Society but also his membership in a half
dozen others from Maine to Georgia.[3] In 1803 he convinced his
brother Francis to donate the two volumes of John Winthrop's journal still in the family's hands together with a "large trunk" of old books
and manuscripts to the Massachusetts society.[4] Six years later, Francis Winthrop, who had caught the historical society enthusiasm
himself, offered the newly organized New-York Historical Society a

bundle of twenty-two more historical manuscripts. The last on his list was "A Modell of Christian Charity."[5]

In the safekeeping of the New-York Historical Society, however, the Model sat for almost thirty more years, inert and unremarked upon. In early 1838 one of the Society's members, George Folsom, a lawyer and amateur historian who was just about to marry into the Winthrop lineage, wrote to the Massachusetts Historical Society to ask if it would be interested in publishing the Model in its *Collections*. Though Folsom apologized that he was "unable to furnish any additional information relative to the interesting relic," the answer came back positive. Later that year, after a disappearance that had lasted more than two centuries, "A Model of Christian Charity" was finally published.[6]

Eclecticism governed the volume of the Massachusetts Historical Society *Collections* in which the Model appeared. It opened with an account of the Society, two poetic odes to New England, "rescued," the editors proudly wrote, from more than 160 years of obscurity, and what was said to be an equally ancient song:

If fresh meat be wanting, to fill up our dish,
We have carrots and turnips as much as we wish;
. . . .
Instead of pottage and puddings and custards and pies,
Our pumpkins and parsnips are common supplies;
We have pumpkins at morning and pumpkins at noon;
If it was not for pumpkins we should be undone.

Bracketing the Model on the other side was a painstakingly detailed history of the origins of the postal service. Attempting to elevate the Model above its companion relics, the editors exalted Winthrop and his peers for "founding deeply and broadly the edifice of such an empire" as the United States had now achieved, "whose whole and true glory was all within their prophetic vision."[7]

But from this promising send-off, the Model almost immediately sank into almost complete obscurity again. It was only reprinted twice before the century's end. The first reprinting, in 1840, was in the newsletter of the American Education Society, a Boston association offering financial assistance to young men from poor families seeking to study for the ministry. Seeing a fellow spirit in Winthrop, the Society passed over the Model's "city upon a hill" and chosen people motifs to single out the document for its "correct views . . . in respect to charitable contributions."[8] With ten volumes to fill out, Edmund Clarence Stedman and Ellen Mackay Hutchinson's *Library of American Literature* reprinted about a third of the Model's text in 1888.[9] That was all.

A handful of historians noted the existence of the Model or, more rarely, extracted a line or two from it—though almost never the "city upon a hill" line. George Bancroft, with his own ten volumes to occupy, quoted generously from it in his *History of the United States* in 1858. John Gorham Palfrey gave it a half a paragraph that same year in his *History of New England*, noting that it "breathes the noblest spirit of philanthropy." Charles F. Richardson's *American Literature, 1607–1885*, on the other hand, told its readers in 1889 that "the industrious Winthrop beguiled the tedium of the voyage by writing a booklet called "A Model of Christian Charity" but that "it need not long detain the literary student."[10] The most widely used school history texts—Noah Webster's *History of the United States* in 1841, Charles A. Goodrich's *History of the United States of America on a Plan Adapted to the Capacity of Youth* in 1852, Edward Eggleston's *A History of the United States and Its People for the Use of Schools* in 1889, Edward Channing's *A Students' History of the United States* in 1904, through David Saville Muzzey's extraordinary textbook success, *An American History* in 1911—gave no mention of the Model's existence. Neither did Woodrow Wilson's *A History of the American People* in 1902.[11]

Beyond the history books, the Model simply didn't exist in public consciousness at all. New England's foremost nineteenth-century champion, Daniel Webster, from whom oratory flowed in awesome volume, never mentioned the text.[12] For the national centennial of 1876, the Massachusetts legislature was asked to commission two statues for the National Statutory Hall being inaugurated in Washington, DC. The legislature nominated Samuel Adams and (after a tussle with those who preferred the less harsh and autocratic governor of the Plymouth colony, William Bradford) John Winthrop. The Winthrop statue shows a dignified, bearded, and heavily beruffled figure with a Bible in one hand and the colony's charter in the other. Nowhere in the commission's report or in the raft of dedicatory speeches was Winthrop's Model thought to be worth mentioning.[13]

The era of the first print publication of "A Model of Christian Charity" should have been an auspicious one. In 1820 New England patriots had turned the two hundredth year of the Plymouth colony's beginnings into a major celebration: an occasion for parades, toasts, a public dinner and ball, and an instantly celebrated one-and-three-quarter-hour oration by Daniel Webster. The fiftieth anniversary of the independence struggle ignited still more enthusiastic memorializations of the nation's past. The first stone of the Bunker Hill Monument (whose completion Daniel Webster was to celebrate with another epically long and stirring oration) was laid in 1825. A decade later, Bostonians rediscovered their Tea Party, an event whose memory had been largely shunted aside by the city's elite who had watched it spin out of their control in 1773—shoving forward one of the crowd's aging survivors for a long-delayed hero's acclamation.[14] But no comparable attention was paid to John Winthrop's Model.

Part of the reason for the document's neglect stemmed from its competition with other print representations of New England's seventeenth-century mission. William Bradford's *History of Plymouth Plantation*, which had come to light in the 1850s, gave a much more emotionally empathetic account of the earliest New England immigrants' sufferings. Winthrop's own *Journal* gave detail to the Massachusetts colonists' struggles to find a stable political and ecclesiastical order.

A still deeper liability of the Model was its immersion in assumptions of immutably hierarchical class relations at a time when those premises had come under increasingly vocal attack in American society. "God almighty in his most holy and wise providence hath so disposed of the condition of mankind, as in all times some must be rich, some poor, some high and eminent in power and dignity, others mean and in subjection" restated a seventeenth-century moral truism. But by 1838 when the Model was first put into print, a year after Andrew Jackson concluded his tumultuous popular remaking of the presidency, that opening sentence could not but seem a relic: jarring and out of place even in the political culture of anti-Jackson New England.

But the most important reason why "A Model of Christian Charity" faded so quickly from sight was that the words and phrases that we now so strongly identify with it and imagine to have drawn the culture's attention to it like a magnet were already, independently, in the air. In an age of nationalism, they had become too ubiquitous, too easily available wholly apart from Winthrop's text for the Model to make any serious impression. Too foreign in parts, it was, in this second respect, too familiar. Phrases on which Winthrop had drawn had become portable, malleable particles of nationalist consciousness that traveled, not only through the oral and print cultures of the United States but far beyond.

"City on a hill" was a particularly placeless, almost infinitely malleable phrase. Every Bible-reading Christian knew its place in the book of Matthew from which Winthrop had drawn it. By the nineteenth century, "city on a hill" had been used in homilies virtually beyond counting. The most common reference of the phrase was to the body of Christian believers, the "visible" church that they composed, their obligation to illuminate the world, and their special vulnerability if they fell short. Into the twentieth century, no secular uses came close to matching this in frequency.

But no simile stays easily within bounds. As the technologies of nationalism multiplied in the nineteenth century, the political possibilities in the motif quickly expanded. To describe the *nation* as a city on a hill was still rare in the United States in the first years of nation making. In none of the records of the early Congress does the simile appear, nor in the ratification conventions called to debate the Constitution.[15] John Adams used the phrase once in a letter from Paris in 1780 admonishing General Nathaniel Greene that the movements of his army were being intensely watched all over Europe. There were more "lies" in circulation there about the fortunes of the war and the course of the American Congress, Adams, warned, than about any royal court on the continent.[16] Beyond Adams, however, none of the other figures who were to assume leadership in the early republic used the phrase at all.

By the 1820s, in a more confident nationalist political culture, orators began to employ the "city on a hill" phrase to expand on a much grander theme. "Our American Republic exists not for herself alone," William Plummer told a July 4th audience in Portsmouth, New Hampshire, in 1828. "She is a city set upon a hill which cannot be hid: a beacon kindled upon the mountain top, to which the nations look for light and guidance, through the storms of revolution, and the thick night of ignorance and despotism, with which so large a portion of mankind is still enveloped. To the broad light of our bright example, the longing eyes of millions are turned, from every quarter of this benighted globe." In a similar vein Paul Dean preached in a Massachusetts Election Day sermon in 1832 that we should view "this vast and mighty republic as a beautiful city set upon an hill seen and admired by the kingdoms of the world, and risen as a sun in the firmament of glory, shedding light and liberty on every region on earth."[17]

Our national unity would not be frayed by annexation of still more territory in the West, Lewis Cass insisted in Congress in 1846: "Our Jerusalem is neither beleaguered nor in danger. It is yet the city upon a hill, glorious in what it is, still more glorious, by the blessing of God, in what it is to be—a landmark, inviting the nations of the world, struggling upon the stormy ocean of political oppression, to follow us to a haven of safety and of rational liberty."[18] In the "golden age" of Independence Day oratory, as some have called the decades between 1820 and 1860, speakers' hunger for the apt metaphor, joined with the Bibles by their inkstands or in their memories, combined to set the simile in political motion. But none of these evoked Winthrop's text or New England's early history.

And from the beginning these patriotic uses of the "city on a hill" phrase jostled with a crowd of others. The nation might be like a city set upon a hill, but every missionary family and every pious college student was a city upon a hill too, the church journals advised. Every member of the Masonic Order and every Oddfellow was a city on a hill. Farmers who practiced scientific agriculture were like a city on a hill, whose powerful example to their neighbors "cannot be hid."[19] New York City's intensely developed commerce made it a city upon a hill. Brooklyn, Denver, Baltimore, Akron, and Virginia City, Nevada, were all heralded as cities on a hill as well.[20]

Temperance societies were cities on a hill. But by the same token, so were breweries, visible everywhere, for evil could be as conspicuous as virtue.[21] The proslavery platform of the New Hampshire Democratic Party was "a city set on a hill," William Lloyd Garrison's *Liberator* fumed. It was "a mountain, a volcano, whose belchings gleam up against the Northern sky, by day and night, and whose devouring lava desolates and withers wherever it flows."[22] In a dime novel western published in 1849, just as the melodrama's villain starts to burn one of his victims alive, he stops to boast, "We shall have light now—like a city set upon a hill—won't we?"[23]

The most flexible of metaphors, it could go most everywhere. English patriots declared that "truly" the English people were "a city upon a hill," a "bright beacon . . . to the surrounding world."[24] Robespierre told the National Convention at the French Revolution's height in 1794 that the mission of France was to "accomplish the destiny of humanity," to be "the model to the nations" of the world. "The moral ideal of the world" the historian Jules Michelet heralded France's position in the early 1830s. France was "the pilot ship of humanity" down the "road of the future," destined to "help every nation be born to liberty."[25] Mid-nineteenth-century Latin American Liberals, momentarily regaining their confidence after the disappointments of the early postindependence years, proclaimed their republics as visible models to the world that were "every day moving closer to the apex of civilization." "All nations are watching us," another writer in the same vein declared. "The cause of Mexico is the cause of the American continent; what's more, it is the cause of humanity."[26]

None of these uses of the "city on a hill" phrase depended on any familiarity with Winthrop's "Model of Christian Charity." The words traveled across all of Bible-reading Christendom and from there, unlinked to their scriptural text, deep into secular and political culture. By the nineteenth century, the act of imagining one's own nation to be a beacon to others, a light illuminating the world's darkness, an example set upon a hill, came with the very rhetoric of nationalism.

If "as a city on a hill" was a mobile metaphor across the transnational rhetorics of civic patriotism, the notion of a chosen people swelled even more quickly and consequentially in the new nationalist cultures. During the Revolutionary War, New England preachers had heralded the new nation as God's "American Israel." They stressed the remarkable "favours of heaven" that gave "incontestable evidence that God Almighty, with all the powers of heaven, are on our side."[27] New

Englanders' conflation of the religious and the national was so stock a part of the region's patriotic culture that Harriet Beecher Stowe incorporated a gentle but sharp-eyed parody of it in her description of "Dolly's 'Fourth'" in small town New England. Between a reading of the Declaration of Independence, which Dolly found deeply stirring, an elaborate Fourth of July oration in which "the bird of our nation . . . flew upward and sunward, waved his pinions, gazed with undaunted eye on the brightness, and did all the other things appointed for the American Eagle to do on the Fourth of July," between the cannon-shot-filled battle reenactment that her brothers had come for and the barely veiled jabs at political opponents in the day's opening prayers, Dolly heard the village minister deliver a fervent "recounting of God's mercies to New England from the beginning, and of his deliverances from her enemies, and of petitions for the glorious future of the United States of America—that they might be chosen vessels, commissioned to bear the light of liberty and religion through all the earth."[28]

Much as the New Englanders cherished the chosen people motif, however, they had no special ownership of it. Andrew Jackson bid the nation farewell in 1837 with the reminder that "Providence has showered on this favored land blessings without number, and has chosen you, as the guardians of freedom, to preserve it for the benefit of the human race."[29] Later that year, Sam Houston reassured the new Republic of Texas that God would govern them "as a chosen people." "Who will, what can, set limits on our onward march?" the Irish American immigrant editor and coiner of the "manifest destiny" phrase, John L. O'Sullivan, asked rhetorically in 1839. "For this blessed mission to the nations of the world, which are shut out from the life-giving light of truth, America has been chosen." We are not just a people, a South Carolina writer, far from New England, took up the theme in 1845: "We are a peculiar people, chosen of the Lord . . . to keep burning the vestal flame of Liberty, as a light unto the feet and a lamp unto the path of the benighted nations, who yet slumber or groan under the bondage of tyranny."[30] By 1862, their loyalties having slid from one nation to another, the editors of the *Christian Observer* in 1862 were sure that the Confederacy "will be the Lord's peculiar people."[31]

None of this was unique to Americans. British nationalists, steeped in a similarly covenantal language, used the same tropes for themselves. Victory over France in the Seven Years War had been celebrated with thanks for God's deliverance of "our Jerusalem . . . [our] British Israel." Providence "was no less watchful, for the preservation of the British nation, than it was of old, for the Jewish," Bishop William Warburton celebrated the armies' success. "What I propose to prove," Thomas Lewis declared in 1793, "is that we of this nation are *blessed* above the rest of the world. . . . There are no people under Heaven who have seen clearer instances of the interposition of Providence on their behalf."[32] Dutch patriots embraced their own variation on the theme of "our Dutch Zion." "Truly never has there been a people, and it is possible there will never be one, which has so much similarity and resemblance with Israel than the people of the Netherlands."[33]

Cultures with a Calvinist past found the idea of a covenant with God easy to imagine, but a Calvinist legacy was not required for a nation to be imagined as God's favored people, chosen (as John Milton had put it) "before any other." "Oh Russia," a nineteenth-century Slavophile writer proclaimed. "You, you are chosen to consummate, to crown the development of humanity, to embody all the various human achievements in one great synthesis."[34] "We Germans are a chosen people which represents mankind and makes everything a universal concern," Friedrich Christoph Perthes enthused to a friend in 1807. "We never were a mere nation." A French writer in *Articles de l'avenir* countered in 1831: "In the new universe formed by Christianity, one people, among all others appears visibly chosen to carry forward the universal emancipation within this temporal state. It is the Frankish people."[35]

The language of divine election was a language of simile. To be chosen was to be especially favored. It was to experience more of the protection of providence from natural disaster and military defeat than any other people elsewhere. It was to be given an especially momentous task in the unfolding of human history. It was to enjoy the special "smiles" of providence. It was to be chosen as a "theater for the display of some of the most astonishing dispensations" of God's favor. To laud the appearance of God's "new Israel" was to ratchet up almost to the breaking point the power of metaphor. But to narrow the space between likeness and fact, to try to make their nations not only engines of public order and happiness but instruments of sacred design—all this raced through the traveling rhetoric of nationalism both within and far beyond the United States.

The point has been made many times. Nationalism slipped into the clothes of a civil religion. But to hitch the special destiny of the nation to the language of a chosen people was, at the same time, to hitch it to no simple, glorious future. The history of Old Testament Israel had fluctuated across every register from triumph to exile and tribulation, from exaltation to the ashes of defeat. Punishments had rained down continually upon it. Taken literally there was no simple reassurance to be found in the claim of chosenness.[36]

Not surprisingly, uses of the phrase splayed all across the spectrum from pride to anger. Thomas Jefferson in 1801 praised the good fortune of "possessing a chosen country," a broad ocean away from the "exterminating havoc" of Europe, "with room enough for our descendants to the thousandth and thousandth generation." An older and more disillusioned John Adams took the opposite tack, lamenting that "we are not a Chosen People, that I know of. . . . We must and we shall go the Way of all the Earth." Robert C. Winthrop, serving as a Whig congressman from Massachusetts during the manifest destiny debates in Congress, scoffed at his opponents in the Democratic Party who professed to find the "finger of God" pointing straight to the annexation of Oregon. Abraham Lincoln, speaking briefly in Trenton in 1861 on his way to his inaugural in Washington, DC, used the chosen people phrase for his first and only time: "I shall be most happy indeed if I shall be an humble instrument in the hands of the Almighty, and of this, his almost chosen people."[37]

In this history of recirculating fragments of biblical quotation and repurposed technologies of nationalism, all vastly more distant from the still half-buried text of 1630 than we have conventionally imagined, the variety of these uses is important. Jefferson seized on the celebratory possibilities of the chosen people motif. Adams used it in lament, Robert Winthrop in sarcasm. But the critical edge that the words of apparent self-congratulation disguised is no less important. Lincoln's phrase, in particular, has been repeated too often and far too glibly. It is worth pausing longer over Lincoln's haunting word: "almost."

CHAPTER 11

From the Top Mast

HOW DOES A CRITIC SPEAK within the self-reaffirming echo chambers of a nationalist culture? Sometimes in direct confrontation. Sometimes in disguise. But often by repurposing one of the circulating commonplaces so that a platitude turns suddenly into a barb and provocation. John Winthrop was no stranger to twists of language of this kind. Inverting the accustomed meaning of "city upon a hill," he had taken a biblical line of encouragement and reworked it into a phrase of high anxiety. To dwell as in a city upon a hill, he had reminded himself and his fellows, was not to dwell on a mountain top of confidence but under the eyes of relentless scrutiny. Anxiety was the price of their chosenness. Break their covenant with themselves and God and the world would never forget their falseness. There was terror beneath the confidence of "A Model of Christian Charity," and warning beneath its benedictions.

In the nineteenth-century age of nationalism, a great deal of Winthrop's conditionality gave way before the inflowing tides of patriotism. Spread-eagle rhetoric set the standard for nationalist oratory. Giants of the age like Daniel Webster learned to make its cadences into anthems of self-congratulation. But the critical impulse did not go away. Some of it was clothed in the terms Winthrop had placed, for very different purposes, in the Model itself.

The double-edged potential within these movable metaphors has often been hard to perceive. The impulse to cut up the literature of American nationalism into truncated, quotable fragments, to thread them along a continuous string so that each of the extracts, from the Puritans to the present, amplifies and reinforces the others, has softened and repolished the words. But amidst the din of self-congratulation, critical turns on the theme of a chosen people dwelling in a city on a hill were never far from sight.

One of the now most celebrated nineteenth-century odes to the new chosen people of modern American times was a passage that Herman Melville injected into his novel of life aboard an American Navy frigate, a book he titled *White-Jacket*. The Americans bear "the ark of the liberties of the world," Melville wrote impassionedly there. They were the world's "predestinated" pioneers: "the Israel of our time." Melville picked up the words from the currents of fervent affirmation around him. What is not so often noticed is that he put them into the top-mast musings of one of American fiction's most striking, critical misfits.

Certainly in the literature of nineteenth-century American nationalism there is no stranger figure than the sailor Melville named "White-Jacket." He took his name from the jacket he had stitched together himself when no proper sailor's pea jacket could be had. Stiffly darned and quilted, with a "Quakerish amplitude" and "tumble-down collar," patched with every kind of pocket for books, biscuits, an extra shirt or two, and other gear, all it needed was waterproofing.[1] But the keeper of the ship's paint room insisted that there was no more paint or tar to be had. So alone among his thousand other black-coated fellow crew members, White-Jacket stood out as conspicuously as a ghost in his sodden, homemade, albino outfit.

In this garb, White-Jacket worked the top-most sails of the U.S. naval frigate *Neversink*. A hundred feet above the ship's main deck and its cannons below, he manned the stays of the royal mainsail. His brethren on the main top, if Melville is to be believed, were an elite cadre of sailors. They read Ulysses and Macbeth, Byron's poetry and Scott's romances. They carried Shakespeare in their pockets. They ribbed lesser sailors who knew only whaling ships and blubber. If they slipped at their tasks they fell in a horrifying instant to splinter their bones on brass and wood below or, like the luckier White-Jacket himself, to crash into the sea with a thunder-boom in his ears and the sensation of death flooding over him in billows, yet still alive. But at other times, White-Jacket would mount the mainmast not for conversation or for ship's duty but, in a "meditative humor," would wrap his strange costume around him and "muse." He was, aloft, the ship's loner, its detached conscience, its aerial ghost, its albatross.

One of White-Jacket's extended monologues was to become one of the widely quoted expressions of what is routinely described as the optimistic, future-confident nationalism of the mid-nineteenth-century United States. "Let us leave the Past," Melville has White-Jacket say. "The Past is the text-book of tyrants; the Future the Bible of the Free." The Future was the proper realm for America.

Escaped from the house of bondage, Israel of old did not follow after the ways of the Egyptians. To her was given an express dispensation; to her were given new things under the sun. And we Americans are the peculiar, chosen people—the Israel of our time; we bear the ark of the liberties of the world. . . . God has predestinated, mankind expects, great things from our race; and great things we feel in our souls. The rest of the nations must soon be in our rear. We are the pioneers of the world; the advance-guard, sent on through the wilderness of untried things, to break a new path in the New World that is ours. . . . Long enough have we been skeptics with regard to ourselves, and doubted whether, indeed, the political Messiah had come. But he has come in *us*, if we would but give utterance to his promptings. And let us always remember that with ourselves, almost for the first time in the history of earth, national selfishness is unbounded philanthropy; for we can not do a good to America but we give alms to the world.[2]

Among the most eloquent passages Melville ever wrote, this hymn to the new chosen people, the American "Israel of our time," quickly went into a circulation wider than the book itself. During the late nineteenth century, when Melville's literary reputation had receded to a low ebb, White-Jacket's lines celebrating the Future were imbedded in the quotation books that circulated in both England and the United States for ministers in need of sermon materials. It did not seem to jar on readers that they were there unlinked from American references and attributed to a different sea-yarn spinner, the British novelist Frederick Marryat. Detached from any American referents, they showed up as Marryat's words in the early twentieth century as American newspaper quotation box filler as well.[3] In the mid-twentieth-century flowering of American studies, the words came back into circulation not merely as Melville's own but as the apotheosis of an emergent national optimism. Here, scores of commentators agreed, was the American Idea distilled to its essence. Here one heard the myth of America, the American creed, the distinctive terms of a nationalism that ran back to the Puritan past and forward to an unbounded future.

White-Jacket did not carry much in the way of a plot. Written in a headlong rush between April and September 1849 ("by the job, as a woodsawyer saws wood," Melville apologized to his friends), the book was a pastiche made up of memories of Melville's own naval shipboard experiences six years before, generously larded with vignettes taken from other writers. Reviewers praised it for its vividly penned glimpses into the social life aboard a man-of-war. Seamen's quirks and habits, the strains and dangers under which they lived, the rituals of the deck and mess hall, the exaggerated character traits a ship's environment incubated, the maelstrom of a sea storm and the dullness of life at anchor: all this Melville offered up with a skilled hand.[4]

But if *White-Jacket* did not have a plot, it had a theme that ran insistently through its pages. That theme was the barbaric exercise of authority in the American naval fleet. The "chosen people" passage that was to be so often extracted as distilling the extraordinary promise of America came at the culmination of three of the angriest chapters Melville would ever write: a condemnation of flogging in the U.S. Navy from which he would not let his readers avert their eyes. Tied and "stripped like a slave," in full sight of the ship's officers and entire crew who were required to witness it, the sailors whom the captain's orders had condemned to punishment were whipped until their backs ran with blood, their bodies leaping and writhing under the cat-of-nine-tails' dozen blows. Still worse was the punishment of being flogged "through the fleet," by which an American sailor could be whipped a dozen times at each flogging station from warship to warship. These savage, body-breaking beatings were not only crimes against the Law of Nature, Melville insisted. They were the barbaric remnants of a feudal order, "monstrous graftings of tyranny" upon a nominally free people. Though flogging remained lawful in the English navy, some of England's most admired naval heroes had proved that the governance of sailors did not require it.[5]

But in the U.S. Navy, Melville wrote in anger, the grip of the past was unyielding. Captains behaved like petty kings and tyrants, fortressed behind the "immutable ceremonies and iron etiquette of a man-of-war." The fleet's commodore domineered over his ships' crews as if he were an ancient emperor or sultan, "far more regal than any descendant of Charlemagne, more haughty than any Mogul of the East."[6] The Past wasn't elsewhere. It lorded its sway over the American navy; it saturated the world White-Jacket lived in.

The Future—the dream of escaping the Past's house of bondage to become the ark of the liberties of the world—was not a celebratory report on an emergent American culture, as it has too often been read. It was a dissent from America: a countervision in Melville's and White-Jacket's outraged imaginations of what America ought to have stood for. It turned the rhetoric of a New Israel on its head to flay the America of fact with the ideals it so blatantly failed to live up to.

Flogging on U.S. naval ships would, in fact, be abolished in the same year that *White-Jacket* was published. But nothing in the heat of Melville's impassioned prose and the sense of betrayal that he vested in the "ark of the liberties of the world" passage suggests he anticipated that step. America, in its barbaric cruelties, was being acted out in the ship far below White-Jacket's feet. The *idea* of America that Melville implored readers to believe in lay elsewhere, in a realm at cross purposes to the institutionalized barbarism Melville himself had witnessed: in the dreams of a lonely top-mast man, America's white-coated misfit, its detached critic, its ghostly albatross.

An edge of discomfort had always been part of the chosen people idea. But Melville's dissent from the top mast differed from Winthrop's call to a life of self-scrutiny. It differed, too, from the generalized laments with which later New England preachers would scourge their people's moral and spiritual failings. The Jeremiad's form was enveloping and yet, ultimately, redemptive. It amassed every sign of a chosen people's accumulating weaknesses, every mark of moral and spiritual failure, every reason why God should lose patience and cut his people off entirely—before offering them one last chance at reform.

Critical nationalism of the sort Melville employed was different. It pressed the gulf between ideal and practice into a deeply cutting contradiction. Its power was dialectical, not merely hortatory. It used the rhetoric of nationalism to try to pierce the billowing conceits of national greatness. To wield the term "chosen people" in nineteenth-century America was, typically, to heap still more timbers on the celebratory bonfires of pride. A nation more blessed than any other was no mean object of affection. But with a different, critical turn of the words, the idea of a chosen people, blind to the hypocrisy of their conceits, could be wielded as a stinging critique.

Neither in his earlier, more celebratory pieces nor in his later, darker writings did Melville use these phrases to take up more broadly the cause of reform. But it should not be surprising that some of the most vivid uses of the "chosen people" motif in nineteenth-century America were penned by those who wielded it against what they took to be the nation's most shameful contradictions.

"The Birth-day of Freedom," not merely for this country "but for the world, for man universally," the freelance radical Orestes Brownson called the day of American independence in a Fourth of July address in 1834. "There was more in that revolution than the American and British armies. The past and the future were there. The spirit of immobility and the spirit of progress met there in terrible conflict; humanity all entire was there." But what had come of that struggle for freedom and the "soul-kindling truth" of equal human rights? Brownson went on. What did equality mean when some lived in luxury and idleness while others were riveted to the chains of labor, when starvation faced the working man, when the gap grew ever wider between "those who produce and are poor and those who produce not and are rich?" The promise of America—"Freedom's chosen land," he would call it in 1840—was the rhetorical set-up. The critical knife came in naming "the worm gnawing into the very heart of that tree of liberty which our fathers have planted."[7]

The radical journalist Margaret Fuller proclaimed the greatness of America in the same double-edged way. "We doubt not the destiny of our country—that she is to accomplish great things for human nature, and be the mother of a nobler race than the world has yet known. . . . But she has been so false to that scheme made out at her nativity, that it is now hard to say which way that destiny points."[8] "What might she be?" a correspondent to the abolitionist *Liberator* echoed the theme. "But for this foul blot [of slavery] . . . she would be as a city on a hill for the admiring gaze of the whole world. *Alas! alas!* that she is . . . blind to the elements of greatness within her."[9]

There was a still more radical stance for antebellum America's critics to take, of course, which was to dissociate themselves from the city on a hill theme altogether. This was William Lloyd Garrison's position well before, in dramatic fury, he publicly burned the Constitution that he called a covenant of death with slavery. "What is there in the character of this American Nation that they should be the especial charge of the Most High? Is it that we have extirpated the races He had planted here at first, with fire-water and sword? . . . Is it that we have promoted this System [of slavery] by blood and this fraud to the utmost of our power, and spread it where it did not exist, and still sigh for new worlds for its fatal victories? . . . And yet, to judge from the words of priests and politicians, we are His chosen people, on whom depend all the hopes of mankind!"[10]

Frederick Douglass, the most eloquent African American orator and writer of his day, took the same line, even after he had broken with Garrison on the efficacy of political action under a blood-stained Constitution. When fugitive slave hunters tracked down Anthony Burns in Boston and tried to force his return to slavery in Virginia, Douglass wrote with irony-dripping anger, "Now let all true patriotic Christian Republicans rejoice and be glad! . . . Let the churches be flung open and the pulpit resound with thanksgiving, that our beloved country has been saved, and that Republican Liberty is still secure, and the example of the model republic still shines refulgently, to the confusion of tyrants and oppressors in Europe."[11]

And yet, even Douglass knew the critical potential of the chosen nation theme. He refused to think that the North could save its virtue simply by dissociating itself from the slave South. That would be akin to a pirate imagining that he could clear his crime by leaping into a longboat and leaving his crewmates and their tormented prisoners behind. Sooner or later, "by fair means or foul means, in quiet or in tumult, in peace or in blood, in judgment or in mercy, slavery is

doomed to cease out of this otherwise goodly land, and liberty is destined to become the settled law of this Republic."[12] This stance was not
a sign of passive resignation to the tides of history; it was not the voice
of a writer unwittingly entangled in the "myth of America," as Sacvan
Bercovitch was to put it.[13] To embrace the nationalist promise and insist that only when the nation's deepest flaw had been excised would
that promise be realized was a tool of powerful edge and potency.

When Abraham Lincoln came as close as he ever would to the chosen
people trope, there is no evidence that he had read Douglass's appeal
to "this otherwise goodly land." "This almost chosen people" was a
phrase of Lincoln's own improvisation. In the long, ceremonial train
ride in early 1861 from Springfield, Illinois, to his inaugural in Washington, DC, during which Lincoln was called on to speak at every
stop, even after his voice had grown hoarse and failed, he never used
the phrase other than in his impromptu remarks at Trenton. You can
read through the entire record of Lincoln's writings, speeches, and remarks, public and private, without ever finding a variation on "chosen people" again.[14]

   Of all the ways in which Lincoln made his own distinctive course
through the crisis of war and disunion, his refusal to join the chorus
of those who were certain they knew God's intentions for the nation
was one of the most striking. The "chosen people" phrase and its halo
of patriotic sentiments erupted with the secession crisis itself, both
in the North and the South. The rhetoric of a redemptive war thundered from pulpits on both sides. "Government is now become
Providential," Horace Bushnell declared. "If there ever was a war undertaken in the name of God in his service, at his command, under
his approbation," a Rhode Island clergyman greeted the coming of
the war, this was surely it. "Our national deliverance has been
wrought out for us, as a world-historical act, by God himself," another Northern preacher heralded the final, bloody end of the war.[15]

In the states of the Southern Confederacy a mirror rhetoric ran just as strongly. The constitution of the Confederate States of America invoked the favor and guidance of almighty God in its very first sentence. "This is a holy war," Southern preachers and politicians declared. The theme of chosenness swelled. "The analogy between the Confederacy and the chosen Hebrew nation was invoked so often as to be transformed into a figure of everyday speech," Drew Faust writes.[16] "The God of Abraham, Isaac and Jacob" was the "God of Jefferson Davis, Robert E. Lee, and Stonewall Jackson," a Confederate camp revivalist exhorted the troops. In both the North and the South, preachers searched the daily war news for signs of God's providential hand at work. A sense of living in Old Testament time, amidst its typological emblems and signs, returned in force.[17]

This was surely God's cause, Lincoln's allies insisted. And yet Lincoln himself was never as certain as they. He believed unyieldingly in the imperative of preserving the union. He refused to compromise on secession or on the demand to open still more room for slavery in the territories, the knotted issues over which the politicians wrangled futilely in the interregnum months between his election and inauguration. When the war came, Lincoln prosecuted it with all the vigor at his disposal, egging on his generals to more aggressive action, wringing his hands at their caution, mourning the bodies that soon piled up in the tens of thousands on the battlefields, but never flinching from adding more.

But that this was God's war, Lincoln was never convinced with the simplicity that others preached. Could one be sure that God was on either side? he confided to those closest to him. Could one know that he willed either side victory? Could anyone be certain that this immense catastrophe, this carnage, was not intended for some still more distant purpose? Could one be sure that these rivers of blood were not God's punishment for the sin of slavery, in which both North and South had been so deeply complicit?

"The Almighty has His own purposes," Lincoln confessed in his second inaugural address. "If God wills that it continue, until all the wealth piled by the bond-man's two hundred and fifty years of unrequited toil shall be sunk, and until every drop of blood drawn with the lash shall be paid by another drawn with the sword," that will would be done. Lincoln was immovable. But his God—"omnipotent, inscrutable, and mysterious," in Richard Carwardine's words—was no cosmic nationalist, no covenant maker, no straightforward chooser of sides.[18]

Holding to this lonely combination of certainty and doubt amidst the eruption of providential nationalism around him, Lincoln went through the war in a kind of a top mast of his own. But of one thing he was certain, that the promises of liberty embedded in the Declaration of Independence were the nation's birthright. He was thinking about the Declaration as he made his way from New York City through Trenton to Philadelphia where he was to speak the next day at Independence Hall. "I have never had a feeling politically that did not spring from the sentiments embodied in the Declaration of Independence," he told a cheering crowd there.[19] He was thinking, as he had since his turn to the Republican Party began, about slavery.

We have too often read Lincoln's "almost chosen people" phrase too naively. We have not seen clearly the difference between Winthrop's anxious hopes of realizing God's providential scheme and the patriotic certainties of the Civil War preachers, and the distance between both these uses of the chosen people trope and Lincoln's strikingly different, critical nationalism. By "almost chosen" as the crisis began to unfold in 1861 he did not mean "not quite." He did not mean that, step by step, the nation might reach that favored place. He did not mean a nation that had been chosen once and then fell away from its promise.

Across a century and a half, we cannot read Lincoln's mind any better than those who fretted and strained to do so at the time. Later, acquiescing in the pressures on his abolitionist flank to weaken the

Confederacy by directly undermining the system of slavery, he seems to have regained momentarily a clearer sense of God's providence in the unexpected maelstrom of the war. The Emancipation Proclamation—Lincoln's pivot to an "emancipation war," as Frederick Douglass called it—seems to have brought a certain catharsis. But in February 1861, none of this was legible in the future: not open war, certainly not a war this grindingly long and consuming of lives, and certainly not abolition of the regime of slave labor. In 1861, what he seems to have meant by "almost chosen" was something much more critical and, even now, more sobering. He meant a nation that might have been chosen—but for the deep, original sin of slavery.

CHAPTER 12

Constructing a City on a Hill in Africa

I N ALL THESE VARIATIONS—fervently celebratory or sharply critical, patriotically enlisted or splattered across a mass of other references—"city on a hill" and "chosen people" circulated through the nations of the nineteenth century. Unrelated to their employment in "A Model of Christian Charity" centuries before, they formed a part of the stock vocabulary of a nationalist age.

There was one event, however, around which something especially close to Winthrop's original use of the "city on a hill" motif cohered. That was not the U.S. Civil War, fraught though it was with attempts to read the hand of God's providence in human events. It was not the Great War for civilization's defense in 1914–18, saturated with talk of divine destiny. It was in discussions of a new, American-made, black republic in Africa: Liberia. Not only did the "city on a hill" phrase flourish with particular exuberance in Liberia, but there, more clearly than anywhere else in the nineteenth and early twentieth centuries, Winthrop's sense of living under the world's scrutiny had its modern parallel.

Liberia did not begin as a nation-making project. It began as a means to offload onto the West African coast those black Americans whom other Americans wanted to be rid of. Although there were some African Americans in the early nineteenth century who envisioned returning to the continent from which their forebears had been stolen, the origins of the American colony in Liberia came from white Americans with, at best, deeply paternalistic relationships with those whom they hoped to colonize.

Free Negroes were the primary point of concern for the Liberia project's originators. An anomalous people in a biracial society, confounding notions that some were naturally suited for mastership and the others for slavery, free blacks raised nightmares of racial discontent and social disorganization among many early nineteenth-century white Americans. Southern slaveholders worried that if free blacks did not themselves ignite resentment and revolt among the region's slaves, their example could not but fuel dangerous ambitions and discontents. Slaveholders in the upper South, where slave labor's profits were diminishing and where some had grown morally queasy about slave ownership itself, were particularly drawn to the colonization idea. For them, the project of establishing a charitable organization that would transport free blacks and emancipated slaves to distant Africa had both a self-exculpatory and self-preservationist appeal.

Southern slaveholders were joined in the colonization project by Northern philanthropists who saw free, poor blacks as in need of aid but who could not imagine them thriving in the cities of the early United States. "A people which are as injurious and dangerous to our social interests, as they are ignorant, vicious and unhappy," the first secretary of the American Colonization Society called them. In the colonizationists' eyes, free blacks constituted "a degraded, despised and oppressed" underclass in the nation's midst. They would do better, the Society organizers insisted, if their return to Africa were organized, underwritten, and managed by those who had their best interests at heart.[1]

On this mission, the American Colonization Society's first shipload of emigrants departed from New York City in 1820. Skirting past the settlements at Sierra Leone that British philanthropists had established for London's black poor and for the slaves who had fled across the British lines during the war for American independence, searching the West African coast for a usable anchorage and a native chiefdom that would tolerate their disembarking, eighty-odd colonizers under the direction of their three white, American Colonization Society agents established a tiny coastal settlement. Within three months, a quarter of them had died of disease.

Relocating the project further south to a site they would rename Providence Island, the Society tried again. This time they soon faced not only disease but an alliance of West African chiefs and an army of several thousand warriors determined to drive the strangers out. Only the unexpected effectiveness of the colonizers' cannon against the tightly massed ranks of the native African warriors, whose use of human walls of fighters proved deadly vulnerable to cannon fire, turned the effort back. But survival was still a close thing. Twenty years later, of the 4,500 emigrants the Society had succeeded in transporting to its Liberian colony to try their luck against disease, hunger, and recurrent war with the native peoples of the coast, fewer than two thousand remained.[2]

Yet in the reports of the American Colonization Society, dismay and disappointment were overwhelmed by a sense of realizing God's promise both for the United States and for Africa. Surely God's hand must have been at work in the ability of so few to cut down so many and send the native armies hurling back. New England's earlier years, Society speakers reminded each other, had been full of trials and disease as well. Above all, the promise of bringing Christianity to Africa was not to be retreated from. Emerging out of the Society's other goals, the task of converting pagan and heathen Africa to Protestant Christianity quickly became its principal rationale. And with it flourished the mission of being a "city on a hill"—not simply an example to the natives beyond the colony's small string of settlements on the

West African coast, but a lighthouse that would illuminate the whole of the African continent.

Tiny though the Liberian venture might be, its destiny could not have been more grandly exalted. By the "wisdom of God's providence," an American Colonization Society speaker expanded on the theme in 1827, a people who could only be a source of malignancy at home were transformed into "a glorious beacon, beaming with broad, and vivid, and constant splendor, indefinitely into the interior of an extensive continent overspread with the darkness of heathenism." They were to be "the means of kindling up on that wide and benighted continent, the beacon lights of science and Christianity."[3] Their moral example would defeat "the night of witchcraft and superstition" that enveloped Africa. It would stamp out the international traffic in slaves at its source.

The project had not only proved "a blessed asylum for a wretched people," the Society's publications insisted. It was "already to the African tribes, like 'a city set upon a hill which cannot be hid.' A thousand barbarians, who have long made merchandise of their brethren, and been regarded themselves, as the objects of a bloody and accursed traffick, come within its gates, and are taught the doctrine of immortality. . . . Heaven forbid that this Colony should perish; for its influence to the most abject, injured and miserable of our race, will be cheering as 'the day-spring from on high,' and salutary as the waters of life."[4] The first Puritan generation in New England had never raised visions this fervent or this expansive.

On the ground, the Liberian venture scarcely lived up to its organizers' high promises. Between the mid-1830s and a brief upward spike of interest in the 1850s, few already free American blacks joined the emigrant boats to Liberia. More and more often the American Colonization Society's vessels carried newly freed slaves who, by the tightening laws of most U.S. slave states, could not be emancipated unless their owners promised to transport them elsewhere. Discouraged by the difficulties of raising funds and controlling at a distance the often autocratic actions of its agents, the American Colonization Society engineered Liberia's reorganization in 1847 as an independent state—the first free black republic in Africa.

But independence did not bring prosperity to Liberia. Its population hardly grew after the 1850s; by the turn of the twentieth century, there were barely twelve thousand Libero Americans clustered in a coastal string of towns on the fringe of the continent. Visions of evangelizing the native masses came to very little effect. The two million or more African peoples living in the territory the Libero Americans claimed as their own had no citizenship rights in the Liberian republic. Only the self-cancelling effects of their internal rivalries kept West Africans from driving the black American colonizers back into the sea—that and the assistance of British and U.S. naval vessels at timely moments.

Economically, Liberia struggled to find a footing in the global economy. Visions of a nation where onetime slaves could become free-standing land cultivators quickly evaporated. Trade in native export goods and government salaries sustained a political and economic elite—prideful and insular, fiercely protective of the race privileges of its lighter-skinned ruling families, and scornful of those over whom they claimed nominal sovereignty. In the capital city, Monrovia, a starkly divided double settlement quickly grew up: on the one side, a Libero American town of broad streets and wood-framed, veranda houses, and, right next door, a much poorer, segregated native town of narrow alleyways and tightly packed bamboo dwellings. Geopolitically Liberia sank quickly into insignificance. A loan for internal improvements negotiated in London through unscrupulous middlemen in 1871 turned out to carry disastrous economic consequences. Into the early twentieth century, Liberian governments were still going hat in hand to European and U.S. creditors hoping for debt relief.

Virtually from the first, moreover, the Liberian venture had been a lightning rod for critics. In 1831 the fiery abolitionist William Lloyd Garrison had decided that the removal of free blacks to Africa was nothing other than a ploy to perpetuate the regime of slavery and had turned in fury against it. "This is our home, and this our country," a free black convention resolved in the same mood early that year. "Here we were born, here we will die." The colonization idea was a fraud and a foe to every American colored man, Frederick Douglass added with his powerful voice. "Our right to stay here is as good as that of . . . any man-stealer in the land." "We say to every colored man, *be a man where you are*. . . . You must be a man here, and force your way to intelligence, wealth, and respectability. If you can't do that here, you can't do it there."[5]

When in the 1850s the aggressiveness of Southern slaveholders' designs for the expansion of slave territory and the tightening fetters of racial restrictions in the North caused some free blacks to think of finding a refuge elsewhere, Douglass insisted that Africa held nothing for American-born people of color but impoverishment and exile. "If we go anywhere," he wrote discouragedly in early 1861, just before war broke out, "let us go to *Hayti*"—to the black revolutionary republic that had overthrown its slave owners and had successfully defended itself against the best armies Napoleon could muster. Haiti was close enough to the shores of the United States that it could continue to vex and disturb American slavery. We can "plant ourselves at the very portals of slavery" and perhaps around that germ organize all twelve million Negroes in the Americas, from the Caribbean islands to the mountain tops of South America. If there was a "city set on an hill" for African Americans, Douglass wrote, it was there, in "this modern land of Canaan," where a free black republic stood as a rebuke to the racist contention that blacks were unfit to administer a government on their own.[6]

But in Liberia itself, despite the nation's critics and setbacks, the "city on a hill" motif flourished extravagantly. There is no evidence that any of the project's founders had read John Winthrop's "Model of Christian Charity." Nowhere else in the nineteenth- and early twentieth-century United States and its dependencies, however, did the "city on a hill" phrase so heavily saturate the rhetoric of politics. To the colonization project's organizers the mission of a new black America in Africa was that, in a sea of African paganism and immorality, it would bring the light of Protestant Christian religion. To the Libero Americans who made the trope their own, the mission of Liberia was that, in a world awash in racial prejudices, their new, black-led nation would demonstrate to the world the Negro's political capacities for self-government.

The notion that a small, economically precarious nation in Africa could refute the assumption that only Europeans and their imperial administrators had the racial capacities for rule may seem quixotic now. But there is no missing the intensity with which the Libero American elite embraced the idea of a New Jerusalem and repurposed it in Africa. God's "special providence has been as unmistakably manifest in Liberia . . . as ever were the pillars of cloud by day and of fire by night to direct Israel's course to the land of promise," Stephen Allen Benson, Liberia's second president, declaimed in 1858. Edward James Roye refurbished the theme in 1870: "God has planted us here, and through all the vicissitudes of our existence, his hand has been plainly, visibly directing our affairs. God has set Liberia, as it were, upon an hill on this continent." William David Coleman, assuming the presidential office in 1900, affirmed: "Our fathers, with the blessing of an all-wise Providence, have laid on these shores the foundation of a great Negro nationality that may in [the] future be the hope of the race and admiration of the world."[7]

Liberia's most celebrated writer in this vein, Edward Blyden, did not have an easy relationship with the Liberian merchant and political elite. A migrant from the Danish West Indies, he spent a brief sojourn in the United States in 1850, long enough to be turned away from the theological seminaries to which he sought enrollment on the grounds that no person of African descent could possibly possess the abilities a theological education required and also to catch wind of the Liberian project. A thorn in the side of the mulatto elite whose color prejudices he felt personally and acutely, he was driven out of Liberia by a lynch mob in 1871 at the height of a political party feud. But for Blyden, too, the natural language of Liberia was providential. As he told American audiences during a recruiting trip in 1862: "In a sense that is not merely constructive and figurative, but truly literal, God says to the black men of this country, with reference to Africa: 'behold, I set the land before you, go up and possess it.'" Theirs was not to be a conquest but a return, an exodus out of captivity, a reclaiming of "consecrated ground."[8]

Most striking of all in the rhetoric of Liberian nationalism was not the Exodus motif but its echo of the Model's theme: that the success or failure of the Liberian nation makers' work could not escape the world's scrutiny. "The eyes of the whole civilized world are upon her, critically observing every step she takes," Liberia's first president, Joseph Jenkins Roberts, warned. "We are more eagerly watched than we have any idea of," Blyden wrote. "The nations are looking to see whether 'order and law, religion and morality, the rights of conscience, the rights of persons, the rights of property, may all be secured' by a government controlled entirely and purely by Negroes."[9]

Liberia might be on the margins of the world, but there, Liberian orators told each other, the very basis of the idea of white racial superiority lay exposed to scrutiny. There as nowhere else, assumptions "of the incapacity of the colored race for self-government" were brought to a test. "Fellow citizens! we stand now on ground never occupied by a people before," Hilary Teage told a Monrovia audience on the eve of Liberian independence, whose declaration he was soon to write.

> However insignificant we may regard ourselves, the eyes of Europe
> and America are upon us, as a germ destined to burst from its

enclosure in the earth . . . and swell to the dimensions of the full-grown tree, or (inglorious fate!) to shrivel, to die, and be buried in oblivion. . . . . Upon you, rely upon it, depends, in a measure you can hardly conceive, the future destiny of your race. You are to give the answer whether the African race is doomed to interminable degradation—a hideous blot on the fair face of creation, a libel upon the dignity of human nature, or incapable to take an honorable rank amongst the great family of nations!

"The experiment we are now making concerns the entire Negro race," others wrote. It would either prove "the old calumnies against the Negro" or be the foundation upon which "an abiding Negro Nationality" would take its rightful place in a racially hostile world.[10]

The Liberian republic was to be a beacon to others. But to dwell in that city upon a hill was to dwell in a site of intense visibility and vulnerability. Each step would be taken under the skeptical eye of its race-demeaning critics. The theme of trial and vulnerability that ran so palpably through Winthrop's "Model of Christian Charity" had no clearer expression in the greater America of the nineteenth and early twentieth centuries than in the nation that a handful of its racial castoffs endeavored to make.

Liberia was a small and distant place. But by the turn of the twentieth century, a sense that the future of the black "race" might turn on its success had begun to infect the imaginations of a new generation of African Americans in the United States as well. Perhaps it was no surprise that Booker T. Washington should have found the project congenial to his conviction that in a prejudiced world the "Negro" must pull himself up by his bootstraps through work, education, and self-help. His own Tuskegee Institute for industrial and agricultural education was often described as a "city on a hill," beaming a gospel of self-reliance far beyond its Alabama setting.[11] By the turn of the twentieth century Tuskegee Institute had begun to dispatch small teams of students and faculty to colonial Africa to help train native Africans in more efficient cotton production techniques. When debt crisis broke over Liberia once again in 1908, Booker T. Washington himself intervened with Presidents Theodore Roosevelt and William Howard Taft to help broker a new loan on much less avaricious terms than the British bankers had granted, secured by what essentially amounted to protectorate status for Liberia: U.S. government control over Liberia's customs revenues and U.S. control over appointments to its army officer corps. Fittingly, not long after Washington's death a clone of his Tuskegee Institute, the Booker T. Washington Agricultural and Industrial Institute, was established by his admirers in Liberia.[12]

Marcus Garvey's vision for a new Liberia was far more flamboyant. Garvey cut a meteoric arc through African America between 1919 and 1923. Preaching a separatist version of Booker T. Washington's gospel of self-help, he drew tens of thousands to the rallies of his Universal Negro Improvement Association. Through chains of factories, publishing houses, retail stores, and steamship lines, the movement promised to create a black-owned economy within an economy that had systematically suppressed and exploited the descendants of Africa. At the apex of this project, Garvey envisioned a massive return to Africa via a recolonization of Liberia. The Liberia that Garvey promised was a nation teaming with new race pride, new emigrants from American racial injustice, and capital raised from the black American masses. "We are coming four hundred million strong" from the United States, South America, and the West Indies, Garvey promised: to reclaim Africa for its people, to reunite a people in exile, and to build "a great state in Africa which . . . will make the Negro race as respectable as the others."[13]

But the most unexpected of those who caught the sense that African Americans' future might, in some critically important way, lie in Liberia's possession was W.E.B. Du Bois. Booker T. Washington's rival, Marcus Garvey's nemesis, the National Association for the

Advancement of Colored People's most eloquent voice for African Americans' claims not simply to a side economy of their own but for full, equal rights within the U.S. nation, Du Bois was an odd figure to enlist in the cause of Pan-Africanism, and he came late to it. It was in watching the First World War spill over Europe in a contest for the spoils of the world's resources that the importance of the global "color line," as Du Bois called it, began to press itself on his acute and restless consciousness.

He helped engineer the first Pan-African Congresses in London and Paris and to write into their manifestos the imperative that Negroes everywhere be recognized as potentially fully civilized peoples. Imperialism needed to be recognized for what it was: a system of monopolization of the world's wealth and resources and exploitation of its black, brown, and yellow labor, all justified by the cant of the impossibility of self-government by people of color. It was with that global struggle in mind that Du Bois sailed for his first glimpse of Africa in 1923. His destination was Liberia.[14]

The breathless reports that Du Bois filed from his four-week stay make a mass of contradictory reading now. Enchanted by the colors, the bare limbs, the sinuous, muscled bodies, the leisure and languor of African life, the deep silences and "great gold globules" of sunlight that enveloped the landscape, Du Bois seemed to have slipped on the robe and slippers of the purest bohemian aesthete. When "primitive men" outpaced those who now thought themselves fittest to rule, he wrote, "there will spring in Africa a civilization without coal, without noise, where machinery will sing and never rush and roar, and where men will sleep and think and dance and lie prone before the rising sons and women will be happy." In this alternative to modern commercial-industrial society, "We shall dream the day away and in cool dawns, in little swift hours, do all our work." This was a view of Liberia from the hammock of a beguiled tourist.[15] In the meantime, Du Bois was working hard to help arrange the massive rubber plantation investment that was to make Liberia for the next fifty years what some critics would call a wholly owned subsidiary of the Firestone Rubber Company.

"The spell of Africa is upon me," Du Bois confessed in the midst of these contradictions. Africa "is a great black bosom where the Spirit longs to die. It is life so burning, so fire encircled that one bursts with terrible soul inflaming life." Can one blame Du Bois for being a little dizzy under its effects? In his circle of New Negro artists and writers, the allure of negritude was powerfully at work in the early 1920s in paint, dance, and prose. Langston Hughes, sailing down the west coast of the African "motherland" in 1923, could not shake from his mind the same images that overpowered Du Bois: the "market flashing with colors, the dark girls in bright bandannas . . . blue green twilight. . . . The hot, heavy African night studded with stars." The ancient "witchery" of Africa, Du Bois wrote, was "burning" in his Massachusetts-born, Harvard-educated blood.[16]

But of one thing Du Bois was certain. Every power in Europe and every white supremacist at home was vitally interested in the failure of Liberia. In Liberia, he wrote, in a soberer mood, "political power has tried to resist the power of modern capital." The outcome was not yet clear. But "if Liberia fails this justifies slavery, serfdom, autocracy and exploitation of a race 'incapable' of self-rule. If Liberia succeeds why should not the Negro succeed in self rule and democratic development and decent industrial organization in Sierra Leone, the Gold Coast, French Africa, South Africa, East Africa, Kenya, the Sudan and Abyssinia?"[17] The eyes of a scornful world were upon Liberia, eager for its every misstep. Du Bois did not need to read "A Model of Christian Charity" to share, more intensely than any of the drum-beating patriots at home, what Winthrop meant by the anxiety of being made "a story and a byword through the world." For all its contradictions and failures, Liberia was an experiment in black political capacity perched on a mountain peak of visibility and vulnerability.

The "city upon a hill" language flowed unforced out of his pen. "We fall down, down to the burning equator, past Guinea and

Gambia, to where the Lion Mountain glares, toward the vast gulf whose sides are lined with silver and gold and ivory," Du Bois wrote. "And now we stand before Liberia—Liberia that is a little thing set upon a hill—thirty or forty thousand square miles and two million folk. But it represents to me the world."[18]

The Carnage of God's Chosen Nations

B Y THE TIME W.E.B. Du Bois set foot in Africa, the conse-quences of nineteenth-century hypernationalism were al-ready marked across the globe. European nation-state consolidation had exploded in 1914 in a war more deliberately and devastatingly organized than any before it. As Du Bois journeyed through France in late 1923, the last of the millions of the war dead were still being dug out of the killing fields. Africa and southern Asia had been carved up virtually to the last acre by the imperial powers. The nations that emerged after 1919 with their empires intact rearranged the losers' spoils, but the new "mandates" they authorized did not fundamen-tally change the character of an empire-dominated world.

Liberia, as Du Bois celebrated it, was an exception to the new imperial order: the sole black republic on the African continent. But at the same time, and in ways far deeper than Du Bois could bring himself to admit, Liberia, too, had been a pawn in the project of em-pire from its very beginning. Its African American settler colonists had imposed their land claims on the African native populations by force, justifying their right to rule the native populations, like impe-rialists everywhere, by their higher level of civilization and more fully developed benevolence. Though formally unrecognized by the

U.S. government until the Civil War, Liberia by the early twentieth century had become for all practical purposes a U.S. overseas colony: an open field for Firestone Rubber and other American investments protected by the U.S. Navy.

The United States' position in the global fields of power had changed radically over the same years as well. At the Liberia colony's founding in 1820, the United States was still an Atlantic-facing nation; its center of population lay just 130 miles west of the national capital at Washington, DC. By the end of the nineteenth century, the territorial limits of the United States had not only reached the Pacific Ocean but were pressing into new locations overseas. Acquisition of the Philippines, Puerto Rico, and Hawaii had been secured; de facto protectorates over Cuba, Nicaragua, the Dominican Republic, and Haiti were about to be put in place. The United States, far less scathed by World War I than the other combatants, came to the Versailles Peace Conference in 1919 as the strongest of the Great Powers, both economically and militarily. It was this accomplished geopolitical reality that made Woodrow Wilson confident that the United States could set the terms of the postwar world order. From a new nation still clinging to the Atlantic rim in 1776, the ascent to global power a century and a third later had been remarkable.

In explaining the dramatic expansion across space of American power in the nineteenth century, historians routinely point to the sense of mission injected into the nation's consciousness by its early Puritan settlers, with Winthrop's "Model of Christian Charity" as its clearest articulation. One of the leading textbooks of the 1970s put the claim succinctly: "This sense of destiny, so eloquently expressed by Winthrop at the dawn of the New World's history, infused and shaped the perception that Americans have ever since had of themselves and their role in the world, a perception apparent in Thomas Jefferson's belief that Americans were the chosen people of a new Israel, in Woodrow Wilson's phrase that the world must be made safe for democracy, and in John F. Kennedy's alarm, sounded in 1961, that 'a new generation of Americans' must be prepared to fight the world-wide battle of 'freedom versus tyranny.'" College students now find the same equation of American great-power ascent with the Puritan past in the widely used *Major Problems in American Foreign Relations*. Placing the "city upon a hill" passage from Winthrop's Model as the very first of the historical documents their readers will encounter, the editors explain that students will find there "the American doctrine of mission and God-favored destiny that the Puritans had etched on American memory."[1]

Other explanations for the dramatic expansion of global ambitions and power, to be sure, quickly supplement the theme of a destiny and mission inherited from the Puritan past. The rivalries for empire on the North American continent, the Southern slaveholders' drive for new soil and territory, Northern industrialists' quest for wider and wider markets, settler hunger for land and property, the racist assumptions that gave Anglo-Americans a sense of their "manifest" right to the continent, and the ideology of endlessly expanding liberty all propelled the expansion of power across space. In these accounts, the nature of the Puritan contribution is not always clear. Some American foreign relations experts take the Model's call to act as a moral example to the world as sharply opposed to the impulse to subdue and civilize it; others, to the contrary, point to the cruel self-righteousness with which the Puritans waged war against their Native American enemies as a legacy that Americans would carry all the way into the wars of the present.[2]

None of these amendments, however, have fully displaced the sense that Winthrop's text—whether literally present or not, whether through its words or its unspoken assumptions—somehow imbued a sense of God's chosenness into the distinctive cultural DNA of imperially expansive America. From Winthrop's "Model of Christian Charity," to John L. O'Sullivan's rhetoric of "manifest destiny," to Albert J. Beveridge's celebration of the Americans' "divine mission" to bring civilization to the Philippines, to Woodrow Wilson's profound

sense of America's righteous place in the world of global affairs—
strung one after another like unalterable station stops on history's
rail line—the story proceeds.[3] The Puritan sense of a nation endowed
with a sacred calling, as Perry Anderson put it, helped ease the "seamless passage to an American imperialism."[4] What difference it might
make to realize that almost none of the writers in this succession had
read—or could have read—Winthrop's Model, or that the analytical
terms themselves—"etched on American memory," "infused" into
the self-perception of Americans, "afforded seamless passage"—are
extremely difficult to pin down, is rarely explored.

In fact, the course of American expansion was carried far less by its
distinctive texts than by circumstances. The colonial American settlements were, from the beginning, parts of an imperial project, born
as projections of English power and linked by commerce to the engine of English economic growth. The first movements toward intra-
colonial solidarity in British North America took place during the
Seven Years War, a decade before the first anticolonial protests, when
a sense of their common Protestant Englishness, vis-à-vis the designs
of the "papist" French and their "savage" Native American allies, drew
the geographically scattered British colonists together. The first empire New England's preachers celebrated was the British empire. The
fall of Quebec and Montreal to English, Scots, and American soldiers
in 1759–60 brought forth a spate of sermons praising the blessings
of providence on "the *British* Israel"—"the wonder and envy of all the
world."[5] Thomas Jefferson's prediction of "an empire of liberty" unrolling across the continent was an appropriation of imperial sentiments already in circulation long before the Revolution itself.

    To this, still more importantly, were added the dynamics of
nationalism itself. There were a few nations in the nineteenth century
that rested content within their borders, but most did not. Even as
the loosely joined early modern empires gave way before the competition of more tightly organized nation-states, the expansive im-

pulses continued. To press the nation's power outward, to expand its political influence and territorial reach, was part of the very project of nationalism. The ambitions of nations that we think of now as small and tidy sprawled across space not long ago: the Dutch Republic (a global maritime force in the seventeenth century), Belgium (whose king claimed a thirteenth of the African land mass as his personal possession at the end of the nineteenth century), Denmark (with colonies and treaty ports across Asia, Africa, and the Caribbean). Other nations were made by spatial aggrandizement, in the way that Prussia aggregated the German empire to itself in the last quarter of the nineteenth century or the role that Piedmont-Sardinia played in the construction of modern Italy. By war, treaty, and population displacement nations pushed across the boundaries of weaker neighbors. The English pressed into Ireland with particularly callous and bloody determination, the French pressed into Alsace, the Germans into Poland, and the Russians deeper into the Caucasus and central Asia. The new nations of the Americas locked each other in territorial wars. In Latin America as in the United States, frontiers between settlers and native peoples were sites of massive land expropriation, population displacement, and endemic violence, punctuated by revolt and campaigns of military "pacification."[6]

The neat conceptual lines that analysts have tried to draw between expansion (the annexation of spatially contiguous territory) and empire (annexation across more distant, discontinuous space) all but dissolve under closer examination. In both, the pressure for territorial enlargement was foundational: to force open new territories for population, to acquire new economic resources, to bid for membership in the ranks of the great powers. Not all nations' projects succeeded in this restless competition for space; there were inevitably more losers than winners. But ambitions for expansion ran hard through the nations of the nineteenth century.

In all this, the American case was no exception. The language with which we still explain the project of expansion—as a great westward "movement" of families, possessions, hopes, and institutions—disguises the forces principally at work. There were, indeed, massive population movements; the trains of Conestoga wagons on the trek west are not a historical fiction, nor were the westward-driven gangs of coffled slaves. But the underlying technologies of nationalist expansion mirrored those of nationalist expansion elsewhere: treaty, purchase, war and threatened war, population infiltration across contested borders, and violent subjection of the native populations. The same processes would have carried Americans into the Caribbean before the Civil War if Southern expansionists' longings for Cuba had not been blocked by Northerners' opposition to the addition of more territory for slavery.[7]

Over all these projects of expansion the voice of providence and "destiny" rang. Russian expansionists talked of their nation's destiny in Asia. French expansionists celebrated their destiny in northern Africa. British writers heralded the "imperial destiny" that beckoned them to India, Africa, and beyond. Not interests or power, they claimed, but the manifest designs of history itself called them, irresistibly, to their new geographic destinies.

What distinguished the case of the United States was not the uniqueness of the expansionists' sense of mission but the weakness of the resistance they faced. The older empires that might have precluded the Americans' race across the continent ceded their claims with unexpectedly little cost to the upstart Americans. Facing slave rebellion and military defeat in France's prize sugar colony in the Caribbean and beleaguered by renewed war with Britain, Napoleon undertook a strategic retreat from the North American continent leaving an initially perplexed President Thomas Jefferson and his openly hostile Federalist opponents with a huge, unexpected gift of western territory.[8] After defeating American efforts to seize the St. Lawrence waterway in the War of 1812, the British were content to let the Americans turn their ambitions elsewhere. Severely weakened by internal revolts and seemingly irresolvable political strife,

1840s Mexico was no match for the U.S. expansionists; its claims to the sparsely populated territory north of the Rio Grande dissolved in decisive military defeat.

This retreat of powers capable of effectively mounting modern technological warfare against U.S. territorial ambitions effectively doomed the Native American peoples, their numbers and resources already massively thinned by the invasion of European diseases. Without the possibility of tactical alliance with one or another of the competing imperial powers, the "middle ground" of potential negotiation and compromise dissolved. Rebellion and resistance continued, but they could not hold off deeper and deeper invasion of Native America, all the more so as the military forces organized in the Civil War were redeployed to subdue the West. Not even the powerful Comanche military presence could stave off the ultimate dispossession of the native population, the expropriation of their land for Euro-American farming, ranching, and mining interests, and the forced relocation of those who resisted.[9]

Each of these campaigns faced resistance from Americans who feared that distance and dispersal would undermine the social basis on which the nation rested. None spoke more forcefully to that point in the first part of the nineteenth century than the New Englanders, where, if anywhere, the Puritan sense of destiny might have been assumed to run most strongly. But there was destiny enough in the system of cultural nationalism to make up for it.

By the time the territorial ambitions of American expansionists had turned to Asia and then back once more to the Caribbean and to Central America, the globe was much more crowded than before and the opportunities more limited. The last phase of imperial expansion, from the slicing up of Africa at the Berlin Conference in 1884 to the First World War, more closely resembled a zero-sum game than the phases before. But the very scarceness of opportunity now made possession of imperial territory an even more prized marker of power and status. If in the early and mid-nineteenth century American policy makers were acting on an impulse deep in a nationalist project that they shared with many others, by the turn of the century they were consciously playing catch-up: trying their best to put down stakes of their own on an imperial board game already teeming with players.

The proponents of American overseas empire were acutely aware of their latecomer's status. "There are points of resemblance in our work to the work which is being done by the British in India and Egypt, by the French in Algiers, by the Dutch in Java, by the Russians in Turkestan, by the Japanese in Formosa," Theodore Roosevelt candidly defended the United States' administration of the Philippines in 1904. There were many reasons to stay in the Philippines, he told Congress, but "our chief reason for continuing to hold them must be that we ought in good faith to try to do our share of the world's work, and this particular piece of work has been imposed upon us." The mission of the United States was not unique; it was to shoulder the duty that a great and civilized power's destiny demanded.[10]

There were distinctions within the practices of empire, to be sure, and there were differences in the terms by which imperial domination was justified. Not all imperial cultures were the same. French defenders of empire emphasized the universality of their *mission civilisatrice* to civilize the world. The Germans tended to talk more particularly of the special gifts of the German peoples for elevating and improving those they ruled. The blood of governance ran in their Teutonic veins and spirit, they reminded each other.[11] American proponents of empire at the end of the nineteenth century borrowed from both, celebrating "the divine mission of America" for "the civilization of the world," and at the same time the special capacities of "our race," the "Teutonic" and "Anglo-Saxon" peoples "in whose blood resided the genius of administration." "Behold" the work of the Dutch in Java, imperialism's gifted orator Senator Albert Beveridge exhorted his

countrymen during the great national debate over Philippine annexation in 1900. "Behold" the work of the Germans in the "fields of
world-regeneration and administration." Behold the English and
"their work all around the world." *"Every progressive nation of Europe
to-day is seeking lands to colonize and governments to administer,"* he
stressed. "The high ordinances of universal and racial morality" called
the United States to that same end.[12]

American proponents of overseas empire, stitching their arguments together out of the rhetoric and rationalizations already in the
air, insisted that they were, at no small cost to themselves, shoulder-
ing their moral duty to mankind: that they were bringing elevation,
improvement, civilization, education, and religion to a world that no
longer imagined that those gifts should only be the possession of the
privileged few. To claim to be "the trustee, under God, of the civilization of the world," to be called to "our saving, regenerating, and
uplifting work," as Beveridge put it, was to latch onto sentiments circulating through all the imperial cultures.[13] To Americans coming
late to the game of overseas empire, the rhetoric of imperial duty and
obligation was a derivative discourse. All the talk of mission they
needed, all the high reminders of destiny and providential responsibility, of their obligations to elevate and civilize their allotment of the
world's people for the world's good, lay ready for the borrowing from
the language of empire burgeoning around them.

The historian of American foreign relations Robert Schulzinger
puts the comparative point acutely: "It is a mistake to think that ideas
such as Manifest Destiny... [were] derived from seventeenth-
century theologians like Cotton Mather or Jonathan Edwards. Instead it makes more sense to consider American messianism a form
of nationalist exuberance which afflicted all of the great powers by the
end of the nineteenth century."[14] In a context this saturated with nationalist mission, there was no need to reach for Winthrop's "Model
of Christian Charity." Reworked into mobile metaphors of destiny,

everything the empire makers might have wanted from it was already at hand.

Perhaps it was all but inevitable that nationalist sentiments screwed to so high a pitch and backed by the massive new organizational efficiencies of the early twentieth-century nation-states should have sheered into war. Perhaps the Great War's origin lay, rather, in a series of catastrophic miscalculations as a chain reaction of alliances, threats, and military mobilizations combusted into war. No one anticipated the catastrophes of the First World War: the cascade of war declarations, the mobilization of armies and war materials and the scale of the battles into which they locked themselves, the melting away of hopes of quick victory into the mud-and-death-soaked hell of trench warfare. What remains most astonishing about the war is not the ability of the belligerent powers to rise to its massive organizational challenges. It is the willingness of the peoples to carry it on so long.

From every side the marshals of war patriotism brought to bear the cultural resources of nationalist righteousness. They were called not simply to their country's defense, the war propagandists thundered, but to "holy war"—"the holiest war in history," the voice of British political liberalism, the Manchester *Guardian* declared. "In August 1914, God called in a voice like thunder," the British army chaplain and popular author Geoffrey Studdert Kennedy insisted: "He called to England. . . . 'Come out! Come out! Come out from home and comfort. Come out to right the wrong. Come out to share my sorrow and help to save the world.'" German pulpits echoed the same call to their fellow countrymen to leave behind the ordinary affairs of the day, to set their petty differences aside, and together shoulder their "awesome duty to destroy every embodiment of evil." The "cause of Germany and the cause of God are synonymous." French war propagandists played the war as a stupendous conflict between "civilization" on the one hand and "savagery," "barbarism," and "beast-liness" on the other.[15]

None of the nations at war described their cause in terms of narrow national interest. From every side, the war nations carried a sense of divine necessity into the battlefields. The British insisted that they were not defending themselves only but the rule of international law and rights of weaker nations. "I do not think any nation entered into a great conflict . . . with a stronger conviction that it is fighting not for aggression, not the maintenance of its own selfish ends, but in defense of principles, the maintenance of which is vital to the civilisation of the world," Prime Minister Herbert Henry Asquith put it at the war's eruption in August 1914. The French declared their obligation to join in a "sacred union" for civilization's defense. The Germans insisted to the world that they had entered the war as a "sacred duty" in defense of Christianity and culture. Every German act was an act of "service" to God and to justice.[16]

It is not clear how deep these words of destiny penetrated the ranks of the soldiers, whose broken limbs and bodies so quickly piled up across what the poet Wilfred Owen would call a "Titan's grave" a thousand miles long that "crossed all Europe like a mystic road."[17] The heavily laden soldiers who fought the war carried more immediate burdens of survival. But a sense of duty, mission, and destiny was not simply a mystification for home-front consumption. It played an inextricable part in the recruitment machinery that fed the war's awesome appetite for soldiers and sustained the rationing and war material production that kept the conflict going so long.

In the midst of this world struggle, in 1916, Winthrop's "Model of Christian Charity" received its first pamphlet publication—indeed, its first full reprinting since 1840. Edited by the Harvard historian Samuel Eliot Morison, it came out as the 207th leaflet in Boston's Old South Church series of historical documents, bound together with the New England Puritans' "Humble Request" of 1630. Morison put the "Humble Request" first. A "little gem of Puritan literature," he called it; it "breathes a spirit of sweetness and humility that was altogether too rare in the early history of Massachusetts." Most of Winthrop's Model, by contrast, was "rather dull reading." But it was "the clearest statement we have of the principles that guided the Puritan leaders" in their venture. It showed their "emphasis on collectivism rather than individualism." It "explains," he cautioned, "much of the rigor and intolerance in the early history of New England."[18]

It would be convenient to imagine that Woodrow Wilson read Winthrop's Model in this form, but he did not. He had already passed over it with only an excerpted line about the Puritans' intentions to establish "a due form of government both civil and ecclesiastical" in his five-volume *History of the American People* in 1903. (John Fiske and Henry Cabot Lodge, two of the fiercest advocates of American cultural imperialism, had passed over it altogether in their own histories as well.)[19] In an address to the New Jersey Historical Society in 1895, Wilson had criticized the historical profession as a whole for concentrating too much of its attention on the history of New England. Better to focus the history books on the westward population thrust across the Appalachian Mountains where Wilson, like Frederick Jackson Turner, thought the nation's history had really begun.[20] Wilson believed deeply in the historical destiny of the American nation. But neither Winthrop's text nor Winthrop's dream of finding a refuge from the world was the wellspring from which he drew it.

The hopeful, idealist presence that Wilson brought to the Peace Conference at the war's end was a point of comment for all the more tired and more deeply war-scarred figures who convened there. The U.S. military forces had come into the war late and from a nation itself barely marked by the war's brutality. They were stronger, younger, and much better fed than the veterans they joined. They were more optimistic, as was Wilson himself. "The eyes of all

the world will be upon you," Wilson instructed the first embark-
ment of U.S. troops in 1917, "because you are in some special sense
the soldiers of freedom." "The mere sight of our men," he was later to
say, the sight "of their vigor, of the confidence that showed itself in
every movement of their stalwart figures and every turn of their
swinging march," made everyone know that "a great moral force had
flung itself into the struggle."[21] He brought to the Peace Conference
a conviction that the United States had entered the war on a basis
unlike that of any of the other combatants, solely on behalf of
"high disinterested purpose," as a "servant" to the world in the cause
of Christianity, civilization, and democracy, as "an instrument in the
hands of God to see that liberty is made secure for mankind."[22]

In fact, variations of the League of Nations idea into which Wilson would ultimately vest these hopes were already in circulation on
both sides of the Atlantic well before 1919. Some looked to the formation of a League to Enforce Peace with arbitration of international
disputes as its capstone—as Wilson's rival in the 1912 election, William Howard Taft, did. Others, most articulately organized on the
British left, proposed scrapping the secret treaty-making system that
had helped precipitate the war for a broader international forum for
foreign policy discussion and armaments controls. Wilson, who kept
a file on all these emerging proposals, was not an original thinker on
any of these matters, historian Thomas Knock notes. "League of Nations" was a British coinage. Refusing to be pinned down prematurely
on the League's details, Wilson left most of the original draft of its
scope and organization to the British ministries' making. His task
was to help synthesize these initiatives and, in the end, to champion
the result with striking intensity and stubbornness.[23]

The special place of the United States in the world's escape
from the barbarism of its war-strewn past was a fixed point in Wilson's
thinking. "I cannot be deprived of the hope that is in me," he had told
a campaign rally as early as 1912, "that we are chosen, and prominently chosen, to show the way to the nations of the world how they

shall walk in the paths of liberty." He told a skeptical U.S. Senate in submitting the Treaty of Versailles to them in 1919 that the nation's new responsibility in world affairs had come through the force of "destiny," "by no plan of our conceiving, but by the hand of God, who led us into this way." In his cross-country speaking trip on the treaty's behalf Wilson told the crowds who came to hear him, "It was America—never let anybody forget this—it was America that saved the world." Now it was America's task to save the peace as well, "to lead the world in the paths of liberty and justice and of right." "For nothing less depends upon us, nothing less than the liberation and salvation of the world."[24]

These were deeply held sentiments, but they fit almost seamlessly into the chosen people rhetoric that already floated above the trenches, the battlefields, and the recruitment rallies. "In the mysterious calling and election of God, Britain is the elect nation of the world to-day," the British war publicist J. Patterson-Smith asserted. "We are God's chosen people, his inheritance, the salt of the earth, His loved ones, His glory, the people He delights in," a fellow writer for the English war cause urged. "Our German God" and "*Gott mit uns!*" were the capsule German phrases. Nothing was clearer in this war, the Berlin preacher, Otto Dibelius, declared, than that "the Lord God had given the German spirit a special and holy mission."[25]

In this context of mass-produced nationalism, Winthrop's "Model of Christian Charity" was irrelevant. Declarations of holy sacrifice and chosenness were everywhere. They saturated the wartime air, productions of the same nationalist forces that were pumping out bombs, shells, and gas masks. They rained down on the battlefields over the dead and mangled and exhausted bodies.

Mary Borden was among the handful of Americans who threw herself into the war at its very outbreak. She poured her family's Chicago-made wealth into the establishment of a field hospital just back of the battle lines in northern France, where she served both as nurse and director. Later, like others who attempted to put the unspeakable experiences of the war into words, she tried to do so in poetry. She began "Where Is Jehovah?" not with an assertion but the question that hung so heavily in the air:

> Where is Jehovah, the God of Israel, with his Ark and his
> Tabernacle and his Pillars of Fire?
> He ought to be here—This place would suit him.
> Here is a people pouring through a wilderness—
> Here are armies camping in a desert— . . .
> It's all in the style of the God of Israel. . . .
> What a chance for His prophets!
> What a playground for miracles!
> A host of men at the end of their strength, fighting death,
> fighting terror, with no one to worship—
> He need but lift his finger—
> Here are his pet properties ready to hand, the thunder, the
> lightning, the clouds and the fire—[26]

But he did not.

How could he when, if the cries and prayers and war appeals were right, he was on every battalion's side? How could he act on behalf of any empire or nation when, in the formulas of nationalism that were on hand in the crisis, God had chosen them all?

PART III

Icon

CHAPTER 14

The Historical
Embarrassments of
New England

O N THE THREE HUNDREDTH anniversary of the Winthrop
expedition's landing in Boston, the city threw itself a mammoth birthday party. The celebration climaxed on September 17, 1930, with a parade of over forty thousand marchers that took almost six hours to pass the million persons who were said to have lined the streets, some of them peering through showers of ticker tape for a glimpse of the spectacle. Rank upon rank of war veterans, some of them survivors of the brutal trench warfare in France, led off the procession. They were followed by scores of school children's groups, rafts of women's and men's fraternal club members, church and civic associations, immigrant and ethnic societies, factory and department store employee groups, police and public servants. Carefully prepared historical floats depicted Winthrop's *Arbella*, the Puritans' landing on the Boston peninsula, Puritan home life and customs, an early town meeting, the Boston Tea Party, the Battles of Lexington and Concord, Massachusetts's ratification of the Constitution, and the founding of the nation's first free public school. From the grand ceremony's tributes to its Puritan founders to its displays of the latest in traffic lights,

up-to-date commercial buildings, and modern oil refinery methods, the Boston Day parade made a bid for recognition of the city's importance all across the nation's past and future.[1]

The day before, in a smaller but equally impressive ceremony, the city had dedicated a new "Founders Memorial" on the Boston Common. Charles Francis Adams, great-great-grandson of the nation's second president, gave the dedicatory oration. A direct descendant of the Winthrops pulled the cord to release the flag draping the monument. The sculptor was one of Boston's favorite sons who had already given the city monuments to Lafayette and the signing of the Declaration of Independence. The "people's poet" Edwin Markham composed an ode for the occasion: "Thus the new epic of the world began / Where there was room for a man to be a man. . . . 'Not a new country only—a new mind!'"[2]

In the focal center of John Francis Paramino's bronze relief, John Winthrop and Boston's first minister, John Wilson, strode confidently up from the shore to shake the hand of the lone-living earlier arrival, William Blaxton, who had agreed to let a part of the 1630 expedition settle around his land and freshwater spring. On the reverse side, fronting Beacon Street, the memorials committee inscribed a line from William Bradford's *History* and these now-famous words of Winthrop's: "For wee must consider that wee shall be as a citty upon a hill. The eies of all people are uppon us, soe that if wee shall deale falsely with our God in this worke we have undertaken, wee shall be made a story and a byword through the world."[3]

It was the first occasion on which any piece of "A Model of Christian Charity" had escaped the history books' and literary anthologies' extracts, the obscure journal and the antiquarian pamphlet. On the Boston Common what is now the most quoted fragment of the text went public, visible to any casual passerby. In the hoopla of that "Boston Week," amidst the skirling bagpipes and marching bands, the three thousand Knights of Columbus paraders, the special radio link that allowed Mayor James Curley to share an amplified real-time conversation with his counterpart in Boston, England, and amidst the other dozen memorial plaques being mounted across the state and the city, it is hard to know how many Bostonians paid attention to Winthrop's words or tried to imagine their meaning. What we do know is that in 1930 Boston's political and cultural elite bid to give them iconic status in their—and the nation's—history.

The Boston tercentennial was not the first time that New Englanders had staged a pageant for themselves or undertaken to fix their place as Founding Fathers of the nation. Cultivation of the region's heritage had been a major project of New England's cultural and literary elite for over a century. Celebration of the two hundredth anniversary of the Pilgrims' landing at Plymouth had been an important undertaking in 1820. Five years later, the fiftieth anniversary of the battle that had opened the War for Independence at Bunker Hill had been an even grander affair. Five thousand persons marched in the great parade; 4,400 sat down for dinner afterward under a field of tents; some 15,000 were said to have strained to hear Daniel Webster's address. The monument that New England's boosters completed near the battle site in 1843 was the nation's tallest and most imposing historical marker until the Washington Monument was finally finished some forty years later.[4]

Still more lasting than parades and monuments were the New Englanders' celebrations of their history in print and speeches. Oration-filled observances of Forefathers' Day on the anniversary of the Pilgrims' landing were sustained annually from 1798 on. Starting with the founding of the New England Society of New York in 1805, elite out-migrants from the region met regularly to congratulate themselves and the exceptional virtues of New England. Most consequential of all was the capture of history-book writing by New England authors and publishers who stamped New England historical self-consciousness into primers and schoolbooks sold across the country.[5]

An essential part of the New England elite's project lay in celebrating the region's distinctiveness and superiority. Writers and artists broadcast idyllic scenes of New England's compact towns, with their village greens and arching elms, steepled churches and whitewashed fences. A pious and orderly folk, conscience-driven and hardworking, transacting their public business in the simple democracy of their town meetings, scornful of pretense but committed to high ideals and widespread learning: part-fiction though it was, this picture of regional distinctiveness spread as far as New England emissaries could carry it.

But these efforts to carve out a place of clearly defined regional character comprised only half the project. The other half, already in full gear by the 1820s, was to insist that the nation itself—or at least its best and most important characteristics—had been formed from seeds planted first in New England. Theirs was not a sectional project only but, in Harlow Sheidley's words, a project of "sectional nationalism"—a bid for Founders' status, for cultural ownership of the American past and leadership of its future.

The notion that any nation has a distinct site of its foundation is a self-serving myth, of course—especially so in the case of a nation as plural and complex in its origins as the United States. The most obvious obstacle to the New Englanders' efforts to write themselves into the role of the nation's founders was that the Virginia settlement had been established first.[6] Planters and profit seekers, indentured laborers, and the first of what was to be the importation of hundreds of thousands of enslaved Africans—all had a better historical claim to Founders' status than the New Englanders. Not all New England orators denied the point. Neither did they deny the way in which the unexpected strength of the alliance between Northern and Southern colonists, thwarting the British hopes to drive the rebellious Americans into fragmented regional camps, had been instrumental in securing the struggle for independence. The New England–born historian George

Bancroft was among the celebrators of that transregionalism theme. The establishment of the Virginia General Assembly in 1619 and the Massachusetts Bay Company's reorganization as a general assembly of the colony's freemen in 1634 flowed equally from the same germ of civic republican instincts, Bancroft wrote. "Thus early did the freemen of Massachusetts unconsciously echo back the voice of the people of Virginia; like the solitary mountain, replying to the thunder, or like deep, calling unto deep." Thus did "the epidemic of America break out."[7]

But much more common among New England writers was to dismiss the Virginia project as a false start, an illegitimate line of descent. The Virginia settlement had its origins not in ideals but in mere self-interest, they emphasized. Dominated by rogues and adventurers, "idle and dissolute persons" with illusions of immediately gotten riches, it was no wonder that Virginia had so quickly descended into "disorder" and "anarchy," that only by accident had its first colonists been intercepted on the brink of abandoning the venture altogether and sailing back to England.[8] It was not just empty coincidence, in their eyes, that in 1820, as New England's boosters descended on Plymouth Rock to celebrate their past, there was nothing left of Jamestown; burned in a rebellion in 1676, then rebuilt, it had been all but abandoned by1699.

The true foundations of the American republic, New England publicists insisted, were laid by the first New Englanders. The American model for constitutional self-government had originated among them. Travel to the nation's capital, H. A. Scudder declared in 1853, and you would "there behold her noblest institutions based upon the principles of that compact originally signed . . . in the cabin of the Mayflower." The struggles that coalesced into the Revolution had begun there as well. "I presume it will be admitted by every philosopher, every honest and judicious politician," the New England Society of Charleston, South Carolina, orator for 1835 affirmed, "that from the character of the first settlers of Virginia and New-York, we should never have existed as an independent nation." Robert C. Winthrop echoed the point in 1839. The influences of Plymouth and New England have "pervaded our Continent. . . . The seeds of the Mayflower . . . have sprung up in every latitude . . . and though so often struck down and crushed beneath the iron tread of arbitrary Power, they are still ineradicably imbedded in every soil." It was the great boon of America that "the corner-stone of our Republican edifice" was quarried out of the old, original, New England rock.[9]

One of the New England elite's prized catches in their desire to insert themselves into American history as the template on which the republic had been built was the young visiting Frenchman, Alexis de Tocqueville. Taken in by Boston's Harvard-educated ministerial and merchant class, Tocqueville concluded after a month in New England that he had discovered, finally, the secret of American democracy. It lay in New England's institutions of town governance. A suggestion given to him by the Boston historian Jared Sparks, it made all the more powerful an impression on an observer used to the political authority of much more highly centralized France. Not in the much-vaunted constitutional system established in 1789 but the institutions of local township deliberation, carried to New England by its earliest Puritan settlers, Tocqueville was sure, lay the seeds of a political democracy inoculated against the excesses that had run riot in Revolutionary France.[10] From these beginnings, "the principles of New England spread first into neighboring states; then, one by one, they reached the most distant states and finished, if I can express myself in this way, by *penetrating* the entire confederation. . . . The civilization of New England has been like those fires kindled on the hilltops that, after spreading warmth around them, light the farthest bounds of the horizon with their brightness." "The whole destiny of America," Tocqueville summed up what he thought he had learned, was "contained in the first Puritan who reached its shores."[11]

The term "Founding Fathers" was not to be invented until the twentieth century.[12] But the yearning of the nineteenth-century New

England elite for Founders' status can hardly be exaggerated. They had a stock of stories and myths at hand. They had the local institutions that Tocqueville idealized and admired. They had the Mayflower Compact and the Battle of Bunker Hill. They had "A Model of Christian Charity," too, if anyone cared to notice.

But assertion of Founders' status by the New Englanders, however fervently they hungered for it, was not the same thing as achieving it. There were deep embarrassments along the path.

The first of those embarrassments was that the place of New England in seventeenth- and eighteenth-century British America was much more marginal than its boosters chose to imagine it. Virginia may have been a colony on the verge of anarchy in its first years, preserved only by imposition of authoritarian rule in the 1610s, but it grew to be the single most important engine of colonial North American economic and demographic growth. By 1775 its capital-intensive, labor-exploiting economy had made it the wealthiest and most populous of the colonies of the nascent United States. The per capita wealth of free white persons in the colonial American South was more than twice that in the middle colonies or New England. Estimates of the relative living standards of common, small farmers are harder to make, but Virginian military recruits were taller on average than New Englanders by the end of the eighteenth century, presumably an indicator that they were better fed. Whatever the case, the disparity in immigrants' destinations is clear. Immigrants looking for opportunities in colonial America sailed for Pennsylvania or, in still greater numbers, the slave South or the West Indies; these were the New World's magnets. After the initial Puritan exodus, they rarely chose New England.[13]

In time, New England's turn to the sea for wealth, through cod fishing, whale oil hunting, shipbuilding, food exports to the West Indian slave and sugar islands and, later, direct traffic in African-captured slaves, revived the region's economy. But on the eve of the

American Revolution, Philadelphia had eclipsed Boston as the colonies' leading seaport. If diversity, toleration, and eagerness for ambitious immigrant populations held the key to the nation's future, its foundations were laid in Penn's colony, not in the thin soils and culturally insular towns of New England.[14]

Political dynamics were more volatile than demographic or economic trends. Had it not been for the quickness of Boston's artisan and sailor crowds to mobilize against new tax impositions, the tacit approval that many of the merchants gave to the eruption of street politics, and the anger in the New England towns over the heavy-handed measures by which the British tried to subdue the protests, the Revolution would not have unrolled in the 1760s and 1770s as it did. New Englanders played a leading role in pressing for resistance and ultimately for independence. But despite the influence of John Adams's writings on the principles of constitutional design, New Englanders did not take a vanguard part in the framing of the Constitution in 1787, whose impetus had come far more strongly from the middle and southern colonies than from New England.

In the decades to come, moreover, the region's devotion to the new government was much less firm than the later New England historians would acknowledge. During "Mr. Madison's War" with Britain in 1812–15, New England authorities not only sharply criticized federal policy as highly injurious to the region's interest but they also publicly discouraged enlistments in the army, refused direct requisitions of their state militias by the War Department, and urged the withholding of taxes and loans to the national government. Representatives from New England were meeting in a secret convention at Hartford to debate outright nullification, perhaps even secession, when the war officially came to an end. But that did not prevent them from presenting a series of constitutional amendments that would have required a two-thirds majority in Congress (that is to say, the assent of New England's representatives) to authorize any future war, any future embargo, and admission of any future state from the territories.

In the wake of the embarrassments of the Hartford affair, the New England elite undertook to make themselves over as if they had been, all along, the nation's cultural bedrock. But the conditionality of New England loyalty did not go away. With the White House locked in a virtually unbroken dynasty of Southern slave holders, with Southern expansionists pressing relentlessly for more territory for slave-labor production, with New England's influence in Congress undergoing steady dilution, and with mounting fears of a "slave power conspiracy" that would ultimately make them "enslaved" to slavery, talk of resistance, even of disunion, ran almost as hard in sectors of New England as in the South right up to the opening shots of the Civil War. Northern victory in that war brought discussion of a breakup of the nation to a close, but the prickly, independent, self-righteous streak in New England politics, and what seemed to others a blatant preference for self- and regional interests over the national good, added further embarrassments to New Englanders' quest for recognition as the nation's Founders.[15]

And then there were the witches, the banished Antinomians, and the Quakers stripped and flogged and hanged in Boston. Witch-hunting frenzies of the sort that so famously consumed Salem, Massachusetts, in 1692–93 were in no way unique to the New England Puritans. Far more persons were executed in spasms of witchcraft accusations in Catholic Salzburg and in Lutheran Sweden in the late seventeenth century than in Massachusetts. In Geneva, public authorities had burned and executed heretics who mistakenly imagined that Calvin's "city of refuge" might be a refuge for them. Still, by the nineteenth century, intolerant, prosecutorial zeal was the skeleton in New England's closet. Critics from other regions knew it, and pressed its embarrassments home. New England writers knew it as well. From

Nathaniel Hawthorne's angry sketch of Puritan zealotry in *The Scarlet Letter* through New England's critical historians of the 1880s and 1890s, whose detailed documentation of their ancestors' religious persecution grew into a literature of apology and purgation, the fierce intolerance of the Puritans was a fixed a point in the public imagination.[16]

In 1883 one of the late nineteenth-century's leading American sculptors, Augustus Saint-Gaudens, was commissioned to cast a statue of one of the prominent early settlers of Springfield, Massachusetts. Reproduced many times over, the sculpture quickly became known simply as "The Puritan." His steepled hat and the great Bible under his arm were not the telltale clues to his identity as much as the "unbending and militant force of the Puritan" that Saint-Gaudens was praised for capturing. A writer in the *Century* declared: "Surely those old searchers for a 'liberty of conscience' that should not include the liberty to differ from themselves could not fail to recognize in this swift-striding, stern-looking old man, clasping his Bible as Moses clasped the tablets of the law, and holding his peaceful walking-stick with as firm a grip as the handle of a sword—surely they could not fail to recognize in him a man after their own hearts."[17]

By the middle years of the nineteenth century, a major flowering of learning and literature had begun to be born from New England's cultural soil. But to the region's critics, the scars of its older mores endured in its unbending rigidity, self-righteousness, and self-repression. New England's founders were a people of "negation," William Carlos Williams put the critical case most vividly as the early twentieth century's culture wars over prohibition and artistic censorship escalated: a people empty and terrorized by the world who, in response, "praised a zero in themselves."[18] The competing stereotypes gained force from their very exaggerations. But however one cut through the storm over the Puritans, by the 1920s their mantle as bearers of liberty to the New World had been severely undermined.

It was left to Samuel Eliot Morison, the young Harvard historian of early America, to sum up the balance. The New England Puritans, he wrote in 1931, were not democrats; they did not believe in religious liberty as later Americans would come to understand it. At root, they were persons who still lived in the Middle Ages, closer in their religious ambitions to St. Augustine than to modern Protestants. It was "moonshine" to think they brought ideas of market price or economic ambition with them. Although they valued the principle of election, they took "heavy precautions . . . against the popular will's having a chance to express itself." They had no faith in the average person's capacity for government. "Even the vaunted town meeting was almost always controlled by the squire, the shipowner, or the money lender." They brought many things of value to their foothold in New England: public spirit, respect for learning and popular education, an aesthetic of usefulness and the fitness of objects to their tasks. But the germs of modern America that nineteenth-century New England historians had emphasized had seeped into the country despite them. "These stern founders had a faith that is not ours."[19]

On all these counts, John Winthrop himself was a particular embarrassment. More vigorously than any of his peers in the colony's early leadership, he had labored to preserve religious orthodoxy in early Massachusetts. He had articulated more clearly than any of the others the closed character of the colony and bounded nature of what the Puritans imagined by liberty. He had spoken more articulately than any other early New Englander in defense of status and authority. In the New Englanders' quest to be recognized as laying the cultural and political foundations of the nation, Winthrop was a liability.

In Winthrop's place New England boosters thrust other figures from the region's past. The Pilgrims, the Massachusetts Bay colony's much smaller and weaker neighbors to the southeast, were early candidates. Less powerful, less prideful, and less self-righteous than the Puritans, the Pilgrims had occupied a side venue in early Puritan history writing. The agreement they signed, after first pledging their loyalty to the British crown, to "combine ourselves into a civil body politic" was not singled out for particular attention until the late eighteenth century. But by the early nineteenth century, the Mayflower Compact was being celebrated by New England historians as the formative act of self-government in American history. An outlier like John Lothrop Motley might dismiss it as an agreement "among a very few individuals." But the much stronger tendency was to see the Constitution, the nation, and the principle of representative government itself as already foreshadowed in that shipboard action.[20]

More striking than the history schoolbooks' singling out of the Pilgrims for a devotion to liberty far stronger than the dogmatic founders of Boston was the rehabilitation of the Puritan colony's most outspoken dissidents. Roger Williams, whose challenges to the ecclesiastical and political orthodox kept Massachusetts Bay in continuous turmoil throughout the early 1630s, was the most prominent case in point. Seeking first to cut his Salem church off from association with all those whom he did not see as truly Christian, Williams finally gave up hope of finding purity this side of heaven and opened his Rhode Island colony to persons of all sorts of religious opinions. Williams himself never relented in his search for truth, but the idea of a New Israel, a state good enough to police the religious opinions of its people, seemed to him the deeper heresy than doctrinal heterodoxy itself. A "turbulent" spirit Williams's critics called him at his trial and banishment in 1635. By the early nineteenth century, however, Williams was already beginning to be set off from his Boston prosecutors as a truly heroic figure in early American history: the first and clearest American articulator of the liberty of conscience.[21]

A later sign of the same tendency was the redemption of Anne Hutchinson, whose religious turbulence Winthrop had found even more dangerous to the colony's safety and good order. Hutchinson was not a clergyman like the Cambridge-educated Roger Williams. She taught private gatherings of other pious New England women.

But when she told the General Court that she knew by an immediate, inner voice which of the ministers and magistrates were truly
Christian enough to be honored with obedience and which were not,
Winthrop could not contain his outrage. "It overthrows all." The court
banished Hutchinson and disarmed her supporters not only to censor
her opinions, as Winthrop and others saw it, but to preserve their very
covenant from being rent in pieces by anarchy.

But in time Anne Hutchinson, too, was raised to a status morally higher than Winthrop's. Charles Francis Adams, whose account
of the affair in 1892 was a model of the new, balanced, scientific history, did not warm to Anne Hutchinson's inner religious certainties.
She was "an ambitious woman, with her head full of Deborahs and
the like, and with a genius for making trouble," Adams wrote. But her
trial was "no trial at all, but a mockery of justice rather,—a bare-faced
inquisitorial proceeding."[22] A generation later, Hutchinson's elevation
to martyrdom in the cause of free speech and women's status was
complete. Funded by the State Federation of Women's Clubs, a statue
of Anne Hutchinson was erected just outside the Massachusetts State
House in 1922. "Courageous exponent of civil liberty and religious
toleration," the inscription ran. The city's only statue of John Winthrop, by contrast, erected in 1880 not far from the State House, had
already been shunted into a less conspicuous site to open more room
for subway construction.[23]

To understand the development of "American thought," the
literary historian Vernon Louis Parrington wrote in his canonical
history of American ideas and literature in 1927, there was no alternative but to begin with the Puritans. But it was with New
England's dissenters, not its "stewards of theocracy," that "the
promise of the [American] future" was to be found. Given the colony's leaders' "patriarchal" social philosophy, their "extreme jealousy of
popular power," and their inability to adjust to new conditions, "New
England democracy owes no debt to her godly magistrates."[24] For
Parrington, Winthrop stood at the beginnings of American history

not as a Founding Father but as a man determined to stave off what America was to become.

Boston's tercentenary celebration of 1930 pulled Winthrop out from these shrouds of embarrassment. Its organizers gave an extract from "A Model of Christian Charity," for the first time, a prominent public place. But they did all this only to celebrate a city vastly more secular and more multicultural than Winthrop had ever imagined. Boston of 1930 was in the hands of its new immigrants. Mayor James Curley, who spearheaded the summer's celebration plans and who presided enthusiastically over its events, was a product of the city's Irish political machine and its mass politics. Corrupt enough to go to jail for helping two of his constituents to cheat on their civil service exams, he was beloved enough to be elected mayor on four different occasions. The tercentenary celebration over which he presided placed the city's new immigrants on full display. The organizers' "racial groups committee" arranged programs by the city's Greek, Syrian, Polish, Armenian, Finn, Ukrainian, and other populations. A Lithuanian group did some "clever tumbling" as they marched in the grand parade, the *Daily Boston Globe* reported. The Chinese built a "wonderfully picturesque float" that stopped the show. The music and steps of the African American marching bands riveted the reporters' eyes. Replicas of the *Arbella* and Puritan home life were swept along in this spectacle of twentieth-century Boston's diversity, tolerance, and modernity.[25]

In the course of celebrating Winthrop as Boston's founder, the tercentenary's organizers remade him into a figure that they would have liked far better than the governor of 1630. In Paramino's bronze relief, Winthrop strides up the hill to shake William Blaxton's hand, while a pair of Indians give silent blessing to the scene. Paramino's Winthrop carries no Bible. A young woman helps lead the way. No "steward of theocracy," this was a generous, open-handed Winthrop, tacitly stripped of his religious convictions, a Winthrop who could have presided comfortably over James Curley's immigrant city.

Paramino credited the leaders of the Massachusetts Art Commission, all of them from old-stock Puritan families, with suggesting the quoted lines from the Model for the memorial's street-facing side.[26] Though they included Winthrop's warning of peril "if we deal falsely in this work," the Model's extracted words no longer evoked a pious English remnant, anxious to make God's purposes visible in a strange world and fearful of their ability to do so. It did not signify a people convinced of their divine chosenness. In the context of the city's grand parade—the Lithuanian American gymnasts, the Syrian American swordsmen, the Irish American organizers, and the orators—the "city upon a hill" phrase meant something much more literal and much closer at hand. Many of the physical hills of Winthrop's Boston had been cut down and redeposited as fill for urban expansion, but Boston remained in literal fact a city of hills. "City upon a hill" in 1930 was a bid to boost the City of Boston's fortunes. It was a bid to release New England from its accumulated embarrassments. It was a slogan for a city admiring itself.

The first, small steps toward iconic status for "A Model of Christian Charity" had begun. But for the New England elite's ambition to be seen as the nation's Founders to be realized—and for Winthrop's text to take on still more weight than the Boston tercentennial's celebrators gave it—it would take other hands and contexts than these.

CHAPTER 15

Puritanism in an Existentialist Key

THE DECADES THAT FINALLY saw the release of the Puritans from the embarrassments of their past were the crisis decades of the Depression and war. And the figure who, more than any other, accomplished this came from Chicago, not Boston. Though he was a commanding presence in Harvard's lecture halls for thirty years, Perry Miller never imagined that he fit into New England manners or Boston civic pride. He entered the field of Puritan studies as an outsider, writing books that initially bewildered his fellow historians and literature scholars. He cultivated a sense of heroic intellectualism and existentialist drama that roiled many of his academic peers. But by his death in 1963, he had written the Puritans into the core story of the development of the "American mind" and had begun, for the first time, to single out Winthrop's "Model of Christian Charity" as one of the central statements in its unfolding.[1]

Perry Miller was a man of poses as well as a scholar of enormous erudition and writerly force. Some of what he said about his own past worked far better as story than as literal truth. Born into a physician's family on Chicago's West Side, he dropped out of the University of Chicago in 1923 to try to soak up some of the real-life experience he felt he had missed by being too young to enlist in World War I. He acted for a while with a theater company in Paterson, New Jersey, wrote a bit for pulp magazines, and then enlisted as a merchant sailor.[2] It was in Africa, unloading American oil drums for export to the Congo, he would later claim, that he caught a "vision" of his life's task: "the mission of expounding what I took to be the innermost propulsion of the United States." There was "a kind of truth" in that story, his widow would patiently explain, mixed with a great deal of fiction— though for decades historians preferred to take Miller's fib as literal fact.[3] What he did decide in the Congo was to go back to college, then to graduate school, and finally to immerse himself in the literature and history of early America.

There was a kind of truth, and a kind of fiction as well, to his subsequent claim that he went on to read every piece of writing produced in colonial New England. But he did read massively across three centuries of American thought and literature. He brought an insatiable appetite to the history of American ideas and a passion for making ideas the fulcrum point of history itself. Pious, disciplined John Winthrop and the gifted, unruly, atheist historian who began Winthrop's incorporation into the center of American history were an oddly matched couple. But between Winthrop's heroic sense of acting on a commission from God and Miller's sense of the heroic act by which Winthrop's Puritans had held up the assumptions of that commission by sheer force of will there turned out to be a powerful synergy. Out of that unlikely pairing the modern life of "A Model of Christian Charity" began.

Perry Miller arrived at Harvard as a visiting graduate student in 1930 at the peak of Boston's tercentenary celebration whose "horrors" of self-congratulatory excesses he thought the city had "barely survived." He had already decided that to fathom the American mind he needed to start at "the beginning of the beginning," where the earliest surviving sources were richest and deepest.[4] That meant starting not with the Virginia project but with New England. And not with Bostonians'

mythmaking but with the massive sermon literature generated in Puritan New England whose legacy, he was soon sure, had coursed
through virtually all American thought and literature thereafter.
Among "the elements that have gone into the making of the 'American mind,'" Miller was writing by the end of the 1930s, the New
England inputs were "the most conspicuous, the most sustained, and
the most fecund." "Without some understanding of the Puritans, it
may safely be said, there is no understanding of America."[5]

In the early 1930s when Miller undertook this task, there was
nothing fashionable in studying the history of "mind," much less the
obscure byways of Puritan theology. For most historians in the 1920s
and 1930s, the serious engines of historical change were the pressures
of material experience. Frederick Jackson Turner had insisted on the
massive significance of the frontier in American history. Charles Beard
had stressed the determinative force of economic interests. Vernon
Louis Parrington's *Main Currents in American Thought* had breasted
much of this trend in 1927, but even Parrington had launched his
chapter on Puritan thought by warning that "unless one keeps in mind
the social forces that found it convenient to array themselves in Puritan garb, the clear meaning of it all will be lost in the fogs of Biblical
disputation."[6]

In the face of all this the young Miller took to the challenge of
explicating the intellectual structure of the New England mind with
the exuberant sense of climbing an unconquered mountain peak. The
indispensable tool the historian needed was to set aside every temptation to translate Puritan social and theological ideas into modern
terms. Those who imagined that democracy had arrived on the first
Pilgrim vessels were wrong, Miller was certain; so were those who saw
only the hand of an oligarchical theocracy in New England's history.
The Boston tercentenary's portrait of bland conviviality distorted the
past most severely of all. To begin at the beginning was, for Miller, to
plunge into a radically foreign frame of thought that ultimately, but
only through a series of wrenching dialectical twists and turns, would

become the template on which the cultures of nineteenth- and twentieth-century America would be forged.

No corner of human thought went unexamined by the Puritans, Miller wrote. Reason, rhetoric, psychology, nature, piety, knowledge, and cosmology all had intricately connecting rooms in the intellectual edifice the Puritan divines constructed. But at the core of the Puritan mind was the idea of the covenant. "We are entered into covenant" in this work, Winthrop had deployed the idea in the Model's closing passages. By covenant, Miller insisted, neither Winthrop nor any of the ministerial elite meant simply "agreement." To argue about how far New England politics fell short of modern democratic standards was to begin from premises that were thoroughly inadequate to understanding the New England Puritans' intentions. A covenant-framed world was not the social contract society John Locke had imagined. A covenant was a pact in which consent and the demands of obedience fused into virtually a single thought and gesture.

The template of covenant thought was stamped across every aspect of early New Englanders' assumptions about their faith, their polity, and their place in history, Miller was arguing by the mid-1930s. God's relationship with the fallible people he had created began with a covenant with Adam. For disobeying God, Adam and all his offspring had been branded with sin. Mercifully, God had recovenanted to bring salvation to those who believed—though without his arbitrary gift of grace at work within their deeply polluted selves they were powerless to enter into any such state. Collectively the New Englanders had made a social covenant with each other to live a moral life of love and obedience, and a political covenant between themselves and the magistrates they elected to rule and lead them. At the pinnacle of this ladder of covenants, God made a covenant with his special peoples, to treat them as his own, rewarding their efforts toward virtue and scourging their failures and backslidings, all the while holding the script of the drama in his own hands.[7]

Worked out by English Puritan writers long before the notion of
a Puritan settlement in North America was seriously entertained in
anyone's mind, the idea of the covenant's myriad, interlocked faces
went on to be elaborated in scores of New England sermons. With
its imperatives of liberty of will and obedience to law, human ability
and human helplessness, all balanced on the sharpest of knife edges,
it commanded the heart of the New England orthodoxy, Miller argued, for over a century.

In Miller's first description of the "marrow" of covenant theology,
Winthrop's Model barely figured at all. Like other historians of New
England, Miller put his emphasis, rather, on John Winthrop's speech
to the General Court on the identity of obedience and liberty, already
quoted and anthologized many times over. Miller slipped about a
third of the Model's text into his own anthology of New England Puritan writings in 1938, but he did so without any special emphasis or
comment.[8]

But in the darkening world context of 1939, Miller found a more
arresting "genius" in Winthrop's text. The "greatness of Winthrop's address aboard the *Arbella*, the daring flight of his imagination," Miller
now emphasized, lay in the audacious way in which Winthrop there
had fused the New England migration with the demands at the very
core of covenant theology. The New England venture would not be a
mere test of the migrants' practicality. It would not be an escape into
an unsettled frontier: a space to do with as they chose. "A Covenant
People are not left at their Liberty, whether they will Love, Fear, Serve,
and Obey the Voice of God in his Commands, or not," a New England
sermon writer had expressed Miller's point. "They are under the highest, and most awful Obligations imaginable to the whole of Covenant duty." In the Model, Miller wrote, Winthrop had urged the same
point even more strongly: the emigration to New England would not
be flight into freedom but a flight into obligation.[9]

In the context of the late 1930s, it is hard to miss the contemporary references in passages like this. The illusion of remaining
free from the catastrophes overcoming Europe was a pipe dream for
a culture born in a deep sense of obligation, Miller implied. But there
was also a profoundly new dimension to "A Model of Christian Charity." Winthrop's text was not simply a programmatic statement. It
was not merely a call to charitable action or the sympathies of love.
Within it was encapsulated the very core of covenant theology. By
yoking the terms of the New Englanders' settlement to the deepest
assumptions of the "Puritan mind," from its understandings of piety
and reason, its rules of logic and rhetoric, its anthropology and politics, and its ladders of authority and covenants, as Miller urged his
readers to understand it, Winthrop had poured the whole of a culture's aspirations into his text. With the Model's words, Winthrop
literally "tied heaven and earth to his enterprise."[10]

Miller was thirty-four years old when he completed this much. But
what was more audacious still was Miller's claim that the New England
Puritans had built this cathedral of assumptions not out of confidence
or dogmatic certainty, but, rather, the reverse: that they had constructed this remarkable synthesis of thought in the face of deepest
anxiety about themselves and the capacities of human reason. Miller
opened his magnum opus, *The New England Mind: The Seventeenth
Century*, not with New England's preachers speaking confidently from
their pulpits but with the terrors of human beings in the face of the
"absolute, incomprehensible, and transcendent sovereignty of God."[11]
As old as Augustine, this strain of doubt and sinfulness, this urgent
sense of the human predicament and hunger for escape, had marked
Christianity for ages. In the Calvinist phase of the Reformation, however, it had erupted again, and in starker terms. The Puritans' God
was not unreasonable in his own being. But to human understandings
he was beyond grasp. He was "hidden, unknowable, and unpredictable,"

"the ultimate secret, the awful mystery," "entirely incomprehensible to man."[12] He was not fully revealed in his scriptures, not even in the inner experience of conversion and regeneration for which the Puritan faithful yearned—for that was always imperfect, dispensed or withheld by God for his own inscrutable reasons. This sense of an ineradicable gulf between God and his faithful, this sense of homelessness and of disharmony with the world in which they lived, was the starting point of Puritan religiosity.

And yet, as Miller portrayed it, New England's elite could not resist the obligation to try to apprehend what they knew could not be apprehended. They tried to pin the mystery of God down to attributes humans might try to understand. They strained to discern the outlines of orderliness in a nature that only God's will ultimately held in place. They tried to anatomize the stages of the overwhelmingly mysterious experience of conversion. They tried to read the divine course of justice in the willfulness and outward chaos of human history. They built their elegantly nested structure of covenants within a universe they knew to be more arbitrarily ruled than they hoped it might be. They wrote God's part as well as their own into the "commission" that framed their flight to North America, even though they could only guess, in anxious hope, that they understood what God's part might be. They imagined that across the awful gulf between divine and human reason they and God might have actually made a covenant, binding on both sides.

As Miller told the story of New England's first three generations, its most gripping drama lay in their efforts to bring as much reason to bear on the "implacable mystery" of God as they could devise. None of the writers of the eighteenth-century Age of Reason would work harder at this than they. Pride in their achievement, though they knew it to be a sin, was built into their circumstances. Still they "could never banish from their minds the consciousness of something mysterious and terrible in life, of something that leaped when least expected, that upset all the regularities of [science] and circumvented the laws of logic, that cut across the rules of justice, of something behind appearances that could not be tamed and brought to heel." They could not forget that behind the covenants, including the one whose terms Winthrop had presumed to state, there "loomed the inconceivable being about whom no man could confidently predict anything, who was not to be relied upon or perfectly trusted, who might day in and day out deal with men in stated forms, and then suddenly strike without warning, scatter the world into fragments with a casual sweep of His hand."[13]

This was Puritanism in a starkly existentialist mood. Its heroism was the heroism of persons who dared to try to bridge the gap between the certainties they longed for and the hubris and potential failure they knew their task invited. Miller did not put the point explicitly in the existentialist philosophers' terms. But like many other mid-twentieth-century intellectuals in Europe and the United States, he participated in the mood of disenchantment that we call, in retrospect, existentialism. A generation before, young rebellious writers had taken their revenge on their culture's dominant conventions by breaking its rules, scoffing at its philistines and moralists, and decamping for the freedoms of artistic bohemia. The attack on the puritanical strain in American culture had been a product of that rebellion. But for many of those who followed in the next generation, for whom the senseless waste and destruction of World War I and then the catastrophic economic and political implosions of the 1930s were formative experiences, personal liberation no longer seemed sufficient. What an honest person needed to realize was that the myth of history as a march toward greater and greater progress and freedom, with God as its optimist in chief, was an illusion. And a dangerous one at that.

Miller's own father had been deeply invested in the prewar social gospel hope of more and more perfect realization of God's designs. But God stood not within history but outside it, Reinhold

Niebuhr was writing in the late 1920s; societies needed to make their way toward justice without the crutch of cosmic reassurance or the conceit of believing they knew God's inner mind. The first English-language translations of Søren Kierkegaard's works began to circulate in the United States in the 1930s, carrying with them their message that "angst," anguish, and anxiety lay far deeper in the structures of the human condition than the steady improvement in faith and circumstances that nineteenth-century writers had heralded.[14] The Puritan sense of divine predestination was different from our modern "sense of things being ordered by blind forces," Miller himself wrote in 1938. "Yet even with this momentous difference in our imagination of the controlling power, the human problem today has more in common with the Puritan understanding of it than at any time for two centuries: how can man live by the lights of humanity in a universe that appears indifferent or even hostile to them?"[15]

Perry Miller resisted the full force of Niebuhr's political and philosophical conclusions.[16] But his students could not miss the existentialist strain in Miller's own teaching. It was through his Harvard mentor, Miller, that historian Arthur Schlesinger Jr. discovered Niebuhr and, through him, what Schlesinger thought to be the foundations for a chastened, less utopian project than the American political left had yet constructed. For Robert Coles, the social psychologist, biographer of America's children of crises, and, in time, a charismatic Harvard lecturer in his own right, the most memorable part of Miller's late 1940s course in the Classics of the Christian Tradition were its readings: Niebuhr, Blaise Pascal, Dietrich Bonhoeffer, Simone Weil, and the newly translated Kierkegaard texts Miller assigned. Decades later, Coles was still telling interviewers about the power they cast on him.[17]

Above all, Perry Miller etched the existentialist mood not only into his syllabi but into the Puritans themselves. His portrait of God's "supreme and awful" essence, beyond any human comprehension, was, as his later critics would point out, as much his own invention as the creation of John Calvin, to whom he attributed it. The work of the existentialist writers was to convince their naive fellow voyagers through the mid-twentieth century that history and optimism could not be counted on; that the world was much less reasonable that they imagined and courage far harder to find. As Miller described them, the Puritans had begun at the opposite philosophical pole; in the midst of what they knew to be life's ultimate incomprehensibility, they had struggled to build in enough handholds for reason and logic for their society to survive. The heroism of the Puritans was not to be found in their efforts at system building, monumental as they were. It lay in their determination to construct as rational a picture of life as they dared without ever forgetting the universe's ultimate impenetrability.

Perry Miller came back from World War II service to stow his military boots and a captured Nazi flag in his Harvard office, to resume his teaching, and to push his histories of the American mind deeper and deeper into the nineteenth century. He plunged into the worlds of Jonathan Edwards, Henry Thoreau, and Ralph Waldo Emerson; Herman Melville and Margaret Fuller; nineteenth-century literary institutions; and the history of the law. But though he spurned any temptation to glue these all to a common theme, he never wholly dropped the existentialist strain.

More and more he saw it written into the very text of Winthrop's "Model of Christian Charity." In what was to become the single most-cited piece he would write, "Errand into the Wilderness," Miller reminded his readers that historical "errands" like those Winthrop and his generation had undertaken came in two sorts. Some were errands that one undertakes for one's self. Others were missions on which one is sent as someone else's errand boy.[18] Winthrop and his peers knew how much self-determination and will they had poured into their own efforts. But they yearned to be on an errand that God, not they, had dictated. They worked as hard as they could to remind each other of the terms of the commission on which they had been dispatched, to read God's mind and purposes in sending them so far from home and England. But being the sorts of Puritans Miller imagined, they could never be fully sure that they had read their commission right. They could never be entirely confident that their city on a hill was not a product of their own mistake or illusion. Even when they felt the hand of God in their good fortune, Miller argued—or, equally, when they felt the hand of God in a disaster that they hoped was proof God still cared enough to chastise them—they could find no certainty.

"In fear and trembling" they had decided to emigrate, temporarily at least, to America.[19] They had publicly declared the terms of their project; they had made their settlement in a conscious act of decision. But who among them could dare to be certain that the grounds on which they had acted were not merely a castle of vanities?

Then and since, many readers of Miller's "Errand" essay have seen it simply as an amplification of the Cold War culture into which it was published in 1956. Miller had always imagined a kind of crusading aspect to the New England project, as if the voyage to America were best perceived as international Calvinism's flank attack on Catholicism itself. By the 1950s the military metaphors had become more insistent. In the New Englanders' inner mind, he began to speculate, perhaps God intended to finally sweep their home country clear of its desperate corruptions and "bring back these temporary colonials to govern England."[20] In that sense, the America of the 1950s seemed never to have left its Puritan starting point. A conviction of acting on a global errand for God appeared to join Dwight D. Eisenhower and John Winthrop in a common, all but timeless, project. What could one imagine of a nation so conceived in righteousness but that it should still be trying to save the world?

But Miller was never a thoroughgoing Cold Warrior and certainly not a spokesman for the business civilization he saw ascendant in Eisenhower's America.[21] Toward the end of "Errand into the

Wilderness," Miller retold the story of a classic circus act. It featured two clowns, one with an ample skirt and the other, hidden underneath, as the first clown's bustle. They race around the stage as one, and then, suddenly, as the first clown veers right, the bustle, heading straight, makes off with a mind of its own. The story told its own moral. America enters history, dispatched on a mission, only to discover that it can't remember anymore what that mission was, or whether it was, like a head-and-bodiless-clown act, just a fool's errand to begin with. After 1660, with the Puritan Revolution in England overthrown and Puritanism's offshoot in America orphaned as a result, the international dimensions of the New England project suddenly became irrelevant. It had become historically irrelevant as well, like a soldier dispatched on a task that his superiors had forgotten. Its ideas "had served their purpose and died."[22]

What is a society to do in such a pinch but to make its purpose up all over again? That was the pattern of American history, Miller wrote in 1954. At some deep level it was discontinuous, glued to no "pre-existing" design, bound only to the necessity of inventing itself anew in a universe that gave it no prefurnished home. It was a "frantic," futile gesture on the historian's part to try "to preserve, just as he at the moment understands it, the distinctive American essence." Indeterminacy and choice were the ground pattern of history. This "complexity is worrisome, imparts not serenity, only anxiety. It keeps us wondering whether we might now be something other, and probably better, than we are had we in the past decided otherwise, and this in turn makes decision in the present even more nerve-wracking." But from that anxiety there was no escape.[23]

How that story worked itself out from Winthrop's first enunciation of its terms forward, Miller himself was never ultimately able to say. His teaching remained as electrifying and terrifying as before. He wrote prolifically, but the comprehensive *History of the American Mind* he mapped out for his publisher eluded him. In the end he had aspired to far too much, he had fought too many inner contradictions, and he was drinking too heavily to complete it. He died of a heart attack at age fifty-eight.

But Miller's part in shaping the lives of "A Model of Christian Charity" was indelible. No other figure before him had done as much to pull that text out of a later culture's forgetfulness and insert it into the nation's beginnings. He put the "city upon a hill" phrase at the core of historians' understanding of Puritanism and put Puritanism, for the first time, at the core of the American story itself. "I am sure," Miller told an audience in 1954, that Winthrop's "Model of Christian Charity" "is known to all of you."[24] To the extent that there was as yet any truth to that claim beyond the specialists in religious history to whom Miller was speaking—to the extent that excavation of the Model from its decades on the margins of American history and its elevation into the status of a foundational text, perhaps *the* foundational text for the nation, had begun—the first steps were largely Perry Miller's work.

But what was foundational about Miller's Model was not its solidity. The Model's achievement, as Miller understood it, was to put on display the extent to which the American covenant was held up by will and aspirations alone. It was a heroic act of mind: an attempt to make reasonable a purpose and a mission about which its own participants could never be entirely confident. In the midst of Eisenhower's America, when one might have thought that Winthrop's Model might fit easily into the certainties of Cold War conversation around it, irony, not certainty, was Miller's passion. Among his most lasting achievements was to begin to put at the foundations of American history a text that, as he urged others to read it, had under its anxieties and aspirations no bedrock foundations at all.

CHAPTER 16

Arguing over the Puritans during the Cold War

A MOOD OF CRISIS SHAPED Perry Miller's portrait of the Puritans. The disillusionments of the generation that had seen the idealism of World War I soar and then disintegrate, that had then seen the nations they thought at the heart of European civilization spiral into an even crueler vortex of war and inhumanity, and finally witnessed peace turn virtually overnight into the armed and hostile standoff that by 1947 was being called the Cold War all left their mark on Miller's work. The Cold War left its marks on the others, too, who, after Miller, began to find their own threads of importance in Winthrop's long-unnoticed text. None of them read "A Model of Christian Charity" as simply a piece of ammunition in a new sort of global and ideological war. But the crises of the Cold War would be imprinted, in one way or another, on virtually every one of the Model's reappropriations for the rest of the century.

These reinventions of the Model were the work of many hands, acting on many different intentions, and they took time to emerge. There is a simpler story, frequently retold, in which John Kennedy's use of Winthrop's "city upon a hill" in a speech in 1961 shot directly into the phrase book of another man of burgeoning political aspirations, Ronald Reagan; but that simplified tale will not stand serious examination. Even Kennedy and his speechwriters did not initially recognize the potential of the Model's story. A sense of Winthrop's "city upon a hill" phrase as encapsulating the very core of the nation's mission to spread its ideas, its alliance networks, and its way of life across the Cold War world seeped, rather, out of many sources in post-1945 American political culture. Some was the work of that culture's boosters, some the work of its fiercest critics.

Desire for a usable national past hung heavily over Cold War America. The project of rediscovering the nation's enduring character had accelerated during World War II, most intensely among the social scientists drawn into the study of human morale. To "know" the enemy not as faceless "beasts" but as products of specific cultural, historical, and anthropological forces took on urgency as an essential tool of modern warfare. So, by the same token, did a deeper knowledge of the values, character, and culture that would keep Americans in the fight. Socioanthropological studies of "the American character" spilled out of World War II. New programs in American studies proliferated in the postwar colleges and universities. In literature departments, specialists in American writing began to assert themselves to shape a canon of American literary works whose depth could rival those of any European nation. The search for foundational texts and foundational ideas accelerated. Colgate University launched a compulsory American studies course for its seniors in 1949. Entitled "The American Idea in the Modern World," its goal was explicitly nationalist: to examine the "American credo, what strengths and weaknesses are inherent in it, and whether it has any value as an example to other countries."[1]

Offshoots of these programs quickly carried the American studies project abroad. The Voice of America did its best to blanket the shortwave radio bands with positive images of American society and culture. The Fulbright program's grants for travel and scholarly exchange were explicitly designed to counteract stereotypes abroad of a culturally superficial, commercially absorbed American society. Perry Miller, who traveled on lectureships to Europe and Japan in 1949–52, came back to worry about "the deep and ubiquitous anti-Americanism" that he had sensed there, a "settled and frozen image of America" that discounted the possibility that it might have any serious ideas or historical lessons for others.[2] When in 1950 Connecticut's U.S. senator William Benton raised a plea for "a Marshall plan of ideas," an understanding that the struggle with the Soviet Union had drawn Americans not only into a political and military contest but an ideological battle for world opinion was fully formed.[3]

Words for that struggle lay already at hand. "You have summoned me on behalf of millions of your fellow Americans to lead a great crusade—for Freedom in America and Freedom in the world," Dwight D. Eisenhower opened his acceptance speech at the Republican National Convention in 1952 in the cadence of Cold War politics.[4] "On America almost alone has fallen the awful responsibility of holding open the door of history against the forces of evil until freedom is born anew all over the world," *Life* magazine's lead editorial writer had put the charge the year before. The "American Proposition" was precious not because it was unique, John Jessup urged, but because it was universal: because "it belongs to all mankind."[5]

In these early Cold War articulations of the American task Winthrop and his Model did not yet have a place. Surveying the history of the American idea of mission in 1950, the Cornell University historian Clinton Rossiter opened with the New England Puritans, but he did not mention "A Model of Christian Charity." Harvey Wish's widely read *Society and Thought in America* in 1950 titled its section on the Puritans not after Winthrop but the New Englanders' radical dissenter, Roger Williams. Virtually none of the popular American history textbooks of the early and mid-1950s thought it important to include a reference to the Model. As late as 1957, Edward M. Burns's *The American Idea of Mission* passed it by without mention.[6]

In most Americans' minds their usable past began with the documents of the Revolution. There, in John Jessup's terms, was where the "American Proposition" was enunciated. There, not in the scattered social experiments of the earlier period, was where an exportable American history began. But a new reckoning with a deeper history was soon to come.

The publication of the second volume of Perry Miller's monumental *The New England Mind* in 1953 and his collection of shorter pieces, *Errand into the Wilderness*, in 1956 helped tilt some of the Cold War quest for a usable past toward New England. Puritan studies after Miller gained an important new foothold in university history and literature departments in ways that southern and middle-colony studies did not begin to match. But at first the Model's sense of mission was not central to it.

What caught 1950s historians' attention, rather, was the New England Puritans' example of the responsible exercise of power in a dangerous world. In 1958, in what quickly became one of the most widely assigned college history books of its generation, Perry Miller's student, Edmund Morgan, published a markedly sympathetic portrait of John Winthrop not as the stubborn theocrat of 1920s and 1930s scholarship but as a man struggling to balance the responsibilities of governance against the eruptive social and religious passions around him. Morgan made very little of "A Model of Christian Charity," but between his lines Morgan made a great deal of the model of Winthrop's life as a lesson in the ethical responsibilities of power. Morally chastened but unwilling to simply flee from the world's burdens and dangers, Morgan's Winthrop emerged from the past as a vital example for the Cold War present.[7]

The year 1958 saw the publication of a second book on early American history, even more widely read than Morgan's. This was Daniel Boorstin's Bancroft Prize–winning *The Americans: The Colonial Experience*. The first in a three-volume sweep through all of American history, it opened not with the Virginia expedition, or the Spanish conquest, or the lives of the continent's native peoples, all of which had much better claims as origin points than Winthrop's venture, but with the founding of the Massachusetts Bay colony. The book's first sentence placed its readers aboard the *Arbella*. By its fifth sentence it was quoting the "eyes of all people" passage from the Model. The book's opening chapter was entitled "A City upon a Hill"—but not with the meaning that phrase was to take on later.[8]

Boorstin was a University of Chicago historian, political critic, and by the 1950s a centrist, pragmatic conservative. As he told the American story, it began not with the American Revolution but with a series of "visions," each of which turned out to be a partial mistake: the New Englanders' vision of a "city upon a hill" where a purified faith might reign; William Penn's vision of a "holy experiment" in peace, toleration, and social harmony in Pennsylvania; and eighteenth-century English philanthropists' vision of a charity colony in Georgia where, with land and discipline, the outcast English poor might flourish. In the founding of each of these, Boorstin wrote, the planners had tried to work too hard against the grain of practical human nature. In each case, experience had overwhelmed the designers' blueprints. America began as visions, as idealized "cities upon a hill"; it concluded, in Boorstin's view, as sobered experience.

This was a line down which Boorstin had already been thinking since the late 1930s. He had graduated from Harvard in 1934 to spend a year at Oxford University amidst the ferment of the British political left. He joined the American Communist Party in 1938 and then left it, shaken, in 1939 when the Soviet Union joined with the Nazi regime in the invasion and dismemberment of Poland.

That experience of being tricked by illusions of perfection stayed with Boorstin for the rest of his career. "Ideology" was the utopianism of modern times, a chastened Boorstin concluded. The "genius" of American politics—if it were wise enough to hang on to it—was its resistance to the dreams of social perfection with which ideologies lured their victims. In *The Lost World of Thomas Jefferson* in 1948 Boorstin had set out to rescue Jefferson from his own abstractions and the generalities of the Declaration of Independence's opening paragraph and recast him as an empiricist, a man of practical science and political experience. Boorstin was unrelentingly critical of the notion that centuries of national experience could be repackaged as the "American idea" and exported to the rest of the world. "To tell people what institution they must have, whether we tell them with the Voice of America or with the Money of America, is the thorough denial of our American heritage," he wrote at the height of the early Cold War. It was to play into the game of tyrannizing abstractions that the ideologues on the other side would surely win.[9]

Boorstin believed his own moral to be simple: the bedrock story of the Americans was the consistency with which they had resisted the temptations of Utopia. In truth, the story he told was more complicated. Had history only been about the pragmatic strain in American culture, he might have begun the documents collection he compiled to supplement *The Americans* with the thoroughly practical example of Benjamin Franklin. But he did not.[10] He read Perry Miller's work with great seriousness. He recognized the utility of Winthrop's strenuous calls for public virtue as essential to a colony's infant years when practical instrumentalism alone would have broken it apart on its fault lines of interest. The story of Boorstin's America was not the story of an insatiably practical people but of a people whose character it was to search for utopias but never to fall wholly under their spell. It was the story of Europeans who imagined they might offer the world profoundly new possibilities for society and then learned to temper their visions in practice. Despite their political differences, Boorstin's moral was not totally unlike Morgan's: a chastened model of practice was the New England Puritans'—and now the nation's—gift to an ideology-wracked world.

The story of John Kennedy's part in injecting a more strenuous reading of "A Model of Christian Charity" into the rhetoric of American politics was different—in part because identification of Winthrop's words with Cold War America was not Kennedy's original intention at all. The occasion was Kennedy's farewell to the state of Massachusetts on the eve of his assumption of the presidency in January 1961. His principal speechwriter, Theodore Sorensen, had much more important projects on his agenda during the months between Kennedy's election and his installation in the White House. The deadline loomed for Kennedy's inaugural address, for which Sorensen would write the instantly famous Cold War pledge: "Let every nation know, whether it wishes us well or ill, that we shall pay any price, bear any burden, meet any hardship, support any friend, oppose any foe to assure the survival and the success of liberty."[11]

Kennedy's speech to the Massachusetts legislature was much more quickly and casually drafted. Faced with the need to say something uplifting to a legislature that had been mired in perpetual corruption scandals since the James Curley era, Sorensen chose to admonish its members with the words of their own colony's founder. "I have been guided," Sorensen had Kennedy say, "by the standard John Winthrop set before his shipmates on the flagship Arabella 331 years ago. . . . 'We must always consider,' he said, 'that we shall be as a city upon a hill—the eyes of all people are upon us.' Today, the eyes of all people are truly upon us—and our governments, in every branch, at every level, national, state and local must be as a city upon a hill—constructed and inhabited by men aware of their grave trust and their great responsibilities."[12]

Asked much later for his inspiration for these words, Sorensen could no longer remember. Sorensen was a serious reader of history. His *Profiles in Courage*, which was issued under Kennedy's name in 1956 and helped catapult the junior Massachusetts senator to national fame, was a roster of courageous dissenting figures in the American past who had stood for conscience against mere popularity. It is possible that the suggestion to use Winthrop's words was passed on to Sorensen, in a blizzard of other suggestions, by one of the Harvard historians who circled around the Kennedy campaign, though the most active of them, Arthur Schlesinger Jr., had proposed a different Winthrop quotation than the one Sorensen chose. He might have taken it from a speech, "The Progressive Spirit in an Age of Conformity," that Illinois senator Paul Douglas had given at a Roosevelt Day dinner in New York City in 1957. An uncowed political progressive in Eisenhower's America, Douglas had used Winthrop's "eyes of all people" phrase to urge upon the Democratic Party the need for a second New Deal: to protect consumers from the exactions of big oil and big business, to democratize an economy in which power and control were excessively concentrated, to eliminate the slums, and to "eradicate" racial and religious discrimination. But if Douglas had been his source, Sorensen left Douglas's progressive political agenda altogether out of what he borrowed. Most likely Sorensen had picked up Winthrop's "eyes of all people" passage from the monument on the Boston Common that Curley himself had helped install in 1930 and by which Sorensen must often have passed.[13]

Whatever its source, Kennedy's referent for Winthrop's "city upon a hill" was not the nation. It was the scandal-enmeshed Boston legislature. "Call for Moral Uplift in Bay State," the *Boston Globe* headlined its account of Kennedy's speech. "Offers a Strict Moral Code for Presidency," the *New York Times* reported it. "Dirty Money in Boston" was the *Atlantic Monthly* story's title.[14] Sorensen used the Model's words only once again, in Kennedy's talk to the Big Brothers of America later in 1961. This time, the context was broader: "Now, I feel that we are a city on a hill and that one of our great responsibilities during these days is to make sure that we in this country set an example to the world ... [by] demonstrating what a free people can do." Still, the practical upshot was narrow: take on responsibility for two or three underprivileged boys or girls; reach out to them so that their lives do not go to waste.[15]

Others, however, wanted more out of Winthrop's words than Kennedy and Sorensen understood them to contain. From Kennedy's address of early 1961 they moved by a kind of folk process into the stock phrases of other speechwriters, acquiring more urgent weight along the way. Cold War culture by then had taken a more strenuous turn. In 1956 the United States had found itself a helpless observer of the Soviet army's suppression of revolt in Hungary, stalemated by the atomic superpowers' sudden new capacity for mutual destruction. The next year the Soviet Union launched the Cold War's first space satellite, setting off alarms that the United States had fallen permanently behind in the race for military superiority. In 1957, with the eyes of the Third World's peoples intent on the United States' handling of its intensifying race "problem," federal troops and the elected state governor had gone face to face in Little Rock, Arkansas, over the Supreme Court's school integration decision.

In the face of these events the mass-circulation *Life* magazine launched a series of essays in May 1960 to promote a wide-ranging debate on the "national purpose." "In this strange era of Communism, megaton weaponry, fractured empires, mushrooming sovereignties and continuing moral, social and technical revolution," its opening statement asked, what explained Americans' apparent retreat into private pursuits of happiness? What would be required to fill the era's "vacuum in the national will?"[16]

Kennedy himself contributed an essay to the series, saturated with a sense of destiny and mission, but he did not invoke the Puritans.[17] It was left, later in 1961, to the director of the Health, Education, and Welfare Department's regional operations in the West,

Albert H. Rosenthal, to make the connection between the mission of modern America and the deep historical ballast of Winthrop's text. "You are graduating into a world of crisis," Rosenthal told the commencement class at Colorado State College at Greeley. In the ongoing struggle for the minds of the world's majority, Rosenthal urged, citing Winthrop through Kennedy, we in the United States "are as a city upon a hill—the eyes of all people are upon us." In this global "war of ideas," if we let our commitments to democracy, to the freedom and dignity of all persons "play their music to the world"—if we show that liberty and a positive program of social wel- fare can be effectively combined—they will resound more loudly than the "tallest rocket or the biggest bomb."[18] The speech that John Kennedy might have been expected to give, Rosenthal gave for him.

From there the formula spread to others. Lyndon Johnson's speechwriters seized on the Winthrop reference in 1964. "America to- night is a city upon a hill" to which the world looks "uncertainly and hopefully" to see "the brightness of nobility which is in man." Rich- ard Nixon retold the *Arbella* story as a more general rhetorical ques- tion in 1971: at this moment of the free world's testing, "do we have the character, the richness in spirit, and the strength in spirit that a nation needs?" George McGovern, running as the conscience candi- date against the Johnson-Nixon War in Vietnam, put the question in essentially the same way in 1972.[19]

Some of the voices in this Cold War chorus of Winthrop refer- ences amplified the charity themes at the Model's heart. "As long as millions of Americans suffer indignity and punishment and depriva- tion because of their color, their poverty, and our inaction," Robert Kennedy urged in 1965, "we know that we are only halfway . . . to the city upon the hill." Hubert Humphrey defended Lyndon Johnson's Great Society programs in the same way during the "War on Poverty" debates of the mid-1960s.[20]

But for most of those who revived the public life of Winthrop's words during the years of the high Cold War, the core issue was not the enduring gap between rich and poor or what obligations charity might take in a new era of economic abundance. It was the need for a national civic renewal at a time of unprecedented global challenge. In these explicit reuses of the Model's language, the "city upon a hill" was the United States as a nation. The "eyes of all people" were the hearts and minds of the nonaligned world. From "A Model of Christian Charity" the speechwriters drew proof that a sense of world-historical mission ran back to the imagined beginning point of American history, that seamless bands of time welded the summons of the present to deep resources in the past.

Scholars followed in the same tracks. Editing the *Life* magazine "National Purpose" series for book publication in 1961, the Harvard historian Oscar Handlin organized it around a series of themes that defined the American way of life: "material well-being," "success and individualism," "the culture of the common man," "democracy," "equality," "freedom." But it was with the "The American Mission" that the book opened; its first document consisted of the final, "city upon a hill" paragraphs of Winthrop's Model.[21] Merle Curti's magisterial *The Growth of American Thought* had not mentioned the Model in 1943. Now in 1966, Daniel Boorstin's *American Primer* for a general audience and Loren Baritz's *Sources of the American Mind* for college students both included generous extracts from the Model. By 1973 the Model had come to lodge firmly in the most influential American literature anthology of its generation, Cleanth Brooks, R.W.B. Lewis, and Robert Penn Warren's *American Literature*.[22] The sociologist Robert Bellah had coined the term "civil religion" in 1967; eight years later, he pitched his anguished report on the broken state of civic culture in terms of the need to make Winthrop's sense of covenant central to Americans' understanding of themselves once more.[23]

Still, increasingly common as encounter with Winthrop's words and story now was, readers might be forgiven a degree of uncertainty about the Model's exact place in the American past. Most one-volume college textbooks through the 1970s still did not squeeze out room to mention it. As late as 1979, the D. C. Heath and John Wiley & Sons U.S. history textbooks ignored Winthrop's Model to give their extended attention to Winthrop's nemesis, Anne Hutchinson.[24] Hutchinson's dissent from Puritan orthodoxy had, in fact, compelled John Kennedy's and Ted Sorensen's attention as well. Asked by *McCall's* magazine in 1958 to expand the sketches in Kennedy's *Profiles in Courage* to include women, they had responded with three vividly told vignettes of women who had refused to bend to the pressures of conformity around them. One of these women of courage was Prudence Crandall, who faced down court orders and the violent, racist mobs that demanded she close the school for the education of free black young women that she had launched in 1830s Connecticut. Their second figure was Jeannette Rankin, the feminist and peace activist who, in the face of intense pressure, had chosen to cast the sole vote in the House of Representatives against war in December 1941 rather than violate the call of her conscience. Their third example of women's heroism was Anne Hutchinson, who, "ruthlessly and unfairly cross-examined" by Winthrop and his fellow magistrates, had stood courageous and unbowed against the wrath of Puritan authority.[25]

The incongruities could seem head spinning. No other early American had demonstrated as fully as Winthrop the courage to use power responsibly, readers of Edmund Morgan's book learned; but in the history textbooks American courage was embodied in Anne Hutchinson's defiance of everything Winthrop stood for, too. The usable American past was encapsulated in the universality of American ideas; it was not to be found in ideas at all, if Daniel Boorstin was to be believed, but in the everyday practice of Americans. "At the heart of our tradition is a spiritual reality," a Pennsylvania Lutheran preacher declared in his Fourth of July sermon in 1973, in a wild conflation of detached and reassembled pieces from the past. "'We the people . . . ,' wrote one of the Founding Fathers, 'are as a city set upon a hill, in the open view of all the earth, the eyes of the world are upon us, because we profess to be a people in covenant with God."[26] In this yearning for consensus and continuity, the deist Jefferson and the Calvinist Winthrop, the war of ideas with Communism, the seventeenth-century settlement of New England, and the revolutionary Declaration of Independence all collapsed into pretty much the same thing.

It was at this entry point that the figure who succeeded Perry Miller as the most closely watched critic and explicator of American literature of his time, and of Winthrop's Model in particular, came onto the scene to declare that "A Model of Christian Charity" had set a trap, a consensual cage from which there was no escape. Even more than Miller, who let others imagine that he had discovered America on the banks of the Congo, Sacvan Bercovitch came to Puritan studies as an outsider. Born in Montreal into a Yiddish-speaking family of left-wing Russian-born Jews, he made his way by a series of zigzags through the disjoined cultural patchworks of twentieth-century immigrant society. He tried the New School for Social Research in New York City and Reed College in Oregon briefly, took an extensive detour to live and work in a socialist kibbutz in Israel, and then returned to graduate from a Montreal night school. Coming again to the United States for graduate work in 1961, he was overwhelmed by the experience of a nation in the grips of Cold War consensus.[27]

By the time Bercovitch's deeply learned and intricately woven readings of American Puritan literature began to appear in the late 1960s, the tenets of that consensus were already under challenge. By the late 1970s, when Bercovitch's reputation was at its peak, any sense of a singular American "national character" seemed to most observers to have fragmented in the upheavals on college campuses, the mass political demonstrations over civil rights and the Vietnam War, and the smoldering anger of black urban neighborhoods. The American studies project was already beginning its disaggregation into a multitude of competing projects: African American and Latino/a studies, women's and gender studies, Native American studies, environmental studies, cultural studies, and more.[28]

But Sacvan Bercovitch never lost his initial sense of a nation organized as no other around its own proposition of itself. In a culture where Martin Luther King Jr.'s severest criticism of America was that it had violated its own ideals, where its anarchist Yippies could dress themselves in flags and Uncle Sam hats, where bringing America back to its senses shaped the deepest passions of its critics, Bercovitch insisted, consensus could hardly be said to have disintegrated. Others in the 1970s were beginning to probe the social and institutional mechanisms through which cultural consensus might be imposed and perpetuated. But for Bercovitch the "America" that both critics and defenders seemed so intent on possessing had always been a rhetorical, not a sociological, construct: a symbolic field, a ritually repeated trope that, by its very nature, remained immune from the flaws of the society and nation it stood for.

For the origins of that enduring "myth of America" you needed only to look at Winthrop's Model, Bercovitch was claiming by the late 1970s. The key part of it was not the "city upon a hill" sentence. It was Winthrop's caution, right on the heels of that promise, that failure to live up to their covenant would bring God's special wrath upon his New England people. For that very promise of God's enduring attention carried reassurance that New England's proto-Americans would not be left to the ordinary forces of history. Every act of censure after Winthrop's sermon, every lament, every twinge of anxiety, could thereafter be construed as reassertion that the American errand was still intact, that their God was still watching out for America. From the sermons of anguish and lament that soon began to pour out of seventeenth-century New England pulpits, to the refusals of Thoreau's *Walden* or the dark, foreboding vision of Melville's *Moby Dick*, to the upheavals shaking Bercovitch's own society and times, dissent in a culture organized rhetorically in this way could only reinforce that culture's original premises. "America" was not a nation like other nations but a "totalistic" symbolic system that co-opted every imagination, that locked its defenders of order and its anguished, radical dissenters in the same embrace.[29]

For Bercovitch, Winthrop's Model not only stood at the beginnings of the unshakable consensus that he had felt so strongly in Cold War America. It stood also for the insatiable appetite he sensed around him to expand the Americans' "imperialism of the word." Winthrop and his cohort, in wrapping their mission in the language of Exodus, had not simply tried to orient themselves by analogy to the history they knew best. They had swallowed the history of the Jews wholly into themselves. "I followed the process of usurpation with 'wild amaze,'" Bercovitch wrote later. "Through a kind of imperialism by interpretation, one scriptural story had been made the colony of another. A wondrous [Jewish] textual world of chronicle and prophesy—of wisdom literature, poetry, legal and moral commandment, heroic saga, even the erotic Song of Songs—had been appropriated from start to end" by a new chosen people.[30]

It was no wonder that a nation consumed by an appetite to engorge the history of others should have been so irresistibly drawn into the Cold War, even into the quagmires of Vietnam. It was not in their wish to be a model to others but in their urge to swallow every world within their reach that the enduring hubris of the Puritans was manifest. From Winthrop on, Bercovitch wrote, "the rhetoric of expansion was prefigured in the American Puritan imagination."[31]

It is hard now to recover the power and authority that Bercovitch cast over the American studies project in the late years of the Cold War, fusing the American Puritans with European theories of cultural hegemony and welding both to an enduring American present. The intellectual virtuosity with which Bercovitch extracted these themes from the Model cannot be discounted. Since Miller there had been nothing comparable in force and imagination. But where Miller's Puritans lived in the face of uncertainty, yearning for connection with the sacred that they knew could never fully be given, Bercovitch's Puritans swelled with self-absorbed, self-imprisoning confidence.

Nonetheless, Bercovitch did perceive, as Miller did not, how Cold War American culture could hold its contradictions together.[32] America could be John Winthrop's nation *and* Anne Hutchinson's nation because, in the dialectical heart of Winthrop's Model, the language of hegemony and the language of dissent were all but inseparable. The very anxieties of Cold War America were the products of the culture's exaggerated confidence.

Most of these readings of Winthrop's text were in place by the time Ronald Reagan began his drive toward the presidency with Winthrop's "city upon a hill" as a key note in his speeches. The Cold War had driven the Model out of the scholarly cloisters and injected it into public speech, catapulting it into a prominence that Winthrop's text had never enjoyed in its first life. The stage for Winthrop's words was no longer the Puritans' quarrel with God. They were lines for America now. They encapsulated the very heart of the "proposition" of America.

But, in truth, not one but a whole raft of Models had been broached for late twentieth-century America. Some offered reassurance to a Cold War nation. Others issued a challenge to more strenuous, mission-imbued action. Still others explained why the nation's blundering action in the world could never be remedied. A few tried to use the Model's example to encourage the responses to poverty that the modern world demanded; most left that aspect of Winthrop's text out altogether. The work of Ronald Reagan and his speechwriters was not only to canonize the "city upon a hill" lines of the Model—which they did with spectacular success. Their task was also to distill and focus this new, late-arriving, long-orphaned addition to the nation's imagined past.

Ronald Reagan's Shining City on a Hill

B Y THE END of the 1970s, the transit of "A Model of Christian Charity" from a regional New England text to a foundational document for America itself was already well under way. The Puritans had begun their remarkable movement from one of history's side theaters into their center-stage role as articulators of the "myth of America." The "city upon a hill" line, employed now with explicit reference to Winthrop's *Arbella* text, had been added to the stock phrases of American presidential rhetoric. But it was Ronald Reagan who gave the Model its modern public life. Reinventing Winthrop's words for the late twentieth century, he seized on two of its sentences, inserted them into the very "beginnings" of U.S. history, and made them parts of a script that virtually every American would be taught by the end of the century.

The result was an extraordinary act of simplification. Miller's notion of a people severely tested by the demands of their covenant, like Bercovitch's sense of a people swallowed whole by a totalizing vision of themselves, was put aside for scholars to worry over. The social ethic at the heart of the Model's plea for charity was left on the cutting room floor. The Winthrop whom Reagan gave to his listeners—detached from the Anne Hutchinson and Roger Williams controversies, detached

233

from Winthrop's contemporaries' disputes over the proper bounds of liberty and authority, detached from every historical context except the "tiny" pitching ship carrying him and his small band across the Atlantic—was the founding articulator of the American promise.

The Model came into the Reagan White House through the chains of happenstance, neglect, and reappropriation that, as we have seen, shaped its history from the first. A four-word snippet of it came out of the Reagan White House as patriotic icon: a foundation stone in the American canon. Ronald Reagan accomplished all of this in part by sheer repetition of the elements in Winthrop's text and story that had caught his imagination. Reagan was a man familiar with scripts and more skilled than any other president of his century in working with them. He knew how to make their cadences into a kind of verbal music. He did not mind the endless loops of repetition by which certain key-words became deeply attached to his political beliefs and persona. From his first ventures into public speaking in the late 1940s through his "Farewell Address" almost half a century later, certain cherished phrases were to echo continuously through his speeches: verbal signatures that he would occupy like comfortable old clothes.

But Reagan did not make an extract from Winthrop's words and story familiar by repetition only. He and his speechwriters did so through a series of reinventions by which Winthrop's "city upon a hill" phrase slowly morphed from a call to battle into a line of reassurance for a kind of cinematic nationalism. Those unsettled by Reagan's transformation from a messenger of Cold War apocalypse to the bland cheerleader of a nation where "it's a sunrise every day"—where at every new moment "something wonderful can happen to you"— often found the move dismaying.[1] But it was a fitting capstone to the Model's story. Even at the height of its public reputation, its ingredients did not stay stable.

Ronald Reagan liked a good historical tale. As a college student, he was later candid enough to admit, he had not cared much for his classes.[2] He had essentially majored in football at small, Disciples of Christ–affiliated Eureka College, not the economics major in which he was officially enrolled. In his middle age, however, he began to read more and more voraciously in history and politics. Eclectic in his choices, he proved an easy mark for the dramatic quotation and fictionalized historical event that circulated through the conservative magazines, speakers' handbooks, and newspapers clippings he devoured. Blood-thirsty, false quotations from Lenin, more savage than anything Lenin ever actually said, put into circulation by witnesses before the congressional committees on un-American activities, struck a powerful chord with Reagan. One of those false quotations still strikes awe in visitors to the Reagan Museum in Simi Valley, California, though its fabrication was pointed out years ago.[3]

Reagan loved to retell the story that he thought Jefferson himself had written about the climactic moment at Independence Hall in July 1776. As the members of the Continental Congress were still fretting about the act of signing the Declaration, an old man had risen in the balcony, shaken his bony finger at the delegates, and called out: "Sign that parchment! . . . Sign, sign if the next moment the noose is around your neck, sign if the hall is ringing with the sound of headman's axe, for that parchment will be the textbook of freedom, the bible of the rights of man forever." An invention of the gothic fiction writer George Leppard in 1847, nothing like this ever happened.[4] Reagan was equally fond of a pledge that John Adams was said to have made on the same occasion—"sink or swim, live or die, survive or perish, I give my hand and my heart to this vote"—which was also an invention of the nineteenth century.[5] He mistook scenes from the World War II movies that he loved for the war's real events.[6]

Much later, on Reagan's entry into the White House, an unidentified staff member assigned to squeeze some of these fabrications out of the new president's speeches, borrowed a copy of the 1838 *Collections* of the Massachusetts Historical Society from the Library of Congress to check out Reagan's "city upon a hill" quotation.[7] But Reagan's version of the *Arbella* story was, except for his shrinking of the ship down to the dimensions of a "tiny" vessel, an accurate rendition of what historians were writing at the time. And the note card extract he made in his own handwriting was accurate virtually word for word: "We shall be as a city upon a hill. The eyes of all people are upon us, so that if we shall deal falsely with our God in this work we have undertaken & so cause him to withdraw his present help from us, we shall be made a story & a byword throughout the world."[8]

It is a commonplace assumption that someone other than Reagan himself must have injected that passage into Reagan's speeches. At some point, it is supposed, a speechwriter fed him the text that he was, by force of repetition, to make iconic of himself and America. But that is not at all likely. After leaving his Hollywood acting career in 1954, Reagan had earned his living for the next ten years as a public speaker, writing out his own material in longhand. In 1969–70, when the "city upon a hill" phrase first showed up in his speeches on four tightly clustered occasions, Reagan was in the California governor's office assisted by a professional speechwriting staff. Its head, Jerry Martin, remembered their collaboration this way: "We would sit down and we would talk." He would pull something out of his full briefcase; he would say "I want to say this." Then "I would write it and he would edit it . . . and [sometimes] put a lot more into it than we had already put in."[9] Pages of these handwritten inserts can still be found in the Reagan archives.[10] The apocryphal "speech from the balcony" story was one of Reagan's own additions, as Martin's accompanying memo to his 1974 American Conservative Union speech draft noted. Martin did not say who put the *Arbella* story and its "city upon a hill" lines into that same speech. But they were not in Martin's first draft. Almost certainly they had come out of Reagan's briefcase as well.[11]

By the time Ronald Reagan opened his campaign for the 1980 presidential election, his signature phrases were being more carefully polished by those who knew the arts of public relations. But even then his speechwriting staff did not know the power of the "city on a hill" line as fully as Reagan himself. From 1981 to 1989, Reagan's principal speechwriter was Anthony Dolan. A former journalist like Martin, Dolan authored Reagan's famous "Evil Empire" speech excoriating the Soviet Union in 1983, and he helped shape hundreds of others. It was Dolan who appropriated the phrase from Isaiah to promise that the United States would become not only a city on a hill but, like biblical Israel itself, "a light unto the nations."[12] By contrast, John Winthrop was a much vaguer presence in Dolan's mind. In his first draft of Reagan's much admired speech at the relighting of the Statue of Liberty torch in 1986, Dolan still did not know the "city upon a hill" quotation by heart.[13] In a draft for an earlier speech in 1983, Dolan confused John Winthrop with Joseph Warren, hero of the Battle of Bunker Hill, whose words Reagan also loved to quote, so they came out as quotations from Joseph Warren and "Joseph" Winthrop. Unnoticed by the White House staff, the two Josephs mistake persisted into the final version.[14] At another point, as a speech was in rewriting, Dolan made a note to be sure to include "the quote from John Wordsworth about the city upon a hill."[15] Modern speechwriters are almost inconceivably busy people, who cannot be expected to keep everything straight. But "city on a hill" was not Dolan's invention.

Nor was it the invention of the other speechwriters who during Reagan's presidency honed the motif with great rhetorical skill. Peggy Noonan, the most gifted of them in this regard, had Reagan confess to the nation in his farewell address in 1989 that just in the past few days "I've been at that window upstairs, [and] I've thought a bit of the 'shining city on a hill'" and what John Winthrop must have meant in using it "to describe the America he imagined." From that launching point Noonan's imagery took flight, from the "little wooden boat," the *Arbella*, to the giant aircraft carrier *Midway*, from the Normandy beaches to the "granite ridge" on which the nation stood.[16] But the core story and its extracted phrase was one that

Reagan's principal writers had been given to work with, not one they owned.

In a radio address that Reagan had written out by hand in 1978, he told his listeners that sorting through his bundles of note cards looking for quotations that spoke most powerfully to the current state of the world, he had chosen three that went to the heart of the American promise: Emma Lazarus's words at the base of the Statue of Liberty, Thomas Jefferson's commitments to small government and the broadest possible sphere for liberty, and Winthrop's words from "A Model of Christian Charity."[17]

Where had Ronald Reagan found the "city upon a hill" lines? The record gives no clear answer. It was certainly not a borrowing from John Kennedy, as scores of accounts have suggested. In the 1960s Reagan did reach eagerly for Kennedy's words and political mantle. He had been deeply moved by Kennedy's pledge that the nation would pay any price for freedom, a phrase Reagan turned back sharply on the Democratic Party's second thoughts on Kennedy's war in Vietnam. In the same vein, Reagan attached himself proudly to Franklin Roosevelt's line from the 1936 Democratic National Convention, that his generation had "a rendezvous with destiny."[18] In 1979 Reagan would put that signature New Deal phrase into his own speech announcing his candidacy for the presidency.[19] But in the farewell address that Kennedy had delivered to the Massachusetts legislature in 1961, Sorensen had used only the first of the Winthrop phrases that Reagan would initially make his own. "We must always consider that we shall be as a city upon a hill—the eyes of all people are upon us," Sorensen had Kennedy say.[20] But Sorensen had cut off the quotation before the phrase that initially meant even more to Reagan: "so that if we shall deal falsely with our God in this work we have undertaken & so cause him to withdraw his present help from us, we shall be made a story & a byword through the world." Reagan could not have copied that from Kennedy.

The most likely source was Daniel Boorstin's *The Americans*, whose first volume had been published in 1958. Reagan was then General Electric's principal goodwill spokesman, making hundreds of speeches a year on behalf of his employer and corporate capitalism generally. Actively on the lookout for usable material, he would copy out a treasured joke and or a quotation that had caught his imagination onto the note cards from which he spoke. On page three of *The Americans*, where it would have been hard for even a casual reader to miss it, Boorstin had printed the full two-sentence Winthrop quotation that Reagan wrote out on his note card. The passage's spelling and punctuation were modernized, but the words were virtually intact.[21]

In Reagan's early uses of Winthrop's words, the second sentence—"if we shall deal falsely with our God"—was every bit as essential as the first one. From Reagan's first recorded use of Winthrop's story through his election eve television address in 1980, the two tightly linked sentences—the claim of world-historical importance and the warning that the promise might turn, overnight, to ashes—were virtually undetachable from one another in Reagan's mind. The frame that united them was a deeply Manichaean reading of the Cold War that Reagan, in his turn from New Deal Democrat to Barry Goldwater Republican in the late 1950s and early 1960s, had imbibed from the anti-Communist calls to arms around him.

Reagan's core theme was the nearness of a tragic misstep from the destiny that Winthrop's words had laid out for America. Threatened by arms and revolutions abroad and sapped from within by the ever-expansive reach of government, liberty itself was under siege. Reagan embraced every prediction of freedom's vulnerability with fearful eagerness. "Freedom has never been so fragile, so near to slipping from our grasp, as it is at this moment," he declared in his celebrated "A Time for Choosing" speech in 1964.[22] A fall as catastrophic as the fall of Rome and Athens threatened to overwhelm the nation.

The clock of history was running out. Time now stood at "high noon," the shoot-out hour. "Where shall we be at five minutes after Twelve?"[23] Reagan loved to grimly repeat the words of an "Ohio doctor" that rattled through the conservative press: "For one shining glorious moment in history, we had the key and open door and the way was there before us. And men threw off the yoke of centuries and thrust forward along that way with such brilliance that for a little while we were the light and the inspiration of the world. And now the key has been thrown away, the door is closing and we are losing the way."[24]

Reagan was in no manner a Calvinist. But a sense of standing at a rendezvous with destiny, at a division point between starkly divergent futures, made Winthrop's "story and a byword" warning intensely real for him. Betray their mission, Reagan warned his audiences, and their ideals would turn to "ashes."[25] One false choice and the United States might be consigned to a "sterile footnote in history."[26]

These forces of stark opposition came home for Reagan in the eruptive political battles of the late 1960s. He had made forceful crackdown on campus protests a centerpiece of his campaign for the California governorship, together with brakes on runaway government spending and mounting welfare budgets. In May 1969 he had sent California Highway Patrol forces into a bloody confrontation with students at the University of California at Berkeley who had tried to turn an occupied piece of university land into an open "People's Park." A campaign television ad script written the previous year had already sketched out Reagan's basic plot. "Speakers . . . mouths open, impassioned speeches . . . professor on strike . . . bearded 'student leader' . . . quick cut of [the Black Panthers' George] Murray putting down the flag, the Constitution, the American people," and then a quick cut again to Governor Reagan at his desk, soberly reminding voters that "for one tick of history's clock we gave the world a shining, golden hope."[27]

Reagan's very first recorded use of the Model's words came in a speech to a fund-raising dinner for the association of Independent

Colleges of Southern California a month after the People's Park occupation began. He repeated the same speech essentially unchanged
on three other college fund-raising occasions over the next year on
behalf of the newly founded Eisenhower College in upstate New York,
his own Eureka College, and the Churches of Christ–sponsored Pepperdine College in 1970. In each case, Reagan began with the tumult
on college campuses. There, he warned his audiences, scenes from the
fall of Rome into barbarism were replaying before one's eyes. Loot-
ing, vandalism, arson, drug use, and demonstrations in the streets ran
rampant. Students were demanding an immediate peace in Vietnam,
a peace that could bring "a thousand years of darkness for generations
yet unborn." Ages of wisdom were being heaved aside. "The jungle
seems to be closing in on this plot we've been trying to civilize for
6,000 years."[28]

But Reagan concluded each of these speeches in the same way.
Not all college students had descended into University of California
at Berkeley–style anarchy. At places like Eisenhower College, or Pepperdine College, or the independent colleges of Southern California
deeper commitments to learning and teaching persisted. Against
the chaos whipped up by Black Power advocates and free-speech
anarchists, each of these institutions stood, as Winthrop's "shining
dream" had promised, as a "city upon a hill." Give to their annual appeals, Reagan pleaded, and John Winthrop's vision might be preserved
from turning to "ashes" in our lifetime.

When in the mid-1970s Reagan took a version of that formula
into the arena of national politics, the structure remained the same.
Moral and patriotic feelings were decaying. Inflation was on the rise.
Government growth was out of control. Capitalism was being blamed
for everything from despoiling the environment to "seducing, if not
outright raping, the customer."[29] "Ideological fanaticism" was running
hard. Abroad, the "terrifying, enormous blackness" of totalitarianism
grew larger every day.[30] At home, "ghosts from the riotous, hate-filled
'60s are stalking the land."[31] But there was a saving remnant who knew

the stark choices that the nation faced. There were Americans who were not ready to let the vision of a city on a hill go: Americans who knew (as he put it to the Conservative Political Action Conference in 1975) that "if we fail to keep our rendezvous with destiny or, as John Winthrop said in 1630, 'Deal falsely with our God,' we shall be made 'a story and byword throughout the world.'"[32]

As in every act of reappropriation, Reagan altered the meaning of Winthrop's words in the very act of possessing them. Winthrop never spelled out the scenario of failure with the vividness that Reagan invested in the "byword" line. Winthrop wrote for a company that had already cast its choice; his deepest fear was that under the scrutiny of their detractors the Puritans might not show that they could live up to the tasks of faith, love, and discipline that their covenant demanded. Reagan urged Americans to *make* a choice, and having made it, stand as a beacon for the world to see. What joined Reagan's and Winthrop's cities on a hill across this chasm of difference was their sense of embattlement—their sense of a people living under probation at a profoundly urgent moment in history.

On the strength of his personal charm and alarmist message, abetted by Jimmy Carter's foreign policy woes and economic failures, Reagan swept into the White House, carrying Winthrop's words with him. "I know I have told before of the moment when the tiny ship *Arabella* bearing settlers to the New World lay off the Massachusetts coast," Reagan reminded the nation in his election eve speech in November 1980.[33] He would tell or refer to that story repeatedly thereafter. But already a repackaging of Reagan's signature extract from the Model was under way.

Perhaps Reagan's public relations managers sensed that a doomsayer president would not have the same political staying power as an alarm-sounding insurgent candidate. Perhaps they recognized that the widely criticized speech on the crisis of morale haunting the land that Jimmy Carter had delivered just the summer before Reagan an-

nounced his candidacy for president had given them an opportunity
to reposition him as a figure of strength and confidence.[34] Perhaps
Reagan's very election had begun to alter the mood within his speechwriting staff. The fervidly Manichaean tone of Reagan's "Evil Empire" speech was still to come. But gradually the Winthrop-quoting
candidate who entered the White House began to be replaced by a
more reassuring, measured, Winthrop-quoting president.

The most striking sign of that transformation was the way in
which the "story and a byword" line all but disappeared from Reagan's
version of Winthrop's words after the election. Reagan used the "byword" sentence in his election eve speech in 1980. In his more than
thirty references to the "city on a hill" afterward, however, he used or
paraphrased the Model's "byword" sentence on only two occasions,
once in a speech to the conservative Heritage Foundation in 1983 and
again in his final radio address to the nation in 1989.[35] But that was
all. The imminence of potential failure, once so prominent in Reagan's
mind, silently fell away.

Just as striking was the manner in which the "city on a hill" image
shifted in his speeches as well. Reagan had been drawn to the word
"shining" for a long while. Could the nation stave off the threats it
faced at every hand, he had asked a television audience in 1968: "Can
we hold open the door to that shining golden tomorrow?"[36] In his Independent Colleges of Southern California speech in 1969 he had
evoked that "shining dream of John Winthrop's." You must take up the
task to restore America as a "shining city on a hill"—"a golden hope
for all mankind," he told a college audience in 1973.[37] But if "shining"
was an old usage, in his White House speechwriters' hands images of
light now burst out everywhere. What flashed through Tony Dolan's
mind at the thought of a "city on a hill" was the scene that caught
visitors' eyes when they glimpsed the floodlights bathing the monuments in Washington, DC. The "city on a hill" was the halls of Congress, the monuments and cemeteries of heroes, and "those lights on
the Potomac." Let us resolve, Dolan wrote for Reagan, that future

generations of visitors to that "city on a hill" would still find those Potomac lights burning.[38]

Dolan was responsible for the addition of another softening line to Reagan's stock phrases. "This kindly, pleasant, greening land we call America," he had Reagan say, apparently oblivious to the fact that it was a paraphrase extracted from William Blake's epic appeal for a new "Jerusalem" to be built "in England's green and pleasant land," set to music as Britain's unofficial national anthem during World War I, and known to the rest of the world as a foundation stone in English rhetorical nationalism.[39] Blake's line, Winthrop's words, and Isaiah's "light unto the nations" were all essentially the same for Dolan, sometimes yoked together virtually in the same sentence.

For others, intent on surrounding the city on a hill with auras of adjectives, "hope" became the hinge word. Reagan's America, they wrote, was "a city of hope," "a land of wonders," a "beacon of hope to oppressed peoples everywhere," a nation whose "future is bright again with collective glow," a "shining city on a hill where all things are possible." "How can anyone in the United States of America in the world today, be scared of anything?" Reagan's speechwriters had him tell the Texas Bar Association in 1984; "we are truly a shining city on a hill."[40]

In these variations, any sense of contingency virtually fell away. Let us go to the American people and remind them of "America's destiny," he told the Republican National Convention in 1988. Let us help them to see, rising through the "dark but dispersing clouds of twentieth-century tragedy . . . that shining city we have seen and labored for and loved so long, a city aglow with the light of human freedom, a light that someday will cast its glow on every dark corner of the world and on every age and generation to come." "Twilight? Twilight?" he told the cheering delegates the next day. "Not in America. . . . That's not possible." "In this springtime of hope," he promised in 1984, "some lights seem eternal; America's is."[41]

It was left to Reagan's most cinematic of speechwriters to complete the transformation of the "city on a hill" line from fragile possibility to an enduring fact. "I've spoken of the shining city on a hill all my political life," Peggy Noonan had Reagan say in his farewell address to the nation, "but I don't know if I ever quite communicated what I saw when I said it. . . . In my mind it was a tall, proud city built on rocks stronger than oceans, windswept, God-blessed, and teeming with people of all kinds living in harmony and peace; a city with free ports that hummed with commerce and creativity. And if there had to be city walls, the walls had doors and the doors were open to anyone with the will and the heart to get there. That's how I saw it, and see it still."[42] But that movie-set city, flooded in light and harmony, was not the way Reagan had seen the "city on a hill" all his political life. It had no resemblance to the "city upon a hill" of Winthrop's "Model of Christian Charity." A rhetoric veined with choice and danger when it caught Reagan's imagination had morphed into a celebration of what already existed.

If in their first instantiation in his rhetoric Reagan had wielded Winthrop's lines as a sword, in their second, pared of their embarrassing "story" and "byword" lines, they became a rhetoric of reassurance. "U.S.A.!, U.S.A.!, U.S.A.!," the delegates to the 1984 Republican National Convention chanted.[43] "America is back," Reagan's campaign ads declared. Threading that theme through all of the American past from the Puritan "Founders" to the present was part of the work the rhetoric did. Hope, Reagan's public-image makers began to realize, was his best selling point. The Jeremiah holding aloft the ticking clock of history had yielded the stage to a cheerleader. Divesting "A Model of Christian Charity" of its early, more ambivalent lives, Reagan's 1980s speechwriters remade it as a foundational text for a nation eager for reassurance of its power and greatness.

Nationalism feeds on the continuous invention of timeless-appearing texts. By the end of the 1980s Reagan's use and reuse had made "a city on a hill" into one of the most widely recognized building blocks in the culture of American nationalism. In a single verbal gesture it

stretched the usable history of the nation back three and a half centuries into the mists of nationalist time. "We who are privileged to be
Americans have had a rendezvous with destiny since the moment in
1630 when John Winthrop, standing on the deck of the tiny *Arbella*
off the coast of Massachusetts, told the little band of Pilgrims, 'We
shall be a city upon a hill,'" Reagan declared at the outset of his 1980
presidential campaign. The Declaration of Independence and the
Constitution became not dramatic punctuation marks in history
but confirmations of a story and a destiny articulated long before.[44]
And yet, even in constructing Winthrop's words as timeless, Reagan
and his writers had changed them not merely once but twice. The
lights and shadows of Cold War Manichaeism were out; contingency was out; the steady glow of hopefulness was in. "We Americans
are keepers of the miracles," Reagan promised in his last radio speech.
"May it ever be so."[45]

CHAPTER 18

Puritan Foundations of an "Exceptionalist" Nation

IN NORMAL TIMES, the work of speechwriters leaves only a shallow mark on history. Phrases swell into currency—"new frontier," "Great Society," or "compassionate conservatism"—and then fade from use. But the impact of Ronald Reagan's speechwriters' labors was different. Within a decade their "shining" version of Winthrop's "city upon a hill" had moved from their storage files of usable quotations into a virtually ubiquitous, mandatory piece of the American civic creed.

Equally striking, although it took time to emerge, was the pairing of Winthrop's phrase with another term of unexpectedly rising importance: "exceptionalism." Reagan's speechwriters had helped Americans to imagine Winthrop as present at the very origin moment of American history. Now in post-Reagan America Winthrop moved into modernity as the man whose "city upon a hill" phrase had caught, for all time, the difference between the United States and every other nation. In the words of Winthrop's "Model of Christian Charity," it was now said, lay the promise of the nation's enduring uniqueness— its exemption not only from the dynamics that shaped the course of other nations but from the rules of history itself.

This was a remarkable apotheosis for a document so deeply embedded in its times and circumstances. But this unexpected conjunction of themes—one wrenched from New England's seventeenth-century past, the other from the theoretical jargon of early twentieth-century Marxism—also revealed something else: a fear that, with the end of the Cold War, the United States might be becoming a more ordinary nation after all.

The first and most striking sign of the new status of "A Model of Christian Charity" was the speed with which Reagan's speech-writers' extracts from it began to appear everywhere: in political rhetoric, op-ed pieces, academic debates, history books, and every-day speech. Before Ronald Reagan arrived in the White House in 1981, presidents and presidential aspirants had invoked Winthrop and his words in a half-dozen instances. Now those gestures became a rhetorical mandate. One might invert the meaning of the "city upon a hill" phrase or transpose its politics. But as almost all presidential aspirants after Reagan learned, one could not do without it.

From 1980 to 2016 virtually every candidate for the presidency found a way to attach his or her prospects to the "city on a hill" phrase. Speechwriters for Democratic candidates initially searched for a critical edge to the words. In his keynote speech to the 1984 Democratic National Convention, Mario Cuomo scored Reagan's tax and social policies for turning the "shining city on a hill" into a tragedy of two starkly divided cities, one for the lucky rich, the other where Americans struggled with lost mortgages, unstable work, and un-stable lives. Michael Dukakis in 1988 placed his emphasis on the Model's theme of a community knit together by love and mutual re-sponsibility, as did Bill Clinton in 1997. Al Gore in 2000 urged that the "city on a hill" lay still farther ahead, at the end of a march toward true justice and equality.[1]

Republican presidential candidates were more Reaganesque in their appropriations of "city upon a hill." John McCain, Sarah Palin,

Mitt Romney, and Rick Santorum all leaned heavily on the phrase as if it were a straightforward synonym for patriotic pride. Newt Gingrich hosted a patriotism-boosting video called *A City upon a Hill: The Spirit of American Exceptionalism.* George W. Bush told a Simon Wiesenthal Center audience in 2000, "I believe our nation is chosen by God and commissioned by history to be a model to the world."[2] By then Democrats, abandoning their stress on the self-critical strain in the "city on a hill" phrase, were falling into the same patriotic formulas. John Kerry boasted that he was John Winthrop's lineal descendant. Barack Obama evoked the "improbable idea called America" that the Puritan dream of building a "city on a hill" had set in motion. Hillary Clinton in 2016 channeled Reagan's Winthrop directly: "The United States is an exceptional nation. I believe we are still Lincoln's last, best hope of Earth. We're still Reagan's shining city on a hill."[3]

As the politicians burnished these extracts from the Model, historians rushed to keep pace with the election results. In the 1970s, mention of Winthrop's "Model of Christian Charity" had been a hit or miss affair in the textbooks that commanded the college history-teaching market. After 1980 textbook formulas quickly began to change. By 1990 it was a very rare U.S. history college textbook that did not include an account of the Model's delivery aboard the *Arbella.* The principal author of the Harcourt Brace textbook of 1996, John Murrin, cautioned that the "city upon a hill" theme "seldom appears in the writings of the other founders." Nonetheless, he and his fellow authors found room to elaborate on it. In 2012, in a miniature gem of narrative compression which managed to survey almost four centuries of history within its 138 pages, Paul S. Boyer's *American History: A Very Short Introduction* allotted almost a half page to a description of Winthrop's "Model of Christian Charity" and its legacy. Anne Hutchinson, the dissenting heroine of pre-1970s U.S. history textbooks, received two sentences.[4]

Outside the college textbook industry, readjustments to the historical narrative were more fiercely contested. Since the Reagan years, conservative critics had worried about the increasingly critical tone they saw in the American history taught to school children. The new prominence of slavery as a foundational (rather than accidental or aberrational) part of colonial and early national American history formed a particular point of alarm. So did the schoolbook writers' new emphases on social history, microhistory, and global history at the expense of politics and statecraft. Revision of the accepted canon of great American texts, as the voices of women, African Americans, Native Americans, and immigrants from Latin America, Asia, and south and central Europe crowded in, added to conservatives' distress. In 2010 the Texas State Board of Education moved to revise the state's high school curricular standards to stress, in place of the social and multicultural emphases of the school history textbooks, the nation's timelessly enduring commitment to liberty, the "free enterprise system," the principles of a "constitutional republic," and the concept of "American exceptionalism."[5]

Four years later, in 2014, Winthrop's Model was pulled into these ongoing "history wars." In a public letter, amplified by the Heartland Institute and other conservative institutions, a retired high school teacher and advanced placement test guide author, Larry Krieger, charged that the revisions proposed by the Advanced Placement exam's administrators threatened fundamentally to undermine the story that high school students had traditionally learned about American history. The flaws of the nation were magnified, Krieger and those who rallied to his position charged. Stories of oppression were given exaggerated prominence. "Internationalists" on the College Board's team of experts had rewritten American history to make it the story not of a special nation but simply a nation like every other. Flaws were in; "American exceptionalism" was out as a test subject. Symbolic of this stealth attack on the American story, they charged, was that John Winthrop and his vision of a "city upon a hill" had been struck from the list of things serious high school students needed to know about the American past.[6]

The College Board denied that Winthrop and the "city upon a hill" line had been scrubbed from its expectations for an Advanced Placement history course, and it quickly put American "exceptionalism" explicitly back into the list of concepts its test takers would need to know. Unsatisfied, the Republican National Committee issued a public rebuke to the new exam guidelines. In Oklahoma, the legislature's Education Committee authored a mandate that all high school U.S. history courses introduce students to a wide array of primary source documents, specifically including Winthrop's "Model of Christian Charity."[7]

Controversy quickly killed the Oklahoma bill. But what almost no one in these fiercely polemical debates bothered to notice was how recently Winthrop's Model had entered into the history curriculum at all. The Winthrop that the conservatives wanted to make sure that high school history students remembered had barely been part of the core narrative thirty-five years earlier. The Mayflower Compact, the persecution of Anne Hutchinson and Roger Williams, and the strains of building a life in cold and barren New England: these were stories with many decades' telling behind them. The idea that the most important thing those New Englanders had brought with them was a dream of being a model of freedom to the world was new: a construction made within the lifetime of those who now fought so fiercely over its place in the history books.

The second phrase at the crux of the history wars, "American exceptionalism," was an even more recent entrant into the political-rhetorical fray. Every school child should know the meaning and root of the term, the leading conservative protagonist in the Advanced Placement exam controversy, Peter Wood, insisted. "Exceptionalism" was the assertion that America was a wholly new kind of nation, founded on the principles of the Declaration of Independence but "harkening back to Governor Winthrop's 1630 sermon calling on the colonists of Massachusetts Bay to create a community that would be 'a city on a hill' for all mankind." Winthrop's "Model of Christian Charity" was "the rock on which the notion of American exceptionalism was built" and from which it had echoed through American political rhetoric ever since, author and columnist Terry Golway put the now-conventional wisdom in 2012.[8] By then the seventeenth-century New England Puritans and the twentieth-century term "exceptionalism" were locked in tight embrace. But it was an extremely recent marriage and an incongruous one at that.

"Exceptionalism," as its ring of jargon might have led one to suspect, began its life not in the context of American nationalism but as a word in the vocabulary of international Marxism. For Marx himself, uncovering the "laws of historical motion" that swept through economics, society, and politics had been a lifetime preoccupation. The Marxist-Leninists of the twentieth century who invented the term "exceptionalism" inherited from Marx not only the idea of universal laws of historical motion but the tactical task of locating each national economy's place in history's long march toward more intense forms of capital accumulation, proletarianization, and class conflict. In the late 1920s, when the Moscow-based Comintern concluded that international capitalism's "third period" of "collapsing stabilization" had begun, some of the leaders of the U.S. Communist Party objected that circumstances in the United States did not yet mirror the general rule. Worse, in light of the temporary divergence of the United States from the norm, they asked for more autonomy from the central party's tactical directives. Summoned to Moscow where their claim of "American exceptionalism" was branded as heresy, the dissidents were ejected from the Comintern. Rule was rule; in history there were no national exceptions.[9]

The term "exceptionalism," coined in this political-historical squabble, quickly vanished from American politics. But in the 1960s it was taken up by a cohort of American sociologists who had had enough exposure to radical politics in the 1930s to know the idea and to sense its new possibilities for a quite different era. Why had the

United States, alone among the tightly interconnected economies in the North Atlantic world, emerged from the catastrophes of the Great Depression and World War II without a strong socialist or labor party? How had it managed to skate past the destructive inner turmoil of other nations and maintain (at least since the Civil War) the conditions for a stable democracy? These were the problems "of what was once known in the Marxist literature as 'American exceptionalism,'" Seymour Martin Lipset wrote in 1963, made newly pressing in the anxieties of the Cold War.[10]

Uncovering the special conditions that had governed U.S. historical development was not a wholly new task, as Lipset and others recognized. Frederick Jackson Turner had famously singled out the frontier as the Americans' temporary escape hatch from the political and economic inequalities etched on other nations' histories; as long as relatively open land had staved off pressure toward urban concentrations of power, wealth, and poverty, settlement on the North American continent had been able to take its own, more fortunate course. The German economic sociologist Werner Sombart had suggested the role of high wages in buying off American workers from the attractions of socialism. Lipset, writing in the 1960s, maintained that the answer lay in the long-term persistence of a distinctive value structure, an enduring American "creed" as Samuel Huntington was to expand the point.[11] These and other variations on the (European) rule and (U.S.) exception scheme oversimplified dramatically. But in their postwar moment they offered a novel term and a new array of explanations for the fortunate fate of the United States vis-à-vis the world that the war had shattered so profoundly. Still more, they offered hope that that historical exemption would endure into the future.

An awkward taint of foreignness, however, hung over the word "exceptionalism." Indeed the very project of discerning the general rules of history from which the United States might be exempt was not easily naturalized in either scholarly or political discourse. Some of the prominent early participants in these debates thought they had

found a use of the term more closely rooted in the American past in
the work of the French visitor to 1830s America, Alexis de Tocqueville. Tocqueville had not used the noun "exceptionalism" but he
had used the adjective "exceptional" to emphasize the "entirely exceptional situation" of the Americans. "No democratic people will
ever be put in the same situation."[12]

Those words, cut and repasted so often that their context became
utterly lost, were to be recycled hundreds of times in the exceptionalism debates. In fact, Tocqueville had meant them as no compliment.
The "exceptional" character of American society appeared only once
in *Democracy in America*'s two volumes, in a chapter explaining why
the Americans had not yet produced any serious works of art or science, and yet why that failure should not reflect on the possibilities
of democracy itself. Being compelled by the "exceptional" circumstances of their settlement to concentrate on purely material necessities, they had not yet had the leisure to pursue other things. But those
conditions and early habits would change. In time, Tocqueville wrote,
Americans would find themselves "less preoccupied by the material
cares of life" and in that liberation from an overwhelming "pursuit of
wealth" they would show that democracies as well as aristocracies
could enlarge their appreciation of "the human mind" to embrace the
sciences and arts.[13] Tocqueville's exceptionalism was not a fixed thing
but a characteristic in motion.

Still, outside the scholarly literature, even with Tocqueville's authority enlisted behind it, the term had little traction in twentieth-
century public rhetoric. Woodrow Wilson had not known the term
"exceptionalism." Ronald Reagan's speechwriters never paired it with
his "city on a hill" theme. Newt Gingrich listed "unique" among the
positive words in politics in his "Language: A Key Mechanism of
Control" in 1993, but "exceptionalism" did not make his list. None
of the social scientists who revived the term "exceptionalism" in the
1960s and 1970s had associated Winthrop or the New England
Puritans with it at all. Daniel Bell penned his acutely perceptive

Public Interest essay of 1975, "The End of American Exceptionalism," as an epitaph for the idea. The "peculiar and unrepeatable combination of historical circumstances" that had made the American
economy and politics "unique" was gone, Bell wrote. "Our mortality
now lies before us."[14]

The George W. Bush administration's response to the fiery destruction of the World Trade Center in 2001 by militarily overwhelming
Afghanistan and, soon thereafter, Iraq, without waiting for any of the
agencies of international law to act, caused a sharp spike in uses of
the term "exceptionalism." Here was a fitting word for a newly assertive, go-it-alone turn in U.S. foreign policy. The term seeped into the
election of 2008, as John McCain pressed home the contrast between
his foreign policy and Barack Obama's more cautious, consultative
impulses. It was in this context, three months into Obama's first term,
that *Time* magazine's White House correspondent, fresh from coverage of the McCain campaign, arranged to pose a question to the
president at a news conference in Strasbourg, France. Do "you subscribe, as many of your predecessors have, to the school of American
exceptionalism that sees America as uniquely qualified to lead the
world, or do you have a slightly different philosophy?" Obama was
clear: "I am enormously proud of my country. . . . [We] remain the
largest economy in the world. We have unmatched military capability. And I think that we have a core set of values that are enshrined in
our Constitution, in our body of law, in our democratic practices, in
our belief in free speech and equality that, though imperfect, are
exceptional." But he didn't get to that response before musing: "I believe in American exceptionalism, just as I suspect that the Brits believe in British exceptionalism and the Greeks believe in Greek
exceptionalism."[15]

Conservative critics pounced gleefully on that sentence, elated
at the opportunity to sharpen the distinction between themselves and
the first African American to be elected president, the first modern

president to have spent part of his childhood outside the United States. "This is not a man who sees America like you and I see America," Sarah Palin had already charged during the 2008 campaign. "We see America as a force of good in this world. We see an America of exceptionalism." After the Strasbourg news conference, those terms of attack became ubiquitous. Mitt Romney opened his presidential bid in 2010 with explicit dissent from Obama's anti-exceptionalism. Newt Gingrich weighed into the Republican Party primary contest with a new book, *A Nation Like No Other: Why American Exceptionalism Matters.*[16] Are we still Ronald Reagan's "shining city on the hill?" each Republican presidential nomination seeker at the Palmetto Forum in 2011 was asked. Proudly they all answered yes. "To deny American exceptionalism is in essence to deny the heart and soul of this nation," Mike Huckabee told an interviewer in 2012 with an explicit swipe at Obama.[17] That year, the Republican Party for the first time in any American political party's history, put a plank on "American exceptionalism" into its platform. In 2016 the Republican Party led off its whole platform with a declaration of faith: "We believe in American exceptionalism. We believe the United States of America is unlike any other nation on earth."[18]

In some ways these were the familiar sounds of nationalism under pressure. To claim that one's country was different from every other country and better than them all comes with the very culture of nationalism. To believe that one's nation has been appointed by history and destiny to follow a path all its own flows almost inevitably from great power status.[19] What was new in the term "exceptionalism" was not its boast of uniqueness. It was not its claim to dispensation from the rules that others nations' delegations to the institutions of international law and justice might decide. It was a claim of exemption from the general rules of history themselves. It was an insistence that departure from the dynamics of every other people's histories flowed through the very core of the nation. In the wake of Obama's Strasbourg news conference, John Bolton, the Bush administration's hawkish undersecretary of state, weighed into the controversy. Obama is "our first post-American president," Bolton claimed. "I said 'post-American' because he is beyond all that patriotism stuff. . . . He's a citizen of the world and he's a citizen of the world in large part because he doesn't believe as we do in American exceptionalism." He doesn't understand that "it started really with Gov. John Winthrop of the Plymouth Bay [sic] Colony."[20]

All words grow more inflamed in a superheated political climate. U.S. political polarization intensified extremely sharply during the Bush-Obama years, and the rhetoric of public argument boiled up to match. Still, only part of the matter was the speed and intensity with which "exceptionalism" was injected into the center of political debate, strapped to Winthrop's "Model of Christian Charity" as if to a booster rocket. What was more remarkable was that this new explosion of talk about the nation's exception from the general rules of change came at a time when the United States was, by almost every measure, becoming more like other, more "normal" nations, not less.

Were one to ask, stepping back from the events of the moment, during what periods America was most different from the rest of the world, three would stand out. Winthrop's seventeenth century would not be one of them. The seventeenth-century Atlantic world was dotted with experiments in settler colonialism, many with a sense of mission as intense as anything preached in Puritan New England. Visitors to Winthrop's Boston would have found a simpler economy and a much more foreshortened social and political hierarchy than in England. But whether their attention had turned to the theology preached from New England's pulpits, to the delicate balance between liberty, conformity, and authority instantiated in its political institutions, to its treatment of the poor, or to the techniques of farming, fishing, and trade on which its economy depended, they would have recognized themselves instantly within a variation on the familiar landscapes of seventeenth-century England.[21]

The Americans' break with British imperial rule in the late eighteenth century marked a much more momentous departure from history's norms. Its hinge point lay not in the Americans' founding of a nation on the basis of a mission or an "idea." The English Puritan Revolution and the French Revolution were much more deeply saturated with foundational ideas and convictions of world-historical mission than the American. The American Revolution's point of departure from the rules of history was that, in a world where nations without monarchs and established social hierarchies were assumed to be inherently unstable, the nascent United States managed to survive intact for most of a century as a republican outlier in a world of monarchs, revolutionary violence, and recurrent civil wars. "A new order of the ages," the phrase Congress ultimately adopted for the new Great Seal, was a statement of aspiration. But by the first decades of the nineteenth century the American republic had become a new and exceptional political fact in the world around it.[22]

A second era in which one could say that the United States was a highly visible outlier among other nations remains a much less comfortable one to remember. These were the middle years of the nineteenth century when the United States stood out against almost all the rest of the world in the depth of its institutionalization of human slavery. Slavery had pervaded the world economy in the late eighteenth century when American independence had been achieved. But by the mid-1850s, the United States was virtually alone not only in preserving a system of plantation slavery that was vitally important in its national economy but in the ambitions of those who dominated American political life to expand it: west through Texas and (when the time should be ripe) Mexico or southeast into a new U.S.-controlled Caribbean. Cuba and Brazil remained slave major powers as well. But everywhere else revulsion against the idea of outright ownership of human beings had brought statutes of abolition or gradual emancipation into force. Wage labor or contract service had become the rule; slavery in the United States, so firmly entrenched that only an appallingly costly war could ultimately destroy its legal foundations, was the exception.[23]

The great leap to world power status between 1865 and World War I might seem a third era in which the nation broke out of history's rules. The speed of American economic growth in the late nineteenth and early twentieth centuries astonished much of the world. The United States overtook Britain as the world's leading producer of manufactured goods in the 1880s; on the eve of World War I, its economy was more than twice the size of its nearest rival.[24] But the processes of more and more intense industrial and capital development that swept through the United States during this era were not unique to it. Capital for railroad and industrial development was internationally mobile, much of it borrowed from the world's financial center, Britain. The world's new armies of uprooted peasants and farm laborers migrated everywhere that labor was in demand. Tens of millions passed by the Statue of Liberty on their way into the United States before World War I and the restrictive Immigration Act of 1924 sharply reduced that flow. But, taking the world's migration patterns as a whole, just as many others made their way to Argentina, Brazil, and Canada, or abandoned their peasant plots in Poland or southern Italy for the swelling industrial and commercial complexes of the Ruhr and the Italian north, or left southern China for agricultural and construction labor in Southeast Asia, or, having made the stake they hoped for in the United States, passed the Statue of Liberty the other way to return home.[25]

By the eve of World War I, widespread suffrage was no longer an American peculiarity. Throughout Europe and the Americas, the bourgeoisie was moving into ascendance. Great nations now routinely had empires of one sort or another. All had incipient welfare-state structures in place, constructed of ingredients they were now beginning more and more rapidly to borrow from one another. In terms of sheer economic size, the U.S. economy outstripped all the others. It was a remarkable testament to the expansive tendencies of the new global economy. But it was not an exception to it.[26]

The twenty years after 1945 were different. In the aftermath of the second "suicide" of Europe, the United States suddenly found itself the sole great power survivor in a war-devastated world. Almost half of all the world's manufactured goods flowed out of U.S. factories. No other nation—not even the still reeling Soviet Union—strode so large on the world scene either as a military force or a model for human progress. The postwar institutions of world governance, economic stabilization, and human rights enforcement, however inadequate to their tasks they might prove to be, were essentially the Americans' undertaking. The United States operated as the keeper of many of the world's ambitions, the generator of consumer goods and desires that seemed to have almost no limit, and the armed policeman self-appointed to keep the world in order. One can exaggerate the point. There were large regions of the globe outside the American sphere: the Soviet Union, China, and much of the decolonizing world. Still, at no other time in twentieth-century world history had the asymmetry of one nation from all the rest been so evident. It was no accident that American social scientists should have first plucked the term "exceptionalism" out of obscurity in this moment.[27]

By the turn of the twenty-first century, when "exceptionalism" went viral, by contrast, the hegemony the United States had commanded fifty years before was visibly diminishing. The U.S. economy was still the world's largest, but the unchallenged economic supremacy it had enjoyed in 1950 was a thing of the past. With the collapse of the Soviet Union after 1989, the military capacity of the United States overshadowed every other nation's. At the turn of the twenty-first century, the United States accounted for over half the world's military spending, but in a newly multipolar world it could no longer impose its terms on the scale it once could.[28] As it did a century ago, the United States draws more immigrants than any other

single country, but the magnetic power of America has sharply defined limits. When respondents in a sixteen-nation global survey in
2005 were asked to name the country where they thought a young
person would have the best chance for a good life, the United States
did not head the great majority of their lists.[29] By the time the exceptionalism debate exploded, the bookstores were filled with titles de-
scribing the declining cultural, economic, and geopolitical hegemony
of the United States: Andrew Bacevich's *The Limits of Power: The End
of American Exceptionalism,* Fareed Zakaria's *The Post-American World,*
Edward Luce's *Time to Start Thinking: America in the Age of Descent.*[30]
The social scientists who probed more closely into the differences between the United States and other nations found a checkerboard of
similarities and contrasts, not a pattern of rule and exception.[31]

In the late seventeenth century, when it became clear that history
had stranded the New Englanders in a backwater of international
Protestantism, the region's ministry began to talk all the more fervently of a "New Israel" in America. When the United States' dis-
proportionately massive share of global power and resources began
to recede at the turn of the twenty-first century, the political speechwriters began to talk more and more fervently of American "exceptionalism." Rhetorics of confidence, they were also rhetorics of
compensation.

But to insist on the "exceptionalist" character of the nation was not
only to resist, by an act of will, these signs of relative decline. It was
not only to rebuke those who foresaw a more "normal" United States
in the world's future. To declare one's enduring faith in exceptionalism was to resist altogether the idea that a nation might tack back and
forth between eras of normality and eras of exception. It was to imagine that American history could be straightened out into a single,
continuous line.

For that task of historical reconstruction, one needed precedents:
earlier figures who had seen a parallel thread of exceptionalism

running through their own times. Those who shaped the eighteenth-century American republic were not a good match. For every figure of the revolutionary generation who believed that independence had shattered the very rules and fetters of the past, there were others watching anxiously to see if the Americans had virtue enough to resist the luxury, corruption, and decay that had overwhelmed republics in the past. Would history catch up with the new nation? Would it fall like other nations from the high moral plane that self-government demanded? The question haunted the new nation's makers.

To reach back to Winthrop's "city upon a hill" as the origins of the American exceptionalist faith was to imagine oneself boring still deeper into the bedrocks of time. Handbook writers on American political culture now routinely did so. ABC-CLIO's three-volume encyclopedia of American political culture ran the idea of "American exceptionalism" in a straight line from Winthrop through Thomas Jefferson and Abraham Lincoln to George W. Bush. The legal "originalist," Steven G. Calabresi, opened his case for the exclusion of foreign precedents from U.S. courts' consideration with the "city upon a hill" quotation from Winthrop.[32] Asked by a National Public Radio interviewer where the idea of American exceptionalism was born, law professor Peter Schuck replied: "Well, it goes back to the eighteenth century, at the very least, and perhaps the earlier colonists: the 'City on a Hill' idea, John Winthrop."[33] The best-selling author Eric Metaxas crystallized those assumptions in 2016: The idea of a singular destiny was "the principal idea of America, the idea that existed before the nation, that gave birth to the nation. . . . We may trace the seed of what we think of as American exceptionalism to the summer of 1630."[34]

Nothing was more deeply on Winthrop's mind in that summer, as we know, than the downward drag of time and his anxiety that the rules of sinful human nature would overwhelm the effort to build an experiment in religious purity on New England soil. Covenanted people had sinned before. Before the second autumn had set in, the Massachusetts authorities had whipped and banished two of their number for foul and slanderous invectives against their government and church order, whipped and fined three others for stealing corn from the native people in whose midst they lived, and a fourth for sexual assault on a native woman. Winthrop carefully noted each instance in his journal. The preachers took up the themes of fallibility and failure with still more earnestness. Drunkenness, worldliness, idleness, and profanity had come in the same boats and in the same human nature as piety. To be a New England Puritan was not to live outside history but within it, within the possibility that the New Englanders would prove that they were no different than others.

The idea of American exceptionalism as it was wielded in the political battles of the Bush-Obama years, by contrast, was an assertion of timelessness: a claim of title to an idea that had always been present in the very soul of America. There was no greater irony in the way in which the "city on a hill" phrase swept into everyday language in early twenty-first-century America than that John Winthrop, steeped in a deep sense of history's power over human events, should have been conscripted into contemporary politics as reassurance that America would be somehow immune from history after all.

CHAPTER 19

Ambivalent Evangelicals

ENTER "CITY ON A HILL" into an internet search, and one trail of referents leads you to "exceptionalism" and discussions of the place of the United States in world affairs and history. Another takes you to Ronald Reagan's policies and speeches. A third pulls you back still deeper in time to John Winthrop and the Massachusetts Bay colony. But by far the most heavily trafficked hyperlinks that spread out from "City on a Hill" sweep you into the culture of twenty-first-century American evangelical Protestantism.

"City on the Hill" is the name of a Christian contemporary pop music series[1] and a new Christian right radio show.[2] In Louisville, Kentucky, the "City on a Hill" studio produces a stream of Christian books and videos, Bible stories and study guides, films, and sermon aids that are said to have already reached 1.3 million people.[3] In Zeeland, Michigan, a former hospital has been renamed "City on a Hill" and repurposed as a hub of evangelical Protestant social organizations: a family social service center, medical clinic, second-hand clothing store, start-up church, and café for fellowship and Bible study.[4] There is a "City on the Hill" music festival in Duluth, Minnesota,[5] a faith-based "City on a Hill" substance abuse recovery center in Garden City, Kansas,[6] and a faith-based "City on a Hill" health clinic and youth center for poor families in central Milwaukee.[7] More than a dozen congregations calling themselves "City on a

Hill Church" dot contemporary America from Brookline, Massachusetts, to Provo, Utah.

Institutions like these mirror the broader landscape of contemporary American evangelical Protestantism. Religion in evangelical Protestant America is spirit led, Gospel driven, biblically centered,
and salvation focused. Gospel music and high-energy preaching pump
through many of its churches. The faces of young families shine out
from their websites. Missions, adult Bible study groups, youth camps,
and charity and service projects absorb and refuel their energies.
The reference point of the "city on a hill" for most evangelical Protestants is not Winthrop or Reagan. It is Matthew 5:14. It marks their
claim to be the direct heirs of Jesus's disciples: the salt of the earth,
the light of the world, believers who build on rock rather than on
sand and whose faith rises above the troubles of a fallen world as a
city upon a hill. They are far closer to the biblical roots of the phrase
than the political and presidential speechwriters. They form clumps
of believers *within* America, consciously apart from much of the
America around them. In this sense they parallel many of those who
joined Winthrop's project, imagining themselves as misfits in a society they thought had gone astray.[8]

"City on a hill" imbues these Americans with a sense of direct,
unmediated relationship to God. But they cannot escape the power
of the nation either. Patriotism saturates most of the cultures of
American evangelical Protestants. It comes through their preachers
and, still more, through the televangelists who dominate Christian
television. It comes through the explicitly Christian histories of the
United States stocked by online Christian book stores and through
the history and social studies texts that dominate the Christian home-
schooling market. It comes through the "City on a Hill" summer
camps where young people can learn how to lobby their state governments on the issues of sexuality, marriage, and public prayer that
ignite the political passions of conservative evangelical Christians.[9] It comes through the God and country rallies many evangelical

church members flock to. It comes through the Republican Party, to which they have become cemented as a powerfully coherent voting bloc.

Still, the relationship of evangelical Protestants to the nation and to the text that for others had come to sum up the special hope and promise of America is more complicated than one might first expect. With a burst of publicity in 2011, Newt and Callista Gingrich joined forces with Citizens United, the conservative political lobby, to release a film entitled *As a City upon a Hill: The Spirit of American Exceptionalism*.[10] But many American evangelical Protestants are not so sure that Winthrop's text stands, in the same way, as a patriotic icon for them. In the story of "A Model of Christian Charity"—its long neglect, its sudden, unexpected arc into prominence, the dismantlement of the text into independently circulating phrases, and the continuous remaking of their meanings—the place of the Model in contemporary evangelical America is, in some ways, the story's most surprising chapter.

Hunger for history and heritage runs strongly through the cultures of American evangelical Protestantism. Since the last quarter of the twentieth century, an ever-expanding genre of explicitly Christian histories of the United States has grown up to meet that desire. Self-help books on faith, family, and personal relationships vastly outsell works of history in Christian book stores. Scenarios of the end of the world sell vastly more copies than backward-looking history books. But providence-saturated histories of the United States form an important niche in the Christian book market.[11]

The first to tap this need was Peter Marshall and David Manuel's *The Light and the Glory*, which the evangelical publishing house Fleming H. Revell brought out in 1977. Neither Marshall nor Manuel was a professional historian when they were struck dumb (as they told it) by the idea that there might be a providential mission for America running all through its history. Their first moment of revelation came in reading Columbus's assertion that "it was the Lord who put into my mind (I could feel his hand upon me)" the idea of sailing west to the Indies. What if that were literally true? What if God had used Columbus to bring Christianity to the Americas, but then had saved that part of the continent that would become the United States for something even grander? What if "God knew what the twentieth century would hold in store?" What if he knew "the totalitarian darkness that would arise out of Europe and Asia, and knew that England alone would never have the spiritual power to stop them?" What if in seventeenth-century New England he had "planted the seeds of light that would make a difference early in the twentieth century," guiding the new nation through the "definite and extremely demanding plan" he had in mind? Writing with the infectious energy of men unearthing a history that they were sure secular culture had deliberately hidden from them, they shaped a providentialist story of colonial and early nineteenth-century America for evangelical readers.[12]

The Light and the Glory was the first modern, best-selling, explicitly Christian history of the United States, but others soon followed. The Virginia preacher Mark Beliles parlayed the success of his America's Providential History (1989) into an accompanying study guide and video, a dozen more books, a Providence Foundation to publish them, a Providential Perspective newsletter to publicize them, and online classes at his Biblical Worldview University.[13] Another amateur historian, David Barton, launched an even larger empire in the late 1980s dedicated to setting the history of the nation's founding on biblical and providentialist foundations. His books and videos were already "ubiquitous" in politically conservative evangelical households, a sociologist found in the 1990s. The new Christian right's 2008 presidential candidate, Mike Huckabee, heralded Barton as "America's greatest historian."[14] Barton's website in early 2017 claimed that he spoke on the biblical origins of the U.S. Constitution to over four hundred audiences a year. History texts for Christian homeschoolers drum home the same message. "Who, knowing the facts of our history, can doubt that the United States of America has been a thought in the mind of God from all eternity?" the *American Republic for Christian Schools* declares.[15]

The seriousness of the quest for a Christian history of the United States can be sensed by hefting *The American Patriot's Bible*, first published in 2009, off any Christian bookstore's shelves. Bound in paper, four choices of leather binding, or army camouflage covers, it contains the whole of the King James Version of the Old and New Testaments, prefaced with a call to action to bring the nation home to its "biblical foundations" and profusely illustrated with figures and events from American history. Exodus 3:10 is paired with a full-page paean to America's Moses, George Washington. Leviticus 25:37 is paired with a long extract from the U.S. Supreme Court judgment upholding released time programs in public schools for religious instruction. Genesis 14:14 ("Now when Abram heard that his brother was taken captive, he armed his three hundred and eighteen trained servants") is paired with a full-page celebration of the Second Amendment's right to bear arms. Deuteronomy 20:4 is illustrated by Franklin Roosevelt's passages on the importance of religion from his 1939 State of the Union Address. Colossians 3:17 is explained as a warning against any temptation to let others "simply exist on handouts from a government agency." Literally hundreds of American figures make cameo appearances in *The American Patriot's Bible*—Grover Cleveland and Andrew Jackson, Irving Berlin and Charlton Heston, Bayard Rustin and Martin Luther King Jr., Stonewall Jackson and Robert E. Lee—each linked to a specific scriptural text, as if prefigured in the Bible itself. An extended passage from Winthrop's Model leads off the book of Micah, with which Winthrop's Model had concluded. The melding of sacred and secular—biblical word, conservative politics, and American history—is complete and seamless.[16]

A year after *The American Patriot's Bible*'s publication, a still more striking expression of the unity of patriotism, faith, and history erupted into Protestant religious culture in the God and country rallies launched by the television and talk radio megastar, Glenn Beck, between 2010 and 2012. A longtime figure on the airwaves, Beck catapulted into fame during the 2008–9 financial meltdown as the Tea Party movement's most visible talking head. Operatic and uninhibited, an unrelenting foe of active government, of the "cancer" of progressive politics and of Barack Obama in particular, a font of tears and bizarre conspiracy theories, he was the enormously successful public face of furious, modern-day, right-wing populism. In 2010, however, he claimed he had had an epiphany. He would stage a mega-rally not to promote his next book (*The Plan*, a manual for resisting the coils of socialism strangling America, he had envisioned it) but to celebrate patriotism, faith, and American history. In the first of his rallies, "Restoring Honor," some hundred thousand persons converged on the site where Martin Luther King Jr. had delivered his "I Have a Dream" speech almost fifty years before to witness Beck ("America's history professor," his radio cohost introduced him), a battalion of preachers, and a corps of honored military veterans celebrate the nation. Some evangelical Protestant preachers grumbled that a Mormon like Beck had no business presiding over a faith-and-nation camp meeting. But those who came by the busload didn't care. "There was piety—endless piety, as speaker after speaker demanded that Americans rededicate themselves to God," Ross Douthat wrote in the *New York Times*. "There was patriotism"; there were "encomiums to the founding fathers." As another observer noted, there were references to "more American historical figures than it's possible to count."[17]

Two years later, in a Dallas stadium, Beck presided over the third of his "Restoring" rallies, this one a three-hour extravaganza dedicated to "Restoring Love." Beck brought to the Dallas Cowboys' arena a desk once used by Abraham Lincoln, one of the first Bibles to be printed at the encouragement of the Continental Congress, a stage full of musicians, and a program of one-day voluntary, government-free service projects for those who came early. There was ugliness in American history as well as glory, Beck admitted. "Manifest destiny" had worked terrible consequences for the continent's native peoples. The billy clubs and water cannons wielded at Selma, Alabama, against African Americans seeking justice were a betrayal of the American promise. But with courage, love, and a sense of history, faithful Americans could join together to "make a shelter from the storm."[18]

To drum home that lesson, Beck's film studio produced a short, accompanying docudrama of Winthrop's "Model of Christian Charity." The studio budget for the video production was not high. Winthrop, with the tangled hair and the piercing eyes of a man transfixed by his faith, sits below the *Arbella*'s decks facing two other Puritans. He has no text in front of him other than a huge Bible. He declaims from memory or perhaps from spontaneous inspiration. "If we shall deal falsely with our God in this work we have undertaken and so cause him to withdraw his present help from us, we shall be made a story and a byword," he begins, as the camera whirls through a sudden jumble of dystopic images: a gallows, a sketch of John Brown at the head of a slave insurrection, fields strewn with the bodies of men killed in combat. To avoid this fate we must be knit together as one man. For if we keep the covenant with our Lord—Winthrop is on his feet now, shouting, his voice a full, impassioned fortissimo—ten of us shall withstand a thousand of our enemies. The Lord will make other plantations like New England. Then, suddenly seated and sotto voce: "We must consider that we shall be as a city upon a hill; the eyes of all people are upon us." A second, longer barrage of dystopic images suddenly breaks in: more soldiers' corpses, images of war, Depression-era soup lines. These cut abruptly to photos of the Statue of Liberty, the sublime beauty of Niagara Falls, and the oratory of Martin Luther King Jr. "Have we kept the covenant?" Winthrop asks as the video ends.[19]

The impassioned visual melodrama of Glenn Beck's rendition of "A Model of Christian Charity" is only part of what makes it significant. Beck's Winthrop script put on vivid display the emotional dualism that cuts through the world he and his fans inhabit. A stark collision of moods, a vertiginous oscillation between a sense of power and a sense of paranoia: this was the theme that Beck's film-makers drew from the Model's story, not the shining optimism of a Ronald Reagan or the certainties of American exceptionalism. Jagged, scene-cutting, emotional contradictions form Beck's retelling of Winthrop's story.

In the larger context of efforts to write a Christian history of the United States, Beck's explicit investment in Winthrop's text and story is not the norm. Marshall and Manuel, eager readers of Perry Miller's essays in Puritan history, had given Puritan New England a central stage in God's drama in America. But by far the larger number of writers who followed Marshall and Manuel in the production of explicitly Christian histories of America quietly eased Winthrop off to the margins of their stories. Evangelist and presidential candidate Pat Robertson gave Winthrop no mention at all in his *America's Dates with Destiny* in 1986. Neither did the best-selling Christian books author Tim LaHaye in his *Faith of Our Founding Fathers: A Comprehensive Study of America's Christian Foundations* in 1987. Mark Beliles's *America's Providential History* in 1989 gave Winthrop only a tiny, cameo role. Gary DeMar's *America's Christian History: The Untold Story* pulled five key dates out of the history of "the early Christian colonies." The year of the Model's writing and the New England Puritans' landing, 1630, was not among them. William Federer's seven-hundred page *America's God and Country Encyclopedia of Quotations* in 1994 gave Winthrop a little over two pages, much of that devoted to a long quotation from "A Model of Christian Charity." But William Bradford and William Penn each received three times as much; John Adams, Benjamin Franklin, and Thomas Jefferson each received five times the space Federer's *Encyclopedia* gave to Winthrop. In the intensely crowded canvas of *The American Patriot's Bible*, Winthrop got a portrait, but no one could have picked him out from the rest as a truly foundational architect of American national consciousness.[20]

The contrast is arresting. In secular histories of the United States and analyses of American political culture, John Winthrop's "Model of Christian Charity" occupies an indispensably central place. In explicitly Christian histories it does not. The marginal location of the Model on history's sidelines is not the result of doubts about the religious character of the nation. "Our nation is chosen by God and commissioned by history to be a model to the world," George W. Bush, the modern evangelical Protestant movement's representative in the White House, declared in a campaign speech in 2000. "God is not on the side of any nation," Bush pulled back his rhetoric in 2004. But that "our part, our calling, is to align our hearts and action with God's plan," he had no doubt.[21] John McCain, positioning himself for the presidential election of 2008 was less qualified: "The Constitution established the United States of America as a Christian nation."[22]

But "A Model of Christian Charity" was not central to these convictions. Part of the reason that evangelical Protestant writers have kept their distance from Winthrop is their concern with government-wielded power. Evangelical Protestants yearn for the state to repress the moral ills they think bedevil their America: pornography, homosexuality, abortion, and the like. Many look to the government to preserve the "Judeo-Christian" character of the nation from those immigrant groups they fear will undermine it. But the thoroughgoing interfusion of church and state power that had been the hallmark of Puritan Massachusetts is not their ideal.

Evangelical Protestant Americans' views of the public welfare functions of governments mirror that concern. Messages of Christian charity permeate the preaching of modern "city on a hill" churches. They sponsor hunger drives and food pantries. Their members respond to general poll questions concerning the poor with still greater sympathy than do their counterparts in white, mainstream Protestant churches. But when it comes to government assistance to the poor, their resistance grows sharper. More than other Americans, they worry about the effects of public welfare on the poor. They would

prefer to see many of its functions taken from government and performed by private, voluntary hands. The system of local, tax-supported
public assistance that prevailed in Winthrop's Massachusetts incor-
porates too strong a hand of public obligation to match their ideal of
charity's reach.[23]

Reflecting evangelical Protestants' concerns that a too active state
already intrudes too much on them, evangelical historians find the
simpler voluntarism of the tiny Plymouth colony much more to their
liking than the religious authoritarianism of the Massachusetts Puritans. They lavish attention on the Pilgrims. Beliles titled his chapter on
Plymouth "The Pilgrims: A Model of Christian Character." William
Federer's encyclopedia of God and country quotations gave the colony's William Bradford more than twice the space of its Winthrop
entry.[24] Mike Huckabee helped produce a DVD on the *Mayflower*
landing and the first Thanksgiving; the conservative Regnery Press
markets a book of eyewitness accounts from the Pilgrim colony. Neither has issued anything comparable for the New England Puritans.[25]

A second, and still more important, reason why John Winthrop
and "A Model of Christian Charity" do not figure more strongly in
evangelical Protestants' accounts of the American past is that their histories have a more important goal to pursue: and that is control over
the historical interpretation of the era of the Revolution and the writing of the Constitution. Constitutional law matters intensely in
modern evangelical Protestant politics. It was a series of Supreme
Court decisions between 1962 and 1973 that shocked the apolitical
subcultures of modern evangelical Protestantism into political alarm
and action. In *Engel* (1962) and *Abington* (1963) the court had barred
state-written prayers and Bible readings from public school class-
rooms. Starting in 1970 and upheld thirteen years later in the U.S.
Supreme Court's *Bob Jones University* judgment, a series of Internal
Revenue Service rulings qualified the autonomy of churches in choosing and excluding persons for membership by holding that private,
religious associations that discriminated on racial lines would forfeit

their tax-exempt status. *Roe v. Wade* (1973) outlawed blanket criminalization of abortion. All these decisions rested on expansive Bill of Rights grounds. Demonstrate that the Constitution and Bill of Rights' drafters understood the nation they were making as an explicitly Christian one, prove that its founding documents ultimately rested not on secular but on Bible-infused ethical principles, and all those decisions might be brought down at once.

This was the cause into which David Barton rushed with his arsenal of lectures, books, and videos aimed at rewriting the religious culture within which the nation's late eighteenth-century Founders had worked. Claiming a library of tens of thousands of original documents and an encyclopedic knowledge of the religious ideas of the Constitution's framers, Barton put together a case for the essentially Christian character of the Constitution and its early amendments that had an enormous resonance in conservative Protestant America. His books and videos endure as a staple of the Christian book market. Glenn Beck gave him copious airtime. Strings of quotations, often wrenched from context, misreadings of texts, by which even the firmest eighteenth-century deist could be made to appear a theologically orthodox Protestant, unevidenced historical anecdotes, and sometimes the retailing of outright fabrications build a powerfully convincing edifice for those alarmed by the Supreme Court's church and state rulings. The evangelical Christian publishing house Thomas Nelson pulled Barton's *Jefferson's Lies* from publication after scholars began to list its most striking errors, but not before it had climbed onto the *New York Times'* best-seller list and into the consciousness of millions of believers.[26]

For Americans who think themselves under siege in an increasingly secular society, taking hold of the history of the Revolution and the early republic is the project that matters. Succeed in that, and the edifice of liberal Supreme Court judgments affecting faith and morals might fall and the Christian America of their imagination be restored. In this context, the earlier political culture of Puritan Massachusetts and Winthrop's Model is beside the point.

But the deepest reason why "A Model of Christian Charity," after its reputational apogee in Cold War and Ronald Reagan's America, has come to occupy so minor a place in Christian rewritings of U.S. history points to the tension between the optimism into which the Model has been enlisted and the sense of history that dominates the subcultures of evangelical Protestant America. Reagan and his speechwriters made the Model into an icon of hope for the nation. To the scholars and writers who worked within the framework of American exceptionalism, the specialness of the United States was a fixed presumption. For both groups, the referent of the "city on a hill" was an America that beamed its virtues, its unmatched wealth of freedoms and possibilities confidently out to the world. But many contemporary evangelical Protestants are not so sure those premises hold. They relish the idea that they are part of a God-driven history. "God has blessed this land," evangelical American writers proclaim. "He has loved America unlike He has loved any nation of the world." Yet profound pessimism runs just beneath this streak of pride. More than secular Americans or members of other religious groups, they see themselves and the nation under attack in contemporary America. Thus the evangelical Protestant political project: not to live out their religious lives in a good and faithful land but to live in resistance to the dominant culture, "to bring this nation back to God."[27]

An acute sense of sin and the world's defects has always run hard through Protestant America. But this sense of sin complicates more acutely than before the notion of being a model to the world. "Our society is crumbling," Jerry Falwell wrote in *Listen America!* in 1980, when the new Christian right was just moving into high gear. "America, our beloved country, is indeed sick." Our "exceptionalism" is being cast into "the dustbin of history," former congressman Tom Tancredo restated the same mood in 2013. "The case for a weary

pessimism grows stronger each day." "We were set up to . . . be a light
to the world," a speaker told an Operation Save America rally in Wichita,
Kansas, in 2016. "But we got drunk with all of the wealth, drunk with
all of the prosperity, and we've forgotten who we are."[28] Evangelical
Protestants tell interviewers their worries that America will go the way
of the Roman Empire, consumed in hedonism and self-pleasure. They
struggle to find their way in "this pluralistic, humanistic, no-name, no-
God, no-nothing nation" they see around them. "Christians are aliens
in America," the director of the antiabortion National Christian Action
Council declared. "This world is not our home."[29]

Where this sense of being pilgrims in a radically imperfect world
comes to its most thoughtful expression, one finds some of the most
acute critiques of the assumption that John Winthrop's "city upon a
hill" ever had anything to do with the modern, secular U.S. nation.
Hillsdale College's Richard Gamble, whose *In Search of the City on a
Hill* in 2012 did more than any historical account before it to cut Winthrop's text down to size, to show its "insignificance" throughout
most of American history and to demonstrate the adventitious way
in which it became, long after the fact and at cross-purposes to Winthrop's own intentions, a symbol of the American nation, wrote both
as a professional historian and a committed evangelical Protestant. "In
Christian theology, it is simply not true that America is the city on a
hill, not now, not ever," Gamble writes. To take the words of Matthew
5:14 seriously is to refuse their political appropriation.[30] The idea of
a "Christian nation" as a whole, other evangelical Protestant historians have written, sets a trap for Christian believers. To imagine a
national-providential history in which the United States is born as an
idea in God's mind, and through which God's hand is to be found in
every turn of its fortunes, is to fall into "idolatry of our nation," the
most distinguished of modern evangelical Protestant historians, Mark
Noll, writes. The God of the New Testament does not choose nations
or especially favor one above another, Noll, Gamble, and others insist.
The true city on a hill lies outside the fallen world of human history.[31]

At the other end of the evangelical Protestant spectrum and among its much more widely popular writers and preachers, this strain of historical pessimism runs headlong toward visions of world-ending catastrophe. Apocalyptic visions of history, though their sources run deep in Christianity, have multiplied manyfold in the last half century.[32] Modern evangelical writers have charted the stages of the Apocalypse, mapped it into phases and dispensations, and visualized its drama in film and fiction. It is not a pretty sight. "New pagan hordes . . . are on the verge of obliterating the last strongholds of civilized humanity," the author and filmmaker Frank Schaeffer warned at the height of his end times prophecy phase. "God has granted America—though she doesn't deserve it—a reprieve from the agenda of paganism," Bob Jones III wrote in the aftermath of George W. Bush's reelection. But still the end remains near for many evangelical Protestants. "I really believe that the pagans, the abortionists, and the feminists, and the gays and the lesbians who are actively trying to make an alternative lifestyle, the ACLU, People for the American Way, all of them who have tried to secularize America . . . I point the finger in their face and say 'you helped this happen,'" Jerry Falwell stated two days after the World Trade Center's destruction on September 11, 2001.[33] End times novels, movies, and videos, Tim LaHaye's *Left Behind* series the most successful among scores of imitators, put the agonies of the world's end in cataclysmic prose and images. On my hotel television screen in Milwaukee, Wisconsin, Donnie Swaggart, heir to the pulpit of his famous televangelist father, is striding in fury across the television stage set. "God hates the idol worship" that has consumed America. He hates the freeloaders and homosexuals and the immigrants who steal Americans' jobs. This nation has become an "insane asylum," Swaggart shouts. God hates the people we have become.[34]

In the complexly compartmentalized world of contemporary American evangelical Protestantism, the foretellers of a divine catastrophe that will swallow up the nation in waves of divine fury are not the only voices. There are churches where optimism is much the stronger message, where purpose and hope are the controlling themes. There are prosperity churches where God is poised to drop riches in your lap. There are churches that put loving service to others first. There are "postmillennial" churches where the end of the world does not come in consuming fury but in gradual, step-by-step realization of God's ultimate grace and justice. Nor is pessimism new to American Christianity. Dilations on the sinfulness of man poured forth from New England Puritan pulpits. The preachers' Jeremiads held the acts of God's people up for relentless examination, listed their failings in detail, and warned that, were his hand not stayed by mercy, an angry God would, in full justice, cast them off.

The Jeremiad was a warning, however, not a map of history's inevitable destination. It was a reminder that the New Englanders lay under the close scrutiny of a God whose very strictness, paradoxically, gave reassurance to New England Puritans that they were still an especially chosen people. There was spiritual anxiety aplenty in Winthrop's world. But the mood swings within contemporary evangelical Protestantism are sharper and more exaggerated. The utopic and the dystopic intercut one another, not only in the images of Glenn Beck's Winthrop video but in the religious cultures that most evangelical Protestants inhabit. Messianic hopes for a sacred America and apocalyptic images of its destruction, a sense of virtuous power and a sense of helplessness—all lie closely intertwined in evangelical Protestant imaginations.

Modern evangelical Protestants cling proudly to the "city on a hill" phrase. They have, to a considerable extent, taken it back from the political speechwriters and rerouted its meanings once more. Although they have largely marginalized Winthrop in their histories of "Christian America," many evangelical Protestants know that Winthrop had used the words before them. In their sense of living as quasi-exiles in their own land, indeed, modern evangelical Protestants echo the mood of many of the early seventeenth-century English Puritans who struck out for New England. But the Puritans' counterparts in contemporary America have no land into which to flee the divine wrath that they fear may be closing in. Their sense of their special place in God's providence and their fear of God's abandonment of the nation in which they live are locked in an antagonistic embrace from which there is no easy escape. In their heightened sense of fear and beleagueredness, they have recast the Model's words once more, this time on far more ambivalent and pessimistic lines than the secular culture that surrounds them.

EPILOGUE

Disembarking from the Arbella

W HAT MAKES A TEXT "TIMELESS"? The answer cannot be that it endures, unchanged through the passage of time. No text ends up as it began. None escapes history. The point is not simply that the meaning of a text erodes. In the very act of reading a text, cherishing, possessing or rejecting it, its meaning is remade. It is, inescapably, always under construction.

The exaggerated swings of the Model's reputation offer a particularly vivid lesson in the ways in which the lives of a text proceed through time. As it took shape in Winthrop's mind, "A Model of Christian Charity" was a reflection on the ways in which social inequality and love might be imagined as fulfilling each other's necessities. It was a plea to Winthrop's fellows in the New England emigration project to set aside prudence and price, to step outside the bounds of market rules and customs when social necessity demanded it. It was a claim to their special place in divine favor and history. It was a stark reminder that their work would proceed under the relentless scrutiny of God and others. It was an intensely personal document whose themes were forged during a critically important span of months in John Winthrop's life. It was a string of extracted quotations and rhetorical commonplaces. It was important enough to copy, correct, and retitle at different times during the seventeenth century. But on the whole, it was quickly forgotten.

A quite different "Model of Christian Charity"—reconceived as the founding statement of an enduring American civic creed—was a twentieth-century invention. That centuries-delayed injection of the Model into the national canon was the product of many different hands and intentions. For Perry Miller, who stood at the head of that enterprise, the Model articulated, above all, the Puritans' heroic gamble with the odds of providential history. For others, the Model set the trap for the nation's enthrallment in an idea of its cosmic self-importance. Ronald Reagan wielded a two-sentence extract from the Model as a weapon in Cold War politics before, quietly abandoning one of those sentences, he turned it into a line of nationalist reassurance. Scholars of American civil religion reimagined the Model as the republic's defining text. Op-ed writers found it a virtually indispensable reference point. In the evangelical Protestant subcultures of modern America, however, contemporaries are not so sure of its relevance to them. This is not simply a history of rival readings of "A Model of Christian Charity": not simply a cacophony of interpretations. The Model is inseparable from its history. It *is* the shifting arguments, uses, angers, and aspirations that, from Winthrop forward, persons have poured into it.

Similar lives of continuous reinvention mark every "timeless" text. The Declaration of Independence holds its greatness because over time it became the touchstone of so many aspirations, far beyond those that Thomas Jefferson and the Declaration's drafting committee envisioned. A literally interpreted statement of grievances against the English Crown and government, prefaced by a quickly controversial opening paragraph of Enlightenment abstractions, would have had no staying power beyond the moment of its enunciation. Legal "originalists" dream of bringing the untainted text of the original Constitution back to life. But the Constitutional document of 1787, its very words saturated with unresolved disputes and papered-over

compromises, was already in motion from the moment of its transmission to Congress. Take away the lives of a text and you take away
the very histories that give them meaning.

A sense of "timelessness" helps to give ballast against the buffet-
ing of events. There is reassurance in its folded sense of time—in the
"traditions" and continuities that have poured with such fertility out
of the imaginations of nationalism's articulators. But the deep, enduring cultures that were said to propel nations down their distinctive
ways were inventions: constructions for their time and moment.
Nations and political cultures, too, have complex lives. They have
multiple, not singular origin points. They emerge not only out of
agreements but out of clashes of ideas. They are always in the making.
They are products of a continuing argument and a continuous reinvention for new contexts and circumstances. "America is a constant
work in progress," Barack Obama put the point, speaking at the foot
of the Edmund Pettus Bridge in Selma, Alabama, where one of those
moments of remaking took place.[1] Without continuous renewal
through deliberation and imagination, nations dissipate. They
crack up. Or, like texts, they disappear.

Certainly the disappearance of texts is a common enough occurrence.
Who now practices the arts of political persuasion by declaiming the
once-electrifying lines of Daniel Webster? Or memorizes the "cross
of gold" speech of William Jennings Bryan? Who in the eighteenth
and nineteenth centuries paused for more than a moment over "A
Model of Christian Charity"? "The afterlife of a document is vagrant,
unpredictable, and often astonishing," Daniel Boorstin once observed.
"The disproportion between the circumstances of the inspiration
and the reach of the product is remarkable and sometimes bizarre."[2]
"A Model of Christian Charity," exhumed from obscurity in the
1930s, reached the peak of its public recognition in Ronald Reagan's
rhetoric and the post-Reagan celebrations of American "exception-

alist" history. In contemporary America, its presence may already be beginning to wane.

In the run-up to the presidential election of 2016, Ronald Reagan's reworking of the Model's "city upon a hill" line seemed still as strong as it had been in the 1980s. Hillary Clinton declared that "if there's one core belief that has guided and inspired me every step of the way, it is this. The United States is an exceptional nation. I believe we are still Lincoln's last, best hope of Earth. We're still Reagan's shining city on a hill. We're still Robert Kennedy's great, unselfish, compassionate country." Marco Rubio launched his bid for the national political stage by ringing the changes on the "city on a hill" line. Ted Cruz pledged to uphold "the American exceptionalism that has made this nation a clarion voice for freedom in the world, a shining city on a hill." Ben Carson and Chris Christie appealed to the enduring truth of the "city on a hill" phrase. Barack Obama and Mitt Romney defended its timeless relevance. Even Rudy Giuliani, in a convention speech laced with grim, catastrophe-strewn descriptions of a crime-ridden America, concluded with the "city on a hill" line.[3]

The one candidate who consistently refused the phrase, even when his rivals taunted him for his demurral, was the candidate who won: Donald Trump. His preferred term was "disaster." The Democratic Congress's Affordable Health Care Act was a "disaster." The federal budget was a "disaster." Banking reform was a "disaster." The Common Core curriculum was a "disaster." U.S. foreign policy was "a complete and total disaster." In the Middle East, despite the lives and money expended, "we have nothing . . . we have nothing." The gross domestic product's growth was "below zero." "We don't have victories anymore." Reagan's America had been a "shining city on a hill," George W. Bush's speechwriter, Peter Wehner, observed; Trump's America was a "dumpster fire." "We're dying. We're dying," Trump told his rallies. "The American dream is dead."[4]

Donald Trump's grimly apocalyptic rhetoric, amplified and secularized for the occasion, echoed a pessimism already strong in the
minds of conservative values voters. It made many evangelical Protestant voters feel as if they were on familiar terms with even as flamboyant an outsider to their ways of faith as Trump. More importantly, the
rhetoric of disaster was the prelude to a promise of a heroic, near-
superhuman action. "I" will repeal and replace Obamacare, Trump
promised in his campaign speeches. "I" will build a wall across the
U.S.-Mexico border. "Nobody builds walls better than me, believe
me." "I" will stop Iran from getting nuclear weapons. "I'll be the greatest jobs president that God ever created." "I will bring [the American
dream] back bigger and better and stronger than ever before." "Nobody can do that like me." "I am your voice!" Trump declared.[5]

There was a "we," too, at the end of Trump's standard stump
speech. "We will make American strong again. We will make America proud again. We will make America safe again. We will make
American great again."[6] But the agent of change, the man who in this
time of disaster was going to turn things around, faster than you would
believe possible, was Donald Trump himself.

Many accidents of history combined to bring Donald Trump's
exaggerated sense of self into the White House. But he may ultimately
signal a broad, new turn in American political culture. His is the language of modern, swift-moving, transactional capitalism. He talks the
talk of the "deal"—the promise of the turnaround artist who can spin
a broken enterprise back to profitability overnight. Historical
references—the sinews of earlier political rhetoric—are virtually
nonexistent in the language of the corporate dealmaker. In Trump's
world there are no historic enemies, only leaders who, if you are naive
at the game, can outsmart and outmaneuver you. At home, "greatness" is promised, but heroes are rare. Trump mentioned Reagan far
less often than any of his Republican opponents. In his campaign
speeches Trump never paused to mention the Founding Fathers, or
James Madison, or Thomas Jefferson, or the Declaration of Indepen-

dence. He rarely mentioned the Constitution except in his pledge to appoint Supreme Court justices in the tradition of Antonin Scalia. The power of American "exceptionalism," the American "idea," or the American political "tradition" never worked their way into his campaign speeches. In the Republican presidential candidates' debates, Chris Christie was moved to say, "I love this country. It's the most exceptional country the world has ever known." Jeb Bush took up the theme: "Look, America still is an exceptional country."[7] Donald Trump did not rise to the bait.[8]

As for the Puritans, in the language of purely transactional politics they belong to a past that has no relevance for the present. The "mystic chords of memory," to which Abraham Lincoln had appealed so eloquently in 1861, were silent in Trump's speeches. Even the note cards of historical quotes and snippets that Ronald Reagan had written out so assiduously by hand were, in this context, relics from another time. Donald Trump may be the United States' first posthistorical president, the first inhabitant of that office to live fully and completely in the present moment of the transaction and the deal.

The formulas of nationalism that bound time together in seamless webs of continuity, which enlisted a deep past, however exaggerated or fictive, may have run their course in the patriotism of the present. The point should not be exaggerated. In the month of Donald Trump's inaugural, Harvard University announced the imminent reopening of its one of its undergraduate colleges, named for John Winthrop. Around the frieze of Winthrop House's common room, not far from the site where John F. Kennedy once lodged, students will now read, elegantly stylized and lifted out of every relevant context: "We shall be as a city upon a hill, the eyes of all people are upon us."[9] Others know the words as well. "We remain—as difficult as we can be with each other, we remain that shining city on the hill," James Comey declared in testimony on his dismissal by Donald Trump as director of the Federal Bureau of Investigation.[10] These may be harbingers of continuing lives for Winthrop's text. Or they may be a set of receding echoes as "A Model of Christian Charity" drifts toward an antiquarian oddity once more, a companion for poetry about pumpkins and parsnips.

The disappearance of the Model from the canon of foundational American texts would not be a complete loss. There is no doubt that "A Model of Christian Charity" has been overused and its historical force overestimated. It has been routinely stripped from context. It has been employed to explain too much, to weld the contemporary American nation to a fragment of its past with too much imagined continuity. The theme of a chosen people, selected out from humankind for a task apart from that of all other peoples, which Winthrop plucked out of his seventeenth-century surroundings, is strewn with tragic consequences. The hubris that endures into the early twenty-first century's clashes of nations and cultures haunts our times still. The Puritans are not to be blamed for this. But a more tempered reckoning with the complex and multiple aspirations that flow into the project of nation making would make us better readers of history than does fixation on an ur-text, a singular core idea, or the imagined "beginning of our consciousness."

But there are two takeaway points from the thoughts that came to Winthrop's mind in the winter and spring of 1630 that are worth saving before we reconsign "A Model of Christian Charity" to the obscurity that surrounded it so long. One is the aching tension in the Model's opening pages between the social fact of inequality and Winthrop's yearnings for a community rooted in love. The New England Puritans never succeeded in working that tension out in ways that satisfied them. But they did not dismiss it. They groped their way through the moral knots and difficulties of dealing with questions of wealth and poverty with a conscious effort that we might let unsettle our own confidence that, in the era of the deal, the incentivized bargain, and widening inequality, we have got the answer right.

The second theme we might take away from the Model is the theme that controls its closing section. Winthrop stitched together the promise and the warning of the Model's "city upon a hill" section from widely separated parts of the Bible, each differently intended. But his borrowing of Old and New Testament voices made no random conflation in Winthrop's mind. Exposure was their common theme. To aspire to be a covenanted people could not be unlinked, the Model warned, from the burdens of visibility. To live not in a permanently shining city, its floodlights guaranteed by God and exceptionalist history, nor in a fortress of unshakable greatness, but to live as if one's society was under the moral scrutiny of the world, as if the eyes of all people were trained on it: What responsibility could be heavier?

The invented texts and stories that nations lay over their messier origins cannot shoulder that burden. Without an honest and searching account of their pasts, nations are at peril. But the "model" a nation makes in the critical eyes of the world, the actions it takes or foregoes, the ideals on which it acts or fails to act, and the people it imagines itself to be: all are made in the present tense. As a small step toward that realization we might do worse than to take a text onto which so many modern yearnings have been projected, from which so many malleable bits of rhetoric have been extracted, around which so many myths have been woven and conflicts waged and put it back, more wisely and humbly, into history.

John Winthrop,
"A Model of Christian Charity":
A Modern Transcription

Note on the text: This modern transcription of "A Model of Christian Charity" attempts to balance faithfulness to the surviving text against a desire to ease modern readers' way through the unfamiliar language of the seventeenth century. The text follows the transcription of the New-York Historical Society with the silent correction of a few minor errors. The copyist's mistakes are left intact, even where the copyist clearly omitted a word, misidentified a biblical text, or, miscounting, ran two passages headed "secondly" right after each other. The original grammar has not been altered. To guide modern readers through the unfamiliar underbrush of seventeenth-century spelling, run-on paragraphing, and inconsistent punctuation, however, this transcription intervenes in three significant ways. The text has been repunctuated and reparagraphed throughout to make its logic and meaning easier to follow. Spellings have been modernized. The section breaks are my own, as discussed in chapter 1. A digital image of the New-York Historical Society's text can be accessed at https://cdm16694.content dm.oclc.org/digital/collection/p16124coll1/id/1907.

For assistance in transcription, I am grateful to Sarah Matherly and Spencer Weinreich. Discovery of the word "Massachusetts" hidden under the partially erased and overwritten "New England" was the work of Edward O'Reilly, Curator and Head of the Manuscript Department, Patricia D. Klingenstein Library, New-York Historical Society.

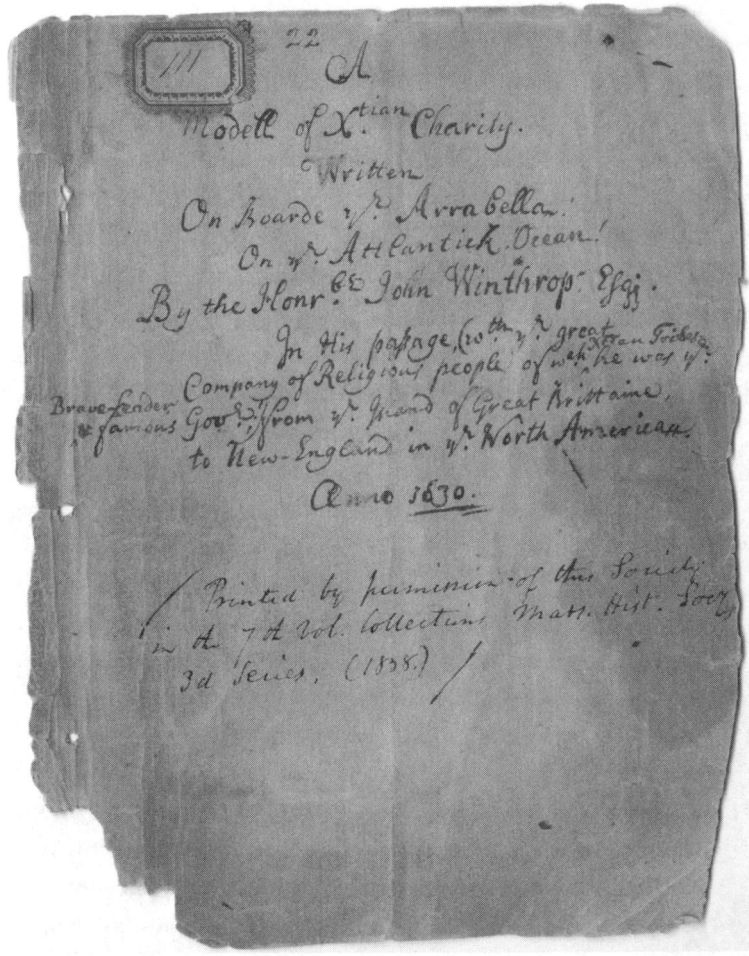

FIGURE 2. Cover sheet to the only surviving copy of "A Modell of Christian Charity," written sometime after the copy itself was made, with additional words interlined still later.

John Winthrop, "A Model of Christian Charity," 1630; from BV Winthrop, John; image #79597d, New-York Historical Society.

Christian Charity
A Model hereof

[I]

God almighty in his most holy and wise providence hath so disposed of the condition of mankind, as in all times some must be rich, some poor, some high and eminent in power and dignity, others mean and in subjection.

The Reason hereof

1 Reason: First, to hold conformity with the rest of his works, being delighted to show forth the glory of his wisdom in the variety and difference of the creatures and the glory of his power in ordering all these differences for the preservation and good of the whole and the glory of his greatness. That as it is the glory of princes to have many officers, so this great king will have many stewards, counting himself more honored in dispensing his gifts to man by man than if he did it by his own immediate hand.

2 Reason: Secondly, that he might have the more occasion to manifest the work of his spirit. First upon the wicked in moderating and restraining them; so that the rich and mighty should not eat up the poor, nor the poor and despised rise up against their superiors and shake off their yoke. 2ly, in the regenerate in exercising his graces in them, as in the great ones, their love, mercy, gentleness, temperance, &c, in the poor and inferior sort, their faith, patience, obedience, &c.

3 Reason: Thirdly, that every man might have need of others, and from hence they might be all knit more nearly together in the bond of brotherly affection.

From hence it appears plainly that no man is made more honorable than another or more wealthy &c. out of any particular and singular respect to himself but for the glory of his creator and the common good of the creature, man. Therefore God still reserves the property of these gifts to himself as Ezek. 16.17. He there calls wealth his gold and his silver, and Prov. 3.9, he claims their service as his due: honor the Lord with thy riches &c.

[II]

All men being thus (by divine providence) ranked into two sorts, rich and poor; under the first are comprehended all such as are able to live comfortably by their own means duly improved; and all others are poor according to the former distribution.

There are two rules whereby we are to walk one towards another: Justice and Mercy. These are always distinguished in their act and in their object, yet may they both concur in the same subject in each respect: as sometimes there may be an occasion of showing mercy to a rich man in some sudden danger or distress, and also doing of mere justice to a poor man in regard of some particular contract &c.

There is likewise a double law by which we are regulated in our conversation one towards another in both the former respects: the law of nature and the law of grace, or the moral law or the law of the gospel, to omit the rule of justice as not properly belonging to this purpose otherwise than it may fall into consideration in some particular cases.

By the first of these laws man as he was enabled so withal is commanded to love his neighbor as himself. Upon this ground stands all the precepts of the moral law, which concerns our dealings with men. To apply this to the works of mercy, this law requires two things: first, that every man afford his help to another in every want or distress. Secondly, that he perform this out of the same affection which makes him careful of his own goods. According to that of our savior, Matth: Whatsoever ye would that men should do to you. This was practiced by Abraham and Lot in entertaining the angels and the old man of Gibeah.

The law of grace or the gospel hath some difference from the former as in these respects: First, the law of nature was given to man in the estate of innocency; this of the gospel in the estate of regeneracy. 2ly, the former propounds one man to another as the same flesh and image of God, this as a brother in Christ also and in the communion of the same spirit, and so teacheth us to put a difference between Christians and others. Do good to all especially to the household of faith. Upon this ground the Israelites were to put a difference between the brethren of such as were strangers, though not of the Canaanites. 3ly, the law of nature could give no rules for dealing with enemies for all are to be considered as friends in the estate of innocency, but the gospel commands love to an enemy. Proof: If thine enemy hunger, feed him; love your enemies, do good to them that hate you. Matth. 5.44.

This law of the gospel propounds likewise a difference of seasons and occasions. There is a time when a Christian must sell all and give to the poor as they did in the apostles' times. There is a time also when a Christian (though they give not all yet) must give beyond their ability, as they of Macedonia: Cor. 2.6. Likewise, community of perils calls for extraordinary liberality, and so doth community in some special service for the church. Lastly, when there is no other means whereby our Christian brother may be relieved in this distress, we must help him beyond our ability rather than tempt God in putting him upon help by miraculous or extraordinary means.

This duty of mercy is exercised in the kinds: giving, lending and forgiving.

Question: What rule shall a man observe in giving in respect of the measure?

Answer: If the time and occasion be ordinary, he is to give out of his abundance. Let him lay aside as God hath blessed him. If the time and occasion be extraordinary, he must be ruled by them, taking this withal, that then a man cannot likely do too much, especially if he may leave himself and his family under probable means of comfortable subsistence.

Objection: A man must lay up for posterity. The fathers lay up for posterity and children, and he is worse than an infidel that provideth not for his own.

Answer: For the first, it is plain that it being spoken by way of comparison it must be meant of the ordinary and usual course of fathers and cannot extend to times and occasions extraordinary. For the other place, the apostle speaks against such as walked inordinately; and it is without question, that he is worse than an infidel who through his own sloth and voluptuousness shall neglect to provide for his family.

Objection: The wise man's eyes are in his head (sayeth Solomon) and foreseeth the plague. Therefore we must forecast and lay up against evil times when he or his may stand in need of all he can gather.

Answer: This very argument Solomon useth to persuade to liberality. Eccle: Cast thy bread upon the waters &c., for thou knowest not what evil may come upon the land. Luke 16: Make you friends of the riches of iniquity. You will ask how this shall be? Very well. For first, he that gives to the poor lends to the Lord and he will repay him even in this life an hundred fold to him or his. The righteous is ever merciful and lendeth, and his seed enjoyeth the blessing. And besides we know what advantage it will be to us in the day of account when many such witnesses shall stand forth for us to witness the improvement of our talent.

And I would know of those who plead so much for laying up for time to come, whether they hold that to be gospel. Matth. 6:19: Lay not up for yourselves treasures upon earth &c. If they acknowledge it, what extent will they allow it? If only to those primitive times, let them consider the reason whereupon our saviour grounds it. The first is that they are subject to the moth, the rust, the thief. Secondly, they will steal away the heart; where the treasure is, there will the heart be also. The reasons are of like force at all times. Therefore the exhortation must be general and perpetual, which always in respect of the love and affection to riches and in regard of the things themselves, when any special service for the church or particular distress of our brother do call for the use of them. Otherwise it is not only lawful but necessary to lay up as Joseph did to have ready upon such occasions as the Lord (whose stewards we are of them) shall call for them from us.

Christ gives us an instance of the first, when he sent his disciples for the ass, and bids them answer the owner thus: the Lord hath need of him. So when the tabernacle was to be built, he sends to his people to call for their silver and gold, &c.; and yields them no other reason but that it was for his work. When Elijah comes to the widow of Sarepta and finds her preparing to make ready her pittance for herself and family, he bids her first provide for him. He challengeth first God's part which she must first give before she must serve her own family. All these teach us that the Lord looks that when he is pleased to call for his right in any thing we have, our own interest we have must stand aside till his turn be served.

For the other, we need look no further than to that of John 1: He who hath this world's goods and seeth his brother to need and shuts up his compassion from him, how dwelleth the love of God in him? Which comes punctually to this conclusion: if thy brother be in want

and thou canst help him, thou needst not make doubt
what thou shouldst do; if thou lovest God thou must
help him.

Question: What rule must we observe in lending?

Answer: Thou must observe whether thy brother hath
present or probable or possible means of repaying thee. If
there be none of these, thou must give him according to
his necessity rather than lend him as he requires. If he
hath present means of repaying thee, thou art to look at
him, not as an act of mercy, but by way of commerce,
wherein thou art to walk by the rule of justice. But, if his
means of repaying thee be only probable or possible, then
is he an object of thy mercy. Thou must lend him, though
there be danger of losing it. Deut. 15.7: If any of thy
brethren be poor &c. thou shalt lend him sufficient. That
men might not shift off this duty by the apparent hazard,
he tells them that though the year of jubilee were at hand
(when he must remit it, if he were not able to repay it
before) yet he must lend him and that cheerfully. It may
not grieve thee to give him (sayeth he) and because some
might object, why so I should soon impoverish myself
and my family? he adds with all thy work, &c. For our
savior, Matth. 5.42: From him that would borrow of thee,
turn not away.

Question: What rule must we observe in forgiving?

Answer: Whether thou didst lend by way of commerce or in
mercy, if he have nothing to pay, thee must forgive him
(except in cause where thou hast a surety or a lawful
pledge). Deut. 15.2. Every seventh year the creditor was
to quit that which he lent to his brother if he were poor,
as appears ver. 8: Save when there shall be no poor with
thee. In all these and like cases Christ was a general rule,
Matth. 7.22: Whatsoever ye would that men should do to
you, do ye the same to them also.

Question: What rule must we observe and walk by in cause of community of peril?

Answer: The same as before, but with more enlargement towards others and less respect towards ourselves and our own right. Hence it was that in the primitive church they sold all, had all things in common; neither did any man say that that which he possessed was his own. Likewise in their return out of the captivity, because the work was great for the restoring of the church and the danger of enemies was common to all, Nehemiah exhorts the Jews to liberality and readiness in remitting their debts to their brethren, and disposeth liberally of his own to such as wanted and stands not upon his own due which he might have demanded of them. Thus did some of our forefathers in times of persecution here in England, and so did many of the faithful in other churches whereof we keep an honorable remembrance of them. And it is to be observed that both in scriptures and latter stories of the churches that such as have been most bountiful to the poor saints, especially in these extraordinary times and occasions, God hath left them highly commended to posterity: as Zacheus, Cornelius, Dorcas, Bishop Hooper, the Cuttler of Brussells and diverse others.

Observe again that the scripture gives no caution to restrain any from being over liberal this way; but all men to the liberal and cheerful practice hereof by the sweetest promises. As to instance one for many. Isaiah 58.6: Is not this the fast that I have chosen to loose the bonds of wickedness, to take off the heavy burdens, to let the oppressed go free and to break every yoke, to deal thy bread to the hungry and to bring the poor that wander into thy house; when thou seest the naked to cover them, &c. Then shall thy light break forth as the morning, and thy health shall grow speedily, thy righteousness shall go before thee, and the glory of the Lord shall embrace thee. Then thou shalt call and the Lord shall answer thee &c.

2.10. If thou power out thy soul to the hungry, then shall thy light spring out in darkness, and the Lord shall guide thee continually, and satisfy thy soul in drought, and make fat thy bones. Thou shalt be like a watered garden, and they shall be of thee that shall build the old waste places &c.

On the contrary, most heavy curses are laid upon such as are straightened towards the Lord and his people. Judg. 5: Curse ye Meroshe because ye came not to help the Lord, &c. Pro: He who shutteth his ears from hearing the cry of the poor, he shall cry and shall not be heard. Matth. 25: Go ye cursed into everlasting fire, &c. I was hungry and ye fed me not. Cor. 2.9.16: He that soweth sparingly shall reap sparingly.

[III]

Having already set forth the practice of mercy according to the rule of God's law, it will be useful to lay open the grounds of it also being the other part of the commandment: and that is the affection from which this exercise of mercy must arise. The apostle tells us that this love is the fulfilling of the law. Not that it is enough to love our brother and so no further, but in regard of the excellency of his parts giving any motion to the other, as the soul to the body and the power it hath to set all the faculties on work in the outward exercise of this duty. As when we bid one make the clock strike, he doth not lay hand on the hammer which is the immediate instrument of the sound but sets on work the first mover or main wheel, knowing that will certainly produce the sound which he intends. So the way to draw men to the works of mercy is not by force of argument from the goodness or necessity of the work: for though this course may enforce a rational mind to some present act of mercy as is frequent in experience, yet it cannot work such a habit in a soul as shall make it prompt upon all occasions to produce the same effect;

but by framing these affections of love in the heart which will as naturally bring forth the other as any cause doth produce the effect.

The definition which the scripture gives us of love is this: love is the bond of perfection. First, it is a bond or ligament. Secondly, it makes the work perfect. There is no body but consists of parts. And that which knits these parts together gives the body its perfection, because it makes each part so contiguous to other as thereby they do mutually participate with each other, both in strength and infirmity, in pleasure and pain. To instance in the most perfect of all bodies: Christ and his church make one body. The several parts of this body considered apart before they were united were as disproportionate and as much disordering as so many contrary qualities or elements. But when Christ comes and by his spirit and love knits all those parts to himself and each to other, it is become the most perfect and best proportioned body in the world. Eph. 4.16: Christ by whom all the body being knit together by every joint for the furniture thereof according to the effectual power which is in the measure of every perfection of parts a glorious body without spot or wrinkle; the ligaments hereof being Christ or his love. For Christ is love. 1 John 4. 8. So this definition is right: love is the bond of perfection.

From hence we may frame these conclusions.

1. First of all true Christians are of one body in Christ 1 Cor. 12.12.13.17: Ye are the body of Christ and members of your part.

2ly. The ligaments of this body which knit together are love.

3ly. No body can be perfect which wants its proper ligament.

4ly. All the parts of this body being thus united are made so contiguous in a special relation as they must needs partake of each others strength and infirmity, joy and sorrow, weal and woe. 1 Cor. 12.26: If one member suffers, all suffer with it; if one be in honor, all rejoice with it.

5*ly.* This sensibleness and sympathy of each others conditions will necessarily infuse into each part a native desire and endeavor to strengthen, defend, preserve, and comfort the other.

To insist a little on this conclusion being the product of all the former, the truth hereof will appear both by precept and pattern. 1 John 3.10: Ye ought to lay down your lives for the brethren. Gal. 6.2: Bear ye one anothers burdens and so fulfill the law of Christ. For patterns we have that first of our savior who, out of his good will in obedience to his father, becoming a part of this body and, being knit with it in the bond of love, found such a native sensibleness of our infirmities and sorrows as he willingly yielded himself to death to ease the infirmities of the rest of his body and so heal their sorrows. From the like sympathy of parts did the apostles and many thousands of the saints lay down their lives for Christ again. The like we may see in the members of this body among themselves. 1 Rom. 9. Paul could have been contented to have been separated from Christ that the Jews might not be cut off from the body. It is very observable which he professeth of his affectionate parting with every member: Who is weak (sayeth he) and I am not weak? Who is offended and I burn not? And again, 2 Cor. 7.13: Therefore we are comforted because ye were comforted (of Epaphroditus he speaketh). Phil. 2.30: That he regarded not his own life to him service. So Phoebe and others are called the servants of the church. Now it is apparent that they served not for wages or by constraint but out of love.

The like we shall find in the histories of the church in all ages: the sweet sympathy of affections which was in the members of this body one towards another, their cheerfulness in serving and suffering together, how liberal they were without repining, harborers without grudging, and helpful without reproaching. And all from hence: they had fervent love amongst them which only make the practice of mercy constant and easy.

The next consideration is how this love comes to be wrought. Adam in his first estate was a perfect model of mankind in all their generations, and in him this love was perfected in regard of the habit. But Adam rent in himself from his creator, rent all his posterity also one from another. Whence it comes that every man is born with this principle in him: to love and seek himself only. And thus a man continueth til Christ comes and takes possession of the soul, and infuseth another principle: love to God and our brother. And this latter having continual supply from Christ, as the head and root by which he is united, get the predominency in the soul, so by little and little expels the former. 1 John. 4.7: Love cometh of God and every one that loveth is born of God. So that this love is the fruit of the new birth, and none can have it but the new creature. Now when this quality is thus formed in the souls of men it works like the spirit upon the dry bones. Ezek. 37: Bone came to bone. It gathers together the scattered bones or perfect old man Adam and knits them into one body again in Christ, whereby a man is become again a living soul.

The third consideration is concerning the exercise of this love, which is twofold, inward or outward. The outward hath been handled in the former preface of this discourse. For unfolding the other we must take in our way that maxim of philosophy, Simile simili gaudet, or like will to like. For as it is things which are carved with disaffection to each other, the ground of it is from a dissimilitude or [   ] arising from the contrary or different nature of the things themselves, so the ground of love is an apprehension of some resemblance in the things loved to that which affects it. This is the cause why the Lord loves the creature, so far as it hath any of his image in it. He loves his elect because they are like himself. He beholds them in his beloved son. So a mother loves her child, because she thoroughly conceives a resemblance of herself in it. Thus it is between the members of Christ: each discerns by the work of the spirit his own image and

resemblance in another, and therefore cannot but love him as
he loves himself.

Now when the soul, which is of a sociable nature, finds any
thing like to itself, it is like Adam when Eve was brought to
him. She must have it one with herself. This is flesh of my
flesh (sayeth she) and bone of my bone. She conceives a great
delight in it; therefore she desires nearness and familiarity
with it. She hath a great propensity to do it good and receives
such content in it, as fearing the miscarriage of her beloved she
bestows it in the inmost closet of her heart. She will not endure
that it shall want any good which she can give it. If by occasion
she be withdrawn from the company of it, she is still looking
towards the place where she left her beloved. If she hear it
groan she is with it presently. If she find it sad and disconsolate
she sighs and mourns with it. She hath no such joy as to see her
beloved merry and thriving. If she see it wronged, she cannot
bear it without passion. She sets no bounds of her affections nor
hath any thought of reward. She finds recompense enough in
the exercise of her love towards it.

We may see this acted to life in Jonathan and David. Jonathan,
a valiant man endued with the spirit of Christ, so soon as he
discovers the same spirit in David had presently his heart knit
to him by this lineament of love; so that it is said he loved him
as his own soul. He takes so great pleasure in him that he
strips himself to adorn his beloved. His father's kingdom was
not so precious to him as his beloved David. David shall have
it with all his heart. Himself desires no more but that he may
be near to him to rejoice in his good. He chooseth to converse
with him in the wilderness even to the hazard of his own life,
rather than with the great courtiers in his father's palace. When
he sees danger towards him, he spares neither care, pains, nor
peril to divert it. When injury was offered his beloved David,
he could not bear it, though from his own father. And when
they must part for a season only, they thought their hearts
would have broke for sorrow, had not their affections found

vent by abundance of tears. Other instances might be brought to show the nature of this affection, as of Ruth and Naomi and many others, but this truth is cleared enough.

If any shall object that it is not possible that love should be bred or upheld without hope of requital, it is granted, but that is not our cause. For this love is always under reward; it never gives, but it always receives with advantage. First, in regard that among the members of the same body, love and affection are reciprocal in a most equal and sweet kind of commerce. 2ly, in regard of the pleasure and content that the exercise of love carries with it, as we may see in the natural body. The mouth is at all the pains to receive and mince the food which serves for the nourishment of all the other parts of the body. Yet it hath no cause to complain. For first, the other parts send back by several passages a due proportion of the same nourishment in a better form for the strengthening and comforting the mouth. 2ly, the labor of the mouth is accompanied with such pleasure and content as far exceeds the pains it takes. So is it in all the labor of love among Christians: the party loving reaps love again as was showed before, which the soul covets more than all the wealth in the world.

2ly, nothing yields more pleasure and content to the soul than when it finds that which it may love fervently. For to love and live beloved is the soul's paradise, both here and in heaven. In the estate of wedlock there be many comforts to bear out the troubles of that condition; but let such as have tried the most say if there be any sweetness in that condition comparable to the exercise of mutual love.

From the former considerations arise these conclusions.

First, this love among Christians is a real thing not imaginary.

2ly.   This love is as absolutely necessary to the being of the body of Christ as the sinews and other ligaments of a natural body are to the being of that body.

3ly.　This love is a divine spiritual nature: free, active,
　　　　strong, courageous, permanent, undervaluing all
　　　　things beneath its proper object. And of all the graces
　　　　this makes us nearer to resemble the virtues of our
　　　　heavenly father.

4ly.　It rests in the love and welfare of its beloved.

For the full, certain knowledge of those truths concerning the
nature, use, and excellency of this grace, that which the holy
ghost hath left recorded 1 Cor. 13. may give full satisfaction.
Which is needful for every true member of this lovely body
of the Lord Jesus to work upon their hearts, by prayer,
meditation, continual exercise at least of the special [　　] of
this grace, til Christ be formed in them and they in him, all in
each other knit together by this bond of love.

[IV]

It rests now to make some application of this discourse by
the present design which gave the occasion of writing of it.
Herein are 4 things to be propounded: first, the persons, 2ly
the work, 3ly the end, 4ly the means.

1.　For the persons, we are a company professing ourselves
　　fellow members of Christ, in which respect only, though
　　we were absent from each other many miles, and had our
　　employments as far distant, yet we ought to account
　　ourselves knit together by this bond of love and live in
　　the exercise of it if we would have comfort of our being
　　in Christ. This was notorious in the practice of the
　　Christians in former times, as is testified of the Waldenses
　　from the mouth of one of the adversaries Aeneas Sylvius,
　　mutuo [　　] pene antequam norint: they use to love any
　　of their own religion even before they were acquainted
　　with them.

2ly.　For the work we have in hand, it is by a mutual consent
　　through a special overruling providence, and a more

than an ordinary approbation of the Churches of Christ,
to seek out a place of cohabitation and consortship under
a due form of government both civil and ecclesiastical.
In such cases as this the care of the public must oversway
all private respects, by which not only consequence,[1] but
mere civil policy doth bind us; for it is a true rule that
particular estates cannot subsist in the ruin of the public.

3ly. The end is to improve our lives, to do more service to
the Lord, the comfort and increase of the body of Christ
whereof we are members, that ourselves and posterity
may be the better preserved from the common corruptions
of this evil world; to serve the Lord, and work out our
salvation under the power and purity of his holy
ordinances.

4ly. For the means whereby this must be effected, they are
2fold. A conformity with the work and end we aim at.
These we see are extraordinary. Therefore we must not
content ourselves with usual ordinary means.
Whatsoever we did, or ought to have done, when we
lived in England, the same must we do, and more also,
where we go. That which the most in their churches
maintain as a truth in profession only, we must bring into
familiar and constant practice, as in this duty of love. We
must love brotherly without dissimulation. We must love
one another with a pure heart fervently. We must bear
one anothers burdens. We must not look only on our own
things, but also on the things of our brethren.

Neither must we think that the Lord will bear with such
failings at our hands as he doth from those among whom we
have lived, and that for 3 reasons.

1. In regard of the more near bond of marriage between
him and us, wherein he hath taken us to be his after a
most strict and peculiar manner, which will make him the

---

1. A later writer changed "consequence" to read "conscience."

more jealous of our love and obedience. So he tells the people of Israel: you only have I known of all the families of the earth, therefore will I punish you for your transgressions.

2ly. Because the Lord will be sanctified in them that come near him. We know that there were many that corrupted the service of the Lord, some setting up altars before his own, others offering both strange fire and strange sacrifices also. Yet there came no fire from heaven, or other sudden judgement upon them as did upon Nadab and Abihu, who yet we may think did not sin presumptuously.

3ly. When God gives a special commission he looks to have it strictly observed in every article. When he gave Saul a commission to destroy Amalek he indented with him upon certain articles; and because he failed in one of the least, and that upon a fair pretense, it lost him the kingdom, which should have been his reward if he had observed his commission.

Thus stands the cause between God and us. We are entered into covenant with him for this work. We have taken out a commission. The Lord hath given us leave to draw our own articles. We have professed to enterprise these actions upon these and these ends. We have hereupon besought him of favor and blessing. Now if the Lord shall please to hear us, and bring us in peace to the place we desire, then hath he ratified this covenant and sealed our commission, will expect a strict performance of the articles contained in it. But if we shall neglect the observation of these articles which are the ends we have propounded and, dissembling with our God, shall fall to embrace this present world and prosecute our carnal intentions, seeking great things for ourselves and our posterity, the Lord will surely break out in wrath against us, be revenged of such a perjured people, and make us know the price of the breach of such a covenant.

Now the only way to avoid this shipwreck and to provide for our posterity is to follow the counsel of Micah: to do justly, to love mercy, to walk humbly with our God. For this end we must be knit together in this work as one man. We must entertain each other in brotherly affection. We must be willing to abridge ourselves of our superfluities for the supply of others necessities. We must uphold a familiar commerce together in all meekness, gentleness, patience, and liberality. We must delight in each other, make others conditions our own, rejoice together, mourn together, labor and suffer together, always having before our eyes our commission and community in the work, our community as members of the same body.

So shall we keep the unity of the spirit in the bond of peace, the Lord will be our God and delight to dwell among us as his own people and will command a blessing upon us in all our ways, so that we shall see much more of his wisdom, power, goodness and truth than formerly we have been acquainted with. We shall find that the God of Israel is among us, when ten of us shall be able to resist a thousand of our enemies, when he shall make us a praise and glory, that men shall say of succeeding plantations, the Lord make it like that of Massachusetts.[2]

For we must consider that we shall be as a city upon a hill; the eyes of all people are upon us. So that if we shall deal falsely with our God in this work we have undertaken and so cause him to withdraw his present help from us, we shall be made a story and a byword through the world. We shall open the mouths of enemies to speak evil of the ways of God and all professors for God's sake. We shall shame the faces of many of God's worthy servants and cause their prayers to be turned into curses upon us til we be consumed out of the good land whither we are a going.

2. "Massachusetts" was washed out and replaced by a later writer with "New England."

And to shut up this discourse with that exhortation of Moses,
that faithful servant of the Lord in his last farewell to Israel,
Deut. 30: Beloved there is now set before us life and good,
death and evil, in that we are commanded this day to love the
Lord our God, and to love one another, to walk in his ways
and to keep his commandments and his ordinance and his
laws and the articles of our covenant with him, that we may
live and be multiplied and that the Lord our God may bless us
in the land whither we go to possess it. But if our hearts shall
turn away so that we will not obey, but shall be seduced and
~~serve~~ worship[3] other Gods, our pleasures, and profits, and
serve them, it is propounded unto us this day, we shall surely
perish out of the good land whither we pass over this vast sea
to possess it.

> Therefore let us choose life,
> that we, and our seed,
> may live, by obeying his
> voice, and cleaving to him,
> for he is our life, and
> our prosperity.

---

3. Correction in the original.

$\mathcal{N}otes$

INTRODUCTION. "The Most Famous Lay Sermon in All of American History"

1. Michael Parker, *John Winthrop: Founding the City upon a Hill* (New York: Routledge, 2014), p. 39.

2. Ronald Reagan, "Election Eve Address: 'A Vision for America,'" Nov. 3, 1980. The American Presidency Project, Gerhard Peters and John Woolley, eds., http://www.presidency.ucsb.edu; Barack Obama, "Commencement Address, University of Massachusetts at Boston," June 2, 2006, Obama Speeches, http://obamaspeeches.com/074-University-of-Massachusetts-at-Boston-Commencement-Address-Obama-Speech.htm.

3. Matthew S. Holland, *Bonds of Affection: Civic Charity and the Making of America— Winthrop, Jefferson, and Lincoln* (Washington, DC: Georgetown University Press, 2007), p. 19; Terry Golway, ed., *American Political Speeches* (New York: Penguin, 2012), p. xxvii; Philip Gorski, *American Covenant: A History of Civil Religion from the Puritans to the Present* (Princeton, NJ: Princeton University Press, 2017). Richard M. Gamble makes the counterargument that "A Model of Christian Charity" did not achieve iconic status until the twentieth century: *In Search of the City on a Hill: The Making and Unmaking of an American Myth* (London: Continuum, 2012).

4. Perry Miller, "The Shaping of the American Character," *New England Quarterly* 28:4 (Dec. 1955): 443.

CHAPTER 1. Writing "A Model of Christian Charity"

1. David D. Hall, *Ways of Writing: The Practice and Politics of Text-Making in Seventeenth-Century New England* (Philadelphia: University of Pennsylvania Press, 2008), chap. 2.

2. Bernard Bailyn, *The Peopling of British North America: An Introduction* (New York: Knopf, 1986); Alison Games, *Migration and the Origins of the English Atlantic World* (Cambridge, MA: Harvard University Press, 1999). The aggregate figures are summarized in Bruce C. Daniels, *New England Nation: The Country the Puritans Built* (New York: Palgrave Macmillan, 2012), table 3.1.

3. Henry Jacie [*sic*] to John Winthrop Jr., c. Feb. 1635, *Winthrop Papers*, 5 vols. (Boston: Massachusetts Historical Society, 1929–47), 3:188.

4. Addition of an extra syllable to the name of the ship that Winthrop and his contemporaries knew as the *Arbella* was also this writer's contribution.

5. Perry Miller, ed., *The American Puritans: Their Prose and Poetry* (Garden City, NY: Doubleday, 1956), p. 79.

6. Draft of Ronald Reagan speech at Eisenhower College, 1969, Edwin Meese Papers, box 283, Hoover Institution Archives, courtesy of Hoover Institution Library and Archives, Stanford University.

7. Jon Butler, Grant Wacker, and Randall Balmer, *Religion in American Life: A Short History*, 2nd ed. (New York: Oxford University Press, 2011), p. 48.

8. *Journal of John Winthrop, 1630–1649*, ed. Richard S. Dunn, James Savage, and Laetitia Yeandle (Cambridge, MA: Harvard University Press,1996), pp. 19, 18, 17, 10.

9. Hugh J. Dawson, "John Winthrop's Rite of Passage: The Origins of the 'Christian Charitie' Discourse," *Early American Literature* 26:3 (1991): 219–31; Hugh J. Dawson, "'Christian Charitie' as Colonial Discourse: Rereading Winthrop's Sermon in Its English Context," *Early American Literature* 33:2 (1998): 117–48. See also Richard M. Gamble, *In Search of the City on a Hill: The Making and Unmaking of an American Myth* (London: Continuum, 2012), chap. 1.

10. Francis J. Bremer, *John Winthrop: America's Forgotten Founding Father* (New York: Oxford University Press, 2003), pp. 173–74.

11. Bremer, *John Winthrop*; Michael Parker, *John Winthrop: Founding the City upon a Hill* (New York: Routledge, 2014).

12. "Address of John Winthrop to the Company of the Massachusetts Bay," *Winthrop Papers*, 2:175.

13. Ibid., 2:176.

14. Ibid.

15. *Journal of John Winthrop*, pp. 725–26.

16. Babette May Levy, *Preaching in the First Half Century of New England History* (Hartford, CT: American Society of Church History, 1945), chap. 5; Harry S. Stout, *The New England Soul: Preaching and Religious Culture in Colonial New England* (New York: Oxford University Press, 2012); Richard Bernard, *The Faithfull Shepheard* (London, 1607), chaps. 5–12.

17. Aware of this difficulty, Abram Van Engen has proposed a scriptural passage that he imagines must have originally prefaced the Model before an incomplete text reached the copyist, but this seems implausible. Abram C. Van Engen, "Origins and Last Farewells: Bible Wars, Textual Form, and the Making of American History," *New England Quarterly* 86:4 (Dec. 2013): 543–92.

18. Stout, *New England Soul*, pp. 14–16; Meredith Marie Neuman, *Jeremiah's Scribes: Creating Sermon Literature in Puritan New England* (Philadelphia: University of Pennsylvania Press, 2013); Levy, *Preaching in the First Half Century*, pp. 81–85. "Social authorship," David D. Hall calls this in his *Ways of Writing*.

19. "Prefatory Remarks," *Collections of the Massachusetts Historical Society* 27 (1838): 32 ("homily"); George E. Ellis, "The Aims and Purposes of the Founders of the Massachusetts Colony," in *Lectures Delivered in a Course at the Lowell Institute . . . on Subjects Relating to the Early History of Massachusetts* (Boston: Massachusetts Historical Society, 1869) ("treatise"); Charles F. Richardson, *American Literature, 1607–1885*, 2 vols. (New York: G. Putnam's Sons, 1889–91), 1:90 ("booklet"); *The Humble Request of the Massachusetts Puritans and A Modell of Christian Charity by John Winthrop 1630*, ed. S. E. Morison, Old South Leaflets no. 207 (Boston, 1916), p. 1 ("tract").

20. For an extended discussion of this theme: David Grayson Allen, *In English Ways: The Movement of Societies and the Transferal of English Local Law and Custom to Massachusetts Bay in the Seventeenth Century* (New York: W. W. Norton, 1982).

21. Susan Hardman Moore, *Pilgrims: New World Settlers and the Call of Home* (New Haven, CT: Yale University Press, 2007), p. 36.

22. *Journal of John Winthrop*, p. 590; *Winthrop Papers*, 4:468–88.

23. *Journal of John Winthrop*, pp. 584–89.

CHAPTER 2. "We Shall Be as a City upon a Hill"

1. "Arguments for the Plantation of New England. Objections Answered: First Draft," *Winthrop Papers*, 5 vols. (Boston: Massachusetts Historical Society, 1929–47), 2:136.

2. Ronald Reagan, "Farewell Address to the Nation," Jan. 11, 1989, The American Presidency Project, Gerhard Peters and John Woolley, eds., http://www.presidency.ucsb .edu.

3. Bernard Bailyn, *The Barbarous Years. The Peopling of British North America: The Conflict of Civilizations, 1600–1675* (New York: Knopf, 2012), chap. 12; Roger Thompson, *Mobility and Migration: East Anglican Founders of New England, 1629–1640* (Amherst: University of Massachusetts Press, 1994); Virginia DeJohn Anderson, *New England's Generation: The Great Migration and the Formation of Society and Culture in the Seventeenth Century* (Cambridge: Cambridge University Press, 1991), chap. 1; David Cressy, *Coming Over: Migration and Communication between England and New England in the Seventeenth Century* (New York: Cambridge University Press, 1987), pp. 46–50.

4. John White et al., *The Planters Plea* (London, 1630); "Sir John Eliot's Copy of the New England Tracts," *Winthrop Papers*, 2:146–47.

5. "Arguments for the Plantation of New England," *Winthrop Papers*, 2:106–49.

6. Karen Ordahl Kupperman, *The Jamestown Project* (Cambridge, MA: Harvard University Press, 2007), p. 227. Bailyn, *Barbarous Years*, chap. 2.

7. Thomas Dudley, "To the Right Honourable; My Very Good Lady, the Lady Bridget Countess of Lincoln," Mar. 12, 1631, in *Massachusetts, or the First Planters of New-England* (Boston, 1696), p. 16.

8. John Winthrop to—, *Winthrop Papers*, 2:123.

9. "Reasons to be Considered, and Objections with Answers," *Winthrop Papers*, 2:139.

10. John Cotton, *God's Promise to His Plantation* (London, 1630), p. 9.

11. Darrett Rutman, *John Winthrop's Decision for America, 1629* (Philadelphia: Lippincott, 1975), pp. 24–25; John Winthrop, "General Conclusions and Particular Considerations," *Winthrop Papers*, 2:133; John Winthrop, "General Conclusions and Particular Considerations: Early Draft," *Winthrop Papers*, 2:126.

12. "General Observations for the Plantation of New England," *Winthrop Papers*, 2:111; John Winthrop to—, *Winthrop Papers*, 2:122.

13. "Reasons to Be Answered, and Objections with Answers," *Winthrop Papers*, 2:139.

14. Thomas Hooker, "The Danger of Desertion," in Thomas Hooker, *Writings in England and Holland*, ed. George H. Williams et al. (Cambridge, MA: Harvard University Press, 1975), pp. 246, 252.

15. John Winthrop to Margaret Winthrop, May 15, 1629, *Winthrop Papers*, 2:91–92.

16. Richard Mather, "Arguments Tending to Prove the Removing from Old England to New . . . ," in Increase Mather, *The Life and Death of that Reverend Man of God, Mr. Richard Mather* (Cambridge, 1670), p. 17.

17. Quoted in Theodore Dwight Bozeman, *To Live Ancient Lives: The Primitivist Dimension in Puritanism* (Chapel Hill: University of North Carolina Press, 1988), p. 111.

18. Peter Bulkeley, *The Gospel-Covenant, or, The Covenant of Grace Opened* (London, 1646); cf. Francis J. Bremer, "To Live Exemplary Lives: Puritans and Puritan Communities as Lofty Lights," *Seventeenth Century* 7:1 (Spring 1992): 27–39.

19. Matt. 5:13–16 (Geneva Bible).

20. James Sharpe, *The Triall of the Protestant Private Spirit* (1630).

21. William Perkins, *A Godly and Learned Exposition of Christ's Sermon in the Mount* (Cambridge, England, 1608), pp. 53–57.

22. Calvin is quoted in Richard M. Gamble, *In Search of the City on a Hill: The Making and Unmaking of an American Myth* (London: Continuum, 2012), p. 56.

23. Richard Baxter, *Church-History of the Government of Bishops and Their Counsels* (London, 1680), p. 483.

24. Patrick Collinson, *The Birthpangs of Protestant England: Religious and Cultural Change in the Sixteenth and Seventeenth Centuries* (Houndmills, UK: Macmillan, 1988), p. 30.

25. John Milton, *Of Reformation in England* (1641), quoted in Gamble, *In Search of the City on a Hill*, p. 69.

26. Perkins, *Godly and Learned Exposition of Christ's Sermon in the Mount*, p. 55.

27. Anthony Horneck, *Several Sermons upon the Fifth of St. Matthew* (London, 1698), pp. 426–27.

28. Edward Howes to John Winthrop Jr., Apr. 3, 1632, *Winthrop Papers*, 3:76.

29. *The Correspondence of John Cotton*, ed. Sargent Bush Jr. (Chapel Hill: University of North Carolina Press, 2001), p. 283.

30. B. E., *A New Dictionary of the Canting Crew in Its Several Tribes* (London, 1699), n.p.

31. Michael P. Winship, "Were There Any Puritans in New England?," *New England Quarterly* 74:1 (Mar. 2001): 118–38.

CHAPTER 3. A Chosen People

1. Francis J. Bremer, *Building a New Jerusalem: John Davenport, a Puritan in Three Worlds* (New Haven, CT: Yale University Press, 2012), pp. 132–34; Frances Rose-Troup, *John White, The Patriarch of Dorchester and the Founder of Massachusetts, 1575–1648* (New York: G. P. Putnam's Sons, 1930), pp. 221–23; and, more generally, David D. Hall, *A Reforming People: Puritanism and the Transformation of Public Life in New England* (New York: Knopf, 2011).

2. John Cotton, *God's Promise to His Plantation* (London, 1630), p. 13.

3. *The Journal of John Winthrop, 1630–1649*, ed. Richard S. Dunn, James Savage, and Laetitia Yeandle (Cambridge, MA: Harvard University Press, 1996), pp. 24, 340–41. For an excellent history of providentialism: Nicholas Guyatt, *Providence and the Invention of the United States, 1607–1876* (New York: Cambridge University Press, 2007).

4. Mason I. Lowance Jr., *The Language of Canaan: Metaphor and Symbol in New England from the Puritans to the Transcendentalists* (Cambridge, MA: Harvard University Press, 1980).

5. "General Considerations for the Plantation in New England," *Winthrop Papers*, 5 vols. (Boston: Massachusetts Historical Society, 1929–47), 2:120.

6. John Winthrop, "General Conclusions and Particular Considerations: Early Draft," *Winthrop Papers*, 2:125.

7. *Journal of John Winthrop*, pp. 440–50.

8. Michael McGiffert, "God's Controversy with Jacobean England," *American Historical Review* 88:5 (Dec. 1983): 1152; John Lyly, *Euphues and His England* (1580), quoted in Dorian Llywelyn, *Sacred Place, Chosen People: Land and National Identity in Welsh Spirituality* (Cardiff: University of Wales Press, 1999), p. 37; Pasi Ihalainen, *Protestant Nations Redefined: Changing Perceptions of National Identity in the Rhetoric of the English, Dutch, and Swedish Public Churches, 1685–1772* (Leiden: Brill, 2005), p. 100.

9. Simon Schama, *The Embarrassment of Riches: An Interpretation of Dutch Culture in the Golden Age* (New York: Knopf, 1987), p. 98.

10. Paul Stevens, "'Leviticus Thinking' and the Rhetoric of Early Modern Colonialism," *Criticism* 35:3 (Summer 1993): 451–52.

11. Robert Montgomery, "Discourse concerning the Designed Establishment of a New Colony to the South of Carolina" (1717), quoted in Charles L. Sanford, *The Quest for Paradise: Europe and the American Moral Imagination* (Urbana: University of Illinois Press, 1961), p. 85.

12. Robert Gray, "A Good Speed to Virginia" (1609), quoted in Alfred A. Cave, "Canaanites in a Promised Land: The American Indian and the Providential Theory of Empire," *American Indian Quarterly* 12:4 (Autumn 1988): 286.

13. Roger Williams, *The Bloudy Tenent Yet More Bloody* (1652), quoted in Perry Miller, *Roger Williams: His Contribution to the American Tradition* (New York: Atheneum, 1965), p. 169.

14. Robert Cushman, *A Relation or Journal of the Beginning and Proceeding of the English Plantation Settled at Plimouth in New England* (1622), quoted in Guyatt, *Providence and the Invention of the United States*, p. 25.

15. Cotton Mather, *Magnalia Christi Americana*, ed. Kenneth B. Murdock (Cambridge, MA: Harvard University Press, 1977), bk. 2, chap. 4.

16. Amos 3:2 (King James Version).

17. Deut. 28:37 (King James Version).

18. Deut. 30:15–19 (Geneva Bible); emphases added.

19. Cotton, *God's Promise to His Plantation*, p. 18.

20. Thomas Hooker, "The Danger of Desertion," in *Thomas Hooker, Writings in England and Holland*, ed. George H. Williams et al. (Cambridge, MA: Harvard University Press, 1975), pp. 245–46; John Winthrop to Margaret Winthrop, May 15, 1629, *Winthrop Papers*, 2:91.

21. "The Humble Request of His Majesty's Loyal Subjects, the Governor and the Company Late Gone for New England" (1630), *Winthrop Papers*, 2:232.

22. Cave, "Canaanites in a Promised Land," pp. 291–92.

23. Thomas Dudley, "To the Right Honourable My Very Good Lady, the Lady Bridget Countess of Lincoln" (1630), in *Massachusetts, or the First Planters of New-England* (Boston, 1696), p. 21

24. *Journal of John Winthrop*, p. 416.

25. Everett Emerson, ed., *Letters from New England: The Massachusetts Bay Colony, 1629–1638* (Amherst: University of Massachusetts Press, 1976), p. 205.

26. John Allin and Thomas Shepard, "Defence of the Answer Made unto the Nine Questions" (1645), in *Massachusetts, or the First Planters of New-England* (Boston, 1696), p. 37.

27. *Journal of John Winthrop*, pp. 675, 672.

28. Ibid., pp. 324–25.

29. Lord Saye and Sele to John Winthrop, July 9, 1640, *Winthrop Papers*, 4:263–67.

30. *Journal of John Winthrop*, p. 334. On the controversy: Karen Ordahl Kupperman, "Errand to the Indies: Puritan Colonization from Providence Island through the Western Design," *William and Mary Quarterly* 45:1 (Jan. 1988): 70–99.

31. *Journal of John Winthrop*, p. 333.

32. Dudley, "To the Right Honourable . . . Countess of Lincoln," p. 24; "General Observations for the Plantation of New England," *Winthrop Papers*, 2:112.

33. Thomas Hooker, "Danger of Desertion," pp. 4, 230–31; Michael P. Winship, "What Puritan Guarantee?," *Early American Literature* 47:2 (2012): 411–20.

34. Peter Bulkeley, *The Gospel-Covenant, or, The Covenant of Grace Opened* (London, 1646), p. 15.

35. Cotton, *God's Promise to His Plantation*, p. 17.

CHAPTER 4. New England in a World of Holy Experiments

1. Donald Worster, *Shrinking the Earth: The Rise and Decline of American Abundance* (New York: Oxford University Press, 2016), chap. 1.

2. J. H. Elliott, *Empires of the Atlantic World: Britain and Spain in America, 1492–1830* (New Haven, CT: Yale University Press, 2006), chap. 7.

3. Jorge Cañizares-Esguerra, "Entangled Histories: Borderlands Historiographies in New Clothes?," *American Historical Review* 112:3 (June 2007): 787–99; Jorge Cañizares-Esguerra,

"Typology in the Atlantic World: Early Modern Readings of Colonization," in *Soundings in Atlantic History: Latent Structures and Intellectual Currents, 1500–1830*, ed. Bernard Bailyn and Patricia L. Denault (Cambridge, MA: Harvard University Press, 2009), pp. 237–264; Thomas O. Beebee, *Millennial Literatures of the Americas, 1492–2002* (New York: Oxford University Press, 2009), chap. 1; Frank Graziano, *The Millennial New World* (New York: Oxford University Press, 1999).

4. John Leddy Phelan, *The Millennial Kingdom of the Franciscans in the New World* (Berkeley: University of California Press, 1970), p. 5.

5. Djelal Kadir, *Columbus and the Ends of the Earth: Europe's Prophetic Rhetoric as Conquering Ideology* (Berkeley: University of California Press, 1992), p. 54.

6. Leonard I. Sweet, "Christopher Columbus and the Millennial Vision of the New World," *Catholic Historical Review* 72:3 (July 1986): 370.

7. Ralph Bauer, "Millennium's Darker Side: The Missionary Utopias of Franciscan New Spain and Puritan New England," in *Finding Colonial Americas*, ed. Carla Mulford and David S. Shields (Newark: University of Delaware Press, 2001), pp. 38–39.

8. Jaime Lara, *City, Temple, Stage: Eschatological Architecture and Liturgical Theatrics in New Spain* (Notre Dame, IN: University of Notre Dame Press, 2004).

9. William Bradford, *Of Plymouth Plantation, 1620–1647*, ed. Samuel Eliot Morison (New York: Modern Library, 1967), p. 296.

10. Graziano, *Millennial New World*, chap. 4.

11. Julia J. S. Sarreal, *The Guaraní and Their Missions: A Socioeconomic History* (Stanford, CA: Stanford University Press, 2014); Sélim Abou, *The Jesuit "Republic" of the Guaranis (1609–1768) and Its Heritage* (New York: Crossroad, 1997).

12. Antonio Ruiz de Montoya, *The Spiritual Conquest Accomplished by the Religious Society of Jesus in the Provinces of Paraguay, Paraná, Uruguay and Tape* (St. Louis, MO: Institute of Jesuit Sources, 1993), p. 109.

13. Guillaume Ansart, "From Voltaire to Raynal and Diderot's *Histoire des deux Indes*: The French *Philosophes* and Colonial America," in *America through European Eyes: British and French Reflections on the New World from the Eighteenth Century to the Present*, ed. Aurelian Craiutu and Jeffrey C. Isaac (University Park: Pennsylvania State University Press, 2009), pp. 71–90.

14. Tim Blanning, *The Pursuit of Glory: Europe, 1648–1815* (New York: Viking, 2007), p. 96.

15. Edward Johnson, *Johnson's Wonder-Working Providence, 1628–1651*, ed. J. Franklin Jameson (New York: Scribner's, 1910), p. 59.

16. Kenneth Shipps, "Puritan Emigration to New England," *New England Historical and Genealogical Register* 135 (1981): 91, n. 43.

17. Simon Schama, *The Embarrassment of Riches: An Interpretation of Dutch Culture in the Golden Age* (New York: Knopf, 1987), pp. 94, 98.

18. Ibid., p. 224.

19. Jean R. Soderlund et al., eds., *William Penn and the Founding of Pennsylvania, 1680–1684: A Documentary History* (Philadelphia: University of Pennsylvania Press, 1983), p. 77.

20. Ibid., pp. 77, 55, 58–65.

21. Voltaire, "On Paraguay," in *The Works of Voltaire*, trans. William F. Fleming (Paris: E. R. Dumont, 1901), vol. 39, p. 269; Edith Philips, *The Good Quaker in French Legend* (Philadelphia: University of Pennsylvania Press, 1932), chap. 4.

22. J. Potter, "The Growth of Population in America, 1700–1760," in *Population in History: Essays in Historical Demography*, ed. D. V. Glass and D.E.C. Eversley (Chicago: Aldine, 1965), p. 638.

CHAPTER 5. Left All Alone in America

1. Thomas Coleman, *The Christians Course and Complaint* (London, 1643), p. 70.

2. *Oliver Cromwell's Letters and Speeches*, ed. Thomas Carlyle, 2 vols. (New York: Harper, 1851), 2:263–64.

3. *Journal of John Winthrop, 1630–1649*, ed. Richard S. Dunn, James Savage, and Laetitia Yeandle (Cambridge, MA: Harvard University Press, 1996), pp. 70, 207; *Records of the Governor and Company of the Massachusetts Bay in New England*, 5 vols., ed. Nathaniel B. Shurtleff (Boston, 1853–54), 1:204.

4. Francis J. Bremer, "Puritan Crisis: New England and the English Civil Wars, 1630–1670" (PhD diss., Columbia University, 1972), chap. 1.

5. David W. Galenson, "The Settlement and Growth of the Colonies: Population, Labor, and Economic Development," in *The Cambridge Economic History of the United States*, vol. 1: *Colonial Era*, ed. Stanley L. Engerman and Robert E. Gallman (Cambridge: Cambridge University Press, 2008), table 4.5.

6. Susan Hardman Moore, *Pilgrims: New World Settlers and the Call of Home* (New Haven, CT: Yale University Press, 2007), pp. 55–56, 70, 82.

7. Bremer, "Puritan Crisis," pp. 115, 217–25.

8. *Journal of John Winthrop*, p. 416.

9. Bremer, "Puritan Crisis," p. 219.

10. Alison Games, *The Web of Empire: English Cosmopolitans in an Age of Expansion, 1560–1660* (New York: Oxford University Press, 2008).

11. Christopher Durston, *Cromwell's Major-Generals: Godly Government during the English Revolution* (Manchester: Manchester University Press, 2001), chap. 8; David Underdown, *Fire from Heaven: The Life of an English Town in the Seventeenth Century* (London: HarperCollins, 1992); David Underdown, *Revel, Riot, and Rebellion: Popular Politics and Culture in England, 1603–1660* (Oxford: Clarendon Press, 1985).

12. Perry Miller, *Errand into the Wilderness* (Cambridge, MA: Harvard University Press, 1956), p. 11.

13. *Journal of John Winthrop*, pp. 353–54.

14. Carla Gardina Pestana, *The English Atlantic in an Age of Revolution, 1640–1661* (Cambridge, MA: Harvard University Press, 2004), pp. 58–59.

15. John Coffey, "The Toleration Controversy during the English Revolution," in *Religion in Revolutionary England*, ed. Christopher Durston and Judith Maltby (Manchester: Manchester University Press, 2006); John Coffey, *Persecution and Toleration in Protestant England, 1558–1689* (Harlow, UK: Longman, 2000); Andrew R. Murphy, *Conscience and Community: Revisiting Toleration and Religious Dissent in Early Modern England and America* (University Park: Pennsylvania State University Press, 2001).

16. *Journal of John Winthrop*, pp. 608, 635.

17. Bremer, "Puritan Crisis," p. 283.

18. William Hooke, *New-Englands Sence of Old-England and Irelands Sorrowes* (London, 1645), p. 19.

19. Nicholas Guyatt, *Providence and the Invention of the United States, 1607–1876* (New York: Cambridge University Press, 2007), p. 33.

20. Galenson, "Settlement and Growth of the Colonies," table 4.5.

21. Edward Johnson, *Johnson's Wonder-Working Providence, 1628–1651*, ed. J. Franklin Jameson (New York: Scribner's, 1910), p. 29; Increase Mather, *Returning unto God the Great Concernment of a Covenant People* (Boston, 1680), p. A2; Jonathan Mitchell, *Nehemiah on the Wall in Troublesome Times* (Cambridge, 1671), p. 19; John Norton, *The Heart of New-England Rent at the Blasphemies of the Present Generation* (London, 1660), p. 79.

22. Urian Oakes, *New-England Pleaded With* (Cambridge, 1673), p. 17; Increase Mather, *The Day of Trouble Is Near* (Cambridge, 1674), p. 26; Samuel Wakeman, "To the Christian Reader," *Sound Repentance the Right Way to Escape Deserved Ruine* (Boston, 1685).

23. Wakeman, "To the Christian Reader"; Increase Mather, *Ichabod, or, A Discourse Shewing What Cause There Is To Fear That the Glory of the Lord Is Departing from New-England* (Boston, 1702), pp. 57, 63.

24. W[illiam] Stoughton, *New-Englands True Interest; Not to Lie* (Cambridge, 1670), p. 10; Mather, *Returning unto God*, pp. A2, 10.

25. Robert Middlekauf, *The Mathers: Three Generations of Puritan Intellectuals, 1596–1728* (New York: Oxford University Press, 1971), p. 101.

26. Oakes, *New-England Pleaded With*, pp. 20–21, 54.

27. Cotton Mather, *Magnalia Christi Americana, Books I and II*, ed. Kenneth B. Murdock (Cambridge, MA: Harvard University Press, 1977), p. 126.

28. Ibid., pp. 129, 92–93, 89, 123, 196; Cotton Mather, *Magnalia Christi Americana*, 2 vols. (Hartford, CT: Andrus, 1855), 1:580.

29. Oakes, *New-England Pleaded With*, p. 25.

CHAPTER 6. Love Is a Bond or Ligament

1. "Arguments for the Plantation of New England," in *Winthrop Papers*, 5 vols. (Boston: Massachusetts Historical Society, 1929–47), 2:106–49; [John Winthrop et al.], *A Short Story of the Rise, Reign and Ruin of the Antinomians, Familists, and Libertines that Infected the Churches of New England* (London, 1644).

2. *The Journal of John Winthrop, 1630–1649*, ed. Richard S. Dunn, James Savage, and Laetitia Yeandle (Cambridge, MA: Harvard University Press, 1996), pp. 584–89.

3. Henry Jacie [*sic*] to John Winthrop Jr., c. Feb. 1635, *Winthrop Papers*, 3:188.

4. John Yates, *A Modell of Divinitie, Catechistically Composed* (London, 1622); James Harrington, *Rota; or, A Model of a Free State or Equall Commonwealth* (London, 1660); James Harrington, *The Art of Law-Giving, Book 3, Shewing a Model Fitted unto the Present State or Balance of This Nation* (London, 1659).

5. *Journal of John Winthrop*, p. 590.

6. Isa. 58:6–8; Deut. 15:7–8 (Geneva Bible).

7. Matt. 5:42; 1 John 3:17 (Geneva Bible).

8. Frances J. Bremer, *John Winthrop: America's Forgotten Founding Father* (New York: Oxford University Press, 2003), p. 179; Abram C. Van Engen, *Sympathetic Puritans: Calvinist Fellow Feeling in Early New England* (New York: Oxford University Press, 2015), p. 26.

9. "An Exhortation, concerning Good Order & Obedience," *Certayne Sermons Appointed by the Queene Majesty, to be Declared and Read* (1562), quoted in Darrett B. Rutman, ed., *John Winthrop's Decision for America: 1629* (Philadelphia: Lippincott, 1975), p. 56; William J. Bouwsma, *John Calvin: A Sixteenth-Century Portrait* (New York: Oxford University Press, 1988), pp. 194, 51, 201.

10. Edmund S. Morgan, "John Winthrop's 'Modell of Christian Charity' in a Wider Context," *Huntington Library Quarterly* 50:2 (Spring 1987): 147.

11. Thomas Smith, *Sir Thomas Smithes Voiage and Entertainment in Rushia* (London, 1605), p. B3.

12. William Ames, *Marrow of Sacred Divinity* (London, 1642), chap. 7.

13. Jonathan Edwards, *Charity and Its Fruits* (1738), in *The Works of Jonathan Edwards*, vol. 8, *Ethical Writings*, ed. Paul Ramsey (New Haven, CT: Yale University Press, 1989), p. 178.

CHAPTER 7. Moralizing the Market Economy

1. Alison Games, *Migration and the Origins of the English Atlantic World* (Cambridge, MA: Harvard University Press, 1999).

2. James E. McWilliams, *Building the Bay Colony: Local Economy and Culture in Early Massachusetts* (Charlottesville: University of Virginia Press, 2007); Margaret Ellen Newell, *From Dependency to Independence: Economic Revolution in Colonial New England* (Ithaca, NY: Cornell University Press, 1998); Virginia DeJohn Anderson, *New England's Generation: The Great Migration and the Formation of Society and Culture in the Seventeenth Century* (Cambridge: Cambridge University Press, 1991), chap. 4; Daniel Vickers, "Competency and Competition: Economic Culture in Early America," *William and Mary Quarterly* 47:1 (Jan. 1990): 3–29. On the pervasiveness of debts and obligation in contemporaneous England: Craig Muldrew, *The Economy of Obligation: The Culture of Credit and Social Relations in Early Modern England* (New York: St. Martin's Press, 1998).

3. Mark Valeri, "Religious Discipline and the Market: Puritans and the Issue of Usury," *William and Mary Quarterly* 54:4 (Oct. 1997): 47–68; Mark Valeri, *Heavenly Merchandize: How Religion Shaped Commerce in Puritan America* (Princeton, NJ: Princeton University Press, 2010); David D. Hall, *A Reforming People: Puritanism and the Transformation of Public Life in New England* (New York: Knopf, 2011), chap. 4.

4. John Winthrop to Margaret Winthrop, Nov. 12, 1629, *Winthrop Papers*, 5 vols. (Boston: Massachusetts Historical Society, 1929–47), 2:168; John Winthrop to Margaret Winthrop, Nov. 24, 1629, ibid., 2:174; John Winthrop to Margaret Winthrop, Feb. 5, 1629/30, ibid., 2:201–2.

5. *Records of the Governor and Company of the Massachusetts Bay in New England*, ed. Nathaniel B. Shurtleff, 5 vols. (Boston, 1853–54), 1:61–64.

6. "Address of John Winthrop to the Company of the Massachusetts Bay," *Winthrop Papers*, 2:175.

7. *Records of the Governor and Company of the Massachusetts Bay*, 1:64–66.

8. "Address of John Winthrop to the Company of the Massachusetts Bay," *Winthrop Papers*, 2:174–77.

9. *Records of the Governor and Company of the Massachusetts Bay*, 1:74, 89, 91, 109.

10. Ibid., 1:223, 307.

11. Ibid., 1:142.

12. *The Journal of John Winthrop, 1630–1649*, ed. Richard S. Dunn, James Savage, and Laetitia Yeandle (Cambridge, MA: Harvard University Press, 1996), pp. 174–75.

13. John White to John Winthrop, Nov. 16, 1636, *Winthrop Papers*, 3:321–23.

14. *Journal of John Winthrop*, p. 308.

15. *Records of the Governor and Company of the Massachusetts Bay*, 1:331.

16. Ibid., 1:260, 283, 284; *Journal of John Winthrop*, pp. 342, 424.

17. Ibid., p. 66.

18. *Records of the Governor and Company of the Massachusetts Bay*, 1:131–33, 253.

19. Bernard Bailyn, ed., *The Apologia of Robert Keayne: The Self-Portrait of a Puritan Merchant* (New York: Harper and Row, 1964); Valeri, *Heavenly Merchandize*, chap. 1.

20. *Journal of John Winthrop*, p. 307.

21. Ibid., p. 308.

22. Valeri, *Heavenly Merchandize*; Mark A. Peterson, *The Price of Redemption: The Spiritual Economy of Puritan New England* (Stanford, CA: Stanford University Press, 1997); Joseph A. Conforti, *Saints and Strangers: New England in British North America* (Baltimore: Johns Hopkins University Press, 2006).

23. Wendy Warren, *New England Bound: Slavery and Colonization in Early America* (New York: Liveright, 2016).

CHAPTER 8. The Poor and the Boundaries of Obligation

1. Bernard Bailyn, ed., *The Apologia of Robert Keayne: The Self-Portrait of a Puritan Merchant* (New York: Harper and Row, 1964), pp. 45–55.

2. Ibid., pp. 6–20.

3. John Winthrop to—[1629], *Winthrop Papers*, 5 vols. (Boston: Massachusetts Historical Society, 1929–47), 2:122.

4. Paul Slack, *Poverty and Policy in Tudor and Stuart England* (London: Longman, 1988); Paul Slack, *From Reformation to Improvement: Public Welfare in Early Modern England* (Oxford: Clarendon Press, 1999), chap. 2; Keith Wrightson and David Levine, *Poverty and Piety in an English Village: Terling, 1525–1700* (New York: Academic Press, 1979); William Hunt, *The Puritan Moment: The Coming of Revolution in an English County* (Cambridge, MA: Harvard University Press, 1983), esp. chap. 6; Steve Hindle, *On the Parish? The Micro-Politics of Poor Relief in Rural England, c. 1550–1750* (Oxford: Clarendon Press, 2004).

5. Slack, *Poverty and Policy*, p. 170.

6. David Underdown, *Fire from Heaven: The Life of an English Town in the Seventeenth Century* (London: Harper Collins, 1992).

7. Slack, *From Reformation to Improvement*, p. 47.

8. Ibid., p. 86.

9. John White to John Winthrop, Nov. 16, 1636, *Winthrop Papers*, 3:322.

10. *Records of the Governor and Company of the Massachusetts Bay in New England*, ed. Nathaniel B. Shurtleff, 5 vols. (Boston, 1853–54), 1:287, 2:173, 164.

11. Marcus W. Jernegan, "The Development of Poor Relief in Colonial New England," *Social Service Review* 5:2 (June 1931): 175–98; Charles R. Lee, "Public Poor Relief and the Massachusetts Community, 1620–1715," *New England Quarterly* 55:4 (Dec. 1982): 564–85; Darrett B. Rutman, *Winthrop's Boston: Portrait of a Puritan Town, 1630–1649* (Chapel Hill: University of North Carolina Press, 1965), chap. 8; Stephen Foster, *Their Solitary Way: The Puritan Social Ethic in the First Century of Settlement in New England* (New Haven, CT: Yale University Press, 1971), chap. 5.

12. *Record Commissioners of the City of Boston, Fourth Report: Dorchester Town Records*, 2nd ed. (Boston, 1883), pp. 317, 237. Online at https://archive.org/details/fourthreportofre04bost.

13. Rutman, *Winthrop's Boston*, p. 230; Lee, "Public Poor Relief," 577, 581.

14. Barry Levy, *Town Born: The Political Economy of New England from Its Founding to the Revolution* (Philadelphia: University of Pennsylvania Press, 2009), pp. 47–48.

15. *Record Commissioners of the City of Boston, Fourth Report: Dorchester Town Records*, pp. 181, 197, 202, 208, 229, 257–58.

16. Ibid., p. 236.

17. Ibid., p. 237.

18. Ibid., pp. 214, 219.

19. Ibid., pp. 203, 207, 211, 212, 261.

20. Ibid., pp. 166, 181–82, 185.

21. Ruth Wallis Herndon, "'Who Died an Expence to This Town': Poor Relief in Eighteenth-Century Rhode Island," in *Down and Out in Early America*, ed. Billy G. Smith (University Park: Pennsylvania State University Press, 2004); Ruth Wallis Herndon, *Unwelcome Americans: Living on the Margin in Early New England* (Philadelphia: University of Pennsylvania Press, 2001).

22. Gary B. Nash, "Poverty and Politics in Early American History," in Smith, *Down and Out in Early America*, chap. 1; Heli Meltsner, *The Poorhouses of Massachusetts: A Cultural and Architectural History* (Jefferson, NC: McFarland, 2012).

23. I. Smith Homans, *History of Boston from 1630 to 1856* (Boston: F. C. Moore, 1856), p. 55; Eric Nellis and Anne Decker Cecere, eds., *The Eighteenth-Century Records of the Boston Overseers of the Poor* (Boston: Colonial Society of Massachusetts, 2007), chap. 3.

24. Priscilla Ferguson Clement, *Welfare and the Poor in the Nineteenth-Century City: Philadelphia, 1800–1854* (Rutherford, NJ: Fairleigh Dickinson University Press, 1985), chap. 2; John K. Alexander, *Render Them Submissive: Responses to Poverty in Philadelphia, 1760–1800* (Amherst: University of Massachusetts Press, 1980); Mara Kaktins, "Almshouses (Poorhouses)," in *The Encyclopedia of Greater Philadelphia*, http://philadelphiaencyclopedia .org/archive/almshouses-poorhouses.

25. Harold Kirker and James Kirker, *Bulfinch's Boston, 1787–1817* (New York: Oxford University Press, 1964); Meltsner, *Poorhouses of Massachusetts*, pp. 90–91. More generally: Christine Leigh Heyrman, "The Fashion among More Superior People: Charity and Social Change in Provincial New England, 1700–1740," *American Quarterly* 34:2 (Summer 1982): 107–24.

CHAPTER 9. Inventing Foundations

1. Gary B. Nash, *First City: Philadelphia and the Forging of Historical Memory* (Philadelphia: University of Pennsylvania Press, 2007), p. 70; Edwin Wolf, *Philadelphia: Portrait of an American City. A Bicentennial History* (Harrisburg, PA: Stackpole Books, 1975); Nicholas Garrison, "A View of the House of Employment, Alms-House, Pennsylvania Hospital, and Part of the City of Philadelphia," 1767, New York Public Library, Digital Collections, https://digitalcollections.nypl.org/items/510d47d9-7ad6-a3d9-e040-e00a18064a99; Benjamin Easburn, "A Plan of the City of Philadelphia, 1776," Free Library of Philadelphia, Digital Collections, https://libwww.freelibrary.org/digital/item/MBEAAA00001.

2. Linda Colley, *Britons: Forging the Nation, 1707–1837* (New Haven, CT: Yale University Press, 1992); David A. Bell, *The Cult of the Nation in France: Inventing Nationalism, 1680–1800* (Cambridge, MA: Harvard University Press, 2001); Simon Schama, *The Embarrassment of Riches: An Interpretation of Dutch Culture in the Golden Age* (New York: Knopf, 1987); Benedict Anderson, *Imagined Communities: Reflections on the Origin and Spread of Nationalism*, rev. ed. (London: Verso, 1983).

3. Bell, *Cult of the Nation*, p. 4.

4. Wim Klooster, *Revolutions in the Atlantic World: A Comparative History*, new ed. (New York: New York University Press, 2018); Felipe Fernández-Armesto, *The Americas: A Hemispheric History* (New York: Modern Library, 2003).

5. John M. Murrin, "A Roof without Walls: The Dilemma of Early American National Identity," in *Beyond Confederation: Origins of the Constitution and American National Identity*, ed. Richard Beeman et al. (Chapel Hill: University of North Carolina Press, 1987); Michael A. McDonnell, "War and Nationhood: Founding Myths and Historical Realities," in *Remembering the Revolution: Memory, History and Nation Making from Independence to the Civil War*, ed. Michael A. McDonnell et al. (Amherst: University of Massachusetts Press, 2013), pp. 19–40.

6. Simon P. Newman, *Parades and the Politics of the Street: Festive Culture in the Early American Republic* (Philadelphia: University of Pennsylvania Press, 1997); Alfred F. Young, *The Shoemaker and the Tea Party: Memory and the American Revolution* (Boston: Beacon Press, 1999); Eric Hobsbawm and Terence Ranger, eds., *The Invention of Tradition* (Cambridge: Cambridge University Press, 1983); Boyd C. Shafer, *Faces of Nationalism: New*

Realities and Old Myths (New York: Harcourt Brace Jovanovich, 1972), chaps. 6–7; Michael Billig, *Banal Nationalism* (London: Sage, 1995); Rachel Tsang and Eric Taylor Woods, eds., *The Cultural Politics of Nationalism and Nation-Building: Ritual and Performance in the Forging of Nations* (London: Routledge, 2014).

7. Hobsbawm and Ranger, *Invention of Tradition*; David Waldstreicher, *In the Midst of Perpetual Fetes: The Making of American Nationalism, 1776–1820* (Chapel Hill: University of North Carolina Press, 1997); Drew Gilpin Faust, *The Creation of Confederate Nationalism: Ideology and Identity in the Civil War South* (Baton Rouge: Louisiana State University Press, 1988); John R. Gillis, ed., *Commemorations: The Politics of National Identity* (Princeton, NJ: Princeton University Press, 1994); Stefan Berger and Christoph Conrad, eds., *The Past as History: National Identity and Historical Consciousness in Modern Europe* (Houndmills, UK: Palgrave Macmillan, 2014).

8. Mona Ozouf, *Festivals and the French Revolution* (Cambridge, MA: Harvard University Press, 1988), p. 9.

9. Mark A. Noll, "The Image of the United States as a Biblical Nation, 1776–1865," in *The Bible in America: Essays in Cultural History*, ed. Nathan O. Hatch and Mark A. Noll (New York: Oxford University Press, 1982), pp. 39–58; Eran Shalev, *American Zion: The Old Testament as a Political Text from the Revolution to the Civil War* (New Haven, CT: Yale University Press, 2013). On Paine: Eric Foner, *Tom Paine and Revolutionary America* (New York: Oxford University Press, 1976).

10. David Ramsey, *An Oration, Delivered on the Anniversary of American Independence, July 4th, 1794* (London, 1795), pp. 5, 17; Samuel Stillman, *An Oration Delivered July 4th, 1789, at the Request of the Inhabitants of the Town of Boston* (Boston, 1789), p. 20; John L. O'Sullivan, "The Great Nation of Futurity," *United States Magazine and Democratic Review* 6:23 (Nov. 1839): 426–30.

11. Ralph V. Turner, *Magna Carta: Through the Ages* (Harlow, UK: Pearson/Longman, 2003).

12. Mona Ozouf, "Liberty, Equality, Fraternity," in *Realms of Memory: Rethinking the French Past*, 3 vols., ed. Pierre Nora (New York: Columbia University Press, 1996–98), 3:77–116.

13. Pauline Maier, *American Scripture: Making the Declaration of Independence* (New York: Knopf, 1997), chap. 4; Newman, *Parades and the Politics of the Street*; Len Travers, *Celebrating the Fourth: Independence Day and the Rise of Nationalism in the Early Republic* (Amherst: University of Massachusetts Press, 1997).

14. Faust, *Creation of Confederate Nationalism*, p. 21.

CHAPTER 10. Mobile Metaphors of Nationalism

1. Malcolm Freiberg, "The Winthrops and Their Papers," *Proceedings of the Massachusetts Historical Society* 80 (1968): 55–70.

2. "Constitution of the Historical Society" and "Introductory Address from the Historical Society to the Public," *Collections of the Massachusetts Historical Society* 1 (1792): 1–4; Louis Leonard Tucker, *The Massachusetts Historical Society: A Bicentennial History, 1791–1991* (Boston: Northeastern University Press, 1995).

3. *Memoirs of Hon. Thomas Lindall Winthrop, LL.D.* (Boston, 1857).

4. "June Meeting, 1872," *Proceedings of the Massachusetts Historical Society* 12 (1871–73): 233–37.

5. "List of 22 Historical Books Dated 1607–1728—Sent F. B. Winthrop to Reverend Samuel Miller, 30 January 1809," New-York Historical Society Archives, Patricia D. Klingenstein Library, New-York Historical Society. For additional details of the Model's

early years: Richard M. Gamble, *In Search of the City on a Hill: The Making and Unmaking of an American Myth* (London: Continuum, 2012), chap. 4.

6. Gamble, *In Search of the City on a Hill*, p. 95. On Folsom: Lyman Horace Weeks, ed., *Prominent Families of New York*, rev. ed. (New York: Historical Company, 1897), p. 221.

7. *Collections of the Massachusetts Historical Society*, 3rd ser., 7 (1838): 29–30, 32, 33–48.

8. *American Quarterly Register* 13:2 (Nov. 1840): 213–20. David F. Allmendinger Jr., "The Strangeness of the American Education Society: Indigent Students and the New Charity, 1815–1840," *History of Education Quarterly* 11:1 (Spring 1971): 3–22.

9. Edmund Clarence Stedman and Ellen Mackay Hutchinson, eds., *A Library of American Literature from the Earliest Settlement to the Present Time*, 10 vols. (New York: W. E. Benjamin, 1888), 1:304–7.

10. John Gorham Palfrey, *History of New England*, vol. 1 (Boston: Little, Brown, 1858), pp. 312–13; Charles F. Richardson, ed., *American Literature, 1607–1885*, 2 vols. (New York: G. P. Putnam's Sons, 1889–91), 1:90–91. Moses Coit Tyler gave a page to the Model in his *A History of American Literature, 1607–1865* (New York: G. P. Putnam's Sons, 1878). On Bancroft: Gamble, *In Search of the City on a Hill*, pp. 102–5.

11. Noah Webster, *History of the United States* (Columbus, OH: J. N. Whiting, 1841); Charles A. Goodrich, *History of the United States of America on a Plan Adapted to the Capacity of Youth* (Boston: Jenks, Hickling, and Swan, 1852); Edward Eggleston, *A History of the United States and Its People for the Use of Schools* (New York: D. Appleton, 1889); Edward Channing, *A Students' History of the United States* (New York: Macmillan, 1904); David Saville Muzzey, *An American History* (Boston: Ginn, 1911); Woodrow Wilson, *A History of the American People* (New York: Harper and Brothers, 1902).

12. *The Writings and Speeches of Daniel Webster*, 18 vols. (Boston: Little, Brown, 1903).

13. Commonwealth of Massachusetts, *Report of the Commission to Procure Memorial Statues for the National Statuary Hall at Washington* (Boston, 1877).

14. Michael G. Kammen, *Mystic Chords of Memory: The Transformation of Tradition in American Culture* (New York: Knopf, 1991); Michael A. McDonnell et al., eds., *Remembering the Revolution: Memory, History, and Nation Making from Independence to the Civil War* (Amherst: University of Massachusetts Press, 2013); Harlow W. Sheidley, *Sectional Nationalism: Massachusetts Conservative Leaders and the Transformation of America, 1815–1836* (Boston: Northeastern University Press, 1998), chap. 5; Alfred F. Young, *The Shoemaker and the Tea Party: Memory and the American Revolution* (Boston: Beacon Press, 1999).

15. *Annals of the Congress on the United States, 1789–1824*, HeinOnline, https://www .heinonline.org/HOL/Index?index=congrec/aoc&collection=congrec; *The Documentary History of the Ratification of the Constitution Digital Edition*, ed. John P. Kaminski et al. (Charlottesville: University of Virginia Press, 2009–2018), http://rotunda.upress.virginia .edu/founders/RNCN.html.

16. John Adams to Nathaniel Greene, Mar. 1780, *The Adams Papers Digital Edition*, ed. C. James Taylor (Charlottesville: University of Virginia Press, 2008), http://www.upress .virginia.edu/content/adams-papers-digital-edition.

17. William Plummer Jr., *An Address Delivered at Portsmouth, N.H, on the Fourth of July, 1828* (Portsmouth, NH, 1828), p. 23; Paul Dean, *A Discourse, Delivered at the Annual Election*, Jan. 4, 1832 (Boston, 1832), p. 34.

18. *Sketch of the Life and Public Services of Gen. Lewis Cass* (Washington, DC, 1848), p. 7.

19. Rev. J. W. Wiley, "The Daughters of China," *The Ladies' Repository* 15 (Mar. 1855); "On Certain Errors of Pious Students in Our Colleges," *Home, the School and the Church, or, The Presbyterian Education Repository* 1 (1850): 79; "Masonic Record," *North American, or,*

Weekly Journal of Politics, Science, and Literature 1 (Oct. 13, 1827): 22; James L. Ridgely, *Oration Delivered in Faneuil Hall, before the Independent Order of Odd Fellows* (Boston, 1845), p. 38; "The Feeding of Cotton Plants," *Southern Cultivator* 8 (April 1850): 49; "Book Farming," *New York Farmer* 8 (June 1835): 170.

20. *New York Mirror*, Dec. 5, 1829, p. 174; "Brooklyn on a Hill," *New York Evangelist* 62 (Feb. 12, 1891): 7; *Proceedings of the National Convention of Insurance Commissioners* (1918), p. 129; "Baltimore and Her Great Railroad," *American Farmer* 2 (Dec. 1867): 178; "Some Things about Akron," *Ohio Farmer* 18 (May 15, 1869): 312; Albert D. Richardson, *Our New States and Territories, Being Notes of a Recent Tour of Observations through Colorado, Utah, Idaho, Nevada, Oregon, Montana, Washington Territory, and California* (New York, 1866), p. 44.

21. Jonathan Kittredge, *An Address Delivered before the Temperance Society of Plymouth, N.H., July 4, 1829* (Boston, 1830), p. 18; Irving Fisher, "Can Prohibition Drive Out Drink?," *Independent*, Jan. 4, 1919, p. 97.

22. "New Hampshire Democracy and Massachusetts Whigism," *Liberator* 16 (Mar. 6, 1846), p. 38.

23. Charles W. Webber, *The Gold Mines of the Gila*, vol. 2 (New York, 1849), p. 175.

24. *The Morality of Public Men: A Second Letter to the Right Hon. the Earl of Derby* (London, 1853), p. 12; [Elizabeth Heyrick], *Appeal to the Hearts and Consciences of British Women* (Leicester, 1828), p. 15.

25. Maximilien Robespierre, "Sur les principes de morale politique qui doivent guider la convention nationale dans l'administration intérieure de la république," in *Oeuvres de Robespierre*, ed. A. Vermorel (Paris, 1866), p. 295. On Michelet: Tzvetan Todorov, *On Human Diversity: Nationalism, Racism, and Exoticism in French Thought* (Cambridge, MA: Harvard University Press, 1993), pp. 210–11. More generally: Tyler Stovall, *Transnational France: The Modern History of a Universal Nation* (Boulder, CO: Westview Press, 2015).

26. James E. Sanders, *The Vanguard of the Atlantic World: Creating Modernity, Nation, and Democracy in Nineteenth-Century Latin America* (Durham, NC: Duke University Press, 2014), pp. 85, 88.

27. Samuel Sherwood, *The Church's Flight into the Wilderness: An Address on the Times* (New York, 1776), pp. 46–47. More generally: James P. Byrd, *Sacred Scripture, Sacred War: The Bible and the American Revolution* (New York: Oxford University Press, 2013); Nicholas Guyatt, *Providence and the Invention of the United States, 1607–1876* (New York: Cambridge University Press, 2007); Mark A. Noll, "The Image of the United States as a Biblical Nation, 1776–1865," in *The Bible in America: Essays in Cultural History*, ed. Nathan O. Hatch and Mark A. Noll (New York: Oxford University Press, 1982), pp. 39–58.

28. Harriet Beecher Stowe, "Poganuc People," in *The Writings of Harriet Beecher Stowe*, 16 vols., Riverside ed. (Boston: Houghton, Mifflin, 1896), 11:139–40.

29. Andrew Jackson, "Farewell Address," Mar. 4, 1837, The American Presidency Project, Gerhard Peters and John Woolley, eds., http://www.presidency.ucsb.edu.

30. William Carey Crane, *Life and Selected Literary Remains of Sam Houston of Texas* (Philadelphia: Lippincott, 1884), p. 287; John L. O'Sullivan, "The Great Nation of Futurity," *United States Magazine and Democratic Review* 6:23 (Nov. 1839): 430; *Charleston Courier*, July 4, 1845, quoted in Merle Curti, *The Roots of American Loyalty* (New York: Columbia University Press, 1946), p. 68.

31. Quoted in Drew Gilpin Faust, *The Creation of Confederate Nationalism: Ideology and Identity in the Civil War South* (Baton Rouge: Louisiana State University Press, 2006), p. 26.

32. Guyatt, *Providence and the Invention of the United States*, p. 66; Mary Anne Perkins, *Nation and Word, 1770–1850: Religious and Metaphorical Language in European National Consciousness* (Aldershot, UK: Ashgate, 1999), p. 165.

33. Pasi Ihalainen, *Protestant Nations Redefined: Changing Perceptions of National Identity in the Rhetoric of the English, Dutch, and Swedish Public Churches, 1685–1772* (Leiden: Brill, 2005), pp. 135–36; Simon Schama, *The Embarrassment of Riches: An Interpretation of Dutch Culture in the Golden Age* (New York: Knopf, 1987), chap. 2; Philip S. Gorski, "The Mosaic Moment: An Early Modernist Critique of Modernist Theories of Nationalism," *American Journal of Sociology* 105:5 (Mar. 2000): 1428–68.

34. Quoted in Michael Lind, *The Next American Nation: The New Nationalism and the Fourth American Revolution* (New York: Free Press, 1996), p. 231.

35. Perkins, *Nation and Word*, p. 146. See also "Chosen Peoples," special issue of *Nations and Nationalism* 5:3 (July 1999); Anthony D. Smith, *Chosen Peoples* (Oxford: Oxford University Press, 2003).

36. Todd Gitlin and Liel Liebovitz, *The Chosen Peoples: America, Israel, and the Ordeals of Divine Election* (New York: Simon and Schuster, 2010), chap. 1.

37. Thomas Jefferson, "Inaugural Address," Mar. 4, 1801, The American Presidency Project, http://www.presidency.ucsb.edu; John Adams to Benjamin Rush, Oct. 22, 1812, in *Old Family Letters* (Philadelphia: Lippincott, 1892), p. 311; Robert C. Winthrop, "The Oregon Question and the Treaty of Washington," Mar. 18, 1844, quoted in Guyatt, *Providence and the Invention of the United States*, p. 222; Abraham Lincoln, "Address to the New Jersey State Senate, Feb. 21, 1861," *Collected Works of Abraham Lincoln*, ed. Roy P. Basler et al., 9 vols. (New Brunswick, NJ: Rutgers University Press, 1953–55), 4:236.

CHAPTER 11. From the Top Mast

1. Herman Melville, *White-Jacket; or, The World in a Man-of-War* (1850), *The Writings of Herman Melville*, Northwestern-Newberry ed., vol. 5 (Evanston, IL: Northwestern University Press, 1970), pp. 3–5

2. Ibid., pp. 150–51.

3. Henry Southgate, ed., *Many Thoughts of Many Minds*, 3rd ed. (London: Griffin, Bone, 1862), p. 468; Elon Foster, *New Cyclopaedia of Prose Illustrations* (New York: Thomas Y. Crowell, 1877), pp. 612–13.

4. *The Letters of Herman Melville*, ed. Merrell R. Davis and William H. Gilman (New Haven, CT: Yale University Press, 1960), p. 106; Willard Thorp, "Historical Note," to Melville, *White-Jacket*.

5. Melville, *White-Jacket*, pp. 138, 297 and, more generally, chaps. 33–36.

6. Ibid., pp. 375, 194.

7. O. A. Brownson, *An Address Delivered at Dedham on the Fifty-Eighth Anniversary of American Independence, July 4, 1834* (Dedham, MA, 1834), pp. 3–4, 10; O. A. Brownson, *An Oration before the Democracy of Worcester and Vicinity, Delivered at Worcester, Mass., July 4, 1840* (Boston, 1840), p. 34.

8. Margaret Fuller, "American Facts," in *Life Without and Life Within: Reviews, Narratives, Essays, and Poems* (Boston, 1859), p. 108.

9. "The Stain on Our National Character," *Liberator*, Apr. 7, 1848, p. 54.

10. American Anti-Slavery Society, *Annual Report* (New York, 1855), p. 13.

11. Frederick Douglass, "Anthony Burns Returned to Slavery," in *Frederick Douglass, Selected Speeches and Writings*, ed. Philip S. Foner (Chicago: Lawrence Hill Books, 1999), p. 281.

12. Frederick Douglass, "The Dred Scott Decision," in Douglass, *Selected Speeches and Writings*, p. 350. More generally: David W. Blight, *Frederick Douglass' Civil War: Keeping Faith in Jubilee* (Baton Rouge: Louisiana State University Press, 1989).

13. Sacvan Bercovitch, *The Puritan Origins of the American Self* (New Haven, CT: Yale University Press, 1975).

14. *Collected Works of Abraham Lincoln*, ed. Roy P. Basler et al., 9 vols. (New Brunswick, NJ: Rutgers University Press, 1953–55), searchable online at https://quod.lib.umich.edu/l/lincoln. Lincoln used the "almost chosen people" phrase in his "Address to the New Jersey State Senate, Feb. 21, 1861," ibid., 4:236.

15. Mark A. Noll, *America's God: From Jonathan Edwards to Abraham Lincoln* (New York: Oxford University Press, 2002), pp. 432, 433; George Rable, *God's Almost Chosen Peoples: A Religious History of the American Civil War* (Chapel Hill: University of North Carolina Press, 2010), p. 55.

16. Drew Gilpin Faust, *The Creation of Confederate Nationalism: Ideology and Identity in the Civil War South* (Baton Rouge: Louisiana State University Press, 1988), p. 29.

17. Harry S. Stout, *Upon the Altar of the Nation: A Moral History of the American Civil War* (New York: Viking, 2006); Nicholas Guyatt, *Providence and the Invention of the United States, 1607–1876* (New York: Cambridge University Press, 2007), chap. 7; Leonard Rogoff, "Who Is Israel? Yankees, Confederates, African Americans, and Jews," *American Jewish Archives Journal* 64:1–2 (2012): 33.

18. Abraham Lincoln, "Second Inaugural Address, Mar. 4, 1865," *Collected Works of Abraham Lincoln*, 8:333; Richard Carwardine, "Lincoln's Religion," in *Our Lincoln: New Perspectives on Lincoln and His World*, ed. Eric Foner (New York: W. W. Norton, 2008), p. 238.

19. Abraham Lincoln, "Address at Independence Hall in Philadelphia, Feb. 22, 1861," *Collected Works of Abraham Lincoln*, 4:240.

CHAPTER 12. Constructing a City on a Hill in Africa

1. Quoted in Richard West, *Back to Africa: A History of Sierra Leone and Liberia* (London: Cape, 1970), pp. 139–40. On the American Colonization Society and its Liberia project: James Ciment, *Another America: The Story of Liberia and the Former Slaves Who Ruled It* (New York: Hill and Wang, 2013); Nicholas Guyatt, "'The Outskirts of Our Happiness': Race and the Lure of Colonization in the Early Republic," *Journal of American History* 95:4 (Mar. 2009): 986–1011; Claude A. Clegg III, *The Price of Liberty: African Americans and the Making of Liberia* (Chapel Hill: University of North Carolina Press, 2004); Charles S. Johnson, *Bitter Canaan: The Story of the Negro Republic* (New Brunswick, NJ: Transaction Books, 1987); Tom W. Shick, *Behold the Promised Land: A History of Afro-American Settler Society in Nineteenth-Century Liberia* (Baltimore: Johns Hopkins University Press, 1980).

2. Tom W. Shick, "A Quantitative Analysis of Liberian Colonization from 1820 to 1843 with Special Reference to Mortality," *Journal of African History* 12:1 (1971): 45–59.

3. "Address Delivered before a Society in North Carolina, Auxiliary to the Society at Washington, for Colonizing the Free People of Colour on the Coast of Africa," *African Repository* 3:3 (May 1827); "Twenty-First Annual Meeting of the American Colonization Society," *African Repository* 14:1 (Jan. 1838).

4. *American Colonization Society, Eighth Annual Report* (Washington, DC, 1825), pp. 13–14.

5. Leslie M. Alexander, *African or American? Black Identity and Political Activism in New York City, 1784–1861* (Urbana: University of Illinois Press, 2008), p.180; Frederick Douglass, "Henry Clay," *North Star*, Jan. 28, 1848; *Frederick Douglass' Paper*, Feb. 26, 1852.

6. Frederick Douglass, "Emigration to Hayti," *Douglass' Monthly*, Jan. 1861; Frederick Douglass, "A Trip to Haiti," *Douglass' Monthly*, May 1861. On Douglass and the emigration movement: David W. Blight, *Frederick Douglass' Civil War: Keeping Faith in Jubilee* (Baton Rouge: Louisiana State University Press, 1989), chap. 6.

7. Joseph Saye Guannu, ed., *The Inaugural Addresses of the Presidents of Liberia: From Joseph Jenkins Roberts to William Richard Tolbert, Jr., 1848 to 1976* (Hicksville, NY: Exposition Press, 1980), pp. 84, 28, 179.

8. Hollis R. Lynch, ed., *Black Spokesman: Selected Published Writings of Edward Wilmot Blyden* (New York: Humanities Press, 1971), pp. 27, 50, 43.

9. Guannu, *Inaugural Addresses of the Presidents of Liberia*, p. 13; Lynch, *Black Spokesman*, p. 79.

10. Hilary Teage, "Liberia Anniversary Oration, Delivered December 1st, 1846, in the Baptist Church of Monrovia," *African Repository* 239: 9 (Sept. 1847); Guannu, *Inaugural Addresses of the Presidents of Liberia*, pp. 63, 78, 87.

11. Booker T. Washington, ed., *Tuskegee and Its People: Their Ideals and Achievements* (New York: Appleton, 1905), p. 56; "Bishop W. T. Vernon on Booker T. Washington," *Chicago Defender*, Apr. 25, 1931, p. 15.

12. Louis R. Harlan, "Booker T. Washington and the White Man's Burden," *American Historical Review* 71:2 (Jan. 1966): 441–67; Louis R. Harlan, *Booker T. Washington: The Wizard of Tuskegee, 1901–1915* (New York: Oxford University Press, 1983), chap. 11.

13. West, *Back to Africa*, p. 267; Ibrahim Sundiata, *Brothers and Strangers: Black Zion, Black Slavery, 1914–1940* (Durham, NC: Duke University Press, 2003), p. 19.

14. W.E.B. Du Bois, "The African Roots of War," *Atlantic Monthly* 115 (May 1915): 707–14. On Du Bois and Africa: David Levering Lewis, *W.E.B. Du Bois: A Biography* (New York: Henry Holt, 2009), chap. 15; Frank Chalk, "Du Bois and Garvey Confront Liberia: Two Incidents of the Coolidge Years," *Canadian Journal of African Studies* 1:2 (Nov. 1967): 135–42; James Campbell, *Middle Passages: African American Journeys to Africa, 1787–2005* (New York: Penguin, 2006), chap. 6.

15. W.E.B. Du Bois, "Little Portraits of Africa," *Crisis*, Apr. 1924, pp. 273–74; W.E.B. Du Bois, *Dusk of Dawn: An Essay toward an Autobiography of a Race Concept* (New York: Schocken Books, 1940), chap. 5; W.E.B. Du Bois, "The Primitive Black Man," *Nation*, Dec. 17, 1924, 675–76.

16. Du Bois, "Little Portraits of Africa"; Langston Hughes, "Ships, Sea, and Africa: Random Impressions of a Sailor on His First Trip down the West Coast of the Motherland," *Crisis*, Dec. 1923, pp. 69–71.

17. W.E.B. Du Bois, "Worlds of Color," *Foreign Affairs* 3:3 (Apr. 1925): 444; W.E.B. Du Bois, "Sensitive Liberia," *Crisis*, May 1924, p. 10.

18. Du Bois, "Worlds of Color," p. 444.

CHAPTER 13. The Carnage of God's Chosen Nations

1. Lloyd C. Gardner, Walter F. LaFeber, and Thomas J. McCormick, *Creation of the American Empire: U.S. Diplomatic History* (Chicago: Rand McNally, 1973), p. 4; Dennis Merrill and Thomas G. Paterson, eds., *Major Problems in American Foreign Relations: Documents and Essays*, vol. 1, *To 1920*, 7th ed. (Boston: Wadsworth, 2010), p. 31.

2. Walter A. McDougall, *Promised Land, Crusader State: The American Encounter with the World since 1776* (Boston: Houghton Mifflin, 1997); Robert Kagan, *Dangerous Nation* (New York: Knopf, 2006); Andrew J. Bacevich, *The Limits of Power: The End of American Exceptionalism* (New York: Metropolitan Books, 2008); Andrew Preston, *Sword of the Spirit, Shield of Faith: Religion in American War and Diplomacy* (New York: Knopf, 2012).

McDougall partially retracted his earlier thesis in "The Unlikely History of American Exceptionalism," *American Interest* 8:4 (Mar.–Apr. 2013): 6–15.

3. John L. O'Sullivan, "Annexation," *United States Magazine and Democratic Review* 17 (July–Aug. 1845): 5–10; Albert J. Beveridge, *The Meaning of the Times and Other Speeches* (Indianapolis: Bobbs-Merrill, 1908), p. 85.

4. Perry Anderson, "Imperium," *New Left Review* 83 (Sept.–Oct. 1983): 6.

5. Thomas Foxcroft, *Grateful Reflexions on the Signal Appearances of Divine Providence for Great Britain and Its Colonies in America* (Boston, 1760), pp. 11, 9. More generally: Nicholas S. Guyatt, *Providence and the Invention of the United States, 1607–1876* (New York: Cambridge University Press, 2007), chap. 2.

6. Jane Burbank and Frederick Cooper, *Empires in World History* (Princeton, NJ: Princeton University Press, 2010); Charles S. Maier, *Among Empires: American Ascendancy and Its Predecessors* (Cambridge, MA: Harvard University Press, 2006).

7. Walter Nugent, *Habits of Empire: A History of American Expansion* (New York: Knopf, 2008); Thomas Bender, *A Nation among Nations: America's Place in World History* (New York: Hill and Wang, 2006), chap. 4; Frank Ninkovitch, *The United States and Imperialism* (Malden, MA: Blackwell, 2001); Walter Johnson, *River of Dark Dreams: Slavery and Empire in the Cotton Kingdom* (Cambridge, MA: Harvard University Press, 2013).

8. Peter J. Kastor and Francois Weil, eds., *Empires of the Imagination: Transatlantic Histories of the Louisiana Purchase* (Charlottesville: University of Virginia Press, 2009).

9. Pekka Hämäläinen, *The Comanche Empire* (New Haven, CT: Yale University Press, 2008).

10. Theodore Roosevelt, "Fourth Annual Message to Congress," Dec. 6, 1904, The American Presidency Project, Gerhard Peters and John Woolley, eds., http://www.presidency.ucsb.edu.

11. Alice L. Conklin, *A Mission to Civilize: The Republican Idea of Empire in France and West Africa, 1895–1930* (Stanford: Stanford University Press, 1997); Sebastian Conrad, *German Colonialism: A Short History* (Cambridge: Cambridge University Press, 2012); Burbank and Cooper, *Empires in World History*; Duncan Bell, "Ideologies of Empire," in *The Oxford Handbook of Political Ideologies*, ed. Michael Freeden and Marc Stears (Oxford: Oxford University Press, 2013).

12. Albert J. Beveridge, "The Star of Empire," in Beveridge, *Meaning of the Times*, pp. 120–21, 131, 133.

13. Albert J. Beveridge, "Speech in the U.S. Senate," *Congressional Record*, Jan. 9, 1900, pp. 704, 712.

14. Robert D. Schulzinger, *American Diplomacy in the Twentieth Century*, 3rd ed. (New York: Oxford University Press, 1994), p. 11.

15. Albert Marrin, *The Last Crusade: The Church of England in the First World War* (Durham, NC: Duke University Press, 1974), pp. 142, 135; Gerhard Besier, ed., *Die protestantischen Kirchen Europas im Ersten Weltkrieg* (Göttingen: Vandenhoeck and Ruprecht, 1984), pp. 157, 17; Alice L. Conklin, Sarah Fishman, and Robert Zaretsky, *France and Its Empire since 1870*, 2nd ed. (New York: Oxford University Press, 2015), p. 132.

16. David Roberts, ed., *Minds at War: Poetry of the First World War in Context* (Burgess Hill, UK: Saxon Books, 1996), p. 46; Besier, *Die protestantischen Kirchen Europas*, pp. 156, 18.

17. Roberts, *Minds at War*, p. 338.

18. Samuel Eliot Morison, ed., *The Humble Request of the Massachusetts Puritans and A Modell of Christian Charity by John Winthrop*, 1630, Old South Leaflets no. 207 (Boston, 1916), pp. 1–2.

19. Woodrow Wilson, *A History of the American People* (New York: Harper and Brothers, 1903); John Fiske, *The Beginnings of New England* (Boston: Houghton Mifflin, 1889); Henry

Cabot Lodge, *A Short History of the English Colonies in America* (New York: Harper and Brothers, 1881).

20. Woodrow Wilson, "The Course of American History," in Woodrow Wilson, *Mere Literature, and Other Essays* (Boston: Houghton, Mifflin, 1896).

21. Woodrow Wilson, "Message to the National Army, Aug. 7, 1917," *The Papers of Woodrow Wilson*, ed. Arthur S. Link et al., 69 vols. (Princeton, NJ: Princeton University Press, 1966–94), 43:380; Woodrow Wilson, "Address to the Senate, July 10, 1919," ibid., 61:427–28.

22. Woodrow Wilson, "Annual Message to Congress, Dec. 4, 1917," ibid., 45:202; Woodrow Wilson, "Remarks to Confederate Veterans, June 5, 1917," ibid., 42:452. See also Richard M. Gamble, *The War for Righteousness: Progressive Christianity, the Great War, and the Rise of the Messianic Nation* (Wilmington, DE: ISI Books, 2003).

23. Thomas J. Knock, *To End All Wars: Woodrow Wilson and the Quest for a New World Order* (Princeton, NJ: Princeton University Press, 1995).

24. Woodrow Wilson, "Campaign Address in Jersey City, May 25, 1912," *Papers of Woodrow Wilson*, 24:443; Woodrow Wilson, "Address to the U.S. Senate, July 10, 1919," ibid., 61:436; Woodrow Wilson, "Speech at Coeur D'Alene, Sept. 12, 1919," ibid., 63:213; Woodrow Wilson "Speech at Pueblo, NM, Sept. 25, 1919," ibid., 63:512.

25. A. J. Hoover, *God, Germany, and Britain in the Great War: A Study in Clerical Nationalism* (New York: Praeger, 1989), pp. 90, 69; Besier, *Die protestantischen Kirchen Europas*, p. 131. See also Philip Jenkins, *The Great and Holy War: How World War I Became a Religious Crusade* (New York: HarperOne, 2014); John F. Piper Jr., *The American Churches in World War I* (Athens: Ohio University Press, 1985).

26. Mary Borden, *The Forbidden Zone* (London: Heinemann, 1929), pp. 183–84.

CHAPTER 14. The Historical Embarrassments of New England

1. *Tercentenary of the Founding of Boston: An Account of the Celebration Marking the Three Hundredth Anniversary of the Settlement of the Site of the City of Boston, Massachusetts, 1930* (Boston: City of Boston Printing Department, 1930). Online at https://archive.org/stream /tercentenaryoffo00bost/tercentenaryoffo00bost_djvu.txt.

2. Edwin Markham, "Ode to Boston," in *Tercentenary of the Founding of Boston*.

3. "Commission Approves Design of Memorial Commemorating Establishment of Boston," *Daily Boston Globe*, Jan. 16, 1930, p. 10.

4. Harlow W. Sheidley, *Sectional Nationalism: Massachusetts Conservative Leaders and the Transformation of America, 1815–1836* (Boston: Northeastern University Press, 1998), pp. 141–45.

5. Joseph A. Conforti, *Imagining New England: Explorations of Regional Identity from the Pilgrims to the Mid-Twentieth Century* (Chapel Hill: University of North Carolina Press, 2001); Stephanie Kermes, *Creating an American Identity: New England, 1789–1825* (New York: Palgrave Macmillan, 2008); Sheidley, *Sectional Nationalism*; John D. Seelye, *Memory's Nation: The Place of Plymouth Rock* (Chapel Hill: University of North Carolina Press, 1998); Lawrence Buell, *New England Literary Culture: From Revolution through Renaissance* (Cambridge: Cambridge University Press, 1986), chap. 8; Ruth Miller Elson, *Guardians of Tradition: American Schoolbooks of the Nineteenth Century* (Lincoln: University of Nebraska Press, 1964), pp. 169–73.

6. Wesley Frank Craven, *The Legend of the Founding Fathers* (New York: New York University Press, 1956).

7. George Bancroft, *History of the United States from the Discovery of the American Continent to the Present Time*, 10 vols. (Boston: Charles Bowen, etc., 1834–74), 1:393–94.

8. Sheidley, *Sectional Nationalism*, p. 126. See also Ann Uhry Abrams, *The Pilgrims and Pocahontas: Rival Myths of American Origins* (Boulder, CO: Westview Press, 1999).

9. Quoted in Seelye, *Memory's Nation*, p. 258; Joshua Barker Whitridge, *An Oration Delivered on the Anniversary of the New-England Society, Charleston, S.C., Delivered December 22, 1835* (Charleston, SC, 1836), p. 15; Robert C. Winthrop, *An Address Delivered before the New England Society in the City of New York, Dec. 23, 1839* (Boston, 1840), pp. 13, 59.

10. Alexis de Tocqueville, *Democracy in America*, 4 vols., trans. James T. Schleifer (Indianapolis: Liberty Fund, 2010), 1:110–14.

11. Ibid., 1:52–53, 2:455. See also George Wilson Pierson, *Tocqueville in America*, abridged ed. (Baltimore: Johns Hopkins University Press, 1996), chap. 8.

12. R. B. Bernstein, *The Founding Fathers Reconsidered* (New York: Oxford University Press, 2009).

13. David W. Galenson, "The Settlement and Growth of the Colonies: Population, Labor, and Economic Development," Daniel Vickers, "The Northern Colonies: Economy and Society, 1600–1775," and Russell E. Menard, "Economic and Social Development of the South," all in Stanley L. Engerman and Robert E. Gallman, *The Cambridge Economic History of the United States*, vol. 1, *The Colonial Era* (Cambridge: Cambridge University Press, 1996); Nicholas Canny, "English Migration into and across the Atlantic in the Seventeenth and Eighteenth Centuries," in *Europeans on the Move: Studies in European Migration, 1500–1800*, ed. Nicholas Canny (Oxford: Oxford University Press, 1994), pp. 39–75.

14. Mark A. Peterson, "Life on the Margins: Boston's Anxieties of Influence in the Atlantic World," in *The Atlantic World: Essays on Slavery, Migration, and Imagination*, ed. Wim Klooster and Alfred Padula (Upper Saddle River, NJ: Pearson/Prentice Hall, 2005), pp. 45–59; Vickers, "Northern Colonies," p. 235; Galenson, "Settlement and Growth of the Colonies," p. 198.

15. Susan-Mary Grant, *North Over South: Northern Nationalism and American Identity in the Antebellum Era* (Lawrence: University Press of Kansas, 2000).

16. John Fiske, *The Beginnings of New England; or, the Puritan Theocracy in Its Relations to Civil and Religious Liberty* (Boston: Houghton, Mifflin, 1889); Charles Francis Adams, *Three Episodes of Massachusetts History* (Boston: Houghton, Mifflin, 1892).

17. Herbert Sherman Houston, "Memorials of Phillips Brooks," *Outlook* 61:1 (Jan. 7, 1899): 61; Kenyon Cox, "Augustus Saint Gaudens," *Century Illustrated Magazine* 35:1 (Nov. 1887): 30.

18. William Carlos Williams, *In the American Grain* (New York: Boni, 1925), pp. 67, 65.

19. Samuel Eliot Morison, "Those Misunderstood Puritans," *Forum and Century* 85 (Mar. 1931): 142–47.

20. Mark L. Sargent, "The Conservative Covenant: The Rise of the Mayflower Compact in American Myth," *New England Quarterly* 61:2 (June 1988): 233–51, esp. p. 248; Seelye, *Memory's Nation*; Peter J. Gomes, "Puritans and Pilgrims: 'Heroes' and 'Villains'" in the Creation of the American Past," *Proceedings of the Massachusetts Historical Society*, 3rd ser., 95 (1983): 1–16.

21. Edmund S. Morgan, *Roger Williams: The Church and the State* (New York: Harcourt, Brace and World, 1967).

22. Adams, *Three Episodes*, pp. 569, 488.

23. Francis J. Bremer, "Remembering—and Forgetting—John Winthrop and the Puritan Founders," *Massachusetts Historical Review* 6 (2004): 38–69.

24. Vernon Louis Parrington, *Main Currents in American Thought*, vol. 1, *The Colonial Mind* (New York: Harcourt, Brace, 1927), pp. 6, vii, 43, 47, 50.

25. *Tercentenary of the Founding of Boston*; "Racial Groups' Tercentenary Program Begins Tomorrow," *Daily Boston Globe*, July 13, 1930, p. B8.

26. None of the printed publications of the Tercentenary Commission included mention of the Model: Samuel Eliot Morison, *Historical Background for the Massachusetts Bay Tercentenary in 1930* (Boston, 1928); Massachusetts Historical Society, *The Founding of Massachusetts: A Selection from the Sources of the History of the Settlement, 1628–1631* (Boston, 1930); Mrs. N. S. Bell, *Pathways of the Puritans* (Framingham, MA, 1930); Massachusetts Department of Education, *Material Suggested for Use in the Schools in Observance of the Tercentenary of Massachusetts Bay Colony* (Boston, 1930).

CHAPTER 15. Puritanism in an Existentialist Key

1. On Perry Miller as a teacher and historian: Edmund S. Morgan, "Perry Miller and the Historians," *Harvard Review* 2:2 (1964): 52–59; Ann Douglas, "The Mind of Perry Miller," *New Republic*, Feb. 3, 1982, pp. 26–30; Nicholas Guyatt, "'An Instrument of National Policy': Perry Miller and the Cold War," *Journal of American Studies* 36:1 (Apr. 2002): 107–49; David Levin, "Perry Miller at Harvard," *Southern Review* 19 (Oct. 1983): 802–16; Kenneth S. Lynn, "Perry Miller," *American Scholar* 52:2 (Spring 1983): 221–27.

2. Albert J. Gelpi, "Perry Miller, 1905–1963," *Harvard Review* 2:2 (1964): 5–7.

3. Perry Miller, *Errand into the Wilderness* (Cambridge, MA: Harvard University Press, 1956), p. viii; Elizabeth Miller to Sanford Searl Jr., quoted in Rivka Maizlish, "Rethinking the Origins of American Studies (with Help from Perry Miller)," *U.S. Intellectual History Blog*, Nov. 13, 2013, https://s-usih.org/2013/11/rethinking-the origin-of-american-studies-with -help-from-perry-miller.

4. Miller, *Errand into the Wilderness*, pp. 16, viii.

5. Perry Miller and Thomas H. Johnson, eds., *The Puritans: A Sourcebook of Their Writings*, 2 vols. (New York: American Book Company, 1938), 1:1.

6. Vernon Louis Parrington, *Main Currents in American Thought*, vol. 1, *The Colonial Mind, 1620–1800* (New York: Harcourt, Brace, 1927), p. 6.

7. Perry Miller, "The Marrow of Puritan Divinity," *Publications of the Colonial Society of Massachusetts* (Feb. 1935), reprinted in Miller, *Errand into the Wilderness*. Miller's full statement came in Perry Miller, *The New England Mind: The Seventeenth Century* (New York: Macmillan, 1939).

8. Miller and Johnson, *Puritans*, 1:195–99.

9. Miller, *New England Mind: The Seventeenth Century*, pp. 477, 483.

10. Ibid., p. 477.

11. Ibid., chap. 1.

12. Ibid., p. 10.

13. Miller, "Marrow of Puritan Divinity," in Miller, *Errand into the Wilderness*, p. 65; Miller, *New England Mind: The Seventeenth Century*, p. 487.

14. George Cotkin, *Existential America* (Baltimore: Johns Hopkins University Press, 2003).

15. Miller and Johnson, *Puritans*, 1:63.

16. For Miller's and Niebuhr's assessments of each other: Perry Miller, "The Great Method," *Nation* 169:6 (Aug. 6, 1949): 138–39; Perry Miller, "The Influence of Reinhold Niebuhr," *Reporter*, May 1, 1958, pp. 39–40; Reinhold Niebuhr, review of Perry Miller, *The New England Mind: From Colony to Province*, *New Republic* 129:5 (Aug. 31, 1953): 18; Reinhold Niebuhr, "Perry Miller and Our Embarrassment," *Harvard Review* 2:2 (1964): 49–51.

17. Arthur M. Schlesinger Jr., *A Life in the Twentieth Century: Innocent Beginnings, 1917–1950* (Boston: Houghton Mifflin, 2000), pp. 161–63; Robert Coles, "Dr. Percy's Hold on Medicine," in *The Last Physician: Walker Percy and the Moral Life of Medicine*, ed. Carl Elliott and John Lantos (Durham, NC: Duke University Press, 1999), p. 12; Robert Coles,

Lives We Carry with Us: Profiles of Moral Courage, ed. David D. Cooper (New York: New Press, 2010).

18. Perry Miller, "Errand into the Wilderness," first delivered as a lecture at Brown University in 1952, reprinted in Miller, *Errand into the Wilderness*. An extensive critical literature soon grew up around the essay. Among the particularly acute contributions: Andrew Delbanco, "The Puritan Errand Re-viewed," *Journal of American Studies* 18:3 (Dec. 1984): 343–60; Theodore Dwight Bozeman, "The Puritans' 'Errand into the Wilderness' Reconsidered," *New England Quarterly* 59:2 (June 1986): 231–51; Theodore Dwight Bozeman, *To Live Ancient Lives: The Primitivist Dimension in Puritanism* (Chapel Hill: University of North Carolina Press, 1988); Gordon S. Wood, "Struggle over the Puritans," *New York Review of Books*, Nov. 9, 1989, pp. 26–34; David D. Hall, "Narrating Puritanism," in *New Directions in American Religious History*, ed. Harry S. Stout and D. G. Hart (New York: Oxford University Press, 1997).

19. Perry Miller, *The New England Mind: From Colony to Province* (Cambridge, MA: Harvard University Press, 1953), p. 25.

20. Miller, "Errand into the Wilderness," in Miller, *Errand into the Wilderness*, p. 11.

21. Perry Miller, "Liberty and Conformity" (1958), in Perry Miller, *The Responsibility of Mind in a Civilization of Machines* (Amherst: University of Massachusetts Press, 1979).

22. Miller, "Errand into the Wilderness," p. 13; Miller, *New England Mind: From Colony to Province*, p. 485.

23. Perry Miller, "The Shaping of the American Character" (1955), in Miller, *Nature's Nation*, pp. 12–13.

24. Perry Miller, "The Social Context of the Covenant" (1953), in Miller, *Responsibility of Mind*, p. 157.

CHAPTER 16. Arguing over the Puritans during the Cold War

1. Philip Gleason, "World War II and the Development of American Studies," *American Quarterly* 36:3 (1984): 343–58; Stephen J. Whitfield, *The Culture of the Cold War* (Baltimore: Johns Hopkins University Press, 1991); Wendy L. Wall, *Inventing the "American Way": The Politics of Consensus from the New Deal to the Civil Rights Movement* (New York: Oxford University Press, 2008); Robert H. Walker, *American Studies in the United States: A Survey of College Programs* (Baton Rouge: Louisiana State University Press, 1958); "The American Studies Movement: A Thirty-Year Retrospective," *American Quarterly* 31:3 (1979): 289–406; Marvin Wachman, "Colgate's Course in the American Idea," *Journal of Higher Education* 26:5 (May 1955): 243.

2. Perry Miller, "What Drove Me Crazy in Europe," *Atlantic Monthly* 187 (Mar. 1951): 41, 45.

3. William Benton, "The Struggle for the Minds and Loyalties of Mankind," *Congressional Record*, Mar. 22, 1950, pp. 3763–65.

4. Dwight D. Eisenhower, "Address Accepting the Presidential Nomination at the Republican National Convention in Chicago," July 11, 1952, The American Presidency Project (hereafter "APP"), Gerhard Peters and John Woolley, eds., http://www.presidency.ucsb.edu.

5. John Jessup, *The Third Estate: Selections from the Writings of John Knox Jessup*, ed. Henry Grunwald (privately printed), pp. 29, 32.

6. Clinton Rossiter, "The American Mission," *American Scholar* 20:1 (Winter 1950/51): 19–28; Harvey Wish, *Society and Thought in America*, vol. 1 (New York: Longmans, Green, 1950), chap. 2; Edward M. Burns, *The American Idea of Mission: Concepts of National Purpose and Destiny* (New Brunswick, NJ: Rutgers University Press, 1957).

7. Edmund S. Morgan, *The Puritan Dilemma: The Story of John Winthrop* (Boston: Little, Brown, 1958); Jon Butler, "In Memoriam: Edmund Sears Morgan," *Perspectives on History*, Dec. 2013, p. 39.

8. Daniel J. Boorstin, *The Americans: The Colonial Experience* (New York: Random House, 1958), bk. 1.

9. John P. Diggins, "The Perils of Naturalism: Some Reflections on Daniel J. Boorstin's Approach to American History," *American Quarterly* 23:2 (May 1971): 153–80; Daniel J. Boorstin, *The Lost World of Thomas Jefferson* (New York: Holt, 1948); Daniel J. Boorstin, *The Genius of American Politics* (Chicago: University of Chicago Press, 1953), p. 187.

10. Daniel J. Boorstin, ed., *An American Primer* (Chicago: University of Chicago Press, 1966).

11. John F. Kennedy, "Inaugural Address," Jan. 20, 1961, APP.

12. "Text of Kennedy's Speech," *New York Times*, Jan. 10, 1961, p. 20.

13. Richard M. Gamble, *In Search of the City on a Hill: The Making and Unmaking of an American Myth* (London: Continuum, 2012), p. 133; Arthur S. Schlesinger Jr. to "Fred," c. Jan. 6, 1961, in John F. Kennedy Papers, Speech Files, Address to the Massachusetts State Legislature, Jan. 9, 1961, https://www.jfklibrary.org/Asset-Viewer/Archives/JFKPOF-034 -001.aspx; "The Progressive Spirit in an Age of Conformity—Address by Senator Douglas," *Congressional Record*, appx., Mar. 2, 1957, pp. A1659–60.

14. "State House Talk Seen as Call for Moral Uplift in Bay State," *Boston Globe*, Jan. 10, 1961, p. 1; "Kennedy Pledges Rule of Integrity," *New York Times*, Jan. 10, 1961, pp. 1ff.; Charles L. Whipple, "Dirty Money in Boston," *Atlantic Monthly*, Mar. 1961, pp. 41–46.

15. John F. Kennedy, "Remarks at a Dinner for the Big Brothers of America," June 7, 1961, APP.

16. John W. Jeffries, "The 'Quest for National Purpose' of 1960," *American Quarterly* 30:4 (Autumn 1978): 451–70; John K. Jessup, "A Noble Framework for a Great Debate," *Life*, May 23, 1960, p. 25.

17. John F. Kennedy, "We Must Climb to the Hilltop," *Life*, Aug. 22, 1960, pp. 70ff.

18. Albert H. Rosenthal, "Ideas Are Weapons," *Congressional Record*, appx., Sept. 6, 1961, pp. A7021–22.

19. Lyndon B. Johnson, "Remarks in Boston at Post Office Square," Oct. 27, 1964, APP; Richard M. Nixon, "Remarks to the 89th Annual International Meeting of the Knights of Columbus in New York City," Aug. 17, 1971, APP; George McGovern, *An American Journey: The Presidential Campaign Speeches of George McGovern* (New York: Randon House, 1974), p. 212.

20. Robert F. Kennedy, "Racial Problems in the North: Speech to the National Council of Christians and Jews," in *RFK: Collected Speeches*, ed. Edwin Guthman and C. Richard Allen (New York: Viking, 1993), p. 158; Hubert Humphrey, "Address to the Citizens Crusade against Poverty," Feb. 10, 1965, *Congressional Record*, Feb. 17, 1965, p. 2824.

21. Oscar Handlin, ed., *American Principles and Issues: The National Purpose* (New York: Holt, Rinehart, and Winston, 1961), pp. 33–34.

22. Merle Curti, *The Growth of American Thought*, 2nd ed. (New York: Harper and Brothers, 1943); Boorstin, *An American Primer*; Loren Baritz, ed., *Sources of the American Mind: A Collection of Documents and Texts in American Intellectual History* (New York: Wiley, 1966); Cleanth Brooks, R.W.B. Lewis, and Robert Penn Warren, eds., *American Literature: The Makers and the Making* (New York: St. Martin's Press, 1973).

23. Robert N. Bellah, "Civil Religion in America," *Daedalus* 96:1 (Winter 1967): 1–21; Robert N. Bellah, *The Broken Covenant: American Civil Religion in Time of Trial* (Chicago: University of Chicago Press, 1975).

24. Thomas A. Bailey and David M. Kennedy, *American Pageant: A History of the Republic*, 6th ed. (Lexington, MA: D. C. Heath, 1979); Charles M. Dollar et al., eds., *America: Changing Times* (New York: Wiley, 1979).

25. John F. Kennedy, "Three Women of Courage," *McCall's*, Jan. 1958.

26. Rev. D. Paul Reaser in the *Congressional Record*, July 20, 1973, p. 25249.

27. Christopher Looby, "Scholar and Exegete: A Tribute to Sacvan Bercovitch," *Early American Literature* 39:1 (2004): 1–9; Sacvan Bercovitch, "Introduction: The Music of America," in his *The Rites of Assent: Transformations in the Symbolic Construction of America* (New York: Routledge, 1993).

28. Doris Friedensohn, "The Mid-Life Crisis of American Studies," *American Quarterly* 31:3 (1979): 372–76.

29. Sacvan Bercovitch, *The American Jeremiad* (Madison: University of Wisconsin Press, 1978); Sacvan Bercovitch, "How the Puritans Won the American Revolution," *Massachusetts Quarterly* 17 (1976): 597–663; Sacvan Bercovitch, "The Rites of Assent: Rhetoric, Ritual, and the Ideology of American Consensus," in *The American Self: Myth, Ideology, and Popular Culture*, ed. Sam B. Girgus (Albuquerque: University of New Mexico Press, 1981), pp. 5–42.

30. Sacvan Bercovitch, "The Biblical Basis of the American Myth," in *The Bible and American Arts and Letters*, ed., Giles Gunn (Minneapolis: Fortress Press, 1983), p. 223; Sacvan Bercovitch, Preface to the 2011 edition of *The Puritan Origins of the American Self*, (New Haven, CT: Yale University Press, 2011), pp. xi–xii.

31. Ibid., p. xix.

32. For important critiques of Bercovitch's work: David Harlan, "A People Blinded from Birth: American History According to Sacvan Bercovitch," *Journal of American History* 78:3 (Dec. 1991): 949–71; Donald Weber et al., "Symposium on *The Puritan Origins of the American Self*," *Early American Literature* 47:2 (2012): 377–441; Michael P. Winship, "What Puritan Guarantee?," *Early American Literature* 47:2 (2012): 411–20.

CHAPTER 17. Ronald Reagan's Shining City on a Hill

1. Ronald Reagan, "Remarks at the Republican National Convention in New Orleans, Louisiana," Aug. 15, 1988, The American Presidency Project (hereafter "APP"), Gerhard Peters and John Woolley, eds., http://www.presidency.ucsb.edu.

2. Reagan, "Remarks at Oath Taking Ceremony, State Capitol Rotunda, Sacramento, CA," Jan. 2, 1967, Ronald Reagan, Governor's Papers, Press Unit, Series III: Speeches, box P17, Ronald Reagan Presidential Library (hereafter "RRPL").

3. Sean Wilentz, *The Age of Reagan: A History, 1974–2008* (New York: Harper, 2008), p. 58. The false quotation was "It would not matter if 3/4 of the human race perished; the important thing is that the remaining 1/4 be communist."

4. Ronald Reagan, "Commencement Address at Eureka College," 1957, Reagan 2020, http://reagan2020.us/speeches/Your_America_to_be_Free.asp; Ronald Reagan, "Remarks to the First Conservative Political Action Conference," Jan. 25, 1974, Reagan 2020, http://reagan2020.us/speeches/City_Upon_A_Hill.asp; George Lippard, "The Unknown Speaker," in Wilmot Brookings Mitchell, ed., *School and College Speaker* (New York: Henry Holt, 1902), pp. 275–78.

5. Ronald Reagan, *The Notes: Ronald Reagan's Private Collection of Stories and Wisdom*, ed. Douglas Brinkley (New York: Harper, 2011), p. 34; William Safire, ed., *Lend Me Your Ears: Great Speeches in History* (New York: Norton, 1992), p. 7.

6. Ken Khachigian, "Memorandum for the President-Elect: First Draft of Inaugural Address," Jan. 4, 1981, Kenneth L. Khachigian Files, box 1, RRPL.

7. Larry Seidler to Tony Dolan, "Corrections in 'Vision of America' Speech," Oct. 29, 1980, Ronald Reagan 1980 Presidential Campaign Papers, Series XXII, Tony Dolan Files, box 865, RRPL.

8. Reagan, *Notes*, p. 7. By this point Reagan had altered Winthrop's "through" to "throughout." In his earliest use of Winthrop's words, in his speeches of 1969–70, he had quoted them correctly.

9. Jerry C. Martin, "Information and Policy Research for Ronald Reagan, 1969–75," an interview conducted by Sarah Sharp for the Government History Documentation Project, Ronald Reagan Gubernatorial Era, Regional Oral History Office, Bancroft Library, University of California at Berkeley, pp. 28–29.

10. Speechwriting Office Files, RRPL; Edwin Meese Papers, Hoover Institution Archives, Stanford University (hereafter "Edwin Meese Papers"). Some of these handwritten texts are collected in Reagan, *In His Own Hand*, ed. Kiron K. Skinner, Annelise Anderson, and Martin Anderson (New York: Free Press, 2001).

11. Jerry R. Martin to Ronald Reagan, Jan. 14, 1974, and "Remarks to the American Conservative Union/Young Americans for Freedom Political Action Conference, Mayflower Hotel, Washington, DC," Jan. 25, 1974, draft, both in Edwin Meese Papers, box 280: RR: Speeches/Drafts/Articles 1970–1974, Hoover Institution Archives, courtesy of Hoover Institution Library and Archives, Stanford University.

12. "Speech to the Board of Governors of the Ronald Reagan Library Foundation," Dec. 14, 1985, draft, White House Office of Speechwriting, Speech Drafts, box 244, RRPL.

13. Anthony Dolan, "Presidential Remarks: Lighting of the Statue of Liberty, Governors' Island, New York," July 3, 1986, draft dated June 29, 1986, Anthony R. Dolan Files, box 44, RRPL.

14. Anthony Dolan, "Remarks at the Heritage Foundation Dinner," Oct. 3, 1983, draft, Dolan Files, box 23, RRPL.

15. Anthony Dolan to Edwin Meese, c. June 1980, Ronald Reagan 1980 Presidential Campaign Papers, 1964–1980, box 867, RRPL.

16. Ronald Reagan, "Farewell Address to the Nation," Jan. 11, 1989, APP.

17. Reagan, *In His Own Hand*, pp. 13–15.

18. Ronald Reagan, "Address to the Employees of Forest Lawn," Nov. 2, 1961, White House Office of Speechwriting, Research Office, Series IV, Subseries C: Reagan Speeches, 1952–1978, box 424, RRPL.

19. Ronald Reagan, "Remarks Announcing Candidacy for the Republican Presidential Nomination," Nov. 13, 1979, APP.

20. "Text of Kennedy's Speech," *New York Times*, Jan. 10, 1961, p. 20.

21. Daniel J. Boorstin, *The Americans: The Colonial Experience* (New York: Random House, 1958), p. 3.

22. Ronald Reagan, "A Time for Choosing" (1964), in *A Time for Choosing: The Speeches of Ronald Reagan, 1961–1982*, ed. Alfred A. Balitzer and Gerald M. Bonetto (Chicago: Regnery, 1983).

23. Ronald Reagan, "Remarks at John F. Kennedy High School, Fremont, CA," June 13, 1973, Edwin Meese Papers, box 282.

24. Reagan, "Speech to the Economic Club of New York, New York City," Jan. 17, 1966, Ronald Reagan 1980 Presidential Campaign Papers, box 873, RRPL.

25. Ronald Reagan, "Remarks at an Eisenhower College Fund Raising Luncheon," Oct. 14, 1969, Gubernatorial Papers, 1966–75, Press Unit—Speeches 8/1/68 to 12/31/72, box P18, RRPL.

26. Ronald Reagan, "Election Eve Address: A Vision for America," Nov. 3, 1980, APP.

27. "Draft—Report to the People Script—Campus Unrest 1968," Edwin Meese Papers, box 284.

28. Ronald Reagan, "Remarks at a Luncheon Sponsored by the Independent Colleges of Southern California, Los Angeles Music Center," May 23, 1969; Ronald Reagan, "Remarks at an Eisenhower College Fund Raising Dinner, Washington, DC," October 14, 1969; Ronald Reagan, "Remarks at a Eureka College Fund Raising Luncheon, Chicago, IL," Oct. 22, 1969; Ronald Reagan, "Address at Pepperdine College," Feb. 9, 1970, all in Gubernatorial Papers, 1966–75, Press Unit—Speeches 8/1/68 to 12/31/72, box P18, RRPL. The second of these speeches is reprinted in Ronald Reagan, *Speaking My Mind: Selected Speeches* (New York: Simon & Schuster, 1989). For yet another version of the same speech: Ronald Reagan, "Commencement Address at Azusa-Pacific College, Azusa, CA," May 5, 1973, Gubernatorial Records, Research Files (Mary Sturgis Tuttle), box G0199, RRPL.

29. Reagan, "Remarks to the First Conservative Political Action Conference."

30. Ronald Reagan, "The New Republican Party: Remarks to the Fourth Annual CPAC Convention," Feb. 6, 1977, Reagan 2020, http://reagan2020.us/speeches/The_New_Republican_Party.asp.

31. Ronald Reagan, *In His Own Hand* (New York: Free Press, 2001), p. 140.

32. Ronald Reagan, "Let Them Go Their Way: Remarks to the 2nd Annual CPAC Convention," Mar. 1, 1975, Reagan 2020, http://reagan2020.us/speeches/Let_Them_Go_Their_Way.asp.

33. Reagan, "Election Eve Address."

34. Jimmy Carter, "Address to the Nation on Energy and Policy Goals," July 15, 1979, APP.

35. Ronald Reagan, "Remarks at a Dinner Marking the 10th Anniversary of the Heritage Foundation," Oct. 8, 1983, APP; Ronald Reagan, "Final Radio Address to the Nation," Jan. 14, 1989, APP.

36. "Draft—Report to the People Script—Campus Unrest 1968."

37. Reagan, "Remarks at a Luncheon Sponsored by the Independent Colleges of Southern California"; Reagan, "Commencement Address at Azusa-Pacific College, Azusa, CA."

38. Anthony Dolan to Edwin Meese, c. June 1980, Ronald Reagan 1980 Presidential Campaign Papers, box 867, RRPL; Reagan, "Election Eve Address."

39. Anthony Dolan, "Election Eve Address: A Vision for America," draft, Ronald Reagan 1980 Presidential Campaign Papers, box 867, RRPL.

40. Reagan, "Election Eve Address"; Ronald Reagan, "Remarks at a Luncheon of the World Affairs Council of Philadelphia," Oct. 15, 1981, APP; Ronald Reagan, "Proclamation 4850—Captive Nations Week," June 30, 1981, APP; Ronald Reagan, "Remarks at the Annual Convention of the National League of Cities in Los Angeles, CA," Nov. 29, 1982, APP; Ronald Reagan, "Address to the Nation on the Eve of the Presidential Election," Nov. 5, 1984, APP; Ronald Reagan, "Remarks to the Annual Convention of the Texas State Bar Association," July 6, 1984, APP.

41. Ronald Reagan, "Remarks at the Welcoming Rally at the Republican National Convention in New Orleans, Louisiana," Aug. 14, 1988, APP; Ronald Reagan, "Remarks at the Republican National Convention in New Orleans, Louisiana," Aug. 15, 1988, APP; Ronald Reagan, "Remarks Accepting the Presidential Nomination at the Republican National Convention in Dallas, Texas," Aug. 23, 1984, APP.

42. Reagan, "Farewell Address to the Nation."

43. Reagan, "Remarks Accepting the Presidential Nomination at the Republican National Convention in Dallas, Texas."

44. Reagan, "Remarks Announcing Candidacy for the Republican Presidential Nomination."
45. Reagan, "Final Radio Address to the Nation."

CHAPTER 18. Puritan Foundations of an "Exceptionalist" Nation

1. Mario Cuomo, "Keynote address at the 1984 Democratic National Convention," American Rhetoric, http://www.americanrhetoric.com/speeches/mariocuomo1984dnc .htm; Michael Dukakis, "Address Accepting the Presidential Nomination at the Democratic National Convention in Atlanta," July 21, 1988, The American Presidency Project (hereafter "APP"), Gerhard Peters and John Woolley, eds., http://www.presidency.ucsb.edu; Bill Clinton, "Remarks to the Democratic Leadership Council," Oct. 27, 1997, APP; Al Gore, "Speech on Martin Luther King, Jr., Day at the Ebenezer Baptist Church, Atlanta," Jan. 17, 2000, Clinton White House, https://clintonwhitehouse4.archives.gov/WH/EOP/OVP /speeches/mlk_other.html.

2. Sarah Palin, *America by Heart: Reflections on Family, Faith, and Flag* (New York: HarperCollins, 2010), chap. 3; Newt Gingrich and Callista Gingrich, *A City upon a Hill: The Spirit of American Exceptionalism* [video] (Washington, DC: Citizens United Productions, 2011); George W. Bush, "Remarks at the Simon Wiesenthal Center in Los Angeles," Mar 6, 2000, APP.

3. Hillary Clinton, "Speech to the American Legion in Cincinnati," Aug. 31, 2016, *Time .com*, http://time.com/4474619/read-hillary-clinton-american-legion-speech.

4. John M. Murrin et al., *Liberty, Equality, Power: A History of the American People* (Fort Worth, TX: Harcourt Brace, 1996), p. 70; Paul S. Boyer, *American History: A Very Short Introduction* (New York: Oxford University Press, 2012), pp. 11–13.

5. "Texas Essential Knowledge and Skills for Social Studies. Subchapter C. High School. United States History Studies since 1877, Beginning with the School Year 2011–12," Texas Education Agency, http://ritter.tea.state.tx.us/rules/tac/chapter113/ch113c.html; Russell Shorto, "How Christian Were the Founders? History Wars: Inside America's Textbook Battles," *New York Times Magazine*, Feb. 14, 2010, pp. 32ff.

6. Larry Krieger and Jane Robbins, "Five Reasons Why the College Board's U.S. History Talking Points Are Wrong," *The Federalist*, Sept. 17, 2014, https://thefederalist.com/2014 /09/17/five-reasons-the-college-boards-u-s-history-talking-points-are-wrong/hat; Stanley Kurtz, "A Hard Left for High-School History," *National Review* 66:20 (Nov. 3, 2014): 25–26; Stanley Kurtz, "Sorry, Still No Exceptionalism in APUSH, *National Review* 66:20 (Nov. 3, 2014): 25–26; Peter Wood, "APUSH: The New, New History," *Academic Questions* 29 (2015): 224–35; "Letter Opposing the 2014 APUSH Framework," National Association of Scholars (NAS), June 2, 2015, https://www.nas.org/images/documents/Historians _Statement.pdf.

7. Republican National Committee, "Resolution Concerning Advanced Placement U.S. History (APUSH)," Aug. 8, 2014, https://prod-static-ngop-pbl.s3.amazonaws.com/docs /RESOLUTION_CONCERNING_ADVANCED_PLACEMENT_US_HISTORY _APUSH.pdf; State of Oklahoma, 55th Legislature, 1st Session, (2015), House Bill 1380, p. 3.

8. Peter Wood, "AP History and Us," NAS, Aug. 6, 2015, https://www.nas.org/articles /ap_history and_us; Terry Golway, ed., *American Political Speeches* (New York: Penguin, 2012), p. xxvi.

9. Daniel T. Rodgers, "Exceptionalism," in *Imagined Histories: American Historians Interpret the Past*, ed. Anthony Molho and Gordon S. Wood (Princeton, NJ: Princeton University Press, 1998), pp. 21–40; Daniel T. Rodgers, "American Exceptionalism Revisited," *Raritan Review* 24 (Fall 2004): 21–47. For acute critiques of exceptionalism: Walter A.

McDougall, "American Exceptionalism . . . Exposed," Foreign Policy Research Institute, Oct. 13, 2012, https://www.fpri.org/article/2012/10/american-exceptionalism-exposed; Richard Gamble, "Reconsidering American Exceptionalism," *The Imaginative Conservative*, Oct. 8, 2013, http://www.theimaginativeconservative.org/2013/10/american -exceptionalism.html; James W. Ceasar, "The Origins and Character of American Exception-alism," *American Political Thought* 1:1 (May 2012): 3–28.

10. Seymour Martin Lipset, *The First New Nation: The United States in Comparative and Historical Perspective* (New York: Basic Books, 1963), p. vii; Seymour Martin Lipset, *American Exceptionalism: A Double-Edged Sword* (New York: Norton, 1996).

11. Samuel P. Huntington, *American Politics: The Promise of Disharmony* (Cambridge, MA: Harvard University Press, 1981).

12. Alexis de Tocqueville, *Democracy in America*, trans. James T. Schleifer, 4 vols. (Indianapolis: Liberty Fund, 2010), 3:767–68. See also Aurelian Craiutu and Jeremy Jennings, "The Third 'Democracy'": Tocqueville's View of America after 1840," *American Political Science Review* 98:3 (Aug. 2004): 391–401.

13. Tocqueville, *Democracy in America*, 3:767–68.

14. Newt Gingrich, *Quotations from Speaker Newt: The Little Red, White, and Blue Book of the Republican Revolution* (New York: Workman, 1995), pp. 172–73; Daniel Bell, "The End of American Exceptionalism," *The Public Interest*, no. 41 (Fall 1975): 197, 205.

15. Barack Obama, "The President's News Conference in Strasbourg," Apr. 4, 2009, APP.

16. Mark Nusbaum, *Sarah Palin: Rendezvous with Liberty* (Maitland, FL: Xulon Press, 2009), p. 296; Mitt Romney, *No Apology: The Case for American Greatness* (New York: St. Martin's Press, 2010), p. 29; Newt Gingrich with Vince Haley, *A Nation Like No Other: Why American Exceptionalism Matters* (Washington, DC: Regnery, 2011).

17. "Presidential Debates: Palmetto Freedom Forum in Columbia, SC," Sept. 5, 2011, APP; Ben Smith and Jonathan Martin, "The New Battle: What It Means to Be an American," *Politico*, Aug. 20, 2010.

18. "2012 Republican Party Platform," Aug. 27, 2012, APP; "2016 Republican Party Platform," Jul. 18, 2016, APP. In the same vein: Richard Lowry and Ramesh Ponnuru, "An Exceptional Debate: The Obama Administration's Assault on American Identity," *National Review*, Mar. 8, 2010, pp. 31–38.

19. In confirmation of the point, the French were simultaneously engaged in their own debate over exceptionalism: Tony Chafer and Emmanuel Godin, eds., *The End of the French Exception? Decline and Revival of the "French Model"* (New York: Palgrave Macmillan, 2010).

20. John R. Bolton, "The First Post-American President and American Sovereignty," *AEI .org*, May 18, 2010, https://www.aei.org/publication/the-first-post-american-president-and -american-sovereignty.

21. David Grayson Allen, *In English Ways: The Movement of Societies and the Transferal of Local Law and Custom to Massachusetts Bay in the Seventeenth Century* (New York: W. W. Norton, 1982).

22. Wim Klooster, *Revolutions in the Atlantic World: A Comparative History*, new ed. (New York: New York University Press, 2018); Jonathan Sperber, *Revolutionary Europe, 1780–1850* (London: Routledge, 2000).

23. David Brion Davis, *Inhuman Bondage: The Rise and Fall of Slavery in the New World* (New York: Oxford University Press, 2006).

24. Paul Bairoch, "International Industrialization Levels from 1750 to 1980," *Journal of European Economic History* 11:2 (Fall 1982): 269–333; Edward J. Davies II, *The United States in World History* (New York: Routledge, 2006), chaps. 4–6.

25. Adam McKeown, "Global Migration, 1846–1940," *Journal of World History* 15:2 (June 2004): 155–89; Dirk Hoerder, *Cultures in Contact: World Migrations in the Second Millennium* (Durham, NC: Duke University Press, 2002).

26. C. A. Bayly, *The Birth of the Modern World, 1780–1914: Global Connections and Comparisons* (Malden, MA: Blackwell, 2004); Daniel T. Rodgers, *Atlantic Crossings: Social Politics in a Progressive Age* (Cambridge, MA: Harvard University Press, 1998).

27. Bairoch, "International Industrialization Levels," p. 301; Charles S. Maier, *Among Empires: American Ascendancy and Its Predecessors* (Cambridge, MA: Harvard University Press, 2016); John A. Thompson, *A Sense of Power* (Ithaca, NY: Cornell University Press, 2015); Alfred E. Eckes Jr. and Thomas W. Zeiler, *Globalization and the American Century* (Cambridge: Cambridge University Press, 2003).

28. William C. Wohlforth, "U.S. Strategy in a Unipolar World," in *America Unrivaled: The Future Balance of Power,* ed. G. John Ikenberry (Ithaca, NY: Cornell University Press, 2002), p. 104.

29. Giovanni Gozzini, "The Global System of International Migrations, 1900 and 2000: A Comparative Approach," *Journal of Global History* 1:3 (Nov. 2006): 321–41; Andrew Kohut and Bruce Stokes, *America against the World: How We Are Different and Why We Are Disliked* (New York: Times Books, 2006), p. 35.

30. Andrew J. Bacevich, *The Limits of Power: The End of American Exceptionalism* (New York: Metropolitan Books, 2008), Fareed Zakaria, *The Post-American World* (New York: Norton, 2008); David S. Mason, *The End of the American Century* (Lanham, MD: Rowman and Littlefield, 2009); Edward Luce, *Time to Start Thinking: America in the Age of Descent* (New York: Atlantic Monthly Press, 2012). For criticism of the "declinist" thesis: Robert Kagan, "Not Fade Away: The Myth of American Decline," *New Republic,* Jan. 11, 2012.

31. Peter Baldwin, *The Narcissism of Minor Differences: How America and Europe Are Alike* (New York: Oxford University Press, 2009); Godfrey Hodgson, *The Myth of American Exceptionalism* (New Haven, CT: Yale University Press, 2009).

32. Michael Shally-Jensen, ed., *American Political Culture: An Encyclopedia,* 4 vols. (Santa Barbara, CA: ABC-CLIO, 2015) 1:41; Steven G. Calabresi, "'A Shining City on a Hill': American Exceptionalism and the Supreme Court's Practice of Relying on Foreign Law," *Boston University Law Review* 86:5 (Dec. 2006): 1335–1416.

33. Peter Schuck, "Origins and Future of U.S. 'Exceptionalism,'" May 2, 2008, *NPR.org,* https://www.npr.org/templates/story/story.php?storyId=90126925. Schuck was promoting his new book: Peter H. Schuck and James Q. Wilson, eds., *Understanding America: The Anatomy of an Exceptional Nation* (New York: PublicAffairs, 2008).

34. Eric Metaxas, *If You Can Keep It: The Forgotten Promise of American Liberty* (New York: Viking, 2016), pp. 186, 188.

CHAPTER 19. Ambivalent Evangelicals

1. Crosswalk.com, https://www.crosswalk.com/culture/music/city-on-a-hill-541246 .html.

2. City on a Hill, Louisville, KY, http://www.cityonahill.tv/city-on-a-hill-radio-show -podc.

3. City on a Hill Radio Show, https://www.cityonahillstudio.com.

4. City on a Hill Ministries, Zeeland, MI, http://www.coahm.org.

5. City on the Hill Music Festival, Duluth, MN, http://cityonthehillmusicfest.com.

6. City on a Hill, Inc., Garden City, KS, http://www.cityonahillinc.com/substance -addiction-garden-city-ks.html.

7. City on a Hill, Milwaukee, WI, http://www.cityonahillmilwaukee.org.

8. Christian Smith et al., *American Evangelicalism: Embattled and Thriving* (Chicago: University of Chicago Press, 1998); Randall Balmer, *Mine Eyes Have Seen the Glory: A Journey into the Evangelical Subculture in America*, 25th Anniversary ed. (New York: Oxford University Press, 2014).

9. For example: NJ Family First, http://www.njfpc.org/programs-2/citizen-builders /city-on-the-hill.

10. Citizens United Productions, A City upon a Hill: The Spirit of American Exceptionalism, http://www.cityuponahill.com.

11. Stephen M. Stookey, "In God We Trust? Evangelical Historiography and the Quest for a Christian America," *Southwestern Journal of Theology* 41:2 (Spring 1999): 41–69; and 41:3 (Summer 1999): 5–37.

12. Peter Marshall and David Manuel, *The Light and the Glory* (Old Tappan, NJ: Fleming H. Revell, 1977), pp. 18, 154, 22.

13. Mark A. Beliles and Stephen K. McDowell, *America's Providential History* (Charlottesville, VA: Providence Foundation, 1989). For more on the Providence Foundation see https://providencefoundation.com.

14. Barton published his books and videos through his own Wallbuilders organization, see https://wallbuilders.com; Ruth Murray Brown, *For a "Christian America": A History of the Religious Right* (Amherst, NY: Prometheus Books, 2002), chap. 13; "Barton's Bunk: Religious Right 'Historian' Hits the Big Time in Tea Party America," *Right Wing Watch: A Project of People for the America Way*, Apr. 18, 2011, http://www.rightwingwatch.org/report /bartons-bunk-religious-right-historian-hits-the-big-time-in-tea-party-america. See also Julie Ingersoll, "Meet the Tea Party's Evangelical Quack," *Salon*, Aug. 23, 2015.

15. Quoted in Jeff Sharlet, "Through a Glass Darkly: How the Christian Right Is Imagining U.S. History," *Harper's Magazine*, Dec. 2006, p. 36.

16. Richard Lee, *The American Patriot's Bible: The Word of God and the Shaping of America* (Nashville: Thomas Nelson, 2009).

17. "The Agitator," *Time*, Sept. 28, 2009, pp. 30–36; Chris Good, "Glenn Beck Comes to Town," *Atlantic*, Aug. 28, 2010; Ross Douthat, "Mr. Beck Goes to Washington," *New York Times*, Aug. 30, 2010; Ross Douthat, *Bad Religion: How We Became a Nation of Heretics* (New York: Free Press, 2012), chap. 8.

18. "Can Glenn Beck Save America?," *Dallas News*, July 2012, http://www.dallasnews .com/news/arlington/2012/07/27/can-glenn-beck-save-america-many-fans-at-arlington -event-think-so; Mercury One, *History of America—A Short Film from Restoring Love* [YouTube video], https://www.youtube.com/watch?v=yf4uuE0SWFE; NXG, *Restoring Love* [YouTube video], https://www.youtube.com/watch?v=jzdqPnylLJk.

19. Mercury One, *John Winthrop and the Journey to America—A Short Film from Restoring Love* [YouTube video], https://www.youtube.com/watch?v=-CaLshwQrTM.

20. Pat Robertson, *America's Dates with Destiny* (Nashville: Thomas Nelson, 1986); Tim LaHaye, *Faith of Our Founding Fathers: A Comprehensive Study of America's Christian Foundations* (Brentwood, TN: Wolgemuth and Hyatt, 1987); Beliles and McDowell, *America's Providential History*; Gary DeMar, *America's Christian History: The Untold Story* (Atlanta: American Vision, 1993); William J. Federer, *America's God and Country Encyclopedia of Quotations* (Coppell, TX: FAME Publishing, 1994).

21. George W. Bush, "Remarks at the Simon Wiesenthal Center in Los Angeles," Mar. 6, 2000, The American Presidency Project, Gerhard Peters and John Woolley, eds., http://www .presidency.ucsb.edu; George W. Bush, "Remarks on the National Day of Prayer, May 6, 2004," The American Presidency Project, http://www.presidency.ucsb.edu.

22. John McCain quoted in Jon Meacham, "A Nation of Christians Is Not a Christian Nation," *New York Times*, Oct. 7, 2007.

23. J. Matthew Wilson, "'Blessed Are the Poor': American Protestantism and Attitudes toward Poverty and Welfare," *Southeastern Political Review* 27:3 (Sept. 1999): 421–37; Daniel Cox et al., *Economic Values Survey 2013*, Public Religion Research Institute, https://www .prri.org/research/economic-values-survey-07-2013; Pew Research Center, *U.S. Religious Landscape Survey: Views About Government Aid to the Poor*, http://www.pewforum.org /religious-landscape-study/views-about-government-aid-to-the-poor.

24. Beliles and McDowell, *America's Providential History*; Federer, *America's God and Country Encyclopedia of Quotations*.

25. The Mayflower and the First Thanksgiving, https://www.amazon.com/Mayflower -First-Thanksgiving-Huckabees-History/dp/B00BE9GKLE; Rod Gragg, *The Pilgrim Chronicles: An Eyewitness History of the Pilgrims and the Founding of Plymouth Colony* (Washington, DC: Regnery, 2013).

26. Garrett Epps, "Genuine Scholars Smack Down an Unruly Colleague," *Atlantic*, Aug. 10, 2012, https://www.theatlantic.com/national/archive/2012/08/genuine-christian -scholars-smack-down-an-unruly-colleague/260994; Jon Meacham, *American Gospel: God, the Founding Fathers, and the Making of a Nation* (New York: Random House, 2007); John Fea, *Was America Founded as a Christian Nation? A Historical Introduction* (Louisville, KY: Westminster John Knox Press, 2011).

27. Michael Lienesch, *Redeeming America: Piety and Politics in the New Christian Right* (Chapel Hill: University of North Carolina Press, 1993), p. 155.

28. Jerry Falwell, *Listen, America!* (Garden City, NY: Doubleday, 1980), pp. 117, 7; Tom Tancredo, "The Vanishing American," *WND*, May 3, 2013, http://www.wnd.com/2013/05 /the-vanishing-american; Miranda Blue, "Return to Wichita: 25 Years after the Summer of Mercy, the Rescue Movement Plots Its Next Steps," *Right Wing Watch*, Oct. 2016, http://www.rightwingwatch.org/report/return-to-wichita-25-years-after-the-summer-of -mercy-the-rescue-movement-plots-its-next-steps.

29. Ruth Murray Brown, *For a "Christian America": A History of the Religious Right* (Amherst, NY: Prometheus Books, 2002), pp. 81–84; Joseph Gimenez quoted in Jeffrey L. Sheler, *Believers: A Journey into Evangelical America* (New York: Viking, 2006), p. 36; Lienesch, *Redeeming America*, p. 172.

30. Richard M. Gamble, *In Search of the City on a Hill: The Making and Unmaking of an American Myth* (London: Continuum, 2012), pp. 169, 183.

31. Mark A. Noll, George M. Marsden, and Nathan O. Hatch, *The Search for Christian America*, expanded ed. (Colorado Springs, CO: Helmers and Howard, 1989); Richard T. Hughes, *Christian America and the Kingdom of God* (Urbana: University of Illinois Press, 2009); Robert Tracy McKenzie, "Metaxas on America as a 'City on a Hill,'" *Faith and History: Thinking Christianly about the American Past* [blog], July 4, 2016, https:// faithandamericanhistory.wordpress.com/2016/07/04/america-as-a-city-on-a-hill. For a nonprovidentialist evangelical history of the United States, see David Edwin Harrell Jr. et al., *Unto a Good Land: A History of the American People* (Grand Rapids, MI: Eerdmans, 2005).

32. Nicholas Guyatt, *Have a Nice Doomsday: Why Millions of Americans Are Looking Forward to the End of the World* (New York: Harper Perennial, 2007); Matthew Avery Sutton, *American Apocalypse: A History of Modern Evangelicalism* (Cambridge, MA: Harvard University Press, 2014).

33. Franky Schaeffer quoted in Lienesch, *Redeeming America*, p. 165; Bob Jones III quoted in Hughes, *Christian America*, p. 159; Jerry Falwell quoted in Michelle Goldberg, *Kingdom Coming: The Rise of Christian Nationalism* (New York: Norton, 2006), p. 8.

34. Accessed 2/14/2017.

EPILOGUE. Disembarking from the *Arbella*

1. Barack Obama, "Remarks Commemorating the 50th Anniversary of the Selma to Montgomery Marches for Voting Rights in Selma, Alabama," Mar. 7, 2015, The American Presidency Project (hereafter "APP"), Gerhard Peters and John Woolley, eds., http://www .presidency.ucsb.edu.

2. Daniel Boorstin, ed., *An American Primer*, 2 vols. (Chicago: University of Chicago Press, 1966), 1:xvii.

3. Hillary Clinton, "Speech to the American Legion, Cleveland, OH," Aug. 31, 2016, transcript at *Time.com*, http://time.com/4474619/read-hillary-clinton-american-legion -speech. On Rubio: Jennifer Rubin, "A Speech for All Times," *Washington Post*, June 27, 2013; Ted Cruz, "Speech at Liberty University, Lynchburg, VA," Mar. 23, 2015, transcript at *Washington Post*, https://www.washingtonpost.com/politics/transcript-ted-cruzs-speech-at -liberty-university/2015/03/23/41c4011a-d168-11e4-a62f-ee745911a4ff_story.html; Dr. Ben and Candy Carson [Facebook post], Mar. 11, 2016, https://www.facebook.com /realbencarson/posts/607001686132968; Chris Christie, "Speech at Saint Anselm College, Goffstown, NH," Jan. 4, 2016, transcript at *Washington Post*, https://www.washingtonpost .com/news/the-fix/wp/2016/01/04/chris-christie-just-made-a-compelling-argument-for -why-republicans-shouldnt-nominate-donald-trump; Barack Obama, "Remarks to the Democratic National Convention in Philadelphia, July 27, 2016," APP; Mitt Romney, "Speech at the University of Utah, Salt Lake City," Mar. 2, 2016, transcript at *Time.com*, http://time.com/4246596/donald-trump-mitt-romney-utah-speech; Rudy Giuliani, "Speech at the Republican National Convention, Cleveland, OH," July 18, 2016, transcript at *Time.com*, http://time.com/4412059/republican-convention-rudy-giuliani-transcript-video.

4. Donald J. Trump, "Remarks Announcing Candidacy for President in New York City," June 16, 2015, APP; Donald J. Trump, "Remarks on Foreign Policy at the National Press Club in Washington, DC," Apr. 27, 2016, APP; Peter Wehner, "From the Shining City on a Hill to America Is a Dumpster Fire," in "What We Saw during the Debate," *New York Times*, Sept. 26, 2016, https://www.nytimes.com/interactive/projects/cp/opinion/clinton-trump -first-debate-election-2016.

5. Ibid.; Donald J. Trump, "Address Accepting the Presidential Nomination at the Republican National Convention in Cleveland, OH," July 21, 2016, APP.

6. Ibid.

7. Chris Christie in "Republican Candidates Debate in North Charleston, SC," Jan. 14, 2016, APP; Jeb Bush in "Republican Candidates Debate in Las Vegas, NV," Dec. 15, 2015, APP.

8. The ghost writers of the book with which Donald Trump bid for the Republican Party presidential nomination in 2012 had called out Barack Obama for waffling on the "exceptionalism" of America. Donald J. Trump, *Time to Get Tough: Make America #1 Again* (Washington, DC: Regnery, 2011), pp. 155–57. But by 2016 "exceptionalism" had dropped out of Trump's own vocabulary.

9. Jill Radsken, "The Return of Winthrop House," *Harvard Gazette*, Jan. 24, 2017.

10. "Full Transcript and Video: James Comey's Testimony on Capitol Hill," *New York Times*, June 8, 2017.

Acknowledgments

Many hands helped shape this book. Students played an essential part as, over the years, they and I have tried to think through the lives of texts, contentions, and ideas. Their insights and puzzlements, even when we did not have "A Model of Christian Charity" as our focus, inform every page of this book.

Institutions played an indispensable role as well. Research for *As a City on a Hill* was launched with a sabbatical grant from Princeton University. At the New-York Historical Society, Ted O'Reilly gave extremely generously of his time and expertise. Ray Wilson at the Ronald Reagan Presidential Library and Dan Hinchen at the Massachusetts Historical Society offered expert guidance through their sources. The initial draft of the book itself was written at the Center for Advanced Study in the Behavioral Sciences at Stanford University: as idyllic a city on a hill as higher education contains. To write in this tranquil yet stimulating setting, gathering ideas on each evening's walk home past the deer and wild turkeys, was a rare and unforgettable privilege.

As the book took shape, audiences became critically important testing grounds for the themes that began to emerge. Participants in the American Studies Workshop and the Works in Progress series of the Shelby Cullom Davis Center for Historical Studies at Princeton University, the Bay Area Seminar in Early American History and Culture, the Center for Advanced Study in the Behavioral Sciences at Stanford University, the Phi Beta Kappa chapter of Temple University, and the Graduate Institute at Geneva gave back generously with responses and suggestions. A casual conversation with my congressman,

Rush Holt, sharpened an idea I had only half formed in my mind. Louis Hyman helped me understand what was at stake in the investors' controversy. My colleagues at Princeton, faculty and graduate students alike, are an unmatched well of ideas and inspiration.

To try to list those whose leads and suggestions enriched the book risks inadvertently missing many others. But I cannot omit noting my especial thanks to Jeremy Adelman, Claire Arcenas, Peter Brown, David Blight, Liam Brockey, Olivier Burton, Henry Cowles, Margarita Fajardo, Matthew Franck, Jonathan Gienapp, Dov Grohsgal, Kristin Hoganson, Dani Holtz, Walter Johnson, Chin Jou, Ariane Leendertz, Aiala Levy, Rivka Maizlish, Jim McClure, Martín Merimón, Ronny Regev, Helmut Reimitz, Sarah Rivett, Mark Sholdice, Melissa Teixeira, Keith Wailoo, and Wendy Warren.

David Hall, James Kloppenberg, Joyce Seltzer, and an anonymous reader for Princeton University Press all offered acute and extremely helpful readings of the book's penultimate draft. Kellen Funk and Alison Isenberg did the same for individual chapters. My especially deep thanks go to four former students, now fine historians in their own right: Brooke Blower, Chris Florio, Sarah Igo, and Lou Masur. Reading the whole manuscript at a particularly important juncture in its composition, they gave back just the blend of encouragement, provocation, and criticism that a writer needs.

At Princeton University Press Brigitta van Rheinberg gave the book a home and provided critically important suggestions to make it better. Sarah Matherly cleaned up my citations and, with additional assistance from Spencer Weinreich, prepared the Model's transcription. Paul Vincent copyedited the book with scrupulous care. On the Princeton University Press staff, Amanda Peery and Debbie Tegarden managed the last stages of the book's preparation with ease and graciousness.

The four teachers to whose memory this book is dedicated taught and inspired in very different ways. William McLoughlin threw open the door to the astonishing wealth of ideas that have saturated the

American past. George Morgan's seminars modeled what it meant not just to know but to think. Edmund Morgan taught the art of surprise: how to notice a puzzle when you stumbled on one and how to find one's way toward an answer. C. Vann Woodward made the link between research, the arts of writing, and serious engagement with the world come alive. Each of these teachers helped shape a young college student and aspiring historian in ways far deeper than they could know.

The last name on this list of acknowledgments is, in every meaningful sense, the first of all. Her eyes read what I have written before any other's. Almost five decades on now, she remains my best, wisest, most honest, and most indispensable reader. For Rene my love and gratitude swell beyond any mere thanks or words.

Index

Blake, William, 144
Blaxton, William, 190, 202
Blyden, Edward, 164–65
Bolton, John, 256–57
Bonhoeffer, Dietrich, 212
Boorstin, Daniel, 221–23, 227, 228, 239, 282
Borden, Mary, 184–85
Boston, 48, 53, 64, 67, 72, 153, 181, 194, 257; in the American Revolution, 196; civic pride of, 203, 204; early ministers of, 50, 83, 105–6, 130, 190; first historical society in, 134; intolerance and dogmatism in, 67, 197–98, 200; merchants of, 104, 105, 107–8; Philadelphia eclipses as leading seaport, 196; political scandals in, 224–25; relief of the poor of, 108, 113, 117, 118, 119; and the tercentennial of its founding, 189–91, 202, 203, 205, 206; Winthrop memorials in, 190, 201, 202
Boston Common "Founders Memorial," 190–91, 202–3, 224
Boston Day parade, 189–91, 203
Boston Tea Party, memorialization of, 137, 189
Boyer, Paul S., 249
Bradford, William, 62, 137, 190, 271, 273
Brazil, 65, 258, 259
Bremer, Francis, 18
British empire, 67, 96, 126, 174, 176, 178–79
Brooks, Cleanth, 227
Brownson, Orestes, 152
Bryan, William Jennings, 282
Buckmaster, Thomas, 111
Bulfinch, Charles, 118
Bulkeley, Peter, 56
Burns, Anthony, 153
Bush, George W., 255, 256, 257, 262, 263, 277, 283; and the chosen people theme, 249, 272
Bush, Jeb, 285
Bushnell, Horace, 154

Cabot, Sebastian, 92
Calabresi, Steven G., 262

California, 236, 240, 241
Calvin, John, 24, 39, 47, 92, 197, 213. See also Calvinism
Calvinism, 24, 47, 49, 52, 65–66, 143, 209, 214, 229, 240
Canaan, 79, 163; as analogue for New World settlements, 48, 49, 50, 53, 60, 61, 68, 81, 101
Canada, 174, 259
capitalism: in early America, 96; in Puritan New England, 96–98
Caribbean, 33, 105, 175, 176, 177, 258
Carson, Ben, 283
Carter, Jimmy, 242–43
Carwardine, Richard, 156
Cass, Lewis, 140
Catholicism: and the Roman Catholic Church as the true "city on a hill," 38; Protestant campaigns against, 20–21, 33, 35, 37, 71–76. See also Franciscans; Jesuits; toleration, religious
Channing, Edward, 136
charity, 108, 123; bounds of obligation of, 94, 115–16, 119–20, 124; centrality of, in the Model, 7, 19, 50, 87–91, 93–95, 97–98; and contemporary evangelical Protestants, 265, 272–73; diminished importance of, in later readings of the Model, 125, 136, 209, 226–27, 233–34; in Puritan England, 109–11; in Puritan sermons, 92–93. See also poor, the; poor relief
Charles I (king of England), 71, 72
chosen people: concept of, 8, 71, 73, 82, 144–45, 158, 172, 231, 249, 272, 278, 286; and cultures of nationalism, 125–26, 141–44; Abraham Lincoln on, 145, 154–57; Herman Melville on, 147–51; in the Model, 7, 30, 44–57, 86, 94, 136; as a tool of criticism, 146–47, 151–52, 153; beyond the U.S., 52–53, 57, 60, 65–66, 70, 125, 143–44, 158, 231; in World War I, 183–85. See also Israel: biblical, analogues of in modern world
Christie, Chris, 283, 285
Chubb, Mercy, 115

352

Index